Collins

ENGLISH

DICTIONARY
& THESAURUS

Published by Collins
An imprint of HarperCollins Publishers
Westerhill Road
Bishopbriggs
Glasgow G64 2QT

Fifth edition 2015

10 9 8 7 6 5 4 3 2 1

© HarperCollins Publishers 2011, 2015

ISBN 978-0-00-810287-6

Collins ® is a registered trademark of
HarperCollins Publishers Limited

www.collinsdictionary.com
www.collins.co.uk

Typeset by MacMillan Publishing
Solutions

Printed in Great Britain by Clays Ltd,
St Ives plc

A catalogue record for this book is
available from the British Library.

If you would like to comment on any
aspect of this book, please contact us
at the given address or online.
E-mail: dictionaries@harpercollins.co.uk

Acknowledgements
We would like to thank those authors
and publishers who kindly gave
permission for copyright material to be
used in the Collins Corpus. We would
also like to thank Times Newspapers
Ltd for providing valuable data.

Contents

Subject field labels

 a

anomaly ❶ [an-**nom**-a-lee] *n, pl* **-lies** something that deviates from the normal, irregularity. **anomalous** *adj*.

Entry words

anomie [an-oh-mee] *n Sociology* lack of social or moral standards. **anomic** [an-**nom**-mik] *adj*.

anon *adv obs* in a short time, soon.

anon. anonymous.

❶ Thesaurus symbols (in entries with matching thesaurus entries)

anonymous ❶ *adj* **1** by someone whose name is unknown or withheld. **2** having no known name. **anonymously** *adv* **anonymity** *n*.

anorak *n* waterproof hooded jacket.

anorexia *n* psychological disorder characterized by fear of becoming fat and refusal to eat (also **anorexia nervosa**). **anorexic** *adj, n*.

another *adj, pron* **1** one more. **2** a different (one).

Part of speech labels

answer ❶ *n* **1** reply to a question, request, letter, etc. **2** solution to a problem. **3** reaction or response. ▷ *v* **4** give an answer (to). **5** be responsible to (a person). **6** respond or react.

Grammatical information

answerable *adj* (foll. by *for* or *to*) responsible for or accountable to.

answering machine device for answering a telephone automatically and recording messages.

ant *n* small insect living in highly organized colonies. **anteater** *n* mammal which feeds on ants by means of a long snout. **ant hill** mound built by ants around their nest.

antacid *n* substance that counteracts acidity, esp. in the stomach.

antagonist ❶ *n* opponent or adversary. **antagonism** *n* open opposition or hostility. **antagonistic** *adj* **antagonize**

Derived words

---

anomalous *adj* = **unusual**, abnormal, eccentric, exceptional, incongruous, inconsistent, irregular, munted (*NZ sl*), odd, peculiar

International English

anomaly *n* = **irregularity**, abnormality, eccentricity, exception, incongruity, inconsistency, oddity, peculiarity

anonymous *adj* **1** = **uncredited**, unacknowledged, unknown, unsigned **2** = **unnamed**, incognito, nameless, unidentified

Sense numbers

answer *n* **1** = **reply**, comeback, defence, rejoinder, response, retort, return, riposte **2** = **solution**, explanation **3** = **reaction**, response ▷ *v* **4** = **reply**, respond, retort, return **6** = **react**, respond

Dictionary & Thesaurus

---------- **DICTIONARY** ----------

v arouse hostility in, annoy.

antalkali [ant-**alk**-a-lie] *n* substance
that neutralizes alkalis.

Antarctic *n* **1 the Antarctic** area
around the South Pole. ▷ *adj* **2** of this
region.

- **SPELLING TIP**
- Almost one in every hundred
- references to the **Antarctic** in the
- Bank of English is written *Antarctic*.
- Note there is a *c* after the *r*.

ante *n* **1** player's stake in poker. ▷ *v*
-teing, **-ted** *or* **-teed 2** place (one's
stake) in poker.

ante- *prefix* before in time or position,
e.g. *antedate*; *antechamber*.

antecedent *n* **1** event or circumstance
happening or existing before another.
▷ *adj* **2** preceding, prior.

antechamber *n* same as ANTEROOM.

antedate *v* precede in time.

antediluvian *adj* **1** of the time before
the biblical Flood. **2** old-fashioned.

antelope *n* deerlike mammal with long
legs and horns.

antenatal *adj* during pregnancy, before
birth.

antenna *n* **1** *pl* **-nae** insect's feeler. **2** *pl*
-nas aerial

antepenultimate *adj* third last.

ante-post *adj* (of a bet) placed
before the runners in a race are
confirmed.

anterior *adj* **1** to the front. **2** earlier.

anteroom *n* small room leading into a
larger one, often used as a waiting
room.

anthem ❶ *n* **1** song of loyalty, esp. to a
country. **2** piece of music for a choir,

---------- **THESAURUS** ----------

answerable *adj* (foll. by *for* or *to*)
= **responsible**, accountable, amenable,
chargeable, liable, subject, to blame

antagonism *n* = **hostility**, antipathy,
conflict, discord, dissension, friction,
opposition, rivalry

antagonist *n* = **opponent**, adversary,
competitor, contender, enemy, foe,
rival

antagonistic *adj* = **hostile**, at odds, at
variance, conflicting, incompatible, in
dispute, opposed, unfriendly

antagonize *v* = **annoy**, anger, get on
one's nerves (*inf*), hassle (*inf*), irritate,
offend

anthem *n* **1** = **song of praise**, paean
2 = **hymn**, canticle, carol, chant,
chorale, psalm

Annotations (right margin):
- Definitions
- Pronunciation help
- Spelling tips and usage notes give advice on good English
- Examples
- Cross-references
- Dictionary sense numbers
- Spelling help (for irregular and difficult forms of word)
- Synonyms
- Key synonyms given first
- Part of speech labels

Abbreviations

adj	adjective	lb(s)	pound(s)
adv	adverb	*lit*	Literary
Afr	African	*masc*	masculine
Anat	Anatomy	*Maths*	Mathematics
arch	Archaic	*n*	noun
Aust	Australian	N	North(ern)
Brit	Britain, British	*NZ*	New Zealand
Canad	Canadian	*obs*	Obsolete
cap.	capital	*offens*	Offensive
conj	conjuction	orig.	originally
dial	Dialect	*pl*	plural
E	East(ern)	*poet*	Poetic
Eng	England, English	*prep*	preposition
e.g.	for example	*pron*	pronoun
esp.	especially	S	South(ern)
etc.	et cetera	*Scot*	Scottish
fem	feminine	*sl*	slang
foll.	followed	US	United States
inf	Informal	usu.	usually
interj	interjection	*v*	verb
kg	kilogram(s)	W	West(ern)
km	kilometre(s)		

a *adj* indefinite article, used before a noun being mentioned for the first time.

A *n, pl* **A's, As** highest grade in an examination. **from A to Z** from start to finish.

Å angstrom unit.

a- *prefix* not or without, e.g. *apolitical*; *amoral*.

A1 *adj informal* first-class, excellent.

AA 1 Alcoholics Anonymous.
2 Automobile Association.

aardvark *n* S African anteater with long ears and snout.

AB 1 able-bodied seaman. 2 Alberta.

aback *adv* **taken aback** startled or disconcerted.

abacus [**ab**-a-cuss] *n* beads on a wire frame, used for doing calculations.

abaft *adj, adv Nautical* closer to the rear of (a ship).

abalone [ab-a-**lone**-ee] *n* edible sea creature with a shell lined with mother of pearl.

abandon ❶ *v* 1 desert or leave (one's wife, children, etc.). 2 give up (hope etc.) altogether. ▷ *n* 3 lack of inhibition.

abandoned *adj* 1 deserted.
2 uninhibited. **abandonment** *n*.

abase *v* humiliate or degrade (oneself). **abasement** *n*.

abashed ❶ *adj* embarrassed and ashamed.

abate ❶ *v* make or become less strong. **abatement** *n*.

abattoir [**ab**-a-twahr] *n* slaughterhouse.

abbess *n* nun in charge of a convent.

abbey ❶ *n* dwelling place of, or a church belonging to, a community of monks or nuns.

abbot *n* head of an abbey of monks.

abbreviate ❶ *v* shorten (a word) by leaving out some letters. **abbreviation** *n* shortened form of a word or words.

ABC *n* 1 alphabet. 2 basics of a subject.

abdicate ❶ *v* give up (the throne or a responsibility). **abdication** *n*.

abdomen *n* part of the body containing the stomach and intestines. **abdominal** *adj*.

abduct ❶ *v* carry off, kidnap. **abduction** *n* **abductor** *n*.

aberration ❶ *n* 1 sudden change from what is normal, accurate, or correct.
2 brief lapse in control of one's thoughts or feelings. **aberrant** *adj* showing aberration.

abet ❶ *v* **abetting, abetted** help or encourage in wrongdoing. **abettor** *n*.

abeyance ❶ *n* **in abeyance** not in use.

abhor ❶ *v* **-horring, -horred** detest utterly. **abhorrent** *adj* hateful,

abandon *v* 1 = **leave**, desert, forsake, strand 2 = **give up**, relinquish, surrender, yield ▷ *n* 3 = **wildness**, recklessness

abandonment *n* 1 = **leaving**, dereliction, desertion, forsaking

abashed *adj* = **embarrassed**, ashamed, chagrined, disconcerted, dismayed, humiliated, mortified, shamefaced, taken aback

abate *v* = **decrease**, decline, diminish, dwindle, fade, lessen, let up, moderate, outspan (*S Afr*), relax, slacken, subside, weaken

abbey *n* = **monastery**, convent, friary, nunnery, priory

abbreviate *v* = **shorten**, abridge, compress, condense, contract, cut, reduce, summarize

abbreviation *n* = **shortening**, abridgment, contraction, reduction

abdicate *v* = **give up**, abandon, quit, relinquish, renounce, resign, step down (*inf*)

abdication *n* = **giving up**, abandonment, quitting, renunciation, resignation, retirement, surrender

abduct *v* = **kidnap**, carry off, seize, snatch (*sl*)

abduction *n* = **kidnapping**, carrying off, seizure

aberration *n* 1 = **oddity**, abnormality, anomaly, defect, irregularity, peculiarity, quirk 2 = **lapse**

abet *v* = **help**, aid, assist, connive at, support

abeyance *n* **in abeyance** = **shelved**, hanging fire, on ice (*inf*), pending, suspended

abhor *v* = **hate**, abominate, detest, loathe, shrink from, shudder at

abhorrent *adj* = **hateful**, abominable,

loathsome. **abhorrence** n.

abide ❶ v **1** endure, put up with. **2** obs stay or dwell, e.g. abide with me. **abide by** v obey (the law, rules, etc.). **abiding** adj lasting.

ability ❶ n, pl **-ties 1** competence, power. **2** talent.

abject ❶ adj **1** utterly miserable. **2** lacking all self-respect. **abjectly** adv.

abjure v deny or renounce on oath.

ablative [ab-lat-iv] n case of nouns in Latin and other languages, indicating source, agent, or instrument of action.

ablaze ❶ adj **1** burning fiercely. **2** emotionally aroused, e.g. ablaze with desire.

able ❶ adj capable, competent. **ably** adv **able-bodied** adj strong and healthy. **able-bodied seaman** seaman who is trained in certain skills.

-able adj suffix able to be acted on as specified, e.g. washable. **-ably** adv suffix **-ability** n suffix.

ablutions pl n act of washing.

ABM antiballistic missile.

abnormal ❶ adj not normal or usual. **abnormally** adv **abnormality** n.

aboard adv, prep on, in, onto, or into (a ship, train, or plane).

abode ❶ n home, dwelling.

abolish ❶ v do away with. **abolition** n **abolitionist** n person who wishes to do away with something, esp. slavery.

A-bomb n short for ATOMIC BOMB.

abominable ❶ adj detestable, very bad. **abominable snowman** large apelike creature said to live in the Himalayas. **abominably** adv.

abomination n **1** someone or something that is detestable. **2** strong dislike.

aborigine [ab-or-**rij**-in-ee], **aboriginal** n original inhabitant of a country or region, esp. (**A-**) Australia. **aboriginal** adj.

abort ❶ v **1** have an abortion or perform an abortion on. **2** have a miscarriage. **3** end a plan or process before completion. **abortion** n **1** operation to end a pregnancy. **2** informal something grotesque. **abortionist** n **1** person in favour of legal abortion. **2** person who performs abortions, esp. illegally. **abortive** adj unsuccessful.

abound ❶ v be plentiful. **abounding** adj.

about ❶ prep **1** concerning, on the

THESAURUS

disgusting, distasteful, hated, horrid, loathsome, offensive, repulsive

abide v **1** = **tolerate**, accept, bear, endure, put up with, stand, suffer

abide by v = **obey**, adhere to, agree to, carry out, comply with, conform to, discharge, follow, fulfil, keep to, observe, submit to

abiding adj = **everlasting**, continuing, enduring, lasting, permanent, persistent, unchanging

ability n **1** = **skill**, aptitude, capability, competence, expertise, proficiency **2** = **talent**

abject adj **1** = **miserable**, deplorable, forlorn, hopeless, pitiable, wretched **2** = **servile**, cringing, degraded, fawning, grovelling, submissive

ablaze adj **1** = **on fire**, aflame, alight, blazing, burning, fiery, flaming, ignited, lighted

able adj = **capable**, accomplished, competent, efficient, proficient, qualified, skilful

able-bodied adj = **strong**, fit, healthy, robust, sound, sturdy

abnormal adj = **unusual**, atypical, exceptional, extraordinary, irregular, munted (NZ sl), odd, peculiar, strange,

uncommon

abnormality n = **oddity**, deformity, exception, irregularity, peculiarity, singularity, strangeness

abode n = **home**, domicile, dwelling, habitat, habitation, house, lodging, pad (sl), quarters, residence

abolish v = **do away with**, annul, cancel, destroy, eliminate, end, eradicate, put an end to, quash, rescind, revoke, stamp out

abolition n = **ending**, cancellation, destruction, elimination, end, extermination, termination, wiping out

abominable adj = **terrible**, despicable, detestable, disgusting, hateful, horrible, horrid, repulsive, revolting, vile

abort v **1** = **terminate** (a pregnancy) **2** = **miscarry 3** = **stop**, arrest, axe (inf), call off, check, end, fail, halt, terminate

abortion n **1** = **termination**, deliberate miscarriage, miscarriage

abortive adj = **failed**, fruitless, futile, ineffectual, miscarried, unsuccessful, useless, vain

abound v = **be plentiful**, flourish, proliferate, swarm, swell, teem, thrive

about prep **1** = **regarding**, as regards,

a

subject of. **2** in or near (a place). ▷ *adv* **3** nearly, approximately. **4** nearby. **about to** shortly going to, e.g. *about to leave*. **not about to** determined not to, e.g. *I'm not about to give up now*. **about-turn** *n* **1** turn to the opposite direction. **2** complete change of attitude.

above ❶ *adv, prep* **1** over or higher (than). **2** greater (than). **3** superior (to). **above board** in the open, without dishonesty.

abracadabra *n* supposedly magic word.

abrasion ❶ *n* scraped area or spot on the skin; graze.

abrasive ❶ *adj* **1** harsh and unpleasant in manner. **2** tending to rub or scrape. ▷ *n* **3** substance for cleaning or polishing by rubbing.

abreast ❶ *adv, adj* side by side. **abreast of** up to date with.

abridge ❶ *v* shorten by using fewer words. **abridgment**, **abridgement** *n*.

abroad ❶ *adv* **1** to or in a foreign country. **2** at large.

abrogate *v* cancel (a law or agreement) formally. **abrogation** *n*.

abrupt ❶ *adj* **1** sudden, unexpected.

2 blunt and rude. **abruptly** *adv* **abruptness** *n*.

abs *pl n informal* abdominal muscles.

abscess [**ab**-sess] *n* inflamed swelling containing pus.

abscond ❶ *v* leave secretly.

abseil [**ab**-sale] *v* go down a steep drop by a rope fastened at the top and tied around one's body.

absent ❶ *adj* **1** not present. **2** lacking. **3** inattentive. ▷ *v* **4** stay away. **absently** *adv* **absence** *n* **1** being away. **2** lack. **absentee** *n* person who should be present but is not. **absenteeism** *n* persistent absence from work or school. **absent-minded** *adj* inattentive or forgetful. **absent-mindedly** *adv*.

absinthe *n* strong green aniseed-flavoured liqueur.

absolute ❶ *adj* **1** complete, perfect. **2** not limited, unconditional. **3** pure, e.g. *absolute alcohol*. **absolute zero** *Physics* lowest possible temperature, −273.15°C. **absolutely** *adv* **1** completely. ▷ *interj* **2** certainly, yes. **absolutism** *n* government by a ruler with unrestricted power.

——————— THESAURUS ———————

concerning, dealing with, on, referring to, relating to **2** = **near**, adjacent to, beside, circa (*used with dates*), close to, nearby ▷ *adv* **3** = **nearly**, almost, approaching, approximately, around, close to, more or less, roughly

above *prep* **1** = **over**, higher than, on top of, upon **2** = **greater than**, beyond, exceeding

abrasion *n* = **graze**, chafe, scrape, scratch, scuff, surface injury

abrasive *adj* **1** = **unpleasant**, caustic, cutting, galling, grating, irritating, rough, sharp **2** = **rough**, chafing, grating, scraping, scratchy

abreast *adv, adj* = **alongside**, beside, side by side

abreast of *adj* = **informed about**, acquainted with, *au courant* (with), *au fait* (with), conversant with, familiar with, in the picture about, in touch with, keeping one's finger on the pulse of, knowledgeable about, up to date with, up to speed with

abridge *v* = **shorten**, abbreviate, condense, cut, decrease, reduce, summarize

abroad *adv* **1** = **overseas**, in foreign lands, out of the country

abrupt *adj* **1** = **sudden**, precipitate, quick, surprising, unexpected **2** = **curt**, brusque, gruff, impatient, rude, short, terse

abscond *v* = **flee**, clear out, disappear, escape, make off, run off, steal away

absence *n* **1** = **nonattendance**, absenteeism, truancy **2** = **lack**, deficiency, need, omission, unavailability, want

absent *adj* **1** = **missing**, away, elsewhere, gone, nonexistent, out **2** = **lacking**, unavailable **3** = **absent-minded**, blank, distracted, inattentive, oblivious, preoccupied, vacant, vague ▷ *v* **4 absent oneself** = **stay away**, keep away, play truant, withdraw

absent-minded *adj* = **vague**, distracted, dreaming, forgetful, inattentive, preoccupied, unaware

absolute *adj* **1** = **total**, complete, outright, perfect, pure, sheer, thorough, utter **2** = **supreme**, full, sovereign, unbounded, unconditional, unlimited, unrestricted

absolutely *adv* **1** = **totally**, completely, entirely, fully, one hundred per cent, perfectly, utterly, wholly

absolve ❶ v declare to be free from blame or sin. **absolution** n.

absorb ❶ v **1** soak up (a liquid). **2** take in. **3** engage the interest of (someone). **absorption** n **absorbent** adj able to absorb liquid. **absorbency** n.

abstain ❶ v **1** choose not to do something. **2** choose not to vote. **abstainer** n **abstention** n abstaining, esp. from voting. **abstinence** n abstaining, esp. from drinking alcohol. **abstinent** adj.

abstemious ❶ [ab-**steem**-ee-uss] adj taking very little alcohol or food. **abstemiousness** n.

abstract ❶ adj **1** existing as a quality or idea rather than a material object.

2 theoretical. **3** (of art) using patterns of shapes and colours rather than realistic likenesses. ▷ n **4** summary. **5** abstract work of art. **6** abstract word or idea. ▷ v **7** summarize. **8** remove. **abstracted** adj lost in thought. **abstractedly** adv **abstraction** n.

abstruse ❶ adj not easy to understand.

absurd ❶ adj incongruous or ridiculous. **absurdly** adv **absurdity** n.

abundant ❶ adj plentiful. **abundantly** adv very, e.g. it is abundantly clear. **abundance** n.

abuse ❶ v **1** use wrongly. **2** ill-treat violently. **3** speak harshly and rudely to. ▷ n **4** prolonged ill-treatment. **5** harsh and vulgar comments. **6** wrong use.

absolution n = **forgiveness**, deliverance, exculpation, exoneration, mercy, pardon, release

absolve v = **forgive**, deliver, exculpate, excuse, let off, pardon, release, set free

absorb v **1** = **soak up**, suck up **2** = **take in**, consume, digest, imbibe, incorporate, receive **3** = **preoccupy**, captivate, engage, engross, fascinate, rivet

absorbed adj **1** = **soaked up 2** = **taken in**, assimilated, digested, incorporated, received **3** = **preoccupied**, captivated, engrossed, fascinated, immersed, involved, lost, rapt, riveted, wrapped up

absorbent adj = **permeable**, porous, receptive, spongy

absorbing adj **3** = **fascinating**, captivating, engrossing, gripping, interesting, intriguing, riveting, spellbinding

absorption n **1** = **soaking up**, sucking up **2** = **taking in**, assimilation, consumption, digestion, incorporation **3** = **concentration**, fascination, immersion, intentness, involvement, preoccupation

abstain v **1** = **refrain**, avoid, decline, deny yourself, desist, fast, forbear, forgo, give up, keep from

abstemious adj = **self-denying**, ascetic, austere, frugal, moderate, sober, temperate

abstention n = **refusal**, abstaining, abstinence, avoidance, forbearance, refraining, self-control, self-denial, self-restraint

abstinence n = **self-denial**, abstemiousness, avoidance,

forbearance, moderation, self-restraint, soberness, teetotalism, temperance

abstinent adj = **self-denying**, abstaining, abstemious, forbearing, moderate, self-controlled, sober, temperate

abstract adj **1** = **indefinite**, general **2** = **theoretical**, hypothetical, notional ▷ n **4** = **summary**, abridgment, digest, epitome, outline, précis, résumé, synopsis ▷ v **7** = **summarize**, abbreviate, abridge, condense, digest, epitomize, outline, précis, shorten **8** = **remove**, detach, extract, isolate, separate, take away, take out, withdraw

abstraction n **1** = **idea**, concept, generalization, notion, thought **2** = **theory**, formula, hypothesis, theorem

abstruse adj = **obscure**, arcane, complex, deep, enigmatic, esoteric, recondite, unfathomable, vague

absurd adj = **ridiculous**, crazy (inf), farcical, foolish, idiotic, illogical, inane, incongruous, irrational, ludicrous, nonsensical, preposterous, senseless, silly, stupid, unreasonable

absurdity n = **ridiculousness**, farce, folly, foolishness, incongruity, joke, nonsense, silliness, stupidity

abundance n = **plenty**, affluence, bounty, copiousness, exuberance, fullness, profusion

abundant adj = **plentiful**, ample, bountiful, copious, exuberant, filled, full, luxuriant, profuse, rich, teeming

abuse v **1** = **misuse 2** = **ill-treat**, damage, exploit, harm, hurt, injure,

abuser n **abusive** adj **abusively** adv **abusiveness** n.

abut v **abutting**, **abutted** be next to or touching.

abuzz adj noisy, busy with activity etc.

abysmal ❶ adj informal extremely bad, awful. **abysmally** adv.

abyss ❶ n very deep hole or chasm.

Ac Chemistry actinium.

AC alternating current.

a/c account.

acacia [a-**kay**-sha] n tree or shrub with yellow or white flowers.

academy ❶ n, pl -**mies 1** society to advance arts or sciences. **2** institution for training in a particular skill. **3** Scot secondary school. **academic** adj **1** of an academy or university. **2** of theoretical interest only. ▷ n **3** lecturer or researcher at a university. **academically** adv **academician** n member of an academy.

acanthus n **1** prickly plant.

2 ornamental carving in the shape of an acanthus leaf.

ACAS Advisory Conciliation and Arbitration Service.

acc. account.

accede ❶ v **1** consent or agree (to). **2** take up (an office or position).

accelerate ❶ v (cause to) move faster. **acceleration** n **accelerator** n pedal in a motor vehicle to increase speed.

accent ❶ n **1** distinctive style of pronunciation of a local, national, or social group. **2** mark over a letter to show how it is pronounced. **3** stress on a syllable or musical note. ▷ v **4** place emphasis on.

accentuate ❶ v stress, emphasize. **accentuation** n.

accept ❶ v **1** receive willingly. **2** agree to. **3** consider to be true. **accepted** adj generally approved. **acceptance** n **acceptable** adj **1** tolerable. **2** satisfactory. **acceptably** adv

---

THESAURUS

maltreat, take advantage of **3** = **insult**, castigate, curse, defame, disparage, malign, rouse on (Aust), scold, vilify ▷ n **4** = **ill-treatment**, damage, exploitation, harm, hurt, injury, maltreatment, manhandling **5** = **insults**, blame, castigation, censure, defamation, derision, disparagement, invective, reproach, scolding, vilification **6** = **misuse**, misapplication

abusive adj **2** = **harmful**, brutal, cruel, destructive, hurtful, injurious, rough **3** = **insulting**, censorious, defamatory, disparaging, libellous, offensive, reproachful, rude, scathing

abysmal adj Inf = **terrible**, appalling, awful, bad, dire, dreadful

abyss n = **pit**, chasm, crevasse, fissure, gorge, gulf, void

academic adj **1** = **scholarly**, bookish, erudite, highbrow, learned, literary, studious **2** = **hypothetical**, abstract, conjectural, impractical, notional, speculative, theoretical ▷ n **3** = **scholar**, academician, don, fellow, lecturer, master, professor, tutor

accede v **1** = **agree**, accept, acquiesce, admit, assent, comply, concede, concur, consent, endorse, grant **2** = **inherit**, assume, attain, come to, enter upon, succeed, succeed to (as heir)

accelerate v = **speed up**, advance,

expedite, further, hasten, hurry, quicken

acceleration n = **speeding up**, hastening, hurrying, quickening, stepping up (inf)

accent n **1** = **pronunciation**, articulation, brogue, enunciation, inflection, intonation, modulation, tone **3** = **emphasis**, beat, cadence, force, pitch, rhythm, stress, timbre ▷ v **4** = **emphasize**, accentuate, stress, underline, underscore

accentuate v = **emphasize**, accent, draw attention to, foreground, highlight, stress, underline, underscore

accept v **1** = **receive**, acquire, gain, get, obtain, secure, take **2** = **agree to**, approve, concur with, consent to, cooperate with **3** = **believe**, admit, recognize

acceptable adj **1** = **tolerable** **2** = **satisfactory**, adequate, admissible, all right, fair, moderate, passable, suitable

acceptance n **1** = **accepting**, acquiring, gaining, getting, obtaining, receipt, securing, taking **2** = **agreement**, acknowledgment, acquiescence, approval, assent, concurrence, consent, cooperation **3** = **belief**, admission, recognition

accepted adj = **agreed**, acknowledged, approved, common, conventional, customary, established, normal,

acceptability n.

access ❶ n 1 means of or right to approach or enter. ▷ v 2 obtain (data) from a computer. **accessible** adj 1 easy to reach. 2 easy to understand. **accessibility** n.

accession n taking up of an office or position.

accessory ❶ n, pl **-ries** 1 supplementary part or object. 2 person involved in a crime although not present when it is committed.

accident ❶ n 1 mishap, usu. one causing injury or death. 2 event happening by chance. **accidental** adj 1 happening by chance or unintentionally. ▷ n 2 Music symbol indicating that a sharp, flat, or natural note is not a part of the key signature. **accidentally** adv **accident-prone** adj often having accidents.

acclaim ❶ v 1 applaud, praise. ▷ n

2 enthusiastic approval. **acclamation** n.

acclimatize ❶ v adapt to a new climate or environment. **acclimatization** n.

accolade ❶ n 1 award, honour, or praise. 2 award of knighthood.

accommodate ❶ v 1 provide with lodgings. 2 have room for. 3 oblige, do a favour for. 4 adapt or adjust (to something). **accommodation** n house or room for living in. **accommodating** adj obliging.

● **SPELLING TIP**
● The Bank of English shows
● that people usually remember
● that **accommodation** and
● **accommodate** have two cs, but they
● often forget that these words have
● two ms as well.

accompany ❶ v **-nying**, **-nied** 1 go along with. 2 occur with. 3 provide a musical accompaniment for.

recognized, traditional

access n 1 = **entrance**, admission, admittance, approach, entry, passage, path, road

accessibility n 1 = **handiness**, availability, nearness, possibility, readiness

accessible adj 1 = **handy**, achievable, at hand, attainable, available, near, nearby, obtainable, reachable

accessory n 1 = **addition**, accompaniment, adjunct, adornment, appendage, attachment, decoration, extra, supplement, trimming
2 = **accomplice**, abettor, assistant, associate (in crime), colleague, confederate, helper, partner

accident n 1 = **misfortune**, calamity, collision, crash, disaster, misadventure, mishap 2 = **chance**, fate, fluke, fortuity, fortune, hazard, luck

accidental adj 1 = **unintentional**, casual, chance, fortuitous, haphazard, inadvertent, incidental, random, unexpected, unforeseen, unlooked-for, unplanned

accidentally adv 1 = **unintentionally**, by accident, by chance, fortuitously, haphazardly, inadvertently, incidentally, randomly, unwittingly

acclaim v 1 = **praise**, applaud, approve, celebrate, cheer, clap, commend, exalt, hail, honour, salute ▷ n
2 = **praise**, acclamation, applause, approval, celebration, commendation,

honour, kudos

acclamation n = **praise**, acclaim, adulation, approval, ovation, plaudit, tribute

acclimatization n = **adaptation**, adjustment, habituation, inurement, naturalization

acclimatize v = **adapt**, accommodate, accustom, adjust, get used to, habituate, inure, naturalize

accolade n 1 = **praise**, acclaim, applause, approval, commendation, compliment, ovation, recognition, tribute

accommodate v 1 = **house**, cater for, entertain, lodge, put up, shelter
3 = **help**, aid, assist, oblige, serve
4 = **adapt**, adjust, comply, conform, fit, harmonize, modify, reconcile, settle

accommodating adj = **helpful**, considerate, cooperative, friendly, hospitable, kind, obliging, polite, unselfish, willing

accommodation n = **housing**, board, digs (Brit inf), house, lodging(s), quarters, shelter

accompaniment n 1 = **supplement**, accessory, companion, complement
2 Music = **backing music**, backing

accompany v 1 = **go with**, attend, chaperon, conduct, convoy, escort, hold (someone's) hand 2 = **occur with**, belong to, come with, follow, go together with, supplement

accompanying adj 2 = **additional**,

accompaniment *n* **1** something that accompanies. **2** *Music* supporting part that goes with a solo. **accompanist** *n*.

accomplice ❶ *n* person who helps another to commit a crime.

accomplish ❶ *v* **1** manage to do. **2** finish. **accomplishment** *n* **1** completion. **2** personal ability or skill. **accomplished** *adj* expert, proficient.

accord ❶ *n* **1** agreement, harmony. ▷ *v* **2** fit in with. **3** grant or give. **of one's own accord** voluntarily.

accordance *n* **in accordance with** conforming to or according to.

according ❶ *adv* **according to 1** as stated by. **2** in conformity with. **accordingly** *adv* **1** in an appropriate manner. **2** consequently.

accordion *n* portable musical instrument played by moving the two sides apart and together, and pressing a keyboard or buttons to produce the notes. **accordionist** *n*.

accost ❶ *v* approach and speak to.

account ❶ *n* **1** report, description.

2 business arrangement making credit available. **3** record of money received and paid out with the resulting balance. **4** person's money held in a bank. **5** importance, value. ▷ *v* **6** judge to be. **on account of** because of. **accountable** *adj* responsible to someone or for something. **accountability** *n* **account for** *v* **1** explain. **2** make up, constitute.

accounting ❶ *n* skill or practice of maintaining and auditing business accounts. **accountant** *n* person who maintains and audits business accounts. **accountancy** *n*.

accoutrements [ak-**koo**-tra-ments] *pl n* clothing and equipment for a particular activity.

accredited ❶ *adj* authorized, officially recognized.

accretion [ak-**kree**-shun] *n* **1** gradual growth. **2** something added.

accrue ❶ *v* **-cruing, -crued** increase gradually. **accrual** *n*.

---

associated, attached, attendant, complementary, related, supplementary

accomplice *n* = **helper**, abettor, accessory, ally, assistant, associate, collaborator, colleague, henchman, partner

accomplish *v* **1** = **do**, achieve, attain, bring about, carry out, effect, execute, fulfil, manage, perform, produce **2** = **finish**, complete

accomplished *adj* = **skilled**, expert, gifted, masterly, polished, practised, proficient, talented

accomplishment *n* **1** = **completion**, bringing about, carrying out, conclusion, execution, finishing, fulfilment, performance

accord *n* **1** = **agreement**, conformity, correspondence, harmony, rapport, sympathy, unison ▷ *v* **2** = **agree**, conform, correspond, fit, harmonize, match, suit, tally

accordingly *adv* **1** = **appropriately**, correspondingly, fitly, properly, suitably **2** = **consequently**, as a result, ergo, hence, in consequence, so, therefore, thus

according to *adv* **1** = **as stated by**, as believed by, as maintained by, in the light of, on the authority of, on the report of **2** = **in keeping with**, after,

after the manner of, consistent with, in accordance with, in compliance with, in line with, in the manner of

accost *v* = **approach**, buttonhole, confront, greet, hail

account *n* **1** = **description**, explanation, narrative, report, statement, story, tale, version **3** = **statement**, balance, bill, books, charge, invoice, reckoning, register, score, tally **5** = **importance**, consequence, honour, note, significance, standing, value, worth ▷ *v* **6** = **consider**, count, estimate, judge, rate, reckon, regard, think, value

accountability *n* = **responsibility**, answerability, chargeability, culpability, liability

accountable *adj* = **responsible**, amenable, answerable, charged with, liable, obligated, obliged

accountant *n* = **auditor**, bean counter (*inf*), book-keeper

account for *v* **1** = **explain**, answer for, clarify, clear up, elucidate, illuminate, justify, rationalize

accredited *adj* = **authorized**, appointed, certified, empowered, endorsed, guaranteed, licensed, official, recognized

accrue *v* = **increase**, accumulate, amass, arise, be added, build up, collect, enlarge, flow, follow, grow

accumulate ❶ v gather together in increasing quantity. **accumulation** n **accumulative** adj **accumulator** n rechargeable electric battery.

accurate ❶ adj exact, correct. **accurately** adv **accuracy** n.

accursed ❶ [a-**curse**-id] adj **1** under a curse. **2** detestable.

accusative n grammatical case indicating the direct object.

accuse ❶ v charge with wrongdoing. **accused** n Law person or people accused of a crime in a court. **accuser** n **accusing** adj **accusation** n **accusatory** adj.

accustom ❶ v make used to. **accustomed** adj **1** usual. **2** used (to). **3** in the habit (of).

ace ❶ n **1** playing card with one symbol on it. **2** informal expert. **3** Tennis unreturnable serve. ▷ adj **4** informal excellent.

acerbic [ass-**sir**-bik] adj harsh or bitter. **acerbity** n.

acetate [**ass**-it-tate] n **1** Chemistry salt or ester of acetic acid. **2** (also **acetate rayon**) synthetic textile fibre.

acetic [ass-**see**-tik] adj of or involving vinegar. **acetic acid** colourless liquid used to make vinegar.

acetone [**ass**-it-tone] n colourless liquid used as a solvent.

acetylene [ass-**set**-ill-een] n colourless flammable gas used in welding metals.

ache ❶ n **1** dull continuous pain. ▷ v **2** be in or cause continuous dull pain. **aching** adj, n **achingly** adv.

achieve ❶ v gain by hard work or ability. **achievement** n something accomplished. **achiever** n.

- **USAGE NOTE**
- Remember the 'ie'. This word is very
- commonly misspelled.

Achilles heel [ak-**kill**-eez] n small but fatal weakness.

Achilles tendon n cord connecting the calf to the heel bone.

achromatic adj **1** colourless. **2** Music with no sharps or flats.

acid ❶ n **1** Chemistry one of a class of compounds, corrosive and sour when dissolved in water, that combine with a

———————————————————————————— THESAURUS ————————

accumulate v = **collect**, accrue, amass, build up, gather, hoard, increase, pile up, store

accumulation n = **collection**, build-up, gathering, heap, hoard, increase, mass, pile, stack, stock, stockpile, store

accuracy n = **exactness**, accurateness, authenticity, carefulness, closeness, correctness, fidelity, precision, strictness, truthfulness, veracity

accurate adj = **exact**, authentic, careful, close, correct, faithful, precise, scrupulous, spot-on (Brit inf), strict, true, unerring

accurately adv = **exactly**, authentically, closely, correctly, faithfully, precisely, scrupulously, strictly, to the letter, truly, unerringly

accursed adj **1** = **cursed**, bewitched, condemned, damned, doomed, hopeless, ill-fated, ill-omened, jinxed, unfortunate, unlucky, wretched **2** = **hateful**, abominable, despicable, detestable, execrable, hellish, horrible

accusation n = **charge**, allegation, complaint, denunciation, incrimination, indictment, recrimination

accuse v = **charge**, blame, censure, denounce, impeach, impute, incriminate, indict

accustom v = **adapt**, acclimatize, acquaint, discipline, exercise, familiarize, train

accustomed adj **1** = **usual**, common, conventional, customary, established, everyday, expected, habitual, normal, ordinary, regular, traditional **2** = **used**, acclimatized, acquainted, adapted, familiar, familiarized, trained **3** = **in the habit of**, given to

ace n **1** = **one**, single point **2** Inf = **expert**, champion, dab hand (Brit inf), fundi (S Afr), master, star, virtuoso, wizard (inf) ▷ adj **4** Inf = **excellent**, awesome (sl), brilliant, fine, great, outstanding, superb

ache n **1** = **pain**, hurt, pang, pounding, soreness, suffering, throbbing ▷ v **2** = **hurt**, pain, pound, smart, suffer, throb, twinge

achieve v = **attain**, accomplish, acquire, bring about, carry out, complete, do, execute, fulfil, gain, get, obtain, perform

achievement n = **accomplishment**, act, deed, effort, exploit, feat, feather in one's cap, stroke

acid adj **4** = **sour**, acerbic, acrid, pungent, tart, vinegary **5** = **sharp**, biting, bitter, caustic, cutting, harsh, trenchant, vitriolic

base to form a salt. **2** *slang* LSD. ▷ *adj*
3 containing acid. **4** sour-tasting.
5 sharp or sour in manner. **acidly** *adv*
acidic *adj* **acidify** *v* **-fying, -fied**.
acidity *n* **Acid (House)** *n* type of
funk-based electronically edited disco
music with hypnotic sound effects.
acid rain rain containing acid from
atmospheric pollution. **acid test**
conclusive test of value.
acknowledge ❶ *v* **1** admit, recognize.
2 indicate recognition of (a person).
3 say one has received.
acknowledgment,
acknowledgement *n*.
acme [**ak**-mee] *n* highest point of
achievement or excellence.
acne [**ak**-nee] *n* pimply skin disease.
acolyte *n* **1** follower or attendant.
2 *Christianity* person who assists a priest.
aconite *n* **1** poisonous plant with
hoodlike flowers. **2** poison obtained
from this plant.
acorn *n* nut of the oak tree.
acoustic *adj* **1** of sound and hearing.
2 (of a musical instrument) not
electronically amplified. **acoustics** *n*

1 science of sounds. ▷ *pl* **2** features
of a room or building determining
how sound is heard within it.
acoustically *adv*.
acquaint ❶ *v* make familiar, inform.
acquainted *adj* **acquaintance** *n*
1 person known. **2** personal
knowledge.
acquiesce ❶ [ak-wee-**ess**] *v* agree to
what someone wants. **acquiescence** *n*
acquiescent *adj*.
acquire ❶ *v* gain, get. **acquisition** *n*
1 thing acquired. **2** act of getting.
acquired taste 1 liking for something
at first considered unpleasant. **2** the
thing liked.
acquisitive ❶ *adj* eager to gain material
possessions. **acquisitiveness** *n*.
acquit ❶ *v* **-quitting, -quitted**
1 pronounce (someone) innocent.
2 behave in a particular way.
acquittal *n*.
acre *n* measure of land, 4840 square
yards. **acreage** [**ake**-er-rij] *n* land area
in acres.
acrid ❶ [**ak**-rid] *adj* pungent, bitter.
acridity *n*.

THESAURUS

---

acidity *n* **4** = **sourness**, acerbity,
pungency, tartness **5** = **sharpness**,
bitterness, harshness
acknowledge *v* **1** = **accept**, admit,
allow, concede, confess, declare, grant,
own, profess, recognize, yield
2 = **greet**, address, hail, notice,
recognize, salute **3** = **reply to**, answer,
notice, react to, recognize, respond to,
return
acknowledged *adj* **1** = **accepted**,
accredited, approved, confessed,
declared, professed, recognized
acknowledgment *n* **1** = **acceptance**,
admission, allowing, confession,
declaration, profession, realization,
yielding **2** = **greeting**, addressing, hail,
hailing, notice, recognition, salutation,
salute **3** = **appreciation**, answer,
credit, gratitude, reaction, recognition,
reply, response, return, thanks
acquaint *v* = **tell**, disclose, divulge,
enlighten, familiarize, inform, let
(someone) know, notify, reveal
acquaintance *n* **1** = **associate**,
colleague, contact **2** = **knowledge**,
awareness, experience, familiarity,
fellowship, relationship, understanding
acquainted with *adj* = **familiar with**,
alive to, apprised of, *au fait* (with),

aware of, conscious of, experienced in,
informed of, knowledgeable about,
versed in
acquiesce *v* = **agree**, accede, accept,
allow, approve, assent, comply, concur,
conform, consent, give in, go along
with, submit, yield
acquiescence *n* = **agreement**,
acceptance, approval, assent,
compliance, conformity, consent,
giving in, obedience, submission,
yielding
acquire *v* = **get**, amass, attain, buy,
collect, earn, gain, gather, obtain,
receive, secure, win
acquisition *n* **1** = **possession**, buy, gain,
prize, property, purchase
2 = **acquiring**, attainment, gaining,
procurement
acquisitive *adj* = **greedy**, avaricious,
avid, covetous, grabbing, grasping,
predatory, rapacious
acquit *v* **1** = **clear**, discharge, free,
liberate, release, vindicate **2** = **behave**,
bear, comport, conduct, perform
acquittal *n* **1** = **clearance**, absolution,
deliverance, discharge, exoneration,
liberation, release, relief, vindication
acrid *adj* = **pungent**, bitter, caustic,
harsh, sharp, vitriolic

a

acrimonious ❶ *adj* bitter in speech or manner. **acrimony** *n*.

acrobat *n* person skilled in gymnastic feats requiring agility and balance. **acrobatic** *adj* **acrobatics** *pl n* acrobatic feats.

acronym *n* word formed from the initial letters of other words, such as NASA.

acrophobia *n* fear of heights.

acropolis [a-**crop**-pol-liss] *n* citadel of an ancient Greek city.

across *adv, prep* **1** from side to side (of). **2** on or to the other side (of). **across the board** applying equally to all.

acrostic *n* lines of writing in which the first or last letters of each line spell a word or saying.

acrylic *n, adj* (synthetic fibre, paint, etc.) made from acrylic acid. **acrylic acid** strong-smelling corrosive liquid.

act ❶ *n* **1** thing done. **2** law or decree. **3** section of a play or opera. **4** one of several short performances in a show. **5** pretended attitude. ▷ *v* **6** do something. **7** behave in a particular way. **8** perform in a play, film, etc. **act of God** unpredictable natural event. **acting** *n* **1** art of an actor. ▷ *adj* **2** temporarily performing the duties of. **action** *n* process of doing something. **active** *adj* moving, working. **actor**,

actress *n* person who acts in a play, film, etc.

ACT Australian Capital Territory.

actinide series *n* series of 15 radioactive elements with increasing atomic numbers from actinium to lawrencium.

actinium *n Chemistry* radioactive chemical element.

action ❶ *n* **1** process of doing something. **2** thing done. **3** lawsuit. **4** operating mechanism. **5** events forming the plot of a story or play. **6** *slang* main activity in a place. **7** minor battle. **actionable** *adj* giving grounds for a lawsuit. **action replay** rerun of an event on a television tape.

active ❶ *adj* **1** moving, working, e.g. *he remained active in public affairs*. **2** busy, energetic. **3** *Grammar* (of a verb) in a form indicating that the subject is performing the action, e.g. *threw* in *Kim threw the ball*. **actively** *adv* **activity** *n* **1** state of being active. **2** *pl* **-ties** leisure pursuit. **activate** *v* make active. **activation** *n* **activator** *n* **activist** *n* person who works energetically to achieve political or social goals. **activism** *n* **active service** military duty in an operational area.

acrimonious *adj* = **bitter**, caustic, irascible, petulant, rancorous, spiteful, splenetic, testy

acrimony *n* = **bitterness**, harshness, ill will, irascibility, rancour, virulence

act *n* **1** = **deed**, accomplishment, achievement, action, exploit, feat, performance, undertaking **2** = **law**, bill, decree, edict, enactment, measure, ordinance, resolution, statute **4** = **performance**, routine, show, sketch, turn **5** = **pretence**, affectation, attitude, front, performance, pose, posture, show ▷ *v* **6** = **do**, carry out, enact, execute, function, operate, perform, take effect, work **8** = **perform**, act out, impersonate, mimic, play, *play or* take the part of, portray, represent

acting *n* **1** = **performance**, characterization, impersonation, performing, playing, portrayal, stagecraft, theatre ▷ *adj* **2** = **temporary**, interim, pro tem, provisional, substitute, surrogate

action *n* **1** = **act**, accomplishment,

achievement, performance **2** = **deed**, accomplishment, achievement, act, exploit, feat **3** = **lawsuit**, case, litigation, proceeding, prosecution, suit **4** = **movement**, activity, functioning, motion, operation, process, working **7** = **battle**, clash, combat, conflict, contest, encounter, engagement, fight, skirmish, sortie

activate *v* = **start**, arouse, energize, galvanize, initiate, mobilize, move, rouse, set in motion, stir

active *adj* **1** = **in operation**, acting, at work, effectual, in action, in force, operative, working **2** = **busy**, animated, bustling, energetic, hard-working, industrious, involved, lively, occupied, on the go (*inf*), on the move, vigorous

activist *n* = **militant**, organizer, partisan

activity *n* **1** = **action**, animation, bustle, exercise, exertion, hustle, labour, motion, movement **2** = **pursuit**, hobby, interest, pastime, project, scheme

actor, actress *n* = **performer**, player, Thespian

actual ❶ *adj* existing in reality. **actually** *adv* really, indeed. **actuality** *n*.
- **USAGE NOTE**
- Avoid using *actual* or *actually* when it adds nothing to the sense of the sentence.

actuary *n, pl* **-aries** statistician who calculates insurance risks. **actuarial** *adj*.

actuate *v* start up (a device).

acuity [ak-**kew**-it-ee] *n* keenness of vision or thought.

acumen ❶ [**ak**-yew-men] *n* ability to make good judgments.

acupuncture *n* medical treatment involving the insertion of needles at various points on the body. **acupuncturist** *n*.

acute ❶ *adj* **1** severe. **2** keen, shrewd. **3** sharp, sensitive. **4** (of an angle) less than 90° ▷ *n* **5** accent (´) over a letter to indicate the quality or length of its sound, as in café **acutely** *adv* **acuteness** *n*.

ad *n informal* advertisement.

AD anno Domini.

adage [**ad**-ij] *n* wise saying, proverb.

adagio [ad-**dahj**-yo] *n, pl* **-gios** *adv Music* (piece to be played) slowly and gracefully.

adamant ❶ *adj* unshakable in determination or purpose. **adamantly** *adv*.

Adam's apple *n* projecting lump of thyroid cartilage at the front of the throat.

adapt ❶ *v* alter for new use or new conditions. **adaptable** *adj* **adaptability** *n* **adaptation** *n* **1** thing produced by adapting something. **2** adapting. **adaptor**, **adapter** *n* device for connecting several electrical appliances to a single socket.

ADC aide-de-camp.

add ❶ *v* **1** combine (numbers or quantities). **2** join (to something). **3** say or write further. **add up** *v* **1** calculate the sum of (two or more numbers). **2** *informal* make sense. **add up to** *v* amount to.

addendum ❶ *n, pl* **-da 1** an addition. **2** appendix to a book etc.

adder *n* small poisonous snake.

addict ❶ *n* **1** person who is unable to stop taking drugs. **2** *informal* person devoted to something. **addicted** *adj* **addiction** *n* **addictive** *adj* causing addiction.

addition ❶ *n* **1** adding. **2** thing added. **in addition** besides, as well.

——————— THESAURUS ———————

actual *adj* = **definite**, concrete, factual, physical, positive, real, substantial, tangible

actually *adv* = **really**, as a matter of fact, indeed, in fact, in point of fact, in reality, in truth, literally, truly

acumen *n* = **judgment**, astuteness, cleverness, ingenuity, insight, intelligence, perspicacity, shrewdness

acute *adj* **1** = **sharp**, excruciating, fierce, intense, piercing, powerful, severe, shooting, violent **2** = **perceptive**, astute, clever, insightful, keen, observant, sensitive, sharp, smart

acuteness *n* **1** = **seriousness**, severity **2** = **perceptiveness**, astuteness, cleverness, discrimination, insight, perspicacity, sharpness

adamant *adj* = **determined**, firm, fixed, obdurate, resolute, stubborn, unbending, uncompromising

adapt *v* = **adjust**, acclimatize, accommodate, alter, change, conform, convert, modify, remodel, tailor

adaptability *n* = **flexibility**, changeability, resilience, versatility

adaptable *adj* = **flexible**, adjustable, changeable, compliant, easy-going, plastic, pliant, resilient, versatile

adaptation *n* **1** = **conversion**, adjustment, alteration, change, modification, transformation, variation, version **2** = **acclimatization**, familiarization, naturalization

add *v* **1** = **count up**, add up, compute, reckon, total, tot up **2** = **include**, adjoin, affix, append, attach, augment, supplement

addendum *n* **1** = **addition**, appendage, attachment, extension, extra **2** = **appendix**, postscript, supplement

addict *n* **1** = **junkie**, fiend (*inf*), freak (*inf*) **2** *Inf* = **fan**, adherent, buff (*inf*), devotee, enthusiast, follower, nut (*sl*)

addicted *adj* **1** = **dependent**, habituated, hooked (*sl*) **2** *Inf* = **devoted**, absorbed, dedicated

addiction *n* **1** = **dependence**, craving, enslavement, habit **2** *Inf* = **obsession**, dedication, devotion

addition *n* **1** = **counting up**, adding up, computation, totalling, totting up

a

additional *adj* **additionally** *adv*

additive *n* something added, esp. to a foodstuff, to improve it or prevent deterioration.

addled *adj* confused or unable to think clearly.

address **❶** *n* **1** place where a person lives. **2** direction on a letter. **3** location. **4** formal public speech. ▷ *v* **5** mark the destination, as on an envelope. **6** speak to. **7** give attention to (a problem, task, etc.). **addressee** *n* person addressed.

● **SPELLING TIP**
● If you spell **address** wrongly, you
● probably miss out one *d*. Remember
● to double the *d* and the *s*.

adduce *v* mention something as evidence or proof.

adenoids [**ad**-in-oidz] *pl n* mass of tissue at the back of the throat. **adenoidal** *adj* having a nasal voice caused by swollen adenoids.

adept **❶** *adj, n* very skilful (person).

adequate **❶** *adj* **1** sufficient, enough. **2** not outstanding. **adequately** *adv* **adequacy** *n*.

à deux [ah **der**] *adv French* of or for two people.

adhere **❶** *v* **1** stick (to). **2** be devoted (to). **adherence** *n* **adherent** *n* devotee, follower. **adhesion** *n* **1** sticking (to). **2** joining together of parts of the body that are normally separate, as after surgery.

adhesive **❶** *n* **1** substance used to stick things together. ▷ *adj* **2** able to stick to things.

ad hoc *adj, adv Latin* for a particular purpose only.

adieu **❶** [a-**dew**] *interj* farewell, goodbye.

ad infinitum *adv Latin* endlessly.

adipose *adj* of or containing fat.

adj. adjective.

adjacent **❶** *adj* **1** near or next (to). **2** having a common boundary. **3** *Geometry* (of a side in a right-angled triangle) lying between a specified angle and the right angle.

adjective *n* word that adds information about a noun or pronoun. **adjectival** *adj*.

adjoin **❶** *v* be next to. **adjoining** *adj*.

adjourn **❶** *v* **1** close (a court) at the end of a session. **2** postpone temporarily. **3** *informal* go elsewhere. **adjournment** *n*.

adjudge *v* declare (to be).

THESAURUS

2 = extra, addendum, additive, appendage, appendix, attachment, augmentation, enlargement, extension, gain, increase, increment, supplement **in addition = as well**, additionally, also, besides, into the bargain, moreover, over and above, to boot, too

additional *adj* = **extra**, added, fresh, further, new, other, spare, supplementary

address *n* **3 = location**, abode, dwelling, home, house, residence, situation, whereabouts **4 = speech**, discourse, dissertation, lecture, oration, sermon, talk ▷ *v* **6 = speak to**, approach, greet, hail, talk to **7 = concentrate on**, apply (oneself) to, attend to, devote (oneself) to, engage in, focus on, take care of

add up *v* **1 = count up**, add, compute, count, reckon, total, tot up

adept *adj* = **skilful**, able, accomplished, adroit, expert, practised, proficient, skilled, versed ▷ *n* = **expert**, dab hand (*Brit inf*), fundi (*S Afr*), genius, hotshot (*inf*), master

adequacy *n* **1 = sufficiency**

2 = fairness, capability, competence, suitability, tolerability

adequate *adj* **1 = enough**, satisfactory, sufficient **2 = fair**, competent, satisfactory, tolerable, up to scratch (*inf*)

adhere *v* **1 = stick**, attach, cleave, cling, fasten, fix, glue, hold fast, paste

adherent *n* = **supporter**, admirer, devotee, disciple, fan, follower, upholder

adhesive *n* **1 = glue**, cement, gum, paste ▷ *adj* **2 = sticky**, clinging, cohesive, gluey, glutinous, tenacious

adieu *interj* = **goodbye**, farewell

adjacent *adj* **1 = next**, adjoining, beside, bordering, close, near, neighbouring, next door, touching

adjoin *v* = **connect**, border, join, link, touch

adjoining *adj* = **connecting**, abutting, adjacent, bordering, neighbouring, next door, touching

adjourn *v* **2 = postpone**, defer, delay, discontinue, interrupt, put off, suspend

adjournment *n* **2 = postponement**, delay, discontinuation, interruption, putting off, suspension

a

adjudicate ⓘ *v* **1** give a formal decision on (a dispute). **2** judge (a competition). **adjudication** *n* **adjudicator** *n*.

adjunct *n* subordinate or additional person or thing.

adjure *v* **1** command (to do). **2** appeal earnestly. **adjuration** *n*.

adjust ⓘ *v* **1** adapt to new conditions. **2** alter slightly so as to be suitable. **adjustable** *adj* **adjuster** *n* **adjustment** *n*.

adjutant [**aj**-oo-tant] *n* army officer in charge of routine administration.

ad-lib ⓘ *v* **-libbing, -libbed 1** improvise a speech etc. without preparation. ▷ *n* **2** improvised remark.

Adm. Admiral(ty).

admin *n informal* administration.

administer ⓘ *v* **1** manage (business affairs). **2** organize and put into practice. **3** give (medicine or treatment).

administrate ⓘ *v* manage (an organization). **administration** *n* **administrative** *adj* **administrator** *n*.

admiral *n* highest naval rank. **Admiralty** *n* former government department in charge of the Royal Navy.

admire ⓘ *v* regard with esteem and approval. **admirable** [**ad**-mer-a-bl] *adj* **admirably** *adv* **admiration** *n* **admirer** *n* **admiring** *adj* **admiringly** *adv*.

admissible ⓘ *adj* allowed to be brought in as evidence in court. **admissibility** *n*.

admission ⓘ *n* **1** permission to enter. **2** permission to join (an organization). **3** entrance fee. **4** confession.

admit ⓘ *v* **-mitting, -mitted 1** confess, acknowledge. **2** concede the truth of. **3** allow in. **admission** *n* permission to enter. **admittance** *n* permission to enter. **admittedly** *adv* it must be agreed.

admixture *n* **1** mixture. **2** ingredient.

admonish ⓘ *v* reprove sternly. **admonition** *n*.

ad nauseam [ad **naw**-zee-am] *adv Latin* to a boring or sickening extent.

ado *n* fuss, trouble.

THESAURUS

adjudicate *v* **1** = **judge**, adjudge, arbitrate, decide, determine, mediate, referee, settle, umpire

adjudication *n* **1** = **judgment**, arbitration, conclusion, decision, finding, pronouncement, ruling, settlement, verdict

adjust *v* **1** = **adapt**, accustom **2** = **alter**, make conform, modify

adjustable *adj* **2** = **alterable**, adaptable, flexible, malleable, modifiable, movable

adjustment *n* **1** = **acclimatization**, orientation, settling in **2** = **alteration**, adaptation, modification, redress, regulation, tuning

ad-lib *v* **1** = **improvise**, busk, extemporize, make up, speak off the cuff, wing it (*inf*)

administer *v* **1, 2** = **manage**, conduct, control, direct, govern, handle, oversee, run, supervise **3** = **give**, apply, dispense, impose, mete out, perform, provide

administration *n* = **management**, application, conduct, control, direction, government, running, supervision

administrative *adj* = **managerial**, directorial, executive, governmental, organizational, regulatory, supervisory

administrator *n* = **manager**, bureaucrat, executive, official, organizer, supervisor

admirable *adj* = **excellent**, commendable, exquisite, fine, laudable, praiseworthy, wonderful, worthy

admiration *n* = **regard**, amazement, appreciation, approval, esteem, praise, respect, wonder

admire *v* = **respect**, appreciate, approve, esteem, look up to, praise, prize, think highly of, value

admirer *n* = **fan**, devotee, disciple, enthusiast, follower, partisan, supporter

admissible *adj* = **permissible**, acceptable, allowable, passable, tolerable

admission *n* **1** = **entrance**, access, admittance, entry **2** = **acceptance**, entrée, entry, initiation, introduction **4** = **confession**, acknowledgment, allowance, declaration, disclosure, divulgence, revelation

admit *v* **1** = **confess**, acknowledge, declare, disclose, divulge, own, reveal **2** = **allow**, agree, grant, let, permit, recognize **3** = **let in**, accept, allow, give access, initiate, introduce, receive, take in

admonish *v* = **reprimand**, berate, chide, rebuke, rouse on (*Aust*), scold, slap on the wrist, tell off (*inf*)

a

adobe [ad-**oh**-bee] *n* sun-dried brick.
adolescence ❶ *n* period between
puberty and adulthood. **adolescent** *n*,
adj (person) between puberty and
adulthood.
Adonis *n* handsome young man.
adopt ❶ *v* 1 take (someone else's child)
as one's own. 2 take up (a plan or
principle). **adoption** *n* **adoptive** *adj*
related by adoption.
adore ❶ *v* 1 love intensely. 2 worship.
3 *informal* like very much, e.g. *I adore
being in the country.* **adorable** *adj*
adoration *n* **adoring** *adj*
adoringly *adv*.
adorn ❶ *v* decorate, embellish.
adornment *n*.
ADP automatic data processing.
adrenal [ad-**reen**-al] *adj* near the
kidneys. **adrenal glands** glands
covering the top of the kidneys.
adrenalin, adrenaline *n* hormone
secreted by the adrenal glands in
response to stress.
adrift ❶ *adj, adv* 1 drifting. 2 without a

clear purpose; aimless.
adroit ❶ *adj* quick and skilful. **adroitly**
adv **adroitness** *n*.
adsorb *v* (of a gas or vapour) condense
and form a thin film on a surface.
adsorbent *adj* **adsorption** *n*.
adulation ❶ *n* uncritical admiration.
adult ❶ *adj* 1 fully grown, mature. ▷ *n*
2 adult person or animal. **adulthood** *n*.
adulterate *v* spoil something by adding
inferior material. **adulteration** *n*.
adultery *n, pl* **-teries** sexual
unfaithfulness of a husband or wife.
adulterer, adulteress *n*
adulterous *adj*.
adv. adverb.
advance ❶ *v* 1 go or bring forward.
2 further (a cause). 3 propose (an idea).
4 lend (a sum of money). ▷ *n* 5 forward
movement. 6 improvement. 7 loan.
▷ *pl* 8 approaches to a person with the
hope of starting a romantic or sexual
relationship. ▷ *adj* 9 done or happening
before an event. **in advance** ahead.
advanced *adj* 1 at a late stage in

———————————————— THESAURUS ————————————————

adolescence *n* = **youth**, boyhood,
childishness, girlhood, immaturity,
minority, teens, youthfulness
adolescent *n* = **youth**, juvenile, minor,
teenager, youngster ▷ *adj* = **young**,
boyish, girlish, immature, juvenile,
puerile, teenage, youthful
adopt *v* 1 = **foster**, take in 2 = **choose**,
assume, espouse, follow, maintain,
take up
adoption *n* 1 = **fostering**, adopting,
taking in 2 = **choice**, appropriation,
assumption, embracing,
endorsement, espousal, selection,
taking up
adorable *adj* 1, 3 = **lovable**, appealing,
attractive, charming, cute, dear,
delightful, fetching, pleasing, sweet
adore *v* 1 = **love**, admire, cherish, dote
on, esteem, honour 2 = **worship**, exalt,
glorify, idolize, revere
adoring *adj* 1 = **loving**, admiring,
affectionate, devoted, doting, fond
adorn *v* = **decorate**, array, embellish,
festoon
adornment *n* = **decoration**, accessory,
embellishment, festoon, frill, frippery,
ornament, supplement, trimming
adrift *adj* 1 = **drifting**, afloat,
unanchored, unmoored 2 = **aimless**,
directionless, goalless, purposeless
adroit *adj* = **skilful**, adept, clever, deft,

dexterous, expert, masterful, neat,
proficient, skilled
adulation *n* = **worship**, fawning,
fulsome praise, servile flattery,
sycophancy
adult *adj* 1 = **fully grown**, full grown,
fully developed, grown-up, mature, of
age, ripe ▷ *n* 2 = **grown-up**, grown or
grown-up person (man or woman),
person of mature age
advance *v* 1 = **progress**, accelerate,
bring forward, come forward, go on,
hasten, make inroads, proceed, speed
2 = **benefit**, further, improve, prosper
3 = **suggest**, offer, present, proffer, put
forward, submit 4 = **lend**, pay
beforehand, supply on credit ▷ *n*
5 = **progress**, advancement,
development, forward movement,
headway, inroads, onward movement
6 = **improvement**, breakthrough,
gain, growth, progress, promotion,
step 7 = **loan**, credit, deposit, down
payment, prepayment, retainer ▷ *pl*
8 = **overtures**, approach, approaches,
moves, proposals, proposition ▷ *adj*
9 = **prior**, beforehand, early, forward, in
front **in advance** = **beforehand**,
ahead, earlier, previously
advanced *adj* = **foremost**, ahead,
avant-garde, forward, higher, leading,
progressive

development. **2** not elementary. **advancement** *n* promotion.
advantage ❶ *n* **1** more favourable position or state. **2** benefit or profit. **3** *Tennis* point scored after deuce. **take advantage of 1** use (a person) unfairly. **2** use (an opportunity). **advantageous** *adj* **advantageously** *adv* **advantaged** *adj* in a superior social or financial position.
advent *n* **1** arrival. **2** (**A-**) season of four weeks before Christmas. **Adventist** *n* member of a Christian sect that believes in the imminent return of Christ.
adventitious *adj* added or appearing accidentally.
adventure ❶ *n* exciting and risky undertaking or exploit. **adventurer**, **adventuress** *n* **1** person who unscrupulously seeks money or power. **2** person who seeks adventures. **adventurous** *adj* **adventurously** *adv*.
adverb *n* word that adds information about a verb, adjective, or other adverb. **adverbial** *adj*.

adversary ❶ [**ad**-verse-er-ree] *n, pl* **-saries** opponent or enemy.
adverse ❶ *adj* **1** unfavourable. **2** antagonistic or hostile. **adversely** *adv* **adversity** *n* very difficult or hard circumstances.
advert ❶ *n informal* advertisement.
advertise ❶ *v* **1** present or praise (goods or services) to the public in order to encourage sales. **2** make (a vacancy, event, etc.) known publicly. **advertisement** *n* public announcement to sell goods or publicize an event. **advertiser** *n* **advertising** *adj, n*.

● SPELLING TIP
● Some verbs can be spelt ending in
● either -*ise* or -*ize*, but **advertise** and
● **advise** always have an *s*.

advice ❶ *n* recommendation as to what to do. **advise** *v* **1** offer advice to. **2** notify (someone). **adviser**, **advisor** *n* **advisable** *adj* prudent, sensible. **advisability** *n* **advisory** *adj* giving advice. **advised** *adj* considered, thought-out, e.g. *ill-advised*. **advisedly** [ad-**vize**-id-lee] *adv* deliberately.

— THESAURUS —

advancement *n* = **promotion**, betterment, gain, improvement, preferment, progress, rise
advantage *n* **1** = **superiority**, ascendancy, dominance, lead, precedence, sway **2** = **benefit**, good, help, profit
advantageous *adj* **1** = **superior**, dominant, dominating, favourable **2** = **beneficial**, convenient, expedient, helpful, of service, profitable, useful, valuable, worthwhile
adventure *n* = **escapade**, enterprise, experience, exploit, incident, occurrence, undertaking, venture
adventurer *n* **1** = **mercenary**, charlatan, fortune-hunter, gambler, opportunist, rogue, speculator **2** = **hero**, daredevil, heroine, knight-errant, traveller, voyager
adventurous *adj* = **daring**, bold, daredevil, enterprising, intrepid, reckless
adversary *n* = **opponent**, antagonist, competitor, contestant, enemy, foe, rival
adverse *adj* **1** = **unfavourable**, contrary, detrimental, inopportune, negative **2** = **hostile**, antagonistic, opposing
adversity *n* = **hardship**, affliction, bad

luck, disaster, distress, hard times, misfortune, reverse, trouble
advert *n Inf* = **advertisement**, ad (*inf*), announcement, blurb, commercial, notice, plug (*inf*), poster
advertise *v* **1** = **publicize**, plug (*inf*), promote, tout **2** = **announce**, make known
advertisement *n* = **advert** (*inf*), ad (*inf*), announcement, blurb, commercial, notice, plug (*inf*), poster
advice *n* = **guidance**, counsel, help, opinion, recommendation, suggestion
advisability *n* = **wisdom**, appropriateness, aptness, desirability, expediency, fitness, propriety, prudence, suitability
advisable *adj* = **wise**, appropriate, desirable, expedient, fitting, politic, prudent, recommended, seemly, sensible
advise *v* **1** = **recommend**, admonish, caution, commend, counsel, prescribe, suggest, urge **2** = **notify**, acquaint, apprise, inform, let (someone) know, make known, report, tell, warn
adviser *n* = **guide**, aide, confidant, consultant, counsellor, guru, helper, mentor, right-hand man
advisory *adj* = **advising**, consultative,

a

● The Bank of English shows that
people sometimes write **advise**
with an *s* where they ought to write
advice with a *c*. The verb is **advise**
and the noun is **advice**.

advocaat *n* liqueur with a raw egg base.
advocate ❶ *v* **1** propose or recommend.
▷ *n* **2** person who publicly supports a
cause. **3** *Scot* barrister. **advocacy** *n*.
adze *n* tool with an arched blade at right
angles to the handle.
aegis [**ee**-jiss] *n* sponsorship, protection.
aeolian harp [ee-**oh**-lee-an] *n* musical
instrument that produces sounds when
the wind passes over its strings.
aeon [**ee**-on] *n* immeasurably long
period of time.
aerate *v* put gas into (a liquid), as when
making a fizzy drink. **aeration** *n*.
aerial *adj* **1** in, from, or operating in the
air. **2** relating to aircraft. ▷ *n* **3** metal
pole, wire, etc., for receiving or
transmitting radio or TV signals.
aero- *combining form* air or aircraft, e.g.
aeronautics.
aerobatics *pl n* stunt flying.
aerobatic *adj*.
aerobics *n* exercises designed to
increase the amount of oxygen in the
blood. **aerobic** *adj* **aerobically** *adv*.
aerodrome *n* small airport.
aerodynamics *n* study of how air flows
around moving solid objects.
aerodynamic *adj*.
aerofoil *n* part of an aircraft, such as the
wing, designed to give lift.
aerogram *n* airmail letter on a single
sheet of paper that seals to form an
envelope.
aeronautics *n* study or practice of
aircraft flight. **aeronautical** *adj*.

aeroplane *n* powered flying vehicle with
fixed wings.
aerosol *n* pressurized can from which a
substance can be dispensed as a fine
spray.
● **USAGE NOTE**
● Be careful not to confuse the spelling
'aer-' with 'air-'.
aerospace *n* **1** earth's atmosphere and
space beyond. ▷ *adj* **2** of rockets or
space vehicles, e.g. *the aerospace
industry*.
aesthetic [iss-**thet**-ik] *adj* relating to the
appreciation of art and beauty.
aesthetics *n* study of art, beauty, and
good taste. **aesthetically** *adv*
aesthete [**eess**-theet] *n* person who
has or affects an extravagant love of
art. **aestheticism** *n*.
aether *n* same as ETHER.
aetiology [ee-tee-**ol**-a-jee] *n* same as
ETIOLOGY.
afar *adv* **from afar** from or at a great
distance.
affable ❶ *adj* friendly and easy to talk to.
affably *adv* **affability** *n*.
affair ❶ *n* **1** event or happening.
2 sexual relationship outside marriage.
3 thing to be done or attended to. ▷ *pl*
4 personal or business interests.
5 matters of public interest.
affect[1] ❶ *v* **1** act on, influence. **2** move
(someone) emotionally.
● **USAGE NOTE**
● Do not confuse *affect* meaning
'influence' with *effect* meaning
'accomplish'.
affect[2] ❶ *v* **1** put on a show of. **2** wear
or use by preference. **affectation** *n*
attitude or manner put on to impress.
affected *adj* **1** displaying affectation.
2 pretended, e.g. *he spoke with*

—————————— THESAURUS ——————————

counselling, helping, recommending
advocate *v* **1** = **recommend**, advise,
argue for, campaign for, champion,
commend, encourage, promote,
propose, support, uphold ▷ *n*
2 = **supporter**, campaigner, champion,
counsellor, defender, promoter,
proponent, spokesman, upholder
3 *Scot* = **lawyer**, attorney, barrister,
counsel, solicitor
affable *adj* = **friendly**, amiable,
amicable, approachable, congenial,
cordial, courteous, genial, pleasant,
sociable, urbane
affair *n* **1** = **event**, activity, business,

episode, happening, incident, matter,
occurrence **2** = **relationship**, amour,
intrigue, liaison, romance
affect[1] *v* **1** = **influence**, act on, alter, bear
upon, change, concern, impinge upon,
relate to **2** = **move**, disturb, overcome,
perturb, stir, touch, upset
affect[2] *v* **1** = **put on**, adopt, aspire to,
assume, contrive, feign, imitate,
pretend, simulate
affectation *n* = **pretence**, act,
artificiality, assumed manners, facade,
insincerity, pose, pretentiousness, show
affected *adj* **1** = **mannered**, contrived,
unnatural **2** = **pretended**, artificial,

affected modesty.

affection ❶ *n* fondness or love.
affectionate *adj* loving.
affectionately *adv*.

affianced [af-**fie**-anst] *adj old-fashioned* engaged to be married.

affidavit [af-fid-**dave**-it] *n* written statement made on oath.

affiliate ❶ *v* (of a group) link up with a larger group. **affiliation** *n*.

affinity ❶ *n, pl* -**ties** **1** close connection or liking. **2** close resemblance. **3** chemical attraction.

affirm ❶ *v* **1** declare to be true. **2** uphold or confirm (an idea or belief).
affirmation *n* **affirmative** *n, adj* (word or phrase) indicating agreement.

affix *v* **1** attach or fasten. ▷ *n* **2** word or syllable added to a word to change its meaning.

afflict ❶ *v* give pain or grief to.
affliction *n*.

affluent ❶ *adj* having plenty of money.
affluence *n* wealth.

afford ❶ *v* **1** have enough money to buy. **2** be able to spare (the time etc.). **3** give

or supply. **affordable** *adj*.

afforest *v* plant trees on.
afforestation *n*.

affray *n* noisy fight, brawl.

affront ❶ *v, n* insult.

Afghan *n* **1** language of Afghanistan. **2** person from Afghanistan. ▷ *adj* **3** of Afghanistan or its language. **Afghan hound** large slim dog with long silky hair.

aficionado [af-fish-yo-**nah**-do] *n, pl* -**dos** enthusiastic fan of something or someone.

afield *adv* **far afield** far away.

aflame ❶ *adj* burning.

afloat *adv, adj* **1** floating. **2** at sea.

afoot ❶ *adv, adj* happening, in operation.

aforesaid, aforementioned *adj* referred to previously.

aforethought *adj* premeditated, e.g. *with malice aforethought*.

a fortiori [eh for-tee-**or**-rye] *adv* for a stronger reason.

Afr. Africa(n).

afraid ❶ *adj* **1** frightened. **2** regretful.

afresh ❶ *adv* again, anew.

THESAURUS

feigned, insincere, phoney *or* phony (*inf*), put-on
affection *n* = **fondness**, attachment, care, feeling, goodwill, kindness, liking, love, tenderness, warmth
affectionate *adj* = **fond**, attached, caring, devoted, doting, friendly, kind, loving, tender, warm-hearted
affiliate *v* = **join**, ally, amalgamate, associate, band together, combine, incorporate, link, unite
affinity *n* **1** = **attraction**, fondness, inclination, leaning, liking, partiality, rapport, sympathy **2** = **similarity**, analogy, closeness, connection, correspondence, kinship, likeness, relationship, resemblance
affirm *v* **1** = **declare**, assert, maintain, state, swear **2** = **confirm**, certify, pronounce, testify
affirmation *n* **1** = **declaration**, assertion, oath, statement **2** = **confirmation**, certification, pronouncement, testimony
affirmative *adj* = **agreeing**, approving, assenting, concurring, confirming, consenting, corroborative, favourable, positive
afflict *v* = **torment**, distress, grieve, harass, hurt, oppress, pain, plague, trouble

affliction *n* = **suffering**, adversity, curse, disease, hardship, misfortune, ordeal, plague, scourge, torment, trial, trouble, woe
affluence *n* = **wealth**, abundance, fortune, opulence, plenty, prosperity, riches
affluent *adj* = **wealthy**, loaded (*sl*), moneyed, opulent, prosperous, rich, well-heeled (*inf*), well-off, well-to-do
afford *v* **2** = **spare**, bear, manage, stand, sustain **3** = **give**, offer, produce, provide, render, supply, yield
affordable *adj* **1** = **inexpensive**, cheap, economical, low-cost, moderate, modest, reasonable
affront *v* = **offend**, anger, annoy, displease, insult, outrage, provoke, slight ▷ *n* = **insult**, offence, outrage, provocation, slap in the face (*inf*), slight, slur
aflame *adj* = **burning**, ablaze, alight, blazing, fiery, flaming, lit, on fire
afoot *adj* = **going on**, abroad, brewing, current, happening, in preparation, in progress, on the go (*inf*), up (*inf*)
afraid *adj* **1** = **scared**, apprehensive, cowardly, faint-hearted, fearful, frightened, nervous **2** = **sorry**, regretful, unhappy
afresh *adv* = **again**, anew, newly, once

African *adj* **1** of Africa. ▷ *n* **2** person from Africa. **African-American** *n* **1** American of African descent. ▷ *adj* **2** of African-Americans. **African violet** house plant with pink or purple flowers and hairy leaves.

Afrikaans *n* language used in S Africa, related to Dutch.

Afrikaner *n* White S African whose mother tongue is Afrikaans.

Afro- *combining form* African, e.g. *Afro-Caribbean*.

aft *adv* at or towards the rear of a ship or aircraft.

after ❶ *prep* **1** following in time or place. **2** in pursuit of. **3** in imitation of. ▷ *conj* **4** at a later time than. ▷ *adv* **5** at a later time. **afters** *pl n informal* dessert.

afterbirth *n* material expelled from the womb after childbirth.

aftercare *n* **1** support given to a person discharged from a hospital or prison. **2** regular care required to keep something in good condition.

aftereffect *n* result occurring some time after its cause.

afterglow *n* **1** glow left after a source of light has gone. **2** pleasant feeling left after an enjoyable experience.

afterlife *n* life after death.

aftermath ❶ *n* results of an event considered together.

afternoon *n* time between noon and evening.

afterpains *pl n* pains caused by the contraction of the womb after childbirth.

aftershave *n* lotion applied to the face after shaving.

afterthought *n* **1** idea occurring later.

2 something added later.

afterwards, afterward *adv* later.

Ag *Chemistry* silver.

again ❶ *adv* **1** once more. **2** in addition.

against ❶ *prep* **1** in opposition or contrast to. **2** in contact with. **3** as a protection from.

agape *adj* **1** (of the mouth) wide open. **2** (of a person) very surprised.

agaric *n* fungus with gills on the underside of the cap, such as a mushroom.

agate [**ag**-git] *n* semiprecious form of quartz with striped colouring.

agave [a-**gave**-vee] *n* tropical American plant with tall flower stalks and thick leaves.

age ❶ *n* **1** length of time a person or thing has existed. **2** time of life. **3** latter part of human life. **4** period of history. **5** long time. ▷ *v* **ageing** or **aging**, **aged 6** make or grow old. **aged** *adj* **1** [**ay**-jid] old. **2** [rhymes with **raged**] being at the age of. **ageing**, **aging** *n, adj* **ageless** *adj* **1** apparently never growing old. **2** seeming to have existed for ever.

age-old *adj* very old.

agency ❶ *n, pl* **-cies 1** organization providing a service. **2** business or function of an agent. **3** *old-fashioned* power or action by which something happens.

agenda ❶ *n* list of things to be dealt with, esp. at a meeting.

agent ❶ *n* **1** person acting on behalf of another. **2** person or thing producing an effect. **agency** *n* organization providing a service.

agent provocateur [**azh**-on prov-vok-at-**tur**] *n, pl* **agents provocateurs**

———————————————— THESAURUS ————

again, once more, over again

after *adv* **5** = **following**, afterwards, behind, below, later, subsequently, succeeding, thereafter

aftermath *n* = **effects**, aftereffects, consequences, end result, outcome, results, sequel, upshot, wake

again *adv* **1** = **once more**, afresh, anew, another time **2** = **also**, besides, furthermore, in addition, moreover

against *prep* **1** = **opposed to**, anti (*inf*), averse to, hostile to, in defiance of, in opposition to, resisting, versus **2** = **beside**, abutting, facing, in contact with, on, opposite to, touching, upon **3** = **in preparation for**, in anticipation

of, in expectation of, in provision for

age 1 = **lifetime**, generation ▷ *n* **3** = **old age**, advancing years, decline (*of life*), majority, maturity, senescence, senility, seniority **4** = **time**, date, day(s), duration, epoch, era, period, span

aged *adj* **1** = **old**, ancient, antiquated, antique, elderly, getting on, grey

agency *n* **1** = **business**, bureau, department, office, organization **3** *Old-fashioned* = **medium**, activity, means, mechanism

agenda *n* = **list**, calendar, diary, plan, programme, schedule, timetable

agent *n* **1** = **representative**, envoy, go-between, negotiator, rep (*inf*),

[**azh**-on prov-vok-at-**tur**] person employed by the authorities to tempt people to commit illegal acts and so be discredited or punished.

agglomeration n confused mass or cluster.

aggrandize v make greater in size, power, or rank. **aggrandizement** n.

aggravate ❶ v **1** make worse. **2** informal annoy. **aggravating** adj **aggravation** n.

● **SPELLING TIP**
● The biggest problem with spelling
● **aggravate** is not how many gs there
● are at the beginning, but that there is
● an a (not an e) in the middle.

aggregate ❶ n **1** total. **2** rock consisting of a mixture of minerals. **3** sand or gravel used to make concrete. ▷ adj **4** gathered into a mass. **5** total or final. ▷ v **6** combine into a whole. **aggregation** n.

aggression ❶ n **1** hostile behaviour. **2** unprovoked attack. **aggressive** adj **1** showing aggression. **2** forceful. **aggressively** adv **aggressiveness** n **aggressor** n.

● **SPELLING TIP**
● The Bank of English shows that
● **aggressive** is quite a common word
● and that agressive is a common way
● of misspelling it.

aggrieved ❶ adj upset and angry.

aggro n slang aggressive behaviour.

aghast ❶ adj overcome with amazement or horror.

agile ❶ adj **1** nimble, quick-moving. **2** mentally quick. **agilely** adv **agility** n.

agin prep dialect against, opposed to.

agitate ❶ v **1** disturb or excite. **2** stir or shake (a liquid). **3** stir up public opinion for or against something. **agitated** adj anxious or worried. **agitatedly** adv **agitation** n **agitator** n.

agitprop n political agitation and propaganda.

aglitter adj sparkling, glittering.

aglow adj glowing.

AGM annual general meeting.

agnostic ❶ n **1** person who believes that it is impossible to know whether God exists. ▷ adj **2** of agnostics. **agnosticism** n.

ago adv in the past.

———————————— **THESAURUS** ————————————

surrogate **2** = **force**, agency, cause, instrument, means, power, vehicle

aggravate v **1** = **make worse**, exacerbate, exaggerate, increase, inflame, intensify, magnify, worsen **2** Inf = **annoy**, bother, get on one's nerves (inf), irritate, nettle, provoke

aggravation n **1** = **worsening**, exacerbation, exaggeration, heightening, increase, inflaming, intensification, magnification **2** Inf = **annoyance**, exasperation, gall, grief (inf), hassle (inf), irritation, provocation

aggregate n **1** = **total**, accumulation, amount, body, bulk, collection, combination, mass, pile, sum, whole ▷ adj **4** = **accumulated**, collected, combined, composite, mixed **5** = **total**, cumulative ▷ v **6** = **combine**, accumulate, amass, assemble, collect, heap, mix, pile

aggression n **1** = **hostility**, antagonism, belligerence, destructiveness, pugnacity **2** = **attack**, assault, injury, invasion, offensive, onslaught, raid

aggressive adj **1** = **hostile**, belligerent, destructive, offensive, pugnacious, quarrelsome **2** = **forceful**, assertive, bold, dynamic, energetic, enterprising,

militant, pushy (inf), vigorous

aggressor n = **attacker**, assailant, assaulter, invader

aggrieved adj = **hurt**, afflicted, distressed, disturbed, harmed, injured, unhappy, wronged

aghast adj = **horrified**, amazed, appalled, astonished, astounded, awestruck, confounded, shocked, startled, stunned

agile adj **1** = **nimble**, active, brisk, lithe, quick, sprightly, spry, supple, swift **2** = **acute**, alert, bright (inf), clever, lively, quick-witted, sharp

agility n **1** = **nimbleness**, litheness, liveliness, quickness, suppleness, swiftness

agitate v **1** = **upset**, disconcert, distract, excite, fluster, perturb, trouble, unnerve, worry **2** = **stir**, beat, convulse, disturb, rouse, shake, toss

agitation n **1** = **turmoil**, clamour, commotion, confusion, disturbance, excitement, ferment, trouble, upheaval **2** = **turbulence**, convulsion, disturbance, shaking, stirring, tossing

agitator n **3** = **troublemaker**, agent provocateur, firebrand, instigator, rabble-rouser, revolutionary, stirrer (inf)

agog ❶ *adj* eager or curious.

agony ❶ *n, pl* **-nies** extreme physical or mental pain. **agonize** *v* **1** worry greatly. **2** (cause to) suffer agony. **agonizing** *adj* **agonizingly** *adv* **agony aunt** journalist who gives advice in an agony column. **agony column** newspaper or magazine feature offering advice on personal problems.

agoraphobia *n* fear of open spaces. **agoraphobic** *n, adj*.

agrarian *adj* of land or agriculture.

agree ❶ *v* **agreeing**, **agreed** **1** be of the same opinion. **2** consent. **3** reach a joint decision. **4** be consistent. **5** (foll. by *with*) be suitable to (one's health or digestion). **agreeable** *adj* **1** pleasant and enjoyable. **2** prepared to consent. **agreeably** *adv* **agreement** *n* **1** agreeing. **2** contract.

agriculture ❶ *n* raising of crops and livestock. **agricultural** *adj* **agriculturalist** *n*.

agrimony *n* yellow-flowered plant with bitter-tasting fruits.

agronomy [ag-**ron**-om-mee] *n* science of soil management and crop production. **agronomist** *n*.

aground ❶ *adv* onto the bottom of shallow water.

ague [**aig**-yew] *n* periodic fever with shivering.

ah *interj* exclamation of pleasure, pain, etc.

aha *interj* exclamation of triumph, surprise, etc.

ahead ❶ *adv* **1** in front. **2** forwards.

ahem *interj* clearing of the throat to attract attention etc.

ahoy *interj* shout used at sea to attract attention.

AI 1 artificial insemination. **2** artificial intelligence.

aid ❶ *v, n* (give) assistance or support.

AID formerly, artificial insemination by donor: see DI.

aide ❶ *n* assistant.

aide-de-camp [**aid**-de-**kom**] *n, pl* **aides-de-camp** [**aid**-de-**kom**] military officer serving as personal assistant to a senior.

AIDS acquired immunodeficiency syndrome, a viral disease that destroys the body's ability to fight infection.

AIH artificial insemination by husband.

ail ❶ *v* **1** trouble, afflict. **2** be ill. **ailing** *adj* **1** sickly. **2** unsuccessful over a long time. **ailment** *n* illness.

aileron [**ale**-er-on] *n* movable flap on an aircraft wing which controls rolling.

aim ❶ *v* **1** point (a weapon or missile) or

agog *adj* = **eager**, avid, curious, enthralled, enthusiastic, excited, expectant, impatient, in suspense

agonize *v* **1** = **suffer**, be distressed, be in agony, be in anguish, go through the mill, labour, strain, struggle, worry

agony *n* = **suffering**, anguish, distress, misery, pain, throes, torment, torture

agree *v* **1** = **concur**, assent, be of the same opinion, comply, consent, see eye to eye **4** = **match**, coincide, conform, correspond, tally

agreeable *adj* **1** = **pleasant**, delightful, enjoyable, gratifying, likable *or* likeable, pleasing, satisfying, to one's taste **2** = **consenting**, amenable, approving, complying, concurring, in accord, onside (*inf*), sympathetic, well-disposed, willing

agreement *n* **1** = **concurrence**, agreeing, assent, compliance, concord, consent, harmony, union, unison **2** = **contract**, arrangement, bargain, covenant, deal (*inf*), pact, settlement, treaty, understanding

agricultural *adj* = **farming**, agrarian, country, rural, rustic

agriculture *n* = **farming**, cultivation, culture, husbandry, tillage

aground *adv* = **beached**, ashore, foundered, grounded, high and dry, on the rocks, stranded, stuck

ahead *adv* **1** = **in front**, at an advantage, at the head, before, in advance, in the lead, leading, to the fore

aid *v* = **help**, assist, encourage, favour, promote, serve, subsidize, support, sustain ▷ *n* = **help**, assistance, benefit, encouragement, favour, promotion, relief, service, support

aide *n* = **assistant**, attendant, helper, right-hand man, second, supporter

ailing *adj* **1** = **ill**, crook (*Aust & NZ sl*), indisposed, infirm, poorly, sick, under the weather (*inf*), unwell, weak

ailment *n* = **illness**, affliction, complaint, disease, disorder, infirmity, malady, sickness

aim *v* **2** = **intend**, attempt, endeavour, mean, plan, point, propose, seek, set one's sights on, strive, try ▷ *n* **4** = **intention**, ambition, aspiration, desire, goal, objective, plan, purpose, target

direct (a blow or remark) at a target. **2** propose or intend. ▷ *n* **3** aiming. **4** intention, purpose. **aimless** *adj* having no purpose. **aimlessly** *adv*.

ain't *not standard* **1** am not. **2** is not. **3** are not. **4** has not. **5** have not.

air ❶ *n* **1** mixture of gases forming the earth's atmosphere. **2** space above the ground, sky. **3** breeze. **4** quality or manner. **5** tune. ▷ *pl* **6** affected manners. ▷ *v* **7** make known publicly. **8** expose to air to dry or ventilate. **on the air** in the act of broadcasting on radio or television. **airless** *adj* stuffy. **air base** centre from which military aircraft operate. **airborne** *adj* **1** carried by air. **2** (of aircraft) flying. **airbrush** *n* atomizer spraying paint by compressed air. **airfield** *n* place where aircraft can land and take off. **air force** branch of the armed forces responsible for air warfare. **air gun** gun fired by compressed air. **air hostess** stewardess on an aircraft. **airlift** *n* **1** transport of troops or cargo by aircraft when other routes are blocked. ▷ *v* **2** transport by airlift. **airlock** *n* **1** air bubble blocking the flow of liquid in a pipe. **2** airtight chamber. **airmail** *n* **1** system of sending mail by aircraft. **2** mail sent in this way. **airman** *n* member of the air force. **air miles** miles of free air travel that can be earned by buying airline tickets and various other products. **airplane** *n* US aeroplane. **airplay** *n* broadcast performances of a record on radio. **airport** *n* airfield for civilian aircraft, with facilities for aircraft maintenance and passengers. **air raid** attack by aircraft. **airship** *n* lighter-than-air self-propelled aircraft. **airsick** *adj* nauseated from travelling in an aircraft. **airspace** *n* atmosphere above a country, regarded as its territory. **airstrip** *n* cleared area where aircraft can take off and land. **airtight** *adj* sealed so that air cannot enter.

air conditioning *n* system that controls the temperature and humidity of the air in a building. **air-conditioned** *adj* **air conditioner** *n*

aircraft *n* any machine that flies, such as an aeroplane. **aircraft carrier** warship for the launching and landing of aircraft.

Airedale *n* large rough-coated terrier.

airing ❶ *n* **1** exposure to air for drying or ventilation. **2** exposure to public debate.

airline *n* company providing scheduled flights for passengers and cargo. **airliner** *n* large passenger aircraft.

airworthy *adj* (of aircraft) fit to fly. **airworthiness** *n*.

airy ❶ *adj* **airier**, **airiest 1** well-ventilated. **2** light-hearted and casual. **airily** *adv*.

aisle ❶ [rhymes with **mile**] *n* passageway separating seating areas in a church, theatre, etc., or row of shelves in a supermarket.

ajar *adj*, *adv* (of a door) partly open.

AK Alaska.

akimbo *adv* **with arms akimbo** with hands on hips and elbows outwards.

akin *adj* **akin to** similar, related.

Al *Chemistry* aluminium.

AL Alabama.

à la *prep* in the manner of.

alabaster *n* soft white translucent stone.

à la carte *adj*, *adv* (of a menu) having dishes individually priced.

alacrity ❶ *n* speed, eagerness.

--- THESAURUS ---

aimless *adj* = **purposeless**, directionless, pointless, random, stray

air *n* **1, 2** = **atmosphere**, heavens, sky **3** = **wind**, breeze, draught, zephyr **4** = **manner**, appearance, atmosphere, aura, demeanour, impression, look, mood **5** = **tune**, aria, lay, melody, song ▷ *pl* **6** = **affectation**, arrogance, haughtiness, hauteur, pomposity, pretensions, superciliousness, swank (*inf*) ▷ *v* **7** = **publicize**, circulate, display, exhibit, express, give vent to, make known, make public, reveal, voice **8** = **ventilate**, aerate, expose, freshen

airborne *adj* = **flying**, floating, gliding, hovering, in flight, in the air, on the wing

airing *n* **1** = **ventilation**, aeration, drying, freshening **2** = **exposure**, circulation, display, dissemination, expression, publicity, utterance, vent

airy *adj* **1** = **well-ventilated**, fresh, light, open, spacious, uncluttered **2** = **light-hearted**, blithe, cheerful, high-spirited, jaunty, lively, sprightly

aisle *n* = **passageway**, alley, corridor, gangway, lane, passage, path

alacrity *n* = **eagerness**, alertness, enthusiasm, promptness, quickness, readiness, speed, willingness, zeal

à la mode *adj* fashionable.

alarm ❶ *n* **1** sudden fear caused by awareness of danger. **2** warning sound. **3** device that gives this. **4** alarm clock. ▷ *v* **5** fill with fear. **alarming** *adj* **alarmingly** *adv* **alarmist** *n* person who alarms others needlessly. **alarm clock** clock which sounds at a set time to wake someone up.

alas *adv* unfortunately, regrettably.

alb *n* long white robe worn by a Christian priest.

albacore *n* tuna found in warm seas, eaten for food.

albatross *n* large sea bird with very long wings.

albeit *conj* even though.

albino *n*, *pl* **-nos** person or animal with white skin and hair and pink eyes. **albinism** *n*.

Albion *n poetic* **1** Britain. **2** England.

album *n* **1** book with blank pages for keeping photographs or stamps in. **2** long-playing record.

albumen *n* egg white.

albumin, albumen *n* protein found in blood plasma, egg white, milk, and muscle.

alchemy *n* medieval form of chemistry concerned with trying to turn base metals into gold and to find the elixir of life. **alchemist** *n*.

alcohol ❶ *n* **1** colourless flammable liquid present in intoxicating drinks. **2** intoxicating drinks generally. **alcoholic** *adj* **1** of alcohol. ▷ *n* **2** person addicted to alcohol. **alcoholism** *n* addiction to alcohol.

alcopop *n informal* alcoholic drink that tastes like a soft drink.

alcove ❶ *n* recess in the wall of a room.

aldehyde *n* one of a group of chemical compounds derived from alcohol by oxidation.

alder *n* tree related to the birch.

alderman *n* formerly, senior member of a local council.

ale *n* kind of beer.

alembic *n* anything that distils or purifies, esp. an obsolete vessel used for distillation.

alert ❶ *adj* **1** watchful, attentive. ▷ *n* **2** warning of danger. ▷ *v* **3** warn of danger. **4** make (someone) aware of (a fact). **on the alert** watchful. **alertness** *n*.

A level *n* (pass in a subject at) the advanced level of the GCE.

alfalfa *n* kind of plant used to feed livestock.

alfresco *adv*, *adj* in the open air.

algae [al-jee] *pl n* plants which live in or near water and have no true stems, leaves, or roots.

algebra *n* branch of mathematics using symbols to represent numbers. **algebraic** *adj*.

ALGOL *n Computers* computer programming language designed for mathematical and scientific purposes.

Algonquin, Algonkin *n* a member of a North American Indian people formerly living along the Lawrence and Ottawa Rivers in Canada.

algorithm *n* logical arithmetical or computational procedure for solving a problem.

alias ❶ *adv* **1** also known as, e.g. *William Bonney, alias Billy the Kid*. ▷ *n* **2** false name.

alibi ❶ *n* **1** plea of being somewhere else when a crime was committed.

THESAURUS

alarm *n* **1** = **fear**, anxiety, apprehension, consternation, fright, nervousness, panic, scare, trepidation **2, 3** = **danger signal**, alarm bell, alert, bell, distress signal, hooter, siren, warning ▷ *v* **5** = **frighten**, daunt, dismay, distress, give (someone) a turn (*inf*), panic, scare, startle, unnerve

alarming *adj* = **frightening**, daunting, distressing, disturbing, scaring, shocking, startling, unnerving

alcoholic *adj* **1** = **intoxicating**, brewed, distilled, fermented, hard, strong ▷ *n* **2** = **drunkard**, dipsomaniac, drinker, drunk, inebriate, tippler, toper, wino (*inf*)

alcove *n* = **recess**, bay, compartment, corner, cubbyhole, cubicle, niche, nook

alert *adj* **1** = **watchful**, attentive, awake, circumspect, heedful, observant, on guard, on one's toes, on the lookout, vigilant, wide-awake ▷ *n* **2** = **warning**, alarm, signal, siren ▷ *v* **3** = **warn**, alarm, forewarn, signal **4** = **inform**, notify

alertness *n* **1** = **watchfulness**, attentiveness, heedfulness, liveliness, vigilance

alias *adv* **1** = **also known as**, also called, otherwise, otherwise known as ▷ *n* **2** = **pseudonym**, assumed name, nom de guerre, nom de plume, pen name, stage name

alibi *n* **2** *Inf* = **excuse**, defence,

2 *informal* excuse; justification.
Alice band *n* band worn across the head to hold the hair back from the face.
alien ⊙ *adj* **1** foreign. **2** repugnant (to). **3** from another world. ▷ *n* **4** foreigner. **5** being from another world. **alienable** *adj Law* able to be transferred to another owner. **alienate** *v* cause to become hostile. **alienation** *n*.
alight¹ ⊙ *v* **1** step out of (a vehicle). **2** land.
alight² ⊙ *adj* **1** on fire. **2** lit up.
align ⊙ [a-**line**] *v* **1** bring (a person or group) into agreement with the policy of another. **2** place in a line. **alignment** *n*.
alike ⊙ *adj* **1** like, similar. ▷ *adv* **2** in the same way.
alimentary *adj* of nutrition. **alimentary canal** food passage in the body.
alimony *n* allowance paid under a court order to a separated or divorced spouse.
A-line *adj* (of a skirt) slightly flared.
aliped [**al**-lee-ped] *n* animal, like the bat, whose toes are joined by membrane that serves as wing.
aliphatic *adj* (of an organic compound) having an open chain structure.

aliquot *Maths* ▷ *adj* **1** of or denoting an exact divisor of a number. ▷ *n* **2** exact divisor.
alive ⊙ *adj* **1** living, in existence. **2** lively. **alive to** aware of. **alive with** swarming with.
alkali [**alk**-a-lie] *n* substance which combines with acid and neutralizes it to form a salt. **alkaline** *adj* **alkalinity** *n* **alkaloid** *n* any of a group of organic compounds containing nitrogen.
all ⊙ *adj* **1** whole quantity or number (of). ▷ *adv* **2** wholly, entirely. **3** (in the score of games) each. **give one's all** make the greatest possible effort. **all in** *adj* **1** exhausted. **2** (of wrestling) with no style forbidden. ▷ *adv* **3** with all expenses included. **all-clear** *n* signal indicating that danger is over. **all right** *adj* **1** adequate, satisfactory. **2** unharmed. ▷ *interj* **3** expression of approval or agreement. **all-rounder** *n* person with ability in many fields.
Allah *n* name of God in Islam.
allay *v* reduce (fear or anger).
allege ⊙ *v* state without proof. **alleged** *adj* **allegedly** [al-**lej**-id-lee] *adv* **allegation** *n* unproved accusation.
allegiance ⊙ *n* loyalty to a person,

—————————————— **THESAURUS** ——————————————

explanation, justification, plea, pretext, reason
alien *adj* **1** = **strange**, exotic, foreign, unfamiliar ▷ *n* **4** = **foreigner**, newcomer, outsider, stranger
alienate *v* = **set against**, disaffect, estrange, make unfriendly, turn away
alienation *n* = **setting against**, disaffection, estrangement, remoteness, separation, turning away
alight¹ *v* **1** = **get off**, descend, disembark, dismount, get down **2** = **land**, come down, come to rest, descend, light, perch, settle, touch down
alight² *adj* **1** = **on fire**, ablaze, aflame, blazing, burning, fiery, flaming, lighted, lit **2** = **lit up**, bright, brilliant, illuminated, shining
align *v* **1** = **ally**, affiliate, agree, associate, cooperate, join, side, sympathize **2** = **line up**, even up, order, range, regulate, straighten
alignment *n* **1** = **alliance**, affiliation, agreement, association, cooperation, sympathy, union **2** = **lining up**, adjustment, arrangement, evening up, order, straightening up

alike *adj* **1** = **similar**, akin, analogous, corresponding, identical, of a piece, parallel, resembling, the same ▷ *adv* **2** = **similarly**, analogously, correspondingly, equally, evenly, identically, uniformly
alive *adj* **1** = **living**, animate, breathing, existing, extant, in existence, in the land of the living (*inf*), subsisting **2** = **lively**, active, alert, animated, energetic, full of life, vital, vivacious
all *adj* **1** = **entire**, complete, each, each and every, every, every bit of, every one of, every single, full, the whole of, total ▷ *adv* **2** = **completely**, altogether, entirely, fully, totally, utterly, wholly
allegation *n* = **claim**, accusation, affirmation, assertion, charge, declaration, statement
allege *v* = **claim**, affirm, assert, charge, declare, maintain, state
alleged *adj* = **stated**, affirmed, asserted, declared, described, designated, ostensible, professed, purported, so-called, supposed, unproved
allegiance *n* = **loyalty**, constancy, devotion, faithfulness, fidelity, obedience

country, or cause.

allegory ❶ *n, pl* **-ries** story with an underlying meaning as well as the literal one. **allegorical** *adj*.

allegretto *n, pl* **-tos** *adv Music* (piece to be played) fairly quickly or briskly.

allegro *n, pl* **-gros** *adv Music* (piece to be played) in a brisk lively manner.

alleluia *interj* same as HALLELUJAH.

allergy ❶ *n, pl* **-gies** extreme sensitivity to a substance, which causes the body to react to it. **allergic** *adj* having or caused by an allergy. **allergic to** having a strong dislike of, e.g. *allergic to work*. **allergen** [al-ler-jen] *n* substance capable of causing an allergic reaction.

alleviate ❶ *v* lessen (pain or suffering). **alleviation** *n*.

alley ❶ *n* **1** narrow street or path. **2** long narrow enclosure in which tenpin bowling or skittles is played.

alliance ❶ *n* **1** state of being allied. **2** formal relationship between countries or groups for a shared purpose.

alligator *n* reptile of the crocodile family, found in the southern US and China.

alliteration *n* use of the same sound at the start of words occurring together. **alliterative** *adj*.

allocate ❶ *v* assign to someone or for a particular purpose. **allocation** *n*.

allopathy [al-**lop**-ath-ee] *n* orthodox method of treating disease, by using drugs that produce an effect opposite to the effect of the disease being treated, as contrasted with homeopathy. **allopathic** *adj*.

allot ❶ *v* **-lotting**, **-lotted** assign as a share or for a particular purpose. **allotment** *n* **1** distribution. **2** portion allotted. **3** small piece of public land rented to grow vegetables on.

allotrope *n* any of two or more physical forms in which an element can exist. **allotropic** *adj* **allotropy** *n*.

allow ❶ *v* **1** permit. **2** set aside. **3** acknowledge (a point or claim). **allow for** *v* take into account. **allowable** *adj* **allowance** *n* **1** amount of money given at regular intervals. **2** amount permitted. **make allowances for 1** treat or judge (someone) less severely because he or she has special problems. **2** take into account.

alloy ❶ *n* **1** mixture of two or more metals. ▷ *v* **2** mix (metals).

allegorical *adj* = **symbolic**, emblematic, figurative, symbolizing

allegory *n* = **symbol**, fable, myth, parable, story, symbolism, tale

allergic *adj* = **sensitive**, affected by, hypersensitive, susceptible

allergy *n* = **sensitivity**, antipathy, hypersensitivity, susceptibility

alleviate *v* = **ease**, allay, lessen, lighten, moderate, reduce, relieve, soothe

alley *n* **1** = **passage**, alleyway, backstreet, lane, passageway, pathway, walk

alliance *n* **1** = **connection**, affiliation, agreement, association, combination, marriage, partnership **2** = **union**, coalition, confederation, federation, league, pact, treaty

allied *adj* = **united**, affiliated, associated, combined, connected, in league, linked, related

allocate *v* = **assign**, allot, allow, apportion, budget, designate, earmark, mete, set aside, share out

allocation *n* = **assignment**, allotment, allowance, lot, portion, quota, ration, share

allot *v* = **assign**, allocate, apportion, budget, designate, earmark, mete, set aside, share out

allotment *n* **2** = **share**, allocation, allowance, grant, portion, quota, ration, stint **3** = **plot**, kitchen garden, patch, tract

allow *v* **1** = **permit**, approve, authorize, enable, endure, let, sanction, stand, suffer, tolerate **2** = **set aside**, allocate, allot, assign, give, grant, provide, spare **3** = **acknowledge**, admit, concede, confess, grant, own

allowable *adj* **1** = **permissible**, acceptable, admissible, all right, appropriate, suitable, tolerable

allowance *n* **2** = **portion**, allocation, amount, grant, lot, quota, ration, share, stint

allow for *v* = **take into account**, consider, make allowances for, make concessions for, make provision for, plan for, provide for, take into consideration

alloy *n* **1** = **mixture**, admixture, amalgam, blend, combination, composite, compound, hybrid ▷ *v* **2** = **mix**, amalgamate, blend, combine, compound, fuse

allspice n spice made from the berries of a tropical American tree.

allude ❶ v (foll. by *to*) refer indirectly to. **allusion** n indirect reference. **allusive** adj.

- **USAGE NOTE**
- *Allude* is followed by *to*. Be careful
- not to confuse this word with *elude*
- meaning 'escape'. Also be careful
- not to confuse *allusion* with *illusion*
- meaning 'fallacy' or 'fantasy'.

allure ❶ n 1 attractiveness. ▷ v 2 entice or attract. **alluring** adj.

alluvium n fertile soil deposited by flowing water. **alluvial** adj.

ally ❶ n, pl **-lies 1** country, person, or group with an agreement to support another. ▷ v **-lying, -lied 2 ally oneself with** join as an ally. **allied** adj.

alma mater n school, university, or college that one attended.

almanac n yearly calendar with detailed information on anniversaries, phases of the moon, etc.

almighty ❶ adj 1 having absolute power. 2 *informal* very great. ▷ n 3 **the Almighty** God.

almond n edible oval-shaped nut which grows on a small tree.

almoner n formerly, a hospital social worker.

almost ❶ adv very nearly.

alms [ahmz] pl n *old-fashioned* charitable donations to the poor.

aloe n 1 plant with fleshy spiny leaves. ▷ pl 2 bitter drug made from aloe leaves. **aloe vera** plant producing a juice used for skin and hair care.

aloft adv 1 in the air. 2 in a ship's rigging.

alone ❶ adj, adv without anyone or anything else.

along prep 1 over part or all the length of. ▷ adv 2 forward. 3 in company with others, e.g. *come along for the ride*. **alongside** prep, adv beside (something).

aloof ❶ adj distant or haughty in manner. **aloofness** n.

alopecia [al-loh-**pee**-sha] n loss of hair.

aloud ❶ adv in an audible voice.

alp n high mountain. **the Alps** high mountain range in S central Europe.

alpaca n 1 Peruvian llama. 2 wool or cloth made from its hair.

alpenstock n iron-tipped stick used by climbers.

alpha n 1 first letter in the Greek alphabet. 2 highest grade in an examination. **alpha and omega** the first and last. **alpha particle** positively charged particle emitted during some radioactive transformations. **alpha ray** stream of alpha particles.

alphabet n set of letters used in writing a language. **alphabetical** adj in the conventional order of the letters of an alphabet. **alphabetically** adv

---

THESAURUS

all right adj **a** = **satisfactory**, acceptable, adequate, average, fair, O.K. or okay (*inf*), standard, up to scratch (*inf*) **b** = **well**, healthy, O.K. or okay (*inf*), safe, sound, unharmed, uninjured, whole

allude v (foll. by *to*) = **refer**, hint, imply, intimate, mention, suggest, touch upon

allure n **1** = **attractiveness**, appeal, attraction, charm, enchantment, enticement, glamour, lure, persuasion, seductiveness, temptation ▷ v **2** = **attract**, captivate, charm, enchant, entice, lure, persuade, seduce, tempt, win over

alluring adj = **attractive**, beguiling, captivating, come-hither, fetching, glamorous, seductive, tempting

allusion n = **reference**, casual remark, hint, implication, innuendo, insinuation, intimation, mention, suggestion

ally n **1** = **partner**, accomplice, associate, cobber (*Aust or old-fashioned NZ inf*), collaborator, colleague, friend, helper ▷ v **2 ally oneself with** = **unite with**, associate with, collaborate with, combine with, join forces with, join with

almighty adj **1** = **all-powerful**, absolute, invincible, omnipotent, supreme, unlimited **2** *Inf* = **great**, enormous, excessive, intense, loud, severe, terrible

almost adv = **nearly**, about, approximately, close to, just about, not quite, on the brink of, practically, virtually

alone adj = **by oneself**, apart, detached, isolated, lonely, lonesome (*chiefly US & Canad*), only, on one's tod (*sl*), separate, single, solitary, unaccompanied

aloof adj = **distant**, detached, haughty, remote, standoffish, supercilious, unapproachable, unfriendly

aloud adv = **out loud**, audibly, clearly, distinctly, intelligibly, plainly

alphabetize v put in alphabetical order. **alphabetization** n.

alphanumeric adj consisting of alphabetical and numerical symbols.

alpine adj **1** of high mountains. **2** (**A-**) of the Alps. ▷ n **3** mountain plant.

already ❶ adv **1** before the present time. **2** sooner than expected.

alright adj, interj all right

● **USAGE NOTE**
● The form *alright*, though very
● common, is still considered by many
● people to be wrong or less acceptable
● than *all right*.

Alsatian n large wolflike dog.

also ❶ adv in addition, too. **also-ran** n loser in a race, competition, or election.

alt. combining form informal alternative, e.g. *alt. rock*.

altar n **1** table used for Communion in Christian churches. **2** raised structure on which sacrifices are offered and religious rites are performed. **altarpiece** n work of art above and behind the altar in some Christian churches.

alter ❶ v make or become different. **alteration** n.

altercation n heated argument.

alter ego n **1** second self. **2** very close friend.

alternate ❶ v **1** (cause to) occur by turns. ▷ adj **2** occurring by turns. **3** every second (one) of a series, e.g. *alternate Fridays*. **alternately** adv **alternation** n **alternator** n electric

generator for producing alternating current. **alternating current** electric current that reverses direction at frequent regular intervals.

alternative ❶ n **1** one of two choices. ▷ adj **2** able to be done or used instead of something else. **3** (of medicine, lifestyle, etc.) not conventional. **alternatively** adv **alternative energy** form of energy derived from a natural source, such as the sun, wind, tides, or waves.

although ❶ conj despite the fact that.

altimeter [al-**tim**-it-er] n instrument that measures altitude.

altitude n height above sea level.

alto n, pl **-tos** Music **1** short for CONTRALTO. **2** (singer with) the highest adult male voice. **3** instrument with the second-highest pitch in its group.

altogether ❶ adv **1** entirely. **2** on the whole. **3** in total.

altruism ❶ n unselfish concern for the welfare of others. **altruist** n **altruistic** adj **altruistically** adv.

alum n double sulphate of aluminium and potassium.

aluminium n Chemistry light silvery-white metal that does not rust.

alumnus [al-**lumm**-nuss] n, pl **-ni** [-nie]Chiefly US graduate of a college. **alumna** [al-**lumm**-na] n fem, pl **-nae** [-nee].

always ❶ adv **1** at all times. **2** for ever. **3** in any case, e.g. *you could always work abroad*.

THESAURUS

---

already adv **1** = **before now**, at present, before, by now, by then, even now, heretofore, just now, previously

also adv = **too**, additionally, and, as well, besides, further, furthermore, in addition, into the bargain, moreover, to boot

alter v = **change**, adapt, adjust, amend, convert, modify, reform, revise, transform, turn, vary

alteration n = **change**, adaptation, adjustment, amendment, conversion, difference, modification, reformation, revision, transformation, variation

alternate v **1** = **change**, act reciprocally, fluctuate, interchange, oscillate, rotate, substitute, take turns ▷ adj **3** = **every other**, alternating, every second

alternative n **1** = **choice**, option, other (of two), preference, recourse, selection, substitute ▷ adj **2** = **different**,

alternate, another, other, second, substitute

alternatively adv = **or**, as an alternative, if not, instead, on the other hand, otherwise

although conj = **though**, albeit, despite the fact that, even if, even though, notwithstanding, while

altogether adv **1** = **completely**, absolutely, fully, perfectly, quite, thoroughly, totally, utterly, wholly **2** = **on the whole**, all in all, all things considered, as a whole, collectively, generally, in general **3** = **in total**, all told, everything included, in all, in sum, taken together

altruistic adj = **selfless**, benevolent, charitable, generous, humanitarian, philanthropic, public-spirited, self-sacrificing, unselfish

always adv **1** = **continually**, consistently, constantly, every time,

alyssum n garden plant with small yellow or white flowers.

am v see BE.

Am Chemistry americium.

AM 1 amplitude modulation. **2** (in Britain) Member of the National Assembly for Wales.

Am. America(n).

a.m. ante meridiem: before noon.

amalgam n **1** blend or combination. **2** alloy of mercury and another metal.

amalgamate ❶ v combine or unite. **amalgamation** n.

amanuensis [am-man-yew-**en**-siss] n, pl **-ses** [-seez] person who writes from dictation.

amaranth n **1** imaginary flower that never fades. **2** lily-like plant with red, green, or purple flowers.

amaryllis n lily-like plant with large red, pink, or white flowers.

amass ❶ v collect or accumulate.

amateur ❶ n **1** person who engages in a sport or activity as a pastime rather than as a profession. ▷ adj **3** not professional. **amateurish** adj lacking skill. **amateurishly** adv **amateurism** n.

amatory adj relating to romantic or sexual love.

amaut, amowt n Canad a hood on an Inuit woman's parka for carrying a child.

amaze ❶ v surprise greatly, astound. **amazing** adj **amazingly** adv **amazement** n.

Amazon n **1** strong and powerful woman. **2** legendary female warrior. **Amazonian** adj.

ambassador ❶ n senior diplomat who represents his or her country in another country. **ambassadorial** adj.

amber n **1** clear yellowish fossil resin. ▷ adj **2** brownish-yellow.

ambergris [**am**-ber-greece] n waxy substance secreted by the sperm whale, used in making perfumes.

ambidextrous adj able to use both hands with equal ease.

ambience, ambiance n atmosphere of a place.

ambient adj surrounding.

ambiguous ❶ adj having more than one possible meaning. **ambiguously** adv **ambiguity** n, pl **-ties**.

ambit n limits or boundary.

ambition ❶ n **1** desire for success. **2** something so desired, goal. **ambitious** adj **ambitiously** adv.

ambivalence ❶ [am-**biv**-a-lenss] n state of feeling two conflicting emotions at the same time. **ambivalent** adj **ambivalently** adv.

—————————— THESAURUS ——————————

invariably, perpetually, repeatedly, twenty-four-seven (inf), without exception **2 = forever**, eternally, evermore

amalgamate v **= combine**, ally, blend, fuse, incorporate, integrate, merge, mingle, unite

amalgamation n **= combination**, blend, coalition, compound, fusion, joining, merger, mixture, union

amass v **= collect**, accumulate, assemble, compile, gather, hoard, pile up

amateur n **1 = nonprofessional**, dabbler, dilettante, layman

amateurish adj **= unprofessional**, amateur, bungling, clumsy, crude, inexpert, unaccomplished

amaze v **= astonish**, alarm, astound, bewilder, dumbfound, shock, stagger, startle, stun, surprise

amazement n **= astonishment**, admiration, bewilderment, confusion, perplexity, shock, surprise, wonder

amazing adj **= astonishing**, astounding, breathtaking, eye-opening, jaw-dropping, overwhelming, staggering, startling, stunning, surprising

ambassador n **= representative**, agent, consul, deputy, diplomat, envoy, legate, minister

ambiguity n **= vagueness**, doubt, dubiousness, equivocation, obscurity, uncertainty

ambiguous adj **= unclear**, dubious, enigmatic, equivocal, inconclusive, indefinite, indeterminate, obscure, vague

ambition n **1 = enterprise**, aspiration, desire, drive, eagerness, longing, striving, yearning, zeal **2 = goal**, aim, aspiration, desire, dream, hope, intent, objective, purpose, wish

ambitious adj **= enterprising**, aspiring, avid, eager, hopeful, intent, purposeful, striving, zealous

ambivalent adj **= undecided**, contradictory, doubtful, equivocal, in two minds, uncertain, unsure, wavering

a

amble ❶ *v* **1** walk at a leisurely pace. ▷ *n* **2** leisurely walk or pace.

ambrosia *n* **1** anything delightful to taste or smell. **2** *Myth* food of the gods. **ambrosial** *adj*.

ambulance *n* motor vehicle designed to carry sick or injured people.

ambulatory *adj* **1** of or relating to walking. **2** able to walk. ▷ *n, pl* **-ries 3** place for walking in, such as a cloister.

ambush ❶ *n* **1** act of waiting in a concealed position to make a surprise attack. **2** attack from a concealed position. ▷ *v* **3** attack from a concealed position.

ameliorate [am-**meal**-yor-rate] *v* make (something) better. **amelioration** *n*.

amen *interj* so be it: used at the end of a prayer.

amenable ❶ [a-**mean**-a-bl] *adj* likely or willing to cooperate.

amend ❶ *v* make small changes to correct or improve (something). **amendment** *n*.

amends ❶ *pl n* **make amends for** compensate for.

amenity ❶ *n, pl* **-ties** useful or enjoyable feature.

American *adj* **1** of the United States of America or the American continent. ▷ *n* **2** person from America or the American continent. **Americanism** *n* expression or custom characteristic of Americans. **Americanize** *v* make American in

outlook, form, etc.

americium *n Chemistry* white metallic element artificially produced from plutonium.

amethyst [am-myth-ist] *n* bluish-violet variety of quartz used as a gemstone.

Amharic *n* official language of Ethiopia.

amiable ❶ *adj* friendly, pleasant-natured. **amiably** *adv* **amiability** *n*.

amicable ❶ *adj* friendly. **amicably** *adv* **amicability** *n*.

amid, amidst ❶ *prep* in the middle of, among. **amidships** *adv* at or towards the middle of a ship.

amino acid [am-**mean**-oh] *n* organic compound found in protein.

amiss ❶ *adv* **1** wrongly, badly. ▷ *adj* **2** wrong, faulty. **take something amiss** be offended by something.

amity *n* friendship.

ammeter *n* instrument for measuring electric current.

ammo *n informal* ammunition.

ammonia *n* **1** strong-smelling alkaline gas containing hydrogen and nitrogen. **2** solution of this in water.

ammonite *n* fossilized spiral shell of an extinct sea creature.

ammunition ❶ *n* **1** bullets, bombs, and shells that can be fired from or as a weapon. **2** facts that can be used in an argument.

amnesia *n* loss of memory. **amnesiac** *adj, n*.

THESAURUS

---

amble *v* **1** = **stroll**, dawdle, meander, mosey (*inf*), ramble, saunter, walk, wander

ambush *n* **1** = **trap**, lying in wait, waylaying ▷ *v* **3** = **trap**, attack, bushwhack (*US*), ensnare, surprise, waylay

amenable *adj* = **receptive**, able to be influenced, acquiescent, agreeable, compliant, open, persuadable, responsive, susceptible

amend *v* = **change**, alter, correct, fix, improve, mend, modify, reform, remedy, revise

amendment *n* = **change**, addendum, addition, alteration, correction, emendation, improvement, modification, reform, remedy, repair, revision

amends *pl n* **make amends for** = **compensate for**, atone for, give satisfaction for, make reparation for,

make restitution for, recompense, redress

amenity *n* = **facility**, advantage, comfort, convenience, service

amiable *adj* = **pleasant**, affable, agreeable, charming, congenial, engaging, friendly, genial, likable *or* likeable, lovable

amicable *adj* = **friendly**, amiable, civil, cordial, courteous, harmonious, neighbourly, peaceful, sociable

amid, amidst *prep* = **in the middle of**, among, amongst, in the midst of, in the thick of, surrounded by

amiss *adv* **1** = **wrongly**, erroneously, improperly, inappropriately, incorrectly, mistakenly, unsuitably ▷ *adj* **2** = **wrong**, awry, faulty, incorrect, mistaken, untoward

ammunition *n* **1** = **munitions**, armaments, explosives, powder, rounds, shells, shot

a

amnesty ❶ *n, pl* **-ties** general pardon for offences against a government.

amniocentesis *n, pl* **-ses** removal of some amniotic fluid to test for possible abnormalities in a fetus.

amniotic fluid *n* fluid surrounding a fetus in the womb.

amoeba [am-**mee**-ba] *n, pl* **-bae** [-bee] **-bas** microscopic single-celled animal able to change its shape.

amok ❶ *adv* **run amok** run about in a violent frenzy.

among, amongst ❶ *prep* **1** in the midst of. **2** in the group or number of. **3** to each of, e.g. *divide it among yourselves*.

amoral [aim-**mor**-ral] *adj* without moral standards. **amorality** *n*.

● **USAGE NOTE**
● *Amoral* is often wrongly used where
● *immoral* is meant. You would use
● *amoral* to talk about people who
● have no moral standards, or about
● a place or situation where moral
● rules do not apply, as in *a violent and*
● *amoral criminal* or *the amoral world of*
● *big business*, while *immoral* should
● be used to talk about the breaking
● of rules, as in *criminal or immoral*
● *activities*.

amorous ❶ *adj* feeling, showing, or relating to sexual love or desire. **amorously** *adv*.

amorphous *adj* **1** without distinct shape. **2** of no recognizable character or type.

amortize *v* pay off (a debt) gradually by periodic transfers to a sinking fund.

amount ❶ *n* **1** extent or quantity. ▷ *v* **2** (foll. by *to*) be equal or add up to.

amour *n* (secret) love affair.

amour-propre [am-**moor-prop**-ra] *n* French self-respect.

amp *n* **1** ampere. **2** *informal* amplifier.

amperage *n* strength of an electric current measured in amperes.

ampere [am-pair] *n* basic unit of electric current.

ampersand *n* the character (&), meaning *and*.

● **USAGE NOTE**
● It is best to avoid using an *ampersand*
● (&) to replace the word *and* in formal
● writing.

amphetamine [am-**fet**-am-mean] *n* drug used as a stimulant.

amphibian *n* **1** animal that lives on land but breeds in water. **2** vehicle that can travel on both land and water.

amphibious *adj* **1** living or operating both on land and in water. **2** relating to a military attack launched from the sea against a shore.

amphitheatre *n* open oval or circular building with tiers of seats rising round an arena.

amphora [am-for-ra] *n, pl* **-phorae** [-for-ree] ancient Greek or Roman jar with two handles and a narrow neck.

ample ❶ *adj* **1** more than sufficient, e.g. *there is already ample evidence*. **2** large, e.g. *ample helpings of stewed pears and pomegranates*. **amply** *adv*.

amplify ❶ *v* **-fying, -fied 1** increase the strength of (a current or sound signal). **2** explain in more detail. **3** increase the size or effect of. **amplification** *n* **amplifier** *n* device used to amplify a current or sound signal.

amplitude *n* greatness of extent.

————— **THESAURUS** —————

amnesty *n* = **general pardon**, absolution, dispensation, forgiveness, immunity, remission (*of penalty*), reprieve

amok *adv* **run amok** = **madly**, berserk, destructively, ferociously, in a frenzy, murderously, savagely, uncontrollably, violently, wildly

among, amongst *prep* **1** = **in the midst of**, amid, amidst, in the middle of, in the thick of, surrounded by, together with, with **2** = **in the group of**, in the class of, in the company of, in the number of, out of **3** = **to each of**, between

amorous *adj* = **loving**, erotic, impassioned, in love, lustful,

passionate, tender

amount *n* **1** = **quantity**, expanse, extent, magnitude, mass, measure, number, supply, volume ▷ *v* **2** (foll. by *to*) = **add up to**, become, come to, develop into, equal, mean, total

ample *adj* **1** = **plenty**, abundant, bountiful, copious, expansive, extensive, full, generous, lavish, plentiful, profuse

amplify *v* **2** = **go into detail**, develop, elaborate, enlarge, expand, explain, flesh out **3** = **expand**, enlarge, extend, heighten, increase, intensify, magnify, strengthen, widen

amply *adv* **1** = **fully**, abundantly, completely, copiously, generously,

a

ampoule *n* small sealed glass vessel containing liquid for injection.

amputate ❶ *v* cut off (a limb or part of a limb) for medical reasons. **amputation** *n* **amputee** *n* person who has had a limb amputated.

amuck ❶ *adv* same as AMOK.

amulet *n* something carried or worn as a protection against evil.

amuse ❶ *v* **1** cause to laugh or smile. **2** entertain or divert. **amusing** *adj* **amusingly** *adv* **amusement** *n* **1** state of being amused. **2** something that amuses.

amylase *n* enzyme, present in saliva, that helps to change starch into sugar.

an *adj* form of **a** used before vowels, and sometimes before *h*, e.g. *an hour*.

- ● **USAGE NOTE**
- ● This form of the indefinite article is
- ● also used with abbreviations which
- ● have a vowel sound when read aloud:
- ● *an MA*. It is
- ● old-fashioned to use *an* before words
- ● like *hotel* or *historic*.

anabolic steroid *n* synthetic steroid hormone used to stimulate muscle and bone growth.

anabolism *n Biology* metabolic process in which body tissues are synthesized from food.

anachronism [an-**nak**-kron-iz-zum] *n* person or thing placed in the wrong historical period or seeming to belong to another time. **anachronistic** *adj*.

anaconda *n* large S American snake which kills by constriction.

anaemia ❶ [an-**neem**-ee-a] *n* deficiency in the number of red blood cells. **anaemic** *adj* **1** having anaemia. **2** pale

and sickly. **3** lacking vitality.

anaerobic *adj Biology* not requiring oxygen.

anaesthetic ❶ [an-niss-**thet**-ik] *n, adj* (substance) causing loss of bodily feeling. **anaesthesia** [an-niss-**theez**-ee-a] *n* loss of bodily feeling. **anaesthetist** [an-**neess**-thet-ist] *n* doctor trained to administer anaesthetics. **anaesthetize** *v*.

Anaglypta *n* ® thick embossed wallpaper, designed to be painted.

anagram *n* word or phrase made by rearranging the letters of another word or phrase.

anal [**ain**-al] *adj* of the anus.

analgesic [an-nal-**jeez**-ik] *n, adj* (drug) relieving pain. **analgesia** *n* absence of pain.

analogous *adj* similar in some respects.

analogue *n* **1** something that is similar in some respects to something else. ▷ *adj* **2** displaying information by means of a dial, e.g. *analogue speedometers*.

analogy ❶ *n, pl* **-gies 1** similarity in some respects. **2** comparison made to show such a similarity. **analogical** *adj* **analogize** *v* **1** use analogy. **2** show analogy between.

analysis ❶ [an-**nal**-liss-iss] *n, pl* **-ses** [-seez] **1** separation of a whole into its parts for study and interpretation. **2** psychoanalysis. **analyse** [**an**-nal-lize] *v* **1** make an analysis of (something). **2** psychoanalyse. **analyst** *n* **1** person skilled in analysis. **2** psychoanalyst. **analytical**, **analytic** *adj* **analytically** *adv*.

——————————————————————— THESAURUS ———————

profusely, richly

amputate *v* = **cut off**, curtail, lop, remove, separate, sever, truncate

amuck same as AMOK.

amuse *v* **2** = **entertain**, charm, cheer, delight, interest, please

amusement *n* **1** = **entertainment**, cheer, enjoyment, fun, merriment, mirth, pleasure **2** = **pastime**, diversion, entertainment, game, hobby, joke, recreation, sport

amusing *adj* **1** = **funny**, comical, droll, humorous, witty **2** = **entertaining**, enjoyable, interesting

anaemic *adj* **2** = **pale**, ashen, colourless, pallid, wan **3** = **feeble**, sickly, weak

anaesthetic *n* = **painkiller**, analgesic,

anodyne, narcotic, opiate, sedative, soporific ▷ *adj* = **pain-killing**, analgesic, anodyne, deadening, dulling, numbing, sedative, soporific

analogy *n* **1** = **similarity**, correlation, correspondence, likeness, parallel, relation, resemblance **2** = **comparison**

analyse *v* **1** = **examine**, evaluate, investigate, research, test, think through, work over

analysis *n* **1** = **examination**, breakdown, dissection, inquiry, investigation, scrutiny, sifting, test

analytical, analytic *adj* **1** = **rational**, inquiring, inquisitive, investigative, logical, organized, problem-solving, systematic

anarchism ❶ n doctrine advocating the abolition of government. **anarchist** n **anarchistic** adj.

anarchy ❶ [an-ark-ee] n 1 lawlessness and disorder. 2 lack of government in a state. **anarchic** adj.

anastigmat n lens corrected for astigmatism. **anastigmatic** adj (of lens) not astigmatic.

anathema [an-**nath**-im-a] n detested person or thing. **anathematize** v curse (a person or thing).

anatomy ❶ n, pl -**mies** 1 science of the structure of the body. 2 physical structure. 3 person's body, e.g. a delicate part of his anatomy. 4 detailed analysis. **anatomical** adj **anatomically** adv **anatomist** n expert in anatomy.

ancestor ❶ n 1 person from whom one is descended. 2 forerunner. **ancestral** adj **ancestry** n lineage or descent.

anchor n 1 heavy hooked device attached to a boat by a cable and dropped overboard to fasten the ship to the sea bottom. 2 source of stability or security. ▷ v 3 fasten with or as if with an anchor. **anchorage** n place where boats can be anchored. **anchorman**, **anchorwoman** n 1 broadcaster in a central studio who links up and presents items from outside camera units and other studios. 2 last person to compete in a relay team.

anchorite n religious recluse.

anchovy [an-chov-ee] n, pl -**vies** small strong-tasting fish.

ancien régime [on-syan ray-**zheem**] n French a former system, esp. the political and social system in France before the 1789 Revolution.

ancient ❶ adj 1 dating from very long ago. 2 very old. **ancients** pl n people who lived very long ago.

ancillary ❶ adj 1 supporting the main work of an organization. 2 used as an extra or supplement.

and ❶ conj 1 in addition to. 2 as a consequence. 3 then, afterwards. **and/or** conj either or both.

andante [an-**dan**-tay] n, adv Music (piece to be played) moderately slowly.

andantino [an-dan-**tee**-no] n, pl -**nos** adv Music (piece to be played) slightly faster or slower than andante.

andiron n iron stand for supporting logs in a fireplace.

androgynous adj having both male and female characteristics.

android n robot resembling a human.

anecdote ❶ n short amusing account of an incident. **anecdotal** adj.

anemometer n instrument for recording wind speed.

anemone [an-**nem**-on-ee] n plant with white, purple, or red flowers.

aneroid barometer n device for measuring air pressure, consisting of a partially evacuated chamber in which variations in pressure cause a pointer on the lid to move.

aneurysm, aneurism [an-new-rizzum] n permanent swelling of a blood vessel.

anew adv 1 once more. 2 in a different way.

angel ❶ n 1 spiritual being believed to be an attendant or messenger of God. 2 person who is kind, pure, or beautiful. **angelic** adj **angelically** adv.

THESAURUS

anarchic adj = **lawless**, chaotic, disorganized, rebellious, riotous, ungoverned

anarchist n = **revolutionary**, insurgent, nihilist, rebel, terrorist

anarchy n = **lawlessness**, chaos, confusion, disorder, disorganization, revolution, riot

anatomy n 2 = **structure**, build, composition, frame, framework, make-up 4 = **examination**, analysis, dissection, division, inquiry, investigation, study

ancestor n = **forefather**, forebear, forerunner, precursor, predecessor

ancient adj = **old**, aged, antique, archaic, old-fashioned, primeval, primordial, timeworn

ancillary adj 1 = **supporting**, auxiliary, secondary, subordinate, subsidiary 2 = **supplementary**, additional, extra

and conj 1 = **also**, along with, as well as, furthermore, in addition to, including, moreover, plus, together with

anecdote n = **story**, reminiscence, short story, sketch, tale, urban legend, urban myth, yarn

angel n 1 = **divine messenger**, archangel, cherub, seraph 2 = **dear**, beauty, darling, gem, jewel, paragon, saint, treasure

angelic adj 1 = **heavenly**, celestial, cherubic, ethereal, seraphic 2 = **pure**, adorable, beautiful, entrancing, lovely,

angelica [an-**jell**-ik-a] n 1 aromatic plant. 2 its candied stalks, used in cookery.

Angelus [**an**-jell-uss] n 1 (in the Roman Catholic Church) prayers recited in the morning, at midday, and in the evening. 2 bell signalling the times of these prayers.

anger ❶ n 1 fierce displeasure or extreme annoyance. ▷ v 2 make (someone) angry.

angina [an-**jine**-a] n heart disorder causing sudden severe chest pains (also **angina pectoris**).

angle¹ ❶ n 1 space between or shape formed by two lines or surfaces that meet. 2 divergence between these, measured in degrees. 3 corner. 4 point of view. ▷ v 5 bend or place (something) at an angle.

angle² ❶ v 1 fish with a hook and line. 2 (foll. by for) try to get by hinting. **angler** n **angling** n.

Anglican n, adj (member) of the Church of England. **Anglicanism** n.

anglicize v make or become English in outlook, form, etc. **Anglicism** n expression or custom characteristic of the English.

Anglo n, pl **-glos** Canad English-speaking Canadian.

Anglo- combining form 1 English, e.g. Anglo-Scottish. 2 British, e.g. Anglo-American.

Anglophile n person who admires England or the English. **Anglophilia** n.

Anglophobe n person who dislikes England or the English. **Anglophobia** n.

Anglo-Saxon n 1 member of any of the W Germanic tribes that settled in England from the fifth century AD. 2 language of the Anglo-Saxons. ▷ adj 3 of the Anglo-Saxons or their language.

angora n 1 variety of goat, cat, or rabbit with long silky hair. 2 hair of the angora goat or rabbit. 3 cloth made from this hair.

Angostura Bitters pl n ® bitter tonic, used as a flavouring in alcoholic drinks.

angry ❶ adj **-grier, -griest** 1 full of anger. 2 inflamed, e.g. an angry wound. **angrily** adv.

angst ❶ n feeling of anxiety.

angstrom n unit of length used to measure wavelengths.

anguish ❶ n great mental pain. **anguished** adj.

angular adj 1 (of a person) lean and bony. 2 having angles. 3 measured by an angle. **angularity** n.

anhydrous adj Chemistry containing no water.

anil n West Indian shrub, from which indigo is obtained.

aniline n colourless oily liquid obtained from coal tar and used for making dyes, plastics, and explosives.

animal ❶ n 1 living creature with specialized sense organs and capable of voluntary motion, esp. one other than a human being. 2 quadruped. ▷ adj 3 of animals. 4 sensual, physical. **animality** n animal instincts of human beings. **animalcule** n microscopic animal.

animate ❶ v 1 give life to. 2 make lively. 3 make a cartoon film of. ▷ adj 4 having life. **animated** adj **animatedly** adv **animation** n 1 technique of making

---

THESAURUS

saintly, virtuous

anger n 1 = **rage**, annoyance, displeasure, exasperation, fury, ire, outrage, resentment, temper, wrath ▷ v 2 = **enrage**, annoy, displease, exasperate, gall, incense, infuriate, madden, outrage, rile, vex

angle¹ n 1 = **intersection**, bend, crook, elbow, nook 3 = **corner**, edge, point 4 = **point of view**, approach, aspect, outlook, perspective, position, side, slant, standpoint, viewpoint

angle² v 1 = **fish**, cast

angry adj 1 = **furious**, annoyed, cross, displeased, enraged, exasperated, incensed, infuriated, irate, mad (inf), outraged, resentful

angst n = **anxiety**, apprehension, unease, worry

anguish n = **suffering**, agony, distress, grief, heartache, misery, pain, sorrow, torment, woe

animal n 2 = **creature**, beast, brute ▷ adj 4 = **physical**, bestial, bodily, brutish, carnal, gross, sensual

animate v 2 = **enliven**, energize, excite, fire, inspire, invigorate, kindle, move, stimulate ▷ adj 4 = **living**, alive, alive and kicking, breathing, live, moving

animated adj 2 = **lively**, ebullient, energetic, enthusiastic, excited, passionate, spirited, vivacious

animation n 2 = **liveliness**, ebullience, energy, enthusiasm, excitement,

cartoon films. **2** liveliness and enthusiasm. **animator** *n*.

animism *n* belief that natural objects possess souls. **animist** *n*, *adj* **animistic** *adj*.

animosity ❶ *n*, *pl* **-ties** hostility, hatred.

animus *n* hatred, animosity.

anion [**an**-eye-on] *n* ion with negative charge.

anise [**an**-niss] *n* plant with liquorice-flavoured seeds.

aniseed *n* liquorice-flavoured seeds of the anise plant.

ankle *n* joint between the foot and leg. **anklet** *n* ornamental chain worn round the ankle.

ankylosis [ang-kill-**loh**-siss] *n* abnormal immobility of a joint, caused by a fibrous growth.

anna *n* former Indian coin worth one sixteenth of rupee.

annals ❶ *pl n* yearly records of events. **annalist** *n*.

anneal *v* toughen (metal or glass) by heating and slow cooling.

annelid *n* worm with a segmented body, such as an earthworm.

annex ❶ *v* **1** seize (territory). **2** take (something) without permission. **3** join or add (something) to something larger. **annexation** *n*.

annexe *n* **1** extension to a building. **2** nearby building used as an extension.

annihilate ❶ *v* destroy utterly. **annihilation** *n*.

anniversary *n*, *pl* **-ries** **1** date on which something occurred in a previous year.

2 celebration of this.

anno Domini *adv Latin* (indicating years numbered from the supposed year of the birth of Christ) in the year of our Lord.

annotate *v* add notes to (a written work). **annotation** *n*.

announce ❶ *v* **1** make known publicly. **2** proclaim. **announcement** *n* **announcer** *n* person who introduces radio or television programmes.

annoy ❶ *v* irritate or displease. **annoyance** *n* **annoying** *adj* **annoyingly** *adv*.

annual ❶ *adj* **1** happening once a year. **2** lasting for a year. ▷ *n* **3** plant that completes its life cycle in a year. **4** book published once every year. **annually** *adv*.

annuity *n*, *pl* **-ties** fixed sum paid every year.

annul ❶ *v* **-nulling**, **-nulled** declare (something, esp. a marriage) invalid. **annulment** *n*.

annular [**an**-new-lar] *adj* ring-shaped.

Annunciation *n Christianity* angel Gabriel's announcement to the Virgin Mary of her conception of Christ.

anode *n Electricity* positive electrode in a battery, valve, etc. **anodize** *v* coat (metal) with a protective oxide film by electrolysis.

anodyne *n* **1** something that relieves pain or distress. ▷ *adj* **2** relieving pain or distress.

anoint ❶ *v* smear with oil as a sign of consecration.

THESAURUS

fervour, passion, spirit, verve, vivacity, zest

animosity *n* = **hostility**, acrimony, antipathy, bitterness, enmity, hatred, ill will, malevolence, malice, rancour, resentment

annals *pl n* = **records**, accounts, archives, chronicles, history

annex *v* **1** = **seize**, acquire, appropriate, conquer, occupy, take over **3** = **join**, add, adjoin, attach, connect, fasten

annihilate *v* = **destroy**, abolish, eradicate, exterminate, extinguish, obliterate, wipe out

announce *v* = **make known**, advertise, broadcast, declare, disclose, proclaim, report, reveal, tell

announcement *n* = **statement**, advertisement, broadcast, bulletin, communiqué, declaration,

proclamation, report, revelation

announcer *n* = **presenter**, broadcaster, commentator, master of ceremonies, newscaster, newsreader, reporter

annoy *v* = **irritate**, anger, bother, displease, disturb, exasperate, get on one's nerves (*inf*), hassle (*inf*), madden, molest, pester, plague, trouble, vex

annoyance *n* = **irritation**, anger, bother, hassle (*inf*), nuisance, trouble

annoying *adj* = **irritating**, disturbing, exasperating, maddening, troublesome

annual *adj* **1** = **yearly**, once a year **2** = **yearlong**

annually *adv* **1** = **yearly**, every year, once a year, per annum, per year

annul *v* = **invalidate**, abolish, cancel, declare *or* render null and void, negate, nullify, repeal, retract

anoint *v* = **consecrate**, anele (*archaic*),

a

anomaly ❶ [an-**nom**-a-lee] *n, pl* **-lies** something that deviates from the normal, irregularity. **anomalous** *adj*.

anomie [**an**-oh-mee] *n Sociology* lack of social or moral standards. **anomic** [an-**nom**-mik] *adj*.

anon *adv obs* in a short time, soon.

anon. anonymous.

anonymous ❶ *adj* **1** by someone whose name is unknown or withheld. **2** having no known name. **anonymously** *adv* **anonymity** *n*.

anorak *n* waterproof hooded jacket.

anorexia *n* psychological disorder characterized by fear of becoming fat and refusal to eat (also **anorexia nervosa**). **anorexic** *adj, n*.

another *adj, pron* **1** one more. **2** a different (one).

answer ❶ *n* **1** reply to a question, request, letter, etc. **2** solution to a problem. **3** reaction or response. ▷ *v* **4** give an answer (to). **5** be responsible to (a person). **6** respond or react. **answerable** *adj* (foll. by *for* or *to*) responsible for or accountable to. **answering machine** device for answering a telephone automatically and recording messages.

ant *n* small insect living in highly organized colonies. **anteater** *n* mammal which feeds on ants by means of a long snout. **ant hill** mound built by ants around their nest.

antacid *n* substance that counteracts acidity, esp. in the stomach.

antagonist ❶ *n* opponent or adversary. **antagonism** *n* open opposition or hostility. **antagonistic** *adj* **antagonize**

v arouse hostility in, annoy.

antalkali [ant-**alk**-a-lie] *n* substance that neutralizes alkalis.

Antarctic *n* **1 the Antarctic** area around the South Pole. ▷ *adj* **2** of this region.

● **SPELLING TIP**
● Almost one in every hundred
● references to the **Antarctic** in the
● Bank of English is written *Antartic*.
● Note there is a *c* after the *r*.

ante *n* **1** player's stake in poker. ▷ *v* **-teing**, **-ted** *or* **-teed 2** place (one's stake) in poker.

ante- *prefix* before in time or position, e.g. *antedate*; *antechamber*.

antecedent *n* **1** event or circumstance happening or existing before another. ▷ *adj* **2** preceding, prior.

antechamber *n* same as ANTEROOM.

antedate *v* precede in time.

antediluvian *adj* **1** of the time before the biblical Flood. **2** old-fashioned.

antelope *n* deerlike mammal with long legs and horns.

antenatal *adj* during pregnancy, before birth.

antenna *n* **1** *pl* **-nae** insect's feeler. **2** *pl* **-nas** aerial.

antepenultimate *adj* third last.

ante-post *adj* (of a bet) placed before the runners in a race are confirmed.

anterior *adj* **1** to the front. **2** earlier.

anteroom *n* small room leading into a larger one, often used as a waiting room.

anthem ❶ *n* **1** song of loyalty, esp. to a country. **2** piece of music for a choir,

───────────────────────────────────── THESAURUS ─────

bless, hallow, sanctify

anomalous *adj* = **unusual**, abnormal, eccentric, exceptional, incongruous, inconsistent, irregular, munted (*NZ sl*), odd, peculiar

anomaly *n* = **irregularity**, abnormality, eccentricity, exception, incongruity, inconsistency, oddity, peculiarity

anonymous *adj* **1** = **uncredited**, unacknowledged, unknown, unsigned **2** = **unnamed**, incognito, nameless, unidentified

answer *n* **1** = **reply**, comeback, defence, rejoinder, response, retort, return, riposte **2** = **solution**, explanation **3** = **reaction**, response ▷ *v* **4** = **reply**, respond, retort, return **6** = **react**, respond

answerable *adj* (foll. by *for* or *to*) = **responsible**, accountable, amenable, chargeable, liable, subject, to blame

antagonism *n* = **hostility**, antipathy, conflict, discord, dissension, friction, opposition, rivalry

antagonist *n* = **opponent**, adversary, competitor, contender, enemy, foe, rival

antagonistic *adj* = **hostile**, at odds, at variance, conflicting, incompatible, in dispute, opposed, unfriendly

antagonize *v* = **annoy**, anger, get on one's nerves (*inf*), hassle (*inf*), irritate, offend

anthem *n* **1** = **song of praise**, paean **2** = **hymn**, canticle, carol, chant, chorale, psalm

usu. set to words from the Bible.

anther *n* part of a flower's stamen containing pollen.

anthology ❶ *n, pl* **-gies** collection of poems or other literary pieces by various authors. **anthologist** *n*.

anthracite *n* hard coal burning slowly with little smoke or flame but intense heat.

anthrax *n* dangerous disease of cattle and sheep, communicable to humans.

anthropocentric *adj* regarding human beings as the most important factor in the universe.

anthropoid *adj* **1** like a human. ▷ *n* **2** ape, such as a chimpanzee, that resembles a human.

anthropology *n* study of human origins, institutions, and beliefs. **anthropological** *adj* **anthropologist** *n*.

anthropomorphic *adj* attributing human form or personality to a god, animal, or object. **anthropomorphism** *n*.

anti *adj, prep informal* opposed (to).

anti- *prefix* **1** against, opposed to, e.g. *anti-war*. **2** opposite to, e.g. *anticlimax*. **3** counteracting, e.g. *antifreeze*.

anti-aircraft *adj* for defence against aircraft attack.

antiballistic missile *n* missile designed to destroy a ballistic missile in flight.

antibiotic *n* **1** chemical substance capable of destroying bacteria. ▷ *adj* **2** of antibiotics.

antibody *n, pl* **-bodies** protein produced in the blood, which destroys bacteria.

Antichrist *n* **1** *New Testament* the antagonist of Christ. **2** any enemy of Christ or Christianity.

anticipate ❶ *v* **1** foresee and act in advance of. **2** look forward to. **3** make use of (something) before receiving it. **anticipation** *n* **anticipatory** *adj*.

anticlimax ❶ *n* disappointing conclusion to a series of events. **anticlimactic** *adj*.

anticlockwise *adv, adj* in the opposite direction to the rotation of the hands of a clock.

antics ❶ *pl n* absurd acts or postures.

anticyclone *n* area of moving air of high pressure in which the winds rotate outwards.

antidote ❶ *n* **1** substance that counteracts a poison. **2** anything that counteracts a harmful condition.

antifreeze *n* liquid added to water to lower its freezing point, used in car radiators.

antigen [an-tee-jen] *n* substance, usu. a toxin, causing the blood to produce antibodies.

antihero *n, pl* **-roes** central character in a book, film, etc., who lacks the traditional heroic virtues.

antihistamine *n* drug used to treat allergies.

antimacassar *n* cloth put over a chairback to prevent soiling.

antimony [an-tim-mon-ee] *n Chemistry* brittle silvery-white metallic element.

antinuclear *adj* opposed to nuclear weapons or nuclear power.

antipasto *n, pl* **-tos** appetizer in an Italian meal.

antipathy ❶ [an-**tip**-a-thee] *n* dislike, hostility. **antipathetic** *adj*.

antiperspirant *n* substance used to reduce or prevent sweating.

antiphon *n* hymn sung in alternate parts by two groups of singers. **antiphonal** *adj*.

antipodes [an-**tip**-pod-deez] *pl n* any two places diametrically opposite one another on the earth's surface. **the Antipodes** Australia and New Zealand. **antipodean** *adj*.

antipyretic *adj* **1** reducing fever. ▷ *n* **2** drug that reduces fever.

antiquary *n, pl* **-quaries** student or collector of antiques or ancient works of art. **antiquarian** *adj* **1** of or relating to antiquities or rare books. ▷ *n*

anthology *n* = **collection**, compendium, compilation, miscellany, selection, treasury

anticipate *v* **1** = **expect**, await, foresee, foretell, predict, prepare for **2** = **look forward to**, hope for

anticipation *n* **1** = **expectation**, expectancy, foresight, forethought, premonition, prescience

anticlimax *n* = **disappointment**, bathos, comedown (*inf*), letdown

antics *pl n* = **clowning**, escapades, horseplay, mischief, playfulness, pranks, tomfoolery, tricks

antidote *n* = **cure**, countermeasure, remedy

antipathy *n* = **hostility**, aversion, bad blood, dislike, enmity, hatred, ill will

2 antiquary. **antiquarianism** n.

antiquated ❶ adj out-of-date.

antique ❶ n **1** object of an earlier period, valued for its beauty, workmanship, or age. ▷ adj **2** made in an earlier period. **3** old-fashioned.

antiquity ❶ n **1** great age. **2** ancient times. **antiquities** pl n objects dating from ancient times.

antiracism n policy of challenging racism and promoting racial tolerance. **antiracist** n, adj.

antirrhinum n two-lipped flower of various colours.

antiscorbutic adj preventing or curing scurvy.

anti-Semitism n discrimination against Jews. **anti-Semite** n person who persecutes or discriminates against Jews. **anti-Semitic** adj.

antiseptic ❶ adj **1** preventing infection by killing germs. ▷ n **2** antiseptic substance.

antisocial ❶ adj **1** avoiding the company of other people. **2** (of behaviour) harmful to society.

antistatic adj reducing the effects of static electricity.

antithesis ❶ [an-**tith**-iss-iss] n, pl **-ses** [-seez] **1** exact opposite. **2** placing together of contrasting ideas or words to produce an effect of balance. **antithetical** adj.

antitoxin n (serum containing) an antibody that acts against a toxin.

antitrades pl n winds blowing in the opposite direction from and above the trade winds.

antitrust adj Aust, S Afr & US (of laws) opposing business monopolies.

antivirus adj protecting computers from viruses.

antler n branched horn of male deer.

antonym n word that means the opposite of another.

anus [**ain**-uss] n opening at the end of the alimentary canal, through which faeces are discharged.

anvil n heavy iron block on which metals are hammered into particular shapes.

anxiety ❶ n, pl **-ties** state of being anxious.

anxious ❶ adj **1** worried and tense. **2** intensely desiring. **anxiety** n **anxiously** adv.

any adj, pron **1** one or some, no matter which. ▷ adv **2** at all, e.g. it isn't any worse. **anybody** pron anyone. **anyhow** adv anyway. **anyone** pron **1** any person. **2** person of any importance. **anything** pron any object, event, or action whatever. **anyway** adv **1** at any rate, nevertheless. **2** in any manner. **anywhere** adv in, at, or to any place.

● **USAGE NOTE**
● It is no longer considered wrong to
● use anyone with a following plural
● form as in Has anyone lost their
● purse?

Anzac n (in World War 1) a soldier serving with the Australian and New Zealand Army Corps.

AOB (on the agenda for a meeting) any other business.

aorta [eh-**or**-ta] n main artery of the body, carrying oxygen-rich blood from the heart.

apace adv lit swiftly.

Apache n, pl **Apaches**, **Apache** Native American of the SW US and N Mexico.

———————————————— THESAURUS ————————————————

antiquated adj = **obsolete**, antique, archaic, dated, old-fashioned, out-of-date, passé

antique n **1** = **period piece**, bygone, heirloom, relic ▷ adj **2** = **vintage**, antiquarian, classic, olden **3** = **old-fashioned**, archaic, obsolete, outdated

antiquity n **1** = **old age**, age, ancientness, elderliness, oldness **2** = **distant past**, ancient times, olden days, time immemorial

antiseptic adj **1** = **hygienic**, clean, germ-free, pure, sanitary, sterile, uncontaminated ▷ n **2** = **disinfectant**, germicide, purifier

antisocial adj **1** = **unsociable**, alienated, misanthropic, reserved, retiring, uncommunicative, unfriendly, withdrawn **2** = **disruptive**, antagonistic, belligerent, disorderly, hostile, menacing, rebellious, uncooperative

antithesis n **1** = **opposite**, contrary, contrast, converse, inverse, reverse

anxiety n = **uneasiness**, angst, apprehension, concern, foreboding, misgiving, nervousness, tension, trepidation, worry

anxious adj **1** = **uneasy**, apprehensive, concerned, fearful, in suspense, nervous, on tenterhooks, tense, troubled, worried **2** = **eager**, desirous, impatient, intent, itching, keen, yearning

apart ❶ *adv* **1** to or in pieces. **2** to or at a distance. **3** individual, distinct. **apart from** other than.

apartheid *n* former official government policy of racial segregation in S Africa.

apartment ❶ *n* **1** room in a building. **2** flat.

apathy ❶ *n* lack of interest or enthusiasm. **apathetic** *adj* **apathetically** *adv*.

ape *n* **1** tailless monkey such as the chimpanzee or gorilla. **2** stupid, clumsy, or ugly man. ▷ *v* **3** imitate. **apeman** *n* extinct primate thought to have been the forerunner of true humans.

aperient [ap-**peer**-ee-ent] *adj* **1** having a mild laxative effect. ▷ *n* **2** mild laxative.

aperitif [ap-per-rit-**teef**] *n* alcoholic drink taken before a meal.

aperture *n* **1** opening or hole. **2** opening in a camera or telescope that controls the amount of light entering it.

apex ❶ *n* highest point.

APEX Advance Purchase Excursion: reduced fare for journeys booked a specified period in advance.

aphasia *n* disorder of the central nervous system that affects the ability to speak and understand words.

aphelion [ap-**heel**-lee-on] *n, pl* -**lia** [-lee-a] point of a planet's orbit that is farthest from the sun.

aphid [**eh**-fid], **aphis** [**eh**-fiss] *n* small insect which sucks the sap from plants.

aphorism *n* short clever saying expressing a general truth.

aphrodisiac [af-roh-**diz**-zee-ak] *n*

1 substance that arouses sexual desire. ▷ *adj* **2** arousing sexual desire.

apiary [**ape**-yar-ee] *n, pl* -**ries** place where bees are kept. **apiarist** *n* beekeeper.

apiculture *n* breeding and care of bees.

apiece ❶ *adv* each, e.g. *they were given two apples apiece*.

aplomb ❶ [ap-**plom**] *n* calm self-possession.

apocalypse *n* **1** end of the world. **2** event of great destruction. **the Apocalypse** book of Revelation, the last book of the New Testament. **apocalyptic** *adj*.

Apocrypha [ap-**pok**-rif-fa] *pl n* **the Apocrypha** collective name for the 14 books of the Old Testament which are not accepted as part of the Hebrew scriptures.

apocryphal ❶ *adj* (of a story) of questionable authenticity.

apogee [**ap**-oh-jee] *n* **1** point of the moon's or a satellite's orbit that is farthest from the earth. **2** highest point.

apolitical *adj* not concerned with political matters.

apologia *n* formal written defence of a cause.

apology ❶ *n, pl* -**gies 1** expression of regret for wrongdoing. **2** (foll. by *for*) poor example (of). **3** same as APOLOGIA. **apologetic** *adj* showing or expressing regret. **apologetically** *adv* **apologetics** *n* branch of theology concerned with the reasoned defence of Christianity. **apologist** *n* person who formally defends a cause. **apologize** *v*

———————— THESAURUS ————————

apart *adv* **1** = **to pieces**, asunder, in bits, in pieces, to bits **2** = **separate**, alone, aside, away, by oneself, isolated, to one side

apart from *prep* = **except for**, aside from, besides, but, excluding, not counting, other than, save

apartment *n* **1** = **room**, accommodation, living quarters, quarters, rooms, suite **2** = **flat**, penthouse, duplex (*US & Canad*)

apathetic *adj* = **uninterested**, cool, indifferent, passive, phlegmatic, unconcerned

apathy *n* = **lack of interest**, coolness, indifference, inertia, nonchalance, passivity, torpor, unconcern

apex *n* = **highest point**, crest, crown,

culmination, peak, pinnacle, point, summit, top

apiece *adv* = **each**, for each, from each, individually, respectively, separately

aplomb *n* = **self-possession**, calmness, composure, confidence, level-headedness, poise, sang-froid, self-assurance, self-confidence

apocryphal *adj* = **dubious**, doubtful, legendary, mythical, questionable, unauthenticated, unsubstantiated

apologetic *adj* = **regretful**, contrite, penitent, remorseful, rueful, sorry

apologize *v* = **say sorry**, ask forgiveness, beg pardon, express regret

apology *n* **1** = **defence**, acknowledgment, confession, excuse, explanation, justification, plea **2** (foll.

make an apology.

● **SPELLING TIP**
● Remember that the correct way to
● spell **apology** is with one *p* and one *l*.

apoplexy *n Medical* stroke. **apoplectic**
adj **1** of apoplexy. **2** *informal* furious.

apostasy [ap-**poss**-stass-ee] *n*, *pl* **-sies**
abandonment of one's religious
faith or other belief. **apostate**
n, *adj*.

a posteriori [eh poss-steer-ee-**or**-rye]
adj involving reasoning from effect to
cause.

Apostle *n* **1** one of the twelve disciples
chosen by Christ to preach his gospel.
2 (**a-**) ardent supporter of a cause or
movement. **apostolic** [ap-poss-**stoll**-
ik] *adj*.

apostrophe [ap-**poss**-trof-fee] *n*
1 punctuation mark (') showing the
omission of a letter or letters in a word,
e.g. *don't*, or forming the possessive,
e.g. *Jill's car*. **2** digression from a speech
to address an imaginary or absent
person or thing.

apothecary *n*, *pl* **-caries** *obs* chemist.

apotheosis ❶ [ap-poth-ee-**oh**-siss] *n*, *pl*
-ses [-seez] **1** perfect example.
2 elevation to the rank of a god.

app *n* computer program designed for a
particular purpose, especially one for a
mobile phone.

appal ❶ *v* **-palling**, **-palled** dismay,
terrify. **appalling** *adj* dreadful, terrible.

● **SPELLING TIP**
● The verb **appal** has two *ps*, but only
● one *l*. If you extend it with an ending
● beginning with a vowel, you must
● add another *l*, as in **appalling**.

apparatus ❶ *n* equipment for a
particular purpose.

apparel [ap-**par**-rel] *n old-fashioned*
clothing.

apparent ❶ *adj* **1** readily seen, obvious.
2 seeming as opposed to real.
apparently *adv*.

● **SPELLING TIP**
● It's quite common to spell
● **apparently** with three *as*, but there
● should only be two - and then an *e*.

apparition ❶ *n* ghost or ghostlike figure.

appeal ❶ *v* **1** make an earnest request.
2 attract, please, or interest.
3 request a review of a lower court's
decision by a higher court. ▷ *n*
4 earnest request for money or help.
5 power to attract, please, or interest
people. **6** request for a review of a
lower court's decision by a higher court.
appealing *adj* **appealingly** *adv*.

appear ❶ *v* **1** become visible or present.
2 seem. **3** be seen in public.
appearance *n* **1** sudden or unexpected
arrival of someone or something at a

—————— THESAURUS ——————

by *for*) = **mockery**, caricature, excuse,
imitation, travesty

Apostle *n* **1** = **evangelist**, herald,
messenger, missionary, preacher **2** (not
cap.) = **supporter**, advocate,
champion, pioneer, propagandist,
proponent

apotheosis *n* **2** = **deification**,
elevation, exaltation, glorification,
idolization

appal *v* = **horrify**, alarm, daunt,
dishearten, dismay, frighten, outrage,
shock, unnerve

appalling *adj* = **horrifying**, alarming,
awful, daunting, dreadful, fearful,
frightful, horrible, shocking, terrifying

apparatus *n* = **equipment**, appliance,
contraption (*inf*), device, gear,
machinery, mechanism, tackle, tools

apparent *adj* **1** = **obvious**, discernible,
distinct, evident, manifest, marked,
unmistakable, visible **2** = **seeming**,
ostensible, outward, superficial

apparently *adv* **2** = **it appears that**, it
seems that, on the face of it, ostensibly,

outwardly, seemingly, superficially

apparition *n* = **ghost**, chimera,
phantom, spectre, spirit, wraith

appeal *v* **1** = **plead**, ask, beg, call upon,
entreat, pray, request **2** = **attract**,
allure, charm, entice, fascinate,
interest, please, tempt ▷ *n* **4** = **plea**,
application, entreaty, petition, prayer,
request, supplication **5** = **attraction**,
allure, beauty, charm, fascination

appealing *adj* **2** = **attractive**, alluring,
charming, desirable, engaging, lekker
(*S Afr sl*), winsome

appear *v* **1** = **come into view**, be
present, come out, come to light, crop
up (*inf*), emerge, occur, show up (*inf*),
surface, turn up **2** = **look (like** *or* **as if)**,
occur, seem, strike one as

appearance *n* **1** = **arrival**, coming,
emergence, introduction, presence
2 a = **look**, demeanour, expression,
figure, form, looks, manner, mien (*lit*)
b = **impression**, front, guise, illusion,
image, outward show, pretence,
semblance

place. **2** an appearing. **3** outward aspect.

appease ⓘ v **1** pacify (a person) by yielding to his or her demands. **2** satisfy or relieve (a feeling). **appeasement** n.

appellant n person who makes an appeal to a higher court.

appellation n name, title.

append ⓘ v join on, add. **appendage** n thing joined on or added.

appendicitis n inflammation of the appendix.

appendix ⓘ n, pl -**dices**, -**dixes**
1 separate additional material at the end of a book. **2** Anat short closed tube attached to the large intestine.

- **USAGE NOTE**
- Extra sections at the end of a book
- are appendices. The plural appendixes is
- used in medicine.

appertain v (foll. by to) **1** belong to. **2** be connected with.

appetite ⓘ n **1** desire for food or drink. **2** liking or willingness. **appetizer** n thing eaten or drunk to stimulate the appetite. **appetizing** adj stimulating the appetite.

applaud ⓘ v **1** show approval of by clapping one's hands. **2** approve

strongly. **applause** n approval shown by clapping one's hands.

apple n round firm fleshy fruit that grows on trees. **in apple-pie order** informal very tidy.

appliance ⓘ n device with a specific function.

applicable ⓘ adj relevant, appropriate. **applicability** n.

applicant ⓘ n person who applies for something.

application ⓘ n **1** formal request. **2** act of applying something to a particular use. **3** diligent effort. **4** act of putting something onto a surface.

applicator n simple device for applying cosmetics, medication, etc.

appliqué [ap-**plee**-kay] n kind of decoration in which one material is cut out and attached to another.

apply ⓘ v -**plying**, -**plied 1** make a formal request. **2** put to practical use. **3** put onto a surface. **4** be relevant or appropriate. **apply oneself** concentrate one's efforts. **applicant** n **application** n formal request. **applied** adj (of a skill, science, etc.) put to practical use.

appoint ⓘ v **1** assign to a job or position.

——— **THESAURUS** ———

appease v **1** = **pacify**, calm, conciliate, mollify, placate, quiet, satisfy, soothe **2** = **ease**, allay, alleviate, calm, relieve, soothe

appeasement n **1** = **pacification**, accommodation, compromise, concession, conciliation, mollification, placation **2** = **easing**, alleviation, lessening, relieving, soothing

appendage n = **attachment**, accessory, addition, supplement

appendix n **1** = **supplement**, addendum, addition, adjunct, appendage, postscript

appetite n **1** = **desire**, craving, demand, hunger, relish, stomach, taste **2** = **liking**, longing, passion, yearning

appetizing adj = **delicious**, appealing, inviting, mouthwatering, palatable, succulent, tasty, tempting

applaud v **1** = **clap**, cheer **2** = **approve**, acclaim, commend, compliment, encourage, extol, praise

applause n = **ovation**, big hand, cheers, clapping, hand

appliance n = **device**, apparatus, gadget, implement, instrument, machine, mechanism, tool

applicable adj = **appropriate**, apt, fitting, pertinent, relevant, suitable, useful

applicant n = **candidate**, claimant, inquirer

application n **1** = **request**, appeal, claim, inquiry, petition, requisition **3** = **effort**, commitment, dedication, diligence, hard work, industry, perseverance

apply v **1** = **request**, appeal, claim, inquire, petition, put in, requisition **2** = **use**, bring to bear, carry out, employ, exercise, exert, implement, practise, utilize **3** = **put on**, cover with, lay on, paint, place, smear, spread on **4** = **be relevant**, be applicable, be appropriate, bear upon, be fitting, fit, pertain, refer, relate

apply oneself v = **try**, be diligent, buckle down (inf), commit oneself, concentrate, dedicate oneself, devote oneself, persevere, work hard

appoint v **1** = **assign**, choose, commission, delegate, elect, name, nominate, select **2** = **decide**, allot, arrange, assign, choose, designate, establish, fix, set **3** = **equip**, fit out,

2 fix or decide, e.g. *appoint a time.*
3 equip or furnish. **appointee** *n*
appointment *n* **1** arrangement to
meet a person. **2** act of placing
someone in a job. **3** the job itself. ▷ *pl*
4 fixtures or fittings.

apportion ⊙ *v* divide out in shares.

apposite ⊙ *adj* suitable, apt. **apposition**
n grammatical construction in which
two nouns or phrases referring to the
same thing are placed one after
another without a conjunction, e.g. *my
son the doctor.*

appraise ⊙ *v* estimate the value or
quality of. **appraisal** *n* **appraising** *adj*
appraisingly *adv.*

appreciate ⊙ *v* **1** value highly. **2** be
aware of and understand. **3** be grateful
for. **4** rise in value. **appreciable** *adj*

enough to be noticed. **appreciably** *adv*
appreciation *n* **appreciative** *adj*
feeling or showing appreciation.
appreciatively *adv.*

apprehend ⊙ *v* **1** arrest and take into
custody. **2** grasp (something) mentally.
apprehension *n* **1** dread, anxiety.
2 arrest. **3** understanding.
apprehensive *adj* fearful or anxious.
apprehensively *adv.*

apprentice ⊙ *n* **1** someone working for
a skilled person for a fixed period in
order to learn his or her trade. ▷ *v*
2 take or place (someone) as an
apprentice. **apprenticeship** *n.*

apprise *v* make aware (of).

appro *n* **on appro** *informal* on approval.

approach ⊙ *v* **1** come near or nearer
(to). **2** make a proposal or suggestion

——————————————————————— THESAURUS ———————

furnish, provide, supply
appointed *adj* **1** = **assigned**, chosen,
delegated, elected, named, nominated,
selected **2** = **decided**, allotted,
arranged, assigned, chosen,
designated, established, fixed, set
3 = **equipped**, fitted out, furnished,
provided, supplied
appointment *n* **1** = **meeting**,
arrangement, assignation, date,
engagement, interview, rendezvous
2 = **selection**, assignment, choice,
election, naming, nomination **3** = **job**,
assignment, office, place, position,
post, situation ▷ *pl* **4** = **fittings**,
fixtures, furnishings, gear, outfit,
paraphernalia, trappings
apportion *v* = **divide**, allocate, allot,
assign, dispense, distribute, dole out,
give out, ration out, share
apposite *adj* = **appropriate**, applicable,
apt, fitting, pertinent, relevant,
suitable, to the point
appraisal *n* = **assessment**, estimate,
estimation, evaluation, judgment,
opinion
appraise *v* = **assess**, estimate, evaluate,
gauge, judge, rate, review, value
appreciable *adj* = **significant**,
considerable, definite, discernible,
evident, marked, noticeable, obvious,
pronounced, substantial
appreciate *v* **1** = **value**, admire, enjoy,
like, prize, rate highly, respect, treasure
2 = **be aware of**, perceive, realize,
recognize, sympathize with, take
account of, understand **3** = **be grateful
for**, be appreciative, be indebted, be

obliged, be thankful for, give thanks for
4 = **increase**, enhance, gain, grow,
improve, rise
appreciation *n* **2** = **awareness**,
admiration, comprehension,
enjoyment, perception, realization,
recognition, sensitivity, sympathy,
understanding **3** = **gratitude**,
acknowledgment, gratefulness,
indebtedness, obligation,
thankfulness, thanks **4** = **increase**,
enhancement, gain, growth,
improvement, rise
appreciative *adj* = **grateful**, beholden,
indebted, obliged, thankful
apprehend *v* **1** = **arrest**, capture,
catch, nick (*sl, chiefly Brit*), seize, take
prisoner **2** = **understand**,
comprehend, conceive, get the
picture, grasp, perceive, realize,
recognize
apprehension *n* **1** = **anxiety**, alarm,
concern, dread, fear, foreboding,
suspicion, trepidation, worry
2 = **arrest**, capture, catching, seizure,
taking **3** = **awareness**,
comprehension, grasp, perception,
understanding
apprehensive *adj* = **anxious**,
concerned, foreboding, nervous,
uneasy, worried
apprentice *n* **1** = **trainee**, beginner,
learner, novice, probationer, pupil,
student
approach *v* **1** = **move towards**, come
close, come near, draw near, near, reach
2 = **make a proposal to**, appeal to,
apply to, make overtures to, sound out

to. **3** begin to deal with (a matter). ▷ *n* **4** approaching or means of approaching. **5** proposal or suggestion made to someone. **6** approximation. **approachable** *adj* **1** friendly. **2** accessible.

approbation *n* approval.

appropriate ❶ *adj* **1** suitable, fitting. ▷ *v* **2** take for oneself. **3** put aside for a particular purpose. **appropriately** *adv* **appropriateness** *n* suitability. **appropriation** *n* act of putting (something) aside for a particular purpose.

approve ❶ *v* **1** consider good or right. **2** authorize, agree to. **approval** *n* **1** consent. **2** favourable opinion. **on approval** (of goods) with an option to be returned without payment if unsatisfactory. **approving** *adj* **approvingly** *adv*.

approx. approximate(ly).

approximate ❶ *adj* **1** almost but not quite exact. ▷ *v* (foll. by *to*) **2** come close to. **3** be almost the same as. **approximately** *adv* **approximation** *n*.

appurtenances *pl n* minor or additional features.

Apr. April.

après-ski [ap-ray-**skee**] *n* social activities after a day's skiing.

apricot *n* **1** yellowish-orange juicy fruit like a small peach. ▷ *adj* **2** yellowish-orange.

April *n* fourth month of the year. **April fool** victim of a practical joke played on April 1 (**April Fools' Day**).

a priori [eh pry-**or**-rye] *adj* involving reasoning from cause to effect.

apron ❶ *n* **1** garment worn over the front of the body to protect the clothes. **2** area at an airport or hangar for manoeuvring and loading aircraft. **3** part of a stage in front of the curtain.

apropos [ap-prop-**poh**] *adj*, *adv* appropriate(ly). **apropos of** with regard to.

apse *n* arched or domed recess, esp. in a church.

apt ❶ *adj* **1** having a specified tendency. **2** suitable. **3** quick to learn. **aptly** *adv* **aptness** *n* **aptitude** *n* natural ability.

APT Advanced Passenger Train.

aqua *adj* short for AQUAMARINE (sense 2).

aqualung *n* mouthpiece attached to air cylinders, worn for underwater swimming.

aquamarine *n* **1** greenish-blue gemstone. ▷ *adj* **2** greenish-blue.

THESAURUS

3 = **set about**, begin work on, commence, embark on, enter upon, make a start, undertake ▷ *n* **4** = **coming**, advance, arrival, drawing near, nearing **5** = **proposal**, appeal, application, invitation, offer, overture, proposition **6** = **likeness**, approximation, semblance

approachable *adj* **1** = **friendly**, affable, congenial, cordial, open, sociable **2** = **accessible**, attainable, reachable

appropriate *adj* **1** = **suitable**, apt, befitting, fitting, pertinent, relevant, to the point, well-suited ▷ *v* **2** = **seize**, commandeer, confiscate, embezzle, filch, impound, misappropriate, pilfer, pocket, steal, take possession of, usurp **3** = **allocate**, allot, apportion, assign, devote, earmark, set aside

approval *n* **1** = **consent**, agreement, assent, authorization, blessing, endorsement, permission, recommendation, sanction **2** = **favour**, acclaim, admiration, applause, appreciation, esteem, good opinion, praise, respect

approve *v* **1** = **favour**, admire, commend, have a good opinion of, like, praise, regard highly, respect **2** = **agree to**, allow, assent to, authorize, consent to, endorse, pass, permit, recommend, sanction

approximate *adj* **1** = **close**, estimated, inexact, loose, near, rough ▷ *v* (foll. by *to*) **2** = **come close**, approach, border on, come near, reach, touch, verge on **3** = **resemble**

approximately *adv* = **almost**, about, around, circa (*used with dates*), close to, in the region of, just about, more or less, nearly, roughly

approximation *n* = **guess**, conjecture, estimate, estimation, guesswork, rough calculation, rough idea

apron *n* **1** = **pinny**, pinafore (*inf*)

apt *adj* **1** = **inclined**, disposed, given, liable, likely, of a mind, prone, ready **2** = **appropriate**, fitting, pertinent, relevant, suitable, to the point **3** = **gifted**, clever, quick, sharp, smart, talented

aptitude *n* = **gift**, ability, capability, faculty, intelligence, proficiency, talent

a

aquaplane *n* **1** board on which a person stands to be towed by a motorboat. ▷ *v* **2** ride on an aquaplane. **3** (of a motor vehicle) skim uncontrollably on a thin film of water.

aquarium *n*, *pl* **aquariums**, **aquaria** **1** tank in which fish and other underwater creatures are kept. **2** building containing such tanks.

Aquarius *n* (the water bearer) eleventh sign of the zodiac.

aquatic *adj* **1** living in or near water. **2** done in or on water. **aquatics** *pl n* water sports.

aquatint *n* print like a watercolour, produced by etching copper.

aqua vitae [**ak**-wa **vee**-tie] *n obs* brandy.

aqueduct *n* structure carrying water across a valley or river.

aqueous *adj* of, like, or containing water.

aquiline *adj* **1** (of a nose) curved like an eagle's beak. **2** of or like an eagle.

Ar *Chemistry* argon.

AR Arkansas.

Arab *n* **1** member of a Semitic people originally from Arabia. ▷ *adj* **2** of the Arabs. **Arabian** *adj* of Arabia or the Arabs. **Arabic** *n* **1** language of the Arabs. ▷ *adj* **2** of Arabic, Arabs, or Arabia. **Arabic numerals** the symbols 1, 2, 3, 4, 5, 6, 7, 8, 9, 0, used to represent numbers.

arabesque [ar-ab-**besk**] *n* **1** ballet position in which one leg is raised behind and the arms are extended. **2** elaborate ornamental design.

arable ❶ *adj* suitable for growing crops on.

arachnid [ar-**rak**-nid] *n* eight-legged invertebrate, such as a spider, scorpion, tick, or mite.

arak *n* same as ARRACK.

Aramaic *n* an ancient Semitic language of the Middle East.

Aran *adj* (of sweaters etc.) knitted in a complicated pattern traditional to the Aran Islands, usu. with natural unbleached wool.

arbiter ❶ *n* **1** person empowered to judge in a dispute. **2** person with influential opinions about something.

arbitrary ❶ *adj* based on personal choice or chance, rather than reason. **arbitrarily** *adv* **arbitrariness** *n*.

● **SPELLING TIP**
● The spelling *arbitary* appears 22
● times in the Bank of English. But the
● correct spelling, **arbitrary**, appears
● 1959 times: it has three *r*s.

arbitration ❶ *n* hearing and settling of a dispute by an impartial referee chosen by both sides. **arbitrate** *v* **arbitrator** *n*.

arboreal [ahr-**bore**-ee-al] *adj* of or living in trees.

arboretum [ahr-bore-**ee**-tum] *n*, *pl* **-ta** [-ta] place where rare trees or shrubs are cultivated.

arboriculture *n* cultivation of trees or shrubs. **arboriculturist** *n*.

arbour *n* glade sheltered by trees.

arbutus [ar-**byew**-tuss] *n*, *pl* **-tuses** evergreen shrub with strawberry-like berries.

arc ❶ *n* **1** part of a circle or other curve. **2** luminous discharge of electricity across a small gap between two electrodes. ▷ *v* **3** form an arc.

arcade ❶ *n* **1** covered passageway lined with shops. **2** set of arches and their supporting columns.

Arcadian *adj* rustic in an idealized way.

arcane ❶ *adj* mysterious and secret.

arch¹ ❶ *n* **1** curved structure supporting a bridge or roof. **2** something curved.

———————— THESAURUS ————————

arable *adj* = **productive**, farmable, fertile, fruitful

arbiter *n* **1** = **judge**, adjudicator, arbitrator, referee, umpire
2 = **authority**, controller, dictator, expert, governor, lord, mana (*NZ*), master, pundit, ruler

arbitrary *adj* = **random**, capricious, chance, erratic, inconsistent, personal, subjective, whimsical

arbitrate *v* = **settle**, adjudicate, decide, determine, judge, mediate, pass judgment, referee, umpire

arbitration *n* = **settlement**, adjudication, decision, determination, judgment

arbitrator *n* = **judge**, adjudicator, arbiter, referee, umpire

arc *n* **1** = **curve**, arch, bend, bow, crescent, half-moon

arcade *n* = **gallery**, cloister, colonnade, portico

arcane *adj* = **mysterious**, esoteric, hidden, occult, recondite, secret

arch¹ *n* **1** = **archway**, curve, dome, span, vault **2** = **curve**, arc, bend, bow, hump, semicircle ▷ *v* **4** = **curve**, arc, bend, bow, bridge, span

3 curved lower part of the foot. ▷ *v* **4** (cause to) form an arch. **archway** *n* passageway under an arch.

arch² ❶ *adj* **1** superior, knowing. **2** coyly playful. **archly** *adv* **archness** *n*.

arch- *combining form* chief, principal, e.g. *archenemy*.

archaeology *n* study of ancient cultures from their physical remains. **archaeological** *adj* **archaeologist** *n*.

archaeopteryx *n* extinct bird with teeth, a long tail, and well-developed wings.

archaic ❶ [ark-**kay**-ik] *adj* **1** ancient. **2** out-of-date. **archaism** [**ark**-kay-iz-zum] *n* archaic word or phrase.

archangel [**ark**-ain-jell] *n* chief angel.

archbishop *n* chief bishop.

archdeacon *n* priest ranking just below a bishop.

archdiocese *n* diocese of an archbishop.

archduke *n* duke of specially high rank. **archduchess** *n fem* **archduchy** *n* territory of an archduke or archduchess.

archer *n* person who shoots with a bow and arrow. **archery** *n*.

archetype ❶ [**ark**-ee-type] *n* **1** perfect specimen. **2** original model. **archetypal** *adj*.

archipelago [ark-ee-**pel**-a-go] *n, pl* **-gos 1** group of islands. **2** sea full of small islands.

architect ❶ *n* person qualified to design and supervise the construction of buildings. **architecture** *n* **1** style in which a building is designed and built. **2** designing and construction of buildings. **architectural** *adj* **architecturally** *adv*.

architrave *n Architecture* **1** beam that rests on columns. **2** moulding round a doorway or window.

archive ❶ [**ark**-ive] *n* **1** (often *pl*) collection of records or documents. **2** place where these are kept. **archival** *adj* **archivist** [**ark**-iv-ist] *n* person in charge of archives.

Arctic ❶ *n* **1 the Arctic** area around the North Pole. ▷ *adj* **2** of this region. **3** (**a-**) *informal* very cold.

ardent ❶ *adj* **1** passionate. **2** eager, zealous. **ardently** *adv* **ardour** *n* **1** passion. **2** enthusiasm, zeal.

arduous ❶ *adj* hard to accomplish, strenuous. **arduously** *adv*.

are¹ *v* see BE.

are² *n* unit of measure, 100 square metres.

area ❶ *n* **1** part or region. **2** size of a two-dimensional surface. **3** subject field. **4** small sunken yard giving access to a basement.

arena ❶ *n* **1** seated enclosure for sports events. **2** area of a Roman amphitheatre where gladiators fought.

arch² *adj* **2** = **playful**, frolicsome, mischievous, pert, roguish, saucy, sly, waggish

archaic *adj* **1** = **old**, ancient, antique, bygone, olden (*arch*), primitive **2** = **old-fashioned**, antiquated, behind the times, obsolete, outmoded, out of date, passé

archetypal *adj* **1** = **typical**, classic, ideal, model, standard **2** = **original**

archetype *n* **1** = **standard**, model, paradigm, pattern, prime example **2** = **original**, prototype

architect *n* = **designer**, master builder, planner

architecture *n* **1** = **structure**, construction, design, framework, make-up, style **2** = **design**, building, construction, planning

archive *n* **1** (often *pl*) = **records**, annals, chronicles, documents, papers, rolls **2** = **record office**, museum, registry, repository

Arctic *adj* **2** = **polar**, far-northern, hyperborean **3** (not cap.) *Inf* = **freezing**, chilly, cold, frigid, frozen, glacial, icy

ardent *adj* **1** = **passionate**, amorous, hot-blooded, impassioned, intense, lusty **2** = **enthusiastic**, avid, eager, keen, zealous

ardour *n* **1** = **passion**, fervour, intensity, spirit, vehemence, warmth **2** = **enthusiasm**, avidity, eagerness, keenness, zeal

arduous *adj* = **difficult**, exhausting, fatiguing, gruelling, laborious, onerous, punishing, rigorous, strenuous, taxing, tiring

area *n* **1** = **region**, district, locality, neighbourhood, part, portion, section, sector, zone **3** = **field**, department, domain, province, realm, sphere, territory

arena *n* **1** = **ring**, bowl, enclosure, field, ground, stadium **2** = **amphitheatre 3** = **sphere**, area, domain, field, province, realm, sector, territory

a

3 sphere of intense activity.

aren't are not.

areola *n, pl* **-lae, -las** small circular area, such as the coloured ring around the human nipple.

arête *n* sharp ridge separating valleys.

argon *n Chemistry* inert gas found in the air.

argosy *n, pl* **-sies** *poetic* large merchant ship.

argot [ahr-go] *n* slang or jargon.

argue ❶ *v* **-guing, -gued 1** try to prove by giving reasons. **2** debate. **3** quarrel, dispute. **arguable** *adj* **arguably** *adv* **argument** *n* **1** quarrel. **2** discussion. **3** point presented for or against something. **argumentation** *n* process of reasoning methodically. **argumentative** *adj* given to arguing.

● **SPELLING TIP**
● There's an *e* at the end of **argue**, but
● you should leave it out when you
● write **argument**. A lot of people get
● that wrong.

argy-bargy *n, pl* **-bargies** *informal* squabbling argument.

aria [ah-ree-a] *n* elaborate song for solo voice, esp. one from an opera.

arid ❶ *adj* **1** parched, dry. **2** uninteresting. **aridity** *n*.

Aries *n* (the ram) first sign of the zodiac.

aright *adv* rightly.

arise ❶ *v* **arising, arose, arisen 1** come about. **2** come into notice. **3** get up.

aristocracy ❶ *n, pl* **-cies 1** highest social class. **2** government by this class. **aristocrat** *n* member of the aristocracy. **aristocratic** *adj* **aristocratically** *adv*.

arithmetic *n* **1** calculation by or of numbers. ▷ *adj* **2** of arithmetic. **arithmetical** *adj* **arithmetically** *adv* **arithmetician** *n*.

ark *n* **1** *Old Testament* boat built by Noah, which survived the Flood. **2** (**A-**) *Judaism* chest containing the writings of Jewish Law.

arm¹ ❶ *n* **1** upper limb from the shoulder to the wrist. **2** sleeve of a garment. **3** side of a chair. **armful** *n* as much as can be held in the arms. **armlet** *n* band worn round the arm. **armchair** *n* upholstered chair with side supports for the arms. **armhole** *n* opening in a garment through which the arm passes. **armpit** *n* hollow under the arm at the shoulder.

arm² ❶ *v* **1** supply with weapons. **2** prepare (a bomb etc.) for use. **arms** *pl n* **1** weapons. **2** military exploits. **3** heraldic emblem.

armada ❶ *n* large number of warships.

armadillo *n, pl* **-los** small S American mammal covered in strong bony plates.

Armageddon *n* **1** *New Testament* final battle between good and evil at the end of the world. **2** catastrophic conflict.

armament ❶ *n* **1** military weapons. **2** preparation for war.

THESAURUS

---

argue *v* **1** = **maintain**, assert, claim, dispute, remonstrate **2** = **debate**, discuss, reason **3** = **quarrel**, bicker, disagree, dispute, fall out (*inf*), fight, squabble

argument *n* **1** = **quarrel**, clash, controversy, disagreement, dispute, feud, fight, row, squabble **2** = **discussion**, debate **3** = **reason**, argumentation, assertion, case, claim, defence, dialectic, ground(s), line of reasoning, logic, plea, polemic, reasoning

argumentative *adj* = **quarrelsome**, belligerent, combative, contentious, contrary, disputatious, litigious, opinionated

arid *adj* **1** = **dry**, barren, desert, parched, sterile, torrid, waterless **2** = **boring**, dreary, dry, dull, tedious, tiresome, uninspired, uninteresting

arise *v* **1** = **happen**, begin, emerge, ensue, follow, occur, result, start, stem

3 = **get up**, get to one's feet, go up, rise, stand up, wake up

aristocracy *n* **1** = **upper class**, elite, gentry, nobility, patricians, peerage, ruling class

aristocrat *n* = **noble**, grandee, lady, lord, patrician, peer, peeress

aristocratic *adj* = **upper-class**, blue-blooded, elite, gentlemanly, lordly, noble, patrician, titled

arm¹ *n* **1** = **upper limb**, appendage, limb

arm² *v* **1** = **equip**, accoutre, array, deck out, furnish, issue with, provide, supply **2** = **prime**

armada *n* = **fleet**, flotilla, navy, squadron

armament *n* **1** = **weapons**, ammunition, arms, guns, materiel, munitions, ordnance, weaponry

armed *adj* **1** = **carrying weapons**, equipped, fitted out, protected **2** = **primed**

a

armature *n* revolving structure in an electric motor or generator, wound with coils carrying the current.

armistice ❶ [**arm**-miss-stiss] *n* agreed suspension of fighting.

armour ❶ *n* **1** metal clothing formerly worn to protect the body in battle. **2** metal plating of tanks, warships, etc. **armoured** *adj* **1** having a protective covering. **2** consisting of armoured vehicles. **armourer** *n* maker, repairer, or keeper of arms or armour. **armoury** *n* place where weapons are stored.

army ❶ *n, pl* **armies 1** military land forces of a nation. **2** great number.

aroma ❶ *n* pleasant smell. **aromatic** *adj* **aromatherapy** *n* massage with fragrant oils to relieve tension.

arose *v* past tense of ARISE.

around ❶ *prep, adv* **1** on all sides (of). **2** from place to place (in). **3** somewhere in or near. **4** approximately.

arouse ❶ *v* **1** stimulate, make active. **2** awaken. **arousal** *n*.

arpeggio [arp-**pej**-ee-oh] *n, pl* **-gios** *Music* notes of a chord played or sung in quick succession.

arr. 1 arranged (by). **2** arrival. **3** arrive(d).

arrack *n* alcoholic drink distilled from grain or rice.

arraign [ar-**rain**] *v* **1** bring (a prisoner) before a court to answer a charge. **2** accuse. **arraignment** *n*.

arrange ❶ *v* **1** plan. **2** agree. **3** put in order. **4** adapt (music) for performance in a certain way. **arrangement** *n*.

arrant *adj* utter, downright.

arras *n* tapestry wall-hanging.

array ❶ *n* **1** impressive display or collection. **2** orderly arrangement, esp. of troops. **3** *poetic* rich clothing. ▷ *v* **4** arrange in order. **5** dress in rich clothing.

arrears *pl n* money owed. **in arrears** late in paying a debt.

arrest ❶ *v* **1** take (a person) into custody. **2** stop the movement or development of.

———————————— THESAURUS ————————————

armistice *n* = **truce**, ceasefire, peace, suspension of hostilities

armour *n* = **protection**, armour plate, covering, sheathing, shield

armoured *adj* = **protected**, armour-plated, bombproof, bulletproof, ironclad, mailed, steel-plated

arms *pl n* **1** = **weapons**, armaments, firearms, guns, instruments of war, ordnance, weaponry **3** = **heraldry**, blazonry, crest, escutcheon, insignia

army *n* **1** = **soldiers**, armed force, legions, military, military force, soldiery, troops **2** = **vast number**, array, horde, host, multitude, pack, swarm, throng

aroma *n* = **scent**, bouquet, fragrance, odour, perfume, redolence, savour, smell

aromatic *adj* = **fragrant**, balmy, perfumed, pungent, redolent, savoury, spicy, sweet-scented, sweet-smelling

around *prep* **1** = **surrounding**, about, encircling, enclosing, encompassing, on all sides of, on every side of **4** = **approximately**, about, circa (*used with dates*), roughly ▷ *adv* **1** = **everywhere**, about, all over, here and there, in all directions, on all sides, throughout **3** = **near**, at hand, close, close at hand, nearby, nigh (*arch or dial*)

arouse *v* **1** = **stimulate**, excite, incite, instigate, provoke, spur, stir up,

summon up, whip up **2** = **awaken**, rouse, waken, wake up

arrange *v* **1** = **plan**, construct, contrive, devise, fix up, organize, prepare **2** = **agree**, adjust, come to terms, compromise, determine, settle **3** = **put in order**, classify, group, line up, order, organize, position, sort **4** = **adapt**, instrument, orchestrate, score

arrangement *n* **1** = **plan**, organization, planning, preparation, provision, schedule **2** = **agreement**, adjustment, compact, compromise, deal, settlement, terms **3** = **order**, alignment, classification, form, organization, structure, system **4** = **adaptation**, instrumentation, interpretation, orchestration, score, version

array *n* **1, 2** = **arrangement**, collection, display, exhibition, formation, line-up, parade, show, supply **3** *Poet* = **clothing**, apparel, attire, clothes, dress, finery, garments, regalia ▷ *v* **4** = **arrange**, display, exhibit, group, parade, range, show **5** = **dress**, adorn, attire, clothe, deck, decorate, festoon

arrest *v* **1** = **capture**, apprehend, catch, detain, nick (*sl, chiefly Brit*), seize, take prisoner **2** = **stop**, block, delay, end, inhibit, interrupt, obstruct, slow, suppress **3** = **grip**, absorb, engage, engross, fascinate, hold, intrigue,

3 catch and hold (the attention). ▷ *n*
4 act of taking a person into custody.
5 slowing or stopping. **arresting** *adj*
attracting attention, striking.

arrive ⊙ *v* **1** reach a place or destination.
2 happen, come. **3** *informal* be born.
4 *informal* attain success. **arrival** *n*
1 arriving. **2** person or thing that has
just arrived.

arrivederci [ar-reeve-a-**der**-chee] *interj*
Italian goodbye.

arrogant ⊙ *adj* proud and overbearing.
arrogantly *adv* **arrogance** *n*.

arrogate *v* claim or seize without
justification.

arrow ⊙ *n* **1** pointed shaft shot from a
bow. **2** arrow-shaped sign or symbol
used to show direction. **arrowhead** *n*
pointed tip of an arrow.

arrowroot *n* nutritious starch obtained
from the root of a W Indian plant.

arse *n taboo* buttocks or anus. **arsehole**
n taboo **1** anus. **2** stupid or annoying
person.

arsenal ⊙ *n* place where arms and
ammunition are made or stored.

arsenic *n* **1** toxic grey element. **2** highly
poisonous compound of this.
arsenical *adj*.

arson *n* crime of intentionally setting
property on fire. **arsonist** *n*.

art ⊙ *n* **1** creation of works of beauty,
esp. paintings or sculpture. **2** works of
art collectively. **3** skill. ▷ *pl*
4 nonscientific branches of knowledge.
artist *n* **1** person who produces works
of art, esp. paintings or sculpture.

2 person skilled at something.
3 artiste. **artiste** *n* professional
entertainer such as a singer or dancer.
artistic *adj* **artistically** *adv* **artistry** *n*
artistic skill. **arty** *adj* **artier**,
artiest *informal* having an affected
interest in art.

artefact *n* something made by human
beings.

arteriosclerosis [art-ear-ee-oh-skler-
oh-siss] *n* hardening of the arteries.

artery *n, pl* **-teries** **1** one of the tubes
carrying blood from the heart. **2** major
road or means of communication.
arterial *adj* **1** of an artery. **2** (of a route)
major.

artesian well [art-**teez**-yan] *n* well
bored vertically so that the water is
forced to the surface by natural
pressure.

Artex *n* ® textured plaster-like covering
for ceilings and walls.

artful ⊙ *adj* cunning, wily. **artfully** *adv*
artfulness *n*.

arthritis *n* painful inflammation of a
joint or joints. **arthritic** *adj, n*.

arthropod *n* animal, such as a spider or
insect, with jointed limbs and a
segmented body.

artic *n informal* articulated lorry.

artichoke *n* flower head of a thistle-like
plant, cooked as a vegetable.

article ⊙ *n* **1** written piece in a magazine
or newspaper. **2** item or object.
3 clause in a document. **4** *Grammar* any
of the words *the, a,* or *an.*

articled *adj* bound (as an apprentice) by

---

occupy ▷ *n* **4** = **capture**, bust (*inf*),
cop (*sl*), detention, seizure
5 = **stopping**, blockage, delay, end,
hindrance, interruption, obstruction,
suppression

arresting *adj* = **striking**, engaging,
impressive, noticeable, outstanding,
remarkable, stunning, surprising

arrival *n* **1** = **coming**, advent,
appearance, arriving, entrance,
happening, occurrence, taking place
2 = **newcomer**, caller, entrant,
incomer, visitor

arrive *v* **1** = **come**, appear, enter, get to,
reach, show up (*inf*), turn up
4 *Inf* = **succeed**, become famous,
make good, make it (*inf*), make the
grade (*inf*)

arrogance *n* = **conceit**, disdainfulness,
haughtiness, high-handedness,

insolence, pride, superciliousness,
swagger

arrogant *adj* = **conceited**, disdainful,
haughty, high-handed, overbearing,
proud, scornful, supercilious

arrow *n* **1** = **dart**, bolt, flight, quarrel,
shaft (*arch*) **2** = **pointer**, indicator

arsenal *n* = **armoury**, ammunition
dump, arms depot, ordnance depot,
stockpile, store, storehouse, supply

art *n* = **skill**, craft, expertise, ingenuity,
mastery, virtuosity

artful *adj* = **cunning**, clever, crafty,
shrewd, sly, smart, wily

article *n* **1** = **piece**, composition,
discourse, essay, feature, item, paper,
story, treatise **2** = **thing**, commodity,
item, object, piece, substance, unit
3 = **clause**, item, paragraph, part,
passage, point, portion, section

a written contract.

articulate ❶ *adj* **1** able to express oneself clearly and coherently. **2** (of speech) clear, distinct. **3** *Zoology* having joints. ▷ *v* **4** speak or say clearly and coherently. **articulately** *adv* **articulated** *adj* jointed. **articulated lorry** large lorry in two separate sections joined by a pivoted bar. **articulation** *n*.

artifact *n* same as ARTEFACT.

artifice ❶ *n* **1** clever trick. **2** cleverness, skill. **artificer** [art-**tiff**-iss-er] *n* craftsman.

artificial ❶ *adj* **1** man-made, not occurring naturally. **2** made in imitation of something natural. **3** not sincere. **artificial insemination** introduction of semen into the womb by means other than sexual intercourse. **artificial intelligence** branch of computer science aiming to produce machines which can imitate intelligent human behaviour. **artificial respiration** method of restarting a person's breathing after it has stopped. **artificially** *adv* **artificiality** *n*.

artillery ❶ *n* **1** large-calibre guns. **2** branch of the army who use these.

artisan ❶ *n* skilled worker, craftsman.

artless ❶ *adj* **1** free from deceit or cunning. **2** natural, unpretentious. **artlessly** *adv*.

arum lily [**air**-rum] *n* plant with a white funnel-shaped leaf surrounding a spike of flowers.

Aryan [**air**-ree-an] *n* **1** (in Nazi Germany) non-Jewish person of the Nordic type. **2** person supposedly of Indo-European descent. ▷ *adj* **3** of Aryans.

as ❶ *conj* **1** while, when. **2** in the way that. **3** that which, e.g. *do as you are told*. **4** since, seeing that. **5** for instance. ▷ *adv, conj* **6** used to indicate amount or extent in comparisons, e.g. *he is as tall as you*. ▷ *prep* **7** in the role of, being, e.g. *as a mother, I am concerned*.

As *Chemistry* arsenic.

ASA Advertising Standards Authority.

asafoetida *n* strong-smelling and bitter plant resin used as a spice in Eastern cookery.

a.s.a.p. as soon as possible.

asbestos *n* fibrous mineral which does not burn. **asbestosis** *n* lung disease caused by inhalation of asbestos fibre.

ASBO *Brit* anti-social behaviour order: a civil order made against a persistently anti-social person.

ascend ❶ *v* go or move up. **ascent** *n* **1** ascending. **2** upward slope. **ascendant** *adj* **1** dominant or influential. ▷ *n* **2** **in the ascendant** increasing in power or influence. **ascendancy** *n* condition of being dominant. **the Ascension** *Christianity* passing of Jesus Christ from earth into heaven.

articulate *adj* **1, 2** = **expressive**, clear, coherent, eloquent, fluent, lucid, well-spoken ▷ *v* **4** = **express**, enunciate, pronounce, say, speak, state, talk, utter, voice

artifice *n* **1** = **trick**, contrivance, device, machination, manoeuvre, stratagem, subterfuge, tactic **2** = **cleverness**, ingenuity, inventiveness, skill

artificial *adj* **1** = **synthetic**, man-made, manufactured, non-natural, plastic **2** = **fake**, bogus, counterfeit, imitation, mock, sham, simulated **3** = **insincere**, affected, contrived, false, feigned, forced, phoney *or* phony (*inf*), unnatural

artillery *n* **1** = **big guns**, battery, cannon, cannonry, gunnery, ordnance

artisan *n* = **craftsman**, journeyman, mechanic, skilled workman, technician

artistic *adj* = **creative**, aesthetic, beautiful, cultured, elegant, refined, sophisticated, stylish, tasteful

artistry *n* = **skill**, brilliance, craftsmanship, creativity, finesse, mastery, proficiency, virtuosity

artless *adj* **1** = **straightforward**, frank, guileless, open, plain **2** = **natural**, plain, pure, simple, unadorned, unaffected, uncontrived, unpretentious

as *conj* **1** = **when**, at the time that, during the time that, just as, while **2** = **in the way that**, in the manner that, like **3** = **what**, that which **4** = **since**, because, considering that, seeing that **5** = **for instance**, like, such as ▷ *prep* **7** = **being**, in the character of, in the role of, under the name of

ascend *v* = **move up**, climb, go up, mount, scale

ascent *n* **1** = **rise**, ascending, ascension, climb, mounting, rising, scaling, upward movement **2** = **upward slope**, gradient, incline, ramp, rise, rising ground

a

ascertain ❶ *v* find out definitely. **ascertainable** *adj* **ascertainment** *n*.

ascetic ❶ [ass-**set**-tik] *n, adj* (person) abstaining from worldly pleasures and comforts. **asceticism** *n*.

ascorbic acid [ass-**core**-bik] *n* vitamin C.

ascribe ❶ *v* attribute, as to a particular origin. **ascription** *n*.

aseptic [eh-**sep**-tik] *adj* free from harmful bacteria. **asepsis** [eh-**sep**-siss] *n* aseptic condition.

asexual [eh-**sex**-yew-al] *adj* without sex. **asexually** *adv*.

ash[1] ❶ *n* **1** powdery substance left when something is burnt. ▷ *pl* **2** remains after burning, esp. of a human body after cremation. **the Ashes** cricket trophy competed for in test matches by England and Australia. **ashen** *adj* pale with shock. **ashtray** *n* receptacle for tobacco ash and cigarette butts. **Ash Wednesday** first day of Lent.

ash[2] *n* tree with grey bark.

ashamed ❶ *adj* feeling shame.

ashlar *n* square block of hewn stone used in building.

ashore ❶ *adv* towards or on land.

ashram *n* religious retreat where a Hindu holy man lives.

Asian *adj* **1** (also **Asiatic**) of the continent of Asia or any of its peoples or languages. **2** of the Indian subcontinent. ▷ *n* **3** person from Asia or a descendant of one. **4** person from the Indian subcontinent or a descendant of one. **Asian pear** apple-shaped pear with crisp juicy flesh.

● **USAGE NOTE**
● Use *Asian* for 'someone who comes
● from Asia'. *Asiatic* in this context can
● be offensive.

aside ❶ *adv* **1** to one side. **2** out of other people's hearing, e.g. *he took me aside to tell me his plans*. ▷ *n* **3** remark not meant to be heard by everyone present.

asinine ❶ [**ass**-in-nine] *adj* stupid, idiotic.

ask ❶ *v* **1** say or write (something) in a form that requires an answer. **2** make a request or demand. **3** invite.

askance [ass-**kanss**] *adv* **look askance at 1** look at with an oblique glance. **2** regard with suspicion.

askew ❶ *adv, adj* to one side, crooked.

aslant *adv, prep* at a slant (to), slanting (across).

asleep ❶ *adj* **1** sleeping. **2** (of limbs) numb.

asp *n* small poisonous snake.

asparagus *n* plant whose shoots are cooked as a vegetable.

aspect ❶ *n* **1** feature or element. **2** position facing a particular direction. **3** appearance or look.

aspen *n* kind of poplar tree.

asperity [ass-**per**-rit-ee] *n* roughness of temper.

aspersion *n* **cast aspersions on** make derogatory remarks about.

asphalt *n* **1** black hard tarlike substance used for road surfaces etc. ▷ *v* **2** cover with asphalt.

asphodel *n* plant with clusters of yellow or white flowers.

———————————————— THESAURUS ————————

ascertain *v* = **find out**, confirm, determine, discover, establish, learn

ascetic *n* = **monk**, abstainer, hermit, nun, recluse ▷ *adj* = **self-denying**, abstinent, austere, celibate, frugal, puritanical, self-disciplined

ascribe *v* = **attribute**, assign, charge, credit, impute, put down, refer, set down

ashamed *adj* = **embarrassed**, distressed, guilty, humiliated, mortified, remorseful, shamefaced, sheepish, sorry

ashen *adj* = **pale**, colourless, grey, leaden, like death warmed up (*inf*), pallid, wan, white

ashore *adv* = **on land**, aground, landwards, on dry land, on the beach, on the shore, shorewards, to the shore

aside *adv* **1** = **to one side**, apart, beside, on one side, out of the way, privately, separately, to the side ▷ *n*

3 = **interpolation**, parenthesis

asinine *adj* = **stupid**, fatuous, foolish, idiotic, imbecilic, moronic, senseless

ask *v* **1** = **inquire**, interrogate, query, question, quiz **2** = **request**, appeal, beg, demand, plead, seek **3** = **invite**, bid, summon

askew *adv* = **crookedly**, aslant, awry, obliquely, off-centre, to one side ▷ *adj* = **crooked**, awry, cockeyed (*inf*), lopsided, oblique, off-centre, skewwhiff (*Brit inf*)

asleep *adj* **1** = **sleeping**, dormant, dozing, fast asleep, napping, slumbering, snoozing (*inf*), sound asleep

aspect *n* **1** = **feature**, angle, facet, side **2** = **position**, outlook, point of view, prospect, scene, situation, view **3** = **appearance**, air, attitude, bearing, condition, demeanour, expression, look, manner

asphyxia ❶ [ass-**fix**-ee-a] *n*
suffocation. **asphyxiate** *v* suffocate.
asphyxiation *n*.

aspic *n* savoury jelly used to coat meat,
eggs, fish, etc.

aspidistra *n* plant with long tapered
leaves.

aspirate *Phonetics* ▷ *v* **1** pronounce with
an *h* sound. ▷ *n* **2** an *h* sound.

aspire ❶ *v* (foll. by *to*) yearn (for), hope
(to do or be). **aspirant** *n* person who
aspires. **aspiration** *n* strong desire or
aim. **aspiring** *adj*.

aspirin *n* **1** drug used to relieve pain and
fever. **2** tablet of this.

ass ❶ *n* **1** donkey. **2** stupid person.

assagai *n* same as ASSEGAI.

assail ❶ *v* attack violently. **assailant** *n*.

assassin ❶ *n* person who murders a
prominent person. **assassinate** *v*
murder (a prominent person).
assassination *n*.

assault ❶ *n* **1** violent attack. ▷ *v*
2 attack violently. **assault course**
series of obstacles used in military
training.

assay *n* **1** analysis of a substance, esp. a
metal, to ascertain its purity. ▷ *v*
2 make such an analysis.

assegai *n* slender spear used in S Africa.

assemble ❶ *v* **1** collect or congregate.
2 put together the parts of (a machine).
assemblage *n* **1** collection or group.
2 assembling. **assembly** *n* **1** *pl* **-blies**
assembled group. **2** assembling.
assembly line sequence of machines
and workers in a factory assembling a
product.

assent ❶ *n* **1** agreement or consent. ▷ *v*
2 agree or consent.

assert ❶ *v* **1** declare forcefully. **2** insist
upon (one's rights etc.). **assert oneself**
put oneself forward forcefully.
assertion *n* **1** positive statement, usu.
made without evidence. **2** act of
asserting. **assertive** *adj* **assertively**
adv **assertiveness** *n*.

assess ❶ *v* **1** judge the worth or
importance of. **2** estimate
the value of (income or property)
for taxation purposes. **assessment** *n*
assessor *n*.

asphyxiate *v* = **suffocate**, choke,
smother, stifle, strangle, strangulate,
throttle

aspiration *n* = **aim**, ambition, desire,
dream, goal, hope, objective, wish

aspire *v* (foll. by *to*) = **aim**, desire, dream,
hope, long, seek, set one's heart on, wish

aspiring *adj* = **hopeful**, ambitious, eager,
longing, wannabe (*inf*), would-be

ass *n* **1** = **donkey**, moke (*sl*) **2** = **fool**,
blockhead, halfwit, idiot, jackass,
numbskull *or* numskull, oaf, twit (*inf*,
chiefly *Brit*)

assail *v* = **attack**, assault, fall upon, lay
into (*inf*), set upon

assailant *n* = **attacker**, aggressor,
assailer, assaulter, invader

assassin *n* = **murderer**, executioner,
hatchet man (*sl*), hit man (*sl*), killer,
liquidator, slayer

assassinate *v* = **murder**, eliminate (*sl*),
hit (*sl*), kill, liquidate, slay, take out (*sl*)

assault *n* **1** = **attack**, charge, invasion,
offensive, onslaught ▷ *v* **2** = **attack**,
beset, fall upon, lay into (*inf*), set about,
set upon, strike at

assemble *v* **1** = **gather**, amass, bring
together, call together, collect, come
together, congregate, meet, muster,
rally **2** = **put together**, build up,
connect, construct, fabricate, fit

together, join, piece together, set up

assembly *n* **1** = **gathering**, collection,
company, conference, congress,
council, crowd, group, mass, meeting
2 = **putting together**, building up,
connecting, construction, piecing
together, setting up

assent *n* **1** = **agreement**, acceptance,
approval, compliance, concurrence,
consent, permission, sanction ▷ *v*
2 = **agree**, allow, approve, consent,
grant, permit

assert *v* **1** = **state**, affirm, declare,
maintain, profess, pronounce, swear
2 = **insist upon**, claim, defend, press,
put forward, stand up for, stress,
uphold **assert oneself** = **be forceful**,
exert one's influence, make one's
presence felt, put oneself forward, put
one's foot down (*inf*)

assertion *n* **1** = **statement**, claim,
declaration, pronouncement
2 = **insistence**, maintenance, stressing

assertive *adj* = **confident**, aggressive,
domineering, emphatic, feisty (*inf*,
chiefly *US & Canad*), forceful, insistent,
positive, pushy (*inf*), strong-willed

assess *v* **1** = **judge**, appraise, estimate,
evaluate, rate, size up (*inf*), value,
weigh **2** = **evaluate**, fix, impose, levy,
rate, tax, value

asset ❶ *n* **1** valuable or useful person or thing. ▷ *pl* **2** property that a person or firm can sell, esp. to pay debts.

asseverate *v* declare solemnly. **asseveration** *n*.

assiduous ❶ *adj* **1** hard-working. **2** done with care. **assiduously** *adv* **assiduity** *n*.

assign ❶ *v* **1** appoint (someone) to a job or task. **2** allot (a task). **3** attribute. **assignation** [ass-sig-**nay**-shun] *n* **1** assigning. **2** secret arrangement to meet. **assignment** *n* **1** task assigned. **2** assigning.

assimilate ❶ *v* **1** learn and understand (information). **2** absorb or be absorbed or incorporated. **assimilable** *adj* **assimilation** *n*.

assist ❶ *v* give help or support. **assistance** *n* **assistant** *n* **1** helper. ▷ *adj* **2** junior or deputy.

assizes *pl n* court sessions formerly held

in each county of England and Wales.

assoc. association.

associate ❶ *v* **1** connect in the mind. **2** mix socially. ▷ *n* **3** partner in business. **4** friend or companion. ▷ *adj* **5** having partial rights or subordinate status, e.g. *associate member*. **association** *n* **1** society or club. **2** associating.

assonance *n* rhyming of vowel sounds but not consonants, as in *time* and *light*. **assonant** *adj*.

assorted ❶ *adj* consisting of various types mixed together. **assortment** *n* assorted mixture.

asst assistant.

assuage [ass-**wage**] *v* relieve (pain, grief, thirst, etc.).

assume ❶ *v* **1** take to be true without proof. **2** take upon oneself, e.g. *he assumed command*. **3** pretend, e.g. *I assumed indifference*. **assumption** *n* **1** thing assumed. **2** assuming.

——————————————— THESAURUS ———————

assessment *n* **1** = **judgment**, appraisal, estimate, evaluation, rating, valuation **2** = **evaluation**, charge, fee, levy, rating, toll, valuation

asset *n* **1** = **benefit**, advantage, aid, blessing, boon, feather in one's cap, help, resource, service ▷ *pl* **2** = **property**, capital, estate, funds, goods, money, possessions, resources, wealth

assiduous *adj* **1** = **diligent**, hard-working, indefatigable, industrious, persevering, persistent, unflagging

assign *v* **1** = **select**, appoint, choose, delegate, designate, name, nominate **2** = **give**, allocate, allot, apportion, consign, distribute, give out, grant **3** = **attribute**, accredit, ascribe, put down

assignation *n* **1** = **selection**, appointment, assignment, choice, delegation, designation, nomination **2** = **secret meeting**, clandestine meeting, illicit meeting, rendezvous, tryst (*arch*)

assignment *n* **1** = **task**, appointment, commission, duty, job, mission, position, post, responsibility

assimilate *v* **1** = **learn**, absorb, digest, take in **2** = **adjust**, adapt, blend in, digest, incorporate, mingle, take in

assist *v* = **help**, abet, aid, cooperate, lend a helping hand, serve, support

assistance *n* = **help**, aid, backing, cooperation, helping hand, support

assistant *n* **1** = **helper**, accomplice, aide, ally, colleague, right-hand man, second, supporter

associate *v* **1** = **connect**, ally, combine, identify, join, link, lump together **2** = **mix**, accompany, consort, hobnob, mingle, socialize ▷ *n* **3** = **partner**, collaborator, colleague, confederate, co-worker **4** = **friend**, ally, cobber (*Aust or old-fashioned NZ inf*), companion, comrade, mate (*inf*)

association *n* **1** = **group**, alliance, band, club, coalition, federation, league, organization, society **2** = **connection**, blend, combination, joining, juxtaposition, mixture, pairing, union

assorted *adj* = **various**, different, diverse, miscellaneous, mixed, motley, sundry, varied

assortment *n* = **variety**, array, choice, collection, jumble, medley, mixture, selection

assume *v* **1** = **take for granted**, believe, expect, fancy, imagine, infer, presume, suppose, surmise, think **2** = **take on**, accept, enter upon, put on, shoulder, take, take over **3** = **put on**, adopt, affect, feign, imitate, impersonate, mimic, pretend to, simulate

assumed *adj* **1** = **taken for granted**, accepted, expected, hypothetical, presumed, presupposed, supposed, surmised **3** = **false**, bogus, counterfeit, fake, fictitious, made-up, make-believe

assure ❶ v 1 promise or guarantee.
2 convince. 3 make (something)
certain. 4 insure against loss of life.
assured adj 1 confident. 2 certain to
happen. **assuredly** [a-**sure**-id-lee] adv
definitely. **assurance** n assuring or
being assured.

astatine n Chemistry radioactive
nonmetallic element.

aster n plant with daisy-like flowers.

asterisk n 1 star-shaped symbol (*) used
in printing or writing to indicate a
footnote etc. ▷ v 2 mark with an
asterisk.

astern adv 1 at or towards the stern of a
ship. 2 backwards.

asteroid n any of the small planets that
orbit the sun between Mars and Jupiter.

asthma [**ass**-ma] n illness causing
difficulty in breathing. **asthmatic**
adj, n.

astigmatism [eh-**stig**-mat-tiz-zum] n
inability of a lens, esp. of the eye, to
focus properly. **astigmatic** adj.

astir adj 1 out of bed. 2 in motion.

astonish ❶ v surprise greatly.
astonishment n **astonishing** adj
astonishingly adv.

astound ❶ v overwhelm with
amazement. **astounding** adj
astoundingly adv.

astrakhan n 1 dark curly fleece of lambs
from Astrakhan in Russia. 2 fabric
resembling this.

astral adj 1 of stars. 2 of the spirit world.

➾**astray** ❶ adv off the right path.

astride adv, prep with a leg on either
side (of).

astringent adj 1 causing contraction of
body tissue. 2 checking the flow of
blood from a cut. 3 severe or harsh. ▷ n
4 astringent substance. **astringency** n.

astro- combining form star.

astrolabe n instrument formerly used to
measure the altitude of stars and
planets.

astrology n study of the alleged
influence of the stars, planets, and
moon on human affairs. **astrologer** n
astrological adj.

astronaut n person trained for
travelling in space.

astronautics n science and technology
of space flight. **astronautical** adj.

astronomy n scientific study of
heavenly bodies. **astronomer** n
astronomical adj 1 very large. 2 of
astronomy. **astronomically** adv.

astrophysics n science of the physical
and chemical properties of stars,
planets, etc. **astrophysical** adj
astrophysicist n.

Astroturf n ® artificial grass.

astute ❶ adj perceptive or shrewd.
astutely adv **astuteness** n.

asunder adv into parts or pieces.

asylum ❶ n 1 refuge or sanctuary. 2 old
name for a mental hospital.

THESAURUS

assumption n 1 = **presumption**, belief,
conjecture, guess, hypothesis,
inference, supposition, surmise
2 = **taking on**, acceptance, acquisition,
adoption, entering upon, putting on,
shouldering, takeover, taking up

assure v 1 = **promise**, certify, confirm,
declare confidently, give one's word to,
guarantee, pledge, swear, vow
2 = **convince**, comfort, embolden,
encourage, hearten, persuade,
reassure 3 = **make certain**, clinch,
complete, confirm, ensure, guarantee,
make sure, seal, secure

assured adj 1 = **confident**, certain,
poised, positive, self-assured, self-
confident, sure of oneself 2 = **certain**,
beyond doubt, confirmed, ensured,
fixed, guaranteed, in the bag (sl),
secure, settled, sure

astonish v = **amaze**, astound, bewilder,
confound, daze, dumbfound, stagger,
stun, surprise

astonishing adj = **amazing**,
astounding, bewildering, breathtaking,
brilliant, jaw-dropping, sensational
(inf), staggering, stunning, surprising

astonishment n = **amazement**, awe,
bewilderment, confusion,
consternation, surprise, wonder,
wonderment

astounding adj = **amazing**,
astonishing, bewildering,
breathtaking, brilliant, impressive, jaw-
dropping, sensational (inf), staggering,
stunning, surprising

astray adv = **off the right track**, adrift,
amiss, lost, off, off course, off the mark

astute adj = **intelligent**, canny, clever,
crafty, cunning, perceptive, sagacious,
sharp, shrewd, subtle

asylum n 1 = **refuge**, harbour, haven,
preserve, retreat, safety, sanctuary,
shelter 2 Old-fashioned = **mental
hospital**, hospital, institution,
madhouse (inf), psychiatric hospital

a

asymmetry *n* lack of symmetry.
asymmetrical, **asymmetric** *adj*.
asymptote [**ass**-im-tote] *n* straight line closely approached but never met by a curve.
at *prep* indicating position in space or time, movement towards an object, etc. e.g. *at midnight; throwing stones at windows*.
At *Chemistry* astatine.
atavism [**at**-a-viz-zum] *n* recurrence of a trait present in distant ancestors.
atavistic *adj*.
ate *v* past tense of EAT.
atelier [**at**-tell-yay] *n* workshop, artist's studio.
atheism ❶ [**aith**-ee-iz-zum] *n* belief that there is no God. **atheist** *n* **atheistic** *adj*.
atherosclerosis *n, pl* **-ses** disease in which deposits of fat cause the walls of the arteries to thicken.
athlete ❶ *n* person trained in or good at athletics. **athletic** *adj* **1** physically fit or strong. **2** of an athlete or athletics. **athletics** *pl n* track-and-field sports such as running, jumping, throwing, etc. **athletically** *adv* **athleticism** *n*.
at-home *n* social gathering in a person's home.
athwart *prep* **1** across. ▷ *adv* **2** transversely.
atigi *n* a type of parka worn by the Inuit in Canada.
atlas *n* book of maps.
atmosphere ❶ *n* **1** mass of gases surrounding a heavenly body, esp. the earth. **2** prevailing tone or mood (of a place etc.). **3** unit of pressure.

atmospheric *adj* **atmospherics** *pl n* radio interference due to electrical disturbance in the atmosphere.
atoll *n* ring-shaped coral reef enclosing a lagoon.
atom ❶ *n* **1** smallest unit of matter which can take part in a chemical reaction. **2** very small amount. **atom bomb** same as ATOMIC BOMB.
atomic *adj* **1** of or using atomic bombs or atomic energy. **2** of atoms. **atomic bomb** bomb in which the energy is provided by nuclear fission. **atomic energy** nuclear energy. **atomic number** number of protons in the nucleus of an atom. **atomic weight** ratio of the mass per atom of an element to one twelfth of the mass of a carbon atom.
atomize *v* reduce to atoms or small particles. **atomizer** *n* device for discharging a liquid in a fine spray.
atonal [eh-**tone**-al] *adj* (of music) not written in an established key. **atonality** *n*.
atone ❶ *v* make amends (for sin or wrongdoing). **atonement** *n*.
atop *prep* on top of.
atrium *n, pl* **atria 1** upper chamber of either half of the heart. **2** central hall extending through several storeys of a modern building. **3** main courtyard of an ancient Roman house.
atrocious ❶ *adj* **1** extremely cruel or wicked. **2** horrifying or shocking. **3** *informal* very bad. **atrociously** *adv* **atrocity** *n* **1** wickedness. **2** *pl* **-ties** act of cruelty.

———————————— THESAURUS ————————————

atheism *n* = **nonbelief**, disbelief, godlessness, heathenism, infidelity, irreligion, paganism, scepticism, unbelief
atheist *n* = **nonbeliever**, disbeliever, heathen, infidel, pagan, sceptic, unbeliever
athlete *n* = **sportsperson**, competitor, contestant, gymnast, player, runner, sportsman, sportswoman
athletic *adj* **1** = **fit**, active, energetic, muscular, powerful, strapping, strong, sturdy
athletics *pl n* = **sports**, contests, exercises, gymnastics, races, track and field events
atmosphere *n* **1** = **air**, aerosphere, heavens, sky **2** = **feeling**, ambience, character, climate, environment, mood, spirit, surroundings, tone

atom *n* **2** = **particle**, bit, dot, speck, spot, trace
atone *v* = **make amends**, compensate, do penance, make redress, make reparation, make up for, pay for, recompense, redress
atonement *n* = **amends**, compensation, penance, recompense, redress, reparation, restitution
atrocious *adj* **1** = **cruel**, barbaric, brutal, fiendish, infernal, monstrous, savage, vicious, wicked **2** = **shocking**, appalling, detestable, grievous, horrible, horrifying, terrible
atrocity *n* **1** = **cruelty**, barbarity, brutality, fiendishness, horror, savagery, viciousness, wickedness **2** = **act of cruelty**, abomination, crime, evil, horror, outrage

atrophy [**at**-trof-fee] *n, pl* **-phies**
  1 wasting away of an organ or part.
  2 failure to grow. ▷ *v* **-phying**, **-phied**
  3 (cause to) waste away.
atropine *n* poisonous alkaloid obtained
  from deadly nightshade.
attach ❶ *v* **1** join, fasten, or connect.
  2 attribute or ascribe, e.g. *he attaches
  great importance to his looks*. **attached**
  adj (foll. by *to*) fond of. **attachment** *n*
  1 act of attaching. **2** fondness.
  3 computer file sent with an email.
attaché [at-**tash**-shay] *n* specialist
  attached to a diplomatic mission.
  attaché case flat rectangular briefcase
  for papers.
attack ❶ *v* **1** launch a physical assault
  (against). **2** criticize. **3** set about (a job
  or problem) with vigour. **4** affect
  adversely. ▷ *n* **5** act of attacking.
  6 sudden bout of illness. **attacker** *n*.
attain ❶ *v* **1** achieve or accomplish (a
  task or aim). **2** reach. **attainable** *adj*

attainment *n* accomplishment.
attar *n* fragrant oil made from roses.
attempt ❶ *v* **1** try, make an effort. ▷ *n*
  2 effort or endeavour.
attend ❶ *v* **1** be present at. **2** go regularly
  to a school, college, etc. **3** look after.
  4 pay attention. **5** apply oneself (to).
  attendance *n* **1** attending. **2** number
  attending. **attendant** *n* **1** person who
  assists, guides, or provides a service.
  ▷ *adj* **2** accompanying. **attention** *n*
  1 concentrated direction of the mind.
  2 consideration. **3** care. **4** alert position
  in military drill. **attentive** *adj* **1** giving
  attention. **2** considerately helpful.
  attentively *adv* **attentiveness** *n*.
attenuated *adj* **1** weakened. **2** thin and
  extended. **attenuation** *n*.
attest *v* affirm the truth of, be proof of.
  attestation *n*.
attic ❶ *n* space or room within the roof
  of a house.
attire ❶ *n* fine or formal clothes.

---

attach *v* **1** = **connect**, add, couple,
  fasten, fix, join, link, secure, stick, tie
  2 = **put**, ascribe, assign, associate,
  attribute, connect
attached *adj* (foll. by *to*) = **fond of**,
  affectionate towards, devoted to, full of
  regard for
attack *v* **1** = **assault**, invade, lay into
  (*inf*), raid, set upon, storm, strike (at)
  2 = **criticize**, abuse, blame, censure,
  have a go (at) (*inf*), put down, vilify ▷ *n*
  5 a = **assault**, campaign, charge,
  foray, incursion, invasion, offensive,
  onslaught, raid, strike **b** = **criticism**,
  abuse, blame, censure, denigration,
  stick (*sl*), vilification **6** = **bout**,
  convulsion, fit, paroxysm, seizure,
  spasm, stroke
attacker *n* **1** = **assailant**, aggressor,
  assaulter, intruder, invader, raider
attain *v* **1** = **achieve**, accomplish,
  acquire, complete, fulfil, gain, get,
  obtain
attainment *n* = **achievement**,
  accomplishment, completion, feat
attempt *v* **1** = **try**, endeavour, seek,
  strive, undertake, venture ▷ *n* **2** = **try**,
  bid, crack (*inf*), effort, go (*inf*), shot
  (*inf*), stab (*inf*), trial
attend *v* **1** = **be present**, appear,
  frequent, go to, haunt, put in an
  appearance, show oneself, turn up,
  visit **3** = **look after**, care for, mind,
  minister to, nurse, take care of, tend

  4 = **pay attention**, hear, heed, listen,
  mark, note, observe, pay heed
  5 attend to = **apply oneself to**,
  concentrate on, devote oneself to, get
  to work on, look after, occupy oneself
  with, see to, take care of
attendance *n* **1** = **presence**,
  appearance, attending, being there
  2 = **turnout**, audience, crowd, gate,
  house, number present
attendant *n* **1** = **assistant**, aide,
  companion, escort, follower, guard,
  helper, servant ▷ *adj*
  2 = **accompanying**, accessory,
  associated, concomitant, consequent,
  related
attention *n* **1** = **concentration**,
  deliberation, heed, intentness, mind,
  scrutiny, thinking, thought
  2 = **notice**, awareness, consciousness,
  consideration, observation,
  recognition, regard **3** = **care**,
  concern, looking after, ministration,
  treatment
attentive *adj* **1** = **careful**, alert, awake,
  concentrating, heedful, intent,
  mindful, observant, studious, watchful
  2 = **considerate**, courteous, helpful,
  kind, obliging, polite, respectful,
  thoughtful
attic *n* = **loft**, garret
attire *n* = **clothes**, apparel, costume,
  dress, garb, garments, outfit, robes,
  wear

a

attired *adj* dressed in a specified way.
attitude ❶ *n* **1** way of thinking and
behaving. **2** posture of the body.
3 *informal* hostile manner.
attorney *n* **1** person legally appointed
to act for another. **2** *US* lawyer.
attract ❶ *v* **1** arouse the interest or
admiration of. **2** draw (something)
closer by exerting a force on it.
attraction *n* **1** power to attract.
2 something that attracts. **attractive**
adj **attractively** *adv* **attractiveness** *n*.
attribute ❶ *v* **1** (usu. foll. by *to*) regard as
belonging to or produced by. ▷ *n*
2 quality or feature representative of a
person or thing. **attributable** *adj*
attribution *n* **attributive** *adj*
Grammar (of an adjective) preceding the
noun modified.
attrition *n* constant wearing down to
weaken or destroy, e.g. *war of attrition*.
attune ❶ *v* adjust or accustom (a person
or thing).
atypical [eh-**tip**-ik-al] *adj* not typical.
Au *Chemistry* gold.
aubergine [**oh**-bur-zheen] *n* dark purple
tropical fruit, cooked and eaten as a
vegetable.
aubrietia [aw-**bree**-sha] *n* trailing plant
with purple flowers.
auburn *adj* (of hair) reddish-brown.
auction *n* **1** public sale in which articles
are sold to the highest bidder. ▷ *v* **2** sell
by auction. **auctioneer** *n* person who
conducts an auction.
audacious ❶ *adj* **1** recklessly bold or

daring. **2** impudent. **audaciously** *adv*
audacity *n*.
audible ❶ *adj* loud enough to be heard.
audibly *adv* **audibility** *n*.
audience ❶ *n* **1** group of spectators or
listeners. **2** formal interview.
audio *adj* **1** of sound or hearing. **2** of or
for the transmission or reproduction of
sound. **audiotypist** *n* typist trained to
type from a dictating machine.
audiovisual *adj* (esp. of teaching aids)
involving both sight and hearing.
audit *n* **1** official examination of
business accounts. ▷ *v* **auditing**,
audited 2 examine (business
accounts) officially. **auditor** *n*.
audition *n* **1** test of a performer's ability
for a particular role or job. ▷ *v* **2** test or
be tested in an audition.
auditorium *n*, *pl* **-toriums**, **-toria** area
of a concert hall or theatre where the
audience sits.
auditory *adj* of or relating to hearing.
au fait [oh **fay**] *adj French* **1** fully
informed. **2** expert.
auf Wiedersehen [owf **vee**-der-zay-
en] *interj German* goodbye.
Aug. August.
auger *n* carpenter's tool for boring holes.
aught *pron old-fashioned* anything
whatever.
augment *v* increase or enlarge.
augmentation *n*.
au gratin [oh **grat**-tan] *adj* covered and
cooked with breadcrumbs and
sometimes cheese.

——————————————————————— THESAURUS ———————————

attitude *n* **1** = **disposition**, approach,
frame of mind, mood, opinion, outlook,
perspective, point of view, position,
stance **2** = **position**, pose, posture,
stance
attract *v* **1** = **appeal to**, charm, enchant
2 = **draw**, allure, entice, lure, pull (*inf*),
tempt
attraction *n* **1** = **appeal**, allure, charm,
enticement, fascination, lure,
magnetism, pull (*inf*), temptation
attractive *adj* = **appealing**, alluring,
charming, fair, fetching,
good-looking, handsome, inviting,
lekker (*S Afr sl*), lovely, pleasant, pretty,
tempting
attribute *v* (usu. foll. by *to*) = **ascribe**,
charge, credit, put down to, set down
to ▷ *n* **2** = **quality**, aspect, character,
characteristic, facet, feature,
peculiarity, property, trait

attune *v* = **accustom**, adapt, adjust,
familiarize, harmonize, regulate
audacious *adj* **1** = **daring**, bold, brave,
courageous, fearless, intrepid, rash,
reckless **2** = **cheeky**, brazen, defiant,
impertinent, impudent, insolent,
presumptuous, shameless
audacity *n* **1** = **daring**, boldness,
bravery, courage, fearlessness, nerve,
rashness, recklessness **2** = **cheek**,
chutzpah (*US & Canad inf*), effrontery,
impertinence, impudence, insolence,
nerve
audible *adj* = **clear**, detectable,
discernible, distinct, hearable,
perceptible
audience *n* **1** = **spectators**, assembly,
crowd, gallery, gathering, listeners,
onlookers, turnout, viewers
2 = **interview**, consultation, hearing,
meeting, reception

augur v be a sign of (future events).
augury n **1** foretelling of the future.
2 pl **-ries** omen.
august adj dignified and imposing.
August n eighth month of the year.
auk n northern sea bird with short wings
and black-and-white plumage.
auld lang syne n times past.
aunt n **1** father's or mother's sister.
2 uncle's wife. **auntie**, **aunty** n, pl
aunties informal aunt. **Aunt Sally**
1 figure used in fairgrounds as a target.
2 target of abuse or criticism.
au pair n young foreign woman who
does housework in return for board and
lodging.
aura ❶ n distinctive air or quality of a
person or thing.
aural adj of or using the ears or hearing.
aureate adj **1** covered with gold, gilded.
2 (of style of writing or speaking)
excessively elaborate.
aureole, aureola n halo.
au revoir [**oh** riv-**vwahr**] interj French
goodbye.
auricle n **1** upper chamber of the heart.
2 outer part of the ear. **auricular** adj.
auriferous adj containing gold.
aurochs n, pl **aurochs** recently extinct
European wild ox.
aurora n, pl **-ras**, **-rae** bands of light
sometimes seen in the sky in polar
regions. **aurora australis** aurora seen
near the South Pole. **aurora borealis**
aurora seen near the North Pole.
auscultation n listening to the internal
sounds of the body, usu. with a
stethoscope, to help with diagnosis.
auspices [**aw**-spiss-siz] pl n **under the**
auspices of with the support and
approval of.
auspicious ❶ adj showing signs of
future success, favourable.
auspiciously adv.
Aussie n, adj informal Australian.
austere ❶ adj **1** stern or severe.
2 ascetic or self-disciplined. **3** severely
simple or plain. **austerely** adv
austerity n.
austral adj southern.
Australasian n, adj (person) from
Australia, New Zealand, and
neighbouring islands.
Australian n, adj (person) from
Australia.
Austrian n, adj (person) from Austria.
autarchy [**aw**-tar-kee] n absolute
power or autocracy.
autarky [**aw**-tar-kee] n policy of
economic self-sufficiency.
authentic ❶ adj known to be real,
genuine. **authentically** adv
authenticity n **authenticate** v
establish as genuine. **authentication** n.
author ❶ n **1** writer of a book etc.
2 originator or creator. **authorship** n.
authority ❶ n, pl **-ties 1** power to
command or control others. **2** (often

━━━━━━━━━━━ **THESAURUS** ━━━━━━━━━━━

aura n = **air**, ambience, atmosphere,
feeling, mood, quality, tone
auspicious adj = **favourable**, bright,
encouraging, felicitous, hopeful,
promising
austere adj **1** = **stern**, forbidding,
formal, serious, severe, solemn, strict
2 = **ascetic**, abstemious, puritanical,
self-disciplined, sober, solemn, strait-
laced, strict **3** = **plain**, bleak, harsh,
simple, spare, Spartan, stark
austerity n **1** = **sternness**, formality,
inflexibility, rigour, seriousness,
severity, solemnity, stiffness, strictness
2 = **asceticism**, puritanism, self-denial,
self-discipline, sobriety **3** = **plainness**,
simplicity, starkness
authentic adj = **genuine**, actual,
authoritative, bona fide, legitimate,
pure, real, true-to-life, valid
authenticity n = **genuineness**,
accuracy, certainty, faithfulness,
legitimacy, purity, truthfulness, validity
author n **1** = **writer**, composer, creator
2 = **creator**, architect, designer,
father, founder, inventor, originator,
producer
authoritarian n = **disciplinarian**,
absolutist, autocrat, despot, dictator,
tyrant ▷ adj = **strict**, autocratic,
dictatorial, doctrinaire, dogmatic,
severe, tyrannical
authoritative adj **1** = **reliable**,
accurate, authentic, definitive,
dependable, trustworthy, valid
2 = **commanding**, assertive,
imperious, imposing, masterly, self-
assured
authority n **1** = **power**, command,
control, direction, influence, mana
(NZ), supremacy, sway, weight **2** (often
pl) = **powers that be**, administration,
government, management,
officialdom, police, the Establishment
3 = **expert**, connoisseur, guru, judge,
master, professional, specialist

pl) person or group having this power.
3 expert in a particular field.
authoritarian n, adj (person) insisting
on strict obedience to authority.
authoritative adj **1** recognized as
being reliable, e.g. the authoritative book
on Shakespeare. **2** possessing authority.
authoritatively adv **authorize** v **1** give
authority to. **2** give permission for.
authorization n.
autism n Psychiatry disorder, usu. of
children, characterized by lack of
response to people and limited ability
to communicate. **autistic** adj.
auto- combining form self-, e.g.
autobiography.
autobahn n German motorway.
autobiography n, pl **-phies** account of
a person's life written by that person.
autobiographical adj
autobiographically adv.
autocrat ❶ n **1** ruler with absolute
authority. **2** dictatorial person.
autocratic adj **autocratically** adv
autocracy n government by an
autocrat.
autocross n motor-racing over a rough
course.
Autocue n ® electronic television
prompting device displaying a speaker's
script, unseen by the audience.
autogiro, autogyro n, pl **-ros** self-
propelled aircraft resembling a
helicopter but with an unpowered rotor.
autograph n **1** handwritten signature
of a (famous) person. ▷ v **2** write one's
signature on or in.
automat n US vending machine.
automate v make (a manufacturing

process) automatic. **automation** n.
automatic ❶ adj **1** (of a device)
operating mechanically by itself. **2** (of a
process) performed by automatic
equipment. **3** done without conscious
thought. **4** (of a firearm) self-loading.
▷ n **5** self-loading firearm. **6** vehicle
with automatic transmission.
automatically adv **automatic
transmission** transmission system in a
motor vehicle in which the gears
change automatically.
automaton n **1** robot. **2** person who
acts mechanically.
automobile n US motor car.
automotive adj relating to motor
vehicles.
autonomy ❶ n self-government.
autonomous adj.
autopsy n, pl **-sies** dissection and
examination of a corpse to determine
the cause of death.
autoroute n French motorway.
autostrada n Italian motorway.
autosuggestion n process in which a
person unconsciously influences his or
her own behaviour or beliefs.
autumn n season between summer and
winter. **autumnal** adj.
auxiliary ❶ adj **1** secondary or
supplementary. **2** supporting. ▷ n, pl
-ries 3 person or thing that
supplements or supports. **auxiliary
verb** verb used to form the tense,
voice, or mood of another, such as will
in I will go.
avail ❶ v **1** be of use or advantage (to).
▷ n **2** use or advantage, esp. in to no
avail. **avail oneself of** make use of.

———————————————————————————— THESAURUS ————————

authorization n **1** = **permission**, a
blank cheque, approval, leave, licence,
permit, warrant
authorize v **1** = **empower**, accredit,
commission, enable, entitle, give
authority **2** = **permit**, allow, approve,
give authority for, license, sanction,
warrant
autocracy n = **dictatorship**,
absolutism, despotism, tyranny
autocrat n **1** = **dictator**, absolutist,
despot, tyrant
autocratic adj = **dictatorial**, absolute,
all-powerful, despotic, domineering,
imperious, tyrannical
automatic adj **1, 2** = **mechanical**,
automated, mechanized, push-button,
self-propelling **3** = **involuntary**,

instinctive, mechanical, natural, reflex,
spontaneous, unconscious, unwilled
autonomous adj = **self-ruling**, free,
independent, self-determining,
self-governing, sovereign
autonomy n = **independence**, freedom,
home rule, self-determination,
self-government, self-rule, sovereignty
auxiliary adj **1** = **supplementary**,
back-up, emergency, fall-back, reserve,
secondary, subsidiary, substitute
2 = **supporting**, accessory, aiding,
ancillary, assisting, helping ▷ n
3 = **helper**, assistant, associate,
backup, companion, reserve,
subordinate, supporter
avail v **1** = **benefit**, aid, assist, be of
advantage, be useful, help, profit ▷ n

available ❶ *adj* obtainable or accessible. **availability** *n*.

avalanche ❶ *n* **1** mass of snow or ice falling down a mountain. **2** sudden overwhelming quantity of anything.

avant-garde ❶ [av-ong-**gard**] *n* **1** group of innovators, esp. in the arts. ▷ *adj* **2** innovative and progressive.

avarice ❶ [**av**-a-riss] *n* greed for wealth. **avaricious** *adj*.

avast *interj Nautical* stop.

avatar *n Hinduism* appearance of a god in animal or human form.

Ave. Avenue.

Ave Maria [**ah**-vay ma-**ree**-a] *n* same as HAIL MARY.

avenge ❶ *v* take revenge in retaliation for (harm done) or on behalf of (a person harmed). **avenger** *n*.

avenue ❶ *n* **1** wide street. **2** road between two rows of trees. **3** way of approach.

aver [av-**vur**] *v* **averring**, **averred** state to be true.

average ❶ *n* **1** typical or normal amount or quality. **2** result obtained by adding quantities together and dividing the total by the number of quantities. ▷ *adj* **3** usual or typical. **4** calculated as an average. ▷ *v* **5** calculate the average of. **6** amount to as an average.

averse ❶ *adj* (usu. foll. by *to*) disinclined or unwilling. **aversion** *n* **1** strong dislike. **2** person or thing disliked.

avert ❶ *v* **1** turn away. **2** ward off.

aviary *n, pl* **aviaries** large cage or enclosure for birds.

aviation ❶ *n* art of flying aircraft. **aviator** *n*.

avid ❶ *adj* **1** keen or enthusiastic. **2** greedy (for). **avidly** *adv* **avidity** *n*.

avocado *n, pl* **-dos** pear-shaped tropical fruit with a leathery green skin and yellowish-green flesh.

avocation *n old-fashioned* **1** occupation. **2** hobby.

avocet *n* long-legged wading bird with a long slender upward-curving bill.

avoid ❶ *v* **1** prevent from happening. **2** refrain from. **3** keep away from. **avoidable** *adj* **avoidance** *n*.

avoirdupois [av-er-de-**poise**] *n* system of weights based on pounds and ounces.

avow ❶ *v* **1** state or affirm. **2** admit

---

2 = **benefit**, advantage, aid, good, help, profit, use

availability *n* = **accessibility**, attainability, handiness, readiness

available *adj* = **accessible**, at hand, at one's disposal, free, handy, on tap, ready, to hand

avalanche *n* **1** = **snow-slide**, landslide, landslip **2** = **flood**, barrage, deluge, inundation, torrent

avant-garde *adj* **2** = **progressive**, experimental, ground-breaking, innovative, pioneering, unconventional

avarice *n* = **greed**, covetousness, meanness, miserliness, niggardliness, parsimony, stinginess

avaricious *adj* = **grasping**, covetous, greedy, mean, miserly, niggardly, parsimonious, stingy

avenge *v* = **get revenge for**, get even for (*inf*), get one's own back, hit back, punish, repay, retaliate

avenue *n* **1** = **street**, boulevard, course, drive, passage, path, road, route, way

average *n* **1** = **usual**, norm, normal, par, standard **2** = **mean**, medium, midpoint ▷ *adj* **3** = **usual**, commonplace, fair, general, normal, ordinary, regular, standard, typical **4** = **mean**, intermediate, median, medium, middle

▷ *v* **6** = **make on average**, balance out to, be on average, do on average, even out to

averse *adj* (usu. foll. by *to*) = **opposed**, disinclined, hostile, ill-disposed, loath, reluctant, unwilling

aversion *n* **1** = **hatred**, animosity, antipathy, disinclination, dislike, hostility, revulsion, unwillingness

avert *v* **1** = **turn away**, turn aside **2** = **ward off**, avoid, fend off, forestall, frustrate, preclude, prevent, stave off

aviator *n* = **pilot**, aeronaut, airman, flyer

avid *adj* **1** = **enthusiastic**, ardent, devoted, eager, fanatical, intense, keen, passionate, zealous **2** = **insatiable**, grasping, greedy, hungry, rapacious, ravenous, thirsty, voracious

avoid *v* **1** = **prevent**, avert **2** = **refrain from**, dodge, duck (out of) (*inf*), eschew, fight shy of, shirk **3** = **keep away from**, bypass, dodge, elude, escape, evade, shun, steer clear of

avoidance *n* **3** = **evasion**, dodging, eluding, escape, keeping away, shunning, steering clear

avowed *adj* **1** = **declared**, open, professed, self-proclaimed, sworn

openly. **avowal** n **avowed** adj
avowedly [a-**vow**-id-lee] adv.
avuncular adj (of a man) friendly, helpful,
and caring towards someone younger.
await ❶ v **1** wait for. **2** be in store for.
awake ❶ v **awaking**, **awoke**, **awoken**
1 emerge or rouse from sleep. **2** (cause
to) become alert. ▷ adj **3** not sleeping.
4 alert.
awaken ❶ v awake. **awakening** n.
award ❶ v **1** give (something, such as a
prize) formally. ▷ n **2** something
awarded, such as a prize.
aware ❶ adj having knowledge,
informed. **awareness** n.
awash adv washed over by water.
away ❶ adv **1** from a place, e.g. go away.
2 to another place, e.g. put that gun
away. **3** out of existence, e.g. fade away.
4 continuously, e.g. laughing away.
▷ adj **5** not present. **6** distant, e.g. two
miles away. **7** Sport played on an

opponent's ground.
awe ❶ n **1** wonder and respect mixed
with dread. ▷ v **2** fill with awe.
awesome adj **1** inspiring awe. **2** slang
excellent or outstanding. **awestruck**
adj filled with awe.
aweigh adj Nautical (of an anchor) no
longer hooked into the bottom.
awful ❶ adj **1** very bad or unpleasant.
2 informal very great. **3** obs inspiring
awe. **awfully** adv **1** in an unpleasant
way. **2** informal very. **awfulness** n.
awhile adv for a brief time.
awkward ❶ adj **1** clumsy or ungainly.
2 embarrassed. **3** difficult to use or
handle. **4** inconvenient. **awkwardly**
adv **awkwardness** n.
awl n pointed tool for piercing wood,
leather, etc.
awning n canvas roof supported by a
frame to give protection against the
weather.

———————————————— THESAURUS ————————

2 = **confessed**, acknowledged,
admitted
await v **1** = **wait for**, abide, anticipate,
expect, look for, look forward to, stay
for **2** = **be in store for**, attend, be in
readiness for, be prepared for, be ready
for, wait for
awake v **1** = **wake up**, awaken, rouse,
wake **2** = **alert**, arouse, kindle,
provoke, revive, stimulate, stir up ▷ adj
3 = **not sleeping**, aroused, awakened,
aware, conscious, wakeful, wide-
awake **4** = **alert**, alive, attentive,
aware, heedful, observant, on the
lookout, vigilant, watchful
awaken v = **awake**, arouse, revive,
rouse, wake
award v **1** = **give**, bestow, confer,
endow, grant, hand out, present ▷ n
2 = **prize**, decoration, gift, grant, trophy
aware adj = **knowing**, acquainted with,
conscious of, conversant with,
enlightened, familiar with, informed, in
the loop, in the picture, knowledgeable,
mindful of
awareness n = **knowledge**,
consciousness, familiarity, perception,
realization, recognition, understanding
away adv **1** = **from here**, abroad, apart,
at a distance, elsewhere, far, from
home, hence, off, remote **2** = **aside**, out
of the way, to one side
4 = **continuously**, incessantly,
interminably, relentlessly, repeatedly,
uninterruptedly, unremittingly ▷ adj

5 = **not present**, abroad, absent,
elsewhere, gone, not at home, not
here, out
awe n **1** = **wonder**, admiration,
amazement, astonishment, dread, fear,
horror, respect, reverence, terror ▷ v
2 = **impress**, amaze, astonish, frighten,
horrify, intimidate, stun, terrify
awesome adj = **awe-inspiring**,
amazing, astonishing, breathtaking,
formidable, impressive, intimidating,
stunning
awful adj **1** = **terrible**, abysmal,
appalling, deplorable, dreadful,
frightful, ghastly, horrendous **3** Obs
= **awe-inspiring**, awesome, fearsome,
majestic, solemn
awfully adv **1** = **badly**, disgracefully,
dreadfully, reprehensibly, unforgivably,
unpleasantly, woefully, wretchedly
2 Inf = **very**, dreadfully, exceedingly,
exceptionally, extremely, greatly,
immensely, terribly
awkward adj **1** = **clumsy**, gauche,
gawky, inelegant, lumbering,
uncoordinated, ungainly
2 = **embarrassed**, ill at ease,
uncomfortable **3** = **difficult**,
cumbersome, troublesome,
unmanageable, unwieldy
4 = **inconvenient**
awkwardness n **1** = **clumsiness**,
gawkiness, inelegance, ungainliness
3 = **unwieldiness**, difficulty
4 = **inconvenience**

awoke v past tense of AWAKE. **awoken**
v past participle of AWAKE.

AWOL [**eh**-woll] adj Military absent
without leave.

awry [a-**rye**] adv, adj **1** with a twist to
one side, askew. **2** amiss.

axe ❶ n **1** tool with a sharp blade for felling
trees or chopping wood. **2** informal
dismissal from employment etc. ▷ v
3 informal dismiss (employees), restrict
(expenditure), or terminate (a project).

axil n angle where the stalk of a leaf joins
a stem.

axiom ❶ n **1** generally accepted
principle. **2** self-evident statement.
axiomatic adj **1** containing axioms.
2 self-evident.

axis ❶ n, pl **axes 1** (imaginary) line round
which a body can rotate or about which
an object or geometrical figure is
symmetrical. **2** one of two fixed lines
on a graph, against which quantities or
positions are measured. **axial** adj.

axle ❶ n shaft on which a wheel or pair of
wheels turns.

axolotl n aquatic salamander of central
America.

ayah n (in parts of the former British
Empire) native maidservant or
nursemaid.

ayatollah n Islamic religious leader in
Iran.

aye, ay interj **1** yes. ▷ n **2** affirmative
vote or voter.

AZ Arizona.

azalea [az-**zale**-ya] n garden shrub
grown for its showy flowers.

azimuth n **1** arc of the sky between the
zenith and the horizon. **2** horizontal
angle of a bearing measured clockwise
from the north.

Aztec n, adj (person) of the race ruling
Mexico before the Spanish conquest in
the 16th century.

azure adj, n (of) the colour of a clear
blue sky.

——————————— THESAURUS ———————————

axe n **1** = **hatchet**, adze, chopper **2** Inf
= **the sack**, dismissal, termination, the
boot (sl), the chop (sl) ▷ v **3** Inf = **cut
back**, cancel, dismiss, dispense with,
eliminate, fire (inf), get rid of, remove,
sack (inf)

axiom n **1** = **principle**, adage, aphorism,

dictum, maxim, precept **2** = **truism**

axiomatic adj **2** = **self-evident**,
accepted, assumed, certain, given,
granted, manifest, understood

axis n **1** = **pivot**, axle, centre line, shaft,
spindle

axle n = **shaft**, axis, pin, pivot, rod, spindle

Bb

B *Chemistry* boron.

Ba *Chemistry* barium.

BA Bachelor of Arts.

baa *v* **baaing, baaed 1** make the characteristic bleating sound of a sheep. ▷ *n* **2** cry made by a sheep.

baas *n S Afr* boss.

babble ❶ *v* **1** talk excitedly or foolishly. **2** (of streams) make a low murmuring sound. ▷ *n* **3** muddled or foolish speech.

babe *n* **1** baby. **2** *slang* an attractive girl.

babel [**babe**-el] *n* confused mixture of noises or voices.

babiche *n Canad* thongs or lacings of rawhide.

baboon *n* large monkey with a pointed face and a long tail.

baby ❶ *n, pl* **-bies 1** very young child or animal. **2** *slang* sweetheart. ▷ *adj* **3** comparatively small of its type. **babyish** *adj* **baby-sit** *v* take care of a child while the parents are out. **baby-sitter** *n*.

baccarat [**back**-a-rah] *n* card game involving gambling.

bacchanalia *n* wild drunken party or orgy.

bach *n NZ* small holiday cottage.

bachelor *n* **1** unmarried man. **2** person who holds the lowest university or college degree, e.g. *a Bachelor of Science*.

- **SPELLING TIP**
- We find *batchelor* spelt with a t **14**
- times in the Bank of English. The
- correct spelling has no *t*: **bachelor**.

bacillus [bass-**ill**-luss] *n, pl* **-li** [-lie] rod-shaped bacterium, esp. one causing disease. **bacillary** *adj* of or caused by bacilli.

back ❶ *n* **1** rear part of the human body, from the neck to the pelvis. **2** spinal column. **3** part or side of an object opposite the front. **4** part of anything less often seen or used. **5** *Ball games* defensive player or position. ▷ *v* **6** (cause to) move backwards. **7** provide money for (a person or enterprise). **8** bet on the success of. **9** (foll. by *onto*) have the back facing towards. ▷ *adj* **10** situated behind, e.g. *back garden*. **11** owing from an earlier date, e.g. *back pay*. ▷ *adv* **12** at, to, or towards the rear. **13** to or towards the original starting point or condition. **backer** *n* person who gives financial support. **backfire** *v* fail to have the desired effect. **background** *n* space behind chief figures of a picture, etc. **backing** *n* **1** support. **2** musical accompaniment for a pop singer. **backlash** *n* sudden and adverse reaction. **backward** *adj* **1** directed towards the rear. **2** retarded in physical, material, or intellectual development. **backwardness** *n* **backwards** *adv* **1** towards the rear. **2** with the back foremost. **3** in the reverse of the usual direction. **back door** secret or underhand means of entry to a job etc. **back down** *v* withdraw an earlier claim. **back number** old issue of a newspaper or magazine. **back out** *v* withdraw (from an agreement). **back room** place where secret research or planning is done. **back up** *v* support. **backup** *n* **1** support or reinforcement. **2** reserve or substitute.

backbencher *n* Member of Parliament who does not hold office in the government or opposition.

backbiting ❶ *n* spiteful talk about an

──────── THESAURUS ────────

babble *v* **1** = **gabble**, burble, chatter, gibber, jabber, prattle, waffle (*inf, chiefly Brit*) **2** = **gurgle** ▷ *n* **3** = **gabble**, burble, drivel, gibberish, waffle (*inf, chiefly Brit*)

baby *n* **1** = **infant**, babe, babe in arms, bairn (*Scot*), child, newborn child ▷ *adj* **3** = **small**, little, mini, miniature, minute, teeny-weeny, tiny, wee

babyish *adj* **1** = **childish**, foolish, immature, infantile, juvenile, puerile, sissy, spoiled

back *n* **1** = **rear**, end, hindquarters **3** = **end**, far end, hind part, rear, reverse, stern, tail end ▷ *v* **7** = **support**, advocate, assist, champion, endorse, promote, sponsor ▷ *adj* **10** = **rear**, end, hind, hindmost, posterior, tail **11** = **previous**, delayed, earlier, elapsed, former, overdue, past

backbiting *n* = **slander**, bitchiness (*sl*), cattiness (*inf*), defamation, disparagement, gossip, malice,

absent person.

backbone ❶ n 1 spinal column.
2 strength of character.

backbreaking ❶ adj (of work or effort)
exhausting.

backchat n informal impudent replies.

backcloth, backdrop n painted
curtain at the back of a stage set.

backdate v make (a document) effective
from a date earlier than its completion.

backfire ❶ v 1 (of a plan) fail to have the
desired effect. 2 (of an engine) make a
loud noise like an explosion.

backgammon n game played with
counters and dice.

background ❶ n 1 events or
circumstances that help to explain
something. 2 person's social class,
education, or experience. 3 part of a
scene or picture furthest from the viewer.

backhand n Tennis, etc. stroke played
with the back of the hand facing the
direction of the stroke. **backhanded**
adj ambiguous or implying criticism,
e.g. a backhanded compliment.
backhander n slang bribe.

backlash ❶ n sudden and adverse
reaction.

backlog ❶ n accumulation of things to
be dealt with.

backpack n 1 rucksack. ▷ v 2 go hiking
with a backpack. **backpacker** n.

back-pedal v retract or modify a
previous statement.

back-seat driver n informal person who
offers unwanted advice.

backside n informal buttocks.

backslide ❶ v relapse into former bad
habits. **backslider** n.

backstage adv, adj behind the stage in
a theatre.

backstairs adj underhand, e.g.
backstairs deals.

backstreet n 1 street far from any main
road. ▷ adj 2 secret or illegal, e.g. a
backstreet abortion.

backstroke n swimming stroke
performed on the back.

backtrack v 1 return by the same route
by which one has come. 2 retract or
reverse one's opinion or policy.

backwash n 1 water washed
backwards by the motion of a boat.
2 repercussion.

backwater n isolated or backward place
or condition.

backwoods pl n remote sparsely
populated area.

bacon n salted or smoked pig meat.

bacteria ❶ pl n, sing **-rium** large group
of microorganisms, many of which
cause disease. **bacterial** adj
bacteriology n study of bacteria.
bacteriologist n.

- **USAGE NOTE**
- Note that the word bacteria is
- already plural and does not need
- an '-s'. The singular form is bacterium.

THESAURUS

spitefulness

backbone n 1 = **spinal column**, spine,
vertebrae, vertebral column
2 = **strength of character**, character,
courage, determination, fortitude, grit,
nerve, pluck, resolution

backbreaking adj = **exhausting**,
arduous, crushing, gruelling, hard,
laborious, punishing, strenuous

back down v = **give in**, accede, admit
defeat, back-pedal, cave in (inf),
concede, surrender, withdraw, yield

backer n = **supporter**, advocate, angel
(inf), benefactor, patron, promoter,
second, sponsor, subscriber

backfire v 1 = **fail**, boomerang,
disappoint, flop (inf), miscarry,
rebound, recoil

background n 1 = **circumstances**,
culture, environment, history, tradition
2 = **upbringing**, education, grounding

backing n 1 = **support**, aid, assistance,
encouragement, endorsement, moral

support, patronage, sponsorship

backlash n = **reaction**, counteraction,
recoil, repercussion, resistance,
response, retaliation

backlog n = **build-up**, accumulation,
excess, hoard, reserve, stock, supply

back out v = **withdraw**, abandon,
cancel, give up, go back on, resign,
retreat

backslide v = **relapse**, go astray, go
wrong, lapse, revert, slip, stray, weaken

backslider n = **relapser**, apostate,
deserter, recidivist, recreant, renegade,
turncoat

back up v = **support**, aid, assist, bolster,
confirm, corroborate, reinforce,
second, stand by, substantiate

backward adj 2 = **slow**, behind, dull,
retarded, subnormal, underdeveloped,
undeveloped

backwards adv 1 = **towards the rear**,
behind, rearward 3 = **in reverse**

bacteria pl n = **microorganisms**, bacilli,

bad ❶ *adj* **worse**, **worst 1** of poor quality. **2** lacking skill or talent. **3** harmful. **4** immoral or evil. **5** naughty or mischievous. **6** rotten or decayed. **7** unpleasant. **badly** *adv* **badness** *n* **bad blood** feeling of intense hatred.

bade *v* a past tense of BID.

badge ❶ *n* emblem worn to show membership, rank, etc.

badger ❶ *n* **1** nocturnal burrowing mammal with a black and white head. ▷ *v* **2** pester or harass.

badinage ❶ [**bad**-in-nahzh] *n* playful and witty conversation.

badminton *n* game played with rackets and a shuttlecock, which is hit back and forth over a high net.

baffle ❶ *v* **1** perplex or puzzle. ▷ *n* **2** device to limit or regulate the flow of fluid, light, or sound. **bafflement** *n*.

bag ❶ *n* **1** flexible container with an opening at one end. **2** handbag or piece of luggage. **3** loose fold of skin under the eyes. **4** *offens* ugly or bad-tempered woman. **5** amount of game killed by a hunter. ▷ *v* **bagging**, **bagged 6** put into a bag. **7** succeed in capturing, killing or scoring, e.g. *he has bagged over 40 goals this season*. **bags of** *informal* lots (of). **baggy** *adj* **-gier**, **-giest** (of clothes) hanging loosely.

bagatelle *n* **1** something of little value. **2** board game in which balls are struck

into holes.

bagel *n* hard ring-shaped bread roll.

baggage ❶ *n* **1** suitcases packed for a journey. **2** *informal* previous knowledge or experience that affects contemporary behaviour, e.g. *ideological baggage*.

bagpipes *pl n* musical wind instrument with reed pipes and an inflatable bag.

bah *interj* expression of contempt or disgust.

bail¹ *n* **1** *Law* money deposited with a court as security for a person's reappearance in court. **2** person giving such security. ▷ *v* **3** pay bail for (a person).

bail², **bale** ❶ *v* (foll. by *out*) **1** remove (water) from (a boat). **2** *informal* help (a person or organization) out of a predicament. **3** make an emergency parachute jump from an aircraft.

bail³ *n Cricket* either of two wooden bars across the tops of the stumps.

bailey *n* outermost wall or court of a castle.

bailiff *n* **1** sheriff's officer who serves writs and summonses. **2** landlord's agent.

bailiwick *n* area a person is interested in or operates in.

bairn *n Scot* child.

bait ❶ *n* **1** piece of food on a hook or in a trap to attract fish or animals. **2** enticement or temptation. ▷ *v* **3** put a

───────────────────────────── THESAURUS ─────────────────

bugs (*sl*), germs, microbes, pathogens, viruses

bad *adj* **1** = **inferior**, defective, faulty, imperfect, inadequate, poor, substandard, unsatisfactory **3** = **harmful**, damaging, dangerous, deleterious, detrimental, hurtful, ruinous, unhealthy **4** = **wicked**, corrupt, criminal, evil, immoral, mean, sinful, wrong **5** = **naughty**, disobedient, mischievous, unruly **6** = **rotten**, decayed, mouldy, off, putrid, rancid, sour, spoiled **7** = **unfavourable**, adverse, distressing, gloomy, grim, troubled, unfortunate, unpleasant

badge *n* = **mark**, brand, device, emblem, identification, insignia, sign, stamp, token

badger *v* **2** = **pester**, bully, goad, harass, hound, importune, nag, plague, torment

badinage *n* = **wordplay**, banter,

mockery, pleasantry, repartee, teasing

badly *adv* **2** = **poorly**, carelessly, imperfectly, inadequately, incorrectly, ineptly, wrongly

baffle *v* **1** = **puzzle**, bewilder, confound, confuse, flummox, mystify, nonplus, perplex, stump

bag *n* **1** = **container**, receptacle, sac, sack ▷ *v* **7** = **catch**, acquire, capture, kill, land, shoot, trap

baggage *n* **1** = **luggage**, accoutrements, bags, belongings, equipment, gear, paraphernalia, suitcases, things

baggy *adj* = **loose**, bulging, droopy, floppy, ill-fitting, oversize, roomy, sagging, slack

bail¹ *n* **1** *Law* = **security**, bond, guarantee, pledge, surety, warranty

bail², **bale** *v* (foll. by *out*) **2** *Inf* = **help**, aid, relieve, rescue, save (someone's) bacon (*inf, chiefly Brit*) ▷ *v* **3** = **escape**, quit, retreat, withdraw

bait *n* **2** = **lure**, allurement, attraction,

piece of food on or in (a hook or trap).
4 persecute or tease.

baize n woollen fabric used to cover
billiard and card tables.

bake v **1** cook by dry heat as in an oven.
2 make or become hardened by heat.
3 informal be extremely hot. **baker** n
person whose business is to make or
sell bread, cakes, etc. **baker's dozen**
thirteen. **bakery** n, pl **-eries** place
where bread, cakes, etc. are baked or
sold. **baking powder** powdered
mixture containing sodium
bicarbonate, used as a raising agent in
baking. **bakeoff** n baking competition.

bakeapple n cloudberry.

bakkie n S Afr small truck.

baksheesh n (in some Eastern
countries) money given as a tip.

balaclava, balaclava helmet n close-
fitting woollen hood that covers the
ears and neck.

balalaika n guitar-like musical
instrument with a triangular body.

balance ❶ n **1** stability of mind or body.
2 state in which a weight or amount is
evenly distributed. **3** amount that
remains, e.g. the balance of what you owe.
4 weighing device. **5** difference
between the credits and debits of an
account. ▷ v **6** weigh in a balance.
7 make or remain steady. **8** consider or
compare. **9** compare or equalize the
money going into or coming out of an
account. **balance of payments**
difference between the payments for
the imports and exports of a country.

balance of power equal distribution of
military and economic power among
countries. **balance of trade** difference
in value between a country's imports
and exports. **balance sheet** statement
showing the financial position of a
business.

balcony ❶ n, pl **-nies 1** platform on the
outside of a building with a rail along
the outer edge. **2** upper tier of seats in
a theatre or cinema.

bald ❶ adj **1** having little or no hair on the
scalp. **2** plain or blunt, e.g. the bald
facts. **3** (of a tyre) having a worn tread.
balding adj becoming bald. **baldly** adv
baldness n.

balderdash ❶ n stupid talk.

bale¹ n **1** large bundle of hay or goods
tightly bound together. ▷ v **2** make or
put into bales.

bale² v same as BAIL².

baleen n whalebone.

baleful adj vindictive or menacing.
balefully adv.

balk, baulk ❶ v **1** be reluctant to (do
something). **2** thwart or hinder.

Balkan adj of any of the countries of the
Balkan Peninsula: Romania, Bulgaria,
Albania, Greece, the former Yugoslavia,
and the European part of Turkey.

ball¹ ❶ n **1** round or nearly round object,
esp. one used in games. **2** single
delivery of the ball in a game. **3** bullet.
4 more or less rounded part of the body,
e.g. the ball of the foot. ▷ pl taboo slang
5 testicles. **6** nonsense. ▷ v **7** form into
a ball, e.g. he balled his fist. **ball**

decoy, enticement, incentive,
inducement, snare, temptation ▷ v
4 = **tease**, annoy, bother, harass, hassle
(inf), hound, irritate, persecute,
torment, wind up (Brit sl)

baked adj **2** = **dry**, arid, desiccated,
parched, scorched, seared, sun-baked,
torrid

balance n **1** = **stability**, composure,
equanimity, poise, self-control, self-
possession, steadiness
2 = **equilibrium**, correspondence,
equity, equivalence, evenness, parity,
symmetry **3** = **remainder**, difference,
residue, rest, surplus ▷ v **6** = **weigh**
7 = **stabilize**, level, match, parallel,
steady **8** = **compare**, assess, consider,
deliberate, estimate, evaluate
9 = **calculate**, compute, settle, square,
tally, total

balcony n **1** = **terrace**, veranda
2 = **upper circle**, gallery, gods

bald adj **1** = **hairless**, baldheaded,
depilated **2** = **plain**, blunt, direct,
forthright, straightforward,
unadorned, unvarnished

balderdash n = **nonsense**, claptrap
(inf), drivel, garbage (inf), gibberish,
hogwash, hot air (inf), kak (S Afr sl),
rubbish

baldness n **1** = **hairlessness**, alopecia
(Path), baldheadedness **2** = **plainness**,
austerity, bluntness, severity, simplicity

balk, baulk v **1** = **recoil**, evade, flinch,
hesitate, jib, refuse, resist, shirk, shrink
from **2** = **foil**, check, counteract, defeat,
frustrate, hinder, obstruct, prevent,
thwart

ball¹ n **1** = **sphere**, drop, globe, globule,
orb, pellet, spheroid

bearings steel balls between moving parts of a machine to reduce friction.
ball cock device with a floating ball and a valve for regulating the flow of water.
ballpoint, **ballpoint pen** n pen with a tiny ball bearing as a writing point.
ball² n formal social function for dancing. **ballroom** n.
ballad n 1 narrative poem or song. 2 slow sentimental song.
ballast ❶ n 1 substance, such as sand, used to stabilize a ship when it is not carrying cargo. 2 crushed rock used for road or railway foundation. ▷ v 3 give stability or weight to.
ballet n 1 classical style of expressive dancing based on conventional steps. 2 theatrical performance of this. **ballerina** n female ballet dancer.
ballistics n study of the flight of projectiles, such as bullets. **ballistic** adj **ballistic missile** missile guided automatically in flight but which falls freely at its target.
balloon ❶ n 1 inflatable rubber bag used as a plaything or decoration. 2 large bag inflated with air or gas, designed to float in the atmosphere with passengers in a basket underneath. ▷ v 3 fly in a balloon. 4 swell or increase rapidly in size, e.g. *his weight ballooned*. **balloonist** n.
ballot ❶ n 1 method of voting secretly. 2 actual vote or paper indicating a person's choice. ▷ v -**loting**, -**loted** 3 vote or ask for a vote from.
ballyhoo ❶ n exaggerated fuss.
balm ❶ n 1 aromatic substance used for healing and soothing. 2 anything that comforts or soothes.

balmy ❶ adj **balmier**, **balmiest** (of weather) mild and pleasant.
baloney n informal nonsense.
balsa [**bawl**-sa] n very light wood from a tropical American tree.
balsam n 1 aromatic resin obtained from various trees and shrubs. 2 soothing ointment. 3 flowering plant.
Baltic adj of the Baltic Sea in N Europe or the states bordering it.
baluster n set of posts supporting a rail. **balustrade** n ornamental rail supported by balusters.
bamboo n tall treelike tropical grass with hollow stems.
bamboozle ❶ v informal 1 cheat or mislead. 2 confuse, puzzle.
ban ❶ v **banning**, **banned** 1 prohibit or forbid officially. ▷ n 2 official prohibition.
banal ❶ [ban-**nahl**] adj ordinary and unoriginal. **banality** n.
banana n yellow crescent-shaped fruit. **banana republic** small politically unstable country whose economy is dominated by foreign interests.
band¹ ❶ n 1 group of musicians playing together. 2 group of people having a common purpose. **bandmaster** n conductor of a band. **bandsman** n **bandstand** n roofed outdoor platform for a band. **band together** v unite.
band² ❶ n 1 strip of some material, used to hold objects. 2 strip of contrasting colour or texture. 3 *Physics* range of frequencies or wavelengths between two limits.

———————————————————————— THESAURUS ———————

ballast n 1 = **counterbalance**, balance, counterweight, equilibrium, sandbag, stability, stabilizer, weight
balloon v 4 = **swell**, billow, blow up, dilate, distend, expand, grow rapidly, inflate, puff out
ballot n 1 = **vote**, election, poll, polling, voting
ballyhoo n = **fuss**, babble, commotion, hubbub, hue and cry, hullabaloo, noise, racket, to-do
balm n 1 = **ointment**, balsam, cream, embrocation, emollient, lotion, salve, unguent 2 = **comfort**, anodyne, consolation, curative, palliative, restorative, solace
balmy adj = **mild**, clement, pleasant, summery, temperate

bamboozle v Inf 1 = **cheat**, con (*inf*), deceive, dupe, fool, hoodwink, swindle, trick ▷ v 2 = **puzzle**, baffle, befuddle, confound, confuse, mystify, perplex, stump
ban v 1 = **prohibit**, banish, bar, block, boycott, disallow, disqualify, exclude, forbid, outlaw ▷ n 2 = **prohibition**, boycott, disqualification, embargo, restriction, taboo
banal adj = **unoriginal**, hackneyed, humdrum, mundane, pedestrian, stale, stereotyped, trite, unimaginative
band¹ n 1 = **ensemble**, combo, group, orchestra 2 = **gang**, body, company, group, party, posse (*inf*)
band² n 1 = **strip**, belt, bond, chain, cord, ribbon, strap

DICTIONARY

bandage ❶ n 1 piece of material used to cover a wound or wrap an injured limb. ▷ v 2 cover with a bandage.

bandanna, bandana n large brightly coloured handkerchief or neckerchief.

B & B bed and breakfast.

bandicoot n ratlike Australian marsupial.

bandit ❶ n robber, esp. a member of an armed gang. **banditry** n.

bandolier n shoulder belt for holding cartridges.

bandwagon n **jump, climb on the bandwagon** join a party or movement that seems assured of success.

bandy adj **-dier, -diest 1** (also **bandy-legged**) having legs curved outwards at the knees. ▷ v **-dying, -died 2** exchange (words) in a heated manner. **3** use (a name, term, etc.) frequently.

bane ❶ n person or thing that causes misery or distress. **baneful** adj.

bang ❶ n **1** short loud explosive noise. **2** hard blow or loud knock. ▷ v **3** hit or knock, esp. with a loud noise. **4** close (a door) noisily. ▷ adv **5** precisely, e.g. *bang in the middle*. **6** with a sudden impact.

banger n **1** informal old decrepit car. **2** slang sausage. **3** firework that explodes loudly.

bangle n bracelet worn round the arm or the ankle.

banish ❶ v **1** send (someone) into exile. **2** drive away, e.g. *she has banished all thoughts of retirement*. **banishment** n.

banisters ❶ pl n railing supported by posts on a staircase.

banjo n, pl **-jos, -joes** guitar-like musical instrument with a circular body.

bank¹ ❶ n **1** institution offering services such as the safekeeping and lending of money. **2** any supply, store, or reserve. ▷ v **3** deposit (cash or cheques) in a bank. **4** transact business with a bank. **banking** n **bank holiday** public holiday when banks are closed by law. **banknote** n piece of paper money. **bank on** v rely on.

bank² ❶ n **1** raised mass, esp. of earth. **2** slope, as of a hill. **3** sloping ground at the side of a river. ▷ v **4** form into a bank. **5** cover (a fire) with ashes and fuel so that it will burn slowly. **6** cause (an aircraft) or (of an aircraft) to tip to one side on turning.

bank³ ❶ n arrangement of switches, keys, oars, etc. in a row or in tiers.

banker n **1** manager or owner of a bank. **2** keeper of the bank in gambling games.

bankrupt ❶ n **1** person declared by a court to be unable to pay his or her debts. ▷ adj **2** financially ruined. **3** completely lacking a particular quality, e.g. *morally bankrupt*. ▷ v **4** make bankrupt. **bankruptcy** n.

banner ❶ n **1** long strip of cloth displaying a slogan, advertisement, etc. **2** placard carried in a demonstration or procession.

THESAURUS

bandage n **1** = **dressing**, compress, gauze, plaster ▷ v **2** = **dress**, bind, cover, swathe

bandit n = **robber**, brigand, desperado, highwayman, marauder, outlaw, thief

bane n = **plague**, bête noire, curse, nuisance, pest, ruin, scourge, torment

bang n **1** = **explosion**, clang, clap, clash, pop, slam, thud, thump **2** = **blow**, bump, cuff, knock, punch, smack, stroke, whack ▷ v **3** = **hit**, belt (inf), clatter, knock, slam, strike, thump ▷ adv **5** = **straight**, precisely, slap, smack **6** = **hard**, abruptly, headlong, noisily, suddenly

banish v **1** = **expel**, deport, eject, evict, exile, outlaw **2** = **get rid of**, ban, cast out, discard, dismiss, oust, remove

banishment n **1** = **expulsion**, deportation, exile, expatriation, transportation

banisters pl n = **railing**, balusters, balustrade, handrail, rail

bank¹ n **1** = **storehouse**, depository, repository **2** = **store**, accumulation, fund, hoard, reserve, reservoir, savings, stock, stockpile ▷ v **3** = **save**, deposit, keep

bank² n **1** = **mound**, banking, embankment, heap, mass, pile, ridge **3** = **side**, brink, edge, margin, shore ▷ v **4** = **pile**, amass, heap, mass, mound, stack **6** = **tilt**, camber, cant, heel, incline, pitch, slant, slope, tip

bank³ n = **row**, array, file, group, line, rank, sequence, series, succession

bankrupt adj **2** = **insolvent**, broke (inf), destitute, impoverished, in queer street, in the red, munted (NZ sl), ruined, wiped out (inf)

bankruptcy n **2** = **insolvency**, disaster, failure, liquidation, ruin

banner n **1** = **flag**, colours, ensign, pennant, standard, streamer

bannisters *pl n* same as BANISTERS.

banns *pl n* public declaration, esp. in a church, of an intended marriage.

banquet ❶ *n* **1** elaborate formal dinner. ▷ *v* **-queting, -queted** **2** hold or take part in a banquet.

banshee *n* (in Irish folklore) female spirit whose wailing warns of a coming death.

bantam *n* small breed of chicken. **bantamweight** *n* boxer weighing up to 118lb (professional) or 54kg (amateur).

banter ❶ *v* **1** tease jokingly. ▷ *n* **2** teasing or joking conversation.

Bantu *n* **1** group of languages of Africa. **2** *offens* Black speaker of a Bantu language.

banyan *n* Indian tree whose branches grow down into the soil forming additional trunks.

baobab [**bay**-oh-bab] *n* African tree with a thick trunk and angular branches.

bap *n Brit* large soft bread roll.

baptism ❶ *n* Christian religious ceremony in which a person is immersed in or sprinkled with water as a sign of being cleansed from sin and accepted into the Church. **baptismal** *adj* **baptize** *v* **1** perform baptism on. **2** give a name to.

Baptist *n* member of a Protestant denomination that believes in adult baptism by immersion.

bar¹ ❶ *n* **1** rigid length of metal, wood, etc. **2** solid, usu. rectangular block, of any material. **3** anything that obstructs

or prevents. **4** counter or room where drinks are served. **5** heating element in an electric fire. **6** place in court where the accused stands during trial. **7** *Music* group of beats repeated throughout a piece of music. ▷ *v* **barring, barred 8** secure with a bar. **9** obstruct. **10** ban or forbid. ▷ *prep* **11** (also **barring**) except for. **the Bar** barristers collectively. **barman**, **barmaid**, **bartender** *n*.

bar² *n* unit of atmospheric pressure.

barachois [bar-ah-**shwah**] *n* (in the Atlantic Provinces of Canada) a shallow lagoon formed by a sand bar.

barb ❶ *n* **1** cutting remark. **2** point facing in the opposite direction to the main point of a fish-hook etc. **barbed** *adj* **barbed wire** strong wire with protruding sharp points.

barbarian ❶ *n* member of a primitive or uncivilized people. **barbaric** *adj* cruel or brutal. **barbarism** *n* condition of being backward or ignorant. **barbarity** *n* **1** state of being barbaric or barbarous. **2** *pl* **-ties** vicious act. **barbarous** *adj* **1** uncivilized. **2** brutal or cruel.

barbecue *n* **1** grill on which food is cooked over hot charcoal, usu. outdoors. **2** outdoor party at which barbecued food is served. ▷ *v* **3** cook (food) on a barbecue.

barber *n* person who cuts men's hair and shaves beards.

barbican *n* walled defence to protect a gate or drawbridge of a fortification.

——————— THESAURUS ———————

2 = **placard**, sign

banquet *n* **1** = **feast**, dinner, meal, repast, revel, treat

banter *v* **1** = **joke**, jest, kid (*inf*), rib (*inf*), taunt, tease ▷ *n* **2** = **joking**, badinage, jesting, kidding (*inf*), repartee, teasing, wordplay

baptism *n* = **christening**, immersion, purification, sprinkling

baptize *v* **1** = **purify**, cleanse, immerse

bar¹ *n* **1** = **rod**, paling, palisade, pole, rail, shaft, stake, stick **3** = **obstacle**, barricade, barrier, block, deterrent, hindrance, impediment, obstruction, stop **4** = **public house**, boozer (*Brit, Aust & NZ inf*), beer parlour (*Canad*), beverage room (*Canad*), canteen, counter, inn, pub (*inf, chiefly Brit*), saloon, tavern, watering hole (*facetious sl*) ▷ *v* **8** = **fasten**, barricade, bolt, latch, lock, secure **9** = **obstruct**,

hinder, prevent, restrain **10** = **exclude**, ban, black, blackball, forbid, keep out, prohibit **the Bar** = **barristers**, body of lawyers, counsel, court, judgment, tribunal

barb *n* **1** = **dig**, affront, cut, gibe, insult, sarcasm, scoff, sneer **2** = **point**, bristle, prickle, prong, quill, spike, spur, thorn

barbarian *n* = **savage**, boor, brute, lout, philistine, yahoo

barbaric *adj* = **brutal**, barbarous, coarse, crude, cruel, fierce, inhuman, savage

barbarous *adj* **1** = **uncivilized**, barbarian, brutish, primitive, rough, rude, savage, uncouth, wild **2** = **brutal**, barbaric, cruel, ferocious, heartless, inhuman, monstrous, ruthless, vicious

barbed *adj* **1** = **cutting**, critical, hostile, hurtful, nasty, pointed, scathing, unkind **2** = **spiked**, hooked, jagged, prickly, spiny, thorny

barbiturate *n* drug used as a sedative.

bard *n lit* poet. **the Bard** William Shakespeare.

bare ❶ *adj* **1** unclothed, naked. **2** without the natural or usual covering. **3** unembellished, simple. **4** just sufficient, e.g. *the bare minimum.* ▷ *v* **5** uncover. **barely** *adv* only just. **bareness** *n*.

bareback *adj, adv* (of horse-riding) without a saddle.

barefaced ❶ *adj* shameless or obvious.

barefoot, barefooted *adj, adv* with the feet uncovered.

bareheaded *adj, adv* with the head uncovered.

bargain ❶ *n* **1** agreement establishing what each party will give, receive, or perform in a transaction. **2** something bought or offered at a low price. ▷ *v* **3** negotiate the terms of an agreement. **into the bargain** besides, in addition. **bargain for** *v* anticipate or take into account.

barge ❶ *n* **1** flat-bottomed boat used to transport freight. ▷ *v* **2** *informal* push violently. **bargee** *n* person in charge of a barge. **barge in, into** *v* interrupt rudely.

barista *n* person who makes and sells coffee in a coffee bar.

baritone *n* (singer with) the second lowest adult male voice.

barium [bare-ee-um] *n Chemistry* soft white metallic element. **barium meal** preparation of barium sulphate swallowed by a patient before an x-ray of the alimentary canal.

bark¹ ❶ *n* **1** loud harsh cry of a dog. ▷ *v* **2** (of a dog) make its typical cry. **3** shout in an angry tone. **barker** *n* person at a fairground who calls loudly to passers-by in order to attract customers.

bark² ❶ *n* **1** tough outer layer of a tree. ▷ *v* **2** scrape or rub off skin.

barking *adj slang* mad.

barley *n* **1** tall grasslike plant cultivated for grain. **2** grain of this plant used in making malt and whisky and in soups. **barley sugar** brittle clear amber-coloured sweet. **barley water** drink made from an infusion of barley.

bar mitzvah *n Judaism* ceremony marking the 13th birthday of a boy, who then assumes full religious obligations.

barmy ❶ *adj* **-mier, -miest** *slang* insane.

barn *n* large building on a farm used for storing grain. **barn dance** informal party with country dancing. **barn owl** owl with pale brown and white plumage. **barnstorm** *v US* tour rural districts putting on shows or making speeches in a political campaign.

barnacle *n* shellfish that lives attached to rocks, ship bottoms, etc. **barnacle goose** goose with a black-and-white head and body.

barney *n informal* noisy fight or argument.

barometer *n* instrument for measuring atmospheric pressure. **barometric** *adj*.

baron *n* **1** member of the lowest rank of nobility. **2** powerful businessman, e.g. *a press baron.* **baroness** *n* **baronial** *adj*.

baronet *n* commoner who holds the lowest hereditary British title.

baroque [bar-**rock**] *n* **1** highly ornate style of art, architecture, or music from the late 16th to the early 18th century. ▷ *adj* **2** ornate in style.

barque [bark] *n* sailing ship, esp. one with three masts.

barrack *v* criticize loudly or shout against (a team or speaker).

———————— **THESAURUS** ————————

bare *adj* **1** = **naked**, nude, stripped, unclad, unclothed, uncovered, undressed, without a stitch on (*inf*) **3** = **plain**, austere, basic, sheer, simple, spare, spartan, stark, unadorned, unembellished

barefaced *adj* = **obvious**, blatant, bold, brazen, flagrant, open, shameless

barely *adv* = **only just**, almost, at a push, by the skin of one's teeth, hardly, just, scarcely

bargain *n* **1** = **agreement**, arrangement, contract, pact, pledge, promise **2** = **good buy**, (cheap) purchase, discount, giveaway, good deal, reduction, snip (*inf*), steal (*inf*) ▷ *v* **3** = **negotiate**, agree, contract, covenant, cut a deal, promise, stipulate, transact

barge *n* **1** = **canal boat**, flatboat, lighter, narrow boat

bark¹ *n* **1** = **yap**, bay, howl, woof, yelp ▷ *v* **2** = **yap**, bay, howl, woof, yelp

bark² *n* **1** = **covering**, casing, cortex (*Anat, bot*), crust, husk, rind, skin

barmy *adj Sl* = **insane**, crazy, daft (*inf*), foolish, idiotic, nuts (*sl*), out of one's mind, stupid

barracks ❶ *pl n* building used to accommodate military personnel.

barracouta *n* large Pacific fish with a protruding lower jaw and strong teeth.

barracuda [bar-rack-**kew**-da] *n* fierce tropical sea fish.

barrage ❶ [**bar**-rahzh] *n* **1** continuous delivery of questions, complaints, etc. **2** continuous artillery fire. **3** artificial barrier across a river to control the water level.

barrel *n* **1** cylindrical container with rounded sides and flat ends. **2** amount that a barrel can hold. **3** tube in a firearm through which the bullet is fired. **barrel organ** musical instrument played by turning a handle.

barren ❶ *adj* **1** (of a woman or female animal) incapable of producing offspring. **2** (of land) unable to support the growth of crops, fruit, etc. **3** unprofitable, e.g. *a barren period*. **barrenness** *n*.

barricade ❶ *n* **1** barrier, esp. one erected hastily for defence. ▷ *v* **2** erect a barricade across (an entrance).

barrier ❶ *n* anything that prevents access, progress, or union. **barrier cream** cream that protects the skin. **barrier reef** long narrow coral reef lying close to the shore.

barrister *n* lawyer qualified to plead in a higher court.

barrow¹ *n* **1** wheelbarrow. **2** movable stall used by street traders.

barrow² *n* mound of earth over a prehistoric tomb.

barter ❶ *v* **1** trade (goods) in exchange for other goods. ▷ *n* **2** trade by the exchange of goods.

basal *adj* **1** of, at, or constituting a base. **2** fundamental.

basalt [**bass**-awlt] *n* dark volcanic rock. **basaltic** *adj*.

bascule *n* drawbridge that operates by a counterbalanced weight.

base¹ ❶ *n* **1** bottom or supporting part of anything. **2** fundamental part. **3** centre of operations, organization, or supply. **4** starting point. **5** chemical compound that combines with an acid to form a salt. **6** *Maths* the number of units in a counting system that is equivalent to one in the next higher counting place. ▷ *v* **7** (foll. by *on* or *upon*) use as a basis (for). **8** (foll. by *at* or *in*) station or place. **baseless** *adj* **basement** *n* partly or wholly underground storey of a building. **base rate** rate of interest as a basis for bank lending rates.

base² ❶ *adj* **1** dishonourable or immoral. **2** of inferior quality or value. **3** debased or counterfeit. **basely** *adv* **baseness** *n*.

baseball *n* **1** team game in which runs are scored by hitting a ball with a bat then running round four bases. **2** ball used for this.

basement *n* partly or wholly underground storey of a building.

bases *n* plural of BASIS.

bash ❶ *informal* ▷ *v* **1** hit violently or forcefully. ▷ *n* **2** heavy blow. **have a bash** *informal* make an attempt.

— THESAURUS —

barracks *pl n* = **camp**, billet, encampment, garrison, quarters

barrage *n* **1** = **torrent**, burst, deluge, hail, mass, onslaught, plethora, stream **2** = **bombardment**, battery, cannonade, fusillade, gunfire, salvo, shelling, volley

barren *adj* **1** = **infertile**, childless, sterile **2** = **unproductive**, arid, desert, desolate, dry, empty, unfruitful, waste

barricade *n* **1** = **barrier**, blockade, bulwark, fence, obstruction, palisade, rampart, stockade ▷ *v* **2** = **bar**, block, blockade, defend, fortify, obstruct, protect, shut in

barrier *n* **a** = **barricade**, bar, blockade, boundary, fence, obstacle, obstruction, wall **b** = **hindrance**, difficulty, drawback, handicap, hurdle, obstacle, restriction, stumbling block

barter *v* **1** = **trade**, bargain, drive a hard bargain, exchange, haggle, sell, swap, traffic

base¹ *n* **1** = **bottom**, bed, foot, foundation, pedestal, rest, stand, support **2** = **basis**, core, essence, heart, key, origin, root, source **3** = **centre**, camp, headquarters, home, post, settlement, starting point, station ▷ *v* **7** (foll. by *on* or *upon*) = **found**, build, construct, depend, derive, establish, ground, hinge **8** (foll. by *at* or *in*) = **place**, locate, post, station

base² *adj* **1** = **dishonourable**, contemptible, despicable, disreputable, evil, immoral, scungy (*Aust & NZ inf*), shameful, sordid, wicked **3** = **counterfeit**, alloyed, debased, fake, forged, fraudulent, impure

bash *Inf* ▷ *v* **1** = **hit**, belt (*inf*), smash,

bashful ⊕ *adj* shy or modest. **bashfully** *adv* **bashfulness** *n*.

basic ⊕ *adj* **1** of or forming a base or basis. **2** elementary or simple. **3** *Chemistry* of or containing a base. **basics** *pl n* fundamental principles, facts, etc. **basically** *adv*.

BASIC *n* computer programming language that uses common English words.

basil *n* aromatic herb used in cooking.

basilica *n* rectangular church with a rounded end and two aisles.

basilisk *n* legendary serpent said to kill by its breath or glance.

basin *n* **1** round open container. **2** sink for washing the hands and face. **3** sheltered area of water where boats may be moored. **4** catchment area of a particular river.

basis ⊕ *n, pl* **-ses** fundamental principles etc. from which something is started or developed.

bask ⊕ *v* **1** lie in or be exposed to something, esp. pleasant warmth. **2** enjoy (approval or favourable conditions).

basket *n* container made of interwoven strips of wood or cane. **basketwork** *n*.

basketball *n* **1** team game in which points are scored by throwing the ball through a high horizontal hoop. **2** ball used for this.

basque *n* tight-fitting bodice for women.

Basque *n, adj* (member or language) of a people living in the W Pyrenees in France and Spain.

bas-relief *n* sculpture in which the figures project slightly from the background.

bass¹ ⊕ [base] *n* **1** (singer with) the lowest adult male voice. **2** *informal* same as BASS GUITAR *or* DOUBLE BASS. ▷ *adj* **3** of the lowest range of musical notes. **bass guitar** electric guitar with same pitch and tuning as a double bass.

bass² *n* edible sea fish.

basset hound *n* smooth-haired dog with short legs and long ears.

bassoon *n* low-pitched woodwind instrument.

bastard ⊕ *n* **1** *offens* obnoxious or despicable person. **2** person born of parents not married to each other. **bastardize** *v* debase or corrupt.

baste¹ *v* moisten (meat) during cooking with hot fat.

baste² *v* sew with loose temporary stitches.

bastion ⊕ *n* **1** projecting part of a fortification. **2** thing or person regarded as defending a principle.

bat¹ ⊕ *n* **1** any of various types of club used to hit the ball in certain sports. ▷ *v* **batting, batted 2** strike with or as if with a bat. **3** *Cricket* take a turn at batting. **batsman** *n Cricket* person who bats or specializes in batting.

bat² *n* nocturnal mouselike flying animal.

bat³ *v* **not bat an eyelid** *informal* show no surprise.

batch ⊕ *n* group of people or things dealt with at the same time.

bated *adj* **with bated breath** in suspense or fear.

bath ⊕ *n* **1** large container in which to wash the body. **2** act of washing in

sock (*sl*), strike, wallop (*inf*)

bashful *adj* = **shy**, blushing, coy, diffident, reserved, reticent, retiring, timid

basic *adj* **1** = **essential**, fundamental, key, necessary, primary, vital **2** = **elementary**, simple

basically *adv* **1** = **essentially**, at heart, fundamentally, inherently, in substance, intrinsically, mostly, primarily

basics *pl n* = **essentials**, brass tacks (*inf*), fundamentals, nitty-gritty (*inf*), nuts and bolts (*inf*), principles, rudiments

basis *n* = **foundation**, base, bottom, footing, ground, groundwork, support

bask *v* **1** = **lie in**, laze, loll, lounge, outspan (*S Afr*), relax, sunbathe

bass¹ *adj* **3** = **deep**, deep-toned, low, low-pitched, resonant, sonorous

bastard *n* **1** *Offens* = **rogue**, blackguard, miscreant, reprobate, scoundrel, villain, wretch **2** = **illegitimate child**, love child, natural child

bastion *n* **1** = **stronghold**, bulwark, citadel, defence, fortress **2** = **tower of strength**, mainstay, prop, rock, support

bat *v* **2** = **hit**, bang, smack, strike, swat, thump, wallop (*inf*), whack

batch *n* = **group**, amount, assemblage, bunch, collection, crowd, lot, pack, quantity, set

bath *n* **2** = **wash**, cleansing, douche, scrubbing, shower, soak, tub ▷ *v* **4** = **wash**, bathe, clean, douse, scrub

such a container. ▷ *pl* **3** public
swimming pool. ▷ *v* **4** wash in a bath.
bathroom *n* room with a bath, sink,
and usu. a toilet.
Bath chair *n* wheelchair for an invalid.
bathe ❶ *v* **1** swim in open water for
pleasure. **2** apply liquid to (the skin or a
wound) in order to cleanse or soothe.
3 (foll. by *in*) fill (with), e.g. *bathed in
sunlight*. ▷ *n* **4** *Brit* instance of bathing.
bather *n*.
bathos [**bay**-thoss] *n* sudden ludicrous
change in speech or writing from a
serious subject to a trivial one.
**bathyscaph, bathyscaphe
bathysphere** *n* deep-sea diving vessel
for observation.
batik [bat-**teek**] *n* **1** process of printing
fabric using wax to cover areas not to
be dyed. **2** fabric printed in this way.
batman *n* officer's servant in the armed
forces.
baton ❶ *n* **1** thin stick used by the
conductor of an orchestra. **2** short bar
transferred in a relay race. **3** police
officer's truncheon.
batrachian [bat-**tray**-kee-an] *n*
1 amphibian, esp. a frog or toad. ▷ *adj*
2 of or relating to frogs and toads.
battalion *n* army unit consisting of
three or more companies.
batten¹ ❶ *n* strip of wood fixed to
something, esp. to hold it in place.
batten down *v* secure with battens.
batten² ❶ *v* **batten on** thrive at the
expense of (someone else).
batter¹ ❶ *v* **1** hit repeatedly. **2** damage

or injure, as by blows, heavy wear, etc.
e.g. *battered by gales*. **battering ram**
large beam used to break down
fortifications.
batter² *n* mixture of flour, eggs, and
milk, used in cooking.
battery ❶ *n, pl* **-teries 1** device that
produces electricity in a torch, radio,
etc. **2** number of similar things
occurring together. **3** *Law* assault by
beating. **4** group of heavy guns
operating as a single unit. ▷ *adj* **5** kept
in series of cages for intensive rearing,
e.g. *battery hens*.
battle ❶ *n* **1** fight between large armed
forces. **2** conflict or struggle. ▷ *v*
3 struggle.
battle-axe *n* **1** *informal* domineering
woman. **2** (formerly) large heavy axe.
battledress *n* ordinary uniform of a
soldier.
battlefield, battleground ❶ *n* place
where a battle is fought.
battlement *n* wall with gaps along the
top for firing through.
battleship ❶ *n* large heavily armoured
warship.
batty ❶ *adj* **-tier, -tiest** *slang* eccentric
or crazy.
bauble ❶ *n* trinket of little value.
baulk ❶ *v* same as BALK.
bauxite *n* claylike substance that is the
chief source of aluminium.
bawdy ❶ *adj* **bawdier, bawdiest** (of
writing etc.) containing humorous
references to sex. **bawdiness** *n*.
bawl ❶ *v* **1** shout or weep noisily. ▷ *n*

─────────────── THESAURUS ───────────────

down, shower, soak
bathe *v* **1** = **swim 2** = **wash**, cleanse,
rinse **3** (foll. by *in*) = **cover**, flood,
immerse, steep, suffuse
baton *n* **1** = **stick**, wand **3** = **truncheon**,
club, rod
batten¹ batten down *v* = **fasten**, board
up, clamp down, cover up, fix, nail
down, secure, tighten
batten² *v* **batten on** = **thrive**, fatten,
flourish, gain, grow, increase, prosper
batter¹ *v* **1** = **beat**, buffet, clobber (*sl*),
pelt, pound, pummel, thrash, wallop
(*inf*)
battery *n* **4** = **artillery**, cannon,
cannonry, gun emplacements, guns
battle *n* **1** = **fight**, action, attack,
combat, encounter, engagement,
hostilities, skirmish **2** = **conflict**,
campaign, contest, crusade, dispute,
struggle ▷ *v* **3** = **struggle**, argue,

clamour, dispute, fight, lock horns,
strive, war
battlefield *n* = **battleground**, combat
zone, field, field of battle, front
battleship *n* = **warship**, gunboat,
man-of-war
batty *adj Sl* = **crazy**, daft (*inf*), dotty
(*sl, chiefly Brit*), eccentric, mad, munted
(*NZ sl*), odd, peculiar, potty (*Brit inf*),
touched
bauble *n* = **trinket**, bagatelle, gewgaw,
gimcrack, knick-knack, plaything, toy,
trifle
baulk SEE BALK.
bawdy *adj* = **rude**, coarse, dirty,
indecent, lascivious, lecherous, lewd,
ribald, salacious, scungy (*Aust & NZ inf*),
smutty
bawl *v* **a** = **shout**, bellow, call, clamour,
howl, roar, yell **b** = **cry**, blubber, sob,
wail, weep

b

2 loud shout or cry.

bay¹ ❶ *n* stretch of coastline that curves inwards.

bay² ❶ *n* **1** recess in a wall. **2** area set aside for a particular purpose, e.g. *loading bay*. **3** compartment in an aircraft, e.g. *bomb bay*. **bay window** window projecting from a wall.

bay³ ❶ *n* **1** deep howl of a hound or wolf. ▷ *v* **2** howl in deep prolonged tones. **at bay 1** forced to turn and face attackers. **2** at a safe distance.

bay⁴ *n* Mediterranean laurel tree. **bay leaf** its dried leaf, used in cooking.

bay⁵ *adj, n* reddish-brown (horse).

bayonet *n* **1** sharp blade that can be fixed to the end of a rifle. ▷ *v* **-neting**, **-neted 2** stab with a bayonet.

bazaar ❶ *n* **1** sale in aid of charity. **2** market area, esp. in Eastern countries.

bazooka *n* portable rocket launcher that fires an armour-piercing projectile.

BB Boys' Brigade.

BBC British Broadcasting Corporation.

BC 1 before Christ. **2** British Columbia.

BCG antituberculosis vaccine.

BD Bachelor of Divinity.

BDS Bachelor of Dental Surgery.

be ❶ *v, present sing 1st person* **am**; *2nd person* **are**; *3rd person* **is**; *present pl* **are**; *past sing 1st person* **was**; *2nd person* **were**; *3rd person* **was**; *past pl* **were**; *present participle* **being**; *past participle* **been 1** exist or live. **2** pay a visit, e.g. *have you been to Spain?* **3** take place, e.g. *my birthday was last Monday*. **4** used as a linking between the subject of a sentence and its complement, e.g. *John is a musician*. **5** forms the progressive present tense, e.g. *the man is running*. **6** forms the passive voice of all transitive verbs, e.g. *a good film is being shown on television tonight*.

Be *Chemistry* beryllium.

BE Bachelor of Engineering.

be- *prefix* **1** surround or cover, e.g. *befog*. **2** affect completely, e.g. *bedazzle*. **3** consider as or cause to be, e.g. *befriend*. **4** provide or cover with, e.g. *bejewelled*. **5** at, for, against, on, or over, e.g. *bewail*.

beach ❶ *n* **1** area of sand or pebbles on a shore. ▷ *v* **2** run or haul (a boat) onto a beach. **beachcomber** *n* person who searches shore debris for anything of worth. **beachhead** *n* beach captured by an attacking army on which troops can be landed.

beacon ❶ *n* **1** fire or light on a hill or tower, used as a warning. **2** lighthouse. **3** radio or other signal used in air navigation.

bead ❶ *n* **1** small piece of plastic, wood, etc., pierced for threading on a string to form a necklace etc. **2** small drop of moisture. **3** small metal knob acting as the sight of a firearm. **beaded** *adj* **beading** *n* strip of moulding used for edging furniture. **beady** *adj* **beadier**, **beadiest** small, round, and glittering, e.g. *beady eyes*.

beagle *n* small hound with short legs and drooping ears.

beak¹ ❶ *n* **1** projecting horny jaws of a bird. **2** *slang* nose. **beaky** *adj* **beakier**, **beakiest**.

beak² *n slang* judge, magistrate, or headmaster.

beaker *n* **1** large drinking cup. **2** lipped glass container used in laboratories.

beam ❶ *n* **1** broad smile. **2** ray of light. **3** narrow flow of electromagnetic radiation or particles. **4** long thick piece of wood, metal, etc., used in building. **5** breadth of a ship at its widest part. ▷ *v* **6** smile broadly. **7** divert or aim (a radio signal, light,

bay¹ *n* = **inlet**, bight, cove, gulf, natural harbour, sound

bay² *n* **2** = **recess**, alcove, compartment, niche, nook, opening

bay³ *n* **1** = **howl**, bark, clamour, cry, yelp ▷ *v* **2** = **howl**, bark, clamour, cry, yelp

bazaar *n* **1** = **fair**, bring-and-buy, fete, sale of work **2** = **market**, exchange, marketplace

be *v* **1** = **exist**, be alive, breathe, inhabit, live

beach *n* **1** = **shore**, coast, sands, seashore, seaside, water's edge

beacon *n* **1** = **signal**, beam, bonfire, flare, sign **2** = **lighthouse**, watchtower

bead *n* **2** = **drop**, bubble, droplet, globule

beady *adj* = **bright**, gleaming, glinting, glittering, sharp, shining

beak¹ *n* **1** = **bill**, mandible, neb (*arch or dial*), nib **2** *Sl* = **nose**, proboscis, snout

beam *n* **1** = **smile**, grin **2** = **ray**, gleam, glimmer, glint, glow, shaft, streak, stream **4** = **rafter**, girder, joist, plank, spar, support, timber ▷ *v* **6** = **smile**, grin **7** = **send out**, broadcast, emit, transmit

b

etc.) in a certain direction.

bean *n* seed or pod of various plants, eaten as a vegetable or used to make coffee etc. **full of beans** *informal* full of energy and vitality. **beansprout** *n* small edible shoot grown from a bean seed.

beanie *n Brit, Aust & NZ* close-fitting woolen hat.

beano *n, pl* **beanos** *Brit slang* celebration or party.

bear¹ ⓥ *v* **bearing**, **bore**, **borne** **1** support or hold up. **2** bring, e.g. *to bear gifts*. **3** *passive* **born** give birth to. **4** produce as by natural growth. **5** tolerate or endure. **6** stand up to, e.g. *his story does not bear scrutiny*. **7** hold in the mind, e.g. *to bear a grudge*. **8** show or be marked with, e.g. *he still bears the scars*. **9** have or be in (relation or comparison), e.g. *her account bears no relation to the facts*. **10** move in a specified direction, e.g. *bring to bear*. **bearable** *adj* **bear down on** *v* **1** press down on. **2** approach (someone) in a determined manner. **bear out** *v* show to be truthful.

bear² *n* large heavy mammal with a shaggy coat. **bear hug** rough tight embrace. **bearskin** *n* tall fur helmet worn by some British soldiers.

beard *n* **1** hair growing on the lower parts of a man's face. ▷ *v* **2** oppose boldly. **bearded** *adj*.

bearer ⓞ *n* person who carries, presents, or upholds something.

bearing ⓞ *n* **1** relevance (to). **2** person's general social conduct. **3** part of a machine that supports another part, esp. one that reduces friction. ▷ *pl* **4** sense of one's own relative position, e.g. *I lost my bearings in the fog*.

beast ⓞ *n* **1** large wild animal. **2** brutal or uncivilized person. **beastly** *adj* unpleasant or disagreeable.

beat ⓞ *v* **beating**, **beat**, **beaten** or **beat** **1** hit hard and repeatedly. **2** move (wings) up and down. **3** throb rhythmically. **4** stir or mix vigorously. **5** *Music* indicate (time) by one's hand or a baton. **6** overcome or defeat. **7** (foll. by *back* or *off*) drive, push, or thrust. **8** *slang* puzzle or baffle. ▷ *n* **9** (sound made by) a stroke or blow. **10** regular throb. **11** assigned route, as of a policeman. **12** basic rhythmic unit in a piece of music. **beat up** *v* injure (someone) by repeated blows or kicks.

beatify [bee-*at*-if-fie] *v* -**fying**, -**fied** *RC Church* declare (a dead person) to be among the blessed in heaven: the first step towards canonization. **beatific** *adj* displaying great happiness. **beatification** *n* **beatitude** *n* *Christianity* any of the blessings on the poor, meek, etc., in the Sermon on the Mount.

━━━━━━━━━━━━━━━━━━━━━━━━━━━ THESAURUS ━━━━━━━━━━

bear¹ *v* **1** = **support**, have, hold, maintain, possess, shoulder, sustain, uphold **2** = **carry**, bring, convey, hump (*Brit sl*), move, take, transport **3, 4** = **produce**, beget, breed, bring forth, engender, generate, give birth to, yield **5** = **tolerate**, abide, allow, brook, endure, permit, put up with (*inf*), stomach, suffer

bearable *adj* **5** = **tolerable**, admissible, endurable, manageable, passable, sufferable, supportable, sustainable

bearer *n* = **carrier**, agent, conveyor, messenger, porter, runner, servant

bearing *n* **1** = **relevance**, application, connection, import, pertinence, reference, relation, significance **2** = **manner**, air, aspect, attitude, behaviour, demeanour, deportment, posture ▷ *pl* **4** = **position**, aim, course, direction, location, orientation, situation, track, way, whereabouts

bear out *v* = **support**, confirm, corroborate, endorse, justify, prove,

substantiate, uphold, vindicate

beast *n* **1** = **animal**, brute, creature **2** = **brute**, barbarian, fiend, monster, ogre, sadist, savage, swine

beastly *adj* = **unpleasant**, awful, disagreeable, horrid, mean, nasty, rotten

beat *v* **1** = **hit**, bang, batter, buffet, knock, pound, strike, thrash **2** = **flap**, flutter **3** = **throb**, palpitate, pound, pulsate, quake, thump, vibrate **6** = **defeat**, conquer, outdo, overcome, overwhelm, surpass, vanquish ▷ *n* **10** = **throb**, palpitation, pulsation, pulse **11** = **route**, circuit, course, path, rounds, way **12** = **rhythm**, accent, cadence, metre, stress, time

beaten *adj* **4** = **stirred**, blended, foamy, frothy, mixed, whipped, whisked **6** = **defeated**, cowed, overcome, overwhelmed, thwarted, vanquished

beat up *v* = **assault**, attack, batter, beat the living daylights out of (*inf*), knock about or around, thrash

beatnik *n* young person in the late 1950s who rebelled against conventional attitudes etc.

beau ❶ [boh] *n, pl* **beaux, beaus 1** boyfriend or admirer. **2** man greatly concerned with his appearance.

Beaufort scale *n* scale for measuring wind speeds.

Beaujolais *n* wine, usu. red, from southern Burgundy in France.

beauteous *adj lit* beautiful.

beautician *n* person who gives beauty treatments professionally.

beautiful ❶ *adj* **1** very attractive to look at. **2** very pleasant. **beautifully** *adv*.

beautify ❶ *v* **-fying, -fied** make beautiful. **beautification** *n*.

beauty ❶ *n, pl* **-ties 1** combination of all the qualities of a person or thing that delight the senses and mind. **2** very attractive woman. **3** *informal* something outstanding of its kind. **beautiful** very attractive to look at. **beauty queen** woman who has been judged the most beautiful in a contest. **beauty spot 1** place of outstanding beauty. **2** small black spot formerly worn on a lady's face as decoration.

beaver *n* **1** amphibious rodent with a big flat tail. **2** (hat made of) its fur. **beaver away** *v* work industriously.

becalmed ❶ *adj* (of a sailing ship) motionless through lack of wind.

became *v* past tense of BECOME.

because ❶ *conj* on account of the fact that. **because of** on account of.

beck¹ *n* **at someone's beck and call** having to be constantly available to do as someone asks.

beck² *n* N English stream.

beckon ❶ *v* summon with a gesture.

become ❶ *v* **-coming, -came, -come 1** come to be. **2** (foll. by *of*) happen to, e.g. *what became of him?* **3** suit, e.g. *that dress really becomes you.* **becoming** *adj* **1** attractive or pleasing. **2** appropriate or proper.

bed ❶ *n* **1** piece of furniture on which to sleep. **2** garden plot. **3** bottom of a river, lake, or sea. **4** layer of rock. ▷ *v* **bedding, bedded 5** plant in a bed. **go to bed with** have sexual intercourse with. **bed and breakfast** overnight accommodation plus breakfast. **bedclothes** *pl n* coverings for a bed. **bed down** *v* go to or put into a place to sleep or rest. **bedpan** *n* shallow bowl used as a toilet by bedridden people. **bedridden** *adj* confined to bed because of illness or old age. **bedrock** *n* **1** solid rock beneath the surface soil. **2** basic facts or principles. **bedroom** *n* **bedsit, bedsitter** *n* furnished sitting room with a bed. **bedspread** *n* top cover on a bed. **bedstead** *n* framework of a bed.

BEd Bachelor of Education.

bedaub *v* smear with something sticky or dirty.

bedding *n* **1** sheets and covers that are used on a bed. **2** litter, such as straw, for animals.

bedeck *v* cover with decorations.

bedevil ❶ [bid-**dev**-ill] *v* **-illing, -illed** harass, confuse, or torment.

THESAURUS

beau *n* **1** = **boyfriend**, admirer, fiancé, lover, suitor, sweetheart **2** = **dandy**, coxcomb, fop, gallant, ladies' man

beautiful *adj* **1** = **attractive**, exquisite, fair, fine, gorgeous, handsome, lekker (*S Afr sl*), lovely **2** = **pleasant**, charming, delightful, pleasing

beautify *v* = **make beautiful**, adorn, decorate, embellish, festoon, garnish, glamorize, ornament

beauty *n* **1** = **attractiveness**, charm, comeliness, elegance, exquisiteness, glamour, grace, handsomeness, loveliness **2** = **belle**, good-looker, lovely (*sl*), stunner (*inf*)

becalmed *adj* = **still**, motionless, settled, stranded, stuck

because *conj* = **since**, as, by reason of, in that, on account of, owing to, thanks to

beckon *v* = **gesture**, bid, gesticulate, motion, nod, signal, summon, wave at

become *v* **1** = **come to be**, alter to, be transformed into, change into, develop into, grow into, mature into, ripen into **3** = **suit**, embellish, enhance, fit, flatter, set off

becoming *adj* **1** = **flattering**, attractive, comely, enhancing, graceful, lekker (*S Afr sl*), neat, pretty, tasteful **2** = **appropriate**, compatible, fitting, in keeping, proper, seemly, suitable, worthy

bed *n* **1** = **bedstead**, berth, bunk, cot, couch, divan **2** = **plot**, area, border, garden, patch, row, strip **3** = **bottom**, base

bedevil *v* = **torment**, afflict, confound, confuse, distress, harass, plague, trouble, vex, worry

bedlam ❶ *n* noisy confused situation.
Bedouin *n, pl* **-in, -ins** member of a
nomadic Arab race.
bedraggled ❶ *adj* untidy, wet, or dirty.
bee¹ *n* insect that makes wax and honey.
have a bee in one's bonnet be
obsessed with an idea. **beehive** *n*
structure in which bees live. **beeswax** *n*
wax secreted by bees, used in
polishes etc.
bee² *n US* social gathering to carry out a
communal task, e.g. *quilting bee*.
Beeb *n informal* the BBC.
beech *n* European tree with a smooth
greyish bark.
beef ❶ *n* **1** flesh of a cow, bull, or ox.
2 *informal* complaint. ▷ *v* **3** *informal*
complain. **beefy** *adj* **beefier, beefiest**
1 like beef. **2** *informal* strong and
muscular. **beefburger** *n* flat grilled or
fried cake of minced beef. **beefeater** *n*
yeoman warder at the Tower of
London. **beef tomato, beefsteak
tomato** large fleshy tomato. **beef up** *v*
make stronger or more effective.
been *v* past participle of BE.
beep *n* **1** high-pitched sound, like that of
a car horn. ▷ *v* **2** (cause to) make this
noise.
beer *n* alcoholic drink brewed from malt
and hops. **beery** *adj*.
beer parlour ❶ *n Canad* tavern.
beet *n* plant with an edible root and

leaves. **beetroot** *n* type of beet plant
with a dark red root.
beetle¹ *n* insect with a hard wing cover
on its back.
beetle² *adj* overhang or jut. **beetling** *adj*
beetle-browed *adj* having bushy or
overhanging eyebrows.
befall ❶ *v old-fashioned* happen to
(someone).
befit ❶ *v* be appropriate or suitable for.
befitting *adj*.
before ❶ *conj, prep, adv* indicating
something earlier in time, in front of, or
preferred to, e.g. *before the war*; *brought
before a judge*; *death before dishonour*.
beforehand *adv* in advance.
befriend ❶ *v* become friends with.
befuddled *adj* stupefied or confused, as
through alcoholic drink.
beg ❶ *v* **begging, begged 1** solicit (for
money or food), esp. in the street. **2** ask
formally or humbly. **beg the question**
assume the thing under examination as
proved. **go begging** be unwanted or
unused.
began *v* past tense of BEGIN.
beget *v* **-getting, -got** *or* **-gat, -gotten**
or **-got** *old-fashioned* **1** cause or create.
2 father.
beggar ❶ *n* **1** person who lives by
begging. **2** *Brit* fellow. ▷ *v* **3** **beggar
description** be impossible to describe.
beggarly *adj*.

THESAURUS

bedlam *n* = **pandemonium**, chaos,
commotion, confusion, furore, tumult,
turmoil, uproar
bedraggled *adj* = **messy**, dirty,
dishevelled, disordered, muddied,
unkempt, untidy
bedridden *adj* = **confined to bed**,
confined, flat on one's back,
incapacitated, laid up (*inf*)
bedrock *n* **1** = **bottom**, bed, foundation,
rock bottom, substratum, substructure
2 = **basics**, basis, core, essentials,
fundamentals, nuts and bolts (*inf*), roots
beefy *adj* **2** *Inf* = **brawny**, bulky, hulking,
muscular, stocky, strapping, sturdy,
thickset
beer parlour *noun* (*Canad*) = **tavern**,
inn, bar, pub (*informal, chiefly Brit*),
public house, watering hole (*facetious
slang*), boozer (*Brit, Austral & NZ
informal*), beverage room (*Canad*),
hostelry, alehouse (*archaic*), taproom
befall *v Old-fashioned* = **happen**, chance,
come to pass, fall, occur, take place,

transpire (*inf*)
befitting *adj* = **appropriate**, apposite,
becoming, fit, fitting, proper, right,
seemly, suitable
before *prep, adv* **a** = **earlier than**, in
advance of, prior to **b** = **ahead of**, in
advance of, in front of **c** = **previously**,
ahead, earlier, formerly, in advance,
sooner **d** = **in front**, ahead
beforehand *adv* = **in advance**, ahead of
time, already, before, earlier, in
anticipation, previously, sooner
befriend *v* = **help**, aid, assist, back,
encourage, side with, stand by,
support, welcome
beg *v* **1** = **scrounge**, bludge (*Aust & NZ*),
cadge, seek charity, solicit charity,
sponge on, touch (someone) for (*sl*)
2 = **implore**, beseech, entreat, petition,
plead, request, solicit
beggar *n* **1** = **tramp**, bag lady (*chiefly
US*), bum (*inf*), down-and-out, pauper,
vagrant
beggarly *adj* **1** = **poor**, destitute,

begin ❶ *v* **-ginning, -gan, -gun 1** start. **2** bring or come into being. **beginner** *n* person who has just started learning to do something. **beginning** *n*.

begone *interj* go away!

begonia *n* tropical plant with waxy flowers.

begot *v* a past of BEGET. **begotten** *v* a past participle of BEGET.

begrudge ❶ *v* **1** envy (someone) the possession of something, e.g. *I don't begrudge him his success*. **2** give or allow unwillingly, e.g. *he begrudged her an apology*.

beguile ❶ [big-**gile**] *v* **1** cheat or mislead. **2** charm or amuse. **beguiling** *adj*.

beguine [big-**geen**] *n* **1** S American dance. **2** music for this.

begum [**bay**-gum] *n* Muslim woman of high rank.

begun *v* past participle of BEGIN.

behalf *n* **on behalf of** in the interest of or for the benefit of.

behave ❶ *v* **1** act or function in a particular way. **2** conduct (oneself) properly. **behaviour** *n* manner of behaving.

behaviour ❶ *n* manner of behaving.

behead *v* remove the head from.

beheld *v* past of BEHOLD.

behemoth [bee-**hee**-moth] *n* huge person or thing.

behest *n* order or earnest request, e.g. *I came at her behest*.

behind ❶ *prep, adv* **1** indicating position to the rear, lateness, responsibility, etc. e.g. *behind the wall*; *behind schedule*; *the reasons behind her departure*. ▷ *n* **2** *informal* buttocks.

behold ❶ *v* **-holding, -held** *old-fashioned* look (at). **beholder** *n*.

beholden ❶ *adj* indebted or obliged.

behove *v* *old-fashioned* be necessary or fitting for.

beige *adj* pale brown.

being ❶ *n* **1** state or fact of existing. **2** something that exists or is thought to exist. **3** human being. ▷ *v* **4** present participle of BE.

belabour *v* attack verbally or physically.

belated ❶ *adj* late or too late. **belatedly** *adv*.

belch ❶ *v* **1** expel wind from the stomach noisily through the mouth. **2** expel or be expelled forcefully, e.g. *smoke belched from the factory*. ▷ *n* **3** act of belching.

——————— **THESAURUS** ———————

impoverished, indigent, needy, poverty-stricken

begin *v* **1** = **start**, commence, embark on, initiate, instigate, institute, prepare, set about **2** = **happen**, appear, arise, come into being, emerge, originate, start

beginner *n* = **novice**, amateur, apprentice, learner, neophyte, starter, trainee, tyro

beginning *n* **1** = **start**, birth, commencement, inauguration, inception, initiation, onset, opening, origin, outset **2** = **seed**, fount, germ, root

begrudge *v* **1** = **resent**, be jealous, envy, grudge

beguile *v* **1** = **fool**, cheat, deceive, delude, dupe, hoodwink, mislead, take for a ride (*inf*), trick **2** = **charm**, amuse, distract, divert, engross, entertain, occupy

beguiling *adj* **2** = **charming**, alluring, attractive, bewitching, captivating, enchanting, enthralling, intriguing

behave *v* **1** = **act**, function, operate, perform, run, work **2** = **conduct oneself properly**, act correctly, keep

one's nose clean, mind one's manners (*inf*)

behaviour *n* = **conduct**, actions, bearing, demeanour, deportment, manner, manners, ways

behind *prep, adv* **1 a** = **after**, at the back of, at the heels of, at the rear of, following, later than **b** = **causing**, at the bottom of, initiating, instigating, responsible for **c** = **after**, afterwards, following, in the wake (of), next, subsequently **d** = **overdue**, behindhand, in arrears, in debt

behold *v* *Old-fashioned* = **look at**, observe, perceive, regard, survey, view, watch, witness

beholden *adj* = **indebted**, bound, grateful, obliged, owing, under obligation

being *n* **1** = **existence**, life, reality **2** = **nature**, entity, essence, soul, spirit, substance **3** = **human being**, creature, individual

belated *adj* = **late**, behindhand, behind time, delayed, late in the day, overdue, tardy

belch *v* **1** = **burp** (*inf*), hiccup **2** = **emit**, discharge, disgorge, erupt, give off,

b

beleaguered ❶ *adj* **1** struggling against difficulties or criticism. **2** besieged by an enemy.

belfry *n, pl* **-fries** part of a tower where bells are hung.

belie *v* **1** show to be untrue. **2** misrepresent.

belief ❶ *n* **1** faith or confidence. **2** opinion. **3** principle accepted as true, often without proof. **believe** *v* **1** accept as true or real. **2** think, assume, or suppose. **3** accept (someone's) statement or opinion as true, e.g. *I don't believe you!* **believe in** be convinced of the truth or existence of. **believable** *adj* **believer** *n*.

Belisha beacon [bill-**lee**-sha] *n* flashing orange globe mounted on a post, marking a pedestrian crossing.

belittle ❶ *v* treat as having little value or importance.

bell *n* **1** hollow, usu. metal, cup-shaped instrument that emits a ringing sound when struck. **2** device that rings or buzzes as a signal. **ring a bell** bring to mind something previously known or experienced. **bell-bottoms** *pl n* trousers that flare from the knee.

belladonna *n* (drug obtained from) deadly nightshade.

belle *n* beautiful woman, esp. the most attractive woman at a function.

belles-lettres [bell-**let**-tra] *n* literary works, esp. essays and poetry.

bellicose *adj* warlike and aggressive.

belligerent ❶ *adj* **1** hostile and aggressive. **2** engaged in war. ▷ *n* **3** person or country engaged in war. **belligerence** *n*.

bellow ❶ *v* **1** make a low deep cry like that of a bull. **2** shout in anger. ▷ *n* **3** loud deep roar.

bellows *pl n* instrument for pumping a stream of air into something.

belly ❶ *n, pl* **-lies 1** part of the body of a vertebrate which contains the intestines. **2** stomach. **3** front, lower, or inner part of something. ▷ *v* **-lying**, **-lied 4** (cause to) swell out. **bellyful** *n slang* more than one can tolerate. **belly laugh** loud deep laugh.

belong ❶ *v* **1** (foll. by *to*) be the property of. **2** (foll. by *to*) be a part or member of. **3** (foll. by *to* or *with*) be classified with. **belongings** *pl n* personal possessions.

beloved ❶ *adj* **1** dearly loved. ▷ *n* **2** person dearly loved.

below ❶ *prep, adv* at or to a position

---

spew forth, vent

beleaguered *adj* **1** = **harassed**, badgered, hassled (*inf*), persecuted, pestered, plagued, put upon, vexed **2** = **besieged**, assailed, beset, blockaded, hemmed in, surrounded

belief *n* **1** = **faith**, assurance, confidence, conviction, trust **2** = **opinion**, feeling, impression, judgment, notion **3** = **faith**, credo, creed, doctrine, dogma, ideology, principles, tenet

believable *adj* **1** = **credible**, authentic, imaginable, likely, plausible, possible, probable, trustworthy

believe *v* **1** = **accept**, be certain of, be convinced of, credit, depend on, have faith in, rely on, swear by, trust **2** = **think**, assume, gather, imagine, judge, presume, reckon, speculate, suppose

belittle *v* = **disparage**, decry, denigrate, deprecate, deride, scoff at, scorn, sneer at

belligerent *adj* **1** = **aggressive**, bellicose, combative, hostile, pugnacious, unfriendly, warlike, warring ▷ *n* **3** = **fighter**, combatant, warring nation

bellow *v* **2** = **shout**, bawl, cry, howl, roar, scream, shriek, yell ▷ *n* **3** = **shout**, bawl, cry, howl, roar, scream, shriek, yell

belly *n* **1, 2** = **stomach**, abdomen, corporation (*inf*), gut, insides (*inf*), paunch, potbelly, tummy ▷ *v* **4** = **swell out**, billow, bulge, fill, spread, swell

bellyful *n Sl* = **surfeit**, enough, excess, glut, plenty, satiety, too much

belong *v* **1** (foll. by *to*) = **be the property of**, be at the disposal of, be held by, be owned by **2** (foll. by *to*) = **be a member of**, be affiliated to, be allied to, be associated with, be included in

belonging *n* **2** = **relationship**, acceptance, affinity, association, attachment, fellowship, inclusion, loyalty, rapport

belongings *pl n* = **possessions**, accoutrements, chattels, effects, gear, goods, paraphernalia, personal property, stuff, things

beloved *adj* **1** = **dear**, admired, adored, darling, loved, pet, precious, prized, treasured, valued, worshipped

below *prep* = **lower than**, inferior, lesser, less than, subject, subordinate ▷ *adv*

b

lower than, under.

belt ❶ *n* **1** band of cloth, leather, etc., worn usu. around the waist. **2** long narrow area, e.g. *a belt of trees*. **3** circular strip of rubber that drives moving parts in a machine. ▷ *v* **4** fasten with a belt. **5** *slang* hit very hard. **6** *slang* move very fast. **belt out** *v* sing (a song) loudly.

bemoan ❶ *v* express sorrow or dissatisfaction about.

bemused ❶ *adj* puzzled or confused.

ben *n Scot & Irish* mountain peak.

bench ❶ *n* **1** long seat. **2** long narrow work table. **the bench 1** judge or magistrate sitting in court, or judges and magistrates collectively. **2** place where substitutes sit during a sports match. **benchmark** *n* criterion by which to measure something.

bend ❶ *v* **bending**, **bent 1** (cause to) form a curve. **2** (often foll. by *down*, etc.) incline the body. **3** (cause to) submit. ▷ *n* **4** curved part. ▷ *pl* **5** *informal* decompression sickness. **bend the rules** *informal* ignore or change rules to suit oneself. **bendy** *adj* **bendier**, **bendiest**.

beneath ❶ *adv, prep* **1** below. **2** not worthy of.

Benedictine *adj* **1** of an order of Christian monks and nuns founded by Saint Benedict. ▷ *n* **2** liqueur first made by Benedictine monks.

benediction *n* prayer for divine blessing. **benedictory** *adj*.

benefactor, benefactress ❶ *n* someone who supports a person or institution by giving money. **benefaction** *n* **1** act of doing good. **2** gift to charity.

benefice *n Christianity* church office providing its holder with an income.

beneficent [bin-**eff**-iss-ent] *adj* charitable or generous. **beneficence** *n*.

beneficial ❶ *adj* helpful or advantageous.

beneficiary ❶ *n, pl* **-ciaries** person who gains or benefits.

benefit ❶ *n* **1** something that improves or promotes. **2** advantage or sake, e.g. *I'm doing this for your benefit*. **3** payment made by a government to a poor, ill, or unemployed person. **4** theatrical performance or sports event to raise money for charity. ▷ *v* **-fiting**, **-fited 5** do or receive good.

benevolence ❶ *n* **1** inclination to do good. **2** act of kindness. **benevolent** *adj* **benevolently** *adv*.

Bengali *n, adj* (member or language) of a people living chiefly in Bangladesh and W Bengal.

benighted *adj* ignorant or uncultured.

benign ❶ [bin-**nine**] *adj* **1** showing kindliness. **2** favourable or propitious. **3** (of a tumour) not threatening to life. **benignly** *adv*.

= **lower**, beneath, down, under, underneath

belt *n* **1** = **waistband**, band, cummerbund, girdle, girth, sash **2** = **zone**, area, district, layer, region, stretch, strip, tract

bemoan *v* = **lament**, bewail, deplore, grieve for, mourn, regret, rue, weep for

bemused *adj* = **puzzled**, at sea, bewildered, confused, flummoxed, muddled, nonplussed, perplexed

bench *n* **1** = **seat**, form, pew, settle, stall **2** = **worktable**, board, counter, table, trestle table, workbench ▷ *n* **the bench 1** = **court**, courtroom, judges, judiciary, magistrates, tribunal

benchmark *n* = **reference point**, criterion, gauge, level, measure, model, norm, par, standard, yardstick

bend *v* **1** = **curve**, arc, arch, bow, turn, twist, veer **2** = **lean**, bow ▷ *n* **4** = **curve**, angle, arc, arch, bow, corner, loop, turn, twist

beneath *adv* **1** = **underneath**, below, in a lower place ▷ *prep* **1** = **under**, below, lower than, underneath **2** = **unworthy of**, below, inferior to, less than, unbefitting

benefactor *n* = **supporter**, backer, donor, helper, patron, philanthropist, sponsor, well-wisher

beneficial *adj* = **helpful**, advantageous, benign, favourable, profitable, useful, valuable, wholesome

beneficiary *n* = **recipient**, heir, inheritor, payee, receiver

benefit *n* **1** = **help**, advantage, aid, asset, assistance, favour, good, profit ▷ *v* **5** = **help**, aid, assist, avail, enhance, further, improve, profit

benevolent *adj* = **kind**, altruistic, benign, caring, charitable, generous, philanthropic

benign *adj* **1** = **kindly**, amiable, friendly, genial, kind, obliging, sympathetic **3** = **harmless**, curable, remediable

b

bent ❶ v **1** past of BEND. ▷ adj **2** curved.
3 slang dishonest or corrupt, e.g. a bent
cop. **4** offens slang homosexual. ▷ n
5 personal inclination or aptitude. **bent
on** determined to pursue (a course of
action).

bento, bento box n thin lightweight
box divided into compartments, which
contain small separate dishes
comprising a Japanese meal.

benumb v **1** make numb or powerless.
2 stupefy (the mind etc.).

benzene n flammable poisonous liquid
used as a solvent, insecticide, etc.

benzine n volatile liquid used as a
solvent.

bequeath ❶ v **1** dispose of (property) as
in a will. **2** hand down. **bequest** n legal
gift of money or property by someone
who has died.

berate ❶ v scold harshly.

berberis n shrub with red berries.

bereaved ❶ adj having recently lost a
close friend or relative through death.
bereavement n.

bereft ❶ adj (foll. by of) deprived.

beret [ber-ray] n round flat close-fitting
brimless cap.

berg¹ n S Afr mountain.

berg² n iceberg.

bergamot n small Asian tree, the fruit of
which yields an oil used in perfumery.

beri-beri n disease caused by vitamin B
deficiency.

berk n Brit, Aust & NZ slang stupid person.

berkelium n Chemistry radioactive
element.

berm n NZ narrow grass strip between
the road and the footpath in a
residential area.

Bermuda shorts pl n shorts that come
down to the knees.

berry n, pl **-ries** small soft stoneless fruit.

berserk ❶ adj **go berserk** become
violent or destructive.

berth ❶ n **1** bunk in a ship or train.
2 place assigned to a ship at a mooring.
▷ v **3** dock (a ship). **give a wide berth
to** keep clear of.

beryl n hard transparent mineral.

beryllium n Chemistry toxic silvery-
white metallic element.

beseech ❶ v **-seeching, -sought** or
-seeched ask earnestly; beg.

beset ❶ v **1** trouble or harass constantly.
2 attack from all sides.

beside ❶ prep **1** at, by, or to the side of.
2 as compared with. **3** away from, e.g.
beside the point. **beside oneself**
overwhelmed or overwrought. **besides**
adv, prep in addition.

besiege ❶ v **1** surround with military
forces. **2** hem in. **3** overwhelm, as with
requests.

— THESAURUS —

bent adj **2** = **curved**, angled, arched,
bowed, crooked, hunched, stooped,
twisted ▷ n **5** = **inclination**, ability,
aptitude, leaning, penchant,
preference, propensity, tendency

bent on adj = **determined to**, disposed
to, fixed on, inclined to, insistent on,
predisposed to, resolved on, set on

bequeath v **1** = **leave**, endow, entrust,
give, grant, will **2** = **hand down**,
bestow, impart, pass on

bequest n = **legacy**, bestowal,
endowment, estate, gift, inheritance,
settlement

berate v = **scold**, castigate, censure,
chide, criticize, harangue, rebuke,
reprimand, reprove, rouse on (Aust), tell
off (inf), upbraid

bereavement n = **loss**, affliction, death,
deprivation, misfortune, tribulation

bereft adj (foll. bu of) = **deprived**,
devoid, lacking, parted from, robbed of,
wanting

berserk adj **go berserk** = **go crazy**, go
mad, go wild, raging, rampage, run

amok, wig out (sl)

berth n **1** = **bunk**, bed, billet, hammock
2 = **anchorage**, dock, harbour, haven,
pier, port, quay, wharf ▷ v **3** = **anchor**,
dock, drop anchor, land, moor, tie up

beseech v = **beg**, ask, call upon, entreat,
implore, plead, pray, solicit

beset v **1** = **plague**, bedevil, harass,
pester, trouble

beside prep **1** = **next to**, abreast of,
adjacent to, alongside, at the side of,
close to, near, nearby, neighbouring

beside oneself adj = **distraught**,
apoplectic, at the end of one's tether,
demented, desperate, frantic, frenzied,
out of one's mind, unhinged

besides adv = **too**, also, as well, further,
furthermore, in addition, into the
bargain, moreover, otherwise, what's
more ▷ prep = **in addition to**, apart
from, barring, excepting, excluding,
other than, over and above, without

besiege v **1, 2** = **surround**, blockade,
encircle, hem in, lay siege to, shut in
3 = **harass**, badger, harry, hassle (inf),

besmirch v **1** tarnish (someone's name or reputation). **2** make dirty; soil. **3** reduce the brightness or lustre of.

besom n broom made of twigs.

besotted ⊙ adj infatuated.

besought v a past of BESEECH.

bespatter v splash, e.g. with dirty water.

bespeak v indicate or suggest. **bespoke** adj **1** (esp. of a suit) made to the customer's specifications, e.g. a bespoke three-piece suit. **2** making or selling such suits, e.g. a bespoke tailor.

best ⊙ adj **1** most excellent of a particular group etc. ▷ adv **2** in a manner surpassing all others. ▷ n **3** the utmost effort, e.g. I did my best. **4** most outstanding or excellent person, thing, or group in a category. ▷ v **5** defeat. **best man** groom's attendant at a wedding. **bestseller** n book or other product that has sold in great numbers. **bestselling** adj.

bestial ⊙ adj **1** brutal or savage. **2** of or like a beast. **bestiality** n.

bestir v cause (oneself) to become active.

bestow ⊙ v present (a gift) or confer (an honour). **bestowal** n.

bestride v have or put a leg on either side of.

bet ⊙ n **1** the act of staking a sum of money or other stake on the outcome of an event. **2** stake risked. **3** course of action, e.g. your best bet is to go by train. ▷ v **betting**, **bet** or **betted 4** make or place (a bet). **5** informal predict.

beta n second letter in the Greek alphabet. **beta-blocker** n drug used to treat high blood pressure and angina. **beta particle** electron or positron emitted by a nucleus during radioactive decay or nuclear fission.

betake v **betake oneself** formal go or move.

betel [bee-tl] n Asian climbing plant, the leaves and nuts of which can be chewed.

bête noire [bet nwahr] n, pl **bêtes noires** person or thing that one particularly dislikes.

betide v happen (to).

betoken ⊙ v indicate or signify.

betray ⊙ v **1** hand over or expose (one's nation, friend, etc.) treacherously to an enemy. **2** disclose (a secret or confidence) treacherously. **3** reveal unintentionally. **betrayal** n **betrayer** n.

betrothed adj engaged to be married. **betrothal** n.

better ⊙ adj **1** more excellent than others. **2** improved or fully recovered in health. ▷ adv **3** in a more excellent manner. **4** in or to a greater degree. ▷ pl n **5** one's superiors. ▷ v **6** improve upon. **get the better of** defeat or outwit. **betterment** n improvement. **better off** in more favourable circumstances, esp. financially. **better-off** adj reasonably wealthy.

between ⊙ prep, adv indicating position in the middle, alternatives, etc.

THESAURUS

---

hound, nag, pester, plague

besotted adj = **infatuated**, doting, hypnotized, smitten, spellbound

best adj **1** = **finest**, foremost, leading, most excellent, outstanding, pre-eminent, principal, supreme, unsurpassed ▷ adv **2** = **most highly**, extremely, greatly, most deeply, most fully ▷ n **4** = **finest**, cream, elite, flower, pick, prime, top

bestial adj **1** = **brutal**, barbaric, beastly, brutish, inhuman, savage

bestow v = **present**, award, commit, give, grant, hand out, impart, lavish

bet n **1** = **gamble**, long shot, risk, speculation, venture, wager **2** = **stake** ▷ v **4** = **gamble**, chance, hazard, risk, speculate, stake, venture, wager

betoken v = **indicate**, bode, denote, promise, represent, signify, suggest

betray v **1** = **be disloyal**, be treacherous, be unfaithful, break one's promise, double-cross (inf), inform on or against, sell out (inf), stab in the back **2, 3** = **give away**, disclose, divulge, let slip, reveal

betrayal n **1** = **disloyalty**, deception, double-cross (inf), sell-out (inf), treachery, treason, trickery **2, 3** = **giving away**, disclosure, divulgence, revelation

better adj **1** = **superior**, excelling, finer, greater, higher-quality, more desirable, preferable, surpassing **2** = **well**, cured, fully recovered, on the mend (inf), recovering, stronger ▷ adv **3** = **in a more excellent manner**, in a superior way, more advantageously, more attractively, more competently, more effectively **4** = **to a greater degree**, more completely, more thoroughly ▷ v **6** = **improve**, enhance, further, raise

between prep = **amidst**, among,

b

betwixt *prep, adv old-fashioned* between.

bevel *n* **1** slanting edge. ▷ *v* **-elling, -elled 2** slope. **3** cut a bevel on (a piece of timber etc.).

beverage ❶ *n* drink.

beverage room ❶ *n Canad* tavern.

bevy ❶ *n, pl* **bevies** flock or group.

bewail ❶ *v* express great sorrow over.

beware ❶ *v* be on one's guard (against).

bewilder ❶ *v* confuse utterly.
  bewildering *adj* **bewilderment** *n*.

bewitch ❶ *v* **1** attract and fascinate.
  2 cast a spell over. **bewitching** *adj*.

beyond ❶ *prep* **1** at or to a point on the other side of. **2** outside the limits or scope of. ▷ *adv* **3** at or to the far side of something. ▷ *n* **4** the unknown, esp. life after death.

bezique *n* card game for two or more players.

bhaji *n, pl* **bhaji, bhajis** Indian deep-fried savoury of chopped vegetables in spiced batter.

bhp brake horsepower.

Bi *Chemistry* bismuth.

bi- *combining form* two or twice, e.g. *bifocal*; *biweekly*.

biannual *adj* occurring twice a year.
  biannually *adv*.

bias ❶ *n* **1** mental tendency, esp.

prejudice. **2** diagonal cut across the weave of a fabric. **3** *Bowls* bulge or weight on one side of a bowl that causes it to roll in a curve. ▷ *v* **-asing, -ased** *or* **-assing, -assed 4** cause to have a bias. **biased, biassed** *adj* **bias binding** strip of material used for binding hems.

bib *n* **1** piece of cloth or plastic worn to protect a young child's clothes when eating. **2** upper front part of dungarees etc.

Bible *n* **1** sacred writings of the Christian religion. **2** (**b-**) book regarded as authoritative. **biblical** *adj*.

bibliography *n, pl* **-phies 1** list of books on a subject. **2** list of sources used in a book etc. **bibliographer** *n*.

bibliophile *n* person who collects or is fond of books.

bibulous *adj* addicted to alcohol.

bicameral *adj* (of a legislature) consisting of two chambers.

bicarbonate *n* salt of carbonic acid.
  bicarbonate of soda powder used in baking or as medicine.

bicentenary, US **bicentennial** *adj* **1** marking a 200th anniversary. ▷ *n, pl* **-naries 2** 200th anniversary.

biceps *n* muscle with two origins, esp. the muscle that flexes the forearm.

bicker ❶ *v* argue over petty matters.

bicycle *n* **1** vehicle with two wheels, one behind the other, pedalled by the rider. ▷ *v* **2** ride a bicycle.

─────────────────────────── THESAURUS ───────

betwixt, in the middle of, mid

beverage *n* = **drink**, liquid, liquor, refreshment

beverage room *noun* (*Canad*) = **tavern**, inn, bar, pub (*informal, chiefly Brit*), public house, watering hole (*facetious slang*), boozer (*Brit, Austral & NZ informal*), beer parlour (*Canad*), hostelry, alehouse (*archaic*), taproom

bevy *n* = **group**, band, bunch (*inf*), collection, company, crowd, gathering, pack, troupe

bewail *v* = **lament**, bemoan, cry over, deplore, grieve for, moan, mourn, regret

beware *v* = **be careful**, be cautious, be wary, guard against, heed, look out, mind, take heed, watch out

bewilder *v* = **confound**, baffle, bemuse, confuse, flummox, mystify, nonplus, perplex, puzzle

bewildered *adj* = **confused**, at a loss, at

sea, baffled, flummoxed, mystified, nonplussed, perplexed, puzzled

bewitch *v* = **enchant**, beguile, captivate, charm, enrapture, entrance, fascinate, hypnotize

bewitched *adj* = **enchanted**, charmed, entranced, fascinated, mesmerized, spellbound, under a spell

beyond *prep* **1** = **past**, above, apart from, at a distance, away from, over **2** = **exceeding**, out of reach of, superior to, surpassing

bias *n* **1** = **prejudice**, favouritism, inclination, leaning, partiality, tendency ▷ *v* **4** = **prejudice**, distort, influence, mana (*NZ*), predispose, slant, sway, twist, warp, weight

biased *adj* **1** = **prejudiced**, distorted, one-sided, partial, slanted, weighted

bicker *v* = **quarrel**, argue, disagree, dispute, fight, row (*inf*), squabble, wrangle

bid ❶ v **bidding**, **bade**, **bidden 1** say (a greeting), e.g. to bid farewell. **2** command. **3** past **bid** offer (an amount) in an attempt to buy something. ▷ n **4** offer of a specified amount. **5** attempt. **bidder** n **biddable** adj obedient. **bidding** n **1** command. **2** invitation.

bide v **bide one's time** wait patiently for an opportunity.

bidet [**bee**-day] n low basin for washing the genital area.

biennial adj **1** occurring every two years. ▷ n **2** plant that completes its life cycle in two years.

bier n stand on which a corpse or coffin rests before burial.

biff slang ▷ n **1** blow with the fist. ▷ v **2** give (someone) such a blow.

bifocals pl n spectacles with lenses permitting near and distant vision. **bifocal** adj having two different focuses.

bifurcate v fork into two branches.

big ❶ adj **bigger**, **biggest 1** of considerable size, height, number, or capacity. **2** important through having power, wealth, etc. **3** elder. **4** generous. ▷ adv **5** on a grand scale, e.g. think big. **bighead** n informal conceited person. **big-headed** adj **big shot**, **bigwig** n informal important person. **big top** informal main tent of a circus or the circus itself.

bigamy n crime of marrying a person while still legally married to someone else. **bigamist** n **bigamous** adj.

bight n **1** long curved shoreline. **2** curve or loop in a rope.

bigot ❶ n person who is intolerant, esp. regarding religion or race. **bigoted** adj **bigotry** n.

bijou [**bee**-zhoo] adj (of a house) small but elegant.

bike n informal bicycle or motorcycle.

bikini n woman's brief two-piece swimming costume.

bilateral adj affecting or undertaken by two parties.

bilberry n bluish-black edible berry.

bile n **1** bitter yellow fluid secreted by the liver. **2** irritability or peevishness.

bilge n **1** informal nonsense. **2** ship's bottom. **3** dirty water that collects in a ship's bilge.

bilingual adj involving or using two languages.

bilious adj **1** sick, nauseous. **2** informal bad-tempered or irritable.

bilk v cheat, esp. by not paying.

bill¹ ❶ n **1** statement of money owed for goods or services supplied. **2** draft of a proposed new law. **3** poster. **4** US & Canad banknote. **5** list of events, such as a theatre programme. ▷ v **6** send or present a bill to. **7** advertise by posters.

bid v **1** = **say**, call, greet, tell, wish **2** = **tell**, ask, command, direct, instruct, order, require **3** = **offer**, proffer, propose, submit, tender ▷ n **4** = **offer**, advance, amount, price, proposal, sum, tender **5** = **attempt**, crack (inf), effort, go (inf), stab (inf), try

bidding n **1** = **order**, beck and call, command, direction, instruction, request, summons

big adj **1** = **large**, enormous, extensive, great, huge, immense, massive, substantial, vast **2** = **important**, eminent, influential, leading, main, powerful, prominent, significant, skookum (Canad) **3** = **grown-up**, adult, elder, grown, mature **4** = **generous**, altruistic, benevolent, gracious, magnanimous, noble, unselfish

bighead n Inf = **boaster**, braggart, know-all (inf)

bigheaded adj Inf = **boastful**, arrogant, cocky, conceited, egotistic, immodest, overconfident, swollen-headed

bigot n = **fanatic**, racist, sectarian, zealot

bigoted adj = **intolerant**, biased, dogmatic, narrow-minded, opinionated, prejudiced, sectarian

bigotry n = **intolerance**, bias, discrimination, dogmatism, fanaticism, narrow-mindedness, prejudice, sectarianism

big shot, **bigwig** n Inf = **important person**, celebrity, dignitary, mogul, personage, somebody, V.I.P.

bill¹ n **1** = **charges**, account, invoice, reckoning, score, statement, tally **2** = **proposal**, measure, piece of legislation, projected law **3** = **advertisement**, bulletin, circular, handbill, hand-out, leaflet, notice, placard, poster **5** = **list**, agenda, card, catalogue, inventory, listing, programme, roster, schedule ▷ v **6** = **charge**, debit, invoice **7** = **advertise**, announce, give advance notice of, post

bill of fare menu. **clean bill of health** favourable account of a person or thing's physical or financial condition. **fit**, **fill the bill** *informal* be suitable or adequate.

bill² ❶ *n* bird's beak. **bill and coo** (of lovers) kiss and whisper amorously.

billabong *n Aust* stagnant pool in an intermittent stream.

billboard *n Chiefly US & Canad* hoarding.

billet ❶ *v* -**leting**, -**leted** 1 assign a lodging to (a soldier). ▷ *n* 2 accommodation for a soldier in civil lodgings.

billet-doux [bill-ee-**doo**] *n, pl* **billets-doux** love letter.

billhook *n* tool with a hooked blade, used for chopping etc.

billiards *n* game played on a table with balls and a cue.

billion *n* 1 one thousand million. 2 formerly, one million million. **billionth** *adj* **billionaire** *n* person who owns at least a billion pounds, dollars, etc.

billow ❶ *n* 1 large sea wave. 2 swelling or surging mass, as of smoke or sound. ▷ *v* 3 rise up or swell out. **billowy**, **billowing** *adj*.

billy, **billycan** *n, pl* -**lies**, -**lycans** metal can or pot for cooking on a camp fire.

billy goat *n* male goat.

biltong *n S Afr* strips of dried meat.

bimbo *n slang* attractive but empty-headed young person, esp. a woman.

bimonthly *adv, adj* 1 every two months. 2 twice a month.

bin *n* 1 container for rubbish or for storing grain, coal, etc. 2 a large container for bulk storage. ▷ *v* 3 put in a rubbish bin.

binary [**bine**-a-ree] *adj* 1 composed of two parts. 2 *Maths, Computers* of or in a counting system with only two digits, o and 1.

bind ❶ *v* **binding**, **bound** 1 make secure

with or as if with a rope. 2 place (someone) under obligation. 3 place under certain constraints, e.g. *bound by the rules*. 4 stick together or cause to stick, e.g. *egg binds fat and flour*. 5 enclose and fasten (the pages of a book) between covers. ▷ *n* 6 *informal* annoying situation. **binder** *n* 1 firm cover for holding loose sheets of paper together. 2 something used to fasten or hold together. 3 *obs* machine for cutting and binding sheaves. **binding** *n* 1 anything that binds or fastens. 2 book cover. ▷ *adj* 3 imposing an obligation or duty.

bindweed *n* plant that twines around a support.

binge ❶ *n informal* bout of excessive indulgence, esp. in drink.

bingo *n* gambling game in which numbers are called out and covered by the players on their individual cards.

binnacle *n* box holding a ship's compass.

binoculars *pl n* optical instrument consisting of two small telescopes joined together. **binocular** *adj* involving both eyes.

binomial *n, adj* (mathematical expression) consisting of two terms.

bio- *combining form* life or living organisms, e.g. *biology*.

biochemistry *n* study of the chemistry of living things. **biochemist** *n*.

biodegradable *adj* capable of being decomposed by natural means.

biodiversity *n* existence of a wide variety of species in their natural environment.

biography ❶ *n, pl* -**phies** account of a person's life by another person. **biographical** *adj* **biographer** *n*.

biological *adj* 1 of or relating to biology. 2 (of a detergent) containing enzymes that remove natural stains. **biological warfare** use of living organisms or their toxic products to kill or disable.

————————————————————— THESAURUS ————

bill² *n* = **beak**, mandible, neb (*arch or dial*), nib

billet *v* 1 = **quarter**, accommodate, berth, station ▷ *n* 2 = **quarters**, accommodation, barracks, lodging

billow *n* 1 = **wave**, breaker, crest, roller, surge, swell, tide ▷ *v* 3 = **surge**, balloon, belly, puff up, rise up, roll, swell

bind *v* 1 = **tie**, fasten, hitch, lash, secure, stick, strap, wrap 2 = **oblige**, compel, constrain, engage, force, necessitate,

require ▷ *n* 6 *Inf* = **nuisance**, bore, difficulty, dilemma, drag (*inf*), pain in the neck (*inf*), quandary, spot (*inf*)

binding *adj* 3 = **compulsory**, indissoluble, irrevocable, mandatory, necessary, obligatory, unalterable

binge *n Inf* = **bout**, bender (*inf*), feast, fling, orgy, spree

biography *n* = **life story**, account, curriculum vitae, CV, life, memoir, profile, record

biology *n* study of living organisms. **biologist** *n*.

biometric *adj* of any automated system using physiological or behavioural traits as a means of identification.

bionic *adj* having a part of the body that is operated electronically.

biopsy *n*, *pl* **-sies** examination of tissue from a living body.

biosphere *n* part of the earth's surface and atmosphere inhabited by living things.

biotechnology *n* use of microorganisms, such as cells or bacteria, in industry and technology.

bioterrorism *n* use of viruses, bacteria, etc., by terrorists. **bioterrorist** *n*.

bipartite *adj* **1** consisting of two parts. **2** affecting or made by two parties.

biped [**bye**-ped] *n* animal with two feet.

biplane *n* aeroplane with two sets of wings, one above the other.

bipolar *adj* **1** having two poles. **2** having two extremes.

birch *n* **1** tree with thin peeling bark. **2** birch rod or twigs used, esp. formerly, for flogging offenders. ▷ *v* **3** flog with a birch.

bird *n* **1** creature with feathers and wings, most types of which can fly. **2** *slang* young woman. **bird flu** form of influenza occurring in poultry caused by a virus capable of spreading to humans. **bird's-eye view 1** view seen from above. **2** general or overall impression.

birdie *n Golf* score of one stroke under par for a hole.

biretta *n* stiff square cap worn by the Catholic clergy.

Biro *n* ® ballpoint pen.

birth ❶ *n* **1** process of bearing young; childbirth. **2** act of being born. **3** origin or beginning. **4** ancestry. **give birth to** bear (offspring). **birth control** any

method of contraception. **birthday** *n* anniversary of the day of one's birth. **birthmark** *n* blemish on the skin formed before birth. **birth rate** ratio of live births to population. **birthright** *n* privileges or possessions that someone is entitled to as soon as he or she is born.

biscuit *n* **1** small flat dry sweet or plain cake. **2** porcelain that has been fired but not glazed. ▷ *adj* **3** pale brown.

bisect ❶ *v* divide into two equal parts.

bisexual *adj* **1** sexually attracted to both men and women. **2** showing characteristics of both sexes. ▷ *n* **3** bisexual person. **bisexuality** *n*.

bishop *n* **1** clergyman who governs a diocese. **2** chessman which is moved diagonally. **bishopric** *n* diocese or office of a bishop.

bismuth *n Chemistry* pinkish-white metallic element.

bison *n*, *pl* **-son** large hairy animal of the cattle family.

bisque¹ *n* thick rich soup made from shellfish.

bisque² *adj* pinkish-tan.

bistro *n*, *pl* **-tros** small restaurant.

bit¹ ❶ *n* **1** small piece, portion, or quantity. **2** short time or distance. **a bit** rather, somewhat. **bit by bit** gradually.

bit² ❶ *n* **1** metal mouthpiece on a bridle. **2** cutting or drilling part of a tool.

bit³ *v* past tense of BITE.

bit⁴ *n Maths, Computers* **1** single digit of binary notation, either 0 or 1. **2** smallest unit of information.

bitch ❶ *n* **1** female dog, fox, or wolf. **2** *offens* spiteful woman. ▷ *v* **3** *informal* complain or grumble. **bitchy** *adj* **bitchier**, **bitchiest**. **bitchiness** *n*.

bite ❶ *v* **biting**, **bit**, **bitten 1** grip, tear, or puncture the skin, as with the teeth or jaws. **2** take firm hold of or act effectively upon. **3** (of corrosive

_____ THESAURUS _____

birth *n* **1** = **childbirth**, delivery, parturition **2** = **nativity 4** = **ancestry**, background, blood, breeding, lineage, parentage, pedigree, stock

bisect *v* = **cut in two**, cross, cut across, divide in two, halve, intersect, separate, split

bit¹ *n* **1** = **piece**, crumb, fragment, grain, morsel, part, scrap, speck

bit² *n* **1** = **curb**, brake, check, restraint, snaffle

bitchy *adj* **2** *Inf* = **spiteful**, backbiting,

catty (*inf*), mean, nasty, snide, vindictive

bite *v* **1** = **cut**, chew, gnaw, nip, pierce, pinch, snap, tear, wound ▷ *n* **5** = **wound**, nip, pinch, prick, smarting, sting, tooth marks **6** = **snack**, food, light meal, morsel, mouthful, piece, refreshment, taste, tucker (*Aust & NZ inf*)

biting *adj* **1** = **piercing**, bitter, cutting, harsh, penetrating, sharp **2** = **sarcastic**, caustic, cutting, incisive,

material) eat away or into. ▷ *n* **4** act of biting. **5** wound or sting inflicted by biting. **6** snack. **biter** *n* **biting** *adj* **1** piercing or keen. **2** sarcastic.

bitter ❶ *adj* **1** having a sharp unpleasant taste. **2** showing or caused by hostility or resentment. **3** extremely cold. ▷ *n* **4** beer with a slightly bitter taste. ▷ *pl* **5** bitter-tasting alcoholic drink. **bitterly** *adv* **bitterness** *n* **bittersweet** *adj* **1** tasting of bitterness and sweetness. **2** pleasant but tinged with sadness.

bittern *n* wading marsh bird with a booming call.

bitty *adj* **-tier**, **-tiest** lacking unity, disjointed. **bittiness** *n*.

bitumen *n* black sticky substance obtained from tar or petrol.

bivalve *n*, *adj* (marine mollusc) with two hinged segments to its shell.

bivouac *n* **1** temporary camp in the open air. ▷ *v* **-acking**, **-acked** **2** camp in a bivouac.

bizarre ❶ *adj* odd or unusual.

Bk *Chemistry* berkelium.

blab ❶ *v* **blabbing**, **blabbed** reveal (secrets) indiscreetly.

blabber *v* talk without thinking.

black ❶ *adj* **1** of the darkest colour, like coal. **2** without light. **3** (**B-**) dark-skinned. **4** without hope. **5** angry or resentful, e.g. *black looks*. **6** unpleasant in a macabre manner, e.g. *black comedy*. **7** (of coffee or tea) without milk or cream. ▷ *n* **8** darkest colour. **9** (**B-**) member of a dark-skinned race. **10** complete darkness. ▷ *v* **11** make black. **12** (of trade unionists) boycott (goods or people). **blackness** *n* **blacken**

v **1** make or become black. **2** defame or slander. **blacking** *n* preparation for giving a black finish to shoes, metals, etc. **black-and-blue** *adj* bruised, as from a beating. **black-and-white** *adj* **1** not in colour. ▷ *n* **in black and white 2** in print or writing. **black box** *informal* flight recorder. **black eye** bruising round the eye. **black hole** *Astronomy* hypothetical region of space from which neither matter nor radiation can escape. **black ice** thin transparent layer of new ice on a road. **black magic** magic used for evil purposes. **Black Maria** police van for transporting prisoners. **black market** illegal trade in goods or currencies. **black pudding** sausage made from blood, suet, etc. **black sheep** person who is regarded as a disgrace by his or her family. **black spot** place on a road where accidents frequently occur. **black widow** American spider, the female of which eats its mate.

blackball *v* exclude from a group.

blackberry *n* small blackish edible fruit.

BlackBerry *n* ® hand-held wireless device incorporating e-mail, browser and mobile-phone functions.

blackbird *n* common European thrush.

blackboard *n* hard black surface used for writing on with chalk.

blackcurrant *n* very small blackish edible fruit that grows in bunches.

blackguard ❶ [**blag**-gard] *n* unprincipled person.

blackhead *n* small black spot on the skin.

blackleg *n* person who continues to work during a strike.

mordant, scathing, stinging, trenchant, vitriolic

bitter *adj* **1** = **sour**, acid, acrid, astringent, harsh, sharp, tart, unsweetened, vinegary **2** = **resentful**, acrimonious, begrudging, hostile, sore, sour, sullen **3** = **freezing**, biting, fierce, intense, severe, stinging

bitterness *n* **1** = **sourness**, acerbity, acidity, sharpness, tartness **2** = **resentment**, acrimony, animosity, asperity, grudge, hostility, rancour, sarcasm

bizarre *adj* = **strange**, eccentric, extraordinary, fantastic, freakish, ludicrous, munted (*NZ sl*), outlandish, peculiar, unusual, weird, zany

blab *v* = **tell**, blurt out, disclose, divulge, give away, let slip, let the cat out of the bag, reveal, spill the beans (*inf*)

black *adj* **1** = **dark**, dusky, ebony, jet, pitch-black, raven, sable, swarthy **4** = **gloomy**, depressing, dismal, foreboding, hopeless, ominous, sad, sombre **5** = **angry**, furious, hostile, menacing, resentful, sullen, threatening ▷ *v* **12** = **boycott**, ban, bar, blacklist

blacken *v* **1** = **darken**, befoul, begrime, cloud, dirty, make black, smudge, soil **2** = **discredit**, defame, denigrate, malign, slander, smear, smirch, vilify

blackguard *n* = **scoundrel**, bastard (*offens*), bounder (*old-fashioned Brit sl*),

b

blacklist ❶ *n* **1** list of people or organizations considered untrustworthy etc. ▷ *v* **2** put on a blacklist.

blackmail ❶ *n* **1** act of attempting to extort money by threats. ▷ *v* **2** (attempt to) obtain money by blackmail.

blackout ❶ *n* **1** extinguishing of all light as a precaution against an air attack. **2** momentary loss of consciousness or memory. **black out** *v* **1** extinguish (lights). **2** lose consciousness or memory temporarily.

blacksmith *n* person who works iron with a furnace, anvil, etc.

blackthorn *n* thorny shrub with white flowers and small sour plumlike fruits.

black-tie *adj* denoting an occasion when a dinner jacket should be worn.

bladder *n* **1** sac in the body where urine is held. **2** hollow bag which may be filled with air or liquid.

blade *n* **1** cutting edge of a weapon or tool. **2** thin flattish part of a propeller, oar, etc. **3** leaf of grass.

blame ❶ *v* **1** consider (someone) responsible for, e.g. *I blame her for the failure.* **2** (foll. by *on*) put responsibility for (something) on (someone), e.g. *she blames the failure on me.* ▷ *n*

3 responsibility for something that is wrong. **4** expression of condemnation. **blameless** *adj* **blameworthy** *adj* deserving blame.

blanch *v* **1** become white or pale. **2** prepare (vegetables etc.) by plunging them in boiling water.

blancmange [blam-**monzh**] *n* jelly-like dessert made with milk.

bland ❶ *adj* **1** dull and uninteresting. **2** smooth in manner. **blandly** *adv*.

blandishments *pl n* flattery intended to coax or persuade.

blank ❶ *adj* **1** not written on. **2** with spaces left for details to be filled in. **3** without decoration. **4** showing no interest or expression, e.g. *a blank stare.* **5** lacking ideas or inspiration, e.g. *his mind went blank.* ▷ *n* **6** empty space. **7** condition of not understanding. **8** cartridge containing no bullet. **blankly** *adv* **blank cheque** **1** signed cheque without the amount payable specified. **2** complete freedom of action. **blank verse** unrhymed verse.

blanket ❶ *n* **1** large thick cloth used as covering for a bed. **2** concealing cover, as of snow. ▷ *adj* **3** applying to a wide group of people, situations, conditions, etc. ▷ *v* **4** cover as with a blanket.

blare ❶ *v* **1** sound loudly and harshly. ▷ *n*

THESAURUS

rascal, rogue, swine, villain

blacklist *v* **2** = **exclude**, ban, bar, boycott, debar, expel, reject, snub

black magic *n* = **witchcraft**, black art, diabolism, necromancy, sorcery, voodoo, wizardry

blackmail *n* **1** = **threat**, extortion, hush money (*sl*), intimidation, ransom ▷ *v* **2** = **threaten**, coerce, compel, demand, extort, hold to ransom, intimidate, squeeze

blackness *n* **1** = **darkness**, duskiness, gloom, murkiness, swarthiness

blackout *n* **2** = **unconsciousness**, coma, faint, loss of consciousness, oblivion, swoon

black sheep *n* = **disgrace**, bad egg (*old-fashioned inf*), dropout, ne'er-do-well, outcast, prodigal, renegade, reprobate

blame *v* **1** = **hold responsible**, accuse, censure, chide, condemn, criticize, find fault with, reproach ▷ *n* **3** = **responsibility**, accountability, accusation, culpability, fault, guilt, liability, onus

blameless *adj* = **innocent**, above suspicion, clean, faultless, guiltless, immaculate, impeccable, irreproachable, perfect, unblemished, virtuous

blameworthy *adj* = **reprehensible**, discreditable, disreputable, indefensible, inexcusable, iniquitous, reproachable, shameful

bland *adj* **1** = **dull**, boring, flat, humdrum, insipid, tasteless, unexciting, uninspiring, vapid

blank *adj* **1** = **unmarked**, bare, clean, clear, empty, void, white **4** = **expressionless**, deadpan, empty, impassive, poker-faced (*inf*), vacant, vague ▷ *n* **6** = **empty space**, emptiness, gap, nothingness, space, vacancy, vacuum, void

blanket *n* **1** = **cover**, coverlet, rug **2** = **covering**, carpet, cloak, coat, layer, mantle, sheet ▷ *v* **4** = **cover**, cloak, coat, conceal, hide, mask, obscure, suppress

blare *v* **1** = **sound out**, blast, clamour, clang, resound, roar, scream, trumpet

2 loud harsh noise.

blarney ❶ *n* flattering talk.

blasé [**blah**-zay] *adj* indifferent or bored through familiarity.

blaspheme ❶ *v* **1** speak disrespectfully of (God or sacred things). **2** utter curses. **blasphemy** *n* **blasphemous** *adj* **blasphemer** *n*.

blast ❶ *n* **1** explosion. **2** sudden strong gust of air or wind. **3** sudden loud sound, as of a trumpet. **4** *US slang* very enjoyable or thrilling experience. ▷ *v* **5** blow up (a rock etc.) with explosives. **6** make a loud harsh noise. **7** criticize severely. ▷ *interj* **8** *slang* expression of annoyance. **blasted** *adj, adv slang* extreme or extremely. **blast furnace** furnace for smelting, using a preheated blast of air. **blastoff** *n* launching of a rocket.

blatant ❶ [**blay**-tant] *adj* glaringly obvious. **blatantly** *adv*.

blather *v, n* same as BLETHER.

blaze¹ ❶ *n* **1** strong fire or flame. **2** very bright light. **3** outburst of passion. ▷ *v* **4** burn or shine brightly. **5** become stirred with anger or excitement.

blaze² *n* **1** mark made on a tree to indicate a route. **2** light-coloured marking on the face of an animal. ▷ *v* **3** mark (a tree etc.) with a blaze.

blaze³ *v* **blaze something abroad** make something widely known.

blazer *n* lightweight jacket, often in the colours of a school etc.

blazon *v* proclaim publicly.

bleach ❶ *v* **1** make or become white or colourless. ▷ *n* **2** bleaching agent.

bleak ❶ *adj* **1** exposed and barren. **2** offering little hope.

bleary ❶ *adj* **-rier, -riest** with eyes dimmed, as by tears or tiredness. **blearily** *adv*.

bleat *v* **1** (of a sheep, goat, or calf) utter its plaintive cry. **2** whine. ▷ *n* **3** cry of sheep, goats, and calves.

bleed ❶ *v* **bleeding, bled 1** lose or emit blood. **2** draw blood from (a person or animal). **3** *informal* obtain money by extortion. **4** draw off or emit liquid or gas.

bleep *n* **1** short high-pitched sound made by an electrical device. ▷ *v* **2** make a bleeping sound. **bleeper** *n* small portable radio receiver that makes a bleeping signal.

blemish ❶ *n* **1** defect or stain. ▷ *v* **2** spoil or tarnish.

───────────────── THESAURUS ─────────

blarney *n* = **flattery**, blandishments, cajolery, coaxing, soft soap (*inf*), spiel, sweet talk (*inf*), wheedling

blasé *adj* = **indifferent**, apathetic, lukewarm, nonchalant, offhand, unconcerned

blaspheme *v* **1** = **profane**, desecrate **2** = **curse**, abuse, damn, execrate, revile, swear

blasphemous *adj* **1** = **irreverent**, godless, impious, irreligious, profane, sacrilegious, ungodly

blasphemy *n* **1** = **irreverence**, desecration, impiety, profanity, sacrilege **2** = **cursing**, execration, profanity, swearing

blast *n* **1** = **explosion**, bang, burst, crash, detonation, discharge, eruption, outburst, salvo, volley **2** = **gust**, gale, squall, storm, strong breeze, tempest **3** = **blare**, blow, clang, honk, peal, scream, toot, wail ▷ *v* **5** = **blow up**, break up, burst, demolish, destroy, explode, put paid to, ruin, shatter

blastoff *n* = **launch**, discharge, expulsion, firing, launching, liftoff, projection, shot

blatant *adj* = **obvious**, brazen, conspicuous, flagrant, glaring, obtrusive, ostentatious, overt

blaze¹ *n* **1** = **fire**, bonfire, conflagration, flames **2** = **glare**, beam, brilliance, flare, flash, gleam, glitter, glow, light, radiance ▷ *v* **4** = **burn**, beam, fire, flame, flare, flash, glare, gleam, glow, shine

bleach *v* **1** = **whiten**, blanch, fade, grow pale, lighten, wash out

bleak *adj* **1** = **exposed**, bare, barren, desolate, unsheltered, weather-beaten, windswept **2** = **dismal**, cheerless, depressing, discouraging, dreary, gloomy, grim, hopeless, joyless, sombre

bleary *adj* = **dim**, blurred, blurry, foggy, fuzzy, hazy, indistinct, misty, murky

bleed *v* **1** = **lose blood**, flow, gush, ooze, run, shed blood, spurt **2** = **draw** or **take blood**, extract, leech **3** *Inf* = **extort**, drain, exhaust, fleece, milk, squeeze

blemish *n* **1** = **mark**, blot, defect, disfigurement, fault, flaw, imperfection, smudge, stain, taint ▷ *v* **2** = **mark**, damage, disfigure, impair, injure, mar, spoil, stain, sully, taint, tarnish

blench *v* shy away, as in fear.
blend ❶ *v* **1** mix or mingle (components or ingredients). **2** look good together. ▷ *n* **3** mixture. **blender** *n* electrical appliance for puréeing vegetables etc.
blende *n* mineral consisting mainly of zinc sulphide.
blenny *n, pl* **-nies** small fish with a tapering scaleless body.
bless ❶ *v* **1** make holy by means of a religious rite. **2** call upon God to protect. **3** give thanks to. **4** endow with health, talent, etc. **blessed** *adj* **1** holy. **2** *RC Church* beatified by the Pope. **3** *euphemistic* damned. **blessing** *n* **1** invoking of divine aid. **2** approval. **3** happy event.
blether *Scot* ▷ *v* **1** talk, esp. foolishly or at length. ▷ *n* **2** conversation. **3** talkative person.
blew *v* past tense of BLOW¹.
blight ❶ *n* **1** person or thing that spoils or prevents growth. **2** withering plant disease. ▷ *v* **3** cause to suffer a blight. **4** frustrate or disappoint.
blighter *n informal* irritating person.
blimey *interj slang* exclamation of surprise or annoyance.
blimp *n* small airship.
blind ❶ *adj* **1** unable to see. **2** unable or unwilling to understand. **3** not determined by reason, e.g. *blind hatred.* ▷ *v* **4** deprive of sight. **5** deprive of good

sense, reason, or judgment. ▷ *n* **6** covering for a window. **7** something that serves to conceal the truth. **blindly** *adv* **blindness** *n* **blind alley** alley open at one end only. **blind date** *informal* prearranged social meeting between two people who have not met. **blind man's buff** game in which a blindfolded person tries to catch and identify other players. **blind spot 1** area of the retina where vision is not experienced. **2** place where vision is obscured. **3** subject about which a person is ignorant.

● **USAGE NOTE**
● The use of *the blind, the disabled,*
● etc. can be offensive and should
● be avoided. Instead you should
● talk about *blind people, disabled*
● *people,* etc.

blindfold *v* **1** prevent (a person) from seeing by covering the eyes. ▷ *n* **2** piece of cloth used to cover the eyes. ▷ *adj, adv* **3** with the eyes covered by a cloth.
blink ❶ *v* **1** close and immediately reopen (the eyes). **2** shine intermittently. ▷ *n* **3** act of blinking. **on the blink** *slang* not working properly.
blinkers *pl n* leather flaps on a horse's bridle to prevent sideways vision. **blinkered** *adj* considering only a narrow point of view.
blip *n* **1** spot of light on a radar screen

— THESAURUS —

blend *v* **1** = **mix**, amalgamate, combine, compound, merge, mingle, unite **2** = **go well**, complement, fit, go with, harmonize, suit ▷ *n* **3** = **mixture**, alloy, amalgamation, combination, compound, concoction, mix, synthesis, union
bless *v* **1** = **sanctify**, anoint, consecrate, dedicate, exalt, hallow, ordain **4** = **endow**, bestow, favour, give, grace, grant, provide
blessed *adj* **1, 2** = **holy**, adored, beatified, divine, hallowed, revered, sacred, sanctified
blessing *n* **1** = **benediction**, benison, commendation, consecration, dedication, grace, invocation, thanksgiving **2** = **approval**, backing, consent, favour, good wishes, leave, permission, sanction, support **3** = **benefit**, favour, gift, godsend, good fortune, help, kindness, service, windfall
blight *n* **1** = **curse**, affliction, bane,

contamination, corruption, evil, plague, pollution, scourge, woe **2** = **disease**, canker, decay, fungus, infestation, mildew, pest, pestilence, rot ▷ *v* **4** = **frustrate**, crush, dash, disappoint, mar, ruin, spoil, undo, wreck
blind *adj* **1** = **sightless**, eyeless, unseeing, unsighted, visionless **2** = **unaware of**, careless, heedless, ignorant, inattentive, inconsiderate, indifferent, insensitive, oblivious, unconscious of **3** = **unreasoning**, indiscriminate, prejudiced ▷ *n* **7** = **cover**, camouflage, cloak, facade, feint, front, mask, masquerade, screen, smoke screen
blindly *adv* **2** = **thoughtlessly**, carelessly, heedlessly, inconsiderately, recklessly, senselessly **3** = **aimlessly**, at random, indiscriminately, instinctively
blink *v* **1** = **wink**, bat, flutter **2** = **flicker**, flash, gleam, glimmer, shine, twinkle, wink **on the blink** *Sl* = **not working**

indicating the position of an object.
2 temporary irregularity in
performance.

bliss ❶ *n* perfect happiness. **blissful** *adj*
blissfully *adv*.

blister ❶ *n* **1** small bubble on the skin.
2 swelling, as on a painted surface. ▷ *v*
3 (cause to) have blisters. **blistering** *adj*
1 (of weather) very hot. **2** (of criticism)
extremely harsh.

blithe ❶ *adj* **1** casual and indifferent.
2 very happy. **blithely** *adv*.

blithering *adj informal* stupid.

blitz ❶ *n* **1** violent and sustained attack
by aircraft. **2** intensive attack or
concerted effort. ▷ *v* **3** attack suddenly
and intensively.

blizzard ❶ *n* blinding storm of wind and
snow.

bloat ❶ *v* cause to swell, as with liquid
or air.

bloater *n* salted smoked herring.

blob ❶ *n* **1** soft mass or drop. **2** indistinct
or shapeless form.

bloc ❶ *n* people or countries combined
by a common interest.

block ❶ *n* **1** large solid piece of wood,
stone, etc. **2** large building of offices,
flats, etc. **3** group of buildings enclosed

by intersecting streets. **4** obstruction
or hindrance. **5** piece of wood or metal
engraved for printing. **6** one of a set of
wooden or plastic cubes used as a toy.
7 *slang* person's head. ▷ *v* **8** obstruct or
impede by introducing an obstacle.
blockage *n* **blockbuster** *n* highly
successful film, novel, etc. **blockhead** *n*
stupid person. **block letter** plain
capital letter.

blockade ❶ *n* **1** sealing off of a place to
prevent the passage of goods. ▷ *v*
2 impose a blockade on.

blog *n* **1** journal published on the
internet. ▷ *v* **blogging**, **blogged**
2 write a journal on the internet.
blogger *n*.

bloke ❶ *n informal* man.

blonde ❶, (*masc*) **blond** *adj*, *n* fair-haired
(person).

blood ❶ *n* **1** red fluid that flows around
the body. **2** bloodshed. **3** race or
kinship. ▷ *v* **4** initiate (a person) to war
or hunting. **in cold blood** done
deliberately. **bloodless** *adj* **1** without
blood or bloodshed. **2** pale. **3** lacking
vitality. **blood bath** massacre.
bloodcurdling *adj* terrifying.
bloodhound *n* large dog formerly used

——————————————————————— THESAURUS ———————

(properly), faulty, malfunctioning, out
of action, out of order, playing up

bliss *n* = **joy**, beatitude, blessedness,
blissfulness, ecstasy, euphoria, felicity,
gladness, happiness, heaven, nirvana,
paradise, rapture

blissful *adj* = **joyful**, ecstatic, elated,
enraptured, euphoric, happy, heavenly
(*inf*), rapturous

blister *n* **1** = **sore**, abscess, boil,
carbuncle, cyst, pimple, pustule,
swelling

blithe *adj* **1** = **heedless**, careless, casual,
indifferent, nonchalant, thoughtless,
unconcerned, untroubled

blitz *n* **1** = **attack**, assault, blitzkrieg,
bombardment, offensive, onslaught,
raid, strike

blizzard *n* = **snowstorm**, blast, gale,
squall, storm, tempest

bloat *v* = **puff up**, balloon, blow up,
dilate, distend, enlarge, expand, inflate,
swell

blob *n* **1** = **drop**, ball, bead, bubble, dab,
droplet, globule, lump, mass

bloc *n* = **group**, alliance, axis, coalition,
faction, league, union

block *n* **1** = **piece**, bar, brick, chunk,

hunk, ingot, lump, mass
4 = **obstruction**, bar, barrier,
hindrance, impediment, jam, obstacle
▷ *v* **8** = **obstruct**, bung up (*inf*), choke,
clog, close, impede, plug, stem the
flow, stop up

blockade *n* **1** = **stoppage**, barricade,
barrier, block, hindrance, impediment,
obstacle, obstruction, restriction,
siege

blockage *n* **8** = **obstruction**, block,
impediment, occlusion, stoppage

blockhead *n* = **idiot**, chump (*inf*),
dunce, fool, nitwit, numbskull *or*
numskull, thickhead, twit (*inf, chiefly
Brit*)

bloke *n Inf* = **man**, chap, character (*inf*),
fellow, guy (*inf*), individual, person

blonde *adj* = **fair**, fair-haired, fair-
skinned, flaxen, golden-haired, light,
tow-headed

blood *n* **1** = **lifeblood**, gore, vital fluid
3 = **family**, ancestry, birth, descent,
extraction, kinship, lineage, relations

bloodcurdling *adj* = **terrifying**,
appalling, chilling, dreadful, fearful,
frightening, hair-raising, horrendous,
horrifying, scaring, spine-chilling

b

for tracking. **blood poisoning** same as SEPTICAEMIA. **blood pressure** pressure exerted by the blood on the inner walls of the blood vessels. **bloodshed** n slaughter or killing. **bloodshot** adj (of an eye) inflamed. **blood sport** sport involving the killing of animals. **bloodstream** n flow of blood round the body. **bloodsucker** n **1** animal that sucks blood. **2** informal person who extorts money from other people. **bloodthirsty** adj taking pleasure in violence. **blood vessel** tube that carries the blood in the body.

bloody ❶ adj **1** covered with blood. **2** marked by much killing. ▷ adj, adv **3** slang extreme or extremely. ▷ v **4** stain with blood. **bloody-minded** adj deliberately unhelpful.

bloom ❶ n **1** blossom on a flowering plant. **2** period when flowers open. **3** flourishing condition. **4** youthful or healthy glow. **5** whitish coating on fruit, leaves, etc. ▷ v **6** (of flowers) open. **7** bear flowers. **8** be in a healthy, glowing condition.

bloomer n informal stupid mistake.

bloomers pl n woman's baggy knickers.

blossom ❶ n **1** flowers of a plant. ▷ v **2** (of plants) flower. **3** come to a promising stage.

blot ❶ n **1** spot or stain. **2** something that spoils. ▷ v **blotting**, **blotted** **3** cause a blemish in or on. **4** soak up (ink) by using blotting paper. **blotter** n **blot out** v darken or hide completely. **blotting paper** soft absorbent paper for soaking up ink.

blotch n discoloured area or stain. **blotchy** adj **blotchier**, **blotchiest**.

blotto adj slang extremely drunk.

blouse n woman's shirtlike garment.

blouson n short loose jacket with a tight waist.

blow¹ ❶ v **blowing**, **blew**, **blown** **1** (of air, the wind, etc.) move. **2** move or be carried as if by the wind. **3** expel (air etc.) through the mouth or nose. **4** cause (a musical instrument) to sound by forcing air into it. **5** burn out (a fuse etc.). **6** slang spend (money) freely. **7** slang use (an opportunity) ineffectively. **blower** n **blowy** adj windy. **blow-dry** v style (the hair) with a hand-held dryer. **blowfly** n fly that lays its eggs in meat. **blowtorch** n small burner producing a very hot flame. **blowout** n **1** sudden loss of air in a tyre. **2** escape of oil or gas from a well. **3** slang filling meal. **blowpipe** n long tube from which darts etc. are shot by blowing. **blow up** v **1** explode. **2** fill with air. **3** informal lose one's temper. **4** exaggerate the importance of. **5** informal enlarge (a photograph).

blow² ❶ n **1** hard hit. **2** sudden setback. **3** attacking action, e.g. a blow for freedom.

THESAURUS

bloodshed n = **killing**, blood bath, blood-letting, butchery, carnage, gore, massacre, murder, slaughter, slaying

bloodthirsty adj = **cruel**, barbarous, brutal, cut-throat, ferocious, gory, murderous, savage, vicious, warlike

bloody adj **1** = **bloodstained**, bleeding, blood-soaked, blood-spattered, gaping, raw **2** = **cruel**, ferocious, fierce, sanguinary, savage

bloom n **2** = **flower**, blossom, blossoming, bud, efflorescence, opening **3** = **prime**, beauty, flourishing, health, heyday, vigour **4** = **glow**, freshness, lustre, radiance ▷ v **6**, **7** = **blossom**, blow, bud, burgeon, open, sprout **8** = **flourish**, develop, fare well, grow, prosper, succeed, thrive, wax

blossom n **1** = **flower**, bloom, bud, floret, flowers ▷ v **2** = **flower**, bloom, burgeon **3** = **grow**, bloom, develop, flourish, mature, progress, prosper, thrive

blot n **1** = **spot**, blotch, mark, patch, smear, smudge, speck, splodge **2** = **stain**, blemish, defect, fault, flaw, scar, spot, taint ▷ v **3** = **stain**, disgrace, mark, smirch, smudge, spoil, spot, sully, tarnish **4** = **soak up**, absorb, dry, take up

blot out v = **obliterate**, darken, destroy, eclipse, efface, obscure, shadow

blow¹ v **2** = **carry**, drive, fling, flutter, move, sweep, waft **3** = **exhale**, breathe, pant, puff **4** = **play**, blare, mouth, pipe, sound, toot, trumpet, vibrate

blow² n **1** = **knock**, bang, clout (inf), punch, smack, sock (sl), stroke, thump, wallop (inf), whack **2** = **setback**, bombshell, calamity, catastrophe, disappointment, disaster, misfortune, reverse, shock

blow up v **1** = **explode**, blast, blow sky-high, bomb, burst, detonate, rupture, shatter **2** = **inflate**, bloat, distend, enlarge, expand, fill, puff up, pump up,

blowie n Aust informal bluebottle.
blown v past participle of BLOW¹.
blowsy adj fat, untidy, and red-faced.
blubber n 1 fat of whales, seals, etc. ▷ v 2 sob without restraint.
bludge v 1 Aust & NZ informal evade work. 2 scrounge. **bludger** n person who scrounges.
bludgeon ❶ n 1 short thick club. ▷ v 2 hit with a bludgeon. 3 force or bully.
blue ❶ n 1 colour of a clear unclouded sky. 2 sportsman representing Oxford or Cambridge University. ▷ pl 3 feeling of depression. 4 type of folk music of Black American origin. ▷ adj **bluer**, **bluest** 5 of the colour blue. 6 depressed. 7 pornographic. **out of the blue** unexpectedly. **bluish** adj **bluebell** n flower with blue bell-shaped flowers. **bluebottle** n large fly with a dark-blue body. **blue cheese** cheese containing a blue mould. **blue-collar** adj denoting manual industrial workers. **blue heeler** Aust & NZ informal dog that controls cattle by biting their heels. **blueprint** n 1 photographic print of a plan. 2 description of how a plan is expected to work. **blue ribbon** first prize in a competition. **bluestocking** n intellectual woman. **bluetongue** n Australian lizard with a blue tongue.
bluff¹ ❶ v 1 pretend to be confident in order to influence (someone). ▷ n 2 act of bluffing.
bluff² ❶ n 1 steep cliff or bank. ▷ adj 2 good-naturedly frank and hearty.
blunder ❶ n 1 clumsy mistake. ▷ v 2 make a blunder. 3 act clumsily.
blunderbuss n obsolete gun with a wide flared muzzle.
blunt ❶ adj 1 not having a sharp edge or point. 2 (of people, speech, etc.) straightforward or uncomplicated. ▷ v 3 make less sharp. **bluntly** adv.
blur ❶ v blurring, blurred 1 make or become vague or less distinct. 2 smear or smudge. ▷ n 3 something vague, hazy, or indistinct. **blurry** adj -rier, -riest.
blurb n promotional description, as on the jacket of a book.
blurt ❶ v (foll. by out) utter suddenly and involuntarily.
blush ❶ v 1 become red in the face, esp. from embarrassment or shame. ▷ n 2 reddening of the face. **blusher** n cosmetic for giving the cheeks a rosy colour.

────────── THESAURUS ──────

swell 3 Inf = **lose one's temper**, become angry, erupt, fly off the handle (inf), hit the roof (inf), rage, see red (inf)
bludgeon n 1 = **club**, cosh (Brit), cudgel, truncheon ▷ v 2 = **club**, beat up, cosh (Brit), cudgel, knock down, strike 3 = **bully**, bulldoze (inf), coerce, force, railroad (inf), steamroller
blue n 1 = **azure**, cobalt, cyan, navy, sapphire, ultramarine ▷ pl 3 = **depression**, doldrums, dumps (inf), gloom, low spirits, melancholy, unhappiness ▷ adj 5 = **azure**, cerulean, cobalt, cyan, navy, sapphire, sky-coloured, ultramarine 6 = **depressed**, dejected, despondent, downcast, low, melancholy, sad, unhappy 7 = **smutty**, indecent, lewd, obscene, risqué, X-rated (inf)
blueprint n = **plan**, design, draft, outline, pattern, pilot scheme, prototype, sketch
bluff¹ v 1 = **deceive**, con, delude, fake, feign, mislead, pretend, pull the wool over someone's eyes ▷ n 2 = **deception**, bluster, bravado, deceit, fraud, humbug, pretence, sham, subterfuge
bluff² n 1 = **precipice**, bank, cliff, crag, escarpment, headland, peak, promontory, ridge ▷ adj 2 = **hearty**, blunt, blustering, genial, good-natured, open, outspoken, plain-spoken
blunder n 1 = **mistake**, bloomer (Brit inf), clanger (inf), error, fault, faux pas, gaffe, howler (inf), inaccuracy, indiscretion, oversight, slip, slip-up (inf) ▷ v 2 = **make a mistake**, botch, bungle, err, put one's foot in it (inf), slip up (inf) 3 = **stumble**, bumble, flounder
blunt adj 1 = **dull**, dulled, edgeless, pointless, rounded, unsharpened 2 = **forthright**, bluff, brusque, frank, outspoken, plain-spoken, rude, straightforward, tactless ▷ v 3 = **dull**, dampen, deaden, numb, soften, take the edge off, water down, weaken
blur v 1 = **make indistinct**, cloud, darken, make hazy, make vague, mask, obscure ▷ n 3 = **indistinctness**, confusion, fog, haze, obscurity
blurt v (foll. by out) = **exclaim**, disclose, let the cat out of the bag, reveal, spill the beans (inf), tell all, utter suddenly
blush v 1 = **turn red**, colour, flush, go red (as a beetroot), redden, turn scarlet ▷ n 2 = **reddening**, colour, flush, glow, pink

b

bluster ❶ v **1** speak loudly or in a bullying way. ▷ n **2** empty threats or protests. **blustery** adj (of weather) rough and windy.

BMA British Medical Association.

B-movie n film originally made as a supporting film, now considered a genre in its own right.

BO informal body odour.

boa n **1** large nonvenomous snake. **2** long scarf of fur or feathers. **boa constrictor** large snake that kills its prey by crushing.

boab [**boh**-ab] n Aust informal short for BAOBAB.

boar n **1** uncastrated male pig. **2** wild pig.

board ❶ n **1** long flat piece of sawn timber. **2** smaller flat piece of rigid material for a specific purpose, e.g. ironing board; chess board. **3** group of people who administer a company, trust, etc. **4** meals provided for money. ▷ pl **5** the stage. ▷ v **6** go aboard (a train, aeroplane, etc.). **7** cover with boards. **8** receive meals and lodgings in return for money. **on board** on or in a ship, aeroplane, etc. **boarder** n pupil who lives at school during the school term. **boarding house** private house that provides meals and accommodation for paying guests. **boarding school** school providing living accommodation for pupils. **boardroom** n room where the board of a company meets.

boast ❶ v **1** speak too proudly about one's talents etc. **2** possess (something to be proud of). ▷ n **3** bragging

statement. **4** something that is bragged about. **boastful** adj.

boat n **1** small vehicle for travelling across water. **2** informal ship. **3** boat-shaped dish, e.g. gravy boat. ▷ v **4** travel in a boat. **boater** n flat straw hat. **boating** n **boat train** train scheduled to take passengers to or from a ship.

boatswain n same as BOSUN.

bob¹ ❶ v **bobbing, bobbed 1** move up and down repeatedly. ▷ n **2** short abrupt movement.

bob² n **1** hairstyle in which the hair is cut short evenly all round the head. **2** weight on a pendulum or plumb line. ▷ v **bobbing, bobbed 3** cut (the hair) in a bob.

bob³ n, pl **bob** Brit informal (formerly) shilling.

bobbin n reel on which thread is wound.

bobble n small ball of material, usu. for decoration.

bobby n, pl **-bies** informal policeman.

bobotie n S Afr dish of curried mince.

bobsleigh n **1** sledge for racing down an icy track. ▷ v **2** ride on a bobsleigh.

bod n informal person.

bode ❶ v be an omen of (good or ill).

bodega n shop in a Spanish-speaking country that sells wine.

bodge v informal make a mess of.

bodice n upper part of a dress.

bodkin n blunt large-eyed needle.

body ❶ n, pl **bodies 1** entire physical structure of an animal or human. **2** trunk or torso. **3** corpse. **4** group regarded as a single entity. **5** main part of anything. **6** separate mass of water or land. **7** person. **8** woman's

———————————————— **THESAURUS** ❶ ————————————————

tinge, rosiness, rosy tint, ruddiness

bluster v **1** = **roar**, bully, domineer, hector, rant, storm ▷ n **2** = **hot air**, bluff, bombast, bravado (inf)

blustery adj = **gusty**, boisterous, inclement, squally, stormy, tempestuous, violent, wild, windy

board n **1** = **plank**, panel, piece of timber, slat, timber **3** = **directors**, advisers, committee, conclave, council, panel, trustees **4** = **meals**, daily meals, provisions, victuals ▷ v **6** = **get on**, embark, enter, mount **8** = **lodge**, put up, quarter, room

boast v **1** = **brag**, blow one's own trumpet, crow, skite (Aust & NZ), strut, swagger, talk big (sl), vaunt **2** = **possess**, be proud of, congratulate

oneself on, exhibit, flatter oneself, pride oneself on, show off ▷ n **3** = **brag**, avowal

boastful adj **1** = **bragging**, cocky, conceited, crowing, egotistical, full of oneself, swaggering, swollen-headed, vaunting

bob¹ v **1** = **duck**, bounce, hop, nod, oscillate, waggle, wobble

bode v = **portend**, augur, be an omen of, forebode, foretell, predict, signify, threaten

bodily adj **1** = **physical**, actual, carnal, corporal, corporeal, material, substantial, tangible

body n **1** = **physique**, build, figure, form, frame, shape **2** = **torso**, trunk **3** = **corpse**, cadaver, carcass, dead body,

one-piece undergarment. **bodily** *adj*
1 relating to the body. ▷ *adv* **2** by taking
hold of the body. **body-board** *n Aust,*
NZ, S Afr & US small polystyrene
surfboard. **bodyguard** *n* person or
group of people employed to protect
someone. **body shop** place where
vehicle bodywork is repaired. **body**
stocking woman's one-piece
undergarment, covering the torso.
bodywork *n* outer shell of a motor
vehicle.

Boer *n* descendant of the Dutch settlers
in S Africa.

boffin ❶ *n Brit informal* **1** scientist or
expert. **2** someone who is clever, but
only in an academic way.

bog ❶ *n* **1** wet spongy ground. **2** *slang*
toilet. **boggy** *adj* **-gier, -giest. bog**
down *v* **bogging, bogged** impede
physically or mentally.

bogan *n Aust dated & NZ slang* youth who
dresses and behaves rebelliously.

bogey, bogy ❶ *n* **1** evil or mischievous
spirit. **2** something that worries or
annoys. **3** *Golf* score of one stroke over
par on a hole.

boggle *v* **1** be surprised, confused, or
alarmed. **2** hesitate when confronted
with a problem. **3** baffle; bewilder;
puzzle, e.g. *it boggles the imagination*.

bogie, bogy *n* set of wheels, as on a
railway carriage.

bog-standard *adj slang* completely
ordinary.

bogus ❶ [**boh**-guss] *adj* not genuine.

bogy *n, pl* **-gies** same as BOGEY or BOGIE.

bohemian *n, adj* (person) leading an
unconventional life.

boil¹ ❶ *v* **1** (cause to) change from a liquid
to a vapour so quickly that bubbles are
formed. **2** reach or cause to reach
boiling point. **3** cook by the process of
boiling. **4** bubble like something
boiling. **5** be extremely angry. ▷ *n*
6 state or action of boiling. **boiler** *n*
piece of equipment which provides hot
water. **boiler suit** one-piece overall.
boiling point temperature at which a
liquid boils.

boil² ❶ *n* red pus-filled swelling on the skin.

boisterous ❶ *adj* **1** noisy and lively.
2 turbulent or stormy.
boisterously *adv*.

bold ❶ *adj* **1** confident and fearless.
2 immodest or impudent. **3** standing
out distinctly. **boldly** *adv* **boldness** *n*.

bole *n* tree trunk.

bolero *n, pl* **-ros 1** (music for) traditional
Spanish dance. **2** short open jacket.

boll *n* rounded seed capsule of cotton,
flax, etc.

bollard *n* **1** short thick post used to
prevent the passage of motor vehicles.
2 post on a quay etc. for securing
mooring lines.

boloney *n* same as BALONEY.

Bolshevik *n* (formerly) Russian
Communist.

bolshie, bolshy *adj informal* difficult or
rebellious.

bolster ❶ *v* **1** support or strengthen. ▷ *n*
2 long narrow pillow.

bolt ❶ *n* **1** sliding metal bar for fastening

---

remains, stiff (*sl*) **4** = **organization**,
association, band, bloc, collection,
company, confederation, congress,
corporation, society **5** = **main part**,
bulk, essence, mass, material, matter,
substance

boffin *n Brit inf* **1** = **expert**, brainbox,
egghead, fundi (*S Afr*), genius,
intellectual, inventor, mastermind

bog *n* **1** = **marsh**, fen, mire, morass,
quagmire, slough, swamp, wetlands,
muskeg (*Canad*)

bogey *n* **1** = **bugbear**, bête noire,
bugaboo, nightmare

bogus *adj* = **fake**, artificial, counterfeit,
false, forged, fraudulent, imitation,
phoney *or* phony (*inf*), sham

bohemian *n* = **nonconformist**, beatnik,
dropout, hippy, iconoclast ▷ *adj*
= **unconventional**, alternative,

artistic, arty (*inf*), left bank,
nonconformist, offbeat, unorthodox

boil¹ *v* **1** = **bubble** **4** = **froth**, bubble,
effervesce, fizz, foam, seethe

boil² *n* = **pustule**, blister, carbuncle,
gathering, swelling, tumour, ulcer

boisterous *adj* **1** = **unruly**, disorderly,
loud, noisy, riotous, rollicking, rowdy,
unrestrained, vociferous, wild

bold *adj* **1** = **fearless**, adventurous,
audacious, brave, courageous, daring,
enterprising, heroic, intrepid, valiant
2 = **impudent**, barefaced, brazen,
cheeky, confident, forward, feisty (*US &*
Canad), insolent, rude, shameless

bolster *v* **1** = **support**, augment, boost,
help, reinforce, shore up, strengthen

bolt *n* **1** = **bar**, catch, fastener, latch,
lock, sliding bar **2** = **pin**, peg, rivet, rod
▷ *v* **6** = **run away**, abscond, dash,

b

a door etc. **2** metal pin which screws into a nut. **3** flash (of lightning). **4** sudden movement, esp. in order to escape. **5** arrow for a crossbow. ▷ *v* **6** run away suddenly. **7** fasten with a bolt. **8** eat hurriedly. **bolt upright** stiff and rigid. **bolt hole** place of escape.

bomb ❶ *n* **1** container fitted with explosive material. **2** *slang* large amount of money. ▷ *v* **3** attack with bombs. **4** move very quickly. **the bomb** nuclear bomb. **bomber** *n* **1** aircraft that drops bombs. **2** person who throws or puts a bomb in a particular place. **bombshell** *n* shocking or unwelcome surprise.

bombard ❶ *v* **1** attack with heavy gunfire or bombs. **2** attack verbally, esp. with questions. **bombardier** *n* noncommissioned rank in the Royal Artillery. **bombardment** *n*.

bombast ❶ *n* pompous language. **bombastic** *adj*.

bona fide ❶ [**bone**-a **fide**-ee] *adj* genuine.

bonanza *n* sudden good luck or wealth.

bonbon *n* sweet.

bond ❶ *n* **1** something that binds, fastens or holds together. **2** something that unites people, e.g. *a bond of friendship*. **3** written or spoken agreement. **4** *Finance* certificate of debt issued to raise funds. **5** *S Afr* conditional pledging of property, esp. a house, as security for the repayment of a loan. ▷ *pl* **6** something that restrains or imprisons. ▷ *v* **7** bind. **bonded** *adj*.

bondage ❶ *n* **1** slavery. **2** subjection to some influence or duty. **3** sexual practice in which one partner is tied or chained up.

bone ❶ *n* **1** any of the hard parts in the body that form the skeleton. ▷ *pl* **2** human skeleton. ▷ *v* **3** remove the bones from (meat for cooking etc.). **boneless** *adj* **bony** *adj* **bonier**, **boniest** **1** having many bones. **2** thin or emaciated. **bone china** porcelain containing powdered bone. **bone-dry** *adj* completely dry. **bone-idle** *adj* extremely lazy. **bone meal** ground bones used as a fertilizer.

bonfire *n* large outdoor fire.

bongo *n*, *pl* **-gos**, **-goes** small drum played with the fingers.

bonhomie [**bon**-om-ee] *n* cheerful friendliness.

bonito [ba-**nee**-toh] *n*, *pl* **-os 1** small tunny-like marine food fish. **2** related fish, whose flesh is dried and flaked and used in Japanese cookery.

bonk *v informal* **1** have sex with. **2** hit. **bonking** *n*.

bonkers *adj slang* crazy.

bon mot [bon **moh**] *n*, *pl* **bons mots** clever and fitting remark.

bonnet *n* **1** metal cover over a vehicle's engine. **2** hat which ties under the chin. **3** *Scot* soft cloth cap.

bonny *adj* **-nier**, **-niest** *Scot* **1** beautiful. **2** good or fine.

bonsai *n*, *pl* **-sai** ornamental miniature tree or shrub.

bonus ❶ *n* something given, paid, or received above what is due or expected.

THESAURUS

escape, flee, fly, make a break (for it), run for it **7** = **lock**, bar, fasten, latch, secure **8** = **gobble**, cram, devour, gorge, gulp, guzzle, stuff, swallow whole, wolf

bomb *n* **1** = **explosive**, device, grenade, mine, missile, rocket, shell, torpedo ▷ *v* **3** = **blow up**, attack, blow sky-high, bombard, destroy, shell, strafe, torpedo

bombard *v* **1** = **bomb**, assault, blitz, fire upon, open fire, pound, shell, strafe **2** = **attack**, assail, beset, besiege, harass, hound, pester

bombardment *n* **1** = **bombing**, assault, attack, barrage, blitz, fusillade, shelling

bombastic *adj* = **grandiloquent**, grandiose, high-flown, inflated, pompous, verbose, wordy

bona fide *adj* = **genuine**, actual, authentic, honest, kosher (*inf*), legitimate, real, true

bond *n* **1** = **fastening**, chain, cord, fetter, ligature, manacle, shackle, tie **2** = **tie**, affiliation, affinity, attachment, connection, link, relation, union **3** = **agreement**, contract, covenant, guarantee, obligation, pledge, promise, word ▷ *v* **6** = **hold together**, bind, connect, fasten, fix together, glue, paste

bondage *n* **1** = **slavery**, captivity, confinement, enslavement, imprisonment, subjugation

bonus *n* = **extra**, dividend, gift, icing on the cake, plus, premium, prize, reward

bony *adj* **2** = **thin**, emaciated, gaunt, lean, scrawny, skin and bone, skinny

bon voyage *interj* phrase used to wish a traveller a pleasant journey.

boo *interj* **1** shout of disapproval. **2** shout to startle someone. ▷ *v* **booing, booed 3** shout 'boo' to show disapproval.

boob *slang* ▷ *n* **1** foolish mistake. **2** female breast. ▷ *v* **3** make a foolish mistake.

boobook [**boo**-book] *n* small spotted Australian brown owl.

booby *n, pl* **-bies** foolish person. **booby prize** prize given for the lowest score in a competition. **booby trap 1** hidden bomb primed to be set off by an unsuspecting victim. **2** trap for an unsuspecting person, intended as a joke.

boogie *v informal* dance to fast pop music.

book ❶ *n* **1** number of pages bound together between covers. **2** long written work. **3** number of tickets, stamps, etc. fastened together. **4** libretto of a musical etc. **5** record of betting transactions. ▷ *pl* **6** record of transactions of a business or society. ▷ *v* **7** reserve (a place, passage, etc.) in advance. **8** record the name of (a person) who has committed an offence. **bookcase** *n* piece of furniture containing shelves for books. **bookish** *adj* **1** fond of reading. **2** forming opinions through reading rather than experience. **booklet** *n* thin book with paper covers.

bookie *n informal* short for BOOKMAKER.

book-keeping *n* systematic recording of business transactions.

book-keeper *n*.

bookmaker *n* person whose occupation is taking bets.

bookmark *v Computers* store (a website) so that one can return to it easily.

bookworm *n* **1** person devoted to reading. **2** small insect that feeds on books.

boom¹ ❶ *v* **1** make a loud deep echoing sound. **2** prosper vigorously and rapidly. ▷ *n* **3** loud deep echoing sound. **4** period of high economic growth. **boomer** *n Aust* large male kangaroo.

boom² *n* **1** pole to which the foot of a sail is attached. **2** pole carrying an overhead microphone. **3** barrier across a waterway.

boomerang *n* **1** curved wooden missile which can be made to return to the thrower. ▷ *v* **2** (of a plan) recoil unexpectedly.

boon¹ ❶ *n* something helpful or beneficial.

boon² ❶ *adj* close or intimate.

boongary [**boong**-gar-ree] *n, pl* **-garies** tree kangaroo of NE Queensland, Australia.

boor ❶ *n* rude or insensitive person. **boorish** *adj*.

boost ❶ *n* **1** encouragement or help. **2** upward thrust or push. **3** increase. ▷ *v* **4** improve. **5** increase. **booster** *n* **1** small additional injection of a vaccine. **2** radio-frequency amplifier to strengthen signals. **3** first stage of a multistage rocket.

boot¹ ❶ *n* **1** outer covering for the foot that extends above the ankle. **2** space

— THESAURUS —

book *n* **1** = **notebook**, album, diary, exercise book, jotter, pad **2** = **work**, publication, title, tome, tract, volume ▷ *v* **7** = **reserve**, arrange for, charter, engage, make reservations, organize, programme, schedule **8** = **note**, enter, list, log, mark down, put down, record, register, write down

booklet *n* = **brochure**, leaflet, pamphlet

boom¹ *v* **1** = **bang**, blast, crash, explode, resound, reverberate, roar, roll, rumble, thunder **2** = **flourish**, develop, expand, grow, increase, intensify, prosper, strengthen, swell, thrive ▷ *n* **3** = **bang**, blast, burst, clap, crash, explosion, roar, rumble, thunder **4** = **expansion**, boost, development, growth, improvement, increase, jump, upsurge, upswing, upturn

boon¹ *n* = **benefit**, advantage, blessing, favour, gift, godsend, manna from heaven, windfall

boon² *adj* = **intimate**, close, special

boorish *adj* = **loutish**, churlish, coarse, crude, oafish, uncivilized, uncouth, vulgar

boost *n* **1** = **help**, encouragement, gee-up, praise, promotion **3** = **rise**, addition, expansion, improvement, increase, increment, jump ▷ *v* **4** = **promote**, advertise, encourage, foster, further, gee up, hype, improve, plug (*inf*), praise **5** = **increase**, add to, amplify, develop, enlarge, expand, heighten, raise

boot¹ *v Inf* **5** = **kick**, drive, drop-kick, knock, punt, put the boot in(to) (*sl*), shove

in a car for luggage. **3** *informal* kick.
4 *slang* dismissal from employment. ▷ *v*
5 *informal* kick. **6** start up (a computer).
bootee *n* baby's soft shoe. **boot camp**
centre for young offenders, with strict
discipline and hard physical exercise.
boot² *n* **to boot** in addition.
booth *n* **1** small partly enclosed cubicle.
2 stall at a fair or market.
bootleg *adj* **1** produced, distributed, or
sold illicitly. ▷ *v* **-legging, -legged**
2 make, carry, or sell (illicit goods).
bootlegger *n*.
booty ❶ *n*, *pl* **-ties** valuable articles
obtained as plunder.
booze *v*, *n informal* (consume) alcoholic
drink. **boozy** *adj* **boozer** *n informal*
1 person who is fond of drinking. **2** pub.
booze-up *n informal* drinking spree.
bop *v* **bopping, bopped** *informal* dance
to pop music.
borage *n* Mediterranean plant with star-
shaped blue flowers.
borax *n* white mineral used in making
glass. **boracic** *adj*.
Bordeaux *n* red or white wine from SW
France.
border ❶ *n* **1** dividing line between
political or geographical regions.
2 band around or along the edge of
something. ▷ *v* **3** provide with a
border. **4** be adjacent to. **5** be nearly
the same as, e.g. *resentment that
borders on hatred*.
bore¹ ❶ *v* **1** make (a hole) with a drill etc.
▷ *n* **2** hole or tunnel drilled in search of
oil, minerals, etc. **3** (diameter of) the
hollow of a gun barrel.
bore² ❶ *v* **1** make weary by being dull or
repetitious. ▷ *n* **2** dull or repetitious

person or thing. **bored** *adj* **boredom** *n*.
bore³ *n* high wave in a narrow estuary,
caused by the tide.
bore⁴ *v* past tense of BEAR¹.
boree [**baw-ree**] *n Aust* same as MYALL.
boric *adj* of or containing boron. **boric
acid** white soluble solid used as a mild
antiseptic.
born *v* **1** a past participle of BEAR¹. ▷ *adj*
2 possessing certain qualities from
birth, e.g. *a born musician*.
born-again *adj* **1** having experienced
conversion, esp. to evangelical
Christianity. **2** showing the enthusiasm
of someone newly converted to a
cause, e.g. *a born-again romantic*.
borne *v* a past participle of BEAR¹.
boron *n Chemistry* element used in
hardening steel.
boronia *n* Australian aromatic flowering
shrub.
borough *n* town or district with its own
council.
borrow ❶ *v* **1** obtain (something)
temporarily. **2** adopt (ideas etc.) from
another source. **borrower** *n*.
borscht, borsch *n* Russian soup based
on beetroot.
borstal *n* (formerly) prison for young
criminals.
borzoi *n* tall dog with a long silky coat.
bosh *n informal* empty talk, nonsense.
Bosnian *n*, *adj* (person) from Bosnia.
bosom ❶ *n* **1** chest of a person, esp. the
female breasts. ▷ *adj* **2** very dear, e.g. *a
bosom friend*.
boss¹ ❶ *n* **1** person in charge of or
employing others. ▷ *v* **2 boss around,
about** be domineering towards. **bossy**
adj **bossier, bossiest**.

THESAURUS

booty *n* = **plunder**, gains, haul, loot,
prey, spoils, swag (*sl*), takings, winnings
border *n* **1** = **frontier**, borderline,
boundary, line, march **2** = **edge**,
bounds, brink, limits, margin, rim,
verge ▷ *v* **3** = **edge**, bind, decorate,
fringe, hem, rim, trim
bore¹ *v* **1** = **drill**, burrow, gouge out,
mine, penetrate, perforate, pierce, sink,
tunnel
bore² *v* **1** = **tire**, be tedious, fatigue, jade,
pall on, send to sleep, wear out, weary
▷ *n* **2** = **nuisance**, anorak (*inf*), pain
(*inf*), yawn (*inf*)
bored *adj* = **fed up**, listless, tired,
uninterested, wearied
boredom *n* = **tedium**, apathy, ennui,

flatness, monotony, sameness,
tediousness, weariness, world-
weariness
boring *adj* = **uninteresting**, dull, flat,
humdrum, mind-numbing,
monotonous, tedious, tiresome
borrow *v* **1** = **take on loan**, bludge (*Aust
& NZ*), cadge, scrounge (*inf*), touch
(someone) for (*sl*), use temporarily
2 = **steal**, adopt, copy, obtain,
plagiarize, take, usurp
bosom *n* **1** = **breast**, bust, chest ▷ *adj*
2 = **intimate**, boon, cherished, close,
confidential, dear, very dear
boss¹ *n* **1** = **head**, chief, director,
employer, gaffer (*inf, chiefly Brit*), leader,
manager, master, supervisor

boss² ⊙ *n* raised knob or stud.

bosun *n* officer responsible for the maintenance of a ship.

bot. 1 botanical. **2** botany.

botany *n* study of plants. **botanical**, **botanic** *adj* **botanist** *n*.

botch ⊙ *v* **1** spoil through clumsiness. **2** repair badly. ▷ *n* **3** (also **botch-up**) badly done piece of work or repair.

both *adj*, *pron* two considered together.

bother ⊙ *v* **1** take the time or trouble. **2** give annoyance or trouble to. **3** pester. ▷ *n* **4** trouble, fuss, or difficulty. ▷ *interj* **5** *Chiefly Brit* exclamation of slight annoyance. **bothersome** *adj*.

bothy *n*, *pl* **-ies** *Chiefly Scot* hut used for temporary shelter.

bottle ⊙ *n* **1** container for holding liquids. **2** *slang* courage. ▷ *v* **3** put in a bottle. **bottle bank** container into which people can throw glass bottles for recycling. **bottle-green** *adj* dark green. **bottleneck** *n* narrow stretch of road where traffic is held up. **bottle tree** Australian tree with a bottle-shaped swollen trunk. **bottle up** *v* restrain (powerful emotion).

bottom ⊙ *n* **1** lowest, deepest, or farthest removed part of a thing. **2** least important or successful position. **3** ground underneath a sea, lake, or river. **4** buttocks. ▷ *adj* **5** lowest or last. **bottomless** *adj* **bottom out** *v*

reach the lowest point and level out.

botulism *n* severe food poisoning.

bouclé *n* looped yarn giving a knobbly effect.

boudoir [boo-dwahr] *n* woman's bedroom or private sitting room.

bouffant [boof-fong] *adj* (of a hairstyle) having extra height through backcombing.

bougainvillea *n* climbing plant with red or purple flowers.

bough *n* large branch of a tree.

bought *v* past of BUY.

- ● **USAGE NOTE**
- ● Be careful not to confuse the past
- ● forms *bought* (from *buy*) with *brought*
- ● (from *bring*).

bouillon [boo-yon] *n* thin clear broth or stock.

boulder *n* large rounded rock.

boulevard *n* wide, usu. tree-lined, street.

bounce ⊙ *v* **1** (of a ball etc.) rebound from an impact. **2** *slang* (of a cheque) be returned uncashed owing to a lack of funds in the account. ▷ *n* **3** act of rebounding. **4** springiness. **5** *informal* vitality or vigour. **bouncer** *n* person employed at a disco etc. to remove unwanted people. **bouncing** *adj* vigorous and robust. **bouncy** *adj* **bouncier**, **bounciest**.

bound¹ ⊙ *v* **1** past of BIND. ▷ *adj* **2** destined or certain. **3** compelled

————————————————— THESAURUS —————————————————

boss² *n* = **stud**, knob, point, protuberance, tip

boss around (also **about**) *v* = **domineer**, bully, dominate, oppress, order, push around (*sl*)

bossy *adj Inf* = **domineering**, arrogant, authoritarian, autocratic, dictatorial, hectoring, high-handed, imperious, overbearing, tyrannical

botch *v* **1** = **spoil**, blunder, bungle, cock up (*Brit sl*), make a pig's ear of (*inf*), mar, mess up, screw up (*inf*) ▷ *n* **3** = **mess**, blunder, bungle, cock-up (*Brit sl*), failure, hash, pig's ear (*inf*)

bother *v* **3** = **trouble**, disturb, harass, hassle (*inf*), inconvenience, pester, plague, worry ▷ *n* **4** = **trouble**, difficulty, fuss, hassle (*inf*), inconvenience, irritation, nuisance, problem, worry

bottleneck *n* = **hold-up**, block, blockage, congestion, impediment, jam, obstacle, obstruction, snarl-up

(*inf, chiefly Brit*)

bottle up *v* = **suppress**, check, contain, curb, keep back, restrict, shut in, trap

bottom *n* **1** = **lowest part**, base, bed, depths, floor, foot, foundation, lower side, sole, underneath, underside **4** = **buttocks**, backside, behind (*inf*), posterior, rear, rump, seat ▷ *adj* **5** = **lowest**, last

bottomless *adj* = **unlimited**, boundless, deep, fathomless, immeasurable, inexhaustible, infinite, unfathomable

bounce *v* **1** = **rebound**, bob, bound, jump, leap, recoil, ricochet, spring ▷ *n* **4** = **springiness**, elasticity, give, recoil, resilience, spring **5** *Inf* = **life**, dynamism, energy, go (*inf*), liveliness, vigour, vivacity, zip (*inf*)

bound¹ *adj* **1** = **tied**, cased, fastened, fixed, pinioned, secured, tied up **2** = **certain**, destined, doomed, fated, sure **3** = **obliged**, beholden, committed, compelled, constrained,

or obliged.

bound² ❶ v **1** move forwards by jumps. ▷ n **2** jump upwards or forwards.

bound³ ❶ v **1** limit or place restrictions on. **2** form a boundary of. ▷ pl n **3** limit, e.g. *his ignorance knows no bounds*. **boundary** n, pl **-aries** dividing line that indicates the farthest limit.

bound⁴ adj going or intending to go towards, e.g. *homeward bound*.

bounder n old-fashioned brit slang morally reprehensible person.

bounty ❶ n, pl **-ties 1** generosity. **2** generous gift or reward. **bountiful**, **bounteous** adj.

bouquet ❶ n **1** bunch of flowers. **2** aroma of wine. **bouquet garni** bunch of herbs tied together and used for flavouring soups etc.

bourbon [**bur**-bn] n whiskey made from maize.

bourgeois ❶ [**boor**-zhwah] adj, n offens middle-class (person). **bourgeoisie** n middle classes.

bourn n (in S Britain) stream.

Bourse [**boorss**] n stock exchange, esp. of Paris.

bout ❶ n **1** period of activity or illness. **2** boxing or wrestling match.

boutique n small clothes shop.

bouzouki n Greek stringed musical instrument.

bovine adj **1** relating to cattle. **2** rather slow and stupid.

bow¹ ❶ [rhymes with **now**] v **1** lower (one's head) or bend (one's knee or body) as a sign of respect or shame. **2** comply or accept. ▷ n **3** movement made when bowing.

bow² [rhymes with **go**] n **1** knot with two loops and loose ends. **2** weapon for shooting arrows. **3** something curved, bent, or arched. **4** long stick stretched with horsehair for playing stringed instruments. **bow-legged** adj having legs that curve outwards at the knees. **bow window** curved bay window.

bow³ ❶ [rhymes with **now**] n front end of a ship.

bowdlerize v remove words regarded as indecent from (a play, novel, etc.). **bowdlerization** n.

bowel n **1** intestine, esp. the large intestine. ▷ pl **2** innermost part.

bower n shady leafy shelter. **bowerbird** n songbird of Australia and New Guinea, the males of which build bower-like display grounds to attract females.

bowie knife n stout hunting knife.

bowl¹ ❶ n **1** round container with an open top. **2** hollow part of an object.

bowl² ❶ n **1** large heavy ball. ▷ pl **2** game played on smooth grass with wooden bowls. ▷ v **3** roll smoothly along the ground. **4** Cricket send (a ball) towards the batsman. **5** Cricket dismiss

──────────── THESAURUS ────────────

duty-bound, forced, pledged, required

bound² v **1** = **leap**, bob, bounce, gambol, hurdle, jump, skip, spring, vault ▷ n **2** = **leap**, bob, bounce, gambol, hurdle, jump, skip, spring, vault

bound³ v **1, 2** = **limit**, confine, demarcate, encircle, enclose, hem in, restrain, restrict, surround ▷ pl n **3** = **boundary**, border, confine, edge, extremity, limit, rim, verge

boundary n = **limits**, barrier, border, borderline, brink, edge, extremity, fringe, frontier, margin

bountiful adj = **generous**, liberal, magnanimous, open-handed, prodigal, unstinting

bounty n **1** = **generosity**, benevolence, charity, kindness, largesse or largess, liberality, philanthropy **2** = **reward**, bonus, gift, present

bouquet n **1** = **bunch of flowers**, buttonhole, corsage, garland, nosegay, posy, spray, wreath **2** = **aroma**,

fragrance, perfume, redolence, savour, scent

bourgeois adj Offens = **middle-class**, conventional, hidebound, materialistic, traditional

bout n **1** = **period**, fit, spell, stint, term, turn **2** = **fight**, boxing match, competition, contest, encounter, engagement, match, set-to, struggle

bow¹ v **1** = **bend**, bob, droop, genuflect, nod, stoop **2** = **give in**, acquiesce, comply, concede, defer, kowtow, relent, submit, succumb, surrender, yield ▷ n **3** = **bending**, bob, genuflexion, kowtow, nod, obeisance

bow³ n = **prow**, beak, fore, head, stem

bowels pl n **1** = **guts**, entrails, innards (inf), insides (inf), intestines, viscera, vitals **2** = **depths**, belly, core, deep, hold, inside, interior

bowl¹ n **1** = **basin**, dish, vessel

bowl² v **4** Cricket = **throw**, fling, hurl, pitch

b

(a batsman) by delivering a ball that breaks his wicket. **6** play bowls.
bowler *n* **bowling** *n* game in which bowls are rolled at a group of pins.

bowler *n* stiff felt hat with a rounded crown.

box¹ ❶ *n* **1** container with a firm flat base and sides. **2** separate compartment in a theatre, stable, etc. **3** place to which mail is sent and from which it is collected or redistributed, e.g. *a post-office box.* ▷ *v* **4** put into a box. **the box** *informal* television. **boxy** *adj* **boxier**, **boxiest** squarish or chunky. **box in** *v* prevent from moving freely. **box jellyfish** highly venomous jellyfish of Australian tropical waters with a cuboidal body. **box junction** road junction marked with yellow lines which may only be entered if the exit is clear. **box lacrosse** *Canad* lacrosse played indoors. **box office** place where theatre or cinema tickets are sold. **box pleat** flat double pleat.

box² ❶ *v* **1** fight (an opponent) in a boxing match. **2** hit (a person's ears) with the fist. **boxer** *n* **1** person who participates in the sport of boxing. **2** medium-sized dog with smooth hair and a short nose. **boxer shorts**, **boxers** *pl n* men's underpants shaped like shorts but with a front opening. **boxing** *n* sport of fighting with the fists.

box³ *n* **1** evergreen tree with shiny leaves. **2** eucalyptus with similar timber and foliage, and with rough bark.

Boxing Day *n* first weekday after Christmas.

boy ❶ *n* male child. **boyish** *adj* **boyhood** *n* **boyfriend** *n* male friend with whom a person is romantically or sexually

involved.

boycott ❶ *v* **1** refuse to deal with (an organization or country). ▷ *n* **2** instance of boycotting.

- ● **SPELLING TIP**
- ● The word **boycott** has two *t*s,
- ● whether or not it has an ending such
- ● as in **boycotting**.

BP blood pressure.
Br *Chemistry* bromine.
bra *n* woman's undergarment for supporting the breasts.

braaivlies, braai *S Afr* ▷ *n* **1** grill on which food is cooked over hot charcoal, usu. outdoors. ▷ *v* **2** cook (food) on in this way.

brace ❶ *n* **1** object fastened to something to straighten or support it. **2** pair, esp. of game birds. ▷ *pl* **3** straps worn over the shoulders to hold up trousers. ▷ *v* **4** steady or prepare (oneself) for something unpleasant. **5** strengthen or fit with a brace. **bracing** *adj* refreshing and invigorating.

bracelet *n* ornamental chain or band for the wrist.
bracken *n* large fern.
bracket *n* **1** pair of characters used to enclose a section of writing. **2** group falling within certain defined limits. **3** support fixed to a wall. ▷ *v* **-eting**, **-eted 4** put in brackets. **5** class together.

brackish *adj* (of water) slightly salty.
bract *n* leaf at the base of a flower.
bradawl *n* small boring tool.
brae *n Scot* hill or slope.
brag ❶ *v* **bragging**, **bragged 1** speak arrogantly and boastfully. ▷ *n* **2** boastful talk or behaviour. **3** card game similar to poker. **braggart** *n* person who boasts loudly.

—————————————————————————— THESAURUS ——————

box¹ *n* **1** = **container**, carton, case, casket, chest, pack, package, receptacle, trunk ▷ *v* **4** = **pack**, package, wrap
box² *v* **1** = **fight**, exchange blows, spar
boxer *n* **1** = **fighter**, prizefighter, pugilist, sparring partner
boy *n* = **lad**, fellow, junior, schoolboy, stripling, youngster, youth
boycott *v* **1** = **embargo**, ban, bar, black, exclude, outlaw, prohibit, refuse, reject
boyfriend *n* = **sweetheart**, admirer, beau, date, lover, man, suitor
boyish *adj* = **youthful**, adolescent,

childish, immature, juvenile, puerile, young
brace *n* **1** = **support**, bolster, bracket, buttress, prop, reinforcement, stay, strut, truss ▷ *v* **5** = **support**, bolster, buttress, fortify, reinforce, steady, strengthen
bracing *adj* = **refreshing**, brisk, crisp, exhilarating, fresh, invigorating, stimulating
brag *v* **1** = **boast**, blow one's own trumpet, bluster, crow, skite (*Aust & NZ*), swagger, talk big (*sl*), vaunt
braggart *n* = **boaster**, bigmouth (*sl*), bragger, show-off (*inf*)

Brahma n Hindu god, the Creator. **Brahman**, **Brahmin** n member of the highest Hindu caste.

braid ❶ v **1** interweave (hair, thread, etc.). ▷ n **2** length of hair etc. that has been braided. **3** narrow ornamental tape of woven silk etc.

Braille n system of writing for the blind, consisting of raised dots interpreted by touch.

brain ❶ n **1** soft mass of nervous tissue in the head. **2** intellectual ability. ▷ v **3** hit (someone) hard on the head. **brainless** adj stupid. **brainy** adj **brainier**, **brainiest** informal clever. **brainchild** n idea produced by creative thought. **braindead** adj **1** having suffered irreversible stoppage of breathing due to brain damage. **2** informal not using or showing intelligence. **brainstorm** n sudden mental aberration. **brain up** v make (something) more intellectually demanding or sophisticated. **brainwash** v cause (a person) to alter his or her beliefs, esp. by methods based on isolation, sleeplessness, etc. **brainwave** n sudden bright idea.

braise v cook slowly in a covered pan with a little liquid.

brake¹ ❶ n **1** device for slowing or stopping a vehicle. ▷ v **2** slow down or stop by using a brake. **brake horsepower** rate at which an engine does work. **brake light** red light at the rear of a motor vehicle that comes on when the brakes are applied.

brake² n area of dense undergrowth.

bramble n **1** prickly shrub that produces blackberries. **2** Scot blackberry.

bran n husks of cereal grain.

branch ❶ n **1** secondary stem of a tree. **2** offshoot or subsidiary part of something larger or more complex. ▷ v **3** (of stems, roots, etc.) divide, then develop in different directions. **branch out** v expand one's interests.

brand ❶ n **1** particular product. **2** particular kind or variety. **3** identifying mark burnt onto the skin of an animal. **4** lit burning piece of wood. ▷ v **5** mark with a brand. **6** denounce as being, e.g. he was branded a fascist. **brand-new** adj absolutely new.

brandish ❶ v wave (a weapon etc.) in a threatening way.

brandy n, pl **-dies** alcoholic spirit distilled from wine. **brandy snap** tube-shaped crisp sweet biscuit.

brash ❶ adj offensively loud, showy, or self-confident. **brashness** n.

brass n **1** alloy of copper and zinc. **2** family of wind instruments made of brass. **3** engraved brass memorial tablet in a church. **4** N English dialect money. **5** informal bold self-confidence. **brassy** adj **brassier**, **brassiest** **1** brazen or flashy. **2** like brass, esp. in colour. **brass hat** informal top-ranking military officer.

brasserie n restaurant serving drinks and cheap meals.

brassica n any plant of the cabbage and turnip family.

brassiere n bra.

brat n unruly child.

bravado ❶ n showy display of self-confidence.

——————— THESAURUS ———————

braid v **1** = **interweave**, entwine, interlace, intertwine, lace, plait, twine, weave

brain n **2** = **intelligence**, intellect, sense, understanding

brainless adj = **stupid**, foolish, idiotic, inane, mindless, senseless, thoughtless, witless

brainwave n = **idea**, bright idea, stroke of genius, thought

brainy adj Inf = **intelligent**, bright, brilliant, clever, smart

brake¹ n **1** = **control**, check, constraint, curb, rein, restraint ▷ v **2** = **slow**, check, decelerate, halt, moderate, reduce speed, slacken, stop

branch n **1** = **bough**, arm, limb, offshoot, shoot, spray, sprig

2 = **division**, chapter, department, office, part, section, subdivision, subsection, wing

brand n **1** = **label**, emblem, hallmark, logo, mark, marker, sign, stamp, symbol, trademark **2** = **kind**, cast, class, grade, make, quality, sort, species, type, variety ▷ v **5** = **mark**, burn, burn in, label, scar, stamp **6** = **stigmatize**, censure, denounce, discredit, disgrace, expose, mark

brandish v = **wave**, display, exhibit, flaunt, flourish, parade, raise, shake, swing, wield

brash adj = **bold**, brazen, cocky, impertinent, impudent, insolent, pushy (inf), rude

bravado n = **swagger**, bluster,

brave ❶ *adj* **1** having or showing courage, resolution, and daring. **2** splendid. ▷ *n* **3** Native American warrior. ▷ *v* **4** confront with resolution or courage. **bravery** *n*.

bravo *interj* well done!

bravura *n* **1** display of boldness or daring. **2** *Music* brilliance of execution.

brawl ❶ *n* **1** noisy fight. ▷ *v* **2** fight noisily.

brawn ❶ *n* **1** physical strength. **2** pressed meat from the head of a pig or calf. **brawny** *adj*.

bray *v* **1** (of a donkey) utter its loud harsh sound. ▷ *n* **2** donkey's loud harsh sound.

braze *v* join (two metal surfaces) with brass.

brazen ❶ *adj* **1** shameless and bold. ▷ *v* **2 brazen it out** overcome a difficult situation boldly or shamelessly. **brazenly** *adv*.

brazier [**bray**-zee-er] *n* portable container for burning charcoal or coal.

brazil nut *n* large three-sided nut of a tropical American tree.

breach ❶ *n* **1** breaking of a promise, obligation, etc. **2** serious quarrel or separation. **3** gap or break. ▷ *v* **4** break (a promise, law, etc.). **5** make a gap in.

bread ❶ *n* **1** food made by baking a mixture of flour and water or milk. **2** *slang* money. **breadwinner** *n* person whose earnings support a family.

breadline *n* **on the breadline** living at subsistence level.

breadth ❶ *n* **1** extent of something from side to side. **2** lack of restriction, esp. of viewpoint or interest.

break ❶ *v* **breaking, broke, broken 1** separate or become separated into two or more pieces. **2** damage or become damaged so as to be inoperative. **3** fail to observe (an agreement etc.). **4** disclose or be disclosed, e.g. *he broke the news*. **5** bring or come to an end, e.g. *the good weather broke at last*. **6** weaken or be weakened, as in spirit. **7** cut through or penetrate, e.g. *silence broken by shouts*. **8** improve on or surpass, e.g. *break a record*. **9** accustom (a horse) to being ridden. **10** (of the male voice) become permanently deeper at puberty. ▷ *n* **11** act or result of breaking. **12** gap or interruption in continuity. **13** sudden rush, esp. to escape. **14** *informal* fortunate opportunity. **15** *Billiards, Snooker* series of successful shots during one turn. **break even** make neither a profit nor a loss. **breakable** *adj* **breakage** *n* **breaker** *n* large wave. **breakaway** *adj, n* **1** (consisting of) a dissenting group who have left a larger unit. ▷ *n* **2** *Aust* stampede of cattle, esp. at the smell of water. **break down**

———————————————————————— THESAURUS ————————————————————————

boastfulness, boasting, bombast, swashbuckling, vaunting

brave *adj* **1** = **courageous**, bold, daring, fearless, heroic, intrepid, plucky, resolute, valiant ▷ *v* **4** = **confront**, defy, endure, face, stand up to, suffer, tackle, withstand

bravery *n* **1** = **courage**, boldness, daring, fearlessness, fortitude, heroism, intrepidity, mettle, pluck, spirit, valour

brawl *n* **1** = **fight**, affray, altercation, clash, dispute, fracas, fray, mêlée, punch-up (*inf*), rumpus, scuffle, skirmish ▷ *v* **2** = **fight**, scrap (*inf*), scuffle, tussle, wrestle

brawn *n* **1** = **muscle**, beef (*inf*), might, muscles, power, strength, vigour

brawny *adj* **1** = **muscular**, beefy (*inf*), hefty (*inf*), lusty, powerful, strapping, strong, sturdy, well-built

brazen *adj* **1** = **bold**, audacious, barefaced, brash, defiant, impudent, insolent, shameless, unabashed, unashamed

breach *n* **1** = **nonobservance**, contravention, infraction, infringement, noncompliance, transgression, trespass, violation **3** = **crack**, cleft, fissure, gap, opening, rift, rupture, split

bread *n* **2** *Sl* = **money**, cash, dough (*sl*), lolly (*Aust & NZ sl*)

breadth *n* **1** = **width**, broadness, latitude, span, spread, wideness **2** = **extent**, compass, expanse, range, scale, scope

break *v* **1** = **separate**, burst, crack, destroy, disintegrate, fracture, fragment, shatter, smash, snap, split, tear **3** = **disobey**, breach, contravene, disregard, infringe, renege on, transgress, violate **4** = **reveal**, announce, disclose, divulge, impart, inform, let out, make public, proclaim, tell **5** = **stop**, abandon, cut, discontinue, give up, interrupt, pause, rest, suspend **6** = **weaken**, demoralize,

b

v **1** cease to function. **2** yield to strong emotion. **3** decompose or separate into component parts. **breakdown** *n* **1** act or instance of breaking down. **2** nervous breakdown. **3** separation of something into its component parts. **break-in** *n* illegal entering of a building, esp. by thieves. **break into** *v* start doing, esp. suddenly, e.g. *she broke into song*. **breakneck** *adj* fast and dangerous. **break off** *v* **1** sever or detach. **2** end (a relationship etc.). **break out** *v* begin or arise suddenly. **breakthrough** *n* important development or discovery. **break up** *v* **1** (cause to) separate. **2** come to an end. **3** (of a school) close for the holidays. **breakwater** *n* wall that extends into the sea to protect a harbour or beach from the force of waves.

breakfast *v, n* (eat) the first meal of the day.

bream *n* freshwater silvery fish.

breast ❶ *n* **1** either of the two soft fleshy milk-secreting glands on a woman's chest. **2** chest. **3** source of human emotions. ▷ *v* **4** *lit* reach the summit of.

breastbone *n* long flat bone in the front of the body, to which most of the ribs are attached. **breast-feed** *v* feed (a baby) with milk from the breast. **breaststroke** *n* swimming stroke in which the arms are extended in front of the head and swept back on either side.

breath ❶ *n* **1** taking in and letting out of air during breathing. **2** air taken in and let out during breathing. **3** slight gust of air. **breathless** *adj* **breathtaking** *adj* causing awe or excitement. **breathe** *v* **1** take in oxygen and give out carbon dioxide. **2** be alive. **3** whisper. **4** impart or instil, e.g. *the move breathed new life into his career*. **breather** *n informal* short rest. **breathing** *n*.

Breathalyser *n* ® device for estimating the amount of alcohol in the breath. **breathalyse** *v*.

bred *v* past of BREED.

breech *n* **1** buttocks. **2** part of a firearm behind the barrel. **breech birth**, **breech delivery** birth of a baby with the feet or buttocks appearing first.

breeches *pl n* trousers extending to just below the knee.

breed ❶ *v* **breeding**, **bred** **1** produce

---

dispirit, subdue, tame, undermine **8** = **beat**, better, exceed, excel, go beyond, outdo, outstrip, surpass, top ▷ *n* **11** = **division**, crack, fissure, fracture, gap, hole, opening, split, tear **12** = **rest**, breather (*inf*), hiatus, interlude, intermission, interruption, interval, let-up (*inf*), lull, pause, respite **14** *Inf* = **stroke of luck**, advantage, chance, fortune, opening, opportunity

breakable *adj* **1** = **fragile**, brittle, crumbly, delicate, flimsy, frail, frangible, friable

breakdown *n* **1** = **collapse**, disintegration, disruption, failure, mishap, stoppage

break down *v* **1** = **collapse**, come unstuck, fail, seize up, stop, stop working **2** = **be overcome**, crack up (*inf*), go to pieces

break-in *n* = **burglary**, breaking and entering, robbery

break off *v* **1** = **detach**, divide, part, pull off, separate, sever, snap off, splinter **2** = **stop**, cease, desist, discontinue, end, finish, halt, pull the plug on, suspend, terminate

break out *v* = **begin**, appear, arise, commence, emerge, happen, occur, set

in, spring up, start

breakthrough *n* = **development**, advance, discovery, find, invention, leap, progress, quantum leap, step forward

break up *v* **1** = **separate**, dissolve, divide, divorce, part, scatter, sever, split **2** = **stop**, adjourn, disband, dismantle, end, suspend, terminate

breast *n* **1** = **bosom**, bust, chest, front, teat, udder

breath *n* **1** = **respiration**, breathing, exhalation, gasp, gulp, inhalation, pant, wheeze

breathe *v* **1** = **inhale and exhale**, draw in, gasp, gulp, pant, puff, respire, wheeze **3** = **whisper**, murmur, sigh

breather *n Inf* = **rest**, break, breathing space, halt, pause, recess, respite

breathless *adj* **1** = **out of breath**, gasping, gulping, panting, short-winded, spent, wheezing

breathtaking *adj* = **amazing**, astonishing, awe-inspiring, exciting, impressive, magnificent, sensational, stunning (*inf*), thrilling

breed *v* **1** = **cultivate**, develop **2** = **reproduce**, bear, bring forth, hatch, multiply, procreate, produce,

new or improved strains of (domestic animals or plants). **2** bear (offspring). **3** bring up, e.g. *he was born and bred in Hull*. **4** produce or be produced, e.g. *breed trouble*. ▷ *n* **5** group of animals etc. within a species that have certain clearly defined characteristics. **6** kind or sort. **breeder** *n* **breeder reactor** nuclear reactor that produces more fissionable material than it uses. **breeding** *n* result of good upbringing or training.

breeze ❶ *n* **1** gentle wind. ▷ *v* **2** move quickly or casually. **breezy** *adj* **breezier**, **breeziest 1** windy. **2** casual or carefree.

breeze block *n* light building brick made of ashes bonded by cement.

Bren gun *n* gas-operated light machine gun.

brent *n* small goose with a dark grey plumage.

brethren *pl n old-fashioned* (used in religious contexts) brothers.

Breton *adj* **1** of Brittany. ▷ *n* **2** person from Brittany. **3** language of Brittany.

breviary *n*, *pl* **-aries** book of prayers to be recited daily by a Roman Catholic priest.

brevity ❶ *n* shortness.

brew ❶ *v* **1** make (beer etc.) by steeping, boiling, and fermentation. **2** prepare (a drink) by infusing. **3** be about to happen or forming, e.g. *trouble was*

brewing. ▷ *n* **4** beverage produced by brewing. **brewer** *n* **brewery** *n*, *pl* **-eries** place where beer etc. is brewed.

briar¹, **brier** *n* **1** European shrub with a hard woody root. **2** tobacco pipe made from this root.

briar² *n* same as BRIER¹.

bribe ❶ *v* **1** offer or give something to someone to gain favour, influence, etc. ▷ *n* **2** something given or offered as a bribe. **bribery** *n*.

bric-a-brac ❶ *n* miscellaneous small ornamental objects.

brick *n* **1** (rectangular block of) baked clay used in building. ▷ *v* **2** (foll. by *up* or *over*) build, enclose, or fill with bricks. **brickbat** *n* blunt criticism. **bricklayer** *n* person who builds with bricks.

bride ❶ *n* woman who has just been or is about to be married. **bridal** *adj* **bridegroom** *n* man who has just been or is about to be married. **bridesmaid** *n* girl who attends a bride at her wedding.

bridge¹ ❶ *n* **1** structure for crossing a river etc. **2** platform from which a ship is steered or controlled. **3** upper part of the nose. **4** dental plate with artificial teeth that is secured to natural teeth. **5** piece of wood supporting the strings of a violin etc. ▷ *v* **6** build a bridge over (something). **7** connect or reduce the distance between. **bridgehead** *n* fortified position at the end of a bridge nearest the enemy. **bridging loan** loan

━━━━━━━━━━━━━━━━━━━━ THESAURUS ━━━━━━━━

propagate **3** = **bring up**, nourish, nurture, raise, rear **4** = **produce**, arouse, bring about, cause, create, generate, give rise to, stir up ▷ *n* **5** = **variety**, pedigree, race, species, stock, strain, type **6** = **kind**, brand, sort, stamp, type, variety

breeding *n* = **refinement**, cultivation, culture, manners, polish, sophistication, urbanity

breeze *n* **1** = **light wind**, air, breath of wind, current of air, draught, gust, waft, zephyr ▷ *v* **2** = **move briskly**, flit, glide, hurry, pass, sail, sweep

breezy *adj* **1** = **windy**, airy, blowy, blustery, fresh, gusty, squally **2** = **carefree**, blithe, casual, easy-going, free and easy, jaunty, light-hearted, lively, sprightly

brevity *n* = **shortness**, briefness, conciseness, crispness, curtness, economy, impermanence, pithiness, succinctness, terseness, transience,

transitoriness

brew *v* **1, 2** = **make** (*beer*), boil, ferment, infuse (*tea*), soak, steep, stew **3** = **develop**, foment, form, gather, start, stir up ▷ *n* **4** = **drink**, beverage, blend, concoction, infusion, liquor, mixture, preparation

bribe *v* **1** = **buy off**, corrupt, grease the palm *or* hand of (*sl*), pay off (*inf*), reward, suborn ▷ *n* **2** = **inducement**, allurement, backhander (*sl*), enticement, kickback (*US*), pay-off (*inf*), sweetener (*sl*)

bribery *n* = **buying off**, corruption, inducement, palm-greasing (*sl*), payola (*inf*)

bric-a-brac *n* = **knick-knacks**, baubles, curios, ornaments, trinkets

bridal *adj* = **matrimonial**, conjugal, connubial, marital, marriage, nuptial, wedding

bridge¹ *n* **1** = **arch**, flyover, overpass, span, viaduct ▷ *v* **7** = **connect**, join, link, span

made to cover the period between two transactions.

bridge² n card game based on whist, played between two pairs.

bridle ❶ n 1 headgear for controlling a horse. **2** something that curbs or restrains. ▷ v **3** show anger or indignation. **4** put a bridle on (a horse). **bridle path** path suitable for riding horses.

Brie [bree] n soft creamy white cheese.

brief ❶ adj 1 short in duration. **2** concise. ▷ n **3** condensed statement or written synopsis. **4** (also **briefing**) set of instructions. ▷ pl **5** men's or women's underpants. ▷ v **6** give information and instructions to (a person). **briefly** adv **briefcase** n small flat case for carrying papers, books, etc.

brier¹, **briar** n wild rose with long thorny stems.

brier² n same as BRIAR¹.

brig n two-masted square-rigged ship.

Brig. Brigadier.

brigade ❶ n 1 army unit smaller than a division. **2** group of people organized

for a certain task. **brigadier** n high-ranking army officer.

brigand ❶ n bandit.

brigantine n two-masted sailing ship.

bright ❶ adj 1 emitting or reflecting much light. **2** (of colours) intense. **3** full of promise. **4** lively or cheerful. **5** clever. **brightly** adv **brightness** n **brighten** v.

brill n edible European flatfish.

brilliant ❶ adj 1 shining with light. **2** (of a colour) vivid. **3** splendid. **4** extremely clever. ▷ n **5** diamond cut so as to increase its sparkle. **brilliance**, **brilliancy** n.

brilliantine n perfumed hair oil.

brim ❶ n 1 upper rim of a cup etc. **2** projecting edge of a hat. ▷ v **brimming**, **brimmed 3** be full to the brim.

brimstone n obs sulphur.

brindled adj brown or grey streaked with a darker colour.

brine n salt water. **briny** adj very salty. **the briny** informal the sea.

bring ❶ v **bringing**, **brought 1** carry,

— THESAURUS —

bridle n **2** = **curb**, check, control, rein, restraint ▷ v **3** = **get angry**, be indignant, bristle, draw (oneself) up, get one's back up, raise one's hackles, rear up

brief adj **1** = **short**, ephemeral, fleeting, momentary, quick, short-lived, swift, transitory ▷ n **3** = **summary**, abridgment, abstract, digest, epitome, outline, précis, sketch, synopsis **4** = **instructions**, conference, directions, guidance, information, preparation, priming, rundown ▷ v **6** = **inform**, advise, explain, fill in (inf), instruct, keep posted, prepare, prime, put (someone) in the picture (inf)

briefly adv = **shortly**, concisely, hastily, hurriedly, in a nutshell, in brief, momentarily, quickly

brigade n **2** = **group**, band, company, corps, force, outfit, squad, team, troop, unit

brigand n = **bandit**, desperado, freebooter, gangster, highwayman, marauder, outlaw, plunderer, robber

bright adj **1, 2** = **shining**, brilliant, dazzling, gleaming, glowing, luminous, lustrous, radiant, shimmering, vivid **5** = **intelligent**, astute, aware, clever, inventive, quick-witted, sharp, smart, wide-awake

brighten v **1** = **light up**, gleam, glow, illuminate, lighten, make brighter, shine

brightness n **1, 2** = **shine**, brilliance, glare, incandescence, intensity, light, luminosity, radiance, vividness **5** = **intelligence**, acuity, cleverness, quickness, sharpness, smartness

brilliance, brilliancy n **1, 2** = **brightness**, dazzle, intensity, luminosity, lustre, radiance, sparkle, vividness **3** = **splendour**, éclat, glamour, grandeur, illustriousness, magnificence **4** = **cleverness**, distinction, excellence, genius, greatness, inventiveness, talent, wisdom

brilliant adj **1, 2** = **shining**, bright, dazzling, glittering, intense, luminous, radiant, sparkling, vivid **3** = **splendid**, celebrated, famous, glorious, illustrious, magnificent, notable, outstanding, superb **4** = **intelligent**, clever, expert, gifted, intellectual, inventive, masterly, penetrating, profound, talented

brim n **1** = **rim**, border, brink, edge, lip, margin, skirt, verge ▷ v **3** = **be full**, fill, fill up, hold no more, overflow, run over, spill, well over

bring v **1** = **take**, bear, carry, conduct,

convey, or take to a designated place or person. **2** cause to happen. **3** *Law* put forward (charges) officially. **bring about** *v* cause to happen. **bring off** *v* succeed in achieving. **bring out** *v* **1** publish or have (a book) published. **2** reveal or cause to be seen. **bring up** *v* **1** rear (a child). **2** mention. **3** vomit (food).

brinjal *n S Afr* dark purple tropical fruit, cooked and eaten as a vegetable.

brink ❶ *n* edge of a steep place. **on the brink of** very near. **brinkmanship** *n* pressing of a dangerous situation to the limit of safety in order to win an advantage.

briquette *n* block of compressed coal dust.

brisk ❶ *adj* **1** lively and quick. **2** invigorating or sharp, e.g. *a brisk breeze*. **3** practical and businesslike. **briskly** *adv*.

brisket *n* beef from the breast of a cow.

bristle ❶ *n* **1** short stiff hair. ▷ *v* **2** (cause to) stand up like bristles. **3** show anger. **bristly** *adj* **bristlier**, **bristliest**.

Brit *n informal* British person.

Brit. **1** Britain. **2** British.

Britannia *n* female warrior personifying Great Britain.

Britannic *adj* of Britain, esp. in *Her Britannic Majesty*.

British *adj* **1** of Great Britain or the British Commonwealth. ▷ *pl n* **2** people of Great Britain.

Briton *n* native or inhabitant of Britain.

brittle ❶ *adj* hard but easily broken. **brittleness** *n*.

broach ❶ *v* **1** introduce (a topic) for discussion. **2** open (a bottle or barrel).

broad ❶ *adj* **1** having great breadth or width. **2** not detailed. **3** extensive, e.g. *broad support*. **4** obvious, e.g. *broad hints*. **5** strongly marked, e.g. *a broad Bristol accent*. ▷ *n* **6** *slang, chiefly US* woman. **broadly** *adv* **broaden** *v* **broadband** *n* telecommunication transmission technique using a wide range of frequencies. **broad bean** thick flat edible bean. **broadcast** *n* programme or announcement on radio or television. **broad-leaved** *adj* (of trees) having broad rather than needle-shaped leaves. **broad-minded** *adj* tolerant. **broadsheet** *n* newspaper in a large format. **broadside** *n* **1** strong verbal or written attack. **2** *Naval* firing of all the guns on one side of a ship at once.

B-road *n* secondary road in Britain.

broadcast ❶ *n* **1** programme or announcement on radio or television.

————————— THESAURUS —————————

convey, deliver, escort, fetch, guide, lead, transfer, transport **2 = cause**, contribute to, create, effect, inflict, occasion, produce, result in, wreak

bring about *v* = **cause**, accomplish, achieve, create, effect, generate, give rise to, make happen, produce

bring off *v* = **accomplish**, achieve, carry off, execute, perform, pull off, succeed

bring up *v* **1** = **rear**, breed, develop, educate, form, nurture, raise, support, teach, train **2** = **mention**, allude to, broach, introduce, move, propose, put forward, raise

brink *n* = **edge**, border, boundary, brim, fringe, frontier, limit, lip, margin, rim, skirt, threshold, verge

brisk *adj* **1** = **lively**, active, bustling, busy, energetic, quick, sprightly, spry, vigorous

briskly *adv* **1** = **quickly**, actively, apace, energetically, promptly, rapidly, readily, smartly

bristle *n* **1** = **hair**, barb, prickle, spine, stubble, thorn, whisker ▷ *v* **2** = **stand up**, rise, stand on end **3** = **be angry**, bridle, flare up, rage, see red, seethe

bristly *adj* = **hairy**, prickly, rough, stubbly

brittle *adj* = **fragile**, breakable, crisp, crumbling, crumbly, delicate, frail, frangible, friable

broach *v* **1** = **bring up**, introduce, mention, open up, propose, raise the subject, speak of, suggest, talk of, touch on **2** = **open**, crack, draw off, pierce, puncture, start, tap, uncork

broad *adj* **1** = **wide**, ample, expansive, extensive, generous, large, roomy, spacious, vast, voluminous, widespread **3** = **general**, all-embracing, comprehensive, encyclopedic, inclusive, overarching, sweeping, wide, wide-ranging

broadcast *n* **1** = **transmission**, programme, show, telecast ▷ *v* **2** = **transmit**, air, beam, cable, put on the air, radio, relay, show, televise **3** = **make public**, advertise, announce, circulate, proclaim, publish, report, spread

broaden *v* = **expand**, develop, enlarge,

▷ v **2** transmit (a programme or announcement) on radio or television. **3** make widely known. **4** scatter (seed etc.). **broadcaster** n **broadcasting** n.

brocade n rich fabric woven with a raised design.

broccoli n type of cabbage with greenish flower heads.

- **SPELLING TIP**
- You might expect a word that
- sounds like **broccoli** to have two
- *l*s at the end, but it has only one
- because it comes from Italian and
- ends with an *i*.

brochure ❶ n booklet that contains information about a product or service.

broderie anglaise n open embroidery on white cotton etc.

broekies [**brook**-eez] *pl n S Afr informal* underpants.

brogue¹ n sturdy walking shoe.

brogue² n strong accent, esp. Irish.

broil *v Aust, NZ, US & Canad* same as GRILL. **broiler** n young tender chicken for roasting.

broke ❶ v **1** past tense of BREAK. ▷ *adj* **2** *informal* having no money.

broken ❶ v **1** past participle of BREAK. ▷ *adj* **2** fractured or smashed. **3** (of the speech of a foreigner) noticeably imperfect, e.g. *broken English*. **brokenhearted** *adj* overwhelmed by grief. **broken home** family where the parents are separated or divorced.

broker ❶ n agent who buys or sells goods, securities, etc. **brokerage** n commission charged by a broker.

brolga n large grey Australian crane with a trumpeting call (also **native companion**) .

brolly n, *pl* **-lies** *informal* umbrella.

bromide n **1** chemical compound used in medicine and photography. **2** boring or meaningless remark.

bromine n *Chemistry* dark red liquid element that gives off a pungent vapour.

bronchus [**bronk**-uss] n, *pl* **bronchi** [**bronk**-eye] either of the two branches of the windpipe. **bronchial** *adj* **bronchitis** n inflammation of the bronchi.

bronco n, *pl* **-cos** (in the US) wild or partially tamed pony.

brontosaurus n very large plant-eating four-footed dinosaur.

bronze ❶ n **1** alloy of copper and tin. **2** statue, medal, etc. made of bronze. ▷ *adj* **3** made of, or coloured like, bronze. ▷ v **4** (esp. of the skin) make or become brown. **Bronze Age** era when bronze tools and weapons were used. **bronze medal** medal awarded as third prize.

brooch n ornament with a pin, worn fastened to clothes.

brood ❶ n **1** number of birds produced at one hatching. **2** all the children of a family. ▷ v **3** (of a bird) sit on or hatch eggs. **4** think long and unhappily. **broody** *adj* **1** moody and sullen. **2** (of a hen) wishing to hatch eggs. **3** *informal* (of a woman) wishing to have a baby.

brook¹ ❶ n small stream.

brook² ❶ v bear or tolerate.

broom n **1** long-handled sweeping

THESAURUS

extend, increase, spread, stretch, supplement, swell, widen

broad-minded *adj* = **tolerant**, free-thinking, indulgent, liberal, open-minded, permissive, unbiased, unbigoted, unprejudiced

broadside n **1** = **attack**, assault, censure, criticism, denunciation, diatribe, swipe **2** *Naval* = **bombardment**

brochure n = **booklet**, advertisement, circular, folder, handbill, hand-out, leaflet, mailshot, pamphlet

broke *adj* **2** *Inf* = **penniless**, bankrupt, bust (*inf*), down and out, impoverished, insolvent, in the red, munted (*NZ sl*), ruined, short, skint (*Brit sl*)

broken *adj* **2** = **smashed**, burst, fractured, fragmented, ruptured,

separated, severed, shattered **3** = **imperfect**, disjointed, halting, hesitating, stammering

brokenhearted *adj* = **heartbroken**, desolate, devastated, disconsolate, grief-stricken, inconsolable, miserable, sorrowful, wretched

broker n = **dealer**, agent, factor, go-between, intermediary, middleman, negotiator

bronze *adj* **3** = **reddish-brown**, brownish, chestnut, copper, rust, tan

brood n **1** = **offspring**, clutch, family, issue, litter, progeny ▷ v **4** = **think upon**, agonize, dwell upon, mope, mull over, muse, obsess, ponder, ruminate

brook¹ n = **stream**, beck, burn, rill, rivulet, watercourse

brook² v = **tolerate**, abide, accept, allow,

b

brush. **2** yellow-flowered shrub.
broomstick n handle of a broom.
bros., Bros. brothers.
broth n soup, usu. containing
vegetables.
brothel n house where men pay to have
sex with prostitutes.
brother ❶ n **1** boy or man with the same
parents as another person. **2** close
friend or comrade. **3** member of a male
religious order. **brotherly** adj
brotherhood n **1** fellowship.
2 association, such as a trade union.
brother-in-law n, pl **brothers-in-law**
1 brother of one's husband or wife.
2 husband of one's sibling.
brought v past of BRING.
brouhaha n loud confused noise.
brow n **1** part of the face from the eyes
to the hairline. **2** eyebrow. **3** top of
a hill.
browbeat ❶ v frighten (someone) with
threats.
brown ❶ n **1** colour of earth or wood.
▷ adj **2** (of bread) made from
wheatmeal or wholemeal flour. **3** of
the colour brown. ▷ v **4** make or
become brown. **brownish** adj
browned-off adj informal bored and
depressed.
brownie n **1** elf said to do household
chores at night. **2** small square nutty
chocolate cake.

Brownie Guide, Brownie n junior
Guide. **Brownie point** credit for being
seen to do the right thing.
browse ❶ v **1** look through (a book or
articles for sale) in a casual manner.
2 nibble on young shoots or leaves. ▷ n
3 instance of browsing. **browser** n
Computers software package that
enables a user to read hypertext, esp .
on the internet.
brucellosis n infectious disease of
animals which can be transmitted to
humans.
bruise ❶ n **1** discoloured area on the skin
caused by an injury. ▷ v **2** cause a bruise
on. **bruiser** n strong tough person.
brumby n Aust **1** wild horse. **2** unruly
person.
brunch n informal breakfast and lunch
combined.
brunette n girl or woman with dark
brown hair.
brunt ❶ n main force or shock of a blow,
attack, etc.
brush¹ ❶ n **1** device made of bristles,
wires, etc. used for cleaning, painting,
etc. **2** brief unpleasant encounter.
3 fox's tail. ▷ v **4** clean, scrub, or paint
with a brush. **5** touch lightly and
briefly. **brush off** v slang dismiss or
ignore (someone). **brush up** v refresh
one's knowledge of (a subject).
brush² ❶ n thick growth of shrubs.

——————————————————— THESAURUS ———————————

bear, countenance, endure, hack (sl),
put up with (inf), stand, stomach,
suffer, support, swallow, thole (dial),
withstand
brother n **1** = **sibling**, blood brother, kin,
kinsman, relation, relative **3** = **monk**,
cleric, friar
brotherhood n **1** = **fellowship**,
brotherliness, camaraderie,
companionship, comradeship,
friendliness, kinship **2** = **association**,
alliance, community, fraternity, guild,
league, order, society, union
brotherly adj = **kind**, affectionate,
altruistic, amicable, benevolent,
cordial, fraternal, friendly, neighbourly,
philanthropic, sympathetic
browbeat v = **bully**, badger, coerce,
dragoon, hector, intimidate, ride
roughshod over, threaten, tyrannize
brown adj **3** = **brunette**, auburn, bay,
bronze, chestnut, chocolate, coffee,
dun, hazel, sunburnt, tan, tanned,
tawny, umber ▷ v **4** = **fry**, cook, grill,

sauté, seal, sear
browse v **1** = **skim**, dip into, examine
cursorily, flip through, glance at, leaf
through, look round, look through,
peruse, scan, survey **2** = **graze**, eat,
feed, nibble
bruise n **1** = **discoloration**, black mark,
blemish, contusion, injury, mark,
swelling ▷ v **2** = **discolour**, damage,
injure, mar, mark, pound
brunt n = **full force**, burden, force,
impact, pressure, shock, strain, stress,
thrust, violence
brush¹ n **1** = **broom**, besom, sweeper
2 = **encounter**, clash, conflict,
confrontation, skirmish, tussle ▷ v
4 = **clean**, buff, paint, polish, sweep,
wash **5** = **touch**, flick, glance, graze,
kiss, scrape, stroke, sweep
brush² n = **shrubs**, brushwood, bushes,
copse, scrub, thicket, undergrowth
brush off v Sl = **ignore**, disdain, dismiss,
disregard, reject, repudiate, scorn,
snub, spurn

b

brushwood *n* cut or broken-off tree branches and twigs.

brush turkey *n* bird of New Guinea and Australia resembling the domestic fowl, with black plumage.

brusque ❶ *adj* blunt or curt in manner or speech. **brusquely** *adv* **brusqueness** *n*.

Brussels sprout *n* vegetable like a tiny cabbage.

brute ❶ *n* **1** brutal person. **2** animal other than man. ▷ *adj* **3** wholly instinctive or physical, like an animal. **4** without reason. **brutish** *adj* of or like an animal. **brutal** *adj* **1** cruel and vicious. **2** extremely honest in speech or manner. **brutally** *adv* **brutality** *n* **brutalize** *v*.

bryony *n* wild climbing hedge plant.

BSc Bachelor of Science.

BSE bovine spongiform encephalopathy: fatal virus disease of cattle.

BSI British Standards Institution.

BST British Summer Time.

Bt Baronet.

bubble ❶ *n* **1** ball of air in a liquid or solid. **2** thin film of liquid forming a ball around air or a gas. **3** transparent dome. **4** something initially very pleasing or successful which suddenly disappears or goes wrong. ▷ *v* **5** form bubbles. **6** move or flow with a gurgling sound. **bubbly** *adj* **-blier**, **-bliest 1** excited and lively. **2** full of bubbles. ▷ *n* **3** *informal* champagne. **bubble over** *v* express an emotion freely.

bubonic plague [bew-**bonn**-ik] *n* acute infectious disease characterized by swellings.

buccaneer ❶ *n* pirate.

buck¹ *n* **1** male of the goat, hare, kangaroo, rabbit, and reindeer. ▷ *v* **2** (of a horse etc.) jump with legs stiff and back arched. **3** *informal* resist or oppose obstinately, e.g. *to buck a trend*. **buckshot** *n* large lead pellets used for shooting game. **buck up** *v* make or become more cheerful.

buck² *n* US, Canad & Aust slang dollar.

buck³ *n* **pass the buck** *informal* shift blame or responsibility onto someone else.

bucket *n* **1** open-topped round container with a handle. ▷ *v* **-eting**, **-eted 2** (also **bucket down**) rain heavily **kick the bucket** *slang* die. **bucketful** *n*.

buckle ❶ *n* **1** clasp for fastening a belt or strap. ▷ *v* **2** fasten or be fastened with a buckle. **3** (cause to) bend out of shape through pressure or heat. **buckle down** *v informal* apply oneself with determination.

buckshee *adj slang* free.

buckteeth *pl n* projecting upper front teeth. **buck-toothed** *adj*.

buckwheat *n* small black grain used for making flour.

bucolic [bew-**koll**-ik] *adj* of the countryside or country life.

bud ❶ *n* **1** swelling on a tree or plant that develops into a leaf or flower. **2** partially opened flower. ▷ *v* **budding**,

---

brush up *v* = **revise**, bone up (*inf*), cram, go over, polish up, read up, refresh one's memory, relearn, study

brusque *adj* = **curt**, abrupt, discourteous, gruff, impolite, sharp, short, surly, terse

brutal *adj* **1** = **cruel**, bloodthirsty, heartless, inhuman, ruthless, savage, uncivilized, vicious **2** = **harsh**, callous, gruff, impolite, insensitive, rough, rude, severe

brutality *n* **1** = **cruelty**, atrocity, barbarism, bloodthirstiness, ferocity, inhumanity, ruthlessness, savagery, viciousness

brute *n* **1** = **savage**, barbarian, beast, devil, fiend, monster, sadist, swine **2** = **animal**, beast, creature, wild animal ▷ *adj* **3** = **physical**, bodily, carnal, fleshly **4** = **mindless**, instinctive, senseless, unthinking

bubble *n* **1, 2** = **air ball**, bead, blister, blob, drop, droplet, globule ▷ *v* **5** = **foam**, boil, effervesce, fizz, froth, percolate, seethe, sparkle **6** = **gurgle**, babble, burble, murmur, ripple, trickle

bubbly *adj* **1** = **lively**, animated, bouncy, elated, excited, happy, merry, sparky **2** = **frothy**, carbonated, effervescent, fizzy, foamy, sparkling

buccaneer *n* = **pirate**, corsair, freebooter, privateer, sea-rover

buckle *n* **1** = **fastener**, catch, clasp, clip, hasp ▷ *v* **2** = **fasten**, clasp, close, hook, secure **3** = **distort**, bend, bulge, cave in, collapse, contort, crumple, fold, twist, warp

bud *n* **1** = **shoot**, embryo, germ, sprout ▷ *v* **3** = **develop**, burgeon, burst forth, grow, shoot, sprout

budding *adj* = **developing**, beginning, burgeoning, embryonic, fledgling,

budded 3 produce buds. **budding** *adj* beginning to develop or grow, e.g. *a budding actor*.

Buddhism *n* eastern religion founded by Buddha. **Buddhist** *n*, *adj*.

buddleia *n* shrub with long spikes of purple flowers.

buddy *n*, *pl* **-dies** *informal* friend.

budge ❶ *v* **1** move slightly. **2** change (an opinion).

budgerigar *n* small cage bird bred in many different-coloured varieties.

budget ❶ *n* **1** financial plan for a period of time. **2** money allocated for a specific purpose. ▷ *v* **-eting, -eted 3** plan the expenditure of (money or time). ▷ *adj* **4** cheap. **the Budget** statement of government's financial plans for the coming year. **budgetary** *adj*.

- **SPELLING TIP**
- A lot of verbs ending in *et* have two
- *t*s when you add an ending like *-ing*,
- but **budget** is not one of them:
- **budgeting** and **budgeted** have a
- single *t*.

budgie *n* *informal* short for BUDGERIGAR.

buff¹ ❶ *n* **1** soft flexible undyed leather. ▷ *adj* **2** dull yellowish-brown. ▷ *v* **3** clean or polish with soft material. **in the buff** *informal* naked.

buff² ❶ *n* *informal* expert on or devotee of a given subject.

buffalo *n* **1** type of cattle. **2** US bison.

buffer¹ ❶ *n* something that lessens shock or protects from damaging impact, circumstances, etc. **buffer**

state small state between two rival powers.

buffer² *n* *Brit informal* stupid or bumbling man.

buffet¹ ❶ [**boof**-ay] *n* **1** counter where drinks and snacks are served. **2** meal at which guests serve themselves from a range of dishes.

buffet² ❶ [**buff**-it] *v* **-feting, -feted 1** knock against or about. **2** hit, esp. with the fist. ▷ *n* **3** blow, esp. with the hand.

buffoon ❶ *n* clown or fool. **buffoonery** *n*.

bug ❶ *n* **1** small insect. **2** *informal* minor illness. **3** small mistake in a computer program. **4** concealed microphone. ▷ *v* **bugging, bugged 5** *informal* irritate (someone). **6** conceal a microphone in (a room or phone).

bugbear ❶ *n* thing that causes obsessive anxiety.

bugger *n* **1** *taboo slang* unpleasant or difficult person or thing. **2** *slang* any person, e.g. *poor old bugger*. **3** person who practises buggery. ▷ *v* **4** *slang* tire. **5** practise buggery with. **bugger off** *v* *taboo slang* go away. **buggery** *n* anal intercourse.

buggy *n*, *pl* **-gies 1** light horse-drawn carriage having two or four wheels. **2** lightweight folding pram.

bugle *n* instrument like a small trumpet. **bugler** *n*.

build ❶ *v* **building, built 1** make, construct, or form by joining parts or materials. **2** establish and develop. ▷ *n*

───────────────── THESAURUS ─────────────

growing, incipient, nascent, potential, promising

budge *v* **1** = **move**, dislodge, push, shift, stir

budget *n* **2** = **allowance**, allocation, cost, finances, funds, means, resources ▷ *v* **3** = **plan**, allocate, apportion, cost, estimate, ration

buff¹ *adj* **2** = **yellowish-brown**, sandy, straw, tan, yellowish ▷ *v* **3** = **polish**, brush, burnish, rub, shine, smooth

buff² *n Inf* = **expert**, addict, admirer, aficionado, connoisseur, devotee, enthusiast, fan, fundi (*S Afr*)

buffer¹ *n* = **safeguard**, bulwark, bumper, cushion, fender, intermediary, screen, shield, shock absorber

buffet¹ *n* **1** = **snack bar**, brasserie, café, cafeteria, refreshment counter, sideboard

buffet² *v* **1, 2** = **batter**, beat, bump, knock, pound, pummel, strike, thump, wallop (*inf*)

buffoon *n* = **clown**, comedian, comic, fool, harlequin, jester, joker, wag

bug *n* **2** *Inf* = **illness**, disease, infection, virus **3** = **fault**, defect, error, flaw, glitch, gremlin ▷ *v* **5** *Inf* = **annoy**, bother, disturb, get on one's nerves (*inf*), hassle (*inf*), irritate, pester, vex **6** = **tap**, eavesdrop, listen in, spy

bugbear *n* = **pet hate**, bane, bête noire, bogey, dread, horror, nightmare

build *v* **1** = **construct**, assemble, erect, fabricate, form, make, put up, raise ▷ *n* **3** = **physique**, body, figure, form, frame, shape, structure

building *n* = **structure**, domicile, dwelling, edifice, house

build-up *n* = **increase**, accumulation,

3 shape of the body. **builder** n **building** n structure with walls and a roof.
building society organization where money can be borrowed or invested.
build-up n gradual increase. **build up** v construct or establish gradually.
built ⊕ v past of BUILD. **built-in** adj incorporated as an integral part. **built-up** adj having many buildings.
bulb ⊕ n **1** same as LIGHT BULB. **2** onion-shaped root which grows into a flower or plant. **bulbous** adj round and fat.
bulge ⊕ n **1** swelling on a normally flat surface. **2** sudden increase in number. ▷ v **3** swell outwards. **bulging** adj.
bulimia n disorder characterized by compulsive overeating followed by vomiting. **bulimic** adj, n.
bulk ⊕ n **1** size or volume, esp. when great. **2** main part. ▷ v **3 bulk large** be or seem important. **in bulk** in large quantities. **bulky** adj.
bulkhead n partition in a ship or aeroplane.
bull¹ ⊕ n male of some animals, such as cattle, elephants, and whales. **bullock** n castrated bull. **bulldog** n thickset dog with a broad head and a muscular body. **bulldozer** n powerful tractor for moving earth. **bulldoze** v **1** demolish or flatten with a bulldozer. **2** informal achieve (something) or persuade (someone) by intimidation, e.g. the new law was bulldozed through parliament. **bullfight** n public show in which a matador kills a bull. **bullfinch** n common European songbird. **bullfrog**

n large American frog with a deep croak. **bull's-eye** n central disc of a target. **bull terrier** terrier with a short smooth coat.
bull² n informal complete nonsense.
bull³ n papal decree.
bullet ⊕ n small piece of metal fired from a gun.
bulletin ⊕ n short official report or announcement.
bullion n gold or silver in the form of bars.
bully ⊕ n, pl **-lies 1** person who hurts, persecutes, or intimidates a weaker person. ▷ v **-lying, -lied 2** hurt, intimidate, or persecute (a weaker person).
bully beef n canned corned beef.
bully-off n Hockey method of restarting play in which opposing players strike their sticks together before trying to hit the ball. **bully off** v Hockey restart play with a bully-off.
bulrush n tall stiff reed.
bulwark ⊕ n **1** wall used as a fortification. **2** person or thing acting as a defence.
bum¹ n slang buttocks or anus. **bumbag** n small bag attached to a belt and worn round the waist.
bum² informal ▷ n **1** disreputable idler. **2** US tramp or hobo. ▷ v **bumming, bummed 3** get by begging. ▷ adj **4** of poor quality.
bumble ⊕ v speak, do, or move in a clumsy way. **bumbling** adj, n.
bumblebee n large hairy bee.

development, enlargement, escalation, expansion, gain, growth
bulbous adj = **bulging**, bloated, convex, rounded, swelling, swollen
bulge n **1** = **swelling**, bump, hump, lump, projection, protrusion, protuberance **2** = **increase**, boost, intensification, rise, surge ▷ v **3** = **swell out**, dilate, distend, expand, project, protrude, puff out, stick out
bulk n **1** = **size**, dimensions, immensity, largeness, magnitude, substance, volume, weight **2** = **main part**, better part, body, lion's share, majority, mass, most, nearly all, preponderance
bulky adj **1** = **large**, big, cumbersome, heavy, hulking, massive, substantial, unwieldy, voluminous, weighty
bulldoze v **1** = **demolish**, flatten, level, raze

bullet n = **projectile**, ball, missile, pellet, shot, slug
bulletin n = **announcement**, account, communication, communiqué, dispatch, message, news flash, notification, report, statement
bully n **1** = **persecutor**, browbeater, bully boy, coercer, cyberbully, intimidator, oppressor, ruffian, tormentor, tough ▷ v **2** = **persecute**, browbeat, coerce, domineer, hector, intimidate, oppress, push around (sl), terrorize, tyrannize
bulwark n **1** = **fortification**, bastion, buttress, defence, embankment, partition, rampart **2** = **defence**, buffer, guard, mainstay, safeguard, security, support
bumbling adj = **clumsy**, awkward, blundering, bungling, incompetent, inefficient, inept, maladroit, muddled

b

bumf, bumph *n informal* official documents or forms.

bump ❶ *v* **1** knock or strike with a jolt. **2** travel in jerks and jolts. ▷ *n* **3** dull thud from an impact or collision. **4** lump on the body caused by a blow. **5** raised uneven part. **bumpy** *adj* **bumpier**, **bumpiest**. **bump into** *v informal* meet (someone) by chance. **bump off** *v informal* murder.

bumper¹ *n* bar on the front and back of a vehicle to protect against damage.

bumper² ❶ *n* **1** glass filled to the brim. ▷ *adj* **2** unusually large or abundant.

bumph *n* same as BUMF.

bumpkin ❶ *n* awkward simple country person.

bumptious ❶ *adj* offensively self-assertive.

bun *n* **1** small sweet bread roll or cake. **2** hair gathered into a bun shape at the back of the head.

bunch ❶ *n* **1** number of things growing, fastened, or grouped together. **2** group, e.g. *a bunch of cowards*. ▷ *v* **3** group or be grouped together in a bunch.

bundle ❶ *n* **1** number of things gathered loosely together. ▷ *v* **2** cause to go roughly or unceremoniously. **bundle up** *v* make into a bundle.

bung *n* **1** stopper for a cask etc. ▷ *v* **2** (foll. by *up*) *informal* close with a bung. **3** *slang* throw (something) somewhere

in a careless manner.

bungalow *n* one-storey house.

bungee jumping, bungy jumping *n* sport of leaping from a high bridge, tower, etc., to which one is connected by a rubber rope.

bungle ❶ *v* **1** spoil through incompetence. ▷ *n* **2** blunder or muddle. **bungler** *n* **bungling** *adj, n*.

bunion *n* inflamed swelling on the big toe.

bunk¹ *n* narrow shelflike bed. **bunk bed** one of a pair of beds constructed one above the other.

bunk² ❶ *n* same as BUNKUM.

bunk³ *n* **do a bunk** *slang* make a hurried and secret departure.

bunker *n* **1** sand-filled hollow forming an obstacle on a golf course. **2** underground shelter. **3** large storage container for coal etc.

bunkum *n* nonsense.

bunny *n, pl* **-nies** child's word for a rabbit.

Bunsen burner *n* gas burner used in laboratories.

bunting¹ *n* decorative flags.

bunting² *n* songbird with a short stout bill.

bunya *n* tall dome-shaped Australian coniferous tree (also **bunya-bunya**).

bunyip *n Aust* legendary monster said to live in swamps and lakes.

buoy ❶ *n* **1** floating marker anchored in

——————————— THESAURUS ———————————

bump *v* **1** = **knock**, bang, collide (with), crash, hit, slam, smash into, strike **2** = **jerk**, bounce, jolt, rattle, shake ▷ *n* **3** = **knock**, bang, blow, collision, crash, impact, jolt, thud, thump **4** = **lump**, bulge, contusion, hump, nodule, protuberance, swelling

bumper² *adj* **2** = **exceptional**, abundant, bountiful, excellent, jumbo (*inf*), massive, whopping (*inf*)

bumpkin *n* = **yokel**, country bumpkin, hick (*inf, chiefly US & Canad*), hillbilly, peasant, rustic

bumptious *adj* = **cocky**, arrogant, brash, conceited, forward, full of oneself, overconfident, pushy (*inf*), self-assertive

bumpy *adj* = **rough**, bouncy, choppy, jarring, jerky, jolting, rutted, uneven

bunch *n* **1** = **number**, assortment, batch, bundle, clump, cluster, collection, heap, lot, mass, pile **2** = **group**, band, crowd, flock, gang,

gathering, party, team ▷ *v* **3** = **group**, assemble, bundle, cluster, collect, huddle, mass, pack

bundle *n* **1** = **bunch**, assortment, batch, collection, group, heap, mass, pile, stack ▷ *v* **2** = **push**, hurry, hustle, rush, shove, thrust

bundle up *v* = **wrap up**, swathe

bungle *v* **1** = **mess up**, blow (*sl*), blunder, botch, foul up, make a mess of, muff, ruin, spoil

bungling *adj* = **incompetent**, blundering, cack-handed (*inf*), clumsy, ham-fisted (*inf*), inept, maladroit

bunk² same as BUNKUM.

bunkum *n* = **nonsense**, balderdash, baloney (*inf*), garbage (*inf*), hogwash, hot air (*inf*), kak (*S Afr sl*), moonshine, poppycock (*inf*), rubbish, stuff and nonsense, twaddle

buoy *n* **1** = **marker**, beacon, float, guide, signal ▷ *v* **3** = **encourage**, boost, cheer, cheer up, hearten, lift,

b

the sea. ▷ v **2** prevent from sinking.
3 encourage or hearten. **buoyant** adj
1 able to float. **2** cheerful or resilient.
buoyancy n.

bur n same as BURR¹.

burble v **1** make a bubbling sound. **2** talk
quickly and excitedly. ▷ n **3** bubbling or
gurgling sound. **4** flow of excited
speech. **5** turbulence in the flow of air.

burden¹ ❶ n **1** heavy load. **2** something
difficult to cope with. ▷ v **3** put a burden
on. **4** oppress. **burdensome** adj.

burden² n **1** theme of a speech etc.
2 chorus of a song.

burdock n weed with prickly burrs.

bureau ❶ n, pl **-reaus, -reaux 1** office
that provides a service. **2** writing desk
with shelves and drawers.

bureaucracy ❶ n, pl **-cies**
1 administrative system based on
complex rules and procedures.
2 excessive adherence to complex
procedures. **bureaucrat** n
bureaucratic adj.

burette n glass tube for dispensing
known volumes of fluids.

burgeon v develop or grow rapidly.

burger n informal hamburger.

burgess n citizen or freeman of a
borough.

burgh n Scottish borough. **burgher** n
citizen.

burglar ❶ n person who enters a
building to commit a crime, esp. theft.
burglary n, pl **-ries. burgle** v.

Burgundy n type of French wine.

burgundy adj dark-purplish red.

burial ❶ n burying of a dead body.

burka n same as BURQA.

burlesque ❶ n **1** artistic work which
satirizes a subject by caricature.
2 bawdy comedy show of the late 19th
and early 20th centuries. ▷ v **3** satirize a
subject by caricature.

burly ❶ adj **-lier, -liest** (of a person)
broad and strong.

burn¹ ❶ v **burning, burnt** or **burned 1** be
or set on fire. **2** destroy or be destroyed
by fire. **3** damage, injure, or mark by
heat. **4** feel strong emotion. **5** to record
data on (a compact disc). ▷ n **6** injury
or mark caused by fire or exposure to
heat. **burner** n part of a stove or lamp
that produces the flame. **burning** adj
1 intense. **2** urgent or crucial.

burn² n Scot small stream.

burnish ❶ v make smooth and shiny by
rubbing.

burnous n long circular cloak with a
hood, worn esp. by Arabs.

————— THESAURUS —————

raise, support, sustain

buoyant adj **1** = **floating**, afloat, light,
weightless **2** = **cheerful**, carefree,
chirpy (inf), happy, jaunty, light-
hearted, upbeat (inf)

burden¹ n **1** = **load**, encumbrance,
weight **2** = **trouble**, affliction,
millstone, onus, responsibility, strain,
weight, worry ▷ v **3** = **weigh down**,
bother, encumber, handicap, load,
oppress, saddle with, tax, worry

bureau n **1** = **office**, agency, branch,
department, division, service **2** = **desk**,
writing desk

bureaucracy n **1** = **government**,
administration, authorities, civil
service, corridors of power, officials, the
system **2** = **red tape**, officialdom,
regulations

bureaucrat n **1** = **official**,
administrator, civil servant,
functionary, mandarin, officer, public
servant

burglar n = **housebreaker**, cat burglar,
filcher, pilferer, robber, sneak thief, thief

burglary n = **breaking and entering**,
break-in, housebreaking, larceny,

robbery, stealing, theft, thieving

burial n = **interment**, funeral

buried adj **1** = **interred**, entombed, laid
to rest **3** = **hidden**, concealed, private,
sequestered, tucked away

burlesque n = **parody**, caricature,
mockery, satire, send-up (Brit inf),
spoof (inf), takeoff (inf), travesty

burly adj = **brawny**, beefy (inf), bulky,
hefty, stocky, stout, sturdy, thickset,
well-built

burn¹ v **1** = **be on fire**, be ablaze,
blaze, flame, flare, glow, go up in
flames, smoke **3** = **set on fire**, char,
ignite, incinerate, kindle, light, parch,
scorch, sear, singe, toast **4** = **be
passionate**, be angry, be aroused, be
inflamed, fume, seethe, simmer,
smoulder

burning adj **1** = **intense**, ardent, eager,
fervent, impassioned, passionate,
vehement **2** = **crucial**, acute,
compelling, critical, essential,
important, pressing, significant,
urgent, vital

burnish v = **polish**, brighten, buff,
furbish, glaze, rub up, shine, smooth

burnt v a past of BURN¹.

burp v, n informal belch.

burqa, burka n long enveloping garment worn by some Muslim women.

burr¹ n head of a plant with prickles or hooks.

burr² n **1** soft trilling sound given to the letter r in some dialects. **2** whirring sound. **3** rough edge left after cutting.

burrawang n Australian plant with fernlike leaves and an edible nut.

burrow ❶ n **1** hole dug in the ground by a rabbit etc. ▷ v **2** dig holes in the ground. **3** delve deeply, e.g. *he burrowed into his coat pocket*.

bursar n treasurer of a school, college, or university. **bursary** n, pl **-ries** scholarship.

burst ❶ v **bursting, burst 1** (cause to) break open or apart noisily and suddenly. **2** come or go suddenly and forcibly. **3** be full to the point of breaking open. ▷ n **4** instance of breaking open suddenly. **5** sudden outbreak or occurrence. **burst into** v give vent to (an emotion) suddenly.

bury ❶ v **burying, buried 1** place in a grave. **2** place in the earth and cover with soil. **3** conceal or hide. **4** occupy (oneself) with deep concentration.

bus n **1** large motor vehicle for carrying passengers. ▷ v **bussing, bussed 2** travel or transport by bus.

busby n, pl **-bies** tall fur hat worn by some soldiers.

bush ❶ n **1** dense woody plant, smaller than a tree. **2** wild uncultivated part of a country. **bushy** adj **bushier, bushiest** (of hair) thick and shaggy. **bushbaby** n small African tree-living mammal with large eyes. **Bushman** n member of a hunting and gathering people of Southern Africa. **bush telegraph** means of spreading gossip.

bushel n obsolete unit of measure equal to 8 gallons.

business ❶ n **1** purchase and sale of goods and services. **2** commercial establishment. **3** trade or profession. **4** proper concern or responsibility. **5** affair, e.g. *it's a dreadful business*. **businesslike** adj efficient and methodical. **businessman, businesswoman** n.

busker n street entertainer. **busk** v act as a busker.

bust¹ ❶ n **1** woman's bosom. **2** sculpture of the head and shoulders.

bust² ❶ informal ▷ v **busting, bust** or **busted 1** burst or break. **2** (of the police) raid (a place) or arrest (someone). ▷ adj **3** broken. **go bust** become bankrupt. **bust-up** n informal **1** serious quarrel. **2** brawl or disturbance.

———————————————————————————— THESAURUS

burrow n **1** = **hole**, den, lair, retreat, shelter, tunnel ▷ v **2** = **dig**, delve, excavate, hollow out, scoop out, tunnel

burst v **1** = **explode**, blow up, break, crack, puncture, rupture, shatter, split, tear apart **2** = **rush**, barge, break, break out, erupt, gush forth, run, spout ▷ n **4** = **explosion**, bang, blast, blowout, break, crack, discharge, rupture, split **5** = **rush**, gush, gust, outbreak, outburst, outpouring, spate, spurt, surge, torrent

bury v **1** = **inter**, consign to the grave, entomb, inhume, lay to rest **2** = **embed**, engulf, submerge **3** = **hide**, conceal, cover, enshroud, secrete, stow away

bush n **1** = **shrub**, hedge, plant, shrubbery, thicket **2** = **the wild**, backwoods, brush, scrub, scrubland, woodland

bushy adj = **thick**, bristling, fluffy, fuzzy, luxuriant, rough, shaggy, unruly

business n **1** = **trade**, bargaining, commerce, dealings, industry, manufacturing, selling, transaction **2** = **establishment**, company, concern, corporation, enterprise, firm, organization, venture **3** = **profession**, career, employment, function, job, line, occupation, trade, vocation, work, yakka (*Aust & NZ inf*) **4** = **concern**, affair, assignment, duty, pigeon (*inf*), problem, responsibility, task

businesslike adj = **efficient**, methodical, orderly, organized, practical, professional, systematic, thorough, well-ordered

businessman n = **executive**, capitalist, employer, entrepreneur, financier, industrialist, merchant, tradesman, tycoon

bust¹ n = **bosom**, breast, chest, front, torso

bust² *Inf* v **1** = **break**, burst, fracture, rupture **2** = **arrest**, catch, fossick (*Aust & NZ*), raid, search **go bust** = **go bankrupt**, become insolvent, be ruined, fail

bustard *n* bird with long strong legs, a heavy body, a long neck, and speckled plumage.

bustle[1] ⓿ *v* 1 hurry with a show of activity or energy. ▷ *n* 2 energetic and noisy activity. **bustling** *adj*.

bustle[2] *n* cushion or framework formerly worn under the back of a woman's skirt to hold it out.

busy ⓿ *adj* **busier**, **busiest** 1 actively employed. 2 crowded or full of activity. ▷ *v* **busying**, **busied** 3 keep (someone, esp. oneself) busy. **busily** *adv* **busybody** *n* meddlesome or nosy person.

but ⓿ *conj* 1 contrary to expectation. 2 in contrast. 3 other than. 4 without it happening. ▷ *prep* 5 except. ▷ *adv* 6 only. **but for** were it not for.

butane [**bew**-tane] *n* gas used for fuel.

butch *adj slang* markedly or aggressively masculine.

butcher ⓿ *n* 1 person who slaughters animals or sells their meat. 2 brutal murderer. ▷ *v* 3 kill and prepare (animals) for meat. 4 kill (people) brutally or indiscriminately. 5 make a mess of. **butcherbird** *n* Australian magpie that impales its prey on thorns. **butchery** *n*.

butler *n* chief male servant.

butt[1] ⓿ *n* 1 thicker end of something. 2 unused end of a cigar or cigarette. 3 *Chiefly US & Canad slang* buttocks.

butt[2] ⓿ *n* 1 person or thing that is the target of ridicule. 2 mound of earth behind a target. ▷ *pl* 3 target range.

butt[3] ⓿ *v* 1 strike with the head or horns. ▷ *n* 2 blow with the head or horns. **butt in** *v* interrupt a conversation.

butt[4] ⓿ *n* large cask.

butter *n* 1 edible fatty solid made by churning cream. ▷ *v* 2 put butter on. **buttery** *adj* **butter up** *v* flatter.

butter bean *n* large pale flat edible bean.

buttercup *n* small yellow flower.

butterfingers *n informal* person who drops things by mistake.

butterfly *n* 1 insect with brightly coloured wings. 2 swimming stroke in which both arms move together in a forward circular action.

buttermilk *n* sourish milk that remains after the butter has been separated from milk.

butterscotch *n* kind of hard brittle toffee.

buttock *n* either of the two fleshy masses that form the human rump.

button *n* 1 small disc or knob sewn to clothing, which can be passed through a slit in another piece of fabric to fasten them. 2 knob that operates a piece of equipment when pressed. ▷ *v* 3 fasten with buttons. **buttonhole** *n* 1 slit in a garment through which a button is passed. 2 flower worn on a lapel. ▷ *v* 3 detain (someone) in conversation.

buttress ⓿ *n* 1 structure to support a wall. ▷ *v* 2 support with, or as if with, a buttress.

THESAURUS

bustle[1] *v* 1 = **hurry**, fuss, hasten, rush, scamper, scurry, scuttle ▷ *n* 2 = **activity**, ado, commotion, excitement, flurry, fuss, hurly-burly, stir, to-do

busy *adj* 1 = **occupied**, active, employed, engaged, hard at work, industrious, on duty, rushed off one's feet, working 2 = **lively**, energetic, exacting, full, hectic, hustling ▷ *v* 3 = **occupy**, absorb, employ, engage, engross, immerse, interest

busybody *n* = **nosy parker** (*inf*), gossip, meddler, snooper, stirrer (*inf*), troublemaker, tattletale (*chiefly US & Canad*)

but *conj* 1 = **however**, further, moreover, nevertheless, on the contrary, on the other hand, still, yet ▷ *prep* 5 = **except**, bar, barring, excepting, excluding, notwithstanding, save, with the exception of ▷ *adv* 6 = **only**, just, merely, simply, singly, solely

butcher *n* 2 = **murderer**, destroyer, killer, slaughterer, slayer ▷ *v* 3 = **slaughter**, carve, clean, cut, cut up, dress, joint, prepare 4 = **kill**, assassinate, cut down, destroy, exterminate, liquidate, massacre, put to the sword, slaughter, slay

butt[1] *n* 1 = **end**, haft, handle, hilt, shaft, shank, stock 2 = **stub**, fag end (*inf*), leftover, tip

butt[2] *n* 1 = **target**, Aunt Sally, dupe, laughing stock, victim

butt[3] *v* 1 = **knock**, bump, poke, prod, push, ram, shove, thrust ▷ *n* 2 = **knock**, bump, poke, prod, push, ram, shove, thrust

butt[4] *n* = **cask**, barrel

butt in *v* = **interfere**, chip in (*inf*), cut in, interrupt, intrude, meddle, put one's oar in, stick one's nose in

buttress *n* 1 = **support**, brace, mainstay, prop, reinforcement, stanchion, strut ▷ *v* 2 = **support**, back up, bolster, prop

b

buxom ❶ *adj* (of a woman) healthily plump and full-bosomed.

buy ❶ *v* **buying, bought 1** acquire by paying money for. **2** be capable of purchasing, e.g. *money can't buy love*. **3** acquire by any exchange or sacrifice. **4** *slang* accept as true. **5** bribe. ▷ *n* **6** thing acquired through payment. **buyer** *n* **1** customer. **2** person employed to buy merchandise.

- **USAGE NOTE**
- Be careful not to confuse the past
- forms *bought* (from *buy*) with *brought*
- (from *bring*).

buzz *n* **1** rapidly vibrating humming sound. **2** *informal* telephone call. **3** *informal* sense of excitement. ▷ *v* **4** make a humming sound. **5** be filled with an air of excitement. **6** *informal* fly an aircraft very low over. **buzzer** *n* **buzz around** *v* move around quickly and busily. **buzz word** jargon word which becomes fashionably popular.

buzzard *n* bird of prey of the hawk family.

by ❶ *prep* **1** indicating the doer of an action, nearness, movement past, time before or during which, etc. e.g. *bitten by a dog; down by the river; driving by the school; in bed by midnight*. ▷ *adv* **2** near. **3** past. **by and by** eventually. **by and large** in general.

bye¹ *n* **1** *Sport* situation where a player or team wins a round by having no opponent. **2** *Cricket* run scored off a ball not touched by the batsman.

bye², bye-bye *interj informal* goodbye.

by-election *n* election held during parliament to fill a vacant seat.

bygone ❶ *adj* **1** past or former. ▷ *pl n* **2 let bygones be bygones** agree to forget past quarrels.

bylaw, bye-law *n* rule made by a local authority.

by-line *n* line under the title of a newspaper or magazine article giving the author's name.

bypass ❶ *n* **1** main road built to avoid a city. **2** operation to divert blood flow away from a damaged part of the heart. ▷ *v* **3** go round or avoid.

by-product *n* secondary or incidental product of a process.

byre *n* shelter for cows.

bystander ❶ *n* person present but not involved.

byte *n* *Computers* group of bits processed as one unit of data.

byway *n* minor road.

byword ❶ *n* person or thing regarded as a perfect example of something.

Byzantine *adj* **1** of Byzantium or the Byzantine Empire. **2** of the style of architecture developed in the Byzantine Empire. **3** complicated.

     THESAURUS

up, reinforce, shore up, strengthen, sustain, uphold

buxom *adj* = **plump**, ample, bosomy, busty, curvaceous, healthy, voluptuous, well-rounded

buy *v* **1** = **purchase**, acquire, get, invest in, obtain, pay for, procure, shop for ▷ *n* **6** = **purchase**, acquisition, bargain, deal

by *prep* **1 a** = **via**, by way of, over **b** = **through**, through the agency of **c** = **near**, along, beside, close to, next to, past ▷ *adv* **2** = **near**, at hand, close, handy, in reach

bygone *adj* **1** = **past**, antiquated, extinct, forgotten, former, lost, of old, olden

bypass *v* **3** = **go round**, avoid, circumvent, depart from, detour round, deviate from, get round, give a wide berth to, pass round

bystander *n* = **onlooker**, eyewitness, looker-on, observer, passer-by, spectator, viewer, watcher, witness

byword *n* = **saying**, adage, maxim, motto, precept, proverb, slogan

C 1 *Chemistry* carbon. 2 Celsius.
3 centigrade. 4 century. 5 the Roman
numeral for 100.

c. circa.

Ca *Chemistry* calcium.

CA 1 California. 2 Chartered
Accountant.

ca. circa.

cab ❶ *n* 1 taxi. 2 enclosed driver's
compartment on a train, lorry, etc.
cabbie, **cabby** *n*, *pl* **-bies** *informal* taxi
driver.

cabal ❶ [kab-**bal**] *n* 1 small group of
political plotters. 2 secret plot.

cabaret [**kab**-a-ray] *n* dancing and
singing show in a nightclub.

cabbage *n* 1 vegetable with a large
head of green leaves. 2 *informal* person
with no mental faculties.

caber *n* tree trunk tossed in competition
at Highland games.

cabin ❶ *n* 1 compartment in a ship or
aircraft. 2 small hut. **cabin boy** boy
who waits on the officers and
passengers of a ship. **cabin cruiser**
motorboat with a cabin.

cabinet ❶ *n* 1 piece of furniture with
drawers or shelves. 2 (**C-**) committee
of senior government ministers.
cabinet-maker *n* person who makes
fine furniture.

cable *n* 1 strong thick rope. 2 bundle of
wires that carries electricity or
electronic signals. 3 telegram sent
abroad. ▷ *v* 4 send (someone) a
message by cable. **cable car** vehicle
pulled up a steep slope by a moving

cable. **cable television** television
service conveyed by cable to
subscribers.

caboodle *n* **the whole
caboodle** *informal* the whole lot.

caboose *n US & Canad* guard's van on a
train.

cabriolet [kab-ree-oh-**lay**] *n* small
horse-drawn carriage with a folding
hood.

cacao [kak-**kah**-oh] *n* tropical tree with
seed pods from which chocolate and
cocoa are made.

cachalot *n* sperm whale.

cache [**kash**] *n* hidden store of weapons
or treasure.

cachet [**kash**-shay] *n* prestige,
distinction.

cachou *n* lozenge eaten to sweeten the
breath.

cack-handed *adj informal* clumsy.

cackle *v* 1 laugh shrilly. 2 (of a hen)
squawk with shrill broken notes. ▷ *n*
3 cackling noise.

cacophony [kak-**koff**-on-ee] *n* harsh
discordant sound. **cacophonous** *adj*.

cactus *n*, *pl* **-tuses**, **-ti** fleshy desert
plant with spines but no leaves.

cad ❶ *n old-fashioned* dishonourable
man. **caddish** *adj*.

cadaver [kad-**dav**-ver] *n* corpse.
cadaverous *adj* pale, thin, and
haggard.

caddie, caddy *n*, *pl* **-dies** 1 person who
carries a golfer's clubs. ▷ *v* **-dying**,
-died 2 act as a caddie.

caddis fly *n* insect whose larva (**caddis
worm**) lives underwater in a
protective case of sand and stones.

caddy *n*, *pl* **-dies** small container
for tea.

cadence [**kade**-enss] *n* 1 rise and fall in
the pitch of the voice. 2 close of a
musical phrase.

cadenza *n* complex solo passage in a
piece of music.

cadet *n* young person training for the

---

cab *n* 1 = **taxi**, hackney carriage,
minicab, taxicab

cabal *n* 1 = **clique**, caucus, conclave,
faction, league, party, set 2 = **plot**,
conspiracy, intrigue, machination,
scheme

cabin *n* 1 = **room**, berth, compartment,
quarters 2 = **hut**, chalet, cottage,
lodge, shack, shanty, shed

cabinet *n* 1 = **cupboard**, case,

chiffonier, closet, commode, dresser,
escritoire, locker 2 (usu. cap.)
= **council**, administration, assembly,
counsellors, ministry

cad *n Old-fashioned* = **scoundrel**,
bounder (*old-fashioned Brit sl*), heel (*sl*),
rat (*inf*), rotter (*sl*, *chiefly Brit*)

caddish *adj Old-fashioned*
= **ungentlemanly**, despicable,
ill-bred, low, unmannerly

armed forces or police.

cadge *v informal* get (something) by taking advantage of someone's generosity. **cadger** *n*.

cadi *n, pl* **-dis** judge in a Muslim community.

cadmium *n Chemistry* bluish-white metallic element used in alloys.

cadre [**kah**-der] *n* small group of people selected and trained to form the core of a political organization or military unit.

caecum [**seek**-um] *n, pl* **-ca** [-ka] pouch at the beginning of the large intestine.

Caerphilly *n* creamy white mild-flavoured cheese.

Caesarean section [see-**zair**-ee-an] *n* surgical incision into the womb to deliver a baby.

caesium *n Chemistry* silvery-white metallic element used in photocells.

caesura [siz-**your**-ra] *n, pl* **-ras**, **-rae** [-ree] pause in a line of verse.

café *n* **1** small or inexpensive restaurant serving light refreshments. **2** *S Afr* corner shop or grocer. **cafeteria** *n* self-service restaurant.

caffeine *n* stimulant found in tea and coffee.

caftan *n* same as KAFTAN.

cage ❶ *n* **1** enclosure of bars or wires, for keeping animals or birds. **2** enclosed platform of a lift in a mine. **caged** *adj* kept in a cage.

cagey ❶ *adj* **cagier**, **cagiest** *informal* reluctant to go into details. **cagily** *adv*.

cagoule [kag-**gool**] *n* lightweight hooded waterproof jacket.

cahoots *pl n* **in cahoots** *informal* conspiring together.

caiman *n* same as CAYMAN.

cairn *n* mound of stones erected as a memorial or marker.

cairngorm *n* yellow or brownish quartz gemstone.

caisson [**kay**-son] *n* watertight chamber used to carry out construction work under water.

cajole ❶ *v* persuade by flattery. **cajolery** *n*.

cake ❶ *n* **1** sweet food baked from a mixture of flour, eggs, etc. **2** flat compact mass of something, such as soap. ▷ *v* **3** form into a hardened mass or crust.

calabash *n* **1** type of large round gourd. **2** bowl made from this.

calamine *n* pink powder consisting chiefly of zinc oxide, used in skin lotions and ointments.

calamity ❶ *n, pl* **-ties** disaster. **calamitous** *adj*.

calciferol *n* substance found in fish oils and used to treat rickets.

calcify *v* **-fying**, **-fied** harden by the depositing of calcium salts. **calcification** *n*.

calcium *n Chemistry* silvery-white metallic element found in bones, teeth, limestone, and chalk.

calculate ❶ *v* **1** solve or find out by a mathematical procedure or by reasoning. **2** aim to have a particular effect. **calculable** *adj* **calculated** *adj* deliberate, premeditated. **calculating** *adj* selfishly scheming. **calculation** *n* **calculator** *n* small electronic device for making calculations.

calculus *n, pl* **-luses 1** branch of mathematics dealing with

---

café *n* = **snack bar**, brasserie, cafeteria, coffee bar, coffee shop, lunchroom, restaurant, tearoom

cage *n* **1** = **enclosure**, pen, pound

cagey *adj Inf* = **wary**, careful, cautious, chary, discreet, guarded, noncommittal, shrewd, wily

cajole *v* = **persuade**, coax, flatter, seduce, sweet-talk (*inf*), wheedle

cake *n* **2** = **block**, bar, cube, loaf, lump, mass, slab ▷ *v* **3** = **encrust**, bake, coagulate, congeal, solidify

calamitous *adj* = **disastrous**, cataclysmic, catastrophic, deadly, devastating, dire, fatal, ruinous, tragic

calamity *n* = **disaster**, cataclysm, catastrophe, misadventure,

misfortune, mishap, ruin, tragedy, tribulation

calculate *v* **1** = **work out**, compute, count, determine, enumerate, estimate, figure, reckon **2** = **plan**, aim, design, intend

calculated *adj* = **deliberate**, considered, intended, intentional, planned, premeditated, purposeful

calculating *adj* = **scheming**, crafty, cunning, devious, Machiavellian, manipulative, sharp, shrewd, sly

calculation 1 = **working out**, answer, computation, estimate, forecast, judgment, reckoning, result **2** = **planning**, contrivance, deliberation, discretion, foresight,

infinitesimal changes to a variable number or quantity. **2** *Pathology* hard deposit in kidney or bladder.

caldron *n* same as CAULDRON.

Caledonian *adj* Scottish.

calendar *n* **1** chart showing a year divided up into months, weeks, and days. **2** system for determining the beginning, length, and division of years. **3** schedule of events or appointments.

calender *n* machine in which paper or cloth is smoothed by passing it between rollers.

calends *pl n* first day of each month in the ancient Roman calendar.

calendula *n* marigold.

calf[1] *n, pl* **calves 1** young cow, bull, elephant, whale, or seal. **2** leather made from calf skin. **calve** *v* give birth to a calf. **calf love** adolescent infatuation.

calf[2] *n, pl* **calves** back of the leg between the ankle and knee.

calibre ❶ [**kal**-lib-ber] *n* **1** person's ability or worth. **2** diameter of the bore of a gun or of a shell or bullet. **calibrate** *v* mark the scale or check the accuracy of (a measuring instrument). **calibration** *n*.

calico *n, pl* **-coes, -cos** white cotton fabric.

californium *n Chemistry* radioactive element produced artificially.

caliph *n History* Muslim ruler.

call ❶ *v* **1** name. **2** shout to attract attention. **3** telephone. **4** summon. **5** (often foll. by *on*) visit. **6** arrange (a meeting, strike, etc.). ▷ *n* **7** cry, shout. **8** animal's or bird's cry. **9** telephone communication. **10** short visit. **11** summons, invitation. **12** need, demand. **caller** *n* **calling** *n* vocation, profession. **call box** kiosk for a public telephone. **call for** *v* require. **call girl** prostitute with whom appointments are made by telephone. **call off** *v* cancel. **call up** *v* **1** summon to serve in the armed forces. **2** cause one to remember.

calligraphy *n* (art of) beautiful handwriting. **calligrapher** *n*.

calliper *n* **1** metal splint for supporting the leg. **2** instrument for measuring diameters.

callisthenics *pl n* light keep-fit exercises. **callisthenic** *adj*.

callous ❶ *adj* showing no concern for other people's feelings. **calloused** *adj* (of skin) thickened and hardened. **callously** *adv* **callousness** *n*.

callow ❶ *adj* young and inexperienced.

callus *n, pl* **-luses** area of thick hardened skin.

calm ❶ *adj* **1** not agitated or excited. **2** not ruffled by the wind. **3** windless. ▷ *n* **4** peaceful state. ▷ *v* **5** (often foll. by *down*) make or become calm. **calmly** *adv* **calmness** *n*.

Calor Gas *n* ® butane gas liquefied under pressure in containers for domestic use.

forethought, precaution

calibre *n* **1** = **worth**, ability, capacity, distinction, merit, quality, stature, talent **2** = **diameter**, bore, gauge, measure

call *v* **1** = **name**, christen, describe as, designate, dub, entitle, label, style, term **2** = **cry**, arouse, hail, rouse, shout, yell **3** = **phone**, ring up (*inf, chiefly Brit*), telephone **4** = **summon**, assemble, convene, gather, muster, rally **5** (often foll. by *on*) = **visit**, drop in on, look in on, look up, see ▷ *n* **7** = **cry**, hail, scream, shout, signal, whoop, yell **11** = **summons**, appeal, command, demand, invitation, notice, order, plea, request **12** = **need**, cause, excuse, grounds, justification, occasion, reason

call for *v* = **require**, demand, entail, involve, necessitate, need, occasion, suggest

calling *n* = **profession**, career, life's work, mission, trade, vocation

callous *adj* = **heartless**, cold, hard-bitten, hardened, hardhearted, insensitive, uncaring, unfeeling

callow *adj* = **inexperienced**, green, guileless, immature, naive, raw, unsophisticated

calm *adj* **1** = **cool**, collected, composed, dispassionate, relaxed, sedate, self-possessed, unemotional **2, 3** = **still**, balmy, mild, quiet, serene, smooth, tranquil, windless ▷ **4** = **peacefulness**, hush, peace, quiet, repose, serenity, stillness ▷ *v* **5** (often foll. by *down*) = **quieten**, hush, mollify, outspan (*S Afr*), placate, relax, soothe

calmness *n* **1** = **coolness**, composure, cool (*sl*), equanimity, impassivity, poise, sang-froid, self-possession

calorie *n* **1** unit of measurement for the energy value of food. **2** unit of heat. **calorific** *adj* of calories or heat.

calumny *n, pl* **-nies** false or malicious statement. **calumniate** *v* make false or malicious statements about.

Calvary *n* place outside the walls of Jerusalem where Jesus was crucified.

calves *n* plural of CALF.

Calvinism *n* theological system of Calvin, stressing predestination and salvation solely by God's grace. **Calvinist** *n, adj* **Calvinistic** *adj*.

calypso *n, pl* **-sos** West Indian song with improvised topical lyrics.

calyx *n, pl* **calyxes**, **calyces** outer leaves that protect a flower bud.

cam *n* device that converts a circular motion to a to-and-fro motion. **camshaft** *n* part of an engine consisting of a rod to which cams are fixed.

camaraderie *n* comradeship.

camber *n* slight upward curve to the centre of a surface.

cambric *n* fine white linen fabric.

camcorder *n* combined portable video camera and recorder.

came *v* past tense of COME.

camel *n* humped mammal that can survive long periods without food or water in desert regions.

camellia [kam-**meal**-ya] *n* evergreen ornamental shrub with white, pink, or red flowers.

Camembert [**kam**-mem-bare] *n* soft creamy French cheese.

cameo *n, pl* **cameos** **1** brooch or ring with a profile head carved in relief. **2** small part in a film or play performed by a well-known actor or actress.

camera *n* apparatus used for taking photographs or pictures for television or cinema. **in camera** in private session. **cameraman** *n* man who operates a camera for television or cinema. **camera phone** mobile phone incorporating a camera.

camiknickers *pl n* woman's

undergarment consisting of knickers attached to a camisole.

camisole *n* woman's bodice-like garment.

camomile *n* aromatic plant, used to make herbal tea.

camouflage ① [kam-moo-flahzh] *n* **1** use of natural surroundings or artificial aids to conceal or disguise something. ▷ *v* **2** conceal by camouflage.

camp¹ ① *n* **1** (place for) temporary lodgings consisting of tents, huts, or cabins. **2** group supporting a particular doctrine. ▷ *v* **3** stay in a camp. **camper** *n* **camp follower** person who supports a particular group without being a member of it.

camp² ① *adj informal* **1** effeminate or homosexual. **2** consciously artificial or affected. **camp it up** *informal* behave in a camp way.

campaign ① *n* **1** series of coordinated activities designed to achieve a goal. **2** number of military operations aimed at achieving an objective. ▷ *v* **3** take part in a campaign.

campanile [camp-an-**neel**-lee] *n* bell tower, usu. one not attached to another building.

campanology *n* art of ringing bells. **campanologist** *n*.

campanula *n* plant with blue or white bell-shaped flowers.

camphor *n* aromatic crystalline substance used medicinally and in mothballs. **camphorated** *adj*.

campion *n* red, pink, or white wild flower.

campus *n, pl* **-puses** grounds of a university or college.

can¹ *v, past* **could** **1** be able to. **2** be allowed to.

can² *n* **1** metal container for food or liquids. ▷ *v* **canning**, **canned** **2** put (something) into a can. **canned** *adj* **1** preserved in a can. **2** (of music) prerecorded. **cannery** *n, pl* **-neries** factory where food is canned.

THESAURUS

4 = **peacefulness**, calm, hush, quiet, repose, restfulness, serenity, stillness, tranquillity

camouflage *n* **1** = **disguise**, blind, cloak, concealment, cover, mask, masquerade, screen, subterfuge ▷ *v* **2** = **disguise**, cloak, conceal, cover, hide, mask, obfuscate, obscure,

screen, veil

camp¹ *n* **1** = **camp site**, bivouac, camping ground, encampment, tents

camp² *adj Inf* **1** = **effeminate** **2** = **affected**, artificial, mannered, ostentatious, posturing

campaign *n* **1** = **operation**, crusade, drive, movement, push **2** = **attack**,

Canada Day n July 1, the anniversary of the day when Canada became the first British colony to receive dominion status.

Canada goose n large greyish-brown N American goose with a black neck and head and a white throat patch.

Canada jay n a large common jay of North America with a grey body, and a white-and-black crestless head.

Canadian n, adj (person) from Canada.

canal ⊙ n 1 artificial waterway. 2 passage in the body. **canalize** v 1 give direction to. 2 convert into a canal.

canapé [**kan**-nap-pay] n small piece of bread or toast with a savoury topping.

canard n false report.

canary n, pl **-ries** small yellow songbird often kept as a pet.

canasta n card game like rummy, played with two packs.

cancan n lively high-kicking dance performed by a female group.

cancel ⊙ v **-celling, -celled** 1 stop (something that has been arranged) from taking place. 2 mark (a cheque or stamp) with an official stamp to prevent further use. **cancellation** n **cancel out** v counterbalance, neutralize.

cancer ⊙ n 1 serious disease resulting from a malignant growth or tumour. 2 malignant growth or tumour. 3 evil influence that spreads dangerously. **cancerous** adj.

Cancer n (the crab) fourth sign of the zodiac. **tropic of Cancer** see TROPIC.

candela [kan-**dee**-la] n unit of luminous intensity.

candelabrum n, pl **-bra** large branched candle holder.

candid ⊙ adj honest and straightforward. **candidly** adv.

candidate ⊙ n 1 person seeking a job or position. 2 person taking an examination. **candidacy**, **candidature** n.

candle n stick of wax enclosing a wick, which is burned to produce light. **candlestick** n holder for a candle. **candlewick** n cotton fabric with a tufted surface.

Candlemas n Christianity February 2, Feast of the Purification of the Virgin Mary.

candour ⊙ n honesty and straightforwardness.

candy n, pl **-dies** US a sweet or sweets. **candied** adj coated with sugar. **candyfloss** n light fluffy mass of spun sugar on a stick. **candy-striped** adj having coloured stripes on a white background.

candytuft n garden plant with clusters of white, pink, or purple flowers.

cane n 1 stem of the bamboo or similar plant. 2 flexible rod used to beat someone. 3 slender walking stick. ▷ v 4 beat with a cane. **cane toad** large toad used to control insects and other pests of sugar-cane plantations.

canine [**kay**-nine] adj 1 of or like a dog. ▷ n 2 sharp pointed tooth between the incisors and the molars.

canister n metal container.

canker ⊙ n 1 ulceration, ulcerous disease. 2 something evil that spreads and corrupts.

cannabis n 1 Asian plant with tough fibres. 2 drug obtained from the dried leaves and flowers of this plant, which can be smoked or chewed.

cannelloni pl n tubular pieces of pasta filled with meat etc.

cannibal n 1 person who eats human flesh. 2 animal that eats others of its own kind. **cannibalism** n **cannibalize** v

————————— **THESAURUS** —————————

expedition, offensive

canal n 1 = **waterway**, channel, conduit, duct, passage, watercourse

cancel v 1 = **call off**, abolish, abort, annul, delete, do away with, eliminate, erase, expunge, obliterate, repeal, revoke

cancellation n 1 = **abandonment**, abolition, annulment, deletion, elimination, repeal, revocation

cancer n 1 = **sickness**, pestilence 2 = **growth**, malignancy, tumour 3 = **corruption**

candid adj = **honest**, blunt, forthright, frank, open, outspoken, plain, straightforward, truthful

candidate n 1 = **contender**, applicant, claimant, competitor, contestant, entrant, nominee, runner

candour n = **honesty**, directness, forthrightness, frankness, openness, outspokenness, straightforwardness, truthfulness

canker n 1 = **disease**, cancer, infection, rot, sore, ulcer 2 = **corruption**, blight, rot, scourge

use parts from (one machine) to repair another.

cannon ❶ *n* **1** large gun on wheels. **2** billiard stroke in which the cue ball hits two balls successively. **cannonade** *n* continuous heavy gunfire. **cannonball** *n* heavy metal ball fired from a cannon. **cannon into** *v* collide with.

cannot can not.

canny ❶ *adj* **-nier, -niest** shrewd, cautious. **cannily** *adv*.

canoe *n* light narrow open boat propelled by a paddle or paddles. **canoeing** *n* sport of rowing in a canoe. **canoeist** *n*.

canon¹ *n* priest serving in a cathedral.

canon² ❶ *n* **1** Church decree regulating morals or religious practices. **2** general rule or standard. **3** list of the works of an author that are accepted as authentic. **4** piece of music in which the same melody is taken up in different parts. **canonical** *adj* **canonize** *v* declare (a person) officially to be a saint. **canonization** *n*.

canoodle *v slang* kiss and cuddle.

canopy ❶ *n, pl* **-pies 1** covering above a bed, door, etc. **2** any large or wide covering. **canopied** *adj* covered with a canopy.

cant¹ ❶ *n* **1** insincere talk. **2** specialized vocabulary of a particular group. ▷ *v* **3** use cant.

cant² ❶ *n* **1** tilted position. ▷ *v* **2** tilt, overturn.

can't can not.

cantaloupe, cantaloup *n* kind of melon with sweet orange flesh.

cantankerous ❶ *adj* quarrelsome, bad-tempered.

cantata [kan-**tah**-ta] *n* musical work consisting of arias, duets, and choruses.

canteen *n* **1** restaurant attached to a workplace or school. **2** box containing a set of cutlery.

canter ❶ *n* **1** horse's gait between a trot and a gallop. ▷ *v* **2** move at a canter.

canticle *n* short hymn with words from the Bible.

cantilever *n* beam or girder fixed at one end only. **cantilever bridge** bridge made of two cantilevers that meet in the middle.

canto [**kan**-toe] *n, pl* **-tos** main division of a long poem.

canton *n* political division of a country, esp. Switzerland.

cantonment [kan-**toon**-ment] *n* military camp.

cantor *n* man employed to lead services in a synagogue.

Canuck *n, adj informal* Canadian.

canvas *n* **1** heavy coarse cloth used for sails and tents, and for oil painting. **2** an oil painting on canvas. **under canvas** in a tent.

canvass ❶ *v* **1** try to get votes or support (from). **2** find out the opinions of (people) by conducting a survey. ▷ *n* **3** canvassing.

canyon *n* deep narrow valley.

caoutchouc [**cow**-chook] *n* raw rubber.

cap ❶ *n* **1** soft close-fitting covering for the head. **2** cap given to player selected for a national team. **3** small lid. **4** small explosive device used in a toy gun. **5** contraceptive device. ▷ *v* **capping, capped 6** cover or top with something. **7** select (a player) for a

---

cannon *n* **1** = **gun**, big gun, field gun, mortar

canny *adj* = **shrewd**, astute, careful, cautious, clever, judicious, prudent, wise

canon² *n* **2** = **rule**, criterion, dictate, formula, precept, principle, regulation, standard, statute, yardstick **3** = **list**, catalogue, roll

canopy *n* **1** = **awning**, covering, shade, sunshade

cant¹ *n* **1** = **hypocrisy**, humbug, insincerity, lip service, pretence, pretentiousness, sanctimoniousness **2** = **jargon**, argot, lingo, patter, slang, vernacular

cant² *v* **2** = **tilt**, angle, bevel, incline, rise, slant, slope

cantankerous *adj* = **bad-tempered**, choleric, contrary, disagreeable, grumpy, irascible, irritable, testy, waspish

canter *n* **1** = **jog**, amble, dogtrot, lope ▷ *v* **2** = **jog**, amble, lope

canvass *v* **1** = **campaign**, electioneer, solicit, solicit votes **2** = **poll**, examine, inspect, investigate, scrutinize, study ▷ *n* **3** = **poll**, examination, investigation, scrutiny, survey, tally

cap *v* **9** = **beat**, better, crown, eclipse, exceed, outdo, outstrip, surpass, top, transcend

national team. **8** impose an upper limit on (a tax). **9** outdo, excel.

CAP (in the EU) Common Agricultural Policy.

cap. capital.

capable ❶ *adj* **1** (foll. by *of*) having the ability (for). **2** competent and efficient. **capably** *adv* **capability** *n, pl* **-ties**.

capacity ❶ *n, pl* **-ties 1** ability to contain, absorb, or hold. **2** maximum amount that can be contained or produced. **3** physical or mental ability. **4** position, function. **capacious** *adj* roomy. **capacitance** *n* (measure of) the ability of a system to store electrical charge. **capacitor** *n* device for storing electrical charge.

caparisoned [kap-**par**-riss-sond] *adj* magnificently decorated.

cape¹ *n* short cloak.

cape² ❶ *n* large piece of land that juts out into the sea.

caper ❶ *n* **1** high-spirited prank. ▷ *v* **2** skip about.

capercaillie, capercailzie [kap-per-**kale**-yee] *n* large black European grouse.

capers *pl n* pickled flower buds of a Mediterranean shrub used in sauces.

capillary [kap-**pill**-a-ree] *n, pl* **-laries 1** very fine blood vessel. ▷ *adj* **2** (of a tube) having a fine bore.

capital¹ ❶ *n* **1** chief city of a country.

2 accumulated wealth. **3** wealth used to produce more wealth. **4** large letter, as used at the beginning of a name or sentence. ▷ *adj* **5** involving or punishable by death. **6** *old-fashioned* excellent. **capitalize** *v* **1** write or print (words) in capitals. **2** convert into or provide with capital. **capitalize on** *v* take advantage of (a situation). **capital gain** profit from the sale of an asset. **capitalism** *n* economic system based on the private ownership of industry.

capital² *n* top part of a pillar.

capitalism ❶ *n* economic system based on the private ownership of industry. **capitalist** *adj* **1** of capitalists or capitalism. **2** supporting capitalism. ▷ *n* **3** supporter of capitalism. **4** person who owns a business.

capitation *n* tax of a fixed amount per person.

capitulate ❶ *v* surrender on agreed terms. **capitulation** *n*.

capon [**kay**-pon] *n* castrated cock fowl fattened for eating.

cappuccino [kap-poo-**cheen**-oh] *n, pl* **-nos** coffee with steamed milk, sprinkled with powdered chocolate.

caprice ❶ [kap-**reess**] *n* sudden change of attitude. **capricious** *adj* tending to have sudden changes of attitude. **capriciously** *adv*.

Capricorn *n* (the goat) tenth sign of the

capability *n* **1** = **ability**, capacity, means, potential, power, qualification(s), wherewithal **2** = **competence**, efficiency, proficiency

capable *adj* **1** = **able**, accomplished, gifted, qualified, talented **2** = **competent**, efficient, proficient

capacious *adj* = **spacious**, broad, commodious, expansive, extensive, roomy, sizable *or* sizeable, substantial, vast, voluminous, wide

capacity *n* **1** = **size**, amplitude, compass, dimensions, extent, magnitude, range, room, scope, space, volume **3** = **ability**, aptitude, aptness, capability, competence, facility, genius, gift **4** = **function**, office, position, post, province, role, sphere

cape² *n* = **headland**, head, peninsula, point, promontory

caper *n* **1** = **escapade**, antic, high jinks, jape, lark (*inf*), mischief, practical joke,

prank, stunt ▷ *v* **2** = **dance**, bound, cavort, frolic, gambol, jump, skip, spring, trip

capital¹ *n* **2** = **money**, assets, cash, finances, funds, investment(s), lolly (*Aust & NZ sl*), means, principal, resources, wealth, wherewithal ▷ *adj* **6** *Old-fashioned* = **first-rate**, excellent, fine, splendid, sterling, superb

capitalism *n* = **private enterprise**, free enterprise, laissez faire *or* laisser faire, private ownership

capitalize on *v* = **take advantage of**, benefit from, cash in on (*inf*), exploit, gain from, make the most of, profit from

capitulate *v* = **give in**, cave in (*inf*), come to terms, give up, relent, submit, succumb, surrender, yield

caprice *n* = **whim**, fad, fancy, fickleness, impulse, inconstancy, notion, whimsy

capricious *adj* = **unpredictable**, changeful, erratic, fickle, fitful,

c

zodiac. **tropic of Capricorn** see
TROPIC.

capsicum n kind of pepper used as a
vegetable or as a spice.

capsize ❶ v overturn accidentally.

capstan n rotating cylinder round
which a ship's rope is wound.

capsule ❶ n **1** soluble gelatine case
containing a dose of medicine.
2 plant's seed case. **3** Anat membrane
surrounding an organ. **4** detachable
crew compartment of a spacecraft.

Capt. Captain.

captain ❶ n **1** commander of a ship or
civil aircraft. **2** middle-ranking naval
officer. **3** junior officer in the army.
4 leader of a team or group. ▷ v **5** be
captain of. **captaincy** n.

caption n **1** title or explanation
accompanying an illustration. ▷ v
2 provide with a caption.

captious adj tending to make trivial
criticisms.

captivate ❶ v attract and hold the
attention of. **captivating** adj.

captive ❶ n **1** person kept in
confinement. ▷ adj **2** kept in
confinement. **3** (of an audience)
unable to leave. **captivity** n.

captor n person who captures a person
or animal.

capture ❶ v **1** take by force. **2** succeed
in representing (something elusive)
artistically. ▷ n **3** capturing.

capuchin [**kap**-yoo-chin] n S American
monkey with thick hair on the top of
its head.

capybara n very large S American
rodent.

car ❶ n **1** motor vehicle designed to
carry a small number of people.
2 passenger compartment of a cable
car, lift, etc. **3** US railway carriage.

carjack v attack (a car driver) to rob
them or to steal the car. **car park** area
or building reserved for parking cars.

carafe [kar-**raff**] n glass bottle for
serving water or wine.

caramel n **1** chewy sweet made from
sugar and milk. **2** burnt sugar, used for
colouring and flavouring food.
caramelize v turn into caramel.

carapace n hard upper shell of tortoises
and crustaceans.

carat n **1** unit of weight of precious
stones. **2** measure of the purity of gold
in an alloy.

caravan n **1** large enclosed vehicle for
living in, designed to be towed by a car
or horse. **2** group travelling together
in Eastern countries. **caravanserai** n
large inn enclosing a courtyard,
providing accommodation for
caravans in Eastern countries.

caraway n plant whose seeds are used
as a spice.

carb n informal short for CARBOHYDRATE.

carbide n compound of carbon with a
metal.

carbine n light automatic rifle.

carbohydrate n any of a large group of
energy-producing compounds in food,
such as sugars and starches.

carbolic acid n disinfectant derived
from coal tar.

carbon n nonmetallic element
occurring as charcoal, graphite, and
diamond, found in all organic matter.
carbonate n salt or ester of carbonic
acid. **carbonated** adj (of a drink)

THESAURUS

impulsive, inconsistent, inconstant,
mercurial, variable, wayward,
whimsical

capsize v = **overturn**, invert, keel over,
tip over, turn over, turn turtle, upset

capsule n **1** = **pill**, lozenge, tablet
2 = **pod**, case, receptacle, seed case,
sheath, shell, vessel

captain n = **leader**, boss, chief,
commander, head, master, skipper

captivate v = **charm**, allure, attract,
beguile, bewitch, enchant, enrapture,
enthral, entrance, fascinate, infatuate,
mesmerize

captive n **1** = **prisoner**, convict,
detainee, hostage, internee, prisoner
of war, slave ▷ adj **2** = **confined**,

caged, enslaved, ensnared,
imprisoned, incarcerated, locked up,
penned, restricted, subjugated

captivity n **2** = **confinement**,
bondage, custody, detention,
imprisonment, incarceration,
internment, slavery

capture v **1** = **catch**, apprehend, arrest,
bag, collar (inf), secure, seize, take,
take prisoner ▷ n **3** = **catching**,
apprehension, arrest, imprisonment,
seizure, taking, taking captive,
trapping

car n **1** = **vehicle**, auto (US), automobile,
jalopy (inf), machine, motor, motorcar,
wheels (inf) **3** US = **(railway)**
carriage, buffet car, cable car, coach,

containing carbon dioxide.
carboniferous *adj* producing coal or carbon. **carbonize** *v* **1** turn into carbon as a result of heating. **2** coat with carbon. **carbon capture** capture of carbon dioxide in the atmosphere, intended to prevent climate change. **carbon copy 1** copy made with carbon paper. **2** very similar person or thing. **carbon dioxide** colourless gas exhaled by people and animals. **carbon footprint** measure of the carbon dioxide produced by an individual or organization. **carbonic acid** weak acid formed from carbon dioxide and water. **carbon-neutral** not affecting the amount of carbon dioxide in the earth's atmosphere. **carbon paper** paper coated on one side with a dark waxy pigment, used to make a copy of something as it is typed or written.

Carborundum *n* ® compound of silicon and carbon, used for grinding and polishing.

carboy *n* large bottle with a protective casing.

carbuncle *n* inflamed boil.

carburettor *n* device which mixes petrol and air in an internal-combustion engine.

carcass, carcase ❶ *n* **1** dead body of an animal. **2** *informal* person's body.

carcinogen *n* substance that produces cancer. **carcinogenic** *adj* **carcinoma** *n* malignant tumour.

card¹ *n* **1** piece of thick stiff paper or cardboard used for identification, reference, or sending greetings or messages. **2** one of a set of cards with a printed pattern, used for playing games. **3** small rectangle of stiff plastic with identifying numbers for use as a credit card, cheque card, or charge card. **4** *old-fashioned* witty or eccentric person. ▷ *pl* **5** any card game, or card games in general. **cardboard** *n* thin stiff board made from paper pulp. **cardsharp** *n* professional card player who cheats.

card² *n* **1** machine or tool for combing wool before spinning. ▷ *v* **2** process with such a machine or tool.

cardamom *n* spice obtained from the seeds of a tropical plant.

cardiac *adj* of the heart. **cardiogram** *n* electrocardiogram. **cardiograph** *n* electrocardiograph. **cardiology** *n* study of the heart and its diseases. **cardiologist** *n* **cardiovascular** *adj* of the heart and the blood vessels.

cardigan *n* knitted jacket.

cardinal ❶ *n* **1** any of the high-ranking clergymen of the RC Church who elect the Pope and act as his counsellors. ▷ *adj* **2** fundamentally important. **cardinal number** number denoting quantity but not order in a group, for example four as distinct from fourth. **cardinal points** the four main points of the compass.

care ❶ *v* **1** be concerned. **2** like (to do something). **3** (foll. by *for*) like, be fond of. **4** (foll. by *for*) look after. ▷ *n* **5** careful attention, caution. **6** protection, charge. **7** trouble, worry. **in, into care** made the legal responsibility of a local authority. **carefree** *adj* **careful** *adj* **carefully** *adv* **carefulness** *n* **careless** *adj* **carelessly** *adv* **carelessness** *n* **caring** *adj*.

careen *v* tilt over to one side.

career ❶ *n* **1** series of jobs in a profession or occupation that a person has through their life. **2** part of a person's life spent in a particular occupation. ▷ *v* **3** rush in an

---

THESAURUS

dining car, sleeping car, van

carcass *n* = **body**, cadaver (*Med*), corpse, dead body, framework, hulk, remains, shell, skeleton

cardinal *adj* **2** = **principal**, capital, central, chief, essential, first, fundamental, key, leading, main, paramount, primary

care *v* **1** = **be concerned**, be bothered, be interested, mind **4** (foll. by *for*) = **look after**, attend, foster, mind, minister to, nurse, protect, provide for, tend, watch over ▷ *n* **5** = **caution**, attention, carefulness, consideration, forethought, heed, management, pains, prudence, vigilance, watchfulness **6** = **protection**, charge, control, custody, guardianship, keeping, management, supervision **7** = **worry**, anxiety, concern, disquiet, perplexity, pressure, responsibility, stress, trouble

career *n* **1** = **occupation**, calling, employment, life's work, livelihood, pursuit, vocation ▷ *v* **3** = **rush**, barrel (along) (*inf, chiefly US & Canad*), bolt, dash, hurtle, race, speed, tear

uncontrolled way. **careerist** n person who seeks advancement by any possible means.

carefree ❶ adj without worry or responsibility.

caress ❶ n **1** gentle affectionate touch or embrace. ▷ v **2** touch gently and affectionately.

caret [kar-rett] n symbol (^) indicating a place in written or printed matter where something is to be inserted.

caretaker ❶ n person employed to look after a place.

careworn adj showing signs of worry.

cargo ❶ n, pl **-goes** goods carried by a ship, aircraft, etc. **cargo pants**, **trousers** pl n loose trousers with a large pocket on each leg.

caribou n, pl **-bou** or **-bous** large N American reindeer.

caricature ❶ n **1** drawing or description of a person that exaggerates features for comic effect. ▷ v **2** make a caricature of.

caries [**care**-reez] n tooth decay.

carillon [kar-**rill**-yon] n **1** set of bells played by keyboard or mechanically. **2** tune played on such bells.

cark v Aust & NZ slang die.

Carmelite n, adj (friar or nun) of the Order of Our Lady of Carmel.

carminative n, adj (drug) able to relieve flatulence.

carmine adj vivid red.

carnage ❶ n extensive slaughter of people.

carnal ❶ adj of a sexual or sensual nature. **carnal knowledge** sexual intercourse.

carnation n cultivated plant with fragrant white, pink, or red flowers.

carnelian n reddish-yellow gemstone.

carnival ❶ n **1** festive period with processions, music, and dancing in the street. **2** travelling funfair.

carnivore n meat-eating animal. **carnivorous** adj.

carob n pod of a Mediterranean tree, used as a chocolate substitute.

carol ❶ n **1** joyful Christmas hymn. ▷ v **-olling, -olled 2** sing carols. **3** sing joyfully.

carotid [kar-**rot**-id] adj, n (of) either of the two arteries supplying blood to the head.

carouse v have a merry drinking party. **carousal** n merry drinking party.

carousel [kar-roo-**sell**] n **1** revolving conveyor belt for luggage or photographic slides. **2** US merry-go-round.

carp[1] n large freshwater fish.

carp[2] ❶ v complain, find fault.

carpal n wrist bone.

carpel n female reproductive organ of a flowering plant.

carpenter ❶ n person who makes or repairs wooden structures. **carpentry** n.

──────────────────────── THESAURUS ────────────

carefree adj = **untroubled**, blithe, breezy, cheerful, easy-going, halcyon, happy-go-lucky, light-hearted

careful adj = **thorough**, cautious, chary, circumspect, conscientious, discreet, meticulous, painstaking, particular, precise, prudent, scrupulous, thoughtful

careless adj = **negligent**, absent-minded, casual, cavalier, forgetful, irresponsible, lackadaisical, neglectful, nonchalant, offhand, slapdash, slipshod, sloppy (inf), thoughtless

carelessness n = **negligence**, irresponsibility, laxity, neglect, omission, slackness, sloppiness (inf), thoughtlessness

caress n **1** = **stroke**, cuddle, embrace, fondling, hug, kiss, pat ▷ v **2** = **stroke**, cuddle, embrace, fondle, hug, kiss, neck (inf), nuzzle, pet

caretaker n = **warden**, concierge, curator, custodian, janitor, keeper, porter, superintendent, watchman

cargo n = **load**, baggage, consignment, contents, freight, goods, merchandise, shipment

caricature n **1** = **parody**, burlesque, cartoon, distortion, farce, lampoon, satire, send-up (Brit inf), takeoff (inf), travesty ▷ v **2** = **parody**, burlesque, distort, lampoon, mimic, mock, ridicule, satirize, send up (Brit inf), take off (inf)

carnage n = **slaughter**, blood bath, bloodshed, butchery, havoc, holocaust, massacre, mass murder, murder, shambles

carnal adj = **sexual**, erotic, fleshly, lascivious, lewd, libidinous, lustful, sensual

carnival n **1** = **festival**, celebration, fair, fete, fiesta, gala, holiday, jamboree, jubilee, merrymaking, revelry

carol n **1** = **song**, chorus, ditty, hymn, lay

carp[2] v = **find fault**, cavil, complain, criticize, pick holes, quibble, reproach

carpenter n = **joiner**, cabinet-maker, woodworker

carpet *n* **1** heavy fabric for covering floors. **2** covering like a carpet. ▷ *v* **carpeting**, **carpeted 3** cover with a carpet. **on the carpet** *informal* being reprimanded. **carpetbagger** *n* politician seeking office in a place where he or she has no connections. **carpet snake** *or* **python** large nonvenomous Australian snake with a carpet-like pattern on its back.

carpus *n, pl* -**pi** set of eight bones of the wrist.

carriage ❶ *n* **1** one of the sections of a train for passengers. **2** way a person holds his or her head and body. **3** four-wheeled horse-drawn vehicle. **4** moving part of a machine that supports and shifts another part. **5** charge made for conveying goods. **carriageway** *n* part of a road along which traffic passes in one direction.

carrier *n* **1** person or thing that carries something. **2** person or animal that does not suffer from a disease but can transmit it to others. **carrier bag** large plastic or paper bag for shopping. **carrier pigeon** homing pigeon used for carrying messages.

carrion *n* dead and rotting flesh. **carrion crow** scavenging European crow.

carrot *n* **1** long tapering orange root vegetable. **2** something offered as an incentive. **carroty** *adj* (of hair) reddish-orange.

carry ❶ *v* -**rying**, -**ried 1** take from one place to another. **2** have with one habitually, in one's pocket etc. **3** transmit (a disease). **4** have as a factor or result. **5** hold (one's head or body) in a specified manner. **6** secure the adoption of (a bill or motion). **7** (of sound) travel a certain distance.

carrycot *n* light portable bed for a baby, with handles and a hood. **carry on** *v* **1** continue. **2** do, run, or take part in. **3** *informal* cause a fuss. **carry out** *v* follow, accomplish. **carry through** *v* bring to completion.

cart *n* **1** open two-wheeled horse-drawn vehicle for carrying goods or passengers. **2** small vehicle pulled or pushed by hand. ▷ *v* **3** carry, usu. with some effort. **carthorse** *n* large heavily built horse. **cartwheel** *n* **1** sideways somersault supported by the hands with legs outstretched. **2** large spoked wheel of a cart.

carte blanche *n French* complete authority.

cartel *n* association of competing firms formed to fix prices.

Carthusian *n, adj* (monk or nun) of a strict monastic order founded in 1084.

cartilage [**kar**-till-ij] *n* strong flexible tissue forming part of the skeleton. **cartilaginous** *adj*.

cartography *n* map making. **cartographer** *n* **cartographic** *adj*.

carton ❶ *n* container made of cardboard or waxed paper.

cartoon ❶ *n* **1** humorous or satirical drawing. **2** sequence of these telling a story. **3** film made by photographing a series of drawings which give the illusion of movement when projected. **cartoonist** *n*.

cartouche, cartouch *n* **1** ornamental tablet or panel in the form of a scroll. **2** oval figure containing royal or divine Egyptian names.

cartridge ❶ *n* **1** casing containing an explosive charge and bullet for a gun. **2** part of the pick-up of a record player that converts the movements of the stylus into electrical signals. **3** sealed container of film, tape, etc. **cartridge**

---

carriage *n* **1** = **vehicle**, cab, coach, conveyance **2** = **bearing**, air, behaviour, comportment, conduct, demeanour, deportment, gait, manner, posture

carry *v* **1** = **transport**, bear, bring, conduct, convey, fetch, haul, lug, move, relay, take, transfer **6** = **win**, accomplish, capture, effect, gain, secure

carry on *v* **1** = **continue**, endure, keep going, last, maintain, perpetuate, persevere, persist **3** *Inf* = **make a fuss**, create (*sl*), misbehave

carry out *v* = **perform**, accomplish, achieve, carry through, effect, execute, fulfil, implement, realize

carton *n* = **box**, case, container, pack, package, packet

cartoon *n* **1** = **drawing**, caricature, lampoon, parody, satire, sketch **2** = **comic strip 3** = **animation**, animated cartoon, animated film

cartridge *n* **1** = **shell**, charge, round **3** = **container**, capsule, case, cassette, cylinder, magazine

paper strong thick drawing paper.
carve ❶ *v* **1** cut to form an object.
2 form (an object or design) by cutting.
3 slice (cooked meat). **carving** *n* **carve
out** *v informal* make or create (a
career).
caryatid [kar-ree-**at**-id] *n* supporting
column in the shape of a female figure.
Casanova *n* promiscuous man.
casbah *n* citadel of a N African city.
cascade ❶ *n* **1** waterfall. **2** something
flowing or falling like a waterfall. ▷ *v*
3 flow or fall in a cascade.
cascara *n* bark of a N American shrub,
used as a laxative.
case¹ ❶ *n* **1** instance, example. **2** matter
for discussion. **3** condition, state of
affairs. **4** set of arguments supporting
an action or cause. **5** person or
problem dealt with by a doctor, social
worker, or solicitor. **6** action, lawsuit.
7 evidence offered in court to support
a claim. **8** *Grammar* form of a noun,
pronoun, or adjective showing its
relation to other words in the
sentence. **in case** so as to allow for the
possibility that.
case² ❶ *n* **1** container, protective
covering. **2** suitcase. ▷ *v* **3** *slang*
inspect (a building) with the intention
of burgling it. **case-hardened** *adj*
having been made callous by
experience.
casein *n* protein found in milk and its
products.
casement *n* window that is hinged on
one side.
cash ❶ *n* **1** banknotes and coins. ▷ *adj*
2 of, for, or paid in cash. ▷ *v* **3** obtain
cash for. **cash-and-carry** *adj* operating

on a basis of cash payment for goods
that are taken away by the buyer. **cash
in on** *v informal* gain profit or
advantage from. **cash register** till
that displays and adds the prices of the
goods sold.
cashew *n* edible kidney-shaped nut.
cashier¹ ❶ *n* person responsible for
handling cash in a bank, shop, etc.
cashier² ❶ *v* dismiss with dishonour
from the armed forces.
cashmere *n* fine soft wool obtained
from goats.
casing *n* protective case, covering.
casino *n, pl* **-nos** public building or room
where gambling games are played.
cask *n* barrel used to hold alcoholic
drink.
casket ❶ *n* **1** small box for valuables.
2 *US* coffin.
Cassandra *n* someone whose
prophecies of doom are unheeded.
cassava *n* starch obtained from the
roots of a tropical American plant,
used to make tapioca.
casserole *n* **1** covered dish in which
food is cooked slowly, usu. in an oven.
2 dish cooked in this way. ▷ *v* **3** cook in
a casserole.
cassette *n* plastic case containing a reel
of film or magnetic tape.
cassia *n* tropical plant whose pods yield
a mild laxative. **cassia bark** cinnamon-
like bark used as a spice.
cassock *n* long tunic, usu. black, worn
by priests.
cassowary *n, pl* **-waries** large flightless
bird of Australia and New Guinea.
cast ❶ *n* **1** actors in a play or film
collectively. **2** object shaped by a

───────────── THESAURUS ─────────────

carve *v* **1, 2** = **cut**, chip, chisel, engrave,
etch, hew, mould, sculpt, whittle
3 = **slice**
cascade *n* **1** = **waterfall**, avalanche,
cataract, deluge, downpour, falls,
flood, fountain, outpouring, shower,
torrent ▷ *v* **3** = **flow**, descend, fall,
flood, gush, overflow, pitch, plunge,
pour, spill, surge, teem, tumble
case¹ *n* **1** = **instance**, example,
illustration, occasion, occurrence,
specimen **3** = **situation**,
circumstance(s), condition, context,
contingency, event, position, state
6 = **lawsuit**, action, dispute,
proceedings, suit, trial
case² *n* **1** = **container**, box, canister,

capsule, carton, casing, chest,
covering, crate, envelope, holder,
jacket, receptacle, sheath, shell,
wrapper
cash *n* **1** = **money**, brass (*N Eng dial*),
coinage, currency, dough (*sl*), funds,
lolly (*Aust & NZ sl*), notes, ready money,
silver
cashier¹ *n* = **teller**, bank clerk, banker,
bursar, clerk, purser, treasurer
cashier² *v* = **dismiss**, discard,
discharge, drum out, expel, give the
boot to (*sl*)
casket *n* **1** = **box**, case, chest, coffer,
jewel box
cast *n* **1** = **actors**, characters, company,
dramatis personae, players, troupe

mould while molten. **3** mould used to shape such as an object. **4** rigid plaster-of-Paris casing for immobilizing broken bones while they heal. **5** sort, kind. **6** slight squint in the eye. ▷ *v* **casting**, **cast 7** select (an actor) to play a part in a play or film. **8** give (a vote). **9** let fall, shed. **10** shape (molten material) in a mould. **11** throw with force. **12** direct (a glance).

castaway *n* shipwrecked person.

casting vote deciding vote used by the chairman of a meeting when the votes on each side are equal. **cast-iron** *adj* **1** made of a hard but brittle type of iron. **2** definite, unchallengeable. **cast-off** *adj*, *n* discarded (person or thing). **cast off** *v* **1** discard (something no longer wanted). **2** untie a ship from a dock. **3** knot and remove (stitches) from the needle in knitting. **cast on** *v* make (stitches) on the needle in knitting.

castanets *pl n* musical instrument, used by Spanish dancers, consisting of curved pieces of hollow wood clicked together in the hand.

caste ❶ *n* **1** any of the hereditary classes into which Hindu society is divided. **2** social rank.

castellated *adj* having battlements.

caster *n* same as CASTOR.

caster sugar *n* finely ground white sugar.

castigate ❶ *v* reprimand severely. **castigation** *n*.

castle ❶ *n* **1** large fortified building, often built as a ruler's residence. **2** rook in chess. **castle in the air**

daydream unlikely to be realized.

castor *n* small swivelling wheel fixed to the bottom of a piece of furniture for easy moving.

castor oil *n* oil obtained from an Indian plant, used as a lubricant and purgative.

castrate ❶ *v* **1** remove the testicles of. **2** deprive of vigour or masculinity. **castration** *n*.

casual ❶ *adj* **1** careless, nonchalant. **2** (of work or workers) occasional. **3** shallow, superficial. **4** for informal wear. **5** happening by chance. ▷ *n* **6** occasional worker. **casually** *adv*

casualty *n* person killed or injured in an accident or war.

casualty ❶ *n*, *pl* **-ties 1** person killed or injured in an accident or war. **2** hospital department treating victims of accidents. **3** person or thing that has suffered as the result of something.

casuistry *n* reasoning that is misleading or oversubtle. **casuist** *n*.

cat ❶ *n* **1** small domesticated furry mammal. **2** related wild mammal, such as the lion or tiger. **catty** *adj* **-tier**, **-tiest** *informal* spiteful. **catkin** *n* drooping flower spike of certain trees. **catcall** *n* derisive whistle or cry. **catfish** *n* fish with whisker-like barbels round the mouth. **catgut** *n* strong cord used to string musical instruments and sports rackets. **catnap** *n*, *v* doze. **cat-o'-nine-tails** *n* whip with nine knotted thongs. **Catseyes** *pl n* ® glass reflectors set in the road to indicate traffic lanes. **cat's**

5 = **type**, complexion, manner, stamp, style ▷ *v* **7**, **8** = **choose**, allot, appoint, assign, name, pick, select **9** = **give out**, deposit, diffuse, distribute, emit, radiate, scatter, shed, spread **10** = **form**, found, model, mould, set, shape **11** = **throw**, fling, hurl, launch, pitch, sling, thrust, toss

caste *n* **2** = **class**, estate, grade, order, rank, social order, status, stratum

castigate *v* = **reprimand**, berate, censure, chastise, criticize, lambast(e), rebuke, rouse on (*Aust*), scold

cast-iron *adj* **2** = **certain**, copper-bottomed, definite, established, fixed, guaranteed, settled

castle *n* **1** = **fortress**, chateau, citadel, keep, palace, stronghold, tower

cast-off *adj* = **unwanted**, discarded, rejected, scrapped, surplus to requirements, unneeded, useless ▷ *n* = **reject**, discard, failure, outcast, second

castrate *v* **1** = **neuter**, emasculate, geld

casual *adj* **1** = **careless**, blasé, cursory, lackadaisical, nonchalant, offhand, relaxed, unconcerned **2** = **occasional**, irregular **4** = **informal**, non-dressy, sporty **5** = **chance**, accidental, incidental, random, unexpected

casualty *n* **1** = **victim**, death, fatality, loss, sufferer, wounded

cat *n* **1** = **feline**, kitty (*inf*), moggy (*sl*), puss (*inf*), pussy (*inf*), tabby

paw person used by another to do unpleasant things for him or her.
catwalk n **1** narrow pathway or platform. **2** narrow platform where models display clothes in a fashion show.
catabolism n breaking down of complex molecules into simple ones.
cataclysm [kat-a-kliz-zum] n **1** violent upheaval. **2** disaster, such as an earthquake. **cataclysmic** adj.
catacombs ❶ [kat-a-koomz] pl n underground burial place consisting of tunnels with recesses for tombs.
catafalque [kat-a-falk] n raised platform on which a body lies in state before or during a funeral.
catalepsy n trancelike state in which the body is rigid. **cataleptic** adj.
catalogue ❶ n **1** book containing details of items for sale. **2** systematic list of items. ▷ v **3** enter (an item) in a catalogue. **4** make a systematic list of.
catalyst n **1** substance that speeds up a chemical reaction without itself changing. **2** person or thing that causes a change. **catalyse** v speed up (a chemical reaction) by a catalyst. **catalysis** n **catalytic** adj.
catamaran n boat with twin parallel hulls.
catapult ❶ n **1** Y-shaped device with a loop of elastic, used by children for firing stones. ▷ v **2** shoot forwards or upwards violently. **3** cause (someone) suddenly to be in a particular situation.

cataract n **1** eye disease in which the lens becomes opaque. **2** opaque area of an eye. **3** large waterfall.
catarrh [kat-tar] n excessive mucus in the nose and throat, during or following a cold. **catarrhal** adj.
catastrophe ❶ [kat-ass-trof-fee] n great and sudden disaster. **catastrophic** adj.
catatonia n form of schizophrenia characterized by stupor, with outbreaks of excitement. **catatonic** adj.
catch ❶ v **catching**, **caught** **1** seize, capture. **2** surprise in an act, e.g. *two boys were caught stealing*. **3** hit unexpectedly. **4** be in time for (a bus, train, etc.). **5** see or hear. **6** be infected with (an illness). **7** entangle. **8** understand, make out. **9** start burning. ▷ n **10** device for fastening a door, window, etc. **11** total number of fish caught. **12** *informal* concealed or unforeseen drawback. **13** *informal* person considered worth having as a husband or wife. **catch it** *informal* be punished. **catching** adj infectious.
catchy adj **catchier**, **catchiest** (of a tune) pleasant and easily remembered.
catchment area area served by a particular school or hospital. **catch on** v *informal* **1** become popular. **2** understand. **catch out** v *informal* trap (someone) in an error or lie.
catchpenny adj designed to have instant appeal without regard for quality. **catch phrase** well-known

— THESAURUS —

catacombs pl n = **vault**, crypt, tomb
catalogue n **1** = **directory**, gazetteer **2** = **list**, index, inventory, record, register, roll ▷ v **3** = **register**, file, index **4** = **list**, alphabetize, classify, inventory, tabulate
catapult n **1** = **sling**, slingshot (US) ▷ v **2, 3** = **shoot**, heave, hurl, pitch, plunge, propel
catastrophe n = **disaster**, adversity, calamity, cataclysm, fiasco, misfortune, tragedy, trouble
catcall n = **jeer**, boo, gibe, hiss, raspberry, whistle
catch v **1** = **seize**, apprehend, arrest, capture, clutch, ensnare, entrap, get, grab, grasp, grip, lay hold of, snare, snatch, take, trap **2** = **discover**, catch in the act, detect, expose, find out, surprise, take unawares, unmask

6 = **contract**, develop, get, go down with, incur, succumb to, suffer from **8** = **make out**, comprehend, discern, get, grasp, hear, perceive, recognize, sense, take in ▷ n **10** = **fastener**, bolt, clasp, clip, latch **12** *Inf* = **drawback**, disadvantage, fly in the ointment, hitch, snag, stumbling block, trap, trick
catching adj = **infectious**, communicable, contagious, transferable, transmittable
catch on v *Inf* **2** = **understand**, comprehend, find out, get the picture, grasp, see, see through, twig (*Brit inf*)
catchword n = **slogan**, byword, motto, password, watchword
catchy adj = **memorable**, captivating, haunting, popular

phrase associated with a particular entertainer. **catch 22** inescapable dilemma. **catch up with** v reach or pass. **catchword** n well-known and frequently used phrase.

catechism [kat-ti-kiz-zum] n instruction on the doctrine of a Christian Church in a series of questions and answers. **catechize** v **1** instruct by using a catechism. **2** question (someone) thoroughly.

category ❶ n, pl **-ries** class, group. **categorical** adj absolutely clear and certain. **categorically** adv **categorize** v put in a category. **categorization** n.

cater ❶ v provide what is needed or wanted, esp. food or services. **caterer** n.

caterpillar n **1** wormlike larva of a moth or butterfly. **2** ® endless track, driven by cogged wheels, used to propel a heavy vehicle.

caterwaul v, n wail, yowl.

catharsis [kath-**thar**-siss] n, pl **-ses 1** relief of strong suppressed emotions. **2** evacuation of the bowels, esp. with a laxative. **cathartic** adj **1** causing catharsis. ▷ n **2** drug that causes catharsis.

cathedral n principal church of a diocese.

Catherine wheel n rotating firework.

catheter [**kath**-it-er] n tube inserted into a body cavity to drain fluid.

cathode n negative electrode, by which electrons leave a circuit. **cathode rays** stream of electrons from a cathode in a vacuum tube. **cathode-ray tube** vacuum tube in which a beam of electrons produces a visible image, used in television receivers etc.

catholic adj **1** (of tastes or interests) covering a wide range. ▷ n, adj **2** (**C-**)

(member) of the Roman Catholic Church. **Catholicism** n.

● **USAGE NOTE**
● Note that the meaning of catholic
● can change depending on whether it
● begins with a capital letter or not.

cation [**kat**-eye-on] n positively charged ion.

cattle ❶ pl n domesticated cows and bulls. **cattle-grid** n grid over a ditch in the road to prevent livestock crossing.

Caucasian, Caucasoid n, adj (member) of the light-skinned racial group of humankind.

caucus n, pl **-cuses 1** local committee or faction of a political party. **2** political meeting to decide future plans.

caudal adj at or near an animal's tail.

caught v past of CATCH.

caul n Anat membrane sometimes covering a child's head at birth.

cauldron, caldron n large pot used for boiling.

cauliflower n vegetable with a large head of white flower buds surrounded by green leaves.

caulk v fill in (cracks) with paste etc.

causal adj of or being a cause. **causally** adv **causation, causality** n relationship of cause and effect.

cause ❶ n **1** something that produces a particular effect. **2** (foll. by for) reason, motive. **3** aim or principle supported by a person or group. ▷ v **4** be the cause of.

cause célèbre [kawz sill-**leb**-ra] n, pl **causes célèbres** [kawz sill-**leb**-ra] controversial legal case or issue.

causeway n raised path or road across water or marshland.

caustic ❶ adj **1** capable of burning by

———————— **THESAURUS** ————————

categorical adj = **absolute**, downright, emphatic, explicit, express, positive, unambiguous, unconditional, unequivocal, unqualified, unreserved

category n = **class**, classification, department, division, grade, grouping, heading, section, sort, type

cater v = **provide**, furnish, outfit, purvey, supply

cattle pl n = **cows**, beasts, bovines, livestock, stock

catty adj Inf = **spiteful**, backbiting, bitchy (inf), malevolent, malicious,

rancorous, shrewish, snide, venomous

cause n **1** = **origin**, agent, beginning, creator, genesis, mainspring, maker, producer, root, source, spring **2** (foll. by for) = **reason**, basis, grounds, incentive, inducement, justification, motivation, motive, purpose **3** = **aim**, belief, conviction, enterprise, ideal, movement, principle ▷ v **4** = **produce**, bring about, create, generate, give rise to, incite, induce, lead to, result in

caustic adj **1** = **burning**, acrid, astringent, biting, corroding,

chemical action. **2** bitter and sarcastic. ▷ *n* **3** caustic substance. **caustically** *adv* **caustic soda** same as SODIUM HYDROXIDE.

cauterize *v* burn (a wound) with heat or a caustic agent to prevent infection. **cauterization** *n*.

caution ❶ *n* **1** care, esp. in the face of danger. **2** warning. ▷ *v* **3** warn, advise. **cautionary** *adj* warning. **cautious** *adj* showing caution. **cautiously** *adv*.

cavalcade ❶ *n* procession of people on horseback or in cars.

cavalier ❶ *adj* **1** showing haughty disregard. ▷ *n* **2** *old-fashioned* gallant gentleman. **3** (**C-**) supporter of Charles I in the English Civil War.

cavalry ❶ *n*, *pl* **-ries** part of the army orig. on horseback, but now often using fast armoured vehicles.

cave ❶ *n* hollow in the side of a hill or cliff. **caving** *n* sport of exploring caves. **cave in** *v* **1** collapse inwards. **2** *informal* yield under pressure. **caveman** *n* **1** prehistoric cave dweller. **2** *informal* man who is primitive in his behaviour.

caveat [**kav**-vee-at] *n* warning.

cavern ❶ *n* large cave. **cavernous** *adj*.

caviar, caviare *n* salted sturgeon roe, regarded as a delicacy.

cavil *v* **-illing**, **-illed 1** make petty objections. ▷ *n* **2** petty objection.

cavity ❶ *n*, *pl* **-ties 1** hollow space. **2** decayed area on a tooth.

cavort *v* skip about.

caw *n* **1** cry of a crow, rook, or raven. ▷ *v* **2** make this cry.

cay *n* low island or bank composed of sand and coral fragments.

cayenne pepper, cayenne *n* hot red spice made from capsicum seeds.

cayman *n*, *pl* **-mans** S American reptile similar to an alligator.

CB Citizens' Band.

CBE Commander of the Order of the British Empire.

CBI Confederation of British Industry.

cc cubic centimetre.

Cd *Chemistry* cadmium.

CD compact disc.

CD-ROM compact disc read-only memory.

Ce *Chemistry* cerium.

cease ❶ *v* bring or come to an end. **ceaseless** *adj* **ceaselessly** *adv* **ceasefire** *n* temporary truce.

cedar *n* **1** evergreen coniferous tree. **2** its wood.

cede ❶ *v* surrender (territory or legal rights).

cedilla *n* character (˛) placed under a *c* in some languages, to show that it is pronounced *s*, not *k*.

ceilidh [**kay**-lee] *n* informal social gathering for singing and dancing, esp. in Scotland.

ceiling *n* **1** inner upper surface of a room. **2** upper limit set on something. **3** upper altitude to which an aircraft can climb.

celandine *n* wild plant with yellow flowers.

———————————————————————————— THESAURUS ———————

corrosive, mordant, vitriolic **2** = **sarcastic**, acrimonious, cutting, pungent, scathing, stinging, trenchant, virulent, vitriolic

caution *n* **1** = **care**, alertness, carefulness, circumspection, deliberation, discretion, forethought, heed, prudence, vigilance, watchfulness **2** = **warning**, admonition, advice, counsel, injunction ▷ *v* **3** = **warn**, admonish, advise, tip off, urge

cautious *adj* = **careful**, cagey (*inf*), chary, circumspect, guarded, judicious, prudent, tentative, wary

cavalcade *n* = **parade**, array, march-past, procession, spectacle, train

cavalier *adj* **1** = **haughty**, arrogant, disdainful, lofty, lordly, offhand, scornful, supercilious

cavalry *n* = **horsemen**, horse, mounted troops

cave *n* = **hollow**, cavern, cavity, den, grotto

cavern *n* = **cave**, hollow, pothole

cavernous *adj* = **deep**, hollow, sunken, yawning

cavity *n* **1** = **hollow**, crater, dent, gap, hole, pit

cease *v* = **stop**, break off, conclude, discontinue, end, finish, halt, leave off, refrain, terminate

ceaseless *adj* = **continual**, constant, endless, eternal, everlasting, incessant, interminable, never-ending, nonstop, perpetual, unremitting

cede *v* = **surrender**, concede, hand over, make over, relinquish, renounce, resign, transfer, yield

celebrate ❶ v **1** hold festivities to mark (a happy event, anniversary, etc.). **2** perform (a religious ceremony). **3** praise publicly. **celebrated** adj well known. **celebration** n **celebrant** n person who performs a religious ceremony. **celebrity** n, pl **-rities 1** famous person. **2** state of being famous.

celeriac [sill-**ler**-ee-ak] n variety of celery with a large turnip-like root.

celerity [sill-**ler**-rit-tee] n swiftness.

celery n vegetable with long green crisp edible stalks.

celestial ❶ adj **1** heavenly, divine. **2** of the sky.

celibate ❶ adj **1** unmarried or abstaining from sex, esp. because of a religious vow of chastity. ▷ n **2** celibate person. **celibacy** n.

cell ❶ n **1** smallest unit of an organism that is able to function independently. **2** small room for a prisoner, monk, or nun. **3** small compartment of a honeycomb etc. **4** small group operating as the core of a larger organization. **5** device that produces electrical energy by chemical reaction. **cellular** adj **1** of or consisting of cells. **2** woven with an open texture. **3** designed for or using cellular radio. **cellular radio** radio communication, used esp. in car phones, based on a network of transmitters each serving a small area. **cell phone**, **cellular phone** telephone operating by radio communication via a network of transmitters each serving a small area.

cellar n **1** underground room for storage. **2** stock of wine.

cello [**chell**-oh] n, pl **-los** large low-pitched instrument of the violin family. **cellist** n.

Cellophane n ® thin transparent cellulose sheeting used as wrapping.

cellulite n fat deposits under the skin alleged to resist dieting.

celluloid n kind of plastic used to make toys and, formerly, photographic film.

cellulose n main constituent of plant cell walls, used in making paper, plastics, etc.

Celsius adj of the temperature scale in which water freezes at 0° and boils at 100°.

Celt [kelt] n person from Scotland, Ireland, Wales, Cornwall, or Brittany. **Celtic** [**kel**-tik, **sel**-tik] n **1** group of languages including Gaelic and Welsh. ▷ adj **2** of the Celts or the Celtic languages.

cement ❶ n **1** fine grey powder mixed with water and sand to make mortar or concrete. **2** something that unites, binds, or joins. **3** material used to fill teeth. ▷ v **4** join, bind, or cover with cement. **5** make (a relationship) stronger.

cemetery ❶ n, pl **-teries** place where dead people are buried.

cenotaph n monument honouring soldiers who died in a war.

censer n container for burning incense.

censor ❶ n **1** person authorized to

—————————————— THESAURUS ——————————————

celebrate v **1** = **rejoice**, commemorate, drink to, keep, kill the fatted calf, observe, put the flags out, toast **2** = **perform**, bless, honour, solemnize

celebrated adj = **well-known**, acclaimed, distinguished, eminent, famous, illustrious, notable, popular, prominent, renowned

celebration n **1** = **festivity**, anniversary, commemoration, festival, gala, jubilee, merrymaking, party, red-letter day, revelry **2** = **honouring**, observance, performance, remembrance, solemnization

celebrity n **1** = **personality**, big name, big shot (inf), dignitary, luminary, star, superstar, V.I.P. **2** = **fame**, distinction, notability, prestige, prominence, renown, reputation, repute, stardom

celestial adj **1** = **heavenly**, angelic, astral, divine, ethereal, spiritual, sublime, supernatural

celibacy n = **chastity**, continence, purity, virginity

cell n **2** = **room**, chamber, compartment, cubicle, dungeon, stall **3** = **compartment**, cavity **4** = **unit**, caucus, core, coterie, group, nucleus

cement 1 n = **mortar**, plaster ▷ n **2** = **glue**, adhesive, gum, paste, sealant ▷ v **4** = **stick together**, attach, bind, bond, combine, glue, join, plaster, seal, unite, weld

cemetery n = **graveyard**, burial ground, churchyard, God's acre, necropolis

censor v **2** = **cut**, blue-pencil, bowdlerize, expurgate

examine films, books, etc., to ban or cut anything considered obscene or objectionable. ▷ *v* **2** ban or cut parts of (a film, book, etc.). **censorship** *n* **censorious** *adj* harshly critical.

censure ❶ *n* **1** severe disapproval. ▷ *v* **2** criticize severely.

census *n*, *pl* **-suses** official count of a population.

cent *n* hundredth part of a monetary unit such as the dollar or euro.

centaur *n* mythical creature with the head, arms, and torso of a man, and the lower body and legs of a horse.

centenary [sen-**teen**-a-ree] *n*, *pl* **-naries** 100th anniversary or its celebration. **centenarian** *n* person at least 100 years old. **centennial** *n* US centenary.

centi- *prefix* **1** one hundredth, e.g. *centimetre*. **2** a hundred, e.g. *centipede*.

centigrade *adj* same as CELSIUS.

● **USAGE NOTE**
● Scientists now use *Celsius* in
● preference to *centigrade*.

centigram, centigramme *n* one hundredth of a gram.

centilitre *n* one hundredth of a litre.

centime [**son**-teem] *n* monetary unit worth one hundredth of a franc.

centimetre *n* one hundredth of a metre.

centipede *n* small wormlike creature with many legs.

central ❶ *adj* **1** of, at, or forming the centre. **2** main, principal. **centrally** *adv* **centrality** *n* **centralism** *n* principle of central control of a country or organization. **centralize** *v* bring under central control. **centralization** *n* **central heating** system for heating a building from one central source of heat. **central processing unit** part of a computer that performs logical and arithmetical operations on the data.

centre ❶ *n* **1** middle point or part. **2** place for a specified activity. **3** person or thing that is a focus of interest. **4** political party or group favouring moderation. **5** *Sport* player who plays in the middle of the field. ▷ *v* **6** put in the centre of something. **central** *adj* **centrist** *n* person favouring political moderation. **centre on** *v* have as a centre or main theme.

centrifugal *adj* moving away from a centre. **centrifuge** *n* machine that separates substances by centrifugal force. **centrifugal force** force that acts outwards on any body that rotates or moves along a curved path.

centripetal *adj* moving towards a centre.

centurion *n* (in ancient Rome) officer commanding 100 men.

century *n*, *pl* **-ries 1** period of 100 years. **2** cricket score of 100 runs.

CEO chief executive officer.

cephalopod [**seff**-a-loh-pod] *n* sea mollusc with a head and tentacles, such as the octopus.

ceramic *n* **1** hard brittle material made by heating clay to a very high temperature. **2** object made of this. ▷ *pl* **3** art of producing ceramic objects. ▷ *adj* **4** made of ceramic.

cereal *n* **1** grass plant with edible grain, such as oat or wheat. **2** this grain. **3** breakfast food made from this grain, eaten mixed with milk.

cerebellum [serr-rib-**bell**-lum] *n*, *pl* **-lums, -la** [-la] back part of the brain.

cerebral [**ser**-rib-ral] *adj* **1** of the brain. **2** intellectual.

————————————————————— THESAURUS —————————

censorious *adj* = **critical**, captious, carping, cavilling, condemnatory, disapproving, disparaging, fault-finding, hypercritical, scathing, severe

censure *n* **1** = **disapproval**, blame, condemnation, criticism, obloquy, rebuke, reprimand, reproach, reproof, stick (*sl*) ▷ *v* **2** = **criticize**, blame, castigate, condemn, denounce, rap over the knuckles, rebuke, reprimand, reproach, rouse on (*Aust*), scold, slap on the wrist

central *adj* **1** = **middle**, inner, interior, mean, median, mid **2** = **main**, chief, essential, focal, fundamental, key, primary, principal

centralize *v* = **unify**, concentrate, condense, incorporate, rationalize, streamline

centre *n* **1** = **middle**, core, heart, hub, kernel, midpoint, nucleus, pivot **3** = **focus** ▷ *v* **6** = **focus**, cluster, concentrate, converge, revolve

ceremonial *adj* **1** = **ritual**, liturgical, ritualistic **2** = **formal**, solemn, stately ▷ *n* **1** = **ritual**, ceremony, rite **2** = **formality**, solemnity

ceremonious *adj* = **formal**, civil, courteous, deferential, dignified, punctilious, solemn, stately, stiff

cerebrum [**serr**-rib-rum] *n, pl* -**brums**, -**bra** [-bra] main part of the brain. **cerebrospinal** *adj* of the brain and spinal cord.

ceremony ❶ *n, pl* -**nies 1** formal act or ritual. **2** formally polite behaviour. **ceremonial** *adj, n* **ceremonially** *adv* **ceremonious** *adj* excessively polite or formal. **ceremoniously** *adv*.

cerise [ser-**reess**] *adj* cherry-red.

cerium *n Chemistry* steel-grey metallic element.

cert *n informal* certainty, e.g. *a dead cert*.

certain ❶ *adj* **1** positive and confident. **2** definite. **3** some but not much. **4** named but not known, e.g. *a certain Miss Watson taught me English*. **certainly** *adv* **certainty** *n* **1** state of being sure. **2** *pl* -**ties** something that is inevitable.

certificate ❶ *n* official document stating the details of a birth, academic course, etc.

certify ❶ *v* -**fying,** -**fied 1** confirm, attest to. **2** guarantee. **3** declare legally insane. **certifiable** *adj* considered legally insane. **certification** *n*.

certitude *n* confidence, certainty.

cervix *n, pl* **cervixes, cervices 1** narrow entrance of the womb. **2** neck. **cervical** *adj*.

cessation *n* ceasing.

cession *n* ceding.

cesspit, cesspool *n* covered tank or pit for sewage.

cetacean [sit-**tay**-shun] *n* fish-shaped

sea mammal such as a whale or dolphin.

cetane [**see**-tane] *n* colourless liquid hydrocarbon, used as a solvent.

cf compare.

Cf *Chemistry* californium.

CFC chlorofluorocarbon.

cg centigram.

CGI computer-generated image(s).

ch. **1** chapter. **2** church.

cha-cha, cha-cha-cha *n* (music for) a modern ballroom dance from Latin America.

chafe ❶ *v* **1** make sore or worn by rubbing. **2** be annoyed or impatient.

chafer *n* large beetle.

chaff¹ ❶ *n* **1** grain husks. **2** something of little worth.

chaff² ❶ *v* tease good-naturedly.

chaffinch *n* small European songbird.

chagrin [**shag**-grin] *n* annoyance and disappointment. **chagrined** *adj* annoyed and disappointed.

chain ❶ *n* **1** flexible length of connected metal links. **2** (usu. pl) anything that restricts or restrains. **3** series of connected facts or events. **4** group of shops, hotels, etc. owned by one firm. ▷ *v* **5** restrict or fasten with or as if with a chain. **chain gang** *US* group of prisoners chained together. **chain mail** same as MAIL². **chain reaction** series of events, each of which causes the next. **chain-smoke** *v* smoke (cigarettes) continuously. **chain smoker**.

chair ❶ *n* **1** seat with a back, for one

———————————————— THESAURUS ————————————————

ceremony *n* **1** = **ritual**, commemoration, function, observance, parade, rite, service, show, solemnities **2** = **formality**, ceremonial, decorum, etiquette, niceties, pomp, propriety, protocol

certain *adj* **1** = **sure**, assured, confident, convinced, positive, satisfied **2** = **definite**, conclusive, decided, established, fixed, incontrovertible, inevitable, irrefutable, known, settled, sure, true, undeniable, unequivocal

certainly *adv* **2** = **definitely**, assuredly, indisputably, indubitably, surely, truly, undeniably, undoubtedly, without doubt

certainty *n* **1** = **sureness**, assurance, confidence, conviction, faith, positiveness, trust, validity **2** = **fact**, banker, reality, sure thing (*inf*), truth

certificate *n* = **document**, authorization, credential(s), diploma, licence, testimonial, voucher, warrant

certify *v* **1** = **confirm**, attest, authenticate, declare, testify, validate, verify **2** = **guarantee**, assure

chafe *v* **1** = **rub**, abrade, rasp, scrape, scratch **2** = **be annoyed**, be impatient, fret, fume, rage, worry

chaff¹ *n* **1** = **husks 2** = **rubbish**, dregs, refuse, remains, trash, waste

chaff² *v* = **tease**, mock, rib (*inf*), ridicule, scoff, taunt

chain *n* **1** = **link**, bond, coupling, fetter, manacle, shackle **3** = **series**, progression, sequence, set, string, succession, train ▷ *v* **5** = **bind**, confine, enslave, fetter, handcuff, manacle, restrain, shackle, tether

chairman *n* = **director**, chairperson,

person. **2** official position of authority. **3** person holding this. **4** professorship. ▷ *v* **5** preside over (a meeting).

chairlift series of chairs suspended from a moving cable for carrying people up a slope. **chairman**, **chairwoman** *n* person in charge of a company's board of directors or a meeting (also **chairperson**).

- **USAGE NOTE**
- *Chairman* can seem inappropriate
- when applied to a woman, while
- *chairwoman* can be offensive. *Chair*
- and *chairperson* can be applied
- to either a man or a woman;
- *chair* is generally preferred to
- *chairperson*.

chaise [**shaze**] *n* light horse-drawn carriage.

chaise longue [**long**] *n* couch with a back and a single armrest.

chalcedony [kal-**sed**-don-ee] *n*, *pl* **-nies** variety of quartz.

chalet *n* **1** kind of Swiss wooden house with a steeply sloping roof. **2** similar house, used as a holiday home.

chalice [**chal**-liss] *n* **1** large goblet. **2** goblet containing the wine at Communion.

chalk *n* **1** soft white rock consisting of calcium carbonate. **2** piece of chalk, often coloured, used for drawing and writing on blackboards. ▷ *v* **3** draw or mark with chalk. **chalky** *adj*.

challenge ❶ *n* **1** demanding or stimulating situation. **2** call to take part in a contest or fight. **3** questioning of a statement of fact. **4** demand by a sentry for identification or a password. ▷ *v* **5** issue a challenge to. **challenged** *adj* disabled as specified, e.g. *physically challenged*;

mentally challenged. **challenger** *n*.

chamber ❶ *n* **1** hall used for formal meetings. **2** legislative or judicial assembly. **3** *old-fashioned* bedroom. **4** compartment, cavity. **5** compartment for a cartridge in a gun. ▷ *pl* **6** set of rooms used as offices by a barrister. **chambermaid** *n* woman employed to clean bedrooms in a hotel. **chamber music** classical music to be performed by a small group of musicians. **chamber pot** bowl for urine, formerly used in bedrooms.

chamberlain *n History* officer who managed the household of a king or nobleman.

chameleon [kam-**meal**-yon] *n* small lizard that changes colour to blend in with its surroundings.

chamfer [**cham**-fer] *v* bevel the edge of.

chamois [**sham**-wah] *n*, *pl* **-ois 1** small mountain antelope. **2** [**sham**-ee] soft suede leather. **3** piece of this, used for cleaning or polishing.

chamomile [**kam**-mo-mile] *n* same as CAMOMILE.

champ[1] *v* chew noisily. **champ at the bit** *informal* be impatient to do something.

champ[2] *n* short for CHAMPION.

champagne *n* sparkling white French wine.

champion ❶ *n* **1** overall winner of a competition. **2** (foll. by *of*) someone who defends a person or cause. ▷ *v* **3** support. ▷ *adj* **4** *dialect* excellent. **championship** *n*.

chance ❶ *n* **1** likelihood, probability. **2** opportunity to do something. **3** risk, gamble. **4** unpredictable element that causes things to happen one way rather than another. ▷ *v* **5** risk, hazard.

chairwoman, master of ceremonies, president, speaker, spokesman

challenge *n* **1** = **trial**, test **2** = **confrontation**, provocation, ultimatum **3** = **question** ▷ *v* **5** = **test**, confront, defy, dispute, object to, question, tackle, throw down the gauntlet

chamber *n* **1** = **hall**, room **2** = **council**, assembly, legislative body, legislature **3** *Old-fashioned* = **bedroom**, apartment, room **4** = **compartment**, cubicle, enclosure

champion *n* **1** = **winner**, conqueror, hero, title holder, victor **2** (foll. by *of*)

= **defender**, backer, guardian, patron, protector, upholder ▷ *v* **3** = **support**, advocate, back, commend, defend, encourage, espouse, fight for, promote, uphold

chance *n* **1** = **probability**, likelihood, odds, possibility, prospect **2** = **opportunity**, occasion, opening, time **3** = **risk**, gamble, hazard, jeopardy, speculation, uncertainty **4** = **luck**, accident, coincidence, destiny, fate, fortune, providence ▷ *v* **5** = **risk**, endanger, gamble, hazard, jeopardize, stake, try, venture, wager

6 (foll. by *to*) do something without planning to. **chancy** *adj* **chancier**, **chanciest** uncertain, risky. **by chance** without planning.

chancel *n* part of a church containing the altar and choir.

chancellery *n, pl* **-leries 1** residence or office of a chancellor. **2** office of an embassy or consulate.

chancellor *n* **1** head of government in some European countries. **2** honorary head of a university. **chancellorship** *n* **Chancellor of the Exchequer** cabinet minister responsible for finance.

Chancery *n* division of the British High Court of Justice.

chancre [shang-ker] *n* small hard growth which is the first sign of syphilis.

chandelier [shan-dill-**eer**] *n* ornamental light with branches and holders for several candles or bulbs.

chandler *n* dealer, esp. in ships' supplies.

change ❶ *n* **1** becoming different. **2** variety or novelty. **3** different set, esp. of clothes. **4** balance received when the amount paid is more than the cost of a purchase. **5** coins of low value. ▷ *v* **6** make or become different. **7** give and receive (something) in return. **8** exchange (money) for its equivalent in a smaller denomination or different currency. **9** put on other clothes. **10** leave one vehicle and board another. **changeable** *adj* changing often. **changeling** *n* child believed to have been exchanged by fairies for another.

channel ❶ *n* **1** band of broadcasting frequencies. **2** means of access or communication. **3** broad strait connecting two areas of sea. **4** bed or course of a river, stream, or canal. **5** groove. ▷ *v* **-nelling**, **-nelled 6** direct or convey through a channel.

chant ❶ *v* **1** utter or sing (a slogan or psalm). ▷ *n* **2** rhythmic or repetitious slogan. **3** psalm that has a short simple melody with several words sung on one note.

chanter *n* (on bagpipes) pipe on which the melody is played.

chanty *n, pl* **-ties** same as SHANTY².

chaos ❶ *n* complete disorder or confusion. **chaotic** *adj* **chaotically** *adv*.

chap ❶ *n informal* man or boy.

chapati, chapatti *n* (in Indian cookery) flat thin unleavened bread.

chapel *n* **1** place of worship with its own altar, within a church. **2** similar place of worship in a large house or institution. **3** Nonconformist place of worship. **4** section of a trade union in the print industry.

chaperone [shap-per-rone] *n* **1** older person who accompanies and supervises a young person or young people on a social occasion. ▷ *v* **2** act as a chaperone to.

chaplain *n* clergyman attached to a chapel, military body, or institution. **chaplaincy** *n, pl* **-cies**.

chaplet *n* garland for the head.

chapped *adj* (of the skin) raw and cracked, through exposure to cold.

chaps *pl n* leather leggings without a

THESAURUS

change *n* **1** = **alteration**, difference, innovation, metamorphosis, modification, mutation, revolution, transformation, transition **2** = **variety**, break (*inf*), departure, diversion, novelty, variation ▷ *v* **6** = **alter**, convert, modify, mutate, reform, reorganize, restyle, shift, transform, vary **7** = **exchange**, barter, convert, interchange, replace, substitute, swap, trade

changeable *adj* = **variable**, erratic, fickle, inconstant, irregular, mobile, mutable, protean, shifting, unsettled, unstable, volatile, wavering

channel *n* **2** = **route**, approach, artery, avenue, canal, conduit, course, duct, means, medium, passage, path, way

3 = **strait 5** = **groove**, furrow, gutter ▷ *v* **6** = **direct**, conduct, convey, guide, transmit

chant *v* **1** = **sing**, carol, chorus, descant, intone, recite, warble ▷ *n* **3** = **song**, carol, chorus, melody, psalm

chaos *n* = **disorder**, anarchy, bedlam, confusion, disorganization, lawlessness, mayhem, pandemonium, tumult

chaotic *adj* = **disordered**, anarchic, confused, deranged, disorganized, lawless, riotous, topsy-turvy, tumultuous, uncontrolled

chap *n Inf* = **fellow**, bloke (*Brit inf*), character, guy (*inf*), individual, man, person

chaperone *n* **1** = **escort**, companion

seat, worn by cowboys.

chapter ➊ *n* **1** division of a book.
2 period in a life or history. **3** sequence
of events, e.g. *chapter of accidents*.
4 branch of a society or club.

char¹ *v* **charring**, **charred** blacken by
partial burning.

char² *informal* ▷ *n* **1** charwoman. ▷ *v*
charring, **charred 2** clean other
people's houses as a job.

char³ *n old-fashioned slang* tea.

char⁴ *n* small troutlike fish.

charabanc [**shar**-rab-bang] *n old-
fashioned* coach for sightseeing.

character ➊ *n* **1** combination of
qualities distinguishing a person,
group, or place. **2** reputation, esp.
good reputation. **3** person
represented in a play, film, or story.
4 unusual or amusing person. **5** letter,
numeral, or symbol used in writing or
printing. **characteristic** *n*
1 distinguishing feature or quality.
▷ *adj* **2** typical. **characteristically** *adv*
characterize *v* **1** be a characteristic of.
2 (foll. by *as*) describe.
characterization *n*.

charade ➊ [shar-**rahd**] *n* **1** absurd
pretence. ▷ *pl* **2** game in which one
team acts out a word or phrase, which

the other team has to guess.

charcoal *n* black substance formed by
partially burning wood.

charge ➊ *v* **1** ask as a price. **2** enter a
debit against a person's account for (a
purchase). **3** accuse formally. **4** make
a rush at or sudden attack upon. **5** fill
(a glass). **6** fill (a battery) with
electricity. **7** command, assign. ▷ *n*
8 price charged. **9** formal accusation.
10 attack. **11** command, exhortation.
12 custody, guardianship. **13** person or
thing entrusted to someone's care.
14 cartridge, shell. **15** amount of
electricity stored in a battery. **in
charge of** in control of. **chargeable**
adj **charger** *n* **1** device for charging an
accumulator. **2** (in the Middle Ages)
warhorse.

chargé d'affaires [**shar**-zhay daf-
fair] *n*, *pl* **chargés d'affaires** head
of a diplomatic mission in the absence
of an ambassador or in a small
mission.

chariot *n* two-wheeled horse-drawn
vehicle used in ancient times in wars
and races. **charioteer** *n* chariot driver.

charisma ➊ [kar-**rizz**-ma] *n* person's
power to attract or influence people.
charismatic [kar-rizz-**mat**-ik] *adj*.

──────────────── THESAURUS ────────

▷ *v* **2** = **escort**, accompany, attend,
protect, safeguard, shepherd, watch
over

chapter *n* **1** = **section**, clause, division,
episode, part, topic **2** = **period**, part,
phase, stage

character *n* **1** = **nature**, attributes,
calibre, complexion, disposition,
personality, quality, temperament,
type **2** = **reputation**, honour,
integrity, rectitude, strength,
uprightness **3** = **role**, part, persona,
portrayal **4** = **eccentric**, card (*inf*),
oddball (*inf*), original **5** = **symbol**,
device, figure, hieroglyph, letter, mark,
rune, sign

characteristic *n* **1** = **feature**,
attribute, faculty, idiosyncrasy, mark,
peculiarity, property, quality, quirk,
trait ▷ *adj* **2** = **typical**, distinctive,
distinguishing, idiosyncratic,
individual, munted (*NZ sl*), peculiar,
representative, singular, special,
symbolic, symptomatic

characterize *v* **1** = **identify**, brand,
distinguish, indicate, mark, represent,
stamp, typify

charade *n* **1** = **pretence**, fake, farce,
pantomime, parody, travesty

charge *v* **3** = **accuse**, arraign, blame,
impeach, incriminate, indict
4 = **attack**, assail, assault, rush,
stampede, storm **5** = **fill**, load
7 = **command**, bid, commit, demand,
entrust, instruct, order, require ▷ *n*
8 = **price**, amount, cost, expenditure,
expense, outlay, payment, rate, toll
9 = **accusation**, allegation,
imputation, indictment **10** = **attack**,
assault, onset, onslaught, rush, sortie,
stampede **11** = **instruction**,
command, demand, direction,
injunction, mandate, order, precept
12 = **care**, custody, duty, office,
responsibility, safekeeping, trust
13 = **ward**

charisma *n* = **charm**, allure, attraction,
lure, magnetism, personality

charismatic *adj* = **charming**, alluring,
attractive, enticing, influential, lekker
(*S Afr sl*), magnetic

charitable *adj* **2**, **3** = **generous**,
beneficent, benevolent, bountiful,
kind, lavish, liberal, philanthropic

charity ❶ n, pl **-ties 1** organization that gives help, such as money or food, to those in need. **2** giving of help to those in need. **3** help given to those in need. **4** kindly attitude towards people. **charitable** adj **charitably** adv.

charlady n same as CHARWOMAN.

charlatan ❶ [**shar**-lat-tan] n person who claims expertise that he or she does not have.

charleston n lively dance of the 1920s.

charlock n weed with hairy leaves and yellow flowers.

charlotte n dessert made with fruit and bread or cake crumbs.

charm ❶ n **1** attractive quality. **2** trinket worn on a bracelet. **3** small object with supposed magical powers. **4** magic spell. ▷ v **5** attract, delight. **6** influence by personal charm. **7** protect or influence as if by magic. **charmer** n **charming** adj attractive. **charmingly** adv.

charnel house n building or vault for the bones of the dead.

chart ❶ n **1** graph, table, or diagram showing information. **2** map of the sea or stars. ▷ v **3** plot the course of. **4** make a chart of. **the charts** informal weekly lists of the bestselling pop records.

charter ❶ n **1** document granting or

demanding certain rights. **2** fundamental principles of an organization. **3** hire of transport for private use. ▷ v **4** hire by charter. **5** grant a charter to. **chartered** adj officially qualified to practise a profession, e.g. chartered accountant.

chartreuse [shar-**trerz**] n sweet-smelling green or yellow liqueur.

charwoman n woman whose job is to clean other people's homes.

chary [**chair**-ee] adj **-rier, -riest** wary, careful. **charily** adv.

chase¹ ❶ v **1** run after quickly in order to catch or drive away. **2** informal rush, run. **3** informal try energetically to obtain. ▷ n **4** chasing, pursuit. **chaser** n milder drink drunk after another stronger one.

chase² v engrave or emboss (metal).

chasm ❶ [**kaz**-zum] n **1** deep crack in the earth. **2** wide difference.

chassis [**shass**-ee] n, pl **-sis** frame, wheels, and mechanical parts of a vehicle.

chaste ❶ adj **1** abstaining from sex outside marriage or altogether. **2** (of style) simple. **chastely** adv **chastity** n.

chasten ❶ [**chase**-en] v subdue by criticism.

chastise ❶ v **1** scold severely. **2** punish

THESAURUS

4 = **kind**, considerate, favourable, forgiving, humane, indulgent, lenient, magnanimous, sympathetic, tolerant, understanding

charity n **2** = **help**, assistance, benefaction, philanthropy, relief **3** = **donations**, contributions, endowment, fund, gift, hand-out, largesse or largess **4** = **kindness**, altruism, benevolence, compassion, fellow feeling, generosity, goodwill, humanity, indulgence

charlatan n = **fraud**, cheat, con man (inf), fake, impostor, phoney or phony (inf), pretender, quack, sham, swindler

charm n **1** = **attraction**, allure, appeal, fascination, magnetism **2** = **trinket** **3** = **talisman**, amulet, fetish **4** = **spell**, enchantment, magic, sorcery ▷ v **5** = **attract**, allure, beguile, bewitch, captivate, delight, enchant, enrapture, entrance, fascinate, mesmerize **6** = **win over**

charming adj = **attractive**, appealing, captivating, cute, delightful, fetching, lekker (S Afr sl), likable or likeable,

pleasing, seductive, winsome

chart n **1** = **table**, blueprint, diagram, graph, plan **2** = **map** ▷ v **3** = **plot**, map out **4** = **outline**, delineate, draft, shape, sketch

charter n **1** = **document**, contract, deed, licence, permit ▷ v **4** = **hire**, commission, employ, lease, rent **5** = **authorize**, sanction

chase¹ v **1** = **pursue**, course, drive, drive away, expel, follow, hound, hunt, put to flight, run after, track ▷ n **4** = **pursuit**, hunt, hunting, race

chasm n **1** = **gulf**, abyss, crater, crevasse, fissure, gap, gorge, ravine

chaste adj **1** = **pure**, immaculate, innocent, modest, unaffected, undefiled, virtuous **2** = **simple**

chasten v = **subdue**, chastise, correct, discipline, humble, humiliate, put in one's place, tame

chastise v **1** = **scold**, berate, castigate, censure, correct, discipline, rouse on (Aust), upbraid **2** = **beat**, flog, lash, lick (inf), punish, scourge, whip

chastity n **1** = **purity**, celibacy,

by beating. **chastisement** n.

chasuble [**chazz**-yew-bl] n long sleeveless robe worn by a priest when celebrating Mass.

chat ❶ n 1 informal conversation. ▷ v **chatting**, **chatted** 2 have an informal conversation. **chatty** adj **-tier**, **-tiest**. **chatroom** n site on the internet where users have group discussions by e-mail.

chateau [**shat**-toe] n, pl **-teaux**, **-teaus** French castle.

chatelaine [**shat**-tell-lane] n (formerly) mistress of a large house or castle.

chattels pl n possessions.

chatter ❶ v 1 speak quickly and continuously about unimportant things. 2 (of a bird or monkey) make rapid repetitive high-pitched noises. 3 (of the teeth) rattle with cold or fear. ▷ n 4 idle talk. **chatterbox** n person who chatters a lot.

chauffeur n person employed to drive a car for someone. **chauffeuse** n fem.

chauvinism [**show**-vin-iz-zum] n irrational belief that one's own country, race, group, or sex is superior. **chauvinist** n, adj **chauvinistic** adj.

chav n Brit informal young working-class person considered to have vulgar tastes.

cheap ❶ adj 1 costing relatively little. 2 of poor quality. 3 not valued highly. 4 mean, despicable. **cheaply** adv **cheapen** v 1 lower the reputation of.

2 reduce the price of. **cheap-jack** n informal person who sells cheap and shoddy goods. **cheapskate** n informal miserly person.

cheat ❶ v 1 act dishonestly to gain profit or advantage. 2 (usu. foll. by on) be unfaithful (to). ▷ n 3 person who cheats. 4 fraud, deception.

check ❶ v 1 examine, investigate. 2 slow the growth or progress of. 3 correspond, agree. ▷ n 4 test to ensure accuracy or progress. 5 break in progress. 6 US cheque. 7 pattern of squares or crossed lines. 8 Chess position of a king under attack. **checked** adj having a pattern of squares. **check in** v register one's arrival. **checkmate** n 1 Chess winning position in which an opponent's king is under attack and unable to escape. 2 utter defeat. ▷ v 3 Chess place the king of (one's opponent) in checkmate. 4 thwart, defeat. **check out** v 1 pay the bill and leave a hotel. 2 examine, investigate. 3 informal have a look at. **checkout** n counter in a supermarket, where customers pay. **checkup** n thorough medical examination.

checkers n US same as DRAUGHTS.

Cheddar n firm orange or yellowy-white cheese.

cheek ❶ n 1 either side of the face below the eye. 2 informal impudence, boldness. ▷ v 3 informal speak impudently to. **cheeky** adj **cheekier**,

continence, innocence, maidenhood, modesty, virginity, virtue

chat n 1 = **talk**, chatter, chinwag (Brit inf), conversation, gossip, heart-to-heart, natter, tête-à-tête ▷ v 2 = **talk**, chatter, gossip, jaw (sl), natter

chatter v 1 = **prattle**, babble, blather, chat, gab (inf), gossip, natter, rabbit (on) (Brit inf), schmooze (sl) ▷ n 4 = **prattle**, babble, blather, chat, gab (inf), gossip, natter

cheap adj 1 = **inexpensive**, bargain, cut-price, economical, keen, low-cost, low-priced, reasonable, reduced 2 = **inferior**, common, poor, second-rate, shoddy, tatty, tawdry, two a penny, worthless 4 = **despicable**, contemptible, mean

cheapen v 1 = **degrade**, belittle, debase, demean, denigrate, discredit, disparage, lower 2 = **devalue**, depreciate

cheat v 1 = **deceive**, beguile, con (inf), defraud, double-cross (inf), dupe, fleece, fool, mislead, rip off (sl), swindle, trick ▷ n 3 = **deceiver**, charlatan, con man (inf), double-crosser (inf), shark, sharper, swindler, trickster 4 = **deception**, deceit, fraud, rip-off (sl), scam (sl), swindle, trickery

check v 1 = **examine**, inquire into, inspect, investigate, look at, make sure, monitor, research, scrutinize, study, test, vet 2 = **stop**, delay, halt, hinder, impede, inhibit, limit, obstruct, restrain, retard ▷ n 4 = **examination**, inspection, investigation, once-over (inf), research, scrutiny, test

cheek n 2 Inf = **impudence**, audacity, chutzpah (US & Canad inf), disrespect, effrontery, impertinence, insolence, lip (sl), nerve, temerity

cheeky adj = **impudent**, audacious, disrespectful, forward, impertinent,

cheekiest impudent, disrespectful.
cheekily *adv* **cheekiness** *n*.
cheep *n* **1** young bird's high-pitched cry.
▷ *v* **2** utter a cheep.
cheer ❶ *v* **1** applaud or encourage with
shouts. **2** make or become happy. ▷ *n*
3 shout of applause or
encouragement. **4** feeling of
happiness. **cheerful** *adj* **cheerfully** *adv*
cheerfulness *n* **cheerless** *adj* dreary,
gloomy. **cheery** *adj* **cheerily** *adv*.
cheerio *interj informal* goodbye.
cheese *n* **1** food made from coagulated
milk curd. **2** block of this. **cheesy** *adj*
cheeseburger *n* hamburger topped
with melted cheese. **cheesecake** *n*
1 dessert with a biscuit-crumb base
covered with a sweet cream-cheese
mixture. **2** *slang* photographs of naked
or near-naked women. **cheesecloth** *n*
light cotton cloth. **cheesed off** bored,
annoyed. **cheeseparing** *adj* mean,
miserly.
cheetah *n* large fast-running spotted
African wild cat.
chef *n* cook in a restaurant.
chef-d'oeuvre [shay-**durv**] *n, pl* **chefs-
d'oeuvre** masterpiece.
chemical *n* **1** substance used in or
resulting from a reaction involving
changes to atoms or molecules. ▷ *adj*
2 of chemistry or chemicals.
chemically *adv*.
chemise [shem-**meez**] *n old-fashioned*
woman's loose-fitting slip.
chemistry ❶ *n* science of the
composition, properties, and reactions
of substances. **chemical** *n* substance
used in or resulting from a reaction
involving changes to atoms or
molecules. **chemist** *n* **1** shop selling
medicines and cosmetics. **2** qualified

dispenser of prescribed medicines.
3 specialist in chemistry.
chemotherapy *n* treatment of
disease, often cancer, using chemicals.
chenille [shen-**neel**] *n* (fabric of) thick
tufty yarn.
cheque *n* written order to one's bank to
pay money from one's account.
cheque book book of detachable
blank cheques issued by a bank.
cheque card plastic card issued by a
bank guaranteeing payment of a
customer's cheques.
chequer *n* **1** piece used in Chinese
chequers. ▷ *pl* **2** game of draughts.
chequered *adj* **1** marked by varied
fortunes, e.g. *a chequered career*.
2 having a pattern of squares.
cherish ❶ *v* **1** cling to (an idea or
feeling). **2** care for.
cheroot [sher-**root**] *n* cigar with both
ends cut flat.
cherry *n, pl* -**ries 1** small red or black
fruit with a stone. **2** tree on which it
grows. ▷ *adj* **3** deep red. **cherry
tomato** miniature tomato.
cherub *n, pl* -**ubs**, -**ubim 1** angel, often
represented as a winged child. **2** sweet
child. **cherubic** [cher-**rew**-bik] *adj*.
chervil *n* aniseed-flavoured herb.
chess *n* game for two players with 16
pieces each, played on a chequered
board of 64 squares. **chessman** *n* piece
used in chess.
chest ❶ *n* **1** front of the body, from neck
to waist. **2** large strong box. **chest of
drawers** piece of furniture consisting
of drawers in a frame.
chesterfield *n* couch with high padded
sides and back.
chestnut *n* **1** reddish-brown edible
nut. **2** tree on which it grows.

———————————— THESAURUS ————————————

insolent, insulting, pert, saucy
cheer *v* **1** = **applaud**, acclaim, clap, hail
2 = **cheer up**, brighten, buoy up,
comfort, encourage, gladden,
hearten, uplift ▷ *n* **3** = **applause**,
acclamation, ovation, plaudits
cheerful *adj* = **happy**, buoyant, cheery,
chirpy (*inf*), enthusiastic, jaunty, jolly,
light-hearted, merry, optimistic,
upbeat (*inf*)
cheerfulness *n* = **happiness**,
buoyancy, exuberance, gaiety,
geniality, good cheer, good humour,
high spirits, jauntiness, light-
heartedness

cheerless *adj* = **gloomy**, bleak,
desolate, dismal, drab, dreary, forlorn,
miserable, sombre, woeful
cheery *adj* = **cheerful**, breezy, carefree,
chirpy (*inf*), genial, good-humoured,
happy, jovial, upbeat (*inf*)
chemist *n* **2** = **pharmacist**, apothecary
(*obs*), dispenser
cherish *v* **1** = **cling to**, cleave to,
encourage, entertain, foster, harbour,
hold dear, nurture, prize, sustain,
treasure **2** = **care for**, comfort, hold
dear, love, nurse, shelter, support
chest *n* **2** = **box**, case, casket, coffer,
crate, strongbox, trunk

3 reddish-brown horse. **4** *informal* old joke. ▷ *adj* **5** (of hair or a horse) reddish-brown.

chesty *adj* **chestier**, **chestiest** *informal* symptomatic of chest disease.

cheval glass [shev-**val**] *n* full-length mirror mounted to swivel within a frame.

Cheviot *n* large British sheep reared for its wool.

chevron [**shev**-ron] *n* V-shaped pattern, esp. on the sleeve of a military uniform to indicate rank.

chew ❶ *v* grind (food) between the teeth. **chewy** *adj* **chewier**, **chewiest** requiring a lot of chewing. **chewing gum** flavoured gum to be chewed but not swallowed. **chew over** *v* consider carefully.

chianti [kee-**ant**-ee] *n* dry red Italian wine.

chiaroscuro [kee-ah-roh-**skew**-roh] *n*, *pl* **-ros** distribution of light and shade in a picture.

chic ❶ [**sheek**] *adj* **1** stylish, elegant. ▷ *n* **2** stylishness, elegance.

chicane [shik-**kane**] *n* obstacle in a motor-racing circuit.

chicanery *n* trickery, deception.

chick *n* **1** baby bird. **2** *slang* young woman. **chickpea** *n* edible yellow pealike seed. **chickweed** *n* weed with small white flowers.

chicken *n* **1** domestic fowl. **2** its flesh, used as food. **3** *slang* coward. ▷ *adj* **4** *slang* cowardly. **chicken feed** *slang* trifling amount of money. **chicken out** *v informal* fail to do something through

cowardice. **chickenpox** *n* infectious disease with an itchy rash.

chicory *n*, *pl* **-ries 1** plant whose leaves are used in salads. **2** root of this plant, used as a coffee substitute.

chide ❶ *v* **chiding**, **chided** *or* **chid**, **chid** *or* **chidden** rebuke, scold.

chief ❶ *n* **1** head of a group of people. ▷ *adj* **2** most important. **chiefly** *adv* **1** especially. **2** mainly. **chieftain** *n* leader of a tribe.

chiffchaff *n* common European warbler.

chiffon [**shif**-fon] *n* fine see-through fabric.

chignon [**sheen**-yon] *n* knot of hair pinned up at the back of the head.

chigoe [**chig**-go] *n* tropical flea that burrows into the skin.

chihuahua [chee-**wah**-wah] *n* tiny short-haired dog.

chilblain *n* inflammation of the fingers or toes, caused by exposure to cold.

child ❶ *n*, *pl* **children 1** young human being, boy or girl. **2** son or daughter. **3** product of an influence or environment, e.g. *a child of the Sixties*. **childhood** *n* **childish** *adj* **1** immature, silly. **2** of or like a child. **childishly** *adv* **childless** *adj* **childlike** *adj* innocent, trustful. **childbirth** *n* giving birth to a child. **child's play** very easy task.

● **USAGE NOTE**
● Note that *childish* has overtones of
● *foolish* while *childlike* suggests an
● *innocent* quality.

chill ❶ *n* **1** a feverish cold. **2** moderate

chew *v* = **bite**, champ, chomp, crunch, gnaw, grind, masticate, munch

chewy *adj* = **tough**, as tough as old boots, leathery

chic *adj* **1** = **stylish**, elegant, fashionable, smart, trendy (*Brit inf*)

chide *v* = **scold**, admonish, berate, censure, criticize, lecture, rebuke, reprimand, reproach, reprove, rouse on (*Aust*), tell off (*inf*), tick off (*inf*)

chief *n* **1** = **head**, boss (*inf*), captain, commander, director, governor, leader, manager, master, principal, ruler ▷ *adj* **2** = **primary**, foremost, highest, key, leading, main, predominant, pre-eminent, premier, prime, principal, supreme, uppermost

chiefly *adv* **1** = **especially**, above all, essentially, primarily, principally

2 = **mainly**, in general, in the main, largely, mostly, on the whole, predominantly, usually

child *n* **1** = **youngster**, babe, baby, bairn (*Scot*), infant, juvenile, kid (*inf*), offspring, toddler, tot

childbirth *n* = **child-bearing**, confinement, delivery, labour, lying-in, parturition, travail

childhood *n* = **youth**, boyhood *or* girlhood, immaturity, infancy, minority, schooldays

childish *adj* **1** = **immature**, foolish, infantile, juvenile, puerile **2** = **young**, boyish *or* girlish, juvenile

childlike *adj* = **innocent**, artless, guileless, ingenuous, naive, simple, trusting

chill *n* **2** = **cold**, bite, coldness, coolness, crispness, frigidity, nip, rawness, coldness. ▷ v **3** make (something) cool or cold. **4** cause (someone) to feel cold or frightened. ▷ adj **5** unpleasantly cold. **chilly** adj **chillier**, **chilliest 1** moderately cold. **2** unfriendly. **chilly-bin** n NZ informal insulated container for carrying food and drink. **chilliness** n **chill out** v informal to relax, esp. after energetic dancing at a rave.

chilli, chili n **1** small red or green hot-tasting capsicum pod, used in cooking. **2** (also **chilli con carne**) hot-tasting Mexican dish of meat, onions, beans, and chilli powder.

chime ❶ n **1** musical ringing sound of a bell or clock. ▷ v **2** make a musical ringing sound. **3** indicate (the time) by chiming. **4** (foll. by with) be consistent with.

chimera [kime-**meer**-a] n **1** unrealistic hope or idea. **2** fabled monster with a lion's head, goat's body, and serpent's tail. **chimerical** adj.

chimney n hollow vertical structure for carrying away smoke from a fire. **chimney breast** walls surrounding the base of a chimney or fireplace. **chimneypot** n short pipe on the top of a chimney. **chimney sweep** person who cleans soot from chimneys.

chimp n informal short for CHIMPANZEE.

chimpanzee n intelligent black African ape.

chin n part of the face below the mouth. **chinwag** n informal chat.

china ❶ n **1** fine earthenware or porcelain. **2** dishes or ornaments made of this. **china clay** same as KAOLIN.

chinchilla n **1** S American rodent bred for its soft grey fur. **2** its fur.

chine n **1** cut of meat including part of the backbone. ▷ v **2** cut (meat) along the backbone.

Chinese adj **1** of China. ▷ n **2** pl **-nese** person from China. **3** any of the languages of China. **Chinese chequers** game played with marbles or pegs on a star-shaped board. **Chinese lantern** collapsible lantern made of thin paper.

chink¹ ❶ n small narrow opening, e.g. a chink of light.

chink² v, n (make) a light ringing sound.

chintz n printed cotton fabric with a glazed finish.

chip ❶ n **1** strip of potato, fried in deep fat. **2** tiny wafer of semiconductor material forming an integrated circuit. **3** counter used to represent money in gambling games. **4** small piece removed by chopping, breaking, etc. **5** mark left where a small piece has been broken off something. ▷ v **chipping, chipped 6** break small pieces from. **have a chip on one's shoulder** informal bear a grudge. **chip in** v informal **1** contribute (money). **2** interrupt with a remark. **chippie** n Brit, Aust & NZ informal carpenter.

chipboard n thin board made of compressed wood particles.

chipmunk n small squirrel-like N American rodent with a striped back.

chipolata n small sausage.

chiropodist [kir-**rop**-pod-ist] n person who treats minor foot complaints. **chiropody** n.

chiropractic [kire-oh-**prak**-tik] n system of treating bodily disorders by manipulation of the spine. **chiropractor** n.

chirp, chirrup ❶ v **1** (of a bird or insect) make a short high-pitched sound. **2** speak in a lively fashion. ▷ n **3** chirping sound. **chirpy** adj **chirpier, chirpiest** informal lively and cheerful.

chisel n **1** metal tool with a sharp end for shaping wood or stone. ▷ v **-elling**,

---

sharpness ▷ v **3** = **cool**, freeze, refrigerate **4** = **dishearten**, dampen, deject, depress, discourage, dismay ▷ adj **5** = **cold**, biting, bleak, chilly, freezing, frigid, raw, sharp, wintry

chilly adj **1** = **cool**, brisk, crisp, draughty, fresh, nippy, penetrating, sharp **2** = **unfriendly**, frigid, hostile, unresponsive, unsympathetic, unwelcoming

chime n **1** = **ring**, clang, jingle, peal, sound, tinkle, toll ▷ v **2** = **ring**, clang,

jingle, peal, sound, tinkle, toll

china n **1** = **pottery**, ceramics, porcelain **2** = **crockery**, service, tableware, ware

chink¹ n **1** = **opening**, aperture, cleft, crack, cranny, crevice, fissure, gap

chip n **4** = **scratch**, fragment, nick, notch, shard, shaving, sliver, wafer ▷ v **6** = **nick**, chisel, damage, gash, whittle

chirp, chirrup v **1** = **tweet**, cheep, peep, pipe, twitter, warble

-elled 2 carve or form with a chisel.

chit¹ *n* short official note, such as a receipt.

chit² *n old-fashioned* pert or impudent girl.

chitchat *n* chat, gossip.

chitterlings *pl n* pig's intestines cooked as food.

chivalry ❶ *n* **1** courteous behaviour, esp. by men towards women. **2** medieval system and principles of knighthood. **chivalrous** *adj*.

chives *pl n* herb with a mild onion flavour.

chivvy *v* **-vying, -vied** *informal* harass, nag.

chlorine *n* strong-smelling greenish-yellow gaseous element, used to disinfect water. **chlorinate** *v* disinfect (water) with chlorine. **chlorination** *n* **chloride** *n* compound of chlorine and another substance.

chlorofluorocarbon *n* any of various gaseous compounds of carbon, hydrogen, chlorine, and fluorine, used in refrigerators and aerosol propellants, some of which break down the ozone in the atmosphere.

chloroform *n* strong-smelling liquid formerly used as an anaesthetic.

chlorophyll *n* green colouring matter of plants, which enables them to convert sunlight into energy.

chock *n* **1** block or wedge used to prevent a heavy object from moving. ▷ *v* **2** secure by a chock. **chock-full, chock-a-block** *adj* completely full.

chocolate *n* **1** sweet food made from cacao seeds. **2** sweet or drink made from this. ▷ *adj* **3** dark brown.

choice ❶ *n* **1** choosing. **2** opportunity or power of choosing. **3** person or thing chosen or that may be chosen. **4** alternative action or possibility. ▷ *adj* **5** of high quality.

choir *n* **1** organized group of singers, esp. in church. **2** part of a church occupied by the choir.

choke ❶ *v* **1** hinder or stop the breathing of (a person) by strangling or smothering. **2** have trouble in breathing. **3** block, clog up. ▷ *n* **4** device controlling the amount of air that is mixed with the fuel in a petrol engine. **choker** *n* tight-fitting necklace. **choke back** *v* suppress (tears or anger).

cholera [kol-ler-a] *n* serious infectious disease causing severe vomiting and diarrhoea.

choleric [kol-ler-ik] *adj* bad-tempered. **choler** *n old-fashioned* bad temper.

cholesterol [kol-**lest**-er-oll] *n* fatty substance found in animal tissue, an excess of which can cause heart disease.

chomp *v* chew noisily.

chook *n Aust & NZ* hen or chicken.

choose ❶ *v* **choosing, chose, chosen 1** select from a number of alternatives. **2** decide (to do something) because one wants to. **choosy** *adj* **choosier, choosiest** *informal* fussy, hard to please.

chop¹ ❶ *v* **chopping, chopped 1** cut with a blow from an axe or knife. **2** cut into pieces. **3** *Boxing, karate* hit (an opponent) with a short sharp blow. ▷ *n* **4** cutting or sharp blow. **5** slice of lamb or pork, usu. with a rib. **chopper** *n* **1** *informal* helicopter. **2** small axe. **3** butcher's cleaver. **4** cycle with very high handlebars. **choppy** *adj* **-pier, -piest** (of the sea) fairly rough.

chop² *v* **chopping, chopped. chop and change** change one's mind repeatedly.

chops *pl n informal* jaws, cheeks.

chopsticks *pl n* pair of thin sticks used to eat Chinese food.

chop suey *n* Chinese dish of chopped meat and vegetables in a sauce.

choral *adj* of a choir.

———————————————— THESAURUS ————————————————

chivalrous *adj* **1** = **courteous**, gallant, gentlemanly, honourable **2** = **valiant**, bold, brave, courageous

chivalry *n* **1** = **courtesy**, gallantry, gentlemanliness, politeness **2** = **knighthood**, courage, knight-errantry

choice *n* **2** = **option**, alternative, pick, preference, say **3** = **selection**, range, variety ▷ *adj* **5** = **best**, elite, excellent, exclusive, prime, rare, select

choke *v* **1** = **strangle**, asphyxiate, gag, overpower, smother, stifle, suffocate, suppress, throttle **3** = **block**, bar, bung, clog, congest, constrict, obstruct, stop

choose *v* = **pick**, adopt, designate, elect, opt for, prefer, select, settle upon

choosy *adj Inf* = **fussy**, discriminating, faddy, fastidious, finicky, particular, picky (*inf*), selective

chop *v* **1** = **cut**, cleave, fell, hack, hew, lop, sever

chorale [kor-**rahl**] n slow stately hymn tune.

chord[1] n Maths straight line joining two points on a curve.

chord[2] n simultaneous sounding of three or more musical notes.

chore ❶ n 1 routine task. 2 unpleasant task.

chorea [kor-**ree**-a] n disorder of the nervous system characterized by uncontrollable brief jerky movements.

choreography n composition of steps and movements for dancing. **choreographer** n **choreographic** adj.

chorister n singer in a choir.

chortle ❶ v 1 chuckle in amusement. ▷ n 2 amused chuckle.

chorus ❶ n, pl -**ruses** 1 large choir. 2 part of a song repeated after each verse. 3 something expressed by many people at once. 4 group of singers or dancers who perform together in a show. ▷ v **chorusing, chorused** 5 sing or say together. **in chorus** in unison.

chose v past tense of CHOOSE. **chosen** v past participle of CHOOSE.

chough [**chuff**] n large black bird of the crow family.

choux pastry [**shoo**] n very light pastry made with eggs.

chow n 1 thick-coated dog with a curled tail, orig. from China. 2 informal food.

chowder n thick soup containing clams or fish.

chow mein n Chinese-American dish of chopped meat or vegetables fried with noodles.

chrism n consecrated oil used for anointing in some churches.

Christ n 1 Jesus of Nazareth, regarded by Christians as the Messiah. ▷ interj 2 taboo slang oath of annoyance or surprise.

christen ❶ v 1 baptize. 2 give a name to. 3 informal use for the first time. **christening** n.

Christendom n all Christian people or Christian countries.

Christian n 1 person who believes in and follows Christ. ▷ adj 2 of Christ or Christianity. 3 kind, good. **Christianity** n religion based on the life and teachings of Christ. **Christian name** person's first name. **Christian Science** religious system which emphasizes spiritual healing.

Christmas ❶ n 1 annual festival on December 25 commemorating the birth of Christ. 2 period around this time. **Christmassy** adj **Christmas box** tip given at Christmas to postmen or tradesmen. **Christmas Day** December 25. **Christmas Eve** December 24. **Christmas tree** evergreen tree or imitation of one, decorated as part of Christmas celebrations.

chromatic adj 1 of colour or colours. 2 Music (of a scale) proceeding by semitones. **chromatically** adv.

chromatography n separation and analysis of the components of a substance by slowly passing it through an adsorbing material.

chromium, chrome n Chemistry grey metallic element used in steel alloys and for electroplating.

chromosome n microscopic gene-carrying body in the nucleus of a cell.

chronic adj 1 (of an illness) lasting a long time. 2 habitual, e.g. chronic drinking. 3 informal of poor quality. **chronically** adv.

chronicle ❶ n 1 record of events in order of occurrence. ▷ v 2 record in or as if in a chronicle. **chronicler** n.

chronology n, pl -**gies** arrangement or list of events in order of occurrence. **chronological** adj **chronologically** adv.

chronometer n timepiece designed to be accurate in all conditions.

chrysalis [**kriss**-a-liss] n insect in the stage between larva and adult, when it is in a cocoon.

THESAURUS

chore n 1 = **task**, duty, errand, job 2 = **burden**

chortle v 1 = **chuckle**, cackle, crow, guffaw ▷ n 2 = **chuckle**, cackle, crow, guffaw

chorus n 1 = **choir**, choristers, ensemble, singers, vocalists 2 = **refrain**, burden, response, strain 3 = **unison**, accord, concert, harmony

christen v 1 = **baptize** 2 = **name**, call, designate, dub, style, term, title

Christmas n = **festive season**, Noel, Xmas (inf), Yule (arch)

chronicle n 1 = **record**, account, annals, diary, history, journal, narrative, register, story ▷ v 2 = **record**, enter, narrate, put on record, recount, register, relate, report, set down, tell

chrysanthemum *n* garden flower with a large head made up of thin petals.

chub *n* freshwater fish of the carp family.

chubby ❶ *adj* **-bier, -biest** plump and round. **chubbiness** *n*.

chuck[1] ❶ *v* **1** *informal* throw. **2** *informal* give up, reject. **3** touch (someone) affectionately under the chin.

chuck[2] *n* **1** cut of beef from the neck to the shoulder. **2** device that holds a workpiece in a lathe or a tool in a drill.

chuckle ❶ *v* **1** laugh softly. ▷ *n* **2** soft laugh.

chuff *v* (of a steam engine) move while making a puffing sound.

chuffed *adj informal* very pleased.

chug *n* **1** short dull sound like the noise of an engine. ▷ *v* **chugging, chugged 2** operate or move with this sound.

chukka, chukker *n* period of play in polo.

chum ❶ *informal* ▷ *n* **1** close friend. ▷ *v* **chumming, chummed 2 chum up with** form a close friendship with. **chummy** *adj* **-mier, -miest**.

chump *n* **1** *informal* stupid person. **2** thick piece of meat. **3** thick block of wood.

chunk ❶ *n* **1** thick solid piece. **2** considerable amount. **chunky** *adj* **chunkier, chunkiest 1** (of a person) broad and heavy. **2** (of an object) large and thick.

church *n* **1** building for public Christian worship. **2** particular Christian denomination. **3** (**C-**) Christians collectively. **4** clergy. **churchgoer** *n* person who attends church regularly. **churchwarden** *n* member of a congregation who assists the vicar. **churchyard** *n* grounds round a church, used as a graveyard.

churlish ❶ *adj* surly and rude.

churn ❶ *n* **1** machine in which cream is shaken to make butter. **2** large container for milk. ▷ *v* **3** stir (cream) vigorously to make butter. **4** move about violently. **churn out** *v informal* produce (things) rapidly in large numbers.

chute[1] [**shoot**] *n* steep slope down which things may be slid.

chute[2] *n informal* short for PARACHUTE.

chutney *n* pickle made from fruit, vinegar, spices, and sugar.

chyle *n* milky fluid formed in the small intestine during digestion.

chyme *n* thick fluid mass of partially digested food that leaves the stomach.

CIA (in the US) Central Intelligence Agency.

cicada [sik-**kah**-da] *n* large insect that makes a high-pitched drone.

cicatrix [**sik**-a-trix] *n*, *pl* **-trices** scar.

CID Criminal Investigation Department.

cider *n* alcoholic drink made from fermented apple juice.

cigar *n* roll of cured tobacco leaves for smoking.

cigarette *n* thin roll of shredded tobacco in thin paper, for smoking.

cilantro *n* the US and Canadian word for CORIANDER.

cilium *n*, *pl* **cilia** *Biology* **1** short thread projecting from a cell, whose rhythmic beating causes movement. **2** eyelash.

cinch [**sinch**] *n informal* easy task.

cinchona [sing-**kone**-a] *n* **1** S American tree with medicinal bark. **2** (drug made from) the dried bark of this tree, which yields quinine.

cinder *n* piece of material that will not burn, left after burning coal.

Cinderella *n* poor, neglected, or unsuccessful person.

cine camera *n* camera for taking moving pictures.

cinema ❶ *n* **1** place for showing films. **2** films collectively. **cinematic** *adj* **cinematograph** *n* combined camera,

————————————— THESAURUS —————————————

chubby *adj* = **plump**, buxom, flabby, podgy, portly, roly-poly, rotund, round, stout, tubby

chuck[1] *v* **1** *Inf* = **throw**, cast, fling, heave, hurl, pitch, sling, toss

chuckle *v* **1** = **laugh**, chortle, crow, exult, giggle, snigger, titter

chum *Inf* ▷ *n* **1** = **friend**, cobber (*Aust or old-fashioned NZ inf*), companion, comrade, crony, mate (*inf*), pal (*inf*)

chunk *n* **1** = **piece**, block, dollop (*inf*),

hunk, lump, mass, nugget, portion, slab

churlish *adj* = **rude**, brusque, harsh, ill-tempered, impolite, sullen, surly, uncivil

churn *v* **4** = **stir up**, agitate, beat, convulse, swirl, toss

cinema *n* **1** = **pictures**, flicks (*sl*), movies **2** = **films**, big screen (*inf*), flicks (*sl*), motion pictures, movies, pictures

printer, and projector.
cinematography n technique of making films. **cinematographer** n.

cineraria n garden plant with daisy-like flowers.

cinerarium n, pl **-raria** place for keeping the ashes of the dead after cremation.

cinnabar n heavy red mineral containing mercury.

cinnamon n spice obtained from the bark of an Asian tree.

- SPELLING TIP
- **Cinnamon** is a tricky word to
- spell. The Bank of English shows
- at least 3 different ways of getting
- it wrong. The correct spelling
- has two *ns* in the middle and
- only one *m*.

cinquefoil n plant with five-lobed leaves.

cipher ❶ [**sife**-er] n **1** system of secret writing. **2** unimportant person. **3** obs numeral zero.

circa [**sir**-ka] prep Latin approximately, about.

circle ❶ n **1** perfectly round geometric figure, line, or shape. **2** group of people sharing an interest or activity. **3** Theatre section of seats above the main level of the auditorium. ▷ v **4** move in a circle (round). **5** enclose in a circle. **circular** adj **circulate** v move round.

circlet n circular ornament worn on the head.

circuit ❶ n **1** complete route or course, esp. a circular one. **2** complete path through which an electric current can flow. **3** periodical journey round a district, as made by judges. **4** motor-racing track. **5** series of sports tournaments. **circuitous** [sir-**kew**-it-

uss] adj indirect and lengthy. **circuitry** [**sir**-kit-tree] n electrical circuit(s).

circular ❶ adj **1** in the shape of a circle. **2** moving in a circle. ▷ n **3** letter for general distribution. **circularity** n.

circulate ❶ v **1** send, go, or pass from place to place or person to person. **2** move about a party, talking to different people. **circulation** n **1** flow of blood around the body. **2** number of copies of a newspaper or magazine sold. **3** sending or moving round. **circulatory** adj.

circum- prefix around, on all sides, e.g. circumlocution.

circumcise v **1** remove the foreskin of. **2** cut or remove the clitoris of. **circumcision** n.

circumference ❶ n **1** boundary of a specified area or shape, esp. of a circle. **2** distance round this.

circumflex n mark (ˆ) over a vowel to show that it is pronounced in a particular way.

circumlocution n indirect way of saying something. **circumlocutory** adj.

circumnavigate v sail right round. **circumnavigation** n.

circumscribe v **1** limit, restrict. **2** draw a line round. **circumscription** n.

circumspect adj cautious and careful not to take risks. **circumspectly** adv **circumspection** n.

circumstance ❶ n (usu. pl) occurrence or condition that accompanies or influences a person or event. **pomp and circumstance** formal display or ceremony. **circumstantial** adj **1** (of evidence) strongly suggesting something but not proving it. **2** very detailed. **circumstantiate** v prove by giving details.

THESAURUS

cipher n **1** = **code**, cryptograph **2** = **nobody**, nonentity

circle n **1** = **ring**, disc, globe, orb, sphere **2** = **group**, clique, club, company, coterie, set, society ▷ v **4** = **go round**, circumnavigate, circumscribe, wheel **5** = **enclose**, circumscribe, encircle, envelop, ring, surround

circuit n **1** = **course**, journey, lap, orbit, revolution, route, tour **4** = **track**

circuitous adj = **indirect**, labyrinthine, meandering, oblique, rambling, roundabout, tortuous, winding

circular adj **1** = **round**, ring-shaped,

rotund, spherical **2** = **orbital**, circuitous, cyclical ▷ n **3** = **advertisement**, notice

circulate v **1** = **spread**, broadcast, disseminate, distribute, issue, make known, promulgate, publicize, publish

circulation n **1** = **bloodstream** **3** = **distribution**, currency, dissemination, spread, transmission

circumference n **1** = **boundary**, border, edge, extremity, limits, outline, perimeter, periphery, rim

circumstance n (usu. pl) = **situation**, condition, contingency, event,

c

circumvent *v* **1** avoid or get round (a rule etc.). **2** outwit. **circumvention** *n*.

circus *n, pl* **-cuses** (performance given by) a travelling company of acrobats, clowns, performing animals, etc.

cirque *n* steep-sided semicircular hollow found in mountainous areas.

cirrhosis [sir-**roh**-siss] *n* serious liver disease, often caused by drinking too much alcohol.

cirrus *n, pl* **-ri** high wispy cloud.

CIS Commonwealth of Independent States.

Cistercian *n, adj* (monk or nun) of a strict Benedictine order.

cistern ⊕ *n* water tank, esp. one that holds water for flushing a toilet.

citadel ⊕ *n* fortress in a city.

cite ⊕ *v* **1** quote, refer to. **2** bring forward as proof. **3** summon to appear before a court of law. **citation** *n* **1** commendation for bravery. **2** summons to appear before a court of law. **3** quotation.

citizen ⊕ *n* **1** native or naturalized member of a state or nation. **2** inhabitant of a city or town. **citizenship** *n* **Citizens' Band** range of radio frequencies for private communication by the public.

citric acid *n* weak acid found in citrus fruits.

citron *n* lemon-like fruit of a small Asian tree.

citrus fruit *n* juicy sharp-tasting fruit such as an orange or lemon.

city ⊕ *n, pl* **-ties** **1** large or important town. **2** town that has received this title from the Crown. **the City** area of London as a financial centre.

civet [**siv**-vit] *n* **1** spotted catlike African mammal. **2** musky fluid from its glands used in perfume.

civic ⊕ *adj* of a city or citizens. **civics** *n* study of the rights and responsibilities of citizenship.

civil ⊕ *adj* **1** relating to the citizens of a state as opposed to the armed forces or the Church. **2** polite, courteous. **civilly** *adv* **civility** *n* polite or courteous behaviour. **civilian** *n, adj* (person) not belonging to the armed forces. **civil law** law relating to private and civilian affairs. **civil service** service responsible for the administration of the government. **civil servant** member of the civil service. **civil war** war between people of the same country.

civilize ⊕ *v* **1** refine or educate (a person). **2** make (a place) more pleasant or more acceptable. **civilization** *n* **1** high level of human cultural and social development. **2** particular society which has reached this level.

civvies *pl n slang* ordinary clothes that are not part of a uniform.

cl centilitre.

Cl *Chemistry* chlorine.

clack *n* **1** sound made by two hard objects striking each other. ▷ *v* **2** make this sound.

clad *v* a past of CLOTHE.

cladding *n* material used to cover the outside of a building.

claim ⊕ *v* **1** assert as a fact. **2** demand as a right. **3** need, require. ▷ *n* **4** assertion that something is true. **5** assertion of a right. **6** something

---

THESAURUS

happening, incident, occurrence, position, state, state of affairs, status

cistern *n* = **tank**, basin, reservoir, sink, vat

citadel *n* = **fortress**, bastion, fortification, keep, stronghold, tower

cite *v* **1** = **quote**, adduce, advance, allude to, enumerate, extract, mention, name, specify

citizen *n* = **inhabitant**, denizen, dweller, resident, subject, townsman

city *n* **1** = **town**, conurbation, metropolis, municipality

civic *adj* = **public**, communal, local, municipal

civil *adj* **1** = **civic**, domestic, municipal, political **2** = **polite**, affable, courteous,

obliging, refined, urbane, well-mannered

civilization *n* **1** = **culture**, advancement, cultivation, development, education, enlightenment, progress, refinement, sophistication **2** = **society**, community, nation, people, polity

civilize *v* **1** = **cultivate**, educate, enlighten, refine, sophisticate, tame

civilized *adj* **1** = **cultured**, educated, enlightened, humane, polite, sophisticated, urbane

claim *v* **1** = **assert**, allege, challenge, insist, maintain, profess, uphold **2** = **demand**, ask, call for, insist, need, require ▷ *n* **4** = **assertion**, affirmation,

claimed as a right. **7** demand for payment in connection with an insurance policy. **claimant** n.

clairvoyance ● n power of perceiving things beyond the natural range of the senses. **clairvoyant** n, adj.

clam n **1** edible shellfish with a hinged shell. ▷ v **clamming**, **clammed 2 clam up** informal stop talking, esp. through nervousness.

clamber ● v climb awkwardly.

clammy ● adj **-mier, -miest** unpleasantly moist and sticky. **clamminess** n.

clamour ● n **1** loud protest. **2** loud persistent noise or outcry. ▷ v **3** make a loud noise or outcry. **clamorous** adj **clamour for** v demand noisily.

clamp ● n **1** tool with movable jaws for holding things together tightly. **2** short for WHEEL CLAMP. ▷ v **3** fasten with a clamp. **4** immobilize (a car) with a wheel clamp. **clamp down on** v **1** become stricter about. **2** suppress.

clan ● n **1** group of families with a common ancestor, esp. among Scottish Highlanders. **2** close group. **clannish** adj (of a group) tending to exclude outsiders.

clandestine ● adj secret and concealed.

clang v **1** make a loud ringing metallic sound. ▷ n **2** ringing metallic sound. **clanger** n informal obvious mistake.

clangour n loud continuous clanging sound. **clangorous** adj.

clank n **1** harsh metallic sound. ▷ v **2** make such a sound.

clap¹ ● v **clapping, clapped 1** applaud by hitting the palms of one's hands sharply together. **2** put quickly or forcibly. **3** strike (someone) lightly with an open hand, for example in greeting. ▷ n **4** act or sound of clapping. **5** sudden loud noise, e.g. a clap of thunder. **clapped out** slang worn out, dilapidated.

clap² n slang gonorrhoea.

clapper n piece of metal inside a bell, which causes it to sound when struck against the side. **clapperboard** n pair of hinged boards clapped together during filming to help in synchronizing sound and picture.

claptrap n informal foolish or pretentious talk.

claque n group of people hired to applaud.

claret [**klar**-rit] n dry red wine from Bordeaux.

clarify ● v **-fying, -fied 1** make (a matter) clear and unambiguous. **2** remove the water from (butter) by heating it. **clarification** n.

clarinet n keyed woodwind instrument with a single reed. **clarinettist** n.

clarion n **1** obsolete high-pitched trumpet. **2** its sound. **clarion call** strong encouragement to do something.

clarity ● n clearness.

clash ● v **1** come into conflict. **2** (of events) happen at the same time. **3** (of colours) look unattractive together. **4** (of objects) make a loud harsh sound by being hit together. ▷ n **5** fight,

———————————— THESAURUS ————————————

allegation, pretension **6 = demand**, application, call, petition, request, requirement

clairvoyant n **= psychic**, diviner, fortune-teller, visionary ▷ adj **= psychic**, extrasensory, second-sighted, telepathic, visionary

clamber v **= climb**, claw, scale, scrabble, scramble, shin

clammy adj **= moist**, close, damp, dank, sticky, sweaty

clamour n **2 = noise**, commotion, din, hubbub, outcry, racket, shouting, uproar

clamp n **1 = vice**, bracket, fastener, grip, press ▷ v **3 = fasten**, brace, fix, make fast, secure

clan n **1 = family**, tribe **2 = group**, brotherhood, faction, fraternity, society

clandestine adj **= secret**, cloak-and-dagger, concealed, covert, furtive, private, stealthy, surreptitious, underground

clap¹ v **1 = applaud**, acclaim, cheer

clarification n **1 = explanation**, elucidation, exposition, illumination, interpretation, simplification

clarify v **1 = explain**, clear up, elucidate, illuminate, interpret, make plain, simplify, throw or shed light on

clarity n **= clearness**, definition, limpidity, lucidity, precision, simplicity, transparency

clash v **1 = conflict**, cross swords, feud, grapple, lock horns, quarrel, war, wrangle **4 = crash**, bang, clang, clank,

argument. **6** fact of two events happening at the same time. **7** loud harsh noise, esp. of things striking together.

clasp ❶ *n* **1** device for fastening things. **2** firm grasp or embrace. ▷ *v* **3** grasp or embrace firmly. **4** fasten with a clasp. **clasp knife** large knife with blades that fold into the handle.

class ❶ *n* **1** group of people sharing a similar social position. **2** system of dividing society into such groups. **3** group of people or things sharing a common characteristic. **4** group of pupils or students taught together. **5** standard of quality. **6** *informal* elegance or excellence, e.g. *a touch of class*. ▷ *v* **7** place in a class.

classic ❶ *adj* **1** being a typical example of something. **2** of lasting interest because of excellence. **3** attractive because of simplicity of form. ▷ *n* **4** author, artist, or work of art of recognized excellence. ▷ *pl* **5** study of ancient Greek and Roman literature and culture. **classical** *adj* **1** of or in a restrained conservative style. **2** denoting serious art music. **3** of or influenced by ancient Greek and Roman culture. **classically** *adv* **classicism** *n* artistic style showing emotional restraint and regularity of form. **classicist** *n*.

classify ❶ *v* **-fying**, **-fied 1** divide into groups with similar characteristics. **2** declare (information) to be officially secret. **classifiable** *adj* **classification** *n*.

classy ❶ *adj* **classier**, **classiest** *informal* stylish and elegant.

clatter *v*, *n* (make) a rattling noise.

clause ❶ *n* **1** section of a legal document. **2** part of a sentence, containing a verb.

claustrophobia *n* abnormal fear of confined spaces. **claustrophobic** *adj*.

clavichord *n* early keyboard instrument.

clavicle *n* same as COLLARBONE.

claw ❶ *n* **1** sharp hooked nail of a bird or beast. **2** similar part, such as a crab's pincer. ▷ *v* **3** tear with claws or nails.

clay *n* fine-grained earth, soft when moist and hardening when baked, used to make bricks and pottery. **clayey** *adj* **clay pigeon** baked clay disc hurled into the air as a target for shooting.

claymore *n* large two-edged sword formerly used by Scottish Highlanders.

clean ❶ *adj* **1** free from dirt or

— THESAURUS —

clatter, jangle, jar, rattle ▷ *n* **5** = **conflict**, brush, collision, confrontation, difference of opinion, disagreement, fight, showdown (*inf*)

clasp *n* **1** = **fastening**, brooch, buckle, catch, clip, fastener, grip, hook, pin **2** = **grasp**, embrace, grip, hold, hug ▷ *v* **3** = **grasp**, clutch, embrace, grip, hold, hug, press, seize, squeeze **4** = **fasten**, connect

class *n* **3** = **group**, category, division, genre, kind, set, sort, type ▷ *v* **7** = **classify**, brand, categorize, designate, grade, group, label, rank, rate

classic *adj* **1** = **typical**, archetypal, characteristic, definitive, exemplary, ideal, model, quintessential, standard **2** = **best**, consummate, finest, first-rate, masterly, world-class ▷ *n* **4** = **standard**, exemplar, masterpiece, model, paradigm, prototype

classical *adj* **1** = **pure**, elegant, harmonious, refined, restrained,

symmetrical, understated, well-proportioned

classification *n* **1** = **categorization**, analysis, arrangement, grading, sorting, taxonomy

classify *v* **1** = **categorize**, arrange, catalogue, grade, pigeonhole, rank, sort, systematize, tabulate

classy *adj* *Inf* = **high-class**, elegant, exclusive, posh (*inf*, *chiefly Brit*), stylish, superior, top-drawer, up-market

clause *n* **1** = **section**, article, chapter, condition, paragraph, part, passage

claw *n* **1** = **nail**, talon **2** = **pincer** ▷ *v* **3** = **scratch**, dig, lacerate, maul, rip, scrape, tear

clean *adj* **1** = **pure**, antiseptic, decontaminated, flawless, hygienic, immaculate, impeccable, purified, spotless, sterile, sterilized, unblemished, uncontaminated, unpolluted **3** = **moral**, chaste, decent, good, honourable, innocent, pure, respectable, upright, virtuous

impurities. **2** not yet used. **3** morally acceptable, inoffensive. **4** (of a reputation or record) free from dishonesty or corruption. **5** complete, e.g. *a clean break*. **6** smooth and regular. ▷ *v* **7** make (something) free from dirt. ▷ *adv* **8** *not standard* completely, e.g. *I clean forgot*. **come clean** *informal* reveal or admit something. **cleaner** *n* **cleanly** *adv* **cleanliness** *n* **clean-cut** *adj* **1** clearly outlined. **2** wholesome in appearance.

cleanse ❶ *v* make clean. **cleanser** *n*.

clear ❶ *adj* **1** free from doubt or confusion. **2** easy to see or hear. **3** able to be seen through. **4** free from darkness or obscurity. **5** free of obstruction. **6** (of weather) free from clouds. **7** (of skin) without blemish. **8** (of money) without deduction. ▷ *adv* **9** in a clear or distinct manner. **10** out of the way, e.g. *he lifted him clear of the deck*. ▷ *v* **11** make or become clear. **12** pass by or over (something) without contact. **13** prove (someone) innocent of a crime or mistake. **14** make as profit. **clearly** *adv* **clearance** *n* **1** clearing. **2** official permission. **3** space between two parts in motion. **clear-cut** *adj* easy to understand, not vague. **clearing** *n* treeless area in a wood. **clear off** *v informal* go away. **clear out** *v* **1** remove and sort the contents of. **2** *informal* go away. **clear-sighted** *adj* having good judgment.

clearway *n* stretch of road on which motorists may stop in an emergency.

cleat *n* **1** wedge. **2** piece of wood or iron with two projecting ends round which ropes are fastened.

cleave¹ *v* **cleaving**, **cleft**, **cleaved** or **clove**, **cleft**, **cleaved** or **cloven** split apart. **cleavage** *n* **1** space between a woman's breasts, as revealed by a low-cut dress. **2** division, split. **cleaver** *n* butcher's heavy knife with a square blade.

cleave² *v* cling or stick.

clef *n Music* symbol at the beginning of a stave to show the pitch.

cleft *n* **1** narrow opening or crack. ▷ *v* **2** a past of CLEAVE¹. **in a cleft stick** in a very difficult position.

clematis *n* climbing plant with large colourful flowers.

clement *adj* (of weather) mild. **clemency** *n* kind or lenient treatment.

clementine *n* small orange citrus fruit.

clench *v* **1** close or squeeze (one's teeth or fist) tightly. **2** grasp firmly.

clerestory [clear-store-ee] *n, pl* **-ries** row of windows at the top of a wall above an adjoining roof.

clergy ❶ *n* priests and ministers as a group. **clergyman** *n*.

cleric *n* member of the clergy.

clerical *adj* **1** of clerks or office work. **2** of the clergy.

clerk *n* employee in an office, bank, or court who keeps records, files, and accounts.

5 = **complete**, conclusive, decisive, entire, final, perfect, thorough, total, unimpaired, whole ▷ *v* **7** = **cleanse**, disinfect, launder, purge, purify, rinse, sanitize, scour, scrub, wash

cleanse *v* = **clean**, absolve, clear, purge, purify, rinse, scour, scrub, wash

cleanser *n* = **detergent**, disinfectant, purifier, scourer, soap, solvent

clear *adj* **1** = **certain**, convinced, decided, definite, positive, resolved, satisfied, sure **2** = **obvious**, apparent, blatant, comprehensible, conspicuous, distinct, evident, manifest, palpable, plain, pronounced, recognizable, unmistakable **3** = **transparent**, crystalline, glassy, limpid, pellucid, see-through, translucent **5** = **unobstructed**, empty, free, open, smooth, unhindered, unimpeded **6** = **bright**, cloudless, fair, fine, light,

luminous, shining, sunny, unclouded **7** = **unblemished**, clean, immaculate ▷ *v* **11** = **unblock**, disentangle, extricate, free, open, rid **12** = **pass over**, jump, leap, miss, vault **13** = **absolve**, acquit, excuse, exonerate, justify, vindicate **14** = **gain**, acquire, earn, make, reap, secure

clear-cut *adj* = **straightforward**, black-and-white, cut-and-dried (*inf*), definite, explicit, plain, precise, specific, unambiguous, unequivocal

clearly *adv* = **obviously**, beyond doubt, distinctly, evidently, markedly, openly, overtly, undeniably, undoubtedly

clergy *n* = **priesthood**, churchmen, clergymen, clerics, holy orders, ministry, the cloth

clergyman *n* = **minister**, chaplain, cleric, man of God, man of the cloth, padre, parson, pastor, priest, vicar

clever ❶ *adj* **1** intelligent, quick at learning. **2** showing skill. **cleverly** *adv* **cleverness** *n*.

clianthus [klee-**anth**-us] *n* Australian or NZ plant with slender scarlet flowers.

cliché [**klee**-shay] *n* expression or idea that is no longer effective because of overuse. **clichéd** *adj*.

click *n* **1** short sharp sound. ▷ *v* **2** make this sound. **3** *informal* (of two people) get on well together. **4** *informal* become suddenly clear. **5** *Computers* press and release (a button on a mouse). **6** *slang* be a success. **7** (also **click on**) *Computers* to select a particular function by pressing a button on a mouse. **click bait** *informal* link on a website intended to lead the user to another website.

client ❶ *n* **1** person who uses the services of a professional person or company. **2** *Computers* a program or work station that requests data from a server. **clientele** [klee-on-**tell**] *n* clients collectively.

cliff ❶ *n* steep rock face, esp. along the sea shore. **cliffhanger** *n* film, game, etc., that is tense and exciting because its outcome is uncertain.

climacteric *n* **1** same as MENOPAUSE. **2** diminishing sex drive and fertility experienced by men in middle age.

climate ❶ *n* **1** typical weather conditions of an area. **2** prevailing trend. **climatic** *adj* **climatically** *adv*.

- **USAGE NOTE**
- *Climatic* is sometimes wrongly used
- where *climactic* is meant. *Climatic*
- should be used to talk about things
- relating to climate; *climactic* is used

- to describe something which forms
- a climax.

climax ❶ *n* **1** most intense point of an experience, series of events, or story. **2** same as ORGASM. ▷ *v* **3** *not universally accepted* reach a climax. **climactic** *adj*.

climb ❶ *v* **1** go up, ascend. **2** rise to a higher point or intensity. ▷ *n* **3** climbing. **4** place to be climbed. **climber** *n* **climb down** *v* retreat from an opinion or position.

clime *n* *poetic* place or its climate.

clinch ❶ *v* **1** settle (an argument or agreement) decisively. ▷ *n* **2** *Boxing, Wrestling* movement in which one competitor holds on to the other to avoid punches. **3** *informal* lover's embrace. **clincher** *n* *informal* something decisive.

cling ❶ *v* **clinging, clung** hold tightly or stick closely. **clingfilm** *n* thin polythene material for wrapping food.

clinic ❶ *n* **1** building where outpatients receive medical treatment or advice. **2** private or specialized hospital. **clinical** *adj* **1** of a clinic. **2** logical and unemotional. **clinically** *adv*.

clink¹ *v, n* (make) a light sharp metallic sound.

clink² *n* *slang* prison.

clinker *n* fused coal left over in a fire or furnace.

clinker-built *adj* (of a boat) made of overlapping planks.

clip¹ ❶ *v* **clipping, clipped 1** cut with shears or scissors. **2** *informal* hit sharply. ▷ *n* **3** short extract of a film. **4** *informal* sharp blow. **clipped** *adj* (of speech) abrupt and disjointed.

— THESAURUS —

clever *adj* **1** = **intelligent**, bright, ingenious, knowledgeable, quick-witted, resourceful, shrewd, smart **2** = **talented**, gifted

cleverness *n* = **intelligence**, ability, brains, ingenuity, quick wits, resourcefulness, shrewdness, smartness

cliché *n* = **platitude**, banality, commonplace, hackneyed phrase, stereotype, truism

client *n* = **customer**, applicant, buyer, consumer, patient, patron, shopper

clientele *n* = **customers**, business, clients, following, market, patronage, regulars, trade

cliff *n* = **rock face**, bluff, crag, escarpment, overhang, precipice, scar, scarp

climactic *adj* **1** = **crucial**, critical, decisive, paramount, peak

climate *n* **2** = **weather**, temperature

climax *n* **1** = **culmination**, height, highlight, high point, peak, summit, top, zenith

climb *v* **1** = **ascend**, clamber, mount, rise, scale, shin up, soar, top

climb down *v* = **back down**, eat one's words, retract, retreat

clinch *v* **1** = **settle**, conclude, confirm, decide, determine, seal, secure, set the seal on, sew up (*inf*)

cling *v* = **stick**, adhere, clasp, clutch, embrace, grasp, grip, hug

clinical *adj* **2** = **unemotional**, analytic, cold, detached, dispassionate, impersonal, objective, scientific

clip¹ *v* **1** = **trim**, crop, curtail, cut, pare,

clippers *pl n* tool for clipping. **clipping** *n* something cut out, esp. an article from a newspaper.

clip² ❶ *n* 1 device for attaching or holding things together. ▷ *v* **clipping**, **clipped** 2 attach or hold together with a clip.

clipper *n* fast commercial sailing ship.

clique ❶ [kleek] *n* small exclusive group. **cliquey** *adj*.

clitoris [klit-or-iss] *n* small sexually sensitive organ at the front of the vulva. **clitoral** *adj*.

cloak ❶ *n* 1 loose sleeveless outer garment. 2 something that covers or conceals. ▷ *v* 3 cover or conceal. **cloakroom** *n* room where coats may be left temporarily.

clobber¹ *v informal* 1 hit. 2 defeat utterly.

clobber² *n informal* belongings, esp. clothes.

cloche [klosh] *n* 1 cover to protect young plants. 2 woman's close-fitting hat.

clock *n* 1 instrument for showing the time. 2 device with a dial for recording or measuring. ▷ *v* 3 record (time) with a stopwatch. **clockwise** *adv, adj* in the direction in which the hands of a clock rotate. **clock in** *or* **on**, **out** *or* **off** *v* register arrival at or departure from work on an automatic time recorder. **clock up** *v* reach (a total). **clockwork** *n* mechanism similar to the kind in a clock, used in wind-up toys. **like clockwork** with complete regularity and precision.

clod *n* 1 lump of earth. 2 stupid person.

cloddish *adj* **clodhopper** *n informal* clumsy or stupid person.

clog ❶ *v* **clogging**, **clogged** 1 obstruct. ▷ *n* 2 wooden or wooden-soled shoe.

cloisonné [klwah-**zon**-nay] *n* design made by filling in a wire outline with coloured enamel.

cloister *n* 1 covered pillared arcade, usu. in a monastery. 2 place of religious seclusion. **cloistered** *adj* sheltered.

clone *n* 1 animal or plant produced artificially from the cells of another animal or plant, and identical to the original. 2 *informal* person who closely resembles another. ▷ *v* 3 produce as a clone.

close¹ ❶ *v* [rhymes with **nose**] 1 shut. 2 prevent access to. 3 end, terminate. 4 bring or come nearer together. ▷ *n* 5 end, conclusion. 6 [rhymes with **dose**] street closed at one end. 7 [rhymes with **dose**] courtyard, quadrangle. **closed-circuit television** television system used within a limited area such as a building. **closed shop** place of work in which all workers must belong to a particular trade union.

close² ❶ *adj* [rhymes with **dose**] 1 near. 2 intimate. 3 careful, thorough. 4 compact, dense. 5 oppressive, stifling. 6 secretive. ▷ *adv* 7 closely, tightly. **closely** *adv* **closeness** *n* **close season** period when it is illegal to kill certain game or fish. **close shave** *informal* narrow escape. **close-up** *n* photograph or film taken at close range.

THESAURUS

prune, shear, shorten, snip 2 *Inf* = **smack**, clout (*inf*), cuff, knock, punch, strike, thump, wallop (*inf*), whack ▷ *n* 4 *Inf* = **smack**, clout (*inf*), cuff, knock, punch, strike, thump, wallop (*inf*), whack

clip² *v* 2 = **attach**, fasten, fix, hold, pin, staple

clique *n* = **group**, cabal, circle, coterie, faction, gang, set

cloak *n* 1 = **cape**, coat, mantle, wrap ▷ *v* 3 = **cover**, camouflage, conceal, disguise, hide, mask, obscure, screen, veil

clog *v* 1 = **obstruct**, block, congest, hinder, impede, jam

close¹ *v* 1 = **shut**, bar, block, lock, plug, seal, secure, stop up 2 = **end**, cease, complete, conclude, finish, shut down, terminate, wind up 4 = **connect**,

come together, couple, fuse, join, unite ▷ *n* 5 = **end**, completion, conclusion, culmination, denouement, ending, finale, finish

close² *adj* 1 = **near**, adjacent, adjoining, at hand, cheek by jowl, handy, impending, nearby, neighbouring, nigh 2 = **intimate**, attached, confidential, dear, devoted, familiar, inseparable, loving 3 = **careful**, detailed, intense, minute, painstaking, rigorous, thorough 4 = **compact**, congested, crowded, dense, impenetrable, jam-packed, packed, tight 5 = **stifling**, airless, heavy, humid, muggy, oppressive, stuffy, suffocating, sweltering 6 = **secretive**, private, reticent, secret, taciturn, uncommunicative

closet n 1 US cupboard. 2 small private room. ▷ adj 3 private, secret. ▷ v **closeting**, **closeted** 4 shut (oneself) away in private.

closure n 1 closing. 2 ending of a debate by immediate vote. 3 a resolution of a significant event or relationship in a person's life.

clot n 1 soft thick lump formed from liquid. 2 informal stupid person. ▷ v **clotting**, **clotted** 3 form soft thick lumps.

cloth ❶ n 1 (piece of) woven fabric. 2 (preceded by the) the clergy.

clothe ❶ v **clothing**, **clothed** or **clad** 1 put clothes on. 2 provide with clothes. **clothes** pl n 1 articles of dress. 2 bed coverings. **clothier** n old-fashioned maker or seller of clothes or cloth. **clothing** n clothes collectively.

cloud ❶ n 1 mass of condensed water vapour floating in the sky. 2 floating mass of smoke, dust, etc. 3 large number of insects etc. in flight. 4 something that threatens or causes gloom. ▷ v 5 (foll. by over) become cloudy. 6 confuse. 7 make gloomy or depressed. **cloudless** adj **cloudy** adj 1 having a lot of clouds. 2 (of liquid) not clear. **cloudburst** n heavy fall of rain. **cloud computing** system in which services stored on the internet are accessible to users on a temporary basis.

cloudberry n creeping plant with white flowers and orange berry-like fruits.

clout ❶ informal ▷ n 1 hard blow. 2 power, influence. ▷ v 3 hit hard.

clove[1] n dried flower bud of a tropical tree, used as a spice.

clove[2] n segment of a bulb of garlic.

clove[3] v a past tense of CLEAVE[1]. **clove hitch** knot used to fasten a rope to a spar.

cloven v a past participle of CLEAVE[1]. **cloven hoof** divided hoof of a cow, goat, etc.

clover n plant with three-lobed leaves. **in clover** in luxury.

clown ❶ n 1 comic entertainer in a circus. 2 amusing person. 3 stupid person. ▷ v 4 behave foolishly. 5 perform as a clown. **clownish** adj.

cloying adj sickeningly sweet.

club ❶ n 1 association of people with common interests. 2 building used by such a group. 3 thick stick used as a weapon. 4 stick with a curved end used to hit the ball in golf. 5 playing card with black three-leaved symbols. ▷ v **clubbing**, **clubbed** 6 hit with a club. **club together** v combine resources for a common purpose.

club foot n deformity of the foot causing inability to put the foot flat on the ground.

cluck n 1 low clicking noise made by a hen. ▷ v 2 make this noise.

clue ❶ n something that helps to solve a mystery or puzzle. **not have a clue** be

closed adj 1 = **shut**, fastened, locked, out of service, sealed 2 = **exclusive**, restricted 3 = **finished**, concluded, decided, ended, over, resolved, settled, terminated

cloth n 1 = **fabric**, material, textiles

clothe v 1 = **dress**, array, attire, cover, drape, garb, robe 2 = **fit out**, equip

clothes pl n 1 = **clothing**, apparel, attire, costume, dress, garb, garments, gear (inf), outfit, wardrobe, wear

clothing n = **clothes**, apparel, attire, costume, dress, garb, garments, gear (inf), outfit, wardrobe, wear

cloud n 1, 2 = **mist**, gloom, haze, murk, vapour ▷ v 5 (foll. by over) = **obscure**, becloud, darken, dim, eclipse, obfuscate, overshadow, shade, shadow, veil 6 = **confuse**, disorient, distort, impair, muddle, muddy the waters

cloudy adj 1 = **dull**, dim, gloomy, leaden, louring or lowering, overcast, sombre, sunless 2 = **opaque**, muddy, murky

clout Inf ▷ n 2 = **influence**, authority, mana (NZ), power, prestige, pull, weight ▷ v 3 = **hit**, clobber (sl), punch, sock (sl), strike, thump, wallop (inf)

clown n 1 = **comedian**, buffoon, comic, fool, harlequin, jester 2 = **joker**, prankster ▷ v 4 = **play the fool**, act the fool, jest, mess about

club n 1 = **association**, fraternity, group, guild, lodge, set, society, union 3 = **stick**, bat, bludgeon, cosh (Brit), cudgel, truncheon ▷ v 6 = **beat**, bash, batter, bludgeon, cosh (Brit), hammer, pummel, strike

clue n = **indication**, evidence, hint, lead, pointer, sign, suggestion, suspicion, trace

clueless adj = **stupid**, dim, dozy (Brit inf), dull, half-witted, simple, slow,

completely baffled. **clueless** adj stupid. **clued-up** adj shrewd and well-informed.

clump ❶ n 1 small group of things or people. 2 dull heavy tread. ▷ v 3 walk heavily. 4 form into clumps.

clumsy ❶ adj **-sier, -siest** 1 lacking skill or physical coordination. 2 badly made or done. **clumsily** adv **clumsiness** n.

clung v past of CLING.

clunk n 1 dull metallic sound. ▷ v 2 make such a sound.

cluster ❶ n 1 small close group. ▷ v 2 gather in clusters.

clutch¹ ❶ v 1 grasp tightly. 2 (foll. by at) try to get hold of. ▷ n 3 device enabling two revolving shafts to be connected and disconnected, esp. in a motor vehicle. 4 tight grasp.

clutch² n 1 set of eggs laid at the same time. 2 small group of things.

clutter ❶ v 1 scatter objects about (a place) untidily. ▷ n 2 untidy mess.

Clydesdale n heavy powerful carthorse.

cm centimetre.

Cm Chemistry curium.

CND Campaign for Nuclear Disarmament.

Co Chemistry cobalt.

CO 1 Colorado. 2 Commanding Officer.

Co. 1 Company. 2 County.

co- prefix together, joint, or jointly, e.g. coproduction.

c/o 1 care of. 2 Book-keeping carried over.

coach ❶ n 1 long-distance bus. 2 railway carriage. 3 large four-wheeled horse-drawn carriage. 4 trainer, instructor. ▷ v 5 train, teach. **coachman** n driver of a horse-drawn coach or carriage.

coagulate [koh-**ag**-yew-late] v change from a liquid to a semisolid mass. **coagulation** n **coagulant** n substance causing coagulation.

coal n black rock consisting mainly of carbon, used as fuel. **coalface** n exposed seam of coal in a mine. **coalfield** n area with coal under the ground. **coal gas** mixture of gases produced from coal, used for heating and lighting. **coal tar** black tar made from coal, used for making drugs and chemical products.

coalesce ❶ [koh-a-**less**] v come together, merge. **coalescence** n.

coalition ❶ [koh-a-**lish**-un] n temporary alliance, esp. between political parties.

coaming n raised frame round a ship's hatchway for keeping out water.

coarse ❶ adj 1 rough in texture. 2 unrefined, indecent. 3 of inferior quality. **coarsely** adv **coarseness** n **coarsen** v **coarse fish** any freshwater fish not of the salmon family.

coast ❶ n 1 place where the land meets the sea. ▷ v 2 move by momentum, without the use of power. 3 proceed without great effort. **coastal** adj **coaster** n 1 small mat placed under a

thick, unintelligent, witless

clump n 1 = **cluster**, bunch, bundle, group, mass ▷ v 3 = **stomp**, lumber, plod, thud, thump, tramp

clumsy adj 1 = **awkward**, bumbling, gauche, gawky, ham-fisted (inf), lumbering, maladroit, ponderous, uncoordinated, ungainly, unwieldy

cluster n 1 = **gathering**, assemblage, batch, bunch, clump, collection, group, knot ▷ v 2 = **gather**, assemble, bunch, collect, flock, group

clutch¹ v 1 = **seize**, catch, clasp, cling to, embrace, grab, grasp, grip, snatch

clutter v 1 = **litter**, scatter, strew ▷ n 2 = **untidiness**, confusion, disarray, disorder, hotchpotch, jumble, litter, mess, muddle

coach n 1 = **bus**, car, charabanc, vehicle 3 = **carriage** 4 = **instructor**, handler, teacher, trainer, tutor ▷ v 5 = **instruct**,

drill, exercise, prepare, train, tutor

coalesce v = **blend**, amalgamate, combine, fuse, incorporate, integrate, merge, mix, unite

coalition n = **alliance**, amalgamation, association, bloc, combination, confederation, conjunction, fusion, merger, union

coarse adj 1 = **rough** 2 = **vulgar**, earthy, improper, indecent, indelicate, ribald, rude, smutty 3 = **crude**, homespun, impure, unfinished, unpolished, unprocessed, unpurified, unrefined

coarseness n 1 = **roughness**, crudity, unevenness 2 = **vulgarity**, bawdiness, crudity, earthiness, indelicacy, ribaldry, smut, uncouthness

coast n 1 = **shore**, beach, border, coastline, seaboard, seaside ▷ v 2 = **cruise**, drift, freewheel, glide, sail, taxi

glass. **2** small ship. **coastguard** n **1** organization that aids ships and swimmers in trouble and prevents smuggling. **2** member of this. **coastline** n outline of a coast.

coat ❶ n **1** outer garment with long sleeves. **2** animal's fur or hair. **3** covering layer, e.g. *a coat of paint.* ▷ v **4** cover with a layer. **coating** n covering layer. **coat of arms** heraldic emblem of a family or institution.

coax ❶ v **1** persuade gently. **2** obtain by persistent coaxing.

coaxial [koh-**ax**-ee-al] adj (of a cable) transmitting by means of two concentric conductors separated by an insulator.

cob n **1** stalk of an ear of maize. **2** thickset type of horse. **3** round loaf of bread. **4** male swan.

cobalt n *Chemistry* brittle silvery-white metallic element.

cobber n *Aust or NZ informal* friend.

cobble n cobblestone. **cobbler** n shoe mender. **cobblestone** n rounded stone used for paving. **cobble together** v put together clumsily.

cobblers pl n *taboo slang* nonsense.

cobia [**koh**-bee-a] n large dark-striped game fish of tropical and subtropical seas.

COBOL n high-level computer programming language for general commercial use.

cobra n venomous hooded snake of Asia and Africa.

cobweb n spider's web.

coca n dried leaves of a S American shrub which contain cocaine.

Coca-Cola n ® dark brown fizzy soft drink.

cocaine n addictive drug used as a narcotic and as an anaesthetic.

coccyx [**kok**-six] n, pl **coccyges** [kok-**sije**-eez] bone at the base of the spinal column.

cochineal n red dye obtained from a Mexican insect, used for food colouring.

cochlea [**kok**-lee-a] n, pl **-leae** [-li-**ee**] spiral tube in the internal ear, which converts sound vibrations into

nerve impulses.

cock n **1** male bird, esp. of domestic fowl. **2** *taboo slang* penis. **3** stopcock. ▷ v **4** draw back (the hammer of a gun) to firing position. **5** lift and turn (part of the body). **cockerel** n young domestic cock. **cock-a-hoop** adj in high spirits. **cock-and-bull story** improbable story.

cockade n feather or rosette worn on a hat as a badge.

cockatiel, cockateel n crested Australian parrot with a greyish-brown and yellow plumage.

cockatoo n crested parrot of Australia or the East Indies.

cocker spaniel n small spaniel.

cockeyed adj **1** *informal* crooked, askew. **2** foolish, absurd.

cockie, cocky n, pl **-kies** *Aust & NZ informal* farmer.

cockle n edible shellfish. **cockleshell** n **1** shell of the cockle. **2** small light boat.

Cockney n **1** native of the East End of London. **2** London dialect.

cockpit n **1** pilot's compartment in an aircraft. **2** driver's compartment in a racing car. **3** site of many battles or contests.

cockroach n beetle-like insect which is a household pest.

cockscomb n same as COXCOMB.

cocksure adj overconfident, arrogant.

cocktail n **1** mixed alcoholic drink. **2** appetizer of seafood or mixed fruits.

cocky ❶ adj **cockier**, **cockiest** conceited and overconfident. **cockily** adv **cockiness** n.

coco n coconut palm.

cocoa n **1** powder made from the seed of the cacao tree. **2** drink made from this powder.

coconut n **1** large hard fruit of a type of palm tree. **2** edible flesh of this fruit.

cocoon n **1** silky protective covering of a silkworm. **2** protective covering. ▷ v **3** wrap up tightly for protection.

cocotte n small fireproof dish in which individual portions of food are cooked.

cod n **1** large food fish of the North Atlantic. **2** any other fish of the same family. **cod-liver oil** oil extracted from

coat n **2** = **fur**, fleece, hair, hide, pelt, skin, wool **3** = **layer**, coating, covering, overlay ▷ v **4** = **cover**, apply, plaster, smear, spread

coax v **1** = **persuade**, allure, cajole,

entice, prevail upon, sweet-talk (*inf*), talk into, wheedle

cocky adj = **overconfident**, arrogant, brash, cocksure, conceited, egotistical, full of oneself, swaggering, vain

fish, rich in vitamins A and D.

COD cash on delivery.

coda [**kode**-a] *n* final part of a musical composition.

coddle *v* **1** pamper, overprotect. **2** cook (eggs) in water just below boiling point.

code ❶ *n* **1** system of letters, symbols, or prearranged signals by which messages can be communicated secretly or briefly. **2** set of principles or rules. ▷ *v* **3** put into code. **codify** [**kode**-if-fie] *v* -**fying**, -**fied** organize (rules or procedures) systematically. **codification** *n*.

codeine [**kode**-een] *n* drug used as a painkiller.

codex *n*, *pl* **codices** volume of manuscripts of an ancient text.

codger *n informal* old man.

codicil [**kode**-iss-ill] *n* addition to a will.

codpiece *n History* bag covering the male genitals, attached to the breeches.

codswallop *n slang* nonsense.

coeducation *n* education of boys and girls together. **coeducational** *adj*.

coefficient *n* **1** *Maths* number or constant placed before and multiplying a quantity. **2** *Physics* number or constant used to calculate the behaviour of a substance under specified conditions.

coelacanth [**seel**-a-kanth] *n* primitive marine fish.

coeliac disease [**seel**-ee-ak] *n* disease which hampers digestion of food.

coequal *adj*, *n* equal.

coerce [koh-**urss**] *v* compel, force. **coercion** *n* **coercive** *adj*.

coeval [koh-**eev**-al] *adj*, *n* contemporary.

coexist *v* exist together, esp. peacefully despite differences. **coexistence** *n*.

coextensive *adj* covering the same area.

C of E Church of England.

coffee *n* **1** drink made from the roasted and ground seeds of a tropical shrub. **2** beanlike seeds of this shrub. ▷ *adj* **3** medium-brown. **coffee bar** café, snack bar. **coffee table** small low table. **coffee-table book** large expensive illustrated book.

coffer *n* **1** chest for valuables. ▷ *pl* **2** store of money.

cofferdam *n* watertight enclosure pumped dry to enable construction work to be done.

coffin *n* box in which a corpse is buried or cremated.

cog *n* **1** one of the teeth on the rim of a gearwheel. **2** unimportant person in a big organization.

cogent ❶ [**koh**-jent] *adj* forcefully convincing. **cogency** *n* **cogently** *adv*.

cogitate ❶ [**koj**-it-tate] *v* think deeply about. **cogitation** *n*.

cognac [**kon**-yak] *n* French brandy.

cognate *adj* derived from a common original form.

cognition *n* act or experience of knowing or acquiring knowledge. **cognitive** *adj*.

cognizance *n* knowledge, understanding. **cognizant** *adj*.

cognomen [kog-**noh**-men] *n*, *pl* -**nomens**, -**nomina** [-**nom**-min-a] **1** nickname. **2** surname.

cognoscenti [kon-yo-**shen**-tee] *pl n* connoisseurs.

cohabit *v* live together as a couple without being married. **cohabitation** *n*.

cohere ❶ *v* **1** hold or stick together. **2** be logically connected or consistent. **coherence** *n* **coherent** *adj* **1** logical and consistent. **2** capable of intelligible speech. **3** sticking together. **coherently** *adv* **cohesion** *n* sticking together. **cohesive** *adj*.

cohort *n* **1** band of associates. **2** tenth part of an ancient Roman legion.

coif *v* **coiffing**, **coiffed** **1** arrange the hair of. ▷ *n* **2** close-fitting cap worn in the Middle Ages.

coiffure *n* hairstyle. **coiffeur**, **coiffeuse** *n* hairdresser.

---

code *n* **1** = **cipher**, cryptograph **2** = **principles**, canon, convention, custom, ethics, etiquette, manners, maxim, regulations, rules, system

cogent *adj* = **convincing**, compelling, effective, forceful, influential, potent, powerful, strong, weighty

cogitate *v* = **think**, consider, contemplate, deliberate, meditate, mull over, muse, ponder, reflect, ruminate

coherent *adj* **1** = **consistent**, logical, lucid, meaningful, orderly, organized, rational, reasoned, systematic **2** = **intelligible**, articulate, comprehensible

coil ❶ v **1** wind in loops. **2** move in a winding course. ▷ n **3** something coiled. **4** single loop of this. **5** coil-shaped contraceptive device inserted in the womb. **6** electrical conductor wound into a spiral.

coin ❶ n **1** piece of metal money. **2** metal currency collectively. ▷ v **3** invent (a word or phrase). **4** make or stamp (coins). **coin it in** informal earn money quickly. **coinage** n **1** coins collectively. **2** word or phrase coined. **3** coining.

coincide ❶ v **1** happen at the same time. **2** agree or correspond exactly. **coincidence** n **1** occurrence of simultaneous or apparently connected events. **2** coinciding. **coincident** adj in agreement. **coincidental** adj resulting from coincidence. **coincidentally** adv.

coir n coconut fibre, used for matting.

coitus [**koh**-it-uss], **coition**[koh-**ish**-un] n sexual intercourse. **coital** adj.

coke¹ n solid fuel left after gas has been distilled from coal.

coke² n slang cocaine.

Coke n ® short for COCA-COLA.

col n high mountain pass.

Col. Colonel.

cola n dark brown fizzy soft drink.

colander n perforated bowl for straining or rinsing foods.

cold ❶ adj **1** lacking heat. **2** lacking affection or enthusiasm. **3** (of a colour) giving an impression of coldness. **4** (of a scent in hunting) faint. **5** slang unconscious, e.g. out cold. ▷ n **6** lack of heat. **7** mild illness causing a runny nose, sneezing, and coughing. **coldly** adv **coldness** n **cold-blooded** adj **1** cruel, unfeeling. **2** having a body temperature that varies according to the surrounding temperature. **cold cream** creamy preparation for softening and cleansing the skin. **cold feet** slang nervousness, fear. **cold-shoulder** v treat with indifference. **cold sore** cluster of blisters near the lips, caused by a virus. **cold war** political hostility between countries without actual warfare.

coleslaw n salad dish of shredded raw cabbage in a dressing.

coley n codlike food fish of the N Atlantic.

colic n severe pains in the stomach and bowels. **colicky** adj.

colitis [koh-**lie**-tiss] n inflammation of the colon.

collaborate ❶ v **1** work with another on a project. **2** cooperate with an enemy invader. **collaboration** n **collaborative** adj **collaborator** n.

collage [kol-**lahzh**] n **1** art form in which various materials or objects are glued onto a surface. **2** picture made in this way.

collapse ❶ v **1** fall down suddenly. **2** fail completely. **3** fold compactly. ▷ n **4** collapsing. **5** sudden failure or breakdown. **collapsible** adj.

---

coil v **1** = **wind**, curl, loop, snake, spiral, twine, twist, wreathe, writhe

coin n **1, 2** = **money**, cash, change, copper, silver, specie ▷ v **3** = **invent**, create, fabricate, make up, originate **4** = **mint**, forge, mould

coincide v **1** = **occur simultaneously**, be concurrent, coexist, synchronize **2** = **agree**, accord, concur, correspond, harmonize, match, square, tally

coincidence n **1** = **chance**, accident, fluke, happy accident, luck, stroke of luck **2** = **coinciding**, concurrence, conjunction, correlation, correspondence

coincidental adj = **chance**, accidental, casual, fluky (inf), fortuitous, unintentional, unplanned

cold adj **1** = **chilly**, arctic, bleak, cool, freezing, frigid, frosty, frozen, icy, wintry **2** = **unfriendly**, aloof, distant, frigid, indifferent, reserved, standoffish ▷ n **6** = **coldness**, chill, frigidity, frostiness, iciness

cold-blooded adj **1** = **callous**, dispassionate, heartless, ruthless, steely, stony-hearted, unemotional, unfeeling

collaborate v **1** = **work together**, cooperate, join forces, participate, play ball (inf), team up **2** = **conspire**, collude, cooperate, fraternize

collaboration n **1** = **teamwork**, alliance, association, cooperation, partnership

collaborator n **1** = **co-worker**, associate, colleague, confederate, partner, team-mate **2** = **traitor**, fraternizer, quisling, turncoat

collapse v **1** = **fall down**, cave in, crumple, fall, fall apart at the seams, give way, subside **2** = **fail**, come to

C

collar ❶ n **1** part of a garment round the neck. **2** band put round an animal's neck. **3** cut of meat from an animal's neck. ▷ v **4** informal seize, arrest. **5** catch in order to speak to. **collarbone** n bone joining the shoulder blade to the breastbone.

collate v gather together, examine, and put in order. **collation** n **1** collating. **2** light meal. **collator** n.

collateral n **1** security pledged for the repayment of a loan. ▷ adj **2** descended from a common ancestor but through different lines. **3** additional but subordinate.

colleague ❶ n fellow worker, esp. in a profession.

collect¹ ❶ v **1** gather together. **2** accumulate (stamps etc.) as a hobby. **3** fetch. **4** receive payments of (taxes etc.). **5** regain control of (oneself). **collected** adj calm and controlled. **collection** n **1** things collected. **2** collecting. **3** sum of money collected. **collective** adj of or done by a group. **collector** n.

collect² n short prayer.

collective ❶ adj **1** of or done by a group. ▷ n **2** group of people working together on an enterprise and sharing the benefits from it. **collective bargaining** negotiation between a trade union and an employer on the wages etc. of the employees. **collectively** adv **collectivism** n theory that the state should own all means of production. **collectivize** v organize according to the theory of collectivism.

colleen n Irish girl.

college n **1** place of higher education. **2** Brit name given to some secondary schools. **3** group of people of the same profession or with special duties. **collegian** n member of a college. **collegiate** adj.

collide ❶ v **1** crash together violently. **2** have an argument. **collision** n.

collie n silky-haired sheepdog.

colliery n, pl **-lieries** coal mine. **collier** n **1** coal miner. **2** coal ship.

collocate v (of words) occur together regularly. **collocation** n.

colloid n suspension of particles in a solution. **colloidal** adj.

colloquial ❶ adj suitable for informal speech or writing. **colloquialism** n colloquial word or phrase.

colloquium n, pl **-quiums, -quia** academic seminar.

colloquy n, pl **-quies** conversation or conference.

collusion n secret or illegal cooperation. **collude** v act in collusion.

collywobbles pl n slang nervousness.

cologne n mild perfume.

colon¹ n punctuation mark (:).

colon² n part of the large intestine connected to the rectum. **colonic** adj.

colonel n senior commissioned army or air-force officer.

colonnade n row of columns.

colony ❶ n, pl **-nies 1** group of people

———————————— THESAURUS ————————————

nothing, fold, founder, go belly-up (inf) ▷ n **4** = **falling down**, cave-in, disintegration, falling apart, ruin, subsidence **5** = **failure**, downfall, flop, slump

collar v **4** Inf = **seize**, apprehend, arrest, capture, catch, grab, nab (inf), nail (inf)

colleague n = **fellow worker**, ally, assistant, associate, collaborator, comrade, helper, partner, team-mate, workmate

collect¹ v **1** = **assemble**, cluster, congregate, convene, converge, flock together, rally **2** = **gather**, accumulate, amass, assemble, heap, hoard, save, stockpile

collected adj = **calm**, composed, cool, poised, self-possessed, serene, unperturbed, unruffled

collection n **1** = **accumulation**, anthology, assembly, assortment, cluster, compilation, group, heap, hoard, mass, pile, set, stockpile, store **3** = **contribution**, alms, offering, offertory

collective adj **1** = **combined**, aggregate, composite, corporate, cumulative, joint, shared, unified, united

collide v **1** = **crash**, clash, come into collision, meet head-on **2** = **conflict**, clash

collision n **1** = **crash**, accident, bump, impact, pile-up (inf), prang (inf), smash **2** = **conflict**, clash, confrontation, encounter, opposition, skirmish

colloquial adj = **informal**, conversational, demotic, everyday, familiar, idiomatic, vernacular

colony n **1** = **settlement**, community,

who settle in a new country but remain under the rule of their homeland. **2** territory occupied by a colony. **3** group of people or animals of the same kind living together. **colonial** adj, n (inhabitant) of a colony. **colonialism** n policy of acquiring and maintaining colonies. **colonist** n settler in a colony. **colonize** v make into a colony. **colonization** n.

Colorado beetle n black-and-yellow beetle that is a serious pest of potatoes.

coloration, colouration n arrangement of colours.

coloratura n Music **1** complicated vocal passage. **2** soprano who specializes in such music.

colossal 0 adj very large.

colossus n, pl **-si**, **-suses 1** huge statue. **2** huge or important person or thing.

colostomy n, pl **-mies** operation to form an opening from the colon onto the surface of the body, for emptying the bowel.

colour 0 n **1** appearance of things as a result of reflecting light. **2** substance that gives colour. **3** complexion. **4** vividness, authenticity. ▷ pl **5** flag of a country or regiment. **6** Sport badge or symbol denoting membership of a team. ▷ v **7** apply colour to. **8** influence (someone's judgment). **9** blush. **coloured** adj **1** having colour.

2 (**C-**) (in S Africa) of mixed White and non-White parentage. **colourful** adj **1** with bright or varied colours. **2** vivid, distinctive. **colourfully** adv **colouring** n **1** application of colour. **2** something added to give colour. **3** complexion. **colourless** adj **1** dull and uninteresting. **2** without colour. **colour-blind** adj unable to distinguish between certain colours.

colt n young male horse.

columbine n garden flower with five petals.

column 0 n **1** pillar. **2** vertical division of a newspaper page. **3** regular feature in a newspaper. **4** vertical arrangement of numbers. **5** narrow formation of troops. **columnist** n journalist who writes a regular feature in a newspaper.

com-, con- prefix together, jointly, e.g. commingle.

coma 0 n state of deep unconsciousness. **comatose** adj **1** in a coma. **2** sound asleep.

comb 0 n **1** toothed implement for arranging the hair. **2** cock's crest. **3** honeycomb. ▷ v **4** use a comb on. **5** search with great care.

combat 0 n, v **-bating**, **-bated** fight, struggle. **combatant** n **1** fighter. ▷ adj **2** fighting. **combative** adj.

combe n same as COOMB.

combine 0 v **1** join together. **2** form a

——————————————————— THESAURUS ———————————

dependency, dominion, outpost, possession, province, satellite state **2** = **territory**

colossal adj = **huge**, enormous, gigantic, immense, mammoth, massive, monumental, prodigious, vast

colour n **1** = **hue**, shade, tint **2** = **pigment**, colorant, dye, paint, tint ▷ v **7** = **paint**, dye, stain, tinge, tint **9** = **blush**, flush, redden

colourful adj **1** = **bright**, brilliant, multicoloured, psychedelic, variegated **2** = **interesting**, distinctive, graphic, lively, picturesque, rich, vivid

colourless adj **1** = **uninteresting**, characterless, dreary, dull, insipid, lacklustre, vapid **2** = **drab**, achromatic, anaemic, ashen, bleached, faded, wan, washed out

column n **1** = **pillar**, obelisk, post, shaft, support, upright **5** = **line**, file, procession, rank, row

coma n = **unconsciousness**, oblivion, stupor, trance

comb v **4** = **untangle**, arrange, dress, groom **5** = **search**, forage, fossick, hunt (Aust & NZ), rake, ransack, rummage, scour, sift

combat n = **fight**, action, battle, conflict, contest, encounter, engagement, skirmish, struggle, war, warfare ▷ v = **fight**, defy, do battle with, oppose, resist, withstand

combatant n **1** = **fighter**, adversary, antagonist, enemy, opponent, soldier, warrior

combination n **1** = **mixture**, amalgamation, blend, coalescence, composite, connection, mix **2** = **association**, alliance, coalition, confederation, consortium, federation, syndicate, union

combine v **1** = **join together**, amalgamate, blend, connect, integrate, link, merge, mix, pool, unite

chemical compound. ▷ *n* **3** association of people or firms for a common purpose. **combination** *n* **1** combining. **2** people or things combined. **3** set of numbers that opens a special lock. ▷ *pl* **4** old-fashioned undergarment with long sleeves and long legs. **combine harvester** machine that reaps and threshes grain in one process.

combo *n, pl* **-bos** small group of jazz musicians.

combustion *n* process of burning. **combustible** *adj* burning easily.

come ❶ *v* **coming**, **came**, **come 1** move towards a place, arrive. **2** occur. **3** reach a specified point or condition. **4** be produced. **5** (foll. by *from*) be born in. **6** become, e.g. *a dream come true*. **come across** *v* **1** meet or find by accident. **2** (often foll. by *as*) give an impression of (being). **comeback** *n informal* **1** return to a former position. **2** retort. **come by** *v* find, obtain. **comedown** *n* **1** decline in status. **2** disappointment. **come into** *v* **1** enter. **2** inherit. **come of** *v* result from. **come to** *v* **1** regain consciousness. **2** amount to (a total figure). **come up** *v* be mentioned, arise. **comeuppance** *n informal*

deserved punishment.

comedy ❶ *n, pl* **-dies 1** humorous play, film, or programme. **2** humorous aspect of events. **comedian**, **comedienne** *n* **1** entertainer who tells jokes. **2** person who performs in comedy.

comely *adj* **-lier**, **-liest** *old-fashioned* nice-looking.

comestibles *pl n formal* food.

comet *n* heavenly body with a long luminous tail.

comfit *n* sugar-coated sweet.

comfort ❶ *n* **1** physical ease or wellbeing. **2** consolation. **3** means of consolation. ▷ *v* **4** soothe, console. **comfortable** *adj* **1** giving comfort. **2** free from pain. **3** *informal* well-off financially. **comfortably** *adv* **comforter** *n* **1** person or thing that comforts. **2** baby's dummy. **3** *Brit* woollen scarf.

comfrey *n* tall plant with bell-shaped flowers.

comfy *adj* **-fier**, **-fiest** *informal* comfortable.

comic ❶ *adj* **1** humorous, funny. **2** of comedy. ▷ *n* **3** comedian. **4** magazine containing strip cartoons. **comical** *adj* amusing. **comically** *adv*.

come *v* **1** = **arrive**, advance, appear, approach, draw near, materialize, move towards, near, reach, show up (*inf*), turn up (*inf*) **2** = **happen**, fall, occur, take place **4** = **result**, arise, be produced, emanate, emerge, flow, issue, originate

come across *v* **1** = **find**, bump into (*inf*), chance upon, discover, encounter, meet, notice, stumble upon, unearth

comeback *n Inf* **1** = **return**, rally, rebound, recovery, resurgence, revival, triumph ▷ *n* **2** = **response**, rejoinder, reply, retaliation, retort, riposte

comedian *n* = **comic**, card (*inf*), clown, funny man, humorist, jester, joker, wag, wit

comedown *n* **1** = **decline**, deflation, demotion, reverse **2** = **disappointment**, anticlimax, blow, humiliation, letdown

comedy *n* **1** = **light entertainment**, farce **2** = **humour**, fun, hilarity, jesting, joking

comeuppance *n Inf* = **punishment**, chastening, deserts, due reward,

recompense, retribution

comfort *n* **1** = **luxury**, cosiness, ease, opulence, snugness, wellbeing **2** = **relief**, compensation, consolation, help, succour, support ▷ *v* **4** = **console**, commiserate with, hearten, reassure, soothe

comfortable *adj* **1** = **pleasant**, agreeable, convenient, cosy, homely, relaxing, restful **2** = **happy**, at ease, at home, contented, gratified, relaxed, serene **3** *Inf* = **well-off**, affluent, in clover (*inf*), prosperous, well-to-do

comforting *adj* = **consoling**, cheering, consolatory, encouraging, heart-warming, reassuring, soothing

comic *adj* **1** = **funny**, amusing, comical, droll, farcical, humorous, jocular, witty ▷ *n* **3** = **comedian**, buffoon, clown, funny man, humorist, jester, wag, wit

comical *adj* = **funny**, amusing, comic, droll, farcical, hilarious, humorous, priceless, side-splitting

coming *adj* **1** = **approaching**, at hand, forthcoming, imminent, impending, in store, near, nigh ▷ *n* **2** = **arrival**, advent, approach

comma n punctuation mark (,).

command ❶ v **1** order. **2** have authority over. **3** deserve and get. **4** look down over. ▷ n **5** authoritative instruction that something must be done. **6** authority to command. **7** knowledge. **8** military or naval unit with a specific function. **9** instruction given to a computer. **commandant** n officer commanding a military group. **commandeer** v **1** seize for military use. **2** take (something to which one is not entitled). **commander** n **1** military officer in command of a group or operation. **2** middle-ranking naval officer. **commander-in-chief** n, pl **commanders-in-chief** supreme commander of a nation's armed forces. **commandment** n command from God, esp. one of the Ten Commandments in the Old Testament. **commando** n, pl **-dos**, **-does** (member of) a military unit trained for swift raids in enemy territory.

commedia dell'arte [kom-**made**-ee-a dell-**art**-tay] n form of improvised comedy popular in Italy in the 16th century, with stock characters and a stereotyped plot.

commemorate ❶ v honour the memory of, e.g. *a series of events to commemorate the end of the Second World War.* **commemoration** n **commemorative** adj.

commence ❶ v begin. **commencement** n **1** beginning; start. **2** *US & Canad* graduation ceremony.

commend ❶ v **1** praise. **2** recommend. **commendable** adj **commendably** adv **commendation** n.

commensurable adj **1** measurable by the same standards. **2** *Maths* **a** having a common factor **b** having units of the same dimensions and being related by whole numbers. **commensurability** n.

commensurate adj corresponding in degree, size, or value.

comment ❶ n **1** remark. **2** talk, gossip. **3** explanatory note. ▷ v **4** make a comment. **commentary** n, pl **-taries** **1** spoken accompaniment to a broadcast or film. **2** series of explanatory notes on a subject. **commentate** v provide a commentary. **commentator** n.

commerce ❶ n **1** buying and selling, trade. **2** *lit* social relations. **commercial** adj **1** of commerce. **2** (of television or radio) paid for by

——————————— THESAURUS ———————————

command v **1** = **order**, bid, charge, compel, demand, direct, require **2** = **have authority over**, control, dominate, govern, handle, head, lead, manage, rule, supervise ▷ n **5** = **order**, commandment, decree, demand, directive, instruction, requirement, ultimatum **6** = **authority**, charge, control, government, mana (*NZ*), management, mastery, power, rule, supervision

commandeer v **1** = **seize**, appropriate, confiscate, requisition, sequester, sequestrate

commander n = **officer**, boss, captain, chief, commanding officer, head, leader

commanding adj **2** = **controlling**, advantageous, decisive, dominant, dominating, superior

commemorate v = **remember**, celebrate, honour, immortalize, pay tribute to, recognize, salute

commemoration n = **remembrance**, ceremony, honouring, memorial service, tribute

commence v = **begin**, embark on, enter upon, initiate, open, originate, start

commend v **1** = **praise**, acclaim, applaud, approve, compliment, extol, speak highly of **2** = **recommend**

commendable adj **1** = **praiseworthy**, admirable, creditable, deserving, estimable, exemplary, laudable, meritorious, worthy

commendation n **1** = **praise**, acclaim, acclamation, approbation, approval, credit, good opinion, panegyric **2** = **recommendation**

comment n **1** = **remark**, observation, statement **3** = **note**, annotation, commentary, explanation, exposition, illustration ▷ v **4** = **remark**, mention, note, observe, point out, say, utter

commentary n **1** = **narration**, description, voice-over **2** = **notes**, analysis, critique, explanation, review, treatise

commentator n = **annotator**, critic, interpreter, reporter, special correspondent, sportscaster

commerce n **1** = **trade**, business, dealing, exchange, traffic

advertisers. **3** having profit as the main aim. ▷ *n* **4** television or radio advertisement. **commercialize** *v* make commercial.

commercialization *n* **commercial traveller** sales representative.

commie *n, adj informal offens* communist.

commingle *v* mix or be mixed.

commis *n, pl* **-mis** apprentice waiter or chef.

commiserate ⊙ *v* (foll. by *with*) express sympathy (for). **commiseration** *n*.

- **SPELLING TIP**
- The most popular way to misspell
- **commiserate** and **commiseration**
- is to double the *s* as well as the *m*.
- There should indeed be two *m*s, but
- only one *s*.

commissar *n* (formerly) official responsible for political education in Communist countries.

commissariat *n* military department in charge of food supplies.

commissary *n, pl* **-saries** *US* shop supplying food or equipment, esp. in a military camp.

commission ⊙ *n* **1** piece of work that an artist is asked to do. **2** duty, task. **3** percentage paid to a salesperson for each sale made. **4** group of people appointed to perform certain duties. **5** committing of a crime. **6** *Military* rank or authority officially given to an officer. ▷ *v* **7** place an order for. **8** *Military* give a commission to. **9** grant authority to. **out of commission** not in working order. **commissioner** *n* **1** appointed official in a government department. **2** member of a commission.

commissionaire *n* uniformed doorman at a hotel, theatre, etc.

commit ⊙ *v* **-mitting, -mitted 1** perform (a crime or error). **2** hand over, allocate. **3** pledge (oneself) to a course of action. **4** send (someone) to prison or hospital. **committal** *n* sending someone to prison or hospital. **commitment** *n* **1** dedication to a cause. **2** responsibility that restricts freedom of action.

- **SPELLING TIP**
- The correct spelling of
- **commitment** has three *m*s
- altogether, but only two *t*s (which
- are not next to each other).
- Although the Bank of English has
- 176 examples of *committment*, with
- three *m*s and three *t*s, this spelling
- is wrong.

committee *n* group of people appointed to perform a specified service or function.

- **SPELLING TIP**
- The commonest misspelling of
- **committee** is *commitee*, with 81
- occurrences in the Bank of English,
- which also has examples of *comittee*.
- The correct spelling is with two *m*s
- and two *t*s.

commode *n* **1** seat with a hinged flap concealing a chamber pot. **2** chest of drawers.

commodious *adj* roomy.

commodity *n, pl* **-ities** article of trade.

commodore *n* senior commissioned officer in the navy.

common ⊙ *adj* **1** occurring often. **2** belonging to two or more people. **3** public, general. **4** lacking in taste or manners. ▷ *n* **5** area of grassy land

commercial *adj* **1** = **mercantile**, trading **3** = **materialistic**, mercenary, profit-making

commiserate *v* (foll. by *with*) = **sympathize**, console, feel for, pity

commission *n* **2** = **duty**, errand, mandate, mission, task **3** = **fee**, cut, percentage, rake-off (*sl*), royalties **4** = **committee**, board, commissioners, delegation, deputation, representatives ▷ *v* **7** = **appoint**, contract, engage, nominate, order, select **9** = **authorize**, delegate, depute, empower

commit *v* **1** = **do**, carry out, enact,

execute, perform, perpetrate **4** = **put in custody**, confine, imprison

commitment *n* **1** = **dedication**, devotion, involvement, loyalty **2** = **responsibility**, duty, engagement, liability, obligation, tie

common *adj* **1** = **average**, commonplace, conventional, customary, everyday, familiar, frequent, habitual, ordinary, regular, routine, standard, stock, usual **2** = **collective**, communal, public **3** = **popular**, accepted, general, prevailing, prevalent, universal, widespread **4** = **vulgar**, coarse, inferior, plebeian

belonging to a community. ▷ *pl*
6 shared food. **House of Commons**,
the Commons lower chamber of the
British parliament. **in common**
shared. **commonly** *adv* **commoner** *n*
person who does not belong to the
nobility. **common-law** *adj* (of a
relationship) regarded as a marriage
through being long-standing.
Common Market European Union.
commonplace *adj* **1** ordinary,
everyday. ▷ *n* **2** trite remark. **common
room** sitting room for students or staff
in a school or college. **common sense**
good practical understanding.
commonwealth *n* **1** state or nation
viewed politically. **2** (**C-**) association of
independent states that used to be
ruled by Britain.
commotion ❶ *n* noisy disturbance.
commune¹ ❶ *n* **1** group of people who
live together and share everything.
2 smallest district of local government
in some countries. **communal** *adj*
shared. **communally** *adv*.
commune² ❶ *v* (foll. by *with*) feel very
close (to), e.g. *communing with nature*.
communion *n* **1** sharing of thoughts
or feelings. **2** (**C-**) Christian ritual of
sharing consecrated bread and wine.
3 religious group with shared beliefs
and practices.
communicate ❶ *v* **1** make known or

share (information, thoughts, or
feelings). **2** receive Communion.
communicable *adj* (of a disease) able
to be passed on. **communicant** *n*
person who receives Communion.
communicating *adj* (of a door) joining
two rooms. **communication** *n*
1 communicating. **2** thing
communicated. ▷ *pl* **3** means of
travelling or sending messages.
communicative *adj* talking freely.
communiqué [kom-**mune**-ik-kay] *n*
official announcement.
communism ❶ *n* **1** belief that all
property and means of production
should be shared by the community.
2 (**C-**) system of state control of the
economy and society in some
countries. **communist** *n*, *adj*
communistic *adj*.
community ❶ *n*, *pl* **-ties 1** all the
people living in one district. **2** group
with shared origins or interests. **3** the
public, society. **community centre**
building used by a community for
activities.
commute ❶ *v* **1** travel daily to and from
work. **2** reduce (a sentence) to a less
severe one. **commuter** *n* person who
commutes to and from work.
commutator *n* device used to change
alternating electric current into direct
current.

———————————————————— THESAURUS ———————

commonplace *adj* **1** = **everyday**,
banal, common, humdrum, mundane,
obvious, ordinary, run-of-the-mill,
widespread ▷ *n* **2** = **cliché**, banality,
platitude, truism
common sense *n* = **good sense**,
gumption (*Brit inf*), horse sense, level-
headedness, native intelligence,
prudence, sound judgment, wit
commotion *n* = **disturbance**, disorder,
excitement, furore, fuss, hue and
cry, rumpus, tumult, turmoil,
upheaval, uproar
communal *adj* = **public**, collective,
general, joint, shared
commune¹ *n* **1** = **community**,
collective, cooperative, kibbutz
commune² *v* (foll. by *with*)
= **contemplate**, meditate on, muse
on, ponder, reflect on
communicate *v* **1** = **make known**,
convey, declare, disclose,
impart, inform, pass on, proclaim,
transmit

communication *n* **1** = **passing on**,
contact, conversation,
correspondence, dissemination, link,
transmission **2** = **message**,
announcement, disclosure, dispatch,
information, news, report, statement,
word
communicative *adj* = **talkative**,
chatty, expansive, forthcoming, frank,
informative, loquacious, open,
outgoing, voluble
communism *n* (also cap.) = **socialism**,
Bolshevism, collectivism, Marxism,
state socialism
communist *n* (also cap.) = **socialist**,
Bolshevik, collectivist, Marxist, Red
(*inf*)
community *n* **1** = **populace**,
commonwealth, residents, society,
state **2** = **public**, general public,
people **3** = **group**, brotherhood,
company, society
commuter *n* = **daily traveller**,
straphanger (*inf*), suburbanite

compact¹ ❶ *adj* **1** closely packed.
2 neatly arranged. **3** concise, brief. ▷ *n*
4 small flat case containing a mirror
and face powder. ▷ *v* **5** pack closely
together. **compactly** *adv*
compactness *n* **compact disc** small
digital audio disc on which the sound
is read by an optical laser system.
compact² ❷ *n* contract, agreement.
companion ❶ *n* **1** person who
associates with or accompanies
someone. **2** woman paid to live with
another woman. **companionable** *adj*
friendly. **companionship** *n*.
companionway *n* ladder linking the
decks of a ship.
company ❶ *n*, *pl* **-nies 1** business
organization. **2** group of actors.
3 small unit of troops. **4** crew of a ship.
5 fact of being with someone.
6 gathering of people. **7** guest or
guests. **8** person's associates.
compare ❶ *v* **1** examine (things) and

point out the resemblances or
differences. **2** (foll. by *to*) declare to be
(like). **3** (foll. by *with*) be worthy of
comparison. **comparable** *adj*
1 worthy of comparison. **2** able to be
compared. **comparability** *n*
comparative *adj* **1** relative.
2 involving comparison.
3 *Grammar* denoting the form of an
adjective or adverb indicating *more*. ▷ *n*
4 *Grammar* comparative form of a
word. **comparatively** *adv*
comparison *n* **1** comparing.
2 similarity or equivalence.
compartment ❶ *n* **1** section of a
railway carriage. **2** separate section.
compass ❶ *n* **1** instrument for
showing direction, with a needle that
points north. **2** limits, range. ▷ *pl*
3 hinged instrument for drawing
circles.
compassion ❶ *n* pity, sympathy.
compassionate *adj*.

THESAURUS
---

compact¹ *adj* **1** = **closely packed**,
compressed, condensed, dense,
pressed together, solid, thick **3** = **brief**,
compendious, concise, succinct, terse,
to the point ▷ *v* **5** = **pack closely**,
compress, condense, cram, stuff, tamp
compact² *n* = **agreement**, arrangement,
bargain, bond, contract, covenant,
deal, pact, treaty, understanding
companion *n* **1** = **friend**, accomplice,
ally, associate, cobber (*Aust or old-
fashioned NZ inf*), colleague, comrade,
consort, mate (*inf*), partner
2 = **escort**, aide, assistant, attendant,
chaperon, squire
companionship *n* **1** = **fellowship**,
camaraderie, company, comradeship,
conviviality, esprit de corps, friendship,
rapport, togetherness
company *n* **1** = **business**, association,
concern, corporation, establishment,
firm, house, partnership, syndicate
5 = **companionship**, fellowship,
presence, society **6** = **group**,
assembly, band, collection,
community, crowd, gathering, party,
set **7** = **guests**, callers, party, visitors
comparable *adj* **1** = **on a par**, a match
for, as good as, commensurate, equal,
equivalent, in a class with,
proportionate, tantamount
2 = **similar**, akin, alike, analogous,
cognate, corresponding, cut from the
same cloth, of a piece, related

comparative *adj* **1** = **relative**, by
comparison, qualified
compare *v* **1** = **weigh**, balance,
contrast, juxtapose, set against **2** (foll.
by *to*) = **liken to**, correlate to, equate
to, identify with, mention in the same
breath as, parallel, resemble **3** (foll. by
with) = **be on a par with**, approach,
bear comparison, be in the same class
as, be the equal of, compete with,
equal, hold a candle to, match
comparison *n* **1** = **contrast**,
distinction, juxtaposition
2 = **similarity**, analogy, comparability,
correlation, likeness, resemblance
compartment *n* **1** = **carriage**
2 = **section**, alcove, bay, berth, booth,
cubbyhole, cubicle, locker, niche,
pigeonhole
compass *n* **2** = **range**, area, boundary,
circumference, extent, field, limit,
reach, realm, scope
compassion *n* = **sympathy**,
condolence, fellow feeling, humanity,
kindness, mercy, pity, sorrow,
tenderness, understanding
compassionate *adj* = **sympathetic**,
benevolent, charitable, humane,
humanitarian, kind-hearted,
merciful, pitying, tender-hearted,
understanding
compatibility *n* = **harmony**, affinity,
agreement, concord, empathy, like-
mindedness, rapport, sympathy

compatible ❶ adj able to exist, work, or be used together. **compatibility** n.

compatriot n fellow countryman or countrywoman.

compel ❶ v -**pelling**, -**pelled** force (to be or do). **compelling** adj **1** convincing. **2** arousing strong interest.

compendium n, pl -**diums**, -**dia** selection of board games in one box. **compendious** adj brief but comprehensive.

compensate ❶ v **1** make amends to (someone), esp. for injury or loss. **2** (foll. by for) cancel out (a bad effect). **compensation** n payment to make up for loss or injury. **compensatory** adj.

compere n **1** person who presents a stage, radio, or television show. ▷ v **2** be the compere of.

compete ❶ v try to win or achieve (a prize, profit, etc.). **competition** n **1** competing. **2** event in which people compete. **3** people against whom one

competes. **competitive** adj **1** involving rivalry. **2** eager to be more successful than other people. **3** offering good value compared with commercial rivals. **competitor** n.

competent ❶ adj having the skill or knowledge to do something well. **competently** adv **competence** n.

compile ❶ v collect and arrange (information), esp. to make a book. **compilation** n **compiler** n.

complacent ❶ adj self-satisfied. **complacently** adv **complacency** n.

complain ❶ v **1** express resentment or displeasure. **2** (foll. by of) say that one is suffering from (an illness). **complaint** n **1** complaining. **2** mild illness. **complainant** n Law plaintiff.

complaisant [kom-**play**-zant] adj willing to please. **complaisance** n.

complement ❶ n **1** thing that completes something. **2** complete amount or number. **3** Grammar word

—————————————— THESAURUS ——————————————

compatible adj = **harmonious**, adaptable, congruous, consistent, in harmony, in keeping, suitable

compel v = **force**, coerce, constrain, dragoon, impel, make, oblige, railroad (inf)

compelling adj **1** = **convincing**, cogent, conclusive, forceful, irrefutable, powerful, telling, weighty **2** = **fascinating**, enchanting, enthralling, gripping, hypnotic, irresistible, mesmeric, spellbinding

compensate v **1** = **recompense**, atone, make amends, make good, refund, reimburse, remunerate, repay **2** (foll. by for) = **cancel (out)**, balance, counteract, counterbalance, make up for, offset, redress

compensation n = **recompense**, amends, atonement, damages, reimbursement, remuneration, reparation, restitution, satisfaction

compete v = **contend**, be in the running, challenge, contest, fight, strive, struggle, vie

competence n = **ability**, capability, capacity, expertise, fitness, proficiency, skill, suitability

competent adj = **able**, adequate, capable, fit, proficient, qualified, suitable

competition n **1** = **rivalry**, opposition, strife, struggle **2** = **contest**, championship, event, head-to-head,

puzzle, quiz, tournament **3** = **opposition**, challengers, field, rivals

competitive adj **1** = **cut-throat**, aggressive, antagonistic, at odds, dog-eat-dog, opposing, rival **2** = **ambitious**, combative

competitor n = **contestant**, adversary, antagonist, challenger, opponent, rival

compilation n = **collection**, accumulation, anthology, assemblage, assortment, treasury

compile v = **put together**, accumulate, amass, collect, cull, garner, gather, marshal, organize

complacency n = **self-satisfaction**, contentment, satisfaction, smugness

complacent adj = **self-satisfied**, contented, pleased with oneself, resting on one's laurels, satisfied, serene, smug, unconcerned

complain v **1** = **find fault**, bemoan, bewail, carp, deplore, groan, grouse, grumble, lament, moan, whine, whinge (inf)

complaint n **1** = **criticism**, charge, grievance, gripe (inf), grouse, grumble, lament, moan, protest **2** = **illness**, affliction, ailment, disease, disorder, malady, sickness, upset

complement n **1** = **completion**, companion, consummation, counterpart, finishing touch,

or words added to a verb to complete the meaning. **4** *Maths* angle added to a specified angle to produce a right angle. ▷ *v* **5** make complete. **complementary** *adj*.
● **USAGE NOTE**
● Avoid confusing this word with
● *compliment*.

complete ❶ *adj* **1** thorough, absolute. **2** finished. **3** having all the necessary parts. ▷ *v* **4** finish. **5** make whole or perfect. **completely** *adv* **completeness** *n* **completion** *n* finishing.

complex ❶ *adj* **1** made up of parts. **2** complicated. ▷ *n* **3** whole made up of parts. **4** group of unconscious feelings that influences behaviour. **complexity** *n*.

complexion ❶ *n* **1** skin of the face. **2** character, nature.

compliance *n* **1** complying. **2** tendency to do what others want. **compliant** *adj*.

complicate ❶ *v* make or become complex or difficult to deal with. **complication** *n*.

complicity *n* fact of being an accomplice in a crime.

compliment ❶ *n* **1** expression of praise. ▷ *pl* **2** formal greetings. ▷ *v* **3** praise. **complimentary** *adj* **1** expressing praise. **2** free of charge.
● **USAGE NOTE**
● Avoid confusing this word with
● *complement*.

compline *n* last service of the day in the Roman Catholic Church.

comply ❶ *v* **-plying, -plied** (foll. by *with*) act in accordance (with).

component ❶ *n, adj* (being) part of a whole.

rounding-off, supplement **2** = **total**, aggregate, capacity, entirety, quota, totality, wholeness ▷ *v* **5** = **complete**, cap (*inf*), crown, round off, set off
complementary *adj* = **completing**, companion, corresponding, interdependent, interrelating, matched, reciprocal
complete *adj* **1** = **total**, absolute, consummate, outright, perfect, thorough, thoroughgoing, utter **2** = **finished**, accomplished, achieved, concluded, ended **3** = **entire**, all, faultless, full, intact, plenary, unbroken, whole ▷ *v* **4** = **finish**, close, conclude, crown, end, finalize, round off, settle, wrap up (*inf*)
completely *adv* **1** = **totally**, absolutely, altogether, entirely, every inch, fully, hook, line and sinker, in full, lock, stock and barrel, one hundred per cent, perfectly, thoroughly, utterly, wholly
completion *n* = **finishing**, bitter end, close, conclusion, culmination, end, fruition, fulfilment
complex *adj* **1** = **compound**, composite, heterogeneous, manifold, multifarious, multiple **2** = **complicated**, convoluted, elaborate, intricate, involved, labyrinthine, tangled, tortuous ▷ *n* **3** = **structure**, aggregate, composite, network, organization, scheme, system **4** = **obsession**, fixation, fixed idea, phobia, preoccupation
complexion *n* **1** = **skin**, colour,

colouring, hue, pigmentation, skin tone **2** = **nature**, appearance, aspect, character, guise, light, look, make-up
complexity *n* **2** = **complication**, elaboration, entanglement, intricacy, involvement, ramification
complicate *v* = **make difficult**, confuse, entangle, involve, muddle, ravel
complicated *adj* = **difficult**, complex, convoluted, elaborate, intricate, involved, perplexing, problematic, puzzling, troublesome
complication *n* **1** = **problem**, difficulty, drawback, embarrassment, obstacle, snag
compliment *n* **1** = **praise**, bouquet, commendation, congratulations, eulogy, flattery, honour, tribute **2** *pl* = **greetings**, good wishes, regards, remembrances, respects, salutation ▷ *v* **3** = **praise**, commend, congratulate, extol, flatter, pay tribute to, salute, speak highly of
complimentary *adj* **1** = **flattering**, appreciative, approving, commendatory, congratulatory, laudatory **2** = **free**, courtesy, donated, gratis, gratuitous, honorary, on the house
comply *v* (foll. by *with*) = **obey**, abide by, acquiesce, adhere to, conform to, follow, observe, submit, toe the line
component *n* = **part**, constituent, element, ingredient, item, piece, unit ▷ *adj* = **constituent**, inherent, intrinsic

comport v behave (oneself) in a specified way.

compose ❶ v **1** put together. **2** be the component parts of. **3** create (a piece of music or writing). **4** calm (oneself). **5** arrange artistically. **composed** adj (of people) in control of their feelings. **composer** n person who writes music. **composition** n way that something is put together or arranged.

composite n, adj (something) made up of separate parts.

composition ❶ n **1** way that something is put together or arranged. **2** work of art, esp. a musical one. **3** essay. **4** composing.

compositor n person who arranges type for printing.

compos mentis adj Latin sane.

compost n decayed plants used as a fertilizer.

composure ❶ n calmness.

compote n fruit stewed with sugar.

compound¹ ❶ n, adj **1** (thing, esp. chemical) made up of two or more combined parts or elements. ▷ v **2** combine or make by combining.

3 intensify, make worse. **compound fracture** fracture in which the broken bone pierces the skin. **compound interest** interest paid on a sum and its accumulated interest.

compound² n fenced enclosure containing buildings.

comprehend ❶ v understand. **comprehensible** adj **comprehension** n **comprehensive** adj **1** of broad scope, fully inclusive. ▷ n **2** comprehensive school. **comprehensive school** secondary school for children of all abilities.

compress ❶ v [kum-**press**] **1** squeeze together. **2** make shorter. ▷ n [**kom**-press] **3** pad applied to stop bleeding or cool inflammation. **compression** n **compressor** n machine that compresses gas or air.

comprise ❶ v be made up of or make up.

compromise ❶ [**kom**-prom-mize] n **1** settlement reached by concessions on each side. ▷ v **2** settle a dispute by making concessions. **3** put in a dishonourable position.

──────────────── THESAURUS ────────────────

compose v **1** = **put together**, build, comprise, constitute, construct, fashion, form, make, make up **3** = **create**, contrive, devise, invent, produce, write **4** = **calm**, collect, control, pacify, placate, quiet, soothe **5** = **arrange**, adjust

composed adj = **calm**, at ease, collected, cool, level-headed, poised, relaxed, sedate, self-possessed, serene, unflappable

composition n **1** = **design**, arrangement, configuration, formation, layout, make-up, organization, structure **3** = **essay**, exercise, literary work, opus, piece, treatise, work **4** = **creation**, compilation, fashioning, formation, formulation, making, production, putting together

composure n = **calmness**, aplomb, equanimity, poise, sang-froid, self-assurance, self-possession, serenity

compound¹ n **1** = **combination**, alloy, amalgam, blend, composite, fusion, medley, mixture, synthesis ▷ v **2** = **combine**, amalgamate, blend, intermingle, mix, synthesize, unite **3** = **intensify**, add to, aggravate, augment, complicate, exacerbate,

heighten, magnify, worsen

comprehend v = **understand**, apprehend, conceive, fathom, grasp, know, make out, perceive, see, take in

comprehensible adj = **understandable**, clear, coherent, conceivable, explicit, intelligible, plain

comprehension n = **understanding**, conception, discernment, grasp, intelligence, perception, realization

comprehensive adj **1** = **broad**, all-embracing, all-inclusive, blanket, complete, encyclopedic, exhaustive, full, inclusive, overarching, thorough

compress v **1** = **squeeze**, concentrate, condense, contract, crush, press, squash **2** = **shorten**, abbreviate, contract

comprise v = **be composed of**, compose, consist of, constitute, contain, embrace, encompass, form, include, make up, take in

compromise n **1** = **give-and-take**, accommodation, adjustment, agreement, concession, settlement, trade-off ▷ v **2** = **meet halfway**, adjust, agree, concede, give and take, go fifty-fifty (inf), settle, strike a balance **3** = **weaken**, discredit, dishonour, embarrass, expose,

comptroller *n* (in titles) financial controller.

compulsion ❶ *n* **1** irresistible urge. **2** forcing by threats or violence. **compulsive** *adj* **compulsively** *adv* **compulsory** *adj* required by rules or laws.

compunction *n* feeling of guilt or shame.

compute ❶ *v* calculate, esp. using a computer. **computation** *n* **computer** *n* electronic machine that stores and processes data. **computerize** *v* **1** adapt (a system) to be handled by computer. **2** store or process in a computer. **computerization** *n*.

comrade ❶ *n* **1** fellow member of a union or socialist political party. **2** companion. **comradeship** *n*.

con¹ ❶ *informal* ▷ *n* **1** short for CONFIDENCE TRICK. ▷ *v* **conning**, **conned 2** deceive, swindle.

con² *n* an argument against **pros and cons** see PRO¹.

con³ *n slang* convict.

concatenation *n* series of linked events.

concave ❶ *adj* curving inwards. **concavity** *n*.

conceal ❶ *v* **1** cover and hide. **2** keep secret. **concealment** *n*.

concede ❶ *v* **1** admit to be true. **2** acknowledge defeat in (a contest or argument). **3** grant as a right.

conceit ❶ *n* **1** too high an opinion of oneself. **2** far-fetched or clever comparison. **conceited** *adj*.

conceive ❶ *v* **1** imagine, think. **2** form in the mind. **3** become pregnant. **conceivable** *adj* imaginable, possible. **conceivably** *adv*.

concentrate ❶ *v* **1** fix one's attention or efforts on something. **2** bring or come together in large numbers in one place. **3** make (a liquid) stronger by removing water from it. ▷ *n* **4** concentrated liquid. **concentration** *n* **1** concentrating. **2** proportion of a substance in a mixture or solution.

concentration camp prison camp for

---

jeopardize, prejudice

compulsion *n* **1** = **urge**, drive, necessity, need, obsession, preoccupation **2** = **force**, coercion, constraint, demand, duress, obligation, pressure, urgency

compulsive *adj* **1** = **irresistible**, compelling, driving, neurotic, obsessive, overwhelming, uncontrollable, urgent

compulsory *adj* = **obligatory**, binding, *de rigueur*, forced, imperative, mandatory, required, requisite

compute *v* = **calculate**, add up, count, enumerate, figure out, reckon, tally, total

comrade *n* **2** = **companion**, ally, associate, cobber (*Aust or old-fashioned NZ inf*), colleague, co-worker, fellow, friend, partner

con¹ *Inf n* **1** = **swindle**, deception, fraud, scam (*sl*), sting (*inf*), trick ▷ *v* **2** = **swindle**, cheat, deceive, defraud, double-cross (*inf*), dupe, hoodwink, rip off (*sl*), trick

concave *adj* = **hollow**, indented

conceal *v* **1** = **hide**, bury, camouflage, cover, disguise, mask, obscure, screen

concede *v* **1** = **admit**, accept, acknowledge, allow, confess, grant, own **2** = **give up**, cede, hand over, relinquish, surrender, yield

conceit *n* **1** = **self-importance**, arrogance, egotism, narcissism, pride, swagger, vanity **2** = **fancy**, fantasy, image, whim, whimsy

conceited *adj* **1** = **self-important**, arrogant, bigheaded (*inf*), cocky, egotistical, full of oneself, immodest, narcissistic, too big for one's boots or breeches, vain

conceivable *adj* = **imaginable**, believable, credible, possible, thinkable

conceive *v* **1** = **imagine**, believe, comprehend, envisage, fancy, suppose, think, understand **2** = **think up**, contrive, create, design, devise, formulate **3** = **become pregnant**, become impregnated

concentrate *v* **1** = **focus one's attention on**, be engrossed in, put one's mind to, rack one's brains **2** = **gather**, accumulate, centre, cluster, collect, congregate, converge, focus, huddle

concentrated *adj* **1** = **intense**, all-out (*inf*), deep, hard, intensive **2** = **condensed**, boiled down, evaporated, reduced, rich, thickened, undiluted

concentration *n* **1** = **focusing**, absorption, application, single-mindedness

civilian prisoners, esp. in Nazi
Germany.

concentric *adj* having the same centre.

concept ⊕ *n* abstract or general idea.
conceptual *adj* of or based on
concepts. **conceptualize** *v* form a
concept of.

conception ⊕ *n* **1** general idea.
2 becoming pregnant.

concern ⊕ *n* **1** anxiety, worry.
2 something that is of importance to
someone. **3** business, firm. ▷ *v*
4 worry (someone). **5** involve
(oneself). **6** be relevant or important
to. **concerned** *adj* **1** interested,
involved. **2** anxious, worried.
concerning *prep* about, regarding.

concert *n* musical entertainment. **in
concert 1** working together. **2** (of
musicians) performing live. **concerted**
adj done together.

concertina *n* **1** small musical
instrument similar to an accordion. ▷ *v*
-naing, -naed 2 collapse or fold up
like a concertina.

concerto [kon-**chair**-toe] *n, pl* **-tos, -ti**
large-scale composition for a solo

instrument and orchestra.

concession ⊕ *n* **1** grant of rights, land,
or property. **2** reduction in price for a
specified category of people.
3 conceding. **4** thing conceded.
concessionary *adj*.

concession road *n Canad* (esp. in
Ontario) one of a series of roads
separating land concessions in a
township.

conch *n* **1** shellfish with a large spiral
shell. **2** its shell.

concierge [kon-see-**airzh**] *n* (in France)
caretaker in a block of flats.

conciliate ⊕ *v* try to end a
disagreement (with). **conciliation** *n*
conciliator *n* **conciliatory** *adj*.

concise ⊕ *adj* brief and to the point.
concisely *adv* **concision**,
conciseness *n*.

conclave *n* **1** secret meeting. **2** private
meeting of cardinals to elect a new
pope.

conclude ⊕ *v* **1** decide by reasoning.
2 end, finish. **3** arrange or settle
finally. **conclusion** *n* **1** decision based
on reasoning. **2** ending. **3** final

───────────────── THESAURUS ─────────────────

concept *n* = **idea**, abstraction,
conception, conceptualization,
hypothesis, image, notion, theory,
view

conception *n* **1** = **idea**, concept,
design, image, notion, plan
2 = **impregnation**, fertilization,
germination, insemination

concern *n* **1** = **worry**, anxiety,
apprehension, burden, care, disquiet,
distress **2** = **business**, affair, interest,
job, responsibility, task **3** = **business**,
company, corporation, enterprise,
establishment, firm, organization ▷ *v*
4 = **worry**, bother, disquiet, distress,
disturb, make anxious, perturb,
trouble **6** = **be relevant to**, affect,
apply to, bear on, interest, involve,
pertain to, regard, touch

concerned *adj* **1** = **involved**, active,
implicated, interested, mixed up, privy
to **2** = **worried**, anxious, bothered,
distressed, disturbed, troubled,
uneasy, upset

concerning *prep* = **regarding**, about,
apropos of, as regards, on the subject
of, re, relating to, respecting,
touching, with reference to

concession *n* **1, 2** = **grant**, adjustment,
allowance, boon, compromise,

indulgence, permit, privilege
3 = **conceding**, acknowledgment,
admission, assent, confession,
surrender, yielding

conciliate *v* = **pacify**, appease, clear
the air, mediate, mollify, placate,
reconcile, soothe, win over

conciliation *n* = **pacification**,
appeasement, mollification, placation,
reconciliation, soothing

conciliatory *adj* = **pacifying**,
appeasing, mollifying, pacific,
peaceable, placatory

concise *adj* = **brief**, compendious,
condensed, laconic, pithy, short,
succinct, terse

conclude *v* **1** = **decide**, assume,
deduce, gather, infer, judge, surmise,
work out **2** = **end**, cease, close,
complete, finish, round off, terminate,
wind up **3** = **accomplish**, bring about,
carry out, effect, pull off

conclusion *n* **1** = **decision**, conviction,
deduction, inference, judgment,
opinion, verdict **2** = **end**, bitter end,
close, completion, ending, finale,
finish, result, termination
3 = **outcome**, consequence,
culmination, end result, result,
upshot

arrangement or settlement.
conclusive *adj* ending doubt,
convincing. **conclusively** *adv*.

concoct ❶ *v* **1** make up (a story or
plan). **2** make by combining
ingredients. **concoction** *n*.

concomitant *adj* existing along with
something else.

concord *n* state of peaceful agreement,
harmony. **concordance** *n* **1** similarity
or consistency. **2** index of words in a
book. **concordant** *adj* agreeing.

concordat *n* pact or treaty.

concourse *n* **1** large open public place
where people can gather. **2** large
crowd.

concrete ❶ *n* **1** mixture of cement,
sand, stone, and water, used in
building. ▷ *v* **2** cover with concrete.
▷ *adj* **3** made of concrete. **4** particular,
specific. **5** real or solid, not abstract.

concubine [**kon**-kew-bine] *n* woman
living with a man as his wife, but not
married to him.

concupiscence [kon-**kew**-piss-enss] *n*
formal lust. **concupiscent** *adj*.

concur ❶ *v* **-curring**, **-curred** agree.
concurrence *n* **concurrent** *adj*

happening at the same time or place.
concurrently *adv* at the same time.

concussion *n* period of
unconsciousness caused by a blow to
the head. **concussed** *adj* having
concussion.

condemn ❶ *v* **1** express disapproval of.
2 sentence, e.g. *he was condemned to
death*. **3** force into an unpleasant
situation. **4** declare unfit for use.
condemnation *n* **condemnatory** *adj*.

condense ❶ *v* **1** make shorter. **2** turn
from gas into liquid. **condensation** *n*
condenser *n Electricity* capacitor.

condescend ❶ *v* **1** behave
patronizingly towards someone.
2 agree to do something, but as if
doing someone a favour.
condescension *n*.

condiment *n* seasoning for food, such
as salt or pepper.

condition ❶ *n* **1** particular state of
being. **2** necessary requirement for
something else to happen.
3 restriction, qualification. **4** state of
health, physical fitness. **5** medical
problem, e.g. *a heart condition*. ▷ *pl*
6 circumstances. ▷ *v* **7** train or

— THESAURUS —

conclusive *adj* = **decisive**, clinching,
convincing, definite, final, irrefutable,
ultimate, unanswerable

concoct *v* **1** = **make up**, contrive,
devise, formulate, hatch, invent, think
up **2** = **prepare**, brew

concoction *n* **2** = **mixture**, blend,
brew, combination, compound,
creation, mix, preparation

concrete *adj* **4** = **specific**, definite,
explicit **5** = **real**, actual, factual,
material, sensible, substantial,
tangible

concur *v* = **agree**, acquiesce, assent,
consent

condemn *v* **1** = **disapprove**, blame,
censure, criticize, damn, denounce,
reproach, reprove, upbraid
2 = **sentence**, convict, damn, doom,
pass sentence on

condemnation *n* **1** = **disapproval**,
blame, censure, denunciation,
reproach, reproof, stricture
2 = **sentence**, conviction, damnation,
doom, judgment

condensation *n* **1** = **abridgment**,
contraction, digest, précis, synopsis
2 = **distillation**, liquefaction,
precipitate, precipitation

condense *v* **1** = **abridge**, abbreviate,
compress, concentrate, epitomize,
shorten, summarize **2** = **concentrate**,
boil down, reduce, thicken

condensed *adj* **1** = **abridged**,
compressed, concentrated, shortened,
shrunken, slimmed-down,
summarized **2** = **concentrated**,
boiled down, reduced, thickened

condescend *v* **1** = **patronize**, talk
down to **2** = **lower oneself**, bend,
deign, humble *or* demean oneself, see
fit, stoop

condescending *adj* **1** = **patronizing**,
disdainful, lofty, lordly, snobbish,
snooty (*inf*), supercilious, superior,
toffee-nosed (*sl, chiefly Brit*)

condition *n* **1** = **state**, circumstances,
lie of the land, position, shape,
situation, state of affairs **2,**
3 = **requirement**, limitation,
prerequisite, proviso, qualification,
restriction, rider, stipulation, terms
4 = **health**, fettle, fitness, kilter, order,
shape, state of health, trim
5 = **ailment**, complaint, infirmity,
malady, problem, weakness ▷ *pl*
6 = **circumstances**, environment,
milieu, situation, surroundings, way of

influence to behave in a particular
way. **8** treat with conditioner.
9 control. **on condition that** only if.
conditional *adj* depending on
circumstances. **conditioner** *n* thick
liquid used when washing to make
hair or clothes feel softer.

condo *n, pl* **-dos** *informal* a
condominium building or apartment.

condolence *n* **1** sympathy, e.g. *a
message of condolence*. ▷ *pl* **2** expression
of sympathy.

condom *n* rubber sheath worn on the
penis or in the vagina during sexual
intercourse to prevent conception or
infection.

condominium *n Aust, US & Canad* block
of flats in which each flat is owned by
the occupant.

condone ● *v* overlook or forgive
(wrongdoing).

condor *n* large vulture of S America.

conducive *adj* (foll. by *to*) likely to lead
(to).

conduct ● *n* **1** management of an
activity. **2** behaviour. ▷ *v* **3** carry out (a
task). **4** behave (oneself). **5** direct
(musicians) by moving the hands or a
baton. **6** lead, guide. **7** transmit (heat
or electricity). **conduction** *n*
transmission of heat or electricity.
conductivity *n* ability to transmit
heat or electricity. **conductive** *adj*
conductor *n* **1** person who conducts
musicians. **2** (*fem* **conductress**)
official on a bus who collects fares.

3 something that conducts heat or
electricity.

conduit [kon-dew-it] *n* channel or tube
for fluid or cables.

cone *n* **1** object with a circular base,
tapering to a point. **2** cone-shaped
ice-cream wafer. **3** plastic cone used
as a traffic marker on the roads.
4 scaly fruit of a conifer tree.

coney *n* same as CONY.

confab *n informal* conversation (also
confabulation).

confection *n* **1** any sweet food.
2 elaborate article of clothing.
confectioner *n* maker or seller of
confectionery. **confectionery** *n*
sweets.

confederate ● *n* **1** member of a
confederacy. **2** accomplice. ▷ *adj*
3 united, allied. ▷ *v* **4** unite in a
confederacy. **confederacy** *n, pl* **-cies**
union of states or people for a
common purpose. **confederation** *n*
alliance of political units.

confer ● *v* **-ferring, -ferred** **1** discuss
together. **2** grant, give. **conference** *n*
meeting for discussion. **conferment** *n*
granting, giving.

confess ● *v* **1** admit (a fault or crime).
2 admit to be true. **3** declare (one's
sins) to God or a priest, in hope of
forgiveness. **confession** *n*
1 something confessed. **2** confessing.
3 declaring one's sins to God or a
priest, in hope of forgiveness.
confessional *n* small stall in which a

life ▷ *v* **7** = **accustom**, adapt, equip,
prepare, ready, tone up, train, work
out

conditional *adj* = **dependent**,
contingent, limited, provisional,
qualified, subject to, with reservations

condone *v* = **overlook**, excuse, forgive,
let pass, look the other way, make
allowance for, pardon, turn a blind
eye to

conduct *n* **1** = **management**,
administration, control, direction,
guidance, handling, organization,
running, supervision **2** = **behaviour**,
attitude, bearing, demeanour,
deportment, manners, ways ▷ *v*
3 = **carry out**, administer, control,
direct, handle, manage, organize,
preside over, run, supervise
4 = **behave**, acquit, act, carry,
comport, deport **6** = **accompany**,

convey, escort, guide, lead, steer,
usher

confederacy *n* = **union**, alliance,
coalition, confederation, federation,
league

confer *v* **1** = **discuss**, consult, converse,
deliberate, discourse, talk **2** = **grant**,
accord, award, bestow, give, hand out,
present

conference *n* = **meeting**, colloquium,
congress, consultation, convention,
discussion, forum, seminar,
symposium

confess *v* **1** = **admit**, acknowledge,
come clean (*inf*), concede, confide,
disclose, divulge, own up **2** = **declare**,
affirm, assert, confirm, profess,
reveal

confession *n* **1, 2** = **admission**,
acknowledgment, disclosure,
exposure, revelation

priest hears confessions. **confessor** *n* priest who hears confessions.

confetti *n* small pieces of coloured paper thrown at weddings.

confidant ❶ *n* person confided in. **confidante** *n fem.*

confide ❶ *v* 1 tell someone (a secret). 2 entrust. **confidence** *n* 1 trust. 2 self-assurance. 3 something confided. **in confidence** as a secret. **confidence trick** swindle involving gaining a person's trust in order to cheat him or her. **confident** *adj* sure, esp. of oneself. **confidently** *adv* **confidential** *adj* 1 private, secret. 2 entrusted with someone's secret affairs. **confidentially** *adv* **confidentiality** *n.*

configuration *n* arrangement of parts.

confine ❶ *v* 1 keep within bounds. 2 restrict the free movement of. **confines** *pl n* boundaries, limits.

confinement *n* 1 being confined. 2 period of childbirth.

confirm ❶ *v* 1 prove to be true. 2 reaffirm, strengthen. 3 administer the rite of confirmation to. **confirmation** *n* 1 confirming. 2 something that confirms. 3 *Christianity* rite that admits a baptized person to full church membership. **confirmed** *adj* firmly established in a habit or condition, e.g. *a confirmed bachelor.*

confiscate ❶ *v* seize (property) by authority. **confiscation** *n.*

conflagration *n* large destructive fire.

conflate *v* combine or blend into a whole. **conflation** *n.*

conflict ❶ *n* 1 disagreement. 2 struggle or fight. ▷ *v* 3 be incompatible.

confluence *n* 1 place where two rivers

---

confidant *n* = **close friend**, alter ego, bosom friend, crony, familiar, intimate

confide *v* 1 = **tell**, admit, confess, disclose, divulge, impart, reveal, whisper 2 = **entrust**, commend, commit, consign

confidence *n* 1 = **trust**, belief, credence, dependence, faith, reliance 2 = **self-assurance**, aplomb, assurance, boldness, courage, firmness, nerve, self-possession **in confidence** = **in secrecy**, between you and me (and the gatepost), confidentially, privately

confident *adj* **a** = **certain**, convinced, counting on, positive, satisfied, secure, sure **b** = **self-assured**, assured, bold, dauntless, fearless, self-reliant

confidential *adj* 1 = **secret**, classified, hush-hush (*inf*), intimate, off the record, private, privy

confidentially *adv* 1 = **in secret**, behind closed doors, between ourselves, in camera, in confidence, personally, privately, sub rosa

confine *v* 1 = **imprison**, cage, enclose, incarcerate, intern, shut up 2 = **restrict**, hem in, hold back, keep, limit

confinement *n* 1 = **imprisonment**, custody, detention, incarceration, internment, porridge (*sl*) 2 = **childbirth**, childbed, labour, lying-in, parturition

confines *pl n* = **limits**, boundaries, bounds, circumference, edge, precincts

confirm *v* 1 = **prove**, authenticate, bear out, corroborate, endorse, ratify, substantiate, validate, verify 2 = **strengthen**, buttress, establish, fix, fortify, reinforce

confirmation *n* 1 = **sanction**, acceptance, agreement, approval, assent, endorsement, ratification 2 = **proof**, authentication, corroboration, evidence, substantiation, testimony, validation, verification

confirmed *adj* = **long-established**, chronic, dyed-in-the-wool, habitual, hardened, ingrained, inveterate, seasoned

confiscate *v* = **seize**, appropriate, commandeer, impound, sequester, sequestrate

confiscation *n* = **seizure**, appropriation, forfeiture, impounding, sequestration, takeover

conflict *n* 1 = **opposition**, antagonism, difference, disagreement, discord, dissension, friction, hostility, strife 2 = **battle**, clash, combat, contest, encounter, fight, strife, war ▷ *v* 3 = **be incompatible**, be at variance, clash, collide, differ, disagree, interfere

conflicting *adj* 1 = **opposing**, antagonistic, discordant 3 = **incompatible**, clashing, contradictory, contrary, inconsistent, paradoxical

join. **2** gathering.

conform ❶ v **1** comply with accepted standards or customs. **2** (foll. by *to* or *with*) be like or in accordance with. **conformist** n, adj (person) complying with accepted standards or customs. **conformity** n compliance with accepted standards or customs.

confound ❶ v **1** astound, bewilder. **2** confuse. **confounded** adj informal damned, e.g. *what a confounded nuisance!*

confront ❶ v come face to face with. **confrontation** n serious argument.

confuse ❶ v **1** mix up. **2** perplex, disconcert. **3** make unclear. **confusion** n.

confute v prove wrong. **confutation** n.

conga n **1** dance performed by a number of people in single file. **2** large single-headed drum played with the hands.

congeal v (of a liquid) become thick and sticky.

congenial ❶ adj **1** pleasant, agreeable. **2** having similar interests and attitudes. **congeniality** n.

congenital ❶ adj (of a condition) existing from birth. **congenitally** adv.

conger n large sea eel.

congested ❶ adj crowded to excess. **congestion** n.

conglomerate n **1** large corporation made up of many companies. **2** thing made up of several different elements. ▷ v **3** form into a mass. ▷ adj **4** made up of several different elements. **conglomeration** n.

congratulate ❶ v express one's pleasure to (someone) at his or her good fortune or success. **congratulations** pl n, interj **congratulatory** adj.

congregate ❶ v gather together in a crowd. **congregation** n people who attend a church. **congregational** adj **Congregationalism** n Protestant denomination in which each church is self-governing. **Congregationalist** adj, n.

congress ❶ n **1** formal meeting for

───── THESAURUS ─────

conform v **1** = **comply**, adapt, adjust, fall in with, follow, obey, toe the line **2** (foll. by *to* or *with*) = **agree**, accord, correspond, harmonize, match, suit, tally

conformist n = **traditionalist**, stick-in-the-mud (inf), yes man

conformity n = **compliance**, conventionality, observance, orthodoxy, traditionalism

confound v **1** = **bewilder**, astound, baffle, dumbfound, flummox, mystify, nonplus, perplex

confront v = **face**, accost, challenge, defy, encounter, oppose, stand up to, tackle

confrontation n = **conflict**, contest, encounter, fight, head-to-head, set-to (inf), showdown (inf)

confuse v **1** = **mix up**, disarrange, disorder, jumble, mingle, muddle, ravel **2** = **bewilder**, baffle, bemuse, faze, flummox, mystify, nonplus, perplex, puzzle

confused adj **1** = **disordered**, chaotic, disorganized, higgledy-piggledy (inf), in disarray, jumbled, mixed up, topsy-turvy, untidy **2** = **bewildered**, at sea, baffled, disorientated, flummoxed, muddled, nonplussed, perplexed, puzzled, taken aback

confusing adj **2** = **bewildering**, baffling, contradictory, disconcerting, misleading, perplexing, puzzling

confusion n **1** = **disorder**, chaos, commotion, jumble, mess, muddle, shambles, turmoil, untidiness, upheaval **2** = **bewilderment**, disorientation, mystification, perplexity, puzzlement

congenial adj **1** = **pleasant**, affable, agreeable, companionable, favourable, friendly, genial, kindly **2** = **compatible**, kindred, like-minded, sympathetic, well-suited

congenital adj = **inborn**, immanent, inbred, inherent, innate, natural

congested adj = **overcrowded**, crowded, teeming

congestion n = **overcrowding**, crowding, jam

congratulate v = **compliment**, pat on the back, wish joy to

congratulations pl n, interj = **good wishes**, best wishes, compliments, felicitations, greetings

congregate v = **come together**, assemble, collect, convene, converge, flock, gather, mass, meet

congregation n = **assembly**, brethren, crowd, fellowship, flock, multitude, throng

congress n **1** = **meeting**, assembly, conclave, conference, convention, discussion. **2** (**C-**) federal parliament of the US. **congressional** adj **Congressman**, **Congresswoman** n member of Congress.

congruent adj **1** similar, corresponding. **2** Geometry identical in shape and size. **congruence** n.

conical adj cone-shaped.

conic section n Geometry figure formed by the intersection of a plane and a cone.

conifer n cone-bearing tree, such as the fir or pine. **coniferous** adj.

conjecture ❶ n, v guess. **conjectural** adj.

conjoined twins pl n the technical name for SIAMESE TWINS.

conjugal ❶ [**kon**-jew-gal] adj of marriage.

conjugate v give the inflections of (a verb). **conjugation** n complete set of inflections of a verb.

conjunction n **1** combination. **2** simultaneous occurrence of events. **3** part of speech joining words, phrases, or clauses.

conjunctivitis n inflammation of the membrane covering the eyeball and inner eyelid. **conjunctiva** n this membrane.

conjuncture n combination of events.

conjure ❶ v **1** perform tricks that appear to be magic. **2** summon (a spirit) by magic. **conjuror**, **conjurer** n **conjure up** v produce as if by magic.

conk n slang nose.

conker n informal nut of the horse chestnut. **conkers** n game played with conkers tied on strings.

conk out v informal **1** (of a machine) break down. **2** fall asleep suddenly.

connect ❶ v **1** join together. **2** put into telephone communication with. **3** associate in the mind. **connection**, **connexion** n **1** relationship, association. **2** link or bond. **3** opportunity to transfer from one public vehicle to another. **4** influential acquaintance. **connective** adj.

conning tower n raised observation tower containing the periscope on a submarine.

connive ❶ v **1** (foll. by at) allow (wrongdoing) by ignoring it. **2** conspire. **connivance** n.

connoisseur ❶ [kon-noss-**sir**] n person with special knowledge of the arts, food, or drink.

connotation n associated idea conveyed by a word. **connote** v.

connubial [kon-**new**-bee-al] adj of marriage.

conquer ❶ v **1** defeat. **2** overcome (a difficulty). **3** take (a place) by force.

THESAURUS

council, legislature, parliament

conjecture n = **guess**, hypothesis, shot in the dark, speculation, supposition, surmise, theory ▷ v = **guess**, hypothesize, imagine, speculate, suppose, surmise, theorize

conjugal adj = **marital**, bridal, connubial, married, matrimonial, nuptial, wedded

conjure v **1** = **perform tricks**, juggle

conjure up v = **bring to mind**, contrive, create, evoke, produce as if by magic, recall, recollect

conjuror, **conjurer** n **1** = **magician**, illusionist, sorcerer, wizard

connect v **1** = **join**, affix, attach, couple, fasten, link, unite

connected adj **1** = **joined**, affiliated, akin, allied, associated, combined, coupled, linked, related, united

connection n **1** = **association**, affinity, bond, liaison, link, relationship, relevance, tie-in **2** = **link**, alliance, association, attachment, coupling, fastening, junction, tie, union

4 = **contact**, acquaintance, ally, associate, friend, sponsor

connivance n **1** = **tacit consent** **2** = **collusion**, abetting, complicity, conspiring

connive v **1** (foll. by at) = **turn a blind eye to**, abet, disregard, let pass, look the other way, overlook, wink at **2** = **conspire**, collude, cook up (inf), intrigue, plot, scheme

connoisseur n = **expert**, aficionado, appreciator, authority, buff (inf), devotee, fundi (S Afr), judge, mana (NZ)

conquer v **1** = **defeat**, beat, crush, get the better of, master, overcome, overpower, overthrow, quell, subjugate, vanquish **3** = **seize**, acquire, annex, obtain, occupy, overrun, win

conqueror n **1** = **winner**, defeater, vanquisher, victor

conquest n **1 a** = **defeat**, mastery, overthrow, rout, triumph, victory **b** = **takeover**, annexation, coup, invasion, occupation, subjugation

conqueror n **conquest** n
1 conquering. **2** person or thing conquered. **3** person whose affections have been won.
consanguinity n formal relationship by blood.
conscience ❶ n sense of right or wrong as regards thoughts and actions. **conscience-stricken** adj feeling anxious or guilty.
conscientious ❶ adj **1** painstaking. **2** governed by conscience. **conscientiously** adv **conscientious objector** person who refuses to serve in the armed forces on moral or religious grounds.
conscious ❶ adj **1** alert and awake. **2** aware. **3** deliberate, intentional. **4** of the part of the mind that determines the choices of action. **consciously** adv **consciousness** n.
conscript n **1** person enrolled for compulsory military service. ▷ v **2** enrol (someone) for compulsory military service. **conscription** n.
consecrate ❶ v **1** make sacred. **2** dedicate to a specific purpose. **consecration** n.
consecutive ❶ adj in unbroken succession. **consecutively** adv.

consensus ❶ n general agreement.
● **SPELLING TIP**
● The Bank of English has 6694
● examples of the word **consensus**
● and another 112 of concensus with
● a c in the middle. The correct
● spelling is **consensus** and it has
● only one c.
consent ❶ n **1** agreement, permission. ▷ v **2** (foll. by to) permit, agree to.
consequence ❶ n **1** result, effect. **2** importance. **consequent** adj resulting. **consequently** adv as a result, therefore. **consequential** adj **1** important. **2** following as a result.
conservative ❶ adj **1** opposing change. **2** moderate, cautious. **3** conventional in style. **4** (**C-**) of the Conservative Party, the British right-wing political party which believes in private enterprise and capitalism. ▷ n **5** conservative person. **6** (**C-**) supporter or member of the Conservative Party. **conservatism** n.
conservatoire [kon-**serv**-a-twahr] n school of music.
conservatory n, pl **-ries 1** room with glass walls and a glass roof, attached to a house. **2** conservatoire.
conserve ❶ v **1** protect from harm,

━━━━━━━━━━━━━━━━ THESAURUS ━━━━━━━━

conscience n = **principles**, moral sense, scruples, sense of right and wrong, still small voice
conscientious adj **1** = **thorough**, careful, diligent, exact, faithful, meticulous, painstaking, particular, punctilious
conscious adj **1** = **alert**, awake, responsive **2** = **aware**, alive to, sensible, sentient **3** = **deliberate**, calculated, intentional, knowing, premeditated, self-conscious, studied, wilful
consciousness n **2** = **awareness**, apprehension, knowledge, realization, recognition, sensibility
consecrate v **1** = **sanctify**, hallow, ordain, venerate **2** = **dedicate**, devote, set apart
consecutive adj = **successive**, in sequence, in turn, running, sequential, succeeding, uninterrupted
consensus n = **agreement**, assent, common consent, concord, general agreement, harmony, unanimity, unity
consent n **1** = **agreement**, acquiescence, approval, assent,

compliance, go-ahead (inf), O.K. or okay (inf), permission, sanction ▷ v **2** = **agree**, acquiesce, allow, approve, assent, concur, permit
consequence n **1** = **result**, effect, end result, issue, outcome, repercussion, sequel, upshot **2** = **importance**, account, concern, import, moment, significance, value, weight
consequent adj = **following**, ensuing, resultant, resulting, subsequent, successive
consequently adv = **as a result**, accordingly, ergo, hence, subsequently, therefore, thus
conservation n **1** = **protection**, guardianship, preservation, safeguarding, safekeeping **2** = **saving**, husbandry, maintenance, upkeep
conservative adj **1** = **traditional**, conventional, die-hard, hidebound, moderate, reactionary **2** = **cautious** **4** (cap.) = **Tory**, right-wing ▷ n **5** = **traditionalist**, die-hard, reactionary, stick-in-the-mud (inf) **6** (cap.) = **Tory**, right-winger
conserve v **1** = **protect**, hoard,

decay, or loss. **2** preserve (fruit) with sugar. ▷ *n* **3** jam containing large pieces of fruit. **conservancy** *n* environmental conservation.
conservation *n* **1** protection of natural resources and the environment. **2** conserving.
conservationist *n* **conservative** *adj* opposing change.
consider ❶ *v* **1** regard as. **2** think about. **3** be considerate of. **4** discuss. **5** look at. **considerable** *adj* large in amount or degree. **considerably** *adv*
considerate *adj* thoughtful towards others. **considerately** *adv*
consideration *n* **1** careful thought. **2** fact that should be considered. **3** thoughtfulness. **4** payment for a service. **considered** *adj* thought out with care. **considering** *prep* taking (a specified fact) into account.
consign ❶ *v* **1** put somewhere. **2** send (goods). **consignee** *n* **consignor** *n* **consignment** *n* shipment of goods.
consist ❶ *v* **1 consist of** be made up of. **2 consist in** have as its main or only feature, e.g. *Freedom consists in being*

master of oneself.
consistent ❶ *adj* **1** unchanging, constant. **2** (foll. by *with*) in agreement. **consistently** *adv*
consistency *n*, *pl* **-cies 1** being consistent. **2** degree of thickness or smoothness.
console¹ ❶ *v* comfort in distress.
consolation *n* **1** consoling. **2** person or thing that consoles.
console² *n* **1** panel of controls for electronic equipment. **2** cabinet for a television or audio equipment. **3** ornamental wall bracket. **4** part of an organ containing the pedals, stops, and keys.
consolidate ❶ *v* **1** make or become stronger or more stable. **2** combine into a whole. **consolidation** *n*.
consommé [kon-**som**-may] *n* thin clear meat soup.
consonant *n* **1** speech sound made by partially or completely blocking the breath stream, such as *b* or *f*. **2** letter representing this. ▷ *adj* **3** (foll. by *with*) agreeing (with). **consonance** *n* agreement, harmony.

husband, keep, nurse, preserve, save, store up, take care of, use sparingly
consider *v* **1** = **think**, believe, deem, hold to be, judge, rate, regard as **2** = **think about**, cogitate, contemplate, deliberate, meditate, ponder, reflect, ruminate, turn over in one's mind, weigh **3** = **bear in mind**, keep in view, make allowance for, reckon with, remember, respect, take into account
considerable *adj* = **large**, appreciable, goodly, great, marked, noticeable, plentiful, sizable *or* sizeable, substantial
considerably *adv* = **greatly**, appreciably, markedly, noticeably, remarkably, significantly, substantially, very much
considerate *adj* = **thoughtful**, attentive, concerned, kindly, mindful, obliging, patient, tactful, unselfish
consideration *n* **1** = **thought**, analysis, deliberation, discussion, examination, reflection, review, scrutiny **2** = **factor**, concern, issue, point **3** = **thoughtfulness**, concern, considerateness, kindness, respect, tact **4** = **payment**, fee, recompense, remuneration, reward, tip

considering *prep* = **taking into account**, in the light of, in view of
consignment *n* = **shipment**, batch, delivery, goods
consist *v* **1 consist of** = **be made up of**, amount to, be composed of, comprise, contain, embody, include, incorporate, involve **2 consist in** = **lie in**, be expressed by, be found *or* contained in, inhere in, reside in
consistency *n* **1** = **constancy**, evenness, regularity, steadfastness, steadiness, uniformity **2** = **texture**, compactness, density, firmness, thickness, viscosity
consistent *adj* **1** = **unchanging**, constant, dependable, persistent, regular, steady, true to type, undeviating **2** (foll. by *with*) = **agreeing**, coherent, compatible, congruous, consonant, harmonious, logical
consolation *n* = **comfort**, cheer, encouragement, help, relief, solace, succour, support
console¹ *v* = **comfort**, calm, cheer, encourage, express sympathy for, soothe
consolidate *v* **1** = **strengthen**, fortify, reinforce, secure, stabilize

consort ❶ v **1** (foll. by with) keep company (with). ▷ n **2** husband or wife of a monarch.

consortium n, pl -**tia** association of business firms.

conspectus n formal survey or summary.

conspicuous ❶ adj **1** clearly visible. **2** noteworthy, striking. **conspicuously** adv.

conspire ❶ v **1** plan a crime together in secret. **2** act together as if by design. **conspiracy** n **1** conspiring. **2** pl -**cies** plan made by conspiring. **conspirator** n **conspiratorial** adj.

constable n police officer of the lowest rank. **constabulary** n, pl -**laries** police force of an area.

constant ❶ adj **1** continuous. **2** unchanging. **3** faithful. ▷ n **4** unvarying quantity. **5** something that stays the same. **constantly** adv **constancy** n.

constellation n group of stars.

consternation ❶ n anxiety or dismay.

constipation n difficulty in defecating. **constipated** adj having constipation.

constituent ❶ n **1** member of a constituency. **2** component part. ▷ adj **3** forming part of a whole.

constituency n, pl -**cies 1** area represented by a Member of Parliament. **2** voters in such an area.

constitute ❶ v **1** be, amount to. **2** form, make up. **constitution** n **1** principles on which a state is governed. **2** physical condition. **3** structure. **constitutional** adj **1** of a constitution. **2** in accordance with a political constitution. **3** being inherent to a person or thing. ▷ n **4** walk taken for exercise. **constitutionally** adv.

constrain ❶ v **1** compel, force. **2** limit, restrict. **constrained** adj embarrassed or unnatural. **constraint** n something that limits or controls a person's actions.

constrict v **1** make narrower by squeezing. **2** limit, restrict. **constriction** n **constrictive** adj **constrictor** n **1** large snake that squeezes its prey to death. **2** muscle that compresses an organ.

————————————————— THESAURUS —————————————————

2 = **combine**, amalgamate, federate, fuse, join, unite

consort v **1** (foll. by with) = **associate**, fraternize, go around with, hang about, around or out with, keep company, mix ▷ n **2** = **spouse**, companion, husband, partner, wife

conspicuous adj **1** = **obvious**, blatant, clear, evident, noticeable, patent, salient **2** = **noteworthy**, illustrious, notable, outstanding, prominent, remarkable, salient, signal, striking

conspiracy n **2** = **plot**, collusion, intrigue, machination, scheme, treason

conspirator n = **plotter**, conspirer, intriguer, schemer, traitor

conspire v **1** = **plot**, contrive, intrigue, machinate, manoeuvre, plan, scheme **2** = **work together**, combine, concur, contribute, cooperate, tend

constant adj **1** = **continuous**, ceaseless, incessant, interminable, nonstop, perpetual, sustained, unrelenting **2** = **unchanging**, even, fixed, invariable, permanent, stable, steady, uniform, unvarying **3** = **faithful**, devoted, loyal, stalwart, staunch, true, trustworthy, trusty

constantly adv **1, 2** = **continuously**, all the time, always, continually, endlessly, incessantly, interminably, invariably, nonstop, perpetually, twenty-four-seven (inf)

consternation n = **dismay**, alarm, anxiety, distress, dread, fear, trepidation

constituent n **1** = **voter**, elector **2** = **component**, element, factor, ingredient, part, unit ▷ adj **3** = **component**, basic, elemental, essential, integral

constitute v **2** = **make up**, compose, comprise, establish, form, found, set up

constitution n **2** = **health**, build, character, disposition, physique **3** = **structure**, composition, form, make-up, nature

constitutional adj **1** = **statutory**, chartered, vested ▷ n **4** = **walk**, airing, stroll, turn

constrain v **1** = **force**, bind, coerce, compel, impel, necessitate, oblige, pressurize **2** = **restrict**, check, confine, constrict, curb, restrain, straiten

constraint n = **restriction**, check, curb, deterrent, hindrance, limitation, rein, restraint

construct ❶ *v* **1** build or put together.
2 *Geometry* draw (a figure).
construction *n* **1** constructing.
2 thing constructed. **3** interpretation.
4 *Grammar* way in which words are
arranged in a sentence, clause, or
phrase. **constructive** *adj* (of advice,
criticism, etc.) useful and helpful.
constructively *adv*.
construe *v* **-struing, -strued** interpret.
consul *n* **1** official representing a state
in a foreign country. **2** one of the two
chief magistrates in ancient Rome.
consular *adj* **consulate** *n* workplace
or position of a consul. **consulship** *n*.
consult ❶ *v* go to for advice or
information. **consultant** *n* **1** specialist
doctor with a senior position in a
hospital. **2** specialist who gives
professional advice. **consultancy** *n*, *pl*
-cies work or position of a consultant.
consultation *n* (meeting for)
consulting. **consultative** *adj* giving
advice.
consume ❶ *v* **1** eat or drink. **2** use up.
3 destroy. **4** obsess. **consumer** *n*
person who buys goods or uses
services. **consumerism** *n* protection

of the rights of consumers.
consumption *n* **1** amount consumed.
2 consuming. **3** purchase of goods and
services. **4** *old-fashioned* tuberculosis.
consumptive *n*, *adj* *old-fashioned*
(person) having tuberculosis.
consummate ❶ [**kon**-sum-mate] *v*
1 make (a marriage) legal by sexual
intercourse. **2** complete or fulfil. ▷ *adj*
[kon-**sum**-mit] **3** supremely skilled.
4 complete, extreme. **consummation** *n*.
cont. continued.
contact ❶ *n* **1** communicating.
2 touching. **3** useful acquaintance.
4 connection between two electrical
conductors in a circuit. ▷ *v* **5** get in
touch with. **contact lens** lens placed on
the eyeball to correct defective vision.
contagion ❶ *n* **1** passing on of disease
by contact. **2** disease spread by
contact. **3** spreading of a harmful
influence. **contagious** *adj* spreading
by contact, catching.
contain ❶ *v* **1** hold or be capable of
holding. **2** consist of. **3** control,
restrain. **container** *n* **1** object used to
hold or store things in. **2** large
standard-sized box for transporting

THESAURUS

construct *v* **1** = **build**, assemble,
compose, create, fashion, form, make,
manufacture, put together, shape
construction *n* **2** = **building**,
composition, creation, edifice
3 = **interpretation**, explanation,
inference, reading, rendering
constructive *adj* = **helpful**, positive,
practical, productive, useful, valuable
consult *v* = **ask**, compare notes, confer,
pick (someone's) brains, question,
refer to, take counsel, turn to
consultant *n* **2** = **specialist**, adviser,
authority, mana (*NZ*)
consultation *n* = **seminar**,
appointment, conference, council,
deliberation, dialogue, discussion,
examination, hearing, interview,
meeting, session
consume *v* **1** = **eat**, devour, eat up,
gobble (up), put away, swallow
2 = **use up**, absorb, dissipate, exhaust,
expend, spend, squander, waste
3 = **destroy**, annihilate, demolish,
devastate, lay waste, ravage
4 = **obsess**, absorb, dominate, eat up,
engross, monopolize, preoccupy
consumer *n* = **buyer**, customer,
purchaser, shopper, user

consummate *v* **2** = **complete**,
accomplish, conclude, crown, end,
finish, fulfil ▷ *adj* **3** = **skilled**,
accomplished, matchless, perfect,
polished, practised, superb, supreme
4 = **complete**, absolute, conspicuous,
extreme, supreme, total, utter
consumption *n* **2** = **using up**,
depletion, diminution, dissipation,
exhaustion, expenditure, loss, waste
4 *Old-fashioned* = **tuberculosis**, T.B.
contact *n* **1** = **communication**,
association, connection **2** = **touch**,
contiguity **3** = **acquaintance**,
connection ▷ *v* **5** = **get or be in touch
with**, approach, call, communicate
with, reach, speak to, write to
contagious *adj* = **infectious**, catching,
communicable, spreading,
transmissible
contain *v* **1** = **hold**, accommodate,
enclose, have capacity for, incorporate,
seat **2** = **include**, comprehend,
comprise, consist of, embody,
embrace, involve **3** = **restrain**, control,
curb, hold back, hold in, keep a tight
rein on, repress, stifle
container *n* **1** = **holder**, receptacle,
repository, vessel

cargo by lorry or ship. **containerize** v pack (cargo) into containers.
containment n prevention of the spread of something harmful.

contaminate ❶ v **1** make impure, pollute. **2** make radioactive.
contaminant n contaminating substance. **contamination** n.

contemn v formal regard with contempt.

contemplate ❶ v **1** think deeply. **2** consider as a possibility. **3** gaze at.
contemplation n **contemplative** adj deeply thoughtful.

contemporary ❶ adj **1** present-day, modern. **2** living or occurring at the same time. **3** of roughly the same age. ▷ n, pl **-raries 4** person or thing living or occurring at the same time as another. **contemporaneous** adj happening at the same time.

- **SPELLING TIP**
- It's easy to miss a syllable out when
- you say **contemporary**. The Bank
- of English shows that syllables get
- lost from spellings too - for example,
- *contempory* is a common mistake. But
- remember that the correct spelling
- ends in *orary*.

contempt ❶ n **1** dislike and disregard. **2** open disrespect for the authority of a court. **contemptible** adj deserving contempt. **contemptuous** adj showing contempt. **contemptuously** adv.

contend ❶ v **1** (foll. by with) deal with. **2** state, assert. **3** compete. **contender** n.

content¹ ❶ n **1** meaning or substance of a piece of writing. **2** amount of a substance in a mixture. ▷ pl **3** what something contains. **4** list of chapters at the front of a book.

content² ❶ adj **1** satisfied with things as they are. **2** willing to accept a proposed course of action. ▷ v **3** make (someone) content. ▷ n **4** happiness and satisfaction. **contented** adj **contentment** n.

contention ❶ n **1** disagreement or dispute. **2** point asserted in argument. **contentious** adj **1** causing disagreement. **2** quarrelsome.

contest ❶ n **1** competition or struggle. ▷ v **2** dispute, object to. **3** fight or compete for. **contestant** n.

———————————————— THESAURUS ————————————————

contaminate v **1** = **pollute**, adulterate, befoul, corrupt, defile, infect, stain, taint, tarnish

contamination n **1** = **pollution**, contagion, corruption, defilement, impurity, infection, poisoning, taint

contemplate v **1** = **think about**, consider, deliberate, meditate, muse over, ponder, reflect upon, ruminate (upon) **2** = **consider**, envisage, expect, foresee, intend, plan, think of **3** = **look at**, examine, eye up, gaze at, inspect, regard, stare at, study, survey, view

contemporary adj **1** = **modern**, à la mode, current, newfangled, present, present-day, recent, up-to-date **2** = **coexisting**, concurrent, contemporaneous ▷ n **4** = **peer**, fellow

contempt n **1** = **scorn**, derision, disdain, disregard, disrespect, mockery, slight

contemptible adj = **despicable**, detestable, ignominious, measly, paltry, pitiful, shameful, worthless

contemptuous adj = **scornful**, arrogant, condescending, derisive, disdainful, haughty, sneering, supercilious, withering

contend v **1** (foll. by with) = **compete**,

clash, contest, fight, jostle, strive, struggle, vie **2** = **argue**, affirm, allege, assert, dispute, hold, maintain

content¹ n **1** = **meaning**, essence, gist, significance, substance **2** = **amount**, capacity, load, measure, size, volume ▷ pl **3** = **constituents**, elements, ingredients, load

content² adj **1** = **satisfied**, agreeable, at ease, comfortable, contented, fulfilled **2** = **willing to accept** ▷ v **3** = **satisfy**, appease, humour, indulge, mollify, placate, please ▷ n **4** = **satisfaction**, comfort, contentment, ease, gratification, peace of mind, pleasure

contented adj **1** = **satisfied**, comfortable, content, glad, gratified, happy, pleased, serene, thankful

contentious adj **2** = **argumentative**, bickering, captious, cavilling, disputatious, quarrelsome, querulous, wrangling

contentment n **1** = **satisfaction**, comfort, content, ease, equanimity, fulfilment, happiness, peace, pleasure, serenity

contest n **1** = **competition**, game, match, tournament, trial ▷ v

context ❶ *n* **1** circumstances of an event or fact. **2** words before and after a word or sentence that help make its meaning clear. **contextual** *adj*.

contiguous *adj* very near or touching.

continent[1] *n* one of the earth's large masses of land. **the Continent** mainland of Europe. **continental** *adj* **continental breakfast** light breakfast of coffee and rolls. **continental quilt** same as DUVET.

continent[2] *adj* **1** able to control one's bladder and bowels. **2** sexually restrained. **continence** *n*.

contingent ❶ *n* **1** group of people that represents or is part of a larger group. ▷ *adj* **2** (foll. by *on*) dependent on (something uncertain). **contingency** *n*, *pl* -**cies** something that may happen.

continue ❶ *v* -**tinuing**, -**tinued** **1** (cause to) remain in a condition or place. **2** carry on (doing something). **3** resume. **4** go on beyond a place. **continual** *adj* **1** constant. **2** recurring frequently. **continually** *adv* **continuance** *n* continuing. **continuation** *n* **1** continuing. **2** part added. **continuity** *n*, *pl* -**ties 1** smooth development or sequence.

2 arrangement of scenes in a film so that they follow each other logically and without breaks. **continuous** *adj* continuing uninterrupted. **continuously** *adv*.

continuo *n*, *pl* -**tinuos** *Music* continuous bass part, usu. played on a keyboard instrument.

continuum *n*, *pl* -**tinua**, -**tinuums** continuous series.

contort *v* twist out of shape. **contortion** *n* **contortionist** *n* performer who contorts his or her body to entertain.

contour *n* **1** outline. **2** (also **contour line**) line on a map joining places of the same height.

contra- *prefix* against or contrasting, e.g. *contraflow*.

contraband ❶ *n*, *adj* smuggled (goods).

contraception *n* prevention of pregnancy by artificial means. **contraceptive** *n* **1** device used or pill taken to prevent pregnancy. ▷ *adj* **2** preventing pregnancy.

contract ❶ *n* **1** (document setting out) a formal agreement. ▷ *v* **2** make a formal agreement (to do something). **3** make or become smaller or shorter. **4** catch (an illness). **5** tighten

——————————— THESAURUS ———————————

2 = **dispute**, argue, call in *or* into question, challenge, debate, doubt, object to, oppose, question **3** = **compete**, contend, fight, strive, vie

contestant *n* = **competitor**, candidate, contender, entrant, participant, player

context *n* **1** = **circumstances**, ambience, background, conditions, frame of reference, situation

contingency *n* = **possibility**, accident, chance, emergency, event, eventuality, happening, incident

continual *adj* **1** = **constant**, frequent, incessant, interminable, unremitting **2** = **recurrent**, regular, repeated

continually *adv* **1** = **constantly**, all the time, always, forever, incessantly, interminably, nonstop, persistently, twenty-four-seven (*inf*) **2** = **repeatedly**

continuation *n* **1** = **continuing**, perpetuation, prolongation, resumption **2** = **addition**, extension, furtherance, postscript, sequel, supplement

continue *v* **1** = **remain**, abide, carry on,

endure, last, live on, persist, stay, survive **2** = **keep on**, carry on, go on, maintain, persevere, persist in, stick at, sustain **3** = **resume**, carry on, pick up where one left off, proceed, recommence, return to, take up

continuing *adj* **1, 2** = **lasting**, enduring, in progress, ongoing, sustained

continuity *n* **1** = **sequence**, cohesion, connection, flow, progression, succession

continuous *adj* = **constant**, extended, prolonged, unbroken, unceasing, undivided, uninterrupted

contraband *n* = **smuggling**, black-marketing, bootlegging, trafficking ▷ *adj* = **smuggled**, banned, bootleg, forbidden, hot (*inf*), illegal, illicit, prohibited, unlawful

contract *n* **1** = **agreement**, arrangement, bargain, commitment, covenant, pact, settlement ▷ *v* **2** = **agree**, bargain, come to terms, commit oneself, covenant, negotiate, pledge **3** = **shorten**, abbreviate, curtail, diminish, dwindle, lessen,

c

(muscles) or (of muscles) be tightened.
contraction n 1 contracting.
2 shortened word. **contractor** n firm
that supplies materials or labour, esp.
for building. **contractual** adj.
contradict ❶ v 1 declare the opposite
of (a statement) to be true. 2 be at
variance with. **contradiction** n
contradictory adj.
contradistinction n distinction made
by contrasting different qualities.
contraflow n flow of traffic going
alongside but in an opposite direction
to the usual flow.
contralto n, pl **-tos** (singer with) the
lowest female voice.
contraption ❶ n strange-looking
device.
contrapuntal adj Music of or in
counterpoint.
contrary ❶ n 1 complete opposite.
▷ adj 2 opposed, completely different.
3 perverse, obstinate. ▷ adv 4 in
opposition. **contrarily** adv

contrariness n **contrariwise** adv.
contrast ❶ n 1 obvious difference.
2 person or thing very different
from another. 3 degree of difference
between colours in a photograph
or television picture. ▷ v 4 compare
in order to show differences.
5 (foll. by with) be very different (from).
contravene v break (a rule or law).
contravention n.
contretemps [kon-tra-tahn] n, pl
-temps embarrassing minor
disagreement.
contribute ❶ v 1 give for a common
purpose or fund. 2 (foll. by to) be partly
responsible (for). 3 write articles for a
publication. **contribution** n
contributor n **contributory** adj.
contrite ❶ adj sorry and apologetic.
contritely adv **contrition** n.
contrive ❶ v 1 make happen. 2 devise
or construct. **contrivance** n 1 device.
2 plan. 3 contriving. **contrived** adj
planned or artificial.

━━━━━━━━━━━━━━━━━━━━━━━━━━━ THESAURUS ━━━━━

narrow, reduce, shrink, shrivel
4 = **catch**, acquire, be afflicted with,
develop, get, go down with, incur
contraction n 1 = **shortening**,
compression, narrowing, reduction,
shrinkage, shrivelling, tightening
2 = **abbreviation**
contradict v 1 = **deny**, challenge, rebut
2 = **be at variance with**, belie,
controvert, fly in the face of, negate
contradiction n 1 = **denial**
2 = **incongruity**, conflict,
contravention, inconsistency,
negation, opposite
contradictory adj 2 = **inconsistent**,
conflicting, contrary, incompatible,
opposed, opposite, paradoxical
contraption n Inf = **device**, apparatus,
contrivance, gadget, instrument,
mechanism
contrary n 1 = **opposite**, antithesis,
converse, reverse ▷ adj 2 = **opposed**,
adverse, clashing, contradictory,
counter, discordant, hostile,
inconsistent, opposite, paradoxical
3 = **perverse**, awkward, cantankerous,
difficult, disobliging, intractable,
obstinate, stroppy (Brit sl),
unaccommodating
contrast n 1 = **difference**, comparison,
disparity, dissimilarity, distinction,
divergence, opposition ▷ v
4 = **compare**, differentiate,

distinguish, set in opposition, set off
5 (foll. by with) = **differ**, oppose
contribute v 1 = **give**, add, bestow,
chip in (inf), donate, provide,
subscribe, supply 2 (foll. by to) = **be
partly responsible for**, be conducive
to, be instrumental in, help, lead to,
tend to
contribution n 1 = **gift**, addition,
donation, grant, input, offering,
subscription
contributor n 1 = **giver**, donor, patron,
subscriber, supporter
contrite adj = **sorry**, chastened,
conscience-stricken, humble,
penitent, regretful, remorseful,
repentant, sorrowful
contrivance n 1 = **device**,
apparatus, appliance,
contraption, gadget, implement,
instrument, invention, machine,
mechanism 2 = **plan**, intrigue,
machination, plot, ruse, scheme,
stratagem, trick
contrive v 1 = **bring about**, arrange,
effect, manage, manoeuvre, plan,
plot, scheme, succeed 2 = **devise**,
concoct, construct, create, design,
fabricate, improvise, invent,
manufacture
contrived adj = **forced**, artificial,
elaborate, laboured, overdone,
planned, strained, unnatural

control ➊ n **1** power to direct something. **2** curb or check. **3** standard of comparison in an experiment. ▷ pl **4** instruments used to operate a machine. ▷ v **-trolling, -trolled 5** have power over. **6** limit, restrain. **7** regulate, operate. **controllable** adj **controller** n.

controversy ➊ n, pl **-sies** fierce argument or debate. **controversial** adj causing controversy.
● **USAGE NOTE**
● Note that the stress used always
● to be on the first syllable, 'kon', but
● is now more often on the second
● syllable, 'trov'.

contumely [**kon**-tume-mill-ee] n lit scornful or insulting treatment.

contusion n formal bruise.

conundrum n riddle.

conurbation n large urban area formed by the growth and merging of towns.

convalesce ➊ v recover after an illness or operation. **convalescence** n **convalescent** n, adj.

convection n transmission of heat in liquids or gases by the circulation of currents. **convector** n heater that gives out hot air.

convene ➊ v gather or summon for a formal meeting. **convener, convenor** n person who calls a meeting.

convenient ➊ adj **1** suitable or opportune. **2** easy to use. **3** nearby. **conveniently** adv **convenience** n **1** quality of being convenient. **2** useful object. **3** euphemistic public toilet.

convent n **1** building where nuns live. **2** school run by nuns.

conventicle n secret or unauthorized religious meeting.

convention ➊ n **1** widely accepted view of proper behaviour. **2** assembly or meeting. **3** formal agreement. **conventional** adj **1** (unthinkingly) following the accepted customs. **2** customary. **3** (of weapons or warfare) not nuclear. **conventionally** adv **conventionality** n.

converge ➊ v meet or join. **convergence** n **convergent** adj.

conversant adj **conversant with** having knowledge or experience of.

converse[1] ➊ v have a conversation. **conversation** n informal talk.

control n **1** = **power**, authority, charge, command, guidance, mana (NZ), management, oversight, supervision, supremacy **2** = **restraint**, brake, check, curb, limitation, regulation ▷ pl **4** = **instruments**, console, control panel, dash, dashboard, dials ▷ v **5** = **have power over**, administer, command, direct, govern, handle, have charge of, manage, manipulate, supervise **6** = **restrain**, check, constrain, contain, curb, hold back, limit, repress, subdue

controversial adj = **disputed**, at issue, contentious, debatable, disputable, open to question, under discussion

controversy n = **argument**, altercation, debate, dispute, quarrel, row, squabble, wrangling

convalescence n = **recovery**, improvement, recuperation, rehabilitation, return to health

convalescent adj = **recovering**, getting better, improving, mending, on the mend, recuperating

convene v = **gather**, assemble, bring together, call, come together, congregate, convoke, meet, summon

convenience n **1** = **usefulness**, accessibility, advantage, appropriateness, availability, benefit, fitness, suitability, utility **2** = **appliance**, amenity, comfort, facility, help, labour-saving device

convenient adj **1** = **suitable**, appropriate, fit, timely **2** = **useful**, handy, helpful, labour-saving, serviceable **3** = **nearby**, accessible, at hand, available, close at hand, handy, just round the corner, within reach

convention n **1** = **custom**, code, etiquette, practice, propriety, protocol, tradition, usage **2** = **assembly**, conference, congress, convocation, council, meeting **3** = **agreement**, bargain, contract, pact, protocol, treaty

conventional adj **1** = **unoriginal**, banal, hackneyed, prosaic, routine, run-of-the-mill, stereotyped **2** = **ordinary**, accepted, customary, normal, orthodox, regular, standard, traditional, usual

converge v = **come together**, coincide, combine, gather, join, meet, merge

conversation n = **talk**, chat, conference, dialogue, discourse, discussion, gossip, tête-à-tête

converse[1] v = **talk**, chat, commune,

conversational *adj* **conversationalist** *n* person with a specified ability at conversation.

converse² ❶ *adj, n* opposite or contrary. **conversely** *adv*.

convert ❶ *v* **1** change in form, character, or function. **2** cause to change in opinion or belief. **3** change (money) into a different currency. **4** *Rugby* make a conversion after (a try). ▷ *n* **5** person who has converted to a different belief or religion. **conversion** *n* **1** (thing resulting from) converting. **2** *Rugby* score made after a try by kicking the ball over the crossbar. **convertible** *adj* **1** capable of being converted. ▷ *n* **2** car with a folding or removable roof.

convex ❶ *adj* curving outwards. **convexity** *n*.

convey ❶ *v* **1** communicate (information). **2** carry, transport. **3** transfer (the title to property). **conveyance** *n* **1** *old-fashioned* vehicle. **2** transfer of the legal title to property. **conveyancing** *n* branch of law dealing with the transfer of ownership of property. **conveyor belt** continuous moving belt for transporting things, esp. in a factory.

convict ❶ *v* **1** declare guilty. ▷ *n* **2** person serving a prison sentence. **conviction** *n* **1** firm belief. **2** instance of being convicted.

convince ❶ *v* persuade by argument or evidence. **convincing** *adj* **convincingly** *adv*.

convivial *adj* sociable, lively. **conviviality** *n*.

convocation *n* **1** calling together. **2** large formal meeting. **convoke** *v* call together.

convoluted *adj* **1** coiled, twisted. **2** (of an argument or sentence) complex and hard to understand. **convolution** *n*.

convolvulus *n* twining plant with funnel-shaped flowers.

convoy *n* group of vehicles or ships travelling together.

convulse ❶ *v* **1** (of part of the body) undergo violent spasms. **2** (of a person) shake violently. **3** *informal* (be) overcome with laughter. **convulsion** *n* **1** violent muscular spasm. ▷ *pl* **2** uncontrollable laughter. **convulsive** *adj*.

cony *n, pl* **conies 1** rabbit. **2** rabbit fur.

coo *v* **cooing, cooed** (of a dove or pigeon) make a soft murmuring sound.

cooee *interj* call to attract attention.

cook *v* **1** prepare (food) by heating. **2** (of food) be cooked. ▷ *n* **3** person who cooks food. **cook the books** falsify accounts. **cooker** *n* **1** apparatus for cooking heated by gas or electricity. **2** apple suitable for cooking. **cookery** *n* art of cooking. **cookie** *n* **1** *US* biscuit. **2** piece of data downloaded from a website to a computer, identifying the user when he or she revisits the website. **cook up** *v* *informal* devise (a story or scheme).

Cooktown orchid *n* purple Australian orchid.

cool ❶ *adj* **1** moderately cold. **2** calm

confer, discourse, exchange views

converse² *adj* = **opposite**, contrary, counter, reverse, reversed, transposed ▷ *n* = **opposite**, antithesis, contrary, obverse, other side of the coin, reverse

conversion *n* **1** = **change**, adaptation, alteration, metamorphosis, modification, reconstruction, remodelling, reorganization, transformation

convert *v* **1** = **change**, adapt, alter, customize, modify, remodel, reorganize, restyle, revise, transform, transpose, turn **2** = **reform**, convince, proselytize ▷ *n* **5** = **neophyte**, disciple, proselyte

convex *adj* = **rounded**, bulging, gibbous, protuberant

convey *v* **1** = **communicate**, disclose, impart, make known, relate, reveal,

tell **2** = **carry**, bear, bring, conduct, fetch, guide, move, send, transport

convict *v* **1** = **find guilty**, condemn, imprison, pronounce guilty, sentence ▷ *n* **2** = **prisoner**, criminal, culprit, felon, jailbird, lag (*sl*)

conviction *n* **1** = **belief**, assurance, certainty, certitude, confidence, creed, faith, opinion, persuasion, principle, tenet, view

convince *v* = **persuade**, assure, bring round, prevail upon, satisfy, sway, win over

convincing *adj* = **persuasive**, cogent, conclusive, credible, impressive, plausible, powerful, telling

convulsion *n* **1** = **spasm**, contraction, cramp, fit, paroxysm, seizure

cool *adj* **1** = **cold**, chilled, chilly, nippy, refreshing **2** = **calm**, collected,

and unemotional. **3** indifferent or unfriendly. **4** *informal* sophisticated or excellent. **5** *informal* (of a large sum of money) without exaggeration, e.g. *a cool million.* ▷ *v* **6** make or become cool. ▷ *n* **7** coolness. **8** *slang* calmness, composure. **coolly** *adv* **coolness** *n* **coolant** *n* fluid used to cool machinery while it is working. **cool drink** *n* S *Afr* nonalcoholic drink. **cooler** *n* container for making or keeping things cool.

coolie *n old-fashioned offens* unskilled Oriental labourer.

coomb, coombe *n* valley.

coop¹ *n* cage or pen for poultry. **coop up** *v* confine in a restricted place.

coop² [**koh**-op] *n* (shop run by) a cooperative society.

cooper *n* person who makes or repairs barrels.

cooperate ❶ *v* work or act together. **cooperation** *n* **cooperative** *adj* **1** willing to cooperate. **2** (of an enterprise) owned and managed collectively. ▷ *n* **3** cooperative organization.

coopt [koh-**opt**] *v* add (someone) to a group by the agreement of the existing members.

coordinate ❶ *v* **1** bring together and cause to work together efficiently. ▷ *n* **2** *Maths* any of a set of numbers defining the location of a point. ▷ *pl* **3** clothes designed to be worn together. **coordination** *n* **coordinator** *n*.

coot *n* **1** small black water bird. **2** foolish person.

cop *slang* ▷ *n* **1** policeman. ▷ *v* **copping, copped 2** take or seize. **cop it** get into trouble or be punished. **cop out** *v* avoid taking responsibility or committing oneself. **cop-out** *n*.

copal *n* resin used in varnishes.

cope¹ ❶ *v* (often foll. by *with*) **1** deal successfully (with). **2** tolerate, endure.

cope² *n* large ceremonial cloak worn by some Christian priests.

cope³ *v* provide with a coping.

copier *n* see COPY.

copilot *n* second pilot of an aircraft.

coping *n* sloping top row of a wall.

copious ❶ [**kope**-ee-uss] *adj* abundant, plentiful. **copiously** *adv*.

copper¹ *n* **1** soft reddish-brown metal. **2** copper or bronze coin. **3** large metal container used to boil water. ▷ *adj* **4** reddish-brown. **copper-bottomed** *adj* financially reliable. **copperplate 1** fine handwriting style. **2** (print taken from) an engraved copper plate.

copper² *n slang* policeman.

coppice, copse *n* small group of trees growing close together.

copra *n* dried oil-yielding kernel of the coconut.

copula *n, pl* **-las, -lae** verb used to link the subject and complement of a sentence, e.g. *become* in *they become chums*.

copulate *v* have sexual intercourse. **copulation** *n*.

copy ❶ *n, pl* **copies 1** thing made to

——————————————— **THESAURUS** ———————————————

composed, relaxed, sedate, self-controlled, self-possessed, unemotional, unruffled **3** = **unfriendly**, aloof, distant, indifferent, lukewarm, offhand, standoffish, unenthusiastic, unwelcoming ▷ *v* **6** = **chill**, cool off, freeze, lose heat, refrigerate ▷ *n* **8** *Sl* = **calmness**, composure, control, poise, self-control, self-discipline, self-possession, temper

cooperate *v* = **work together**, collaborate, combine, conspire, coordinate, join forces, pool resources, pull together

cooperation *n* = **teamwork**, collaboration, combined effort, esprit de corps, give-and-take, unity

cooperative *adj* **1** = **helpful**, accommodating, obliging,

onside (*inf*), responsive, supportive **2** = **shared**, collective, combined, joint

coordinate *v* **1** = **bring together**, harmonize, integrate, match, organize, synchronize, systematize

cope¹ *v* (often foll. by *with*) **1** = **manage**, carry on, get by (*inf*), hold one's own, make the grade, struggle through, survive ▷ *v* **2** = **deal with**, contend with, grapple with, handle, struggle with, weather, wrestle with

copious *adj* = **abundant**, ample, bountiful, extensive, full, lavish, plentiful, profuse

copy *n* **1** = **reproduction**, counterfeit, duplicate, facsimile, forgery, imitation, likeness, model, replica ▷ *v* **5** = **reproduce**, counterfeit, duplicate, replicate, transcribe **6** = **imitate**, act

look exactly like another. **2** single specimen of a book etc. **3** material for printing. **4** suitable material for a newspaper article. ▷ *v* **copying**, **copied 5** make a copy of. **6** act or try to be like. **copier** *n* machine that copies. **copybook** *n* **blot one's copybook** *informal* spoil one's reputation. **copyright** *n* **1** exclusive legal right to reproduce and control a book, work of art, etc. ▷ *v* **2** take out a copyright on. ▷ *adj* **3** protected by copyright. **copywriter** *n* person who writes advertising copy.

coquette *n* woman who flirts. **coquettish** *adj*.

coracle *n* small round boat of wicker covered with skins.

coral *n* **1** hard substance formed from the skeletons of very small sea animals. ▷ *adj* **2** orange-pink.

cor anglais *n, pl* **cors anglais** woodwind instrument similar to the oboe.

corbel *n* stone or timber support sticking out of a wall.

cord ❶ *n* **1** thin rope or thick string. **2** cordlike structure in the body. **3** corduroy. **4** *US* electrical flex. ▷ *pl* **5** corduroy trousers. ▷ *adj* **6** (also **corded**) (of fabric) ribbed.

cordate *adj* heart-shaped.

cordial ❶ *adj* **1** warm and friendly. ▷ *n* **2** drink with a fruit base. **cordially** *adv* **cordiality** *n*.

cordite *n* explosive used in guns and bombs.

cordon ❶ *n* chain of police, soldiers, etc., guarding an area. **cordon off** *v* form a cordon round.

cordon bleu [**bluh**] *adj* (of cookery or cooks) of the highest standard.

corduroy *n* cotton fabric with a velvety ribbed surface.

core ❶ *n* **1** central part of certain fruits, containing the seeds. **2** central or essential part. **3** region of a nuclear

reactor that contains fissionable material. ▷ *v* **4** remove the core from.

corella *n* white Australian cockatoo.

co-respondent *n* person with whom someone being sued for divorce is claimed to have committed adultery.

corgi *n* short-legged sturdy dog.

coriander *n* **1** plant grown for its aromatic seeds and leaves. **2** its dried seeds, used as a flavouring.

cork *n* **1** thick light bark of a Mediterranean oak. **2** piece of this used as a stopper. ▷ *v* **3** seal with a cork. **corked** *adj* (of wine) spoiled through having a decayed cork. **corkage** *n* restaurant's charge for serving wine bought elsewhere. **corkscrew** *n* **1** spiral metal tool for pulling corks from bottles. ▷ *adj* **2** like a corkscrew in shape.

corm *n* bulblike underground stem of certain plants.

cormorant *n* large dark-coloured long-necked sea bird.

corn¹ ❶ *n* **1** cereal plant such as wheat or oats. **2** grain of such plants. **3** *US* maize. **4** *slang* something unoriginal or oversentimental. **corny** *adj* **cornier**, **corniest** *slang* unoriginal or oversentimental. **cornflakes** *pl n* breakfast cereal made from toasted maize. **cornflour** *n* fine maize flour *NZ* fine wheat flour. **cornflower** *n* plant with blue flowers.

corn² *n* painful hard skin on the toe.

corncrake *n* brown bird with a harsh cry.

cornea [**korn-ee-a**] *n, pl* **-neas**, **-neae** transparent membrane covering the eyeball. **corneal** *adj*.

corned beef *n* beef preserved in salt.

cornelian *n* same as CARNELIAN.

corner ❶ *n* **1** area or angle where two converging lines or surfaces meet. **2** place where two streets meet. **3** sharp bend in a road. **4** remote place. **5** *Sport* free kick or shot from

like, ape, behave like, emulate, follow, mimic, mirror, repeat

cord *n* **1** = **rope**, line, string, twine

cordial *adj* **1** = **warm**, affable, agreeable, cheerful, congenial, friendly, genial, hearty, sociable

cordon *n* = **chain**, barrier, line, ring

cordon off *v* = **surround**, close off, encircle, enclose, fence off, isolate, picket, separate

core *n* **1** = **kernel**, pith **2** = **centre**, crux, essence, gist, heart, nub, nucleus

corner *n* **1** = **angle**, bend, crook, joint **4** = **space**, hideaway, hide-out, nook, retreat ▷ *v* **6** = **trap**, run to earth **8** = **monopolize**, dominate, engross, hog (*sl*)

corny *adj Sl* = **unoriginal**, hackneyed, old-fashioned, old hat, stale, stereotyped, trite

the corner of the field. ▷ v **6** force into a difficult or inescapable position. **7** (of a vehicle) turn a corner. **8** obtain a monopoly of. **cornerstone** n **1** indispensable part or basis. **2** stone at the corner of a wall.

cornet n **1** brass instrument similar to the trumpet. **2** cone-shaped ice-cream wafer.

cornice [**korn**-iss] n decorative moulding round the top of a wall.

Cornish pl n, adj (people) of Cornwall. **Cornish pasty** pastry case with a filling of meat and vegetables.

cornucopia [korn-yew-**kope**-ee-a] n **1** great abundance. **2** symbol of plenty, consisting of a horn overflowing with fruit and flowers.

corolla n petals of a flower collectively.

corollary [kor-**oll**-a-ree] n, pl **-laries** idea, fact, or proposition which is the natural result of something else.

corona [kor-**rone**-a] n, pl **-nas**, **-nae** **1** ring of light round the moon or sun. **2** long cigar with blunt ends.

coronary [**kor**-ron-a-ree] adj **1** of the arteries surrounding the heart. ▷ n, pl **-naries 2** coronary thrombosis. **coronary thrombosis** condition in which the flow of blood to the heart is blocked by a blood clot.

coronation n ceremony of crowning a monarch.

coroner n official responsible for the investigation of violent, sudden, or suspicious deaths.

coronet n small crown.

corpora n plural of CORPUS.

corporal[1] n noncommissioned officer in an army.

corporal[2] adj of the body. **corporal punishment** physical punishment, such as caning.

corporation ❶ n **1** large business or company. **2** city or town council. **3** informal large paunch. **corporate** adj **1** of business corporations. **2** shared by a group.

corporeal [kore-**pore**-ee-al] adj physical or tangible.

corps ❶ [kore] n, pl **corps 1** military unit with a specific function. **2** organized body of people.

corpse ❶ n dead body.

corpulent adj fat or plump. **corpulence** n.

corpus n, pl **corpora** collection of writings, esp. by a single author.

corpuscle n red or white blood cell.

corral US ▷ n **1** enclosure for cattle or horses. ▷ v **-ralling**, **-ralled 2** put in a corral.

correct ❶ adj **1** free from error, true. **2** in accordance with accepted standards. ▷ v **3** put right. **4** indicate the errors in. **5** rebuke or punish. **6** make conform to a standard. **correctly** adv **correctness** n **correction** n **1** correcting. **2** alteration correcting something. **3** punishment. **corrective** adj intended to put right something wrong.

correlate v place or be placed in a mutual relationship. **correlation** n.

correspond ❶ v **1** be consistent or

——————————— **THESAURUS** ———————————

corporation n **1** = **business**, association, corporate body, society **2** = **town council**, civic authorities, council, municipal authorities **3** Inf = **paunch**, beer belly (inf), middle-age spread (inf), potbelly, spare tyre (Brit sl), spread (inf)

corps n **1** = **team**, band, company, detachment, division, regiment, squadron, troop, unit

corpse n = **body**, cadaver, carcass, remains, stiff (sl)

correct adj **1** = **true**, accurate, exact, faultless, flawless, O.K. or okay (inf), precise, right **2** = **proper**, acceptable, appropriate, fitting, kosher (inf), O.K. or okay (inf), seemly, standard ▷ v **3** = **rectify**, adjust, amend, cure, emend, redress, reform, remedy, right

5 = **punish**, admonish, chasten, chastise, chide, discipline, rebuke, reprimand, reprove, rouse on (Aust)

correction n **2** = **rectification**, adjustment, alteration, amendment, emendation, improvement, modification **3** = **punishment**, admonition, castigation, chastisement, discipline, reformation, reproof

correctly adv = **rightly**, accurately, perfectly, precisely, properly, right

correctness n **1** = **truth**, accuracy, exactitude, exactness, faultlessness, fidelity, preciseness, precision, regularity **2** = **decorum**, civility, good breeding, propriety, seemliness

correspond v **1** = **be consistent**, accord, agree, conform, fit,

C

compatible (with). **2** be the same or similar. **3** communicate by letter.
corresponding *adj* **correspondingly** *adv* **correspondence** *n*
1 communication by letters. **2** letters so exchanged. **3** relationship or similarity. **correspondence course** study conducted by post.
correspondent *n* **1** person employed by a newspaper etc. to report on a special subject or from a foreign country. **2** letter writer.
corridor ❶ *n* **1** passage in a building or train. **2** strip of land or airspace providing access through foreign territory.
corrie *n Scot* circular hollow on a hillside.
corrigendum [kor-rij-**end**-um] *n, pl* **-da** error to be corrected.
corroborate ❶ *v* support (a fact or opinion) by giving proof. **corroboration** *n* **corroborative** *adj*.
corroboree *n Aust* Aboriginal gathering or dance.
corrode ❶ *v* **1** eat or be eaten away by chemical action or rust. **2** destroy gradually. **corrosion** *n* **corrosive** *adj*.
corrugate *v* fold into alternate grooves and ridges. **corrugated** *adj*.
corrupt ❶ *adj* **1** open to or involving bribery. **2** morally depraved. **3** (of a text or data) unreliable through errors or alterations. ▷ *v* **4** make corrupt.

corruptly *adv* **corruption** *n* **corruptible** *adj*.
corsage [kor-**sahzh**] *n* small bouquet worn on the bodice of a dress.
corsair *n* **1** pirate. **2** pirate ship.
corselet *n* **1** one-piece undergarment combining a corset and bra. **2** piece of armour to cover the trunk.
corset ❶ *n* women's close-fitting undergarment worn to shape the torso.
cortege [kor-**tayzh**] *n* funeral procession.
cortex *n, pl* **-tices** *Anat* outer layer of the brain or other internal organ. **cortical** *adj*.
cortisone *n* steroid hormone used to treat various diseases.
corundum *n* hard mineral used as an abrasive.
coruscate *v formal* sparkle. **coruscation** *n*.
corvette *n* lightly armed escort warship.
cos¹, cos lettuce *n* long crisp-leaved lettuce.
cos² *Maths* cosine.
cosh *n* **1** heavy blunt weapon. ▷ *v* **2** hit with a cosh.
cosine [**koh**-sine] *n* (in trigonometry) ratio of the length of the adjacent side to that of the hypotenuse in a right-angled triangle.
cosmetic ❶ *n* **1** preparation used to

——————————————————————————————— THESAURUS ———————————————

harmonize, match, square, tally **3** = **communicate**, exchange letters, keep in touch, write
correspondence *n* **1, 2** = **letters**, communication, mail, post, writing **3** = **relation**, agreement, coincidence, comparison, conformity, correlation, harmony, match, similarity
correspondent *n* **1** = **reporter**, contributor, journalist **2** = **letter writer**, pen friend *or* pal
corresponding *adj* **1, 2** = **related**, analogous, answering, complementary, equivalent, matching, reciprocal, similar
corridor *n* **1** = **passage**, aisle, alley, hallway, passageway
corroborate *v* = **support**, authenticate, back up, bear out, confirm, endorse, ratify, substantiate, validate
corrode *v* **1** = **eat away**, consume, corrupt, erode, gnaw, oxidize, rust,

wear away
corrosive *adj* **1** = **corroding**, caustic, consuming, erosive, virulent, vitriolic, wasting, wearing
corrupt *adj* **1** = **dishonest**, bent (*sl*), bribable, crooked (*inf*), fraudulent, unprincipled, unscrupulous, venal **2** = **depraved**, debased, degenerate, dissolute, profligate, vicious **3** = **distorted**, altered, doctored, falsified ▷ *v* **4 a** = **bribe**, buy off, entice, fix (*inf*), grease (someone's) palm (*sl*), lure, suborn **b** = **deprave**, debauch, pervert, subvert
corruption *n* **1** = **dishonesty**, bribery, extortion, fraud, shady dealings (*inf*), unscrupulousness, venality **2** = **depravity**, decadence, evil, immorality, perversion, vice, wickedness **3** = **distortion**, doctoring, falsification
corset *n* **1** = **girdle**, belt, bodice
cosmetic *adj* **2** = **beautifying**,

improve the appearance of a person's skin. ▷ *adj* **2** improving the appearance only.

cosmic ❶ *adj* of the whole universe. **cosmic rays** electromagnetic radiation from outer space.

cosmonaut *n* Russian name for an astronaut.

cosmopolitan ❶ *adj* **1** composed of people or elements from many countries. **2** having lived and travelled in many countries. ▷ *n* **3** cosmopolitan person. **cosmopolitanism** *n*.

cosmos *n* the universe. **cosmogony** *n* study of the origin of the universe. **cosmology** *n* study of the origin and nature of the universe. **cosmological** *adj*.

Cossack *n* member of a S Russian people famous as horsemen and dancers.

cosset *v* **cosseting, cosseted** pamper.

cost ❶ *n* **1** amount of money, time, labour, etc., required for something. ▷ *pl* **2** expenses of a lawsuit. ▷ *v* **costing, cost 3** have as its cost. **4** involve the loss or sacrifice of. **costly** *adj* **-lier, -liest 1** expensive. **2** involving great loss or sacrifice. **costliness** *n* **cost of living** average cost of the basic necessities of life.

costal *adj* of the ribs.

costermonger *n* person who sells fruit and vegetables from a street barrow.

costive *adj old-fashioned* having or causing constipation.

costume ❶ *n* **1** style of dress of a particular place or time, or for a particular activity. **2** clothes worn by an actor or performer. **costumier** *n* maker or seller of costumes. **costume jewellery** inexpensive artificial

jewellery worn for fun.

cosy ❶ *adj* **-sier, -siest 1** warm and snug. **2** intimate, friendly. ▷ *n* **3** cover for keeping things warm, e.g. *a tea cosy*. **cosily** *adv* **cosiness** *n*.

cot¹ *n* **1** baby's bed with high sides. **2** small portable bed. **cot death** unexplained death of a baby while asleep.

cot² *n* **1** *lit* small cottage. **2** cote.

cote *n* shelter for birds or animals.

coterie [**kote**-er-ee] *n* exclusive group, clique.

cotoneaster [kot-tone-ee-**ass**-ter] *n* garden shrub with red berries.

cottage ❶ *n* small house in the country. **cottager** *n* **cottage cheese** soft mild white cheese. **cottage industry** craft industry in which employees work at home. **cottage pie** dish of minced meat topped with mashed potato.

cotter *n* pin or wedge used to secure machine parts.

cotton *n* **1** white downy fibre covering the seeds of a tropical plant. **2** cloth or thread made from this. **cottony** *adj* **cotton on (to)** *v informal* understand. **cotton wool** fluffy cotton used for surgical dressings etc.

cotyledon [kot-ill-**ee**-don] *n* first leaf of a plant embryo.

couch *n* **1** piece of upholstered furniture for seating more than one person. ▷ *v* **2** express in a particular way. **couch potato** *slang* lazy person whose only hobby is watching television.

couchette [koo-**shett**] *n* bed converted from seats on a train or ship.

couch grass *n* quickly spreading grassy weed.

cougar [**koo**-gar] *n* puma.

cough ❶ *v* **1** expel air from the lungs abruptly and noisily. ▷ *n* **2** act or sound

---

nonessential, superficial, surface

cosmic *adj* = **universal**, stellar

cosmopolitan *adj* **2** = **sophisticated**, broad-minded, catholic, open-minded, universal, urbane, well-travelled, worldly-wise ▷ *n* **3** = **man** *or* **woman of the world**, jet-setter, sophisticate

cost *n* **1** = **price**, amount, charge, damage (*inf*), expense, outlay, payment, worth ▷ *v* **3** = **sell at**, come to, command a price of, set (someone) back (*inf*) **4** = **lose**, do disservice to, harm, hurt, injure

costly *adj* **1** = **expensive**, dear,

exorbitant, extortionate, highly-priced, steep (*inf*), stiff **2** = **damaging**, catastrophic, deleterious, disastrous, harmful, loss-making, ruinous

costume *n* **1** = **outfit**, apparel, attire, clothing, dress, ensemble, garb, livery, uniform

cosy *adj* **1** = **snug**, comfortable, comfy (*inf*), homely, sheltered, tucked up, warm **2** = **intimate**, friendly

cottage *n* = **cabin**, chalet, hut, lodge, shack

cough *v* **1** = **clear one's throat**, bark, hack ▷ *n* **2** = **frog** *or* **tickle in one's**

of coughing. **3** illness which causes coughing. **cough up** v *informal* hand over or pay (money).

could v past tense of CAN[1].

couldn't could not.

coulomb [**koo**-lom] n SI unit of electric charge.

coulter [**kole**-ter] n blade at the front of a ploughshare.

council ❶ n **1** group meeting for discussion or consultation. **2** local governing body of a town or region. ▷ *adj* **3** of or by a council. **councillor** n member of a council. **council tax** tax based on the value of property, to fund local services.

counsel ❶ n **1** advice or guidance. **2** discussion or consultation. **3** barrister or barristers. ▷ v **-selling**, **-selled 4** give guidance to. **5** urge, recommend. **counsellor** n.

count[1] ❶ v **1** say numbers in order. **2** find the total of. **3** be important. **4** regard as. **5** take into account. ▷ n **6** counting. **7** number reached by counting. **8** *Law* one of a number of charges. **countless** *adj* too many to count. **count on** v rely or depend on. **count out** v **1** exclude. **2** declare (a boxer) defeated when he has not risen from the floor within ten seconds.

count[2] n European nobleman.

countdown n counting backwards to zero of the seconds before an event.

countenance n **1** (expression of) the face. ▷ v **2** allow or tolerate.

counter[1] n **1** long flat surface in a bank or shop, on which business is transacted. **2** small flat disc used in board games.

counter[2] ❶ v **1** oppose, retaliate against. ▷ *adv* **2** in the opposite direction. **3** in direct contrast. ▷ n **4** opposing or retaliatory action.

counter[3] n apparatus for counting things.

counter- *prefix* **1** opposite, against, e.g. *counterattack*. **2** complementary, corresponding, e.g. *counterpart*.

counteract ❶ v act against or neutralize. **counteraction** n.

counterattack n, v attack in response to an attack.

counterbalance ❶ n **1** weight or force balancing or neutralizing another. ▷ v **2** act as a counterbalance to.

counterblast n aggressive response to a verbal attack.

counterclockwise *adv, adj* US anticlockwise.

counterespionage n activities to counteract enemy espionage.

counterfeit ❶ *adj* **1** fake, forged. ▷ n **2** fake, forgery. ▷ v **3** fake, forge.

counterfoil n part of a cheque or receipt kept as a record.

counterintelligence n activities designed to frustrate enemy espionage.

countermand ❶ v cancel (a previous order).

——————————————————————— THESAURUS ————————

throat, bark, hack

council n **1, 2** = **governing body**, assembly, board, cabinet, committee, conference, congress, convention, panel, parliament

counsel n **1** = **advice**, direction, guidance, information, recommendation, suggestion, warning **3** = **legal adviser**, advocate, attorney, barrister, lawyer, solicitor ▷ v **4** = **advise**, instruct, warn **5** = **urge**, advocate, exhort, recommend

count[1] v **1** = **enumerate 2** = **add (up)**, calculate, compute, number, reckon, tally, tot up **3** = **matter**, be important, carry weight, rate, signify, tell, weigh **4** = **consider**, deem, judge, look upon, rate, regard, think **5** = **take into account** *or* **consideration**, include, number among ▷ n **6** = **calculation**, computation, enumeration, numbering, poll **7** = **sum**, reckoning,

tally

counter[2] v **1** = **retaliate**, answer, hit back, meet, oppose, parry, resist, respond, ward off ▷ *adv* **3** = **opposite to**, against, at variance with, contrariwise, conversely, in defiance of, versus

counteract v = **act against**, foil, frustrate, negate, neutralize, offset, resist, thwart

counterbalance v **2** = **offset**, balance, compensate, make up for, set off

counterfeit *adj* **1** = **fake**, bogus, false, forged, imitation, phoney *or* phony (*inf*), sham, simulated ▷ n **2** = **fake**, copy, forgery, fraud, imitation, phoney *or* phony (*inf*), reproduction, sham ▷ v **3** = **fake**, copy, fabricate, feign, forge, imitate, impersonate, pretend, sham, simulate

countermand v = **cancel**, annul, override, repeal, rescind, retract,

counterpane n bed covering.
counterpart ❶ n person or thing complementary to or corresponding to another.
counterpoint n Music **1** technique of combining melodies. **2** part or melody so combined.
counterpoise n, v counterbalance.
counterproductive adj having an effect opposite to the one intended.
countersign v sign (a document already signed by someone) as confirmation.
countersink v drive (a screw) into a shaped hole so that its head is below the surface.
countertenor n male alto.
countess n **1** woman holding the rank of count or earl. **2** wife or widow of a count or earl.
country ❶ n, pl **-tries 1** nation. **2** nation's territory. **3** nation's people. **4** part of the land away from cities. **5** person's native land. **countrified** adj rustic in manner or appearance. **country and western**, **country music** popular music based on American White folk music. **country dancing** British folk dancing in rows or circles. **countryman**, **countrywoman** n **1** person from one's native land. **2** person who lives in the country. **countryside** n land away from cities.
county ❶ n, pl **-ties 1** division of a country. ▷ adj **2** informal upper-class.

coup ❶ [koo] n **1** successful action. **2** coup d'état.
coup de grâce [koo de **grahss**] n final or decisive action.
coup d'état [koo day-**tah**] n sudden violent overthrow of a government.
coupé [koo-pay] n sports car with two doors and a sloping fixed roof.
couple ❶ n **1** two people who are married or romantically involved. **2** two partners in a dance or game. ▷ v **3** connect, associate. **4** lit have sexual intercourse. **a couple 1** a pair. **2** informal a few. **couplet** n two consecutive lines of verse, usu. rhyming and of the same metre. **coupling** n device for connecting things, such as railway carriages.
coupon ❶ n **1** piece of paper entitling the holder to a discount or gift. **2** detachable order form. **3** football pools entry form.
courage ❶ n ability to face danger or pain without fear. **courageous** adj **courageously** adv.
courgette n type of small vegetable marrow.
courier ❶ n **1** person employed to look after holiday-makers. **2** person employed to deliver urgent messages.
course ❶ n **1** series of lessons or medical treatment. **2** onward movement in space or time. **3** route or direction taken. **4** area where golf is played or a race is run. **5** any of the

reverse, revoke
counterpart n = **opposite number**, complement, equal, fellow, match, mate, supplement, tally, twin
countless adj = **innumerable**, endless, immeasurable, incalculable, infinite, legion, limitless, myriad, numberless, untold
count on v = **depend on**, bank on, believe (in), lean on, pin one's faith on, reckon on, rely on, take for granted, take on trust, trust
country n **1** = **nation**, commonwealth, kingdom, people, realm, state **2** = **territory**, land, region, terrain **3** = **people**, citizens, community, inhabitants, nation, populace, public, society **4** = **countryside**, backwoods, farmland, green belt, outback (Aust & NZ), provinces, sticks (inf)
countryside n = **country**, farmland, green belt, outback (Aust & NZ),

outdoors, sticks (inf)
county n **1** = **province**, shire
coup n **1** = **masterstroke**, accomplishment, action, deed, exploit, feat, manoeuvre, stunt
couple n **1** = **pair**, two, twosome ▷ v **3** = **link**, connect, hitch, join, marry, pair, unite, wed, yoke
coupon n **1** = **slip**, card, certificate, ticket, token, voucher
courage n = **bravery**, daring, fearlessness, gallantry, heroism, mettle, nerve, pluck, resolution, valour
courageous adj = **brave**, bold, daring, fearless, gallant, gritty, intrepid, lion-hearted, stouthearted, valiant
courier n **1** = **guide**, representative **2** = **messenger**, bearer, carrier, envoy, runner
course n **1** = **classes**, curriculum, lectures, programme, schedule **2** = **progression**, development, flow,

successive parts of a meal.
6 continuous layer of masonry at one level in a building. **7** mode of conduct or action. **8** natural development of events. ▷ *v* **9** (of liquid) run swiftly. **10** hunt with hounds that follow the quarry by sight and not scent. **of course** as expected, naturally. **courser** *n lit* swift horse.

court ❶ *n* **1** body which decides legal cases. **2** place where it meets. **3** marked area for playing a racket game. **4** courtyard. **5** residence, household, or retinue of a sovereign. ▷ *v* **6** *old-fashioned* try to gain the love of. **7** try to win the favour of. **8** invite, e.g. *to court disaster*. **courtier** *n* attendant at a royal court. **courtly** *adj* **-lier, -liest** ceremoniously polite. **courtliness** *n* **courtship** *n* courting of an intended spouse or mate. **court martial** *n, pl* **courts martial** court for trying naval or military offences. **court shoe** woman's low-cut shoe without straps or laces. **courtyard** *n* paved space enclosed by buildings or walls.

courtesan [kor-tiz-**zan**] *n History* mistress or high-class prostitute.

courtesy ❶ *n* **1** politeness, good manners. **2** *pl* **-sies** courteous act. **(by) courtesy of** by permission of. **courteous** *adj* polite. **courteously** *adv*.

cousin *n* child of one's uncle or aunt.

couture [koo-**toor**] *n* high-fashion designing and dressmaking. **couturier** *n* person who designs women's fashion clothes.

cove ❶ *n* small bay or inlet.

coven [**kuv**-ven] *n* meeting of witches.

covenant ❶ [**kuv**-ven-ant] *n* **1** formal agreement to make an annual (charitable) payment. ▷ *v* **2** agree by a covenant.

Coventry *n* **send someone to Coventry** punish someone by refusing to speak to them.

cover ❶ *v* **1** place something over, to protect or conceal. **2** extend over or lie on the surface of. **3** travel over. **4** keep a gun aimed at. **5** insure against loss or risk. **6** include. **7** report (an event) for a newspaper. **8** be enough to pay for. ▷ *n* **9** anything that covers. **10** outside of a book or magazine. **11** pretext or disguise. **12** individual table setting. **13** insurance. **14** shelter

movement, order, progress, sequence, unfolding **3** = **route**, direction, line, passage, path, road, track, trajectory, way **4** = **racecourse**, cinder track, circuit **7** = **procedure**, behaviour, conduct, manner, method, mode, plan, policy, programme **8** = **period**, duration, lapse, passage, passing, sweep, term, time ▷ *v* **9** = **run**, flow, gush, race, speed, stream, surge **10** = **hunt**, chase, follow, pursue **of course** = **naturally**, certainly, definitely, indubitably, needless to say, obviously, undoubtedly, without a doubt

court *n* **1** = **law court**, bar, bench, tribunal **4** = **courtyard**, cloister, piazza, plaza, quad (*inf*), quadrangle, square, yard **5 a** = **palace**, hall, manor, royal household **b** = **retinue**, attendants, cortege, entourage, suite, train ▷ *v* **6** *Old-fashioned* = **woo**, date, go (out) with, run after, serenade, set one's cap at, take out, walk out with **7** = **cultivate**, curry favour with, fawn upon, flatter, pander to, seek, solicit **8** = **invite**, attract, bring about, incite, prompt, provoke, seek

courteous *adj* = **polite**, affable, attentive, civil, gallant, gracious, refined, respectful, urbane, well-mannered

courtesy *n* **1** = **politeness**, affability, civility, courteousness, gallantry, good manners, graciousness, urbanity **2** = **favour**, indulgence, kindness

courtier *n* = **attendant**, follower, squire

courtly *adj* = **ceremonious**, chivalrous, dignified, elegant, formal, gallant, polished, refined, stately, urbane

courtyard *n* = **yard**, enclosure, quad, quadrangle

cove *n* = **bay**, anchorage, inlet, sound

covenant *n* **1** = **promise**, agreement, arrangement, commitment, contract, pact, pledge ▷ *v* **2** = **promise**, agree, contract, pledge, stipulate, undertake

cover *v* **1** = **envelop**, cloak, coat, conceal, encase, enshroud, hide, mask, obscure, overlay, put on, shroud, veil, wrap **2** = **submerge**, engulf, flood, overrun, wash over **3** = **travel over**, cross, pass through *or* over, traverse **7** = **report**, describe, investigate, narrate, relate, tell of,

or protection. **coverage** n amount or extent covered. **coverlet** n bed cover. **cover charge** fixed service charge in a restaurant.

covert adj **1** concealed, secret. ▷ n **2** thicket giving shelter to game birds or animals. **covertly** adv.

covet ❶ v **coveting**, **coveted** long to possess (what belongs to someone else). **covetous** adj **covetousness** n.

covey [**kuv**-vee] n small flock of grouse or partridge.

cow¹ ❶ n **1** mature female of cattle and of certain other mammals, such as the elephant or seal. **2** informal, offens a disagreeable woman. **cowboy** n **1** (in the US) ranch worker who herds and tends cattle, usu. on horseback. **2** informal irresponsible or unscrupulous worker. **cowpat** n pool of cow dung. **cowpox** n disease of cows, the virus of which is used in the smallpox vaccine.

cow² v intimidate, subdue.

coward ❶ n person who lacks courage. **cowardly** adj **cowardice** n lack of courage.

cower ❶ v cringe in fear.

cowl n **1** loose hood. **2** monk's hooded robe. **3** cover on a chimney to increase ventilation.

cowling n cover on an engine.

cowrie n brightly-marked sea shell.

cowslip n small yellow wild flower.

cox n **1** coxswain. ▷ v **2** act as cox of (a boat).

coxcomb n **1** comb of a domestic cock. **2** informal conceited dandy.

coxswain [**kok**-sn] n person who steers a rowing boat.

coy ❶ adj affectedly shy or modest. **coyly** adv **coyness** n.

coyote [koy-**ote**-ee] n prairie wolf of N America.

coypu n beaver-like aquatic rodent, bred for its fur.

cozen v lit cheat, trick.

CPU Computers central processing unit.

Cr Chemistry chromium.

crab n **1** edible shellfish with ten legs, the first pair modified into pincers. **2** crab louse. **crab louse** parasitic louse living in the pubic area of humans.

crab apple n small sour apple.

crabbed adj **1** (of handwriting) hard to read. **2** (also **crabby**) bad-tempered.

crack ❶ v **1** break or split partially. **2** break with a sharp noise. **3** (cause to) make a sharp noise. **4** (of the voice) become harsh or change pitch suddenly. **5** break down or yield under strain. **6** hit suddenly. **7** force (a safe) open. **8** solve (a code or problem). **9** tell (a joke). ▷ n **10** sudden sharp noise. **11** narrow gap. **12** sharp blow.

THESAURUS

---

write up ▷ n **9** = **covering**, canopy, case, coating, envelope, jacket, lid, top, wrapper **11** = **disguise**, camouflage, concealment, facade, front, mask, pretext, screen, smoke screen, veil **13** = **insurance**, compensation, indemnity, protection, reimbursement **14** = **protection**, defence, guard, shelter, shield

covet v = **long for**, aspire to, crave, desire, envy, lust after, set one's heart on, yearn for

covetous adj = **envious**, acquisitive, avaricious, close-fisted, grasping, greedy, jealous, rapacious, yearning

coward n = **wimp** (inf), chicken (sl), scaredy-cat (inf), yellow-belly (sl)

cowardice n = **faint-heartedness**, fearfulness, spinelessness, weakness

cowardly adj = **faint-hearted**, chicken (sl), craven, fearful, scared, soft, spineless, timorous, weak, yellow (inf)

cowboy n **1** = **rancher**, cattleman, drover, gaucho (S Amer), herdsman,

stockman, wrangler (US)

cower v = **cringe**, draw back, flinch, grovel, quail, shrink, tremble

coy adj = **shy**, bashful, demure, modest, reserved, retiring, shrinking, timid

crack v **1** = **break**, burst, cleave, fracture, snap, splinter, split **2**, **3** = **snap**, burst, crash, detonate, explode, pop **5** = **give in**, break down, collapse, give way, go to pieces, lose control, succumb, yield **6** = **hit**, clip (inf), clout (inf), cuff, slap, smack, whack **8** = **solve**, decipher, fathom, get the answer to, work out ▷ n **10** = **snap**, burst, clap, crash, explosion, pop, report **11** = **break**, chink, cleft, cranny, crevice, fissure, fracture, gap, rift **12** = **blow**, clip (inf), clout (inf), cuff, slap, smack, whack **13** Inf = **joke**, dig, funny remark, gag (inf), jibe, quip, wisecrack, witticism ▷ adj **15** Inf = **first-class**, ace, choice, elite, excellent, first-rate, hand-picked, superior, world-class

13 *informal* gibe, joke. **14** *slang* highly addictive form of cocaine. ▷ *adj* **15** *informal* first-rate, excellent, e.g. *a crack shot.* **cracking** *adj* **1** very fast, e.g. *a cracking pace.* **2** very good. **crackdown** *n* severe disciplinary measures. **crack down on** *v* take severe measures against. **crack up** *v informal* have a physical or mental breakdown.

cracker *n* **1** thin dry biscuit. **2** decorated cardboard tube, pulled apart with a bang, containing a paper hat and a joke or toy. **3** small explosive firework. **4** *slang* an outstanding thing or person.

crackers *adj slang* insane.

crackle *v* **1** make small sharp popping noises. ▷ *n* **2** crackling sound. **crackling** *n* **1** crackle. **2** crisp skin of roast pork.

crackpot *n, adj informal* eccentric (person).

cradle ❶ *n* **1** baby's bed on rockers. **2** place where something originates. **3** supporting structure. ▷ *v* **4** hold gently as if in a cradle.

craft ❶ *n* **1** occupation requiring skill with the hands. **2** skill or ability. **3** *pl* **craft** boat, ship, aircraft, or spaceship. ▷ *v* **4** make skilfully. **crafty** **craftier**, **craftiest** skilled in deception. **craftily** *adv* **craftiness** *n* **craftsman**, **craftswoman** *n* skilled worker. **craftsmanship** *n*.

crag ❶ *n* steep rugged rock. **craggy** *adj*.

cram ❶ *v* **cramming**, **crammed** **1** force into too small a space. **2** fill too full. **3** study hard just before an examination.

cramp¹ ❶ *n* **1** painful muscular contraction. **2** clamp for holding masonry or timber together. ▷ *v* **3** affect with a cramp.

cramp² ❶ *v* confine, restrict. **cramped** *adj* **1** closed in. **2** (of handwriting) small and irregular.

crampon *n* spiked plate strapped to a boot for climbing on ice.

cranberry *n* sour edible red berry.

crane *n* **1** machine for lifting and moving heavy weights. **2** large wading bird with a long neck and legs. ▷ *v* **3** stretch (one's neck) to see something.

crane fly *n* long-legged insect with slender wings.

cranesbill *n* plant with pink or purple flowers.

cranium *n, pl* **-niums**, **-nia 1** skull. **2** part of the skull enclosing the brain. **cranial** *adj*.

crank *n* **1** arm projecting at right angles from a shaft, for transmitting or converting motion. **2** *informal* eccentric person. ▷ *v* **3** turn with a crank. **4** start (an engine) with a crank. **cranky** *adj* **crankier**, **crankiest** *informal* **1** eccentric. **2** bad-tempered. **crankshaft** *n* shaft driven by a crank.

cranny ❶ *n, pl* **-nies** narrow opening.

———————— THESAURUS ————————

crackdown *n* = **suppression**, clampdown, crushing, repression

cracked *adj* = **broken**, chipped, damaged, defective, faulty, flawed, imperfect, split

cradle *n* **1** = **crib**, bassinet, cot, Moses basket **2** = **birthplace**, beginning, fount, fountainhead, origin, source, spring, wellspring ▷ *v* **4** = **hold**, lull, nestle, nurse, rock, support

craft *n* **1** = **occupation**, business, employment, handicraft, pursuit, trade, vocation, work, yakka (*Aust & NZ inf*) **2** = **skill**, ability, aptitude, art, artistry, expertise, ingenuity, know-how (*inf*), technique, workmanship **3** = **vessel**, aircraft, boat, plane, ship, spacecraft

craftsman *n* = **skilled worker**, artisan, maker, master, smith, technician, wright

craftsmanship *n* = **workmanship**, artistry, expertise, mastery, technique

crafty *adj* = **cunning**, artful, calculating, devious, sharp, shrewd, sly, subtle, wily

crag *n* = **rock**, bluff, peak, pinnacle, tor

cram *v* **1** = **stuff**, compress, force, jam, pack in, press, shove, squeeze **3** = **study**, bone up (*inf*), mug up (*sl*), revise, swot

cramp¹ *n* **1** = **spasm**, ache, contraction, convulsion, pain, pang, stitch, twinge

cramp² *v* = **restrict**, constrain, hamper, handicap, hinder, impede, inhibit, obstruct

cramped *adj* **1** = **closed in**, confined, congested, crowded, hemmed in, overcrowded, packed, uncomfortable

cranny *n* = **crevice**, chink, cleft, crack, fissure, gap, hole, opening

crap *slang* ▷ *n* **1** rubbish, nonsense. **2** *taboo* faeces. ▷ *v* **crapping**, **crapped 3** *taboo* defecate. **crappy** *adj*.

crape *n* same as CREPE.

craps *n* gambling game played with two dice.

crash ❶ *n* **1** collision involving a vehicle or vehicles. **2** sudden loud smashing noise. **3** financial collapse. ▷ *v* **4** (cause to) collide violently with a vehicle, a stationary object, or the ground. **5** (cause to) make a loud smashing noise. **6** (cause to) fall with a crash. **7** collapse or fail financially. **8** *informal* gate-crash. **crash barrier** safety barrier along a road or racetrack. **crash course** short, very intensive course in a particular subject. **crash helmet** protective helmet worn by a motorcyclist. **crash-land** *v* (of an aircraft) land in an emergency, causing damage. **crash-landing** *n*.

crass ❶ *adj* stupid and insensitive. **crassly** *adv* **crassness** *n*.

crate ❶ *n* **1** large wooden container for packing goods. ▷ *v* **2** put in a crate.

crater ❶ *n* **1** very large hole in the ground or in the surface of the moon. **2** mouth of a volcano.

cravat *n* man's scarf worn like a tie.

crave ❶ *v* **1** desire intensely. **2** beg or plead for. **craving** *n*.

craven *adj* cowardly.

craw *n* **stick in one's craw** *informal* be difficult for one to accept.

crawfish *n* same as CRAYFISH.

crawl ❶ *v* **1** move on one's hands and knees. **2** move very slowly. **3** (foll. by *to*) flatter in order to gain some advantage. **4** feel as if covered with crawling creatures. ▷ *n* **5** crawling motion or pace. **6** overarm swimming stroke. **crawler** *n*.

crayfish *n* **1** edible freshwater shellfish like a lobster. **2** any similar shellfish, e.g. the spiny lobster.

crayon *v*, *n* (draw or colour with) a stick or pencil of coloured wax or clay.

craze ❶ *n* short-lived fashion or enthusiasm. **crazed** *adj* **1** wild and uncontrolled. **2** (of porcelain) having fine cracks. **crazy** *adj* **crazier**, **craziest 1** ridiculous. **2** (foll. by *about*) very fond (of). **3** insane. **craziness** *n* **crazy paving** paving made of irregularly shaped slabs of stone.

creak ❶ *v*, *n* (make) a harsh squeaking sound. **creaky** *adj* **creakier**, **creakiest**.

cream ❶ *n* **1** fatty part of milk. **2** food or cosmetic resembling cream in consistency. **3** best part (of something). ▷ *adj* **4** yellowish-white.

crash *n* **1** = **collision**, accident, bump, pile-up (*inf*), prang (*inf*), smash, wreck **2** = **smash**, bang, boom, clang, clash, clatter, din, racket, thunder **3** = **collapse**, debacle, depression, downfall, failure, ruin ▷ *v* **4** = **collide**, bump (into), crash-land (*an aircraft*), drive into, have an accident, hit, plough into, wreck **6** = **hurtle**, fall headlong, give way, lurch, overbalance, plunge, topple **7** = **collapse**, be ruined, fail, fold, fold up, go belly up (*inf*), go bust (*inf*), go to the wall, go under

crass *adj* = **insensitive**, boorish, gross, indelicate, oafish, stupid, unrefined, witless

crate *n* **1** = **container**, box, case, packing case, tea chest

crater *n* **1** = **hollow**, depression, dip

crave *v* **1** = **long for**, desire, hanker after, hope for, lust after, want, yearn for **2** = **beg**, ask, beseech, entreat, implore, petition, plead for, pray for, seek, solicit, supplicate

craving *n* **1** = **longing**, appetite, desire, hankering, hope, hunger, thirst, yearning, yen (*inf*)

crawl *v* **1, 2** = **creep**, advance slowly, inch, slither, worm one's way, wriggle, writhe **3** (foll. by *to*) = **grovel**, creep, fawn, humble oneself, toady **4** = **be full of**, be alive, be overrun (*sl*), swarm, teem

craze *n* = **fad**, enthusiasm, fashion, infatuation, mania, rage, trend, vogue

crazy *adj* **1** = **ridiculous**, absurd, foolish, idiotic, ill-conceived, ludicrous, nonsensical, preposterous, senseless **2** (foll. by *about*) = **fanatical**, devoted, enthusiastic, infatuated, mad, passionate, wild (*inf*) **3** = **insane**, crazed, demented, deranged, mad, nuts (*sl*), out of one's mind, unbalanced

creak *v*, *n* = **squeak**, grate, grind, groan, scrape, scratch, screech

cream *n* **2** = **lotion**, cosmetic, emulsion, essence, liniment, oil, ointment, paste, salve, unguent

▷ *v* **5** beat to a creamy consistency.
6 remove the cream from. **creamer** *n* powdered milk substitute for use in coffee. **creamery** *n*, *pl* **-eries** place where dairy products are made or sold. **creamy** *adj* **creamier**, **creamiest**. **cream cheese** rich soft white cheese. **cream off** *v* take the best part from. **cream of tartar** purified tartar used in baking powder.

crease ❶ *n* **1** line made by folding or pressing. **2** wrinkle or furrow. **3** *Cricket* line marking the bowler's and batsman's positions. ▷ *v* **4** crush or line.

create ❶ *v* **1** make, cause to exist. **2** appoint to a new rank or position. **3** *slang* make an angry fuss. **creation** *n* **creative** *adj* **1** imaginative or inventive. ▷ *n* **2** person who is creative professionally. **creativity** *n* **creator** *n* **1** person who creates. **2** (**C-**) God.

creature ❶ *n* **1** animal, person, or other being. **2** person controlled by another.

crèche *n* place where small children are looked after while their parents are working, shopping, etc.

credence [**kreed**-enss] *n* belief in the truth or accuracy of a statement.

credentials ❶ *pl n* document giving evidence of a person's identity or qualifications.

credible ❶ *adj* **1** believable. **2** trustworthy. **credibly** *adv* **credibility** *n*.

credit ❶ *n* **1** system of allowing customers to receive goods and pay later. **2** reputation for trustworthiness in paying debts. **3** money at one's disposal in a bank account. **4** side of an account book on which such sums are entered. **5** (source or cause of) praise or approval. **6** influence or reputation based on the good opinion of others. **7** belief or trust. ▷ *pl* **8** list of people responsible for the production of a film, programme, or record. ▷ *v* **crediting**, **credited 9** enter as a credit in an account. **10** (foll. by *with*) attribute (to). **11** believe. **creditable**

3 = **best**, elite, flower, pick, prime ▷ *adj* **4** = **off-white**, yellowish-white
creamy *adj* **1** = **milky**, buttery **2** = **smooth**, rich, soft, velvety
crease *n* **1**, **2** = **line**, corrugation, fold, groove, ridge, wrinkle ▷ *v* **4** = **wrinkle**, corrugate, crumple, double up, fold, rumple, screw up
create *v* **1** = **make**, bring about, cause, compose, devise, formulate, invent, lead to, occasion, originate, produce, spawn **2** = **appoint**, constitute, establish, install, invest, make, set up
creation *n* **a** = **making**, conception, development, establishment, formation, foundation, generation, genesis, inception, institution, procreation, production, setting up **b** = **invention**, achievement, brainchild (*inf*), concoction, handiwork, magnum opus, *pièce de résistance*, production
creative *adj* = **imaginative**, artistic, clever, gifted, ingenious, inspired, inventive, original, visionary
creativity *n* = **imagination**, cleverness, ingenuity, inspiration, inventiveness, originality
creator *n* **1** = **maker**, architect, author, designer, father, inventor, originator, prime mover
creature *n* **1** = **living thing**, animal, beast, being, brute, human being, individual, man, mortal, person, soul, woman
credentials *pl n* = **certification**, authorization, document, licence, papers, passport, reference(s), testimonial
credibility *n* = **believability**, integrity, plausibility, reliability, trustworthiness
credible *adj* **1** = **believable**, conceivable, imaginable, likely, plausible, possible, probable, reasonable, thinkable **2** = **reliable**, dependable, honest, sincere, trustworthy, trusty
credit *n* **1** = **deferred payment**, hire-purchase, (the) H.P., the slate (*inf*), tick (*inf*) **5** = **praise**, acclaim, acknowledgment, approval, commendation, honour, kudos, recognition, tribute **6** = **prestige**, esteem, good name, influence, mana (*NZ*), position, regard, reputation, repute, standing, status **7** = **belief**, confidence, credence, faith, reliance, trust ▷ *v* **10** (foll. by *with*) = **attribute to**, ascribe to, assign to, impute to **11** = **believe**, accept, have faith in, rely on, trust
creditable *adj* = **praiseworthy**, admirable, commendable,

adj praiseworthy. **creditably** *adv*
creditor *n* person to whom money is owed. **credit card** card allowing a person to buy on credit. **credit crunch** period during which there is a sudden reduction in the availability of credit from banks, mortgage lenders, etc.
credo *n*, *pl* **-dos** creed.
credulous ❶ *adj* too willing to believe. **credulity** *n*.
creed ❶ *n* statement or system of (Christian) beliefs or principles.
creek ❶ *n* **1** narrow inlet or bay. **2** *Aust*, *NZ*, *US & Canad* small stream.
creel *n* wicker basket used by anglers.
creep ❶ *v* **creeping**, **crept 1** move quietly and cautiously. **2** crawl with the body near to the ground. **3** have a crawling sensation on the skin, from fear or disgust. **4** (of a plant) grow along the ground or over rocks. ▷ *n* **5** creeping movement. **6** *slang* obnoxious or servile person. **give one the creeps** *informal* make one feel fear or disgust. **creeper** *n* creeping plant. **creepy** *adj* **creepier**, **creepiest** *informal* causing a feeling of fear or disgust. **creepy-crawly** *n*, *pl* **-crawlies** *informal* insect, viewed with fear or disgust.
cremate *v* burn (a corpse) to ash. **cremation** *n* **crematorium** *n* building where corpses are cremated.
crème de menthe *n* peppermint-flavoured liqueur.
crenellated *adj* having battlements.
creole *n* **1** language developed from a mixture of languages. **2** (**C-**) native-born

W Indian or Latin American of mixed European and African descent.
creosote *n* **1** dark oily liquid made from coal tar and used for preserving wood. ▷ *v* **2** treat with creosote.
crepe [**krayp**] *n* **1** fabric or rubber with a crinkled texture. **2** very thin pancake. **crepe paper** *paper with a crinkled texture*.
crept *v* past of CREEP.
crepuscular *adj* *lit* of or like twilight.
Cres. Crescent.
crescendo [krish-**end**-oh] *n*, *pl* **-dos 1** gradual increase in loudness, esp. in music. ▷ *adv* **2** gradually getting louder.
crescent ❶ *n* **1** (curved shape of) the moon as seen in its first or last quarter. **2** crescent-shaped street. ▷ *adj* **3** crescent-shaped.
cress *n* plant with strong-tasting leaves, used in salads.
crest ❶ *n* **1** top of a mountain, hill, or wave. **2** tuft or growth on a bird's or animal's head. **3** heraldic design used on a coat of arms and elsewhere. ▷ *v* **4** come to or be at the top of. **crested** *adj* **crestfallen** *adj* disheartened.
cretin *n* **1** *informal* stupid person. **2** *obs* person afflicted with physical and mental retardation caused by a thyroid deficiency. **cretinism** *n* **cretinous** *adj*.
cretonne *n* heavy printed cotton fabric used in furnishings.
crevasse *n* deep open crack in a glacier.
crevice ❶ *n* narrow crack or gap in rock.
crew¹ ❶ *n* **1** people who work on a ship or aircraft. **2** group of people working

————————— **THESAURUS** —————————

honourable, laudable, reputable, respectable, worthy
credulity *n* = **gullibility**, blind faith, credulousness, naivety
creed *n* = **belief**, articles of faith, catechism, credo, doctrine, dogma, principles
creek *n* **1** = **inlet**, bay, bight, cove, firth or frith (*Scot*) **2** *Aust & NZ*, *US*, & *Canadian* = **stream**, bayou, brook, rivulet, runnel, tributary, watercourse
creep *v* **1** = **sneak**, approach unnoticed, skulk, slink, steal, tiptoe **2** = **crawl**, glide, slither, squirm, wriggle, writhe ▷ *n* **6** *Sl* = **bootlicker** (*inf*), crawler (*sl*), sneak, sycophant, toady ▷ *pl* **give one the creeps** *Inf* = **disgust**, frighten, make one's hair stand on end, make one squirm, repel, repulse, scare

creeper *n* = **climbing plant**, rambler, runner, trailing plant, vine (*chiefly US*)
creepy *adj* *Inf* = **disturbing**, eerie, frightening, hair-raising, macabre, menacing, scary (*inf*), sinister
crescent *n* **1** = **meniscus**, new moon, sickle
crest *n* **1** = **top**, apex, crown, highest point, peak, pinnacle, ridge, summit **2** = **tuft**, comb, crown, mane, plume **3** = **emblem**, badge, bearings, device, insignia, symbol
crestfallen *adj* = **disappointed**, dejected, depressed, despondent, discouraged, disheartened, downcast, downhearted
crevice *n* = **gap**, chink, cleft, crack, cranny, fissure, hole, opening, slit
crew¹ *n* **1** = **(ship's) company**, hands,

together. **3** *informal* any group of people. ▷ *v* **4** serve as a crew member (on). **crew cut** man's closely cropped haircut.

crew² *v old-fashioned* past tense of CROW².

crewel *n* fine worsted yarn used in embroidery.

crib ❶ *n* **1** piece of writing stolen from elsewhere. **2** translation or list of answers used by students, often illicitly. **3** baby's cradle. **4** rack for fodder. **5** short for CRIBBAGE. ▷ *v* **cribbing, cribbed 6** copy (someone's work) dishonestly.

cribbage *n* card game for two to four players.

crick *n* **1** muscle spasm or cramp in the back or neck. ▷ *v* **2** cause a crick in.

cricket¹ *n* outdoor game played with bats, a ball, and wickets by two teams of eleven. **cricketer** *n*.

cricket² *n* chirping insect like a grasshopper.

cried *v* past of CRY.

crier *n* (formerly) official who made public announcements (also **town crier**).

crime ❶ *n* **1** unlawful act. **2** unlawful acts collectively. **3** *informal* disgraceful act. **criminal** *n* **1** person guilty of a crime. ▷ *adj* **2** of crime. **3** *informal* deplorable. **criminalize** *v* **1** make (an activity) criminal. **2** treat (a person) as a criminal. **criminally** *adv* **criminality** *n* **criminology** *n* study of crime. **criminologist** *n*.

crimp *v* **1** fold or press into ridges. **2** curl (hair) tightly.

crimson *adj* deep purplish-red.

cringe ❶ *v* **1** flinch in fear. **2** behave in a submissive or timid way.

crinkle *v, n* wrinkle, crease, or fold. **crinkly** *adj*.

crinoline *n* hooped petticoat.

cripple ❶ *n* **1** person who is lame or disabled. **2** person with a mental or social problem, e.g. *an emotional cripple*. ▷ *v* **3** make lame or disabled. **4** damage (something).

crisis ❶ *n, pl* **-ses 1** crucial stage, turning point. **2** time of extreme trouble.

crisp ❶ *adj* **1** fresh and firm. **2** dry and brittle. **3** clean and neat. **4** (of weather) cold but invigorating. **5** clear and sharp. **6** lively or brisk. ▷ *n* **7** very thin slice of potato fried till crunchy. ▷ *v* **8** make or become crisp. **crisply** *adv* **crispness** *n* **crispy** *adj* **crispier**, **crispiest** hard and crunchy. **crispbread** *n* thin dry biscuit.

crisscross *v* **1** move in or mark with a crosswise pattern. ▷ *adj* **2** (of lines) crossing in different directions.

criterion ❶ *n, pl* **-ria** standard of judgment.

(ship's) complement **2** = **team**, corps, gang, posse, squad **3** *Inf* = **crowd**, band, bunch (*inf*), gang, horde, mob, pack, set

crib *n* **2** = **translation**, key **3** = **cradle**, bassinet, bed, cot **4** = **manger**, rack, stall ▷ *v* **6** = **copy**, cheat, pirate, plagiarize, purloin, steal

crime *n* **1** = **offence**, felony, misdeed, misdemeanour, transgression, trespass, unlawful act, violation **2** = **lawbreaking**, corruption, illegality, misconduct, vice, wrongdoing

criminal *n* **1** = **lawbreaker**, convict, crook (*inf*), culprit, felon, offender, sinner, villain ▷ *adj* **2** = **unlawful**, corrupt, crooked (*inf*), illegal, illicit, immoral, lawless, wicked, wrong **3** *Inf* = **disgraceful**, deplorable, foolish, preposterous, ridiculous, scandalous, senseless

cringe *v* **1** = **shrink**, cower, draw back, flinch, recoil, shy, wince **2** = **grovel**, bootlick (*inf*), crawl, creep, fawn, kowtow, pander to, toady

cripple *v* **3** = **disable**, hamstring, incapacitate, lame, maim, paralyse, weaken **4** = **damage**, destroy, impair, put out of action, put paid to, ruin, spoil

crippled *adj* **3** = **disabled**, handicapped, incapacitated, laid up (*inf*), lame, paralysed

crisis *n* **1** = **critical point**, climax, crunch (*inf*), crux, culmination, height, moment of truth, turning point **2** = **emergency**, deep water, dire straits, meltdown (*inf*), panic stations (*inf*), plight, predicament, trouble

crisp *adj* **1** = **firm**, crispy, crunchy, fresh **2** = **brittle**, crumbly **3** = **clean**, neat, smart, spruce, tidy, trim, well-groomed, well-pressed **4** = **bracing**, brisk, fresh, invigorating, refreshing

criterion *n* = **standard**, bench mark, gauge, measure, principle, rule, test, touchstone, yardstick

critic ❶ *n* **1** professional judge of any of the arts. **2** person who finds fault. **critical** *adj* **1** very important or dangerous. **2** very seriously ill or injured. **3** fault-finding. **4** able to examine and judge carefully. **5** of a critic or criticism. **critically** *adv* **criticism** *n* **1** fault-finding. **2** analysis of a work of art. **criticize** *v* **1** find fault with. **2** analyse. **critique** *n* critical essay.

croak ❶ *v* **1** (of a frog or crow) give a low hoarse cry. **2** utter or speak with a croak. **3** *slang* die. ▷ *n* **4** low hoarse sound. **croaky** *adj* hoarse.

Croatian [kroh-**ay**-shun], **Croat** *adj* **1** of Croatia. ▷ *n* **2** person from Croatia. **3** dialect of Serbo-Croat spoken in Croatia.

crochet [**kroh**-shay] *v* **-cheting**, **-cheted 1** make by looping and intertwining yarn with a hooked needle. ▷ *n* **2** work made in this way.

crock¹ *n* earthenware pot or jar. **crockery** *n* dishes.

crock² *n informal* old or decrepit person or thing.

crocodile *n* **1** large amphibious tropical reptile. **2** a line of people, esp. schoolchildren, walking two by two. **crocodile tears** insincere show of grief.

crocus *n, pl* **-cuses** small plant with yellow, white, or purple flowers in spring.

croft *n* small farm worked by one family in Scotland. **crofter** *n*.

croissant [**krwah**-son] *n* rich flaky crescent-shaped roll.

cromlech *n* circle of prehistoric standing stones.

crone *n* witchlike old woman.

crony *n, pl* **-nies** close friend.

crook ❶ *n* **1** *informal* criminal. **2** bent or curved part. **3** hooked pole. ▷ *v* **4** bend or curve. ▷ *adj* **5** *Aust & NZ slang* unwell, injured **go crook** *Aust & NZ slang* become angry. **crooked** *adj* **1** bent or twisted. **2** set at an angle. **3** *informal* dishonest.

croon ❶ *v* sing, hum, or speak in a soft low tone. **crooner** *n* male singer of sentimental ballads.

crop ❶ *n* **1** cultivated plant. **2** season's total yield of produce. **3** group of things appearing at one time. **4** (handle of) a whip. **5** pouch in a bird's gullet. **6** very short haircut. ▷ *v* **cropping, cropped 7** cut very short. **8** produce or harvest as a crop. **9** (of animals) feed on (grass). **cropper** *n* **come a cropper** *informal* have a disastrous failure or heavy fall. **crop-top** *n* short T-shirt or vest that reveals the wearer's midriff. **crop up** *v informal* happen unexpectedly.

THESAURUS

critic *n* **1** = **judge**, analyst, authority, commentator, connoisseur, expert, mana (*NZ*), pundit, reviewer **2** = **fault-finder**, attacker, detractor, knocker (*inf*)

critical *adj* **1** = **crucial**, all-important, decisive, pivotal, precarious, pressing, serious, urgent, vital **3** = **disparaging**, captious, censorious, derogatory, disapproving, fault-finding, nagging, nit-picking (*inf*), scathing **4** = **analytical**, discerning, discriminating, fastidious, judicious, penetrating, perceptive

criticism *n* **1** = **fault-finding**, bad press, censure, character assassination, disapproval, disparagement, flak (*inf*), stick (*sl*) **2** = **analysis**, appraisal, appreciation, assessment, comment, commentary, critique, evaluation, judgment

criticize *v* **1** = **find fault with**, carp, censure, condemn, disapprove of, disparage, knock (*inf*), put down, slate (*inf*)

croak *v* **1, 2** = **squawk**, caw, grunt, utter *or* speak huskily, wheeze

crook *n* **1** *Inf* = **criminal**, cheat, racketeer, robber, rogue, shark, swindler, thief, villain

crooked *adj* **1** = **bent**, curved, deformed, distorted, hooked, irregular, misshapen, out of shape, twisted, warped, zigzag **2** = **at an angle**, askew, awry, lopsided, off-centre, skewwhiff (*Brit inf*), slanting, squint, uneven **3** *Inf* = **dishonest**, bent (*sl*), corrupt, criminal, fraudulent, illegal, shady (*inf*), underhand, unlawful

croon *v* = **sing**, hum, purr, warble

crop *n* **2** = **produce**, fruits, gathering, harvest, reaping, vintage, yield ▷ *v* **7** = **cut**, clip, lop, pare, prune, shear, snip, trim **9** = **graze**, browse, nibble

crop up *v Inf* = **happen**, appear, arise, emerge, occur, spring up, turn up

croquet [**kroh**-kay] n game played on a lawn in which balls are hit through hoops.

croquette [kroh-**kett**] n fried cake of potato, meat, or fish.

crosier n same as CROZIER.

cross ❶ v 1 move or go across (something). 2 meet and pass. 3 draw two lines across (a cheque) to make it payable only into a bank account. 4 mark with a cross. 5 (with *out*) delete with a cross or lines. 6 place (one's arms or legs) crosswise. 7 make the sign of the cross on (oneself). 8 challenge or oppose. 9 cross-fertilize. ▷ n 10 structure, symbol, or mark of two intersecting lines. 11 such a structure of wood as a means of execution. 12 representation of the Cross as an emblem of Christianity. 13 crossbred animal or plant. 14 mixture of two things. 15 hindrance or misfortune, e.g. *that's my cross to bear.* ▷ adj 16 angry, annoyed. 17 lying or placed across. **the Cross** *Christianity* the cross on which Christ was crucified. **crossing** n 1 place where a street may be crossed safely. 2 place where one thing crosses another. 3 journey across water. **crossly** adv **crossness** n **crossbar** n horizontal bar across goalposts or on a bicycle. **cross-bench** n seat in Parliament for a member belonging to neither the government nor the opposition. **crossbow** n weapon consisting of a bow fixed across a wooden stock. **crossbred** adj bred from two different types of animal or plant. **crossbreed** n crossbred animal or plant. **crosscheck** v check using a different method. **cross-country** adj, adv 1 by way of open country or fields. ▷ n 2 race across open ground. **cross-examine** v *Law* question (a witness for

the opposing side) to check his or her testimony. **cross-examination** n **cross-eyed** adj with eyes looking towards each other. **cross-fertilize** v fertilize (an animal or plant) from one of a different kind. **cross-fertilization** n **crossfire** n gunfire crossing another line of fire. **cross-ply** adj (of a tyre) having the fabric cords in the outer casing running diagonally. **cross-purposes** pl n **at cross-purposes** misunderstanding each other. **cross-reference** n reference within a text to another part. **crossroads** n place where roads intersect. **cross section** 1 (diagram of) a surface made by cutting across something. 2 representative sample. **crosswise** adj, adv 1 across. 2 in the shape of a cross. **crossword puzzle**, **crossword** n puzzle in which words suggested by clues are written into a grid of squares.

crosswalk n *Canad* place marked where pedestrians may cross a road.

crotch n part of the body between the tops of the legs.

crotchet n musical note half the length of a minim.

crotchety adj *informal* bad-tempered.

crouch ❶ v 1 bend low with the legs and body close. ▷ n 2 this position.

croup¹ [**kroop**] n throat disease of children, with a cough.

croup² [**kroop**] n hind quarters of a horse.

croupier [**kroop**-ee-ay] n person who collects bets and pays out winnings at a gambling table in a casino.

crouton n small piece of fried or toasted bread served in soup.

crow¹ n large black bird with a harsh call. **as the crow flies** in a straight line. **crow's feet** wrinkles at the corners of the eyes. **crow's nest** lookout platform at the top of a ship's

──────── THESAURUS ────────

cross v 1 = **go across**, bridge, cut across, extend over, move across, pass over, span, traverse 2 = **intersect**, crisscross, intertwine 5 (with *out*) = **strike off** *or* **out**, blue-pencil, cancel, delete, eliminate, score off *or* out 8 = **oppose**, block, impede, interfere, obstruct, resist 9 = **interbreed**, blend, crossbreed, cross-fertilize, cross-pollinate, hybridize, intercross, mix, mongrelize ▷ n 12 = **crucifix**, rood 14 = **mixture**, amalgam, blend,

combination 15 = **trouble**, affliction, burden, grief, load, misfortune, trial, tribulation, woe, worry ▷ adj 16 = **angry**, annoyed, grumpy, ill-tempered, in a bad mood, irascible, put out, short 17 = **transverse**, crosswise, diagonal, intersecting, oblique

cross-examine v = **question**, grill (*inf*), interrogate, pump, quiz

crouch v 1 = **bend down**, bow, duck, hunch, kneel, squat, stoop

mast **stone the crows!** *Brit & Aust slang*
expression of surprise, dismay, etc.
crow² ❶ *v* **1** (of a cock) make a shrill
squawking sound. **2** boast or gloat.
3 (of a baby) utter cries of pleasure.
crowbar *n* iron bar used as a lever.
crowd ❶ *n* **1** large group of people or
things. **2** particular group of people.
▷ *v* **3** gather together in large numbers.
4 press together in a confined space.
5 fill or occupy fully. **crowdfunding** *n*
practice of funding a project by getting
small donations from many
supporters, often via the internet.
crown ❶ *n* **1** monarch's headdress of
gold and jewels. **2** wreath for the head,
given as an honour. **3** top of the head
or of a hill. **4** artificial cover for a broken
or decayed tooth. **5** former British coin
worth 25 pence. ▷ *v* **6** put a crown on
the head of (someone) to proclaim him
or her monarch. **7** put on or form the
top of. **8** put the finishing touch to (a
series of events). **9** attach a crown to
(a tooth). **10** *informal* hit on the head.
the Crown power of the monarchy.
crown court local criminal court in
England and Wales. **crown jewels**
jewellery used by a sovereign on state
occasions. **crown-of-thorns** *n* starfish
with a spiny outer covering that feeds
on living coral. **crown prince**, **crown
princess** heir to a throne.
crozier *n* bishop's hooked staff.
crucial ❶ *adj* **1** very important. **2** *slang*
excellent. **crucially** *adv*.
crucible *n* pot in which metals are melted.
crucify ❶ *v* **-fying, -fied 1** put to death
by fastening to a cross. **2** *informal*
punish severely. **crucifix** *n* model of
Christ on the Cross. **crucifixion** *n*
crucifying. **the Crucifixion**
Christianity crucifying of Christ.
cruciform *adj* cross-shaped.
crude ❶ *adj* **1** rough and simple.
2 tasteless, vulgar. **3** in a natural or
unrefined state. **crude oil** unrefined
petroleum. **crudely** *adv* **crudity**,
crudeness *n*.
cruel ❶ *adj* **1** delighting in others' pain.
2 causing pain or suffering. **cruelly** *adv*
cruelty *n*.
cruet *n* small container for salt, pepper,
etc., at table.

———————— THESAURUS ————————

crow² *v* **2** = **gloat**, blow one's own
trumpet, boast, brag, exult, skite (*Aust
& NZ*), strut, swagger, triumph
crowd *n* **1** = **multitude**, army, horde,
host, mass, mob, pack, swarm, throng
2 = **group**, bunch (*inf*), circle, clique,
lot, set ▷ *v* **3** = **flock**, congregate,
gather, mass, stream, surge, swarm,
throng **4** = **squeeze**, bundle, congest,
cram, pack, pile
crowded *adj* = **packed**, busy,
congested, cramped, full, jam-packed,
swarming, teeming
crown *n* **1** = **coronet**, circlet, diadem,
tiara **2** = **laurel wreath**, garland,
honour, laurels, prize, trophy, wreath
3 = **high point**, apex, crest, pinnacle,
summit, tip, top ▷ *v* **6** = **honour**,
adorn, dignify, festoon **8** = **cap**, be the
climax *or* culmination of, complete,
finish, perfect, put the finishing touch
to, round off, top **10** *Inf* = **strike**, belt
(*inf*), biff (*sl*), box, cuff, hit over the
head, punch
Crown *n* = **monarchy**, royalty,
sovereignty
crucial *adj* **1** = **vital**, central, critical,
decisive, essential, high-priority,
important, momentous, pivotal,
pressing, urgent
crucify *v* **1** = **execute**, persecute,
torment, torture
crude *adj* **1** = **primitive**, clumsy,
makeshift, rough, rough-and-ready,
rudimentary, unpolished **2** = **vulgar**,
coarse, dirty, gross, indecent, obscene,
scungy (*Aust & NZ inf*), smutty,
tasteless, uncouth **3** = **unrefined**,
natural, raw, unprocessed
crudely *adv* **2** = **vulgarly**, bluntly,
coarsely, impolitely, roughly, rudely,
tastelessly
crudity, crudeness *n* **1** = **roughness**,
clumsiness **2** = **vulgarity**, coarseness,
impropriety, indecency, indelicacy,
obscenity, smuttiness
cruel *adj* **1** = **brutal**, barbarous, callous,
hard-hearted, heartless, inhumane,
malevolent, sadistic, spiteful, unkind,
vicious
cruelly *adv* **1** = **brutally**, barbarously,
callously, heartlessly, in cold blood,
mercilessly, pitilessly, sadistically,
spitefully **2** = **bitterly**, deeply,
fearfully, grievously, monstrously,
severely
cruelty *n* **1** = **brutality**, barbarity,
callousness, depravity, fiendishness,
inhumanity, mercilessness,
ruthlessness, spitefulness

cruise ❶ *n* **1** sail for pleasure. ▷ *v* **2** sail from place to place for pleasure. **3** (of a vehicle) travel at a moderate and economical speed. **cruiser** *n* **1** fast warship. **2** motorboat with a cabin. **cruiserweight** *n* same as LIGHT HEAVYWEIGHT. **cruise missile** low-flying guided missile.

crumb ❶ *n* **1** small fragment of bread or other dry food. **2** small amount. **crumby** *adj* **crumbier**, **crumbiest**.

crumble ❶ *v* **1** break into fragments. **2** fall apart or decay. ▷ *n* **3** pudding of stewed fruit with a crumbly topping. **crumbly** *adj* **-blier**, **-bliest**.

crummy *adj* **-mier**, **-miest** *slang* of poor quality.

crumpet *n* **1** round soft yeast cake, eaten buttered. **2** *slang* sexually attractive women collectively.

crumple ❶ *v* **1** crush, crease. **2** collapse, esp. from shock. **crumpled** *adj*.

crunch ❶ *v* **1** bite or chew with a noisy crushing sound. **2** make a crisp or brittle sound. ▷ *n* **3** crunching sound. **4** *informal* critical moment. **crunchy** *adj*.

crupper *n* strap that passes from the back of a saddle under a horse's tail.

crusade ❶ *n* **1** medieval Christian war to recover the Holy Land from the Muslims. **2** vigorous campaign in favour of a cause. ▷ *v* **3** take part in a crusade. **crusader** *n*.

cruse *n* small earthenware jug or pot.

crush ❶ *v* **1** compress so as to injure, break, or crumple. **2** break into small pieces. **3** defeat or humiliate utterly. ▷ *n* **4** dense crowd. **5** *informal* infatuation. **6** drink made by crushing fruit.

crust ❶ *n* **1** hard outer part of something, esp. bread. **2** solid outer shell of the earth. ▷ *v* **3** cover with or form a crust. **crusty** *adj* **crustier**, **crustiest 1** having a crust. **2** irritable.

crustacean *n* hard-shelled, usu. aquatic animal with several pairs of legs, such as the crab or lobster.

crutch *n* **1** long sticklike support with a rest for the armpit, used by a lame person. **2** person or thing that gives support. **3** crotch.

crux *n, pl* **cruxes** crucial or decisive point.

cry ❶ *v* **crying**, **cried 1** shed tears. **2** call or utter loudly. ▷ *n, pl* **cries 3** fit of weeping. **4** loud utterance. **5** urgent appeal, e.g. *a cry for help*. **crying** *adj* **a crying shame** something demanding immediate attention. **crybaby** *n* person, esp. a child, who cries too readily. **cry off** *v informal* withdraw from an arrangement. **cry out for** *v* need urgently.

cryogenics *n* branch of physics concerned with very low temperatures. **cryogenic** *adj*.

crypt *n* vault under a church, esp. one

cruise *n* **1** = **sail**, boat trip, sea trip, voyage ▷ *v* **2** = **sail**, coast, voyage **3** = **travel along**, coast, drift, keep a steady pace

crumb *n* = **bit**, fragment, grain, morsel, scrap, shred, *soupçon*

crumble *v* **1** = **crush**, fragment, granulate, grind, pound, powder, pulverize **2** = **disintegrate**, collapse, decay, degenerate, deteriorate, fall apart, go to pieces, go to wrack and ruin, tumble down

crumple *v* **1** = **crush**, crease, rumple, screw up, wrinkle **2** = **collapse**, break down, cave in, fall, give way, go to pieces

crunch *v* **1** = **chomp**, champ, chew noisily, grind, munch ▷ *n* **4** *Inf* = **critical point**, crisis, crux, emergency, moment of truth, test

crusade *n* **2** = **campaign**, cause, drive, movement, push

crush *v* **1** = **squash**, break, compress, press, pulverize, squeeze **3 a** = **overcome**, conquer, overpower, overwhelm, put down, quell, stamp out, subdue **b** = **humiliate**, abash, mortify, put down (*sl*), quash, shame ▷ *n* **4** = **crowd**, huddle, jam

crust *n* **1** = **layer**, coating, covering, shell, skin, surface

crusty *adj* **1** = **crispy**, hard **2** = **irritable**, cantankerous, cross, gruff, prickly, short-tempered, testy

cry *v* **1** = **weep**, blubber, shed tears, snivel, sob **2** = **shout**, bawl, bellow, call out, exclaim, howl, roar, scream, shriek, yell ▷ *n* **3** = **weeping**, blubbering, snivelling, sob, sobbing, weep **4** = **shout**, bellow, call, exclamation, howl, roar, scream, screech, shriek, yell **5** = **appeal**, plea

cry off *v Inf* = **back out**, excuse oneself, quit, withdraw

used as a burial place.

cryptic *adj* obscure in meaning, secret. **cryptically** *adv* **cryptography** *n* art of writing in and deciphering codes.

crystal *n* 1 (single grain of) a symmetrically shaped solid formed naturally by some substances. 2 very clear and brilliant glass, usu. with the surface cut in many planes. 3 tumblers, vases, etc., made of crystal. ▷ *adj* 4 bright and clear. **crystalline** *adj* 1 of or like crystal or crystals. 2 clear. **crystallize** *v* 1 make or become definite. 2 form into crystals. **crystallization** *n* **crystal meth** *informal* highly addictive narcotic with dangerous side effects.

Cs *Chemistry* caesium.

CS gas *n* gas causing tears and painful breathing, used to control civil disturbances.

CT Connecticut.

Cu *Chemistry* copper.

cu. cubic.

cub ❶ *n* 1 young wild animal such as a bear or fox. 2 (C-) Cub Scout. ▷ *adj* 3 young or inexperienced, e.g. *a cub reporter*. ▷ *v* **cubbing**, **cubbed** 4 give birth to cubs. **Cub Scout** member of a junior branch of the Scout Association.

cubbyhole *n* small enclosed space or room.

cube *n* 1 object with six equal square sides. 2 number resulting from multiplying a number by itself twice. ▷ *v* 3 cut into cubes. 4 find the cube of (a number). **cubic** *adj* 1 having three dimensions. 2 cube-shaped. 3 involving the cubes of numbers. **cubism** *n* style of art in which objects are represented by geometrical shapes. **cubist** *adj*, *n* **cube root** number whose cube is a given number.

cubicle *n* enclosed part of a large room, screened for privacy.

cubit *n* old measure of length based on the length of the forearm.

cuckold *n* 1 man whose wife has been unfaithful. ▷ *v* 2 be unfaithful to (one's husband).

cuckoo *n* 1 migratory bird with a characteristic two-note call, which lays its eggs in the nests of other birds. ▷ *adj* 2 *informal* insane or foolish. **cuckoo spit** white frothy mass produced on plants by larvae.

cucumber *n* long green-skinned fleshy fruit used in salads.

cud *n* partially digested food which a ruminant brings back into its mouth to chew again. **chew the cud** think deeply.

cuddle ❶ *v*, *n* hug. **cuddle up** *v* lie close to and hug someone. **cuddly** *adj*.

cudgel ❶ *n* short thick stick used as a weapon.

cue¹ ❶ *n* 1 signal to an actor or musician to begin speaking or playing. 2 signal or reminder. ▷ *v* **cueing**, **cued** 3 give a cue to.

cue² *n* 1 long tapering stick used in billiards, snooker, or pool. ▷ *v* **cueing**, **cued** 2 hit (a ball) with a cue.

cuff¹ *n* end of a sleeve. **off the cuff** *informal* without preparation. **cuff link** one of a pair of decorative fastenings for shirt cuffs.

cuff² *v* 1 hit with an open hand. ▷ *n* 2 blow with an open hand.

cuisine [quiz-**zeen**] *n* style of cooking.

cul-de-sac ❶ *n* road with one end blocked off.

culinary *adj* of kitchens or cookery.

cull *v* 1 choose, gather. 2 remove or kill (inferior or surplus animals) from a herd. ▷ *n* 3 culling.

culminate ❶ *v* reach the highest point or climax. **culmination** *n*.

culottes *pl n* women's knee-length trousers cut to look like a skirt.

culpable ❶ *adj* deserving blame. **culpability** *n*.

culprit ❶ *n* person guilty of an offence or misdeed.

━━━━━━━━━━━ THESAURUS ━━━━━━━━━━━

cub *n* 1 = **young**, offspring, whelp

cuddle *v* = **hug**, bill and coo, cosset, embrace, fondle, pet, snuggle

cudgel *n* = **club**, baton, bludgeon, cosh (*Brit*), stick, truncheon

cue¹ *n* = **prompt**, catchword
1 2 = **signal**, hint, reminder, sign, suggestion

cul-de-sac *n* = **dead end**, blind alley

culminate *v* = **end up**, climax, close,

come to a climax, come to a head, conclude, finish, wind up

culmination *n* = **climax**, acme, conclusion, consummation, finale, peak, pinnacle, zenith

culpable *adj* = **blameworthy**, at fault, found wanting, guilty, in the wrong, to blame, wrong

culprit *n* = **offender**, criminal, evildoer, felon, guilty party, miscreant,

cult ❶ n 1 specific system of worship.
2 sect devoted to the beliefs of a cult.
3 devotion to a person, idea, or
activity. 4 popular fashion.

cultivate ❶ v 1 prepare (land) to grow
crops. 2 grow (plants). 3 develop or
improve (something). 4 try to develop
a friendship with (someone).
cultivated adj well-educated.
cultivation n **cultivator** n farm
implement for breaking up soil.

culture ❶ n 1 ideas, customs, and art of
a particular society. 2 particular
society. 3 developed understanding of
the arts. 4 development by special
training. 5 cultivation of plants or
rearing of animals. 6 growth of
bacteria for study. ▷ v 7 grow
(bacteria) for study. **cultural** adj
cultured adj showing good taste or
manners. **cultured pearl** pearl
artificially grown in an oyster shell.

culvert ❶ n drain under a road or railway.

cum prep with, e.g. a kitchen-cum-dining
room.

cumbersome, cumbrous ❶ adj
1 awkward because of size or shape.
2 difficult because of complexity.

cumin, cummin n sweet-smelling
seeds of a Mediterranean plant, used
in cooking.

cummerbund n wide sash worn round
the waist.

cumquat n same as KUMQUAT.

cumulative [kew-myew-la-tiv] adj
increasing steadily.

cumulus [kew-myew-luss] n, pl -li thick
white or dark grey cloud.

cuneiform [kew-nif-form] n, adj
(written in) an ancient system of
writing using wedge-shaped
characters.

cunjevoi n 1 Aust plant of tropical Asia
and Australia with small flowers,
cultivated for its edible rhizome. 2 sea
squirt.

cunning ❶ adj 1 clever at deceiving.
2 ingenious. ▷ n 3 cleverness at
deceiving. 4 ingenuity. **cunningly** adv.

cup ❶ n 1 small bowl-shaped drinking
container with a handle. 2 contents of
a cup. 3 (competition with) a cup-
shaped trophy given as a prize.
4 hollow rounded shape. ▷ v **cupping**,
cupped 5 form (one's hands) into the
shape of a cup. 6 hold in cupped
hands. **cupful** n **cup tie** eliminating
match between two teams in a cup
competition.

cupboard ❶ n piece of furniture or
alcove with a door, for storage.

Cupid n Roman god of love, represented
as a winged boy with a bow and arrow.

cupidity [kew-pid-it-ee] n greed for
money or possessions.

cupola [kew-pol-la] n domed roof or
ceiling.

cupreous adj of copper.

cur n lit 1 mongrel dog. 2 contemptible
person.

curaçao [kew-rah-so] n orange-
flavoured liqueur.

────────────────── THESAURUS ──────────────────

transgressor, wrongdoer
cult n 2 = **sect**, clique, faction, religion,
school 3 = **devotion**, idolization,
worship
cultivate v 1 = **farm**, plant, plough,
tend, till, work 3 = **develop**, foster,
improve, promote, refine 4 = **court**,
dance attendance upon, run after,
seek out
cultivation n 1 = **farming**, gardening,
husbandry, planting, ploughing,
tillage 3 = **development**,
encouragement, fostering,
furtherance, nurture, patronage,
promotion, support
cultural adj = **artistic**, civilizing,
edifying, educational, enlightening,
enriching, humane, liberal
culture n 1 = **civilization**, customs,
lifestyle, mores, society, way of life
3 = **refinement**, education,

enlightenment, good taste,
sophistication, urbanity 5 = **farming**,
cultivation, husbandry
cultured adj = **refined**, educated,
enlightened, highbrow, sophisticated,
urbane, well-informed, well-read
culvert n = **drain**, channel, conduit,
gutter, watercourse
cumbersome adj 1 = **awkward**, bulky,
burdensome, heavy, unmanageable,
unwieldy, weighty
cunning adj 1 = **crafty**, artful, devious,
Machiavellian, sharp, shifty, sly, wily
2 = **skilful**, imaginative, ingenious ▷ n
3 = **craftiness**, artfulness,
deviousness, guile, slyness, trickery
4 = **skill**, artifice, cleverness, ingenuity,
subtlety
cup n 1 = **mug**, beaker, bowl, chalice,
goblet, teacup 3 = **trophy**
cupboard n = **cabinet**, press

curare [kew-**rah**-ree] *n* poisonous resin of a S American tree, used as a muscle relaxant in medicine.

curate *n* clergyman who assists a parish priest. **curacy** [**kew**-rah-see] *n*, *pl* -**cies** work or position of a curate.

curative *adj*, *n* (something) able to cure.

curator *n* person in charge of a museum or art gallery. **curatorship** *n*.

curb ❶ *n* **1** something that restrains. **2** strap under a horse's jaw, used to check it. ▷ *v* **3** control, restrain.

curd *n* coagulated milk, used to make cheese. **curdle** *v* turn into curd, coagulate.

cure ❶ *v* **1** get rid of (an illness or problem). **2** make (someone) well again. **3** preserve by salting, smoking, or drying. ▷ *n* **4** (treatment causing) curing of an illness or person. **5** remedy or solution. **curable** *adj*.

curette *n* **1** surgical instrument for scraping tissue from body cavities. ▷ *v* **2** scrape with a curette. **curettage** *n*.

curfew *n* **1** law ordering people to stay inside their homes after a specific time at night. **2** time set as a deadline by such a law.

Curia *n*, *pl* -**riae** court and government of the Roman Catholic Church.

curie *n* standard unit of radioactivity.

curio [**kew**-ree-oh] *n*, *pl* -**rios** rare or unusual object valued as a collector's item.

curious ❶ *adj* **1** eager to learn or know. **2** eager to find out private details.

3 unusual or peculiar. **curiously** *adv* **curiosity** *n* **1** eagerness to know or find out. **2** *pl* -**ties** rare or unusual object.

curium [**kew**-ree-um] *n* *Chemistry* radioactive element artificially produced from plutonium.

curl ❶ *n* **1** curved piece of hair. **2** curved spiral shape. ▷ *v* **3** make (hair) into curls or (of hair) grow in curls. **4** make into a curved spiral shape. **curly** *adj* **curler** *n* pin or small tube for curling hair. **curling** *n* game like bowls, played with heavy stones on ice.

curlew *n* long-billed wading bird.

curlicue *n* ornamental curl or twist.

curmudgeon *n* bad-tempered person.

currajong *n* same as KURRAJONG.

currant *n* **1** small dried grape. **2** small round berry, such as a redcurrant.

current ❶ *adj* **1** of the immediate present. **2** most recent, up-to-date. **3** commonly accepted. ▷ *n* **4** flow of water or air in one direction. **5** flow of electricity. **6** general trend. **currently** *adv* **currency** *n*, *pl* -**cies** **1** money in use in a particular country. **2** general acceptance or use. **current account** bank account from which money may be drawn at any time by cheque or computerized card.

curriculum *n*, *pl* -**la**, -**lums** all the courses of study offered by a school or college. **curriculum vitae** [**vee**-tie] outline of someone's educational and professional history, prepared for

---

curb *n* **1** = **restraint**, brake, check, control, deterrent, limitation **2** = **rein**, bridle ▷ *v* **3** = **restrain**, check, control, hinder, impede, inhibit, restrict, retard, suppress

cure *v* **1, 2** = **make better**, correct, ease, heal, mend, relieve, remedy, restore **3** = **preserve**, dry, pickle, salt, smoke ▷ *n* **4** = **remedy**, antidote, medicine, nostrum, panacea, treatment

curiosity *n* **1** = **inquisitiveness**, interest, nosiness (*inf*), prying, snooping (*inf*) **2** = **oddity**, freak, novelty, phenomenon, rarity, sight, spectacle, wonder

curious *adj* **1** = **inquiring**, inquisitive, interested, questioning, searching **2** = **inquisitive**, meddling, nosy (*inf*), prying **3** = **unusual**, bizarre, extraordinary, munted (*NZ sl*),

mysterious, novel, odd, peculiar, rare, strange, unexpected

curl *n* **2** = **twist**, coil, kink, ringlet, spiral, whorl ▷ *v* **4** = **twirl**, bend, coil, curve, loop, spiral, turn, twist, wind

curly *adj* = **curling**, crinkly, curled, frizzy, fuzzy, wavy, winding

currency *n* **1** = **money**, coinage, coins, lolly (*Aust & NZ sl*), notes **2** = **acceptance**, circulation, exposure, popularity, prevalence, vogue

current *adj* **1** = **present**, contemporary, present-day **2** = **up-to-date**, fashionable, in fashion, in vogue, trendy (*Brit inf*) **3** = **prevalent**, accepted, common, customary, in circulation, popular, topical, widespread ▷ *n* **4** = **flow**, course, draught, jet, progression, river, stream, tide, undertow **6** = **mood**,

job applications.

- **SPELLING TIP**
- You possibly read the word
- **curriculum** more often than you
- have to write it. It's easy not to
- notice that the only letter that is
- doubled is the r in the middle.

curry[1] n, pl **-ries 1** Indian dish of meat or vegetables in a hot spicy sauce. ▷ v **-rying**, **-ried 2** prepare (food) with mixture of hot spices. **curry powder** mixture of spices for making curry.

curry[2] v **-rying**, **-ried 1** groom (a horse). **2** dress (leather). **curry favour** ingratiate oneself with an important person. **currycomb** n ridged comb for grooming a horse.

curse ❶ v **1** swear (at). **2** ask a supernatural power to cause harm to. ▷ n **3** swearword. **4** (result of) a call to a supernatural power to cause harm to someone. **5** something causing trouble or harm. **cursed** adj **1** under a curse. **2** (foll. by with) having (something unfortunate).

cursive adj, n (handwriting) done with joined letters.

cursor n movable point of light that shows a specific position on a visual display unit.

cursory adj quick and superficial. **cursorily** adv.

curt ❶ adj brief and rather rude. **curtly** adv **curtness** n.

curtail ❶ v **1** cut short. **2** restrict. **curtailment** n.

curtain ❶ n **1** piece of cloth hung at a window or opening as a screen. **2** hanging cloth separating the audience and the stage in a theatre.

3 fall or closing of the curtain at the end, or the rise or opening of the curtain at the start of a theatrical performance. **4** something forming a barrier or screen. ▷ pl **5** informal death, the end. ▷ v **6** provide with curtains. **7** (foll. by off) separate by a curtain. **curtain call** return to the stage by performers to receive applause.

curtsy, curtsey n, pl **-sies**, **-seys 1** woman's gesture of respect made by bending the knees and bowing the head. ▷ v **-sying**, **-sied** or **-seying**, **-seyed 2** make a curtsy.

curve ❶ n **1** continuously bending line with no straight parts. **2** something that curves or is curved. ▷ v **3** form or move in a curve. **curvy** adj **curvier**, **curviest**. **curvaceous** adj informal (of a woman) having a shapely body. **curvature** n curved shape. **curvilinear** adj consisting of or bounded by a curve.

cushion ❶ n **1** bag filled with soft material, to make a seat more comfortable. **2** something that provides comfort or absorbs shock. **3** padded edge of a billiard, snooker, or pool table. ▷ v **4** lessen the effects of. **5** protect from injury or shock.

cushy ❶ adj **cushier**, **cushiest** informal easy, e.g. a cushy job.

cusp n **1** pointed end, esp. on a tooth. **2** Astrology division between houses or signs of the zodiac.

cuss informal ▷ n **1** curse, oath. **2** annoying person. ▷ v **3** swear (at). **cussed** [**kuss**-id] adj informal obstinate.

custard n sweet yellow sauce made

atmosphere, feeling, tendency, trend, undercurrent

curse v **1** = **swear**, blaspheme, cuss (inf), take the Lord's name in vain **2** = **damn**, anathematize, excommunicate ▷ n **3** = **oath**, blasphemy, expletive, obscenity, swearing, swearword **4** = **denunciation**, anathema, ban, excommunication, hoodoo (inf), jinx **5** = **affliction**, bane, hardship, plague, scourge, torment, trouble

cursed adj **1** = **damned**, accursed, bedevilled, doomed, ill-fated

curt adj = **short**, abrupt, blunt, brief, brusque, gruff, monosyllabic, succinct, terse

curtail v **1** = **cut short**, cut back, decrease, diminish, dock, lessen, reduce, shorten, truncate

curtain n **1** = **hanging**, drape (chiefly US)

curve n **1, 2** = **bend**, arc, curvature, loop, trajectory, turn ▷ v **3** = **bend**, arc, arch, coil, hook, spiral, swerve, turn, twist, wind

curved adj = **bent**, arched, bowed, rounded, serpentine, sinuous, twisted

cushion n **1** = **pillow**, beanbag, bolster, hassock, headrest, pad ▷ v **4** = **soften**, dampen, deaden, muffle, stifle, suppress

cushy adj Inf = **easy**, comfortable, soft, undemanding

from milk and eggs.

custody ❶ n **1** keeping safe.
2 imprisonment prior to being tried.
custodial adj **custodian** n person in charge of a public building.

custom ❶ n **1** long-established activity or action. **2** usual habit. **3** regular use of a shop or business. ▷ pl **4** duty charged on imports or exports.
5 government department which collects these. **6** area at a port, airport, or border where baggage and freight are examined for dutiable goods. **customary** adj **1** usual.
2 established by custom. **customarily** adv **customer** n **1** person who buys goods or services. **2** informal person who behaves in a specified way, e.g. a cool customer. **custom-built**, **custom-made** adj made to the specifications of an individual customer.

cut ❶ v **cutting**, **cut 1** open up, penetrate, wound, or divide with a sharp instrument. **2** divide. **3** trim or shape by cutting. **4** abridge, shorten.
5 reduce, restrict. **6** informal hurt the feelings of. **7** pretend not to recognize.
8 informal not attend (classes). **9** grow (teeth) through the gums. **10** call a halt to a shooting sequence in a film.
11 move quickly to another scene in a film. **12** divide (a pack of cards) at random. ▷ n **13** act of cutting.

14 stroke or incision made by cutting.
15 piece cut off. **16** reduction.
17 deletion in a text, film, or play.
18 informal share, esp. of profits.
19 style in which hair or a garment is cut. **cut and dried** informal settled in advance. **cutback** n decrease or reduction. **cut back (on)** v decrease or reduce. **cut in** v **1** interrupt. **2** obstruct another vehicle in overtaking it. **cut off** v **1** separate. **2** stop the supply of. **cut out** v **1** shape by cutting. **2** delete, remove. **3** informal stop doing (something). **4** (of an engine) cease to operate suddenly. **5** be cut out for be suited for or to. **cut-price** adj at a reduced price. **cut up** v **1** cut into pieces. **2** be cut up informal be very upset.

cutaneous [kew-**tane**-ee-uss] adj of the skin.

cute ❶ adj **1** appealing or attractive. ❶
2 informal clever or shrewd. **cutely** adv **cuteness** n.

cuticle [**kew**-tik-kl] n skin at the base of a fingernail or toenail.

cutlass n curved one-edged sword formerly used by sailors.

cutlery n knives, forks, and spoons.
cutler n maker of cutlery.

cutlet n **1** small piece of meat like a chop. **2** flat croquette of chopped meat or fish.

---

custody n **1** = **safekeeping**, care, charge, keeping, protection, supervision **2** = **imprisonment**, confinement, detention, incarceration

custom n **1** = **tradition**, convention, policy, practice, ritual, rule, usage
2 = **habit**, practice, procedure, routine, way, wont **3** = **customers**, patronage, trade ▷ pl **4** = **duty**, import charges, tariff, tax, toll

customary adj = **usual**, accepted, accustomed, common, conventional, established, normal, ordinary, routine, traditional

customer n **1** = **client**, buyer, consumer, patron, purchaser, regular (inf), shopper

cut v **1** = **penetrate**, chop, pierce, score, sever, slash, slice, slit, wound
2 = **divide**, bisect, dissect, slice, split
3 = **shape**, carve, chisel, clip, fashion, form, hew, lop, mow, pare, prune, sculpt, shave, snip, trim, whittle
4 = **abridge**, abbreviate, condense,

curtail, delete, shorten **5** = **reduce**, contract, cut back, decrease, diminish, lower, slash, slim (down) **6** Inf = **hurt**, insult, put down, snub, sting, wound
7 = **ignore**, avoid, cold-shoulder, slight, spurn, turn one's back on ▷ n
14 = **incision**, gash, laceration, nick, slash, slit, stroke, wound
16 = **reduction**, cutback, decrease, fall, lowering, saving **18** Inf = **share**, percentage, piece, portion, section, slice **19** = **style**, fashion, look, shape

cutback n = **reduction**, cut, decrease, economy, lessening, retrenchment

cute adj **1** = **appealing**, attractive, charming, delightful, engaging, lekker (S Afr sl), lovable

cut in v **1** = **interrupt**, break in, butt in, intervene, intrude

cut off v **1** = **separate**, isolate, sever
2 = **interrupt**, disconnect, intercept

cut out v **3** Inf = **stop**, cease, give up, refrain from

cutter *n* **1** person or tool that cuts. **2** any of various small fast boats.

cut-throat ❶ *adj* **1** fierce or relentless. ▷ *n* **2** murderer. **3** razor with a long folding blade.

cutting ❶ *n* **1** article cut from a newspaper or magazine. **2** piece cut from a plant from which to grow a new plant. **3** passage cut through high ground for a road or railway. ▷ *adj* **4** (of a remark) hurtful. **cutting edge** leading position in any field.

cuttlefish *n* squidlike sea mollusc.

CV curriculum vitae.

cwm [**koom**] *n* (in Wales) valley.

cwt hundredweight.

cyanide *n* extremely poisonous chemical compound.

cyanosis *n* blueness of the skin, caused by a deficiency of oxygen in the blood.

cyber- *combining form* computers, e.g. *cyberspace.*

cyberbully *n* person who bullies another person via electronic technology such as mobile phones and social media. **cyberbullying** *n.*

cybernetics *n* branch of science in which electronic and mechanical systems are studied and compared to biological systems.

cyberspace *n* place said to contain all the data stored in computers.

cybersquatting *n* registering an internet domain name belonging to another person in the hope of selling it to them for a profit. **cybersquatter** *n.*

cyclamen [**sik**-la-men] *n* plant with red, pink, or white flowers.

cycle ❶ *v* **1** ride a bicycle. ▷ *n* **2** bicycle. **3** *US* motorcycle. **4** complete series of recurring events. **5** time taken for one such series. **6** single complete movement in an electrical, electronic, or mechanical process. **7** set of plays, songs, or poems about a figure or event. **cyclical**, **cyclic** *adj* occurring in cycles. **cyclist** *n* person who rides a bicycle.

cyclone *n* violent wind moving clockwise round a central area.

cyclotron *n* apparatus that accelerates charged particles by means of a strong vertical magnetic field.

cygnet *n* young swan.

cylinder *n* **1** solid or hollow body with straight sides and circular ends. **2** container with this shape. **3** chamber within which the piston moves in an internal-combustion engine. **cylindrical** *adj.*

cymbal *n* percussion instrument consisting of a brass plate which is struck against another or hit with a stick.

Cymric [**kim**-rik] *adj* Welsh.

cynic ❶ [**sin**-ik] *n* person who believes that people always act selfishly. **cynical** *adj* **cynically** *adv* **cynicism** *n.*

cynosure [**sin**-oh-zyure] *n* centre of attention.

cypher *n* same as CIPHER.

cypress *n* evergreen tree with dark green leaves.

Cypriot *n, adj* (person) from Cyprus.

cyst [**sist**] *n* (abnormal) sac in the body containing fluid or soft matter. **cystic** *adj* **cystitis** [siss-**tite**-iss] *n* inflammation of the bladder.

cytology [site-**ol**-a-jee] *n* study of plant and animal cells. **cytological** *adj* **cytologist** *n.*

cytoplasm *n* protoplasm of a cell excluding the nucleus.

czar [**zahr**] *n* same as TSAR.

Czech *n, adj* **1** (person) from the Czech Republic. ▷ *n* **2** language of the Czech Republic.

———————————————————— THESAURUS ————————————

cut-throat *adj* **1** = **competitive**, dog-eat-dog, fierce, relentless, ruthless, unprincipled ▷ *n* **2** = **murderer**, assassin, butcher, executioner, hit man (*sl*), killer

cutting *adj* **4** = **hurtful**, barbed, caustic, malicious, sarcastic, scathing, vitriolic, wounding

cycle *n* **4, 5** = **era**, circle, period, phase, revolution, rotation

cynic *n* = **sceptic**, doubter, misanthrope, misanthropist, pessimist, scoffer

Dd

d *Physics* density.

D 1 *Chemistry* deuterium. **2** the Roman numeral for 500.

d. 1 *Brit* (before decimalization) penny. **2** died.

dab¹ ❶ *v* **dabbing, dabbed 1** pat lightly. **2** apply with short tapping strokes. ▷ *n* **3** small amount of something soft or moist. **4** light stroke or tap. **dab hand** *informal* person who is particularly good at something.

dab² *n* small flatfish with rough scales.

dabble ❶ *v* **1** be involved in something superficially. **2** splash about. **dabbler** *n*.

dace *n* small freshwater fish.

dacha *n* country cottage in Russia.

dachshund *n* dog with a long body and short legs.

dad *n informal* father.

Dada, Dadaism *n* early 20th-century artistic movement that systematically used arbitrary and absurd concepts. **Dadaist** *n, adj.*

daddy *n, pl* **-dies** *informal* father.

daddy-longlegs *n informal* crane fly.

dado [**day**-doe] *n, pl* **-does, -dos** lower part of an interior wall, below a rail, decorated differently from the upper part.

daffodil *n* yellow trumpet-shaped flower that blooms in spring.

daft ❶ *adj informal* foolish or crazy.

dagga *n S Afr informal* cannabis.

dagger ❶ *n* short knifelike weapon with a pointed blade.

daguerreotype [dag-**gair**-oh-type] *n* type of early photograph produced on chemically treated silver.

dahlia [**day**-lya] *n* brightly coloured garden flower.

Dáil Éireann [**doil air**-in], **Dáil** *n* lower chamber of parliament in the Irish Republic.

daily ❶ *adj* **1** occurring every day or every weekday. ▷ *adv* **2** every day. ▷ *n, pl* **-lies 3** daily newspaper. **4** *Brit informal* person who cleans other people's houses.

dainty ❶ *adj* **-tier, -tiest 1** delicate or elegant. ▷ *n, pl* **-ties 2** small cake or sweet. **daintily** *adv*.

daiquiri [**dak**-eer-ee] *n* iced drink containing rum, lime juice, and sugar.

dairy *n, pl* **dairies 1** place for the processing or sale of milk and its products. **2** *NZ* small shop selling groceries and milk often outside normal trading hours. ▷ *adj* **3** of milk or its products. **dairy cattle** cows kept mainly for their milk. **dairy farm** farm where cows are kept mainly for their milk. **dairymaid** *n* (formerly) woman employed to milk cows. **dairyman** *n* man employed to look after cows.

dais [**day**-iss] *n* raised platform in a hall, used by a speaker.

daisy *n, pl* **-sies** small wild flower with a yellow centre and white petals. **daisy chain** string of daisies joined together by their stems to make a necklace. **daisywheel** *n* flat disc in a word processor with radiating spokes for printing letters.

Dalai Lama *n* chief lama and (until 1959) ruler of Tibet.

dale *n* (esp. in N England) valley.

dally *v* **-lying, -lied 1** waste time. **2** (foll. by *with*) deal frivolously (with). **dalliance** *n* flirtation.

Dalmatian *n* large dog with a white coat and black spots.

dam¹ ❶ *n* **1** barrier built across a river to create a lake. **2** lake created by this.

THESAURUS

dab¹ *v* **1** = **pat**, tap, touch **2** = **daub**, stipple ▷ *n* **3** = **spot**, bit, drop, pat, smudge, speck **4** = **pat**, flick, stroke, tap, touch

dabble *v* **1** = **play at**, dip into, potter, tinker, trifle (with) **2** = **splash**, dip

daft *adj Inf* = **foolish**, absurd, asinine, crackpot (*inf*), crazy, idiotic, insane, silly, stupid, witless

dagger *n* = **knife**, bayonet, dirk, stiletto

daily *adj* **1** = **everyday**, diurnal, quotidian ▷ *adv* **2** = **every day**, day by day, once a day

dainty *adj* **1** = **delicate**, charming, elegant, exquisite, fine, graceful, neat, petite, pretty

dam¹ *n* **1** = **barrier**, barrage, embankment, obstruction, wall

▷ *v* **damming**, **dammed 3** build a dam across (a river).

dam² *n* mother of an animal such as a sheep or horse.

damage ❶ *v* **1** harm, spoil. ▷ *n* **2** harm to a person or thing. **3** *informal* cost, e.g. *what's the damage?* ▷ *pl* **4** money awarded as compensation for injury or loss.

damask *n* fabric with a pattern woven into it, used for tablecloths etc.

dame ❶ *n* **1** *slang* woman. **2 (D-)** title of a woman who has been awarded the OBE or another order of chivalry.

damn ❶ *interj* **1** *slang* exclamation of annoyance. ▷ *adv, adj* **2** (also **damned**) *slang* extreme(ly). ▷ *v* **3** condemn as bad or worthless. **4** (of God) condemn to hell. **damnable** *adj* annoying. **damnably** *adv* **damnation** *interj, n* **damning** *adj* proving or suggesting guilt, e.g. *a damning report*.

damp ❶ *adj* **1** slightly wet. ▷ *n* **2** slight wetness, moisture. ▷ *v* (also **dampen**) **3** make damp. **4** (foll. by *down*) reduce the intensity of (feelings or actions). **damply** *adv* **dampness** *n* **damper** *n* **1** movable plate to regulate the draught in a fire. **2** pad in a piano that deadens the vibration of each string. **put a damper on** have a depressing or inhibiting effect on. **damp course**, **damp-proof course** layer of water-resistant material built into the foot of a wall to stop moisture rising.

damsel *n* old-fashioned young woman.

damson *n* small blue-black plumlike fruit.

dan *n Martial arts* **1** any of the 10 black-belt grades of proficiency. **2** competitor entitled to a dan grading.

dance ❶ *v* **1** move the feet and body rhythmically in time to music. **2** perform (a particular dance). **3** skip or leap. **4** move rhythmically. ▷ *n* **5** series of steps and movements in time to music. **6** social meeting arranged for dancing. **dancer** *n*.

D and C *n Medical* dilatation and curettage: a minor operation in which the neck of the womb is stretched and the lining of the womb scraped, to clear the womb or remove tissue for diagnosis.

dandelion *n* yellow-flowered wild plant.

dander *n* **get one's dander up** *slang* become angry.

dandle *v* move (a child) up and down on one's knee.

dandruff *n* loose scales of dry dead skin shed from the scalp.

dandy *n, pl* **-dies 1** man who is overconcerned with the elegance of his appearance. ▷ *adj* **-dier, -diest 2** *informal* very good. **dandified** *adj*.

Dane *n* person from Denmark. **Danish** *n, adj* (language) of Denmark. **Danish blue** strong white cheese with blue veins. **Danish pastry** iced puff

──────────────── THESAURUS ────────────────

▷ *v* **3** = **block up**, barricade, hold back, obstruct, restrict

damage *v* **1** = **harm**, hurt, impair, injure, ruin, spoil, weaken, wreck ▷ *n* **2** = **harm**, destruction, detriment, devastation, hurt, injury, loss, suffering **3** *Inf* = **cost**, bill, charge, expense ▷ *pl* **4** = **compensation**, fine, reimbursement, reparation, satisfaction

damaging *adj* = **harmful**, deleterious, detrimental, disadvantageous, hurtful, injurious, ruinous

dame *n* **2** (with cap.) = **noblewoman**, baroness, dowager, *grande dame*, lady, peeress

damn *v* **3** = **criticize**, blast, censure, condemn, denounce, put down **4** = **sentence**, condemn, doom

damnation *n* **4** = **condemnation**, anathema, damning, denunciation, doom

damned *adj* **3** = **detestable**, confounded, hateful, infernal, loathsome **4** = **doomed**, accursed, condemned, lost

damp *adj* **1** = **moist**, clammy, dank, dewy, drizzly, humid, soggy, sopping, wet ▷ *n* **2** = **moisture**, dampness, dankness, drizzle ▷ *v* **3** = **moisten**, dampen, wet **4** (foll. by *down*) = **curb**, allay, check, diminish, dull, inhibit, lessen, moderate, pour cold water on, reduce, restrain, stifle

damper *n* **put a damper on** = **discourage**, be a wet blanket (*inf*), hinder, pour cold water on (*inf*), restrain

dance *v* **1** = **prance**, jig, trip, whirl **3** = **skip**, hop ▷ *n* **6** = **ball**, disco, discotheque, hop (*inf*), knees-up (*Brit inf*), social

pastry filled with fruit, almond paste, etc.

danger ❶ *n* **1** possibility of being injured or killed. **2** person or thing that may cause injury or harm. **3** likelihood that something unpleasant will happen. **danger money** extra money paid for doing dangerous work. **dangerous** *adj* **dangerously** *adv.*

dangle ❶ *v* **1** hang loosely. **2** display as an enticement.

dank *adj* unpleasantly damp and chilly.

dapper ❶ *adj* (of a man) neat in appearance and slight in build.

dappled *adj* **1** marked with spots of a different colour. **2** covered in patches of light and shadow. **dapple-grey** *n* horse with a grey coat and darker coloured spots.

Darby and Joan *n* happily married elderly couple. **Darby and Joan Club** club for elderly people.

dare ❶ *v* **1** be courageous enough to try (to do something). **2** challenge to do something risky. ▷ *n* **3** challenge to do something risky. **I dare say** probably. **daring** *adj* **1** willing to take risks. ▷ *n* **2** courage to do dangerous things.

daringly *adv* **daredevil** *adj, n* recklessly bold (person).

dark ❶ *adj* **1** having little or no light. **2** (of a colour) reflecting little light. **3** (of hair or skin) brown or black. **4** gloomy, sad. **5** sinister, evil. **6** secret, e.g. *keep it dark*. ▷ *n* **7** absence of light. **8** night. **in the dark** not knowing, uninformed. **darkly** *adv* **darkness** *n* **darken** *v* **dark age** period of ignorance or barbarism. **Dark Ages** period of European history between 500 and 1000 AD. **dark horse** person about whom little is known. **darkroom** *n* darkened room for processing photographic film.

darling ❶ *n* **1** much-loved person. **2** favourite, e.g. *the darling of the financial press*. ▷ *adj* **3** much-loved.

darn¹ ❶ *v* **1** mend (a garment) with a series of interwoven stitches. ▷ *n* **2** patch of darned work.

darn² *interj, adv, adj, v* euphemistic damn.

dart ❶ *n* **1** small narrow pointed missile that is thrown or shot, esp. in the game of darts. **2** sudden quick movement. **3** tapered tuck made in dressmaking. ▷ *pl* **4** game in which darts are thrown at a circular

---

THESAURUS

dancer *n* = **ballerina**, Terpsichorean

danger *n* **1, 2** = **peril**, hazard, jeopardy, menace, pitfall, risk, threat

dangerous *adj* = **perilous**, breakneck, chancy (*inf*), hazardous, insecure, precarious, risky, safe

dangerously *adv* = **perilously**, alarmingly, hazardously, precariously, recklessly, riskily, unsafely

dangle *v* **1** = **hang**, flap, hang down, sway, swing, trail

dapper *adj* = **neat**, natty (*inf*), smart, soigné, spruce, spry, trim, well-groomed, well turned out

dare *v* **1** = **risk**, hazard, make bold, presume, venture **2** = **challenge**, defy, goad, provoke, taunt, throw down the gauntlet ▷ *n* **3** = **challenge**, provocation, taunt

daredevil *adj* = **daring**, adventurous, audacious, bold, death-defying, madcap, reckless ▷ *n* = **adventurer**, desperado, exhibitionist, madcap, show-off (*inf*), stunt man

daring *adj* **1** = **brave**, adventurous, audacious, bold, daredevil, fearless, intrepid, reckless, venturesome ▷ *n* **2** = **bravery**, audacity, boldness,

bottle (*Brit sl*), courage, fearlessness, nerve (*inf*), pluck, temerity

dark *adj* **1** = **dim**, dingy, murky, shadowy, shady, sunless, unlit **3** = **brunette**, black, dark-skinned, dusky, ebony, sable, swarthy **4** = **gloomy**, bleak, dismal, grim, morose, mournful, sad, sombre **5** = **evil**, foul, infernal, sinister, vile, wicked **6** = **secret**, concealed, hidden, mysterious ▷ *n* **7** = **darkness**, dimness, dusk, gloom, murk, obscurity, semi-darkness **8** = **night**, evening, nightfall, night-time, twilight

darken *v* = **make dark**, blacken, dim, obscure, overshadow

darkness *n* = **dark**, blackness, duskiness, gloom, murk, nightfall, shade, shadows

darling *n* **1** = **beloved**, dear, dearest, love, sweetheart, truelove ▷ *adj* **3** = **beloved**, adored, cherished, dear, precious, treasured

darn¹ *v* **1** = **mend**, cobble up, patch, repair, sew up, stitch ▷ *n* **2** = **mend**, invisible repair, patch, reinforcement

dart *v* **5** = **dash**, fly, race, run, rush, shoot, spring, sprint, tear

d

numbered board. ▷ v **5** move or direct quickly and suddenly.

Darwinism n theory of the origin of animal and plant species by evolution. **Darwinian**, **Darwinist** adj, n.

dash ❶ v **1** move quickly. **2** hurl or crash. **3** frustrate (someone's hopes). ▷ n **4** sudden quick movement. **5** small amount. **6** mixture of style and courage. **7** punctuation mark (–) indicating a change of subject. **8** longer symbol used in Morse code. **dashing** adj stylish and attractive. **dashboard** n instrument panel in a vehicle. **dash off** v write or produce quickly.

dastardly adj wicked and cowardly.

dasyure [**dass**-ee-your] n small marsupial of Australia, New Guinea, and adjacent islands.

data ❶ n **1** information consisting of observations, measurements, or facts. **2** numbers, digits, etc., stored by a computer. **data base** store of information that can be easily handled by a computer. **data capture** process for converting information into a form that can be handled by a computer. **data processing** series of operations performed on data, esp. by a computer, to extract or interpret information.

- **USAGE NOTE**
- *Data* is a Latin plural word but it is
- generally used as a singular word
- in English.

date¹ ❶ n **1** specified day of the month. **2** particular day or year when an

event happened. **3** *informal* appointment, esp. with a person of the opposite sex. **4** *informal* person with whom one has a date. ▷ v **5** mark with the date. **6** assign a date of occurrence to. **7** become old-fashioned. **8** (foll. by *from*) originate from, e.g. *the church dates from Norman times*. **dated** adj old-fashioned. **dateline** n *Journalism* information about the place and time a story was written, placed at the top of the article. **Date Line** line, approx. equal to 180°, on the east side of which the date is one day earlier than on the west.

date² n dark-brown sweet-tasting fruit of the date palm. **date palm** tall palm grown in tropical regions for its fruit.

dative n (in certain languages) the form of the noun that expresses the indirect object.

datum ❶ n, pl **data** single piece of information in the form of a fact or statistic.

daub ❶ v smear or spread quickly or clumsily.

daughter n **1** female child. **2** woman who comes from a certain place or is connected with a certain thing, e.g. *daughter of the Catholic church*. **daughterly** adj **daughter-in-law** n, pl **daughters-in-law** son's or daughter's wife.

daunting ❶ adj intimidating or worrying. **dauntless** adj fearless.

dauphin [**doe**-fan] n (formerly) eldest son of the king of France.

THESAURUS

dash v **1** = **rush**, bolt, fly, hurry, race, run, speed, sprint, tear **2** = **throw**, cast, fling, hurl, slam, sling **3** = **frustrate**, blight, foil, ruin, spoil, thwart, undo ▷ n **4** = **rush**, dart, race, run, sortie, sprint, spurt **5** = **little**, bit, drop, hint, pinch, soupçon, sprinkling, tinge, touch **6** = **style**, brio, élan, flair, flourish, panache, spirit, verve

dashing adj = **stylish**, debonair, elegant, flamboyant, jaunty, showy, smart, sporty

data n **1** = **information**, details, facts, figures, statistics

date¹ n **3** *Inf* = **appointment**, assignation, engagement, meeting, rendezvous, tryst **4** *Inf* = **partner**, escort, friend ▷ v **6** = **put a date on**,

assign a date to, fix the period of **7** = **become old-fashioned**, be dated, show one's age **8** (foll. by *from*) = **come from**, bear a date of, belong to, exist from, originate in

dated adj = **old-fashioned**, obsolete, old hat, outdated, outmoded, out of date, passé, unfashionable

daub v = **smear**, coat, cover, paint, plaster, slap on (*inf*)

daunting adj = **intimidating**, alarming, demoralizing, disconcerting, discouraging, disheartening, frightening, off-putting (*Brit inf*), unnerving

dauntless adj = **fearless**, bold, doughty, gallant, indomitable, intrepid, resolute, stouthearted, undaunted, unflinching

d

davenport n 1 small writing table with drawers. 2 Aust, US & Canad large couch.

davit [**dav**-vit] n crane, usu. one of a pair, at a ship's side, for lowering and hoisting a lifeboat.

Davy Jones's locker n the sea, considered as a grave for sailors.

Davy lamp n miner's lamp designed to prevent it from igniting gas.

dawdle ❶ v walk slowly, lag behind. **dawdler** n.

dawn ❶ n 1 daybreak. 2 beginning (of something). ▷ v 3 begin to grow light. 4 begin to develop or appear. 5 (foll. by on) become apparent (to).

day ❶ n 1 period of 24 hours. 2 period of light between sunrise and sunset. 3 part of a day occupied with regular activity, esp. work. 4 period or point in time. 5 time of success. **daybreak** n time in the morning when light first appears. **day centre** place providing meals etc., where elderly or disabled people can spend the day. **daydream** n 1 pleasant fantasy indulged in while awake. ▷ v 2 indulge in idle fantasy. **daydreamer** n **daylight** n light from the sun. **daylight robbery** informal blatant overcharging. **daylight-saving time** time set one hour ahead of the local standard time, to provide an extra hour of light in the evening in summer.

day release system in which workers go to college one day a week. **day return** reduced fare for a journey to a place and back again on the same day. **day room** communal living-room in a hospital or similar institution. **day-to-day** adj routine.

daze ❶ v 1 stun, by a blow or shock. ▷ n 2 state of confusion or shock. **dazed** adj.

dazzle ❶ v 1 impress greatly. 2 blind temporarily by sudden excessive light. ▷ n 3 bright light that dazzles. **dazzling** adj **dazzlingly** (cut) adv.

dB, db decibel(s).

DC 1 direct current. 2 District of Columbia.

DD Doctor of Divinity.

D-day n day selected for the start of some operation, orig. the Allied invasion of Europe in 1944.

DDT n kind of insecticide.

DE Delaware.

de- prefix indicating: 1 removal, e.g. dethrone. 2 reversal, e.g. declassify. 3 departure, e.g. decamp.

deacon n Christianity 1 ordained minister ranking immediately below a priest. 2 (in some Protestant churches) lay official who assists the minister.

deactivate v make (a bomb etc.) harmless or inoperative.

dead ❶ adj 1 no longer alive. 2 no longer in use. 3 numb, e.g. my leg has

---

THESAURUS

dawdle v = **waste time**, dally, delay, drag one's feet or heels, hang about, idle, loaf, loiter, trail

dawn n 1 = **daybreak**, cockcrow, crack of dawn, daylight, morning, sunrise, sunup 2 = **beginning**, advent, birth, emergence, genesis, origin, rise, start ▷ v 3 = **grow light**, break, brighten, lighten 4 = **begin**, appear, develop, emerge, originate, rise, unfold 5 (foll. by on) = **hit**, become apparent, come into one's head, come to mind, occur, register (inf), strike

day n 1 = **twenty-four hours** 2 = **daytime**, daylight 4 = **point in time**, date, time 5 = **time**, age, epoch, era, heyday, period, zenith

daybreak n = **dawn**, break of day, cockcrow, crack of dawn, first light, morning, sunrise, sunup

daydream n 1 = **fantasy**, dream, fancy, imagining, pipe dream, reverie, wish ▷ v 2 = **fantasize**, dream, envision, fancy, imagine, muse

daylight n = **sunlight**, light of day, sunshine

daze v 1 = **stun**, benumb, numb, paralyse, shock, stupefy ▷ n 2 = **shock**, bewilderment, confusion, distraction, stupor, trance, trancelike state

dazed adj = **shocked**, bewildered, confused, disorientated, dizzy, muddled, punch-drunk, staggered, stunned

dazzle v 1 = **impress**, amaze, astonish, bowl over (inf), overpower, overwhelm, take one's breath away 2 = **blind**, bedazzle, blur, confuse, daze ▷ n 3 = **splendour**, brilliance, glitter, magnificence, razzmatazz (sl), sparkle

dazzling adj 1 = **splendid**, brilliant, glorious, sensational (inf), stunning, virtuoso 2 = **brilliant**, glittering, scintillating, sparkling

dead adj 1 = **deceased**, defunct, departed, extinct, late, passed away, perished 2 = **not working**, inactive,

gone dead. **4** complete, absolute, e.g. *dead silence.* **5** *informal* very tired. **6** (of a place) lacking activity. ▷ *n* **7** period during which coldness or darkness is most intense, e.g. *in the dead of night.* ▷ *adv* **8** extremely. **9** suddenly, e.g. *I stopped dead.* **the dead** dead people. **dead set** firmly decided, e.g. *he really was dead set against it.* **deadbeat** *n informal* lazy useless person. **dead beat** *informal* exhausted. **dead end** **1** road with one end blocked off. **2** situation in which further progress is impossible. **dead heat** tie for first place between two participants in a contest. **deadline** *n* time limit. **deadlock** *n* point in a dispute at which no agreement can be reached. **deadlocked** *adj* **dead loss** *informal* useless person or thing. **deadly** *adj* likely to cause death. **deadpan** *adj*, *adv* showing no emotion or expression. **dead reckoning** method of establishing one's position using the distance and direction travelled. **dead weight** heavy weight. **dead wood** *informal* useless people or things.

deaden ❶ *v* make less intense.

deadly ❶ *adj* **-lier, -liest** **1** likely to cause death. **2** *informal* extremely boring. ▷ *adv* **3** extremely. **deadly**

nightshade plant with poisonous black berries.

deaf ❶ *adj* unable to hear. **deaf to** refusing to listen to or take notice of. **deafen** *v* make deaf, esp. temporarily. **deafness** *n* **deaf-mute** *n* person unable to hear or speak.

- ● **USAGE NOTE**
- ● The use of *the deaf, the disabled,* etc.
- ● can be offensive and should be
- ● avoided. Instead you should talk
- ● about *deaf people, disabled people,*
- ● etc.

deal¹ ❶ *n* **1** agreement or transaction. **2** kind of treatment, e.g. *a fair deal.* **3** large amount. ▷ *v* **dealing, dealt** [delt] **4** inflict (a blow) on. **5** *Cards* give out (cards) to the players. **dealer** *n* **1** person whose business involves buying and selling. **2** *slang* person who sells illegal drugs. **3** *Cards* person who gives out the cards. **dealings** *pl n* transactions or business relations. **deal in** *v* buy or sell (goods). **deal out** *v* distribute. **deal with** *v* **1** take action on. **2** be concerned with.

deal² *n* plank of fir or pine wood.

dean *n* **1** chief administrative official of a college or university faculty. **2** chief administrator of a cathedral. **deanery** *n, pl* **-eries** **1** office or residence of a

━━━━━━━━━━━━━━ THESAURUS ━━━━━━━━━━━

inoperative, stagnant, unemployed, useless **3** = **numb**, inert, paralysed **4** = **total**, absolute, complete, outright, thorough, unqualified, utter **5** *Inf* = **exhausted**, dead beat (*inf*), spent, tired, worn out **6** = **boring**, dull, flat, uninteresting ▷ *n* **7** = **middle**, depth, midst ▷ *adv* **8** = **exactly**, absolutely, completely, directly, entirely, totally

deaden *v* = **reduce**, alleviate, blunt, cushion, diminish, dull, lessen, muffle, smother, stifle, suppress, weaken

deadline *n* = **time limit**, cutoff point, limit, target date

deadlock *n* = **impasse**, dead heat, draw, gridlock, stalemate, standoff, standstill, tie

deadly *adj* **1** = **lethal**, dangerous, death-dealing, deathly, fatal, malignant, mortal **2** *Inf* = **boring**, dull, mind-numbing, monotonous, tedious, tiresome, uninteresting, wearisome

deadpan *adj* = **expressionless**, blank,

impassive, inexpressive, inscrutable, poker-faced, straight-faced

deaf *adj* = **hard of hearing**, stone deaf, without hearing **deaf to** = **oblivious**, indifferent, unconcerned, unhearing, unmoved

deafen *v* = **make deaf**, din, drown out, split *or* burst the eardrums

deafening *adj* = **ear-piercing**, booming, ear-splitting, overpowering, piercing, resounding, ringing, thunderous

deal¹ *n* **1** = **agreement**, arrangement, bargain, contract, pact, transaction, understanding **3** = **amount**, degree, extent, portion, quantity, share

dealer *n* **1** = **trader**, merchant, purveyor, supplier, tradesman, wholesaler

deal in *v* = **sell**, bargain, buy and sell, do business, negotiate, stock, trade, traffic

deal out *v* = **distribute**, allot, apportion, assign, dispense, dole out, give, mete out, share

dean. **2** parishes of a dean.

dear ⊕ *n* **1** someone regarded with affection. ▷ *adj* **2** much-loved. **3** costly. **dearly** *adv* **dearness** *n*.

dearth ⊕ [**dirth**] *n* inadequate amount, scarcity.

death ⊕ *n* **1** permanent end of life in a person or animal. **2** instance of this. **3** ending, destruction. **deathly** *adj*, *adv* like death, e.g. *a deathly silence*; *deathly pale*. **deathless** *adj* everlasting, because of fine qualities. **deathbed** *n* bed where a person is about to die or has just died. **death certificate** document signed by a doctor certifying the death of a person and giving the cause of death if known. **death duty** former name for INHERITANCE TAX. **death knell** something that heralds death or destruction. **death mask** cast taken from the face of a person who has recently died. **death row** *US* part of a prison where convicts awaiting execution are held. **death's-head** *n* human skull or a representation of one. **deathtrap** *n* place or vehicle considered very unsafe. **death warrant** official authorization for a death sentence. **deathwatch beetle** beetle that bores into wood and makes a tapping sound.

deb *n informal* debutante.

debacle ⊕ [day-**bah**-kl] *n* disastrous failure, collapse, or defeat.

debar *v* prevent, bar.

debase ⊕ *v* lower in value, quality, or character. **debasement** *n*.

debate ⊕ *n* **1** discussion. **2** formal discussion of a proposition, at the end of which people vote on whether to accept it. ▷ *v* **3** discuss formally. **4** consider (a course of action). **debatable** *adj* not absolutely certain.

debauch ⊕ [dib-**bawch**] *v* make (someone) bad or corrupt, esp. sexually. **debauched** *adj* immoral, sexually corrupt. **debauchery** *n*.

debenture *n* long-term bond bearing fixed interest, issued by a company or a government agency.

debilitate *v* weaken, make feeble. **debilitation** *n* **debility** *n* weakness, infirmity.

debit *n* **1** acknowledgment of a sum owing by entry on the left side of an account. ▷ *v* **debiting**, **debited 2** charge (an account) with a debt. **3** record as a debit. **debit card** card that allows users to pay for goods and services from a current bank or building society account.

debonair ⊕ *adj* (of a man) charming and refined.

debouch *v* move out from a narrow place to a wider one.

debrief ⊕ *v* receive a report from (a soldier, diplomat, etc.) after an event. **debriefing** *n*.

debris ⊕ [**deb**-ree] *n* fragments of something destroyed.

deal with *v* **1** = **handle**, attend to, cope with, get to grips with, manage, see to, take care of, treat **2** = **be concerned with**, consider

dear *n* **1** = **beloved**, angel, darling, loved one, precious, treasure ▷ *adj* **2** = **beloved**, cherished, close, favourite, intimate, precious, prized, treasured **3** = **expensive**, at a premium, costly, high-priced, overpriced, pricey (*inf*)

dearth *n* = **scarcity**, deficiency, inadequacy, insufficiency, lack, paucity, poverty, shortage, want

death *n* **1, 2** = **dying**, demise, departure, end, exit, passing **3** = **destruction**, downfall, extinction, finish, ruin, undoing

deathly *adj* = **deathlike**, ghastly, grim, pale, pallid, wan

debacle *n* = **disaster**, catastrophe, collapse, defeat, fiasco, reversal, rout

debase *v* = **degrade**, cheapen, devalue, lower, reduce

debatable *adj* = **doubtful**, arguable, controversial, dubious, moot, problematical, questionable, uncertain

debate *n* **1** = **discussion**, argument, contention, controversy, dispute ▷ *v* **3** = **discuss**, argue, dispute, question **4** = **consider**, deliberate, ponder, reflect, ruminate, weigh

debauchery *n* = **depravity**, dissipation, dissoluteness, excess, indulgence, intemperance, lewdness, overindulgence

debonair *adj* = **elegant**, charming, courteous, dashing, refined, smooth, suave, urbane, well-bred

debrief *v* = **interrogate**, cross-examine, examine, probe, question, quiz

debris *n* = **remains**, bits, detritus, fragments, rubble, ruins, waste, wreckage

debt ❶ n something owed, esp. money. **bad debt** debt that is unlikely to be repaid. **debt of honour** debt that is morally but not legally binding. **in debt** owing money. **debtor** n.

debug v 1 informal find and remove defects in (a computer program). 2 remove concealed microphones from (a room or telephone).

debunk ❶ v informal expose the falseness of.

debut ❶ [**day**-byoo] n first public appearance of a performer. **debutante** [**day**-byoo-tont] n young upper-class woman being formally presented to society.

Dec. December.

decade n period of ten years.

decadence ❶ [**dek**-a-denss] n deterioration in morality or culture. **decadent** adj.

decaffeinated [dee-**kaf**-fin-ate-id] adj (of coffee, tea, or cola) with caffeine removed.

decagon n geometric figure with ten sides. **decagonal** adj.

decahedron [deck-a-**heed**-ron] n solid figure with ten faces.

Decalogue n the Ten Commandments.

decamp v depart secretly or suddenly.

decant v 1 pour (a liquid) from one container to another. 2 rehouse (people) while their homes are being renovated. **decanter** n stoppered bottle for wine or spirits.

decapitate ❶ v behead. **decapitation** n.

decathlon n athletic contest with ten events. **decathlete** n.

decay ❶ v 1 become weaker or more corrupt. 2 rot. ▷ n 3 process of decaying. 4 state brought about by this process.

decease ❶ n formal death. **deceased** adj formal dead. **the deceased** dead person.

deceive ❶ v 1 mislead by lying. 2 be unfaithful to (one's sexual partner). **deceiver** n **deceit** n behaviour intended to deceive. **deceitful** adj.

decelerate v slow down. **deceleration** n.

December n twelfth month of the year.

decent ❶ adj 1 (of a person) polite and morally acceptable. 2 fitting or proper. 3 conforming to conventions of sexual behaviour. 4 informal kind. **decently** adv **decency** n, pl **-cies**.

THESAURUS

debt n = **debit**, commitment, liability, obligation ▷ n **in debt** = **owing**, in arrears, in the red (inf), liable

debtor n = **borrower**, mortgagor

debunk v Inf = **expose**, cut down to size, deflate, disparage, mock, ridicule, show up

debut n = **introduction**, beginning, bow, coming out, entrance, first appearance, initiation, presentation

decadence n = **degeneration**, corruption, decay, decline, deterioration, dissipation, dissolution

decadent adj = **degenerate**, abandoned, corrupt, decaying, declining, dissolute, immoral, self-indulgent

decapitate v = **behead**, execute, guillotine

decay v 1 = **decline**, crumble, deteriorate, disintegrate, dwindle, shrivel, wane, waste away, wither 2 = **rot**, corrode, decompose, perish, putrefy ▷ n 3 = **decline**, collapse, degeneration, deterioration, fading, failing, wasting, withering 4 = **rot**, caries, decomposition, gangrene,

putrefaction

decease n Formal = **death**, demise, departure, dying, release

deceased adj Formal = **dead**, defunct, departed, expired, former, late, lifeless

deceit n = **dishonesty**, cheating, chicanery, deception, fraud, lying, pretence, treachery, trickery

deceitful adj = **dishonest**, deceptive, false, fraudulent, sneaky, treacherous, two-faced, untrustworthy

deceive v 1 = **take in** (inf), cheat, con (inf), dupe, fool, hoodwink, mislead, swindle, trick

deceiver n 1 = **liar**, cheat, con man (inf), double-dealer, fraud, impostor, swindler, trickster

decency n = **respectability**, civility, correctness, courtesy, decorum, etiquette, modesty, propriety

decent adj 2 = **proper**, appropriate, becoming, befitting, fitting, seemly, suitable 3 = **respectable**, chaste, decorous, modest, proper, pure 4 Inf = **kind**, accommodating, courteous, friendly, generous, gracious, helpful, obliging, thoughtful

decentralize v reorganize into smaller local units. **decentralization** n.

deception ❶ n 1 deceiving. 2 something that deceives, trick. **deceptive** adj likely or designed to deceive. **deceptively** adv **deceptiveness** n.

deci- combining form one tenth.

decibel n unit for measuring the intensity of sound.

decide ❶ v 1 (cause to) reach a decision. 2 settle (a contest or question). **decided** adj 1 unmistakable. 2 determined. **decidedly** adv **decision** n judgment, conclusion, or resolution.

deciduous adj (of a tree) shedding its leaves annually.

decimal n 1 fraction written in the form of a dot followed by one or more numbers. ▷ adj 2 relating to or using powers of ten. 3 expressed as a decimal. **decimalize** v change (a system or number) to the decimal system. **decimalization** n **decimal currency** system of currency in which the units are parts or powers of ten. **decimal point** dot between the unit and the fraction of a number in the decimal system. **decimal system** number system with a base of ten, in which numbers are expressed by combinations of the digits 0 to 9.

decimate ❶ v destroy or kill a large proportion of. **decimation** n.

decipher ❶ v work out the meaning of (something illegible or in code). **decipherable** adj.

decision ❶ n 1 judgment, conclusion, or resolution. 2 act of making up one's mind. 3 firmness of purpose. **decisive** adj 1 having a definite influence, e.g. the decisive factor. 2 having the ability to make quick decisions. **decisively** adv **decisiveness** n.

deck ❶ n 1 area of a ship that forms a floor. 2 similar area in a bus. 3 platform that supports the turntable and pick-up of a record player. 4 US pack (of cards). **deck chair** folding chair made of canvas over a wooden frame. **deck hand** sailor assigned duties on the deck of a ship. **decking** n wooden platform in a garden. **deck out** v decorate.

declaim ❶ v 1 speak loudly and dramatically. 2 protest loudly. **declamation** n **declamatory** adj.

declare ❶ v 1 state firmly and forcefully. 2 announce officially. 3 acknowledge for tax purposes. **declaration** n **declaratory** adj.

declassify v state officially that (information or a document) is no longer secret. **declassification** n.

declension n Grammar changes in the form of nouns, pronouns, or adjectives to show case, number, and gender.

——————————— THESAURUS ———————————

deception n 1 = **trickery**, cunning, deceit, fraud, guile, legerdemain, treachery 2 = **trick**, bluff, decoy, hoax, illusion, lie, ruse, subterfuge

deceptive adj = **misleading**, ambiguous, deceitful, dishonest, false, fraudulent, illusory, unreliable

decide v 1 = **reach** or **come to a decision**, choose, conclude, determine, make up one's mind, resolve 2 = **adjudge**, adjudicate

decidedly adv 2 = **definitely**, clearly, distinctly, downright, positively, unequivocally, unmistakably

decimate v = **devastate**, ravage, wreak havoc on

decipher v = **figure out** (inf), crack, decode, deduce, interpret, make out, read, solve

decision n 1 = **judgment**, arbitration, conclusion, finding, resolution, ruling, sentence, verdict 3 = **decisiveness**, determination, firmness, purpose,

resolution, resolve, strength of mind or will

decisive adj 1 = **crucial**, conclusive, critical, fateful, influential, momentous, significant 2 = **resolute**, decided, determined, firm, forceful, incisive, strong-minded, trenchant

deck out v = **decorate**, adorn, array, beautify, clothe, dress, embellish, festoon

declaim v 1 = **orate**, harangue, hold forth, lecture, proclaim, rant, recite, speak 2 = **protest against**, attack, decry, denounce, inveigh, rail

declaration n 1 = **statement**, acknowledgment, affirmation, assertion, avowal, disclosure, protestation, revelation, testimony 2 = **announcement**, edict, notification, proclamation, profession, pronouncement

declare v 1 = **state**, affirm, announce, assert, claim, maintain, proclaim, profess, pronounce, swear, utter

decline ❶ v **1** become smaller, weaker, or less important. **2** refuse politely to accept or do. **3** *Grammar* list the inflections of (a noun, pronoun, or adjective). ▷ n **4** gradual weakening or loss.

declivity n, pl **-ties** downward slope.

declutch v disengage the clutch of a motor vehicle.

decoct v extract the essence from (a substance) by boiling. **decoction** n.

decode ❶ v convert from code into ordinary language. **decoder** n.

décolleté [day-**kol**-tay] adj (of a woman's garment) low-cut. **décolletage** [day-**kol**-tazh] n low-cut dress or neckline.

decommission v dismantle (a nuclear reactor, weapon, etc.) which is no longer needed.

decompose ❶ v be broken down through chemical or bacterial action. **decomposition** n.

decompress v **1** free from pressure. **2** return (a diver) to normal atmospheric pressure. **decompression** n **decompression sickness** severe pain and difficulty in breathing, caused by a sudden change in atmospheric pressure.

decongestant n medicine that relieves nasal congestion.

decontaminate v make safe by removing poisons, radioactivity, etc. **decontamination** n.

decor [**day**-core] n style in which a room or house is decorated.

decorate ❶ v **1** make more attractive by adding something ornamental. **2** paint or wallpaper. **3** award a (military) medal to. **decoration** n **decorative** adj **decorator** n.

decorous ❶ [**dek**-a-russ] adj polite, calm, and sensible in behaviour. **decorously** adv.

decorum ❶ [dik-**core**-um] n polite and socially correct behaviour.

decoy ❶ n **1** person or thing used to lure someone into danger. **2** dummy bird or animal, used to lure game within shooting range. ▷ v **3** lure away by means of a trick.

decrease ❶ v **1** make or become less. ▷ n **2** lessening, reduction. **3** amount by which something has decreased.

decree ❶ n **1** law made by someone in authority. **2** court judgment. ▷ v **3** order by decree. **decree absolute** final court order in a divorce case,

———————————————— THESAURUS ————————————————

decline v **1 a** = **lessen**, decrease, diminish, dwindle, ebb, fade, fall off, shrink, wane, weaken
b = **deteriorate**, decay, degenerate, sink, worsen **2** = **refuse**, abstain, avoid, reject, say `no', turn down ▷ n **4** = **deterioration**, decay, degeneration, downturn, drop, dwindling, failing, falling off, lessening, recession, slump, weakening, worsening

decode v = **decipher**, crack, decrypt, interpret, solve, unscramble, work out

decompose v = **rot**, break up, crumble, decay, fall apart, fester, putrefy

decor n = **decoration**, colour scheme, furnishing style, ornamentation

decorate v **1** = **adorn**, beautify, embellish, festoon, grace, ornament, trim **2** = **do up** (inf), colour, furbish, paint, paper, renovate, wallpaper **3** = **pin a medal on**, cite, confer an honour on or upon

decoration n **1** = **adornment**, beautification, elaboration, embellishment, enrichment, ornamentation, trimming

2 = **ornament**, bauble, frill, garnish, trimmings **3** = **medal**, award, badge, ribbon, star

decorative adj = **ornamental**, beautifying, fancy, nonfunctional, pretty

decorous adj = **proper**, becoming, correct, decent, dignified, fitting, polite, seemly, well-behaved

decorum n = **propriety**, decency, dignity, etiquette, good manners, politeness, protocol, respectability

decoy n **1** = **lure**, bait, enticement, inducement, pretence, trap ▷ v **3** = **lure**, deceive, ensnare, entice, entrap, seduce, tempt

decrease v **1** = **lessen**, cut down, decline, diminish, drop, dwindle, lower, reduce, shrink, subside ▷ n **2** = **lessening**, contraction, cutback, decline, dwindling, falling off, loss, reduction, subsidence

decree n **1** = **law**, act, command, edict, order, proclamation, ruling, statute ▷ v **3** = **order**, command, demand, ordain, prescribe, proclaim, pronounce, rule

which leaves the parties free to remarry. **decree nisi** court order in a divorce case, which will become absolute unless valid reasons are produced to oppose it.

decrepit ❶ *adj* weakened or worn out by age or long use. **decrepitude** *n*.

decretal *n RC Church* papal decree.

decriminalize *v* make (an illegal act) no longer a crime. **decriminalization** *n*.

decry ❶ *v* **-crying, -cried** express disapproval of.

dedicate ❶ *v* **1** commit (oneself or one's time) wholly to a special purpose or cause. **2** inscribe or address (a book etc.) to someone as a tribute. **dedicated** *adj* devoted to a particular purpose or cause. **dedication** *n*.

deduce ❶ *v* reach (a conclusion) by reasoning from evidence. **deducible** *adj*.

deduct ❶ *v* subtract. **deductible** *adj*.

deduction ❶ *n* **1** deducting. **2** something that is deducted. **3** deducing. **4** conclusion reached by deducing. **deductive** *adj*.

deed ❶ *n* **1** something that is done. **2** legal document. **deed box** strong box in which legal documents are stored. **deed poll** *Law* deed made by one party only, esp. to change one's name.

deejay *n informal* disc jockey.

deem *v* consider, judge.

deep ❶ *adj* **1** extending or situated far down, inwards, backwards, or sideways. **2** of a specified dimension downwards, inwards, or backwards, e.g. *three inches deep*. **3** difficult to understand. **4** of great intensity. **5** (foll. by *in*) absorbed in (an activity). **6** (of a colour) strong or dark. **7** low in pitch. **the deep** *poetic* the sea. **deeply** *adv* profoundly or intensely (also **deep down**). **deepen** *v* **deep-freeze** *n* same as FREEZER. **deep-fry** *v* cook in hot oil deep enough to cover the food completely. **deep-rooted** *adj* (of an idea or belief) firmly fixed or held. **deep-seated** *adj* (of a problem, fear, etc.) affecting one strongly.

deer *n, pl* **deer** large wild animal, the male of which has antlers. **deerstalker** *n* cloth hat with peaks at the back and front and earflaps.

deface ❶ *v* deliberately spoil the appearance of. **defacement** *n*.

THESAURUS

decrepit *adj* **a** = **weak**, aged, doddering, feeble, frail, infirm **b** = **worn-out**, battered, beat-up (*inf*), broken-down, dilapidated, ramshackle, rickety, run-down, tumbledown, weather-beaten

decry *v* = **condemn**, belittle, criticize, denigrate, denounce, discredit, disparage, put down, run down

dedicate *v* **1** = **devote**, commit, give over to, pledge, surrender **2** = **inscribe**, address

dedicated *adj* = **devoted**, committed, enthusiastic, purposeful, single-minded, wholehearted, zealous

dedication *n* **1** = **devotion**, adherence, allegiance, commitment, faithfulness, loyalty, single-mindedness, wholeheartedness **2** = **inscription**, address, message

deduce *v* = **conclude**, draw, gather, glean, infer, reason, take to mean, understand

deduct *v* = **subtract**, decrease by, knock off (*inf*), reduce by, remove, take away, take off

deduction *n* **1, 2** = **subtraction**, decrease, diminution, discount, reduction, withdrawal **4** = **conclusion**, assumption, finding, inference, reasoning, result

deed *n* **1** = **action**, achievement, act, exploit, fact, feat, performance **2** = **document**, contract, title

deep *adj* **1** = **wide**, bottomless, broad, far, profound, unfathomable, yawning **3** = **mysterious**, abstract, abstruse, arcane, esoteric, hidden, obscure, recondite, secret **4** = **intense**, extreme, grave, great, profound, serious (*inf*), unqualified **5** (foll. by *in*) = **absorbed**, engrossed, immersed, lost, preoccupied, rapt **6** = **dark**, intense, rich, strong, vivid **7** = **low**, bass, booming, low-pitched, resonant, sonorous ▷ *n* **the deep** *Poet* = **ocean**, briny (*inf*), high seas, main, sea

deepen *v* **1** = **dig out**, excavate, hollow, scoop out **4** = **intensify**, grow, increase, magnify, reinforce, strengthen

deeply *adv* **4** = **intensely**, acutely, completely, gravely, profoundly, seriously, severely, thoroughly, to the core, to the heart, to the quick

deface *v* = **vandalize**, damage, deform, disfigure, mar, mutilate, spoil, tarnish

de facto ❶ *adv* **1** in fact. ▷ *adj*
2 existing in fact, whether legally recognized or not.
defame ❶ *v* attack the good reputation of. **defamation** *n* **defamatory** [dif-**fam**-a-tree] *adj*.
default ❶ *n* **1** failure to do something. **2** *Computers* instruction to a computer to select a particular option unless the user specifies otherwise. ▷ *v* **3** fail to fulfil an obligation. **by default** (happening) only because something else has not happened.
in default of in the absence of. **defaulter** *n*.
defeat ❶ *v* **1** win a victory over. **2** thwart, frustrate. ▷ *n* **3** defeating. **defeatism** *n* ready acceptance or expectation of defeat. **defeatist** *adj, n*.
defecate *v* discharge waste from the body through the anus. **defecation** *n*.
defect ❶ *n* **1** imperfection, blemish. ▷ *v* **2** desert one's cause or country to join the opposing forces. **defective** *adj* imperfect, faulty. **defection** *n*

defector *n*.
defence ❶ *n* **1** resistance against attack. **2** argument in support of something. **3** a country's military resources. **4** defendant's case in a court of law. **5** *Sport* players whose chief task is to stop the opposition scoring. **defenceless** *adj*.
defend ❶ *v* **1** protect from harm or danger. **2** support in the face of criticism. **3** represent (a defendant) in court. **4** *Sport* protect (a title) against a challenge. **defendant** *n* person accused of a crime. **defender** *n* **defensible** *adj* capable of being defended because believed to be right. **defensibility** *n* **defensive** *adj* **1** intended for defence. **2** overanxious to protect oneself against (threatened) criticism. **on the defensive** protecting oneself, esp. against (threatened) criticism. **defensively** *adv*.
defer[1] ❶ *v* **-ferring, -ferred** delay (something) until a future time. **deferment, deferral** *n*.

de facto *adv* **1** = **in fact**, actually, in effect, in reality, really ▷ *adj*
2 = **actual**, existing, real
defame *v* = **slander**, bad-mouth (*sl, chiefly US & Canad*), cast aspersions on, denigrate, discredit, disparage, knock (*inf*), libel, malign, smear
default *n* **1** = **failure**, deficiency, dereliction, evasion, lapse, neglect, nonpayment, omission ▷ *v* **3** = **fail**, dodge, evade, neglect
defeat *v* **1** = **beat**, conquer, crush, master, overwhelm, rout, trounce, vanquish, wipe the floor with (*inf*)
2 = **frustrate**, baffle, balk, confound, foil, get the better of, ruin, thwart ▷ *n*
3 = **conquest**, beating, overthrow, pasting (*sl*), rout
defeatist *adj* = **pessimistic** ▷ *n*
= **pessimist**, prophet of doom, quitter
defect *n* **1** = **imperfection**, blemish, blotch, error, failing, fault, flaw, spot, taint ▷ *v* **2** = **desert**, abandon, change sides, go over, rebel, revolt, walk out on (*inf*)
defection *n* = **desertion**, apostasy, rebellion
defective *adj* = **faulty**, broken, deficient, flawed, imperfect, not working, on the blink (*sl*), out of order
defector *n* = **deserter**, apostate,

renegade, turncoat
defence *n* **1** = **protection**, cover, guard, immunity, resistance, safeguard, security, shelter
2 = **argument**, excuse, explanation, justification, plea, vindication
3 = **shield**, barricade, bulwark, buttress, fortification, rampart
4 = **plea**, alibi, denial, rebuttal, testimony
defenceless *adj* = **helpless**, exposed, naked, powerless, unarmed, unguarded, unprotected, vulnerable, wide open
defend *v* **1** = **protect**, cover, guard, keep safe, preserve, safeguard, screen, shelter, shield **2** = **support**, champion, endorse, justify, speak up for, stand up for, stick up for (*inf*), uphold, vindicate
defendant *n* = **the accused**, defence, offender, prisoner at the bar, respondent
defender *n* **1** = **protector**, bodyguard, escort, guard **2** = **supporter**, advocate, champion, sponsor
defensive *adj* **1** = **on guard**, protective, watchful
defer[1] *v* = **postpone**, delay, hold over, procrastinate, put off, put on ice (*inf*), shelve, suspend

defer² ❶ v **-ferring, -ferred** (foll.
by to) comply with the wishes (of).
deference n polite and respectful
behaviour. **deferential** adj
deferentially adv.
defiance ❶ n see DEFY.
deficient ❶ adj 1 lacking some
essential thing or quality.
2 inadequate in quality or quantity.
deficiency n, pl **-cies** 1 state of being
deficient. 2 lack, shortage.
deficiency disease condition, such as
scurvy, caused by a lack of vitamins or
other nutrients. **deficit** n amount by
which a sum of money is too small.
defile¹ v treat (something sacred or
important) without respect.
defilement n.
defile² n narrow valley or pass.
define ❶ v 1 state precisely the
meaning of. 2 show clearly the outline
of. **definable** adj **definite** adj 1 firm,
clear, and precise. 2 having precise
limits. 3 known for certain. **definite
article** the word the. **definitely** adv

definition n 1 statement of the
meaning of a word or phrase.
2 quality of being clear and distinct.
definitive adj 1 providing an
unquestionable conclusion. 2 being
the best example of something.
definitively adv.
deflate ❶ v 1 (cause to) collapse
through the release of air. 2 take away
the self-esteem or conceit from.
3 Economics cause deflation of (an
economy). **deflation** n 1 Economics
reduction in economic activity
resulting in lower output and
investment. 2 feeling of sadness
following excitement. **deflationary**
adj.
deflect ❶ v (cause to) turn aside from a
course. **deflection** n **deflector** n.
deflower v lit deprive (a woman) of her
virginity.
defoliate v deprive (a plant) of its
leaves. **defoliant** n **defoliation** n.
deforestation n destruction of all the
trees in an area.

─────── **THESAURUS** ───────

defer² v (foll. by to) = **comply**, accede,
bow, capitulate, give in, give way to,
submit, yield
deference n = **respect**, attention,
civility, consideration, courtesy,
honour, politeness, regard,
reverence
deferential adj = **respectful**,
ingratiating, obedient, obeisant,
obsequious, polite, reverential,
submissive
defiance n = **resistance**, confrontation,
contempt, disobedience, disregard,
insolence, insubordination, opposition,
rebelliousness
defiant adj = **resisting**, audacious,
bold, daring, disobedient, insolent,
insubordinate, mutinous, provocative,
rebellious
deficiency n 1 = **failing**, defect,
demerit, fault, flaw, frailty,
imperfection, shortcoming, weakness
2 = **lack**, absence, dearth, deficit,
scarcity, shortage
deficient adj 1 = **lacking**, inadequate,
insufficient, meagre, scant, scarce,
short, skimpy, wanting
2 = **unsatisfactory**, defective, faulty,
flawed, impaired, imperfect,
incomplete, inferior, weak
deficit n = **shortfall**, arrears, deficiency,
loss, shortage

define v 1 = **describe**, characterize,
designate, explain, expound,
interpret, specify, spell out 2 = **mark
out**, bound, circumscribe, delineate,
demarcate, limit, outline
definite adj 1, 2 = **clear**, black-and-
white, cut-and-dried (inf), exact,
fixed, marked, particular, precise,
specific 3 = **certain**, assured, decided,
guaranteed, positive, settled, sure
definitely adv = **certainly**, absolutely,
categorically, clearly, positively, surely,
undeniably, unmistakably,
unquestionably, without doubt
definition n 1 = **explanation**,
clarification, elucidation, exposition,
statement of meaning 2 = **sharpness**,
clarity, contrast, distinctness, focus,
precision
definitive adj 1 = **final**, absolute,
complete, conclusive, decisive
2 = **authoritative**, exhaustive,
perfect, reliable, ultimate
deflate v 1 = **collapse**, empty, exhaust,
flatten, puncture, shrink
2 = **humiliate**, chasten, disconcert,
dispirit, humble, mortify, put down
(sl), squash 3 Economics = **reduce**,
depress, devalue, diminish
deflect v = **turn aside**, bend, deviate,
diverge, glance off, ricochet, swerve,
veer

d

deform ❶ v put out of shape or spoil the appearance of. **deformation** n **deformed** adj **deformity** n, pl **-ties** 1 Pathology distortion of a body part. 2 state of being deformed.

defraud ❶ v cheat out of money, property, etc.

defray v provide money for (costs or expenses).

defrock v deprive (a priest) of priestly status.

defrost v 1 make or become free of ice. 2 thaw (frozen food) by removing it from a freezer.

deft ❶ adj quick and skilful in movement. **deftly** adv **deftness** n.

defunct ❶ adj no longer existing or operative.

defuse v 1 remove the fuse of (an explosive device). 2 remove the tension from (a situation).

defy ❶ v **-fying, -fied** 1 resist openly and boldly. 2 make impossible, e.g. the condition of the refugees defied description. **defiance** n open resistance or disobedience. **defiant** adj.

degenerate ❶ adj 1 having deteriorated to a lower mental, moral, or physical level. ▷ n 2 degenerate person. ▷ v 3 become degenerate. **degeneracy** n degenerate behaviour. **degeneration** n **degenerative** adj (of a disease or condition) getting steadily worse.

degrade ❶ v 1 reduce to dishonour or disgrace. 2 reduce in status or quality. 3 Chemistry decompose into smaller molecules. **degrading** adj **degradation** n.

degree ❶ n 1 stage in a scale of relative amount or intensity. 2 academic award given by a university or college on successful completion of a course. 3 unit of measurement for temperature, angles, or latitude and longitude.

dehumanize v 1 deprive of human qualities. 2 make (an activity) mechanical or routine. **dehumanization** n.

dehumidifier n device for removing moisture from the air.

dehydrate v remove water from (food) to preserve it. **be dehydrated** become weak through losing too much water from the body. **dehydration** n.

de-ice v free of ice. **de-icer** n.

deify [**day**-if-fie] v **-fying, -fied** treat or worship as a god. **deification** n.

deign [**dane**] v agree (to do something), but as if doing someone a favour.

deism [**dee**-iz-zum] n belief in god but not in divine revelation. **deist** n.

deity ❶ [**dee**-it-ee] n, pl **-ties** 1 god or goddess. 2 state of being divine.

déjà vu [**day**-zhah **voo**] n feeling of having experienced before something that is actually happening now.

dejected ❶ adj unhappy. **dejectedly** adv **dejection** n.

---

deflection n = **deviation**, bend, divergence, swerve

deform v = **distort**, buckle, contort, deface, disfigure, gnarl, maim, mangle, mar, misshape, mutilate, ruin, spoil, twist, warp

deformity n = **abnormality**, defect, disfigurement, malformation

defraud v = **cheat**, con (inf), diddle (inf), embezzle, fleece, pilfer, rip off (sl), swindle, trick

deft adj = **skilful**, adept, adroit, agile, dexterous, expert, neat, nimble, proficient

defunct adj = **dead**, bygone, deceased, departed, expired, extinct, gone, inoperative, invalid, nonexistent, obsolete, out of commission

defy v 1 = **resist**, brave, confront, disregard, flout, scorn, slight, spurn

degenerate adj 1 = **depraved**, corrupt, debauched, decadent, dissolute, immoral, low, perverted ▷ v 3 = **worsen**, decay, decline, decrease, deteriorate, fall off, lapse, sink, slip

degradation n 1 = **disgrace**, discredit, dishonour, humiliation, ignominy, mortification, shame
2 = **deterioration**, decline, degeneration, demotion, downgrading

degrade v 1 = **demean**, debase, discredit, disgrace, dishonour, humble, humiliate, shame
2 = **demote**, downgrade, lower

degrading adj 1 = **demeaning**, dishonourable, humiliating, infra dig (inf), shameful, undignified, unworthy

degree n 1 = **stage**, grade, notch, point, rung, step, unit

deity n 1 = **god**, divinity, goddess, godhead, idol, immortal, supreme being

dejected adj = **downhearted**, crestfallen, depressed, despondent,

de jure ● *adv, adj* according to law.
dekko *n Brit & Aust slang* **have a dekko** have a look.
delay ● *v* **1** put off to a later time. **2** slow up or cause to be late. ▷ *n* **3** act of delaying. **4** interval of time between events.
delectable *adj* delightful, very attractive. **delectation** *n formal* great pleasure.
delegate ● *n* **1** person chosen to represent others, esp. at a meeting. ▷ *v* **2** entrust (duties or powers) to someone. **3** appoint as a delegate. **delegation** *n* **1** group chosen to represent others. **2** delegating.
delete ● *v* remove (something written or printed). **deletion** *n*.
deleterious [del-lit-**eer**-ee-uss] *adj* harmful, injurious.

Delft *n* type of earthenware, orig. from Delft in the Netherlands, usu. with blue decoration on a white background (also **delftware**).
deli *n informal* delicatessen.
deliberate ● *adj* **1** planned in advance, intentional. **2** careful and unhurried. ▷ *v* **3** think something over. **deliberately** *adv* **deliberation** *n* **deliberative** *adj*.
delicate ● *adj* **1** fine or subtle in quality or workmanship. **2** having a fragile beauty. **3** (of a taste etc.) pleasantly subtle. **4** easily damaged. **5** requiring tact. **delicately** *adv* **delicacy** *n* **1** being delicate. **2** *pl* **-cies** something particularly good to eat.
delicatessen *n* shop selling imported or unusual foods, often already cooked or prepared.

———————— **THESAURUS** ————————

disconsolate, disheartened, downcast, glum, miserable, sad
dejection *n* = **low spirits**, depression, despair, despondency, doldrums, downheartedness, gloom, melancholy, sadness, sorrow, unhappiness
de jure *adv* = **legally**, by right, rightfully
delay *v* **1** = **put off**, defer, hold over, postpone, procrastinate, shelve, suspend **2** = **hold up**, bog down, detain, hinder, hold back, impede, obstruct, set back, slow down ▷ *n* **3** = **putting off**, deferment, postponement, procrastination, suspension **4** = **hold-up**, hindrance, impediment, interruption, interval, setback, stoppage, wait
delegate *n* **1** = **representative**, agent, ambassador, commissioner, deputy, envoy, legate ▷ *v* **2** = **entrust**, assign, consign, devolve, give, hand over, pass on, transfer **3** = **appoint**, accredit, authorize, commission, depute, designate, empower, mandate
delegation *n* **1** = **deputation**, commission, contingent, embassy, envoys, legation, mission **2** = **devolution**, assignment, commissioning, committal
delete *v* = **remove**, cancel, cross out, efface, erase, expunge, obliterate, rub out, strike out
deliberate *adj* **1** = **intentional**, calculated, conscious, planned, prearranged, premeditated,

purposeful, wilful **2** = **unhurried**, careful, cautious, circumspect, measured, methodical, ponderous, slow, thoughtful ▷ *v* **3** = **consider**, cogitate, consult, debate, discuss, meditate, ponder, reflect, think, weigh
deliberately *adv* **1** = **intentionally**, by design, calculatingly, consciously, in cold blood, knowingly, on purpose, wilfully, wittingly
deliberation *n* = **consideration**, calculation, circumspection, conference, consultation, debate, discussion, forethought, meditation, reflection, thought
delicacy *n* **1 a** = **fineness**, accuracy, daintiness, elegance, exquisiteness, lightness, precision, subtlety **b** = **fragility**, flimsiness, frailty, slenderness, tenderness, weakness **c** = **sensitivity**, sensitiveness, tact **2** = **treat**, dainty, luxury, savoury, titbit
delicate *adj* **1** = **fine**, deft, elegant, exquisite, graceful, precise, skilled, subtle **3** = **subtle**, choice, dainty, delicious, fine, savoury, tender **4** = **fragile**, flimsy, frail, slender, slight, tender, weak **5** = **considerate**, diplomatic, discreet, sensitive, tactful
delicately *adv* **1** = **finely**, daintily, deftly, elegantly, exquisitely, gracefully, precisely, skilfully, subtly **5** = **tactfully**, diplomatically, sensitively

delicious ❶ *adj* very appealing to taste or smell. **deliciously** *adv*.

delight ❶ *n* **1** (source of) great pleasure. ▷ *v* **2** please greatly. **3** (foll. by *in*) take great pleasure (in). **delightful** *adj* **delightfully** *adv*.

delimit *v* mark or lay down the limits of. **delimitation** *n*.

delineate [dill-**lin**-ee-ate] *v* **1** show by drawing. **2** describe in words. **delineation** *n*.

delinquent ❶ *n* **1** someone, esp. a young person, who repeatedly breaks the law. ▷ *adj* **2** repeatedly breaking the law. **delinquency** *n*, *pl* **-cies**.

delirium ❶ *n* **1** state of excitement and mental confusion, often with hallucinations. **2** great excitement. **delirium tremens** [**treh**-menz] trembling and hallucinations caused by chronic alcoholism. **delirious** *adj* **deliriously** *adv*.

deliver ❶ *v* **1** carry (goods etc.) to a destination. **2** hand over. **3** aid in the birth of. **4** present (a lecture or speech). **5** release or rescue. **6** strike (a blow). **deliverance** *n* rescue from captivity or evil. **delivery** *n*, *pl* **-eries** **1** delivering. **2** something that is delivered. **3** act of giving birth to a baby. **4** style in public speaking.

dell *n* small wooded hollow.

Delphic *adj* ambiguous, like the ancient Greek oracle at Delphi.

delphinium *n* large garden plant with blue flowers.

delta *n* **1** fourth letter in the Greek alphabet. **2** flat area at the mouth of some rivers where the main stream splits up into several branches.

delude ❶ *v* deceive.

deluge ❶ [**del**-lyooj] *n* **1** great flood. **2** torrential rain. **3** overwhelming number. ▷ *v* **4** flood. **5** overwhelm.

delusion ❶ *n* **1** mistaken idea or belief. **2** state of being deluded. **delusive** *adj*.

━━━ THESAURUS ━━━━

delicious *adj* = **delectable**, appetizing, choice, dainty, lekker (*S Afr sl*), mouthwatering, savoury, scrumptious (*inf*), tasty, toothsome

delight *n* **1** = **pleasure**, ecstasy, enjoyment, gladness, glee, happiness, joy, rapture ▷ *v* **2** = **please**, amuse, charm, cheer, enchant, gratify, thrill **3** (foll. by *in*) = **take pleasure in**, appreciate, enjoy, feast on, like, love, relish, revel in, savour

delighted *adj* = **pleased**, ecstatic, elated, enchanted, happy, joyous, jubilant, overjoyed, thrilled

delightful *adj* = **pleasant**, agreeable, charming, delectable, enchanting, enjoyable, pleasurable, rapturous, thrilling

delinquent *n* **1** = **criminal**, culprit, lawbreaker, miscreant, offender, villain, wrongdoer

delirious *adj* **1** = **mad**, crazy, demented, deranged, incoherent, insane, raving, unhinged **2** = **ecstatic**, beside oneself, carried away, excited, frantic, frenzied, hysterical, wild

delirium *n* **1** = **madness**, derangement, hallucination, insanity, raving **2** = **frenzy**, ecstasy, fever, hysteria, passion

deliver *v* **1** = **carry**, bear, bring, cart, convey, distribute, transport **2** = **hand over**, commit, give up, grant, make

over, relinquish, surrender, transfer, turn over, yield **4** = **give**, announce, declare, present, read, utter **5** = **release**, emancipate, free, liberate, loose, ransom, rescue, save **6** = **strike**, administer, aim, deal, direct, give, inflict, launch

deliverance *n* = **release**, emancipation, escape, liberation, ransom, redemption, rescue, salvation

delivery *n* **1** = **handing over**, consignment, conveyance, dispatch, distribution, surrender, transfer, transmission **3** = **childbirth**, confinement, labour, parturition **4** = **speech**, articulation, elocution, enunciation, intonation, utterance

delude *v* = **deceive**, beguile, dupe, fool, hoodwink, kid (*inf*), mislead, take in (*inf*), trick

deluge *n* **1** = **flood**, cataclysm, downpour, inundation, overflowing, spate, torrent **3** = **rush**, avalanche, barrage, flood, spate, torrent ▷ *v* **4** = **flood**, douse, drench, drown, inundate, soak, submerge, swamp **5** = **overwhelm**, engulf, inundate, overload, overrun, swamp

delusion *n* **1** = **misconception**, error, fallacy, false impression, fancy, hallucination, illusion, misapprehension, mistake

de luxe ❶ *adj* rich or sumptuous, superior in quality.

delve ❶ *v* **1** research deeply (for information). **2** *old-fashioned* dig.

demagnetize *v* remove magnetic properties from.

demagogue ❶ *n* political agitator who appeals to the prejudice and passions of the mob. **demagogic** *adj* **demagogy** *n*.

demand ❶ *v* **1** request forcefully. **2** require as just, urgent, etc. **3** claim as a right. ▷ *n* **4** forceful request. **5** *Economics* willingness and ability to purchase goods and services. **6** something that requires special effort or sacrifice. **demanding** *adj* requiring a lot of time or effort.

demarcation ❶ *n formal* establishing limits or boundaries, esp. between the work performed by different trade unions.

demean ❶ *v* **demean oneself** do something unworthy of one's status or character.

demeanour ❶ *n* way a person behaves.

demented ❶ *adj* mad. **dementedly** *adv* **dementia** [dim-**men**-sha] *n* state of serious mental deterioration.

demerara sugar *n* brown crystallized cane sugar.

demerger *n* separation of two or more companies which have previously been merged.

demerit *n* fault, disadvantage.

demesne [dim-**mane**] *n* **1** land surrounding a house. **2** *Law* possession of one's own property or land.

demi- *combining form* half.

demigod *n* **1** being who is part mortal, part god. **2** godlike person.

demijohn *n* large bottle with a short neck, often encased in wicker.

demilitarize *v* remove the military forces from. **demilitarization** *n*.

demimonde *n* **1** (esp. in the 19th century) class of women considered to be outside respectable society because of promiscuity. **2** group considered not wholly respectable.

demise ❶ *n* **1** eventual failure (of something successful). **2** *formal* death.

demist *v* remove condensation from (a windscreen). **demister** *n*.

demo *n, pl* **demos** *informal* **1** demonstration, organized expression of public opinion. **2** demonstration record or tape.

demob *v informal* demobilize.

demobilize *v* release from the armed forces. **demobilization** *n*.

democracy ❶ *n, pl* **-cies 1** government by the people or their elected representatives. **2** state governed in this way. **democrat** *n* **1** advocate of democracy. **2** (**D-**) member or supporter of the Democratic Party in the US. **democratic** *adj* **1** of democracy. **2** upholding democracy. **3** (**D-**) of the Democratic Party, the more liberal of the two main political parties in the US. **democratically** *adv*.

———————————— **THESAURUS** ————————————

de luxe *adj* = **luxurious**, costly, exclusive, expensive, grand, opulent, select, special, splendid, superior

delve *v* **1** = **research**, burrow, explore, ferret out, forage, investigate, look into, probe, rummage, search

demagogue *n* = **agitator**, firebrand, rabble-rouser

demand *v* **1** = **request**, ask, challenge, inquire, interrogate, question **2** = **require**, call for, cry out for, entail, involve, necessitate, need, want **3** = **claim**, exact, expect, insist on, order ▷ *n* **4** = **request**, inquiry, order, question, requisition **5** *Economics* = **need**, call, claim, market, requirement, want

demanding *adj* = **difficult**, challenging, exacting, hard, taxing, tough, trying, wearing

demarcation *n Formal* = **delimitation**, differentiation, distinction, division, separation

demean *v* = **lower**, abase, debase, degrade, descend, humble, stoop

demeanour *n* = **behaviour**, air, bearing, carriage, comportment, conduct, deportment, manner

demented *adj* = **mad**, crazed, crazy, deranged, frenzied, insane, maniacal, unbalanced, unhinged

demise *n* **1** = **failure**, collapse, downfall, end, fall, ruin **2** *Formal* = **death**, decease, departure

democracy *n* **1** = **self-government 2** = **republic**, commonwealth

democratic *adj* **1, 2** = **self-governing**, autonomous, egalitarian, popular, populist, representative

d

demography *n* study of population statistics, such as births and deaths. **demographer** *n* **demographic** *adj*.

demolish ❶ *v* **1** knock down or destroy (a building). **2** disprove (an argument). **demolisher** *n* **demolition** *n*.

demon ❶ *n* **1** evil spirit. **2** person who does something with great energy or skill, e.g. *I worked like a demon*. **demonic** *adj* evil. **demoniac**, **demoniacal** *adj* **1** appearing to be possessed by a devil. **2** frenzied. **demoniacally** *adv* **demonology** *n* study of demons.

demonetize *v* withdraw from use as currency. **demonetization** *n*.

demonstrate ❶ *v* **1** show or prove by reasoning or evidence. **2** display and explain the workings of. **3** reveal the existence of. **4** show support or opposition by public parades or rallies. **demonstrable** *adj* able to be proved. **demonstrably** *adv* **demonstration** *n* **1** organized expression of public opinion. **2** explanation or display of how something works. **3** proof. **demonstrative** *adj* tending to show one's feelings unreservedly. **demonstratively** *adv* **demonstrator** *n* **1** person who demonstrates how a device or machine works. **2** person who takes part in a public demonstration.

demoralize ❶ *v* undermine the morale of. **demoralization** *n*.

demote ❶ *v* reduce in status or rank. **demotion** *n*.

demotic *adj* of the common people.

demur ❶ *v* **-murring, -murred 1** show reluctance. ▷ *n* **2 without demur** without objecting.

demure ❶ *adj* quiet, reserved, and rather shy. **demurely** *adv* **demureness** *n*.

demystify *v* remove the mystery from. **demystification** *n*.

den ❶ *n* **1** home of a wild animal. **2** small secluded room in a home. **3** place where people indulge in criminal or immoral activities, e.g. *a den of thieves*.

denarius *n, pl* **-narii** ancient Roman silver coin, often called a penny in translation.

denationalize *v* transfer (an industry) from public to private ownership. **denationalization** *n*.

denature *v* **1** change the nature of. **2** make (alcohol) unfit to drink.

dengue fever, dengue [**deng**-gee] *n* infectious tropical fever.

— THESAURUS —

demolish *v* **1** = **knock down**, bulldoze, destroy, dismantle, flatten, level, raze, tear down

demolition *n* **1** = **knocking down**, bulldozing, destruction, explosion, levelling, razing, tearing down, wrecking

demon *n* **1** = **evil spirit**, devil, fiend, ghoul, goblin, malignant spirit **2** = **wizard**, ace (*inf*), fiend, master

demoniac, demoniacal *adj* **2** = **frenzied**, crazed, frantic, frenetic, furious, hectic, maniacal, manic

demonic *adj* = **evil**, devilish, diabolic, diabolical, fiendish, hellish, infernal, satanic

demonstrable *adj* = **provable**, evident, irrefutable, obvious, palpable, self-evident, unmistakable, verifiable

demonstrate *v* **1** = **prove**, display, exhibit, indicate, manifest, show, testify to **2** = **show how**, describe, explain, illustrate, make clear, teach **4** = **march**, parade, picket, protest, rally

demonstration *n* **1** = **march**, mass lobby, parade, picket, protest, rally, sit-in **2** = **explanation**, description, exposition, presentation, test, trial **3** = **proof**, confirmation, display, evidence, exhibition, expression, illustration, testimony

demoralize *v* = **dishearten**, deject, depress, discourage, dispirit, undermine, unnerve, weaken

demote *v* = **downgrade**, degrade, kick downstairs (*sl*), lower in rank, relegate

demur *v* **1** = **object**, balk, dispute, hesitate, protest, refuse, take exception, waver ▷ *n* **2 without demur** = **without objection**, without a qualm, without compunction, without hesitation, without misgivings, without protest

demure *adj* = **shy**, diffident, modest, reserved, reticent, retiring, sedate, unassuming

den *n* **1** = **lair**, cave, cavern, haunt, hide-out, hole, shelter **2** = **study**, cubbyhole, hideaway, retreat, sanctuary, sanctum

denial ❶ *n* see DENY.

denier [**den**-yer] *n* unit of weight used to measure the fineness of nylon or silk.

denigrate ❶ *v* criticize unfairly. **denigration** *n* **denigrator** *n*.

denim *n* 1 hard-wearing cotton fabric, usu. blue. ▷ *pl* 2 jeans made of denim.

denizen *n* inhabitant.

denominate ❶ *v* give a specific name to. **denomination** *n* 1 group having a distinctive interpretation of a religious faith. 2 unit in a system of weights, values, or measures. **denominational** *adj* **denominator** *n* number below the line in a fraction.

denote ❶ *v* 1 be a sign of. 2 have as a literal meaning. **denotation** *n*.

denouement [day-**noo**-mon] *n* final outcome or solution in a play or book.

denounce ❶ *v* 1 speak vehemently against. 2 give information against. **denunciation** *n* open condemnation.

dense ❶ *adj* 1 closely packed. 2 difficult to see through. 3 stupid. **densely** *adv* **density** *n, pl* **-ties** 1 degree to which something is filled or occupied. 2 measure of the compactness of a substance, expressed as its mass per unit volume.

dent ❶ *n* 1 hollow in the surface of something, made by hitting it. ▷ *v* 2 make a dent in.

dental *adj* of teeth or dentistry. **dental**

floss waxed thread used to remove food particles from between the teeth. **dental surgeon** dentist. **dentate** *adj* having teeth or teethlike notches. **dentifrice** [**den**-tif-riss] *n* paste or powder for cleaning the teeth. **dentine** [**den**-teen] *n* hard dense tissue forming the bulk of a tooth. **dentist** *n* person qualified to practise dentistry. **dentition** *n* typical arrangement of teeth in a species. **denture** *n* false tooth.

dentist *n* person qualified to practise dentistry. **dentistry** *n* branch of medicine concerned with the teeth and gums.

denude *v* remove the covering or protection from. **denudation** *n*.

denunciation *n* see DENOUNCE.

deny ❶ *v* **-nying, -nied** 1 declare to be untrue. 2 refuse to give or allow. 3 refuse to acknowledge. **deniable** *adj* **denial** *n* 1 statement that something is not true. 2 rejection of a request.

deodorize *v* remove or disguise the smell of. **deodorization** *n* **deodorant** *n* substance applied to the body to mask the smell of perspiration.

deoxyribonucleic acid *n* same as DNA.

depart ❶ *v* 1 leave. 2 differ, deviate. **departed** *adj euphemistic* dead. **the departed** *euphemistic* a dead person. **departure** *n*.

THESAURUS

denial *n* 1 = **negation**, contradiction, dissent, renunciation, repudiation, retraction 2 = **refusal**, prohibition, rebuff, rejection, repulse, veto

denigrate *v* = **disparage**, bad-mouth (*sl, chiefly US & Canad*), belittle, knock (*inf*), malign, rubbish (*inf*), run down, slander, vilify

denomination *n* 1 = **religious group**, belief, creed, persuasion, school, sect 2 = **unit**, grade, size, value

denote *v* 1 = **indicate**, betoken, designate, express, imply, mark, mean, show, signify

denounce *v* 1 = **condemn**, attack, censure, revile, stigmatize, vilify 2 = **accuse**, denunciate

dense *adj* 1 = **thick**, close-knit, compact, condensed, heavy, impenetrable, solid 2 = **opaque** 3 = **stupid**, dozy (*Brit inf*), dull, dumb (*inf*), obtuse, slow-witted, stolid,

thick, thick-witted

density *n* 1 = **tightness**, compactness, consistency, denseness, impenetrability, solidity, thickness 2 = **mass**, bulk

dent *n* 1 = **hollow**, chip, crater, depression, dimple, dip, impression, indentation, pit ▷ *v* 2 = **make a dent in**, gouge, hollow, press in, push in

deny *v* 1 = **contradict**, disagree with, disprove, rebuff, rebut, refute 2 = **refuse**, begrudge, disallow, forbid, reject, turn down, withhold 3 = **renounce**, disclaim, disown, recant, repudiate, retract

depart *v* 1 = **leave**, absent (oneself), disappear, exit, go, go away, quit, retire, retreat, withdraw 2 = **change**, deviate, differ, digress, diverge, stray, swerve, turn aside, vary, veer

d

department ❶ *n* **1** specialized division of a large organization. **2** major subdivision of the administration of a government. **3** administrative division of France and some other countries. **4** *informal* task for which someone is responsible, e.g. *gardening is my department.* **departmental** *adj* **department store** large shop selling many kinds of goods.

depend ❶ *v* (foll. by *on*) **1** put trust (in). **2** be influenced or determined (by). **3** rely (on) for income or support. **dependable** *adj* **dependably** *adv* **dependability** *n* **dependant** *n* person who depends on another for financial support. **dependence** *n* state of being dependent. **dependency** *n, pl* **-cies** **1** country controlled by another country. **2** overreliance on another person or on a drug. **dependent** *adj* depending on someone or something.

● **SPELLING TIP**
● The words **dependant** and
● **dependent** are easy to confuse.
● The first, ending in *-ant*, is a noun
● meaning a person who is dependent
● (adjective ending in *-ent*) on
● someone else.

depict ❶ *v* **1** produce a picture of. **2** describe in words. **depiction** *n*.
depilatory [dip-**pill**-a-tree] *n, pl* **-tories** *adj* (substance) designed to remove unwanted hair.
deplete ❶ *v* **1** use up. **2** reduce in number. **depletion** *n*.
deplore ❶ *v* condemn strongly. **deplorable** *adj* very bad or unpleasant.
deploy ❶ *v* organize (troops or resources) into a position ready for immediate action. **deployment** *n*.
deponent *n Law* person who makes a statement on oath.
depopulate *v* reduce the population of. **depopulation** *n*.
deport ❶ *v* remove forcibly from a country. **deport oneself** behave in a specified way. **deportation** *n* **deportee** *n*.
deportment *n* way in which a person moves or stands.
depose ❶ *v* **1** remove from an office or position of power. **2** *Law* testify on oath.
deposit ❶ *v* **1** put down. **2** entrust for safekeeping, esp. to a bank. **3** lay down naturally. ▷ *n* **4** sum of money

—————————————————————— THESAURUS ——————————

department *n* **1** = **section**, branch, bureau, division, office, station, subdivision, unit
departure *n* **1** = **leaving**, exit, exodus, going, going away, leave-taking, removal, retirement, withdrawal **2** = **change**, deviation, difference, digression, divergence, innovation, novelty, shift, variation, whole new ball game (*inf*)
depend *v* (foll. by *on*) **1** = **trust in**, bank on, count on, lean on, reckon on, rely upon, turn to ▷ *v* **2** = **be determined by**, be based on, be contingent on, be subject to, be subordinate to, hang on, hinge on, rest on, revolve around
dependable *adj* **1** = **reliable**, faithful, reputable, responsible, staunch, steady, sure, trustworthy, trusty, unfailing
dependent *adj* = **determined**, conditional, contingent, depending, influenced, subject
depict *v* **1** = **draw**, delineate, illustrate, outline, paint, picture, portray, sketch **2** = **describe**, characterize, narrate, outline, represent
depiction *n* **1** = **representation**,

delineation, picture, portrayal, sketch **2** = **description**
deplete *v* **1** = **use up**, consume, drain, empty, exhaust, expend, impoverish **2** = **reduce**, lessen
deplorable *adj* = **terrible**, disgraceful, grievous, lamentable, pitiable, regrettable, sad, scandalous, shameful, unfortunate, wretched
deplore *v* = **disapprove of**, abhor, censure, condemn, denounce, object to, take a dim view of
deploy *v* = **position**, arrange, set out, station, use, utilize
deployment *n* = **position**, arrangement, organization, spread, stationing, use, utilization
deport *v* = **expel**, banish, exile, expatriate, extradite, oust ▷ *v* **deport oneself** = **behave**, acquit oneself, act, bear oneself, carry oneself, comport oneself, conduct oneself, hold oneself
depose *v* **1** = **remove from office**, demote, dethrone, dismiss, displace, oust **2** *Law* = **testify**, avouch, declare, make a deposition
deposit *v* **1** = **put**, drop, lay, locate, place **2** = **store**, bank, consign,

paid into a bank account. **5** money given in part payment for goods or services. **6** accumulation of sediments, minerals, etc. **deposit account** bank account that earns interest. **depositary** n, pl **-taries** person to whom something is entrusted for safety. **depositor** n **depository** n, pl **-tories** store for furniture etc.

deposition n **1** Law sworn statement of a witness used in court in his or her absence. **2** deposing. **3** depositing. **4** something deposited.

depot ⊕ [dep-oh] n **1** building where goods or vehicles are kept when not in use. **2** Chiefly US bus or railway station.

depraved ⊕ adj morally bad. **depravity** n.

deprecate v express disapproval of. **deprecation** n **deprecatory** adj.

depreciate ⊕ v **1** decline in value or price. **2** criticize. **depreciation** n.

depredation n plundering.

depress ⊕ v **1** make sad. **2** lower (prices or wages). **3** push down. **depressing** adj **depressingly** adv **depressant** n, adj (drug) able to reduce nervous activity. **depression** n **1** mental state in which a person has feelings of gloom and inadequacy. **2** economic condition in which there is high unemployment and low output and investment. **3** area of low air pressure. **4** sunken place. **the Depression** the worldwide economic depression of the early 1930s. **depressive** adj **1** tending to cause depression. ▷ n **2** person who suffers from depression.

deprive ⊕ v (foll. by of) prevent from (having or enjoying). **deprivation** n **deprived** adj lacking adequate living conditions, education, etc.

dept department.

depth ⊕ n **1** distance downwards, backwards, or inwards. **2** intensity of emotion. **3** profundity of character or thought. **4** intensity of colour. ▷ pl

---

THESAURUS

entrust, lodge ▷ n **5** = **down payment**, instalment, part payment, pledge, retainer, security, stake **6** = **sediment**, accumulation, dregs, lees, precipitate, silt

depot n **1** = **storehouse**, depository, repository, warehouse **2** Chiefly US = **bus station**, garage, terminus

depraved adj = **corrupt**, degenerate, dissolute, evil, immoral, sinful, vicious, vile, wicked

depravity n = **corruption**, debauchery, evil, immorality, sinfulness, vice, wickedness

depreciate v **1** = **decrease**, deflate, devalue, lessen, lose value, lower, reduce **2** = **disparage**, belittle, denigrate, deride, detract, run down, scorn, sneer at

depreciation n **1** = **devaluation**, deflation, depression, drop, fall, slump **2** = **disparagement**, belittlement, denigration, deprecation, detraction

depress v **1** = **sadden**, deject, discourage, dishearten, dispirit, make despondent, oppress, weigh down **2** = **lower**, cheapen, depreciate, devalue, diminish, downgrade, lessen, reduce **3** = **press down**, flatten, level, lower, push down

depressed adj **1** = **low-spirited**, blue, dejected, despondent, discouraged, dispirited, downcast, downhearted, fed up, sad, unhappy **2** = **lowered**, cheapened, depreciated, devalued, weakened **3** = **sunken**, concave, hollow, indented, recessed

depressing adj **1** = **bleak**, discouraging, disheartening, dismal, dispiriting, gloomy, harrowing, sad, saddening

depression n **1** = **low spirits**, dejection, despair, despondency, downheartedness, dumps (inf), gloominess, melancholy, sadness, the blues **2** = **recession**, economic decline, hard or bad times, inactivity, slump, stagnation **4** = **hollow**, bowl, cavity, dent, dimple, dip, indentation, pit, valley

deprivation n = **want**, denial, destitution, dispossession, hardship, need, privation, removal, withdrawal, withholding

deprive v (foll. by of) = **withhold**, bereave, despoil, dispossess, rob, strip

deprived adj = **poor**, bereft, destitute, disadvantaged, down at heel, in need, lacking, needy

depth n **1** = **deepness**, drop, extent, measure **3** = **profoundness**, astuteness, discernment, insight, penetration, profundity, sagacity, wisdom

5 remote inaccessible place, e.g. *the depths of the Universe.* **6** most severe point, e.g. *in the depths of the Depression; the depths of their anguish.* **depth charge** bomb used to attack submarines by exploding at a preset depth of water.

depute ❶ *v* appoint (someone) to act on one's behalf. **deputation** *n* body of people appointed to represent others. **deputize** *v* act as deputy. **deputy** *n, pl* **-ties** person appointed to act on behalf of another.

derail *v* cause (a train) to go off the rails. **derailment** *n*.

derailleur [dee-**rail**-yer] *n* type of gear-change mechanism for bicycles.

deranged ❶ *adj* **1** insane or uncontrolled. **2** in a state of disorder. **derangement** *n*.

derby¹ [**der**-bee] *n, pl* **-bies** *US* bowler hat.

derby² [**dah**-bee] *n, pl* **-bies** sporting event between teams from the same area. **the Derby** annual horse race run at Epsom Downs.

deregulate *v* remove regulations or controls from. **deregulation** *n*.

derelict ❶ *adj* **1** unused and falling into ruins. ▷ *n* **2** social outcast, vagrant. **dereliction** *n* state of being abandoned. **dereliction of duty** failure to do one's duty.

derestrict *v* make (a road) free from speed limits.

deride ❶ *v* treat with contempt or ridicule. **derision** *n* **derisive** *adj* mocking, scornful. **derisory** *adj* too small or inadequate to be

considered seriously.

de rigueur [de rig-**gur**] *adj* required by fashion.

derive ❶ *v* (foll. by *from*) take or develop (from). **derivation** *n* **derivative** *adj* **1** based on other sources, not original. ▷ *n* **2** word, idea, etc., derived from another. **3** *Maths* rate of change of one quantity in relation to another.

dermatitis *n* inflammation of the skin.

dermatology *n* branch of medicine concerned with the skin. **dermatologist** *n*.

derogate *v* (foll. by *from*) detract from. **derogation** *n*.

derogatory ❶ [dir-**rog**-a-tree] *adj* intentionally offensive.

derrick *n* **1** simple crane. **2** framework erected over an oil well.

derring-do *n old-fashioned or lit* spirited bravery, boldness.

derringer *n* small large-bored pistol.

derv *n* diesel oil, when used for road transport.

dervish *n* member of a Muslim religious order noted for a frenzied whirling dance.

desalination *n* process of removing salt, esp. from sea water.

descale *v* remove a hard coating from inside (a kettle or pipe).

descant *n Music* **1** tune played or sung above a basic melody. ▷ *adj* **2** denoting the highest member in a family of musical instruments, e.g. *descant clarinets.*

descend ❶ *v* **1** move down (a slope etc.). **2** move to a lower level, pitch, etc. **3** (foll. by *to*) stoop to (unworthy behaviour). **4** (foll. by *on*) visit

———————————————————————— THESAURUS ——————————

deputation *n* = **delegation**, commission, embassy, envoys, legation

deputize *v* = **stand in for**, act for, take the place of, understudy

deputy *n* = **substitute**, delegate, legate, lieutenant, number two, proxy, representative, second-in-command, surrogate

deranged *adj* **1** = **mad**, crazed, crazy, demented, distracted, insane, irrational, unbalanced, unhinged

derelict *adj* **1** = **abandoned**, deserted, dilapidated, discarded, forsaken, munted (*NZ sl*), neglected, ruined ▷ *n* **2** = **tramp**, bag lady, down-and-out, outcast, vagrant

deride *v* = **mock**, disdain, disparage,

insult, jeer, ridicule, scoff, scorn, sneer, taunt

derisory *adj* = **ridiculous**, contemptible, insulting, laughable, ludicrous, outrageous, preposterous

derivation *n* = **origin**, beginning, foundation, root, source

derive *v* (foll. by *from*) = **come from**, arise from, emanate from, flow from, issue from, originate from, proceed from, spring from, stem from

derogatory *adj* = **disparaging**, belittling, defamatory, offensive, slighting, uncomplimentary, unfavourable, unflattering

descend *v* **1** = **move down**, drop, fall, go down, plummet, plunge, sink,

unexpectedly. **be descended from** be connected by a blood relationship to.
descendant n person or animal descended from an individual, race, or species. **descendent** adj descending. **descent** n 1 descending. 2 downward slope. 3 derivation from an ancestor.

describe ❶ v 1 give an account of (something or someone) in words. 2 trace the outline of (a circle etc.). **description** n 1 statement that describes something or someone. 2 sort, e.g. flowers of every description. **descriptive** adj **descriptively** adv.

descry v **-scrying, -scried** 1 catch sight of. 2 discover by looking carefully.

desecrate v damage or insult (something sacred). **desecration** n.

desegregate v end racial segregation in. **desegregation** n.

deselect v Brit Politics refuse to select (an MP) for re-election. **deselection** n.

desensitize v make less sensitive.

desert¹ ❶ n region with little or no vegetation because of low rainfall.

desert² ❶ v 1 abandon (a person or place) without intending to return. 2 Military leave (a post or duty) with no intention of returning. **deserter** n **desertion** n.

deserts pl n **get one's just deserts** get the punishment one deserves.

deserve ❶ v be entitled to or worthy of. **deserved** adj rightfully earned. **deservedly** [dee-**zerv**-id-lee] adv **deserving** adj worthy of help, praise, or reward.

deshabille [day-zab-**beel**] n state of being partly dressed.

desiccate v remove most of the water from. **desiccation** n.

● SPELLING TIP
● The word **desiccate** has two cs
● because it comes from the Latin
● word siccus, which means 'dry'.

design ❶ v 1 work out the structure or form of (something), by making a sketch or plans. 2 plan and make artistically. 3 intend for a specific purpose. ▷ n 4 sketch, plan, or preliminary drawing. 5 arrangement or features of an artistic or decorative

d

THESAURUS

subside, tumble 2 = **slope**, dip, incline, slant 3 = **lower oneself**, degenerate, deteriorate, stoop 4 (foll. by on) = **attack**, arrive, invade, raid, swoop ▷ v **be descended from** = **originate from**, be handed down from, be passed down from, derive from, issue from, proceed from, spring from

descent n 1 = **coming down**, drop, fall, plunge, swoop 2 = **slope**, declivity, dip, drop, incline, slant 3 = **ancestry**, extraction, family tree, genealogy, lineage, origin, parentage

describe v 1 = **relate**, depict, explain, express, narrate, portray, recount, report, tell 2 = **trace**, delineate, draw, mark out, outline

description n 1 = **account**, depiction, explanation, narrative, portrayal, report, representation, sketch 2 = **kind**, brand, category, class, order, sort, type, variety

descriptive adj 1 = **graphic**, detailed, explanatory, expressive, illustrative, pictorial, picturesque, vivid

desert¹ n = **wilderness**, solitude, waste, wasteland, wilds

desert² v 1 = **abandon**, abscond, forsake, jilt, leave, leave stranded, maroon, quit, strand, walk out on (inf)

deserted adj = **abandoned**, derelict, desolate, empty, forsaken, neglected, unoccupied, vacant

deserter n = **defector**, absconder, escapee, fugitive, renegade, runaway, traitor, truant

desertion n = **abandonment**, absconding, apostasy, betrayal, defection, dereliction, escape, evasion, flight, relinquishment

deserve v = **merit**, be entitled to, be worthy of, earn, justify, rate, warrant

deserved adj = **well-earned**, due, earned, fitting, justified, merited, proper, rightful, warranted

deserving adj = **worthy**, commendable, estimable, laudable, meritorious, praiseworthy, righteous

design v 1 = **plan**, draft, draw, outline, sketch, trace 2 = **create**, conceive, fabricate, fashion, invent, originate, think up 3 = **intend**, aim, mean, plan, propose, purpose ▷ n 4 = **plan**, blueprint, draft, drawing, model, outline, scheme, sketch 5 = **arrangement**, construction, form, organization, pattern, shape, style 7 = **intention**, aim, end, goal, object, objective, purpose, target

d

work. **6** finished artistic or decorative creation art of designing. **7** intention, e.g. *by design*. **designedly** [dee-**zine**-id-lee] *adv* intentionally. **designer** *n* **1** person who draws up original sketches or plans from which things are made. ▷ *adj* **2** designed by a well-known designer. **designing** *adj* cunning and scheming.

designate ❶ [**dez**-zig-nate] *v* **1** give a name to. **2** select (someone) for an office or duty. ▷ *adj* **3** appointed but not yet in office, e.g. *the Prime Minister designate*. **designation** *n* name.

desire ❶ *v* **1** want very much. ▷ *n* **2** wish, longing. **3** sexual appetite. **4** person or thing desired. **desirable** *adj* **1** worth having. **2** arousing sexual desire. **desirability** *n* **desirous of** having a desire for.

desist ❶ *v* (foll. by *from*) stop (doing something).

desk *n* **1** piece of furniture with a writing surface and drawers. **2** service counter in a public building. **3** section of a newspaper covering a specific subject, e.g. *the sports desk*. **desktop**

adj (of a computer) small enough to use at a desk. **desktop publishing** means of publishing reports etc. using a desktop computer and a laser printer.

desolate ❶ *adj* **1** uninhabited and bleak. **2** very sad. ▷ *v* **3** deprive of inhabitants. **4** make (someone) very sad. **desolation** *n*.

despair ❶ *n* **1** total loss of hope. ▷ *v* **2** lose hope.

despatch ❶ *v*, *n* same as DISPATCH.

desperado ❶ *n*, *pl* **-does**, **-dos** reckless person ready to commit any violent illegal act.

desperate ❶ *adj* **1** in despair and reckless. **2** (of an action) undertaken as a last resort. **3** having a strong need or desire. **desperately** *adv* **desperation** *n*.

- ● SPELLING TIP
- ● It's often difficult to decide
- ● whether to write an *a* or an *e* when
- ● it doesn't seem to affect a word's
- ● pronunciation. An example in
- ● the Bank of English is *desparate*,
- ● which should, of course, be spelt
- ● **desperate**.

_____ THESAURUS _____

designate *v* **1** = **name**, call, dub, entitle, label, style, term **2** = **appoint**, assign, choose, delegate, depute, nominate, select

designation *n* = **name**, description, label, mark, title

designer *n* **1** = **creator**, architect, deviser, inventor, originator, planner

desirable *adj* **1** = **agreeable**, advantageous, advisable, beneficial, good, preferable, profitable, worthwhile **2** = **attractive**, adorable, alluring, fetching, glamorous, lekker (*S Afr sl*), seductive, sexy (*inf*)

desire *v* **1** = **want**, crave, hanker after, hope for, long for, set one's heart on, thirst for, wish for, yearn for ▷ *n* **2** = **wish**, aspiration, craving, hankering, hope, longing, thirst, want **3** = **lust**, appetite, libido, passion

desist *v* (foll. by *from*) = **stop**, break off, cease, discontinue, end, forbear, leave off, pause, refrain from

desolate *adj* **1** = **uninhabited**, bare, barren, bleak, dreary, godforsaken, solitary, wild **2** = **miserable**, dejected, despondent, disconsolate, downcast, forlorn, gloomy, wretched ▷ *v* **3** = **lay**

waste, depopulate, despoil, destroy, devastate, lay low, pillage, plunder, ravage, ruin **4** = **deject**, depress, discourage, dishearten, dismay, distress, grieve

desolation *n* **1** = **bleakness**, barrenness, isolation, solitude **2** = **misery**, anguish, dejection, despair, distress, gloom, sadness, woe, wretchedness

despair *n* **1** = **despondency**, anguish, dejection, depression, desperation, gloom, hopelessness, misery, wretchedness ▷ *v* **2** = **lose hope**, give up, lose heart

despairing *adj* = **hopeless**, dejected, desperate, despondent, disconsolate, frantic, grief-stricken, inconsolable, miserable, wretched

despatch see DISPATCH

desperado *n* = **criminal**, bandit, lawbreaker, outlaw, villain

desperate *adj* **1** = **reckless**, audacious, daring, frantic, furious, risky **2** = **grave**, drastic, extreme, urgent

desperately *adv* **2** = **badly**, appallingly, dangerously, fearfully, frightfully, gravely, hopelessly, perilously, seriously, severely

despise ● v regard with contempt.
  despicable adj deserving contempt.
  despicably adv.
despite ● prep in spite of.
despoil v formal plunder. **despoliation** n.
despondent ● adj unhappy.
  despondently adv **despondency** n.
despot ● n person in power who acts
  unfairly or cruelly. **despotic** adj
  despotically adv **despotism** n unfair
  or cruel government or behaviour.
dessert n sweet course served at the
  end of a meal. **dessertspoon** n spoon
  between a tablespoon and a teaspoon
  in size.
destabilize v make (a country or
  government) politically or
  economically unstable.
  destabilization n.
destination ● n place to which
  someone or something is going.
destined ● [**dess**-tind] adj 1 certain to be
  or to do something, e.g. destined to fail.
  2 heading towards a specific destination,
  e.g. destined for eastern Europe.
destiny ● n, pl **-nies** 1 future marked

out for a person or thing. 2 the power
  that predetermines the course of
  events.
destitute ● adj having no money or
  possessions. **destitution** n.
destroy ● v 1 ruin, demolish. 2 put an
  end to. 3 kill (an animal). **destroyer** n
  1 small heavily armed warship.
  2 person or thing that destroys.
destruction ● n 1 destroying.
  2 cause of ruin. **destructible** adj able
  to be destroyed. **destructive** adj
  (capable of) causing destruction.
  destructively adv **destructiveness** n.
desuetude [diss-**syoo**-it-tude] n
  condition of not being in use.
desultory [**dez**-zl-tree] adj 1 jumping
  from one thing to another, disconnected.
  2 random. **desultorily** adv.
detach ● v disengage and separate.
  detachable adj **detached** adj 1 (of a
  house) not joined to another house.
  2 showing no emotional involvement.
  detachment n 1 lack of emotional
  involvement. 2 small group of
  soldiers.

THESAURUS

desperation n a = **misery**, agony,
  anguish, despair, hopelessness,
  trouble, unhappiness, worry
  b = **recklessness**, foolhardiness,
  frenzy, impetuosity, madness, rashness
despicable adj = **contemptible**,
  detestable, disgraceful, hateful, mean,
  scungy (Aust & NZ inf), shameful,
  sordid, vile, worthless, wretched
despise v = **look down on**, abhor,
  detest, loathe, revile, scorn
despite prep = **in spite of**, against,
  even with, in the face of, in the teeth
  of, notwithstanding, regardless of,
  undeterred by
despondency n = **dejection**,
  depression, despair, desperation,
  gloom, low spirits, melancholy,
  misery, sadness
despondent adj = **dejected**, depressed,
  disconsolate, disheartened, dispirited,
  downhearted, glum, in despair, sad,
  sorrowful
despot n = **tyrant**, autocrat, dictator,
  oppressor
despotic adj = **tyrannical**,
  authoritarian, autocratic, dictatorial,
  domineering, imperious, oppressive
despotism n = **tyranny**, autocracy,
  dictatorship, oppression,
  totalitarianism

destination n = **journey's end**, haven,
  resting-place, station, stop, terminus
destined adj = **fated**, bound, certain,
  doomed, intended, meant,
  predestined
destiny n 1 = **fortune**, doom, fate, lot,
  portion 2 = **fate**, fortune, karma,
  kismet
destitute adj = **penniless**, down and
  out, impoverished, indigent,
  insolvent, moneyless, penurious,
  poor, poverty-stricken
destroy v 1, 2 = **ruin**, annihilate, crush,
  demolish, devastate, eradicate,
  shatter, wipe out, wreck
destruction n 1 = **ruin**, annihilation,
  demolition, devastation, eradication,
  extermination, havoc, slaughter,
  wreckage
destructive adj = **damaging**,
  calamitous, catastrophic, deadly,
  devastating, fatal, harmful, lethal,
  ruinous
detach v = **separate**, cut off,
  disconnect, disengage, divide,
  remove, sever, tear off, unfasten
detached adj 1 = **separate**,
  disconnected, discrete, unconnected
  2 = **uninvolved**, disinterested,
  dispassionate, impartial, impersonal,
  neutral, objective, reserved, unbiased

detail ❶ *n* **1** individual piece of information. **2** unimportant item. **3** small individual features of something, considered collectively. **4** *Chiefly military* (personnel assigned) a specific duty. ▷ *v* **5** list fully. **6** *Chiefly military* assign to a specific duty.

detain ❶ *v* **1** delay (someone). **2** hold (someone) in custody. **detainee** *n* **detainment** *n*.

detect ❶ *v* **1** notice. **2** discover, find. **detectable** *adj* **detection** *n* **detective** *n* policeman or private agent who investigates crime. **detector** *n* instrument used to find something, e.g. *a metal detector*.

detente [day-**tont**] *n* easing of tension between nations.

detention ❶ *n* **1** imprisonment. **2** form of punishment in which a pupil is detained after school.

deter ❶ *v* **-terring, -terred** discourage (someone) from doing something by instilling fear or doubt. **deterrent** *n* **1** something that deters. **2** weapon, esp. nuclear, intended to deter attack.

▷ *adj* **3** tending to deter. **deterrence** *n*.

detergent ❶ *n* chemical substance for washing clothes or dishes.

deteriorate ❶ *v* become worse. **deterioration** *n*.

determine ❶ *v* **1** settle (an argument or a question) conclusively. **2** find out the facts about. **3** make a firm decision (to do something). **determinant** *n* factor that determines. **determinate** *adj* definitely limited or fixed. **determination** *n* **1** being determined or resolute. **2** determining. **determined** *adj* firmly decided, unable to be dissuaded. **determinedly** *adv* **determiner** *n Grammar* word that determines the object to which a noun phrase refers, e.g. *all*. **determinism** *n* theory that human choice is not free, but decided by past events. **determinist** *n*, *adj* **deterministic** *adj*.

detest ❶ *v* dislike intensely. **detestable** *adj* **detestation** *n*.

dethrone *v* remove from a throne or position of power.

——————————————————————— THESAURUS ——————

detachment *n* **1** = **indifference**, aloofness, coolness, impartiality, neutrality, nonchalance, objectivity, remoteness, unconcern **2** = **unit**, body, force, party, patrol, squad, task force

detail *n* **2** = **fine point**, nicety, particular, triviality **3** = **point**, aspect, component, element, fact, factor, feature, particular, respect **4** *Chiefly mil* = **party**, assignment, body, detachment, duty, fatigue, force, squad ▷ *v* **5** = **list**, catalogue, enumerate, itemize, recite, recount, rehearse, relate, tabulate **6** *Chiefly mil* = **appoint**, allocate, assign, charge, commission, delegate, send

detailed *adj* **1** = **comprehensive**, blow-by-blow, exhaustive, full, intricate, minute, particular, thorough

detain *v* **1** = **delay**, check, hinder, hold up, impede, keep back, retard, slow up (*or* down) **2** = **hold**, arrest, confine, intern, restrain

detect *v* **1** = **notice**, ascertain, identify, note, observe, perceive, recognize, spot **2** = **discover**, find, track down, uncover, unmask

detective *n* = **investigator**, cop (*sl*), gumshoe (*US sl*), private eye, private

investigator, sleuth (*inf*)

detention *n* **1** = **imprisonment**, confinement, custody, incarceration

deter *v* = **discourage**, dissuade, frighten, inhibit from, intimidate, prevent, put off, stop, talk out of

detergent *n* = **cleaner**, cleanser

deteriorate *v* = **decline**, degenerate, go downhill (*inf*), lower, slump, worsen

determination *n* **1** = **resolution**, dedication, doggedness, fortitude, perseverance, persistence, resolve, single-mindedness, steadfastness, tenacity, willpower

determine *v* **1** = **settle**, conclude, decide, end, finish, ordain, regulate **2** = **find out**, ascertain, detect, discover, establish, learn, verify, work out **3** = **decide**, choose, elect, make up one's mind, resolve

determined *adj* = **resolute**, dogged, firm, intent, persevering, persistent, single-minded, steadfast, tenacious, unwavering

deterrent *n* **1** = **discouragement**, check, curb, disincentive, hindrance, impediment, obstacle, restraint

detest *v* = **hate**, abhor, abominate, despise, dislike intensely, loathe, recoil from

detonate ❶ v explode. **detonation** n
detonator n small amount of
explosive, or a device, used to set off
an explosion.

detour ❶ n route that is not the most
direct one.

detox v, n informal (undergo) treatment
to rid the body of poisonous
substances.

detoxify v **-fying, -fied** remove poison
from. **detoxification** n.

detract ❶ v (foll. by from) make
(something) seem less good.
detractor n **detraction** n.

detriment ❶ n disadvantage or
damage. **detrimental** adj
detrimentally adv.

detritus [dit-**trite**-uss] n **1** loose mass
of stones and silt worn away from
rocks. **2** debris.

de trop [de **troh**] adj French unwanted,
unwelcome.

detumescence n subsidence of
swelling. **detumescent** adj.

deuce [**dyewss**] n **1** Tennis score
of forty all. **2** playing card with
two symbols or dice with two
spots.

deuterium n isotope of hydrogen
twice as heavy as the normal atom.

Deutschmark [**doytch**-mark],
Deutsche Mark[**doytch**-a] n former
monetary unit of Germany.

devalue v **-valuing, -valued 1** reduce
the exchange value of (a currency).
2 reduce the value of (something or
someone). **devaluation** n.

devastate ❶ v destroy. **devastated** adj
shocked and extremely upset.
devastation n.

develop ❶ v **1** grow or bring to a
later, more elaborate, or more
advanced stage. **2** come or bring into
existence. **3** build houses or factories
on (an area of land). **4** produce
(photographs) by making negatives or
prints from a film. **developer** n
1 person who develops property.
2 chemical used to develop
photographs or films. **development** n
1 developing. **2** product of developing.
3 event or incident that changes a
situation. **4** area of land that has been
developed. **developmental** adj
developing country poor or
nonindustrial country that is trying to
develop its resources by
industrialization.

deviate ❶ v **1** differ from others
in belief or thought. **2** depart
from one's previous behaviour.
deviation n **deviant** n, adj
(person) deviating from what is
considered acceptable behaviour.
deviance n.

device ❶ n **1** machine or tool used
for a specific task. **2** scheme or plan.
**leave someone to his, her own
devices** let someone do as he or she
wishes.

THESAURUS

detonate v = **explode**, blast, blow up,
discharge, set off, trigger

detour n = **diversion**, bypass, indirect
course, roundabout way

detract v (foll. by from) = **lessen**,
devaluate, diminish, lower, reduce,
take away from

detriment n = **damage**, disadvantage,
disservice, harm, hurt, impairment,
injury, loss

detrimental adj = **damaging**, adverse,
deleterious, destructive,
disadvantageous, harmful,
prejudicial, unfavourable

devastate v = **destroy**, demolish, lay
waste, level, ravage, raze, ruin, sack,
wreck

devastation n = **destruction**,
demolition, desolation, havoc, ruin

develop v **1** = **advance**, amplify,
augment, broaden, elaborate,
enlarge, evolve, expand, flourish,
grow, mature, progress, prosper, ripen
2 = **form**, breed, establish, generate,
invent, originate

development n **1** = **growth**, advance,
evolution, expansion, improvement,
increase, progress, spread **3** = **event**,
happening, incident, occurrence,
result, turn of events, upshot

deviant n = **pervert**, freak, misfit ▷ adj
= **perverted**, kinky (sl), sick (inf),
twisted, warped

deviate v = **differ**, depart, diverge,
stray, swerve, veer, wander

deviation n = **departure**, digression,
discrepancy, disparity, divergence,
inconsistency, irregularity, shift,
variation

device n **1** = **gadget**, apparatus,
appliance, contraption, implement,
instrument, machine, tool **2** = **ploy**,
gambit, manoeuvre, plan, scheme,
stratagem, trick, wile

devil ❶ *n* **1** evil spirit. **2** evil person. **3** person, e.g. *poor devil*. **4** daring person, e.g. *be a devil!* **5** *informal* something difficult or annoying, e.g. *a devil of a long time*. ▷ *v* **-illing**, **-illed 6** prepare (food) with a highly flavoured spiced mixture. **the Devil** *Theology* chief spirit of evil and enemy of God. **devilish** *adj* **1** cruel or unpleasant. ▷ *adv* **2** (also **devilishly**) *informal* extremely. **devilment** *n* mischievous conduct. **devilry** *n* mischievousness. **devil-may-care** *adj* carefree and cheerful. **devil's advocate** person who takes an opposing or unpopular point of view for the sake of argument.

devious ❶ *adj* **1** insincere and dishonest. **2** indirect. **deviously** *adv* **deviousness** *n*.

devise ❶ *v* work out (something) in one's mind.

devoid ❶ *adj* (foll. by *of*) completely lacking (in).

devolve *v* (foll. by *on* or *to*) pass (power or duties) or (of power or duties) be passed to a successor or substitute. **devolution** *n* transfer of authority from a central government to regional governments.

devote ❶ *v* apply or dedicate to a particular purpose. **devoted** *adj* showing loyalty or devotion. **devotedly** *adv* **devotee** [dev-vote-tee] *n* **1** person who is very enthusiastic about something. **2** zealous follower of a religion. **devotion** *n* **1** strong affection for or loyalty to someone or something. **2** religious zeal. ▷ *pl* **3** prayers. **devotional** *adj*.

devour ❶ *v* **1** eat greedily. **2** (of an emotion) engulf and destroy. **3** read eagerly.

devout ❶ *adj* deeply religious. **devoutly** *adv*.

dew *n* drops of water that form on the ground at night from vapour in the air. **dewy** *adj* **dewier**, **dewiest**. **dewy-eyed** *adj* innocent and inexperienced.

dewlap *n* loose fold of skin hanging under the throat in dogs, cattle, etc.

dexterity ❶ *n* **1** skill in using one's hands. **2** mental quickness. **dexterous** *adj* **dexterously** *adv*.

dextrin, dextrine *n* sticky substance obtained from starch, used as a thickening agent in food.

dextrose *n* glucose occurring in fruit, honey, and the blood of animals.

───────────────── THESAURUS ─────────────────

devil *n* **1** = **brute**, beast, demon, fiend, monster, ogre, terror **2** = **scamp**, rascal, rogue, scoundrel **3** = **person**, beggar, creature, thing, wretch ▷ *n* **the Devil** *Theology* = **Satan**, Beelzebub, Evil One, Lucifer, Mephistopheles, Old Nick (*inf*), Prince of Darkness

devilish *adj* **1** = **fiendish**, atrocious, damnable, detestable, diabolical, hellish, infernal, satanic, wicked

devious *adj* **1** = **sly**, calculating, deceitful, dishonest, double-dealing, insincere, scheming, surreptitious, underhand, wily **2** = **indirect**, circuitous, rambling, roundabout

devise *v* = **work out**, conceive, construct, contrive, design, dream up, formulate, invent, think up

devoid *adj* (foll. by *of*) = **lacking**, bereft, deficient, destitute, empty, free from, wanting, without

devote *v* = **dedicate**, allot, apply, assign, commit, give, pledge, reserve, set apart

devoted *adj* = **dedicated**, ardent, committed, constant, devout,

faithful, loyal, staunch, steadfast, true

devotee *n* **1** = **enthusiast**, adherent, admirer, aficionado, buff (*inf*), fan, fanatic, supporter **2** = **follower**, disciple

devotion *n* **1** = **dedication**, adherence, affection, allegiance, attachment, commitment, constancy, faithfulness, fidelity, fondness, love, loyalty, passion **2** = **devoutness**, godliness, holiness, piety, reverence, spirituality ▷ *pl* **3** = **prayers**, church service, divine office, religious observance

devour *v* **1** = **eat**, consume, gobble, gulp, guzzle, polish off (*inf*), swallow, wolf **2** = **destroy**, annihilate, consume, ravage, waste, wipe out **3** = **enjoy**, read compulsively *or* voraciously, take in

devout *adj* = **religious**, godly, holy, orthodox, pious, prayerful, pure, reverent, saintly

dexterity *n* **1** = **skill**, adroitness, deftness, expertise, finesse, nimbleness, proficiency, touch **2** = **cleverness**, ability, aptitude, ingenuity

dg decigram.

DH Department of Health.

dhal, dal n curry made from lentils or beans.

dharma n **1** *Hinduism* moral law or behaviour. **2** *Buddhism* ideal truth.

dhoti n, pl **-tis** long loincloth worn by men in India.

dhow n Arab sailing ship.

DI donor insemination: method of making a woman pregnant by transferring sperm from a man other than her regular partner using artificial means.

di- prefix **1** twice, two, or double, e.g. *dicotyledon.* **2** containing two specified atoms or groups of atoms, e. g. *carbon dioxide.*

diabetes [die-a-**beet**-eez] n disorder in which an abnormal amount of urine containing an excess of sugar is excreted. **diabetic** n **1** person who has diabetes. ▷ adj **2** of or having diabetes. **3** suitable for people with diabetes.

diabolic ❶ adj of the Devil. **diabolical** adj informal extremely bad, e.g. *the conditions were diabolical.* **diabolically** adv **diabolism** n witchcraft, devil worship.

diaconate n position or period of office of a deacon.

diacritic n sign above or below a character to indicate phonetic value or stress.

diadem n old-fashioned crown.

diaeresis n, pl **-ses** mark (¨) placed over a vowel to show that it is pronounced separately from the preceding one, for example in *Noël.*

diagnosis ❶ [die-ag-**no**-siss] n, pl **-ses** [-seez] discovery and identification of diseases from the examination of symptoms. **diagnose** v **diagnostic** adj.

diagonal ❶ adj **1** from corner to corner.

2 slanting. ▷ n **3** diagonal line. **diagonally** adv.

diagram ❶ n sketch showing the form or workings of something. **diagrammatic** adj.

dial n **1** face of a clock or watch. **2** graduated disc on a measuring instrument. **3** control on a radio or television set used to change the station. **4** numbered disc on the front of some telephones. ▷ v **dialling**, **dialled 5** operate the dial or buttons on a telephone in order to contact (a number). **dialling tone** continuous sound heard on picking up a telephone, indicating that a number can be dialled.

dialect ❶ n form of a language spoken in a particular area. **dialectal** adj.

dialectic n logical debate by question and answer to resolve differences between two views. **dialectical** adj.

dialogue ❶ n **1** conversation between two people, esp. in a book, film, or play. **2** discussion between representatives of two nations or groups. **dialogue box** n small window on a computer screen prompting the user to ent er information.

dialysis [die-**al**-iss-iss] n *Medical* filtering of blood through a membrane to remove waste products.

diamagnetism n phenomenon exhibited by substances that are repelled by both poles of a magnet.

diamanté [die-a-**man**-tee] adj decorated with artificial jewels or sequins.

diameter n (length of) a straight line through the centre of a circle or sphere. **diametric**, **diametrical** adj **1** of a diameter. **2** completely opposed, e.g. *the diametric opposite.* **diametrically** adv.

d

THESAURUS

diabolical adj Inf = **dreadful**, abysmal, appalling, atrocious, hellish, outrageous, shocking, terrible

diagnose v = **identify**, analyse, determine, distinguish, interpret, pinpoint, pronounce, recognize

diagnosis n = **analysis**, conclusion, examination, investigation, opinion, scrutiny

diagonal adj **1** = **crossways**, cross, crosswise **2** = **slanting**, angled, oblique

diagonally adv **1** = **crosswise**, cornerwise **2** = **aslant**, at an angle, obliquely

diagram n = **plan**, chart, drawing, figure, graph, representation, sketch

dialect n = **language**, brogue, idiom, jargon, patois, provincialism, speech, vernacular

dialogue n **1** = **conversation**, communication, discourse, exchange **2** = **discussion**, conference

diamond *n* **1** exceptionally hard, usu. colourless, precious stone. **2** *Geometry* figure with four sides of equal length forming two acute and two obtuse angles. **3** playing card marked with red diamond-shaped symbols. **4** *Baseball* the playing field. **diamond jubilee** sixtieth anniversary of an event. **diamond wedding** sixtieth anniversary of a wedding.

diapason [die-a-**pay**-zon] *n* **1** either of two stops found throughout the range of a pipe organ. **2** range of an instrument or voice.

diaper *n US & Canad* towelling cloth to absorb baby's excrement.

diaphanous [die-**af**-fan-ous] *adj* fine and almost transparent.

diaphoretic *n, adj* (drug) causing sweating.

diaphragm [die-a-fram] *n* **1** muscular partition that separates the abdominal cavity and chest cavity. **2** contraceptive device placed over the neck of the womb.

diarrhoea [die-a-**ree**-a] *n* frequent discharge of abnormally liquid faeces.

- **SPELLING TIP**
- It's possibly because people don't
- write the word **diarrhoea** very
- often that there's only one example
- of *diarhoea*, with only one *r*, in the
- Bank of English. Or is it because it's
- such a difficult word to spell, we
- always look it up to get it right?

diary ❶ *n, pl* **-ries** (book for) a record of daily events, appointments, or observations. **diarist** *n* person who writes a diary.

Diaspora [die-**ass**-spore-a] *n* **1** dispersion of the Jews after the Babylonian conquest of Palestine. **2** (**d-**) dispersion of people originally of one nation.

diastole [die-**ass**-stoh-lee] *n* dilation of the chambers of the heart. **diastolic** *adj*.

diatomic *adj* containing two atoms.

diatonic *adj Music* of a regular major or minor scale.

diatribe *n* bitter critical attack.

dibble *n* small hand tool used to make holes in the ground for seeds or plants.

dice *n, pl* **dice 1** small cube each of whose sides has a different number of spots (1 to 6), used in games of chance. **2** game played with dice. ▷ *v* **3** cut (food) into small cubes. **dice with death** take a risk. **dicey** *adj* **dicier**, **diciest** *informal* dangerous or risky.

dichotomy [die-**kot**-a-mee] *n, pl* **-mies** division into two opposed groups or parts.

dick *n taboo slang* penis. **clever dick** person who likes to show how clever he or she is.

Dickensian *adj* denoting poverty, distress, and exploitation as depicted in Dickens's novels.

dicky¹ *n, pl* **dickies** false shirt front. **dicky-bird** *n* child's word for a bird.

dicky² ❶ *adj* **dickier**, **dickiest** *informal* shaky or weak, e.g. *a dicky heart*.

Dictaphone *n* ® tape recorder for recording dictation for subsequent typing.

dictate ❶ *v* **1** say aloud for someone else to write down. **2** (foll. by *to*) seek to impose one's will on (other people). ▷ *n* **3** authoritative command. **4** guiding principle. **dictation** *n* **dictator** *n* **1** ruler who has complete power. **2** person in power who acts unfairly or cruelly. **dictatorship** *n* **dictatorial** *adj* like a dictator.

——————————————————————————— THESAURUS ———————

diary *n* = **journal**, appointment book, chronicle, daily record, engagement book, Filofax ®

dicky² *adj Inf* = **weak**, fluttery, shaky, shonky (*Aust & NZ inf*), unreliable, unsound, unsteady

dictate *v* **1** = **speak**, read out, say, utter **2** (foll. by *to*) = **order**, command, decree, demand, direct, impose, lay down the law, pronounce ▷ *n* **3** = **command**, decree, demand, direction, edict, fiat, injunction, order **4** = **principle**, code, law, rule

dictator *n* **1** = **absolute ruler**, autocrat, despot **2** = **tyrant**, oppressor

dictatorial *adj* **a** = **absolute**, arbitrary, autocratic, despotic, totalitarian, tyrannical, unlimited, unrestricted **b** = **domineering**, authoritarian, bossy (*inf*), imperious, oppressive, overbearing

dictatorship *n* **1** = **absolute rule**, absolutism, autocracy, despotism, totalitarianism **2** = **tyranny**, authoritarianism

diction ❶ *n* manner of pronouncing words and sounds.

dictionary ❶ *n, pl* **-aries 1** book consisting of an alphabetical list of words with their meanings. **2** similar book giving equivalent words in two languages. **3** alphabetically ordered reference book of terms relating to a particular subject.

dictum *n, pl* **-tums, -ta 1** formal statement. **2** popular saying.

did *v* past tense of DO¹.

didactic *adj* **1** intended to instruct. **2** overeager to instruct. **didactically** *adv*.

diddle *v informal* swindle.

didgeridoo *n Music* Australian Aboriginal deep-toned wind instrument.

didn't did not.

die¹ ❶ *v* **dying, died 1** (of a person, animal, or plant) cease all biological activity permanently. **2** (of something inanimate) cease to exist or function. **be dying for to do something** *informal* be eager for or to do something. **die down** *v* lose strength or power by degrees. **die-hard** *n* person who resists change.

die² *n* **1** shaped block used to cut or form metal. **2** same as DICE (sense 1).

dieldrin *n* highly toxic insecticide.

dielectric *n* **1** substance which does not conduct electricity well, insulator. ▷ *adj* **2** not conducting electricity well.

dieresis [die-**air**-iss-iss] *n, pl* **-ses** [-seez]same as DIAERESIS.

diesel *n* **1** diesel engine. **2** vehicle driven by a diesel engine. **3** diesel oil. **diesel engine** internal-combustion engine in which oil is ignited by compression. **diesel oil** fuel obtained from petroleum distillation.

diet¹ ❶ *n* **1** food that a person or animal regularly eats. **2** specific range of foods, to control weight or for health reasons. ▷ *v* **3** follow a special diet so as to lose weight. ▷ *adj* **4** (of food) suitable for a weight-reduction diet. **dietary** *adj* **dietary fibre** fibrous substances in fruit and vegetables that aid digestion. **dieter** *n* **dietetic** *adj* prepared for special dietary requirements. **dietetics** *n* study of diet and nutrition. **dietician** *n* person who specializes in dietetics.

diet² ❶ *n* parliament of some countries.

differ ❶ *v* **1** be unlike. **2** disagree. **difference** *n* **1** state of being unlike. **2** disagreement. **3** remainder left after subtraction. **different** *adj* **1** unlike. **2** unusual. **differently** *adv*.

- **USAGE NOTE**
- The accepted idiom is *different from* but *different to* is also used. *Different than* is used in America.

———— THESAURUS ————

diction *n* = **pronunciation**, articulation, delivery, elocution, enunciation, fluency, inflection, intonation, speech

dictionary *n* = **wordbook**, glossary, lexicon, vocabulary

die¹ *v* **1** = **pass away**, breathe one's last, cark (*Aust & NZ sl*), croak (*sl*), expire, give up the ghost, kick the bucket (*sl*), peg out (*inf*), perish, snuff it (*sl*) **2** = **stop**, break down, fade out or away, fail, fizzle out, halt, lose power, peter out, run down ▷ *v* **be dying for to do something** *Inf* = **long for**, ache for, be eager for, desire, hunger for, pine for, yearn for

die-hard *n* = **reactionary**, fanatic, old fogey, stick-in-the-mud (*inf*)

diet¹ *n* **1** = **food**, fare, nourishment, nutriment, provisions, rations, sustenance, tucker (*Aust & NZ inf*), victuals **2** = **regime**, abstinence, fast, regimen ▷ *v* **3** = **slim**, abstain, eat sparingly, fast, lose weight

diet² *n* = **council**, chamber, congress, convention, legislature, meeting, parliament

differ *v* **1** = **be dissimilar**, contradict, contrast, depart from, diverge, run counter to, stand apart, vary **2** = **disagree**, clash, contend, debate, demur, dispute, dissent, oppose, take exception, take issue

difference *n* **1** = **dissimilarity**, alteration, change, contrast, discrepancy, disparity, diversity, variation, variety **2** = **disagreement**, argument, clash, conflict, contretemps, debate, dispute, quarrel **3** = **remainder**, balance, rest, result

different *adj* **1** = **unlike**, altered, changed, contrasting, disparate, dissimilar, divergent, diverse, inconsistent, opposed, sundry, varied, various **2** = **unusual**, atypical, distinctive, extraordinary, munted (*NZ sl*), peculiar, singular, special, strange, uncommon

d

differential ❶ *adj* **1** of or using a difference. **2** *Maths* involving differentials. ▷ *n* **3** factor that differentiates between two comparable things. **4** *Maths* tiny difference between values in a scale. **5** difference between rates of pay for different types of work. **differential calculus** branch of calculus concerned with derivatives and differentials. **differential gear** mechanism in a road vehicle that allows one driving wheel to rotate faster than the other when cornering. **differentiate** *v* **1** perceive or show the difference (between). **2** make (one thing) distinct from other such things. **differentiation** *n*.

difficult ❶ *adj* **1** requiring effort or skill to do or understand. **2** not easily pleased. **difficulty** *n*, *pl* **-ties**.

diffident ❶ *adj* lacking self-confidence. **diffidence** *n* **diffidently** *adv*.

diffract *v* cause to undergo diffraction. **diffraction** *n Physics* **1** deviation in the direction of a wave at the edge of an obstacle in its path. **2** formation of light and dark fringes by the passage of light through a small aperture.

diffuse *v* **1** spread over a wide area. ▷ *adj* **2** widely spread. **3** lacking concision. **diffusely** *adv* **diffusion** *n*.

dig ❶ *v* **digging**, **dug** **1** cut into, break up, and turn over or remove (earth), esp. with a spade. **2** excavate (a hole or tunnel) by digging. **3** (foll. by *out* or *up*) find by effort or searching. **4** (foll. by *in* or *into*) thrust or jab. ▷ *n* **5** digging. **6** archaeological excavation. **7** thrust or poke. **8** spiteful remark. ▷ *pl* **9** *informal* lodgings. **digger** *n* machine used for digging.

digest ❶ *v* **1** subject to a process of digestion. **2** absorb mentally. ▷ *n* **3** shortened version of a book, report, or article. **digestible** *adj* **digestion** *n* (body's system for) breaking down food into easily absorbed substances. **digestive** *adj* **digestive biscuit** biscuit made from wholemeal flour.

digit [**dij**-it] *n* **1** finger or toe. **2** numeral from 0 to 9. **digital** *adj* **1** displaying information as numbers rather than with hands and a dial, e.g. *a digital clock*. **2** representing data as a series of numerical values. **digital recording** sound-recording process that converts audio or analogue signals into a series of pulses. **digital television** television in which the picture is transmitted in digital form and then decoded. **digitally** *adv*.

digitalis *n* drug made from foxglove leaves, used as a heart stimulant.

— THESAURUS —

differentiate *v* **1** = **distinguish**, contrast, discriminate, make a distinction, mark off, separate, set off *or* apart, tell apart **2** = **make different**, adapt, alter, change, convert, modify, transform

difficult *adj* **1 a** = **hard**, arduous, demanding, formidable, laborious, onerous, strenuous, uphill **b** = **problematical**, abstruse, baffling, complex, complicated, intricate, involved, knotty, obscure **2** = **troublesome**, demanding, fastidious, fussy, hard to please, perverse, refractory, unaccommodating

difficulty *n* **1** = **laboriousness**, arduousness, awkwardness, hardship, strain, strenuousness, tribulation

diffidence *n* = **shyness**, bashfulness, hesitancy, insecurity, modesty, reserve, self-consciousness, timidity

diffident *adj* = **shy**, bashful, doubtful, hesitant, insecure, modest, reserved, self-conscious, timid, unassertive, unassuming

dig *v* **1, 2** = **excavate**, burrow, delve, hollow out, mine, quarry, scoop, tunnel **3** (foll. by *out* or *up*) = **find**, delve, dig down, discover, expose, fossick (*Aust & NZ*), go into, investigate, probe, research, search, uncover, unearth, uproot **4** (foll. by *in* or *into*) = **poke**, drive, jab, prod, punch, thrust ▷ *n* **7** = **poke**, jab, prod, punch, thrust **8** = **cutting remark**, barb, crack (*sl*), gibe, insult, jeer, sneer, taunt, wisecrack (*inf*)

digest *v* **1** = **ingest**, absorb, assimilate, dissolve, incorporate **2** = **take in**, absorb, consider, contemplate, grasp, study, understand ▷ *n* **3** = **summary**, abridgment, abstract, epitome, précis, résumé, synopsis

digestion *n* = **ingestion**, absorption, assimilation, conversion, incorporation, transformation

dignity ❶ *n, pl* **-ties 1** serious, calm, and controlled behaviour or manner. **2** quality of being worthy of respect. **3** sense of self-importance. **dignify** *v* **-fying**, **-fied** add distinction to. **dignitary** *n, pl* **-taries** person of high official position.

digress ❶ *v* depart from the main subject in speech or writing. **digression** *n*.

dihedral *adj* having or formed by two intersecting planes.

dike *n* same as DYKE.

diktat *n* dictatorial decree.

dilapidated ❶ *adj* (of a building) having fallen into ruin. **dilapidation** *n*.

dilate ❶ *v* make or become wider or larger. **dilation**, **dilatation** *n*.

dilatory ❶ [**dill**-a-tree] *adj* tending or intended to waste time. **dilatoriness** *n*.

dildo *n, pl* **-dos** object used as a substitute for an erect penis.

dilemma ❶ *n* situation offering a choice between two equally undesirable alternatives.

dilettante ❶ [dill-it-**tan**-tee] *n, pl* **-tantes**, **-tanti** person whose interest in a subject is superficial rather than serious. **dilettantism** *n*.

diligent ❶ *adj* **1** careful and persevering in carrying out duties. **2** carried out with care and perseverance. **diligently** *adv* **diligence** *n*.

dill *n* sweet-smelling herb.

dilly-dally *v* **-lying**, **-lied** *informal* dawdle, waste time.

dilute ❶ *v* **1** make (a liquid) less concentrated, esp. by adding water. **2** make (a quality etc.) weaker in force. ▷ *adj* **3** (of a liquid) thin and watery. **dilution** *n*.

diluvial, **diluvian** *adj* of a flood, esp. the great Flood described in the Old Testament.

dim ❶ *adj* **dimmer**, **dimmest 1** badly lit. **2** not clearly seen. **3** unintelligent. ▷ *v* **dimming**, **dimmed 4** make or become dim. **take a dim view of** disapprove of. **dimly** *adv* **dimness** *n* **dimmer** *n* device for dimming an electric light.

dime *n* coin of the US and Canada, worth ten cents.

THESAURUS

dignified *adj* = **distinguished**, formal, grave, imposing, noble, reserved, solemn, stately

dignitary *n* = **public figure**, bigwig (*inf*), high-up (*inf*), notable, personage, pillar of society, V.I.P., worthy

dignity *n* **1** = **decorum**, courtliness, grandeur, gravity, loftiness, majesty, nobility, solemnity, stateliness **2** = **honour**, eminence, importance, rank, respectability, standing, status **3** = **self-importance**, pride, self-esteem, self-respect

digress *v* = **wander**, depart, deviate, diverge, drift, get off the point *or* subject, go off at a tangent, ramble, stray

digression *n* = **departure**, aside, detour, deviation, divergence, diversion, straying, wandering

dilapidated *adj* = **ruined**, broken-down, crumbling, decrepit, in ruins, munted (*NZ sl*), ramshackle, rickety, run-down, tumbledown

dilate *v* = **enlarge**, broaden, expand, puff out, stretch, swell, widen

dilatory *adj* = **time-wasting**, delaying, lingering, procrastinating, slow, sluggish, tardy, tarrying

dilemma *n* = **predicament**, difficulty, mess, plight, problem, puzzle, quandary, spot (*inf*)

dilettante *n* = **amateur**, aesthete, dabbler, trifler

diligence *n* = **application**, attention, care, industry, laboriousness, perseverance

diligent *adj* = **hard-working**, assiduous, attentive, careful, conscientious, industrious, painstaking, persistent, studious, tireless

dilute *v* **1** = **water down**, adulterate, cut, make thinner, thin (out), weaken **2** = **reduce**, attenuate, decrease, diffuse, diminish, lessen, mitigate, temper, weaken

dim *adj* **1** = **poorly lit**, cloudy, dark, grey, overcast, shadowy, tenebrous **2** = **unclear**, bleary, blurred, faint, fuzzy, ill-defined, indistinct, obscured, shadowy **3** = **stupid**, dense, dozy (*Brit inf*), dull, dumb (*inf*), obtuse, slow on the uptake (*inf*), thick ▷ *v* **4** = **dull**, blur, cloud, darken, fade, obscure **take a dim view of** = **disapprove of**, be displeased with, be sceptical of, look askance at, reject, suspect, take exception to, view with disfavour

dimension ❶ n **1** measurement of the size of something in a particular direction. **2** aspect, factor.

diminish ❶ v make or become smaller, fewer, or less. **diminished responsibility** Law mental derangement which makes a person unaware that he or she is committing a crime. **diminution** n **diminutive** adj **1** very small. ▷ n **2** word or affix which implies smallness or unimportance. **diminutiveness** n.

diminuendo n Music gradual decrease in loudness.

dimple n **1** small natural dent, esp. in the cheeks or chin. ▷ v **2** produce dimples by smiling. **dimpled** adj.

dimwit n informal stupid person. **dim-witted** adj.

din ❶ n **1** loud unpleasant confused noise. ▷ v **dinning**, **dinned 2** (foll. by into) instil (something) into someone by constant repetition.

dinar [**dee**-nahr] n monetary unit of various Balkan, Middle Eastern, and North African countries.

dine ❶ v eat dinner. **diner** n **1** person eating a meal. **2** Chiefly US small cheap restaurant. **dining car** railway coach where meals are served. **dining room** room where meals are eaten.

ding-dong n **1** sound of a bell. **2** informal lively quarrel or fight.

dinghy [**ding**-ee] n, pl **-ghies** small boat, powered by sails, oars, or a motor.

dingo n, pl **-goes** Australian wild dog (also **native dog**).

dingy ❶ [**din**-jee] adj **-gier**, **-giest** dull and drab. **dinginess** n.

dinkum adj Aust & NZ informal genuine or right.

dinky adj **-kier**, **-kiest** Brit & Aust informal small and neat.

dinner ❶ n main meal of the day, eaten either in the evening or at midday. **dinner jacket** man's semiformal black evening jacket.

dinosaur n extinct gigantic prehistoric reptile.

dint n **by dint of** by means of.

diocese [**die**-a-siss] n district over which a bishop has control. **diocesan** adj.

diode n semiconductor device for converting alternating current to direct current.

Dionysian [die-on-**niz**-zee-an] adj wild or unrestrained.

dioptre [die-**op**-ter] n unit for measuring the refractive power of a lens.

diorama n miniature three-dimensional scene, in which models of figures are seen against a three-dimensional background.

dioxide n oxide containing two oxygen atoms per molecule.

dip ❶ v **dipping**, **dipped 1** plunge quickly or briefly into a liquid. **2** slope downwards. **3** switch (car headlights) from the main to the lower beam. **4** lower briefly. ▷ n **5** dipping. **6** brief swim. **7** liquid chemical in which farm animals are dipped to rid them of insects. **8** depression in a landscape. **9** creamy mixture into which pieces of food are dipped before being eaten. **dip into** v read passages at random from (a book or journal).

Dip Ed Diploma in Education.

diphtheria [dif-**theer**-ya] n contagious disease producing fever and difficulty in breathing and swallowing.

————————————————————————— THESAURUS —————————————————————————

dimension n **1** = **measurement**, amplitude, bulk, capacity, extent, proportions, size, volume

diminish v = **decrease**, curtail, cut, decline, die out, dwindle, lessen, lower, recede, reduce, shrink, subside, wane

diminutive adj **1** = **small**, little, mini, miniature, minute, petite, tiny, undersized

din n **1** = **noise**, clamour, clatter, commotion, crash, pandemonium, racket, row, uproar ▷ v **2** (foll. by into) = **instil**, drum into, go on at, hammer into, inculcate, instruct, teach

dine v = **eat**, banquet, feast, lunch, sup

dingy adj = **dull**, dark, dim, drab, dreary, gloomy, murky, obscure, sombre

dinner n = **meal**, banquet, feast, main meal, repast, spread (inf)

dip v **1** = **plunge**, bathe, douse, duck, dunk, immerse **2** = **slope**, decline, descend, drop (down), fall, lower, sink, subside ▷ n **5** = **plunge**, douche, drenching, ducking, immersion, soaking **6** = **bathe**, dive, plunge, swim **8** = **hollow**, basin, concavity, depression, hole, incline, slope

dip into v = **sample**, browse, glance at, peruse, skim

diphthong *n* union of two vowel sounds in a single compound sound.

diploma *n* qualification awarded by a college on successful completion of a course.

diplomacy ❶ *n* **1** conduct of the relations between nations by peaceful means. **2** tact or skill in dealing with people. **diplomat** *n* official engaged in diplomacy. **diplomatic** *adj* **1** of diplomacy. **2** tactful in dealing with people. **diplomatic immunity** freedom from legal action and taxation which diplomats have in the country where they are working. **diplomatically** *adv*.

dipper *n* **1** ladle used for dipping. **2** (also **ousel**, **ouzel**) songbird that lives by a river.

diprotodont [die-**pro**-toe-dont] *n* marsupial with fewer than three upper incisor teeth on each side of the jaw.

dipsomania *n* compulsive craving for alcohol. **dipsomaniac** *n*, *adj*.

dipstick *n* notched rod dipped into a container to measure the level of a liquid.

diptych [**dip**-tik] *n* painting on two hinged panels.

dire ❶ *adj* disastrous, urgent, or terrible.

direct ❶ *adj* **1** (of a route) shortest, straight. **2** without anyone or

anything intervening. **3** likely to have an immediate effect. **4** honest, frank. ▷ *adv* **5** in a direct manner. ▷ *v* **6** lead and organize. **7** tell (someone) to do something. **8** tell (someone) the way to a place. **9** address (a letter, package, remark, etc.). **10** provide guidance to (actors, cameramen, etc.) in (a play or film). **directly** *adv* **1** in a direct manner. **2** at once. ▷ *conj* **3** as soon as. **directness** *n* **direct current** electric current that flows in one direction only. **direct debit** order given to a bank by an account-holder to pay an amount of money directly from the account to a specified person or company. **direct object** noun or pronoun receiving the direct action of the verb, e.g. *a book* in *I bought you a book*. **director** *n* person or thing that directs or controls.

directory *n* book listing names, addresses, and telephone numbers.

direct speech reporting of what someone has said by quoting his or her exact words. **direct tax** tax paid by the person or organization on which it is levied.

direction ❶ *n* **1** course or line along which a person or thing moves, points, or lies. **2** management or guidance. ▷ *pl* **3** instructions for doing something or for reaching a place. **directional** *adj*.

directive ❶ *n* instruction, order.

d

———————— THESAURUS ————————

diplomacy *n* **1** = **statesmanship**, international negotiation, statecraft **2** = **tact**, artfulness, craft, delicacy, discretion, finesse, savoir-faire, skill, subtlety

diplomat *n* = **negotiator**, conciliator, go-between, mediator, moderator, politician, tactician

diplomatic *adj* **2** = **tactful**, adept, discreet, polite, politic, prudent, sensitive, subtle

dire *adj* **a** = **disastrous**, awful, calamitous, catastrophic, horrible, ruinous, terrible, woeful **b** = **desperate**, critical, crucial, drastic, extreme, now or never, pressing, urgent

direct *adj* **1** = **straight**, nonstop, not crooked, shortest, through, unbroken, uninterrupted **2** = **first-hand**, face-to-face, head-on, immediate, personal **4** = **straightforward**, blunt, candid,

downright, explicit, frank, honest, open, plain, plain-spoken, point-blank, straight, unambiguous, unequivocal, upfront (*inf*) ▷ *v* **6** = **control**, conduct, guide, handle, lead, manage, oversee, run, supervise **7** = **order**, bid, charge, command, demand, dictate, instruct **8** = **guide**, indicate, lead, point in the direction of, point the way, show **9** = **address**, label, mail, route, send

direction *n* **1** = **way**, aim, bearing, course, line, path, road, route, track **2** = **management**, administration, charge, command, control, guidance, leadership, order, supervision ▷ *pl* **3** = **instructions**, briefing, guidance, guidelines, plan, recommendation, regulations

directive *n* = **order**, command, decree, edict, injunction, instruction, mandate, regulation, ruling

director ❶ *n* **1** person or thing that directs or controls. **2** member of the governing board of a business etc. **3** person responsible for the artistic and technical aspects of the making of a film etc. **directorial** *adj* **directorship** *n* **directorate** *n* **1** board of directors. **2** position of director. **director-general** *n*, *pl* **directors-general** person in overall charge of a large organization.

directory *n*, *pl* **-tories 1** book listing names, addresses, and telephone numbers. **2** *Computers* area of a disk containing the names and locations of the files it currently holds.

dirge ❶ *n* slow sad song of mourning.

dirigible [**dir**-rij-jib-bl] *adj* **1** able to be steered. ▷ *n* **2** airship.

dirk *n* dagger, formerly worn by Scottish Highlanders.

dirndl *n* full gathered skirt.

dirt ❶ *n* **1** unclean substance, filth. **2** earth, soil. **3** obscene speech or writing. **4** *informal* harmful gossip. **dirt-cheap** *adj*, *adv* at a very low price. **dirt track** racetrack made of packed earth or cinders.

dirty ❶ *adj* **dirtier, dirtiest 1** covered or marked with dirt. **2** unfair or dishonest. **3** obscene. **4** displaying dislike or anger, e.g. *a dirty look*. ▷ *v* **dirtying, dirtied 5** make dirty. **dirtiness** *n*.

dis- *prefix* indicating: **1** reversal, e.g. *disconnect*. **2** negation or lack, e.g. *dissimilar*; *disgrace*. **3** removal or release, e.g. *disembowel*.

disable ❶ *v* make ineffective, unfit, or incapable. **disabled** *adj* lacking a physical power, such as the ability to walk. **disablement** *n* **disability** *n*, *pl* **-ties 1** condition of being disabled. **2** something that disables someone.
- **USAGE NOTE**
- The use of *the disabled*, *the blind*
- etc. can be offensive and should be
- avoided. Instead you should talk
- about *disabled people*, *blind people*,
- etc.

disabuse *v* (foll. by *of*) rid (someone) of a mistaken idea.

disadvantage ❶ *n* unfavourable or harmful circumstance. **disadvantageous** *adj* **disadvantaged** *adj* socially or economically deprived.

disaffected *adj* having lost loyalty to or affection for someone or something. **disaffection** *n*.

disagree ❶ *v* **-greeing, -greed 1** argue or have different opinions. **2** be

directly *adv* **1** = **straight**, by the shortest route, exactly, in a beeline, precisely, unswervingly, without deviation **2** = **at once**, as soon as possible, forthwith, immediately, promptly, right away, straightaway

director *n* **1, 2** = **controller**, administrator, chief, executive, governor, head, leader, manager, supervisor

dirge *n* = **lament**, dead march, elegy, funeral song, requiem, threnody

dirt *n* **1** = **filth**, dust, grime, impurity, muck, mud **2** = **soil**, clay, earth, loam **3** = **obscenity**, indecency, pornography, sleaze, smut

dirty *adj* **1** = **filthy**, foul, grimy, grubby, messy, mucky, muddy, polluted, soiled, unclean **2** = **dishonest**, crooked, fraudulent, illegal, treacherous, unfair, unscrupulous, unsporting **3** = **obscene**, blue, indecent, pornographic, salacious, scungy (*Aust & NZ inf*), sleazy, smutty **4** = **angry**, annoyed, bitter, choked, indignant, offended, resentful,

scorching ▷ *v* **5** = **soil**, blacken, defile, foul, muddy, pollute, smirch, spoil, stain

disability *n* **1** = **handicap**, affliction, ailment, complaint, defect, disorder, impairment, infirmity, malady

disable *v* = **handicap**, cripple, damage, enfeeble, immobilize, impair, incapacitate, paralyse, render *or* declare incapable

disabled *adj* = **handicapped**, crippled, incapacitated, infirm, lame, paralysed, weakened

disadvantage *n* = **drawback**, damage, detriment, disservice, downside, handicap, harm, hurt, inconvenience, injury, loss, nuisance, snag, trouble

disagree *v* **1** = **differ (in opinion)**, argue, clash, cross swords, dispute, dissent, object, quarrel, take issue with **3** = **conflict**, be dissimilar, contradict, counter, differ, diverge, run counter to, vary **2** (foll. by *with*) = **make ill**, bother, discomfort, distress, hurt, nauseate, sicken, trouble, upset

different, conflict. **3** (foll. by *with*) cause physical discomfort (to), e.g. *curry disagrees with me*. **disagreement** *n* **1** refusal or failure to agree. **2** difference between results, totals, etc. which shows that they cannot all be true. **3** argument. **disagreeable** *adj* **1** unpleasant. **2** (of a person) unfriendly or unhelpful. **disagreeably** *adv*.

disallow ❶ *v* reject as untrue or invalid; cancel.

disappear ❶ *v* **1** cease to be visible. **2** go away or become lost, esp. without explanation. **3** cease to exist. **disappearance** *n*.

disappoint ❶ *v* **1** fail to meet the expectations or hopes of. **2** prevent the fulfilment of (a plan, etc.); frustrate. **disappointment** *n* **1** feeling of being disappointed. **2** person or thing that disappoints.

disapprobation *n* disapproval.

disapprove ❶ *v* (foll. by *of*) consider wrong or bad. **disapproval** *n*.

disarm ❶ *v* **1** deprive of weapons. **2** win the confidence or affection of. **3** (of a country) decrease the size of one's armed forces. **disarmament** *n* **disarming** *adj* removing hostility or suspicion. **disarmingly** *adv*.

disarrange ❶ *v* throw into disorder. **disarrangement** *n*.

disarray ❶ *n* **1** confusion and lack of discipline. **2** extreme untidiness. ▷ *v* **3** throw into confusion.

disassociate *v* same as DISSOCIATE. **disassociation** *n*.

disaster ❶ *n* **1** occurrence that causes great distress or destruction. **2** project etc. that fails. **disastrous** *adj* **disastrously** *adv*.

disavow *v* deny connection with or responsibility for. **disavowal** *n*.

d

disagreeable *adj* **1** = **nasty**, disgusting, displeasing, distasteful, objectionable, obnoxious, offensive, repugnant, repulsive, unpleasant **2** = **ill-natured**, bad-tempered, churlish, difficult, disobliging, irritable, rude, surly, unpleasant

disagreement *n* **1** = **argument**, altercation, clash, conflict, dispute, dissent, quarrel, row, squabble **2** = **incompatibility**, difference, discrepancy, disparity, dissimilarity, divergence, incongruity, variance

disallow *v* = **reject**, disavow, dismiss, disown, rebuff, refuse, repudiate

disappear *v* **1** = **vanish**, evanesce, fade away, pass, recede **2** = **cease**, die out, dissolve, evaporate, leave no trace, melt away, pass away, perish

disappearance *n* **1** = **vanishing**, eclipse, evanescence, passing **2** = **going**, departure, evaporation, melting

disappoint *v* = **let down**, disenchant, disgruntle, dishearten, disillusion, dismay, dissatisfy, fail

disappointed *adj* = **let down**, cast down, despondent, discouraged, disenchanted, disgruntled, dissatisfied, downhearted, frustrated

disappointing *adj* = **unsatisfactory**, depressing, disconcerting, discouraging, inadequate, insufficient, sad, sorry

disappointment *n* **1** = **frustration**, chagrin, discontent, discouragement, disenchantment, disillusionment, dissatisfaction, regret **2** = **letdown**, blow, calamity, choker (*inf*), misfortune, setback

disapproval *n* = **displeasure**, censure, condemnation, criticism, denunciation, dissatisfaction, objection, reproach

disapprove *v* (foll. by *of*) = **condemn**, deplore, dislike, find unacceptable, frown on, look down one's nose at (*inf*), object to, reject, take a dim view of, take exception to

disarm *v* **1** = **render defenceless**, disable **2** = **win over**, persuade, set at ease **3** = **demilitarize**, deactivate, demobilize, disband

disarmament *n* **3** = **arms reduction**, arms limitation, de-escalation, demilitarization, demobilization

disarming *adj* **2** = **charming**, irresistible, likable *or* likeable, persuasive, winning

disarrange *v* = **disorder**, confuse, disorganize, disturb, jumble (up), mess (up), scatter, shake (up), shuffle, muss (*US & Canad*)

disarray *n* **1** = **confusion**, disorder, disorganization, disunity, indiscipline, unruliness **2** = **untidiness**, chaos, clutter, hotchpotch, jumble, mess, muddle, shambles

disaster *n* **1** = **catastrophe**, adversity, calamity, cataclysm, misfortune, ruin, tragedy, trouble

disband v (cause to) cease to function as a group.

disbelieve ❶ v **1** reject as false. **2** (foll. by *in*) have no faith (in). **disbelief** n.

disburse v pay out. **disbursement** n.

disc n **1** flat circular object. **2** gramophone record. **3** *Anat* circular flat structure in the body, esp. between the vertebrae. **4** *Computers* same as DISK. **disc brake** brake in which two plates rub against a flat disc. **disc jockey** person who introduces and plays pop records on a radio programme or at a disco.

discard ❶ v get rid of (something or someone) as useless or undesirable.

discern v see or be aware of (something) clearly. **discernible** adj **discernibly** adv **discerning** adj having good judgment. **discernment** n.

discharge ❶ v **1** release, allow to go. **2** dismiss (someone) from duty or employment. **3** fire (a gun). **4** pour forth, send out. **5** meet the demands of (a duty or responsibility). **6** relieve oneself of (a debt). ▷ n **7** substance that comes out from a place. **8** discharging.

disciple ❶ [diss-**sipe**-pl] n follower of the doctrines of a teacher, esp. Jesus Christ.

discipline ❶ n **1** practice of imposing strict rules of behaviour. **2** area of academic study. ▷ v **3** attempt to improve the behaviour of (oneself or another) by training or rules. **4** punish. **disciplined** adj able to behave and work in a controlled way. **disciplinarian** n person who practises strict discipline. **disciplinary** adj.

disclaim v deny (responsibility for or knowledge of something). **disclaimer** n statement denying responsibility.

disclose ❶ v **1** make known. **2** allow to be seen. **disclosure** n.

disco n, pl **-cos 1** nightclub where people dance to amplified pop records. **2** occasion at which people dance to amplified pop records. **3** mobile equipment for providing music for a disco.

discography n, pl **-phies** classified list of gramophone records.

discolour ❶ v change in colour, fade. **discoloration** n.

discomfit v make uneasy or confused. **discomfiture** n.

━━━━━━━━━━━━━━━━━━━ **THESAURUS** ━━━━━━

disastrous adj = **terrible**, calamitous, cataclysmic, catastrophic, devastating, fatal, ruinous, tragic

disbelief n = **scepticism**, distrust, doubt, dubiety, incredulity, mistrust, unbelief

discard v = **get rid of**, abandon, cast aside, dispense with, dispose of, drop, dump (*inf*), jettison, reject, throw away *or* out

discharge v **1** = **release**, allow to go, clear, free, liberate, pardon, set free **2** = **dismiss**, cashier, discard, expel, fire (*inf*), oust, remove, sack (*inf*) **3** = **fire**, detonate, explode, let loose (*inf*), let off, set off, shoot **4** = **pour forth**, dispense, emit, exude, give off, leak, ooze, release **5** = **carry out**, accomplish, do, execute, fulfil, observe, perform **6** = **pay**, clear, honour, meet, relieve, satisfy, settle, square up ▷ n **7** = **emission**, excretion, ooze, pus, secretion, seepage, suppuration **8 a** = **release**, acquittal, clearance, liberation, pardon **b** = **dismissal**, demobilization, ejection **c** = **firing**, blast, burst, detonation, explosion, report, salvo, shot, volley

disciple n = **follower**, adherent, apostle, devotee, pupil, student, supporter

disciplinarian n = **authoritarian**, despot, martinet, stickler, taskmaster, tyrant

discipline n **1** = **training**, conduct, control, orderliness, practice, regimen, regulation, restraint, self-control, strictness **2** = **field of study**, area, branch of knowledge, course, curriculum, speciality, subject ▷ v **3** = **train**, bring up, drill, educate, exercise, prepare **4** = **punish**, bring to book, castigate, chasten, chastise, correct, penalize, reprimand, reprove

disclose v **1** = **make known**, broadcast, communicate, confess, divulge, let slip, publish, relate, reveal **2** = **show**, bring to light, expose, lay bare, reveal, uncover, unveil

disclosure n **1** = **revelation**, acknowledgment, admission, announcement, confession, declaration, divulgence, leak, publication

discolour v = **stain**, fade, mark, soil, streak, tarnish, tinge

discomfort ❶ *n* inconvenience, distress, or mild pain.
discommode *v* cause inconvenience to.
discompose *v* disturb, upset. **discomposure** *n*.
disconcert ❶ *v* embarrass or upset.
disconnect ❶ *v* **1** undo or break the connection between (two things). **2** stop the supply of electricity or gas of. **disconnected** *adj* (of speech or ideas) not logically connected. **disconnection** *n*.
disconsolate ❶ *adj* sad beyond comfort. **disconsolately** *adv*.
discontent ❶ *n* lack of contentment. **discontented** *adj* **discontentedly** *adv*.
discontinue ❶ *v* come or bring to an end. **discontinuous** *adj* characterized by interruptions. **discontinuity** *n*.

discord ❶ *n* **1** lack of agreement or harmony between people. **2** harsh confused sounds. **discordant** *adj* **discordance** *n*.
discotheque *n* same as DISCO.
discount ❶ *v* **1** take no account of (something) because it is considered to be unreliable, prejudiced, or irrelevant. **2** deduct (an amount) from the price of something. ▷ *n* **3** deduction from the full price of something.
discountenance *v* make (someone) ashamed or confused.
discourage ❶ *v* **1** deprive of the will to persist in something. **2** oppose by expressing disapproval. **discouraging** *adj* **discouragement** *n*.
discourse ❶ *n* **1** conversation. **2** formal treatment of a subject in

---

THESAURUS

discomfort *n* **a** = **uneasiness**, annoyance, distress, hardship, irritation, nuisance, trouble **b** = **pain**, ache, hurt, irritation, malaise, soreness
disconcert *v* = **disturb**, faze, fluster, perturb, rattle (*inf*), take aback, unsettle, upset, worry
disconcerting *adj* = **disturbing**, alarming, awkward, bewildering, confusing, distracting, embarrassing, off-putting (*Brit inf*), perplexing, upsetting
disconnect *v* **1** = **cut off**, detach, disengage, divide, part, separate, sever, take apart, uncouple
disconnected *adj* = **illogical**, confused, disjointed, incoherent, jumbled, mixed-up, rambling, unintelligible
disconsolate *adj* = **inconsolable**, crushed, dejected, desolate, forlorn, grief-stricken, heartbroken, miserable, wretched
discontent *n* = **dissatisfaction**, displeasure, envy, regret, restlessness, uneasiness, unhappiness
discontented *adj* = **dissatisfied**, disaffected, disgruntled, displeased, exasperated, fed up, unhappy, vexed
discontinue *v* = **stop**, abandon, break off, cease, drop, end, give up, quit, suspend, terminate
discord *n* **1** = **disagreement**, conflict, dissension, disunity, division, friction, incompatibility, strife
2 = **disharmony**, cacophony, din,

dissonance, harshness, jarring, racket, tumult
discordant *adj* **1** = **disagreeing**, at odds, clashing, conflicting, contradictory, contrary, different, incompatible **2** = **inharmonious**, cacophonous, dissonant, grating, harsh, jarring, shrill, strident
discount *v* **1** = **leave out**, brush off (*sl*), disbelieve, disregard, ignore, overlook, pass over **2** = **deduct**, lower, mark down, reduce, take off ▷ *n* **3** = **deduction**, concession, cut, rebate, reduction
discourage *v* **1** = **dishearten**, dampen, deject, demoralize, depress, dispirit, intimidate, overawe, put a damper on **2** = **put off**, deter, dissuade, inhibit, prevent, talk out of
discouraged *adj* **1** = **put off**, crestfallen, deterred, disheartened, dismayed, dispirited, downcast, down in the mouth, glum
discouragement *n* **1** = **loss of confidence**, dejection, depression, despair, despondency, disappointment, dismay, downheartedness **2** = **deterrent**, damper, disincentive, hindrance, impediment, obstacle, opposition, setback
discouraging *adj* **1** = **disheartening**, dampening, daunting, depressing, disappointing, dispiriting, off-putting (*Brit inf*), unfavourable
discourse *n* **1** = **conversation**, chat, communication, dialogue, discussion,

speech or writing. ▷v **3** (foll. by *on*)
speak or write (about) at length.

discourteous ❶ *adj* showing bad
manners. **discourteously** *adv*
discourtesy *n*.

discover ❶ *v* **1** be the first to find or
to find out about. **2** learn about
for the first time. **3** find after study
or search. **discoverer** *n* **discovery** *n*,
pl **-eries 1** discovering. **2** person,
place, or thing that has been
discovered.

discredit ❶ *v* **1** damage the reputation
of. **2** cause (an idea) to be disbelieved
or distrusted. ▷*n* **3** damage to
someone's reputation. **discreditable**
adj bringing shame.

discreet ❶ *adj* **1** careful to avoid
embarrassment, esp. by keeping
confidences secret. **2** unobtrusive.
discreetly *adv*.

discrepancy ❶ *n*, *pl* **-cies** conflict
or variation between facts,

figures, or claims.

discrete *adj* separate, distinct.

discretion ❶ [diss-**kresh**-on] *n*
1 quality of behaving in a discreet way.
2 freedom or authority to make
judgments and decide what to do.
discretionary *adj*.

discriminate ❶ *v* **1** (foll. by *against* or
in favour of) single out (a particular
person or group) for worse or better
treatment than others. **2** (foll. by
between) recognize or understand the
difference (between). **discriminating**
adj showing good taste and judgment.
discrimination *n* **discriminatory** *adj*
based on prejudice.

discursive *adj* passing from one topic
to another.

discus *n* heavy disc-shaped object
thrown in sports competitions.

discuss ❶ *v* **1** consider (something) by
talking it over. **2** treat (a subject) in
speech or writing. **discussion** *n*.

——————————————— THESAURUS ———————————————

seminar, speech, talk **2** = **speech**,
dissertation, essay, homily, lecture,
oration, sermon, treatise ▷*v* **3** (foll. by
on) = **hold forth**, expatiate, speak, talk

discourteous *adj* = **rude**, bad-
mannered, boorish, disrespectful,
ill-mannered, impolite, insolent,
offhand, ungentlemanly, ungracious

discourtesy *n* = **rudeness**, bad
manners, disrespectfulness,
impertinence, impoliteness, incivility,
insolence

discover *v* **1** = **find**, come across, come
upon, dig up, locate, turn up, uncover,
unearth **2, 3** = **find out**, ascertain,
detect, learn, notice, perceive, realize,
recognize, uncover

discovery *n* **1** = **finding**, detection,
disclosure, exploration, location,
revelation, uncovering
2 = **breakthrough**, find, innovation,
invention, secret

discredit *v* **1** = **disgrace**, bring into
disrepute, defame, dishonour,
disparage, slander, smear, vilify
2 = **doubt**, challenge, deny, disbelieve,
discount, dispute, distrust, mistrust,
question ▷*n* **3** = **disgrace**, dishonour,
disrepute, ignominy, ill-repute,
scandal, shame, stigma

discreditable *adj* **1** = **disgraceful**,
dishonourable, ignominious,
reprehensible, scandalous, shameful,
unworthy

discreet *adj* **1** = **tactful**, careful,
cautious, circumspect, considerate,
diplomatic, guarded, judicious,
prudent, wary

discrepancy *n* = **disagreement**,
conflict, contradiction, difference,
disparity, divergence, incongruity,
inconsistency, variation

discretion *n* **1** = **tact**, carefulness,
caution, consideration, diplomacy,
judiciousness, prudence, wariness
2 = **choice**, inclination, pleasure,
preference, volition, will

discriminate *v* **1** (foll. by *against* or
in favour of) = **show prejudice**, favour,
show bias, single out, treat as inferior,
treat as superior, treat differently,
victimize **2** (foll. by *between*)
= **differentiate**, distinguish, draw a
distinction, segregate, separate, tell
the difference

discriminating *adj* = **discerning**,
cultivated, fastidious, particular,
refined, selective, tasteful

discrimination *n* **1** = **prejudice**, bias,
bigotry, favouritism, intolerance,
unfairness **2** = **discernment**,
judgment, perception, refinement,
subtlety, taste

discuss *v* = **talk about**, argue, confer,
consider, converse, debate, deliberate,
examine

discussion *n* = **talk**, analysis,
argument, conference, consultation,

d

disdain ❶ n 1 feeling of superiority and dislike. ▷ v 2 refuse with disdain. **disdainful** adj **disdainfully** adv.

disease ❶ n illness, sickness. **diseased** adj.

disembark ❶ v get off a ship, aircraft, or bus. **disembarkation** n.

disembodied adj 1 lacking a body. 2 seeming not to be attached to or coming from anyone.

disembowel v -elling, -elled remove the entrails of.

disenchanted ❶ adj disappointed and disillusioned. **disenchantment** n.

disenfranchise v deprive (someone) of the right to vote or of other rights of citizenship.

disengage ❶ v release from a connection. **disengagement** n.

disentangle ❶ v release from entanglement or confusion. **disentanglement** n.

disequilibrium n loss or absence of stability or balance.

disestablish v remove state support from (a church etc.). **disestablishment** n.

disfavour ❶ n disapproval or dislike.

disfigure ❶ v spoil the appearance of. **disfigurement** n.

disfranchise v same as DISENFRANCHISE.

disgorge ❶ v empty out, discharge.

disgrace ❶ n 1 condition of shame, loss of reputation, or dishonour. 2 shameful person or thing. ▷ v 3 bring shame upon (oneself or others). **disgraceful** adj **disgracefully** adv.

disgruntled ❶ adj sulky or discontented. **disgruntlement** n.

disguise ❶ v 1 change the appearance or manner in order to conceal the identity of (someone or something). 2 misrepresent (something) in order to obscure its actual nature or meaning. ▷ n 3 mask, costume, or manner that disguises. 4 state of being disguised.

THESAURUS

---

conversation, debate, deliberation, dialogue, discourse

disdain n 1 = **contempt**, arrogance, derision, haughtiness, scorn, superciliousness ▷ v 2 = **scorn**, deride, disregard, look down on, reject, slight, sneer at, spurn

disdainful adj = **contemptuous**, aloof, arrogant, derisive, haughty, proud, scornful, sneering, supercilious, superior

disease n = **illness**, affliction, ailment, complaint, condition, disorder, infection, infirmity, malady, sickness

diseased adj = **sick**, ailing, crook (Aust & NZ sl), infected, rotten, sickly, unhealthy, unsound, unwell, unwholesome

disembark v = **land**, alight, arrive, get off, go ashore, step out of

disenchanted adj = **disillusioned**, cynical, disappointed, indifferent, jaundiced, let down, sick of, soured

disenchantment n = **disillusionment**, disappointment, disillusion, rude awakening

disengage v = **release**, disentangle, extricate, free, loosen, set free, unloose, untie

disentangle v = **untangle**, disconnect, disengage, extricate, free, loose, unravel

disfavour n = **disapproval**, disapprobation, dislike, displeasure

disfigure v = **damage**, blemish, deface, deform, distort, mar, mutilate, scar

disgorge v = **vomit**, discharge, eject, empty, expel

disgrace n 1 = **shame**, degradation, dishonour, disrepute, ignominy, infamy, odium, opprobrium 2 = **stain**, blemish, blot, reproach, scandal, slur, stigma ▷ v 3 = **bring shame upon**, degrade, discredit, dishonour, humiliate, shame, sully, taint

disgraceful adj = **shameful**, contemptible, detestable, dishonourable, disreputable, ignominious, scandalous, shocking, unworthy

disgruntled adj = **discontented**, annoyed, displeased, dissatisfied, grumpy, irritated, peeved, put out, vexed

disguise v 1 = **hide**, camouflage, cloak, conceal, cover, mask, screen, shroud, veil 2 = **misrepresent**, fake, falsify ▷ n 3 = **costume**, camouflage, cover, mask, screen, veil 4 = **facade**, deception, dissimulation, front, pretence, semblance, trickery, veneer

disguised adj 1 = **in disguise**, camouflaged, covert, incognito, masked, undercover 2 = **fake**, false, feigned

disgust ❶ n 1 great loathing or distaste. ▷ v 2 sicken, fill with loathing. **disgusted** adj **disgusting** adj **disgustingly** adv.

dish ❶ n 1 shallow container used for holding or serving food. 2 particular kind of food. 3 short for DISH AERIAL. 4 informal attractive person. **dish aerial** aerial consisting of a concave disc-shaped reflector, used esp. for satellite television. **dishcloth** n cloth for washing dishes. **dish out** v informal distribute. **dish up** v informal serve (food).

dishabille [diss-a-**beel**] n same as DESHABILLE.

disharmony n lack of agreement, discord.

dishearten ❶ v weaken or destroy the hope, courage, or enthusiasm of.

dishevelled ❶ adj (of a person's hair, clothes, or general appearance) disordered and untidy.

dishonest ❶ adj not honest or fair. **dishonestly** adv **dishonesty** n.

dishonour ❶ v 1 treat with disrespect. 2 refuse to cash (a cheque). ▷ n 3 lack of respect. 4 state of shame or disgrace. 5 something that causes a loss of honour. **dishonourable** adj **dishonourably** adv.

disillusion v 1 destroy the illusions or false ideas of. ▷ n 2 (also **disillusionment**) state of being disillusioned.

disincentive n something that acts as a deterrent.

disinclined ❶ adj unwilling, reluctant. **disinclination** n.

disinfect ❶ v rid of harmful germs, chemically. **disinfectant** n substance that destroys harmful germs. **disinfection** n.

disinformation n false information intended to mislead.

disingenuous adj not sincere. **disingenuously** adv.

disinherit ❶ v Law deprive (an heir) of inheritance. **disinheritance** n.

disintegrate ❶ v break up. **disintegration** n.

disinter v -**terring**, -**terred** 1 dig up. 2 reveal, make known. **disinterment** n.

disgust n 1 = **loathing**, abhorrence, aversion, dislike, distaste, hatred, nausea, repugnance, repulsion, revulsion ▷ v 2 = **sicken**, displease, nauseate, offend, put off, repel, revolt

disgusted adj = **sickened**, appalled, nauseated, offended, repulsed, scandalized

disgusting adj = **sickening**, foul, gross, loathsome, nauseating, offensive, repellent, repugnant, revolting

dish n 1 = **bowl**, plate, platter, salver 2 = **food**, fare, recipe

dishearten v = **discourage**, cast down, deject, depress, deter, dismay, dispirit, put a damper on

dishevelled adj = **untidy**, bedraggled, disordered, messy, ruffled, rumpled, tousled, uncombed, unkempt

dishonest adj = **deceitful**, bent (sl), cheating, corrupt, crooked (inf), disreputable, double-dealing, false, lying, treacherous

dishonesty n = **deceit**, cheating, chicanery, corruption, fraud, treachery, trickery, unscrupulousness

dishonour v 1 = **disgrace**, debase, debauch, defame, degrade, discredit, shame, sully ▷ n 4 = **disgrace**, discredit, disrepute, ignominy, infamy, obloquy, reproach, scandal, shame 5 = **insult**, abuse, affront, discourtesy, indignity, offence, outrage, sacrilege, slight

dishonourable adj 4 = **shameful**, contemptible, despicable, discreditable, disgraceful, ignominious, infamous, scandalous 5 = **untrustworthy**, blackguardly, corrupt, disreputable, shameless, treacherous, unprincipled, unscrupulous

disillusioned adj = **disenchanted**, disabused, disappointed, enlightened, undeceived

disinclination n = **reluctance**, aversion, dislike, hesitance, objection, opposition, repugnance, resistance, unwillingness

disinclined adj = **reluctant**, averse, hesitating, loath, not in the mood, opposed, resistant, unwilling

disinfect v = **sterilize**, clean, cleanse, decontaminate, deodorize, fumigate, purify, sanitize

disinfectant n = **antiseptic**, germicide, sterilizer

disinherit v Law = **cut off**, disown, dispossess, oust, repudiate

disintegrate v = **break up**, break apart, crumble, fall apart, go to pieces, separate, shatter, splinter

disinterested ❶ *adj* free from bias or involvement. **disinterest** *n*.

● **USAGE NOTE**
● People sometimes use *disinterested*
● where they mean *uninterested*. If you
● want to say that someone shows
● a lack of interest, use *uninterested*.
● *Disinterested* would be used in a
● sentence such as *We asked him to*
● *decide because he was a disinterested*
● *observer.*

disjointed ❶ *adj* having no coherence, disconnected.

disjunction *n* disconnection, separation. **disjunctive** *adj*.

disk *n Computers* storage device, consisting of a stack of plates coated with a magnetic layer, which rotates rapidly as a single unit.

dislike ❶ *v* 1 consider unpleasant or disagreeable. ▷ *n* 2 feeling of not liking something or someone.

dislocate *v* 1 displace (a bone or joint) from its normal position.

2 disrupt or shift out of place. **dislocation** *n*.

dislodge ❶ *v* remove (something) from a previously fixed position.

disloyal ❶ *adj* not loyal, deserting one's allegiance. **disloyalty** *n*.

dismal ❶ *adj* 1 gloomy and depressing. 2 *informal* of poor quality. **dismally** *adv*.

dismantle ❶ *v* take apart piece by piece.

dismay ❶ *v* 1 fill with alarm or depression. ▷ *n* 2 alarm mixed with sadness.

dismember ❶ *v* 1 remove the limbs of. 2 cut to pieces. **dismemberment** *n*.

dismiss ❶ *v* 1 remove (an employee) from a job. 2 allow (someone) to leave. 3 put out of one's mind. 4 (of a judge) state that (a case) will not be brought to trial. **dismissal** *n* **dismissive** *adj* scornful, contemptuous.

dismount *v* get off a horse or bicycle.

disinterest *n* = **impartiality**, detachment, fairness, neutrality

disinterested *adj* = **impartial**, detached, dispassionate, even-handed, impersonal, neutral, objective, unbiased, unprejudiced

disjointed *adj* = **incoherent**, confused, disconnected, disordered, rambling

dislike *v* 1 = **be averse to**, despise, detest, disapprove, hate, loathe, not be able to bear *or* abide *or* stand, object to, take a dim view of ▷ *n* 2 = **aversion**, animosity, antipathy, disapproval, disinclination, displeasure, distaste, enmity, hostility, repugnance

dislodge *v* = **displace**, disturb, extricate, force out, knock loose, oust, remove, uproot

disloyal *adj* = **treacherous**, faithless, false, subversive, traitorous, two-faced, unfaithful, untrustworthy

disloyalty *n* = **treachery**, breach of trust, deceitfulness, double-dealing, falseness, inconstancy, infidelity, treason, unfaithfulness

dismal *adj* 1 = **gloomy**, bleak, cheerless, dark, depressing, discouraging, dreary, forlorn, sombre, wretched

dismantle *v* = **take apart**, demolish, disassemble, strip, take to pieces

dismay *v* 1 = **alarm**, appal, daunt, discourage, dishearten, dispirit, distress, frighten, horrify, paralyse, put off, scare, terrify, unnerve ▷ *n* 2 = **alarm**, anxiety, apprehension, consternation, discouragement, dread, fear, horror, trepidation

dismember *v* 1 = **amputate** 2 = **cut into pieces**, dissect, sever

dismiss *v* 1 = **sack** (*inf*), axe (*inf*), cashier, discharge, fire (*inf*), give notice to, give (someone) their marching orders, lay off, remove 2 = **let go**, disperse, dissolve, free, release, send away 3 = **put out of one's mind**, banish, discard, dispel, disregard, lay aside, reject, set aside

dismissal *n* 1 = **the sack** (*inf*), expulsion, marching orders (*inf*), notice, removal, the boot (*sl*), the push (*sl*)

disobedience *n* = **defiance**, indiscipline, insubordination, mutiny, noncompliance, nonobservance, recalcitrance, revolt, unruliness, waywardness

disobedient *adj* = **defiant**, contrary, disorderly, insubordinate, intractable, naughty, refractory, undisciplined, unruly, wayward

disobey ❶ v neglect or refuse to obey.
disobedient adj **disobedience** n.
disobliging adj unwilling to help.
disorder ❶ n **1** state of untidiness and disorganization. **2** public violence or rioting. **3** an illness. **disordered** adj untidy. **disorderly** adj **1** untidy and disorganized. **2** uncontrolled, unruly.
disorganize v disrupt the arrangement or system of. **disorganization** n.
disorientate, disorient v cause (someone) to lose his or her bearings. **disorientation** n.
disown ❶ v deny any connection with (someone).
disparage ❶ v speak contemptuously of. **disparagement** n.
disparate adj completely different. **disparity** n, pl **-ties** inequality or difference.
dispassionate ❶ adj not influenced by emotion. **dispassionately** adv.
dispatch ❶ v **1** send off to a destination or to perform a task. **2** carry out (a duty or a task) with speed. **3** old-fashioned kill. ▷ n **4** official communication or report,

sent in haste. **5** report sent to a newspaper by a correspondent.
dispatch rider motorcyclist who carries dispatches.
dispel ❶ v **-pelling, -pelled** destroy or remove.
dispense ❶ v **1** distribute in portions. **2** prepare and distribute (medicine). **3** administer (the law etc.). **dispensable** adj not essential. **dispensation** n **1** dispensing. **2** exemption from an obligation. **dispenser** n **dispensary** n, pl **-saries** place where medicine is dispensed. **dispense with** v do away with, manage without.
disperse ❶ v **1** scatter over a wide area. **2** (cause to) leave a gathering. **3** separate (light) into its different wavelengths. **dispersal, dispersion** n.
dispirit ❶ v make downhearted. **dispirited** adj **dispiriting** adj.
displace ❶ v **1** move from the usual location. **2** remove from office. **displacement** n **displaced person** person forced from his or her home or country, esp. by war.

———————————— THESAURUS ————————————

disobey v = **refuse to obey**, contravene, defy, disregard, flout, ignore, infringe, rebel, violate
disorder n **1** = **untidiness**, chaos, clutter, confusion, disarray, jumble, mess, muddle, shambles **2** = **disturbance**, commotion, riot, turmoil, unrest, unruliness, uproar **3** = **illness**, affliction, ailment, complaint, disease, malady, sickness
disorderly adj **1** = **untidy**, chaotic, confused, disorganized, higgledy-piggledy (inf), jumbled, messy, shambolic (inf) **2** = **unruly**, disruptive, indisciplined, lawless, riotous, rowdy, tumultuous, turbulent, ungovernable
disorganized = **muddled**, chaotic, confused, disordered, haphazard, jumbled, unsystematic
disown v = **deny**, cast off, disavow, disclaim, reject, renounce, repudiate
disparage v = **run down**, belittle, denigrate, deprecate, deride, malign, put down, ridicule, slander, vilify
dispassionate adj = **unemotional**, calm, collected, composed, cool, detached, disinterested, impersonal, imperturbable, serene, unruffled
dispatch v **1** = **send**, consign, dismiss, hasten **2** = **carry out**, discharge,

dispose of, finish, perform, settle **3** Old-fashioned = **murder**, assassinate, execute, kill, slaughter, slay ▷ n **5** = **message**, account, bulletin, communication, communiqué, news, report, story
dispel v = **drive away**, banish, chase away, dismiss, disperse, eliminate, expel
dispense v **1** = **distribute**, allocate, allot, apportion, assign, deal out, dole out, share **2** = **prepare**, measure, mix, supply **3** = **administer**, apply, carry out, discharge, enforce, execute, implement, operate ▷ v **dispense with** = **do without**, abolish, abstain from, brush aside, cancel, dispose of, do away with, forgo, get rid of, give up
disperse v **1** = **scatter**, broadcast, diffuse, disseminate, distribute, spread, strew **2** = **break up**, disband, dissolve, scatter, separate
dispirited adj = **disheartened**, crestfallen, dejected, depressed, despondent, discouraged, downcast, gloomy, glum, sad
displace v **1** = **move**, disturb, misplace, shift, transpose **2** = **replace**, oust, succeed, supersede, supplant, take the place of

display ● v 1 make visible or noticeable. ▷ n 2 displaying. 3 something displayed. 4 exhibition. 5 electronic device for representing information visually. 6 *Zoology* pattern of behaviour an animal uses to draw attention to itself when courting, defending its territory, etc.

displease ● v annoy or upset. **displeasure** n.

disport v **disport oneself** indulge oneself in pleasure.

dispose ● v place in a certain order. **disposed** adj 1 willing or eager. 2 having an attitude as specified, e.g. *he felt well disposed towards her*. **disposable** adj 1 designed to be thrown away after use. 2 available for use, e.g. *disposable income*. **disposal** n getting rid of something. **at one's disposal** available for use. **disposition** n 1 person's usual temperament. 2 desire or tendency to do something. 3 arrangement.

dispose of v 1 throw away, get rid of. 2 deal with (a problem etc.). 3 kill.

dispossess v (foll. by *of*) deprive (someone) of (a possession). **dispossessed** adj **dispossession** n.

disproportion ● n lack of proportion or equality. **disproportionate** adj **disproportionately** adv.

disprove ● v show (an assertion or claim) to be incorrect.

dispute ● n 1 disagreement, argument. ▷ v 2 argue about (something). 3 doubt the validity of. 4 fight over possession of.

disqualify ● v stop (someone) officially from taking part in something for wrongdoing. **disqualification** n.

disquiet ● n 1 feeling of anxiety. ▷ v 2 make (someone) anxious. **disquietude** n.

disquisition n detailed explanation of a subject.

THESAURUS

display v 1 = **show**, demonstrate, disclose, exhibit, expose, flaunt, flourish, manifest, parade, present, reveal, show off, vaunt ▷ n 2, 3 = **exhibition**, array, demonstration, presentation, show 4 = **show**, pageant, parade, spectacle

displease v = **annoy**, anger, irk, irritate, offend, pique, put out, upset, vex

displeasure n = **annoyance**, anger, disapproval, dissatisfaction, distaste, indignation, irritation, resentment

disposable adj 1 = **throwaway**, biodegradable, nonreturnable 2 = **available**, consumable, expendable

disposal n = **throwing away**, discarding, dumping (*inf*), ejection, jettisoning, removal, riddance, scrapping ▷ n **at one's disposal** = **available**, at one's service, consumable, expendable, free for use

dispose v = **arrange**, array, distribute, group, marshal, order, place, put

dispose of v 1 = **get rid of**, destroy, discard, dump (*inf*), jettison, scrap, throw out *or* away, unload 2 = **deal with**, decide, determine, end, finish with, settle

disposition n 1 = **character**, constitution, make-up, nature, spirit, temper, temperament 2 = **tendency**, bent, bias, habit, inclination, leaning, proclivity, propensity 3 = **arrangement**, classification, distribution, grouping, ordering, organization, placement

disproportion n = **inequality**, asymmetry, discrepancy, disparity, imbalance, lopsidedness, unevenness

disproportionate adj = **unequal**, excessive, inordinate, out of proportion, unbalanced, uneven, unreasonable

disprove v = **prove false**, contradict, discredit, expose, give the lie to, invalidate, negate, rebut, refute

dispute n 1 = **disagreement**, altercation, argument, conflict, contention, controversy, debate, dissension, feud, quarrel ▷ v 2 = **argue**, clash, cross swords, debate, quarrel, squabble 3 = **doubt**, challenge, contest, contradict, deny, impugn, question, rebut

disqualification n = **ban**, elimination, exclusion, ineligibility, rejection

disqualified adj = **ineligible**, debarred, eliminated, knocked out, out of the running

disqualify v = **ban**, debar, declare ineligible, preclude, prohibit, rule out

disquiet n 1 = **uneasiness**, alarm, anxiety, concern, disturbance, foreboding, nervousness, trepidation,

disregard ❶ v **1** give little or no attention to. ▷ n **2** lack of attention or respect.

disrepair ❶ n condition of being worn out or in poor working order.

disrepute ❶ n loss or lack of good reputation. **disreputable** adj having or causing a bad reputation.

disrespect ❶ n lack of respect. **disrespectful** adj **disrespectfully** adv.

disrobe v undress.

disrupt ❶ v interrupt the progress of. **disruption** n **disruptive** adj.

dissatisfied ❶ adj not pleased or contented. **dissatisfaction** n.

dissect ❶ v **1** cut open (a corpse) to examine it. **2** examine critically and minutely. **dissection** n.

dissemble v conceal one's real motives or emotions by pretence.

disseminate ❶ v spread (information). **dissemination** n.

dissent ❶ v **1** disagree.
2 Christianity reject the doctrines of an established church. ▷ n
3 disagreement.
4 Christianity separation from an established church. **dissension** n **dissenter** n **dissentient** adj dissenting.

dissertation ❶ n **1** written thesis, usu. required for a higher university degree. **2** long formal speech.

disservice ❶ n harmful action.

dissident ❶ n **1** person who disagrees with and criticizes the government. ▷ adj **2** disagreeing with the government. **dissidence** n.

dissimilar ❶ adj not alike, different. **dissimilarity** n.

— THESAURUS —

worry ▷ v **2** = **make uneasy**, bother, concern, disturb, perturb, trouble, unsettle, upset, worry

disregard v **1** = **ignore**, brush aside or away, discount, make light of, neglect, overlook, pass over, pay no heed to, turn a blind eye to ▷ n
2 = **inattention**, contempt, disdain, disrespect, indifference, neglect, negligence, oversight

disrepair n = **dilapidation**, collapse, decay, deterioration, ruination

disreputable adj = **discreditable**, dishonourable, ignominious, infamous, louche, notorious, scandalous, shady (inf), shameful

disrepute n = **discredit**, disgrace, dishonour, ignominy, ill repute, infamy, obloquy, shame, unpopularity

disrespect n = **contempt**, cheek, impertinence, impoliteness, impudence, insolence, irreverence, lack of respect, rudeness, sauce

disrespectful adj = **contemptuous**, cheeky, discourteous, impertinent, impolite, impudent, insolent, insulting, irreverent, rude

disrupt v = **disturb**, break up or into, confuse, disorder, disorganize, interfere with, interrupt, intrude, spoil, unsettle, upset

disruption n = **disturbance**, interference, interruption, stoppage

disruptive adj = **disturbing**, disorderly, distracting, troublesome, unruly, unsettling, upsetting

dissatisfaction n = **discontent**,

annoyance, chagrin, disappointment, displeasure, frustration, irritation, resentment, unhappiness

dissatisfied adj = **discontented**, disappointed, disgruntled, displeased, fed up, frustrated, unhappy, unsatisfied

dissect v **1** = **cut up** or **apart**, anatomize, dismember, lay open
2 = **analyse**, break down, explore, inspect, investigate, research, scrutinize, study

disseminate v = **spread**, broadcast, circulate, disperse, distribute, publicize, scatter

dissension n **1** = **disagreement**, conflict, discord, dispute, dissent, friction, quarrel, row, strife

dissent v **1** = **disagree**, differ, object, protest, refuse, withhold assent or approval ▷ n **3** = **disagreement**, discord, dissension, objection, opposition, refusal, resistance

dissenter n = **objector**, dissident, nonconformist

dissertation n **1** = **thesis**, critique, discourse, disquisition, essay, exposition, treatise

disservice n = **bad turn**, harm, injury, injustice, unkindness, wrong

dissident n **1** = **protester**, agitator, dissenter, rebel ▷ adj **2** = **dissenting**, disagreeing, discordant, heterodox, nonconformist

dissimilar adj = **different**, disparate, divergent, diverse, heterogeneous, unlike, unrelated, various

dissimulate *v* conceal one's real feelings by pretence. **dissimulation** *n*.

dissipate ❶ *v* **1** waste or squander. **2** scatter, disappear. **dissipated** *adj* showing signs of overindulgence in alcohol and other physical pleasures. **dissipation** *n*.

dissociate ❶ *v* regard or treat as separate. **dissociate oneself from** deny or break an association with. **dissociation** *n*.

dissolute ❶ *adj* leading an immoral life.

dissolution ❶ *n* **1** official breaking up of an organization or institution, such as Parliament. **2** official ending of a formal agreement, such as a marriage.

dissolve ❶ *v* **1** (cause to) become liquid. **2** break up or end officially. **3** break down emotionally, e.g. *she dissolved into tears*.

dissonance *n* lack of agreement or harmony. **dissonant** *adj*.

dissuade ❶ *v* deter (someone) by persuasion from doing something. **dissuasion** *n*.

distaff *n* rod on which wool etc. is wound for spinning. **distaff side** female side of a family.

distance ❶ *n* **1** space between two points. **2** state of being apart. **3** remoteness in manner. **the distance** most distant part of the visible scene. **distance oneself from** separate oneself mentally from. **distant** *adj* **1** far apart. **2** separated by a specified distance. **3** remote in manner. **distantly** *adv*.

distaste ❶ *n* dislike, disgust. **distasteful** *adj* unpleasant, offensive. **distastefully** *adv*.

distemper[1] *n* highly contagious viral disease of dogs.

distemper[2] *n* paint mixed with water, glue, etc., used for painting walls.

distend *v* (of part of the body) swell. **distension** *n*.

distil ❶ *v* **-tilling, -tilled 1** subject to or obtain by distillation. **2** give off (a substance) in drops. **3** extract the essence of. **distillation** *n* **1** process of evaporating a liquid and condensing its vapour. **2** (also **distillate**) concentrated essence. **distiller** *n* person or company that makes strong alcoholic drink, esp. whisky. **distillery** *n, pl* **-leries** place where a strong alcoholic drink, esp. whisky, is made.

dissipate *v* **1** = **squander**, consume, deplete, expend, fritter away, run through, spend, waste **2** = **disperse**, disappear, dispel, dissolve, drive away, evaporate, scatter, vanish

dissipation *n* = **debauchery**, dissoluteness, excess, extravagance, indulgence, intemperance, prodigality, profligacy, wantonness, waste

dissociate *v* = **separate**, detach, disconnect, distance, divorce, isolate, segregate, set apart ▷ *v* **dissociate oneself from** = **break away from**, break off from, part company from, quit

dissolute *adj* = **immoral**, debauched, degenerate, depraved, dissipated, profligate, rakish, wanton, wild

dissolution *n* **1** = **breaking up**, disintegration, division, parting, separation **2** = **adjournment**, discontinuation, end, finish, suspension, termination

dissolve *v* **1** = **melt**, deliquesce, fuse, liquefy, soften, thaw **2** = **end**, break up, discontinue, suspend, terminate,

wind up

dissuade *v* = **deter**, advise against, discourage, put off, remonstrate, talk out of, warn

distance *n* **1** = **space**, extent, gap, interval, length, range, span, stretch **3** = **reserve**, aloofness, coldness, coolness, remoteness, restraint, stiffness ▷ *v* **distance oneself from** = **separate oneself from**, be distanced from, dissociate oneself from

distant *adj* **1** = **far-off**, abroad, apart, far, faraway, far-flung, outlying, out-of-the-way, remote, separate **3** = **reserved**, aloof, cool, reticent, standoffish, unapproachable, unfriendly, withdrawn

distaste *n* = **dislike**, aversion, disgust, horror, loathing, odium, repugnance, revulsion

distasteful *adj* = **unpleasant**, disagreeable, objectionable, offensive, repugnant, repulsive, uninviting, unpalatable, unsavoury

distil *v* **1, 3** = **extract**, condense, purify, refine

distinct ❶ *adj* **1** not the same. **2** easily sensed or understood. **3** clear and definite. **distinctly** *adv* **distinction** *n* **1** act of distinguishing. **2** distinguishing feature. **3** state of being different. **4** special honour, recognition, or fame. **distinctive** *adj* easily recognizable. **distinctively** *adv* **distinctiveness** *n*.

distinguish ❶ *v* **1** (usu. foll. by *between*) make, show, or recognize a difference (between). **2** be a distinctive feature of. **3** make out by hearing, seeing, etc. **distinguishable** *adj* **distinguished** *adj* **1** dignified in appearance. **2** highly respected.

distort ❶ *v* **1** misrepresent (the truth or facts). **2** twist out of shape.

3 *Electronics* reproduce or amplify (a signal) inaccurately. **distortion** *n*.

distract ❶ *v* **1** draw the attention of (a person) away from something. **2** entertain. **distracted** *adj* unable to concentrate, preoccupied. **distraction** *n*.

distrait [diss-**tray**] *adj* absent-minded or preoccupied.

distraught ❶ [diss-**trawt**] *adj* extremely anxious or agitated.

distress ❶ *n* **1** extreme unhappiness. **2** great physical pain. **3** poverty. ▷ *v* **4** upset badly. **distressed** *adj* **1** extremely upset. **2** in financial difficulties. **3** (of furniture or fabric) made to look old. **distressing** *adj* **distressingly** *adv*.

—————————————————————————————— THESAURUS ————

distinct *adj* **1** = **different**, detached, discrete, individual, separate, unconnected **3** = **definite**, clear, decided, evident, marked, noticeable, obvious, palpable, unmistakable, well-defined

distinction *n* **1** = **differentiation**, discernment, discrimination, perception, separation **2** = **feature**, characteristic, distinctiveness, individuality, mark, particularity, peculiarity, quality **3** = **difference**, contrast, differential, division, separation **4** = **excellence**, eminence, fame, greatness, honour, importance, merit, prominence, repute

distinctive *adj* = **characteristic**, idiosyncratic, individual, original, peculiar, singular, special, typical, unique

distinctly *adv* **3** = **definitely**, clearly, decidedly, markedly, noticeably, obviously, patently, plainly, unmistakably

distinguish *v* **1** (usu. foll. by *between*) = **differentiate**, ascertain, decide, determine, discriminate, judge, tell apart, tell the difference **2** = **characterize**, categorize, classify, mark, separate, set apart, single out **3** = **make out**, discern, know, perceive, pick out, recognize, see, tell

distinguished *adj* **2** = **eminent**, acclaimed, celebrated, famed, famous, illustrious, noted, renowned, well-known

distort *v* **1** = **misrepresent**, bias, colour, falsify, pervert, slant, twist **2** = **deform**, bend, buckle, contort,

disfigure, misshape, twist, warp

distortion *n* **1** = **misrepresentation**, bias, falsification, perversion, slant **2** = **deformity**, bend, buckle, contortion, crookedness, malformation, twist, warp

distract *v* **1** = **divert**, draw away, sidetrack, turn aside **2** = **amuse**, beguile, engross, entertain, occupy

distracted *adj* = **agitated**, at sea, flustered, harassed, in a flap (*inf*), perplexed, puzzled, troubled

distraction *n* **1** = **diversion**, commotion, disturbance, interference, interruption **2** = **entertainment**, amusement, diversion, pastime, recreation

distraught *adj* = **frantic**, agitated, beside oneself, desperate, distracted, distressed, out of one's mind, overwrought, worked-up

distress *n* **1** = **worry**, grief, heartache, misery, pain, sorrow, suffering, torment, wretchedness **2** = **pain**, suffering, torment **3** = **need**, adversity, difficulties, hardship, misfortune, poverty, privation, trouble ▷ *v* **4** = **upset**, disturb, grieve, harass, sadden, torment, trouble, worry

distressed *adj* **1** = **upset**, agitated, distracted, distraught, tormented, troubled, worried, wretched **2** = **poverty-stricken**, destitute, down at heel, indigent, needy, poor, straitened

distressing *adj* **1** = **upsetting**, disturbing, harrowing, heart-breaking, painful, sad, worrying

distribute ❶ v **1** hand out or deliver. **2** share out. **distribution** n **1** distributing. **2** arrangement or spread. **distributor** n **1** wholesaler who distributes goods to retailers in a specific area. **2** device in a petrol engine that sends the electric current to the spark plugs. **distributive** adj.

district ❶ n area of land regarded as an administrative or geographical unit. **district nurse** nurse who attends to patients in their homes.

distrust ❶ v **1** regard as untrustworthy. ▷ n **2** feeling of suspicion or doubt. **distrustful** adj.

disturb ❶ v **1** intrude on. **2** worry, make anxious. **3** change the position or shape of. **disturbance** n **disturbing** adj **disturbingly** adv **disturbed** adj Psychiatry emotionally upset or maladjusted.

disunite v cause disagreement among. **disunity** n.

disuse ❶ n state of being no longer used. **disused** adj.

ditch ❶ n **1** narrow channel dug in the earth for drainage or irrigation. ▷ v **2** slang abandon.

dither ❶ v **1** be uncertain or indecisive. ▷ n **2** state of indecision or agitation. **ditherer** n **dithery** adj.

ditto n, pl **-tos 1** the same. ▷ adv **2** in the same way.

ditty n, pl **-ties** short simple poem or song.

diuretic [die-yoor-**et**-ik] n drug that increases the flow of urine.

diurnal [die-**urn**-al] adj happening during the day or daily.

diva n distinguished female singer.

divan n **1** low backless bed. **2** backless sofa or couch.

dive ❶ v **diving**, **dived 1** plunge headfirst into water. **2** (of a submarine or diver) submerge under water. **3** fly in a steep nose-down descending path. **4** move quickly in a specified direction. **5** (foll. by in or into) start doing (something) enthusiastically. ▷ n **6** diving. **7** steep nose-down descent. **8** slang disreputable bar or club. **diver** n **1** person who works or explores underwater. **2** person who dives for sport. **3** water bird that swims and dives. **dive bomber** military aircraft designed to release bombs during a dive. **diving bell** diving apparatus with an open bottom, supplied with compressed air from above. **diving board** platform from which swimmers may dive. **diving suit** diver's waterproof suit, with a helmet and air supply.

---

distribute v **1** = **hand out**, circulate, convey, deliver, pass round **2** = **share**, allocate, allot, apportion, deal, dispense, dole out

distribution n **1 a** = **delivery**, dealing, handling, mailing, transportation **b** = **sharing**, allocation, allotment, apportionment, division **2** = **classification**, arrangement, grouping, organization, placement

district n = **area**, locale, locality, neighbourhood, parish, quarter, region, sector, vicinity

distrust v **1** = **suspect**, be suspicious of, be wary of, disbelieve, doubt, mistrust, question, smell a rat (inf) ▷ n **2** = **suspicion**, disbelief, doubt, misgiving, mistrust, question, scepticism, wariness

disturb v **1** = **interrupt**, bother, butt in on, disrupt, interfere with, intrude on, pester **2** = **upset**, alarm, distress, fluster, harass, perturb, trouble, unnerve, unsettle, worry **3** = **muddle**, disarrange, disorder

disturbance n **1** = **interruption**, annoyance, bother, distraction, intrusion **2** = **disorder**, brawl, commotion, fracas, fray, rumpus

disturbed adj Psychiatry = **unbalanced**, disordered, maladjusted, neurotic, troubled, upset

disturbing adj **2** = **worrying**, alarming, disconcerting, distressing, frightening, harrowing, startling, unsettling, upsetting

disuse n = **neglect**, abandonment, decay, idleness

ditch n **1** = **channel**, drain, dyke, furrow, gully, moat, trench, watercourse ▷ v **2** Sl = **get rid of**, abandon, discard, dispose of, drop, dump (inf), jettison, scrap, throw out or overboard

dither v **1** = **vacillate**, faff about (Brit inf), hesitate, hum and haw, shillyshally (inf), teeter, waver ▷ n **2** = **flutter**, flap (inf), fluster, tizzy (inf)

dive v **1-3** = **plunge**, descend, dip, drop, duck, nose-dive, plummet, swoop ▷ n **6** = **plunge**, jump, leap **7** = **nose dive**,

diverge ❶ v **1** separate and go in different directions. **2** deviate (from a prescribed course). **divergence** n **divergent** adj.

divers adj old-fashioned various.

diverse ❶ adj **1** having variety, assorted. **2** different in kind. **diversity** n, pl **-ties 1** quality of being different or varied. **2** range of difference. **diversify** v **-fying, -fied. diversification** n.

divert ❶ v **1** change the direction of. **2** entertain, distract the attention of. **diversion** n **1** official detour used by traffic when a main route is closed. **2** something that distracts someone's attention. **3** diverting. **4** amusing pastime. **diversionary** adj.

divest v **1** strip (of clothes). **2** deprive (of a role or function).

divide ❶ v **1** separate into parts. **2** share or be shared out in parts. **3** (cause to) disagree. **4** keep apart, be a boundary between. **5** calculate how many times (one number) can be contained in (another). ▷ n **6** division, split. **dividend** n **1** sum of money representing part of the profit made, paid by a company to its shareholders.

2 extra benefit. **3** number to be divided by another number. **divider** n **1** screen used to divide a room into separate areas. ▷ pl **2** compasses with two pointed arms, used for measuring or dividing lines.

divine ❶ adj **1** of God or a god. **2** godlike. **3** informal splendid. ▷ v **4** discover (something) by intuition or guessing. **divinely** adv **divination** n art of discovering future events, as though by supernatural powers. **divinity** n **1** study of religion. **2** pl **-ties** god. **3** state of being divine. **divining rod** forked twig said to move when held over ground in which water or metal is to be found.

division ❶ n **1** dividing, sharing out. **2** one of the parts into which something is divided. **3** mathematical operation of dividing. **4** difference of opinion. **5** several departments in an organization that are grouped together. **divisional** adj of a division in an organization. **divisible** adj **divisibility** n **divisive** [div-**vice**-iv] adj tending to cause disagreement. **divisor** n number to be divided into another number.

——————————————————— THESAURUS ———————————————————

descent, drop, plummet, plunge, swoop
diverge v **1** = **separate**, branch, divide, fork, part, split, spread **2** = **deviate**, depart, digress, meander, stray, turn aside, wander

diverse adj **1** = **various**, assorted, manifold, miscellaneous, of every description, several, sundry, varied **2** = **different**, discrete, disparate, dissimilar, distinct, divergent, separate, unlike, varying

diversify v = **vary**, branch out, change, expand, have a finger in every pie, spread out

diversion n **1** = **detour**, departure, deviation, digression **2** = **distraction 4** = **pastime**, amusement, entertainment, game, recreation, relaxation, sport

diversity n **1** = **difference**, distinctiveness, diverseness, heterogeneity, multiplicity **2** = **range**, variety

divert v **1** = **redirect**, avert, deflect, switch, turn aside **2 a** = **entertain**, amuse, beguile, delight, gratify, regale **b** = **distract**, draw or lead away from, lead astray, sidetrack

diverting adj **2** = **entertaining**, amusing, beguiling, enjoyable, fun, humorous, pleasant

divide v **1** = **separate**, bisect, cut (up), part, partition, segregate, split **2** = **share**, allocate, allot, deal out, dispense, distribute **3** = **cause to disagree**, break up, come between, estrange, split

dividend n **1** = **bonus**, cut (inf), divvy (inf), portion, share, surplus **2** = **gain**, extra, plus

divine adj **1, 2** = **heavenly**, angelic, celestial, godlike, holy, spiritual, superhuman, supernatural **3** Inf = **wonderful**, beautiful, excellent, glorious, marvellous, perfect, splendid, superlative ▷ v **4** = **infer**, apprehend, deduce, discern, guess, perceive, suppose, surmise

divinity n **1** = **theology**, religion, religious studies **2** = **god** or **goddess**, deity, guardian spirit, spirit **3** = **godliness**, deity, divine nature, holiness, sanctity

divisible adj = **dividable**, separable
division n **1** = **separation**, cutting up, dividing, partition, splitting

divorce ❶ *n* **1** legal ending of a marriage. **2** any separation, esp. a permanent one. ▷ *v* **3** legally end one's marriage (to). **4** separate, consider separately. **divorcée**, (*masc*) **divorcé** *n* person who is divorced.

divot *n* small piece of turf.

divulge ❶ *v* make known, disclose. **divulgence** *n*.

divvy *v* **-vying, -vied** (foll. by *up*) *informal* divide and share.

Diwali *n* annual Hindu festival honouring Lakshmi, the goddess of wealth.

Dixie *n* southern states of the US (also **Dixieland**).

DIY *Brit, Aust & NZ* do-it-yourself.

dizzy ❶ *adj* **-zier, -ziest 1** having or causing a whirling sensation. **2** mentally confused. ▷ *v* **-zying, -zied 3** make dizzy. **dizzily** *adv* **dizziness** *n*.

DJ 1 disc jockey. **2** dinner jacket.

djinni *n, pl* **djinn** same as JINNI.

dl decilitre.

dm decimetre.

DM Deutschmark.

DNA *n* deoxyribonucleic acid, the main constituent of the chromosomes of all living things.

D-notice *n Brit* official notice sent to newspapers etc., prohibiting publication of certain security information.

do¹ ❶ *v* **does, doing, did, done 1** perform or complete (a deed or action). **2** be adequate, e.g. *that one will do*. **3** provide, serve. **4** make (hair) neat or attractive. **5** suit or improve, e.g. *that style does nothing for you*. **6** find the answer to (a problem or puzzle). **7** cause, produce, e.g. *it does no harm to think ahead*. **8** give, grant, e.g. *do me a favour*. **9** work at, as a course of study or a job. **10** mimic. **11** *informal* cheat or rob. **12** *slang* use (illegal drugs). **13** used to form questions, e.g. *how do you know?* **14** used to intensify positive statements and commands, e.g. *I do like port; do go on*. **15** used to form negative statements and commands, e.g. *I do not know her well; do not get up*. **16** used to replace an earlier verb, e.g. *he gets paid more than I do*. ▷ *n, pl* **dos, do's 17** *informal* party, celebration. **do away with** *v* get rid of. **do down** *v* belittle, criticize. **do for** *v informal* cause the death or ruin of. **do-gooder** *n informal* well-intentioned but naive or impractical person. **do in** *v slang* **1** kill. **2** exhaust. **do-it-yourself** *n* constructing and repairing things oneself. **do up** *v* **1** fasten. **2** decorate and repair. **do with** *v* find useful or benefit from, e.g. *I could do with a rest*. **do without** *v* manage without.

do² *n, pl* **dos** same as DOH.

Doberman pinscher, Doberman *n* large dog with a black-and-tan coat.

dob in *v* **dobbing, dobbed** *Aust & NZ informal* **1** inform against. **2** contribute to a fund.

docile ❶ *adj* (of a person or animal) easily controlled. **docilely** *adv* **docility** *n*.

---

up **2** = **share**, allotment, apportionment **4** = **disagreement**, difference of opinion, discord, rupture, split, variance **5** = **part**, branch, category, class, department, group, section

divorce *n* **1** = **separation**, annulment, dissolution, split-up ▷ *v* **3** = **separate**, disconnect, dissociate, dissolve (*marriage*), divide, part, sever, split up

divulge *v* = **make known**, confess, declare, disclose, let slip, proclaim, reveal, tell

dizzy *adj* **1** = **giddy**, faint, light-headed, off balance, reeling, shaky, swimming, wobbly, woozy (*inf*) **2** = **confused**, at sea, befuddled, bemused, bewildered, dazed, dazzled, muddled

do¹ *v* **1** = **perform**, accomplish, achieve, carry out, complete, execute **2** = **be adequate**, be sufficient, cut the mustard, pass muster, satisfy, suffice **4** = **get ready**, arrange, fix, look after, prepare, see to **6** = **solve**, decipher, decode, figure out, puzzle out, resolve, work out **7** = **cause**, bring about, create, effect, produce ▷ *n* **17** *Inf* = **event**, affair, function, gathering, occasion, party **do without** = **manage without**, abstain from, dispense with, forgo, get along without, give up, kick (*inf*)

do away with *v* = **get rid of**, abolish, discard, discontinue, eliminate, put an end to, put paid to, remove

docile *adj* = **submissive**, amenable, biddable, compliant, manageable, obedient, pliant

docility *n* = **submissiveness**, compliance, manageability, meekness, obedience

d

dock¹ ❶ n 1 enclosed area of water where ships are loaded, unloaded, or repaired. ▷ v 2 bring or be brought into dock. 3 link (two spacecraft) or (of two spacecraft) be linked together in space. **docker** n person employed to load and unload ships. **dockyard** n place where ships are built or repaired.

dock² ❶ v 1 deduct money from (a person's wages). 2 remove part of (an animal's tail) by cutting through the bone.

dock³ ❶ n enclosed space in a court of law where the accused person sits or stands.

dock⁴ ❶ n weed with broad leaves.

docket n label on a package or other delivery, stating contents, delivery instructions, etc.

doctor ❶ n 1 person licensed to practise medicine. 2 person who has been awarded a doctorate. ▷ v 3 alter in order to deceive. 4 poison or drug (food or drink). 5 informal castrate (an animal). **doctoral** adj **doctorate** n highest academic degree in any field of knowledge.

doctrine ❶ [dock-trin] n 1 body of teachings of a religious, political, or philosophical group. 2 principle or body of principles that is taught or advocated. **doctrinal** adj of doctrines. **doctrinaire** adj stubbornly insistent on the application of a theory without regard to practicality.

document ❶ n 1 piece of paper providing an official record of something. ▷ v 2 record or report

(something) in detail. 3 support (a claim) with evidence. **documentation** n.

documentary n, pl **-ries** 1 film or television programme presenting the facts about a particular subject. ▷ adj 2 (of evidence) based on documents.

docu-soap n television documentary series presenting the lives of the people filmed as entertainment.

dodder v move unsteadily. **doddery** adj.

doddle n informal something easily accomplished.

dodecagon [doe-**deck**-a-gon] n geometric figure with twelve sides.

dodecahedron [doe-deck-a-**heed**-ron] n solid figure with twelve faces.

dodge ❶ v 1 avoid (a blow, being seen, etc.) by moving suddenly. 2 evade by cleverness or trickery. ▷ n 3 cunning or deceitful trick. **dodger** n **dodgy** adj **dodgier**, **dodgiest** informal 1 dangerous, risky. 2 untrustworthy.

Dodgem n ® small electric car driven and bumped against similar cars in a rink at a funfair.

dodo n, pl **dodos**, **dodoes** large flightless extinct bird.

doe n female deer, hare, or rabbit.

does v third person singular of the present tense of DO¹.

doesn't does not.

doff v take off or lift (one's hat) in polite greeting.

dog ❶ n 1 domesticated four-legged mammal of many different breeds. 2 related wild mammal, such as the

━━━━━━━━━━━━━━━━━━━━━━ THESAURUS ━━━━━━

dock¹ n 1 = **wharf**, harbour, pier, quay, waterfront ▷ v 2 = **moor**, anchor, berth, drop anchor, land, put in, tie up 3 Of spacecraft = **link up**, couple, hook up, join, rendezvous, unite

dock² v 1 = **deduct**, decrease, diminish, lessen, reduce, subtract, withhold 2 = **cut off**, clip, crop, curtail, cut short, shorten

doctor n 1 = **G.P.**, general practitioner, medic (inf), medical practitioner, physician ▷ v 3 = **change**, alter, disguise, falsify, misrepresent, pervert, tamper with 4 = **add to**, adulterate, cut, dilute, mix with, spike, water down

doctrinaire adj = **dogmatic**, biased, fanatical, inflexible, insistent, opinionated, rigid

doctrine n = **teaching**, article of faith, belief, conviction, creed, dogma, opinion, precept, principle, tenet

document n 1 = **paper**, certificate, record, report ▷ v 3 = **support**, authenticate, certify, corroborate, detail, substantiate, validate, verify

dodge v 1 = **duck**, dart, sidestep, swerve, turn aside 2 = **evade**, avoid, elude, get out of, shirk ▷ n 3 = **trick**, device, ploy, ruse, scheme, stratagem, subterfuge, wheeze (Brit sl)

dog n 1 = **hound**, canine, cur, man's best friend, pooch (sl) ▷ v 5 = **trouble**, follow, haunt, hound, plague, pursue, track, trail **go to the dogs** Inf = **go to ruin**, degenerate, deteriorate, go down the drain, go to pot

dingo or coyote. **3** male animal of the dog family. **4** *informal* person, e.g. *you lucky dog!* ▷ v **dogging, dogged 5** follow (someone) closely. **6** trouble, plague. **the dogs** *Brit informal* greyhound racing. **go to the dogs** *informal* go to ruin physically or morally. **let sleeping dogs lie** leave things undisturbed. **doggy, doggie** *n,* *pl* **-gies** child's word for a dog. **doggy bag** bag in which leftovers from a meal may be taken away. **dogcart** *n* light horse-drawn two-wheeled cart. **dog collar 1** collar for a dog. **2** *informal* white collar fastened at the back, worn by members of the clergy. **dog days** hottest part of the summer. **dog-eared** *adj* **1** (of a book) having pages folded down at the corner. **2** shabby, worn. **dog-end** *n informal* cigarette end. **dogfight** *n* close-quarters combat between fighter aircraft. **dogfish** *n* small shark. **doghouse** *n US* kennel. **in the doghouse** *informal* in disgrace. **dogleg** *n* sharp bend. **dog paddle** swimming stroke in which the hands are paddled in imitation of a swimming dog. **dog rose** wild rose with pink or white flowers. **dog-tired** *adj informal* exhausted.

doge [**doje**] *n* (formerly) chief magistrate of Venice or Genoa.

dogged ❶ [**dog**-gid] *adj* obstinately determined. **doggedly** *adv* **doggedness** *n.*

doggerel *n* poorly written poetry, usu. comic.

doggo *adv* **lie doggo** *informal* hide and keep quiet.

dogma ❶ *n* doctrine or system of doctrines proclaimed by authority as true. **dogmatic** *adj* habitually stating one's opinions forcefully or arrogantly. **dogmatically** *adv* **dogmatism** *n.*

dogsbody *n, pl* **-bodies** *informal* person who carries out boring tasks for others.

doh *n Music* in tonic sol-fa, first degree of any major scale.

doily *n, pl* **-lies** decorative lacy paper mat, laid on a plate.

Dolby *n* ® system used in tape recorders that reduces noise level on recorded or broadcast sound.

doldrums ❶ *pl n* **1** depressed state of mind. **2** state of inactivity. **3** area of sea round the equator where there is hardly any wind.

dole ❶ *n* **1** *informal* money received from the state while unemployed. ▷ v **2** (foll. by *out*) distribute in small quantities. **on the dole** *Brit informal* receiving unemployment benefit.

doleful *adj* dreary, unhappy. **dolefully** *adv* **dolefulness** *n.*

doll *n* **1** small model of a human being, used as a toy. **2** *slang* pretty girl or young woman. **doll up** *v slang* dress up smartly or showily.

dollar *n* standard monetary unit of the US, Canada, and various other countries.

dollop ❶ *n informal* lump (of food).

dolly *n, pl* **-lies 1** child's word for a doll. **2** wheeled support on which a camera may be moved.

dolman sleeve *n* sleeve that is very wide at the armhole, tapering to a tight wrist.

dolmen *n* prehistoric monument consisting of a horizontal stone supported by vertical stones.

dolomite *n* mineral consisting of calcium magnesium carbonate.

dolorous *adj* sad, mournful.

dolphin *n* sea mammal of the whale family, with a beaklike snout. **dolphinarium** *n* aquarium for dolphins.

dolt ❶ *n* stupid person. **doltish** *adj.*

domain *n* **1** field of knowledge or activity. **2** land under one ruler or

---

THESAURUS

dogged *adj* = **determined**, indefatigable, obstinate, persistent, resolute, steadfast, stubborn, tenacious, unflagging, unshakable

dogma *n* = **doctrine**, belief, credo, creed, opinion, teachings

dogmatic *adj* = **opinionated**, arrogant, assertive, doctrinaire, emphatic, obdurate, overbearing

doldrums *n* **1** = **depression**, dumps (*inf*), gloom, malaise **2** = **inactivity**,

listlessness

dole *n* **1** *Inf* = **benefit**, allowance, gift, grant, hand-out, pogey (*Canad*) ▷ v **2** (foll. by *out*) = **give out**, allocate, allot, apportion, assign, dispense, distribute, hand out

dollop *n Inf* = **lump**, helping, portion, scoop, serving

dolt *n* = **idiot**, ass, blockhead, chump (*inf*), clot (*Brit inf*), dope (*inf*), dunce, fool, oaf

government. **3** *Computers* group of computers with the same name on the internet. **4** *NZ* public park.

dome *n* **1** rounded roof built on a circular base. **2** something shaped like this. **domed** *adj*.

domestic ❶ *adj* **1** of one's own country or a specific country, e.g. *domestic and foreign policy*. **2** of the home or family. **3** enjoying running a home. **4** (of an animal) kept as a pet or to produce food. ▷ *n* **5** person whose job is to do housework in someone else's house. **domestically** *adv* **domesticity** *n* **domesticate** *v* **1** bring or keep (a wild animal or plant) under control or cultivation. **2** accustom (someone) to home life. **domestication** *n* **domestic science** study of household skills.

domicile [**dom**-miss-ile] *n* place where one lives. **domiciliary** *adj*.

dominant ❶ *adj* **1** having authority or influence. **2** main, chief. **dominance** *n*.

dominate ❶ *v* **1** control or govern. **2** tower above (surroundings). **3** be very significant in. **domination** *n*.

domineering ❶ *adj* forceful and arrogant.

Dominican *n*, *adj* (friar or nun) of an order founded by Saint Dominic.

dominion ❶ *n* **1** control or authority. **2** land governed by one ruler or government. **3** (formerly) self-governing division of the British Empire.

domino *n*, *pl* **-noes 1** small rectangular block marked with dots, used in dominoes. ▷ *pl* **2** game in which dominoes with matching halves are laid together.

don¹ ❶ *v* **donning**, **donned** put on (clothing).

don² **n* **1 *Brit* member of the teaching staff at a university or college. **2** Spanish gentleman or nobleman. **3** head of a Mafia family. **donnish** *adj* serious and academic.

donate ❶ *v* give, esp. to a charity or organization. **donation** *n* **1** donating. **2** thing donated. **donor** *n* **1** *Medical* person who gives blood or organs for use in the treatment of another person. **2** person who makes a donation.

done *v* **1** past participle of DO¹. ▷ *adj* **2** completed. **3** used up. **4** socially acceptable. **5** *informal* cheated, tricked.

doner kebab *n* see KEBAB.

Don Juan *n* man who has seduced many women.

donkey *n* long-eared member of the horse family. **donkey jacket** man's long thick jacket with a waterproof panel across the shoulders. **donkey's years** *informal* a long time. **donkey-work** *n* tedious hard work.

Don Quixote [**don** kee-**hoe**-tee] *n* impractical idealist.

don't do not.

doodle *v* **1** scribble or draw aimlessly. ▷ *n* **2** shape or picture drawn aimlessly.

domestic *adj* **1** = **native**, indigenous, internal **2** = **home**, family, household, private **3** = **home-loving**, domesticated, homely, housewifely, stay-at-home **4** = **domesticated**, house-trained, pet, tame, trained ▷ *n* **5** = **servant**, char (*inf*), charwoman, daily, help, maid

dominant *adj* **1** = **controlling**, assertive, authoritative, commanding, governing, ruling, superior, supreme **2** = **main**, chief, predominant, pre-eminent, primary, principal, prominent

dominate *v* **1** = **control**, direct, govern, have the whip hand over, monopolize, rule, tyrannize **2** = **tower above**, loom over, overlook, stand head and shoulders above, stand over, survey

domination *n* **1** = **control**, ascendancy, authority, command, influence, mana (*NZ*), power, rule, superiority, supremacy

domineering *adj* = **overbearing**, arrogant, authoritarian, bossy (*inf*), dictatorial, high-handed, imperious, oppressive, tyrannical

dominion *n* **1** = **control**, authority, command, jurisdiction, mana (*NZ*), power, rule, sovereignty, supremacy **2** = **kingdom**, country, domain, empire, realm, territory

don¹ *v* = **put on**, clothe oneself in, dress in, get into, pull on, slip on *or* into

donate *v* = **give**, contribute, make a gift of, present, subscribe

donation *n* **2** = **contribution**, gift, grant, hand-out, offering, present, subscription

donor *n* **2** = **giver**, benefactor, contributor, donator, philanthropist

doom ❶ *n* **1** death or a terrible fate. ▷ *v* **2** destine or condemn to death or a terrible fate. **doomsday** *n* **1** *Christianity* day on which the Last Judgment will occur. **2** any dreaded day.

door ❶ *n* **1** hinged or sliding panel for closing the entrance to a building, room, etc. **2** entrance. **doorjamb**, **doorpost** *n* vertical post forming one side of a door frame. **doorman** *n* man employed to be on duty at the entrance to a large public building. **doormat** *n* **1** mat for wiping dirt from shoes before going indoors. **2** *informal* person who offers little resistance to ill-treatment. **door-to-door** *adj* **1** (of selling) from one house to the next. **2** (of a journey) direct. **doorway** *n* opening into a building or room.

dope ❶ *n* **1** *slang* illegal drug, usu. cannabis. **2** medicine, drug. **3** *informal* stupid person. ▷ *v* **4** give a drug to, esp. in order to improve performance in a race. **dopey**, **dopy** *adj* **1** half-asleep, drowsy. **2** *slang* silly.

doppelgänger *n Legend* ghostly double of a living person.

Doppler effect *n* change in the apparent frequency of a sound or light wave as a result of relative motion between the observer and the source.

Doric *adj* **1** of a style of ancient Greek architecture. ▷ *n* **2** country dialect, esp. a Scots one.

dormant ❶ *adj* temporarily quiet, inactive, or not being used. **dormancy** *n*.

dormer, dormer window *n* window that sticks out from a sloping roof.

dormitory *n, pl* **-ries 1** large room, esp. at a school, containing several beds. ▷ *adj* **2** (of a town or suburb) having many inhabitants who travel to work in a nearby city.

dormouse *n, pl* **-mice** small mouselike rodent with a furry tail.

dorp *n S Afr* small town.

dorsal *adj* of or on the back.

dory *n, pl* **-ries 1** (also **John Dory**) spiny-finned edible sea fish. **2** same as WALLEYE.

dose ❶ *n* **1** specific quantity of a medicine taken at one time. **2** *informal* something unpleasant to experience, e.g. *a dose of the jitters*. ▷ *v* **3** give a dose to. **dosage** *n* size of a dose.

dosh *n slang* money.

doss *v* **doss down** *Brit & Aust slang* sleep in an uncomfortable place. **dosshouse** *n Brit slang* cheap lodging house for homeless people.

dossier [**doss**-ee-ay] *n* collection of documents about a subject or person.

dot ❶ *n* **1** small round mark. **2** shorter symbol used in Morse code. ▷ *v* **dotting**, **dotted 3** mark with a dot. **4** scatter, spread around. **on the dot** at exactly the arranged time. **dotty** *adj* **-tier**, **-tiest** *slang* rather eccentric. **dotcom**, **dot.com** *n* company that does most of its business on the internet.

dote ❶ *v* **dote on** love to an excessive degree. **dotage** *n* weakness as a result of old age. **doting** *adj*.

dotterel *n* rare kind of plover.

dottle *n* tobacco left in a pipe after smoking.

THESAURUS

doom *n* **1** = **destruction**, catastrophe, downfall, fate, fortune, ruin ▷ *v* **2** = **condemn**, consign, damn, destine, sentence

doomed *adj* = **condemned**, bewitched, cursed, fated, hopeless, ill-fated, ill-omened, luckless, star-crossed

door *n* = **opening**, doorway, entrance, entry, exit

dope *n* **1** *Sl* = **drug**, narcotic, opiate **3** *Inf* = **idiot**, dimwit (*inf*), dunce, fool, nitwit (*inf*), numbskull *or* numskull, simpleton, twit (*inf, chiefly Brit*) ▷ *v* **4** = **drug**, anaesthetize, knock out, narcotize, sedate, stupefy

dormant *adj* = **inactive**, asleep, hibernating, inert, inoperative, latent, sleeping, slumbering, suspended

dose *n* **1** = **quantity**, dosage, draught, measure, portion, potion, prescription

dot *n* **1** = **spot**, fleck, jot, mark, point, speck, speckle ▷ *v* **3** = **spot**, dab, dabble, fleck, speckle, sprinkle, stipple, stud **on the dot** = **on time**, exactly, on the button (*inf*), precisely, promptly, punctually, to the minute

dotage *n* = **senility**, decrepitude, feebleness, imbecility, old age, second childhood, weakness

dote *v* **dote on** = **adore**, admire, hold dear, idolize, lavish affection on, prize, treasure

doting *adj* = **adoring**, devoted, fond, foolish, indulgent, lovesick

double ❶ *adj* **1** as much again in number, amount, size, etc. **2** composed of two equal or similar parts. **3** designed for two users, e.g. *double room.* **4** folded in two. ▷ *adv* **5** twice over. ▷ *n* **6** twice the number, amount, size, etc. **7** person who looks almost exactly like another. ▷ *pl* **8** game between two pairs of players. ▷ *v* **9** make or become twice as much or as many. **10** bend or fold (material etc.). **11** play two parts. **12** turn sharply. **at, on the double** quickly or immediately. **doubly** *adv* **double agent** spy employed by two enemy countries at the same time. **double-barrelled** *adj* **1** (of a gun) having two barrels. **2** (of a surname) having two hyphenated parts. **double bass** stringed instrument, largest and lowest member of the violin family. **double-breasted** *adj* (of a jacket or coat) having overlapping fronts. **double-check** *v* make certain by checking again. **double chin** fold of fat under the chin. **double cream** thick cream with a high fat content. **double-cross** *v* **1** cheat or betray. ▷ *n* **2** double-crossing. **double-dealing** *n* treacherous or deceitful behaviour. **double-decker** *n* **1** bus with two passenger decks one on top of the other. ▷ *adj* **2** *informal* (of a sandwich) made from three slices of bread with two fillings. **double Dutch** *informal* incomprehensible talk, gibberish. **double-edged** *adj* **1** (of a remark) malicious in intent though apparently complimentary. **2** (of a knife) having a cutting edge on each side of the blade. **double glazing** two panes of glass in a window, fitted to reduce heat loss. **double-jointed** *adj* (of a person) having unusually flexible joints. **double-park** *v* park (a vehicle) alongside another, causing an obstruction. **double standard** set of principles that allows greater freedom to one person or group than to another. **double take** esp. in comedy, delayed reaction by a person to a remark or situation. **double talk** deceptive or ambiguous talk. **double whammy** *informal* devastating setback made up of two elements.

double entendre [doob-bl on-**tond**-ra] *n* word or phrase that can be interpreted in two ways, one of which is rude.

doublet [**dub**-lit] *n History* man's close-fitting jacket, with or without sleeves.

doubloon *n* former Spanish gold coin.

doubt ❶ *n* **1** uncertainty about the truth, facts, or existence of something. **2** unresolved difficulty or point. ▷ *v* **3** question the truth of. **4** distrust or be suspicious of (someone). **doubter** *n* **doubtful** *adj* **1** unlikely. **2** feeling doubt. **doubtfully** *adv* **doubtless** *adv* probably or certainly.

douche [**doosh**] *n* **1** (instrument for applying) a stream of water directed onto or into the body for cleansing or medical purposes. ▷ *v* **2** cleanse or treat by means of a douche.

dough *n* **1** thick mixture of flour and water or milk, used for making bread

————————————————————— THESAURUS —————————————————————

double *adj* **1** = **twice**, duplicate, twofold **2** = **dual**, coupled, in pairs, paired, twin ▷ *n* **7** = **twin**, clone, dead ringer (*sl*), doppelgänger, duplicate, lookalike, replica, spitting image (*inf*) ▷ *v* **9** = **multiply**, duplicate, enlarge, grow, increase, magnify **at** *or* **on the double** = **quickly**, at full speed, briskly, immediately, posthaste, without delay

double-cross *v* **1** = **betray**, cheat, defraud, hoodwink, mislead, swindle, trick, two-time (*inf*)

doubt *n* **1** = **uncertainty**, apprehension, distrust, hesitancy, hesitation, indecision, irresolution, lack of conviction, misgiving, mistrust, qualm, scepticism, suspense, suspicion ▷ *v* **3** = **be uncertain**, be dubious, demur **4** = **suspect**, discredit, distrust, fear, lack confidence in, mistrust, query, question

doubtful *adj* **1** = **unlikely**, debatable, dubious, equivocal, improbable, problematic(al), questionable, unclear **2** = **unsure**, distrustful, hesitating, in two minds (*inf*), sceptical, suspicious, tentative, uncertain, unconvinced, wavering

doubtless *adv* **a** = **probably**, apparently, most likely, ostensibly, presumably, seemingly, supposedly **b** = **certainly**, assuredly, indisputably, of course, surely, undoubtedly, unquestionably, without doubt

etc. **2** *slang* money. **doughy** *adj*
doughier, **doughiest**. **doughnut** *n*
small cake of sweetened dough fried
in deep fat.

doughty [**dowt**-ee] *adj* **-tier**,
-tiest *old-fashioned* brave and
determined.

dour ⊕ [**doo**-er] *adj* sullen and
unfriendly. **dourness** *n*.

douse [rhymes with **mouse**] *v* **1** drench
with water or other liquid. **2** put out
(a light).

dove *n* **1** bird with a heavy body, small
head, and short legs. **2** *Politics* person
opposed to war. **dovecote**, **dovecot** *n*
structure for housing pigeons.

dovetail *n* **1** joint containing wedge-
shaped tenons. ▷ *v* **2** fit together
neatly.

dowager *n* widow possessing property
or a title obtained from her husband.

dowdy ⊕ *adj* **-dier**, **-diest** dull and old-
fashioned. **dowdily** *adv* **dowdiness** *n*.

dowel *n* wooden or metal peg that fits
into two corresponding holes to join
two adjacent parts.

dower *n* life interest in a part of her
husband's estate allotted to a widow
by law.

down¹ ⊕ *prep*, *adv* **1** indicating
movement to or position in a lower
place. ▷ *adv* **2** indicating completion
of an action, lessening of intensity,
etc. e.g. *calm down*. ▷ *adj* **3** depressed,
unhappy. ▷ *v* **4** *informal* drink quickly.

have a down on *informal* feel hostile
towards. **down under** *informal* (in or
to) Australia or New Zealand.

downward *adj*, *adv* (descending) from
a higher to a lower level, condition, or
position. **downwards** *adv* from a
higher to a lower level, condition, or
position. **down-and-out** *n* **1** person
who is homeless and destitute. ▷ *adj*
2 without any means of support.
down-to-earth *adj* sensible or
practical.

down² *n* soft fine feathers. **downy** *adj*.

downbeat *adj* **1** *informal* gloomy.
2 relaxed.

downcast ⊕ *adj* **1** sad, dejected. **2** (of
the eyes) directed downwards.

downfall ⊕ *n* (cause of) a sudden loss
of position or reputation.

downgrade ⊕ *v* reduce in importance
or value.

downhearted ⊕ *adj* sad and
discouraged.

downhill *adj* **1** going or sloping
down. ▷ *adv* **2** towards the bottom
of a hill. **go downhill** *informal*
deteriorate.

Downing Street *n informal* British
prime minister or government.

download *v* **1** transfer (data) from the
memory of one computer to that of
another. ▷ *n* **2** file transferred in such
a way.

downpour ⊕ *n* heavy fall of rain.

downright ⊕ *adj*, *adv* extreme(ly).

— THESAURUS —

dour *adj* = **gloomy**, dismal, dreary,
forbidding, grim, morose, sour, sullen,
unfriendly

dowdy *adj* = **frumpy**, dingy, drab,
frowzy, old-fashioned, shabby,
unfashionable

down¹ *adj* **3** = **depressed**, dejected,
disheartened, downcast, low,
miserable, sad, unhappy ▷ *v* **4** *Inf* =
swallow, drain, drink (down),
gulp, put away, toss off **have a down
on** *Inf* = **be antagonistic** *or* **hostile
to**, bear a grudge towards, be
prejudiced against, be set against,
have it in for (*sl*)

down-and-out *n* **1** = **tramp**, bag lady,
beggar, derelict, dosser (*Brit sl*),
pauper, vagabond, vagrant ▷ *adj*
2 = **destitute**, derelict, impoverished,
on one's uppers (*inf*), penniless,
short, without two pennies to rub
together (*inf*)

downcast *adj* **1** = **dejected**,
crestfallen, depressed, despondent,
disappointed, disconsolate,
discouraged, disheartened, dismayed,
dispirited

downfall *n* = **ruin**, collapse,
comeuppance (*sl*), destruction,
disgrace, fall, overthrow, undoing

downgrade *v* = **demote**, degrade,
humble, lower *or* reduce in rank, take
down a peg (*inf*)

downhearted *adj* = **dejected**,
crestfallen, depressed, despondent,
discouraged, disheartened, dispirited,
downcast, sad, unhappy

downpour *n* = **rainstorm**, cloudburst,
deluge, flood, inundation, torrential
rain

downright *adj* = **complete**, absolute,
out-and-out, outright, plain,
thoroughgoing, total, undisguised,
unqualified, utter

downs *pl n* low grassy hills, esp. in S England.

Down's syndrome *n* genetic disorder characterized by a flat face, slanting eyes, and mental retardation.

downstage *adv, adj* to or at the front part of the stage.

downstairs *adv* **1** to or on a lower floor. ▷ *n* **2** lower or ground floor.

downtown *n US, Canad & NZ* **1** the central or lower part of a city, especially the main commercial area. ▷ *adv* **2** towards, to, or into this area.

downtrodden ❶ *adj* oppressed and lacking the will to resist.

dowry *n, pl* **-ries** property brought by a woman to her husband at marriage.

dowse [rhymes with **cows**] *v* search for underground water or minerals using a divining rod. **dowser** *n*.

doxology *n, pl* **-gies** short hymn of praise to God.

doyen [**doy**-en] *n* senior member of a group, profession, or society. **doyenne** [doy-**en**] *n fem*.

doyley *n* same as DOILY.

doze ❶ *v* **1** sleep lightly or briefly. ▷ *n* **2** short sleep. **dozy** *adj* **dozier**, **doziest 1** feeling sleepy. **2** *informal* stupid. **doze off** *v* fall into a light sleep.

dozen *adj, n* twelve. **dozenth** *adj*.

DPP Director of Public Prosecutions.

Dr 1 Doctor. **2** Drive.

drab ❶ *adj* **drabber**, **drabbest 1** dull and dreary. **2** dull brown. **drabness** *n*.

drachm [**dram**] *n Brit* one eighth of a fluid ounce.

drachma *n, pl* **-mas**, **-mae** former monetary unit of Greece.

draconian *adj* severe, harsh.

draft ❶ *n* **1** plan, sketch, or drawing of something. **2** preliminary outline of a book, speech, etc. **3** written order for payment of money by a bank. **4** *US & Aust* selection for compulsory military service. ▷ *v* **5** draw up an outline or plan of. **6** send (people) from one place to another to do a specific job. **7** *US & Aust* select for compulsory military service.

drag ❶ *v* **dragging**, **dragged 1** pull with force, esp. along the ground. **2** trail on the ground. **3** persuade or force (oneself or someone else) to go somewhere. **4** (foll. by *on* or *out*) last or be prolonged tediously. **5** search (a river) with a dragnet or hook. **6** *Computers* move (an image) on the screen by use of the mouse. ▷ *n* **7** person or thing that slows up progress. **8** *informal* tedious thing or person. **9** *slang* women's clothes worn by a man. **10** resistance to the motion of a body passing through air or a liquid. **dragnet** *n* net used to scour the bottom of a pond or river to search for something. **drag race** race in which specially built cars or motorcycles are timed over a measured course.

dragoman *n, pl* **-mans**, **-men** (in some Middle Eastern countries) professional interpreter or guide.

dragon *n* **1** mythical fire-breathing monster like a huge lizard. **2** *informal* fierce woman. **dragonfly** *n* brightly coloured insect with a long slender body and two pairs of wings.

dragoon ❶ *n* **1** heavily armed cavalryman. ▷ *v* **2** coerce, force.

——————————————————————— THESAURUS ——————

down-to-earth *adj* = **sensible**, matter-of-fact, no-nonsense, plain-spoken, practical, realistic, sane, unsentimental

downtrodden *adj* = **oppressed**, exploited, helpless, subjugated, subservient, tyrannized

downward *adj* = **descending**, declining, earthward, heading down, sliding, slipping

doze *v* **1** = **nap**, kip (*Brit sl*), nod off (*inf*), sleep, slumber, snooze (*inf*) ▷ *n* **2** = **nap**, catnap, forty winks (*inf*), kip (*Brit sl*), shuteye (*sl*), siesta, snooze (*inf*)

drab *adj* **1** = **dull**, dingy, dismal, dreary, flat, gloomy, shabby, sombre

draft *n* **1** = **outline**, abstract, plan, rough, sketch, version **3** = **order**, bill (*of exchange*), cheque, postal order ▷ *v* **5** = **outline**, compose, design, draw, draw up, formulate, plan, sketch

drag *v* **1** = **pull**, draw, haul, lug, tow, trail, tug **4** (foll. by *on* or *out*) = **last**, draw out, extend, keep going, lengthen, persist, prolong, protract, spin out, stretch out ▷ *n* **8** *Inf* = **nuisance**, annoyance, bore, bother, pain (*inf*), pest

dragoon *v* **2** = **force**, browbeat, bully, coerce, compel, constrain, drive, impel, intimidate, railroad (*inf*)

d

drain ❶ *n* **1** pipe or channel that carries off water or sewage. **2** cause of a continuous reduction in energy or resources. ▷ *v* **3** draw off or remove liquid from. **4** flow away or filter off. **5** drink the entire contents of (a glass or cup). **6** make constant demands on (energy or resources), exhaust. **drainage** *n* **1** system of drains. **2** process or method of draining. **draining board** sloping grooved surface at the side of a sink, used for draining washed dishes. **drainpipe** *n* **1** pipe for carrying off rainwater or sewage. ▷ *pl* **2** trousers with very narrow legs.

drake *n* male duck.

dram *n* **1** small amount of a strong alcoholic drink, esp. whisky. **2** one sixteenth of an ounce.

drama ❶ *n* **1** serious play for theatre, television, or radio. **2** plays collectively. **3** writing, producing, or acting in plays. **4** situation that is exciting or highly emotional. **dramatic** *adj* **1** of or like drama. **2** behaving flamboyantly. **dramatically** *adv* **dramatist** *n* person who writes plays. **dramatize** *v* **1** rewrite (a book) in the form of a play. **2** express (something) in a dramatic or exaggerated way. **dramatization** *n*.

dramatis personae [drah-mat-tiss per-**soh**-nigh] *pl n* characters in a play.

dramaturgy *n* art and technique of the theatre. **dramaturge** *n*

1 playwright. **2** literary adviser to a theatre, film company, etc. **dramaturgical, dramaturgic** *adj*.

drank *v* past tense of DRINK.

drape ❶ *v* **1** cover with material, usu. in folds. **2** place casually. ▷ *n* **3** *Aust, US & Canad* curtain. **draper** *n Brit, Aust & NZ* person who sells fabrics and sewing materials. **drapery** *n, pl* **-peries 1** fabric or clothing arranged and draped. **2** fabrics and cloth collectively.

drastic ❶ *adj* strong and severe. **drastically** *adv*.

draught ❶ *n* **1** current of cold air, esp. in an enclosed space. **2** portion of liquid to be drunk, esp. medicine. **3** gulp or swallow. **4** one of the flat discs used in the game of draughts. ▷ *pl* **5** game for two players using a chessboard and twelve draughts each. ▷ *adj* **6** (of an animal) used for pulling heavy loads. **draughty** *adj* **draughtier, draughtiest** exposed to draughts of air. **draughtsman** *n* **1** person employed to prepare detailed scale drawings of machinery, buildings, etc. **2** person skilled in drawing. **draughtsmanship** *n* **draught beer** beer stored in a cask.

draw ❶ *v* **drawing, drew, drawn 1** sketch (a figure, picture, etc.) with a pencil or pen. **2** pull (a person or thing) closer to or further away from a place. **3** move in a specified direction, e.g. *the car drew near.* **4** take from a

———————— **THESAURUS** ————————

drain *n* **1** = **pipe**, channel, conduit, culvert, ditch, duct, sewer, sink, trench **2** = **reduction**, depletion, drag, exhaustion, sap, strain, withdrawal ▷ *v* **3** = **remove**, bleed, draw off, dry, empty, pump off *or* out, tap, withdraw **4** = **flow out**, effuse, exude, leak, ooze, seep, trickle, well out **5** = **drink up**, finish, gulp down, quaff, swallow **6** = **exhaust**, consume, deplete, dissipate, empty, sap, strain, use up

drama *n* **1** = **play**, dramatization, show, stage show **3** = **theatre**, acting, dramaturgy, stagecraft **4** = **excitement**, crisis, histrionics, scene, spectacle, turmoil

dramatic *adj* **1 a** = **theatrical**, dramaturgical, Thespian **b** = **exciting**, breathtaking, climactic, electrifying, melodramatic, sensational,

suspenseful, tense, thrilling **c** = **powerful**, expressive, impressive, moving, striking, vivid

dramatist *n* = **playwright**, dramaturge, screenwriter, scriptwriter

dramatize *v* **2** = **exaggerate**, lay it on (thick) (*sl*), overdo, overstate, play to the gallery

drape *v* **1** = **cover**, cloak, fold, swathe, wrap

drastic *adj* = **extreme**, desperate, dire, forceful, harsh, radical, severe, strong

draught *n* **1** = **breeze**, current, flow, movement, puff **2** = **drink**, cup, dose, potion, quantity

draw *v* **1** = **sketch**, depict, design, map out, mark out, outline, paint, portray, trace **2** = **pull**, drag, haul, tow, tug **4** = **take out**, extract, pull out **5** = **attract**, allure, elicit, entice, evoke,

source, e.g. *draw money from bank accounts*. **5** attract, interest. **6** formulate or decide, e.g. *to draw conclusions*. **7** (of two teams or contestants) finish a game with an equal number of points. ▷ *n* **8** raffle or lottery. **9** contest or game ending in a tie. **10** event, act, etc., that attracts a large audience. **drawing** *n* **1** picture or plan made by means of lines on a surface. **2** art of making drawings. **drawing pin** short tack with a broad smooth head. **drawing room** *old-fashioned* room where visitors are received and entertained. **drawback** *n* disadvantage. **drawbridge** *n* bridge that may be raised to prevent access or to enable vessels to pass. **draw out** *v* **1** encourage (someone) to talk freely. **2** make longer. **drawstring** *n* cord run through a hem around an opening, so that when it is pulled tighter, the opening closes. **draw up** *v* **1** prepare and write out (a contract). **2** (of a vehicle) come to a stop.

drawer *n* **1** sliding box-shaped part of a piece of furniture, used for storage. ▷ *pl* **2** *old-fashioned* undergarment worn on the lower part of the body.

drawl *v* **1** speak slowly, with long vowel sounds. ▷ *n* **2** drawling manner of speech.

drawn ❶ *v* **1** past participle of DRAW. ▷ *adj* **2** haggard, tired, or tense in appearance.

dray *n* low cart used for carrying heavy loads.

dread ❶ *v* **1** anticipate with apprehension or fear. ▷ *n* **2** great fear. **dreadful** *adj* **1** very disagreeable or shocking. **2** extreme, e.g. *a dreadful anticlimax*. **dreadfully** *adv*.

dreadlocks *pl n* hair worn in the Rastafarian style of tightly twisted strands.

dream ❶ *n* **1** imagined series of events experienced in the mind while asleep. **2** daydream. **3** cherished hope. **4** *informal* wonderful person or thing. ▷ *v* **dreaming, dreamed** or **dreamt 5** see imaginary pictures in the mind while asleep. **6** (often foll. by *of* or *about*) have an image (of) or fantasy (about). **7** (foll. by *of*) consider the possibility (of). ▷ *adj* **8** ideal, e.g. *a dream house*. **dreamer** *n* **dreamy** *adj* **dreamier, dreamiest 1** vague or impractical. **2** *informal* wonderful. **dreamily** *adv* **dream team** *informal* group of people with the ideal combination of talents. **dream up** *v* invent by imagination and ingenuity.

dreary ❶ *adj* **drearier, dreariest** dull, boring. **drearily** *adv* **dreariness** *n*.

induce, influence, invite, persuade **6 = deduce**, derive, infer, make, take ▷ *n* **9 = tie**, dead heat, deadlock, impasse, stalemate **10 = attraction**, enticement, lure, pull (*inf*)

drawback *n* **= disadvantage**, deficiency, difficulty, downside, flaw, handicap, hitch, snag, stumbling block

drawing *n* **1 = picture**, cartoon, depiction, illustration, outline, portrayal, representation, sketch, study

drawn *adj* **2 = tense**, haggard, pinched, stressed, tired, worn

draw out *v* **2 = extend**, drag out, lengthen, make longer, prolong, protract, spin out, stretch, string out

draw up *v* **1 = draft**, compose, formulate, frame, prepare, write out **2 = halt**, bring to a stop, pull up, stop

dread *v* **1 = fear**, cringe at, have cold feet (*inf*), quail, shrink from, shudder, tremble ▷ *n* **2 = fear**, alarm, apprehension, dismay, fright, horror, terror, trepidation

dreadful *adj* **1 = terrible**, abysmal, appalling, atrocious, awful, fearful, frightful, hideous, horrible, shocking

dream *n* **1 = vision**, delusion, hallucination, illusion, imagination, trance **2 = daydream**, fantasy, pipe dream **3 = ambition**, aim, aspiration, desire, goal, hope, wish **4** *Inf* **= delight**, beauty, gem, joy, marvel, pleasure, treasure ▷ *v* **6** (often foll. by *of* or *about*) **= daydream**, build castles in the air *or* in Spain, conjure up, envisage, fantasize, imagine, stargaze, visualize

dreamer *n* **2 = idealist**, daydreamer, escapist, utopian, visionary, Walter Mitty

dreamy *adj* **2 = vague**, absent, abstracted, daydreaming, faraway, pensive, preoccupied, with one's head in the clouds

dreary *adj* **= dull**, boring, drab, humdrum, monotonous, tedious, tiresome, uneventful, wearisome

dredge¹ v clear or search (a river bed or harbour) by removing silt or mud. **dredger** n boat fitted with machinery for dredging. **dredge up** v informal remember (something) obscure or half-forgotten.

dredge² v sprinkle (food) with flour etc.

dregs ❶ pl n **1** solid particles that settle at the bottom of some liquids. **2** most despised elements, e.g. the dregs of society.

drench ❶ v make completely wet.

Dresden china, Dresden n delicate decorative porcelain made near Dresden in Germany.

dress ❶ n **1** one-piece garment for a woman or girl, consisting of a skirt and bodice and sometimes sleeves. **2** complete style of clothing. ▷ v **3** put clothes on. **4** put on formal clothes. **5** apply a protective covering to (a wound). **6** arrange or prepare. **dressing** n **1** sauce for salad. **2** covering for a wound. **dressing-down** n informal severe scolding. **dressing gown** coat-shaped garment worn over pyjamas or nightdress. **dressing room** room used for changing clothes, esp. backstage in a theatre. **dressing table** piece of bedroom furniture with a mirror and drawers. **dressy** adj **dressier**, **dressiest** (of clothes) elegant. **dress circle** first gallery in a theatre. **dressmaker** n person who makes women's clothes. **dressmaking** n **dress rehearsal** last rehearsal of a play or show, using costumes, lighting, etc. **dress up** v **1** put on glamorous or stylish clothes. **2** put on fancy dress. **3** make (something) seem better than it really is, e.g. to dress up profits.

dressage [dress-ahzh] n training of a horse to perform manoeuvres in response to the rider's body signals.

dresser¹ n piece of furniture with shelves and with cupboards, for storing or displaying dishes.

dresser² n Theatre person employed to assist actors with their costumes.

drew v past tense of DRAW.

drey n squirrel's nest.

dribble ❶ v **1** (allow to) flow in drops. **2** allow saliva to trickle from the mouth. **3** Sport propel (a ball) by repeatedly tapping it with the foot, hand, or a stick. ▷ n **4** small quantity of liquid falling in drops. **5** dribbling. **dribbler** n.

driblet n small amount.

dribs and drabs pl n informal small occasional amounts.

dried v past of DRY.

drier¹ adj a comparative of DRY.

drier² n same as DRYER.

driest adj a superlative of DRY.

drift ❶ v **1** be carried along by currents of air or water. **2** move aimlessly from one place or activity to another. **3** (of snow) pile up in heaps. ▷ n **4** something piled up by the wind or current, such as a snowdrift. **5** general movement or development. **6** point, meaning, e.g. catch my drift? **drifter** n **1** person who moves aimlessly from place to place or job to job. **2** fishing boat equipped with drift nets. **drift net** fishing net that is allowed to drift with the tide. **driftwood** n wood floating on or washed ashore by the sea.

d

THESAURUS

dregs pl n **1** = **sediment**, deposit, dross, grounds, lees, resi, residuum, scum, waste **2** = **scum**, good-for-nothings, rabble, ragtag and bobtail, riffraff

drench v = **soak**, drown, flood, inundate, saturate, souse, steep, swamp, wet

dress n **1** = **frock**, gown, outfit, robe **2** = **clothing**, apparel, attire, clothes, costume, garb, garments, togs ▷ v **3** = **put on**, attire, change, clothe, don, garb, robe, slip on or into **5** = **bandage**, bind up, plaster, treat **6** = **arrange**, adjust, align, get ready, prepare, straighten

dressmaker n = **seamstress**, couturier, tailor

dribble v **1** = **run**, drip, drop, fall in drops, leak, ooze, seep, trickle **2** = **drool**, drivel, slaver, slobber

drift v **1** = **float**, be carried along, coast, go (aimlessly), meander, stray, waft, wander **3** = **pile up**, accumulate, amass, bank up, drive, gather ▷ n **4** = **pile**, accumulation, bank, heap, mass, mound **6** = **meaning**, direction, gist, import, intention, purport, significance, tendency, thrust

drill[1] ❶ n 1 tool or machine for boring holes. 2 strict and often repetitious training. 3 *informal* correct procedure. ▷ v 4 bore a hole in (something) with or as if with a drill. 5 teach by rigorous exercises or training.

drill[2] n 1 machine for sowing seed in rows. 2 small furrow for seed. ▷ v 3 sow (seed) in drills or furrows.

drill[3] n hard-wearing cotton cloth.

drily adv see DRY.

drink v **drinking**, **drank**, **drunk** 1 swallow (a liquid). 2 consume alcohol, esp. to excess. ▷ n 3 (portion of) a liquid suitable for drinking. 4 alcohol, or its habitual or excessive consumption. **drinkable** adj **drinker** n **drink-driving** adj, n (of) driving a car after drinking alcohol. **drink in** v pay close attention to. **drink to** v drink a toast to.

drip ❶ v **dripping**, **dripped** 1 (let) fall in drops. ▷ n 2 falling of drops of liquid. 3 sound made by falling drops. 4 *informal* weak dull person. 5 *Medical* device by which a solution is passed in small drops through a tube into a vein. **drip-dry** adj denoting clothing that will dry free of creases if hung up when wet. **drip-feed** v feed (someone) a liquid drop by drop, usu. through a vein.

dripping n fat that comes from meat while it is being roasted or fried.

drive ❶ v **driving**, **drove**, **driven** 1 guide the movement of (a vehicle). 2 transport in a vehicle. 3 goad into a specified state. 4 push or propel. 5 *Sport* hit (a ball) very hard and straight. 6 make (people or animals) go to or from a place. ▷ n 7 journey by car, van, etc. 8 (also **driveway**) path for vehicles connecting a building to a public road. 9 united effort towards a common goal, e.g. *a recruitment drive*. 10 energy and ambition. 11 *Psychology* motive or interest, e.g. *sex drive*. 12 means by which power is transmitted in a mechanism. **driver** n **drive at** v *informal* intend or mean, e.g. *what was he driving at?* **drive-in** adj, n (denoting) a cinema, restaurant, etc., used by people in their cars. **driving licence** official document authorizing a person to drive a motor vehicle.

drivel ❶ n 1 foolish talk. ▷ v **-elling**, **-elled** 2 speak foolishly.

drizzle ❶ n 1 very light rain. ▷ v 2 rain lightly. **drizzly** adj **-zlier**, **-zliest**.

droll ❶ adj quaintly amusing. **drolly** adv **drollery** n.

dromedary [**drom**-mid-er-ee] n, pl **-daries** camel with a single hump.

———————————————————————————————————— THESAURUS ——————

drifter n 1 = **wanderer**, beachcomber, bum (*inf*), hobo (*US*), itinerant, rolling stone, vagrant

drill[1] n 1 = **boring tool**, bit, borer, gimlet 2 = **training**, discipline, exercise, instruction, practice, preparation, repetition ▷ v 4 = **bore**, penetrate, perforate, pierce, puncture, sink in 5 = **train**, coach, discipline, exercise, instruct, practise, rehearse, teach

drink v 1 = **swallow**, gulp, guzzle, imbibe, quaff, sip, suck, sup 2 = **booze** (*inf*), hit the bottle (*inf*), tipple, tope ▷ n 3 = **beverage**, cup, draught, glass, liquid, potion, refreshment 4 = **alcohol**, booze (*inf*), hooch or hootch (*inf, chiefly US & Canad*), liquor, spirits, the bottle (*inf*)

drip v 1 = **drop**, dribble, exude, plop, splash, sprinkle, trickle ▷ n 2 = **drop**, dribble, leak, trickle 4 *Inf* = **weakling**, mummy's boy (*inf*), namby-pamby, softie (*inf*), weed (*inf*), wet (*Brit inf*)

drive v 1 = **operate**, direct, guide, handle, manage, motor, ride, steer, travel 3 = **goad**, coerce, constrain, force, press, prod, prompt, spur 4 = **push**, hurl, impel, propel, ram, send, thrust 6 = **herd**, urge ▷ n 7 = **run**, excursion, jaunt, journey, outing, ride, spin (*inf*), trip 9 = **campaign**, action, appeal, crusade, effort, push (*inf*) 10 = **initiative**, ambition, energy, enterprise, get-up-and-go (*inf*), motivation, vigour, zip (*inf*)

drivel n 1 = **nonsense**, garbage (*inf*), gibberish, hogwash, hot air (*inf*), kak (*S Afr sl*), poppycock (*inf*), rubbish, trash, twaddle, waffle (*inf, chiefly Brit*) ▷ v 2 = **babble**, blether, gab (*inf*), prate, ramble, waffle (*inf, chiefly Brit*)

drizzle n 1 = **fine rain**, Scotch mist ▷ v 2 = **rain**, shower, spot or spit with rain, spray, sprinkle

droll adj = **amusing**, comical, entertaining, funny, humorous, jocular, waggish, whimsical

drone¹ n male bee.

drone² ❶ v, n (make) a monotonous low dull sound. **drone on** v talk for a long time in a monotonous tone.

drongo n, pl **-gos** tropical songbird with a glossy black plumage, a forked tail, and a stout bill.

drool ❶ v 1 (foll. by over) show excessive enthusiasm (for). 2 allow saliva to flow from the mouth.

droop ❶ v hang downwards loosely. **droopy** adj **droopier**, **droopiest**.

drop ❶ v **dropping**, **dropped** 1 (allow to) fall vertically. 2 decrease in amount, strength, or value. 3 (of ground) go down to a lower level. 4 mention (a hint or name) casually. 5 drive (someone or something) to a place. 6 discontinue. ▷ n 7 small quantity of liquid forming a round shape. 8 any small quantity of liquid. 9 decrease in amount, strength, or value. 10 vertical distance that something may fall. ▷ pl 11 liquid medication applied in small drops. **droplet** n **droppings** pl n faeces of certain animals, such as rabbits or birds. **drop in**, **by** v pay someone a casual visit. **drop kick** (in rugby etc.) kick in which the ball is dropped from the hands and kicked as it hits the ground. **drop off** v 1 informal fall asleep.

2 same as DROP (sense 5) 3 grow smaller or less. **dropout** n 1 person who rejects conventional society. 2 person who does not complete a course of study. **drop out (of)** v abandon or withdraw from (a school, job, etc.).

dropsy n illness in which watery fluid collects in the body.

dross n 1 scum formed on the surfaces of molten metals. 2 anything worthless.

drought ❶ n prolonged shortage of rainfall.

drove¹ v past tense of DRIVE.

drove² ❶ n very large group, esp. of people. **drover** n person who drives sheep or cattle.

drown ❶ v 1 die or kill by immersion in liquid. 2 forget (one's sorrows) temporarily by drinking alcohol. 3 drench thoroughly. 4 make (a sound) inaudible by being louder.

drowse ❶ v be sleepy, dull, or sluggish. **drowsy** adj **drowsily** adv **drowsiness** n.

drubbing n utter defeat in a contest etc.

drudge ❶ n 1 person who works hard at uninteresting tasks. ▷ v 2 work at such tasks. **drudgery** n.

d

THESAURUS

drone² v = **hum**, buzz, purr, thrum, vibrate, whirr ▷ n = **hum**, buzz, murmuring, purr, thrum, vibration, whirring

drool v 1 (foll. by over) = **gloat over**, dote on, gush, make much of, rave about (inf) 2 = **dribble**, drivel, salivate, slaver, slobber, water at the mouth

droop v = **sag**, bend, dangle, drop, fall down, hang (down), sink

drop v 1 = **fall**, descend, plummet, plunge, sink, tumble 2 = **diminish**, decline, fall, plummet 6 = **discontinue**, axe (inf), give up, kick (inf), quit, relinquish ▷ n 7 = **droplet**, bead, bubble, drip, globule, pearl, tear 8 = **dash**, mouthful, shot (inf), sip, spot, tot, trace, trickle 9 = **decrease**, cut, decline, deterioration, downturn, fall-off, lowering, reduction, slump 10 = **fall**, descent, plunge

drop off v 1 Inf = **fall asleep**, doze

(off), have forty winks (inf), nod (off), snooze (inf) 3 = **decrease**, decline, diminish, dwindle, fall off, lessen, slacken

drop out (of) v = **leave**, abandon, fall by the wayside, give up, quit, stop, withdraw

drought n = **dry spell**, aridity, dehydration, dryness

drove² n = **herd**, collection, company, crowd, flock, horde, mob, multitude, swarm, throng

drown v 3 = **drench**, deluge, engulf, flood, go under, immerse, inundate, sink, submerge, swamp 4 = **overpower**, deaden, muffle, obliterate, overcome, overwhelm, stifle, swallow up, wipe out

drowsy adj = **sleepy**, dopey (sl), dozy, half asleep, heavy, lethargic, somnolent, tired, torpid

drudge n 1 = **menial**, dogsbody (inf), factotum, servant, skivvy (chiefly Brit), slave, toiler, worker

d

drug ❶ n **1** substance used in the treatment or prevention of disease. **2** chemical substance, esp. a narcotic, taken for the effects it produces. ▷ v **drugging, drugged 3** give a drug to (a person or animal) to cause sleepiness or unconsciousness. **4** mix a drug with (food or drink). **drugstore** n US pharmacy where a wide range of goods are available.

Druid n member of an ancient order of Celtic priests. **Druidic, Druidical** adj.

drum ❶ n **1** percussion instrument sounded by striking a membrane stretched across the opening of a hollow cylinder. **2** cylindrical object or container. ▷ v **drumming, drummed 3** play (music) on a drum. **4** tap rhythmically or regularly. **drummer** n **drum into** v instil into (someone) by constant repetition. **drum machine** synthesizer programmed to reproduce the sound of percussion instruments. **drum major** person in charge of a marching band. **drum out (of)** v force to leave (an organization). **drumstick** n **1** stick used for playing a drum. **2** lower joint of the leg of a cooked chicken etc. **drum up** v obtain (support or business) by making requests or canvassing.

drunk ❶ v **1** past participle of DRINK. ▷ adj **2** intoxicated with alcohol to the extent of losing control over normal functions. **3** overwhelmed by a strong influence or emotion, e.g. drunk with success. ▷ n **4** person who is drunk or who frequently gets drunk.

drunkard n person who frequently gets drunk. **drunken** adj **1** drunk or frequently drunk. **2** caused by or relating to alcoholic intoxication. **drunkenly** adv **drunkenness** n.

dry ❶ adj **drier, driest** or **dryer, dryest 1** lacking moisture. **2** having little or no rainfall. **3** informal thirsty. **4** (of wine) not sweet. **5** uninteresting, e.g. a dry book. **6** (of humour) subtle and sarcastic. **7** prohibiting the sale of alcohol, e.g. a dry town. ▷ v **drying, dried 8** make or become dry. **9** preserve (food) by removing the moisture. **drily, dryly** adv **dryness** n **dryer** n apparatus for removing moisture. **dry-clean** v clean (clothes etc.) with chemicals rather than water. **dry-cleaner** n **dry-cleaning** n **dry dock** dock that can be pumped dry to permit work on a ship's bottom. **dry ice** solid carbon dioxide. **dry out** v **1** make or become dry. **2** (cause to) undergo treatment for alcoholism. **dry rot** crumbling and drying of timber, caused by certain fungi. **dry run** informal rehearsal. **dry-stone** adj (of a wall) made without mortar. **dry up** v **1** dry (washed dishes) with a tea towel. **2** stop being productive. **3** informal stop speaking.

dryad n wood nymph.

DSc Doctor of Science.

DSS Department of Social Security.

————————————————————————— THESAURUS —————————

drudgery n = **menial labour**, donkey-work, fag (inf), grind (inf), hard work, labour, skivvying (Brit), slog, toil

drug n **1** = **medication**, medicament, medicine, physic, poison, remedy **2** = **dope** (sl), narcotic, opiate, stimulant ▷ v **3** = **dose**, administer a drug, anaesthetize, deaden, dope (sl), knock out, medicate, numb, poison, stupefy, treat

drum v **4** = **beat**, pulsate, rap, reverberate, tap, tattoo, throb **drum into** v = **drive home**, din into, hammer away, harp on, instil into, reiterate

drunk adj **2** = **intoxicated**, drunken, inebriated, legless (inf), merry (Brit inf), plastered (sl), tipsy, under the influence (inf) ▷ n **4** = **drunkard**, alcoholic, boozer (inf), inebriate, lush (sl), wino (inf)

drunkard n = **drinker**, alcoholic, dipsomaniac, drunk, lush (sl), tippler, wino (inf)

drunkenness n = **intoxication**, alcoholism, bibulousness, dipsomania, inebriation, insobriety, intemperance

dry adj **1** = **dehydrated**, arid, barren, desiccated, dried up, parched, thirsty **5** = **dull**, boring, dreary, monotonous, plain, tedious, tiresome, uninteresting **6** = **sarcastic**, deadpan, droll, low-key, sly ▷ v **8** = **dehydrate**, dehumidify, desiccate, drain, make dry, parch, sear

dry out v **1** = **become dry**, harden, shrivel up, wilt, wither, wizen

DT's *informal* delirium tremens.

dual ❶ *adj* having two parts, functions, or aspects. **duality** *n* **dualism** *n* state of having or being believed to have two distinct parts or aspects. **dual carriageway** *Brit, Aust & NZ* road on which traffic travelling in opposite directions is separated by a central strip of grass or concrete.

dub¹ *v* **dubbing**, **dubbed** give (a person or place) a name or nickname.

dub² *v* **dubbing**, **dubbed 1** provide (a film) with a new soundtrack, esp. in a different language. **2** provide (a film or tape) with a soundtrack. ▷ *n* **3** style of reggae record production involving exaggeration of instrumental parts, echo, etc.

dubbin *n* thick grease applied to leather to soften and waterproof it.

dubious ❶ [**dew**-bee-uss] *adj* feeling or causing doubt. **dubiously** *adv* **dubiety** [dew-**by**-it-ee] *n*.

ducal [**duke**-al] *adj* of a duke.

ducat [**duck**-it] *n* former European gold or silver coin.

duchess *n* **1** woman who holds the rank of duke. **2** wife or widow of a duke.

duchy *n*, *pl* **duchies** territory of a duke or duchess.

duck¹ *n* **1** water bird with short legs, webbed feet, and a broad blunt bill. **2** its flesh, used as food. **3** female of this bird. **4** *Cricket* score of nothing. **duckling** *n* baby duck. **duck-billed platypus** *or* **duckbill** see PLATYPUS.

duck² ❶ *v* **1** move (the head or body) quickly downwards, to avoid being seen or to dodge a blow. **2** plunge suddenly under water. **3** *informal* dodge (a duty or responsibility).

duct *n* **1** tube, pipe, or channel through which liquid or gas is conveyed. **2** bodily passage conveying secretions or excretions.

ductile *adj* (of a metal) able to be shaped into sheets or wires.

dud ❶ *informal* ▷ *n* **1** ineffectual person or thing. ▷ *adj* **2** bad or useless, e.g. *dud cheques*.

dude *n* *US informal* **1** man. **2** *old-fashioned* dandy. **3** any person.

dudgeon ❶ *n* **in high dudgeon** angry, resentful.

due ❶ *adj* **1** expected or scheduled to be present or arrive. **2** owed as a debt. **3** fitting, proper. ▷ *n* **4** something that is owed or required. ▷ *pl* **5** charges for membership of a club or organization. ▷ *adv* **6** directly or exactly, e.g. *due south*. **due to** attributable to or caused by.

duel ❶ *n* **1** formal fight with deadly weapons between two people, to settle a quarrel. ▷ *v* **duelling**, **duelled 2** fight in a duel. **duellist** *n*.

duenna *n* (esp. in Spain) elderly woman acting as chaperone to a young woman.

duet *n* piece of music for two performers.

duff *adj chiefly brit* broken or useless. **duff up** *v Brit informal* beat (someone) severely.

THESAURUS

dual *adj* = **twofold**, binary, double, duplex, duplicate, matched, paired, twin

dubious *adj* **a** = **unsure**, doubtful, hesitant, sceptical, uncertain, unconvinced, undecided, wavering **b** = **suspect**, fishy (*inf*), questionable, suspicious, unreliable, untrustworthy

duck² *v* **1** = **bob**, bend, bow, crouch, dodge, drop, lower, stoop **2** = **plunge**, dip, dive, douse, dunk, immerse, souse, submerge, wet **3** *Inf* = **dodge**, avoid, escape, evade, shirk, shun, sidestep

dud *Inf* ▷ *n* **1** = **failure**, flop (*inf*), washout (*inf*) ▷ *adj* **2** = **useless**, broken, duff (*Brit inf*), failed, inoperative, worthless

dudgeon *n* **in high dudgeon** = **indignant**, angry, choked, fuming, offended, resentful, vexed

due *adj* **1** = **expected**, scheduled **2** = **payable**, in arrears, outstanding, owed, owing, unpaid **3** = **fitting**, appropriate, deserved, justified, merited, proper, rightful, suitable, well-earned ▷ *n* **4** = **right(s)**, comeuppance (*sl*), deserts, merits, privilege ▷ *pl* **5** = **membership fee**, charge, charges, contribution, fee, levy ▷ *adv* **6** = **directly**, dead, exactly, straight, undeviatingly

duel *n* **1** = **fight**, affair of honour, clash, competition, contest, encounter, engagement, head-to-head, single

d

duffel, duffle *n* short for DUFFEL COAT. **duffel bag** cylindrical canvas bag fastened with a drawstring. **duffel coat** wool coat with toggle fastenings, usu. with a hood.

duffer *n informal* dull or incompetent person.

dug¹ *v* past of DIG.

dug² *n* teat or udder.

dugite [**doo**-gyte] *n* medium-sized Australian venomous snake.

dugong *n* whalelike mammal of tropical waters.

dugout *n* **1** (at a sports ground) covered bench where managers and substitutes sit. **2** canoe made by hollowing out a log. **3** *Military* covered excavation to provide shelter.

duke *n* **1** nobleman of the highest rank. **2** prince or ruler of a small principality or duchy. **dukedom** *n*.

dulcet [**dull**-sit] *adj* (of a sound) soothing or pleasant.

dulcimer *n* tuned percussion instrument consisting of a set of strings stretched over a sounding board and struck with hammers.

dull ❶ *adj* **1** not interesting. **2** (of an ache) not acute. **3** (of weather) not bright or clear. **4** lacking in spirit. **5** not very intelligent. **6** (of a blade) not sharp. ▷ *v* **7** make or become dull. **dullness** *n* **dully** *adv* **dullard** *n* dull or stupid person.

dulse *n* seaweed with large red edible fronds.

duly ❶ *adv* **1** in a proper manner. **2** at the proper time.

dumb ❶ *adj* **1** lacking the power to speak. **2** silent. **3** *informal* stupid. **dumbly** *adv* **dumbness** *n* **dumbbell** *n* short bar with a heavy ball or disc at each end, used for physical exercise. **dumbfounded** *adj* speechless with astonishment. **dumb show** meaningful gestures without speech. **dumbwaiter** *n* **1** lift for carrying food etc. between floors. **2** stand for holding food at a dining table.

dumdum *n* soft-nosed bullet that expands on impact and causes serious wounds.

dummy ❶ *n, pl* **-mies 1** figure representing the human form, used for displaying clothes etc. **2** copy of an object, often lacking some essential feature of the original. **3** rubber teat for a baby to suck. **4** *slang* stupid person. ▷ *adj* **5** imitation, substitute. **dummy run** rehearsal.

dump ❶ *v* **1** drop or let fall in a careless manner. **2** *informal* get rid of (someone or something no longer wanted). **3** dispose of (nuclear waste). **4** market (goods) in bulk and at low prices, esp. abroad. ▷ *n* **5** place where waste materials are left. **6** *informal* dirty unattractive place.

---

combat ▷ *v* **2** = **fight**, clash, compete, contend, contest, lock horns, rival, struggle, vie with

dull *adj* **1** = **boring**, dreary, flat, humdrum, monotonous, plain, run-of-the-mill, tedious, uninteresting **3** = **cloudy**, dim, dismal, gloomy, leaden, overcast **4** = **lifeless**, apathetic, blank, indifferent, listless, passionless, unresponsive **5** = **stupid**, dense, dim-witted (*inf*), dozy (*Brit inf*), slow, thick, unintelligent **6** = **blunt**, blunted, unsharpened ▷ *v* **7** = **relieve**, allay, alleviate, blunt, lessen, moderate, soften, take the edge off

duly *adv* **1** = **properly**, accordingly, appropriately, befittingly, correctly, decorously, deservedly, fittingly, rightfully, suitably **2** = **on time**, at the proper time, punctually

dumb *adj* **1, 2** = **mute**, mum, silent, soundless, speechless, tongue-tied, voiceless, wordless **3** *Inf* = **stupid**,

asinine, dense, dim-witted (*inf*), dull, foolish, thick, unintelligent

dumbfounded *adj* = **amazed**, astonished, astounded, flabbergasted (*inf*), lost for words, nonplussed, overwhelmed, speechless, staggered, stunned

dummy *n* **1** = **model**, figure, form, manikin, mannequin **2** = **copy**, counterfeit, duplicate, imitation, sham, substitute **4** *Sl* = **fool**, blockhead, dunce, idiot, nitwit (*inf*), numbskull *or* numskull, oaf, simpleton ▷ *adj* **5** = **imitation**, artificial, bogus, fake, false, mock, phoney *or* phony (*inf*), sham, simulated

dump *v* **1** = **drop**, deposit, fling down, let fall, throw down **2** *Inf* = **get rid of**, dispose of, ditch (*sl*), empty out, jettison, scrap, throw away *or* out, tip, unload ▷ *n* **5** = **rubbish tip**, junkyard, refuse heap, rubbish heap, tip **6** *Inf* = **pigsty**, hole (*inf*), hovel, mess, slum

7 *Military* place where weapons or supplies are stored. **down in the dumps** *informal* depressed and miserable.

dumpling *n* **1** small ball of dough cooked and served with stew. **2** round pastry case filled with fruit.

dumpy *adj* **dumpier**, **dumpiest** short and plump.

dun¹ *adj* brownish-grey.

dun² *v* **dunning**, **dunned 1** demand payment from (a debtor). ▷ *n* **2** demand for payment.

dunce ❶ *n* person who is stupid or slow to learn.

dunderhead *n* slow-witted person.

dune *n* mound or ridge of drifted sand.

dung *n* faeces from animals such as cattle.

dungarees *pl n* trousers with a bib attached.

dungeon ❶ *n* underground prison cell.

dunk *v* **1** dip (a biscuit or bread) in a drink or soup before eating it. **2** put (something) in liquid.

dunlin *n* small sandpiper with a brown back.

duo *n*, *pl* **duos 1** pair of performers. **2** *informal* pair of closely connected people.

duodenum [dew-oh-**deen**-um] *n*, *pl* **-na**, **-nums** first part of the small intestine, just below the stomach. **duodenal** *adj*.

duologue *n* (in drama) conversation between only two speakers.

dupe *v* **1** deceive or cheat. ▷ *n* **2** person who is easily deceived.

duple *adj Music* having two beats in a bar.

duplex *n US & Canad* apartment on two floors.

duplicate ❶ *adj* **1** copied exactly from an original. ▷ *n* **2** exact copy. ▷ *v* **3** make an exact copy of. **4** do again (something that has already been done). **duplication** *n* **duplicator** *n*.

duplicity *n* deceitful behaviour.

durable ❶ *adj* long-lasting. **durability** *n* **durable goods**, **durables** *pl n* goods that require infrequent replacement.

duration ❶ *n* length of time that something lasts.

duress ❶ *n* compulsion by use of force or threats.

during *prep* throughout or within the limit of (a period of time).

dusk ❶ *n* time just before nightfall, when it is almost dark. **dusky** *adj* **duskier**, **duskiest 1** dark in colour. **2** shadowy. **duskiness** *n*.

dust ❶ *n* **1** small dry particles of earth, sand, or dirt. ▷ *v* **2** remove dust from (furniture) by wiping. **3** sprinkle (something) with a powdery substance. **duster** *n* cloth used for dusting. **dusty** *adj* **dustier**, **dustiest** covered with dust. **dustbin** *n* large container for household rubbish. **dust bowl** dry area in which the surface soil is exposed to wind

---

THESAURUS

dunce *n* = **simpleton**, blockhead, duffer (*inf*), dunderhead, ignoramus, moron, nincompoop, numbskull *or* numskull, thickhead

dungeon *n* = **prison**, cage, cell, oubliette, vault

duplicate *adj* **1** = **identical**, corresponding, matched, matching, twin, twofold ▷ *n* **2** = **copy**, carbon copy, clone, double, facsimile, photocopy, replica, reproduction ▷ *v* **3** = **copy**, clone, double, replicate, reproduce **4** = **repeat**

durability *n* = **durableness**, constancy, endurance, imperishability, permanence, persistence

durable *adj* = **long-lasting**, dependable, enduring, hard-wearing, persistent, reliable, resistant, strong, sturdy, tough

duration *n* = **length**, extent, period, span, spell, stretch, term, time

duress *n* = **pressure**, coercion, compulsion, constraint, threat

dusk *n* = **twilight**, dark, evening, eventide, gloaming (*Scot or poet*), nightfall, sundown, sunset

dusky *adj* **1** = **dark**, dark-complexioned, sable, swarthy **2** = **dim**, cloudy, gloomy, murky, obscure, shadowy, shady, tenebrous, twilit

dust *n* **1** = **grime**, grit, particles, powder ▷ *v* **3** = **sprinkle**, cover, dredge, powder, scatter, sift, spray, spread

dusty *adj* = **dirty**, grubby, sooty, unclean, unswept

dutiful *adj* = **conscientious**, devoted, obedient, respectful, reverential, submissive

erosion. **dustcart** n lorry for collecting household rubbish. **dust jacket** removable paper cover used to protect a book. **dustman** n Brit man whose job is to collect household rubbish. **dustpan** n short-handled shovel into which dust is swept from floors. **dustsheet** n Brit large cloth cover to protect furniture from dust. **dust-up** n informal fight or argument.

Dutch adj 1 of the Netherlands. ▷ n 2 language of the Netherlands. **go Dutch** informal share the expenses on an outing. **Dutch auction** auction in which the price is gradually lowered until a buyer is found. **Dutch barn** farm building with a steel frame and a curved roof. **Dutch courage** false courage gained from drinking alcohol. **Dutch elm disease** fungal disease of elm trees.

duty ❶ n, pl **-ties** 1 work or a task performed as part of one's job. **2** task that a person feels morally bound to do. **3** government tax on imports. **on duty** at work. **dutiable** adj (of goods) requiring payment of duty. **dutiful** adj doing what is expected. **dutifully** adv **duty-bound** adj morally obliged. **duty-free** adj, adv with exemption from customs or excise duties.

duvet [**doo**-vay] n kind of quilt used in bed instead of a top sheet and blankets.

DVD Digital Versatile (or Video) Disk.

DVT deep-vein thrombosis.

dwarf ❶ n, pl **dwarfs**, **dwarves** **1** person who is smaller than average. **2** (in folklore) small ugly manlike creature, often possessing magical powers. ▷ adj **3** (of an animal or plant) much smaller than the usual size for the species. ▷ v **4** cause (someone or something) to seem small by being much larger.

dwell ❶ v **dwelling**, **dwelt** or **dwelled** live, reside. **dweller** n **dwelling** n place of residence. **dwell on, upon** v think, speak, or write at length about.

dwindle ❶ v grow less in size, strength, or number.

Dy Chemistry dysprosium.

dye ❶ n 1 colouring substance. **2** colour produced by dyeing. ▷ v **dyeing**, **dyed 3** colour (hair or fabric) by applying a dye. **dyer** n **dyed-in-the-wool** adj uncompromising or unchanging in opinion.

dying ❶ v present participle of DIE¹.

dyke¹ n wall built to prevent flooding.

dyke² n slang lesbian.

dynamic ❶ adj **1** full of energy, ambition, and new ideas. **2** Physics of energy or forces that produce motion. **dynamically** adv **dynamism** n great energy and enthusiasm.

dynamics n **1** branch of mechanics concerned with the forces that change or produce the motions of bodies. ▷ pl **2** forces that produce change in a system.

——————————————————————————— THESAURUS ——————————

duty n 1 = **responsibility**, assignment, function, job, obligation, role, task, work, yakka (Aust & NZ inf) **2** = **loyalty**, allegiance, deference, obedience, respect, reverence **3** = **tax**, excise, levy, tariff, toll **on duty** = **at work**, busy, engaged, on active service

dwarf n 1 = **midget**, Lilliputian, pygmy or pigmy, Tom Thumb ▷ adj **3** = **miniature**, baby, bonsai, diminutive, small, tiny, undersized ▷ v **4** = **tower above** or **over**, diminish, dominate, overshadow

dwell v = **live**, abide, inhabit, lodge, reside

dwelling n = **home**, abode, domicile,

habitation, house, lodging, quarters, residence

dwindle v = **lessen**, decline, decrease, die away, diminish, fade, peter out, shrink, subside, taper off, wane

dye n 1 = **colouring**, colorant, colour, pigment, stain, tinge, tint ▷ v **3** = **colour**, pigment, stain, tinge, tint

dying adj = **expiring**, at death's door, failing, in extremis, moribund, not long for this world

dynamic adj 1 = **energetic**, forceful, go-ahead, go-getting (inf), high-powered, lively, powerful, storming (inf), vital

dynamite *n* **1** explosive made of nitroglycerine. **2** *informal* dangerous or exciting person or thing. ▷ *v* **3** blow (something) up with dynamite.

dynamo *n*, *pl* **-mos** device for converting mechanical energy into electrical energy.

dynasty ❶ *n*, *pl* **-ties** sequence of hereditary rulers. **dynastic** *adj* **dynast** *n* hereditary ruler.

dysentery *n* infection of the intestine causing severe diarrhoea.

dysfunction *n* **1** *Medical* disturbance or abnormality in the function of an organ or part. **2** (of a family) failure to show the characteristics accepted as normal. **dysfunctional** *adj*.

dyslexia *n* disorder causing impaired ability to read. **dyslexic** *adj*.

dysmenorrhoea *n* painful menstruation.

dyspepsia *n* indigestion. **dyspeptic** *adj*.

dysprosium *n* *Chemistry* metallic element of the lanthanide series.

dystopia *n* imaginary place where everything is as bad as it can be.

dystrophy [**diss**-trof-fee] *n* see MUSCULAR DYSTROPHY.

dwindle *v* = **lessen**, decline, decrease, die away, diminish, fade, peter out, shrink, subside, taper off, wane

dye *n* **1** = **colouring**, colorant, colour, pigment, stain, tinge, tint ▷ *v* **3** = **colour**, pigment, stain, tinge, tint

dying *adj* = **expiring**, at death's door, failing, *in extremis*, moribund, not long for this world

dynamic *adj* **1** = **energetic**, forceful, go-ahead, go-getting (*inf*), high-powered, lively, powerful, storming (*inf*), vital

dynasty *n* = **empire**, government, house, regime, rule, sovereignty

dynasty *n* = **empire**, government, house, regime, rule, sovereignty

E 1 East(ern). 2 *slang* ecstasy (the drug).
e- *prefix* electronic, e.g. *e-mail*.
each ⊙ *adj, pron* every (one) taken separately.
eager ⊙ *adj* showing or feeling great desire, keen. **eagerly** *adv* **eagerness** *n*.
eagle *n* 1 large bird of prey with keen eyesight. 2 *Golf* score of two strokes under par for a hole. **eaglet** *n* young eagle.
ear¹ ⊙ *n* 1 organ of hearing, esp. the external part of it. 2 sensitivity to musical or other sounds. **earache** *n* pain in the ear. **earbash** *v Aust & NZ informal* talk incessantly. **eardrum** *n* thin piece of skin inside the ear which enables one to hear sounds. **earmark** *v* 1 set (something) aside for a specific purpose. ▷ *n* 2 distinguishing mark. **earphone** *n* receiver for a radio etc., held to or put in the ear. **ear-piercing** *adj* deafening. **earplug** *n* piece of soft material placed in the ear to keep out water or noise. **earring** *n* ornament for the lobe of the ear. **earshot** *n*

hearing range.
ear² *n* head of corn.
earl *n* British nobleman ranking next below a marquess. **earldom** *n*.
early ⊙ *adj, adv* **-lier, -liest** 1 before the expected or usual time. 2 in the first part of a period. 3 in a period far back in time.
earn ⊙ *v* 1 obtain by work or merit. 2 (of investments etc.) gain (interest). **earnings** *pl n* money earned.
earnest¹ ⊙ *adj* serious and sincere. **in earnest** seriously. **earnestly** *adv*.
earnest² ⊙ *n* part payment given in advance, esp. to confirm a contract.
earth ⊙ *n* 1 planet that we live on. 2 land, the ground. 3 soil. 4 fox's hole. 5 wire connecting an electrical apparatus with the earth. ▷ *v* 6 connect (a circuit) to earth. **come down to earth** return to reality from a daydream. **earthen** *adj* made of baked clay or earth. **earthenware** *n* pottery made of baked clay. **earthly** *adj* conceivable or possible, e.g. *no earthly reason.* **earthy** *adj* 1 coarse or crude. 2 of or like earth. **earthquake** *n* violent vibration of the earth's surface. **earthwork** *n* fortification made of earth. **earthworm** *n* worm which burrows in the soil.
earwig *n* small insect with a pincer-like tail.

——————————————————————— THESAURUS ——————

each *adj* = **every** ▷ *pron* = **every one**, each and every one, each one, one and all
eager *adj* = **keen**, agog, anxious, athirst, avid, enthusiastic, fervent, hungry, impatient, longing
eagerness *n* = **keenness**, ardour, enthusiasm, fervour, hunger, impatience, thirst, yearning, zeal
ear¹ *n* 2 = **sensitivity**, appreciation, discrimination, taste
early *adj* 1 = **premature**, advanced, forward, untimely 3 = **primitive**, primeval, primordial, undeveloped, young ▷ *adv* 1 = **too soon**, ahead of time, beforehand, in advance, in good time, prematurely
earmark *v* 1 = **set aside**, allocate, designate, flag, label, mark out, reserve
earn *v* 1 = **deserve**, acquire, attain, be entitled to, be worthy of, merit, rate, warrant, win 2 = **make**, bring in,

collect, gain, get, gross, net, receive
earnest¹ *adj* = **serious**, grave, intent, resolute, resolved, sincere, solemn, thoughtful **in earnest** = **in seriousness**, in sincerity, in truth
earnest² *n* = **down payment**, assurance, deposit, earnest money (*Law*), foretaste, guarantee, pledge, promise, security, token
earnings *pl n* = **income**, pay, proceeds, profits, receipts, remuneration, salary, takings, wages
earth *n* 1 = **world**, globe, orb, planet, sphere 2, 3 = **soil**, clay, dirt, ground, land, turf
earthenware *n* = **crockery**, ceramics, pots, pottery, terracotta
earthly *adj* = **possible**, conceivable, feasible, imaginable, likely, practical
earthy *adj* 1 = **crude**, bawdy, coarse, raunchy (*sl*), ribald, robust, uninhibited, unsophisticated

ease ❶ n **1** freedom from difficulty, discomfort, or worry. **2** rest or leisure, e.g. *at one's ease*. ▷ v **3** give bodily or mental ease to. **4** lessen (severity, tension, pain, etc.). **5** move carefully or gradually. **ease off** v become less severe.

easel n frame to support an artist's canvas or a blackboard.

east n **1** (direction towards) the part of the horizon where the sun rises. **2** region lying in this direction. ▷ adj **3** to or in the east. **4** (of a wind) from the east. ▷ adv **5** in, to, or towards the east. **easterly** adj **eastern** adj **easterner** n person from the east of a country or area. **eastward** adj, adv **eastwards** adv.

Easter n Christian spring festival commemorating the Resurrection of Jesus Christ. **Easter egg** chocolate egg given at Easter.

easy ❶ adj **easier, easiest 1** not needing much work or effort. **2** free from pain, care, or anxiety. **3** easy-going. **easily** adv **easiness** n **easy chair** comfortable armchair. **easy-going** adj relaxed in attitude, tolerant.

eat ❶ v **eating, ate, eaten 1** take (food) into the mouth and swallow it. **2** have a meal. **3** (foll. by *away* or *up*) destroy. **eatable** adj fit or suitable for eating.

eau de Cologne [oh de kol-**lone**] n French light perfume.

eaves pl n overhanging edges of a roof.

eavesdrop ❶ v **-dropping, -dropped** listen secretly to a private conversation. **eavesdropper** n **eavesdropping** n.

e-banking n use of the internet for banking transactions.

ebb ❶ v **1** (of tide water) flow back. **2** fall away or decline, e.g. *her anger ebbed away*. ▷ n **3** flowing back of the tide. **at a low ebb** in a state of weakness.

Ebola virus disease n severe infectious disease characterized by fever, vomiting, and internal bleeding.

ebony n, pl **-onies 1** hard black wood. ▷ adj **2** deep black.

e-book n book in electronic form, for reading on a computer, mobile phone, or e-reader.

ebullient adj full of enthusiasm or excitement. **ebullience** n.

EC 1 European Commission. **2** European Community: a former name for the European Union.

eccentric ❶ adj **1** odd or unconventional. **2** (of circles) not having the same centre. ▷ n **3** eccentric person. **eccentrically** adv **eccentricity** n.

THESAURUS
---

ease n **1 a** = **effortlessness**, easiness, facility, readiness, simplicity **b** = **peace of mind**, comfort, content, happiness, peace, quiet, serenity, tranquillity **2** = **leisure**, relaxation, repose, rest, restfulness ▷ v **3** = **comfort**, calm, outspan (*S Afr*), relax, soothe **4** = **relieve**, alleviate, lessen, lighten, soothe **5** = **move carefully**, edge, inch, manoeuvre, slide, slip

easily adv **1** = **without difficulty**, comfortably, effortlessly, readily, smoothly, with ease, with one hand tied behind one's back

easy adj **1** = **not difficult**, a piece of cake (*inf*), child's play (*inf*), effortless, no trouble, painless, plain sailing, simple, straightforward, uncomplicated, undemanding **2** = **carefree**, comfortable, cushy (*inf*), leisurely, peaceful, quiet, relaxed, serene, tranquil, untroubled **3** = **tolerant**, easy-going, indulgent, lenient, mild, permissive, unoppressive

easy-going adj = **relaxed**, carefree, casual, easy, even-tempered, happy-go-lucky, laid-back (*inf*),

nonchalant, placid, tolerant, undemanding

eat v **1** = **consume**, chew, devour, gobble, ingest, munch, scoff (*sl*), swallow **2** = **have a meal**, dine, feed, take nourishment **3** (foll. by *away*) (*up*) = **destroy**, corrode, decay, dissolve, erode, rot, waste away, wear away

eavesdrop v = **listen in**, earwig (*inf*), monitor, overhear, snoop (*inf*), spy

ebb v **1** = **flow back**, go out, recede, retire, retreat, subside, wane, withdraw **2** = **decline**, decrease, diminish, dwindle, fade away, fall away, flag, lessen, peter out ▷ n **3** = **flowing back**, going out, low tide, low water, retreat, subsidence, wane, withdrawal

eccentric adj **1** = **odd**, freakish, idiosyncratic, irregular, munted (*NZ sl*), outlandish, peculiar, quirky, strange, unconventional ▷ n **3** = **crank** (*inf*), character (*inf*), nonconformist, oddball (*inf*), weirdo *or* weirdie (*inf*)

eccentricity n **1** = **oddity**, abnormality, caprice, capriciousness, foible, idiosyncrasy, irregularity, peculiarity, quirk

ecclesiastic ❶ *n* **1** clergyman. ▷ *adj*
2 (also **ecclesiastical**) of the Christian
Church or clergy.

ECG electrocardiogram.

echelon [**esh**-a-lon] *n* **1** level of power or
responsibility. **2** *Military* formation in
which units follow one another but are
spaced out sideways to allow each a
line of fire ahead.

echidna [ik-**kid**-na] *n, pl* **-s**, **-nae** [-nee]
mammal with a protective layer of
spines, found in Australia and New
Guinea (also **spiny anteater**).

echo ❶ *n, pl* **-oes 1** repetition of sounds
by reflection of sound waves off a
surface. **2** close imitation. ▷ *v* **-oing**,
-oed 3 repeat or be repeated as an
echo. **4** imitate (what someone else
has said). **echo sounder** sonar.

éclair *n* finger-shaped pastry filled with
cream and covered with chocolate.

éclat [ake-**lah**] *n* **1** brilliant success.
2 splendour.

eclectic *adj* selecting from various
styles, ideas, or sources. **eclecticism** *n*.

eclipse ❶ *n* **1** temporary obscuring of
reflected light from one star or planet
as it passes through the shadow of
another. ▷ *v* **2** surpass or outclass.
ecliptic *n* apparent path of the sun.

eco- *combining form* ecology or
ecological, e.g. *ecotourism*.

ecological *adj* **1** of ecology. **2** intended
to protect the environment, e.g. *an
ecological approach to agriculture*.
ecologically *adv* **ecology** *n* study of the
relationships between living things and
their environment. **ecologist** *n*.

e-commerce, ecommerce *n* business

transactions done on the internet.

economy ❶ *n, pl* **-mies 1** system of
interrelationship of money, industry,
and employment in a country. **2** careful
use of money or resources to avoid
waste. **economic** *adj* **1** of economics.
2 profitable. **3** *informal* inexpensive or
cheap. **economics** *n* **1** social science
concerned with the production and
consumption of goods and services.
▷ *pl* **2** financial aspects. **economical**
adj not wasteful, thrifty. **economically**
adv **economist** *n* specialist in economics.
economize *v* reduce expense or waste.

ecosystem *n* system involving
interactions between a community and
its environment.

ecru *adj* pale creamy-brown.

ecstasy ❶ *n* **1** state of intense delight.
2 *slang* powerful drug that can produce
hallucinations. **ecstatic** *adj*
ecstatically *adv.*

- ● **SPELLING TIP**
- ● People get confused about how
- ● many cs there are in **ecstasy**. The
- ● Bank of English has 119 occurrences
- ● of *ecstacy*, but 3379 of the correct
- ● spelling **ecstasy**.

ECT electroconvulsive therapy.

ectoplasm *n Spiritualism* substance that
supposedly is emitted from the body of
a medium during a trance.

ecumenical *adj* of the Christian Church
throughout the world, esp. with regard
to its unity.

eczema [**ek**-sim-a] *n* skin disease
causing intense itching.

ed. 1 edition. **2** editor.

Edam *n* round Dutch cheese with a

────────────────────── THESAURUS ────

ecclesiastic *n* **1** = **clergyman**,
churchman, cleric, holy man, man of
the cloth, minister, parson, pastor,
priest ▷ *adj* **2** (also **ecclesiastical**)
= **clerical**, divine, holy, pastoral,
priestly, religious, spiritual

echo *n* **1** = **repetition**, answer,
reverberation **2** = **copy**, imitation,
mirror image, parallel, reflection,
reiteration, reproduction ▷ *v*
3 = **repeat**, resound, reverberate
4 = **copy**, ape, imitate, mirror, parallel,
recall, reflect, resemble

eclipse *n* **1** = **obscuring**, darkening,
dimming, extinction, shading ▷ *v*
2 = **surpass**, exceed, excel, outdo,
outshine, put in the shade (*inf*), transcend

economic *adj* **1** = **financial**, commercial,

industrial **2** = **profitable**, money-
making, productive, profit-making,
remunerative, viable **3** *Inf* = **inexpensive**,
cheap, low-priced, modest, reasonable

economical *adj* = **thrifty**, careful,
cost-effective, efficient, frugal, money-
saving, prudent, scrimping, sparing

economize *v* = **cut back**, be economical,
be frugal, draw in one's horns, retrench,
save, scrimp, tighten one's belt

economy *n* **2** = **thrift**, frugality,
husbandry, parsimony, prudence,
restraint

ecstasy *n* **1** = **rapture**, bliss, delight,
elation, euphoria, fervour, joy, seventh
heaven

ecstatic *adj* **1** = **rapturous**, blissful,
elated, enraptured, entranced,

red waxy cover.

eddy ❶ n, pl **eddies** 1 circular movement of air, water, etc. ▷ v **eddying**, **eddied** 2 move with a circular motion.

edelweiss [**ade**-el-vice] n alpine plant with white flowers.

Eden n 1 Bible garden in which Adam and Eve were placed at the Creation. 2 place of delight or contentment.

edge ❶ n 1 border or line where something ends or begins. 2 cutting side of a blade. 3 sharpness of tone. ▷ v 4 provide an edge or border for. 5 push (one's way) gradually. **have the edge on** have an advantage over. **on edge** nervous or irritable. **edgeways** adv with the edge forwards or uppermost. **edging** n anything placed along an edge to finish it. **edgy** adj nervous or irritable.

edible ❶ adj fit to be eaten. **edibility** n.

edict ❶ [**ee**-dikt] n order issued by an authority.

edifice ❶ [**ed**-if-iss] n large building.

edify ❶ [**ed**-if-fie] v **-fying**, **-fied** improve morally by instruction. **edification** n.

edit ❶ v prepare (a book, film, etc.) for publication or broadcast. **edition** n 1 number of copies of a new publication printed at one time. 2 single television or radio programme which forms part of a series. **editor** n 1 person who edits.

2 person in charge of one section of a newspaper or magazine. **editorial** n 1 newspaper article stating the opinion of the editor. ▷ adj 2 of editing or editors.

educate ❶ v 1 teach. 2 provide schooling for. **education** n **educational** adj **educationally** adv **educationalist** n expert in the theory of education. **educative** adj educating.

Edwardian adj of the reign of King Edward VII of Great Britain and Ireland (1901–10).

EEG electroencephalogram.

eel n snakelike fish.

eerie ❶ adj **eerier**, **eeriest** uncannily frightening or disturbing. **eerily** adv.

efface ❶ v 1 remove by rubbing. 2 make (oneself) inconspicuous. **effacement** n.

effect ❶ n 1 change or result caused by someone or something. 2 condition of being operative, e.g. the law comes into effect next month. 3 overall impression. ▷ pl 4 personal belongings. 5 lighting, sounds, etc. to accompany a film or a broadcast. ▷ v 6 cause to happen, accomplish. **effective** adj 1 producing a desired result. 2 operative. 3 impressive. **effectively** adv **effectual** adj producing the intended result. **effectually** adv.

———— THESAURUS ————

euphoric, in seventh heaven, joyous, on cloud nine (inf), overjoyed

eddy n 1 = **swirl**, counter-current, undertow, vortex, whirlpool ▷ v 2 = **swirl**, whirl

edge n 1 = **border**, boundary, brink, fringe, limit, outline, perimeter, rim, side, verge ▷ v 4 = **border**, fringe, hem 5 = **inch**, creep, ease, sidle, steal **have the edge on** = **have the advantage over**, have ascendancy over, have dominance over, have superiority over, have the upper hand over **on edge** = **nervous**, apprehensive, edgy, ill at ease, impatient, irritable, keyed up, on tenterhooks, tense, wired (sl)

edgy adj = **nervous**, anxious, ill at ease, irritable, keyed up, on edge, on tenterhooks, restive, tense, wired (sl)

edible adj = **eatable**, digestible, fit to eat, good, harmless, palatable, wholesome

edict n = **decree**, act, command, injunction, law, order, proclamation, ruling

edifice n = **building**, construction, erection, house, structure

edify v = **instruct**, educate, enlighten,

guide, improve, inform, nurture, school, teach

edit v = **revise**, adapt, condense, correct, emend, polish, rewrite

edition n 1 = **version**, copy, impression, issue, number, printing, volume 2 = **programme** (TV, Radio)

educate v 1 = **teach**, discipline, enlighten, improve, inform, instruct, school, train, tutor

educated adj = **taught**, coached, informed, instructed, knowledgeable, learned, schooled, tutored

education n = **teaching**, development, discipline, enlightenment, instruction, nurture, schooling, training, tuition

educational adj = **instructive**, cultural, edifying, educative, enlightening, improving, informative

eerie adj = **frightening**, creepy (inf), ghostly, mysterious, scary (inf), spooky (inf), strange, uncanny, unearthly, weird

efface v 1 = **obliterate**, blot out, cancel, delete, destroy, eradicate, erase, rub out, wipe out

effect n 1 = **result**, conclusion,

● **USAGE NOTE**
● Note the difference between *effect*
● meaning 'accomplish' and *affect*
● meaning 'influence'.

effeminate ❶ *adj* (of a man) displaying characteristics thought to be typical of a woman. **effeminacy** *n*.

effervescent ❶ *adj* **1** (of a liquid) giving off bubbles of gas. **2** (of a person) lively and enthusiastic. **effervescence** *n*.

effete ❶ [if-**feet**] *adj* powerless, feeble.

efficacious ❶ *adj* producing the intended result. **efficacy** *n*.

efficient ❶ *adj* functioning effectively with little waste of effort. **efficiently** *adv* **efficiency** *n*.

effigy ❶ [ef-fij-ee] *n*, *pl* **-gies** image or likeness of a person.

efflorescence *n* flowering.

effluent ❶ *n* liquid discharged as waste.

effluvium *n*, *pl* **-via** unpleasant smell, as of decaying matter or gaseous waste.

effort ❶ *n* **1** physical or mental exertion. **2** attempt. **effortless** *adj* **effortlessly** *adv*.

effrontery ❶ *n* brazen impudence.

effusion ❶ *n* **1** unrestrained outburst. **2** sudden pouring out of light or liquid.

effusive *adj* openly emotional, demonstrative. **effusively** *adv* **effusiveness** *n*.

EFTA European Free Trade Association.

EFTPOS electronic funds transfer at point of sale.

e.g. for example.

egalitarian *adj* **1** upholding the equality of all people. ▷ *n* **2** person who holds egalitarian beliefs. **egalitarianism** *n*.

egg¹ *n* **1** oval or round object laid by the females of birds and other creatures, containing a developing embryo. **2** hen's egg used as food. **3** (also **egg cell**) ovum. **egghead** *n informal* intellectual person. **eggplant** *n US, Canad, & Aust* aubergine. **eggshell** *n* hard covering round the egg of a bird or animal. **egg timer** *n* device used for measuring the time needed to boil an egg.

egg² ❶ *v* **egg on** encourage or incite, esp. to do wrong.

ego ❶ *n*, *pl* **egos 1** the conscious mind of an individual. **2** self-esteem. **egoism**,

— THESAURUS —

consequence, end result, event, outcome, upshot **2 = operation**, action, enforcement, execution, force, implementation **3 = impression**, essence, impact, sense, significance, tenor ▷ *pl* **4 = belongings**, gear, goods, paraphernalia, possessions, property, things ▷ *v* **6 = bring about**, accomplish, achieve, complete, execute, fulfil, perform, produce

effective *adj* **1 = efficient**, active, adequate, capable, competent, productive, serviceable, useful **2 = in operation**, active, current, in effect, in force, operative **3 = powerful**, cogent, compelling, convincing, forceful, impressive, persuasive, telling

effeminate *adj* **= womanly**, camp (*inf*), feminine, sissy, soft, tender, unmanly, weak, womanish

effervescent *adj* **1 = bubbling**, carbonated, fizzy, foaming, frothy, sparkling **2 = lively**, animated, bubbly, ebullient, enthusiastic, exuberant, irrepressible, vivacious

effete *adj* **= decadent**, dissipated, enfeebled, feeble, ineffectual, spoiled, weak

efficacious *adj* **= effective**, adequate, efficient, operative, potent, powerful,

productive, successful, useful

efficiency *n* **= competence**, adeptness, capability, economy, effectiveness, power, productivity, proficiency

efficient *adj* **= competent**, businesslike, capable, economic, effective, organized, productive, proficient, well-organized, workmanlike

effigy *n* **= likeness**, dummy, figure, guy, icon, idol, image, picture, portrait, representation, statue

effluent *n* **= waste**, effluvium, pollutant, sewage

effort *n* **1 = exertion**, application, elbow grease (*facetious*), endeavour, energy, pains, struggle, toil, trouble, work, yakka (*Aust & NZ inf*) **2 = attempt**, endeavour, essay, go (*inf*), shot (*inf*), stab (*inf*), try

effortless *adj* **= easy**, painless, plain sailing, simple, smooth, uncomplicated, undemanding

effrontery *n* **= insolence**, arrogance, audacity, brazenness, cheek (*inf*), impertinence, impudence, nerve, presumption, temerity

effusive *adj* **= demonstrative**, ebullient, expansive, exuberant, gushing, lavish, unreserved, unrestrained

egg² *v* **egg on = encourage**, exhort,

egotism n **1** excessive concern for one's own interests. **2** excessively high opinion of oneself. **egotist**, **egoist** n **egotistic**, **egoistic** adj **egocentric** adj self-centred.

egregious [ig-**greej**-uss] adj outstandingly bad.

egress ⓘ [**ee**-gress] n **1** departure. **2** way out.

egret [**ee**-grit] n lesser white heron.

Egyptian adj **1** relating to Egypt. ▷ n **2** person from Egypt.

Egyptology n study of the culture of ancient Egypt.

Eid n Muslim festival at the end of Ramadan.

eider n Arctic duck. **eiderdown** n quilt (orig. stuffed with eider feathers).

eight adj, n **1** one more than seven. ▷ n **2** eight-oared boat. **3** its crew. **eighth** adj, n (of) number eight in a series. **eighteen** adj, n eight and ten. **eighteenth** adj, n **eighty** adj, n eight times ten. **eightieth** adj, n.

Eire n Ireland or the Republic of Ireland.

eisteddfod [ice-**sted**-fod] n Welsh festival with competitions in music and other performing arts.

either adj, pron **1** one or the other (of two). **2** each of two. ▷ conj **3** used preceding two or more possibilities joined by or. ▷ adv **4** likewise, e.g. I don't eat meat and he doesn't either.

● **USAGE NOTE**
● When either is followed by a plural
● noun, it is acceptable to make the
● verb plural too: Either of these books
● are useful.

ejaculate v **1** eject (semen). **2** utter abruptly. **ejaculation** n.

eject ⓘ v force out, expel. **ejection** n **ejector** n **ejector seat** n seat in an aircraft that ejects the occupant in an emergency.

eke out ⓘ v **1** make (a supply) last by frugal use. **2** make (a living) with difficulty.

elaborate ⓘ adj **1** with a lot of fine detail. ▷ v **2** expand upon. **elaborately** adv **elaboration** n.

élan [ale-**an**] n style and vigour.

eland [**eel**-and] n large antelope of southern Africa.

elapse ⓘ v (of time) pass by.

elastane noun synthetic fibre that is able to return to its normal shape after being stretched.

elastic ⓘ adj **1** capable of resuming normal shape after distortion. **2** adapting easily to change. **3** made of elastic. ▷ n **4** tape or fabric containing interwoven strands of flexible rubber. **elasticity** n **elastic band** rubber band.

elated ⓘ v extremely happy and excited. **elatedly** adv **elation** n.

elbow ⓘ n **1** joint between the upper arm and the forearm. **2** part of a garment that covers this. ▷ v **3** shove or

─── **THESAURUS** ───

goad, incite, prod, prompt, push, spur, urge

egocentric adj = **self-centred**, egoistic, egoistical, egotistic, egotistical, selfish

egoism, egotism n **1** = **self-centredness**, self-absorption, self-interest, selfishness **2** = **conceit**, narcissism, self-esteem, self-importance, vanity

egotist, egoist n = **egomaniac**, bighead (inf), boaster, braggart, narcissist

egotistic, egoistic adj **1** = **self-centred**, egocentric, self-absorbed **2** = **conceited**, boasting, full of oneself, narcissistic, self-important, vain

egress n **1** = **departure**, exit, exodus, withdrawal **2** = **exit**, way out

eject v = **throw out**, banish, drive out, evict, expel, oust, remove, turn out

ejection n = **expulsion**, banishment, deportation, eviction, exile, removal

eke out v **1** = **be sparing with**, economize on, husband, stretch out

elaborate adj **1** = **detailed**, complex, complicated, intricate, involved ▷ v **2** = **expand (upon)**, add detail, amplify, develop, embellish, enlarge, flesh out

elapse v = **pass**, glide by, go by, lapse, roll by, slip away

elastic adj **1** = **flexible**, plastic, pliable, pliant, resilient, rubbery, springy, stretchy, supple, tensile **2** = **adaptable**, accommodating, adjustable, compliant, flexible, supple, tolerant, variable, yielding

elated adj = **joyful**, cock-a-hoop, delighted, ecstatic, euphoric, exhilarated, gleeful, jubilant, overjoyed

elation n = **joy**, bliss, delight, ecstasy, euphoria, exhilaration, glee, high spirits, jubilation, rapture

elbow n **1** = **joint**, angle ▷ v **3** = **push**, jostle, knock, nudge, shove

strike with the elbow. **elbow grease** vigorous physical labour. **elbow room** sufficient room to move freely.

elder¹ ❶ *adj* **1** older. ▷ *n* **2** older person. **3** (in certain Protestant Churches) lay officer. **elderly** *adj* (fairly) old. **eldest** *adj* oldest.

elder² *n* small tree with white flowers and black berries.

El Dorado [el dor-**rah**-doe] *n* fictitious country rich in gold.

eldritch *adj Scot* weird, uncanny.

elect ❶ *v* **1** choose by voting. **2** decide (to do something). ▷ *adj* **3** appointed but not yet in office, e.g. *president elect*. **election** *n* **1** choosing of representatives by voting. **2** act of choosing. **electioneering** *n* active participation in a political campaign. **elective** *adj* **1** chosen by election. **2** optional. **elector** *n* someone who has the right to vote in an election. **electoral** *adj* **electorate** *n* people who have the right to vote.

electricity ❶ *n* **1** form of energy associated with stationary or moving electrons or other charged particles. **2** electric current or charge. **electric** *adj* **1** produced by, transmitting, or powered by electricity. **2** exciting or tense. **electrical** *adj* using or concerning electricity. **electrician** *n* person trained to install and repair electrical equipment. **electrics** *pl n* electric appliances. **electric chair** *US* chair in which criminals who have been sentenced to death are electrocuted. **electric shock** effect of an electric current passing through the body.

electrify ❶ *v* **-fying, -fied 1** adapt for operation by electric power. **2** charge with electricity. **3** startle or excite intensely. **electrification** *n*.

electro- *combining form* operated by or caused by electricity.

electrocardiograph *n* instrument for recording the electrical activity of the heart. **electrocardiogram** *n* tracing

produced by this.

electroconvulsive therapy *n* treatment of severe mental disorders by passing an electric current through the brain.

electrocute *v* kill or injure by electricity. **electrocution** *n*.

electrode *n* conductor through which an electric current enters or leaves a battery, vacuum tube, etc.

electrodynamics *n* branch of physics concerned with the interactions between electrical and mechanical forces.

electroencephalograph [ill-lek-tro-en-**sef**-a-loh-graf] *n* instrument for recording the electrical activity of the brain. **electroencephalogram** *n* tracing produced by this.

electrolysis [ill-lek-**troll**-iss-iss] *n* **1** conduction of electricity by an electrolyte, esp. to induce chemical change. **2** destruction of living tissue such as hair roots by an electric current.

electrolyte *n* solution or molten substance that conducts electricity. **electrolytic** *adj*.

electromagnet *n* magnet containing a coil of wire through which an electric current is passed. **electromagnetic** *adj* **electromagnetism** *n*.

electron *n* elementary particle in all atoms that has a negative electrical charge. **electron microscope** microscope that uses electrons, rather than light, to produce a magnified image. **electronvolt** *n* unit of energy used in nuclear physics.

electronic *adj* **1** (of a device) dependent on the action of electrons. **2** (of a process) using electronic devices. **electronic mail** see E-MAIL. **electronic publishing** publication of information on discs etc., so that it can be accessed by computer. **electronics** *n* technology concerned with the development of electronic devices and circuits.

electroplate *v* coat with silver etc. by electrolysis.

───────────────────── THESAURUS ─────────────

elbow room *n* = **scope**, freedom, latitude, leeway, play, room, space

elder¹ *adj* **1** = **older**, first-born, senior ▷ *n* **2** = **older person**, senior

elect *v* **1** = **choose**, appoint, determine, opt for, pick, prefer, select, settle on, vote

election *n* = **voting**, appointment, choice, judgment, preference, selection, vote

elector *n* = **voter**, constituent, selector

electric *adj* **2** = **charged**, dynamic, exciting, rousing, stimulating, stirring, tense, thrilling

electrify *v* **3** = **startle**, astound, excite, galvanize, invigorate, jolt, shock, stir, thrill

elegant ❶ *adj* **1** pleasing or graceful in dress, style, or design. **2** cleverly simple and clear, e.g. *an elegant summary*. **elegance** *n* **elegantly** *adv*.

elegy [**el**-lij-ee] *n, pl* **-egies** mournful poem, esp. a lament for the dead. **elegiac** *adj* mournful or plaintive.

element ❶ *n* **1** component part. **2** substance which cannot be separated into other substances by ordinary chemical techniques. **3** section of people within a larger group, e.g. *the rowdy element*. **4** heating wire in an electric kettle, stove, etc. ▷ *pl* **5** basic principles of something. **6** weather conditions, esp. wind, rain, and cold. **in one's element** in a situation where one is happiest. **elemental** *adj* of primitive natural forces or passions. **elementary** *adj* simple and straightforward. **elementary particle** entity that is less complex than an atom.

elephant *n* huge four-footed thick-skinned animal with ivory tusks and a long trunk. **elephantine** *adj* unwieldy, clumsy. **elephantiasis** [el-lee-fan-**tie**-a-siss] *n* disease with hardening of the skin and enlargement of the legs etc.

elevate ❶ *v* **1** raise in rank or status. **2** lift up. **elevated** *adj* **1** higher than normal, e.g. *elevated cholesterol levels*. **2** (of ideas or pursuits) dignified or of a high rank. **elevation** *n* **1** raising.

2 height above sea level. **3** scale drawing of one side of a building. **elevator** *n Aust, US & Canad* lift for carrying people.

eleven *adj, n* **1** one more than ten. ▷ *n* **2** *Sport* team of eleven people. **eleventh** *adj, n* (of) number eleven in a series. **elevenses** *n informal* mid-morning snack. **eleventh hour** the last moment.

elf *n, pl* **elves** (in folklore) small mischievous fairy. **elfin** *adj* small and delicate.

elicit ❶ *v* **1** bring about (a response or reaction), e.g. *her remarks elicited a sharp retort*. **2** find out (information) by careful questioning.

elide *v* omit (a vowel or syllable) from a spoken word. **elision** *n*.

eligible ❶ *adj* **1** meeting the requirements or qualifications needed. **2** desirable as a spouse. **eligibility** *n*.

eliminate ❶ *v* **1** get rid of. **2** remove (a team or competitor) from a contest, esp. following a defeat. **elimination** *n*.

elision *n* see ELIDE.

elite ❶ [ill-**eet**] *n* most powerful, rich, or gifted members of a group. **elitism** *n* belief that society should be governed by a small group of superior people. **elitist** *n, adj*.

elixir ❶ [ill-**ix**-er] *n* imaginary liquid that can prolong life or turn base metals into gold.

THESAURUS

elegance *n* **1** = **style**, dignity, exquisiteness, grace, gracefulness, grandeur, luxury, refinement, taste

elegant *adj* **1** = **stylish**, chic, delicate, exquisite, fine, graceful, handsome, polished, refined, tasteful

element *n* **1** = **component**, constituent, factor, ingredient, part, section, subdivision, unit ▷ *pl* **5** = **basics**, essentials, foundations, fundamentals, nuts and bolts (*inf*), principles, rudiments **6** = **weather conditions**, atmospheric conditions, powers of nature

elementary *adj* = **simple**, clear, easy, plain, rudimentary, straightforward, uncomplicated

elevate *v* **1** = **promote**, advance, aggrandize, exalt, prefer, upgrade **2** = **raise**, heighten, hoist, lift, lift up, uplift

elevated *adj* **2** = **high-minded**,

dignified, exalted, grand, high-flown, inflated, lofty, noble, sublime

elevation *n* **1** = **promotion**, advancement, aggrandizement, exaltation, preferment, upgrading **2** = **altitude**, height

elicit *v* **1** = **bring about**, bring forth, bring out, bring to light, call forth, cause, derive, evolve, give rise to **2** = **obtain**, draw out, evoke, exact, extort, extract, wrest

eligible *adj* **1** = **qualified**, acceptable, appropriate, desirable, fit, preferable, proper, suitable, worthy

eliminate *v* **1** = **get rid of**, cut out, dispose of, do away with, eradicate, exterminate, remove, stamp out, take out

elite *n* = **best**, aristocracy, cream, flower, nobility, pick, upper class

elitist *adj* = **snobbish**, exclusive, selective

elixir *n* = **panacea**, nostrum

Elizabethan *adj* of the reign of Elizabeth I of England (1558–1603).

elk *n* large deer of N Europe and Asia.

ellipse *n* oval shape. **elliptical** *adj* **1** oval-shaped. **2** (of speech or writing) obscure or ambiguous.

ellipsis [ill-**lip**-siss] *n, pl* **-ses** omission of letters or words in a sentence.

elm *n* tree with serrated leaves.

elocution ❶ *n* art of speaking clearly in public. **elocutionist** *n*.

elongate ❶ [eel-long-gate] *v* make or become longer. **elongation** *n*.

elope ❶ *v* (of two people) run away secretly to get married. **elopement** *n*.

eloquence ❶ *n* fluent powerful use of language. **eloquent** *adj* **eloquently** *adv*.

else ❶ *adv* **1** in addition or more, e.g. *what else can I do?* **2** other or different, e.g. *it was unlike anything else that had happened.* **elsewhere** *adv* in or to another place.

elucidate ❶ *v* make (something difficult) clear. **elucidation** *n*.

elude ❶ *v* **1** escape from by cleverness or quickness. **2** baffle. **elusive** *adj* difficult to catch or remember.

elver *n* young eel.

elves *n* plural of ELF.

Elysium [ill-**liz**-zee-um] *n* **1** *Greek myth* (also **Elysian fields**) dwelling place of the blessed after death. **2** state or place of perfect bliss.

emaciated ❶ [im-**mace**-ee-ate-id] *adj* abnormally thin. **emaciation** *n*.

e-mail, email *n* **1** (also **electronic mail**) sending of messages between computer terminals. ▷ *v* **2** communicate in this way.

emanate ❶ [**em**-a-nate] *v* issue, proceed from a source. **emanation** *n*.

emancipate ❶ *v* free from social, political, or legal restraints. **emancipation** *n*.

emasculate *v* deprive of power. **emasculation** *n*.

embalm ❶ *v* preserve (a corpse) from decay by the use of chemicals etc.

embankment *n* man-made ridge that carries a road or railway or holds back water.

embargo ❶ *n, pl* **-goes 1** order by a government prohibiting trade with a country. ▷ *v* **-going, -goed 2** put an embargo on.

embark ❶ *v* **1** board a ship or aircraft. **2** (foll. by *on*) begin (a new project). **embarkation** *n*.

THESAURUS

elocution *n* = **diction**, articulation, declamation, delivery, enunciation, oratory, pronunciation, speech, speechmaking

elongate *v* = **make longer**, draw out, extend, lengthen, prolong, protract, stretch

elope *v* = **run away**, abscond, bolt, decamp, disappear, escape, leave, run off, slip away, steal away

eloquence *n* = **expressiveness**, expression, fluency, forcefulness, oratory, persuasiveness, rhetoric, way with words

eloquent *adj* = **expressive**, articulate, fluent, forceful, moving, persuasive, silver-tongued, stirring, vivid, well-expressed

elsewhere *adv* = **in** *or* **to another place**, abroad, away, hence (*arch*), not here, somewhere else

elucidate *v* = **clarify**, clear up, explain, explicate, expound, illuminate, illustrate, make plain, shed *or* throw light upon, spell out

elude *v* **1** = **escape**, avoid, dodge, duck (*inf*), evade, flee, get away from, outrun **2** = **baffle**, be beyond (someone),

confound, escape, foil, frustrate, puzzle, stump, thwart

elusive *adj* **a** = **slippery**, difficult to catch, shifty, tricky **b** = **indefinable**, fleeting, intangible, subtle, transient, transitory

emaciated *adj* = **skeletal**, cadaverous, gaunt, haggard, lean, pinched, scrawny, thin, undernourished, wasted

emanate *v* = **flow**, arise, come forth, derive, emerge, issue, originate, proceed, spring, stem

emancipate *v* = **free**, deliver, liberate, release, set free, unchain, unfetter

emancipation *n* = **freedom**, deliverance, liberation, liberty, release

embalm *v* = **preserve**, mummify

embargo *n* **1** = **ban**, bar, boycott, interdiction, prohibition, restraint, restriction, stoppage ▷ *v* **2** = **ban**, bar, block, boycott, prohibit, restrict, stop

embark *v* **1** = **go aboard**, board ship, take ship **2** (foll. by *on*) = **begin**, commence, enter, launch, plunge into, set about, set out, start, take up

embarrass ● v cause to feel self-conscious or ashamed. **embarrassed** adj **embarrassing** adj **embarrassment** n.

- **SPELLING TIP**
- There are 32 examples of the
- misspelling *embarras* in the Bank
- of English and another mistake,
- *embarassment*, occurs 64 times. Both
- these words should have two rs and
- two ss.

embassy n, pl **-sies 1** offices or official residence of an ambassador. **2** ambassador and his staff.

embattled adj having a lot of difficulties.

embed v **-bedding, -bedded** fix firmly in something solid.

embellish ● v **1** decorate. **2** embroider (a story). **embellishment** n.

ember n glowing piece of wood or coal in a dying fire.

embezzle ● v steal money that has been entrusted to one. **embezzlement** n **embezzler** n.

embittered ● adj feeling anger as a result of misfortune. **embitterment** n.

emblazon [im-**blaze**-on] v **1** decorate with bright colours. **2** proclaim or publicize (something).

emblem ● n object or design that symbolizes a quality, type, or group. **emblematic** adj.

embody ● v **-bodying, -bodied 1** be an example or expression of. **2** comprise, include. **embodiment** n.

embolden ● v encourage (someone).

embolism n blocking of a blood vessel by a blood clot or air bubble. **embolus** n, pl **-li** material, such as a blood clot, that blocks a blood vessel.

embossed adj (of a design or pattern) standing out from a surface.

embrace ● v **1** clasp in the arms, hug. **2** accept (an idea) eagerly. **3** comprise. ▷ n **4** act of embracing.

embrasure n **1** door or window having splayed sides so that the opening is larger on the inside. **2** opening like this in a fortified wall, for shooting through.

embrocation n lotion for rubbing into the skin to relieve pain.

embroider v **1** decorate with needlework. **2** make (a story) more interesting with fictitious detail. **embroidery** n.

embroil ● v involve (a person) in

e

THESAURUS

embarrass v = **shame**, discomfit, disconcert, distress, fluster, humiliate, mortify, show up (*inf*)

embarrassed adj = **ashamed**, awkward, blushing, discomfited, disconcerted, humiliated, mortified, red-faced, self-conscious, sheepish

embarrassing adj = **humiliating**, awkward, compromising, discomfiting, disconcerting, mortifying, sensitive, shameful, toe-curling (*sl*), uncomfortable

embarrassment n = **shame**, awkwardness, bashfulness, distress, humiliation, mortification, self-consciousness, showing up (*inf*)

embellish v **1** = **decorate**, adorn, beautify, enhance, enrich, festoon, ornament **2** = **elaborate**, embroider

embellishment n **1** = **decoration**, adornment, enhancement, enrichment, exaggeration, ornament, ornamentation **2** = **elaboration**, embroidery

embezzle v = **misappropriate**, appropriate, filch, misuse, peculate, pilfer, purloin, rip off (*sl*), steal

embezzlement n = **misappropriation**, appropriation, filching, fraud, misuse, peculation, pilfering, stealing, theft

embittered adj = **resentful**, angry, bitter, disaffected, disillusioned, rancorous, soured, with a chip on one's shoulder (*inf*)

emblem n = **symbol**, badge, crest, image, insignia, mark, sign, token

embodiment n **1** = **personification**, epitome, example, exemplar, expression, incarnation, representation, symbol

embody v **1** = **personify**, exemplify, manifest, represent, stand for, symbolize, typify **2** = **incorporate**, collect, combine, comprise, contain, include

embolden v = **encourage**, fire, inflame, invigorate, rouse, stimulate, stir, strengthen

embrace v **1** = **hug**, clasp, cuddle, envelop, hold, seize, squeeze, take *or* hold in one's arms **2** = **accept**, adopt, espouse, seize, take on board, take up, welcome **3** = **include**, comprehend, comprise, contain, cover, encompass, involve, take in ▷ n **4** = **hug**, clasp, clinch (*sl*), cuddle, squeeze

embroil v = **involve**, enmesh, ensnare, entangle, implicate, incriminate,

problems. **embroilment** n.

embryo ❶ [**em**-bree-oh] n, pl **-bryos**
1 unborn creature in the early stages of
development. **2** something at an
undeveloped stage. **embryonic** adj at
an early stage. **embryology** n scientific
study of embryos.

emend ❶ v remove errors from.
emendation n.

emerald n **1** bright green precious
stone. ▷ adj **2** bright green.

emerge ❶ v **1** come into view. **2** (foll. by
from) come out of. **3** become known.
emergence n **emergent** adj.

emergency ❶ n, pl **-cies** sudden
unforeseen occurrence needing
immediate action.

emeritus [im-**mer**-rit-uss] adj retired,
but retaining an honorary title, e.g.
emeritus professor.

emery n hard mineral used for
smoothing and polishing. **emery
board** cardboard strip coated with
crushed emery, for filing the nails.

emetic [im-**met**-ik] n **1** substance that
causes vomiting. ▷ adj **2** causing
vomiting.

EMF electromotive force.

emigrate ❶ v go and settle in another
country. **emigrant** n **emigration** n.

émigré [**em**-mig-gray] n someone who
has left his native country for political
reasons.

eminent ❶ adj distinguished, well-
known. **eminently** adv **eminence** n
1 position of superiority or fame. **2** (**E-**)
title of a cardinal.

emir [em-**meer**] n Muslim ruler. **emirate**
n his country.

emissary n, pl **-saries** agent sent on a
mission by a government.

emit ❶ v **emitting**, **emitted 1** give out
(heat, light, or a smell). **2** utter.
emission n.

emollient adj **1** softening, soothing. ▷ n
2 substance which softens or soothes
the skin.

emolument n formal fees or wages from
employment.

emoticon [i-**mote**-i-kon] n
Computers symbol depicting a smile or
other facial expression, used in e-mail.

emotion ❶ n strong feeling. **emotional**
adj readily affected by or appealing to
the emotions. **emotionally** adv
emotive adj tending to arouse emotion.

empathy n ability to understand
someone else's feelings as if they were
one's own. **empathize** v.

emperor n ruler of an empire. **empress**
n fem.

emphasis ❶ n, pl **-ses 1** special
importance or significance. **2** stress on
a word or phrase in speech. **emphasize**
v **emphatic** adj showing emphasis.
emphatically adv.

---

mire, mix up

embryo n **2** = **germ**, beginning, nucleus,
root, rudiment

emend v = **revise**, amend, correct, edit,
improve, rectify

emendation n = **revision**, amendment,
correction, editing, improvement,
rectification

emerge v **1** = **come into view**, appear,
arise, come forth, surface **2** (foll. by
from) = **issue**, emanate, rise, spring up
3 = **become apparent**, become
known, come out, come out in the
wash, come to light, crop up, transpire

emergency n = **crisis**, danger, difficulty,
extremity, necessity, plight,
predicament, quandary, scrape (inf)

emigrate v = **move abroad**, migrate,
move

emigration n = **departure**, exodus,
migration

eminence n **1** = **prominence**, distinction,
esteem, fame, greatness, importance,
note, prestige, renown, repute

eminent adj = **prominent**, celebrated,
distinguished, esteemed, famous, high-
ranking, illustrious, noted, renowned,
well-known

emission n **1** = **giving off** or **out**,
discharge, ejection, exhalation,
radiation, shedding, transmission

emit v **1** = **give off**, cast out, discharge,
eject, emanate, exude, radiate, send
out, transmit

emotion n = **feeling**, ardour,
excitement, fervour, passion,
sensation, sentiment, vehemence,
warmth

emotional adj **a** = **sensitive**,
demonstrative, excitable, hot-blooded,
passionate, sentimental,
temperamental **b** = **moving**, affecting,
emotive, heart-warming, poignant,
sentimental, stirring, touching

emotive adj = **sensitive**, controversial,
delicate, touchy

emphasis n **1** = **importance**, accent,
attention, force, priority, prominence,

emphysema [em-fiss-**see**-ma] *n* condition in which the air sacs of the lungs are grossly enlarged, causing breathlessness.

empire ❶ *n* **1** group of territories under the rule of one state or person. **2** large organization that is directed by one person or group.

empirical ❶ *adj* relying on experiment or experience, not on theory. **empirically** *adv* **empiricism** *n* doctrine that all knowledge derives from experience. **empiricist** *n*.

emplacement *n* prepared position for a gun.

employ ❶ *v* **1** hire (a person). **2** provide work or occupation for. **3** use. ▷ *n* **4** **in the employ of** doing regular paid work for. **employee** *n* **employer** *n* **employment** *n* **1** state of being employed. **2** work done by a person to earn money.

emporium ❶ *n, pl* **-riums**, **-ria** *old-fashioned* large general shop.

empower ❶ *v* enable, authorize.

empress *n* see EMPEROR.

empty ❶ *adj* **-tier**, **-tiest 1** containing nothing. **2** unoccupied. **3** without purpose or value. **4** (of words) insincere. ▷ *v* **-tying**, **-tied 5** make or become empty. **empties** *pl n* empty boxes, bottles, etc. **emptiness** *n*.

empyrean [em-pie-**ree**-an] *n poetic* heavens or sky.

EMS European Monetary System.

emu *n* large Australian flightless bird with long legs.

EMU European Monetary Union.

emulate ❶ *v* attempt to equal or surpass by imitating. **emulation** *n*.

emulsion *n* **1** light-sensitive coating on photographic film. **2** type of water-based paint. ▷ *v* **3** paint with emulsion paint. **emulsify** *v* **-fying**, **-fied** (of two liquids) join together or join (two liquids) together. **emulsifier** *n*.

enable ❶ *v* provide (a person) with the means, opportunity, or authority (to do something). **enabling act** legislative act giving certain powers to

significance, stress, weight **2** = **stress**, accent

emphasize *v* **1** = **highlight**, accentuate, dwell on, give priority to, lay stress on, play up, press home, stress, underline **2** = **stress**, accentuate, lay stress on

emphatic *adj* = **forceful**, categorical, definite, insistent, positive, pronounced, resounding, unequivocal, unmistakable, vigorous

empire *n* **1** = **kingdom**, commonwealth, domain, realm

empirical *adj* = **first-hand**, experiential, experimental, observed, practical, pragmatic

employ *v* **1** = **hire**, commission, engage, enlist, retain, take on **2** = **keep busy**, engage, fill, make use of, occupy, take up, use up **3** = **use**, apply, bring to bear, exercise, exert, make use of, ply, put to use, utilize

employed *adj* **1** = **working**, active, busy, engaged, in a job, in employment, in work, occupied

employee *n* = **worker**, hand, job-holder, staff member, wage-earner, workman

employer *n* = **boss** (*inf*), company, firm, gaffer (*inf, chiefly Brit*), owner, patron, proprietor

employment *n* **1 a** = **taking on**, engagement, enlistment, hire, retaining **b** = **use**, application, exercise,

exertion, utilization **2** = **job**, line, occupation, profession, trade, vocation, work, yakka (*Aust & NZ inf*)

emporium *n Old-fashioned* = **shop**, bazaar, market, mart, store, warehouse

empower *v* = **enable**, allow, authorize, commission, delegate, entitle, license, permit, qualify, sanction, warrant

emptiness *n* **1, 2** = **bareness**, blankness, desolation, vacancy, vacuum, void, waste **3** = **purposelessness**, banality, futility, hollowness, inanity, meaninglessness, senselessness, vanity, worthlessness **4** = **insincerity**, cheapness, hollowness, idleness

empty *adj* **1, 2** = **bare**, blank, clear, deserted, desolate, hollow, unfurnished, uninhabited, unoccupied, vacant, void **3** = **purposeless**, banal, fruitless, futile, hollow, inane, meaningless, senseless, vain, worthless **4** = **insincere**, cheap, hollow, idle ▷ *v* **5** = **evacuate**, clear, drain, exhaust, pour out, unload, vacate, void

emulate *v* = **imitate**, compete with, copy, echo, follow, mimic, rival

enable *v* = **allow**, authorize, empower, entitle, license, permit, qualify, sanction, warrant

a person or organization.

enact ❶ v **1** establish by law. **2** perform (a story or play) by acting. **enactment** n.

enamel n **1** glasslike coating applied to metal etc. to preserve the surface. **2** hard white coating on a tooth. ▷ v **-elling, -elled 3** cover with enamel.

enamoured ❶ adj inspired with love.

en bloc adv French as a whole, all together.

encamp ❶ v set up in a camp. **encampment** n.

encapsulate ❶ v **1** summarize. **2** enclose as in a capsule.

encase v enclose or cover completely. **encased** adj.

encephalitis [en-sef-a-**lite**-iss] n inflammation of the brain.

encephalogram n short for ELECTROENCEPHALOGRAM.

enchant ❶ v delight and fascinate. **enchanting** adj **enchantment** n **enchanter** n **enchantress** n fem.

enchilada n Mexican dish of a tortilla filled with meat, served with chilli sauce.

encircle v form a circle around. **encirclement** n.

enclave n part of a country entirely surrounded by foreign territory.

enclose ❶ v **1** surround completely. **2** include along with something else. **enclosure** n **enclosed order** Christian religious order whose members do not go into the outside world.

encomium n, pl **-miums, -mia** formal expression of praise.

encompass ❶ v **1** surround. **2** include comprehensively.

encore interj **1** again, once more. ▷ n **2** extra performance due to enthusiastic demand.

encounter ❶ v **1** meet unexpectedly. **2** be faced with. ▷ n **3** unexpected meeting. **4** game or battle.

encourage ❶ v **1** inspire with confidence. **2** spur on. **encouraging** adj **encouragement** n.

encroach ❶ v intrude gradually on a person's rights or land. **encroachment** n.

encrust v cover with a layer of something.

encumber ❶ v hinder or impede. **encumbrance** n something that impedes or is burdensome.

encyclical [en-**sik**-lik-kl] n letter sent by the Pope to all bishops.

encyclopedia, encyclopaedia n book or set of books containing facts about many subjects, usu. in alphabetical

enact v **1 = establish**, authorize, command, decree, legislate, ordain, order, proclaim, sanction **2 = perform**, act out, depict, play, play the part of, portray, represent

enamoured adj **= in love**, captivated, charmed, enraptured, fond, infatuated, smitten, taken

encampment n **= camp**, base, bivouac, camping ground, camp site, cantonment, quarters, tents

encapsulate v **1 = sum up**, abridge, compress, condense, digest, epitomize, précis, summarize

enchant v **= fascinate**, beguile, bewitch, captivate, charm, delight, enrapture, enthral, ravish

enchanting adj **= fascinating**, alluring, attractive, bewitching, captivating, charming, delightful, entrancing, lekker (S Afr sl), lovely, pleasant

enclose v **1 = surround**, bound, encase, encircle, fence, hem in, shut in, wall in **2 = send with**, include, insert, put in

encompass v **1 = surround**, circle, encircle, enclose, envelop, ring

2 = include, admit, comprise, contain, cover, embrace, hold, incorporate, take in

encounter v **1 = meet**, bump into (inf), chance upon, come upon, run across **2 = face**, confront, experience ▷ n **3 = meeting**, brush, confrontation, rendezvous **4 = battle**, clash, conflict, contest, head-to-head, run-in (inf)

encourage v **1 = inspire**, buoy up, cheer, comfort, console, embolden, hearten, reassure, support **2 = spur**, advocate, egg on, foster, incite, promote, prompt, urge

encouragement n **1 = inspiration**, cheer, reassurance, support **2 = incitement**, promotion, stimulation, stimulus

encouraging adj **1 = promising**, bright, cheerful, comforting, good, heartening, hopeful, reassuring, rosy

encroach v **= intrude**, impinge, infringe, invade, make inroads, overstep, trespass, usurp

encumber v **= burden**, hamper, handicap, hinder, impede, inconvenience, obstruct,

order. **encyclopedic**, **encyclopaedic** *adj* comprehensive.

end ❶ *n* **1** furthest point or part. **2** limit. **3** last part of something. **4** fragment. **5** death or destruction. **6** purpose. **7** *Sport* either of the two defended areas of a playing field. ▷ *v* **8** bring or come to a finish. **make ends meet** have just enough money for one's needs. **ending** *n* **endless** *adj* endways. **endways** *adv* having the end forwards or upwards. **end product** final result of a process, esp. in manufacturing.

endanger ❶ *v* put in danger.

endear ❶ *v* cause to be liked. **endearing** *adj* **endearment** *n* affectionate word or phrase.

endeavour ❶ *v* **1** try. ▷ *n* **2** effort.

endemic *adj* present within a localized area or peculiar to a particular group of people.

endive *n* curly-leaved plant used in salads.

endocardium *n* lining membrane of the cavities of the heart.

endocrine *adj* relating to the glands which secrete hormones directly into the bloodstream.

endogenous [en-**dodge**-in-uss] *adj* originating from within.

endorphin *n* chemical occurring in the brain, which has a similar effect to morphine.

endorse ❶ *v* **1** give approval to. **2** sign the back of (a cheque). **3** record a conviction on (a driving licence). **endorsement** *n*.

endow ❶ *v* provide permanent income for. **endowed with** provided with. **endowment** *n*.

endure ❶ *v* **1** bear (hardship) patiently. **2** last for a long time. **endurable** *adj* **endurance** *n* act or power of enduring. **enduring** *adj* long-lasting.

enema [en-im-a] *n* medicine injected into the rectum to empty the bowels.

THESAURUS

saddle, weigh down

end *n* **1, 2** = **extremity**, boundary, edge, extent, extreme, limit, point, terminus, tip **3** = **finish**, cessation, close, closure, conclusion, culmination, denouement, ending, expiration, expiry, finale, resolution, stop, termination **4** = **remnant**, butt, fragment, leftover, oddment, remainder, scrap, stub **5** = **destruction**, death, demise, doom, extermination, extinction, ruin **6** = **purpose**, aim, goal, intention, object, objective, point, reason ▷ *v* **8** = **finish**, cease, close, conclude, culminate, stop, terminate, wind up

endanger *v* = **put at risk**, compromise, imperil, jeopardize, put in danger, risk, threaten

endearing *adj* = **attractive**, captivating, charming, cute, engaging, lekker (*S Afr sl*), lovable, sweet, winning

endearment *n* = **loving word**, sweet nothing

endeavour *v* **1** = **try**, aim, aspire, attempt, labour, make an effort, strive, struggle, take pains ▷ *n* **2** = **effort**, attempt, enterprise, trial, try, undertaking, venture

ending *n* = **finish**, cessation, close, completion, conclusion, culmination, denouement, end, finale

endless *adj* = **eternal**, boundless, continual, everlasting, incessant, infinite, interminable, unlimited

endorse *v* **1** = **approve**, advocate, authorize, back, champion, promote, ratify, recommend, support **2** = **sign**, countersign

endorsement *n* **1** = **approval**, advocacy, approbation, authorization, backing, favour, ratification, recommendation, seal of approval, support **2** = **signature**, countersignature

endow *v* = **provide**, award, bequeath, bestow, confer, donate, finance, fund, give

endowment *n* = **provision**, award, benefaction, bequest, donation, gift, grant, legacy

endurable *adj* **1** = **bearable**, acceptable, sufferable, sustainable, tolerable

endurance *n* **1** = **staying power**, fortitude, patience, perseverance, persistence, resolution, stamina, strength, tenacity, toleration **2** = **permanence**, continuity, durability, duration, longevity, stability

endure *v* **1** = **bear**, cope with, experience, stand, suffer, sustain, undergo, withstand **2** = **last**, continue, live on, persist, remain, stand, stay, survive

enduring *adj* = **long-lasting**, abiding, constant, continuing, lasting, perennial, persistent, steadfast, unfaltering,

enemy ❶ n, pl **-mies** hostile person or nation, opponent.

energy ❶ n, pl **-gies** 1 capacity for intense activity. 2 capacity to do work and overcome resistance. 3 source of power, such as electricity. **energetic** adj **energetically** adv **energize** v give vigour to. **energy drink** soft drink supposed to boost the drinker's energy levels.

enervate v deprive of strength or vitality. **enervated** adj **enervation** n.

enfant terrible [on-fon ter-**reeb**-la] n, pl **enfants terribles** French clever but unconventional or indiscreet person.

enfeeble v weaken. **enfeebled** adj **enfeeblement** n.

enfold v 1 cover by wrapping something around. 2 embrace.

enforce ❶ v 1 impose obedience (to a law etc.). 2 impose (a condition). **enforceable** adj **enforcement** n.

enfranchise v grant (a person) the right to vote. **enfranchised** adj **enfranchisement** n.

engage ❶ v 1 take part, participate. 2 involve (a person or his or her attention) intensely. 3 employ (a person). 4 begin a battle with. 5 bring (a mechanism) into operation.

engaged adj 1 pledged to be married. 2 in use. **engagement** n **engaging** adj charming.

engender ❶ v produce, cause to occur.

engine ❶ n 1 any machine which converts energy into mechanical work. 2 railway locomotive.

engineer ❶ n 1 person trained in any branch of engineering. ▷ v 2 plan in a clever manner. 3 design or construct as an engineer.

engineering n profession of applying scientific principles to the design and construction of engines, cars, buildings, or machines.

English n 1 official language of Britain, the US, most of the Commonwealth, and certain other countries. ▷ adj 2 relating to England. **the English** the people of England.

engorge v Pathology clog with blood. **engorgement** n.

engrave ❶ v 1 carve (a design) onto a hard surface. 2 fix deeply in the mind. **engraver** n **engraving** n print made from an engraved plate.

engross ❶ [en-**groce**] v occupy the attention of (a person) completely. **engrossing** adj.

engulf ❶ v cover or surround completely.

————————————————————— THESAURUS —————

unwavering

enemy n = **foe**, adversary, antagonist, competitor, opponent, rival, the opposition, the other side

energetic adj = **vigorous**, active, animated, dynamic, forceful, indefatigable, lively, strenuous, tireless

energy n 1, 2 = **vigour**, drive, forcefulness, get-up-and-go (inf), liveliness, pep, stamina, verve, vitality

enforce v = **impose**, administer, apply, carry out, execute, implement, insist on, prosecute, put into effect

engage v 1 = **participate**, embark on, enter into, join, set about, take part, undertake 2 = **preoccupy**, absorb, captivate, engross, fix, grip, involve, occupy 3 = **employ**, appoint, enlist, enrol, hire, retain, take on 4 = **begin battle with**, assail, attack, encounter, fall on, join battle with, meet, take on 5 = **set going**, activate, apply, bring into operation, energize, switch on

engaged adj 1 = **betrothed** (arch), affianced, pledged, promised, spoken

for 2 = **occupied**, busy, employed, in use, tied up, unavailable

engaging adj = **charming**, agreeable, attractive, fetching (inf), lekker (S Afr sl), likable or likeable, pleasing, winning, winsome

engender v = **produce**, breed, cause, create, generate, give rise to, induce, instigate, lead to

engine n 1 = **machine**, mechanism, motor

engineer v 2 = **bring about**, contrive, create, devise, effect, mastermind, plan, plot, scheme

engrave v 1 = **carve**, chisel, cut, etch, inscribe 2 = **fix**, embed, impress, imprint, ingrain, lodge

engraving n = **carving**, etching, inscription, plate, woodcut

engross v = **absorb**, engage, immerse, involve, occupy, preoccupy

engrossed adj = **absorbed**, caught up, enthralled, fascinated, gripped, immersed, lost, preoccupied, rapt, riveted

engulf v = **immerse**, envelop, inundate, overrun, overwhelm, submerge,

enhance ❶ v increase in quality, value, or attractiveness. **enhancement** n.

enigma ❶ n puzzling thing or person. **enigmatic** adj **enigmatically** adv.

enjoin v order (someone) to do something.

enjoy ❶ v 1 take joy in. 2 have the benefit of. 3 experience. **enjoyable** adj **enjoyment** n.

enlarge ❶ v 1 make or grow larger. 2 (foll. by on) speak or write about in greater detail. **enlargement** n.

enlighten ❶ v give information to. **enlightened** adj 1 guided by rational thought. 2 tolerant and unprejudiced. **enlightenment** n.

enlist ❶ v 1 enter the armed forces. 2 obtain the support of. **enlistment** n.

enliven ❶ v make lively or cheerful.

en masse adv French in a group, all together, as a whole.

enmeshed adj deeply involved, e.g. enmeshed in turmoil.

enmity ❶ n, pl -ties ill will, hatred.

ennoble ❶ v make noble, elevate.

ennui [on-**nwee**] n boredom, dissatisfaction.

enormous ❶ adj very big, vast. **enormously** adv **enormity** n, pl -ties 1 great wickedness. 2 gross offence. 3 informal great size.

enough ❶ adj 1 as much or as many as necessary. ▷ n 2 sufficient quantity. ▷ adv 3 sufficiently. 4 fairly or quite, e.g. that's a common enough experience.

en passant [on pass-**on**] adv French in passing, by the way.

enquire ❶ v same as INQUIRE. **enquiry** n.

enraptured adj filled with delight and fascination.

THESAURUS

swallow up, swamp

enhance v = **improve**, add to, boost, heighten, increase, lift, reinforce, strengthen, swell

enigma n = **mystery**, conundrum, problem, puzzle, riddle, teaser

enigmatic adj = **mysterious**, ambiguous, cryptic, equivocal, inscrutable, obscure, puzzling, unfathomable

enjoy v 1 = **take pleasure in** or **from**, appreciate, be entertained by, be pleased with, delight in, like, relish 2 = **have**, be blessed or favoured with, experience, have the benefit of, own, possess, reap the benefits of, use

enjoyable adj 1 = **pleasurable**, agreeable, delightful, entertaining, gratifying, pleasant, satisfying, to one's liking

enjoyment n 1 = **pleasure**, amusement, delectation, delight, entertainment, fun, gratification, happiness, joy, relish

enlarge v 1 = **increase**, add to, amplify, broaden, expand, extend, grow, magnify, swell, widen 2 (foll. by on) = **expand on**, descant on, develop, elaborate on, expatiate on, give further details about

enlighten v = **inform**, advise, cause to understand, counsel, edify, educate, instruct, make aware, teach

enlightened adj 1 = **informed**, aware, civilized, cultivated, educated, knowledgeable, sophisticated 2 = **open-minded**, reasonable,

tolerant, unbiased

enlightenment n 1 = **understanding**, awareness, comprehension, education, insight, instruction, knowledge, learning, wisdom

enlist v 1 = **join up**, enrol, enter (into), join, muster, register, sign up, volunteer 2 = **obtain**, engage, procure, recruit

enliven v = **cheer up**, animate, excite, inspire, invigorate, pep up, rouse, spark, stimulate, vitalize

enmity n = **hostility**, acrimony, animosity, bad blood, bitterness, hatred, ill will, malice

ennoble v = **dignify**, aggrandize, elevate, enhance, exalt, glorify, honour, magnify, raise

enormity n 1 = **wickedness**, atrocity, depravity, monstrousness, outrageousness, vileness, villainy 2 = **atrocity**, abomination, crime, disgrace, evil, horror, monstrosity, outrage 3 Inf = **hugeness**, greatness, immensity, magnitude, vastness

enormous adj = **huge**, colossal, gigantic, gross, immense, mammoth, massive, mountainous, tremendous, vast

enough adj 1 = **sufficient**, abundant, adequate, ample, plenty ▷ n 2 = **sufficiency**, abundance, adequacy, ample supply, plenty, right amount ▷ adv 3 = **sufficiently**, abundantly, adequately, amply, reasonably, satisfactorily, tolerably

enquire SEE INQUIRE.

enquiry SEE INQUIRY.

enrich ❶ v 1 improve in quality. 2 make wealthy or wealthier. **enriched** adj **enrichment** n.

enrol ❶ v **-rolling, -rolled** (cause to) become a member. **enrolment** n.

en route ❶ adv French on the way.

ensconce v settle firmly or comfortably.

ensemble ❶ [on-**som**-bl] n 1 all the parts of something taken together. 2 complete outfit of clothes. 3 company of actors or musicians. 4 Music group of musicians playing together.

enshrine v cherish or treasure.

enshroud v cover or hide as with a shroud.

ensign ❶ n 1 naval flag. 2 banner. 3 US naval officer.

enslave v make a slave of (someone). **enslavement** n.

ensnare v catch in or as if in a snare.

ensue ❶ v come next, result. **ensuing** adj.

en suite adv French connected to a bedroom and entered directly from it.

ensure ❶ v 1 make certain or sure. 2 make safe or protect.

ENT Medical ear, nose, and throat.

entablature n Architecture part of a classical temple above the columns, with an architrave, frieze, and cornice.

entail ❶ v 1 bring about or impose inevitably. 2 Law restrict (ownership of property) to designated heirs.

entangle ❶ v catch or involve in or as if in a tangle. **entanglement** n.

entente [on-**tont**] n friendly understanding between nations.

enter ❶ v 1 come or go in. 2 join. 3 become involved in, take part in. 4 record (an item) in a journal etc. 5 begin. **entrance** n 1 way into a place. 2 act of entering. 3 right of entering. **entrant** n person who enters a university, contest, etc. **entry** n, pl **-tries** 1 entrance. 2 entering. 3 item entered in a journal etc.

enteric [en-**ter**-ik] adj intestinal. **enteritis** [en-ter-**rite**-iss] n inflammation of the intestine, causing diarrhoea.

enterprise ❶ n 1 company or firm. 2 bold or difficult undertaking. 3 boldness and energy. **enterprising** adj full of boldness and initiative.

entertain ❶ v 1 amuse. 2 receive as a guest. 3 consider (an idea).

———————————————— THESAURUS ————

enrich v 1 = **enhance**, augment, develop, improve, refine, supplement 2 = **make rich**, make wealthy

enrol v = **enlist**, accept, admit, join up, recruit, register, sign up or on, take on

enrolment n = **enlistment**, acceptance, admission, engagement, matriculation, recruitment, registration

en route adv French = **on** or **along the way**, in transit, on the road

ensemble n 1 = **whole**, aggregate, collection, entirety, set, sum, total, totality 2 = **outfit**, costume, get-up (inf), suit 3 = **group**, band, cast, chorus, company, troupe

ensign n 1, 2 = **flag**, banner, colours, jack, pennant, pennon, standard, streamer

ensue v = **follow**, arise, come next, derive, flow, issue, proceed, result, stem

ensure v 1 = **make certain**, certify, confirm, effect, guarantee, make sure, secure, warrant 2 = **protect**, guard, make safe, safeguard, secure

entail v 1 = **involve**, bring about, call for, demand, give rise to, necessitate, occasion, require

entangle v = **tangle**, catch, embroil, enmesh, ensnare, entrap, implicate, snag, snare, trap

enter v 1 = **come** or **go in** or **into**, arrive, make an, pass into, penetrate, pierce 2 = **join**, enlist, enrol 3 = **start**, commence, embark upon, set out on, take up 4 = **record**, inscribe, list, log, note, register, set down, take down

enterprise n 1 = **firm**, business, company, concern, establishment, operation 2 = **undertaking**, adventure, effort, endeavour, operation, plan, programme, project, venture 3 = **initiative**, adventurousness, boldness, daring, drive, energy, enthusiasm, resourcefulness

enterprising adj = **resourceful**, adventurous, bold, daring, energetic, enthusiastic, go-ahead, intrepid, spirited

entertain v 1 = **amuse**, charm, cheer, delight, please, regale 2 = **show hospitality to**, accommodate, be host to, harbour, have company, lodge, put up, treat 3 = **consider**, conceive, contemplate, imagine, keep in mind, think about

entertainer n **entertaining** adj **entertainment** n.

enthral ❶ [en-**thrawl**] v -**thralling**, -**thralled** hold the attention of. **enthralling** adj.

enthrone v **1** place (someone) on a throne. **2** praise or honour (something). **enthronement** n.

enthusiasm ❶ n ardent interest, eagerness. **enthuse** v (cause to) show enthusiasm. **enthusiast** n ardent supporter of something. **enthusiastic** adj **enthusiastically** adv.

entice ❶ v attract by exciting hope or desire, tempt. **enticing** adj **enticement** n.

entire ❶ adj including every detail, part, or aspect of something. **entirely** adv **entirety** n.

entitle ❶ v **1** give a right to. **2** give a title to. **entitlement** n.

entity ❶ n, pl -**ties** separate distinct thing.

entomb v **1** place (a corpse) in a tomb. **2** serve as a tomb for. **entombment** n.

entomology n study of insects. **entomological** adj **entomologist** n.

entourage ❶ [**on**-toor-ahzh] n group of people who assist an important person.

entozoon [en-toe-**zoe**-on] n, pl -**zoa** [-**zoe**-a] internal parasite. **entozoic** adj.

entr'acte [on-**tract**] n interval between acts of a play etc.

entrails ❶ pl n **1** intestines. **2** innermost parts of something.

entrance¹ ❶ n see ENTER.

entrance² ❶ v **1** delight. **2** put into a trance. **entrancing** adj.

entrap v **1** trick into difficulty etc. **2** catch in a trap, or catch as if in a trap. **entrapment** n.

entreat ❶ v ask earnestly. **entreaty** n, pl -**ties** earnest request.

entrecôte [**on**-tra-coat] n beefsteak cut from between the ribs.

entrée [**on**-tray] n **1** dish served before a main course. **2** main course. **3** right of admission.

entrench ❶ v **1** establish firmly. **2** establish in a fortified position with trenches. **entrenched** adj **entrenchment** n.

---

entertaining adj **1** = **enjoyable**, amusing, cheering, diverting, funny, humorous, interesting, pleasant, pleasurable

entertainment n **1** = **enjoyment**, amusement, fun, leisure activity, pastime, pleasure, recreation, sport, treat

enthral v = **fascinate**, captivate, charm, enchant, enrapture, entrance, grip, mesmerize

enthusiasm n = **keenness**, eagerness, fervour, interest, passion, relish, zeal, zest

enthusiast n = **lover**, aficionado, buff (inf), devotee, fan, fanatic, follower, supporter

enthusiastic adj = **keen**, avid, eager, fervent, passionate, vigorous, wholehearted, zealous

entice v = **attract**, allure, cajole, coax, lead on, lure, persuade, seduce, tempt

entire adj = **whole**, complete, full, gross, total

entirely adv = **completely**, absolutely, altogether, fully, in every respect, thoroughly, totally, utterly, wholly

entitle v **1** = **give the right to**, allow, authorize, empower, enable, license, permit **2** = **call**, christen, dub, label,

name, term, title

entity n = **thing**, being, creature, individual, object, organism, substance

entourage n = **retinue**, associates, attendants, company, court, escort, followers, staff, train

entrails pl n **1** = **intestines**, bowels, guts, innards (inf), insides (inf), offal, viscera

entrance¹ n **1** = **way in**, access, door, doorway, entry, gate, opening, passage **2** = **appearance**, arrival, coming in, entry, introduction **3** = **admission**, access, admittance, entrée, entry, permission to enter

entrance² v **1** = **enchant**, bewitch, captivate, charm, delight, enrapture, enthral, fascinate **2** = **mesmerize**, hypnotize, put in a trance

entrant n = **competitor**, candidate, contestant, entry, participant, player

entreaty n = **plea**, appeal, earnest request, exhortation, petition, prayer, request, supplication

entrenched adj **1** = **fixed**, deep-rooted, deep-seated, ineradicable, ingrained, rooted, set, unshakable, well-established

entrepreneur ❶ *n* business person who attempts to make a profit by risk and initiative.

entropy [en-trop-ee] *n* **1** lack of organization. **2** *Physics* unavailability of the heat energy of a system for mechanical work.

entrust ❶ *v* put into the care or protection of.

entwine ❶ *v* twist together or around.

E number *n* any of a series of numbers with the prefix E indicating a specific food additive recognized by the EU.

enumerate ❶ *v* name one by one. **enumeration** *n*.

enunciate ❶ *v* **1** pronounce clearly. **2** state precisely or formally. **enunciation** *n*.

enuresis [en-yoo-reece-iss] *n* involuntary discharge of urine, esp. during sleep. **enuretic** *adj*.

envelop ❶ *v* enveloping, enveloped wrap up, enclose. **envelopment** *n*.

envelope ❶ *n* folded gummed paper cover for a letter.

environment ❶ [en-vire-on-ment] *n* **1** external conditions and surroundings in which people, animals, or plants live. **2** natural world of land, sea, air, plants, and animals. **environmental** *adj*

environmentalist *n* person concerned with the protection of the natural environment.

- ● **SPELLING TIP**
- ● For every thousand correct
- ● appearances of the word
- ● **environment** in the Bank of English,
- ● there is one *enviroment*, without the
- ● middle *n*.

environs ❶ *pl n* surrounding area, esp. of a town.

envisage ❶ *v* conceive of as a possibility.

envoy ❶ *n* **1** messenger. **2** diplomat ranking below an ambassador.

envy ❶ *n* **1** feeling of discontent aroused by another's good fortune. ▷ *v* **-vying**, **-vied 2** grudge (another's good fortune, success, or qualities). **enviable** *adj* arousing envy, fortunate. **envious** *adj* full of envy.

enzyme *n* any of a group of complex proteins that act as catalysts in specific biochemical reactions.

Eolithic *adj* of the early part of the Stone Age.

epaulette *n* shoulder ornament on a uniform.

ephedrine [eff-fid-dreen] *n* alkaloid used for treatment of asthma and hay fever.

———————————————— THESAURUS ————————————————

entrepreneur *n* = **businessman** or **businesswoman**, impresario, industrialist, magnate, tycoon

entrust *v* = **give custody of**, assign, commit, confide, delegate, deliver, hand over, turn over

entry *n* **1** = **way in**, access, door, doorway, entrance, gate, opening, passage **2** = **coming in**, appearance, entering, entrance, initiation, introduction **3** = **admission**, access, entrance, entrée, permission to enter

entwine *v* = **twist**, interlace, interweave, knit, plait, twine, weave, wind

enumerate *v* = **list**, cite, itemize, mention, name, quote, recite, recount, relate, spell out

enunciate *v* **1** = **pronounce**, articulate, enounce, say, sound, speak, utter, vocalize, voice **2** = **state**, declare, proclaim, promulgate, pronounce, propound, publish

envelop *v* = **enclose**, cloak, cover, encase, encircle, engulf, shroud, surround, wrap

envelope *n* = **wrapping**, case, casing, cover, covering, jacket, wrapper

enviable *adj* = **desirable**, advantageous, favoured, fortunate, lucky, privileged, to die for (*inf*)

envious *adj* = **covetous**, green with envy, grudging, jealous, resentful

environment *n* **1** = **surroundings**, atmosphere, background, conditions, habitat, medium, setting, situation

environmental *adj* **2** = **ecological**, green

environmentalist *n* = **conservationist**, ecologist, green

environs *pl n* = **surrounding area**, district, locality, neighbourhood, outskirts, precincts, suburbs, vicinity

envisage *v* = **imagine**, conceive (of), conceptualize, contemplate, envision, fancy, foresee, picture, see, think up, visualize

envoy *n* **1** = **messenger**, agent, courier, delegate, emissary, intermediary, representative **2** = **diplomat**, ambassador

envy *n* **1** = **covetousness**, enviousness, jealousy, resentfulness, resentment ▷ *v* **2** = **covet**, be envious (of), begrudge, be jealous (of), grudge, resent

ephemeral ❶ *adj* short-lived.
epic *n* **1** long poem, book, or film about heroic events or actions. ▷ *adj* **2** very impressive or ambitious.
epicene *adj* **1** common to both sexes. **2** effeminate.
epicentre *n* point on the earth's surface immediately above the origin of an earthquake.
epicure *n* person who enjoys good food and drink. **epicurism** *n* **epicurean** *adj* **1** devoted to sensual pleasures, esp. food and drink. ▷ *n* **2** epicure. **epicureanism** *n*.
epidemic ❶ *n* **1** widespread occurrence of a disease. **2** rapid spread of something.
epidermis *n* outer layer of the skin.
epidural [ep-pid-**dure**-al] *adj, n* (of) spinal anaesthetic injected to relieve pain during childbirth.
epiglottis *n* thin flap that covers the opening of the larynx during swallowing.
epigram ❶ *n* short witty remark or poem. **epigrammatic** *adj*.
epigraph *n* **1** quotation at the start of a book. **2** inscription.
epilepsy *n* disorder of the nervous system causing loss of consciousness and sometimes convulsions. **epileptic** *adj* **1** of or having epilepsy. ▷ *n* **2** *old-fashioned* person who has epilepsy.
epilogue ❶ *n* short speech or poem at the end of a literary work, esp. a play.
Epiphany *n* Christian festival held on January 6 commemorating the manifestation of Christ to the Magi.

episcopal [ip-**piss**-kop-al] *adj* of or governed by bishops. **episcopalian** *adj* **1** advocating Church government by bishops. ▷ *n* **2** advocate of such Church government.
episode ❶ *n* **1** incident in a series of incidents. **2** section of a serialized book, television programme, etc. **episodic** *adj* occurring at irregular intervals.
epistemology [ip-iss-stem-**ol**-a-jee] *n* study of the source, nature, and limitations of knowledge. **epistemological** *adj* **epistemologist** *n*.
epistle ❶ *n* letter, esp. of an apostle. **epistolary** *adj*.
epitaph ❶ *n* **1** commemorative inscription on a tomb. **2** commemorative speech or passage.
epithet ❶ *n* descriptive word or name.
epitome ❶ [ip-**pit**-a-mee] *n* typical example. **epitomize** *v* be the epitome of.
epoch ❶ [**ee**-pok] *n* period of notable events. **epoch-making** *adj* extremely important.
eponymous [ip-**pon**-im-uss] *adj* after whom a book, play, etc. is named. **eponymously** *adv*.
EPOS electronic point of sale.
Epsom salts *pl n* medicinal preparation of magnesium sulphate and water, used to empty the bowels.
equable ❶ [**ek**-wab-bl] *adj* even-tempered. **equably** *adv*.
equal ❶ *adj* **1** identical in size, quantity, degree, etc. **2** having identical rights or

e

THESAURUS

ephemeral *adj* = **brief**, fleeting, momentary, passing, short-lived, temporary, transient, transitory
epidemic *n* **1** = **plague**, contagion, outbreak **2** = **spread**, growth, upsurge, wave
epigram *n* = **witticism**, aphorism, bon mot, quip
epilogue *n* = **conclusion**, coda, concluding speech, postscript
episode *n* **1** = **event**, adventure, affair, escapade, experience, happening, incident, matter, occurrence **2** = **part**, chapter, instalment, passage, scene, section
epistle *n* = **letter**, communication, message, missive, note
epitaph *n* **1** = **monument**, inscription
epithet *n* = **name**, appellation,

description, designation (*sl*), nickname, sobriquet, tag, title
epitome *n* = **personification**, archetype, embodiment, essence, quintessence, representation, type, typical example
epitomize *v* = **typify**, embody, exemplify, illustrate, personify, represent, symbolize
epoch *n* = **era**, age, date, period, time
equable *adj* = **even-tempered**, calm, composed, easy-going, imperturbable, level-headed, placid, serene, unflappable (*inf*)
equal *adj* **1** = **identical**, alike, corresponding, equivalent, regular, symmetrical, the same, uniform **3** = **even**, balanced, evenly matched, fifty-fifty (*inf*), level pegging (*Brit inf*)

status. **3** evenly balanced. **4** (foll. by *to*) having the necessary ability (for). ▷ *n*
5 person or thing equal to another. ▷ *v*
equalling, **equalled 6** be equal to.
equally *adv* **equality** *n* state of being equal. **equalize** *v* **1** make or become equal. **2** reach the same score as one's opponent. **equalization** *n* **equal opportunity** nondiscrimination as to sex, race, etc. in employment.

equanimity *n* calmness of mind.

equate ❶ *v* make or regard as equivalent. **equation** *n* **1** mathematical statement that two expressions are equal. **2** act of equating. **3** representation of a chemical reaction using symbols of the elements.

equator *n* imaginary circle round the earth, equidistant from the poles. **equatorial** *adj*.

equerry [**ek**-kwer-ee] *n*, *pl* -**ries** officer who acts as an attendant to a member of a royal family.

equestrian *adj* of horses and riding.

equidistant *adj* equally distant.

equilateral *adj* having equal sides.

equilibrium ❶ *n*, *pl* -**ria** steadiness or stability.

equine *adj* of or like a horse.

equinox *n* time of year when day and night are of equal length. **equinoctial** *adj*.

equip ❶ *v* **equipping**, **equipped** provide with supplies, components, etc. **equipment** *n* **1** set of tools or devices used for a particular purpose. **2** act of equipping.

equipoise *n* perfect balance.

equitation *n* riding and horsemanship.

equity ❶ *n*, *pl* -**ties 1** fairness. **2** legal system, founded on the principles of natural justice, that supplements common law. ▷ *pl* **3** interest of ordinary shareholders in a company. **equitable** *adj* fair and reasonable. **equitably** *adv*.

equivalent ❶ *adj* **1** equal in value. **2** having the same meaning or result. ▷ *n* **3** something that is equivalent. **equivalence** *n*.

equivocal ❶ *adj* **1** ambiguous. **2** deliberately misleading. **3** of doubtful character or sincerity. **equivocally** *adv* **equivocate** *v* use vague or ambiguous language to mislead people. **equivocation** *n*.

er *interj* sound made when hesitating in speech.

Er *Chemistry* erbium.

ER Queen Elizabeth.

era ❶ *n* period of time considered as distinctive.

eradicate ❶ *v* destroy completely. **eradication** *n*.

---

4 (foll. by *to*) = **capable of**, competent to, fit for, good enough for, ready for, strong enough, suitable for, up to ▷ *n*
5 = **match**, counterpart, equivalent, rival, twin ▷ *v* **6** = **match**, amount to, be tantamount to, correspond to, equate, level, parallel, tie with

equality *n* **1** = **sameness**, correspondence, equivalence, evenness, identity, likeness, similarity, uniformity **2** = **fairness**, egalitarianism, equal opportunity, parity

equalize *v* **1** = **make equal**, balance, equal, even up, level, match, regularize, smooth, square, standardize

equate *v* = **make** *or* **be equal**, be commensurate, compare, correspond with *or* to, liken, mention in the same breath, parallel

equation *n* **2** = **equating**, comparison, correspondence, parallel

equilibrium *n* = **stability**, balance, equipoise, evenness, rest, steadiness, symmetry

equip *v* = **supply**, arm, array, fit out, furnish, kit out, provide, stock

equipment *n* **1** = **apparatus**, accoutrements, gear, paraphernalia, stuff, supplies, tackle, tools

equitable *adj* = **fair**, even-handed, honest, impartial, just, proper, reasonable, unbiased

equivalence *n* = **equality**, correspondence, evenness, likeness, parity, sameness, similarity

equivalent *adj* **1, 2** = **equal**, alike, commensurate, comparable, corresponding, interchangeable, of a piece, same, similar, tantamount ▷ *n* **3** = **equal**, counterpart, match, opposite number, parallel, twin

equivocal *adj* **1** = **ambiguous**, indefinite, indeterminate, oblique, obscure, uncertain, vague **2** = **misleading**, evasive

era *n* = **age**, date, day *or* days, epoch, generation, period, time

eradicate *v* = **wipe out**, annihilate, destroy, eliminate, erase, exterminate,

erase ❶ v **1** destroy all traces of, e.g. *he could not erase the memory of his earlier defeat*. **2** rub out. **3** remove sound or information from (a magnetic tape or disk). **eraser** n object for erasing something written. **erasure** n **1** erasing. **2** place or mark where something has been erased.

erbium n *Chemistry* metallic element of the lanthanide series.

ere prep, conj poetic before.

e-reader n portable device for reading books in electronic form.

erect ❶ v **1** build. **2** found or form. ▷ adj **3** upright. **4** (of the penis, clitoris, or nipples) rigid as a result of sexual excitement. **erectile** adj capable of becoming erect from sexual excitement. **erection** n.

erg n unit of work or energy.

ergo adv therefore.

ergonomics n study of the relationship between workers and their environment. **ergonomic** adj **1** designed to minimize effort. **2** of ergonomics.

ergot n **1** fungal disease of cereal. **2** dried fungus used in medicine.

erica n genus of plants including heathers.

ermine n **1** stoat in northern regions. **2** its white winter fur.

erne, ern n fish-eating sea eagle.

Ernie n Brit machine that randomly selects winning numbers of Premium Bonds.

erode ❶ v wear away. **erosion** n.

erogenous [ir-**roj**-in-uss] adj sensitive to sexual stimulation.

erotic ❶ adj relating to sexual pleasure or desire. **eroticism** n **erotica** n sexual literature or art.

err ❶ v **1** make a mistake. **2** sin. **erratum** n, pl **-ta** error in writing or printing. **erroneous** adj incorrect, mistaken. **erroneously** adv **error** n mistake, inaccuracy, or misjudgment.

errand ❶ n short trip to do something for someone.

errant adj behaving in a manner considered to be unacceptable.

erratic ❶ adj irregular or unpredictable. **erratically** adv.

error ❶ n mistake, inaccuracy, or misjudgment.

ersatz [**air**-zats] adj made in imitation, e.g. *ersatz coffee*.

Erse n **1** Gaelic. ▷ adj **2** of or relating to the Gaelic language.

erstwhile ❶ adj former.

erudite ❶ [**air**-rude-ite] adj having great academic knowledge. **erudition** n.

erupt ❶ v **1** eject (steam, water, or volcanic material) violently. **2** burst forth suddenly and violently. **3** (of a blemish) appear on the skin. **eruption** n.

erysipelas [err-riss-**sip**-pel-ass] n acute skin infection causing purplish patches.

THESAURUS

extinguish, get rid of, obliterate, remove, root out

erase v **1** = **remove**, blot, cancel, delete, expunge, obliterate **2** = **wipe out**, rub out

erect v **1** = **build**, construct, put up, raise, set up **2** = **found**, create, establish, form, initiate, institute, organize, set up ▷ adj **3** = **upright**, elevated, perpendicular, straight, vertical **4** = **stiff**

erode v = **wear down** or **away**, abrade, consume, corrode, destroy, deteriorate, disintegrate, eat away, grind down

erosion n = **deterioration**, abrasion, attrition, destruction, disintegration, eating away, grinding down, wearing down or away

erotic adj = **sexual**, amatory, carnal, lustful, seductive, sensual, sexy (inf), voluptuous

err v **1** = **make a mistake**, blunder, go wrong, miscalculate, misjudge, mistake, slip up (inf)

errand n = **job**, charge, commission, message, mission, task

erratic adj = **unpredictable**, changeable, inconsistent, irregular, shonky (Aust & NZ inf), uneven, unreliable, unstable, variable, wayward

erroneous adj = **incorrect**, fallacious, false, faulty, flawed, invalid, mistaken, shonky (Aust & NZ inf), unsound, wrong

error n = **mistake**, bloomer (Brit inf), blunder, howler (inf), miscalculation, oversight, slip, solecism

erstwhile adj = **former**, bygone, late, old, once, one-time, past, previous, sometime

erudite adj = **learned**, cultivated, cultured, educated, knowledgeable, scholarly, well-educated, well-read

erupt v **1, 2** = **explode**, belch forth, blow up, burst out, gush, pour forth, spew forth or out, spout, throw off **3** = **break out**, appear

eruption n **1, 2** = **explosion**, discharge, ejection, flare-up, outbreak, outburst

erythema [err-rith-**theme**-a] *n* patchy inflammation of the skin.

erythrocyte [ir-**rith**-roe-site] *n* red blood cell of vertebrates that transports oxygen and carbon dioxide.

Es *Chemistry* einsteinium.

escalate ❶ *v* increase in extent or intensity. **escalation** *n*.

escalator *n* moving staircase.

escalope [ess-kal-lop] *n* thin slice of meat, esp. veal.

escapade ❶ *n* mischievous adventure.

escape ❶ *v* **1** get free (of). **2** avoid, e.g. *escape attention*. **3** (of a gas, liquid, etc.) leak gradually. **4** be forgotten by, e.g. *the figure escapes me.* ▷ *n* **5** act of escaping. **6** means of relaxation. **escapee** *n* person who has escaped. **escapism** *n* taking refuge in fantasy to avoid unpleasant reality. **escapologist** *n* entertainer who specializes in freeing himself from confinement. **escapology** *n*.

escarpment *n* steep face of a ridge or mountain.

eschatology [ess-cat-**tol**-loh-jee] *n* branch of theology concerned with the end of the world. **eschatological** *adj*.

escheat [iss-**cheat**]*Law* ▷ *n* **1** private possessions that become state property in the absence of an heir. ▷ *v* **2** attain such property.

eschew [iss-**chew**] *v* abstain from, avoid.

escort ❶ *n* **1** people or vehicles accompanying another person for protection or as an honour. **2** person who accompanies a person of the opposite sex to a social event. ▷ *v* **3** act as an escort to.

escritoire [ess-kree-**twahr**] *n* type of writing desk.

escudo [ess-**kyoo**-doe] *n*, *pl* **-dos** former monetary unit of Portugal.

escutcheon *n* shield with a coat of arms. **blot on one's escutcheon** stain on one's honour.

Eskimo *n* **1** a member of a group of peoples inhabiting N Canada, Greenland, Alaska, and E Siberia, having a material culture adapted to an extremely cold climate. **2** their language.

- **● USAGE NOTE**
- *Eskimo* is considered by many people
- to be offensive, and in North America
- the term *Inuit* is often used.

ESN *obs* educationally subnormal.

esoteric [ee-so-**ter**-rik] *adj* understood by only a small number of people with special knowledge.

ESP extrasensory perception.

esp. especially.

espadrille [**ess**-pad-drill] *n* light canvas shoe with a braided cord sole.

espalier [ess-**pal**-yer] *n* **1** shrub or fruit tree trained to grow flat. **2** trellis for this.

esparto *n*, *pl* **-tos** grass used for making rope etc.

especial ❶ *adj formal* special. **especially** *adv* particularly.

Esperanto *n* universal artificial language.

espionage ❶ [**ess**-pyon-ahzh] *n* spying.

esplanade *n* wide open road used as a public promenade.

espouse ❶ *v* adopt or give support to

——————————————————————————— THESAURUS ———

3 = **inflammation**, outbreak, rash

escalate *v* = **increase**, expand, extend, grow, heighten, intensify, mount, rise

escapade *n* = **adventure**, antic, caper, prank, scrape (*inf*), stunt

escape *v* **1** = **get away**, abscond, bolt, break free *or* out, flee, fly, make one's getaway, run away *or* off, slip away
2 = **avoid**, dodge, duck, elude, evade, pass, shun, slip **3** = **leak**, emanate, exude, flow, gush, issue, pour forth, seep ▷ *n* **5** = **getaway**, break, break-out, flight **6** = **relaxation**, distraction, diversion, pastime, recreation

escort *n* **1** = **guard**, bodyguard, convoy, cortege, entourage, retinue, train
2 = **companion**, attendant, beau, chaperon, guide, partner ▷ *v*

3 = **accompany**, chaperon, conduct, guide, lead, partner, shepherd, usher

especial *adj Formal* = **exceptional**, noteworthy, outstanding, principal, special, uncommon, unusual

especially *adv* = **exceptionally**, conspicuously, markedly, notably, outstandingly, remarkably, specially, strikingly, uncommonly, unusually

espionage *n* = **spying**, counter-intelligence, intelligence, surveillance, undercover work

espousal *n* = **support**, adoption, advocacy, backing, championing, defence, embracing, promotion, taking up

espouse *v* = **support**, adopt, advocate, back, champion, embrace, promote,

(a cause etc.). **espousal** n.

espresso n, pl **-sos** strong coffee made by forcing steam or boiling water through ground coffee beans.

esprit [ess-**pree**] n spirit, liveliness, or wit. **esprit de corps** [de **core**] pride in and loyalty to a group.

espy v **espying**, **espied** catch sight of.

Esq. esquire.

esquire n courtesy title placed after a man's name.

essay ❶ n 1 short literary composition. 2 short piece of writing on a subject done as an exercise by a student. ▷ v 3 attempt. **essayist** n.

essence ❶ n 1 most important feature of a thing which determines its identity. 2 concentrated liquid used to flavour food. **essential** adj 1 vitally important. 2 basic or fundamental. ▷ n 3 something fundamental or indispensable. **essentially** adv.

est. 1 established. 2 estimate(d).

establish ❶ v 1 set up on a permanent basis. 2 make secure or permanent in a certain place, job, etc. 3 prove. 4 cause to be accepted. **establishment** n 1 act of establishing. 2 commercial or other institution. **the Establishment** group of people having authority within a society.

estate ❶ n 1 landed property. 2 large area of property development, esp. of new houses or factories. 3 property of a deceased person. **estate agent** agent concerned with the valuation, lease, and sale of property. **estate car** car with a rear door and luggage space behind the rear seats.

esteem ❶ n 1 high regard. ▷ v 2 think highly of. 3 judge or consider.

ester n Chemistry compound produced by the reaction between an acid and an alcohol.

estimate ❶ v 1 calculate roughly. 2 form an opinion about. ▷ n 3 approximate calculation. 4 statement from a workman etc. of the likely charge for a job. 5 opinion. **estimable** adj worthy of respect. **estimation** n considered opinion.

estranged adj no longer living with one's spouse. **estrangement** n.

estuary ❶ n, pl **-aries** mouth of a river.

THESAURUS

stand up for, take up, uphold

essay n 1 = **composition**, article, discourse, dissertation, paper, piece, tract, treatise ▷ v 3 = **attempt**, aim, endeavour, try, undertake

essence n 1 = **fundamental nature**, being, core, heart, nature, quintessence, soul, spirit, substance 2 = **concentrate**, distillate, extract, spirits, tincture

essential adj 1 = **vital**, crucial, important, indispensable, necessary, needed, requisite 2 = **fundamental**, basic, cardinal, elementary, innate, intrinsic, main, principal ▷ n 3 = **prerequisite**, basic, fundamental, must, necessity, rudiment, sine qua non

establish v 1 = **create**, constitute, form, found, ground, inaugurate, institute, settle, set up 3 = **prove**, authenticate, certify, confirm, corroborate, demonstrate, substantiate, verify

establishment n 1 = **creation**, formation, foundation, founding, inauguration, installation, institution, organization, setting up 2 = **organization**, business, company, concern, corporation, enterprise, firm, institution, outfit (inf) **the Establishment** = **the authorities**, ruling class, the powers that be, the system

estate n 1 = **lands**, area, domain, holdings, manor, property, homestead (US & Canad) 3 = **property**, assets, belongings, effects, fortune, goods, possessions, wealth

esteem n 1 = **respect**, admiration, credit, estimation, good opinion, honour, regard, reverence, veneration ▷ v 2 = **respect**, admire, love, prize, regard highly, revere, think highly of, treasure, value 3 = **consider**, believe, deem, estimate, judge, reckon, regard, think, view

estimate v 1 = **calculate roughly**, assess, evaluate, gauge, guess, judge, number, reckon, value 2 = **form an opinion**, believe, conjecture, consider, judge, rank, rate, reckon, surmise ▷ n 3 = **approximate calculation**, assessment, ballpark figure (inf), guess, guesstimate (inf), judgment, valuation 5 = **opinion**, appraisal, assessment, belief, estimation, judgment

estimation n = **opinion**, appraisal, appreciation, assessment, belief, consideration, considered opinion, judgment, view

estuary n = **inlet**, creek, firth, fjord, mouth

ETA estimated time of arrival.

e-tail *n* selling of goods via the internet.

et al. 1 and elsewhere. **2** and others.

etc. et cetera.

- ● **USAGE NOTE**
- ● *Etc.* means 'and the rest' so you do
- ● not need to write *and etc.* Note the
- ● spelling; it comes from the Latin *et*
- ● *cetera.*

et cetera ❶ [et **set**-ra] *Latin* **1** and the rest, and others. **2** or the like. **etceteras** *pl n* miscellaneous extra things or people.

etch ❶ *v* **1** wear away or cut the surface of (metal, glass, etc.) with acid. **2** imprint vividly (on someone's mind). **etching** *n* picture printed from an etched metal plate.

eternal ❶ *adj* **1** without beginning or end. **2** unchanging. **eternally** *adv* **eternity** *n* **1** infinite time. **2** seemingly endless period of time. **3** timeless existence after death. **eternity ring** ring given as a token of lasting affection.

ethane *n* odourless flammable gas obtained from natural gas and petroleum.

ether *n* **1** colourless sweet-smelling liquid used as an anaesthetic. **2** region above the clouds. **ethereal** [eth-**eer**-ee-al] *adj* extremely delicate.

ethic ❶ *n* moral principle. **ethical** *adj* **ethically** *adv* **ethics** *n* **1** code of behaviour. **2** study of morals.

Ethiopian *adj* **1** of Ethiopia, its people, or their languages. ▷ *n* **2** person from Ethiopia.

ethnic ❶ *adj* **1** relating to a people or group that shares a culture, religion, or language. **2** belonging or relating to such a group, esp. one that is a minority

group in a particular place. **ethnic cleansing** practice, by the dominant ethnic group in an area, of removing other ethnic groups by expulsion or extermination. **ethnology** *n* study of human races. **ethnological** *adj* **ethnologist** *n*.

ethos [**eeth**-oss] *n* distinctive spirit and attitudes of a people, culture, etc.

ethyl [**eeth**-ile] *adj* of, consisting of, or containing the hydrocarbon group C_2H_5. **ethylene** *n* poisonous gas used as an anaesthetic and as fuel.

etiolate [**ee**-tee-oh-late] *v* **1** become pale and weak. **2** *Botany* whiten through lack of sunlight.

etiology *n* study of the causes of diseases.

etiquette ❶ *n* conventional code of conduct.

étude [**ay**-tewd] *n* short musical composition for a solo instrument, esp. intended as a technical exercise.

etymology *n, pl* **-gies** study of the sources and development of words. **etymological** *adj* **etymologist** *n*.

Eu *Chemistry* europium.

EU European Union.

eucalyptus, eucalypt *n* tree, mainly grown in Australia, that provides timber, gum, and medicinal oil from the leaves.

Eucharist [**yew**-kar-ist] *n* **1** Christian sacrament commemorating Christ's Last Supper. **2** consecrated elements of bread and wine. **Eucharistic** *adj*.

eugenics [yew-**jen**-iks] *n* study of methods of improving the human race.

eulogy *n, pl* **-gies** speech or writing in praise of a person. **eulogize** *v* praise (a person or thing) highly in speech or writing. **eulogist** *n* **eulogistic** *adj*.

———————————————————————————— THESAURUS ————————————————

et cetera *Latin* = **and so on**, and others, and so forth, and the like, and the rest, et al.

etch *v* **1** = **cut**, carve, eat into, engrave, impress, imprint, inscribe, stamp

etching *n* = **print**, carving, engraving, impression, imprint, inscription

eternal *adj* **1** = **everlasting**, endless, immortal, infinite, never-ending, perpetual, timeless, unceasing, unending **2** = **permanent**, deathless, enduring, immutable, imperishable, indestructible, lasting, unchanging

eternity *n* **1** = **infinity**, ages, endlessness, immortality, perpetuity,

timelessness **3** = **the afterlife**, heaven, paradise, the hereafter, the next world

ethical *adj* = **moral**, conscientious, fair, good, honourable, just, principled, proper, right, upright, virtuous

ethics *pl n* **1** = **moral code**, conscience, morality, moral philosophy, moral values, principles, rules of conduct, standards

ethnic *adj* = **cultural**, folk, indigenous, national, native, racial, traditional

etiquette *n* = **good** or **proper behaviour**, civility, courtesy, decorum, formalities, manners, politeness, propriety, protocol

eunuch *n* castrated man, esp. (formerly) a guard in a harem.

euphemism *n* inoffensive word or phrase substituted for one considered offensive or upsetting. **euphemistic** *adj* **euphemistically** *adv*.

euphony *n*, *pl* **-nies** pleasing sound. **euphonious** *adj* pleasing to the ear. **euphonium** *n* brass musical instrument, tenor tuba.

euphoria ❶ *n* sense of elation. **euphoric** *adj*.

Eurasian *adj* **1** of Europe and Asia. **2** of mixed European and Asian parentage. ▷ *n* **3** person of Eurasian parentage.

eureka [yew-**reek**-a] *interj* exclamation of triumph at finding something.

euro *n*, *pl* **euros** unit of the single currency of the European Union.

Eurodollar *n* US dollar as part of a European holding.

Euroland *n* the countries within the European Union that have adopted the euro.

European *n*, *adj* (person) from Europe. **European Union** association of a number of European nations with some shared monetary and political goals.

europium *n Chemistry* silvery-white element of the lanthanide series.

Eurozone same as EUROLAND.

Eustachian tube *n* passage leading from the ear to the throat.

euthanasia *n* act of killing someone painlessly, esp. to relieve his or her suffering.

eV electronvolt.

evacuate ❶ *v* **1** send (someone) away from a place of danger. **2** empty. **evacuation** *n* **evacuee** *n*.

evade ❶ *v* **1** get away from or avoid. **2** elude. **evasion** *n* **evasive** *adj* not straightforward, e.g. *an evasive answer*. **evasively** *adv*.

evaluate ❶ *v* find or judge the value of. **evaluation** *n*.

evanescent *adj* quickly fading away. **evanescence** *n*.

evangelical *adj* **1** of or according to gospel teaching. **2** of certain Protestant sects which maintain the doctrine of salvation by faith. ▷ *n* **3** member of an evangelical sect. **evangelicalism** *n*.

evangelist *n* **1** writer of one of the four gospels. **2** travelling preacher. **evangelism** *n* teaching and spreading of the Christian gospel. **evangelize** *v* preach the gospel. **evangelization** *n*.

evaporate ❶ *v* **1** change from a liquid or solid to a vapour. **2** disappear. **evaporation** *n* **evaporated milk** thick unsweetened tinned milk.

eve ❶ *n* **1** evening or day before some special event. **2** period immediately before an event. **evensong** *n* evening prayer.

even ❶ *adj* **1** flat or smooth. **2** (foll. by *with*) on the same level (as). **3** constant. **4** calm. **5** equally balanced. **6** divisible by two. ▷ *adv* **7** equally. **8** simply. **9** nevertheless. ▷ *v* **10** make even.

evening ❶ *n* **1** end of the day or early part of the night. ▷ *adj* **2** of or in the evening. **evening class** educational class for adults, held during the

euphoria *n* = **elation**, ecstasy, exaltation, exhilaration, intoxication, joy, jubilation, rapture

evacuate *v* **1** = **clear**, abandon, desert, forsake, leave, move out, pull out, quit, vacate, withdraw

evade *v* **1** = **avoid**, dodge, duck, elude, escape, get away from, sidestep, steer clear of **2** = **avoid answering**, equivocate, fend off, fudge, hedge, parry

evaluate *v* = **assess**, appraise, calculate, estimate, gauge, judge, rate, reckon, size up (*inf*), weigh

evaporate *v* **1** = **dry up**, dry, vaporize **2** = **disappear**, dematerialize, dissolve, fade away, melt away, vanish

evasion *n* **1** = **avoidance**, dodging, escape **2** = **deception**, equivocation, evasiveness, prevarication

evasive *adj* = **deceptive**, cagey (*inf*), equivocating, indirect, oblique, prevaricating, shifty, slippery

eve *n* **1** = **night before**, day before, vigil **2** = **brink**, edge, point, threshold, verge

even *adj* **1** = **level**, flat, horizontal, parallel, smooth, steady, straight, true, uniform **2** (foll. by *with*) = **equal**, comparable, fifty-fifty (*inf*), identical, level, like, matching, neck and neck, on a par, similar, tied **3** = **regular**, constant, smooth, steady, unbroken, uniform, uninterrupted, unvarying, unwavering **4** = **calm**, composed, cool, even-tempered, imperturbable, placid, unruffled, well-balanced

evening *n* **1** = **dusk**, gloaming (*Scot or poet*), twilight

evening. **evening dress** attire for a formal occasion during the evening.
event ❶ n **1** anything that takes place. **2** planned and organized occasion. **3** contest in a sporting programme. **eventful** adj full of exciting incidents.
eventing n riding competitions, usu. involving cross-country, jumping, and dressage.
eventual ❶ adj ultimate. **eventually** adv **eventuality** n possible event.
ever ❶ adv **1** at any time. **2** always. **evergreen** n, adj (tree or shrub) having leaves throughout the year. **everlasting** adj **1** eternal. **2** lasting for an indefinitely long period. **evermore** adv for all time to come.
every ❶ adj **1** each without exception. **2** all possible. **everybody** pron every person. **everyday** adj usual or ordinary. **everyone** pron every person.

everything pron **everywhere** adv in all places.
evict ❶ v legally expel (someone) from his or her home. **eviction** n.
evidence ❶ n **1** ground for belief. **2** matter produced before a lawcourt to prove or disprove a point. **3** sign, indication. ▷ v **4** demonstrate, prove. **in evidence** conspicuous. **evident** adj easily seen or understood. **evidently** adv **evidential** adj of, serving as, or based on evidence. **evidentially** adv.
evil ❶ n **1** wickedness. **2** wicked deed. ▷ adj **3** harmful. **4** morally bad. **5** very unpleasant. **evilly** adv **evildoer** n wicked person. **evil eye** look superstitiously supposed to have the power of inflicting harm.
evince v make evident.
eviscerate v disembowel. **evisceration** n.

━━━━━━━━ ━━━━━━━━ THESAURUS ━━━━━━━━

event n **1** = **incident**, affair, business, circumstance, episode, experience, happening, occasion, occurrence **3** = **competition**, bout, contest, game, tournament
eventful adj = **exciting**, active, busy, dramatic, full, lively, memorable, remarkable
eventual adj = **final**, concluding, overall, ultimate
eventuality n = **possibility**, case, chance, contingency, event, likelihood, probability
eventually adv = **in the end**, after all, at the end of the day, finally, one day, some time, ultimately, when all is said and done
ever adv **1** = **at any time**, at all, at any period, at any point, by any chance, in any case, on any occasion **2** = **always**, at all times, constantly, continually, evermore, for ever, perpetually, twenty-four-seven (inf)
everlasting adj **1** = **eternal**, endless, immortal, indestructible, never-ending, perpetual, timeless, transitory
evermore adv = **for ever**, always, eternally, ever, to the end of time
every adj = **each**, all, each one
everybody pron = **everyone**, all and sundry, each one, each person, every person, one and all, the whole world
everyday adj = **ordinary**, common, customary, mundane, routine, run-of-the-mill, stock, usual, workaday
everyone pron = **everybody**, all and

sundry, each one, each person, every person, one and all, the whole world
everything pron = **all**, each thing, the lot, the whole lot
everywhere adv = **to** or **in every place**, all around, all over, far and wide or near, high and low, in every nook and cranny, the world over, ubiquitously
evict v = **expel**, boot out (inf), eject, kick out (inf), oust, remove, throw out, turf out (inf), turn out
evidence n **1, 2** = **proof**, confirmation, corroboration, demonstration, grounds, substantiation, testimony **3** = **sign**, indication ▷ v **4** = **show**, demonstrate, display, exhibit, indicate, prove, reveal, signify, witness
evident adj = **obvious**, apparent, clear, manifest, noticeable, perceptible, plain, unmistakable, visible
evidently adv = **obviously**, clearly, manifestly, plainly, undoubtedly, unmistakably, without question
evil n **1** = **wickedness**, badness, depravity, malignity, sin, vice, villainy, wrongdoing **2** = **harm**, affliction, disaster, hurt, ill, injury, mischief, misfortune, suffering, woe ▷ adj **3** = **harmful**, calamitous, catastrophic, destructive, dire, disastrous, pernicious, ruinous **4** = **wicked**, bad, depraved, immoral, malevolent, malicious, sinful, villainous **5** = **offensive**, foul, noxious, pestilential, unpleasant, vile

evoke ❶ v call or summon up (a memory, feeling, etc.). **evocation** n **evocative** adj.

evolve ❶ v **1** develop gradually. **2** (of an animal or plant species) undergo evolution. **evolution** n **1** gradual change in the characteristics of living things over successive generations, esp. to a more complex form. **2** gradual development. **evolutionary** adj.

ewe n female sheep.

ewer n large jug with a wide mouth.

ex n informal former wife or husband.

ex- prefix **1** out of, outside, from, e.g. exodus. **2** former, e.g. ex-wife.

exacerbate [ig-zass-er-bate] v make (pain, emotion, or a situation) worse. **exacerbation** n.

exact ❶ adj **1** correct and complete in every detail. **2** precise, as opposed to approximate. ▷ v **3** demand (payment or obedience). **exactly** adv precisely, in every respect. **exactness, exactitude** n **exacting** adj making rigorous or excessive demands.

exaggerate ❶ v **1** regard or represent as greater than is true. **2** make greater or more noticeable. **exaggeratedly** adv **exaggeration** n.

● SPELLING TIP
● Some apparently tricky words, like
● **exaggerate** for example, appear
● wrongly spelt relatively rarely in
● the Bank of English. Similarly,
● there is only one occurrence of
● exagerration, instead of the correct
● **exaggeration**.

exalt ❶ v **1** praise highly. **2** raise to a higher rank. **exalted** adj **exaltation** n.

exam n short for EXAMINATION.

examine ❶ v **1** look at closely. **2** test the knowledge of. **3** ask questions of. **examination** n **1** examining. **2** test of a candidate's knowledge or skill. **examinee** n person who sits an exam. **examiner** n person who sets or marks an exam.

example ❶ n **1** specimen typical of its group. **2** instance that illustrates a fact or opinion. **3** person or thing worthy of imitation. **4** punishment regarded as a warning to others.

THESAURUS

---

evoke v = **arouse**, awaken, call, give rise to, induce, recall, rekindle, stir up, summon up

evolution n **2** = **development**, expansion, growth, increase, maturation, progress, unfolding, working out

evolve v **1** = **develop**, expand, grow, increase, mature, progress, unfold, work out

exact adj **1** = **correct**, faultless, right, true, unerring **2** = **accurate**, definite, precise, specific ▷ v **3** = **demand**, claim, command, compel, extort, extract, force

exacting adj = **demanding**, difficult, hard, harsh, rigorous, severe, strict, stringent, taxing, tough

exactly adv **a** = **precisely**, accurately, correctly, explicitly, faithfully, scrupulously, truthfully, unerringly **b** = **in every respect**, absolutely, indeed, precisely, quite, specifically, to the letter

exactness, exactitude n **1** = **scrupulousness**, rigorousness, strictness, veracity **2** = **accuracy**, correctness, precision

exaggerate v = **overstate**, amplify, embellish, embroider, enlarge, overemphasize, overestimate

exaggeration n = **overstatement**, amplification, embellishment, enlargement, hyperbole, overemphasis, overestimation

exalt v **1** = **praise**, acclaim, extol, glorify, idolize, set on a pedestal, worship **2** = **raise**, advance, elevate, ennoble, honour, promote, upgrade

exaltation n **1** = **praise**, acclaim, glorification, idolization, reverence, tribute, worship **2** = **rise**, advancement, elevation, ennoblement, promotion, upgrading

exalted adj **1** = **high-ranking**, dignified, eminent, grand, honoured, lofty, prestigious

examination n **1** = **inspection**, analysis, exploration, interrogation, investigation, research, scrutiny, study, test **2** = **questioning**, inquiry, inquisition, probe, quiz, test

examine v **1** = **inspect**, analyse, explore, investigate, peruse, scrutinize, study, survey **2** = **test**, question, quiz **3** = **question**, cross-examine, grill (inf), inquire, interrogate

example n **2** = **specimen**, case, illustration, instance, sample **3** = **model**, archetype, ideal, paradigm, paragon, prototype, standard **4** = **warning**, caution, lesson

exasperate 𝟎 v cause great irritation to. **exasperation** n.

excavate 𝟎 v **1** unearth buried objects from (a piece of land) methodically to learn about the past. **2** make (a hole) in solid matter by digging. **excavation** n **excavator** n large machine used for digging.

exceed 𝟎 v **1** be greater than. **2** go beyond (a limit). **exceedingly** adv very.

excel 𝟎 v **-celling, -celled 1** be superior to. **2** be outstandingly good at something. **excellent** adj exceptionally good. **excellence** n.

Excellency n title used to address a high-ranking official, such as an ambassador.

except 𝟎 prep **1** (sometimes foll. by for) other than, not including. ▷ v **2** not include. **except that** but for the fact that. **excepting** prep except. **exception** n **1** excepting. **2** thing that is excluded from or does not conform to the general rule. **exceptionable** adj causing offence. **exceptional** adj **1** not ordinary. **2** much above the average. **exceptionally** adv.

excerpt 𝟎 n passage taken from a book, speech, etc.

excess 𝟎 n **1** state or act of exceeding the permitted limits. **2** immoderate amount. **3** amount by which a thing exceeds the permitted limits. **excessive** adj **excessively** adv.

exchange 𝟎 v **1** give or receive (something) in return for something else. ▷ n **2** act of exchanging. **3** thing given or received in place of another. **4** centre in which telephone lines are interconnected. **5** Finance place where securities or commodities are traded. **6** transfer of sums of money of equal value between different currencies. **exchangeable** adj **exchange rate** rate at which the currency unit of one country may be exchanged for that of another.

Exchequer n Brit government

━━━━━━━━━━━━━━━━━━━━━━━━━━━━━━━━ THESAURUS ━━━━━━

exasperate v = **irritate**, anger, annoy, enrage, incense, inflame, infuriate, madden, pique

exasperation n = **irritation**, anger, annoyance, fury, pique, provocation, rage, wrath

excavate v **1** = **unearth**, dig out, dig up, mine, quarry, uncover **2** = **dig**, burrow, delve, tunnel

exceed v **1** = **surpass**, beat, better, cap (inf), eclipse, outdo, outstrip, overtake, pass, top **2** = **go over the limit of**, go over the top, overstep

exceedingly adv = **extremely**, enormously, exceptionally, extraordinarily, hugely, superlatively, surpassingly, unusually, very

excel v **1** = **be superior**, beat, eclipse, outdo, outshine, surpass, transcend **2** = **be good**, be proficient, be skilful, be talented, shine, show talent

excellence n = **high quality**, distinction, eminence, goodness, greatness, merit, pre-eminence, superiority, supremacy

excellent adj = **outstanding**, brilliant, exquisite, fine, first-class, first-rate, good, great, superb, superlative, world-class

except prep **1** (sometimes foll. by for) = **apart from**, barring, besides, but, excepting, excluding, omitting, other than, saving, with the exception of ▷ v **2** = **exclude**, leave out, omit, pass over

exception n **1** = **exclusion**, leaving out, omission, passing over **2** = **special case**, anomaly, deviation, freak, inconsistency, irregularity, oddity, peculiarity

exceptional adj **1** = **unusual**, abnormal, atypical, extraordinary, irregular, munted (NZ sl), odd, peculiar, special, strange **2** = **remarkable**, excellent, extraordinary, marvellous, outstanding, phenomenal, prodigious, special, superior

excerpt n = **extract**, fragment, part, passage, piece, quotation, section, selection

excess n **1** = **overindulgence**, debauchery, dissipation, dissoluteness, extravagance, intemperance, prodigality **2** = **surfeit**, glut, overload, superabundance, superfluity, surplus, too much

excessive adj = **immoderate**, disproportionate, exaggerated, extreme, inordinate, overmuch, superfluous, too much, undue, unfair, unreasonable

exchange v **1** = **interchange**, barter, change, convert into, swap, switch, trade ▷ n **2** = **interchange**, barter, quid pro quo, reciprocity, substitution, swap, switch, tit for tat, trade

department in charge of state money.

excise¹ *n* tax on goods produced for the home market.

excise² *v* cut out or away. **excision** *n*.

excite ❶ *v* **1** arouse to strong emotion. **2** arouse or evoke (an emotion). **3** arouse sexually. **excitement** *n* **excitable** *adj* easily excited. **excitability** *n* **exciting** *adj*.

exclaim ❶ *v* speak suddenly, cry out. **exclamation** *n* **exclamation mark** punctuation mark (!) used after exclamations. **exclamatory** *adj*.

exclude ❶ *v* **1** keep out, leave out. **2** leave out of consideration. **exclusion** *n* **exclusive** *adj* **1** excluding everything else. **2** not shared. **3** catering for a privileged minority. ▷ *n* **4** story reported in only one newspaper. **exclusively** *adv* **exclusivity**, **exclusiveness** *n*.

excommunicate ❶ *v* exclude from membership and the sacraments of the Church. **excommunication** *n*.

excoriate *v* **1** censure severely. **2** strip skin from. **excoriation** *n*.

excrement *n* waste matter discharged from the body.

excrescence *n* lump or growth on the surface of an animal or plant. **excrescent** *adj*.

excrete *v* discharge (waste matter) from the body. **excretion** *n* **excreta** [ik-**skree**-ta] *n* excrement. **excretory** *adj*.

excruciating ❶ *adj* **1** agonizing. **2** hard to bear, e.g. *he spoke at excruciating length*. **excruciatingly** *adv*.

exculpate ❶ *v* free from blame or guilt.

excursion ❶ *n* short journey, esp. for pleasure.

excuse ❶ *n* **1** explanation offered to justify (a fault etc.). ▷ *v* **2** put forward a reason or justification for (a fault etc.). **3** forgive (a person) or overlook (a fault etc.). **4** make allowances for. **5** exempt. **6** allow to leave. **excusable** *adj*.

ex-directory *adj* not listed in a telephone directory by request.

execrable [**eks**-sik-rab-bl] *adj* of very poor quality.

execute ❶ *v* **1** put (a condemned

THESAURUS

excitable *adj* = **nervous**, emotional, highly strung, hot-headed, mercurial, quick-tempered, temperamental, volatile, wired (*sl*)

excite *v* **1, 2** = **arouse**, animate, galvanize, inflame, inspire, provoke, rouse, stir up **3** = **thrill**, electrify, titillate

excitement *n* = **agitation**, action, activity, animation, commotion, furore, passion, thrill

exciting *adj* = **stimulating**, dramatic, electrifying, exhilarating, rousing, sensational, stirring, thrilling

exclaim *v* = **cry out**, call out, declare, proclaim, shout, utter, yell

exclamation *n* = **cry**, call, interjection, outcry, shout, utterance, yell

exclude *v* **1** = **keep out**, ban, bar, boycott, disallow, forbid, prohibit, refuse, shut out **2** = **leave out**, count out, eliminate, ignore, omit, pass over, reject, rule out, set aside

exclusion *n* **1** = **ban**, bar, boycott, disqualification, embargo, prohibition, veto **2** = **elimination**, omission, rejection

exclusive *adj* **1, 2** = **sole**, absolute, complete, entire, full, total, undivided, whole **3** = **select**, chic, cliquish, fashionable, posh (*inf, chiefly Brit*),

restricted, snobbish, up-market

excommunicate *v* = **expel**, anathematize, ban, banish, cast out, denounce, exclude, repudiate

excruciating *adj* **1** = **agonizing**, harrowing, intense, piercing, severe, violent **2** = **unbearable**, insufferable

exculpate *v* = **absolve**, acquit, clear, discharge, excuse, exonerate, pardon, vindicate

excursion *n* = **trip**, day trip, expedition, jaunt, journey, outing, pleasure trip, ramble, tour

excusable *adj* = **forgivable**, allowable, defensible, justifiable, pardonable, permissible, understandable, warrantable

excuse *n* **1** = **justification**, apology, defence, explanation, grounds, mitigation, plea, reason, vindication ▷ *v* **2** = **justify**, apologize for, defend, explain, mitigate, vindicate **3, 4** = **forgive**, acquit, exculpate, exonerate, make allowances for, overlook, pardon, tolerate, turn a blind eye to **5** = **free**, absolve, discharge, exempt, let off, release, relieve, spare

execute *v* **1** = **put to death**, behead, electrocute, guillotine, hang, kill, shoot **2** = **carry out**, accomplish, administer, discharge, effect, enact, implement,

person) to death. **2** carry out or accomplish. **3** produce (a work of art). **4** render (a legal document) effective, as by signing. **execution** n **executioner** n.

executive ❶ n **1** person or group in an administrative position. **2** branch of government responsible for carrying out laws etc. ▷ adj **3** having the function of carrying out plans, orders, laws, etc. **4** of the most expensive or exclusive type, e.g. *executive housing*.

executor, executrix n person appointed to perform the instructions of a will.

exegesis [eks-sij-**jee**-siss] n, pl **-ses** [-seez] explanation of a text, esp. of the Bible.

exemplar ❶ n **1** person or thing to be copied, model. **2** example. **exemplary** adj **1** being a good example. **2** serving as a warning. **3** fit for imitation; model, e.g. *an exemplary performance*.

exemplify ❶ v **-fying, -fied 1** show an example of. **2** be an example of. **exemplification** n.

exempt ❶ adj **1** not subject to an obligation etc. ▷ v **2** release from an obligation etc. **exemption** n.

exequies [**eks**-sik-wiz] pl n funeral rites.

exercise ❶ n **1** activity to train the body or mind. **2** set of movements or tasks designed to improve or test a person's ability. **3** performance of a function. ▷ v **4** make use of, e.g. *to exercise one's rights*. **5** take exercise or perform exercises.

exert ❶ v use (influence, authority, etc.) forcefully or effectively. **exert oneself** make a special effort. **exertion** n.

exeunt [**eks**-see-unt] *Latin* they go out: used as a stage direction.

exfoliate v peel in scales or layers.

ex gratia [eks **gray**-sha] adj given as a favour where no legal obligation exists.

exhale v breathe out. **exhalation** n.

exhaust ❶ v **1** tire out. **2** use up. **3** discuss (a subject) thoroughly. ▷ n **4** gases ejected from an engine as waste products. **5** pipe through which an engine's exhaust fumes pass.

— THESAURUS —

perform, prosecute

execution n **1** = **killing**, capital punishment, hanging **2** = **carrying out**, accomplishment, administration, enactment, enforcement, implementation, operation, performance, prosecution

executioner n = **killer**, assassin, exterminator, hangman, hit man (*sl*), liquidator, murderer, slayer

executive n **1** = **administrator**, director, manager, official **2** = **administration**, directorate, directors, government, hierarchy, leadership, management ▷ adj **3** = **administrative**, controlling, decision-making, directing, governing, managerial

exemplary adj **1** = **ideal**, admirable, commendable, excellent, fine, good, model, praiseworthy **2** = **warning**, cautionary

exemplify v **1** = **show**, demonstrate, display, embody, exhibit, illustrate, represent, serve as an example of

exempt adj **1** = **immune**, excepted, excused, free, not liable, released, spared ▷ v **2** = **grant immunity**, absolve, discharge, excuse, free, let off, release, relieve, spare

exemption n = **immunity**, absolution, discharge, dispensation, exception,

exoneration, freedom, release

exercise n **1** = **exertion**, activity, effort, labour, toil, training, work, work-out **2** = **task**, drill, lesson, practice, problem **3** = **use**, application, discharge, fulfilment, implementation, practice, utilization ▷ v **4** = **put to use**, apply, bring to bear, employ, exert, use, utilize **5** = **train**, practise, work out

exert v = **use**, apply, bring to bear, employ, exercise, make use of, utilize, wield **exert oneself** = **make an effort**, apply oneself, do one's best, endeavour, labour, strain, strive, struggle, toil, work

exertion n = **effort**, elbow grease (*facetious*), endeavour, exercise, industry, strain, struggle, toil

exhaust v **1** = **tire out**, debilitate, drain, enervate, enfeeble, fatigue, sap, weaken, wear out **2** = **use up**, consume, deplete, dissipate, expend, run through, spend, squander, waste

exhausted adj **1** = **worn out**, all in (*sl*), debilitated, done in (*inf*), drained, fatigued, knackered (*sl*), spent, tired out **2** = **used up**, consumed, depleted, dissipated, expended, finished, spent, squandered, wasted

exhausting adj **1** = **tiring**, backbreaking, debilitating, gruelling, laborious, punishing, sapping,

exhaustible *adj* **exhaustion** *n*
1 extreme tiredness. **2** exhausting.
exhaustive *adj* comprehensive.
exhaustively *adv*.
exhibit ❶ *v* **1** display to the public.
2 show (a quality or feeling). ▷ *n*
3 object exhibited to the public.
4 *Law* document or object produced in
court as evidence. **exhibitor** *n*
exhibition *n* **1** public display of art,
skills, etc. **2** exhibiting. **exhibitionism**
n **1** compulsive desire to draw attention
to oneself. **2** compulsive desire to
display one's genitals in public.
exhibitionist *n*.
exhilarate *v* make lively and cheerful.
exhilaration *n*.

● **SPELLING TIP**
● It may surprise you that it's the
● vowels, not the consonants, that
● are a problem when people try to
● spell **exhilarate** or **exhilaration**.
● They often make the mistake of
● writing an *e* instead of an *a* in the
● middle.

exhort ❶ *v* urge earnestly.
exhortation *n*.
exhume ❶ [ig-**zyume**] *v* dig up
(something buried, esp. a corpse).
exhumation *n*.
exigency ❶ *n*, *pl* **-cies** urgent demand or
need. **exigent** *adj*.
exiguous *adj* scanty or meagre.

exile ❶ *n* **1** prolonged, usu. enforced,
absence from one's country. **2** person
banished or living away from his or her
country. ▷ *v* **3** expel from one's country.
exist ❶ *v* **1** have being or reality. **2** eke
out a living. **3** live. **existence** *n*
existent *adj*.

● **SPELLING TIP**
● People often write *-ance* at the end
● of a word when it should be *-ence*.
● The Bank of English shows this is
● the case for *existance* which occurs
● 43 times. However, the correct
● spelling **existence** is over 350 times
● commoner.

existential *adj* of or relating to
existence, esp. human existence.
existentialism *n* philosophical
movement stressing the personal
experience and responsibility of the
individual, who is seen as a free agent.
existentialist *adj*, *n*.
exit ❶ *n* **1** way out. **2** going out.
3 actor's going off stage. ▷ *v* **4** go out.
5 go offstage: used as a stage
direction.
exocrine *adj* relating to a gland, such as
the sweat gland, that secretes
externally through a duct.
exodus ❶ [**eks**-so-duss] *n* departure of a
large number of people.
ex officio [eks off-**fish**-ee-oh] *adv*, *adj*
Latin by right of position or office.

THESAURUS

---

strenuous, taxing
exhaustion *n* **1** = **tiredness**,
debilitation, fatigue, weariness
2 = **depletion**, consumption,
emptying, using up
exhaustive *adj* = **thorough**, all-
embracing, complete, comprehensive,
extensive, full-scale, in-depth, intensive
exhibit *v* **1** = **display**, parade, put on
view, show **2** = **show**, demonstrate,
express, indicate, manifest, reveal
exhibition *n* **1** = **display**,
demonstration, exposition,
performance, presentation,
representation, show, spectacle
exhilarating *adj* = **exciting**,
breathtaking, enlivening, invigorating,
stimulating, thrilling
exhort *v* = **urge**, advise, beseech, call
upon, entreat, persuade, press, spur
exhume *v* = **dig up**, disentomb, disinter,
unearth
exigency *n* = **need**, constraint, demand,
necessity, requirement

exile *n* **1** = **banishment**, deportation,
expatriation, expulsion **2** = **expatriate**,
deportee, émigré, outcast, refugee ▷ *v*
3 = **banish**, deport, drive out, eject,
expatriate, expel
exist *v* **1** = **be**, be present, occur
2 = **survive**, eke out a living, get along
or by, keep one's head above water, stay
alive, subsist **3** = **live**, endure
existence *n* **1** = **being**, actuality
2 = **subsistence**, survival **3** = **life**
existent *adj* **1** = **in existence**, existing,
extant, present, standing
2 = **surviving 3** = **alive**, living
exit *n* **1** = **way out**, door, gate, outlet
2 = **departure**, exodus, farewell, going,
goodbye, leave-taking, retreat,
withdrawal ▷ *v* **4** = **depart**, go away,
go out, leave, make tracks, retire,
retreat, take one's leave, withdraw
5 = **go offstage** (*Theatre*)
exodus *n* = **departure**, evacuation, exit,
flight, going out, leaving, migration,
retreat, withdrawal

exonerate ❶ v free from blame or a criminal charge. **exoneration** n.

exorbitant ❶ adj (of prices, demands, etc.) excessive, immoderate. **exorbitantly** adv.

exorcize ❶ v expel (evil spirits) by prayers and religious rites. **exorcism** n **exorcist** n.

exotic ❶ adj 1 having a strange allure or beauty. 2 originating in a foreign country. ▷ n 3 non-native plant. **exotically** adv **exotica** pl n (collection of) exotic objects.

expand ❶ v 1 make or become larger. 2 spread out. 3 (foll. by on) enlarge (on). 4 become more relaxed, friendly, and talkative. **expansion** n **expansionism** n policy of expanding the economy or territory of a country. **expansionist** adj **expanse** n uninterrupted wide area. **expansive** adj 1 wide or extensive. 2 friendly and talkative.

expatiate [iks-**pay**-shee-ate] v (foll. by on) speak or write at great length (on). **expatiation** n.

expatriate ❶ [eks-**pat**-ree-it] adj 1 living outside one's native country. ▷ n 2 person living outside his or her native country. **expatriation** n.

expect ❶ v 1 regard as probable. 2 look forward to, await. 3 require as an obligation. **expectancy** n 1 something expected on the basis of an average, e.g. life expectancy. 2 feeling of anticipation. **expectant** adj 1 expecting or hopeful. 2 pregnant. **expectantly** adv **expectation** n 1 act or state of expecting. 2 something looked forward to. 3 attitude of anticipation or hope.

expectorate v spit out (phlegm etc.). **expectoration** n **expectorant** n medicine that helps to bring up phlegm from the respiratory passages.

expedient ❶ [iks-**pee**-dee-ent] n 1 something that achieves a particular purpose. ▷ adj 2 suitable to the circumstances, appropriate. **expediency** n.

exonerate v = **clear**, absolve, acquit, discharge, exculpate, excuse, justify, pardon, vindicate

exorbitant adj = **excessive**, extortionate, extravagant, immoderate, inordinate, outrageous, preposterous, unreasonable

exorcize v = **drive out**, cast out, deliver (from), expel, purify

exotic adj 1 = **unusual**, colourful, fascinating, glamorous, mysterious, strange, striking, unfamiliar 2 = **foreign**, alien, external, imported, naturalized

expand v 1 = **increase**, amplify, broaden, develop, enlarge, extend, grow, magnify, swell, widen 2 = **spread (out)**, diffuse, stretch (out), unfold, unfurl, unravel, unroll 3 (foll. by on) = **go into detail about**, amplify, develop, elaborate on, embellish, enlarge on, expatiate on, expound on, flesh out

expanse n = **area**, breadth, extent, range, space, stretch, sweep, tract

expansion n 1 = **increase**, amplification, development, enlargement, growth, magnification 2 = **spread**, opening out

expansive adj 1 = **wide**, broad, extensive, far-reaching, voluminous, wide-ranging, widespread

2 = **talkative**, affable, communicative, effusive, friendly, loquacious, open, outgoing, sociable, unreserved

expatriate adj 1 = **exiled**, banished, emigrant, émigré ▷ n 2 = **exile**, emigrant, émigré, refugee

expect v 1 = **think**, assume, believe, imagine, presume, reckon, suppose, surmise, trust 2 = **look forward to**, anticipate, await, contemplate, envisage, hope for, predict, watch for 3 = **require**, call for, demand, insist on, want

expectant adj 1 = **expecting**, anticipating, apprehensive, eager, hopeful, in suspense, ready, watchful 2 = **pregnant**, expecting (inf), gravid

expectation n 2 = **probability**, assumption, belief, conjecture, forecast, likelihood, presumption, supposition 3 = **anticipation**, apprehension, expectancy, hope, promise, suspense

expediency n = **suitability**, advisability, benefit, convenience, pragmatism, profitability, prudence, usefulness, utility

expedient n 1 = **means**, contrivance, device, makeshift, measure, method, resort, scheme, stopgap ▷ adj 2 = **advantageous**, appropriate, beneficial, convenient, effective,

expedite ❶ v hasten the progress of.
expedition n 1 organized journey, esp.
for exploration. 2 people and
equipment comprising an expedition.
3 pleasure trip or excursion.
expeditionary adj relating to an
expedition, esp. a military one.
expeditious adj done quickly and
efficiently.
expel ❶ v -pelling, -pelled 1 drive out
with force. 2 dismiss from a school etc.
permanently. **expulsion** n.
expend ❶ v spend, use up. **expendable**
adj able to be sacrificed to achieve an
objective. **expenditure** n 1 something
expended, esp. money. 2 amount
expended. **expense** n 1 cost. 2 (cause
of) spending. ▷ pl 3 charges, outlay
incurred. **expense account**
arrangement by which an employee's
expenses are refunded by the employer.
expensive adj high-priced.
experience ❶ n 1 direct personal

participation. 2 particular incident,
feeling, etc. that a person has
undergone. 3 accumulated knowledge.
▷ v 4 participate in. 5 be affected by
(an emotion). **experienced** adj skilful
from extensive participation.
experiment ❶ n 1 test to provide
evidence to prove or disprove a theory.
2 attempt at something new. ▷ v
3 carry out an experiment.
experimental adj **experimentally** adv
experimentation n.
expert ❶ n 1 person with extensive skill
or knowledge in a particular field. ▷ adj
2 skilful or knowledgeable. **expertise**
[eks-per-**teez**] n special skill or
knowledge. **expertly** adv.
expiate v make amends for. **expiation** n.
expire ❶ v 1 finish or run out. 2 breathe
out. 3 lit die. **expiration** n **expiry** n
end, esp. of a contract period.
explain ❶ v 1 make clear and intelligible.
2 account for. **explanation** n

THESAURUS

helpful, opportune, practical, suitable,
useful
expedition n 1 = **journey**, excursion,
mission, quest, safari, tour, trek,
voyage
expel v 1 = **drive out**, belch, cast out,
discharge, eject, remove, spew
2 = **dismiss**, ban, banish, drum out,
evict, exclude, exile, throw out, turf out
(inf)
expend v = **spend**, consume, dissipate,
exhaust, go through, pay out, use (up)
expendable adj = **dispensable**,
inessential, nonessential, replaceable,
unimportant, unnecessary
expenditure n = **spending**,
consumption, cost, expense,
outgoings, outlay, output, payment
expense n 1 = **cost**, charge,
expenditure, loss, outlay, payment,
spending
expensive adj = **dear**, costly, exorbitant,
extravagant, high-priced, lavish,
overpriced, steep (inf), stiff
experience n 1 = **participation**,
contact, exposure, familiarity,
involvement 2 = **event**, adventure,
affair, encounter, episode, happening,
incident, occurrence 3 = **knowledge**,
practice, training ▷ v 4 = **undergo**,
encounter, endure, face, feel, go
through, live through, sample, taste
experienced adj = **knowledgeable**,
accomplished, expert, practised,

seasoned, tested, tried, veteran,
well-versed
experiment n 1 = **test**, examination,
experimentation, investigation,
procedure, proof, research 2 = **trial**,
trial run ▷ v 3 = **test**, examine,
investigate, put to the test, research,
sample, try, verify
experimental adj = **test**, exploratory,
pilot, preliminary, probationary,
provisional, speculative, tentative,
trial, trial-and-error
expert n 1 = **master**, authority,
connoisseur, dab hand (Brit inf), fundi
(S Afr), guru, mana (NZ), past master,
professional, specialist, virtuoso ▷ adj
2 = **skilful**, adept, adroit, experienced,
masterly, practised, professional,
proficient, qualified, virtuoso
expertise n = **skill**, adroitness,
command, facility, judgment, know-
how (inf), knowledge, mastery,
proficiency
expire v 1 = **finish**, cease, close, come to
an end, conclude, end, lapse, run out,
stop, terminate 2 = **breathe out**, emit,
exhale, expel 3 Lit = **die**, cark (Aust & NZ
sl), depart, kick the bucket (inf), pass
away or on, perish
explain v 1 = **make clear** or **plain**,
clarify, clear up, define, describe,
elucidate, expound, resolve, teach
2 = **account for**, excuse, give a reason
for, justify

explanatory adj.

expletive [iks-**plee**-tiv] n swearword.

explicable adj able to be explained.
  explicate v formal explain.
  explication n.

explicit ❶ adj 1 precisely and clearly
  expressed. 2 shown in realistic detail.
  explicitly adv.

explode ❶ v 1 burst with great violence,
  blow up. 2 react suddenly with
  emotion. 3 increase rapidly. 4 show (a
  theory etc.) to be baseless. **explosion** n
  explosive adj 1 tending to explode. ▷ n
  2 substance that causes explosions.

exploit ❶ v 1 take advantage of for one's
  own purposes. 2 make the best use of.
  ▷ n 3 notable feat or deed.
  exploitation n **exploiter** n.

explore ❶ v 1 investigate. 2 travel into
  (unfamiliar regions), esp. for scientific
  purposes. **exploration** n **exploratory**
  adj **explorer** n.

expo n, pl **expos** informal exposition,
  large public exhibition.

exponent ❶ n 1 person who advocates
  an idea, cause, etc. 2 skilful performer,
  esp. a musician.

exponential adj informal very rapid.
  exponentially adv.

export n 1 selling or shipping of goods
  to a foreign country. 2 product shipped
  or sold to a foreign country. ▷ v 3 sell or
  ship (goods) to a foreign country.
  exporter n.

expose ❶ v 1 uncover or reveal. 2 make
  vulnerable, leave unprotected.
  3 subject (a photographic film) to light.
  expose oneself display one's sexual
  organs in public. **exposure** n
  1 exposing. 2 lack of shelter from the
  weather, esp. the cold. 3 appearance
  before the public, as on television.
  4 Photography act of exposing film or
  plates to light. 5 Photography intensity
  of light falling on a film or plate
  multiplied by the time of the exposure.

exposé [iks-**pose**-ay] n bringing of a
  crime, scandal, etc. to public notice.

exposition n see EXPOUND.

expostulate v (foll. by with) reason
  (with), esp. to dissuade.
  expostulation n.

expound ❶ v explain in detail.
  exposition n 1 explanation. 2 large

─────────────────── THESAURUS ───────────────

explanation n 1 = **description**,
  clarification, definition, elucidation,
  illustration, interpretation 2 = **reason**,
  account, answer, excuse, justification,
  motive, vindication

explanatory adj 1 = **descriptive**,
  illustrative, interpretive

explicit adj 1 = **clear**, categorical,
  definite, frank, precise, specific,
  straightforward, unambiguous

explode v 1 = **blow up**, burst, detonate,
  discharge, erupt, go off, set off, shatter
  4 = **disprove**, debunk, discredit, give
  the lie to, invalidate, refute, repudiate

exploit v 1 = **take advantage of**, abuse,
  manipulate, milk, misuse, play on or
  upon 2 = **make the best use of**,
  capitalize on, cash in on (inf), profit by
  or from, use, utilize ▷ n 3 = **feat**,
  accomplishment, achievement,
  adventure, attainment, deed,
  escapade, stunt

exploitation n 1 = **misuse**, abuse,
  manipulation, using

exploration n 1 = **investigation**,
  analysis, examination, fossick (Aust &
  NZ), inquiry, inspection, research,
  scrutiny, search 2 = **expedition**,
  reconnaissance, survey, tour,
  travel, trip

explore v 1 = **investigate**, examine,
  fossick (Aust & NZ), inquire into, inspect,
  look into, probe, research, search
  2 = **travel**, reconnoitre, scout, survey,
  tour

explosion n 1 = **bang**, blast, burst,
  clap, crack, detonation, discharge,
  report 2 = **outburst**, eruption, fit,
  outbreak

explosive adj 1 = **unstable**, volatile

exponent n 1 = **advocate**, backer,
  champion, defender, promoter,
  proponent, supporter, upholder
  2 = **performer**, player

expose v 1 = **uncover**, display, exhibit,
  present, reveal, show, unveil 2 = **make
  vulnerable**, endanger, imperil,
  jeopardize, lay open, leave open,
  subject

exposed adj 1 = **unconcealed**, bare, on
  display, on show, on view, revealed,
  uncovered 2 = **vulnerable**, in peril, laid
  bare, open, susceptible, unprotected,
  unsheltered, wide open

exposure n 1 = **publicity**, display,
  exhibition, presentation, revelation,
  showing, uncovering, unveiling

expound v = **explain**, describe,
  elucidate, interpret, set forth, spell out,
  unfold

public exhibition.
express ❶ *v* **1** put into words. **2** show (an emotion). **3** indicate by a symbol or formula. **4** squeeze out (juice etc.). ▷ *adj* **5** explicitly stated. **6** (of a purpose) particular. **7** of or for rapid transportation of people, mail, etc. ▷ *n* **8** fast train or bus stopping at only a few stations. ▷ *adv* **9** by express delivery. **expression** *n* **1** expressing. **2** word or phrase. **3** showing or communication of emotion. **4** look on the face that indicates mood. **5** *Maths* variable, function, or some combination of these. **expressionless** *adj* **expressive** *adj* **expressiveness** *n*.
expressionism *n* early 20th-century artistic movement which sought to express emotions rather than represent the physical world. **expressionist** *n*, *adj*.
expropriate *v* deprive an owner of (property). **expropriation** *n*.
expulsion ❶ *n* see EXPEL.
expunge [iks-**sponge**] *v* delete, erase, blot out.
expurgate [**eks**-per-gate] *v* remove objectionable parts from (a book etc.).
exquisite ❶ *adj* **1** of extreme beauty or delicacy. **2** sensitive or discriminating, e.g. *exquisite manners*. **3** intense in feeling. **exquisitely** *adv*.
ex-serviceman *n* man who has served in the armed forces.
extant *adj* still existing.
extemporize *v* speak, perform, or compose without preparation.
extend ❶ *v* **1** draw out or be drawn out, stretch. **2** last for a certain time. **3** (foll. by *to*) include. **4** increase in size or scope. **5** offer, e.g. *extend one's sympathy*. **extendable** *adj* **extension** *n* **1** room or rooms added to an existing building. **2** additional telephone connected to the same line as another. **3** extending. **extensive** *adj* having a large extent, widespread. **extensor** *n* muscle that extends a part of the body. **extent** *n* range over which something extends, area.

SPELLING TIP
Lots of nouns in English end with *-tion*, but **extension** is not one of them.

extenuate ❶ *v* make (an offence or fault) less blameworthy. **extenuating** *adj* **extenuation** *n*.
exterior ❶ *n* **1** part or surface on the outside. **2** outward appearance. ▷ *adj* **3** of, on, or coming from the outside.

THESAURUS

express *v* **1** = **state**, articulate, communicate, declare, phrase, put into words, say, utter, voice, word **2** = **show**, convey, exhibit, intimate, make known, reveal **3** = **represent**, indicate, signify, stand for, symbolize ▷ *adj* **5** = **explicit**, categorical, clear, definite, distinct, plain, unambiguous **6** = **specific**, clear-cut, especial, particular, singular, special **7** = **fast**, direct, high-speed, nonstop, rapid, speedy, swift
expression *n* **1** = **statement**, announcement, communication, declaration, utterance **2** = **phrase**, idiom, locution, remark, term, turn of phrase, word **3** = **indication**, demonstration, exhibition, manifestation, representation, show, sign, symbol, token **4** = **look**, air, appearance, aspect, countenance, face
expressive *adj* = **vivid**, eloquent, moving, poignant, striking, telling
exquisite *adj* **1** = **beautiful**, attractive, comely, dainty, delicate, elegant, fine, lovely, pleasing **3** = **intense**, acute, keen, sharp
extend *v* **1** = **make longer**, drag out, draw out, lengthen, prolong, spin out, spread out, stretch **2** = **last**, carry on, continue, go on **4** = **widen**, add to, augment, broaden, enhance, enlarge, expand, increase, supplement **5** = **offer**, confer, impart, present, proffer
extension *n* **1** = **annexe**, addition, appendage, appendix, supplement **3** = **lengthening**, broadening, development, enlargement, expansion, increase, spread, widening
extensive *adj* = **wide**, broad, far-flung, far-reaching, large-scale, pervasive, spacious, vast, voluminous, widespread
extent *n* = **size**, amount, area, breadth, expanse, length, stretch, volume, width
extenuating *adj* = **mitigating**, justifying, moderating, qualifying
exterior *n* **1** = **outside**, coating, covering, facade, face, shell, skin, surface ▷ *adj* **3** = **outside**, external, outer, outermost, outward, surface

exterminate ❶ v destroy (animals or people) completely. **extermination** n **exterminator** n.

external ❶ adj of, situated on, or coming from the outside. **externally** adv **externalize** v express (feelings) in words or actions.

extinct ❶ adj 1 having died out. 2 (of a volcano) no longer liable to erupt. **extinction** n.

extinguish ❶ v 1 put out (a fire or light). 2 remove or destroy entirely. **extinguisher** n.

extirpate [**eks**-ter-pate] v destroy utterly.

extol ❶ v **-tolling, -tolled** praise highly.

extort ❶ v get (something) by force or threats. **extortion** n **extortionate** adj (of prices) excessive.

extra ❶ adj 1 more than is usual, expected or needed. ▷ n 2 additional person or thing. 3 something for which an additional charge is made. 4 Films actor hired for crowd scenes. 5 Cricket run not scored off the bat. ▷ adv 6 unusually or exceptionally.

extra- prefix outside or beyond an area or scope, e.g. extrasensory; extraterritorial.

extract ❶ v 1 pull out by force. 2 remove. 3 derive. 4 copy out (an article, passage, etc.) from a publication. ▷ n 5 something

extracted, such as a passage from a book etc. 6 preparation containing the concentrated essence of a substance, e.g. beef extract. **extraction** n **extractor** n **extractor fan** device for removing stale air or fumes from a room.

extracurricular adj taking place outside the normal school timetable.

extradite v send (an accused person) back to his or her own country for trial. **extradition** n.

extramural adj connected with but outside the normal courses of a university or college.

extraneous ❶ [iks-**train**-ee-uss] adj irrelevant.

extraordinary ❶ adj 1 very unusual. 2 (of a meeting) specially arranged to deal with a particular subject. **extraordinarily** adv.

extrapolate [iks-**trap**-a-late] v 1 infer (something not known) from the known facts. 2 Maths estimate (a value of a function or measurement) beyond the known values by the extension of a curve. **extrapolation** n.

extrasensory adj **extrasensory perception** supposed ability to obtain information other than through the normal senses.

extraterrestrial adj of or from outside the earth's atmosphere.

THESAURUS

exterminate v = **destroy**, abolish, annihilate, eliminate, eradicate

external adj = **outer**, exterior, outermost, outside, outward, surface

extinct adj 1 = **dead**, defunct, gone, lost, vanished

extinction n 1 = **dying out**, abolition, annihilation, destruction, eradication, extermination, obliteration, oblivion

extinguish v 1 = **put out**, blow out, douse, quench, smother, snuff out, stifle 2 = **destroy**, annihilate, eliminate, end, eradicate, exterminate, remove, wipe out

extol v = **praise**, acclaim, commend, eulogize, exalt, glorify, sing the praises of

extort v = **force**, blackmail, bully, coerce, extract, squeeze

extortionate adj = **exorbitant**, excessive, extravagant, inflated, outrageous, preposterous, sky-high, unreasonable

extra adj 1 **a** = **additional**, added,

ancillary, auxiliary, further, more, supplementary **b** = **surplus**, excess, leftover, redundant, spare, superfluous, unused ▷ n 2 = **addition**, accessory, attachment, bonus, extension, supplement ▷ adv 6 = **exceptionally**, especially, extraordinarily, extremely, particularly, remarkably, uncommonly, unusually

extract v 1 = **pull out**, draw, pluck out, pull, remove, take out, uproot, withdraw 3 = **derive**, draw, elicit, glean, obtain ▷ n 5 = **passage**, citation, clipping, cutting, excerpt, quotation, selection 6 = **essence**, concentrate, distillation, juice

extraneous adj = **irrelevant**, beside the point, immaterial, inappropriate, off the subject, unconnected, unrelated

extraordinary adj 1 = **unusual**, amazing, exceptional, fantastic, outstanding, phenomenal, remarkable, strange, uncommon

extravagant ❶ *adj* **1** spending money excessively. **2** going beyond reasonable limits. **extravagance** *n* **extravaganza** *n* elaborate and lavish entertainment, display, etc.

- **SPELLING TIP**
- Make sure that **extravagant** ends
- in -*ant*, even though -*ent* sounds like
- a possibility.

extreme ❶ *adj* **1** of a high or the highest degree or intensity. **2** severe. **3** immoderate. **4** farthest or outermost. ▷ *n* **5** either of the two limits of a scale or range. **extremely** *adv* **extremism** *n* behaviour or beliefs that are immoderate. **extremist** *n* **1** person who favours immoderate methods. ▷ *adj* **2** holding extreme opinions. **extremity** *n*, *pl* -**ties 1** farthest point. **2** extreme condition, as of misfortune. ▷ *pl* **3** hands and feet. **extreme sport** sport with a high risk of injury or death.

extricate ❶ *v* free from complication or difficulty. **extrication** *n*.

extrinsic *adj* not contained or included within. **extrinsically** *adv*.

extrovert ❶ *adj* **1** lively and outgoing. **2** concerned more with external reality than inner feelings. ▷ *n* **3** extrovert person. **extroversion** *n*.

extrude *v* squeeze or force out. **extrusion** *n*.

exuberant ❶ *adj* **1** high-spirited. **2** growing luxuriantly. **exuberance** *n* **exuberantly** *adv*.

exude *v* **1** (of a liquid or smell) seep or flow out slowly and steadily. **2** make apparent by mood or behaviour, e.g. *exude confidence*.

exult ❶ *v* be joyful or jubilant. **exultation** *n* **exultant** *adj*.

eye ❶ *n* **1** organ of sight. **2** external part of an eye. **3** (often pl) ability to see. **4** attention, e.g. *his new shirt caught my eye*. **5** ability to judge or appreciate, e.g. *a good eye for detail*. **6** one end of a sewing needle. **7** small area of calm at the centre of a hurricane. **8** dark spot on a potato from which a stem grows. ▷ *v* **eyeing** *or* **eying**, **eyed 9** look at carefully or warily. **eyeless** *adj* **eyelet** *n* **1** small hole for a lace or cord to be passed through. **2** ring that strengthens this. **eyeball** *n* ball-shaped part of the eye. **eyebrow** *n* line of hair on the bony ridge above the eye. **eye-catching** *adj* attracting attention. **eyeful** *n informal* **1** view. **2** attractive sight, esp. a woman. **eyeglass** *n* lens for aiding defective

---

THESAURUS

extravagant *adj* **1** = **wasteful**, lavish, prodigal, profligate, spendthrift **2** = **excessive**, outrageous, over the top (*sl*), preposterous, reckless, unreasonable

extreme *adj* **1** = **maximum**, acute, great, highest, intense, severe, supreme, ultimate, utmost **2** = **severe**, drastic, harsh, radical, rigid, strict, uncompromising **3** = **excessive**, fanatical, immoderate, radical **4** = **farthest**, far-off, most distant, outermost, remotest ▷ *n* **5** = **limit**, boundary, edge, end, extremity, pole

extremely *adv* **1** = **very**, awfully (*inf*), exceedingly, exceptionally, extraordinarily, severely, terribly, uncommonly, unusually

extremist *n* **1** = **fanatic**, die-hard, radical, zealot

extremity *n* **1** = **limit**, border, boundary, edge, extreme, frontier, pinnacle, tip **2** = **crisis**, adversity, dire straits, disaster, emergency, exigency, trouble ▷ *pl* **3** = **hands and feet**, fingers and toes, limbs

extricate *v* = **free**, disengage, disentangle, get out, release, remove, rescue, wriggle out of

extrovert *adj* **1** = **outgoing**, exuberant, gregarious, sociable

exuberant *adj* **1** = **high-spirited**, animated, cheerful, ebullient, energetic, enthusiastic, lively, spirited, vivacious **2** = **luxuriant**, abundant, copious, lavish, plentiful, profuse

exult *v* = **be joyful**, be overjoyed, celebrate, jump for joy, rejoice

eye *n* **1** = **eyeball**, optic (*inf*) **5** = **appreciation**, discernment, discrimination, judgment, perception, recognition, taste ▷ *v* **9** = **look at**, check out (*inf*), contemplate, inspect, study, survey, view, watch

eyesight *n* = **vision**, perception, sight

eyesore *n* = **mess**, blemish, blot, disfigurement, horror, monstrosity, sight (*inf*)

eyewitness *n* = **observer**, bystander, onlooker, passer-by, spectator, viewer, witness

vision. **eyelash** *n* short hair that grows out from the eyelid. **eyelid** *n* fold of skin that covers the eye when it is closed. **eyeliner** *n* cosmetic used to outline the eyes. **eye-opener** *n informal* something startling or revealing. **eye shadow** coloured cosmetic worn on the upper eyelids.

eyesight *n* ability to see. **eyesore** *n* ugly object. **eyetooth** *n* canine tooth. **eyewash** *n informal* nonsense. **eyewitness** *n* person who was present at an event and can describe what happened.

eyrie *n* **1** nest of an eagle. **2** high isolated place.

e

f *Music* forte.

F 1 Fahrenheit. **2** farad.
3 *Chemistry* fluorine. **4** franc(s).

f. and the following (page).

fa *n* same as FAH.

FA Football Association.

fable ❶ *n* **1** story with a moral. **2** false or fictitious account. **3** legend or myth. **fabled** *adj* made famous in legend. **fabulous** *adj*.

fabric ❶ *n* **1** knitted or woven cloth. **2** framework or structure.

fabricate ❶ *v* **1** make up (a story or lie). **2** make or build. **fabrication** *n*.

fabulous ❶ *adj* **1** *informal* excellent. **2** astounding. **3** told of in fables. **fabulously** *adv*.

facade [fas-**sahd**] *n* **1** front of a building. **2** (false) outward appearance.

face ❶ *n* **1** front of the head. **2** facial expression. **3** distorted expression. **4** outward appearance. **5** front or main side. **6** dial of a clock. **7** exposed area of coal or ore in a mine. **8** dignity, self-respect. ▷ *v* **9** look or turn towards. **10** be opposite. **11** be confronted by. **12** provide with a surface. **set one's face against** oppose determinedly. **faceless** *adj* impersonal, anonymous. **face-lift** *n* operation to tighten facial skin, to remove wrinkles. **face-saving** *adj* maintaining dignity or self-respect. **face up to** *v* accept (an unpleasant fact or reality). **face value** apparent worth or meaning.

facet ❶ *n* **1** aspect. **2** surface of a cut gem.

facetious ❶ [fas-**see**-shuss] *adj* funny or trying to be funny, esp. at inappropriate times. **facetiously** *adv*.

facia *n*, *pl* **-ciae** same as FASCIA.

facial *adj* **1** of the face. ▷ *n* **2** beauty treatment for the face.

facile ❶ [fas-**sile**] *adj* **1** (of a remark, argument, etc.) superficial and

---

THESAURUS

fable *n* **1** = **story**, allegory, legend, myth, parable, tale **2, 3** = **fiction**, fabrication, fantasy, invention, tall story (*inf*), urban legend, urban myth, yarn (*inf*)

fabric *n* **1** = **cloth**, material, stuff, textile, web **2** = **framework**, constitution, construction, foundations, make-up, organization, structure

fabricate *v* **1** = **make up**, concoct, devise, fake, falsify, feign, forge, invent, trump up **2** = **build**, assemble, construct, erect, form, make, manufacture, shape

fabrication *n* **1** = **forgery**, concoction, fake, falsehood, fiction, invention, lie, myth **2** = **construction**, assembly, building, erection, manufacture, production

fabulous *adj* **1** *Inf* = **wonderful**, brilliant, fantastic (*inf*), marvellous, out-of-this-world (*inf*), sensational (*inf*), spectacular, superb
2 = **astounding**, amazing, breathtaking, inconceivable, incredible, phenomenal, unbelievable **3** = **legendary**, apocryphal, fantastic, fictitious, imaginary, invented, made-up, mythical, unreal

facade *n* **2** = **appearance**, exterior, face, front, guise, mask, pretence, semblance, show

face *n* **1** = **countenance**, features, mug (*sl*), visage **2** = **expression**, appearance, aspect, look **3** = **scowl**, frown, grimace, pout, smirk **4** = **side**, exterior, front, outside, surface **8** = **self-respect**, authority, dignity, honour, image, prestige, reputation, standing, status ▷ *v* **10** = **look onto**, be opposite, front onto, overlook **11** = **confront**, brave, come up against, deal with, encounter, experience, meet, oppose, tackle **12** = **coat**, clad, cover, dress, finish

faceless *adj* = **impersonal**, anonymous, remote

facet *n* **1** = **aspect**, angle, face, part, phase, plane, side, slant **2** = **surface**

facetious *adj* = **funny**, amusing, comical, droll, flippant, frivolous, humorous, jocular, playful, tongue in cheek

face up to *v* = **accept**, acknowledge, come to terms with, confront, cope with, deal with, meet head-on, tackle

facile *adj* **1** = **superficial**, cursory, glib, hasty, shallow, slick showing lack of real thought. **2** easily performed or achieved.

facilitate ⓘ v make easy. **facilitation** n.

facility ⓘ n, pl -**ties** **1** skill. **2** easiness. ▷ pl **3** means or equipment for an activity.

facing n **1** lining or covering for decoration or reinforcement. ▷ pl **2** contrasting collar and cuffs on a jacket.

facsimile ⓘ [fak-**sim**-ill-ee] n exact copy. **facsimile transmission** same as FAX (sense 1).

fact ⓘ n **1** event or thing known to have happened or existed. **2** provable truth. **fact of life** inescapable, often unpleasant, truth. **facts of life** details of sex and reproduction. **factual** adj.

faction¹ ⓘ n **1** (dissenting) minority group within a larger body. **2** dissension. **factious** adj of or producing factions.

faction² n dramatized presentation of a factual event.

factitious adj artificial.

factor ⓘ n **1** element contributing to a result. **2** Maths one of the integers multiplied together to give a given number. **3** level on a scale of measurement, e.g. suntan oil with a factor of 5. **4** Scot property manager. **factorial** n product of all the integers from one to a given number. **factorize** v calculate the factors of (a number).

factory ⓘ n, pl -**ries** building where goods are manufactured. **factory**

farm farm on which animals are reared using modern industrial methods. **factory ship** ship that processes fish caught by a fleet.

factotum n person employed to do all sorts of work.

faculty ⓘ n, pl -**ties** **1** physical or mental ability. **2** department in a university or college.

fad ⓘ n **1** short-lived fashion. **2** whim. **faddy**, **faddish** adj.

fade ⓘ v **1** (cause to) lose brightness, colour, or strength. **2** vanish slowly. **fade-in**, **-out** n gradual increase or decrease, as of vision or sound in a film or broadcast.

faeces [**fee**-seez] pl n waste matter discharged from the anus. **faecal** [**fee**-kl] adj.

faff v (often foll. by about) Brit informal dither or fuss.

fag¹ n **1** informal boring task. **2** young public schoolboy who does menial chores for a senior boy. ▷ v **3** do menial chores in a public school.

fag² n slang cigarette. **fag end 1** last and worst part. **2** slang cigarette stub.

fag³ n US offens male homosexual.

faggot¹ n **1** ball of chopped liver, herbs, and bread. **2** bundle of sticks for fuel.

faggot² n US & Aust offens male homosexual.

fah n Music (in tonic sol-fa) fourth degree of any major scale.

———————— THESAURUS ————————

facilitate v = **promote**, expedite, forward, further, help, make easy, pave the way for, speed up

facility n **1, 2** = **ease**, ability, adroitness, dexterity, efficiency, effortlessness, fluency, proficiency, skill ▷ pl **3** = **equipment**, advantage, aid, amenity, appliance, convenience, means, opportunity, resource

facsimile n = **copy**, carbon copy, duplicate, fax, photocopy, print, replica, reproduction, transcript

fact n **1** = **event**, fait accompli, act, deed, happening, incident, occurrence, performance **2** = **truth**, certainty, reality

faction¹ n **1** = **group**, bloc, cabal, clique, contingent, coterie, gang, party, set, splinter group **2** = **dissension**, conflict, disagreement, discord, disunity, division, infighting, rebellion

factor n **1** = **element**, aspect, cause, component, consideration, influence, item, part

factory n = **works**, mill, plant

factual adj = **true**, authentic, correct, exact, genuine, precise, real, true-to-life

faculty n **1** = **ability**, aptitude, capacity, facility, power, propensity, skill **2** = **department**, school

fad n **1** = **craze**, fashion, mania, rage, trend, vogue **2** = **whim**

fade v **1** = **pale**, bleach, discolour, lose colour, wash out **2** = **dwindle**, decline, die away, disappear, dissolve, melt away, vanish, wane

faded adj **1** = **discoloured**, bleached, dull, indistinct, pale, washed out

fading adj **2** = **declining**, decreasing, disappearing, dying, on the decline, vanishing

Fahrenheit [far-ren-hite] *adj* of a temperature scale with the freezing point of water at 32° and the boiling point at 212°.

faïence [**fie**-ence] *n* tin-glazed earthenware.

fail ❶ *v* 1 be unsuccessful. 2 stop operating. 3 be or judge to be below the required standard in a test. 4 disappoint or be useless to (someone). 5 neglect or be unable to do (something). 6 go bankrupt. ▷ *n* 7 instance of not passing an exam or test. **without fail** 1 regularly. 2 definitely. **failing** *n* 1 weak point. ▷ *prep* 2 in the absence of. **failure** *n* 1 act or instance of failing. 2 unsuccessful person or thing. **fail-safe** *adj* designed to return to a safe condition if something goes wrong.

fain *adv obs* gladly.

faint ❶ *adj* 1 lacking clarity, brightness, or volume. 2 feeling dizzy or weak. 3 lacking conviction or force. ▷ *v* 4 lose consciousness temporarily. ▷ *n* 5 temporary loss of consciousness.

faint-hearted *adj* lacking courage and confidence.

fair[1] ❶ *adj* 1 unbiased and reasonable. 2 in agreement with rules. 3 light in colour. 4 beautiful. 5 quite good, e.g. *a fair attempt*. 6 quite large, e.g. *a fair amount of money*. 7 (of weather) fine. ▷ *adv* 8 fairly. 9 absolutely. **fairly** *adv* 1 moderately. 2 to a great degree or extent. 3 as deserved, reasonably. **fairness** *n* **fair copy** neat copy, without mistakes or alterations, of a piece of writing. **fair game** person regarded as a justifiable target for criticism or ridicule. **fair play** conventional standard of honourable behaviour. **fairway** *n Golf* smooth area between the tee and the green. **fair-weather** *adj* unreliable in difficult situations, e.g. *a fair-weather friend*.

fair[2] ❶ *n* 1 travelling entertainment with sideshows, rides, and amusements. 2 exhibition of commercial or industrial products. **fairground** *n* open space used for a fair.

─────────── **THESAURUS** ───────────

fail *v* 1 = **be unsuccessful**, bite the dust, break down, come to grief, come unstuck, fall, fizzle out (*inf*), flop (*inf*), founder, miscarry, misfire 2 = **give out**, cark (*Aust & NZ sl*), conk out (*inf*), cut out, die, peter out, stop working 4, 5 = **disappoint**, abandon, desert, forget, forsake, let down, neglect, omit 6 = **go bankrupt**, become insolvent, close down, fold (*inf*), go broke (*inf*), go bust (*inf*), go into receivership, go out of business, go to the wall, go under **without fail** 1 = **regularly**, like clockwork, religiously 2 = **dependably**, conscientiously, constantly, without exception

failing *n* 1 = **weakness**, blemish, defect, deficiency, drawback, fault, flaw, imperfection, shortcoming ▷ *prep* 2 = **in the absence of**, in default of, lacking

failure *n* 1 a = **lack of success**, breakdown, collapse, defeat, downfall, fiasco, miscarriage, overthrow b = **bankruptcy**, crash, downfall, insolvency, liquidation, ruin 2 = **loser**, black sheep, dead duck (*sl*), disappointment, dud (*inf*), flop (*inf*), nonstarter, washout (*inf*)

faint *adj* 1 = **dim**, distant, faded, indistinct, low, muted, soft, subdued, vague 2 = **dizzy**, exhausted, giddy, light-headed, muzzy, weak, woozy (*inf*) 3 = **slight**, feeble, remote, unenthusiastic, weak ▷ *v* 4 = **pass out**, black out, collapse, flake out (*inf*), keel over (*inf*), lose consciousness, swoon (*lit*) ▷ *n* 5 = **blackout**, collapse, swoon (*lit*), unconsciousness

fair[1] *adj* 1, 2 = **unbiased**, above board, equitable, even-handed, honest, impartial, just, lawful, legitimate, proper, unprejudiced 3 = **light**, blond, blonde, fair-haired, flaxen-haired, towheaded 4 = **beautiful**, bonny, comely, handsome, lovely, pretty 5 = **respectable**, adequate, average, decent, moderate, O.K. *or* okay (*inf*), passable, reasonable, satisfactory, tolerable 7 = **fine**, bright, clear, cloudless, dry, sunny, unclouded

fair[2] *n* 1 = **carnival**, bazaar, festival, fete, gala, show

fairly *adv* 1 = **moderately**, adequately, pretty well, quite, rather, reasonably, somewhat, tolerably 2 = **positively**, absolutely, really 3 = **deservedly**, equitably, honestly, impartially, justly, objectively, properly, without fear or favour

fairness *n* = **impartiality**, decency, disinterestedness, equitableness,

fairing n curved metal structure fitted round part of a car, aircraft, etc. to reduce drag.

Fair Isle n intricate multicoloured knitted pattern.

fairy ❶ n, pl **fairies 1** imaginary small creature with magic powers. **2** offens male homosexual. **fairy godmother** person who helps in time of trouble. **fairyland** n **fairy lights** small coloured electric bulbs used as decoration. **fairy penguin** small penguin with a bluish head and back, found on the Australian coast. **fairy ring** ring of dark grass caused by fungi. **fairy tale, story 1** story about fairies or magic. **2** unbelievable story or explanation.

fait accompli [**fate** ak-**kom**-plee] n French something already done that cannot be altered.

faith ❶ n **1** strong belief, esp. without proof. **2** religion. **3** complete confidence or trust. **4** allegiance to a person or cause. **faithful** adj **1** loyal. **2** maintaining sexual loyalty to one's lover or spouse. **3** consistently reliable. **4** accurate in detail. **faithfully** adv **faithless** adj disloyal or dishonest. **faith-healing** n healing of bodily ailments by religious rather than medical means. **faith-healer** n.

fake ❶ v **1** cause something not genuine to appear real or more valuable by fraud. **2** pretend to have (an illness, emotion, etc.). ▷ n **3** person, thing, or act that is not genuine. ▷ adj **4** not genuine.

fakir [**fay**-keer] n **1** member of any Islamic religious order. **2** Hindu holy man.

falcon n small bird of prey. **falconry** n **1** art of training falcons. **2** sport of hunting with falcons. **falconer** n.

fall ❶ v **falling, fell, fallen 1** drop from a higher to a lower place through the force of gravity. **2** collapse to the ground. **3** decrease in number or quality. **4** slope downwards. **5** die in battle. **6** be captured. **7** pass into a specified condition. **8** (of the face) take on a sad expression. **9** occur. **10** yield to temptation. ▷ n **11** falling. **12** thing or amount that falls. **13** decrease in value or number. **14** decline in power or influence. **15** capture or overthrow. **16** US autumn. ▷ pl **17** waterfall. **fall flat** fail utterly. **fall behind** v **1** fail to keep up. **2** be in arrears with a payment etc. **fall for** v **1** informal fall in love with. **2** be deceived by (a lie or trick). **fall guy 1** informal victim of a confidence trick. **2** scapegoat. **fall in** v **1** collapse. **2** (of a soldier etc.) take his or her place in a formation. **fall in with** v **1** meet with and join. **2** agree with or support a

— THESAURUS —

equity, justice, legitimacy, rightfulness

fairy n **1** = **sprite**, brownie, elf, leprechaun, peri, pixie

fairy tale, story n **1** = **folk tale**, romance **2** = **lie**, cock-and-bull story (inf), fabrication, fiction, invention, tall story, untruth, urban legend, urban myth

faith n **1, 3** = **confidence**, assurance, conviction, credence, credit, dependence, reliance, trust **2** = **religion**, belief, church, communion, creed, denomination, dogma, persuasion **4** = **allegiance**, constancy, faithfulness, fidelity, loyalty

faithful adj **1-3** = **loyal**, constant, dependable, devoted, reliable, staunch, steadfast, true, trusty **4** = **accurate**, close, exact, precise, strict, true

faithless adj = **disloyal**, false, fickle, inconstant, traitorous, treacherous, unfaithful, unreliable

fake v **1** = **counterfeit**, copy, fabricate, forge **2** = **sham**, feign, pretend, put on, simulate ▷ n **3** = **impostor**, charlatan, copy, forgery, fraud, hoax, imitation, reproduction, sham ▷ adj **4** = **artificial**, counterfeit, false, forged, imitation, mock, phoney or phony (inf), sham

fall v **1, 2** = **descend**, cascade, collapse, dive, drop, plummet, plunge, sink, subside, tumble **3** = **decrease**, decline, diminish, drop, dwindle, go down, lessen, slump, subside **4** = **slope**, fall away, incline **5** = **die**, be killed, cark (Aust & NZ sl), meet one's end, perish **6** = **be overthrown**, capitulate, pass into enemy hands, succumb, surrender **9** = **occur**, befall, chance, come about, come to pass, happen, take place **10** = **lapse**, err, go astray, offend, sin, transgress, trespass ▷ n **11** = **descent**, dive, drop, nose dive, plummet, plunge, slip, tumble **13** = **decrease**, cut, decline, dip, drop, lessening,

person or idea. **fallout** n radioactive particles spread as a result of a nuclear explosion. **fall out** v **1** informal stop being friendly, disagree. **2** (of a soldier etc.) leave his or her place in a formation. **fall through** v fail. **fall to** v **1** (of a task or duty) become (someone's) responsibility. **2** begin some activity.

fallacy ❶ n, pl -cies **1** false belief. **2** unsound reasoning. **fallacious** adj.

fallen v past participle of FALL.

fallible ❶ adj (of a person) liable to make mistakes. **fallibility** n.

Fallopian tube n either of a pair of tubes through which egg cells pass from the ovary to the womb.

fallow¹ ❶ adj (of land) ploughed but left unseeded to regain fertility.

fallow² adj light yellowish-brown. **fallow deer** reddish-brown deer with white spots in summer.

false ❶ adj **1** not true or correct. **2** artificial, fake. **3** deceptive, e.g. false promises. **4** forced or insincere, e.g. false cheer. **falsely** adv **falseness** n **falsity** n, pl -ties **1** state of being false.

2 lie. **falsehood** n **1** quality of being untrue. **2** lie.

falsetto n, pl -tos voice pitched higher than one's natural range.

falsify ❶ v -fying, -fied alter fraudulently. **falsification** n.

falter ❶ v **1** be hesitant, weak, or unsure. **2** lose power momentarily. **3** utter hesitantly. **4** move unsteadily. **faltering** adj.

fame ❶ n state of being widely known or recognized. **famed** adj famous.

familiar ❶ adj **1** well-known. **2** frequent or common. **3** intimate, friendly. **4** too friendly. ▷ n **5** demon supposed to attend a witch. **6** friend. **familiarly** adv **familiarity** n, pl -ties. **familiarize** v acquaint fully with a particular subject. **familiarization** n.

family ❶ n, pl -lies **1** group of parents and their children. **2** one's spouse and children. **3** one's children. **4** group descended from a common ancestor. **5** group of related objects or beings. ▷ adj **6** suitable for parents and children together. **familial** adj **family doctor** informal same as GENERAL

lowering, reduction, slump **14, 15** = **collapse**, capitulation, defeat, destruction, downfall, overthrow, ruin

fallacy n **1** = **error**, delusion, falsehood, flaw, misapprehension, misconception, mistake, untruth

fallible adj = **imperfect**, erring, frail, ignorant, uncertain, weak

fall out v **1** Inf = **argue**, clash, come to blows, differ, disagree, fight, quarrel, squabble

fallow¹ adj = **uncultivated**, dormant, idle, inactive, resting, unplanted, unused

false adj **1** = **incorrect**, erroneous, faulty, inaccurate, inexact, invalid, mistaken, wrong **2** = **artificial**, bogus, counterfeit, fake, forged, imitation, sham, simulated **3** = **untrue**, deceitful, deceptive, fallacious, fraudulent, hypocritical, lying, misleading, trumped up, unreliable, unsound, untruthful

falsehood n **1** = **untruthfulness**, deceit, deception, dishonesty, dissimulation, mendacity **2** = **lie**, fabrication, fib, fiction, story, untruth

falsify v = **alter**, counterfeit, distort, doctor, fake, forge, misrepresent, tamper with

falter v **1** = **hesitate**, vacillate, waver **3** = **stutter**, stammer **4** = **stumble**, totter

faltering adj **1** = **hesitant**, irresolute, tentative, timid, uncertain, weak **3** = **stammering**, broken

fame n = **prominence**, celebrity, glory, honour, renown, reputation, repute, stardom

familiar adj **1** = **well-known**, recognizable **2** = **common**, accustomed, customary, frequent, ordinary, routine **3** = **friendly**, amicable, close, easy, intimate, relaxed **4** = **disrespectful**, bold, forward, impudent, intrusive, presumptuous

familiarity n **1** = **acquaintance**, awareness, experience, grasp, understanding **3** = **friendliness**, ease, informality, intimacy, openness, sociability **4** = **disrespect**, boldness, forwardness, presumption

familiarize v = **accustom**, habituate, instruct, inure, school, season, train

family n **1, 2** = **relations**, folk (inf), household, kin, kith and kin, one's nearest and dearest, one's own flesh and blood, relatives **4** = **clan**, dynasty, house, race, tribe **5** = **group**,

PRACTITIONER. **family name** surname, esp. when seen as representing a family's good reputation. **family planning** control of the number of children in a family by the use of contraception. **family tree** chart showing the relationships between individuals in a family over many generations.

famine ❶ n severe shortage of food.

famished ❶ adj very hungry.

famous ❶ adj very well-known. **famously** adv informal excellently.

fan¹ ❶ n 1 hand-held or mechanical object used to create a current of air for ventilation or cooling. ▷ v **fanning**, **fanned 2** blow or cool with a fan. **3** spread out like a fan. **fanbase** n body of admirers of a particular pop singer, sports team, etc. **fan belt** belt that drives a cooling fan in a car engine. **fan heater** heater which uses a fan to spread warmed air through a room. **fanlight** n semicircular window over a door or window.

fan² ❶ n informal devotee of a pop star, sport, or hobby.

fanatic ❶ n person who is excessively enthusiastic about something. **fanatical** adj **fanatically** adv **fanaticism** n.

fancy ❶ adj **-cier**, **-ciest 1** elaborate, not plain. **2** (of prices) higher than usual. ▷ n, pl **-cies 3** sudden irrational liking or desire. **4** uncontrolled imagination. ▷ v **-cying**, **-cied 5** informal be sexually attracted to. **6** informal have a wish for. **7** picture in the imagination. **8** suppose. **fancy oneself** informal have a high opinion of oneself. **fancier** n person who is interested in and often breeds plants or animals, e.g. a pigeon fancier. **fanciful** adj 1 not based on fact. **2** excessively elaborate. **fancifully** adv **fancy dress** party costume representing a historical figure, animal, etc. **fancy-free** adj not in love. **fancy goods** small decorative gifts.

fandango n, pl **-gos** lively Spanish dance.

fanfare n short loud tune played on brass instruments.

fang n 1 snake's tooth which injects poison. **2** long pointed tooth.

fanny n, pl **-nies** slang 1 Brit taboo female genitals. **2** US buttocks.

fantasia n musical composition of an improvised nature.

fantastic ❶ adj 1 informal very good. **2** unrealistic or absurd. **3** strange or difficult to believe. **fantastically** adv.

fantasy ❶ n, pl **-sies 1** far-fetched notion. **2** imagination unrestricted by

——————————————— THESAURUS ———————————————

class, genre, network, subdivision, system

famine n = **hunger**, dearth, scarcity, starvation

famished adj = **starving**, ravenous, voracious

famous adj = **well-known**, acclaimed, celebrated, distinguished, eminent, illustrious, legendary, noted, prominent, renowned

fan¹ n 1 = **blower**, air conditioner, ventilator ▷ v 2 = **blow**, air-condition, cool, refresh, ventilate

fan² n Inf = **supporter**, admirer, aficionado, buff (inf), devotee, enthusiast, follower, lover

fanatic n = **extremist**, activist, bigot, militant, zealot

fanatical adj = **obsessive**, bigoted, extreme, fervent, frenzied, immoderate, overenthusiastic, passionate, wild, zealous

fanciful adj 1 = **unreal**, imaginary, mythical, romantic, visionary, whimsical, wild

fancy adj 1 = **elaborate**, baroque, decorative, embellished, extravagant, intricate, ornamental, ornate ▷ n 3 = **whim**, caprice, desire, humour, idea, impulse, inclination, notion, thought, urge 4 = **delusion**, chimera, daydream, dream, fantasy, vision ▷ v 5 Inf = **be attracted to**, be captivated by, like, lust after, take a liking to, take to 6 Inf = **wish for**, crave, desire, hanker after, hope for, long for, thirst for, yearn for 7, 8 = **suppose**, believe, conjecture, imagine, reckon, think, think likely

fantasize v = **daydream**, dream, envision, imagine

fantastic adj 1 Inf = **wonderful**, awesome (sl), excellent, first-rate, marvellous, sensational (inf), superb 2 = **unrealistic**, extravagant, far-fetched, ludicrous, ridiculous, wild 3 = **strange**, absurd, cock-and-bull (inf), fanciful, grotesque, implausible, incredible, outlandish, preposterous, unlikely

fantasy n 1, 3 = **daydream**, dream, flight of fancy, illusion, mirage, pipe

reality. **3** daydream. **4** fiction with a large fantasy content. **fantasize** v indulge in daydreams.

fanzine [**fan**-zeen] n magazine produced by fans of a specific interest, football club, etc., for fellow fans.

FAQ Computers frequently asked question or questions.

far ⊕ adv **farther** or **further**, **farthest** or **furthest 1** at, to, or from a great distance. **2** at or to a remote time. **3** very much. ▷ adj **4** remote in space or time. **faraway** adj **1** very distant. **2** absent-minded. **Far East** East Asia. **far-fetched** adj hard to believe. **far-flung** adj **1** distributed over a wide area. **2** very distant. **far-reaching** adj extensive in influence, effect, or range. **far-sighted** adj having or showing foresight and wisdom.

farad n unit of electrical capacitance.

farce ⊕ n **1** boisterous comedy. **2** ludicrous situation. **farcical** adj ludicrous. **farcically** adv.

fare ⊕ n **1** charge for a passenger's journey. **2** passenger. **3** food provided. ▷ v **4** get on (as specified), e.g. we fared badly. **fare stage 1** section of a bus journey for which a set charge is made. **2** bus stop marking the end of such a section.

farewell ⊕ interj **1** goodbye. ▷ n **2** act of saying goodbye and leaving. ▷ v NZ say goodbye.

farinaceous adj containing starch or having a starchy texture.

farm ⊕ n **1** area of land for growing crops or rearing livestock. **2** area of land or water for growing or rearing a specified animal or plant, e.g. fish farm. ▷ v **3** cultivate (land). **4** rear (stock). **farmer** n **farmers' market** market at which farm produce is sold directly to the public by the producer. **farm hand** person employed to work on a farm. **farmhouse** n **farm out** v send (work) to be done by others. **farmstead** n farm and its buildings. **farmyard** n.

farrago [far-**rah**-go] n, pl **-gos**, **-goes** jumbled mixture of things.

farrier n person who shoes horses.

farrow n **1** litter of piglets. ▷ v **2** (of a sow) give birth.

fart taboo ▷ n **1** emission of gas from the anus. ▷ v **2** emit gas from the anus.

farther, farthest adv, adj see FAR.

farthing n former British coin equivalent to a quarter of a penny.

farthingale n obs hoop worn under skirts in the Elizabethan period.

fascia [**fay**-shya] n, pl **-ciae**, **-cias 1** outer surface of a dashboard. **2** flat surface above a shop window.

fascinate ⊕ v **1** attract and interest strongly. **2** make motionless from fear or awe. **fascinating** adj **fascination** n.

● **SPELLING TIP**
● Remember that there is a silent c
● after the s in **fascinate**, **fascinated**,
● and **fascinating**.

THESAURUS

dream, reverie, vision **2** = **imagination**, creativity, fancy, invention, originality

far adv **1** = **a long way**, afar, a good way, a great distance, deep, miles **3** = **much**, considerably, decidedly, extremely, greatly, incomparably, very much ▷ adj **4** = **remote**, distant, faraway, far-flung, far-off, outlying, out-of-the-way

farce n **1** = **comedy**, buffoonery, burlesque, satire, slapstick **2** = **mockery**, joke, nonsense, parody, sham, travesty

farcical adj = **ludicrous**, absurd, comic, derisory, laughable, nonsensical, preposterous, ridiculous, risible

fare n **1** = **charge**, price, ticket money **3** = **food**, provisions, rations, sustenance, victuals ▷ v **4** = **get on**, do, get along, make out, manage, prosper

farewell n **2** = **goodbye**, adieu, departure, leave-taking, parting, sendoff (inf), valediction

far-fetched adj = **unconvincing**, cock-and-bull (inf), fantastic, implausible, incredible, preposterous, unbelievable, unlikely, unrealistic

farm n **1** = **smallholding**, croft (Scot), farmstead, grange, homestead, plantation, ranch (chiefly N Amer) ▷ v **3** = **cultivate**, plant, work

fascinate v **1** = **entrance**, absorb, beguile, captivate, engross, enthral, hold spellbound, intrigue **2** = **transfix**, rivet

fascinating adj **1** = **captivating**, alluring, compelling, engaging, engrossing, enticing, gripping, intriguing, irresistible, riveting

fascination n **1** = **attraction**, allure, charm, enchantment, lure, magic, magnetism, pull

fascism [**fash**-iz-zum] n right-wing totalitarian political system characterized by state control and extreme nationalism. **fascist** adj, n.

fashion ❶ n **1** style in clothes, hairstyle, etc., popular at a particular time. **2** way something happens or is done. ▷ v **3** form or make into a particular shape. **fashionable** adj currently popular. **fashionably** adv.

fast¹ ❶ adj **1** (capable of) acting or moving quickly. **2** done in or lasting a short time. **3** adapted to or allowing rapid movement. **4** (of a clock or watch) showing a time later than the correct time. **5** dissipated. **6** firmly fixed, fastened, or shut. **7** (of colours and dyes) not likely to fade. ▷ adv **8** quickly. **9** soundly, deeply, e.g. *fast asleep*. **10** tightly and firmly. **pull a fast one** informal trick or deceive someone. **fast food** food, such as hamburgers, prepared and served very quickly. **fast lane 1** outside lane on a motorway. **2** quickest but most competitive route to success. **fast-track** adj **1** taking the quickest but most competitive route to success, e. g. *fast-track executives*. ▷ v **2** speed up the progress of (a project or person).

fast² ❶ v **1** go without food, esp. for religious reasons. ▷ n **2** period of fasting.

fasten ❶ v **1** make or become firmly fixed or joined. **2** close by fixing in place or locking. **3** (foll. by *on*) direct (one's attention) towards. **fastener**, **fastening** n device that fastens.

fastidious adj **1** very fussy about details. **2** excessively concerned with cleanliness. **fastidiously** adv **fastidiousness** n.

fastness n fortress, safe place.

fat ❶ adj **fatter**, **fattest 1** having excess flesh on the body. **2** (of meat) containing a lot of fat. **3** thick. **4** profitable. ▷ n **5** extra flesh on the body. **6** oily substance obtained from animals or plants. **fatness** n **fatten** v (cause to) become fat. **fatty** adj **fattier**, **fattiest** containing fat. **fathead** n informal stupid person. **fat-headed** adj **fat stock** livestock fattened and ready for market.

fatal ❶ adj causing death or ruin. **fatally** adv **fatality** n, pl **-ties** death caused by an accident or disaster.

fatalism n belief that all events are predetermined and people are powerless to change their destinies. **fatalist** n **fatalistic** adj.

fate ❶ n **1** power supposed to predetermine events. **2** inevitable fortune that befalls a person or thing. **fated** adj **1** destined. **2** doomed to death or destruction. **fateful** adj

————————————————————— THESAURUS —————————————————————

fashion n **1** = **style**, craze, custom, fad, look, mode, rage, trend, vogue **2** = **method**, manner, mode, style, way ▷ v **3** = **make**, construct, create, forge, form, manufacture, mould, shape

fashionable adj = **popular**, à la mode, chic, in (inf), in vogue, modern, stylish, trendy (Brit inf), up-to-date, with it (inf)

fast¹ adj **1-3** = **quick**, brisk, fleet, flying, hasty, nippy (Brit inf), rapid, speedy, swift **5** = **dissipated**, dissolute, extravagant, loose, profligate, reckless, self-indulgent, wanton, wild **6** = **fixed**, close, fastened, firm, immovable, secure, sound, steadfast, tight ▷ adv **8** = **quickly**, hastily, hurriedly, in haste, like lightning, rapidly, speedily, swiftly **9** = **soundly**, deeply, firmly, fixedly, securely, tightly

fast² v **1** = **go hungry**, abstain, deny oneself, go without food ▷ n **2** = **fasting**, abstinence

fasten v **1, 2** = **fix**, affix, attach, bind, connect, join, link, secure, tie

fat adj **1** = **overweight**, corpulent, heavy, obese, plump, podgy, portly, rotund, stout, tubby **2** = **fatty**, adipose, greasy, oily, oleaginous ▷ n **5** = **fatness**, blubber, bulk, corpulence, flab, flesh, obesity, paunch

fatal adj **a** = **lethal**, deadly, final, incurable, killing, malignant, mortal, terminal **b** = **disastrous**, baleful, baneful, calamitous, catastrophic, ruinous

fatality n = **death**, casualty, loss, mortality

fate n **1** = **destiny**, chance, divine will, fortune, kismet, nemesis, predestination, providence **2** = **fortune**, cup, horoscope, lot, portion, stars

fated adj **1** = **destined**, foreordained, inescapable, inevitable, predestined, preordained, sure, written **2** = **doomed**

having important, usu. disastrous, consequences.

father ❶ *n* **1** male parent. **2** person who founds a line or family. **3** man who starts, creates, or invents something. **4** (**F-**) God. **5** (**F-**) title of some priests. ▷ *v* **6** be the father of (offspring). **fatherhood** *n* **fatherless** *adj* **fatherly** *adj* **father-in-law** *n, pl* **fathers-in-law** father of one's husband or wife. **fatherland** *n* one's native country.

fathom ❶ *n* **1** unit of measurement of the depth of water, equal to six feet. ▷ *v* **2** understand. **fathomable** *adj* **fathomless** *adj* too deep or difficult to fathom.

fatigue ❶ [fat-**eeg**] *n* **1** extreme physical or mental tiredness. **2** weakening of a material due to stress. **3** soldier's nonmilitary duty. ▷ *pl* **4** soldier's clothing for nonmilitary duty. ▷ *v* **5** tire out.

fatuous ❶ *adj* foolish. **fatuously** *adv* **fatuity** *n, pl* **-ties 1** foolish thoughtlessness. **2** fatuous remark.

faucet ❶ [**faw**-set] *n US & Canad* valve with handle, plug etc. to regulate or stop flow of fluid.

fault ❶ *n* **1** responsibility for something wrong. **2** defect or flaw. **3** mistake or error. **4** *Geology* break in layers of rock. **5** *Tennis, Squash, etc.* invalid serve. ▷ *v* **6** criticize or blame. **at fault** guilty of error. **find fault with** seek out minor imperfections in. **to a fault** excessively. **faulty** *adj* **faultless** *adj* **faultlessly** *adv*.

faun *n* (in Roman legend) creature with a human face and torso and a goat's horns and legs.

fauna *n, pl* **-nas, -nae** animals of a given place or time.

faux pas [foe pah] *n, pl* **faux pas** social blunder.

favour ❶ *n* **1** approving attitude. **2** act of goodwill or generosity. **3** partiality. ▷ *v* **4** prefer. **5** regard or treat with especial kindness. **6** support or advocate. **favourable** *adj* **favourite** *n* preferred person or thing.

THESAURUS

fateful *adj* **a** = **crucial**, critical, decisive, important, portentous, significant **b** = **disastrous**, deadly, destructive, fatal, lethal, ominous, ruinous

father *n* **1** = **daddy** (*inf*), dad (*inf*), old man (*inf*), pa (*inf*), papa (*old-fashioned inf*), pater, pop (*inf*) **2** = **forefather**, ancestor, forebear, predecessor, progenitor **3** = **founder**, architect, author, creator, inventor, maker, originator, prime mover **5** (with cap.) = **priest**, padre (*inf*), pastor ▷ *v* **6** = **sire**, beget, get, procreate

fatherland *n* = **homeland**, motherland, native land

fatherly *adj* **1** = **paternal**, affectionate, benevolent, benign, kindly, patriarchal, protective, supportive

fathom *v* **2** = **understand**, comprehend, get to the bottom of, grasp, interpret

fatigue *n* **1** = **tiredness**, heaviness, languor, lethargy, listlessness ▷ *v* **5** = **tire**, drain, exhaust, knacker (*sl*), take it out of (*inf*), weaken, wear out, weary

fatten *v* = **grow fat**, expand, gain weight, put on weight, spread, swell, thicken

fatty *adj* = **greasy**, adipose, fat, oily, oleaginous, rich

fatuous *adj* = **foolish**, brainless, idiotic, inane, ludicrous, mindless, moronic, silly, stupid, witless

faucet *n* (US & Canad) = **tap**, spout, spigot, stopcock, valve

fault *n* **1** = **responsibility**, accountability, culpability, liability **2** = **flaw**, blemish, defect, deficiency, failing, imperfection, shortcoming, weakness, weak point **3** = **mistake**, blunder, error, indiscretion, lapse, oversight, slip ▷ *v* **6** = **criticize**, blame, censure, find fault with, hold (someone) responsible, impugn **at fault** = **guilty**, answerable, blamable, culpable, in the wrong, responsible, to blame **find fault with** = **criticize**, carp at, complain, pick holes in, pull to pieces, quibble, take to task **to a fault** = **excessively**, immoderately, in the extreme, overmuch, unduly

faultless 1 *adj* = **flawless**, foolproof, impeccable, model, perfect, unblemished ▷ *adj* **2** = **correct**, exemplary

faulty *adj* **1** = **defective**, broken, damaged, flawed, impaired, imperfect, malfunctioning, out of order **2** = **incorrect**, unsound

favour *n* **1** = **approval**, approbation, backing, good opinion, goodwill,

favourable ⊙ *adj* **1** encouraging or advantageous. **2** giving consent. **3** useful or beneficial. **favourably** *adv*.

favourite ⊙ *adj* **1** most liked. ▷ *n* **2** preferred person or thing. **3** *Sport* competitor expected to win. **favouritism** *n* practice of giving special treatment to a person or group.

fawn¹ ⊙ *n* **1** young deer. ▷ *adj* **2** light yellowish-brown.

fawn² ⊙ *v* **1** (foll. by *on*) seek attention from (someone) by insincere flattery. **2** (of a dog) try to please by a show of extreme affection.

fax *n* **1** electronic system for sending facsimiles of documents by telephone. **2** document sent by this system. ▷ *v* **3** send (a document) by this system.

faze *v informal* disconcert or fluster.

FBI *US* Federal Bureau of Investigation.

FC Football Club.

Fe *Chemistry* iron.

fealty *n* (in feudal society) subordinate's loyalty to his ruler or lord.

fear ⊙ *n* **1** distress or alarm caused by impending danger or pain. **2** something that causes distress. ▷ *v* **3** be afraid of (something or someone). **fear for** feel anxiety about something. **fearful** *adj* **1** feeling fear. **2** causing fear. **3** *informal* very unpleasant. **fearfully** *adv* **fearless** *adj* **fearlessly** *adv* **fearsome** *adj* terrifying.

feasible ⊙ *adj* able to be done, possible. **feasibly** *adv* **feasibility** *n*.

feast ⊙ *n* **1** lavish meal. **2** something extremely pleasing. **3** annual religious celebration. ▷ *v* **4** eat a feast. **5** give a feast to. **6** (foll. by *on*) eat a large amount of. **feast one's eyes on** look at (someone or something) with a great deal of pleasure.

feat ⊙ *n* remarkable, skilful, or daring action.

————————————————— THESAURUS —————

patronage, support **2 = good turn**, benefit, boon, courtesy, indulgence, kindness, service ▷ *v* **4, 5 = prefer**, incline towards, indulge, reward, side with, smile upon **6 = support**, advocate, approve, champion, commend, encourage

favourable *adj* **1, 3 = advantageous**, auspicious, beneficial, encouraging, helpful, opportune, promising, propitious, suitable **2 = positive**, affirmative, agreeable, approving, encouraging, enthusiastic, reassuring, sympathetic

favourably *adv* **1, 3 = advantageously**, auspiciously, conveniently, fortunately, opportunely, profitably, to one's advantage, well **2 = positively**, approvingly, enthusiastically, helpfully, with approval

favourite *adj* **1 = preferred**, best-loved, choice, dearest, esteemed, favoured ▷ *n* **2 = darling**, beloved, blue-eyed boy (*inf*), idol, pet, teacher's pet, the apple of one's eye

fawn¹ *adj* **2 = beige**, buff, greyish-brown, neutral

fawn² *v* **1** (foll. by *on*) **= ingratiate oneself**, crawl, creep, curry favour, dance attendance, flatter, grovel, kowtow, pander to

fawning *adj* **1 = obsequious**, crawling, cringing, deferential, flattering, grovelling, servile, sycophantic

fear *n* **1 = dread**, alarm, apprehensiveness, fright, horror, panic, terror, trepidation **2 = bugbear**, bête noire, bogey, horror, nightmare, spectre ▷ *v* **3 = be afraid**, dread, shake in one's shoes, shudder at, take fright, tremble at ▷ *v* **fear for = worry about**, be anxious about, feel concern for

fearful *adj* **1 = scared**, afraid, alarmed, frightened, jumpy, nervous, timid, timorous, uneasy **2, 3 = frightful**, awful, dire, dreadful, gruesome, hair-raising, horrendous, horrific, terrible

fearfully *adv* **1 = nervously**, apprehensively, diffidently, timidly, timorously, uneasily

fearless *adj* **= brave**, bold, courageous, dauntless, indomitable, intrepid, plucky, unafraid, undaunted, valiant

fearsome *adj* **= terrifying**, awe-inspiring, daunting, formidable, frightening, horrifying, menacing, unnerving

feasible *adj* **= possible**, achievable, attainable, likely, practicable, reasonable, viable, workable

feast *n* **1 = banquet**, dinner, repast, spread (*inf*), treat **2 = treat**, delight, enjoyment, gratification, pleasure **3 = festival**, celebration, fete, holiday, holy day, red-letter day, saint's day ▷ *v* **4 = eat one's fill**, gorge, gormandize, indulge, overindulge, pig out (*sl*) **5 = wine and dine**

feat *n* **= accomplishment**,

feather n 1 one of the barbed shafts forming the plumage of birds. ▷ v 2 fit or cover with feathers. 3 turn (an oar) edgeways. **feather in one's cap** achievement one can be pleased with. **feather one's nest** make one's life comfortable. **feathered** adj **feathery** adj **featherbedding** n practice of working deliberately slowly so that more workers are employed than are necessary. **featherweight** n 1 boxer weighing from 118lb or 53.5kg (professional), 119lb or 54kg (amateur), up to 126lb or 57kg. 2 insignificant person or thing.

feature ❶ n 1 part of the face, such as the eyes. 2 prominent or distinctive part. 3 special article in a newspaper or magazine. 4 main film in a cinema programme. ▷ v 5 have as a feature or be a feature in. 6 give prominence to. **featureless** adj.

Feb. February.

febrile [fee-brile] adj 1 very active and nervous, e.g. increasingly febrile activity at the Stock Exchange. 2 feverish.

February n second month of the year.

feckless ❶ adj ineffectual or irresponsible.

fecund adj fertile. **fecundity** n.

fed ❶ v past of FEED. **fed up** informal bored, dissatisfied.

federal ❶ adj 1 of a system in which power is divided between one central government and several regional governments. 2 of the central government of a federation. **federalism** n **federalist** n **federate** v unite in a federation. **federation** n 1 union of several states, provinces, etc. 2 association.

fedora [fid-**or**-a] n man's soft hat with a brim.

fee ❶ n 1 charge paid to be allowed to do something. 2 payment for professional services.

feeble ❶ adj 1 lacking physical or mental power. 2 unconvincing. **feebleness** n **feebly** adv **feeble-minded** adj unable to think or understand effectively.

feed ❶ v **feeding**, **fed** 1 give food to. 2 give (something) as food. 3 eat. 4 supply or prepare food for. 5 supply (what is needed). ▷ n 6 act of feeding. 7 food, esp. for babies or animals. 8 informal meal. **feeder** n 1 baby's bib. 2 device used to feed an animal, child, or sick person. 3 road or railway line linking outlying areas to the main traffic network. **feedback** n 1 information received in response to something done. 2 return of part of the output of an electrical circuit or loudspeaker to its source.

feel ❶ v **feeling**, **felt** 1 have a physical or emotional sensation of. 2 become

achievement, act, attainment, deed, exploit, performance

feathers pl n 1 = **plumage**, down, plumes

feature n 2 = **aspect**, characteristic, facet, factor, hallmark, peculiarity, property, quality, trait 3 = **article**, column, item, piece, report, story 4 = **highlight**, attraction, main item, speciality ▷ v 6 = **spotlight**, emphasize, foreground, give prominence to, play up, present, star

features pl n 1 = **face**, countenance, lineaments, physiognomy

feckless adj = **irresponsible**, good-for-nothing, hopeless, incompetent, ineffectual, shiftless, worthless

federation n = **union**, alliance, amalgamation, association, coalition, combination, league, syndicate

fed up adj Inf = **dissatisfied**, bored, depressed, discontented, down in the mouth, glum, sick and tired, tired

fee n = **charge**, bill, payment, remuneration, toll

feeble adj 1 = **weak**, debilitated, doddering, effete, frail, infirm, puny, sickly, weedy (inf) 2 = **flimsy**, inadequate, insufficient, lame, paltry, pathetic, poor, tame, thin, unconvincing

feebleness n 1 = **weakness**, effeteness, frailty, infirmity, languor, lassitude, sickliness

feed v 1, 2, 4 = **cater for**, nourish, provide for, provision, supply, sustain, victual, wine and dine 3 = **eat**, devour, exist on, live on, partake of ▷ n 7 = **food**, fodder, pasturage, provender 8 Inf = **meal**, feast, nosh (sl), repast, spread (inf)

feel v 1 = **experience**, be aware of, notice, observe, perceive 2 = **touch**, caress, finger, fondle, handle, manipulate, paw, stroke 3 = **sense**, be convinced, intuit 4 = **believe**, consider, deem, hold, judge, think ▷ n

aware of or examine by touch. **3** sense by intuition. **4** believe. ▷ *n* **5** act of feeling. **6** impression. **7** way something feels. **8** sense of touch. **9** instinctive aptitude. **feeler** *n* **1** organ of touch in some animals. **2** remark made to test others' opinion. **feeling** *n* **1** emotional reaction. **2** intuitive understanding. **3** opinion. **4** sympathy, understanding. **5** ability to experience physical sensations. **6** sensation experienced. ▷ *pl* **7** emotional sensitivities. **feel like** wish for, want. **feel for** *v* **1** attempt to find by touch alone. **2** have sympathy or compassion for someone in trouble. **feel up to** *v* be fit or energetic enough to.

feet *n* plural of FOOT.

feign [fane] *v* pretend. **feigned** *adj*.

feint[1] [faint] *n* **1** sham attack or blow meant to distract an opponent. ▷ *v* **2** make a feint.

feint[2] [faint] *n* narrow lines on ruled paper.

feisty ❶ *adj* **1** *inf* lively, resilient, and self-reliant. **2** *US & Canad* frisky. **3** *US & Canad* irritable.

feldspar *n* hard mineral that is the main constituent of igneous rocks.

felicity *n* **1** happiness. **2** *pl* **-ties** appropriate expression or style. **felicitations** *pl n* congratulations. **felicitous** *adj*.

feline *adj* **1** of cats. **2** catlike. ▷ *n* **3** member of the cat family.

fell[1] *v* past tense of FALL.

fell[2] ❶ *v* **1** cut down (a tree). **2** knock down.

fell[3] *adj* **in one fell swoop** in a single action or occurrence.

fell[4] *n* *Scot & N English* a mountain, hill, or moor.

fell[5] *n* animal's skin or hide with its hair.

felloe *n* (segment of) the rim of a wheel.

fellow ❶ *n* **1** *old-fashioned* man or boy. **2** comrade or associate. **3** person in the same group or condition. **4** member of a learned society or the governing body of a college. ▷ *adj* **5** in the same group or condition. **fellowship** *n* **1** sharing of aims or interests. **2** group with shared aims or interests. **3** feeling of friendliness. **4** paid research post in a college or university. **fellow feeling** sympathy between people who have undergone the same experience. **fellow traveller** Communist sympathizer who is not a Communist Party member.

felon *n* *Criminal law* (formerly) person guilty of a felony. **felony** *n*, *pl* **-nies** serious crime. **felonious** *adj*.

felspar *n* same as FELDSPAR.

felt[1] *v* past of FEEL.

felt[2] *n* matted fabric made by bonding fibres by pressure. **felt-tip pen** pen with a writing point made from pressed fibres.

fem. feminine.

female *adj* **1** of the sex which bears offspring. **2** (of plants) producing fruits. ▷ *n* **3** female person or animal.

feminine ❶ *adj* **1** having qualities traditionally regarded as suitable for, or typical of, women. **2** of women. **3** belonging to a particular class of grammatical inflection in some languages. **femininity** *n* **feminism** *n* advocacy of equal rights for women. **feminist** *n*, *adj*.

─────────────────────────── **THESAURUS** ───────────

6 = impression, air, ambience, atmosphere, feeling, quality, sense
7 = texture, finish, surface, touch
feeler *n* **1 = antenna**, tentacle, whisker
2 = approach, advance, probe
feeling *n* **1 = emotion**, ardour, fervour, intensity, passion, sentiment, warmth
2 = impression, hunch, idea, inkling, notion, presentiment, sense, suspicion
3 = opinion, inclination, instinct, point of view, view **4 = sympathy**, compassion, concern, empathy, pity, sensibility, sensitivity, understanding
5 = sense of touch, perception, sensation **6 = atmosphere**, air, ambience, aura, feel, mood, quality

feisty *adjective* (*Informal*) = **fiery**, spirited, bold, plucky, vivacious
fell[1] *v* **1 = cut down**, cut, hew **2 = knock down**, demolish, level
fellow *n* **1** *Old-fashioned* = **man**, bloke (*Brit inf*), chap (*inf*), character, guy (*inf*), individual, person **2**,
3 = associate, colleague, companion, comrade, partner, peer
fellowship *n* **1, 3 = camaraderie**, brotherhood, companionship, sociability **2 = society**, association, brotherhood, club, fraternity, guild, league, order
feminine *adj* **1, 2 = womanly**, delicate, gentle, ladylike, soft, tender

femme fatale ❶ [**fam** fat-**tahl**] *n, pl* **femmes fatales** alluring woman who leads men into dangerous situations by her charm.

femur [**fee**-mer] *n* thighbone. **femoral** *adj* of the thigh.

fen ❶ *n* low-lying flat marshy land. **fenland** *n*.

fence ❶ *n* **1** barrier of posts linked by wire or wood, enclosing an area. **2** obstacle for a horse to jump in steeplechasing or showjumping. **3** *slang* dealer in stolen property. ▷ *v* **4** enclose with or as if with a fence. **5** fight with swords as a sport. **6** avoid a question. **fencing** *n* **1** sport of fighting with swords. **2** material for making fences. **fencer** *n*.

fend *v* **fend for oneself** provide for oneself. **fend off** *v* defend oneself against (verbal or physical attack).

fender *n* **1** low metal frame in front of a fireplace. **2** soft but solid object hung over a ship's side to prevent damage when docking. **3** *US & Canad* the part of a car body that surrounds the wheels.

feng shui [fung **shway**] *n* Chinese art of deciding the best design of a building, etc., in order to bring good luck.

Fenian [**feen**-yan] *n* member of a 19th-century Irish revolutionary organization founded to fight for an independent Ireland.

fennel *n* fragrant plant whose seeds, leaves, and root are used in cookery.

fenugreek *n* Mediterranean plant grown for its heavily scented seeds.

feoff [feef] *n History* same as FIEF.

feral *adj* wild.

ferment ❶ *n* **1** commotion, unrest. ▷ *v* **2** undergo or cause to undergo fermentation. **fermentation** *n* reaction in which an organic molecule splits into simpler substances, esp. the conversion of sugar to alcohol.

fermium *n Chemistry* element artificially produced by neutron bombardment of plutonium.

fern *n* flowerless plant with fine fronds.

ferocious ❶ *adj* savagely fierce or cruel. **ferocity** *n*.

ferret ❶ *n* **1** tamed polecat used to catch rabbits or rats. ▷ *v* **ferreting**, **ferreted 2** hunt with ferrets. **3** search around. **ferret out** *v* find by searching.

ferric, ferrous *adj* of or containing iron.

Ferris wheel *n* large vertical fairground wheel with hanging seats for riding in.

ferrule *n* metal cap to strengthen the end of a stick.

ferry ❶ *n, pl* **-ries 1** boat for transporting people and vehicles. **2** route or service operated by such a boat. ▷ *v* **-rying, -ried 3** carry by ferry. **4** convey (goods or people). **ferryboat** *n* **ferryman** *n*.

fertile ❶ *adj* **1** capable of producing young, crops, or vegetation. **2** highly productive, e.g. *a fertile mind*. **fertility** *n* **fertilize** *v* **1** provide (an animal or plant) with sperm or pollen to bring about fertilization. **2** supply (soil) with nutrients. **fertilization** *n* **fertilizer** *n* substance added to the soil to increase its productivity.

f

---

femme fatale *n* = **seductress**, enchantress, siren, vamp (*inf*)

fen *n* = **marsh**, bog, morass, quagmire, slough, swamp, muskeg (*Canad*)

fence *n* **1** = **barrier**, barricade, defence, hedge, palisade, railings, rampart, wall ▷ *v* **4** = **enclose**, bound, confine, encircle, pen, protect, surround **6** = **evade**, dodge, equivocate, flannel (*Brit inf*), parry

ferment *n* **1** = **commotion**, disruption, excitement, frenzy, furore, stir, tumult, turmoil, unrest, uproar

ferocious *adj* = **fierce**, bloodthirsty, brutal, cruel, predatory, rapacious, ravening, ruthless, savage, vicious, violent, wild

ferocity *n* = **savagery**, bloodthirstiness, brutality, cruelty, fierceness, viciousness, wildness

ferret out *v* = **track down**, dig up, discover, elicit, root out, search out, trace, unearth

ferry *n* **1** = **ferry boat**, packet, packet boat ▷ *v* **3, 4** = **carry**, chauffeur, convey, run, ship, shuttle, transport

fertile *adj* = **productive**, abundant, fecund, fruitful, luxuriant, plentiful, prolific, rich, teeming

fertility *n* = **fruitfulness**, abundance, fecundity, luxuriance, productiveness, richness

fertilizer *n* = **compost**, dressing, dung, manure

fervent, fervid ❶ *adj* intensely passionate and sincere. **fervently** *adv* **fervour** *n* intensity of feeling.

fescue *n* pasture and lawn grass with stiff narrow leaves.

fester ❶ *v* **1** grow worse and increasingly hostile, e.g. *the bitterness which had been festering beneath the surface.* **2** (of a wound) form pus. **3** rot and decay, e.g. *rubbish festered in the heat.*

festival ❶ *n* **1** organized series of special events or performances. **2** day or period of celebration. **festive** *adj* of or like a celebration. **festivity** *n, pl* **-ties 1** happy celebration. ▷ *pl* **2** celebrations.

festoon ❶ *v* hang decorations in loops.

feta *n* white salty Greek cheese.

fetal *adj* see FETUS.

fetch ❶ *v* **1** go after and bring back. **2** be sold for. **3** *informal* deal (a blow). **fetching** *adj* attractive. **fetch up** *v informal* arrive or end up.

fete [**fate**] *n* **1** gala, bazaar, etc., usu. held outdoors. ▷ *v* **2** honour or entertain regally.

fetid *adj* stinking.

fetish ❶ *n* **1** form of behaviour in which sexual pleasure is derived from looking at or handling an inanimate object. **2** thing with which one is excessively concerned. **3** object believed to have magical powers. **fetishism** *n*

fetishist *n* **fetishize** *or* **fetishise** *v*.

fetlock *n* projection behind and above a horse's hoof.

fetter *n* **1** chain or shackle for the foot. ▷ *pl* **2** restrictions. ▷ *v* **3** restrict. **4** bind in fetters.

fettle *n* state of health or spirits.

fetus, foetus [**fee**-tuss] *n, pl* **-tuses** embryo of a mammal in the later stages of development. **fetal**, **foetal** *adj*.

feu *n* (in Scotland) right of use of land in return for a fixed annual payment.

feud ❶ *n* **1** long bitter hostility between two people or groups. ▷ *v* **2** carry on a feud.

feudalism *n* medieval system in which people held land from a lord, and in return worked and fought for him. **feudal** *adj* of or like feudalism.

fever ❶ *n* **1** (illness causing) high body temperature. **2** nervous excitement. **fevered** *adj* **feverish** *adj* **1** suffering from fever. **2** in a state of nervous excitement. **feverishly** *adv* **fever pitch** state of great excitement.

few ❶ *adj* not many. **a few** a small number. **quite a few, a good few** several.

● **USAGE NOTE**
● *Few(er)* is used of things that can
● be counted: *Fewer than five visits.*
● Compare *less*, which is used for
● quantity: *It uses less sugar.*

————————————————————— THESAURUS —————————

fervent, fervid *adj* = **intense**, ardent, devout, earnest, enthusiastic, heartfelt, impassioned, passionate, vehement

fervour *n* = **intensity**, ardour, enthusiasm, excitement, passion, vehemence, warmth, zeal

fester *v* **1** = **intensify**, aggravate, smoulder **2** = **suppurate**, ulcerate **3** = **putrefy**, decay

festival *n* **1** = **celebration**, carnival, entertainment, fête, gala, jubilee **2** = **holy day**, anniversary, commemoration, feast, fete, fiesta, holiday, red-letter day, saint's day

festive *adj* = **celebratory**, cheery, convivial, happy, jovial, joyful, joyous, jubilant, merry

festivity *n* (often *pl*) = **celebration**, entertainment, festival, party

festoon *v* = **decorate**, array, deck, drape, garland, hang, swathe, wreathe

fetch *v* **1** = **bring**, carry, convey, deliver, get, go for, obtain, retrieve, transport **2** = **sell for**, bring in, earn, go for, make, realize, yield

fetching *adj* = **attractive**, alluring, captivating, charming, cute, enticing, winsome

fetish *n* **1, 2** = **fixation**, mania, obsession, thing (*inf*) **3** = **talisman**, amulet

feud *n* **1** = **hostility**, argument, conflict, disagreement, enmity, quarrel, rivalry, row, vendetta ▷ *v* **2** = **quarrel**, bicker, clash, contend, dispute, fall out, row, squabble, war

fever *n* **1** = **delirium 2** = **excitement**, agitation, ferment, fervour, frenzy, restlessness

feverish *adj* **1** = **hot**, febrile, fevered, flushed, inflamed, pyretic (*Med*) **2** = **excited**, agitated, frantic, frenetic, frenzied, overwrought, restless

few *adj* = **not many**, meagre, negligible, rare, scanty, scarcely any, sparse, sporadic

fey *adj* **1** whimsically strange. **2** having the ability to look into the future.

fez *n, pl* **fezzes** brimless tasselled cap, orig. from Turkey.

ff *Music* fortissimo.

ff. and the following (pages).

fiancé [fee-**on**-say] *n* man engaged to be married. **fiancée** *n fem*.

fiasco ⊕ *n, pl* **-cos, -coes** ridiculous or humiliating failure.

fiat [**fee**-at] *n* **1** arbitrary order. **2** official permission.

fib ⊕ *n* **1** trivial lie. ▷ *v* **fibbing, fibbed 2** tell a lie. **fibber** *n*.

fibre ⊕ *n* **1** thread that can be spun into yarn. **2** threadlike animal or plant tissue. **3** fibrous material in food. **4** strength of character. **5** essential substance or nature. **fibrous** *adj* **fibreboard** *n* building material made of compressed wood. **fibreglass** *n* material made of fine glass fibres, used as insulation. **fibre optics** transmission of information by light along very thin flexible fibres of glass.

fibrillation *n* uncontrollable twitching of muscles, esp. those in the heart.

fibroid [**fibe**-royd] *adj* **1** *Anat* (of structures or tissues) containing or resembling fibres. ▷ *n* **2** benign tumour composed of fibrous connective tissue. **fibrositis** [fibe-roh-**site**-iss] *n* inflammation of the tissues

of muscle sheaths.

fibula [**fib**-yew-la] *n, pl* **-lae, -las** slender outer bone of the lower leg. **fibular** *adj*.

fiche [**feesh**] *n* sheet of film for storing publications in miniaturized form.

fickle ⊕ *adj* changeable, inconstant. **fickleness** *n*.

fiction ⊕ *n* **1** literary works of the imagination, such as novels. **2** invented story. **fictional** *adj* **fictionalize** *v* turn into fiction. **fictitious** *adj* **1** not genuine. **2** of or in fiction.

fiddle ⊕ *n* **1** violin. **2** *informal* dishonest action or scheme. ▷ *v* **3** play the violin. **4** falsify (accounts). **5** move or touch something restlessly. **fiddling** *adj* trivial. **fiddly** *adj* **-lier, -liest** awkward to do or use. **fiddlesticks** *interj* expression of annoyance or disagreement.

fidelity ⊕ *n* **1** faithfulness. **2** accuracy in detail. **3** quality of sound reproduction.

fidget ⊕ *v* **1** move about restlessly. ▷ *n* **2** person who fidgets. ▷ *pl* **3** restlessness. **fidgety** *adj*.

fiduciary [fid-**yew**-she-er-ee]*Law* ▷ *n, pl* **-aries 1** person bound to act for someone else's benefit, as a trustee. ▷ *adj* **2** of a trust or trustee.

fie *interj obs or facetious* exclamation of disapproval.

———————— THESAURUS ————————

fiasco *n* = **flop** (*inf*), catastrophe, cock-up (*Brit sl*), debacle, disaster, failure, mess, washout (*inf*)

fib *n* **1** = **lie**, fiction, story, untruth, white lie

fibre *n* = **thread**, filament, pile, strand, texture, wisp **4** = **strength of character**, resolution, stamina, strength, toughness **5** = **essence**, nature, quality, spirit, substance

fickle *adj* = **changeable**, capricious, faithless, inconstant, irresolute, temperamental, unfaithful, variable, volatile

fiction *n* **1** = **tale**, fantasy, legend, myth, novel, romance, story, yarn (*inf*) **2** = **lie**, cock and bull story (*inf*), fabrication, falsehood, invention, tall story, untruth, urban legend, urban myth

fictional *adj* = **imaginary**, invented, legendary, made-up, nonexistent, unreal

fictitious *adj* **1** = **false**, bogus,

fabricated, imaginary, invented, made-up, make-believe, mythical, untrue

fiddle *n* **1** = **violin 2** *Inf* = **fraud**, fix, racket, scam (*sl*), swindle ▷ *v* **4** = **cheat**, cook the books (*inf*), diddle (*inf*), fix, swindle, wangle (*inf*) **5** = **fidget**, finger, interfere with, mess about *or* around, play, tamper with, tinker

fiddling *adj* = **trivial**, futile, insignificant, pettifogging, petty, trifling

fidelity *n* **1** = **loyalty**, allegiance, constancy, dependability, devotion, faithfulness, staunchness, trustworthiness **2** = **accuracy**, closeness, correspondence, exactness, faithfulness, precision, scrupulousness

fidget *v* **1** = **move restlessly**, fiddle (*inf*), fret, squirm, twitch ▷ *pl n* **3** = **restlessness**, fidgetiness, jitters (*inf*), nervousness, unease, uneasiness

fidgety *adj* = **restless** (*inf*), impatient,

fief [**feef**] *n History* land granted by a lord in return for war service.

field ● *n* **1** enclosed piece of agricultural land. **2** marked off area for sports. **3** area rich in a specified natural resource. **4** all the competitors in a competition. **5** all the competitors except the favourite. **6** battlefield. **7** sphere of knowledge or activity. **8** place away from the laboratory or classroom where practical work is done. **9** background, as of a flag. **10** area over which electric, gravitational, or magnetic force is exerted. ▷ *v* **11** *Sport* catch and return (a ball). **12** send (a player or team) on to the field. **13** play as a fielder. **14** deal with (a question) successfully. **fielder** *n Sport* player whose task is to field the ball. **field day** day or time of exciting activity. **field events** throwing and jumping events in athletics. **fieldfare** *n* type of large thrush. **field glasses** binoculars. **field hockey** *US* hockey played on grass, as distinguished from ice hockey. **field marshal** army officer of the highest rank. **fieldmouse** *n, pl* **-mice** nocturnal mouse that lives in fields and woods. **field sports** hunting, shooting, and fishing. **fieldwork** *n* investigation made in the field as opposed to the classroom or the laboratory.

fiend ● [**feend**] *n* **1** evil spirit. **2** cruel or wicked person. **3** *informal* person devoted to something, e.g. *fitness*

fiend. **fiendish** *adj* **fiendishly** *adv*.

fierce ● *adj* **1** wild or aggressive. **2** intense or strong. **fiercely** *adv* **fierceness** *n*.

fiery ● [**fire**-ee] *adj* **fierier**, **fieriest** **1** consisting of or like fire. **2** easily angered. **3** (of food) very spicy.

fiesta *n* religious festival, carnival.

FIFA [**fee**-fa] Fédération Internationale de Football Association (International Association Football Federation).

fife *n* small high-pitched flute.

fifteen *adj, n* **1** five and ten. ▷ *n* **2** Rugby Union team. **fifteenth** *adj, n*.

fifth *adj, n* **1** (of) number five in a series. ▷ *n* **2** one of five equal parts of something. **fifth column** group secretly helping the enemy.

fifty *adj, n, pl* **-ties** five times ten. **fifty-fifty** *informal* ▷ *adv* **1** equally divided, e.g. *they split the profits fifty-fifty.* ▷ *adj* **2** having an equal chance of happening or not happening, e.g. *a fifty-fifty chance of success.* **fiftieth** *adj, n*.

fig *n* **1** soft pear-shaped fruit. **2** tree bearing it. **fig leaf 1** representation of the leaf of a fig tree, used to cover the genitals of a nude statue or painting. **2** anything used to conceal something thought to be shameful.

fig. **1** figurative(ly). **2** figure.

fight ● *v* **fighting**, **fought 1** struggle (against) in battle or physical combat. **2** struggle to overcome someone or obtain something. **3** carry on (a battle or contest). **4** make (one's way)

━━━━━━━━━━━━━━━━━━━━━━ THESAURUS ━━━

jittery (*inf*), jumpy, nervous, on edge, restive, uneasy

field *n* **1** = **meadow**, grassland, green, lea (*poet*), pasture **4** = **competitors**, applicants, candidates, competition, contestants, entrants, possibilities, runners **7** = **speciality**, area, department, discipline, domain, line, province, territory ▷ *v* **11** *Sport* = **retrieve**, catch, pick up, return, stop **14** = **deal with**, deflect, handle, turn aside

fiend *n* **1** = **demon**, devil, evil spirit **2** = **brute**, barbarian, beast, ghoul, monster, ogre, savage **3** *Inf* = **enthusiast**, addict, fanatic, freak (*inf*), maniac

fiendish *adj* **1** = **devilish**, diabolical, hellish, infernal, satanic **2** = **wicked**, cruel, malignant, monstrous, unspeakable

fierce *adj* **1** = **wild**, brutal, cruel, dangerous, ferocious, fiery, furious, menacing, powerful, raging, savage, stormy, strong, tempestuous, vicious, violent **2** = **intense**, cut-throat, keen, relentless, strong

fiercely *adv* = **ferociously**, furiously, passionately, savagely, tempestuously, tigerishly, tooth and nail, viciously, with no holds barred

fiery *adj* **1** = **burning**, ablaze, afire, aflame, blazing, flaming, on fire **2** = **excitable**, fierce, hot-headed, impetuous, irascible, irritable, passionate

fight *v* **1** = **battle**, box, clash, combat, do battle, grapple, spar, struggle, tussle, wrestle **2** = **oppose**, contest, defy, dispute, make a stand against, resist, stand up to, withstand **3** = **engage in**, carry on, conduct,

somewhere with difficulty. ▷ *n*
5 aggressive conflict between two
(groups of) people. **6** quarrel or
contest. **7** resistance. **8** boxing
match. **fighter** *n* **1** boxer.
2 determined person. **3** aircraft
designed to destroy other aircraft.
fight off *v* **1** drive away (an attacker).
2 struggle to avoid.
figment *n* **figment of one's**
imagination imaginary thing.
figure ❶ *n* **1** numerical symbol.
2 amount expressed in numbers.
3 bodily shape. **4** well-known person.
5 representation in painting or
sculpture of a human form. **6** diagram
or illustration. **7** set of movements in
dancing or skating. **8** *Maths* any
combination of lines, planes, points, or
curves. ▷ *pl* **9** calculations with
numbers. ▷ *v* **10** calculate (sums or
amounts). **11** *US & Aust* consider,
conclude. **12** (usu. foll. by *in*) be
included (in). **figure of speech**
expression in which words do not have
their literal meaning. **figurative** *adj* (of
language) abstract, imaginative, or
symbolic. **figuratively** *adv* **figurine** *n*
statuette. **figurehead** *n* **1** nominal
leader. **2** carved bust at the bow of a
ship. **figure out** *v* solve or understand.
filament *n* **1** fine wire in a light bulb
that gives out light. **2** fine thread.
filbert *n* hazelnut.

filch ❶ *v* steal (small amounts).
file¹ ❶ *n* **1** box or folder used to keep
documents in order. **2** documents in a
file. **3** information about a person or
subject. **4** line of people one behind
the other. **5** *Computers* organized
collection of related material. ▷ *v*
6 place (a document) in a file. **7** place
(a legal document) on official record.
8 bring a lawsuit, esp. for divorce.
9 walk or march in a line. **filing**
cabinet piece of office furniture with
deep drawers used for storing
documents.
file² ❶ *n* **1** tool with a roughened blade
for smoothing or shaping. ▷ *v* **2** shape
or smooth with a file. **filings** *pl n*
shavings removed by a file.
filial *adj* of or befitting a son or
daughter.
filibuster *n* **1** obstruction of legislation
by making long speeches. **2** person
who filibusters. ▷ *v* **3** obstruct
(legislation) with such delaying
tactics.
filigree *n* **1** delicate ornamental work of
gold or silver wire. ▷ *adj* **2** made of
filigree.
Filipino [fill-lip-**pee**-no] *adj* **1** of the
Philippines. ▷ *n* **2** (*fem* **Filipina**) person
from the Philippines.
fill ❶ *v* **1** make or become full. **2** occupy
completely. **3** plug (a gap). **4** satisfy
(a need). **5** hold and perform the

─── **THESAURUS** ───

prosecute, wage ▷ *n* **5, 6** = **battle**,
clash, conflict, contest, dispute, duel,
encounter, struggle, tussle
7 = **resistance**, belligerence, militancy,
pluck, spirit
fighter *n* **1** = **boxer**, prize fighter,
pugilist
fight off *v* **1** = **repel**, beat off, drive
away, keep *or* hold at bay, repress,
repulse, resist, stave off, ward off
figure *n* **1** = **number**, character, digit,
numeral, symbol **2** = **amount**, cost,
price, sum, total, value **3** = **shape**,
body, build, frame, physique,
proportions **4** = **character**, big name,
celebrity, dignitary, personality
5, 6 = **diagram**, design, drawing,
illustration, representation, sketch ▷ *v*
10 = **calculate**, compute, count,
reckon, tally, tot up, work out **12** (usu.
foll. by *in*) = **feature**, act, appear, be
featured, contribute to, play a part
figurehead *n* **1** = **front man**,

mouthpiece, puppet, titular *or*
nominal head
figure out *v* = **understand**, calculate,
comprehend, compute, decipher,
fathom, make out, reckon, see, work
out
filch *v* = **steal**, embezzle,
misappropriate, pilfer, pinch (*inf*),
take, thieve, walk off with
file¹ *n* = **folder**, case, data, documents,
dossier, information, portfolio ▷ *n*
4 = **line**, column, queue, row ▷ *v*
6 = **put in place**, document, enter,
pigeonhole **7** = **register**, record
9 = **march**, parade, troop
file² *v* **2** = **smooth**, abrade, polish, rasp,
rub, scrape, shape
fill *v* **1** = **stuff**, cram, crowd, glut, pack,
stock, supply, swell **2** = **saturate**,
charge, imbue, impregnate, pervade,
suffuse **3** = **plug**, block, bung, close,
cork, seal, stop **5** = **perform**, carry
out, discharge, execute, fulfil, hold,

duties of (a position). **6** appoint to (a job or position). **one's fill** sufficient for one's needs or wants. **filler** *n* substance that fills a gap or increases bulk. **fill in** *v* **1** complete (a form or drawing). **2** act as a substitute. **3** *informal* give (a person) fuller details. **filling** *n* **1** substance that fills a gap or cavity, esp. in a tooth. ▷ *adj* **2** (of food) substantial and satisfying. **filling station** garage selling petrol, oil, etc.

fillet *n* **1** boneless piece of meat or fish. ▷ *v* **filleting, filleted 2** remove the bones from.

fillip *n* something that adds stimulation or enjoyment.

filly *n, pl* **-lies** young female horse.

film ❶ *n* **1** sequence of images projected on a screen, creating the illusion of movement. **2** story told in such a sequence of images. **3** thin strip of light-sensitive cellulose used to make photographic negatives and transparencies. **4** thin sheet or layer. ▷ *v* **5** photograph with a movie or video camera. **6** make a film of (a scene, story, etc.). **7** cover or become covered with a thin layer. ▷ *adj* **8** connected with films or the cinema. **filmy** *adj* **filmier, filmiest** very thin, delicate. **film strip** set of pictures on a strip of film, projected separately

as individual slides.

filter ❶ *n* **1** material or device permitting fluid to pass but retaining solid particles. **2** device that blocks certain frequencies of sound or light. **3** traffic signal that allows vehicles to turn either left or right while the main signals are at red. ▷ *v* **4** remove impurities from (a substance) with a filter. **5** pass slowly or faintly. **filter tip** (cigarette with) a built-in filter to reduce the amount of nicotine etc. inhaled by a smoker.

filth ❶ *n* **1** disgusting dirt. **2** offensive material or language. **filthy** *adj* **filthier, filthiest. filthily** *adv* **filthiness** *n*.

filtrate *n* **1** filtered gas or liquid. ▷ *v* **2** remove impurities with a filter. **filtration** *n*.

fin *n* **1** projection from a fish's body enabling it to balance and swim. **2** vertical tailplane of an aircraft.

finagle [fin-**nay**-gl] *v* get or achieve by craftiness or trickery.

final ❶ *adj* **1** at the end. **2** having no possibility of further change, action, or discussion. ▷ *n* **3** deciding contest between winners of previous rounds in a competition. ▷ *pl* **4** last examinations in an educational course. **finally** *adv* **finality** *n* **finalist** *n*

---

occupy **one's fill** = **sufficient**, all one wants, ample, enough, plenty

filler *n* = **padding**, makeweight, stopgap

fill in *v* **1** = **complete**, answer, fill out (*US*), fill up **2** = **replace**, deputize, represent, stand in, sub, substitute, take the place of **3** *Inf* = **inform**, acquaint, apprise, bring up to date, give the facts *or* background

filling *n* **1** = **stuffing**, contents, filler, inside, insides, padding, wadding ▷ *adj* **2** = **satisfying**, ample, heavy, square, substantial

film *n* **1, 2** = **movie**, flick (*sl*), motion picture **4** = **layer**, coating, covering, dusting, membrane, skin, tissue ▷ *v* **5, 6** = **photograph**, shoot, take, video, videotape

filter *n* **1** = **sieve**, gauze, membrane, mesh, riddle, strainer ▷ *v* **4** = **purify**, clarify, filtrate, refine, screen, sieve, sift, strain, winnow **5** = **trickle**, dribble, escape, exude, leak, ooze, penetrate, percolate, seep

filth *n* **1** = **dirt**, excrement, grime, muck, refuse, sewage, slime, sludge, squalor **2** = **obscenity**, impurity, indecency, pornography, smut, vulgarity

filthy *adj* **1** = **dirty**, begrimed, blackened, foul, grimy, grubby, muddy, polluted, putrid, slimy, squalid, unclean **2** = **obscene**, corrupt, depraved, impure, indecent, lewd, licentious, pornographic, smutty

final *adj* **1** = **last**, closing, concluding, latest, terminal, ultimate **2** = **conclusive**, absolute, decided, definite, definitive, incontrovertible, irrevocable, settled

finale *n* = **ending**, climax, close, conclusion, culmination, denouement, epilogue

finalize *v* = **complete**, clinch, conclude, decide, settle, tie up, work out, wrap up (*inf*)

finally *adv* = **in conclusion**, at last, at length, at long last, eventually, in summary, in the end, lastly, to conclude, ultimately

competitor in a final. **finalize** v put into final form. **finale** [fin-**nah**-lee] n concluding part of a dramatic performance or musical work.

finance ❶ v **1** provide or obtain funds for. ▷ n **2** system of money, credit, and investment. **3** management of money, loans, or credits. **4** (provision of) funds. ▷ pl **5** money resources. **financial** adj **financially** adv **financier** n person involved in large-scale financial business. **financial year** twelve-month period used for financial calculations.

finch n, pl **finches** small songbird with a short strong beak.

find ❶ v **finding**, **found 1** discover by chance. **2** discover by search or effort. **3** become aware of. **4** consider to have a particular quality. **5** experience (a particular feeling). **6** Law pronounce (the defendant) guilty or not guilty. **7** provide, esp. with difficulty. ▷ n **8** person or thing found, esp. when valuable. **finder** n **finding** n conclusion from an investigation. **find out** v **1** gain knowledge of. **2** detect (a crime, deception, etc.).

fine¹ ❶ adj **1** very good. **2** (of weather) clear and dry. **3** in good health. **4** satisfactory. **5** of delicate workmanship. **6** thin or slender. **7** in small particles. **8** very small, e.g. fine print. **9** subtle or abstruse, e.g. a fine distinction. **finely** adv **fineness** n **finery** n showy clothing. **fine art** art produced to appeal to the sense of beauty. **fine-tune** v make small adjustments to (something) so that it works really well.

fine² ❶ n **1** payment imposed as a penalty. ▷ v **2** impose a fine on.

finesse ❶ [fin-**ness**] n **1** delicate skill. **2** subtlety and tact.

finger ❶ n **1** one of the four long jointed parts of the hand. **2** part of a glove that covers a finger. **3** something that resembles a finger in shape or function. **4** quantity of liquid in a glass as deep as a finger is wide. ▷ v **5** touch or handle with the fingers. **fingering** n technique of using the fingers in playing a musical instrument. **fingerboard** n part of a stringed instrument against which the strings are pressed. **finger bowl** small bowl of water for diners to rinse their hands in at the table. **fingerprint** n **1** impression of the ridges on the tip of the finger. ▷ v **2** take the fingerprints of (someone). **fingerstall** n cover to protect an injured finger.

finial n Architecture ornament at the apex of a gable or spire.

f

---

finance v **1** = **fund**, back, bankroll (US), guarantee, pay for, subsidize, support, underwrite ▷ n **2** = **economics**, accounts, banking, business, commerce, investment, money

finances pl n **5** = **resources**, affairs, assets, capital, cash, funds, money, wherewithal

financial adj = **economic**, fiscal, monetary, pecuniary

find v **1** = **discover**, come across, encounter, hit upon, locate, meet, recognize, spot, uncover **2**, **3** = **realise**, detect, discover, learn, note, notice, observe, perceive ▷ n **8** = **discovery**, acquisition, asset, bargain, catch, good buy

find out v **1** = **learn**, detect, discover, note, observe, perceive, realize **2** = **detect**, catch, disclose, expose, reveal, uncover, unmask

fine¹ adj **1** = **excellent**, accomplished, exceptional, exquisite, first-rate, magnificent, masterly, outstanding, splendid, superior **2** = **sunny**, balmy, bright, clear, clement, cloudless, dry, fair, pleasant **4** = **satisfactory**, acceptable, all right, convenient, good, O.K. or okay (inf), suitable **5** = **delicate**, dainty, elegant, expensive, exquisite, fragile, quality **6** = **slender**, diaphanous, flimsy, gauzy, gossamer, light, sheer, thin **9** = **subtle**, abstruse, acute, hairsplitting, minute, nice, precise, sharp

fine² n **1** = **penalty**, damages, forfeit, punishment ▷ v **2** = **penalize**, mulct, punish

finery n = **splendour**, frippery, gear (inf), glad rags (inf), ornaments, showiness, Sunday best, trappings, trinkets

finesse n **1** = **skill**, adeptness, adroitness, craft, sophistication **2** = **subtlety**, delicacy, diplomacy, discretion, tact

finger v **5** = **touch**, feel, fiddle with (inf), handle, manipulate, maul, paw (inf), toy with

finicky *adj* **1** excessively particular, fussy. **2** overelaborate.

finis *n Latin* end: used at the end of a book.

finish ❶ *v* **1** bring to an end, stop. **2** use up. **3** bring to a desired or completed condition. **4** put a surface texture on (wood, cloth, or metal). **5** defeat or destroy. ▷ *n* **6** end, last part. **7** death or defeat. **8** surface texture. **finishing school** private school for girls that teaches social graces.

finite ❶ [**fine**-ite] *adj* having limits in space, time, or size.

Finn *n* native of Finland. **Finnish** *adj* **1** of Finland. ▷ *n* **2** official language of Finland.

finnan haddock, haddie *n* smoked haddock.

fiord *n* same as FJORD.

fipple flute *n* end-blown flute with a plug (**fipple**) at the mouthpiece, such as a recorder.

fir *n* pyramid-shaped tree with needle-like leaves and erect cones.

fire ❶ *n* **1** state of combustion producing heat, flames, and smoke. **2** burning coal or wood, or a gas or electric device, used to heat a room. **3** uncontrolled destructive burning. **4** shooting of guns. **5** intense passion, ardour. ▷ *v* **6** operate (a weapon) so that a bullet or missile is released. **7** *informal* dismiss from employment. **8** bake (ceramics etc.) in a kiln. **9** (of an internal-combustion engine) start. **10** excite. **firearm** *n* rifle, pistol, or

shotgun. **fireball** *n* **1** ball of fire at the centre of an explosion. **2** large bright meteor. **3** *slang* energetic person.

firebrand *n* person who causes unrest.

firebreak *n* strip of cleared land to stop the advance of a fire. **firebrick** *n* heat-resistant brick used for lining furnaces, fireplaces, etc. **fire brigade** organized body of people whose job is to put out fires. **firecracker** *n* firework which produces a loud bang. **firedamp** *n* explosive gas, composed mainly of methane, formed in mines. **fire drill** rehearsal of procedures for escape from a fire. **fire engine** vehicle with apparatus for extinguishing fires. **fire escape** metal staircase or ladder down the outside of a building for escape in the event of fire. **firefighter** *n* member of a fire brigade. **firefly** *n, pl* **-flies** beetle that glows in the dark. **fireguard** *n* protective grating in front of a fire. **fire irons** tongs, poker, and shovel for tending a domestic fire. **fireplace** *n* recess in a room for a fire. **fire power** *Military* amount a weapon or unit can fire. **fire raiser** person who deliberately starts fires. **fire station** building where firefighters are stationed. **fire trap** building which could easily catch fire or which would be difficult to escape from if it did. **firewall** *n Computers* computer that prevents unauthorized access to a computer ne twork from the internet. **firework** *n* **1** device containing chemicals that is ignited to produce

——————————————— THESAURUS ——

finish *v* **1** = **stop**, cease, close, complete, conclude, end, round off, terminate, wind up, wrap up (*inf*) **2** = **consume**, devour, dispose of, eat, empty, exhaust, use up **3** = **perfect**, polish, refine **4** = **coat**, gild, lacquer, polish, stain, texture, veneer, wax **5** = **destroy**, bring down, defeat, dispose of, exterminate, overcome, put an end to, put paid to, rout, ruin ▷ *n* **6** = **end**, cessation, close, completion, conclusion, culmination, denouement, finale, run-in **7** = **defeat**, annihilation, curtains (*inf*), death, end, end of the road, ruin **8** = **surface**, lustre, patina, polish, shine, smoothness, texture

finite *adj* = **limited**, bounded, circumscribed, delimited, demarcated, restricted

fire *n* **1, 3** = **flames**, blaze, combustion, conflagration, inferno **4** = **bombardment**, barrage, cannonade, flak, fusillade, hail, salvo, shelling, sniping, volley **5** = **passion**, ardour, eagerness, enthusiasm, excitement, fervour, intensity, sparkle, spirit, verve, vigour ▷ *v* **6** = **shoot**, detonate, discharge, explode, let off, pull the trigger, set off, shell **7** *Inf* = **dismiss**, cashier, discharge, make redundant, sack (*inf*), show the door **10** = **inspire**, animate, enliven, excite, galvanize, impassion, inflame, rouse, stir

firebrand *n* = **rabble-rouser**, agitator, demagogue, incendiary, instigator, tub-thumper

fireworks *pl n* **2** = **pyrotechnics**, illuminations **3** *Inf* = **trouble**, hysterics, rage, row, storm, uproar

spectacular explosions and coloured sparks. ▷ *pl* **2** show of fireworks. **3** *informal* outburst of temper. **firing line** leading or most vulnerable position. **firing squad** group of soldiers ordered to execute an offender by shooting.

firm¹ ❶ *adj* **1** not soft or yielding. **2** securely in position. **3** definite. **4** having determination or strength. ▷ *adv* **5** in an unyielding manner, e.g. *hold firm*. ▷ *v* **6** make or become firm. **firmly** *adv* **firmness** *n*.

firm² ❶ *n* business company.

firmament *n lit* sky or the heavens.

first ❶ *adj* **1** earliest in time or order. **2** graded or ranked above all others. ▷ *n* **3** person or thing coming before all others. **4** outset or beginning. **5** first-class honours degree at university. **6** lowest forward gear in a motor vehicle. ▷ *adv* **7** before anything else. **8** for the first time. **firstly** *adv* **first aid** immediate medical assistance given in an emergency. **first-class** *adj* **1** of the highest class or grade. **2** excellent. **first-foot** *Scot* ▷ *n*, *pl* **first-foots 1** first person to enter a house in the New Year. ▷ *v* **2** visit (someone) as a first-foot. **first-footing** *n* **first-hand** *adj*, *adv* (obtained) directly from the original source. **first mate** officer of a merchant ship second in command to the captain. **first person** *Grammar* category of verbs and pronouns used by a speaker to refer to himself or herself. **first-rate** *adj* excellent. **first refusal** right to buy something before it is offered to others. **first-strike** *adj* (of a nuclear missile) for use in an opening attack to destroy enemy weapons.

First Nations *pl n Canad* Canadian aboriginal communities.

First Peoples *pl n Canad* a collective term for the Native Canadian peoples, the Inuit, and the Métis.

firth *n* narrow inlet of the sea.

fiscal *adj* **1** of government finances, esp. taxes. ▷ *n* **2** short for PROCURATOR FISCAL.

fish ❶ *n*, *pl* **fish**, **fishes 1** cold-blooded vertebrate with gills, that lives in water. **2** its flesh as food. ▷ *v* **3** try to catch fish. **4** fish in (a particular area of water). **5** (foll. by *for*) grope for and find with difficulty. **6** (foll. by *for*) seek indirectly. **fisherman** *n* person who catches fish for a living or for pleasure. **fishery** *n*, *pl* **-eries** area of the sea used for fishing. **fishing** *n* job or pastime of catching fish. **fishy** *adj* **fishier**, **fishiest 1** of or like fish. **2** *informal* suspicious or questionable. **fishfinger** *n* oblong piece of fish covered in breadcrumbs. **fishmeal** dried ground fish used as animal feed or fertilizer. **fishmonger** *n* seller of fish. **fishnet** *n* open mesh fabric resembling netting. **fishwife** *n*, *pl* **-wives** coarse scolding woman.

firm¹ *adj* **1** = **hard**, dense, inflexible, rigid, set, solid, solidified, stiff, unyielding **2** = **secure**, embedded, fast, fixed, immovable, rooted, stable, steady, tight, unshakable **3** = **definite 4** = **determined**, adamant, inflexible, resolute, resolved, set on, unbending, unshakable, unyielding

firm² *n* = **company**, association, business, concern, conglomerate, corporation, enterprise, organization, partnership

firmly *adv* = **securely**, immovably, like a rock, resolutely, staunchly, steadfastly, steadily, tightly, unchangeably, unflinchingly, unshakably, unwaveringly

firmness *n* **1** = **hardness**, inelasticity, inflexibility, resistance, rigidity, solidity, stiffness **4** = **resolve**, constancy, inflexibility, resolution, staunchness, steadfastness

first *adj* **1** = **earliest**, cardinal, elementary, fundamental, initial, introductory, key, maiden, opening, original, premier, primary, primordial, rudimentary **2** = **foremost**, chief, head, highest, leading, pre-eminent, prime, principal, ruling ▷ *n* **4** = **start**, beginning, commencement, inception, introduction, outset, starting point ▷ *adv* **7** = **to begin with**, at the beginning, at the outset, beforehand, firstly, initially, in the first place, to start with

first-rate *adj* = **excellent**, crack (*sl*), elite, exceptional, first class, outstanding, superb, superlative, top-notch (*inf*), world-class

fishy *adj* **1** = **fishlike**, piscatorial, piscatory, piscine **2** *Inf* = **suspicious**, dodgy (*Brit, Aust & NZ inf*), dubious, funny (*inf*), implausible, odd, questionable, suspect, unlikely

fishplate *n* metal plate holding rails together.

fission *n* **1** splitting. **2** *Biology* asexual reproduction involving a division into two or more equal parts. **3** splitting of an atomic nucleus with the release of a large amount of energy. **fissionable** *adj* **fissile** *adj* **1** capable of undergoing nuclear fission. **2** tending to split.

fissure ❶ [**fish**-er] *n* long narrow cleft or crack.

fist *n* clenched hand. **fisticuffs** *pl n* fighting with the fists.

fistula [**fist**-yew-la] *n* long narrow ulcer.

fit¹ ❶ *v* **fitting, fitted** **1** be appropriate or suitable for. **2** be of the correct size or shape (for). **3** adjust so as to make appropriate. **4** try (clothes) on and note any adjustments needed. **5** make competent or ready. **6** correspond with the facts or circumstances. ▷ *adj* **7** appropriate. **8** in good health. **9** worthy or deserving. ▷ *n* **10** way in which something fits. **fitness** *n* **fitted** *adj* **1** designed for excellent fit, e.g. *a fitted suit*. **2** (of a kitchen, bathroom, etc.) having equipment and furniture built or selected to suit the measurements of the room. **3** (of a carpet) covering a floor completely. **fitter** *n* **1** person skilled in the installation and adjustment of machinery. **2** person who fits garments. **fitting** *adj* **1** appropriate,

suitable. ▷ *n* **2** accessory or part. **3** trying on of clothes for size. ▷ *pl* **4** furnishings and accessories in a building. **fitment** *n* **1** accessory attached to a machine. **2** detachable part of the furnishings of a room. **fit in** *v* **1** give a place or time to. **2** belong or conform. **fit out** *v* provide with the necessary equipment.

fit² ❶ *n* **1** sudden attack or convulsion, such as an epileptic seizure. **2** sudden short burst or spell.

fitful ❶ *adj* occurring in irregular spells. **fitfully** *adv*.

five *adj, n* one more than four. **fiver** *n* *informal* five-pound note. **fives** *n* ball game resembling squash but played with bats or the hands.

fix ❶ *v* **1** make or become firm, stable, or secure. **2** repair. **3** place permanently. **4** settle definitely. **5** direct (the eyes etc.) steadily. **6** *informal* unfairly influence the outcome of. ▷ *n* **7** *informal* difficult situation. **8** ascertaining of the position of a ship by radar etc. **9** *slang* injection of a narcotic drug. **fixed** *adj* **fixedly** [**fix**-id-lee] *adv* steadily. **fixer** *n* **1** solution used to make a photographic image permanent. **2** *slang* person who arranges things. **fix up** *v* **1** arrange. **2** provide (with).

fixation ❶ *n* obsessive interest in something. **fixated** *adj* obsessed.

━━━━━━━━━━━━━━━━━━━━━━━━ THESAURUS ━━━━━━

fissure *n* = **crack**, breach, cleft, crevice, fault, fracture, opening, rift, rupture, split

fit¹ *v* **1, 2** = **suit**, accord, belong, conform, correspond, match, meet, tally **3** = **adapt**, adjust, alter, arrange, customize, modify, shape, tweak (*inf*) **5** = **equip**, arm, fit out, kit out, prepare, provide ▷ *adj* **7** = **appropriate**, apt, becoming, correct, fitting, proper, right, seemly, suitable **8** = **healthy**, able-bodied, hale, in good shape, robust, strapping, trim, well

fit² *n* **1** = **seizure**, attack, bout, convulsion, paroxysm, spasm **2** = **outbreak**, bout, burst, outburst, spell

fitful *adj* = **irregular**, broken, desultory, disturbed, inconstant, intermittent, spasmodic, sporadic, uneven

fitness *n* **7** = **appropriateness**, aptness, competence, eligibility,

propriety, readiness, suitability **8** = **health**, good condition, good health, robustness, strength, vigour, wellness

fitting *adj* **1** = **appropriate**, apposite, becoming, correct, decent, proper, right, seemly, suitable ▷ *n* **2** = **accessory**, attachment, component, part, piece, unit

fix *v* **1** = **fasten**, attach, bind, connect, link, secure, stick, tie **2** = **repair**, correct, mend, patch up, put to rights, see to **3** = **place**, embed, establish, implant, install, locate, plant, position, set **4** = **decide**, agree on, arrange, arrive at, determine, establish, set, settle, specify **5** = **focus**, direct **6** *Inf* = **rig**, fiddle (*inf*), influence, manipulate ▷ *n* **7** *Inf* = **predicament**, difficulty, dilemma, embarrassment, mess, pickle (*inf*), plight, quandary

fixation *n* = **obsession**, complex, hang-up (*inf*), infatuation, mania,

fixative *n* liquid used to preserve or hold things in place.

fixture *n* **1** permanently fitted piece of household equipment. **2** person whose presence seems permanent. **3** sports match or the date fixed for it.

fizz ❶ *v* **1** make a hissing or bubbling noise. **2** give off small bubbles. ▷ *n* **3** hissing or bubbling noise. **4** releasing of small bubbles of gas by a liquid. **5** effervescent drink. **fizzy** *adj* **fizzier, fizziest. fizziness** *n*.

fizzle *v* make a weak hissing or bubbling sound. **fizzle out** *v informal* come to nothing, fail.

fjord [fee-**ord**] *n* long narrow inlet of the sea between cliffs, esp. in Norway.

FL Florida.

flab *n informal* unsightly body fat.

flabbergasted ❶ *adj* completely astonished.

flabby ❶ *adj* **-bier, -biest 1** having flabby flesh. **2** loose or limp. **flabbiness** *n*.

flaccid [**flas**-sid] *adj* soft and limp. **flaccidity** *n*.

flag[1] ❶ *n* **1** piece of cloth attached to a pole as an emblem or signal. ▷ *v* **flagging, flagged 2** mark with a flag or sticker. **3** (often foll. by *down*) signal (a vehicle) to stop by waving the arm. **flag day** day on which small stickers are sold in the streets for charity. **flagpole, flagstaff** *n* pole for a flag.

flagship *n* **1** admiral's ship. **2** most important product of an organization.

flag[2] ❶ *v* **flagging, flagged** lose enthusiasm or vigour.

flag[3], **flagstone** *n* flat paving-stone. **flagged** *adj* paved with flagstones.

flag[4] *n* any of various plants with sword-shaped leaves, esp. the iris.

flagellate [**flaj**-a-late] *v* whip, esp. in religious penance or for sexual pleasure. **flagellation** *n* **flagellant** *n* person who whips himself or herself.

flagellum [flaj-**jell**-lum] *n*, *pl* **-la** [-la] **-lums 1** *Biology* whiplike outgrowth from a cell that acts as an organ of movement. **2** *Botany* long thin shoot.

flageolet [flaj-a-**let**] *n* small instrument like a recorder.

flagon *n* **1** wide bottle for wine or cider. **2** narrow-necked jug for liquid.

flagrant ❶ [**flayg**-rant] *adj* openly outrageous. **flagrantly** *adv* **flagrancy** *n*.

flail ❶ *v* **1** wave about wildly. **2** beat or thrash. ▷ *n* **3** tool formerly used for threshing grain by hand.

flair ❶ *n* **1** natural ability. **2** stylishness.

flak *n* **1** anti-aircraft fire. **2** *informal* severe criticism.

flake ❶ *n* **1** small thin piece, esp. chipped off something. **2** *Aust, NZ & US informal* unreliable person. ▷ *v* **3** peel off in flakes. **flaky** *adj* **flakier, flakiest. flake out** *v informal* collapse or fall asleep from exhaustion.

f

---

preoccupation, thing (*inf*)

fixed *adj* **3 = immovable**, established, permanent, rigid, rooted, secure, set **4 = definite**, agreed, arranged, decided, established, planned, resolute, resolved, settled, unwavering

fix up *v* **1 = arrange**, agree on, fix, organize, plan, settle, sort out **2 = provide**, arrange for, bring about, lay on

fizz *v* **1, 2 = bubble**, effervesce, fizzle, froth, hiss, sparkle, sputter

fizzy *adj* **= bubbly**, bubbling, carbonated, effervescent, gassy, sparkling

flabbergasted *adj* **= astonished**, amazed, astounded, dumbfounded, lost for words, overwhelmed, speechless, staggered, stunned

flabby *adj* **1 = baggy 2 = limp**, drooping, flaccid, floppy, loose, pendulous, sagging

flag[1] *n* **1 = banner**, colours, ensign, pennant, pennon, standard, streamer

▷ *v* **2 = mark**, indicate, label, note **3** (often foll. by *down*) **= hail**, signal, warn, wave

flag[2] *v* **= weaken**, abate, droop, fade, languish, peter out, sag, wane, weary, wilt

flagging *adj* **= weakening**, declining, deteriorating, fading, faltering, waning, wilting

flagrant *adj* **= outrageous**, barefaced, blatant, brazen, glaring, heinous, scandalous, shameless

flail *v* **1 = windmill 2 = thrash**, beat, thresh

flair *n* **1 = ability**, aptitude, faculty, feel, genius, gift, knack, mastery, talent **2 = style**, chic, dash, discernment, elegance, panache, stylishness, taste

flake *n* **1 = chip**, layer, peeling, scale, shaving, sliver, wafer ▷ *v* **3 = chip**, blister, peel off

flake out *v Inf* **= collapse**, faint, keel over, pass out

flambé [**flahm**-bay] *v* **flambéing**, **flambéed** cook or serve (food) in flaming brandy.

flamboyant ❶ *adj* **1** behaving in a very noticeable, extravagant way. **2** very bright and showy. **flamboyance** *n*.

flame ❶ *n* **1** luminous burning gas coming from burning material. ▷ *v* **2** burn brightly. **3** become bright red. **old flame** *informal* former sweetheart.

flamenco *n*, *pl* **-cos 1** rhythmical Spanish dance accompanied by a guitar and vocalist. **2** music for this dance.

flamingo *n*, *pl* **-gos, -goes** large pink wading bird with a long neck and legs.

flammable *adj* easily set on fire. **flammability** *n*.

flan *n* open sweet or savoury tart.

flange *n* projecting rim or collar.

flank ❶ *n* **1** part of the side between the hips and ribs. **2** side of a body of troops. ▷ *v* **3** be at or move along the side of.

flannel *n* **1** small piece of cloth for washing the face. **2** soft woollen fabric for clothing. **3** *informal* evasive talk. ▷ *pl* **4** trousers made of flannel. ▷ *v* **-nelling, -nelled 5** *informal* talk evasively. **flannelette** *n* cotton imitation of flannel.

flap ❶ *v* **flapping, flapped 1** move back and forwards or up and down. ▷ *n* **2** action or sound of flapping. **3** piece of something attached by one edge only. **4** hinged section of an aircraft's wing that is raised and lowered to control the speed. **5** *informal* state of excitement or panic.

flapjack *n* chewy biscuit made with oats.

flare ❶ *v* **1** blaze with a sudden unsteady flame. **2** *informal* (of temper, violence, or trouble) break out suddenly. **3** (of a skirt or trousers) become wider towards the hem. ▷ *n* **4** sudden unsteady flame. **5** signal light. ▷ *pl* **6** flared trousers. **flared** *adj* (of a skirt or trousers) becoming wider towards the hem.

flash ❶ *n* **1** sudden burst of light or flame. **2** sudden occurrence (of intuition or emotion). **3** very short time. **4** brief unscheduled news announcement. **5** *Photography* small bulb that produces an intense flash of light. ▷ *adj* **6** (also **flashy**) vulgarly showy. ▷ *v* **7** (cause to) burst into flame. **8** (cause to) emit light suddenly or intermittently. **9** move very fast. **10** come rapidly (to mind or view). **11** *informal* display ostentatiously. **12** *slang* expose oneself indecently. **flasher** *n slang* man who exposes himself indecently. **flashback** *n* scene in a book, play, or film, that shows earlier events. **flash drive** portable computer hard drive and data storage device. **flash flood** sudden short-lived flood. **flashlight** *n US* torch. **flash point 1** critical point beyond which a situation will inevitably erupt into violence. **2** lowest temperature at which vapour given off by a liquid can ignite.

flashing *n* watertight material used to cover joins in a roof.

flask *n* **1** same as VACUUM FLASK. **2** flat bottle for carrying alcoholic drink in the pocket. **3** narrow-necked bottle.

flat¹ ❶ *adj* **flatter, flattest 1** level and horizontal. **2** even and smooth. **3** (of a tyre) deflated. **4** outright. **5** fixed. **6** without variation or emotion. **7** (of a

———————————————————————————— THESAURUS ————————————

flamboyant *adj* **1** = **theatrical**, dashing, extravagant, ostentatious, swashbuckling **2** = **showy**, brilliant, colourful, dazzling, elaborate, florid, glamorous, glitzy (*sl*), ornate

flame *n* **1** = **fire**, blaze ▷ *v* **2** = **burn**, blaze, flare, flash, glare, glow, shine

flank *n* **1** = **side**, hip, loin, thigh

flap *v* **1** = **flutter**, beat, flail, shake, thrash, vibrate, wag, wave ▷ *n* **2** = **flutter**, beating, shaking, swinging, swish, waving **5** *Inf* = **panic**, agitation, commotion, fluster, state (*inf*), sweat (*inf*), tizzy (*inf*)

flare *v* **1** = **blaze**, burn up, flicker, glare ▷ *n* **4** = **flame**, blaze, burst, flash,

flicker, glare

flash *n* **1** = **gleam**, blaze, burst, dazzle, flare, flicker, shimmer, spark, streak **3** = **moment**, instant, jiffy (*inf*), second, split second, trice, twinkling of an eye ▷ *adj* **6** (also **flashy**) = **showy**, flamboyant, garish, gaudy, glitzy (*sl*), jazzy (*inf*), ostentatious, snazzy (*inf*), tacky (*inf*), tasteless, vulgar ▷ *v* **7** = **blaze**, flare **8** = **gleam**, flicker, glare, shimmer, sparkle, twinkle **9** = **speed**, dart, dash, fly, race, shoot, streak, whistle, zoom **11** *Inf* = **show**, display, exhibit, expose, flaunt, flourish

flat¹ *adj* **1, 2** = **even**, horizontal, level, levelled, low, smooth **3** = **punctured**,

drink) no longer fizzy. **8** (of a battery) with no electrical charge.
9 *Music* below the true pitch. ▷ *adv* **10** in or into a flat position. **11** completely or absolutely. **12** exactly. **13** *Music* too low in pitch. ▷ *n* **14** flat surface.
15 *Music* symbol lowering the pitch of a note by a semitone. **16** punctured car tyre. **17** level ground. **18** mudbank exposed at low tide. **flat out** with maximum speed or effort. **flatly** *adv*
flatness *n* **flatten** *v* **flatfish** *n* sea fish, such as the sole, which has a flat body.
flat-footed *adj* **1** having a less than usually arched instep. **2** clumsy or insensitive. **flat racing** horse racing over level ground with no jumps.

flat² ❶ *n* set of rooms for living in which are part of a larger building. **flatlet** *n* small flat. **flatmate** *n* person with whom one shares a flat.

flatter ❶ *v* **1** praise insincerely. **2** show to advantage. **3** make (a person) appear more attractive in a picture than in reality. **flatterer** *n* **flattery** *n*.

flattie *n NZ & S Afr informal* flat tyre.

flatulent *adj* suffering from or caused by too much gas in the intestines. **flatulence** *n*.

flaunt ❶ *v* display (oneself or one's possessions) arrogantly.

- **USAGE NOTE**
- Be careful not to confuse this with
- *flout* meaning 'disobey'.

flautist [**flaw**-tist] *n* flute player.

flavour ❶ *n* **1** distinctive taste.
2 distinctive characteristic or quality. ▷ *v* **3** give flavour to. **flavouring** *n* substance used to flavour food. **flavourless** *adj*.

flaw ❶ *n* **1** imperfection or blemish.
2 mistake that makes a plan or argument invalid. **flawed** *adj* **flawless** *adj*.

flax *n* **1** plant grown for its stem fibres and seeds. **2** its fibres, spun into linen thread. **flaxen** *adj* (of hair) pale yellow.

flay *v* **1** strip the skin off. **2** criticize severely.

flea *n* small wingless jumping bloodsucking insect. **flea market** market for cheap goods. **fleapit** *n informal* shabby cinema or theatre.

fleck *n* **1** small mark, streak, or speck. ▷ *v* **2** speckle.

fled *v* past of FLEE.

fledged *adj* **1** (of young birds) able to fly.
2 (of people) fully trained. **fledgling**, **fledgeling** *n* **1** young bird. ▷ *adj* **2** new or inexperienced.

flee ❶ *v* **fleeing**, **fled** run away (from).

fleece *n* **1** sheep's coat of wool.
2 sheepskin used as a lining for coats etc. **3** warm polyester fabric. **4** jacket or top made of this fabric. ▷ *v* **5** defraud or overcharge. **fleecy** *adj* made of or like fleece.

---

blown out, burst, collapsed, deflated, empty **4** = **absolute**, categorical, downright, explicit, out-and-out, positive, unequivocal, unqualified
6 = **dull**, boring, dead, lacklustre, lifeless, monotonous, tedious, tiresome, uninteresting ▷ *adv*
11 = **completely**, absolutely, categorically, exactly, point blank, precisely, utterly **flat out** = **at full speed**, all out, at full tilt, for all one is worth, hell for leather (*inf*)

flat² *n* = **apartment**, rooms, duplex (*US & Canad*)

flatten *v* = **level**, compress, even out, iron out, raze, smooth off, squash, trample

flatter *v* **1** = **praise**, butter up, compliment, pander to, soft-soap (*inf*), sweet-talk (*inf*), wheedle
2 = **suit**, become, do something for, enhance, set off, show to advantage

flattery *n* **1** = **obsequiousness**,

adulation, blandishments, fawning, servility, soft-soap (*inf*), sweet-talk (*inf*), sycophancy

flaunt *v* = **show off**, brandish, display, exhibit, flash about, flourish, parade, sport (*inf*)

flavour *n* **1** = **taste**, aroma, flavouring, piquancy, relish, savour, seasoning, smack, tang, zest **2** = **quality**, character, essence, feel, feeling, style, tinge, tone ▷ *v* **3** = **season**, ginger up, imbue, infuse, leaven, spice

flaw *n* **1** = **weakness**, blemish, chink in one's armour, defect, failing, fault, imperfection, weak spot

flawed *adj* **1** = **damaged**, blemished, defective, faulty, imperfect
2 = **unsound**, erroneous

flawless *adj* = **perfect**, faultless, impeccable, spotless, unblemished, unsullied

flee *v* = **run away**, bolt, depart, escape, fly, make one's getaway, scarper

fleet¹ ❶ *n* **1** number of warships organized as a unit. **2** number of vehicles under the same ownership.
fleet² ❶ *adj* swift in movement. **fleeting** *adj* rapid and soon passing. **fleetingly** *adv*.
Fleet Street *n* **1** street in London where many newspaper offices were formerly situated. **2** British national newspapers collectively.
Flemish *n* **1** one of two official languages of Belgium. ▷ *adj* **2** of Flanders, in Belgium.
flesh ❶ *n* **1** soft part of a human or animal body. **2** *informal* excess fat. **3** meat of animals as opposed to fish or fowl. **4** thick soft part of a fruit or vegetable. **5** human body as opposed to the soul. **in the flesh** in person, actually present. **one's own flesh and blood** one's family. **flesh-coloured** *adj* yellowish-pink. **fleshly** *adj* **1** carnal. **2** worldly. **fleshy** *adj* **fleshier**, **fleshiest 1** plump. **2** like flesh. **flesh wound** wound affecting only superficial tissue.
fleur-de-lys, fleur-de-lis [flur-de-**lee**] *n, pl* **fleurs-de-lys, fleurs-de-lis** heraldic lily with three petals.
flew *v* past tense of FLY¹.
flex ❶ *n* **1** flexible insulated electric cable. ▷ *v* **2** bend. **flexible** *adj* **1** easily bent. **2** adaptable. **flexibly** *adv* **flexibility** *n* **flexitime** *n* system permitting variation in starting and finishing times of work.
flick ❶ *v* **1** touch or move with the finger or hand in a quick movement. **2** move with a short sudden movement, often repeatedly, e.g. *the windscreen wipers flicked back and forth*. ▷ *n* **3** tap or quick stroke. ▷ *pl* **4** *slang* the cinema. **flick knife** knife with a spring-loaded blade which shoots out when a button is pressed. **flick through** *v* look at (a book or magazine) quickly or idly.
flicker ❶ *v* **1** shine unsteadily or intermittently. **2** move quickly to and fro. ▷ *n* **3** unsteady brief light. **4** brief faint indication.
flier *n* see FLY¹.
flight¹ ❶ *n* **1** journey by air. **2** act or manner of flying through the air. **3** group of birds or aircraft flying together. **4** aircraft flying on a scheduled journey. **5** set of stairs between two landings. **6** stabilizing feathers or plastic fins on an arrow or dart. **flightless** *adj* (of certain birds or insects) unable to fly. **flight deck 1** crew compartment in an airliner. **2** runway deck on an aircraft carrier. **flight lieutenant** junior commissioned officer in an air force. **flight of fancy** imaginative but impractical idea. **flight recorder** electronic device in an aircraft storing information about its flight.
flight² ❶ *n* act of running away.
flighty *adj* **flightier**, **flightiest** frivolous and fickle.
flimsy ❶ *adj* **-sier, -siest 1** not strong or substantial. **2** thin. **3** not very convincing. **flimsily** *adv* **flimsiness** *n*.

(*Brit sl*), take flight, take off (*inf*), take to one's heels, turn tail
fleet¹ *n* **1** = **navy**, armada, flotilla, task force
fleet² *adj* = **swift**, fast, flying, mercurial, meteoric, nimble, nimble-footed, quick, rapid, speedy, winged
fleeting *adj* = **momentary**, brief, ephemeral, passing, short-lived, temporary, transient, transitory
flesh *n* **1** = **meat**, tissue **2** = **fat**, brawn, weight **5** = **physical nature**, carnality, flesh and blood, human nature **one's own flesh and blood** = **family**, blood, kin, kinsfolk, kith and kin, relations, relatives
flexible *adj* **1** = **pliable**, elastic, lithe, plastic, pliant, springy, stretchy, supple **2** = **adaptable**, adjustable, discretionary, open, variable
flick *v* **1** = **strike**, dab, flip, hit, tap, touch **flick through** *v* = **browse**, flip through, glance at, skim, skip, thumb
flicker *v* **1** = **twinkle**, flare, flash, glimmer, gutter, shimmer, sparkle **2** = **flutter**, quiver, vibrate, waver ▷ *n* **3** = **glimmer**, flare, flash, gleam, spark **4** = **trace**, breath, glimmer, iota, spark
flight¹ *n* **1** = **journey**, trip, voyage **2** = **aviation**, aeronautics, flying **3** = **flock**, cloud, formation, squadron, swarm, unit
flight² *n* = **escape**, departure, exit, exodus, fleeing, getaway, retreat, running away
flimsy *adj* **1** = **fragile**, delicate, frail, insubstantial, makeshift, rickety, shaky **2** = **thin**, gauzy, gossamer, light, sheer, transparent **3** = **unconvincing**, feeble, implausible, inadequate, pathetic, poor, unsatisfactory, weak

flinch ● v draw back or wince, as from pain. **flinch from** v shrink from or avoid.

fling ● v flinging, flung 1 throw, send, or move forcefully or hurriedly. ▷ n 2 spell of self-indulgent enjoyment. 3 brief romantic or sexual relationship. **fling oneself into** (start to) do with great vigour.

flint n 1 hard grey stone. 2 piece of this. 3 small piece of an iron alloy, used in cigarette lighters. **flinty** adj 1 cruel. 2 of or like flint. **flintlock** n obsolete gun in which the powder was lit by a spark from a flint.

flip ● v flipping, flipped 1 throw (something small or light) carelessly. 2 turn (something) over. 3 throw (a coin) so that it turns over in the air. 4 (also **flip one's lid**) slang fly into an emotional state. ▷ n 5 snap or tap. ▷ adj 6 informal flippant. **flipper** n 1 limb of a sea animal adapted for swimming. 2 one of a pair of paddle-like rubber devices worn on the feet to help in swimming. **flipchart** n large pad of paper mounted on a stand, used in giving lectures etc. **flip-flop** n rubber-soled sandal held on by a thong between the big toe and the next toe. **flip through** v look at (a book or magazine) quickly or idly.

flippant ● adj treating serious things lightly. **flippancy** n.

flirt ● v 1 behave as if sexually attracted to someone. 2 consider lightly, toy (with). ▷ n 3 person who flirts. **flirtation** n **flirtatious** adj.

flit v flitting, flitted 1 move lightly and rapidly. 2 Scot move house. 3 informal depart hurriedly and secretly. ▷ n 4 act of flitting.

float ● v 1 rest on the surface of a liquid. 2 move lightly and freely. 3 move about aimlessly. 4 launch (a company). 5 offer for sale on the stock market. 6 allow (a currency) to fluctuate against other currencies. ▷ n 7 light object used to help someone or something float. 8 indicator on a fishing line that moves when a fish bites. 9 decorated lorry in a procession. 10 small delivery vehicle. 11 sum of money used for minor expenses or to provide change. **floating** adj 1 moving about, changing, e.g. floating population. 2 (of a voter) not committed to one party.

flock¹ ● n 1 number of animals of one kind together. 2 large group of people. 3 Christianity congregation. ▷ v 4 gather in a crowd.

flock² n 1 wool or cotton waste used as stuffing. ▷ adj 2 (of wallpaper) with a velvety raised pattern.

floe n sheet of floating ice.

flog ● v flogging, flogged 1 beat with a whip or stick. 2 slang sell. **flogging** n.

flood ● n 1 overflow of water onto a normally dry area. 2 large amount of water. 3 rising of the tide. ▷ v 4 cover or become covered with water. 5 fill to

flinch v = **recoil**, cower, cringe, draw back, quail, shirk, shrink, shy away, wince

fling v 1 = **throw**, cast, catapult, heave, hurl, propel, sling, toss ▷ n 2 = **binge** (inf), bash, good time, party, rave-up (Brit sl), spree

flip v 1-3 = **toss**, flick, spin, throw ▷ n 5 = **snap**

flippant adj = **frivolous**, cheeky, disrespectful, glib, impertinent, irreverent, offhand, superficial

flirt v 1 = **chat up** (inf), lead on, make advances, make eyes at, make sheep's eyes at, philander 2 = **toy with**, consider, dabble in, entertain, expose oneself to, give a thought to, play with, trifle with ▷ n 3 = **tease**, coquette, heart-breaker, philanderer

flirtatious adj 1 = **teasing**, amorous, come-hither, coquettish, coy, enticing, provocative, sportive

float v 1 = **be buoyant**, bob, sail 2 = **glide**, hang, hover, move gently, slide, slip along 3 = **drift** 4 = **launch**, get going, promote, set up

floating adj 1 = **free**, fluctuating, movable, unattached, variable, wandering

flock¹ n 1 = **herd**, colony, drove, flight, gaggle, skein 2 = **crowd**, collection, company, gathering, group, herd, host, mass 3 Christianity = **congregation** ▷ v 4 = **gather**, collect, congregate, converge, crowd, herd, huddle, mass, throng

flog v 1 = **beat**, flagellate, flay, lash, scourge, thrash, trounce, whack, whip

flood n 1 = **overflow**, deluge, downpour, inundation 2 = **torrent**, flow, rush, stream 3 = **tide**, spate ▷ v 4 = **immerse**, drown, engulf, inundate,

overflowing. **6** come in large numbers or quantities. **7** supply excess petrol to (an engine) so that it does not work properly. **floodgate** *n* gate used to control the flow of water. **floodlight** *n* **1** lamp that casts a broad intense beam of light. ▷ *v* **-lighting, -lit** **2** illuminate by floodlight.

floor ❶ *n* **1** lower surface of a room. **2** level of a building. **3** flat bottom surface. **4** (right to speak in) a legislative hall. ▷ *v* **5** knock down. **6** *informal* disconcert or defeat. **floored** *adj* covered with a floor. **flooring** *n* material for floors. **floorboard** *n* long plank used for making floors. **floor show** entertainment in a nightclub.

floozy *n, pl* **-zies** *old-fashioned slang* disreputable woman.

flop ❶ *v* **flopping, flopped** **1** bend, fall, or collapse loosely or carelessly. **2** *informal* fail. ▷ *n* **3** *informal* failure. **4** flopping movement. **floppy** *adj* **floppier, floppiest** hanging downwards, loose. **floppy disk** *Computers* flexible magnetic disk that stores information.

flora *n* plants of a given place or time.

floral ❶ *adj* consisting of or decorated with flowers.

floret [**flaw**-ret] *n* small flower forming part of a composite flower head.

floribunda *n* type of rose whose flowers grow in large clusters.

florid ❶ *adj* **1** with a red or flushed complexion. **2** ornate.

florin *n* former British coin equivalent to ten pence.

florist *n* seller of flowers.

floss *n* **1** fine silky fibres. **2** see DENTAL FLOSS.

flotation *n* launching or financing of a business enterprise.

flotilla *n* small fleet or fleet of small ships.

flotsam ❶ *n* floating wreckage. **flotsam and jetsam** **1** odds and ends. **2** homeless or vagrant people.

flounce¹ *v* **1** go with emphatic movements. ▷ *n* **2** flouncing movement.

flounce² *n* ornamental frill on a garment.

flounder¹ ❶ *v* **1** move with difficulty, as in mud. **2** behave or speak in a bungling or hesitating manner.

flounder² *n* edible flatfish.

flour *n* **1** powder made by grinding grain, esp. wheat. ▷ *v* **2** sprinkle with flour. **floury** *adj*.

flourish ❶ *v* **1** be active, successful, or widespread. **2** be at the peak of development. **3** wave (something) dramatically. ▷ *n* **4** dramatic waving motion. **5** ornamental curly line in writing. **flourishing** *adj*.

flout ❶ [rhymes with **out**] *v* deliberately disobey (a rule, law, etc.).
- **USAGE NOTE**
- Be careful not to confuse this with
- *flaunt* meaning 'display'.

flow ❶ *v* **1** (of liquid) move in a stream. **2** (of blood or electricity) circulate. **3** proceed smoothly. **4** hang loosely. **5** be abundant. ▷ *n* **6** act, rate, or

———————————————— THESAURUS ————————

overwhelm, pour over, submerge, surge, swamp **5** = **overflow**, fill, saturate

floor *n* **2** = **tier**, level, stage, storey ▷ *v* **5** = **knock down**, deck (*sl*), prostrate **6** *Inf* = **disconcert**, baffle, bewilder, confound, defeat, dumbfound, perplex, puzzle, stump, throw (*inf*)

flop *v* **1** = **fall**, collapse, dangle, droop, drop, sag, slump **2** *Inf* = **fail**, come unstuck, fall flat, fold (*inf*), founder, go belly-up (*sl*), misfire ▷ *n* **3** *Inf* = **failure**, debacle, disaster, fiasco, nonstarter, washout (*inf*)

floppy *adj* **1** = **droopy**, baggy, flaccid, limp, loose, pendulous, sagging, soft

floral *adj* = **flowery**, flower-patterned

florid *adj* **1** = **flushed**, blowsy, rubicund, ruddy **2** = **ornate**, baroque,

flamboyant, flowery, high-flown, overelaborate

flotsam *n* = **debris**, detritus, jetsam, junk, odds and ends, wreckage

flounder¹ *v* **1** = **struggle**, fumble, grope, stumble, thrash, toss

flourish *v* **1, 2** = **thrive**, bloom, blossom, boom, flower, grow, increase, prosper, succeed **3** = **wave**, brandish, display, flaunt, shake, wield ▷ *n* **4** = **wave** **5** = **ornamentation**, curlicue, decoration, embellishment, plume, sweep

flout *v* = **defy**, laugh in the face of, mock, scoff at, scorn, sneer at, spurn

flow *v* **1** = **pour**, cascade, flood, gush, rush, stream, surge, sweep **2** = **run**, circulate, course, move, roll **3** = **issue**, arise, emanate, emerge, proceed,

manner of flowing. **7** continuous stream or discharge. **flow chart** diagram showing a sequence of operations in a process.

flower ❶ *n* **1** part of a plant that produces seeds. **2** plant grown for its colourful flowers. **3** best or finest part. ▷ *v* **4** produce flowers, bloom. **5** reach full growth or maturity. **in flower** with flowers open. **flowered** *adj* decorated with a floral design. **flowery** *adj* **1** decorated with a floral design. **2** (of language or style) elaborate. **flowerbed** *n* piece of ground for growing flowers.

flown ❶ *v* past participle of FLY¹.

fl. oz. fluid ounce(s).

flu *n* short for INFLUENZA.

fluctuate ❶ *v* change frequently and erratically. **fluctuation** *n*.

flue *n* passage or pipe for smoke or hot air.

fluent ❶ *adj* **1** able to speak or write with ease. **2** spoken or written with ease. **fluently** *adv* **fluency** *n*.

fluff ❶ *n* **1** soft fibres. **2** *informal* mistake. ▷ *v* **3** make or become soft and puffy. **4** *informal* make a mistake. **fluffy** *adj* **fluffier**, **fluffiest**.

fluid ❶ *n* **1** substance able to flow and change its shape; a liquid or a gas. ▷ *adj* **2** able to flow or change shape easily. **fluidity** *n* **fluid ounce** one twentieth of a pint.

fluke¹ ❶ *n* accidental stroke of luck. **fluky** *adj*.

fluke² *n* **1** flat triangular point of an anchor. **2** lobe of a whale's tail.

fluke³ *n* parasitic worm.

flume *n* **1** narrow sloping channel for water. **2** enclosed water slide at a swimming pool.

flummox *v* puzzle or confuse.

fling *v* past of FLING.

flunk *v US, Aust & NZ informal* fail.

flunky, flunkey *n*, *pl* **flunkies**, **flunkeys 1** servile person. **2** manservant who wears a livery.

fluorescence *n* emission of light from a substance bombarded by particles, such as electrons, or by radiation. **fluorescent** *adj* **fluorescent lamp** lamp in which ultraviolet radiation causes the chemical lining of a glass tube to glow. **fluoresce** *v* exhibit fluorescence.

fluoride *n* compound containing fluorine. **fluoridate** *v* add fluoride to (water) as protection against tooth decay. **fluoridation** *n*.

fluorine *n Chemistry* toxic yellow gas, most reactive of all the elements.

flurry ❶ *n*, *pl* **-ries 1** sudden commotion. **2** gust of rain or wind or fall of snow. ▷ *v* **-rying, -ried 3** confuse.

flush¹ ❶ *v* **1** blush or cause to blush. **2** send water through (a toilet or pipe) so as to clean it. **3** elate. ▷ *n* **4** blush. **5** rush of water. **6** excitement or elation. **flushed** *adj*.

flush² ❶ *adj* **1** level with the surrounding surface. **2** *informal* having plenty of money.

———————————— THESAURUS ————————————

result, spring ▷ *n* **6** = **course**, current, drift, flood, flux, outpouring, spate, tide **7** = **stream**

flower *n* **1, 2** = **bloom**, blossom, efflorescence **3** = **elite**, best, cream, pick ▷ *v* **4** = **bloom**, blossom, flourish, open, unfold **5** = **mature**

flowery *adj* **2** = **ornate**, baroque, embellished, fancy, florid, high-flown

fluctuate *v* = **change**, alternate, oscillate, seesaw, shift, swing, vary, veer, waver

fluency *n* **1** = **smoothness**, articulateness **2** = **ease**, assurance, command, control, facility, readiness, slickness

fluent *adj* **1** = **flowing**, articulate, natural, smooth, voluble, well-versed **2** = **effortless**, easy

fluff *n* **1** = **fuzz**, down, nap, pile ▷ *v* **4** *Inf* = **mess up** (*inf*), bungle, make a mess off, muddle, spoil

fluffy *adj* **1** = **soft**, downy, feathery, fleecy, fuzzy

fluid *n* **1** = **liquid**, liquor, solution ▷ *adj* **2** = **liquid**, flowing, liquefied, melted, molten, runny, watery

fluke¹ *n* = **stroke of luck**, accident, chance, coincidence, lucky break, quirk of fate, serendipity

flurry *n* **1** = **commotion**, ado, bustle, disturbance, excitement, flutter, fuss, stir **2** = **gust**, squall

flush¹ *v* **1** = **blush**, colour, glow, go red, redden **2** = **rinse out**, cleanse, flood, hose down, wash out ▷ *n* **4** = **blush**, colour, glow, redness, rosiness

flush² *adj* **1** = **level**, even, flat, square, true **2** *Inf* = **wealthy**, in the money

flush³ ❶ *v* drive out of a hiding place.

flush⁴ *n* (in card games) hand all of one suit.

fluster ❶ *v* **1** make nervous or upset. ▷ *n* **2** nervous or upset state.

flute *n* **1** wind instrument consisting of a tube with sound holes and a mouth hole in the side. **2** tall narrow wineglass. **fluted** *adj* having decorative grooves. **fluting** *n* design of decorative grooves.

flutter ❶ *v* **1** wave rapidly. **2** flap the wings. **3** move quickly and irregularly. **4** (of the heart) beat abnormally quickly. ▷ *n* **5** flapping movement. **6** nervous agitation. **7** *informal* small bet. **8** abnormally fast heartbeat.

fluvial [**flew**-vee-al] *adj* of rivers.

flux *n* **1** constant change or instability. **2** flow or discharge. **3** substance mixed with metal to assist in fusion. **4** *Physics* strength of a field in a given area.

fly¹ ❶ *v* **flying**, **flew**, **flown 1** move through the air on wings or in an aircraft. **2** control the flight of. **3** float, flutter, display, or be displayed in the air. **4** transport or be transported by air. **5** move quickly or suddenly. **6** (of time) pass rapidly. **7** flee. ▷ *n*, *pl* **flies 8** (often pl) fastening at the front of trousers. **9** flap forming the entrance to a tent. ▷ *pl* **10** space above a stage, used for storage. **flyer**, **flier** *n* **1** small advertising leaflet. **2** aviator. **fly-by-night** *adj informal* unreliable or untrustworthy. **flyleaf** *n* blank leaf at the beginning or end of a book. **flyover** *n* road passing over another by a bridge. **fly-past** *n* ceremonial flight

of aircraft. **flywheel** *n* heavy wheel regulating the speed of a machine.

fly² *n*, *pl* **flies** two-winged insect. **flycatcher** *n* small insect-eating songbird. **fly-fishing** *n* fishing with an artificial fly as a lure. **flypaper** *n* paper with a sticky poisonous coating, used to kill flies. **flyweight** *n* boxer weighing up to 112lb or 51kg (professional) or 106lb or 48kg up to 112lb or 51kg (amateur).

fly³ *adj slang* sharp and cunning.

flying ❶ *adj* hurried and brief. **flying boat** aircraft fitted with floats instead of landing wheels. **flying colours** conspicuous success, e.g. *pass with flying colours*. **flying fish** fish with winglike fins used for gliding above the water. **flying fox** large fruit-eating bat. **flying officer** junior officer in an air force. **flying phalanger** phalanger with black-striped greyish fur, which moves with gliding leaps. **flying saucer** unidentified disc-shaped flying object, supposedly from outer space. **flying squad** small group of police, soldiers, etc., ready to act quickly. **flying start** very good start.

Fm *Chemistry* fermium.

FM 1 frequency modulation. **2** (in Scotland) First Minister.

foal *n* **1** young of a horse or related animal. ▷ *v* **2** give birth to a foal.

foam ❶ *n* **1** mass of small bubbles on a liquid. **2** frothy saliva. **3** light spongelike solid used for insulation, packing, etc. ▷ *v* **4** produce foam. **5** be very angry, e.g. *he makes me foam at the mouth*. **foamy** *adj* **foamier**, **foamiest**.

fob *n* **1** short watch chain. **2** small pocket in a waistcoat.

THESAURUS

(*inf*), moneyed, rich, well-heeled (*inf*), well-off

flush³ *v* = **drive out**, discover, disturb, put to flight, rouse, start, uncover

flushed *adj* **1** = **blushing**, crimson, embarrassed, glowing, hot, red, rosy, ruddy

fluster *v* **1** = **upset**, agitate, bother, confuse, disturb, perturb, rattle (*inf*), ruffle, unnerve ▷ *n* **2** = **turmoil**, disturbance, dither, flap (*inf*), flurry, flutter, furore, state (*inf*)

flutter *v* **2** = **beat**, flap **3** = **tremble**, quiver, ripple, waver **4** = **palpitate** ▷ *n* **5** = **vibration**, quiver, shiver, shudder, tremble, tremor, twitching **6** = **agitation**, commotion, confusion,

dither, excitement, fluster, state (*inf*) **8** = **palpitation**

fly¹ *v* **1** = **take wing**, flit, flutter, hover, sail, soar, wing **2** = **pilot**, control, manoeuvre, operate **3** = **display**, flap, float, flutter, show, wave **5** = **rush**, career, dart, dash, hurry, race, shoot, speed, sprint, tear **6** = **pass**, elapse, flit, glide, pass swiftly, roll on, run its course, slip away **7** = **flee**, escape, get away, run for it, skedaddle (*inf*), take to one's heels

flying *adj* = **hurried**, brief, fleeting, hasty, rushed, short-lived, transitory

foam *n* **1** = **froth**, bubbles, head, lather, spray, spume, suds ▷ *v* **4** = **bubble**, boil, effervesce, fizz, froth, lather

fob off v **fobbing**, **fobbed 1** pretend to satisfy (a person) with lies or excuses. **2** sell or pass off (inferior goods) as valuable.

fo'c's'le n same as FORECASTLE.

focus ❶ n, pl **-cuses**, **-ci** [-sye] **1** point at which light or sound waves converge. **2** state of an optical image when it is clearly defined. **3** state of an instrument producing such an image. **4** centre of interest or activity. ▷ v **-cusing**, **-cused** or **-cussing**, **-cussed 5** bring or come into focus. **6** concentrate (on). **focal** adj of or at a focus. **focal length** distance from a lens or a mirror to its focal point. **focal point 1** point where the object seen in a lens or a mirror is in perfect focus. **2** centre of interest or attention. **focus group** group of people gathered by a market-research company to discuss and assess a product or service.

fodder n feed for livestock.

foe ❶ n enemy, opponent.

foetid adj same as FETID.

foetus n, pl **-tuses** same as FETUS.

fog ❶ n **1** mass of condensed water vapour in the lower air, often greatly reducing visibility. **2** blurred area on a developed photograph. ▷ v **fogging**, **fogged 3** cover with steam. **foggy** adj **foggier**, **foggiest**. **fogbound** adj prevented from operating by fog. **foghorn** n large horn sounded to warn ships in fog.

fogey, **fogy** n, pl **-geys**, **-gies** old-fashioned person.

foible n minor weakness or slight peculiarity.

foil¹ ❶ v ruin (someone's plan).

foil² ❶ n **1** metal in a thin sheet. **2** anything which sets off another

thing to advantage.

foil³ n light slender flexible sword tipped with a button.

foist ❶ v (foll. by on or upon) force or impose on.

fold¹ ❶ v **1** bend so that one part covers another. **2** interlace (the arms). **3** clasp (in the arms). **4** Cooking mix gently. **5** informal fail or go bankrupt. ▷ n **6** folded piece or part. **7** mark, crease, or hollow made by folding. **folder** n piece of folded cardboard for holding loose papers.

fold² n **1** enclosure for sheep. **2** church or its members.

foliage n leaves. **foliaceous** adj of or like leaves. **foliation** n process of producing leaves.

folio n, pl **-lios 1** sheet of paper folded in half to make two leaves of a book. **2** book made up of such sheets. **3** page number.

folk ❶ n **1** people in general. **2** race of people. **3** informal folk music. ▷ pl **4** relatives. **folksy** adj simple and unpretentious. **folk dance** traditional country dance. **folklore** n traditional beliefs and stories of a people. **folk music 1** music handed down from generation to generation. **2** piece written in the style of such music. **folk song 1** song handed down among the common people. **2** modern song like this. **folk singer**.

follicle n small cavity in the body, esp. one from which a hair grows.

follow ❶ v **1** go or come after. **2** accompany. **3** be a logical or natural consequence of. **4** keep to the course or track of. **5** act in accordance with. **6** accept the ideas or beliefs of.

THESAURUS

focus n **4** = **centre**, focal point, heart, hub, target ▷ v **6** = **concentrate**, aim, centre, direct, fix, pinpoint, spotlight, zoom in

foe n = **enemy**, adversary, antagonist, opponent, rival

fog n **1** = **mist**, gloom, miasma, murk, peasouper (inf), smog

foggy adj **1** = **misty**, cloudy, dim, hazy, indistinct, murky, smoggy, vaporous

foil¹ v = **thwart**, balk, counter, defeat, disappoint, frustrate, nullify, stop

foil² n **2** = **contrast**, antithesis, complement

foist v (foll. by on or upon) = **impose**, fob off, palm off, pass off, sneak in,

unload

fold¹ v **1** = **bend**, crease, double over **5** Inf = **go bankrupt**, collapse, crash, fail, go bust (inf), go to the wall, go under, shut down ▷ n **7** = **crease**, bend, furrow, overlap, pleat, wrinkle

folder n = **file**, binder, envelope, portfolio

folk n **1** = **people 2** = **race**, clan, tribe ▷ pl **4** = **family**, kin, kindred

follow v **1** = **come after**, come next, succeed, supersede, supplant, take the place of **2** = **accompany**, attend, escort, tag along **3** = **result**, arise, develop, ensue, flow, issue, proceed, spring **4** = **pursue**, chase, dog, hound,

7 understand. 8 have a keen interest in. 9 choose to receive messages or blogs posted online by a particular person. **follower** n disciple or supporter. **following** adj 1 about to be mentioned. 2 next in time. ▷ n 3 group of supporters. ▷ prep 4 as a result of. **follow-on** n Cricket immediate second innings forced on a team scoring a set number of runs fewer than its opponents in the first innings. **follow through** v 1 continue an action or series of actions until finished. 2 Sport continue a stroke, kick, etc. after striking the ball. **follow up** v 1 investigate. 2 do a second, often similar, thing after (a first). **follow-up** n something done to reinforce an initial action.

folly ❶ n, pl **-lies** 1 foolishness. 2 foolish action or idea. 3 useless extravagant building.

foment [foam-**ent**] v encourage or stir up (trouble).

fond ❶ adj 1 tender, loving. 2 unlikely to be realized, e.g. a fond hope. **fond of** having a liking for. **fondly** adv **fondness** n.

fondant n (sweet made from) flavoured paste of sugar and water.

fondle ❶ v caress.

fondue n Swiss dish of a hot melted cheese sauce into which pieces of bread are dipped.

font n bowl in a church for baptismal water.

fontanelle n soft membranous gap between the bones of a baby's skull.

food ❶ n what one eats, solid nourishment. **foodie** n informal gourmet. **foodbank** n charity that provides food to people in financial trouble. **food chain** Ecology series of living organisms each member of which feeds on another in the chain and is in turn eaten. **food poisoning** illness caused by eating contaminated food. **food processor** machine for chopping, liquidizing, or mixing food. **foodstuff** n substance used as food.

fool¹ ❶ n 1 person lacking sense or judgment. 2 person made to appear ridiculous. 3 History jester, clown. ▷ v 4 deceive (someone). **foolish** adj unwise, silly, or absurd. **foolishly** adv **foolishness** n **foolery** n foolish behaviour. **fool around** v act or play irresponsibly or aimlessly. **foolproof** adj unable to fail. **fool's paradise** state of happiness based on false hopes or beliefs.

fool² n dessert of puréed fruit mixed with cream.

foolhardy ❶ adj recklessly adventurous. **foolhardiness** n.

—————————————— THESAURUS ——————

hunt, shadow, stalk, track, trail 5 = **obey**, be guided by, conform, heed, observe 7 = **understand**, appreciate, catch on (inf), comprehend, fathom, grasp, realize, take in 8 = **be interested in**, cultivate, keep abreast of, support

follower n = **supporter**, adherent, apostle, devotee, disciple, fan, pupil

following adj 2 = **next**, consequent, ensuing, later, subsequent, succeeding, successive ▷ n 3 = **supporters**, clientele, coterie, entourage, fans, retinue, suite, train

folly n 1 = **foolishness**, imprudence, indiscretion, lunacy, madness, nonsense, rashness, stupidity

fond adj 1 = **loving**, adoring, affectionate, amorous, caring, devoted, doting, indulgent, tender, warm 2 = **foolish**, deluded, delusive, empty, naive, overoptimistic, vain **fond of** = **keen on**, addicted to, attached to, enamoured of, having a soft spot for, hooked on, into (inf), partial to

fondle v = **caress**, cuddle, dandle, pat, pet, stroke

fondness n 1 = **liking**, affection, attachment, devotion, fancy, love, partiality, penchant, soft spot, taste, weakness

food n = **nourishment**, cuisine, diet, fare, grub (sl), nutrition, rations, refreshment

fool¹ n 1 = **simpleton**, blockhead, dunce, halfwit, idiot, ignoramus, imbecile (inf), numbskull or numskull, twit (inf, chiefly Brit) 2 = **dupe**, fall guy (inf), laughing stock, mug (Brit sl), stooge (sl), sucker (sl) 3 Hist = **clown**, buffoon, harlequin, jester ▷ v 4 = **deceive**, beguile, con (inf), delude, dupe, hoodwink, mislead, take in, trick

foolhardy adj = **rash**, hot-headed, impetuous, imprudent, irresponsible, reckless

foolish adj = **unwise**, absurd, ill-judged, imprudent, injudicious, senseless, silly

foolishness n = **stupidity**, absurdity, folly, imprudence, indiscretion,

foolscap _n_ size of paper, 34.3 × 43.2 centimetres.

foot ❶ _n, pl_ **feet** **1** part of the leg below the ankle. **2** unit of length of twelve inches (0.3048 metre). **3** lowest part of anything. **4** unit of poetic rhythm. **foot it** _informal_ walk. **foot the bill** pay the entire cost. **footage** _n_ amount of film used. **foot-and-mouth disease** infectious viral disease of sheep, cattle, etc. **football** _n_ game played by two teams kicking a ball in an attempt to score goals. **footbridge** _n_ bridge for pedestrians. **footfall** _n_ sound of a footstep. **foothills** _pl n_ hills at the foot of a mountain. **foothold** _n_ **1** secure position from which progress may be made. **2** small place giving a secure grip for the foot. **footlights** _pl n_ lights across the front of a stage. **footloose** _adj_ free from ties. **footman** _n_ male servant in uniform. **footnote** _n_ note printed at the foot of a page. **footpath** _n_ **1** narrow path for walkers only. **2** _Aust_ raised space alongside a road, for pedestrians. **footplate** _n_ platform in the cab of a locomotive for the driver. **footprint** _n_ mark left by a foot. **footstep** _n_ **1** step in walking. **2** sound made by walking. **footstool** _n_ low stool used to rest the feet on while sitting. **footwear** _n_ anything worn to cover the feet. **footwork** _n_ skilful use of the feet, as in sport or dancing.

football _n_ **1** game played by two teams of eleven players kicking a ball in an attempt to score goals, soccer. **2** any of various similar games, such as rugby. **3** ball used for this. **footballer** _n_ **football pools** form of gambling on the results of football matches.

footing ❶ _n_ **1** basis or foundation. **2** relationship between people. **3** secure grip by or for the feet.

footle _v_ _informal_ loiter aimlessly. **footling** _adj_ trivial.

footsie _n_ _informal_ flirtation involving the touching together of feet.

fop _n_ man excessively concerned with fashion. **foppery** _n_ **foppish** _adj_.

for _prep_ **1** indicating a person intended to benefit from or receive something, span of time or distance, person or thing represented by someone, etc. e.g. _a gift for you; for five miles; playing for his country_. ▷ _conj_ **2** because. **for it** _informal_ liable for punishment or blame.

forage ❶ [**for**-ridge] _v_ **1** search about (for). ▷ _n_ **2** food for cattle or horses.

foray ❶ _n_ **1** brief raid or attack. **2** first attempt or new undertaking.

forbear[1] ❶ _v_ cease or refrain (from doing something). **forbearance** _n_ tolerance, patience.

forbear[2] _n_ same as FOREBEAR.

forbid ❶ _v_ prohibit, refuse to allow. **forbidden** _adj_ **forbidden fruit** anything attractive because prohibited. **forbidding** _adj_ severe, threatening.

force ❶ _n_ **1** strength or power. **2** compulsion. **3** _Physics_ influence tending to produce a change in a physical system. **4** mental or moral strength. **5** person or thing with strength or influence. **6** vehemence or

irresponsibility, silliness, weakness

foolproof _adj_ = **infallible**, certain, guaranteed, safe, sure-fire (_inf_)

footing _n_ **1** = **basis**, foundation, groundwork **2** = **relationship**, grade, position, rank, standing, status

footstep _n_ **1** = **step** **2** = **footfall**, tread

forage _v_ **1** = **search**, cast about, explore, hunt, rummage, scour, seek ▷ _n_ **2** = **fodder**, feed, food, provender

foray _n_ **1** = **raid**, incursion, inroad, invasion, sally, sortie, swoop

forbear[1] _v_ = **refrain**, abstain, cease, desist, hold back, keep from, restrain oneself, stop

forbearance _n_ = **patience**, long-suffering, resignation, restraint, self-control, temperance, tolerance

forbid _v_ = **prohibit**, ban, disallow, exclude, outlaw, preclude, rule out, veto

forbidden _adj_ = **prohibited**, banned, outlawed, proscribed, taboo, vetoed

forbidding _adj_ = **threatening**, daunting, frightening, hostile, menacing, ominous, sinister, unfriendly

force _n_ **1** = **power**, energy, impulse, might, momentum, pressure, strength, vigour **2** = **compulsion**, arm-twisting (_inf_), coercion, constraint, duress, pressure, violence **6** = **intensity**, emphasis, fierceness, vehemence, vigour **7** = **army**, host, legion, patrol, regiment, squad, troop, unit ▷ _v_ **8** = **compel**, coerce, constrain,

intensity. **7** group of people organized for a particular task or duty. ▷ *v* **8** compel, make (someone) do something. **9** acquire or produce through effort, strength, etc. **10** propel or drive. **11** break open. **12** impose or inflict. **13** cause to grow at an increased rate. **in force 1** having legal validity. **2** in great numbers.

forced *adj* **1** compulsory. **2** false or unnatural. **3** due to an emergency.

force-feed *v* **-feeding**, **-fed** compel (a person or animal) to swallow food.

forceful *adj* **1** emphatic and confident. **2** effective. **forcefully** *adv* **forcible** *adj* **1** involving physical force or violence. **2** strong and emphatic. **forcibly** *adv*.

forcemeat *n* mixture of chopped ingredients used for stuffing.

forceps *pl n* surgical pincers.

ford *n* **1** shallow place where a river may be crossed. ▷ *v* **2** cross (a river) at a ford. **fordable** *adj*.

fore *adj* **1** in, at, or towards the front. ▷ *n* **2** front part. ▷ *interj* **3** golfer's shouted warning to a person in the path of a ball. **to the fore** in a conspicuous position.

fore- *prefix* **1** before in time or rank, e.g. *forefather*. **2** at the front, e.g. *forecourt*.

fore-and-aft *adj* located at both ends of a ship.

forearm¹ *n* arm from the wrist to the elbow.

forearm² *v* prepare beforehand.

forebear ❶ *n* ancestor.

foreboding ❶ *n* feeling that something bad is about to happen.

forecast ❶ *v* **-casting**, **-cast** *or* **-casted** **1** predict (weather, events, etc.). ▷ *n* **2** prediction.

forecastle [**foke**-sl] *n* raised front part of a ship.

foreclose *v* take possession of (property bought with borrowed money which has not been repaid). **foreclosure** *n*.

forecourt *n* courtyard or open space in front of a building.

forefather ❶ *n* ancestor.

forefinger *n* finger next to the thumb.

forefoot *n* either of the front feet of an animal.

forefront ❶ *n* **1** most active or prominent position. **2** very front.

foregather *v* meet together or assemble.

forego ❶ *v* same as FORGO.

foregoing ❶ *adj* going before, preceding. **foregone conclusion** inevitable result.

foreground *n* part of a view, esp. in a picture, nearest the observer.

forehand *n Tennis, etc.* stroke played with the palm of the hand facing forward.

forehead *n* part of the face above the eyebrows.

foreign ❶ *adj* **1** not of, or in, one's own country. **2** relating to or connected

————————— THESAURUS —————————

dragoon, drive, impel, make, oblige, press, pressurize **10** = **push**, propel, thrust **11** = **break open**, blast, prise, wrench, wrest **in force 1** = **valid**, binding, current, effective, in operation, operative, working **2** = **in great numbers**, all together, in full strength

forced *adj* **1** = **compulsory**, conscripted, enforced, involuntary, mandatory, obligatory **2** = **false**, affected, artificial, contrived, insincere, laboured, stiff, strained, unnatural, wooden

forceful *adj* **2** = **powerful**, cogent, compelling, convincing, dynamic, effective, persuasive

forcible *adj* **1** = **violent**, aggressive, armed, coercive **2** = **compelling**, energetic, forceful, potent, powerful, strong, weighty

forebear *n* = **ancestor**, father,

forefather, forerunner, predecessor

foreboding *n* = **dread**, anxiety, apprehension, apprehensiveness, chill, fear, misgiving, premonition, presentiment

forecast *v* **1** = **predict**, anticipate, augur, divine, foresee, foretell, prophesy ▷ *n* **2** = **prediction**, conjecture, guess, prognosis, prophecy

forefather *n* = **ancestor**, father, forebear, forerunner, predecessor

forefront *n* **1** = **foreground**, centre, fore, prominence **2** = **lead**, front, spearhead, vanguard

forego SEE FORGO

foregoing *adj* = **preceding**, above, antecedent, anterior, former, previous, prior

foreign *adj* **1, 2** = **external**, exotic, imported, remote **3** = **alien**, strange, unfamiliar, unknown

with other countries. **3** unfamiliar, strange. **4** in an abnormal place or position, e.g. *foreign matter*. **foreigner** n **foreign minister**, **secretary** government minister who deals with other countries. **foreign office** ministry that deals with other countries.

foreknowledge n knowledge of something before it actually happens.

foreleg n either of the front legs of an animal.

forelock n lock of hair over the forehead. **tug the forelock** behave servilely or obsequiously.

foreman n **1** person in charge of a group of workers. **2** leader of a jury.

foremast n mast nearest the bow of a ship.

foremost ① adj, adv first in time, place, or importance.

forename n first name.

forenoon n morning.

forensic [for-ren-sik] adj used in or connected with courts of law. **forensic medicine** use of medical knowledge for the purposes of the law.

foreordain v determine events in the future.

forepaw n either of the front feet of a land mammal that does not have hooves.

foreplay n sexual stimulation before intercourse.

forerunner ① n person or thing that goes before, precursor.

foresail n main sail on the foremast of a ship.

foresee ① v see or know beforehand.

foreseeable adj.

● **SPELLING TIP**
● There are 665 occurrences of the
● word **unforeseen** in the Bank of
● English. The misspelling *unforsen*
● occurs 50 times.

foreshadow ① v show or indicate beforehand.

foreshore n part of the shore between high- and low-tide marks.

foreshorten v represent (an object) in a picture as shorter than it really is, in accordance with perspective.

foresight ① n ability to anticipate and provide for future needs.

foreskin n fold of skin covering the tip of the penis.

forest n large area with a thick growth of trees. **forested** adj **forestry** n **1** science of planting and caring for trees. **2** management of forests. **forester** n person skilled in forestry.

forestall v prevent or guard against in advance.

foretaste n early limited experience of something to come.

foretell ① v tell or indicate beforehand.

forethought ① n thoughtful planning for future events.

forever, for ever ① adv **1** without end. **2** at all times. **3** *informal* for a long time.

forewarn ① v warn beforehand.

foreword n introduction to a book.

forfeit ① [for-fit] n **1** thing lost or given up as a penalty for a fault or mistake. ▷ v **2** lose as a forfeit. ▷ adj **3** lost as a forfeit. **forfeiture** n.

forgather v same as FOREGATHER.

f

— THESAURUS —

foreigner n = **alien**, immigrant, incomer, stranger

foremost adj = **leading**, chief, highest, paramount, pre-eminent, primary, prime, principal, supreme

forerunner n = **precursor**, harbinger, herald, prototype

foresee v = **predict**, anticipate, envisage, forecast, foretell, prophesy

foreshadow v = **indicate**, augur, forebode, portend, prefigure, presage, promise, signal

foresight n = **forethought**, anticipation, far-sightedness, precaution, preparedness, prescience, prudence

foretell v = **predict**, forecast, forewarn, presage, prognosticate, prophesy

forethought n = **anticipation**,

far-sightedness, foresight, precaution, providence, provision, prudence

forever, for ever adv **1** = **evermore**, always, endlessly, eternally, for all time, for keeps, in perpetuity **2** = **constantly**, all the time, continually, incessantly, interminably, perpetually, twenty-four-seven (*inf*), unremittingly **3** *Inf* = **till the cows come home**, till Doomsday (*inf*)

forewarn v = **caution**, advise, alert, apprise, give fair warning, put on guard, tip off

forfeit n **1** = **penalty**, damages, fine, forfeiture, loss, mulct ▷ v **2** = **lose**, be deprived of, be stripped of, give up, relinquish, renounce, say goodbye to, surrender

forgave *v* past tense of FORGIVE.

forge[1] ❶ *n* **1** place where metal is worked, smithy. **2** furnace for melting metal. ▷ *v* **3** make a fraudulent imitation of (something). **4** shape (metal) by heating and hammering it. **5** create (an alliance etc.).

forge[2] *v* advance steadily. **forge ahead** increase speed or take the lead.

forgery ❶ *n, pl* **-ries 1** illegal copy of something. **2** crime of making an illegal copy. **forger** *n*.

forget ❶ *v* **-getting, -got, -gotten 1** fail to remember. **2** neglect. **3** leave behind by mistake. **forgetful** *adj* tending to forget. **forgetfulness** *n* **forget-me-not** *n* plant with clusters of small blue flowers.

forgive ❶ *v* **-giving, -gave, -given** cease to blame or hold resentment against, pardon. **forgiveness** *n* **forgivable** *adj* able to be forgiven. **forgiving** *adj* willing to forgive.

forgo ❶ *v* do without or give up.

forgot ❶ *v* past tense of FORGET. **forgotten** *v* past participle of FORGET.

fork ❶ *n* **1** tool for eating food, with prongs and a handle. **2** large similarly-shaped tool for digging or lifting. **3** point where a road, river, etc. divides into branches. **4** one of the branches. ▷ *v* **5** pick up, dig, etc. with a fork. **6** branch. **7** take one or other branch at a fork in the road. **forked** *adj* **fork-lift truck** vehicle with a forklike device at the front which can be raised or lowered to move loads. **fork out** *v informal* pay.

forlorn ❶ *adj* lonely and unhappy. **forlorn hope** hopeless enterprise. **forlornly** *adv*.

form ❶ *n* **1** shape or appearance. **2** mode in which something appears. **3** type or kind. **4** printed document with spaces for details. **5** physical or mental condition. **6** previous record of an athlete, racehorse, etc. **7** class in school. **8** procedure or etiquette. **9** bench. **10** hare's nest. ▷ *v* **11** give a (particular) shape to or take a (particular) shape. **12** come or bring into existence. **13** make or be made. **14** train. **15** acquire or develop. **16** be an element of. **formation** *n* structure or shape. **formless** *adj*.

---

forge[1] *v* **3** = **fake**, copy, counterfeit, falsify, feign, imitate **4** = **shape**, fashion, mould, work **5** = **create**, construct, devise, form, frame, make

forgery *n* **1** = **fake**, counterfeit, falsification, imitation, phoney *or* phony (*inf*), sham **2** = **falsification**, coining, counterfeiting, fraudulence, fraudulent imitation

forget *v* **1** = **omit**, overlook **2** = **neglect**, lose sight of **3** = **leave behind**

forgetful *adj* = **absent-minded**, careless, inattentive, neglectful, oblivious, unmindful, vague

forgive *v* = **excuse**, absolve, acquit, condone, exonerate, let bygones be bygones, let off (*inf*), pardon

forgiveness *n* = **pardon**, absolution, acquittal, amnesty, exoneration, mercy, remission

forgiving *adj* = **lenient**, clement, compassionate, forbearing, magnanimous, merciful, soft-hearted, tolerant

forgo *v* = **give up**, abandon, do without, relinquish, renounce, resign, surrender, waive, yield

forgotten *adj* = **unremembered**, bygone, left behind, lost, omitted, past, past recall

fork *v* **6** = **branch**, bifurcate, diverge, divide, part, split

forked *adj* **6** = **branching**, angled, bifurcate(d), branched, divided, pronged, split, zigzag

forlorn *adj* = **miserable**, disconsolate, down in the dumps (*inf*), helpless, hopeless, pathetic, pitiful, unhappy, woebegone, wretched

form *n* **1** = **shape**, appearance, structure **2** = **formation**, configuration, pattern **3** = **type**, kind, sort, style, variety **4** = **document**, application, paper, sheet **5** = **condition**, fettle, fitness, health, shape, trim **7** = **class**, grade, rank **8** = **procedure**, convention, custom, etiquette, protocol ▷ *v* **11** = **arrange**, combine, draw up, organize **12** = **take shape**, appear, become visible, come into being, crystallize, grow, materialize, rise **13** = **make**, build, construct, create, fashion, forge, mould, produce, shape **15** = **develop**, acquire, contract, cultivate, pick up **16** = **constitute**, compose, comprise, make up

formal ❶ *adj* **1** of or characterized by established conventions of ceremony and behaviour. **2** of or for formal occasions. **3** stiff in manner. **4** organized. **5** symmetrical. **formally** *adv* **formalism** *n* concern with outward appearances and structure at the expense of content. **formalist** *n*, *adj* **formality** *n*, *pl* **-ties 1** requirement of custom or etiquette. **2** necessary procedure without real importance. **formalize** *v* make official or formal.

formaldehyde [for-**mal**-de-hide] *n* colourless pungent gas used to make the disinfectant and preservative formalin. **formalin** *n* solution of formaldehyde in water, used as a disinfectant or a preservative for biological specimens.

format ❶ *n* **1** size and shape of a publication. **2** style in which something is arranged. ▷ *v* **-matting**, **-matted 3** arrange in a format.

formation ❶ *n* **1** forming. **2** thing formed. **3** structure or shape. **4** arrangement of people or things acting as a unit.

formative ❶ *adj* **1** of or relating to development. **2** shaping.

former ❶ *adj* of an earlier time, previous. **the former** first mentioned of two. **formerly** *adv*.

Formica *n* ® kind of laminated sheet used to make heat-resistant surfaces.

formic acid *n* acid derived from ants.

formidable ❶ *adj* **1** frightening because difficult to overcome or manage. **2** extremely impressive. **formidably** *adv*.

formula ❶ *n*, *pl* **-las**, **-lae 1** group of numbers, letters, or symbols expressing a scientific or mathematical rule. **2** method or rule for doing or producing something. **3** set form of words used in religion, law, etc. **4** specific category of car in motor racing. **5** *US* powder used to produce a milky drink for babies. **formulaic** *adj* **formulate** *v* plan or describe precisely and clearly. **formulation** *n*.

fornicate *v* have sexual intercourse without being married. **fornication** *n* **fornicator** *n*.

forsake ❶ *v* **-saking**, **-sook**, **-saken 1** withdraw support or friendship from. **2** give up, renounce.

forsooth *adv obs* indeed.

forswear *v* **-swearing**, **-swore**, **-sworn** renounce or reject.

forsythia [for-**syth**-ee-a] *n* shrub with yellow flowers in spring.

fort ❶ *n* fortified building or place. **hold the fort** *informal* keep things going during someone's absence.

forte¹ ❶ [**for**-tay] *n* thing at which a person excels.

THESAURUS
---

formal *adj* **1** = **conventional**, correct, solemn **2** = **official**, ceremonial, ritualistic **3** = **stiff**, affected, precise, unbending

formality *n* **1** = **convention**, correctness, custom, decorum, etiquette, procedure, protocol, rite **2** = **ritual**, red tape

format *n* **1** = **layout**, construction, form, make-up, plan **2** = **arrangement**, appearance, look, style, type

formation *n* **1** = **development**, constitution, establishment, forming, generation, genesis, manufacture, production **3, 4** = **arrangement**, configuration, design, grouping, pattern, structure

formative *adj* **1** = **developmental 2** = **influential**

former *adj* = **previous**, earlier, erstwhile, one-time, prior

formerly *adv* = **previously**, at one time, before, lately, once

formidable *adj* **1** = **intimidating**, daunting, dismaying, fearful, frightful, terrifying **2** = **impressive**, awesome, great, mighty, powerful, redoubtable, terrific, tremendous

formula *n* **2** = **method**, blueprint, precept, principle, procedure, recipe, rule

formulate *v* **a** = **devise**, develop, forge, invent, map out, originate, plan, work out **b** = **define**, detail, express, frame, give form to, set down, specify, systematize

forsake *v* **1** = **desert**, abandon, disown, leave in the lurch, strand **2** = **give up**, forgo, relinquish, renounce, set aside, surrender, yield

fort *n* = **fortress**, blockhouse, camp, castle, citadel, fortification, garrison, stronghold **hold the fort** *Inf* = **carry on**, keep things on an even keel, stand in, take over the reins

forte¹ *n* = **speciality**, gift, long suit (*inf*), métier, strength, strong point, talent

forte² [**for**-tay] *adv Music* loudly.

forth ❶ *adv* forwards, out, or away. **and so forth** and so on.

forthcoming ❶ *adj* **1** about to appear or happen. **2** available. **3** (of a person) communicative.

forthright ❶ *adj* direct and outspoken.

forthwith ❶ *adv* at once.

fortieth *adj*, *n* see FORTY.

fortify ❶ *v* **-fying**, **-fied 1** make (a place) defensible, as by building walls. **2** strengthen. **3** add vitamins etc. to (food). **4** add alcohol to (wine) to make sherry or port. **fortification** *n*.

fortissimo *adv Music* very loudly.

fortitude ❶ *n* courage in adversity or pain.

fortnight *n* two weeks. **fortnightly** *adv*, *adj*.

FORTRAN *n Computers* programming language for mathematical and scientific purposes.

fortress ❶ *n* large fort or fortified town.

fortuitous [for-**tyew**-it-uss] *adj* happening by (lucky) chance. **fortuitously** *adv*.

fortunate ❶ *adj* **1** having good luck. **2** occurring by good luck. **fortunately** *adv*.

fortune ❶ *n* **1** luck, esp. when favourable. **2** power regarded as influencing human destiny. **3** wealth, large sum of money. ▷ *pl* **4** person's destiny. **fortunate** *adj* having good luck. **fortune-teller** *n* person who claims to predict the future of others.

forty *adj*, *n*, *pl* **-ties** four times ten. **fortieth** *adj*, *n* **forty winks** short light sleep.

forum *n* meeting or medium for open discussion or debate.

forward ❶ *adj* **1** directed or moving ahead. **2** in, at, or near the front. **3** presumptuous. **4** well developed or advanced. **5** relating to the future. ▷ *n* **6** attacking player in various team games, such as football or hockey. ▷ *adv* **7** forwards. ▷ *v* **8** send (a letter etc.) on to an ultimate destination. **9** advance or promote. **forwards** *adv* **1** towards or at a place further ahead in space or time. **2** towards the front.

forwent *v* past tense of FORGO.

fossick *v Aust & NZ* search, esp. for gold or precious stones.

fossil *n* **1** hardened remains of a prehistoric animal or plant preserved in rock. ▷ *adj* **2** of, like, or being a fossil. **fossil fuel** fuel such as coal or oil that is formed from the decayed remains of prehistoric animals or plants. **fossilize**

———————————————————————————— THESAURUS —————————

forth *adv* = **forward**, ahead, away, onward, out, outward

forthcoming *adj* **1** = **approaching**, coming, expected, future, imminent, impending, prospective, upcoming **2** = **available**, accessible, at hand, in evidence, obtainable, on tap (*inf*), ready **3** = **communicative**, chatty, expansive, free, informative, open, sociable, talkative, unreserved

forthright *adj* = **outspoken**, blunt, candid, direct, frank, open, plain-spoken, straightforward, upfront (*inf*)

forthwith *adv* = **at once**, directly, immediately, instantly, quickly, right away, straightaway, without delay

fortification *n* **1** = **defence**, bastion, fastness, fort, fortress, protection, stronghold **2** = **strengthening**, reinforcement

fortify *v* **1** = **protect**, buttress, reinforce, shore up **2** = **strengthen**, augment, support

fortitude *n* = **courage**, backbone, bravery, fearlessness, grit, perseverance, resolution, strength, valour

fortress *n* = **castle**, citadel, fastness, fort, redoubt, stronghold

fortunate *adj* **1** = **lucky**, favoured, in luck, jammy (*Brit sl*), successful, well-off **2** = **providential**, advantageous, convenient, expedient, favourable, felicitous, fortuitous, helpful, opportune, timely

fortunately *adv* = **luckily**, by a happy chance, by good luck, happily, providentially

fortune *n* **1** = **luck**, chance **2** = **fate**, destiny, kismet, providence **3** = **wealth**, affluence, opulence, possessions, property, prosperity, riches, treasure ▷ *pl* **4** = **destiny**, lot

forward *adj* **1** = **leading**, advance, head **2** = **front**, first, foremost **3** = **presumptuous**, bold, brash, brazen, cheeky, familiar, impertinent, impudent, pushy (*inf*) **4** = **well-developed**, advanced, precocious, premature ▷ *adv* **7** = **forth**, ahead, on, onward ▷ *v* **8** = **send**, dispatch, post, send on **9** = **promote**, advance, assist, expedite, further, hasten, hurry

v **1** turn into a fossil. **2** become out-of-date or inflexible.

foster ❶ *v* **1** promote the growth or development of. **2** bring up (a child not one's own). ▷ *adj* **3** of or involved in fostering a child, e.g. *foster parents*. **fostering** *n*.

fought *v* past of FIGHT.

foul ❶ *adj* **1** loathsome or offensive. **2** stinking or dirty. **3** (of language) obscene or vulgar. **4** unfair. **5** very bad-tempered. ▷ *n* **6** *Sport* violation of the rules. ▷ *v* **7** make dirty or polluted. **8** make or become entangled or clogged. **9** *Sport* commit a foul against (an opponent). **fall foul of** come into conflict with. **foul-mouthed** *adj* habitually using foul language. **foul play** unfair conduct, esp. involving violence.

found¹ *v* past of FIND.

found² ❶ *v* **1** establish or bring into being. **2** lay the foundation of. **3** (foll. by *on* or *upon*) have a basis (in). **founder** *n* **founder member** one of the original members of a club or organization, often someone involved in setting it up.

found³ *v* **1** cast (metal or glass) by melting and setting in a mould. **2** make (articles) by this method.

foundation ❶ *n* **1** basis or base. **2** part of a building or wall below the ground. **3** act of founding. **4** institution supported by an endowment. **5** cosmetic used as a base for make-up.

founder ❶ *v* **1** break down or fail. **2** (of a ship) sink. **3** stumble or fall.

foundling *n* abandoned baby.

foundry *n*, *pl* **-ries** place where metal is melted and cast.

fount¹ *n* **1** *lit* fountain. **2** source.

fount² *n* set of printing type of one style and size.

fountain ❶ *n* **1** jet of water. **2** structure from which such a jet spurts. **3** source. **fountainhead** *n* original source. **fountain pen** pen supplied with ink from a container inside it.

four *adj*, *n* **1** one more than three. ▷ *n* **2** (crew of) four-oared rowing boat. **on all fours** on hands and knees. **four-letter word** short obscene word referring to sex or excrement. **four-poster** *n* bed with four posts supporting a canopy. **foursome** *n* group of four people. **foursquare** *adv* **1** squarely or firmly. ▷ *adj* **2** solid and strong. **3** forthright.

fourteen *adj*, *n* four and ten. **fourteenth** *adj*, *n*.

fourth *adj*, *n* **1** (of) number four in a series. ▷ *n* **2** quarter. **fourthly** *adv* **fourth dimension** time. **fourth estate** the press.

fowl *n* **1** domestic cock or hen. **2** any bird used for food or hunted as game.

fox *n* **1** reddish-brown bushy-tailed animal of the dog family. **2** its fur. **3** cunning person. ▷ *v* **4** *informal* perplex or deceive. **foxy** *adj* **foxier**, **foxiest** of or like a fox, esp. in craftiness. **foxglove** *n* tall plant with purple or white flowers. **foxhole** *n* *Military* small pit dug for protection. **foxhound** *n* dog bred for hunting foxes. **fox terrier** small short-haired terrier. **foxtrot** *n* **1** ballroom dance

foster *v* **1** = **promote**, cultivate, encourage, feed, nurture, stimulate, support, uphold **2** = **bring up**, mother, nurse, raise, rear, take care of

foul *adj* **1** = **offensive**, abhorrent, despicable, detestable, disgraceful, scandalous, shameful, wicked **2** = **dirty**, fetid, filthy, malodorous, nauseating, putrid, repulsive, squalid, stinking, unclean **3** = **obscene**, abusive, blue, coarse, indecent, lewd, profane, scurrilous, vulgar **4** = **unfair**, crooked, dishonest, fraudulent, shady (*inf*), underhand, unscrupulous ▷ *v* **7** = **dirty**, besmirch, contaminate, defile, pollute, stain, sully, taint

found² *v* **1** = **establish**, constitute, create, inaugurate, institute, organize,

originate, set up, start

foundation *n* **1** = **basis**, base, bedrock, bottom, footing, groundwork **2** = **substructure**, underpinning **3** = **setting up**, endowment, establishment, inauguration, institution, organization, settlement

founder *n* = **initiator**, architect, author, beginner, father, inventor, originator ▷ *v* **1** = **fail**, break down, collapse, come to grief, come unstuck, fall through, miscarry, misfire **2** = **sink**, be lost, go down, go to the bottom, submerge **3** = **stumble**, lurch, sprawl, stagger, trip

fountain *n* **1** = **jet**, spout, spray, spring **2** = **fount**, font, well **3** = **source**, cause, derivation, fount, fountainhead, origin, wellspring

with slow and quick steps. **2** music for this.

foyer ❶ [**foy**-ay] *n* entrance hall in a theatre, cinema, or hotel.

Fr 1 *Chemistry* francium. **2** Father.

Fr. Franc.

fracas ❶ [**frak**-ah] *n*, *pl* **-cas** noisy quarrel.

fracking *n* extraction of gas or oil from rock by forcing liquid into the rock at high pressure.

fraction ❶ *n* **1** numerical quantity that is not a whole number. **2** fragment, piece. **3** *Chemistry* substance separated by distillation. **fractional** *adj* **fractionally** *adv*.

fractious ❶ *adj* easily upset and angered.

fracture ❶ *n* **1** breaking, esp. of a bone. ▷ *v* **2** break.

fragile ❶ *adj* **1** easily broken or damaged. **2** in a weakened physical state. **fragility** *n*.

fragment ❶ *n* **1** piece broken off. **2** incomplete piece. ▷ *v* **3** break into pieces. **fragmentary** *adj* **fragmentation** *n*.

fragrant ❶ *adj* sweet-smelling. **fragrance** *n* **1** pleasant smell. **2** perfume, scent.

frail ❶ *adj* **1** physically weak. **2** easily

damaged. **frailty** *n*, *pl* **-ties** physical or moral weakness.

frame ❶ *n* **1** structure giving shape or support. **2** enclosing case or border, as round a picture. **3** person's build. **4** individual exposure on a strip of film. **5** individual game of snooker in a match. ▷ *v* **6** put together, construct. **7** put into words. **8** put into a frame. **9** *slang* incriminate (a person) on a false charge. **frame of mind** mood or attitude. **frame-up** *n slang* false incrimination. **framework** *n* supporting structure.

franc *n* monetary unit of Switzerland and various African countries (formerly France and Belgium).

franchise *n* **1** right to vote. **2** authorization to sell a company's goods.

Franciscan *n*, *adj* (friar or nun) of the order founded by St. Francis of Assisi.

francium *n Chemistry* radioactive metallic element.

Franco- *combining form* of France or the French.

frank ❶ *adj* **1** honest and straightforward in speech or attitude. ▷ *n* **2** official mark on a letter permitting delivery. ▷ *v* **3** put such a mark on (a letter). **frankly** *adv* **frankness** *n*.

———————————————————————————— THESAURUS ————————————————————————————

foyer *n* = **entrance hall**, antechamber, anteroom, lobby, reception area, vestibule

fracas *n* = **brawl**, affray (*Law*), disturbance, mêlée, riot, rumpus, scuffle, skirmish

fraction *n* **1** = **percentage 2** = **piece**, part, portion, section, segment, share, slice

fractious *adj* = **irritable**, captious, cross, petulant, querulous, testy, tetchy, touchy

fracture *n* **1** = **break**, crack ▷ *v* **2** = **break**, crack, rupture, splinter, split

fragile *adj* **1** = **delicate**, breakable, brittle, dainty, fine, flimsy, frangible **2** = **weak**, frail

fragment *n* **1** = **chip**, bit, particle, scrap, shred, sliver **2** = **piece**, portion ▷ *v* **3** = **break**, break up, come apart, come to pieces, crumble, disintegrate, shatter, splinter, split up

fragmentary *adj* **1** = **broken**, bitty, disconnected, scattered, scrappy **2** = **incomplete**, incoherent, partial, piecemeal, sketchy

fragrance *n* **1** = **smell**, aroma,

bouquet, redolence, sweet odour **2** = **perfume**, scent

fragrant *adj* = **aromatic**, balmy, odorous, perfumed, redolent, sweet-scented, sweet-smelling

frail *adj* **1** = **weak**, feeble, fragile, infirm, puny **2** = **delicate**, flimsy, insubstantial, vulnerable

frailty *n* = **weakness**, fallibility, feebleness, frailness, infirmity, susceptibility

frame *n* **1** = **casing**, construction, framework, shell, structure **3** = **physique**, anatomy, body, build, carcass ▷ *v* **6** = **construct**, assemble, build, make, manufacture, put together **7** = **devise**, compose, draft, draw up, formulate, map out, sketch **8** = **mount**, case, enclose, surround **frame of mind** = **mood**, attitude, disposition, humour, outlook, state, temper

framework *n* = **structure**, foundation, frame, groundwork, plan, shell, skeleton, the bare bones

frank *adj* **1** = **honest**, blunt, candid, direct, forthright, open, outspoken,

frankfurter *n* smoked sausage.
frankincense *n* aromatic gum resin burned as incense.
frantic ⊙ *adj* **1** distracted with rage, grief, joy, etc. **2** hurried and disorganized. **frantically** *adv*.
frappé *adj* (of drinks) chilled.
fraternal ⊙ *adj* of a brother, brotherly. **fraternally** *adv* **fraternity** *n*, *pl* **-ties 1** group of people with shared interests, aims, etc. **2** brotherhood. **3** *US* male social club at college. **fraternize** *v* associate on friendly terms. **fraternization** *n* **fratricide** *n* **1** crime of killing one's brother. **2** person who does this.
Frau [rhymes with **how**] *n*, *pl* **Fraus, Frauen** German title, equivalent to *Mrs*. **Fräulein froy-***line*, *n*, *pl* **-leins, -lein** German title, equivalent to *Miss*.
fraud ⊙ *n* **1** (criminal) deception, swindle. **2** person who acts in a deceitful way. **fraudulent** *adj* **fraudulence** *n*.
fraught [**frawt**] *adj* tense or anxious. **fraught with** involving, filled with.
fray¹ *n* noisy quarrel or conflict.
fray² ⊙ *v* **1** make or become ragged at the edge. **2** become strained.
frazzle *n informal* exhausted state. **frazzled** *adj informal* exhausted and irritable.
freak ⊙ *n* **1** abnormal person or thing. **2** person who is excessively enthusiastic about something. ▷ *adj* **3** abnormal. **freakish** *adj* **freak out** *v*

informal (cause to) be in a heightened emotional state. **freaky** *adj* **freakier, freakiest** *informal* weird, peculiar.
freckle *n* small brown spot on the skin. **freckled** *adj* marked with freckles.
free ⊙ *adj* **freer, freest 1** able to act at will, not compelled or restrained. **2** not subject (to). **3** independent. **4** provided without charge. **5** generous, lavish. **6** not in use. **7** (of a person) not busy. **8** not fixed or joined. **9** (of a translation) not exact or literal. ▷ *v* **freeing, freed 10** release, liberate. **11** remove (obstacles, pain, etc.) from. **12** make available or usable. **a free hand** unrestricted freedom to act. **freely** *adv* **free-and-easy** *adj* casual and tolerant. **freebooter** *n* pirate. **free enterprise** economic system in which businesses compete for profit with little state control. **free fall** part of a parachute descent before the parachute opens. **free-for-all** *n informal* brawl. **freehand** *adj* drawn without guiding instruments. **freehold** *n* tenure of land for life without restrictions. **freeholder** *n* **free house** public house not bound to sell only one brewer's products. **freelance** *adj*, *n* (of) a self-employed person doing specific pieces of work for various employers. **freeloader** *n slang* habitual scrounger. **freeman** *n* person who has been given the freedom of a city. **free-market** *adj* denoting an economic system in which

plain-spoken, sincere, straightforward, truthful
frantic *adj* **1** = **distraught**, at the end of one's tether, berserk, beside oneself, desperate, distracted, fraught (*inf*), furious, wild **2** = **hectic**, frenetic, frenzied (*sl*)
fraternity *n* **1** = **association**, brotherhood, circle, club, company, guild, league, union **2** = **companionship**, brotherhood, camaraderie, fellowship, kinship
fraternize *v* = **associate**, consort, cooperate, hobnob, keep company, mingle, mix, socialize
fraud *n* **1** = **deception**, chicanery, deceit, double-dealing, duplicity, sharp practice, swindling, treachery, trickery **2** = **impostor**, charlatan, fake, hoaxer, phoney *or* phony (*inf*), pretender, swindler

fraudulent *adj* = **deceitful**, crooked (*inf*), dishonest, double-dealing, duplicitous, sham, swindling, treacherous
fray² *v* **1** = **wear thin**, wear
freak *n* **1** = **oddity**, aberration, anomaly, malformation, monstrosity, weirdo *or* weirdie (*inf*) **2** = **enthusiast**, addict, aficionado, buff (*inf*), devotee, fan, fanatic, fiend (*inf*), nut (*sl*) ▷ *adj* **3** = **abnormal**, exceptional, unparalleled, unusual
free *adj* **1** = **allowed**, able, clear, permitted, unimpeded, unrestricted **2, 3** = **at liberty**, at large, footloose, independent, liberated, loose, on the loose, unfettered **4** = **complimentary**, for free (*inf*), for nothing, free of charge, gratis, gratuitous, on the house, unpaid, without charge **5** = **generous**, lavish,

supply and demand regulate prices, wages, etc. **free-range** *adj* kept or produced in natural conditions. **free-standing** *adj* not attached to or supported by another object. **free-style** *n* competition, esp. in swimming, in which each participant uses the style of his or her choice. **freethinker** *n* person who forms his or her ideas independently of authority, esp. on religious matters. **free verse** unrhymed verse without a fixed rhythm. **freeway** *n Chiefly US* motorway. **freewheel** *v* travel downhill on a bicycle without pedalling. **free will 1** ability to make choices that are not externally determined. **2** ability to make a decision without outside coercion, e.g. *she left of her own free will.*

- **USAGE NOTE**
- *Free of* means 'not subject to': *free of*
- *charge. Free from* suggests a change
- of circumstances: *They were free from*
- *danger.*

-free *combining form* without, e.g. *a trouble-free journey.*

freedom ❶ *n* **1** being free. **2** exemption or immunity, e.g. *freedom from hunger.* **3** right or privilege of unlimited access, e.g. *the freedom of the city.*

Freemason *n* member of a secret fraternity pledged to help each other. **Freemasonry** *n.*

freesia *n* plant with fragrant tubular flowers.

freeze ❶ *v* **freezing, froze, frozen 1** change from a liquid to a solid by the reduction of temperature, as water to ice. **2** preserve (food etc.) by extreme

cold. **3** (cause to) be very cold. **4** become motionless with fear, shock, etc. **5** fix (prices or wages) at a particular level. **6** ban the exchange or collection of (loans, assets, etc.). ▷ *n* **7** period of very cold weather. **8** freezing of prices or wages. **freezer** *n* insulated cabinet for cold-storage of perishable foods. **freeze-dry** *v* preserve (food) by rapid freezing and drying in a vacuum. **freeze-frame** *n* single frame from a film or video recording shown as a still photograph. **freezing** *adj informal* very cold. **freezing point** temperature below which a liquid turns into a solid.

freight ❶ [frate] *n* **1** commercial transport of goods. **2** cargo transported. **3** cost of this. ▷ *v* **4** send by freight. **freighter** *n* ship or aircraft for transporting goods.

French *n* **1** language of France, also spoken in parts of Belgium, Canada, and Switzerland. ▷ *adj* **2** of France, its people, or their language. **French bean** green bean whose pods are eaten. **French bread** white bread in a long thin crusty loaf. **French-Canadian** *adj* of or from the part of Canada where French is spoken. **French dressing** salad dressing of oil and vinegar. **French fries** potato chips. **French horn** brass wind instrument with a coiled tube. **French letter** *Slang* condom. **French polish** shellac varnish for wood. **French window** window extending to floor level, used as a door.

French fries potato chips.

━━━━━━━━━━━━━━━━━━━━ THESAURUS ━━━━━━

liberal, unsparing, unstinting **6** = **available**, empty, spare, unoccupied, unused, vacant **7** = **idle**, unemployed ▷ *v* **10** = **release**, deliver, let out, liberate, loose, set free, turn loose, unchain, untie **11** = **clear**, cut loose, disengage, disentangle, extricate, rescue

freedom *n* **1** = **liberty**, deliverance, emancipation, independence, release **3** = **licence**, blank cheque, carte blanche, discretion, free rein, latitude, opportunity

free-for-all *n Inf* = **fight**, brawl, dust-up (*inf*), fracas, mêlée, riot, row, scrimmage

freely *adv* **1** = **willingly**, of one's own

accord, of one's own free will, spontaneously, voluntarily, without prompting **5** = **abundantly**, amply, copiously, extravagantly, lavishly, liberally, unstintingly

freeze *v* **1** = **ice over** *or* **up**, harden, stiffen **3** = **chill 5, 6** = **suspend**, fix, hold up, inhibit, stop

freezing *adj Inf* = **icy**, arctic, biting, bitter, chill, frosty, glacial, raw, wintry

freight *n* **1** = **transportation**, carriage, conveyance, shipment **2** = **cargo**, burden, consignment, goods, load, merchandise, payload

frenzied *adj* = **uncontrolled**, distracted, feverish, frantic, frenetic, furious, rabid, wild

French horn brass wind instrument with a coiled tube.

frenetic [frin-**net**-ik] *adj* uncontrolled, excited. **frenetically** *adv*.

frenzy ❶ *n, pl* **-zies 1** violent mental derangement. **2** wild excitement. **frenzied** *adj* **frenziedly** *adv*.

frequent ❶ *adj* **1** happening often. **2** habitual. ▷ *v* **3** visit habitually. **frequently** *adv* **frequency** *n, pl* **-cies 1** rate of occurrence. **2** *Physics* number of times a wave repeats itself in a given time.

fresco *n, pl* **-coes, -cos** watercolour painting done on wet plaster on a wall.

fresh ❶ *adj* **1** newly made, acquired, etc. **2** novel, original. **3** most recent. **4** further, additional. **5** (of food) not preserved. **6** (of water) not salty. **7** (of weather) brisk or invigorating. **8** not tired. **9** *informal* impudent. **freshly** *adv* **freshness** *n* **freshen** *v* **1** make or become fresh or fresher. **2** (foll. by *up*) refresh oneself, esp. by washing. **3** (of the wind) increase. **fresher, freshman** *n* first-year student. **freshwater** *adj* of or living in fresh water.

fret¹ ❶ *v* **fretting, fretted 1** be worried. **2** rub or wear away. ▷ *n* **3** worried state. **fretful** *adj* irritable.

fret² *n* small bar on the fingerboard of a guitar etc.

fretwork *n* decorative carving in wood. **fret saw** fine saw with a narrow blade, used for fretwork.

Freudian [**froy**-dee-an] *adj* of or relating to the psychoanalyst Sigmund Freud or his theories. **Freudian slip** action or error which may reveal an unconscious wish.

Fri. Friday.

friable [**fry**-a-bl] *adj* easily crumbled. **friability** *n*.

friar *n* member of a male Roman Catholic religious order. **friary** *n, pl* **-ries** house of friars.

fricassee *n* stewed meat served in a thick white sauce.

fricative *n* **1** consonant produced by friction of the breath through a partially open mouth, such as (f) or (z). ▷ *adj* **2** relating to or being a fricative.

friction ❶ *n* **1** resistance met with by a body moving over another. **2** rubbing. **3** clash of wills or personalities. **frictional** *adj*.

Friday *n* sixth day of the week. **Good Friday** Friday before Easter.

fridge *n* apparatus in which food and drinks are kept cool.

fried *v* past of FRY¹.

friend ❶ *n* **1** person whom one knows well and likes. **2** supporter or ally. **3** (**F-**) Quaker. ▷ *v* **4** add (a person) as a contact on a social networking site. **friendly** *adj* **-lier, -liest 1** showing or expressing liking. **2** not hostile, on the same side. ▷ *n, pl* **-lies 3** *Sport* match played for its own sake and not as part of a competition. **-friendly** *combining*

THESAURUS

frenzy *n* **1** = **fury**, derangement, hysteria, paroxysm, passion, rage, seizure

frequent *adj* **1** = **persistent**, recurrent, repeated **2** = **habitual**, common, customary, everyday, familiar, usual ▷ *v* **3** = **visit**, attend, hang out at (*inf*), haunt, patronize

frequently *adv* **1** = **often**, many times, much, not infrequently, repeatedly **2** = **habitually**, commonly

fresh *adj* **1** = **new**, different **2** = **novel**, original **3** = **recent**, modern, up-to-date **4** = **additional**, added, auxiliary, extra, further, more, other, supplementary **5** = **natural**, unprocessed **7** = **invigorating**, bracing, brisk, clean, cool, crisp, pure, refreshing, unpolluted **8** = **lively**, alert, energetic, keen, refreshed, sprightly, spry, vigorous **9** *Inf* = **cheeky**, disrespectful, familiar,

forward, impudent, insolent, presumptuous

freshen *v* **1, 2** = **refresh**, enliven, freshen up, liven up, restore, revitalize

fret¹ *v* **1** = **worry**, agonize, brood, lose sleep over, obsess about, upset *or* distress oneself

fretful *adj* = **irritable**, crotchety (*inf*), edgy, fractious, querulous, short-tempered, testy, touchy, uneasy

friction *n* **2** = **rubbing**, abrasion, chafing, grating, rasping, resistance, scraping **3** = **hostility**, animosity, bad blood, conflict, disagreement, discord, dissension, resentment

friend *n* **1** = **companion**, buddy (*inf*), chum (*inf*), comrade, mate (*inf*), pal, playmate **2** = **supporter**, ally, associate, patron, well-wisher

friendly *adj* **1** = **amiable**, affectionate, amicable, close, cordial, familiar, helpful, intimate, neighbourly, on

form good or easy for the person or thing specified, e.g. *user-friendly*.
friendly fire *n Military* firing by one's own side, esp when it harms one's own personnel. **friendly society** association of people who pay regular dues in return for pensions, sickness benefits, etc. **friendliness** *n* **friendless** *adj* **friendship** *n*.

fries *pl n* see FRY[1] (sense 3).

Friesian [**free**-zhan] *n* breed of black-and-white dairy cattle.

frieze [**freeze**] *n* ornamental band on a wall.

frigate [**frig**-it] *n* medium-sized fast warship.

fright ❶ *n* **1** sudden fear or alarm. **2** sudden alarming shock. **3** *informal* grotesque person. **frighten** *v* **1** scare or terrify. **2** force (someone) to do something from fear. **frightening** *adj* **frighteningly** *adv* **frightful** *adj* **1** horrifying. **2** *informal* very great. **frightfully** *adv*.

frigid ❶ [**frij**-id] *adj* **1** (of a woman) sexually unresponsive. **2** very cold. **3** excessively formal. **frigidity** *n*.

frill *n* **1** gathered strip of fabric attached at one edge. ▷ *pl* **2** superfluous decorations or details. **frilled** *adj* **frilled lizard** large tree-living Australian lizard with an erectile fold of skin round the neck. **frilly** *adj*.

fringe ❶ *n* **1** hair cut short and hanging over the forehead. **2** ornamental edge of hanging threads, tassels, etc.

3 outer edge. **4** less important parts of an activity or group. ▷ *v* **5** decorate with a fringe. ▷ *adj* **6** (of theatre) unofficial or unconventional. **fringed** *adj* **fringe benefit** benefit given in addition to a regular salary.

frippery *n, pl* **-peries 1** useless ornamentation. **2** trivia.

Frisian *n* **1** language spoken in the NW Netherlands and adjacent islands. **2** speaker of this language. ▷ *adj* **3** of this language or its speakers.

frisk ❶ *v* **1** move or leap playfully. **2** *informal* search (a person) for concealed weapons etc. ▷ *n* **3** playful movement. **4** *informal* instance of searching a person. **frisky** *adj* **friskier, friskiest** lively or high-spirited. **friskily** *adv*.

frisson [**frees**-sonn] *n* shiver of fear or excitement.

fritter *n* piece of food fried in batter.

fritter away ❶ *v* waste.

frivolous ❶ *adj* **1** not serious or sensible. **2** enjoyable but trivial. **frivolity** *n, pl* **-ties**.

frizz *v* form (hair) into stiff wiry curls. **frizzy** *adj* **frizzier, frizziest**.

frizzle *v* cook or heat until crisp and shrivelled.

fro *adv* away, only in *to and fro*.

frock *n* dress. **frock coat** man's skirted coat as worn in the 19th century.

frog *n* smooth-skinned tailless amphibian with long back legs used for jumping. **frog in one's throat**

THESAURUS

good terms, pally (*inf*), sociable, sympathetic, welcoming

friendship *n* **1** = **friendliness**, affection, amity, attachment, concord, familiarity, goodwill, harmony, intimacy

fright *n* **1, 2** = **fear**, alarm, consternation, dread, horror, panic, scare, shock, trepidation

frighten *v* **1** = **scare**, alarm, petrify, shock, startle, terrify, unnerve **2** = **intimidate**, terrorize

frightful *adj* **1** = **terrifying**, alarming, awful, dreadful, fearful, ghastly, horrendous, horrible, terrible, traumatic

frigid *adj* **1** = **unresponsive 2** = **cold**, arctic, frosty, frozen, glacial, icy, wintry **3** = **formal**, aloof, austere, forbidding, unapproachable, unfeeling

frills *pl n* **2** = **trimmings**, additions,

bells and whistles, embellishments, extras, frippery, fuss, ornamentation, ostentation

fringe *n* **2** = **border**, edging, hem, trimming **3** = **edge**, borderline, limits, margin, outskirts, perimeter, periphery ▷ *adj* **6** = **unofficial**, unconventional, unorthodox

frisk *v* **1** = **frolic**, caper, cavort, gambol, jump, play, prance, skip, trip **2** *Inf* = **search**, check, inspect, run over, shake down (*US sl*)

frisky *adj* = **lively**, coltish, frolicsome, high-spirited, kittenish, playful, sportive

fritter away *v* = **waste**, dissipate, idle away, misspend, run through, spend like water, squander

frivolous *adj* **1** = **flippant**, childish, foolish, idle, juvenile, puerile, silly, superficial **2** = **trivial**, footling (*inf*),

phlegm on the vocal cords, hindering speech. **frogman** n swimmer with a rubber suit and breathing equipment for working underwater. **frogmarch** v force (a resisting person) to move by holding his arms. **frogspawn** n jelly-like substance containing frog's eggs.

frolic ❶ v **-icking, -icked 1** run and play in a lively way. ▷ n **2** lively and merry behaviour. **frolicsome** adj playful.

from prep indicating the point of departure, source, distance, cause, change of state, etc.

frond n long leaf or leaflike part of a fern, palm, or seaweed.

front ❶ n **1** fore part. **2** position directly before or ahead. **3** seaside promenade. **4** battle line or area. **5** Meteorology dividing line between two different air masses. **6** outward appearance. **7** informal cover for another, usu. criminal, activity. **8** group with a common goal. **9** particular field of activity, e.g. on the economic front. ▷ adj **10** of or at the front. ▷ v **11** face (onto). **12** be a front of or for. **13** be the presenter of (a television show). **frontal** adj **frontage** n facade of a building. **front bench** parliamentary leaders of the government or opposition. **front-bencher** n **frontrunner** n informal person regarded as most likely to win a race, election, etc.

frontier ❶ n **1** area of a country bordering on another. **2** edge of the settled area of a country. ▷ pl **3** limit of knowledge in a particular field.

frontispiece n illustration facing the title page of a book.

frost ❶ n **1** white frozen dew or mist. **2** atmospheric temperature below freezing point. ▷ v **3** become covered with frost. **frosted** adj (of glass) having a rough surface to make it opaque. **frosting** n Chiefly US sugar icing. **frosty** adj **frostier, frostiest 1** characterized or covered by frost. **2** unfriendly. **frostily** adv **frostiness** n **frostbite** n destruction of tissue, esp. of the fingers or ears, by cold. **frostbitten** adj.

froth ❶ n **1** mass of small bubbles. **2** trivial but superficially attractive ideas or entertainment. ▷ v **3** foam. **frothy** adj **frothier, frothiest**.

frown ❶ v **1** wrinkle one's brows in worry, anger, or thought. **2** look disapprovingly (on). ▷ n **3** frowning expression.

frowsty adj stale or musty.

frowzy, frowsy adj **-zier, -ziest** or **-sier, -siest** dirty or unkempt.

froze ❶ v past tense of FREEZE. **frozen** v past participle of FREEZE.

FRS Fellow of the Royal Society.

fructify v **-fying, -fied** (cause to) bear fruit. **fructification** n.

fructose n crystalline sugar occurring in many fruits.

frugal ❶ [froo-gl] adj **1** thrifty, sparing. **2** meagre and inexpensive. **frugally** adv **frugality** n.

fruit ❶ n **1** part of a plant containing seeds, esp. if edible. **2** any plant

minor, petty, shallow, trifling, unimportant

frolic v **1** = **play**, caper, cavort, frisk, gambol, lark, make merry, romp, sport ▷ n **2** = **revel**, antic, game, lark, romp, spree

front n **1** = **foreground**, frontage **2** = **forefront**, head, lead, vanguard **4** = **front line 6** = **exterior**, facade, face **7** Inf = **cover**, blind, cover-up, disguise, mask, pretext ▷ adj **10** = **foremost**, first, head, lead, leading, topmost ▷ v **11** = **face onto**, look over or onto, overlook

frontier n **1, 2** = **boundary**, borderline, edge, limit, perimeter, verge

frost n **1** = **hoarfrost**, rime **2** = **freeze**

frosty adj **1** = **cold**, chilly, frozen, icy, wintry **2** = **unfriendly**, discouraging, frigid, off-putting (Brit inf),

standoffish, unenthusiastic, unwelcoming

froth n **1** = **foam**, bubbles, effervescence, head, lather, scum, spume, suds ▷ v **3** = **fizz**, bubble over, come to a head, effervesce, foam, lather

frown v **1** = **scowl**, glare, glower, knit one's brows, look daggers, lour or lower **2** = **disapprove of**, discourage, dislike, look askance at, take a dim view of

frozen adj = **icy**, arctic, chilled, frigid, frosted, icebound, ice-cold, ice-covered, numb

frugal adj **1** = **thrifty**, abstemious, careful, economical, niggardly, parsimonious, prudent, sparing

fruit n **2** = **produce**, crop, harvest, product, yield **3** (often pl) = **result**,

product useful to man. **3** (often pl) result of an action or effort. ▷ v **4** bear fruit. **fruiterer** n person who sells fruit. **fruitful** adj useful or productive. **fruitfully** adv **fruitless** adj useless or unproductive. **fruitlessly** adv **fruity** adj **fruitier**, **fruitiest 1** of or like fruit. **2** (of a voice) mellow. **3** informal mildly bawdy. **fruitcake** n cake containing dried fruit. **fruit fly 1** small fly that feeds on and lays its eggs in plant tissues. **2** similar fly that feeds on plant sap, decaying fruit, etc., and is widely used in genetics experiments. **fruit machine** coin-operated gambling machine. **fruit salad, cocktail** dish consisting of pieces of different kinds of fruit.

fruition ❶ [froo-**ish**-on] n fulfilment of something worked for or desired.

frump n dowdy woman. **frumpy** adj **frumpier**, **frumpiest**.

frustrate ❶ v **1** upset or anger. **2** hinder or prevent. **frustrated** adj **frustrating** adj **frustration** n.

frustum n, pl **-tums**, **-ta** Geometry part of a cone or pyramid contained between the base and a plane parallel to the base that intersects the solid.

fry¹ v **frying**, **fried 1** cook or be cooked in fat or oil. ▷ n, pl **fries 2** (also **fry-up**) dish of fried food. ▷ pl **3** potato chips. **frying pan** shallow pan used for frying food. **out of the frying pan into the fire** from a bad situation into a worse one.

fry² pl n young fishes. **small fry** young or insignificant people.

ft. 1 foot. **2** feet.

fuchsia [**fyew**-sha] n ornamental shrub with hanging flowers.

fuck taboo ▷ v **1** have sexual intercourse (with). ▷ n **2** act of sexual intercourse. ▷ interj **3** expression of strong disgust or anger. **fuck off** v taboo slang go away. **fuck up** v taboo slang make a mess of (something).

fuddle v **1** cause to be intoxicated or confused. ▷ n **2** confused state. **fuddled** adj.

fuddy-duddy ❶ adj, n, pl **-dies** informal old-fashioned (person).

fudge¹ n soft caramel-like sweet.

fudge² ❶ v **1** make (an issue) less clear deliberately. **2** avoid making a firm statement or decision.

fuel ❶ n **1** substance burned or treated to produce heat or power. **2** something that intensifies (a feeling etc.). ▷ v **fuelling**, **fuelled 3** provide with fuel.

fug n hot stale atmosphere. **fuggy** adj **fuggier**, **fuggiest**.

fugitive ❶ [**fyew**-jit-iv] n **1** person who flees, esp. from arrest or pursuit. ▷ adj **2** fleeing. **3** transient.

fugue [**fyewg**] n musical composition in which a theme is repeated in different parts.

Führer n German leader: title used by Hitler as Nazi dictator.

-ful adj suffix **1** full of or characterized by, e.g. painful; restful. **2** able or tending to, e.g. useful. ▷ n suffix **3** as much as will fill the thing specified, e.g. mouthful.

fulcrum n, pl **-crums**, **-cra** pivot about which a lever turns.

——————————————— THESAURUS ———————

advantage, benefit, consequence, effect, end result, outcome, profit, return, reward

fruitful adj = **useful**, advantageous, beneficial, effective, productive, profitable, rewarding, successful, worthwhile

fruition n = **fulfilment**, attainment, completion, materialization, maturity, perfection, realization, ripeness

fruitless adj = **useless**, futile, ineffectual, pointless, profitless, unavailing, unproductive, unprofitable, unsuccessful, vain

frustrate v **2** = **thwart**, balk, block, check, counter, defeat, disappoint, foil, forestall, nullify, stymie

frustration n **1** = **annoyance**, disappointment, dissatisfaction, grievance, irritation, resentment, vexation **2** = **obstruction**, blocking, circumvention, foiling, thwarting

fuddy-duddy n Inf = **conservative**, (old) fogey, square (inf), stick-in-the-mud (inf), stuffed shirt (inf)

fudge² v **1** = **misrepresent**, equivocate, flannel (Brit inf) **2** = **stall**, hedge

fuel n **2** = **incitement**, provocation

fugitive n **1** = **runaway**, deserter, escapee, refugee ▷ adj **3** = **momentary**, brief, ephemeral, fleeting, passing, short-lived, temporary, transient, transitory

fulfil ❶ *v* **-filling, -filled 1** bring about the achievement of (a desire or promise). **2** carry out (a request or order). **3** do what is required. **fulfilment** *n* **fulfil oneself** *v* achieve one's potential.

full¹ ❶ *adj* **1** containing as much or as many as possible. **2** abundant in supply. **3** having had enough to eat. **4** plump. **5** complete, whole. **6** (of a garment) of ample cut. **7** (of a sound or flavour) rich and strong. ▷ *adv* **8** completely. **9** directly. **10** very. **fully** *adv* **fullness** *n* **in full** without shortening. **full back** defensive player in various sports. **full-blooded** *adj* vigorous or enthusiastic. **full-blown** *adj* fully developed. **full board** provision by a hotel of a bed and all meals. **full-bodied** *adj* having a full rich flavour or quality. **full house 1** theatre filled to capacity. **2** (in bingo) set of numbers needed to win. **full-length** *adj* **1** (of a mirror, portrait, etc.) showing the whole human body. **2** not abridged. **full moon** phase of the moon when it is visible as a fully illuminated disc. **full-scale** *adj* **1** (of a plan) of actual size. **2** using all resources. **full stop** punctuation mark (.) at the end of a sentence and after

abbreviations. **full time** (in football, rugby, etc.) end of the game. **full-time** *adj* for all of the normal working week. **full up** filled to capacity.

full² *v* clean, shrink, and press cloth. **fuller** *n* **fuller's earth** absorbent clay used for clarifying oils and fats, fulling cloth, etc.

fulmar *n* Arctic sea bird.

fulminate *v* (foll. by *against*) criticize or denounce angrily. **fulmination** *n*.

fulsome ❶ *adj* distastefully excessive or insincere.

fumble ❶ *v* **1** handle awkwardly. **2** say awkwardly. ▷ *n* **3** act of fumbling.

fume ❶ *v* **1** be very angry. **2** give out smoke or vapour. **3** treat with fumes. ▷ *pl n* **4** pungent smoke or vapour.

fumigate ❶ [**fyew**-mig-gate] *v* disinfect with fumes. **fumigation** *n*.

fun ❶ *n* enjoyment or amusement. **make fun of** mock or tease. **funny** *adj* **funnier, funniest 1** comical, humorous. **2** odd. **funny bone** part of the elbow where the nerve is near the surface. **funnily** *adv*.

function ❶ *n* **1** purpose something exists for. **2** way something works. **3** large or formal social event. **4** *Maths* quantity whose value depends on the varying value of

---

fulfil *v* **1** = **achieve**, accomplish, realise **2** = **carry out**, complete, perform, satisfy **3** = **comply with**, answer, conform to, fill, meet, obey, observe

full¹ *adj* **1** = **filled**, brimming, complete, loaded, saturated, stocked **2** = **extensive**, abundant, adequate, ample, generous, plentiful **3** = **satiated**, replete **4** = **plump**, buxom, curvaceous, rounded, voluptuous **5** = **comprehensive**, exhaustive **6** = **voluminous**, baggy, capacious, large, loose, puffy **7** = **rich**, clear, deep, distinct, loud, resonant, rounded **in full** = **completely**, in its entirety, in total, without exception

fullness *n* **1** = **fill**, saturation **2** = **plenty**, abundance, adequateness, ampleness, copiousness, profusion, sufficiency **3** = **satiety 7** = **richness**, clearness, loudness, resonance, strength

full-scale *adj* **2** = **major**, all-out, comprehensive, exhaustive, in-depth, sweeping, thorough, thoroughgoing,

wide-ranging

fully *adv* **5** = **totally**, altogether, completely, entirely, in all respects, one hundred per cent, perfectly, thoroughly, utterly, wholly

fulsome *adj* = **extravagant**, excessive, immoderate, inordinate, insincere, sycophantic, unctuous

fumble *v* **1** = **grope**, feel around, flounder, scrabble

fume *v* **1** (*inf*) = **rage**, rant, see red (*inf*), seethe, smoulder, storm ▷ *pl n* **4** = **smoke**, exhaust, gas, pollution, smog, vapour

fumigate *v* = **disinfect**, clean out *or* up, cleanse, purify, sanitize, sterilize

fun *n* = **enjoyment**, amusement, entertainment, jollity, merriment, mirth, pleasure, recreation, sport **make fun of** = **mock**, lampoon, laugh at, parody, poke fun at, ridicule, satirize, send up (*Brit inf*)

function *n* **1** = **purpose**, *raison d'être*, business, duty, job, mission, responsibility, role, task

another. **5** sequence of operations performed by a computer at a key stroke. ▷ *v* **6** operate or work. **7** (foll. by *as*) fill the role of. **functional** *adj* **1** of or as a function. **2** practical rather than decorative. **3** in working order. **functionally** *adv* **functionary** *n*, *pl* **-aries** official.

fund ❶ *n* **1** stock of money for a special purpose. **2** supply or store. ▷ *pl* **3** money resources. ▷ *v* **4** provide money to. **funding** *n*.

fundamental ❶ *adj* **1** essential or primary. **2** basic. ▷ *n* **3** basic rule or fact. **fundamentally** *adv* **fundamentalism** *n* literal or strict interpretation of a religion. **fundamentalist** *n*, *adj*.

fundi *n S Afr* expert or boffin.

funeral ❶ *n* ceremony of burying or cremating a dead person. **funeral director** undertaker. **funeral parlour** place where the dead are prepared for burial or cremation.

funerary *adj* of or for a funeral.

funereal [fyew-**neer**-ee-al] *adj* gloomy or sombre.

funfair *n* entertainment with machines to ride on and stalls.

fungus *n*, *pl* **-gi**, **-guses** plant without leaves, flowers, or roots, such as a mushroom or mould. **fungal**, **fungous** *adj* **fungicide** *n* substance that destroys fungi.

funicular [fyew-**nik**-yew-lar] *n* cable railway on a mountainside or cliff.

funk¹ *n* style of dance music with a strong beat. **funky** *adj* **funkier**,

funkiest (of music) having a strong beat.

funk² *informal* ▷ *n* **1** nervous or fearful state. ▷ *v* **2** avoid (doing something) through fear.

funnel ❶ *n* **1** cone-shaped tube for pouring liquids into a narrow opening. **2** chimney of a ship or locomotive. ▷ *v* **-nelling**, **-nelled 3** (cause to) move through or as if through a funnel. **funnel-web** *n Aust* large poisonous black spider that builds funnel-shaped webs.

funny ❶ *adj* see FUN.

fur *n* **1** soft hair of a mammal. **2** animal skin with the fur left on. **3** garment made of this. **4** whitish coating on the tongue or inside a kettle. ▷ *v* **5** cover or become covered with fur. **furry** *adj* **furrier**, **furriest**. **furrier** *n* dealer in furs.

furbish *v* smarten up.

furcate *v* **1** divide into two parts. ▷ *adj* **2** forked, branching.

furious ❶ *adj* **1** very angry. **2** violent or unrestrained. **furiously** *adv*.

furl *v* roll up and fasten (a sail, umbrella, or flag). **furled** *adj*.

furlong *n* eighth of a mile.

furlough [**fur**-loh] *n* leave of absence from military duty.

furnace *n* **1** enclosed chamber containing a very hot fire. **2** *informal* very hot place.

furnish ❶ *v* **1** provide (a house or room) with furniture. **2** supply, provide. **furnishings** *pl n* furniture, carpets, and fittings. **furniture** *n* large

————————————————————————————— THESAURUS —————————————

3 = **reception**, affair, do (*inf*), gathering, social occasion ▷ *v*
6 = **work**, go, operate, perform, run
7 (foll. by *as*) = **act as**, behave as, do duty as
functional *adj* **2** = **practical**, hard-wearing, serviceable, useful, utilitarian
3 = **working**, operative
fund *n* **1** = **kitty**, pool **2** = **reserve**, stock, store, supply ▷ *v* **4** = **finance**, pay for, subsidize, support
fundamental *adj* **1** = **essential**, cardinal, central, key, primary, principal **2** = **basic**, elementary, rudimentary, underlying ▷ *n*
3 = **principle**, axiom, cornerstone, law, rudiment, rule
funds *pl n* **3** = **money**, capital, cash, finance, ready money, resources,

savings, the wherewithal
funeral *n* = **burial**, cremation, interment, obsequies
funnel *v* **3** = **channel**, conduct, convey, direct, filter, move, pass, pour
funny *adj* **1** = **humorous**, amusing, comic, comical, droll, entertaining, hilarious, riotous, side-splitting, witty
2 = **peculiar**, curious, mysterious, odd, queer, strange, suspicious, unusual, weird
furious *adj* **1** = **angry**, beside oneself, enraged, fuming, incensed, infuriated, livid (*inf*), raging, up in arms
2 = **violent**, fierce, intense, savage, turbulent, unrestrained, vehement
furnish *v* **1** = **decorate**, equip, fit out, stock **2** = **supply**, give, grant, hand out, offer, present, provide

movable articles such as chairs and wardrobes.

furore ❶ [fyew-**ror**-ee] *n* very excited or angry reaction.

furrow ❶ *n* **1** trench made by a plough. **2** groove, esp. a wrinkle on the forehead. ▷ *v* **3** make or become wrinkled. **4** make furrows in.

further ❶ *adv* **1** in addition. **2** to a greater distance or extent. ▷ *adj* **3** additional. **4** more distant. ▷ *v* **5** assist the progress of. **further education** education beyond school other than at a university. **furthest** *adv* **1** to the greatest distance or extent. ▷ *adj* **2** most distant. **furtherance** *n* **furthermore** *adv* besides. **furthermost** *adj* most distant.

furtive ❶ *adj* sly and secretive. **furtively** *adv*.

fury ❶ *n, pl* **-ries 1** wild anger. **2** uncontrolled violence. **3** person with a violent temper.

furze *n* gorse.

fuse¹ *n* cord containing an explosive for detonating a bomb.

fuse² *n* **1** safety device for electric circuits, containing a wire that melts and breaks the connection when the circuit is overloaded. ▷ *v* **2** (cause to) fail as a result of a blown fuse. **3** equip (a plug) with a fuse. **4** join or combine. **5** unite by melting. **6** melt with heat.

fuselage [fyew-zill-lahzh] *n* body of an aircraft.

fusible *adj* capable of being melted.

fusilier [fyew-zill-**leer**] *n* soldier of certain regiments.

fusillade [fyew-zill-**lade**] *n* **1** continuous discharge of firearms. **2** outburst of criticism, questions, etc.

fusion *n* **1** melting. **2** product of fusing. **3** (also **nuclear fusion**) combination of the nucleus of two atoms with the release of energy. **4** something new created by a mixture of qualities, ideas, or things. **5** popular music blending styles, esp. jazz and funk. ▷ *adj* **6** of a style of cooking that combines traditional Western techniques and ingredients with those used in Eastern cuisine.

fuss ❶ *n* **1** needless activity or worry. **2** complaint or objection. **3** great display of attention. ▷ *v* **4** make a fuss. **fussy** *adj* **fussier**, **fussiest 1** inclined to fuss. **2** overparticular. **3** overelaborate. **fussily** *adv* **fussiness** *n*.

fusty ❶ *adj* **-tier**, **-tiest 1** stale-smelling. **2** behind the times. **fustiness** *n*.

furniture *n* = **household goods**, appliances, fittings, furnishings, goods, possessions, things (*inf*)

furore *n* = **commotion**, disturbance, hullabaloo, outcry, stir, to-do, uproar

furrow *n* **1** = **groove**, channel, hollow, line, rut, seam, trench **2** = **wrinkle**, crease ▷ *v* **3** = **wrinkle**, corrugate, crease, draw together, knit

further *adv* **1** = **in addition**, additionally, also, besides, furthermore, into the bargain, moreover, to boot ▷ *adj* **3** = **additional**, extra, fresh, more, new, other, supplementary ▷ *v* **5** = **promote**, advance, assist, encourage, forward, help, lend support to, work for

furthermore *adv* = **besides**, additionally, as well, further, in addition, into the bargain, moreover, to boot, too

furthest *adj* **2** = **most distant**, extreme, farthest, furthermost, outmost, remotest, ultimate

furtive *adj* = **sly**, clandestine, conspiratorial, secretive, sneaky, stealthy, surreptitious, underhand, under-the-table

fury *n* **1** = **anger**, frenzy, impetuosity, madness, passion, rage, wrath **2** = **violence**, ferocity, fierceness, force, intensity, savagery, severity, vehemence

fuss *n* **1** = **bother**, ado, commotion, excitement, hue and cry, palaver, stir, to-do **2** = **argument**, complaint, furore, objection, row, squabble, trouble ▷ *v* **4** = **worry**, fidget, flap (*inf*), fret, get worked up, take pains

fussy *adj* **1** = **difficult**, hard to please **2** = **particular**, choosy (*inf*), fastidious, finicky, nit-picking (*inf*), pernickety, picky (*inf*) **3** = **overelaborate**, busy, cluttered, overworked, rococo

fusty *adj* **1** = **stale**, airless, damp, mildewed, mouldering, mouldy, musty, stuffy

futile ❶ [**fyew**-tile] *adj* unsuccessful or useless. **futility** *n*.

futon [**foo**-tonn] *n* Japanese padded quilt, laid on the floor as a bed.

future ❶ *n* **1** time to come. **2** what will happen. **3** prospects. ▷ *adj* **4** yet to come or be. **5** of or relating to time to come. **6** (of a verb tense) indicating that the action specified has not yet taken place. **futuristic** *adj* of a design appearing to belong to some future time.

fuzz¹ ❶ *n* mass of fine or curly hairs or fibres. **fuzzy** *adj* **fuzzier**, **fuzziest 1** of, like, or covered with fuzz. **2** blurred or indistinct. **3** (of hair) tightly curled. **fuzzily** *adv* **fuzziness** *n*.

fuzz² *n slang* police.

fwd forward.

———————————————————————— THESAURUS ————————

futile *adj* = **useless**, fruitless, ineffectual, unavailing, unprofitable, unsuccessful, vain, worthless

future *n* **1** = **time to come**, hereafter **3** = **prospect**, expectation, outlook ▷ *adj* **4, 5** = **forthcoming**, approaching, coming, fated, impending, later, subsequent, to come

fuzzy *adj* **1** = **fluffy**, downy, woolly **2** = **indistinct**, bleary, blurred, distorted, ill-defined, out of focus, unclear, vague **3** = **frizzy**

g 1 gram(s). **2** (acceleration due to) gravity.

Ga *Chemistry* gallium.

GA Georgia.

gab *n, v* **gabbing**, **gabbed** *informal* talk or chatter. **gift of the gab** eloquence. **gabby** *adj* **-bier**, **-biest** *informal* talkative.

gabardine, gaberdine *n* strong twill cloth used esp. for raincoats.

gabble 𝟙 *v* **1** speak rapidly and indistinctly. ▷ *n* **2** rapid indistinct speech.

gable *n* triangular upper part of a wall between sloping roofs. **gabled** *adj*.

gad 𝟙 *v* **gadding**, **gadded**. **gad about, around** go around in search of pleasure. **gadabout** *n* pleasure-seeker.

gadfly *n* **1** fly that bites cattle. **2** constantly annoying person.

gadget 𝟙 *n* small mechanical device or appliance. **gadgetry** *n* gadgets.

gadoid [**gay**-doid] *adj* **1** of the cod family of marine fishes. ▷ *n* **2** gadoid fish.

gadolinium *n* *Chemistry* silvery-white metallic element.

Gael [**gayl**] *n* speaker of Gaelic. **Gaelic** [**gal**-lik, **gay**-lik] *n* **1** any of the Celtic languages of Ireland and the Scottish Highlands. ▷ *adj* **2** of the Gaels or their language.

gaff¹ *n* stick with an iron hook for landing large fish.

gaff² *n* **blow the gaff** *slang* divulge a secret.

gaffe 𝟙 *n* social blunder.

gaffer 𝟙 *n* **1** *informal* foreman or boss. **2** old man.

gag¹ 𝟙 *v* **gagging, gagged 1** choke or retch. **2** stop up the mouth of (a person) with cloth etc. **3** deprive of free speech. ▷ *n* **4** cloth etc. put into or tied across the mouth.

gag² 𝟙 *n informal* joke.

gaga [**gah**-gah] *adj slang* **1** senile. **2** foolishly doting.

gage *n, v US* gauge.

gaggle *n* **1** *informal* disorderly crowd. **2** flock of geese.

gaiety 𝟙 *n* **1** cheerfulness. **2** merrymaking. **gaily** *adv* **1** merrily. **2** colourfully.

gain 𝟙 *v* **1** acquire or obtain. **2** increase or improve. **3** reach. **4** (of a watch or clock) be or become too fast. ▷ *n* **5** profit or advantage. **6** increase or improvement. **gainful** *adj* useful or

---

gabble *v* **1** = **prattle**, babble, blabber, gibber, gush, jabber, spout ▷ *n* **2** = **gibberish**, babble, blabber, chatter, drivel, prattle, twaddle

gadabout *n* = **pleasure-seeker**, rambler, rover, wanderer

gadget *n* = **device**, appliance, contraption (*inf*), contrivance, gizmo (*sl, chiefly US*), instrument, invention, thing, tool

gaffe *n* = **blunder**, bloomer (*inf*), clanger (*inf*), faux pas, howler, indiscretion, lapse, mistake, slip, solecism

gaffer *n* **1** *Inf* = **manager**, boss (*inf*), foreman, overseer, superintendent, supervisor **2** = **old man**, granddad, greybeard, old boy (*inf*), old fellow, old-timer (*US*)

gag¹ *v* **1** = **retch**, heave, puke (*sl*), spew, throw up (*inf*), vomit **3** = **suppress**, curb, muffle, muzzle, quiet, silence, stifle, stop up

gag² *n Inf* = **joke**, crack (*sl*), funny (*inf*), hoax, jest, wisecrack (*inf*), witticism

gaiety *n* **1** = **cheerfulness**, blitheness, exhilaration, glee, high spirits, jollity, light-heartedness, merriment, mirth **2** = **merrymaking**, conviviality, festivity, fun, jollification, revelry

gaily *adv* **1** = **cheerfully**, blithely, gleefully, happily, joyfully, light-heartedly, merrily **2** = **colourfully**, brightly, brilliantly, flamboyantly, flashily, gaudily, showily

gain *v* **1** = **acquire**, attain, capture, collect, gather, get, land, secure **2** = **improve**, advance, increase, pick up, profit **3** = **reach**, arrive at, attain, come to, get to ▷ *n* **5** = **profit**, advantage, benefit, dividend, return, yield **6** = **increase**, advance, growth, improvement, progress, rise

profitable. **gainfully** adv **gain on**,
upon v get nearer to or catch up with.

gainsay ❶ v **-saying**, **-said** deny or
contradict.

gait ❶ n manner of walking.

gaiter n cloth or leather covering for the
lower leg.

gal n slang girl.

gal. gallon.

gala ❶ [**gah**-la] n **1** festival.
2 competitive sporting event.

galaxy n, pl **-axies 1** system of stars.
2 gathering of famous people. **3** (**G-**)
Milky Way. **galactic** adj.

gale ❶ n **1** strong wind. **2** informal loud
outburst.

gall¹ ❶ [**gawl**] n **1** informal impudence.
2 bitter feeling. **3** bile. **gall bladder**
sac attached to the liver, storing bile.
gallstone n hard mass formed in the
gall bladder or its ducts.

gall² ❶ [**gawl**] v **1** annoy. **2** make sore
by rubbing. ▷ n **3** sore caused by
rubbing. **galling** adj annoying or
bitterly humiliating.

gall³ [**gawl**] n abnormal outgrowth on a
tree or plant.

gallant ❶ adj **1** brave and noble.
2 (of a man) attentive to women.
gallantly adv **gallantry** n **1** showy,
attentive treatment of women.
2 bravery.

galleon n large three-masted sailing
ship of the 15th–17th centuries.

gallery n, pl **-ries 1** room or building for

displaying works of art. **2** balcony in a
church, theatre, etc. **3** passage in a
mine. **4** covered walk with side
openings. **5** long narrow room
for a specific purpose, e.g. shooting
gallery.

galley n **1** kitchen of a ship or aircraft.
2 History ship propelled by oars, usu.
rowed by slaves. **galley slave 1** slave
forced to row in a galley. **2** informal
drudge.

Gallic adj **1** French. **2** of ancient Gaul.
Gallicism n French word or idiom.

gallinaceous adj of an order of birds
including poultry, pheasants, and
grouse.

gallium n Chemistry soft grey metallic
element used in semiconductors.

gallivant ❶ v go about in search of
pleasure.

gallon n liquid measure of eight pints,
equal to 4.55 litres.

gallop ❶ n **1** horse's fastest pace.
2 galloping. ▷ v **galloping**, **galloped**
3 go or ride at a gallop. **4** move or
progress rapidly.

  ● **SPELLING TIP**
  ● Although **gallop** has two ls,
  ● remember that **galloping** and
  ● **galloped** have only one p.

gallows n wooden structure used for
hanging criminals.

Gallup poll n public opinion poll carried
out by questioning a cross section of
the population.

THESAURUS

gainful adj = **profitable**, advantageous,
beneficial, fruitful, lucrative,
productive, remunerative, rewarding,
useful, worthwhile

gainsay v = **contradict**, contravene,
controvert, deny, disagree with,
dispute, rebut, retract

gait n = **walk**, bearing, carriage, pace,
step, stride, tread

gala n **1** = **festival**, carnival,
celebration, festivity, fete, jamboree,
pageant

gale n **1** = **storm**, blast, cyclone,
hurricane, squall, tempest, tornado,
typhoon **2** Inf = **outburst**, burst,
eruption, explosion, fit, howl,
outbreak, paroxysm, peal, shout,
shriek, storm

gall¹ n **1** Inf = **impudence**, brazenness,
cheek (inf), chutzpah (US & Canad inf),
effrontery, impertinence, insolence,
nerve (inf) **2** = **bitterness**, acrimony,

animosity, bile, hostility, rancour

gall² v **1** = **annoy**, exasperate, irk,
irritate, provoke, rankle, vex
2 = **scrape**, abrade, chafe, irritate

gallant adj **1** = **brave**, bold,
courageous, heroic, honourable,
intrepid, manly, noble, valiant
2 = **courteous**, attentive, chivalrous,
gentlemanly, gracious, noble, polite

gallantry n **1** = **courtesy**,
attentiveness, chivalry, courteousness,
gentlemanliness, graciousness,
nobility, politeness **2** = **bravery**,
boldness, courage, heroism,
intrepidity, manliness, spirit, valour

galling adj = **annoying**, bitter,
exasperating, irksome, irritating,
provoking, vexatious

gallivant v = **wander**, gad about,
ramble, roam, rove

gallop v **3, 4** = **run**, bolt, career, dash,
hurry, race, rush, speed, sprint

galore ❶ *adv* in abundance, e.g. *presents galore.*

galoshes *pl n* waterproof overshoes.

galumph *v informal* leap or move about clumsily.

galvanic ❶ *adj* **1** of or producing an electric current generated by chemical means. **2** *informal* stimulating or startling. **galvanize** *v* **1** stimulate into action. **2** coat (metal) with zinc. **galvanometer** *n* instrument for measuring small electric currents.

gambit *n* **1** opening line or move intended to secure an advantage. **2** *Chess* opening move involving the sacrifice of a pawn.

gamble ❶ *v* **1** play games of chance to win money. **2** act on the expectation of something. ▷ *n* **3** risky undertaking. **4** bet or wager. **gambler** *n* **gambling** *n*.

gamboge [gam-**boje**] *n* gum resin used as a yellow pigment and purgative.

gambol ❶ *v* **-bolling, -bolled 1** jump about playfully, frolic. ▷ *n* **2** frolic.

- ● **SPELLING TIP**
- ● Although the pronunciation is the
- ● same as 'gamble', both the verb
- ● and the noun **gambol** must always
- ● contain an *o*.

game¹ ❶ *n* **1** amusement or pastime. **2** contest for amusement. **3** single period of play in a contest. **4** score needed to win a contest. **5** animals or birds hunted for sport or food. **6** their flesh. **7** scheme or trick. ▷ *pl* **8** athletic contests. ▷ *v* **9** gamble. ▷ *adj* **10** brave. **11** willing. **gamely** *adv* **gaming** *n* gambling. **gamey, gamy** *adj*

gamier, gamiest having the smell or flavour of game. **gamekeeper** *n* person employed to breed game and prevent poaching. **gamer** *n* person who plays computer games.

gamesmanship *n* art of winning by cunning practices without actually cheating.

game² ❶ *adj Brit, Aust & NZ* lame, crippled.

gamete [**gam**-eet] *n Biology* reproductive cell.

gamin *n* street urchin.

gamine [**gam**-een] *n* slim boyish young woman.

gamma *n* third letter of the Greek alphabet. **gamma ray** electromagnetic ray of shorter wavelength and higher energy than an x-ray.

gammon *n* **1** cured or smoked ham. **2** hindquarter of a side of bacon.

gammy *adj* **-mier, -miest** same as GAME².

gamp *n informal* umbrella.

gamut ❶ *n* whole range or scale (of music, emotions, etc.).

gander *n* **1** male goose. **2** *informal* quick look.

gang ❶ *n* **1** (criminal) group. **2** organized group of workmen. **gangland** *n* criminal underworld. **gang up** *v* form an alliance (against).

galore *adv* = **in abundance**, all over the place, aplenty, everywhere, in great quantity, in numbers, in profusion, to spare

galvanize *v* **1** = **stimulate**, electrify, excite, inspire, invigorate, jolt, provoke, spur, stir

gamble *v* **1** = **bet**, game, have a flutter (*inf*), play, punt, wager **2** = **risk**, chance, hazard, speculate, stick one's neck out (*inf*), take a chance ▷ *n* **3** = **risk**, chance, leap in the dark, lottery, speculation, uncertainty, venture **4** = **bet**, flutter (*inf*), punt, wager

gambol *v* **1** = **frolic**, caper, cavort, frisk, hop, jump, prance, skip ▷ *n* **2** = **frolic**, caper, hop, jump, prance, skip

game¹ *n* **1** = **pastime**, amusement, distraction, diversion, entertainment,

lark, recreation, sport **2** = **match**, competition, contest, event, head-to-head, meeting, tournament **5** = **wild animals**, prey, quarry **7** = **scheme**, design, plan, plot, ploy, stratagem, tactic, trick ▷ *adj* **10** = **brave**, courageous, gallant, gritty, intrepid, persistent, plucky, spirited, feisty (*US & Canad*) **11** = **willing**, desirous, eager, interested, keen, prepared, ready

game² *adj* = **disabled**, bad, crippled, deformed, gammy (*Brit sl*), incapacitated, injured, lame, maimed

gamut *n* = **range**, area, catalogue, compass, field, scale, scope, series, sweep

gang *n* = **group**, band, clique, club, company, coterie, crowd, mob, pack, squad, team

gangling ❶ *adj* lanky and awkward.

ganglion *n* **1** group of nerve cells. **2** small harmless tumour.

gangplank *n* portable bridge for boarding or leaving a ship.

gangrene *n* decay of body tissue as a result of disease or injury. **gangrenous** *adj*.

gangsta rap *n* style of music portraying life in Black ghettos in the US.

gangster ❶ *n* member of a criminal gang.

gangue *n* valueless material in an ore.

gangway *n* **1** passage between rows of seats. **2** gangplank. **3** opening in a ship's side for a gangplank.

gannet *n* **1** large sea bird. **2** *slang* greedy person.

gantry *n, pl* **-tries** structure supporting something such as a crane or rocket.

gaol [**jayl**] *n* same as JAIL.

gap ❶ *n* **1** break or opening. **2** interruption or interval. **3** divergence or difference. **gappy** *adj*.

gape ❶ *v* **1** stare in wonder. **2** open the mouth wide. **3** be or become wide open. **gaping** *adj*.

garage *n* **1** building used to house cars. **2** place for the refuelling, sale, and repair of cars. ▷ *v* **3** put or keep a car in a garage.

garb *n* **1** clothes. ▷ *v* **2** clothe.

garbage ❶ *n* rubbish.

garbled ❶ *adj* (of a story etc.) jumbled

and confused.

garden *n* **1** piece of land for growing flowers, fruit, or vegetables. ▷ *pl* **2** ornamental park. ▷ *v* **3** cultivate a garden. **gardener** *n* **gardening** *n* **garden centre** place selling plants and gardening equipment.

gardenia [gar-**deen**-ya] *n* **1** large fragrant white waxy flower. **2** shrub bearing this.

garfish *n* **1** freshwater fish with a long body and very long toothed jaws. **2** sea fish with similar characteristics.

gargantuan *adj* huge.

gargle *v* **1** wash the throat with (a liquid) by breathing out slowly through the liquid. ▷ *n* **2** liquid used for gargling. **3** act or sound of gargling.

gargoyle *n* waterspout carved in the form of a grotesque face, esp. on a church.

garish ❶ *adj* crudely bright or colourful. **garishly** *adv* **garishness** *n*.

garland ❶ *n* **1** wreath of flowers worn or hung as a decoration. ▷ *v* **2** decorate with garlands.

garlic *n* pungent bulb of a plant of the onion family, used in cooking.

garment *n* **1** article of clothing. ▷ *pl* **2** clothes.

garner ❶ *v* collect or store.

garnet *n* red semiprecious stone.

garnish ❶ *v* **1** decorate (food). ▷ *n* **2** decoration for food.

garret *n* attic in a house.

————————————————————————————— THESAURUS ————

gangling *adj* = **tall**, angular, awkward, lanky, rangy, rawboned, spindly

gangster *n* = **racketeer**, crook (*inf*), hood (*US sl*), hoodlum (*chiefly US*), mobster (*US sl*)

gap *n* **1** = **opening**, break, chink, cleft, crack, hole, space **2** = **interval**, breathing space, hiatus, interlude, intermission, interruption, lacuna, lull, pause, respite **3** = **difference**, disagreement, disparity, divergence, inconsistency

gape *v* **1** = **stare**, gawk, gawp (*Brit sl*), goggle, wonder **3** = **open**, crack, split, yawn

gaping *adj* **3** = **wide**, broad, cavernous, great, open, vast, wide open, yawning

garbage *n* = **waste**, refuse, rubbish, trash (*chiefly US*)

garbled *adj* = **jumbled**, confused, distorted, double-Dutch,

incomprehensible, mixed up, unintelligible

garish *adj* = **gaudy**, brash, brassy, flashy, loud, showy, tacky (*inf*), tasteless, vulgar

garland *n* **1** = **wreath**, bays, chaplet, crown, festoon, honours, laurels ▷ *v* **2** = **adorn**, crown, deck, festoon, wreathe

garments *pl n* = **clothes**, apparel, attire, clothing, costume, dress, garb, gear (*sl*), outfit, uniform

garner *v* = **collect**, accumulate, amass, gather, hoard, save, stockpile, store, stow away

garnish *v* **1** = **decorate**, adorn, embellish, enhance, ornament, set off, trim ▷ *n* **2** = **decoration**, adornment, embellishment, enhancement, ornamentation, trimming

garrison ❶ *n* **1** troops stationed in a town or fort. **2** fortified place. ▷ *v* **3** station troops in.

garrotte, garotte *n* **1** Spanish method of execution by strangling. **2** cord or wire used for this. ▷ *v* **3** kill by this method. **4** strangle.

garrulous ❶ *adj* talkative. **garrulously** *adv*.

garter *n* band worn round the leg to hold up a sock or stocking. **the Garter** highest order of British knighthood.

gas *n, pl* **gases, gasses 1** airlike substance that is not liquid or solid. **2** fossil fuel in the form of a gas, used for heating. **3** gaseous anaesthetic. **4** *US & Canad* petrol. **5** poisonous gas used in warfare. ▷ *v* **gassing, gassed 6** poison or render unconscious with gas. **7** *informal* talk idly or boastfully. **gassy** *adj* **-sier, -siest** filled with gas. **gaseous** *adj* of or like gas. **gasbag** *n* *informal* person who talks too much. **gas chamber** airtight room which is filled with poison gas to kill people or animals. **gasholder, gasometer** [gas-**som**-it-er] *n* large tank for storing gas. **gasify** *v* **-fying, -fied** change into a gas. **gasification** *n* **gas mask** mask with a chemical filter to protect the wearer against poison gas. **gasworks** *n* plant where coal gas is made.

gash ❶ *v* **1** make a long deep cut in. ▷ *n* **2** long deep cut.

gasket *n* piece of rubber etc. placed between the faces of a metal joint to act as a seal.

gasoline *n* *US* petrol.

gasp ❶ *v* **1** draw in breath sharply or with difficulty. **2** utter breathlessly.

3 (foll. by *for*) crave. ▷ *n* **4** convulsive intake of breath.

gastric *adj* of the stomach. **gastric band** adjustable band fitted inside the stomach to reduce its capacity and help weight loss. **gastritis** *n* inflammation of the stomach lining. **gastroenteritis** *n* inflammation of the stomach and intestines.

gastronomy *n* art of good eating. **gastronomic** *adj*.

gastropod *n* mollusc, such as a snail, with a single flattened muscular foot.

gate ❶ *n* **1** movable barrier, usu. hinged, in a wall or fence. **2** opening with a gate. **3** any entrance or way in. **4** (entrance money paid by) those attending a sporting event. **5** exit at an airport by which passengers get to an aircraft. **gate-crash** *v* enter (a party) uninvited. **gatehouse** *n* building at or above a gateway. **gateway** *n* **1** entrance with a gate. **2** means of access, e.g. *Mumbai, gateway to India*.

gâteau [gat-toe] *n, pl* **-teaux** [-toes] rich elaborate cake.

gather ❶ *v* **1** assemble. **2** collect gradually. **3** increase gradually. **4** learn from information given. **5** pick or harvest. **6** draw (material) into small tucks or folds. **gathers** *pl n* gathered folds in material. **gathering** *n* assembly.

GATT General Agreement on Tariffs and Trade.

gauche ❶ [gohsh] *adj* socially awkward. **gaucheness** *n*.

gaucho [gow-choh] *n, pl* **-chos** S American cowboy.

gaudy ❶ *adj* **gaudier, gaudiest** vulgarly

garrison *n* **1** = **troops**, armed force, command, detachment, unit **2** = **fort**, base, camp, encampment, fortification, fortress, post, station, stronghold ▷ *v* **3** = **station**, assign, position, post, put on duty

garrulous *adj* = **talkative**, chatty, gossiping, loquacious, prattling, verbose, voluble

gash *v* **1** = **cut**, gouge, lacerate, slash, slit, split, tear, wound ▷ *n* **2** = **cut**, gouge, incision, laceration, slash, slit, split, tear, wound

gasp *v* **1** = **gulp**, blow, catch one's breath, choke, pant, puff ▷ *n* **4** = **gulp**, exclamation, pant, puff, sharp intake of breath

gate *n* **1-3** = **barrier**, door, entrance, exit, gateway, opening, passage, portal

gather *v* **1, 2** = **assemble**, accumulate, amass, collect, garner, mass, muster, stockpile **3** = **intensify**, deepen, expand, grow, heighten, increase, rise, swell, thicken **4** = **learn**, assume, conclude, deduce, hear, infer, surmise, understand **5** = **pick**, cull, garner, glean, harvest, pluck, reap, select **6** = **fold**, pleat, tuck

gathering *n* = **assembly**, company, conclave, congress, convention, crowd, group, meeting

gauche *adj* = **awkward**, clumsy, ill-mannered, inelegant, tactless, unsophisticated

gaudy *adj* = **garish**, bright, flashy, loud, showy, tacky (*inf*), tasteless, vulgar

bright or colourful. **gaudily** adv
gaudiness n.

gauge ① [**gayj**] v **1** estimate or judge.
2 measure the amount or condition of.
▷ n **3** measuring instrument. **4** scale
or standard of measurement.
5 distance between the rails of a
railway track. **6** capacity or extent.

● **SPELLING TIP**
● The vowels in **gauge** are often
● confused so that the misspelling guage
● is common in the Bank of English.

Gaul n **1** native of ancient Gaul.
2 Frenchman.

gaunt ① adj **1** lean and haggard. **2** (of a
place) desolate or bleak. **gauntness** n.

gauntlet¹ n **1** heavy glove with a long
cuff. **2** medieval armoured glove. **throw
down the gauntlet** offer a challenge.

gauntlet² n **run the gauntlet** be exposed
to criticism or unpleasant treatment.

gauze n transparent loosely-woven
fabric, often used for surgical
dressings. **gauzy** adj.

gave v past tense of GIVE.

gavel [**gav**-el] n small hammer banged
on a table by a judge, auctioneer, or
chairman to call for attention.

gavotte n **1** old formal dance. **2** music
for this.

gawk ① v **1** stare stupidly. ▷ n **2** clumsy
awkward person. **gawky** adj **gawkier**,
gawkiest clumsy or awkward.
gawkiness n.

gawp v slang stare stupidly.

gay ① adj **1** homosexual. **2** carefree and
merry. **3** colourful. ▷ n **4** homosexual.
gayness n homosexuality.

● **USAGE NOTE**
● The meaning 'homosexual' is now
● the most frequent use of gay, which
● retains the meaning 'happy' only in
● older books.

gaze ① v **1** look fixedly. ▷ n **2** fixed look.

gazebo [gaz-**zee**-boh] n, pl -**bos**, -**boes**
summerhouse with a good view.

gazelle n small graceful antelope.

gazette ① n official publication
containing announcements.
gazetteer n (part of) a book that lists
and describes places.

gazump v Brit & Aust raise the price of a
property after verbally agreeing it with
(a prospective buyer).

gazunder v Brit reduce an offer on a
property immediately before
exchanging contracts having earlier
agreed a higher price with the seller.

GB Great Britain.

GBH grievous bodily harm.

GC George Cross.

GCE 1 General Certificate of Education.
2 pass in a GCE examination.

GCSE 1 General Certificate of Secondary
Education. **2** pass in a GCSE
examination.

Gd Chemistry gadolinium.

Ge Chemistry germanium.

gear ① n **1** set of toothed wheels
connecting with another or with a
rack to change the direction or speed
of transmitted motion. **2** mechanism
for transmitting motion by gears.
3 setting of a gear to suit engine
speed, e.g. first gear. **4** clothing or
belongings. **5** equipment. ▷ v
6 prepare or organize for something.
in, **out of gear** with the gear
mechanism engaged or disengaged.
gearbox n case enclosing a set of
gears in a motor vehicle. **gear lever**
lever for changing gears in a motor
vehicle. **gear up** v prepare for an
activity.

gecko n, pl **geckos**, **geckoes** small
tropical lizard.

⎯⎯⎯⎯⎯⎯⎯⎯⎯⎯⎯⎯⎯⎯⎯⎯⎯ **THESAURUS** ⎯⎯⎯

gauge v **1** = **judge**, adjudge, appraise,
assess, estimate, evaluate, guess,
rate, reckon, value **2** = **measure**,
ascertain, calculate, check, compute,
count, determine, weigh ▷ n **3**,
4 = **indicator**, criterion, guide,
guideline, measure, meter, standard,
test, touchstone, yardstick

gaunt adj **1** = **thin**, angular, bony,
haggard, lean, pinched, scrawny,
skinny, spare

gawky adj **2** = **awkward**, clumsy,
gauche, loutish, lumbering, maladroit,
ungainly

gay adj **1** = **homosexual**, lesbian, queer
(inf, derog) **2** = **cheerful**, blithe,
carefree, jovial, light-hearted, lively,
merry, sparkling **3** = **colourful**, bright,
brilliant, flamboyant, flashy, rich,
showy, vivid ▷ n **4** = **homosexual**,
lesbian

gaze v **1** = **stare**, gape, look, regard,
view, watch, wonder ▷ n **2** = **stare**,
fixed look, look

gazette n = **newspaper**, journal,
news-sheet, paper, periodical

gear n **1** = **cog**, cogwheel, gearwheel
2 = **mechanism**, cogs, machinery,

gee *interj US informal* mild exclamation of surprise, admiration, etc.

geebung [**gee**-bung] *n* **1** Australian tree or shrub with an edible but tasteless fruit. **2** fruit of this tree.

geek *n informal* boring, unattractive person.

geese *n* plural of GOOSE.

geezer *n informal* man.

Geiger counter [**guy**-ger] *n* instrument for detecting and measuring radiation.

geisha [**gay**-sha] *n, pl* -**sha**, -**shas** (in Japan) professional female companion for men.

gel [**jell**] *n* **1** jelly-like substance, esp. one used to secure a hairstyle. ▷ *v* **gelling**, **gelled 2** form a gel. **3** *informal* take on a definite form.

gelatine ❶ [**jel**-at-teen], **gelatin** *n* **1** substance made by boiling animal bones. **2** edible jelly made of this. **gelatinous** [jel-**at**-in-uss] *adj* of or like jelly.

geld *v* castrate. **gelding** *n* castrated horse.

gelignite *n* type of dynamite used for blasting.

gem ❶ *n* **1** precious stone or jewel. **2** highly valued person or thing. **gemfish** *n* Australian food fish with a delicate flavour.

Gemini *n* (the twins) third sign of the zodiac.

gen *n informal* information. **gen up on** *v* **genning**, **genned** *informal* make or become fully informed about.

gendarme [**zhohn**-darm] *n* member of the French police force.

gender *n* **1** state of being male or female. **2** *Grammar* classification of nouns in certain languages as masculine, feminine, or neuter.

gene [**jean**] *n* part of a cell which determines inherited characteristics.

genealogy [jean-ee-**al**-a-gee] *n, pl* -**gies** (study of) the history and descent of a family or families. **genealogical** *sadj* **genealogist** *n*.

genera [**jen**-er-a] *n* plural of GENUS.

general ❶ *adj* **1** common or widespread. **2** of or affecting all or most. **3** not specific. **4** including or dealing with various or miscellaneous items. **5** highest in authority or rank, e.g. *general manager*. ▷ *n* **6** very senior army officer. **in general** mostly or usually. **generally** *adv* **generality** *n, pl* -**ties 1** general principle. **2** state of being general. **generalize** *v* **1** draw general conclusions. **2** speak in generalities. **3** make widely known or used. **generalization** *n* **general election** election in which representatives are chosen for every constituency. **general practitioner** nonspecialist doctor serving a local area.

generalissimo *n, pl* -**mos** supreme commander of combined armed forces.

generate ❶ *v* produce or bring into being. **generation** *n* all the people born about the same time. **generative** *adj* capable of producing. **generator** *n* machine for converting mechanical energy into electrical energy.

generation ❶ *n* **1** all the people born about the same time. **2** successive stage in descent of people or animals.

—————— **THESAURUS** ——————

works **4** = **clothing**, clothes, costume, dress, garments, outfit, togs, wear **5** = **equipment**, accoutrements, apparatus, instruments, paraphernalia, supplies, tackle, tools ▷ *v* **6** = **equip**, adapt, adjust, fit

gelatinous *adj* = **jelly-like**, glutinous, gummy, sticky, viscous

gem *n* **1** = **precious stone**, jewel, stone **2** = **prize**, jewel, masterpiece, pearl, treasure

general *adj* **1** = **common**, accepted, broad, extensive, popular, prevalent, public, universal, widespread **2**, **4** = **universal**, across-the-board, blanket, collective, comprehensive, indiscriminate, miscellaneous, overall, overarching, sweeping, total **3** = **imprecise**, approximate, ill-defined, indefinite, inexact, loose, unspecific, vague

generally *adv* = **usually**, as a rule, by and large, commonly, customarily, extensively, normally, on the whole, ordinarily, popularly, publicly, typically, universally, widely

generate *v* = **produce**, breed, cause, create, engender, give rise to, make, propagate

generation *n* **1** = **age group**, breed, crop **2**, **3** = **age**, epoch, era, period, time **4** = **production**, creation, formation, genesis, propagation, reproduction

3 average time between two generations (about 30 years). **4** generating.

generic ❶ [jin-**ner**-ik] *adj* of a class, group, or genus. **generically** *adv*.

generous ❶ *adj* **1** free in giving. **2** free from pettiness. **3** plentiful. **generously** *adv* **generosity** *n*.

genesis ❶ [**jen**-iss-iss] *n*, *pl* **-eses** [-iss-eez] beginning or origin.

genetic [jin-**net**-tik] *adj* of genes or genetics. **genetics** *n* study of heredity and variation in organisms. **geneticist** *n* **genetic engineering** alteration of the genetic structure of an organism for a particular purpose. **genetic fingerprinting** use of a person's unique DNA pattern for identification.

Geneva Convention *n* international agreement establishing a code for wartime treatment of the sick, wounded, and prisoners of war.

genial ❶ [**jean**-ee-al] *adj* cheerful and friendly. **genially** *adv* **geniality** *n*.

genie [**jean**-ee] *n* (in fairy tales) servant who appears by magic and grants wishes.

genital *adj* of the sexual organs or reproduction. **genitals**, **genitalia** [jen-it-**ail**-ya] *pl n* external sexual organs.

genitive *n* grammatical case indicating possession or association.

genius ❶ [**jean**-yuss] *n* **1** (person with) exceptional ability in a particular field. **2** person considered as exerting influence of a certain sort.

genocide [**jen**-no-side] *n* murder of a race of people.

genre ❶ [**zhohn**-ra] *n* style of literary, musical, or artistic work.

gent *n informal* gentleman. **gents** *n* men's public toilet.

genteel ❶ *adj* affectedly proper and polite. **genteelly** *adv* **gentility** *n* **1** noble birth or ancestry. **2** polite and well-mannered behaviour.

gentian [**jen**-shun] *n* mountain plant with deep blue flowers. **gentian violet** violet dye used as an antiseptic.

gentile *adj*, *n* non-Jewish (person).

gentle ❶ *adj* **1** mild or kindly. **2** not rough or severe. **3** gradual. **4** easily controlled, tame. **gentleness** *n* **gently** *adv* **gentlefolk**, **gentlefolks** *pl n* people of good breeding. **gentleman** *n* **1** polite well-bred man. **2** man of high social position. **3** polite name for a man. **gentlemanly** *adj* **gentlewoman** *n fem*.

gentry ❶ *n* people just below the nobility in social rank. **gentrification**

———————————————————————————————— **THESAURUS** —————————

generic *adj* = **collective**, blanket, common, comprehensive, general, inclusive, universal, wide

generosity *n* **1** = **unselfishness**, beneficence, bounty, charity, goodness, kindness, largesse *or* largess, liberality, munificence, open-handedness **2** = **nobleness**, high-mindedness, magnanimity

generous *adj* **1** = **liberal**, beneficent, bountiful, charitable, hospitable, kind, lavish, open-handed, unstinting **2** = **unselfish**, big-hearted, good, high-minded, lofty, magnanimous, noble **3** = **plentiful**, abundant, ample, copious, full, lavish, liberal, rich, unstinting

genesis *n* = **beginning**, birth, creation, formation, inception, origin, start

genial *adj* = **cheerful**, affable, agreeable, amiable, congenial, friendly, good-natured, jovial, pleasant, warm

geniality *n* = **cheerfulness**, affability, agreeableness, amiability, conviviality, cordiality, friendliness, good cheer, joviality, warmth

genius *n* **1** = **master**, brainbox, expert, fundi (*S Afr*), hotshot (*inf*), maestro, mastermind, virtuoso, whiz (*inf*)

genre *n* = **type**, category, class, group, kind, sort, species, style

genteel *adj* = **refined**, courteous, cultured, elegant, gentlemanly, ladylike, polite, respectable, urbane, well-mannered

gentle *adj* **1** = **mild**, compassionate, humane, kindly, meek, placid, sweet-tempered, tender **2** = **moderate**, light, mild, muted, slight, soft, soothing **3** = **gradual**, easy, imperceptible, light, mild, moderate, slight, slow **4** = **tame**, biddable, broken, docile, manageable, placid, tractable

gentlemanly *adj* **1** = **polite**, civil, courteous, gallant, genteel, honourable, refined, urbane, well-mannered

gentleness *n* **1, 2** = **tenderness**, compassion, kindness, mildness, softness, sweetness

gentry *n* = **upper class**, aristocracy, elitey, upper crust (*inf*)

n taking-over of a traditionally working-class area by middle-class incomers. **gentrify** *v* **-fying, -fied**.

genuflect *v* bend the knee as a sign of reverence or deference. **genuflection, genuflexion** *n*.

genuine ❶ *adj* **1** not fake, authentic. **2** sincere. **genuinely** *adv* **genuineness** *n*.

genus [**jean**-uss] *n*, *pl* **genera 1** group into which a family of animals or plants is divided. **2** kind, type.

geocentric *adj* **1** having the earth as a centre. **2** measured as from the earth's centre.

geodesic *adj* **1** of the geometry of curved surfaces. ▷ *n* **2** shortest line between two points on a curve.

geodesy *n* study of the shape and size of the earth.

geography *n* **1** study of the earth's physical features, climate, population, etc. **2** physical features of a region. **geographer** *n* **geographical, geographic** *adj* **geographically** *adv*.

geology *n* **1** study of the earth's origin, structure, and composition. **2** geological features of an area. **geological** *adj* **geologically** *adv* **geologist** *n*.

geometry *n* branch of mathematics dealing with points, lines, curves, and surfaces. **geometric, geometrical** *adj* **geometrically** *adv* **geometrician** *n*.

Geordie *n* **1** person from, or dialect of, Tyneside. ▷ *adj* **2** of Tyneside or its dialect.

George Cross *n* British award for bravery.

georgette [jor-**jet**] *n* fine silky fabric.

Georgian *adj* of the time of any of the kings of Britain called George, esp. 1714–1830.

geostationary *adj* (of a satellite) orbiting so as to remain over the same point of the earth's surface.

geothermal *adj* of or using the heat in the earth's interior.

geranium *n* cultivated plant with red, pink, or white flowers.

gerbil [**jer**-bill] *n* burrowing desert rodent of Asia and Africa.

geriatrics *n* branch of medicine dealing with old age and its diseases. **geriatric** *adj*, *n* old (person). **geriatrician** *n*.

germ ❶ *n* **1** microbe, esp. one causing disease. **2** beginning from which something may develop. **3** simple structure that can develop into a complete organism. **germicide** *n* substance that kills germs.

German *n* **1** language of Germany, Austria, and part of Switzerland. **2** person from Germany. ▷ *adj* **3** of Germany or its language. **Germanic** *adj* **German measles** contagious disease accompanied by a cough, sore throat, and red spots. **German shepherd dog** Alsatian.

germane ❶ *adj* **germane to** relevant to.

germanium *n Chemistry* brittle grey element that is a semiconductor.

German measles contagious disease accompanied by a cough, sore throat, and red spots.

germinate ❶ *v* (cause to) sprout or begin to grow. **germination** *n* **germinal** *adj* **1** of or in the earliest stage of development. **2** of germs.

gerontology *n* study of ageing and the problems of elderly people. **gerontologist** *n*.

gerrymandering *n* division of voting constituencies in order to give an unfair advantage to one party.

gerund [**jer**-rund] *n* noun formed from a verb, such as *living*.

Gestapo *n* secret state police of Nazi Germany.

gestation *n* **1** (period of) carrying of young in the womb between conception and birth. **2** developing of a plan or idea in the mind.

--- THESAURUS ---

genuine *adj* **1** = **authentic**, actual, bona fide, legitimate, real, the real McCoy, true, veritable **2** = **sincere**, candid, earnest, frank, heartfelt, honest, unaffected, unfeigned

germ *n* **1** = **microbe**, bacterium, bug (*inf*), microorganism, virus **2** = **beginning**, embryo, origin, root, rudiment, seed, source, spark **3** = **embryo**, seed

germane *adj* = **relevant**, apposite, appropriate, apropos, connected, fitting, material, pertinent, related, to the point *or* purpose

germinate *v* = **sprout**, bud, develop, generate, grow, originate, shoot, swell, vegetate

gesticulate ❶ *v* make expressive movements with the hands and arms. **gesticulation** *n*.

gesture ❶ *n* **1** movement to convey meaning. **2** thing said or done to show one's feelings. ▷ *v* **3** gesticulate.

get ❶ *v* **getting**, **got 1** obtain or receive. **2** bring or fetch. **3** contract (an illness). **4** capture or seize. **5** (cause to) become as specified, e.g. *get wet*. **6** understand. **7** (often foll. by *to*) come (to) or arrive (at). **8** go on board (a plane, bus, etc.). **9** persuade. **10** receive a broadcast signal. **11** *informal* annoy. **12** *informal* have the better of. **13** be revenged on. **get across** *v* (cause to) be understood. **get at** *v* **1** gain access to. **2** imply or mean. **3** criticize. **getaway** *adj*, *n* (used in) escape. **get by** *v* manage in spite of difficulties. **get off** *v* **1** leave (a bus, train, etc.). **2** (cause to) avoid the consequences of, or punishment for, an action. **get off with** *v informal* start a romantic or sexual relationship with. **get on** *v* **1** board (a bus, train, etc.). **2** be friends with. **3** (foll. by *with*) continue to do. **4** grow old. **get over** *v* recover from. **get through** *v* **1** (cause to)

succeed. **2** use up (money or supplies). **get through to** *v* **1** make (a person) understand. **2** contact by telephone. **get-up** *n informal* costume. **get up to** *v* be involved in.

geyser [**geez**-er] *n* **1** spring that discharges steam and hot water. **2** domestic gas water heater.

ghastly ❶ *adj* **-lier**, **-liest 1** *informal* unpleasant. **2** deathly pale. **3** *informal* unwell. **4** *informal* horrible. **ghastliness** *n*.

ghat *n* **1** (in India) steps leading down to a river. **2** (in India) place of cremation. **3** mountain pass.

ghee [**gee**] *n* (in Indian cookery) clarified butter.

gherkin *n* small pickled cucumber.

ghetto *n*, *pl* **-tos**, **-toes** slum area inhabited by a deprived minority. **ghetto-blaster** *n informal* large portable cassette recorder or CD player.

ghillie *n* same as GILLIE.

ghost ❶ *n* **1** disembodied spirit of a dead person. **2** faint trace. **3** faint secondary image on a television screen. ▷ *v* **4** ghostwrite. **ghost gum** *Aust* eucalyptus with white trunk and branches. **ghostly** *adj* **ghost**

─────────────────────── THESAURUS ───────────────────────

gesticulate *v* = **signal**, gesture, indicate, make a sign, motion, sign, wave

gesture *n* **1** = **signal**, action, gesticulation, indication, motion, sign **2** = **signal**, indication, sign ▷ *v* **3** = **signal**, gesticulate, indicate, motion, sign, wave

get *v* **1** = **obtain**, acquire, attain, gain, land, net, pick up, procure, receive, secure, win **2** = **bring**, fetch **3** = **contract**, catch, come down with, fall victim to, take **4** = **capture**, grab, lay hold of, nab (*inf*), seize, take **5** = **become**, come to be, grow, turn **6** = **understand**, catch, comprehend, fathom, follow, perceive, see, take in, work out **9** = **persuade**, convince, induce, influence, prevail upon **11** *Inf* = **annoy**, bug (*inf*), gall, irritate, upset, vex

get across *v* = **communicate**, bring home to, convey, impart, make clear *or* understood, put over, transmit

get at *v* **1** = **gain access to**, acquire, attain, come to grips with, get hold of, reach **2** = **imply**, hint, intend, lead up

to, mean, suggest **3** = **criticize**, attack, blame, find fault with, nag, pick on

getaway *n* = **escape**, break, break-out, flight

get by *v* = **manage**, cope, exist, fare, get along, keep one's head above water, make both ends meet, survive

get off *v* **1** = **leave**, alight, depart, descend, disembark, dismount, escape, exit

get on *v* **1** = **board**, ascend, climb, embark, mount **2** = **be friendly**, be compatible, concur, get along, hit it off (*inf*)

get over *v* = **recover from**, come round, get better, mend, pull through, rally, revive, survive

ghastly *Inf* ▷ *adj* **1**, **4** = **horrible**, dreadful, frightful, gruesome, hideous, horrendous, loathsome, shocking, terrible, terrifying

ghost *n* **1** = **spirit**, apparition, phantom, soul, spectre, spook (*inf*), wraith **2** = **trace**, glimmer, hint, possibility, semblance, shadow, suggestion

town deserted town. **ghostwrite** v write (a book or article) on behalf of another person who is credited as the author. **ghostwriter** n.

ghoul ❶ [**gool**] n **1** person with morbid interests. **2** demon that eats corpses. **ghoulish** adj.

GHQ Military General Headquarters.

GI n informal US soldier.

giant ❶ n **1** mythical being of superhuman size. **2** very large person or thing. **3** person of exceptional ability or importance. ▷ adj **4** huge. **giantess** n fem.

gibber ❶ [**jib**-ber] v speak or utter rapidly and unintelligibly. **gibberish** n rapid unintelligible talk.

gibbet [**jib**-bit] n gallows for displaying executed criminals.

gibbon [**gib**-bon] n agile tree-dwelling ape of S Asia.

gibbous adj (of the moon) more than half but less than fully illuminated.

gibe ❶ [**jibe**] v, n same as JIBE[1].

giblets [**jib**-lets] pl n gizzard, liver, heart, and neck of a fowl.

gidday, g'day interj Aust & NZ expression of greeting.

giddy ❶ adj **-dier, -diest 1** having or causing a feeling of dizziness. **2** happy and excited. **giddily** adv **giddiness** n.

gift ❶ n **1** present. **2** natural talent. ▷ v **3** make a present of. **gifted** adj talented.

gig[1] n **1** single performance by pop or jazz musicians. ▷ v **gigging, gigged 2** play a gig or gigs.

gig[2] n informal short for GIGABYTE.

gig[3] n **1** light two-wheeled horse-drawn carriage. **2** long light rowing boat.

giga- prefix **1** denoting 10⁹, e.g. gigavolt. **2** Computers denoting 2³⁰, e.g. gigabyte.

gigabyte n Computers 1024 megabytes.

gigantic ❶ adj enormous.

giggle ❶ v **1** laugh nervously or foolishly. ▷ n **2** such a laugh. **3** informal amusing person or thing. **giggly** adj.

gigolo [**jig**-a-lo] n, pl **-los** man paid by an older woman to be her escort or lover.

gigot n leg of lamb or mutton.

gild ❶ v **gilding, gilded** or **gilt 1** put a thin layer of gold on. **2** make falsely attractive.

gill[1] [**gill**] n radiating structure beneath the cap of a mushroom.

gill[2] [**jill**] n liquid measure of quarter of a pint, equal to 0.142 litres.

gillie n (in Scotland) attendant for hunting or fishing.

gills [**gillz**] pl n breathing organs in fish and other water creatures.

gillyflower n fragrant flower.

gilt[1] v **1** past of GILD. ▷ adj **2** covered with a thin layer of gold. ▷ n **3** thin layer of gold used as decoration. **gilt-edged** adj denoting government stocks on which interest payments and final repayments are guaranteed.

gilt[2] n young female pig.

gimbals pl n set of pivoted rings which allow nautical instruments to remain horizontal at sea.

gimcrack [**jim**-krak] adj **1** showy but cheap. **2** shoddy.

gimlet [**gim**-let] n small tool with a screwlike tip for boring holes in wood. **gimlet-eyed** adj having a piercing glance.

g

THESAURUS

ghostly adj **1** = **supernatural**, eerie, ghostlike, phantom, spectral, spooky (inf), unearthly, wraithlike

ghoulish adj **1** = **macabre**, disgusting, grisly, gruesome, morbid, sick (inf), unwholesome

giant n **1, 2** = **ogre**, colossus, monster, titan ▷ adj **4** = **huge**, colossal, enormous, gargantuan, gigantic, immense, mammoth, titanic, vast

gibberish n = **nonsense**, babble, drivel, gobbledegook (inf), mumbo jumbo, twaddle

gibe v, n see JIBE[1].

giddiness n **1** = **dizziness**, faintness, light-headedness, vertigo

giddy adj **1** = **dizzy**, dizzying, faint, light-headed, reeling, unsteady, vertiginous

gift n **1** = **donation**, bequest, bonus, contribution, grant, hand-out, legacy, offering, present **2** = **talent**, ability, capability, capacity, flair, genius, knack, power

gifted adj = **talented**, able, accomplished, brilliant, capable, clever, expert, ingenious, masterly, skilled

gigantic adj = **enormous**, colossal, giant, huge, immense, mammoth, stupendous, titanic, tremendous

giggle v **1** n **2** = **laugh**, cackle, chortle, chuckle, snigger, titter, twitter

gild v **2** = **embellish**, adorn, beautify, brighten, coat, dress up, embroider, enhance, ornament

gimmick ❶ *n* something designed to attract attention or publicity. **gimmickry** *n* **gimmicky** *adj*.

gin¹ *n* alcoholic drink flavoured with juniper berries.

gin² *n* **1** wire noose used to trap small animals. **2** machine for separating seeds from raw cotton.

ginger *n* **1** root of a tropical plant, used as a spice. **2** light orange-brown colour. **gingery** *adj* **ginger ale**, **beer** fizzy ginger-flavoured soft drink. **gingerbread** *n* moist cake flavoured with ginger. **ginger group** group within a larger group that agitates for a more active policy. **ginger nut**, **snap** crisp ginger-flavoured biscuit.

gingerly ❶ *adv* **1** cautiously. ▷ *adj* **2** cautious.

gingham *n* cotton cloth, usu. checked or striped.

gingivitis [jin-jiv-**vite**-iss] *n* inflammation of the gums.

ginkgo [**gink**-go] *n, pl* **-goes** ornamental Chinese tree.

ginseng [**jin**-seng] *n* (root of) a plant believed to have tonic and energy-giving properties.

Gipsy *n, pl* **-sies** same as GYPSY.

giraffe *n* African ruminant mammal with a spotted yellow skin and long neck and legs.

gird ❶ *v* **girding**, **girded** *or* **girt** **1** put a belt round. **2** secure with or as if with a belt. **3** surround. **gird (up) one's loins** prepare for action.

girder *n* large metal beam.

girdle¹ ❶ *n* **1** woman's elastic corset. **2** belt. **3** *Anat* encircling structure or part. ▷ *v* **4** surround or encircle.

girdle² *n Scot* griddle.

girl ❶ *n* **1** female child. **2** young woman. **3** girlfriend. **4** *informal* any woman. **girlhood** *n* **girlish** *adj* **girlie** *adj informal* featuring photographs of naked or scantily clad women. **girlfriend** *n* **1** girl or woman with whom a person is romantically or sexually involved. **2** female friend. **Girl Guide** same as GUIDE.

giro [**jire**-oh] *n, pl* **-ros** **1** system of transferring money within a post office or bank directly from one account to another. **2** *informal* social security payment by giro cheque.

girt *v* a past of GIRD.

girth ❶ *n* **1** measurement round something. **2** band round a horse to hold the saddle in position.

gist ❶ *v* [**jist**] *n* substance or main point of a matter.

give ❶ *v* **giving**, **gave**, **given** **1** present (something) to another person. **2** transfer in exchange or payment. **3** impart. **4** attribute. **5** administer. **6** be a source of. **7** utter or emit. **8** sacrifice or devote. **9** organize or host. **10** concede. **11** yield or break under pressure. ▷ *n* **12** resilience or elasticity. **give away** *v* **1** donate as a gift. **2** reveal. **3** hand over (a bride) formally to her spouse in a marriage ceremony. **giveaway** *n* **1** something that reveals hidden

———————————— THESAURUS ————————————

gimmick *n* = **stunt**, contrivance, device, dodge, ploy, scheme

gingerly *adv* **1** = **cautiously**, carefully, charily, circumspectly, hesitantly, reluctantly, suspiciously, timidly, warily

gird *v* **3** = **surround**, encircle, enclose, encompass, enfold, hem in, ring

girdle¹ *n* **2** = **belt**, band, cummerbund, sash, waistband ▷ *v* **4** = **surround**, bound, encircle, enclose, encompass, gird, ring

girl *n* **1, 2** = **female child**, damsel (*arch*), daughter, lass, lassie (*inf*), maid (*arch*), maiden (*arch*), miss

girth *n* **1** = **circumference**, bulk, measure, size

gist *n* = **point**, core, essence, force, idea, meaning, sense, significance, substance

give *v* **1** = **present**, award, contribute, deliver, donate, grant, hand over *or* out, provide, supply **3, 7** = **announce**, communicate, issue, notify, pronounce, transmit, utter **6** = **produce**, cause, engender, make, occasion **8** = **devote**, hand over, relinquish **10** = **concede**, allow, grant **11** = **surrender**, yield

give away *v* **2** = **reveal**, betray, disclose, divulge, expose, leak, let out, let slip, uncover

give in *v* = **admit defeat**, capitulate, cave in (*inf*), collapse, concede, quit, submit, succumb, surrender, yield

give off *v* = **emit**, discharge, exude, produce, release, send out, throw out

give out *v* **2** = **emit**, discharge, exude, produce, release, send out, throw out

feelings or intentions. ▷ *adj* **2** very cheap or free. **give in** *v* admit defeat. **give off** *v* emit. **give out** *v* **1** distribute. **2** emit. **3** come to an end or fail. **give over** *v* **1** set aside for a specific purpose. **2** *informal* cease. **give up** *v* **1** abandon. **2** acknowledge defeat.

gizzard *n* part of a bird's stomach.

glacé [**glass**-say] *adj* preserved in a thick sugary syrup.

glacier *n* slow-moving mass of ice formed by accumulated snow. **glacial** *adj* **1** of ice or glaciers. **2** very cold. **3** unfriendly. **glaciated** *adj* covered with or affected by glaciers. **glaciation** *n*.

glad ❶ *adj* **gladder**, **gladdest** **1** pleased and happy. **2** causing happiness. **glad to** very willing to (do something). **the glad eye** *informal* inviting or seductive glance. **gladly** *adv* **gladness** *n* **gladden** *v* make glad. **gladsome** *adj* old-fashioned joyous or cheerful. **glad rags** *informal* best clothes.

glade *n* open space in a forest.

gladiator *n* (in ancient Rome) man trained to fight in arenas to provide entertainment.

gladiolus *n*, *pl* **-lus**, **-li**, **-luses** garden plant with sword-shaped leaves.

glamour ❶ *n* alluring charm or fascination. **glamorous** *adj* alluring. **glamorize** *v*.

● **SPELLING TIP**
● People often forget to drop the *u*
● in **glamour** when they add *ous*.
● That's why there are 124 occurrences
● of *glamourous* in the Bank of
● English. But the correct spelling is
● **glamorous**.

glance ❶ *v* **1** look rapidly or briefly. **2** glint or gleam. ▷ *n* **3** brief look. **glancing** *adj* hitting at an oblique angle. **glance off** *v* strike and be deflected off (an object) at an oblique angle.

gland *n* **1** organ that produces and secretes substances in the body. **2** similar organ in a plant. **glandular** *adj* **glandular fever** infectious viral disease characterized by fever and swollen lymph nodes.

glare ❶ *v* **1** stare angrily. **2** be unpleasantly bright. ▷ *n* **3** angry stare. **4** unpleasant brightness. **glaring** *adj* **1** conspicuous. **2** unpleasantly bright. **glaringly** *adv*.

glasnost *n* policy of openness and accountability, esp., formerly, in the USSR.

glass ❶ *n* **1** hard brittle, usu. transparent substance consisting of metal silicates or similar compounds. **2** tumbler. **3** its contents. **4** objects made of glass. **5** mirror. **6** barometer. ▷ *pl* **7** spectacles. **glassy** *adj* **1** like glass. **2** expressionless. **glassiness** *n* **glasshouse** *n* **1** greenhouse. **2** *informal* army prison.

THESAURUS

give up *v* **1** = **abandon**, call it a day *or* night, cease, desist, leave off, quit, relinquish, renounce, stop **2** = **surrender**, cave in (*inf*)

glad *adj* **1** = **happy**, contented, delighted, gratified, joyful, overjoyed, pleased **2** = **pleasing**, cheerful, cheering, gratifying, pleasant

gladden *v* = **please**, cheer, delight, gratify, hearten

gladly *adv* = **happily**, cheerfully, freely, gleefully, readily, willingly, with pleasure

gladness *n* = **happiness**, cheerfulness, delight, gaiety, glee, high spirits, joy, mirth, pleasure

glamorous *adj* = **elegant**, attractive, dazzling, exciting, fascinating, glittering, glossy, prestigious, smart

glamour *n* = **charm**, allure, appeal, attraction, beauty, enchantment, fascination, prestige

glance *v* **1** = **peek**, glimpse, look, peep, scan, view **2** = **gleam**, flash, glimmer, glint, glisten, glitter, reflect, shimmer, shine, twinkle ▷ *n* **3** = **peek**, dekko (*sl*), glimpse, look, peep, view

glare *v* **1** = **scowl**, frown, glower, look daggers, lour *or* lower **2** = **dazzle**, blaze, flame, flare ▷ *n* **3** = **scowl**, black look, dirty look, frown, glower, lour *or* lower **4** = **dazzle**, blaze, brilliance, flame, glow

glaring *adj* **1** = **conspicuous**, blatant, flagrant, gross, manifest, obvious, outrageous, unconcealed **2** = **dazzling**, blazing, bright, garish, glowing

glassy *adj* **1** = **transparent**, clear, glossy, shiny, slippery, smooth **2** = **expressionless**, blank, cold, dull, empty, fixed, glazed, lifeless, vacant

glaucoma n eye disease.
glaze ❶ v **1** fit or cover with glass.
2 cover with a protective shiny
coating. **3** cover (food) with
beaten egg or milk before cooking.
4 become glassy. ▷ n **5** transparent
coating. **6** substance used for this.
glazier n person who fits windows
with glass.
gleam ❶ n **1** small beam or glow of
light. **2** brief or faint indication. ▷ v
3 emit a gleam. **gleaming** adj.
glean v **1** gather (facts etc.) bit by bit.
2 gather (the useful remnants of a
crop) after harvesting. **gleaner** n.
glee ❶ n triumph and delight. **gleeful**
adj **gleefully** adv.
glen n deep narrow valley.
glengarry n, pl **-ries** brimless Scottish
cap with a crease down the crown.
glib ❶ adj **glibber**, **glibbest** fluent but
insincere or superficial. **glibly** adv
glibness n.
glide ❶ v **1** move easily and smoothly.
2 (of an aircraft) move without the use
of engines. **3** pass gradually and
imperceptibly. ▷ n **4** smooth easy
movement. **glider** n **1** aircraft without
an engine which floats on air currents.
2 flying phalanger. **gliding** n sport of
flying gliders.

glimmer ❶ v **1** shine faintly, flicker.
▷ n **2** faint gleam. **3** faint indication.
glimpse ❶ n **1** brief or incomplete view.
2 vague indication. ▷ v **3** catch a
glimpse of.
glint v **1** gleam brightly. ▷ n **2** bright
gleam.
glissade n **1** gliding step in ballet.
2 controlled slide down a snow slope.
▷ v **3** perform a glissade.
glissando n Music slide between two
notes in which all intermediate notes
are played.
glisten ❶ v gleam by reflecting light.
glitch ❶ n small problem that
stops something from working
properly.
glitter ❶ v **1** shine with bright flashes.
2 be showy. ▷ n **3** sparkle or brilliance.
4 superficial glamour. **5** tiny pieces of
shiny decorative material.
glitzy adj **glitzier**, **glitziest** slang
showily attractive.
gloaming n twilight.
gloat ❶ v (often foll. by over) regard
one's own good fortune or the
misfortune of others with smug or
malicious pleasure.
glob n rounded mass of thick fluid.

————— THESAURUS —————

glaze v **2** = **coat**, enamel, gloss, lacquer,
polish, varnish ▷ n **5, 6** = **coat**, enamel,
finish, gloss, lacquer, lustre, patina,
polish, shine, varnish
gleam n **1** = **glow**, beam, flash,
glimmer, ray, sparkle **2** = **trace**, flicker,
glimmer, hint, inkling, suggestion ▷ v
3 = **shine**, flash, glimmer, glint, glisten,
glitter, glow, shimmer, sparkle
glee n = **delight**, elation, exhilaration,
exuberance, exultation, joy,
merriment, triumph
gleeful adj = **delighted**, cock-a-hoop,
elated, exuberant, exultant, joyful,
jubilant, overjoyed, triumphant
glib adj = **smooth**, easy, fluent,
insincere, plausible, quick, ready, slick,
suave, voluble
glide v **1** = **slide**, coast, drift, float, flow,
roll, run, sail, skate, slip **3** = **slip**, drift,
slide
glimmer v **1** = **flicker**, blink, gleam,
glisten, glitter, glow, shimmer, shine,
sparkle, twinkle ▷ n **2** = **gleam**, blink,
flicker, glow, ray, shimmer, sparkle,
twinkle **3** = **trace**, flicker, gleam, hint,
inkling, suggestion

glimpse n **1** = **look**, glance, peek, peep,
sight, sighting ▷ v **3** = **catch sight of**,
espy, sight, spot, spy, view
glint v **1** = **gleam**, flash, glimmer,
glitter, shine, sparkle, twinkle ▷ n
2 = **gleam**, flash, glimmer, glitter,
shine, sparkle, twinkle, twinkling
glisten v = **gleam**, flash, glance, glare,
glimmer, glint, glitter, shimmer, shine,
sparkle, twinkle
glitch n = **problem**, blip, difficulty,
gremlin, hitch, interruption,
malfunction, snag
glitter v **1** = **shine**, flash, glare, gleam,
glimmer, glint, glisten, shimmer,
sparkle, twinkle ▷ n **3** = **shine**,
brightness, flash, glare, gleam, radiance,
sheen, shimmer, sparkle **4** = **glamour**,
display, gaudiness, pageantry, show,
showiness, splendour, tinsel
gloat v (often foll. by over) = **relish**,
crow, drool, exult, glory, revel in, rub it
in (inf), triumph
global adj **1** = **worldwide**,
international, universal, world
2 = **comprehensive**, all-inclusive,
exhaustive, general, total, unlimited

globe ❶ *n* **1** sphere with a map of the earth on it. **2** spherical object. **3** *S Afr* light bulb. **the globe** the earth. **global** *adj* **1** worldwide. **2** total or comprehensive. **globalization** *n* process by which a company, etc., expands to operate internationally. **global warming** increase in the overall temperature worldwide believed to be caused by the greenhouse effect. **globally** *adv* **globetrotter** *n* habitual worldwide traveller. **globetrotting** *n*, *adj*.

globule ❶ *n* small round drop. **globular** *adj*.

globulin *n* simple protein found in living tissue.

glockenspiel *n* percussion instrument consisting of small metal bars played with hammers.

gloom ❶ *n* **1** melancholy or depression. **2** darkness. **gloomy** *adj* **gloomier**, **gloomiest**. **gloomily** *adv*.

glory ❶ *n*, *pl* **-ries 1** praise or honour. **2** splendour. **3** praiseworthy thing. **4** adoration or worship. ▷ *v* **-rying**, **-ried 5** (foll. by *in*) triumph or exalt. **glorify** *v* **-fying**, **-fied 1** make (something) seem more worthy than it is. **2** praise. **3** worship. **glorification** *n* **glorious** *adj* **1** brilliantly beautiful.

2 delightful. **3** full of or conferring glory. **gloriously** *adv* **glory hole** *informal* untidy cupboard or storeroom.

gloss¹ ❶ *n* **1** surface shine or lustre. **2** superficially attractive appearance. **3** paint or cosmetic giving a shiny finish. ▷ *v* **4** make glossy. **glossy** *adj* **-sier**, **-siest 1** smooth and shiny. **2** (of a magazine) printed on shiny paper. **3** superficially attractive or sophisticated. **glossily** *adv* **glossiness** *n* **gloss over** *v* (try to) cover up or pass over (a fault or error).

gloss² ❶ *n* **1** explanatory comment added to the text of a book. ▷ *v* **2** add glosses to.

glossary *n*, *pl* **-ries** list of special or technical words with definitions.

glottis *n*, *pl* **-tises**, **-tides** vocal cords and the space between them. **glottal** *adj* **glottal stop** speech sound made by closing and then opening the glottis.

glove *n* covering for the hand with individual sheaths for each finger and the thumb. **gloved** *adj* covered by a glove or gloves. **glove compartment** small storage area in the dashboard of a car.

THESAURUS

globe *n* **2** = **sphere**, ball, orb **the globe** = **earth**, planet, world

globule *n* = **droplet**, bead, bubble, drop, particle, pearl, pellet

gloom *n* **1** = **depression**, dejection, despondency, low spirits, melancholy, sorrow, unhappiness, woe **2** = **darkness**, blackness, dark, dusk, murk, obscurity, shade, shadow, twilight

gloomy *adj* **1** = **depressing**, bad, cheerless, crestfallen, dejected, disheartening, dispirited, downcast, downhearted, dreary, glum, melancholy, miserable, morose, pessimistic, sad, sombre **2** = **dark**, black, dim, dismal, dreary, dull, grey, murky, sombre

glorify *v* **1** = **enhance**, aggrandize, dignify, elevate, ennoble, magnify **2** = **praise**, celebrate, eulogize, extol, sing *or* sound the praises of **3** = **worship**, adore, bless, exalt, honour, idolize, pay homage to, revere, venerate

glorious *adj* **1** = **splendid**, beautiful,

brilliant, dazzling, gorgeous, shining, superb **2** = **delightful**, excellent, fine, gorgeous, marvellous, wonderful **3** = **famous**, celebrated, distinguished, eminent, honoured, illustrious, magnificent, majestic, renowned

glory *n* **1** = **honour**, dignity, distinction, eminence, fame, praise, prestige, renown **2** = **splendour**, grandeur, greatness, magnificence, majesty, nobility, pageantry, pomp ▷ *v* **5** (foll. by *in*) = **triumph**, exalt, pride oneself, relish, revel, take delight

gloss¹ *n* **1, 2** = **shine**, brightness, gleam, lustre, patina, polish, sheen, veneer

gloss² *n* **1** = **comment**, annotation, commentary, elucidation, explanation, footnote, interpretation, note, translation ▷ *v* **2** = **interpret**, annotate, comment, elucidate, explain, translate

glossy *adj* **1** = **shiny**, bright, glassy, glazed, lustrous, polished, shining, silky

glow ❶ *v* **1** emit light and heat without flames. **2** shine. **3** have a feeling of wellbeing or satisfaction. **4** (of a colour) look warm. **5** be hot. ▷ *n* **6** glowing light. **7** warmth of colour. **8** feeling of wellbeing. **glow-worm** *n* insect giving out a green light.

glower ❶ [rhymes with **power**] *v*, *n* scowl.

gloxinia *n* tropical plant with large bell-shaped flowers.

glucose *n* kind of sugar found in fruit.

glue ❶ *n* **1** natural or synthetic sticky substance used as an adhesive. ▷ *v* **gluing** or **glueing**, **glued 2** fasten with glue. **3** (foll. by *to*) pay full attention to, e.g. *her eyes were glued to the TV*. **gluey** *adj* **glue-sniffing** *n* inhaling of glue fumes for intoxicating or hallucinatory effects.

glum ❶ *adj* **glummer**, **glummest** sullen or gloomy. **glumly** *adv*.

glut ❶ *n* **1** excessive supply. ▷ *v* **glutting**, **glutted 2** oversupply. **3** feed or fill to excess.

gluten [**gloo**-ten] *n* protein found in cereal grain.

glutinous [**gloo**-tin-uss] *adj* sticky or gluey.

glutton ❶ *n* **1** greedy person. **2** person with a great capacity for something. **gluttonous** *adj* **gluttony** *n*.

glycerine, **glycerin** [**gliss**-ser-in] *n* colourless sweet liquid used widely in chemistry and industry.

glycerol [**gliss**-ser-ol] *n* technical name for GLYCERINE.

gm gram.

GM 1 genetically modified. **2** grant-maintained.

G-man *n*, *pl* **G-men** *US slang* FBI agent.

GMO genetically modified organism.

GMT Greenwich Mean Time.

gnarled ❶ *adj* rough, twisted, and knobbly.

gnash *v* grind (the teeth) together in anger or pain.

gnat *n* small biting two-winged fly.

gnaw ❶ *v* **gnawing**, **gnawed**, **gnawed** or **gnawn 1** bite or chew steadily. **2** (foll. by *at*) cause constant distress (to). **gnawing** *adj*.

gneiss *n* coarse-grained metamorphic rock.

gnome *n* **1** imaginary creature like a little old man. **2** *facetious* international banker or financier.

gnomic [**no**-mik] *adj* of pithy sayings.

Gnosticism *n* religious movement believing in intuitive spiritual knowledge. **Gnostic** *n*, *adj*.

GNP Gross National Product.

gnu [**noo**] *n* oxlike S African antelope.

go ❶ *v* **going**, **went**, **gone 1** move to or from a place. **2** be in regular attendance at. **3** depart. **4** function. **5** be, do, or become as specified. **6** contribute to a result, e.g. *it just goes to show*. **7** be allotted to a specific purpose or recipient. **8** be sold. **9** blend or harmonize. **10** fail or break down. **11** elapse. **12** be got rid of. **13** attend. **14** reach or exceed certain limits, e.g. *she's gone too far this time*.

━━━━━━━━━━━━━━━━━━━━━━━━━━━━ THESAURUS ━━━━━

glow *v* **1** = **smoulder**, burn **2** = **shine**, brighten, burn, gleam, glimmer, redden ▷ *n* **6** = **light**, burning, gleam, glimmer, luminosity, phosphorescence **7** = **radiance**, brightness, brilliance, effulgence, splendour, vividness

glower *v* = **scowl**, frown, give a dirty look, glare, look daggers, lour *or* lower ▷ *n* = **scowl**, black look, dirty look, frown, glare, lour *or* lower

glue *n* **1** = **adhesive**, cement, gum, paste

glum *adj* = **gloomy**, crestfallen, dejected, doleful, low, morose, pessimistic, sullen

glut *n* **1** = **surfeit**, excess, oversupply, plethora, saturation, superfluity, surplus ▷ *v* **2, 3** = **saturate**, choke, clog, deluge, flood, inundate, overload, oversupply

glutton *n* **1** = **gourmand**, gannet (*sl*), pig (*inf*)

gluttonous *adj* = **greedy**, insatiable, ravenous, voracious

gluttony *n* = **greed**, greediness, voracity

gnarled *adj* = **twisted**, contorted, knotted, knotty, rough, rugged, weather-beaten, wrinkled

gnaw *v* **1** = **bite**, chew, munch, nibble

go *v* **1** = **move**, advance, journey, make for, pass, proceed, set off, travel **3** = **leave**, depart, make tracks, move out, slope off, withdraw **4** = **function**, move, operate, perform, run, work **6** = **contribute**, lead to, serve, tend, work towards **9** = **harmonize**, agree, blend, chime, complement, correspond, fit, match, suit **11** = **elapse**, expire, flow, lapse, pass,

15 be acceptable. **16** carry authority. ▷ n **17** attempt. **18** verbal attack. **19** turn. **20** *informal* energy or vigour. **make a go of** be successful at. **on the go** active and energetic. **go-ahead** *adj* enterprising or ambitious. **go back on** *v* break (a promise etc.). **go-between** *n* intermediary. **go for** *v* **1** *informal* choose. **2** attack. **3** apply to equally. **go-getter** *n* energetically ambitious person. **go-go dancer** scantily dressed erotic dancer. **go off** *v* **1** stop functioning. **2** explode. **3** ring or sound. **4** occur as specified. **5** *informal* become stale or rotten. **6** *informal* stop liking. **go out** *v* **1** go to entertainments or social functions. **2** be romantically involved (with). **3** be extinguished. **4** (of a broadcast) be transmitted. **go over** *v* examine or check. **go-slow** *n* deliberate slowing of work-rate as an industrial protest. **go through** *v* **1** suffer or undergo. **2** examine or search.

goad ❶ *v* **1** provoke (someone) to take some kind of action, usu. in anger. ▷ *n* **2** spur or provocation. **3** spiked stick for driving cattle.

goal ❶ *n* **1** *Sport* posts through which the ball or puck has to be propelled to score. **2** score made in this way. **3** aim or purpose. **goalie** *n informal* goalkeeper. **goalkeeper** *n* player whose task is to stop shots entering the goal. **goalpost** *n* one of the two posts supporting the crossbar of a goal. **move the goalposts** change the aims of an activity to ensure the desired result.

goat *n* **1** sure-footed ruminant animal with horns. **2** foolish person. **get someone's goat** *slang* annoy someone. **goatee** *n* pointed tuftlike beard.

gob *n* **1** lump of a soft substance. **2** *slang* mouth.

gobbet *n* lump, esp. of food.

gobble¹ ❶ *v* eat hastily and greedily.

gobble² *n* **1** rapid gurgling cry of the male turkey. ▷ *v* **2** make this noise.

gobbledegook, gobbledygook ❶ *n* unintelligible (official) language or jargon.

goblet *n* drinking cup without handles.

goblin *n* (in folklore) small malevolent creature.

goby *n, pl* **-by, -bies** small spiny-finned fish.

god ❶ *n* **1** spirit or being worshipped as having supernatural power. **2** object of worship, idol. **3** (**G-**) (in monotheistic religions) the Supreme Being, creator and ruler of the universe. **the gods** top balcony in a theatre. **goddess** *n fem* **godlike** *adj* **godly** *adj* devout or pious. **godliness** *n* **god-fearing** *adj* pious and devout. **godforsaken** *adj* desolate or dismal. **godsend** *n* something unexpected but welcome.

godetia *n* plant with showy flowers.

godparent *n* person who promises at a child's baptism to bring the child up as a Christian. **godchild** *n* child for whom a person stands as godparent. **goddaughter** *n* **godfather** *n* **1** male godparent. **2** head of a criminal, esp. Mafia, organization. **godmother** *n* **godson** *n*.

godwit *n* shore bird with long legs and an upturned bill.

goer *n* person who attends something regularly, e.g. *filmgoer*.

gogga *n S Afr informal* any small insect.

goggle *v* **1** (of the eyes) bulge. **2** stare. **goggles** *pl n* protective spectacles. **gogglebox** *n slang* television set.

━━━━━━━━━━━━━━━━ THESAURUS ━━━━━━━━━━━━━━━━

slip away ▷ n **17, 19** = **attempt**, bid, crack (*inf*), effort, shot (*inf*), try, turn **20** *Inf* = **energy**, drive, force, life, spirit, verve, vigour, vitality, vivacity

goad *v* **1** = **provoke**, drive, egg on, exhort, incite, prod, prompt, spur ▷ *n* **2** = **provocation**, impetus, incentive, incitement, irritation, spur, stimulus, urge

goal *n* **3** = **aim**, ambition, end, intention, object, objective, purpose, target

gobble¹ *v* = **devour**, bolt, cram, gorge, gulp, guzzle, stuff, swallow, wolf

gobbledegook, gobbledygook *n* = **nonsense**, babble, cant, gabble, gibberish, hocus-pocus, jargon, mumbo jumbo, twaddle

godforsaken *adj* = **desolate**, abandoned, bleak, deserted, dismal, dreary, forlorn, gloomy, lonely, remote, wretched

godlike *adj* = **divine**, celestial, heavenly, superhuman, transcendent

godly *adj* = **devout**, god-fearing, good, holy, pious, religious, righteous, saintly

Goidelic *adj, n* (of) the group of Celtic languages consisting of Scottish Gaelic, Irish Gaelic, and Manx.

going *n* **1** condition of the ground for walking or riding over. **2** speed or progress. **3** departure. ▷ *adj* **4** thriving. **5** current or accepted. **going-over** *n, pl* **goings-over 1** *informal* investigation or examination. **2** scolding or thrashing. **goings-on** *pl n* mysterious or unacceptable events.

goitre [**goy**-ter] *n* swelling of the thyroid gland in the neck.

go-kart *n* small low-powered racing car.

gold *n* **1** yellow precious metal. **2** coins or articles made of this. **3** colour of gold. **4** wealth. ▷ *adj* **5** made of gold. **6** gold-coloured. **goldcrest** *n* small bird with a yellow crown. **gold-digger** *n* **1** person who digs for gold. **2** *informal* woman who uses her sexual attractions to get money from a man. **goldfinch** *n* kind of finch, the male of which has yellow-and-black wings. **goldfish** *n* orange fish kept in ponds or aquariums. **gold leaf** thin gold sheet used for gilding. **gold medal** medal given to the winner of a competition or race. **gold rush** migration of people to a territory where gold has been found. **goldsmith** *n* dealer in or maker of gold articles.

golden ❶ *adj* **1** made of gold. **2** gold-coloured. **3** very successful or promising. **golden eagle** large mountain eagle of the N hemisphere.

golden goal *Soccer* first goal scored in extra time, which wins the match for the side scoring it. **golden handshake** *informal* payment to a departing employee. **golden mean** middle course between extremes. **golden rule** important principle. **golden wattle** Australian plant with yellow flowers that yields a useful gum and bark. **golden wedding** fiftieth wedding anniversary.

golf *n* **1** outdoor game in which a ball is struck with clubs into a series of holes. ▷ *v* **2** play golf. **golfer** *n*.

golliwog *n* soft black-faced doll.

golly *interj* exclamation of mild surprise.

goloshes *pl n* same as GALOSHES.

gonad *n* organ producing reproductive cells, such as a testicle or ovary.

gondola *n* **1** long narrow boat used in Venice. **2** suspended cabin of a cable car, airship, etc. **gondolier** *n* person who propels a gondola.

gone ❶ *v* past participle of GO. **goner** *n* *informal* person or thing beyond help or recovery.

gong *n* **1** rimmed metal disc that produces a note when struck. **2** *slang* medal.

gonorrhoea [gon-or-**ree**-a] *n* venereal disease with a discharge from the genitals.

good ❶ *adj* **better**, **best 1** giving pleasure. **2** morally excellent. **3** beneficial. **4** kindly. **5** talented. **6** well-behaved. **7** valid. **8** reliable. **9** financially sound. **10** complete or full. ▷ *n* **11** benefit. **12** positive moral

———————————————— THESAURUS ————————————————

godsend *n* = **blessing**, boon, manna, stroke of luck, windfall

go for *v* **1** *Inf* = **favour**, admire, be attracted to, be fond of, choose, like, prefer **2** = **attack**, assail, assault, launch oneself at, rush upon, set about *or* upon, spring upon

golden *adj* **2** = **yellow**, blond, blonde, flaxen **3** = **successful**, excellent, favourable, flourishing, glorious, halcyon, happy, opportune, promising, prosperous, rich

good *adj* **1** = **excellent**, acceptable, admirable, fine, first-class, first-rate, great, pleasing, satisfactory, splendid, superior **2** = **honourable**, admirable, ethical, honest, moral, praiseworthy, righteous, trustworthy, upright, virtuous, worthy **3** = **favourable**,

advantageous, beneficial, convenient, fitting, helpful, profitable, suitable, useful, wholesome **4** = **kind**, altruistic, benevolent, charitable, friendly, humane, kind-hearted, kindly, merciful, obliging **5** = **expert**, able, accomplished, adept, adroit, clever, competent, proficient, skilled, talented **6** = **well-behaved**, dutiful, obedient, orderly, polite, well-mannered **7** = **valid**, authentic, bona fide, genuine, legitimate, proper, real, true **10** = **full**, adequate, ample, complete, considerable, extensive, large, substantial, sufficient ▷ *n* **11** = **benefit**, advantage, gain, interest, profit, use, usefulness, welfare, wellbeing **12** = **virtue**, excellence, goodness, merit, morality, rectitude,

qualities. ▷ pl **13** merchandise.
14 property. **as good as** virtually. **for good** permanently. **goodness** n
goodly adj considerable. **goody** n, pl **-dies 1** informal hero in a book or film.
2 enjoyable thing. **goody-goody** adj, n smugly virtuous (person). **good-for-nothing** adj, n irresponsible or worthless (person). **Good Friday** Friday before Easter, observed by Christians as a commemoration of the Crucifixion. **good-natured** adj tolerant and kindly. **Good Samaritan** person who helps another in distress.
goodwill n **1** kindly feeling. **2** value of a business in reputation etc. over and above its tangible assets.

● **USAGE NOTE**
● Note that good is an adjective. To
● modify a verb, use well: She did well.

goodbye ❶ interj, n expression used on parting.
gooey adj **gooier**, **gooiest** informal **1** sticky and soft. **2** sentimental.
goof informal ▷ n **1** mistake. **2** stupid person. ▷ v **3** make a mistake. **goofy** adj **goofier**, **goofiest**.
google v search for (something on the internet) using a search engine.
googly n, pl **-lies** Cricket ball that spins unexpectedly from off to leg on the bounce.
goon n **1** informal stupid person. ·

2 Chiefly US hired thug.
goosander n type of duck.
goose n, pl **geese 1** web-footed bird like a large duck. **2** female of this bird. **3** silly person. **goose flesh**, **pimples** bumpy condition of the skin and bristling of the hair due to cold or fright. **goose step** march step in which the leg is raised rigidly.
gooseberry n **1** edible yellowy-green berry. **2** informal unwanted third person accompanying a couple.
gopher [go-fer] n American burrowing rodent.
gore¹ ❶ n blood from a wound.
gore² ❶ v pierce with horns.
gore³ n tapering piece of material in a garment, sail, or umbrella.
gorge ❶ n **1** deep narrow valley. ▷ v **2** eat greedily. **make one's gorge rise** cause feelings of disgust or nausea.
gorgeous ❶ adj **1** strikingly beautiful or attractive. **2** informal very pleasant. **gorgeously** adv.
gorgon n terrifying or repulsive woman.
Gorgonzola n sharp-flavoured blue-veined Italian cheese.
gorilla n largest of the apes, found in Africa.
gormless adj informal stupid.
gorse n prickly yellow-flowered shrub.

———————— **THESAURUS** ————————

right, righteousness, worth ▷ pl **13** = **merchandise**, commodities, stock, stuff, wares **14** = **property**, belongings, chattels, effects, gear, paraphernalia, possessions, things, trappings **for good** = **permanently**, finally, for ever, irrevocably, once and for all
goodbye interj = **farewell**, adieu ▷ n = **parting**, adieu, farewell, leave-taking
good-for-nothing adj = **worthless**, feckless, idle, irresponsible, useless ▷ n = **layabout**, black sheep, idler, ne'er-do-well, skiver (Brit sl), slacker (inf), waster, wastrel
goodly adj = **considerable**, ample, large, significant, sizable or sizeable, substantial, tidy (inf)
goodness n **2** = **virtue**, honesty, honour, integrity, merit, morality, probity, rectitude, righteousness, uprightness **3** = **benefit**, advantage,

salubriousness, wholesomeness
4 = **kindness**, benevolence, friendliness, generosity, goodwill, humaneness, kind-heartedness, kindliness, mercy
goodwill n **1** = **friendliness**, amity, benevolence, friendship, heartiness, kindliness
gore¹ n = **blood**, bloodshed, butchery, carnage, slaughter
gore² v = **pierce**, impale, transfix, wound
gorge n **1** = **ravine**, canyon, chasm, cleft, defile, fissure, pass ▷ v **2** = **overeat**, cram, devour, feed, glut, gobble, gulp, guzzle, stuff, wolf
gorgeous adj **1** = **beautiful**, dazzling, elegant, magnificent, ravishing, splendid, stunning (inf), sumptuous, superb **2** Inf = **pleasing**, delightful, enjoyable, exquisite, fine, glorious, good, lovely

gory ❶ *adj* **gorier, goriest 1** horrific or bloodthirsty. **2** involving bloodshed.

gosh *interj* exclamation of mild surprise or wonder.

goshawk *n* large hawk.

gosling *n* young goose.

gospel ❶ *n* **1** (**G-**) any of the first four books of the New Testament. **2** doctrine held to be of great importance. **3** unquestionable truth. **4** Black religious music originating in the churches of the Southern US.

gossamer *n* **1** very fine fabric. **2** filmy cobweb.

gossip ❶ *n* **1** idle talk, esp. about other people. **2** person who engages in gossip. ▷ *v* **gossiping, gossiped 3** engage in gossip. **gossipy** *adj*.

got *v* past of GET. **have got** possess. **have got to** need or be required to.

Goth *n* member of an East Germanic people who invaded the Roman Empire.

Gothic *adj* **1** (of architecture) of or in the style common in Europe from the 12th–16th centuries, with pointed arches. **2** of or in an 18th-century literary style characterized by gloom and the supernatural. **3** (of print) using a heavy ornate typeface. **4** barbarous.

gotten *v* US past participle of GET.

gouache *n* (painting using) watercolours mixed with glue.

Gouda *n* mild-flavoured Dutch cheese.

gouge ❶ [gowj] *v* **1** scoop or force out. **2** cut (a hole or groove) in (something). ▷ *n* **3** hole or groove. **4** chisel with a curved cutting edge.

goulash [goo-lash] *n* rich stew seasoned with paprika.

gourd [goord] *n* **1** fleshy fruit of a climbing plant. **2** its dried shell, used as a container.

gourmand [goor-mand] *n* person who is very keen on food and drink.

gourmet ❶ [goor-may] *n* connoisseur of food and drink.

gout [gowt] *n* disease causing inflammation of the joints. **gouty** *adj*.

govern ❶ *v* **1** rule, direct, or control. **2** exercise restraint over (temper etc.). **3** decide or determine. **governable** *adj* **governance** *n* governing. **governess** *n* woman teacher in a private household. **government** *n* **1** executive policy-making body of a state. **2** exercise of political authority over a country or state. **3** system by which a country or state is ruled. **governmental** *adj* **governor** *n* **1** official governing a province or state. **2** senior administrator of a society, institution, or prison. **3** chief executive of a US state. **4** *informal* person's father or employer. **governor general** representative of the Crown in a Commonwealth country.

- **SPELLING TIP**
- In the Bank of English, there are
- hundreds of examples of *goverment*
- without its middle *n*. Remember it
- has two *n*s: **government**.

gown ❶ *n* **1** woman's long formal dress. **2** surgeon's overall. **3** official robe worn by judges, clergymen, etc.

THESAURUS

gory *adj* = **bloodthirsty**, blood-soaked, bloodstained, bloody, murderous, sanguinary

gospel *n* **2** = **doctrine**, credo, creed, message, news, revelation, tidings **3** = **truth**, certainty, fact, the last word

gossip *n* **1** = **idle talk**, blether, chinwag (*Brit inf*), chitchat, hearsay, scandal, small talk, tittle-tattle **2** = **busybody**, chatterbox (*inf*), chatterer, gossipmonger, scandalmonger, tattler, telltale, tattletale (*chiefly US & Canad*) ▷ *v* **3** = **chat**, blether, gabble, jaw (*sl*), prate, prattle, tattle

gouge *v* **1, 2** = **scoop**, chisel, claw, cut, dig (out), hollow (out) ▷ *n* **3** = **gash**, cut, furrow, groove, hollow, scoop, scratch, trench

gourmet *n* = **connoisseur**, bon vivant, epicure, foodie (*inf*), gastronome

govern *v* **1** = **rule**, administer, command, control, direct, guide, handle, lead, manage, order **2** = **restrain**, check, control, curb, discipline, hold in check, master, regulate, subdue, tame

government *n* **1** = **executive**, administration, ministry, powers-that-be, regime **2** = **rule**, administration, authority, governance, mana (*NZ*), sovereignty, statecraft

governor *n* **1, 2** = **leader**, administrator, chief, commander, controller, director, executive, head, manager, ruler

gown *n* **1** = **dress**, frock **3** = **robe**, costume, garb, garment, habit

goy *n*, *pl* **goyim**, **goys** *slang* Jewish word for a non-Jew.

GP general practitioner.

GPO General Post Office.

GPS Global Positioning System: a satellite-based navigation system.

grab *v* **grabbing**, **grabbed** **1** grasp suddenly, snatch. **2** take (food, drink, or rest) hurriedly. **3** seize illegally. ▷ *n* **4** sudden snatch. **5** mechanical device for gripping.

grace ❶ *n* **1** beauty and elegance. **2** polite, kind behaviour. **3** goodwill or favour. **4** courtesy or decency. **5** delay granted. **6** free favour of God shown towards man. **7** short prayer of thanks for a meal. **8** (**G-**) title of a duke, duchess, or archbishop. ▷ *pl* **9** (**G-**) (in Greek mythology) three sister goddesses, givers of charm and beauty. ▷ *v* **10** honour. **11** add grace to. **graceful** *adj* **gracefully** *adv* **graceless** *adj* **gracious** *adj* **1** kind and courteous. **2** condescendingly polite. **3** elegant. **graciously** *adv* **grace note** *Music* note ornamenting a melody.

grade ❶ *n* **1** place on a scale of quality, rank, or size. **2** mark or rating. **3** *US* & *Aust* class in school. ▷ *v* **4** arrange in grades. **5** assign a grade to. **make the grade** succeed. **gradation** *n* **1** (stage in) a series of degrees or steps. **2** arrangement in stages.

gradient ❶ *n* (degree of) slope.

gradual ❶ *adj* occurring, developing, or moving in small stages. **gradually** *adv*.

graduate ❶ *v* **1** receive a degree or diploma. **2** (often foll. by *to*) change by degrees. **3** group by type or quality. **4** mark (a container etc.) with units of measurement. ▷ *n* **5** holder of a degree. **graduation** *n*.

graffiti [graf-**fee**-tee] *pl n* words or drawings scribbled or sprayed on walls etc.

● **SPELLING TIP**
● People get confused about the
● number of *f*s and *t*s in **graffiti**. The
● favourite misspelling in the Bank
● of English is *grafitti*. The correct
● spelling has two *f*s and only one *t*.

graft¹ ❶ *n* **1** surgical transplant of skin or tissue. **2** shoot of a plant set in the stalk of another. ▷ *v* **3** transplant (living tissue) surgically. **4** insert (a plant shoot) in another stalk.

graft² *informal* ▷ *n* **1** hard work. **2** obtaining of money by misusing one's position. ▷ *v* **3** work hard. **grafter** *n*.

grail *n* same as HOLY GRAIL.

grain ❶ *n* **1** seedlike fruit of a cereal plant. **2** cereal plants in general. **3** small hard particle. **4** very small amount. **5** arrangement of fibres, as in

——————————————— THESAURUS ———————————————

grab *v* **1** = **snatch**, capture, catch, catch or take hold of, clutch, grasp, grip, pluck, seize, snap up

grace *n* **1** = **elegance**, attractiveness, beauty, charm, comeliness, ease, gracefulness, poise, polish, refinement, tastefulness **2, 4** = **manners**, consideration, decency, decorum, etiquette, propriety, tact **3** = **goodwill**, benefaction, benevolence, favour, generosity, goodness, kindliness, kindness **5** = **indulgence**, mercy, pardon, reprieve **7** = **prayer**, benediction, blessing, thanks, thanksgiving ▷ *v* **10** = **honour**, dignify, favour **11** = **enhance**, adorn, decorate, embellish, enrich, ornament, set off

graceful *adj* **1** = **elegant**, beautiful, charming, comely, easy, pleasing, tasteful

gracious *adj* **1** = **kind**, charitable, civil, considerate, cordial, courteous, friendly, polite, well-mannered

grade *n* **1-3** = **level**, category (*US* & *Aust*), class, degree, echelon, group, rank, stage ▷ *v* **4, 5** = **classify**, arrange, class, group, order, range, rank, rate, sort

gradient *n* = **slope**, bank, declivity, grade, hill, incline, rise

gradual *adj* = **steady**, gentle, graduated, piecemeal, progressive, regular, slow, unhurried

gradually *adv* = **steadily**, by degrees, gently, little by little, progressively, slowly, step by step, unhurriedly

graduate *v* **3** = **classify**, arrange, grade, group, order, rank, sort **4** = **mark off**, calibrate, grade, measure out, proportion, regulate

graft¹ *n* **2** = **shoot**, bud, implant, scion, splice, sprout ▷ *v* **3, 4** = **transplant**, affix, implant, ingraft, insert, join, splice

grain *n* **1** = **seed**, grist, kernel **2** = **cereals**, corn **4** = **bit**, fragment, granule, modicum, morsel, particle,

wood. **6** texture or pattern resulting from this. ▷ *v* **7** paint in imitation of the grain of wood or leather. **go against the grain** be contrary to one's natural inclination. **grainy** *adj*.

gram, gramme *n* metric unit of mass equal to one thousandth of a kilogram.

gramineous, graminaceous *adj* of or like grass.

graminivorous *adj* (of animals) feeding on grass.

grammar *n* **1** branch of linguistics dealing with the form, function, and order of words. **2** use of words. **3** book on the rules of grammar. **grammarian** *n* **grammatical** *adj* according to the rules of grammar. **grammatically** *adv* **grammar school** esp. formerly, a secondary school providing an education with a strong academic bias.

gramme *n* same as GRAM.

gramophone *n* old-fashioned type of record player.

grampus *n*, *pl* **-puses** dolphin-like mammal.

gran *n informal* grandmother.

granary *n*, *pl* **-ries 1** storehouse for grain. **2** region that produces a large amount of grain.

grand ❶ *adj* **1** large or impressive, imposing. **2** ambitious or important. **3** dignified or haughty. **4** *informal* excellent. **5** (of a total) final. ▷ *n* **6** *slang* thousand pounds or dollars. **7** grand piano. **grandchild** *n* child of one's child. **granddaughter** *n* female grandchild. **grandfather** *n* male grandparent. **grandfather clock** tall standing clock with a pendulum and wooden case. **grandmother** *n* female grandparent. **grandparent** *n* parent of one's parent. **grand piano** large

harp-shaped piano with the strings set horizontally. **grand slam** winning of all the games or major tournaments in a sport in one season. **grandson** *n* male grandchild. **grandstand** *n* terraced block of seats giving the best view at a sports ground.

grandee *n* **1** Spanish nobleman of the highest rank. **2** person of high station.

grandeur ❶ *n* **1** magnificence. **2** nobility or dignity.

grandiloquent *adj* using pompous language. **grandiloquence** *n*.

grandiose ❶ *adj* **1** imposing. **2** pretentiously grand. **grandiosity** *n*.

Grand Prix [gron **pree**] *n* international formula motor race.

grange *n* country house with farm buildings.

granite [**gran**-nit] *n* very hard igneous rock often used in building.

granivorous *adj* feeding on grain or seeds.

granny, grannie *n*, *pl* **-nies** *informal* grandmother. **granny flat** flat in or added to a house, suitable for an elderly parent.

grant ❶ *v* **1** consent to fulfil (a request). **2** give formally. **3** admit. ▷ *n* **4** sum of money provided by a government for a specific purpose, such as education. **take for granted 1** accept as true without proof. **2** take advantage of without due appreciation.

Granth *n* sacred scripture of Sikhism.

granule ❶ *n* small grain. **granular** *adj* of or like grains. **granulated** *adj* (of sugar) in the form of coarse grains. **granulation** *n*.

grape *n* small juicy green or purple berry, eaten raw or used to produce wine, raisins, currants, or sultanas. **grapeshot** *n* bullets which scatter

———————————————————————— THESAURUS ————

piece, scrap, speck, trace
5, 6 = **texture**, fibre, nap, pattern, surface, weave

grand *adj* **1** = **impressive**, grandiose, great, imposing, large, magnificent, regal, splendid, stately, sublime **4** *Inf* = **excellent**, fine, first-class, great (*inf*), outstanding, smashing (*inf*), splendid, wonderful

grandeur *n* = **splendour**, dignity, magnificence, majesty, nobility, pomp, stateliness, sublimity

grandiose *adj* **1** = **imposing**, grand, impressive, lofty, magnificent,

majestic, monumental, stately
2 = **pretentious**, affected, bombastic, extravagant, flamboyant, high-flown, ostentatious, pompous, showy

grant *v* **1** = **consent to**, accede to, agree to, allow, permit **2** = **give**, allocate, allot, assign, award, donate, hand out, present **3** = **admit**, acknowledge, concede ▷ *n* **4** = **award**, allowance, donation, endowment, gift, hand-out, present, subsidy

granule *n* = **grain**, atom, crumb, fragment, molecule, particle, scrap, speck

when fired. **grapevine** n 1 grape-bearing vine. 2 *informal* unofficial way of spreading news.

grapefruit n large round yellow citrus fruit.

graph n drawing showing the relation of different numbers or quantities plotted against a set of axes.

graphic ❶ adj 1 vividly descriptive. 2 of or using drawing, painting, etc. **graphics** pl n diagrams, graphs, etc., esp. as used on a television programme or computer screen. **graphically** adv.

graphite n soft black form of carbon, used in pencil leads.

graphology n study of handwriting. **graphologist** n.

grapnel n device with several hooks, used to grasp or secure things.

grapple ❶ v 1 try to cope with (something difficult). 2 come to grips with (a person). ▷ n 3 grapnel. **grappling iron** grapnel.

grasp ❶ v 1 grip something firmly. 2 understand. 3 try to seize. ▷ n 4 grip or clasp. 5 understanding. 6 total rule or possession. **grasping** adj greedy or avaricious.

grass n 1 common type of plant with jointed stems and long narrow leaves, including cereals and bamboo. 2 lawn. 3 pasture land. 4 *slang* marijuana. 5 *slang* person who informs, esp. on

criminals. ▷ v 6 cover with grass. 7 (often foll. by on) *slang* inform on. **grassy** adj **-sier, -siest**. **grasshopper** n jumping insect with long hind legs. **grass roots** 1 ordinary members of a group, as distinct from its leaders. 2 essentials. **grassroots** adj **grass snake** harmless European snake. **grass tree** Australian plant with stiff grasslike leaves and small white flowers. **grass widow** wife whose husband is absent for a time.

grate¹ ❶ v 1 rub into small bits on a rough surface. 2 scrape with a harsh rasping noise. 3 annoy. **grater** n **grating** adj 1 harsh or rasping. 2 annoying.

grate² n framework of metal bars for holding fuel in a fireplace. **grating** n framework of metal bars covering an opening.

grateful ❶ adj feeling or showing gratitude. **gratefully** adv **gratefulness** n.

gratify ❶ v **-fying, -fied** 1 satisfy or please. 2 indulge (a desire or whim). **gratification** n.

gratis adv, adj free, for nothing.

gratitude ❶ n feeling of being thankful for a favour or gift.

gratuitous ❶ [grat-**tyoo**-it-uss] adj 1 unjustified, e.g. *gratuitous violence*. 2 given free. **gratuitously** adv.

THESAURUS

graphic adj 1 = **vivid**, clear, detailed, explicit, expressive, lively, lucid, striking 2 = **pictorial**, diagrammatic, visual

grapple v 1 = **deal with**, address oneself to, confront, get to grips with, tackle, take on, wrestle 2 = **grip**, clutch, grab, grasp, seize, struggle, wrestle

grasp v 1, 3 = **grip**, catch, clasp, clinch, clutch, grab, grapple, hold, lay *or* take hold of, seize, snatch 2 = **understand**, catch on, catch *or* get the drift of, comprehend, get, realize, see, take in ▷ n 4 = **grip**, clasp, clutches, embrace, hold, possession, tenure 5 = **understanding**, awareness, comprehension, grip, knowledge, mastery 6 = **control**, power, reach, scope

grasping adj = **greedy**, acquisitive, avaricious, covetous, rapacious

grate¹ v 2 = **scrape**, creak, grind, rasp, rub, scratch 3 = **annoy**, exasperate,

get on one's nerves (*inf*), irritate, jar, rankle, set one's teeth on edge

grateful adj = **thankful**, appreciative, beholden, indebted, obliged

gratification n = **satisfaction**, delight, enjoyment, fulfilment, indulgence, pleasure, relish, reward, thrill

gratify v = **please**, delight, give pleasure, gladden, humour, requite, satisfy

grating¹ adj 1 = **harsh**, discordant, jarring, raucous, strident 2 = **irritating**, annoying, displeasing, offensive, unpleasant

grating² n = **grille**, grate, grid, gridiron, lattice, trellis

gratitude n = **thankfulness**, appreciation, gratefulness, indebtedness, obligation, recognition, thanks

gratuitous adj 1 = **unjustified**, baseless, causeless, groundless, needless, superfluous, uncalled-for, unmerited, unnecessary,

gratuity ❶ [grat-**tyoo**-it-ee] *n, pl* **-ties**
money given for services rendered, tip.

grave¹ ❶ *n* hole for burying a corpse.
the grave death. **gravestone** *n* stone
marking a grave. **graveyard** *n*
cemetery.

grave² *adj* **1** causing concern.
2 serious and solemn. **3** important.
gravely *adv*.

grave³ [rhymes with **halve**] *n* accent
(`) over a vowel to indicate a special
pronunciation.

gravel *n* **1** mixture of small stones and
coarse sand. **2** small rough stones in
the kidneys or bladder. ▷ *v* **-elling**,
-elled 3 cover with gravel. **gravelled**
adj covered with gravel. **gravelly** *adj*
1 covered with gravel. **2** rough-
sounding.

graven [**grave**-en] *adj* carved or
engraved.

gravid [**grav**-id] *adj Medical* pregnant.

gravitate *v* **1** be influenced or drawn
towards. **2** *Physics* move by gravity.
gravitation *n* **gravitational** *adj*.

gravity ❶ *n, pl* **-ties 1** force of
attraction of one object for another,
esp. of objects to the earth.
2 seriousness or importance.
3 solemnity.

gravy *n, pl* **-vies 1** juices from meat in
cooking. **2** sauce made from these.

gray *adj Chiefly US* grey.

grayling *n* fish of the salmon family.

graze¹ ❶ *v* feed on grass. **grazier** *n*
person who feeds cattle for market.
grazing *n* land on which grass for
livestock is grown.

graze² ❶ *v* **1** scratch or scrape the skin.
2 touch lightly in passing. ▷ *n* **3** slight
scratch or scrape.

grease ❶ *n* **1** soft melted animal fat.
2 any thick oily substance. ▷ *v* **3** apply
grease to. **greasy** *adj* **greasier**,
greasiest 1 covered with or
containing grease. **2** unctuous in
manner. **greasiness** *n* **grease gun**
appliance for injecting oil or grease
into machinery. **greasepaint** *n*
theatrical make-up.

great ❶ *adj* **1** large in size or number.
2 extreme or more than usual.
3 important. **4** pre-eminent.
5 *informal* excellent. **the greats** the
most successful people in a particular
field. **great-** *prefix* one generation
older or younger than, e.g. *great-
grandfather*. **greatly** *adv* **greatness** *n*
greatcoat *n* heavy overcoat. **Great
Dane** very large dog with short
smooth hair.

greave *n* piece of armour for the shin.

grebe *n* diving water bird.

Grecian [**gree**-shan] *adj* of ancient
Greece.

greed ❶ *n* excessive desire for food,
wealth, etc. **greedy** *adj* **greedier**,
greediest. **greedily** *adv* **greediness** *n*.

━━━━━━━━━━━━━━━━ THESAURUS ━━━━━━

unwarranted, wanton **2 = voluntary**,
complimentary, free, gratis,
spontaneous, unasked-for, unpaid,
unrewarded

grave¹ *n* = **tomb**, burying place,
crypt, mausoleum, pit, sepulchre,
vault

grave² **1** *adj* = **critical**, acute,
dangerous, pressing, serious, severe,
threatening **2** *adj* = **serious**, dignified,
dour, earnest, sober, solemn, sombre,
unsmiling **3** *adj* = **important**, serious,
urgent

graveyard *n* = **cemetery**, burial
ground, charnel house, churchyard,
necropolis

gravity *n* **2** = **importance**, acuteness,
momentousness, perilousness,
seriousness, severity, significance,
urgency, weightiness **3** = **solemnity**,
dignity, earnestness, seriousness,
sobriety

graze¹ *v* = **feed**, browse, crop, pasture

graze² *v* **1** = **scratch**, abrade, chafe,
scrape, skin **2** = **touch**, brush, glance
off, rub, scrape, shave, skim ▷ *n*
3 = **scratch**, abrasion, scrape

greasy *adj* **1** = **fatty**, oily, oleaginous,
slimy, slippery

great *adj* **1** = **large**, big, enormous,
gigantic, huge, immense, prodigious,
vast, voluminous **3** = **important**,
critical, crucial, momentous, serious,
significant **4** = **famous**, eminent,
illustrious, noteworthy, outstanding,
prominent, remarkable, renowned
5 *Inf* = **excellent**, fantastic (*inf*),
fine, marvellous (*inf*), superb,
terrific (*inf*), tremendous (*inf*),
wonderful

greatly *adv* **1, 2** = **very much**,
considerably, enormously, exceedingly,
hugely, immensely, remarkably,
tremendously, vastly

greed *n* = **gluttony**, acquisitiveness,
avarice, avidity, covetousness, craving,

Greek *n* **1** language of Greece. **2** person from Greece. ▷ *adj* **3** of Greece, the Greeks, or the Greek language.

green ❶ *adj* **1** of a colour between blue and yellow. **2** characterized by green plants or foliage. **3** of or concerned with environmental issues. **4** unripe. **5** envious or jealous. **6** immature or gullible. ▷ *n* **7** colour between blue and yellow. **8** area of grass kept for a special purpose. **9** person concerned with environmental issues. ▷ *pl* **10** green vegetables. ▷ *v* **11** make or become green. **greenness** *n* **greenish**, **greeny** *adj* **greenery** *n* vegetation. **green belt** protected area of open country around a town. **greenfinch** *n* European finch with dull green plumage in the male. **green fingers** skill in gardening. **greenfly** *n* green aphid, a common garden pest. **greengage** *n* sweet green plum. **greengrocer** *n* shopkeeper selling vegetables and fruit. **greenhorn** *n* novice. **greenhouse** *n* glass building for rearing plants. **greenhouse effect** rise in the temperature of the earth caused by heat absorbed from the sun being unable to leave the atmosphere. **greenhouse gas** gas that contributes to the greenhouse effect. **green light** **1** signal to go. **2** permission to proceed with something. **greenroom** *n* room for actors when offstage. **greenshank** *n* large European sandpiper.

Greenwich Mean Time *n* local time of the 0° meridian passing through Greenwich, England: the basis for calculating times throughout the world.

greet ❶ *v* **1** meet with expressions of welcome. **2** receive in a specified manner. **3** be immediately noticeable to. **greeting** *n*.

gregarious ❶ *adj* **1** fond of company. **2** (of animals) living in flocks or herds.

Gregorian calendar *n* calendar introduced by Pope Gregory XIII and still widely used.

Gregorian chant *n* same as PLAINSONG.

gremlin *n* imaginary being blamed for mechanical malfunctions.

grenade *n* small bomb thrown by hand or fired from a rifle. **grenadier** *n* soldier of a regiment formerly trained to throw grenades.

grenadine [gren-a-**deen**] *n* syrup made from pomegranates.

grew *v* past tense of GROW.

grey ❶ *adj* **1** of a colour between black and white. **2** (of hair) partly turned white. **3** dismal or dark. **4** dull or boring. ▷ *n* **5** grey colour. **6** grey or white horse. **greying** *adj* (of hair) turning grey. **greyish** *adj* **greyness** *n* **grey matter** *informal* brains.

greyhound *n* swift slender dog used in racing.

greylag *n* large grey goose.

grid *n* **1** network of horizontal and vertical lines, bars, etc. **2** national network of electricity supply cables.

griddle *n* flat iron plate for cooking.

gridiron *n* **1** frame of metal bars for grilling food. **2** American football pitch.

gridlock ❶ *n* situation where traffic is not moving. **gridlocked** *adj*.

grief ❶ *n* deep sadness. **come to grief** end unsuccessfully. **grieve** *v* (cause to) feel grief. **grievance** *n* real or imaginary cause for complaint. **grievous** *adj* **1** very severe or painful. **2** very serious.

— THESAURUS —

desire, edacity, esurience, gormandizing, hunger, longing, selfishness, voracity

greedy *adj* = **gluttonous**, acquisitive, avaricious, avid, covetous, craving, desirous, gormandizing, grasping, hungry, insatiable, piggish, rapacious, ravenous, selfish, voracious

green *adj* **2** = **leafy**, grassy, verdant **3** (with cap.) = **ecological**, conservationist, environment-friendly, non-polluting, ozone-friendly **5** = **jealous**, covetous, envious, grudging, resentful **6** = **inexperienced**, gullible, immature, naive, new, raw, untrained, wet behind the ears (*inf*) ▷ *n* **8** = **lawn**, common, sward, turf

greet *v* **1, 2** = **welcome**, accost, address, compliment, hail, meet, receive, salute

gregarious *adj* **1** = **outgoing**, affable, companionable, convivial, cordial, friendly, sociable, social

grey *adj* **3** = **dismal**, dark, depressing, dim, drab, dreary, dull, gloomy **4** = **characterless**, anonymous, colourless, dull

grief *n* = **sadness**, anguish, distress, heartache, misery, regret, remorse, sorrow, suffering, woe

griffin n mythical monster with an eagle's head and wings and a lion's body.

grill n **1** device on a cooker that radiates heat downwards. **2** grilled food. **3** gridiron. **4** grillroom. ▷ v **5** cook under a grill. **6** question relentlessly. **grilling** n relentless questioning. **grillroom** n restaurant serving grilled foods.

grille, grill n grating over an opening.

grilse [**grillss**] n salmon on its first return from the sea to fresh water.

grim ⊕ adj **grimmer, grimmest 1** stern. **2** harsh or forbidding. **3** very unpleasant. **4** harshly ironic or sinister. **grimly** adv **grimness** n.

grimace ⊕ n **1** ugly or distorted facial expression of pain, disgust, etc. ▷ v **2** make a grimace.

grimalkin n old female cat.

grime ⊕ n **1** ingrained dirt. ▷ v **2** make very dirty. **grimy** adj **griminess** n.

grin v **grinning, grinned 1** smile broadly, showing the teeth. ▷ n **2** broad smile.

grind ⊕ v **grinding, ground 1** crush or rub to a powder. **2** smooth or sharpen by friction. **3** scrape together with a harsh noise. **4** oppress. **5** informal work or study hard. ▷ n **6** informal hard work. **7** act or sound of grinding. **grind out** v produce in a routine or uninspired manner. **grindstone** n stone used for grinding.

grip ⊕ n **1** firm hold or grasp. **2** way in which something is grasped. **3** mastery or understanding. **4** US travelling bag. **5** handle. ▷ v **gripping, gripped 6** grasp or hold tightly. **7** affect strongly. **8** hold the interest or attention of. **gripping** adj.

gripe v **1** informal complain persistently. ▷ n **2** informal complaint. **3** sudden intense bowel pain.

grisly ⊕ adj **-lier, -liest** horrifying or ghastly.

grist n grain for grinding. **grist to one's mill** something which can be turned to advantage.

gristle n tough stringy animal tissue found in meat. **gristly** adj.

grit ⊕ n **1** rough particles of sand. **2** courage. **3** coarse sandstone. ▷ pl **4** coarsely ground grain. ▷ v **gritting, gritted 5** spread grit on (an icy road etc.). **6** clench or grind (the teeth). **gritty** adj **-tier, -tiest. gritter** n **grittiness** n.

grizzle v informal whine or complain.

grizzled adj grey-haired.

grizzly n, pl **-zlies** large American bear (also **grizzly bear**).

groan ⊕ n **1** deep sound of grief or pain. **2** informal complaint. ▷ v **3** utter a groan. **4** informal complain.

———————————————————— THESAURUS ————————

grievance n = **complaint**, axe to grind, gripe (inf), injury, injustice

grieve v = **mourn**, afflict, complain, deplore, distress, hurt, injure, lament, pain, regret, rue, sadden, suffer, weep, wound

grievous adj **1** = **severe**, dreadful, grave, harmful, painful

grim adj **1, 2** = **forbidding**, formidable, harsh, merciless, ruthless, severe, sinister, stern, terrible

grimace n **1** = **scowl**, face, frown, sneer ▷ v **2** = **scowl**, frown, lour or lower, make a face or faces, sneer

grime n **1** = **dirt**, filth, grot (sl), smut, soot

grind v **1** = **crush**, abrade, granulate, grate, mill, pound, powder, pulverize, triturate **2** = **smooth**, polish, sand, sharpen, whet **3** = **scrape**, gnash, grate ▷ n **6** Inf = **hard work**, chore, drudgery, labour, sweat (inf), toil

grip n **1** = **control**, clasp, clutches, domination, hold, influence, mana (NZ), possession, power **3** = **understanding**, command, comprehension, grasp, mastery ▷ v **6** = **grasp**, clasp, clutch, hold, seize, take hold of **8** = **engross**, absorb, enthral, entrance, fascinate, hold, mesmerize, rivet

gripping adj **8** = **fascinating**, compelling, engrossing, enthralling, entrancing, exciting, riveting, spellbinding, thrilling

grisly adj = **gruesome**, appalling, awful, dreadful, ghastly, horrible, macabre, shocking, terrifying

grit n **1** = **gravel**, dust, pebbles, sand **2** = **courage**, backbone, determination, fortitude, guts (inf), perseverance, resolution, spirit, tenacity ▷ v **6** = **grind**, clench, gnash, grate

groan n **1** = **moan**, cry, sigh, whine **2** Inf = **complaint**, gripe (inf), grouse, grumble, objection, protest ▷ v **3** = **moan**, cry, sigh, whine **4** Inf

5 (usu. foll. by *beneath*) (*under*) be weighed down (by).

groat *n History* fourpenny piece.

groats *pl n* hulled and crushed grain of various cereals.

grocer *n* shopkeeper selling foodstuffs.

grocery *n*, *pl* **-ceries 1** business or premises of a grocer. ▷ *pl* **2** goods sold by a grocer.

grog *n* spirit, usu. rum, and water.

groggy ❶ *adj* **-gier, -giest** *informal* faint, shaky, or dizzy.

groin *n* **1** place where the legs join the abdomen. **2** edge made by the intersection of two vaults.

grommet *n* **1** ring or eyelet. **2** *Medical* tube inserted in the ear to drain fluid from the middle ear.

groom ❶ *n* **1** person who looks after horses. **2** bridegroom. **3** officer in a royal household. ▷ *v* **4** make or keep one's clothes and appearance neat and tidy. **5** brush or clean a horse. **6** train (someone) for a future role.

groove ❶ *n* **1** long narrow channel in a surface. **2** spiral channel in a gramophone record. **3** routine. **grooved** *adj* **groovy** *adj* **groovier, grooviest** *dated slang* attractive or exciting.

grope ❶ *v* feel about or search uncertainly. **groping** *n*.

grosbeak *n* finch with a large powerful bill.

grosgrain [**grow**-grain] *n* heavy ribbed silk or rayon fabric.

gross ❶ *adj* **1** flagrant. **2** vulgar. **3** *slang* disgusting or repulsive. **4** repulsively fat. **5** total, without deductions. ▷ *n* **6** twelve dozen. ▷ *v* **7** make as total revenue before deductions. **grossly** *adv* **grossness** *n*.

grotesque ❶ [grow-**tesk**] *adj* **1** strangely distorted. **2** absurd. ▷ *n* **3** grotesque person or thing. **4** artistic style mixing distorted human, animal, and plant forms. **grotesquely** *adv*.

grotto *n*, *pl* **-toes, -tos 1** small picturesque cave. **2** construction imitating a cave.

grotty *adj* **-tier, -tiest** *informal* nasty or in bad condition.

grouch *informal* ▷ *v* **1** grumble or complain. ▷ *n* **2** person who is always complaining. **3** persistent complaint. **grouchy** *adj*.

ground¹ ❶ *n* **1** surface of the earth. **2** soil. **3** area used for a specific purpose, e.g. *rugby ground*. **4** position in an argument or controversy. **5** background colour of a painting. ▷ *pl* **6** enclosed land round a house. **7** reason or motive. **8** coffee dregs. ▷ *adj* **9** on or of the ground. ▷ *v* **10** base or establish. **11** instruct in the basics.

g

THESAURUS

= **complain**, bemoan, gripe (*inf*), grouse, grumble, lament, object

groggy *adj Inf* = **dizzy**, confused, dazed, faint, shaky, unsteady, weak, wobbly

groom *n* **1** = **stableman**, hostler *or* ostler (*arch*), stableboy ▷ *v* **4** = **smarten up**, clean, preen, primp, spruce up, tidy **5** = **rub down**, brush, clean, curry, tend **6** = **train**, coach, drill, educate, make ready, nurture, prepare, prime, ready

groove *n* **1** = **indentation**, channel, cut, flute, furrow, hollow, rut, trench, trough

grope *v* = **feel**, cast about, fish, flounder, forage, fumble, scrabble, search

gross *adj* **1** = **blatant**, flagrant, grievous, heinous, rank, sheer, unmitigated, utter **2** = **vulgar**, coarse, crude, indelicate, obscene, offensive **4** = **fat**, corpulent, hulking, obese, overweight **5** = **total**, aggregate, before deductions, before tax, entire, whole ▷ *v* **7** = **earn**, bring in, make,

rake in (*inf*), take

grotesque *adj* **1** = **deformed**, distorted **2** = **unnatural**, bizarre, fantastic, freakish, outlandish, preposterous, strange

ground¹ *n* **1, 2** = **earth**, dry land, land, soil, terra firma, terrain, turf **3** = **stadium**, arena, field, park (*inf*), pitch ▷ *pl* **6** = **land**, estate, fields, gardens, terrain, territory **7** = **reason**, basis, cause, excuse, foundation, justification, motive, occasion, pretext, rationale **8** = **dregs**, deposit, lees, sediment ▷ *v* **10** = **base**, establish, fix, found, set, settle **11** = **instruct**, acquaint with, familiarize with, initiate, teach, train, tutor

groundless *adj* = **unjustified**, baseless, empty, idle, uncalled-for, unfounded, unwarranted

groundwork *n* = **preliminaries**, foundation, fundamentals, preparation, spadework, underpinnings

12 ban an aircraft or pilot from flying. **13** run (a ship) aground. **14** place on the ground. **groundless** adj without reason. **grounding** n basic knowledge of a subject. **ground-breaking** adj innovative. **ground floor** floor of a building level with the ground. **groundnut** n peanut. **groundsheet** n waterproof sheet put on the ground under a tent. **groundsman** n person employed to maintain a sports ground or park. **groundswell** n rapidly developing general feeling or opinion. **groundwork** n preliminary work.

ground² v past of GRIND. **ground beef** finely chopped beef used in beefburgers etc.

groundsel [grounce-el] n yellow-flowered weed.

group ❶ n **1** number of people or things regarded as a unit. **2** small band of musicians or singers. ▷ v **3** place or form into a group. **group captain** middle-ranking air force officer.

grouper n large edible sea fish.

grouse¹ n **1** stocky game bird. **2** its flesh.

grouse² ❶ v **1** grumble or complain. ▷ n **2** complaint.

grout n **1** thin mortar. ▷ v **2** fill up with grout.

grove ❶ n small group of trees.

grovel ❶ [grov-el] v **-elling**, **-elled** **1** behave humbly in order to win a superior's favour. **2** crawl on the floor.

grow ❶ v **growing**, **grew**, **grown** **1** develop physically. **2** (of a plant) exist. **3** cultivate (plants). **4** increase in size or degree. **5** originate. **6** become gradually, e.g. it was growing dark. **growth** n **1** growing. **2** increase. **3** something grown or growing. **4** tumour. **grown** adj developed or advanced. **grown-up** adj, n adult. **grow on** v become more acceptable to. **grow up** v mature.

growl v **1** make a low rumbling sound. **2** utter with a growl. ▷ n **3** growling sound.

groyne n wall built out from the shore to control erosion.

grub ❶ n **1** legless insect larva. **2** slang food. ▷ v **grubbing**, **grubbed 3** search carefully for something by digging or by moving things about. **4** dig up the surface of (soil).

grubby ❶ adj **-bier**, **-biest** dirty. **grubbiness** n.

grudge ❶ v **1** be unwilling to give or allow. ▷ n **2** resentment. **grudging** adj **grudgingly** adv.

gruel n thin porridge.

gruelling ❶ adj exhausting or severe.

─────────── THESAURUS ───────────

group n **1** = **set**, band, bunch, cluster, collection, crowd, gang, pack, party ▷ v **3** = **arrange**, bracket, class, classify, marshal, order, sort

grouse² v **1** = **complain**, bellyache (sl), carp, gripe (inf), grumble, moan, whine, whinge (inf) ▷ n **2** = **complaint**, grievance, gripe (inf), grouch (inf), grumble, moan, objection, protest

grove n = **wood**, coppice, copse, covert, plantation, spinney, thicket

grovel v **1** = **humble oneself**, abase oneself, bow and scrape, crawl, creep, cringe, demean oneself, fawn, kowtow, toady **2** = **crawl**, creep

grow v **1** = **increase**, develop, enlarge, expand, get bigger, multiply, spread, stretch, swell **3** = **cultivate**, breed, farm, nurture, produce, propagate, raise **4** = **improve**, advance, flourish, progress, prosper, succeed, thrive **5** = **originate**, arise, issue, spring, stem **6** = **become**, come to be, get, turn

grown-up adj = **mature**, adult, fully-grown, of age ▷ n = **adult**, man, woman

growth n **1, 2** = **increase**, development, enlargement, expansion, multiplication, proliferation, stretching **3** = **progress**, advance, expansion, improvement, prosperity, rise, success **4** = **tumour**, lump

grub n **1** = **larva**, caterpillar, maggot **2** Sl = **food**, nosh (sl), rations, sustenance, tucker (Aust & NZ inf), victuals ▷ v **3** = **search**, ferret, forage, fossick (Aust & NZ), hunt, rummage, scour, uncover, unearth **4** = **dig up**, burrow, pull up, root (inf)

grubby adj = **dirty**, filthy, grimy, messy, mucky, scruffy, scungy (Aust & NZ inf), seedy, shabby, sordid, squalid, unwashed

grudge v **1** = **resent**, begrudge, complain, covet, envy, mind ▷ n **2** = **resentment**, animosity, antipathy, bitterness, dislike, enmity, grievance, rancour

gruelling adj = **exhausting**, arduous, backbreaking, demanding, laborious, punishing, severe, strenuous, taxing, tiring

gruesome ❶ *adj* causing horror and disgust.

gruff ❶ *adj* rough or surly in manner or voice. **gruffly** *adv* **gruffness** *n*.

grumble ❶ *v* **1** complain. **2** rumble. ▷ *n* **3** complaint. **4** rumble. **grumbler** *n* **grumbling** *adj*, *n*.

grumpy ❶ *adj* **grumpier**, **grumpiest** bad-tempered. **grumpily** *adv* **grumpiness** *n*.

grunge *n* **1** style of rock music with a fuzzy guitar sound. **2** deliberately untidy and uncoordinated fashion style.

grunt *v* **1** make a low short gruff sound, like a pig. ▷ *n* **2** pig's sound. **3** gruff noise.

Gruyère [**grew**-yair] *n* hard yellow Swiss cheese with holes.

gryphon *n* same AS GRIFFIN.

G-string *n* small strip of cloth covering the genitals and attached to a waistband.

G-suit *n* close-fitting pressurized garment worn by the crew of high-speed aircraft.

GT gran turismo, used of a sports car.

guanaco [gwah-**nah**-koh] *n*, *pl* -**cos** S American animal related to the llama.

guano [**gwah**-no] *n* dried sea-bird manure, used as fertilizer.

guarantee ❶ *n* **1** formal assurance, esp. in writing, that a product will meet certain standards. **2** something that makes a specified condition or outcome certain. **3** guarantor. **4** guaranty. ▷ *v* -**teeing**, -**teed** **5** give a guarantee. **6** secure against risk etc. **7** ensure. **guarantor** *n* person who gives or is bound by a guarantee.

guaranty *n*, *pl* -**ties 1** pledge of responsibility for fulfilling another person's obligations in case of default. **2** thing given as security for a guaranty.

guard ❶ *v* **1** watch over to protect or to prevent escape. **2** protect (a right or privilege). ▷ *n* **3** person or group that guards. **4** official in charge of a train. **5** protection. **6** screen for enclosing anything dangerous. **7** posture of defence in sports such as boxing or fencing. ▷ *pl* **8** (**G**-) regiment with ceremonial duties. **guarded** *adj* cautious or noncommittal. **guardedly** *adv* **guard against** *v* take precautions against. **guardhouse**, **guardroom** *n* military police office for holding prisoners. **guardian** *n* keeper or protector. **guardsman** *n* member of the Guards.

guardian ❶ *n* **1** keeper or protector. **2** person legally responsible for a child, mentally ill person, etc. **guardianship** *n*.

guava [**gwah**-va] *n* yellow-skinned tropical American fruit.

gubernatorial *adj* US of or relating to a governor.

gudgeon[1] *n* small freshwater fish.

gudgeon[2] *n* socket for a hinge or rudder.

guelder-rose [**geld**-er-rose] *n* shrub with clusters of white flowers.

———————————— **THESAURUS** ————————————

gruesome *adj* = **horrific**, ghastly, grim, grisly, horrible, macabre, shocking, terrible

gruff *adj* **a** = **surly**, bad-tempered, brusque, churlish, grumpy, rough, rude, sullen, ungracious **b** = **hoarse**, croaking, guttural, harsh, husky, low, rasping, rough, throaty

grumble *v* **1** = **complain**, bleat, carp, gripe (*inf*), grouch (*inf*), grouse, moan, whine, whinge (*inf*) **2** = **rumble**, growl, gurgle, murmur, mutter, roar ▷ *n* **3** = **complaint**, grievance, gripe (*inf*), grouch (*inf*), grouse, moan, objection, protest **4** = **rumble**, growl, gurgle, murmur, muttering, roar

grumpy *adj* = **irritable**, bad-tempered, cantankerous, crotchety (*inf*), peevish, sulky, sullen, surly, testy

guarantee *n* **1** = **assurance**, bond, certainty, pledge, promise, security, surety, warranty, word of honour ▷ *v* **5-7** = **ensure**, assure, certify, make certain, pledge, promise, secure, vouch for, warrant

guard *v* **1, 2** = **watch over**, defend, mind, preserve, protect, safeguard, secure, shield ▷ *n* **3** = **protector**, custodian, defender, lookout, picket, sentinel, sentry, warder, watch, watchman **5, 6** = **protection**, buffer, defence, safeguard, screen, security, shield

guarded *adj* = **cautious**, cagey (*inf*), careful, circumspect, noncommittal, prudent, reserved, reticent, suspicious, wary

guardian *n* **1** = **keeper**, champion, curator, custodian, defender, guard, protector, warden

Guernsey [**gurn**-zee] n breed of dairy cattle.

guerrilla, guerilla ❶ n member of an unofficial armed force fighting regular forces.

guess ❶ v 1 estimate or draw a conclusion without proper knowledge. 2 estimate correctly by guessing. 3 US & Canad suppose. ▷ n 4 estimate or conclusion reached by guessing. **guesswork** n process or results of guessing.

guest ❶ n 1 person entertained at another's house or at another's expense. 2 invited performer or speaker. 3 customer at a hotel or restaurant. ▷ v 4 appear as a visiting player or performer. **guesthouse** n boarding house.

guff n slang nonsense.

guffaw n 1 crude noisy laugh. ▷ v 2 laugh in this way.

guide ❶ n 1 person who conducts tour expeditions. 2 person who shows the way. 3 book of instruction or information. 4 model for behaviour. 5 something used to gauge something or to help in planning one's actions. 6 (G-) member of an organization for girls equivalent to the Scouts. ▷ v 7 act as a guide for. 8 control, supervise, or influence. **guidance** n leadership, instruction, or advice. **guidebook** n handbook with information for visitors to a place.

guided missile missile whose flight is controlled electronically. **guide dog** dog trained to lead a blind person.

guideline n set principle for doing something.

guild ❶ n 1 organization or club. 2 History society of men in the same trade or craft.

guilder n former monetary unit of the Netherlands.

guile ❶ [gile] n cunning or deceit. **guileful** adj **guileless** adj.

guillemot [gil-lee-mot] n black-and-white diving sea bird.

guillotine n 1 machine for beheading people. 2 device for cutting paper or sheet metal. 3 method of preventing lengthy debate in parliament by fixing a time for taking the vote. ▷ v 4 behead by guillotine. 5 limit debate by the guillotine.

guilt ❶ n 1 fact or state of having done wrong. 2 remorse for wrongdoing. **guiltless** adj innocent. **guilty** adj **guiltier, guiltiest** 1 responsible for an offence or misdeed. 2 feeling or showing guilt. **guiltily** adv.

guinea n 1 former British monetary unit worth 21 shillings (1.05 pounds). 2 former gold coin of this value. **guinea fowl** bird related to the pheasant. **guinea pig** 1 tailless S American rodent, commonly kept as a pet. 2 informal person used for experimentation.

————————— THESAURUS —————————

guerrilla, guerilla n = **freedom fighter**, partisan, underground fighter

guess v 1 = **estimate**, conjecture, hypothesize, predict, speculate, work out 3 Chiefly US = **suppose**, believe, conjecture, fancy, imagine, judge, reckon, suspect, think ▷ n 4 = **supposition**, conjecture, hypothesis, prediction, shot in the dark, speculation, theory

guesswork n = **speculation**, conjecture, estimation, supposition, surmise, theory

guest n 1, 3 = **visitor**, boarder, caller, company, lodger, visitant

guidance n = **advice**, counselling, direction, help, instruction, leadership, management, teaching

guide ❶ n 1, 2 = **escort**, adviser, conductor, counsellor, guru, leader, mentor, teacher, usher 3 = **guidebook**, catalogue, directory, handbook,

instructions, key, manual 4 = **model**, example, ideal, inspiration, paradigm, standard 5 = **pointer**, beacon, guiding light, landmark, lodestar, marker, sign, signpost ▷ v 7 = **lead**, accompany, conduct, direct, escort, shepherd, show the way, usher 8 = **supervise**, advise, command, control, counsel, direct, handle, influence, instruct, manage, manoeuvre, oversee, steer, superintend, teach, train

guild n 1 = **society**, association, brotherhood, club, company, corporation, fellowship, fraternity, league, lodge, order, organization, union

guile n = **cunning**, artifice, cleverness, craft, deceit, slyness, trickery, wiliness

guilt n 1 = **culpability**, blame, guiltiness, misconduct, responsibility, sinfulness, wickedness, wrongdoing 2 = **remorse**, contrition, guilty

guise ❶ [rhymes with **size**] *n* **1** false appearance. **2** external appearance.

guitar *n* stringed instrument with a flat back and a long neck, played by plucking or strumming. **guitarist** *n*.

Gulag *n* system or department that silences dissidents, esp. in the former Soviet Union.

gulch *n US & Canad* a narrow ravine cut by a fast stream.

gulf ❶ *n* **1** large deep bay. **2** chasm. **3** large difference in opinion or understanding. **Gulf Stream** warm ocean current flowing from the Gulf of Mexico towards NW Europe.

gull¹ *n* long-winged sea bird.

gull² *v* cheat or deceive.

gullet *n* muscular tube through which food passes from the mouth to the stomach.

gullible ❶ *adj* easily tricked. **gullibility** *n*.

gully ❶ *n, pl* **-lies** channel cut by running water.

gulp ❶ *v* **1** swallow hastily. **2** gasp. ▷ *n* **3** gulping. **4** thing gulped.

gum¹ *n* firm flesh in which the teeth are set. **gummy** *adj* **-mier, -miest** toothless. **gumboil** *n* abscess on the gum.

gum² ❶ *n* **1** sticky substance obtained from certain trees. **2** adhesive. **3** chewing gum. **4** gumdrop. **5** gumtree. ▷ *v* **gumming, gummed 6** stick with gum. **gummy** *adj* **-mier, -miest**. **gumboots** *pl n* Wellington boots. **gumdrop** *n* hard jelly-like

sweet. **gumtree** *n* eucalypt tree.

gumption ❶ *n informal* **1** resourcefulness. **2** courage.

gun ❶ *n* **1** weapon with a metal tube from which missiles are fired by explosion. **2** device from which a substance is ejected under pressure. **3** member of a shooting party. ▷ *v* **gunning, gunned 4** cause (an engine) to run at high speed. **jump the gun** act prematurely. **gunner** *n* artillery soldier. **gunnery** *n* use or science of large guns. **gunboat** *n* small warship. **guncotton** *n* form of cellulose nitrate used as an explosive. **gun dog** dog used to retrieve game. **gun down** *v* shoot (a person). **gun for** *v* seek or pursue vigorously. **gunman** *n* armed criminal. **gunmetal** *n* **1** alloy of copper, tin, and zinc. ▷ *adj* **2** dark grey. **gunpowder** *n* explosive mixture of potassium nitrate, sulphur, and charcoal. **gunrunning** *n* smuggling of guns and ammunition. **gunrunner** *n* **gunshot** *n* **1** shot or range of a gun. **2** sound of a gun being fired.

gunge *n informal* sticky unpleasant substance. **gungy** *adj* **-gier, -giest**.

gunk *n informal* slimy or filthy substance.

gunny *n* strong coarse fabric used for sacks.

gunwale, gunnel [**gun**-nel] *n* top of a ship's side.

guppy *n, pl* **-pies** small colourful aquarium fish.

THESAURUS

conscience, regret, self-reproach, shame, stigma

guiltless *adj* = **innocent**, blameless, clean (*sl*), irreproachable, pure, sinless, spotless, squeaky-clean, untainted

guilty *adj* **1** = **culpable**, at fault, blameworthy, reprehensible, responsible, sinful, to blame, wrong **2** = **remorseful**, ashamed, conscience-stricken, contrite, regretful, rueful, shamefaced, sheepish, sorry

guise *n* **1** = **disguise**, pretence, semblance **2** = **form**, appearance, aspect, demeanour, mode, shape

gulf *n* **1** = **bay**, bight, sea inlet **2** = **chasm**, abyss, gap, opening, rift, separation, split, void

gullible *adj* = **naive**, born yesterday, credulous, innocent, simple, trusting,

unsuspecting, wet behind the ears (*inf*)

gully *n* = **channel**, ditch, gutter, watercourse

gulp *v* **1** = **swallow**, devour, gobble, guzzle, quaff, swig (*inf*), swill, wolf **2** = **gasp**, choke, swallow ▷ *n* **4** = **swallow**, draught, mouthful, swig (*inf*)

gum² *n* **1** = **resin 2** = **glue**, adhesive, cement, paste ▷ *v* **6** = **stick**, affix, cement, glue, paste

gumption *n Inf* **1** = **resourcefulness**, acumen, astuteness, common sense, enterprise, initiative, mother wit, savvy (*sl*), wit(s)

gun *n* **1** = **firearm**, handgun, piece (*sl*), shooter (*sl*)

gunman *n* = **terrorist**, bandit, gunslinger (*US sl*), killer

gurdwara *n* Sikh place of worship.
gurgle ❶ *v, n* (make) a bubbling noise.
Gurkha *n* person, esp. a soldier, belonging to a Hindu people of Nepal.
gurnard *n* spiny armour-headed sea fish.
guru ❶ *n* **1** Hindu or Sikh religious teacher or leader. **2** leader or adviser.
gush ❶ *v* **1** flow out suddenly and profusely. **2** express admiration effusively. ▷ *n* **3** sudden copious flow. **4** sudden surge of strong feeling. **gusher** *n* spurting oil well. **gushing** *adj*.
gusset *n* piece of material sewn into a garment to strengthen it.
gust ❶ *n* **1** sudden blast of wind. **2** sudden burst of rain, anger, etc. ▷ *v* **3** blow in gusts. **gusty** *adj*.
gustation *n* act of tasting or the faculty of taste. **gustatory** *adj*.
gusto ❶ *n* enjoyment or zest.
gut ❶ *n* **1** intestine. **2** *informal* fat stomach. **3** short for CATGUT. ▷ *pl* **4** internal organs. **5** *informal* courage. **6** *informal* essential part. ▷ *v* **gutting**, **gutted 7** remove the guts from. **8** (of a fire) destroy the inside of (a building). ▷ *adj* **9** basic or instinctive, e.g. *a gut reaction*. **gutless** *adj informal* cowardly. **gutsy** *adj* **-sier**, **-siest** *informal* **1** courageous. **2** vigorous or robust, e.g. *a gutsy performance*. **3** greedy. **gutted** *adj informal* disappointed and upset.
gutta-percha *n* whitish rubbery substance obtained from an Asian tree.

gutter ❶ *n* **1** shallow channel for carrying away water from a roof or roadside. ▷ *v* **2** (of a candle) burn unsteadily, with wax running down the sides. **the gutter** degraded or criminal environment. **guttering** *n* material for gutters. **gutter press** newspapers that rely on sensationalism. **guttersnipe** *n* neglected slum child.
guttural ❶ [gut-ter-al] *adj* **1** (of a sound) produced at the back of the throat. **2** (of a voice) harsh-sounding.
guy[1] ❶ *n* **1** *informal* man or boy. **2** effigy of Guy Fawkes burnt on November 5 (**Guy Fawkes Day**). ▷ *v* **3** make fun of.
guy[2] *n* **1** rope or chain to steady or secure something. ▷ *v* **2** secure or guide with a guy. **guyrope** *n*.
guzzle ❶ *v* eat or drink greedily.
gybe [jibe] *v* **1** (of a fore-and-aft sail) swing suddenly from one side to the other. **2** (of a boat) change course by letting the sail gybe.
gym *n* **1** gymnasium. **2** gymnastics. **gymslip** *n* tunic or pinafore formerly worn by schoolgirls.
gymkhana [jim-**kah**-na] *n* horse-riding competition.
gymnasium *n* large room with equipment for physical training. **gymnast** *n* expert in gymnastics. **gymnastic** *adj* **gymnastics** *pl n* exercises to develop strength and agility.
gynaecology [guy-nee-**kol**-la-jee] *n* branch of medicine dealing with

———————————————————— THESAURUS ————————————

gurgle *v* = **murmur**, babble, bubble, lap, plash, purl, ripple, splash ▷ *n* = **murmur**, babble, purl, ripple
guru *n* **2** = **teacher**, authority, leader, mana (*NZ*), master, mentor, sage, Svengali, tutor
gush *v* **1** = **flow**, cascade, flood, pour, run, rush, spout, spurt, stream **2** = **enthuse**, babble, chatter, effervesce, effuse, overstate, spout ▷ *n* **3, 4** = **stream**, cascade, flood, flow, jet, rush, spout, spurt, torrent
gust *n* **1** = **blast**, blow, breeze, puff, rush, squall **2** = **rush**, blast ▷ *v* **3** = **blow**, blast, squall
gusto *n* = **relish**, delight, enjoyment, enthusiasm, fervour, pleasure, verve, zeal
gut *n* **2** *Inf* = **paunch**, belly, potbelly, spare tyre (*Brit sl*) ▷ *pl* **4** = **intestines**, belly, bowels, entrails, innards (*inf*),

insides (*inf*), stomach, viscera **5** *Inf* = **courage**, audacity, backbone, bottle (*sl*), daring, mettle, nerve, pluck, spirit ▷ *v* **7** = **disembowel**, clean **8** = **ravage**, clean out, despoil, empty ▷ *adj* **9** = **instinctive**, basic, heartfelt, intuitive, involuntary, natural, spontaneous, unthinking, visceral
gutsy *adj Inf* **1** = **brave**, bold, courageous, determined, gritty, indomitable, plucky, resolute, spirited, feisty (*US & Canad*)
gutter *n* **1** = **drain**, channel, conduit, ditch, sluice, trench, trough
guttural *adj* = **throaty**, deep, gravelly, gruff, hoarse, husky, rasping, rough, thick
guy[1] *n* **1** *Inf* = **man**, bloke (*Brit inf*), chap, fellow, lad, person
guzzle *v* = **devour**, bolt, cram, drink, gobble, stuff (oneself), swill, wolf

diseases and conditions specific to women. **gynaecological** *adj* **gynaecologist** *n*.

gyp *n* **give someone gyp** *slang* cause someone severe pain.

gypsophila *n* garden plant with small white flowers.

gypsum *n* chalklike mineral used to make plaster of Paris.

Gypsy ❶ *n*, *pl* **-sies** member of a travelling people found throughout Europe.

gyrate [jire-**rate**] *v* rotate or spiral about a point or axis. **gyration** *n* **gyratory** *adj* gyrating.

gyrfalcon [**jur**-fawl-kon] *n* large rare falcon.

gyro *n*, *pl* **-ros** short for GYROSCOPE.

gyrocompass *n* compass using a gyroscope.

gyroscope [**jire**-oh-skohp] *n* disc rotating on an axis that can turn in any direction, so the disc maintains the same position regardless of the movement of the surrounding structure. **gyroscopic** *adj*.

g

───────── THESAURUS ─────────

Gypsy *n* = **traveller**, Bohemian, nomad, rambler, roamer, Romany, rover, wanderer

Hh

H *Chemistry* hydrogen.

habeas corpus [**hay**-bee-ass **kor**-puss] *n* writ ordering a prisoner to be brought before a court.

haberdasher *n Brit, Aust & NZ* dealer in small articles used for sewing. **haberdashery** *n*.

habiliments *pl n* clothes.

habit ❶ *n* **1** established way of behaving. **2** addiction to a drug. **3** costume of a monk or nun. **4** woman's riding costume. **habitual** *adj* done regularly and repeatedly.

habitable ❶ *adj* fit to be lived in. **habitat** *n* natural home of an animal or plant. **habitation** *n* (occupation of) a dwelling place.

habitual ❶ *adj* done regularly and repeatedly. **habitually** *adv*.

habituate *v* accustom. **habituation** *n* **habitué** [hab-**it**-yew-ay] *n* frequent visitor to a place.

hacienda [hass-ee-**end**-a] *n* ranch or large estate in Latin America.

hack¹ ❶ *v* **1** cut or chop violently. **2** *Brit and NZ informal* tolerate. **hacking** *adj* (of a cough) dry, painful, and harsh.

hack² ❶ *n* **1** (inferior) writer or journalist. **2** horse kept for riding. **hackwork** *n* dull repetitive work.

hacker *n slang* computer enthusiast, esp. one who breaks into the computer system of a company or government.

hackles *pl n* **make one's hackles rise** make one feel angry or hostile.

hackney *n* taxi.

hackneyed ❶ [**hak**-need] *adj* (of a word or phrase) unoriginal and overused.

hacksaw *n* small saw for cutting metal.

had *v* past of HAVE.

haddock *n* edible sea fish.

Hades [**hay**-deez] *n Greek myth* underworld home of the dead.

hadj *n* same as HAJJ.

haematite [**hee**-ma-tite] *n* type of iron ore, reddish-brown when powdered.

haematology *n* study of blood and its diseases. **haematologist** *n*.

haemo- *combining form* blood.

haemoglobin [hee-moh-**globe**-in] *n* protein found in red blood cells which carries oxygen.

haemophilia [hee-moh-**fill**-lee-a] *n* hereditary illness in which the blood does not clot. **haemophiliac** *n*.

haemorrhage [**hem**-or-ij] *n* **1** heavy bleeding. ▷ *v* **2** bleed heavily.

● **SPELLING TIP**
● The Bank of English shows that
● the most usual mistake in spelling
● **haemorrhage** is to miss out the
● second *h*, which is silent.

haemorrhoids [**hem**-or-oydz] *pl n* swollen veins in the anus (also **piles**).

hafnium *n Chemistry* metallic element found in zirconium ores.

haft *n* handle of an axe, knife, or dagger.

hag ❶ *n* ugly old woman. **hag-ridden** *adj* distressed or worried.

haggard ❶ *adj* looking tired and ill.

haggis *n* Scottish dish made from sheep's offal, oatmeal, suet, and seasonings, boiled in a bag made from the sheep's stomach.

haggle ❶ *v* bargain or wrangle over a price.

━━━━━━━━━━━━━ THESAURUS ━━━━━━━

habit *n* **1** = **mannerism**, custom, practice, proclivity, propensity, quirk, tendency, way **2** = **addiction**, dependence

habitation *n* **a** = **occupation**, inhabitance, occupancy, tenancy **b** = **dwelling**, abode, domicile, home, house, living quarters, lodging, quarters, residence

habitual *adj* = **customary**, accustomed, familiar, normal, regular, routine, standard, traditional, usual

hack¹ *v* **1** = **cut**, chop, hew, lacerate, mangle, mutilate, slash

hack² *n* **1** = **scribbler**, literary hack **2** = **horse**, crock, nag

hackneyed *adj* = **unoriginal**, clichéd, commonplace, overworked, stale, stereotyped, stock, threadbare, tired, trite

hag *n* = **witch**, crone, harridan

haggard *adj* = **gaunt**, careworn, drawn, emaciated, pinched, thin, wan

haggle *v* = **bargain**, barter, beat down

hagiography *n, pl* **-phies** writing about the lives of the saints. **hagiographer** *n*.

ha-ha *interj* representation of the sound of laughter.

haiku [**hie**-koo] *n, pl* **-ku** Japanese verse form in 17 syllables.

hail¹ ❶ *n* **1** (shower of) small pellets of ice. **2** large number of insults, missiles, blows, etc. ▷ *v* **3** fall as or like hail. **hailstone** *n*.

hail² ❶ *v* **1** call out to, greet. **2** stop (a taxi) by waving. **3** acknowledge publicly, e.g. *he was hailed as a hero*. **hail from** *v* come originally from. **Hail Mary** *RC Church* prayer to the Virgin Mary.

hair ❶ *n* **1** threadlike growth on the skin. **2** such growths collectively, esp. on the head. **hairy** *adj* **hairier**, **hairiest** **1** covered with hair. **2** *slang* dangerous or exciting. **hairiness** *n* **hairless** *adj* **hairdo** *n informal* hairstyle. **hairdresser** *n* person who cuts and styles hair. **hairdressing** *n* **hairgrip** *n* small, tightly bent metal hairpin. **hairline** *n* **1** edge of hair at the top of the forehead. ▷ *adj* **2** very fine or narrow. **hairpiece** *n* section of false hair added to a person's real hair. **hairpin** *n* U-shaped wire used to hold the hair in place. **hairpin bend** very sharp bend in a road. **hair-raising** *adj* frightening or exciting. **hair's-breadth** *n* extremely small margin or distance. **hair shirt** shirt made of horsehair cloth worn against the skin as a penance. **hairsplitting** *n, adj* making petty distinctions. **hairstyle** *n* cut and arrangement of a person's hair.

hajj *n* pilgrimage a Muslim makes to Mecca. **hajji** *n* Muslim who has made a pilgrimage to Mecca.

hake *n* **1** edible fish of the cod family. **2** *Aust* same as BARRACOUTA.

halal *n* meat from animals slaughtered according to Muslim law.

halberd *n* spear with an axe blade.

halcyon ❶ [**hal**-see-on] *adj* peaceful and happy. **halcyon days** time of peace and happiness.

hale ❶ *adj* healthy, robust, e.g. *hale and hearty*.

half ❶ *n, pl* **halves** **1** either of two equal parts. **2** *informal* half-pint of beer etc. **3** half-price ticket. ▷ *adj* **4** denoting one of two equal parts. ▷ *adv* **5** to the extent of half. **6** partially. **half-and-half** *adj* half one thing and half another thing. **halfback** *n Sport* player positioned immediately behind the forwards. **half-baked** *adj informal* not properly thought out. **half board** (in a hotel) bed, breakfast, and evening meal. **half-brother**, **half-sister** *n* brother *or* sister related through one parent only. **half-caste** *n offens* person with parents of different races. **half-cocked** *adj* **go off half-cocked, (at)**

hail¹ **1** = **shower**, rain, storm **2** = **barrage**, bombardment, downpour, volley ▷ *v* **3** = **shower**, batter, beat down upon, bombard, pelt, rain, rain down on

hail² *v* **1** = **salute**, greet, welcome **2** = **flag down**, signal to, wave down **3** = **acclaim**, acknowledge, applaud, cheer, honour ▷ *v* **hail from** = **come from**, be a native of, be born in, originate in

hair *n* **2** = **locks**, head of hair, mane, mop, shock, tresses

hairdresser *n* = **stylist**, barber, coiffeur *or* coiffeuse

hair-raising *adj* = **frightening**, alarming, bloodcurdling, horrifying, scary, shocking, spine-chilling, terrifying

hairstyle *n* = **haircut**, coiffure, cut, hairdo, style

hairy *adj* **1** = **shaggy**, bushy, furry, hirsute, stubbly, unshaven, woolly **2** *Sl* = **dangerous**, difficult, hazardous, perilous, risky

halcyon *adj* = **peaceful**, calm, gentle, quiet, serene, tranquil, undisturbed

halcyon (days) = **happy**, carefree, flourishing, golden, palmy, prosperous

hale *adj* = **healthy**, able-bodied, fit, flourishing, in the pink, robust, sound, strong, vigorous, well

half *n* **1** = **equal part**, fifty per cent, hemisphere, portion, section ▷ *adj* **4** = **partial**, halved, limited, moderate ▷ *adv* **5** = **partially**, in part, partly

half-baked *adj Inf* = **poorly planned**, ill-conceived, ill-judged, impractical, short-sighted, unformed, unthought-out *or* -through

half-hearted *adj* = **unenthusiastic**, apathetic, indifferent, lacklustre, listless, lukewarm, perfunctory, tame

halfway *adv* = **midway**, to *or* in the middle ▷ *adj* = **midway**, central, equidistant, intermediate, mid, middle

halfwit *n* = **fool**, airhead (*sl*), dunderhead, idiot, imbecile (*inf*), moron, numbskull *or* numskull, simpleton, twit (*inf, chiefly Brit*)

half-cock fail because of inadequate preparation. **half-day** n day when a person works only in the morning or only in the afternoon. **half-hearted** adj unenthusiastic. **half-heartedly** adv **half-life** n time taken for half the atoms in radioactive material to decay. **half-mast** n halfway position of a flag on a mast as a sign of mourning. **half-moon** n moon when half its face is illuminated. **half-nelson** n wrestling hold in which one wrestler's arm is pinned behind his back by his opponent. **half-pipe** large U-shaped ramp used for skateboarding, snowboarding, etc. **half-term** n holiday midway through a school term. **half-timbered** adj (of a house) having an exposed wooden frame filled in with plaster. **half-time** n Sport short rest period between two halves of a game. **halftone** n illustration showing lights and shadows by means of very small dots. **halfway** adv, adj at or to half the distance. **halfwit** n foolish or stupid person. **halfwitted** adj.

halfpenny [**hayp**-nee] n former British coin worth half an old penny.

halibut n large edible flatfish.

halitosis n unpleasant-smelling breath.

hall ❶ n 1 (also **hallway**) entrance passage. 2 large room or building for public meetings, dances, etc. 3 large country house.

hallelujah [hal-ee-**loo**-ya] interj exclamation of praise to God.

hallmark ❶ n 1 typical feature. 2 mark indicating the amount of tested gold and silver. ▷ v 3 stamp with a hallmark.

hallo interj same as HELLO.

halloo interj shout used to call hounds at a hunt.

hallowed adj regarded as holy.

Halloween, Hallowe'en n October 31, celebrated by children by dressing up as ghosts, witches, etc.

hallucinate ❶ v seem to see something that is not really there. **hallucination** n **hallucinatory** adj **hallucinogen** n drug that causes hallucinations. **hallucinogenic** adj.

halo ❶ [**hay**-loh] n, pl **-loes**, **-los** 1 ring of light round the head of a sacred figure. 2 circle of refracted light round the sun or moon.

halogen [**hal**-oh-jen] n Chemistry any of a group of nonmetallic elements including chlorine and iodine.

halt ❶ v 1 come or bring to a stop. ▷ n 2 temporary stop. 3 minor railway station without a building. **halting** adj hesitant, uncertain, e.g. in a halting voice. **haltingly** adv.

halter n strap round a horse's head with a rope to lead it with. **halterneck** n woman's top or dress with a strap fastened at the back of the neck.

halve ❶ v 1 divide in half. 2 reduce by half.

halves n plural of HALF.

halyard n rope for raising a ship's sail or flag.

ham¹ n smoked or salted meat from a pig's thigh. **ham-fisted** adj clumsy.

ham² informal ▷ n 1 amateur radio operator. 2 actor who overacts. ▷ v **hamming**, **hammed** 3 **ham it up** overact.

hamburger n minced beef shaped into a flat disc, cooked and usu. served in a bread roll.

hamlet n small village.

——————————————————— THESAURUS ———————

hall n 1 = **entrance hall**, corridor, entry, foyer, lobby, passage, passageway, vestibule 2 = **meeting place**, assembly room, auditorium, chamber, concert hall

hallmark n 1 = **indication**, sure sign, telltale sign 2 = **seal**, device, endorsement, mark, sign, stamp, symbol

hallucination n = **illusion**, apparition, delusion, dream, fantasy, figment of the imagination, mirage, vision

halo n = **ring of light**, aura, corona, nimbus, radiance

halt v 1 a = **stop**, break off, cease, come to an end, desist, rest, stand still, wait b = **hold back**, block, bring to an end, check, curb, cut short, end, nip in the bud, terminate ▷ n 2 = **stop**, close, end, pause, standstill, stoppage

halting adj = **faltering**, awkward, hesitant, laboured, stammering, stumbling, stuttering

halve v 1 = **bisect**, cut in half, divide equally, share equally, split in two

hammer ❶ *n* **1** tool with a heavy metal head and a wooden handle, used to drive in nails etc. **2** part of a gun which causes the bullet to be fired. **3** heavy metal ball on a wire, thrown as a sport. **4** auctioneer's mallet. **5** striking mechanism in a piano. ▷ *v* **6** hit (as if) with a hammer. **7** *informal* punish or defeat utterly. **go at it hammer and tongs** do something, esp. argue, very vigorously. **hammerhead** *n* shark with a wide flattened head. **hammer out** *v* settle (differences) with great effort. **hammertoe** *n* condition in which a toe is permanently bent at the joint.

hammock *n* hanging bed made of canvas or net.

hamper¹ ❶ *v* make it difficult for (someone or something) to move or progress.

hamper² *n* **1** large basket with a lid. **2** selection of food and drink packed as a gift.

hamster *n* small rodent with a short tail and cheek pouches.

- **SPELLING TIP**
- The word **hamster** appears 750
- times in the Bank of English. The
- misspelling *hampster*, with a *p*,
- appears 13 times.

hamstring *n* **1** tendon at the back of the knee. ▷ *v* **2** make it difficult for (someone) to take any action. **hamstrung** *adj*.

hand ❶ *n* **1** part of the body at the end of the arm, consisting of a palm, four fingers, and a thumb. **2** style of handwriting. **3** round of applause. **4** manual worker. **5** pointer on a dial, esp. on a clock. **6** cards dealt to a player in a card game. **7** unit of length of four inches used to measure horses. ▷ *v* **8** pass, give. **have a hand in** be involved in. **lend a hand** help. **out of hand 1** beyond control. **2** definitely and finally, e.g. *the idea was rejected out of hand*. **to hand**, **at hand**, **on hand** nearby. **win hands down** win easily. **handbag** *n* woman's small bag for carrying personal articles in. **handbill** *n* small printed notice. **handbook** *n* small reference or instruction book. **handcuff** *n* **1** one of a linked pair of metal rings designed to be locked round a prisoner's wrists by the police. ▷ *v* **2** put handcuffs on. **handheld** *adj* **1** (of a computer) small enough to be held in the hand. ▷ *n* **2** computer small enough to be held in the hand. **hand-me-downs** *pl n informal* clothes that someone has finished with and passed on to someone else. **hand-out** *n* **1** clothing, food, or money given to a needy person. **2** written information given out at a talk etc. **hand-pick** *v* select carefully for a particular purpose. **handrail** *n* rail alongside a stairway, to provide support. **handset** *n* telephone mouthpiece and earpiece in a single unit. **hands-free** *adj, n* (of) a device allowing the user to make and receive phone calls without holding the handset. **hands-on** *adj* involving practical experience of equipment. **handstand** *n* act of supporting the body on the hands in an upside-down position. **hand-to-hand** *adj* (of combat) at close quarters. **hand-to-mouth** *adj* having barely enough food or money to live on. **handwriting** *n* (style of) writing by hand. **handwritten** *adj*.

h & c hot and cold (water).

handful ❶ *n* **1** amount that can be held in the hand. **2** small number. **3** *informal* person or animal that is difficult to control.

hammer *v* **6** = **hit**, bang, beat, drive, knock, strike, tap **7** *Inf* = **defeat**, beat, drub, run rings around (*inf*), thrash, trounce, wipe the floor with (*inf*)

hamper¹ *v* = **hinder**, frustrate, hamstring, handicap, impede, interfere with, obstruct, prevent, restrict

hand *n* **1** = **palm**, fist, mitt (*sl*), paw (*inf*) **2** = **penmanship**, calligraphy, handwriting, script **3** = **round of applause**, clap, ovation **4** = **worker**, artisan, craftsman, employee, hired man, labourer, operative, workman ▷ *v* **8** = **give**, deliver, hand over, pass **to, at** *or* **on hand** = **nearby**, at one's fingertips, available, close, handy, near, ready, within reach

handbook *n* = **guidebook**, guide, instruction book, manual

handcuff *n* **1** = **shackle**, cuff (*inf*), fetter, manacle ▷ *v* **2** = **shackle**, cuff (*inf*), fetter, manacle

handful *n* **2** = **few**, small number, smattering, sprinkling

handicap ⓘ n 1 physical or mental disability. 2 something that makes progress difficult. 3 contest in which the competitors are given advantages or disadvantages in an attempt to equalize their chances. 4 advantage or disadvantage given. ▷ v 5 make it difficult for (someone) to do something. **handicapped** adj.

handicraft ⓘ n objects made by hand.

handiwork ⓘ n something that one has made or done oneself, e.g. I looked up to admire my handiwork.

handkerchief n small square of fabric used to wipe the nose.

● **SPELLING TIP**
● People often forget to write a d in
● **handkerchief**, probably because
● they don't say it or hear it either.

handle ⓘ n 1 part of an object that is held so that it can be used. ▷ v 2 hold, feel, or move with the hands. 3 control or deal with. **handler** n person who controls an animal. **handlebars** pl n curved metal bar used to steer a cycle.

handsome ⓘ adj 1 (esp. of a man) good-looking. 2 large or generous, e.g. a handsome profit. **handsomely** adv.

handy ⓘ adj **handier**, **handiest** 1 convenient, useful. 2 good at manual work. **handily** adv **handyman** n man who is good at making or repairing things.

hang ⓘ v **hanging**, **hung** 1 attach or be attached at the top with the lower part free. 2 (of cloth or clothing) fall or flow in a particular way. 3 past **hanged** suspend or be suspended by the neck until dead. 4 fasten to a wall. **get the hang of** informal begin to understand. **hanger** n curved piece of wood, wire, or plastic, with a hook, for hanging up clothes (also **coat hanger**). **hanger-on** n, pl **hangers-on** unwanted follower. **hanging** n 1 execution by hanging. 2 decorative drapery hung on a wall. **hang about, around** v 1 stand about idly. 2 (foll. by with) spend a lot of time in the company (of). **hang back** v hesitate, be reluctant. **hangman** n man who executes people by hanging. **hangover** n headache and nausea as a result of drinking too much alcohol. **hang-up** n informal emotional or psychological problem.

hangar n large shed for storing aircraft.

hangdog ⓘ adj guilty, ashamed, e.g. a hangdog look.

hang-glider n glider with a light framework from which the pilot hangs in a harness. **hang-gliding** n.

hank ⓘ n coil, esp. of yarn.

——————— THESAURUS ———————

handicap n 1 = **disability**, defect, impairment 2 = **disadvantage**, barrier, drawback, hindrance, impediment, limitation, obstacle, restriction, stumbling block 3 = **advantage**, head start ▷ v 5 = **hinder**, burden, encumber, hamper, hamstring, hold back, impede, limit, restrict

handicraft n = **craftsmanship**, art, craft, handiwork, skill, workmanship

handiwork n = **creation**, achievement, design, invention, product, production

handle n 1 = **grip**, haft, hilt, stock ▷ v 2 = **hold**, feel, finger, grasp, pick up, touch 3 = **control**, cope with, deal with, direct, guide, manage, manipulate, manoeuvre

hand-out n 1 = **charity**, alms, dole, pogey (Canad) 2 = **leaflet**, bulletin, circular, literature (inf), mailshot, press release

handsome adj 1 = **good-looking**, attractive, comely, dishy (inf, chiefly Brit), elegant, gorgeous, personable 2 = **generous**, abundant, ample, considerable, large, liberal, plentiful, sizable or sizeable

handwriting n = **penmanship**, calligraphy, hand, scrawl, script

handy adj 1 a = **convenient**, accessible, at hand, at one's fingertips, available, close, nearby, on hand, within reach b = **useful**, convenient, easy to use, helpful, manageable, neat, practical, serviceable, user-friendly 2 = **skilful**, adept, adroit, deft, dexterous, expert, proficient, skilled

hang v 1 = **suspend**, dangle, droop 3 = **execute**, lynch, string up (inf) **get the hang of** Inf = **grasp**, comprehend, understand

hang back v = **be reluctant**, demur, hesitate, hold back, recoil

hangdog adj = **guilty**, cowed, cringing, defeated, downcast, furtive, shamefaced, wretched

hangover n = **aftereffects**, morning after (inf)

hang-up n Inf = **preoccupation**, block, difficulty, inhibition, obsession, problem, thing (inf)

hank n = **coil**, length, loop, piece, roll, skein

hanker ❶ v (foll. by *after*) desire intensely. **hankering** n.

hanky, hankie n, pl **hankies** informal handkerchief.

hanky-panky n informal illicit sexual relations.

hansom cab, hansom n (formerly) two-wheeled horse-drawn carriage for hire.

haphazard ❶ adj not organized or planned. **haphazardly** adv.

hapless adj unlucky.

happen ❶ v **1** take place, occur. **2** chance (to be or do something). **happening** n event, occurrence.

happy ❶ adj **-pier, -piest 1** feeling or causing joy. **2** lucky, fortunate. **3** willing (to do something). **happily** adv **happiness** n **happy-go-lucky** adj carefree and cheerful.

hara-kiri n (formerly, in Japan) ritual suicide by disembowelling.

harangue ❶ v **1** address angrily or forcefully. ▷ n **2** angry or forceful speech.

harass ❶ v annoy or trouble constantly. **harassed** adj **harassment** n.

- ● **SPELLING TIP**
- ● The commonest misspelling
- ● of **harass** is *harrass*. There should
- ● be only one r, but it's obviously
- ● difficult to remember: there are
- ● 232 instances of *harrassment* in
- ● the Bank of English and 10 of
- ● *harrasment*. The correct spelling is
- ● **harassment**.

harbinger [har-binj-a] n someone or something that announces the approach of something, e.g. *a harbinger of doom*.

harbour ❶ n **1** sheltered port. ▷ v **2** maintain secretly in the mind. **3** give shelter or protection to.

hard ❶ adj **1** firm, solid, or rigid. **2** difficult. **3** requiring a lot of effort. **4** unkind, unfeeling. **5** causing pain, sorrow, or hardship. **6** (of water) containing calcium salts which stop soap lathering freely. **7** (of a drug) strong and addictive. ▷ adv **8** with

---

THESAURUS

hanker v (foll. by *after*) = **desire**, crave, hunger, itch, long, lust, pine, thirst, yearn

haphazard adj = **unsystematic**, aimless, casual, disorganized, hit or miss (*inf*), indiscriminate, slapdash

happen v **1** = **occur**, come about, come to pass, develop, result, take place, transpire (*inf*) **2** = **chance**, turn out

happening n = **event**, affair, episode, experience, incident, occurrence, proceeding

happily adv **1** = **joyfully**, blithely, cheerfully, gaily, gleefully, joyously, merrily **2** = **luckily**, fortunately, opportunely, providentially **3** = **willingly**, freely, gladly, with pleasure

happiness n **1** = **joy**, bliss, cheerfulness, contentment, delight, ecstasy, elation, jubilation, pleasure, satisfaction

happy adj **1** = **joyful**, blissful, cheerful, content, delighted, ecstatic, elated, glad, jubilant, merry, overjoyed, pleased, thrilled **2** = **fortunate**, advantageous, auspicious, favourable, lucky, timely

happy-go-lucky adj = **carefree**, blithe, easy-going, light-hearted, nonchalant, unconcerned, untroubled

harangue v **1** = **rant**, address, declaim, exhort, hold forth, lecture, spout (*inf*) ▷ n **2** = **speech**, address, declamation,

diatribe, exhortation, tirade

harass v = **annoy**, bother, harry, hassle (*inf*), hound, persecute, pester, plague, trouble, vex

harassed adj = **hassled** (*inf*), careworn, distraught, strained, tormented, troubled, under pressure, vexed, worried

harassment n = **hassle** (*inf*), annoyance, bother, irritation, nuisance, persecution, pestering, trouble

harbour n **1** = **port**, anchorage, haven ▷ v **2** = **maintain**, cling to, entertain, foster, hold, nurse, nurture, retain **3** = **shelter**, hide, protect, provide refuge, shield

hard adj **1** = **tough**, firm, inflexible, rigid, rocklike, solid, stiff, strong, unyielding **2** = **difficult**, complicated, intricate, involved, knotty, perplexing, puzzling, thorny **3** = **strenuous**, arduous, backbreaking, exacting, exhausting, laborious, rigorous, tough **4** = **harsh**, callous, cold, cruel, hardhearted, pitiless, stern, unfeeling, unkind, unsympathetic **5** = **grim**, disagreeable, distressing, grievous, intolerable, painful, unpleasant ▷ adv **8, 9** = **energetically**, fiercely, forcefully, forcibly, heavily, intensely, powerfully, severely, sharply, strongly, vigorously, violently, with all one's might, with might and main great energy or effort. **9** with great intensity. **hard up** *informal* short of money. **harden** *v* **hardness** *n* **hardship** *n* **1** suffering. **2** difficult circumstances. **hard-and-fast** *adj* (of rules) fixed and not able to be changed. **hard-bitten** *adj* tough and determined. **hard-boiled** *adj* **1** (of an egg) boiled until solid. **2** *informal* tough, unemotional. **hard cash** notes and coins, as opposed to cheques or credit cards. **hard copy** computer output printed on paper. **hard core** the members of a group who most resist change. **hard-core** *adj* **1** (of pornography) showing sexual acts in explicit detail. **2** extremely committed, fanatical. **hard disk** *Computers* inflexible disk in a sealed container. **hard drive** *Computers* mechanism that handles the reading, writing, and storage of data on the hard disk. **hard-headed** *adj* shrewd, practical. **hardhearted** *adj* unsympathetic, uncaring. **hard line** uncompromising policy. **hard-line** *adj* **hard-liner** *n* **hard of hearing** unable to hear properly. **hard sell** aggressive sales technique. **hard shoulder** surfaced verge at the edge of a motorway for emergency stops.

hardback *n* book with a stiff cover.

hardboard *n* thin stiff board made of compressed sawdust and wood chips.

hardly ⓘ *adv* **1** scarcely or not at all. **2** with difficulty.

hardware *n* **1** metal tools or implements. **2** machinery used in a computer system. **3** heavy military equipment, such as tanks and missiles.

hardwood *n* wood of a deciduous tree such as oak or ash.

hardy ⓘ *adj* **hardier, hardiest** able to stand difficult conditions. **hardiness** *n*.

hare *n* **1** animal like a large rabbit, with longer ears and legs. ▷ *v* **2** (usu. foll. by *off*) run (away) quickly. **harebell** *n* blue bell-shaped flower. **harebrained** *adj* foolish or impractical. **harelip** *n* slight split in the upper lip.

harem *n* (apartments of) a Muslim man's wives and concubines.

haricot bean, haricot [har-rik-oh] *n* small pale edible bean, usu. sold dried.

hark *v* *old-fashioned* listen. **hark back** *v* return (to an earlier subject).

harlequin *n* **1** stock comic character with a diamond-patterned costume and mask. ▷ *adj* **2** in many colours.

harlot *n* *lit* prostitute.

harm ⓘ *v* **1** injure physically, mentally, or morally. ▷ *n* **2** physical, mental, or moral injury. **harmful** *adj* **harmless** *adj*.

harmonica *n* small wind instrument played by sucking and blowing.

——————— THESAURUS ———————

hard-bitten *adj Inf* = **tough**, cynical, hard-nosed (*inf*), matter-of-fact, practical, realistic

hard-boiled *adj* **2** *Inf* = **tough**, cynical, hard-nosed (*inf*), matter-of-fact, practical, realistic, unsentimental

harden *v* **1** = **solidify**, bake, cake, freeze, set, stiffen

hard-headed *adj* = **shrewd**, level-headed, practical, pragmatic, realistic, sensible, tough, unsentimental

hardhearted *adj* = **unsympathetic**, callous, cold, hard, heartless, insensitive, uncaring, unfeeling

hardiness *n* = **resilience**, resolution, robustness, ruggedness, sturdiness, toughness

hardly *adv* **1** = **barely**, just, only just, scarcely **2** = **with difficulty**

hardship *n* = **suffering**, adversity, difficulty, misfortune, need, privation, tribulation

hard up *adj Inf* = **poor**, broke (*inf*), impecunious, impoverished, on the

breadline, out of pocket, penniless, short, skint (*Brit sl*), strapped for cash (*inf*)

hardy *adj* = **strong**, robust, rugged, sound, stout, sturdy, tough

harm *v* **1** = **injure**, abuse, damage, hurt, ill-treat, maltreat, ruin, spoil, wound ▷ *n* **2** = **injury**, abuse, damage, hurt, ill, loss, mischief, misfortune

harmful *adj* = **injurious**, damaging, deleterious, destructive, detrimental, hurtful, noxious, pernicious

harmless *adj* = **innocuous**, gentle, innocent, inoffensive, nontoxic, safe, unobjectionable

harmonious *adj* **1** = **compatible**, agreeable, consonant **2 a** = **friendly**, agreeable, amicable, compatible, congenial, cordial, sympathetic ▷ *adj* **b** = **melodious**, concordant, dulcet, mellifluous, musical, sweet-sounding, tuneful

harmonize *v* **2** = **go together**, agree, blend, coordinate, correspond, match, tally, tone in with

harmonium n keyboard instrument like a small organ.

harmony ❶ n, pl **-nies 1** peaceful agreement and cooperation. **2** pleasant combination of notes sounded at the same time. **harmonious** adj **1** consisting of parts that blend together well. **2** of harmony. **harmoniously** adv **harmonic** adj of harmony. **harmonics** n science of musical sounds. **harmonize** v **1** sing or play in harmony. **2** blend well together. **harmonization** n.

harness ❶ n **1** arrangement of straps for attaching a horse to a cart or plough. **2** set of straps fastened round someone's body to attach something, e.g. a safety harness. ▷ v **3** put a harness on. **4** control (something) in order to make use of it.

harp n large triangular stringed instrument played with the fingers. **harpist** n **harp on about** v talk about continuously.

harpoon n **1** barbed spear attached to a rope used for hunting whales. ▷ v **2** spear with a harpoon.

harpsichord n stringed keyboard instrument.

harpy n, pl **-pies** nasty or bad-tempered woman.

harridan n nagging or vicious woman.

harrier n cross-country runner.

harrow n **1** implement used to break up lumps of soil. ▷ v **2** draw a harrow over.

harrowing ❶ adj very distressing.

harry ❶ v **-rying, -ried** keep asking (someone) to do something, pester.

harsh ❶ adj **1** severe and difficult to cope with. **2** unkind, unsympathetic. **3** extremely hard, bright, or rough. **harshly** adv **harshness** n.

hart n adult male deer.

hartebeest n large African antelope.

harum-scarum adj reckless.

harvest ❶ n **1** (season for) the gathering of crops. **2** crops gathered. ▷ v **3** gather (a ripened crop). **harvester** n.

has v third person singular of the present tense of HAVE. **has-been** n informal person who is no longer popular or successful.

hash¹ ❶ n dish of diced cooked meat and vegetables reheated. **make a hash of** informal spoil, do badly.

hash² n informal hashish.

hash³, hashmark n character (#) used to precede a number. **hashtag** n (on Twitter) word or phrase preceded by a hash, indicating the topic of the post.

hashish [hash-eesh] n drug made from the cannabis plant, smoked for its intoxicating effects.

hasp n clasp that fits over a staple and is secured by a bolt or padlock, used as a fastening.

hassle ❶ informal ▷ n **1** trouble, bother. **2** long argument. ▷ v **3** bother or annoy.

hassock n cushion for kneeling on in church.

haste ❶ n (excessive) quickness. **make haste** hurry, rush. **hasten** v (cause to)

---

harmony n **1** = **agreement**, accord, amicability, compatibility, concord, cooperation, friendship, peace, rapport, sympathy **2** = **tunefulness**, euphony, melody, tune, unison

harness n **1** = **tack 2** = **equipment**, gear, tackle ▷ v **4** = **exploit**, channel, control, employ, mobilize, utilize

harrowing adj = **distressing**, agonizing, disturbing, gut-wrenching, heart-rending, nerve-racking, painful, terrifying, tormenting, traumatic

harry v = **pester**, badger, bother, chivvy, harass, hassle (inf), plague

harsh adj **1, 2** = **severe**, austere, cruel, Draconian, drastic, hard, pitiless, punitive, ruthless, stern, tough **3** = **raucous**, discordant, dissonant, grating, guttural, rasping, rough, strident

harshly adv **1, 2** = **severely**, brutally, cruelly, roughly, sternly, strictly

harshness n **1, 2** = **severity**, asperity, brutality, rigour, roughness, sternness

harvest n **1** = **gathering**, harvesting, harvest-time, reaping **2** = **crop**, produce, yield ▷ v **3** = **gather**, mow, pick, pluck, reap

hash¹ n **make a hash of** Inf = **mess up**, botch, bungle, make a pig's ear of (inf), mishandle, mismanage, muddle

hassle Inf ▷ n **1** = **trouble**, bother, difficulty, grief (inf), inconvenience, problem **2** = **argument**, bickering, disagreement, dispute, fight, quarrel, row, squabble ▷ v **3** = **bother**, annoy, badger, bug (inf), harass, hound, pester

haste n = **speed**, alacrity, hurry, impetuosity, quickness, rapidity, rush, swiftness, urgency, velocity

hasten v = **rush**, dash, fly, hurry (up), make haste, race, scurry, speed

hurry. **hasty** *adj* **hastier**, **hastiest** (too) quick. **hastily** *adv*.

hat *n* covering for the head, often with a brim, usu. worn to give protection from the weather. **keep something under one's hat** keep something secret. **hat trick** any three successive achievements, esp. in sport.

hatch[1] ❶ *v* **1** (cause to) emerge from an egg. **2** devise (a plot).

hatch[2] *n* **1** hinged door covering an opening in a floor or wall. **2** opening in the wall between a kitchen and a dining area. **3** door in an aircraft or spacecraft. **hatchback** *n* car with a lifting door at the back. **hatchway** *n* opening in the deck of a ship.

hatchet *n* small axe. **bury the hatchet** become reconciled. **hatchet job** malicious verbal or written attack. **hatchet man** *informal* person carrying out unpleasant tasks for an employer.

hate ❶ *v* **1** dislike intensely. **2** be unwilling (to do something). ▷ *n* **3** intense dislike. **4** person or thing hated. **hateful** *adj* causing or deserving hate. **hater** *n* **hatred** *n* intense dislike.

haughty ❶ *adj* **-tier**, **-tiest** proud, arrogant. **haughtily** *adv* **haughtiness** *n*.

haul ❶ *v* **1** pull or drag with effort. ▷ *n* **2** hauling. **3** amount gained by effort or

theft. **long haul** something that takes a lot of time and effort. **haulage** *n* (charge for) transporting goods. **haulier** *n* firm or person that transports goods by road.

haulm [**hawm**] *n* stalks of beans, peas, or potatoes collectively.

haunch *n* human hip or fleshy hindquarter of an animal.

haunt ❶ *v* **1** visit in the form of a ghost. **2** remain in the memory or thoughts of. ▷ *n* **3** place visited frequently. **haunted** *adj* **1** frequented by ghosts. **2** worried. **haunting** *adj* memorably beautiful or sad. **hauntingly** *adv*.

haute couture [**oat** koo-**ture**] *n French* high fashion.

hauteur [oat-**ur**] *n* haughtiness.

Havana *n* fine-quality cigar made in Cuba.

have ❶ *v* **has**, **having**, **had 1** possess, hold. **2** receive, take, or obtain. **3** experience or be affected by. **4** (foll. by *to*) be obliged, must, e.g. *I had to go.* **5** cause to be done. **6** give birth to. **7** *slang* cheat or outwit. **8** used to form past tenses (with a past participle), e.g. *we have looked*; *she had done enough.* **have it out** *informal* settle a matter by argument. **haves and have-nots** *informal* rich people and poor people. **have on** *v* **1** wear. **2** *informal* tease or trick. **have up** *v* bring to trial.

THESAURUS

hastily *adv* = **quickly**, hurriedly, impetuously, precipitately, promptly, rapidly, speedily

hasty *adj* = **speedy**, brisk, hurried, impetuous, impulsive, precipitate, prompt, rapid, swift, urgent

hatch[1] *v* **1** = **incubate**, breed, bring forth, brood **2** = **devise**, conceive, concoct, contrive, cook up (*inf*), design, dream up (*inf*), think up

hate *v* **1** = **detest**, abhor, despise, dislike, loathe, recoil from **2** = **be unwilling**, be loath, be reluctant, be sorry, dislike, feel disinclined, shrink from ▷ *n* **3** = **dislike**, animosity, antipathy, aversion, detestation, enmity, hatred, hostility, loathing

hateful *adj* = **despicable**, abhorrent, detestable, horrible, loathsome, obnoxious, odious, offensive, repellent, repugnant, repulsive

hatred *n* = **dislike**, animosity, antipathy, aversion, detestation, enmity, hate, repugnance, revulsion

haughty *adj* = **proud**, arrogant, conceited, contemptuous, disdainful, imperious, scornful, snooty (*inf*), stuck-up (*inf*), supercilious

haul *v* **1** = **drag**, draw, heave, lug, pull, tug ▷ *n* **3** = **yield**, booty, catch, gain, harvest, loot, spoils, takings

haunt *v* **2** = **plague**, obsess, possess, prey on, recur, stay with, torment, trouble, weigh on ▷ *n* **3** = **meeting place**, rendezvous, stamping ground

haunted *adj* **1** = **possessed**, cursed, eerie, ghostly, jinxed, spooky (*inf*) **2** = **preoccupied**, obsessed, plagued, tormented, troubled, worried

haunting *adj* = **evocative**, nostalgic, persistent, poignant, unforgettable

have *v* **1** = **possess**, hold, keep, obtain, own, retain **2** = **receive**, accept, acquire, gain, get, obtain, procure, secure, take **3** = **experience**, endure, enjoy, feel, meet with, suffer, sustain, undergo **4** (foll. by *to*) = **be obliged**, be bound, be compelled, be forced, have

haven ⊕ *n* place of safety.

haver *v dialect* talk nonsense. **havers** *pl n Scot* nonsense.

haversack *n* canvas bag carried on the back or shoulder.

havoc ⊕ *n* disorder and confusion.

haw *n* hawthorn berry.

hawk¹ *n* 1 bird of prey with a short hooked bill and very good eyesight. 2 *Politics* supporter or advocate of warlike policies. **hawkish**, **hawklike** *adj* **hawk-eyed** *adj* having very good eyesight.

hawk² *v* offer (goods) for sale in the street or door-to-door. **hawker** *n*.

hawk³ *v* cough noisily.

hawser *n* large rope used on a ship.

hawthorn *n* thorny shrub or tree.

hay ⊕ *n* grass cut and dried as fodder. **hay fever** allergy to pollen, causing sneezing and watery eyes. **haystack** *n* large pile of stored hay. **haywire** *adj* **go haywire** *informal* not function properly.

hazard ⊕ *n* 1 something that could be dangerous. ▷ *v* 2 put in danger. 3 make (a guess). **hazardous** *adj*.

haze ⊕ *n* mist, often caused by heat. **hazy** *adj* **hazier**, **haziest** 1 not clear, misty. 2 confused or vague.

hazel *n* 1 small tree producing edible nuts. ▷ *adj* 2 (of eyes) greenish-brown. **hazelnut** *n*.

HB (on pencils) hard-black.

H-bomb *n* hydrogen bomb.

he *pron* refers to: 1 male person or animal. 2 person or animal of unspecified sex.

He *Chemistry* helium.

HE His (or Her) Excellency.

head ⊕ *n* 1 upper or front part of the body, containing the sense organs and the brain. 2 mind and mental abilities. 3 upper or most forward part of anything. 4 person in charge of a group, organization, or school. 5 pus-filled tip of a spot or boil. 6 white froth

h

THESAURUS

got to, must, ought, should **6 = give birth to**, bear, beget, bring forth, deliver **7** *Sl* **= cheat**, deceive, dupe, fool, outwit, swindle, take in (*inf*), trick

haven *n* **= sanctuary**, asylum, refuge, retreat, sanctum, shelter

have on *v* **1 = wear**, be clothed in, be dressed in **2** *Inf* **= tease**, deceive, kid (*inf*), pull someone's leg, take the mickey, trick, wind up (*Brit sl*)

havoc *n* **= disorder**, chaos, confusion, disruption, mayhem, shambles

haywire *adj* **go haywire** *Inf* **= malfunction**, break down, fail, go wrong

hazard *n* **1 = danger**, jeopardy, peril, pitfall, risk, threat ▷ *v* **2 = jeopardize**, endanger, expose, imperil, risk, threaten **3 = conjecture**, advance, offer, presume, throw out, venture, volunteer

hazardous *adj* **= dangerous**, dicey (*inf, chiefly Brit*), difficult, insecure, perilous, precarious, risky, unsafe

haze *n* **= mist**, cloud, fog, obscurity, vapour

hazy *adj* **1 = misty**, cloudy, dim, dull, foggy, overcast **2 = vague**, fuzzy, ill-defined, indefinite, indistinct, muddled, nebulous, uncertain, unclear

head *n* **1 = skull**, crown, loaf (*sl*), nut (*sl*), pate **2 = mind**, brain, brains (*inf*), intellect, intelligence, thought, understanding **3 = top**, crest, crown, peak, pinnacle, summit, tip **4 = leader**,

boss (*inf*), captain, chief, commander, director, manager, master, principal, supervisor ▷ *adj* **10 = chief**, arch, first, leading, main, pre-eminent, premier, prime, principal, supreme ▷ *v* **11 = lead**, be or go first, cap, crown, lead the way, precede, top **12 = be in charge of**, command, control, direct, govern, guide, lead, manage, run **13 = make for**, aim, go to, make a beeline for, point, set off for, set out, start towards, steer, turn **go to one's head = excite**, intoxicate, make conceited, puff up

head over heels = completely, intensely, thoroughly, uncontrollably, utterly, wholeheartedly

headache *n* **1 = migraine**, head (*inf*), neuralgia **2 = problem**, bane, bother, inconvenience, nuisance, trouble, vexation, worry

heading *n* **= title**, caption, headline, name, rubric

headlong *adv* **1 = headfirst**, head-on **2 = hastily**, heedlessly, helter-skelter, hurriedly, pell-mell, precipitately, rashly, thoughtlessly ▷ *adj* **1 = headfirst**, head-on **2 = hasty**, breakneck, dangerous, impetuous, impulsive, inconsiderate, precipitate, reckless, thoughtless

headstrong *adj* **= obstinate**, foolhardy, heedless, impulsive, perverse, pig-headed, self-willed, stubborn, unruly, wilful

on beer. **7** *pl* **head** person or animal considered as a unit. **8** headline or heading. **9** *informal* headache. ▷ *adj* **10** chief, principal. ▷ *v* **11** be at the top or front of. **12** be in charge of. **13** move (in a particular direction). **14** hit (a ball) with the head. **15** provide with a heading. **go to one's head** make one drunk or conceited. **head over heels (in love)** very much in love. **not make head nor tail of** not understand. **off one's head** *slang* foolish or insane. **heads** *adv informal* with the side of a coin which has a portrait of a head on it uppermost. **header** *n* **1** striking a ball with the head. **2** headlong fall. **heading** *n* title written or printed at the top of a page. **heady** *adj* **headier**, **headiest** intoxicating or exciting. **headache** *n* **1** continuous pain in the head. **2** cause of worry or annoyance. **headboard** *n* vertical board at the top end of a bed. **headdress** *n* decorative head covering. **head-hunt** *v* (of a company) approach and offer a job to (a person working for a rival company). **head-hunting** *n* **head-hunter** *n* **headland** *n* area of land jutting out into the sea. **headlight** *n* powerful light on the front of a vehicle. **headline** *n* **1** title at the top of a newspaper article, esp. on the front page. ▷ *pl* **2** main points of a news broadcast. **headlong** *adv, adj* **1** with the head first. **2** hastily. **head-on** *adv, adj* **1** front foremost. **2** direct(ly) and uncompromising(ly). **headphones** *pl n* two small loudspeakers held against the ears by a strap. **headquarters** *pl n* centre from which

operations are directed. **head start** advantage in a competition. **headstone** *n* memorial stone on a grave. **headstrong** *adj* self-willed, obstinate. **head teacher** person in charge of a school. **headway** *n* progress. **headwind** *n* wind blowing against the course of an aircraft or ship. **heal ❶** *v* make or become well. **healer** *n* **healing** *n, adj*. **health ❶** *n* normal (good) condition of someone's body. **health centre** surgery and offices of the doctors in a district. **health food** natural food, organically grown and free from additives. **health visitor** nurse who visits elderly people and mothers of newborn babies in their homes. **healthy** *adj* **healthier**, **healthiest** **1** having good health. **2** of or producing good health. **3** functioning well, sound. **healthily** *adv*. **heap ❶** *n* **1** pile of things one on top of another. **2** (also **heaps**) large number or quantity. ▷ *v* **3** gather into a pile. **4** (foll. by *on*) give liberally (to), e.g. *Keegan heaped praise on his team*. **hear ❶** *v* **hearing**, **heard 1** perceive (a sound) by ear. **2** listen to. **3** learn or be informed. **4** *Law* try (a case). **hear! hear!** exclamation of approval or agreement. **hearer** *n* **hearing** *n* **1** ability to hear. **2** trial of a case. **within hearing** close enough to be heard. **hearken** *v obs* listen. **hearsay ❶** *n* gossip, rumour. **hearse** *n* funeral car used to carry a coffin.

————————————————————— THESAURUS ————

headway *n* = **advance**, improvement, progress, progression, way

heady *adj* **a** = **intoxicating**, inebriating, potent, strong **b** = **exciting**, exhilarating, stimulating, thrilling

heal *v* = **cure**, make well, mend, regenerate, remedy, restore, treat

health *n* **a** = **condition**, constitution, fettle, shape, state **b** = **wellbeing**, fitness, good condition, healthiness, robustness, soundness, strength, vigour

healthy *adj* **1** = **well**, active, fit, hale and hearty, in fine fettle, in good shape (*inf*), in the pink, robust, strong **2** = **wholesome**, beneficial, hygienic, invigorating, nourishing, nutritious, salubrious, salutary

heap *n* **1** = **pile**, accumulation, collection, hoard, lot, mass, mound, stack **2** (also **heaps**) = **a lot**, great deal, load(s) (*inf*), lots (*inf*), mass, plenty, pot(s) (*inf*), stack(s), tons ▷ *v* **3** = **pile**, accumulate, amass, collect, gather, hoard, stack **4** (foll. by *on*) = **confer**, assign, bestow, load, shower upon

hear *v* **1** = **perceive**, catch, overhear **2** = **listen to 3** = **learn**, ascertain, discover, find out, gather, get wind of (*inf*), pick up **4** *Law* = **try**, examine, investigate, judge

hearing *n* **2** = **inquiry**, industrial tribunal, investigation, review, trial

hearsay *n* = **rumour**, gossip, idle talk, report, talk, tittle-tattle, word of mouth

heart ❶ *n* **1** organ that pumps blood round the body. **2** centre of emotions, esp. love. **3** courage, spirit. **4** central or most important part. **5** figure representing a heart. **6** playing card with red heart heart-shaped symbols. **break someone's heart** cause someone great grief. **by heart** from memory. **set one's heart on something** greatly desire something. **take something to heart** be upset about something. **hearten** *v* encourage, make cheerful. **heartening** *adj* **heartless** *adj* cruel, unkind. **heartlessly** *adv* **hearty** *adj* **heartier**, **heartiest 1** substantial, nourishing. **2** friendly, enthusiastic. **3** strongly felt. **heartily** *adv* **heart attack** sudden severe malfunction of the heart. **heart failure** sudden stopping of the heartbeat. **heart-rending** *adj* causing great sorrow. **heart-throb** *n slang* very attractive man, esp. a film or pop star. **heart-to-heart** *adj, n* intimate (conversation).

heartache ❶ *n* intense anguish.

heartbeat *n* one complete pulsation of the heart.

heartbreak ❶ *n* intense grief. **heartbreaking** *adj* **heartbroken** *adj*.

heartburn *n* burning sensation in the chest caused by indigestion.

heartfelt ❶ *adj* felt sincerely or strongly.

hearth *n* floor of a fireplace.

heat ❶ *v* **1** make or become hot. ▷ *n* **2** state of being hot. **3** energy transferred as a result of a difference in temperature. **4** hot weather. **5** intensity of feeling. **6** preliminary eliminating contest in a competition. **on, in heat** (of some female animals) ready for mating. **heated** *adj* angry and excited. **heatedly** *adv* **heater** *n* **heating** *n* **heatstroke** *n* same as SUNSTROKE. **heat wave** spell of unusually hot weather.

heath *n* area of open uncultivated land.

heathen ❶ *adj, n* (of) a person who does not believe in an established religion.

heather *n* low-growing plant with small purple, pinkish, or white flowers, growing on heaths and mountains.

heave ❶ *v* **1** lift with effort. **2** throw (something heavy). **3** utter (a sigh). **4** rise and fall. **5** vomit. **6** *past* **hove** *Nautical* move in a specified direction. ▷ *n* **7** heaving. **heave to** *v* (of a ship) stop moving.

heaven ❶ *n* **1** place believed to be the home of God, where good people go

heart *n* **2** = **nature**, character, disposition, soul, temperament **3** = **courage**, bravery, fortitude, pluck, purpose, resolution, spirit, will **4** = **centre**, core, hub, middle, nucleus, quintessence **by heart** = **by memory**, by rote, off pat, parrot-fashion (*inf*), pat, word for word

heartache *n* = **sorrow**, agony, anguish, despair, distress, grief, heartbreak, pain, remorse, suffering, torment, torture

heartbreak *n* = **grief**, anguish, desolation, despair, misery, pain, sorrow, suffering

heartbreaking *adj* = **sad**, agonizing, distressing, gut-wrenching, harrowing, heart-rending, pitiful, poignant, tragic

heartfelt *adj* = **sincere**, deep, devout, earnest, genuine, honest, profound, unfeigned, wholehearted

heartily *adv* **2, 3** = **enthusiastically**, eagerly, earnestly, resolutely, vigorously, zealously

heartless *adj* = **cruel**, callous, cold, hard, hardhearted, merciless, pitiless, uncaring, unfeeling

heart-rending *adj* = **moving**, affecting, distressing, gut-wrenching, harrowing,

heartbreaking, poignant, sad, tragic

hearty *adj* **1** = **substantial**, ample, filling, nourishing, sizable *or* sizeable, solid, square **2** = **friendly**, back-slapping, ebullient, effusive, enthusiastic, genial, jovial, warm

heat *v* **1** = **warm up**, make hot, reheat ▷ *n* **2** = **hotness**, high temperature, warmth **5** = **passion**, excitement, fervour, fury, intensity, vehemence

heated *adj* = **impassioned**, angry, excited, fierce, frenzied, furious, intense, passionate, stormy, vehement

heathen *adj* = **pagan**, godless, idolatrous, irreligious ▷ *n* = **pagan**, infidel, unbeliever

heave *v* **1** = **lift**, drag (up), haul (up), hoist, pull (up), raise, tug **2** = **throw**, cast, fling, hurl, pitch, send, sling, toss **3** = **sigh**, groan, puff **5** = **vomit**, be sick, gag, retch, spew, throw up (*inf*)

heaven *n* **1** = **paradise**, bliss, Elysium *or* Elysian fields (*Greek myth*), hereafter, life everlasting, next world, nirvana (*Buddhism, Hinduism*), Zion (*Christianity*) **2** = **happiness**, bliss, ecstasy, paradise, rapture, seventh heaven, utopia **the heavens** = **sky**, ether, firmament

when they die. **2** place or state of bliss. **the heavens** sky. **heavenly** adj **1** of or like heaven. **2** of or occurring in space. **3** wonderful or beautiful.

heavy ❶ adj **heavier**, **heaviest 1** of great weight. **2** having a high density. **3** great in degree or amount. **4** (of breathing) deep and loud. **5** (of food) solid and difficult to digest. **6** informal (of a situation) serious. **heavily** adv **heaviness** n **heavy-duty** adj made to withstand hard wear. **heavy industry** large-scale production of raw material or machinery. **heavy metal** very loud rock music featuring guitar riffs. **heavy water** water formed of oxygen and deuterium. **heavyweight** n boxer weighing over 175lb (professional) or 81kg (amateur).

Hebrew n **1** member of an ancient Semitic people. **2** ancient language of the Hebrews. **3** its modern form, used in Israel. ▷ adj **4** of the Hebrews.

heckle ❶ v interrupt (a public speaker) with comments, questions, or taunts. **heckler** n.

hectare n one hundred ares or 10 000 square metres (2.471 acres).

hectic ❶ adj rushed or busy.

hector v bully. **hectoring** adj, n.

hedge ❶ n **1** row of bushes forming a barrier or boundary. ▷ v **2** be evasive or noncommittal. **3** (foll. by against)

protect oneself (from). **hedgerow** n bushes forming a hedge. **hedge sparrow** small brownish songbird.

hedgehog n small mammal with a protective covering of spines.

hedonism n doctrine that pleasure is the most important thing in life. **hedonist** n **hedonistic** adj.

heed ❶ n **1** careful attention. ▷ v **2** pay careful attention to. **heedless** adj **heedless of** taking no notice of.

heel¹ ❶ n **1** back part of the foot. **2** part of a shoe supporting the heel. **3** slang contemptible person. ▷ v **4** repair the heel of (a shoe). **heeler** n Aust & NZ dog that herds cattle by biting at their heels.

heel² ❶ v (foll. by over) lean to one side.

hefty ❶ adj **heftier**, **heftiest 1** large, heavy, or strong. **2** (of a fine or bill) involving a large sum of money.

hegemony [hig-**em**-on-ee] n political domination.

Hegira n Mohammed's flight from Mecca to Medina in 622 AD.

heifer [**hef**-fer] n young cow.

height ❶ n **1** distance from base to top. **2** distance above sea level. **3** highest degree or topmost point. **heighten** v make or become higher or more intense. **heightened** adj.

heinous adj evil and shocking.

⎯⎯⎯⎯⎯⎯⎯⎯⎯⎯ THESAURUS ⎯⎯⎯⎯⎯⎯⎯⎯⎯⎯

heavenly adj **1** = **celestial**, angelic, blessed, divine, holy, immortal **3** = **wonderful**, beautiful, blissful, delightful, divine (inf), exquisite, lovely, ravishing, sublime

heavily adv **1** = **ponderously**, awkwardly, clumsily, weightily **2** = **densely**, closely, compactly, thickly **3** = **considerably**, a great deal, copiously, excessively, to excess, very much

heaviness n **1** = **weight**, gravity, heftiness, ponderousness

heavy adj **1** = **weighty**, bulky, hefty, massive, ponderous **3** = **considerable**, abundant, copious, excessive, large, profuse

heckle v = **jeer**, barrack (inf), boo, disrupt, interrupt, shout down, taunt

hectic adj = **frantic**, animated, chaotic, feverish, frenetic, heated, turbulent

hedge n **1** = **hedgerow** ▷ v **2** = **dodge**, duck, equivocate, evade, flannel (Brit inf), prevaricate, sidestep, temporize **3** (foll. by against) = **insure**, cover,

guard, protect, safeguard, shield

heed n **1** = **care**, attention, caution, mind, notice, regard, respect, thought ▷ v **2** = **pay attention to**, bear in mind, consider, follow, listen to, note, obey, observe, take notice of

heedless adj = **careless**, foolhardy, inattentive, oblivious, thoughtless, unmindful

heel¹ n **3** Sl = **swine**, bounder (old-fashioned Brit sl), cad (Brit inf), rotter (sl, chiefly Brit)

heel² (foll. by over) v = **lean over**, keel over, list, tilt

hefty adj **1** = **big**, burly, hulking, massive, muscular, robust, strapping, strong

height n **1, 2** = **altitude**, elevation, highness, loftiness, stature, tallness **3 a** = **culmination**, climax, limit, maximum, ultimate **b** = **peak**, apex, crest, crown, pinnacle, summit, top, zenith

heighten v = **intensify**, add to, amplify, enhance, improve, increase, magnify, sharpen, strengthen

heir ❶ *n* person entitled to inherit property or rank. **heiress** *n fem* **heir apparent** person whose right to inherit cannot be defeated. **heirloom** *n* object that has belonged to a family for generations. **heir presumptive** heir whose right may be defeated by the birth of a closer relative.

hejab *n* same as HIJAB.

held *v* past of HOLD¹.

helical *adj* spiral.

helices [**hell**-iss-seez] *n* plural of HELIX.

helicopter *n* aircraft lifted and propelled by rotating overhead blades. **heliport** *n* airport for helicopters.

heliograph *n* signalling apparatus that uses a mirror to reflect the sun's rays.

heliotrope *n* **1** plant with purple flowers. ▷ *adj* **2** light purple.

helium [**heel**-ee-um] *n Chemistry* very light colourless odourless gas.

helix [**heel**-iks] *n*, *pl* **helices**, **helixes** spiral.

hell ❶ *n* **1** place believed to be where wicked people go when they die. **2** place or state of wickedness, suffering, or punishment. **hell for leather** at great speed. **hellish** *adj* **hellbent** *adj* (foll. by on) intent.

hellebore *n* plant with white flowers that bloom in winter.

Hellenic *adj* of the (ancient) Greeks or their language.

hello ❶ *interj* expression of greeting or surprise.

helm ❶ *n* tiller or wheel for steering a ship. **at the helm** in a position of leadership or control.

helmet *n* hard hat worn for protection.

help ❶ *v* **1** make something easier, better, or quicker for (someone). **2** improve (a situation). **3** refrain from, e.g. *I can't help smiling.* ▷ *n* **4** assistance or support. **5** person who gives assistance. **help oneself 1** take something, esp. food or drink, without being served. **2** *informal* steal something. **helper** *n* **helpful** *adj* **helpfully** *adv* **helpfulness** *n* **helping** *n* single portion of food. **helpless** *adj* weak or incapable. **helplessly** *adv* **helplessness** *n* **helpline** *n* telephone line set aside for callers to contact an organization for help with a problem. **helpmate** *n* companion and helper, esp. a husband or wife.

helter-skelter ❶ *adj* **1** haphazard and careless. ▷ *adv* **2** in a haphazard and careless manner. ▷ *n* **3** high spiral slide at a fairground.

hem ❶ *n* **1** bottom edge of a garment, folded under and stitched down. ▷ *v* **hemming**, **hemmed 2** provide with a hem. **hem in** *v* surround and prevent from moving. **hemline** *n* level to which the hem of a skirt hangs.

heir *n* = **successor**, beneficiary, heiress (*fem*), inheritor, next in line

hell *n* **1** = **underworld**, abyss, fire and brimstone, Hades (*Greek myth*), hellfire, inferno, nether world **2** = **torment**, agony, anguish, misery, nightmare, ordeal, suffering, wretchedness

hellish *adj* **1** = **devilish**, damnable, diabolical, fiendish, infernal

hello *interj* = **hi** (*inf*), gidday (*Aust & NZ*), good afternoon, good evening, good morning, greetings, how do you do?, welcome

helm *n* = **tiller**, rudder, wheel **at the helm** = **in charge**, at the wheel, in command, in control, in the driving seat, in the saddle

help *v* **1** = **aid**, abet, assist, cooperate, lend a hand, succour, support **2** = **improve**, alleviate, ameliorate, ease, facilitate, mitigate, relieve **3** = **refrain from**, avoid, keep from, prevent, resist ▷ *n* **4** = **assistance**, advice, aid, cooperation, guidance, helping hand, support

helper *n* **1** = **assistant**, aide, ally, attendant, collaborator, helpmate, mate, right-hand man, second, supporter

helpful *adj* **a** = **useful**, advantageous, beneficial, constructive, practical, profitable, timely **b** = **cooperative**, accommodating, considerate, friendly, kind, neighbourly, supportive, sympathetic

helping *n* = **portion**, dollop (*inf*), piece, ration, serving

helpless *adj* = **powerless**, disabled, impotent, incapable, infirm, paralysed, weak

helter-skelter *adj* **1** = **haphazard**, confused, disordered, higgledy-piggledy (*inf*), hit-or-miss, jumbled, muddled, random, topsy-turvy ▷ *adv* **2** = **carelessly**, anyhow, hastily, headlong, hurriedly, pell-mell, rashly, recklessly, wildly

hem *n* **1** = **edge**, border, fringe, margin, trimming

he-man *n informal* strong virile man.
hemisphere *n* half of a sphere, esp. the earth. **hemispherical** *adj*.
hemlock *n* poison made from a plant with spotted stems and small white flowers.
hemp *n* **1** (also **cannabis**) Asian plant with tough fibres. **2** its fibre, used to make canvas and rope. **3** narcotic drug obtained from hemp.
hen ❶ *n* **1** female domestic fowl. **2** female of any bird. **hen night**, **party** party for women only. **henpecked** *adj* (of a man) dominated by his wife.
henbane *n* poisonous plant with sticky hairy leaves.
hence ❶ *conj* **1** for this reason. ▷ *adv* **2** from this time. **henceforth**, **henceforward** *adv* from now on.
henchman ❶ *n* attendant or follower.
henna *n* **1** reddish dye made from a shrub or tree. ▷ *v* **2** dye (the hair) with henna.
henry *n*, *pl* **-ry**, **-ries**, **-rys** unit of electrical inductance.
hepatitis *n* inflammation of the liver.
heptagon *n* geometric figure with seven sides. **heptagonal** *adj*.
heptathlon *n* athletic contest for women, involving seven events.
her *pron* **1** refers to a female person or animal or anything personified as feminine when the object of a sentence or clause. ▷ *adj* **2** belonging to her.
herald ❶ *n* **1** person who announces important news. **2** forerunner. ▷ *v* **3** signal the approach of. **heraldry** *n* study of coats of arms and family trees. **heraldic** *adj*.

herb *n* plant used for flavouring in cookery, and in medicine. **herbal** *adj* **herbalist** *n* person who grows or specializes in the use of medicinal herbs. **herbaceous** *adj* (of a plant) soft-stemmed. **herbaceous border** flowerbed containing perennials rather than annuals. **herbicide** *n* chemical used to destroy plants, esp. weeds. **herbivore** *n* animal that eats only plants. **herbivorous** [her-**biv**-or-uss] *adj*.
herculean [her-kew-**lee**-an] *adj* requiring great strength or effort.
herd ❶ *n* **1** group of animals feeding and living together. **2** large crowd of people. ▷ *v* **3** collect into a herd. **herdsman** *n* man who looks after a herd of animals.
here ❶ *adv* in, at, or to this place or point. **hereabouts** *adv* near here. **hereafter** *adv* after this point or time. **the hereafter** life after death. **hereby** *adv* by means of or as a result of this. **herein** *adv* in this place, matter, or document. **hereinafter** *adv Law* from this point oxn in this document, matter, or case. **heretofore** *adv Law* until now. **herewith** *adv* with this.
heredity ❶ [hir-**red**-it-ee] *n* passing on of characteristics from one generation to another. **hereditary** *adj* **1** passed on genetically from one generation to another. **2** passed on by inheritance.

● **SPELLING TIP**
● There are several ways to misspell
● **hereditary**. The problems always
● come after the *t*, where there should
● be three more letters: *-ary*.

hem in *v* = **surround**, beset, circumscribe, confine, enclose, restrict, shut in
hence *conj* **1** = **therefore**, ergo, for this reason, on that account, thus
henchman *n* = **attendant**, associate, bodyguard, follower, minder (*sl*), right-hand man, sidekick (*sl*), subordinate, supporter
henpecked *adj* = **dominated**, browbeaten, bullied, meek, subjugated, timid
herald *n* **1** = **messenger**, crier **2** = **forerunner**, harbinger, indication, omen, precursor, sign, signal, token ▷ *v* **3** = **indicate**, foretoken, portend,

presage, promise, show, usher in
herd *n* **1** = **flock**, drove **2** = **crowd**, collection, horde, mass, mob, multitude, swarm, throng ▷ *v* **3** = **congregate**, assemble, collect, flock, gather, huddle, muster, rally
hereafter *adv* = **in future**, from now on, hence, henceforth, henceforward **the hereafter** = **afterlife**, life after death, next world
hereditary *adj* **1** = **genetic**, inborn, inbred, inheritable, transmissible **2** = **inherited**, ancestral, traditional
heredity *n* = **genetics**, constitution, genetic make-up, inheritance

heresy ❶ [**herr**-iss-ee] *n, pl* **-sies** opinion contrary to accepted opinion or belief. **heretic** [**herr**-it-ik] *n* person who holds unorthodox opinions. **heretical** [hir-**ret**-ik-al] *adj*.

heritage ❶ *n* **1** something inherited. **2** anything from the past, considered as the inheritance of present-day society.

hermaphrodite [her-**maf**-roe-dite] *n* animal, plant, or person with both male and female reproductive organs.

hermetic *adj* sealed so as to be airtight. **hermetically** *adv*.

hermit ❶ *n* person living in solitude, esp. for religious reasons. **hermitage** *n* home of a hermit. **hermit crab** small crab that lives in the shells of other shellfish.

hernia *n* protrusion of an organ or part through the lining of the surrounding body cavity.

hero ❶ *n, pl* **heroes** **1** principal character in a film, book, etc. **2** man greatly admired for his exceptional qualities or achievements. **heroine** *n fem* **heroic** *adj* **1** courageous. **2** of or like a hero. **heroics** *pl n* extravagant behaviour. **heroically** *adv* **heroism** [**herr**-oh-izz-um] *n*.

heroin *n* highly addictive drug derived from morphine.

heron *n* long-legged wading bird.

herpes [**her**-peez] *n* any of several inflammatory skin diseases, including shingles and cold sores.

Herr [**hair**] *n, pl* **Herren** German term of address equivalent to *Mr*.

herring *n* important food fish of northern seas. **herringbone** *n* pattern of zigzag lines.

hers *pron* something belonging to her.

herself *pron* emphatic or reflexive form of SHE or HER.

hertz *n, pl* **hertz** *Physics* unit of frequency.

hesitate ❶ *v* **1** be slow or uncertain in doing something. **2** be reluctant (to do something). **hesitation** *n* **hesitant** *adj* undecided or wavering. **hesitantly** *adv* **hesitancy** *n*.

hessian *n* coarse jute fabric.

hetero- *combining form* other, different, e.g. *heterosexual*.

heterodox *adj* differing from accepted doctrines or beliefs. **heterodoxy** *n*.

heterogeneous [het-er-oh-**jean**-ee-uss] *adj* composed of diverse elements. **heterogeneity** *n*.

heterosexual *n, adj* (person) sexually attracted to members of the opposite sex. **heterosexuality** *n*.

het up *adj informal* agitated or anxious.

heuristic [**hew**-rist-ik] *adj* involving learning by investigation.

hew ❶ *v* **hewing**, **hewed**, **hewed** or **hewn 1** cut with an axe. **2** carve from a substance.

hexagon *n* geometrical figure with six sides. **hexagonal** *adj*.

hexagram *n* star formed by extending the sides of a regular hexagon to meet at six points.

hey *interj* expression of surprise or for catching attention. **hey presto!** exclamation used by conjurors at the climax of a trick.

h

THESAURUS

heresy *n* = **unorthodoxy**, apostasy, dissidence, heterodoxy, iconoclasm

heretic *n* = **nonconformist**, apostate, dissenter, dissident, renegade, revisionist

heretical *adj* = **unorthodox**, heterodox, iconoclastic, idolatrous, impious, revisionist

heritage *n* **1** = **inheritance**, bequest, birthright, endowment, legacy

hermit *n* = **recluse**, anchorite, loner (*inf*), monk

hero *n* **1** = **leading man**, protagonist **2** = **idol**, champion, conqueror, star, superstar, victor

heroic *adj* = **courageous**, brave, daring, fearless, gallant, intrepid, lion-hearted, valiant

heroine *n* **1** = **leading lady**, diva, prima donna, protagonist

heroism *n* **1** = **bravery**, courage, courageousness, fearlessness, gallantry, intrepidity, spirit, valour

hesitant *adj* = **uncertain**, diffident, doubtful, half-hearted, halting, irresolute, reluctant, unsure, vacillating, wavering

hesitate *v* **1** = **waver**, delay, dither, doubt, hum and haw, pause, vacillate, wait **2** = **be reluctant**, balk, be unwilling, demur, hang back, scruple, shrink from, think twice

hesitation *n* **1** = **indecision**, delay, doubt, hesitancy, irresolution, uncertainty, vacillation **2** = **reluctance**, misgiving(s), qualm(s), scruple(s), unwillingness

hew *v* **1** = **cut**, axe, chop, hack, lop, split **2** = **carve**, fashion, form, make, model, sculpt, sculpture, shape, smooth

heyday ❶ *n* time of greatest success, prime.

Hf *Chemistry* hafnium.

Hg *Chemistry* mercury.

HGV (formerly) heavy goods vehicle.

hi *interj informal* hello.

HI Hawaii.

hiatus ❶ [hie-**ay**-tuss] *n, pl* **-tuses**, **-tus** pause or interruption in continuity.

hibernate *v* (of an animal) pass the winter as if in a deep sleep. **hibernation** *n*.

Hibernian *adj poetic* Irish.

hibiscus *n, pl* **-cuses** tropical plant with large brightly coloured flowers.

hiccup, hiccough *n* **1** spasm of the breathing organs with a sharp coughlike sound. **2** *informal* small problem, hitch. ▷ *v* **3** make a hiccup.

hick *n US & Aust informal* unsophisticated country person.

hickory *n, pl* **-ries 1** N American nut-bearing tree. **2** its wood.

hide¹ ❶ *v* **hiding**, **hid**, **hidden 1** put (oneself or an object) somewhere difficult to see or find. **2** keep secret. ▷ *n* **3** place of concealment, esp. for a bird-watcher. **hiding** *n* state of concealment, e.g. *in hiding*. **hidden agenda** motives or intentions concealed from others who might object to them. **hideaway** *n* private place. **hide-out** *n* place to hide in.

hide² ❶ *n* skin of an animal. **hiding** *n slang* severe beating. **hidebound** *adj* unwilling to accept new ideas.

hideous ❶ [**hid**-ee-uss] *adj* ugly, revolting. **hideously** *adv*.

hie *v* **hying** *or* **hieing**, **hied** *obs* hurry.

hierarchy ❶ [**hire**-ark-ee] *n, pl* **-chies** system of people or things arranged in a graded order. **hierarchical** *adj*.

hieroglyphic [hire-oh-**gliff**-ik] *adj* **1** of a form of writing using picture symbols, as used in ancient Egypt. ▷ *n* **2** symbol that is difficult to decipher. **3** (also **hieroglyph**) symbol representing an object, idea, or sound.

hi-fi *n* **1** set of high-quality sound-reproducing equipment. ▷ *adj* **2** high-fidelity.

higgledy-piggledy *adv, adj* in a muddle.

high ❶ *adj* **1** of a great height. **2** far above ground or sea level. **3** being at its peak. **4** greater than usual in intensity or amount. **5** (of a sound) acute in pitch. **6** (of food) slightly decomposed. **7** of great importance, quality, or rank. **8** *informal* under the influence of alcohol or drugs. ▷ *adv* **9** at or to a high level. ▷ *n* **10 on a high** *informal* very excited and happy, (as if) intoxicated by alcohol or drugs. **highly** *adv* **highly strung** nervous and easily upset. **Highness** *n* title used to address or refer to a royal person. **High-Church** *adj* belonging to a section within the Church of England stressing the importance of ceremony and ritual. **high commissioner** senior diplomatic representative sent by one

——————————————————————— THESAURUS ————————

heyday *n* = **prime**, bloom, pink, prime of life, salad days

hiatus *n* = **pause**, break, discontinuity, gap, interruption, interval, respite, space

hidden *adj* = **concealed**, clandestine, covert, latent, secret, under wraps, unseen, veiled

hide¹ *v* **1 a** = **go into hiding**, go to ground, go underground, hole up, lie low, take cover **b** = **conceal**, camouflage, cloak, cover, disguise, mask, obscure, secrete, shroud, stash (*inf*), veil **2** = **suppress**, draw a veil over, hush up, keep dark, keep secret, keep under one's hat, withhold

hide² *n* = **skin**, pelt

hidebound *adj* = **conventional**, narrow-minded, rigid, set in one's ways, strait-laced, ultraconservative

hideous *adj* = **ugly**, ghastly, grim, grisly, grotesque, gruesome, monstrous, repulsive, revolting, unsightly

hide-out *n* = **hiding place**, den, hideaway, lair, shelter

hiding *n* = **beating**, drubbing, licking (*inf*), spanking, thrashing, walloping (*inf*), whipping

hierarchy *n* = **grading**, pecking order, ranking

high *adj* **1, 2** = **tall**, elevated, lofty, soaring, steep, towering **4** = **extreme**, excessive, extraordinary, great, intensified, sharp, strong **5** = **high-pitched**, acute, penetrating, piercing, piping, sharp, shrill, strident **7** = **important**, arch, chief, eminent, exalted, powerful, superior, skookum (*Canad*) **8** *Inf* = **intoxicated**, stoned (*sl*), tripping (*inf*) ▷ *adv* **9** = **aloft**, at great height, far up, way up

Commonwealth country to another. **higher education** education at colleges and universities. **high explosive** extremely powerful chemical explosive, such as TNT. **high-fidelity** *adj* able to reproduce sound with little or no distortion. **high-flown** *adj* (of language) extravagant or pretentious. **high-handed** *adj* excessively forceful. **high jump** athletic event in which competitors attempt to jump over a high bar. **high-minded** *adj* having high moral principles. **high-powered** *adj* dynamic and energetic. **high priest** head of a cult. **high priestess** *n fem* **high-rise** *adj* (of a building) having many storeys. **high school** secondary school. **high-spirited** *adj* lively, fun-loving. **high tea** early evening meal consisting of a cooked dish, bread, cakes, and tea. **high technology** use of advanced electronic processes in industry. **high time** latest possible time.

highball *n US* tall drink of whiskey with soda water or ginger ale and ice.

highbrow ❶ *adj, n* intellectual and serious (person).

highchair *n* long-legged chair with a tray attached, used by a very young child at mealtimes.

highfalutin [hie-fa-**loot**-in] *adj informal* pompous or pretentious.

Highland *adj* of the Highlands, a mountainous region of N Scotland.

Highlander *n*.

highlands *pl n* area of high ground.

highlight ❶ *n* **1** outstanding part or feature. **2** light-toned area in a painting or photograph. **3** lightened streak in the hair. ▷ *v* **4** give emphasis to.

highway *n US & Canad* main road for fast-moving traffic. **Highway Code** regulations and recommendations applying to all road users.

highwayman *n* (formerly) robber, usu. on horseback, who robbed travellers at gunpoint.

hijab, **hejab** *n* covering for the head and face, worn by some Muslim women.

hijack ❶ *v* seize control of (an aircraft or other vehicle) while travelling. **hijacker** *n* **hijacking** *n*.

hike ❶ *n* **1** long walk in the country, esp. for pleasure. **2** rise in price. ▷ *v* **3** go for a long walk. **4** (foll. by *up*) pull (up) or raise. **hiker** *n*.

hilarious ❶ *adj* very funny. **hilariously** *adv* **hilarity** *n*.

hill ❶ *n* raised part of the earth's surface, less high than a mountain. **hilly** *adj* **hillier**, **hilliest**. **hillock** *n* small hill. **hillbilly** *n, pl* **-billies** *US* unsophisticated country person.

hilt ❶ *n* handle of a sword or knife. **to the hilt**, **up to the hilt** to the full.

him *pron* refers to a male person or animal when the object of a sentence or clause. **himself** *pron* emphatic or reflexive form of HE or HIM.

h

---

highbrow *adj* = **intellectual**, bookish, cultivated, cultured, sophisticated ▷ *n* = **intellectual**, aesthete, egghead (*inf*), scholar

high-flown *adj* = **extravagant**, elaborate, exaggerated, florid, grandiose, inflated, lofty, overblown, pretentious

high-handed *adj* = **dictatorial**, despotic, domineering, imperious, oppressive, overbearing, tyrannical, wilful

highlight *n* **1** = **high point**, climax, feature, focal point, focus, high spot, peak ▷ *v* **4** = **emphasize**, accent, accentuate, bring to the fore, show up, spotlight, stress, underline

highly *adv* **4** = **extremely**, exceptionally, greatly, immensely, tremendously, vastly, very, very much **highly strung** = **nervous**, edgy, excitable, neurotic,

sensitive, stressed, temperamental, tense, wired (*sl*)

hijack *v* = **seize**, commandeer, expropriate, take over

hike *n* **1** = **walk**, march, ramble, tramp, trek ▷ *v* **3** = **walk**, back-pack, ramble, tramp **4** (foll. by *up*) = **raise**, hitch up, jack up, lift, pull up

hilarious *adj* = **funny**, amusing, comical, entertaining, humorous, rollicking, side-splitting, uproarious

hilarity *n* = **merriment**, amusement, exhilaration, glee, high spirits, jollity, laughter, mirth

hill *n* = **mount**, fell, height, hillock, hilltop, knoll, mound, tor

hillock *n* = **mound**, hummock, knoll

hilly *adj* = **mountainous**, rolling, undulating

hilt *n* = **handle**, grip, haft, handgrip

hind¹ ⊙ *adj* **hinder**, **hindmost** situated at the back. **hindsight** *n* ability to understand, after something has happened, what should have been done.

hind² *n* female deer.

hinder ⊙ *v* get in the way of. **hindrance** *n*.

Hinduism *n* dominant religion of India, which involves the worship of many gods and a belief in reincarnation. **Hindu** *n* **1** person who practises Hinduism. ▷ *adj* **2** of Hinduism. **Hindi** *n* language of N central India. **Hindustani** *n* group of N Indian languages including Hindi and Urdu.

hinge ⊙ *n* **1** device for holding together two parts so that one can swing freely. ▷ *v* **2** (foll. by *on*) depend (on). **3** fit a hinge to.

hint ⊙ *n* **1** indirect suggestion. **2** piece of advice. **3** small amount. ▷ *v* **4** suggest indirectly.

hinterland *n* land lying behind a coast or near a city, esp. a port.

hip¹ *n* either side of the body between the waist and the thigh.

hip² *n* rosehip.

hip³ *adj* **hipper**, **hippest** *slang* aware of or following the latest trends.

hip-hop *n* pop-culture movement of the 1980s, comprising rap music, graffiti, and break dancing.

hippie *adj*, *n* same as HIPPY.

hippo *n*, *pl* **-pos** *informal* hippopotamus.

Hippocratic oath *n* oath taken by doctors to observe a code of medical ethics.

hippodrome *n* music hall, variety theatre, or circus.

hippopotamus *n*, *pl* **-muses**, **-mi** large African mammal with thick wrinkled skin, living near rivers.

hippy ⊙ *adj*, *n*, *pl* **-pies** (esp. in the 1960s) (of) a person whose behaviour and dress imply a rejection of conventional values.

hire ⊙ *v* **1** pay to have temporary use of. **2** employ for wages. ▷ *n* **3** hiring. **for hire** available to be hired. **hireling** *n* person who works only for wages. **hire-purchase** *n* system of purchase by which the buyer pays for goods by instalments.

hirsute [**her**-suit] *adj* hairy.

his *pron*, *adj* (something) belonging to him.

Hispanic *adj* Spanish or Latin-American.

hiss ⊙ *n* **1** sound like that of a long *s* (as an expression of contempt). ▷ *v* **2** utter a hiss. **3** show derision or anger towards.

histamine [**hiss**-ta-meen] *n* substance released by the body tissues in allergic reactions.

histogram *n* statistical graph in which the frequency of values is represented by vertical bars of varying heights and widths.

histology *n* study of the tissues of an animal or plant. **histological** *adj*.

history ⊙ *n*, *pl* **-ries** **1** (record or account of) past events and developments. **2** study of these. **3** record of someone's past. **historian** *n* writer of history. **historic** *adj* famous or significant in

——————————————————— THESAURUS ———————————————————

hinder *v* = **obstruct**, block, check, delay, encumber, frustrate, hamper, handicap, hold up *or* back, impede, interrupt, stop

hinder, hindmost *adj* = **last**, final, furthest, furthest behind, rearmost, trailing

hindrance *n* = **obstacle**, barrier, deterrent, difficulty, drawback, handicap, hitch, impediment, obstruction, restriction, snag, stumbling block

hinge *v* **2** (foll. by *on*) = **depend on**, be contingent on, hang on, pivot on, rest on, revolve around, turn on

hint *n* **1** = **indication**, allusion, clue, implication, innuendo, insinuation, intimation, suggestion **2** = **advice**, help, pointer, suggestion, tip **3** = **trace**, dash, suggestion, suspicion, tinge,

touch, undertone ▷ *v* **4** = **suggest**, imply, indicate, insinuate, intimate

hippy *n* = **bohemian**, beatnik, dropout

hire *v* **1** = **rent**, charter, engage, lease, let **2** = **employ**, appoint, commission, engage, sign up, take on ▷ *n* **3** = **rental**

hiss *n* **1 a** = **sibilation**, buzz, hissing **b** = **catcall**, boo, jeer ▷ *v* **2** = **whistle**, sibilate, wheeze, whirr, whiz **3** = **jeer**, boo, deride, hoot, mock

historic *adj* = **significant**, epoch-making, extraordinary, famous, ground-breaking, momentous, notable, outstanding, remarkable

historical *adj* **2** = **factual**, actual, attested, authentic, documented, real

history *n* **1 a** = **chronicle**, account, annals, narrative, recital, record, story **b** = **the past**, antiquity, olden days, yesterday, yesteryear

h

history. **historical** *adj* **1** occurring in the past. **2** based on history. **historically** *adv*.

histrionic *adj* excessively dramatic. **histrionics** *pl n* excessively dramatic behaviour.

hit ❶ *v* **hitting**, **hit 1** strike, touch forcefully. **2** come into violent contact with. **3** affect badly. **4** reach (a point or place). ▷ *n* **5** hitting. **6** successful record, film, etc. **7** *Computers* single visit to a website. **hit it off** *informal* get on well together. **hit the road** *informal* start a journey. **hit-and-miss**, **hit-or-miss** *adj* sometimes successful and sometimes not. **hit-and-run** *adj* denoting a motor-vehicle accident in which a driver drives away without stopping. **hit man** hired assassin. **hit on** *v* think of (an idea).

hitch ❶ *n* **1** minor problem. ▷ *v* **2** *informal* obtain (a lift) by hitchhiking. **3** fasten with a knot or tie. **4** (foll. by *up*) pull up with a jerk. **get hitched** *slang* get married. **hitchhike** *v* travel by obtaining free lifts. **hitchhiker** *n*.

hi-tech *adj* using sophisticated technology.

hither ❶ *adv* *old-fashioned* to or towards this place. **hitherto** *adv* until this time.

HIV human immunodeficiency virus, the cause of AIDS.

hive *n* same as BEEHIVE. **hive of activity** place where people are very busy. **hive off** *v* separate from a larger group.

hives *n* allergic reaction in which itchy red or whitish patches appear on the skin.

HM Her (or His) Majesty.

HMI Her (or His) Majesty's Inspector (of schools).

HMS Her (or His) Majesty's Ship.

HMSO Her (or His) Majesty's Stationery Office.

HNC Higher National Certificate.

HND Higher National Diploma.

Ho *Chemistry* holmium.

hoard ❶ *n* **1** store hidden away for future use. ▷ *v* **2** save or store. **hoarder** *n*.

hoarding *n* large board for displaying advertisements.

hoarfrost *n* white ground frost.

hoarse ❶ *adj* **1** (of a voice) rough and unclear. **2** having a rough and unclear voice. **hoarsely** *adv* **hoarseness** *n*.

hoary *adj* **hoarier**, **hoariest 1** grey or white(-haired). **2** very old.

hoax ❶ *n* **1** deception or trick. ▷ *v* **2** deceive or play a trick upon. **hoaxer** *n*.

hob *n* flat top part of a cooker, or a separate flat surface, containing gas or electric rings for cooking on.

hobble *v* **1** walk lamely. **2** tie the legs of (a horse) together.

hit *v* **1** = **strike**, bang, beat, clout (*inf*), knock, slap, smack, thump, wallop (*inf*), whack **2** = **collide with**, bang into, bump, clash with, crash against, run into, smash into **3** = **affect**, damage, devastate, impact on, influence, leave a mark on, overwhelm, touch **4** = **reach**, accomplish, achieve, arrive at, attain, gain ▷ *n* **5** = **stroke**, belt (*inf*), blow, clout (*inf*), knock, rap, slap, smack, wallop (*inf*) **6** = **success**, sensation, smash (*inf*), triumph, winner **hit it off** *Inf* = **get on (well) with**, be on good terms, click (*sl*), get on like a house on fire (*inf*)

hit-and-miss, **hit-or-miss** *adj* = **haphazard**, aimless, casual, disorganized, indiscriminate, random, undirected, uneven

hitch *n* **1** = **problem**, catch, difficulty, drawback, hindrance, hold-up, impediment, obstacle, snag ▷ *v* **2** *Inf*

= **hitchhike**, thumb a lift **3** = **fasten**, attach, connect, couple, harness, join, tether, tie **4** (foll. by *up*) = **pull up**, jerk, tug, yank

hitherto *adv* = **previously**, heretofore, so far, thus far, until now

hit on *v* = **think up**, arrive at, discover, invent, light upon, strike upon, stumble on

hoard *n* **1** = **store**, accumulation, cache, fund, pile, reserve, stash, stockpile, supply, treasure-trove ▷ *v* **2** = **save**, accumulate, amass, collect, gather, lay up, put by, stash away (*inf*), stockpile, store

hoarse *adj* **1** = **rough**, croaky, grating, gravelly, gruff, guttural, husky, rasping, raucous, throaty

hoax *n* **1** = **trick**, con (*inf*), deception, fraud, practical joke, prank, spoof (*inf*), swindle ▷ *v* **2** = **deceive**, con (*sl*), dupe, fool, hoodwink, swindle, take in (*inf*), trick

hobby ❶ *n, pl* **-bies** activity pursued in one's spare time. **hobbyhorse** *n* **1** favourite topic. **2** toy horse.

hobgoblin *n* mischievous goblin.

hobnail boots *pl n* heavy boots with short nails in the soles.

hobnob ❶ *v* **-nobbing, -nobbed** (foll. by *with*) be on friendly terms (with).

hobo *n, pl* **-bos** *US & Aust* tramp or vagrant.

Hobson's choice *n* the choice of taking what is offered or nothing at all.

hock¹ *n* joint in the back leg of an animal such as a horse that corresponds to the human ankle.

hock² *n* white German wine.

hock³ *v informal* pawn. **in hock** *informal* in debt.

hockey *n* **1** team game played on a field with a ball and curved sticks. **2** *US & Canad* ice hockey.

hocus-pocus *n* trickery.

hod *n* open wooden box attached to a pole, for carrying bricks or mortar.

hoe *n* **1** long-handled tool used for loosening soil or weeding. ▷ *v* **2** scrape or weed with a hoe.

hog *n* **1** castrated male pig. **2** *informal* greedy person. ▷ *v* **hogging, hogged** **3** *informal* take more than one's share of. **go the whole hog** *slang* do something thoroughly or unreservedly. **hogshead** *n* large cask. **hogwash** *n informal* nonsense.

Hogmanay *n* (in Scotland) New Year's Eve.

ho-ho *interj* representation of the sound of laughter.

hoick *v* raise abruptly and sharply.

hoi polloi *n* the ordinary people.

hoist ❶ *v* **1** raise or lift up. ▷ *n* **2** device for lifting things.

hoity-toity *adj informal* arrogant or haughty.

hokum *n US slang* **1** rubbish, nonsense. **2** stereotyped sentimentality in a film or play.

hold¹ ❶ *v* **holding, held** **1** keep or support in or with the hands or arms. **2** arrange for (a meeting, party, etc.) to take place. **3** consider to be as specified, e.g. *who are you holding responsible?* **4** maintain in a specified position or state. **5** have the capacity for. **6** *informal* wait, esp. on the telephone. **7** reserve (a room etc.). **8** restrain or keep back. **9** own, possess. **10** (cause to) remain committed to (a promise etc.). **11** believe. ▷ *n* **12** act or way of holding. **13** controlling influence. **14** something to hold onto for support. **holder** *n* **holding** *n* property, such as land or stocks and shares. **holdall** *n* large strong travelling bag. **hold forth** *v* speak for a long time. **hold-up** *n* **1** armed robbery. **2** delay. **hold up** *v* **hold with** *v* approve of, e.g. *I don't hold with this theory*.

hold² *n* cargo compartment in a ship or aircraft.

hole ❶ *n* **1** area hollowed out in a solid. **2** opening or hollow. **3** animal's burrow. **4** *informal* unattractive place. **5** *informal*

──────── THESAURUS ────────

hobby *n* = **pastime**, diversion, (leisure) activity, leisure pursuit, relaxation

hobnob *v* (foll. by *with*) = **socialize**, associate, consort, fraternize, hang about, hang out (*inf*), keep company, mingle, mix

hoist *v* **1** = **raise**, elevate, erect, heave, lift ▷ *n* **2** = **lift**, crane, elevator, winch

hold¹ *v* **1** = **grasp**, clasp, cling, clutch, cradle, embrace, enfold, grip **2** = **convene**, call, conduct, preside over, run **5** = **accommodate**, contain, have a capacity for, seat, take **8** = **restrain**, confine, detain, impound, imprison **9** = **own**, have, keep, maintain, occupy, possess, retain **11** = **consider**, assume, believe, deem, judge, presume, reckon, regard, think ▷ *n* **12** = **grip**, clasp, grasp **13** = **control**, influence, mana (*NZ*), mastery **14** = **foothold**, footing, support

hold forth *v* = **speak**, declaim,

discourse, go on, lecture, preach, spiel (*inf*), spout (*inf*)

hold-up *n* **1** = **robbery**, mugging (*inf*), stick-up (*sl, chiefly US*), theft **2** = **delay**, bottleneck, hitch, setback, snag, stoppage, traffic jam, wait

hold up *v* **1** = **rob**, mug (*inf*), waylay **2** = **delay**, detain, hinder, retard, set back, slow down, stop

hold with *v* = **approve of**, agree to *or* with, be in favour of, countenance, subscribe to, support

hole *n* **1** = **cavity**, cave, cavern, chamber, hollow, pit **2** = **opening**, aperture, breach, crack, fissure, gap, orifice, perforation, puncture, tear, vent **3** = **burrow**, den, earth, lair, shelter **4** *Inf* = **hovel**, dive (*sl*), dump (*inf*), slum **5** *Inf* = **predicament**, dilemma, fix (*inf*), hot water (*inf*), jam (*inf*), mess, scrape (*inf*), spot (*inf*), tight spot

difficult situation. ▷ *v* **6** make holes in. **7** hit (a golf ball) into the target hole. **holey** *adj* **hole up** *v informal* go into hiding.

holiday ❶ *n* **1** time spent away from home for rest or recreation. **2** day or other period of rest from work or studies.

holiness ❶ *n* **1** state of being holy. **2** (H-) title used to address or refer to the Pope.

holistic *adj* considering the complete person, physically and mentally, in the treatment of an illness. **holism** *n*.

holler *v*, *n informal* shout, yell.

hollow ❶ *adj* **1** having a hole or space inside. **2** (of a sound) as if echoing in a hollow place. **3** without any real value or worth. ▷ *n* **4** cavity or space. **5** dip in the land. ▷ *v* **6** form a hollow in. **hollowly** *adv* **hollowness** *n*.

holly *n* evergreen tree with prickly leaves and red berries.

hollyhock *n* tall garden plant with spikes of colourful flowers.

holmium *n Chemistry* silver-white metallic element, the compounds of which are highly magnetic.

holm oak *n* evergreen oak tree with prickly leaves.

holocaust ❶ *n* destruction or loss of life on a massive scale.

hologram *n* three-dimensional photographic image.

holograph *n* document handwritten by the author.

holography *n* science of using lasers to produce holograms. **holographic** *adj*.

holster *n* leather case for a pistol, hung from a belt.

holt *n* otter's lair.

holy ❶ *adj* **-lier**, **-liest** **1** of God or a god. **2** devout or virtuous. **holier-than-thou** *adj* self-righteous. **Holy Communion** *Christianity* service in which people take bread and wine in remembrance of the death and resurrection of Jesus Christ. **Holy Grail** (in medieval legend) the bowl used by Jesus Christ at the Last Supper. **holy orders** status of an ordained Christian minister. **Holy Spirit**, **Ghost** *Christianity* one of the three aspects of God. **Holy Week** *Christianity* week before Easter.

homage ❶ *n* show of respect or honour towards someone or something.

homburg *n* man's soft felt hat with a dented crown and a stiff upturned brim.

home ❶ *n* **1** place where one lives. **2** place where one was born or grew up. **3** institution for the care of the elderly, orphans, etc. ▷ *adj* **4** of one's home, birthplace, or native country. **5** *Sport* played on one's own ground. ▷ *adv* **6** to or at home. ▷ *v* **7** (foll. by *in* or *in on*) direct towards (a point or target). **at home** at ease. **bring home to** make clear to. **home and dry** *informal* safe or successful. **homeless** *adj* **1** having nowhere to live. ▷ *pl n* **2** people who have nowhere to live. **homelessness** *n* **homely** *adj* **1** simple, ordinary, and comfortable. **2** *US* unattractive. **homeliness** *n* **home page** *Computers* introductory information about a website with hyperlinks to further pages. **homeward** *adj*, *adv* **homewards** *adv*

---

holiday *n* **1** = **vacation**, break, leave, recess, time off **2** = **festival**, celebration, feast, fete, gala

holiness *n* **1** = **sanctity**, divinity, godliness, piety, purity, righteousness, sacredness, saintliness, spirituality

hollow *adj* **1** = **empty**, unfilled, vacant, void **2** = **toneless**, deep, dull, low, muted, reverberant **3** = **worthless**, fruitless, futile, meaningless, pointless, useless, vain ▷ *n* **4** = **cavity**, basin, bowl, crater, depression, hole, pit, trough **5** = **valley**, dale, dell, dingle, glen ▷ *v* **6** = **scoop**, dig, excavate, gouge

holocaust *n* = **genocide**, annihilation, conflagration, destruction, devastation, massacre

holy *adj* **1** = **sacred**, blessed, consecrated, hallowed, sacrosanct, sanctified, venerable **2** = **devout**, god-fearing, godly, pious, pure, religious, righteous, saintly, virtuous

homage *n* = **respect**, adoration, adulation, deference, devotion, honour, reverence, worship

home *n* **1** = **dwelling**, abode, domicile, habitation, house, pad (*sl*), residence **2** = **birthplace**, home town ▷ *adj* **4** = **domestic**, familiar, internal, local, native **at home** = **at ease**, comfortable, familiar, relaxed **bring home to** = **make clear**, drive home, emphasize, impress upon, press home

home-brew n beer made at home.
home economics study of subjects concerned with running a home. **home help** person employed by a local authority to do housework in an elderly or disabled person's home. **home-made** adj made at home or on the premises. **Home Office** government department responsible for law and order, immigration, and other domestic matters. **Home Secretary** head of the Home Office. **home truths** unpleasant facts told to a person about himself or herself.

homeland ❶ n country from which a person's ancestors came.

homeopathy [home-ee-**op**-ath-ee] n treatment of disease by small doses of a drug that produces symptoms of the disease in healthy people. **homeopath** n person who practises homeopathy. **homeopathic** [home-ee-oh-**path**-ik] adj.

homesick adj sad because missing one's home and family. **homesickness** n.

homestead n **1** a house or estate and the adjoining land and buildings, esp. on a farm. **2** land assigned to a N American settler.

homework n school work done at home.

homicide ❶ n **1** killing of a human being. **2** person who kills someone. **homicidal** adj.

homily ❶ n, pl -**lies** speech telling people how they should behave.

homing pigeon n pigeon trained to return home after travelling great distances, kept for racing.

hominid n man or any extinct forerunner of man.

hominoid adj, n manlike (animal).

homo- combining form same, like, e.g. homosexual.

homogeneous ❶ [home-oh-**jean**-ee-uss] adj formed of similar parts. **homogeneity** n **homogenize** v **1** break up fat globules in (milk or cream) to distribute them evenly. **2** make homogeneous.

homograph n word spelt the same as another, but with a different meaning.

homologous [hom-**ol**-log-uss] adj having a related or similar position or structure.

homonym n word spelt or pronounced the same as another, but with a different meaning.

homophobia n hatred or fear of homosexuals. **homophobic** adj.

homophone n word pronounced the same as another, but with a different meaning or spelling.

Homo sapiens [hoe-moh **sap**-ee-enz] n human beings as a species.

homosexual n, adj (person) sexually attracted to members of the same sex. **homosexuality** n.

Hon. Honourable.

hone ❶ v sharpen.

honest ❶ adj **1** truthful and moral. **2** open and sincere. **honestly** adv **honesty** n **1** quality of being honest. **2** plant with silvery seed pods.

honey n **1** sweet edible sticky substance made by bees from nectar. **2** term of endearment. **honeyed** adj poetic

─────────────── THESAURUS ───────────────

homeland n = **native land**, country of origin, fatherland, mother country, motherland

homeless adj **1** = **destitute**, displaced, dispossessed, down-and-out ▷ pl n **2** = **vagrants**, squatters

homely adj **1** = **comfortable**, cosy, friendly, homespun, modest, ordinary, plain, simple, welcoming

homicidal adj = **murderous**, deadly, lethal, maniacal, mortal

homicide n **1** = **murder**, bloodshed, killing, manslaughter, slaying **2** = **murderer**, killer, slayer

homily n = **sermon**, address, discourse, lecture, preaching

homogeneity n = **uniformity**, consistency, correspondence, sameness, similarity

homogeneous adj = **uniform**, akin, alike, analogous, comparable, consistent, identical, similar, unvarying

homosexual n = **gay**, lesbian ▷ adj = **gay**, lesbian

hone v = **sharpen**, edge, file, grind, point, polish, whet

honest adj **1** = **trustworthy**, ethical, honourable, law-abiding, reputable, scrupulous, truthful, upright, virtuous **2** = **open**, candid, direct, forthright, frank, plain, sincere, upfront (inf)

honestly adv **1** = **ethically**, by fair means, cleanly, honourably, lawfully, legally **2** = **frankly**, candidly, in all sincerity, plainly, straight (out), to one's face, truthfully

honesty n **1** = **integrity**, honour, incorruptibility, morality, probity,

flattering or soothing, e.g. *honeyed words*. **honeycomb** *n* waxy structure of six-sided cells in which honey is stored by bees in a beehive. **honeydew melon** melon with a yellow skin and sweet pale flesh. **honey-eater** *n* small Australasian songbird with a brushlike tongue used for extracting nectar from flowers. **honeymoon** *n* holiday taken by a newly married couple. **honeysuckle** *n* **1** climbing shrub with sweet-smelling flowers. **2** Australian tree or shrub with flowers in dense spikes.

honk *n* **1** sound made by a car horn. **2** sound made by a goose. ▷ *v* **3** (cause to) make this sound.

honour ❶ *n* **1** sense of honesty and fairness. **2** (award given out of) respect. **3** pleasure or privilege. ▷ *pl* **4** university degree of a higher standard than an ordinary degree. ▷ *v* **5** give praise and attention to. **6** give an award to (someone) out of respect. **7** accept or pay (a cheque or bill). **8** keep (a promise). **do the honours** act as host or hostess by pouring drinks or giving out food. **honourable** *adj* **1** worthy of respect or esteem. **2** (**H-**) denoting a title of respect placed before the names of some members of the nobility, judges, etc. **honourably** *adv* **honorary** *adj* **1** held or given only as an honour. **2** unpaid. **honorific** *adj* showing respect.

hooch [rhymes with **smooch**] *n US slang* alcoholic drink, esp. illicitly distilled spirits.

hood¹ *n* **1** head covering, often attached to a coat or jacket. **2** folding roof of a convertible car or a pram. **3** *US & Aust* car bonnet. **hooded** *adj* **1** (of a garment) having a hood. **2** (of eyes) having heavy eyelids that appear to be half-closed.

hood² *n slang* hoodlum.

hoodie *n informal* **1** hooded sweatshirt. **2** young person who wears a hooded sweatshirt.

hoodlum *n slang* violent criminal, gangster.

hoodoo *n, pl* -**doos** (cause of) bad luck.

hoodwink ❶ *v* trick, deceive.

hooey *n slang* nonsense.

hoof *n, pl* **hooves**, **hoofs** horny covering of the foot of a horse, deer, etc. **hoof it** *slang* walk.

hoo-ha *n* fuss or commotion.

hook ❶ *n* **1** curved piece of metal, plastic, etc., used to hang, hold, or pull something. **2** short swinging punch. ▷ *v* **3** fasten or catch (as if) with a hook. **hooked** *adj* **1** bent like a hook. **2** (foll. by *on*) *slang* addicted (to) or obsessed (with). **hooker** *n* **1** *slang* prostitute. **2** *Rugby* player who uses his feet to get the ball in a scrum. **hook-up** *n* linking of radio or television stations. **hookworm** *n* blood-sucking worm with hooked mouthparts.

hookah *n* oriental pipe in which smoke is drawn through water and a long tube.

THESAURUS

rectitude, scrupulousness, trustworthiness, truthfulness, uprightness, virtue **2** = **frankness**, bluntness, candour, openness, outspokenness, sincerity, straightforwardness

honorary *adj* **1** = **nominal**, complimentary, in name *or* title only, titular, unofficial **2** = **unpaid**

honour *n* **1** = **integrity**, decency, fairness, goodness, honesty, morality, probity, rectitude **2 a** = **tribute**, accolade, commendation, homage, praise, recognition **b** = **prestige**, credit, dignity, distinction, fame, glory, renown, reputation, respect **3** = **privilege**, compliment, credit, pleasure ▷ *v* **5** = **respect**, adore, appreciate, esteem, prize, value

6 = **acclaim**, commemorate, commend, decorate, praise **7** = **pay**, accept, acknowledge, pass, take **8** = **fulfil**, be true to, carry out, discharge, keep, live up to, observe

honourable *adj* **1** = **respected**, creditable, estimable, reputable, respectable, virtuous

hoodwink *v* = **deceive**, con (*inf*), delude, dupe, fool, mislead, swindle, trick

hook *n* **1** = **fastener**, catch, clasp, link, peg ▷ *v* **3 a** = **fasten**, clasp, fix, secure **b** = **catch**, ensnare, entrap, snare, trap

hooked *adj* **1** = **bent**, aquiline, curved, hook-shaped **2** (foll. by *on*) *Sl* = **addicted**, devoted, enamoured, obsessed, taken, turned on (*sl*)

h

hooligan ❶ *n* rowdy young person. **hooliganism** *n*.

hoon *n Aust & NZ slang* loutish youth who drives irresponsibly.

hoop ❶ *n* rigid circular band, used esp. as a child's toy or for animals to jump through in the circus. **hoop pine** Australian tree or shrub with flowers in dense spikes. **jump, be put through the hoops** go through an ordeal or test.

hoopla *n* fairground game in which hoops are thrown over objects in an attempt to win them.

hoopoe [hoop-oo] *n* bird with a pinkish-brown plumage and a fanlike crest.

hooray *interj* same as HURRAH.

hoot ❶ *n* **1** sound of a car horn. **2** cry of an owl. **3** cry of derision. **4** *informal* amusing person or thing. ▷ *v* **5** sound (a car horn). **6** jeer or yell contemptuously (at someone). **hooter** *n* **1** device that hoots. **2** *slang* nose.

Hoover *n* **1** ® vacuum cleaner. ▷ *v* **2** (**h-**) clean with a vacuum cleaner.

hooves *n* a plural of HOOF.

hop¹ ❶ *v* **hopping, hopped 1** jump on one foot. **2** move in short jumps. **3** *informal* move quickly. ▷ *n* **4** instance of hopping. **5** *informal* dance. **6** short journey, esp. by air. **hop it** *slang* go away. **catch someone on the hop** *informal* catch someone unprepared.

hop² *n* (often *pl*) climbing plant, the dried flowers of which are used to make beer.

hope ❶ *v* **1** want (something) to happen or be true. ▷ *n* **2** expectation of something desired. **3** thing that gives cause for hope or is desired. **hopeful** *adj*

1 having, expressing, or inspiring hope. ▷ *n* **2** person considered to be on the brink of success. **hopefully** *adv* **1** in a hopeful manner. **2** it is hoped. **hopefulness** *n* **hopeless** *adj* **hopelessly** *adv* **hopelessness** *n*.

hopper *n* container for storing substances such as grain or sand.

hopscotch *n* children's game of hopping in a pattern drawn on the ground.

horde ❶ *n* large crowd.

horizon ❶ *n* **1** apparent line that divides the earth and the sky. ▷ *pl* **2** limits of scope, interest, or knowledge. **on the horizon** likely or about to happen or appear. **horizonless** *adj*.

horizontal ❶ *adj* parallel to the horizon, level, flat. **horizontally** *adv*.

hormone *n* **1** substance secreted by certain glands which stimulates certain organs of the body. **2** synthetic substance with the same effect. **hormonal** *adj*.

horn *n* **1** one of a pair of bony growths sticking out of the heads of cattle, sheep, etc. **2** substance of which horns are made. **3** musical instrument with a tube or pipe of brass fitted with a mouthpiece. **4** device on a vehicle sounded as a warning. **horned** *adj* **horny** *adj* **hornier, horniest 1** of or like horn. **2** *slang* (easily) sexually aroused. **hornbeam** *n* tree with smooth grey bark. **hornbill** *n* bird with a bony growth on its large beak. **hornpipe** *n* (music for) a solo dance, traditionally performed by sailors.

hornblende *n* mineral containing aluminium, calcium, sodium, magnesium, and iron.

—— THESAURUS ——

hooligan *n* = **delinquent**, lager lout, ruffian, vandal, yob *or* yobbo (*Brit sl*)

hooliganism *n* = **delinquency**, disorder, loutishness, rowdiness, vandalism, violence

hoop *n* = **ring**, band, circlet, girdle, loop, round, wheel

hoot *n* **1** = **toot 2** = **cry**, call **3** = **catcall**, boo, hiss, jeer ▷ *v* **6** = **jeer**, boo, hiss, howl down

hop¹ *v* **2** = **jump**, bound, caper, leap, skip, spring, trip, vault ▷ *n* **4** = **jump**, bounce, bound, leap, skip, spring, step, vault

hope *v* **1** = **desire**, aspire, cross one's fingers, long, look forward to, set one's heart on ▷ *n* **2** = **belief**, ambition,

assumption, confidence, desire, dream, expectation, longing

hopeful *adj* **1 a** = **optimistic**, buoyant, confident, expectant, looking forward to, sanguine **b** = **promising**, auspicious, bright, encouraging, heartening, reassuring, rosy

hopefully *adv* **1** = **optimistically**, confidently, expectantly

hopeless *adj* = **impossible**, futile, no-win, pointless, unattainable, useless, vain

horde *n* = **crowd**, band, drove, gang, host, mob, multitude, pack, swarm, throng

horizon *n* **1** = **skyline**, vista

horizontal *adj* = **level**, flat, parallel

hornet *n* large wasp with a severe sting.

horoscope *n* **1** prediction of a person's future based on the positions of the planets, sun, and moon at his or her birth. **2** diagram of the positions of the planets, sun, and moon at a particular time and place.

horrendous *adj* very unpleasant and shocking. **horrendously** *adv*.

horrible ❶ *adj* **1** disagreeable, unpleasant. **2** causing horror. **horribly** *adv*.

horrid ❶ *adj* **1** disagreeable, unpleasant. **2** *informal* nasty.

horrify ❶ *v* **-fying, -fied** cause to feel horror or shock. **horrifying** *adj* **horrifyingly** *adv* **horrific** *adj* causing horror. **horrifically** *adv*.

horror ❶ *n* (thing or person causing) terror or hatred. **horrible** *adj* disagreeable, unpleasant.

hors d'oeuvre [**or durv**] *n* appetizer served before a main meal.

horse ❶ *n* **1** large animal with hooves, a mane, and a tail, used for riding and pulling carts etc. **2** piece of gymnastic equipment used for vaulting over. **(straight) from the horse's mouth** from the original source. **horsey**, **horsy** *adj* **horsier**, **horsiest 1** very keen on horses. **2** of or like a horse. **horse around** *v informal* play roughly or boisterously. **horsebox** *n* trailer used for transporting horses. **horse chestnut 1** tree with broad leaves and inedible large brown shiny nuts in spiky cases. **2** the nut. **horsefly** *n* large bloodsucking fly. **horsehair** *n* hair from the tail or mane of a horse. **horse**

laugh loud coarse laugh. **horseman**, **horsewoman** *n* **1** person skilled in riding. **2** person riding a horse. **horsemanship** *n* **horseplay** *n* rough or rowdy play. **horsepower** *n* unit of power (equivalent to 745.7 watts), used to measure the power of an engine. **horseradish** *n* strong-tasting root of a plant, usu. made into a sauce. **horse sense** common sense. **horseshoe** *n* protective U-shaped piece of iron nailed to a horse's hoof, regarded as a symbol of good luck.

horticulture *n* art or science of cultivating gardens. **horticultural** *adj* **horticulturalist**, **horticulturist** *n*.

hosanna *interj* exclamation of praise to God.

hose¹ *n* **1** flexible pipe for conveying liquid. ▷ *v* **2** water with a hose.

hose² *n* stockings, socks, and tights. **hosiery** *n* stockings, socks, and tights collectively.

hoser *n* **1** *US sl* a person who swindles or deceives others. **2** *Canad sl* an unsophisticated, esp. rural, person.

hospice [**hoss**-piss] *n* nursing home for the terminally ill.

hospital *n* place where people who are ill are looked after and treated. **hospitalize** *v* send or admit to hospital. **hospitalization** *n*.

hospitality ❶ *n* kindness in welcoming strangers or guests. **hospitable** *adj* welcoming to strangers or guests.

host¹ ❶ *n* **1** (*fem* **hostess**) person who entertains guests, esp. in his own home. **2** place or country providing the

---

THESAURUS

horrible *adj* **1** = **dreadful**, awful, cruel, disagreeable, horrid, mean, nasty, terrible, unpleasant **2** = **terrifying**, appalling, dreadful, frightful, ghastly, grim, grisly, gruesome, hideous, repulsive, revolting, shocking

horrid *adj* **1** = **unpleasant**, awful, disagreeable, dreadful, horrible, terrible **2** *Inf* = **unkind**, beastly (*inf*), cruel, mean, nasty

horrific *adj* = **horrifying**, appalling, awful, dreadful, frightful, ghastly, grisly, horrendous, shocking, terrifying

horrify *v* = **shock**, alarm, appal, dismay, frighten, intimidate, make one's hair stand on end, outrage, petrify, scare, sicken, terrify

horror *n* = **terror**, alarm, aversion, consternation, detestation, disgust,

dread, fear, fright, hatred, loathing, odium, panic, repugnance, revulsion

horse *n* **1** = **nag**, colt, filly, gee-gee (*sl*), mare, mount, stallion, steed (*arch or lit*)

horseman, horsewoman *n* = **rider**, equestrian

horseplay *n* = **rough-and-tumble**, buffoonery, clowning, fooling around, high jinks, pranks, romping, skylarking (*inf*)

hospitable *adj* = **welcoming**, cordial, friendly, generous, gracious, kind, liberal, sociable

hospitality *n* = **welcome**, conviviality, cordiality, friendliness, neighbourliness, sociability, warmth

host¹ *n* **1** = **master of ceremonies**, entertainer, innkeeper, landlord *or* landlady, proprietor **3** = **presenter**,

facilities for an event. **3** compere of a show. **4** animal or plant on which a parasite lives. **5** *Computers* computer connected to others on a network. ▷ *v* **6** be the host of.

host² ❶ *n* large number.

Host *n Christianity* bread used in Holy Communion.

hostage ❶ *n* person who is illegally held prisoner until certain demands are met by other people.

hostel *n* building providing accommodation at a low cost for travellers, homeless people, etc.

hostelry *n, pl* **-ries** *old-fashioned or facetious* inn, pub.

hostile ❶ *adj* **1** unfriendly. **2** (foll. by *to*) opposed (to). **3** of an enemy. **hostility** *n, pl* **-ties 1** unfriendly and aggressive feelings or behaviour. ▷ *pl* **2** acts of warfare.

hot ❶ *adj* **hotter, hottest 1** having a high temperature. **2** strong, spicy. **3** (of news) very recent. **4** (of a contest) fiercely fought. **5** (of a temper) quick to rouse. **6** liked very much, e.g. *a hot favourite*. **7** *slang* stolen. **in hot water** *informal* in trouble. **in the hot seat** *informal* in a difficult and responsible position. **hotly** *adv* **hotting** *n informal* practice of stealing fast cars and putting on a show of skilful but dangerous driving. **hotter** *n* **hot air** *informal* empty talk. **hot-blooded** *adj* passionate or excitable. **hot dog** long roll split lengthways with a hot frankfurter inside. **hot-headed** *adj* rash, having a hot temper. **hotline** *n*

direct telephone link for emergency use. **hot-water bottle** rubber container filled with hot water, used for warming a bed.

hotbed *n* any place encouraging a particular activity, e.g. *hotbeds of unrest*.

hotchpotch ❶ *n* jumbled mixture.

hotel *n* commercial establishment providing lodging and meals. **hotelier** *n* owner or manager of a hotel.

hotfoot *adv informal* quickly and eagerly. **hotfoot it** *informal* go quickly and eagerly.

hothouse *n* greenhouse.

hotplate *n* **1** heated metal surface on an electric cooker. **2** portable device for keeping food warm.

hotpot *n* casserole of meat and vegetables, topped with potatoes.

Hottentot *n* (member of) a race of people of South Africa, now almost extinct.

hound ❶ *n* **1** hunting dog. ▷ *v* **2** pursue relentlessly.

hour *n* **1** twenty-fourth part of a day, sixty minutes. **2** time of day. ▷ *pl* **3** period regularly appointed for work or business. **hourly** *adj, adv* **1** (happening) every hour. **2** frequent(ly). **hourglass** *n* device with two glass compartments, containing a quantity of sand that takes an hour to trickle from the top section to the bottom one.

houri *n Islam* any of the nymphs of paradise.

---

anchorman *or* anchorwoman, compere (*Brit*) ▷ *v* **6** = **present**, compere (*Brit*), front (*inf*), introduce

host² *n* = **multitude**, army, array, drove, horde, legion, myriad, swarm, throng

hostage *n* = **prisoner**, captive, pawn

hostile *adj* **1** = **unfriendly**, antagonistic, belligerent, contrary, ill-disposed, opposed, rancorous **2** (foll. by *to*) = **inhospitable**, adverse, unsympathetic, unwelcoming

hostility *n* **1** = **unfriendliness**, animosity, antipathy, enmity, hatred, ill will, malice, opposition, resentment ▷ *pl* **2** = **warfare**, conflict, fighting, war

hot *adj* **1** = **heated**, boiling, roasting, scalding, scorching, searing, steaming, sultry, sweltering, torrid, warm **2** = **spicy**, biting, peppery, piquant,

pungent, sharp **3** = **new**, fresh, just out, latest, recent, up to the minute **4** = **passionate**, fierce, fiery, intense, raging, stormy, violent **6** = **popular**, approved, favoured, in demand, in vogue, sought-after

hot air *n Inf* = **empty talk**, bombast, claptrap (*inf*), guff (*sl*), verbiage, wind

hot-blooded *adj* = **passionate**, ardent, excitable, fiery, impulsive, spirited, temperamental, wild

hotchpotch *n* = **mixture**, farrago, jumble, medley, *melange*, mess, mishmash, potpourri

hot-headed *adj* = **rash**, fiery, foolhardy, hasty, hot-tempered, impetuous, quick-tempered, reckless, volatile

hound *v* **2** = **harass**, badger, goad, harry, impel, persecute, pester, provoke

house ❶ n **1** building used as a home. **2** building used for some specific purpose, e.g. *the opera house*. **3** business firm. **4** law-making body or the hall where it meets. **5** family or dynasty. **6** theatre or cinema audience. ▷ v **7** give accommodation to. **8** contain or cover. ▷ adj **9** (of wine) sold in a restaurant at a lower price than wines on the wine list. **get on like a house on fire** *informal* get on very well together. **on the house** *informal* provided free by the management. **housing** n **1** (providing of) houses. **2** protective case or covering of a machine. **house arrest** confinement to one's home rather than in prison. **houseboat** n stationary boat used as a home. **housebound** adj unable to leave one's house, usu. because of illness. **housebreaker** n burglar. **house-breaking** n **housecoat** n woman's long loose coat-shaped garment for wearing at home. **household** n all the people living in a house. **household name**, **word** very well-known person or thing. **householder** n person who owns or rents a house. **housekeeper** n person employed to run someone else's household. **housekeeping** n (money for) running a household. **housemaid** n female servant employed to do housework. **houseman** n junior hospital doctor. **house-proud** adj excessively concerned with the appearance of one's house. **house-train** v train (a pet) to urinate and defecate outside. **house-warming** n party to celebrate

moving into a new home. **housewife** n woman who runs her own household and does not have a job. **housewifely** adj **housework** n work of running a home, such as cleaning, cooking, and shopping.

House music, House n funk-based disco music with fragments of other recordings edited in electronically.

hove v *Nautical* a past of HEAVE.

hovea n Australian plant with purple flowers.

hovel ❶ n small dirty house or hut.

hover ❶ v **1** (of a bird etc.) remain suspended in one place in the air. **2** loiter. **3** be in a state of indecision. **hovercraft** n vehicle which can travel over both land and sea on a cushion of air.

how ❶ adv **1** in what way, by what means. **2** to what degree, e.g. *I know how hard it is*. **however** adv **1** nevertheless. **2** by whatever means. **3** no matter how, e.g. *however much it hurt, he could do it*.

howdah n canopied seat on an elephant's back.

howitzer n large gun firing shells at a steep angle.

howl ❶ n **1** loud wailing cry. **2** loud burst of laughter. ▷ v **3** utter a howl. **howler** n *informal* stupid mistake.

hoyden n wild or boisterous girl.

HP, h.p. 1 hire-purchase. **2** horsepower.

HQ headquarters.

hr hour.

HRH Her (or His) Royal Highness.

HRT hormone replacement therapy.

HTML hypertext markup language: text description language used on the internet.

---

house n **1** = **home**, abode, domicile, dwelling, habitation, homestead, pad (*sl*), residence **3** = **firm**, business, company, organization, outfit (*inf*) **4** = **assembly**, Commons, legislative body, parliament **5** = **dynasty**, clan, family, tribe ▷ v **7** = **accommodate**, billet, harbour, lodge, put up, quarter, take in **8** = **contain**, cover, keep, protect, sheathe, shelter, store **on the house** *Inf* = **free**, for nothing, gratis

household n = **family**, home, house

householder n = **occupant**, homeowner, resident, tenant

housing n **1** = **accommodation**, dwellings, homes, houses **2** = **case**,

casing, container, cover, covering, enclosure, sheath

hovel n = **hut**, cabin, den, hole, shack, shanty, shed

hover v **1** = **float**, drift, flutter, fly, hang **2** = **linger**, hang about **3** = **waver**, dither, fluctuate, oscillate, vacillate

however adv **1** = **nevertheless**, after all, anyhow, but, nonetheless, notwithstanding, still, though, yet

howl n **1** = **cry**, bawl, bay, clamour, groan, roar, scream, shriek, wail ▷ v **3** = **cry**, bawl, bellow, roar, scream, shriek, wail, weep, yell

howler n *Inf* = **mistake**, bloomer (*Brit inf*), blunder, boob (*Brit sl*), clanger (*inf*), error, malapropism

h

hub ❶ *n* **1** centre of a wheel, through which the axle passes. **2** central point of activity.

hubble-bubble *n* same as HOOKAH.

hubbub *n* confused noise of many voices.

hubby *n*, *pl* **-bies** *informal* husband.

hubris [**hew**-briss] *n formal* pride, arrogance.

huckster *n* person using aggressive methods of selling.

huddle ❶ *v* **1** hunch (oneself) through cold or fear. **2** crowd closely together. ▷ *n* **3** small group. **4** *informal* impromptu conference.

hue ❶ *n* colour, shade.

hue and cry *n* public outcry.

huff *n* **1** passing mood of anger or resentment. ▷ *v* **2** blow or puff heavily. **huffy** *adj* **huffier**, **huffiest**. **huffily** *adv*.

hug ❶ *v* **hugging**, **hugged 1** clasp tightly in the arms, usu. with affection. **2** keep close to (the ground, kerb, etc.). ▷ *n* **3** tight or fond embrace.

huge ❶ *adj* very big. **hugely** *adv*.

huh *interj* exclamation of derision, bewilderment, or inquiry.

hula *n* swaying Hawaiian dance. **Hula Hoop®** plastic hoop twirled round the body by gyrating the hips.

hulk ❶ *n* **1** body of an abandoned ship. **2** *offens* large heavy person or thing. **hulking** *adj* bulky, unwieldy.

hull ❶ *n* **1** main body of a boat. **2** leaves round the stem of a strawberry, raspberry, etc. ▷ *v* **3** remove the hulls from.

hullabaloo *n*, *pl* **-loos** loud confused noise or clamour.

hullo *interj* same as HELLO.

hum ❶ *v* **humming**, **hummed 1** make a low continuous vibrating sound. **2** sing with the lips closed. **3** *slang* (of a place) be very busy. ▷ *n* **4** humming sound. **hummingbird** *n* very small American bird whose powerful wings make a humming noise as they vibrate.

human ❶ *adj* **1** of or typical of people. ▷ *n* **2** human being. **humanly** *adv* by human powers or means. **human being** man, woman, or child. **humane** *adj* kind or merciful. **humanity** *n* human race. **human nature** ordinary human behaviour, esp. when less than perfect. **human race** all men, women, and children collectively. **human rights** basic rights of people to liberty, justice, etc.

humane ❶ *adj* kind or merciful. **humanely** *adv*.

humanism *n* belief in human effort rather than religion. **humanist** *n* **humanistic** *adj*.

humanitarian ❶ *n*, *adj* (person) having the interests of humankind at heart. **humanitarianism** *n*.

humanity ❶ *n*, *pl* **-ties 1** human race. **2** the quality of being human. **3** kindness or mercy. ▷ *pl* **4** study of literature, philosophy, and the arts.

————————————————— THESAURUS ————————

hub *n* **2** = **centre**, core, focal point, focus, heart, middle, nerve centre

huddle *v* **1** = **curl up**, crouch, hunch up **2** = **crowd**, cluster, converge, flock, gather, press, throng ▷ *n* **4** *Inf* = **conference**, confab (*inf*), discussion, meeting, powwow

hue *n* = **colour**, dye, shade, tinge, tint, tone

hug *v* **1** = **clasp**, cuddle, embrace, enfold, hold close, squeeze, take in one's arms ▷ *n* **3** = **embrace**, bear hug, clasp, clinch (*sl*), squeeze

huge *adj* = **enormous**, colossal, gigantic, immense, large, mammoth, massive, monumental, tremendous, vast

hulk *n* **1** = **wreck**, frame, hull, shell, shipwreck **2** *Offens* = **oaf**, lout, lubber, lump (*inf*)

hull *n* **1** = **frame**, body, casing, covering, framework

hum *v* **1** = **drone**, buzz, murmur, purr, throb, thrum, vibrate, whir **3** *Sl* = **be busy**, bustle, buzz, pulsate, pulse, stir

human *adj* **1** = **mortal**, manlike ▷ *n* **2** = **human being**, creature, individual, man *or* woman, mortal, person, soul

humane *adj* = **kind**, benign, compassionate, forgiving, good-natured, merciful, sympathetic, tender, understanding

humanitarian *n* = **philanthropist**, altruist, benefactor, Good Samaritan ▷ *adj* = **philanthropic**, altruistic, benevolent, charitable, compassionate, humane, public-spirited

humanity *n* **1** = **human race**, Homo sapiens, humankind, man, mankind, people **2** = **human nature**, mortality **3** = **kindness**, charity, compassion, fellow feeling, kind-heartedness, mercy, philanthropy, sympathy

humanize ❶ v make human or humane. **humanization** n.

humankind n human race.

humanoid n, adj (robot or creature) resembling a human being in appearance.

humble ❶ adj **1** conscious of one's failings. **2** modest, unpretentious. **3** unimportant. ▷ v **4** cause to feel humble, humiliate. **humbly** adv.

humbug ❶ n **1** hard striped peppermint sweet. **2** nonsense. **3** dishonest person.

humdinger n slang excellent person or thing.

humdrum ❶ adj ordinary, dull.

humerus [**hew**-mer-uss] n, pl **-meri** [-mer-rye] bone from the shoulder to the elbow.

humid ❶ adj damp and hot. **humidity** n **humidify** v **-fying**, **-fied**. **humidifier** n device for increasing the amount of water vapour in the air in a room.

humiliate ❶ v lower the dignity or hurt the pride of. **humiliating** adj **humiliation** n.

humility ❶ n quality of being humble.

hummock n very small hill.

humour ❶ n **1** ability to say or perceive things that are amusing. **2** amusing quality in a situation, film, etc. **3** state of mind, mood. **4** old-fashioned fluid in the body. ▷ v **5** be kind and indulgent to. **humorous** adj **humorously** adv **humorist** n writer or entertainer who uses humour in his or her work. **humourless** adj.

● **SPELLING TIP**
● A lot of people simply add
● *-ous* to the noun **humour** to make
● *humourous*, but this is a mistake;
● you have to drop the second *u*
● when you write **humorous** or
● **humorist**.

hump ❶ n **1** raised piece of ground. **2** large lump on the back of an animal or person. ▷ v **3** slang carry or heave. **get, take the hump** informal be annoyed, sulk. **humpback** n offens hunchback. **humpbacked** adj **humpback, humpbacked bridge** road bridge with a sharp slope on each side.

humus [**hew**-muss] n decomposing vegetable and animal mould in the soil.

Hun n **1** member of the Asian people who invaded the Roman Empire in the 4th and 5th centuries AD. **2** informal offens (in World War 1) German.

THESAURUS

humanize v = **civilize**, educate, enlighten, improve, soften, tame

humble adj **1** = **modest**, meek, self-effacing, unassuming, unostentatious, unpretentious **2** = **modest**, lowly, mean, obscure, ordinary, plebeian, poor, simple, undistinguished ▷ v **4** = **humiliate**, chasten, crush, disgrace, put (someone) in their place, subdue, take down a peg (inf)

humbug n **2** = **nonsense**, baloney (inf), cant, claptrap (inf), hypocrisy, kak (S Afr sl), quackery, rubbish **3** = **fraud**, charlatan, con man (inf), faker, impostor, phoney or phony (inf), swindler, trickster

humdrum adj = **dull**, banal, boring, dreary, monotonous, mundane, ordinary, tedious, tiresome, uneventful

humid adj = **damp**, clammy, dank, moist, muggy, steamy, sticky, sultry, wet

humidity n = **damp**, clamminess, dampness, dankness, moistness, moisture, mugginess, wetness

humiliate v = **embarrass**, bring low, chasten, crush, degrade, humble, mortify, put down, put (someone) in their place, shame

humiliating adj = **embarrassing**, crushing, degrading, humbling, ignominious, mortifying, shaming

humiliation n = **embarrassment**, degradation, disgrace, dishonour, humbling, ignominy, indignity, loss of face, mortification, put-down, shame

humility n = **modesty**, humbleness, lowliness, meekness, submissiveness, unpretentiousness

humorist n = **comedian**, card (inf), comic, funny man, jester, joker, wag, wit

humorous adj **1**, **2** = **funny**, amusing, comic, comical, droll, entertaining, jocular, playful, waggish, witty

humour n **1**, **2** = **funniness**, amusement, comedy, drollery, facetiousness, fun, jocularity, ludicrousness **3** = **mood**, disposition, frame of mind, spirits, temper ▷ v **5** = **indulge**, accommodate, flatter, go along with, gratify, mollify, pander to

hump n **1** = **lump**, bulge, bump, mound, projection, protrusion, protuberance, swelling ▷ v **3** Sl = **carry**, heave, hoist, lug, shoulder

hunch ❶ n 1 feeling or suspicion not based on facts. ▷ v 2 draw (one's shoulders) up or together. **hunchback** n offens person with an abnormal curvature of the spine. **hunchbacked** adj.

hundred adj, n 1 ten times ten. ▷ n 2 (often pl) large but unspecified number. **hundredth** adj, n **hundredweight** n Brit unit of weight of 112 pounds (50.8 kilograms).

hung v 1 past of HANG. ▷ adj 2 (of a parliament or jury) with no side having a clear majority. **hung over** informal suffering the effects of a hangover.

Hungarian adj 1 of Hungary. ▷ n 2 person from Hungary. 3 language of Hungary.

hunger ❶ n 1 discomfort or weakness from lack of food. 2 lack of food that causes suffering or death, e.g. refugees dying of hunger. 3 desire or craving. ▷ v 4 (foll. by for) want very much. **hunger march** procession of protest by the unemployed. **hunger strike** refusal of all food, as a means of protest.

hungry ❶ adj **hungrier**, **hungriest** 1 desiring food. 2 (foll. by for) having a desire or craving (for). **hungrily** adv.

hunk ❶ n 1 large piece. 2 slang sexually attractive man.

hunt ❶ v 1 seek out and kill (wild animals) for food or sport. 2 (foll. by for) search (for). ▷ n 3 hunting. 4 (party organized for) hunting wild animals for sport. **hunter** n person or animal that hunts wild animals for food or sport. **hunting** n **huntsman** n man who hunts wild animals, esp. foxes.

hurdle ❶ n 1 Sport light barrier for jumping over in some races. 2 problem or difficulty. ▷ pl 3 race involving hurdles. ▷ v 4 jump over (something). **hurdler** n.

hurdy-gurdy n, pl **-dies** mechanical musical instrument, such as a barrel organ.

hurl ❶ v throw or utter forcefully.

hurling, **hurley** n Irish game like hockey.

hurly-burly n loud confusion.

hurrah, **hurray** interj exclamation of joy or applause.

hurricane ❶ n very strong, often destructive, wind or storm. **hurricane lamp** paraffin lamp with a glass covering.

hurry ❶ v **-rying**, **-ried** 1 (cause to) move or act very quickly. ▷ n 2 doing something quickly or the need to do something quickly. **hurried** adj **hurriedly** adv.

hurt ❶ v **hurting**, **hurt** 1 cause physical or mental pain to. 2 be painful. 3 informal feel pain. ▷ n 4 physical or

---

hunch n 1 = **feeling**, idea, impression, inkling, intuition, premonition, presentiment, suspicion ▷ v 2 = **draw in**, arch, bend, curve

hunger n 1 = **appetite**, emptiness, hungriness, ravenousness 2 = **starvation**, famine 3 = **desire**, ache, appetite, craving, itch, lust, thirst, yearning ▷ v 4 = **want**, ache, crave, desire, hanker, itch, long, thirst, wish, yearn

hungry adj 1 = **empty**, famished, peckish (inf, chiefly Brit), ravenous, starved, starving, voracious 2 (foll. by for) = **eager**, athirst, avid, covetous, craving, desirous, greedy, keen, yearning

hunk n 1 = **lump**, block, chunk, mass, nugget, piece, slab, wedge

hunt v 1 = **stalk**, chase, hound, pursue, track, trail 2 (foll. by for) = **search**, ferret about, forage, fossick (Aust & NZ), look, scour, seek ▷ n 3 = **search**, chase, hunting, investigation, pursuit, quest

hurdle n 1 = **fence**, barricade, barrier 2 = **obstacle**, barrier, difficulty, handicap, hazard, hindrance, impediment, obstruction, stumbling block

hurl v = **throw**, cast, fling, heave, launch, let fly, pitch, propel, sling, toss

hurricane n = **storm**, cyclone, gale, tempest, tornado, twister (US inf), typhoon

hurried adj = **hasty**, brief, cursory, perfunctory, quick, rushed, short, speedy, swift

hurry v 1 = **rush**, dash, fly, get a move on (inf), make haste, scoot, scurry, step on it (inf) ▷ n 2 = **haste**, flurry, quickness, rush, speed, urgency

hurt v 1 a = **harm**, bruise, damage, disable, impair, injure, mar, spoil, wound b = **upset**, annoy, distress, grieve, pain, sadden, wound 2 = **ache**, be sore, be tender, burn, smart, sting, throb ▷ n 4 = **distress**, discomfort, pain, pang, soreness, suffering

mental pain. **hurtful** adj unkind.

hurtle ❶ v move quickly or violently.

husband ❶ n **1** a man to whom a person is married. ▷ v **2** use economically. **husbandry** n **1** farming. **2** management of resources.

hush ❶ v **1** make or be silent. ▷ n **2** stillness or silence. **hushed** adj **hush-hush** adj informal secret. **hush money** slang money given to someone to ensure that something is kept secret. **hush up** v suppress information about.

husk n **1** outer covering of certain seeds and fruits. ▷ v **2** remove the husk from.

husky¹ ❶ adj **huskier**, **huskiest 1** slightly hoarse. **2** informal big and strong. **huskily** adv.

husky² n, pl **huskies** Arctic sledge dog with thick hair and a curled tail.

hussar [hoo-**zar**] n History lightly armed cavalry soldier.

hussy n, pl **-sies** immodest or promiscuous woman.

hustings pl n political campaigns and speeches before an election.

hustle ❶ v **1** push about, jostle. ▷ n **2** lively activity or bustle.

hut ❶ n small house, shelter, or shed.

hutch n cage for pet rabbits etc.

hyacinth n sweet-smelling spring flower that grows from a bulb.

hyaena n same as HYENA.

hybrid ❶ n **1** offspring of two plants or animals of different species. **2** anything of mixed origin. **3** vehicle powered by an internal-combustion engine and another source of power. ▷ adj **4** of mixed origin. **5** of a vehicle powered by more than one source.

hydra n mythical many-headed water serpent.

hydrangea n ornamental shrub with clusters of pink, blue, or white flowers.

hydrant n outlet from a water main with a nozzle for a hose.

hydrate n **1** chemical compound of water with another substance. ▷ v **2** treat or impregnate with water.

hydraulic adj operated by pressure forced through a pipe by a liquid such as water or oil. **hydraulics** n study of the mechanical properties of fluids as they apply to practical engineering. **hydraulically** adv.

hydro¹ n, pl **hydros** hotel offering facilities for hydropathy.

hydro² adj **1** short for HYDROELECTRIC. **2** Canad electricity as supplied to a residence, business, institution, etc.

hydro- combining form **1** water, e.g. hydroelectric. **2** hydrogen, e.g. hydrochloric acid.

hydrocarbon n compound of hydrogen and carbon.

hydrocephalus n accumulation of fluid within the cavities of the brain, causing enlargement of the head in children.

hydrochloric acid n strong colourless acid used in many industrial and laboratory processes.

hydrodynamics n branch of science concerned with the mechanical properties of fluids.

hydroelectric adj of the generation of electricity by water pressure.

hydrofoil n fast light boat with its hull raised out of the water on one or more pairs of fins.

hydrogen n Chemistry light flammable colourless gas that combines with oxygen to form water. **hydrogen bomb** extremely powerful bomb in which

h

hurtful adj = **unkind**, cruel, cutting, damaging, destructive, malicious, nasty, spiteful, upsetting, wounding

hurtle v = **rush**, charge, crash, fly, plunge, race, shoot, speed, stampede, tear

husband n **1** = **partner**, better half (hum), mate, spouse ▷ v **2** = **economize**, budget, conserve, hoard, save, store

husbandry n **1** = **farming**, agriculture, cultivation, tillage **2** = **thrift**, economy, frugality

hush v **1** = **quieten**, mute, muzzle, shush, silence ▷ n **2** = **quiet**, calm, peace, silence, stillness, tranquillity

hush-hush adj Inf = **secret**, classified, confidential, restricted, top-secret, under wraps

husky¹ adj **1** = **hoarse**, croaky, gruff, guttural, harsh, raucous, rough, throaty **2** Inf = **muscular**, burly, hefty, powerful, rugged, stocky, strapping, thickset

hustle v **1** = **jostle**, elbow, force, jog, push, shove

hut n = **shed**, cabin, den, hovel, lean-to, shanty, shelter

hybrid n **1** = **crossbreed**, cross, half-breed, mongrel **2** = **mixture**, amalgam, composite, compound, cross

h

energy is released by fusion of hydrogen nuclei to give helium nuclei. **hydrogen peroxide** colourless liquid used as a hair bleach and as an antiseptic.

hydrology n study of the distribution, conservation, and use of the water of the earth and its atmosphere.

hydrolysis [hie-**drol**-iss-iss] n decomposition of a chemical compound reacting with water.

hydrometer [hie-**drom**-it-er] n instrument for measuring the density of a liquid.

hydropathy n method of treating disease by the use of large quantities of water both internally and externally. **hydropathic** adj.

hydrophobia n **1** rabies. **2** fear of water.

hydroplane n light motorboat that skims the water.

hydroponics n method of growing plants in water rather than soil.

hydrotherapy n Medical treatment of certain diseases by exercise in water.

hyena n scavenging doglike mammal of Africa and S Asia.

hygiene ❶ n **1** principles and practice of health and cleanliness. **2** study of these principles. **hygienic** adj **hygienically** adv.

hymen n membrane partly covering the opening of a girl's vagina, which breaks before puberty or at the first occurrence of sexual intercourse.

hymn ❶ n Christian song of praise sung to God or a saint. **hymnal** n book of hymns (also **hymn book**).

hype ❶ n **1** intensive or exaggerated publicity or sales promotion. ▷ v **2** promote (a product) using intensive or exaggerated publicity.

hyper adj informal overactive or overexcited.

hyper- prefix over, above, excessively, e.g. hyperactive.

hyperbola [hie-**per**-bol-a] n

Geometry curve produced when a cone is cut by a plane at a steeper angle to its base than its side.

hyperbole [hie-**per**-bol-ee] n deliberate exaggeration for effect. **hyperbolic** adj.

hyperlink Computers ▷ n link from a hypertext file that gives users instant access to related material in another file.

hypermarket n huge self-service store.

hypersensitive adj **1** extremely sensitive to certain drugs, extremes of temperature, etc. **2** very easily upset.

hypersonic adj having a speed of at least five times the speed of sound.

hypertension n very high blood pressure.

hyperventilation n increase in the rate of breathing, sometimes resulting in cramp and dizziness. **hyperventilate** v.

hyphen n punctuation mark (-) indicating that two words or syllables are connected. **hyphenated** adj (of two words or syllables) having a hyphen between them. **hyphenation** n.

hypnosis ❶ n artificially induced state of relaxation in which the mind is more than usually receptive to suggestion. **hypnotic** adj of or (as if) producing hypnosis. **hypnotically** adv **hypnotism** n inducing hypnosis in someone. **hypnotist** n **hypnotize** v.

hypo- prefix beneath, less than, e.g. hypothermia.

hypoallergenic adj (of cosmetics) not likely to cause an allergic reaction.

hypochondria n undue preoccupation with one's health. **hypochondriac** n.

hypocrisy ❶ [hip-**ok**-rass-ee] n, pl -**sies** (instance of) pretence of having standards or beliefs that are contrary to one's real character or actual behaviour. **hypocrite** [**hip**-oh-krit] n person who pretends to be what he or she is not.

——————————————— THESAURUS ———————————————

hygiene n **1** = **cleanliness**, sanitation

hygienic adj = **clean**, aseptic, disinfected, germ-free, healthy, pure, sanitary, sterile

hymn n = **song of praise**, anthem, carol, chant, paean, psalm

hype n **1** = **publicity**, ballyhoo (inf), brouhaha, plugging (inf), promotion, razzmatazz (sl)

hypnotic adj = **mesmerizing**, mesmeric, sleep-inducing, soothing, soporific, spellbinding

hypnotize v = **mesmerize**, put in a trance, put to sleep

hypocrisy n = **insincerity**, cant, deceitfulness, deception, duplicity, pretence

hypocrite n = **fraud**, charlatan, deceiver, impostor, phoney or phony (inf), pretender

hypocritical adj = **insincere**, canting, deceitful, duplicitous, false, fraudulent, phoney or phony (inf), sanctimonious, two-faced

hypocritical *adj* **hypocritically** *adv*.

hypodermic *adj*, *n* (denoting) a syringe or needle used to inject a drug beneath the skin.

hypotension *n* very low blood pressure.

hypotenuse [hie-**pot**-a-news] *n* side of a right-angled triangle opposite the right angle.

hypothermia *n* condition in which a person's body temperature is dangerously low as a result of prolonged exposure to severe cold.

hypothesis ❶ [hie-**poth**-iss-iss] *n, pl* **-ses** [-seez] suggested but unproved explanation of something.

hypothesize *v* **hypothetical** *adj* based on assumption rather than fact or reality. **hypothetically** *adv*.

hyssop *n* sweet-smelling herb used in folk medicine.

hysterectomy *n, pl* **-mies** surgical removal of the womb.

hysteria ❶ *n* state of uncontrolled excitement, anger, or panic. **hysteric** *n* **1** hysterical person. **hysterical** *adj* **1** in a state of hysteria. **2** *informal* wildly funny. **hysterically** *adv* **hysterics** *pl n* **1** attack of hysteria. **2** *informal* uncontrollable laughter.

Hz hertz.

——————————————— THESAURUS ———————————————

hypothesis *n* = **assumption**, postulate, premise, proposition, supposition, theory, thesis

hypothetical *adj* = **theoretical**, academic, assumed, conjectural, imaginary, putative, speculative, supposed

hysteria *n* = **frenzy**, agitation, delirium, hysterics, madness, panic

hysterical *adj* **1** = **frenzied**, crazed, distracted, distraught, frantic, overwrought, raving **2** *Inf* = **hilarious**, comical, side-splitting, uproarious

I¹ *pron* used by a speaker or writer to refer to himself or herself as the subject of a verb.

I² *Chemistry* iodine. **1** the Roman numeral for one.

IA Iowa.

IBA Independent Broadcasting Authority.

Iberian *adj* of Iberia, the peninsula comprising Spain and Portugal.

ibex [**ibe**-eks] *n* wild goat with large backward-curving horns.

ibid. (referring to a book, page, or passage already mentioned) in the same place.

ibis [**ibe**-iss] *n* large wading bird with long legs.

ICBM intercontinental ballistic missile.

ice ⓘ *n* **1** frozen water. **2** portion of ice cream. ▷ *v* **3** (foll. by *up* or *over*) become covered with ice. **4** cover with icing. **break the ice** create a relaxed atmosphere, esp. between people meeting for the first time. **iced** *adj* **1** covered with icing. **2** (of a drink) containing ice. **icy** *adj* **icier**, **iciest** **1** very cold. **2** covered with ice. **3** aloof and unfriendly. **icily** *adv* **iciness** *n* **Ice Age** period when much of the earth's surface was covered in glaciers. **iceberg** *n* large floating mass of ice. **icebox** *n* US refrigerator. **icebreaker** *n* ship designed to break a channel through ice. **icecap** *n* mass of ice

permanently covering an area. **ice cream** sweet creamy frozen food. **ice cube** small square block of ice added to a drink to cool it. **ice floe** sheet of ice floating in the sea. **ice hockey** team game like hockey played on ice with a puck. **ice lolly** flavoured ice on a stick. **ice pick** pointed tool for breaking ice. **ice skate** boot with a steel blade fixed to the sole, to enable the wearer to glide over ice. **ice-skate** *v* **ice-skater** *n*.

Icelandic *adj* **1** of Iceland. ▷ *n* **2** language of Iceland. **Icelander** *n*.

ichthyology [ik-thi-**ol**-a-jee] *n* scientific study of fish. **ichthyological** *adj* **ichthyologist** *n*.

icicle *n* tapering spike of ice hanging where water has dripped.

icing *n* mixture of sugar and water etc., used to cover and decorate cakes. **icing sugar** finely ground sugar for making icing.

icon *n* **1** picture of Christ or another religious figure, regarded as holy in the Orthodox Church. **2** picture on a computer screen representing a function that can be activated by moving the cursor over it. **3** person regarded as a sex symbol or as a symbol of a belief or cultural movement.

iconoclast *n* person who attacks established ideas or principles. **iconoclastic** *adj* **iconoclasm** *n*.

id *n* *Psychoanalysis* the mind's instinctive unconscious energies.

ID 1 Idaho. **2** identification.

idea ⓘ *n* **1** plan or thought formed in the mind. **2** thought of something, e.g. *the idea overwhelms me.* **3** belief or opinion.

ideal ⓘ *adj* **1** most suitable. **2** perfect. ▷ *n* **3** conception of something that is perfect. **4** perfect person or thing. **ideally** *adv* **idealism** *n* tendency to seek perfection in everything. **idealist** *n*

THESAURUS

icy *adj* **1** = **cold**, biting, bitter, chill, chilly, freezing, frosty, ice-cold, raw
2 = **slippery**, glassy, slippy (*inf or dial*)
3 = **unfriendly**, aloof, cold, distant, frigid, frosty, unwelcoming

idea *n* **1** = **intention**, aim, object, objective, plan, purpose **2** = **thought**, concept, impression, perception
3 = **belief**, conviction, notion, opinion, teaching, view

ideal *adj* **2** = **perfect**, archetypal, classic, complete, consummate, model, quintessential, supreme ▷ *n* **4** = **model**,

last word, paradigm, paragon, pattern, perfection, prototype, standard

idealist *n* = **romantic**, dreamer, Utopian, visionary

idealistic *adj* = **perfectionist**, impracticable, optimistic, romantic, starry-eyed, Utopian, visionary

idealize *v* = **romanticize**, apotheosize, ennoble, exalt, glorify, magnify, put on a pedestal, worship

ideally *adv* = **in a perfect world**, all things being equal, if one had one's way

idealistic *adj* **idealize** *v* regard or portray as perfect or nearly perfect. **idealization** *n*.

idem *pron, adj Latin* the same: used to refer to an article, chapter, or book already quoted.

identical ❶ *adj* exactly the same. **identically** *adv*.

identify ❶ *v* **-fying, -fied 1** prove or recognize as being a certain person or thing. **2** (foll. by *with*) understand and sympathize with (a person or group that one regards as being similar or similarly situated). **3** treat as being the same. **identifiable** *adj* **identification** *n*.

Identikit *n* ® composite picture, assembled from descriptions given, of a person wanted by the police.

identity ❶ *n, pl* **-ties 1** state of being a specified person or thing. **2** individuality or personality. **3** state of being the same. **identity theft** fraudulent use of another person's name to set up a bank account or obtain credit.

ideology *n, pl* **-gies** body of ideas and beliefs of a group, nation, etc. **ideological** *adj* **ideologically** *adv* **ideologist** *n*.

ides *n* (in the Ancient Roman calendar) the 15th of March, May, July, or October, or the 13th of other months.

idiocy ❶ *n* utter stupidity.

idiom ❶ *n* **1** group of words which when used together have a different meaning from the words individually, e.g. *raining cats and dogs*. **2** way of expression natural or peculiar to a language or group. **idiomatic** *adj* **idiomatically** *adv*.

idiosyncrasy ❶ *n, pl* **-sies** personal peculiarity of mind, habit, or behaviour. **idiosyncratic** *adj*.

idiot ❶ *n* **1** foolish or stupid person. **2** *offens* mentally retarded person. **idiotic** *adj* **idiotically** *adv*.

idle ❶ *adj* **1** not doing anything. **2** not willing to work, lazy. **3** not being used. **4** useless or meaningless, e.g. *an idle threat*. ▷ *v* **5** (usu. foll. by *away*) spend (time) doing very little. **6** (of an engine) run slowly with the gears disengaged. **idleness** *n* **idler** *n* **idly** *adv*.

idol ❶ [**ide**-ol] *n* **1** object of excessive devotion. **2** image of a god as an object of worship. **idolatry** [ide-**ol**-a-tree] *n* worship of idols. **idolatrous** *adj* **idolize** *v* love or admire excessively. **idolization** *n*.

identical *adj* = **alike**, duplicate, indistinguishable, interchangeable, matching, twin

identification *n* **1** = **recognition**, naming, pinpointing **2** = **sympathy**, association, connection, empathy, fellow feeling, involvement, rapport, relationship

identify *v* **1** = **recognize**, diagnose, make out, name, pick out, pinpoint, place, put one's finger on (*inf*), spot **2** (foll. by *with*) = **relate to**, associate with, empathize with, feel for, respond to

identity *n* **1, 2** = **existence**, individuality, personality, self **3** = **sameness**, correspondence, unity

idiocy *n* = **foolishness**, asininity, fatuousness, imbecility, inanity, insanity, lunacy, senselessness

idiom *n* **1** = **phrase**, expression, turn of phrase **2** = **language**, jargon, parlance, style, vernacular

idiosyncrasy *n* = **peculiarity**, characteristic, eccentricity, mannerism, oddity, quirk, trick

idiot *n* **1** = **fool**, chump, cretin, dunderhead, halfwit, imbecile, moron, nincompoop, numbskull *or* numskull, simpleton, twit (*inf, chiefly Brit*)

idiotic *adj* **1** = **foolish**, asinine, crazy, daft (*inf*), foolhardy, harebrained, insane, moronic, senseless, stupid

idle *adj* **1** = **inactive**, redundant, unemployed, unoccupied **2** = **lazy**, good-for-nothing, indolent, lackadaisical, shiftless, slothful, sluggish **3** = **unused**, vacant **4** = **useless**, fruitless, futile, groundless, ineffective, pointless, unavailing, unsuccessful, vain, worthless ▷ *v* **5** (usu. foll. by *away*) = **laze**, dally, dawdle, kill time, loaf, loiter, lounge, potter

idleness *n* **1** = **inactivity**, inaction, leisure, time on one's hands, unemployment **2** = **laziness**, inertia, shiftlessness, sloth, sluggishness, torpor

idol *n* **1** = **hero**, beloved, darling, favourite, pet, pin-up (*sl*) **2** = **graven image**, deity, god

idolatry *n* = **adoration**, adulation, exaltation, glorification

idolize *v* = **worship**, adore, dote upon, exalt, glorify, hero-worship, look up to, love, revere, venerate

idyll ❶ [**id**-ill] *n* scene or time of great peace and happiness. **idyllic** *adj* **idyllically** *adv*.

i.e. that is to say.

if ❶ *conj* **1** on the condition or supposition that. **2** whether. **3** even though. ▷ *n* **4** uncertainty or doubt, e.g. *no ifs, ands, or buts*. **iffy** *adj informal* doubtful, uncertain.

igloo *n, pl* **-loos** dome-shaped Inuit house made of snow and ice.

igneous [**ig**-nee-uss] *adj* (of rock) formed as molten rock cools and hardens.

ignite ❶ *v* catch fire or set fire to.

ignition *n* **1** system that ignites the fuel-and-air mixture to start an engine. **2** igniting.

ignoble *adj* dishonourable. **ignobly** *adv*.

ignominy ❶ [**ig**-nom-in-ee] *n* humiliating disgrace. **ignominious** *adj* **ignominiously** *adv*.

ignoramus *n, pl* **-muses** ignorant person.

ignorant ❶ *adj* **1** lacking knowledge. **2** rude through lack of knowledge of good manners. **ignorance** *n* lack of knowledge or education.

ignore ❶ *v* refuse to notice, disregard deliberately. **ignorantly** *adv*.

iguana *n* large tropical American lizard.

ikebana [eek-a-**bah**-na] *n* Japanese art of flower arrangement.

ikon *n* same as ICON.

IL Illinois.

ileum *n* lowest part of the small intestine.

ilex *n* any of a genus of trees or shrubs that includes holly.

ilium *n, pl* **-ia** uppermost and widest of the three sections of the hipbone. **iliac** *adj*.

ilk *n* type, e.g. *others of his ilk*.

ill ❶ *adj* **1** not in good health. **2** harmful or unpleasant, e.g. *ill effects*. ▷ *n* **3** evil, harm. ▷ *adv* **4** badly. **5** hardly, with difficulty, e.g. *I can ill afford to lose him*. **ill at ease** uncomfortable, unable to relax. **illness** *n* **ill-advised** *adj* **1** badly thought out. **2** unwise. **ill-bred** *adj* lacking good manners, rude. **ill-disposed** *adj* (often foll. by *towards*) unfriendly, unsympathetic. **ill-fated** *adj* doomed to end unhappily. **ill-favoured** *adj* ugly, unattractive. **ill-gotten** *adj* obtained dishonestly, e.g. *ill-gotten gains*. **ill-health** *n* condition of being unwell. **ill-mannered** *adj* having bad manners. **ill-starred** *adj* ill-fated, unlucky. **ill-tempered** *adj* displaying bad temper. **ill-timed** *adj* done or happening at an unsuitable time. **ill-treat** *v* treat cruelly. **ill-treatment** *n* **ill will** unkind feeling, hostility.

illegal ❶ *adj* against the law. **illegally** *adv* **illegality** *n, pl* **-ties**.

———————————————— THESAURUS ——————

idyllic *adj* = **idealized**, charming, halcyon, heavenly, ideal, picturesque, unspoiled

if *conj* **1** = **provided**, assuming, on condition that, providing, supposing

ignite *v* **a** = **catch fire**, burn, burst into flames, flare up, inflame, take fire **b** = **set fire to**, kindle, light, set alight, torch

ignominious *adj* = **humiliating**, discreditable, disgraceful, dishonourable, indecorous, inglorious, shameful, sorry, undignified

ignominy *n* = **disgrace**, discredit, dishonour, disrepute, humiliation, infamy, obloquy, shame, stigma

ignorance *n* **1** = **unawareness**, inexperience, innocence, unconsciousness, unfamiliarity

ignorant *adj* **1** = **uninformed**, illiterate, inexperienced, innocent, oblivious, unaware, unconscious, uneducated, unenlightened, uninitiated, unwitting **2** = **insensitive**, crass, half-baked (*inf*), rude

ignore *v* = **overlook**, discount, disregard, neglect, pass over, reject, take no notice of, turn a blind eye to

ill *adj* **1** = **unwell**, ailing, crook (*Aust & NZ sl*), diseased, indisposed, infirm, off-colour, poorly (*inf*), sick, under the weather (*inf*), unhealthy **2** = **harmful**, bad, damaging, deleterious, detrimental, evil, foul, injurious, unfortunate ▷ *n* **3** = **harm**, affliction, hardship, hurt, injury, misery, misfortune, trouble, unpleasantness, woe ▷ *adv* **4** = **badly**, inauspiciously, poorly, unfavourably, unfortunately, unluckily **5** = **hardly**, barely, by no means, scantily

ill-advised *adj* **1** = **misguided**, ill-considered, ill-judged, injudicious **2** = **unwise**, foolhardy, imprudent, incautious, rash, reckless, thoughtless

ill-disposed *adj* (often foll. by *towards*) = **unfriendly**, antagonistic, disobliging, hostile, inimical, uncooperative, unwelcoming

illegal *adj* = **unlawful**, banned, criminal, felonious, forbidden, illicit, outlawed, prohibited, unauthorized, unlicensed

illegible ● *adj* unable to be read or deciphered. **illegibility** *n*.

illegitimate ● *adj* **1** born of parents not married to each other. **2** not lawful. **illegitimacy** *n*.

illiberal *adj* narrow-minded, intolerant.

illicit ● *adj* **1** illegal. **2** forbidden or disapproved of by society.

illiterate ● *n, adj* (person) unable to read or write. **illiteracy** *n*.

illogical ● *adj* **1** unreasonable. **2** not logical. **illogicality** *n*.

illuminate ● *v* **1** light up. **2** make clear, explain. **3** decorate with lights. **4** *History* decorate (a manuscript) with designs of gold and bright colours. **illumination** *n* **illuminating** *adj*.

illusion ● *n* deceptive appearance or belief. **illusionist** *n* conjuror. **illusory** *adj*

seeming to be true, but actually false.

illustrate ● *v* **1** explain by use of examples. **2** provide (a book or text) with pictures. **3** be an example of. **illustration** *n* **1** picture or diagram. **2** example. **3** art of illustrating. **illustrative** *adj* **illustrator** *n*.

illustrious ● *adj* famous and distinguished.

IM instant messaging: communication in real time through the transmission of messages over a computer network.

image ● *n* **1** mental picture of someone or something. **2** impression people have of a person, organization, etc. **3** representation of a person or thing in a work of art. **4** optical reproduction of someone or something, for example in a mirror. **5** person or thing that looks

---

THESAURUS

illegality *n* = **crime**, felony, illegitimacy, lawlessness, wrong

illegible *adj* = **indecipherable**, obscure, scrawled, unreadable

illegitimate *adj* **1** = **born out of wedlock**, bastard **2** = **unlawful**, illegal, illicit, improper, unauthorized

ill-fated *adj* = **doomed**, hapless, ill-omened, ill-starred, luckless, star-crossed, unfortunate, unhappy, unlucky

illicit *adj* **1** = **illegal**, criminal, felonious, illegitimate, prohibited, unauthorized, unlawful, unlicensed **2** = **forbidden**, clandestine, furtive, guilty, immoral, improper

illiterate *adj* = **uneducated**, ignorant, uncultured, untaught, untutored

ill-mannered *adj* = **rude**, badly behaved, boorish, churlish, discourteous, impolite, insolent, loutish, uncouth

illness *n* **1** = **sickness**, affliction, ailment, disease, disorder, infirmity, malady

illogical *adj* = **irrational**, absurd, inconsistent, invalid, meaningless, senseless, shonky (*Aust & NZ inf*), unreasonable, unscientific, unsound

ill-treat *v* = **abuse**, damage, harm, injure, maltreat, mishandle, misuse, oppress

illuminate *v* **1** = **light up**, brighten **2** = **clarify**, clear up, elucidate, enlighten, explain, interpret, make clear, shed light on

illuminating *adj* **2** = **informative**, enlightening, explanatory, helpful, instructive, revealing

illumination *n* **1** = **light**, brightness, lighting, radiance **2** = **enlightenment**, clarification, insight, revelation

illusion *n* **a** = **fantasy**, chimera, daydream, figment of the imagination, hallucination, mirage, will-o'-the-wisp **b** = **misconception**, deception, delusion, error, fallacy, misapprehension

illusory *adj* = **unreal**, chimerical, deceptive, delusive, fallacious, false, hallucinatory, mistaken, sham

illustrate *v* **1** = **demonstrate**, bring home, elucidate, emphasize, explain, point up, show

illustrated *adj* **2** = **pictorial**, decorated, graphic

illustration *n* **1** = **picture**, decoration, figure, plate, sketch **2** = **example**, case, instance, specimen

illustrious *adj* = **famous**, celebrated, distinguished, eminent, glorious, great, notable, prominent, renowned

ill will *n* = **hostility**, animosity, bad blood, dislike, enmity, hatred, malice, rancour, resentment, venom

image *n* **1, 2** = **concept**, idea, impression, mental picture, perception **3** = **representation**, effigy, figure, icon, idol, likeness, picture, portrait, statue **5** = **replica**, counterpart, (dead) ringer (*sl*), doppelgänger, double, facsimile, spitting image (*inf*)

imaginable *adj* = **possible**, believable, comprehensible, conceivable, credible, likely, plausible

imaginary *adj* = **fictional**, fictitious, hypothetical, illusory, imagined, invented, made-up, nonexistent, unreal

almost exactly like another. **6** figure of speech, esp. a metaphor or simile. **imagery** *n* images collectively, esp. in the arts.

imagine ❶ *v* **1** form a mental image of. **2** think, believe, or guess. **imaginable** *adj* **imaginary** *adj* existing only in the imagination. **imagination** *n* **1** ability to make mental images of things that may not exist in real life. **2** creative mental ability. **imaginative** *adj* having or showing a lot of creative mental ability. **imaginatively** *adv*.

● **SPELLING TIP**
● Remembering that an *e* changes to
● an *a* to form **imagination** is a good
● way of getting **imaginary** right,
● because it has an *a* instead of an *e*
● too.

imago [im-**may**-go] *n, pl* **imagoes**, **imagines** [im-**maj**-in-ees] sexually mature adult insect.

imam *n* **1** leader of prayers in a mosque. **2** title of some Islamic leaders.

IMAX ® [**eye**-max] *n* film projection process which produces an image ten times larger than standard.

imbalance *n* lack of balance or proportion.

imbecile ❶ [**imb**-ess-eel] *n* **1** stupid person. **2** *offens* mentally retarded person. ▷ *adj* **3** (also **imbecilic**) stupid or senseless. **imbecility** *n*.

imbed *v* same as EMBED.

imbibe ❶ *v* **1** drink (alcoholic drinks). **2** *lit* absorb (ideas etc.).

imbroglio ❶ [imb-**role**-ee-oh] *n, pl* **-ios** confusing and complicated situation.

imbue *v* **-buing, -bued** (usu. foll. by *with*) fill or inspire with (ideals or principles).

IMF International Monetary Fund.

imitate ❶ *v* **1** take as a model. **2** copy the voice and mannerisms of, esp. for entertainment. **imitation** *n* **1** copy of an original. **2** imitating. ▷ *adj* **3** made to look like a material of superior quality, e.g. *imitation leather*. **imitative** *adj* **imitator** *n*.

immaculate ❶ *adj* **1** completely clean or tidy. **2** completely flawless. **immaculately** *adv*.

immanent *adj* present within and throughout something. **immanence** *n*.

immaterial ❶ *adj* not important, not relevant.

immature ❶ *adj* **1** not fully developed. **2** lacking wisdom or stability because of youth. **immaturity** *n*.

———————————————— THESAURUS ————————————————

imagination *n* **2** = **creativity**, enterprise, ingenuity, invention, inventiveness, originality, resourcefulness, vision

imaginative *adj* = **creative**, clever, enterprising, ingenious, inspired, inventive, original

imagine *v* **1** = **envisage**, conceive, conceptualize, conjure up, picture, plan, think of, think up, visualize **2** = **believe**, assume, conjecture, fancy, guess (*inf, chiefly US & Canad*), infer, suppose, surmise, suspect, take it, think

imbecile *n* **1** = **idiot**, chump, cretin, fool, halfwit, moron, numbskull *or* numskull, thickhead, twit (*inf, chiefly Brit*) ▷ *adj* **3** (also **imbecilic**) = **stupid**, asinine, fatuous, feeble-minded, foolish, idiotic, moronic, thick, witless

imbibe *v* **1** = **drink**, consume, knock back (*inf*), quaff, sink (*inf*), swallow, swig (*inf*) **2** *Lit* = **absorb**, acquire, assimilate, gain, gather, ingest, receive, take in

imbroglio *n* = **complication**, embarrassment, entanglement, involvement, misunderstanding, quandary

imitate *v* **1** = **follow**, emulate, mirror, simulate **2** = **copy**, ape, echo, mimic, repeat

imitation *n* **1** = **replica**, fake, forgery, impersonation, impression, reproduction, sham, substitution **2** = **mimicry**, counterfeiting, duplication, likeness, resemblance, simulation ▷ *adj* **3** = **artificial**, dummy, ersatz, man-made, mock, phoney *or* phony (*inf*), reproduction, sham, simulated, synthetic

imitative *adj* **1** = **derivative**, second-hand, simulated, unoriginal **2** = **parrot-like**, copycat (*inf*), mimetic

imitator *n* **2** = **impersonator**, copier, copycat (*inf*), impressionist, mimic, parrot

immaculate *adj* **1** = **clean**, neat, spick-and-span, spotless, spruce, squeaky-clean **2** = **pure**, above reproach, faultless, flawless, impeccable, perfect, unblemished, unexceptionable, untarnished

immaterial *adj* = **irrelevant**, extraneous, inconsequential, inessential, insignificant, of no importance, trivial, unimportant

immature *adj* **1** = **young**, adolescent, undeveloped, unformed, unripe

immeasurable *adj* too great to be measured. **immeasurably** *adv*.

immediate ❶ *adj* 1 occurring at once. 2 next or nearest in time, space, or relationship. **immediately** *adv* **immediacy** *n*.

immemorial *adj* **since, from time immemorial** longer than anyone can remember.

immense ❶ *adj* extremely large. **immensely** *adv* to a very great degree. **immensity** *n*.

immerse ❶ *v* 1 involve deeply, engross, e.g. *immersed in his work*. 2 plunge (something or someone) into liquid. **immersion** *n* **immersion heater** electrical device in a domestic hot-water tank for heating water.

immigration ❶ *n* coming to a foreign country in order to settle there. **immigrate** *v* **immigrant** *n* person who comes to a foreign country in order to settle there.

imminent ❶ *adj* about to happen. **imminently** *adv* **imminence** *n*.

immobile ❶ *adj* 1 not moving. 2 unable to move. **immobility** *n* **immobilize** *v* make unable to move or work.

immoderate ❶ *adj* excessive or unreasonable.

immodest *adj* 1 behaving in an indecent or improper manner. 2 behaving in a boastful or conceited manner. **immodesty** *n*.

immolate *v* kill as a sacrifice. **immolation** *n*.

immoral ❶ *adj* 1 morally wrong, corrupt. 2 sexually depraved or promiscuous. **immorality** *n*.

● **USAGE NOTE**
● Do not confuse *immoral* with *amoral*,
● which means 'having no moral
● standards'.

immortal ❶ *adj* 1 living forever. 2 famous for all time. ▷ *n* 3 person whose fame will last for all time. 4 immortal being. **immortality** *n* **immortalize** *v*.

immovable, immoveable ❶ *adj* 1 unable to be moved. 2 unwilling to

---

2 = **childish**, callow, inexperienced, infantile, juvenile, puerile

immaturity *n* 1 = **unripeness**, greenness, imperfection, rawness, unpreparedness 2 = **childishness**, callowness, inexperience, puerility

immediate *adj* 1 = **instant**, instantaneous 2 = **nearest**, close, direct, near, next

immediately *adv* 1 = **at once**, directly, forthwith, instantly, now, promptly, right away, straight away, this instant, without delay

immense *adj* = **huge**, colossal, enormous, extensive, gigantic, great, massive, monumental, stupendous, tremendous, vast

immensity *n* = **size**, bulk, enormity, expanse, extent, greatness, hugeness, magnitude, vastness

immerse *v* 1 = **engross**, absorb, busy, engage, involve, occupy, take up 2 = **plunge**, bathe, dip, douse, duck, dunk, sink, submerge

immersion *n* 1 = **involvement**, absorption, concentration, preoccupation 2 = **dipping**, dousing, ducking, dunking, plunging, submerging

immigrant *n* = **settler**, incomer, newcomer

imminent *adj* = **near**, at hand, close, coming, forthcoming, gathering,

impending, in the pipeline, looming

immobile *adj* = **stationary**, at a standstill, at rest, fixed, immovable, motionless, rigid, rooted, static, still, stock-still, unmoving

immobility *n* = **stillness**, fixity, inertness, motionlessness, stability, steadiness

immobilize *v* = **paralyse**, bring to a standstill, cripple, disable, freeze, halt, stop, transfix

immoderate *adj* = **excessive**, exaggerated, exorbitant, extravagant, extreme, inordinate, over the top (*sl*), undue, unjustified, unreasonable

immoral *adj* 1 = **wicked**, bad, corrupt, sinful, unethical, unprincipled, wrong 2 = **depraved**, debauched, dissolute, indecent

immorality *n* 1 = **wickedness**, corruption, sin, wrong 2 = **depravity**, debauchery, dissoluteness, vice

immortal *adj* 1 = **eternal**, deathless, enduring, everlasting, imperishable, lasting, perennial, undying ▷ *n* 3 = **great**, genius, hero 4 = **god**, goddess

immortality *n* 1 = **eternity**, everlasting life, perpetuity 2 = **fame**, celebrity, glory, greatness, renown

immortalize *v* 2 = **commemorate**, celebrate, exalt, glorify

immovable, immoveable *adj* 1 = **fixed**, firm, immutable, jammed,

change one's opinions or beliefs. **3** not affected by feeling, emotionless. **immovability**, **immoveability** n **immovably**, **immoveably** adv.

immune ❶ adj **1** protected against a specific disease. **2** (foll. by to) secure (against). **3** (foll. by from) exempt (from). **immunity**, pl **-ties 1** ability to resist disease. **2** freedom from prosecution, tax, etc. **immunize** v make immune to a disease. **immunization** n.

immunodeficiency n deficiency in or breakdown of a person's ability to fight diseases.

immunology n branch of medicine concerned with the study of immunity. **immunological** adj **immunologist** n.

immure v lit imprison.

immutable [im-**mute**-a-bl] adj unchangeable. **immutability** n.

imp ❶ n **1** (in folklore) mischievous small creature with magical powers. **2** mischievous child.

impact ❶ n **1** strong effect. **2** (force of) a collision. ▷ v **3** have a strong effect on. **4** press firmly into something.

impair ❶ v weaken or damage. **impairment** n.

impala [imp-**ah**-la] n southern African antelope.

impale v pierce with a sharp object.

impalpable adj difficult to define or understand.

impart ❶ v **1** communicate (information). **2** give, e.g. butter imparts a full rich taste to a cake.

impartial ❶ adj not favouring one side or the other. **impartially** adv **impartiality** n.

impassable ❶ adj (of a road etc.) impossible to travel through or over.

impasse ❶ [am-pass] n situation in which progress is impossible.

impassible adj impassive or unmoved.

impassioned ❶ adj full of emotion.

impassive adj showing no emotion, calm. **impassively** adv.

impasto n **1** paint applied thickly, so that brush marks are evident. **2** technique of painting in this way.

impatient ❶ adj **1** irritable at any delay or difficulty. **2** restless (to have or do something). **impatiently** adv **impatience** n.

impeach ❶ v charge with a serious crime

secure, set, stable, stationary, stuck **2** = **inflexible**, adamant, obdurate, resolute, steadfast, unshakable, unwavering, unyielding

immune adj **1** = **protected**, clear, free, resistant **2** = **invulnerable**, proof (against), safe, unaffected **3** = **exempt**

immunity n **1** = **resistance**, immunization, protection **2** = **exemption**, amnesty, freedom, indemnity, invulnerability, licence, release

immunize v = **vaccinate**, inoculate, protect, safeguard

imp n **1** = **demon**, devil, sprite **2** = **rascal**, brat, minx, rogue, scamp

impact n **1** = **effect**, consequences, impression, influence, repercussions, significance **2** = **collision**, blow, bump, contact, crash, jolt, knock, smash, stroke, thump

impair v = **worsen**, blunt, damage, decrease, diminish, harm, hinder, injure, lessen, reduce, undermine, weaken

impaired adj = **damaged**, defective, faulty, flawed, imperfect, shonky (Aust & NZ inf), unsound

impart v **1** = **communicate**, convey, disclose, divulge, make known, pass

on, relate, reveal, tell **2** = **give**, accord, afford, bestow, confer, grant, lend, yield

impartial adj = **neutral**, detached, disinterested, equitable, even-handed, fair, just, objective, open-minded, unbiased, unprejudiced

impartiality n = **neutrality**, detachment, disinterestedness, dispassion, equity, even-handedness, fairness, objectivity, open-mindedness

impassable adj = **blocked**, closed, impenetrable, obstructed

impasse n = **deadlock**, dead end, stalemate, standoff, standstill

impassioned adj = **intense**, animated, fervent, fiery, heated, inspired, passionate, rousing, stirring

impatience n **1** = **irritability**, intolerance, quick temper, shortness, snappiness **2** = **restlessness**, agitation, anxiety, eagerness, edginess, fretfulness, nervousness, uneasiness

impatient adj **1** = **irritable**, demanding, hot-tempered, intolerant, quick-tempered, snappy, testy **2** = **restless**, eager, edgy, fretful, straining at the leash

impeach v = **charge**, accuse, arraign, indict

against the state. **impeachment** n.

impeccable ⊙ adj without fault, excellent. **impeccably** adv.

impecunious ⊙ adj penniless, poor.

impedance [imp-**eed**-anss] n Electricity measure of the opposition to the flow of an alternating current.

impede ⊙ v hinder in action or progress. **impediment** n something that makes action, speech, or progress difficult. **impedimenta** pl n objects impeding progress, esp. baggage or equipment.

impel ⊙ v -**pelling**, -**pelled** push or force (someone) to do something.

impending ⊙ adj (esp. of something bad) about to happen.

impenetrable ⊙ adj 1 impossible to get through. 2 impossible to understand.

imperative ⊙ adj 1 extremely urgent, vital. 2 Grammar denoting a mood of verbs used in commands. ▷ n 3 Grammar imperative mood.

imperceptible ⊙ adj too slight or gradual to be noticed. **imperceptibly** adv.

imperfect ⊙ adj 1 having faults or mistakes. 2 not complete.

3 Grammar denoting a tense of verbs describing continuous, incomplete, or repeated past actions. ▷ 4 Grammar imperfect tense. **imperfection** n.

imperial ⊙ adj 1 of or like an empire or emperor. 2 denoting a system of weights and measures formerly used in Britain. **imperialism** n rule by one country over many others. **imperialist** adj, n.

imperil ⊙ v -**illing**, -**illed** put in danger.

imperious adj proud and domineering.

impersonal ⊙ adj 1 not relating to any particular person, objective. 2 lacking human warmth or sympathy. 3 Grammar (of a verb) without a personal subject, e.g. it is snowing. **impersonality** n.

impersonate ⊙ v 1 pretend to be (another person). 2 copy the voice and mannerisms of, esp. for entertainment. **impersonation** n **impersonator** n.

impertinent ⊙ adj disrespectful or rude. **impertinently** adv **impertinence** n.

imperturbable ⊙ adj calm, not

impeccable adj = **faultless**, blameless, flawless, immaculate, irreproachable, perfect, squeaky-clean, unblemished, unimpeachable

impecunious adj = **poor**, broke (inf), destitute, down and out, indigent, insolvent, penniless, poverty-stricken

impede v = **hinder**, block, check, disrupt, hamper, hold up, obstruct, slow (down), thwart

impediment n = **obstacle**, barrier, difficulty, encumbrance, hindrance, obstruction, snag, stumbling block

impel v = **force**, compel, constrain, drive, induce, oblige, push, require

impending adj = **looming**, approaching, coming, forthcoming, gathering, imminent, in the pipeline, near, upcoming

impenetrable adj 1 = **impassable**, dense, impermeable, impervious, inviolable, solid, thick

2 = **incomprehensible**, arcane, enigmatic, inscrutable, mysterious, obscure, unfathomable, unintelligible

imperative adj 1 = **urgent**, crucial, essential, pressing, vital

imperceptible adj = **undetectable**, faint, indiscernible, invisible, microscopic, minute, slight, small, subtle, tiny

imperfect adj = **flawed**, damaged, defective, faulty, impaired, incomplete, limited, unfinished

imperfection n 1 = **fault**, blemish, defect, deficiency, failing, flaw, frailty, shortcoming, taint, weakness

imperial adj 1 = **royal**, kingly, majestic, princely, queenly, regal, sovereign

imperil v = **endanger**, expose, jeopardize, risk

impersonal adj 2 = **detached**, aloof, cold, dispassionate, formal, inhuman, neutral, remote

impersonate v 1 = **pretend to be**, masquerade as, pass oneself off as, pose as (inf) 2 = **imitate**, ape, do (inf), mimic, take off (inf)

impersonation n 2 = **imitation**, caricature, impression, mimicry, parody, takeoff (inf)

impertinence n = **rudeness**, brazenness, cheek (inf), disrespect, effrontery, front, impudence, insolence, nerve (inf), presumption

impertinent adj = **rude**, brazen, cheeky (inf), disrespectful, impolite, impudent, insolent, presumptuous

imperturbable adj = **calm**, collected, composed, cool, nerveless, self-possessed, serene, unexcitable, unflappable (inf), unruffled

excitable; unruffled.

impervious ❶ *adj* (foll. by *to*) **1** not letting (water etc.) through. **2** not influenced by (a feeling, argument, etc.).

impetigo [imp-it-**tie**-go] *n* contagious skin disease.

impetuous ❶ *adj* done or acting without thought, rash. **impetuously** *adv* **impetuosity** *n*.

impetus ❶ [imp-it-uss] *n*, *pl* **-tuses** **1** incentive, impulse. **2** force that starts a body moving.

impinge ❶ *v* (foll. by *on*) affect or restrict.

impious ❶ [imp-ee-uss] *adj* showing a lack of respect or reverence.

impish ❶ *adj* mischievous.

implacable ❶ *adj* not prepared to be appeased, unyielding. **implacably** *adv* **implacability** *n*.

implant ❶ *n* **1** *Medical* something put into someone's body, usu. by surgical operation, e.g. *silicone implants*. ▷ *v* **2** put (something) into someone's body,

usu. by surgical operation. **3** fix firmly in someone's mind. **implantation** *n*.

implement ❶ *v* **1** carry out (instructions etc.). ▷ *n* **2** tool, instrument. **implementation** *n*.

implicate ❶ *v* show to be involved, esp. in a crime. **implication** *n* something implied.

implicit ❶ *adj* **1** expressed indirectly. **2** absolute and unquestioning, e.g. *implicit support*. **implicitly** *adv*.

implode *v* collapse inwards.

implore ❶ *v* beg earnestly.

imply ❶ *v* **-plying, -plied 1** indicate by hinting, suggest. **2** involve as a necessary consequence.

impolite ❶ *adj* showing bad manners.

impolitic *adj* unwise or inadvisable.

imponderable *n*, *adj* (something) impossible to assess.

import ❶ *v* **1** bring in (goods) from another country. ▷ *n* **2** something imported. **3** importance. **4** meaning. **importation** *n* **importer** *n*.

━━━━━━━━━━━━━━━━━━━━━━━━━━━━━━━ THESAURUS ━━━━

impervious *adj* **1** (foll. by *to*) = **sealed**, impassable, impenetrable, impermeable, resistant **2** = **unaffected**, immune, invulnerable, proof against, unmoved, untouched

impetuosity *n* = **haste**, impulsiveness, precipitateness, rashness

impetuous *adj* = **rash**, hasty, impulsive, precipitate, unthinking

impetus *n* **1** = **incentive**, catalyst, goad, impulse, motivation, push, spur, stimulus **2** = **force**, energy, momentum, power

impinge *v* (foll. by *on*) = **affect**, bear upon, have a bearing on, impact, influence, relate to, touch

impious *adj* = **sacrilegious**, blasphemous, godless, irreligious, irreverent, profane, sinful, ungodly, unholy, wicked

impish *adj* = **mischievous**, devilish, puckish, rascally, roguish, sportive, waggish

implacable *adj* = **unyielding**, inflexible, intractable, merciless, pitiless, unbending, uncompromising, unforgiving

implant *v* **2** = **insert**, fix, graft **3** = **instil**, inculcate, infuse

implement *v* **1** = **carry out**, bring about, complete, effect, enforce, execute, fulfil, perform, realize ▷ *n* **2** = **tool**, apparatus, appliance, device,

gadget, instrument, utensil

implicate *v* = **incriminate**, associate, embroil, entangle, include, inculpate, involve

implication *n* = **suggestion**, inference, innuendo, meaning, overtone, presumption, significance

implicit *adj* **1** = **implied**, inferred, latent, tacit, taken for granted, undeclared, understood, unspoken **2** = **absolute**, constant, firm, fixed, full, steadfast, unqualified, unreserved, wholehearted

implied *adj* **1** = **unspoken**, hinted at, implicit, indirect, suggested, tacit, undeclared, unexpressed, unstated

implore *v* = **beg**, beseech, entreat, importune, plead with, pray

imply *v* **1** = **hint**, insinuate, intimate, signify, suggest **2** = **entail**, indicate, involve, mean, point to, presuppose

impolite *adj* = **bad-mannered**, discourteous, disrespectful, ill-mannered, insolent, loutish, rude, uncouth

import *v* **1** = **bring in**, introduce ▷ *n* **3** = **importance**, consequence, magnitude, moment, significance, substance, weight **4** = **meaning**, drift, gist, implication, intention, sense, significance, thrust

important ❶ *adj* **1** of great significance or value. **2** having influence or power. **importance** *n*.

importunate ❶ *adj* persistent or demanding. **importune** *v* harass with persistent requests. **importunity** *n*, *pl* **-ties**.

impose ❶ *v* **1** force the acceptance of. **2** (foll. by *on*) take unfair advantage (of). **imposing** *adj* grand, impressive. **imposition** *n* **1** imposing. **2** unreasonable demand.

impossible ❶ *adj* **1** not able to be done or to happen. **2** absurd or unreasonable. **impossibly** *adv* **impossibility** *n*, *pl* **-ties**.

imposter, impostor *n* person who cheats or swindles by pretending to be someone else.

imposture *n* deception, esp. by pretending to be someone else.

impotent ❶ [imp-a-tent] *adj* **1** powerless. **2** (of a man) incapable of sexual intercourse. **impotence** *n* **impotently** *adv*.

impound *v* take legal possession of, confiscate.

impoverish ❶ *v* make poor or weak. **impoverishment** *n*.

impracticable ❶ *adj* incapable of being put into practice.

impractical ❶ *adj* not sensible.

imprecation *n* curse.

impregnable ❶ *adj* impossible to break into. **impregnability** *n*.

impregnate ❶ *v* **1** saturate, spread all through. **2** make pregnant. **impregnation** *n*.

impresario *n*, *pl* **-ios** person who runs theatre performances, concerts, etc.

● **SPELLING TIP**
● Don't be fooled into spelling
● **impresario** as *impressario*, which
● occurs 33 times in the Bank of
● English. The correct spelling has only
● one *s*.

---

importance *n* **1** = **significance**, concern, consequence, import, interest, moment, substance, usefulness, value, weight **2** = **prestige**, distinction, eminence, esteem, influence, mana (*NZ*), prominence, standing, status

important *adj* **1** = **significant**, far-reaching, momentous, seminal, serious, substantial, urgent, weighty **2** = **powerful**, eminent, high-ranking, influential, noteworthy, pre-eminent, prominent, skookum (*Canad*)

importunate *adj Formal* = **persistent**, demanding, dogged, insistent, pressing, urgent

impose *v* **1** = **establish**, decree, fix, institute, introduce, levy, ordain **2** (foll. by *on*) = **inflict**, saddle (someone) with, take advantage of

imposing *adj* = **impressive**, commanding, dignified, grand, majestic, stately, striking

imposition *n* **1** = **application**, introduction, levying **2** = **intrusion**, liberty, presumption

impossibility *n* **1** = **hopelessness**, impracticability, inability

impossible *adj* **1** = **inconceivable**, impracticable, out of the question, unachievable, unattainable, unobtainable, unthinkable **2** = **absurd**, ludicrous, outrageous, preposterous, unreasonable

imposter, impostor *n* = **impersonator**, charlatan, deceiver, fake, fraud, phoney *or* phony (*inf*), pretender, sham, trickster

impotence *n* **1** = **powerlessness**, feebleness, frailty, helplessness, inability, incapacity, incompetence, ineffectiveness, paralysis, uselessness, weakness

impotent *adj* **1** = **powerless**, feeble, frail, helpless, incapable, incapacitated, incompetent, ineffective, paralysed, weak

impoverish *v* = **bankrupt**, beggar, break, ruin

impoverished *adj* = **poor**, bankrupt, destitute, impecunious, needy, on one's uppers, penurious, poverty-stricken

impracticable *adj* = **unfeasible**, impossible, out of the question, unachievable, unattainable, unworkable

impractical *adj* = **unworkable**, impossible, impracticable, inoperable, nonviable, unrealistic, wild

impregnable *adj* = **invulnerable**, impenetrable, indestructible, invincible, secure, unassailable, unbeatable, unconquerable

impregnate *v* **1** = **saturate**, infuse, permeate, soak, steep, suffuse **2** = **fertilize**, inseminate, make pregnant

impress ❶ v 1 affect strongly, usu.
favourably. 2 stress, emphasize.
3 imprint, stamp. **impression** n
1 effect, esp. a strong or favourable one.
2 vague idea. 3 impersonation for
entertainment. 4 mark made by
pressing. **impressionable** adj easily
impressed or influenced.
impressionist n person who
impersonates other people for
entertainment. **impressive** adj making
a strong impression, esp. through size,
importance, or quality.
Impressionism n art style that gives a
general effect or mood rather than
form or structure. **Impressionist** n
Impressionistic adj.
impressive ❶ adj making a strong
impression, esp. through size,
importance, or quality.
imprimatur [imp-rim-**ah**-ter] n official
approval to print a book.
imprint ❶ n 1 mark made by printing or

stamping. 2 publisher's name and
address on a book. ▷ v 3 produce (a
mark) by printing or stamping. 4 fix
firmly in someone's mind.
imprison ❶ v put in prison.
imprisonment n.
improbable ❶ adj not likely to be true
or to happen. **improbability** n, pl **-ties**.
improbity n dishonesty or wickedness.
impromptu ❶ adj without planning or
preparation.
improper ❶ adj 1 indecent. 2 incorrect
or irregular. **improper fraction**
fraction in which the numerator is
larger than the denominator, as in 5/3.
impropriety ❶ [imp-roe-**pry**-a-tee] n, pl
-ties unsuitable or slightly improper
behaviour.
improve ❶ v make or become better.
improvement n.
improvident ❶ adj not planning for
future needs. **improvidence** n.
improvise ❶ v 1 make use of whatever

————————————————————— THESAURUS ——————

impress v 1 = **excite**, affect, inspire,
make an impression, move, stir, strike,
touch 2 = **stress**, bring home to,
emphasize, fix, inculcate, instil into
3 = **imprint**, emboss, engrave, indent,
mark, print, stamp
impression n 1 = **effect**, feeling, impact,
influence, reaction 2 = **idea**, belief,
conviction, feeling, hunch, notion,
sense, suspicion 3 = **imitation**,
impersonation, parody, send-up (Brit
inf), takeoff (inf) 4 = **mark**, dent, hollow,
imprint, indentation, outline, stamp
impressionable adj = **suggestible**,
gullible, ingenuous, open, receptive,
responsive, sensitive, susceptible,
vulnerable
impressive adj = **grand**, awesome,
dramatic, exciting, moving, powerful,
stirring, striking
imprint n 1 = **mark**, impression,
indentation, sign, stamp ▷ v 3 = **fix**,
engrave, etch, impress, print, stamp
imprison v = **jail**, confine, detain,
incarcerate, intern, lock up, put away,
send down (inf)
imprisoned adj = **jailed**, behind bars,
captive, confined, incarcerated, in jail,
inside (sl), locked up, under lock and key
imprisonment n = **custody**,
confinement, detention, incarceration,
porridge (sl)
improbability n = **doubt**, dubiety,
uncertainty, unlikelihood

improbable adj = **doubtful**, dubious,
fanciful, far-fetched, implausible,
questionable, unconvincing, unlikely,
weak
impromptu adj = **unprepared**, ad-lib,
extemporaneous, improvised, offhand,
off the cuff (inf), spontaneous,
unrehearsed, unscripted
improper adj 1 = **indecent**, risqué,
smutty, suggestive, unbecoming,
unseemly, untoward, vulgar
2 = **inappropriate**, out of place,
uncalled-for, unfit, unsuitable,
unwarranted
impropriety n = **indecency**, bad taste,
incongruity, vulgarity
improve v a = **enhance**, ameliorate,
better, correct, help, rectify, touch up,
upgrade b = **progress**, advance,
develop, make strides, pick up, rally, rise
improvement n a = **enhancement**,
advancement, betterment
b = **progress**, advance, development,
rally, recovery, upswing
improvident adj = **imprudent**, careless,
negligent, prodigal, profligate, reckless,
short-sighted, spendthrift,
thoughtless, wasteful
improvisation n 1 = **makeshift**, ad-lib,
expedient 2 = **spontaneity**, ad-libbing,
extemporizing, invention
improvise v 1 = **concoct**, contrive,
devise, throw together
2 = **extemporize**, ad-lib, busk, invent,

materials are available. **2** make up (a piece of music, speech, etc.) as one goes along. **improvisation** *n*.

imprudent ❶ *adj* not sensible or wise. **imprudence** *n*.

impudent ❶ *adj* cheeky, disrespectful. **impudently** *adv* **impudence** *n*.

impugn [imp-**yoon**] *v* challenge the truth or validity of.

impulse ❶ *n* **1** sudden urge to do something. **2** short electrical signal passing along a wire or nerve or through the air. **on impulse** suddenly and without planning. **impulsive** *adj* acting or done without careful consideration. **impulsively** *adv*.

impunity ❶ [imp-**yoon**-it-ee] *n* **with impunity** without punishment.

impure ❶ *adj* **1** having dirty or unwanted substances mixed in. **2** immoral, obscene. **impurity** *n, pl* **-ties**.

impute ❶ *v* attribute responsibility to. **imputation** *n*.

in *prep* **1** indicating position inside, state or situation, etc. e.g. *in the net; in tears*. ▷ *adv* **2** indicating position inside, entry into, etc. e.g. *she stayed in; come*

in. ▷ *adj* **3** fashionable. **inward** *adj* **1** directed towards the middle. **2** situated within. **3** spiritual or mental. ▷ *adv* **4** (also **inwards**) towards the inside or middle. **inwardly** *adv*.

In *Chemistry* indium.

IN Indiana.

in. inch.

in-[1] *prefix* **1** not, non-, e.g. *incredible*. **2** lack of, e.g. *inexperience*.

in-[2] *prefix* in, into, towards, within, on, e.g. *infiltrate*.

inability *n* lack of means or skill to do something.

inaccessible ❶ *adj* **1** impossible or very difficult to reach. **2** difficult to understand or appreciate. **inaccessibility** *n*.

inaccurate ❶ *adj* not correct. **inaccuracy** *n, pl* **-cies**.

inaction *n* doing nothing. **inactive** *adj* **inactivity** *n*.

inadequate ❶ *adj* **1** not enough. **2** not good enough. **inadequacy** *n, pl* **-cies**.

inadmissible *adj* not allowable or acceptable.

---

play it by ear (*inf*), speak off the cuff (*inf*), wing it (*inf*)

imprudent *adj* = **unwise**, careless, foolhardy, ill-advised, ill-considered, ill-judged, injudicious, irresponsible, rash, reckless

impudence *n* = **boldness**, audacity, brazenness, cheek (*inf*), effrontery, impertinence, insolence, nerve (*inf*), presumption, shamelessness

impudent *adj* = **bold**, audacious, brazen, cheeky (*inf*), impertinent, insolent, presumptuous, rude, shameless

impulse *n* **1** = **urge**, caprice, feeling, inclination, notion, whim, wish

impulsive *adj* = **instinctive**, devil-may-care, hasty, impetuous, intuitive, passionate, precipitate, rash, spontaneous

impunity *n* **with impunity** = **without punishment**, at liberty, with freedom, with immunity, with licence, with permission

impure *adj* **1 a** = **unclean**, contaminated, defiled, dirty, infected, polluted, tainted **b** = **unrefined**, adulterated, debased, mixed **2** = **immoral**, corrupt, indecent, lascivious, lewd, licentious,

obscene, unchaste

impurity *n* **1** = **contamination**, defilement, dirtiness, infection, pollution, taint

imputation *n* = **blame**, accusation, aspersion, censure, insinuation, reproach, slander, slur

inaccessible *adj* **1** = **out of reach**, impassable, out of the way, remote, unapproachable, unattainable, unreachable

inaccuracy *n* = **error**, defect, erratum, fault, lapse, mistake

inaccurate *adj* = **incorrect**, defective, erroneous, faulty, imprecise, mistaken, out, shonky (*Aust & NZ inf*), unreliable, unsound, wrong

inactive *adj* = **unused**, dormant, idle, inoperative, unemployed, unoccupied

inactivity *n* = **immobility**, dormancy, hibernation, inaction, passivity, unemployment

inadequacy *n* **1** = **shortage**, dearth, insufficiency, meagreness, paucity, poverty, scantiness **2** = **deficiency**, defect, failing, imperfection, inability, incapacity, incompetence, ineffectiveness, shortcoming, weakness

inadequate *adj* **1** = **insufficient**, meagre, scant, sketchy, sparse

inadvertent *adj* unintentional.
  inadvertently *adv.*
inalienable *adj* not able to be taken
  away, e.g. *an inalienable right.*
inamorata, (*masc*) **inamorato** *n, pl*
  -s *lit* lover.
inane ❶ *adj* senseless, silly. **inanity** *n, pl*
  -ties.
inanimate ❶ *adj* not living.
inapplicable *adj* not suitable or relevant.
inappropriate *adj* not suitable.
inapt *adj* not apt or fitting.
inarticulate *adj* unable to express
  oneself clearly or well.
inasmuch as *conj* because or in so far as.
inattentive *adj* not paying attention.
  inattention *n.*
inaudible *adj* not loud enough to be
  heard. **inaudibly** *adv.*
inaugurate ❶ *v* **1** open or begin the use
  of, esp. with ceremony. **2** formally
  establish (a new leader) in office.
  inaugural *adj* **inauguration** *n.*
inauspicious *adj* unlucky, likely to have
  an unfavourable outcome.
inboard *adj* (of a boat's engine) inside
  the hull.
inborn ❶ *adj* existing from birth, natural.
inbox *n* (on a computer) place in which

incoming email messages are stored.
inbred ❶ *adj* **1** produced as a result of
  inbreeding. **2** inborn or ingrained.
inbreeding *n* breeding of animals or
  people that are closely related.
inbuilt *adj* present from the start.
Inc. *US & Aust* (of a company) incorporated.
incalculable ❶ *adj* too great to be
  estimated.
in camera *adv* see CAMERA.
incandescent *adj* glowing with heat.
  incandescence *n.*
incantation ❶ *n* ritual chanting of
  magic words or sounds.
incapable *adj* **1** (foll. by *of*) unable (to do
  something). **2** incompetent.
incapacitate ❶ *v* deprive of strength or
  ability. **incapacity** *n.*
incarcerate ❶ *v* imprison.
  incarceration *n.*
incarnate ❶ *adj* in human form, e.g. *she
  is evil incarnate.* **incarnation** *n*
  Incarnation *n Christianity* God's coming
  to earth in human form as Jesus Christ.
incendiary [in-**send**-ya-ree] *adj* **1** (of a
  bomb, attack, etc.) designed to cause
  fires. ▷ *n, pl* **-aries 2** bomb designed to
  cause fires.
incense¹ ❶ *v* make very angry.

———————————————————————— THESAURUS ————————————

  2 = **deficient**, faulty, found wanting,
  incapable, incompetent, not up to
  scratch (*inf*), unqualified
inadvertently *adv* = **unintentionally**,
  accidentally, by accident, by mistake,
  involuntarily, mistakenly, unwittingly
inane *adj* = **senseless**, empty, fatuous,
  frivolous, futile, idiotic, mindless, silly,
  stupid, vacuous
inanimate *adj* = **lifeless**, cold, dead,
  defunct, extinct, inert
inaugural *adj* **1** = **first**, initial,
  introductory, maiden, opening
inaugurate *v* **1** = **launch**, begin,
  commence, get under way, initiate,
  institute, introduce, set in motion
  2 = **invest**, induct, install
inauguration *n* **1** = **launch**, initiation,
  institution, opening, setting up
  2 = **investiture**, induction, installation
inborn *adj* = **natural**, congenital,
  hereditary, inbred, ingrained, inherent,
  innate, instinctive, intuitive, native
inbred *adj* **2** = **innate**, constitutional,
  deep-seated, ingrained, inherent,
  native, natural
incalculable *adj* = **countless**,
  boundless, infinite, innumerable,

  limitless, numberless, untold, vast
incantation *n* = **chant**, charm, formula,
  invocation, spell
incapacitate *v* = **disable**, cripple,
  immobilize, lay up (*inf*), paralyse, put
  out of action (*inf*)
incapacitated *adj* = **indisposed**, *hors de
  combat*, immobilized, laid up (*inf*), out
  of action (*inf*), unfit
incapacity *n* = **inability**, impotence,
  inadequacy, incapability,
  incompetency, ineffectiveness,
  powerlessness, unfitness, weakness
incarcerate *v* = **imprison**, confine,
  detain, impound, intern, jail *or* gaol,
  lock up, throw in jail
incarceration *n* = **imprisonment**,
  captivity, confinement, detention,
  internment
incarnate *adj* = **personified**, embodied,
  typified
incarnation *n* = **embodiment**,
  epitome, manifestation,
  personification, type
incense¹ *v* = **anger**, enrage, inflame,
  infuriate, irritate, madden, make one's
  hackles rise, rile (*inf*)
incensed *adj* = **angry**, enraged, fuming,

incense² *n* substance that gives off a sweet perfume when burned.

incentive ❶ *n* something that encourages effort or action.

inception ❶ *n* beginning.

incessant ❶ *adj* never stopping; continual, e.g. *incessant squawking*. **incessantly** *adv*.

incest *n* sexual intercourse between two people too closely related to marry. **incestuous** *adj*.

inch *n* **1** unit of length equal to one twelfth of a foot or 2.54 centimetres. **2** amount of rainfall equal to what would cover a surface with water one inch deep. e.g. *five inches of rain*. ▷ *v* **3** move slowly and gradually.

inchoate [in-**koe**-ate] *adj* just begun and not yet properly developed.

incidence *n* extent or frequency of occurrence.

incident ❶ *n* **1** something that happens. **2** event involving violence.

incidental ❶ *adj* occurring in connection with or resulting from something more important. **incidentally** *adv* **incidental music** background music for a film or play.

incinerate ❶ *v* burn to ashes. **incineration** *n* **incinerator** *n* furnace for burning rubbish.

incipient ❶ *adj* just starting to appear or happen.

incise ❶ *v* cut into with a sharp tool. **incision** *n* **incisive** *adj* direct and forceful. **incisor** *n* front tooth, used for biting into food.

incite ❶ *v* stir up, provoke. **incitement** *n*.

incivility ❶ *n, pl* **-ties** rudeness or a rude remark.

inclement ❶ *adj* (of weather) stormy or severe. **inclemency** *n*.

incline ❶ *v* **1** lean, slope. **2** (cause to) have a certain disposition or tendency. ▷ *n* **3** slope. **inclination** *n* **1** liking, tendency, or preference. **2** slope.

include ❶ *v* **1** have as part of the whole. **2** put in as part of a set or group.

THESAURUS

---

furious, indignant, infuriated, irate, maddened, steamed up (*sl*), up in arms

incentive *n* = **encouragement**, bait, carrot (*inf*), enticement, inducement, lure, motivation, spur, stimulus

inception *n* = **beginning**, birth, commencement, dawn, initiation, origin, outset, start

incessant *adj* = **endless**, ceaseless, constant, continual, eternal, interminable, never-ending, nonstop, perpetual, unceasing, unending

incessantly *adv* = **endlessly**, ceaselessly, constantly, continually, eternally, interminably, nonstop, perpetually, persistently, twenty-four-seven (*inf*)

incident *n* **1** = **happening**, adventure, episode, event, fact, matter, occasion, occurrence **2** = **disturbance**, clash, commotion, confrontation, contretemps, scene

incidental *adj* = **secondary**, ancillary, minor, nonessential, occasional, subordinate, subsidiary

incidentally *adv* = **parenthetically**, by the bye, by the way, in passing

incinerate *v* = **burn up**, carbonize, char, cremate, reduce to ashes

incipient *adj* = **beginning**, commencing, developing, embryonic, inchoate, nascent, starting

incision *n* = **cut**, gash, notch, opening, slash, slit

incisive *adj* = **penetrating**, acute, keen, perspicacious, piercing, trenchant

incite *v* = **provoke**, encourage, foment, inflame, instigate, spur, stimulate, stir up, urge, whip up

incitement *n* = **provocation**, agitation, encouragement, impetus, instigation, prompting, spur, stimulus

incivility *n* = **rudeness**, bad manners, boorishness, discourteousness, discourtesy, disrespect, ill-breeding, impoliteness

inclement *adj* = **stormy**, foul, harsh, intemperate, rough, severe, tempestuous

inclination *n* **1** = **tendency**, disposition, liking, partiality, penchant, predilection, predisposition, proclivity, proneness, propensity **2** = **slope**, angle, gradient, incline, pitch, slant, tilt

incline *v* **1** = **slope**, lean, slant, tilt, tip, veer **2** = **predispose**, influence, persuade, prejudice, sway ▷ *n* **3** = **slope**, ascent, descent, dip, grade, gradient, rise

inclined *adj* **2** = **disposed**, apt, given, liable, likely, minded, predisposed, prone, willing

include *v* **1** = **contain**, comprise, cover, embrace, encompass, incorporate, involve, subsume, take in **2** = **introduce**, add, enter, insert

inclusion *n* **inclusive** *adj* including everything (specified). **inclusively** *adv.*

incognito ❶ [in-kog-**nee**-toe] *adj, adv* **1** having adopted a false identity. ▷ *n, pl* **-tos 2** false identity.

incoherent ❶ *adj* unclear and impossible to understand. **incoherence** *n* **incoherently** *adv.*

income ❶ *n* amount of money earned from work, investments, etc. **income support** (formerly, in Britain) allowance paid by the government to people with a very low income. **income tax** personal tax levied on annual income.

incoming ❶ *adj* **1** coming in. **2** about to come into office.

incommode *v* cause inconvenience to.

incommunicado *adj, adv* deprived of communication with other people.

incomparable ❶ *adj* beyond comparison, unequalled. **incomparably** *adv.*

incompatible ❶ *adj* inconsistent or

conflicting. **incompatibility** *n.*

incompetent ❶ *adj* **1** not having the necessary ability or skill to do something. ▷ *n* **2** incompetent person. **incompetence** *n.*

inconceivable ❶ *adj* extremely unlikely, unimaginable.

inconclusive ❶ *adj* not giving a final decision or result.

incongruous ❶ *adj* inappropriate or out of place. **incongruously** *adv* **incongruity** *n, pl* **-ties**.

inconsequential *adj* unimportant, insignificant.

inconsiderable ❶ *adj* **not inconsiderable** fairly large.

inconsiderate ❶ *adj* not considering other people.

inconsistent ❶ *adj* **1** changeable in behaviour or mood. **2** containing contradictory elements, e.g. *witnesses told inconsistent stories.* **3** not in accordance, e.g. *the outburst was*

─────────── THESAURUS ───────────

inclusion *n* **2** = **addition**, incorporation, insertion

inclusive *adj* = **comprehensive**, across-the-board, all-embracing, blanket, general, global, overarching, sweeping, umbrella

incognito *adj* **1** = **in disguise**, disguised, under an assumed name, unknown, unrecognized

incoherence *n* = **unintelligibility**, disjointedness, inarticulateness

incoherent *adj* = **unintelligible**, confused, disjointed, disordered, inarticulate, inconsistent, jumbled, muddled, rambling, stammering, stuttering

income *n* = **revenue**, earnings, pay, proceeds, profits, receipts, salary, takings, wages

incoming *adj* **1** = **arriving**, approaching, entering, homeward, landing, returning **2** = **new**

incomparable *adj* = **unequalled**, beyond compare, inimitable, matchless, peerless, superlative, supreme, transcendent, unmatched, unparalleled, unrivalled

incompatible *adj* = **inconsistent**, conflicting, contradictory, incongruous, mismatched, unsuited

incompetence *n* = **ineptitude**, inability, inadequacy, incapability, incapacity, ineffectiveness, unfitness, uselessness

incompetent *adj* **1** = **inept**, bungling, floundering, incapable, ineffectual, inexpert, unfit, useless

inconceivable *adj* = **unimaginable**, beyond belief, incomprehensible, incredible, mind-boggling (*inf*), out of the question, unbelievable, unheard-of, unthinkable

inconclusive *adj* = **indecisive**, ambiguous, indeterminate, open, unconvincing, undecided, up in the air (*inf*), vague

incongruity *n* = **inappropriateness**, conflict, discrepancy, disparity, incompatibility, inconsistency, unsuitability

incongruous *adj* = **inappropriate**, discordant, improper, incompatible, out of keeping, out of place, unbecoming, unsuitable

inconsiderable *adj* **not inconsiderable** = **large**, appreciable, goodly, great, marked, noticeable, plentiful, sizable *or* sizeable, substantial

inconsiderate *adj* = **selfish**, indelicate, insensitive, rude, tactless, thoughtless, unkind, unthinking

inconsistency *n* **1** = **unreliability**, fickleness, instability, unpredictability, unsteadiness **2, 3** = **incompatibility**, disagreement, discrepancy, disparity, divergence, incongruity, variance

inconsistent *adj* **1** = **changeable**, capricious, erratic, fickle, inconstant,

inconsistent with his image.
inconsistency n, pl **-cies**.
inconsolable ❶ adj very distressed.
inconsolably adv.
inconspicuous ❶ adj not easily noticed
or seen. **inconspicuously** adv.
inconstant adj liable to change one's
loyalties or opinions.
incontestable adj impossible to deny or
argue with.
incontinent adj unable to control one's
bladder or bowels. **incontinence** n.
incontrovertible ❶ adj impossible to
deny or disprove.
inconvenience ❶ n 1 trouble or
difficulty. ▷ v 2 cause trouble or
difficulty to. **inconvenient** adj.
incorporate ❶ v include or be included as
part of a larger unit. **incorporation** n.
incorporeal adj without material form.
incorrigible ❶ adj beyond correction or
reform. **incorrigibly** adv.
incorruptible ❶ adj 1 too honest to be
bribed or corrupted. 2 not subject to
decay.
increase ❶ v 1 make or become

greater in size, number, etc. ▷ n
2 rise in number, size, etc. 3 amount
by which something increases.
on the increase becoming more
common. **increasingly** adv.
incredible ❶ adj 1 hard to believe or
imagine. 2 informal marvellous,
amazing. **incredibly** adv.
incredulous ❶ adj not willing to believe
something. **incredulity** n.
increment ❶ n increase in money or
value, esp. a regular salary increase.
incremental adj.
incriminate ❶ v make (someone) seem
guilty of a crime. **incriminating** adj.
incubate [**in**-cube-ate] v 1 (of a bird)
hatch (eggs) by sitting on them.
2 grow (bacteria). 3 (of bacteria)
remain inactive in an animal or
person before causing disease.
incubation n **incubator** n
1 heated enclosed apparatus for
rearing premature babies.
2 apparatus for artificially hatching
birds' eggs.
incubus [**in**-cube-uss] n, pl **-bi**, **-buses**

——— THESAURUS ———

unpredictable, unstable, unsteady,
variable **2, 3** = **incompatible**, at odds,
conflicting, contradictory, discordant,
incongruous, irreconcilable, out of step
inconsolable adj = **heartbroken**,
brokenhearted, desolate, despairing
inconspicuous adj = **unobtrusive**,
camouflaged, hidden, insignificant,
ordinary, plain, unassuming,
unnoticeable, unostentatious
incontrovertible adj = **indisputable**,
certain, established, incontestable,
indubitable, irrefutable, positive, sure,
undeniable, unquestionable
inconvenience n 1 = **trouble**,
awkwardness, bother, difficulty,
disadvantage, disruption, disturbance,
fuss, hindrance, nuisance ▷ v
2 = **trouble**, bother, discommode,
disrupt, disturb, put out, upset
inconvenient adj = **troublesome**,
awkward, bothersome,
disadvantageous, disturbing,
inopportune, unsuitable, untimely
incorporate v = **include**, absorb,
assimilate, blend, combine, integrate,
merge, subsume
incorrigible adj = **incurable**, hardened,
hopeless, intractable, inveterate,
irredeemable, unreformed
incorruptible adj 1 = **honest**, above

suspicion, straight, trustworthy,
upright 2 = **imperishable**, everlasting,
undecaying
increase v 1 = **grow**, advance, boost,
develop, enlarge, escalate, expand,
extend, multiply, raise, spread, swell ▷ n
2 = **growth**, development,
enlargement, escalation, expansion,
extension, gain, increment, rise, upturn
increasingly adv = **progressively**, more
and more
incredible adj 1 = **implausible**, beyond
belief, far-fetched, improbable,
inconceivable, preposterous,
unbelievable, unimaginable,
unthinkable 2 Inf = **amazing**,
astonishing, astounding, extraordinary,
prodigious, sensational (inf), wonderful
incredulity n = **disbelief**, distrust,
doubt, scepticism
incredulous adj = **disbelieving**,
distrustful, doubtful, dubious,
sceptical, suspicious, unbelieving,
unconvinced
increment n = **increase**, accrual,
addition, advancement, augmentation,
enlargement, gain, step up,
supplement
incriminate v = **implicate**, accuse,
blame, charge, impeach, inculpate,
involve

1 (in folklore) demon believed to have sex with sleeping women. **2** nightmarish burden or worry.

inculcate *v* fix in someone's mind by constant repetition. **inculcation** *n*.

inculpate *v* cause (someone) to be blamed for a crime.

incumbent *n* **1** person holding a particular office or position. ▷ *adj* **2** holding a particular office or position, e.g. *the incumbent president*. **3 it is incumbent on** it is the duty of. **incumbency** *n, pl* **-cies**.

incur ⊕ *v* **-curring**, **-curred** cause (something unpleasant) to happen.

incurable ⊕ *adj* **1** not able to be cured. **2** not willing or able to change, e.g. *an incurable romantic*. **incurably** *adv*.

incurious *adj* showing no curiosity or interest.

incursion *n* sudden brief invasion.

indebted ⊕ *adj* **1** owing gratitude for help or favours. **2** owing money. **indebtedness** *n*.

indecent ⊕ *adj* **1** morally or sexually offensive. **2** unsuitable or unseemly, e.g. *indecent haste*. **indecently** *adv* **indecency** *n* **indecent assault** sexual attack which does not include rape. **indecent exposure** showing of one's genitals in public.

indecipherable *adj* impossible to read.

indecisive ⊕ *adj* unable to make decisions. **indecision** *n*.

indeed ⊕ *adv* **1** really, certainly. ▷ *interj* **2** expression of indignation or surprise.

indefatigable *adj* never getting tired. **indefatigably** *adv*.

indefensible ⊕ *adj* **1** unable to be justified. **2** impossible to defend.

indefinable *adj* difficult to describe or explain.

indefinite ⊕ *adj* **1** without exact limits, e.g. *for an indefinite period*. **2** vague, unclear. **indefinite article** *Grammar* the word *a* or *an*. **indefinitely** *adv*.

indelible ⊕ *adj* **1** impossible to erase or remove. **2** making indelible marks. **indelibly** *adv*.

indelicate ⊕ *adj* offensive or embarrassing.

indemnify ⊕ *v* **-ifying**, **-ified 1** secure against loss, damage, or liability. **2** compensate for loss or damage.

indemnity ⊕ *n, pl* **-ties 1** insurance against loss or damage. **2** compensation for loss or damage.

indent *v* **1** start (a line of writing) further from the margin than the other lines. **2** order (goods) using a special order form. **indented** *adj* having indentations

incur *v* = **earn**, arouse, bring (upon oneself), draw, expose oneself to, gain, meet with, provoke

incurable *adj* **1** = **fatal**, inoperable, irremediable, terminal

indebted *adj* **1** = **grateful**, beholden, obligated, obliged, under an obligation **2** = **in debt**, owing money

indecency *n* **1** = **obscenity**, immodesty, impropriety, impurity, indelicacy, lewdness, licentiousness, pornography, vulgarity

indecent *adj* **1** = **lewd**, crude, dirty, filthy, immodest, improper, impure, licentious, pornographic, salacious, scungy (*Aust & NZ inf*) **2** = **unbecoming**, in bad taste, indecorous, unseemly, vulgar

indecision *n* = **hesitation**, dithering, doubt, indecisiveness, shillyshallying (*inf*), uncertainty, vacillation, wavering

indecisive *adj* = **hesitating**, dithering, faltering, in two minds (*inf*), tentative, uncertain, undecided, vacillating, wavering

indeed *adv* **1** = **really**, actually, certainly, in truth, truly, undoubtedly

indefensible *adj* **1** = **unforgivable**, inexcusable, unjustifiable, unpardonable, untenable, unwarrantable, wrong

indefinite *adj* = **unclear**, doubtful, equivocal, ill-defined, imprecise, indeterminate, inexact, uncertain, unfixed, vague

indefinitely *adv* = **endlessly**, ad infinitum, continually, for ever

indelible *adj* **1** = **permanent**, enduring, indestructible, ineradicable, ingrained, lasting

indelicate *adj* = **offensive**, coarse, crude, embarrassing, immodest, risqué, rude, suggestive, tasteless, vulgar

indemnify *v* **1** = **insure**, guarantee, protect, secure, underwrite **2** = **compensate**, reimburse, remunerate, repair, repay

indemnity *n* **1** = **insurance**, guarantee, protection, security **2** = **compensation**, redress, reimbursement, remuneration, reparation, restitution

along the edge. **indentation** *n* dent in a surface or edge.

indenture *n* **1** contract, esp. one binding an apprentice to his or her employer. ▷ *v* **2** bind (an apprentice) by indenture.

independent ❶ *adj* **1** free from the control or influence of others. **2** separate. **3** financially self-reliant. **4** capable of acting for oneself or on one's own. ▷ *n* **5** politician who does represent any political party.
independently *adv* **independence** *n*.

- **SPELLING TIP**
- People often get confused about
- how to spell **independent**. It is spelt
- *independant* 44 times in the Bank of
- English. It should be spelt with an *e* at
- the end in the same way as the noun
- it is related to: **independent** and
- **independence**.

in-depth *adj* detailed, thorough.

indescribable ❶ *adj* too intense or extreme for words. **indescribably** *adv*.

indestructible ❶ *adj* not able to be destroyed.

indeterminate ❶ *adj* uncertain in extent, amount, or nature. **indeterminacy** *n*.

index *n, pl* **indices** [**in**-diss-eez] **1** alphabetical list of names or subjects dealt with in a book. **2** file or catalogue used to find things. **3** system by which changes in the value of something can be measured.

▷ *v* **4** provide (a book) with an index. **5** enter in an index. **6** make index-linked. **index finger** finger next to the thumb. **index-linked** *adj* (of pensions, wages, etc.) rising or falling in line with the cost of living.

Indian *n, adj* **1** (person) from India. **2** Native American. **Indian summer** period of warm sunny weather in autumn.

indicate ❶ *v* **1** be a sign or symptom of. **2** point out. **3** state briefly. **4** use the indicators in a car to show that it is going to turn left or right. **5** (of a measuring instrument) show a reading of. **indication** *n* **indicative** [in-**dik**-a-tiv] *adj* **1** (foll. by *of*) suggesting, e.g. *outer mess is indicative of inner confusion*. **2** *Grammar* denoting a mood of verbs used to make a statement. ▷ *n* **3** *Grammar* indicative mood. **indicator** *n* **1** something acting as a sign or indication. **2** flashing light on a vehicle showing the driver's intention to turn. **3** dial or gauge.

indices *n* plural of INDEX.

indict ❶ [in-**dite**] *v* formally charge with a crime. **indictable** *adj* **indictment** *n* **1** indication of how bad something is, e.g. *that's a pretty sad indictment of the UN*. **2** formal charge.

indie *adj informal* (of rock music) released by an independent record company.

independence *n* **1** = **freedom**, autonomy, liberty, self-reliance, self-rule, self-sufficiency, sovereignty

independent *adj* **1** = **free**, autonomous, liberated, self-determining, self-governing, separate, sovereign, unconstrained, uncontrolled **3** = **self-sufficient**, liberated, self-contained, self-reliant, self-supporting

independently *adv* = **separately**, alone, autonomously, by oneself, individually, on one's own, solo, unaided

indescribable *adj* = **unutterable**, beyond description, beyond words, indefinable, inexpressible

indestructible *adj* = **permanent**, enduring, everlasting, immortal, imperishable, incorruptible, indelible, indissoluble, lasting, unbreakable

indeterminate *adj* = **uncertain**, imprecise, indefinite, inexact,

undefined, unfixed, unspecified, unstipulated, vague

indicate *v* **1** = **signify**, betoken, denote, imply, manifest, point to, reveal, suggest **2** = **point out**, designate, specify **5** = **show**, display, express, read, record, register

indication *n* **1** = **sign**, clue, evidence, hint, inkling, intimation, manifestation, mark, suggestion, symptom

indicative *adj* **1** (foll. by *of*) = **suggestive**, pointing to, significant, symptomatic

indicator *n* **1** = **sign**, guide, mark, pointer, signal, symbol **3** = **gauge**, dial, meter

indict *v* = **charge**, accuse, arraign, impeach, prosecute, summon

indictment *n* **2** = **charge**, accusation, allegation, impeachment, prosecution, summons

indifferent ❶ *adj* **1** showing no interest or concern. **2** of poor quality.
indifference *n* **indifferently** *adv*.

indigenous [in-dij-in-uss] *adj* born in or natural to a country.

indigent *adj* extremely poor.
indigence *n*.

indigestion ❶ *n* (discomfort or pain caused by) difficulty in digesting food.
indigestible *adj*.

indignation ❶ *n* anger at something unfair or wrong. **indignant** *adj* feeling or showing indignation.
indignantly *adv*.

indignity ❶ *n*, *pl* **-ties** embarrassing or humiliating treatment.

indigo *adj* **1** deep violet-blue. ▷ *n* **2** dye of this colour.

indirect ❶ *adj* **1** done or caused by someone or something else. **2** not by a straight route. **indirectly** *adv* **indirect object** *Grammar* person or thing indirectly affected by the action of a verb, e.g. *Amy* in *I bought Amy a bag*.
indirect speech same as REPORTED SPEECH. **indirect tax** tax, such as VAT, added to the price of something.

indiscernible *adj* not able to be seen or discerned clearly.

indiscreet ❶ *adj* incautious or tactless in revealing secrets. **indiscreetly** *adv* **indiscretion** *n*.

indiscriminate ❶ *adj* showing lack of careful thought.

indispensable ❶ *adj* absolutely essential.

● SPELLING TIP
● For every twenty examples of the
● word **indispensable** in the Bank
● of English, there is one example
● of the misspelling *indispensible*. So
● remember that it ends in *-able*.

indisposed ❶ *adj* unwell, ill.
indisposition *n*.

indisputable ❶ *adj* beyond doubt.
indisputably *adv*.

indissoluble *adj* permanent.

indistinct ❶ *adj* unable to be seen or heard clearly.

indium *n Chemistry* soft silvery-white metallic element.

individual ❶ *adj* **1** characteristic of or meant for a single person or thing. **2** separate, distinct. **3** distinctive, unusual. ▷ *n* **4** single person or thing.
individually *adv* **individuality** *n*

— THESAURUS —

indifference *n* **1** = **disregard**, aloofness, apathy, coldness, coolness, detachment, inattention, negligence, nonchalance, unconcern

indifferent *adj* **1** = **unconcerned**, aloof, callous, cold, cool, detached, impervious, inattentive, uninterested, unmoved, unsympathetic
2 = **mediocre**, moderate, no great shakes (*inf*), ordinary, passable, so-so (*inf*), undistinguished

indigestion *n* = **heartburn**, dyspepsia, upset stomach

indignant *adj* = **resentful**, angry, disgruntled, exasperated, incensed, irate, peeved (*inf*), riled, scornful, up in arms (*inf*)

indignation *n* = **resentment**, anger, exasperation, pique, rage, scorn, umbrage

indignity *n* = **humiliation**, affront, dishonour, disrespect, injury, insult, opprobrium, slight, snub

indirect *adj* **1** = **incidental**, secondary, subsidiary, unintended **2** = **circuitous**, long-drawn-out, meandering, oblique, rambling, roundabout, tortuous, wandering

indiscreet *adj* = **tactless**, impolitic, imprudent, incautious, injudicious, naive, rash, reckless, unwise

indiscretion *n* = **mistake**, error, faux pas, folly, foolishness, gaffe, lapse, slip

indiscriminate *adj* = **random**, careless, desultory, general, uncritical, undiscriminating, unsystematic, wholesale

indispensable *adj* = **essential**, crucial, imperative, key, necessary, needed, requisite, vital

indisposed *adj* = **ill**, ailing, crook (*Aust & NZ sl*), poorly (*inf*), sick, under the weather, unwell

indisposition *n* = **illness**, ailment, ill health, sickness

indisputable *adj* = **undeniable**, beyond doubt, certain, incontestable, incontrovertible, indubitable, irrefutable, unquestionable

indistinct *adj* = **unclear**, blurred, faint, fuzzy, hazy, ill-defined, indeterminate, shadowy, undefined, vague

individual *adj* **1** = **personal**, characteristic, exclusive, own, special, specific **3** = **distinctive**, idiosyncratic, munted (*NZ sl*), particular, peculiar, singular, unique ▷ *n* **4** = **person**, being, character, creature, soul, unit

individualism n principle of living one's life in one's own way. **individualist** n **individualistic** adj.

indoctrinate ❶ v teach (someone) to accept a doctrine or belief uncritically. **indoctrination** n.

Indo-European adj, n (of) a family of languages spoken in most of Europe and much of Asia, including English, Russian, and Hindi.

indolent ❶ adj lazy. **indolence** n.

indomitable ❶ adj too strong to be defeated or discouraged. **indomitably** adv.

indoor adj inside a building. **indoors** adv.

indubitable ❶ [in-**dew**-bit-a-bl] adj beyond doubt, certain. **indubitably** adv.

induce ❶ v 1 persuade or influence. 2 cause. 3 Medical cause (a woman) to go into labour or bring on (labour) by the use of drugs etc. **inducement** n something used to persuade someone to do something.

induct v formally install (someone, esp. a clergyman) in office.

inductance n property of an electric circuit creating voltage by a change of current.

induction n 1 reasoning process by which general conclusions are drawn from particular instances. 2 Medical process of inducing labour. 3 process by which electrical or magnetic properties are produced by the proximity of an electrified or magnetic object. 4 formal introduction into an office or position. **inductive** adj **induction coil** transformer for producing a high voltage from a low voltage.

induction course training course to help familiarize someone with a new job.

indulge ❶ v 1 allow oneself pleasure, e.g. indulging in rich foods. 2 allow (someone) to have or do everything he or she wants. **indulgence** n 1 something allowed because it gives pleasure. 2 act of indulging oneself or someone else. 3 liberal or tolerant treatment. **indulgent** adj **indulgently** adv.

industrial ❶ adj of, used in, or employed in industry. **industrialize** v develop large-scale industry in (a country or region). **industrialization** n **industrialism** n social organization based on large-scale manufacturing industry rather than trade or farming. **industrialist** n person who owns or controls large amounts of money or

---

THESAURUS

individualist n = **maverick**, freethinker, independent, loner, lone wolf, nonconformist, original

individuality n 3 = **distinctiveness**, character, originality, personality, separateness, singularity, uniqueness

individually adv 2 = **separately**, apart, independently, one at a time, one by one, singly

indoctrinate v = **train**, brainwash, drill, ground, imbue, initiate, instruct, school, teach

indoctrination n = **training**, brainwashing, drilling, grounding, inculcation, instruction, schooling

indolent adj = **lazy**, idle, inactive, inert, languid, lethargic, listless, slothful, sluggish, workshy

indomitable adj = **invincible**, bold, resolute, staunch, steadfast, unbeatable, unconquerable, unflinching, unyielding

indubitable adj = **certain**, incontestable, incontrovertible, indisputable, irrefutable, obvious, sure, undeniable, unquestionable

induce v 1 = **persuade**, convince, encourage, incite, influence, instigate, prevail upon, prompt, talk into 2 = **cause**, bring about, effect, engender, generate, give rise to, lead to, occasion, produce

inducement n = **incentive**, attraction, bait, carrot (inf), encouragement, incitement, lure, reward

indulge v 1 = **gratify**, feed, give way to, pander to, satisfy, yield to 2 = **spoil**, cosset, give in to, go along with, humour, mollycoddle, pamper

indulgence n 1 = **luxury**, extravagance, favour, privilege, treat 2 = **gratification**, appeasement, fulfilment, satiation, satisfaction 3 = **tolerance**, forbearance, patience, understanding

indulgent adj 3 = **lenient**, compliant, easy-going, forbearing, kindly, liberal, permissive, tolerant, understanding

industrialist n = **capitalist**, big businessman, captain of industry, magnate, manufacturer, tycoon

industrious adj = **hard-working**, busy, conscientious, diligent, energetic, persistent, purposeful, tireless, zealous

property in industry. **industrial action** ways in which workers can protest about their conditions, e.g. by striking or working to rule. **industrial estate** area of land set aside for factories and warehouses. **industrial relations** relations between management and workers.

industry ❶ *n, pl* **-tries 1** manufacture of goods. **2** branch of this, e.g. *the music industry*. **3** quality of working hard. **industrial** *adj* of, used in, or employed in industry. **industrious** *adj* hard-working.

inebriate ❶ *n, adj* (person who is) habitually drunk. **inebriated** *adj* drunk. **inebriation** *n*.

inedible *adj* not fit to be eaten.

ineducable [in-**ed**-yuke-a-bl] *adj* incapable of being educated, esp. through mental retardation.

ineffable *adj* too great for words. **ineffably** *adv*.

ineffectual ❶ *adj* having very little effect.

inefficient ❶ *adj* unable to perform a task or function to the best advantage. **inefficiency** *n*.

inelegant *adj* lacking elegance or refinement.

ineligible ❶ *adj* not qualified for or entitled to something.

ineluctable *adj* impossible to avoid.

inept ❶ *adj* clumsy, lacking skill. **ineptitude** *n*.

inequality ❶ *n, pl* **-ties 1** state or quality of being unequal. **2** instance of this.

inequitable *adj* unfair. **inequity** *n, pl* **-ties**.

ineradicable *adj* impossible to remove.

inert ❶ *adj* **1** without the power of motion or resistance. **2** chemically unreactive. **inertly** *adv* **inertness** *n*.

inertia ❶ *n* **1** feeling of unwillingness to do anything. **2** *Physics* tendency of a body to remain still or continue moving unless a force is applied to it. **inertia reel seat belt** car seat belt in which the belt is free to unwind from a metal drum except when the drum locks because of sudden braking. **inertia selling** practice of sending householders unrequested goods followed by a bill if the goods are not returned.

inescapable ❶ *adj* unavoidable.

inestimable ❶ *adj* too great to be estimated. **inestimably** *adv*.

inevitable ❶ *adj* unavoidable, sure to happen. **the inevitable** something that cannot be prevented. **inevitably** *adv* **inevitability** *n*.

inexorable ❶ *adj* unable to be prevented from continuing or progressing. **inexorably** *adv*.

industry *n* **1, 2** = **business**, commerce, manufacturing, production, trade **3** = **effort**, activity, application, diligence, labour, tirelessness, toil, zeal

inebriated *adj* = **drunk**, half-cut (*inf*), intoxicated, legless (*inf*), merry (*Brit inf*), paralytic (*inf*), plastered (*sl*), tight (*inf*), tipsy, under the influence (*inf*)

ineffectual *adj* = **weak**, feeble, impotent, inadequate, incompetent, ineffective, inept

inefficiency *n* = **incompetence**, carelessness, disorganization, muddle, slackness, sloppiness

inefficient *adj* = **incompetent**, disorganized, ineffectual, inept, wasteful, weak

ineligible *adj* = **unqualified**, disqualified, ruled out, unacceptable, unfit, unsuitable

inept *adj* = **incompetent**, bumbling, bungling, clumsy, inexpert, maladroit

ineptitude *n* = **incompetence**, clumsiness, inexpertness, unfitness

inequality *n* **1** = **disparity**, bias, difference, disproportion, diversity, irregularity, prejudice, unevenness

inert *adj* **1** = **inactive**, dead, dormant, immobile, lifeless, motionless, static, still, unresponsive **2** = **unreactive**

inertia *n* **1** = **inactivity**, apathy, immobility, lethargy, listlessness, passivity, sloth, unresponsiveness

inescapable *adj* = **unavoidable**, certain, destined, fated, ineluctable, inevitable, inexorable, sure

inestimable *adj* = **incalculable**, immeasurable, invaluable, precious, priceless, prodigious

inevitable *adj* = **unavoidable**, assured, certain, destined, fixed, ineluctable, inescapable, inexorable, sure

inevitably *adv* = **unavoidably**, as a result, automatically, certainly, necessarily, of necessity, perforce, surely, willy-nilly

inexorable *adj* = **unrelenting**, inescapable, relentless, remorseless, unbending, unyielding

inexperienced ❶ adj having no knowledge or experience of a particular situation, activity, etc. **inexperience** n.

inexpert adj lacking skill.

inexplicable ❶ adj impossible to explain. **inexplicably** adv.

in extremis adv Latin **1** in great difficulty. **2** on the point of death.

inextricable adj **1** impossible to escape from. **2** impossible to disentangle or separate. **inextricably** adv.

infallible ❶ adj never wrong. **infallibly** adv **infallibility** n.

infamous ❶ [in-fam-uss] adj well-known for something bad. **infamously** adv **infamy** n.

infant ❶ n very young child. **infancy** n **1** early childhood. **2** early stage of development. **infantile** adj childish.

infanta n **1** (formerly) daughter of a king of Spain or Portugal. **2** wife of an infante.

infante n (formerly) any son of a king of Spain or Portugal, except the heir to the throne.

infanticide n **1** murder of an infant.

2 person guilty of this.

infantry n soldiers who fight on foot.

infatuate ❶ v inspire with intense unreasoning passion. **infatuated** adj **infatuation** n.

infect ❶ v **1** affect with a disease. **2** affect with a feeling. **infection** n **infectious** adj **1** (of a disease) spreading without actual contact. **2** spreading from person to person, e.g. *infectious enthusiasm*.

infer ❶ v **-ferring, -ferred** work out from evidence. **inference** n.

inferior ❶ adj **1** lower in quality, position, or status. ▷ n **2** person of lower position or status. **inferiority** n **inferiority complex** Psychiatry disorder arising from a feeling of inferiority to others, characterized by aggressiveness or extreme shyness.

infernal ❶ adj **1** of hell. **2** informal irritating. **infernally** adv.

inferno n, pl **-nos** intense raging fire.

infertile ❶ adj **1** unable to produce offspring. **2** (of soil) barren, not productive. **infertility** n.

THESAURUS

---

inexperience n = **unfamiliarity**, callowness, greenness, ignorance, newness, rawness

inexperienced adj = **immature**, callow, green, new, raw, unpractised, untried, unversed

inexplicable adj = **unaccountable**, baffling, enigmatic, incomprehensible, insoluble, mysterious, mystifying, strange, unfathomable, unintelligible

inextricably adv **2** = **inseparably**, indistinguishably, intricately

infallibility n = **perfection**, impeccability, omniscience, supremacy, unerringness

infallible adj = **sure**, certain, dependable, foolproof, reliable, sure-fire (inf), trustworthy, unbeatable, unfailing

infamous adj = **notorious**, disreputable, ignominious, ill-famed

infancy n **2** = **beginnings**, cradle, dawn, inception, origins, outset, start

infant n = **baby**, babe, bairn (Scot), child, toddler, tot

infantile adj = **childish**, babyish, immature, puerile

infatuate v = **obsess**, bewitch, captivate, enchant, enrapture, fascinate

infatuated adj = **obsessed**, besotted, bewitched, captivated, carried away,

enamoured, enraptured, fascinated, possessed, smitten (inf), spellbound

infatuation n = **obsession**, crush (inf), fixation, madness, passion, thing (inf)

infect v **1** = **contaminate**, affect, blight, corrupt, defile, poison, pollute, taint

infection n **1** = **contamination**, contagion, corruption, defilement, poison, pollution, virus

infectious adj **1** = **catching**, communicable, contagious, spreading, transmittable, virulent

infer v = **deduce**, conclude, derive, gather, presume, surmise, understand

inference n = **deduction**, assumption, conclusion, presumption, reading, surmise

inferior adj **1** = **lower**, lesser, menial, minor, secondary, subordinate, subsidiary ▷ n **2** = **underling**, junior, menial, subordinate

inferiority n **a** = **inadequacy**, deficiency, imperfection, insignificance, mediocrity, shoddiness, worthlessness **b** = **subservience**, abasement, lowliness, subordination

infernal adj **1** = **devilish**, accursed, damnable, damned, diabolical, fiendish, hellish, satanic

infertile adj = **barren**, sterile, unfruitful, unproductive

infest ⓞ v inhabit or overrun in unpleasantly large numbers. **infestation** n.

infidel n 1 person with no religion. 2 person who rejects a particular religion, esp. Christianity or Islam.

infidelity n, pl **-ties** (act of) sexual unfaithfulness to one's husband, wife, or lover.

infield n 1 Cricket area of the field near the pitch. 2 Baseball area of the playing field enclosed by the base lines.

infighting n quarrelling within a group.

infiltrate ⓞ v enter gradually and secretly. **infiltration** n **infiltrator** n.

infinite ⓞ [**in**-fin-it] adj without any limit or end. **infinitely** adv **infinity** n endless space, time, or number.

infinitesimal ⓞ adj extremely small.

infinitive [in-**fin**-it-iv] n Grammar form of a verb not showing tense, person, or number, e.g. to sleep.

infinity ⓞ n endless space, time, or number.

infirm ⓞ adj physically or mentally weak. **infirmity** n, pl **-ties**.

infirmary n, pl **-ries** hospital.

in flagrante delicto [in flag-**grant**-ee dee-**lick**-toe] adv while committing the offence.

inflame ⓞ v make angry or excited. **inflamed** adj (of part of the body) red, swollen, and painful because of infection. **inflammation** n.

inflammable ⓞ adj easily set on fire.

inflammatory ⓞ adj likely to provoke anger.

inflate ⓞ v 1 expand by filling with air or gas. 2 cause economic inflation in. **inflatable** adj 1 able to be inflated. ▷ n 2 plastic or rubber object which can be inflated.

inflation ⓞ n 1 inflating. 2 increase in prices and fall in the value of money. **inflationary** adj.

inflection, inflexion n 1 change in the pitch of the voice. 2 Grammar change in the form of a word to show grammatical use.

inflexible ⓞ adj 1 unwilling to be persuaded, obstinate. 2 (of a policy etc.) firmly fixed, unalterable. 3 incapable of being bent. **inflexibly** adv **inflexibility** n.

inflict ⓞ v impose (something unpleasant) on. **infliction** n.

inflorescence n Botany arrangement of flowers on a stem.

inflow n 1 something, such as liquid or gas, that flows in. 2 flowing in, influx.

━━━━━━━━━━━━━━━━━━━━ THESAURUS ━━━━━━

infertility n = **sterility**, barrenness, infecundity, unproductiveness

infest v = **overrun**, beset, invade, penetrate, permeate, ravage, swarm, throng

infested adj = **overrun**, alive, crawling, ravaged, ridden, swarming, teeming

infiltrate v = **penetrate**, filter through, insinuate oneself, make inroads (into), percolate, permeate, pervade, sneak in (inf)

infinite adj = **never-ending**, boundless, eternal, everlasting, illimitable, immeasurable, inexhaustible, limitless, measureless, unbounded

infinitesimal adj = **microscopic**, insignificant, minuscule, minute, negligible, teeny, tiny, unnoticeable

infinity n = **eternity**, boundlessness, endlessness, immensity, vastness

infirm adj = **frail**, ailing, debilitated, decrepit, doddering, enfeebled, failing, feeble, weak

infirmity n = **frailty**, decrepitude, ill health, sickliness, vulnerability

inflame v = **enrage**, anger, arouse, excite, incense, infuriate, madden,

provoke, rouse, stimulate

inflamed adj = **sore**, fevered, hot, infected, red, swollen

inflammable adj = **flammable**, combustible, incendiary

inflammation n = **soreness**, painfulness, rash, redness, tenderness

inflammatory adj = **provocative**, explosive, fiery, intemperate, like a red rag to a bull, rabble-rousing

inflate v 1 = **expand**, bloat, blow up, dilate, distend, enlarge, increase, puff up or out, pump up, swell

inflation n 1 = **expansion**, enlargement, escalation, extension, increase, rise, spread, swelling

inflexibility n 1 = **obstinacy**, intransigence, obduracy

inflexible adj 1 = **obstinate**, implacable, intractable, obdurate, resolute, set in one's ways, steadfast, stubborn, unbending, uncompromising 3 = **inelastic**, hard, rigid, stiff, taut

inflict v = **impose**, administer, apply, deliver, levy, mete or deal out, visit, wreak

infliction n = **imposition**, administration, perpetration, wreaking

influence ❶ *n* **1** effect of one person or thing on another. **2** (person with) the power to have such an effect. ▷ *v* **3** have an effect on. **influential** *adj*.

influenza *n* contagious viral disease causing headaches, muscle pains, and fever.

influx ❶ *n* arrival or entry of many people or things.

info *n informal* information.

inform ❶ *v* **1** tell. **2** give incriminating information to the police. **informant** *n* person who gives information. **information** *n* knowledge or facts. **informative** *adj* giving useful information. **information superhighway** worldwide network of computers transferring information at high speed. **information technology** use of computers and electronic technology to store and communicate information. **informer** *n* person who informs to the police.

informal ❶ *adj* **1** relaxed and friendly. **2** appropriate for everyday life or use. **informally** *adv* **informality** *n*.

infra dig *adj informal* beneath one's dignity.

infrared *adj* of or using rays below the red end of the visible spectrum.

infrastructure *n* basic facilities, services, and equipment needed for a country or organization to function properly.

infrequent ❶ *adj* not happening often. **infrequently** *adv*.

infringe ❶ *v* **1** break (a law or agreement). **2** (foll. by *on*) interfere (with), encroach (on). **infringement** *n*.

infuriate ❶ *v* make very angry.

infuse *v* **1** fill (with an emotion or quality). **2** soak to extract flavour. **infusion** *n* **1** infusing. **2** liquid obtained by infusing.

ingenious ❶ [in-**jean**-ee-uss] *adj* showing cleverness and originality. **ingeniously** *adv* **ingenuity** [in-jen-**new**-it-ee] *n*.

ingénue [**an**-jay-new] *n* naive young woman, esp. as a role played by an actress.

ingenuous ❶ [in-**jen**-new-uss] *adj* unsophisticated and trusting. **ingenuously** *adv*.

i

influence *n* **1** = **effect**, hold, magnetism, power, spell, sway, weight **2** = **power**, ascendancy, authority, clout (*inf*), control, domination, importance, leverage, mana (*NZ*), mastery, prestige, pull (*inf*) ▷ *v* **3** = **affect**, control, direct, guide, manipulate, sway

influential *adj* = **important**, authoritative, instrumental, leading, potent, powerful, significant, telling, weighty

influx *n* = **arrival**, incursion, inrush, inundation, invasion, rush

inform *v* **1** = **tell**, advise, communicate, enlighten, instruct, notify, teach, tip off **2** = **betray**, blow the whistle on (*inf*), denounce, grass (*Brit sl*), incriminate, inculpate, shop (*sl, chiefly Brit*), squeal (*sl*)

informal *adj* **1** = **relaxed**, casual, colloquial, cosy, easy, familiar, natural, simple, unofficial

informality *n* **1** = **familiarity**, casualness, ease, naturalness, relaxation, simplicity

information *n* = **facts**, data, intelligence, knowledge, message, news, notice, report

informative *adj* = **instructive**, chatty, communicative, edifying, educational, enlightening, forthcoming, illuminating, revealing

informer *n* = **betrayer**, accuser, Judas, sneak, stool pigeon

infrequent *adj* = **occasional**, few and far between, once in a blue moon, rare, sporadic, uncommon, unusual

infringe *v* **1** = **break**, contravene, disobey, transgress, violate

infringement *n* **1** = **contravention**, breach, infraction, transgression, trespass, violation

infuriate *v* = **enrage**, anger, exasperate, incense, irritate, madden, provoke, rile

infuriating *adj* = **annoying**, exasperating, galling, irritating, maddening, mortifying, provoking, vexatious

ingenious *adj* = **creative**, bright, brilliant, clever, crafty, inventive, original, resourceful, shrewd

ingenuity *n* = **originality**, cleverness, flair, genius, gift, inventiveness, resourcefulness, sharpness, shrewdness

ingenuous *adj* = **naive**, artless, guileless, honest, innocent, open, plain, simple, sincere, trusting, unsophisticated

ingest v take (food or liquid) into the body. **ingestion** n.

inglenook n corner by a fireplace.

inglorious adj dishonourable, shameful.

ingot n oblong block of cast metal.

ingrained adj firmly fixed.

ingratiate ⊕ v try to make (oneself) popular with someone. **ingratiating** adj **ingratiatingly** adv.

ingratitude n lack of gratitude or thanks.

ingredient ⊕ n component of a mixture or compound.

ingress n act or right of entering.

ingrowing adj (of a toenail) growing abnormally into the flesh.

inhabit ⊕ v **-habiting**, **-habited** live in. **inhabitable** adj **inhabitant** n.

inhale ⊕ v breathe in (air, smoke, etc.). **inhalation** n **inhalant** [in-**hale**-ant] n medical preparation inhaled to help breathing problems. **inhaler** n container for an inhalant.

inherent ⊕ adj existing as an inseparable part. **inherently** adv.

inherit ⊕ v **-heriting**, **-herited** 1 receive (money etc.) from someone who has died. 2 receive (a characteristic) from an earlier generation. 3 receive from a predecessor. **inheritance** n **inheritance tax** tax paid on property left at death. **inheritor** n.

inhibit ⊕ v **-hibiting**, **-hibited** 1 restrain (an impulse or desire). 2 hinder or prevent (action). **inhibited** adj **inhibition** n feeling of fear or embarrassment that stops one from behaving naturally.

inhospitable ⊕ adj 1 not welcoming, unfriendly. 2 difficult to live in, harsh.

inhuman ⊕ adj 1 cruel or brutal. 2 not human.

inhumane ⊕ adj cruel or brutal. **inhumanity** n.

inimical ⊕ adj unfavourable or hostile.

inimitable ⊕ adj impossible to imitate, unique.

iniquity ⊕ n, pl **-ties** 1 injustice or wickedness. 2 wicked act. **iniquitous** adj.

initial ⊕ adj 1 first, at the beginning. ▷ n 2 first letter, esp. of a person's name. ▷ v

——————————————————————————— THESAURUS ———————————

ingratiate v = **pander to**, crawl, curry favour, fawn, flatter, grovel, insinuate oneself, toady

ingratiating adj = **sycophantic**, crawling, fawning, flattering, humble, obsequious, servile, toadying, unctuous

ingredient n = **component**, constituent, element, part

inhabit v = **live**, abide, dwell, occupy, populate, reside

inhabitant n = **dweller**, citizen, denizen, inmate, native, occupant, occupier, resident, tenant

inhabited adj = **populated**, colonized, developed, occupied, peopled, settled, tenanted

inhale v = **breathe in**, draw in, gasp, respire, suck in

inherent adj = **innate**, essential, hereditary, inborn, inbred, ingrained, inherited, intrinsic, native, natural

inherit v 1 = **be left**, come into, fall heir to, succeed to

inheritance n 1 = **legacy**, bequest, birthright, heritage, patrimony

inhibit v 1 = **restrain**, check, constrain, curb, discourage, hold back or in 2 = **hinder**, check, frustrate, hold back, impede, obstruct, prevent

inhibited adj 1 = **shy**, constrained, guarded, repressed, reserved, reticent, self-conscious, subdued

inhibition n = **shyness**, block, hang-up (inf), reserve, restraint, reticence, self-consciousness

inhospitable adj 1 = **unfriendly**, cool, uncongenial, unreceptive, unsociable, unwelcoming, xenophobic 2 = **bleak**, barren, desolate, forbidding, godforsaken, hostile

inhuman adj 1 = **cruel**, barbaric, brutal, cold-blooded, heartless, merciless, pitiless, ruthless, savage, unfeeling

inhumane adj = **cruel**, brutal, heartless, pitiless, unfeeling, unkind, unsympathetic

inhumanity n = **cruelty**, atrocity, barbarism, brutality, heartlessness, pitilessness, ruthlessness, unkindness

inimical adj = **hostile**, adverse, antagonistic, ill-disposed, opposed, unfavourable, unfriendly, unwelcoming

inimitable adj = **unique**, consummate, incomparable, matchless, peerless, unparalleled, unrivalled

iniquitous adj = **wicked**, criminal, evil, immoral, reprehensible, sinful, unjust

iniquity n = **wickedness**, abomination, evil, injustice, sin, wrong

initial adj 1 = **first**, beginning, incipient, introductory, opening, primary

-tialling, -tialled 3 sign with one's initials. **initially** adv.

initiate ❶ v 1 begin or set going. 2 admit (someone) into a closed group. 3 instruct in the basics of something. ▷ n 4 recently initiated person. **initiation** n **initiator** n.

initiative ❶ n 1 first step, commencing move. 2 ability to act independently.

inject ❶ v 1 put (a fluid) into the body with a syringe. 2 introduce (a new element), e.g. try to inject a bit of humour. **injection** n.

injudicious adj showing poor judgment, unwise.

injunction ❶ n court order not to do something.

injure ❶ v hurt physically or mentally. **injury** n, pl **-ries**. **injury time** Sport playing time added at the end of a match to compensate for time spent treating injured players. **injurious** adj.

injustice ❶ n 1 unfairness. 2 unfair action.

ink n 1 coloured liquid used for writing or printing. ▷ v 2 (foll. by in) mark in ink (something already marked in pencil). **inky** adj **inkier**, **inkiest** 1 dark or black. 2 covered in ink.

inkling ❶ n slight idea or suspicion.

inlaid adj 1 set in another material so that the surface is smooth. 2 made like this, e.g. an inlaid table.

inland ❶ adj, adv in or towards the interior of a country, away from the sea. **Inland Revenue** government department that collects taxes.

in-laws pl n one's husband's or wife's family.

inlay n inlaid substance or pattern.

inlet ❶ n 1 narrow strip of water extending from the sea into the land. 2 valve etc. through which liquid or gas enters.

inmate n person living in an institution such as a prison.

inmost ❶ adj innermost.

inn ❶ n pub or small hotel, esp. in the country. **innkeeper** n.

innards pl n informal 1 internal organs. 2 working parts of a machine.

innate ❶ adj being part of someone's nature, inborn.

inner ❶ adj 1 happening or located inside. 2 relating to private feelings, e.g. the inner self. 3 of a group with most power within a larger organization, e.g. the inner circle.

i

THESAURUS

initially adv 1 = **at first**, at or in the beginning, first, firstly, originally, primarily

initiate v 1 = **begin**, commence, get under way, kick off (inf), launch, open, originate, set in motion, start 2 = **induct**, indoctrinate, introduce, invest 3 = **instruct**, acquaint with, coach, familiarize with, teach, train ▷ n 4 = **novice**, beginner, convert, entrant, learner, member, probationer

initiation n 2 = **introduction**, debut, enrolment, entrance, inauguration, induction, installation, investiture

initiative n 1 = **first step**, advantage, first move, lead 2 = **resourcefulness**, ambition, drive, dynamism, enterprise, get-up-and-go (inf), leadership

inject v 1 = **vaccinate**, inoculate 2 = **introduce**, bring in, infuse, insert, instil

injection n 1 = **vaccination**, inoculation, jab (inf), shot (inf) 2 = **introduction**, dose, infusion, insertion

injunction n = **order**, command, exhortation, instruction, mandate, precept, ruling

injure v = **hurt**, damage, harm, impair, ruin, spoil, undermine, wound

injured adj = **hurt**, broken, crook (Aust & NZ sl), damaged, disabled, undermined, weakened, wounded

injury n = **harm**, damage, detriment, disservice, hurt, ill, trauma (Path), wound, wrong

injustice n 1 = **unfairness**, bias, discrimination, inequality, inequity, iniquity, oppression, partisanship, prejudice, wrong

inkling n = **suspicion**, clue, conception, hint, idea, indication, intimation, notion, suggestion, whisper

inland adj = **interior**, domestic, internal, upcountry

inlet n 1 = **bay**, bight, creek, firth or frith (Scot), fjord, passage

inmost adj = **deepest**, basic, central, essential, innermost, intimate, personal, private, secret

innate adj = **inborn**, congenital, constitutional, essential, inbred, ingrained, inherent, instinctive, intuitive, native, natural

inner adj 1 = **inside**, central, interior, internal, inward, middle 2 = **hidden**,

innermost *adj* furthest inside. **inner city** parts of a city near the centre, esp. having social and economic problems.

innings *n* **1** *Sport* player's or side's turn of batting. **2** period of opportunity.

innocent ⊙ *adj* **1** not guilty of a crime. **2** without experience of evil. **3** without malicious intent. ▷ *n* **4** innocent person, esp. a child. **innocently** *adv* **innocence** *n*.

innocuous *adj* not harmful. **innocuously** *adv*.

● **SPELLING TIP**
● Always make sure there are two *n*s
● in **innocuous**. It is more common to
● miss out an *n* than to double the *c* by
● mistake.

innovation ⊙ *n* **1** new idea or method. **2** introduction of new ideas or methods. **innovate** *v* **innovative** *adj* **innovator** *n*.

innuendo ⊙ *n, pl* **-does** (remark making) an indirect reference to something rude or unpleasant.

innumerable ⊙ *adj* too many to be counted.

innumerate *adj* having no understanding of mathematics or science. **innumeracy** *n*.

inoculate *v* protect against disease by injecting with a vaccine. **inoculation** *n*.

● **SPELLING TIP**
● The verb **inoculate** has only one *n*
● and one *c*. There are 235 occurrences
● of the correct spelling of the noun
● **inoculation** in the Bank of English,
● with lots of different misspellings.
● The most popular one, *innoculation*,
● occurs 31 times.

inoffensive *adj* causing no harm or annoyance.

inoperable *adj* (of a tumour or cancer) unable to be surgically removed.

inoperative *adj* not working or functioning.

inopportune *adj* badly timed, unsuitable.

inordinate ⊙ *adj* excessive. **inordinately** *adv*.

inorganic ⊙ *adj* **1** not having the characteristics of living organisms. **2** of chemical substances that do not contain carbon.

inpatient *n* patient who stays in a hospital for treatment.

input *n* **1** resources put into a project etc. **2** data fed into a computer. ▷ *v* **-putting, -put 3** enter (data) in a computer.

inquest ⊙ *n* **1** official inquiry into a sudden death. **2** *inf* investigation or discussion.

inquietude *n* restlessness or anxiety.

inquire ⊙ *v* seek information or ask (about). **inquirer** *n* **inquiry** *n, pl* **-ries**

——————————————————————— THESAURUS ———————————

intimate, personal, private, repressed, secret, unrevealed

innkeeper *n* = **publican**, host *or* hostess, hotelier, landlord *or* landlady, mine host

innocence *n* **1** = **guiltlessness**, blamelessness, clean hands, incorruptibility, probity, purity, uprightness, virtue **2** = **naivety**, artlessness, credulousness, gullibility, inexperience, ingenuousness, simplicity, unworldliness **3** = **harmlessness**, innocuousness, inoffensiveness

innocent *adj* **1** = **not guilty**, blameless, guiltless, honest, in the clear, uninvolved **2** = **naive**, artless, childlike, credulous, gullible, ingenuous, open, simple, unworldly **3** = **harmless**, innocuous, inoffensive, unobjectionable, well-intentioned, well-meant

innovation *n* **1** = **modernization**, alteration, change, departure,

newness, novelty, variation

innuendo *n* = **insinuation**, aspersion, hint, implication, imputation, intimation, overtone, suggestion, whisper

innumerable *adj* = **countless**, beyond number, incalculable, infinite, multitudinous, myriad, numberless, numerous, unnumbered, untold

inordinate *adj* = **excessive**, disproportionate, extravagant, immoderate, intemperate, preposterous, unconscionable, undue, unreasonable, unwarranted

inorganic *adj* **1** = **artificial**, chemical, man-made

inquest *n* = **inquiry**, inquisition, investigation, probe

inquire *v* = **investigate**, ask, examine, explore, look into, make inquiries, probe, query, question, research

inquiry *n* **1** = **question**, query **2** = **investigation**, examination,

1 question. **2** investigation.

inquisition ❶ n **1** thorough investigation. **2** (**I-**) *History* organization within the Catholic Church for suppressing heresy. **inquisitor** n **inquisitorial** adj.

inquisitive ❶ adj **1** excessively curious about other people's affairs. **2** eager to learn. **inquisitively** adv.

inquorate adj without enough people present to make a quorum.

inroads pl n **make inroads into** start affecting or reducing, e.g. *Italy could make inroads into its interest burden*.

ins. inches.

insalubrious adj unpleasant, unhealthy, or sordid.

insane ❶ adj **1** mentally ill. **2** stupidly irresponsible. **insanely** adv **insanity** n.

insanitary ❶ adj dirty or unhealthy.

insatiable ❶ [in-**saysh**-a-bl] adj unable to be satisfied.

inscribe ❶ v write or carve words on. **inscription** n words inscribed.

inscrutable ❶ adj mysterious, enigmatic. **inscrutably** adv **inscrutability** n.

insect n small animal with six legs and usu. wings, such as an ant or fly. **insecticide** n substance for killing

insects. **insectivorous** adj insect-eating.

insecure ❶ adj **1** anxious, not confident. **2** not safe or well-protected.

insemination n putting semen into a woman's or female animal's body to try to make her pregnant. **inseminate** v.

insensate adj **1** without sensation, unconscious. **2** unfeeling.

insensible ❶ adj **1** unconscious, without feeling. **2** (foll. by *to* or *of*) not aware (of) or affected (by). **insensibility** n.

insensitive ❶ adj unaware of or ignoring other people's feelings. **insensitivity** n.

inseparable ❶ adj **1** (of two people) spending most of the time together. **2** (of two things) impossible to separate.

- **SPELLING TIP**
- The word **inseparable** occurs in
- the Bank of English 914 times. The
- misspelling *inseperable*, with an *e*
- instead of an *a* in the middle, appears
- 6 times.

insert ❶ v **1** put inside or include. ▷ n **2** something inserted. **insertion** n.

inset n small picture inserted within a larger one.

inshore adj **1** close to the shore. ▷ adj, adv **2** towards the shore.

exploration, inquest, interrogation, probe, research, study, survey

inquisition n **1** = **investigation**, cross-examination, examination, grilling (*inf*), inquest, inquiry, questioning, third degree (*inf*)

inquisitive adj **1** = **prying**, curious, nosy (*inf*), probing **2** = **inquiring**, curious, questioning

insane adj **1** = **mad**, crazed, crazy, demented, deranged, mentally ill, out of one's mind **2** = **stupid**, daft (*inf*), foolish, idiotic, impractical, irrational, irresponsible, preposterous, senseless

insanitary adj = **unhealthy**, dirty, disease-ridden, filthy, infested, insalubrious, polluted, unclean, unhygienic

insanity n **1** = **madness**, delirium, dementia, mental disorder, mental illness **2** = **stupidity**, folly, irresponsibility, lunacy, senselessness

insatiable adj = **unquenchable**, greedy, intemperate, rapacious, ravenous, voracious

inscribe v = **carve**, cut, engrave, etch,

impress, imprint

inscription n = **engraving**, dedication, legend, words

inscrutable adj **a** = **mysterious**, hidden, incomprehensible, inexplicable, unexplainable, unfathomable, unintelligible **b** = **enigmatic**, blank, deadpan, impenetrable, poker-faced (*inf*), unreadable

insecure adj **1** = **anxious**, afraid, uncertain, unsure **2** = **unsafe**, defenceless, exposed, unguarded, unprotected, vulnerable, wide-open

insensible adj **2** (foll. by *to* or *of*) = **unaware**, impervious, oblivious, unaffected, unconscious, unmindful

insensitive adj = **unfeeling**, callous, hardened, indifferent, thick-skinned, tough, uncaring, unconcerned

inseparable adj **1** = **devoted**, bosom, close, intimate **2** = **indivisible**, indissoluble

insert v **1** = **enter**, embed, implant, introduce, place, put, stick in

insertion n = **inclusion**, addition, implant, interpolation, introduction, supplement

inside ❶ *prep* **1** in or to the interior of.
▷ *adj* **2** on or of the inside. **3** by or from
someone within an organization, e.g.
inside information. ▷ *adv* **4** on, in, or to
the inside, indoors. **5** *slang* in(to)
prison. ▷ *n* **6** inner side, surface, or
part. ▷ *pl* **7** *informal* stomach and
bowels. **inside out** with the inside
facing outwards. **know inside out**
know thoroughly. **insider** *n* member of
a group who has privileged knowledge
about it.

insidious ❶ *adj* subtle or unseen but
dangerous. **insidiously** *adv*.

insight ❶ *n* deep understanding.

insignia ❶ [in-**sig**-nee-a] *n*, *pl* **-nias**, **-nia**
badge or emblem of honour or office.

insignificant ❶ *adj* not important.
insignificance *n*.

insincere ❶ *adj* showing false feelings,
not genuine. **insincerely** *adv*

insincerity *n*, *pl* **-ties**.

insinuate ❶ *v* **1** suggest indirectly.
2 work (oneself) into a position by
gradual manoeuvres. **insinuation** *n*.

insipid ❶ *adj* lacking interest, spirit, or
flavour. **insipidity** *n*.

insist ❶ *v* demand or state firmly.
insistent *adj* **1** making persistent
demands. **2** demanding attention.
insistently *adv* **insistence** *n*.

in situ *adv*, *adj Latin* in its original
position.

in so far as, insofar as *prep* to the
extent that.

insole *n* inner sole of a shoe or boot.

insolent ❶ *adj* rude and disrespectful.
insolence *n* **insolently** *adv*.

insoluble ❶ *adj* **1** incapable of being
solved. **2** incapable of being dissolved.

insolvent ❶ *adj* unable to pay one's
debts. **insolvency** *n*.

inside *adj* **2** = **inner**, interior, internal,
inward **3** = **confidential**, classified,
exclusive, internal, private, restricted,
secret ▷ *adv* **4** = **indoors**, under cover,
within ▷ *n* **6** = **interior**, contents ▷ *pl*
7 *Inf* = **stomach**, belly, bowels,
entrails, guts, innards (*inf*), viscera,
vitals

insidious *adj* = **stealthy**, deceptive, sly,
smooth, sneaking, subtle,
surreptitious

insight *n* = **understanding**,
awareness, comprehension,
discernment, judgment, observation,
penetration, perception, perspicacity,
vision

insignia *n* = **badge**, crest, emblem,
symbol

insignificance *n* = **unimportance**,
inconsequence, irrelevance,
meaninglessness, pettiness, triviality,
worthlessness

insignificant *adj* = **unimportant**,
inconsequential, irrelevant,
meaningless, minor, nondescript,
paltry, petty, trifling, trivial

insincere *adj* = **deceitful**, dishonest,
disingenuous, duplicitous, false,
hollow, hypocritical, lying, two-faced,
untruthful

insincerity *n* = **deceitfulness**,
dishonesty, dissimulation, duplicity,
hypocrisy, pretence, untruthfulness

insinuate *v* **1** = **imply**, allude, hint,
indicate, intimate, suggest
2 = **ingratiate**, curry favour, get in

with, worm *or* work one's way in

insinuation *n* **1** = **implication**, allusion,
aspersion, hint, innuendo, slur,
suggestion

insipid *adj* **a** = **bland**, anaemic,
characterless, colourless, prosaic,
uninteresting, vapid, wishy-washy (*inf*)
b = **tasteless**, bland, flavourless,
unappetizing, watery

insist *v* **a** = **demand**, lay down the law,
put one's foot down (*inf*), require
b = **state**, assert, aver, claim,
maintain, reiterate, repeat,
swear, vow

insistence *n* = **persistence**, emphasis,
importunity, stress

insistent *adj* = **persistent**, dogged,
emphatic, importunate, incessant,
persevering, unrelenting, urgent

insolence *n* = **rudeness**, boldness,
cheek (*inf*), disrespect, effrontery,
impertinence, impudence

insolent *adj* = **rude**, bold,
contemptuous, impertinent,
impudent, insubordinate,
insulting

insoluble *adj* **1** = **inexplicable**, baffling,
impenetrable, indecipherable,
mysterious, unaccountable,
unfathomable, unsolvable

insolvency *n* = **bankruptcy**, failure,
liquidation, ruin

insolvent *adj* = **bankrupt**, broke (*inf*),
failed, gone bust (*inf*), gone to the
wall, in receivership, munted (*NZ sl*),
ruined

insomnia ❶ *n* inability to sleep.
insomniac *n*.

insomuch *adv* (foll. by *as* or *that*) to such
an extent.

insouciant *adj* carefree and
unconcerned. **insouciance** *n*.

inspect *v* check closely or officially.
inspection *n* **inspector** *n* **1** person
who inspects. **2** high-ranking police
officer.

inspire ❶ *v* **1** fill with enthusiasm,
stimulate. **2** arouse (an emotion).
inspiration *n* **1** creative influence
or stimulus. **2** brilliant idea.
inspirational *adj*.

inst. instant (this month).

instability ❶ *n* lack of steadiness or
reliability.

install ❶ *v* **1** put in and prepare
(equipment) for use. **2** place (a person)
formally in a position or rank.
installation *n* **1** installing.

2 equipment installed. **3** place
containing equipment for a particular
purpose, e.g. *oil installations*.

instalment ❶ *n* any of the portions of a
thing presented or a debt paid in
successive parts.

instance ❶ *n* **1** particular example. ▷ *v*
2 mention as an example. **for instance**
as an example.

instant ❶ *n* **1** very brief time.
2 particular moment. ▷ *adj*
3 happening at once. **4** (of foods)
requiring little preparation. **instantly**
adv.

instantaneous ❶ *adj* happening at
once. **instantaneously** *adv*.

instead ❶ *adv* as a replacement or
substitute. **instead of** in place of, as an
alternative to.

instep *n* **1** part of the foot forming the
arch between the ankle and toes.
2 part of a shoe etc. covering this.

i

insomnia *n* = **sleeplessness**,
wakefulness

inspect *v* = **examine**, check, go over *or*
through, investigate, look over,
scrutinize, survey, vet

inspection *n* = **examination**, check,
checkup, investigation, once-over
(*inf*), review, scrutiny, search,
survey

inspector *n* **1** = **examiner**, auditor,
censor, investigator, overseer,
scrutinizer, superintendent,
supervisor

inspiration *n* **1** = **influence**, muse, spur,
stimulus **2** = **revelation**, creativity,
illumination, insight

inspire *v* **1** = **stimulate**, animate,
encourage, enliven, galvanize, gee up,
influence, spur **2** = **arouse**, enkindle,
excite, give rise to, produce

inspired *adj* **1** = **uplifted**, elated,
enthused, exhilarated, stimulated

inspiring *adj* **1, 2** = **uplifting**, exciting,
exhilarating, heartening, moving,
rousing, stimulating, stirring

instability *n* = **unpredictability**,
changeableness, fickleness,
fluctuation, impermanence,
inconstancy, insecurity, unsteadiness,
variability, volatility

install *v* **1** = **set up**, fix, lay, lodge, place,
position, put in, station **2** = **induct**,
establish, inaugurate, institute,
introduce, invest

installation *n* **1** **a** = **setting up**,

establishment, fitting, instalment,
placing, positioning **b** = **induction**,
inauguration, investiture
2 = **equipment**, machinery, plant,
system

instalment *n* = **portion**, chapter,
division, episode, part, repayment,
section

instance *n* **1** = **example**, case,
illustration, occasion, occurrence,
situation ▷ *v* **2** = **quote**, adduce, cite,
mention, name, specify

instant *n* **1** = **second**, flash, jiffy (*inf*),
moment, split second, trice, twinkling
of an eye (*inf*) **2** = **juncture**, moment,
occasion, point, time ▷ *adj*
3 = **immediate**, direct, instantaneous,
on-the-spot, prompt, quick, split-
second **4** = **precooked**, convenience,
fast, ready-mixed

instantaneous *adj* = **immediate**,
direct, instant, on-the-spot,
prompt

instantaneously *adv* = **immediately**,
at once, instantly, in the twinkling of an
eye (*inf*), on the spot, promptly,
straight away

instantly *adv* **3** = **immediately**, at
once, directly, instantaneously,
now, right away, straight away, this
minute

instead *adv* = **rather**, alternatively, in
lieu, in preference, on second thoughts,
preferably **instead of** = **in place of**, in
lieu of, rather than

instigate ⊙ *v* cause to happen.
instigation *n* **instigator** *n*.
instil ⊙ *v* **-stilling, -stilled** introduce (an idea etc.) gradually into someone's mind.
instinct ⊙ *n* inborn tendency to behave in a certain way. **instinctive** *adj* **instinctively** *adv*.
institute ⊙ *n* **1** organization set up for a specific purpose, esp. research or teaching. **2** building where such an organization is situated. ▷ *v* **3** start or establish, e.g. *He instituted parliamentary reform*.
institution ⊙ *n* **1** large important organization such as a university or bank. **2** hospital etc. for people with special needs. **3** long-established custom. **institutional** *adj* **institutionalize** *v* place someone in an institution.
instruct ⊙ *v* **1** order to do something.

2 teach (someone) how to do something. **instruction** *n* **1** order to do something. **2** teaching. ▷ *pl* **3** information on how to do or use something. **instructive** *adj* informative or helpful. **instructor** *n*.
instrument ⊙ *n* **1** tool used for particular work. **2** object played to produce a musical sound. **3** measuring device to show height, speed, etc. **4** *informal* someone or something used to achieve an aim. **instrumental** *adj* **1** (foll. by *in*) having an important function (in). **2** played by or composed for musical instruments.
instrumentalist *n* player of a musical instrument. **instrumentation** *n* **1** set of instruments in a car etc. **2** arrangement of music for instruments.
insubordinate ⊙ *adj* not submissive to

—————————————————————— THESAURUS ——————

instigate *v* = **provoke**, bring about, incite, influence, initiate, prompt, set off, start, stimulate, trigger
instigation *n* = **prompting**, behest, bidding, encouragement, incitement, urging
instigator *n* = **ringleader**, agitator, leader, motivator, prime mover, troublemaker
instil *v* = **introduce**, engender, imbue, implant, inculcate, infuse, insinuate
instinct *n* = **intuition**, faculty, gift, impulse, knack, predisposition, proclivity, talent, tendency
instinctive *adj* = **inborn**, automatic, inherent, innate, intuitive, involuntary, natural, reflex, spontaneous, unpremeditated, visceral
instinctively *adv* = **intuitively**, automatically, by instinct, involuntarily, naturally, without thinking
institute *n* **1** = **society**, academy, association, college, foundation, guild, institution, school ▷ *v* **2** = **establish**, fix, found, initiate, introduce, launch, organize, originate, pioneer, set up, start
institution *n* **1** = **establishment**, academy, college, foundation, institute, school, society **3** = **custom**, convention, law, practice, ritual, rule, tradition
institutional *adj* **3** = **conventional**, accepted, established, formal, orthodox
instruct *v* **1** = **order**, bid, charge,

command, direct, enjoin, tell
2 = **teach**, coach, drill, educate, ground, school, train, tutor
instruction *n* **1** = **order**, command, demand, directive, injunction, mandate, ruling **2** = **teaching**, coaching, education, grounding, guidance, lesson(s), schooling, training, tuition ▷ *pl* **3** = **orders**, advice, directions, guidance, information, key, recommendations, rules
instructive *adj* = **informative**, edifying, educational, enlightening, helpful, illuminating, revealing, useful
instructor *n* **2** = **teacher**, adviser, coach, demonstrator, guide, mentor, trainer, tutor
instrument *n* **1** = **tool**, apparatus, appliance, contraption (*inf*), device, gadget, implement, mechanism **4** *Inf* = **means**, agency, agent, mechanism, medium, organ, vehicle
instrumental *adj* **1** (foll. by *in*) = **active**, contributory, helpful, influential, involved, useful
insubordinate *adj* = **disobedient**, defiant, disorderly, mutinous, rebellious, recalcitrant, refractory, undisciplined, ungovernable, unruly
insubordination *n* = **disobedience**, defiance, indiscipline, insurrection, mutiny, rebellion, recalcitrance, revolt

authority. **insubordination** n.

insubstantial ❶ adj flimsy, fine, or slight.

insufferable ❶ adj unbearable.

insular ❶ adj not open to new ideas, narrow-minded. **insularity** n.

insulate ❶ v 1 prevent or reduce the transfer of electricity, heat, or sound by surrounding or lining with a nonconducting material. 2 isolate or set apart. **insulation** n **insulator** n.

insulin [in-syoo-lin] n hormone produced in the pancreas that controls the amount of sugar in the blood.

insult ❶ v 1 behave rudely to, offend. ▷ n 2 insulting remark or action. **insulting** adj.

insuperable ❶ adj impossible to overcome.

insupportable ❶ adj 1 impossible to tolerate. 2 impossible to justify.

insurance ❶ n 1 agreement by which one makes regular payments to a company who pay an agreed sum if damage, loss, or death occurs. 2 money paid to or by an insurance company. 3 means of protection.

insure v protect by insurance.

insurance policy contract of insurance.

insurgent ❶ n, adj (person) in revolt against an established authority. **insurgency** n.

insurmountable ❶ adj impossible to overcome, e.g. an insurmountable problem.

insurrection ❶ n rebellion.

intact ❶ adj not changed or damaged in any way.

intaglio [in-**tah**-lee-oh] n, pl -**lios** (gem carved with) an engraved design.

intake n amount or number taken in.

intangible adj not clear or definite enough to be seen or felt easily, e.g. an intangible quality.

integer n positive or negative whole number or zero.

integral ❶ adj 1 being an essential part of a whole. ▷ n 2 Maths sum of a large number of very small quantities.

integrate ❶ v 1 combine into a whole. 2 amalgamate (a religious or racial group) into a community. **integration**

THESAURUS

insubstantial adj = **flimsy**, feeble, frail, poor, slight, tenuous, thin, weak

insufferable adj = **unbearable**, detestable, dreadful, impossible, insupportable, intolerable, unendurable

insular adj = **narrow-minded**, blinkered, circumscribed, inward-looking, limited, narrow, parochial, petty, provincial

insulate v 2 = **isolate**, close off, cocoon, cushion, cut off, protect, sequester, shield

insult v 1 = **offend**, abuse, affront, call names, put down, slander, slight, snub ▷ n 2 = **abuse**, affront, aspersion, insolence, offence, put-down, slap in the face (inf), slight, snub

insulting adj = **offensive**, abusive, contemptuous, degrading, disparaging, insolent, rude, scurrilous

insuperable adj = **insurmountable**, impassable, invincible, unconquerable

insupportable adj 1 = **intolerable**, insufferable, unbearable, unendurable 2 = **unjustifiable**, indefensible, untenable

insurance n = **protection**, assurance, cover, guarantee, indemnity, safeguard, security, warranty

insure v = **protect**, assure, cover, guarantee, indemnify, underwrite, warrant

insurgent n = **rebel**, insurrectionist, mutineer, revolutionary, rioter ▷ adj = **rebellious**, disobedient, insubordinate, mutinous, revolting, revolutionary, riotous, seditious

insurmountable adj = **insuperable**, hopeless, impassable, impossible, invincible, overwhelming, unconquerable

insurrection n = **rebellion**, coup, insurgency, mutiny, revolt, revolution, riot, uprising

intact adj = **undamaged**, complete, entire, perfect, sound, unbroken, unharmed, unimpaired, unscathed, whole

integral adj 1 = **essential**, basic, component, constituent, fundamental, indispensable, intrinsic, necessary

integrate v 1 = **combine**, amalgamate, assimilate, blend, fuse, incorporate, join, merge, unite 2 = **unite**, amalgamate, incorporate

integration n 1 = **combining**, amalgamation, assimilation, blending, fusing, incorporation, mixing

n **integrated circuit** tiny electronic circuit on a silicon chip.

integrity ❶ *n* **1** quality of having high moral principles. **2** quality of being united.

intellect ❶ *n* power of thinking and reasoning. **intellectual** *adj* **1** of or appealing to the intellect. **2** clever, intelligent. ▷ *n* **3** intellectual person. **intellectually** *adv* **intellectualism** *n*.

intelligent ❶ *adj* **1** able to understand, learn, and think things out quickly. **2** (of a computerized device) able to initiate or modify action in the light of ongoing events. **intelligence** *n* **1** quality of being intelligent. **2** secret government or military information. **3** people or department collecting such information. **intelligently** *adv* **intelligence quotient** a measure of the intelligence of a person calculated by dividing the person's mental age by his or her actual age and multiplying the result by 100.

intelligentsia ❶ *n* intellectual or cultured people in a society.

intelligible ❶ *adj* able to be understood.

intelligibility *n*.

intemperate ❶ *adj* **1** unrestrained, uncontrolled, e.g. *intemperate language*. **2** drinking alcohol to excess. **intemperance** *n*.

intend ❶ *v* **1** propose or plan (to do something). **2** have as one's purpose. **intended** *adj* **1** planned or future. ▷ *n* **2** *informal* person whom one is to marry.

intense ❶ *adj* **1** of great strength or degree. **2** deeply emotional. **intensity** *n* **intensify** *v* **-fying, -fied** make or become more intense. **intensification** *n*.

intensive ❶ *adj* using or needing concentrated effort or resources. **intensively** *adv* **intensive care** thorough supervised treatment of an acutely ill patient in a hospital.

intent ❶ *n* **1** intention. **2** intention to commit a crime. ▷ *adj* **3** paying close attention. **intently** *adv* **intentness** *n* **intent on doing something** determined to do something. **to all intents and purposes** in almost every respect.

————————————————— THESAURUS ——————————

2 = **unification**, amalgamation, incorporation

integrity *n* **1** = **honesty**, goodness, honour, incorruptibility, principle, probity, purity, rectitude, uprightness, virtue **2** = **soundness**, coherence, cohesion, completeness, unity, wholeness

intellect *n* = **intelligence**, brains (*inf*), judgment, mind, reason, sense, understanding

intellectual *adj* **2** = **scholarly**, bookish, cerebral, highbrow, intelligent, studious, thoughtful ▷ *n* **3** = **academic**, egghead (*inf*), highbrow, thinker

intelligence *n* **1** = **understanding**, acumen, brain power, brains (*inf*), cleverness, comprehension, intellect, perception, sense **2** = **information**, data, facts, findings, knowledge, news, notification, report

intelligent *adj* **1** = **clever**, brainy (*inf*), bright, enlightened, perspicacious, quick-witted, sharp, smart, well-informed

intelligentsia *n* = **intellectuals**, highbrows, literati

intelligible *adj* = **understandable**, clear, comprehensible, distinct, lucid, open, plain

intemperate *adj* **1** = **excessive**, extreme, immoderate, profligate, self-indulgent, unbridled, unrestrained, wild

intend *v* = **plan**, aim, have in mind *or* view, mean, propose, purpose

intense *adj* **1** = **extreme**, acute, deep, excessive, fierce, great, powerful, profound, severe **2** = **passionate**, ardent, fanatical, fervent, fierce, heightened, impassioned, vehement

intensify *v* = **increase**, add to, aggravate, deepen, escalate, heighten, magnify, redouble, reinforce, sharpen, strengthen

intensity *n* **2** = **force**, ardour, emotion, fanaticism, fervour, fierceness, passion, strength, vehemence

intensive *adj* = **concentrated**, comprehensive, demanding, exhaustive, in-depth, thorough, thoroughgoing

intent *n* **1** = **intention**, aim, design, end, goal, meaning, object, objective, plan, purpose ▷ *adj* **3** = **intense**, absorbed, attentive, engrossed, preoccupied, rapt, steadfast, watchful

intention ⊕ *n* something intended.
intentional *adj* planned in advance,
deliberate. **intentionally** *adv*.

inter ⊕ [in-**ter**] *v* -**terring**, -**terred** bury
(a corpse). **interment** *n*.

inter- *prefix* between or among, e.g.
international.

interact *v* act on or in close relation
with each other. **interaction** *n*
interactive *adj*.

interbreed *v* breed within a related
group.

intercede ⊕ *v* try to end a dispute
between two people or groups.
intercession *n*.

intercept ⊕ *v* seize or stop in transit.
interception *n* **interceptor** *n*.

interchange ⊕ *v* 1 (cause to) exchange
places. ▷ *n* 2 motorway junction.
interchangeable *adj*.

Intercity *adj* ® denoting a fast train
(service) travelling between cities.

intercom *n* internal communication
system with loudspeakers.

intercommunion *n* association
between Churches, involving mutual
reception of Holy Communion.

intercontinental *adj* travelling
between or linking continents.

intercourse ⊕ *n* 1 sexual intercourse.
2 communication or dealings between
people or groups.

interdenominational *adj* among or
involving more than one denomination
of the Christian Church.

interdiction, interdict *n* formal order
forbidding something.

interdisciplinary *adj* involving more
than one branch of learning.

interest ⊕ *n* 1 desire to know or hear
more about something. **2** something in
which one is interested. **3** (often pl)
advantage, benefit, e.g. *acting in the
interests of the oil company*. **4** sum paid
for the use of borrowed money.
5 (often pl) right or share. ▷ *v* **6** arouse
the interest of. **interested** *adj* **1** feeling
or showing interest. **2** involved in or
affected by something. **interesting** *adj*
interestingly *adv*.

interface ⊕ *n* 1 area where two things
interact or link. **2** circuit linking a
computer and another device.

interfaith *adj* relating to or involving
different religions.

interfere ⊕ *v* 1 try to influence other
people's affairs where one is not
involved or wanted. **2** (foll. by *with*)
clash (with). **3** (foll. by *with*)
euphemistic abuse (a child) sexually.
interfering *adj* **interference** *n*
1 interfering. **2** *Radio* interruption of
reception by atmospherics or
unwanted signals.

interferon *n* protein that stops the
development of an invading virus.

THESAURUS

intention *n* = **purpose**, aim, design,
end, goal, idea, object, objective, point,
target

intentional *adj* = **deliberate**,
calculated, intended, meant, planned,
premeditated, wilful

intentionally *adv* = **deliberately**,
designedly, on purpose, wilfully

inter *v* = **bury**, entomb, lay to rest

intercede *v* = **mediate**, arbitrate,
intervene, plead

intercept *v* = **seize**, block, catch, cut off,
head off, interrupt, obstruct, stop

interchange *v* **1** = **switch**, alternate,
exchange, reciprocate, swap ▷ *n*
2 = **junction**, intersection

interchangeable *adj* **1** = **identical**,
equivalent, exchangeable, reciprocal,
synonymous

intercourse *n* **1** = **sexual intercourse**,
carnal knowledge, coitus, copulation,
sex (*inf*) **2** = **communication**,
commerce, contact, dealings

interest *n* **1** = **curiosity**, attention,
concern, notice, regard **2** = **hobby**,
activity, diversion, pastime,
preoccupation, pursuit **3** (often pl)
= **advantage**, benefit, good, profit
5 (often pl) = **stake**, claim,
investment, right, share ▷ *v*
6 = **arouse one's curiosity**, attract,
catch one's eye, divert, engross,
fascinate, intrigue

interested *adj* **1** = **curious**, attracted,
drawn, excited, fascinated, keen
2 = **involved**, concerned, implicated

interesting *adj* **6** = **intriguing**,
absorbing, appealing, attractive,
compelling, engaging, engrossing,
gripping, stimulating, thought-
provoking

interface *n* **1** = **connection**, border,
boundary, frontier, link

interfere *v* **1** = **intrude**, butt in,
intervene, meddle, stick one's oar in
(*inf*), tamper **2** (foll. by *with*) = **conflict**,
clash, hamper, handicap, hinder,
impede, inhibit, obstruct

interim ❶ *adj* **1** temporary or provisional. ▷ *n* **2 in the interim** in the intervening time.

interior ❶ *n* **1** inside. **2** inland region. ▷ *adj* **3** inside, inner. **4** mental or spiritual.

interject *v* make (a remark) suddenly or as an interruption. **interjection** *n*.

interlace *v* join together as if by weaving.

interleave *v* insert between other leaves, for example blank leaves in a book.

interlink *v* connect together.

interlock *v* join firmly together.

interlocutor [in-ter-**lok**-yew-ter] *n* person who takes part in a conversation.

interloper ❶ [**in**-ter-lope-er] *n* person in a place or situation where he or she has no right to be.

interlude ❶ *n* short rest or break in an activity or event.

intermarry *v* (of families, races, or religions) become linked by marriage. **intermarriage** *n*.

intermediary ❶ *n, pl* **-ries** person trying to create agreement between others.

intermediate ❶ *adj* coming between two points or extremes.

intermezzo [in-ter-**met**-so] *n, pl* **-zos** short piece of music, esp. one performed between the acts of an opera.

interminable ❶ *adj* seemingly endless

because boring. **interminably** *adv*.

intermingle *v* mix together.

intermission ❶ *n* interval between parts of a play, film, etc.

intermittent ❶ *adj* occurring at intervals. **intermittently** *adv*.

intern ❶ *v* **1** imprison, esp. during a war. ▷ *n* **2** *Chiefly US* trainee doctor in a hospital. **internment** *n* **internee** *n* person who is interned.

internal ❶ *adj* **1** of or on the inside. **2** within a country or organization. **3** spiritual or mental. **internally** *adv*

internal-combustion engine engine powered by the explosion of a fuel-and-air mixture within the cylinders.

international ❶ *adj* **1** of or involving two or more countries. ▷ *n* **2** game or match between teams of different countries. **3** player in such a match. **internationally** *adv*.

internecine *adj* mutually destructive.

internet, Internet ❶ *n* large international computer network.

interplanetary *adj* of or linking planets.

interplay *n* action and reaction of two things upon each other.

Interpol International Criminal Police Organization.

interpolate [in-**ter**-pole-ate] *v* insert (a comment or passage) into (a conversation or text). **interpolation** *n*.

interference *n* **1 a** = **intrusion**, intervention, meddling, prying **b** = **conflict**, clashing, collision, obstruction, opposition

interim *adj* **1** = **temporary**, acting, caretaker, improvised, makeshift, provisional, stopgap

interior *n* **1** = **inside**, centre, core, heart ▷ *adj* **3** = **inside**, inner, internal, inward **4** = **mental**, hidden, inner, intimate, personal, private, secret, spiritual

interloper *n* = **trespasser**, gate-crasher (*inf*), intruder, meddler

interlude *n* = **interval**, break, breathing space, delay, hiatus, intermission, pause, respite, rest, spell, stoppage

intermediary *n* = **mediator**, agent, broker, go-between, middleman

intermediate *adj* = **middle**, halfway, in-between (*inf*), intervening, mid, midway, transitional

interment *n* = **burial**, funeral

interminable *adj* = **endless**, ceaseless, everlasting, infinite, long-drawn-out, long-winded, never-ending, perpetual, protracted

intermission *n* = **interval**, break, interlude, pause, recess, respite, rest, stoppage

intermittent *adj* = **periodic**, broken, fitful, irregular, occasional, spasmodic, sporadic

intern *v* **1** = **imprison**, confine, detain, hold, hold in custody

internal *adj* **1** = **inner**, inside, interior **2** = **domestic**, civic, home, in-house, intramural

international *adj* **1** = **universal**, cosmopolitan, global, intercontinental, worldwide

Internet *n* = **information superhighway**, cyberspace, the net (*inf*), the web (*inf*), World Wide Web

interpose ❶ *v* **1** insert between or among things. **2** say as an interruption.

interpret ❶ *v* **1** explain the meaning of. **2** translate orally from one language into another. **3** convey the meaning of (a poem, song, etc.) in performance. **interpretation** *n* **interpreter** *n*.

interregnum *n*, *pl* **-nums**, **-na** interval between reigns.

interrelate *v* connect (two or more things) to each other. **interrelation** *n*.

interrogate ❶ *v* question closely. **interrogation** *n* **interrogative** *adj* **1** questioning. ▷ *n* **2** word used in asking a question, such as *how* or *why*. **interrogator** *n*.

interrupt ❶ *v* **1** break into (a conversation etc.). **2** stop (a process or activity) temporarily. **interruption** *n*.

intersect ❶ *v* **1** (of roads) meet and cross. **2** divide by passing across or through. **intersection** *n*.

interspersed *adj* scattered (among, between, or on).

interstellar *adj* between or among stars.

interstice [in-**ter**-stiss] *n* small crack or gap between things.

intertwine *v* twist together.

interval ❶ *n* **1** time between two particular moments or events. **2** break between parts of a play, concert, etc. **3** difference in pitch between musical notes. **at intervals 1** repeatedly. **2** with spaces left between.

intervene ❶ *v* **1** involve oneself in a situation, esp. to prevent conflict. **2** happen so as to stop something. **intervention** *n*.

interview ❶ *n* **1** formal discussion, esp. between a job-seeker and an employer. **2** questioning of a well-known person about his or her career, views, etc., by a reporter. ▷ *v* **3** conduct an interview with. **interviewee** *n* **interviewer** *n*.

interweave *v* weave together.

intestate *adj* not having made a will. **intestacy** *n*.

intestine *n* (often *pl*) lower part of the alimentary canal between the stomach and the anus. **intestinal** *adj*.

intimate¹ ❶ *adj* **1** having a close personal relationship. **2** personal or private. **3** (of knowledge) extensive and detailed. **4** (foll. by *with*) euphemistic

---

THESAURUS

interpose *v* **1** = **insert 2** = **interrupt**, interject, put one's oar in

interpret *v* **1** = **explain**, decipher, decode, elucidate, make sense of **2** = **translate**, construe **3** = **render**

interpretation *n* **1** = **explanation**, analysis, clarification, elucidation, exposition **2** = **translation 3** = **version**, portrayal, rendition

interpreter *n* **1** = **commentator 2** = **translator**

interrogate *v* = **question**, cross-examine, examine, grill (*inf*) investigate, pump, quiz

interrogation *n* = **questioning**, cross-examination, examination, grilling (*inf*), inquiry, inquisition, third degree (*inf*)

interrupt *v* **1** = **intrude**, barge in (*inf*), break in, butt in, disturb, heckle, interfere (with) **2** = **suspend**, break off, cut short, delay, discontinue, hold up, lay aside, stop

interruption *n* **2** = **stoppage**, break, disruption, disturbance, hitch, intrusion, pause, suspension

intersection *n* **1** = **junction**, crossing, crossroads, interchange

interval *n* **1** = **break**, delay, gap, pause, respite, rest, space, spell **2** = **interlude**, intermission

intervene *v* **1** = **step in** (*inf*), arbitrate, intercede, interfere, intrude, involve oneself, mediate, take a hand (*inf*) **2** = **happen**, befall, come to pass, ensue, occur, take place

intervention *n* **1** = **mediation**, agency, interference, intrusion

interview *n* **2** = **meeting**, audience, conference, consultation, dialogue, press conference, talk ▷ *v* **3** = **question**, examine, interrogate, talk to

interviewer *n* **3** = **questioner**, examiner, interrogator, investigator, reporter

intestine *n* (often *pl*) = **guts**, bowels, entrails, innards (*inf*), insides (*inf*), viscera

intimacy *n* **1** = **familiarity**, closeness **2** = **confidentiality**

intimate¹ *adj* **1** = **close**, bosom, confidential, dear, near, thick (*inf*) **2** = **private**, confidential, personal, secret **3** = **detailed**, deep, exhaustive, first-hand, immediate, in-depth, profound, thorough **5** = **snug**, comfy

having a sexual relationship (with).
5 having a friendly quiet atmosphere.
▷ *n* **6** close friend. **intimately** *adv*
intimacy *n, pl* **-cies**.
intimate² ❶ *v* **1** hint at or suggest.
2 announce. **intimation** *n*.
intimidate ❶ *v* subdue or influence
by fear. **intimidating** *adj*
intimidation *n*.
into *prep* **1** indicating motion towards
the centre, result of a change, division,
etc. e.g. *into the valley; turned into a
madman; cut into pieces*. **2** *informal*
interested in.
intolerable *adj* more than can be
endured. **intolerably** *adv*.
intolerant *adj* refusing to accept
practices and beliefs different from
one's own. **intolerance** *n*.
intonation *n* sound pattern produced
by variations in the voice.
intone ❶ *v* speak or recite in an
unvarying tone of voice.
in toto *adv Latin* totally, entirely.

intoxicate ❶ *v* **1** make drunk. **2** excite
to excess. **intoxicant** *n* intoxicating
drink. **intoxication** *n*.
intractable *adj* **1** (of a person) difficult
to control. **2** (of a problem or issue)
difficult to deal with.
intranet *n Computers* internal network
that makes use of internet
technology.
intransigent ❶ *adj* refusing to change
one's attitude. **intransigence** *n*.
intransitive *adj* (of a verb) not taking a
direct object.
intrauterine *adj* within the womb.
intravenous [in-tra-**vee**-nuss] *adj* into
a vein. **intravenously** *adv*.
intrepid ❶ *adj* fearless, bold.
intrepidity *n*.
intricate ❶ *adj* **1** involved or
complicated. **2** full of fine detail.
intricately *adv* **intricacy** *n, pl* **-cies**.
intrigue ❶ *v* **1** make interested or curious.
2 plot secretly. ▷ *n* **3** secret plotting.
4 secret love affair. **intriguing** *adj*.

———————————————————————————— THESAURUS ———————

(*inf*), cosy, friendly, warm ▷ *n*
6 = **friend**, close friend, cobber (*Aust or
old-fashioned NZ inf*), confidant or
confidante, (constant) companion,
crony
intimate² *v* **1** = **suggest**, hint, imply,
indicate, insinuate **2** = **announce**,
communicate, declare, make known,
state
intimately *adv* **1** = **confidingly**,
affectionately, confidentially, familiarly,
personally, tenderly, warmly **3** = **in
detail**, fully, inside out, thoroughly, very
well
intimation *n* **1** = **hint**, allusion,
indication, inkling, insinuation,
reminder, suggestion, warning
2 = **announcement**, communication,
declaration, notice
intimidate *v* = **frighten**, browbeat,
bully, coerce, daunt, overawe, scare,
subdue, terrorize, threaten
intimidation *n* = **bullying**, arm-
twisting (*inf*), browbeating, coercion,
menaces, pressure, terrorization,
threat(s)
intone *v* = **recite**, chant
intoxicated *adj* **1** = **drunk**, drunken,
inebriated, legless (*inf*), paralytic (*inf*),
plastered (*sl*), tipsy, under the influence
2 = **euphoric**, dizzy, ecstatic, elated,
enraptured, excited, exhilarated, high
(*inf*)

intoxicating *adj* **1** = **alcoholic**, strong
2 = **exciting**, exhilarating, heady,
thrilling
intoxication *n* **1** = **drunkenness**,
inebriation, insobriety, tipsiness
2 = **excitement**, delirium, elation,
euphoria, exhilaration
intransigent *adj* = **uncompromising**,
hard-line, intractable, obdurate,
obstinate, stiff-necked, stubborn,
unbending, unyielding
intrepid *adj* = **fearless**, audacious, bold,
brave, courageous, daring, gallant,
plucky, stouthearted, valiant
intricacy *n* **1** = **complexity**,
complication, convolutions
2 = **elaborateness**
intricate *adj* **1** = **complicated**,
complex, convoluted, involved,
labyrinthine, tangled, tortuous
2 = **elaborate**, fancy
intrigue *v* **1** = **interest**, attract,
fascinate, rivet, titillate **2** = **plot**,
connive, conspire, machinate,
manoeuvre, scheme ▷ *n* **3** = **plot**,
chicanery, collusion, conspiracy,
machination, manoeuvre, scheme,
stratagem, wile **4** = **affair**, amour,
intimacy, liaison, romance
intriguing *adj* **1** = **interesting**,
beguiling, compelling, diverting,
exciting, fascinating, tantalizing,
titillating

intrinsic ❶ *adj* essential to the basic nature of something. **intrinsically** *adv*.

introduce ❶ *v* **1** present (someone) by name (to another person). **2** present (a radio or television programme). **3** bring forward for discussion. **4** bring into use. **5** insert. **introduction** *n* **1** presentation of one person to another. **2** preliminary part or treatment. **introductory** *adj*.

introspection ❶ *n* examination of one's own thoughts and feelings. **introspective** *adj*.

introvert ❶ *n* person concerned more with his or her thoughts and feelings than with the outside world. **introverted** *adj* **introversion** *n*.

intrude ❶ *v* come in or join in without being invited. **intruder** *n* **intrusion** *n* **intrusive** *adj*.

intuition ❶ *n* instinctive knowledge or insight without conscious reasoning. **intuitive** *adj* **intuitively** *adv*.

Inuit *n* Eskimo of North America or Greenland.

Inuk *n* a member of any Inuit people.

Inuktitut *n* *Canad* the language of the Inuit.

inundate ❶ *v* **1** flood. **2** overwhelm. **inundation** *n*.

inured *adj* accustomed, esp. to hardship or danger.

invade ❶ *v* **1** enter (a country) by military force. **2** enter in large numbers. **3** disturb (someone's privacy). **invader** *n*.

invalid¹ ❶ *adj, n* **1** disabled or chronically ill (person). ▷ *v* **2** (often foll. by *out*) dismiss from active service because of illness or injury. **invalidity** *n*.

invalid² ❶ *adj* **1** having no legal force. **2** (of an argument etc.) not valid because based on a mistake. **invalidate** *v* make or show to be invalid.

invaluable ❶ *adj* of very great value or worth.

intrinsic *adj* = **inborn**, basic, built-in, congenital, constitutional, essential, fundamental, inbred, inherent, native, natural

introduce *v* **1** = **present**, acquaint, familiarize, make known **3** = **bring up**, advance, air, broach, moot, put forward, submit **4** = **bring in**, establish, found, initiate, institute, launch, pioneer, set up, start **5** = **insert**, add, inject, put in, throw in (*inf*)

introduction *n* **2** = **opening**, foreword, intro (*inf*), lead-in, preamble, preface, prelude, prologue

introductory *adj* **4** = **preliminary**, first, inaugural, initial, opening, preparatory

introspective *adj* = **inward-looking**, brooding, contemplative, introverted, meditative, pensive

introverted *adj* = **introspective**, inner-directed, inward-looking, self-contained, withdrawn

intrude *v* = **interfere**, butt in, encroach, infringe, interrupt, meddle, push in, trespass

intruder *n* = **trespasser**, gate-crasher (*inf*), infiltrator, interloper, invader, prowler

intrusion *n* = **invasion**, encroachment, infringement, interference, interruption, trespass

intrusive *adj* = **interfering**, impertinent, importunate, meddlesome, nosy (*inf*), presumptuous, pushy (*inf*), uncalled-for, unwanted

intuition *n* = **instinct**, hunch, insight, perception, presentiment, sixth sense

intuitive *adj* = **instinctive**, innate, spontaneous, untaught

inundate *v* **1** = **flood**, drown, engulf, immerse, overflow, submerge, swamp **2** = **overwhelm**, overrun

invade *v* **1** = **attack**, assault, burst in, descend upon, encroach, infringe, make inroads, occupy, raid, violate **2** = **infest**, overrun, permeate, pervade, swarm over

invader *n* **1** = **attacker**, aggressor, plunderer, raider, trespasser

invalid¹ *adj* = **disabled**, ailing, bedridden, frail, ill, infirm, sick ▷ *n* = **patient**, convalescent, valetudinarian

invalid² *adj* **1** = **null and void**, inoperative, void **2** = **unsound**, fallacious, false, illogical, irrational, shonky (*Aust & NZ inf*), unfounded, worthless

invalidate *v* **1** = **nullify**, annul, cancel, overthrow, undermine

invaluable *adj* = **precious**, inestimable, priceless, valuable, worth one's *or* its weight in gold

invasion ❶ n 1 invading. 2 intrusion, e.g. *an invasion of privacy*.
invective ❶ n abusive speech or writing.
inveigh [in-**vay**] v (foll. by *against*) criticize strongly.
inveigle v coax by cunning or trickery.
invent ❶ v 1 think up or create (something new). 2 make up (a story, excuse, etc.). **invention** n 1 something invented. 2 ability to invent. **inventive** adj creative and resourceful. **inventiveness** n **inventor** n.
inventory ❶ [**in**-ven-tree] n, pl **-tories** detailed list of goods or furnishings.
inverse ❶ adj 1 reversed in effect, sequence, direction, etc. 2 *Maths* linking two variables in such a way that one increases as the other decreases. **inversely** adv.
invert ❶ v turn upside down or inside out. **inversion** n **inverted commas** quotation marks.

invertebrate n animal with no backbone.
invest ❶ v 1 spend (money, time, etc.) on something with the expectation of profit. 2 (foll. by *with*) give (power or rights) to, e.g. *invested with the powers of government*. **investment** n 1 money invested. 2 something invested in. **investor** n **invest in** v buy.
investigate ❶ v inquire into, examine. **investigation** n **investigative** adj **investigator** n.
investiture ❶ n formal installation of a person in an office or rank.
inveterate ❶ adj firmly established in a habit or condition, e.g. *an inveterate gambler*.
invidious adj likely to cause resentment.
invigilate ❶ [in-**vij**-il-late] v supervise people sitting an examination. **invigilator** n.
invigorate ❶ v give energy to, refresh.

———————————————————————— THESAURUS ————

invasion n 1 = **attack**, assault, campaign, foray, incursion, inroad, offensive, onslaught, raid 2 = **intrusion**, breach, encroachment, infraction, infringement, usurpation, violation
invective n = **abuse**, censure, denunciation, diatribe, tirade, tongue-lashing, vilification, vituperation
invent v 1 = **create**, coin, conceive, design, devise, discover, formulate, improvise, originate, think up 2 = **make up**, concoct, cook up (*inf*), fabricate, feign, forge, manufacture, trump up
invention n 1 a = **creation**, brainchild (*inf*), contraption, contrivance, design, device, discovery, gadget, instrument b = **fiction**, fabrication, falsehood, fantasy, forgery, lie, untruth, yarn 2 = **creativity**, genius, imagination, ingenuity, inventiveness, originality, resourcefulness
inventive adj = **creative**, fertile, imaginative, ingenious, innovative, inspired, original, resourceful
inventor n = **creator**, architect, author, coiner, designer, maker, originator
inventory n = **list**, account, catalogue, file, record, register, roll, roster
inverse adj 1 = **opposite**, contrary, converse, reverse, reversed, transposed

invert v = **overturn**, reverse, transpose, upset, upturn
invest v 1 = **spend**, advance, devote, lay out, put in, sink 2 (foll. by *with*) = **empower**, authorize, charge, license, sanction, vest
investigate v = **examine**, explore, go into, inquire into, inspect, look into, probe, research, study
investigation n = **examination**, exploration, inquest, inquiry, inspection, probe, review, search, study, survey
investigator n = **examiner**, inquirer, (private) detective, private eye (*inf*), researcher, sleuth
investiture n = **installation**, enthronement, inauguration, induction, ordination
investment n 1 = **stake**, ante (*inf*), contribution 2 = **transaction**, speculation, venture
inveterate adj = **long-standing**, chronic, confirmed, deep-seated, dyed-in-the-wool, entrenched, habitual, hardened, incorrigible, incurable
invigilate v = **watch over**, conduct, keep an eye on, oversee, preside over, run, superintend, supervise
invigorate v = **refresh**, energize, enliven, exhilarate, fortify, galvanize, liven up, revitalize, stimulate

invincible ⊕ adj impossible to defeat. **invincibility** n.

inviolable ⊕ adj unable to be broken or violated.

inviolate ⊕ adj unharmed, unaffected.

invisible ⊕ adj not able to be seen. **invisibly** adv **invisibility** n.

invite ⊕ v 1 request the company of. 2 ask politely for. 3 encourage or provoke, e.g. *the two works inevitably invite comparison*. ▷ n 4 *informal* invitation. **inviting** adj tempting, attractive. **invitation** n.

in-vitro adj happening outside the body in an artificial environment, e.g. *in-vitro fertilization*.

invoice v, n (present with) a bill for goods or services supplied.

invoke ⊕ v 1 put (a law or penalty) into operation. 2 prompt or cause (a certain feeling). 3 call on (a god or spirit) for help, inspiration, etc. **invocation** n.

involuntary ⊕ adj not done consciously, unintentional. **involuntarily** adv.

involve ⊕ v 1 include as a necessary part. 2 affect, concern. 3 implicate (a person). **involved** adj 1 complicated. 2 concerned, taking part. **involvement** n.

invulnerable ⊕ adj not able to be

wounded or harmed.

inward adj, adv see IN.

iodine n *Chemistry* bluish-black element used in medicine and photography. **iodize** v treat with iodine.

ion n electrically charged atom. **ionic** adj **ionize** v change into ions. **ionization** n **ionosphere** n region of ionized air in the upper atmosphere that reflects radio waves.

iota [eye-**oh**-ta] n 1 ninth letter in the Greek alphabet. 2 very small amount.

IOU n signed paper acknowledging debt.

IPA International Phonetic Alphabet.

ipecacuanha [ip-pee-kak-yoo-**an**-na], **ipecac** [**ip**-pee-kak] n drug made from the dried roots of a S American plant, used to cause vomiting.

iPod n ® pocket-sized device used to play digital music files.

ipso facto adv *Latin* by that very fact.

IQ intelligence quotient.

Ir *Chemistry* iridium.

IRA Irish Republican Army.

Iranian n, adj (person) from Iran.

Iraqi n, adj (person) from Iraq.

irascible adj easily angered. **irascibility** n.

irate ⊕ adj very angry.

ire n *lit* anger.

THESAURUS

invincible adj = **unbeatable**, impregnable, indestructible, indomitable, insuperable, invulnerable, unassailable, unconquerable

inviolable adj = **sacrosanct**, hallowed, holy, inalienable, sacred, unalterable

inviolate adj = **intact**, entire, pure, unbroken, undefiled, unhurt, unpolluted, unsullied, untouched, whole

invisible adj = **unseen**, imperceptible, indiscernible

invitation n 1 = **request**, call, invite (*inf*), summons

invite v 1 = **request**, ask, beg, bid, summon 2 = **ask for** (*inf*) 3 = **encourage**, attract, court, entice, provoke, tempt

inviting adj = **tempting**, alluring, appealing, attractive, enticing, lekker (*S Afr sl*), mouthwatering, seductive, welcoming

invocation n 3 = **appeal**, entreaty, petition, prayer, supplication

invoke v 1 = **apply**, implement, initiate, put into effect, resort to, use 3 = **call**

upon, appeal to, beg, beseech, entreat, implore, petition, pray, supplicate

involuntary adj = **unintentional**, automatic, instinctive, reflex, spontaneous, unconscious, uncontrolled, unthinking

involve v 1 = **entail**, imply, mean, necessitate, presuppose, require 2 = **concern**, affect, draw in, implicate, touch

involved adj 1 = **complicated**, complex, confusing, convoluted, elaborate, intricate, labyrinthine, tangled, tortuous 2 = **concerned**, caught (up), implicated, mixed up in or with, participating, taking part

involvement n 2, 3 = **connection**, association, commitment, interest, participation

invulnerable adj = **safe**, impenetrable, indestructible, insusceptible, invincible, proof against, secure, unassailable

irate adj = **angry**, annoyed, cross, enraged, furious, incensed, indignant, infuriated, livid

iridescent *adj* having shimmering changing colours like a rainbow. **iridescence** *n*.

iridium *n Chemistry* very hard corrosion-resistant metal.

iris *n* **1** coloured circular membrane of the eye containing the pupil. **2** tall plant with purple, yellow, or white flowers.

Irish *adj* of Ireland. **Irish coffee** hot coffee mixed with whiskey and topped with cream.

irk *v* irritate, annoy. **irksome** *adj* irritating, annoying.

iron ❶ *n* **1** strong silvery-white metallic element, widely used for structural and engineering purposes. **2** appliance used, when heated, to press clothes. **3** metal-headed golf club. ▷ *pl* **4** chains, restraints. ▷ *adj* **5** made of iron. **6** strong, inflexible, e.g. *iron will*. ▷ *v* **7** smooth (clothes or fabric) with an iron. **ironbark** *n* Australian eucalyptus with hard rough bark. **ironing** *n* clothes to be ironed. **ironing board** long cloth-covered board with folding legs, for ironing clothes on. **Iron Age** era when iron tools were used. **iron out** *v* settle (a problem) through discussion.

ironic, ironical ❶ *adj* **1** using irony. **2** odd or amusing because the opposite of what one would expect. **ironically** *adv*.

ironmonger *n* shopkeeper or shop dealing in hardware. **ironmongery** *n*.

ironstone *n* rock consisting mainly of iron ore.

irony ❶ *n*, *pl* **-nies 1** mildly sarcastic use of words to imply the opposite of what is said. **2** aspect of a situation that is odd or amusing because the opposite of what one would expect.

irradiate *v* subject to or treat with radiation. **irradiation** *n*.

irrational ❶ *adj* not based on or not using logical reasoning. **irrational number** *Maths* any real number that cannot be expressed as the ratio of two integers, such as π.

irreconcilable *adj* not able to be resolved or settled, e.g. *irreconcilable differences*. **irreconcilability** *n*.

irredeemable *adj* not able to be reformed or corrected.

irreducible *adj* impossible to put in a simpler form.

irrefutable ❶ *adj* impossible to deny or disprove.

irregular ❶ *adj* **1** not regular or even. **2** not conforming to accepted practice. **3** (of a word) not following the typical pattern of formation in a language. **irregularly** *adv* **irregularity** *n*, *pl* **-ties**.

irrelevant ❶ *adj* not connected with the matter in hand. **irrelevantly** *adv* **irrelevance** *n*.

━━━━━━━━━━━━━━━━ THESAURUS ━━━━━━━

iron *adj* **5** = **ferrous**, ferric **6** = **inflexible**, adamant, hard, implacable, indomitable, steely, strong, tough, unbending

ironic, ironical *adj* **1** = **sarcastic**, double-edged, mocking, sardonic, satirical, with tongue in cheek, wry **2** = **paradoxical**, incongruous

iron out *v* = **settle**, clear up, get rid of, put right, reconcile, resolve, smooth over, sort out, straighten out

irony *n* **1** = **sarcasm**, mockery, satire **2** = **paradox**, incongruity

irrational *adj* = **illogical**, absurd, crazy, nonsensical, preposterous, unreasonable

irrefutable *adj* = **undeniable**, certain, incontestable, incontrovertible, indisputable, indubitable, sure, unquestionable

irregular *adj* **1 a** *adj* = **variable**, erratic, fitful, haphazard, occasional, random, spasmodic, sporadic, unsystematic **b** = **uneven**, asymmetrical, bumpy, crooked, jagged, lopsided, ragged, rough **2** = **unconventional**, abnormal, exceptional, extraordinary, munted (*NZ sl*), peculiar, unofficial, unorthodox, unusual

irregularity *n* **1 a** = **uncertainty**, desultoriness, disorganization, haphazardness **b** = **unevenness**, asymmetry, bumpiness, jaggedness, lopsidedness, raggedness, roughness **2** = **abnormality**, anomaly, oddity, peculiarity, unorthodoxy

irrelevant *adj* = **unconnected**, beside the point, extraneous, immaterial, impertinent, inapplicable, inappropriate, neither here nor there, unrelated

irreparable ⊕ *adj* not able to be repaired or put right. **irreparably** *adv*.

irreplaceable *adj* impossible to replace.

irrepressible ⊕ *adj* lively and jolly. **irrepressibly** *adv*.

irreproachable ⊕ *adj* blameless, faultless. **irreproachably** *adv*.

irresistible ⊕ *adj* too attractive or strong to resist. **irresistibly** *adv*.

irresolute *adj* unable to make decisions. **irresolution** *n*.

irrespective of *prep* without taking account of.

irresponsible ⊕ *adj* **1** not showing or not done with due care for the consequences of one's actions or attitudes. **2** not capable of accepting responsibility. **irresponsibility** *n*.

irretrievable *adj* impossible to put right or make good. **irretrievably** *adv*.

irreverent ⊕ *adj* not showing due respect. **irreverence** *n*.

irreversible ⊕ *adj* not able to be reversed or put right again, e.g. *irreversible change*. **irreversibly** *adv*.

irrevocable ⊕ *adj* not possible to change or undo. **irrevocably** *adv*.

irrigate ⊕ *v* supply (land) with water by artificial channels or pipes. **irrigation** *n*.

irritate ⊕ *v* **1** annoy, anger. **2** cause (a body part) to itch or become inflamed. **irritable** *adj* easily annoyed. **irritability** *n* **irritably** *adv* **irritant** *n*, *adj* (person or thing) causing irritation. **irritation** *n*.

is *v* third person singular present tense of BE.

ISA Individual Savings Account.

isinglass [**ize**-ing-glass] *n* kind of gelatine obtained from some freshwater fish.

Islam *n* **1** Muslim religion teaching that there is one God and that Mohammed is his prophet. **2** Muslim countries and civilization. **Islamic** *adj*.

island ⊕ *n* piece of land surrounded by water. **islander** *n* person who lives on an island.

isle *n poetic* island. **islet** *n* small island.

-ism *n suffix* indicating: **1** political or religious belief, e.g. *Communism*; *Buddhism*. **2** characteristic quality, e.g. *cynicism*. **3** an action, e.g. *criticism*. **4** prejudice on the basis specified, e.g. *racism*.

isobar [**ice**-oh-bar] *n* line on a map connecting places of equal atmospheric pressure.

isolate ⊕ *v* **1** place apart or alone. **2** *Chemistry* obtain (a substance) in uncombined form. **isolation** *n*

THESAURUS

irreparable *adj* = **beyond repair**, incurable, irremediable, irretrievable, irreversible

irrepressible *adj* = **ebullient**, boisterous, buoyant, effervescent, unstoppable

irreproachable *adj* = **blameless**, beyond reproach, faultless, impeccable, innocent, perfect, pure, unimpeachable

irresistible *adj* = **overwhelming**, compelling, compulsive, overpowering, urgent

irresponsible *adj* **1** = **thoughtless**, careless, immature, reckless, scatterbrained, shiftless, shonky (*Aust & NZ inf*), unreliable, untrustworthy

irreverent *adj* = **disrespectful**, cheeky (*inf*), flippant, iconoclastic, impertinent, impudent, mocking, tongue-in-cheek

irreversible *adj* = **irrevocable**, final, incurable, irreparable, unalterable

irrevocable *adj* = **fixed**, fated, immutable, irreversible, predestined, predetermined, settled, unalterable

irrigate *v* = **water**, flood, inundate, moisten, wet

irritable *adj* = **bad-tempered**, cantankerous, crotchety (*inf*), ill-tempered, irascible, oversensitive, prickly, testy, tetchy, touchy

irritate *v* **1** = **annoy**, anger, bother, exasperate, get on one's nerves (*inf*), infuriate, needle (*inf*), nettle, rankle with, try one's patience **2** = **rub**, chafe, inflame, pain

irritation *n* **1** = **annoyance**, anger, displeasure, exasperation, indignation, resentment, testiness, vexation **2** = **nuisance**, drag (*inf*), pain in the neck (*inf*), thorn in one's flesh

island *n* = **isle**, ait *or* eyot (*dial*), atoll, cay *or* key, islet

isolate *v* **1** = **separate**, cut off, detach, disconnect, insulate, segregate, set apart

isolationism *n* policy of not participating in international affairs. **isolationist** *n*, *adj*.

isomer [**ice**-oh-mer] *n* substance whose molecules contain the same atoms as another but in a different arrangement.

isometric *adj* relating to muscular contraction without shortening of the muscle. **isometrics** *pl n* isometric exercises.

isosceles triangle [ice-**soss**-ill-eez] *n* triangle with two sides of equal length.

isotherm [**ice**-oh-therm] *n* line on a map connecting points of equal temperature.

isotope [**ice**-oh-tope] *n* one of two or more atoms with the same number of protons in the nucleus but a different number of neutrons.

ISP internet service provider.

Israeli *n*, *pl* -**lis**, -**li** *adj* (person) from Israel.

issue ❶ *n* **1** topic of interest or discussion. **2** reason for quarrelling. **3** particular edition of a magazine or newspaper. **4** outcome or result. **5** *Law* child or children. ▷ *v* **6** make (a statement etc.) publicly. **7** supply officially (with). **8** produce and make available. **9** (foll. by *from*) come out of. **take issue with** disagree with.

-ist *n suffix* indicating: **1** person who performs a particular action, e.g. *exorcist*. **2** person who does a particular type of work, e.g. *physicist*. ▷ *adj suffix*, *n suffix* indicating: **3** (of) a person who holds a particular political or religious belief, e.g. *Communist*; *Buddhist*. **4** (of) a person who is prejudiced on the basis specified, e.g. *racist*.

isthmus [**iss**-muss] *n*, *pl* -**muses** narrow strip of land connecting two areas of land.

it *pron* **1** refers to a nonhuman, animal, plant, or inanimate object. **2** refers to a thing mentioned or being discussed. **3** used as the subject of impersonal verbs, e.g. *it's windy*. **4** *informal* crucial or ultimate point. **its** *adj*, *pron* belonging to it. **it's 1** it is. **2** it has. **itself** *pron* emphatic form of IT.

- **SPELLING TIP**
- Many people find **its** and **it's**
- confusing. But it's quite simple
- really. **It's** only needs an apostrophe
- when it is used as the informal short
- form of 'it is' or 'it has'.

IT information technology.

Italian *n* **1** language of Italy and one of the languages of Switzerland. **2** person from Italy. ▷ *adj* **3** of Italy.

italic *adj* (of printing type) sloping to the right. **italics** *pl n* this type, used for emphasis. **italicize** *v* put in italics.

itch ❶ *n* **1** skin irritation causing a desire to scratch. **2** restless desire. ▷ *v* **3** have an itch. **itchy** *adj* **itchier**, **itchiest**.

item ❶ *n* **1** single thing in a list or collection. **2** piece of information. **itemize** *v* make a list of.

iterate *v* repeat. **iteration** *n*.

— THESAURUS —

isolated *adj* **1** = **remote**, hidden, lonely, off the beaten track, out-of-the-way, secluded

isolation *n* **1** = **separation**, detachment, remoteness, seclusion, segregation, solitude

issue *n* **1** = **topic**, matter, point, question, subject **2** = **problem**, bone of contention **3** = **edition**, copy, number, printing **4** = **outcome**, consequence, effect, end result, result, upshot **5** *Law* = **children**, descendants, heirs, offspring, progeny ▷ *v* **6** = **announce**, broadcast **8** = **give out**, circulate, deliver, distribute, publish, put out, release **take issue with** = **disagree with**, challenge, dispute, object to, oppose, raise an objection to, take exception to

itch *n* **1** = **irritation**, itchiness, prickling, tingling **2** = **desire**, craving, hankering, hunger, longing, lust, passion, yearning, yen (*inf*) ▷ *v* **3 a** = **prickle**, irritate, tickle, tingle **b** = **long**, ache, crave, hanker, hunger, lust, pine, yearn

item *n* **1** = **detail**, article, component, entry, matter, particular, point, thing **2** = **report**, account, article, bulletin, dispatch, feature, note, notice, paragraph, piece

itinerant ❶ *adj* travelling from place to place, e.g. *Itinerant workers are a growing concern among poverty activists.*

itinerary ❶ *n, pl* **-aries** detailed plan of a journey.

ITV Independent Television.

IUD intrauterine device: a coil-shaped contraceptive fitted into the womb.

IVF in-vitro fertilization.

ivory *n* **1** hard white bony substance forming the tusks of elephants. ▷ *adj* **2** yellowish-white. **ivory tower** remoteness from the realities of everyday life, e.g. *These boffins need to step out of their ivory tower and engage with real people.*

ivy *n, pl* **ivies** evergreen climbing plant.

—————— THESAURUS ——————————————————————————

itinerant *adj* = **wandering**, migratory, nomadic, peripatetic, roaming, roving, travelling, vagrant

itinerary *n* = **schedule**, programme, route, timetable

Jj

J joule(s).

jab ❶ v **jabbing, jabbed** 1 poke sharply. ▷ n 2 quick punch or poke. 3 *informal* injection.

jabber ❶ v 1 talk rapidly or incoherently. ▷ n 2 rapid or incoherent talk.

jabot [**zhab**-oh] n frill or ruffle on the front of a blouse or shirt.

jacaranda n tropical tree with sweet-smelling wood.

jack ❶ n 1 device for raising a motor vehicle or other heavy object. 2 playing card with a picture of a pageboy. 3 *Bowls* small white bowl aimed at by the players. 4 socket in electrical equipment into which a plug fits. 5 flag flown at the bow of a ship, showing nationality. 6 piece used in the game of jacks. ▷ pl 7 game in which pieces are thrown and picked up between bounces of a ball. **jack in** v *slang* abandon. **jack-in-the-box** n toy consisting of a figure on a spring in a box. **jack of all trades** person who can do many kinds of work. **jack up** v raise with a jack.

jackal n doglike wild animal of Africa and Asia.

jackass n 1 fool. 2 male of the ass. **laughing jackass** same as KOOKABURRA.

jackboot n 1 high military boot. 2 oppressive military rule.

jackdaw n black-and-grey bird of the crow family.

jacket ❶ n 1 short coat. 2 skin of a baked potato. 3 outer paper cover on a hardback book. **jacket potato** potato baked in its skin.

jackknife v 1 (of an articulated lorry) go out of control so that the trailer swings round at a sharp angle to the cab. ▷ n 2 large clasp knife. 3 dive with a sharp bend at the waist in mid-air.

jackpot ❶ n largest prize that may be won in a game. **hit the jackpot** be very successful through luck.

jack rabbit n American hare with long hind legs and large ears.

Jacobean [jak-a-**bee**-an] *adj* of the reign of James I of England.

Jacobite n supporter of James II of England and his descendants.

Jacquard [**jak**-ard] n fabric in which the design is incorporated into the weave.

Jacuzzi [jak-**oo**-zee] n ® circular bath with a device that swirls the water.

jade n 1 ornamental semiprecious stone, usu. dark green. ▷ *adj* 2 bluish-green.

jaded ❶ *adj* tired and unenthusiastic.

Jaffa n large orange with a thick skin.

jagged [**jag**-gid] *adj* having an uneven edge with sharp points.

jaguar n large S American spotted cat.

jail ❶ n 1 prison. ▷ v 2 send to prison. **jailer** n **jailbird** n *informal* person who has often been in prison.

jalopy [jal-**lop**-ee] n, pl **-lopies** *informal* old car.

jam¹ ❶ v **jamming, jammed** 1 pack tightly into a place. 2 crowd or congest. 3 make or become stuck. 4 *Radio* block (another station) with impulses of equal wavelength. 5 play a jam session. ▷ n 6 hold-up of traffic. 7 *informal* awkward situation. **jam on**

jab v 1 = **poke**, dig, lunge, nudge, prod, punch, stab, thrust ▷ n 2 = **poke**, dig, lunge, nudge, prod, punch, stab, thrust

jabber v 1 = **chatter**, babble, blether, gabble, mumble, prate, rabbit (on) (*Brit inf*), ramble, yap (*inf*)

jacket n 3 = **cover**, wrapper

jackpot n = **prize**, award, bonanza, reward, winnings

jack up v = **lift**, elevate, hoist, lift up, raise

jaded *adj* = **tired**, exhausted, fatigued, spent, weary

jagged *adj* = **uneven**, barbed, craggy,

indented, ragged, serrated, spiked, toothed

jail n 1 = **prison**, nick (*Brit sl*), penitentiary (*US*), reformatory, slammer (*sl*) ▷ v 2 = **imprison**, confine, detain, incarcerate, lock up, send down

jailer n = **guard**, keeper, warden, warder

jam¹ v 1 = **pack**, cram, force, press, ram, squeeze, stuff, wedge 2 = **crowd**, congest, crush, throng 3 = **stick**, block, clog, obstruct, stall ▷ n 7 *Inf* = **predicament**, deep water, fix (*inf*), hole (*sl*), hot water, pickle (*inf*), tight spot, trouble

the brakes apply brakes fiercely.
jam-packed *adj* filled to capacity.
jam session informal rock or jazz
performance.
jam² *n* food made from fruit boiled with
sugar.
jamb *n* side post of a door or window
frame.
jamboree ❶ *n* large gathering or
celebration.
jammy *adj* **-mier**, **-miest** *slang* lucky.
Jan. January.
jangle ❶ *v* **1** (cause to) make a harsh
ringing noise. **2** (of nerves) be
upset or irritated. ▷ *n* **3** harsh ringing
noise.
janitor ❶ *n* caretaker of a school or other
building.
January *n* first month of the year.
japan *n* **1** very hard varnish, usu. black.
▷ *v* **-panning**, **-panned 2** cover with
this varnish.
Japanese *n*, *adj* (native or language) of
Japan.
jape *n* old-fashioned joke or prank.
japonica *n* shrub with red flowers.
jar¹ ❶ *n* **1** wide-mouthed container, usu.
round and made of glass. **2** *informal*
glass of beer.
jar² ❶ *v* **jarring**, **jarred 1** have a
disturbing or unpleasant effect. **2** be in
conflict. **3** jolt or bump. ▷ *n* **4** jolt or
shock.
jardiniere *n* ornamental plant pot.
jargon ❶ *n* **1** specialized technical
language of a particular subject.
2 pretentious language.
jasmine *n* shrub with sweet-smelling
yellow or white flowers.

jasper *n* red, yellow, dark green, or
brown variety of quartz.
jaundice ❶ *n* disease marked by
yellowness of the skin. **jaundiced** *adj*
1 (of an attitude or opinion) bitter or
cynical. **2** having jaundice.
jaunt ❶ *n* **1** short journey for pleasure.
▷ *v* **2** make such a journey.
jaunty ❶ *adj* **-tier**, **-tiest 1** sprightly and
cheerful. **2** smart. **jauntily** *adv*.
javelin *n* light spear thrown in sports
competitions.
jaw ❶ *n* **1** one of the bones in which the
teeth are set. **2** lower part of the face.
▷ *pl* **3** mouth. **4** gripping part of a
tool. **5** narrow opening of a gorge or
valley. ▷ *v* **6** *slang* talk lengthily.
jawbone *n* lower jaw of a person or
animal.
jay *n* bird with a pinkish body and blue-
and-black wings.
jaywalking *n* crossing the road in a
careless or dangerous manner.
jaywalker *n*.
jazz ❶ *n* kind of music with an exciting
rhythm, usu. involving improvisation.
and all that jazz *slang* and other
related things. **jazzy** *adj* **-zier**, **-ziest**
1 flashy or showy. **2** of or like jazz. **jazz
up** *v* make more lively.
JCB *n* ® construction machine with a
shovel at the front and an excavator at
the rear.
jealous ❶ *adj* **1** fearful of losing a partner
or possession to a rival. **2** envious.
3 suspiciously watchful. **jealously** *adv*
jealousy *n*, *pl* **-sies**.
jeans ❶ *pl n* casual denim trousers.
Jeep *n* ® four-wheel-drive motor vehicle.

--- **THESAURUS** ---

jamboree *n* = **festival**, carnival,
celebration, festivity, fete, revelry
jangle *v* **1** = **rattle**, chime, clank, clash,
clatter, jingle, vibrate
janitor *n* = **caretaker**, concierge,
custodian, doorkeeper, porter
jar¹ *n* **1** = **pot**, container, crock, jug,
pitcher, urn, vase
jar² *v* **1** = **irritate**, annoy, get on one's
nerves (*inf*), grate, irk, nettle, offend
3 = **jolt**, bump, convulse, rattle, rock,
shake, vibrate ▷ *n* **4** = **jolt**, bump,
convulsion, shock, vibration
jargon *n* **1** = **parlance**, argot, idiom, usage
jaundiced *adj* **1 a** = **bitter**, envious,
hostile, jealous, resentful, spiteful,
suspicious **b** = **cynical**, sceptical
jaunt *n* **1** = **outing**, airing, excursion,

expedition, ramble, stroll, tour, trip
jaunty *adj* **1** = **sprightly**, buoyant,
carefree, high-spirited, lively, perky,
self-confident, sparky
jaw *v* **6** *Sl* = **talk**, chat, chatter, gossip,
spout
jazz up *v* = **enliven**, animate, enhance,
improve
jazzy *adj* **1** = **flashy**, fancy, gaudy, snazzy
(*inf*)
jealous *adj* **1** = **possessive**, mistrustful,
protective **2** = **envious**, covetous,
desirous, green, grudging, resentful
3 = **suspicious**, vigilant, wary, watchful
jealousy *n* **1** = **possessiveness**,
mistrust **2** = **envy**, covetousness,
resentment, spite **3** = **suspicion**
jeans *pl n* = **denims**

jeer ❶ v **1** scoff or deride. ▷ n **2** cry of derision.

Jehovah n God. **Jehovah's Witness** member of a Christian sect believing that the end of the world is near.

jejune adj **1** simple or naive. **2** dull or boring.

jell ❶ v **1** form into a jelly-like substance. **2** take on a definite form.

jelly n, pl **-lies 1** soft food made of liquid set with gelatine. **2** jam made from fruit juice and sugar. **jellied** adj prepared in a jelly.

jellyfish n small jelly-like sea animal.

jemmy n, pl **-mies** short steel crowbar used by burglars.

jenny n, pl **-nies** female ass or wren.

jeopardy ❶ n danger. **jeopardize** v place in danger.

jerboa n small mouselike rodent with long hind legs.

jerk ❶ v **1** move or throw abruptly. ▷ n **2** sharp or abruptly stopped movement. **3** slang contemptible person. **jerky** adj **jerkier**, **jerkiest** sudden or abrupt. **jerkily** adv **jerkiness** n.

jerkin n sleeveless jacket.

Jerry n Brit slang German or Germans collectively.

jerry-built ❶ adj built badly using flimsy materials.

jerry can n flat-sided can for carrying petrol etc.

jersey n **1** knitted jumper. **2** machine-knitted fabric. **3** (**J-**) breed of cow.

Jerusalem artichoke n small yellowish-white root vegetable.

jest ❶ n, v joke. **jester** n History professional clown at court.

Jesuit [**jezz**-yoo-it] n member of the Society of Jesus, a Roman Catholic order.

Jesus n **1** (also **Jesus Christ**, **Jesus of Nazareth**) ?4 BC–?29 AD, founder of Christianity, believed by Christians to be the Son of God. ▷ interj **2** taboo slang oath used to express intense surprise, dismay, etc.

jet¹ ❶ n **1** aircraft driven by jet propulsion. **2** stream of liquid or gas, esp. one forced from a small hole. **3** nozzle from which gas or liquid is forced. ▷ v **jetting**, **jetted 4** fly by jet aircraft. **jet lag** fatigue caused by crossing time zones in an aircraft. **jet propulsion** propulsion by thrust provided by a jet of gas or liquid. **jet-propelled** adj **jet set** rich and fashionable people who travel the world for pleasure.

jet² ❶ n hard black mineral. **jet-black** adj glossy black.

jetsam n goods thrown overboard to lighten a ship.

jettison ❶ v **-soning**, **-soned 1** abandon. **2** throw overboard.

jetty ❶ n, pl **-ties 1** small pier. **2** structure built from a shore to protect a harbour.

Jew n **1** person whose religion is Judaism. **2** descendant of the ancient Hebrews. **Jewess** n fem now often offens **Jewish** adj **Jewry** n Jews collectively. **jew's-harp** n musical instrument held between the teeth and played by plucking a metal strip with one's finger.

---

jeer v **1** = **mock**, barrack, deride, gibe, heckle, ridicule, scoff, taunt ▷ n **2** = **mockery**, abuse, boo, catcall, derision, gibe, ridicule, taunt

jell v **1** = **solidify**, congeal, harden, set, thicken **2** = **take shape**, come together, crystallize, materialize

jeopardize v = **endanger**, chance, expose, gamble, imperil, risk, stake, venture

jeopardy n = **danger**, insecurity, peril, risk, vulnerability

jerk v **1** = **tug**, jolt, lurch, pull, thrust, twitch, wrench, yank ▷ n **2** = **tug**, jolt, lurch, pull, thrust, twitch, wrench, yank

jerky adj = **bumpy**, convulsive, jolting, jumpy, shaky, spasmodic

jerry-built adj = **ramshackle**, cheap, defective, flimsy, rickety, shabby, slipshod, thrown together

jest n = **joke**, bon mot, crack (sl), jape, pleasantry, prank, quip, wisecrack (inf), witticism ▷ v = **joke**, kid (inf), mock, quip, tease

jester n Hist = **clown**, buffoon, fool, harlequin

jet¹ n **2** = **stream**, flow, fountain, gush, spout, spray, spring **3** = **nozzle**, atomizer, sprayer, sprinkler ▷ v **4** = **fly**, soar, zoom

jet-black adj = **black**, coal-black, ebony, inky, pitch-black, raven, sable

jettison v **1** = **abandon**, discard, dump, scrap **2** = **throw overboard**, eject, expel, unload

jetty n **1** = **pier**, dock, quay, wharf **2** = **breakwater**, groyne, mole

jewel ❶ n **1** precious stone. **2** special person or thing. **jeweller** n dealer in jewels. **jewellery** n objects decorated with precious stones.

jewfish n Aust freshwater catfish.

Jezebel n shameless or scheming woman.

jib¹ n triangular sail set in front of a mast.

jib² ❶ v **jibbing, jibbed** (of a horse, person, etc.) stop and refuse to go on. **jib at** v object to (a proposal etc.).

jib³ n projecting arm of a crane or derrick.

jibe¹ ❶ n, v taunt or jeer.

jibe² v same as GYBE.

jiffy n, pl **-fies** informal very short period of time.

jig ❶ n **1** type of lively dance. **2** music for it. **3** device that holds a component in place for cutting etc. ▷ v **jigging, jigged 4** dance a jig. **5** make jerky up-and-down movements.

jiggery-pokery n informal trickery or mischief.

jiggle v move up and down with short jerky movements.

jigsaw n **1** (also **jigsaw puzzle**) picture cut into interlocking pieces, which the user tries to fit together again. **2** mechanical saw for cutting along curved lines.

jihad n Islamic holy war against unbelievers.

jilt v leave or reject (one's lover).

jingle ❶ n **1** catchy verse or song used in a radio or television advert. **2** gentle ringing noise. ▷ v **3** (cause to) make a gentle ringing sound.

jingoism n aggressive nationalism. **jingoistic** adj.

jinks pl n **high jinks** boisterous merrymaking.

jinni n, pl **jinn** spirit in Muslim mythology.

jinx ❶ n **1** person or thing bringing bad luck. ▷ v **2** be or put a jinx on.

jitters ❶ pl n worried nervousness. **jittery** adj nervous.

jive n **1** lively dance of the 1940s and '50s. ▷ v **2** dance the jive.

job ❶ n **1** occupation or paid employment. **2** task to be done. **3** performance of a task. **4** informal difficult task. **5** informal crime, esp. robbery. **jobbing** adj doing individual jobs for payment. **jobless** adj, pl n unemployed (people). **Jobcentre, job centre** n government office displaying information about available jobs. **job lot** assortment sold together. **job sharing** splitting of one post between two people working part-time.

Job's comforter n person who adds to distress while pretending to give sympathy.

jockey n **1** (professional) rider of racehorses. ▷ v **2 jockey for position** manoeuvre to obtain an advantage.

jockstrap n belt with a pouch to support the genitals, worn by male athletes.

jocose [joke-**kohss**] adj playful or humorous. **jocosely** adv.

jocular ❶ adj **1** fond of joking. **2** meant as a joke. **jocularity** n **jocularly** adv.

jocund [**jok**-kund] adj lit merry or cheerful.

jodhpurs pl n riding trousers, loose-fitting above the knee but tight below.

j

———————— THESAURUS ————————

jewel n **1** = **gemstone**, ornament, rock (sl), sparkler (inf) **2** = **rarity**, collector's item, find, gem, humdinger (sl), pearl, treasure, wonder

jewellery n = **jewels**, finery, gems, ornaments, regalia, treasure, trinkets

jib² v = **refuse**, balk, recoil, retreat, shrink, stop short

jibe¹ n = **taunt**, jeering, mockery, ridicule, scoffing, scorn, sneering ▷ v = **taunt**, jeer, make fun of, mock, poke fun at, ridicule, scoff, scorn, sneer

jig v **4** = **skip**, bob, bounce, caper, prance, wiggle

jingle n **1** = **song**, chorus, ditty, melody, tune **2** = **rattle**, clink, reverberation, ringing, tinkle ▷ v **3** = **ring**, chime, clink, jangle, rattle, tinkle

jinx n **1** = **curse**, hex (US & Canad inf), hoodoo (inf), nemesis ▷ v **2** = **curse**, bewitch, hex (US & Canad inf)

jitters pl n = **nerves**, anxiety, butterflies (in one's stomach) (inf), cold feet (inf), fidgets, nervousness, the shakes (inf)

jittery adj = **nervous**, agitated, anxious, fidgety, jumpy, shaky, trembling, wired (sl)

job n **1** = **occupation**, business, calling, career, employment, livelihood, profession, vocation **2** = **task**, assignment, chore, duty, enterprise, errand, undertaking, venture, work

jobless adj = **unemployed**, idle, inactive, out of work, unoccupied

jocular adj = **humorous**, amusing, droll, facetious, funny, joking, jovial, playful, sportive, teasing, waggish

jog ❶ v **jogging, jogged 1** run at a gentle pace, esp. for exercise. **2** nudge slightly. ▷ n **3** slow run. **jog someone's memory** remind someone of something. **jogger** n **jogging** n.

joggle v shake or move jerkily.

john n US slang toilet.

John Dory n European dory with a deep compressed body, spiny dorsal fins, and massive jaws.

Johnny Canuck n Canad **1** an informal name for a Canadian. **2** a personification of Canada.

joie de vivre ❶ [jwah de **veev**-ra] n French enjoyment of life.

join ❶ v **1** become a member (of). **2** become part of. **3** come into someone's company. **4** take part (in). **5** come or bring together. **6** connect (two points). ▷ n **7** place where two things are joined. **join in** v take part in. **join up** v enlist in the armed services. **joined-up** adj integrated by an overall strategy, e.g. joined-up government.

joiner n maker of finished woodwork. **joinery** n joiner's work.

joint ❶ adj **1** shared by two or more. ▷ n **2** place where bones meet but can move. **3** junction of two or more parts or objects. **4** piece of meat for roasting. **5** slang house or place, esp. a disreputable bar or nightclub. **6** slang marijuana cigarette. ▷ v **7** divide meat into joints. **8** provide with a joint. **out of joint 1** disorganized. **2** dislocated. **jointed** adj **jointly** adv **joint-stock company** firm whose capital is jointly owned by shareholders.

joist n horizontal beam that helps support a floor or ceiling.

jojoba [hoe-**hoe**-ba] n shrub whose seeds yield oil used in cosmetics.

joke ❶ n **1** thing said or done to cause laughter. **2** amusing or ridiculous person or thing. ▷ v **3** make jokes. **jokey** adj **jokingly** adv **joker** n **1** person who jokes. **2** slang fellow. **3** extra card in a pack, counted as any other in some games.

jolly ❶ adj **-lier, -liest 1** (of a person) happy and cheerful. **2** (of an occasion) merry and festive. ▷ adv **3** informal extremely. ▷ v **-lying, -lied 4 jolly along** try to keep (someone) cheerful by flattery or coaxing. **jollity** n **jollification** n merrymaking.

jolt ❶ n **1** unpleasant surprise or shock. **2** sudden jerk or bump. ▷ v **3** surprise or shock. **4** move or shake with a jerk.

Jonah n person believed to bring bad luck to those around him or her.

jonquil n fragrant narcissus.

josh v Chiefly US slang tease.

joss stick n stick of incense giving off a sweet smell when burnt.

jostle ❶ v **1** knock or push against. **2** compete with someone.

jot ❶ v **jotting, jotted 1** write briefly. ▷ n **2** very small amount. **jotter** n notebook. **jottings** pl n notes jotted down.

joual n nonstandard Canadian French dialect, esp. as associated with ill-educated speakers.

joule [**jool**] n Physics unit of work or energy.

————————————————————— THESAURUS —

jog v **1** = **run**, canter, lope, trot **2** = **nudge**, prod, push, shake, stir

joie de vivre n French = **enthusiasm**, ebullience, enjoyment, gusto, relish, zest

join v **1** = **enrol**, enlist, enter, sign up **5, 6** = **connect**, add, append, attach, combine, couple, fasten, link, unite

joint adj **1** = **shared**, collective, combined, communal, cooperative, joined, mutual, united ▷ n **3** = **junction**, connection, hinge, intersection, nexus, node ▷ v **7** = **divide**, carve, cut up, dissect, segment, sever

jointly adv = **collectively**, as one, in common, in conjunction, in league, in partnership, mutually, together

joke n **1** = **jest**, gag (inf), jape, prank, pun, quip, wisecrack (inf), witticism **2** = **laughing stock**, buffoon, clown ▷ v **3** = **jest**, banter, kid (inf), mock, play the fool, quip, taunt, tease

joker n **1** = **comedian**, buffoon, clown, comic, humorist, jester, prankster, trickster, wag, wit

jolly adj **1** = **happy**, cheerful, chirpy (inf), genial, jovial, merry, playful, sprightly, upbeat (inf)

jolt n **1** = **surprise**, blow, bolt from the blue, bombshell, setback, shock **2** = **jerk**, bump, jar, jog, jump, lurch, shake, start ▷ v **3** = **surprise**, discompose, disturb, perturb, stagger, startle, stun **4** = **jerk**, jar, jog, jostle, knock, push, shake, shove

jostle v **1** = **push**, bump, elbow, hustle, jog, jolt, shake, shove

jot v **1** = **note down**, list, record, scribble ▷ n **2** = **bit**, fraction, grain, morsel, scrap, speck

journal ⓘ *n* 1 daily newspaper or magazine. 2 daily record of events. **journalese** *n* superficial style of writing, found in some newspapers. **journalism** *n* writing in or editing of newspapers and magazines. **journalist** *n* **journalistic** *adj*.

journey ⓘ *n* 1 act or process of travelling from one place to another. 2 time taken or distance travelled in a journey. ▷ *v* 3 travel.

journeyman *n* qualified craftsman employed by another.

joust *History* ▷ *n* 1 combat with lances between two mounted knights. ▷ *v* 2 fight on horseback using lances.

jovial ⓘ *adj* happy and cheerful. **jovially** *adv* **joviality** *n*.

jowl¹ *n* 1 lower jaw. ▷ *pl* 2 cheeks.

jowl² *n* fatty flesh hanging from the lower jaw.

joy ⓘ *n* 1 feeling of great delight or pleasure. 2 cause of this feeling. **joyful** *adj* **joyless** *adj* **joyous** *adj* extremely happy and enthusiastic. **joyriding** *n* driving for pleasure, esp. in a stolen car. **joyride** *n* **joyrider** *n* **joystick** *n* control device for an aircraft or computer.

JP Justice of the Peace.

JPEG [**jay**-peg] *Computing* 1 standard compressed file format used for pictures. 2 picture held in this file format.

Jr Junior.

JSA jobseeker's allowance: in Britain, a payment made to unemployed people.

jubilant ⓘ *adj* feeling or expressing great joy. **jubilantly** *adv* **jubilation** *n*.

jubilee ⓘ *n* special anniversary, esp. 25th (**silver jubilee**) or 50th (**golden jubilee**).

Judaism *n* religion of the Jews, based on the Old Testament and the Talmud. **Judaic** *adj*.

Judas *n* person who betrays a friend.

judder *v* 1 vibrate violently. ▷ *n* 2 violent vibration.

judge ⓘ *n* 1 public official who tries cases and passes sentence in a court of law. 2 person who decides the outcome of a contest. 3 person of reliable opinion on a subject. ▷ *v* 4 act as a judge. 5 appraise critically. 6 consider something to be the case. **judgment**, **judgement** *n* 1 opinion reached after careful thought. 2 verdict of a judge. 3 ability to appraise critically. **Judgment Day** occasion of the Last Judgment by God at the end of the world. **judgmental**, **judgemental** *adj*.

judicial ⓘ *adj* 1 of or by a court or judge. 2 showing or using judgment. **judicially** *adv*.

---

journal *n* 1 = **newspaper**, daily, gazette, magazine, monthly, periodical, weekly 2 = **diary**, chronicle, log, record

journalist *n* = **reporter**, broadcaster, columnist, commentator, correspondent, hack, journo (*sl*), pressman

journey *n* 1 = **trip**, excursion, expedition, odyssey, pilgrimage, tour, trek, voyage ▷ *v* 3 = **travel**, go, proceed, roam, rove, tour, traverse, trek, voyage, wander

jovial *adj* = **cheerful**, animated, cheery, convivial, happy, jolly, merry, mirthful

joy *n* 1 = **delight**, bliss, ecstasy, elation, gaiety, glee, pleasure, rapture, satisfaction

joyful *adj* = **delighted**, elated, enraptured, glad, gratified, happy, jubilant, merry, pleased

joyless *adj* = **unhappy**, cheerless, depressed, dismal, dreary, gloomy, miserable, sad

joyous *adj* = **joyful**, festive, merry, rapturous

jubilant *adj* = **overjoyed**, elated, enraptured, euphoric, exuberant, exultant, thrilled, triumphant

jubilation *n* = **joy**, celebration, ecstasy, elation, excitement, exultation, festivity, triumph

jubilee *n* = **celebration**, festival, festivity, holiday

judge *n* 1 = **magistrate**, beak (*Brit sl*), justice 2 = **referee**, adjudicator, arbiter, arbitrator, moderator, umpire 3 = **critic**, arbiter, assessor, authority, connoisseur, expert ▷ *v* 4 = **adjudicate**, arbitrate, decide, mediate, referee, umpire 5 = **consider**, appraise, assess, esteem, estimate, evaluate, rate, value

judgment, **judgement** *n* 1 = **opinion**, appraisal, assessment, belief, diagnosis, estimate, finding, valuation, view 2 = **verdict**, arbitration, decision, decree, finding, ruling, sentence 3 = **sense**, acumen, discernment, discrimination, prudence, shrewdness, understanding, wisdom

judicial *adj* 1 = **legal**, official

judiciary *n* system of courts and judges.

judicious ❶ *adj* well-judged and sensible. **judiciously** *adv*.

judo *n* sport in which two opponents try to throw each other to the ground.

jug ❶ *n* container for liquids, with a handle and small spout. **jugged hare** hare stewed in an earthenware pot.

juggernaut *n* **1** large heavy lorry. **2** any irresistible destructive force.

juggle ❶ *v* **1** throw and catch (several objects) so that most are in the air at the same time. **2** manipulate (figures, situations, etc.) to suit one's purposes. **juggler** *n*.

jugular, jugular vein *n* one of three large veins of the neck that return blood from the head to the heart.

juice ❶ *n* **1** liquid part of vegetables, fruit, or meat. **2** *informal* petrol. ▷ *pl* **3** fluids secreted by an organ of the body. **juicy** *adj* **juicier**, **juiciest 1** full of juice. **2** interesting.

jujitsu *n* Japanese art of wrestling and self-defence.

juju *n* W African magic charm or fetish.

jukebox *n* coin-operated machine on which records, CDs, or videos can be played.

Jul. July.

julep *n* sweet alcoholic drink.

Julian calendar *n* calendar introduced by Julius Caesar, in which leap years occurred every fourth year.

julienne *adj* **1** (of vegetables or meat) cut into thin shreds. ▷ *n* **2** clear soup containing thinly shredded vegetables.

July *n* seventh month of the year.

jumble ❶ *n* **1** confused heap or state. **2** articles for a jumble sale. ▷ *v* **3** mix in a disordered way. **jumble sale** sale of miscellaneous second-hand items.

jumbo ❶ *adj* **1** *informal* very large. ▷ *n* **2** (also **jumbo jet**) large jet airliner.

jump ❶ *v* **1** leap or spring into the air using the leg muscles. **2** move quickly and suddenly. **3** jerk with surprise. **4** increase suddenly. **5** change the subject abruptly. **6** *informal* attack without warning. **7** pass over or miss out (intervening material). ▷ *n* **8** act of jumping. **9** sudden rise. **10** break in continuity. **11** step or degree. **jump the gun** act prematurely. **jump the queue** not wait one's turn. **jumpy** *adj* **jumpier**, **jumpiest** nervous. **jump at** *v* accept (a chance etc.) gladly. **jumped-up** *adj* arrogant because of recent promotion. **jump jet** fixed-wing jet that can take off and land vertically. **jump leads** electric cables to connect a flat car battery to an external battery to aid starting an engine. **jump on** *v* attack suddenly and forcefully. **jump suit** one-piece garment of trousers and top.

jumper¹ ❶ *n* sweater or pullover.

jumper² *n* person or animal that jumps.

Jun. 1 June. **2** Junior.

———————— THESAURUS ————————

judicious *adj* = **sensible**, astute, careful, discriminating, enlightened, prudent, shrewd, thoughtful, well-judged, wise

jug *n* = **container**, carafe, crock, ewer, jar, pitcher, urn, vessel

juggle *v* **2** = **manipulate**, alter, change, manoeuvre, modify

juice *n* **1** = **liquid**, extract, fluid, liquor, nectar, sap

juicy *adj* **1** = **moist**, lush, succulent **2** = **interesting**, colourful, provocative, racy, risqué, sensational, spicy (*inf*), suggestive, vivid

jumble *n* **1** = **muddle**, clutter, confusion, disarray, disorder, mess, mishmash, mixture ▷ *v* **3** = **mix**, confuse, disorder, disorganize, mistake, muddle, shuffle

jumbo *adj* **1** *Inf* = **giant**, gigantic, huge, immense, large, oversized

jump *v* **1** = **leap**, bounce, bound, hop, hurdle, skip, spring, vault **3** = **recoil**, flinch, jerk, start, wince **4** = **increase**, advance, ascend, escalate, rise, surge **7** = **miss**, avoid, evade, omit, skip ▷ *n* **8** = **leap**, bound, hop, skip, spring, vault **9** = **rise**, advance, increase, increment, upsurge, upturn **10** = **interruption**, break, gap, hiatus, lacuna, space

jumped-up *adj* = **conceited**, arrogant, insolent, overbearing, pompous, presumptuous

jumper¹ *n* = **sweater**, jersey, pullover, woolly

jumpy *adj* = **nervous**, agitated, anxious, apprehensive, fidgety, jittery (*inf*), on edge, restless, tense, wired (*sl*)

junction ❶ *n* place where routes, railway lines, or roads meet.

juncture ❶ *n* point in time, esp. a critical one.

June *n* sixth month of the year.

jungle *n* **1** tropical forest of dense tangled vegetation. **2** confusion or mess. **3** place of intense struggle for survival.

junior ❶ *adj* **1** of lower standing. **2** younger. ▷ *n* **3** junior person. **junior school** school for children between seven and eleven.

juniper *n* evergreen shrub with purple berries.

junk¹ ❶ *n* **1** discarded or useless objects. **2** *informal* rubbish. **3** *slang* narcotic drug, esp. heroin. **junkie**, **junky** *n*, *pl* **junkies** *slang* drug addict. **junk food** snack food of low nutritional value. **junk mail** unwanted mail advertising goods or services.

junk² *n* flat-bottomed Chinese sailing boat.

junket *n* **1** excursion by public officials paid for from public funds. **2** sweetened milk set with rennet. **3** feast. **junketing** *n*.

junta *n* group of military officers holding power in a country, esp. after a coup.

Jupiter *n* **1** king of the Roman gods. **2** largest of the planets.

juridical *adj* of law or the administration of justice.

jurisdiction ❶ *n* **1** right or power to administer justice and apply laws. **2** extent of this right or power. **3** authority in general.

jurisprudence *n* science or philosophy of law.

jurist *n* expert in law.

jury *n*, *pl* **-ries 1** group of people sworn to deliver a verdict in a court of law. **2** judges of a competition. **juror** *n* member of a jury.

just ❶ *adv* **1** very recently. **2** at this instant. **3** merely, only. **4** exactly. **5** barely. **6** really. ▷ *adj* **7** fair or impartial in action or judgment. **8** proper or right. **justice** *n* **1** quality of being just. **2** judicial proceedings. **3** magistrate. **justify** *v* prove right or reasonable. **justly** *adv* **justness** *n*.

justice ❶ *n* **1** quality of being just. **2** judicial proceedings. **3** judge or magistrate. **justice of the peace** person who is authorized to act as a judge in a local court of law.

justify ❶ *v* **-fying, -fied 1** prove right or reasonable. **2** explain the reasons for an action. **3** align (text) so the margins are straight. **justifiable** *adj* **justifiably** *adv* **justification** *n*.

jut ❶ *v* **jutting, jutted** project or stick out.

jute *n* plant fibre, used for rope, canvas, etc.

THESAURUS

junction *n* = **connection**, coupling, linking, union

juncture *n* = **moment**, occasion, point, time

junior *adj* **1** = **lower**, inferior, lesser, minor, secondary, subordinate **2** = **younger**

junk¹ *n* **1, 2** = **rubbish**, clutter, debris, litter, odds and ends, refuse, scrap, trash, waste

jurisdiction *n* **1, 3** = **authority**, command, control, influence, power, rule **2** = **range**, area, bounds, compass, field, province, scope, sphere

just *adv* **1** = **recently**, hardly, lately, only now, scarcely **3** = **merely**, by the skin of one's teeth, only, simply, solely **4** = **exactly**, absolutely, completely, entirely, perfectly, precisely ▷ *adj* **7** = **fair**, conscientious, equitable, fair-minded, good, honest, upright,

virtuous **8** = **fitting**, appropriate, apt, deserved, due, justified, merited, proper, rightful

justice *n* **1** = **fairness**, equity, honesty, integrity, law, legality, legitimacy, right **3** = **judge**, magistrate

justifiable *adj* = **reasonable**, acceptable, defensible, excusable, legitimate, sensible, understandable, valid, warrantable

justification *n* = **reason**, basis, defence, excuse, explanation, grounds, rationalization, vindication, warrant

justify *v* **1, 2** = **explain**, defend, exculpate, excuse, exonerate, support, uphold, vindicate, warrant

justly *adv* = **properly**, correctly, equitably, fairly, lawfully

jut *v* = **stick out**, bulge, extend, overhang, poke, project, protrude

juvenile ❶ *adj* **1** young. **2** of or suitable for young people. **3** immature and rather silly. ▷ *n* **4** young person or child. **juvenilia** *pl n* works produced in an author's youth. **juvenile delinquent** young person guilty of a crime.
juxtapose ❶ *v* put side by side. **juxtaposition** *n*.

—————————————————— THESAURUS ——————————

juvenile *adj* **1** = **young**, youthful
3 = **immature**, babyish, callow, childish, inexperienced, infantile, puerile ▷ *n* **4** = **child**, adolescent, boy, girl, infant, minor, youth
juxtaposition *n* = **proximity**, closeness, contact, nearness, propinquity, vicinity

K 1 *Chemistry* potassium. **2** *informal* thousand(s).

Kabloona *n* (in Canada) a person who is not of Inuit ancestry, esp. a White person.

Kaffir [**kaf**-fer] *n S Afr offens obs* Black African.

kaftan *n* **1** long loose Eastern garment. **2** woman's dress resembling this.

kai *n NZ informal* food.

kaiser [**kize**-er] *n History* German or Austro-Hungarian emperor.

kak *n S Afr slang* **1** faeces. **2** rubbish.

Kalashnikov *n* Russian-made automatic rifle.

kale *n* cabbage with crinkled leaves.

kaleidoscope *n* **1** tube-shaped toy containing loose coloured pieces reflected by mirrors so that intricate patterns form when the tube is twisted. **2** complicated or rapidly changing set of colours, circumstances, etc. **kaleidoscopic** *adj*.

kalends *pl n* same as CALENDS.

kamik *n Canad* a traditional Inuit boot made of caribou hide or sealskin.

kamikaze ❶ [kam-mee-**kah**-zee] *n* **1** (in World War II) Japanese pilot who performed a suicide mission. ▷ *adj* **2** (of an action) undertaken in the knowledge that it will kill or injure the person performing it.

kangaroo *n, pl* **-roos** Australian marsupial which moves by jumping with its powerful hind legs. **kangaroo court** unofficial court set up by a group to discipline its members. **kangaroo paw** Australian plant with green-and-red flowers.

kaolin *n* fine white clay used to make porcelain and in some medicines.

kapok *n* fluffy fibre from a tropical tree, used to stuff cushions etc.

kaput [kap-**poot**] *adj informal* ruined or broken.

karaoke *n* form of entertainment in which people sing over a prerecorded backing tape.

karate *n* Japanese system of unarmed combat using blows with the feet, hands, elbows, and legs.

karma *n Buddhism, Hinduism* person's actions affecting his or her fate in the next reincarnation.

karoo *n S Afr* high arid plateau.

kart *n* same as GO-KART.

kasbah *n* same as CASBAH.

katydid *n* large green grasshopper of N America.

kauri *n* large NZ conifer that yields valuable timber and resin.

kayak *n* **1** Inuit canoe made of sealskins stretched over a frame. **2** fibreglass or canvas-covered canoe of this design.

kazoo *n, pl* **-zoos** cigar-shaped metal musical instrument that produces a buzzing sound when the player hums into it.

KBE Knight Commander of the Order of the British Empire.

kbyte *Computers* kilobyte.

kcal kilocalorie.

kea *n* large brownish-green parrot of NZ.

kebab *n* **1** dish of small pieces of meat grilled on skewers. **2** (also **doner kebab**) grilled minced lamb served in a split slice of unleavened bread.

kedgeree *n* dish of fish with rice and eggs.

keel ❶ *n* main lengthways timber or steel support along the base of a ship. **keel over** *v* **1** turn upside down. **2** *informal* collapse suddenly. **on an even keel** working or progressing smoothly.

keen¹ ❶ *adj* **1** eager or enthusiastic. **2** intense or strong. **3** intellectually acute. **4** (of the senses) capable of recognizing small distinctions. **5** sharp. **6** cold and penetrating. **7** competitive. **keenly** *adv* **keenness** *n*.

———— THESAURUS ————

kamikaze *adj* **2** = **self-destructive**, foolhardy, suicidal

keel over *v* **2** *Inf* = **collapse**, black out (*inf*), faint, pass out

keen¹ *adj* **1** = **eager**, ardent, avid, enthusiastic, impassioned, zealous **2** = **intense 3** = **astute**, canny, clever, perceptive, quick, shrewd, wise **5** = **sharp**, cutting, incisive, razor-like

keen² ❶ v wail over the dead.

keep ❶ v **keeping, kept 1** have or retain possession of. **2** take temporary charge of. **3** store. **4** stay or cause to stay (in, on, or at a place or position). **5** continue or persist. **6** support financially. **7** detain (someone). **8** look after or maintain. **9** (of food) remain good. ▷ n **10** cost of food and everyday expenses. **11** central tower of a castle. **keeper** n **1** person who looks after animals in a zoo. **2** person in charge of a museum or collection. **3** short for GOALKEEPER. **keeping** n care or charge. **in, out of keeping with** appropriate or inappropriate for. **keep fit** exercises designed to promote physical fitness. **keepsake** n gift treasured for the sake of the giver. **keep up** v maintain at the current level. **keep up with** v maintain a pace set by (someone). **keep up with the Joneses** informal compete with friends or neighbours in material possessions.

keg ❶ n small metal beer barrel.

kelp n large brown seaweed.

kelvin n SI unit of temperature. **Kelvin scale** temperature scale starting at absolute zero (−273.15° Celsius).

ken v **kenning, kenned** or **kent** Scot know. **beyond one's ken** beyond one's range of knowledge.

kendo n Japanese sport of fencing using wooden staves.

kennel n **1** hutlike shelter for a dog. ▷ pl **2** place for breeding, boarding, or training dogs.

kept v past of KEEP.

keratin n fibrous protein found in the hair and nails.

kerb n stone edging to a footpath. **kerb crawling** act of driving slowly beside a pavement to pick up a prostitute.

kerchief n piece of cloth worn over the head or round the neck.

kerfuffle n informal commotion or disorder.

kernel ❶ n **1** seed of a nut, cereal, or fruit stone. **2** central and essential part of something.

kerosene n US & Canad another name for PARAFFIN.

kestrel n type of small falcon.

ketch n two-masted sailing ship.

ketchup n thick cold sauce, usu. made of tomatoes.

kettle n container with a spout and handle used for boiling water. **a different kettle of fish** something entirely different. **kettledrum** n large bowl-shaped metal drum.

key¹ ❶ n **1** device for operating a lock by moving a bolt. **2** device turned to wind a clock, operate a machine, etc. **3** any of a set of levers or buttons pressed to operate a typewriter, computer, or musical keyboard instrument. **4** Music set of related notes. **5** something crucial in providing an explanation or interpretation. **6** means of achieving a desired end. **7** list of explanations of codes, symbols, etc. ▷ adj **8** of great importance. ▷ v **9** (also **key in**) enter (text) using a keyboard. **keyed up** very excited or nervous.

— THESAURUS —

keen² v = **lament**, bewail, grieve, mourn, wail, weep

keenness n = **eagerness**, ardour, enthusiasm, fervour, intensity, passion, zeal, zest

keep v **1** = **retain**, conserve, control, hold, maintain, possess, preserve **2** = **look after**, care for, guard, maintain, manage, mind, protect, tend, watch over **3** = **store**, carry, deposit, hold, place, stack, stock **6** = **support**, maintain, provide for, subsidize, sustain **7** = **detain**, delay, hinder, hold back, keep back, obstruct, prevent, restrain ▷ n **10** = **board**, food, living, maintenance **11** = **tower**, castle

keeper n **2** = **guardian**, attendant, caretaker, curator, custodian, guard, preserver, steward, warden

keeping n = **care**, charge, custody, guardianship, possession, protection, safekeeping **in keeping with** = **in agreement with**, complying with, conforming to, corresponding to, in accord with, in balance with, in harmony with, in proportion with

keepsake n = **souvenir**, memento, relic, reminder, symbol, token

keep up v = **maintain**, continue, keep pace, preserve, sustain

keg n = **barrel**, cask, drum, vat

kernel n **2** = **essence**, core, germ, gist, nub, pith, substance

key¹ n **1** = **opener**, latchkey **5** = **answer**, explanation, solution ▷ adj **8** = **essential**, crucial, decisive, fundamental, important, leading, main, major, pivotal, principal ▷ v **9** (also **key in**) = **type**, enter, input, keyboard

key² *n* same as CAY.

keyboard *n* **1** set of keys on a piano, computer, etc. **2** musical instrument played using a keyboard. ▷ *v* **3** enter (text) using a keyboard.

keyhole *n* opening for inserting a key into a lock. **keyhole surgery** surgery performed through a narrow hole cut in the body.

keynote ❶ *adj* **1** central or dominating. ▷ *n* **2** dominant idea of a speech etc. **3** basic note of a musical key.

keyring *n* decorative metal ring for keeping keys on.

keystone *n* **1** most important part of a process, organization, etc. **2** central stone of an arch which locks the others in position.

kg kilogram(s).

KG Knight of the Order of the Garter.

KGB *n* (formerly) Soviet secret police.

khaki *adj* **1** dull yellowish-brown. ▷ *n* **2** hard-wearing fabric of this colour used for military uniforms.

khan *n* title of respect in Afghanistan and central Asia.

kHz kilohertz.

kibbutz *n, pl* **kibbutzim** communal farm or factory in Israel.

kibosh *n* **put the kibosh on** *slang* put a stop to.

kick ❶ *v* **1** drive, push, or strike with the foot. **2** (of a gun) recoil when fired. **3** *informal* object or resist. **4** *informal* free oneself of (an addiction). **5** *Rugby* score with a kick. ▷ *n* **6** thrust or blow with the foot. **7** recoil of a gun. **8** *informal* excitement or thrill. **kickback** *n* money paid illegally for favours done. **kick off** *v* **1** start a game

of football. **2** *informal* begin. **kickoff** *n*

kick out *v* dismiss or expel forcibly.

kick-start *v* **1** start (a motorcycle) by kicking a pedal. **2** do something bold or drastic in order to begin or improve the performance of something. ▷ *n* **3** (also **kick-starter**) pedal on a motorcycle that is kicked downwards to start the engine. **kick up** *v informal* create (a fuss).

kid¹ ❶ *n* **1** (also **kiddie**) *informal* child. **2** young goat. **3** leather made from the skin of a young goat. **treat, handle someone with kid gloves** treat someone with great tact in order not to upset them.

kid² ❶ *v* **kidding, kidded** *informal* tease or deceive (someone).

kidnap ❶ *v* **-napping, -napped** seize and hold (a person) to ransom. **kidnapper** *n* **kidnapping** *n*.

kidney *n* **1** either of the pair of organs that filter waste products from the blood to produce urine. **2** animal kidney used as food. **kidney bean** reddish-brown kidney-shaped bean, edible when cooked.

kill ❶ *v* **1** cause the death of. **2** *informal* cause (someone) pain or discomfort. **3** put an end to. **4** pass (time). ▷ *n* **5** act of killing. **6** animals or birds killed in a hunt. **killer** *n* killing *informal* ▷ *adj* **1** very tiring. **2** very funny. ▷ *n* **3** sudden financial success. **killjoy** *n* person who spoils others' pleasure.

kiln *n* oven for baking, drying, or processing pottery, bricks, etc.

kilo *n* short for KILOGRAM.

---

keynote *n* **1** = **heart**, centre, core, essence, gist, substance, theme

kick *v* **1** = **boot**, punt **4** *Inf* = **give up**, abandon, desist from, leave off, quit, stop ▷ *n* **8** *Inf* = **thrill**, buzz (*sl*), pleasure, stimulation

kick off *v* **2** *Inf* = **begin**, commence, get the show on the road, initiate, open, start

kick out *v Inf* = **dismiss**, eject, evict, expel, get rid of, remove, sack (*inf*)

kid¹ *n* **1** (also **kiddie**) *Inf* = **child**, baby, bairn, infant, teenager, tot, youngster, youth

kid² *v Inf* = **tease**, delude, fool, hoax, jest, joke, pretend, trick, wind up (*Brit sl*)

kidnap *v* = **abduct**, capture, hijack, hold to ransom, seize

kill *v* **1** = **slay**, assassinate, butcher, destroy, execute, exterminate, liquidate, massacre, murder, slaughter **3** = **suppress**, extinguish, halt, quash, quell, scotch, smother, stifle, stop

killer *n* = **assassin**, butcher, cut-throat, executioner, exterminator, gunman, hit man (*sl*), murderer, slayer

killing *Inf* ▷ *adj* **1** = **tiring**, debilitating, exhausting, fatiguing, punishing **2** = **hilarious**, comical, ludicrous, uproarious ▷ *n* **3** = **bonanza**, bomb (*sl*), cleanup (*inf*), coup, gain, profit, success, windfall

killjoy *n* = **spoilsport**, dampener, wet blanket (*inf*)

kilo- *combining form* one thousand, e.g. *kilometre*.

kilobyte *n Computers* 1024 units of information.

kilocalorie *n* one thousand calories.

kilogram, kilogramme *n* one thousand grams.

kilohertz *n* one thousand hertz.

kilojoule *n* one thousand joules.

kilometre *n* one thousand metres.

kilowatt *n Electricity* one thousand watts. **kilowatt-hour** *n* unit of energy equal to the work done by a power of one thousand watts in an hour.

kilt *n* knee-length pleated tartan skirt worn orig. by Scottish Highlanders. **kilted** *adj*.

kimono [kim-**moan**-no] *n, pl* **-nos** 1 loose wide-sleeved Japanese robe, fastened with a sash. 2 European dressing gown resembling this.

kin, kinsfolk ❶ *n* person's relatives collectively. **kinship** *n* 1 blood relationship. 2 state of having common characteristics. **kinsman, kinswoman** *n* relative.

kind¹ ❶ *adj* considerate, friendly, and helpful. **kindness** *n* **kindly** *adj* **-lier, -liest** 1 having a warm-hearted nature. 2 pleasant or agreeable. ▷ *adv* 3 in a considerate way. 4 please, e.g. *will you kindly be quiet!* **kindliness** *n* **kind-hearted** *adj*.

kind² ❶ *n* 1 class or group with common characteristics. 2 essential nature or character. **in kind** 1 (of payment) in goods rather than money. 2 with something similar. **kind of** to a certain extent.

- ● **USAGE NOTE**
- ● Note the singular/plural usage: *this*
- ● (or *that*) *kind of dog; these* (or *those*)
- ● *kinds of dog.* In the second, plural
- ● example, you can also say *these kinds*
- ● *of dogs.*

kindergarten *n* class or school for children of about four to six years old.

kindle ❶ *v* 1 set (a fire) alight. 2 (of a fire) start to burn. 3 arouse or be aroused. **kindling** *n* dry wood or straw for starting fires.

kindred ❶ *adj* 1 having similar qualities. 2 related by blood or marriage. ▷ *n* 3 same as KIN.

kindy, kindie *n, pl* **-dies** *Aust & NZ informal* kindergarten.

kine *pl n obs* cows or cattle.

kinetic [kin-**net**-ik] *adj* relating to or caused by motion.

king ❶ *n* 1 male ruler of a monarchy. 2 ruler or chief. 3 best or most important of its kind. 4 piece in chess that must be defended. 5 playing card with a picture of a king on it. **kingship** *n* **kingdom** *n* 1 state ruled by a king or queen. 2 division of the natural world. **king prawn** large prawn, fished commercially in Australian waters. **king-size, king-sized** *adj* larger than standard size.

kingfisher *n* small bird with a bright greenish-blue and orange plumage, that dives for fish.

kingpin *n* most important person in an organization.

— THESAURUS —

kin, kinsfolk *n* = **family**, kindred, relations, relatives

kind¹ *adj* = **considerate**, benign, charitable, compassionate, courteous, friendly, generous, humane, kindly, obliging, philanthropic, tender-hearted

kind² *n* 1 = **class**, brand, breed, family, set, sort, species, variety

kind-hearted *adj* = **sympathetic**, altruistic, compassionate, considerate, generous, good-natured, helpful, humane, kind, tender-hearted

kindle *v* 1 = **set fire to**, ignite, inflame, light 3 = **arouse**, awaken, induce, inspire, provoke, rouse, stimulate, stir

kindliness *n* 1 = **kindness**, amiability, benevolence, charity, compassion, friendliness, gentleness, humanity, kind-heartedness

kindly *adj* 1 = **benevolent**, benign, compassionate, good-natured, helpful, kind, pleasant, sympathetic, warm ▷ *adv* 3 = **benevolently**, agreeably, cordially, graciously, politely, tenderly, thoughtfully

kindness *n* = **goodwill**, benevolence, charity, compassion, generosity, humanity, kindliness, philanthropy, understanding

kindred *adj* 1 = **similar**, akin, corresponding, like, matching, related ▷ *n* 2 = **family**, kin, kinsfolk, relations, relatives

king *n* 1 = **ruler**, emperor, monarch, sovereign

kingdom *n* 1 = **country**, nation, realm, state, territory

kink ❶ *n* **1** twist or bend in rope, wire, hair, etc. **2** *informal* quirk in someone's personality. **kinky** *adj* **kinkier, kinkiest 1** *slang* given to unusual sexual practices. **2** full of kinks.

kiosk ❶ *n* **1** small booth selling drinks, cigarettes, newspapers, etc. **2** public telephone box.

kip *n, v* **kipping, kipped** *informal* sleep.

kipper *n* cleaned, salted, and smoked herring.

kirk *n Scot* church.

Kirsch *n* brandy made from cherries.

kismet *n* fate or destiny.

kiss ❶ *v* **1** touch with the lips in affection or greeting. **2** join lips with a person in love or desire. ▷ *n* **3** touch with the lips. **kisser** *n slang* mouth or face. **kissagram** *n* greetings service in which a messenger kisses the person celebrating. **kiss of life** mouth-to-mouth resuscitation.

kist *n S Afr* large wooden chest.

kit ❶ *n* **1** outfit or equipment for a specific purpose. **2** set of pieces of equipment sold ready to be assembled. **kitbag** *n* bag for a soldier's or traveller's belongings. **kit out** *v* **kitting, kitted** provide with clothes or equipment needed for a particular activity.

kitchen *n* room used for cooking. **kitchenette** *n* small kitchen. **kitchen garden** garden for growing vegetables, herbs, etc.

kite *n* **1** light frame covered with a thin material flown on a string in the wind. **2** large hawk with a forked tail. **Kite mark** official mark on articles approved by the British Standards Institution.

kith *n* **kith and kin** friends and relatives.

kitsch *n* art or literature with popular sentimental appeal.

kitten *n* young cat. **kittenish** *adj* lively and flirtatious.

kittiwake *n* type of seagull.

kitty *n, pl* **-ties 1** communal fund. **2** total amount wagered in certain gambling games.

kiwi *n* **1** *NZ* flightless bird with a long beak and no tail. **2** *informal* New Zealander. **kiwi fruit** edible fruit with a fuzzy brownish skin and green flesh.

kJ kilojoule(s).

klaxon *n* loud horn used on emergency vehicles as a warning signal.

kleptomania *n* compulsive tendency to steal. **kleptomaniac** *n*.

kloof *n S Afr* mountain pass or gorge.

km kilometre(s).

knack ❶ *n* **1** skilful way of doing something. **2** innate ability.

knacker *n* buyer of old horses for killing.

knackered *adj slang* **1** extremely tired. **2** no longer functioning.

knapsack *n* soldier's or traveller's bag worn strapped on the back.

knave ❶ *n* **1** jack at cards. **2** *obs* dishonest man.

knead ❶ *v* **1** work (dough) into a smooth mixture with the hands. **2** squeeze or press with the hands.

knee *n* **1** joint between thigh and lower leg. **2** lap. **3** part of a garment covering the knee. ▷ *v* **kneeing, kneed 4** strike or push with the knee. **kneecap** *n* **1** bone in front of the knee. ▷ *v* **2** shoot in the kneecap. **kneejerk** *adj* (of a reply or reaction) automatic and predictable. **knees-up** *n informal* party.

kneel ❶ *v* **kneeling, kneeled** *or* **knelt** fall or rest on one's knees.

———————————————— **THESAURUS** ————————————————

kink *n* **1** = **twist**, bend, coil, wrinkle **2** *Inf* = **quirk**, eccentricity, fetish, foible, idiosyncrasy, vagary, whim

kinky *adj* **1** *Sl* = **perverted**, depraved, deviant, unnatural, warped **2** = **twisted**, coiled, curled, tangled

kinship *n* **1** = **relation**, consanguinity, kin, ties of blood **2** = **similarity**, affinity, association, connection, correspondence, relationship

kiosk *n* **1** = **booth**, bookstall, counter, newsstand, stall, stand

kiss *v* **1, 2** = **osculate**, neck (*inf*), peck (*inf*) ▷ *n* **3** = **osculation**, peck (*inf*), smacker (*sl*)

kit *n* **1** = **equipment**, apparatus, gear, paraphernalia, tackle, tools

kit out *v* = **equip**, accoutre, arm, deck out, fit out, fix up, furnish, provide with, supply

knack *n* **1** = **skill**, trick **2** = **gift**, ability, aptitude, capacity, expertise, facility, propensity, skill, talent

knave *n* **2** *Obs* = **rogue**, blackguard, bounder (*old-fashioned Brit sl*), rascal, rotter (*sl, chiefly Brit*), scoundrel, villain

knead *v* **2** = **squeeze**, form, manipulate, massage, mould, press, rub, shape, work

kneel *v* = **genuflect**, stoop

knell ❶ *n* **1** sound of a bell, esp. at a funeral or death. **2** portent of doom.
knew *v* past tense of KNOW.
knickerbockers *pl n* loose-fitting short trousers gathered in at the knee.
knickers ❶ *pl n* woman's or girl's undergarment covering the lower trunk and having legs or legholes.
knick-knack ❶ *n* trifle or trinket.
knife ❶ *n, pl* **knives 1** cutting tool or weapon consisting of a sharp-edged blade with a handle. ▷ *v* **2** cut or stab with a knife. **knife edge** critical point in the development of a situation.
knight *n* **1** man who has been given a knighthood. **2** *History* man who served his lord as a mounted armoured soldier. **3** chess piece shaped like a horse's head. ▷ *v* **4** award a knighthood to.
  knighthood *n* honorary title given to a man by the British sovereign. **knightly** *adj*.
knit ❶ *v* **knitting, knitted** *or* **knit 1** make (a garment) by interlocking a series of loops in wool or other yarn. **2** join closely together. **3** draw (one's eyebrows) together. **knitting** *n* **knitwear** *n* knitted clothes, such as sweaters.
knives *n, pl* of KNIFE.
knob ❶ *n* **1** rounded projection, such as a switch on a radio. **2** rounded handle on a door or drawer. **3** small amount of butter. **knobbly** *adj* covered with small bumps.

knock ❶ *v* **1** give a blow or push to. **2** rap audibly on the knuckles. **3** make or drive by striking. **4** *informal* criticize adversely. **5** (of an engine) make a regular banging noise as a result of a fault. ▷ *n* **6** blow or rap. **7** knocking sound. **8** misfortune, rejection, or setback. **knocker** *n* metal fitting for knocking on a door. **knock about**, **around** *v* **1** wander or spend time aimlessly. **2** hit or kick brutally. **knockabout** *adj* (of comedy) boisterous. **knock back** *v informal* **1** drink quickly. **2** cost. **3** reject or refuse. **knock down** *v* **1** demolish. **2** reduce the price of. **knockdown** *adj* (of a price) very low. **knock-knees** *pl n* legs that curve in at the knees. **knock-kneed** *adj* **knock off** *v* **1** *informal* cease work. **2** *informal* make or do (something) hurriedly or easily. **3** take (a specified amount) off a price. **4** *informal* steal. **knock-on effect** indirect result of an action or decision. **knock out** *v* **1** render (someone) unconscious. **2** *informal* overwhelm or amaze. **3** defeat in a knockout competition. **knockout** *n* **1** blow that renders an opponent unconscious. **2** competition from which competitors are progressively eliminated. **3** *informal* overwhelmingly attractive person or thing. **knock up** *v* **1** *informal* assemble (something) quickly. **2** *informal* waken. **3** *slang* make pregnant. **knock-up** *n* practice session at tennis, squash, or badminton.
knoll *n* small rounded hill.

---

knell *n* **1** = **ringing**, chime, peal, sound, toll
knickers *pl n* = **underwear**, bloomers, briefs, broekies (*S Afr inf*), drawers, panties, smalls
knick-knack *n* = **trinket**, bagatelle, bauble, bric-a-brac, plaything, trifle
knife *n* **1** = **blade**, cutter ▷ *v* **2** = **cut**, lacerate, pierce, slash, stab, wound
knit *v* **2** = **join**, bind, fasten, intertwine, link, tie, unite, weave **3** = **wrinkle**, crease, furrow, knot, pucker
knob *n* **1** = **lump**, bump, hump, knot, projection, protrusion, stud
knock *v* **1** = **hit**, belt (*inf*), cuff, punch, smack, strike, thump **2** = **rap 4** *Inf* = **criticize**, abuse, belittle, censure, condemn, denigrate, deprecate, disparage, find fault, run down ▷ *n*

6 = **blow**, clip, clout (*inf*) cuff, rap, slap, smack, thump **8** = **setback**, defeat, failure, rebuff, rejection, reversal
knockabout *adj* = **boisterous**, farcical, riotous, rollicking, slapstick
knock about, around *v* **1** = **wander**, ramble, range, roam, rove, travel **2** = **hit**, abuse, batter, beat up (*inf*), maltreat, manhandle, maul, mistreat, strike
knock down *v* **1** = **demolish**, destroy, fell, level, raze
knock off *v* **1** *Inf* = **stop work**, clock off, clock out, finish **4** *Inf* = **steal**, nick (*sl, chiefly Brit*), pinch, rob, thieve
knockout *n* **1** = **killer blow**, coup de grâce, KO or K.O. (*sl*) **3** *Inf* = **success**, hit, sensation, smash, smash hit, triumph, winner

k

knot ❶ *n* **1** fastening made by looping and pulling tight strands of string, cord, or rope. **2** tangle (of hair). **3** small cluster or huddled group. **4** round lump or spot in timber. **5** feeling of tightness, caused by tension or nervousness. **6** unit of speed used by ships, equal to one nautical mile per hour. ▷ *v* **knotting**, **knotted 7** tie with or into a knot. **knotty** *adj* **-tier**, **-tiest 1** full of knots. **2** puzzling or difficult.

know ❶ *v* **knowing**, **knew**, **known 1** be or feel certain of the truth of (information etc.). **2** be acquainted with. **3** have a grasp of or understand (a skill or language). **4** be aware of. **in the know** *informal* informed or aware. **knowable** *adj* **knowing** *adj* suggesting secret knowledge. **knowingly** *adv* **1** deliberately. **2** in a way that suggests secret knowledge. **knowledge** *n* facts or experiences known by a person. **know-all** *n offens* person who acts as if knowing more than other people. **know-how** *n informal* ingenuity, aptitude, or skill.

knowledge ❶ *n* **1** facts or experiences known by a person. **2** state of knowing. **3** specific information on a subject. **knowledgeable**, **knowledgable** *adj* intelligent or well-informed. **knowledgeably**, **knowledgably** *adv*.

knuckle *n* **1** bone at the finger joint. **2** knee joint of a calf or pig. **near the knuckle** *informal* rather rude or offensive. **knuckle-duster** *n* metal appliance worn on the knuckles to add force to a blow. **knuckle under** *v* yield or submit.

KO knockout.

koala *n* tree-dwelling Australian marsupial with dense grey fur (also **native bear**).

kohl *n* cosmetic powder used to darken the edges of the eyelids.

kook *n US informal* eccentric person. **kooky** *adj* **kookier**, **kookiest**.

kookaburra *n* large Australian kingfisher with a cackling cry.

kopeck *n* former Russian monetary unit, one hundredth of a rouble.

kopje, **koppie** *n S Afr* small hill.

Koran *n* sacred book of Islam.

Korean *adj* **1** of North or South Korea or their language. ▷ *n* **2** person from North or South Korea. **3** language of North and South Korea.

kosher [koh-sher] *adj* **1** conforming to Jewish religious law, esp. (of food) to Jewish dietary law. **2** *informal* legitimate or authentic. ▷ *n* **3** kosher food.

kowtow *v* be servile (towards).

kph kilometres per hour.

Kr *Chemistry* krypton.

kraal *n S* African village surrounded by a strong fence.

Kremlin *n* central government of Russia and, formerly, the Soviet Union.

krill *n*, *pl* **krill** small shrimplike sea creature.

krona *n*, *pl* **kronor** standard monetary unit of Sweden.

krone [kroh-na] *n*, *pl* **-ner** [-ner] standard monetary unit of Norway and Denmark.

krypton *n Chemistry* colourless gas present in the atmosphere and used in fluorescent lights.

KS Kansas.

kudos [kyoo-doss] *n* fame or credit.

k

─────── THESAURUS ───────

knot *n* **1** = **connection**, bond, joint, ligature, loop, tie **3** = **cluster**, bunch, clump, collection ▷ *v* **7** = **tie**, bind, loop, secure, tether

know *v* **1** = **understand**, comprehend, feel certain, notice, perceive, realize, recognize, see **2** = **be acquainted with**, be familiar with, have dealings with, have knowledge of, recognize

know-how *n Inf* = **capability**, ability, aptitude, expertise, ingenuity, knack, knowledge, savoir-faire, skill, talent

knowing *adj* = **meaningful**, expressive, significant

knowingly *adv* **1** = **deliberately**,

consciously, intentionally, on purpose, purposely, wilfully, wittingly

knowledge *n* **1** = **learning**, education, enlightenment, erudition, instruction, intelligence, scholarship, wisdom **2** = **acquaintance**, familiarity, intimacy

knowledgeable *adj* **a** = **intelligent**, educated, erudite, learned, scholarly **b** = **well-informed**, *au fait*, aware, clued-up (*inf*), cognizant, conversant, experienced, familiar, in the know (*inf*), in the loop

known *adj* = **famous**, acknowledged, avowed, celebrated, noted, recognized, well-known

kudu *n* African antelope with spiral horns.

kugel [**koog**-el] *n S Afr* rich, fashion-conscious, materialistic young woman.

Ku Klux Klan *n* secret organization of White Protestant Americans who use violence against African-Americans and Jews.

kumara *n NZ* tropical root vegetable with yellow flesh.

kumquat [**kumm**-kwott] *n* citrus fruit resembling a tiny orange.

kung fu *n* Chinese martial art combining hand, foot, and weapon techniques.

kurrajong *n* Australian tree or shrub with tough fibrous bark.

kW kilowatt.

kWh kilowatt-hour.

KY Kentucky.

l litre.

L 1 large. **2** learner (driver). **3** the Roman numeral for fifty.

L. lake.

la n Music same as LAH.

La Chemistry lanthanum.

LA Louisiana.

lab n informal short for LABORATORY.

Lab. Labour.

label ⊕ n **1** piece of card or other material fixed to an object to show its ownership, destination, etc. **2** brief descriptive term. ▷ v **-elling, -elled 3** give a label to. **4** describe in a phrase.

labia pl n, sing **labium** four liplike folds of skin forming part of the female genitals. **labial** [**lay**-bee-al] adj of the lips.

laboratory n, pl **-ries** building or room designed for scientific research or for the teaching of practical science.

laborious ⊕ adj involving great prolonged effort. **laboriously** adv.

labour ⊕ n **1** physical work or exertion. **2** workers in industry. **3** final stage of pregnancy, leading to childbirth. ▷ v **4** work hard. **5** make one's way with

difficulty. **6** stress to excess or too persistently. **7** be at a disadvantage because of a mistake or false belief. **laboured** adj uttered or done with difficulty. **labourer** n person who labours, esp. someone doing manual work for wages. **Labour Party** major British political party advocating social equality.

labrador n large retriever dog with a gold, brown, or black coat.

laburnum n ornamental tree with yellow hanging flowers.

labyrinth ⊕ [**lab**-er-inth] n **1** complicated network of passages. **2** any complex system. **3** interconnecting cavities in the internal ear. **labyrinthine** adj.

lace ⊕ n **1** delicate decorative fabric made from threads woven into an open weblike pattern. **2** cord drawn through eyelets and tied. ▷ v **3** fasten with laces. **4** thread a cord or string through holes in something. **5** add a small amount of alcohol, a drug, etc. to (food or drink). **lacy** adj fine, like lace. **lace-ups** pl n shoes which fasten with laces.

lacerate ⊕ [**lass**-er-rate] v tear (flesh). **laceration** n.

lachrymose adj **1** tearful. **2** sad.

lack ⊕ n **1** shortage or absence of something needed or wanted. ▷ v **2** need or be short of (something).

lackadaisical ⊕ adj **1** lacking vitality and purpose. **2** lazy and careless in a dreamy way.

lackey ⊕ n **1** servile follower.

THESAURUS

label n **1** = **tag**, marker, sticker, ticket ▷ v **3** = **tag**, mark, stamp

laborious adj = **hard**, arduous, backbreaking, exhausting, onerous, strenuous, tiring, tough, wearisome

labour n **1** = **work**, industry, toil, yakka (Aust & NZ inf) **2** = **workers**, employees, hands, labourers, workforce **3** = **childbirth**, delivery, parturition ▷ v **4** = **work**, endeavour, slave, strive, struggle, sweat (inf), toil **6** = **overemphasize**, dwell on, elaborate, go on about, overdo, strain **7** = **be disadvantaged**, be a victim of, be burdened by, suffer

laboured adj = **difficult**, awkward, forced, heavy, stiff, strained

labourer n = **worker**, blue-collar worker, drudge, hand, manual worker, navvy (Brit inf)

labyrinth n **1, 2** = **maze**, intricacy, jungle, tangle

lace n **1** = **netting**, filigree, openwork **2** = **cord**, bootlace, shoelace, string, tie ▷ v **3** = **fasten**, bind, do up, thread, tie **4** = **intertwine**, interweave, twine **5** = **mix in**, add to, fortify, spike

lacerate v = **tear**, claw, cut, gash, mangle, rip, slash, wound

laceration n = **cut**, gash, rent, rip, slash, tear, wound

lack n **1** = **shortage**, absence, dearth, deficiency, need, scarcity, want ▷ v **2** = **need**, be deficient in, be short of, be without, miss, require, want

lackadaisical adj **1** = **lethargic**, apathetic, dull, half-hearted, indifferent, languid, listless **2** = **lazy**, abstracted, dreamy, idle, indolent, inert

lackey n **1** = **hanger-on**, flatterer,

2 uniformed male servant.

lacklustre ❶ *adj* lacking brilliance or vitality.

laconic ❶ *adj* using only a few words, terse. **laconically** *adv*.

lacquer *n* 1 hard varnish for wood or metal. 2 clear sticky substance sprayed onto the hair to hold it in place. **lacquered** *adj*.

lacrimal [**lack**-rim-al] *adj* of tears or the glands which produce them.

lacrosse *n* sport in which teams catch and throw a ball using long sticks with a pouched net at the end, in an attempt to score goals.

lactation *n* secretion of milk by female mammals to feed young. **lactic** *adj* of or derived from milk. **lactose** *n* white crystalline sugar found in milk.

lacuna [lak-**kew**-na] *n*, *pl* **-nae** gap or missing part, esp. in a document or series.

lad ❶ *n* boy or young man. **laddish** *adj informal* behaving in a macho or immature manner.

ladder *n* 1 frame of two poles connected by horizontal steps used for climbing. 2 system with ascending stages, e.g. *the social ladder*. 3 line of stitches that have come undone in tights or stockings. ▷ *v* 4 have or cause to have such a line of undone stitches.

laden ❶ *adj* 1 loaded. 2 burdened.

la-di-da, lah-di-dah *adj informal* affected or pretentious.

ladle *n* 1 spoon with a long handle and a large bowl, used for serving soup etc. ▷ *v* 2 serve out.

lady ❶ *n*, *pl* **-dies** 1 woman regarded as having characteristics of good breeding

or high rank. 2 polite term of address for a woman. 3 (**L-**) title of some female members of the nobility. **Our Lady** the Virgin Mary. **Lady Day** Feast of the Annunciation, March 25. **ladies, ladies' room** *n* women's public toilet. **lady-in-waiting** *n*, *pl* **ladies-in-waiting** female servant of a queen or princess.

ladykiller *n informal* man who is or thinks he is irresistible to women.

ladylike *adj* polite and dignified.

Ladyship *n* title used to address a Lady.

ladybird *n* small red beetle with black spots.

lag¹ ❶ *v* **lagging, lagged** 1 go too slowly, fall behind. ▷ *n* 2 delay between events. **laggard** *n* person who lags behind.

lag² *v* **lagging, lagged** wrap (a boiler, pipes, etc.) with insulating material. **lagging** *n* insulating material.

lag³ *n* **old lag** *slang* convict.

lager *n* light-bodied beer.

lagoon *n* body of water cut off from the open sea by coral reefs or sand bars.

lah *n Music* (in tonic sol-fa) sixth degree of any major scale.

laid ❶ *v* past of LAY¹. **laid-back** *adj informal* relaxed.

lain *v* past participle of LIE².

lair ❶ *n* 1 resting place of an animal. 2 *informal* hiding place.

laird *n* Scottish landowner.

laissez-faire ❶ [less-ay-**fair**] *n* principle of nonintervention, esp. by a government in commercial affairs.

laity [**lay**-it-ee] *n* people who are not members of the clergy.

lake¹ ❶ *n* expanse of water entirely surrounded by land. **lakeside** *n*.

lake² *n* red pigment.

minion, sycophant, toady, yes man 2 = **manservant**, attendant, flunky, footman, valet

lacklustre *adj* = **flat**, drab, dull, leaden, lifeless, muted, prosaic, uninspired, vapid

laconic *adj* = **terse**, brief, concise, curt, monosyllabic, pithy, short, succinct long-winded

lad *n* = **boy**, fellow, guy (*inf*), juvenile, kid (*inf*), youngster, youth

laden *adj* = **loaded**, burdened, charged, encumbered, full, weighed down

lady *n* 1 = **gentlewoman**, dame 2 = **woman**, female

ladykiller *n Inf* = **womanizer**, Casanova, Don Juan, heartbreaker, ladies' man,

libertine, philanderer, rake, roué

ladylike *adj* = **refined**, elegant, genteel, modest, polite, proper, respectable, sophisticated, well-bred

lag¹ *v* 1 = **hang back**, dawdle, delay, linger, loiter, straggle, tarry, trail

laggard *n* = **straggler**, dawdler, idler, loiterer, slowcoach (*Brit inf*), sluggard, snail

laid-back *adj Inf* = **relaxed**, casual, easy-going, free and easy, unflappable (*inf*), unhurried

lair *n* 1 = **nest**, burrow, den, earth, hole

laissez-faire *n* = **nonintervention**, free enterprise, free trade

lake¹ *n* = **pond**, lagoon, loch (*Scot*), lough (*Irish*), mere, reservoir, tarn

lama *n* Buddhist priest in Tibet or Mongolia.

lamb *n* **1** young sheep. **2** its meat. ▷ *v* **3** (of sheep) give birth to a lamb or lambs. **lambskin** *n* **lambswool** *n*.

lambast, lambaste *v* **1** beat or thrash. **2** reprimand severely.

lambent *adj lit* (of a flame) flickering softly.

lame ❶ *adj* **1** having an injured or disabled leg or foot. **2** (of an excuse) unconvincing. ▷ *v* **3** make lame. **lamely** *adv* **lameness** *n* **lame duck** person or thing unable to cope without help.

lamé [**lah**-may] *n, adj* (fabric) interwoven with gold or silver thread.

lament ❶ *v* **1** feel or express sorrow (for). ▷ *n* **2** passionate expression of grief. **3** song of grief. **lamentable** *adj* very disappointing. **lamentation** *n* **lamented** *adj* grieved for.

laminate *v* **1** make (a sheet of material) by sticking together thin sheets. **2** cover with a thin sheet of material. **3** split or beat into thin sheets. ▷ *n* **4** laminated sheet. **laminated** *adj*.

lamington *n Aust & NZ* sponge cake coated with a sweet frosting.

Lammas *n* August 1, formerly a harvest festival.

lamp *n* device which produces light from electricity, oil, or gas. **lamppost** *n* post supporting a lamp in the street. **lampshade** *n*.

lampoon ❶ *n* **1** humorous satire ridiculing someone. ▷ *v* **2** satirize or ridicule.

lamprey *n* eel-like fish with a round sucking mouth.

lance *n* **1** long spear used by a mounted soldier. ▷ *v* **2** pierce (a boil or abscess) with a lancet. **lancer** *n* formerly, cavalry soldier armed with a lance. **lance corporal** noncommissioned army officer of the lowest rank.

lanceolate *adj* narrow and tapering to a point at each end.

lancet *n* **1** pointed two-edged surgical knife. **2** narrow window in the shape of a pointed arch.

land ❶ *n* **1** solid part of the earth's surface. **2** ground, esp. with reference to its type or use. **3** rural or agricultural area. **4** property consisting of land. **5** country or region. ▷ *v* **6** come or bring to earth after a flight, jump, or fall. **7** go or take from a ship at the end of a voyage. **8** come to or touch shore. **9** come or bring to some point or condition. **10** *informal* obtain. **11** take (a hooked fish) from the water. **12** *informal* deliver (a punch). **landed** *adj* possessing or consisting of lands. **landless** *adj* **land line** telecommunications wire or cable laid over land. **landward** *adj* **1** nearest to or facing the land. ▷ *adv* **2** (also **landwards**) towards land. **landfall** *n* ship's first landing after a voyage. **landfill** *n* disposing of rubbish by covering it with earth. **landlocked** *adj* completely surrounded by land. **landlord** *n* person who rents out land, houses, etc. **landmark** *n* prominent object in or feature of a landscape. **land mine** explosive device laid in the ground. **landscape** *n* extensive piece of inland scenery seen from one place. **land up** *v* arrive at a final point or condition.

landau [**lan**-daw] *n* four-wheeled carriage with two folding hoods.

landing *n* **1** floor area at the top of a flight of stairs. **2** bringing or coming to

lame *adj* **1** = **disabled**, crippled, game, handicapped, hobbling, limping **2** = **unconvincing**, feeble, flimsy, inadequate, pathetic, poor, thin, unsatisfactory, weak

lament *v* **1** = **bemoan**, bewail, complain, deplore, grieve, mourn, regret, sorrow, wail, weep ▷ *n* **2** = **complaint**, lamentation, moan, wailing **3** = **dirge**, elegy, requiem, threnody

lamentable *adj* = **regrettable**, deplorable, distressing, grievous, mournful, tragic, unfortunate, woeful

lampoon *n* **1** = **satire**, burlesque, caricature, parody, send-up (*Brit inf*), skit, takeoff (*inf*) ▷ *v* **2** = **ridicule**, caricature, make fun of, mock, parody, satirize, send up (*Brit inf*), take off (*inf*)

land *n* **1** = **ground**, dry land, earth, terra firma **2** = **soil**, dirt, ground, loam **3** = **countryside**, farmland **4** = **property**, estate, grounds, realty, homestead (*US & Canad*) **5** = **country**, district, nation, province, region, territory, tract ▷ *v* **6** = **alight**, arrive, come to rest, touch down **7** = **disembark 8** = **dock 10** *Inf* = **obtain**, acquire, gain, get, secure, win

land. **3** (also **landing stage**) place where people or goods go onto or come off a boat. **landing gear** undercarriage of an aircraft.

landlord, landlady ❶ *n* **1** person who rents out land, houses, etc. **2** owner or manager of a pub or boarding house.

landlubber *n* person who is not experienced at sea.

landmark ❶ *n* **1** prominent object in or feature of a landscape. **2** event, decision, etc. considered as an important development.

landscape ❶ *n* **1** extensive piece of inland scenery seen from one place. **2** picture of it. ▷ *v* **3** improve natural features of (a piece of land). **landscape gardener** person who designs gardens or parks so that they look attractive.

landslide ❶ *n* **1** (also **landslip**) falling of soil, rock, etc. down the side of a mountain. **2** overwhelming electoral victory.

lane ❶ *n* **1** narrow road. **2** area of road for one stream of traffic. **3** specified route followed by ships or aircraft. **4** strip of a running track or swimming pool for use by one competitor.

language ❶ *n* **1** system of sounds, symbols, etc. for communicating thought. **2** particular system used by a nation or people. **3** style or method of expression. **4** specialized words used by a particular group. **5** (also **programming language**) system of words and symbols for computer programming.

languid ❶ *adj* lacking energy or enthusiasm. **languidly** *adv*.

languish ❶ *v* **1** suffer neglect or hardship. **2** lose or diminish in strength or vigour. **3** pine (for). **languishing** *adj*.

languor [lang-ger] *n* **1** state of dreamy relaxation. **2** laziness or weariness. **languorous** *adj*.

lank ❶ *adj* **1** (of hair) straight and limp. **2** thin or gaunt. **lanky** *adj* ungracefully tall and thin. **lankiness** *n*.

lanolin *n* grease from sheep's wool used in ointments etc.

lantern *n* **1** light in a transparent protective case. **2** structure on top of a dome which lets in light. **3** upper part of a lighthouse that houses the light. **lantern jaw** long thin jaw. **lantern-jawed** *adj*.

lanthanum *n* Chemistry silvery-white metallic element. **lanthanide series** class of 15 elements chemically related to lanthanum.

lanyard *n* **1** cord worn round the neck to hold a knife or whistle. **2** Nautical short rope.

lap[1] *n* part between the waist and knees of a person when sitting. **in the lap of luxury** in conditions of great comfort and wealth. **laptop** *adj* (of a computer) small enough to fit on a user's lap.

lap[2] ❶ *n* **1** single circuit of a racecourse or track. **2** stage of a journey. ▷ *v* **lapping, lapped 3** overtake an opponent so as to be one or more circuits ahead.

lap[3] ❶ *v* **lapping, lapped** (of waves) beat softly against (a shore etc.). **lap up** *v* **1** drink by scooping up with the tongue. **2** accept (information or attention) eagerly.

━━━━━━━━━━━━━━━━━━━━ THESAURUS ━━━━

landlord *n* **1** = **owner**, freeholder, lessor, proprietor **2** = **innkeeper**, host, hotelier

landmark *n* **1** = **feature**, monument **2** = **milestone**, turning point, watershed

landscape *n* **1** = **scenery**, countryside, outlook, panorama, prospect, scene, view, vista

landslide *n* **1** = **landslip**, avalanche, rockfall

land up *v* = **end up**, turn up, wind up

lane *n* **1** = **road**, alley, footpath, passageway, path, pathway, street, way

language *n* **1** = **speech**, communication, discourse, expression, parlance, talk **2** = **tongue**, dialect, patois, vernacular

languid *adj* **a** = **lethargic**, dull, heavy, sluggish, torpid **b** = **lazy**, indifferent, lackadaisical, languorous, listless, unenthusiastic

languish *v* **1** = **waste away**, be abandoned, be neglected, rot, suffer **2** = **decline**, droop, fade, fail, faint, flag, weaken, wilt, wither **3** = **pine**, desire, hanker, hunger, long, yearn

lank *adj* **1** = **limp**, lifeless, straggling **2** = **thin**, emaciated, gaunt, lean, scrawny, skinny, slender, slim, spare

lanky *adj* = **gangling**, angular, bony, gaunt, rangy, spare, tall

lap[2] *n* **1** = **circuit**, circle, loop, orbit, tour

lap[3] *v* = **ripple**, gurgle, plash, purl, splash, swish, wash **lap up** *v* **1** = **drink**, lick, sip, sup

lapel [lap-**pel**] n part of the front of a coat or jacket folded back towards the shoulders.

lapidary adj of or relating to stones.

lapis lazuli [**lap**-iss **lazz**-yoo-lie] n bright blue gemstone.

Lapp n, adj (member or language) of a people living chiefly in N Scandinavia.

lapse ⊙ n 1 temporary drop in a standard, esp. through forgetfulness or carelessness. 2 instance of bad behaviour by someone usually well-behaved. 3 break in occurrence or usage. ▷ v 4 drop in standard. 5 end or become invalid, esp. through disuse. 6 drift (into a condition or habit). 7 abandon religious faith. 8 (of time) slip away. **lapsed** adj.

lapwing n plover with a tuft of feathers on the head.

larboard adj, n old-fashioned port (side of a ship).

larceny n, pl -**nies** Law theft.

larch n deciduous coniferous tree.

lard n 1 soft white fat obtained from a pig. ▷ v 2 insert strips of bacon in (meat) before cooking. 3 decorate (speech or writing) with strange words unnecessarily.

larder n storeroom for food.

large ⊙ adj 1 great in size, number, or extent. 2 comprehensive. **at large** 1 in general. 2 free, not confined. 3 fully. **largely** adv **largish** adj **large-scale** adj wide-ranging or extensive.

largesse, largess [lar-**jess**] n generous giving, esp. of money.

largo n, pl -**gos** adv Music (piece to be played) in a slow and dignified manner.

lariat n 1 US & Canad another word for LASSO. 2 rope for tethering animals.

lark¹ n small brown songbird, skylark.

lark² ⊙ n informal 1 harmless piece of mischief or fun. 2 unnecessary activity or job. **lark about** v play pranks.

larkspur n plant with spikes of blue, pink, or white flowers with spurs.

larrikin n Aust or NZ old-fashioned slang mischievous or unruly person.

larva n, pl -**vae** insect in an immature stage, often resembling a worm. **larval** adj.

larynx n, pl **larynges** part of the throat containing the vocal cords. **laryngeal** adj **laryngitis** n inflammation of the larynx.

lasagne, lasagna [laz-**zan**-ya] n 1 pasta in wide flat sheets. 2 dish made from layers of lasagne, meat, and cheese.

lascivious [lass-**iv**-ee-uss] adj showing or producing sexual desire. **lasciviously** adv.

laser [**lay**-zer] n device that produces a very narrow intense beam of light, used for cutting very hard materials and in surgery etc.

lash¹ ⊙ n 1 eyelash. 2 sharp blow with a whip. 3 flexible end of a whip. ▷ v 4 hit with a whip. 5 (of rain or waves) beat forcefully against. 6 attack verbally, scold. 7 flick or wave sharply to and fro. 8 urge as with a whip. **lash out** v 1 make a sudden physical or verbal attack. 2 informal spend (money) extravagantly.

---

lapse n 1 = **mistake**, error, failing, fault, negligence, omission, oversight, slip 2 = **indescretion** 3 = **interval**, break, breathing space, gap, intermission, interruption, lull, pause ▷ v 4 = **drop**, decline, degenerate, deteriorate, fall, sink, slide, slip 5 = **end**, expire, run out, stop, terminate

lapsed adj 5 = **expired**, discontinued, ended, finished, invalid, out of date, run out

large adj 1 = **big**, considerable, enormous, gigantic, great, huge, immense, massive, monumental, sizable or sizeable, substantial, vast **at large** 1 = **in general**, as a whole, chiefly, generally, in the main, mainly 2 = **free**, at liberty, on the loose, on the run, unconfined 3 = **fully**, at length, exhaustively, greatly, in full detail

largely adv = **mainly**, as a rule, by and large, chiefly, generally, mostly, predominantly, primarily, principally, to a great extent

large-scale adj = **wide-ranging**, broad, extensive, far-reaching, global, sweeping, vast, wholesale, wide

lark² Inf n 1 = **prank**, caper, escapade, fun, game, jape, mischief **lark about** v = **play**, caper, cavort, have fun, make mischief

lash¹ n 2 = **blow**, hit, stripe, stroke, swipe (inf) ▷ v 4 = **whip**, beat, birch, flog, scourge, thrash 5 = **pound**, beat, buffet, dash, drum, hammer, smack, strike 6 = **censure**, attack, blast, criticize, put down, rouse on (Aust), scold, slate (inf, chiefly Brit), tear into (inf), upbraid

lash² ⓿ v fasten or bind tightly with cord etc.

lashings pl n old-fashioned large amounts.

lass, lassie ⓿ n girl.

Lassa fever n serious African disease with high fever and muscular pains.

lassitude n physical or mental weariness.

lasso [lass-**oo**] n, pl -**sos**, -**soes** 1 rope with a noose for catching cattle and horses. ▷ v -**soing**, -**soed** 2 catch with a lasso.

last¹ ⓿ adj, adv 1 coming at the end or after all others. 2 most recent(ly). ▷ adj 3 only remaining. ▷ n 4 last person or thing. **lastly** adv **last-ditch** adj done as a final resort. **Last Judgment** God's verdict on the destinies of all humans at the end of the world. **last post** army bugle-call played at sunset or funerals. **last straw** small irritation or setback that, coming after others, is too much to bear. **last word** 1 final comment in an argument. 2 most recent or best example of something.

last² ⓿ v 1 continue. 2 be sufficient for (a specified amount of time). 3 remain fresh, uninjured, or unaltered. **lasting** adj.

last³ n model of a foot on which shoes and boots are made or repaired.

lat. latitude.

latch ⓿ n 1 fastening for a door with a bar and lever. 2 lock which can only be opened from the outside with a key. ▷ v 3 fasten with a latch. **latch onto** v become attached to (a person or idea).

late ⓿ adj 1 after the normal or expected time. 2 towards the end of a period. 3 being at an advanced time. 4 recently dead. 5 recent. 6 former. ▷ adv 7 after the normal or expected time. 8 at a relatively advanced age. 9 recently. **lately** adv in recent times. **lateness** n **latish** adj, adv **latecomer** n.

latent ⓿ adj hidden and not yet developed. **latency** n.

lateral ⓿ [**lat**-ter-al] adj of or relating to the side or sides. **laterally** adv **lateral thinking** way of solving problems by apparently illogical methods.

latex n milky fluid found in some plants, esp. the rubber tree, used in making rubber.

lath n thin strip of wood used to support plaster, tiles, etc.

lathe n machine for turning wood or metal while it is being shaped.

lather ⓿ n 1 froth of soap and water. 2 frothy sweat. 3 informal state of agitation. ▷ v 4 make frothy. 5 rub with soap until lather appears.

Latin n 1 language of the ancient Romans. ▷ adj 2 of or in Latin. 3 of a people whose language derives from Latin. 4 of the Roman Catholic Church. **Latin America** parts of South and

———————————————— THESAURUS ————

lash² v = **fasten**, bind, make fast, secure, strap, tie

lass, lassie n = **girl**, damsel, maid, maiden, young woman

last¹ adj 1 = **final**, at the end, closing, concluding, hindmost, rearmost, terminal, ultimate 2 = **most recent**, latest

last² v 1 = **continue**, abide, carry on, endure, keep on, persist, remain 3 = **survive**, stand up

lasting adj 1,3 = **continuing**, abiding, durable, enduring, long-standing, long-term, perennial, permanent

latch n 1 = **fastening**, bar, bolt, catch, hasp, hook, lock ▷ v 3 = **fasten**, bar, bolt, make fast, secure

late adj 1 = **overdue**, behind, behindhand, belated, delayed, last-minute, tardy 4 = **dead**, deceased, defunct, departed, former, past 5 = **recent**, advanced, fresh, modern, new ▷ adv 7 = **belatedly**, at the last

minute, behindhand, behind time, dilatorily, tardily

lately adv = **recently**, in recent times, just now, latterly, not long ago, of late

lateness n 1 = **delay**, belatedness, tardiness

latent adj = **hidden**, concealed, dormant, invisible, potential, undeveloped, unrealized

later adv 7 = **afterwards**, after, by and by, in a while, in time, later on, subsequently, thereafter

lateral adj = **sideways**, edgeways, flanking

latest adj 5 = **up-to-date**, current, fashionable, modern, most recent, newest, up-to-the-minute

lather n 1 = **froth**, bubbles, foam, soapsuds, suds 3 Inf = **fluster**, dither, flap (inf), fuss, state (inf), sweat, tizzy (inf) ▷ v 4 = **froth**, foam 5 = **soap**

Central America whose official language is Spanish or Portuguese. **Latin American** n, adj.

latitude ❶ n **1** angular distance measured in degrees N or S of the equator. **2** scope for freedom of action or thought. ▷ pl **3** regions considered in relation to their distance from the equator. **latitudinal** adj.

latrine n toilet in a barracks or camp.

latter ❶ adj **1** second of two. **2** later. **3** recent. **latterly** adv **latter-day** adj modern.

- **USAGE NOTE**
- *Latter* is used for the last mentioned
- of two items. When there are more,
- use *last-named*.

lattice ❶ [**lat**-iss] n **1** framework of intersecting strips of wood, metal, etc. **2** gate, screen, etc. formed of such a framework. **latticed** adj.

laud ❶ v praise or glorify. **laudable** adj praiseworthy. **laudably** adv **laudatory** adj praising or glorifying.

laudanum [**lawd**-a-num] n opium-based sedative.

laugh ❶ v **1** make inarticulate sounds with the voice expressing amusement, merriment, or scorn. **2** utter or express with laughter. ▷ n **3** act or instance of laughing. **4** *informal* person or thing causing amusement. **laughable** adj ridiculously inadequate. **laughter** n sound or action of laughing. **laughing gas** nitrous oxide as an anaesthetic. **laughing stock** object of general

derision. **laugh off** v treat (something serious or difficult) lightly.

launch¹ ❶ v **1** put (a ship or boat) into the water, esp. for the first time. **2** begin (a campaign, project, etc.). **3** put a new product on the market. **4** send (a missile or spacecraft) into space or the air. ▷ n **5** launching. **launcher** n **launch into** v start doing something enthusiastically. **launch out** v start doing something new.

launch² n open motorboat.

launder v **1** wash and iron (clothes and linen). **2** make (illegally obtained money) seem legal by passing it through foreign banks or legitimate businesses. **laundry** n, pl **-dries 1** clothes etc. for washing or which have recently been washed. **2** place for washing clothes and linen. **Launderette** n ® shop with coin-operated washing and drying machines.

laureate [**lor**-ee-at] adj see POET LAUREATE.

laurel ❶ n **1** glossy-leaved shrub, bay tree. ▷ pl **2** wreath of laurel, an emblem of victory or merit.

lava n molten rock thrown out by volcanoes, which hardens as it cools.

lavatory ❶ n, pl **-ries** toilet.

lavender n **1** shrub with fragrant flowers. ▷ adj **2** bluish-purple. **lavender water** light perfume made from lavender.

lavish ❶ adj **1** great in quantity or

———— THESAURUS ————

latitude n **2** = **scope**, elbowroom, freedom, laxity, leeway, liberty, licence, play, space

latter adj **1** = **second 2** = **later**, closing, concluding, last, last-mentioned

latterly adv **3** = **recently**, lately, of late

lattice n = **grid**, grating, grille, trellis

laudable adj = **praiseworthy**, admirable, commendable, creditable, excellent, meritorious, of note, worthy

laugh v **1** = **chuckle**, be in stitches, chortle, giggle, guffaw, snigger, split one's sides, titter ▷ n **3** = **chuckle**, chortle, giggle, guffaw, snigger, titter **4** *Inf* **a** = **clown**, card (*inf*), entertainer, hoot (*inf*), scream (*inf*) **b** = **joke**, hoot (*inf*), lark

laughable adj = **ridiculous**, absurd, derisory, farcical, ludicrous, nonsensical, preposterous, risible

laughing stock n = **figure of fun**, Aunt

Sally (*Brit*), butt, target, victim

laugh off v = **disregard**, brush aside, dismiss, ignore, minimize, pooh-pooh, shrug off

laughter n = **amusement**, glee, hilarity, merriment, mirth

launch¹ v **2** = **begin**, commence, embark upon, inaugurate, initiate, instigate, introduce, open, start **4** = **propel**, discharge, dispatch, fire, project, send off, set in motion

laurels pl n **2** = **glory**, credit, distinction, fame, honour, praise, prestige, recognition, renown

lavatory ❶ n = **toilet**, bathroom, cloakroom (*Brit*), latrine, loo (*Brit inf*), powder room, privy, (public) convenience, washroom, water closet, W.C.

lavish adj **1** = **plentiful**, abundant, copious, profuse, prolific **2** = **generous**,

richness. **2** giving or spending generously. **3** extravagant. ▷ *v* **4** give or spend generously. **lavishly** *adv*.

law ❶ *n* **1** rule binding on a community. **2** system of such rules. **3** *informal* police. **4** invariable sequence of events in nature. **5** general principle deduced from facts. **lawful** *adj* allowed by law. **lawfully** *adv* **lawless** *adj* breaking the law, esp. in a violent way. **lawlessness** *n* **law-abiding** *adj* obeying the laws. **law-breaker** *n* **Law Lords** members of the House of Lords who sit as the highest court of appeal. **lawsuit** *n* court case brought by one person or group against another.

lawn[1] *n* area of tended and mown grass. **lawn mower** machine for cutting grass. **lawn tennis** tennis, esp. when played on a grass court.

lawn[2] *n* fine linen or cotton fabric.

lawrencium *n Chemistry* element artificially produced from californium.

lawyer ❶ *n* professionally qualified legal expert.

lax ❶ *adj* not strict. **laxity** *n*.

laxative *n, adj* (medicine) inducing the emptying of the bowels.

lay[1] ❶ *v* **laying, laid 1** cause to lie, e.g. *Mary laid a clean towel carefully on the grass*. **2** devise or prepare, e.g. *She would lay her plans*. **3** set in a particular place or position, e.g. *He laid a wreath at the*

graveside. **4** attribute (blame). **5** put forward (a plan, argument, etc.). **6** (of a bird or reptile) produce eggs. **7** place (a bet), e.g. *I'll lay money he's already gone home*. **8** arrange (a table) for a meal. **lay aside** *v* **1** abandon or reject. **2** put aside (one thing) in order to take up another. **3** store for future use. **lay bare** reveal or explain, e.g. *a century of neurophysiology has now laid bare the structure of the brain*. **lay-by** *n* stopping place for traffic beside a road. **lay down** *v* **1** set down. **2** sacrifice. **3** formulate (a rule). **4** store (wine). **lay hold of** seize or grasp. **lay in** *v* accumulate and store. **lay into** *v informal* attack or scold severely. **lay off** *v* dismiss staff during a slack period. **lay-off** *n* **lay on** *v* provide or supply. **lay oneself open** make oneself vulnerable (to criticism or attack). **lay open** reveal or disclose. **lay out** *v* **1** arrange or spread out. **2** prepare (a corpse) for burial. **3** *informal* spend money, esp. lavishly. **4** *informal* knock unconscious. **layout** *n* arrangement, esp. of matter for printing or of a building. **lay up** *v* **1** *informal* confine through illness. **2** store for future use. **lay waste** devastate.

lay[2] ❶ *v* past tense of LIE[2]. **layabout** *n* lazy person.

lay[3] ❶ *adj* **1** of or involving people who are not clergymen. **2** nonspecialist.

——————————————— THESAURUS ———————————————

bountiful, free, liberal, munificent, open-handed, unstinting
  3 = **extravagant**, exaggerated, excessive, immoderate, prodigal, unrestrained, wasteful, wild ▷ *v*
  4 = **spend**, deluge, dissipate, expend, heap, pour, shower, squander, waste
law *n* **1** = **rule**, act, command, commandment, decree, edict, order, ordinance, regulation, statute
  2 = **constitution**, charter, code
  5 = **principle**, axiom, canon, precept
law-abiding *adj* = **obedient**, compliant, dutiful, good, honest, honourable, lawful, orderly, peaceable
law-breaker *n* = **criminal**, convict, crook (*inf*), culprit, delinquent, felon (*formerly criminal law*), miscreant, offender, villain, wrongdoer
lawful *adj* = **legal**, authorized, constitutional, legalized, legitimate, licit, permissible, rightful, valid, warranted
lawless *adj* = **disorderly**, anarchic,

chaotic, rebellious, riotous, unruly, wild
lawsuit *n* = **case**, action, dispute, industrial tribunal, litigation, proceedings, prosecution, suit, trial
lawyer *n* = **legal adviser**, advocate, attorney, barrister, counsel, counsellor, solicitor
lax *adj* = **slack**, careless, casual, lenient, negligent, overindulgent, remiss, slapdash, slipshod
lay[1] *v* **1, 3** = **place**, deposit, leave, plant, position, put, set, set down, spread
  2 = **devise**, concoct, contrive, design, hatch, plan, plot, prepare, work out
  4 = **attribute**, allocate, allot, ascribe, assign, impute **5** = **put forward**, advance, bring forward, lodge, offer, present, submit **6** = **produce**, bear, deposit **7** = **bet**, gamble, give odds, hazard, risk, stake, wager **8** = **arrange**, organize, set out
lay[3] *adj* **1** = **nonclerical**, secular
  2 = **nonspecialist**, amateur, inexpert, nonprofessional

layman, **laywoman** n **1** person who is not a member of the clergy. **2** person without specialist knowledge.

lay⁴ ❶ n short narrative poem designed to be sung.

layer ❶ n **1** single thickness of some substance, as a cover or coating on a surface. **2** laying hen. **3** shoot of a plant pegged down or partly covered with earth to encourage root growth. ▷ v **4** form a layer. **5** propagate plants by layers. **layered** adj.

layette n clothes for a newborn baby.

laze v **1** be idle or lazy. ▷ n **2** time spent lazing.

lazy ❶ adj **lazier**, **laziest 1** not inclined to work or exert oneself. **2** done in a relaxed manner without much effort. **3** (of movement) slow and gentle. **lazily** adv **laziness** n **lazybones** n informal lazy person.

lb pound (weight).

lbw Cricket leg before wicket.

lea n poetic meadow.

leach ❶ v remove or be removed from a substance by a liquid passing through it.

lead¹ ❶ v **leading**, **led 1** guide or conduct. **2** cause to feel, think, or behave in a certain way. **3** be the most important person or thing in. **4** be, go, or play first. **5** (of a road, path, etc.) go towards. **6** control or direct. **7** (foll. by to) result in. **8** pass or spend (one's life). ▷ n **9** first or most prominent place. **10** example or leadership. **11** amount by which a person or group is ahead of another. **12** clue. **13** length of leather or chain attached to a dog's collar to control it. **14** principal role or actor in a film, play, etc. **15** most important news story in a newspaper. **16** cable bringing current to an electrical device. ▷ adj **17** acting as a leader or lead. **leader** n person who leads. **leading** adj **1** principal. **2** in the first position. **leading light** important person in an organization. **leading question** question worded to prompt the answer desired. **lead-in** n introduction to a subject. **lead on** v lure or entice, esp. into wrongdoing. **lead up to** v act as a preliminary to.

lead² n **1** soft heavy grey metal. **2** (in a pencil) graphite. **3** lead weight on a line, used for sounding depths of water. ▷ pl **4** strips of lead used as a roof covering. ▷ v **5** cover or secure with lead. **leaded** adj (of windows) made from many small panes of glass held together by lead strips. **leaden** adj **1** heavy or sluggish. **2** dull grey. **3** made from lead.

THESAURUS

lay⁴ n = **poem**, ballad, lyric, ode, song

layabout n = **idler**, couch potato (sl), good-for-nothing, loafer, lounger, ne'er-do-well, skiver (Brit sl), wastrel

layer n **1** = **tier**, row, seam, stratum, thickness

layman, **laywoman** n **2** = **nonprofessional**, amateur, lay person, outsider

lay off v = **dismiss**, discharge, let go, make redundant, pay off

lay-off n = **unemployment**, discharge, dismissal

lay on v = **provide**, cater (for), furnish, give, purvey, supply

layout n = **arrangement**, design, format, formation, outline, plan

lay out v **1** = **arrange**, design, display, exhibit, plan, spread out **3** Inf = **spend**, disburse, expend, fork out (sl), invest, pay, shell out (inf) **4** Inf = **knock out**, knock for six (inf), knock unconscious, KO or K.O. (sl)

lazy adj **1** = **idle**, inactive, indolent, inert, slack, slothful, slow, workshy **3** = **lethargic**, drowsy, languid, languorous, sleepy, slow-moving, sluggish, somnolent, torpid

leach v = **extract**, drain, filter, percolate, seep, strain

lead¹ v **1** = **guide**, conduct, escort, pilot, precede, show the way, steer, usher **2** = **cause**, dispose, draw, incline, induce, influence, persuade, prevail, prompt **3** = **command**, direct, govern, head, manage, preside over, supervise **4** = **be ahead (of)**, blaze a trail, come first, exceed, excel, outdo, outstrip, surpass, transcend **7** (foll. by to) = **result in**, bring on, cause, contribute to, produce **8** = **live**, experience, have, pass, spend, undergo ▷ n **9** = **first place**, precedence, primacy, priority, supremacy, vanguard **10** = **example**, direction, guidance, leadership, model **11** = **advantage**, edge, margin, start **12** = **clue**, hint, indication, suggestion **14** = **leading role**, principal, protagonist, title role ▷ adj **17** = **main**, chief, first, foremost, head, leading, premier, primary, prime, principal

leader ❶ n 1 person who leads. 2 (also **leading article**) article in a newspaper expressing editorial views. 3 principal first violinist of an orchestra. **leadership** n.

leaf ❶ n, pl **leaves** 1 flat usu. green blade attached to the stem of a plant. 2 single sheet of paper in a book. 3 very thin sheet of metal. 4 extending flap on a table. **leafy** adj **leafless** adj **leaf mould** rich soil composed of decayed leaves. **leaf through** v turn pages without reading them.

leaflet ❶ n 1 sheet of printed matter for distribution. 2 small leaf.

league¹ ❶ n 1 association promoting the interests of its members. 2 association of sports clubs organizing competitions between its members. 3 informal class or level.

league² n obs measure of distance, about three miles.

leak ❶ n 1 hole or defect that allows the escape or entrance of liquid, gas, radiation, etc. 2 liquid etc. that escapes or enters. 3 disclosure of secrets. ▷ v 4 let liquid etc. in or out. 5 (of liquid etc.) find its way through a leak. 6 disclose secret information. **leakage** n act or instance of leaking. **leaky** adj.

lean¹ ❶ v **leaning**, **leaned** or **leant** 1 rest against. 2 bend or slope from an upright position. 3 tend (towards). **leaning** n tendency. **lean on** v 1 informal threaten or intimidate. 2 depend on for help or advice. **lean-to** n shed built against an existing wall.

lean² ❶ adj 1 thin but healthy-looking. 2 (of meat) lacking fat. 3 unproductive. ▷ n 4 lean part of meat. **leanness** n.

leap ❶ v **leaping**, **leapt** or **leaped** 1 make a sudden powerful jump. ▷ n 2 sudden powerful jump. 3 abrupt increase, as in costs or prices. **leapfrog** n game in which a player vaults over another bending down. **leap year** year with February 29 as an extra day.

learn ❶ v **learning**, **learned** or **learnt** 1 gain skill or knowledge by study, practice, or teaching. 2 memorize

——————————————————————— THESAURUS ———————————

leader n 1 = **principal**, boss (inf), captain, chief, chieftain, commander, director, guide, head, ringleader, ruler

leadership n 1 = **authority**, command, control, direction, domination, guidance, influence, initiative, mana (NZ), management, pre-eminence, running, superintendency, supremacy

leading adj 1 = **principal**, chief, dominant, first, foremost, greatest, highest, main, primary

lead on v = **entice**, beguile, deceive, draw on, lure, seduce, string along (inf), tempt

lead up to v = **introduce**, pave the way, prepare for

leaf n 1 = **frond**, blade 2 = **page**, folio, sheet **leaf through** v = **skim**, browse, flip, glance, riffle, thumb (through)

leaflet n 1 = **booklet**, brochure, circular, pamphlet

league¹ n 1 = **association**, alliance, coalition, confederation, consortium, federation, fraternity, group, guild, partnership, union 3 Inf = **class**, category, level

leak n 1 = **hole**, aperture, chink, crack, crevice, fissure, opening, puncture 2 = **leakage**, drip, percolation, seepage 3 = **disclosure**, divulgence ▷ v 5 = **escape**, drip, exude, ooze, pass, percolate, seep, spill, trickle

6 = **disclose**, divulge, give away, let slip, make known, make public, pass on, reveal, tell

leaky adj 1 = **leaking**, cracked, holey, perforated, porous, punctured, split

lean¹ v 1 = **rest**, be supported, prop, recline, repose 2 = **bend**, heel, incline, slant, slope, tilt, tip 3 = **tend**, be disposed to, be prone to, favour, prefer **lean on** 2 = **depend on**, count on, have faith in, rely on, trust

lean² adj 1 = **trim**, angular, bony, rangy, skinny, slender, slim, spare, thin, wiry 3 = **poor**, barren, meagre, scanty, unfruitful, unproductive

leaning n = **tendency**, bent, bias, disposition, inclination, partiality, penchant, predilection, proclivity, propensity

leap v 1 = **jump**, bounce, bound, hop, skip, spring ▷ n 2 = **jump**, bound, spring, vault 3 = **rise**, change, escalation, increase, surge, upsurge, upswing

learn v 1 = **master**, grasp, pick up 2 = **memorize**, commit to memory, get off pat, learn by heart 3 = **discover**, ascertain, detect, discern, find out, gather, hear, understand

learned adj = **scholarly**, academic, erudite, highbrow, intellectual, versed, well-informed, well-read

(something). **3** find out or discover.
learned *adj* **1** erudite, deeply read.
2 showing much learning. **learner** *n*
learning *n* knowledge got by study.
lease ⊕ *n* **1** contract by which land or
property is rented for a stated time by
the owner to a tenant. ▷ *v* **2** let or rent
by lease. **new lease of life** prospect of
renewed energy, health, or happiness.
leasehold *n*, *adj* (land or property) held
on lease. **leaseholder** *n*.
leash ⊕ *n* lead for a dog.
least ⊕ *adj* **1** superlative of LITTLE.
2 smallest. ▷ *n* **3** smallest one. ▷ *adv*
4 in the smallest degree.
leather ⊕ *n* **1** material made from
specially treated animal skins. ▷ *adj*
2 made of leather. ▷ *v* **3** beat or thrash.
leathery *adj* like leather, tough.
leave¹ ⊕ *v* **leaving, left 1** go away from.
2 allow to remain, accidentally or
deliberately. **3** cause to be or remain in
a specified state. **4** discontinue
membership of. **5** permit. **6** entrust.
7 bequeath. **leavings** *pl n* something
remaining, such as refuse. **leave out** *v*
exclude or omit.
leave² ⊕ *n* **1** permission to be absent
from work or duty. **2** period of such
absence. **3** permission to do
something. **4** formal parting.
leaven [**lev**-ven] *n* **1** substance that
causes dough to rise. **2** influence that

produces a gradual change. ▷ *v* **3** raise
with leaven. **4** spread through and
influence (something).
lecherous ⊕ [**letch**-er-uss] *adj* (of a
man) having or showing excessive
sexual desire. ▷ *lecher* *n* **lechery** *n*.
lectern *n* sloping reading desk, esp. in a
church.
lecture ⊕ *n* **1** informative talk to an
audience on a subject. **2** lengthy
rebuke or scolding. ▷ *v* **3** give a talk.
4 scold. **lecturer** *n* **lectureship** *n*
appointment as a lecturer.
led *v* past of LEAD¹.
LED light-emitting diode.
ledge ⊕ *n* **1** narrow shelf sticking out
from a wall. **2** shelflike projection from
a cliff etc.
ledger *n* book of debit and credit
accounts of a firm. **ledger line**
Music short line above or below the staff
for notes outside the range of the staff.
lee ⊕ *n* **1** sheltered part or side. ▷ *adj*
2 away from the wind. **leeward** *adj*, *n*
1 (on) the lee side. ▷ *adv* **2** towards this
side. **leeway** *n* **1** room for free
movement within limits. **2** sideways
drift of a boat or plane.
leech *n* **1** species of bloodsucking worm.
2 person who lives off others.
leek *n* vegetable of the onion family with
a long bulb and thick stem.
leer ⊕ *v* **1** look or grin at in a sneering or

——————— **THESAURUS** ———————

learner *n* **1** = **beginner**, apprentice,
neophyte, novice, tyro
learning *n* = **knowledge**, culture,
education, erudition, information, lore,
scholarship, study, wisdom
lease *v* **2** = **hire**, charter, let, loan, rent
leash *n* = **lead**, rein, tether
least *adj* **1, 2** = **smallest**, fewest, lowest,
meanest, minimum, poorest, slightest,
tiniest
leathery *adj* = **tough**, hard, rough
leave¹ *v* **1** = **depart**, decamp, disappear,
exit, go, go away, make tracks, move,
pull out, quit, retire, slope off, withdraw
2 = **forget**, leave behind, mislay
3 = **cause**, deposit, generate, produce,
result in **4** = **give up**, abandon, drop,
relinquish, renounce, surrender
6 = **entrust**, allot, assign, cede,
commit, consign, give over, refer
7 = **bequeath**, hand down, will
leave² *n* **1, 2** = **holiday**, furlough, leave of
absence, sabbatical, time off, vacation
3 = **permission**, allowance,

authorization, concession, consent,
dispensation, freedom, liberty,
sanction **4** = **departure**, adieu,
farewell, goodbye, leave-taking,
parting, retirement, withdrawal
leave out *v* = **omit**, cast aside,
disregard, exclude, ignore, neglect,
overlook, reject
lecherous *adj* = **lustful**, lascivious, lewd,
libidinous, licentious, prurient, randy
(*inf*, *chiefly Brit*), salacious
lecture *n* **1** = **talk**, address, discourse,
instruction, lesson, speech **2** = **telling
off**, dressing-down (*inf*), rebuke,
reprimand, reproof, scolding, talking-to
(*inf*) ▷ *v* **3** = **talk**, address, discourse,
expound, hold forth, speak, spout,
teach **4** = **tell off**, admonish, berate,
castigate, censure, reprimand, reprove,
rouse on (*Aust*), scold (*inf*)
ledge *n* **1** = **shelf**, mantle, projection, sill
2 = **ridge**, step
leer *n*, *v* = **grin**, gloat, goggle, ogle,
smirk, squint, stare

suggestive manner. ▷ n **2** sneering or suggestive look or grin.

leery adj informal suspicious or wary (of).

lees ❶ pl n sediment of wine.

left¹ ❶ adj **1** of the side that faces west when the front faces north. ▷ adv **2** on or towards the left. ▷ n **3** left hand or part. **4** Politics people supporting socialism rather than capitalism. **leftist** n, adj (person) of the political left. **left-handed** adj **1** more adept with the left hand than with the right. **2** done with the left hand. **3** designed for use by the left hand. **left-wing** adj **1** socialist. **2** belonging to the more radical part of a political party. **left-winger** n.

left² v past of LEAVE¹.

leftover ❶ n unused portion of food or material.

leg ❶ n **1** one of the limbs on which a person or animal walks, runs, or stands. **2** part of a garment covering the leg. **3** structure that supports, such as one of the legs of a table. **4** stage of a journey. **5** Sport (part of) one game or race in a series. **6** Cricket part of the field to the left of a right-handed batsman. **pull someone's leg** tease someone. **leggy** adj having long legs. **legless** adj **1** without legs. **2** slang very drunk. **leggings** pl n **1** covering of leather or other material for the legs. **2** close-fitting trousers for women or children.

legacy ❶ n, pl -**cies 1** thing left in a will. **2** thing handed down to a successor.

legal ❶ adj **1** established or permitted by law. **2** relating to law or lawyers. **legally** adv **legalistic** adj showing strict adherence to the letter of the law. **legality** n **legalize** v make legal. **legalization** n.

legate n messenger or representative, esp. from the Pope. **legation** n **1** diplomatic minister and his staff. **2** official residence of a diplomatic minister.

legatee n recipient of a legacy.

legato [leg-**ah**-toe] n, pl -**tos** adv Music (piece to be played) smoothly.

legend ❶ n **1** traditional story or myth. **2** traditional literature. **3** famous person or event. **4** stories about such a person or event. **5** inscription. **6** explanation of symbols on a map etc. **legendary** adj **1** famous. **2** of or in legend.

legerdemain [lej-er-de-**main**] n **1** sleight of hand. **2** cunning deception.

legible ❶ adj easily read. **legibility** n **legibly** adv.

legion ❶ n **1** large military force. **2** large number. **3** association of veterans. **4** infantry unit in the Roman army. **legionary** adj, n **legionnaire** n member of a legion. **legionnaire's disease** serious bacterial disease similar to pneumonia.

legislate ❶ v make laws. **legislation** n

——————————————— THESAURUS ———————————————

lees pl n = **sediment**, deposit, dregs, grounds

leeway n **1** = **room**, elbowroom, latitude, margin, play, scope, space

left¹ adj **1** = **left-hand**, larboard (Naut), port

leftover n = **remnant**, oddment, scrap

left-wing adj **1** = **socialist**, communist, left, leftist, radical, red (inf)

leg n **1** = **limb**, lower limb, member, pin (inf), stump (inf) **3** = **support**, brace, prop, upright **4** = **stage**, lap, part, portion, section, segment, stretch **pull someone's leg** = **tease**, fool, kid (inf), make fun of, trick, wind up (Brit sl)

legacy n = **bequest**, estate, gift, heirloom, inheritance

legal adj **1** = **lawful**, allowed, authorized, constitutional, legitimate, licit, permissible, sanctioned, valid **2** = **judicial**, forensic, judiciary, juridical

legality n = **lawfulness**, legitimacy, rightfulness, validity

legalize v = **permit**, allow, approve, authorize, decriminalize, legitimate, legitimize, license, sanction, validate

legend n **1** = **myth**, fable, fiction, folk tale, saga, story, tale **3** = **celebrity**, luminary, megastar (inf), phenomenon, prodigy **5** = **inscription**, caption, motto

legendary adj **1** = **famous**, celebrated, famed, illustrious, immortal, renowned, well-known **2** = **mythical**, apocryphal, fabled, fabulous, fictitious, romantic, traditional

legible adj = **readable**, clear, decipherable, distinct, easy to read, neat

legion n **1** = **army**, brigade, company, division, force, troop **2** = **multitude**, drove, horde, host, mass, myriad, number, throng

legislation n **1** = **lawmaking**, enactment, prescription, regulation

1 legislating. 2 laws made. **legislative** adj **legislator** n maker of laws. **legislature** n body of people that makes, amends, or repeals laws.

legitimate ❶ adj 1 authorized by or in accordance with law. 2 fairly deduced. 3 born to parents married to each other. ▷ v 4 make legitimate. **legitimacy** n **legitimately** adv **legitimize** v make legitimate, legalize. **legitimization** n.

Lego n ® construction toy of plastic bricks fitted together by studs.

leguaan n large S African lizard.

legume n 1 pod of a plant of the pea or bean family. ▷ pl 2 peas or beans. **leguminous** adj (of plants) pod-bearing.

lei n (in Hawaii) garland of flowers.

leisure ❶ n time for relaxation or hobbies. **at one's leisure** when one has time. **leisurely** adj 1 deliberate, unhurried. ▷ adv 2 slowly. **leisured** adj with plenty of spare time. **leisure centre** building with facilities such as a swimming pool, gymnasium, and café

leitmotif [lite-mote-eef] n Music recurring theme associated with a person, situation, or thought.

lekker adj S Afr slang 1 attractive or nice. 2 tasty.

lemming n rodent of arctic regions, reputed to run into the sea and drown during mass migrations.

lemon n 1 yellow oval fruit that grows on trees. 2 slang useless or defective person or thing. ▷ adj 3 pale-yellow. **lemonade** n lemon-flavoured soft drink, often fizzy. **lemon curd** creamy spread made of lemons, butter, etc. **lemon sole** edible flatfish.

lemur n nocturnal animal like a small monkey, found in Madagascar.

lend ❶ v **lending**, **lent** 1 give the temporary use of. 2 provide (money) temporarily, often for interest. 3 add (a quality or effect), e.g. her presence lent beauty to the scene. **lend itself to** be suitable for. **lender** n.

length ❶ n 1 extent or measurement from end to end. 2 period of time for which something happens. 3 quality of being long. 4 piece of something narrow and long. **at length** 1 at last. 2 in full detail. **lengthy** adj very long or tiresome. **lengthily** adv **lengthen** v make or become longer. **lengthways**, **lengthwise** adj, adv.

lenient ❶ [lee-nee-ent] adj tolerant, not strict or severe. **leniency** n **leniently** adv.

lens n, pl **lenses** 1 piece of glass or similar material with one or both sides curved, used to bring together or spread light rays in cameras, spectacles, telescopes, etc. 2 transparent structure in the eye that focuses light.

THESAURUS

2 = **law**, act, bill, charter, measure, regulation, ruling, statute

legislative adj = **law-making**, judicial, law-giving

legislator n = **lawmaker**, lawgiver

legislature n = **parliament**, assembly, chamber, congress, senate

legitimate adj 1 = **lawful**, authentic, authorized, genuine, kosher (inf), legal, licit, rightful 2 = **reasonable**, admissible, correct, justifiable, logical, sensible, valid, warranted, well-founded ▷ v 4 = **legitimize**, authorize, legalize, permit, pronounce lawful, sanction

legitimize v = **legalize**, authorize, permit, sanction

leisure n = **spare time**, ease, freedom, free time, liberty, recreation, relaxation, rest

leisurely adj 1 = **unhurried**, comfortable, easy, gentle, lazy, relaxed, slow

lend v 2 = **loan**, advance 3 = **give**, add, bestow, confer, grant, impart, provide, supply **lend itself to** = **be appropriate**, be serviceable, suit

length n 1 = **distance**, extent, longitude, measure, reach, span 2 = **duration**, period, space, span, stretch, term 4 = **piece**, measure, portion, section, segment ▷ n **at length** 1 = **at last**, at long last, eventually, finally, in the end 2 = **in detail**, completely, fully, in depth, thoroughly, to the full

lengthen v = **extend**, continue, draw out, elongate, expand, increase, prolong, protract, spin out, stretch

lengthy adj = **long**, drawn-out, extended, interminable, long-drawn-out, long-winded, prolonged, protracted, tedious

lenient adj = **merciful**, compassionate, forbearing, forgiving, indulgent, kind, sparing, tolerant

lent v past of LEND.

Lent n period from Ash Wednesday to Easter Saturday. **Lenten** adj of, in, or suitable to Lent.

lentil n edible seed of a leguminous Asian plant.

lento n, pl **-tos** adv Music (piece to be played) slowly.

Leo n (the lion) fifth sign of the zodiac.

leonine adj like a lion.

leopard n large spotted carnivorous animal of the cat family. **leopardess** n fem.

leotard n tight-fitting garment covering most of the body, worn for dancing or exercise.

leper n 1 offens person suffering from leprosy. 2 ignored or despised person.

lepidoptera pl n order of insects with four wings covered with fine gossamer scales, as moths and butterflies. **lepidopterous** adj **lepidopterist** n person who studies or collects butterflies or moths.

leprechaun n mischievous elf of Irish folklore.

leprosy n disease attacking the nerves and skin, resulting in loss of feeling in the affected parts. **leprous** adj.

lesbian ① n 1 homosexual woman. ▷ adj **2** of homosexual women. **lesbianism** n.

lese-majesty [lezz-**maj**-est-ee] n **1** treason. **2** taking of liberties against people in authority.

lesion n **1** structural change in an organ of the body caused by illness or injury. **2** injury or wound.

less ① adj 1 smaller in extent, degree, or duration. **2** not so much.

3 comparative of LITTLE. ▷ pron **4** smaller part or quantity. ▷ adv **5** to a smaller extent or degree. ▷ prep **6** after deducting, minus. **lessen** v make or become smaller or not as much. **lesser** adj not as great in quantity, size, or worth.

● **USAGE NOTE**
● Avoid confusion with few(er). Less is
● used with amounts that cannot be
● counted: less time; less fuss. Few(er) is
● used of things that can be counted.

lessee n person to whom a lease is granted.

lesson ① n 1 single period of instruction in a subject. **2** content of this. **3** experience that teaches. **4** portion of Scripture read in church.

lest conj **1** so as to prevent any possibility that. **2** for fear that.

let¹ ① v letting, let 1 allow, enable, or cause. **2** used as an auxiliary to express a proposal, command, threat, or assumption. **3** grant use of for rent, lease. **4** allow to escape. ▷ n **5** act of letting property. **let alone** not to mention. **let down** v **1** disappoint. **2** lower. **3** deflate. **letdown** n disappointment. **let off** v **1** excuse from (a duty or punishment). **2** fire or explode (a weapon). **3** emit (gas, steam, etc.). **let on** v informal reveal (a secret). **let out** v **1** emit. **2** release. **3** rent out. **let up** v diminish or stop. **let-up** n lessening.

let² n 1 Tennis minor infringement or obstruction of the ball requiring a replay of the point. **2** hindrance.

lethal ① adj deadly.

lethargy ① n 1 sluggishness or dullness. **2** abnormal lack of energy. **lethargic**

————————————————————— THESAURUS —————————

lesbian adj **2** = **homosexual**, gay

less adj **1** = **smaller**, shorter ▷ prep **6** = **minus**, excepting, lacking, subtracting, without

lessen v = **reduce**, contract, decrease, diminish, ease, lower, minimize, narrow, shrink

lesser adj = **lower**, inferior, less important, minor, secondary

lesson n **1** = **class**, coaching, instruction, period, schooling, teaching, tutoring **3** = **example**, deterrent, message, moral

let¹ v **1** = **allow**, authorize, entitle, give permission, give the go-ahead, permit, sanction, tolerate **3** = **lease**, hire, rent

let² n **2** = **hindrance**, constraint, impediment, interference, obstacle, obstruction, prohibition, restriction

let down v **1** = **disappoint**, disenchant, disillusion, dissatisfy, fail, fall short, leave in the lurch, leave stranded

letdown n = **disappointment**, anticlimax, blow, comedown (inf), setback, washout (inf)

lethal adj = **deadly**, dangerous, destructive, devastating, fatal, mortal, murderous, virulent

lethargic adj = **sluggish**, apathetic, drowsy, dull, languid, listless, sleepy, slothful

lethargy n = **sluggishness**, apathy,

adj **lethargically** adv.

letter ❶ n 1 written message, usu. sent by post. 2 alphabetical symbol. 3 strict meaning (of a law etc.). ▷ pl 4 literary knowledge or ability. **lettered** adj learned. **lettering** n **letter bomb** explosive device in a parcel or letter that explodes on opening. **letter box** 1 slot in a door through which letters are delivered. 2 box in a street or post office where letters are posted. **letterhead** n printed heading on stationery giving the sender's name and address.

lettuce n plant with large green leaves used in salads.

leucocyte [**loo**-koh-site] n white blood cell.

leukaemia [loo-**kee**-mee-a] n disease caused by uncontrolled overproduction of white blood cells.

levee n US natural or artificial river embankment.

level ❶ adj 1 horizontal. 2 having an even surface. 3 of the same height as something else. 4 equal to or even with (someone or something else). 5 not going above the top edge of (a spoon etc.). 6 not irregular. ▷ v **-elling, -elled** 7 make even or horizontal. 8 make equal in position or status. 9 direct (a gun, accusation, etc.) at. 10 raze to the ground. ▷ n 11 horizontal line or

surface. 12 device for showing or testing if something is horizontal. 13 position on a scale. 14 standard or grade. 15 flat area of land. **on the level** informal honest or trustworthy. **level crossing** point where a railway line and road cross. **level-headed** adj not apt to be carried away by emotion.

lever ❶ n 1 handle used to operate machinery. 2 bar used to move a heavy object or to open something. 3 rigid bar pivoted about a fulcrum to transfer a force to a load. 4 means of exerting pressure to achieve an aim. ▷ v 5 prise or move with a lever. **leverage** n 1 action or power of a lever. 2 influence or strategic advantage.

leveraged buyout n takeover bid in which a small company uses its assets, and those of the target company, to raise the loans required to finance the takeover.

leveret [**lev**-ver-it] n young hare.

leviathan [lev-**vie**-ath-an] n 1 sea monster. 2 anything huge or formidable.

Levis pl n ® denim jeans.

levitation n raising of a solid body into the air supernaturally. **levitate** v rise or cause to rise into the air.

levity ❶ n, pl **-ties** inclination to make a joke of serious matters.

levy ❶ [**lev**-vee] v **levying, levied** 1 impose and collect (a tax). 2 raise

---

THESAURUS

drowsiness, inertia, languor, lassitude, listlessness, sleepiness, sloth

let off v 1 = **excuse**, absolve, discharge, exempt, exonerate, forgive, pardon, release, spare 2 = **fire**, detonate, discharge, explode 3 = **emit**, exude, give off, leak, release

let on v Inf = **reveal**, admit, disclose, divulge, give away, let the cat out of the bag (inf), make known, say

let out v 1 = **emit**, give vent to, produce 2 = **release**, discharge, free, let go, liberate

letter n 1 = **message**, communication, dispatch, epistle, line, missive, note 2 = **character**, sign, symbol

let up v = **stop**, abate, decrease, diminish, ease (up), moderate, outspan (S Afr), relax, slacken, subside

let-up n = **lessening**, break, breathing space, interval, lull, pause, remission, respite, slackening

level adj 1 = **horizontal**, flat 2 = **even**, consistent, plain, smooth, uniform

4 = **equal**, balanced, commensurate, comparable, equivalent, even, neck and neck, on a par, proportionate ▷ v 7 = **flatten**, even off or out, plane, smooth 8 = **equalize**, balance, even up 9 = **direct**, aim, focus, point, train 10 = **destroy**, bulldoze, demolish, devastate, flatten, knock down, pull down, raze, tear down ▷ n 14 = **position**, achievement, degree, grade, rank, stage, standard, standing, status **on the level** Inf = **honest**, above board, fair, genuine, square, straight

level-headed adj = **calm**, balanced, collected, composed, cool, sensible, steady, unflappable (inf)

lever n 1, 2 = **handle**, bar ▷ v 5 = **prise**, force

leverage n 2 = **influence**, authority, clout (inf), mana (NZ), pull (inf), weight

levity n = **light-heartedness**, facetiousness, flippancy, frivolity, silliness, skittishness, triviality

levy v 1 = **impose**, charge, collect,

(troops). ▷ *n, pl* **levies 3** imposition or collection of taxes. **4** money levied. **5** troops conscripted for service.

lewd ❶ *adj* lustful or indecent. **lewdly** *adv* **lewdness** *n*.

lexicon *n* **1** dictionary. **2** vocabulary of a language. **lexical** *adj* relating to the vocabulary of a language. **lexicographer** *n* writer of dictionaries. **lexicography** *n*.

LGV large goods vehicle.

Li *Chemistry* lithium.

liable ❶ *adj* **1** legally obliged or responsible. **2** given to or at risk from a condition. **liability** *n* **1** hindrance or disadvantage. **2** state of being liable. **3** financial obligation.

liaise ❶ *v* establish and maintain communication (with). **liaison** *n* **1** communication and contact between groups. **2** secret or adulterous relationship.

- ● **SPELLING TIP**
- ● A lot of people forget to include a
- ● second *i* in **liaise**. They make the
- ● same mistake when they write *liason*,
- ● which occurs 58 times in the Bank of
- ● English and which should, of course,
- ● be **liaison**.

liar ❶ *n* person who tells lies.

lib *n informal* short for LIBERATION.

libation [lie-**bay**-shun] *n* drink poured as an offering to the gods.

libel ❶ *n* **1** published statement falsely damaging a person's reputation. ▷ *v* **-belling, -belled 2** falsely damage the reputation of (someone). **libellous** *adj*.

liberal ❶ *adj* **1** having social and political views that favour progress and reform. **2** generous. **3** tolerant. **4** abundant. **5** (of education) designed to develop general cultural interests. ▷ *n* **6** person who has liberal ideas or opinions. **liberally** *adv* **liberalism** *n* belief in democratic reforms and individual freedom. **liberality** *n* generosity. **liberalize** *v* make (laws, a country, etc.) less restrictive. **liberalization** *n* **Liberal Democrat** member of the Liberal Democrats, a British political party favouring a regulated market or mixed economy.

liberate ❶ *v* set free. **liberation** *n* **liberator** *n*.

libertarian *n* **1** believer in freedom of thought and action. ▷ *adj* **2** having such a belief.

───────────────────── THESAURUS ─────────

demand, exact **2** = **conscript**, call up, mobilize, muster, raise ▷ *n* **3** = **imposition**, assessment, collection, exaction, gathering **4** = **tax**, duty, excise, fee, tariff, toll

lewd *adj* = **indecent**, bawdy, lascivious, libidinous, licentious, lustful, obscene, pornographic, smutty, wanton

liability *n* **1** = **disadvantage**, burden, drawback, encumbrance, handicap, hindrance, inconvenience, millstone, nuisance **2** = **responsibility**, accountability, answerability, culpability **3** = **debt**, debit, obligation

liable *adj* **1** = **responsible**, accountable, answerable, obligated **2** = **vulnerable**, exposed, open, subject, susceptible

liaise *v* = **communicate**, keep contact, link, mediate

liaison *n* **1** = **communication**, connection, contact, hook-up, interchange **2** = **affair**, amour, entanglement, fling, intrigue, love affair, romance

liar *n* = **falsifier**, fabricator, fibber, perjurer

libel *n* **1** = **defamation**, aspersion, calumny, denigration, smear ▷ *v*

2 = **defame**, blacken, malign, revile, slur, smear, vilify

libellous *adj* = **defamatory**, derogatory, false, injurious, malicious, scurrilous, untrue

liberal *adj* **1** = **progressive**, libertarian, radical, reformist **2** = **generous**, beneficent, bountiful, charitable, kind, open-handed, open-hearted, unstinting **3** = **tolerant**, broad-minded, indulgent, permissive **4** = **abundant**, ample, bountiful, copious, handsome, lavish, munificent, plentiful, profuse, rich

liberality *n* **2** = **generosity**, beneficence, benevolence, bounty, charity, kindness, largesse *or* largess, munificence, philanthropy **3** = **broad-mindedness**, latitude, liberalism, libertarianism, permissiveness, toleration

liberate *v* = **free**, deliver, emancipate, let loose, let out, release, rescue, set free

liberation *n* = **freeing**, deliverance, emancipation, freedom, liberty, release

liberator *n* = **deliverer**, emancipator, freer, redeemer, rescuer, saviour

libertine ❶ [**lib**-er-teen] n morally dissolute person.

liberty ❶ n, pl **-ties 1** freedom. **2** act or comment regarded as forward or socially unacceptable. **at liberty 1** free. **2** having the right. **take liberties** be presumptuous.

libido ❶ [lib-**ee**-doe] n, pl **-dos 1** psychic energy. **2** emotional drive, esp. of sexual origin. **libidinal** adj **libidinous** adj lustful.

Libra n (the scales) seventh sign of the zodiac.

library n, pl **-braries 1** room or building where books are kept. **2** collection of books, records, etc. for consultation or borrowing. **3** set of books published in a series. **librarian** n keeper of or worker in a library. **librarianship** n.

libretto n, pl **-tos**, **-ti** words of an opera. **librettist** n.

lice n a plural of LOUSE.

licence ❶ n **1** document giving official permission to do something. **2** formal permission. **3** disregard of conventions for effect, e.g. poetic licence. **4** excessive liberty. **license** v grant a licence to. **licensed** adj **licensee** n holder of a licence, esp. to sell alcohol.

license plate n the US and Canadian term for NUMBERPLATE.

licentiate n person licensed as competent to practise a profession.

licentious ❶ adj sexually unrestrained or promiscuous. **licentiousness** n.

lichen n small flowerless plant forming a crust on rocks, trees, etc.

licit adj lawful, permitted.

lick ❶ v **1** pass the tongue over. **2** touch lightly or flicker round. **3** slang defeat. **4** slang thrash. ▷ n **5** licking. **6** small amount (of paint etc.). **7** informal blow. **8** informal fast pace.

licorice n same as LIQUORICE.

lid n **1** movable cover. **2** short for EYELID.

lido [**lee**-doe] n, pl **-dos** open-air centre for swimming and water sports.

lie¹ ❶ v lying, lied **1** make a deliberately false statement. **2** give a false impression. ▷ n **3** deliberate falsehood. **white lie** see WHITE.

lie² ❶ v lying, lay, lain **1** place oneself or be in a horizontal position. **2** be situated. **3** be or remain in a certain state or position. **4** exist or be found. ▷ n **5** way something lies. **lie-down** n rest. **lie in** v remain in bed late into the morning. **lie-in** n long stay in bed in the morning.

● **USAGE NOTE**
● Note that the past of lie is lay: She lay
● on the beach all day. Do not confuse
● with the main verb lay meaning
● 'put'.

lied [leed] n, pl **lieder** Music setting for voice and piano of a romantic poem.

liege [leej] adj **1** bound to give or receive feudal service. ▷ n **2** lord.

lien n right to hold another's property until a debt is paid.

─────────────── **THESAURUS** ───────────────

libertine n = **reprobate**, debauchee, lecher, profligate, rake, roué, sensualist, voluptuary, womanizer

liberty n **1** = **freedom**, autonomy, emancipation, immunity, independence, liberation, release, self-determination, sovereignty **2** = **impertinence**, impropriety, impudence, insolence, presumption **at liberty 1** = **free**, on the loose **2** = **unrestricted**

libidinous adj = **lustful**, carnal, debauched, lascivious, lecherous, randy (inf, chiefly Brit), sensual, wanton

licence n **1** = **certificate**, charter, permit, warrant **2** = **permission**, authority, authorization, blank cheque, carte blanche, dispensation, entitlement, exemption, immunity, leave, liberty, right **3** = **freedom**, independence, latitude, leeway, liberty **4** = **laxity**, excess, immoderation, indulgence, irresponsibility

license v = **permit**, accredit, allow, authorize, certify, empower, sanction, warrant

licentious adj = **promiscuous**, abandoned, debauched, dissolute, immoral, lascivious, lustful, sensual, wanton

lick v **1** = **taste**, lap, tongue **2** = **flicker**, dart, flick, play over, ripple, touch **3** Inf = **beat**, defeat, master, outdo, outstrip, overcome, rout, trounce, vanquish ▷ n **6** = **dab**, bit, stroke, touch **8** Sl = **pace**, clip (inf), rate, speed

lie¹ v **1** = **fib**, dissimulate, equivocate, fabricate, falsify, prevaricate, tell untruths ▷ n **3** = **falsehood**, deceit, fabrication, fib, fiction, invention, prevarication, untruth

lie² v **1** = **recline**, loll, lounge, repose, rest, sprawl, stretch out **2** = **be situated**, be, be placed, exist **3** = **be**, remain **4** = **exist**

lieu [lyew] *n* **in lieu of** instead of.
lieutenant [lef-**ten**-ant] *n* **1** junior officer in the army or navy. **2** main assistant.
life ❶ *n, pl* **lives 1** state of living beings, characterized by growth, reproduction, and response to stimuli. **2** period between birth and death or between birth and the present time. **3** living person. **4** way of living. **5** sentence of imprisonment for life. **6** amount of time something is active or functions. **7** biography. **8** liveliness or high spirits. **9** living beings collectively. **lifeless** *adj* **1** dead. **2** not lively or exciting. **3** unconscious. **lifelike** *adj* **lifelong** *adj* lasting all of a person's life. **lifer** *n informal* prisoner sentenced to imprisonment for life. **life belt, jacket** buoyant device to keep afloat a person in danger of drowning. **lifeblood** *n* **1** blood vital to life. **2** vital thing for success or development. **lifeboat** *n* boat used for rescuing people at sea. **life cycle** series of changes undergone by each generation of an animal or plant. **lifeguard** *n* person who saves people from drowning. **lifeline** *n* **1** means of contact or support. **2** rope used in rescuing a person in danger. **life science** any science concerned with living organisms, such as biology, botany, or zoology. **life-size, life-sized** *adj* representing actual size. **lifestyle** *n* particular attitudes, habits, etc.

life-support *adj* (of equipment or treatment) necessary to keep a person alive. **lifetime** *n* length of time a person is alive.
lift ❶ *v* **1** move upwards in position, status, volume, etc. **2** revoke or cancel. **3** take (plants) out of the ground for harvesting. **4** disappear. **5** make or become more cheerful. **6** *informal* plagiarize (music or writing). ▷ *n* **7** cage raised and lowered in a vertical shaft to transport people or goods. **8** ride in a car etc. as a passenger. **9** *informal* feeling of cheerfulness. **10** lifting. **liftoff** *n* moment a rocket leaves the ground.
ligament *n* band of tissue joining bones.
ligature *n* **1** link, bond, or tie. **2** *Printing* two or more joined letters.
light¹ ❶ *n* **1** electromagnetic radiation by which things are visible. **2** source of this, lamp. **3** anything that lets in light, such as a window. **4** aspect or view. **5** mental vision. **6** brightness of countenance. **7** means of setting fire to. ▷ *pl* **8** traffic lights. ▷ *adj* **9** bright. **10** (of a colour) pale. ▷ *v* **lighting, lighted** *or* **lit 11** ignite. **12** illuminate or cause to illuminate. **13** guide by a light. **lighten** *v* make less dark. **lighting** *n* apparatus for and use of artificial light in theatres, films, etc. **light bulb** glass part of an electric lamp. **lighthouse** *n* tower with a light to guide ships. **lightship** *n* moored ship used as a

———————————————————————————— THESAURUS ————

life *n* **1** = **being**, sentience, vitality **2** = **existence**, being, lifetime, span, time **4** = **behaviour**, conduct, life style, way of life **7** = **biography**, autobiography, confessions, history, life story, memoirs, story **8** = **liveliness**, animation, energy, high spirits, spirit, verve, vigour, vitality, vivacity, zest
lifeless *adj* **1** = **dead**, deceased, defunct, extinct, inanimate **2** = **dull**, colourless, flat, lacklustre, lethargic, listless, sluggish, wooden **3** = **unconscious**, comatose, dead to the world (*inf*), insensible
lifelike *adj* = **realistic**, authentic, exact, faithful, natural, true-to-life, vivid
lifelong *adj* = **long-lasting**, enduring, lasting, long-standing, perennial, persistent
lifetime *n* = **existence**, career, day(s), span, time

lift *v* **1** = **raise**, draw up, elevate, hoist, pick up, uplift, upraise **2** = **revoke**, annul, cancel, countermand, end, remove, rescind, stop, terminate **4** = **disappear**, be dispelled, disperse, dissipate, vanish ▷ *n* **7** = **elevator** (*chiefly US*) **8** = **ride**, drive, run **9** *Inf* = **boost**, encouragement, fillip, gee-up, pick-me-up, shot in the arm (*inf*)
light¹ *n* **1** = **brightness**, brilliance, glare, gleam, glint, glow, illumination, luminosity, radiance, shine **2** = **lamp**, beacon, candle, flare, lantern, taper, torch **4** = **aspect**, angle, context, interpretation, point of view, slant, vantage point, viewpoint **7** = **match**, flame, lighter ▷ *adj* **9** = **bright**, brilliant, illuminated, luminous, lustrous, shining, well-lit **10** = **pale**, bleached, blond, blonde, faded, fair, pastel ▷ *v* **11** = **ignite**, inflame, kindle

lighthouse. **light up** v **1** illuminate.
2 make or become cheerful. **3** light a
cigarette or pipe. **light year**
Astronomy distance light travels in one
year, about six million million miles.
light² ❶ adj **1** not heavy, weighing
relatively little. **2** relatively low in
strength, amount, density, etc.
3 lacking sufficient weight. **4** not
clumsy. **5** not serious or profound.
6 easily digested. **7** free from care,
cheerful. ▷ adv **8** with little equipment
or luggage. ▷ v **lighting**, **lighted**, **lit**
9 (esp. of birds) settle after flight.
10 come (upon) by chance. **lightly** adv
lightness n **lighten** v **1** make less heavy
or burdensome. **2** make more cheerful
or lively. **light-fingered** adj skilful at
stealing. **light-headed** adj feeling faint,
dizzy. **light-hearted** adj carefree. **light
heavyweight** boxer weighing up to
175lb (professional) or 81kg (amateur).
lightweight n, adj **1** (person) of little
importance. ▷ n **2** boxer weighing up to
135lb (professional) or 60kg (amateur).
lighter¹ n device for lighting cigarettes
etc.
lighter² n flat-bottomed boat for
unloading ships.
lightning n **1** visible discharge of
electricity in the atmosphere. ▷ adj
2 fast and sudden. **lightning
conductor** metal rod attached to the
top of a building to divert lightning
safely to earth.

- **SPELLING TIP**
- Do not confuse this noun with the
- verb 'lighten', which has the form
- 'lightening'. The Bank of English
- shows that people often make the
- mistake of writing *lightening*, when
- they mean the noun **lightning**,
- which doesn't have an *e* in the
- middle.

lights pl n lungs of animals as animal
food.
ligneous adj of or like wood.
lignite [**lig**-nite] n woody textured rock
used as fuel.
like¹ ❶ prep, conj, adj, pron indicating
similarity, comparison, etc. **liken** v
compare. **likeness** n **1** resemblance.
2 portrait. **likewise** adv similarly.
like² ❶ v **1** find enjoyable. **2** be fond of.
3 prefer, choose, or wish. **likeable**,
likable adj **liking** n **1** fondness, e.g. *a
liking for blue cheese.* **2** preference.
likely ❶ adj **1** tending or inclined.
2 probable. **3** hopeful, promising. ▷ adv
4 probably. **not likely** informal

───── THESAURUS ─────

12 = **illuminate**, brighten, light up
light² adj **1** = **insubstantial**, airy,
buoyant, flimsy, portable, slight
2 = **weak**, faint, gentle, indistinct, mild,
moderate, slight, soft
3 = **underweight 4** = **nimble**, agile,
graceful, lithe, sprightly, sylphlike
5 = **insignificant**, inconsequential,
inconsiderable, scanty, slight, small,
trifling, trivial **6** = **digestible**, frugal,
modest **7** = **light-hearted**, frivolous ▷ v
9 = **settle**, alight, land, perch
10 = **come across**, chance upon,
discover, encounter, find, happen upon,
hit upon, stumble on
lighten¹ v = **brighten**, become light,
illuminate, irradiate, light up
lighten² v **1** = **ease**, allay, alleviate,
ameliorate, assuage, lessen, mitigate,
reduce, relieve **2** = **cheer**, brighten,
buoy up, lift, perk up, revive
light-headed adj = **faint**, dizzy, giddy,
hazy, vertiginous, woozy (*inf*)
light-hearted adj = **carefree**, blithe,
cheerful, happy-go-lucky, jolly, jovial,
playful, upbeat (*inf*)
lightly adv **2 a** = **gently**, delicately,

faintly, slightly, softly **b** = **moderately**,
sparingly, sparsely, heavily
7 = **carelessly**, breezily, flippantly,
frivolously, heedlessly, thoughtlessly
lightweight adj **1** = **unimportant**,
inconsequential, insignificant, paltry,
petty, slight, trifling, trivial, worthless
like¹ adj = **similar**, akin, alike, analogous,
corresponding, equivalent, identical,
parallel, same
like² v **1** = **enjoy**, be fond of, be keen on,
be partial to, delight in, go for, love,
relish, revel in **2** = **admire**, appreciate,
approve, cherish, esteem, hold dear,
prize, take to **3** = **wish**, care to, choose,
desire, fancy, feel inclined, prefer, want
likeable, **likable** adj = **attractive**,
agreeable, amiable, appealing,
charming, engaging, lekker *S Afr sl*,
nice, pleasant, sympathetic
likelihood n = **probability**, chance,
possibility, prospect
likely adj **1** = **inclined**, apt, disposed,
liable, prone, tending **2** = **probable**,
anticipated, expected, odds-on, on the
cards, to be expected **3** = **promising**,
hopeful, up-and-coming

definitely not. **likelihood** n probability.

lilac n 1 shrub with pale mauve or white flowers. ▷ adj 2 light-purple.

Lilliputian [lil-lip-**pew**-shun] adj tiny.

Lilo n, pl **-los** ® inflatable rubber mattress.

lilt n 1 pleasing musical quality in speaking. 2 jaunty rhythm. 3 graceful rhythmic motion. ▷ v 4 speak with a lilt. **lilting** adj.

lily n, pl **lilies** plant which grows from a bulb and has large, often white, flowers. **lily of the valley** small plant with fragrant white flowers.

limb ❶ n 1 arm, leg, or wing. 2 main branch of a tree. **out on a limb** in a dangerous or isolated position.

limber adj pliant or supple. **limber up** v loosen stiff muscles by exercising.

limbo¹ n, pl **-bos** supposed region intermediate between Heaven and Hell for the unbaptized. **in limbo** not knowing the result or next stage of something and powerless to influence it.

limbo² n, pl **-bos** West Indian dance in which dancers lean backwards to pass under a bar.

lime¹ ❶ n calcium compound used as a fertilizer or in making cement. **limelight** n glare of publicity. **limestone** n sedimentary rock used in building.

lime² n small green citrus fruit. **lime-green** adj greenish-yellow.

lime³ n deciduous tree with heart-shaped leaves and fragrant flowers.

limerick [**lim**-mer-ik] n humorous verse of five lines.

limey n US slang British person.

limit ❶ n 1 ultimate extent, degree, or amount of something. 2 boundary or edge. ▷ v **-iting, -ited** 3 restrict or confine. **limitation** n **limitless** adj **limited company** company whose shareholders' liability for debts is restricted. **limited edition** edition of a book, record, etc. which has been restricted to a particular number of copies.

limn v represent in drawing or painting.

limousine n large luxurious car.

limp¹ ❶ v 1 walk with an uneven step. 2 proceed with difficulty. ▷ n 3 limping walk.

limp² ❶ adj 1 without firmness or stiffness. 2 lacking strength or energy. **limply** adv.

limpet n shellfish which sticks tightly to rocks.

limpid adj 1 clear or transparent. 2 easy to understand. **limpidity** n.

linchpin, lynchpin n 1 pin to hold a wheel on its axle. 2 essential person or thing.

linctus n, pl **-tuses** syrupy cough medicine.

linden n same as LIME³.

line¹ ❶ n 1 long narrow mark. 2 indented mark or wrinkle. 3 continuous length without breadth. 4 boundary or limit.

━━━━━━━━━━━━━━━━━━━━ THESAURUS ━━━━━━━━━

liken v = **compare**, equate, match, parallel, relate, set beside

likeness n 1 = **resemblance**, affinity, correspondence, similarity 2 = **portrait**, depiction, effigy, image, picture, representation

likewise adv = **similarly**, in like manner, in the same way

liking n 1 = **fondness**, affection, love, soft spot, weakness 2 = **preference**, inclination, partiality, penchant, taste

limb n 1 = **part**, appendage, arm, extremity, leg, member, wing 2 = **branch**, bough, offshoot, projection, spur

limelight n = **publicity**, attention, celebrity, fame, prominence, public eye, recognition, stardom, the spotlight

limit n 1 = **end**, breaking point, deadline, ultimate 2 = **boundary**, border, edge, frontier, perimeter ▷ v 3 = **restrict**, bound, check, circumscribe, confine,

curb, ration, restrain

limitation n 3 = **restriction**, check, condition, constraint, control, curb, qualification, reservation, restraint

limited adj = **restricted**, bounded, checked, circumscribed, confined, constrained, controlled, curbed, finite

limitless adj 2 = **infinite**, boundless, countless, endless, inexhaustible, unbounded, unlimited, untold, vast

limp¹ v 1, 2 = **hobble**, falter, hop, shamble, shuffle ▷ n 3 = **lameness**, hobble

limp² adj 1 = **floppy**, drooping, flabby, flaccid, pliable, slack, soft

line¹ n 1 = **stroke**, band, groove, mark, score, scratch, streak, stripe 2 = **wrinkle**, crease, crow's foot, furrow, mark 4 = **boundary**, border, borderline, edge, frontier, limit 7 = **string**, cable, cord, rope, thread, wire 12 = **trajectory**, course, direction,

5 mark on a sports ground showing divisions of a pitch or track. **6** edge or contour of a shape. **7** string or wire for a particular use. **8** telephone connection. **9** wire or cable for transmitting electricity. **10** shipping company. **11** railway track. **12** course or direction of movement. **13** course or method of action. **14** prescribed way of thinking. **15** field of interest or activity. **16** row or queue of people. **17** class of goods. **18** row of words. **19** unit of verse. **20** military formation. ▷ *pl* **21** words of a theatrical part. **22** school punishment of writing out a sentence a specified number of times. ▷ *v* **23** mark with lines. **24** be or form a border or edge. **in line for** likely to receive. **in line with** in accordance with. **line dancing** form of dancing performed by rows of people to country and western music. **line-up** *n* people or things assembled for a particular purpose. **line up** *v* form or organize a line-up.

line² ❶ *n* **1** give a lining to. **2** cover the inside of.

lineage [**lin**-ee-ij] *n* descent from an ancestor. **lineal** *adj* in direct line of descent.

lineament *n* facial feature.

linear [**lin**-ee-er] *adj* of or in lines.

linen *n* **1** cloth or thread made from flax. **2** sheets, tablecloths, etc.

liner¹ *n* large passenger ship or aircraft.

liner² *n* something used as a lining.

linesman *n* **1** (in some sports) an official who helps the referee or umpire. **2** person who maintains railway, electricity, or telephone lines.

ling¹ *n* slender food fish.

ling² *n* heather.

linger ❶ *v* **1** delay or prolong departure. **2** continue in a weakened state for a long time before dying or disappearing. **3** spend a long time doing something.

lingering *adj*.

lingerie [**lan**-zher-ee] *n* women's underwear or nightwear.

lingo *n, pl* **-goes** *informal* foreign or unfamiliar language or jargon.

lingua franca *n, pl* **lingua francas**, **linguae francae** language used for communication between people of different mother tongues.

lingual *adj* **1** of the tongue. **2** (of a sound) made by the tongue.

linguist *n* **1** person skilled in foreign languages. **2** person who studies linguistics. **linguistic** *adj* of languages. **linguistics** *n* scientific study of language.

liniment *n* medicated liquid rubbed on the skin to relieve pain or stiffness.

lining *n* **1** layer of cloth attached to the inside of a garment etc. **2** inner covering of anything.

link ❶ *n* **1** any of the rings forming a chain. **2** person or thing forming a connection. ▷ *v* **3** connect with or as if with links. **4** connect by association. **linkage** *n* **link-up** *n* joining together of two systems or groups.

links *pl n* golf course, esp. one by the sea.

linnet *n* songbird of the finch family.

lino *n* short for LINOLEUM.

linoleum *n* floor covering of hessian or jute with a smooth decorative coating of powdered cork.

Linotype *n* ® typesetting machine which casts lines of words in one piece.

linseed *n* seed of the flax plant.

lint *n* soft material for dressing a wound.

lintel *n* horizontal beam at the top of a door or window.

lion *n* **1** large animal of the cat family, the male of which has a shaggy mane. **2** courageous person. **lioness** *n fem* **the lion's share** the biggest part. **lionize** *v* treat as a celebrity. **lion-hearted** *adj* brave.

THESAURUS

path, route, track **15** = **occupation**, area, business, calling, employment, field, job, profession, specialization, trade **16** = **row**, column, file, procession, queue, rank ▷ *pl n* **21** = **words**, part, script ▷ *v* **23** = **mark**, crease, furrow, rule, score **24** = **border**, bound, edge, fringe **in line for** = **due for**, in the running for

line² *v* = **fill**, ceil, cover, face, interline

lined *adj* **1** = **ruled**, feint **2** = **wrinkled**, furrowed, wizened, worn

line-up *n* = **arrangement**, array, row, selection, team

linger *v* **1** = **stay**, hang around, loiter, remain, stop, tarry, wait **3** = **delay**, dally, dawdle, drag one's feet *or* heels, idle, take one's time

link *n* **2** = **connection**, affinity, association, attachment, bond, relationship, tie-up ▷ *v* **3** = **connect**, attach, bind, couple, fasten, join, tie, unite **4** = **associate**, bracket, connect, identify, relate

lip ❶ n 1 either of the fleshy edges of the mouth. 2 rim of a jug etc. 3 slang impudence. **lip-reading** n method of understanding speech by interpreting lip movements. **lip-read** v **lip service** insincere tribute or respect. **lipstick** n cosmetic in stick form, for colouring the lips.

liposuction n surgical operation in which body fat is removed.

liquefy v **-fying, -fied** make or become liquid. **liquefaction** n.

liqueur [lik-**cure**] n flavoured and sweetened alcoholic spirit.

liquid ❶ n 1 substance in a physical state which can change shape but not size. ▷ adj 2 of or being a liquid. 3 transparent and shining. 4 flowing smoothly. 5 (of assets) in the form of money or easily converted into money. **liquidize** v make or become liquid. **liquidizer** n kitchen appliance that liquidizes food. **liquidity** n state of being able to meet financial obligations.

liquidate ❶ v 1 pay (a debt). 2 dissolve a company and share its assets among creditors. 3 wipe out or kill. **liquidation** n **liquidator** n official appointed to liquidate a business.

liquor ❶ n 1 alcoholic drink, esp. spirits. 2 liquid in which food has been cooked.

liquorice [**lik**-ker-iss] n black substance used in medicine and as a sweet.

lira n, pl **-re, -ras** monetary unit of Turkey and formerly of Italy.

lisle [rhymes with **mile**] n strong fine cotton thread or fabric.

lisp n 1 speech defect in which s and z are pronounced th. ▷ v 2 speak or utter with a lisp.

lissom, lissome adj supple, agile.

list¹ ❶ n 1 item-by-item record of names or things, usu. written one below another. ▷ v 2 make a list of. 3 include in a list. **listed building** building protected from demolition or alteration because of its historical or architectural interest.

list² ❶ v 1 (of a ship) lean to one side. ▷ n 2 leaning to one side.

listen ❶ v 1 concentrate on hearing something. 2 heed or pay attention to. **listener** n **listen in** v listen secretly, eavesdrop.

listeriosis n dangerous form of food poisoning.

listing n 1 list or an entry in a list. ▷ pl 2 lists of films, concerts, etc. printed in newspapers and magazines.

listless ❶ adj lacking interest or energy. **listlessly** adv.

lists pl n field of combat in a tournament. **enter the lists** engage in a conflict.

lit v past of LIGHT¹ or LIGHT².

litany n, pl **-nies 1** prayer with responses from the congregation. 2 any tedious recital.

literacy ❶ n ability to read and write.

literal ❶ adj 1 according to the explicit meaning of a word or text, not figurative. 2 (of a translation) word for word. 3 dull or unimaginative. 4 actual, true. **literally** adv.

literary ❶ adj 1 of or knowledgeable about literature. 2 (of a word) formal,

⸻ **THESAURUS** ⸻

lip n 2 = **edge**, brim, brink, margin, rim 3 Sl = **impudence**, backchat (inf), cheek (inf), effrontery, impertinence, insolence

liquid n 1 = **fluid**, juice, solution ▷ adj 2 = **fluid**, aqueous, flowing, melted, molten, runny 5 Of assets = **convertible**, negotiable

liquidate v 1 = **pay**, clear, discharge, honour, pay off, settle, square 2 = **dissolve**, abolish, annul, cancel, terminate 3 = **kill**, destroy, dispatch, eliminate, exterminate, get rid of, murder, wipe out (inf)

liquor n 1 = **alcohol**, booze (inf), drink, hard stuff (inf), spirits, strong drink 2 = **juice**, broth, extract, liquid, stock

list¹ n 1 = **inventory**, catalogue, directory, index, record, register, roll,

series, tally ▷ v 2, 3 = **itemize**, catalogue, enter, enumerate, record, register, tabulate

list² v 1 = **lean**, careen, heel over, incline, tilt, tip ▷ n 2 = **tilt**, cant, leaning, slant

listen v 1 = **hear**, attend, lend an ear, prick up one's ears 2 = **pay attention**, heed, mind, obey, observe, take notice

listless adj = **languid**, apathetic, indifferent, indolent, lethargic, sluggish

literacy n = **education**, knowledge, learning

literal adj 1 = **explicit**, precise, strict 2 = **exact**, accurate, close, faithful, verbatim, word for word 4 = **actual**, bona fide, genuine, plain, real, simple, true, unvarnished

literary adj 1 = **well-read**, bookish, erudite, formal, learned, scholarly not colloquial. **literariness** n.

literate ❶ adj **1** able to read and write.
2 educated. **literati** pl n literary people.

literature ❶ n **1** written works such as
novels, plays, and poetry. **2** books and
writings of a country, period, or subject.
3 printed matter on a subject.

lithe ❶ adj flexible or supple, pliant.

lithium n Chemistry chemical element,
the lightest known metal.

litho n, pl **-thos 1** short for LITHOGRAPH.
▷ adj **2** short for LITHOGRAPHIC.

lithography [lith-**og**-ra-fee] n method
of printing from a metal or stone
surface in which the printing areas are
made receptive to ink. **lithograph** n
1 print made by lithography. ▷ v
2 reproduce by lithography.
lithographer n **lithographic** adj.

litigate ❶ v **1** bring or contest a law suit.
2 engage in legal action. **litigant** n
person involved in a lawsuit. **litigation**
n legal action. **litigious** [lit-**ij**-uss] adj
frequently going to law.

litmus n blue dye turned red by acids and
restored to blue by alkalis. **litmus
paper** paper impregnated with litmus.
litmus test something which is
regarded as a simple and accurate test
of a particular thing.

litotes [lie-**toe**-teez] n ironical
understatement used for effect.

litre n unit of liquid measure equal to 1.76
pints.

litter ❶ n **1** untidy rubbish dropped in
public places. **2** group of young animals
produced at one birth. **3** straw etc. as
bedding for an animal. **4** dry material
to absorb a cat's excrement. **5** bed or

seat on parallel sticks for carrying
people. ▷ v **6** strew with litter. **7** scatter
or be scattered about untidily. **8** give
birth to young.

little ❶ adj **1** small or smaller than
average. **2** young. ▷ adv **3** not a lot.
4 hardly. **5** not much or often. ▷ n
6 small amount, extent, or duration.
little by little by small degrees.

littoral adj **1** of or by the seashore. ▷ n
2 coastal district.

liturgy n, pl **-gies** prescribed form of
public worship. **liturgical** adj.

live¹ ❶ v **1** be alive. **2** remain in life or
existence. **3** exist in a specified way,
e.g. we live well. **4** reside. **5** continue or
last. **6** subsist. **7** enjoy life to the full.
liver n person who lives in a specified
way. **live down** v wait till people forget
a past mistake or misdeed. **live-in** adj
resident. **live together** v (of an
unmarried couple) share a house and
have a sexual relationship. **live up to** v
meet (expectations). **live with** v
tolerate.

live² ❶ adj **1** living, alive. **2** (of a
broadcast) transmitted during the
actual performance. **3** (of a
performance) done in front of an
audience. **4** (of a wire, circuit, etc.)
carrying an electric current. **5** causing
interest or controversy. **6** capable of
exploding. **7** glowing or burning. ▷ adv
8 in the form of a live performance.
lively adj **1** full of life or vigour.
2 animated. **3** vivid. **liveliness** n **liven
up** v make (more) lively. **live wire
1** informal energetic person. **2** wire
carrying an electric current.

THESAURUS

literate adj **2** = **educated**, informed,
knowledgeable

literature n = **writings**, lore

lithe adj = **supple**, flexible, limber,
lissom(e), loose-limbed, pliable

litigant n = **claimant**, party, plaintiff

litigate v = **sue**, go to court, press
charges, prosecute

litigation n = **lawsuit**, action, case,
prosecution

litter n **1** = **rubbish**, debris, detritus,
garbage (chiefly US), muck, refuse, trash
2 = **brood**, offspring, progeny, young
▷ v **6** = **clutter**, derange, disarrange,
disorder, mess up, muss (US & Canad)
7 = **scatter**, strew

little adj **1** = **small**, diminutive,
miniature, minute, petite, short, tiny,

wee **2** = **young**, babyish, immature,
infant, undeveloped ▷ adv **4** = **hardly**,
barely **5** = **rarely**, hardly ever, not
often, scarcely, seldom ▷ n **6** = **bit**,
fragment, hint, particle, speck, spot,
touch, trace

live¹ v **1** = **exist**, be, be alive, breathe
4 = **dwell**, abide, inhabit, lodge,
occupy, reside, settle **5** = **persist**, last,
prevail **6** = **survive**, endure, get along,
make ends meet, subsist, support
oneself **7** = **thrive**, flourish, prosper

live² adj **1** = **living**, alive, animate,
breathing **5** = **topical**, burning,
controversial, current, hot, pertinent,
pressing, prevalent **7** = **burning**, active,
alight, blazing, glowing, hot, ignited,
smouldering

livelihood ❶ *n* occupation or employment.

liver *n* **1** organ secreting bile. **2** animal liver as food. **liverish** *adj* **1** having a disorder of the liver. **2** touchy or irritable.

liverwort *n* plant resembling seaweed or leafy moss.

livery ❶ *n, pl* **-eries 1** distinctive dress, esp. of a servant or servants. **2** distinctive design or colours of a company. **liveried** *adj* **livery stable** stable where horses are kept at a charge or hired out.

lives *n* plural of LIFE.

livestock *n* farm animals.

livid ❶ *adj* **1** *informal* angry or furious. **2** bluish-grey.

living ❶ *adj* **1** possessing life, not dead or inanimate. **2** currently in use or existing. **3** of everyday life, e.g. *living conditions*. ▷ *n* **4** condition of being alive. **5** manner of life. **6** financial means. **7** church office yielding annual income. **living room** room in a house used for relaxation and entertainment. **living wage** wage adequate for a worker to live on in reasonable comfort.

lizard *n* four-footed reptile with a long body and tail.

llama *n* woolly animal of the camel family used as a beast of burden in S America.

LLB Bachelor of Laws.

lo *interj* old-fashioned look!

loach *n* carplike freshwater fish.

load ❶ *n* **1** burden or weight. **2** amount carried. **3** source of worry. **4** amount of electrical energy drawn from a source. ▷ *pl* **5** *informal* lots. ▷ *v* **6** put a load on or into. **7** burden or oppress. **8** supply in abundance. **9** cause to be biased. **10** put ammunition into (a weapon). **11** put film into (a camera). **12** transfer (a program) into computer memory. **a load of** *informal* a quantity of. **loaded** *adj* **1** (of a question) containing a hidden trap or implication. **2** (of dice) dishonestly weighted. **3** *slang* wealthy. **4** *slang* drunk.

loaf¹ ❶ *n, pl* **loaves 1** shaped mass of baked bread. **2** shaped mass of food. **3** *slang* head, esp. as the source of common sense, e.g. *use your loaf*.

loaf² ❶ *v* idle, loiter. **loafer** *n*.

loam *n* fertile soil.

loan ❶ *n* **1** money lent at interest. **2** lending. **3** thing lent. ▷ *v* **4** lend. **loan shark** person who lends money at an extremely high interest rate.

loath, loth ❶ [rhymes with **both**] *adj* unwilling or reluctant (to).
- ● USAGE NOTE
- ● Distinguish between *loath* 'reluctant'
- ● and *loathe* 'be disgusted by'.

loathe ❶ *v* hate, be disgusted by.

———————————————— THESAURUS ————————

livelihood *n* = **occupation**, bread and butter (*inf*), employment, job, living, work, yakka (*Aust & NZ inf*)

lively *adj* **1** = **vigorous**, active, agile, alert, brisk, energetic, keen, perky, quick, sprightly **2** = **animated**, cheerful, chirpy (*inf*), sparky, spirited, upbeat (*inf*), vivacious **3** = **vivid**, bright, colourful, exciting, forceful, invigorating, refreshing, stimulating

liven up *v* = **stir**, animate, brighten, buck up (*inf*), enliven, perk up, rouse

livery *n* **1** = **costume**, attire, clothing, dress, garb, regalia, suit, uniform

livid *adj* **1** *Inf* = **angry**, beside oneself, enraged, fuming, furious, incensed, indignant, infuriated, outraged **2** = **discoloured**, black-and-blue, bruised, contused, purple

living *adj* **1** = **alive**, active, breathing, existing **2** = **current**, active, contemporary, extant, in use ▷ *n* **4** = **existence**, being, existing, life,

subsistence **5** = **lifestyle**, way of life

load *n* **1** = **cargo**, consignment, freight, shipment **3** = **burden**, albatross, encumbrance, millstone, onus, trouble, weight, worry ▷ *v* **6** = **fill**, cram, freight, heap, pack, pile, stack, stuff **7** = **burden**, encumber, oppress, saddle with, weigh down, worry **10** *Firearms* = **make ready**, charge, prime

loaded *adj* **1** = **tricky**, artful, insidious, manipulative, prejudicial **3** *Sl* = **rich**, affluent, flush (*inf*), moneyed, wealthy, well-heeled (*inf*), well off, well-to-do

loaf¹ *n* **2** = **lump**, block, cake, cube, slab **3** *Sl* = **head**, gumption (*Brit inf*), nous (*Brit sl*), sense

loaf² *v* = **idle**, laze, lie around, loiter, lounge around, take it easy

loan *n* **1-3** = **advance**, credit ▷ *v* **4** = **lend**, advance, let out

loath, loth *adj* = **unwilling**, averse, disinclined, opposed, reluctant

loathe *v* = **hate**, abhor, abominate,

loathing n **loathsome** adj.

loaves n plural of LOAF[1].

lob Sport ▷ n **1** ball struck or thrown in a high arc. ▷ v **lobbing**, **lobbed 2** strike or throw (a ball) in a high arc.

lobby ❶ n, pl **-bies 1** corridor into which rooms open. **2** group which tries to influence legislators. **3** hall in a legislative building to which the public has access. ▷ v **-bying**, **-bied 4** try to influence (legislators) in the formulation of policy. **lobbyist** n.

lobe n **1** rounded projection. **2** soft hanging part of the ear. **3** subdivision of a body organ. **lobed** adj.

lobelia n garden plant with blue, red, or white flowers.

lobotomy n, pl **-mies** surgical incision into a lobe of the brain to treat mental disorders.

lobster n shellfish with a long tail and claws, which turns red when boiled. **lobster pot** basket-like trap for catching lobsters.

local ❶ adj **1** of or existing in a particular place. **2** confined to a particular place. ▷ n **3** person belonging to a particular district. **4** informal pub close to one's home. **locally** adv **locality** n **1** neighbourhood or area. **2** site. **localize** v restrict to a particular place. **locale** [loh-**kahl**] n scene of an event. **local anaesthetic** anaesthetic which produces loss of feeling in one part of the body. **local authority** governing body of a county or district. **local**

government government of towns, counties, and districts by locally elected political bodies.

locate ❶ v **1** discover the whereabouts of. **2** situate or place. **location** n **1** site or position. **2** act of discovering where something is. **3** site of a film production away from the studio. **4** S Afr Black African or coloured township.

loch n Scot **1** lake. **2** long narrow bay.

loci n plural of LOCUS.

lock[1] ❶ n **1** appliance for fastening a door, case, etc. **2** section of a canal shut off by gates between which the water level can be altered to aid boats moving from one level to another. **3** extent to which a vehicle's front wheels will turn. **4** interlocking of parts. **5** mechanism for firing a gun. **6** wrestling hold. ▷ v **7** fasten or become fastened securely. **8** become or cause to become fixed or united. **9** become or cause to become immovable. **10** embrace closely. **lockout** n closing of a workplace by an employer to force workers to accept terms. **locksmith** n person who makes and mends locks. **lockup** n **1** prison. **2** garage or storage place away from the main premises. **lock up** v **1** imprison. **2** secure (a building) by locking.

lock[2] ❶ n strand of hair.

locker n small cupboard with a lock.

locket n small hinged pendant for a portrait etc.

lockjaw n tetanus.

despise, detest, dislike

loathing n = **hatred**, abhorrence, antipathy, aversion, detestation, disgust, repugnance, repulsion, revulsion

loathsome adj = **hateful**, abhorrent, detestable, disgusting, nauseating, obnoxious, odious, offensive, repugnant, repulsive, revolting, vile

lobby n **1** = **corridor**, entrance hall, foyer, hallway, passage, porch, vestibule **2** = **pressure group** ▷ v **4** = **campaign**, influence, persuade, press, pressure, promote, push, urge

local adj **1** = **regional**, provincial **2** = **restricted**, confined, limited ▷ n **3** = **resident**, inhabitant, native

locality n **1** = **neighbourhood**, area, district, neck of the woods (inf), region, vicinity **2** = **site**, locale, location, place,

position, scene, setting, spot

localize v = **restrict**, circumscribe, confine, contain, delimit, limit

locate v **1** = **find**, come across, detect, discover, pin down, pinpoint, track down, unearth **2** = **place**, establish, fix, put, seat, set, settle, situate

location n **1** = **site**, locale, place, point, position, situation, spot, venue

lock[1] n **1** = **fastening**, bolt, clasp, padlock ▷ v **7** = **fasten**, bolt, close, seal, secure, shut **8** = **unite**, engage, entangle, entwine, join, link **9** = **clench**, freeze **10** = **embrace**, clasp, clutch, encircle, enclose, grasp, hug, press

lock[2] n = **strand**, curl, ringlet, tress, tuft

lockup n **1** = **prison**, cell, jail or gaol

lock up v **1** = **imprison**, cage, confine, detain, incarcerate, jail, put behind bars, shut up

locomotive *n* 1 self-propelled engine for pulling trains. ▷ *adj* 2 of locomotion. **locomotion** *n* action or power of moving.

locum *n* temporary stand-in for a doctor or clergyman.

locus [**loh**-kuss] *n*, *pl* **loci** [**loh**-sigh] 1 area or place where something happens. 2 *Maths* set of points or lines satisfying one or more specified conditions.

locust *n* 1 destructive African insect that flies in swarms and eats crops. 2 N American tree with prickly branches.

lode *n* vein of ore. **lodestar** *n* star used in navigation or astronomy as a point of reference. **lodestone** *n* magnetic iron ore.

lodge ❶ *n* 1 gatekeeper's house. 2 house or cabin used occasionally by hunters, skiers, etc. 3 porters' room in a university or college. 4 local branch of some societies. 5 beaver's home. ▷ *v* 6 live in another's house at a fixed charge. 7 stick or become stuck (in a place). 8 leave for safety or storage. 9 make (a complaint etc.) formally. **lodger** *n* **lodging** *n* 1 temporary residence. ▷ *pl* 2 rented room or rooms in another person's house.

loft *n* 1 space between the top storey and roof of a building. 2 gallery in a church etc. 3 room over a stable used to store hay. ▷ *v* 4 *Sport* strike, throw, or kick (a ball) high into the air.

lofty ❶ *adj* **loftier, loftiest** 1 of great height. 2 exalted or noble. 3 haughty. **loftily** *adv* haughtily. **loftiness** *n*.

log¹ ❶ *n* 1 portion of a felled tree stripped of branches. 2 detailed record of a

journey of a ship, aircraft, etc. ▷ *v* **logging, logged** 3 saw logs from a tree. 4 record in a log. **logging** *n* work of cutting and transporting logs. **logbook** *n* book recording the details about a car or a ship's journeys. **log in, out** *v* gain entrance to or leave a computer system by keying in a special command.

log² *n* short for LOGARITHM.

loganberry *n* purplish-red fruit, similar to a raspberry.

logarithm *n* one of a series of arithmetical functions used to make certain calculations easier. **logarithmic** *adj*.

loggerheads ❶ *pl n* **at loggerheads** quarrelling, disputing.

loggia [**loj**-ya] *n* covered gallery at the side of a building.

logic ❶ *n* 1 philosophy of reasoning. 2 particular system of reasoning. 3 reasoned thought or argument. **logical** *adj* 1 of logic. 2 capable of or using clear valid reasoning. 3 reasonable. **logically** *adv* **logician** *n*.

logistics *n* detailed planning and organization of a large, esp. military, operation. **logistical, logistic** *adj* **logistically** *adv*.

logo [**loh**-go] *n*, *pl* **-os** company emblem or similar device.

loin *n* 1 part of the body between the ribs and the hips. 2 cut of meat from this part of an animal. ▷ *pl* 3 hips and inner thighs. 4 *euphemistic* genitals. **loincloth** *n* piece of cloth covering the loins only.

loiter ❶ *v* stand or wait aimlessly or idly.

loll ❶ *v* 1 lounge lazily. 2 hang loosely.

━━━━━━━━━━━━━━━━━━━━━━━━━━━━━ THESAURUS ━━━━━

lodge *n* 1 = **gatehouse** 2 = **cabin**, chalet, cottage, hut, shelter 4 = **society**, branch, chapter, club, group ▷ *v* 6 = **stay**, board, room 7 = **stick**, come to rest, imbed, implant 9 = **register**, file, put on record, submit

lodger *n* 6 = **tenant**, boarder, paying guest, resident

lodging *n* 1 = **accommodation**, residence, shelter 2 *pl* = **rooms**, abode, apartments, digs (*Brit inf*), quarters

lofty *adj* 1 = **high**, elevated, raised, soaring, towering 2 = **noble**, dignified, distinguished, elevated, exalted, grand, illustrious, renowned 3 = **haughty**, arrogant, condescending, disdainful, patronizing, proud, supercilious

log¹ *n* 1 = **stump**, block, chunk, trunk 2 = **record**, account, journal, logbook ▷ *v* 3 = **chop**, cut, fell, hew 4 = **record**, chart, note, register, set down

loggerheads *pl n* **at loggerheads** = **quarrelling**, at daggers drawn, at each other's throats, at odds, feuding, in dispute, opposed

logic *n* 3 = **reason**, good sense, sense

logical *adj* 2 = **rational**, clear, cogent, coherent, consistent, sound, valid, well-organized 3 = **reasonable**, plausible, sensible, wise

loiter *v* = **linger**, dally, dawdle, dilly-dally (*inf*), hang about or around, idle, loaf, skulk

loll *v* 1 = **lounge**, loaf, outspan (*S Afr*),

lollipop *n* **1** boiled sweet on a small wooden stick. **2** ice lolly. **lollipop man, lady** *informal* person holding a circular sign on a pole, who controls traffic so that children may cross the road safely.

lollop *v* move clumsily.

lolly *n, pl* **-ies** **1** *informal* lollipop or ice lolly. **2** *Aust & NZ informal* sweet. **3** *slang* money.

lone ❶ *adj* **1** solitary. **2** isolated. **lonely** *adj* **1** sad because alone. **2** resulting from being alone. **3** unfrequented. **loneliness** *n* **loner** *n informal* person who prefers to be alone.

lonesome ❶ *adj Chiefly US & Canad* another word for LONELY.

long¹ ❶ *adj* **1** having length, esp. great length, in space or time. ▷ *adv* **2** for a certain time. **3** for an extensive period. **4** a considerable amount of time, e.g. *long ago*. **longways, longwise** *adv* lengthways. **longboat** *n* largest boat carried on a ship. **longbow** *n* large powerful bow. **long-distance** *adj* going between places far apart. **long face** glum expression. **longhand** *n* ordinary writing, not shorthand or typing. **long johns** *informal* long underpants. **long jump** contest of jumping the farthest distance from a fixed mark. **long-life** *adj* (of milk, batteries, etc.) lasting longer than the regular kind. **long-lived** *adj* living or lasting for a long

time. **long-range** *adj* **1** extending into the future. **2** (of vehicles, weapons, etc.) designed to cover great distances. **long shot** competitor, undertaking, or bet with little chance of success. **long-sighted** *adj* able to see distant objects in focus but not nearby ones. **long-standing** *adj* existing for a long time. **long-suffering** *adj* enduring trouble or unhappiness without complaint. **long-term** *adj* lasting or effective for a long time. **long wave** radio wave with a wavelength of over 1000 metres. **long-winded** *adj* speaking or writing at tedious length.

long² ❶ *v* have a strong desire (for). **longing** *n* yearning. **longingly** *adv*.

long. longitude.

longevity [lon-**jev**-it-ee] *n* long life.

longitude *n* distance east or west from a standard meridian. **longitudinal** *adj* **1** of length or longitude. **2** lengthways.

longshoreman *n* a man employed in the loading or unloading of ships.

loo *n informal* toilet.

loofah *n* sponge made from the dried pod of a gourd.

look ❶ *v* **1** direct the eyes or attention (towards). **2** have the appearance of being. **3** face in a particular direction. **4** search (for). **5** hope (for). ▷ *n* **6** instance of looking. **7** view or sight. **8** (often pl) appearance. **look after** *v*

---

recline, relax, slouch, slump, sprawl **2 = droop**, dangle, drop, flap, flop, hang, sag

lone *adj* **1 = solitary**, one, only, single, sole, unaccompanied

loneliness *n* = **solitude**, desolation, isolation, seclusion

lonely *adj* **1 = alone**, abandoned, companionless, destitute, forlorn, forsaken, friendless, isolated, lone, lonesome (*chiefly US & Canad*), single, solitary, withdrawn **3 = desolate**, deserted, godforsaken, isolated, out-of-the-way, remote, secluded, unfrequented, uninhabited

loner *n Inf* = **individualist**, lone wolf, maverick, outsider, recluse

lonesome *adj* (*chiefly US & Canad*) = **lonely**, companionless, desolate, dreary, forlorn, friendless, gloomy

long¹ *adj* **1 a = elongated**, expanded, extended, extensive, far-reaching, lengthy, spread out, stretched **b = prolonged**, interminable, lengthy,

lingering, long-drawn-out, protracted, sustained

long² *v* = **desire**, crave, hanker, itch, lust, pine, want, wish, yearn

longing *n* = **desire**, ambition, aspiration, craving, hope, itch, thirst, urge, wish, yearning, yen (*inf*)

long-lived *adj* = **long-lasting**, enduring

long-standing *adj* = **established**, abiding, enduring, fixed, long-established, long-lasting, time-honoured

long-suffering *adj* = **uncomplaining**, easy-going, forbearing, forgiving, patient, resigned, stoical, tolerant

long-winded *adj* = **rambling**, lengthy, long-drawn-out, prolix, prolonged, repetitious, tedious, tiresome, verbose, wordy

look *v* **1 = see**, behold (*arch*), consider, contemplate, examine, eye, gaze, glance, observe, scan, study, survey, view, watch **2 = seem**, appear, look like, strike one as **3 = face**, front,

take care of. **lookalike** *n* person who is the double of another. **look down on** *v* treat as inferior or unimportant. **look forward to** *v* anticipate with pleasure. **look-in** *n informal* chance to participate. **look in** *v informal* pay a short visit. **looking glass** mirror. **look on** *v* **1** be a spectator. **2** consider or regard. **lookout** *n* **1** act of watching for danger or for an opportunity. **2** guard. **3** place for watching. **4** *informal* worry or concern. **5** chances or prospect. **look out** *v* be careful. **look up** *v* **1** discover or confirm by checking in a book. **2** improve. **3** visit. **look up to** *v* respect.

loom¹ *n* machine for weaving cloth.

loom² ❶ *v* **1** appear dimly. **2** seem ominously close.

loon *n* diving bird.

loonie *n Canad sl* **1** a Canadian dollar coin with a loon bird on one of its faces. **2** the Canadian currency.

loony *slang* ▷ *adj* **loonier, looniest 1** foolish or insane. ▷ *n, pl* **loonies 2** foolish or insane person.

loop ❶ *n* **1** rounded shape made by a curved line or rope crossing itself. **2** closed circuit through which an electronic signal can circulate. **3** continuous strip of film or tape. **4** set of instructions to be repeatedly performed in a computer program. ▷ *v* **5** form or fasten with a loop. **loop the loop** fly or be flown in a complete vertical circle. **loophole** *n* means of evading a rule without breaking it.

loose ❶ *adj* **1** not tight, fastened, fixed, or tense. **2** vague. **3** dissolute or promiscuous. ▷ *adv* **4** in a loose manner. ▷ *v* **5** free. **6** unfasten. **7** slacken. **8** let fly (an arrow, bullet, etc.). **at a loose end** bored, with nothing to do. **on the loose** free from confinement. **loosely** *adv* **looseness** *n* **loosen** *v* make loose. **loosen up** *v* relax, stop worrying. **loose-leaf** *adj* allowing the addition or removal of pages.

loot ❶ *n, v* **1** plunder. ▷ *n* **2** *informal* money. **looter** *n* **looting** *n*.

lop *v* **lopping, lopped 1** cut away twigs and branches. **2** chop off.

lope *v* **1** run with long easy strides. ▷ *n* **2** loping stride.

---

overlook **4** = **search**, forage, fossick (*Aust & NZ*), hunt, seek **5** = **hope**, anticipate, await, expect, reckon on ▷ *n* **7** = **glimpse**, examination, gaze, glance, inspection, observation, peek, sight, view **8** (often *pl*) = **appearance**, air, aspect, bearing, countenance, demeanour, expression, manner, semblance

look after *v* = **take care of**, attend to, care for, guard, keep an eye on, mind, nurse, protect, supervise, take charge of, tend

look down on *v* = **disdain**, contemn, despise, scorn, sneer, spurn

look forward to *v* = **anticipate**, await, expect, hope for, long for, look for, wait for

lookout *n* **1** = **watch**, guard, readiness, vigil **2** = **watchman**, guard, sentinel, sentry **3** = **watchtower**, observation post, observatory, post **4** *Inf* = **concern**, business, worry

look out *v* = **be careful**, beware, keep an eye out, pay attention, watch out

look up *v* **1** = **research**, find, hunt for, search for, seek out, track down **2** = **improve**, get better, perk up, pick up, progress, shape up (*inf*) **3** = **visit**, call on, drop in on (*inf*), look in on **look**

up to *v* = **respect**, admire, defer to, esteem, honour, revere

loom² *v* **1** = **appear**, bulk, emerge, hover, take shape **2** = **threaten**, impend, menace

loop *n* **1** = **curve**, circle, coil, curl, ring, spiral, twirl, twist, whorl ▷ *v* **5** = **twist**, coil, curl, knot, roll, spiral, turn, wind round

loophole *n* = **let-out**, escape, excuse

loose *adj* **1 a** = **slack**, easy, relaxed, sloppy **b** = **free**, insecure, unattached, unbound, unfastened, unfettered, unrestricted, untied **2** = **vague**, ill-defined, imprecise, inaccurate, indistinct, inexact, rambling, random **3** = **promiscuous**, abandoned, debauched, dissipated, dissolute, fast, immoral, profligate ▷ *v* **5, 6** = **free**, detach, disconnect, liberate, release, set free, unfasten, unleash, untie

loosen *v* **a** = **free**, liberate, release, set free **b** = **untie**, detach, separate, undo, unloose

loosen up *v* = **relax**, ease up *or* off, go easy (*inf*), let up, outspan (*S Afr*), soften

loot *n* **1** = **plunder**, booty, goods, haul, prize, spoils, swag (*sl*) ▷ *v* **1** = **plunder**, despoil, pillage, raid, ransack, ravage,

lop-eared *adj* having drooping ears.
lopsided ❶ *adj* greater in height, weight, or size on one side.
loquacious *adj* talkative. **loquacity** *n*.
lord ❶ *n* **1** person with power over others, such as a monarch or master. **2** male member of the nobility. **3** *History* feudal superior. **4** (**L-**) God or Jesus. **5** (**L-**) title given to certain male officials and peers. **House of Lords** unelected upper chamber of the British parliament. **lord it over** act in a superior manner towards. **the Lord's Prayer** prayer taught by Christ to his disciples. **lordly** *adj* imperious, proud. **Lordship** *n* title of some male officials and peers.
lore ❶ *n* body of traditions on a subject.
lorgnette [lor-**nyet**] *n* pair of spectacles mounted on a long handle.
lorry *n, pl* **-ries** large vehicle for transporting loads by road.
lose ❶ *v* **losing, lost 1** come to be without, esp. by accident or carelessness. **2** fail to keep or maintain. **3** be deprived of. **4** get rid of. **5** fail to get or make use of. **6** be defeated in a competition etc. **7** fail to perceive or understand. **8** go astray or allow to go astray. **9** be or become engrossed, e.g. *lost in thought.* **10** die or be destroyed. **11** (of a clock etc.) run slow (by a specified amount). **loser** *n* **1** person or

thing that loses. **2** *informal* person who seems destined to fail. **loss** *n* **1** losing. **2** that which is lost. **lost** *adj* unable to find one's way.

● **SPELLING TIP**
● The verb **lose** (*I don't want to lose my*
● *hair*) should not be confused with
● **loose**, which, although existing
● as a verb, is more often used as an
● adjective (*a loose tooth*) or adverb (*to*
● *work loose*).

loss ❶ *n* **1** losing. **2** that which is lost. **3** damage resulting from losing. **at a loss 1** confused or bewildered. **2** not earning enough to cover costs. **loss leader** item sold at a loss to attract customers.
lost ❶ *v* **1** past of LOSE. ▷ *adj* **2** unable to find one's way. **3** unable to be found. **4** bewildered or confused. **5** (foll. by *on*) not used, noticed, or understood by. **6** no longer possessed or existing.
lot ❶ *pron* **1** great number. ▷ *n* **2** collection of people or things. **3** fate or destiny. **4** one of a set of objects drawn at random to make a selection or choice. **5** item at auction. **6** *US* area of land. ▷ *pl* **7** *informal* great numbers or quantities. **a lot** *informal* a great deal. **bad lot** disreputable person. **the lot** entire amount or number.
loth ❶ *adj* same as LOATH.
lotion ❶ *n* medical or cosmetic liquid for

rifle, rob, sack
lopsided *adj* = **crooked**, askew, asymmetrical, awry, cockeyed, disproportionate, skewwhiff (*Brit inf*), squint, unbalanced, uneven, warped
lord *n* **1** = **master**, commander, governor, leader, liege, overlord, ruler, superior **2** = **nobleman**, earl, noble, peer, viscount **4** (with cap.) = **Jesus Christ**, Christ, God, Jehovah, the Almighty **lord it over** = **order around**, boss around (*inf*), domineer, pull rank, put on airs, swagger
lordly *adj* = **proud**, arrogant, condescending, disdainful, domineering, haughty, high-handed, imperious, lofty, overbearing
lore *n* = **traditions**, beliefs, doctrine, sayings, teaching, wisdom
lose *v* **1** = **mislay**, drop, forget, misplace **2, 5** = **forfeit**, miss, pass up (*inf*), yield **3** = **be deprived of 6** = **be defeated**, come to grief, lose out
loser *n* = **failure**, also-ran, dud (*inf*),

flop (*inf*)
loss *n* **1** = **losing**, defeat, failure, forfeiture, mislaying, squandering, waste **2** = **deficit**, debit, debt, deficiency, depletion **3** = **damage**, cost, destruction, harm, hurt, injury, ruin **at a loss 1** = **confused**, at one's wits' end, baffled, bewildered, helpless, nonplussed, perplexed, puzzled, stumped
lost *adj* **2, 4** = **off-course**, adrift, astray, at sea, disoriented, off-track **3** = **missing**, disappeared, mislaid, misplaced, vanished
lot *n* **2** = **collection**, assortment, batch, bunch (*inf*), consignment, crowd, group, quantity, set **3** = **destiny**, accident, chance, doom, fate, fortune **a lot** *Inf* = **plenty**, abundance, a great deal, heap(s), load(s) (*inf*), masses (*inf*), piles (*inf*), scores, stack(s)
loth see LOATH.
lotion *n* = **cream**, balm, embrocation, liniment, salve, solution

use on the skin.

lottery ❶ *n, pl* **-teries 1** method of raising money by selling tickets that win prizes by chance. **2** gamble.

lotto *n* game of chance like bingo.

lotus *n* **1** legendary plant whose fruit induces forgetfulness. **2** Egyptian water lily.

loud ❶ *adj* **1** relatively great in volume. **2** capable of making much noise. **3** insistent and emphatic. **4** unpleasantly patterned or colourful. **loudly** *adv* **loudness** *n* **loudspeaker** *n* instrument for converting electrical signals into sound.

lough *n Irish* loch.

lounge ❶ *n* **1** living room in a private house. **2** (also **lounge bar**) more expensive bar in a pub. **3** area for waiting in an airport. ▷ *v* **4** sit, lie, or stand in a relaxed manner. **lounge suit** man's suit for daytime wear.

lour *v* same as LOWER².

louse *n* **1** *pl* **lice** wingless parasitic insect. **2** *pl* **louses** unpleasant person. **lousy** *adj* **lousier, lousiest 1** *slang* mean or unpleasant. **2** bad, inferior. **3** unwell. **4** infested with lice.

lout ❶ *n* crude, oafish, or aggressive person. **loutish** *adj*.

louvre [**loo**-ver] *n* one of a set of parallel slats slanted to admit air but not rain. **louvred** *adj*.

lovage *n* European plant used for flavouring food.

love ❶ *v* **1** have a great affection for. **2** feel sexual passion for. **3** enjoy (something) very much. ▷ *n* **4** great affection. **5** sexual passion. **6** wholehearted liking for something. **7** beloved person. **8** *Tennis, Squash, etc.* score of nothing. **fall in love** become in love. **in love (with)** feeling a strong emotional (and sexual) attraction (for). **make love (to)** have sexual intercourse (with). **lovable, loveable** *adj* **loveless** *adj* **lovely** *adj* **-lier, -liest 1** very attractive. **2** highly enjoyable. **lover** *n* **1** person having a sexual relationship outside marriage. **2** person in love. **3** someone who loves a specified person or thing. **loving** *adj* affectionate, tender. **lovingly** *adv* **love affair** romantic or sexual relationship between two people who are not married to each other. **lovebird** *n* small parrot. **love child** *euphemistic* child of an unmarried couple. **love life** person's romantic or sexual relationships. **lovelorn** *adj* miserable because of unhappiness in love. **lovemaking** *n*.

low[1] ❶ *adj* **1** not tall, high, or elevated. **2** of little or less than the usual amount, degree, quality, or cost. **3** coarse or vulgar. **4** dejected. **5** ill. **6** not loud. **7** deep in pitch. **8** (of a gear) providing a

———————————————— THESAURUS ————————————————

lottery *n* **1** = **raffle**, draw, sweepstake **2** = **gamble**, chance, hazard, risk, toss-up (*inf*)

loud *adj* **1** = **noisy**, blaring, booming, clamorous, deafening, ear-splitting, forte (*Music*), resounding, thundering, tumultuous, vociferous **4** = **garish**, brash, flamboyant, flashy, gaudy, glaring, lurid, showy

lounge *v* **4** = **relax**, laze, lie about, loaf, loiter, loll, outspan (*S Afr*), sprawl, take it easy

lout *n* = **oaf**, boor, dolt, yob *or* yobbo (*Brit sl*)

lovable, loveable *adj* = **endearing**, adorable, amiable, charming, cute, delightful, enchanting, likable *or* likeable, lovely, sweet

love *v* **1** = **adore**, cherish, dote on, hold dear, idolize, prize, treasure, worship **3** = **enjoy**, appreciate, delight in, like, relish, savour, take pleasure in ▷ *n* **4** = **affection**, adoration, attachment, devotion, infatuation, tenderness,

warmth **5** = **passion**, ardour **6** = **liking**, devotion, enjoyment, fondness, inclination, partiality, relish, soft spot, taste, weakness **7** = **beloved**, darling, dear, dearest, lover, sweetheart, truelove **in love (with)** = **enamoured**, besotted, charmed, enraptured, infatuated, smitten

love affair *n* = **romance**, affair, amour, intrigue, liaison, relationship

lovely *adj* **1** = **beautiful**, adorable, attractive, charming, comely, exquisite, graceful, handsome, lekker (*S Afr sl*), pretty **2** = **enjoyable**, agreeable, delightful, engaging, lekker (*S Afr sl*), nice, pleasant, pleasing

lover *n* **1, 2** = **sweetheart**, admirer, beloved, boyfriend *or* girlfriend, flame (*inf*), mistress, suitor

loving *adj* = **affectionate**, amorous, dear, devoted, doting, fond, tender, warm-hearted

low[1] *adj* **1** = **small**, little, short, squat, stunted **2** = **inferior**, deficient,

relatively low speed. ▷ *adv* **9** in or to a low position, level, or degree. ▷ *n* **10** low position, level, or degree. **11** area of low atmospheric pressure, depression. **lowly** *adj* modest, humble. **lowliness** *n* **lowbrow** *n, adj* (person) with nonintellectual tastes and interests. **Low Church** section of the Anglican Church stressing evangelical beliefs and practices. **lowdown** *n informal* inside information. **low-down** *adj informal* mean, underhand, or dishonest. **low-key** *adj* subdued, restrained, not intense. **lowland** *n* **1** low-lying country. ▷ *pl* **2** (**L-**) less mountainous parts of Scotland. **low profile** position or attitude avoiding prominence or publicity. **low-spirited** *adj* depressed.

low² *n* **1** cry of cattle, moo. ▷ *v* **2** moo.

lower¹ ❶ *adj* **1** below one or more other things. **2** smaller or reduced in amount or value. ▷ *v* **3** cause or allow to move down. **4** behave in a way that damages one's respect. **5** lessen. **lower case** small, as distinct from capital, letters.

lower², lour ❶ *v* (of the sky or weather) look gloomy or threatening. **lowering** *adj*.

loyal ❶ *adj* faithful to one's friends, country, or government. **loyally** *adv*

loyalty *n* **loyalty card** swipe card issued by a supermarket or chain store to a cust omer, used to record credit points awarded for money spent in the s tore. **loyalist** *n*.

lozenge *n* **1** medicated tablet held in the mouth until it dissolves. **2** four-sided diamond-shaped figure.

LP *n* record playing approximately 20–25 minutes each side.

L-plate *n* sign on a car being driven by a learner driver.

Lr *Chemistry* lawrencium.

LSD lysergic acid diethylamide, a hallucinogenic drug.

Lt Lieutenant.

Ltd Limited (Liability).

Lu *Chemistry* lutetium.

lubricate ❶ [**loo**-brik-ate] *v* oil or grease to lessen friction. **lubricant** *n* lubricating substance, such as oil. **lubrication** *n*.

lubricious [loo-**brish**-uss] *adj lit* lewd.

lucerne *n* fodder plant like clover, alfalfa.

lucid ❶ *adj* **1** clear and easily understood. **2** able to think clearly. **3** bright and clear. **lucidly** *adv* **lucidity** *n*.

Lucifer *n* Satan.

luck ❶ *n* **1** fortune, good or bad. **2** good fortune. **lucky** *adj* having or bringing good luck. **lucky dip** game in which prizes are picked from a tub at random.

---

inadequate, poor, second-rate, shoddy **3** = **coarse**, common, crude, disreputable, rough, rude, undignified, vulgar **4** = **dejected**, depressed, despondent, disheartened, downcast, down in the dumps (*inf*), fed up, gloomy, glum, miserable **5** = **ill**, debilitated, frail, stricken, weak **6** = **quiet**, gentle, hushed, muffled, muted, soft, subdued, whispered

lowdown *n Inf* = **information**, gen (*Brit inf*), info (*inf*), inside story, intelligence

lower¹ *adj* **1** = **under**, inferior, junior, lesser, minor, secondary, second-class, smaller, subordinate **2** = **reduced**, curtailed, decreased, diminished, lessened ▷ *v* **3** = **drop**, depress, fall, let down, sink, submerge, take down **5** = **lessen**, cut, decrease, diminish, minimize, prune, reduce, slash

lower², lour *v* = **darken**, be brewing, blacken, cloud up *or* over, loom, menace, threaten

low-key *adj* = **subdued**, muted, quiet, restrained, toned down, understated

lowly *adj* = **humble**, meek, mild, modest, unassuming

low-spirited *adj* = **depressed**, dejected, despondent, dismal, down, down-hearted, fed up, low, miserable, sad

loyal *adj* = **faithful**, constant, dependable, devoted, dutiful, staunch, steadfast, true, trustworthy, trusty, unwavering

loyalty *n* = **faithfulness**, allegiance, constancy, dependability, devotion, fidelity, staunchness, steadfastness, trustworthiness

lubricate *v* = **oil**, grease, smear

lucid *adj* **1** = **clear**, comprehensible, explicit, intelligible, transparent **2** = **clear-headed**, *compos mentis*, all there, in one's right mind, rational, sane **3** = **translucent**, clear, crystalline, diaphanous, glassy, limpid, pellucid, transparent

luck *n* **1** = **fortune**, accident, chance, destiny, fate **2** = **good fortune**, advantage, blessing, godsend, prosperity, serendipity, success, windfall

luckily adv fortunately. **luckless** adj having bad luck.

lucrative ❶ adj very profitable.

lucre ❶ [**loo**-ker] n **filthy lucre** facetious money.

Luddite n person opposed to change in industrial methods.

luderick n Australian fish, usu. black or dark brown in colour.

ludicrous ❶ adj absurd or ridiculous. **ludicrously** adv.

ludo n game played with dice and counters on a board.

luff v sail (a ship) towards the wind.

lug¹ v **lugging**, **lugged** carry or drag with great effort.

lug² n **1** projection serving as a handle. **2** informal ear.

luggage ❶ n traveller's cases, bags, etc.

lugubrious ❶ [loo-**goo**-bree-uss] adj mournful, gloomy. **lugubriously** adv.

lugworm n large worm used as bait.

lukewarm ❶ adj **1** moderately warm, tepid. **2** indifferent or half-hearted.

lull ❶ v **1** soothe (someone) by soft sounds or motions. **2** calm (fears or suspicions) by deception. ▷ n **3** brief time of quiet in a storm etc.

lullaby n, pl **-bies** quiet song to send a child to sleep.

lumbago [lum-**bay**-go] n pain in the lower back. **lumbar** adj relating to the lower back.

lumber¹ ❶ n **1** unwanted disused household articles. **2** Chiefly US sawn timber. ▷ v **3** informal burden with something unpleasant. **lumberjack** n US man who fells trees and prepares logs for transport.

lumber² ❶ v move heavily and awkwardly. **lumbering** adj.

luminous ❶ adj reflecting or giving off light. **luminosity** n **luminary** n **1** famous person. **2** lit heavenly body giving off light. **luminescence** n emission of light at low temperatures by any process other than burning. **luminescent** adj.

lump¹ ❶ n **1** shapeless piece or mass. **2** swelling. **3** informal awkward or stupid person. ▷ v **4** consider as a single group. **lump in one's throat** tight dry feeling in one's throat, usu. caused by great emotion. **lumpish** adj stupid or clumsy. **lumpy** adj **lump sum** relatively large sum of money paid at one time.

lump² v **lump it** informal tolerate or put up with it.

lunar adj relating to the moon.

lunatic ❶ adj **1** foolish and irresponsible. ▷ n **2** foolish or annoying person. **3** old-fashioned insane person. **lunacy** n.

————————————————— THESAURUS —————

luckily adv = **fortunately**, favourably, happily, opportunely, propitiously, providentially

lucky adj = **fortunate**, advantageous, blessed, charmed, favoured, jammy (Brit sl), successful

lucrative adj = **profitable**, advantageous, fruitful, productive, remunerative, well-paid

lucre n **filthy lucre** Facetious = **money**, gain, lolly (Aust & NZ sl), mammon, pelf, profit, riches, spoils, wealth

ludicrous adj = **ridiculous**, absurd, crazy, farcical, laughable, nonsensical, outlandish, preposterous, silly

luggage n = **baggage**, bags, cases, gear, impedimenta, paraphernalia, suitcases, things

lugubrious adj = **gloomy**, doleful, melancholy, mournful, sad, serious, sombre, sorrowful, woebegone

lukewarm adj **1** = **tepid**, warm **2** = **half-hearted**, apathetic, cool, indifferent, unenthusiastic, unresponsive

lull v **1** = **calm**, allay, pacify, quell, soothe, subdue, tranquillize ▷ n **3** = **respite**, calm, hush, let-up (inf), pause, quiet, silence

lumber¹ n **1** = **junk**, clutter, jumble, refuse, rubbish, trash ▷ v **3** Inf = **burden**, encumber, land, load, saddle

lumber² v = **plod**, shamble, shuffle, stump, trudge, trundle, waddle

lumbering adj = **awkward**, clumsy, heavy, hulking, ponderous, ungainly

luminous adj = **bright**, glowing, illuminated, luminescent, lustrous, radiant, shining

lump¹ n **1** = **piece**, ball, chunk, hunk, mass, nugget **2** = **swelling**, bulge, bump, growth, hump, protrusion, tumour ▷ v **4** = **group**, collect, combine, conglomerate, consolidate, mass, pool

lumpy adj = **bumpy**, knobbly, uneven

lunacy n **1** = **foolishness**, absurdity, craziness, folly, foolhardiness, madness, stupidity **3** Old-fashioned = **insanity**, dementia, derangement, madness, mania, psychosis

lunatic adj **1** = **irrational**, crackbrained, crackpot (inf), crazy, daft, deranged,

lunch *n* **1** meal taken in the middle of the day. ▷ *v* **2** eat lunch. **luncheon** *n* formal lunch. **luncheon meat** tinned ground mixture of meat and cereal. **luncheon voucher** voucher for a certain amount, given to an employee and accepted by some restaurants as payment for a meal.

lung *n* organ that allows an animal or bird to breathe air: humans have two lungs in the chest. **lungfish** *n* freshwater bony fish with an air-breathing lung of South America and Australia.

lunge ❶ *n* **1** sudden forward motion. **2** thrust with a sword. ▷ *v* **3** move with or make a lunge.

lupin *n* garden plant with tall spikes of flowers.

lupine *adj* like a wolf.

lupus *n* ulcerous skin disease.

lurch¹ ❶ *v* **1** tilt or lean suddenly to one side. **2** stagger. ▷ *n* **3** lurching movement.

lurch² *n* **leave someone in the lurch** abandon someone in difficulties.

lurcher *n* crossbred dog trained to hunt silently.

lure ❶ *v* **1** tempt or attract by the promise of reward. ▷ *n* **2** person or thing that lures. **3** brightly-coloured artificial angling bait. **4** feathered decoy for attracting a falcon.

lurid ❶ *adj* **1** vivid in shocking detail, sensational. **2** glaring in colour.

luridly *adv* **luridness** *n*.

lurk ❶ *v* **1** lie hidden or move stealthily, esp. for sinister purposes. **2** be latent.

luscious ❶ [**lush**-uss] *adj* **1** extremely pleasurable to taste or smell. **2** very attractive.

lush¹ ❶ *adj* **1** (of grass etc.) growing thickly and healthily. **2** opulent.

lush² *n slang* alcoholic.

lust ❶ *n* **1** strong sexual desire. **2** any strong desire. ▷ *v* **3** have passionate desire (for). **lustful** *adj* **lusty** *adj* vigorous, healthy. **lustily** *adv*.

lustre ❶ *n* **1** gloss, sheen. **2** splendour or glory. **3** metallic pottery glaze. **lustrous** *adj* shining, luminous.

lute *n* ancient guitar-like musical instrument with a body shaped like a half pear.

lutetium [loo-**tee**-shee-um] *n Chemistry* silvery-white metallic element.

Lutheran *adj* of Martin Luther (1483–1546), German Reformation leader, his doctrines, or a Church following these doctrines.

lux *n, pl* **lux** unit of illumination.

luxuriant *adj* **1** rich and abundant. **2** very elaborate. **luxuriance** *n* **luxuriantly** *adv*.

luxuriate *v* **1** take self-indulgent pleasure (in). **2** flourish.

luxury ❶ *n, pl* **-ries 1** enjoyment of rich, very comfortable living. **2** enjoyable but not essential thing. ▷ *adj* **3** of or

---

insane, mad ▷ *n* **3** *Old-fashioned* = **madman**, maniac, nutcase (*sl*), psychopath

lunge *n* **1** = **pounce**, charge, spring, swing **2** = **thrust**, jab ▷ *v* **3 a** = **pounce**, charge, dive, leap **b** = **thrust**, jab

lurch¹ *v* **1** = **tilt**, heave, heel, lean, list, pitch, rock, roll **2** = **stagger**, reel, stumble, sway, totter, weave

lure *v* **1** = **tempt**, allure, attract, draw, ensnare, entice, invite, seduce ▷ *n* **2** = **temptation**, allurement, attraction, bait, carrot (*inf*), enticement, inducement

lurid *adj* **1** = **sensational**, graphic, melodramatic, shocking, vivid **2** = **glaring**, intense

lurk *v* **1** = **hide**, conceal oneself, lie in wait, prowl, skulk, slink, sneak

luscious *adj* **1** = **delicious**, appetizing, juicy, mouth-watering, palatable, succulent, sweet, toothsome

lush¹ *adj* **1** = **abundant**, dense, flourishing, green, rank, verdant **2** = **luxurious**, elaborate, extravagant, grand, lavish, opulent, ornate, palatial, plush (*inf*), sumptuous

lust *n* **1** = **lechery**, lasciviousness, lewdness, sensuality **2** = **desire**, appetite, craving, greed, longing, passion, thirst ▷ *v* **3** = **desire**, covet, crave, hunger for *or* after, want, yearn

lustre *n* **1** = **sparkle**, gleam, glint, glitter, gloss, glow, sheen, shimmer, shine **2** = **glory**, distinction, fame, honour, prestige, renown

lusty *adj* = **vigorous**, energetic, healthy, hearty, powerful, robust, strong, sturdy, virile

luxurious *adj* = **sumptuous**, comfortable, expensive, lavish, magnificent, opulent, plush (*inf*), rich, splendid

luxury *n* **1** = **opulence**, affluence,

providing luxury. **luxurious** *adj* full of luxury, sumptuous. **luxuriously** *adv*.

LV luncheon voucher.

lychee [lie-**chee**] *n* Chinese fruit with a whitish juicy pulp.

lych gate *n* roofed gate to a churchyard.

Lycra *n* ® elastic fabric used for tight-fitting garments, such as swimsuits.

lye *n* caustic solution made from wood ash.

lying ❶ *v* present participle of LIE¹ *or* LIE². **lying-in** *n* old-fashioned period of confinement during childbirth.

lymph *n* colourless bodily fluid consisting mainly of white blood cells. **lymphatic** *adj* **lymph node** mass of tissue that helps to fight infection in the body by killing bacteria.

lymphocyte *n* type of white blood cell.

lynch *v* put to death without a trial.

lynx *n* animal of the cat family with tufted ears and a short tail.

lyre *n* ancient musical instrument like a U-shaped harp. **lyrebird** *n* pheasant-like Australian bird the male of which spreads its tail out into the shape of a lyre.

lyric ❶ *adj* **1** (of poetry) expressing personal emotion in songlike style. **2** like a song. ▷ *n* **3** short poem in a songlike style. ▷ *pl* **4** words of a popular song. **lyrical** *adj* **1** lyric. **2** enthusiastic. **lyricism** *n* **lyricist** *n* person who writes the words of songs or musicals.

———————————————————————————————— THESAURUS ————

hedonism, richness, splendour, sumptuousness **2** = **extravagance**, extra, frill, indulgence, treat

lying *n* **1** = **dishonesty**, deceit, mendacity, perjury, untruthfulness ▷ *adj* **2** = **deceitful**, dishonest, false, mendacious, perfidious, treacherous, two-faced, untruthful

lyrical *adj* **2** = **enthusiastic**, carried away, ecstatic, effusive, impassioned, inspired, poetic, rapturous, rhapsodic

Mm

m 1 metre(s). **2** mile(s). **3** minute(s).
M 1 Motorway. **2** pl **MM** Monsieur.
3 mega-. **4** the Roman numeral for
1000.

m 1 male. **2** married. **3** masculine.
4 meridian. **5** month.

ma n informal mother.

MA 1 Master of Arts. **2** Massachusetts.

ma'am n madam.

mac n informal mackintosh.

macabre ❶ [mak-**kahb**-ra] adj strange
and horrible, gruesome.

macadam n road surface of pressed
layers of small broken stones.
macadamize v pave (a road) with
macadam.

macaque [mac-**kahk**] n monkey of
Asia and Africa with cheek pouches
and either a short tail or no tail.

macaroni n pasta in short tube
shapes.

macaroon n small biscuit or cake made
with ground almonds.

macaw n large tropical American
parrot.

mace¹ n **1** ceremonial staff of office.
2 medieval weapon with a spiked
metal head.

mace² n spice made from the dried husk
of the nutmeg.

macerate [**mass**-er-ate] v soften by
soaking. **maceration** n.

Mach [**mak**] n short for MACH NUMBER.

machete [mash-**ett**-ee] n broad heavy
knife used for cutting or as a weapon.

Machiavellian ❶ [mak-ee-a-**vel**-yan]
adj unprincipled, crafty, and
opportunist.

machinations [mak-in-**nay**-shunz] pl
n cunning plots and ploys.

machine ❶ n **1** apparatus, usu. powered
by electricity, designed to perform a
particular task. **2** vehicle, such as a car
or aircraft. **3** controlling system of an
organization. ▷ v **4** make or produce by
machine. **machinery** n **1** machines or
machine parts collectively. **2** standard
procedures of an organization.

machinist n person who operates a
machine. **machine gun** automatic gun
that fires rapidly and continuously.
machine-gun v fire at with such a gun.
machine language instructions for a
computer in binary code that require no
conversion or translation by the
computer. **machine-readable** adj (of
data) in a form suitable for processing
by a computer.

machismo [mak-**izz**-moh] n
exaggerated or strong masculinity.

Mach number [**mak**] n **1**.

macho ❶ [**match**-oh] adj strongly or
exaggeratedly masculine.

mack n informal mackintosh.

mackerel n edible sea fish with blue
and silver stripes.

mackintosh, macintosh n
1 waterproof raincoat of rubberized
cloth. **2** any raincoat.

macramé [mak-**rah**-mee] n
ornamental work of knotted cord.

macro- combining form large, long, or
great, e.g. macroscopic.

macrobiotics n dietary system
advocating whole grains and
vegetables grown without chemical
additives. **macrobiotic** adj.

macrocosm n **1** the universe. **2** any
large complete system.

mad ❶ adj **madder**, **maddest**
1 mentally deranged, insane. **2** very
foolish. **3** informal angry. **4** frantic.

——————— THESAURUS ———————

macabre adj = **gruesome**, dreadful,
eerie, frightening, ghastly, ghostly,
ghoulish, grim, grisly, morbid

Machiavellian adj = **scheming**,
astute, crafty, cunning, cynical,
double-dealing, opportunist, sly,
underhand, unscrupulous

machine n **1** = **appliance**, apparatus,
contraption, contrivance, device,
engine, instrument, mechanism, tool
3 = **system**, machinery, organization,
setup (inf), structure

machinery n **1** = **equipment**,
apparatus, gear, instruments, tackle,
tools

macho adj = **manly**, chauvinist,
masculine, virile

mad adj **1** = **insane**, non compos mentis,
crazy (inf), demented, deranged, nuts
(sl), of unsound mind, out of one's
mind, psychotic, raving, unhinged,
unstable **2** = **foolish**, absurd, asinine,

5 (foll. by *about* or *on*) very enthusiastic (about). **like mad** *informal* with great energy, enthusiasm, or haste. **madly** *adv* **1** with great speed and energy. **2** *informal* extremely or excessively. **madness** *n* **madden** *v* infuriate or irritate. **maddening** *adj* **maddeningly** *adv* **madman**, **madwoman** *n*.

madam *n* **1** polite form of address to a woman. **2** *informal* precocious or conceited girl.

madame [mad-**dam**] *n*, *pl* **mesdames** [may-**dam**] French title equivalent to *Mrs*.

madcap ❶ *adj* foolish or reckless.

madder *n* **1** climbing plant. **2** red dye made from its root.

made *v* past of MAKE. **have (got) it made** *informal* be assured of success.

Madeira [mad-**deer**-a] *n* fortified white wine. **Madeira cake** rich sponge cake.

mademoiselle [mad-mwah-**zel**] *n*, *pl* **mesdemoiselles** [maid-mwah-**zel**] French title equivalent to *Miss*.

madhouse *n* **1** *informal* place filled with uproar or confusion. **2** *old-fashioned* mental hospital.

Madonna *n* **1** the Virgin Mary.

2 picture or statue of her.

madrigal *n* 16th–17th-century part song for unaccompanied voices.

maelstrom ❶ [**male**-strom] *n* **1** great whirlpool. **2** turmoil.

maestro ❶ [**my**-stroh] *n*, *pl* **-tri**, **-tros** **1** outstanding musician or conductor. **2** any master of an art.

mae west *n* inflatable life jacket.

Mafia *n* international secret criminal organization founded in Sicily. **mafioso** *n*, *pl* **-sos**, **-si** member of the Mafia.

magazine ❶ *n* **1** periodical publication with articles by different writers. **2** television or radio programme made up of short nonfictional items. **3** appliance for automatically supplying cartridges to a gun or slides to a projector. **4** storehouse for explosives or arms.

magenta [maj-**jen**-ta] *adj* deep purplish-red.

maggot *n* larva of an insect. **maggoty** *adj*.

Magi [**maje**-eye] *pl n* wise men from the East who came to worship the infant Jesus.

magic ❶ *n* **1** supposed art of invoking

———————— THESAURUS ————————

daft (*inf*), foolhardy, irrational, nonsensical, preposterous, senseless, wild **3** *Inf* = **angry**, berserk, enraged, furious, incensed, livid (*inf*), pissed (*taboo sl*), pissed off (*taboo sl*), wild **4** = **frenzied**, excited, frenetic, uncontrolled, unrestrained, wild **5** = **enthusiastic**, ardent, avid, crazy (*inf*), fanatical, impassioned, infatuated, wild **like mad** *Inf* = **energetically**, enthusiastically, excitedly, furiously, rapidly, speedily, violently, wildly

madcap *adj* = **reckless**, crazy, foolhardy, hare-brained, imprudent, impulsive, rash, thoughtless

madden *v* = **infuriate**, annoy, derange, drive one crazy, enrage, incense, inflame, irritate, upset

madly *adv* **1** = **energetically**, excitedly, furiously, like mad (*inf*), recklessly, speedily, wildly **2** *Inf* = **passionately**, desperately, devotedly, intensely, to distraction

madman, madwoman *n* = **lunatic**, maniac, nutcase (*sl*), psycho (*sl*), psychopath

madness *n* **1** = **insanity**, aberration,

craziness, delusion, dementia, derangement, distraction, lunacy, mania, mental illness, psychopathy, psychosis, wildness **2** = **foolishness**, absurdity, daftness (*inf*), folly, foolhardiness, idiocy, nonsense, preposterousness

maelstrom *n* **1** = **whirlpool**, vortex **2** = **turmoil**, chaos, confusion, disorder, tumult, upheaval

maestro *n* **1** = **virtuoso 2** = **master**, expert, fundi (*S Afr*), genius

magazine *n* **1** = **journal**, pamphlet, periodical **4** = **storehouse**, arsenal, depot, store, warehouse

magic *n* **1** = **sorcery**, black art, enchantment, necromancy, witchcraft, wizardry **2** = **conjuring**, illusion, legerdemain, prestidigitation, sleight of hand, trickery **3** = **charm**, allurement, enchantment, fascination, glamour, magnetism, power ▷ *adj* **4** (also **magical**) = **miraculous**, bewitching, charming, enchanting, entrancing, fascinating, spellbinding **5** *Inf* = **marvellous**

magician *n* **1** = **conjuror** or **conjuror**, illusionist **2** = **sorcerer**, enchanter or

supernatural powers to influence events. **2** conjuring tricks done to entertain. **3** mysterious quality or power. ▷ *adj* **4** (also **magical**) of, using, or like magic. **5** *informal* wonderful, marvellous. **magically** *adv* **magician** *n* **1** conjuror. **2** person with magic powers.

magistrate ❶ *n* **1** public officer administering the law. **2** justice of the peace. **magisterial** *adj* **1** commanding or authoritative. **2** of a magistrate.

magma *n* molten rock inside the earth's crust.

magnanimous ❶ *adj* noble and generous. **magnanimously** *adv* **magnanimity** *n*.

magnate ❶ *n* influential or wealthy person, esp. in industry.

magnesia *n* white tasteless substance used as an antacid and a laxative; magnesium oxide.

magnesium *n Chemistry* silvery-white metallic element.

magnet ❶ *n* **1** piece of iron or steel capable of attracting iron and pointing north when suspended. **2** person or thing that exerts a great attraction. **magnetic** *adj* **1** having the properties of a magnet. **2** powerfully attractive. **magnetically** *adv* **magnetism** *n* **1** magnetic property. **2** powerful personal charm. **3** science of magnetic properties. **magnetize** *v*

1 make into a magnet. **2** attract strongly. **magnetic field** area around a magnet in which its power of attraction is felt. **magnetic north** direction in which a compass needle points. **magnetic tape** plastic strip coated with a magnetic substance for recording sound or video signals.

magneto [mag-**nee**-toe] *n, pl* **-tos** apparatus for ignition in an internal-combustion engine.

magnificent ❶ *adj* **1** splendid or impressive. **2** excellent. **magnificently** *adv* **magnificence** *n*.

magnify ❶ *v* **-fying, -fied 1** increase in apparent size, as with a lens. **2** exaggerate. **magnification** *n* **magnifying glass** convex lens used to produce an enlarged image of an object.

magnitude ❶ *n* relative importance or size.

magnolia *n* shrub or tree with showy white or pink flowers.

magnum *n* large wine bottle holding about 1.5 litres.

magnum opus *n* greatest single work of art or literature of a particular artist.

magpie *n* **1** black-and-white bird. **2** any of various similar Australian birds, e.g. the butcherbird.

Magyar *n* **1** member of the main ethnic group in Hungary. **2** Hungarian

---

THESAURUS

enchantress, necromancer, warlock, witch, wizard
magisterial *adj* **1** = **authoritative**, commanding, lordly, masterful
magistrate *n* **1** = **judge 2** = **justice of the peace**, J.P., justice
magnanimity *n* = **generosity**, benevolence, big-heartedness, largesse *or* largess, nobility, selflessness, unselfishness
magnanimous *adj* = **generous**, big-hearted, bountiful, charitable, kind, noble, selfless, unselfish
magnate *n* = **tycoon**, baron, big hitter (*inf*), captain of industry, heavy hitter (*inf*), mogul, plutocrat
magnetic *adj* **2** = **attractive**, captivating, charismatic, charming, fascinating, hypnotic, irresistible, lekker (*S Afr sl*), mesmerizing, seductive
magnetism *n* **2** = **charm**, allure, appeal, attraction, charisma, drawing

power, magic, pull, seductiveness
magnification *n* **1** = **increase**, amplification, enlargement, expansion, heightening
2 = **intensification**, enhancement
magnificence *n* = **splendour**, brilliance, glory, grandeur, majesty, nobility, opulence, stateliness, sumptuousness
magnificent *adj* **1** = **splendid**, glorious, gorgeous, imposing, impressive, majestic, regal, sublime, sumptuous **2** = **excellent**, brilliant, fine, outstanding, splendid, superb
magnify *v* **1** = **enlarge**, amplify, blow up (*inf*), boost, dilate, expand, heighten, increase **2** = **exaggerate**, inflate, intensify, overemphasize, overplay, overstate
magnitude *n* **a** = **importance**, consequence, greatness, moment, note, significance, weight **b** = **size**, amount, amplitude, extent, mass,

language. ▷ adj **3** of the Magyars.

maharajah n former title of some Indian princes. **maharani**, **maharanee** n fem.

maharishi n Hindu religious teacher or mystic.

mahatma n Hinduism person revered for holiness and wisdom.

mah jong, mah-jongg n Chinese table game for four, played with tiles bearing different designs.

mahogany n hard reddish-brown wood of several tropical trees.

mahout [ma-**howt**] n (in India and the East Indies) elephant driver or keeper.

maid ❶ n **1** (also **maidservant**) female servant. **2** lit young unmarried woman.

maiden ❶ n **1** lit young unmarried woman. ▷ adj **2** unmarried. **3** first, e.g. maiden voyage. **maid** n female servant. **maidenly** adj modest. **maidenhair** n fern with delicate fronds. **maidenhead** n virginity. **maiden name** woman's surname before marriage. **maiden over** Cricket over in which no runs are scored.

mail¹ n **1** letters and packages transported and delivered by the post office. **2** postal system. **3** single collection or delivery of mail. **4** train, ship, or aircraft carrying mail. **5** same as E-MAIL. ▷ v **6** send by mail. **7** contact (a person) by e-mail. **8** send (a message) by e-mail. **mailing list** n register of names and addresses to which information and advertising

material is sent by post or electronic mail. **mail order** system of buying goods by post. **mailshot** n posting of advertising material to many selected people at once.

mail² n flexible armour of interlaced rings or links.

mailbox n **1** US & Canad box into which letters are delivered or placed for collection. **2** computer directory in which e-mail messages are stored.

mailman n person who collects or delivers mail.

maim ❶ v cripple or mutilate.

main ❶ adj **1** chief or principal. ▷ n **2** principal pipe or line carrying water, gas, or electricity. ▷ pl **3** main distribution network for water, gas, or electricity. **in the main** on the whole. **mainly** adv for the most part, chiefly. **mainframe** n, adj Computers (denoting) a high-speed general-purpose computer. **mainland** n stretch of land which forms the main part of a country. **mainmast** n chief mast of a ship. **mainsail** n largest sail on a mainmast. **mainspring** n **1** chief cause or motive. **2** chief spring of a watch or clock. **mainstay** n **1** chief support. **2** rope securing a mainmast. **mainstream** adj (of) a prevailing cultural trend.

maintain ❶ v **1** continue or keep in existence. **2** keep up or preserve. **3** support financially. **4** assert. **maintenance** n **1** maintaining.

---

quantity, volume

maid n **1** (also **maidservant**) = **servant**, housemaid, maidservant, serving-maid **2** Lit = **girl**, damsel, lass, lassie (inf), maiden, wench

maiden n **1** Lit = **girl**, damsel, lass, lassie (inf), maid, virgin, wench ▷ adj **2** = **unmarried**, unwed **3** = **first**, inaugural, initial, introductory

maidenly adj = **modest**, chaste, decent, decorous, demure, pure, virginal

mail¹ n **1** = **letters**, correspondence **1-3** = **post** ▷ v **6** = **post**, dispatch, forward, send

maim v = **cripple**, disable, hurt, injure, mutilate, wound

main adj **1** = **chief**, central, essential, foremost, head, leading, pre-eminent, primary, principal ▷ n **2** = **conduit**, cable, channel, duct, line, pipe **in the**

main = **on the whole**, for the most part, generally, in general, mainly, mostly

mainly adv = **chiefly**, for the most part, in the main, largely, mostly, on the whole, predominantly, primarily, principally

mainstay n **1** = **pillar**, anchor, backbone, bulwark, buttress, prop

mainstream adj = **conventional**, accepted, current, established, general, orthodox, prevailing, received

maintain v **1** = **continue**, carry on, perpetuate, prolong, retain, sustain **2** = **keep up**, care for, preserve **3** = **look after**, provide for, support, take care of **4** = **assert**, avow, claim, contend, declare, insist, profess, state

maintenance n **1** = **continuation**, carrying-on, perpetuation, prolongation **2** = **upkeep**, care,

2 upkeep of a building, car, etc.
3 provision of money for a separated or divorced spouse.

maisonette n flat with more than one floor.

maître d'hôtel [**met**-ra dote-**tell**] n French head waiter.

maize n type of corn with spikes of yellow grains.

Maj. Major.

majesty ❶ n, pl **-ties 1** stateliness or grandeur. **2** supreme power. **majestic** adj **majestically** adv.

majolica n type of ornamented Italian pottery.

major ❶ adj **1** greater in number, quality, or extent. **2** significant or serious. ▷ n **3** middle-ranking army officer. **4** scale in music, e.g. the C major scale. **5** US & Canad principal field of study at a university etc.

▷ v **6** (foll. by in) US, Canad, Aust & NZ do one's principal study in (a particular subject). **majorette** n one of a group of girls who practise formation marching and baton twirling.

major-domo n, pl **-domos** chief steward of a great household. **major-general** n senior military officer. **majorship** n.

majority ❶ n, pl **-ties 1** greater number. **2** number by which the votes on one side exceed those on the other. **3** largest party voting together. **4** state of being legally an adult.

make ❶ v **making, made 1** create, construct, or establish. **2** cause to do or be. **3** bring about or produce. **4** perform (an action). **5** appoint. **6** serve as or become. **7** amount to. **8** earn. ▷ n **9** brand, type, or style. **make do** manage with an inferior

— THESAURUS —

conservation, keeping, nurture, preservation, repairs **3** = **allowance**, alimony, keep, support

majestic adj **1** = **grand**, grandiose, impressive, magnificent, monumental, regal, splendid, stately, sublime, superb

majesty n **1** = **grandeur**, glory, magnificence, nobility, pomp, splendour, stateliness

major adj **1** = **main**, bigger, chief, greater, higher, leading, senior, supreme **2** = **important**, critical, crucial, great, notable, outstanding, serious, significant

majority n **1** = **most**, best part, bulk, greater number, mass, preponderance **4** = **adulthood**, manhood or womanhood, maturity, seniority

make v **1** = **create**, assemble, build, construct, fashion, form, manufacture, produce, put together, synthesize **2** = **force**, cause, compel, constrain, drive, impel, induce, oblige, prevail upon, require **3** = **produce**, accomplish, bring about, cause, create, effect, generate, give rise to, lead to **4** = **perform**, carry out, do, effect, execute **7** = **amount to**, add up to, compose, constitute, form **8** = **earn**, clear, gain, get, net, obtain, win ▷ n **9** = **brand**, kind, model, sort, style, type, variety

make for v = **head for**, aim for, be bound for, head towards

make it v Inf = **succeed**, arrive (inf), crack it (inf), get on, prosper

make off with v = **steal**, abduct, carry off, filch, kidnap, nick (sl, chiefly Brit), pinch (inf), run away or off with

make out v **1** = **see**, detect, discern, discover, distinguish, perceive, recognize **2** = **understand**, comprehend, decipher, fathom, follow, grasp, work out **3** = **write out**, complete, draw up, fill in or out **4** = **pretend**, let on, make as if or though **5** = **claim**, assert **6** Inf = **fare**, get on, manage

maker n **1** = **manufacturer**, builder, constructor, producer

makeshift adj = **temporary**, expedient, provisional, stopgap, substitute

make up v **1** = **form**, compose, comprise, constitute **3** = **invent**, coin, compose, concoct, construct, create, devise, dream up, formulate, frame, originate **4** = **complete**, fill, supply **5** (foll. by for) = **compensate for**, atone for, make amends for **6** = **settle**, bury the hatchet, call it quits, reconcile

make-up n **1** = **cosmetics**, face (inf), greasepaint (Theatre), paint (inf), powder **2** = **structure**, arrangement, assembly, composition, configuration, constitution, construction, format, organization **3** = **nature**, character, constitution, disposition, temperament

alternative. **make it** *informal* be successful. **on the make** *informal* out for profit or conquest. **maker** *n*
1 person or company that makes something. **2** (**M-**) title given to God.
making *n* **1** creation or production. ▷ *pl* **2** necessary requirements or qualities. **make-believe** *n* fantasy or pretence. **make for** *v* head towards.
make off with *v* steal or abduct.
make out *v* **1** manage to see or hear (something), perceive. **2** understand.
3 write out (a cheque). **4** pretend.
5 attempt to establish or prove.
6 *informal* manage or fare, e.g. *how did you make out in the competition?*
makeshift *adj* serving as a temporary substitute. **make up** *v* **1** form or constitute. **2** prepare. **3** invent.
4 supply what is lacking, complete.
5 (foll. by *for*) compensate (for).
6 settle a quarrel. **7** apply cosmetics.
make-up *n* **1** cosmetics. **2** way something is made. **3** mental or physical constitution. **makeweight** *n* something unimportant added to make up a lack.
mako *n, pl* **makos** powerful shark of the Atlantic and Pacific Oceans.
mal- *combining form* bad or badly, e.g. *malformation.*
malachite [**mal**-a-kite] *n* green mineral.
maladjusted ⊕ *adj Psychology* unable to meet the demands of society. **maladjustment** *n*.
maladministration ⊕ *n* inefficient or dishonest administration.

maladroit ⊕ [mal-a-**droyt**] *adj* clumsy or awkward.
malady ⊕ [**mal**-a-dee] *n, pl* **-dies** disease or illness.
malaise ⊕ [mal-**laze**] *n* **1** something wrong which affects a section of society or area of activity. **2** vague feeling of unease, illness, or depression.
malapropism *n* comical misuse of a word by confusion with one which sounds similar.
malaria *n* infectious disease caused by the bite of some mosquitoes. **malarial** *adj*.
Malay *n* **1** member of a people of Malaysia or Indonesia. **2** language of this people. ▷ *adj* **3** of the Malays or their language. **Malayan** *adj, n*.
malcontent ⊕ *n* discontented person.
male ⊕ *adj* **1** of the sex which can fertilize female reproductive cells. ▷ *n* **2** male person or animal. **maleness** *n* **male chauvinism** belief, held by some men, that men are superior to women. **male chauvinist** (characteristic of) a man who believes that men are superior to women.
malediction [mal-lid-**dik**-shun] *n* curse.
malefactor ⊕ [**mal**-if-act-or] *n* criminal or wrongdoer.
malevolent ⊕ [mal-**lev**-a-lent] *adj* wishing evil to others. **malevolently** *adv* **malevolence** *n*.
malfeasance [mal-**fee**-zanss] *n* misconduct, esp. by a public official.

———————————— THESAURUS ————————————

making *n* **1** = **creation**, assembly, building, composition, construction, fabrication, manufacture, production *pl* **2** = **beginnings**, capability, capacity, essence, ingredients, material, potential, qualities
maladjusted *adj Psychol* = **disturbed**, alienated, neurotic, unstable
maladministration *n* = **mismanagement**, corruption, dishonesty, incompetence, inefficiency, malpractice, misrule
maladroit *adj* = **clumsy**, awkward, cack-handed (*inf*), ham-fisted *or* ham-handed (*inf*), inept, inexpert, unskilful
malady *n* = **disease**, affliction, ailment, complaint, disorder, illness, infirmity,

sickness
malaise *n* **2** = **unease**, anxiety, depression, disquiet, melancholy
malcontent *n* = **troublemaker**, agitator, mischief-maker, rebel, stirrer (*inf*)
male *adj* **1** = **masculine**, manly, virile
malefactor *n* = **wrongdoer**, criminal, delinquent, evildoer, miscreant, offender, villain
malevolence *n* = **malice**, hate, hatred, ill will, nastiness, rancour, spite, vindictiveness
malevolent *adj* = **spiteful**, hostile, ill-natured, malicious, malign, vengeful, vindictive
malformation *n* = **deformity**, distortion, misshapenness

malformed ❶ *adj* misshapen or deformed. **malformation** *n*.

malfunction ❶ *v* **1** function imperfectly or fail to function. ▷ *n* **2** defective functioning or failure to function.

malice ❶ [**mal**-iss] *n* desire to cause harm to others. **malice aforethought** *Law* deliberate intention to do something unlawful. **malicious** *adj* **maliciously** *adv*.

malign ❶ [mal-**line**] *v* **1** slander or defame. ▷ *adj* **2** evil in influence or effect. **malignity** [mal-**lig**-nit-tee] *n* evil disposition.

malignant ❶ [mal-**lig**-nant] *adj* **1** seeking to harm others. **2** (of a tumour) harmful and uncontrollable. **malignancy** *n*.

malinger [mal-**ling**-ger] *v* feign illness to avoid work. **malingerer** *n*.

mall [**mawl**] *n* street or shopping area closed to vehicles.

mallard *n* wild duck.

malleable ❶ [**mal**-lee-a-bl] *adj* **1** capable of being hammered or pressed into shape. **2** easily influenced. **malleability** *n*.

mallet *n* **1** (wooden) hammer. **2** stick with a head like a hammer, used in croquet or polo.

mallow *n* plant with pink or purple flowers.

malnutrition *n* inadequate nutrition.

malodorous ❶ [mal-**lode**-or-uss] *adj* bad-smelling.

malpractice ❶ *n* immoral, illegal, or unethical professional conduct.

malt *n* **1** grain, such as barley, prepared for use in making beer or whisky. **2** malt whisky. ▷ *v* **3** make into or make with malt. **malty** *adj* **malted milk** drink made from powdered milk with malted cereals. **malt whisky** whisky made from malted barley.

Maltese *adj* **1** of Malta or its language. ▷ *n* **2** *pl* **-tese** person from Malta. **3** language of Malta. **Maltese cross** cross with triangular arms that taper towards the centre.

maltreat ❶ *v* treat badly. **maltreatment** *n*.

malware *n* *Computers* program designed specifically to damage or disrupt a system, such as a virus.

mama [mam-**ma**] *n* old-fashioned mother.

mamba *n* deadly S African snake.

mamma *n* same as MAMA.

mammal *n* animal of the type that suckles its young. **mammalian** *adj*.

mammary *adj* of the breasts or milk-producing glands.

mammon *n* wealth regarded as a source of evil.

mammoth ❶ *n* **1** extinct elephant-like mammal. ▷ *adj* **2** colossal.

man ❶ *n*, *pl* **men 1** adult male. **2** human being or person. **3** mankind. **4** manservant. **5** (usu. *pl*) member of the armed forces who is not an officer. **6** piece used in chess etc.

THESAURUS

malformed *adj* = **misshapen**, abnormal, crooked, deformed, distorted, irregular, twisted

malfunction *v* **1** = **break down**, fail, go wrong ▷ *n* **2** = **fault**, breakdown, defect, failure, flaw, glitch

malice *n* = **spite**, animosity, enmity, evil intent, hate, hatred, ill will, malevolence, vindictiveness

malicious *adj* = **spiteful**, ill-disposed, ill-natured, malevolent, rancorous, resentful, vengeful

malign *v* **1** = **disparage**, abuse, defame, denigrate, libel, run down, slander, smear, vilify ▷ *adj* **2** = **evil**, bad, destructive, harmful, hostile, injurious, malevolent, malignant, pernicious, wicked

malignant *adj* **1** = **hostile**, destructive, harmful, hurtful, malevolent, malign, pernicious, spiteful

2 = **uncontrollable**, cancerous, dangerous, deadly, fatal, irremediable

malleable *adj* **1** = **workable**, ductile, plastic, soft, tensile **2** = **manageable**, adaptable, biddable, compliant, impressionable, pliable, tractable

malodorous *adj* = **smelly**, fetid, mephitic, nauseating, noisome, offensive, putrid, reeking, stinking

malpractice *n* = **misconduct**, abuse, dereliction, mismanagement, negligence

maltreat *v* = **abuse**, bully, harm, hurt, ill-treat, injure, mistreat

mammoth *adj* **2** = **colossal**, enormous, giant, gigantic, huge, immense, massive, monumental, mountainous, prodigious

man *n* **1** = **male**, bloke (*Brit inf*), chap (*inf*), gentleman, guy (*inf*)

2 = **human**, human being, individual,

▷ *v* **manning**, **manned 7** supply with sufficient people for operation or defence. **man in the street** average person. **manhood** *n* **mankind** *n* human beings collectively. **manly** *adj* **-lier**, **-liest** (possessing qualities) appropriate to a man. **manliness** *n* **manned** *adj* having a human personnel or crew. **mannish** *adj* like a man. **man-hour** *n* work done by one person in one hour. **man-made** *adj* made artificially.

mana *n* NZ authority, influence.

manacle ❶ [**man**-a-kl] *n*, *v* handcuff or fetter.

manage ❶ *v* **1** succeed in doing. **2** be in charge of, administer. **3** handle or control. **4** cope with (financial) difficulties. **manageable** *adj* **management** *n* **1** managers collectively. **2** administration or organization. **manager**, **manageress** *n* person in charge of a business, institution, actor, sports team, etc. **managerial** *adj*.

mañana [man-**yah**-na] *adv*, *n* Spanish **1** tomorrow. **2** some later (unspecified) time.

manatee *n* large tropical plant-eating aquatic mammal.

mandarin *n* **1** high-ranking government official. **2** kind of small orange.

Mandarin Chinese, Mandarin *n* official language of China.

mandate ❶ *n* **1** official or authoritative command. **2** authorization or instruction from an electorate to its representative or government. ▷ *v* **3** give authority to. **mandatory** *adj* compulsory.

mandible *n* lower jawbone or jawlike part.

mandolin *n* musical instrument with four pairs of strings.

mandrake *n* plant with a forked root, formerly used as a narcotic.

mandrel *n* shaft on which work is held in a lathe.

mandrill *n* large blue-faced baboon.

mane *n* **1** long hair on the neck of a horse, lion, etc. **2** long thick human hair.

manful ❶ *adj* determined and brave. **manfulness** *n*.

manfully ❶ *adv* bravely and determinedly.

manganese *n* Chemistry brittle greyish-white metallic element.

mange *n* skin disease of domestic animals.

mangelwurzel *n* variety of beet used as cattle food.

manger *n* eating trough in a stable or barn.

mangetout [**mawnzh**-too] *n* variety of pea with an edible pod.

mangle[1] ❶ *v* **1** destroy by crushing and twisting. **2** spoil.

mangle[2] *n* **1** machine with rollers for squeezing water from washed clothes. ▷ *v* **2** put through a mangle.

——————————————— THESAURUS ———————————————

person, soul **3** = **mankind**, Homo sapiens, humanity, humankind, human race, people **4** = **manservant**, attendant, retainer, servant, valet ▷ *v* **7** = **staff**, crew, garrison, occupy, people

manacle *n* = **handcuff**, bond, chain, fetter, iron, shackle ▷ *v* = **handcuff**, bind, chain, fetter, put in chains, shackle

manage *v* **1** = **succeed**, accomplish, arrange, contrive, effect, engineer **2** = **administer**, be in charge (of), command, conduct, direct, handle, run, supervise **3** = **handle**, control, manipulate, operate, use **4** = **cope**, carry on, get by (*inf*), make do, muddle through, survive

manageable *adj* **3 a** = **docile**, amenable, compliant, submissive **b** = **easy**, handy, user-friendly

management *n* **1** = **directors**, administration, board, employers, executive(s) **2** = **administration**, command, control, direction, handling, operation, running, supervision

manager *n* = **supervisor**, administrator, boss (*inf*), director, executive, governor, head, organizer

mandate *n* **1** = **command**, commission, decree, directive, edict, instruction, order

mandatory *adj* = **compulsory**, binding, obligatory, required, requisite

manfully *adv* = **bravely**, boldly, courageously, determinedly, gallantly, hard, resolutely, stoutly, valiantly

mangle *v* **1** = **crush**, deform, destroy, disfigure, distort, mutilate, tear **2** = **spoil**, ruin, wreck

mango n, pl **-goes, -gos** tropical fruit with sweet juicy yellow flesh.

mangrove n tropical tree with exposed roots, which grows beside water.

mangy ❶ adj **mangier, mangiest** 1 having mange. 2 scruffy or shabby.

manhandle ❶ v treat roughly.

manhole n hole with a cover, through which a person can enter a drain or sewer.

manhunt n organized search, usu. by police, for a wanted man or a fugitive.

mania ❶ n 1 extreme enthusiasm. 2 madness. **maniac** n 1 mad person. 2 informal person who has an extreme enthusiasm for something. **maniacal** [man-**eye**-a-kl] adj.

manic adj 1 extremely excited or energetic. 2 affected by mania. **manic-depressive** adj, n Psychiatry (person afflicted with) a mental disorder that causes mood swings from extreme euphoria to deep depression.

manicure n 1 cosmetic care of the fingernails and hands. ▷ v 2 care for (the fingernails and hands) in this way. **manicurist** n.

manifest ❶ adj 1 easily noticed, obvious. ▷ v 2 show plainly. 3 be evidence of. ▷ n 4 list of cargo or passengers for customs. **manifestly** adv **manifestation** n.

manifesto n, pl **-tos, -toes** declaration of policy as issued by a political party.

manifold ❶ adj 1 numerous and varied. ▷ n 2 pipe with several outlets, esp. in an internal-combustion engine.

manikin, mannikin n 1 little man or dwarf. 2 model of the human body.

manila, manilla n strong brown paper used for envelopes.

manipulate ❶ v 1 handle skilfully. 2 control cleverly or deviously. **manipulation** n **manipulative** adj **manipulator** n.

manna n 1 Bible miraculous food which sustained the Israelites in the wilderness. 2 windfall.

mannequin n 1 woman who models clothes at a fashion show. 2 life-size dummy of the human body used to fit or display clothes.

manner ❶ n 1 way a thing happens or is done. 2 person's bearing or behaviour. 3 type or kind. 4 custom

---

THESAURUS

mangy adj 2 = **scruffy**, dirty, moth-eaten, scungy (Aust & NZ inf), seedy, shabby, shoddy, squalid

manhandle v = **rough up**, knock about or around, maul, paw (inf)

manhood n = **manliness**, masculinity, virility

mania n 1 = **obsession**, craze, fad (inf), fetish, fixation, passion, preoccupation, thing (inf) 2 = **madness**, delirium, dementia, derangement, insanity, lunacy

maniac n 1 = **madman** or **madwoman**, lunatic, psycho (sl), psychopath 2 Inf = **fanatic**, enthusiast, fan, fiend (inf), freak (inf)

manifest adj 1 = **obvious**, apparent, blatant, clear, conspicuous, evident, glaring, noticeable, palpable, patent ▷ v 2 = **display**, demonstrate, exhibit, expose, express, reveal, show

manifestation n = **display**, demonstration, exhibition, expression, indication, mark, show, sign, symptom

manifold adj 1 = **numerous**, assorted, copious, diverse, many, multifarious, multiple, varied, various

manipulate v 1 = **work**, handle, operate, use 2 = **influence**, control, direct, engineer, manoeuvre

mankind n = **people**, Homo sapiens, humanity, humankind, human race, man

manliness n = **virility**, boldness, bravery, courage, fearlessness, masculinity, valour, vigour

manly adj = **virile**, bold, brave, courageous, fearless, manful, masculine, strapping, strong, vigorous

man-made adj = **artificial**, ersatz, manufactured, mock, synthetic

manner n 1 = **way**, method, mode 2 = **behaviour**, air, aspect, bearing, conduct, demeanour 3 = **type**, brand, category, form, kind, sort, variety 4 = **style**, custom, fashion

mannered adj = **affected**, artificial, pretentious, stilted

mannerism n = **habit**, characteristic, foible, idiosyncrasy, peculiarity, quirk, trait, trick

manners pl n 5 = **behaviour**, conduct, courtesy, decorum, demeanour, etiquette, politeness, p's and q's, refinement

or style. ▷ *pl* **5** (polite) social
behaviour. **mannered** *adj* affected.
mannerism *n* person's distinctive
habit or trait. **mannerly** *adj* having
good manners, polite.

mannikin *n* same as MANIKIN.

manoeuvre ❶ [man-**noo**-ver] *n*
1 skilful movement. **2** contrived,
complicated, and possibly deceptive
plan or action. ▷ *pl* **3** military or naval
exercises. ▷ *v* **4** manipulate or
contrive skilfully or cunningly.
5 perform manoeuvres.
manoeuvrable *adj*.

manor *n* large country house and its
lands. **manorial** *adj*.

manpower *n* available number of
workers.

manqué [**mong**-kay] *adj* would-be, e.g.
an actor manqué

mansard roof *n* roof with a break in its
slope, the lower part being steeper
than the upper.

manse *n* house provided for a minister
in some religious denominations.

manservant *n, pl* **menservants** male
servant, esp. a valet.

mansion ❶ *n* large house.

manslaughter *n* unlawful but
unintentional killing of a person.

mantel *n* structure round a fireplace.
mantelpiece, mantel shelf *n* shelf
above a fireplace.

mantilla *n* (in Spain) a lace scarf
covering a woman's head and
shoulders.

mantis *n, pl* **-tises, -tes** carnivorous
insect like a grasshopper.

mantle ❶ *n* **1** loose cloak. **2** covering.
3 responsibilities and duties which go

with a particular job or position.
4 incandescent gauze round a gas jet.

mantra *n Hinduism, Buddhism* any
sacred word or syllable used as an
object of concentration.

manual ❶ *adj* **1** of or done with the
hands. **2** by human labour rather than
automatic means. ▷ *n* **3** handbook.
4 organ keyboard. **manually** *adv*.

manufacture ❶ *v* **1** process or make
(goods) on a large scale using
machinery. **2** invent or concoct
(an excuse etc.). ▷ *n* **3** process
of manufacturing goods.
manufacturer *n*.

manure ❶ *n* **1** animal excrement used
as a fertilizer. ▷ *v* **2** fertilize (land) with
this.

manuscript *n* **1** book or document,
orig. one written by hand. **2** copy for
printing.

Manx *adj* **1** of the Isle of Man or its
inhabitants. ▷ *n* **2** almost extinct
language of the Isle of Man. **Manx cat**
tailless breed of cat.

many ❶ *adj* **more, most 1** numerous.
▷ *n* **2** large number.

Maoism *n* form of Marxism advanced
by Mao Tse-tung in China. **Maoist** *n*,
adj.

Māori *n* **1** member of the indigenous
race of New Zealand. **2** language of
the Māoris. ▷ *adj* **3** of the Māoris or
their language.

map *n* **1** representation of the earth's
surface or some part of it, showing
geographical features. **2** *Maths* (also
mapping) same as FUNCTION (sense 4)
v **mapping, mapped 3** make a map
of. **4** *Maths* represent or transform

————————————————————————————————— THESAURUS —————————————————

manoeuvre *n* **1** = **movement**,
exercise, operation **2** = **stratagem**,
dodge, intrigue, machination, ploy,
ruse, scheme, subterfuge, tactic, trick
▷ *v* **4** = **manipulate**, contrive,
engineer, machinate, pull strings,
scheme, wangle (*inf*) **5** = **move**,
deploy, exercise

mansion *n* = **residence**, hall, manor,
seat, villa

mantle *n* **1** = **cloak**, cape, hood, shawl,
wrap **2** = **covering**, blanket, canopy,
curtain, pall, screen, shroud, veil

manual *adj* **1** = **hand-operated**
2 = **human**, physical ▷ *n* **3** = **handbook**,
bible, guide, instructions

manufacture *v* **1** = **make**, assemble,

build, construct, create, mass-
produce, produce, put together, turn
out **2** = **concoct**, cook up (*inf*),
devise, fabricate, invent, make up,
think up, trump up ▷ *n* **3** = **making**,
assembly, construction, creation,
production

manufacturer *n* = **maker**, builder,
constructor, creator, industrialist,
producer

manure *n* **1** = **compost**, droppings,
dung, excrement, fertilizer, kak (*S Afr
sl*), muck, ordure

many *adj* **1** = **numerous**, abundant,
countless, innumerable, manifold,
myriad, umpteen (*inf*), various
▷ *n* **2** = **a lot**, heaps (*inf*), lots (*inf*),

(a function, figure, or set). **map out** v plan.

maple n tree with broad leaves, a variety of which (**sugar maple**) yields sugar. **maple syrup** very sweet syrup made from the sap of the sugar maple.

maple sugar n US & Canad sugar made from the sap of the sugar maple.

mar ❶ v **marring**, **marred** spoil or impair.

Mar. March.

marabou n **1** large black-and-white African stork. **2** its soft white down, used to trim hats etc.

maraca [mar-**rak**-a] n shaken percussion instrument made from a gourd containing dried seeds etc.

maraschino cherry [mar-rass-**kee**-no] n cherry preserved in a cherry liqueur with a taste like bitter almonds.

marathon n **1** long-distance race of 26 miles 385 yards (42.195 kilometres). **2** long or arduous task.

marauding ❶ adj wandering or raiding in search of plunder. **marauder** n.

marble n **1** kind of limestone with a mottled appearance, which can be highly polished. **2** slab of or sculpture in this. **3** small glass ball used in playing marbles. ▷ pl **4** game of rolling these at one another. **marbled** adj having a mottled appearance like marble. **marbling** n.

marcasite n crystals of iron pyrites, used in jewellery.

march¹ ❶ v **1** walk with a military step. **2** make (a person or group) proceed. **3** progress steadily. ▷ n **4** action of marching. **5** steady progress. **6** distance covered by marching. **7** piece of music, as for a march. **marcher** n.

march² n border or frontier.

March n third month of the year.

marchioness [marsh-on-**ness**] n **1** woman holding the rank of marquis. **2** wife or widow of a marquis.

Mardi Gras [**mar**-dee **grah**] n festival of Shrove Tuesday, celebrated in some cities with great revelry.

mare n female horse or zebra. **mare's nest** discovery which proves worthless.

margarine n butter substitute made from animal or vegetable fats.

marge n informal margarine.

margin ❶ n **1** edge or border. **2** blank space round a printed page. **3** additional amount or one greater than necessary. **4** limit. **marginal** adj **1** insignificant, unimportant. **2** near a limit. **3** Politics (of a constituency) won by only a small margin. ▷ n **4** Politics marginal constituency. **marginally** adv.

marguerite n large daisy.

marigold n plant with yellow or orange flowers.

marijuana ❶ [mar-ree-**wah**-na] n dried flowers and leaves of the cannabis plant, used as a drug, esp. in cigarettes.

marimba n Latin American percussion instrument resembling a xylophone.

marina n harbour for yachts and other pleasure boats.

marinade n **1** seasoned liquid in which fish or meat is soaked before cooking. ▷ v **2** same as MARINATE. **marinate** v soak in marinade.

marine ❶ adj **1** of the sea or shipping. **2** used at or found in the sea. ▷ n **3** soldier trained for land and sea combat. **4** country's shipping or fleet. **mariner** [**mar**-in-er] n sailor.

marionette n puppet worked with strings.

---

plenty, scores

mar v = **spoil**, blemish, damage, detract from, disfigure, hurt, impair, ruin, scar, stain, taint, tarnish

marauder n = **raider**, bandit, brigand, buccaneer, outlaw, plunderer

march¹ v **1** = **walk**, pace, parade, stride, strut **3** = **file** ▷ n **4** = **walk**, routemarch, trek **5** = **progress**, advance, development, evolution, progression

margin n **1** = **edge**, border, boundary, brink, perimeter, periphery, rim, side, verge

marginal adj **1** = **insignificant**, minimal, minor, negligible, slight, small **2** = **borderline**, bordering, on the edge, peripheral

marijuana n = **cannabis**, dope (sl), grass (sl), hemp, pot (sl)

marine adj = **nautical**, maritime, naval, seafaring, seagoing

mariner n = **sailor**, salt, sea dog,

marital ❶ *adj* relating to marriage.

maritime ❶ *adj* **1** relating to shipping.
2 of, near, or living in the sea.

marjoram *n* aromatic herb used for seasoning food and in salads.

mark¹ ❶ *n* **1** line, dot, scar, etc. visible on a surface. **2** distinguishing sign or symbol. **3** written or printed symbol. **4** letter or number used to grade academic work. **5** indication of position. **6** indication of some quality. **7** target or goal. ▷ *v* **8** make a mark on. **9** characterize or distinguish. **10** indicate. **11** pay attention to. **12** notice or watch. **13** grade (academic work). **14** stay close to (a sporting opponent) to hamper his or her play. **mark time 1** move the feet up and down as if marching, without moving forward. **2** wait for something more interesting to happen. **marked** *adj* noticeable. **markedly** [**mark**-id-lee] *adv* **marker** *n* **1** object used to show the position of something. **2** (also **marker pen**) thick felt-tipped pen for drawing and colouring. **marking** *n*.

mark² *n* same as DEUTSCHMARK.

market ❶ *n* **1** assembly or place for buying and selling. **2** demand for goods. ▷ *v* **-keting, -keted 3** offer or produce for sale. **on the market** for sale. **marketable** *adj* **marketing** *n* part of a business that controls the way that goods or services are sold. **market garden** place where fruit and vegetables are grown for sale. **market maker** *Stock Exchange*

person who uses a firm's money to create a market for a stock.
marketplace *n* **1** market.
2 commercial world. **market research** research into consumers' needs and purchases.

marksman ❶ *n* person skilled at shooting. **marksmanship** *n*.

marl *n* soil formed of clay and lime, used as fertilizer.

marlin *n* large food and game fish of warm and tropical seas, with a very long upper jaw.

marlinespike, marlinspike [**mar**-lin-spike] *n* pointed hook used to separate strands of rope.

marmalade *n* jam made from citrus fruits.

marmoreal [mar-**more**-ee-al] *adj* of or like marble.

marmoset *n* small bushy-tailed monkey.

marmot *n* burrowing rodent.

maroon¹ *adj* reddish-purple.

maroon² ❶ *v* **1** abandon ashore, esp. on an island. **2** isolate without resources.

marquee *n* large tent used for a party or exhibition.

marquess [**mar**-kwiss] *n Brit* nobleman of the rank below a duke.

marquetry *n* ornamental inlaid work of wood.

marquis *n* (in various countries) nobleman of the rank above a count.

marquise [mar-**keez**] *n* same as MARCHIONESS.

———————— THESAURUS ————————

seafarer, seaman

marital *adj* = **matrimonial**, conjugal, connubial, nuptial

maritime *adj* **1** = **nautical**, marine, naval, oceanic, seafaring **2** = **coastal**, littoral, seaside

mark¹ *n* **1** = **spot**, blemish, blot, line, scar, scratch, smudge, stain, streak **2** = **sign**, badge, device, emblem, flag, hallmark, label, token **3** = **symbol 6** = **criterion**, measure, norm, standard, yardstick **7** = **target**, aim, goal, object, objective, purpose ▷ *v* **8** = **scar**, blemish, blot, scratch, smudge, stain, streak **9** = **distinguish**, brand, characterize, denote, exemplify, flag, identify, illustrate, label, show, stamp **11** = **pay attention**, attend, mind, pay heed

12 = **observe**, note, notice, watch

13 = **grade**, appraise, assess, correct, evaluate

marked *adj* = **noticeable**, blatant, clear, conspicuous, decided, distinct, obvious, patent, prominent, pronounced, striking

markedly *adv* = **noticeably**, clearly, considerably, conspicuously, decidedly, distinctly, obviously, strikingly

market *n* **1** = **fair**, bazaar, mart ▷ *v* **3** = **sell**, retail, vend

marketable *adj* **2** = **sought after**, in demand, saleable, wanted

marksman *n* = **sharpshooter**, crack shot (*inf*), good shot

maroon² *v* **1** = **abandon**, desert, leave **2** = **strand**, leave high and dry (*inf*)

marriage *n* **1** = **matrimony**, wedlock

marram grass n grass that grows on sandy shores.

marrow n 1 fatty substance inside bones. 2 long thick striped green vegetable with whitish flesh.

marry ❶ v **-rying, -ried** 1 take as a husband or wife. 2 join or give in marriage. 3 unite closely. **marriage** n 1 state of being married. 2 wedding. 3 close union or relationship. **marriageable** adj.

Mars n 1 Roman god of war. 2 fourth planet from the sun.

Marsala [mar-**sah**-la] n dark sweet wine.

Marseillaise [mar-say-**yaze**] n French national anthem.

marsh ❶ n low-lying wet land. **marshy** adj **marshier, marshiest**.

marshal ❶ n 1 officer of the highest rank. 2 official who organizes ceremonies or events. 3 US law officer. ▷ v **-shalling, -shalled** 4 arrange in order. 5 assemble. 6 conduct with ceremony. **marshalling yard** railway depot for goods trains.

marshmallow n spongy pink or white sweet.

marsupial [mar-**soop**-ee-al] n animal that carries its young in a pouch, such as a kangaroo.

mart n market.

Martello tower n round tower for coastal defence.

marten n 1 weasel-like animal. 2 its fur.

martial ❶ adj of war, warlike. **martial art** any of various philosophies and techniques of self-defence, orig. Eastern, such as karate. **martial law** law enforced by military authorities in times of danger or emergency.

Martian [**marsh**-an] adj 1 of Mars. ▷ n 2 supposed inhabitant of Mars.

martin n bird with a slightly forked tail.

martinet ❶ n person who maintains strict discipline.

martingale n strap from the reins to the girth of a horse, preventing it from throwing up its head.

martini n cocktail of vermouth and gin.

martyr ❶ n 1 person who dies or suffers for his or her beliefs. ▷ v 2 make a martyr of. **be a martyr to** be constantly suffering from. **martyrdom** n.

marvel ❶ v **-velling, -velled** 1 be filled with wonder. ▷ n 2 wonderful thing. **marvellous** adj 1 amazing. 2 wonderful. **marvellously** adv.

Marxism n political philosophy of Karl Marx. **Marxist** n, adj.

marzipan n paste of ground almonds, sugar, and egg whites.

masc. masculine.

mascara n cosmetic for darkening the eyelashes.

mascot n person, animal, or thing supposed to bring good luck.

masculine ❶ adj 1 relating to males. 2 manly. 3 Grammar of the gender of nouns that includes some male animate things. **masculinity** n.

maser n device for amplifying microwaves.

mash n 1 a soft pulpy mass. 2 informal mashed potatoes. 3 bran or meal mixed with warm water as food for horses etc. ▷ v 4 crush into a soft mass.

——————— THESAURUS ———————

2 = **wedding**, nuptials 3 = **match**

marry v 1 = **wed**, get hitched (sl), tie the knot (inf) 3 = **unite**, ally, bond, join, knit, link, merge, unify, yoke

marsh n = **swamp**, bog, fen, morass, quagmire, slough, muskeg (Canad)

marshal v 4 = **arrange**, align, array, draw up, line up, order, organize 5 = **group**, deploy 6 = **conduct**, escort, guide, lead, shepherd, usher

marshy adj = **swampy**, boggy, quaggy, waterlogged, wet

martial adj = **military**, bellicose, belligerent, warlike

martinet n = **disciplinarian**, stickler

martyrdom n 1 = **persecution**, ordeal, suffering

marvel v 1 = **wonder**, be amazed, be awed, gape ▷ n 2 = **wonder**, miracle, phenomenon, portent, prodigy

marvellous adj 1 = **amazing**, astonishing, astounding, breathtaking, brilliant, extraordinary, jaw-dropping, miraculous, phenomenal, prodigious, spectacular, stupendous 2 = **excellent**, fabulous (inf), fantastic (inf), great (inf), splendid, superb, terrific (inf), wonderful

masculine adj 1 = **male**, manlike, mannish 2 = **manly**, virile

mask ⊕ *n* **1** covering for the face, as a disguise or protection. **2** behaviour that hides one's true feelings. ▷ *v* **3** cover with a mask. **4** hide or disguise. **masking tape** adhesive tape used to protect surfaces surrounding an area to be painted.

masochism [**mass**-oh-kiz-zum] *n* condition in which (sexual) pleasure is obtained from feeling pain or from being humiliated. **masochist** *n* **masochistic** *adj* **masochistically** *adv*.

mason *n* **1** person who works with stone. **2** (**M-**) Freemason. **Masonic** *adj* of Freemasonry. **masonry** *n* **1** stonework. **2** (**M-**) Freemasonry.

masque [**mask**] *n* History 16th–17th-century form of dramatic entertainment.

masquerade ⊕ [mask-er-**aid**] *n* **1** deceptive show or pretence. **2** party at which masks and costumes are worn. ▷ *v* **3** pretend to be someone or something else.

mass ⊕ *n* **1** coherent body of matter. **2** large quantity or number. **3** *Physics* amount of matter in a body. ▷ *adj* **4** large-scale. **5** involving many people. ▷ *v* **6** form into a mass. **massed** *adj* **the masses** ordinary people. **massive** *adj* large and heavy. **massively** *adv* **mass-market** *adj* for

or appealing to a large number of people. **mass media** means of communication to many people, such as television and newspapers. **mass-produce** *v* manufacture (standardized goods) in large quantities. **mass production** manufacturing of standardized goods in large quantities.

Mass *n* service of the Eucharist, esp. in the RC Church.

massacre ⊕ [**mass**-a-ker] *n* **1** indiscriminate killing of large numbers of people. ▷ *v* **2** kill in large numbers.

massage ⊕ [**mass**-ahzh] *n* **1** rubbing and kneading of parts of the body to reduce pain or stiffness. ▷ *v* **2** give a massage to. **masseur** [mass-**ur**], (*fem*) **masseuse** [mass-**uz**] *n* person who gives massages.

massif [**mass**-seef] *n* connected group of mountains.

mast[1] *n* tall pole for supporting something, esp. a ship's sails. **masthead** *n* **1** *Nautical* head of a mast. **2** name of a newspaper printed at the top of the front page.

mast[2] *n* fruit of the beech, oak, etc., used as pig fodder.

mastectomy [mass-**tek**-tom-ee] *n*, *pl* **-mies** surgical removal of a breast.

master ⊕ *n* **1** person in control, such as an employer or an owner of slaves or

⸻ THESAURUS ⸻

mask *n* **1** = **disguise**, camouflage, cover, veil **2** = **front**, facade, guise, screen ▷ *v* **4** = **disguise**, camouflage, cloak, conceal, cover, hide, obscure, screen, veil

masquerade *n* **1** = **pretence**, cloak, cover-up, deception, disguise, mask, pose, screen, subterfuge **2** = **masked ball**, fancy dress party, revel ▷ *v* **3** = **pose**, disguise, dissemble, dissimulate, impersonate, pass oneself off, pretend (to be)

mass *n* **1** = **piece**, block, chunk, hunk, lump **2** = **lot**, bunch, collection, heap, load, pile, quantity, stack **3** = **size**, bulk, greatness, magnitude ▷ *adj* **4** = **large-scale**, extensive, general, indiscriminate, wholesale, widespread ▷ *v* **6** = **gather**, accumulate, assemble, collect, congregate, rally, swarm, throng

massacre *n* **1** = **slaughter**, annihilation, blood bath, butchery,

carnage, extermination, holocaust, murder ▷ *v* **2** = **slaughter**, butcher, cut to pieces, exterminate, kill, mow down, murder, wipe out

massage *n* **1** = **rub-down**, manipulation ▷ *v* **2** = **rub down**, knead, manipulate

massive *adj* = **huge**, big, colossal, enormous, gigantic, hefty, immense, mammoth, monumental, whopping (*inf*)

master *n* **1** = **head**, boss (*inf*), chief, commander, controller, director, governor, lord, manager, ruler **2** = **expert**, ace (*inf*), doyen, fundi (*S Afr*), genius, maestro, past master, virtuoso, wizard **5** = **teacher**, guide, guru, instructor, tutor ▷ *adj* **8** = **main**, chief, foremost, leading, predominant, prime, principal ▷ *v* **9** = **learn**, get the hang of (*inf*), grasp **10** = **overcome**, conquer, defeat, tame, triumph over, vanquish

animals. **2** expert. **3** great artist.
4 original thing from which copies are made. **5** male teacher. **6** (**M-**) title of a boy. ▷ *adj* **7** overall or controlling. **8** main or principal. ▷ *v* **9** acquire knowledge of or skill in. **10** overcome. **masterful** *adj* **1** domineering. **2** showing great skill. **masterly** *adj* showing great skill. **mastery** *n* **1** expertise. **2** control or command. **master key** key that opens all the locks of a set. **mastermind** *v* **1** plan and direct (a complex task). ▷ *n* **2** person who plans and directs a complex task. **master of ceremonies** person who presides over a public ceremony, formal dinner, or entertainment, introducing the events and performers. **masterpiece** *n* outstanding work of art. **masterstroke** *n* outstanding piece of strategy, skill, or talent.

mastic *n* **1** gum obtained from certain trees. **2** putty-like substance used as a filler, adhesive, or seal.

masticate *v* chew. **mastication** *n*.

mastiff *n* large dog.

mastitis *n* inflammation of a breast or udder.

mastodon *n* extinct elephant-like mammal.

mastoid *n* projection of the bone behind the ear. **mastoiditis** *n* inflammation of this area.

masturbate *v* fondle the genitals (of). **masturbation** *n*.

mat¹ *n* **1** piece of fabric used as a floor covering or to protect a surface. **2** thick tangled mass. ▷ *v* **matting**, **matted 3** tangle or become tangled into a dense mass. **on the mat** *informal* summoned for a reprimand. **matted** *adj*.

mat² *adj* same as MATT.

matador *n* man who kills the bull in bullfights.

match¹ ❶ *n* **1** contest in a game or sport. **2** person or thing exactly like, equal to, or in harmony with another. **3** marriage. ▷ *v* **4** be exactly like, equal to, or in harmony with. **5** put in competition (with). **6** find a match for. **7** join (in marriage). **matchless** *adj* unequalled. **matchmaker** *n* person who schemes to bring about a marriage. **matchmaking** *n, adj*.

match² *n* small stick with a tip which ignites when scraped on a rough surface. **matchbox** *n* **matchstick** *n* **1** wooden part of a match. ▷ *adj* **2** (of drawn figures) thin and straight. **matchwood** *n* small splinters.

mate¹ ❶ *n* **1** *informal* friend. **2** *informal* common British and Australian term of address between males. **3** associate or colleague, e.g. *running mate; team-mate*. **4** sexual partner of an animal. **5** officer in a merchant ship. **6** tradesman's assistant. ▷ *v* **7** pair (animals) or (of animals) be paired for reproduction.

mate² *n, v Chess* checkmate.

masterful *adj* **1** = **domineering**, arrogant, bossy (*inf*), high-handed, imperious, overbearing, overweening **2** = **skilful**, adroit, consummate, expert, fine, first-rate, masterly, superlative, supreme, world-class

masterly *adj* = **skilful**, adroit, consummate, crack (*inf*), expert, first-rate, masterful, supreme, world-class

mastermind *v* **1** = **plan**, conceive, devise, direct, manage, organize ▷ *n* **2** = **organizer**, architect, brain(s) (*inf*), director, engineer, manager, planner

masterpiece *n* = **classic**, jewel, magnum opus, pièce de résistance, tour de force

mastery *n* **1** = **expertise**, finesse, know-how (*inf*), proficiency, prowess, skill, virtuosity **2** = **control**,

ascendancy, command, domination, superiority, supremacy, upper hand, whip hand

match¹ *n* **1** = **game**, bout, competition, contest, head-to-head, test, trial **2** = **equal**, counterpart, peer, rival **3** = **marriage**, alliance, pairing, partnership ▷ *v* **4** = **correspond**, accord, agree, fit, go with, harmonize, tally **5** = **rival**, compare, compete, emulate, equal, measure up to

matchless *adj* = **unequalled**, incomparable, inimitable, superlative, supreme, unmatched, unparalleled, unrivalled, unsurpassed

mate¹ *n* **1** *Inf* = **friend**, buddy (*inf*), chum (*inf*), comrade, crony, pal (*inf*) **3** = **colleague**, associate, companion **6** = **assistant**, helper, subordinate ▷ *v* **7** = **pair**, breed, couple

material ❶ *n* **1** substance of which a thing is made. **2** cloth. **3** information on which a piece of work may be based. ▷ *pl* **4** things needed for an activity. ▷ *adj* **5** of matter or substance. **6** not spiritual. **7** affecting physical wellbeing. **8** relevant. **materially** *adv* considerably.
materialism *n* **1** excessive interest in or desire for money and possessions. **2** belief that only the material world exists. **materialist** *adj, n*
materialistic *adj* **materialize** *v* **1** actually happen. **2** come into existence or view. **materialization** *n*.
maternal ❶ *adj* **1** of a mother. **2** related through one's mother. **maternity** *n* **1** motherhood. ▷ *adj* **2** of or for pregnant women, e.g. *maternity leave*.
matey ❶ *adj informal* friendly or intimate.
math *n US & Canad* mathematics.
mathematics *n* science of number, quantity, shape, and space. **mathematical** *adj* **mathematically** *adv* **mathematician** *n*.
maths *n informal* mathematics.
matinée [**mat**-in-nay] *n* afternoon performance in a theatre or cinema.
matins *pl n* early morning service in various Christian Churches.
matriarch [**mate**-ree-ark] *n* female head of a tribe or family. **matriarchal** *adj* **matriarchy** *n, pl* **-archies** society governed by a female, in which

descent is traced through the female line.
matrices [**may**-triss-eez] *n* plural of MATRIX.
matricide *n* **1** crime of killing one's mother. **2** person who does this.
matriculate *v* enrol or be enrolled in a college or university. **matriculation** *n*.
matrimony ❶ *n* marriage. **matrimonial** *adj*.
matrix [**may**-trix] *n, pl* **matrices** **1** substance or situation in which something originates, takes form, or is enclosed. **2** mould for casting. **3** *Maths* rectangular array of numbers or elements.
matron *n* **1** staid or dignified married woman. **2** woman who supervises the domestic or medical arrangements of an institution. **3** former name for NURSING OFFICER. **matronly** *adj* (of a woman) middle-aged and plump.
matt *adj* dull, not shiny.
matter ❶ *n* **1** substance of which something is made. **2** physical substance. **3** event, situation, or subject. **4** written material in general. **5** pus. ▷ *v* **6** be of importance. **what's the matter?** what is wrong? **matter-of-fact** *adj* unimaginative or emotionless. **matter-of-factly** *adv* **matter-of-factness** *n*.
matting *n* coarsely woven fabric used as a floor-covering and packing material.
mattock *n* large pick with one of its blade ends flattened for loosening soil.

————————————————————————————— THESAURUS —————

material *n* **1** = **substance**, matter, stuff **2** = **cloth**, fabric **3** = **information**, data, evidence, facts, notes ▷ *adj* **5** = **tangible**, concrete, palpable, substantial **6** = **physical**, bodily, corporeal **8** = **relevant**, applicable, apposite, apropos, germane, pertinent
materialize *v* **1** = **occur**, come about, come to pass, happen **2** = **appear**, take shape, turn up
materially *adv* = **significantly**, essentially, gravely, greatly, much, seriously, substantially
maternal *adj* **1** = **motherly**
maternity *n* **1** = **motherhood**, motherliness
matey *adj Inf* = **friendly**, chummy (*inf*), hail-fellow-well-met, intimate, pally (*inf*), sociable, thick (*inf*)

matrimonial *adj* = **marital**, conjugal, connubial, nuptial
matrimony *n* = **marriage**, nuptials, wedding ceremony, wedlock
matted *adj* **3** = **tangled**, knotted, tousled, uncombed
matter *n* **1** = **substance**, material, stuff **2** = **body** **3** = **situation**, affair, business, concern, event, incident, proceeding, question, subject, topic ▷ *v* **6** = **be important**, carry weight, count, make a difference, signify **what's the matter?** = **problem**, complication, difficulty, distress, trouble, worry
matter-of-fact *adj* = **unsentimental**, deadpan, down-to-earth, emotionless, mundane, plain, prosaic, sober, unimaginative

mattress n large stuffed flat case, often with springs, used on or as a bed.
mature ⓘ adj **1** fully developed or grown-up. **2** ripe. ▷ v **3** make or become mature. **4** (of a bill or bond) become due for payment. **maturity** n state of being mature. **maturation** n process of becoming mature.
maudlin ⓘ adj foolishly or tearfully sentimental.
maul ⓘ v **1** handle roughly. **2** beat or tear.
maunder v talk or act aimlessly or idly.
mausoleum [maw-so-**lee**-um] n stately tomb.
mauve adj pale purple.
maverick ⓘ n, adj independent and unorthodox (person).
maw n animal's mouth, throat, or stomach.
mawkish ⓘ adj foolishly sentimental. **mawkishness** n.
max. maximum.
maxim ⓘ n general truth or principle.
maximum ⓘ adj, n, pl **-mums**, **-ma** greatest possible (amount or number). **maximal** adj maximum. **maximize** v increase to a maximum. **maximization** n.
may v, past tense **might** used as an auxiliary to express possibility, permission, opportunity, etc. **maybe** adv perhaps, possibly.

● **USAGE NOTE**
● In very careful usage may is used
● in preference to can for asking
● permission. Might is used to express
● a more tentative request: May/
● might I ask a favour?

May n **1** fifth month of the year. **2** (**m-**) same as HAWTHORN. **mayfly** n short-lived aquatic insect. **maypole** n pole set up for dancing round on May 1 to celebrate spring.
maybe ⓘ adv perhaps, possibly.
Mayday n international radio distress signal.
mayhem ⓘ n violent destruction or confusion.
mayonnaise n creamy sauce of egg yolks, oil, and vinegar.

● **SPELLING TIP**
● There are two ns to remember
● in the middle of **mayonnaise**
● - possibly a good reason for the
● increasing use of the abbreviation
● 'mayo'.

mayor n head of a municipality. **mayoress** n **1** mayor's wife. **2** female mayor. **mayoralty** n, pl **-ties** (term of) office of a mayor.
maze ⓘ n **1** complex network of paths or lines designed to puzzle. **2** any confusing network or system.
mazurka n **1** lively Polish dance. **2** music for this.
MB 1 Bachelor of Medicine. **2** Manitoba.
MBE Member of the Order of the British Empire.
MC Master of Ceremonies.
MCC Marylebone Cricket Club.
Md Chemistry mendelevium.
MD 1 Doctor of Medicine. **2** Managing Director. **3** Maryland.
MDMA n same as ECSTASY (sense 2).

───── **THESAURUS** ─────

mature adj **1** = **grown-up**, adult, full-grown, fully fledged, of age **2** = **ripe**, mellow, ready, seasoned ▷ v **3** = **develop**, age, bloom, blossom, come of age, grow up, mellow, ripen
maturity n = **adulthood**, experience, manhood or womanhood, ripeness, wisdom
maudlin adj = **sentimental**, mawkish, overemotional, slushy (inf), soppy (Brit inf), tearful, weepy (inf)
maul v **1** = **ill-treat**, abuse, batter, manhandle, molest **2** = **tear**, claw, lacerate, mangle
maverick n = **rebel**, dissenter, eccentric, heretic, iconoclast, individualist, nonconformist, protester, radical ▷ adj = **rebel**, dissenting, eccentric, heretical,

iconoclastic, individualistic, nonconformist, radical
mawkish adj = **sentimental**, emotional, maudlin, schmaltzy (sl), slushy (inf), soppy (Brit inf)
maxim n = **saying**, adage, aphorism, axiom, dictum, motto, proverb, rule
maximum adj = **greatest**, highest, most, paramount, supreme, topmost, utmost ▷ n = **top**, ceiling, height, peak, pinnacle, summit, upper limit, utmost, zenith
maybe adv = **perhaps**, perchance (arch), possibly
mayhem n = **chaos**, commotion, confusion, destruction, disorder, fracas, havoc, trouble, violence
maze n **1** = **labyrinth 2** = **web**, confusion, imbroglio, tangle

MDT (in the US and Canada) Mountain Daylight Time.

me¹ *pron* objective form of I¹.

me² *n Music* (in tonic sol-fa) third degree of any major scale.

ME 1 myalgic encephalomyelitis: painful muscles and general weakness sometimes persisting long after a viral illness. **2** Maine.

mead *n* alcoholic drink made from honey.

meadow ⊕ *n* piece of grassland. **meadowsweet** *n* plant with dense heads of small fragrant flowers.

meagre ⊕ *adj* scanty or insufficient.

meal¹ *n* **1** occasion when food is served and eaten. **2** the food itself. **make a meal of** *informal* perform (a task) with an unnecessary amount of effort. **meals-on-wheels** *n* service taking hot meals to elderly or infirm people in their own homes. **meal ticket** *slang* person or situation providing a source of livelihood or income.

meal² *n* grain ground to powder. **mealy** *adj* **mealier**, **mealiest**. **mealy-mouthed** *adj* not outspoken enough.

mealie *n S Afr* maize.

mean¹ ⊕ *v* **meaning**, **meant 1** intend to convey or express. **2** signify,

denote, or portend. **3** intend. **4** have importance as specified. **meaning** *n* sense, significance. **meaningful** *adj* important or significant. **meaningfully** *adv* **meaningfulness** *n* **meaningless** *adj* **meaninglessly** *adv* **meaninglessness** *n*.

mean² ⊕ *adj* **1** miserly, ungenerous, or petty. **2** despicable or callous. **3** *Chiefly US informal* bad-tempered. **meanly** *adv* **meanness** *n* **meanie** *n informal* unkind or miserly person.

mean³ ⊕ *n* **1** middle point between two extremes. **2** average. ▷ *pl* **3** method by which something is done. **4** money. ▷ *adj* **5** intermediate in size or quantity. **6** average. **by all means** certainly. **by no means** in no way. **means test** inquiry into a person's means to decide on eligibility for financial aid.

meander ⊕ [mee-**and**-er] *v* **1** follow a winding course. **2** wander aimlessly. ▷ *n* **3** winding course.

meant *v* past of MEAN¹.

meantime ⊕ *n* **1** intervening period. ▷ *adv* **2** meanwhile.

meanwhile *adv* **1** during the intervening period. **2** at the same time.

meadow *n* = **field**, grassland, lea (*poet*), pasture

meagre *adj* = **insubstantial**, inadequate, measly, paltry, poor, puny, scanty, slight, small

mean¹ *v* **1** = **express**, convey, imply, indicate **2** = **signify**, denote, represent, spell, stand for, symbolize **3** = **intend**, aim, aspire, design, desire, plan, set out, want, wish

mean² *adj* **1** = **miserly**, mercenary, niggardly, parsimonious, penny-pinching, stingy, tight-fisted, ungenerous **2** = **dishonourable**, callous, contemptible, despicable, hard-hearted, petty, shabby, shameful, sordid, vile

mean³ *n* **1** = **middle**, balance, compromise, happy medium, midpoint ▷ *adj* **6** = **average**, norm, standard

meander *v* **1** = **wind**, snake, turn, zigzag **2** = **wander**, ramble, stroll ▷ *n* **3** = **curve**, bend, coil, loop, turn, twist, zigzag

meaning *n* = **sense**, connotation, drift, gist, message, significance, substance

meaningful *adj* = **significant**, important, material, purposeful, relevant, useful, valid, worthwhile

meaningless *adj* = **pointless**, empty, futile, inane, inconsequential, insignificant, senseless, useless, vain, worthless

meanness *n* **1** = **miserliness**, niggardliness, parsimony, selfishness, stinginess **2** = **pettiness**, disgracefulness, ignobility, narrow-mindedness, shabbiness, shamefulness

means *pl n* **3** = **method**, agency, instrument, medium, mode, process, way **4** = **money**, affluence, capital, fortune, funds, income, lolly (*Aust & NZ sl*), resources, wealth, wherewithal **by all means** = **certainly**, definitely, doubtlessly, of course, surely **by no means** = **in no way**, definitely not, not in the least, on no account

meantime *adv* **2** = **at the same time**, concurrently, in the interim,

measles ⓘ n infectious disease producing red spots. **measly** adj **-lier**, **-liest** informal meagre.

measure ⓘ n 1 size or quantity. 2 graduated scale etc. for measuring size or quantity. 3 unit of size or quantity. 4 extent. 5 action taken. 6 law. 7 poetical rhythm. ▷ v 8 determine the size or quantity of. 9 be (a specified amount) in size or quantity. **measurable** adj **measured** adj 1 slow and steady. 2 carefully considered. **measurement** n 1 measuring. 2 size. **measure up to** v fulfil (expectations or requirements).

meat ⓘ n animal flesh as food. **meaty** adj **meatier**, **meatiest** 1 (tasting) of or like meat. 2 brawny. 3 full of significance or interest.

Mecca n 1 holy city of Islam. 2 place that attracts visitors.

mechanic ⓘ n person skilled in repairing or operating machinery. **mechanics** n scientific study of motion and force. **mechanical** adj 1 of or done by machines. 2 (of an action) without thought or feeling. **mechanically** adv.

mechanism ⓘ n 1 way a machine works. 2 piece of machinery. 3 process or technique, e.g. defence mechanism. **mechanistic** adj

mechanize v 1 equip with machinery. 2 make mechanical or automatic. 3 Military equip (an army) with armoured vehicles. **mechanization** n.

med. 1 medical. 2 medicine. 3 medieval. 4 medium.

medal n piece of metal with an inscription etc., given as a reward or memento. **medallion** n 1 disc-shaped ornament worn on a chain round the neck. 2 large medal. 3 circular decorative device in architecture. **medallist** n winner of a medal.

meddle ⓘ v interfere annoyingly. **meddler** n **meddlesome** adj.

media n 1 a plural of MEDIUM. 2 the mass media collectively. **media event** event that is staged for or exploited by the mass media.

● **USAGE NOTE**
● Although media is a plural noun,
● there is an increasing tendency
● to use it as a singular noun, as in
● the use of this media and the media
● is obsessed with celebrities. This is
● probably because a lot of people
● do not realize the '-a' ending is a
● plural one.

mediaeval [med-ee-**eve**-al] adj same as MEDIEVAL.

medial [**mee**-dee-al] adj of or in the middle.

m

——————— THESAURUS ———————

simultaneously

measly adj Inf = **meagre**, miserable, paltry, pathetic, pitiful, poor, puny, scanty, skimpy

measurable adj = **quantifiable**, assessable, perceptible, significant

measure n 1 = **quantity**, allotment, allowance, amount, portion, quota, ration, share 2 = **gauge**, metre, rule, scale, yardstick 5 = **action**, act, deed, expedient, manoeuvre, means, procedure, step 6 = **law**, act, bill, resolution, statute 7 = **rhythm**, beat, cadence, metre, verse ▷ v 8 = **quantify**, assess, calculate, calibrate, compute, determine, evaluate, gauge, weigh

measured adj 1 = **steady**, dignified, even, leisurely, regular, sedate, slow, solemn, stately, unhurried 2 = **considered**, calculated, deliberate, reasoned, sober, studied, well-thought-out

measurement n 1 = **calculation**, assessment, calibration,

computation, evaluation, mensuration, valuation

measure up to v = **fulfil the expectations**, be equal to, be suitable, come up to scratch (inf), fit or fill the bill, make the grade (inf)

meat n = **food**, flesh, tucker (Aust & NZ inf)

meaty adj 2 = **brawny**, beefy (inf), burly, heavily built, heavy, muscular, solid, strapping, sturdy 3 = **interesting**, meaningful, profound, rich, significant, substantial

mechanical adj 1 = **automatic**, automated 2 = **unthinking**, automatic, cursory, impersonal, instinctive, involuntary, perfunctory, routine, unfeeling

mechanism n 2 = **machine**, apparatus, appliance, contrivance, device, instrument, tool 3 = **process**, agency, means, method, methodology, operation, procedure, system, technique, way

meddle v = **interfere**, butt in,

median *adj*, *n* middle (point or line).

mediate ❶ [**mee**-dee-ate] *v* intervene in a dispute to bring about agreement. **mediation** *n* **mediator** *n*.

medic *n informal* doctor or medical student.

medical *adj* 1 of the science of medicine. ▷ *n* 2 *informal* medical examination. **medically** *adv* **medicament** [mid-**dik**-a-ment] *n* a medicine. **medicate** *v* treat with a medicinal substance. **medication** *n* (treatment with) a medicinal substance.

medicine ❶ *n* 1 substance used to treat disease. 2 science of preventing, diagnosing, or curing disease. **medicinal** [med-**diss**-in-al] *adj* having therapeutic properties. **medical** *adj* **medicinally** *adv* **medicine man** witch doctor.

medieval [med-ee-**eve**-al] *adj* of the Middle Ages.

mediocre ❶ [mee-dee-**oak**-er] *adj* 1 average in quality. 2 second-rate. **mediocrity** [mee-dee-**ok**-rit-ee] *n* 1 state of being mediocre. 2 *pl* **-rities** mediocre person.

meditate ❶ *v* 1 reflect deeply, esp. on spiritual matters. 2 think about or plan. **meditation** *n* **meditative** *adj* **meditatively** *adv* **meditator** *n*.

Mediterranean *adj* of (the area around) the Mediterranean Sea, between S Europe, N Africa, and SW Asia.

medium ❶ *adj* 1 midway between extremes, average. ▷ *n*, *pl* **-dia**, **-diums** 2 middle state, degree, or condition. 3 intervening substance producing an effect. 4 means of communicating news or information to the public, such as radio or newspapers. 5 person who can supposedly communicate with the dead. 6 surroundings or environment. 7 category of art according to the material used. **medium wave** radio wave with a wavelength between 100 and 1000 metres.

medlar *n* apple-like fruit of a small tree, eaten when it begins to decay.

medley ❶ *n* 1 miscellaneous mixture. 2 musical sequence of different tunes.

medulla [mid-**dull**-la] *n*, *pl* **-las**, **-lae** marrow, pith, or inner tissue.

meek ❶ *adj* submissive or humble. **meekly** *adv* **meekness** *n*.

meerkat *n* S African mongoose.

meerschaum [**meer**-shum] *n* 1 white substance like clay. 2 tobacco pipe with a bowl made of this.

————————————————————————— THESAURUS ——————————————

intervene, intrude, pry, tamper

meddlesome *adj* = **interfering**, intrusive, meddling, mischievous, officious, prying

mediate *v* = **intervene**, arbitrate, conciliate, intercede, reconcile, referee, step in (*inf*), umpire

mediation *n* = **arbitration**, conciliation, intercession, intervention, reconciliation

mediator *n* = **negotiator**, arbiter, arbitrator, go-between, honest broker, intermediary, middleman, peacemaker, referee, umpire

medicinal *adj* = **therapeutic**, curative, healing, medical, remedial, restorative

medicine *n* 1 = **remedy**, cure, drug, medicament, medication, nostrum

mediocre *adj* 1 = **average**, indifferent, middling, ordinary, passable, pedestrian, run-of-the-mill, so-so (*inf*), undistinguished 2 = **second-rate**, inferior

mediocrity *n* 1 a = **insignificance**, indifference, ordinariness,

unimportance b = **inferiority**

meditate *v* 1 = **reflect**, cogitate, consider, contemplate, deliberate, muse, ponder, ruminate, think 2 = **plan**, have in mind, intend, purpose, scheme

meditation *n* = **reflection**, cogitation, contemplation, musing, pondering, rumination, study, thought

medium *adj* 1 = **average**, fair, intermediate, mean, median, mediocre, middle, middling, midway ▷ *n* 2 = **middle**, average, centre, compromise, mean, midpoint 3 = **means**, agency, channel, instrument, mode, organ, vehicle, way 5 = **spiritualist**, channeller 6 = **environment**, atmosphere, conditions, milieu, setting, surroundings

medley *n* 1 = **mixture**, assortment, farrago, hotchpotch, jumble, *melange*, miscellany, mishmash, mixed bag (*inf*), potpourri

meek *adj* = **submissive**, acquiescent,

meet¹ ❶ *v* **meeting**, **met 1** come together (with). **2** come into contact (with). **3** be at the place of arrival of. **4** make the acquaintance of. **5** satisfy (a need etc.). **6** experience. ▷ *n* **7** sports meeting. **8** assembly of a hunt. **meeting** *n* **1** coming together. **2** assembly.

● **USAGE NOTE**
● *Meet* is only followed by *with* in the
● context of misfortune: *I met his son;*
● *I met with an accident.*

meet² *adj obs* fit or suitable.
meg *n Computers informal* short for MEGABYTE.
mega *adj slang* extremely good, great, or successful.
mega- *combining form* **1** denoting one million, e.g. *megawatt.* **2** very great, e. g. *megastar.*
megabyte *n Computers* 220 or 1 048 576 bytes.
megahertz *n, pl* **-hertz** one million hertz.
megalith *n* great stone, esp. as part of a prehistoric monument. **megalithic** *adj.*
megalomania *n* craving for or mental delusions of power. **megalomaniac** *adj, n.*
megaphone *n* cone-shaped instrument used to amplify the voice.
megapode *n* bird of Australia, New Guinea, and adjacent islands.

megaton *n* explosive power equal to that of one million tons of TNT.
meiosis [my-**oh**-siss] *n* type of cell division in which reproductive cells are produced, each containing half the chromosome number of the parent nucleus.
melamine *n* colourless crystalline compound used in making synthetic resins.
melancholy ❶ [**mel**-an-kol-lee] *n* **1** sadness or gloom. ▷ *adj* **2** sad or gloomy. **melancholia** [mel-an-**kole**-lee-a] *n* state of depression. **melancholic** *adj, n.*
melange [may-**lahnzh**] *n* mixture.
melanin *n* dark pigment found in the hair, skin, and eyes of humans and animals.
Melba toast *n* very thin crisp toast.
mêlée ❶ [**mel**-lay] *n* noisy confused fight or crowd.
mellifluous ❶ [mel-**lif**-flew-uss] *adj* (of sound) smooth and sweet.
mellow ❶ *adj* **1** soft, not harsh. **2** kind-hearted, esp. through maturity. **3** (of fruit) ripe. ▷ *v* **4** make or become mellow.
melodrama ❶ *n* **1** play full of extravagant action and emotion. **2** overdramatic behaviour or emotion. **melodramatic** *adj.*

m

——————— THESAURUS ———————

compliant, deferential, docile, gentle, humble, mild, modest, timid, unassuming, unpretentious
meekness *n* = **submissiveness**, acquiescence, compliance, deference, docility, gentleness, humility, mildness, modesty, timidity
meet¹ *v* **1** = **gather**, assemble, collect, come together, congregate, convene, muster **2 a** = **encounter**, bump into, chance on, come across, confront, contact, find, happen on, run across, run into **b** = **converge**, come together, connect, cross, intersect, join, link up, touch **5** = **fulfil**, answer, come up to, comply with, discharge, match, measure up to, satisfy **6** = **experience**, bear, encounter, endure, face, go through, suffer, undergo
meeting *n* **1** = **encounter**, assignation, confrontation, engagement, introduction, rendezvous, tryst **2** = **conference**, assembly, conclave, congress, convention, gathering, get-together

(*inf*), reunion, session
melancholy *n* **1** = **sadness**, dejection, depression, despondency, gloom, low spirits, misery, sorrow, unhappiness ▷ *adj* **2** = **sad**, depressed, despondent, dispirited, downhearted, gloomy, glum, miserable, mournful, sorrowful
mêlée *n* = **fight**, brawl, fracas, free-for-all (*inf*), rumpus, scrimmage, scuffle, set-to (*inf*), skirmish, tussle
mellifluous *adj* = **sweet**, dulcet, euphonious, honeyed, silvery, smooth, soft, soothing, sweet-sounding
mellow *adj* **1** = **soft**, delicate **3** = **ripe**, full-flavoured, mature, rich, sweet ▷ *v* **4** = **mature**, develop, improve, ripen, season, soften, sweeten
melodious *adj* **1** = **sweet-sounding**, dulcet, euphonious **2** = **musical**, harmonious, melodic, tuneful
melodramatic *adj* **2** = **theatrical**, blood-and-thunder, extravagant, histrionic, overdramatic,

melody ❶ *n, pl* **-dies 1** series of musical notes which make a tune. **2** sweet sound. **melodic** [mel-**lod**-ik] *adj* **1** of melody. **2** melodious. **melodious** [mel-**lode**-ee-uss] *adj* **1** pleasing to the ear. **2** tuneful.

melon *n* large round juicy fruit with a hard rind.

melt ❶ *v* **1** (cause to) become liquid by heat. **2** dissolve. **3** disappear. **4** blend (into). **5** soften through emotion. **meltdown** *n* (in a nuclear reactor) melting of the fuel rods, with the possible release of radiation. **melting pot** place or situation in which many races, ideas, etc., are mixed.

member ❶ *n* **1** individual making up a body or society. **2** limb. **membership** *n* **Member of Parliament** person elected to parliament.

membrane *n* thin flexible tissue in a plant or animal body. **membranous** *adj*.

memento ❶ *n, pl* **-tos, -toes** thing serving to remind, souvenir.

memo *n, pl* **memos** short for MEMORANDUM.

memoir ❶ [**mem**-wahr] *n* **1** biography or historical account based on personal knowledge. ▷ *pl* **2** collection of these. **3** autobiography.

memorable ❶ *adj* worth

remembering, noteworthy. **memorably** *adv* **memorabilia** *pl n* objects connected with famous people or events.

memorandum ❶ *n, pl* **-dums, -da 1** written record or communication within a business. **2** note of things to be remembered.

memory ❶ *n, pl* **-ries 1** ability to remember. **2** sum of things remembered. **3** particular recollection. **4** length of time one can remember. **5** commemoration. **6** part of a computer which stores information. **memorable** *adj* **memorize** *v* commit to memory. **memorial** *n* **1** something serving to commemorate a person or thing. ▷ *adj* **2** serving as a memorial. **memory card** small removable data storage device, used in mobile phones, digital cameras, etc.

memsahib *n* (formerly, in India) term of respect used for a European married woman.

men *n* plural of MAN.

menace ❶ *n* **1** threat. **2** *informal* nuisance. ▷ *v* **3** threaten, endanger. **menacing** *adj* **menacingly** *adv*.

ménage [may-**nahzh**] *n* household.

menagerie [min-**naj**-er-ee] *n* collection of wild animals for exhibition.

— THESAURUS —

overemotional, sensational

melody *n* **1** = **tune**, air, music, song, strain, theme **2** = **tunefulness**, euphony, harmony, melodiousness, musicality

melt *v* **1, 2** = **dissolve**, fuse, liquefy, soften, thaw **3** = **disappear**, disperse, dissolve, evanesce, evaporate, fade, vanish **5** = **soften**, disarm, mollify, outspan (*S Afr*), relax

member *n* **1** = **representative**, associate, fellow **2** = **limb**, appendage, arm, extremity, leg, part

membership *n* **1** = **members**, associates, body, fellows

memento *n* = **souvenir**, keepsake, memorial, relic, remembrance, reminder, token, trophy

memoir *n* **1** = **account**, biography, essay, journal, life, monograph, narrative, record, register *pl* **3** = **autobiography**, diary, experiences, journals, life story, memories, recollections, reminiscences

memorable *adj* = **noteworthy**, celebrated, famous, historic, momentous, notable, remarkable, significant, striking, unforgettable

memorandum *n* **1** = **note**, communication, jotting, memo, message, minute **2** = **reminder**

memorial *n* **1** = **monument**, memento, plaque, record, remembrance, souvenir ▷ *adj* **2** = **commemorative**, monumental

memorize *v* = **remember**, commit to memory, learn, learn by heart, learn by rote

memory *n* **1** = **recall**, retention **3** = **recollection**, remembrance, reminiscence **5** = **commemoration**, honour, remembrance

menace *n* **1** = **threat**, intimidation, warning **2** *Inf* = **nuisance**, annoyance, pest, plague, troublemaker ▷ *v* **3** = **threaten**, bully, frighten, intimidate, loom, lour *or* lower, terrorize

mend ❶ v 1 repair or patch. 2 recover or heal. 3 make or become better. ▷ n 4 mended area. **on the mend** regaining health.

mendacity ❶ n (tendency to) untruthfulness. **mendacious** adj.

mendelevium n Chemistry artificially produced radioactive element.

mendicant adj 1 begging. ▷ n 2 beggar.

menfolk pl n men collectively, esp. the men of a particular family.

menhir [**men**-hear] n single upright prehistoric stone.

menial ❶ [**mean**-nee-al] adj 1 involving boring work of low status. ▷ n 2 domestic servant.

meningitis [men-in-**jite**-iss] n inflammation of the membranes of the brain.

meniscus n 1 curved surface of a liquid. 2 crescent-shaped lens.

menopause n time when a woman's menstrual cycle ceases. **menopausal** adj.

menstruation n approximately monthly discharge of blood and cellular debris from the womb of a nonpregnant woman. **menstruate** v **menstrual** adj.

mensuration n measuring, esp. in geometry.

mental ❶ adj 1 of, in, or done by the mind. 2 of or for mental illness. 3 informal insane. **mentally** adv **mentality** n, pl **-ties** way of thinking.

menthol n organic compound found in peppermint, used medicinally.

mention ❶ v 1 refer to briefly. 2 acknowledge. ▷ n 3 brief reference to a person or thing. 4 acknowledgment.

mentor ❶ n adviser or guide.

menu ❶ n 1 list of dishes to be served, or from which to order. 2 Computers list of options displayed on a screen.

MEP Member of the European Parliament.

mercantile ❶ adj of trade or traders.

Mercator projection [mer-**kate**-er] n method of map-making in which latitude and longitude form a rectangular grid.

mercenary ❶ adj 1 influenced by greed. 2 working merely for reward. ▷ n, pl **-aries** 3 hired soldier.

mercerized adj (of cotton) given lustre by treating with chemicals.

merchandise ❶ n commodities.

m

———————— THESAURUS ————————

menacing adj = **threatening**, forbidding, frightening, intimidating, looming, louring or lowering, ominous

mend v 1 = **repair**, darn, fix, patch, refit, renew, renovate, restore, retouch 2 = **heal**, convalesce, get better, recover, recuperate 3 = **improve**, ameliorate, amend, correct, emend, rectify, reform, revise ▷ n 4 = **repair**, darn, patch, stitch **on the mend** = **convalescent**, getting better, improving, recovering, recuperating

mendacious adj = **lying**, deceitful, deceptive, dishonest, duplicitous, fallacious, false, fraudulent, insincere, untruthful

menial adj 1 = **unskilled**, boring, dull, humdrum, low-status, routine ▷ n 2 = **servant**, attendant, dogsbody (inf), drudge, flunky, lackey, skivvy (chiefly Brit), underling

mental adj 1 = **intellectual**, cerebral 3 Inf = **insane**, deranged, disturbed, mad, mentally ill, psychotic, unbalanced, unstable

mentality n = **attitude**, cast of mind, character, disposition, make-up, outlook, personality, psychology

mentally adv 1 = **in the mind**, in one's head, intellectually, inwardly, psychologically

mention v 1 = **refer to**, bring up, declare, disclose, divulge, intimate, point out, reveal, state, touch upon ▷ n 3 = **reference**, allusion, indication, observation, remark 4 = **acknowledgment**, citation, recognition, tribute

mentor n = **guide**, adviser, coach, counsellor, guru, instructor, teacher, tutor

menu n 1 = **bill of fare**, carte du jour, tariff (chiefly Brit)

mercantile adj = **commercial**, trading

mercenary adj 1 = **greedy**, acquisitive, avaricious, grasping, money-grubbing (inf), sordid, venal ▷ n 3 = **hireling**, soldier of fortune

merchandise n = **goods**, commodities, produce, products, stock, wares

merchant ⊕ *n* person engaged in trade, wholesale trader. **merchandise** *n* commodities. **merchant bank** bank dealing mainly with businesses and investment. **merchantman** *n* trading ship. **merchant navy** ships or crew engaged in a nation's commercial shipping.

mercury ⊕ *n* **1** *Chemistry* silvery liquid metal. **2** (**M-**) *Roman myth* messenger of the gods. **3** (**M-**) planet nearest the sun. **mercurial** [mer-**cure**-ee-al] *adj* lively, changeable.

mercy ⊕ *n, pl* **-cies 1** compassionate treatment of an offender or enemy who is in one's power. **2** merciful act. **merciful** *adj* compassionate. **2** giving relief. **mercifully** *adv* **merciless** *adj* **mercilessly** *adv*.

mere¹ ⊕ *adj* nothing more than, e.g. *mere chance*. **merely** *adv*.

mere² *n obs* lake.

meretricious ⊕ *adj* superficially or garishly attractive but of no real value.

merganser [mer-**gan**-ser] *n* large crested diving duck.

merge ⊕ *v* combine or blend. **merger** *n* combination of business firms into one.

meridian *n* imaginary circle of the earth passing through both poles.

meringue [mer-**rang**] *n* **1** baked mixture of egg whites and sugar.

2 small cake of this.

merino *n, pl* **-nos 1** breed of sheep with fine soft wool. **2** this wool.

merit ⊕ *n* **1** excellence or worth. ▷ *pl* **2** admirable qualities. ▷ *v* **-iting, -ited 3** deserve. **meritorious** *adj* deserving praise. **meritocracy** [mer-it-**tok**-rass-ee] *n* rule by people of superior talent or intellect.

merlin *n* small falcon.

mermaid *n* imaginary sea creature with the upper part of a woman and the lower part of a fish.

merry ⊕ *adj* **-rier, -riest 1** cheerful or jolly. **2** *informal* slightly drunk. **merrily** *adv* **merriment** *n* **merry-go-round** *n* roundabout. **merrymaking** *n* noisy, cheerful celebrations or fun.

mescaline *n* hallucinogenic drug obtained from the tops of mescals. **mescal** [mess-**kal**] *n* spineless globe-shaped cactus of Mexico and the SW of the USA.

mesdames *n*plural of MADAME.

mesdemoiselles *n*plural of MADEMOISELLE.

mesembryanthemum *n* low-growing plant with bright daisy-like flowers.

mesh ⊕ *n* **1** network or net. **2** (open space between) strands forming a network. ▷ *v* **3** (of gear teeth) engage.

                               THESAURUS

merchant *n* = **tradesman**, broker, dealer, purveyor, retailer, salesman, seller, shopkeeper, supplier, trader, trafficker, vendor, wholesaler

merciful *adj* **1** = **compassionate**, clement, forgiving, generous, gracious, humane, kind, lenient, sparing, sympathetic, tender-hearted

merciless *adj* = **cruel**, barbarous, callous, hard-hearted, harsh, heartless, pitiless, ruthless, unforgiving

mercurial *adj* = **lively**, active, capricious, changeable, impulsive, irrepressible, mobile, quicksilver, spirited, sprightly, unpredictable, volatile

mercy *n* **1** = **compassion**, clemency, forbearance, forgiveness, grace, kindness, leniency, pity **2** = **blessing**, boon, godsend

mere¹ *adj* = **simple**, bare, common, nothing more than, plain, pure, sheer

meretricious *adj* = **trashy**, flashy, garish, gaudy, gimcrack, showy, tawdry, tinsel

merge *v* = **combine**, amalgamate,

blend, coalesce, converge, fuse, join, meet, mingle, mix, unite

merger *n* = **union**, amalgamation, coalition, combination, consolidation, fusion, incorporation

merit *n* **1** = **worth**, advantage, asset, excellence, goodness, integrity, quality, strong point, talent, value, virtue ▷ *v* **3** = **deserve**, be entitled to, be worthy of, earn, have a right to, rate, warrant

meritorious *adj* = **praiseworthy**, admirable, commendable, creditable, deserving, excellent, good, laudable, virtuous, worthy

merriment *n* **1** = **fun**, amusement, festivity, glee, hilarity, jollity, joviality, laughter, mirth, revelry

merry *adj* **1** = **cheerful**, blithe, carefree, convivial, festive, happy, jolly, joyous **2** *Inf* = **tipsy**, happy, mellow, squiffy (*Brit inf*), tiddly (*sl, chiefly Brit*)

mesh *n* **1** = **net**, netting, network, tracery, web ▷ *v* **3** = **engage**, combine, connect, coordinate, dovetail, harmonize, interlock, knit

mesmerize ❶ v **1** hold spellbound. **2** obs hypnotize. **mesmerizing** adj.

meso- combining form middle or intermediate, e.g. mesosphere.

meson [**mee**-zon] n elementary atomic particle.

mess ❶ n **1** untidy or dirty confusion. **2** trouble or difficulty. **3** place where servicemen eat. **4** group of servicemen who regularly eat together. ▷ v **5** muddle or dirty. **6** (foll. by about) potter about. **7** (foll. by with) interfere with. **8** (of servicemen) eat in a group.

message ❶ n **1** communication sent. **2** meaning or moral. **messenger** n bearer of a message. **get the message** informal understand.

Messiah n **1** Jews' promised deliverer. **2** Christ. **Messianic** adj.

messieurs n plural of MONSIEUR.

Messrs [**mess**-erz] n plural of MR.

messy ❶ adj **messier**, **messiest** dirty, confused, or untidy. **messily** adv.

met v past of MEET¹.

Met adj, n informal Meteorological (Office).

metabolism [met-**tab**-oh-liz-zum] n chemical processes of a living body. **metabolic** adj **metabolize** v produce or be produced by metabolism.

metal n **1** chemical element, such as iron or copper, that is malleable and capable of conducting heat and electricity. **2** short for ROAD METAL. **3** informal short for HEAVY METAL. ▷ adj **4** made of metal. **metallic** adj

metallurgy n scientific study of the structure, properties, extraction, and refining of metals. **metallurgical** adj **metallurgist** n **metalwork** n **1** craft of making objects from metal. **2** metal part of something.

metamorphosis ❶ [met-a-**more**-foss-is] n, pl **-phoses** [-foss-eez] change of form or character. **metamorphic** adj (of rocks) changed in texture or structure by heat and pressure. **metamorphose** v transform.

metaphor ❶ n figure of speech in which a term is applied to something it does not literally denote in order to imply a resemblance, e.g. he is a lion in battle. **metaphorical** adj **metaphorically** adv.

metaphysics n branch of philosophy concerned with being and knowing. **metaphysical** adj.

mete ❶ v (usu. with out) deal out as punishment.

meteor ❶ n small fast-moving heavenly body, visible as a streak of incandescence if it enters the earth's atmosphere. **meteoric** [meet-ee-**or**-rik] adj **1** of a meteor. **2** brilliant and very rapid, e.g. his meteoric rise to power. **meteorite** n meteor that has fallen to earth.

m

───────── **THESAURUS** ─────────

mesmerize v **1** = **entrance**, captivate, enthral, fascinate, grip, hold spellbound, hypnotize

mess n **1** = **disorder**, chaos, clutter, confusion, disarray, disorganization, hotchpotch, jumble, litter, shambles, untidiness **2** = **difficulty**, deep water, dilemma, fix (inf), hole (inf), jam (inf), muddle, pickle (inf), plight, predicament, tight spot ▷ v **5** = **dirty**, clutter, disarrange, dishevel, muck up (Brit sl), muddle, pollute, scramble, muss (US & Canad) **6** (foll. by about) = **potter**, amuse oneself, dabble, fool (about or around), muck about (inf), play about or around, trifle **7** (foll. by with) = **interfere**, fiddle (inf), meddle, play, tamper, tinker

message n **1** = **communication**, bulletin, communiqué, dispatch, letter, memorandum, note, tidings, word **2** = **point**, idea, import, meaning, moral, purport, theme

messenger n = **courier**, carrier, delivery boy, emissary, envoy, errand-boy, go-between, herald, runner

messy adj = **untidy**, chaotic, cluttered, confused, dirty, dishevelled, disordered, disorganized, muddled, shambolic, sloppy (inf)

metamorphosis n = **transformation**, alteration, change, conversion, mutation, transmutation

metaphor n = **figure of speech**, allegory, analogy, image, symbol, trope

metaphorical adj = **figurative**, allegorical, emblematic, symbolic

mete v = **distribute**, administer, apportion, assign, deal, dispense, dole, portion

meteoric adj **2** = **spectacular**, brilliant, dazzling, fast, overnight,

meteorology n study of the earth's atmosphere, esp. for weather forecasting. **meteorological** adj **meteorologist** n.

meter n **1** instrument for measuring and recording something, such as the consumption of gas or electricity. ▷ v **2** measure by meter.

methamphetamine n variety of amphetamine used for its stimulant action.

methane n colourless inflammable gas.

methanol n colourless poisonous liquid used as a solvent and fuel (also **methyl alcohol**).

methinks v, past tense **methought** obs it seems to me.

method ❶ n **1** way or manner. **2** technique. **3** orderliness. **methodical** adj orderly. **methodically** adv **methodology** n, pl **-gies** particular method or procedure.

Methodist n **1** member of any of the Protestant churches originated by John Wesley and his followers. ▷ adj **2** of Methodists or their Church. **Methodism** n.

meths n informal methylated spirits.

methyl n (compound containing) a saturated hydrocarbon group of atoms. **methylate** v mix with methyl alcohol, a liquid used as a solvent and fuel.

methylated spirits n alcohol with methanol added, used as a solvent and for heating.

meticulous ❶ adj very careful about details. **meticulously** adv.

métier [**met**-ee-ay] n **1** profession or trade. **2** one's strong point.

metonymy [mit-**on**-im-ee] n figure of speech in which one thing is replaced by another associated with it, such as 'the Crown' for 'the queen'.

metre n **1** basic unit of length equal to about 1.094 yards (100 centimetres). **2** rhythm of poetry. **metric** adj of the decimal system of weights and measures based on the metre. **metric ton** same as TONNE. **metrical** adj **1** of measurement. **2** of poetic metre.

metrication n conversion to the metric system.

metro n, pl **metros** underground railway system, esp. in Paris.

metronome n instrument which marks musical time by means of a ticking pendulum.

metropolis [mit-**trop**-oh-liss] n chief city of a country or region. **metropolitan** adj of a metropolis.

mettle ❶ n courage or spirit. **on one's mettle** roused to making one's best efforts.

mew n **1** cry of a cat. ▷ v **2** utter this cry.

mews n yard or street orig. of stables, now often converted into houses.

Mexican adj **1** of Mexico. ▷ n **2** person from Mexico.

mezzanine [**mez**-zan-een] n intermediate storey, esp. between the ground and first floor.

mezzo-soprano [**met**-so-] n voice or singer between a soprano and contralto (also **mezzo**).

mezzotint [**met**-so-tint] n **1** method of engraving by scraping the roughened surface of a metal plate. **2** print so made.

mg milligram(s).

Mg Chemistry magnesium.

Mgr 1 manager. **2** Monseigneur. **3** Monsignor.

MHz megahertz.

mi n Music same as ME².

MI 1 Military Intelligence. **2** Michigan.

MI5 Military Intelligence, section five: British Government counterintelligence agency.

MI6 Military Intelligence, section six: British Government intelligence and espionage agency.

miaow [mee-**ow**] n, v same as MEW.

miasma [mee-**azz**-ma] n unwholesome or foreboding atmosphere.

———————— THESAURUS ————————

rapid, speedy, sudden, swift

method n **1** = **manner**, approach, mode, modus operandi, procedure, process, routine, style, system, way **2** = **technique 3** = **orderliness**, order, organization, pattern, planning, purpose, regularity, system

methodical adj = **orderly**, businesslike, deliberate, disciplined, meticulous, organized, precise, regular, structured, systematic

meticulous adj = **thorough**, exact, fastidious, fussy, painstaking, particular, precise, punctilious, scrupulous, strict

mettle n = **courage**, bravery, fortitude, gallantry, life, nerve, pluck, resolution,

mica [**my**-ka] n glasslike mineral used as an electrical insulator.

mice n plural of MOUSE.

Michaelmas [**mik**-kl-mass] n September 29, feast of St Michael the archangel. **Michaelmas daisy** garden plant with small daisy-shaped flowers.

mickey n **take the mickey (out of)** informal tease.

micro n, pl **-cros** short for MICROCOMPUTER or MICROPROCESSOR.

micro- combining form **1** small or minute, e.g. microcopy. **2** denoting a millionth part, e.g. microsecond.

microbe ● n minute organism, esp. one causing disease. **microbial** adj.

microbiology n branch of biology involving the study of microorganisms. **microbiological** adj **microbiologist** n.

microchip n small wafer of silicon containing electronic circuits.

microcircuit n miniature electronic circuit, esp. an integrated circuit.

microcomputer n computer with a central processing unit contained in one or more silicon chips.

microcosm n **1** miniature representation of something. **2** man regarded as epitomizing the universe.

microdot n photographic copy of a document reduced to pinhead size.

microelectronics n branch of electronics concerned with microcircuits. **microelectronic** adj.

microfiche [**my**-kroh-feesh] n microfilm in sheet form.

microfilm n miniaturized recording of books or documents on a roll of film.

microlight, microlite n very small light private aircraft with large wings.

micrometer [**my**-**krom**-it-er] n instrument for measuring very small distances or angles.

micron [**my**-kron] n one millionth of a metre.

microorganism n organism of microscopic size.

microphone n instrument for amplifying or transmitting sounds.

microprocessor n integrated circuit acting as the central processing unit in a small computer.

microscope ● n instrument with lens(es) which produces a magnified image of a very small object. **microscopic** adj **1** too small to be seen except with a microscope. **2** very small. **3** of a microscope. **microscopically** adv **microscopy** n use of a microscope.

microstructure n structure on a microscopic scale, esp. of a metal or a cell.

microsurgery n intricate surgery using a special microscope and miniature precision instruments.

microwave n **1** electromagnetic wave with a wavelength of a few centimetres, used in radar and cooking. **2** microwave oven. ▷ v **3** cook in a microwave oven. **microwave oven** oven using microwaves to cook food quickly.

micturate v urinate. **micturition** n.

mid adj intermediate, middle. **midnight** n twelve o'clock at night. **mid-off** n Cricket fielding position on the off side closest to the bowler. **mid-on** n Cricket fielding position on the on side closest to the bowler. **midway** adj, adv halfway.

midair n some point above ground level, in the air.

midday ● n noon.

midden n dunghill or rubbish heap.

middle ● adj **1** equidistant from two extremes. **2** medium, intermediate. ▷ n **3** middle point or part. **middle age** period of life between youth and old age. **middle-aged** adj **Middle Ages** period from about 1000 AD to the 15th century. **middle class** social class of business and professional people. **middle-class** adj **middle ear** sound-conducting part of the ear immediately inside the eardrum. **Middle East** area around the eastern Mediterranean up to and including Iran. **middleman** n trader who buys

m

spirit, valour, vigour

microbe n = **microorganism**, bacillus, bacterium, bug (inf), germ, virus

microscopic adj **1, 2** = **tiny**, imperceptible, infinitesimal, invisible, minuscule, minute, negligible

midday n = **noon**, noonday,

twelve o'clock

middle adj **1** = **central**, halfway, intermediate, intervening, mean, median, mid **2** = **medium** ▷ n **3** = **centre**, focus, halfway point, heart, midpoint, midsection, midst

middle-class adj = **bourgeois**,

from the producer and sells to the consumer. **middle-of-the-road** *adj* **1** politically moderate. **2** (of music) generally popular. **middleweight** *n* boxer weighing up to 16olb (professional) or 75kg (amateur).

middling ❶ *adj* **1** mediocre. **2** moderate. ▷ *adv* **3** moderately.

midfield *n Soccer* area between the two opposing defences.

midge *n* small mosquito-like insect.

midget ❶ *n* very small person or thing.

midland *n* **1** middle part of a country. ▷ *pl* **2** (**M-**) central England.

midnight ❶ *n* twelve o'clock at night.

midriff *n* middle part of the body.

midshipman *n* naval officer of the lowest commissioned rank.

midst ❶ *n* **in the midst of 1** surrounded by. **2** at a point during.

midsummer *n* **1** middle of summer. **2** summer solstice. **Midsummer's Day, Midsummer Day** June 24.

midtown *n US & Canad* the centre of a town.

midway ❶ *adj*, *adv* halfway.

midwife *n* trained person who assists at childbirth. **midwifery** [mid-**wiff**-fer-ree] *n*.

midwinter *n* **1** middle or depth of winter. **2** winter solstice.

mien [**mean**] *n lit* person's bearing, demeanour, or appearance.

miffed *adj informal* offended or upset.

might¹ *v* past tense of MAY.

- **USAGE NOTE**
- Both *might* and *may* can be used to
- express a tentative request: *Might/*
- *may I ask a favour?*

might² ❶ *n* power or strength. **with might and main** energetically or forcefully. **mighty** *adj* **mightier**, **mightiest 1** powerful. **2** important. ▷ *adv* **3** *US & Aust informal* very. **mightily** *adv*.

mignonette [min-yon-**net**] *n* grey-green plant with sweet-smelling flowers.

migraine [**mee**-grain] *n* severe headache, often with nausea and visual disturbances.

migrate ❶ *v* **1** move from one place to settle in another. **2** (of animals) journey between different habitats at specific seasons. **migration** *n* **migrant** *n* **1** person or animal that moves from one place to another. ▷ *adj* **2** moving from one place to another, e.g. *migrant workers*. **migratory** *adj* (of an animal) migrating every year.

mikado *n*, *pl* **-dos** *old-fashioned* Japanese emperor.

mike *n informal* microphone.

milch [**miltch**] *adj* (of a cow) giving milk.

mild ❶ *adj* **1** not strongly flavoured. **2** gentle. **3** calm or temperate. **mildly** *adv* **mildness** *n*.

————————————————————————————————— THESAURUS ———————

conventional, traditional

middling *adj* **1** = **mediocre**, indifferent, run-of-the-mill, so-so (*inf*), tolerable, unexceptional, unremarkable **2** = **moderate**, adequate, all right, average, fair, medium, modest, O.K. *or* okay (*inf*), ordinary, passable, serviceable

midget *n* = **dwarf**, pygmy *or* pigmy, shrimp (*inf*), Tom Thumb

midnight *n* = **twelve o'clock**, dead of night, middle of the night, the witching hour

midst *n* **in the midst of 1** = **among**, amidst, in the middle of, in the thick of, surrounded by **2** = **during**

midway *adj*, *adv* = **halfway**, betwixt and between, in the middle

might² *n* = **power**, energy, force, strength, vigour **with might and main** = **forcefully**, lustily, manfully, mightily, vigorously

mightily *adv* = **powerfully**, energetically, forcefully, lustily,

manfully, strongly, vigorously

mighty *adj* **1** = **powerful**, forceful, lusty, robust, strapping, strong, sturdy, vigorous

migrant *n* **1** = **wanderer**, drifter, emigrant, immigrant, itinerant, nomad, rover, traveller ▷ *adj* **2** = **travelling**, drifting, immigrant, itinerant, migratory, nomadic, roving, shifting, transient, vagrant, wandering

migrate *v* **1** = **move**, emigrate, journey, roam, rove, travel, trek, voyage, wander

migration *n* = **wandering**, emigration, journey, movement, roving, travel, trek, voyage

migratory *adj* = **nomadic**, itinerant, migrant, peripatetic, roving, transient

mild *adj* **1** = **bland**, smooth **2** = **gentle**, calm, docile, easy-going, equable, meek, peaceable, placid **3** = **temperate**, balmy, calm,

mildew n destructive fungus on plants or things exposed to damp. **mildewed** adj.

mile n unit of length equal to 1760 yards or 1.609 kilometres. **mileage** n 1 distance travelled in miles. 2 miles travelled by a motor vehicle per gallon of petrol. 3 informal usefulness of something. **mileometer** [mile-**om**-it-er] n device that records the number of miles a vehicle has travelled. **milestone** n 1 significant event. 2 stone marker showing the distance to a certain place.

milieu ❶ [meal-**yer**] n, pl **milieux**, **milieus** [meal-**yerz**] environment or surroundings.

militant ❶ adj aggressive or vigorous in support of a cause. **militancy** n **militantly** adv.

military ❶ adj 1 of or for soldiers, armies, or war. ▷ n 2 armed services. **militarily** adv **militarism** n belief in the use of military force and methods. **militarist** n **militaristic** adj **militarized** adj.

militate ❶ v (usu. with against or for) have a strong influence or effect.

militia [mill-**ish**-a] n military force of trained citizens for use in emergency only. **militiaman** n.

milk ❶ n 1 white fluid produced by female mammals to feed their young. 2 milk of cows, goats, etc., used by humans as food. 3 fluid in some plants. ▷ v 4 draw milk from. 5 exploit (a person or situation). **milking** n **milky** adj **milkier**, **milkiest**. **Milky Way** luminous band of stars stretching across the night sky. **milk float** small electrically powered vehicle used to deliver milk to houses. **milkmaid** n (esp. in former times) woman who milks cows.

milkman n man who delivers milk to people's houses. **milk round** 1 route along which a milkman regularly delivers milk. 2 regular series of visits to colleges made by recruitment officers from industry. **milkshake** n frothy flavoured cold milk drink. **milksop** n feeble man. **milk teeth** first set of teeth in young children.

mill ❶ n 1 factory. 2 machine for grinding, processing, or rolling. ▷ v 3 grind, press, or process in or as if in a mill. 4 cut fine grooves across the edges of (coins). 5 move in a confused manner. **miller** n person who works in a mill.

millennium [mill-**en**-nee-um] n, pl -**nia** [-nee-a]-**niums** 1 period of a thousand years. 2 future period of peace and happiness. **millennium bug** computer problem caused by the date change at the beginning of the 21st century.

● **SPELLING TIP**
● If you spell **millennium** with only
● one n, you are not alone: there are
● 338 occurrences of this in the Bank
● of English. The correct spelling has
● two ls and two ns.

millet n a cereal grass.

milli- combining form denoting a thousandth part, e.g. millisecond.

milliard n Brit one thousand millions.

millibar n unit of atmospheric pressure.

milligram, milligramme n thousandth part of a gram.

millilitre n thousandth part of a litre.

millimetre n thousandth part of a metre.

milliner n maker or seller of women's hats. **millinery** n.

million n one thousand thousands. **millionth** adj, n **millionaire** n person

──── **THESAURUS** ────

moderate, tranquil, warm

mildness n = **gentleness**, calmness, clemency, docility, moderation, placidity, tranquillity, warmth

milieu n = **surroundings**, background, element, environment, locale, location, scene, setting

militant adj = **aggressive**, active, assertive, combative, vigorous

military adj 1 = **warlike**, armed, martial, soldierly ▷ n 2 = **armed**

forces, army, forces, services

militate v **militate against** = **counteract**, be detrimental to, conflict with, counter, oppose, resist, tell against, weigh against

milk v 5 = **exploit**, extract, pump, take advantage of

mill n 1 = **factory**, foundry, plant, works 2 = **grinder**, crusher ▷ v 3 = **grind**, crush, grate, pound,

who owns at least a million pounds, dollars, etc.

millipede *n* small animal with a jointed body and many pairs of legs.

millstone ❶ *n* flat circular stone for grinding corn. **millstone round one's neck** heavy burden of responsibility or obligation.

millwheel *n* waterwheel that drives a mill.

milometer [mile-**om**-it-er] *n* same as MILEOMETER.

milt *n* sperm of fish.

mime ❶ *n* 1 acting without the use of words. 2 performer who does this. ▷ *v* 3 act in mime. 4 perform as if singing or playing music that is prerecorded.

mimic ❶ *v* **-icking, -icked** 1 imitate (a person or manner), esp. for satirical effect. ▷ *n* 2 person or animal that is good at mimicking. **mimicry** *n*.

mimosa *n* shrub with fluffy yellow flowers and sensitive leaves.

min. 1 minimum. 2 minute(s).

Min. 1 Minister. 2 Ministry.

minaret *n* tall slender tower of

a mosque.

minatory *adj* threatening or menacing.

mince ❶ *v* 1 cut or grind into very small pieces. 2 walk or speak in an affected manner. 3 soften or moderate (one's words). ▷ *n* 4 minced meat. **mincer** *n* machine for mincing meat. **mincing** *adj* affected in manner. **mincemeat** *n* sweet mixture of dried fruit and spices. **mince pie** pie containing mincemeat.

mind ❶ *n* 1 thinking faculties. 2 memory or attention. 3 intention. 4 sanity. ▷ *v* 5 take offence at. 6 pay attention to. 7 take care of. 8 be cautious or careful about (something). **change one's mind** alter one's decision or opinion. **in one's mind's eye** in one's imagination. **make up one's mind** reach a decision. **minded** *adj* having an inclination as specified, e.g. *politically minded.* **minder** *n informal* aide or bodyguard. **mindful** *adj* 1 heedful. 2 keeping aware. **mindless** *adj* 1 stupid. 2 requiring no thought. 3 careless.

mine¹ *pron* belonging to me.

mine² ❶ *n* 1 deep hole for digging out coal, ores, etc. 2 bomb placed under the ground or in water. 3 profitable source, e.g. *a mine of information.* ▷ *v* 4 dig for minerals. 5 dig (minerals)

━━━━━━━━━━━━━━━━━━━━ ━━━━━━ THESAURUS ━━━━━━

powder 5 = **swarm**, crowd, throng

millstone *n* 1 = **grindstone**, quernstone **millstone round one's neck** = **burden**, affliction, albatross, encumbrance, load, weight

mime *v* 3 = **act out**, gesture, represent, simulate

mimic *v* 1 = **imitate**, ape, caricature, do (*inf*), impersonate, parody, take off (*inf*) ▷ *n* 2 = **imitator**, caricaturist, copycat (*inf*), impersonator, impressionist

mimicry *n* = **imitation**, burlesque, caricature, impersonation, mimicking, mockery, parody, take-off (*inf*)

mince *v* 1 = **cut**, chop, crumble, grind, hash 3 = **tone down**, moderate, soften, spare, weaken

mincing *adj* = **affected**, camp (*inf*), dainty, effeminate, foppish, precious, pretentious, sissy

mind *n* 1 = **intelligence**, brain(s) (*inf*), grey matter (*inf*), intellect, reason, sense, understanding, wits

2 = **memory**, recollection, remembrance 3 = **intention**, desire, disposition, fancy, inclination, leaning, notion, urge, wish 4 = **sanity**, judgment, marbles (*inf*), mental balance, rationality, reason, senses, wits ▷ *v* 5 = **take offence**, be affronted, be bothered, care, disapprove, dislike, object, resent 6 = **pay attention**, heed, listen to, mark, note, obey, observe, pay heed to, take heed 7 = **guard**, attend to, keep an eye on, look after, take care of, tend, watch 8 = **be careful**, be cautious, be on (one's) guard, be wary, take care, watch **make up one's mind** = **decide**, choose, determine, resolve

mindful *adj* 1 = **conscious**, heedful 2 = **aware**, alert, alive to, careful, wary, watchful

mindless *adj* 1 = **unthinking**, foolish, idiotic, inane, moronic, stupid, thoughtless, witless

mine² *n* 1 = **pit**, colliery, deposit,

from a mine. **6** place explosive mines in or on. **miner** n person who works in a mine. **mining** n **minefield** n area of land or water containing mines. **minesweeper** n ship for clearing away mines.

mineral n **1** naturally occurring inorganic substance, such as metal. ▷ adj **2** of, containing, or like minerals. **mineralogy** [min-er-**al**-a-jee] n study of minerals. **mineralogist** n **mineral water** water containing dissolved mineral salts or gases.

minestrone [min-ness-**strone**-ee] n soup containing vegetables and pasta.

mingle ❶ v **1** mix or blend. **2** come into association (with).

mingy adj **-gier, -giest** informal miserly.

mini n, adj **1** (something) small or miniature. **2** short (skirt).

mini- combining form smaller or shorter than usual, e.g. mini-budget; minidress.

miniature ❶ n **1** small portrait, model, or copy. ▷ adj **2** small-scale. **miniaturist** n **miniaturize** v make to a very small scale. **miniaturization** n.

minibar n selection of drinks and confectionery provided in a hotel room.

minibus n small bus.

minicab n ordinary car used as a taxi.

minicomputer n computer smaller than a mainframe but more powerful than a microcomputer.

minidisc n small recordable compact disc.

minim n Music note half the length of a semibreve.

minimum ❶ adj, n, pl **-mums, -ma** least possible (amount or number). **minimal** adj minimum. **minimally** adv **minimize** v **1** reduce to a minimum. **2** belittle. **minimization** n.

minion ❶ n servile assistant.

miniseries n TV programme shown in several parts, often on consecutive days.

miniskirt n very short skirt.

minister ❶ n **1** head of a government department. **2** diplomatic representative. **3** clergyman. ▷ v **4** (foll. by to) attend to the needs of. **ministerial** adj **ministration** n giving of help. **ministry** n, pl **-tries 1** profession or duties of a clergyman. **2** ministers collectively. **3** government department.

mink n **1** stoatlike animal. **2** its highly valued fur.

minnow n small freshwater fish.

minor ❶ adj **1** lesser. **2** Music (of a scale) having a semitone between the second and third notes. ▷ n **3** person regarded legally as a child. **4** Music minor scale. **minority** n, pl **-ties 1** lesser number. **2** smaller party voting together. **3** group in a minority in any state.

minster n cathedral or large church.

minstrel ❶ n medieval singer or musician.

THESAURUS

excavation, shaft **3** = **source**, abundance, fund, hoard, reserve, stock, store, supply, treasury, wealth ▷ v **4, 5** = **dig up**, dig for, excavate, extract, hew, quarry, unearth

miner n = **coalminer**, collier (Brit), pitman (Brit)

mingle v **1** = **mix**, blend, combine, intermingle, interweave, join, merge, unite **2** = **associate**, consort, fraternize, hang about or around, hobnob, rub shoulders (inf), socialize

miniature adj **2** = **small**, diminutive, little, minuscule, minute, scaled-down, tiny, toy

minimal adj = **minimum**, least, least possible, nominal, slightest, smallest, token

minimize v **1** = **reduce**, curtail, decrease, diminish, miniaturize, prune, shrink **2** = **play down**,

belittle, decry, deprecate, discount, disparage, make light or little of, underrate

minimum adj = **least**, least possible, lowest, minimal, slightest, smallest ▷ n = **least**, lowest, nadir

minion n = **follower**, flunky, hanger-on, henchman, hireling, lackey, underling, yes man

minister n **3** = **clergyman**, cleric, parson, pastor, preacher, priest, rector, vicar ▷ v **4** = **attend to**, administer, cater to, pander to, serve, take care of, tend

ministry n **1** = **holy orders 2** = **the priesthood**, the church **3** = **department**, bureau, council, office, quango

minor adj **1** = **small**, inconsequential, insignificant, lesser, petty, slight, trivial, unimportant

minstrel n = **musician**, bard, singer,

mint¹ *n* **1** plant with aromatic leaves used for seasoning and flavouring. **2** sweet flavoured with this.

mint² ❶ *n* **1** place where money is coined. ▷ *v* **2** make (coins).

minuet [min-new-**wet**] *n* **1** stately dance. **2** music for this.

minus *prep, adj* **1** indicating subtraction. ▷ *adj* **2** less than zero. ▷ *n* **3** sign (–) denoting subtraction or a number less than zero.

minuscule ❶ [**min**-niss-skyool] *adj* very small.

● **SPELLING TIP**
● The pronunciation of **minuscule**
● often influences the way people
● spell it. It's spelt *miniscule* 121 times
● in the Bank of English, but it should
● only one *i* and two *us*.

minute¹ ❶ [**min**-it] *n* **1** 60th part of an hour or degree. **2** moment. ▷ *pl* **3** record of the proceedings of a meeting. ▷ *v* **4** record in the minutes.

minute² ❶ [my-**newt**] *adj* **1** very small. **2** precise. **minutely** *adv* **minutiae** [my-**new**-shee-eye] *pl n* trifling or precise details.

minx ❶ *n* bold or flirtatious girl.

miracle ❶ *n* **1** wonderful supernatural event. **2** marvel. **miraculous** *adj*

miraculously *adv* **miracle play** medieval play based on a sacred subject.

mirage ❶ [mir-**rahzh**] *n* optical illusion, esp. one caused by hot air.

mire ❶ *n* **1** swampy ground. **2** mud.

mirror ❶ *n* **1** coated glass surface for reflecting images. ▷ *v* **2** reflect in or as if in a mirror. **mirror image** image or object that has left and right reversed as if seen in a mirror.

mirth ❶ *n* laughter, merriment, or gaiety. **mirthful** *adj* **mirthless** *adj* **mirthlessly** *adv*.

mis- *prefix* wrong(ly), bad(ly).

misadventure ❶ *n* unlucky chance.

misanthrope ❶ [**miz**-zan-thrope] *n* person who dislikes people in general. **misanthropic** [miz-zan-**throp**-ik] *adj* **misanthropy** [miz-**zan**-throp-ee] *n*.

misapplication *n* use of something for the wrong purpose.

misapprehend ❶ *v* misunderstand. **misapprehensive** *adj*.

misapprehension ❶ *n* misunderstanding.

misappropriate ❶ *v* take and use (money) dishonestly. **misappropriation** *n*.

━━━━━━━━━━━━━━━━━━━━━━━━ **THESAURUS** ━━━━━

songstress, troubadour

mint² *v* **2** = **make**, cast, coin, produce, punch, stamp, strike

minuscule *adj* = **tiny**, diminutive, infinitesimal, little, microscopic, miniature, minute

minute¹ *n* **2** = **moment**, flash, instant, jiffy (*inf*), second, tick (*Brit inf*), trice ▷ *pl* **3** = **record**, memorandum, notes, proceedings, transactions, transcript

minute² *adj* **1** = **small**, diminutive, infinitesimal, little, microscopic, miniature, minuscule, tiny **2** = **precise**, close, critical, detailed, exact, exhaustive, meticulous, painstaking, punctilious

minutiae *pl n* = **details**, finer points, niceties, particulars, subtleties, trifles, trivia

minx *n* = **flirt**, coquette, hussy

miracle *n* **2** = **wonder**, marvel, phenomenon, prodigy

miraculous *adj* **2** = **wonderful**, amazing, astonishing, astounding, extraordinary, incredible, phenomenal, prodigious, unaccountable, unbelievable

mirage *n* = **illusion**, hallucination, optical illusion

mire *n* **1** = **swamp**, bog, marsh, morass, quagmire, muskeg (*Canad*) **2** = **mud**, dirt, muck, ooze, slime

mirror *n* **1** = **looking-glass**, glass, reflector ▷ *v* **2** = **reflect**, copy, echo, emulate, follow

mirth *n* = **merriment**, amusement, cheerfulness, fun, gaiety, glee, hilarity, jollity, joviality, laughter, revelry

mirthful *adj* = **merry**, blithe, cheerful, cheery, festive, happy, jolly, jovial, light-hearted, playful, sportive

misadventure *n* = **misfortune**, accident, bad luck, calamity, catastrophe, debacle, disaster, mishap, reverse, setback

misanthropic *adj* = **antisocial**, cynical, malevolent, unfriendly

misapprehend *v* = **misunderstand**, misconstrue, misinterpret, misread, mistake

misapprehension *n* = **misunderstanding**, delusion, error, fallacy, misconception, misinterpretation, mistake

misappropriate *v* = **steal**, embezzle,

misbehave v behave badly.
misbehaviour n.

miscalculate ⊙ v calculate or judge wrongly. **miscalculation** n.

miscarriage ⊙ n 1 spontaneous premature expulsion of a fetus from the womb. 2 failure, e.g. *a miscarriage of justice*. **miscarry** v 1 have a miscarriage. 2 fail.

miscast v -**casting**, -**cast** cast (a role or actor) in (a play or film) inappropriately.

miscegenation [miss-ij-in-**nay**-shun] n interbreeding of races.

miscellaneous ⊙ [miss-sell-**lane**-ee-uss] adj mixed or assorted. **miscellany** [miss-**sell**-a-nee] n mixed assortment.

mischance ⊙ n unlucky event.

mischief ⊙ n 1 annoying but not malicious behaviour. 2 inclination to tease. 3 harm. **mischievous** [miss-chiv-uss] adj 1 full of mischief. 2 intended to cause harm. **mischievously** adv.

miscible [**miss**-sib-bl] adj able to be mixed.

misconception ⊙ n wrong idea or belief. **misconceived** adj.

misconduct ⊙ n immoral or unethical behaviour.

misconstrue v interpret wrongly. **misconstruction** n.

miscreant ⊙ [**miss**-kree-ant] n wrongdoer.

misdeed ⊙ n wrongful act.

misdemeanour ⊙ n minor wrongdoing.

misdirect v give (someone) wrong directions or instructions. **misdirection** n.

miser ⊙ n person who hoards money and hates spending it. **miserly** adj.

miserable ⊙ adj 1 very unhappy, wretched. 2 causing misery. 3 squalid. 4 mean. **miserably** adv **misery** n, pl -**eries** 1 great unhappiness. 2 *informal* complaining person.

——— THESAURUS ———

misspend, misuse, peculate, pocket

miscalculate v = **misjudge**, blunder, err, overestimate, overrate, slip up, underestimate, underrate

miscarriage n 2 = **failure**, breakdown, error, mishap, perversion

miscarry v 2 = **fail**, come to grief, fall through, go awry, go pear-shaped (*inf*), go wrong, misfire

miscellaneous adj = **mixed**, assorted, diverse, jumbled, motley, sundry, varied, various

miscellany n = **assortment**, anthology, collection, hotchpotch, jumble, medley, *mélange*, mixed bag, mixture, potpourri, variety

mischance n = **misfortune**, accident, calamity, disaster, misadventure, mishap

mischief n 1 = **misbehaviour**, impishness, monkey business (*inf*), naughtiness, shenanigans (*inf*), trouble, waywardness 3 = **harm**, damage, evil, hurt, injury, misfortune, trouble

mischievous adj 1 = **naughty**, impish, playful, puckish, rascally, roguish, sportive, troublesome, wayward 2 = **malicious**, damaging, destructive, evil, harmful, hurtful, spiteful, vicious, wicked

misconception n = **delusion**, error, fallacy, misapprehension,

misunderstanding

misconduct n = **immorality**, impropriety, malpractice, mismanagement, wrongdoing

miscreant n = **wrongdoer**, blackguard, criminal, rascal, reprobate, rogue, scoundrel, sinner, vagabond, villain

misdeed n = **offence**, crime, fault, misconduct, misdemeanour, sin, transgression, wrong

misdemeanour n = **offence**, fault, infringement, misdeed, peccadillo, transgression

miser n = **hoarder**, cheapskate (*inf*), niggard, penny-pincher (*inf*), Scrooge, skinflint

miserable adj 1 = **unhappy**, dejected, depressed, despondent, disconsolate, forlorn, gloomy, sorrowful, woebegone, wretched
2 = **despicable**, deplorable, lamentable, shameful, sordid, sorry
3 = **squalid**, wretched

miserly adj = **mean**, avaricious, grasping, niggardly, parsimonious, penny-pinching (*inf*), stingy, tightfisted, ungenerous

misery n 1 = **unhappiness**, anguish, depression, desolation, despair, distress, gloom, grief, sorrow, suffering, torment, woe 2 *Inf* = **moaner**, killjoy, pessimist, prophet of doom, sourpuss (*inf*), spoilsport,

misfire ❶ v 1 (of a firearm or engine) fail to fire correctly. 2 (of a plan) fail to turn out as intended.

misfit ❶ n person not suited to his or her social environment.

misfortune ❶ n (piece of) bad luck.

misgiving ❶ n feeling of fear or doubt.

misguided ❶ adj mistaken or unwise.

mishandle ❶ v handle badly or inefficiently.

mishap ❶ n minor accident.

mishear v hear (what someone says) wrongly.

mishmash n confused collection or mixture.

misinform ❶ v give incorrect information to. **misinformation** n.

misinterpret ❶ v understand or represent (something) wrongly. **misinterpretation** n.

misjudge ❶ v judge wrongly or unfairly. **misjudgment**, **misjudgement** n.

mislay ❶ v lose (something) temporarily.

mislead ❶ v give false or confusing information to. **misleading** adj **misleadingly** adv.

mismanage v organize or run (something) badly. **mismanagement** n.

misnomer [miss-**no**-mer] n 1 incorrect or unsuitable name. 2 use of this.

misogyny [miss-**oj**-in-ee] n hatred of women. **misogynist** n.

misplace ❶ v 1 mislay. 2 put in the wrong place. 3 give (trust or affection) inappropriately.

misprint ❶ n printing error.

mispronounce v pronounce (a word) wrongly. **mispronunciation** n.

misquote ❶ v quote inaccurately. **misquotation** n.

misread v 1 misinterpret (a situation etc.). 2 read incorrectly.

misrepresent ❶ v represent wrongly or inaccurately. **misrepresentation** n.

misrule ❶ v 1 govern inefficiently or unjustly. ▷ n 2 inefficient or unjust government.

miss ❶ v 1 fail to notice, hear, hit, reach, find, or catch. 2 not be in time for. 3 notice or regret the absence of. 4 avoid. 5 (of an engine) misfire. ▷ n 6 fact or instance of missing. **missing** adj lost or absent. **miss out** v 1 leave out or overlook. 2 (foll. by on) fail to take part in (something enjoyable or beneficial).

Miss n title of a girl or unmarried woman.

━━━━━━━━━━━━━━━━━━━━━━━━━━ THESAURUS ━━━━━━━━

wet blanket (inf)

misfire v 2 = **fail**, fall through, go pear-shaped (inf), go wrong, miscarry

misfit n = **nonconformist**, eccentric, fish out of water (inf), oddball (inf), square peg (in a round hole) (inf)

misfortune n = **bad luck**, adversity, hard luck, ill luck, infelicity

misgiving n = **unease**, anxiety, apprehension, distrust, doubt, qualm, reservation, suspicion, trepidation, uncertainty, worry

misguided adj = **unwise**, deluded, erroneous, ill-advised, imprudent, injudicious, misplaced, mistaken, unwarranted

mishandle v = **mismanage**, botch, bungle, make a mess of, mess up (inf), muff

mishap n = **accident**, calamity, misadventure, mischance, misfortune

misinform v = **mislead**, deceive, misdirect, misguide

misinterpret v = **misunderstand**, distort, misapprehend, misconceive, misconstrue, misjudge, misread,

misrepresent, mistake

misjudge v = **miscalculate**, overestimate, overrate, underestimate, underrate

mislay v = **lose**, lose track of, misplace

mislead v = **deceive**, delude, fool, hoodwink, misdirect, misguide, misinform, take in (inf)

misleading adj = **confusing**, ambiguous, deceptive, disingenuous, evasive, false

misplace v 1 = **lose**, lose track of, mislay

misprint n = **mistake**, corrigendum, erratum, literal, typo (inf)

misquote v = **misrepresent**, falsify, twist

misrepresent v = **distort**, disguise, falsify, misinterpret

misrule n 2 = **disorder**, anarchy, chaos, confusion, lawlessness, turmoil

miss v 1 = **omit**, leave out, let go, overlook, pass over, skip 3 = **long for**, pine for, yearn for 4 = **avoid**, escape, evade ▷ n 6 = **mistake**, blunder, error,

missal n book containing the prayers and rites of the Mass.

misshapen ❶ adj badly shaped, deformed.

missile ❶ n 1 rocket with an exploding warhead, used as a weapon. **2** object or weapon thrown, shot, or launched at a target.

mission ❶ n 1 specific task or duty. **2** task or duty that a person believes he or she must achieve. **3** group of people sent on a mission. **4** building in which missionaries work. **5** S Afr long and difficult process. **missionary** n, pl **-aries** person sent abroad to do religious and social work.

missive ❶ n letter.

misspell v spell (a word) wrongly.

misspent ❶ adj wasted or misused.

missus, missis n informal one's wife or the wife of the person addressed or referred to.

mist ❶ n 1 thin fog. **2** fine spray of liquid. **misty** adj **mistier**, **mistiest** **1** full of mist. **2** dim or obscure. **mist over** v 1 (also **mist up**) (of glass) become covered with small drops of moisture causing a misty effect. **2** (of eyes) fill up with tears.

mistake ❶ n 1 error or blunder. ▷ v **-taking**, **-took**, **-taken** **2** misunderstand. **3** confuse (a person or thing) with another. **mistaken** adj wrong in judgment or opinion. **mistakenly** adv.

Mister n polite form of address to a man.

mistime ❶ v do (something) at the wrong time.

mistletoe n evergreen plant with white berries growing as a parasite on trees.

mistral n strong dry northerly wind of S France.

mistreat ❶ v treat (a person or animal) badly.

mistress ❶ n 1 woman who has a continuing sexual relationship with a married man. **2** woman in control of people or animals. **3** female teacher.

mistrial n Law trial made void because of some error.

mistrust ❶ v 1 have doubts or suspicions about. ▷ n 2 lack of trust. **mistrustful** adj.

misunderstand ❶ v fail to understand properly. **misunderstanding** n.

m

———————— THESAURUS ————————

failure, omission, oversight

misshapen adj = **deformed**, contorted, crooked, distorted, grotesque, malformed, twisted, warped

missile n = **rocket**, projectile, weapon

missing adj = **absent**, astray, lacking, left out, lost, mislaid, misplaced, unaccounted-for

mission n 1 = **task**, assignment, commission, duty, errand, job, quest, undertaking **2** = **vocation**

missionary n = **evangelist**, apostle, preacher

missive n = **letter**, communication, dispatch, epistle, memorandum, message, note, report

misspent adj = **wasted**, dissipated, imprudent, profitless, squandered

mist n 1 = **fog**, cloud, film, haze, smog, spray, steam, vapour

mistake n 1 = **error**, blunder, erratum, fault, faux pas, gaffe, howler (inf), miscalculation, oversight, slip ▷ v **2** = **misunderstand**, misapprehend, misconstrue, misinterpret, misjudge, misread **3** = **confuse with**, mix up with, take for

mistaken adj = **wrong**, erroneous, false, faulty, inaccurate, incorrect, misguided, unsound, wide of the mark

mistakenly adv = **incorrectly**, by mistake, erroneously, fallaciously, falsely, inaccurately, misguidedly, wrongly

mistimed adj = **inopportune**, badly timed, ill-timed, untimely

mistreat v = **abuse**, harm, ill-treat, injure, knock about or around, maltreat, manhandle, misuse, molest

mistress n 1 = **lover**, concubine, girlfriend, kept woman, paramour

mistrust v 1 = **doubt**, be wary of, distrust, fear, suspect ▷ n **2** = **suspicion**, distrust, doubt, misgiving, scepticism, uncertainty, wariness

mistrustful adj = **suspicious**, chary, cynical, distrustful, doubtful, fearful, hesitant, sceptical, uncertain, wary

misty adj 1 = **foggy**, blurred, cloudy, dim, hazy, indistinct, murky, obscure, opaque, overcast

misunderstand v = **misinterpret**, be at cross-purposes, get the wrong end of the stick, misapprehend, misconstrue,

misuse ❶ *n* **1** incorrect, improper, or careless use. ▷ *v* **2** use wrongly. **3** treat badly.

mite *n* **1** very small spider-like animal. **2** very small thing or amount. **a mite** somewhat.

mitigate ❶ *v* make less severe. **mitigating** *adj* **mitigation** *n*.

mitosis *n* type of cell division in which the nucleus divides into two nuclei which each contain the same number of chromosomes as the original nucleus.

mitre [**my**-ter] *n* **1** bishop's pointed headdress. **2** joint between two pieces of wood bevelled to meet at right angles. ▷ *v* **3** join with a mitre joint.

mitt *n* **1** short for MITTEN. **2** *slang* hand. **3** baseball catcher's glove.

mitten *n* glove with one section for the thumb and one for the four fingers together.

mix ❶ *v* **1** combine or blend into one mass. **2** form (something) by mixing. **3** be sociable. ▷ *n* **4** mixture. **mixed** *adj* **mixed blessing** something that has advantages as well as disadvantages. **mixed grill** dish of several kinds of grilled meat, tomatoes, and mushrooms. **mix up** *v* **1** confuse. **2** make into a mixture. **mixed up** *adj* **mix-up** *n* **mixer** *n*

1 kitchen appliance used for mixing foods. **2** *informal* person considered in relation to his or her ability to mix socially, e.g. *a good mixer.* **3** nonalcoholic drink, e.g. tonic water, that is mixed with an alcoholic drink.

mixture *n* **1** something mixed. **2** combination.

mizzenmast *n* (on a vessel with three or more masts) third mast from the bow.

mks units *pl n* metric system of units based on the metre, kilogram, and second.

ml millilitre(s).

Mlle *pl* **Mlles** Mademoiselle.

mm millimetre(s).

MM plural of M (sense 1).

Mme *pl* **Mmes** Madame.

Mn *Chemistry* manganese.

MN Minnesota.

mnemonic [nim-**on**-ik] *n, adj* (something, such as a rhyme) intended to help the memory.

mo *n, pl* **mos** *informal* short for MOMENT.

Mo *Chemistry* molybdenum.

MO 1 Medical Officer. **2** Missouri.

moan ❶ *n* **1** low cry of pain. **2** *informal* grumble. ▷ *v* **3** make or utter with a moan. **4** *informal* grumble. **moaner** *n*.

moat *n* deep wide ditch, esp. round a castle.

———————————————————————————— THESAURUS ————————

misjudge, misread, mistake

misunderstanding *n* = **mistake**, error, misconception, misinterpretation, misjudgment, mix-up

misuse *n* **1** = **waste**, abuse, desecration, misapplication, squandering ▷ *v* **3** = **waste**, abuse, desecrate, misapply, prostitute, squander

mitigate *v* = **ease**, extenuate, lessen, lighten, moderate, soften, subdue, temper

mitigation *n* = **relief**, alleviation, diminution, extenuation, moderation, remission

mix *v* **1, 2** = **combine**, blend, cross, fuse, intermingle, interweave, join, jumble, merge, mingle **3** = **socialize**, associate, consort, fraternize, hang out (*inf*), hobnob, mingle ▷ *n* **4** = **mixture**, alloy, amalgam, assortment, blend, combination, compound, fusion, medley

mixed *adj* **1, 2** = **combined**, amalgamated, blended, composite, compound, joint, mingled, united **4** = **varied**, assorted, cosmopolitan, diverse, heterogeneous, miscellaneous, motley

mixed up *adj* = **confused**, at sea, bewildered, distraught, disturbed, maladjusted, muddled, perplexed, puzzled, upset

mixture *n* **1** = **assortment**, jumble, medley, mix, potpourri, variety **2** = **blend**, amalgam, brew, compound, fusion

mix up *v* **1** = **confuse**, confound, muddle **2** = **combine**, blend, mix

mix-up *n* = **confusion**, mess, mistake, misunderstanding, muddle, tangle

moan *n* **1** = **groan**, lament, sigh, sob, wail, whine **2** *Inf* = **grumble**, complaint, gripe (*inf*), grouch (*inf*), grouse, protest, whine ▷ *v* **3** = **groan**, lament, sigh, sob, whine **4** *Inf* = **grumble**, bleat, carp, complain,

mob ❶ n 1 disorderly crowd. 2 slang gang. ▷ v **mobbing**, **mobbed** 3 surround in a mob to acclaim or attack.

mobile ❶ adj 1 able to move. ▷ n 2 same as MOBILE PHONE. 3 hanging structure designed to move in air currents. **mobile phone** cordless phone powered by batteries. **mobility** n.

mobilize ❶ v 1 (of the armed services) prepare for active service. 2 organize for a purpose. **mobilization** n.

moccasin n soft leather shoe.

- ● **SPELLING TIP**
- ● One **moccasin** has a double c, but
- ● only one s. The plural, **moccasins**,
- ● has two ss, but they are not
- ● together.

mocha [**mock**-a] n 1 kind of strong dark coffee. 2 flavouring made from coffee and chocolate.

mock ❶ v 1 make fun of. 2 mimic. ▷ adj 3 sham or imitation. **mocks** pl n informal (in England and Wales) practice exams taken before public exams. **put the mockers on** informal ruin the chances of success of. **mockery** n 1 derision. 2 inadequate or worthless attempt. **mocking** adj **mockingbird** n N American bird which imitates other birds' songs. **mockingly** adv **mock orange** shrub with white fragrant flowers. **mock-up**

n full-scale model for test or study.

mod¹ n member of a group of young people, orig. in the mid-1960s, who were very clothes-conscious and rode motor scooters.

mod² n annual Highland Gaelic meeting with musical and literary competitions.

MOD Ministry of Defence.

mod. 1 moderate. 2 modern.

mod cons pl n informal modern conveniences, such as heating and hot water.

mode ❶ n 1 method or manner. 2 current fashion.

model ❶ n 1 (miniature) representation. 2 pattern. 3 person or thing worthy of imitation. 4 person who poses for an artist or photographer. 5 person who wears clothes to display them to prospective buyers. ▷ adj 6 excellent or perfect, e.g. a model husband. ▷ v **-elling**, **-elled** 7 make a model of. 8 mould. 9 plan or create according to a model or models. 10 display (clothing) as a model. **modelling** n.

modem [**mode**-em] n device for connecting two computers by a telephone line.

moderate ❶ adj 1 not extreme. 2 self-restrained. 3 average. ▷ n 4 person of

groan, grouse, whine, whinge (inf)

mob n 1 = **crowd**, drove, flock, horde, host, mass, multitude, pack, swarm, throng 2 Sl = **gang**, crew (inf), group, lot, set ▷ v 3 = **surround**, crowd around, jostle, set upon, swarm around

mobile adj 1 = **movable**, itinerant, moving, peripatetic, portable, travelling, wandering

mobilize v 1 = **call to arms**, activate, call up, marshal 2 = **prepare**, get or make ready, organize, rally, ready

mock v 1 = **laugh at**, deride, jeer, make fun of, poke fun at, ridicule, scoff, scorn, sneer, taunt, tease 2 = **mimic**, ape, caricature, imitate, lampoon, parody, satirize, send up (Brit inf) ▷ adj 3 = **imitation**, artificial, dummy, fake, false, feigned, phoney or phony (inf), pretended, sham, spurious

mockery n 1 = **derision**, contempt, disdain, disrespect, insults, jeering, ridicule, scoffing, scorn 2 = **farce**, apology (inf), disappointment,

joke, letdown

mocking adj 1 = **scornful**, contemptuous, derisive, disdainful, disrespectful, sarcastic, sardonic, satirical, scoffing

mode n 1 = **method**, form, manner, procedure, process, style, system, technique, way 2 = **fashion**, craze, look, rage, style, trend, vogue

model n 1 = **representation**, copy, dummy, facsimile, image, imitation, miniature, mock-up, replica 2 = **pattern**, example, original, paradigm, prototype, standard 3 = **ideal**, archetype, paragon 4 = **sitter**, poser, subject ▷ v 8 = **shape**, carve, design, fashion, form, mould, sculpt 10 = **show off**, display, sport (inf), wear

moderate adj 1 = **middle-of-the-road**, limited 2 = **restrained**, controlled, gentle, mild, modest, reasonable, steady 3 = **average**, fair, indifferent, mediocre, middling, ordinary, passable, so-so (inf),

moderate views. ▷ *v* **5** make or
become less violent or extreme.
moderately *adv* **moderation** *n*
moderator *n* **1** (Presbyterian Church)
minister appointed to preside over a
Church court, general assembly, etc.
2 person who presides over a public or
legislative assembly.
modern ❶ *adj* **1** of present or recent
times. **2** up-to-date. **modern
languages** languages spoken in
present-day Europe, with the
exception of English. **modern
pentathlon** athletic contest
consisting of five different events.
modernity *n* **modernism** *n* (support
of) modern tendencies, thoughts, or
styles. **modernist** *adj*, *n* **modernize** *v*
bring up to date. **modernization** *n*.
modest ❶ *adj* **1** not vain or boastful.
2 not excessive. **3** not showy. **4** shy.
modestly *adv* **modesty** *n*.
modicum ❶ *n* small quantity.
modify ❶ *v* **-fying, -fied 1** change
slightly. **2** tone down. **3** (of a word)
qualify (another word). **modifier** *n*
word that qualifies the sense of
another. **modification** *n*.
modish ❶ [*mode*-ish] *adj* in fashion.
modulate ❶ *v* **1** vary in tone. **2** adjust.
3 change the key of (music).
modulation *n* **modulator** *n*.
module *n* **1** self-contained unit, section,

or component with a specific function.
2 short study course that together
with other such courses counts
towards a qualification. **modular** *adj*.
modus operandi [*mode*-uss op-er-
an-die] *n Latin* method of operating.
modus vivendi [*mode*-uss viv-**venn**-
die] *n Latin* working arrangement
between conflicting interests.
moggy, moggie *n, pl* **-gies** *slang* cat.
mogul ❶ [**moh**-gl] *n* important or
powerful person.
MOH Medical Officer of Health.
mohair *n* **1** fine hair of the Angora
goat. **2** yarn or fabric made from this.
mohican *n* punk hairstyle with shaved
sides and a stiff central strip of hair,
often brightly coloured.
moiety [**moy**-it-ee] *n, pl* **-ties** half.
moiré [**mwahr**-ray] *adj* **1** having a
watered or wavelike pattern. ▷ *n*
2 any fabric that has such a pattern.
moist ❶ *adj* slightly wet. **moisten** *v*
make or become moist. **moisture** *n*
liquid diffused as vapour or condensed
in drops. **moisturize** *v* add moisture
to (the skin etc.). **moisturizer** *n*.
moke *n* **1** *slang* donkey. **2** *Aust &
NZ* horse of inferior quality.
molar *n* large back tooth used for
grinding.
molasses *n* dark syrup, a by-product of
sugar refining.

— THESAURUS —

unexceptional ▷ *v* **5** = **lessen**, control,
curb, ease, modulate, regulate,
restrain, soften, subdue, temper, tone
down
moderation *n* **2** = **restraint**, fairness,
reasonableness, temperance
modern *adj* **1** = **current**,
contemporary, present-day, recent
2 = **up-to-date**, fresh, new,
newfangled, novel
modernity *n* **2** = **novelty**, currency,
freshness, innovation, newness
modernize *v* **2** = **update**, make over,
rejuvenate, remake, remodel, renew,
renovate, revamp
modest *adj* **1, 4** = **shy**, bashful, coy,
demure, diffident, reserved, reticent,
retiring, self-effacing **2** = **moderate**,
fair, limited, middling, small
3 = **unpretentious**, ordinary,
unexceptional
modesty *n* **1, 4** = **reserve**, bashfulness,
coyness, demureness, diffidence,
humility, reticence, shyness, timidity

modicum *n* = **little**, bit, crumb, drop,
fragment, scrap, shred, touch
modification *n* **1** = **change**,
adjustment, alteration, qualification,
refinement, revision, variation
modify *v* **1** = **change**, adapt, adjust,
alter, convert, reform, remodel, revise,
rework **2** = **tone down**, ease, lessen,
lower, moderate, qualify, restrain,
soften, temper
modish *adj* = **fashionable**,
contemporary, current, in, smart,
stylish, trendy (*Brit inf*), up-to-the-
minute, voguish
modulate *v* **1** = **vary 2** = **adjust**,
attune, balance, regulate **3** = **tune**
mogul *n* = **tycoon**, baron, big hitter
(*inf*), big noise (*inf*), big shot (*inf*),
heavy hitter (*inf*), magnate, V.I.P.
moist *adj* = **damp**, clammy, dewy,
humid, soggy, wet
moisten *v* = **dampen**, damp,
moisturize, soak, water, wet
moisture *n* = **damp**, dew, liquid,

mole¹ n small dark raised spot on the skin.

mole² n 1 small burrowing mammal. 2 informal spy who has infiltrated and become a trusted member of an organization. **molehill** n small mound of earth thrown up by a burrowing mole. **make a mountain out of a molehill** exaggerate an unimportant matter out of all proportion.

mole³ n unit of amount of substance.

mole⁴ n 1 breakwater. 2 harbour protected by this.

molecule ❶ [**mol**-lik-kyool] n 1 simplest freely existing chemical unit, composed of two or more atoms. 2 very small particle. **molecular** [mol-**lek**-yew-lar] adj.

molest ❶ v 1 interfere with sexually. 2 annoy or injure. **molester** n **molestation** n.

moll n slang gangster's female accomplice.

mollify ❶ v -fying, -fied pacify or soothe. **mollification** n.

mollusc n soft-bodied, usu. hard-shelled, animal, such as a snail or oyster.

mollycoddle ❶ v pamper.

Molotov cocktail n petrol bomb.

molten adj liquefied or melted.

molybdenum [mol-**lib**-din-um] n Chemistry hard silvery-white metallic element.

mom n Chiefly US & Canad an informal

word for MOTHER.

moment ❶ n 1 short space of time. 2 (present) point in time. **momentary** adj lasting only a moment. **momentarily** adv.

- ● **USAGE NOTE**
- ● Note that some American speakers
- ● use momentarily to mean 'soon'
- ● rather than 'for a moment'.

momentous ❶ [moh-**men**-tuss] adj of great significance.

momentum ❶ [moh-**men**-tum] n 1 impetus to go forward, develop, or get stronger. 2 impetus of a moving body. 3 product of a body's mass and velocity.

Mon. Monday.

monarch ❶ n sovereign ruler of a state. **monarchical** adj **monarchist** n supporter of monarchy. **monarchy** n, pl **-chies** government by or a state ruled by a sovereign.

monastery ❶ n, pl **-teries** residence of a community of monks. **monastic** adj 1 of monks, nuns, or monasteries. 2 simple and austere. **monasticism** n.

monatomic adj consisting of single atoms.

Monday n second day of the week.

monetary ❶ adj of money or currency. **monetarism** n 1 theory that inflation is caused by an increase in the money supply. 2 economic policy based on this theory. **monetarist** n, adj.

m

water, wetness

molecule n 2 = **particle**, jot, speck

molest v 1 = **abuse**, ill-treat, interfere with, maltreat 2 = **annoy**, attack, badger, beset, bother, disturb, harass, harm, hurt, persecute, pester, plague, torment, worry

mollify v = **pacify**, appease, calm, conciliate, placate, quiet, soothe, sweeten

mollycoddle v = **pamper**, baby, cosset, indulge, spoil

moment n 1 = **instant**, flash, jiffy (inf), second, split second, trice, twinkling 2 = **time**, juncture, point, stage

momentarily adv 1 = **briefly**, for a moment, temporarily

momentary adj = **short-lived**, brief, fleeting, passing, short, temporary, transitory

momentous adj = **significant**, critical, crucial, fateful, historic, important, pivotal, vital, weighty

momentum n 1, 2 = **impetus**, drive, energy, force, power, propulsion, push, strength, thrust

monarch n = **ruler**, emperor or empress, king, potentate, prince or princess, queen, sovereign

monarchy n a = **sovereignty**, autocracy, kingship, monocracy b = **kingdom**, empire, principality, realm

monastery n = **abbey**, cloister, convent, friary, nunnery, priory

monastic adj 1 = **monkish**, cloistered, contemplative, hermit-like, reclusive, secluded, sequestered, withdrawn 2 = **ascetic**

monetary adj = **financial**, budgetary,

money ❶ *n* medium of exchange, coins or banknotes. **moneyed, monied** *adj* rich. **moneylender** *n* person who lends money at a high rate of interest as a living.

Mongolian *n* **1** person from Mongolia. **2** language of Mongolia. ▷ *adj* **3** of Mongolia or its language.

mongolism *n offens* Down's syndrome. **mongol** *n, adj offens* (person) affected by this.

mongoose *n, pl* **-gooses** stoatlike mammal of Asia and Africa that kills snakes.

mongrel ❶ *n* **1** animal, esp. a dog, of mixed breed. **2** something arising from a variety of sources. ▷ *adj* **3** of mixed breed or origin.

monitor ❶ *n* **1** person or device that checks, controls, warns, or keeps a record of something. **2** pupil assisting a teacher with duties. **3** television set used in a studio to check what is being transmitted. **4** type of large lizard. ▷ *v* **5** watch and check on.

monk ❶ *n* member of an all-male religious community bound by vows. **monkish** *adj* **monkshood** *n* poisonous plant with hooded flowers.

monkey ❶ *n* **1** long-tailed primate. **2** mischievous child. ▷ *v* **3** (usu. foll. by *about* or *around*) meddle or fool. **monkey nut** peanut. **monkey puzzle** coniferous tree with sharp stiff leaves. **monkey wrench** wrench with adjustable jaws.

mono *adj* **1** short for MONOPHONIC. ▷ *n* **2** monophonic sound.

mono- *combining form* single, e.g. *monosyllable.*

monochrome *adj* **1** *Photography* black-and-white. **2** in only one colour.

monocle [**mon**-a-kl] *n* eyeglass for one eye only.

monocotyledon [mon-no-kot-ill-**leed**-on] *n* flowering plant with a single embryonic seed leaf.

monocular *adj* having or for one eye only.

monogamy *n* custom of being married to one person at a time. **monogamous** *adj.*

monogram *n* design of combined letters, esp. a person's initials. **monogrammed** *adj* marked with such a design.

monograph *n* book or paper on a single subject.

monolith ❶ *n* large upright block of stone. **monolithic** *adj.*

monologue ❶ *n* **1** long speech by one person. **2** dramatic piece for one performer.

monomania *n* obsession with one thing. **monomaniac** *n, adj.*

monophonic *adj* (of a system of broadcasting, recording, or reproducing sound) using only one channel between source and loudspeaker.

monoplane *n* aeroplane with one pair of wings.

monopoly ❶ *n* **1** *pl* **-lies** exclusive possession of or right to do something. **2** (**M-**) ® board game for four to six players who deal in 'property' as they move around the board. **monopolist** *n* **monopolistic** *adj* **monopolize** *v* have or take exclusive possession of.

monorail *n* single-rail railway.

monosodium glutamate *n* white crystalline substance used as a food additive to enhance protein flavours.

monosyllable *n* word of one syllable. **monosyllabic** *adj.*

monotheism *n* belief in only one God. **monotheistic** *adj.*

THESAURUS

capital, cash, fiscal, pecuniary

money *n* = **cash**, capital, coin, currency, hard cash, legal tender, lolly (*Aust & NZ sl*), readies (*inf*), riches, silver, wealth

mongrel *n* **1** = **crossbreed**, cross, half-breed **2** = **hybrid** ▷ *adj* **3** = **hybrid**, crossbred

monitor *n* **1** = **watchdog**, guide, invigilator, supervisor **2** = **prefect** (*Brit*) ▷ *v* **5** = **check**, follow, keep an eye on, keep tabs on, keep track of, observe, survey, watch

monk *n* = **friar**, brother (*loosely*)

monkey *n* **1** = **simian**, primate **2** = **rascal**, devil, imp, rogue, scamp ▷ *v* **3** (usu. foll. by *about* or *around*) = **fool**, meddle, mess, play, tinker

monolithic *adj* = **huge**, colossal, impenetrable, intractable, massive, monumental, solid

monologue *n* **1** = **speech**, harangue, lecture, sermon **2** = **soliloquy**

monopolize *v* = **control**, corner the market in, dominate, hog (*sl*), keep to

monotone ❶ *n* unvaried pitch in speech or sound. **monotonous** *adj* tedious due to lack of variety. **monotonously** *adv* **monotony** *n* wearisome routine, dullness.

monoxide *n* oxide that contains one oxygen atom per molecule.

Monseigneur [mon-sen-**nyur**] *n, pl* **Messeigneurs** [may-sen-**nyur**] title of French prelates.

monsieur [muss-**syur**] *n, pl* **messieurs** [may-**syur**] French title of address equivalent to *sir* or *Mr*.

Monsignor *n RC Church* title attached to certain offices.

monsoon *n* **1** seasonal wind of SE Asia. **2** rainy season accompanying this.

monster ❶ *n* **1** imaginary, usu. frightening, beast. **2** huge person, animal, or thing. **3** very wicked person. ▷ *adj* **4** huge. **monstrosity** *n, pl* **-ities** large ugly thing. **monstrous** *adj* **1** unnatural or ugly. **2** outrageous or shocking. **3** huge. **monstrously** *adv*.

monstrance *n RC Church* container in which the consecrated Host is exposed for adoration.

montage [**mon**-tahzh] *n* **1** (making of) a picture composed from pieces of others. **2** method of film editing incorporating several shots to form a single image.

month *n* **1** one of the twelve divisions of the calendar year. **2** period of four weeks. **monthly** *adj* **1** happening or payable once a month. ▷ *adv* **2** once a month. ▷ *n, pl* **-lies 3** monthly magazine.

monument ❶ *n* something, esp. a building or statue, that commemorates something. **monumental** *adj* **1** large, impressive, or lasting. **2** of or being a monument. **3** *informal* extreme. **monumentally** *adv informal* extremely.

moo *n* **1** long deep cry of a cow. ▷ *v* **2** make this noise.

mooch *v slang* loiter about aimlessly.

mood[1] ❶ *n* temporary (gloomy) state of mind. **moody** *adj* **moodier, moodiest** **1** sullen or gloomy. **2** changeable in mood. **moodily** *adv* **moodiness** *n*.

mood[2] *n Grammar* form of a verb indicating whether it expresses a fact, wish, supposition, or command.

moon ❶ *n* **1** natural satellite of the earth. **2** natural satellite of any planet. ▷ *v* **3** (foll. by *about* or *around*) be idle in a listless or dreamy way. **moonless** *adj* **moony** *adj informal* dreamy or listless. **moonbeam** *n* ray of moonlight. **moonlight** *n* **1** light from the moon. ▷ *adj* **2** illuminated by the moon, e.g. *a moonlight drive*. ▷ *v* **3** *informal* work at a secondary job,

m

oneself, take over

monotonous *adj* = **tedious**, boring, dull, humdrum, mind-numbing, repetitive, tiresome, unchanging, wearisome

monotony *n* = **tedium**, boredom, monotonousness, repetitiveness, routine, sameness, tediousness

monster *n* **1** = **freak**, monstrosity, mutant **2** = **giant**, colossus, mammoth, titan **3** = **brute**, beast, demon, devil, fiend, villain ▷ *adj* **4** = **huge**, colossal, enormous, gigantic, immense, mammoth, massive, stupendous, tremendous

monstrosity *n* = **eyesore**, freak, horror, monster

monstrous *adj* **1** = **unnatural**, fiendish, freakish, frightful, grotesque, gruesome, hideous, horrible **2** = **outrageous**, diabolical, disgraceful, foul, inhuman, intolerable, scandalous, shocking **3** = **huge**, colossal, enormous,

immense, mammoth, massive, prodigious, stupendous, tremendous

monument *n* = **memorial**, cairn, cenotaph, commemoration, gravestone, headstone, marker, mausoleum, shrine, tombstone

monumental *adj* **1** = **important**, awesome, enormous, epoch-making, historic, majestic, memorable, significant, unforgettable **3** *Inf* = **immense**, colossal, great, massive, staggering

mood[1] *n* = **state of mind**, disposition, frame of mind, humour, spirit, temper

moody *adj* **1** = **sulky**, gloomy, glum, ill-tempered, irritable, morose, pissed (*taboo sl*), pissed off (*taboo sl*), sad, sullen, temperamental, touchy **2** = **changeable**, capricious, erratic, fickle, flighty, impulsive, mercurial, temperamental, unpredictable, volatile

moon *n* **1, 2** = **satellite** ▷ *v* **3** = **idle**, daydream, languish, mope, waste time

esp. illegally. **moonlit** adj **moonshine** n **1** illicitly distilled whisky. **2** nonsense. **moonstone** n translucent semiprecious stone. **moonstruck** adj slightly mad or odd.

moor¹ ❶ n tract of open uncultivated ground covered with grass and heather. **moorhen** n small black water bird. **moorland** n.

moor² ❶ v secure (a ship) with ropes etc. **mooring** n **1** place for mooring a ship. ▷ pl **2** ropes etc. used in mooring a ship.

Moor n member of a Muslim people of NW Africa who ruled Spain between the 8th and 15th centuries. **Moorish** adj.

moose n large N American deer.

moot ❶ adj **1** debatable, e.g. a moot point. ▷ v **2** bring up for discussion.

mop ❶ n **1** long stick with twists of cotton or a sponge on the end, used for cleaning. **2** thick mass of hair. ▷ v **mopping**, **mopped 3** clean or soak up with or as if with a mop.

mope ❶ v be gloomy and apathetic.

moped n light motorized cycle.

mopoke n small spotted owl of Australia and New Zealand.

moraine n accumulated mass of debris deposited by a glacier.

moral ❶ adj **1** concerned with right and wrong conduct. **2** based on a sense of

right and wrong. **3** (of support or a victory) psychological rather than practical. ▷ n **4** lesson to be obtained from a story or event. ▷ pl **5** principles of behaviour with respect to right and wrong. **morally** adv **moralist** n person with a strong sense of right and wrong. **moralistic** adj **morality** n **1** good moral conduct. **2** moral goodness or badness. **morality play** medieval play with a moral lesson. **moralize** v make moral pronouncements.

morale ❶ [mor-**rahl**] n degree of confidence or hope of a person or group.

morass ❶ n **1** marsh. **2** mess.

moratorium ❶ n, pl **-ria**, **-riums** legally authorized ban or delay.

moray n large voracious eel.

morbid ❶ adj **1** unduly interested in death or unpleasant events. **2** gruesome. **morbidly** adv.

mordant ❶ adj **1** sarcastic or scathing. ▷ n **2** substance used to fix dyes.

more ❶ adj **1** greater in amount or degree. **2** comparative of MUCH or MANY **3** additional or further. ▷ adv **4** to a greater extent. **5** in addition. ▷ pron **6** greater or additional amount or number. **moreover** adv in addition to what has already been said.

────────────────────────── THESAURUS ──────────────

moor¹ n = **moorland**, fell (Brit), heath

moor² v = **tie up**, anchor, berth, dock, lash, make fast, secure

moot adj **1** = **debatable**, arguable, contestable, controversial, disputable, doubtful, undecided, unresolved, unsettled ▷ v **2** = **bring up**, broach, propose, put forward, suggest

mop n **1** = **squeegee**, sponge, swab **2** = **mane**, shock, tangle, thatch ▷ v **3** = **clean up**, soak up, sponge, swab, wash, wipe

mope v = **brood**, fret, languish, moon, pine, pout, sulk

moral adj **1, 2** = **good**, decent, ethical, high-minded, honourable, just, noble, principled, right, virtuous ▷ n **4** = **lesson**, meaning, message, point, significance

morale n = **confidence**, esprit de corps, heart, self-esteem, spirit

morality n **1** = **integrity**, decency, goodness, honesty, justice, righteousness, virtue **2** = **standards**,

conduct, ethics, manners, morals, mores, philosophy, principles

morals pl n **5** = **morality**, behaviour, conduct, ethics, habits, integrity, manners, mores, principles, scruples, standards

morass n **1** = **marsh**, bog, fen, quagmire, slough, swamp, muskeg (Canad) **2** = **mess**, confusion, mix-up, muddle, tangle

moratorium n = **postponement**, freeze, halt, standstill, suspension

morbid adj **1** = **unwholesome**, ghoulish, gloomy, melancholy, sick, sombre, unhealthy **2** = **gruesome**, dreadful, ghastly, grisly, hideous, horrid, macabre

mordant adj **1** = **sarcastic**, biting, caustic, cutting, incisive, pungent, scathing, stinging, trenchant

more adj **1** = **extra**, added, additional, further, new, new-found, other, supplementary ▷ adv **4** = **to a greater extent**, better, further, longer

morel *n* edible mushroom with a pitted cap.

mores [**more**-rayz] *pl n* customs and conventions embodying the fundamental values of a community.

Moreton Bay bug *n* Australian flattish edible shellfish.

morganatic marriage *n* marriage of a person of high rank to a lower-ranking person whose status remains unchanged.

morgue ❶ *n* mortuary.

moribund ❶ *adj* without force or vitality.

Mormon *n* member of a religious sect founded in the USA.

morn *n poetic* morning.

mornay *adj* served with a cheese sauce, e.g. *sole mornay*.

morning ❶ *n* part of the day before noon. **the morning after** *informal* the aftereffects of overindulgence, hangover. **morning coat** frock coat. **morning dress** formal day dress for men, comprising a morning coat, grey trousers, and a top hat. **morning-glory** *n* plant with trumpet-shaped flowers which close in the late afternoon. **morning sickness** nausea shortly after rising, often experienced in early pregnancy.

Moroccan *adj* 1 of Morocco. ▷ *n* 2 person from Morocco.

morocco *n* goatskin leather.

moron ❶ *n* 1 *informal* foolish or stupid person. 2 (formerly) person with a low intelligence quotient. **moronic** *adj*.

morose ❶ [mor-**rohss**] *adj* sullen or moody. **morosely** *adv*.

morphine, morphia *n* drug extracted from opium, used as an anaesthetic and sedative.

morphology *n* science of forms and structures of organisms or words. **morphological** *adj*.

morris dance *n* traditional English folk dance performed by men.

morrow *n poetic* next day.

Morse *n* former system of signalling in which letters of the alphabet are represented by combinations of short and long signals.

morsel ❶ *n* small piece, esp. of food.

mortal ❶ *adj* 1 subject to death. 2 causing death. ▷ *n* 3 human being. **mortally** *adv* **mortality** *n* 1 state of being mortal. 2 great loss of life. 3 death rate. **mortal sin** *RC Church* sin meriting damnation.

mortar *n* 1 small cannon with a short range. 2 mixture of lime, sand, and water for holding bricks and stones together. 3 bowl in which substances are pounded. **mortarboard** *n* square academic cap.

mortgage *n* 1 conditional pledging of property, esp. a house, as security for the repayment of a loan. 2 the loan itself. ▷ *v* 3 pledge (property) as

—————————— THESAURUS ——————————

moreover *adv* = **furthermore**, additionally, also, as well, besides, further, in addition, too

morgue *n* = **mortuary**

moribund *adj* = **declining**, on its last legs, stagnant, waning, weak

morning *n* = **dawn**, a.m., break of day, daybreak, forenoon, morn (*poet*), sunrise

moron *n* 1 *Inf* = **fool**, blockhead, cretin, dunce, dunderhead, halfwit, idiot, imbecile, oaf

moronic *adj* 1 = **idiotic**, cretinous, foolish, halfwitted, imbecilic, mindless, stupid, unintelligent

morose *adj* = **sullen**, depressed, dour, gloomy, glum, ill-tempered, moody, sour, sulky, surly, taciturn

morsel *n* = **piece**, bit, bite, crumb, mouthful, part, scrap, *soupçon*, taste, titbit

mortal *adj* 1 = **human**, ephemeral, impermanent, passing, temporal, transient, worldly 2 = **fatal**, deadly, death-dealing, destructive, killing, lethal, murderous, terminal ▷ *n* 3 = **human being**, being, earthling, human, individual, man, person, woman

mortality *n* 1 = **humanity**, impermanence, transience 2 = **killing**, bloodshed, carnage, death, destruction, fatality

mortification *n* 1 = **humiliation**, annoyance, chagrin, discomfiture, embarrassment, shame, vexation 2 = **discipline**, abasement, chastening, control, denial, subjugation 3 = **gangrene**, corruption, festering

mortified *adj* 1 = **humiliated**, ashamed, chagrined, chastened, crushed, deflated, embarrassed, humbled, shamed

security thus. **mortgagee** n creditor in a mortgage. **mortgagor**, **mortgager** n debtor in a mortgage.

mortice, mortise [**more**-tiss] n hole in a piece of wood or stone shaped to receive a matching projection on another piece. **mortice lock** lock set into a door.

mortify ⓘ v **-fying**, **-fied 1** humiliate. **2** subdue by self-denial. **3** (of flesh) become gangrenous. **mortification** n.

mortuary ⓘ n, pl **-aries** building where corpses are kept before burial or cremation.

mosaic [mow-**zay**-ik] n design or decoration using small pieces of coloured stone or glass.

Mosaic adj of Moses.

Moselle n light white German wine.

mosque n Muslim temple.

mosquito n, pl **-toes**, **-tos** blood-sucking flying insect.

moss n small flowerless plant growing in masses on moist surfaces. **mossy** adj **mossier**, **mossiest**.

most ⓘ n **1** greatest number or degree. ▷ adj **2** greatest in number or degree. **3** superlative of MUCH or MANY. ▷ adv **4** in the greatest degree. **mostly** adv for the most part, generally.

MOT, MOT test n compulsory annual test of the roadworthiness of vehicles over a certain age.

mote n tiny speck.

motel n roadside hotel for motorists.

motet [moh-**tet**] n short sacred choral song.

moth ⓘ n nocturnal insect like a butterfly. **mothball** n **1** small ball of camphor or naphthalene used to repel moths from stored clothes. ▷ v **2** store (something operational) for future use. **3** postpone (a project etc.). **moth-eaten** adj **1** decayed or scruffy. **2** eaten or damaged by moth larvae.

mother ⓘ n **1** female parent. **2** head of a female religious community. ▷ adj **3** native or inborn, e.g. mother wit. ▷ v **4** look after as a mother. **motherhood** n **motherly** adj **motherless** adj **mother country**, **motherland** country where one was born. **mother-in-law** n, pl **mothers-in-law** mother of one's husband or wife. **mother of pearl** iridescent lining of certain shells. **mother tongue** one's native language.

motif ⓘ [moh-**teef**] n (recurring) theme or design.

motion ⓘ n **1** process, action, or way of moving. **2** proposal in a meeting. **3** evacuation of the bowels. ▷ v **4** direct (someone) by gesture. **motionless** adj not moving. **motion picture** cinema film.

motive ⓘ n **1** reason for a course of action. ▷ adj **2** causing motion. **motivate** v give incentive to. **motivation** n.

——————————————————————————— **THESAURUS** ———————

mortify v **1** = **humiliate**, chagrin, chasten, crush, deflate, embarrass, humble, shame **2** = **discipline**, abase, chasten, control, deny, subdue **3** Of flesh = **putrefy**, cark (Aust & NZ sl), deaden, die, fester

mortuary n = **morgue**, funeral parlour

mostly adv = **generally**, as a rule, chiefly, largely, mainly, on the whole, predominantly, primarily, principally, usually

moth-eaten adj **1** = **decayed**, decrepit, dilapidated, ragged, shabby, tattered, threadbare, worn-out

mother n **1** = **parent**, dam, ma (inf), mater, mum (Brit inf), mummy (Brit inf), mom (US & Canad) ▷ adj **3** = **native**, inborn, innate, natural ▷ v **4** = **nurture**, care for, cherish, nurse, protect, raise, rear, tend

motherly adj **4** = **maternal**, affectionate, caring, comforting, loving, protective, sheltering

motif n **a** = **theme**, concept, idea, leitmotif, subject **b** = **design**, decoration, ornament, shape

motion n **1** = **movement**, flow, locomotion, mobility, move, progress, travel **2** = **proposal**, proposition, recommendation, submission, suggestion ▷ v **4** = **gesture**, beckon, direct, gesticulate, nod, signal, wave

motionless adj = **still**, fixed, frozen, immobile, paralysed, standing, static, stationary, stock-still, transfixed, unmoving

motivate v = **inspire**, arouse, cause, drive, induce, move, persuade, prompt, stimulate, stir

motivation n **1** = **incentive**, incitement, inducement, inspiration, motive, reason, spur, stimulus

motive n **1** = **reason**, ground(s), incentive, inducement, inspiration, object, purpose, rationale, stimulus

motley ⊙ *adj* **1** miscellaneous. **2** multicoloured.

motocross *n* motorcycle race over a rough course.

motor *n* **1** engine, esp. of a vehicle. **2** machine that converts electrical energy into mechanical energy. **3** car. ▷ *v* **4** travel by car. **motorist** *n* driver of a car. **motorized** *adj* equipped with a motor or motor transport. **motorbike** *n* **motorboat** *n* **motorcade** *n* procession of cars carrying important people. **motorcar** *n* **motorcycle** *n* **motorcyclist** *n* **motor scooter** light motorcycle with small wheels and an enclosed engine. **motorway** *n* main road for fast-moving traffic.

mottled ⊙ *adj* marked with blotches.

motto ⊙ *n*, *pl* **-toes**, **-tos 1** saying expressing an ideal or rule of conduct. **2** verse or maxim in a paper cracker.

mould¹ ⊙ *n* **1** hollow container in which metal etc. is cast. **2** shape, form, or pattern. **3** nature or character. ▷ *v* **4** shape. **5** influence or direct. **moulding** *n* moulded ornamental edging.

mould² ⊙ *n* fungal growth caused by dampness. **mouldy** *adj* **mouldier**, **mouldiest 1** stale or musty. **2** dull or boring.

mould³ ⊙ *n* loose soil. **moulder** *v* decay into dust.

moult *v* **1** shed feathers, hair, or skin to make way for new growth. ▷ *n* **2** process of moulting.

mound ⊙ *n* **1** heap, esp. of earth or stones. **2** small hill.

mount ⊙ *v* **1** climb or ascend. **2** get up on (a horse etc.). **3** increase or accumulate. **4** fix on a support or backing. **5** organize, e.g. *mount a campaign*. ▷ *n* **6** backing or support on which something is fixed. **7** horse for riding. **8** hill.

mountain ⊙ *n* **1** hill of great size. **2** large heap. **mountainous** *adj* **1** full of mountains. **2** huge. **mountaineer** *n* person who climbs mountains. **mountaineering** *n* **mountain bike** bicycle with straight handlebars and heavy-duty tyres, for cycling over rough terrain. **mountain lion** same as PUMA.

mountebank *n* charlatan or fake.

Mountie *n informal* member of the Royal Canadian Mounted Police.

mourn ⊙ *v* feel or express sorrow for (a dead person or lost thing). **mourner** *n* **mournful** *adj* sad or dismal. **mournfully** *adv* **mourning** *n* **1** grieving. **2** conventional symbols of grief for death, such as the wearing of black.

motley *adj* **1** = **miscellaneous**, assorted, disparate, heterogeneous, mixed, varied **2** = **multicoloured**, chequered, variegated

mottled *adj* = **blotchy**, dappled, flecked, piebald, speckled, spotted, stippled, streaked

motto *n* **1** = **saying**, adage, dictum, maxim, precept, proverb, rule, slogan, tag-line, watchword

mould¹ *n* **1** = **cast**, pattern, shape **2** = **design**, build, construction, fashion, form, format, kind, pattern, shape, style **3** = **nature**, calibre, character, kind, quality, sort, stamp, type ▷ *v* **4** = **shape**, construct, create, fashion, forge, form, make, model, sculpt, work **5** = **influence**, affect, control, direct, form, make, shape

mould² *n* = **fungus**, blight, mildew

mould³ *n* = **soil**, dirt, earth, humus, loam

mouldy *adj* **1** = **stale**, bad, blighted, decaying, fusty, mildewed, musty, rotten

mound *n* **1** = **heap**, drift, pile, rick, stack **2** = **hill**, bank, dune, embankment, hillock, knoll, rise

mount *v* **1** = **ascend**, clamber up, climb, go up, scale **2** = **get (up) on**, bestride, climb onto, jump on **3** = **increase**, accumulate, build, escalate, grow, intensify, multiply, pile up, swell ▷ *n* **6** = **backing**, base, frame, setting, stand, support **7** = **horse**, steed (*lit*)

mountain *n* **1** = **peak**, alp, berg (*S Afr*), fell (*Brit*), mount **2** = **heap**, abundance, mass, mound, pile, stack, ton

mountainous *adj* **1** = **high**, alpine, highland, rocky, soaring, steep, towering, upland **2** = **huge**, daunting, enormous, gigantic, great, immense, mammoth, mighty, monumental

mourn *v* = **grieve**, bemoan, bewail, deplore, lament, rue, wail, weep

mournful *adj* **a** = **sad**, melancholy, piteous, plaintive, tragic, unhappy, woeful **b** = **dismal**,

mouse *n, pl* **mice 1** small long-tailed rodent. **2** timid person. **3** *Computers* hand-held device for moving the cursor without keying. **mouser** *n* cat used to catch mice. **mousy** *adj* **mousier**, **mousiest 1** like a mouse, esp. in hair colour. **2** meek and shy.

moussaka *n* dish made with meat, aubergines, and tomatoes, topped with cheese sauce.

mousse *n* **1** dish of flavoured cream whipped and set. **2** foamy substance applied to the hair before styling to hold the style.

moustache *n* hair on the upper lip.

mouth ❶ *n* **1** opening in the head for eating and issuing sounds. **2** lips. **3** entrance. **4** point where a river enters the sea. **5** opening. ▷ *v* **6** form (words) with the lips without speaking. **7** speak or utter insincerely, esp. in public. **mouthful** *n* **1** amount of food or drink put into the mouth at any one time when eating or drinking. **2** word, phrase, or name that is difficult to say. **mouth organ** same as HARMONICA. **mouthpiece** *n* **1** part of a telephone into which a person speaks. **2** part of a wind instrument into which the player blows. **3** spokesperson. **mouthwash** *n* medicated liquid for gargling and cleansing the mouth.

move ❶ *v* **1** change in place or position. **2** change (one's house etc.). **3** take action. **4** stir the emotions of. **5** incite. **6** suggest (a proposal) formally. ▷ *n* **7** moving. **8** action towards some goal. **movable**, **moveable** *adj* **movement** *n* **1** action or process of moving. **2** group with a common aim. **3** division of a piece of music. **4** moving parts of a machine. **moving** *adj* arousing or touching the emotions. **movingly** *adv*.

movie ❶ *n informal* cinema film.

mow ❶ *v* **mowing**, **mowed**, **mowed** or **mown** cut (grass or crops). **mower** *n* **mow down** *v* kill in large numbers.

mozzarella [mot-sa-**rel**-la] *n* moist white cheese originally made in Italy from buffalo milk.

MP 1 Member of Parliament. **2** Military Police(man).

MP3 *Computing* Motion Picture Expert Group-1, Audio Layer-3: a digital compression format used to compress audio files to a fraction of their original size without loss of sound quality. **MP3 player** small portable device for playing MP3 files downloaded from the internet or transferred from a CD.

MPEG [**em**-peg] *Computing* Motion Picture Expert Group: standard compressed file format used for audio and video files.

──────────────────────── THESAURUS ────────

disconsolate, downcast, gloomy, grieving, heavy-hearted, lugubrious, miserable, rueful, sombre

mourning *n* **1** = **grieving**, bereavement, grief, lamentation, weeping, woe **2** = **black**, sackcloth and ashes, widow's weeds

mouth *n* **1** = **maw**, gob (*sl, esp. Brit*), jaws **2** = **lips 3** = **door**, entrance, gateway, inlet **5** = **opening**, aperture, orifice

mouthful *n* **1** = **taste**, bit, bite, little, morsel, sample, spoonful, swallow

mouthpiece *n* **3** = **spokesperson**, agent, delegate, representative, spokesman or spokeswoman

movable *adj* **1** = **portable**, detachable, mobile, transferable, transportable

move *v* **1** = **change**, advance, budge, go, proceed, progress, shift, stir, switch, transfer, transpose **2** = **relocate**, leave, migrate, pack one's bags (*inf*), quit, remove **3** = **drive**, activate, operate, propel,

shift, start, turn **4** = **touch**, affect, excite, impress, inspire, rouse **5** = **prompt**, cause, incite, induce, influence, motivate, persuade **6** = **propose**, advocate, put forward, recommend, suggest, urge ▷ *n* **7** = **transfer**, relocation, removal, shift **8** = **action**, manoeuvre, measure, ploy, step, stratagem, stroke, turn

movement *n* **1** = **motion**, action, activity, change, development, flow, manoeuvre, progress, stirring **2** = **group**, campaign, crusade, drive, faction, front, grouping, organization, party **3** *Music* = **section**, division, part, passage **4** = **workings**, action, machinery, mechanism, works

movie *n Inf* = **film**, feature, flick (*sl*), picture

moving *adj* = **emotional**, affecting, inspiring, pathetic, persuasive, poignant, stirring, touching

mow *v* = **cut**, crop, scythe, shear, trim

mpg miles per gallon.

mph miles per hour.

Mr Mister.

Mrs *n* title of a married woman.

Ms [**mizz**] *n* title used instead of Miss or Mrs.

MS 1 *pl* **MSS** manuscript. **2** multiple sclerosis. **3** Mississippi.

MSc Master of Science.

MSM mainstream media.

MSP Member of the Scottish Parliament.

MSS manuscripts.

Mt Mount.

MT Montana.

much ❶ *adj* **more**, **most 1** large amount or degree of. ▷ *n* **2** large amount or degree. ▷ *adv* **more**, **most 3** to a great degree. **4** nearly. **much of a muchness** very similar.

mucilage [**mew**-sill-ij] *n* gum or glue.

muck ❶ *n* **1** dirt, filth. **2** manure. **3** *slang* something of poor quality, rubbish. **mucky** *adj* **muckier**, **muckiest**. **muck about** *v slang* waste time or misbehave. **muck in** *v slang* share a task with other people. **muck out** *v* clean (a byre, stable, etc.). **muckraking** *n* seeking out and exposing scandal relating to well-known people. **muckraker** *n* **muck up** *v slang* ruin or spoil.

mucus [**mew**-kuss] *n* slimy secretion of the mucous membranes. **mucous** *adj* **mucous membrane** tissue lining body cavities or passages.

mud ❶ *n* wet soft earth. **muddy** *adj* **-dier**, **-diest 1** covered or filled with mud. **2** not clear or bright, e.g. *muddy brown*. ▷ *v* **-dying**, **-dies 3** make muddy. **4** make (a situation or issue) less clear. **mud flat** area of low muddy land that is covered by the sea only at high tide. **mudguard** *n* cover over a wheel to prevent mud or water being thrown up by it. **mudpack** *n* cosmetic paste to improve the complexion.

muddle ❶ *v* **1** (often foll. by *up*) confuse. **2** mix up. ▷ *n* **3** state of confusion.

muesli [**mewz**-lee] *n* mixture of grain, nuts, and dried fruit, eaten with milk.

muezzin [moo-**ezz**-in] *n* official who summons Muslims to prayer.

muff¹ *n* tube-shaped covering to keep the hands warm.

muff² *v* bungle (an action).

muffin *n* **1** light round flat yeast cake. **2** small cup-shaped sweet bread roll.

muffle ❶ *v* wrap up for warmth or to deaden sound. **muffler** *n* scarf.

mufti *n* civilian clothes worn by a person who usually wears a uniform.

mug¹ *n* large drinking cup.

mug² ❶ *n* **1** *slang* face. **2** *slang* gullible person. ▷ *v* **mugging**, **mugged 3** *informal* attack in order to rob. **mugger** *n* **mugging** *n* **mug shot** *informal* photograph of the face of a suspect or criminal, held in a police file.

mug³ ❶ *v* **mugging**, **mugged** (foll. by *up*) *informal* study hard.

THESAURUS

mow down *v* = **massacre**, butcher, cut down, cut to pieces, shoot down, slaughter

much *adj* **1** = **great**, abundant, a lot of, ample, considerable, copious, plenty of, sizable *or* sizeable, substantial ▷ *n* **2** = **a lot**, a good deal, a great deal, heaps (*inf*), loads (*inf*), lots (*inf*), plenty ▷ *adv* **3** = **greatly**, a great deal, a lot, considerably, decidedly, exceedingly

muck *n* **1** = **dirt**, filth, gunge (*inf*), mire, mud, ooze, slime, sludge **2** = **manure**, dung, kak (*S Afr sl*), ordure

muck up *v Sl* = **ruin**, blow (*sl*), botch, bungle, make a mess of, make a pig's ear of (*inf*), mess up, muff, spoil

mucky *adj* **1** = **dirty**, begrimed, filthy, grimy, messy, muddy

mud *n* = **dirt**, clay, mire, ooze, silt, slime, sludge

muddle *v* **1** = **confuse**, befuddle, bewilder, confound, daze, disorient, perplex, stupefy **2** = **jumble**, disarrange, disorder, disorganize, mess, mix up, scramble, spoil, tangle ▷ *n* **3** = **confusion**, chaos, disarray, disorder, disorganization, jumble, mess, mix-up, predicament, tangle

muddy *adj* **1** = **dirty**, bespattered, boggy, grimy, marshy, mucky, mud-caked, quaggy, soiled, swampy

muffle *v* **a** = **wrap up**, cloak, cover, envelop, shroud, swaddle, swathe **b** = **deaden**, muzzle, quieten, silence, soften, stifle, suppress

mug¹ *n* = **cup**, beaker, pot, tankard

mug² *n* **1** *Sl* = **face**, countenance, features, visage **2** *Sl* = **fool**, chump (*inf*), easy *or* soft touch (*sl*), simpleton, sucker (*sl*) ▷ *v* **3** *Inf* = **attack**, assault, beat up, rob, set about *or* upon

mug³ *v* (foll. by *up*) *Inf* = **study**, bone up on (*inf*), burn the midnight oil (*inf*),

muggins *n informal* stupid or gullible person.

muggy ❶ *adj* **-gier, -giest** (of weather) damp and stifling.

mujaheddin, mujahedeen [moo-ja-hed-**deen**] *pl n* fundamentalist Muslim guerrillas.

mulatto [mew-**lat**-toe] *n, pl* **-tos, -toes** child of one Black and one White parent.

mulberry *n* **1** tree whose leaves are used to feed silkworms. **2** purple fruit of this tree.

mulch *n* **1** mixture of wet straw, leaves, etc., used to protect the roots of plants. ▷ *v* **2** cover (land) with mulch.

mule¹ *n* offspring of a horse and a donkey. **mulish** *adj* obstinate. **muleteer** *n* mule driver.

mule² *n* backless shoe or slipper.

mull ❶ *v* think (over) or ponder. **mulled** *adj* (of wine or ale) flavoured with sugar and spices and served hot.

mullah *n* Muslim scholar, teacher, or religious leader.

mullet *n* edible sea fish.

mulligatawny *n* soup made with curry powder.

mullion *n* vertical dividing bar in a window. **mullioned** *adj* having mullions.

mulloway *n* large Australian sea fish, valued for sport and food.

multi- *combining form* many, e.g. *multicultural; multistorey.*

multicoloured *adj* having many different colours.

multifarious ❶ [mull-tee-**fare**-ee-uss] *adj* having many various parts.

multilateral *adj* of or involving more than two nations or parties.

multilingual *adj* speaking or written in more than two languages.

multimillionaire *n* person who owns several million pounds, dollars, etc.

multinational *adj* **1** operating in several countries. **2** involving people from several countries. ▷ *n* **3** large company operating in several countries.

multiple ❶ *adj* **1** having many parts. ▷ *n* **2** quantity which contains another an exact number of times. **multiply** *v* **1** increase in number, quantity, or degree. **2** add (a number) to itself a given number of times. **3** increase in number by reproduction. **multiple-choice** *adj* having a number of possible given answers out of which the correct one must be chosen. **multiple sclerosis** chronic progressive disease of the nervous system, resulting in speech and visual disorders, tremor, and partial paralysis.

multiplex *n* **1** purpose-built complex containing several cinemas and usu. restaurants and bars. ▷ *adj* **2** having many elements, complex.

multiplicity *n, pl* **-ties** large number or great variety.

multiply ❶ *v* **-plying, -plied 1** (cause to) increase in number, quantity, or degree. **2** add (a number or quantity) to itself a given number of times. **3** increase in number by reproduction. **multiplication** *n* **multiplicand** *n Maths* number to be multiplied. **multiplier** *n Maths* number by which another number is multiplied.

multipurpose *adj* having many uses, e.g. *a multipurpose vehicle.*

multiracial *adj* made up of people from many races, e.g. *a multiracial society.*

multitude ❶ *n* **1** great number. **2** great crowd. **multitudinous** *adj* very numerous.

mum¹ *n informal* mother.

mum² *adj* **keep mum** remain silent.

mumble *v* **1** speak indistinctly, mutter. ▷ *n* **2** indistinct utterance.

mumbo jumbo *n* **1** meaningless language. **2** foolish religious ritual or incantation.

mummer *n* actor in a folk play or mime.

cram (*inf*), swot (*Brit inf*)

muggy *adj* = **humid**, clammy, close, moist, oppressive, sticky, stuffy, sultry

mull *v* = **ponder**, consider, contemplate, deliberate, meditate, reflect on, ruminate, think over, weigh

multifarious *adj* = **diverse**, different, legion, manifold, many, miscellaneous, multiple, numerous,

sundry, varied

multiple *adj* **1** = **many**, manifold, multitudinous, numerous, several, sundry, various

multiply *v* **1** = **increase**, build up, expand, extend, proliferate, spread **3** = **reproduce**, breed, propagate

multitude *n* **2** = **mass**, army, crowd, horde, host, mob, myriad,

mummy¹ *n, pl* **-mies** body embalmed and wrapped for burial in ancient Egypt. **mummified** *adj* (of a body) preserved as a mummy.

mummy² *n, pl* **-mies** child's word for MOTHER.

mumps *n* infectious disease with swelling in the glands of the neck.

munch ❶ *v* chew noisily and steadily.

mundane ❶ *adj* **1** everyday. **2** earthly.

municipal ❶ *adj* relating to a city or town. **municipality** *n, pl* **-ities 1** city or town with local self-government. **2** governing body of this.

munificent [mew-**niff**-fiss-sent] *adj* very generous. **munificence** *n*.

muniments [**mew**-nim-ments] *pl n* title deeds or similar documents.

munitions [mew-**nish**-unz] *pl n* military stores.

munted *adj NZ slang* **1** destroyed or ruined. **2** abnormal or peculiar.

mural [**myoor**-al] *n* painting on a wall.

murder ❶ *n* **1** unlawful intentional killing of a human being. ▷ *v* **2** kill in this way. **murderer**, **murderess** *n* **murderous** *adj*.

murk ❶ *n* thick darkness. **murky** *adj* **murkier**, **murkiest 1** dark or gloomy. **2** suspicious or shady.

murmur ❶ *v* **-muring**, **-mured 1** speak or say in a quiet indistinct way. **2** complain.

▷ *n* **3** continuous low indistinct sound. **4** complaint, e.g. *she went without a murmur*. **5** abnormal soft blowing sound heard made by the heart.

murrain [**murr**-rin] *n* cattle plague.

muscle ❶ *n* **1** tissue in the body which produces movement by contracting. **2** strength or power. **muscular** *adj* **1** with well-developed muscles. **2** of muscles. **muscular dystrophy** disease with wasting of the muscles. **muscle in** *v informal* force one's way in.

muse ❶ *v* ponder quietly.

Muse *n* **1** *Greek myth* one of nine goddesses, each of whom inspired an art or science. **2** (**m-**) force that inspires a creative artist.

museum *n* building where natural, artistic, historical, or scientific objects are exhibited and preserved. **museum piece** *informal* very old object or building.

mush¹ ❶ *n* **1** soft pulpy mass. **2** *informal* cloying sentimentality. **mushy** *adj* **mushier**, **mushiest**.

mush² *interj* order to dogs in sled team to advance.

mushroom *n* **1** edible fungus with a stem and cap. ▷ *v* **2** grow rapidly. **mushroom cloud** large mushroom-shaped cloud produced by a nuclear explosion.

THESAURUS

swarm, throng

munch *v* = **chew**, champ, chomp, crunch

mundane *adj* **1** = **ordinary**, banal, commonplace, day-to-day, everyday, humdrum, prosaic, routine, workaday **2** = **earthly**, mortal, secular, temporal, terrestrial, worldly

municipal *adj* = **civic**, public, urban

municipality *n* **1** = **town**, borough, city, district, dorp (*S Afr*), township

murder *n* **1** = **killing**, assassination, bloodshed, butchery, carnage, homicide, manslaughter, massacre, slaying ▷ *v* **2** = **kill**, assassinate, bump off (*sl*), butcher, eliminate (*sl*), massacre, slaughter, slay

murderer *n* = **killer**, assassin, butcher, cut-throat, hit man (*sl*), homicide, slaughterer, slayer

murderous *adj* **2** = **deadly**, bloodthirsty, brutal, cruel, cut-throat,

ferocious, lethal, savage

murky *adj* **1** = **dark**, cloudy, dim, dull, gloomy, grey, misty, overcast

murmur *v* **1** = **mumble**, mutter, whisper **2** = **grumble**, complain, moan (*inf*) ▷ *n* **3** = **drone**, buzzing, humming, purr, whisper

muscle *n* **1** = **tendon**, sinew **2** = **strength**, brawn, clout (*inf*), forcefulness, might, power, stamina, weight **muscle in** *v Inf* = **impose oneself**, butt in, force one's way in

muscular *adj* **1** = **strong**, athletic, powerful, robust, sinewy, strapping, sturdy, vigorous

muse *v* = **ponder**, brood, cogitate, consider, contemplate, deliberate, meditate, mull over, reflect, ruminate

mushy *adj* **1** = **soft**, pulpy, semi-solid, slushy, squashy, squelchy, squidgy (*inf*) **2** *Inf* = **sentimental**, maudlin, mawkish, saccharine, schmaltzy (*sl*),

music ● *n* **1** art form using a melodious and harmonious combination of notes. **2** written or printed form of this. **musical** *adj* **1** of or like music. **2** talented in or fond of music. **3** pleasant-sounding. ▷ *n* **4** play or film with songs and dancing. **musically** *adv* **musician** *n* **musicianship** *n* **musicology** *n* scientific study of music. **musicologist** *n* **music centre** combined record or CD player, radio, and cassette player. **music hall** variety theatre.

musk *n* scent obtained from a gland of the musk deer or produced synthetically. **musky** *adj* **muskier**, **muskiest**. **muskrat** *n* **1** N American beaver-like rodent. **2** its fur.

muskeg ● *n Canad* bog or swamp.

musket *n History* long-barrelled gun. **musketeer** *n* **musketry** *n* (use of) muskets.

Muslim *n* **1** follower of the religion of Islam. ▷ *adj* **2** of or relating to Islam.

muslin *n* fine cotton fabric.

musquash *n* muskrat fur.

muss ● *v US & Canad inf* to make untidy.

mussel *n* edible shellfish with a dark hinged shell.

must¹ ● *v* **1** used as an auxiliary to express obligation, certainty, or resolution. ▷ *n* **2** essential or necessary thing.

must² *n* newly pressed grape juice.

mustang *n* wild horse of SW USA.

mustard *n* **1** paste made from the powdered seeds of a plant, used as a condiment. **2** the plant. **mustard gas** poisonous gas causing blistering burns and blindness.

muster ● *v* **1** summon up (strength, energy, or support). **2** assemble. ▷ *n* **3** assembly of military personnel. **pass muster** be acceptable.

musty ● *adj* **mustier**, **mustiest** smelling mouldy and stale. **mustiness** *n*.

mutable ● [mew-tab-bl] *adj* liable to change. **mutability** *n*.

mutation ● [mew-**tay**-shun] *n* (genetic) change. **mutate** [mew-**tate**] *v* (cause to) undergo mutation. **mutant** [**mew**-tant] *n* mutated animal, plant, etc.

mute ● *adj* **1** silent. **2** unable to speak. ▷ *n* **3** person who is unable to speak. **4** *Music* device to soften the tone of an instrument. **muted** *adj* **1** (of sound or colour) softened. **2** (of a reaction) subdued. **mutely** *adv*.

mutilate ● [**mew**-till-ate] *v* **1** deprive of a limb or other part. **2** damage (a book or text). **mutilated** *adj* **mutilation** *n*.

mutiny ● [mew-tin-ee] *n, pl* **-nies** **1** rebellion against authority, esp. by soldiers or sailors. ▷ *v* **-nying, -nied** **2** commit mutiny. **mutineer** *n* **mutinous** *adj*.

mutt *n slang* **1** stupid person. **2** mongrel dog.

————— THESAURUS —————

sloppy (*inf*), slushy (*inf*)

musical *adj* **1** = **melodious**, dulcet, euphonious, harmonious, lyrical, melodic, sweet-sounding, tuneful

muskeg *n Canad* = **swamp**, bog, marsh, quagmire, moss (*Scot & Northern English dialect*), slough, fen, mire, morass, everglade(s) (*US*), pakihi (*NZ*)

muss *v US & Canad Inf* = **mess (up)**, disarrange, dishevel, ruffle, rumple, make untidy, tumble

must¹ *n* **2** = **necessity**, essential, fundamental, imperative, prerequisite, requirement, requisite, *sine qua non*

muster *v* **2** = **assemble**, call together, convene, gather, marshal, mobilize, rally, summon ▷ *n* **3** = **assembly**, collection, congregation, convention, gathering, meeting, rally, roundup

musty *adj* = **stale**, airless, dank, fusty,

mildewed, mouldy, old, smelly, stuffy

mutable *adj* = **changeable**, adaptable, alterable, fickle, inconsistent, inconstant, unsettled, unstable, variable, volatile

mutation *n* = **change**, alteration, evolution, metamorphosis, modification, transfiguration, transformation, variation

mute *adj* **1, 2** = **silent**, dumb, mum, speechless, unspoken, voiceless, wordless

mutilate *v* **1** = **maim**, amputate, cut up, damage, disfigure, dismember, injure, lacerate, mangle **2** = **distort**, adulterate, bowdlerize, censor, cut, damage, expurgate

mutiny *n* **1** = **rebellion**, disobedience, insubordination, insurrection, revolt, revolution, riot, uprising ▷ *v* **2** = **rebel**, disobey, resist, revolt, rise up

mutter ❶ v 1 utter or speak indistinctly. 2 grumble. ▷ n 3 muttered sound or grumble. **muttering** n.

mutton n flesh of sheep, used as food.

mutual ❶ [**mew**-chew-al] adj 1 felt or expressed by each of two people about the other. 2 common to both or all. **mutually** adv.

Muzak n ® recorded light music played in shops etc.

muzzle ❶ n 1 animal's mouth and nose. 2 cover for these to prevent biting. 3 open end of a gun. ▷ v 4 prevent from being heard or noticed. 5 put a muzzle on.

muzzy adj -zier, -ziest 1 confused or muddled. 2 blurred or hazy.

mW milliwatt(s).

MW 1 megawatt(s). 2 medium wave.

my adj belonging to me.

myall n Australian acacia with hard scented wood.

mycology n study of fungi.

mynah n Asian bird which can mimic human speech.

myopia [my-**oh**-pee-a] n short-sightedness. **myopic** [my-**op**-ik] adj **myopically** adv.

myriad ❶ [**mir**-ree-ad] adj 1 innumerable. ▷ n 2 large indefinite number.

myrrh [**mur**] n aromatic gum used in perfume, incense, and medicine.

myrtle [**mur**-tl] n flowering evergreen shrub.

myself pron emphatic or reflexive form of I¹ or ME¹.

mystery ❶ n, pl -teries 1 strange or inexplicable event or phenomenon. 2 obscure or secret thing. 3 story or film that arouses suspense. **mysterious** adj **mysteriously** adv.

mystic ❶ n 1 person who seeks spiritual knowledge. ▷ adj 2 mystical. **mystical** adj having a spiritual or religious significance beyond human understanding. **mysticism** n.

mystify ❶ v -fying, -fied bewilder or puzzle. **mystification** n.

mystique ❶ [miss-**steek**] n aura of mystery or power.

myth ❶ n 1 tale with supernatural characters, usu. of how the world and mankind began. 2 untrue idea or explanation. 3 imaginary person or object. **mythical**, **mythic** adj **mythology** n 1 myths collectively. 2 study of myths. **mythological** adj.

myxomatosis [mix-a-mat-**oh**-siss] n contagious fatal viral disease of rabbits.

——————————— THESAURUS ———————————

mutter v 2 = **grumble**, complain, grouse, mumble, murmur, rumble

mutual adj 1 = **reciprocal**, requited, returned 2 = **shared**, common, interchangeable, joint

muzzle n 1 = **jaws**, mouth, nose, snout 2 = **gag**, guard ▷ v 4 = **suppress**, censor, curb, gag, restrain, silence, stifle

myriad adj 1 = **innumerable**, countless, immeasurable, incalculable, multitudinous, untold ▷ n 2 = **multitude**, army, horde, host, swarm

mysterious adj 1 = **strange**, arcane, enigmatic, inexplicable, inscrutable, mystifying, perplexing, puzzling, secret, uncanny, unfathomable, weird 2 = **secretive**, cloak-and-dagger, covert, furtive

mystery n 1 = **puzzle**, conundrum, enigma, problem, question, riddle, secret, teaser

mystic adj 2 = **supernatural**, inscrutable, metaphysical, mysterious, occult, otherworldly, paranormal, preternatural, transcendental

mystify v = **puzzle**, baffle, bewilder, confound, confuse, flummox, nonplus, perplex, stump

mystique n = **fascination**, awe, charisma, charm, glamour, magic, spell

myth n 1 = **legend**, allegory, fable, fairy story, fiction, folk tale, saga, story 2 = **illusion**, delusion, fancy, fantasy, figment, imagination, superstition, tall story

mythical adj 2 = **imaginary**, fictitious, invented, made-up, make-believe, nonexistent, pretended, unreal, untrue 3 = **legendary**, fabled, fabulous, fairy-tale, mythological

mythology n 1 = **legend**, folklore, lore, tradition

Nn

n *adj* **1** indefinite number (of), e.g. *there are n ways of doing this.* ▷ *n* **2** *Maths* number whose value is not stated, e.g. *two to the power n.* **nth** *adj.*

N 1 *Chemistry* nitrogen. **2** *Physics* newton(s). **3** North(ern). **4** nuclear, e.g. *N test.*

n. 1 neuter. **2** noun. **3** number.

Na *Chemistry* sodium.

n/a, N.A. not applicable: used to indicate that a question on a form is not relevant to the person filling it in.

Naafi *n* canteen or shop for military personnel.

naan *n* same as NAN BREAD.

nab ❶ *v* **nabbing, nabbed** *informal* **1** arrest (someone). **2** catch (someone) in wrongdoing.

nabob [**nay**-bob] *n informal* rich or important person.

nacelle [nah-**sell**] *n* streamlined enclosure on an aircraft, esp. one housing an engine.

nacre [**nay**-ker] *n* mother of pearl. **nacreous** *adj.*

nadir ❶ *n* **1** point in the sky opposite the zenith. **2** lowest point.

naevus ❶ [**nee**-vuss] *n, pl* **-vi** birthmark or mole.

naff ❶ *adj slang* lacking quality or taste, e.g. *one of the naffest songs ever.*

nag¹ ❶ *v* **nagging, nagged 1** scold or find fault constantly. **2** be a constant source of discomfort or worry to. ▷ *n* **3** person who nags. **nagging** *adj, n.*

nag² ❶ *n informal* old horse.

naiad [**nye**-ad] *n, pl* **naiads, naiades** [**nye**-ad-deez] *Greek myth* water nymph.

nail ❶ *n* **1** pointed piece of metal with a head, hit with a hammer to join two objects together. **2** hard covering of the upper tips of the fingers and toes. ▷ *v* **3** attach (something) with nails. **4** *informal* catch or arrest. **hit the nail on the head** say something exactly correct. **on the nail** at once, esp. in *pay on the nail.* **nailfile** *n* small metal file used to smooth or shape the finger or toe nails. **nail varnish, polish** cosmetic lacquer applied to the finger or toe nails.

naive ❶ [nye-**eev**] *adj* **1** innocent and gullible. **2** simple and lacking sophistication. **naively** *adv* **naivety, naïveté** [nye-**eev**-tee] *n.*

naked ❶ *adj* **1** without clothes. **2** not concealed, e.g. *naked hostility.* **3** without any covering, e.g. *naked flame.* **the naked eye** the eye unassisted by any optical instrument. **nakedly** *adv* **nakedness** *n.*

namby-pamby ❶ *adj* sentimental or insipid.

────────── THESAURUS ──────────

nab *v Inf* **1** = **apprehend**, arrest, capture, catch, collar (*inf*) ▷ *v* **2** = **catch**, apprehend, arrest, capture, collar (*inf*), grab, seize

nadir *n* **2** = **bottom**, depths, lowest point, minimum, rock bottom

naevus *n* = **birthmark**, mole

naff *adj Sl* = **bad**, duff (*Brit inf*), inferior, low-grade, poor, rubbishy, second-rate, shabby, shoddy, worthless

nag¹ *v* **1** = **scold**, badger (*inf*), henpeck, upbraid **2** = **worry**, annoy, harass, hassle, irritate, pester, plague ▷ *n* **3** = **scold**, harpy, shrew, tartar, virago

nag² *n Inf* = **horse**, hack

nagging *adj* **1** = **irritating**, scolding, shrewish **2** = **worrying**, persistent

nail *v* **3** = **fasten**, attach, fix, hammer, join, pin, secure, tack

naive *adj* **1** = **gullible**, callow, credulous, green, innocent, trusting, unsuspicious, wet behind the ears (*inf*) **2** = **unsophisticated**, artless, guileless, ingenuous, innocent, simple, unworldly

naivety, naïveté *n* **1** = **gullibility**, callowness, credulity, innocence **2** = **simplicity**, artlessness, guilelessness, inexperience, ingenuousness, innocence, naturalness

naked *adj* **1** = **nude**, bare, exposed, starkers (*inf*), stripped, unclothed, undressed, without a stitch on (*inf*)

nakedness *n* **1** = **nudity**, bareness, undress

namby-pamby *adj* = **feeble**, insipid, sentimental, spineless, vapid, weak,

DICTIONARY

name ❶ n 1 word by which a person or thing is known. 2 reputation, esp. a good one. 3 famous person, e.g. *a big name in the music business.* ▷ v 4 give a name to. 5 refer to by name. 6 fix or specify. **call someone names, a name** insult someone by using rude words to describe him or her. **in name only** not possessing the powers implied by his, her, or its title, e.g. *ruler in name only.* **nameless** adj 1 without a name. 2 unspecified. 3 too horrible to be mentioned. **namely** adv that is to say. **name day** RC Church feast day of a saint whose name one bears. **name-dropping** n referring to famous people as if they were friends, in order to impress others. **name-dropper** n **nameplate** n small sign on or by a door giving the occupant's name and, sometimes, profession. **namesake** n person with the same name as another.

nan bread n slightly leavened Indian bread in a large flat leaf shape.

nancy, nancy boy n effeminate or homosexual boy or man.

nanny n, pl **-nies** 1 woman whose job is looking after young children. ▷ v 2 be too protective towards. **nanny goat** female goat.

nano- combining form denoting one thousand millionth, e.g. *nanosecond.*

nap¹ ❶ n 1 short sleep. ▷ v **napping, napped** 2 have a short sleep.

nap² ❶ n raised fibres of velvet or similar cloth.

nap³ n 1 card game similar to whist.

2 *Horse racing* tipster's choice for a certain winner. ▷ v **napping, napped** 3 name (a horse) as a certain winner.

napalm n 1 highly inflammable jellied petrol, used in bombs. ▷ v 2 attack (people or places) with napalm.

nape n back of the neck.

naphtha n liquid mixture distilled from coal tar or petroleum, used as a solvent and in petrol. **naphthalene** n white crystalline product distilled from coal tar or petroleum, used in disinfectants, mothballs, and explosives.

napkin ❶ n piece of cloth or paper for wiping the mouth or protecting the clothes while eating.

nappy n, pl **-pies** piece of absorbent material fastened round a baby's lower torso to absorb urine and faeces.

narcissism ❶ n exceptional interest in or admiration for oneself. **narcissistic** adj.

narcissus n, pl **-cissi** yellow, orange, or white flower related to the daffodil.

narcotic ❶ n, adj (of) a drug, such as morphine or opium, which produces numbness and drowsiness, used medicinally but addictive. **narcosis** n effect of a narcotic.

nark ❶ slang ▷ v 1 annoy. ▷ n 2 informer or spy. 3 someone who complains in an irritating manner. **narky** adj **narkier, narkiest** slang irritable or complaining.

THESAURUS

weedy (*inf*), wimpish or wimpy (*inf*), wishy-washy (*inf*)

name n 1 = **title**, designation, epithet, handle (*sl*), nickname, sobriquet, term 2 = **fame**, distinction, eminence, esteem, honour, note, praise, renown, repute ▷ v 4 = **call**, baptize, christen, dub, entitle, label, style, term 6 = **nominate**, appoint, choose, designate, select, specify

named adj = **called**, baptized, christened, dubbed, entitled, known as, labelled, styled, termed

nameless adj 1 = **anonymous**, unnamed, untitled 2 = **unknown**, incognito, obscure, undistinguished, unheard-of, unsung 3 = **horrible**, abominable, indescribable, unmentionable, unspeakable, unutterable

namely adv = **specifically**, to wit, viz.

nap¹ n 1 = **sleep**, catnap, forty winks (*inf*), kip (*Brit sl*), rest, siesta ▷ v 2 = **sleep**, catnap, doze, drop off (*inf*), kip (*Brit sl*), nod off (*inf*), rest, snooze (*inf*)

nap² n = **weave**, down, fibre, grain, pile

napkin n = **serviette**, cloth

narcissism n = **egotism**, self-love, vanity

narcotic n = **drug**, anaesthetic, analgesic, anodyne, opiate, painkiller, sedative, tranquillizer ▷ adj = **sedative**, analgesic, calming, hypnotic, painkilling, soporific

nark *Sl* v 1 = **annoy**, bother, exasperate, get on one's nerves (*inf*), irritate, nettle

narrate ❶ v **1** tell (a story). **2** speak the words accompanying and telling what is happening in a film or TV programme. **narration** n **narrator** n **narrative** n **1** account, story. ▷ adj **2** telling a story, e.g. *a narrative poem*.

narrow ❶ adj **1** small in breadth in comparison to length. **2** limited in range, extent, or outlook. **3** with little margin, e.g. *a narrow escape*. ▷ v **4** make or become narrow. **5** (often foll. by *down*) limit or restrict. **narrows** pl n narrow part of a strait, river, or current. **narrowly** adv **narrowness** n **narrow boat** long bargelike canal boat. **narrow-gauge** adj (of a railway) having less than the standard distance of 56½ inches between the rails. **narrow-minded** adj intolerant or bigoted. **narrow-mindedness** n.

narwhal n arctic whale with a long spiral tusk.

NASA US National Aeronautics and Space Administration.

nasal adj **1** of the nose. **2** (of a sound) pronounced with air passing through the nose. **3** (of a voice) characterized by nasal sounds. **nasally** adv.

nascent adj starting to grow or develop.

nasturtium n plant with yellow, red, or orange trumpet-shaped flowers.

nasty ❶ adj **-tier**, **-tiest** **1** unpleasant. **2** (of an injury) dangerous or painful.

3 spiteful or unkind. ▷ n, pl **-ties** **4** something unpleasant. **nastily** adv **nastiness** n.

nat. 1 national. **2** nationalist.

natal [**nay**-tal] adj of or relating to birth.

nation ❶ n people of one or more cultures or races organized as a single state. **national** adj **1** of or serving a national as a whole. **2** characteristic of a particular nation. **nationality** n fact of being a citizen of a particular nation. **nationwide** adj covering all of a nation.

national ❶ adj **1** of or serving a nation as a whole. **2** characteristic of a particular nation. ▷ n **3** citizen of a nation. **nationally** adv **national anthem** official patriotic song of a nation. **National Curriculum** curriculum of subjects taught in state schools in England and Wales since 1989. **national debt** total outstanding debt of a country's government. **national grid** network of high-voltage power lines linking power stations. **National Health Service** system of national medical services financed mainly by taxation. **national insurance** state insurance scheme providing payments to the unemployed, sick, and retired. **national park** area of countryside protected by a government for its natural or environmental importance. **national service** compulsory military service.

_____ THESAURUS _____

narrate v **1** = **tell**, chronicle, describe, detail, recite, recount, relate, report

narration n **1** = **telling**, description, explanation, reading, recital, relation

narrative n **1** = **story**, account, chronicle, history, report, statement, tale

narrator n **1** = **storyteller**, author, chronicler, commentator, reporter, writer

narrow adj **1** = **thin**, attenuated, fine, slender, slim, spare, tapering **2** = **insular**, dogmatic, illiberal, intolerant, narrow-minded, partial, prejudiced, small-minded **3** = **limited**, close, confined, constricted, contracted, meagre, restricted, tight ▷ v **4** = **tighten**, constrict, limit, reduce

narrowly adv **3** = **just**, barely, by the skin of one's teeth, only just, scarcely

narrow-minded adj = **intolerant**, bigoted, hidebound, illiberal, opinionated, parochial, prejudiced, provincial, small-minded

nastiness n **3** = **unpleasantness**, malice, meanness, spitefulness

nasty adj **1** = **objectionable**, disagreeable, loathsome, obnoxious, offensive, unpleasant, vile **2** = **painful**, bad, critical, dangerous, serious, severe **3** = **spiteful**, despicable, disagreeable, distasteful, malicious, mean, unpleasant, vicious, vile

nation n = **country**, people, race, realm, society, state, tribe

national adj **1** = **nationwide**, countrywide, public, widespread ▷ n **3** = **citizen**, inhabitant, native, resident, subject

nationalism ❶ *n* **1** policy of national independence. **2** patriotism, sometimes to an excessive degree. **nationalist** *n*, *adj* **nationalistic** *adj* fiercely or excessively patriotic.

nationality ❶ *n*, *pl* **-ities 1** fact of being a citizen of a particular nation. **2** group of people of the same race, e.g. *young men of all nationalities*.

nationalize *v* put (an industry or a company) under state control. **nationalization** *n*.

native ❶ *adj* **1** relating to a place where a person was born. **2** born in a specified place. **3** (foll. by *to*) originating (in). **4** inborn. ▷ *n* **5** person born in a specified place. **6** indigenous animal or plant. **7** member of the original race of a country. **Native American** (person) descended from the original inhabitants of the American continent. **native bear** *Aust* same as KOALA. **native companion** *Aust* same as BROLGA. **native dog** *Aust* dingo.

Nativity *n Christianity* birth of Jesus Christ.

NATO North Atlantic Treaty Organization.

natter ❶ *informal* ▷ *v* **1** talk idly or chatter. ▷ *n* **2** long idle chat.

natty ❶ *adj* **-tier, -tiest** *informal* smart and spruce.

natural ❶ *adj* **1** normal or to be expected. **2** genuine or spontaneous.

3 of, according to, existing in, or produced by nature. **4** not created by human beings. **5** not synthetic. **6** (of a parent) not adoptive. **7** (of a child) illegitimate. **8** *Music* not sharp or flat, e.g. *B natural*. ▷ *n* **9** person with an inborn talent or skill. **10** *Music* symbol cancelling the effect of a previous sharp or flat. **naturally** *adv* **1** of course. **2** in a natural or normal way. **3** instinctively. **naturalness** *n* **natural gas** gas found below the ground, used mainly as a fuel. **natural history** study of animals and plants in the wild. **natural number** positive integer, such as 1, 2, 3, etc. **natural philosophy** old-fashioned physics. **natural science** science dealing with the physical world, such as physics, biology or geology. **natural selection** process by which only creatures and plants well adapted to their environment survive.

naturalism ❶ *n* movement in art and literature advocating detailed realism. **naturalistic** *adj*.

naturalist ❶ *n* student of natural history.

naturalize *v* give citizenship to (a person born in another country). **naturalization** *n*.

nature ❶ *n* **1** whole system of the existence, forces, and events of the physical world that are not controlled by human beings. **2** fundamental or

---

THESAURUS

nationalism *n* **2** = **patriotism**, allegiance, chauvinism, jingoism, loyalty

nationality *n* **1** = **nation**, birth, race **2** = **race**, birth

nationwide *adj* = **national**, countrywide, general, widespread

native *adj* **1, 2** = **local**, domestic, home, indigenous **3** (foll. by *to*) = **indigenous 4** = **inborn**, congenital, hereditary, inbred, ingrained, innate, instinctive, intrinsic, natural ▷ *n* **5** = **inhabitant**, citizen, countryman, dweller, national, resident **7** = **aborigine**

natter *Inf v* **1** = **gossip**, blether, chatter, gabble, jaw (*sl*), prattle, rabbit (on) (*Brit inf*), talk ▷ *n* **2** = **gossip**, chat, chinwag (*Brit inf*), chitchat, conversation, gab (*inf*), jaw (*sl*), prattle, talk

natty *Inf adj* = **smart**, dapper, elegant, fashionable, neat, snazzy (*inf*),

spruce, stylish, trim

natural *adj* **1** = **normal**, common, everyday, legitimate, logical, ordinary, regular, typical, usual **2** = **unaffected**, genuine, ingenuous, open, real, simple, spontaneous, unpretentious, unsophisticated **3** = **innate**, characteristic, essential, inborn, inherent, instinctive, intuitive, native **5** = **pure**, organic, plain, unrefined, whole

naturalist *n* = **biologist**, botanist, ecologist, zoologist

naturalistic *adj* = **realistic**, lifelike, true-to-life

naturally *adv* **1** = **of course**, certainly **2** = **genuinely**, normally, simply, spontaneously, typically, unaffectedly, unpretentiously **3** = **spontaneously**

nature *n* **1** = **creation**, cosmos, earth, environment, universe, world **2** = **make-up**, character, complexion,

essential qualities. **3** kind or sort.
natural *adj* normal or to be expected.
naturism *n* nudism. **naturist** *n*.
naught *n lit* nothing.
naughty ❶ *adj* **-tier, -tiest**
1 disobedient or mischievous.
2 mildly indecent. **naughtily** *adv*
naughtiness *n*.
nausea ❶ [**naw**-zee-a] *n* feeling of
being about to vomit. **nauseate** *v*
1 make (someone) feel sick. **2** disgust.
nauseous *adj* **1** as if about to vomit.
2 sickening.
nautical ❶ *adj* of the sea or ships.
nautical mile 1852 metres (6076.12
feet).
nautilus *n, pl* **-luses, -li** shellfish with
many tentacles.
naval ❶ *adj* see NAVY.
nave *n* long central part of a church.
navel *n* hollow in the middle of the
abdomen where the umbilical cord
was attached. **navel orange** sweet
orange with a navel-like hollow at the
top.
navigate ❶ *v* **1** direct or plot the path
or position of a ship, aircraft, or car.
2 travel over or through. **navigation** *n*
navigational *adj* **navigator** *n*
navigable *adj* **1** wide, deep, or safe
enough to be sailed through. **2** able to
be steered.
navvy ❶ *n, pl* **-vies** labourer employed
on a road or a building site.

navy ❶ *n, pl* **-vies 1** branch of a
country's armed services comprising
warships with their crews and
organization. **2** warships of a nation.
▷ *adj* **3** navy-blue. **naval** *adj* of or
relating to a navy or ships. **navy-blue**
adj very dark blue.
nay *interj obs* no.
Nazi *n* **1** member of the fascist National
Socialist Party, which came to power
in Germany in 1933 under Adolf Hitler.
▷ *adj* **2** of or relating to the Nazis.
Nazism *n*.
Nb *Chemistry* niobium.
NB 1 New Brunswick. **2** note well.
NC North Carolina.
NCO noncommissioned officer.
Nd *Chemistry* neodymium.
ND North Dakota.
Ne *Chemistry* neon.
NE 1 Nebraska. **2** northeast(ern).
Neanderthal [nee-**an**-der-tahl] *adj* of
a type of primitive man that lived in
Europe before 12 000 BC.
neap tide *n* tide at the first and last
quarters of the moon when there is
the smallest rise and fall in tidal level.
near ❶ *prep, adv, adj* **1** indicating a place
or time not far away. ▷ *adj* **2** almost
being the thing specified, e.g. *a near
disaster.* ▷ *v* **3** draw close (to). **nearly**
adv almost. **nearness** *n* **nearby** *adj* not
far away. **Near East** same as MIDDLE
EAST. **nearside** *n* side of a vehicle that is

---

constitution, essence **3 = kind**,
category, description, sort, species,
style, type, variety
naughty *adj* **1 = disobedient**, bad,
impish, misbehaved, mischievous,
refractory, wayward, wicked,
worthless **2 = obscene**, improper,
lewd, ribald, risqué, smutty, vulgar
nausea *n* **= sickness**, biliousness,
queasiness, retching, squeamishness,
vomiting
nauseate *v* **1, 2 = sicken**, disgust,
offend, repel, repulse, revolt, turn
one's stomach
nauseous *adj* **2 = sickening**,
abhorrent, disgusting, distasteful,
nauseating, offensive, repugnant,
repulsive, revolting
nautical *adj* **= maritime**, marine, naval
naval *adj* **= nautical**, marine, maritime
navigable *adj* **1 = passable**, clear,
negotiable, unobstructed
2 = sailable, controllable, dirigible

navigate *v* **1 = sail**, drive, guide,
handle, manoeuvre, pilot, steer
2 = voyage
navigation *n* **= sailing**, seamanship,
voyaging
navigator *n* **= pilot**, mariner, seaman
navvy *n* **= labourer**, worker, workman
navy *n* **2 = fleet**, armada, flotilla
near *adj* **1 = close**, adjacent, adjoining,
approaching, forthcoming, imminent,
impending, in the offing, looming,
nearby, neighbouring, nigh,
upcoming
nearby *adj* **= neighbouring**, adjacent,
adjoining, convenient, handy
nearly *adv* **= almost**, approximately, as
good as, just about, practically,
roughly, virtually, well-nigh
nearness *n* **1 = closeness**,
accessibility, availability, handiness,
proximity, vicinity
near-sighted *adj* **= short-sighted**,
myopic

nearer the kerb. **near-sighted** *adj* (of a person) short-sighted.

neat ❶ *adj* **1** tidy and clean. **2** smoothly or competently done. **3** undiluted. **4** *US & Canad* good or pleasing. **neatly** *adv* **neatness** *n* **neaten** *v* make neat.

nebula [**neb**-yew-la] *n*, *pl* **-lae** [-lee] *Astronomy* hazy cloud of particles and gases. **nebular** *adj*.

nebulous ❶ *adj* vague, indistinct. **nebulosity** *n*.

NEC National Executive Committee.

necessary ❶ *adj* **1** needed to obtain the desired result, e.g. *the necessary skills*. **2** certain or unavoidable, e.g. *the necessary consequences*.

necessaries *pl n* essential items, e.g. *the necessaries of life*. **necessarily** *adv* **necessitate** *v* compel or require. **necessitous** *adj* very needy. **necessity** *n*, *pl* **-ties 1** circumstances that inevitably require a certain result. **2** something needed. **3** great poverty.

● **SPELLING TIP**
● There are 41 examples of the
● misspelling *neccessary* in the
● Bank of English; single letters
● throughout (*necesary*) are also
● popular. The correct spelling,
● **necessary**, has one *c* and two *s*s. W
● hen you add *un-* at the beginning,
● you end up with a double *n* too:
● **unnecessary**.

neck *n* **1** part of the body joining the head to the shoulders. **2** part of a garment round the neck. **3** long narrow part of a bottle or violin. ▷ *v* **4** *slang* kiss and cuddle. **neck and neck** absolutely level in a race or competition. **stick one's neck out** *informal* risk criticism or ridicule by speaking one's mind. **neckerchief** *n* piece of cloth worn tied round the neck. **necklace** *n* decorative piece of jewellery worn around the neck. **neckline** *n* shape or position of the upper edge of a dress or top. **neck of the woods** *informal* particular area. **necktie** *n US* same as TIE (sense 5).

necromancy ❶ [**neck**-rome-man-see] *n* **1** communication with the dead. **2** sorcery. **necromancer** *n*.

necrophilia *n* sexual attraction for or intercourse with dead bodies.

necropolis ❶ [neck-**rop**-pol-liss] *n* cemetery.

necrosis *n Biology*, *Medical* death of cells in the body.

nectar *n* **1** sweet liquid collected from flowers by bees. **2** drink of the gods. **3** any delicious drink.

nectarine *n* smooth-skinned peach.

née [**nay**] *prep* indicating the maiden name of a married woman.

———————————— **THESAURUS** ————————————

neat *adj* **1** = **tidy**, orderly, shipshape, smart, spick-and-span, spruce, systematic, trim **2** = **elegant**, adept, adroit, deft, dexterous, efficient, graceful, nimble, skilful, stylish **3** = **undiluted**, pure, straight, unmixed

neatly *adv* **1** = **tidily**, daintily, fastidiously, methodically, smartly, sprucely, systematically **2** = **elegantly**, adeptly, adroitly, deftly, dexterously, efficiently, expertly, gracefully, nimbly, skilfully

neatness *n* **1** = **tidiness**, daintiness, orderliness, smartness, spruceness, trimness **2** = **elegance**, adroitness, deftness, dexterity, efficiency, grace, nimbleness, skill, style

nebulous *adj* = **vague**, confused, dim, hazy, imprecise, indefinite, indistinct, shadowy, uncertain, unclear

necessarily *adv* **2** = **certainly**, automatically, compulsorily, incontrovertibly, inevitably, inexorably, naturally, of necessity, undoubtedly

necessary *adj* **1** = **needed**, compulsory, essential, imperative, indispensable, mandatory, obligatory, required, requisite, vital **2** = **certain**, fated, inescapable, inevitable, inexorable, unavoidable

necessitate *v* = **compel**, call for, coerce, constrain, demand, force, impel, oblige, require

necessities *pl n* = **essentials**, exigencies, fundamentals, needs, requirements

necessity *n* **1** = **inevitability**, compulsion, inexorableness, obligation **2** = **essential**, desideratum, fundamental, need, prerequisite, requirement, requisite, *sine qua non*

necromancy *n* **2** = **magic**, black magic, divination, enchantment, sorcery, witchcraft, wizardry

necropolis *n* = **cemetery**, burial ground, churchyard, graveyard

need ❶ *v* **1** require or be in want of. **2** be obliged (to do something). ▷ *n* **3** condition of lacking something. **4** requirement or necessity. **5** poverty. **needs** *adv* (preceded or foll. by *must*) necessarily. **needy** *adj* **needier**, **neediest** poor, in need of financial support. **needful** *adj* necessary or required. **needless** *adj* unnecessary. **needlessly** *adv*.

needle ❶ *n* **1** thin pointed piece of metal with an eye through which thread is passed for sewing. **2** long pointed rod used in knitting. **3** pointed part of a hypodermic syringe. **4** small pointed part in a record player that touches the record and picks up the sound signals, stylus. **5** pointer on a measuring instrument or compass. **6** long narrow stiff leaf. **7** *informal* intense rivalry or ill-feeling, esp. in a sports match. ▷ *v* **8** *informal* goad or provoke. **needlecord** *n* finely-ribbed corduroy. **needlepoint** *n* embroidery done on canvas.

needlework *n* sewing and embroidery.

ne'er ❶ *adv lit* poetic contraction of NEVER, e.g. *ne'er the twain shall meet*.

ne'er-do-well ❶ *n* useless or lazy person.

nefarious ❶ [nif-**fair**-ee-uss] *adj* wicked.

negate ❶ *v* **1** invalidate. **2** deny the existence of. **negation** *n*.

negative ❶ *adj* **1** expressing a denial or refusal. **2** lacking positive qualities. **3** (of an electrical charge) having the same electrical charge as an electron. **4** *Medical* indicating the absence of a condition for which a test was made. ▷ *n* **5** negative word or statement. **6** *Photography* image with a reversal of tones or colours from which positive prints are made.

neglect ❶ *v* **1** take no care of. **2** fail (to do something) through carelessness. **3** disregard. ▷ *n* **4** neglecting or being neglected. **neglectful** *adj*.

negligee, négligée [**neg**-lee-zhay] *n*

————————————————————— THESAURUS —————————

need *v* **1** = **require**, call for, demand, entail, lack, miss, necessitate, want ▷ *n* **3** = **lack**, inadequacy, insufficiency, paucity, shortage **4** = **requirement**, demand, desideratum, essential, necessity, requisite **5** = **poverty**, deprivation, destitution, penury

needed *adj* **1** = **necessary**, called for, desired, lacked, required, wanted

needful *adj* = **necessary**, essential, indispensable, needed, required, requisite, stipulated, vital

needle *v* **8** *Inf* = **irritate**, annoy, get on one's nerves (*inf*), goad, harass, nag, pester, provoke, rile, taunt

needless *adj* = **unnecessary**, gratuitous, groundless, pointless, redundant, superfluous, uncalled-for, unwanted, useless

needlework *n* = **embroidery**, needlecraft, sewing, stitching, tailoring

needy *adj* = **poor**, deprived, destitute, disadvantaged, impoverished, penniless, poverty-stricken, underprivileged

ne'er-do-well *n* = **layabout**, black sheep, good-for-nothing, idler, loafer, loser, skiver (*Brit sl*), wastrel

nefarious *adj* = **wicked**, criminal,

depraved, evil, foul, heinous, infernal, villainous

negate *v* **1** = **invalidate**, annul, cancel, countermand, neutralize, nullify, obviate, reverse, wipe out **2** = **deny**, contradict, disallow, disprove, gainsay (*arch or lit*), oppose, rebut, refute

negation *n* **1** = **cancellation**, neutralization, nullification **2** = **denial**, contradiction, converse, disavowal, inverse, opposite, rejection, renunciation, reverse

negative *adj* **1** = **contradictory**, contrary, denying, dissenting, opposing, refusing, rejecting, resisting **2** = **pessimistic**, cynical, gloomy, jaundiced, uncooperative, unenthusiastic, unwilling ▷ *n* **5** = **contradiction**, denial, refusal

neglect *v* **2** = **forget**, be remiss, evade, omit, pass over, shirk, skimp **3** = **disregard**, disdain, ignore, overlook, rebuff, scorn, slight, spurn ▷ *n* **4** = **negligence**, carelessness, dereliction, failure, laxity, oversight, slackness

neglected *adj* **1** = **abandoned**, derelict, overgrown **3** = **disregarded**, unappreciated, underestimated, undervalued

neglectful *adj* **2** = **careless**, heedless,

woman's lightweight usu. lace-trimmed dressing gown.

negligence ❶ *n* neglect or carelessness. **negligent** *adj* **negligently** *adv*.

negligible ❶ *adj* so small or unimportant as to be not worth considering.

negotiate ❶ *v* **1** discuss in order to reach (an agreement). **2** succeed in passing round or over (a place or problem). **negotiation** *n* **negotiator** *n* **negotiable** *adj*.

Negro *n, pl* **-groes** *old-fashioned, offens* member of any of the Black peoples originating in Africa. **Negroid** *adj* of or relating to the Negro race.

neigh *n* **1** loud high-pitched sound made by a horse. ▷ *v* **2** make this sound.

neighbour ❶ *n* person who lives or is situated near another. **neighbouring** *adj* situated nearby. **neighbourhood** *n* **1** district. **2** surroundings. **3** people of a district. **neighbourhood watch** scheme in which the residents of an area keep an eye on each other's property as a means of preventing crime. **neighbourly** *adj* kind, friendly, and helpful.

neither *adj, pron* **1** not one nor the other. ▷ *conj* **2** not.

- **USAGE NOTE**
- When *neither* is followed by a plural
- noun it is acceptable to make the
- verb plural too: *Neither of these books*
- *are useful*.

nelson *n* wrestling hold in which a

wrestler places his arm(s) under his opponent's arm(s) from behind and exerts pressure with his palms on the back of his opponent's neck.

nematode, nematode worm *n* slender cylindrical unsegmented worm.

nemesis ❶ [**nem**-miss-iss] *n, pl* **-ses** retribution or vengeance.

neo- *combining form* new, recent, or a modern form of, e.g. *neoclassicism*.

neoclassicism *n* late 18th- and early 19th-century style of art and architecture, based on ancient Roman and Greek models. **neoclassical** *adj*.

neocolonialism *n* political control yielded by one country over another through control of its economy. **neocolonial** *adj*.

neodymium *n Chemistry* silvery-white metallic element of lanthanide series.

Neolithic *adj* of the later Stone Age.

neologism [nee-**ol**-a-jiz-zum] *n* newly-coined word or an established word used in a new sense.

neon *n Chemistry* colourless odourless gaseous element used in illuminated signs and lights.

neonatal *adj* relating to the first few weeks of a baby's life.

neophyte *n* **1** beginner or novice. **2** new convert.

nephew *n* son of one's sister or brother.

nephritis [nif-**frite**-tiss] *n* inflammation of a kidney.

nepotism ❶ [**nep**-a-tiz-zum] *n* favouritism in business shown to relatives and friends.

THESAURUS

inattentive, indifferent, lax, negligent, remiss, thoughtless, uncaring

negligence *n* = **carelessness**, dereliction, disregard, inattention, indifference, laxity, neglect, slackness, thoughtlessness

negligent *adj* = **careless**, forgetful, heedless, inattentive, neglectful, remiss, slack, slapdash, thoughtless, unthinking

negligible *adj* = **insignificant**, imperceptible, inconsequential, minor, minute, small, trifling, trivial, unimportant

negotiable *adj* **1** = **debatable**, variable

negotiate *v* **1** = **deal**, arrange, bargain, conciliate, cut a deal, debate, discuss, mediate, transact, work out **2** = **get round**, clear, cross, get over, get past, pass, surmount

negotiation *n* **1** = **bargaining**, arbitration, debate, diplomacy, discussion, mediation, transaction, wheeling and dealing (*inf*)

negotiator *n* **1** = **mediator**, ambassador, delegate, diplomat, honest broker, intermediary, moderator

neighbourhood *n* **1, 2** = **district**, community, environs, locale, locality, quarter, region, vicinity

neighbouring *adj* = **nearby**, adjacent, adjoining, bordering, connecting, near, next, surrounding

neighbourly *adj* = **helpful**, considerate, friendly, harmonious, hospitable, kind, obliging, sociable

nemesis *n* = **retribution**, destiny, destruction, fate, vengeance

nepotism *n* = **favouritism**, bias,

Neptune *n* **1** Roman god of the sea. **2** eighth planet from the sun.

neptunium *n Chemistry* synthetic radioactive metallic element.

nerd, nurd ❶ *n slang* **1** boring person obsessed with a particular subject. **2** stupid and feeble person.

nerve ❶ *n* **1** cordlike bundle of fibres that conducts impulses between the brain and other parts of the body. **2** bravery and determination. **3** *inf* impudence. ▷ *pl* **4** anxiety or tension. **5** ability or inability to remain calm in a difficult situation. **get on someone's nerves** irritate someone. **nerve oneself** prepare oneself (to do something difficult or unpleasant). **nerveless** *adj* **1** numb, without feeling. **2** fearless. **nervy** *adj* **nervier**, **nerviest** excitable or nervous. **nerve centre** place from which a system or organization is controlled. **nerve gas** poisonous gas which affects the nervous system. **nerve-racking** *adj* very distressing or harrowing.

nervous ❶ *adj* **1** apprehensive or worried. **2** of or relating to the nerves. **nervously** *adv* **nervousness** *n* **nervous breakdown** mental illness in which the sufferer ceases to function properly. **nervous system** brain, spinal column and nerves, which together control thought, feeling and movement.

ness *n* headland, cape.

nest ❶ *n* **1** place or structure in which birds or certain animals lay eggs or give birth to young. **2** secluded place. **3** set of things of graduated sizes designed to fit together. ▷ *v* **4** make or inhabit a nest. **5** (of a set of objects) fit one inside another. **nest egg** fund of money kept in reserve.

nestle ❶ *v* **1** snuggle. **2** be in a sheltered position.

nestling ❶ *n* bird too young to leave the nest.

net¹ ❶ *n* **1** fabric of meshes of string, thread, or wire with many openings. **2** piece of net used to protect or hold things or to trap animals. **3** (in certain sports) piece of net over which the ball or shuttlecock must be hit. **4** goal in soccer or hockey. **5** strategy intended to trap people, e.g. *he had slipped through a police net*. ▷ *v* **netting**, **netted 6** catch (a fish or animal) in a net. **the Net** short for INTERNET. **netting** *n* material made of net.

netball *n* team game in which a ball has to be thrown through a net hanging from a ring at the top of a pole.

net², nett ❶ *adj* **1** left after all deductions. **2** (of weight) excluding the wrapping or container. **3** final or

partiality, patronage, preferential treatment

nerd, nurd *n Sl* **1** = **bore**, anorak (*inf*), dork (*sl*), geek (*inf*), obsessive, train spotter (*inf*)

nerve *n* **2** = **bravery**, bottle (*Brit sl*), courage, daring, fearlessness, grit, guts (*inf*), pluck, resolution, will **3** *Inf* = **impudence**, audacity, boldness, brazenness, cheek (*inf*), impertinence, insolence, temerity **nerve oneself** = **brace oneself**, fortify oneself, gee oneself up, steel oneself

nerveless *adj* **1** = **calm**, composed, controlled, cool, impassive, imperturbable, self-possessed, unemotional **2** = **fearless**, brave, courageous, daring, gutsy (*sl*), plucky, unafraid

nerve-racking *adj* = **tense**, difficult, distressing, frightening, gut-wrenching, harrowing, stressful, trying, worrying

nerves *pl* = **tension**, anxiety, butterflies (in one's stomach) (*inf*), cold feet (*inf*), fretfulness, nervousness, strain, stress, worry

nervous *adj* **1** = **apprehensive**, anxious, edgy, fearful, jumpy, on edge, tense, uneasy, uptight (*inf*), wired (*sl*), worried

nervousness *n* **1** = **anxiety**, agitation, disquiet, excitability, fluster, tension, touchiness, worry

nervy *adj* = **anxious**, agitated, fidgety, jittery (*inf*), jumpy, nervous, on edge, tense, wired (*sl*)

nest *n* **2** = **refuge**, den, haunt, hideaway, retreat **nest egg** = **reserve**, cache, deposit, fall-back, fund(s), savings, store

nestle *v* **1** = **snuggle**, cuddle, curl up, huddle, nuzzle

nestling *n* = **chick**, fledgling

net¹ *n* **1** = **mesh**, lattice, netting, network, openwork, tracery, web ▷ *v* **6** = **catch**, bag, capture, enmesh, ensnare, entangle, trap

net², nett *adj* **1** = **take-home**, after taxes, clear, final ▷ *v* **4** = **earn**,

conclusive, e.g. *the net result.* ▷ *v*
netting, netted 4 yield or earn as a
clear profit.

nether ❶ *adj* lower. **nethermost** *adj*
lowest.

nettle ❶ *n* plant with stinging hairs on
the leaves. **nettled** *adj* irritated or
annoyed. **nettle rash** skin condition
in which itchy red or white raised
patches appear.

network ❶ *n* **1** system of intersecting
lines, roads, etc. **2** interconnecting
group or system. **3** (in broadcasting)
group of stations that all transmit the
same programmes simultaneously.
4 *Computers* system of interconnected
circuits. ▷ *v* **5** broadcast (a
programme) over a network.

neural *adj* of a nerve or the nervous
system.

neuralgia *n* severe pain along a nerve.

neuritis [nyoor-**rite**-tiss] *n*
inflammation of a nerve or nerves.

neurology *n* scientific study of the
nervous system. **neurological** *adj*
neurologist *n*.

neuron, neurone *n* cell specialized to
conduct nerve impulses.

neurosis ❶ *n, pl* **-ses** mental disorder
producing hysteria, anxiety,
depression, or obsessive behaviour.
neurotic *adj* **1** emotionally unstable.
2 suffering from neurosis. ▷ *n*
3 neurotic person.

neurosurgery *n* branch of surgery
concerned with the nervous system.

neurosurgical *adj* **neurosurgeon** *n.*

neuter ❶ *adj* **1** belonging to a
particular class of grammatical
inflections in some languages. **2** (of
an animal) sexually underdeveloped.
▷ *v* **3** castrate (an animal).

neutral ❶ *adj* **1** taking neither side in a
war or dispute. **2** of or belonging to a
neutral party or country. **3** not
displaying emotions or opinions. **4** (of
a colour) not definite or striking. ▷ *n*
5 neutral person or nation. **6** neutral
gear. **neutrality** *n* **neutralize** *v* make
ineffective or neutral. **neutral gear**
position of the controls of a gearbox
that leaves the gears unconnected to
the engine.

neutrino [new-**tree**-no] *n, pl* **-nos**
elementary particle with no mass or
electrical charge.

neutron *n* electrically neutral
elementary particle of about the same
mass as a proton. **neutron bomb**
nuclear bomb designed to kill people
and animals while leaving buildings
virtually undamaged.

never ❶ *adv* at no time. **never-ending**
adj long and boring. **nevermore** *adv* lit
never again. **nevertheless** *adv* in spite
of that.

never-never *n informal* hire-purchase.
never-never land imaginary idyllic
place.

new ❶ *adj* **1** not existing before.
2 recently acquired. **3** having lately
come into some state. **4** additional.

THESAURUS

accumulate, bring in, clear, gain,
make, realize, reap

nether *adj* = **lower**, below, beneath,
bottom, inferior, under, underground

nettled *adj* = **irritated**, annoyed,
exasperated, galled, harassed,
incensed, peeved, put out, riled, vexed

network *n* **1, 2** = **system**,
arrangement, complex, grid,
labyrinth, lattice, maze, organization,
structure, web **4** *Computers* = **web**,
system

neurosis *n* = **obsession**, abnormality,
affliction, derangement, instability,
maladjustment, mental illness,
phobia

neurotic *adj* **1** = **unstable**, abnormal,
compulsive, disturbed, maladjusted,
manic, nervous, obsessive,
unhealthy

neuter *v* **3** = **castrate**, doctor (*inf*),

emasculate, fix (*inf*), geld, spay

neutral *adj* **1** = **unbiased**, even-
handed, impartial, nonaligned,
nonpartisan, uncommitted,
uninvolved, unprejudiced
4 = **indeterminate**, dull, indistinct,
intermediate, undefined

neutrality *n* **1** = **impartiality**,
detachment, nonalignment,
noninterference, noninvolvement,
nonpartisanship

neutralize *v* = **counteract**, cancel,
compensate for, counterbalance,
frustrate, negate, nullify, offset,
undo

never *adv* = **at no time**, not at all, on no
account, under no circumstances

nevertheless *adv* = **nonetheless**, but,
even so, (even) though, however,
notwithstanding, regardless, still, yet

new *adj* **1** = **modern**, contemporary,

5 (foll. by *to*) unfamiliar. ▷ *adv*
6 recently. **newness** *n* **New Age** late 1980s philosophy characterized by a belief in alternative medicine and spiritualism. **newbie** *informal* ▷ *n* person new to a job, club, etc.
newborn *adj* recently or just born.
newcomer *n* recent arrival or participant. **newfangled** *adj* objectionably or unnecessarily modern.
new-found *adj* newly or recently discovered. **newly** *adv* **newlyweds** *pl n* recently married couple. **new moon** moon when it appears as a narrow crescent at the beginning of its cycle.
New Testament part of the Christian Bible dealing with life and teachings of Christ and his followers. **new town** town planned and built as a complete unit. **New World** the Americas; the western hemisphere. **New Year** (holiday marking) the first day or days of the year.
newel *n* post at the top or bottom of a flight of stairs that supports the handrail.
news ❶ *n* **1** important or interesting new happenings. **2** information about such events reported in the mass media.
3 television or radio programme presenting such information. **newsy** *adj* full of news. **newsagent** *n* shopkeeper who sells newspapers and magazines.
newsflash *n* brief important news item, which interrupts a radio or television programme. **newsletter** *n* bulletin issued periodically to members of a group. **newspaper** *n* weekly or daily publication containing news.
newsprint *n* inexpensive paper used for

newspapers. **newsreader**, **newscaster** *n* person who reads the news on the television or radio. **newsreel** *n* short film giving news. **newsroom** *n* room where news is received and prepared for publication or broadcasting.
newsworthy *adj* sufficiently interesting to be reported as news.
newt *n* small amphibious creature with a long slender body and tail.
newton *n* unit of force.
next ❶ *adj*, *adv* **1** immediately following. **2** nearest. **next door** *adj*, *adv* (often hyphenated) in, at, or to the adjacent house or flat. **next-of-kin** *n* closest relative.
nexus *n*, *pl* **nexus** connection or link.
NF Newfoundland.
NH New Hampshire.
NHS National Health Service.
Ni *Chemistry* nickel.
NI 1 *Brit* National Insurance.
2 Northern Ireland.
nib *n* writing point of a pen.
nibble ❶ *v* **1** take little bites (of). ▷ *n*
2 little bite. **3** light meal.
nibs *n* **his, her nibs** *slang* mock title of respect.
nice ❶ *adj* **1** pleasant. **2** kind, e.g. *a nice gesture*. **3** good or satisfactory, e.g. *they made a nice job of it*. **4** subtle, e.g. *a nice distinction*. **nicely** *adv* **niceness** *n*.
- **USAGE NOTE**
- The adjective *nice* has been so
- overused that it has lost a lot of
- its effectiveness. It is therefore
- better to use a more interesting
- or descriptive word in its place
- wherever possible.

——————————————————— THESAURUS ———————

current, fresh, ground-breaking, latest, novel, original, recent, state-of-the-art, unfamiliar, up-to-date
3 = **changed**, altered, improved, modernized, redesigned, renewed, restored **4** = **extra**, added, more, new-found, supplementary
newcomer *n* = **novice**, arrival, beginner, Johnny-come-lately (*inf*), parvenu
newfangled *adj* = **new**, contemporary, fashionable, gimmicky, modern, novel, recent, state-of-the-art
newly *adv* = **recently**, anew, freshly, just, lately, latterly
newness *n* **1** = **novelty**, freshness, innovation, oddity, originality, strangeness, unfamiliarity, uniqueness
news *n* **1, 2** = **information**, bulletin,

communiqué, exposé, gossip, hearsay, intelligence, latest (*inf*), report, revelation, rumour, story
newsworthy *adj* = **interesting**, important, notable, noteworthy, remarkable, significant, stimulating
next *adj* **1** = **following**, consequent, ensuing, later, subsequent, succeeding **2** = **nearest**, adjacent, adjoining, closest, neighbouring ▷ *adv*
1 = **afterwards**, following, later, subsequently, thereafter
nibble *v* **1** = **bite**, eat, gnaw, munch, nip, peck, pick at ▷ *n* **2** = **taste**, crumb, morsel, peck, soupçon, titbit
3 = **snack**, bite
nice *adj* **1** = **pleasant**, agreeable, attractive, charming, delightful, good,

nicety ❶ *n, pl* **-ties 1** subtle point.
2 refinement or delicacy.

niche ❶ [**neesh**] *n* **1** hollow area in a wall. **2** suitable position for a particular person.

nick ❶ *v* **1** make a small cut in. **2** *slang* steal. **3** *slang* arrest. ▷ *n* **4** small cut. **5** *slang* prison or police station. **in good nick** *informal* in good condition. **in the nick of time** just in time.

nickel *n* **1** *Chemistry* silvery-white metal often used in alloys. **2** US coin worth five cents.

nickelodeon *n* US early type of jukebox.

nicker *n, pl* **nicker** *Brit slang* pound sterling.

nickname ❶ *n* **1** familiar name given to a person or place. ▷ *v* **2** call by a nickname.

nicotine *n* poisonous substance found in tobacco.

nictitate *v* blink. **nictitating membrane** (in reptiles, birds, and some mammals) thin fold of skin that can be drawn across the eye beneath the eyelid.

niece *n* daughter of one's sister or brother.

nifty ❶ *adj* **-tier**, **-tiest** *informal* neat or smart.

niggard ❶ *n* stingy person. **niggardly** *adj*.

nigger *n offens* Black person.

niggle ❶ *v* **1** worry slightly.

2 continually find fault (with). ▷ *n*
3 small worry or doubt.

nigh *adv, prep lit* near.

night ❶ *n* **1** time of darkness between sunset and sunrise. **2** evening.
3 period between going to bed and morning. **4** nightfall or dusk. **5** an evening designated for a specified activity, e.g. *parents' night*. ▷ *adj* **6** of, occurring, or working at night, e.g. *the night shift*. **nightly** *adj, adv* (happening) each night. **nightcap** *n* **1** drink taken just before bedtime.
2 soft cap formerly worn in bed. **nightclub** *n* establishment for dancing, music, etc., open late at night. **nightdress** *n* woman's loose dress worn in bed. **nightfall** *n* approach of darkness. **nightgown** *n* loose garment worn in bed; nightdress or nightshirt. **nightie** *n informal* nightdress. **nightingale** *n* small bird with a musical song usu. heard at night. **nightjar** *n* nocturnal bird with a harsh cry. **nightlife** *n* entertainment and social activities available at night in a town or city. **night-light** *n* dim light left on overnight. **nightmare** *n* **1** very bad dream. **2** very unpleasant experience. **nightmarish** *adj* **night safe** safe built into the outside wall of a bank, which customers can deposit money in when the bank is closed.

night school place where adults can attend educational courses in the

---

THESAURUS

pleasurable **2** = **kind**, courteous, friendly, likable *or* likeable, polite, well-mannered **3** = **neat**, dainty, fine, tidy, trim **4** = **subtle**, careful, delicate, fastidious, fine, meticulous, precise, strict

nicely *adv* **1** = **pleasantly**, acceptably, agreeably, attractively, charmingly, delightfully, pleasurably, well
2 = **kindly**, amiably, commendably, courteously, politely **3** = **neatly**, daintily, finely, tidily, trimly

nicety *n* = **subtlety**, daintiness, delicacy, discrimination, distinction, nuance, refinement

niche *n* **1** = **alcove**, corner, hollow, nook, opening, recess **2** = **position**, calling, pigeonhole (*inf*), place, slot (*inf*), vocation

nick *v* **1** = **cut**, chip, dent, mark, notch, scar, score, scratch, snick **2** *Sl* = **steal**, pilfer, pinch (*inf*), swipe (*sl*) ▷ *n*

4 = **cut**, chip, dent, mark, notch, scar, scratch

nickname *n* **1** = **pet name**, diminutive, epithet, label, sobriquet

nifty *adj Inf* = **neat**, attractive, chic, deft, pleasing, smart, stylish

niggard *n* = **miser**, cheapskate (*inf*), Scrooge, skinflint

niggardly *adj* = **stingy**, avaricious, frugal, grudging, mean, miserly, parsimonious, tightfisted, ungenerous

niggle *v* **1** = **worry**, annoy, irritate, rankle **2** = **criticize**, carp, cavil, find fault, fuss

niggling *adj* **1** = **persistent**, gnawing, irritating, troubling, worrying
2 = **petty**, finicky, fussy, nit-picking (*inf*), pettifogging, picky (*inf*), quibbling

night *n* **1** = **darkness**, dark, night-time
3 = **night-time**

evenings. **nightshade** n plant with bell-shaped flowers which are often poisonous. **nightshirt** n long loose shirt worn in bed. **night-time** n time from sunset to sunrise.

nihilism [**nye**-ill-liz-zum] n rejection of all established authority and institutions. **nihilist** n **nihilistic** adj.

nil ❶ n nothing, zero.

nimble ❶ adj 1 agile and quick. 2 mentally alert or acute. **nimbly** adv.

nimbus n, pl **-bi**, **-buses** 1 dark grey rain cloud. 2 halo.

nincompoop ❶ n informal stupid person.

nine adj, n one more than eight. **ninth** adj, n (of) number nine in a series. **ninepins** n game of skittles.

nineteen adj, n ten and nine. **talk nineteen to the dozen** talk very fast. **nineteenth** adj, n **nineteenth hole** slang bar in a golf clubhouse.

ninety adj, n ten times nine. **ninetieth** adj, n.

niobium n Chemistry white superconductive metallic element.

nip¹ ❶ v **nipping**, **nipped** 1 informal hurry. 2 pinch or squeeze. 3 bite lightly. 4 (of the cold) cause pain. ▷ n 5 pinch or light bite. 6 sharp coldness, e.g. a nip in the air. **nippy** adj **-pier**, **-piest** 1 frosty or chilly. 2 informal quick or nimble. **nipper** n informal small child.

nip² ❶ n small alcoholic drink.

nipple n 1 projection in the centre of a breast. 2 small projection through which oil or grease can be put into a machine or component.

niqab n type of veil covering the whole head except the eyes, worn by some Muslim women.

nirvana ❶ [near-**vah**-na] n Buddhism, Hinduism absolute spiritual enlightenment and bliss.

nisi [**nye**-sigh] adj see DECREE NISI.

Nissen hut n tunnel-shaped military hut made of corrugated steel.

nit ❶ n 1 egg or larva of a louse. 2 informal short for NITWIT. **nit-picking** adj informal overconcerned with insignificant detail, esp. to find fault. **nitwit** n informal stupid person.

nitrogen [**nite**-roj-jen] n Chemistry colourless odourless gas that forms four fifths of the air. **nitric**, **nitrous**, **nitrogenous** adj of or containing nitrogen. **nitrate** n compound of nitric acid, used as a fertilizer. **nitroglycerine**, **nitroglycerin** n explosive liquid. **nitric acid** corrosive liquid widely used in industry. **nitrous oxide** anaesthetic gas.

nitty-gritty ❶ n informal basic facts.

NJ New Jersey.

NM New Mexico.

NNE north-northeast.

NNW north-northwest.

no ❶ interj 1 expresses denial, disagreement, or refusal. ▷ adj 2 not any, not a. ▷ adv 3 not at all. ▷ n, pl **noes**, **nos** 4 answer or vote of 'no'. 5 person who answers or votes 'no'.

───────── THESAURUS ─────────

nightfall n = **evening**, dusk, sundown, sunset, twilight

nightly adj = **nocturnal**, night-time ▷ adv = **every night**, each night, night after night, nights (inf)

nightmare n 1 = **bad dream**, hallucination 2 = **ordeal**, horror, torment, trial, tribulation

nil n = **nothing**, love, naught, none, zero

nimble adj 1 = **agile**, brisk, deft, dexterous, lively, quick, sprightly, spry, swift

nimbly adv 1 = **quickly**, briskly, deftly, dexterously, easily, readily, smartly, spryly, swiftly

nincompoop n Inf = **idiot**, blockhead, chump, fool, nitwit (inf), numbskull or numskull, twit (inf, chiefly Brit)

nip¹ v 2 = **pinch**, squeeze, tweak 3 = **bite**

nip² n = **dram**, draught, drop, mouthful, shot (inf), sip, snifter (inf)

nipper n Inf = **child**, baby, boy, girl, infant, kid (inf), tot

nippy adj 1 = **chilly**, biting, sharp 2 Inf = **quick**, active, agile, fast, nimble, spry

nirvana n Buddhism, Hinduism = **paradise**, bliss, joy, peace, serenity, tranquillity

nit-picking adj Inf = **fussy**, captious, carping, finicky, hairsplitting, pedantic, pettifogging, quibbling

nitty-gritty n Inf = **basics**, brass tacks (inf), core, crux, essentials, fundamentals, gist, substance

nitwit n Inf = **fool**, dimwit (inf), dummy (sl), halfwit, nincompoop, oaf, simpleton

no interj 1 = **never**, nay, not at all, no way ▷ n 4 = **refusal**, denial, negation, rejection

no-ball n (in cricket or rounders) improperly bowled ball. **no-claims bonus**, **no-claim bonus** reduction in the cost of an insurance policy made if no claims have been made in a specified period. **no-go area** district barricaded off so that the police or army can enter only by force. **no-man's-land** n land between boundaries, esp. contested land between two opposing forces. **no-one**, **no one** pron nobody.

● **USAGE NOTE**
● When no-one refers to 'people in
● general' it may be followed by a
● plural: No-one finished their drink.

no. number.

No¹, Noh n, pl **No**, **Noh** Japanese classical drama, using music and dancing.

No² Chemistry nobelium.

n.o. Cricket not out.

nob ❶ n slang person of wealth or social distinction.

nobble ❶ v slang **1** attract the attention of (someone) in order to talk to him or her. **2** bribe or threaten.

nobelium n Chemistry artificially-produced radioactive element.

Nobel Prize [no-**bell**] n prize awarded annually for outstanding achievement in various fields.

noble ❶ adj **1** showing or having high moral qualities. **2** of the nobility. **3** impressive and magnificent. ▷ n **4** member of the nobility. **nobility** n **1** quality of being noble. **2** class of people holding titles and high social rank. **nobly** adv **nobleman**, **noblewoman** n **noble gas**

Chemistry any of a group of very unreactive gases, including helium and neon.

noblesse oblige [no-**bless** oh-**bleezh**] n often ironic supposed obligation of the nobility to be honourable and generous.

nobody ❶ pron **1** no person. ▷ n, pl **-bodies 2** person of no importance.

nock n notch on an arrow or a bow for the bowstring.

nocturnal ❶ adj **1** of the night. **2** active at night.

nocturne n short dreamy piece of music.

nod ❶ v **nodding**, **nodded 1** lower and raise (one's head) briefly in agreement or greeting. **2** let one's head fall forward with sleep. ▷ n **3** act of nodding. **nod off** v informal fall asleep.

noddle n informal the head.

node n **1** point on a plant stem from which leaves grow. **2** point at which a curve crosses itself. **nodal** adj.

nodule n **1** small knot or lump. **2** rounded mineral growth on the root of a plant. **nodular** adj.

Noel, Noël n Christmas.

nog n alcoholic drink containing beaten egg.

noggin ❶ n **1** informal head. **2** small quantity of an alcoholic drink.

noise ❶ n sound, usu. a loud or disturbing one. **be noised abroad** be rumoured. **noisy** adj **noisier**, **noisiest 1** making a lot of noise. **2** full of noise. **noisily** adv **noiseless** adj **noiselessly** adv.

noisome ❶ adj **1** (of smells) offensive. **2** harmful or poisonous.

n

THESAURUS

nob n Sl = **aristocrat**, big hitter (inf), bigwig (inf), heavy hitter (inf), toff (Brit sl), V.I.P.

nobble v Sl **2** = **bribe**, get at, influence, intimidate, win over

nobility n **1** = **integrity**, honour, incorruptibility, uprightness, virtue **2** = **aristocracy**, elite, lords, nobles, patricians, peerage, upper class

noble adj **1** = **worthy**, generous, honourable, magnanimous, upright, virtuous **2** = **aristocratic**, blue-blooded, highborn, lordly, patrician, titled **3** = **impressive**, dignified, distinguished, grand, great, imposing, lofty, splendid, stately ▷ n **4** = **lord**, aristocrat, nobleman, peer

nobody pron **1** = **no-one** ▷ n **2** = **nonentity**, cipher, lightweight (inf), menial

nocturnal adj = **nightly**, night-time

nod v **1** = **acknowledge**, bow, gesture, indicate, signal **2** = **sleep**, doze, drowse, nap ▷ n **3** = **gesture**, acknowledgment, greeting, indication, sign, signal

noggin n Inf **1** = **head**, block (inf), nut (sl) ▷ n **2** = **cup**, dram, mug, nip, tot

noise n **1** = **sound**, clamour, commotion, din, hubbub, racket, row, uproar

noiseless adj = **silent**, hushed, inaudible, mute, quiet, soundless, still

noisome adj **1** = **offensive**, disgusting, fetid, foul, malodorous, noxious,

nomad ❶ *n* member of a tribe with no fixed dwelling place, wanderer. **nomadic** *adj*.

nom de plume ❶ *n, pl* **noms de plume** pen name.

nomenclature ❶ [no-**men**-klatch-er] *n* system of names used in a particular subject.

nominal ❶ *adj* **1** in name only. **2** very small in comparison with real worth. **nominally** *adv*.

nominate ❶ *v* **1** suggest as a candidate. **2** appoint to an office or position. **nomination** *n* **nominee** *n* candidate. **nominative** *n* form of a noun indicating the subject of a verb.

non- *prefix* indicating: **1** negation, e.g. *nonexistent*. **2** refusal or failure, e.g. *noncooperation*. **3** exclusion from a specified class, e.g. *nonfiction*. **4** lack or absence, e.g. *nonevent*.

nonage *n* **1** *Law* state of being under full legal age for various actions. **2** any period of immaturity.

nonagenarian *n* person aged between ninety and ninety-nine.

nonaggression *n* policy of not attacking other countries.

nonagon *n* geometric figure with nine sides. **nonagonal** *adj*.

nonalcoholic *adj* containing no alcohol.

nonaligned ❶ *adj* (of a country) not part of a major alliance or power bloc. **nonalignment** *n*.

nonbelligerent *adj* (of a country) not taking part in a war.

nonce *n* **for the nonce** for the present. **nonce word** word coined for a single occasion.

nonchalant ❶ [**non**-shall-ant] *adj* casually unconcerned or indifferent. **nonchalantly** *adv* **nonchalance** *n*.

noncombatant ❶ *n* member of the armed forces whose duties do not include fighting.

noncommissioned officer *n* (in the armed forces) a subordinate officer, risen from the ranks.

noncommittal ❶ *adj* not committing oneself to any particular opinion.

non compos mentis ❶ *adj* of unsound mind.

nonconductor *n* substance that is a poor conductor of heat, electricity, or sound.

nonconformist ❶ *n* **1** person who does not conform to generally

putrid, smelly, stinking **2** = **poisonous**, bad, harmful, pernicious, pestilential, unhealthy, unwholesome

noisy *adj* = **loud**, boisterous, cacophonous, clamorous, deafening, ear-splitting, strident, tumultuous, uproarious, vociferous

nomad *n* = **wanderer**, drifter, itinerant, migrant, rambler, rover, vagabond

nomadic *adj* = **wandering**, itinerant, migrant, peripatetic, roaming, roving, travelling, vagrant

nom de plume *n* = **pseudonym**, alias, assumed name, nom de guerre, pen name

nomenclature *n* = **terminology**, classification, codification, phraseology, taxonomy, vocabulary

nominal *adj* **1** = **so-called**, formal, ostensible, professed, puppet, purported, supposed, theoretical, titular **2** = **small**, inconsiderable, insignificant, minimal, symbolic, token, trifling, trivial

nominate *v* **1** = **suggest**, propose, recommend **2** = **name**, appoint, assign,

choose, designate, elect, select

nomination *n* **1** = **suggestion**, proposal, recommendation **2** = **choice**, appointment, designation, election, selection

nominee *n* = **candidate**, aspirant, contestant, entrant, protégé, runner

nonaligned *adj* = **neutral**, impartial, uncommitted, undecided

nonchalance *n* = **indifference**, calm, composure, equanimity, imperturbability, sang-froid, self-possession, unconcern

nonchalant *adj* = **casual**, blasé, calm, careless, indifferent, insouciant, laid-back (*inf*), offhand, unconcerned, unperturbed

noncombatant *n* = **civilian**, neutral, nonbelligerent

noncommittal *adj* = **evasive**, cautious, circumspect, equivocal, guarded, neutral, politic, temporizing, tentative, vague, wary

non compos mentis *adj* = **insane**, crazy, deranged, mentally ill, unbalanced, unhinged

nonconformist *n* **1** = **maverick**, dissenter, eccentric, heretic,

accepted patterns of behaviour or thought. **2** (**N-**) member of a Protestant group separated from the Church of England. ▷ adj **3** (of behaviour or ideas) not conforming to accepted patterns. **nonconformity** n.

noncontributory adj denoting a pension scheme for employees, the premiums of which are paid entirely by the employer.

non-cooperation n refusal to do more than is legally or contractually required of one.

nondescript ❶ adj lacking outstanding features.

none ❶ pron **1** not any. **2** no-one. **nonetheless** adv despite that, however.

- ● **USAGE NOTE**
- ● Although none means 'not one', and
- ● can take a singular verb, it more
- ● often takes a plural: None of them
- ● are mine.

nonentity ❶ [non-**enn**-tit-tee] n, pl **-ties** insignificant person or thing.

nonessential adj not absolutely necessary.

nonevent ❶ n disappointing or insignificant occurrence.

nonexistent ❶ adj not existing, imaginary. **nonexistence** n.

nonferrous adj **1** denoting metal other than iron. **2** not containing iron.

nonflammable adj not easily set on fire.

nonintervention n refusal to intervene in the affairs of others.

noniron adj not requiring ironing.

non-nuclear adj not involving or using nuclear power or weapons.

nonpareil [non-par-**rail**] n person or thing that is unsurpassed.

nonpartisan adj not supporting any single political party.

nonpayment n failure to pay money owed.

nonplussed adj perplexed.

non-profit-making adj not run with the intention of making a profit.

nonproliferation n limitation of the production or spread of something, such as nuclear weapons.

nonrepresentational adj Art abstract.

nonresident n person who does not live in a particular country or place.

nonsectarian adj not confined to any specific religion.

nonsense ❶ n **1** something that has or makes no sense. **2** absurd language. **3** foolish behaviour. **nonsensical** adj.

non sequitur [**sek**-wit-tur] n statement with little or no relation to what preceded it.

nonsmoker n **1** person who does not smoke. **2** train carriage or compartment in which smoking is forbidden. **nonsmoking**, **no-smoking** adj denoting an area in which smoking is forbidden.

nonstandard adj denoting language that is not regarded as correct by educated native speakers.

nonstarter ❶ n person or idea that has little chance of success.

nonstick adj coated with a substance that food will not stick to when cooked.

nonstop ❶ adj, adv without a stop.

nontoxic adj not poisonous.

iconoclast, individualist, protester, radical, rebel

nonconformity n **1** = **dissent**, eccentricity, heresy, heterodoxy

nondescript adj = **ordinary**, commonplace, dull, featureless, run-of-the-mill, undistinguished, unexceptional, unremarkable

none pron = **not any**, nil, nobody, no-one, nothing, not one, zero

nonentity n = **nobody**, cipher, lightweight (inf), mediocrity, small fry

nonetheless adv = **nevertheless**, despite that, even so, however, in spite of that, yet

nonevent n = **flop** (inf), disappointment, dud (inf), failure,

fiasco, washout

nonexistent adj = **imaginary**, chimerical, fictional, hypothetical, illusory, legendary, mythical, unreal

nonsense n **1, 2** = **rubbish**, balderdash, claptrap (inf), double Dutch (Brit inf), drivel, gibberish, hot air (inf), stupidity, tripe (inf), twaddle

nonsensical adj = **senseless**, absurd, crazy, foolish, inane, incomprehensible, irrational, meaningless, ridiculous, silly

nonstarter n = **dead loss**, dud (inf), lemon (inf), loser, no-hoper (inf), turkey (inf), washout (inf)

nonstop adj = **continuous**, constant, endless, incessant, interminable,

nonunion *adj* **1** (of a company) not employing trade union members. **2** (of a person) not belonging to a trade union.

nonviolent *adj* using peaceful methods to bring about change. **nonviolence** *n*.

nonvoting *adj* (of shares in a company) not entitling the owner to vote at company meetings.

noodles *pl n* long thin strips of pasta.

nook ❶ *n* **1** corner or recess. **2** sheltered place.

noon ❶ *n* twelve o'clock midday. **noonday** *adj* happening at noon.

noose *n* loop in the end of a rope, tied with a slipknot.

nor *conj* and not.

Nordic *adj* of Scandinavia or its typically tall blond and blue-eyed people.

norm ❶ *n* standard that is regarded as usual, e.g. *These values were the norm, not the exception*.

normal ❶ *adj* **1** usual, regular, or typical. **2** free from mental or physical disorder. ▷ *n* **3** usual or regular state, degree or form. **normally** *adv* **normality** *n* **normalize** *v* **1** make or become normal. **2** make comply with a standard. **normalization** *n* **normative** *adj* of or setting a norm or standard.

Norman *n* **1** person from Normandy in N France, esp. one of the people who conquered England in 1066. **2** (also **Norman French**) medieval Norman and English dialect of French. ▷ *adj* **3** of the Normans or their dialect of French. **4** of Normandy. **5** of a style of architecture used in Britain from the Norman Conquest until the 12th century, with massive masonry walls and rounded arches.

Norse *n*, *adj* (language) of ancient and medieval Norway. **Norseman** *n* Viking.

north ❶ *n* **1** direction towards the North Pole, opposite south. **2** area lying in or towards the north. ▷ *adj* **3** to or in the north. **4** (of a wind) from the north. ▷ *adv* **5** in, to, or towards the north. **northerly** *adj* **northern** *adj* **northerner** *n* person from the north of a country or area. **northward** *adj*, *adv* **northwards** *adv* **northeast** *n*, *adj*, *adv* (in or to) direction between north and east. **northwest** *n*, *adj*, *adv* (in or to) direction between north and west. **North Pole** northernmost point on the earth's axis.

Norwegian *adj* **1** of Norway, its language, or its people. ▷ *n* **2** language of Norway. **3** person from Norway.

nos. numbers.

nose ❶ *n* **1** organ of smell, used also in breathing. **2** sense of smell. **3** front part of a vehicle. **4** distinctive smell of a wine, perfume, etc. **5** instinctive skill in finding something, e.g. *a nose for a bargain*. ▷ *v* **6** move forward slowly and carefully. **7** pry or snoop. **nosebag** *n* bag containing feed fastened round a horse's head. **nosebleed** *n* bleeding from the nose. **nose dive** sudden drop. **nosegay** *n* small bunch of flowers. **nose out** *v* discover by searching or prying. **nosey**, **nosy** *adj* **nosier**, **nosiest** *informal* prying or inquisitive. **nosiness** *n*.

relentless, unbroken, uninterrupted ▷ *adv* = **continuously**, ceaselessly, constantly, endlessly, incessantly, interminably, perpetually, relentlessly, twenty-four-seven (*inf*)

nook *n* = **niche**, alcove, corner, cubbyhole, hide-out, opening, recess, retreat

noon *n* = **midday**, high noon, noonday, noontide, twelve noon

norm *n* = **standard**, average, benchmark, criterion, par, pattern, rule, yardstick

normal *adj* **1** = **usual**, average, common, conventional, natural, ordinary, regular, routine, standard, typical **2** = **sane**, rational, reasonable, well-adjusted

normality *n* **1** = **regularity**, conventionality, naturalness **2** = **sanity**, balance, rationality, reason

normally *adv* **1** = **usually**, as a rule, commonly, generally, habitually, ordinarily, regularly, typically

north *adj* **3** = **northern**, Arctic, boreal, northerly, polar ▷ *adv* **5** = **northward(s)**, northerly

nose *n* **1** = **snout**, beak, bill, hooter (*sl*), proboscis ▷ *v* **6** = **ease forward**, nudge, nuzzle, push, shove **7** = **pry**, meddle, snoop (*inf*)

nosh *slang* ▷ *n* **1** food. ▷ *v* **2** eat.
 nosh-up *n slang* large meal.
nostalgia ❶ *n* sentimental longing for
 the past. **nostalgic** *adj*.
nostril *n* one of the two openings at the
 end of the nose.
nostrum ❶ *n* **1** quack medicine.
 2 favourite remedy.
not *adv* expressing negation, refusal, or
 denial.
nota bene [**note**-a **ben**-nay] note well,
 take note.
notable ❶ [**note**-a-bl] *adj* **1** worthy of
 being noted, remarkable. ▷ *n* **2** person
 of distinction. **notably** *adv* **notability**
 [note-a-**bill**-lit-tee] *n*.
notary, notary public [**note**-a-ree] *n*,
 pl **-ries** person authorized to witness
 the signing of legal documents.
notation ❶ [no-**tay**-shun] *n*
 1 representation of numbers or
 quantities in a system by a series of
 symbols. **2** set of such symbols.
notch ❶ *n* **1** V-shaped cut. **2** *informal*
 step or level. ▷ *v* **3** make a notch in.

 4 (foll. by *up*) score or achieve.
note ❶ *n* **1** short letter. **2** brief
 comment or record. **3** banknote.
 4 (symbol for) a musical sound. **5** hint
 or mood. ▷ *v* **6** notice, pay attention
 to. **7** record in writing. **8** remark upon.
 noted *adj* well-known. **notebook** *n*
 book for writing in. **notebook
 computer** small portable computer.
 notelet *n* small folded card with a
 design on the front, used for writing
 informal letters. **notepaper** *n* paper
 used for writing letters. **noteworthy**
 adj worth noting, remarkable.
nothing ❶ *pron* **1** not anything.
 2 matter of no importance. **3** figure o.
 ▷ *adv* **4** not at all. **nothingness** *n*
 1 nonexistence. **2** insignificance.
notice ❶ *n* **1** observation or attention.
 2 sign giving warning or an
 announcement. **3** advance
 notification of intention to end a
 contract of employment. **4** review in a
 newspaper of a book or play. ▷ *v*
 5 observe, become aware of. **6** point

━━━━━━━━━━ **THESAURUS** ━━━━━━━━━━

nosegay *n* = **posy**, bouquet
nosey, nosy *adj* = **inquisitive**, curious,
 eavesdropping, interfering, intrusive,
 meddlesome, prying, snooping (*inf*)
nostalgia *n* = **reminiscence**,
 homesickness, longing, pining,
 regretfulness, remembrance,
 wistfulness, yearning
nostalgic *adj* = **sentimental**,
 emotional, homesick, longing,
 maudlin, regretful, wistful
nostrum *n* **1** = **panacea**, elixir
 2 = **medicine**, cure, drug, potion,
 remedy, treatment
notability *n* **2** = **fame**, celebrity,
 distinction, eminence, esteem, renown
notable *adj* **1** = **remarkable**,
 conspicuous, extraordinary,
 memorable, noteworthy,
 outstanding, rare, striking,
 uncommon, unusual ▷ *n*
 2 = **celebrity**, big name, dignitary,
 luminary, personage, V.I.P.
notably *adv* **1** = **particularly**,
 especially, outstandingly, strikingly
notation *n* **2** = **signs**, characters,
 code, script, symbols, system
notch *n* **1** = **cut**, cleft, incision,
 indentation, mark, nick, score **2** *Inf*
 = **level**, degree, grade, step ▷ *v*
 3 = **cut**, indent, mark, nick, score,
 scratch

notch up *v* = **register**, achieve, gain,
 make, score
note *n* **1, 2** = **message**, comment,
 communication, epistle, jotting,
 letter, memo, memorandum, minute,
 remark, reminder ▷ *v* **6** = **see**, notice,
 observe, perceive **7** = **mark**, denote,
 designate, indicate, record, register
 8 = **mention**, remark
notebook *n* = **jotter**, diary, exercise
 book, journal
noted *adj* = **famous**, acclaimed,
 celebrated, distinguished, eminent,
 illustrious, notable, prominent,
 renowned, well-known
noteworthy *adj* = **remarkable**,
 exceptional, extraordinary, important,
 notable, outstanding, significant,
 unusual
nothing *pron* **1** = **nothingness**,
 emptiness, nullity, void **3** = **nought**,
 nil, zero
nothingness *n* **1** = **oblivion**,
 nonbeing, nonexistence, nullity
 2 = **insignificance**, unimportance,
 worthlessness
notice *n* **1** = **interest**, cognizance,
 consideration, heed, note,
 observation, regard
 2 = **announcement**, advice,
 communication, instruction,
 intimation, news, notification, order,

n

out or remark upon. **noticeable** *adj*
easily seen or detected, appreciable.
noticeably *adv* **notice board** board
on which notices are displayed.
noticeable ❶ *adj* easily seen or
detected, appreciable.
notify ❶ *v* **-fying, -fied** inform.
notification *n* **notifiable** *adj* having
to be reported to the authorities.
notion ❶ *n* **1** idea or opinion. **2** whim.
notional *adj* speculative, imaginary,
or unreal.
notorious ❶ *adj* well known for
something bad. **notoriously** *adv*
notoriety *n*.
notwithstanding ❶ *prep* **1** in spite of.
▷ *adv* **2** nevertheless.
nougat *n* chewy sweet containing nuts
and fruit.
nought ❶ *n* **1** figure 0. **2** nothing.
noughties *informal* ▷ *pl n* decade from
2000 to 2009.
noun *n* word that refers to a person,
place, or thing.
nourish ❶ *v* **1** feed. **2** encourage or
foster (an idea or feeling).
nourishment *n* **nourishing** *adj*
providing the food necessary for life
and growth.

nous *n old-fashioned slang* common
sense.
nouveau riche [**noo**-voh **reesh**] *n, pl*
nouveaux riches [**noo**-voh **reesh**]
person who has recently become rich
and is regarded as vulgar.
nouvelle cuisine [**noo**-vell kwee-
zeen] *n* style of preparing and
presenting food with light sauces and
unusual combinations of flavours.
Nov. November.
nova *n, pl* **-vae, -vas** star that suddenly
becomes brighter and then gradually
decreases to its original brightness.
novel¹ ❶ *n* long fictitious story in book
form. **novelist** *n* writer of novels.
novelette *n* short novel, esp. one
regarded as trivial or sentimental.
novella *n, pl* **-las, -lae** short novel.
novel² ❶ *adj* fresh, new, or original.
novelty *n* **1** newness. **2** something
new or unusual. **3** cheap toy or
trinket.
November *n* eleventh month of the
year.
novena [no-**vee**-na] *n, pl* **-nas** *RC
Church* set of prayers or services on
nine consecutive days.
novice ❶ [**nov**-viss] *n* **1** beginner.

warning ▷ *v* **5** = **observe**, detect,
discern, distinguish, mark, note,
perceive, see, spot
noticeable *adj* = **obvious**, appreciable,
clear, conspicuous, evident, manifest,
perceptible, plain, striking
notification *n* = **announcement**,
advice, declaration, information,
intelligence, message, notice,
statement, warning
notify *v* = **inform**, advise, alert,
announce, declare, make known,
publish, tell, warn
notion *n* **1** = **idea**, belief, concept,
impression, inkling, opinion,
sentiment, view **2** = **whim**, caprice,
desire, fancy, impulse, inclination,
wish
notional *adj* = **speculative**, abstract,
conceptual, hypothetical, imaginary,
theoretical, unreal
notoriety *n* = **scandal**, dishonour,
disrepute, infamy, obloquy,
opprobrium
notorious *adj* = **infamous**,
dishonourable, disreputable,
opprobrious, scandalous
notoriously *adv* = **infamously**,

dishonourably, disreputably,
opprobriously, scandalously
notwithstanding *prep* **1** = **despite**, in
spite of
nought *n* **1** = **zero**, nil **2** = **nothing**, nil,
zero
nourish *v* **1** = **feed**, nurse, nurture,
supply, sustain, tend **2** = **encourage**,
comfort, cultivate, foster, maintain,
promote, support
nourishing *adj* = **nutritious**,
beneficial, nutritive, wholesome
nourishment *n* = **food**, nutriment,
nutrition, sustenance
novel¹ *n* = **story**, fiction, narrative,
romance, tale
novel² *adj* = **new**, different, fresh,
innovative, original, strange,
uncommon, unfamiliar, unusual
novelty *n* **1** = **newness**, freshness,
innovation, oddity, originality,
strangeness, surprise, unfamiliarity,
uniqueness **2** = **gimmick**, curiosity,
gadget **3** = **knick-knack**, bauble,
memento, souvenir, trifle, trinket
novice *n* **1** = **beginner**, amateur,
apprentice, learner, newcomer,
probationer, pupil, trainee

2 person who has entered a religious order but has not yet taken vows.

novitiate, noviciate n **1** period of being a novice. **2** part of a monastery or convent where the novices live.

now ❶ adv **1** at or for the present time. **2** immediately. ▷ conj **3** seeing that, since. **just now** very recently. **now and again, then** occasionally. **nowadays** adv in these times.

Nowell n same as NOEL.

nowhere adv not anywhere.

noxious ❶ adj **1** poisonous or harmful. **2** extremely unpleasant.

nozzle n projecting spout through which fluid is discharged.

Np Chemistry neptunium.

nr near.

NS Nova Scotia.

NSPCC National Society for the Prevention of Cruelty to Children.

NSW New South Wales.

NT 1 National Trust **2** New Testament **3** Northern Territory.

nuance ❶ [**new**-ahnss] n subtle difference in colour, meaning, or tone.

nub n point or gist (of a story etc.).

nubile ❶ [**new**-bile] adj (of a young woman) **1** sexually attractive. **2** old enough to get married.

nuclear adj **1** of nuclear weapons or energy. **2** of a nucleus, esp. the nucleus of an atom. **nuclear energy** energy released as a result of nuclear fission or fusion. **nuclear family** family consisting only of parents and their offspring. **nuclear fission** splitting of an atomic nucleus. **nuclear fusion** combination of two nuclei to form a heavier nucleus with the release of energy. **nuclear power** power produced by a nuclear reactor. **nuclear reaction** change in structure and energy content of an atomic nucleus by interaction with another nucleus or particle. **nuclear reactor** device in which a nuclear reaction is maintained and controlled to produce nuclear energy. **nuclear weapon** weapon whose force is due to uncontrolled nuclear fusion or fission. **nuclear winter** theoretical period of low temperatures and little light after a nuclear war.

nucleic acid n complex compound, such as DNA or RNA, found in all living cells.

nucleonics n branch of physics dealing with the applications of nuclear energy.

nucleus ❶ n, pl **-clei 1** centre, esp. of an atom or cell. **2** central thing around which others are grouped.

nude ❶ adj **1** naked. ▷ n **2** naked figure in painting, sculpture, or photography. **nudity** n **nudism** n practice of not wearing clothes. **nudist** n.

nudge ❶ v **1** push gently, esp. with the elbow. ▷ n **2** gentle push or touch.

nugatory [**new**-gat-tree] adj **1** of little value. **2** not valid.

nugget ❶ n **1** small lump of gold in its natural state. **2** something small but valuable. ▷ v **3** NZ & S Afr polish footwear.

nuisance ❶ n something or someone that causes annoyance or bother.

nuke slang ▷ v **1** attack with nuclear weapons. ▷ n **2** nuclear weapon.

n

now adv **1** = **nowadays**, any more, at the moment **2** = **immediately**, at once, instantly, promptly, straightaway **now and again** or **then** = **occasionally**, from time to time, infrequently, intermittently, on and off, sometimes, sporadically

nowadays adv = **now**, any more, at the moment, in this day and age, today

noxious adj **1** = **harmful**, deadly, destructive, foul, hurtful, injurious, poisonous, unhealthy, unwholesome

nuance n = **subtlety**, degree, distinction, gradation, nicety, refinement, shade, tinge

nubile adj **2** = **marriageable**, ripe (inf)

nucleus n **2** = **centre**, basis, core, focus, heart, kernel, nub, pivot

nude adj **1** = **naked**, bare, disrobed, stark-naked, stripped, unclad, unclothed, undressed, without a stitch on (inf)

nudge v, n = **push**, bump, dig, elbow, jog, poke, prod, shove, touch

nudity n = **nakedness**, bareness, deshabille, nudism, undress

nugget n = **lump**, chunk, clump, hunk, mass, piece

nuisance n = **problem**, annoyance, bother, drag (inf), hassle (inf), inconvenience, irritation, pain in the neck, pest, trouble

null ❶ *adj* **null and void** not legally valid. **nullity** *n* **nullify** *v* **-fying**, **-fied** **1** make ineffective. **2** cancel.

numb ❶ *adj* **1** without feeling, as through cold, shock, or fear. ▷ *v* **2** make numb. **numbly** *adv* **numbness** *n* **numbskull** *n* stupid person.

number ❶ *n* **1** sum or quantity. **2** word or symbol used to express a sum or quantity, numeral. **3** numeral or string of numerals used to identify a person or thing. **4** one of a series, such as a copy of a magazine. **5** song or piece of music. **6** group of people. **7** *Grammar* classification of words depending on how many persons or things are referred to. ▷ *v* **8** count. **9** give a number to. **10** amount to. **11** include in a group. **numberless** *adj* too many to be counted. **number crunching** *Computers* large-scale processing of numerical data. **number one** *informal* **1** oneself. **2** bestselling pop record in any one week. ▷ *adj* **3** first in importance or quality. **numberplate** *n* plate on a car showing the registration number.

numeral ❶ *n* word or symbol used to express a sum or quantity.

numerate *adj* able to do basic arithmetic. **numeracy** *n*.

numeration *n* act or process of numbering or counting.

numerator *n* *Maths* number above the line in a fraction.

numerical *adj* measured or expressed in numbers. **numerically** *adv*.

numerology *n* study of numbers and their supposed influence on human affairs.

numerous ❶ *adj* existing or happening in large numbers.

numinous *adj* **1** arousing religious or spiritual emotions. **2** mysterious or awe-inspiring.

numismatist *n* coin collector. **numismatics** *n* study or collection of coins. **numismatic** *adj*.

numskull *n* same as NUMBSKULL.

nun ❶ *n* female member of a religious order. **nunnery** *n*, *pl* **-neries** convent.

nuncio ❶ *n*, *pl* **-cios** *RC Church* pope's ambassador.

nuptial ❶ *adj* relating to marriage. **nuptials** *pl n* wedding.

nurse ❶ *n* **1** person employed to look after sick people, usu. in a hospital. **2** (also **nursemaid**, **nursery nurse**) woman employed to look after children. ▷ *v* **3** look after (a sick person). **4** breast-feed (a baby). **5** try to cure (an ailment). **6** harbour or foster (a feeling). **nursing home** private hospital or home for old people. **nursing officer** administrative head of the nursing staff of a hospital.

null *adj* **null and void** = **invalid**, inoperative, useless, valueless, void, worthless

nullify *v* = **invalidate**, counteract, negate, neutralize, obviate, render null and void ▷ *v* = **cancel**, veto

nullity *n* = **nonexistence**, invalidity, powerlessness, uselessness, worthlessness

numb *adj* **1** = **unfeeling**, benumbed, dead, deadened, frozen, immobilized, insensitive, paralysed, torpid ▷ *v* **2** = **deaden**, benumb, dull, freeze, immobilize, paralyse

number *n* **1** = **quantity**, aggregate, amount, collection **2** = **numeral**, character, digit, figure, integer **4** = **issue**, copy, edition, imprint, printing **6** = **throng**, collection, crowd, horde, multitude ▷ *v* **8** = **calculate**, account, add, compute, count, enumerate, include, reckon, total

numberless *adj* = **infinite**, countless,

endless, innumerable, multitudinous, myriad, unnumbered, untold

numbness *n* = **deadness**, dullness, insensitivity, paralysis, torpor

numbskull *n* = **fool**, blockhead, clot (*Brit inf*), dolt, dummy (*sl*), dunce, oaf, twit (*inf*)

numeral *n* = **number**, digit, figure, integer

numerous *adj* = **many**, abundant, copious, plentiful, profuse, several, thick on the ground

nuncio *n* *RC Church* = **ambassador**, envoy, legate, messenger

nunnery *n* = **convent**, abbey, cloister, house

nuptial *adj* = **marital**, bridal, conjugal, connubial, matrimonial

nuptials *pl n* = **wedding**, marriage, matrimony

nurse *v* **3** = **look after**, care for, minister to, tend, treat **4** = **breast-feed**, feed, nourish, nurture, suckle, wet-nurse **6** = **foster**, cherish,

nursery ❶ *n, pl* **-ries** **1** room where children sleep or play. **2** place where children are taken care of while their parents are at work. **3** place where plants are grown for sale.
nurseryman *n* person who raises plants for sale. **nursery rhyme** short traditional verse or song for children. **nursery school** school for children from 3 to 5 years old. **nursery slopes** gentle ski slopes for beginners.

nurture ❶ *n* **1** act or process of promoting the development of a child or young plant. ▷ *v* **2** promote or encourage the development of.

nut ❶ *n* **1** fruit consisting of a hard shell and a kernel. **2** small piece of metal that screws onto a bolt. **3** (also **nutcase**) *slang* insane or eccentric person. **4** *slang* head. **nuts** *adj slang* insane or eccentric. **nuts and bolts** *informal* essential or practical details. **nutshell** *n* **in a nutshell** in essence, briefly. **nutty** *adj* **-tier, -tiest** **1** containing or resembling nuts. **2** *slang* insane or eccentric. **nutter** *n slang* insane person. **nutcracker** *n* device for cracking the shells of nuts. **nuthatch** *n* small songbird. **nutmeg** *n* spice made from the seed of a tropical tree.

nutria [**new**-tree-a] *n* fur of the coypu.

nutrient [**new**-tree-ent] *n* substance that provides nourishment.

nutriment [**new**-tree-ment] *n* food or nourishment required by all living things to grow and stay healthy.

nutrition ❶ [new-**trish**-shun] *n* **1** process of taking in and absorbing nutrients. **2** process of being nourished. **3** study of nutrition. **nutritional** *adj* **nutritious, nutritive** *adj* nourishing.

nuzzle ❶ *v* push or rub gently with the nose or snout.

NV Nevada.

NW northwest(ern).

NWT Northwest Territories.

NY New York.

nylon *n* **1** synthetic material used for clothing etc. ▷ *pl* **2** stockings made of nylon.

nymph ❶ *n* **1** mythical spirit of nature, represented as a beautiful young woman. **2** larva of certain insects, resembling the adult form.

nymphet *n* sexually precocious young girl.

nymphomaniac *n* woman with an abnormally intense sexual desire. **nymphomania** *n* abnormally intense sexual desire in women.

NZ New Zealand.

n

———————— THESAURUS ————————

cultivate, encourage, harbour, preserve, promote, succour, support
nursery *n* **2** = **crèche**, kindergarten, playgroup
nurture *n* **1** = **development**, discipline, education, instruction, rearing, training, upbringing ▷ *v* **2** = **develop**, bring up, discipline, educate, instruct, rear, school, train
nut *n* **3** (also **nutcase**) *Sl* = **madman**, crank (*inf*), lunatic, maniac, nutcase

(*sl*), psycho (*sl*) **4** *Sl* = **head**, brain, mind, reason, senses
nutrition *n* **1, 2** = **food**, nourishment, nutriment, sustenance
nutritious *adj* = **nourishing**, beneficial, health-giving, invigorating, nutritive, strengthening, wholesome
nuzzle *v* = **snuggle**, burrow, cuddle, fondle, nestle, pet
nymph *n* **1** = **sylph**, dryad, naiad

O¹ 1 *Chemistry* oxygen. **2** Old. **3** same as
NOUGHT (sense 1).

O² *interj* same as OH.

o' *prep informal* of, e.g. *a cup o' tea*.

oaf *n* stupid or clumsy person. **oafish**
adj.

oak *n* **1** deciduous forest tree. **2** its
wood, used for furniture. **oaken** *adj*
oak apple brownish lump found on
oak trees.

oakum *n* fibre obtained by unravelling
old rope.

OAP old-age pensioner.

oar *n* pole with a broad blade, used
for rowing a boat. **oarsman**,
oarswoman *n*.

oasis *n, pl* **-ses** fertile area in a desert.

oast *n* oven for drying hops. **oast
house** building containing oasts.

oat *n* **1** hard cereal grown as food. ▷ *pl*
2 grain of this cereal. **sow one's wild
oats** have many sexual relationships
when young. **oaten** *adj* **oatcake** *n* thin
flat biscuit of oatmeal. **oatmeal** *n*

1 coarse flour made from oats. ▷ *adj*
2 pale brownish-cream.

oath ❶ *n* **1** solemn promise, esp. to be
truthful in court. **2** swearword.

obbligato [ob-lig-**gah**-toe] *n, pl* **-tos**
Music essential part or
accompaniment.

obdurate ❶ *adj* hardhearted or
stubborn. **obduracy** *n*.

OBE Officer of the Order of the British
Empire.

obedient ❶ *adj* obeying or willing to
obey. **obedience** *n* **obediently** *adv*.

obeisance [oh-**bay**-sanss] *n* **1** attitude
of respect. **2** bow or curtsy.

obelisk ❶ [ob-**bill**-isk] *n* four-sided
stone column tapering to a pyramid at
the top.

obese ❶ [oh-**beess**] *adj* very fat.
obesity *n*.

obey ❶ *v* carry out instructions or orders.

obfuscate ❶ *v* make (something)
confusing. **obfuscation** *n*.

obituary *n, pl* **-aries** announcement of
someone's death, esp. in a newspaper.
obituarist *n*.

object¹ ❶ *n* **1** physical thing. **2** focus of
thoughts or action. **3** aim or purpose.
4 *Grammar* word that a verb or
preposition affects. **no object** not a
hindrance.

object² ❶ *v* express disapproval.
objection *n* **objectionable** *adj*
unpleasant. **objector** *n*.

—————————————————————— THESAURUS ———————————

oaf *n* = **dolt**, blockhead, clod, dunce,
fool, goon, idiot, lout, moron,
numbskull *or* numskull

oafish *adj* = **stupid**, dense, dim-witted
(*inf*), doltish, dumb (*inf*), loutish,
moronic, thick

oath *n* **1** = **promise**, affirmation,
avowal, bond, pledge, vow, word
2 = **swearword**, blasphemy, curse,
expletive, profanity

obdurate *adj* = **stubborn**, dogged,
hard-hearted, immovable, implacable,
inflexible, obstinate, pig-headed,
unyielding

obedience *n* = **submissiveness**,
acquiescence, compliance, docility,
observance, respect, reverence,
subservience

obedient *adj* = **submissive**,
acquiescent, biddable, compliant,
deferential, docile, dutiful, respectful,
subservient, well-trained

obelisk *n* = **column**, monolith,

monument, needle, pillar, shaft

obese *adj* = **fat**, corpulent, gross, heavy,
overweight, paunchy, plump, portly,
rotund, stout, tubby

obesity *n* = **fatness**, bulk, corpulence,
grossness, portliness, stoutness,
tubbiness

obey *v* = **carry out**, abide by, act upon,
adhere to, comply, conform, follow,
heed, keep, observe

obfuscate *v* = **confuse**, befog, cloud,
darken, muddy the waters, obscure,
perplex

object¹ *n* **1** = **thing**, article, body,
entity, item, phenomenon **2** = **target**,
focus, recipient, victim **3** = **purpose**,
aim, design, end, goal, idea, intention,
objective, point

object² *v* = **protest**, argue against,
demur, draw the line (at something),
expostulate, oppose, take exception

objection *n* = **protest**, counter-
argument, demur, doubt, opposition,

objective ❶ n **1** aim or purpose. ▷ adj
2 not biased. **3** existing in the real
world outside the human mind.
objectively adv **objectivity** n.

objet d'art [**ob**-zhay **dahr**] n, pl **objets
d'art** small object of artistic value.

oblation n religious offering.

oblige ❶ v **1** compel (someone) morally
or by law to do something. **2** do a
favour for (someone). **obliging** adj
ready to help other people. **obligingly**
adv **obligated** adj obliged to do
something. **obligation** n **1** duty.
2 indebtedness for a favour.
obligatory adj required by a rule or
law.

oblique ❶ [oh-**bleak**] adj **1** slanting.
2 indirect. ▷ n **3** the symbol (/).
obliquely adv **oblique angle** angle

that is not a right angle.

obliterate ❶ v wipe out, destroy.
obliteration n.

oblivious ❶ adj unaware. **oblivion** n
1 state of being forgotten. **2** state of
being unaware or unconscious.

oblong adj **1** having two long sides,
two short sides, and four right angles.
▷ n **2** oblong figure.

obloquy ❶ [**ob**-lock-wee] n, pl **-quies**
1 verbal abuse. **2** discredit.

obnoxious ❶ adj offensive.
obnoxiousness n.

oboe n double-reeded woodwind
instrument. **oboist** n.

obscene ❶ adj **1** portraying sex
offensively. **2** disgusting. **obscenity** n.

obscure ❶ adj **1** not well known.
2 hard to understand. **3** indistinct. ▷ v

——————— THESAURUS ———————

remonstrance, scruple
objectionable adj = **unpleasant**,
deplorable, disagreeable, intolerable,
obnoxious, offensive, regrettable,
repugnant, unseemly
objective n **1** = **purpose**, aim,
ambition, end, goal, intention, mark,
object, target ▷ adj **2** = **unbiased**,
detached, disinterested,
dispassionate, even-handed, fair,
impartial, impersonal, open-minded,
unprejudiced
objectively adv **2** = **impartially**,
disinterestedly, dispassionately,
even-handedly, with an open mind
objectivity n **2** = **impartiality**,
detachment, disinterestedness,
dispassion
obligation n **1** = **duty**, accountability,
burden, charge, compulsion, liability,
requirement, responsibility
obligatory adj = **compulsory**, binding,
de rigueur, essential, imperative,
mandatory, necessary, required,
requisite, unavoidable
oblige v **1** = **compel**, bind, constrain,
force, impel, make, necessitate,
require **2** = **do (someone) a favour** or
a kindness, accommodate, benefit,
gratify, indulge, please
obliging adj = **cooperative**,
accommodating, agreeable,
considerate, good-natured, helpful,
kind, polite, willing
oblique adj **1** = **slanting**, angled,
aslant, sloping, tilted **2** = **indirect**,
backhanded, circuitous, implied,
roundabout, sidelong

obliterate v = **destroy**, annihilate, blot
out, efface, eradicate, erase, expunge,
extirpate, root out, wipe out
obliteration n = **annihilation**,
elimination, eradication, extirpation,
wiping out
oblivion n **1** = **neglect**, abeyance,
disregard, forgetfulness
2 = **unconsciousness**, insensibility,
obliviousness, unawareness
oblivious adj = **unaware**, forgetful,
heedless, ignorant, insensible,
neglectful, negligent, regardless,
unconcerned, unconscious, unmindful
obloquy n **1** = **abuse**, aspersion,
attack, blame, censure, criticism,
invective, reproach, slander,
vilification **2** = **disgrace**, discredit,
dishonour, humiliation, ignominy,
infamy, shame, stigma
obnoxious adj = **offensive**,
disagreeable, insufferable, loathsome,
nasty, nauseating, objectionable,
odious, repulsive, revolting, unpleasant
obscene adj **1** = **indecent**, dirty, filthy,
immoral, improper, lewd, offensive,
pornographic, salacious, scungy (Aust
& NZ inf) **2** = **disgusting**, atrocious,
evil, heinous, loathsome, outrageous,
shocking, sickening, vile, wicked
obscenity n **1** = **indecency**,
coarseness, dirtiness, impropriety,
lewdness, licentiousness,
pornography, smut **2** = **atrocity**,
abomination, affront, blight, evil,
offence, outrage, wrong
obscure adj **1** = **little-known**, humble,
lowly, out-of-the-way, remote,

4 make (something) obscure.
obscurity n.
obsequies [**ob**-sick-weez] pl n funeral
rites.
obsequious ❶ [ob-**seek**-wee-uss] adj
overattentive in order to gain favour.
obsequiousness n.
observe ❶ v **1** see or notice. **2** watch
(someone or something) carefully.
3 remark. **4** act according to (a law or
custom). **observation** n **1** action or
habit of observing. **2** remark.
3 detailed examination of something
before analysis, diagnosis, or
interpretation, e.g. *you may be admitted
to hospital for observation*. **4** facts
learned from observing. **5** ability to
notice things, e.g. *she has good powers
of observation*. **observer** n **observable**
adj **observance** n **1** observing of a

custom. **2** ritual or ceremony.
observant adj quick to notice things.
observatory n building equipped for
studying the weather and the stars.
obsess ❶ v preoccupy (someone)
compulsively. **obsessed** adj **obsessive**
adj **obsession** n **obsessional** adj.
obsidian n dark glassy volcanic rock.
obsolete ❶ adj no longer in use; out of
date. **obsolescent** adj becoming
obsolete. **obsolescence** n.
obstacle ❶ n something that makes
progress difficult.
obstetrics n branch of medicine
concerned with pregnancy and
childbirth. **obstetric** adj **obstetrician**
n doctor who specializes in obstetrics.
obstinate ❶ adj **1** stubborn. **2** difficult
to remove or change. **obstinately** adv
obstinacy n.

——————————————————————————— THESAURUS ———————————————————————————

undistinguished, unheard-of,
unknown **2** = **vague**, ambiguous,
arcane, confusing, cryptic, enigmatic,
esoteric, mysterious, opaque,
recondite, unclear **3** = **dark**, blurred,
cloudy, dim, faint, gloomy, indistinct,
murky, shadowy ▷ v **4** = **conceal**,
cover, disguise, hide, obfuscate,
screen, veil
obscurity n **1** = **insignificance**,
lowliness, unimportance
3 = **darkness**, dimness, dusk, gloom,
haze, shadows
obsequious adj = **sycophantic**,
cringing, deferential, fawning,
flattering, grovelling, ingratiating,
servile, submissive, unctuous
observable adj **1** = **noticeable**,
apparent, detectable, discernible,
evident, obvious, perceptible,
recognizable, visible
observance n **1** = **carrying out**,
compliance, fulfilment, honouring,
performance
observant adj = **attentive**, alert,
eagle-eyed, perceptive, quick, sharp-
eyed, vigilant, watchful, wide-awake
observation n **1** = **study**,
examination, inspection, monitoring,
review, scrutiny, surveillance,
watching **2** = **comment**, note,
opinion, pronouncement, reflection,
remark, thought, utterance
observe v **1** = **see**, detect, discern,
discover, note, notice, perceive, spot,
witness **2** = **watch**, check, keep an
eye on (inf), keep track of, look at,

monitor, scrutinize, study, survey,
view **3** = **remark**, comment, mention,
note, opine, say, state **4** = **carry out**,
abide by, adhere to, comply, conform
to, follow, heed, honour, keep, obey,
respect
observer n **1, 2** = **spectator**, beholder,
bystander, eyewitness, fly on the wall,
looker-on, onlooker, viewer, watcher,
witness
obsessed adj = **preoccupied**,
dominated, gripped, haunted, hung
up on (sl), infatuated, troubled
obsession n = **preoccupation**,
complex, fetish, fixation, hang-up
(inf), infatuation, mania, phobia,
thing (inf)
obsessive adj = **compulsive**,
besetting, consuming, gripping,
haunting
obsolescent adj = **becoming
obsolete**, ageing, declining, dying
out, on the wane, on the way out, past
its prime, waning
obsolete adj = **out of date**, antiquated,
archaic, discarded, disused, extinct,
old, old-fashioned, outmoded, passé
obstacle n = **difficulty**, bar, barrier,
block, hindrance, hitch, hurdle,
impediment, obstruction, snag,
stumbling block
obstinacy n **1** = **stubbornness**,
doggedness, inflexibility,
intransigence, obduracy, persistence,
pig-headedness, tenacity, wilfulness
obstinate adj **1** = **stubborn**,
determined, dogged, inflexible,

obstreperous ❶ *adj* unruly, noisy.

obstruct ❶ *v* 1 block with an obstacle. 2 make (progress) difficult. **obstruction** *n* **obstructive** *adj*.

obtain ❶ *v* 1 acquire intentionally. 2 be customary. **obtainable** *adj*.

obtrude ❶ *v* push oneself or one's ideas on others. **obtrusion** *n* **obtrusive** *adj* unpleasantly noticeable. **obtrusively** *adv*.

obtuse ❶ *adj* 1 mentally slow. 2 *Maths* (of an angle) between 90° and 180° 3 not pointed. **obtuseness** *n*.

obverse *n* 1 opposite way of looking at an idea. 2 main side of a coin or medal.

obviate ❶ *v* make unnecessary.

obvious ❶ *adj* easy to see or understand, evident. **obviously** *adv*.

ocarina *n* small oval wind instrument.

occasion ❶ *n* 1 time at which a particular thing happens. 2 reason, e.g. *no occasion for complaint*. 3 special event. ▷ *v* 4 cause. **occasional** *adj* happening sometimes. **occasionally** *adv*.

SPELLING TIP

● The commonest misspelling of
● **occasion** is *occassion*, with 44
● occurrences in the Bank of English.
● There are also examples of *ocasion*
● and *ocassion*. The correct spelling
● has two *c*s and one *s*.

Occident *n lit* the West. **Occidental** *adj*.

occiput [**ox**-sip-put] *n Anat* back of the head or skull.

occlude *v* 1 obstruct. 2 close off. **occlusion** *n* **occluded front** *Meteorology* front formed when a cold front overtakes a warm front and warm air rises.

occult ❶ *adj* 1 relating to the supernatural. 2 beyond ordinary human understanding. 3 secret or mysterious. **the occult** knowledge or study of the supernatural.

occupant ❶ *n* person occupying a specified place. **occupancy** *n* (length of) a person's stay in a specified place.

THESAURUS

intractable, intransigent, pig-headed, refractory, self-willed, strong-minded, wilful

obstreperous *adj* = **unruly**, disorderly, loud, noisy, riotous, rowdy, turbulent, unmanageable, wild

obstruct *v* 1 = **block**, bar, barricade 2 = **impede**, check, hamper, hinder, restrict, stop, thwart

obstruction *n* 1 = **obstacle**, bar, barricade, barrier, blockage 2 = **difficulty**, hindrance, impediment

obstructive *adj* 1 = **blocking** 2 = **unhelpful**, awkward, delaying, difficult, hindering, restrictive, stalling, uncooperative

obtain *v* 1 = **get**, achieve, acquire, attain, earn, gain, land, procure, secure 2 = **exist**, be in force, be prevalent, be the case, hold, prevail

obtainable *adj* 1 = **available**, achievable, attainable, on tap (*inf*), to be had

obtrusive *adj* = **noticeable**, blatant, obvious, prominent, protruding, protuberant, sticking out

obtuse *adj* 1 = **stupid**, dense, dull, dumb (*inf*), slow, stolid, thick, uncomprehending

obviate *v* = **preclude**, avert, prevent, remove

obvious *adj* = **evident**, apparent, clear,

conspicuous, distinct, indisputable, manifest, noticeable, plain, self-evident, undeniable, unmistakable

obviously *adv* = **clearly**, manifestly, of course, palpably, patently, plainly, undeniably, unmistakably, unquestionably, without doubt

occasion *n* 1 = **time**, instance, moment, occurrence, point, stage 2 = **reason**, call, cause, excuse, ground(s), justification, motive, prompting, provocation 3 = **event**, affair, celebration, experience, happening, occurrence ▷ *v* 4 = **cause**, bring about, engender, generate, give rise to, induce, inspire, lead to, produce, prompt, provoke

occasional *adj* = **infrequent**, incidental, intermittent, irregular, odd, rare, sporadic, uncommon

occasionally *adv* = **sometimes**, at times, from time to time, irregularly, now and again, once in a while, periodically

occult *adj* = **supernatural**, arcane, esoteric, magical, mysterious, mystical

occupancy *n* = **tenancy**, possession, residence, tenure, use

occupant *n* = **inhabitant**, incumbent, indweller, inmate, lessee, occupier, resident, tenant

O

occupation ❶ *n* **1** profession.
2 activity that occupies one's time.
3 control of a country by a foreign
military power. **4** being occupied.
occupational *adj* **occupational
hazard** unpleasant thing that occurs
due to one's job. **occupational
therapy** purposeful activities,
designed to aid recovery from
illness etc.

occupy ❶ *v* **-pying, -pied 1** live or work
in (a building). **2** take up the attention
of (someone). **3** take up (space or
time). **4** take possession of (a place)
by force. **5** hold (an office or position).
occupant *n* **occupation** *n* profession.
occupier *n*.

occur ❶ *v* **-curring, -curred 1** happen.
2 exist. **occur to** come to the mind of.
occurrence *n* **1** something that
occurs. **2** fact of occurring.

● **SPELLING TIP**
● Rather surprisingly, there are no
● examples in the Bank of English
● where **occurrence** has been spelt
● with only one *c*. However, there are
● 85 examples of *occurence*, with only
● one *r*, as opposed to 2013 instances
● where the word is spelt correctly:
● **occurrence**.

ocean *n* **1** vast area of sea between
continents. **2** large quantity or
expanse. **oceanic** *adj* **oceanography**
n scientific study of the oceans.
oceanographer *n* **ocean-going** *adj*
able to sail on the open sea.

ocelot [**oss**-ill-lot] *n* American wild cat
with a spotted coat.

oche [**ok**-kee] *n Darts* mark on the floor
behind which a player must stand.

ochre [**oak**-er] *adj, n* brownish-yellow
(earth).

o'clock *adv* used after a number to
specify an hour.

Oct. October.

octagon *n* geometric figure with eight
sides. **octagonal** *adj*.

octahedron [ok-ta-**heed**-ron] *n, pl*
-drons, -dra three-dimensional
geometric figure with eight faces.

octane *n* hydrocarbon found in petrol.
octane rating measure of petrol
quality.

octave *n Music* (interval between the
first and) eighth note of a scale.

octavo *n, pl* **-vos** book size in which the
sheets are folded into eight leaves.

octet *n* **1** group of eight performers.
2 music for such a group.

October *n* tenth month of the year.

octogenarian *n* person aged between
eighty and eighty-nine.

octopus *n, pl* **-puses** sea creature with
a soft body and eight tentacles.

ocular *adj* relating to the eyes or sight.

OD *informal* ▷ *n* **1** overdose. ▷ *v* **OD'ing,
OD'd 2** take an overdose.

odd ❶ *adj* **1** unusual. **2** occasional.
3 leftover or additional. **4** not divisible
by two. **5** not part of a set. **odds** *pl n*
1 (ratio showing) the probability of
something happening. **2** likelihood.
at odds in conflict. **odds and ends**
small miscellaneous items. **oddity** *n*
odd person or thing. **oddly** *adv*
oddness *n* quality of being odd.

THESAURUS

occupation *n* **1** = **profession**,
business, calling, employment, job,
line (of work), pursuit, trade, vocation,
walk of life **3** = **invasion**, conquest,
seizure, subjugation

occupied *adj* **1** = **inhabited**, lived-in,
peopled, settled, tenanted **2** = **busy**,
employed, engaged, working **3** = **in
use**, engaged, full, taken, unavailable

occupy *v* **1** = **live in**, dwell in, inhabit,
own, possess, reside in **2** = **take up**,
divert, employ, engage, engross,
involve, monopolize, preoccupy, tie up
3 = **fill**, cover, permeate, pervade, take
up **4** = **invade**, capture, overrun,
seize, take over

occur *v* **1** = **happen**, befall, come
about, crop up (*inf*), take place, turn
up (*inf*) **2** = **exist**, appear, be found, be

present, develop, manifest itself, show
itself **occur to** = **come to mind**, cross
one's mind, dawn on, enter one's
head, spring to mind, strike one,
suggest itself

occurrence *n* **1** = **incident**, adventure,
affair, circumstance, episode, event,
happening, instance **2** = **existence**,
appearance, development,
manifestation, materialization

odd *adj* **1** = **unusual**, bizarre,
extraordinary, freakish, irregular,
munted (*NZ sl*), peculiar, rare,
remarkable, singular, strange
2 = **occasional**, casual, incidental,
irregular, periodic, random, sundry,
various **3** = **spare**, leftover, remaining,
solitary, surplus **5** = **unmatched**,
unpaired

oddball n informal eccentric person.
oddments pl n things left over.
ode n lyric poem, usu. addressed to a particular subject.
odium ❶ [**oh**-dee-um] n widespread dislike. **odious** adj offensive.
odour ❶ n particular smell. **odorous** adj **odourless** adj.
odyssey [**odd**-iss-ee] n long eventful journey.
OECD Organization for Economic Cooperation and Development.
oedema [id-**deem**-a] n, pl -**mata** Medical abnormal swelling.
o'er prep, adv poetic over.
oesophagus [ee-**soff**-a-guss] n, pl -**gi** passage between the mouth and stomach.
oestrogen [**ee**-stra-jen] n female hormone that controls the reproductive cycle.
of prep **1** belonging to. **2** consisting of. **3** connected with. **4** characteristic of.
off ❶ prep **1** away from. ▷ adv **2** away. **3** so as to stop or disengage. ▷ adj

4 not operating. **5** cancelled. **6** not up to the usual standard. **7** (of food) gone bad. ▷ n **8** Cricket side of the field to which the batsman's feet point.
offbeat adj unusual or eccentric. **off chance** slight possibility. **off colour** slightly ill. **offline 1** disconnected from a computer or the internet. ▷ adv **2** while not connected to a computer or the internet. **off-message** adj (esp. of a politician) not following the official Party line. **off-putting** adj rather unpleasant or disturbing.
offal n edible organs of an animal, such as liver or kidneys.
offcut n piece remaining after the required parts have been cut out.
offend ❶ v **1** hurt the feelings of, insult. **2** disgust. **3** commit a crime. **offender** n **offence** n **1** (cause of) hurt feelings or annoyance. **2** illegal act. **offensive** adj **1** disagreeable. **2** insulting. **3** aggressive. ▷ n **4** position or action of attack.

THESAURUS

oddity n **a** = **misfit**, crank (inf), maverick, oddball (inf) **b** = **irregularity**, abnormality, anomaly, eccentricity, freak, idiosyncrasy, peculiarity, quirk
oddments pl n = **leftovers**, bits, fag ends, fragments, offcuts, remnants, scraps, snippets
odds pl n **1** = **probability 2** = **chances**, likelihood **at odds** = **in conflict**, at daggers drawn, at loggerheads, at sixes and sevens, at variance, out of line
odds and ends pl n = **scraps**, bits, bits and pieces, debris, oddments, remnants
odious adj = **offensive**, detestable, horrid, loathsome, obnoxious, repulsive, revolting, unpleasant
odour n = **smell**, aroma, bouquet, essence, fragrance, perfume, redolence, scent, stench, stink
odyssey n = **journey**, crusade, pilgrimage, quest, trek, voyage
off adv **2** = **away**, apart, aside, elsewhere, out ▷ adj **5** = **cancelled**, finished, gone, postponed, unavailable **7** = **bad**, mouldy, rancid, rotten, sour, turned
offbeat adj = **unusual**, eccentric, left-field (inf), novel, outré, strange, unconventional, unorthodox, way-out (inf)

off colour adj = **ill**, crook (Aust & NZ sl), out of sorts, peaky, poorly (inf), queasy, run down, sick, under the weather (inf), unwell
offence n **1 a** = **insult**, affront, hurt, indignity, injustice, outrage, slight, snub **b** = **annoyance**, anger, displeasure, indignation, pique, resentment, umbrage, wrath **2** = **crime**, fault, misdeed, misdemeanour, sin, transgression, trespass, wrongdoing
offend v **1** = **insult**, affront, annoy, displease, hurt (someone's) feelings, outrage, slight, snub, upset, wound
offended adj **1** = **resentful**, affronted, disgruntled, displeased, outraged, piqued, put out (inf), smarting, stung, upset
offender n **3** = **criminal**, crook, culprit, delinquent, lawbreaker, miscreant, sinner, transgressor, villain, wrongdoer
offensive adj **1** = **disgusting**, disagreeable, nauseating, obnoxious, odious, repellent, revolting, unpleasant, vile **2** = **insulting**, abusive, discourteous, disrespectful, impertinent, insolent, objectionable, rude **3** = **attacking**, aggressive, invading ▷ n **4** = **attack**, campaign, drive, onslaught, push (inf)

o

offer ❶ v **1** present (something) for acceptance or rejection. **2** provide. **3** be willing (to do something). **4** present for sale. **5** propose as payment. ▷ n **6** something offered. **7** instance of offering something. **offering** n thing offered. **offertory** n Christianity **1** offering of the bread and wine for Communion. **2** collection of money at Communion.

offhand ❶ adj **1** (also **offhanded**) casual, curt. ▷ adv **2** without preparation.

office ❶ n **1** room or building where people work at desks. **2** department of a commercial organization. **3** formal position of responsibility. **4** place where tickets or information can be obtained. **5** religious ceremony. **officer** n **1** person in authority in the armed services. **2** member of the police force. **3** person with special responsibility in an organization.

official ❶ adj **1** of a position of authority. **2** approved or arranged by someone in authority. **3** formal. ▷ n **4** person who holds a position of authority. **officially** adv **officialdom** n officials collectively. **Official Receiver** person who deals with the affairs of a bankrupt company.

officiate ❶ v act in an official role.

officious ❶ adj interfering unnecessarily.

offing ❶ n area of the sea visible from the shore. **in the offing** likely to happen soon.

off-licence n shop licensed to sell alcohol for drinking elsewhere.

off-load v get rid of (something).

offset ❶ v cancel out, compensate for.

offshoot ❶ n **1** something developed from something else. **2** shoot growing on the main stem of a plant.

offside adj, adv Sport (positioned) illegally ahead of the ball.

offspring ❶ n, pl **offspring** child.

often ❶ adv frequently, much of the time. **oft** adv poetic often.

ogle ❶ v stare at (someone) lustfully.

ogre ❶ n **1** giant that eats human flesh. **2** monstrous or cruel person.

oh interj exclamation of surprise, pain, etc.

OH Ohio.

ohm n unit of electrical resistance.

OHMS On Her or His Majesty's Service.

oil ❶ n **1** viscous liquid, insoluble in water and usu. flammable. **2** same as

——————————————— THESAURUS ———————

o

offer v **1** = **propose**, advance, submit, suggest **2** = **provide**, afford, furnish, present **3** = **volunteer**, come forward, offer one's services **5** = **proffer**, bid, tender ▷ n **6** = **proposal**, bid, tender **7** = **suggestion**, proposition, submission

offering n = **contribution**, donation, gift, hand-out, present, sacrifice, subscription

offhand adj **1** (also **offhanded**) = **casual**, aloof, brusque, careless, curt, glib ▷ adv **2** = **impromptu**, ad lib, extempore, off the cuff (inf)

office n **3** = **post**, function, occupation, place, responsibility, role, situation

officer n **3** = **official**, agent, appointee, executive, functionary, office-holder, representative

official adj **2** = **authorized**, accredited, authentic, certified, legitimate, licensed, sanctioned **3** = **formal**, proper ▷ n **4** = **officer**, agent, bureaucrat, executive, functionary, office bearer, representative

officiate v = **preside**, chair, conduct, manage, oversee, serve, superintend

officious adj = **interfering**, dictatorial, intrusive, meddlesome, obtrusive, overzealous, pushy (inf), self-important

offing n in the offing = **imminent**, in prospect, on the horizon, upcoming

off-putting adj = **discouraging**, daunting, disconcerting, dispiriting, disturbing, formidable, intimidating, unnerving, unsettling

offset v = **cancel out**, balance out, compensate for, counteract, counterbalance, make up for, neutralize

offshoot n **1** = **by-product**, adjunct, appendage, development, spin-off

offspring n a = **child**, descendant, heir, scion, successor ▷ pl n b = **children**, brood, descendants, family, heirs, issue, progeny, young

often adv = **frequently**, generally, repeatedly, time and again

ogle v = **leer**, eye up (inf)

ogre n **1** = **giant 2** = **monster**, bogeyman, bugbear, demon, devil, spectre

oil v **5** = **lubricate**, grease

PETROLEUM. **3** petroleum derivative, used as a fuel or lubricant. ▷ *pl* **4** oil-based paints used in art. ▷ *v* **5** lubricate (a machine) with oil. **oily** *adj* **oilcloth** *n* waterproof material. **oilfield** *n* area containing oil reserves. **oil rig** platform constructed for drilling oil wells. **oilskin** *n* (garment made from) waterproof material. **oil well** well bored into the earth or sea bed to a supply of oil.

ointment ❶ *n* greasy substance used for healing skin or as a cosmetic.

OK Oklahoma.

O.K., okay ❶ *informal* ▷ *interj* **1** expression of approval. ▷ *adj, adv* **2** in satisfactory condition. ▷ *v* **3** approve (something). ▷ *n* **4** approval.

okapi [ok-**kah**-pee] *n* African animal related to the giraffe but with a shorter neck.

okra *n* tropical plant with edible green pods.

old ❶ *adj* **1** having lived or existed for a long time. **2** of a specified age, e.g. *two years old.* **3** former. **olden** *adj* old, e.g. *in the olden days.* **oldie** *n informal* old but popular song or film. **old age pensioner** retired person receiving an allowance from the government. **old boy, girl** former pupil of a school. **old-fashioned** *adj* no longer commonly used or valued. **old guard** group of people in an organization who have traditional values. **old hand** skilled and experienced person. **old hat** boring because so familiar. **old maid** elderly unmarried woman. **old master** European painter or painting from the period 1500–1800. **Old**

Nick *informal* the Devil. **old school tie** system of mutual help between former pupils of public schools. **Old Testament** part of the Bible recording Hebrew history. **Old World** world as it was known before the discovery of the Americas.

oleaginous [ol-lee-**aj**-in-uss] *adj* oily, producing oil.

oleander [ol-lee-**ann**-der] *n* Mediterranean flowering evergreen shrub.

olfactory *adj* relating to the sense of smell.

oligarchy [**ol**-lee-gark-ee] *n, pl* **-chies 1** government by a small group of people. **2** state governed this way. **oligarchic**, **oligarchical** *adj*.

olive *n* **1** small green or black fruit used as food or pressed for its oil. **2** tree on which this fruit grows. ▷ *adj* **3** greyish-green. **olive branch** peace offering.

Olympic Games *pl n* four-yearly international sports competition. **Olympic** *adj*.

OM Order of Merit.

ombudsman *n* official who investigates complaints against government organizations.

omega *n* last letter in the Greek alphabet.

omelette *n* dish of eggs beaten and fried.

● **SPELLING TIP**
● You don't hear it in the
● pronunciation, but there is an *e*
● after the *m* in **omelette**.

omen ❶ *n* happening or object thought to foretell success or misfortune. **ominous** *adj* worrying, seeming to foretell misfortune.

THESAURUS

oily *adj* = **greasy**, fatty, oleaginous
ointment *n* = **lotion**, balm, cream, embrocation, emollient, liniment, salve, unguent
O.K., okay *Inf interj* **1** = **all right**, agreed, right, roger, very good, very well, ya (*S Afr*), yebo (*S Afr inf*), yes ▷ *adj, adv* **2** = **fine**, acceptable, adequate, all right, good, in order, permitted, satisfactory, up to scratch (*inf*) ▷ *v* **3** = **approve**, agree to, authorize, endorse, give the green light, rubber-stamp (*inf*), sanction ▷ *n* **4** = **approval**, agreement, assent, authorization, consent, go-ahead (*inf*), green light, permission,

sanction, say-so (*inf*), seal of approval
old *adj* **1** = **aged**, ancient, antediluvian, antiquated, antique, decrepit, elderly, mature, senile, timeworn, venerable **3** = **former**, earlier, erstwhile, one-time, previous
old-fashioned *adj* = **out of date**, behind the times, dated, obsolescent, obsolete, old hat, outdated, outmoded, passé, unfashionable
omen *n* = **sign**, foreboding, indication, portent, premonition, presage, warning
ominous *adj* = **threatening**, fateful, foreboding, inauspicious, portentous, sinister, unpromising, unpropitious

omit ❶ v **omitting, omitted 1** leave out. **2** neglect (to do something). **omission** n **1** something that has been left out or passed over. **2** an act of missing out or failing to do something, e.g. *we regret the omission of these and the names of other fine artists.*

omnibus n **1** several books or TV or radio programmes made into one. **2** *old-fashioned* bus.

omnipotent ❶ [om-**nip**-a-tent] adj having unlimited power. **omnipotence** n.

omnipresent adj present everywhere. **omnipresence** n.

omniscient ❶ [om-**niss**-ee-ent] adj knowing or seeming to know everything. **omniscience** n.

omnivorous [om-**niv**-vor-uss] adj **1** eating food obtained from both animals and plants. **2** taking in everything indiscriminately. **omnivore** n animal that eats any type of food.

on prep **1** indicating position above, attachment, closeness, etc. e.g. *lying on the ground; a puppet on a string; on the coast.* ▷ adv **2** in operation. **3** attached to or in contact with. **4** continuing. **5** forwards. ▷ adj **6** operating. **7** taking place. ▷ n **8** *Cricket* side of the field on which the batsman stands. **online** adj **1** connected to a computer or the internet. ▷ adj **2** while connected to a computer or the internet. **on-message** adj (esp. of a politician) following the official Party line.

ON Ontario.

ONC Ordinary National Certificate.

once ❶ adv **1** on one occasion.

2 formerly. ▷ conj **3** as soon as. ▷ n **4** one occasion. **at once 1** immediately. **2** simultaneously. **once-over** n *informal* quick examination.

oncogene [**on**-koh-jean] n gene that can cause cancer when abnormally activated.

oncoming ❶ adj approaching from the front.

OND Ordinary National Diploma.

one ❶ adj **1** single, lone. **2** only. ▷ n **3** number or figure 1. **4** single unit. ▷ pron **5** any person. **oneness** n unity. **oneself** pron reflexive form of ONE. **one-armed bandit** fruit machine operated by a lever on one side. **one-liner** n witty remark. **one-night stand** sexual encounter lasting one night. **one-sided** adj considering only one point of view. **onesie** n one-piece garment consisting of a long-sleeved top with trousers, and a zip up the front. **one-way** adj allowing movement in one direction only.

onerous ❶ [**own**-er-uss] adj (of a task) difficult to carry out.

ongoing ❶ adj in progress, continuing.

onion n strongly flavoured edible bulb.

onlooker ❶ n person who watches without taking part.

only ❶ adj **1** alone of its kind. ▷ adv **2** exclusively. **3** merely. **4** no more than. ▷ conj **5** but.

- **USAGE NOTE**
- The use of *only* to connect sentences
- is rather informal: *I would come only*
- *I'm busy.* In formal use *only* is placed
- directly before the words it modifies:
- *The club opens only on Thursdays* but in
- everyday use this becomes: *The club*
- *only opens on Thursdays.*

— THESAURUS —

omission n = **exclusion**, failure, lack, neglect, oversight

omit v **1** = **leave out**, drop, eliminate, exclude, pass over, skip **2** = **forget**, neglect, overlook

omnipotence n = **supremacy**, invincibility, mastery

omnipotent adj = **almighty**, all-powerful, supreme

omniscient adj = **all-knowing**, all-wise

once adv **2** = **at one time**, formerly, long ago, once upon a time, previously **at once 1** = **immediately**, directly, forthwith, instantly, now, right away, straight away, this (very) minute **2** = **simultaneously**, at the same

time, together

oncoming adj = **approaching**, advancing, forthcoming, looming

onerous adj = **difficult**, burdensome, demanding, exacting, hard, heavy, laborious, oppressive, taxing

one-sided adj = **biased**, lopsided, partial, partisan, prejudiced, unfair, unjust

ongoing adj = **in progress**, continuous, developing, evolving, progressing, unfinished, unfolding

onlooker n = **observer**, bystander, eyewitness, looker-on, spectator, viewer, watcher, witness

only adj **1** = **sole**, exclusive, individual, lone, single, solitary, unique ▷ adv

o.n.o. or near(est) offer.

onomatopoeia [on-a-mat-a-**pee**-a] *n* use of a word which imitates the sound it represents, such as *hiss*. **onomatopoeic** *adj*.

onset ❶ *n* beginning.

onslaught ❶ *n* violent attack.

onto *prep* **1** to a position on. **2** aware of, e.g. *she's onto us*.

ontology *n* branch of philosophy concerned with existence. **ontological** *adj*.

onus ❶ [**own**-uss] *n, pl* **onuses** responsibility or burden.

onward ❶ *adj* **1** directed or moving forward. ▷ *adv* **2** (also **onwards**) ahead, forward.

onyx *n* type of quartz with coloured layers.

oodles *pl n informal* great quantities.

oolite [**oh**-a-lite] *n* limestone made up of tiny grains of calcium carbonate.

oops *interj* exclamation of surprise or apology.

ooze¹ ❶ *v* **1** flow slowly. **2** overflow with (a quality). ▷ *n* **3** sluggish flow. **oozy** *adj*.

ooze² *n* soft mud at the bottom of a lake or river.

op *n informal* operation.

op. opus.

opal *n* iridescent precious stone.

opalescent *adj* iridescent like an opal.

opaque ❶ *adj* **1** not able to be seen through, not transparent. **2** hard to understand. **opacity** *n*.

op. cit. [**op sit**] in the work cited.

OPEC Organization of Petroleum-Exporting Countries.

open ❶ *adj* **1** not closed. **2** not covered. **3** unfolded. **4** ready for business. **5** free from obstruction, accessible. **6** unrestricted. **7** not finalized. **8** frank. ▷ *v* **9** (cause to) become open. **10** begin. ▷ *n* **11** *Sport* competition which all may enter. **in the open** outdoors. **opener** *n* tool for opening cans and bottles. **openly** *adv* without concealment. **opening** *n* **1** beginning. **2** opportunity. **3** hole. ▷ *adj* **4** first. **open air** outdoors. **open-and-shut case** problem that is easily solved. **opencast mining** mining at the surface and not underground. **open day** day on which a school or college is open to the public. **open-ended** *adj* without definite limits. **open-handed** *adj* generous. **open-hearted** *adj* **1** generous. **2** frank. **open-heart surgery** surgery on the heart during which the blood circulation is maintained by machine. **open house** hospitality to visitors at any time. **open letter** letter to an individual

○

---

3 = **merely**, barely, just, purely, simply

onset *n* = **beginning**, inception, outbreak, start

onslaught *n* = **attack**, assault, blitz, charge, offensive, onrush, onset

onus *n* = **burden**, liability, load, obligation, responsibility, task

onward *adv* **2** (also **onwards**) = **ahead**, beyond, forth, forward, in front, on

ooze¹ *v* **1** = **seep**, drain, dribble, drip, escape, filter, leak

ooze² *n* = **mud**, alluvium, mire, silt, slime, sludge

opaque *adj* **1** = **cloudy**, dim, dull, filmy, hazy, impenetrable, murky

open *adj* **1** = **unclosed**, agape, ajar, gaping, uncovered, unfastened, unlocked, yawning **3** = **extended**, unfolded, unfurled **5** = **accessible**, available, free, public, unoccupied, vacant **6** = **unrestricted** **7** = **unresolved**, arguable, debatable, moot, undecided, unsettled **8** = **frank**, candid, guileless, honest, sincere,

transparent ▷ *v* **9** = **unfasten**, expand, spread (out), unblock, uncork, uncover, undo, unfold, unfurl, unlock, unroll, untie, unwrap **10** = **start**, begin, commence, inaugurate, initiate, kick off (*inf*), launch, set in motion

open-handed *adj* = **generous**, bountiful, free, lavish, liberal, munificent, unstinting

opening *n* **1** = **beginning**, commencement, dawn, inception, initiation, launch, outset, start **2** = **opportunity**, chance, look-in (*inf*), occasion, vacancy **3** = **hole**, aperture, chink, cleft, crack, fissure, gap, orifice, perforation, slot, space ▷ *adj* **4** = **first**, beginning, inaugural, initial, introductory, maiden, primary

openly *adv* = **candidly**, forthrightly, frankly, overtly, plainly, unhesitatingly, unreservedly

open-minded *adj* = **unprejudiced**, broad-minded, impartial, liberal, reasonable, receptive, tolerant, unbiased, undogmatic

that the writer makes public in a newspaper or magazine. **open-minded** *adj* receptive to new ideas. **open-plan** *adj* (of a house or office) having few interior walls. **open prison** prison with minimal security. **open verdict** coroner's verdict not stating the cause of death.

opera¹ *n* drama in which the text is sung to an orchestral accompaniment. **operatic** *adj* **operetta** *n* light-hearted comic opera. **opera glasses** small binoculars used by theatre audiences.

opera² *n* a plural of OPUS.

operate ❶ *v* **1** (cause to) work. **2** direct. **3** perform an operation. **operator** *n* **operation** *n* **1** method or procedure of working. **2** action or series of actions. **3** medical procedure in which the body is worked on to repair a damaged part. **4** military campaign. **operational** *adj* **1** in working order. **2** relating to an operation. **operative** [op-rat-tiv] *adj* **1** working. **2** having particular significance. ▷ *n* **3** worker with a special skill.

ophthalmic *adj* relating to the eye. **ophthalmia** *n* inflammation of the eye. **ophthalmology** *n* study of the eye and its diseases. **ophthalmologist** *n* **ophthalmoscope** *n* instrument for examining the interior of the eye.

ophthalmic optician see OPTICIAN.

opiate [oh-pee-ate] *n* **1** narcotic drug containing opium. **2** thing producing a stupefying effect.

opinion ❶ *n* **1** personal belief or judgment. **2** judgment given by an expert. **opinionated** *adj* having strong opinions. **opine** *v old-fashioned* express an opinion. **opinion poll** see POLL (sense 1).

opium [oh-pee-um] *n* addictive narcotic drug made from poppy seeds.

opossum *n* small marsupial of America or Australia.

opponent ❶ *n* person one is working against in a contest, battle, or argument.

opportunity ❶ *n*, *pl* **-ties 1** favourable time or condition. **2** good chance. **opportunity shop** *Aust & NZ* shop selling second-hand clothes, sometimes for charity (also **op-shop**). **opportune** *adj* happening at a suitable time. **opportunist** *n, adj* (person) doing whatever is advantageous without regard for principles. **opportunism** *n*.

● **SPELLING TIP**
● Lots of people forget that
● **opportunity**, which is a very
● common word, has two *p*s.

oppose ❶ *v* **1** work against. **2** contrast. **be opposed to** disagree with or disapprove of. **opposite** *adj* situated on the other side. **opposition** *n*

———————————— THESAURUS ————————

operate *v* **1** = **handle**, be in charge of, manage, use, work **2** = **manoeuvre 3** = **work**, act, function, go, perform, run

operation *n* **1** = **procedure**, process **2** = **action**, course, exercise, motion, movement, performance

operational *adj* **1** = **working**, functional, going, operative, prepared, ready, up and running, usable, viable, workable

operative *adj* **1** = **in force**, active, effective, functioning, in operation, operational ▷ *n* **3** = **worker**, artisan, employee, labourer

operator *n* **1, 2** = **worker**, conductor, driver, handler, mechanic, operative, practitioner, technician

opinion *n* **1** = **belief**, assessment, feeling, idea, impression, judgment, point of view, sentiment, theory, view

opinionated *adj* = **dogmatic**, bigoted,

cocksure, doctrinaire, overbearing, pig-headed, prejudiced, single-minded

opponent *n* = **adversary**, antagonist, challenger, competitor, contestant, enemy, foe, rival

opportune *adj* = **timely**, advantageous, appropriate, apt, auspicious, convenient, favourable, fitting, suitable, well-timed

opportunism *n* = **expediency**, exploitation, pragmatism, unscrupulousness

opportunity *n* = **chance**, moment, occasion, opening, scope, time

oppose *v* **1** = **fight**, block, combat, counter, defy, resist, take issue with, take on, thwart, withstand

opposed *adj* **1** = **against**, antagonistic, averse, clashing, conflicting, contrary, dissentient, hostile

opposing *adj* **1** = **conflicting**, contrary, enemy, hostile, incompatible,

1 obstruction or hostility. **2** group opposing another. **3** political party not in power.

opposite ❶ *adj* **1** situated on the other side. **2** facing. **3** completely different. ▷ *n* **4** person or thing that is opposite. ▷ *prep* **5** facing. ▷ *adv* **6** on the other side.

oppress ❶ *v* **1** control by cruelty or force. **2** depress. **oppression** *n* **oppressor** *n* **oppressive** *adj* **1** tyrannical. **2** depressing. **3** (of weather) hot and humid. **oppressively** *adv*.

opprobrium [op-**probe**-ree-um] *n* state of being criticized severely for wrong one has done. **opprobrious** *adj*.

opt ❶ *v* show a preference, choose. **opt out** *v* choose not to be part (of).

optic *adj* relating to the eyes or sight. **optics** *n* science of sight and light. **optical** *adj* **optical character reader** device that electronically reads and stores text. **optical fibre** fine glass-fibre tube used to transmit information.

optician *n* **1** (also **ophthalmic optician**) person qualified to prescribe glasses. **2** (also **dispensing optician**) person who supplies and fits glasses.

optician *n* person who supplies and fits glasses.

optimism ❶ *n* tendency to take the most hopeful view. **optimist** *n* **optimistic** *adj* **optimistically** *adv*.

optimum ❶ *n, pl* **-ma**, **-mums** **1** best possible conditions. ▷ *adj* **2** most favourable. **optimal** *adj* **optimize** *v* make the most of.

option ❶ *n* **1** choice. **2** thing chosen. **3** right to buy or sell something at a specified price within a given time. **optional** *adj* possible but not compulsory.

optometrist [op-**tom**-met-trist] *n* person qualified to prescribe glasses. **optometry** *n*.

opulent ❶ [**op**-pew-lent] *adj* **1** having or indicating wealth. **2** abundant. **opulence** *n*.

opus ❶ [**oh**-puss] *n, pl* **opuses**, **opera** artistic creation, esp. a musical work.

or *conj* used to join alternatives, e.g. *tea or coffee*.

OR Oregon.

———————————————— **THESAURUS** ————————————————

opposite, rival
opposite *adj* **2** = **facing**, fronting **3** = **different**, antithetical, conflicting, contrary, contrasted, reverse, unlike ▷ *n* **4** = **reverse**, antithesis, contradiction, contrary, converse, inverse
opposition *n* **1** = **hostility**, antagonism, competition, disapproval, obstruction, prevention, resistance, unfriendliness **2** = **opponent**, antagonist, competition, foe, other side, rival
oppress *v* **1** = **subjugate**, abuse, maltreat, persecute, subdue, suppress, wrong **2** = **depress**, afflict, burden, dispirit, harass, sadden, torment, vex
oppressed *adj* **1** = **downtrodden**, abused, browbeaten, disadvantaged, harassed, maltreated, tyrannized, underprivileged
oppression *n* **1** = **subjugation**, abuse, brutality, cruelty, injury, injustice, maltreatment, persecution, subjection, tyranny
oppressive *adj* **1** = **tyrannical**, brutal, cruel, despotic, harsh, inhuman, repressive, severe, unjust **3** = **stifling**,

airless, close, muggy, stuffy, sultry
oppressor *n* = **persecutor**, autocrat, bully, despot, scourge, slave-driver, tormentor, tyrant
opt *v* = **choose**, decide (on), elect, go for, plump for, prefer
optimistic *adj* = **hopeful**, buoyant, cheerful, confident, encouraged, expectant, positive, rosy, sanguine
optimum *adj* **2** = **ideal**, best, highest, optimal, peak, perfect, superlative
option *n* **1** = **choice**, alternative, preference, selection
optional *adj* = **voluntary**, discretionary, elective, extra, open, possible
opulence *n* **1** = **wealth**, affluence, luxuriance, luxury, plenty, prosperity, riches **2** = **abundance**, copiousness, cornucopia, fullness, profusion, richness, superabundance
opulent *adj* **1** = **rich**, affluent, lavish, luxurious, moneyed, prosperous, sumptuous, wealthy, well-off, well-to-do **2** = **abundant**, copious, lavish, luxuriant, plentiful, profuse, prolific
opus *n* = **work**, brainchild, composition, creation, *oeuvre*, piece, production

oracle ❶ *n* **1** shrine of an ancient god. **2** prophecy, often obscure, revealed at a shrine. **3** person believed to make infallible predictions. **oracular** *adj*.

oral ❶ *adj* **1** spoken. **2** of or for the mouth. **3** (of a drug) to be taken by mouth. ▷ *n* **4** spoken examination. **orally** *adv*.

orange *n* **1** reddish-yellow citrus fruit. ▷ *adj* **2** reddish-yellow. **orangeade** *n* orange-flavoured, usu. fizzy drink. **orangery** *n* greenhouse for growing orange trees.

Orangeman *n* member of a society in Ireland for the upholding of Protestantism.

orang-utan, orang-utang *n* large reddish-brown ape with long arms.

orator ❶ [**or**-rat-tor] *n* skilful public speaker. **oration** *n* formal speech.

oratorio [or-rat-**tor**-ee-oh] *n, pl* **-rios** musical composition for choir and orchestra, usu. with a religious theme.

oratory¹ ❶ [**or**-rat-tree] *n* art of making speeches. **oratorical** *adj*.

oratory² *n, pl* **-ries** small private chapel.

orb ❶ *n* **1** ceremonial decorated sphere with a cross on top, carried by a monarch. **2** globe.

orbit ❶ *n* **1** curved path of a planet, satellite, or spacecraft around another body. **2** sphere of influence. ▷ *v* **orbiting, orbited 3** move in an orbit around. **4** put (a satellite or spacecraft) into orbit. **orbital** *adj*.

Orcadian *n* **1** person from the Orkneys. ▷ *adj* **2** of the Orkneys.

orchard *n* area where fruit trees are grown.

orchestra ❶ *n* **1** large group of musicians, esp. playing a variety of instruments. **2** (also **orchestra pit**) area of a theatre in front of the stage, reserved for the musicians. **orchestral** *adj* **orchestrate** *v* **1** arrange (music) for orchestra. **2** organize (something) to produce a particular result. **orchestration** *n*.

orchid *n* plant with flowers that have unusual lip-shaped petals.

ordain ❶ *v* **1** make (someone) a member of the clergy. **2** order or establish with authority.

ordeal ❶ *n* painful or difficult experience.

order ❶ *n* **1** instruction to be carried out. **2** methodical arrangement or sequence. **3** established social system. **4** condition of a law-abiding society. **5** request for goods to be supplied. **6** goods so supplied. **7** written instruction to pay money.

━━━━━━━━━━━━━━━━━━━━ THESAURUS ━━━━

oracle *n* **2** = **prophecy**, divination, prediction, prognostication, revelation **3** = **authority**, adviser, guru, mana (*NZ*), mastermind, mentor, pundit, wizard

oral *adj* **1** = **spoken**, verbal, vocal

oration *n* = **speech**, address, discourse, harangue, homily, lecture

orator *n* = **public speaker**, declaimer, lecturer, rhetorician, speaker

oratorical *adj* = **rhetorical**, bombastic, declamatory, eloquent, grandiloquent, high-flown, sonorous

oratory¹ *n* = **eloquence**, declamation, elocution, grandiloquence, public speaking, rhetoric, speech-making

orb *n* **2** = **sphere**, ball, circle, globe, ring

orbit *n* **1** = **path**, circle, course, cycle, revolution, rotation, trajectory **2** = **sphere of influence**, ambit, compass, domain, influence, range, reach, scope, sweep ▷ *v* **3** = **circle**, circumnavigate, encircle, revolve around

orchestrate *v* **1** = **score**, arrange **2** = **organize**, arrange, coordinate, put together, set up, stage-manage

ordain *v* **1** = **appoint**, anoint, consecrate, invest, nominate **2** = **order**, decree, demand, dictate, fix, lay down, legislate, prescribe, rule, will

ordeal *n* = **hardship**, agony, anguish, baptism of fire, nightmare, suffering, test, torture, trial, tribulation(s)

order *n* **1** = **instruction**, command, decree, dictate, direction, directive, injunction, law, mandate, regulation, rule **2 a** = **sequence**, arrangement, array, grouping, layout, line-up, method, organization, pattern, progression, series, structure, system **b** = **tidiness**, neatness, orderliness, regularity, symmetry **4** = **peace**, calm, control, discipline, law, law and order, quiet, tranquillity **5** = **request**, application, booking, commission, requisition, reservation **8** = **class**, caste, grade, position, rank, status **10** = **kind**, class, family, genre, ilk,

8 social class. **9** group of similar plants or animals. **10** kind, sort. **11** religious society of monks or nuns. **12** group of people who have been awarded an honour. ▷ *v* **13** give an instruction to. **14** request (something) to be supplied. **15** arrange methodically. **in order 1** appropriate or fitting. **2** so that it is possible.

orderly *adj* **1** well-organized. **2** well-behaved. ▷ *n, pl* **-lies 3** male hospital attendant. **4** soldier attending an officer. **orderliness** *n*.

ordinal number *n* number showing a position in a series, e.g. *first; second*.

ordinance *n* official rule or order.

ordinary ❶ *adj* **1** usual or normal. **2** dull or commonplace. **ordinarily** *adv* **ordinary seaman** navy rank equivalent to an army private.

ordination *n* act of making someone a member of the clergy.

ordnance *n* weapons and military supplies. **Ordnance Survey** official organization making maps of Britain.

ordure *n* excrement.

ore *n* (rock containing) a mineral which yields metal.

oregano [or-rig-**gah**-no] *n* sweet-smelling herb used in cooking.

organ ❶ *n* **1** part of an animal or plant that has a particular function, such as the heart or lungs. **2** musical keyboard instrument in which notes are produced by forcing air through pipes. **3** means of conveying information, esp. a newspaper. **organist** *n* organ player. **organ-grinder** *n* formerly, a person who played a barrel organ in the streets.

organdie *n* fine cotton fabric.

organic ❶ *adj* **1** of or produced from animals or plants. **2** grown without artificial fertilizers or pesticides, e.g. *organic fruit, vegetables and products*. **3** *Chemistry* relating to compounds of carbon. **4** (of change or development) gradual and natural. **5** organized systematically. **organically** *adv*

organism *n* **1** any living animal or plant. **2** organized body or system.

organize ❶ *v* **1** make arrangements for. **2** arrange systematically. **organization** *n* **1** group of people working together. **2** act of organizing. **3** method of arrangement. **organizational** *adj* **organized** *adj* **organizer** *n*.

orgasm *n* most intense point of sexual pleasure. **orgasmic** *adj*.

orgy ❶ *n, pl* **-gies 1** party involving promiscuous sexual activity. **2** unrestrained indulgence, e.g. *an orgy of destruction*. **orgiastic** *adj*.

sort, type **11** = **community**, association, brotherhood, company, fraternity ▷ *v* **13** = **command**, bid, charge, decree, demand, direct, instruct, require **14** = **request**, apply for, book, reserve, send away for **15** = **arrange**, catalogue, classify, group, marshal, organize, sort out, systematize

orderly *adj* **1** = **well-organized**, businesslike, in order, methodical, neat, regular, scientific, shipshape, systematic, tidy **2** = **well-behaved**, controlled, disciplined, law-abiding, peaceable, quiet, restrained

ordinarily *adv* = **usually**, as a rule, commonly, customarily, generally, habitually, in general, normally

ordinary *adj* **1** = **usual**, common, conventional, everyday, normal, regular, routine, standard, stock, typical **2** = **commonplace**, banal, humble, humdrum, modest, mundane, plain, run-of-the-mill, unremarkable, workaday

organ *n* **1** = **part**, element, structure, unit **3** = **medium**, forum, mouthpiece, vehicle, voice

organic *adj* **1** = **natural**, animate, biological, live, living **5** = **systematic**, integrated, methodical, ordered, organized, structured

organism *n* **1** = **creature**, animal, being, body, entity **2** = **structure**

organization *n* **1** = **group**, association, body, company, confederation, corporation, institution, outfit (*inf*), syndicate **2** = **management**, construction, coordination, direction, organizing, planning, running, structuring **3** = **structure**, arrangement, chemistry, composition, format, make-up, pattern, unity

organize *v* **1** = **plan**, arrange, coordinate, marshal, put together, run, set up, take care of **2** = **put in order**, arrange, classify, group, systematize

orgy *n* **1** = **revel**, bacchanalia, carousal,

oriel window n upper window built out from a wall.

orient, orientate ❶ v **1** position (oneself) according to one's surroundings. **2** position (a map) in relation to the points of the compass. **orientation** n **orienteering** n sport in which competitors hike over a course using a compass and map.

Orient n **the Orient** lit East Asia. **Oriental** adj **1** of the Orient. **2** (o-) eastern. ▷ n **3** person from the Orient. **Orientalist** n specialist in the languages and history of the Far East.

orifice ❶ [or-rif-fiss] n opening or hole.

origami [or-rig-**gah**-mee] n Japanese decorative art of paper folding.

origin ❶ n **1** point from which something develops. **2** ancestry. **original** adj **1** first or earliest. **2** new, not copied or based on something else. **3** able to think up new ideas. ▷ n **4** first version, from which others are copied. **original sin** human imperfection and mortality as a result of Adam's disobedience. **originality** n **originally** adv **originate** v come or

bring into existence. **origination** n **originator** n.

oriole n tropical or American songbird.

ormolu n gold-coloured alloy used for decoration.

ornament ❶ n **1** decorative object. **2** decorations collectively. **3** person regarded as an asset to a group. ▷ v **4** decorate. **ornamental** adj **ornamentation** n.

ornate ❶ adj highly decorated, elaborate.

ornithology n study of birds. **ornithological** adj **ornithologist** n.

orphan n **1** child whose parents are dead. ▷ v **2** deprive of parents. **orphanage** n children's home for orphans. **orphaned** adj having no living parents.

orrery n, pl **-ries** mechanical model of the solar system.

orris n **1** kind of iris. **2** (also **orris root**) fragrant root used for perfume.

orthodontics n branch of dentistry concerned with correcting irregular teeth. **orthodontist** n.

orthodox ❶ adj conforming to established views. **orthodoxy** n

———————— THESAURUS ————————

debauch, revelry, Saturnalia **2 = spree**, binge (inf), bout, excess, indulgence, overindulgence, splurge, surfeit

orient, orientate v **1 = adjust**, acclimatize, adapt, align, familiarize **2 = get one's bearings**

orientation n **1 = adjustment**, acclimatization, adaptation, assimilation, familiarization, introduction, settling in **2 = position**, bearings, direction, location

orifice n **= opening**, aperture, cleft, hole, mouth, pore, rent, vent

origin n **1 = root**, base, basis, derivation, foundation, fount, fountainhead, inception, launch, source, start, wellspring **2 = beginning**, birth, creation, emergence, genesis

original adj **1 = first**, earliest, initial, introductory, opening, primary, starting **2 = new**, fresh, ground-breaking, innovative, novel, seminal, unprecedented, unusual **3 = creative**, fertile, imaginative, ingenious, inventive, resourceful ▷ n **4 = prototype**, archetype, master, model, paradigm, pattern, precedent, standard

originality n **2, 3 = novelty**, creativity,

freshness, imagination, ingenuity, innovation, inventiveness, newness, unorthodoxy

originally adv **1 = initially**, at first, first, in the beginning, to begin with

originate v **a = begin**, arise, come, derive, emerge, result, rise, spring, start, stem **b = introduce**, bring about, create, formulate, generate, institute, launch, pioneer

originator n **= creator**, architect, author, father or mother, founder, inventor, maker, pioneer

ornament n **1 = decoration**, accessory, bauble, knick-knack, trinket **2 = trimming**, adornment, embellishment, festoon ▷ v **4 = decorate**, adorn, beautify, embellish, festoon, grace, prettify

ornamental adj **1 = decorative**, attractive, beautifying, embellishing, for show, showy

ornamentation n **1 = decoration**, adornment, elaboration, embellishment, embroidery, frills, ornateness

ornate adj **= elaborate**, baroque, busy, decorated, fancy, florid, fussy, ornamented, overelaborate, rococo

orthodox adj **= established**, accepted,

Orthodox Church dominant Christian Church in Eastern Europe.

orthography n correct spelling. **orthographic** adj.

orthopaedics n branch of medicine concerned with disorders of the bones or joints. **orthopaedic** adj.

oryx n large African antelope.

Os Chemistry osmium.

OS 1 Ordnance Survey. **2** outsize(d).

Oscar n award in the form of a statuette given for achievements in films.

oscillate ① [oss-ill-late] v **1** swing back and forth. **2** waver. **3** (of an electric current) vary between values. **oscillation** n **oscillator** n **oscilloscope** [oss-**sill**-oh-scope] n instrument that shows the shape of a wave on a cathode-ray tube.

osier [oh-zee-er] n **1** willow tree. **2** willow branch used in basketwork.

osmium n Chemistry heaviest known metallic element.

osmosis n **1** movement of a liquid through a membrane from a lower to a higher concentration. **2** process of subtle influence. **osmotic** adj.

osprey n large fish-eating bird of prey.

ossify ① v **-fying, -fied 1** (cause to) become bone, harden. **2** become inflexible. **ossification** n.

ostensible ① adj apparent, seeming. **ostensibly** adv.

ostentation ① n pretentious display. **ostentatious** adj **ostentatiously** adv.

osteopathy n medical treatment involving manipulation of the joints. **osteopath** n.

osteoporosis n brittleness of the bones, caused by lack of calcium.

ostler n History stableman at an inn.

ostracize ① v exclude (a person) from a group. **ostracism** n.

ostrich n large African bird that runs fast but cannot fly.

OT Old Testament.

OTC Officers' Training Corps.

other ① adj **1** remaining in a group of which one or some have been specified. **2** different from the ones specified or understood. **3** additional. ▷ n **4** other person or thing. **otherwise** conj **1** or else, if not. ▷ adv **2** differently, in another way. **3** in other respects. **otherworldly** adj concerned with spiritual rather than practical matters.

otiose [oh-tee-oze] adj not useful, e.g. otiose language.

otter n small brown freshwater mammal that eats fish.

ottoman n, pl **-mans** storage chest with a padded lid for use as a seat. **Ottoman** n, adj History (member) of the former Turkish empire.

oubliette [oo-blee-**ett**] n dungeon entered only by a trapdoor.

ouch interj exclamation of sudden pain.

ought v used to express: **1** obligation, e.g. you ought to pay. **2** advisability, e.g. you ought to diet. **3** probability,

approved, conventional, customary, official, received, traditional, well-established

orthodoxy n = **conformity**, authority, conventionality, received wisdom, traditionalism

oscillate v **1** = **swing**, seesaw, sway, vibrate **2** = **waver**, fluctuate, vacillate, vary

oscillation n **1** = **swing**, variation **2** = **wavering**, fluctuation, instability, vacillation

ossify v **2** = **harden**, solidify, stiffen

ostensible adj = **apparent**, outward, pretended, professed, purported, seeming, so-called, superficial, supposed

ostensibly adv = **apparently**, on the face of it, professedly, seemingly, supposedly

ostentation n = **display**, affectation,

exhibitionism, flamboyance, flashiness, flaunting, parade, pomp, pretentiousness, show, showing off (inf)

ostentatious adj = **pretentious**, brash, conspicuous, flamboyant, flashy, gaudy, loud, obtrusive, showy

ostracism n = **exclusion**, banishment, exile, isolation, rejection

ostracize v = **exclude**, banish, cast out, cold-shoulder, exile, give (someone) the cold shoulder, reject, send to Coventry, shun

other adj **1** = **spare 2** = **different**, alternative, contrasting, dissimilar, distinct, diverse, separate, unrelated, variant **3** = **additional**, added, auxiliary, extra, further, more, supplementary

otherwise conj **1** = **or else**, if not, or then ▷ adv **2** = **differently**, any other way, contrarily

e.g. *you ought to know by then*.

Ouija board *n* ® lettered board on which supposed messages from the dead are spelt out.

ounce ❶ *n* **1** unit of weight equal to one sixteenth of a pound (28.4 grams). **2** a small amount.

our *adj* belonging to us. **ours** *pron* thing(s) belonging to us. **ourselves** *pron* emphatic and reflexive form of WE or US.

ousel *n* see DIPPER.

oust ❶ *v* force (someone) out, expel.

out ❶ *adv, adj* **1** denoting movement or distance away from, a state of being used up or extinguished, public availability, etc. e.g. *oil was pouring out; turn the light out; her new book is out.* ▷ *v* **2** *informal* name (a public figure) as being homosexual. **out of** at or to a point outside. **out-of-date** *adj* old-fashioned. **out-of-the-way** *adj* remote. **outer** *adj* **1** on the outside. **2** further from the middle. **outermost** *adj* furthest out. **outer space** space beyond the earth's atmosphere. **outing** *n* leisure trip. **outward** *adj* **1** apparent. **2** of the outside. **3** away from a place. ▷ *adv* **4** (also **outwards**) away from somewhere. **outwardly** *adv*.

out- *prefix* **1** surpassing, e.g. *outlive; outdistance*. **2** outside, away, e.g.

outpatient; outgrowth.

outback *n* remote bush country of Australia.

outbid *v* offer a higher price than.

outboard motor *n* engine externally attached to the stern of a boat.

outbreak ❶ *n* sudden occurrence (of something unpleasant).

outbuilding *n* outhouse.

outburst ❶ *n* **1** sudden expression of emotion. **2** sudden period of violent activity.

outcast ❶ *n* person rejected by a particular group.

outclass ❶ *v* surpass in quality.

outcome ❶ *n* result.

outcrop *n* part of a rock formation that sticks out of the earth.

outcry ❶ *n, pl* **-cries** vehement or widespread protest.

outdated ❶ *adj* old-fashioned.

outdo ❶ *v* surpass in performance.

outdoors ❶ *adv* **1** in(to) the open air. ▷ *n* **2** the open air. **outdoor** *adj*.

outface *v* subdue or disconcert (someone) by staring.

outfall *n* mouth of a river or drain.

outfield *n* Cricket area far from the pitch.

outfit ❶ *n* **1** matching set of clothes. **2** *informal* group of people working together. **3** kit for a job. **outfitter** *n* *old-fashioned* supplier of men's clothes.

———————————————— THESAURUS ————————————————

ounce *n* **2** = **shred**, atom, crumb, drop, grain, scrap, speck, trace

oust *v* = **expel**, depose, dislodge, displace, dispossess, eject, throw out, topple, turn out, unseat

out *adj* **1 a** = **away**, abroad, absent, elsewhere, gone, not at home, outside **b** = **extinguished**, at an end, dead, ended, exhausted, expired, finished, used up

outbreak *n* = **eruption**, burst, epidemic, explosion, flare-up, outburst, rash, upsurge

outburst *n* **1** = **outpouring**, paroxysm, spasm, surge **2** = **outbreak**, eruption, explosion, flare-up

outcast *n* = **pariah**, castaway, exile, leper, *persona non grata*, refugee, vagabond, wretch

outclass *v* = **surpass**, eclipse, excel, leave standing (*inf*), outdo, outshine, outstrip, overshadow, run rings around (*inf*)

outcome *n* = **result**, conclusion,

consequence, end, issue, payoff (*inf*), upshot

outcry *n* = **protest**, clamour, commotion, complaint, hue and cry, hullaballoo, outburst, uproar

outdated *adj* = **old-fashioned**, antiquated, archaic, obsolete, outmoded, out of date, passé, unfashionable

outdo *v* = **surpass**, beat, best, eclipse, exceed, get the better of, outclass, outmanoeuvre, overcome, top, transcend

outdoor *adj* = **open-air**, alfresco, out-of-door(s), outside

outer *adj* **1** = **external**, exposed, exterior, outside, outward, surface **2** = **peripheral**, outlying

outfit *n* **1** = **costume**, clothes, ensemble, garb, get-up (*inf*), kit, suit **2** *Inf* = **group**, company, crew, organization, setup (*inf*), squad, team, unit

outflank v 1 get round the side of (an enemy army). 2 outdo (someone).
outgoing ❶ adj 1 leaving. 2 sociable. **outgoings** pl n expenses.
outgrow v become too large or too old for. **outgrowth** n 1 natural development. 2 thing growing out from a main body.
outhouse n building near a main building.
outlandish ❶ adj extremely unconventional.
outlast v last longer than.
outlaw ❶ n 1 History criminal deprived of legal protection, bandit. ▷ v 2 make illegal. 3 History make (someone) an outlaw. **outlawed** adj.
outlay ❶ n expenditure.
outlet ❶ n 1 means of expressing emotion. 2 market for a product. 3 place where a product is sold. 4 opening or way out.
outline ❶ n 1 short general explanation. 2 line defining the shape of something. ▷ v 3 summarize. 4 show the general shape of.

outlive ❶ v 1 live longer than. 2 live through (an unpleasant experience).
outlook ❶ n 1 attitude. 2 probable outcome. 3 view.
outlying ❶ adj distant from the main area.
outmanoeuvre v get an advantage over.
outmoded ❶ adj no longer fashionable or accepted.
outnumber v exceed in number.
outpatient n patient who does not stay in hospital overnight.
outport n Canad isolated fishing village, esp. in Newfoundland.
outpost n outlying settlement.
outpouring ❶ n 1 great amount produced very rapidly. 2 passionate outburst.
output ❶ n 1 amount produced. 2 power, voltage, or current delivered by an electrical circuit. 3 Computers data produced. ▷ v 4 Computers produce (data) at the end of a process.
outrage ❶ n 1 great moral indignation. 2 gross violation of morality. ▷ v

---

THESAURUS

outgoing adj 1 = **leaving**, departing, former, retiring, withdrawing 2 = **sociable**, approachable, communicative, expansive, extrovert, friendly, gregarious, open, warm
outgoings pl n = **expenses**, costs, expenditure, outlay, overheads
outing n = **trip**, excursion, expedition, jaunt, spin (inf)
outlandish adj = **strange**, bizarre, exotic, fantastic, far-out (sl), freakish, outré, preposterous, unheard-of, weird
outlaw n 1 Hist = **bandit**, brigand, desperado, fugitive, highwayman, marauder, outcast, robber ▷ v 2 = **forbid**, ban, bar, disallow, exclude, prohibit, proscribe 3 Hist = **put a price on (someone's) head**
outlay n = **expenditure**, cost, expenses, investment, outgoings, spending
outlet n 1 = **release**, vent 3 = **shop**, market, store 4 = **opening**, avenue, channel, duct, exit, release
outline n 1 = **summary**, recapitulation, résumé, rundown, synopsis, thumbnail sketch 2 = **shape**, configuration, contour, delineation, figure, form, profile,

silhouette ▷ v 3 = **summarize**, adumbrate 4 = **draft**, delineate, plan, rough out, sketch (in), trace
outlive v 1 = **survive**, outlast
outlook n 1 = **attitude**, angle, frame of mind, perspective, point of view, slant, standpoint, viewpoint 2 = **prospect**, expectations, forecast, future
outlying adj = **remote**, distant, far-flung, out-of-the-way, peripheral, provincial
outmoded adj = **old-fashioned**, anachronistic, antiquated, archaic, obsolete, out-of-date, outworn, passé, unfashionable
out-of-date adj = **old-fashioned**, antiquated, dated, expired, invalid, lapsed, obsolete, outmoded, outworn, passé
outpouring n 1 = **stream**, cascade, effusion, flow, spate, spurt, torrent
output n 1 = **production**, achievement, manufacture, productivity, yield
outrage n 1 = **indignation**, anger, fury, hurt, resentment, shock, wrath 2 = **violation**, abuse, affront, desecration, indignity, insult, offence, sacrilege, violence ▷ v 3 = **offend**,

3 offend morally. **outrageous** adj
1 shocking. **2** offensive.
outrageously adv.
outré [oo-tray] adj shockingly
eccentric.
outrider n motorcyclist acting as an
escort.
outrigger n stabilizing frame
projecting from a boat.
outright ❶ adj, adv **1** absolute(ly).
2 open(ly) and direct(ly).
outrun v **1** run faster than. **2** exceed.
outsell v be sold in greater quantities
than.
outset ❶ n beginning.
outshine v surpass (someone) in
excellence.
outside ❶ prep, adj, adv **1** indicating
movement to or position on the
exterior. ▷ adj **2** unlikely, e.g. an
outside chance. **3** coming from outside.
▷ n **4** external area or surface.
outsider n **1** person outside a specific
group. **2** contestant thought unlikely
to win.
outsize, outsized ❶ adj very large or

larger than normal.
outskirts ❶ pl n outer areas, esp. of a
town.
outsmart v informal outwit.
outspan v S Afr relax.
outspoken ❶ adj **1** tending to say
what one thinks. **2** said openly.
outstanding ❶ adj **1** excellent. **2** still
to be dealt with or paid.
outstay v overstay.
outstretched adj stretched out as far
as possible.
outstrip ❶ v **1** surpass. **2** go faster
than.
outtake n unreleased take from a
recording session, film, or TV
programme.
outvote v defeat by getting more votes
than.
outweigh ❶ v **1** be more important,
significant, or influential than. **2** be
heavier than.
outwit ❶ v -witting, -witted get the
better of (someone) by cunning.
outworn ❶ adj no longer in use.
ouzel [ooze-el] n see DIPPER.

————— THESAURUS —————

affront, incense, infuriate, madden,
scandalize, shock
outrageous adj **1** = **unreasonable**,
exorbitant, extravagant, immoderate,
preposterous, scandalous, shocking,
steep (inf) **2** = **atrocious**, disgraceful,
flagrant, heinous, iniquitous,
nefarious, offensive, shocking,
unspeakable, villainous, wicked
outré adj = **eccentric**, bizarre,
fantastic, freakish, odd, off-the-wall
(sl), outlandish, unconventional,
weird
outright adj **1** = **absolute**, complete,
out-and-out, perfect, thorough,
thoroughgoing, total, unconditional,
unmitigated, unqualified **2** = **direct**,
definite, flat, straightforward,
unequivocal, unqualified ▷ adv
1 = **absolutely**, completely,
straightforwardly, thoroughly, to the
full **2** = **openly**, overtly
outset n = **beginning**,
commencement, inauguration,
inception, kickoff (inf), onset,
opening, start
outside adj **1** = **external**, exterior,
extraneous, outer, outward
2 = **remote**, distant, faint, marginal,
slight, slim, small, unlikely ▷ n
4 = **exterior**, facade, face, front, skin,

surface, topside
outsider n **1** = **interloper**, incomer,
intruder, newcomer, odd one out,
stranger
outsize, outsized adj = **extra-large**,
giant, gigantic, huge, jumbo (inf),
mammoth, monster, oversized
outskirts pl n = **edge**, boundary,
environs, periphery, suburbia, suburbs
outspoken adj **1** = **forthright**, abrupt,
blunt, explicit, frank, open,
unceremonious **2** = **plain-spoken**,
unequivocal
outstanding adj **1** = **excellent**,
exceptional, great, important,
impressive, special, superior,
superlative **2** = **unpaid**, due, payable,
pending, remaining, uncollected,
unsettled
outstrip v **1** = **surpass**, better, eclipse,
exceed, excel, outdo, transcend
2 = **overtake**
outweigh v **1** = **override**, cancel (out),
compensate for, eclipse, prevail over,
take precedence over, tip the scales
outwit v = **outsmart** (inf), cheat, dupe,
get the better of, outfox,
outmanoeuvre, outthink, put one over
on (inf), swindle, take in (inf)
outworn adj = **outdated**, antiquated,
discredited, disused, hackneyed,

ouzo [**ooze**-oh] *n* strong aniseed-flavoured spirit from Greece.

ova *n* plural of OVUM.

oval ❶ *adj* **1** egg-shaped. ▷ *n* **2** anything that is oval in shape.

ovary *n, pl* **-ries 1** female egg-producing organ. **2** part of a plant containing the ovules. **ovarian** *adj*.

ovation ❶ *n* enthusiastic round of applause.

oven *n* heated compartment or container for cooking or for drying or firing ceramics.

over ❶ *prep, adv* **1** indicating position on the top of, movement to the other side of, amount greater than, etc. e.g. *a room over the garage; climbing over the fence; over fifty pounds*. ▷ *adj* **2** finished. ▷ *n* **3** *Cricket* series of six balls bowled from one end. **overly** *adv* excessively.

over- *prefix* **1** too much, e.g. *overeat*. **2** above, e.g. *overlord*. **3** on top, e.g. *overshoe*.

overact *v* act in an exaggerated way.

overall ❶ *adj, adv* **1** in total. ▷ *n* **2** coat-shaped protective garment. ▷ *pl* **3** protective garment consisting of trousers with a jacket or bib and braces attached.

overarm *adj, adv* (thrown) with the arm above the shoulder.

overawe ❶ *v* affect (someone) with an overpowering sense of awe.

overbalance ❶ *v* lose balance.

overbearing ❶ *adj* unpleasantly forceful.

overblown ❶ *adj* excessive.

overboard *adv* from a boat into the water. **go overboard** go to extremes, esp. in enthusiasm.

overcast ❶ *adj* (of the sky) covered by clouds.

overcharge ❶ *v* charge too much.

overcoat *n* heavy coat.

overcome ❶ *v* **1** gain control over after an effort. **2** (of an emotion) affect strongly. **3** defeat (someone) in a conflict.

overcrowded *adj* containing more people or things than is desirable. **overcrowding** *n*.

overdo ❶ *v* **1** do to excess. **2** exaggerate (something). **3** cook too long. **overdo it** do something to a greater degree than is advisable.

overdose *n* **1** excessive dose of a drug. ▷ *v* **2** take an overdose.

overdraft *n* **1** overdrawing. **2** amount overdrawn.

overdraw *v* withdraw more money than is in (one's bank account). **overdrawn** *adj* **1** having overdrawn one's account. **2** (of an account) in debit.

overdressed *adj* dressed too elaborately or formally.

obsolete, outmoded, out-of-date, worn-out

oval *adj* **1** = **elliptical**, egg-shaped, ovoid

ovation *n* = **applause**, acclaim, acclamation, big hand, cheers, clapping, plaudits, tribute

over *prep* **1 a** = **on top of**, above, on, upon **b** = **more than**, above, exceeding, in excess of **c** = **above**, aloft, on high, overhead **d** = **extra**, beyond, in addition, in excess, left over ▷ *adj* **2** = **finished**, accomplished, bygone, closed, completed, concluded, done (with), ended, gone, past, wrapped up

overall *adj* **1** = **total**, all-embracing, blanket, complete, comprehensive, general, global, inclusive, overarching ▷ *adv* **1** = **in general**, on the whole

overawe *v* = **intimidate**, abash, alarm, daunt, frighten, scare, terrify

overbalance *v* = **topple over**, capsize, keel over, overturn, slip, tip over, tumble, turn turtle

overbearing *adj* = **dictatorial**, arrogant, bossy (*inf*), domineering, haughty, high-handed, imperious, supercilious, superior

overblown *adj* = **excessive**, disproportionate, immoderate, inflated, overdone, over the top, undue

overcast *adj* = **cloudy**, dismal, dreary, dull, grey, leaden, louring *or* lowering, murky

overcharge *v* = **cheat**, diddle (*inf*), fleece, rip off (*sl*), short-change, sting (*inf*), surcharge

overcome *v* **1** = **surmount**, master, overpower, overwhelm, prevail, subdue, subjugate, triumph over **3** = **conquer**, beat, defeat, vanquish ▷ *adj* **2** = **affected**, at a loss for words, bowled over (*inf*), overwhelmed, speechless, swept off one's feet

overdo *v* **1** = **go overboard** (*inf*), belabour, overindulge, overreach

overdrive n 1 very high gear in a motor vehicle. 2 state of great activity or excitement.

overdue ⊕ adj still due after the time allowed.

overestimate v estimate too highly.

overflow ⊕ v 1 flow over. 2 be filled beyond capacity. ▷ n 3 something that overflows. 4 outlet for excess liquid. 5 excess amount.

overgrown adj thickly covered with plants and weeds.

overhang ⊕ v 1 project beyond something. ▷ n 2 overhanging part.

overhaul ⊕ v 1 examine and repair. 2 overtake. ▷ n 3 examination and repair.

overhead ⊕ adv, adj above one's head. **overheads** pl n general cost of maintaining a business.

overhear v hear (a speaker or remark) unintentionally or without the speaker's knowledge.

overjoyed ⊕ adj extremely pleased.

overkill n treatment that is greater than required.

overland adj, adv by land.

overlap v 1 share part of the same space or period of time (as). ▷ n 2 part or area overlapping.

overlay v cover with a thin layer.

overleaf adv on the back of the current page.

overload v 1 put too large a load on or in. ▷ n 2 excessive load.

overlook ⊕ v 1 fail to notice. 2 ignore. 3 look at from above.

overman v provide with too many staff.

overmuch adv, adj too much.

overnight adj, adv 1 (taking place) during one night. 2 (happening) very quickly.

overpower ⊕ v 1 subdue or overcome (someone). 2 make helpless or ineffective. **overpowering** adj.

overrate ⊕ v have too high an opinion of.

overreach v **overreach oneself** fail by trying to be too clever.

overreact v react more strongly than is necessary.

override ⊕ v 1 overrule. 2 replace.

overrule ⊕ v 1 reverse the decision of (a person with less power). 2 reverse (someone else's decision).

overrun ⊕ v 1 conquer rapidly. 2 spread over (a place) rapidly.

————————————————————— THESAURUS —————————————————————

2 = **exaggerate**, gild the lily, overstate **overdo it** = **overwork**, bite off more than one can chew, burn the candle at both ends (inf), overload oneself, strain or overstrain oneself, wear oneself out

overdone adj 2 = **excessive**, exaggerated, fulsome, immoderate, inordinate, overelaborate, too much, undue, unnecessary 3 = **overcooked**, burnt, charred, dried up, spoiled

overdue adj = **late**, behindhand, behind schedule, belated, owing, tardy, unpunctual

overflow v 1 = **spill**, brim over, bubble over, pour over, run over, well over ▷ n 5 = **surplus**, overabundance, spilling over

overhang v 1 = **project**, extend, jut, loom, protrude, stick out

overhaul v 1 = **check**, do up (inf), examine, inspect, recondition, repair, restore, service 2 = **overtake**, catch up with, get ahead of, pass ▷ n 3 = **checkup**, check, examination, going-over (inf), inspection, reconditioning, service

overhead adv = **above**, aloft, in the sky, on high, skyward, up above, upward ▷ adj = **aerial**, overhanging, upper

overheads pl n = **running costs**, operating costs

overjoyed adj = **delighted**, cock-a-hoop, elated, euphoric, jubilant, on cloud nine (inf), over the moon (inf), thrilled

overlook v 1 = **miss**, disregard, forget, neglect, omit, pass 2 = **ignore**, condone, disregard, excuse, forgive, make allowances for, pardon, turn a blind eye to, wink at 3 = **have a view of**, look over or out on

overpower v = **overwhelm**, conquer, crush, defeat, master, overcome, overthrow, vanquish ▷ v 2 = **subdue**, quell, subjugate

overpowering adj = **overwhelming**, forceful, invincible, irrefutable, irresistible, powerful, strong

overrate v = **overestimate**, exaggerate, overvalue

override v 1 = **overrule**, annul, cancel, countermand, nullify, outweigh 2 = **supersede**

overrule v = **reverse**, alter, annul, cancel, countermand, override, overturn, repeal, rescind, veto

overrun v 1 = **overwhelm**, invade, occupy, rout 2 = **spread over**, choke,

3 extend beyond a set limit.

overseas *adv, adj* to, of, or from a distant country.

oversee ❶ *v* watch over from a position of authority. **overseer** *n*.

overshadow ❶ *v* **1** reduce the significance of (a person or thing) by comparison. **2** sadden the atmosphere of.

overshoe *n* protective shoe worn over an ordinary shoe.

overshoot *v* go beyond (a mark or target).

oversight ❶ *n* mistake caused by not noticing something.

oversleep *v* sleep beyond the intended time.

overspill *n* rehousing of people from crowded cities in smaller towns.

overstate *v* state too strongly. **overstatement** *n*.

overstay *v* **overstay one's welcome** stay longer than one's host or hostess would like.

overstep *v* go beyond (a certain limit).

overt ❶ *adj* open, not hidden. **overtly** *adv*.

overtake ❶ *v* **1** move past (a vehicle or person) travelling in the same

direction. **2** come upon suddenly or unexpectedly.

overtax *v* **1** put too great a strain on. **2** tax too heavily.

overthrow ❶ *v* **1** defeat and replace. ▷ *n* **2** downfall, destruction.

overtime *n, adv* **1** (paid work done) in addition to one's normal working hours. ▷ *n* **2** period of extra time in a contest or game.

overtone ❶ *n* additional meaning.

overture ❶ *n* **1** *Music* orchestral introduction. ▷ *pl* **2** opening moves in a new relationship.

overturn ❶ *v* **1** turn upside down. **2** overrule (a legal decision). **3** overthrow (a government).

overview *n* general survey.

overweening *adj* excessive or immoderate.

overweight ❶ *adj* weighing more than is healthy.

overwhelm ❶ *v* **1** overpower, esp. emotionally. **2** defeat by force. **overwhelming** *adj* **overwhelmingly** *adv*.

overwork ❶ *v* **1** work too much. **2** use too much. ▷ *n* **3** excessive work.

THESAURUS

infest, inundate, permeate, ravage, swarm over **3** = **exceed**, go beyond, overshoot, run over *or* on

overseer *n* = **supervisor**, boss (*inf*), chief, foreman, master, superintendent

overshadow *v* **1** = **outshine**, dominate, dwarf, eclipse, leave *or* put in the shade, surpass, tower above **2** = **spoil**, blight, mar, put a damper on, ruin, temper

oversight *n* = **mistake**, blunder, carelessness, error, fault, lapse, neglect, omission, slip

overt *adj* = **open**, blatant, manifest, observable, obvious, plain, public, unconcealed, undisguised

overtake *v* **1** = **pass**, catch up with, get past, leave behind, outdistance, outdo, outstrip, overhaul **2** = **befall**, engulf, happen, hit, overwhelm, strike

overthrow *v* **1** = **defeat**, bring down, conquer, depose, dethrone, oust, overcome, overpower, topple, unseat, vanquish ▷ *n* **2** = **downfall**, defeat, destruction, dethronement, fall, ousting, undoing, unseating

overtone *n* = **hint**, connotation, implication, innuendo, intimation,

nuance, sense, suggestion, undercurrent

overture *n* **1** *Music* = **introduction**, opening, prelude ▷ *pl* **2** = **approach**, advance, invitation, offer, proposal, proposition

overturn *v* **1** = **tip over**, capsize, keel over, overbalance, topple, upend, upturn **3** = **overthrow**, bring down, depose, destroy, unseat

overweight *adj* = **fat**, bulky, chubby, chunky, corpulent, heavy, hefty, obese, plump, portly, stout, tubby (*inf*)

overwhelm *v* **1** = **overcome**, bowl over (*inf*), devastate, knock (someone) for six (*inf*), stagger, sweep (someone) off his *or* her feet, take (someone's) breath away **2** = **destroy**, crush, cut to pieces, massacre, overpower, overrun, rout

overwhelming *adj* **1** = **overpowering**, breathtaking, crushing, devastating, irresistible, shattering, stunning, towering

overwork *v* **1** = **strain oneself**, burn the midnight oil, sweat (*inf*), work one's fingers to the bone **2** = **overuse**, exhaust, exploit, fatigue, oppress, wear out, weary

overwrought ❶ *adj* nervous and agitated.

oviduct *n* tube through which eggs are conveyed from the ovary.

ovine *adj* of or like a sheep.

ovoid [**oh**-void] *adj* egg-shaped.

ovulate [**ov**-yew-late] *v* release an egg cell from an ovary. **ovulation** *n*.

ovule *n* plant part that contains the egg cell and becomes the seed after fertilization.

ovum [**oh**-vum] *n*, *pl* **ova** unfertilized egg cell.

owe ❶ *v* **1** be obliged to pay (a sum of money) to (a person). **2** feel an obligation to do. **owe to** have as a result of. **owing to** as a result of.

owl *n* night bird of prey. **owlish** *adj*.

own ❶ *adj* **1** used to emphasize possession, e.g. *my own idea.* ▷ *pron* **2** thing(s) belonging to a particular person. ▷ *v* **3** possess. **4** acknowledge. **hold one's own** be able to deal successfully with a situation. **on one's own 1** without help. **2** alone. **owner** *n* **ownership** *n* **own up** *v* confess.

ox *n*, *pl* **oxen** castrated bull.

oxalic acid *n* poisonous acid found in many plants.

Oxbridge *n* universities of Oxford and Cambridge.

Oxfam Oxford Committee for Famine Relief.

oxide *n* compound of oxygen and one other element. **oxidize** *v* combine chemically with oxygen, as in burning or rusting. **oxidation** *n* oxidizing.

oxygen *n Chemistry* gaseous element essential to life and combustion. **oxygenate** *v* add oxygen to.

oxymoron [ox-see-**more**-on] *n* figure of speech that combines two apparently contradictory ideas, e.g. *cruel kindness.*

oyez *interj History* shouted three times by a public crier, listen.

oyster *n* edible shellfish. **oystercatcher** *n* wading bird with black-and-white feathers.

oz. ounce.

Oz *n slang* Australia.

ozone *n* **1** strong-smelling form of oxygen. **2** bracing seaside air. **ozone layer** layer of ozone in the upper atmosphere that filters out ultraviolet radiation.

———————————————————— THESAURUS ——————————

overwrought *adj* = **agitated**, distracted, excited, frantic, keyed up, on edge, overexcited, tense, uptight (*inf*), wired (*sl*)

owe *v* **1** = **be in debt**, be in arrears **2** = **be obligated** *or* **indebted**

owing to *prep* = **because of**, as a result of, on account of

own *adj* **1** = **personal**, individual, particular, private ▷ *v* **3** = **possess**, be in possession of, enjoy, have, hold, keep, retain **4** = **acknowledge**, admit, allow,

concede, confess, grant, recognize **hold one's own** = **keep going**, compete, keep one's end up, keep one's head above water **on one's own 1** = **unaided**, unassisted, under one's own steam **2** = **alone**, by oneself, independently, singly **own up** *v* = **confess**, admit, come clean, tell the truth

owner *n* **3** = **possessor**, holder, landlord *or* landlady, proprietor

ownership *n* **3** = **possession**, dominion, title

Pp

p penny or pence.
P 1 *Chemistry* phosphorus. **2** parking.
p. *pl* **pp.** page.
Pa *Chemistry* protactinium.
PA 1 Pennsylvania. **2** personal assistant. **3** public-address system.
p.a. each year.
pace¹ ❶ *n* **1** single step in walking. **2** length of a step. **3** rate of progress. ▷ *v* **4** walk up and down, esp. in anxiety. **5** (foll. by *out*) cross or measure with steps. **keep pace with** advance at the same rate as. **pace oneself** do something at a steady rate. **pacemaker** *n* **1** electronic device surgically implanted in a person with heart disease to regulate the heartbeat. **2** person who, by taking the lead early in a race, sets the pace for the rest of the competitors.
pace² *prep* with due respect to: used to express polite disagreement.
pachyderm [pak-ee-durm] *n* thick-skinned animal such as an elephant.
pacifier *n US & Canad* a baby's dummy or teething ring.
pacifist ❶ *n* person who refuses on principle to take part in war.

pacifism *n* refusal to take part in war.
pacify ❶ *v* **-fying, -fied** soothe, calm. **pacification** *n*.
pack ❶ *v* **1** put (clothes etc.) together in a suitcase or bag. **2** put (goods) into containers or parcels. **3** fill with people or things. ▷ *n* **4** bag carried on a person's or animal's back. **5** *Chiefly US* same as PACKET. **6** set of playing cards. **7** group of dogs or wolves that hunt together. **8** group of people who do things together. **packing** *n* material, such as paper or plastic, used to protect packed goods. **pack ice** mass of floating ice in the sea. **pack in** *v informal* stop doing, e.g. *I packed in the job*. **pack off** *v* send away. **pack up** *v* **1** put (one's belongings) in a case, bag, etc. **2** *informal* stop (doing something), e.g. *I'd packed up smoking*. **3** *informal* (of a machine) break down.
package ❶ *n* **1** small parcel. **2** (also **package deal**) deal in which separate items are presented together as a unit. ▷ *v* **3** put into a package. **packaging** *n* **package holiday** holiday in which everything is arranged by one company for a fixed price.
packet ❶ *n* **1** small container (and contents). **2** small parcel. **3** *slang* large sum of money. **packet boat** (formerly) boat carrying mail, goods, or passengers on a fixed short route.
packhorse *n* horse used for carrying goods.
packsack *n* a US and Canadian word for HAVERSACK.

p

———————— THESAURUS ————————

pace¹ *n* **1** = **step**, gait, stride, tread, walk **3** = **speed**, rate, tempo, velocity ▷ *v* **4** = **stride**, march, patrol, pound **5** (foll. by *out*) = **measure**, count, mark out, step
pacifist *n* = **peace lover**, conscientious objector, dove
pacify *v* = **calm**, allay, appease, assuage, mollify, placate, propitiate, soothe
pack *v* **1** = **package**, bundle, load, store, stow **2, 3** = **cram**, compress, crowd, fill, jam, press, ram, stuff ▷ *n* **4** = **bundle**, back pack, burden, kitbag, knapsack, load, parcel, rucksack **5** *Chiefly US* = **packet**, package **8** = **group**, band, bunch, company, crowd, flock, gang, herd, mob, troop **pack in** *v Inf* = **stop**, cease, chuck (*inf*),

give up *or* over, kick (*inf*) **pack off** *v* = **send away**, dismiss, send packing (*inf*)
package *n* **1** = **parcel**, box, carton, container, packet **2** (also **package deal**) = **unit**, combination, whole ▷ *v* **3** = **pack**, box, parcel (up), wrap
packet *n* **1** = **container**, bag, carton **2** = **package**, parcel **3** *Sl* = **fortune**, bomb (*Brit sl*), king's ransom (*inf*), pile (*inf*), small fortune, tidy sum (*inf*)
pack in *v Inf* = **stop**, cease, chuck (*inf*), give up, kick, *over*
pack off *v* = **send away**, dismiss, send packing (*inf*)
pack up *v* **1** = **put away**, store **2** *Inf* = **stop**, finish, give up, pack in (*Brit inf*) **3** *Inf* = **break down**, conk out (*inf*), fail

pact ❶ n formal agreement.

pad ❶ n **1** piece of soft material used for protection, support, absorption of liquid, etc. **2** number of sheets of paper fastened at the edge. **3** fleshy underpart of an animal's paw. **4** place for launching rockets. **5** slang home. ▷ v **padding**, **padded 6** protect or fill with soft material. **7** walk with soft steps. **padding** n **1** soft material used to pad something. **2** unnecessary words put into a speech or written work to make it longer. **pad out** v add unnecessary words to (a speech or written work) to make it longer.

paddle¹ ❶ n **1** short oar with a broad blade at one or each end. ▷ v **2** move (a canoe etc.) with a paddle. **paddle steamer** ship propelled by paddle wheels. **paddle wheel** wheel with crosswise blades that strike the water successively to propel a ship.

paddle² ❶ v walk barefoot in shallow water.

paddock n small field or enclosure for horses.

paddy n informal fit of temper.

paddy field n field where rice is grown (also **paddy**).

pademelon, paddymelon [**pad**-ee-mel-an] n small Australian wallaby.

padlock n **1** detachable lock with a hinged hoop fastened over a ring on the object to be secured. ▷ v **2** fasten (something) with a padlock.

padre [**pah**-dray] n chaplain to the armed forces.

paean [**pee**-an] n song of triumph or thanksgiving.

paediatrics n branch of medicine concerned with diseases of children. **paediatrician** n.

paedophilia n condition of being sexually attracted to children. **paedophile** n person who is sexually attracted to children.

paedophile n person who is sexually attracted to children. **paedophilia** n.

paella [pie-**ell**-a] n Spanish dish of rice, chicken, shellfish, and vegetables.

pagan ❶ n, adj (person) not belonging to one of the world's main religions. **paganism** n.

page¹ ❶ n **1** (one side of) a sheet of paper forming a book etc. **2** screenful of information from a website.

page² ❶ n **1** (also **pageboy**) small boy who attends a bride at her wedding. **2** History boy in training for knighthood. ▷ v **3** summon (someone) by bleeper or loudspeaker, in order to pass on a message.

pageant ❶ n parade or display of people in costume, usu. illustrating a scene from history. **pageantry** n.

paginate v number the pages of (a book etc.). **pagination** n.

pagoda n pyramid-shaped Asian temple or tower.

paid v past of PAY. **put paid to** informal end or destroy, e.g. the recession put paid to most of our long-term plans.

pail n (contents of) a bucket.

——————————— THESAURUS ———————————

pact n = **agreement**, alliance, bargain, covenant, deal, treaty, understanding

pad n **1** = **cushion**, buffer, protection, stuffing, wad **2** = **writing pad**, block, jotter **3** = **paw**, foot, sole **5** Sl = **home**, apartment, flat, place ▷ v **6** = **pack**, cushion, fill, protect, stuff **7** = **sneak**, creep, go barefoot, steal

pad out v = **lengthen**, elaborate, fill out, flesh out, protract, spin out, stretch

padding n **1** = **filling**, packing, stuffing, wadding **2** = **waffle** (inf, chiefly Brit), hot air (inf), verbiage, verbosity, wordiness

paddle¹ n **1** = **oar**, scull ▷ v **2** = **row**, propel, pull, scull

paddle² v = **wade**, slop, splash (about)

pagan n = **heathen**, idolater, infidel, polytheist ▷ adj = **heathen**, idolatrous, infidel, polytheistic

page¹ n **1** = **folio**, leaf, sheet, side

page² n **1** = **attendant**, bellboy (US), pageboy **2** Hist = **squire** ▷ v **3** = **call**, send for, summon

pageant n = **show**, display, parade, procession, spectacle, tableau

pageantry n = **spectacle**, display, grandeur, parade, pomp, show, splendour, theatricality

pain ❶ *n* **1** physical or mental suffering. ▷ *pl* **2** trouble, effort, e.g. *Taylor was at pains to reassure Wright*. ▷ *v* **3** cause (someone) mental or physical suffering. **on pain of** subject to the penalty of. **painful** *adj* **painfully** *adv* **painless** *adj* **painlessly** *adv* **painkiller** *n* drug that relieves pain.

painstaking ❶ *adj* extremely thorough and careful.

paint ❶ *n* **1** coloured substance, spread on a surface with a brush or roller. ▷ *v* **2** colour or coat with paint. **3** use paint to make a picture of. **painter** *n* **painting** *n*.

painter *n* rope at the front of a boat, for tying it up.

pair ❶ *n* **1** set of two things matched for use together. **2** two people, animals, or things used or grouped together. ▷ *v* **3** group or be grouped in twos.

- **USAGE NOTE**
- *Pair* is followed by a singular verb if
- it refers to a unit: *A pair of shoes was*
- *on the floor*, and by a plural verb if it
- refers to two individuals: *That pair*
- *are good friends*.

paisley pattern *n* pattern of small curving shapes, used in fabric.

pajamas *pl n US* pyjamas.

Pakistani *n, adj* (person) from Pakistan.

pal ❶ *n informal* friend.

palace *n* **1** residence of a king, bishop, etc. **2** large grand building.

paladin *n History* knight who did battle for a monarch.

palaeography [pal-ee-**og**-ra-fee] *n* study of ancient manuscripts.

Palaeolithic [pal-ee-oh-**lith**-ik] *adj* of the Old Stone Age.

palaeontology [pal-ee-on-**tol**-a-jee] *n* study of past geological periods and fossils. **palaeontologist** *n*.

palatable ❶ *adj* **1** pleasant to taste. **2** acceptable or satisfactory, e.g. *that option is not very palatable*.

palate ❶ *n* **1** roof of the mouth. **2** sense of taste.

palatial ❶ *adj* like a palace, magnificent.

palaver ❶ [pal-**lah**-ver] *n* time-wasting fuss.

pale¹ ❶ *adj* **1** light, whitish. **2** whitish in the face, esp. through illness or shock. ▷ *v* **3** become pale. **pale in, by comparison with** appear inferior when compared with.

─── **THESAURUS** ───

pain *n* **1 a** = **hurt**, ache, discomfort, irritation, pang, soreness, tenderness, throb, twinge **b** = **suffering**, agony, anguish, distress, heartache, misery, torment, torture ▷ *pl* **2** = **trouble**, bother, care, diligence, effort ▷ *v* **3 a** = **hurt**, smart, sting, throb **b** = **distress**, agonize, cut to the quick, grieve, hurt, sadden, torment, torture

painful *adj* **1** = **sore**, aching, agonizing, smarting, tender **2** = **difficult**, arduous, hard, laborious, troublesome, trying **3** = **distressing**, disagreeable, distasteful, grievous, unpleasant

painfully *adv* = **distressingly**, clearly, dreadfully, sadly, unfortunately

painkiller *n* = **analgesic**, anaesthetic, anodyne, drug

painless *adj* = **simple**, easy, effortless, fast, quick

painstaking *adj* = **thorough**, assiduous, careful, conscientious, diligent, meticulous, scrupulous

paint *n* **1** = **colouring**, colour, dye, pigment, stain, tint ▷ *v* **2** = **coat**, apply, colour, cover, daub **3** = **depict**, draw, picture, portray, represent, sketch

pair *n* **2** = **couple**, brace, duo, twins ▷ *v* **3** = **couple**, bracket, join, match (up), team, twin

pal *n Inf* = **friend**, buddy (*inf*), chum (*inf*), cobber (*Aust or old-fashioned NZ inf*), companion, comrade, crony, mate (*inf*)

palatable *adj* **1** = **delicious**, appetizing, lekker (*S Afr sl*), luscious, mouthwatering, tasty

palate *n* **2** = **taste**, appetite, stomach

palatial *adj* = **magnificent**, grand, imposing, majestic, opulent, regal, splendid, stately

palaver *n* = **fuss**, business (*inf*), carry-on (*inf, chiefly Brit*), pantomime (*inf, chiefly Brit*), performance (*inf*), rigmarole, song and dance (*Brit inf*), to-do

pale¹ *adj* **1** = **white**, ashen, bleached, colourless, faded, light **2** = **ashen**, pallid, pasty, wan, white ▷ *v* **3** = **become pale**, blanch, go white, lose colour, whiten

pale² ❶ *n* wooden or metal post used in fences. **beyond the pale** outside the limits of social convention.

palette *n* artist's flat board for mixing colours on. **palette knife** spatula with a broad flat flexible blade, used in painting or cookery.

palindrome *n* word or phrase that reads the same backwards as forwards.

paling *n* wooden or metal post used in fences.

palisade *n* fence made of wooden posts driven into the ground.

pall¹ ❶ *n* **1** cloth spread over a coffin. **2** dark cloud (of smoke). **3** depressing oppressive atmosphere. **pallbearer** *n* person who helps to carry the coffin at a funeral.

pall² ❶ *v* become boring.

palladium *n Chemistry* silvery-white element of the platinum metal group.

pallet¹ *n* portable platform for storing and moving goods.

pallet² *n* straw-filled mattress or bed.

palliasse *n* straw-filled mattress.

palliate *v* lessen the severity of (something) without curing it. **palliative** *adj* **1** giving temporary or partial relief. ▷ *n* **2** something, for example a drug, that palliates.

pallid ❶ *adj* pale, esp. because ill or weak. **pallor** *n*.

pally *adj* **-lier, -liest** *informal* on friendly terms.

palm¹ ❶ *n* inner surface of the hand. **palm off** *v* get rid of (an unwanted thing or person), esp. by deceit. **palmtop** *n* computer small enough to be held in the hand.

palm² *n* tropical tree with long pointed leaves growing out of the top of a straight trunk. **Palm Sunday** Sunday before Easter.

palmistry *n* fortune-telling from lines on the palm of the hand. **palmist** *n*.

palomino *n, pl* **-nos** gold-coloured horse with a white mane and tail.

palpable ❶ *adj* **1** obvious, e.g. *a palpable hit*. **2** so intense as to seem capable of being touched, e.g. *the tension is almost palpable*. **palpably** *adv*.

palpate *v Medical* examine (an area of the body) by touching.

palpitate ❶ *v* **1** (of the heart) beat rapidly. **2** flutter or tremble. **palpitation** *n*.

palsy [**pawl**-zee] *n* paralysis. **palsied** *adj* affected with palsy.

paltry ❶ *adj* **-trier, -triest** insignificant.

pampas *pl n* vast grassy plains in S America. **pampas grass** tall grass with feathery ornamental flower branches.

pamper ❶ *v* treat (someone) with great indulgence, spoil.

pamphlet ❶ *n* thin paper-covered booklet. **pamphleteer** *n* writer of pamphlets.

pan¹ ❶ *n* **1** wide long-handled metal container used in cooking. **2** bowl of a toilet. ▷ *v* **panning, panned 3** sift gravel from (a river) in a pan to search for gold. **4** *informal* criticize harshly. **pan out** *v* result.

pan² ❶ *v* **panning, panned** (of a film camera) be moved slowly so as to

--- THESAURUS ---

pale² *n* = **post**, paling, palisade, picket, slat, stake, upright **beyond the pale** = **unacceptable**, barbaric, forbidden, improper, inadmissible, indecent, irregular, not done, out of line, unseemly, unspeakable, unsuitable

pall¹ *n* **2** = **cloud**, mantle, shadow, shroud, veil **3** = **gloom**, check, damp, damper

pall² *v* = **become boring**, become dull, become tedious, cloy, jade, sicken, tire, weary

pallid *adj* = **pale**, anaemic, ashen, colourless, pasty, wan

palm off *v* = **fob off**, foist off, pass off

palpable *adj* **1** = **obvious**, clear, conspicuous, evident, manifest, plain, unmistakable, visible

palpitate *v* = **beat**, flutter, pound, pulsate, throb, tremble

paltry *adj* = **insignificant**, contemptible, despicable, inconsiderable, meagre, mean, measly, minor, miserable, petty, poor, puny, slight, small, trifling, trivial, unimportant, worthless

pamper *v* = **spoil**, coddle, cosset, indulge, mollycoddle, pet

pamphlet *n* = **booklet**, brochure, circular, leaflet, tract

pan¹ *n* **1** = **pot**, container, saucepan ▷ *v* **3** = **sift out**, look for, search for **4** *Inf* = **criticize**, censure, knock (*inf*), slam (*sl*), tear into (*inf*)

pan² *v* = **move**, follow, sweep, track

cover a whole scene or follow a moving object.

pan- *combining form* all, e.g. *pan-American*.

panacea ❶ [pan-a-**see**-a] *n* remedy for all diseases or problems.

panache ❶ [pan-**ash**] *n* confident elegant style.

panama hat, panama *n* man's straw hat.

panatella *n* long slender cigar.

pancake *n* thin flat circle of fried batter. **Pancake Day** Shrove Tuesday, when people traditionally eat pancakes. **pancake landing** landing in which an aircraft comes down to a height of a few feet and then drops flat onto the ground. **pancake roll** small pancake filled with Chinese-style vegetables and rolled up.

panchromatic *adj Photography* sensitive to light of all colours.

pancreas [**pang**-kree-ass] *n* large gland behind the stomach that produces insulin and helps digestion. **pancreatic** *adj*.

panda *n* large black-and-white bearlike mammal from China. **panda car** police patrol car.

pandemic *adj* (of a disease) occurring over a wide area.

pandemonium ❶ *n* wild confusion, uproar.

pander ❶ *n* person who procures a sexual partner for someone. **pander to** *v* indulge (a person or his or her desires).

p & p postage and packing.

pane *n* sheet of glass in a window or door.

panegyric [pan-ee-**jire**-ik] *n* formal

speech or piece of writing in praise of someone or something.

panel *n* **1** flat distinct section of a larger surface, for example in a door. **2** group of people as a team in a quiz etc. **3** list of jurors, doctors, etc. **4** board or surface containing switches and controls to operate equipment. ▷ *v* **-elling, -elled 5** cover or decorate with panels. **panelling** *n* panels collectively, esp. on a wall. **panellist** *n* member of a panel. **panel beater** person who repairs damage to car bodies.

pang ❶ *n* sudden sharp feeling of pain or sadness.

pangolin *n* animal of tropical countries with a scaly body and a long snout for eating ants and termites (also **scaly anteater**).

panic ❶ *n* **1** sudden overwhelming fear, often affecting a whole group of people. ▷ *v* **-icking, -icked 2** feel or cause to feel panic. **panicky** *adj* **panic-stricken** *adj*.

panicle *n* loose, irregularly branched cluster of flowers.

panini *n, pl* **-ni** *or* **-nis** Italian bread usu. served grilled with a filling.

pannier *n* **1** bag fixed on the back of a cycle. **2** basket carried by a beast of burden.

panoply ❶ [**pan**-a-plee] *n* magnificent array.

panorama ❶ *n* **1** wide unbroken view of a scene. **2** picture of a scene unrolled so as to appear continuous. **panoramic** *adj*.

pansy *n, pl* **-sies 1** small garden flower with velvety purple, yellow, or white petals. **2** *offens* effeminate or homosexual man.

P

---

panacea *n* = **cure-all**, nostrum, universal cure

panache *n* = **style**, dash, élan, flamboyance

pandemonium *n* = **uproar**, bedlam, chaos, confusion, din, hullabaloo, racket, rumpus, turmoil

pander to *v* = **indulge**, cater to, gratify, play up to (*inf*), please, satisfy

pang *n* = **twinge**, ache, pain, prick, spasm, stab, sting

panic *n* **1** = **fear**, alarm, fright, hysteria, scare, terror ▷ *v* **2** = **go to pieces**,

alarm, become hysterical, lose one's nerve, scare, unnerve

panic-stricken *adj* = **frightened**, frightened out of one's wits, hysterical, in a cold sweat (*inf*), panicky, scared, scared stiff, terrified

panoply *n* = **array**, attire, dress, garb, regalia, trappings

panorama *n* **1** = **view**, prospect, vista

panoramic *adj* **1** = **wide**, comprehensive, extensive, overall, sweeping

pant ❶ *v* breathe quickly and noisily after exertion.

pantaloons *pl n* baggy trousers gathered at the ankles.

pantechnicon *n* large van for furniture removals.

pantheism *n* **1** belief that God is present in everything. **2** willingness to worship all gods. **pantheist** *n* **pantheistic** *adj*.

pantheon *n* (in ancient Greece and Rome) temple built to honour all the gods.

panther *n* leopard, esp. a black one.

panties *pl n* women's underpants.

pantile *n* roofing tile with an S-shaped cross section.

pantomime *n* **1** play based on a fairy tale, performed at Christmas time. **2** same as MIME (sense 1) **3** confused or farcical situation.

pantry *n*, *pl* **-tries** small room or cupboard for storing food.

pants ❶ *pl n* **1** undergarment for the lower part of the body. **2** *US & Canad* trousers.

pap *n* **1** soft food for babies or invalids. **2** worthless entertainment or information.

papacy [**pay**-pa-see] *n*, *pl* **-cies** position or term of office of a pope. **papal** *adj* of the pope.

paparazzo [pap-a-**rat**-so] *n*, *pl* **-razzi** photographer specializing in candid photographs of famous people.

papaya [pa-**pie**-ya] *n* large sweet West Indian fruit.

paper ❶ *n* **1** material made in sheets from wood pulp or other fibres. **2** printed sheet of this. **3** newspaper. **4** set of examination questions. **5** article or essay. ▷ *pl* **6** personal documents. ▷ *v* **7** cover (walls) with wallpaper. **on paper** in theory, as opposed to fact, e.g. *this system looks good on paper but it is*

expensive. **paperback** *n* book with covers made of flexible card. **paper money** banknotes, rather than coins. **paperweight** *n* heavy decorative object placed on top of loose papers. **paperwork** *n* clerical work, such as writing reports and letters.

papier-mâché [**pap**-yay **mash**-ay] *n* material made from paper mixed with paste and moulded when moist.

papist *n*, *adj offens* Roman Catholic.

papoose *n* Native American child.

paprika *n* mild powdered seasoning made from red peppers.

Pap smear, test *n* same as SMEAR TEST.

papyrus [pap-**ire**-uss] *n*, *pl* **-ri**, **-ruses** **1** tall water plant. **2** (manuscript written on) a kind of paper made from this plant.

par ❶ *n* **1** usual or average condition, e.g. *feeling under par*. **2** *Golf* expected standard score. **3** face value of stocks and shares. **on a par with** equal to.

para- *combining form* beside, beyond, e.g. *parameter; parapsychology*.

parable ❶ *n* story that illustrates a religious teaching.

parabola [par-**ab**-bol-a] *n* regular curve resembling the course of an object thrown forward and up. **parabolic** *adj*.

paracetamol *n* mild pain-relieving drug.

parachute *n* **1** large fabric canopy that slows the descent of a person or object from an aircraft. ▷ *v* **2** land or drop by parachute. **parachutist** *n*.

parade ❶ *n* **1** procession or march. **2** street or promenade. ▷ *v* **3** display or flaunt. **4** march in procession. **parade ground** place where soldiers assemble regularly for inspection or display.

THESAURUS

pant *v* = **puff**, blow, breathe, gasp, heave, wheeze

pants *pl n* **1** = **underpants**, boxer shorts, briefs, broekies (*S Afr inf*), drawers, knickers, panties **2** *US, Canad, Aust & NZ* = **trousers**, slacks

paper *n* **3** = **newspaper**, daily, gazette, journal **5** = **essay**, article, dissertation, report, treatise ▷ *pl* **6** = **documents**, archive, certificates,

deeds, diaries, dossier, file, letters, records ▷ *v* **7** = **wallpaper**, hang

par *n* **1** = **average**, level, mean, norm, standard, usual

parable *n* = **lesson**, allegory, fable, moral tale, story

parade *n* **1** = **procession**, array, cavalcade, march, pageant ▷ *v* **3** = **flaunt**, display, exhibit, show off (*inf*) **4** = **march**, process

paradigm ❶ [par-a-dime] n example or model.

paradise ❶ n 1 heaven. 2 place or situation that is near-perfect.

paradox ❶ n 1 person or thing made up of contradictory elements. 2 statement that seems self-contradictory but may be true. **paradoxical** adj **paradoxically** adv.

paraffin n liquid mixture distilled from petroleum and used as a fuel or solvent.

● **SPELLING TIP**
● People have trouble remembering
● whether the r or the f is doubled
● in **paraffin**, but according to the
● Bank of English, the most popular
● mistake is to decide on neither, as
● in parafin.

paragliding n cross-country gliding wearing a parachute shaped like wings.

paragon ❶ n model of perfection.

paragraph ❶ n section of a piece of writing starting on a new line.

parakeet n small long-tailed parrot.

parallax n apparent change in an object's position due to a change in the observer's position.

parallel ❶ adj 1 separated by an equal distance at every point. 2 exactly corresponding. ▷ n 3 line separated from another by an equal distance at every point. 4 thing with similar features to another. 5 line of latitude. ▷ v 6 correspond to.

parallelogram n four-sided geometric figure with opposite sides parallel.

paralysis ❶ n inability to move or feel, because of damage to the nervous system. **paralyse** v 1 affect with paralysis. 2 make temporarily unable to move or take action. **paralytic** n, adj 1 (person) affected with paralysis. ▷ adj 2 informal very drunk.

paramedic n person working in support of the medical profession. **paramedical** adj.

parameter ❶ [par-**am**-it-er] n limiting factor, boundary.

paramilitary adj organized on military lines.

paramount ❶ adj of the greatest importance.

paramour n old-fashioned lover, esp. of a person married to someone else.

paranoia ❶ n 1 mental illness causing delusions of grandeur or persecution. 2 informal intense fear or suspicion. **paranoid**, **paranoiac** adj, n.

paranormal adj beyond scientific explanation. **the paranormal** paranormal events or matters.

parapet n low wall or railing along the edge of a balcony or roof.

paraphernalia ❶ n personal belongings or bits of equipment.

paraphrase ❶ v 1 put (a statement or text) into other words. ▷ n 2 expression of a statement or text in other words.

p

THESAURUS

paradigm n = **model**, example, ideal, pattern

paradise n 1 = **heaven**, Elysian fields, Happy Valley (Islam), Promised Land 2 = **bliss**, delight, felicity, heaven, utopia

paradox n 2 = **contradiction**, anomaly, enigma, oddity, puzzle

paradoxical adj = **contradictory**, baffling, confounding, enigmatic, puzzling

paragon n = **model**, epitome, exemplar, ideal, nonpareil, pattern, quintessence

paragraph n = **section**, clause, item, part, passage, subdivision

parallel adj 1 = **equidistant**, alongside, side by side 2 = **matching**, analogous, corresponding, like, resembling, similar ▷ n 4 = **similarity**, analogy, comparison, likeness, resemblance

paralyse v 1 = **disable**, cripple,

incapacitate, lame 2 = **immobilize**, freeze, halt, numb, petrify, stun

paralysis n = **immobility**, palsy

paralytic adj 1 = **paralysed**, crippled, disabled, incapacitated, lame, palsied

parameter n = **limit**, framework, limitation, restriction, specification

paramount adj = **principal**, cardinal, chief, first, foremost, main, primary, prime, supreme

paranoid adj 1 = **mentally ill**, deluded, disturbed, manic, neurotic, paranoiac, psychotic 2 Inf = **suspicious**, fearful, nervous, worried

paraphernalia n = **equipment**, apparatus, baggage, belongings, effects, gear, stuff, tackle, things, trappings

paraphrase v 1 = **reword**, express in other words or one's own words, rephrase, restate ▷ n 2 = **rewording**, rephrasing, restatement

paraplegia [par-a-**pleej**-ya] n paralysis of the lower half of the body. **paraplegic** adj, n.

parapsychology n study of mental phenomena such as telepathy.

Paraquat n ® extremely poisonous weedkiller.

parasite ❶ n 1 animal or plant living in or on another. 2 person who lives at the expense of others. **parasitic** adj.

parasol n umbrella-like sunshade.

paratroops pl n troops trained to be dropped by parachute into a battle area. **paratrooper** n member of the paratroops.

parboil v boil until partly cooked.

parcel ❶ n 1 something wrapped up, package. ▷ v -**celling**, -**celled** 2 (often foll. by up) wrap up. **parcel out** v divide into parts.

parch ❶ v 1 make very hot and dry. 2 make thirsty.

parchment n thick smooth writing material made from animal skin.

pardon ❶ v 1 forgive, excuse. ▷ n 2 forgiveness. 3 official release from punishment for a crime. **pardonable** adj.

pare ❶ v 1 cut off the skin or top layer of. 2 (often foll. by down) reduce in size or amount. **paring** n piece pared off.

parent ❶ n father or mother. **parental** adj **parenthood** n **parentage** n ancestry or family. **parenting** n activity of bringing up children.

parenthesis [par-**en**-thiss-iss] n, pl -**ses** 1 word or sentence inserted into a passage, marked off by brackets or dashes. ▷ pl 2 round brackets, ( ).

parenthetical adj.

par excellence adv beyond comparison, e.g. he is a travel writer par excellence.

pariah ❶ [par-**rye**-a] n social outcast.

parietal [par-**rye**-it-al] adj of the walls of a body cavity such as the skull.

parish ❶ n area that has its own church and clergyman. **parishioner** n inhabitant of a parish.

parity ❶ n equality or equivalence.

park ❶ n 1 area of open land for recreational use by the public. 2 area containing a number of related enterprises, e.g. a business park. 3 area of private land around a large country house. ▷ v 4 stop and leave (a vehicle) temporarily. **parking meter** coin-operated device beside a parking space that indicates how long a vehicle may be parked there. **parking ticket** notice of a fine served on a motorist for a parking offence.

parka n long jacket with a quilted lining and a fur-trimmed hood.

parkade n Canad a building used as a car park.

parkette n Canad a small public park.

parking lot n US & Canad area or building where vehicles may be left for a time.

Parkinson's disease n progressive disorder of the central nervous system which causes impaired muscular coordination and tremor (also **Parkinsonism**).

parky adj **parkier**, **parkiest** informal (of the weather) chilly.

parlance ❶ n particular way of speaking, idiom.

━━━━━━━━━━━━━━━━━━━━━━━━━ THESAURUS ━━━━━━

parasite n 2 = **sponger**, bloodsucker (inf), hanger-on, leech, scrounger (inf)

parasitic adj = **scrounging** (inf), bloodsucking (inf), sponging (inf)

parcel n 1 = **package**, bundle, pack ▷ v 2 (often foll. by up) = **wrap**, do up, pack, package, tie up

parch v 1 = **dry up**, dehydrate, desiccate, evaporate, shrivel, wither

pardon v 1 = **forgive**, absolve, acquit, excuse, exonerate, let off (inf), overlook ▷ n 2 = **forgiveness**, absolution, exoneration 3 = **acquittal**, amnesty

pardonable adj = **forgivable**, excusable, minor, understandable, venial

pare v 1 = **peel**, clip, cut, shave, skin, trim 2 (often foll. by down) = **cut back**, crop, cut, decrease, dock, reduce

parent n = **father** or **mother**, procreator, progenitor, sire

parentage n = **family**, ancestry, birth, descent, lineage, pedigree, stock

pariah n = **outcast**, exile, undesirable, untouchable

parish n = **community**, church, congregation, flock

parity n = **equality**, consistency, equivalence, uniformity, unity

park n 3 = **parkland**, estate, garden, grounds, woodland

parlance n = **language**, idiom, jargon, phraseology, speech, talk, tongue

parley n **1** meeting between leaders or representatives of opposing forces to discuss terms. ▷ v **2** have a parley.

parliament ⓘ n law-making assembly of a country. **parliamentary** adj **parliamentarian** n expert in parliamentary procedures.

parlour ⓘ n old-fashioned living room for receiving visitors.

parlous ⓘ adj old-fashioned dangerous.

Parmesan n hard strong-flavoured Italian cheese, used grated on pasta dishes and soups.

parochial ⓘ adj **1** narrow in outlook. **2** of a parish. **parochialism** n.

parody ⓘ n, pl **-dies 1** exaggerated and amusing imitation of someone else's style. ▷ v **-dying, -died 2** make a parody of.

parole n **1** early freeing of a prisoner on condition that he or she behaves well. ▷ v **2** put on parole. **on parole** (of a prisoner) released on condition that he or she behaves well.

paroxysm ⓘ n **1** uncontrollable outburst of rage, delight, etc. **2** spasm or convulsion of coughing, pain, etc.

parquet [**par**-kay] n **1** floor covering made of wooden blocks arranged in a geometric pattern. ▷ v **2** cover with parquet. **parquetry** n.

parricide n **1** crime of killing either of one's parents. **2** person who does this.

parrot ⓘ n **1** tropical bird with a short hooked beak and an ability to imitate human speech. ▷ v **-roting, -roted 2** repeat (someone else's words) without thinking.

parry ⓘ v **-rying, -ried 1** ward off (an attack). **2** cleverly avoid (an awkward question). ▷ n **3** parrying.

parse [parz] v analyse (a sentence) in terms of grammar.

parsimony ⓘ n extreme caution in spending money. **parsimonious** adj.

parsley n herb used for seasoning and decorating food.

parsnip n long tapering cream-coloured root vegetable.

parson ⓘ n parish priest in the Church of England. **parsonage** n parson's house. **parson's nose** rump of a cooked fowl.

part ⓘ n **1** one of the pieces that make up a whole. **2** one of several equal divisions. **3** actor's role. **4** (often pl) region, area. **5** component of a vehicle or machine. ▷ v **6** divide or separate. **7** (of people) leave each other. **part and parcel of** necessary part of. **take someone's part** support someone in an argument etc. **take (something) in good part** respond to (teasing or criticism) with good humour. **parting** n **1** occasion when one person leaves another. **2** line of scalp between sections of hair combed in opposite directions. **3** dividing or separating. **partly** adv not completely. **part of speech** particular

p

parliament n = **assembly**, congress, convention, council, legislature, senate

parliamentary adj = **governmental**, law-making, legislative

parlour n Old-fashioned = **sitting room**, drawing room, front room, living room, lounge

parlous adj Old-fashioned = **dangerous**, hazardous, risky

parochial adj **1** = **provincial**, insular, limited, narrow, narrow-minded, petty, small-minded

parody n **1** = **takeoff**, burlesque, caricature, satire, send-up (Brit inf), skit, spoof (inf) ▷ v **2** = **take off**, burlesque, caricature, do a takeoff of (inf), satirize, send up (Brit inf)

paroxysm n **2** = **outburst**, attack, convulsion, fit, seizure, spasm

parrot v **2** = **repeat**, copy, echo, imitate, mimic

parry v **1** = **ward off**, block, deflect, rebuff, repel, repulse **2** = **evade**, avoid, dodge, sidestep

parsimonious adj = **mean**, close, frugal, miserly, niggardly, penny-pinching (inf), stingy, tightfisted

parson n = **clergyman**, churchman, cleric, minister, pastor, preacher, priest, vicar

part n **1** = **piece**, bit, fraction, fragment, portion, scrap, section, share **2** = **division**, branch, component, constituent, member, unit **3** = **role**, character, lines **4** (often pl) = **region**, area, district, neighbourhood, quarter, vicinity ▷ v **6** = **divide**, break, come apart, detach, rend, separate, sever, split, tear **7** = **leave**, depart, go, go away, separate, split up, withdraw

grammatical class of words, such as noun or verb. **part time** for less than the full working week. **part-time** adj occupying or working less than the full working week. **part with** v give away, hand over.

partake ❶ v -**taking**, -**took**, -**taken** 1 (foll. by of) take (food or drink). 2 (foll. by in) take part in.

partial ❶ adj 1 not complete. 2 prejudiced. **partial to** having a liking for. **partiality** n **partially** adv.

participate ❶ v become actively involved. **participant** n **participation** n.

participle n form of a verb used in compound tenses or as an adjective, e.g. worried; worrying.

particle ❶ n 1 extremely small piece or amount. 2 Physics minute piece of matter, such as a proton or electron.

particular ❶ adj 1 relating to one person or thing, not general. 2 exceptional or special. 3 very exact. 4 difficult to please, fastidious. ▷ n 5 item of information, detail.

6 separate distinct item as opposed to a generalization, e.g. to go from the general to the particular. **particularly** adv **particularize** v give details about.

partisan ❶ n 1 strong supporter of a party or group. 2 guerrilla, member of a resistance movement. ▷ adj 3 prejudiced or one-sided.

partition ❶ n 1 screen or thin wall that divides a room. 2 division of a country into independent parts. ▷ v 3 divide with a partition.

partner ❶ n 1 either member of a couple in a relationship or activity. 2 member of a business partnership. ▷ v 3 be the partner of. **partnership** n joint business venture between two or more people.

partridge n game bird of the grouse family.

parturition n act of giving birth.

party ❶ n, pl -**ties** 1 social gathering for pleasure. 2 group of people travelling or working together. 3 group of people with a common political aim. 4 person or people forming one side in

——————————— THESAURUS ———————————

partake v 1 (foll. by of) = **consume**, eat, take 2 (foll. by in) = **participate in**, engage in, share in, take part in

partial adj 1 = **incomplete**, imperfect, uncompleted, unfinished 2 = **biased**, discriminatory, one-sided, partisan, prejudiced, unfair, unjust

partiality n = **bias**, favouritism, preference, prejudice

partially adv = **partly**, fractionally, incompletely, in part, not wholly, somewhat

participant n = **participator**, contributor, member, player

participate v = **take part**, be involved in, join in, partake, perform, share

participation n = **taking part**, contribution, involvement, joining in, partaking, sharing in

particle n 1 = **bit**, grain, iota, jot, mite, piece, scrap, shred, speck

particular adj 1 = **specific**, distinct, exact, peculiar, precise, special 2 = **special**, especial, exceptional, marked, notable, noteworthy, remarkable, singular, uncommon, unusual 4 = **fussy**, choosy (inf), demanding, fastidious, finicky, pernickety (inf), picky (inf) ▷ n 5 = **detail**, circumstance, fact, feature, item, specification

particularly adv 1 = **specifically**, distinctly, especially, explicitly, expressly, in particular 2 = **especially**, exceptionally, notably, singularly, uncommonly, unusually

parting n 1 = **going**, farewell, goodbye 3 = **division**, breaking, rift, rupture, separation, split

partisan n 1 = **supporter**, adherent, devotee, upholder 2 = **underground fighter**, guerrilla, resistance fighter ▷ adj 3 = **prejudiced**, biased, interested, one-sided, partial, sectarian

partition n 1 = **screen**, barrier, wall 2 = **division**, segregation, separation ▷ v 3 = **separate**, divide, screen

partly adv = **partially**, slightly, somewhat

partner n 1 = **spouse**, consort, husband or wife, mate, significant other (US inf) 2 = **associate**, colleague

partnership n = **company**, alliance, cooperative, firm, house, society, union

party n 1 = **get-together** (inf), celebration, do (inf), festivity, function, gathering, reception, social gathering 2 = **group**, band, company, crew, gang, squad, team, unit

a lawsuit or dispute. ▷ v **5** celebrate, have fun. **party line 1** official view of a political party. **2** telephone line shared by two or more subscribers. **party wall** common wall separating adjoining buildings.

parvenu [**par**-ven-new] n person newly risen to a position of power or wealth.

pascal n unit of pressure.

paschal [**pass**-kal] adj of the Passover or Easter.

pashmina [pash-**mee**-na] n shawl or scarf made from fine soft goat's wool.

pass ❶ v **1** go by, past, or through. **2** move or extend in a particular direction. **3** be successful in (a test or examination). **4** spend (time) or (of time) go by. **5** give, hand. **6** be inherited by. **7** Sport hit, kick, or throw (the ball) to another player. **8** (of a law-making body) agree to (a law). **9** announce (a sentence or verdict) officially. **10** exceed. **11** choose not to answer a question or not to take one's turn in a game. **12** discharge (urine etc.) from the body. **13** come to an end. ▷ n **14** successful result in a test or examination. **15** Sport transfer of a ball. **16** narrow gap through mountains. **17** permit or licence. **make a pass at** informal make sexual advances to. **pass for** be accepted as.

passable adj **1** (just) acceptable. **2** (of a road) capable of being travelled along. **passing** adj **1** brief or transitory. **2** cursory or casual. **pass away** v die. **pass out** v informal faint. **pass over** v take no notice of, disregard. **pass up** v informal fail to take advantage of (something).

passage ❶ n **1** channel or opening providing a way through. **2** hall or corridor. **3** section of a book etc. **4** journey by sea. **5** act of passing from one place or condition to another. **6** right or freedom to pass. **passageway** n passage or corridor.

passbook n book issued by a bank or building society for keeping a record of deposits and withdrawals.

passé [**pas**-say] adj out-of-date.

passenger ❶ n **1** person travelling in a vehicle driven by someone else. **2** member of a team who does not pull his or her weight.

passer-by ❶ n, pl **passers-by** person who is walking past something or someone.

passerine adj belonging to the order of perching birds.

passim adv Latin everywhere, throughout.

passion ❶ n **1** intense sexual love. **2** any strong emotion. **3** great enthusiasm. **4** (**P-**) Christianity the

---

THESAURUS

3 = **faction**, camp, clique, coterie, league, set, side

pass v **1** = **go by** or **past**, elapse, go, lapse, move, proceed, run **3** = **qualify**, do, get through, graduate, succeed **4** = **spend**, fill, occupy, while away **5** = **give**, convey, deliver, hand, send, transfer **8** = **approve**, accept, decree, enact, legislate, ordain, ratify **10** = **exceed**, beat, go beyond, outdo, outstrip, overtake, surpass **13** = **end**, blow over, cease, go ▷ n **16** = **gap**, canyon, gorge, ravine, route **17** = **licence**, authorization, passport, permit, ticket, warrant

passable adj **1** = **adequate**, acceptable, all right, average, fair, mediocre, so-so (inf), tolerable

passage n **1** = **way**, alley, avenue, channel, course, path, road, route **2** = **corridor**, hall, lobby, vestibule **3** = **extract**, excerpt, piece, quotation, reading, section, text **4** = **journey**, crossing, trek, trip, voyage **6** = **safe-conduct**,

freedom, permission, right

passageway n = **corridor**, aisle, alley, hall, hallway, lane, passage

pass away v = **die**, cark (Aust & NZ sl), expire, kick the bucket (sl), pass on, pass over, shuffle off this mortal coil, snuff it (inf)

passé adj = **out-of-date**, dated, obsolete, old-fashioned, old hat, outdated, outmoded, unfashionable

passenger n **1** = **traveller**, fare, rider

passer-by n = **bystander**, onlooker, witness

passing adj **1** = **momentary**, brief, ephemeral, fleeting, short-lived, temporary, transient, transitory **2** = **superficial**, casual, cursory, glancing, quick, short

passion n **1** = **love**, ardour, desire, infatuation, lust **2** = **emotion**, ardour, excitement, feeling, fervour, fire, heat, intensity, warmth, zeal **3** = **mania**, bug (inf), craving, craze, enthusiasm, fascination, obsession

P

suffering of Christ. **passionate** adj
passionately adv **passionflower** n
tropical American plant. **passion fruit**
edible fruit of the passionflower.
Passion play play about Christ's
suffering.

passive ⊕ adj **1** not playing an active
part. **2** submissive and receptive to
outside forces. **3** Grammar (of a verb)
in a form indicating that the subject
receives the action, e.g. was jeered in he
was jeered by the crowd. **passively** adv
passivity n **passive resistance**
resistance to a government, law, etc.
by nonviolent acts. **passive smoking**
inhalation of smoke from others'
cigarettes by a nonsmoker.

Passover n Jewish festival
commemorating the sparing of the
Jews in Egypt.

passport n official document granting
permission to travel abroad.

password ⊕ n secret word or phrase
that ensures admission.

past ⊕ adj **1** of the time before the
present. **2** ended, gone by.
3 Grammar (of a verb tense) indicating
that the action specified took place
earlier. ▷ n **4** period of time before the
present. **5** person's earlier life, esp. a
disreputable period. **6** Grammar past
tense. ▷ adv **7** ago. **8** by, along. ▷ prep
9 beyond. **past it** informal unable to
do the things one could do when
younger. **past master** person with
great talent or experience in a

particular subject.

pasta n type of food, such as spaghetti,
that is made in different shapes from
flour and water.

paste ⊕ n **1** moist soft mixture, such as
toothpaste. **2** adhesive, esp. for
paper. **3** smooth preparation of fish
etc. for spreading on bread. **4** pastry
dough. **5** shiny glass used to make
imitation jewellery. ▷ v **6** fasten with
paste. **pasting** n informal **1** heavy
defeat. **2** strong criticism.
pasteboard n stiff thick paper.

pastel ⊕ n **1** coloured chalk crayon for
drawing. **2** picture drawn in pastels.
3 pale delicate colour. ▷ adj **4** pale and
delicate in colour.

pasteurize v sterilize by heating.
pasteurization n.

pastiche ⊕ [pass-**teesh**] n work of art
that mixes styles or copies the style of
another artist.

pastille n small fruit-flavoured and
sometimes medicated sweet.

pastime ⊕ n activity that makes time
pass pleasantly.

pastor ⊕ n clergyman in charge of a
congregation. **pastoral** adj **1** of or
depicting country life. **2** of a
clergyman or his duties. ▷ n **3** poem or
picture portraying country life.

pastrami n highly seasoned smoked beef.

pastry n, pl **-ries 1** baking dough made
of flour, fat, and water. **2** cake or pie.

pasture ⊕ n grassy land for farm
animals to graze on.

————————————————————— THESAURUS —————

passionate adj **1** = **loving**, amorous,
ardent, erotic, hot, lustful
2 = **emotional**, ardent, eager, fervent,
fierce, heartfelt, impassioned,
intense, strong

passive adj **1, 2** = **submissive**,
compliant, docile, inactive, quiescent,
receptive

pass out v Inf = **faint**, become
unconscious, black out (inf), lose
consciousness

pass over v = **disregard**, ignore,
overlook, take no notice of

pass up v Inf = **miss**, abstain, decline,
forgo, give (something) a miss (inf),
let slip, neglect

password n = **signal**, key word,
watchword

past adj **1** = **former**, ancient, bygone,
early, olden, previous **2** = **over**, done,
ended, finished, gone ▷ n **4** = **former**

times, days gone by, long ago, olden
days **5** = **background**, history, life,
past life ▷ prep **9** = **beyond**, across, by,
over

paste n **2** = **adhesive**, cement, glue,
gum ▷ v **6** = **stick**, cement, glue, gum

pastel adj **4** = **pale**, delicate, light,
muted, soft

pastiche n = **medley**, blend, hotchpotch,
melange, miscellany, mixture

pastime n = **activity**, amusement,
diversion, entertainment, game,
hobby, recreation

pastor n = **clergyman**, churchman,
ecclesiastic, minister, parson, priest,
rector, vicar

pastoral adj **1** = **rustic**, bucolic,
country, rural **2** = **ecclesiastical**,
clerical, ministerial, priestly

pasture n = **grassland**, grass, grazing,
meadow

pasty¹ ❶ [**pay**-stee] *adj* **pastier**, **pastiest** (of a complexion) pale and unhealthy.

pasty² [**pass**-tee] *n, pl* **pasties** round of pastry folded over a savoury filling.

pat¹ ❶ *v* **patting, patted 1** tap lightly. ▷ *n* **2** gentle tap or stroke. **3** small shaped mass of butter etc.

pat² ❶ *adj* quick, ready, or glib. **off pat** learned thoroughly.

patch ❶ *n* **1** piece of material sewn on a garment. **2** small contrasting section. **3** plot of ground. **4** protective pad for the eye. ▷ *v* **5** mend with a patch. **patchy** *adj* **patchier, patchiest** of uneven quality or intensity. **patch up** *v* **1** repair clumsily. **2** make up (a quarrel). **patchwork** *n* needlework made of pieces of different materials sewn together.

pate *n old-fashioned* head.

pâté [**pat**-ay] *n* spread of finely minced liver etc.

patella *n, pl* **-lae** kneecap.

patent ❶ *n* **1** document giving the exclusive right to make or sell an invention. ▷ *adj* **2** open to public inspection, e.g. *letters patent*. **3** obvious. **4** protected by a patent. ▷ *v* **5** obtain a patent for. **patently** *adv* obviously. **patent leather** leather processed to give a hard glossy surface.

paternal ❶ *adj* **1** fatherly. **2** related through one's father. **paternity** *n* fact or state of being a father.

paternalism *n* authority exercised in a way that limits individual responsibility. **paternalistic** *adj*.

path ❶ *n* **1** surfaced walk or track. **2** course or direction. **3** course of action.

pathetic ❶ *adj* **1** causing feelings of pity or sadness. **2** distressingly inadequate. **pathetically** *adv*.

pathname *n Computers* file name listing the sequence of directories leading to a particular file or directory.

pathogen *n* thing that causes disease. **pathogenic** *adj*.

pathology *n* scientific study of diseases. **pathological** *adj* **1** of pathology. **2** *informal* compulsively motivated. **pathologist** *n*.

pathos ❶ *n* power of arousing pity or sadness.

patient ❶ *adj* **1** enduring difficulties or delays calmly. ▷ *n* **2** person receiving medical treatment. **patience** *n* **1** quality of being patient. **2** card game for one.

patina *n* **1** fine layer on a surface. **2** sheen of age on woodwork.

patio *n, pl* **-tios** paved area adjoining a house.

patois [**pat**-wah] *n, pl* **patois** [**pat**-wahz] regional dialect.

patriarch *n* **1** male head of a family or tribe. **2** highest-ranking bishop in Orthodox Churches. **patriarchal** *adj* **patriarchy** *n, pl* **-chies** society in which men have most of the power.

patrician *n* **1** member of the nobility. ▷ *adj* **2** of noble birth.

p

———————————— THESAURUS ————————————

pasty¹ *adj* = **pale**, anaemic, pallid, sickly, wan

pat¹ *v* **1** = **stroke**, caress, fondle, pet, tap, touch ▷ *n* **2** = **stroke**, clap, tap

pat² *adj* = **glib**, automatic, easy, facile, ready, simplistic, slick, smooth **off pat** = **perfectly**, exactly, faultlessly, flawlessly, precisely

patch *n* **1** = **reinforcement**, piece of material **2** = **spot**, bit, scrap, shred, small piece **3** = **plot**, area, ground, land, tract ▷ *v* **5** = **mend**, cover, reinforce, repair, sew up

patchy *adj* = **uneven**, erratic, fitful, irregular, sketchy, spotty, variable

patent *n* **1** = **copyright**, licence ▷ *adj* **3** = **obvious**, apparent, clear, evident, glaring, manifest

paternal *adj* **1** = **fatherly**, concerned, protective, solicitous

paternity *n* = **fatherhood**

path *n* **1** = **way**, footpath, road, track, trail **2** = **course**, direction, road, route, way

pathetic *adj* **1** = **sad**, affecting, distressing, gut-wrenching, heart-rending, moving, pitiable, plaintive, poignant, tender, touching

pathos *n* = **sadness**, pitifulness, plaintiveness, poignancy

patience *n* **1** = **forbearance**, calmness, restraint, serenity, sufferance, tolerance

patient *adj* **1** = **long-suffering**, calm, enduring, persevering, philosophical, resigned, stoical, submissive, uncomplaining ▷ *n* **2** = **sick person**, case, invalid, sufferer

patricide n 1 crime of killing one's father. 2 person who does this.

patrimony n, pl **-nies** property inherited from ancestors.

patriot ❶ n person who loves his or her country and supports its interests. **patriotic** adj **patriotism** n.

patrol ❶ n 1 regular circuit by a guard. 2 person or small group patrolling. 3 unit of Scouts or Guides. ▷ v **-trolling, -trolled** 4 go round on guard, or reconnoitring. **patrol car** police car used for patrolling streets.

patron ❶ n 1 person who gives financial support to charities, artists, etc. 2 regular customer of a shop, pub, etc. **patronage** n support given by a patron. **patronize** v 1 treat in a condescending way. 2 be a patron of. **patronizing** adj **patron saint** saint regarded as the guardian of a country or group.

patronymic n name derived from one's father or a male ancestor.

patter¹ ❶ v 1 make repeated soft tapping sounds. ▷ n 2 quick succession of taps.

patter² ❶ n glib rapid speech.

pattern ❶ n 1 arrangement of repeated parts or decorative designs. 2 regular way that something is done. 3 diagram or shape used as a guide to make something. **patterned** adj decorated with a pattern.

patty n, pl **-ties** small round meat pie.

paucity ❶ n 1 scarcity. 2 smallness of amount or number.

paunch ❶ n protruding belly.

pauper ❶ n very poor person.

pause ❶ v 1 stop for a time. 2 hesitate. ▷ n 3 stop or rest in speech or action. 4 Music continuation of a note or rest beyond its normal length.

pave ❶ v form (a surface) with stone or brick. **pavement** n paved path for pedestrians.

pavilion n 1 building on a playing field etc. 2 building for housing an exhibition etc.

pavlova n meringue cake topped with whipped cream and fruit.

paw ❶ n 1 animal's foot with claws and pads. ▷ v 2 scrape with the paw or hoof. 3 informal touch in a rough or overfamiliar way.

pawl n pivoted lever shaped to engage with a ratchet to prevent motion in a particular direction.

━━━━━━━━━━━━━━━━━━━━━━ THESAURUS ━━━━━━━━━

patriot n = **nationalist**, chauvinist, loyalist

patriotic adj = **nationalistic**, chauvinistic, jingoistic, loyal

patriotism n = **nationalism**, jingoism

patrol n 1 = **policing**, guarding, protecting, vigilance, watching 2 = **guard**, patrolman, sentinel, watch, watchman ▷ v 4 = **police**, guard, inspect, keep guard, keep watch, safeguard

patron n 1 = **supporter**, backer, benefactor, champion, friend, helper, philanthropist, sponsor 2 = **customer**, buyer, client, frequenter, habitué, shopper

patronage n = **support**, aid, assistance, backing, help, promotion, sponsorship

patronize v 1 = **talk down to**, look down on 2 a = **support**, back, fund, help, maintain, promote, sponsor b = **be a customer** or **client of**, do business with, frequent, shop at

patronizing adj 1 = **condescending**, disdainful, gracious, haughty, snobbish, supercilious, superior

patter¹ v 1 = **tap**, beat, pat, pitter-patter ▷ n 2 = **tapping**, pattering, pitter-patter

patter² n = **spiel**, line, pitch (inf)

pattern n 1 = **design**, arrangement, decoration, device, figure, motif 2 = **order**, method, plan, sequence, system 3 = **plan**, design, diagram, guide, original, stencil, template

paucity n = **scarcity**, dearth, deficiency, lack, rarity, scantiness, shortage, sparseness

paunch n = **belly**, pot, potbelly, spare tyre (Brit sl)

pauper n = **down-and-out**, bankrupt, beggar, mendicant, poor person

pause v 1 = **stop briefly**, break, cease, delay, halt, have a breather (inf), interrupt, rest, take a break, wait ▷ n 3 = **stop**, break, breather (inf), cessation, gap, halt, interlude, intermission, interval, lull, respite, rest, stoppage

pave v = **cover**, concrete, floor, surface, tile

paw v 3 Inf = **manhandle**, grab, handle roughly, maul, molest

P

pawn¹ ❶ v deposit (an article) as security for money borrowed. **in pawn** deposited as security with a pawnbroker. **pawnbroker** n lender of money on goods deposited.

pawn² ❶ n **1** chessman of the lowest value. **2** person manipulated by someone else.

pawpaw n same as PAPAYA.

pay ❶ v **paying**, **paid** **1** give money etc. in return for goods or services. **2** settle a debt or obligation. **3** compensate (for). **4** give. **5** be profitable to. ▷ n **6** wages or salary. **payment** n **1** act of paying. **2** money paid. **payable** adj due to be paid. **payee** n person to whom money is paid or due. **paying guest** lodger. **pay off** v **1** pay (debt) in full. **2** turn out successfully. **pay out** v **1** spend. **2** release (a rope) bit by bit. **paywall** n system preventing a user from accessing certain information on a website unless a fee is paid.

PAYE pay as you earn: system by which income tax is paid by an employer straight to the government.

payload n **1** passengers or cargo of an aircraft. **2** explosive power of a missile etc.

payola n informal bribe to get special treatment, esp. to promote a commercial product.

payroll n list of employees who receive regular pay.

Pb Chemistry lead.

pc per cent.

PC **1** personal computer. **2** Police Constable. **3** politically correct. **4** Privy Councillor.

Pd Chemistry palladium.

PDA personal digital assistant.

PE **1** physical education. **2** Prince Edward Island.

pea n **1** climbing plant with seeds growing in pods. **2** its seed, eaten as a vegetable. **peasouper** n informal thick fog.

peace ❶ n **1** calm, quietness. **2** absence of anxiety. **3** freedom from war. **4** harmony between people. **peaceable** adj inclined towards peace. **peaceably** adv **peaceful** adj **peacefully** adv **peacemaker** n person who brings about peace, esp. between others.

peach n **1** soft juicy fruit with a stone and a downy skin. **2** informal very pleasing person or thing. ▷ adj **3** pinkish-orange.

peacock n large male bird with a brilliantly coloured fanlike tail. **peahen** n fem **peafowl** n peacock or peahen.

peak ❶ n **1** pointed top, esp. of a mountain. **2** point of greatest development etc. **3** projecting piece

pawn¹ v = **hock** (inf, chiefly US), deposit, mortgage, pledge

pawn² n **2** = **tool**, cat's-paw, instrument, plaything, puppet, stooge (sl)

pay v **1, 2** = **reimburse**, give, remit, remunerate, requite, reward, settle **3** = **compensate**, recompense **4** = **give**, bestow, extend, grant, hand out, present **5** = **be profitable**, benefit, be worthwhile, make a return, make money, repay ▷ n **6** = **wages**, allowance, earnings, fee, income, payment, recompense, reimbursement, remuneration, reward, salary, stipend

payable adj = **due**, outstanding, owed, owing

payment n **1** = **paying**, discharge, remittance, settlement **2** = **wage**, advance, deposit, fee, hire, instalment, premium, remittance, remuneration, reward

pay off v **1** = **settle**, clear, discharge, pay in full, square **2** = **succeed**, be effective, work

pay out v **1** = **spend**, disburse, expend, fork out or over or up (sl), shell out (inf)

peace n **1** = **stillness**, calm, calmness, hush, quiet, repose, rest, silence, tranquillity **2** = **serenity**, calm, composure, contentment, repose **3** = **truce**, armistice, treaty **4** = **harmony**, accord, agreement, concord

peaceable adj = **peace-loving**, conciliatory, friendly, gentle, mild, peaceful, unwarlike

peaceful adj **1** = **calm**, placid, quiet, restful, serene, still, tranquil, undisturbed **3** = **peace-loving**, conciliatory, peaceable, unwarlike **4** = **at peace**, amicable, friendly, harmonious, nonviolent

peacemaker n = **mediator**, arbitrator, conciliator, pacifier

peak n **1** = **point**, apex, brow, crest, pinnacle, summit, tip, top **2** = **high point**, acme, climax, crown, culmination, zenith ▷ v **4** = **culminate**, climax, come to a head

p

on the front of a cap. ▷ v **4** form or reach a peak. ▷ adj **5** of or at the point of greatest demand. **peaked** adj **peaky** adj **peakier**, **peakiest** pale and sickly.

peal ❶ n **1** long loud echoing sound, esp. of bells or thunder. ▷ v **2** sound with a peal or peals.

peanut n **1** pea-shaped nut that ripens underground. ▷ pl **2** informal trifling amount of money.

pear n sweet juicy fruit with a narrow top and rounded base.

pearl n hard round shiny object found inside some oyster shells and used as a jewel. **pearly** adj **pearlier**, **pearliest**. **pearl barley** barley ground into small round grains.

peasant ❶ n farmer or farmworker of a low social class. **peasantry** n peasants collectively.

pease pudding n dish of boiled split peas.

peat n decayed vegetable material found in bogs, used as fertilizer or fuel.

pebble n small roundish stone. **pebbly** adj **pebblier**, **pebbliest**. **pebble dash** coating for exterior walls consisting of small stones set in plaster.

pecan [**pee**-kan] n edible nut of a N American tree.

peccadillo ❶ n, pl **-loes**, **-los** trivial misdeed.

peck¹ ❶ v **1** strike or pick up with the beak. **2** informal kiss quickly. ▷ n **3** pecking movement. **peckish** adj informal slightly hungry. **peck at** v nibble, eat reluctantly. **pecking order** order of seniority or power in a group.

peck² n fourth part of a bushel, 2 gallons.

pectin n substance in fruit that makes jam set.

pectoral adj **1** of the chest or thorax. ▷ n **2** pectoral muscle or fin.

peculiar ❶ adj **1** strange. **2** distinct, special. **3** belonging exclusively to. **peculiarity** n, pl **-ties 1** oddity, eccentricity. **2** distinguishing trait.

pecuniary adj relating to, or consisting of, money.

pedagogue ❶ n schoolteacher, esp. a pedantic one.

pedal n **1** foot-operated lever used to control a vehicle or machine, or to modify the tone of a musical instrument. ▷ v **-alling**, **-alled 2** propel (a bicycle) by using its pedals.

pedant ❶ n person who is excessively concerned with details and rules, esp. in academic work. **pedantic** adj **pedantry** n.

peddle ❶ v sell (goods) from door to door. **peddler** n person who sells illegal drugs.

pederast n man who has homosexual relations with boys. **pederasty** n.

pedestal ❶ n base supporting a column, statue, etc.

pedestrian ❶ n **1** person who walks. ▷ adj **2** dull, uninspiring. **pedestrian crossing** place marked where

━━━━━━━━━━━━━━━━━━━━━━━━━━━━━━━ THESAURUS ━━━━━

peal n **1** = **ring**, blast, chime, clang, clap, crash, reverberation, roar, rumble ▷ v **2** = **ring**, chime, crash, resound, roar, rumble

peasant n = **rustic**, countryman

peccadillo n = **misdeed**, error, indiscretion, lapse, misdemeanour, slip

peck¹ v **1** = **pick**, dig, hit, jab, poke, prick, strike, tap

peculiar adj **1** = **odd**, abnormal, bizarre, curious, eccentric, extraordinary, freakish, funny, munted (NZ sl), offbeat, outlandish, outré, quaint, queer, singular, strange, uncommon, unconventional, unusual, weird **2** = **specific**, characteristic, distinctive, particular, special, unique

peculiarity n **1** = **eccentricity**, abnormality, foible, idiosyncrasy, mannerism, oddity, quirk

2 = **characteristic**, attribute, feature, mark, particularity, property, quality, trait

pedagogue n = **teacher**, instructor, master or mistress, schoolmaster or schoolmistress

pedant n = **hairsplitter**, nit-picker (inf), quibbler

pedantic adj = **hairsplitting**, academic, bookish, donnish, formal, fussy, nit-picking (inf), particular, precise, punctilious

pedantry n = **hairsplitting**, punctiliousness, quibbling

peddle v = **sell**, flog (sl), hawk, market, push (inf), trade

pedestal n = **support**, base, foot, mounting, plinth, stand

pedestrian n **1** = **walker**, foot-traveller ▷ adj **2** = **dull**, banal, boring, commonplace, humdrum, mediocre,

pedestrians may cross a road.
pedestrian precinct (shopping) area for pedestrians only.

pedicure *n* medical or cosmetic treatment of the feet.

pedigree ❶ *n* register of ancestors, esp. of a purebred animal.

pediment *n* triangular part over a door etc.

pedlar ❶ *n* person who sells goods from door to door.

pedometer [pid-**dom**-it-er] *n* instrument which measures the distance walked.

pee *informal* ▷ *v* **peeing, peed 1** urinate. ▷ *n* **2** urine. **3** act of urinating.

peek ❶ *v, n* peep or glance.

peel ❶ *v* **1** remove the skin or rind of (a vegetable or fruit). **2** (of skin or a surface) come off in flakes. ▷ *n* **3** rind or skin. **peelings** *pl n*.

peep¹ ❶ *v* **1** look slyly or quickly. ▷ *n* **2** peeping look. **Peeping Tom** man who furtively watches women undressing.

peep² ❶ *v* **1** make a small shrill noise. ▷ *n* **2** small shrill noise.

peer¹ ❶ *n* **1** (*fem* **peeress**) member of the nobility. **2** person of the same status, age, etc. **peerage** *n* **1** whole body of peers. **2** rank of a peer. **peerless** *adj* unequalled, unsurpassed. **peer group** group of people of similar age, status, etc.

peer² ❶ *v* look closely and intently.

peeved *adj informal* annoyed.

peevish ❶ *adj* fretful or irritable. **peevishly** *adv*.

peewit *n* same as LAPWING.

peg ❶ *n* **1** pin or clip for joining, fastening, marking, etc. **2** hook or knob for hanging things on. ▷ *v* **pegging, pegged 3** fasten with pegs. **4** stabilize (prices). **off the peg** (of clothes) ready-to-wear, not tailor-made.

peignoir [**pay**-nwahr] *n* woman's light dressing gown.

pejorative ❶ [pij-**jor**-a-tiv] *adj* (of words etc.) with an insulting or critical meaning.

Pekingese, Pekinese *n, pl* **-ese** small dog with a short wrinkled muzzle.

pelargonium *n* plant with red, white, or pink flowers.

pelican *n* large water bird with a pouch beneath its bill for storing fish. **pelican crossing** road crossing with pedestrian-operated traffic lights.

pellagra *n* disease caused by lack of vitamin B.

pellet *n* small ball of something.

pell-mell *adv* in utter confusion, headlong.

pellucid *adj* very clear.

pelmet *n* ornamental drapery or board, concealing a curtain rail.

pelt¹ ❶ *v* **1** throw missiles at. **2** run fast, rush. **3** rain heavily. **at full pelt** at top speed.

mundane, ordinary, prosaic, run-of-the-mill, uninspired

pedigree *n* = **lineage**, ancestry, blood, breed, descent, extraction, family, family tree, genealogy, line, race, stock

pedlar *n* = **seller**, door-to-door salesman, hawker, huckster, vendor

peek *v* = **glance**, eyeball (*sl*), look, peep ▷ *n* = **glance**, glimpse, look, look-see (*sl*), peep

peel *v* **1** = **skin**, pare, strip off **2** = **flake off**, scale ▷ *n* **3** = **skin**, peeling, rind

peep¹ *v* **1** = **peek**, eyeball (*sl*), look, sneak a look, steal a look ▷ *n* **2** = **look**, glimpse, look-see (*sl*), peek

peep² *v* **1** = **tweet**, cheep, chirp, squeak ▷ *n* **2** = **tweet**, cheep, chirp, squeak

peer¹ *n* **1** = **noble**, aristocrat, lord, nobleman **2** = **equal**, compeer, fellow, like

peer² *v* = **squint**, gaze, inspect, peep, scan, snoop, spy

peerage *n* **1** = **aristocracy**, lords and ladies, nobility, peers

peerless *adj* = **unequalled**, beyond compare, excellent, incomparable, matchless, outstanding, unmatched, unparalleled, unrivalled

peevish *adj* = **irritable**, cantankerous, childish, churlish, cross, crotchety (*inf*), fractious, fretful, grumpy, petulant, querulous, snappy, sulky, sullen, surly

peg *v* **3** = **fasten**, attach, fix, join, secure

pejorative *adj* = **derogatory**, deprecatory, depreciatory, disparaging, negative, uncomplimentary, unpleasant

pelt¹ *v* **1** = **throw**, batter, bombard, cast, hurl, pepper, shower, sling, strike **2** = **rush**, belt (*sl*), charge, dash, hurry, run fast, shoot, speed, tear **3** = **pour**, bucket down (*inf*), rain cats and dogs (*inf*), rain hard, teem

p

pelt² ❶ *n* skin of a fur-bearing animal.
pelvis *n* framework of bones at the base of the spine, to which the hips are attached. **pelvic** *adj*.
pen¹ ❶ *n* **1** instrument for writing in ink. ▷ *v* **penning**, **penned 2** write or compose. **pen friend** friend with whom a person corresponds without meeting. **penknife** *n* small knife with blade(s) that fold into the handle. **pen name** name used by a writer instead of his or her real name.
pen² ❶ *n* **1** small enclosure for domestic animals. ▷ *v* **penning**, **penned 2** put or keep in a pen. **penned in** trapped or confined.
pen³ *n* female swan.
penal ❶ [pee-nal] *adj* of or used in punishment. **penalize** *v* **1** impose a penalty on. **2** handicap, hinder. **penalty** *n*, *pl* **-ties 1** punishment for a crime or offence. **2** *Sport* handicap or disadvantage imposed for breaking a rule.
penance ❶ *n* voluntary self-punishment to make amends for wrongdoing.
pence *n* a plural of PENNY.
penchant ❶ [pon-shon] *n* inclination or liking.
pencil *n* **1** thin cylindrical instrument containing graphite, for writing or

drawing. ▷ *v* **-cilling**, **-cilled 2** draw, write, or mark with a pencil.
pendant *n* ornament worn on a chain round the neck.
pendent *adj* hanging.
pending ❶ *prep* **1** while waiting for. ▷ *adj* **2** not yet decided or settled.
pendulous *adj* hanging, swinging.
pendulum *n* suspended weight swinging to and fro, esp. as a regulator for a clock.
penetrate ❶ *v* **1** find or force a way into or through. **2** arrive at the meaning of. **penetrable** *adj* capable of being penetrated. **penetrating** *adj* **1** (of a sound) loud and unpleasant. **2** quick to understand. **penetration** *n*.
penguin *n* flightless black-and-white Antarctic sea bird.
penicillin *n* antibiotic drug effective against a wide range of diseases and infections.
peninsula *n* strip of land nearly surrounded by water. **peninsular** *adj*.
penis *n* organ of copulation and urination in male mammals.
penitent ❶ *adj* **1** feeling sorry for having done wrong. ▷ *n* **2** someone who is penitent. **penitence** *n* **penitentiary** *n*, *pl* **-ries 1** *US* prison. ▷ *adj* **2** (also **penitential**) relating to penance.

━━━━━━━━━━━━━━━━━ THESAURUS ━━━━━━━

pelt² *n* = **coat**, fell, hide, skin
pen¹ *v* **2** = **write**, compose, draft, draw up, jot down **pen name** = **pseudonym**, nom de plume
pen² *n* **1** = **enclosure**, cage, coop, fold, hutch, pound, sty ▷ *v* **2** = **enclose**, cage, confine, coop up, fence in, hedge, shut up *or* in
penal *adj* = **disciplinary**, corrective, punitive
penalize *v* **1** = **punish**, discipline, impose a penalty on **2** = **handicap**
penalty *n* **1** = **punishment**, fine, forfeit, price *Sport* = **handicap**
penance *n* = **atonement**, penalty, reparation, sackcloth and ashes
penchant *n* = **liking**, bent, bias, fondness, inclination, leaning, partiality, predilection, proclivity, propensity, taste, tendency

pending *adj* **2** = **undecided**, awaiting, imminent, impending, in the balance, undetermined, unsettled
penetrate *v* **1** = **pierce**, bore, enter, go through, prick, stab **2** = **grasp**, comprehend, decipher, fathom, figure out (*inf*), get to the bottom of, suss (out) (*sl*), work out
penetrating *adj* **1** = **sharp**, carrying, harsh, piercing, shrill **2** = **perceptive**, acute, astute, incisive, intelligent, keen, perspicacious, quick, sharp, sharp-witted, shrewd
penetration *n* **1** = **piercing**, entrance, entry, incision, puncturing **2** = **perception**, acuteness, astuteness, insight, keenness, sharpness, shrewdness
penitence *n* **1** = **repentance**, compunction, contrition, regret, remorse, shame, sorrow
penitent *adj* **1** = **repentant**, abject, apologetic, conscience-stricken, contrite, regretful, remorseful, sorry

pennant ❶ n long narrow flag.

pennon n triangular or tapering flag.

penny ❶ n, pl **pence**, **pennies 1** British bronze coin worth one hundredth of a pound. **2** former British coin worth one twelfth of a shilling. **penniless** adj very poor. **penny-pinching** adj excessively careful with money.

penology [pee-**nol**-a-jee] n study of punishment and prison management.

pension¹ ❶ n regular payment to people above a certain age, retired employees, widows, etc. **pensionable** adj **pensioner** n person receiving a pension. **pension off** v force (someone) to retire from a job and pay him or her a pension.

pension² [**pon**-syon] n boarding house in Europe.

pensive ❶ adj deeply thoughtful, often with a tinge of sadness.

pentagon n **1** geometric figure with five sides. **2** (**P-**) headquarters of the US military. **pentagonal** adj.

pentagram, pentacle n five-pointed star.

pentameter [pen-**tam**-it-er] n line of poetry with five metrical feet.

Pentateuch [**pent**-a-tyuke] n first five books of the Old Testament.

Pentecost n Christian festival celebrating the descent of the Holy Spirit to the apostles, Whitsuntide. **Pentecostal** adj of a Christian group that has a charismatic and fundamentalist approach to Christianity.

penthouse n flat built on the roof or top floor of a building.

pent-up ❶ adj (of an emotion) not released, repressed.

penultimate adj second last.

penumbra n, pl **-brae**, **-bras 1** (in an eclipse) the partially shadowed region which surrounds the full shadow. **2** partial shadow. **penumbral** adj.

penury ❶ n extreme poverty. **penurious** adj.

peony n, pl **-nies** garden plant with showy red, pink, or white flowers.

people ❶ pl n **1** persons generally. **2** the community. **3** one's family. ▷ n **4** race or nation. ▷ v **5** provide with inhabitants.

pep n informal high spirits, energy, or enthusiasm. **pep pill** informal tablet containing a stimulant drug. **pep talk** informal talk designed to increase confidence and enthusiasm. **pep up** v **pepping**, **pepped** stimulate, invigorate.

pepper ❶ n **1** sharp hot condiment made from the fruit of an East Indian climbing plant. **2** colourful tropical fruit used as a vegetable, capsicum. ▷ v **3** season with pepper. **4** sprinkle, dot. **5** pelt with missiles. **peppery** adj **1** tasting of pepper. **2** irritable. **peppercorn** n dried berry of the pepper plant. **peppercorn rent** low or nominal rent. **pepper mill** small hand mill used to grind peppercorns.

peppermint n **1** plant that yields an oil with a strong sharp flavour. **2** sweet flavoured with this.

peptic adj relating to digestion or the digestive juices. **peptic ulcer** ulcer in the stomach or duodenum.

per prep for each. **as per** in accordance with.

perambulate v walk through or about (a place). **perambulation** n **perambulator** n pram.

P

---

pennant n = **flag**, banner, ensign, pennon, streamer

penniless adj = **poor**, broke (inf), destitute, dirt-poor (inf), down and out, flat broke (inf), impecunious, impoverished, indigent, penurious, poverty-stricken, skint (Brit sl), stony-broke (Brit sl)

pension¹ n = **allowance**, annuity, benefit, superannuation

pensioner n = **senior citizen**, O.A.P., retired person

pensive adj = **thoughtful**, contemplative, dreamy, meditative, musing, preoccupied, reflective, sad, serious, solemn, wistful

pent-up adj = **suppressed**, bottled up, curbed, held back, inhibited, repressed, smothered, stifled

penury n = **poverty**, beggary, destitution, indigence, need, privation, want

people pl n **1** = **persons**, humanity, mankind, men and women, mortals **2** = **nation**, citizens, community, folk, inhabitants, population, public **3** = **family**, clan, race, tribe ▷ v **5** = **inhabit**, colonize, occupy, populate, settle

pepper n **1** = **seasoning**, flavour, spice ▷ v **4** = **sprinkle**, dot, fleck, spatter, speck **5** = **pelt**, bombard, shower

per annum *adv Latin* in each year.

per capita *adj*, *adv Latin* of or for each person.

perceive ❶ *v* **1** become aware of (something) through the senses. **2** understand. **perception** *n*.

percentage *n* proportion or rate per hundred. **per cent** in each hundred.

perceptible ❶ *adj* discernible, recognizable. **perceptibly** *adv*.

perception ❶ *n* **1** act of perceiving. **2** intuitive judgment. **perceptive** *adj*.

perch¹ ❶ *n* **1** resting place for a bird. ▷ *v* **2** alight, rest, or place on or as if on a perch.

perch² *n* edible freshwater fish.

perchance *adv old-fashioned* perhaps.

percipient *adj* quick to notice things, observant.

percolate *v* **1** pass or filter through small holes. **2** spread gradually. **3** make (coffee) or (of coffee) be made in a percolator. **percolation** *n* **percolator** *n* coffeepot in which boiling water is forced through a tube and filters down through coffee.

percussion ❶ *n* **1** striking of one thing against another. **2** *Music* percussion instruments collectively.

percussionist *n* **percussion instrument** musical instrument played by being struck, such as drums or cymbals.

perdition *n* spiritual ruin.

peregrination *n* travels, roaming.

peregrine falcon *n* falcon with dark upper parts and a light underside.

peremptory ❶ *adj* authoritative, imperious.

perennial ❶ *adj* **1** lasting through many years. ▷ *n* **2** plant lasting more than two years. **perennially** *adv*.

perestroika *n* (formerly, in the USSR) policy of restructuring the economy and political system.

perfect ❶ *adj* **1** having all the essential elements. **2** faultless. **3** correct, precise. **4** utter or absolute. **5** excellent. **6** *Grammar* denoting a tense of verbs describing completed actions. ▷ *n* **7** *Grammar* perfect tense. ▷ *v* **8** improve. **9** make fully correct. **perfectly** *adv* **perfection** *n* state of being perfect. **perfectionist** *n* person who demands the highest standards of excellence. **perfectionism** *n*.

perfidious ❶ *adj* treacherous, disloyal. **perfidy** *n*.

———————————————————————— THESAURUS ———————

perceive *v* **1** = **see**, behold, discern, discover, espy, make out, note, notice, observe, recognize, spot
2 = **understand**, comprehend, gather, grasp, learn, realize, see, suss (out) (*sl*)

perceptible *adj* = **visible**, apparent, appreciable, clear, detectable, discernible, evident, noticeable, observable, obvious, recognizable, tangible

perception *n* **1** = **understanding**, awareness, conception, consciousness, feeling, grasp, idea, impression, notion, sensation, sense

perceptive *adj* = **observant**, acute, alert, astute, aware, percipient, perspicacious, quick, sharp

perch¹ *n* **1** = **resting place**, branch, pole, post ▷ *v* **2** = **sit**, alight, balance, land, rest, roost, settle

percussion *n* **1** = **impact**, blow, bump, clash, collision, crash, knock, smash, thump

peremptory *adj* = **imperious**, authoritative, bossy (*inf*), dictatorial, dogmatic, domineering, overbearing

perennial *adj* **1** = **lasting**, abiding, constant, continual, enduring, incessant, persistent, recurrent

perfect *adj* **1** = **complete**, absolute, consummate, entire, finished, full, sheer, unmitigated, utter, whole
2 = **faultless**, flawless, immaculate, impeccable, pure, spotless, unblemished **3** = **exact**, accurate, correct, faithful, precise, true, unerring **5** = **excellent**, ideal, splendid, sublime, superb, superlative, supreme ▷ *v* **8** = **improve**, develop, polish, refine

perfection *n* = **completeness**, exactness, excellence, exquisiteness, faultlessness, integrity, maturity, perfectness, precision, purity, sublimity, superiority, wholeness

perfectionist *n* = **stickler**, precisionist, purist

perfectly *adv* **2** = **flawlessly**, faultlessly, ideally, impeccably, superbly, supremely, wonderfully
4 = **completely**, absolutely, altogether, fully, quite, thoroughly, totally, utterly, wholly

perfidious *adj* = **treacherous**, disloyal, double-dealing, traitorous, two-faced, unfaithful

perforate ❶ v make holes in. **perforation** n.

perforce adv of necessity.

perform ❶ v **1** carry out (an action). **2** act, sing, or present a play before an audience. **3** fulfil (a request etc.). **performance** n **performer** n.

perfume ❶ n **1** liquid cosmetic worn for its pleasant smell. **2** fragrance. ▷ v **3** give a pleasant smell to. **perfumed** adj **perfumer** n person who makes or sells perfume. **perfumery** n perfumes in general.

perfunctory ❶ adj done only as a matter of routine, superficial. **perfunctorily** adv.

pergola n arch or framework of trellis supporting climbing plants.

perhaps ❶ adv **1** possibly, maybe. **2** approximately.

pericardium n, pl **-dia** membrane enclosing the heart.

perigee n point in the orbit of the moon or a satellite that is nearest the earth.

perihelion n, pl **-lia** point in the orbit of a planet or comet that is nearest to the sun.

peril ❶ n great danger. **perilous** adj **perilously** adv.

perimeter ❶ [per-**rim**-it-er] n (length of) the outer edge of an area.

perinatal adj of or in the weeks shortly before or after birth.

period ❶ n **1** particular portion of time. **2** single occurrence of menstruation. **3** division of time at school etc. when a particular subject is taught. **4** US full stop. ▷ adj **5** (of furniture, dress, a play, etc.) dating from or in the style of an earlier time. **periodic** adj recurring at intervals. **periodic table** Chemistry chart of the elements, arranged to show their relationship to each other. **periodical** n **1** magazine issued at regular intervals. ▷ adj **2** periodic.

peripatetic [per-rip-a-**tet**-ik] adj travelling about from place to place.

periphery ❶ [per-**if**-er-ee] n, pl **-eries** **1** boundary or edge. **2** fringes of a field of activity. **peripheral** [per-**if**-er-al] adj **1** unimportant, not central. **2** of or on the periphery. ▷ n **3** any extra device that can be attached to or put in a computer.

periscope n instrument used, esp. in submarines, to give a view of objects on a different level.

perish ❶ v **1** be destroyed or die. **2** decay, rot. **perishable** adj liable to rot quickly. **perishing** adj informal very cold.

peritoneum [per-rit-toe-**nee**-um] n, pl **-nea**, **-neums** membrane lining the internal surface of the abdomen. **peritonitis** [per-rit-tone-**ite**-iss] n inflammation of the peritoneum.

THESAURUS

perforate v = **pierce**, bore, drill, penetrate, punch, puncture

perform v **1, 3** = **carry out**, accomplish, achieve, complete, discharge, do, execute, fulfil, pull off, work **2** = **present**, act, enact, play, produce, put on, represent, stage

performance n **1, 3** = **carrying out**, accomplishment, achievement, act, completion, execution, fulfilment, work, yakka (Aust & NZ inf) **2** = **presentation**, acting, appearance, exhibition, gig (inf), play, portrayal, production, show

performer n **2** = **artiste**, actor or actress, player, Thespian, trouper

perfume n **2** = **fragrance**, aroma, bouquet, odour, scent, smell

perfunctory adj = **offhand**, cursory, heedless, indifferent, mechanical, routine, sketchy, superficial

perhaps adv **1** = **maybe**, conceivably, feasibly, it may be, perchance (arch), possibly

peril n = **danger**, hazard, jeopardy, menace, risk, uncertainty

perilous adj = **dangerous**, hazardous, precarious, risky, threatening, unsafe

perimeter n = **boundary**, ambit, border, bounds, circumference, confines, edge, limit, margin, periphery

period n **1** = **time**, interval, season, space, span, spell, stretch, term, while

periodic adj = **recurrent**, cyclical, intermittent, occasional, regular, repeated, sporadic

periodical n **1** = **publication**, journal, magazine, monthly, paper, quarterly, weekly

peripheral adj **1** = **incidental**, inessential, irrelevant, marginal, minor, secondary, unimportant **2** = **outermost**, exterior, external, outer, outside

perish v **1 a** = **be destroyed**, cark (Aust & NZ sl), collapse, decline, disappear, fall, vanish **b** = **die**, be

periwinkle[1] *n* small edible shellfish, the winkle.

periwinkle[2] *n* plant with trailing stems and blue flowers.

perjury ● [**per**-jer-ee] *n, pl* **-juries** act or crime of lying while under oath in a court. **perjure oneself** commit perjury.

perk ● *n informal* incidental benefit gained from a job, such as a company car.

perk up *v* cheer up. **perky** *adj* **perkier, perkiest** lively or cheerful.

perm *n* **1** long-lasting curly hairstyle produced by treating the hair with chemicals. ▷ *v* **2** give (hair) a perm.

permafrost *n* permanently frozen ground.

permanent ● *adj* lasting forever. **permanence** *n* **permanently** *adv*.

permanganate *n* a salt of an acid of manganese.

permeate ● *v* pervade or pass through the whole of (something). **permeable** *adj* able to be permeated, esp. by liquid.

permit ● *v* **-mitting, -mitted 1** give permission, allow. ▷ *n* **2** document giving permission to do something.

permission *n* authorization to do something. **permissible** *adj*

permissive *adj* (excessively) tolerant, esp. in sexual matters. **permissiveness** *n*.

permutation *n* **1** any of the ways a number of things can be arranged or combined. **2** *Maths* arrangement of a number of quantities in every possible order. **3** fixed combination for selections of results on football pools.

pernicious ● *adj* **1** wicked. **2** extremely harmful, deadly.

pernickety ● *adj informal* (excessively) fussy about details.

peroration *n* concluding part of a speech, usu. summing up the main points.

peroxide *n* **1** hydrogen peroxide used as a hair bleach. **2** oxide containing a high proportion of oxygen.

perpendicular ● *adj* **1** at right angles to a line or surface. **2** upright or vertical. ▷ *n* **3** line or plane at right angles to another.

perpetrate ● *v* commit or be responsible for (a wrongdoing). **perpetration** *n* **perpetrator** *n*.

——————————————————————— THESAURUS ———

p

killed, expire, lose one's life, pass away **2** = **rot**, decay, decompose, disintegrate, moulder, waste

perishable *adj* = **short-lived**, decaying, decomposable

perjury *n* = **lying under oath**, bearing false witness, false statement, forswearing, giving false testimony **perjure oneself** = **commit perjury**, bear false witness, forswear, give false testimony, lie under oath, swear falsely

perk *n Inf* = **bonus**, benefit, extra, fringe benefit, perquisite, plus

permanence *n* = **continuity**, constancy, continuance, durability, endurance, finality, indestructibility, perpetuity, stability

permanent *adj* = **lasting**, abiding, constant, enduring, eternal, everlasting, immutable, perpetual, persistent, stable, steadfast, unchanging

permeate *v* = **pervade**, charge, fill, imbue, impregnate, infiltrate, penetrate, saturate, spread through

permissible *adj* = **permitted**, acceptable, allowable, all right,

authorized, lawful, legal, legitimate, O.K. *or* okay (*inf*)

permission *n* = **authorization**, allowance, approval, assent, consent, dispensation, go-ahead (*inf*), green light, leave, liberty, licence, sanction

permissive *adj* = **tolerant**, easy-going, forbearing, free, indulgent, lax, lenient, liberal

permit *v* **1** = **allow**, authorize, consent, enable, entitle, give leave *or* permission, give the green light to, grant, let, license, sanction ▷ *n* **2** = **licence**, authorization, pass, passport, permission, warrant

pernicious *adj* **1** = **wicked**, bad, evil **2** = **deadly**, damaging, dangerous, destructive, detrimental, fatal, harmful, hurtful, malign, poisonous

pernickety *adj Inf* = **fussy**, exacting, fastidious, finicky, overprecise, particular, picky (*inf*)

perpendicular *adj* **1, 2** = **upright**, at right angles to, on end, plumb, straight, vertical

perpetrate *v* = **commit**, carry out, do, enact, execute, perform, wreak

perpetual ⊙ *adj* **1** lasting forever.
2 continually repeated. **perpetually**
adv **perpetuate** *v* cause to continue or
be remembered. **perpetuation** *n*
perpetuity *n* eternity. **in perpetuity**
forever.
perplex ⊙ *v* puzzle, bewilder.
perplexity *n*, *pl* **-ties**.
perquisite ⊙ *n formal* same as PERK.
perry *n*, *pl* **-ries** alcoholic drink made
from fermented pears.
per se [per **say**] *adv* Latin in itself.
persecute ⊙ *v* **1** treat cruelly because
of race, religion, etc. **2** subject to
persistent harassment. **persecution** *n*
persecutor *n*.
persevere ⊙ *v* keep making an effort
despite difficulties. **perseverance** *n*.
Persian *adj* **1** of ancient Persia or
modern Iran, their people, or their
languages. ▷ *n* **2** person from modern
Iran, Iranian. **Persian carpet**,
rug hand-made carpet *or* rug with
flowing or geometric designs in rich
colours. **Persian cat** long-haired
domestic cat.

persiflage [**per**-sif-flahzh] *n* light
frivolous talk or writing.
persimmon *n* sweet red tropical fruit.
persist ⊙ *v* **1** continue to be or happen,
last. **2** continue in spite of obstacles
or objections. **persistent** *adj*
persistently *adv* **persistence** *n*.
person ⊙ *n* **1** human being. **2** body of a
human being. **3** *Grammar* form of
pronouns and verbs that shows if a
person is speaking, spoken to, or
spoken of. **personal** *adj* individual,
private. **personality** *n* distinctive
character. **in person** actually present.
● **USAGE NOTE**
● *Person* is generally used in the
● singular and *people* is used to
● indicate more than one. The plural
● *persons* is restricted to formal
● notices.
persona [per-**soh**-na] *n*, *pl* **-nae** [-nee]
someone's personality as presented to
others.
personable ⊙ *adj* pleasant in
appearance and personality.
personage ⊙ *n* important person.

THESAURUS

perpetual *adj* **1** = **everlasting**,
endless, eternal, infinite, lasting,
never-ending, perennial, permanent,
unchanging, unending **2** = **continual**,
constant, continuous, endless,
incessant, interminable, never-
ending, persistent, recurrent,
repeated
perpetuate *v* = **maintain**,
immortalize, keep going,
preserve
perplex *v* = **puzzle**, baffle, bewilder,
confound, confuse, mystify,
stump
perplexing *adj* = **puzzling**, baffling,
bewildering, complex, complicated,
confusing, difficult, enigmatic, hard,
inexplicable, mystifying
perplexity *n* = **puzzlement**,
bafflement, bewilderment,
confusion, difficulty, fix (*inf*),
incomprehension, mystery,
mystification, paradox
perquisite same as PERK.
persecute *v* **1** = **victimize**, afflict,
ill-treat, maltreat, oppress, pick on,
torment, torture **2** = **harass**, annoy,
badger, bother, hassle (*inf*), pester,
tease
perseverance *n* = **persistence**,
determination, diligence, doggedness,

endurance, pertinacity, resolution,
tenacity
persevere *v* = **keep going**, carry on,
continue, go on, hang on, persist,
remain, stick at *or* to
persist *v* **1** = **continue**, carry on, keep
up, last, linger, remain **2** = **persevere**,
continue, insist, stand firm
persistence *n* = **determination**,
doggedness, endurance, grit,
perseverance, pertinacity, resolution,
tenacity, tirelessness
persistent *adj* **1** = **continuous**,
constant, continual, endless,
incessant, never-ending, perpetual,
repeated **2** = **determined**, dogged,
obdurate, obstinate, persevering,
pertinacious, steadfast, steady,
stubborn, tenacious, tireless,
unflagging
person *n* **1** = **individual**, being, body,
human, soul **in person** = **personally**,
bodily, in the flesh, oneself
personable *adj* = **pleasant**, agreeable,
amiable, attractive, charming, good-
looking, handsome, lekker (*S Afr sl*),
likable *or* likeable, nice
personage *n* = **personality**, big shot
(*inf*), celebrity, dignitary, luminary,
megastar (*inf*), notable, public figure,
somebody, V.I.P.

p

personal ❶ *adj* **1** individual or private.
2 of the body, e.g. *personal hygiene*.
3 (of a remark etc.) offensive.
personalize *v* **personalized** *adj*
personally *adv* **1** directly, not by
delegation to others. **2** in one's own
opinion. **personal assistant** person
employed to help someone, esp. with
secretarial and administrative work.
personal column newspaper column
containing personal messages and
advertisements. **personal computer**
small computer used for word
processing or computer games.
personal pronoun pronoun like *I* or
she that stands for a definite person.
personal stereo very small portable
cassette player with headphones.
personality ❶ *n, pl* **-ties 1** person's
distinctive characteristics. **2** celebrity.
▷ *pl* **3** personal remarks, e.g. *the
discussion degenerated into personalities*.
personify ❶ *v* **-fying, -fied 1** give
human characteristics to. **2** be an
example of, typify. **personification** *n*.

personnel ❶ *n* people employed in an
organization.
perspective ❶ *n* **1** view of the relative
importance of situations or facts.
2 method of drawing that gives the
effect of solidity and relative distances
and sizes. **3** appearance of objects or
buildings relative to each other.
Perspex *n* ® transparent acrylic
substitute for glass.
perspicacious ❶ *adj* having quick
mental insight. **perspicacity** *n*.
perspire ❶ *v* sweat. **perspiration** *n*.
persuade ❶ *v* **1** make (someone) do
something by argument, charm, etc.
2 convince. **persuasion** *n* **1** act of
persuading. **2** way of thinking or
belief. **persuasive** *adj*.
pert ❶ *adj* saucy and cheeky.
pertain ❶ *v* belong or be relevant (to).
pertinacious *adj* very persistent and
determined. **pertinacity** *n*.
pertinent ❶ *adj* relevant. **pertinence** *n*.
perturb ❶ *v* disturb greatly.
perturbation *n*.

——— THESAURUS ———

personal *adj* **1** = **private**, exclusive,
individual, intimate, own, particular,
peculiar, special **3** = **offensive**,
derogatory, disparaging, insulting,
nasty
personality *n* **1** = **nature**, character,
disposition, identity, individuality,
make-up, temperament
2 = **celebrity**, famous name,
household name, megastar (*inf*),
notable, personage, star
personally *adv* **1** = **by oneself**, alone,
independently, on one's own, solely
2 = **in one's opinion**, for one's part,
from one's own viewpoint, in one's
books, in one's own view
personification *n* **2** = **embodiment**,
epitome, image, incarnation,
portrayal, representation
personify *v* **2** = **embody**, epitomize,
exemplify, represent, symbolize, typify
personnel *n* = **employees**, helpers,
human resources, people, staff,
workers, workforce
perspective *n* **1** = **objectivity**,
proportion, relation, relative
importance, relativity
perspicacious *adj* = **perceptive**,
acute, alert, astute, discerning, keen,
percipient, sharp, shrewd
perspiration *n* = **sweat**, moisture,
wetness

perspire *v* = **sweat**, exude, glow, pour
with sweat, secrete, swelter
persuade *v* **1** = **talk into**, bring round
(*inf*), coax, entice, impel, incite,
induce, influence, sway, urge, win
over **2** = **convince**, cause to believe,
satisfy
persuasion *n* **1** = **urging**, cajolery,
enticement, inducement, wheedling
2 = **creed**, belief, conviction, credo,
faith, opinion, tenet, views
persuasive *adj* = **convincing**, cogent,
compelling, credible, effective,
eloquent, forceful, influential,
plausible, sound, telling, valid,
weighty
pert *adj* = **impudent**, bold, cheeky,
forward, impertinent, insolent, sassy
(*US inf*), saucy
pertain *v* = **relate**, apply, befit, belong,
be relevant, concern, refer, regard
pertinent *adj* = **relevant**, applicable,
apposite, appropriate, apt, fit, fitting,
germane, material, proper, to the
point
perturb *v* = **disturb**, agitate, bother,
disconcert, faze, fluster, ruffle,
trouble, unsettle, vex, worry
perturbed *adj* = **disturbed**, agitated,
anxious, disconcerted, flustered,
shaken, troubled, uncomfortable,
uneasy, worried

p

DICTIONARY

peruse ❶ v read in a careful or leisurely manner. **perusal** n.

pervade ❶ v spread right through (something). **pervasive** adj.

perverse ❶ adj deliberately doing something different from what is thought normal or proper. **perversely** adv **perversity** n.

pervert ❶ v 1 use or alter for a wrong purpose. 2 lead into abnormal (sexual) behaviour. ▷ n 3 person who practises sexual perversion. **perversion** n 1 sexual act or desire considered abnormal. 2 act of perverting.

pervious adj able to be penetrated, permeable.

peseta [pa-**say**-ta] n former monetary unit of Spain.

peso [**pay**-so] n, pl **pesos** monetary unit of Argentina, Mexico, etc.

pessary n, pl **-ries** 1 appliance worn in the vagina, either to prevent conception or to support the womb. 2 vaginal suppository.

pessimism ❶ n tendency to expect the worst in all things. **pessimist** n **pessimistic** adj **pessimistically** adv.

pest ❶ n 1 annoying person. 2 insect or animal that damages crops. **pesticide** n chemical for killing insect pests.

pester ❶ v annoy or nag continually.

pestilence ❶ n deadly epidemic disease. **pestilent** adj 1 annoying, troublesome. 2 deadly. **pestilential** adj.

pestle n club-shaped implement for grinding things to powder in a mortar.

pet ❶ n 1 animal kept for pleasure and companionship. 2 person favoured or indulged. ▷ adj 3 kept as a pet. 4 particularly cherished. ▷ v **petting**, **petted** 5 treat as a pet. 6 pat or stroke affectionately. 7 informal kiss and caress erotically.

THESAURUS

peruse v = **read**, browse, check, examine, eyeball (sl), inspect, scan, scrutinize, study

pervade v = **spread through**, charge, fill, imbue, infuse, penetrate, permeate, suffuse

pervasive adj = **widespread**, common, extensive, general, omnipresent, prevalent, rife, ubiquitous, universal

perverse adj = **stubborn**, contrary, cussed (inf), disobedient, dogged, headstrong, intractable, intransigent, obdurate, obstinate, pig-headed, rebellious, refractory, stiff-necked, troublesome, wayward, wilful

perversion n 1 = **deviation**, aberration, abnormality, debauchery, depravity, immorality, kink (Brit inf), kinkiness (sl), unnaturalness, vice 2 = **distortion**, corruption, falsification, misinterpretation, misrepresentation, twisting

perversity n = **contrariness**, contradictoriness, intransigence, obduracy, refractoriness, waywardness, wrong-headedness

pervert v 1 = **distort**, abuse, falsify, garble, misrepresent, misuse, twist, warp 2 = **corrupt**, debase, debauch, degrade, deprave, lead astray ▷ n 3 = **deviant**, degenerate, weirdo or weirdie (inf)

pessimism n = **gloominess**, dejection, depression, despair, despondency, distrust, gloom, hopelessness, melancholy

pessimist n = **wet blanket** (inf), cynic, defeatist, killjoy, prophet of doom, worrier

pessimistic adj = **gloomy**, bleak, cynical, dark, dejected, depressed, despairing, despondent, glum, hopeless, morose

pest n 1 = **nuisance**, annoyance, bane, bother, drag (inf), irritation, pain (inf), thorn in one's flesh, trial, vexation 2 = **infection**, blight, bug, epidemic, pestilence, plague, scourge

pester v = **annoy**, badger, bedevil, be on one's back (sl), bother, bug (inf), harass, harry, hassle (inf), nag, plague, torment

pestilence n = **plague**, epidemic, visitation

pestilent adj 1 = **annoying**, bothersome, irksome, irritating, tiresome, vexing 2 = **harmful**, detrimental, evil, injurious, pernicious

pestilential adj 2 = **deadly**, dangerous, destructive, detrimental, harmful, hazardous, injurious, pernicious

pet n 2 = **favourite**, darling, idol, jewel, treasure ▷ adj 4 = **favourite**, cherished, dearest, dear to one's heart, favoured ▷ v 5 = **pamper**, baby, coddle, cosset, mollycoddle, spoil 6 = **fondle**, caress, pat, stroke 7 Inf

petal *n* one of the brightly coloured outer parts of a flower. **petalled** *adj*.

petard *n* **hoist with one's own petard** being the victim of one's own schemes.

peter out ❶ *v* gradually come to an end.

petite ❶ *adj* (of a woman) small and dainty.

petition ❶ *n* **1** formal request, esp. one signed by many people and presented to parliament. ▷ *v* **2** present a petition to. **petitioner** *n*.

petrel *n* sea bird with a hooked bill and tubular nostrils.

petrify ❶ *v* **-fying, -fied 1** frighten severely. **2** turn to stone. **petrification** *n*.

petrochemical *n* substance, such as acetone, obtained from petroleum.

petrodollar *n* money earned by a country by exporting petroleum.

petrol *n* flammable liquid obtained from petroleum, used as fuel in internal-combustion engines. **petrol bomb** home-made incendiary device consisting of a bottle filled with petrol. **petrol station** place selling petrol, oil, etc.

petroleum *n* thick dark oil found underground.

petticoat *n* woman's skirt-shaped undergarment.

pettifogging *adj* excessively concerned with unimportant detail.

petty ❶ *adj* **-tier, -tiest 1** unimportant, trivial. **2** small-minded. **3** on a small scale, e.g. *petty crime*. **pettiness** *n* **petty cash** cash kept by a firm to pay minor expenses. **petty officer** noncommissioned officer in the navy.

petulant ❶ *adj* childishly irritable or peevish. **petulance** *n* **petulantly** *adv*.

petunia *n* garden plant with funnel-shaped flowers.

pew *n* **1** fixed benchlike seat in a church. **2** *informal* chair, seat.

pewter *n* greyish metal made of tin and lead.

pH *Chemistry* measure of the acidity of a solution.

phalanger *n* long-tailed Australian tree-dwelling marsupial.

phalanx *n*, *pl* **phalanxes, phalanges** closely grouped mass of people.

phallus *n*, *pl* **-luses, -li** penis, esp. as a symbol of reproductive power in primitive rites. **phallic** *adj*.

phantasm *n* unreal vision, illusion. **phantasmal** adj.

phantasmagoria *n* shifting medley of dreamlike figures.

phantasy *n*, *pl* **-sies** same as FANTASY.

phantom ❶ *n* **1** ghost. **2** unreal vision.

Pharaoh [**fare**-oh] *n* title of the ancient Egyptian kings.

Pharisee *n* **1** member of an ancient Jewish sect teaching strict observance of Jewish traditions. **2** self-righteous hypocrite.

pharmaceutical *adj* of pharmacy.

pharmacology *n* study of drugs. **pharmacological** *adj* **pharmacologist** *n*.

pharmacopoeia [far-ma-koh-**pee**-a] *n* book with a list of and directions for the use of drugs.

pharmacy *n*, *pl* **-cies 1** preparation and dispensing of drugs and medicines. **2** pharmacist's shop. **pharmacist** *n* person qualified to prepare and sell drugs and medicines.

———————————— THESAURUS ————————————

= **cuddle**, canoodle (*sl*), kiss, neck (*inf*), smooch (*inf*), snog (*Brit sl*)

peter out *v* = **die out**, dwindle, ebb, fade, fail, run out, stop, taper off, wane

petite *adj* = **small**, dainty, delicate, elfin, little, slight

petition *n* **1** = **appeal**, entreaty, plea, prayer, request, solicitation, suit, supplication ▷ *v* **2** = **appeal**, adjure, ask, beg, beseech, entreat, plead, pray, solicit, supplicate

petrify *v* **1** = **terrify**, horrify, immobilize, paralyse, stun, stupefy, transfix **2** = **fossilize**, calcify, harden, turn to stone

petty *adj* **1** = **trivial**, contemptible,

inconsiderable, insignificant, little, measly (*inf*), negligible, paltry, slight, small, trifling, unimportant **2** = **small-minded**, mean, mean-minded, shabby, spiteful, ungenerous

petulance *n* = **sulkiness**, bad temper, ill humour, irritability, peevishness, pique, sullenness

petulant *adj* = **sulky**, bad-tempered, huffy, ill-humoured, moody, peevish, sullen

phantom *n* **1** = **spectre**, apparition, ghost, phantasm, shade (*lit*), spirit, spook (*inf*), wraith **2** = **illusion**, figment of the imagination, hallucination, vision

pharynx [**far**-rinks] *n*, *pl* **pharynges**, **pharynxes** cavity forming the back part of the mouth. **pharyngeal** *adj* **pharyngitis** [far-rin-**jite**-iss] *n* inflammation of the pharynx.

phase ❶ *n* **1** any distinct or characteristic stage in a development or chain of events. ▷ *v* **2** arrange or carry out in stages or to coincide with something else. **phase in**, **out** *v* introduce *or* discontinue gradually.

PhD Doctor of Philosophy.

pheasant *n* game bird with bright plumage.

phenobarbitone *n* drug inducing sleep or relaxation.

phenol *n* chemical used in disinfectants and antiseptics.

phenomenon ❶ *n*, *pl* **-ena 1** anything appearing or observed. **2** remarkable person or thing. **phenomenal** *adj* extraordinary, outstanding. **phenomenally** *adv*.

phew *interj* exclamation of relief, surprise, etc.

phial *n* small bottle for medicine etc.

philadelphus *n* shrub with sweet-scented flowers.

philanderer ❶ *n* man who flirts or has many casual love affairs. **philandering** *adj*, *n*.

philanthropy ❶ *n* practice of helping people less well-off than oneself.

philanthropic *adj* **philanthropist** *n*.

philately [fill-**lat**-a-lee] *n* stamp collecting. **philatelist** *n*.

philharmonic *adj* (in names of orchestras etc.) music-loving.

philippic *n* bitter or impassioned speech of denunciation, invective.

philistine *adj*, *n* boorishly uncultivated (person). **philistinism** *n*.

philology *n* science of the structure and development of languages. **philological** *adj* **philologist** *n*.

philosophy ❶ *n*, *pl* **-phies 1** study of the meaning of life, knowledge, thought, etc. **2** theory or set of ideas held by a particular philosopher. **3** person's outlook on life. **philosopher** *n* person who studies philosophy. **philosophical**, **philosophic** *adj* **1** of philosophy. **2** calm in the face of difficulties or disappointments. **philosophically** *adv* **philosophize** *v* discuss in a philosophical manner.

philtre *n* magic drink supposed to arouse love in the person who drinks it.

phishing [**fish**-ing] *n* practice of tricking computer users into revealing their financial data in order to defraud them.

phlebitis [fleb-**bite**-iss] *n* inflammation of a vein.

THESAURUS

phase *n* **1** = **stage**, chapter, development, juncture, period, point, position, step, time

phase out *v* = **wind down**, close, ease off, eliminate, pull out, remove, run down, terminate, wind up, withdraw

phenominal *adj* **2** = **extraordinary**, exceptional, fantastic, marvellous, miraculous, outstanding, prodigious, remarkable, unusual

phenomenon *n* **1** = **occurrence**, circumstance, episode, event, fact, happening, incident **2** = **wonder**, exception, marvel, miracle, prodigy, rarity, sensation

philanderer *n* = **womanizer**, Casanova, Don Juan, flirt, ladies' man, lady-killer (*inf*), Lothario, playboy, stud (*sl*), wolf (*inf*)

philanthropic *adj* = **humanitarian**, beneficent, benevolent, charitable, generous, humane, kind, kind-hearted, munificent, public-spirited

philanthropist *n* = **humanitarian**,

benefactor, contributor, donor, giver, patron

philanthropy *n* = **humanitarianism**, beneficence, benevolence, brotherly love, charitableness, charity, generosity, kind-heartedness

philistine *adj* = **uncultured**, boorish, ignorant, lowbrow, tasteless, uncultivated, uneducated, unrefined ▷ *n* = **boor**, barbarian, ignoramus, lout, lowbrow, vulgarian, yahoo

philosopher *n* = **thinker**, logician, metaphysician, sage, theorist, wise man

philosophical, philosophic *adj* **1** = **rational**, abstract, logical, sagacious, theoretical, thoughtful, wise **2** = **stoical**, calm, collected, composed, cool, serene, tranquil, unruffled

philosophy *n* **1** = **thought**, knowledge, logic, metaphysics, rationalism, reasoning, thinking, wisdom **2, 3** = **outlook**, beliefs,

P

phlegm [**flem**] n thick yellowish substance formed in the nose and throat during a cold.

phlegmatic ❶ [fleg-**mat**-ik] adj not easily excited, unemotional. **phlegmatically** adv.

phlox n, pl **phlox**, **phloxes** flowering garden plant.

phobia ❶ n intense and unreasoning fear or dislike. **phobic** adj.

phoenix n legendary bird said to set fire to itself and rise anew from its ashes.

phone ❶ n, v informal telephone. **phonecard** n card used to operate certain public telephones. **phone-in** n broadcast in which telephone comments or questions from the public are transmitted live.

phonetic adj 1 of speech sounds. 2 (of spelling) written as it is sounded. **phonetics** n science of speech sounds. **phonetically** adv.

phoney, phony ❶ informal ▷ adj **phonier, phoniest 1** not genuine. **2** insincere. ▷ n, pl **phoneys**, **phonies 3** phoney person or thing.

phonograph n US old-fashioned record player.

phonology n study of the speech sounds in a language.

phosgene [**foz**-jean] n poisonous gas used in warfare.

phosphorescence n faint glow in the dark. **phosphorescent** adj.

phosphorus n Chemistry toxic flammable nonmetallic element which appears luminous in the dark. **phosphate** n 1 compound of phosphorus. 2 fertilizer containing phosphorus.

photo n, pl **photos** short for PHOTOGRAPH. **photo finish** finish of a

race in which the contestants are so close that a photograph is needed to decide the result.

photo- combining form light, e.g. photometer.

photocell n cell which produces a current or voltage when exposed to light or other electromagnetic radiation.

photocopy n, pl -**copies 1** photographic reproduction. ▷ v -**copying, -copied 2** make a photocopy of. **photocopier** n.

photoelectric adj using or worked by electricity produced by the action of light.

Photofit n ® picture made by combining photographs of different facial features.

photogenic adj always looking attractive in photographs.

photograph ❶ n 1 picture made by the chemical action of light on sensitive film. ▷ v 2 take a photograph of. **photographer** n **photographic** adj **photography** n art of taking photographs.

photogravure n process in which an etched metal plate for printing is produced by photography.

photometer [foe-**tom**-it-er] n instrument for measuring the intensity of light.

photon n quantum of electromagnetic radiation energy, such as light, having both particle and wave behaviour.

photostat n copy made by photocopying machine.

photosynthesis n process by which a green plant uses sunlight to build up carbohydrate reserves. **photosynthesize** v.

———————————————————— **THESAURUS** ————————————————————

convictions, doctrine, ideology, principles, tenets, thinking, values, viewpoint, world view

phlegmatic adj = **unemotional**, apathetic, impassive, indifferent, placid, stoical, stolid, undemonstrative, unfeeling

phobia n = **terror**, aversion, detestation, dread, fear, hatred, horror, loathing, repulsion, revulsion, thing (inf)

phone n Inf = **telephone**, blower (inf) ▷ v Inf = **call**, get on the blower (inf), give someone a call, give

someone a ring (inf, chiefly Brit), give someone a tinkle (Brit inf), make a call, ring (up) (inf, chiefly Brit), telephone

phoney, phony Inf adj 1 = **fake**, bogus, counterfeit, ersatz, false, imitation, pseudo (inf), sham ▷ n 3 = **fake**, counterfeit, forgery, fraud, impostor, pseud (inf), sham

photograph n 1 = **picture**, photo (inf), print, selfie (inf), shot, snap (inf), snapshot, transparency ▷ v 2 = **take a picture of**, film, record, shoot, snap (inf), take (someone's) picture

phrase ❶ n 1 group of words forming a unit of meaning, esp. within a sentence. 2 short effective expression. ▷ v 3 express in words. **phrasal verb** phrase consisting of a verb and an adverb or preposition, with a meaning different from the parts, such as *take in* meaning *deceive*. **phrase book** book containing frequently used expressions and their equivalent in a foreign language.

phraseology ❶ n, pl **-gies** way in which words are used.

phrenology n formerly, the study of the shape and size of the skull as a means of finding out a person's character and mental ability. **phrenologist** n.

phut adv **go phut** informal (of a machine) break down.

phylactery n, pl **-teries** leather case containing religious texts, worn by Jewish men.

phylum n, pl **-la** major taxonomic division of animals and plants that contains one or more classes.

physical ❶ adj 1 of the body, as contrasted with the mind or spirit. 2 of material things or nature. 3 of physics. **physically** adv **physical education** training and practice in sports and gymnastics. **physical geography** branch of geography dealing with the features of the earth's surface.

physician ❶ n doctor of medicine.

physics n science of the properties of matter and energy. **physicist** n person skilled in or studying physics.

physio n 1 short for PHYSIOTHERAPY. 2 pl **physios** short for PHYSIOTHERAPIST.

physiognomy [fiz-ee-**on**-om-ee] n face.

physiology n science of the normal function of living things. **physiological** adj **physiologist** n.

physiotherapy n treatment of disease or injury by physical means such as massage, rather than by drugs. **physiotherapist** n.

physique ❶ n person's bodily build and muscular development.

pi n 1 sixteenth letter in the Greek alphabet. 2 *Maths* ratio of the circumference of a circle to its diameter.

pianissimo adv *Music* very quietly.

piano¹ n, pl **pianos** musical instrument with strings which are struck by hammers worked by a keyboard (also **pianoforte**). **pianist** n **Pianola** n ® mechanically played piano.

piano² adv *Music* quietly.

piazza n square or marketplace, esp. in Italy.

pibroch [**pee**-brok] n form of bagpipe music.

pic n, pl **pics**, **pix** informal photograph or illustration.

picador n mounted bullfighter with a lance.

picaresque adj denoting a type of fiction in which the hero, a rogue, has a series of adventures.

piccalilli n pickle of vegetables in mustard sauce.

piccolo n, pl **-los** small flute.

pick¹ ❶ v 1 choose. 2 remove (flowers or fruit) from a plant. 3 take hold of and move with the fingers. 4 provoke (a fight etc.) deliberately. 5 steal from (someone's pocket). 6 open (a lock) by means other than a key. ▷ n 7 choice, e.g. *take your pick*. 8 best part. **pick-me-up** n informal stimulating drink, tonic. **pick on** v continually treat unfairly. **pick out** v recognize,

P

THESAURUS

phrase n 1 = **expression**, group of words, idiom, remark, saying ▷ v 3 = **express**, put, put into words, say, voice, word

phraseology n = **wording**, choice of words, expression, idiom, language, parlance, phrase, phrasing, speech, style, syntax

physical adj 1 = **bodily**, corporal, corporeal, earthly, fleshly, incarnate, mortal 2 = **material**, natural, palpable, real, solid, substantial, tangible

physician n = **doctor**, doc (inf), doctor of medicine, general practitioner, G.P., M.D., medic (inf), medical practitioner

physique n = **build**, body, constitution, figure, form, frame, shape, structure

pick¹ v 1 = **select**, choose, decide upon, elect, fix upon, hand-pick, opt for, settle upon, single out 2 = **gather**, collect, harvest, pluck, pull 4 = **provoke**, incite, instigate, start 6 = **open**, break into, break open, crack, force ▷ n 7 = **choice**, decision, option, preference, selection 8 = **the best**, elect, elite, the cream

distinguish. **pick up** v **1** raise, lift. **2** collect. **3** improve, get better. **4** learn as one goes along. **5** become acquainted with for a sexual purpose. **pick-up** n **1** small truck. **2** casual acquaintance made for a sexual purpose. **3** device for conversion of vibrations into electrical signals, as in a record player.

pick² n tool with a curved iron crossbar and wooden shaft, for breaking up hard ground or rocks.

pickaxe n large pick.

picket ❶ n **1** person or group standing outside a workplace to deter would-be workers during a strike. **2** sentry or sentries posted to give warning of an attack. **3** pointed stick used as part of a fence. ▷ v **4** form a picket outside (a workplace). **picket line** line of people acting as pickets.

pickings pl n money easily acquired.

pickle ❶ n **1** food preserved in vinegar or salt water. **2** informal awkward situation. ▷ v **3** preserve in vinegar or salt water. **pickled** adj **1** preserved in vinegar or salt water. **2** informal drunk.

pickpocket n thief who steals from someone's pocket.

picnic ❶ n **1** informal meal out of doors. **2** informal easy task. ▷ v **-nicking, -nicked 3** have a picnic.

picot [**peek**-oh] n any of pattern of small loops, as on lace.

Pict n member of an ancient race of N Britain. **Pictish** adj.

pictograph n picture or symbol standing for word or group of words, as in written Chinese.

pictorial ❶ adj **1** of or in painting or pictures. ▷ n **2** newspaper etc. with many pictures.

picture ❶ n **1** drawing or painting. **2** photograph. **3** mental image. **4** description or account of a situation. **5** beautiful or picturesque object. **6** image on a TV screen. ▷ pl **7** cinema. ▷ v **8** visualize, imagine. **9** represent in a picture. **picturesque** adj **1** (of a place or view) pleasant to look at. **2** (of language) forceful, vivid. **picture rail** narrow piece of wood near the top of a wall from which pictures are hung. **picture window** large window made of a single sheet of glass.

piddle v informal urinate.

piddling adj informal small or unimportant.

pidgin n language, not a mother tongue, made up of elements of two or more other languages.

pie n dish of meat, fruit, etc. baked in pastry. **pie chart** circular diagram with sectors representing quantities.

P

———————————————————————————— THESAURUS ————————

picket n **1** = **protester**, demonstrator, picketer **2** = **lookout**, guard, patrol, sentinel, sentry, watch **3** = **stake**, pale, paling, post, stanchion, upright ▷ v **4** = **blockade**, boycott, demonstrate

pickle n **2** Inf = **predicament**, bind (inf), difficulty, dilemma, fix (inf), hot water (inf), jam (inf), quandary, scrape (inf), tight spot ▷ v **3** = **preserve**, marinade, steep

pick-me-up n Inf = **tonic**, bracer (inf), refreshment, restorative, shot in the arm (inf), stimulant

pick on v = **torment**, badger, bait, bully, goad, hector, tease

pick out v = **identify**, discriminate, distinguish, make out, perceive, recognize, tell apart

pick up v **1** = **lift**, gather, grasp, raise, take up, uplift **2** = **collect**, call for, get **3** = **recover**, be on the mend, get

better, improve, mend, rally, take a turn for the better, turn the corner **4** = **learn**, acquire, get the hang of (inf), master

picnic n **1** = **excursion**, outdoor meal, outing

pictorial adj **1** = **graphic**, illustrated, sque, representational, scenic

picture n **1** = **representation**, drawing, engraving, illustration, image, likeness, painting, portrait, print, sketch **2** = **photograph** **4** = **description**, account, depiction, image, impression, report ▷ pl **7** = **flicks** (sl), movies (US inf) ▷ v **8** = **imagine**, conceive of, envision, see, visualize **9** = **represent**, depict, draw, illustrate, paint, photograph, show, sketch

picturesque adj **1** = **interesting**, attractive, beautiful, charming, pretty, quaint, scenic, striking **2** = **vivid**, colourful, graphic

piebald ⊕ *n, adj* (horse) with irregular black-and-white markings.

piece ⊕ *n* **1** separate bit or part. **2** instance, e.g. *a piece of luck*. **3** example, specimen. **4** literary or musical composition. **5** coin. **6** small object used in draughts, chess, etc. **piece together** *v* make or assemble bit by bit.

pièce de résistance [**pyess** de ray-**ziss**-tonss] *n* French most impressive item.

piecemeal ⊕ *adv* a bit at a time.

piecework *n* work paid for according to the quantity produced.

pied *adj* having markings of two or more colours.

pied-à-terre [**pyay** da **tair**] *n, pl* **pieds-à-terre** [**pyay** da **tair**] small flat or house for occasional use.

pie-eyed *adj slang* drunk.

pier ⊕ *n* **1** platform on stilts sticking out into the sea. **2** pillar, esp. one supporting a bridge.

pierce ⊕ *v* **1** make a hole in or through with a sharp instrument. **2** make a way through. **piercing** *adj* **1** (of a sound) shrill and high-pitched. **2** (of wind or cold) fierce, penetrating.

Pierrot [**pier**-roe] *n* pantomime clown with a whitened face.

piety ⊕ *n, pl* **-ties** deep devotion to God and religion.

piffle *n informal* nonsense.

pig ⊕ *n* **1** animal kept and killed for pork, ham, and bacon. **2** *informal* greedy, dirty, or rude person. **piglet** *n* young pig. **piggish**, **piggy** *adj*

1 *informal* dirty. **2** greedy. **3** stubborn.

piggery *n, pl* **-geries** place for keeping and breeding pigs. **piggy bank** child's bank shaped like a pig with a slot for coins. **pig-headed** *adj* obstinate. **pig iron** crude iron produced in a blast furnace.

pigeon¹ ⊕ *n* bird with a heavy body and short legs, sometimes trained to carry messages. **pigeonhole** *n* **1** compartment for papers in a desk etc. ▷ *v* **2** classify. **3** put aside and do nothing about. **pigeon-toed** *adj* with the feet or toes turned inwards.

pigeon² *n informal* concern or responsibility.

piggyback *n* **1** ride on someone's shoulders. ▷ *adv* **2** carried on someone's shoulders.

pigment ⊕ *n* colouring matter, paint or dye. **pigmentation** *n*.

Pigmy *n, pl* **-mies** same as PYGMY.

pigsty *n, pl* **-sties** **1** pen for pigs. **2** untidy place.

pigtail *n* plait of hair hanging from the back or either side of the head.

pike¹ *n* large predatory freshwater fish.

pike² *n History* long-handled spear.

pikelet *n Aust & NZ* small thick pancake.

piker *n Aust & NZ slang* shirker.

pilaster *n* square column, usu. set in a wall.

pilau, pilaf pilaff *n* Middle Eastern dish of meat, fish, or poultry boiled with rice, spices, etc.

pilchard *n* small edible sea fish of the herring family.

P

THESAURUS

piebald *adj* = **pied**, black and white, brindled, dappled, flecked, mottled, speckled, spotted

piece *n* **1** = **bit**, chunk, fragment, morsel, part, portion, quantity, segment, slice **4** = **work**, article, composition, creation, item, study, work of art

piecemeal *adv* = **bit by bit**, by degrees, gradually, little by little

pier *n* **1** = **jetty**, landing place, promenade, quay, wharf **2** = **pillar**, buttress, column, pile, post, support, upright

pierce *v* **1** = **penetrate**, bore, drill, enter, perforate, prick, puncture, spike, stab, stick into

piercing *adj* **1** = **penetrating**, ear-splitting, high-pitched, loud, sharp,

shrill **2** = **cold**, arctic, biting, bitter, freezing, nippy, wintry

piety *n* = **holiness**, faith, godliness, piousness, religion, reverence

pig *n* **1** = **hog**, boar, porker, sow, swine **2** *Inf* = **slob** (*sl*), boor, brute, glutton, swine

pigeonhole *n* **1** = **compartment**, cubbyhole, locker, niche, place, section ▷ *v* **2** = **classify**, categorize, characterize, compartmentalize, ghettoize, label, slot (*inf*) **3** = **put off**, defer, postpone, shelve

pig-headed *adj* = **stubborn**, contrary, inflexible, mulish, obstinate, self-willed, stiff-necked, unyielding

pigment *n* = **colour**, colouring, dye, paint, stain, tincture, tint

pile¹ ❶ *n* **1** number of things lying on top of each other. **2** *informal* large amount. **3** large building. ▷ *v* **4** collect into a pile. **5** (foll. by *in* or *out*) move in a group. **pile-up** *n informal* traffic accident involving several vehicles.

pile² ❶ *n* beam driven into the ground, esp. as a foundation for building.

pile³ ❶ *n* fibres of a carpet or a fabric, esp. velvet, that stand up from the weave.

piles *pl n* swollen veins in the rectum, haemorrhoids.

pilfer ❶ *v* steal in small quantities.

pilgrim ❶ *n* person who journeys to a holy place. **pilgrimage** *n*.

pill ❶ *n* small ball of medicine swallowed whole. **the pill** pill taken by a woman to prevent pregnancy. **pillbox** *n* **1** small box for pills. **2** small concrete fort.

pillage ❶ *v* **1** steal property by violence in war. ▷ *n* **2** violent seizure of goods, esp. in war.

pillar ❶ *n* **1** upright post, usu. supporting a roof. **2** strong supporter. **pillar box** red pillar-shaped letter box in the street.

pillion *n* seat for a passenger behind the rider of a motorcycle.

pillory ❶ *n, pl* **-ries 1** *History* frame with holes for the head and hands in which an offender was locked and exposed to public abuse. ▷ *v* **-rying**, **-ried 2** ridicule publicly.

pillow *n* **1** stuffed cloth bag for supporting the head in bed. ▷ *v* **2** rest as if on a pillow. **pillowcase**, **pillowslip** *n* removable cover for a pillow.

pilot ❶ *n* **1** person qualified to fly an aircraft or spacecraft. **2** person employed to steer a ship entering or leaving a harbour. ▷ *adj* **3** experimental and preliminary. ▷ *v* **4** act as the pilot of. **5** guide, steer. **pilot light** small flame lighting the main one in a gas appliance. **pilot officer** most junior commissioned rank in certain air forces.

pimento *n, pl* **-tos** mild-tasting red pepper.

pimp *n* **1** man who gets customers for a prostitute in return for a share of his or her earnings. ▷ *v* **2** act as a pimp.

pimpernel *n* wild plant with small star-shaped flowers.

pimple ❶ *n* small pus-filled spot on the skin. **pimply** *adj*.

pin ❶ *n* **1** short thin piece of stiff wire with a point and head, for fastening things. **2** wooden or metal peg or stake. ▷ *v* **pinning**, **pinned 3** fasten with a pin. **4** seize and hold fast. **pin down** *v* **1** force (someone) to make a decision, take action, etc. **2** define

———————————————— THESAURUS ————————

pile¹ *n* **1** = **heap**, accumulation, berg (*S Afr*), collection, hoard, mass, mound, mountain, stack **2** *Inf* = **a lot**, great deal, ocean, quantity, stacks **3** = **building**, edifice, erection, structure ▷ *v* **4** = **collect**, accumulate, amass, assemble, gather, heap, hoard, stack **5** (foll. by *in* or *out*) = **crowd**, crush, flock, flood, jam, pack, rush, stream

pile² *n* = **foundation**, beam, column, pillar, post, support, upright

pile³ *n* = **nap**, down, fibre, fur, hair, plush

pile-up *n Inf* = **collision**, accident, crash, multiple collision, smash, smash-up (*inf*)

pilfer *v* = **steal**, appropriate, embezzle, filch, knock off (*sl*), lift (*inf*), nick (*sl, chiefly Brit*), pinch (*inf*), purloin, snaffle (*Brit inf*), swipe (*sl*), take

pilgrim *n* = **traveller**, wanderer, wayfarer

pilgrimage *n* = **journey**, excursion, expedition, mission, tour, trip

pill *n* = **tablet**, capsule, pellet **the pill** = **oral contraceptive**

pillage *v* **1** = **plunder**, despoil, loot, maraud, raid, ransack, ravage, sack ▷ *n* **2** = **plunder**, marauding, robbery, sack, spoliation

pillar *n* **1** = **support**, column, pier, post, prop, shaft, stanchion, upright **2** = **supporter**, leader, leading light (*inf*), mainstay, upholder

pillory *v* **2** = **ridicule**, brand, denounce, stigmatize

pilot *n* **1** = **airman**, aviator, flyer **2** = **helmsman**, navigator, steersman ▷ *adj* **3** = **trial**, experimental, model, test ▷ *v* **4, 5** = **fly**, conduct, direct, drive, guide, handle, navigate, operate, steer

pimple *n* = **spot**, boil, plook (*Scot*), pustule, zit (*sl*)

pin *v* **3** = **fasten**, affix, attach, fix, join, secure **4** = **hold fast**, fix, hold down, immobilize, pinion

clearly. **pin money** small amount earned to buy small luxuries. **pins and needles** *informal* tingling sensation in a part of the body. **pin tuck** narrow ornamental fold in shirt etc. **pin-up** *n* picture of a sexually attractive person, esp. (partly) naked.

PIN personal identification number: number used with a credit or debit card to withdraw money, confirm a purchase, etc.

pinafore *n* **1** apron. **2** dress with a bib top.

pinball *n* electrically operated table game in which a small ball is shot through various hazards.

pince-nez [panss-**nay**] *n, pl* **pince-nez** glasses kept in place only by a clip on the bridge of the nose.

pincers *pl n* **1** tool consisting of two hinged arms, for gripping. **2** claws of a lobster etc.

pinch ❶ *v* **1** squeeze between finger and thumb. **2** cause pain by being too tight. **3** *informal* steal. **4** *informal* arrest. ▷ *n* **5** act of pinching. **6** as much as can be taken up between the finger and thumb. **at a pinch** if absolutely necessary. **feel the pinch** have to economize.

pinchbeck *n* alloy of zinc and copper, used as imitation gold.

pincushion *n* small cushion in which pins are stuck ready for use.

pine¹ *n* **1** evergreen coniferous tree. **2** its wood. **pine cone** woody seed case of the pine tree. **pine marten** wild mammal of the coniferous forests of Europe and Asia.

pine² ❶ *v* **1** (foll. by *for*) feel great longing (for). **2** become thin and ill through grief etc.

pineal gland [**pin**-ee-al] *n* small cone-shaped gland at the base of the brain.

pineapple *n* large tropical fruit with juicy yellow flesh and a hard skin.

ping *v, n* (make) a short high-pitched sound. **pinger** *n* device, esp. a timer, that makes a pinging sound.

Ping-Pong *n* ® table tennis.

pinion¹ ❶ *n* **1** bird's wing. ▷ *v* **2** immobilize (someone) by tying or holding his or her arms.

pinion² *n* small cogwheel.

pink ❶ *n* **1** pale reddish colour. **2** fragrant garden plant. ▷ *adj* **3** of the colour pink. ▷ *v* **4** (of an engine) make a metallic noise because not working properly, knock. **in the pink** in good health.

pinking shears *pl n* scissors with a serrated edge that give a wavy edge to material to prevent fraying.

pinnace *n* ship's boat.

pinnacle ❶ *n* **1** highest point of success etc. **2** mountain peak. **3** small slender spire.

pinnate *adj* (of compound leaves) having leaflets growing opposite each other in pairs.

pinpoint ❶ *v* **1** locate or identify exactly. ▷ *adj* **2** exact.

pinprick *n* small irritation or annoyance.

pinstripe *n* **1** very narrow stripe in fabric. **2** the fabric itself.

pint *n* liquid measure, 1/8 gallon (.568 litre).

pintail *n* greyish-brown duck with a pointed tail.

Pinyin *n* system for representing Chinese in Roman letters.

pioneer ❶ *n* **1** explorer or early settler of a new country. **2** originator or

---

pinch *v* **1** = **squeeze**, compress, grasp, nip, press **2** = **hurt**, cramp, crush, pain **3** *Inf* = **steal**, filch, knock off (*sl*), lift (*inf*), nick (*sl, chiefly Brit*), pilfer, purloin, snaffle (*Brit inf*), swipe (*sl*) ▷ *n* **5** = **squeeze**, nip

pin down *v* **1** = **force**, compel, constrain, make, press, pressurize **2** = **determine**, identify, locate, name, pinpoint, specify

pine² *v* **1** (foll. by *for*) = **long**, ache, crave, desire, eat one's heart out over, hanker, hunger for, thirst for, wish for, yearn for **2** = **waste**, decline, fade, languish, sicken

pinion¹ *v* **2** = **immobilize**, bind, chain, fasten, fetter, manacle, shackle, tie

pink *adj* **3** = **rosy**, flushed, reddish, rose, roseate, salmon

pinnacle *n* **2** = **peak**, apex, crest, crown, height, summit, top, vertex, zenith

pinpoint **1** *v* = **identify**, define, distinguish, locate

pioneer *n* **1** = **settler**, colonist, explorer **2** = **founder**, developer, innovator, leader, trailblazer ▷ *v* **3** = **develop**, create, discover, establish, initiate, instigate, institute, invent, originate, show the way, start

developer of something new. ▷ v **3** be the pioneer or leader of.

pious ❶ *adj* deeply religious, devout.

pip¹ *n* small seed in a fruit.

pip² *n* **1** high-pitched sound used as a time signal on radio. **2** spot on a playing card, dice, etc. **3** *informal* star on a junior army officer's shoulder showing rank.

pip³ *n* **give someone the pip** *Brit, NZ & S Afr slang* annoy.

pipe ❶ *n* **1** tube for conveying liquid or gas. **2** tube with a small bowl at the end for smoking tobacco. **3** tubular musical instrument. ▷ *pl* **4** bagpipes. ▷ *v* **5** play on a pipe. **6** utter in a shrill tone. **7** convey by pipe. **8** decorate with piping. **piper** *n* player on a pipe or bagpipes. **piping** *n* **1** system of pipes. **2** decoration of icing on a cake etc. **3** fancy edging on clothes etc. **piping hot** extremely hot. **pipe cleaner** piece of wire coated with tiny tufts of yarn for cleaning the stem of a tobacco pipe. **piped music** recorded music played as background music in public places. **pipe down** *v informal* stop talking. **pipe dream** fanciful impossible plan. **pipeline** *n* **1** long pipe for transporting oil, water, etc. **2** means of communication. **in the pipeline** in preparation. **pipe up** *v* speak suddenly or shrilly.

pipette *n* slender glass tube used to transfer or measure fluids.

pipit *n* small brownish songbird.

pippin *n* type of eating apple.

piquant ❶ [**pee**-kant] *adj* **1** having a pleasant spicy taste. **2** mentally stimulating. **piquancy** *n*.

pique ❶ [**peek**] *n* **1** feeling of hurt pride, baffled curiosity, or resentment. ▷ *v* **2** hurt the pride of. **3** arouse (curiosity).

piqué [**pee**-kay] *n* stiff ribbed cotton fabric.

piquet [pik-**ket**] *n* card game for two.

piranha *n* small fierce freshwater fish of tropical America.

pirate ❶ *n* **1** sea robber. **2** person who illegally publishes or sells work owned by someone else. **3** person or company that broadcasts illegally. ▷ *v* **4** sell or reproduce (artistic work etc.) illegally. **piracy** *n* **piratical** *adj*.

pirouette *v, n* (make) a spinning turn balanced on the toes of one foot.

piscatorial *adj* of fishing or fishes.

Pisces *pl n* (the fishes) twelfth sign of the zodiac.

piss *taboo* ▷ *v* **1** urinate. ▷ *n* **2** act of urinating. **3** urine.

pistachio *n, pl* **-chios** edible nut of a Mediterranean tree.

piste [**peest**] *n* ski slope.

pistil *n* seed-bearing part of a flower.

pistol *n* short-barrelled handgun.

piston *n* cylindrical part in an engine that slides to and fro in a cylinder.

pit ❶ *n* **1** deep hole in the ground. **2** coal mine. **3** dent or depression. **4** servicing and refuelling area on a motor-racing track. **5** same as ORCHESTRA PIT. ▷ *v* **pitting, pitted 6** mark with small dents or scars. **pit one's wits against** compete against in a test or contest. **pit bull terrier** strong muscular terrier with a short coat.

pitapat *adv* **1** with quick light taps. ▷ *n* **2** such taps.

————————————————————— THESAURUS —————————

pious *adj* = **religious**, devout, God-fearing, godly, holy, reverent, righteous, saintly

pipe *n* **1** = **tube**, conduit, duct, hose, line, main, passage, pipeline ▷ *v* **5** = **play**, sound **6** = **whistle**, cheep, peep, sing, warble **7** = **convey**, channel, conduct

pipe down *v Inf* = **be quiet**, hold one's tongue, hush, quieten down, shush, shut one's mouth, shut up (*inf*)

pipeline *n* **1** = **tube**, conduit, duct, passage, pipe

piquant *adj* **1** = **spicy**, biting, pungent, savoury, sharp, tangy, tart, zesty **2** = **interesting**, lively, provocative, scintillating, sparkling, stimulating

pique *n* **1** = **resentment**, annoyance, displeasure, huff, hurt feelings, irritation, offence, umbrage, wounded pride ▷ *v* **2** = **displease**, affront, annoy, get (*inf*), irk, irritate, nettle, offend, rile, sting **3** = **arouse**, excite, rouse, spur, stimulate, stir, whet

piracy *n* **1** = **robbery**, buccaneering, freebooting, stealing, theft

pirate *n* **1** = **buccaneer**, corsair, freebooter, marauder, raider **2** = **plagiarist**, cribber (*inf*), infringer, plagiarizer ▷ *v* **4** = **copy**, appropriate, crib (*inf*), plagiarize, poach, reproduce, steal

pit *n* **1** = **hole**, abyss, cavity, chasm, crater, dent, depression, hollow ▷ *v*

p

pitch¹ ❶ v **1** throw, hurl. **2** set up (a tent). **3** fall headlong. **4** (of a ship or plane) move with the front and back going up and down alternately. **5** set the level or tone of. ▷ n **6** area marked out for playing sport. **7** degree or angle of slope. **8** degree of highness or lowness of a (musical) sound. **9** act or manner of throwing a ball. **10** place where a street or market trader regularly sells. **11** *informal* persuasive sales talk. **pitched battle** fierce fight. **pitch in** v join in enthusiastically. **pitch into** v *informal* attack.

pitch² ❶ n dark sticky substance obtained from tar. **pitch-black**, **pitch-dark** adj very dark.

pitchblende n mineral composed largely of uranium oxide, yielding radium.

pitcher n large jug with a narrow neck.

pitchfork n **1** large long-handled fork for lifting hay. ▷ v **2** thrust abruptly or violently.

pitfall ❶ n hidden difficulty or danger.

pith ❶ n **1** soft white lining of the rind of oranges etc. **2** essential part. **3** soft tissue in the stems of certain plants. **pithy** adj **pithier**, **pithiest** short and full of meaning.

pithead n top of a mine shaft and the buildings and hoisting gear around it.

piton [**peet**-on] n metal spike used in climbing to secure a rope.

pitta bread, pitta n flat slightly leavened bread, orig. from the Middle East.

pittance ❶ n very small amount of money.

pitter-patter n **1** sound of light rapid taps or pats, as of raindrops. ▷ v **2** make such a sound.

pituitary n, pl **-taries** gland at the base of the brain, that helps to control growth (also **pituitary gland**).

pity ❶ n, pl **pities 1** sympathy or sorrow for others' suffering. **2** regrettable fact. ▷ v **pitying**, **pitied 3** feel pity for. **piteous**, **pitiable** adj arousing pity. **pitiful** adj **1** arousing pity. **2** woeful, contemptible. **pitifully** adv **pitiless** adj feeling no pity or mercy.

pivot ❶ n **1** central shaft on which something turns. ▷ v **2** provide with or

6 = **scar**, dent, indent, mark, pockmark

pitch¹ v **1** = **throw**, cast, chuck (inf), fling, heave, hurl, lob (inf), sling, toss **2** = **set up**, erect, put up, raise, settle **3** = **fall**, dive, drop, topple, tumble **4** = **toss**, lurch, plunge, roll ▷ n **6** = **sports field**, field of play, ground, park (US & Canad) **7** = **slope**, angle, degree, dip, gradient, height, highest point, incline, level, point, summit, tilt **8** = **tone**, modulation, sound, timbre **11** *Inf* = **sales talk**, patter, spiel (inf)

pitch-black adj = **jet-black**, dark, inky, pitch-dark, unlit

pitch in v = **help**, chip in (inf), contribute, cooperate, do one's bit, join in, lend a hand, participate

pitch into v *Inf* = **attack**, assail, assault, get stuck into (inf), tear into (inf)

piteous adj = **pathetic**, affecting, distressing, gut-wrenching, harrowing, heartbreaking, heart-rending, moving, pitiable, pitiful, plaintive, poignant, sad

pitfall n = **danger**, catch, difficulty, drawback, hazard, peril, snag, trap

pith n **2** = **essence**, core, crux, gist, heart, kernel, nub, point, quintessence, salient point

pithy adj = **succinct**, brief, cogent, concise, epigrammatic, laconic, pointed, short, terse, to the point, trenchant

pitiful adj **1** = **pathetic**, distressing, grievous, gut-wrenching, harrowing, heartbreaking, heart-rending, piteous, pitiable, sad, wretched **2** = **contemptible**, abject, base, low, mean, miserable, paltry, shabby, sorry

pitiless adj = **merciless**, callous, cold-blooded, cold-hearted, cruel, hardhearted, heartless, implacable, relentless, ruthless, unmerciful

pittance n = **peanuts** (sl), chicken feed (sl), drop, mite, slave wages, trifle

pity n **1** = **compassion**, charity, clemency, fellow feeling, forbearance, kindness, mercy, sympathy **2** = **shame**, bummer (sl), crying shame, misfortune, sin ▷ v **3** = **feel sorry for**, bleed for, feel for, grieve for, have compassion for, sympathize with, weep for

pivot n **1** = **axis**, axle, centre, fulcrum, heart, hinge, hub, kingpin, spindle, swivel ▷ v **2** = **turn**, revolve, rotate, spin, swivel, twirl

P

turn on a pivot. **pivotal** *adj* of crucial importance.

pix *n informal* a plural of PIC.

pixel *n* smallest constituent element of an image, as on a visual display unit.

pixie ❶ *n* (in folklore) fairy.

pizza *n* flat disc of dough covered with a wide variety of savoury toppings and baked.

pizzazz *n informal* attractive combination of energy and style.

pizzicato [pit-see-**kah**-toe] *adj Music* played by plucking the string of a violin etc. with the finger.

pl. 1 place. **2** plural.

placard ❶ *n* notice that is carried or displayed in public.

placate ❶ *v* make (someone) stop feeling angry or upset. **placatory** *adj*.

place ❶ *n* **1** particular part of an area or space. **2** particular town, building, etc. **3** position or point reached. **4** open square lined with houses. **5** seat or space. **6** duty or right. **7** position of employment. **8** usual position. ▷ *v* **9** put in a particular place. **10** identify, put in context. **11** make (an order, bet, etc.). **be placed** (of a competitor in a race) be among the first three. **take place** happen, occur. **placement** *n* **1** arrangement. **2** temporary employment. **3** process of finding

someone a job or a home. **place setting** cutlery, crockery, and glassware laid for one person at a meal.

placebo [plas-**see**-bo] *n, pl* -**bos**, -**boes** sugar pill etc. given to an unsuspecting patient instead of an active drug.

placenta [plass-**ent**-a] *n, pl* -**tas**, -**tae** organ formed in the womb during pregnancy, providing nutrients for the fetus. **placental** *adj*.

placid ❶ *adj* not easily excited or upset, calm. **placidity** *n*.

plagiarize ❶ [**play**-jer-ize] *v* steal ideas, passages, etc. from (someone else's work) and present them as one's own. **plagiarism** *n* **plagiarist** *n*.

plague ❶ *n* **1** fast-spreading fatal disease. **2** *History* bubonic plague. **3** widespread infestation. ▷ *v* **plaguing, plagued 4** trouble or annoy continually.

plaice *n* edible European flatfish.

plaid *n* **1** long piece of tartan cloth worn as part of Highland dress. **2** tartan cloth or pattern.

plain ❶ *adj* **1** easy to see or understand. **2** expressed honestly and clearly. **3** without decoration or pattern. **4** not beautiful. **5** simple, ordinary. ▷ *n* **6** large stretch of level country. **plainly** *adv* **plainness** *n* **plain clothes**

pivotal *adj* = **crucial**, central, critical, decisive, vital

pixie *n* = **elf**, brownie, fairy, sprite

placard *n* = **notice**, advertisement, bill, poster

placate *v* = **calm**, appease, assuage, conciliate, humour, mollify, pacify, propitiate, soothe

place *n* **1** = **spot**, area, location, point, position, site, venue, whereabouts **3** = **position**, grade, rank, station, status **6** = **duty**, affair, charge, concern, function, prerogative, responsibility, right, role **7** = **job**, appointment, employment, position, post ▷ *v* **9** = **put**, deposit, install, lay, locate, position, rest, set, situate, stand, station, stick (*inf*) **10** = **identify**, know, put one's finger on, recognize, remember **take place** = **happen**, come about, go on, occur, transpire (*inf*)

placid *adj* = **calm**, collected, composed, equable, even-tempered,

imperturbable, serene, tranquil, unexcitable, unruffled, untroubled

plagiarism *n* = **copying**, borrowing, cribbing (*inf*), infringement, piracy, theft

plagiarize *v* = **copy**, borrow, crib (*inf*), lift (*inf*), pirate, steal

plague *n* **1** = **disease**, epidemic, infection, pestilence **3** = **affliction**, bane, blight, curse, evil, scourge, torment ▷ *v* **4** = **pester**, annoy, badger, bother, harass, harry, hassle (*inf*), tease, torment, torture, trouble, vex

plain *adj* **1** = **clear**, comprehensible, distinct, evident, manifest, obvious, overt, patent, unambiguous, understandable, unmistakable, visible **2** = **straightforward**, blunt, candid, direct, downright, forthright, frank, honest, open, outspoken, upfront (*inf*) **3** = **unadorned**, austere, bare, basic, severe, simple, Spartan, stark, unembellished, unfussy,

ordinary clothes, as opposed to uniform. **plain sailing** easy progress. **plain speaking** saying exactly what one thinks.

plainsong *n* unaccompanied singing, esp. in a medieval church.

plaintiff *n* person who sues in a court of law.

plaintive ❶ *adj* sad, mournful. **plaintively** *adv*.

plait [platt] *n* **1** intertwined length of hair. ▷ *v* **2** intertwine separate strands in a pattern.

plan ❶ *n* **1** way thought out to do or achieve something. **2** diagram showing the layout or design of something. ▷ *v* **planning**, **planned 3** arrange beforehand. **4** make a diagram of. **planner** *n*.

plane¹ ❶ *n* **1** an aircraft. **2** *Maths* flat surface. **3** level of attainment etc. ▷ *adj* **4** perfectly flat or level. ▷ *v* **5** glide or skim.

plane² *n* **1** tool for smoothing wood. ▷ *v* **2** smooth (wood) with a plane.

plane³ *n* tree with broad leaves.

planet *n* large body in space that revolves round the sun or another star. **planetary** *adj*.

planetarium *n*, *pl* **-iums**, **-ia** building where the movements of the stars, planets, etc. are shown by projecting lights on the inside of a dome.

plangent [plan-jent] *adj* (of sounds) mournful and resounding.

plank *n* long flat piece of sawn timber.

plankton *n* minute animals and plants floating in the surface water of a sea or lake.

plant ❶ *n* **1** living organism that grows in the ground and has no power to move. **2** equipment or machinery used in industrial processes. **3** factory or other industrial premises. ▷ *v* **4** put in the ground to grow. **5** place firmly in position. **6** *informal* put (a person) secretly in an organization to spy. **7** *informal* hide (stolen goods etc.) on a person to make him or her seem guilty. **planter** *n* **1** owner of a plantation. **2** ornamental pot for house plants.

plantain¹ *n* low-growing wild plant with broad leaves.

plantain² *n* tropical fruit like a green banana.

plantation *n* **1** estate for the cultivation of tea, tobacco, etc. **2** wood of cultivated trees.

plaque *n* **1** inscribed commemorative stone or metal plate. **2** filmy deposit on teeth that causes decay.

plasma *n* **1** clear liquid part of blood. **2** *Physics* hot ionized gas containing positive ions and free electrons. **plasma screen** type of high-resolution flat screen on a television or visual display unit.

plaster ❶ *n* **1** mixture of lime, sand, etc. for coating walls. **2** adhesive strip of material for dressing cuts etc. ▷ *v* **3** cover with plaster. **4** coat thickly. **plastered** *adj slang* drunk. **plasterboard** *n* thin rectangular

P

unornamented **4** = **ugly**, ill-favoured, no oil painting (*inf*), not beautiful, unattractive, unlovely, unprepossessing **5** = **ordinary**, common, commonplace, everyday, simple, unaffected, unpretentious ▷ *n* **6** = **flatland**, grassland, plateau, prairie, steppe, veld

plaintive *adj* = **sorrowful**, heart-rending, mournful, pathetic, piteous, pitiful, sad

plan *n* **1** = **scheme**, design, method, plot, programme, proposal, strategy, suggestion, system **2** = **diagram**, blueprint, chart, drawing, layout, map, representation, sketch ▷ *v* **3** = **devise**, arrange, contrive, design, draft, formulate, organize, outline, plot, scheme, think out

plane¹ *n* **1** = **aeroplane**, aircraft, jet **2** *Maths* = **flat surface**, level surface **3** = **level**, condition, degree, position ▷ *adj* **4** = **level**, even, flat, horizontal, regular, smooth ▷ *v* **5** = **skim**, glide, sail, skate

plant *n* **1** = **vegetable**, bush, flower, herb, shrub, weed **2** = **machinery**, apparatus, equipment, gear **3** = **factory**, foundry, mill, shop, works, yard ▷ *v* **4** = **sow**, put in the ground, scatter, seed, transplant **5** = **place**, establish, fix, found, insert, put, set

plaster *n* **1** = **mortar**, gypsum, plaster of Paris, stucco **2** = **bandage**, adhesive plaster, dressing, Elastoplast, sticking plaster ▷ *v* **4** = **cover**, coat, daub, overlay, smear, spread

sheets of cardboard held together with plaster, used to cover interior walls etc. **plaster of Paris** white powder which dries to form a hard solid when mixed with water, used for sculptures and casts for broken limbs.

plastic ❶ *n* **1** synthetic material that can be moulded when soft but sets in a hard long-lasting shape. **2** credit cards etc. as opposed to cash. ▷ *adj* **3** made of plastic. **4** easily moulded, pliant. **plasticity** *n* ability to be moulded. **plastic bullet** solid PVC cylinder fired by police in riot control. **plastic explosive** jelly-like explosive substance. **plastic surgery** repair or reconstruction of missing or malformed parts of the body.

Plasticine *n* ® soft coloured modelling material used esp. by children.

plate ❶ *n* **1** shallow dish for holding food. **2** flat thin sheet of metal, glass, etc. **3** thin coating of metal on another metal. **4** dishes or cutlery made of gold or silver. **5** illustration, usu. on fine quality paper, in a book. **6** *informal* set of false teeth. ▷ *v* **7** cover with a thin coating of gold, silver, or other metal. **plateful** *n* **plate glass** glass in thin sheets, used for mirrors and windows. **plate tectonics** study of the structure of the earth's crust, esp. the movement of layers of rocks.

plateau ❶ *n, pl* **-teaus, -teaux 1** area of level high land. **2** stage when there is no change or development.

platelet *n* minute particle occurring in blood of vertebrates and involved in clotting of blood.

platen *n* **1** roller of a typewriter, against which the paper is held. **2** plate in a printing press by which the paper is pressed against the type.

platform ❶ *n* **1** raised floor. **2** raised area in a station from which passengers board trains. **3** structure in the sea which holds machinery, stores, etc. for drilling an oil well. **4** programme of a political party.

platinum *n Chemistry* valuable silvery-white metal. **platinum blonde** woman with silvery-blonde hair.

platitude ❶ *n* remark that is true but not interesting or original. **platitudinous** *adj*.

platonic *adj* friendly or affectionate but not sexual.

platoon ❶ *n* smaller unit within a company of soldiers.

platteland *n S Afr* rural district.

platter ❶ *n* large dish.

platypus *n* Australian egg-laying amphibious mammal, with dense fur, webbed feet, and a ducklike bill (also **duck-billed platypus, duckbill**).

plaudits ❶ *pl n* expressions of approval.

plausible ❶ *adj* **1** apparently true or reasonable. **2** persuasive but insincere. **plausibly** *adv* **plausibility** *n*.

play ❶ *v* **1** occupy oneself in (a game or recreation). **2** compete against in a game or sport. **3** behave carelessly. **4** act (a part) on the stage. **5** perform

━━━━━━━━━━━━━━━━━━━━━━━━━━━━ THESAURUS ━━━━━━

plastic *adj* **4** = **pliant**, ductile, flexible, mouldable, pliable, soft, supple

plate *n* **1** = **platter**, dish, trencher (*arch*) **2** = **layer**, panel, sheet, slab **5** = **illustration**, lithograph, print ▷ *v* **7** = **coat**, cover, gild, laminate, overlay

plateau *n* **1** = **upland**, highland, table, tableland **2** = **levelling off**, level, stability, stage

platform *n* **1** = **stage**, dais, podium, rostrum, stand **4** = **policy**, manifesto, objective(s), party line, principle, programme

platitude *n* = **cliché**, banality, commonplace, truism

platoon *n* = **squad**, company, group, outfit (*inf*), patrol, squadron, team

platter *n* = **plate**, dish, salver, tray, trencher (*arch*)

plaudits *pl n* = **approval**, acclaim, acclamation, applause, approbation, praise

plausible *adj* **1** = **believable**, conceivable, credible, likely, persuasive, possible, probable, reasonable, tenable **2** = **glib**, smooth, smooth-talking, smooth-tongued, specious

play *v* **1** = **amuse oneself**, entertain oneself, fool, have fun, revel, romp, sport, trifle **2** = **compete**, challenge, contend against, participate, take on, take part **4** = **act**, act the part of, perform, portray, represent ▷ *n* **8** = **drama**, comedy, dramatic piece, farce, pantomime, piece, show, stage show, tragedy **9** = **amusement**, diversion, entertainment, fun, game,

P

on (a musical instrument). **6** cause (a radio, record player, etc.) to give out sound. **7** move lightly or irregularly, flicker. ▷ *n* **8** story performed on stage or broadcast. **9** activities children take part in for amusement. **10** playing of a game. **11** conduct, e.g. *fair play*. **12** (scope for) freedom of movement. **player** *n* **playful** *adj* lively. **play back** *v* listen to or watch (something recorded). **play down** *v* minimize the importance of. **playground** *n* outdoor area for children to play on, esp. one with swings etc. or adjoining a school. **playgroup** *n* regular meeting of very young children for supervised play. **playhouse** *n* theatre. **playing card** one of a set of 52 cards used in card games. **playing field** extensive piece of ground for sport. **play-lunch** *n Aust & NZ* child's mid-morning snack at school. **play off** *v* set (two people) against each other for one's own ends. **play on** *v* exploit or encourage (someone's sympathy or weakness). **playpen** *n* small portable enclosure in which a young child can safely be left to play. **playschool** *n* nursery group for young children. **plaything** *n* **1** toy. **2** person regarded or treated as a toy. **play up** *v* **1** give prominence to. **2** cause trouble. **playwright** *n* author of plays.

playboy ❶ *n* rich man who lives only for pleasure.

plaza *n* **1** open space or square. **2** modern shopping complex.

PLC, plc Public Limited Company.

plea ❶ *n* **1** serious or urgent request, entreaty. **2** statement of a prisoner or defendant. **3** excuse.

plead ❶ *v* **1** ask urgently or with deep feeling. **2** give as an excuse. **3** *Law* declare oneself to be guilty or innocent of a charge made against one.

pleasant ❶ *adj* pleasing, enjoyable. **pleasantly** *adv* **pleasantry** *n*, *pl* **-tries** polite or joking remark.

please ❶ *v* **1** give pleasure or satisfaction to. ▷ *adv* **2** polite word of request. **pleasant** *adj* pleasing, enjoyable. **please oneself** do as one likes. **pleased** *adj* **pleasing** *adj* giving pleasure or satisfaction. **pleasure** *n* **1** feeling of happiness and satisfaction. **2** something that causes this.

THESAURUS

pastime, recreation, sport **12** = **space**, elbowroom, latitude, leeway, margin, room, scope

playboy *n* = **womanizer**, ladies' man, lady-killer (*inf*), philanderer, rake, roué

play down *v* = **minimize**, gloss over, make light of, make little of, soft-pedal (*inf*), underplay, underrate

player *n* **2** = **sportsman** *or* **sportswoman**, competitor, contestant, participant **4** = **performer**, actor *or* actress, entertainer, Thespian, trouper **5** = **musician**, artist, instrumentalist, performer, virtuoso

playful *adj* = **lively**, frisky, impish, merry, mischievous, spirited, sportive, sprightly, vivacious

play on *v* = **take advantage of**, abuse, capitalize on, exploit, impose on, trade on

plaything *n* **1** = **toy**, amusement, game, pastime, trifle

play up *v* **1** = **emphasize**, accentuate, highlight, stress, underline **2** = **be awkward**, be disobedient, be stroppy (*Brit sl*), give trouble, misbehave

plea *n* **1** = **appeal**, entreaty, intercession, petition, prayer, request, suit, supplication **3** = **excuse**, defence, explanation, justification

plead *v* **1**, **2** = **appeal**, ask, beg, beseech, entreat, implore, petition, request

pleasant *adj* = **pleasing**, affable, agreeable, amiable, amusing, charming, congenial, delightful, engaging, enjoyable, fine, friendly, genial, lekker (*S Afr sl*), likable *or* likeable, lovely, nice, pleasurable

pleasantry *n* = **joke**, badinage, banter, jest, quip, witticism

please *v* **1** = **delight**, amuse, entertain, gladden, gratify, humour, indulge, satisfy, suit

pleased *adj* **1** = **happy**, chuffed (*Brit sl*), contented, delighted, euphoric, glad, gratified, over the moon (*inf*), satisfied, thrilled

pleasing *adj* = **enjoyable**, agreeable, charming, delightful, engaging, gratifying, likable *or* likeable, pleasurable, satisfying

pleasurable *adj* = **enjoyable**, agreeable, delightful, fun, good, lekker (*S Afr sl*), lovely, nice, pleasant

p

pleasure ⓞ *n* **1** feeling of happiness and satisfaction. **2** something that causes this. **pleasurable** *adj* giving pleasure. **pleasurably** *adv*.

pleat *n* **1** fold made by doubling material back on itself. ▷ *v* **2** arrange (material) in pleats.

plebeian ⓞ [pleb-**ee**-an] *adj* **1** of the lower social classes. **2** vulgar or rough. ▷ *n* **3** (also **pleb**) member of the lower social classes.

plebiscite [**pleb**-iss-ite] *n* decision by direct voting of the people of a country.

plectrum *n*, *pl* **-trums**, **-tra** small implement for plucking the strings of a guitar etc.

pledge ⓞ *n* **1** solemn promise. **2** something valuable given as a guarantee that a promise will be kept or a debt paid. ▷ *v* **3** promise solemnly. **4** bind by or as if by a pledge, e.g. *pledge to secrecy*.

plenary *adj* (of a meeting) attended by all members.

plenipotentiary *adj* **1** having full powers. ▷ *n*, *pl* **-aries 2** diplomat or representative having full powers.

plenitude *n* completeness, abundance.

plenteous *adj* plentiful.

plenty ⓞ *n* **1** large amount or number. **2** quite enough. **plentiful** *adj* existing in large amounts or numbers. **plentifully** *adv*.

pleonasm *n* use of more words than necessary.

plethora ⓞ *n* excess.

pleurisy *n* inflammation of the membrane covering the lungs.

pliable ⓞ *adj* **1** easily bent. **2** easily influenced. **pliability** *n*.

pliant ⓞ *adj* pliable. **pliancy** *n*.

pliers *pl n* tool with hinged arms and jaws for gripping.

plight¹ ⓞ *n* difficult or dangerous situation.

plight² *v* **plight one's troth** *old-fashioned* promise to marry.

Plimsoll line *n* mark on a ship showing the level water should reach when the ship is fully loaded.

plimsolls *pl n* rubber-soled canvas shoes.

plinth *n* slab forming the base of a statue, column, etc.

PLO Palestine Liberation Organization.

plod ⓞ *v* **plodding**, **plodded 1** walk with slow heavy steps. **2** work slowly but determinedly. **plodder** *n*.

plonk¹ *v* put (something) down heavily and carelessly.

plonk² *n informal* cheap inferior wine.

plop *n* **1** sound of an object falling into water without a splash. ▷ *v* **plopping**, **plopped 2** make this sound.

━━━━━━━━━━━━━━━━━━━━━━━━━━━ THESAURUS ━━━━━━

pleasure *n* **1, 2** = **happiness**, amusement, bliss, delectation, delight, enjoyment, gladness, gratification, joy, satisfaction

plebian *adj* **1, 2** = **common**, base, coarse, low, lower-class, proletarian, uncultivated, unrefined, vulgar, working-class ▷ *n* **3** (also **pleb**) = **commoner**, common man, man in the street, pleb, prole (*offens*), proletarian

pledge *n* **1** = **promise**, assurance, covenant, oath, undertaking, vow, warrant, word **2** = **guarantee**, bail, collateral, deposit, pawn, security, surety ▷ *v* **3** = **promise**, contract, engage, give one's oath, give one's word, swear, vow

plentiful *adj* = **abundant**, ample, bountiful, copious, generous, lavish, liberal, overflowing, plenteous, profuse

plenty *n* **1** = **lots** (*inf*), abundance, enough, great deal, heap(s) (*inf*), masses, pile(s) (*inf*), plethora, quantity, stack(s)

plethora *n* = **excess**, glut, overabundance, profusion, superabundance, surfeit, surplus

pliable *adj* **1** = **flexible**, bendable, bendy, malleable, plastic, pliant, supple **2** = **compliant**, adaptable, docile, easily led, impressionable, pliant, receptive, responsive, susceptible, tractable

pliant *adj* **a** = **flexible**, bendable, bendy, plastic, pliable, supple **b** = **impressionable**, biddable, compliant, easily led, pliable, susceptible, tractable

plight¹ *n* = **difficulty**, condition, jam (*inf*), predicament, scrape (*inf*), situation, spot (*inf*), state, trouble

plod *v* **1** = **trudge**, clump, drag, lumber, tramp, tread **2** = **slog**, grind (*inf*), labour, persevere, plough through, plug away (*inf*), soldier on, toil

plot¹ ❶ *n* **1** secret plan to do something illegal or wrong. **2** story of a film, novel, etc. ▷ *v* **plotting**, **plotted** **3** plan secretly, conspire. **4** mark the position or course of (a ship or aircraft) on a map. **5** mark and join up (points on a graph).

plot² ❶ *n* small piece of land.

plough ❶ *n* **1** agricultural tool for turning over soil. ▷ *v* **2** turn over (earth) with a plough. **3** (usu with *through*) move or work through slowly and laboriously. **ploughman** *n* **ploughman's lunch** snack lunch of bread and cheese with pickle. **ploughshare** *n* blade of a plough.

plover *n* shore bird with a straight bill and long pointed wings.

ploy ❶ *n* manoeuvre designed to gain an advantage.

pluck ❶ *v* **1** pull or pick off. **2** pull out the feathers of (a bird for cooking). **3** sound the strings of (a guitar etc.) with the fingers or a plectrum. ▷ *n* **4** courage. **plucky** *adj* **pluckier**, **pluckiest** brave. **pluckily** *adv* **pluck up** *v* summon up (courage).

plug ❶ *n* **1** thing fitting into and filling a hole. **2** device connecting an appliance to an electricity supply. **3** *informal* favourable mention of a product etc., to encourage people to buy it. ▷ *v* **plugging**, **plugged 4** block

or seal (a hole or gap) with a plug. **5** *informal* advertise (a product etc.) by constant repetition. **plug away** *v* *informal* work steadily. **plug in** *v* connect (an electrical appliance) to a power source by pushing a plug into a socket.

plum ❶ *n* **1** oval usu. dark red fruit with a stone in the middle. ▷ *adj* **2** dark purplish-red. **3** very desirable.

plumage *n* bird's feathers.

plumb ❶ *v* **1** understand (something obscure). **2** test with a plumb line. ▷ *adv* **3** exactly. **plumb the depths of** experience the worst extremes of (an unpleasant quality or emotion). **plumber** *n* person who fits and repairs pipes and fixtures for water and drainage systems. **plumbing** *n* pipes and fixtures used in water and drainage systems. **plumb in** *v* connect (an appliance such as a washing machine) to a water supply. **plumb line** string with a weight at the end, used to test the depth of water or to test whether something is vertical.

plume ❶ *n* feather, esp. one worn as an ornament.

plummet ❶ *v* **-meting**, **-meted** plunge downward.

plump¹ ❶ *adj* moderately or attractively fat. **plumpness** *n* **plump up** *v* make (a pillow) fuller or rounded.

━━━━━━━━━━━━ THESAURUS ━━━━━━━━━━━━

plot¹ *n* **1** = **plan**, cabal, conspiracy, intrigue, machination, scheme, stratagem **2** = **story**, action, narrative, outline, scenario, story line, subject, theme ▷ *v* **3** = **devise**, collude, conceive, concoct, conspire, contrive, cook up, design, hatch, intrigue, lay (*inf*), machinate, manoeuvre, plan, scheme **4** = **chart**, calculate, locate, map, mark, outline

plot² *n* = **patch**, allotment, area, ground, lot, parcel, tract

plough *v* **2** = **turn over**, cultivate, dig, till **3** (usu. with *through*) = **forge**, cut, drive, plunge, press, push, wade

ploy *n* = **tactic**, device, dodge, manoeuvre, move, ruse, scheme, stratagem, trick, wile

pluck *v* **1** = **pull out** *or* off, collect, draw, gather, harvest, pick **3** = **strum**, finger, pick, twang ▷ *n* **4** = **courage**, backbone, boldness, bottle (*Brit sl*), bravery, grit, guts (*inf*), nerve

plucky *adj* **4** = **courageous**, bold,

brave, daring, game, gutsy (*sl*), have-a-go (*inf*), intrepid, feisty (*US & Canad*)

plug *n* **1** = **stopper**, bung, cork, spigot **3** *Inf* = **mention**, advert (*Brit inf*), advertisement, hype, publicity, push ▷ *v* **4** = **seal**, block, bung, close, cork, fill, pack, stop, stopper, stop up, stuff **5** *Inf* = **mention**, advertise, build up, hype, promote, publicize, push **plug away** *v* *Inf* = **slog**, grind (*inf*), labour, peg away, plod, toil

plum *adj* **3** = **choice**, best, first-class, prize

plumb *v* **1** = **delve**, explore, fathom, gauge, go into, penetrate, probe, unravel ▷ *adv* **3** = **exactly**, bang, precisely, slap, spot-on (*Brit inf*) **plumb line** = **weight**, lead, plumb bob, plummet

plume *n* = **feather**, crest, pinion, quill

plummet *v* = **plunge**, crash, descend, dive, drop down, fall, nose-dive, tumble

plump¹ *adj* = **chubby**, corpulent, dumpy, fat, podgy, roly-poly, rotund, round, stout, tubby

P

plump² ❶ v sit or fall heavily and suddenly. **plump for** v choose, vote for.

plunder ❶ v 1 take by force, esp. in time of war. ▷ n 2 things plundered, spoils.

plunge ❶ v 1 put or throw forcibly or suddenly (into). 2 descend steeply. ▷ n 3 plunging, dive. **take the plunge** informal embark on a risky enterprise. **plunger** n rubber suction cup used to clear blocked pipes. **plunge into** v become deeply involved in.

plunk v pluck the strings of (a banjo etc.) to produce a twanging sound.

pluperfect n, adj Grammar (tense) expressing an action completed before a past time, e.g. had gone in his wife had gone already.

plural adj 1 of or consisting of more than one. ▷ n 2 word indicating more than one.

pluralism n existence and toleration of a variety of peoples, opinions, etc. in a society. **pluralist** n **pluralistic** adj.

plus ❶ prep, adj 1 indicating addition. ▷ adj 2 more than zero. 3 positive. 4 advantageous. ▷ n 5 sign (+) denoting addition. 6 advantage.

plus fours pl n trousers gathered in at the knee.

plush ❶ n 1 fabric with long velvety pile. ▷ adj 2 (also **plushy**) luxurious.

Pluto n 1 Greek god of the underworld. 2 farthest planet from the sun, reclassified as a dwarf planet in 2006.

plutocrat n person who is powerful because of being very rich. **plutocracy** n **plutocratic** adj.

plutonium n Chemistry radioactive metallic element used esp. in nuclear reactors and weapons.

pluvial adj of or caused by the action of rain.

ply¹ ❶ v **plying**, **plied** 1 work at (a job or trade). 2 use (a tool). 3 (of a ship) travel regularly along or between. **ply with** v supply with or subject to persistently.

ply² ❶ n thickness of wool, fabric, etc.

plywood n board made of thin layers of wood glued together.

Pm Chemistry promethium.

PM prime minister.

p.m. 1 after noon. 2 postmortem.

PMS premenstrual syndrome.

PMT premenstrual tension.

pneumatic adj worked by or inflated with wind or air.

pneumonia n inflammation of the lungs.

Po Chemistry polonium.

PO 1 postal order. 2 Post Office.

poach¹ ❶ v 1 catch (animals) illegally on someone else's land. 2 encroach on or steal something belonging to someone else. **poacher** n.

poach² v simmer (food) gently in liquid.

pocket ❶ n 1 small bag sewn into clothing for carrying things. 2 pouchlike container, esp. for catching balls at the edge of a snooker table. 3 isolated or distinct group or area. ▷ v **pocketing**, **pocketed** 4 put into one's pocket. 5 take secretly or dishonestly. ▷ adj 6 small. **out of pocket** having made a loss. **pocket money** 1 small regular allowance given to children by parents. 2 money for small personal expenses.

———————————————————————————————————— **THESAURUS** ——————

plump² v = **flop**, drop, dump, fall, sink, slump **plump for** v = **choose**, back, come down in favour of, favour, opt for, side with, support

plunder v 1 = **loot**, pillage, raid, ransack, rifle, rob, sack, strip ▷ n 2 = **loot**, booty, ill-gotten gains, pillage, prize, spoils, swag (sl)

plunge v 1 = **throw**, career, cast, charge, dash, hurtle, jump, pitch, rush, tear 2 = **descend**, dip, dive, drop, fall, nose-dive, plummet, sink, tumble ▷ n 3 = **dive**, descent, drop, fall, jump

plus prep 1 = **and**, added to, coupled with, with ▷ n 6 = **advantage**, asset, benefit, bonus, extra, gain, good point

plush adj 2 = **luxurious**, de luxe, lavish, luxury, opulent, rich, sumptuous

ply¹ v 1 = **work at**, carry on, exercise, follow, practise, pursue 2 = **use**, employ, handle, manipulate, wield

ply² n = **thickness**, fold, layer, leaf, sheet, strand

poach¹ v 2 = **encroach**, appropriate, infringe, intrude, trespass

pocket n 2 = **pouch**, bag, compartment, receptacle, sack ▷ v 5 = **steal**, appropriate, filch, lift (inf), pilfer, purloin, take ▷ adj 6 = **small**, abridged, compact, concise, little, miniature, portable

pockmarked *adj* (of the skin) marked with hollow scars where diseased spots have been.

pod ❶ *n* long narrow seed case of peas, beans, etc.

podcast *n* **1** audio file that can be downloaded to a computer, music player, etc. ▷ *v* **2** create such files and make them available for downloading.

podgy ❶ *adj* **podgier**, **podgiest** short and fat.

podium ❶ *n*, *pl* **-diums**, **-dia** small raised platform for a conductor or speaker.

poem ❶ *n* imaginative piece of writing in rhythmic lines.

poep *n Aust & NZ slang* emission of gas from the anus.

poesy *n obs* poetry.

poet ❶ *n* writer of poems. **poetry** *n* **1** poems. **2** art of writing poems. **3** beautiful or pleasing quality. **poetic**, **poetical** *adj* of or like poetry. **poetically** *adv* **poetic justice** suitable reward or punishment for someone's past actions. **poetic licence** freedom from the normal rules of language and truth, as in poetry. **poet laureate** poet appointed by the British sovereign to write poems on important occasions.

po-faced *adj* wearing a disapproving stern expression.

pogey ❶ *n Canad sl* money received from the state while out of work.

pogo stick *n* pole with steps for the feet and a spring at the bottom, so that the user can bounce up, down, and along on it.

pogrom *n* organized persecution and massacre.

poignant ❶ *adj* sharply painful to the feelings. **poignancy** *n*.

poinsettia *n* Central American shrub widely grown for its clusters of scarlet leaves, which resemble petals.

point ❶ *n* **1** main idea in a discussion, argument, etc. **2** aim or purpose. **3** detail or item. **4** characteristic. **5** particular position, stage, or time. **6** dot indicating decimals. **7** full stop. **8** sharp end. **9** headland. **10** unit for recording a value or score. **11** one of the direction marks of a compass. **12** movable rail used to change a train to other rails. **13** electrical socket. ▷ *pl* **14** electrical contacts in the distributor of an engine. ▷ *v* **15** show the direction or position of something or draw attention to it by extending a finger or other pointed object towards it. **16** direct or face towards. **17** finish or repair the joints in brickwork with mortar. **18** (of a gun dog) show where game is by standing rigidly with the muzzle towards it. **on the point of**

pod *n* = **shell**, hull, husk, shuck

podgy *adj* = **tubby**, chubby, dumpy, fat, plump, roly-poly, rotund, stout

podium *n* = **platform**, dais, rostrum, stage

poem *n* = **verse**, lyric, ode, rhyme, song, sonnet

poet *n* = **bard**, lyricist, rhymer, versifier

poetic, poetical *adj* = **lyrical**, elegiac, lyric, metrical

poetry *n* **1** = **verse**, poems, rhyme, rhyming

pogey *n Canad Sl* = **benefits**, the dole (*Brit & Austral*), welfare, social security, unemployment benefit, state benefit, allowance

poignancy *n* = **sharpness**, bitterness, intensity, keenness, pathos, sadness

poignant *adj* = **moving**, bitter, distressing, gut-wrenching, heart-rending, intense, painful, pathetic, sad, touching

point *n* **1** = **essence**, crux, drift, gist, heart, import, meaning, nub, pith, question, subject, thrust **2** = **aim**, end, goal, intent, intention, motive, object, objective, purpose, reason **3** = **item**, aspect, detail, feature, particular **4** = **characteristic**, aspect, attribute, quality, respect, trait **5** = **place**, instant, juncture, location, moment, position, site, spot, stage, time, very minute **7** = **full stop**, dot, mark, period, stop **8** = **end**, apex, prong, sharp end, spike, spur, summit, tip, top **9** = **headland**, cape, head, promontory **10** = **unit**, score, tally ▷ *v* **15** = **indicate**, call attention to, denote, designate, direct, show, signify **16** = **aim**, direct, level, train

point-blank *adj* **1** = **direct**, blunt, downright, explicit, express, plain ▷ *adv* **3** = **directly**, bluntly, candidly, explicitly, forthrightly, frankly, openly, plainly, straight

pointed *adj* **1** = **sharp**, acute, barbed, edged **2** = **cutting**, acute, biting, incisive, keen, penetrating, pertinent, sharp, telling

p

very shortly going to. **pointed** *adj*
1 having a sharp end. **2** (of a remark)
obviously directed at a particular
person. **pointedly** *adv* **pointer** *n*
1 helpful hint. **2** indicator on a
measuring instrument. **3** breed of gun
dog. **pointless** *adj* meaningless,
irrelevant. **point-blank** *adj* **1** fired at a
very close target. **2** (of a remark or
question) direct, blunt. ▷ *adv*
3 directly or bluntly. **point duty**
control of traffic by a policeman at a
road junction. **point of view** way of
considering something. **point-to-
point** *n* horse race across open
country.

poise ❶ *n* calm dignified manner.
poised *adj* **1** absolutely ready.
2 behaving with or showing poise.

poison ❶ *n* **1** substance that kills or
injures when swallowed or absorbed.
▷ *v* **2** give poison to. **3** have a harmful
or evil effect on, spoil. **poisoner** *n*
poisonous *adj* **poison-pen letter**
malicious anonymous letter.

poke ❶ *v* **1** jab or prod with one's finger,
a stick, etc. **2** thrust forward or out.
▷ *n* **3** poking. **poky** *adj* **pokier**,
pokiest small and cramped.

poker¹ *n* metal rod for stirring a fire.

poker² *n* card game in which players bet
on the hands dealt. **poker-faced** *adj*
expressionless.

polar *adj* of or near either of the earth's
poles. **polar bear** white bear that lives
in the regions around the North Pole.

polarize *v* **1** form or cause to form into
groups with directly opposite views.
2 *Physics* restrict (light waves) to
certain directions of vibration.
polarization *n*.

Polaroid *n* ® **1** plastic which polarizes
light and so reduces glare. **2** camera
that develops a print very quickly
inside itself.

polder *n* land reclaimed from the sea.

pole¹ ❶ *n* long rounded piece of wood
etc. **pole vault** event in which
competitors try to clear a high bar
with the aid of a flexible long pole.

pole² ❶ *n* **1** point furthest north or
south on the earth's axis of rotation.
2 either of the opposite ends of a
magnet or electric cell. **pole position**
advantageous starting position. **Pole
Star** star nearest to the North Pole in
the northern hemisphere.

poleaxe *v* hit or stun with a heavy
blow.

polecat *n* small animal of the weasel
family.

polemic [pol-**em**-ik] *n* fierce attack on
or defence of a particular opinion,
belief, etc. **polemical** *adj*.

police ❶ *n* **1** organized force in a state
which keeps law and order. ▷ *v*
2 control or watch over with police or
a similar body. **policeman**,
policewoman *n* member of a police
force. **police dog** dog trained to help
the police. **police state** state or
country in which the government

━━━━━━━━━━━━━━━━━━━━━━━━━━━━━━ THESAURUS ━━━━━━━

pointer *n* **1** = **hint**, advice, caution,
information, recommendation,
suggestion, tip **2** = **indicator**, guide,
hand, needle

pointless *adj* = **senseless**, absurd,
aimless, fruitless, futile, inane,
irrelevant, meaningless, silly, stupid,
useless

poise *n* = **composure**, aplomb,
assurance, calmness, cool (*sl*), dignity,
presence, sang-froid, self-possession

poised *adj* **1** = **ready**, all set, prepared,
standing by, waiting **2** = **composed**,
calm, collected, dignified, self-
confident, self-possessed, together
(*inf*)

poison *n* **1** = **toxin**, bane, venom ▷ *v*
2 = **murder**, give (someone) poison,
kill **3** = **corrupt**, contaminate, defile,
deprave, infect, pervert, pollute,
subvert, taint, undermine, warp

poisonous *adj* **1** = **toxic**, deadly, fatal,
lethal, mortal, noxious, venomous,
virulent **3** = **evil**, baleful, corrupting,
malicious, noxious, pernicious

poke *v* **1** = **jab**, dig, nudge, prod, push,
shove, stab, stick, thrust ▷ *n* **3** = **jab**,
dig, nudge, prod, thrust

poky *adj* = **small**, confined, cramped,
narrow, tiny

pole¹ *n* = **rod**, bar, mast, post, shaft,
spar, staff, stick

pole² *n* **1** = **extremity**, antipode, limit,
terminus

police *n* **1** = **the law** (*inf*), boys in blue
(*inf*), constabulary, fuzz (*sl*), police
force, the Old Bill (*sl*) ▷ *v* **2** = **control**,
guard, patrol, protect, regulate,
watch

policeman, policewoman *n* = **cop**
(*sl*), bobby (*inf*), constable, copper (*sl*),
fuzz (*sl*), officer

controls people's freedom by means of esp. secret police. **police station** office of the police force of a district.

policy¹ ❶ n, pl **-cies** plan of action adopted by a person, group, or state.

policy² n, pl **-cies** document containing an insurance contract.

polio n disease affecting the spinal cord, which often causes paralysis (also **poliomyelitis**).

polish ❶ v 1 make smooth and shiny by rubbing. **2** make more nearly perfect. ▷ n **3** substance used for polishing. **4** shine or gloss. **5** pleasing elegant style. **polished** adj **1** accomplished. **2** done or performed well or professionally. **polish off** v finish completely, dispose of.

Polish adj **1** of Poland, its people, or their language. ▷ n **2** official language of Poland.

polite ❶ adj **1** showing consideration for others in one's manners, speech, etc. **2** socially correct or refined. **politely** adv **politeness** n.

politic ❶ adj wise and likely to prove advantageous.

politics ❶ n **1** winning and using of power to govern society. **2** (study of) the art of government. **3** person's beliefs about how a country should be governed. **political** adj of the state, government, or public administration. **politically** adv **politically correct** (of

language) intended to avoid any implied prejudice. **political prisoner** person imprisoned because of his or her political beliefs. **politician** n person actively engaged in politics, esp. a member of parliament.

polka n **1** lively 19th-century dance. **2** music for this. **polka dots** pattern of bold spots on fabric.

poll ❶ n **1** (also **opinion poll**) questioning of a random sample of people to find out general opinion. **2** voting. **3** number of votes recorded. ▷ v **4** receive (votes). **5** question in an opinion poll. **pollster** n person who conducts opinion polls. **polling booth** compartment in which a voter can mark his or her ballot paper in private. **polling station** building where people vote in an election. **poll tax** tax levied on every adult person.

pollarded adj (of a tree) growing very bushy because its top branches have been cut short.

pollen n fine dust produced by flowers to fertilize other flowers. **pollinate** v fertilize with pollen. **pollen count** measure of the amount of pollen in the air, esp. as a warning to people with hay fever.

pollute ❶ v contaminate with something poisonous or harmful. **pollution** n **pollutant** n something that pollutes.

THESAURUS

p

policy¹ n = **procedure**, action, approach, code, course, custom, plan, practice, rule, scheme

polish v **1** = **shine**, brighten, buff, burnish, rub, smooth, wax **2** = **perfect**, brush up, enhance, finish, improve, refine, touch up ▷ n **3** = **varnish**, wax **4** = **sheen**, brightness, finish, glaze, gloss, lustre **5** = **style**, breeding, class (inf), elegance, finesse, finish, grace, refinement

polished adj **1** = **accomplished**, adept **2** = **professional**, expert, fine, masterly, skilful, superlative

polite adj **1** = **mannerly**, civil, complaisant, courteous, gracious, respectful, well-behaved, well-mannered **2** = **refined**, civilized, cultured, elegant, genteel, polished, sophisticated, well-bred

politeness n **1** = **courtesy**, civility, courteousness, decency, etiquette,

mannerliness

politic adj = **wise**, advisable, diplomatic, expedient, judicious, prudent, sensible

political adj = **governmental**, parliamentary, policy-making

politician n = **statesman**, legislator, Member of Parliament, M.P., office bearer, public servant

politics n **2** = **statesmanship**, affairs of state, civics, government, political science

poll n **1** (also **opinion poll**) = **canvass**, census, sampling, survey **2** = **vote**, ballot, count, voting **3** = **figures**, returns, tally ▷ v **4** = **tally**, register **5** = **question**, ballot, canvass, interview, sample, survey

pollute v = **contaminate**, dirty, foul, infect, poison, soil, spoil, stain, taint

pollution n = **contamination**, corruption, defilement, dirtying, foulness, impurity, taint, uncleanness

polo n game like hockey played by teams of players on horseback. **polo neck** sweater with tight turned-over collar. **polo shirt** cotton short-sleeved shirt with a collar and three-button opening at the neck.

polonaise n **1** old stately dance. **2** music for this.

polonium n Chemistry radioactive element that occurs in trace amounts in uranium ores.

poltergeist n spirit believed to move furniture and throw objects around.

poltroon n obs utter coward.

poly- combining form many, much.

polyandry n practice of having more than one husband at the same time.

polyanthus n garden primrose.

polychromatic adj many-coloured.

polyester n synthetic material used to make plastics and textile fibres.

polygamy [pol-**ig**-a-mee] n practice of having more than one husband or wife at the same time. **polygamous** adj **polygamist** n.

polyglot n, adj (person) able to speak or write several languages.

polygon n geometrical figure with three or more angles and sides. **polygonal** adj.

polygraph n instrument for recording pulse rate and perspiration, used esp. as a lie detector.

polyhedron n, pl **-drons, -dra** solid figure with four or more sides.

polymath n person of great and varied learning.

polymer n chemical compound with large molecules made of simple molecules of the same kind. **polymerize** v form into polymers. **polymerization** n.

polynomial adj **1** of two or more names or terms. ▷ n **2** mathematical expression consisting of the sum of a number of terms.

polyp n **1** small simple sea creature with a hollow cylindrical body. **2** small growth on a mucous membrane.

polyphonic adj Music consisting of several melodies played simultaneously.

polystyrene n synthetic material used esp. as white rigid foam for packing and insulation.

polytechnic n formerly, college offering courses in many subjects at and below degree level.

polytheism n belief in many gods. **polytheist** n **polytheistic** adj.

polythene n light plastic used for bags etc.

polyunsaturated adj of a group of fats that do not form cholesterol in the blood.

polyurethane n synthetic material used esp. in paints.

pom n Aust & NZ slang person from England (also **pommy**).

pomade n perfumed oil put on the hair to make it smooth and shiny.

pomander n (container for) a mixture of sweet-smelling petals, herbs, etc.

pomegranate n round tropical fruit with a thick rind containing many seeds in a red pulp.

Pomeranian n small dog with long straight hair.

pommel n **1** raised part on the front of a saddle. **2** knob at the top of a sword hilt.

pommy n, pl **-mies** Aust & NZ slang person from Britain (also **pom**).

pomp ❶ n stately display or ceremony.

pompom n decorative ball of tufted wool, silk, etc.

pompous ❶ adj foolishly serious and grand, self-important. **pompously** adv **pomposity** n.

ponce n offens **1** effeminate man. **2** pimp. **ponce around** v act stupidly, waste time.

poncho n, pl **-chos** loose circular cloak with a hole for the head.

pond ❶ n small area of still water. **pondweed** n plant that grows in ponds.

THESAURUS

pomp n **a** = **show**, display, grandiosity, ostentation **b** = **ceremony**, flourish, grandeur, magnificence, pageant, pageantry, splendour, state

pomposity n = **self-importance**, affectation, airs, grandiosity, pompousness, portentousness, pretension, pretentiousness

pompous adj **a** = **grandiloquent**, boastful, bombastic, high-flown, inflated **b** = **self-important**, arrogant, grandiose, ostentatious, pretentious, puffed up, showy

pond n = **pool**, duck pond, fish pond, millpond, small lake, tarn

ponder ❶ v think thoroughly or deeply (about).

ponderous ❶ adj 1 serious and dull. 2 heavy and unwieldy. 3 (of movement) slow and clumsy. **ponderously** adv.

pong v, n informal (give off) a strong unpleasant smell.

pontiff ❶ n the Pope. **pontificate** v 1 state one's opinions as if they were the only possible correct ones. ▷ n 2 period of office of a Pope.

pontoon¹ n floating platform supporting a temporary bridge.

pontoon² n gambling card game.

pony n, pl **ponies** small horse. **ponytail** n long hair tied in one bunch at the back of the head. **pony trekking** pastime of riding ponies cross-country.

poodle n dog with curly hair often clipped fancifully.

poof n offens homosexual man.

pooh interj exclamation of disdain, contempt, or disgust. **pooh-pooh** v express disdain or scorn for.

pool¹ ❶ n 1 small body of still water. 2 puddle of spilt liquid. 3 swimming pool.

pool² ❶ n 1 shared fund or group of workers or resources. 2 game like snooker. ▷ pl 3 short for FOOTBALL POOLS. ▷ v 4 put in a common fund.

poop n raised part at the back of a sailing ship.

poor ❶ adj 1 having little money and few possessions. 2 less, smaller, or weaker than is needed or expected. 3 inferior. 4 unlucky, pitiable. **poorly** adv 1 in a poor manner. ▷ adj 2 not in good health.

pop¹ ❶ v **popping, popped** 1 make or cause to make a small explosive sound. 2 informal go, put, or come unexpectedly or suddenly. ▷ n 3 small explosive sound. 4 nonalcoholic fizzy drink. **popcorn** n grains of maize heated until they puff up and burst.

pop² n 1 music of general appeal, esp. to young people. ▷ adj 2 popular. **pop art** movement in modern art that uses the methods, styles, and themes of popular culture and mass media.

pop³ n informal father.

Pope ❶ n head of the Roman Catholic Church. **popish** adj offens Roman Catholic.

popeyed adj staring in astonishment.

popinjay n conceited or talkative person.

poplar n tall slender tree.

poplin n ribbed cotton material.

poppadom n thin round crisp Indian bread.

poppet n term of affection for a small child or sweetheart.

THESAURUS

ponder v = **think**, brood, cogitate, consider, contemplate, deliberate, meditate, mull over, muse, reflect, ruminate

ponderous adj 1 = **dull**, heavy, long-winded, pedantic, tedious 2 = **unwieldy**, bulky, cumbersome, heavy, huge, massive, weighty 3 = **clumsy**, awkward, heavy-footed, lumbering

pontificate v 1 = **expound**, hold forth, lay down the law, preach, pronounce, sound off

pool¹ n 1 = **pond**, lake, mere, puddle, tarn 3 = **swimming pool**, swimming bath

pool² n 1 **a** = **kitty**, bank, funds, jackpot, pot **b** = **syndicate**, collective, consortium, group, team, trust ▷ v 4 = **combine**, amalgamate, join forces, league, merge, put together, share

poor adj 1 = **impoverished**, broke (inf), destitute, down and out, hard up (inf), impecunious, indigent, needy, on the breadline, penniless, penurious, poverty-stricken, short, skint (Brit sl), stony-broke (Brit sl) 2 = **meagre**, deficient, inadequate, incomplete, insufficient, lacking, measly, scant, scanty, skimpy 3 = **inferior**, below par, low-grade, mediocre, no great shakes (inf), rotten (inf), rubbishy, second-rate, substandard, unsatisfactory 4 = **unfortunate**, hapless, ill-fated, pitiable, unlucky, wretched

poorly adv 1 = **badly**, inadequately, incompetently, inexpertly, insufficiently, unsatisfactorily, unsuccessfully ▷ adj 2 = **ill**, below par, crook (Aust & NZ sl), off colour, rotten (inf), seedy (inf), sick, under the weather (inf), unwell

pop¹ v 1 = **burst**, bang, crack, explode, go off, snap ▷ n 3 = **bang**, burst, crack, explosion, noise, report

Pope n = **Holy Father**, Bishop of Rome, pontiff, Vicar of Christ

p

poppy *n, pl* **-pies 1** plant with a large red flower. **2** artificial red poppy worn to mark Remembrance Sunday.

poppycock *n informal* nonsense.

Popsicle ® *n US & Canad* an ice lolly.

populace ❶ *n* the ordinary people.

popular ❶ *adj* **1** widely liked and admired. **2** of or for the public in general. **popularly** *adv* **popularity** *n* **popularize** *v* **1** make popular. **2** make (something technical or specialist) easily understood.

populate ❶ *v* **1** live in, inhabit. **2** fill with inhabitants. **population** *n* **1** all the people who live in a particular place. **2** the number of people living in a particular place. **populous** *adj* densely populated.

populist *n, adj* (person) appealing to the interests or prejudices of ordinary people. **populism** *n*.

porbeagle *n* kind of shark.

porcelain *n* **1** fine china. **2** objects made of it.

porch *n* covered approach to the entrance of a building.

porcine *adj* of or like a pig.

porcupine *n* animal covered with long pointed quills.

pore ❶ *n* tiny opening in the skin or in the surface of a plant.

pore over *v* make a careful study or examination of (a book, map, etc.).

pork *n* pig meat. **porker** *n* pig raised for food.

porn, porno *n, adj informal* short for PORNOGRAPHY *or* PORNOGRAPHIC.

pornography ❶ *n* writing, films, or pictures designed to be sexually exciting. **pornographer** *n* producer of pornography. **pornographic** *adj*.

porous ❶ *adj* allowing liquid to pass through gradually. **porosity** *n*.

porphyry [por-fir-ee] *n* reddish rock with large crystals in it.

porpoise *n* fishlike sea mammal.

porridge *n* **1** breakfast food made of oatmeal cooked in water or milk. **2** *slang* term in prison.

port¹ ❶ *n* (town with) a harbour.

port² *n* left side of a ship or aircraft when facing the front of it.

port³ *n* strong sweet wine, usu. red.

port⁴ *n* **1** opening in the side of a ship. **2** porthole.

portable ❶ *adj* easily carried. **portability** *n*.

portage *n* (route for) transporting boats and supplies overland between navigable waterways.

portal *n* large imposing doorway or gate.

portcullis *n* grating suspended above a castle gateway, that can be lowered to block the entrance.

portend ❶ *v* be a sign of.

portent ❶ *n* sign of a future event. **portentous** *adj* **1** of great or ominous significance. **2** pompous, self-important.

P

——————— THESAURUS ———————

populace *n* = **people**, general public, hoi polloi, masses, mob, multitude

popular *adj* **1** = **well-liked**, accepted, approved, fashionable, favourite, in, in demand, in favour, liked, sought-after **2** = **common**, conventional, current, general, prevailing, prevalent, universal

popularity *n* **1** = **favour**, acceptance, acclaim, approval, currency, esteem, regard, vogue

popularize *v* **1** = **make popular**, disseminate, give currency to, give mass appeal, make available to all, spread, universalize

populate *v* **1** = **inhabit**, colonize, live in, occupy, settle

population *n* **1** = **inhabitants**, community, denizens, folk, natives, people, residents, society

populous *adj* = **populated**, crowded, heavily populated, overpopulated, packed, swarming, teeming

pore *n* = **opening**, hole, orifice, outlet

pore over *v* = **study**, examine, peruse, ponder, read, scrutinize

pornographic *adj* = **obscene**, blue, dirty, filthy, indecent, lewd, salacious, scungy (*Aust & NZ inf*), smutty

pornography *n* = **obscenity**, dirt, filth, indecency, porn (*inf*), smut

porous *adj* = **permeable**, absorbent, absorptive, penetrable, spongy

port¹ *n* = **harbour**, anchorage, haven, seaport

portable *adj* = **light**, compact, convenient, easily carried, handy, manageable, movable

portend *v* = **foretell**, augur, betoken, bode, foreshadow, herald, indicate, predict, prognosticate, promise, warn of

portent *n* = **omen**, augury, forewarning, indication, prognostication, sign, warning

porter¹ ❶ *n* **1** man who carries luggage. **2** hospital worker who transfers patients between rooms etc.

porter² ❶ *n* doorman or gatekeeper of a building.

portfolio *n, pl* **-os** **1** (flat case for carrying) examples of an artist's work. **2** area of responsibility of a government minister. **3** list of investments held by an investor.

porthole *n* small round window in a ship or aircraft.

portico *n, pl* **-coes, -cos** porch or covered walkway with columns supporting the roof.

portion ❶ *n* **1** part or share. **2** helping of food for one person. **3** destiny or fate. **portion out** *v* divide into shares.

portly ❶ *adj* **-lier, -liest** rather fat.

portmanteau *n, pl* **-teaus, -teaux** **1** *old-fashioned* large suitcase that opens into two compartments. ▷ *adj* **2** combining aspects of different things.

portrait ❶ *n* **1** picture of a person. **2** lifelike description.

portray ❶ *v* describe or represent by artistic means, as in writing or film. **portrait** *n* picture of a person. **portrayal** *n*.

Portuguese *adj* **1** of Portugal, its people, or their language. ▷ *n* **2** person from Portugal. **3** language of Portugal and Brazil. **Portuguese man-of-war** sea creature resembling a jellyfish, with stinging tentacles.

pose ❶ *v* **1** place in or take up a particular position to be photographed or drawn. **2** behave in an affected way. **3** raise (a problem). **4** ask (a question). ▷ *n* **5** position while posing. **6** behaviour adopted for effect. **pose as** pretend to be. **poser** *n* **1** puzzling question. **2** *informal* person who likes to be seen in trendy clothes in fashionable places. **3** poseur. **poseur** *n* person who behaves in an affected way to impress others.

posh ❶ *adj informal* **1** smart, luxurious. **2** affectedly upper-class.

posit ❶ [**pozz**-it] *v* lay down as a basis for argument.

position ❶ *n* **1** place. **2** usual or expected place. **3** way in which something is placed or arranged. **4** attitude, point of view. **5** social standing. **6** job. ▷ *v* **7** place. **positional** *adj*.

THESAURUS

portentous *adj* **1** = **significant**, crucial, fateful, important, menacing, momentous, ominous **2** = **pompous**, ponderous, self-important, solemn

porter¹ *n* **1** = **baggage attendant**, bearer, carrier

porter² *n* = **doorman**, caretaker, concierge, gatekeeper, janitor

portion *n* **1 a** = **part**, bit, fragment, morsel, piece, scrap, section, segment **b** = **share**, allocation, allotment, allowance, lot, measure, quantity, quota, ration **2** = **helping**, piece, serving **3** = **destiny**, fate, fortune, lot, luck **portion out** *v* = **divide**, allocate, allot, apportion, deal, distribute, dole out, share out

portly *adj* = **stout**, burly, corpulent, fat, fleshy, heavy, large, plump

portrait *n* **1** = **picture**, image, likeness, painting, photograph, representation **2** = **description**, characterization, depiction, portrayal, profile, thumbnail sketch

portray *v* **a** = **represent**, depict, draw, figure, illustrate, paint, picture, sketch **b** = **describe**, characterize, depict, put in words **c** = **play**, act the part of, represent

pose *v* **1** = **position**, model, sit **2** = **put on airs**, posture, show off (*inf*) ▷ *n* **5** = **posture**, attitude, bearing, position, stance **6** = **act**, affectation, air, facade, front, mannerism, posturing, pretence **pose as** *v* = **impersonate**, masquerade as, pass oneself off as, pretend to be, profess to be

posh *adj Inf* **1** = **smart**, classy (*sl*), grand, luxurious, ritzy (*sl*), stylish, swanky (*inf, chiefly Brit*), swish (*inf, chiefly Brit*) **2** = **upper-class**, high-class, up-market

posit *v* = **put forward**, advance, assume, postulate, presume, propound, state

position *n* **1** = **place**, area, bearings, locale, location, point, post, situation, spot, station, whereabouts **3** = **posture**, arrangement, attitude, pose, stance **4** = **attitude**, belief, opinion, outlook, point of view, slant, stance, view, viewpoint **5** = **status**, importance, place, prestige, rank,

positive ❶ *adj* **1** feeling no doubts, certain. **2** confident, hopeful. **3** helpful, providing encouragement. **4** absolute, downright. **5** *Maths* greater than zero. **6** (of an electrical charge) having a deficiency of electrons. **7** *Medical* indicating the presence of a condition for which a test was made. **positively** *adv* **positive discrimination** provision of special opportunities for a disadvantaged group.

positivism *n* philosophical system which accepts only things that can be seen or proved. **positivist** *n, adj.*

positron *n* Physics particle with same mass as electron but positive charge.

posse [**poss**-ee] *n* **1** *US* group of men organized to maintain law and order. **2** *informal* group or gang.

possess ❶ *v* **1** have as one's property. **2** (of a feeling, belief, etc.) have complete control of, dominate. **possessed** *adj* **possessor** *n* **possession** *n* **1** state of possessing, ownership. ▷ *pl* **2** things a person possesses. **possessive** *adj* **1** wanting all the attention or love of another person. **2** (of a word) indicating the person or thing that something belongs to. **possessiveness** *n.*

possible ❶ *adj* **1** able to exist, happen, or be done. **2** worthy of consideration. ▷ *n* **3** person or thing that might be suitable or chosen. **possibility** *n, pl* **-ties. possibly** *adv* perhaps, not necessarily.

possum *n* **1** same as OPOSSUM. **2** *Aust & NZ* same as PHALANGER. **play possum** pretend to be dead or asleep to deceive an opponent.

post¹ ❶ *n* **1** official system of delivering letters and parcels. **2** (single collection or delivery of) letters and parcels sent by this system. ▷ *v* **3** send by post. **keep someone posted** supply someone regularly with the latest information. **postage** *n* charge for sending a letter or parcel by post. **postal** *adj* **postal order** written money order sent by post and cashed at a post office by the person who receives it. **postbag** *n* **1** postman's bag. **2** post received by a magazine, famous person, etc. **postbox** *n* same as LETTER BOX (sense 2). **postcode** *n* system of letters and numbers used to aid the sorting of mail. **postie** *Aust, NZ & Scot informal* postman. **postman**, **postwoman** *n* person who collects and delivers post. **postmark** *n* official mark stamped on letters showing

— THESAURUS —

reputation, standing, station, stature **6** = **job**, duty, employment, occupation, office, place, post, role, situation ▷ *v* **7** = **place**, arrange, lay out, locate, put, set, stand

positive *adj* **1, 2** = **certain**, assured, confident, convinced, sure **3** = **helpful**, beneficial, constructive, practical, productive, progressive, useful **4 a** = **definite**, absolute, categorical, certain, clear, conclusive, decisive, explicit, express, firm, real **b** = **absolute**, complete, consummate, downright, out-and-out, perfect, thorough, utter

positively *adv* **1, 4** = **definitely**, absolutely, assuredly, categorically, certainly, emphatically, firmly, surely, unequivocally, unquestionably

possess *v* **1** = **have**, enjoy, hold, own **2** = **dominate**, control, seize, take over

possessed *adj* **2** = **crazed**, berserk, demented, frenzied, obsessed, raving

possession *n* **1** = **ownership**, control, custody, hold, occupation, tenure, title ▷ *pl* **2** = **property**, assets,

belongings, chattels, effects, estate, things

possessive *adj* **1** = **jealous**, controlling, covetous, dominating, domineering, overprotective, selfish

possibility *n* **1 a** = **likelihood**, chance, hope, liability, odds, probability, prospect, risk **b** = **feasibility**, likelihood, potentiality, practicability, workableness **2** (often *pl*) = **potential**, capabilities, potentiality, promise, prospects, talent

possible *adj* **1 a** = **conceivable**, credible, hypothetical, imaginable, likely, potential **b** = **likely**, hopeful, potential, probable, promising **c** = **feasible**, attainable, doable, practicable, realizable, viable, workable

possibly *adv* = **perhaps**, maybe, perchance (*arch*)

post¹ *n* **1** = **mail**, collection, delivery, postal service ▷ *v* **3** = **send**, dispatch, mail, transmit **keep someone posted** = **notify**, advise, brief, fill in on (*inf*), inform, report to

place and date of posting.

postmaster, **postmistress** n official in charge of a post office. **post office** place where postal business is conducted. **post shop** NZ shop providing postal services.

post² ❶ n **1** length of wood, concrete, etc. fixed upright to support or mark something. ▷ v **2** put up (a notice) in a public place.

post³ ❶ n **1** job. **2** position to which someone, esp. a soldier, is assigned for duty. **3** military establishment. ▷ v **4** send (a person) to a new place to work. **5** put (a guard etc.) on duty.

post- prefix after, later than, e.g. postwar.

postcard n card for sending a message by post without an envelope.

postdate v write a date on (a cheque) that is later than the actual date.

poster ❶ n large picture or notice stuck on a wall.

poste restante n French post-office department where a traveller's letters are kept until called for.

posterior n **1** buttocks. ▷ adj **2** behind, at the back of.

posterity ❶ n future generations, descendants.

postern n small back door or gate.

postgraduate n person with a degree who is studying for a more advanced qualification.

posthaste adv with great speed.

posthumous [**poss**-tume-uss] adj **1** occurring after one's death. **2** published after the author's death. **posthumously** adv.

postilion, **postillion** n History person riding one of a pair or team of horses

drawing a carriage.

postmortem n medical examination of a body to establish the cause of death.

postnatal adj occurring after childbirth.

postpone ❶ v put off to a later time. **postponement** n.

postscript ❶ n passage added at the end of a letter.

postulant n candidate for admission to a religious order.

postulate ❶ v assume to be true as the basis of an argument or theory. **postulation** n.

posture ❶ n **1** position or way in which someone stands, walks, etc. ▷ v **2** behave in an exaggerated way to get attention.

posy n, pl **-sies** small bunch of flowers.

pot¹ ❶ n **1** round deep container. **2** teapot. ▷ pl **3** informal a lot. ▷ v **potting**, **potted 4** plant in a pot. **5** Snooker hit (a ball) into a pocket. **potted** adj **1** grown in a pot. **2** (of meat or fish) cooked or preserved in a pot. **3** informal abridged. **potbelly** n bulging belly. **potsherd** n broken fragment of pottery. **pot shot** shot taken without aiming carefully. **potting shed** shed where plants are potted.

pot² n slang cannabis.

potable [**pote**-a-bl] adj drinkable.

potash n white powdery substance obtained from ashes and used as fertilizer.

potassium n Chemistry silvery metallic element.

potato n, pl **-toes** roundish starchy vegetable that grows underground.

P

post² n **1** = **support**, column, picket, pillar, pole, shaft, stake, upright ▷ v **2** = **put up**, affix, display, pin up

post³ n **1** = **job**, appointment, assignment, employment, office, place, position, situation **2** = **station**, beat, place, position ▷ v **4** = **station**, assign, place, position, put, situate

poster n = **notice**, advertisement, announcement, bill, placard, public notice, sticker

posterity n **a** = **future**, succeeding generations **b** = **descendants**, children, family, heirs, issue, offspring, progeny

postpone v = **put off**, adjourn, defer,

delay, put back, put on the back burner (inf), shelve, suspend

postscript n = **P.S.**, addition, afterthought, supplement

postulate v = **presuppose**, assume, hypothesize, posit, propose, suppose, take for granted, theorize

posture n **1** = **bearing**, attitude, carriage, disposition, set, stance ▷ v **2** = **show off**, affect, pose, put on airs (inf)

pot¹ n **1** = **container**, bowl, pan, vessel

potency n = **power**, effectiveness, force, influence, mana (NZ), might, strength

potato chip *n* the US and Canadian term for CRISP.

poteen *n* (in Ireland) illegally made alcoholic drink.

potent ❶ *adj* **1** having great power or influence. **2** (of a male) capable of having sexual intercourse. **potency** *n*.

potentate *n* ruler or monarch.

potential ❶ *adj* **1** possible but not yet actual. ▷ *n* **2** ability or talent not yet fully used. **3** *Electricity* level of electric pressure. **potentially** *adv* **potentiality** *n, pl* **-ties**.

pothole *n* **1** hole in the surface of a road. **2** deep hole in a limestone area. **potholing** *n* sport of exploring underground caves. **potholer** *n*.

potion ❶ *n* dose of medicine or poison.

potluck *n* **take potluck** accept whatever happens to be available.

potoroo *n, pl* **-roos** Australian leaping rodent.

potpourri [po-**poor**-ee] *n* **1** fragrant mixture of dried flower petals. **2** assortment or medley.

pottage *n* thick soup or stew.

potter¹ *n* person who makes pottery.

potter² ❶ *v* be busy in a pleasant but aimless way.

pottery ❶ *n, pl* **-ries 1** articles made from baked clay. **2** place where they are made. **3** craft of making such articles.

potty¹ *adj* **-tier, -tiest** *informal* **1** crazy or silly. **2** trivial.

potty² *n, pl* **-ties** bowl used by a small child as a toilet.

pouch ❶ *n* **1** small bag. **2** baglike pocket of skin on an animal.

pouf, pouffe [poof] *n* large solid cushion used as a seat.

poulterer *n* person who sells poultry.

poultice [**pole**-tiss] *n* moist dressing, often heated, applied to inflamed skin.

poultry *n* domestic fowls.

pounce ❶ *v* **1** spring upon suddenly to attack or capture. ▷ *n* **2** pouncing.

pound¹ *n* **1** monetary unit of Britain and some other countries. **2** unit of weight equal to 0.454 kg.

pound² ❶ *v* **1** hit heavily and repeatedly. **2** crush to pieces or powder. **3** (of the heart) throb heavily. **4** run heavily.

pound³ ❶ *n* enclosure for stray animals or officially removed vehicles.

poundage *n* charge of so much per pound of weight or sterling.

pour ❶ *v* **1** flow or cause to flow out in a stream. **2** rain heavily. **3** come or go in large numbers.

pout ❶ *v* **1** thrust out one's lips, look sulky. ▷ *n* **2** pouting look.

pouter *n* pigeon that can puff out its crop.

poverty ❶ *n* **1** state of being without enough food or money. **2** lack of,

P

————————— THESAURUS —————————

potent *adj* = **powerful**, authoritative, commanding, dominant, dynamic, forceful, influential, mighty, strong, vigorous

potential *adj* **1** = **possible**, dormant, future, hidden, inherent, latent, likely, promising ▷ *n* **2** = **ability**, aptitude, capability, capacity, possibility, potentiality, power, wherewithal

potion *n* = **concoction**, brew, dose, draught, elixir, mixture, philtre

potter² *v* = **mess about**, dabble, footle (*inf*), tinker

pottery *n* **1** = **ceramics**, earthenware, stoneware, terracotta

pouch *n* **1** = **bag**, container, pocket, purse, sack

pounce *v* **1** = **spring**, attack, fall upon, jump, leap at, strike, swoop ▷ *n* **2** = **spring**, assault, attack, bound, jump, leap, swoop

pound² *v* **1** = **beat**, batter, belabour, clobber (*sl*), hammer, pummel, strike, thrash, thump **2** = **crush**, powder, pulverize **3** = **pulsate**, beat, palpitate, pulse, throb **4** = **stomp** (*inf*), march, thunder, tramp

pound³ *n* = **enclosure**, compound, pen, yard

pour *v* **1** = **flow**, course, decant, emit, gush, let flow, run, rush, spew, spill, splash, spout, stream **2** = **rain**, bucket down (*inf*), pelt (down), teem **3** = **stream**, crowd, swarm, teem, throng

pout *v* **1** = **sulk**, glower, look petulant, pull a long face ▷ *n* **2** = **sullen look**, glower, long face

poverty *n* **1** = **pennilessness**, beggary, destitution, hardship, indigence, insolvency, need, penury, privation, want **2** = **scarcity**, dearth, deficiency, insufficiency, lack, paucity, shortage

poverty-stricken *adj* = **penniless**, broke (*inf*), destitute, down and out, flat broke (*inf*), impecunious, impoverished, indigent, poor

scarcity. **poverty-stricken** *adj* very poor. **poverty trap** situation of being unable to raise one's living standard because any extra income would result in state benefits being reduced.

POW prisoner of war.

powder ❶ *n* **1** substance in the form of tiny loose particles. **2** medicine or cosmetic in this form. ▷ *v* **3** apply powder to. **powdered** *adj* in the form of a powder, e.g. *powdered milk*. **powdery** *adj* **powder puff** soft pad used to apply cosmetic powder to the skin. **powder room** ladies' toilet.

power ❶ *n* **1** ability to do or act. **2** strength. **3** position of authority or control. **4** person or thing having authority. **5** *Maths* product from continuous multiplication of a number by itself. **6** *Physics* rate at which work is done. **7** electricity supply. **8** particular form of energy, e.g. *nuclear power*. **powered** *adj* having or operated by mechanical or electrical power. **powerful** *adj* **powerless** *adj* **power cut** temporary interruption in the supply of electricity. **power point** socket on a wall for plugging in electrical appliances. **power station**

installation for generating and distributing electric power. **power steering** type of steering on vehicles in which the turning of the steering wheel is assisted by power from the engine.

powwow *n* talk, conference.

pox *n* **1** disease in which skin pustules form. **2** *informal* syphilis.

pp 1 past participle. **2** (in signing a document) for and on behalf of. **3** *Music* pianissimo.

pp. pages.

PQ Quebec.

Pr *Chemistry* praseodymium.

PR 1 proportional representation. **2** public relations.

practicable ❶ *adj* capable of being done successfully. **practicability** *n*.

practical ❶ *adj* **1** involving experience or actual use rather than theory. **2** concerned with everyday matters. **3** sensible, useful, and effective. **4** good at making or doing things. **5** in effect though not in name. ▷ *n* **6** examination in which something has to be done or made. **practically** *adv* **practicality** *n*, *pl* **-ties**. **practical joke** trick intended to make someone look foolish.

powder *n* **1** = **dust**, fine grains, loose particles, talc ▷ *v* **3** = **dust**, cover, dredge, scatter, sprinkle, strew

powdery *adj* = **fine**, crumbly, dry, dusty, grainy, granular

power *n* **1** = **ability**, capability, capacity, competence, competency, faculty, potential **2** = **strength**, brawn, energy, force, forcefulness, intensity, might, muscle, potency, vigour **3** = **control**, ascendancy, authority, command, dominance, domination, dominion, influence, mana (*NZ*), mastery, prerogative, privilege, rule

powerful *adj* **2** = **strong**, energetic, mighty, potent, strapping, sturdy, vigorous **3 a** = **controlling**, authoritative, commanding, dominant, influential, prevailing, skookum (*Canad*) **b** = **persuasive**, cogent, compelling, convincing, effectual, forceful, impressive, storming, striking, telling, weighty

powerless *adj* **1** = **defenceless**, dependent, ineffective, subject, tied,

unarmed, vulnerable **2** = **weak**, debilitated, disabled, feeble, frail, helpless, impotent, incapable, incapacitated, ineffectual

practicability *n* = **feasibility**, advantage, possibility, practicality, use, usefulness, viability

practicable *adj* = **feasible**, achievable, attainable, doable, possible, viable

practical *adj* **1** = **functional**, applied, empirical, experimental, factual, pragmatic, realistic, utilitarian **2** = **ordinary**, businesslike, down-to-earth, hard-headed, matter-of-fact, realistic **3** = **sensible**, doable, feasible, practicable, serviceable, useful, workable **4** = **skilled**, accomplished, efficient, experienced, proficient

practically *adv* **2** = **realistically**, matter-of-factly **3** = **sensibly**, clearly, rationally, reasonably **5** = **almost**, all but, basically, essentially, fundamentally, in effect, just about, nearly, very nearly, virtually, well-nigh

p

practice ❶ *n* **1** something done regularly or habitually. **2** repetition of something so as to gain skill. **3** doctor's or lawyer's place of work. **in practice** what actually happens as distinct from what is supposed to happen. **put into practice** carry out, do.

- ● SPELLING TIP
- ● It is extremely common for people
- ● to confuse the noun, **practice**,
- ● which has a c at the end, and the
- ● verb **practise**, which has a n s.

practise ❶ *v* **1** do repeatedly so as to gain skill. **2** take part in, follow (a religion etc.). **3** work at, e.g. *practise medicine*. **4** do habitually. **practice** *n* something done regularly or habitually.

practitioner *n* person who practises a profession.

pragmatic ❶ *adj* concerned with practical consequences rather than theory. **pragmatism** *n* **pragmatist** *n*.

prairie *n* a treeless grassy plain of the central US and S Canada. **prairie dog** rodent that lives in burrows in the N American prairies.

praise ❶ *v* **1** express approval or admiration of (someone or something). **2** express honour and thanks to (one's God). ▷ *n* **3** something said or written to show approval or admiration. **sing someone's praises** praise someone highly. **praiseworthy** *adj.*

praline [**prah**-leen] *n* sweet made of nuts and caramelized sugar.

pram *n* four-wheeled carriage for a baby, pushed by hand.

prance ❶ *v* walk with exaggerated bouncing steps.

prang *v, n old-fashioned slang* (have) a crash in a car or aircraft.

prank ❶ *n* mischievous trick.

praseodymium [pray-zee-oh-**dim**-ee-um] *n Chemistry* silvery-white metallic element of the lanthanide series.

prat *n offens* stupid person.

prattle ❶ *v* **1** chatter in a childish or foolish way. ▷ *n* **2** childish or foolish talk.

prawn *n* edible shellfish like a large shrimp.

praxis *n* practice as opposed to theory.

pray ❶ *v* **1** say prayers. **2** ask earnestly, entreat. **prayer** *n* **1** thanks or appeal addressed to one's God. **2** set form of words used in praying. **3** earnest request.

pre- *prefix* before, beforehand, e.g. *prenatal; prerecorded; preshrunk.*

preach ❶ *v* **1** give a talk on a religious theme as part of a church service. **2** speak in support of (an idea, principle, etc.). **preacher** *n.*

————————————————————— THESAURUS —————————

practice *n* **1** = **custom**, habit, method, mode, routine, rule, system, tradition, usage, way, wont **2** = **rehearsal**, drill, exercise, preparation, repetition, study, training **3** = **profession**, business, career, vocation, work, yakka (*Aust & NZ inf*)

practise *v* **1** = **rehearse**, drill, exercise, go over, go through, prepare, repeat, study, train **2** = **follow**, observe, perform **3** = **work at**, carry on, engage in, pursue

pragmatic *adj* = **practical**, businesslike, down-to-earth, hard-headed, realistic, sensible, utilitarian

praise *v* **1** = **approve**, acclaim, admire, applaud, cheer, compliment, congratulate, eulogize, extol, honour, laud **2** = **give thanks to**, adore, bless, exalt, glorify, worship ▷ *n* **3 a** = **approval**, acclaim, acclamation, approbation, commendation, compliment, congratulation, eulogy, plaudit, tribute **b** = **thanks**, adoration, glory, homage, worship

praiseworthy *adj* **1** = **creditable**, admirable, commendable, laudable, meritorious, worthy

prance *v* = **dance**, caper, cavort, frisk, gambol, parade, romp, show off (*inf*), skip, stalk, strut, swagger, swank (*inf*)

prank *n* = **trick**, escapade, jape, lark (*inf*), practical joke

prattle *v* **1** = **chatter**, babble, blather, blether, gabble, jabber, rabbit (on) (*Brit inf*), waffle (*inf, chiefly Brit*), witter (*inf*)

pray *v* **1** = **say one's prayers**, offer a prayer, recite the rosary **2** = **beg**, adjure, ask, beseech, entreat, implore, petition, plead, request, solicit

prayer *n* **1** = **orison**, devotion, invocation, supplication **2** = **litany** **3** = **plea**, appeal, entreaty, petition, request, supplication

preach *v* **1** = **deliver a sermon**, address, evangelize **2** = **lecture**, advocate, exhort, moralize, sermonize

preamble ❶ *n* introductory part to something said or written.

prearranged *adj* arranged beforehand.

prebendary *n, pl* **-daries** clergyman who is a member of the chapter of a cathedral.

precarious ❶ *adj* insecure, unsafe, likely to fall or collapse. **precariously** *adv*.

precaution ❶ *n* action taken in advance to prevent something bad happening. **precautionary** *adj*.

precede ❶ *v* go or be before. **precedence** [**press**-ee-denss] *n* formal order of rank or position. **take precedence over** be more important than. **precedent** *n* previous case or occurrence regarded as an example to be followed.

precentor *n* person who leads the singing in a church.

precept ❶ *n* rule of behaviour.

precinct ❶ *n* **1** area in a town closed to traffic. **2** enclosed area round a building, e.g. *cathedral precinct*. **3** *US* administrative

area of a city. ▷ *pl* **4** surrounding region.

precious ❶ *adj* **1** of great value and importance. **2** loved and treasured. **3** (of behaviour) affected, unnatural. **precious metal** gold, silver, or platinum. **precious stone** rare mineral, such as a ruby, valued as a gem.

precipice ❶ *n* very steep cliff or rockface. **precipitous** *adj* sheer.

precipitate ❶ *v* **1** cause to happen suddenly. **2** condense and fall as snow or rain. **3** *Chemistry* cause to be deposited in solid form from a solution. **4** throw headlong. ▷ *adj* **5** done rashly or hastily. ▷ *n* **6** *Chemistry* substance precipitated from a solution. **precipitately** *adv* **precipitation** *n* **1** precipitating. **2** rain, snow, etc.

précis ❶ [**pray**-see] *n, pl* **précis 1** short written summary of a longer piece. ▷ *v* **2** make a précis of.

precise ❶ *adj* **1** exact, accurate in every detail. **2** strict in observing rules or standards. **precisely** *adv* **precision** *n*.

preacher *n* **1** = **clergyman**, evangelist, minister, missionary, parson

preamble *n* = **introduction**, foreword, opening statement *or* remarks, preface, prelude

precarious *adj* = **dangerous**, dodgy (*Brit, Aust & NZ inf*), hazardous, insecure, perilous, risky, shaky, shonky (*Aust & NZ inf*), tricky, unreliable, unsafe, unsure

precaution *n* = **safeguard**, care, caution, forethought, protection, safety measure, wariness

precede *v* = **go before**, antedate, come first, head, introduce, lead, preface

precedence *n* = **priority**, antecedence, pre-eminence, primacy, rank, seniority, superiority, supremacy

precedent *n* = **instance**, antecedent, example, model, paradigm, pattern, prototype, standard

preceding *adj* = **previous**, above, aforementioned, aforesaid, earlier, foregoing, former, past, prior

precept *n* = **rule**, canon, command, commandment, decree, instruction, law, order, principle, regulation, statute

precinct *n* **1** = **area**, district, quarter, section, sector, zone **2** = **enclosure**,

confine, limit

precious *adj* **1** = **valuable**, costly, dear, expensive, fine, invaluable, priceless, prized **2** = **loved**, adored, beloved, cherished, darling, dear, prized, treasured **3** = **affected**, artificial, overnice, overrefined, twee (*Brit inf*)

precipice *n* = **cliff**, bluff, crag, height, rock face

precipitate *v* **1** = **quicken**, accelerate, advance, bring on, expedite, hasten, hurry, speed up, trigger **4** = **throw**, cast, fling, hurl, launch, let fly ▷ *adj* **5** = **hasty**, abrupt, breakneck, brief, headlong, heedless, impetuous, impulsive, precipitous, quick, rapid, rash, reckless, rushing, sudden, swift, unexpected, without warning

precipitous *adj* = **sheer**, abrupt, dizzy, high, perpendicular, steep

précis *n* **1** = **summary**, abridgment, outline, résumé, synopsis ▷ *v* **2** = **summarize**, abridge, outline, shorten, sum up

precise *adj* **1** = **exact**, absolute, accurate, correct, definite, explicit, express, particular, specific, strict **2** = **strict**, careful, exact, fastidious, finicky, formal, meticulous, particular, punctilious, rigid, scrupulous, stiff

p

preclude ❶ v make impossible to happen.

precocious ❶ adj having developed or matured early or too soon. **precocity** n.

precognition n alleged ability to foretell the future.

preconceived ❶ adj (of an idea) formed without real experience or reliable information. **preconception** n.

precondition n something that must happen or exist before something else can.

precursor ❶ n something that precedes and is a signal of something else, forerunner.

predate v **1** occur at an earlier date than. **2** write a date on (a document) that is earlier than the actual date.

predatory ❶ [pred-a-tree] adj habitually hunting and killing other animals for food. **predator** n predatory animal.

predecease v die before (someone else).

predecessor ❶ n **1** person who precedes another in an office or position. **2** ancestor.

predestination ❶ n belief that future events have already been decided by God or fate. **predestined** adj.

predetermined ❶ adj decided in advance.

predicament ❶ n embarrassing or difficult situation.

predicate n **1** Grammar part of a sentence in which something is said about the subject, e.g. went home in I went home. ▷ v **2** declare or assert. **predicated on** based on. **predicative** adj of or in the predicate of a sentence.

predict ❶ v tell about in advance, prophesy. **predictable** adj **predictive** adj (of a word processer or cell phone) able to complete words after only part of a word has been keyed. **prediction** n.

predilection ❶ n preference or liking.

predispose ❶ v **1** influence (someone) in favour of something. **2** make (someone) susceptible to something. **predisposition** n.

predominate ❶ v be the main or controlling element. **predominance** n **predominant** adj **predominantly** adv.

───────── THESAURUS ─────────

precisely adv **1** = **exactly**, absolutely, accurately, correctly, just so, plumb (inf), smack (inf), square, squarely, strictly

precision n **1** = **exactness**, accuracy, care, meticulousness, particularity, preciseness

preclude v = **prevent**, check, debar, exclude, forestall, inhibit, obviate, prohibit, rule out, stop

precocious adj = **advanced**, ahead, bright, developed, forward, quick, smart

preconceived adj = **presumed**, forejudged, prejudged, presupposed

preconception n = **preconceived idea** or **notion**, bias, notion, predisposition, prejudice, presupposition

precursor n **a** = **herald**, forerunner, harbinger, vanguard **b** = **forerunner**, antecedent, forebear, predecessor

predatory adj = **hunting**, carnivorous, predacious, raptorial

predecessor n **1** = **previous job holder**, antecedent, forerunner, precursor **2** = **ancestor**, antecedent, forebear, forefather

predestination n = **fate**, destiny, foreordainment, foreordination, predetermination

predestined adj = **fated**, doomed, meant, preordained

predetermined adj = **prearranged**, agreed, fixed, preplanned, set

predicament n = **fix** (inf), dilemma, hole (sl), jam (inf), mess, pinch, plight, quandary, scrape (inf), situation, spot (inf)

predict v = **foretell**, augur, divine, forecast, portend, prophesy

predictable adj = **likely**, anticipated, certain, expected, foreseeable, reliable, sure

prediction n = **prophecy**, augury, divination, forecast, prognosis, prognostication

predilection n = **liking**, bias, fondness, inclination, leaning, love, partiality, penchant, preference, propensity, taste, weakness

predispose v **1** = **incline**, affect, bias, dispose, influence, lead, prejudice, prompt

predominant adj = **main**, ascendant, chief, dominant, leading, paramount, prevailing, prevalent, prime, principal

pre-eminent ❶ *adj* excelling all others, outstanding. **pre-eminence** *n*.

pre-empt ❶ *v* prevent an action by doing something which makes it pointless or impossible. **pre-emption** *n* **pre-emptive** *adj*.

preen ❶ *v* (of a bird) clean or trim (feathers) with the beak. **preen oneself 1** smarten oneself. **2** show self-satisfaction.

prefab *n* prefabricated house.

prefabricated *adj* (of a building) manufactured in shaped sections for rapid assembly on site.

preface ❶ [**pref**-iss] *n* **1** introduction to a book. ▷ *v* **2** serve as an introduction to (a book, speech, etc.). **prefatory** *adj*.

prefect *n* **1** senior pupil in a school, with limited power over others. **2** senior administrative officer in some countries. **prefecture** *n* office or area of authority of a prefect.

prefer ❶ *v* **-ferring, -ferred 1** like better. **2** *Law* bring (charges) before a court. **preferable** *adj* more desirable. **preferably** *adv* **preference** *n* **preferential** *adj* showing preference. **preferment** *n* promotion or advancement.

prefigure *v* represent or suggest in advance.

prefix *n* **1** letter or group of letters put at the beginning of a word to make a new word, such as *un-* in *unhappy*. ▷ *v* **2** put as an introduction or prefix (to).

pregnant ❶ *adj* **1** carrying a fetus in the womb. **2** full of meaning or significance, e.g. *a pregnant pause*. **pregnancy** *n, pl* **-cies**.

prehensile *adj* capable of grasping.

prehistoric ❶ *adj* of the period before written history begins. **prehistory** *n*.

prejudge ❶ *v* judge beforehand without sufficient evidence.

prejudice ❶ *n* **1** unreasonable or unfair dislike or preference. ▷ *v* **2** cause (someone) to have a prejudice. **3** harm, cause disadvantage to. **prejudicial** *adj* harmful, disadvantageous.

● **SPELLING TIP**
● There are examples in the Bank
● of English of **prejudice** being
● misspelt as *predjudice*, with an extra
● *d*. Although *d* often combines with
● *g* in English, it is not necessary
● before *j*.

prelate [**prel**-it] *n* bishop or other churchman of high rank.

THESAURUS

predominate *v* = **prevail**, be most noticeable, carry weight, hold sway, outweigh, overrule, overshadow

pre-eminent *adj* = **outstanding**, chief, distinguished, excellent, foremost, incomparable, matchless, predominant, renowned, superior, supreme

pre-empt *v* = **anticipate**, appropriate, assume, usurp

preen *v* = **clean**, plume **preen oneself 1** = **smarten**, dress up, spruce up, titivate **2** = **pride oneself**, congratulate oneself

preface *n* **1** = **introduction**, foreword, preamble, preliminary, prelude, prologue ▷ *v* **2** = **introduce**, begin, open, prefix

prefer *v* **1** = **like better**, be partial to, choose, desire, fancy, favour, go for, incline towards, opt for, pick

preferable *adj* = **better**, best, chosen, favoured, more desirable, superior

preferably *adv* **1** = **rather**, by choice, first, in *or* for preference, sooner

preference *n* **1** = **first choice**, choice, desire, favourite, option, partiality, pick, predilection, selection

preferential *adj* = **privileged**, advantageous, better, favoured, special

preferment *n* = **promotion**, advancement, elevation, exaltation, rise, upgrading

pregnant *adj* **1** = **expectant**, big *or* heavy with child, expecting (*inf*), in the club (*Brit sl*), with child **2** = **meaningful**, charged, eloquent, expressive, loaded, pointed, significant, telling, weighty

prehistoric *adj* = **earliest**, early, primeval, primitive, primordial

prejudge *v* = **jump to conclusions**, anticipate, presume, presuppose

prejudice *n* **1 a** = **discrimination**, bigotry, chauvinism, injustice, intolerance, narrow-mindedness, unfairness **b** = **bias**, partiality, preconceived notion, preconception, prejudgment ▷ *v* **2** = **bias**, colour, distort, influence, poison, predispose, slant **3** = **harm**, damage, hinder, hurt, impair, injure, mar, spoil, undermine

prejudiced 1 *adj* = **biased**, bigoted, influenced, intolerant, narrow-minded, one-sided, opinionated, unfair

P

preliminary ❶ *adj* **1** happening before and in preparation, introductory. ▷ *n, pl* **-naries 2** preliminary remark, contest, etc.

prelude ❶ [**prel**-yewd] *n* **1** introductory movement in music. **2** event preceding and introducing something else.

premarital *adj* occurring before marriage.

premature ❶ *adj* **1** happening or done before the normal or expected time. **2** (of a baby) born before the end of the normal period of pregnancy. **prematurely** *adv*.

premedication *n* drugs given to prepare a patient for a general anaesthetic.

premeditated ❶ *adj* planned in advance. **premeditation** *n*.

premenstrual *adj* occurring or experienced before a menstrual period, e.g. *premenstrual tension*.

premier ❶ *n* **1** prime minister. ▷ *adj* **2** chief, leading. **premiership** *n*.

première *n* first performance of a play, film, etc.

premise, premiss ❶ *n* statement assumed to be true and used as the basis of reasoning.

premises ❶ *pl n* house or other building and its land.

premium ❶ *n* **1** additional sum of money, as on a wage or charge. **2** (regular) sum paid for insurance. **at a premium** in great demand because scarce. **premium bonds** savings certificates issued by the government, on which no interest is paid but cash prizes can be won.

premonition ❶ *n* feeling that something unpleasant is going to happen; foreboding. **premonitory** *adj*.

prenatal *adj* before birth, during pregnancy.

preoccupy ❶ *v* **-pying, -pied** fill the thoughts or attention of (someone) to the exclusion of other things. **preoccupation** *n*.

preordained *adj* decreed or determined in advance.

prep. 1 preparatory. **2** preposition.

prepacked *adj* sold already wrapped.

──────────────────── THESAURUS ────────

prejudicial *adj* = **harmful**, damaging, deleterious, detrimental, disadvantageous, hurtful, injurious, unfavourable

preliminary *adj* **1** = **first**, initial, introductory, opening, pilot, prefatory, preparatory, prior, test, trial ▷ *n* **2** = **introduction**, beginning, opening, overture, preamble, preface, prelude, start

prelude *n* **1** = **overture 2** = **introduction**, beginning, foreword, preamble, preface, prologue, start

premature *adj* **1** **a** = **hasty**, ill-timed, overhasty, previous (*inf*), rash, too soon, untimely **b** = **early**

premeditated *adj* = **planned**, calculated, conscious, considered, deliberate, intentional, wilful

premier *n* **1** = **head of government**, chancellor, chief minister, P.M., prime minister ▷ *adj* **2** = **chief**, first, foremost, head, highest, leading, main, primary, prime, principal

première *n* = **first night**, debut, opening

premise, premiss *n* = **assumption**, argument, assertion, hypothesis,

postulation, presupposition, proposition, supposition

premises *pl n* = **building**, establishment, place, property, site

premium *n* **1** = **bonus**, bounty, fee, perk (*Brit inf*), perquisite, prize, reward **at a premium** = **in great demand**, hard to come by, in short supply, rare, scarce

premonition *n* = **feeling**, foreboding, hunch, idea, intuition, presentiment, suspicion

preoccupation *n* **a** = **obsession**, bee in one's bonnet, fixation **b** = **absorption**, absent-mindedness, abstraction, daydreaming, immersion, reverie, woolgathering

preoccupied *adj* = **absorbed**, absent-minded, distracted, engrossed, immersed, lost in, oblivious, rapt, wrapped up

preparation *n* **1** = **groundwork**, getting ready, preparing **2** = **arrangement**, measure, plan, provision **3** = **mixture**, compound, concoction, medicine

preparatory *adj* = **introductory**, opening, prefatory, preliminary, primary

prepaid *adj* paid for in advance.
prepare ❶ *v* make or get ready.
prepared *adj* 1 willing. 2 ready.
preparation *n* 1 preparing.
2 something done in readiness for
something else. 3 mixture prepared
for use as a cosmetic, medicine, etc.
preparatory [prip-**par**-a-tree] *adj*
preparing for. **preparatory school**
private school for children going on to
public school.
preponderance ❶ *n* greater force,
amount, or influence. **preponderant** *adj*.
preposition *n* word used before a noun
or pronoun to show its relationship
with other words, such as *by* in *go by
bus*. **prepositional** *adj*.

- USAGE NOTE
- It used to be considered incorrect
- to end a sentence with a
- preposition, as in *New York is a*
- *place I'd love to go to*. However, this
- practice is now widely accepted,
- and in many cases, where it gives
- a more natural-sounding sentence,
- it may even be the preferred
- form: *New York is a place to which
- I'd love to go* would sound very
- awkward.

prepossessing ❶ *adj* making a
favourable impression, attractive.
preposterous ❶ *adj* utterly absurd.
prep school *n* short for PREPARATORY
SCHOOL.
prepuce [**pree**-pyewss] *n* retractable

fold of skin covering the tip of the
penis, foreskin.
prerecorded *adj* recorded in advance
to be played or broadcast later.
prerequisite ❶ *n, adj* (something)
required before something else is
possible.
prerogative ❶ *n* special power or
privilege.

- ● SPELLING TIP
- ● The way **prerogative** is often
- ● pronounced is presumably the reaso
- ● n why *perogative* is a common way of
- ● misspelling it.

pres. 1 present (time). 2 presidential.
Pres. President.
presage [**press**-ij] *v* be a sign or
warning of.
Presbyterian *n, adj* (member) of a
Protestant church governed by lay
elders. **Presbyterianism** *n*.
presbytery *n, pl* **-teries** 1 *Presbyterian
Church* local church court. 2 *RC
Church* priest's house.
prescience ❶ [**press**-ee-enss] *n*
knowledge of events before they
happen. **prescient** *adj*.
prescribe ❶ *v* 1 recommend the use of
(a medicine). 2 lay down as a rule.
prescription *n* written instructions
from a doctor for the making up and
use of a medicine. **prescriptive** *adj*
laying down rules.
presence ❶ *n* 1 fact of being in a
specified place. 2 impressive dignified

p

prepare *v* = **make** *or* **get ready**, adapt,
adjust, arrange, practise, prime, train,
warm up
prepared *adj* 1 = **willing**, disposed,
inclined 2 = **ready**, arranged, in order,
in readiness, primed, set
preponderance *n* = **predominance**,
dominance, domination,
extensiveness, greater numbers,
greater part, lion's share, mass,
prevalence, supremacy
prepossessing *adj* = **attractive**,
appealing, charming, engaging,
fetching, good-looking, handsome,
likable *or* likeable, pleasing
preposterous *adj* = **ridiculous**,
absurd, crazy, incredible, insane,
laughable, ludicrous, nonsensical, out
of the question, outrageous,
unthinkable
prerequisite *n* = **requirement**,
condition, essential, must, necessity,

precondition, qualification, requisite,
sine qua non ▷ *adj* = **required**,
essential, indispensable, mandatory,
necessary, obligatory, requisite, vital
prerogative *n* = **right**, advantage,
due, exemption, immunity, liberty,
privilege
prescribe *v* 2 = **order**, decree, dictate,
direct, lay down, ordain, recommend,
rule, set, specify, stipulate
prescription *n* = **instruction**,
direction, formula, recipe
presence *n* 1 = **being**, attendance,
existence, inhabitance, occupancy,
residence 2 = **personality**, air,
appearance, aspect, aura, bearing,
carriage, demeanour, poise, self-
assurance
presence of mind *n* = **level-
headedness**, calmness, composure,
cool (*sl*), coolness, self-possession,
wits

appearance. **presence of mind** ability
to act sensibly in a crisis.
present¹ ❶ *adj* **1** being in a specified
place. **2** existing or happening now.
3 *Grammar* (of a verb tense) indicating
that the action specified is taking
place now. ▷ *n* **4** present time or
tense. **presence** *n* **1** fact of being in a
specified place. **2** impressive dignified
appearance. **presently** *adv* **1** soon.
2 *US & Scot* now.
present² ❶ *n* **1** something given to
bring pleasure to another person. ▷ *v*
2 introduce formally or publicly.
3 introduce and compère (a TV or radio
show). **4** cause, e.g. *present a difficulty*.
5 give, award. **presentation** *n*
presentable *adj* attractive, neat, fit
for people to see. **presenter** *n* person
introducing a TV or radio show.
presentiment [priz-**zen**-tim-ent] *n*
sense of something unpleasant about
to happen.
preserve ❶ *v* **1** keep from being
damaged, changed, or ended. **2** treat
(food) to prevent it decaying. ▷ *n*
3 area of interest restricted to a
particular person or group. **4** fruit
preserved by cooking in sugar. **5** area
where game is kept for private
hunting or fishing. **preservation** *n*
preservative *n* chemical that
prevents decay.

preshrunk *adj* (of fabric or a garment)
having been shrunk during manufacture
so that further shrinkage will not
occur when washed.
preside ❶ *v* be in charge, esp. of a
meeting.
president *n* **1** head of state in
countries without a king or queen.
2 head of a society, institution, etc.
presidential *adj* of or pertaining to a
president or the office of a president.
presidency *n, pl* **-cies** office, dignity,
or term of a president, esp. the
president of the US.
press¹ ❶ *v* **1** apply force or weight to.
2 squeeze. **3** smooth by applying
pressure or heat. **4** urge insistently.
5 crowd, push. ▷ *n* **6** printing
machine. **pressed for** short of, e.g.
pressed for time. **the press 1** news
media collectively, esp. newspapers.
2 reporters, journalists. **pressing** *adj*
urgent. **press box** room at a sports
ground reserved for reporters. **press
conference** interview for reporters
given by a celebrity. **press release**
official announcement or account of a
news item supplied to the press. **press
stud** fastener in which one part with a
projecting knob snaps into a hole on
another part.
press² *v* **press into service** force to be
involved or used. **press gang**

present¹ *adj* **1** = **here**, at hand, near,
nearby, ready, there **2** = **current**,
contemporary, existent, existing,
immediate, present-day ▷ *n* **4** = **now**,
here and now, the present moment,
the time being, today
present² *n* **1** = **gift**, boon, donation,
endowment, grant, gratuity, hand-
out, offering, prezzie (*inf*) ▷ *v*
2 = **introduce**, acquaint with, make
known **3** = **put on**, display, exhibit,
give, show, stage **5** = **give**, award,
bestow, confer, grant, hand out, hand
over
presentable *adj* = **decent**, acceptable,
becoming, fit to be seen, O.K. *or* okay
(*inf*), passable, respectable,
satisfactory, suitable
presentation *n* **1** = **giving**, award,
bestowal, conferral, donation,
offering **3** = **performance**,
demonstration, display, exhibition,
production, show
presently *adv* **1** = **soon**, anon (*arch*),

before long, by and by, shortly
preservation *n* **1** = **protection**,
conservation, maintenance,
safeguarding, safekeeping, safety,
salvation, support
preserve *v* **1 a** = **protect**, care for,
conserve, defend, keep, safeguard,
save, shelter, shield **b** = **maintain**,
continue, keep, keep up, perpetuate,
sustain, uphold ▷ *n* **3** = **area**, domain,
field, realm, sphere
preside *v* = **run**, administer, chair,
conduct, control, direct, govern, head,
lead, manage, officiate
press¹ *v* **1** = **compress**, crush, depress,
force down, jam, mash, push, squeeze
2 = **hug**, clasp, crush, embrace, fold in
one's arms, hold close, squeeze
3 = **smooth**, flatten, iron **4** = **urge**,
beg, entreat, exhort, implore,
petition, plead, pressurize **5** = **crowd**,
flock, gather, herd, push, seethe,
surge, swarm, throng **the press**
1 = **newspapers**, Fleet Street, fourth

History group of men used to capture men and boys and force them to join the navy.

press-up *n* exercise in which the body is raised from and lowered to the floor by straightening and bending the arms.

pressure ❶ *n* 1 force produced by pressing. 2 urgent claims or demands, e.g. *working under pressure*. 3 *Physics* force applied to a surface per unit of area. ▷ *v* 4 persuade forcefully. **bring pressure to bear on** use influence or authority to persuade. **pressurize** *v* **pressure cooker** airtight pot which cooks food quickly by steam under pressure. **pressure group** group that tries to influence policies, public opinion, etc.

prestidigitation *n* skilful quickness with the hands, conjuring.

prestige ❶ *n* high status or respect resulting from success or achievements. **prestigious** *adj*.

presto *adv Music* very quickly.

prestressed *adj* (of concrete) containing stretched steel wires to strengthen it.

presume ❶ *v* 1 suppose to be the case. 2 dare (to). **presumably** *adv* one supposes (that). **presumption** *n* 1 basis on which an assumption is made. 2 bold insolent behaviour. 3 strong probability. **presumptuous** *adj* doing things one has no right or authority to do. **presumptive** *adj* assumed to be true or valid until the contrary is proved.

presuppose ❶ *v* need as a previous condition in order to be true. **presupposition** *n*.

pretend ❶ *v* claim or give the appearance of (something untrue) to deceive or in play. **pretender** *n* person who makes a false or disputed claim to a position of power. **pretence** *n* behaviour intended to deceive, pretending. **pretentious** *adj* making (unjustified) claims to special merit or importance. **pretension** *n*.

preternatural *adj* beyond what is natural, supernatural.

---

estate, news media, the papers 2 = **journalists**, columnists, correspondents, reporters

pressing *adj* = **urgent**, crucial, high-priority, imperative, important, importunate, serious, vital

pressure *n* 1 = **force**, compressing, compression, crushing, squeezing, weight 2 **a** = **power**, coercion, compulsion, constraint, force, influence, mana (*NZ*), sway **b** = **stress**, burden, demands, hassle (*inf*), heat, load, strain, urgency

prestige *n* = **status**, credit, distinction, eminence, fame, honour, importance, kudos, renown, reputation, standing

prestigious *adj* = **celebrated**, eminent, esteemed, great, illustrious, important, notable, prominent, renowned, respected

presumably *adv* = **it would seem**, apparently, in all likelihood, in all probability, on the face of it, probably, seemingly

presume *v* 1 = **believe**, assume, conjecture, guess (*inf, chiefly US & Canad*), infer, postulate, suppose, surmise, take for granted, think 2 = **dare**, go so far, make so bold, take the liberty, venture

presumption *n* 1 = **basis** 2 = **cheek** (*inf*), audacity, boldness, effrontery, gall (*inf*), impudence, insolence, nerve (*inf*) 3 = **probability**, chance, likelihood

presumptuous *adj* = **pushy** (*inf*), audacious, bold, forward, insolent, overconfident, too big for one's boots, uppish (*Brit inf*)

presuppose *v* = **presume**, assume, imply, posit, postulate, take as read, take for granted

presupposition *n* = **assumption**, belief, preconception, premise, presumption, supposition

pretence *n* **a** = **deception**, acting, charade, deceit, falsehood, feigning, sham, simulation, trickery **b** = **show**, affectation, artifice, display, façade, veneer

pretend *v* **a** = **feign**, affect, allege, assume, fake, falsify, impersonate, profess, sham, simulate **b** = **make believe**, act, imagine, make up, suppose

pretension *n* **a** = **claim**, aspiration, assumption, demand, pretence, profession **b** = **affectation**, airs, conceit, ostentation, pretentiousness, self-importance, show, snobbery

pretentious *adj* = **affected**, conceited, grandiloquent, grandiose, high-flown,

p

pretext ❶ n false reason given to hide the real one.

pretty ❶ adj **-tier**, **-tiest** 1 pleasing to look at. ▷ adv 2 fairly, moderately, e.g. *I'm pretty certain*. **prettily** adv **prettiness** n **sitting pretty** in a favourable state.

pretzel n brittle salted biscuit.

prevail ❶ v 1 gain mastery. 2 be generally established. **prevailing** adj 1 widespread. 2 predominant. **prevalence** n **prevalent** adj widespread, common.

prevaricate ❶ v avoid giving a direct or truthful answer. **prevarication** n.

prevent ❶ v keep from happening or doing. **preventable** adj **prevention** n **preventive** adj, n.

preview ❶ n 1 advance showing of a film or exhibition before it is shown to the public. ▷ v 2 view in advance.

previous ❶ adj coming or happening before. **previously** adv.

prey ❶ n 1 animal hunted and killed for food by another animal. 2 victim. **bird of prey** bird that kills and eats other birds or animals. **prey on** v 1 hunt and kill for food. 2 worry, obsess.

price ❶ n 1 amount of money for which a thing is bought or sold. 2 unpleasant thing that must be endured to get something desirable. ▷ v 3 fix or ask the price of. **priceless** adj 1 very valuable. 2 *informal* very funny. **pricey** adj **pricier**, **priciest** *informal* expensive.

prick ❶ v 1 pierce lightly with a sharp point. 2 cause to feel mental pain. 3 (of an animal) make (the ears) stand erect. ▷ n 4 sudden sharp pain caused by pricking. 5 mark made by pricking. 6 remorse. 7 *taboo slang* penis. **prick up one's ears** listen intently.

— THESAURUS —

inflated, mannered, ostentatious, pompous, puffed up, showy, snobbish

pretext n = **guise**, cloak, cover, excuse, ploy, pretence, ruse, show

pretty adj 1 = **attractive**, beautiful, bonny, charming, comely, fair, good-looking, lekker (*S Afr sl*), lovely ▷ adv 2 = **fairly**, kind of (*inf*), moderately, quite, rather, reasonably, somewhat

prevail v 1 = **win**, be victorious, overcome, overrule, succeed, triumph 2 = **be widespread**, abound, be current, be prevalent, exist generally, predominate

prevailing adj 1 = **widespread**, common, current, customary, established, fashionable, general, in vogue, ordinary, popular, prevalent, usual 2 = **predominating**, dominant, main, principal, ruling

prevalent adj = **common**, current, customary, established, frequent, general, popular, universal, usual, widespread

prevaricate v = **evade**, beat about the bush, cavil, deceive, dodge, equivocate, flannel (*Brit inf*), hedge

prevent v = **stop**, avert, avoid, foil, forestall, frustrate, hamper, hinder, impede, inhibit, obstruct, obviate, preclude, thwart

prevention n = **elimination**, avoidance, deterrence, precaution, safeguard, thwarting

preventive adj **a** = **protective**,

counteractive, deterrent, precautionary **b** = **hindering**, hampering, impeding, obstructive ▷ n **a** = **protection**, deterrent, prevention, remedy, safeguard, shield **b** = **hindrance**, block, impediment, obstacle, obstruction

preview n 1 = **sample**, advance showing, foretaste, sneak preview, taster, trailer

previous adj = **earlier**, erstwhile, foregoing, former, past, preceding, prior

previously adv = **before**, beforehand, earlier, formerly, hitherto, in the past, once

prey n 1 = **quarry**, game, kill 2 = **victim**, dupe, fall guy (*inf*), mug (*Brit sl*), target

price n 1 = **cost**, amount, charge, damage (*inf*), estimate, expense, fee, figure, rate, value, worth 2 = **consequences**, cost, penalty, toll ▷ v 3 = **evaluate**, assess, cost, estimate, rate, value

priceless adj 1 = **valuable**, costly, dear, expensive, invaluable, precious 2 *Inf* = **hilarious**, amusing, comic, droll, funny, rib-tickling, side-splitting

pricey adj *Inf* 1 = **expensive**, costly, dear, high-priced, steep (*inf*)

prick v 1 = **pierce**, jab, lance, perforate, punch, puncture, stab ▷ n 5 = **puncture**, hole, perforation, pinhole, wound

prickle ● *n* **1** thorn or spike on a plant. ▷ *v* **2** have a tingling or pricking sensation. **prickly** *adj* **prickly heat** itchy rash occurring in hot moist weather.

pride ● *n* **1** feeling of pleasure and satisfaction when one has done well. **2** too high an opinion of oneself. **3** sense of dignity and self-respect. **4** something that causes one to feel pride. **5** group of lions. **pride of place** most important position. **pride oneself on** feel pride about.

priest ● *n* **1** (in the Christian church) a person who can administer the sacraments and preach. **2** (in some other religions) an official who performs religious ceremonies. **priestess** *n fem* **priesthood** *n* **priestly** *adj*.

prig ● *n* self-righteous person who acts as if superior to others. **priggish** *adj* **priggishness** *n*.

prim ● *adj* **primmer**, **primmest** formal, proper, and rather prudish. **primly** *adv*.

prima ballerina *n* leading female ballet dancer.

primacy *n, pl* **-cies 1** state of being first in rank, grade, etc. **2** office of an archbishop.

prima donna *n* **1** leading female opera singer. **2** *informal* temperamental person.

primaeval *adj* same as PRIMEVAL.

prima facie [**prime**-a **fay**-shee] *adv* Latin as it seems at first.

primal *adj* of basic causes or origins.

primary ● *adj* **1** chief, most important. **2** being the first stage, elementary. **primarily** *adv* **primary colours** (in physics) red, green, and blue or (in art) red, yellow, and blue, from which all other colours can be produced by mixing. **primary school** school for children from five to eleven years.

primate¹ *n* member of an order of mammals including monkeys and humans.

primate² *n* archbishop.

prime ● *adj* **1** main, most important. **2** of the highest quality. ▷ *n* **3** time when someone is at his or her best or most vigorous. ▷ *v* **4** give (someone) information in advance to prepare them for something. **5** prepare (a surface) for painting. **6** prepare (a gun, pump, etc.) for use. **primer** *n* special paint applied to bare wood etc. before the main paint. **Prime Minister** leader of a government. **prime number** number that can be divided exactly only by itself and one. **prime time** peak viewing time on television.

primer *n* special paint applied to bare wood etc. before the main paint.

THESAURUS

prickle *n* **1** = **spike**, barb, needle, point, spine, spur, thorn ▷ *v* **2** = **tingle**, itch, smart, sting

prickly *adj* **1** = **spiny**, barbed, bristly, thorny **2** = **itchy**, crawling, scratchy, sharp, smarting, stinging, tingling

pride *n* **1** = **satisfaction**, delight, gratification, joy, pleasure **2** = **conceit**, arrogance, egotism, hubris, self-importance, vanity **3** = **self-respect**, dignity, honour, self-esteem, self-worth **4** = **gem**, jewel, pride and joy, treasure

priest *n* **1** = **clergyman**, cleric, curate, divine, ecclesiastic, father, minister, pastor, vicar

prig *n* = **goody-goody** (*inf*), prude, puritan, stuffed shirt (*inf*)

priggish *adj* = **self-righteous**, goody-goody (*inf*), holier-than-thou, prim, prudish, puritanical

prim *adj* = **prudish**, demure, fastidious, fussy, priggish, prissy (*inf*), proper, puritanical, strait-laced

primarily *adv* **1** = **chiefly**, above all, essentially, fundamentally, generally, largely, mainly, mostly, principally **2** = **at first**, at *or* from the start, first and foremost, initially, in the beginning, in the first place, originally

primary *adj* **1** = **chief**, cardinal, first, greatest, highest, main, paramount, prime, principal **2** = **elementary**, introductory, rudimentary, simple

prime *adj* **1** = **main**, chief, leading, predominant, pre-eminent, primary, principal **2** = **best**, choice, excellent, first-class, first-rate, highest, quality, select, top ▷ *n* **3** = **peak**, bloom, flower, height, heyday, zenith ▷ *v* **4** = **inform**, brief, clue in (*inf*), coach, fill in (*inf*), get ready, make ready, notify, prepare, tell, train

P

primeval ❶ [prime-**ee**-val] *adj* of the earliest age of the world.

primitive ❶ *adj* **1** of an early simple stage of development. **2** basic, crude, e.g. *a primitive hut*.

primogeniture *n* system under which the eldest son inherits all his parents' property.

primordial *adj* existing at or from the beginning.

primrose *n* pale yellow spring flower.

primula *n* type of primrose with brightly coloured flowers.

Primus *n* ® portable cooking stove used esp. by campers.

prince ❶ *n* **1** male member of a royal family, esp. the son of the king or queen. **2** male ruler of a small country. **princely** *adj* **1** of or like a prince. **2** generous, lavish, or magnificent. **prince consort** husband of a reigning queen. **Prince of Wales** eldest son of the British sovereign. **princess** *n* female member of a royal family, esp. the daughter of the king or queen. **Princess Royal** title sometimes given to the eldest daughter of the British sovereign.

principal ❶ *adj* **1** main, most important. ▷ *n* **2** head of a school or college. **3** person taking a leading part in something. **4** sum of money lent on which interest is paid. **principally** *adv* **principal boy** leading male role in pantomime, played by a woman.

- USAGE NOTE
- Distinguish the spellings of
- *principal* and *principle*. These
- are different words but often
- confused.

principality *n, pl* **-ties** territory ruled by a prince.

principle ❶ *n* **1** moral rule guiding behaviour. **2** general or basic truth, e.g. *the principle of equality*. **3** scientific law concerning the working of something. **in principle** in theory but not always in practice. **on principle** because of one's beliefs.

- USAGE NOTE
- Distinguish the spellings of
- *principle* and *principal*. These
- are different words but often
- confused.

print ❶ *v* **1** reproduce (a newspaper, book, etc.) in large quantities by mechanical or electronic means. **2** reproduce (text or pictures) by pressing ink onto paper etc. **3** write in letters that are not joined up. **4** stamp (fabric) with a design. **5** *Photography* produce (pictures) from negatives. ▷ *n* **6** printed words etc. **7** printed copy of a painting. **8** printed lettering. **9** photograph. **10** printed fabric. **11** mark left on a surface by something that has pressed against it. **out of print** no longer available from a publisher. **printer** *n* **1** person or company engaged in printing. **2** machine that prints. **3** machine connected to a computer that prints out results on paper. **printing** *n* **printed circuit** electronic circuit with wiring printed on an insulating base. **print-out** *n* printed information from a computer.

———— THESAURUS ————

primeval *adj* = **earliest**, ancient, early, first, old, prehistoric, primal, primitive, primordial

primitive *adj* **1** = **early**, elementary, first, original, primary, primeval, primordial **2** = **crude**, rough, rudimentary, simple, unrefined

prince *n* **2** = **ruler**, lord, monarch, sovereign

princely *adj* **1** = **regal**, imperial, majestic, noble, royal, sovereign **2** = **generous**, bounteous, gracious, lavish, liberal, munificent, open-handed, rich

principal *adj* **1** = **main**, cardinal, chief, essential, first, foremost, key, leading, paramount, pre-eminent, primary, prime ▷ *n* **2** = **headmaster** *or*

headmistress, dean, head (*inf*), head teacher, master *or* mistress, rector **3** = **star**, lead, leader **4** = **capital**, assets, money

principle *n* **1** = **morals**, conscience, integrity, probity, scruples, sense of honour **2** = **rule**, canon, criterion, doctrine, dogma, fundamental, law, maxim, precept, standard, truth **in principle** = **in theory**, ideally, theoretically

print *v* **1** = **publish 2** = **imprint**, impress, issue, mark, stamp ▷ *n* **6** = **publication**, book, magazine, newspaper, newsprint, periodical, printed matter **7** = **reproduction**, copy **9** = **photograph**, photo (*inf*), picture

prior¹ ❶ *adj* earlier. **prior to** before.

prior² ❷ *n* head monk in a priory.
prioress *n* deputy head nun in a convent. **priory** *n, pl* **-ries** place where certain orders of monks or nuns live.

priority ❶ *n, pl* **-ties 1** most important thing that must be dealt with first. **2** right to be or go before others.

prise *v* force open by levering.

prism *n* transparent block usu. with triangular ends and rectangular sides, used to disperse light into a spectrum or refract it in optical instruments. **prismatic** *adj* **1** of or shaped like a prism. **2** (of colour) as if produced by refraction through a prism, rainbow-like.

prison ❶ *n* building where criminals and accused people are held. **prisoner** *n* person held captive. **prisoner of war** serviceman captured by an enemy in wartime.

prissy *adj* **-sier, -siest** prim, correct, and easily shocked. **prissily** *adv*.

pristine ❶ *adj* clean, new, and unused.

private ❶ *adj* **1** for the use of one person or group only. **2** secret. **3** personal, unconnected with one's work. **4** owned or paid for by individuals rather than by the government. **5** quiet, not likely to be disturbed. ▷ *n* **6** soldier of the lowest rank. **privately** *adv* **privacy** *n* **private company** limited company that does not issue shares for public subscription. **private detective** person hired by a client to do detective work. **private member's bill** law proposed by a Member of Parliament who is not a government minister. **private parts** *euphemistic* genitals. **private school** school controlled by a private body, accepting mostly fee-paying pupils. **private sector** part of a country's economy not controlled or financially supported by the government.

privateer *n* **1** *History* privately owned armed vessel authorized by the government to take part in a war. **2** captain of such a ship.

privation *n* loss or lack of the necessities of life.

privatize *v* sell (a publicly owned company) to individuals or a private company. **privatization** *n*.

privet *n* bushy evergreen shrub used for hedges.

privilege ❶ *n* **1** advantage or favour that only some people have. **2** rare opportunity to do something which gives great satisfaction. **privileged** *adj* enjoying a special right or immunity.

● **SPELLING TIP**
● Although the Bank of English
● shows that people find it difficult to
● decide whether to use *is* or *es* when
● spelling **privilege**, the commonest
● mistake is to insert an extra *d* to
● make *priviledge*. The adjective,
● **privileged**, should not have a *d* in
● the middle either.

privy ❶ *adj* **1** sharing knowledge of something secret. ▷ *n, pl* **privies 2** *obs* toilet, esp. an outside one. **Privy Council** private council of the British monarch.

─────── **THESAURUS** ───────

prior¹ *adj* = **earlier**, foregoing, former, preceding, pre-existing, previous
prior to = **before**, earlier than, preceding, previous to

priority *n* **2** = **precedence**, pre-eminence, preference, rank, right of way, seniority

priory *n* = **monastery**, abbey, convent, nunnery, religious house

prison *n* = **jail**, clink (*sl*), confinement, cooler (*sl*), dungeon, jug (*sl*), lockup, nick (*Brit sl*), penitentiary (*US*), slammer (*sl*)

prisoner *n* = **captive**, con (*sl*), convict, detainee, hostage, internee, jailbird, lag (*sl*)

pristine *adj* = **new**, immaculate, pure, uncorrupted, undefiled, unspoiled, unsullied, untouched, virginal

privacy *n* **5** = **seclusion**, isolation, retirement, retreat, solitude

private *adj* **1** = **exclusive**, individual, intimate, own, personal, reserved, special **2** = **secret**, clandestine, confidential, covert, hush-hush (*inf*), off the record, unofficial **5** = **separate**, isolated, secluded, secret, sequestered, solitary, withdrawn

privilege *n* **1** = **right**, advantage, claim, concession, due, entitlement, freedom, liberty, prerogative

privileged *adj* = **special**, advantaged, elite, entitled, favoured, honoured

privy *adj* **1** = **secret**, confidential, private ▷ *n* **2** *Obs* = **lavatory**, latrine, outside toilet

p

prize¹ ❶ *n* **1** reward given for success in a competition etc. ▷ *adj* **2** winning or likely to win a prize. **prizefighter** *n* boxer who fights for money. **prizefight** *n*.

prize² ❶ *v* value highly.

prize³ *v* same as PRISE.

pro¹ *adv, prep* in favour of. **pros and cons** arguments for and against.

pro² *n, pl* **pros** *informal* **1** professional. **2** prostitute.

pro- *prefix* **1** in favour of, e.g. *pro-Russian*. **2** instead of, e.g. *pronoun*.

proactive *adj* tending to initiate change rather than reacting to events.

probable ❶ *adj* likely to happen or be true. **probably** *adv* **probability** *n, pl* **-ties**.

probate *n* **1** process of proving the validity of a will. **2** certificate stating that a will is genuine.

probation ❶ *n* **1** system of dealing with law-breakers, esp. juvenile ones, by placing them under supervision. **2** period when someone is assessed for suitability for a job etc. **probationer** *n* person on probation. **probationary** *adj* **probation officer** person who supervises offenders placed on probation.

probe ❶ *v* **1** search into or examine closely. ▷ *n* **2** surgical instrument used to examine a wound, cavity, etc.

3 thorough inquiry.

probiotic *n* **1** bacterium that protects the body from harmful bacteria. ▷ *adj* **2** relating to probiotics, e.g. *probiotic yogurts*.

probity *n* honesty, integrity.

problem ❶ *n* **1** something difficult to deal with or solve. **2** question or puzzle set for solution. **problematic**, **problematical** *adj*.

proboscis [pro-**boss**-iss] *n* **1** long trunk or snout. **2** elongated mouth of some insects.

procedure ❶ *n* way of doing something, esp. the correct or usual one. **procedural** *adj*.

proceed ❶ *v* **1** start or continue doing. **2** *formal* walk, go. **3** start a legal action. **4** arise from. **proceeds** *pl n* money obtained from an event or activity. **proceedings** *pl n* **1** organized or related series of events. **2** minutes of a meeting. **3** legal action. **procedure** *n* way of doing something, esp. the correct or usual one.

process ❶ *n* **1** series of actions or changes. **2** method of doing or producing something. ▷ *v* **3** handle or prepare by a special method of manufacture. **processed** *adj* (of food) treated to prevent it decaying. **processor** *n* *Computers* same as CENTRAL PROCESSING UNIT.

────────────────────────── THESAURUS ──────────────────────────

prize¹ *n* **1** = **reward**, accolade, award, haul, honour, jackpot, purse, stakes, trophy, winnings ▷ *adj* **2** = **champion**, award-winning, best, first-rate, outstanding, top, winning

prize² *v* = **value**, cherish, esteem, hold dear, treasure

probability *n* = **likelihood**, chance(s), expectation, liability, likeliness, odds, prospect

probable *adj* = **likely**, apparent, credible, feasible, plausible, possible, presumable, reasonable

probably *adv* = **likely**, doubtless, maybe, most likely, perchance (*arch*), perhaps, possibly, presumably

probation *n* **2** = **trial period**, apprenticeship, trial

probe *v* **1 a** = **examine**, explore, go into, investigate, look into, scrutinize, search **b** = **explore**, feel around, poke, prod ▷ *n* **3** = **examination**, detection, exploration, inquiry, investigation, scrutiny, study

problem *n* **1** = **difficulty**, complication, dilemma, dispute, predicament, quandary, trouble **2** = **puzzle**, conundrum, enigma, poser, question, riddle

procedure *n* = **method**, action, conduct, course, custom, modus operandi, policy, practice, process, routine, strategy, system

proceed *v* **1** = **go on**, carry on, continue, go ahead, move on, press on, progress **4** = **arise**, come, derive, emanate, flow, issue, originate, result, spring, stem

proceedings *pl n* **2** = **business**, account, affairs, archives, doings, minutes, records, report, transactions

proceeds *pl n* = **income**, earnings, gain, products, profit, returns, revenue, takings, yield

process *n* **1** = **development**, advance, evolution, growth, movement, progress, progression **2** = **procedure**, action, course, manner, means,

procession ⊕ n line of people or vehicles moving forward together in order.

proclaim ⊕ v declare publicly. **proclamation** n.

proclivity n, pl **-ties** inclination, tendency.

procrastinate ⊕ v put off taking action, delay. **procrastination** n **procrastinator** n.

procreate v formal produce offspring. **procreation** n.

procurator fiscal n (in Scotland) law officer who acts as public prosecutor and coroner.

procure ⊕ v 1 get, provide. 2 obtain (people) to act as prostitutes. **procurement** n **procurer**, **procuress** n person who obtains people to act as prostitutes.

prod ⊕ v **prodding**, **prodded** 1 poke with something pointed. 2 goad (someone) to take action. ▷ n 3 prodding.

prodigal ⊕ adj recklessly extravagant, wasteful. **prodigality** n.

prodigy ⊕ n, pl **-gies** 1 person with some marvellous talent. 2 wonderful thing. **prodigious** adj 1 very large, immense. 2 wonderful. **prodigiously** adv.

produce ⊕ v 1 bring into existence. 2 present to view, show. 3 make, manufacture. 4 present on stage, film, or television. ▷ n 5 food grown for sale. **producer** n 1 person with control over the making of a film, record, etc. 2 person or company that produces something.

product ⊕ n 1 something produced. 2 number resulting from multiplication. **production** n 1 producing. 2 things produced. 3 presentation of a play, opera, etc. **productive** adj 1 producing large quantities. 2 useful, profitable. **productivity** n.

THESAURUS

measure, method, operation, performance, practice, system ▷ v **3 = handle**

procession n = **parade**, cavalcade, cortege, file, march, train

proclaim v = **declare**, advertise, announce, circulate, herald, indicate, make known, profess, publish

procrastinate v = **delay**, dally, drag one's feet (inf), gain time, play for time, postpone, put off, stall, temporize

procure v 1 = **obtain**, acquire, buy, come by, find, gain, get, pick up, purchase, score (sl), secure, win

prod v 1 = **poke**, dig, drive, jab, nudge, push, shove 2 = **prompt**, egg on, goad, impel, incite, motivate, move, rouse, spur, stimulate, urge ▷ n 3 **a** = **poke**, dig, jab, nudge, push, shove **b** = **prompt**, cue, reminder, signal, stimulus

prodigal adj = **extravagant**, excessive, immoderate, improvident, profligate, reckless, spendthrift, wasteful

prodigious adj 1 = **huge**, colossal, enormous, giant, gigantic, immense, massive, vast 2 = **wonderful**, amazing, exceptional, extraordinary, fabulous, fantastic (inf), marvellous, phenomenal, remarkable, staggering

prodigy n 1 = **genius**, mastermind, talent, whizz (inf), wizard

2 = **wonder**, marvel, miracle, phenomenon, sensation

produce v 1 = **bring forth**, bear, beget, breed, bring about, cause, deliver, effect, generate, give rise to 2 = **show**, advance, demonstrate, exhibit, offer, present 3 = **make**, compose, construct, create, develop, fabricate, invent, manufacture 4 = **present**, direct, do, exhibit, mount, put on, show, stage ▷ n 5 = **fruit and vegetables**, crop, greengrocery, harvest, product, yield

producer n 1 = **director**, impresario 2 = **maker**, cockie (Aust & NZ inf), farmer, grower, manufacturer

product n 1 **a** = **goods**, artefact, commodity, creation, invention, merchandise, produce, work **b** = **result**, consequence, effect, outcome, upshot

production n 1 = **producing**, construction, creation, fabrication, formation, making, manufacture, manufacturing 3 = **presentation**, direction, management, staging

productive adj 1 = **fertile**, creative, fecund, fruitful, inventive, plentiful, prolific, rich 2 = **useful**, advantageous, beneficial, constructive, effective, profitable, rewarding, valuable, worthwhile

p

profane ❶ *adj* **1** showing disrespect for religion or holy things. **2** (of language) coarse, blasphemous. ▷ *v* **3** treat (something sacred) irreverently, desecrate. **profanation** *n* act of profaning. **profanity** *n*, *pl* **-ties** profane talk or behaviour, blasphemy.

profess ❶ *v* **1** state or claim (something as true), sometimes falsely. **2** have as one's belief or religion. **professed** *adj* supposed.

profession ❶ *n* **1** type of work, such as being a doctor, that needs special training. **2** all the people employed in a profession, e.g. *the legal profession*. **3** declaration of a belief or feeling. **professional** *adj* **1** working in a profession. **2** taking part in an activity, such as sport or music, for money. **3** very competent. ▷ *n* **4** person who works in a profession. **5** person paid to take part in sport,

music, etc. **professionally** *adv* **professionalism** *n*.

professor ❶ *n* teacher of the highest rank in a university. **professorial** *adj* **professorship** *n*.

proffer *v* offer.

proficient ❶ *adj* skilled, expert. **proficiency** *n*.

profile ❶ *n* **1** outline, esp. of the face, as seen from the side. **2** brief biographical sketch.

profit ❶ *n* **1** money gained. **2** benefit obtained. ▷ *v* **3** gain or benefit. **profitable** *adj* making profit. **profitably** *adv* **profitability** *n* **profiteer** *n* person who makes excessive profits at the expense of the public. **profiteering** *n*.

profligate ❶ *adj* **1** recklessly extravagant. **2** shamelessly immoral. ▷ *n* **3** profligate person. **profligacy** *n*.

productivity *n* = **output**, production, work rate, yield

profane *adj* **1** = **sacrilegious**, disrespectful, godless, impious, impure, irreligious, irreverent, sinful, ungodly, wicked **2** = **crude**, blasphemous, coarse, filthy, foul, obscene, vulgar ▷ *v* **3** = **desecrate**, commit sacrilege, debase, defile, violate

profanity *n* **a** = **swearing**, curse, cursing, irreverence, obscenity **b** = **sacrilege**, blasphemy, impiety, profaneness

profess *v* **1 a** = **state**, admit, affirm, announce, assert, avow, confess, declare, proclaim, vouch **b** = **claim**, allege, fake, feign, make out, pretend, purport

professed *adj* = **supposed**, alleged, ostensible, pretended, purported, self-styled, so-called, would-be

profession *n* **1** = **occupation**, business, calling, career, employment, office, position, sphere, vocation **3** = **declaration**, affirmation, assertion, avowal, claim, statement

professional *adj* **3** = **expert**, adept, competent, efficient, experienced, masterly, proficient, qualified, skilled ▷ *n* **4, 5** = **expert**, adept, fundi (*S Afr*), guru, maestro, master, past master, pro (*inf*), specialist, virtuoso

professor *n* = **don** (*Brit*), fellow (*Brit*), prof (*inf*)

proficient *adj* = **skilled**, able, accomplished, adept, capable, competent, efficient, expert, gifted, masterly, skilful

profile *n* **1** = **outline**, contour, drawing, figure, form, side view, silhouette, sketch **2** = **biography**, characterization, sketch, thumbnail sketch, vignette

profit *n* **1** = **earnings**, gain, proceeds, receipts, return, revenue, takings, yield **2** = **benefit**, advancement, advantage, gain, good, use, value ▷ *v* **3 a** = **make money**, earn, gain **b** = **benefit**, be of advantage to, gain, help, improve, promote, serve

profitable *adj* **a** = **money-making**, commercial, cost-effective, fruitful, lucrative, paying, remunerative, worthwhile **b** = **beneficial**, advantageous, fruitful, productive, rewarding, useful, valuable, worthwhile

profiteer *n* = **racketeer**, exploiter

profligate *adj* **1** = **extravagant**, immoderate, improvident, prodigal, reckless, spendthrift, wasteful **2** = **depraved**, debauched, degenerate, dissolute, immoral, licentious, shameless, wanton, wicked, wild ▷ *n* **3 a** = **spendthrift**, squanderer, waster, wastrel **b** = **degenerate**, debauchee, libertine, rake, reprobate, roué

DICTIONARY

pro forma *adj Latin* prescribing a set form.

profound ❶ *adj* **1** showing or needing great knowledge. **2** strongly felt, intense. **profoundly** *adv* **profundity** *n, pl* **-ties**.

profuse ❶ *adj* plentiful. **profusion** *n*.

progeny ❶ [proj-in-ee] *n, pl* **-nies** children. **progenitor** [pro-**jen**-it-er] *n* ancestor.

progesterone *n* hormone which prepares the womb for pregnancy and prevents further ovulation.

prognosis ❶ *n, pl* **-noses 1** doctor's forecast about the progress of an illness. **2** any forecast.

prognostication *n* forecast or prediction.

program *n* **1** sequence of coded instructions for a computer. ▷ *v* **-gramming, -grammed 2** arrange (data) so that it can be processed by a computer. **3** feed a program into (a computer). **programmer** *n* **programmable** *adj*.

programme ❶ *n* **1** planned series of events. **2** broadcast on radio or television. **3** list of items or performers in an entertainment.

progress ❶ *n* **1** improvement, development. **2** movement forward. ▷ *v* **3** become more advanced or skilful. **4** move forward. **in progress** taking place. **progression** *n* **1** act of progressing, advance. **2** sequence of numbers in which each differs from the next by a fixed ratio. **progressive** *adj* **1** favouring political or social reform. **2** happening gradually. **progressively** *adv*.

prohibit ❶ *v* forbid or prevent from happening. **prohibition** *n* **1** act of forbidding. **2** ban on the sale or drinking of alcohol. **prohibitive** *adj* (of prices) too high to be affordable. **prohibitively** *adv*.

project ❶ *n* **1** planned scheme to do or examine something over a period. ▷ *v* **2** make a forecast based on known data. **3** make (a film or slide) appear on a screen. **4** communicate (an impression). **5** stick out beyond a surface or edge. **projector** *n* apparatus for projecting photographic images, films, or slides on a screen. **projection** *n* **projectionist** *n* person who operates a projector.

THESAURUS

profound *adj* **1** = **wise**, abstruse, deep, learned, penetrating, philosophical, sagacious, sage **2** = **sincere**, acute, deeply felt, extreme, great, heartfelt, intense, keen

profuse *adj* = **plentiful**, abundant, ample, bountiful, copious, luxuriant, overflowing, prolific

progeny *n* = **children**, descendants, family, issue, lineage, offspring, race, stock, young

prognosis *n* **1** = **diagnosis** **2** = **forecast**, prediction, prognostication, projection

programme *n* **1** = **schedule**, agenda, curriculum, line-up, list, listing, order of events, plan, syllabus, timetable **2** = **show**, broadcast, performance, presentation, production

progress *n* **1** = **development**, advance, breakthrough, gain, growth, headway, improvement **2** = **movement**, advance, course, headway, passage ▷ *v* **3** = **develop**, advance, gain, grow, improve **4** = **move on**, advance, continue, go forward, make headway, proceed, travel **in progress** = **going on**, being done, happening, occurring, proceeding, taking place, under way

progression *n* **1** = **progress**, advance, advancement, furtherance, gain, headway, movement forward

progressive *adj* **1** = **enlightened**, advanced, avant-garde, forward-looking, liberal, modern, radical, reformist, revolutionary **2** = **growing**, advancing, continuing, developing, increasing, ongoing

prohibit *v* **a** = **forbid**, ban, debar, disallow, outlaw, proscribe, veto **b** = **prevent**, hamper, hinder, impede, restrict, stop

prohibition *n* **1** = **prevention**, ban, bar, boycott, constraint, embargo, exclusion, injunction, interdict, obstruction, proscription, restriction, veto

prohibitive *adj* = **exorbitant**, excessive, extortionate, steep (*inf*)

project *n* **1** = **scheme**, activity, assignment, enterprise, job, occupation, plan, task, undertaking, venture, work ▷ *v* **2** = **forecast**, calculate, estimate, extrapolate, gauge, predict, reckon **5** = **stick out**, bulge, extend, jut, overhang, protrude, stand out

p

projectile ❶ n object thrown as a weapon or fired from a gun.

prolapse n slipping down of an internal organ of the body from its normal position. **prolapsed** adj.

prole adj, n offens proletarian.

proletariat ❶ [pro-lit-**air**-ee-at] n working class. **proletarian** adj, n.

proliferate ❶ v grow or reproduce rapidly. **proliferation** n.

prolific ❶ adj very productive. **prolifically** adv.

prolix adj (of speech or a piece of writing) overlong and boring. **prolixity** n.

prologue ❶ n introduction to a play or book.

prolong ❶ v make (something) last longer. **prolongation** n.

prom n short for PROMENADE or PROMENADE CONCERT.

promenade ❶ n **1** paved walkway along the seafront at a holiday resort. ▷ v, n **2** old-fashioned (take) a leisurely walk. **promenade concert** concert at which part of the audience stands rather than sits.

promethium [pro-**meeth**-ee-um] n Chemistry artificial radioactive element of the lanthanide series.

prominent ❶ adj **1** very noticeable. **2** famous, widely known. **prominently** adv **prominence** n.

promiscuous ❶ adj having many casual sexual relationships. **promiscuity** n.

promise ❶ v **1** say that one will definitely do or not do something. **2** show signs of, seem likely. ▷ n **3** undertaking to do or not to do something. **4** indication of future success. **show promise** seem likely to succeed. **promising** adj likely to succeed or turn out well. **promissory note** written promise to pay a sum of money to a particular person on a certain date or on demand.

promo n, pl **-mos** informal short video film made to promote a pop record.

promontory ❶ n, pl **-ries** point of high land jutting out into the sea.

——————————— **THESAURUS**

projectile n = **missile**, bullet, rocket, shell

projection n **2** = **forecast**, calculation, computation, estimate, estimation, extrapolation, reckoning **5** = **protrusion**, bulge, ledge, overhang, protuberance, ridge, shelf

proletarian adj = **working-class**, common, plebeian ▷ n = **worker**, commoner, man of the people, pleb, plebeian, prole (offens)

proletariat n = **working class**, commoners, hoi polloi, labouring classes, lower classes, plebs, proles (offens), the common people, the masses

proliferate v = **increase**, breed, expand, grow rapidly, multiply

proliferation n = **multiplication**, expansion, increase, spread

prolific adj = **productive**, abundant, copious, fecund, fertile, fruitful, luxuriant, profuse

prologue n = **introduction**, foreword, preamble, preface, prelude

prolong v = **lengthen**, continue, delay, drag out, draw out, extend, perpetuate, protract, spin out, stretch

promenade n **1** = **walkway**, esplanade, parade, prom ▷ v **2** Old-fashioned = **stroll**, saunter, walk

prominence n **1** = **conspicuousness**, markedness **2** = **fame**, celebrity, distinction, eminence, importance, name, prestige, reputation

prominent adj **1** = **noticeable**, conspicuous, eye-catching, obtrusive, obvious, outstanding, pronounced **2** = **famous**, distinguished, eminent, foremost, important, leading, main, notable, renowned, top, well-known

promiscuous adj = **licentious**, abandoned, debauched, fast, immoral, libertine, loose, wanton, wild

promise v **1** = **guarantee**, assure, contract, give one's word, pledge, swear, take an oath, undertake, vow, warrant **2** = **seem likely**, augur, betoken, indicate, look like, show signs of, suggest ▷ n **3** = **guarantee**, assurance, bond, commitment, oath, pledge, undertaking, vow, word **4** = **potential**, ability, aptitude, capability, capacity, talent

promising adj **a** = **encouraging**, auspicious, bright, favourable, hopeful, likely, propitious, reassuring, rosy **b** = **talented**, able, gifted, rising

promontory n = **point**, cape, foreland, head, headland

promote ● v 1 help to make (something) happen or increase. 2 raise to a higher rank or position. 3 encourage the sale of by advertising. **promoter** n person who organizes or finances an event etc. **promotion** n **promotional** adj.

prompt ● v 1 cause (an action). 2 remind (an actor or speaker) of words that he or she has forgotten. ▷ adj 3 done without delay. ▷ adv 4 exactly, e.g. six o'clock prompt. **promptly** adv immediately, without delay. **promptness** n **prompter** n person offstage who prompts actors.

promulgate ● v 1 put (a law etc.) into effect by announcing it officially. 2 make widely known. **promulgation** n **promulgator** n.

prone ● adj 1 (foll. by to) likely to do or be affected by (something). 2 lying face downwards.

prong ● n one spike of a fork or similar instrument. **pronged** adj.

pronoun n word, such as she or it, used to replace a noun. **pronominal** adj.

pronounce ● v 1 form the sounds of (words or letters), esp. clearly or in a particular way. 2 declare formally or officially. **pronounceable** adj

pronounced adj very noticeable. **pronouncement** n formal announcement. **pronunciation** n way in which a word or language is pronounced.

● **SPELLING TIP**
● The noun **pronunciation**, which
● appears in the Bank of English 823
● times, is spelt pronounciation 21
● times, probably because of the way
● **pronounce** is spelt. Remember,
● there is no o between the n and
● the u.

pronto adv informal at once.

proof ● n 1 evidence that shows that something is true or has happened. 2 copy of something printed, such as the pages of a book, for checking before final production. 3 Photography trial print from a negative. ▷ adj 4 able to withstand, e.g. proof against criticism. 5 denoting the strength of an alcoholic drink, e.g. seventy proof. **proofread** v read and correct (printer's proofs). **proofreader** n.

prop¹ ● v **propping, propped** 1 support (something) so that it stays upright or in place. ▷ n 2 pole, beam, etc. used as a support.

promote v 1 = **help**, advance, aid, assist, back, boost, encourage, forward, foster, gee up, support 2 = **raise**, elevate, exalt, upgrade 3 = **advertise**, hype, plug (inf), publicize, push, sell

promotion n 1 = **encouragement**, advancement, boosting, furtherance, support 2 = **rise**, advancement, elevation, exaltation, honour, move up, preferment, upgrading 3 = **publicity**, advertising, plugging (inf)

prompt v 1 = **cause**, elicit, give rise to, occasion, provoke 2 = **remind**, assist, cue, help out ▷ adj 3 = **immediate**, early, instant, quick, rapid, speedy, swift, timely ▷ adv 4 = **exactly**, on the dot, promptly, punctually, sharp

promulgate v 2 = **make known**, broadcast, circulate, communicate, disseminate, make public, proclaim, promote, publish, spread

prone adj 1 (foll. by to) = **liable**, apt, bent, disposed, given, inclined, likely, predisposed, subject, susceptible, tending 2 = **face down**, flat, horizontal, prostrate, recumbent

prong n = **point**, spike, tine

pronounce v 1 = **say**, accent, articulate, enunciate, sound, speak 2 = **declare**, affirm, announce, decree, deliver, proclaim

pronounced adj = **noticeable**, conspicuous, decided, definite, distinct, evident, marked, obvious, striking

pronouncement n = **announcement**, declaration, decree, dictum, edict, judgment, proclamation, statement

pronunciation n = **intonation**, accent, articulation, diction, enunciation, inflection, speech, stress

proof n 1 = **evidence**, authentication, confirmation, corroboration, demonstration, substantiation, testimony, verification ▷ adj 4 = **impervious**, impenetrable, repellent, resistant, strong

prop¹ v 1 = **support**, bolster, brace, buttress, hold up, stay, sustain, uphold ▷ n 2 = **support**, brace, buttress, mainstay, stanchion, stay

P

prop² *n* movable object used on the set of a film or play.

prop³ *n informal* propeller.

propaganda ❶ *n* (organized promotion of) information to assist or damage the cause of a government or movement. **propagandist** *n*.

propagate ❶ *v* **1** spread (information and ideas). **2** reproduce, breed, or grow. **propagation** *n*.

propane *n* flammable gas found in petroleum and used as a fuel.

propel ❶ *v* **-pelling, -pelled** cause to move forward. **propellant** *n* **1** something that provides or causes propulsion. **2** gas used in an aerosol spray. **propeller** *n* revolving shaft with blades for driving a ship or aircraft. **propulsion** *n* **1** method by which something is propelled. **2** act of propelling or state of being propelled.

propensity ❶ *n, pl* **-ties** natural tendency.

proper ❶ *adj* **1** real or genuine. **2** appropriate. **3** suited to a particular purpose. **4** correct in behaviour. **5** excessively moral. **6** *informal* complete. **properly** *adv* **proper noun** name of a person or place, as in *David* or *Iceland*.

property ❶ *n, pl* **-ties 1** something owned. **2** possessions collectively.

3 land or buildings owned by somebody. **4** quality or attribute.

prophet ❶ *n* **1** person supposedly chosen by God to spread His word. **2** person who predicts the future. **prophetic** *adj* **prophetically** *adv* **prophecy** *n, pl* **-cies 1** prediction. **2** message revealing God's will. **prophesy** *v* **-sying, -sied** foretell.

prophylactic *n, adj* (drug) used to prevent disease.

propitiate ❶ *v* appease, win the favour of. **propitiation** *n* **propitious** *adj* favourable or auspicious.

proponent *n* person who argues in favour of something.

proportion ❶ *n* **1** relative size or extent. **2** correct relation between connected parts. **3** part considered with respect to the whole. ▷ *pl* **4** dimensions or size. ▷ *v* **5** adjust in relative amount or size. **in proportion 1** comparable in size, rate of increase, etc. **2** without exaggerating. **proportional, proportionate** *adj* being in proportion. **proportionally, proportionately** *adv* **proportional representation** representation of political parties in parliament in proportion to the votes they win.

— THESAURUS —

propaganda *n* = **information**, advertising, disinformation, hype, promotion, publicity

propagate *v* **1** = **spread**, broadcast, circulate, disseminate, promote, promulgate, publish, transmit **2** = **reproduce**, beget, breed, engender, generate, increase, multiply, procreate, produce

propel *v* = **drive**, force, impel, launch, push, send, shoot, shove, thrust

propensity *n* = **tendency**, bent, inclination, liability, penchant, predisposition, proclivity

proper *adj* **2, 3** = **suitable**, appropriate, apt, becoming, befitting, fit, fitting, right **4** = **correct**, accepted, conventional, established, formal, orthodox, precise, right **5** = **polite**, decent, decorous, genteel, gentlemanly, ladylike, mannerly, respectable, seemly

property *n* **2** = **possessions**, assets, belongings, capital, effects, estate, goods, holdings, riches, wealth **3** = **land**, estate, freehold, holding,

real estate **4** = **quality**, attribute, characteristic, feature, hallmark, trait

prophecy *n* = **prediction**, augury, divination, forecast, prognostication, second sight, soothsaying

prophesy *v* = **predict**, augur, divine, forecast, foresee, foretell, prognosticate

prophet *n* **2** = **soothsayer**, diviner, forecaster, oracle, prophesier, seer, sibyl

propitious *adj* = **favourable**, auspicious, bright, encouraging, fortunate, happy, lucky, promising

proportion *n* **1** = **relative amount**, ratio, relationship **2** = **balance**, congruity, correspondence, harmony, symmetry **3** = **part**, amount, division, fraction, percentage, quota, segment, share ▷ *pl n* **4** = **dimensions**, capacity, expanse, extent, size, volume

proportional, proportionate *adj* = **balanced**, commensurate, compatible, consistent, corresponding, equitable, even, in proportion

propose ❶ v **1** put forward for consideration. **2** nominate. **3** intend or plan (to do). **4** make an offer of marriage. **proposal** n **proposition** n **1** offer. **2** statement or assertion. **3** Maths theorem. **4** informal thing to be dealt with. ▷ v **5** informal ask (someone) to have sexual intercourse.

propound v put forward for consideration.

proprietor n owner of a business establishment. **proprietress** n fem **proprietary** adj **1** made and distributed under a trade name. **2** denoting or suggesting ownership.

propriety ❶ n, pl **-ties 1** quality of being appropriate or fitting. **2** correct conduct.

propulsion ❶ n see PROPEL.

pro rata adv, adj Latin in proportion.

prorogue v suspend (parliament) without dissolving it. **prorogation** n.

prosaic ❶ [pro-**zay**-ik] adj lacking imagination, dull. **prosaically** adv.

proscenium n, pl **-nia**, **-niums** arch in a theatre separating the stage from the auditorium.

proscribe ❶ v prohibit, outlaw.

proscription n **proscriptive** adj.

prose n ordinary speech or writing in contrast to poetry.

Prosecco n sparkling Italian white wine, usually dry.

prosecute ❶ v **1** bring a criminal charge against. **2** continue to do. **prosecution** n **prosecutor** n.

proselyte [**pross**-ill-ite] n recent convert. **proselytize** [**pross**-ill-it-ize] v attempt to convert.

prosody [**pross**-a-dee] n study of poetic metre and techniques.

prospect ❶ n **1** something anticipated, e.g. the prospect of defeat. **2** old-fashioned view from a place. ▷ pl **3** probability of future success. ▷ v **4** explore, esp. for gold. **prospective** adj **1** future. **2** expected. **prospector** n **prospectus** n booklet giving details of a university, company, etc.

prosper ❶ v be successful. **prosperity** n success and wealth. **prosperous** adj.

prostate n gland in male mammals that surrounds the neck of the bladder.

prosthesis [pross-**theess**-iss] n, pl **-ses** [-seez] artificial body part, such as a limb or breast. **prosthetic** adj.

THESAURUS

proposal n **1** = **suggestion**, bid, offer, plan, presentation, programme, project, recommendation, scheme

propose v **1** = **put forward**, advance, present, submit, suggest **2** = **nominate**, name, present, recommend **3** = **intend**, aim, design, have in mind, mean, plan, scheme **4** = **offer marriage**, ask for someone's hand (in marriage), pop the question (inf)

proposition n **1** = **proposal**, plan, recommendation, scheme, suggestion ▷ v **5** Inf = **make a pass at**, accost, make an improper suggestion, solicit

propriety n **1** = **correctness**, aptness, fitness, rightness, seemliness **2** = **decorum**, courtesy, decency, etiquette, manners, politeness, respectability, seemliness

propulsion n = **drive**, impetus, impulse, propelling force, push, thrust

prosaic adj = **dull**, boring, everyday, humdrum, matter-of-fact, mundane, ordinary, pedestrian, routine, trite, unimaginative

proscribe v **a** = **prohibit**, ban, embargo, forbid, interdict

b = **outlaw**, banish, deport, exclude, exile, expatriate, expel, ostracize

prosecute v **1** = **put on trial**, arraign, bring to trial, indict, litigate, sue, take to court, try

prospect n **1** = **expectation**, anticipation, future, hope, odds, outlook, probability, promise **2** Old-fashioned = **view**, landscape, outlook, scene, sight, spectacle, vista ▷ pl n **3** = **likelihood**, chance, possibility ▷ v **4** = **look for**, fossick (Aust & NZ), search for, seek

prospective adj **1** = **future** **2** = **expected**, anticipated, coming, destined, forthcoming, imminent, intended, likely, possible, potential

prospectus n = **catalogue**, list, outline, programme, syllabus, synopsis

prosper v = **succeed**, advance, do well, flourish, get on, progress, thrive

prosperity n **a** = **success**, good fortune **b** = **wealth**, affluence, fortune, luxury, plenty, prosperousness, riches

prosperous adj **a** = **successful**, booming, doing well, flourishing,

P

prostitute ❶ *n* **1** person who offers sexual intercourse in return for payment. ▷ *v* **2** make a prostitute of. **3** offer (oneself or one's talents) for unworthy purposes. **prostitution** *n*.

prostrate ❶ *adj* **1** lying face downwards. **2** physically or emotionally exhausted. ▷ *v* **3** lie face downwards. **4** exhaust physically or emotionally. **prostration** *n*.

protactinium *n Chemistry* toxic radioactive metallic element.

protagonist ❶ *n* **1** supporter of a cause. **2** leading character in a play or a story.

protea [**pro**-tee-a] *n* African shrub with showy flowers.

protean [pro-**tee**-an] *adj* constantly changing.

protect ❶ *v* defend from trouble, harm, or loss. **protection** *n* **protectionism** *n* policy of protecting industries by taxing competing imports. **protectionist** *n*, *adj* **protective** *adj* **1** giving protection, e.g. *protective clothing*. **2** tending or wishing to protect someone. **protector** *n* **1** person or thing that protects. **2** regent. **protectorate** *n* **1** territory largely controlled by a stronger state. **2** (period of) rule of a regent.

protégé (*fem*) **protégée** [**pro**-ti-zhay] *n* person who is protected and helped by another.

protein *n* any of a group of complex organic compounds that are essential for life.

pro tempore *adv*, *adj* for the time being (also **pro tem**).

protest ❶ *n* **1** declaration or demonstration of objection. ▷ *v* **2** object, disagree. **3** assert formally. **protester** *n* **protestation** *n* strong declaration.

Protestant *n* **1** follower of any of the Christian churches that split from the Roman Catholic Church in the sixteenth century. ▷ *adj* **2** of or relating to such a church. **Protestantism** *n*.

protium *n* most common isotope of hydrogen.

proto- *combining form* first, e.g. *protohuman*.

protocol ❶ *n* rules of behaviour for formal occasions.

proton *n* positively charged particle in the nucleus of an atom.

protoplasm *n* substance forming the living contents of a cell.

prototype ❶ *n* original or model to be copied or developed.

protozoan [pro-toe-**zoe**-an] *n*, *pl* **-zoa** microscopic one-celled creature.

THESAURUS

fortunate, lucky, thriving **b** = **wealthy**, affluent, moneyed, rich, well-heeled (*inf*), well-off, well-to-do

prostitute *n* **1** = **whore**, call girl, fallen woman, harlot, hooker (*US sl*), loose woman, pro (*sl*), scrubber (*Brit & Aust sl*), streetwalker, strumpet, tart (*inf*), trollop ▷ *v* **3** = **cheapen**, debase, degrade, demean, devalue, misapply, pervert, profane

prostrate *adj* **1** = **prone**, flat, horizontal **2** = **exhausted**, dejected, depressed, desolate, drained, inconsolable, overcome, spent, worn out ▷ *v* **4** = **exhaust**, drain, fatigue, sap, tire, wear out, weary

protagonist *n* **1** = **supporter**, advocate, champion, exponent **2** = **leading character**, central character, hero *or* heroine, principal

protect *v* = **keep safe**, defend, guard, look after, preserve, safeguard, save, screen, shelter, shield, stick up for (*inf*), support, watch over

protection *n* **a** = **safety**, aegis, care, custody, defence, protecting, safeguard, safekeeping, security **b** = **safeguard**, barrier, buffer, cover, guard, screen, shelter, shield

protector *n* **1** = **defender**, bodyguard, champion, guard, guardian, patron

protest *n* **1** = **objection**, complaint, dissent, outcry, protestation, remonstrance ▷ *v* **2** = **object**, complain, cry out, demonstrate, demur, disagree, disapprove, express disapproval, oppose, remonstrate **3** = **assert**, affirm, attest, avow, declare, insist, maintain, profess

protestation *n* = **declaration**, affirmation, avowal, profession, vow

protester *n* = **demonstrator**, agitator, rebel

protocol *n* = **code of behaviour**, conventions, customs, decorum, etiquette, manners, propriety

prototype *n* = **original**, example, first, model, pattern, standard, type

protract ❶ v lengthen or extend. **protracted** adj **protractor** n instrument for measuring angles.

protrude ❶ v stick out, project. **protrusion** n.

protuberant ❶ adj swelling out, bulging. **protuberance** n.

proud ❶ adj 1 feeling pleasure and satisfaction. 2 feeling honoured. 3 thinking oneself superior to other people. 4 dignified. **proudly** adv.

prove ❶ v **proving**, **proved**, **proved** or **proven** 1 establish the validity of. 2 demonstrate, test. 3 be found to be. **proven** adj known from experience to work.

provenance [**prov**-in-anss] n place of origin.

provender n old-fashioned fodder.

proverb ❶ n short saying that expresses a truth or gives a warning. **proverbial** adj.

provide ❶ v make available. **provider** n **provided that**, **providing** on condition that. **provide for** v 1 take precautions (against). 2 support financially.

providence ❶ n God or nature seen as a protective force that arranges people's lives. **provident** adj 1 thrifty. 2 showing foresight. **providential** adj lucky.

province ❶ n 1 area governed as a unit of a country or empire. 2 area of learning, activity, etc. ▷ pl 3 parts of a country outside the capital. **provincial** adj 1 of a province or the provinces. 2 unsophisticated and narrow-minded. ▷ n 3 unsophisticated person. 4 person from a province or the provinces. **provincialism** n narrow-mindedness and lack of sophistication.

provision ❶ n 1 act of supplying something. 2 something supplied.

———————— THESAURUS ————————

protracted adj = **extended**, dragged out, drawn-out, long-drawn-out, prolonged

protrude v = **stick out**, bulge, come through, extend, jut, obtrude, project, stand out

protrusion n = **projection**, bulge, bump, lump, outgrowth, protuberance

protuberance n = **bulge**, bump, excrescence, hump, knob, lump, outgrowth, process, prominence, protrusion, swelling

proud adj 1 = **satisfied**, content, glad, gratified, pleased, well-pleased 3 = **conceited**, arrogant, boastful, disdainful, haughty, imperious, lordly, overbearing, self-satisfied, snobbish, supercilious

prove v 1 = **verify**, authenticate, confirm, demonstrate, determine, establish, justify, show, substantiate 2 = **test**, analyse, assay, check, examine, try 3 = **turn out**, come out, end up, result

proven adj = **established**, attested, confirmed, definite, proved, reliable, tested, verified

proverb n = **saying**, adage, dictum, maxim, saw

proverbial adj = **conventional**, acknowledged, axiomatic, current, famed, famous, legendary, notorious, traditional, typical, well-known

provide v = **supply**, add, afford, bring, cater, equip, furnish, give, impart, lend, outfit, present, produce, purvey, render, serve, stock up, yield **provide for** v 1 = **take precautions**, anticipate, forearm, plan ahead, plan for, prepare for 2 = **support**, care for, keep, maintain, sustain, take care of

provided that, **providing** conj = **on condition that**, as long as, given

providence n = **fate**, destiny, fortune

provident adj 1 = **thrifty**, economical, frugal, prudent 2 = **foresighted**, careful, cautious, discreet, far-seeing, forearmed, shrewd, vigilant, well-prepared, wise

providential adj = **lucky**, fortuitous, fortunate, happy, heaven-sent, opportune, timely

province n 1 = **region**, colony, department, district, division, domain, patch, section, zone 2 = **area**, business, capacity, concern, duty, field, function, line, responsibility, role, sphere

provincial adj 1 = **rural**, country, homespun, local, rustic 2 = **parochial**, hick (inf, chiefly US & Canad), insular, limited, narrow, narrow-minded, small-minded, small-town (chiefly US), unsophisticated ▷ n 3 = **yokel**, country cousin, hayseed (US & Canad inf), hick (inf, chiefly US & Canad), rustic

provision n 1 = **supplying**, catering, equipping, furnishing, providing 3 Law = **condition**, clause, demand,

P

3 *Law* condition incorporated in a document. ▷ *pl* **4** food. ▷ *v* **5** supply with food. **provisional** *adj* temporary or conditional. **provisionally** *adv*.

proviso ⊕ [pro-**vize**-oh] *n, pl* **-sos**, **-soes** condition, stipulation.

provoke ⊕ *v* **1** deliberately anger. **2** cause (an adverse reaction). **provocation** *n* **provocative** *adj*.

provost *n* **1** head of certain university colleges. **2** chief councillor of a Scottish town. **provost marshal** head of military police.

prow *n* bow of a vessel.

prowess ⊕ *n* **1** superior skill or ability. **2** bravery, fearlessness.

prowl ⊕ *v* **1** move stealthily around a place as if in search of prey or plunder. ▷ *n* **2** prowling. **prowler** *n*.

proximity ⊕ *n* **1** nearness in space or time. **2** nearness or closeness in a series. **proximate** *adj*.

proxy ⊕ *n, pl* **proxies 1** person authorized to act on behalf of someone else. **2** authority to act on behalf of someone else.

prude ⊕ *n* person who is excessively

modest, prim, or proper. **prudish** *adj* **prudery** *n*.

prudent ⊕ *adj* cautious, discreet, and sensible. **prudence** *n* **prudential** *adj* *old-fashioned* prudent.

prune¹ *n* dried plum.

prune² ⊕ *v* **1** cut off dead parts or excessive branches from (a tree or plant). **2** shorten, reduce.

prurient *adj* excessively interested in sexual matters. **prurience** *n*.

pry ⊕ *v* **prying, pried** make an impertinent or uninvited inquiry into a private matter.

PS postscript.

psalm ⊕ *n* sacred song. **psalmist** *n* writer of psalms.

Psalter *n* book containing (a version of) psalms from the Bible. **psaltery** *n, pl* **-ries** ancient instrument played by plucking strings.

PSBR public sector borrowing requirement.

psephology [sef-**fol**-a-jee] *n* statistical study of elections.

pseud *n informal* pretentious person.

pseudo- ⊕ *combining form* false, pretending, or unauthentic, e.g. *pseudoclassical*.

— THESAURUS —

proviso, requirement, rider, stipulation, term ▷ *pl* **4** = **food**, comestibles, eatables, edibles, fare, foodstuffs, rations, stores, supplies, tucker (*Aust & NZ inf*), victuals

provisional *adj* **a** = **temporary**, interim **b** = **conditional**, contingent, limited, qualified, tentative

proviso *n* = **condition**, clause, qualification, requirement, rider, stipulation

provocation *n* **1** = **offence**, affront, annoyance, challenge, dare, grievance, indignity, injury, insult, taunt **2** = **cause**, grounds, incitement, motivation, reason, stimulus

provocative *adj* **1** = **offensive**, annoying, galling, goading, insulting, provoking

provoke *v* **1** = **anger**, aggravate (*inf*), annoy, enrage, hassle (*inf*), incense, infuriate, irk, irritate, madden, rile, troll **2** = **rouse**, bring about, cause, elicit, evoke, incite, induce, occasion, produce, promote, prompt, stir

prowess *n* **1** = **skill**, ability, accomplishment, adeptness, aptitude, excellence, expertise,

genius, mastery, talent **2** = **bravery**, courage, daring, fearlessness, heroism, mettle, valiance, valour

prowl *v* **1** = **move stealthily**, skulk, slink, sneak, stalk, steal

proximity *n* = **nearness**, closeness

proxy *n* **1** = **representative**, agent, delegate, deputy, factor, substitute

prudence *n* **a** = **care**, caution, vigilance, wariness **b** = **discretion** **c** = **common sense**, good sense, judgment, wisdom

prudent *adj* **a** = **careful**, canny, cautious, discerning, judicious, shrewd, vigilant, wary **b** = **discreet**, politic **c** = **sensible**, wise

prudish *adj* = **prim**, old-maidish (*inf*), priggish, prissy (*inf*), proper, puritanical, starchy (*inf*), strait-laced, stuffy, Victorian

prune² *v* **1** = **cut**, clip, dock, shape, snip, trim **2** = **reduce**, shorten

pry *v* = **be inquisitive**, be nosy (*inf*), interfere, intrude, meddle, poke, snoop (*inf*)

psalm *n* = **hymn**, chant

pseudo- *combining form* = **false**, artificial, fake, imitation, mock,

pseudonym ❶ *n* fictitious name adopted esp. by an author. **pseudonymous** *adj*.

psittacosis *n* disease of parrots that can be transmitted to humans.

psoriasis [so-**rye**-a-siss] *n* skin disease with reddish spots and patches covered with silvery scales.

psyche ❶ [**sye**-kee] *n* human mind or soul.

psychedelic *adj* **1** denoting a drug that causes hallucinations. **2** having vivid colours and complex patterns similar to those experienced during hallucinations.

- **SPELLING TIP**
- The main problem with
- **psychedelic** is which vowel
- follows the *ch*; it should be *e* of
- course.

psychiatry ❶ *n* branch of medicine concerned with mental disorders. **psychiatric** *adj* **psychiatrist** *n*.

psychic ❶ *adj* (also **psychical**) **1** having mental powers which cannot be explained by natural laws. **2** relating to the mind. ▷ *n* **3** person with psychic powers.

psycho *n, pl* **-chos** *informal* psychopath.

psycho- *combining form* mind, mental processes, e.g. *psychology; psychosomatic*.

psychoanalysis *n* method of treating mental and emotional disorders by discussion and analysis of one's thoughts and feelings. **psychoanalyse** *v* **psychoanalyst** *n*.

psychology ❶ *n, pl* **-gies 1** study of human and animal behaviour.

2 *informal* person's mental make-up.

psychologist *n* **psychological** *adj* **1** of or affecting the mind. **2** of psychology. **psychological moment** most appropriate time for producing a desired effect. **psychological warfare** military application of psychology, esp. to influence morale in time of war. **psychologically** *adv*.

psychopath ❶ *n* person afflicted with a personality disorder causing him or her to commit antisocial or violent acts. **psychopathic** *adj*.

psychosis ❶ *n, pl* **-ses** severe mental disorder in which the sufferer's contact with reality becomes distorted. **psychotic** *adj*.

psychosomatic *adj* (of a physical disorder) thought to have psychological causes.

psychotherapy *n* treatment of nervous disorders by psychological methods. **psychotherapeutic** *adj* **psychotherapist** *n*.

psych up *v* prepare (oneself) mentally for a contest or task.

pt 1 part. **2** point.

Pt *Chemistry* platinum.

PT *old-fashioned* physical training.

pt. pint.

PTA Parent-Teacher Association.

ptarmigan [**tar**-mig-an] *n* bird of the grouse family which turns white in winter.

pterodactyl [terr-roe-**dak**-til] *n* extinct flying reptile with batlike wings.

PTO please turn over.

ptomaine [**toe**-main] *n* any of a group of poisonous alkaloids found in decaying matter.

Pu *Chemistry* plutonium.

THESAURUS

phoney *or* phony (*inf*), pretended, sham, spurious

pseudonym *n* = **false name**, alias, assumed name, incognito, nom de plume, pen name

psyche *n* = **soul**, anima, individuality, mind, personality, self, spirit

psychiatrist *n* = **psychotherapist**, analyst, headshrinker (*sl*), psychoanalyst, psychologist, shrink (*sl*), therapist

psychic *adj* (also **psychical**)
1 = **supernatural**, mystic, occult ▷ *adj*
2 = **mental**, psychological, spiritual

psychological *adj* **1** = **mental**, cerebral, cognitive, intellectual

psychology *n* **1** = **behaviourism**, science of mind, study of personality
2 *Inf* = **way of thinking**, attitude, mental make-up, mental processes, thought processes, what makes one tick

psychopath *n* = **madman**, lunatic, maniac, nutcase (*sl*), nutter (*Brit sl*), psychotic, sociopath

psychotic *adj* = **mad**, certifiable, demented, deranged, insane, lunatic, mental (*sl*), *non compos mentis*, unbalanced

P

pub ❶ *n* building with a bar licensed to sell alcoholic drinks.

puberty ❶ [**pew**-ber-tee] *n* beginning of sexual maturity. **pubertal** *adj*.

pubescent *adj* **1** reaching or having reached puberty. **2** covered with fine short hairs or down, as some plants and animals. **pubescence** *n*.

pubic [**pew**-bik] *adj* of the lower abdomen, e.g. *pubic hair*.

pubis *n*, *pl* -**bes** one of the three sections of the hipbone that forms part of the pelvis.

public ❶ *adj* **1** of or concerning the people as a whole. **2** for use by everyone. **3** well-known. **4** performed or made openly. ▷ *n* **5** the community, people in general. **publicly** *adv* **public company** limited company whose shares may be purchased by the public. **public house** pub. **public relations** promotion of a favourable opinion towards an organization among the public. **public school** private fee-paying school in Britain. **public sector** part of a country's economy controlled and financially supported by the government. **public-spirited** *adj* having or showing an active interest in the good of the community.

publican *n* person who owns or runs a pub.

publicity ❶ *n* **1** process or information used to arouse public attention. **2** public interest so aroused. **publicize** *v* advertise. **publicist** *n* person, esp. a press agent or journalist, who publicizes something.

publish ❶ *v* **1** produce and issue (printed matter) for sale. **2** announce formally or in public. **publication** *n* **publisher** *n*.

puce *adj* purplish-brown.

puck[1] *n* small rubber disc used in ice hockey.

puck[2] *n* mischievous or evil spirit. **puckish** *adj*.

pucker ❶ *v* **1** gather into wrinkles. ▷ *n* **2** wrinkle or crease.

pudding ❶ *n* **1** dessert, esp. a cooked one served hot. **2** savoury dish with pastry or batter, e.g. *steak-and-kidney pudding*. **3** sausage-like mass of meat, e.g. *black pudding*.

puddle *n* small pool of water, esp. of rain.

pudenda *pl n* human external genital organs, esp. of a female.

puerile ❶ *adj* silly and childish.

puerperal [pew-**er**-per-al] *adj* concerning the period following childbirth.

puff ❶ *n* **1** (sound of) a short blast of breath, wind, etc. **2** act of inhaling cigarette smoke. ▷ *v* **3** blow or

---

pub *n* = **tavern**, bar, inn, beer parlour (*Canad*), beverage room (*Canad*)

puberty *n* = **adolescence**, pubescence, teens

public *adj* **1** = **general**, civic, common, national, popular, social, state, universal, widespread **2** = **open**, accessible, communal, unrestricted **3** = **well-known**, important, prominent, respected **4** = **known**, acknowledged, obvious, open, overt, patent, plain ▷ *n* **5** = **people**, citizens, community, electorate, everyone, nation, populace, society

publication *n* **1** = **pamphlet**, brochure, issue, leaflet, magazine, newspaper, periodical, title **2** = **announcement**, broadcasting, declaration, disclosure, notification, proclamation, publishing, reporting

publicity *n* **1** = **advertising**, attention, boost, hype, plug (*inf*), press, promotion

publicize *v* = **advertise**, hype, make

known, play up, plug (*inf*), promote, push

public-spirited *adj* = **altruistic**, charitable, humanitarian, philanthropic, unselfish

publish *v* **1** = **put out**, issue, print, produce **2** = **announce**, advertise, broadcast, circulate, disclose, divulge, proclaim, publicize, reveal, spread

pucker *v* **1** = **wrinkle**, contract, crease, draw together, gather, knit, purse, screw up, tighten ▷ *n* **2** = **wrinkle**, crease, fold

pudding *n* **1** = **dessert**, afters (*Brit inf*), pud (*inf*), sweet

puerile *adj* = **childish**, babyish, foolish, immature, juvenile, silly, trivial

puff *n* **1** = **blast**, breath, draught, gust, whiff **2** = **smoke**, drag (*sl*), pull ▷ *v* **3** = **blow**, breathe, exhale, gasp, gulp, pant, wheeze **4** = **smoke**, drag (*sl*), draw, inhale, pull at *or* on, suck **6** = **swell**, bloat, dilate, distend, expand, inflate

breathe in short quick draughts.
4 take draws at (a cigarette). **5** send
out in small clouds. **6** swell. **out of
puff** out of breath. **puffy** adj **puff
adder** large venomous African viper.
puffball n ball-shaped fungus. **puff
pastry** light flaky pastry.

puffin n black-and-white sea bird with
a brightly-coloured beak.

pug n small snub-nosed dog. **pug nose**
short stubby upturned nose.

pugilist ⊕ [pew-jil-ist] n boxer.
pugilism n **pugilistic** adj.

pugnacious adj ready and eager to
fight. **pugnacity** n.

puissance n showjumping
competition that tests a horse's ability
to jump large obstacles.

puke slang ▷ v **1** vomit. ▷ n **2** act of
vomiting. **3** vomited matter.

pukka adj Anglo-Indian **1** properly done,
constructed, etc. **2** genuine, real.

pulchritude n lit beauty.

pull ⊕ v **1** exert force on (an object) to
move it towards the source of the
force. **2** strain or stretch. **3** remove or
extract. **4** attract. ▷ n **5** act of pulling.
6 force used in pulling. **7** act of taking
in drink or smoke. **8** informal power,
influence. **pull oneself
together** informal regain one's self-
control. **pull in** v **1** (of a vehicle or
driver) draw in to the side of the road
or stop. **2** reach a destination.
3 attract in large numbers. **4** slang
arrest. **pull off** v informal succeed in
performing. **pull out** v **1** (of a vehicle
or driver) move away from the side of

the road or move out to overtake.
2 (of a train) depart. **3** withdraw.
4 remove by pulling. **pull through** v
survive or recover, esp. after a serious
illness. **pull up** v **1** (of a vehicle or
driver) stop. **2** remove by the roots.
3 reprimand.

pullet n young hen.

pulley n wheel with a grooved rim in
which a belt, chain, or piece of rope
runs in order to lift weights by a
downward pull.

Pullman n, pl **-mans** luxurious railway
coach.

pullover n sweater that is pulled on
over the head.

pulmonary adj of the lungs.

pulp ⊕ n **1** soft wet substance made
from crushed or beaten matter.
2 flesh of a fruit. **3** poor-quality books
and magazines. ▷ v **4** reduce to pulp.

pulpit n raised platform for a preacher.

pulsar n small dense star which emits
regular bursts of radio waves.

pulse¹ ⊕ n **1** regular beating of blood
through the arteries at each
heartbeat. **2** any regular beat or
vibration. **pulsate** v throb, quiver.
pulsation n.

pulse² n edible seed of a pod-bearing
plant such as a bean or pea.

pulverize ⊕ v **1** reduce to fine
pieces. **2** destroy completely.
pulverization n.

puma n large American wild cat with a
greyish-brown coat.

pumice [pumm-iss] n light porous
stone used for scouring.

P

THESAURUS

pugilist n = **boxer**, fighter,
prizefighter

pull v **1** = **draw**, drag, haul, jerk,
tow, trail, tug, yank **2** = **strain**,
dislocate, rip, sprain, stretch, tear,
wrench **3** = **extract**, draw out,
gather, pick, pluck, remove, take
out, uproot **4** = **attract**, draw, entice,
lure, magnetize ▷ n **5** = **tug**, jerk,
twitch, yank **7** = **puff**, drag (sl),
inhalation **8** Inf = **influence**, clout
(inf), mana (NZ), muscle, power,
weight

pull off v Inf = **succeed**, accomplish,
carry out, do the trick, manage

pull out v **2** = **depart**, leave, quit
3 = **withdraw**, evacuate, retreat

pull through v = **survive**, get better,
rally, recover

pull up v **1** = **stop**, brake, halt
3 = **reprimand**, admonish, bawl out
(inf), rap over the knuckles, read the
riot act, rebuke, reprove, rouse on
(Aust), slap on the wrist, tear
(someone) off a strip (Brit inf), tell off
(inf)

pulp n **1** = **paste**, mash, mush
2 = **flesh**, soft part ▷ v **4** = **crush**,
mash, pulverize, squash

pulsate v = **throb**, beat, palpitate,
pound, pulse, quiver, thump

pulse¹ n **1** = **beat**, beating, pulsation,
throb, throbbing **2** = **vibration**,
rhythm

pulverize v **1** = **crush**, granulate,
grind, mill, pound **2** = **defeat**,
annihilate, crush, demolish, destroy,
flatten, smash, wreck

pummel ❶ v **-melling, -melled** strike repeatedly with or as if with the fists.

pump¹ ❶ n **1** machine used to force a liquid or gas to move in a particular direction. ▷ v **2** raise or drive with a pump. **3** supply in large amounts. **4** operate or work in the manner of a pump. **5** extract information from.

pump² n light flat-soled shoe.

pumpernickel n sour black bread made of coarse rye flour.

pumpkin n large round fruit with an orange rind, soft flesh, and many seeds.

pun ❶ n **1** use of words to exploit double meanings for humorous effect. ▷ v **punning, punned 2** make puns.

punch¹ ❶ v **1** strike at with a clenched fist. ▷ n **2** blow with a clenched fist. **3** informal effectiveness or vigour. **punchy** adj **punchier, punchiest** forceful. **punch-drunk** adj dazed by or as if by repeated blows to the head. **punch line** line of a joke or funny story that gives it its point. **punch-up** n informal fight or brawl.

punch² ❶ n **1** tool or machine for shaping, piercing, or engraving. ▷ v **2** pierce, cut, stamp, shape, or drive with a punch.

punch³ n drink made from a mixture of wine, spirits, fruit, sugar, and spices.

punctilious ❶ adj **1** paying great attention to correctness in etiquette. **2** careful about small details.

punctual ❶ adj arriving or taking place at the correct time. **punctuality** n **punctually** adv.

punctuate ❶ v **1** put punctuation marks in. **2** interrupt at frequent intervals. **punctuation** n (use of) marks such as commas, colons, etc. in writing, to assist in making the sense clear. **punctuation mark** any of the signs used in punctuation, such as a comma.

puncture ❶ n **1** small hole made by a sharp object, esp. in a tyre. ▷ v **2** pierce a hole in.

pundit n expert who speaks publicly on a subject.

pungent ❶ adj having a strong sharp bitter flavour. **pungency** n.

punish ❶ v cause (someone) to suffer or undergo a penalty for some wrongdoing. **punishing** adj harsh or difficult. **punishment** n penalty or sanction given for any crime or offence.

punitive ❶ [pew-nit-tiv] adj relating to punishment.

punk n **1** anti-Establishment youth movement and style of rock music of the late 1970s. **2** follower of this music. **3** worthless person.

punkah n fan made of palm leaves.

punnet n small basket for fruit.

punt¹ n **1** open flat-bottomed boat propelled by a pole. ▷ v **2** travel in a punt.

punt² Sport ▷ n **1** kick of a ball before it touches the ground when dropped

─────── THESAURUS ───────

pummel v = **beat**, batter, hammer, pound, punch, strike, thump

pump v **2** = **drive**, force, inject, push **3** = **supply**, pour, send **5** = **interrogate**, cross-examine, probe, quiz

pun n **1** = **play on words**, double entendre, quip, witticism

punch¹ v **1** = **hit**, belt (inf), bop (inf), box, pummel, smash, sock (sl), strike, swipe (inf) ▷ n **2** = **blow**, bop (inf), hit, jab, sock (sl), swipe (inf), wallop (inf) **3** Inf = **effectiveness**, bite, drive, forcefulness, impact, verve, vigour

punch² v **2** = **pierce**, bore, cut, drill, perforate, prick, puncture, stamp

punctilious adj **1** = **formal**, proper **2** = **particular**, exact, finicky, fussy, meticulous, nice, precise, strict

punctual adj = **on time**, exact, on the dot, precise, prompt, timely

punctuate v **2** = **interrupt**, break, intersperse, pepper, sprinkle

puncture n **1 a** = **hole**, break, cut, damage, leak, nick, opening, slit **b** = **flat tyre**, flat ▷ v **2** = **pierce**, bore, cut, nick, penetrate, perforate, prick, rupture

pungent adj = **strong**, acrid, bitter, hot, peppery, piquant, sharp, sour, spicy, tart

punish v = **discipline**, castigate, chasten, chastise, correct, penalize, sentence

punishing adj = **hard**, arduous, backbreaking, exhausting, gruelling, strenuous, taxing, tiring, wearing

punishment n = **penalty**, chastening, chastisement, correction, discipline, penance, retribution

punitive adj = **retaliatory**, in reprisal, retaliative

from the hands. ▷ *v* **2** kick (a ball) in this way.

punt³ *n* monetary unit of the Irish Republic.

punter ❶ *n* **1** person who bets. **2** any member of the public.

puny ❶ *adj* **-nier, -niest** small and feeble.

pup *n* young of certain animals, such as dogs and seals.

pupa [**pew**-pa] *n*, *pl* **-pae, -pas** insect at the stage of development between a larva and an adult. **pupal** *adj*.

pupil¹ ❶ *n* person who is taught by a teacher.

pupil² *n* round dark opening in the centre of the eye.

puppet ❶ *n* **1** small doll or figure moved by strings or by the operator's hand. **2** person or country controlled by another. **puppeteer** *n*.

puppy *n*, *pl* **-pies** young dog. **puppy fat** fatty tissue in a child or adolescent, usu. disappearing with maturity.

purchase ❶ *v* **1** obtain by payment. ▷ *n* **2** thing that is bought. **3** act of buying. **4** leverage, grip. **purchaser** *n*.

purdah *n* Muslim and Hindu custom of keeping women in seclusion, with clothing that conceals them completely when they go out.

pure ❶ *adj* **1** unmixed, untainted. **2** innocent. **3** complete, e.g. *pure delight*. **4** concerned with theory only, e.g. *pure mathematics*. **purely** *adv* **purity** *n* **purify** *v* **-fying, -fied** make or become pure. **purification** *n* **purist** *n* person obsessed with strict obedience to the traditions of a subject.

purée [**pure**-ray] *n* **1** pulp of cooked food. ▷ *v* **-réeing, -réed 2** make into a purée.

purgatory *n* **1** place or state of temporary suffering. **2** (**P-**) *RC Church* place where souls of the dead undergo punishment for their sins before being admitted to Heaven. **purgatorial** *adj*.

purge ❶ *v* **1** rid (a thing or place) of (unwanted things or people). ▷ *n* **2** purging. **purgative** *n*, *adj* (medicine) designed to cause defecation.

Puritan ❶ *n* **1** *History* member of the English Protestant group who wanted simpler church ceremonies. **2** (**p-**) person with strict moral and religious principles. **puritanical** *adj* **puritanism** *n*.

purl *n* **1** stitch made by knitting a plain stitch backwards. ▷ *v* **2** knit in purl.

purlieus [**per**-lyooz] *pl n lit* outskirts.

———————————— **THESAURUS** ————————————

punter *n* **1** = **gambler**, backer, better **2** = **person**, man in the street

puny *adj* = **feeble**, frail, little, sickly, stunted, tiny, weak

pupil¹ *n* = **learner**, beginner, disciple, novice, schoolboy *or* schoolgirl, student

puppet *n* **1** = **marionette**, doll **2** = **pawn**, cat's-paw, instrument, mouthpiece, stooge, tool

purchase *v* **1** = **buy**, acquire, come by, gain, get, obtain, pay for, pick up, score (*sl*) ▷ *n* **2** = **buy**, acquisition, asset, gain, investment, possession, property **4** = **grip**, foothold, hold, leverage, support

pure *adj* **1 a** = **unmixed**, authentic, flawless, genuine, natural, real, simple, straight, unalloyed **b** = **clean**, germ-free, neat, sanitary, spotless, squeaky-clean, sterilized, uncontaminated, unpolluted, untainted, wholesome **2** = **innocent**, blameless, chaste, impeccable, modest, squeaky-clean, uncorrupted, unsullied, virginal, virtuous **3** = **complete**, absolute, outright, sheer, thorough, unmitigated, unqualified, utter

purge *v* **1** = **get rid of**, do away with, eradicate, expel, exterminate, remove, wipe out ▷ *n* **2** = **removal**, ejection, elimination, eradication, expulsion

purify *v* **a** = **clean**, clarify, cleanse, decontaminate, disinfect, refine, sanitize, wash **b** = **absolve**, cleanse, redeem, sanctify

puritan *n* **2** = **moralist**, fanatic, prude, rigorist, zealot

puritanical *adj* **2** = **strict**, ascetic, austere, moralistic, narrow-minded, prudish, severe, strait-laced

purity *n* **1** = **cleanness**, cleanliness, immaculateness, pureness, wholesomeness **2** = **innocence**, chastity, decency, honesty, integrity, virginity, virtue

P

purloin ❶ *v* steal.

purple *adj*, *n* (of) a colour between red and blue.

purport ❶ *v* **1** claim (to be or do something). ▷ *n* **2** apparent meaning, significance.

purpose ❶ *n* **1** reason for which something is done or exists. **2** determination. **3** practical advantage or use, e.g. *use the time to good purpose*. **purposeful** *adj* with a definite purpose, determined. **purposely** *adv* intentionally (also **on purpose**).

purr *v* **1** (of cats) make low vibrant sound, usu. when pleased. ▷ *n* **2** this sound.

purse ❶ *n* **1** small bag for money. **2** *US & Canad* handbag. **3** financial resources. **4** prize money. ▷ *v* **5** draw (one's lips) together into a small round shape. **purser** *n* ship's officer who keeps the accounts.

pursue ❶ *v* **1** chase. **2** follow (a goal). **3** engage in. **4** continue to discuss or ask about (something). **pursuer** *n* **pursuit** *n* **1** act of pursuing.

2 occupation or pastime.

purulent [**pure**-yoo-lent] *adj* of or containing pus.

purvey ❶ *v* supply (provisions). **purveyor** *n*.

purview *n* scope or range of activity or outlook.

pus *n* yellowish matter produced by infected tissue.

push ❶ *v* **1** move or try to move by steady force. **2** drive or spur (oneself or another person) to do something. **3** *informal* sell (drugs) illegally. ▷ *n* **4** act of pushing. **5** drive or determination. **6** special effort. **the push** *slang* dismissal from a job or relationship. **pusher** *n* person who sells illegal drugs. **pushy** *adj* **pushier**, **pushiest** too assertive or ambitious. **push-bike** *n informal*

---

purloin *v* = **steal**, appropriate, filch, nick (*sl, chiefly Brit*), pilfer, pinch (*inf*), swipe (*sl*), thieve

purport *v* **1** = **claim**, allege, assert, profess ▷ *n* **2** = **significance**, drift, gist, idea, implication, import, meaning

purpose *n* **1 a** = **aim**, ambition, desire, end, goal, hope, intention, object, plan, wish **b** = **reason**, aim, idea, intention, object, point
2 = **determination**, firmness, persistence, resolution, resolve, single-mindedness, tenacity, will

purposely *adv* (also **on purpose**) = **deliberately**, consciously, expressly, intentionally, knowingly, with intent

purse *n* **1** = **pouch**, money-bag, wallet **3** = **money**, exchequer, funds, lolly (*Aust & NZ inf*), means, resources, treasury, wealth ▷ *v* **5** = **pucker**, contract, pout, press together, tighten

pursue *v* **1** = **follow**, chase, dog, hound, hunt, hunt down, run after, shadow, stalk, tail (*inf*), track **2** = **try for**, aim for, desire, seek, strive for, work towards **3** = **engage in**, carry on, conduct, perform, practise **4** = **continue**, carry on, keep on,

maintain, persevere in, persist in, proceed

pursuit *n* **1** = **pursuing**, chase, hunt, quest, search, seeking, trailing
2 = **occupation**, activity, hobby, interest, line, pastime, pleasure

purvey *v* = **supply**, cater, deal in, furnish, provide, sell, trade in

push *v* **1** = **shove**, depress, drive, press, propel, ram, thrust **2** = **urge**, encourage, gee up, hurry, impel, incite, persuade, press, spur ▷ *n* **4** = **shove**, butt, nudge, thrust **5** = **drive**, ambition, dynamism, energy, enterprise, go (*inf*), initiative, vigour, vitality **the push** *Sl* = **dismissal**, discharge, one's cards (*inf*), the boot (*sl*), the sack (*inf*)

pushover *n Inf* **1** = **piece of cake** (*Brit inf*), breeze (*US & Canad inf*), child's play (*inf*), cinch (*sl*), doddle (*Brit sl*), picnic (*inf*), plain sailing, walkover (*inf*) ▷ *n* **2** = **sucker** (*sl*), easy game (*inf*), easy *or* soft mark (*inf*), mug (*Brit sl*), soft touch (*sl*), walkover (*inf*)

pushy *adj* **2** = **forceful**, ambitious, assertive, bold, brash, bumptious, obtrusive, presumptuous, self-assertive

bicycle. **pushchair** n folding chair on wheels for a baby. **pushover** n informal **1** something easily achieved. **2** person or team easily taken advantage of or defeated.

pusillanimous adj timid and cowardly. **pusillanimity** n.

puss, pussy n, pl **pusses**, **pussies** informal cat.

pussyfoot ⊕ v informal **1** move about stealthily. **2** behave too cautiously.

pustule n pimple containing pus.

put ⊕ v **putting, put 1** cause to be (in a position, state, or place). **2** estimate or judge. **3** express. **4** throw (the shot) in the shot put. ▷ n **5** throw in putting the shot. **put about** v make widely known. **put across** v express successfully. **put down** v **1** make a written record of. **2** repress (a rebellion). **3** put (an animal) to death. **4** slang belittle or humiliate. **put-down** n cruelly crushing remark. **put off** v **1** postpone. **2** evade (a person) by delay. **3** disconcert. **4** repel. **put out** v annoy or anger. **put over** v informal communicate (facts or information). **put up** v **1** erect. **2** accommodate. **3** offer. **4** nominate. **put up with** v tolerate. **put-upon** adj taken advantage of.

putative [**pew**-tat-iv] adj reputed, supposed.

putrid ⊕ adj rotten and foul-smelling. **putrefy** v **-fying, -fied** rot and produce an offensive smell. **putrefaction** n **putrescent** adj rotting.

putsch n sudden violent attempt to remove a government from power.

putt Golf ▷ n **1** stroke on the putting green to roll the ball into or near the hole. ▷ v **2** strike (the ball) in this way. **putter** n golf club for putting. **putting green** Golf area of closely mown grass around the hole.

putty n paste used to fix glass into frames and fill cracks in woodwork.

puzzle ⊕ v **1** perplex and confuse or be perplexed or confused. ▷ n **2** problem that cannot be easily solved. **3** toy, game, or question that requires skill or ingenuity to solve. **puzzlement** n **puzzled** adj **puzzling** adj.

PVC polyvinyl chloride: plastic material used in clothes etc.

Pygmy n, pl **-mies 1** member of one of the very short peoples of Equatorial Africa. **2** (**p-**) very small person or thing. ▷ adj **3** (**p-**) very small.

pygmy adj **1** very small. ▷ n, pl **-mies** very small person or thing.

pyjamas pl n loose-fitting trousers and top worn in bed.

pylon n steel tower-like structure supporting electrical cables.

P

THESAURUS

pussyfoot v Inf **2 = hedge**, beat about the bush, be noncommittal, equivocate, flannel (Brit inf), hum and haw, prevaricate, sit on the fence

put v **1 = place**, deposit, lay, position, rest, set, settle, situate **3 = express**, phrase, state, utter, word **4 = throw**, cast, fling, heave, hurl, lob, pitch, toss

put down v **1 = record**, enter, set down, take down, write down **2 = repress**, crush, quash, quell, stamp out, suppress **3 = put to sleep**, destroy, do away with, put out of its misery **4** Sl **= humiliate**, disparage, mortify, shame, slight, snub

put off v **1 = postpone**, defer, delay, hold over, put on the back burner (inf), take a rain check on (US & Canad inf) **3 = disconcert**, confuse, discomfit, dismay, faze, nonplus, perturb, throw (inf), unsettle **4 = discourage**,

dishearten, dissuade

putrid adj **= rotten**, bad, decayed, decomposed, off, putrefied, rancid, rotting, spoiled

put up v **1 = build**, construct, erect, fabricate, raise **2 = accommodate**, board, house, lodge, take in **3 = submit**, offer, present **4 = nominate**, propose, put forward, recommend **put up with** v **= stand**, abide, bear, endure, stand for, swallow, take, tolerate

puzzle v **1 = perplex**, baffle, bewilder, confound, confuse, mystify, stump ▷ n **2, 3 = problem**, conundrum, enigma, mystery, paradox, poser, question, riddle

puzzling adj **= perplexing**, abstruse, baffling, bewildering, enigmatic, incomprehensible, involved, mystifying

pyorrhoea [pire-**ree**-a] *n* disease of the gums and tooth sockets which causes bleeding of the gums and the formation of pus.

pyramid *n* **1** solid figure with a flat base and triangular sides sloping upwards to a point. **2** building of this shape, esp. an ancient Egyptian one. **pyramidal** *adj*.

pyre *n* pile of wood for burning a corpse on.

Pyrex *n* ® heat-resistant glassware.

pyromania *n* uncontrollable urge to set things on fire. **pyromaniac** *n*.

pyrotechnics *n* **1** art of making fireworks. **2** firework display. **pyrotechnic** *adj*.

Pyrrhic victory [**pir**-ik] *n* victory in which the victor's losses are as great as those of the defeated.

python *n* large nonpoisonous snake that crushes its prey.

QC Queen's Counsel.
QED which was to be shown or proved.
QLD Queensland.
QM Quartermaster.
qr. 1 quarter. 2 quire.
qt. quart.
q.t. n **on the q.t.** *informal* secretly.
qua [kwah] *prep* in the capacity of.
quack¹ *v* 1 (of a duck) utter a harsh guttural sound. 2 make a noise like a duck. ▷ *n* 3 sound made by a duck.
quack² ❶ *n* 1 unqualified person who claims medical knowledge. 2 *informal* doctor.
quad *n* 1 see QUADRANGLE (sense 1) 2 *informal* quadruplet. ▷ *adj* 3 short for QUADRAPHONIC. **quad bike** vehicle like a small motorcycle with four large wheels, designed for agricultural and sporting uses.
quadrangle *n* 1 (also **quad**) rectangular courtyard with buildings on all four sides. 2 geometric figure consisting of four points connected by four lines. **quadrangular** *adj*.
quadrant *n* 1 quarter of a circle. 2 quarter of a circle's circumference. 3 instrument for measuring the altitude of the stars.
quadraphonic *adj* using four independent channels to reproduce or record sound.

quadratic *Maths* ▷ *n* 1 equation in which the variable is raised to the power of two, but nowhere raised to a higher power. ▷ *adj* 2 of the second power.
quadrennial *adj* 1 occurring every four years. 2 lasting four years.
quadri- *combining form* four, e.g. *quadrilateral*.
quadrilateral *adj* 1 having four sides. ▷ *n* 2 polygon with four sides.
quadrille *n* square dance for four couples.
quadriplegia *n* paralysis of all four limbs. **quadriplegic** *adj*.
quadruped *n* any animal with four legs, such as a dog.
quadruple *v* 1 multiply by four. ▷ *adj* 2 four times as much or as many. 3 consisting of four parts.
quadruplet *n* one of four offspring born at one birth.
quaff ❶ [kwoff] *v* drink heartily or in one draught.
quagga *n, pl* **-ga, -gas** recently extinct zebra, striped only on the head and shoulders.
quagmire ❶ [kwog-mire] *n* soft wet area of land.
quail¹ *n, pl* **quail, quails** small game bird of the partridge family.
quail² ❶ *v* shrink back with fear.
quaint ❶ *adj* attractively unusual, esp. in an old-fashioned style. **quaintly** *adv*.
quake ❶ *v* 1 shake or tremble with or as if with fear. ▷ *n* 2 *informal* earthquake.
Quaker *n* member of a Christian sect, the Society of Friends. **Quakerism** *n*.
qualify ❶ *v* **-fying, -fied** 1 provide or be provided with the abilities necessary for a task, office, or duty. 2 moderate

q

——————————— THESAURUS ———————————

quack² *n* 1 = **charlatan**, fake, fraud, humbug, impostor, mountebank, phoney *or* phony (*inf*)
quaff *v* = **drink**, down, gulp, imbibe, swallow, swig (*inf*)
quagmire *n* = **bog**, fen, marsh, mire, morass, quicksand, slough, swamp, muskeg (*Canad*)
quail² *v* = **shrink**, blanch, blench, cower, cringe, falter, flinch, have cold feet (*inf*), recoil, shudder
quaint *adj* = **old-fashioned**, antiquated, old-world, picturesque
quake *v* 1 = **shake**, move, quiver, rock, shiver, shudder, tremble, vibrate

qualification *n* 2 = **attribute**, ability, aptitude, capability, eligibility, fitness, quality, skill, suitability 3 = **condition**, caveat, limitation, modification, proviso, requirement, reservation, rider, stipulation
qualified *adj* 1 = **capable**, able, adept, competent, efficient, experienced, expert, fit, practised, proficient, skilful, trained 2 = **restricted**, bounded, conditional, confined, contingent, limited, modified, provisional, reserved
qualify *v* 1 = **certify**, empower, equip, fit, permit, prepare, ready, train

or restrict (a statement). **3** be classified as, e.g. *their romance hardly qualifies as news.* **4** reach the later stages of a competition, as by being successful in earlier rounds. **5** *Grammar* modify the sense of a word. **qualified** *adj* **qualifier** *n* **qualification** *n* **1** official record of achievement in a course or examination. **2** quality or skill needed for a particular activity. **3** condition that modifies or limits. **4** act of qualifying.

quality ❶ *n, pl* **-ties 1** degree or standard of excellence. **2** distinguishing characteristic or attribute. **3** basic character or nature of something. ▷ *adj* **4** excellent or superior. **5** (of a newspaper) concentrating on detailed and serious accounts of the news, business affairs and the arts. **qualitative** *adj* of or relating to quality. **quality control** checking of the relative quality of products, usu. by testing samples.

qualm ❶ [kwahm] *n* **1** pang of conscience. **2** sudden sensation of misgiving.

quandary ❶ *n, pl* **-ries** difficult situation or dilemma.

quandong [kwon-dong] *n* **1** small Australian tree with edible fruit and nuts used in preserves. **2** Australian tree with pale timber.

quango *n, pl* **-gos** quasi-autonomous nongovernmental organization: any partly independent official body set up by a government.

quanta *n* plural of QUANTUM.

quantify *v* **-fying, -fied** discover or express the quantity of. **quantifiable**

adj **quantification** *n*.

quantity ❶ *n, pl* **-ties 1** specified or definite amount or number. **2** aspect of anything that can be measured, weighed, or counted. **3** large amount. **quantitative** *adj* of or relating to quantity. **quantity surveyor** person who estimates the cost of the materials and labour necessary for a construction job.

quantum *n, pl* **-ta 1** desired or required amount, esp. a very small one. **2** *Physics* smallest amount of some physical property, such as energy, that a system can possess. **quantum leap, jump** *informal* sudden large change, increase, or advance. **quantum theory** physics theory based on the idea that energy of electrons is discharged in discrete quanta.

quarantine *n* **1** period of isolation of people or animals to prevent the spread of disease. ▷ *v* **2** isolate in or as if in quarantine.

quark *n Physics* subatomic particle thought to be the fundamental unit of matter.

quarrel ❶ *n* **1** angry disagreement. **2** cause of dispute. ▷ *v* **-relling, -relled 3** have a disagreement or dispute. **quarrelsome** *adj*.

quarry¹ *n, pl* **-ries 1** place where stone is dug from the surface of the earth. ▷ *v* **-rying, -ried 2** extract (stone) from a quarry.

quarry² ❶ *n, pl* **-ries** person or animal that is being hunted.

quart *n* unit of liquid measure equal to two pints.

————————— THESAURUS —————————

2 = moderate, diminish, ease, lessen, limit, reduce, regulate, restrain, restrict, soften, temper

quality *n* **1 = excellence**, calibre, distinction, grade, merit, position, rank, standing, status **2 = characteristic**, aspect, attribute, condition, feature, mark, property, trait **3 = nature**, character, kind, make, sort

qualm *n* **1 = compunction**, scruple, twinge *or* pang of conscience **2 = misgiving**, anxiety, apprehension, disquiet, doubt, hesitation, uneasiness

quandary *n* **= difficulty**, cleft stick, dilemma, impasse, plight,

predicament, puzzle, strait

quantity *n* **1 = amount**, lot, number, part, sum, total **2 = size**, bulk, capacity, extent, length, magnitude, mass, measure, volume

quarrel *n* **1 = disagreement**, argument, brawl, breach, contention, controversy, dispute, dissension, feud, fight, row, squabble, tiff ▷ *v* **3 = disagree**, argue, bicker, brawl, clash, differ, dispute, fall out (*inf*), fight, row, squabble

quarrelsome *adj* **= argumentative**, belligerent, combative, contentious, disputatious, pugnacious

quarry² *n* **= prey**, aim, game, goal, objective, prize, victim

quarter ❶ *n* **1** one of four equal parts of something. **2** fourth part of a year. **3** *informal* unit of weight equal to 4 ounces. **4** region or district of a town or city. **5** *US* 25-cent piece. **6** mercy or pity, as shown towards a defeated opponent. **7** either of two phases of the moon when it appears as a semicircle. **8** (sometimes pl) unspecified people or group of people, e.g. *the highest quarters*. ▷ *pl* **9** lodgings. ▷ *v* **10** divide into four equal parts. **11** billet or be billeted in lodgings. **quarterly** *adj* **1** occurring, due, or issued at intervals of three months. ▷ *n, pl* **-lies 2** magazine issued every three months. ▷ *adv* **3** once every three months.
quarterback *n* player in American football who directs attacking play.
quarter day any of the four days in the year when certain payments become due. **quarterdeck** *n Nautical* rear part of the upper deck of a ship. **quarterfinal** *n* round before the semifinal in a competition. **quarterlight** *n* small triangular window in the door of a car. **quartermaster** *n* military officer responsible for accommodation, food, and equipment.
quartet *n* **1** group of four performers. **2** music for such a group. **3** any group of four people or things.
quarto *n, pl* **-tos** book size in which the sheets are folded into four leaves.
quartz *n* hard glossy mineral. **quartz clock, watch** very accurate clock *or* watch operated by a vibrating crystal of quartz.
quasar [**kway**-zar] *n* any of a class of extremely distant starlike objects that emit powerful radio waves.
quash ❶ *v* **1** annul or make void. **2** subdue forcefully and completely.
quasi- ❶ [**kway**-zie] *combining form* almost but not really, e.g. *quasi-religious*; *a quasi-scholar*.
quassia [**kwosh**-a] *n* tropical American tree, the wood of which yields a substance used in insecticides.
quaternary *adj* having four parts.
quatrain *n* stanza or poem of four lines.
quatrefoil *n* **1** leaf composed of four leaflets. **2** *Architecture* carved ornament having four arcs arranged about a common centre.
quaver ❶ *v* **1** (of a voice) quiver or tremble. ▷ *n* **2** *Music* note half the length of a crotchet. **3** tremulous sound or note.
quay [**kee**] *n* wharf built parallel to the shore.
queasy ❶ *adj* **-sier**, **-siest 1** having the feeling that one is about to vomit. **2** feeling or causing uneasiness. **queasily** *adv* **queasiness** *n*.
queen ❶ *n* **1** female sovereign who is the official ruler or head of state. **2** wife of a king. **3** woman, place, or thing considered to be the best of her or its kind. **4** *slang* effeminate male homosexual. **5** only fertile female in a colony of bees, wasps, or ants. **6** the most powerful piece in chess. **queen it** *informal* behave in an overbearing manner. **queenly** *adj* **Queen Mother** widow of a former king who is also the mother of the current monarch. **Queen's Counsel** barrister or advocate appointed Counsel to the Crown.

q

quarter *n* **4** = **district**, area, locality, neighbourhood, part, place, province, region, side, zone **6** = **mercy**, clemency, compassion, forgiveness, leniency, pity ▷ *pl* **9** = **lodgings**, abode, barracks, billet, chambers, dwelling, habitation, residence, rooms ▷ *v* **11** = **accommodate**, billet, board, house, lodge, place, post, station
quash *v* **1** = **annul**, cancel, invalidate, overrule, overthrow, rescind, reverse, revoke **2** = **suppress**, beat, crush, overthrow, put down, quell, repress, squash, subdue
quasi- *combining form* = **pseudo-**, apparent, seeming, semi-, so-called, would-be
quaver *v* **1** = **tremble**, flicker, flutter, quake, quiver, shake, vibrate, waver ▷ *n* **3** = **trembling**, quiver, shake, tremble, tremor, vibration
queasy *adj* **1** = **sick**, bilious, green around the gills (*inf*), ill, nauseated, off colour, squeamish, upset **2** = **uneasy**, anxious, fidgety, ill at ease, restless, troubled, uncertain, worried
queen *n* **1** = **sovereign**, consort, monarch, ruler **3** = **ideal**, model, star

Queensberry rules *pl n* **1** code of rules followed in modern boxing. **2** *informal* gentlemanly conduct, esp. in a dispute.

queer ❶ *adj* **1** not normal or usual. **2** dubious or suspicious. **3** faint, giddy, or queasy. **4** *offens* homosexual. ▷ *n* **5** *offens* homosexual. **queer someone's pitch** *informal* spoil someone's chances of something. **in queer street** *informal* in debt or facing bankruptcy.

quell ❶ *v* **1** suppress. **2** overcome.

quench ❶ *v* **1** satisfy (one's thirst). **2** put out or extinguish.

quern *n* stone hand mill for grinding corn.

querulous ❶ [**kwer**-yoo-luss] *adj* complaining or whining. **querulously** *adv*.

query ❶ *n, pl* **-ries 1** question, esp. one raising doubt. **2** question mark. ▷ *v* **-rying, -ried 3** express uncertainty, doubt, or an objection concerning (something).

quest ❶ *n* **1** long and difficult search. ▷ *v* **2** (foll. by *for* or *after*) go in search of.

question ❶ *n* **1** form of words addressed to a person in order to obtain an answer. **2** point at issue. **3** difficulty or uncertainty. ▷ *v* **4** put a question or questions to (a person).

5 express uncertainty about. **in question** under discussion. **out of the question** impossible.

questionable *adj* of disputable value or authority. **questionably** *adv*

questionnaire *n* set of questions on a form, used to collect information from people. **question mark 1** punctuation mark (?) written at the end of questions. **2** a doubt or uncertainty, e.g. *a question mark still hangs over their success*. **question master** chairman of a radio or television quiz or panel game. **question time** (in a parliament) period when MPs can question government ministers.

● **SPELLING TIP**
● There are 28 occurrences of the
● misspelling *questionaire* (with only
● one *n*) in the Bank of English. The
● correct spelling, **questionnaire**,
● has two *n*s, and appears in the Bank
● of English over 3000 times.

queue ❶ *n* **1** line of people or vehicles waiting for something. ▷ *v* **queuing** or **queueing, queued 2** (often foll. by *up*) form or remain in a line while waiting.

quibble ❶ *v* **1** make trivial objections. ▷ *n* **2** trivial objection.

quiche [**keesh**] *n* savoury flan with an egg custard filling to which vegetables etc. are added.

━━━━━━━━━━━━━━━━━━━━━ THESAURUS ━━━━━

queer *adj* **1** = **strange**, abnormal, curious, droll, extraordinary, funny, munted (*NZ sl*), odd, peculiar, uncommon, unusual, weird **3** = **faint**, dizzy, giddy, light-headed, queasy

quell *v* **1, 2** = **suppress**, conquer, crush, defeat, overcome, overpower, put down, quash, subdue, vanquish

quench *v* **1** = **satisfy**, allay, appease, sate, satiate, slake **2** = **put out**, crush, douse, extinguish, smother, stifle, suppress

querulous *adj* = **complaining**, captious, carping, critical, discontented, dissatisfied, fault-finding, grumbling, peevish, whining

query *n* **1** = **question**, doubt, inquiry, objection, problem, suspicion ▷ *v* **3** = **doubt**, challenge, disbelieve, dispute, distrust, mistrust, question, suspect

quest *n* **1** = **search**, adventure, crusade, enterprise, expedition,

fossick (*Aust & NZ*), hunt, journey, mission

question *n* **2** = **issue**, motion, point, point at issue, proposal, proposition, subject, theme, topic **3** = **difficulty**, argument, contention, controversy, dispute, doubt, problem, query ▷ *v* **4** = **ask**, cross-examine, examine, inquire, interrogate, interview, probe, quiz **5** = **dispute**, challenge, disbelieve, doubt, mistrust, oppose, query, suspect **in question** = **under discussion**, at issue, in doubt, open to debate **out of the question** = **impossible**, inconceivable, unthinkable

questionable *adj* = **dubious**, controversial, debatable, dodgy (*Brit, Aust & NZ inf*), doubtful, iffy (*inf*), moot, suspect, suspicious

queue *n* **1** = **line**, chain, file, sequence, series, string, train

quibble *v* **1** = **split hairs**, carp, cavil ▷ *n* **2** = **objection**, cavil, complaint, criticism, nicety, niggle

quick ❶ *adj* **1** speedy, fast. **2** lasting or taking a short time. **3** alert and responsive. **4** easily excited or aroused. ▷ *n* **5** area of sensitive flesh under a nail. ▷ *adv* **6** *informal* in a rapid manner. **cut someone to the quick** hurt someone's feelings deeply. **quickly** *adv* **quicken** *v* **1** make or become faster. **2** make or become more lively. **3** (of a fetus) reach the stage of development where its movements can be felt. **quickie** *n* *informal* anything done or made hurriedly. **quicklime** *n* white solid used in the manufacture of glass and steel. **quicksand** *n* deep mass of loose wet sand that sucks anything on top of it into it. **quicksilver** *n* mercury. **quickstep** *n* fast modern ballroom dance.

quid¹ *n*, *pl* **quid** *Brit slang* pound (sterling).

quid² *n* piece of tobacco for chewing.

quid pro quo *n*, *pl* **quid pro quos** one thing, esp. an advantage or object, given in exchange for another.

quiescent [kwee-**ess**-ent] *adj* quiet, inactive, or dormant. **quiescence** *n*.

quiet ❶ *adj* **1** with little noise. **2** calm or tranquil. **3** untroubled. **4** private or low-key. ▷ *n* **5** quietness. ▷ *v* **6** make or become quiet. **on the quiet** without other people knowing, secretly. **quietly** *adv* **quietness** *n* **quieten** *v* (often foll. by *down*) make or

become quiet. **quietude** *n* quietness, peace, or tranquillity.

quietism *n* passivity and calmness of mind towards external events. **quietist** *n*, *adj*.

quietus *n* **1** release from life; death. **2** discharge or settlement of debts or duties.

quiff *n* tuft of hair brushed up above the forehead.

quill *n* **1** pen made from the feather of a bird's wing or tail. **2** stiff hollow spine of a hedgehog or porcupine. **3** large stiff feather in a bird's wing or tail.

quilt ❶ *n* padded covering for a bed. **quilted** *adj* consisting of two layers of fabric with a layer of soft material between them.

quin *n* short for QUINTUPLET.

quince *n* acid-tasting pear-shaped fruit.

quinine *n* bitter drug used as a tonic and formerly to treat malaria.

quinquennial *adj* **1** occurring every five years. **2** lasting five years.

quinquereme *n* ancient Roman galley with five banks of oars.

quinsy *n* inflammation of the throat or tonsils.

quintessence ❶ *n* most perfect representation of a quality or state. **quintessential** *adj*.

quintet *n* **1** group of five performers. **2** music for such a group.

quintuple *v* **1** multiply by five. ▷ *adj*

THESAURUS

quick *adj* **1** = **fast**, brisk, express, fleet, hasty, rapid, speedy, swift **2** = **brief**, cursory, hasty, hurried, perfunctory **3** = **intelligent**, acute, alert, astute, bright (*inf*), clever, perceptive, quick-witted, sharp, shrewd, smart **4** = **excitable**, irascible, irritable, passionate, testy, touchy

quicken *v* **1** = **speed**, accelerate, expedite, hasten, hurry, impel, precipitate **2** = **invigorate**, arouse, energize, excite, incite, inspire, revive, stimulate, vitalize

quickly *adv* = **swiftly**, abruptly, apace, briskly, fast, hastily, hurriedly, promptly, pronto (*inf*), rapidly, soon, speedily

quiet *adj* **1** = **silent**, hushed, inaudible, low, noiseless, peaceful, soft, soundless **2, 3** = **calm**, mild, peaceful, placid, restful, serene, smooth,

tranquil **4** = **undisturbed**, isolated, private, secluded, sequestered, unfrequented ▷ *n* **5** = **peace**, calmness, ease, quietness, repose, rest, serenity, silence, stillness, tranquillity

quieten *v* (often foll. by *down*) = **silence**, compose, hush, muffle, mute, quell, quiet, stifle, still, stop, subdue

quietly *adv* **1** = **silently**, in an undertone, inaudibly, in silence, mutely, noiselessly, softly **2** = **calmly**, mildly, patiently, placidly, serenely

quilt *n* = **bedspread**, continental quilt, counterpane, coverlet, duvet, eiderdown

quintessence *n* = **essence**, distillation, soul, spirit

quintessential *adj* = **ultimate**, archetypal, definitive, typical

q

2 five times as much or as many.
3 consisting of five parts. ▷ n
4 quantity or number five times as great as another.

quintuplet n one of five offspring born at one birth.

quip ❶ n 1 witty saying. ▷ v **quipping**, **quipped** 2 make a quip.

quire n set of 24 or 25 sheets of paper.

quirk ❶ n 1 peculiarity of character.
2 unexpected twist or turn, e.g. a quirk of fate. **quirky** adj **quirkier**, **quirkiest**.

quisling n traitor who aids an occupying enemy force.

quit ❶ v **quitting**, **quit 1** stop (doing something). **2** give up (a job). **3** depart from. **quitter** n person who lacks perseverance. **quits** adj informal on an equal footing.

quite ❶ adv 1 somewhat, e.g. she's quite pretty. **2** absolutely, e.g. you're quite right. **3** in actuality, truly. ▷ interj 4 expression of agreement.

quiver¹ ❶ v 1 shake with a tremulous movement. ▷ n 2 shaking or trembling.

quiver² n case for arrows.

quixotic ❶ [kwik-**sot**-ik] adj romantic and unrealistic. **quixotically** adv.

quiz ❶ n, pl **quizzes 1** entertainment in which the knowledge of the players is tested by a series of questions. ▷ v **quizzing**, **quizzed 2** investigate

by close questioning. **quizzical** adj questioning and mocking, e.g. a quizzical look. **quizzically** adv.

quod n Brit slang jail.

quoin n 1 external corner of a building. **2** small wedge.

quoit n 1 large ring used in the game of quoits. ▷ pl 2 game in which quoits are tossed at a stake in the ground in attempts to encircle it.

quondam adj formal of an earlier time; former.

quorum n minimum number of people required to be present at a meeting before any transactions can take place. **quorate** adj having or being a quorum.

quota ❶ n 1 share that is due from, due to, or allocated to a group or person. **2** prescribed number or quantity allowed, required, or admitted.

quote ❶ v 1 repeat (words) exactly from (an earlier work, speech, or conversation). **2** state (a price) for goods or a job of work. ▷ n **3** informal quotation. **quotable** adj **quotation** n 1 written or spoken passage repeated exactly in a later work, speech, or conversation. **2** act of quoting. **3** estimate of costs submitted by a contractor to a prospective client. **quotation marks** raised commas used in writing to mark the beginning and

q

quip n 1 = **joke**, gibe, jest, pleasantry, retort, riposte, sally, wisecrack (inf), witticism

quirk n 1 = **peculiarity**, aberration, characteristic, eccentricity, foible, habit, idiosyncrasy, kink, mannerism, oddity, trait

quirky adj = **odd**, eccentric, idiosyncratic, offbeat, peculiar, unusual

quit v 1 = **stop**, abandon, cease, discontinue, drop, end, give up, halt **2** = **resign**, abdicate, go, leave, pull out, retire, step down (inf) **3** = **depart**, go, leave, pull out

quite adv 1 = **somewhat**, fairly, moderately, rather, reasonably, relatively **2** = **absolutely**, completely, entirely, fully, perfectly, totally, wholly **3** = **truly**, in fact, in reality, in truth, really

quiver¹ v 1 = **shake**, oscillate, quake,

quaver, shiver, shudder, tremble, vibrate ▷ n 2 = **shake**, oscillation, shiver, shudder, tremble, tremor, vibration

quixotic adj = **unrealistic**, dreamy, fanciful, idealistic, impractical, romantic

quiz n 1 = **examination**, investigation, questioning, test ▷ v 2 = **question**, ask, examine, interrogate, investigate

quizzical adj = **mocking**, arch, questioning, sardonic, teasing

quota n 1 = **share**, allowance, assignment, part, portion, ration, slice, whack (inf)

quotation n 1 = **passage**, citation, excerpt, extract, quote (inf), reference **3** = **estimate**, charge, cost, figure, price, quote (inf), rate, tender

quote v 1 = **repeat**, cite, detail, instance, name, recall, recite, recollect, refer to

end of a quotation or passage of speech.

quoth *v obs* said.

quotidian *adj* **1** daily. **2** commonplace.

quotient *n* result of the division of one number or quantity by another.

Quran *n* same as KORAN.

q.v. which see: used to refer a reader to another item in the same book.

qwerty, QWERTY keyboard *n* standard English language typewriter or computer keyboard.

Rr

r 1 radius. **2** ratio. **3** right.

R 1 Queen. **2** King. **3** River.

Ra *Chemistry* radium.

RA 1 Royal Academy. **2** Royal Artillery.

rabbi [**rab**-bye] *n, pl* **-bis** Jewish spiritual leader. **rabbinical** *adj*.

rabbit *n* small burrowing mammal with long ears. **rabbit on** *v* **rabbiting**, **rabbited** *informal* talk too much.

rabble ❶ *n* disorderly crowd of noisy people. **rabble-rouser** *n* person who stirs up the feelings of the mob.

Rabelaisian *adj* characterized by broad, often bawdy humour and sharp satire.

rabid ❶ *adj* **1** fanatical. **2** having rabies. **rabidly** *adv*.

rabies [**ray**-beez] *n* usu. fatal viral disease transmitted by dogs and certain other animals.

RAC Royal Automobile Club.

raccoon *n* small N American mammal with a long striped tail.

race¹ ❶ *n* **1** contest of speed. **2** any competition or rivalry, e.g. *the arms race*. **3** rapid current or channel. ▷ *pl* **4** meeting for horse racing. ▷ *v* **5** compete with in a race. **6** run swiftly. **7** (of an engine) run faster than normal. **racer** *n* **racecourse** *n* **racehorse** *n* **racetrack** *n*.

race² ❶ *n* group of people of common ancestry with distinguishing physical features, such as skin colour. **racial** *adj*

racism, **racialism** *n* hostile attitude or behaviour to members of other races, based on a belief in the innate superiority of one's own race. **racist**, **racialist** *adj, n*.

raceme [rass-**eem**] *n* cluster of flowers along a central stem, as in the foxglove.

rack¹ ❶ *n* **1** framework for holding particular articles, such as coats or luggage. **2** straight bar with teeth on its edge, to work with a cogwheel. **3** *History* instrument of torture that stretched the victim's body. ▷ *v* **4** cause great suffering to. **rack one's brains** try very hard to remember.

rack² *n* **go to rack and ruin** be destroyed.

racket¹ ❶ *n* **1** noisy disturbance. **2** occupation by which money is made illegally. **3** *slang* business or occupation. ▷ *v* **-eting**, **-eted 4** (often foll. by *about* or *around*) make a commotion.

racket², **racquet** *n* bat with strings stretched in an oval frame, used in tennis etc. **rackets** *n* ball game played in a paved walled court.

racketeer *n* person making illegal profits. **racketeering** *n*.

raconteur [rak-on-**tur**] *n* skilled storyteller.

racoon *n* same as RACCOON.

racy ❶ *adj* **racier**, **raciest 1** slightly shocking. **2** spirited or lively. **racily** *adv*.

radar *n* device for tracking distant objects by bouncing high-frequency radio pulses off them.

raddled *adj* (of a person) unkempt or run-down in appearance.

radial *adj* **1** spreading out from a common central point. **2** of a radius. **3** (also **radial-ply**) (of a tyre) having

---

THESAURUS ▷

rabble *n* = **mob**, canaille, crowd, herd, horde, swarm, throng

rabid *adj* **1** = **fanatical**, extreme, fervent, irrational, narrow-minded, zealous **2** = **mad**, hydrophobic

race¹ *n* **1, 2** = **contest**, chase, competition, dash, pursuit, rivalry ▷ *v* **5** = **compete**, contest, run **6** = **run**, career, dart, dash, fly, gallop, hurry, speed, tear, zoom

race² *n* = **people**, blood, folk, nation, stock, tribe, type

racial *adj* = **ethnic**, ethnological, folk,

genealogical, genetic, national, tribal

rack¹ *n* **1** = **frame**, framework, stand, structure ▷ *v* **4** = **torture**, afflict, agonize, crucify, harrow, oppress, pain, torment

racket¹ *n* **1** = **noise**, clamour, din, disturbance, fuss, outcry, pandemonium, row **2** = **fraud**, scheme

racy *adj* **1** = **risqué**, bawdy, blue, naughty, near the knuckle (*inf*), smutty, suggestive **2** = **lively**, animated, energetic, entertaining, exciting, sparkling, spirited

flexible sides strengthened with radial cords.

radian *n* unit for measuring angles, equal to 57.296°.

radiant ❶ *adj* **1** looking happy. **2** shining. **3** emitted as radiation, e.g. *radiant heat.* **4** emitting radiation. **radiantly** *adv* **radiance** *n*.

radiate ❶ *v* **1** spread out from a centre. **2** show (an emotion or quality) to a great degree. **3** emit or be emitted as radiation. **radiator** *n* **1** arrangement of pipes containing hot water or steam to heat a room. **2** tubes containing water as cooling apparatus for a car engine.

radiation *n* **1** transmission of energy from one body to another. **2** particles or waves emitted in nuclear decay. **3** process of radiating. **radiation sickness** illness caused by overexposure to radioactive material or x-rays.

radical ❶ *adj* **1** fundamental. **2** thorough. **3** advocating fundamental change. ▷ *n* **4** person advocating fundamental (political) change. **5** number expressed as the root of another. **6** group of atoms which acts as a unit during chemical reactions. **radically** *adv* **radicalism** *n*.

radicle *n* small or developing root.

radii *n* a plural of RADIUS.

radio *n, pl* **-dios** **1** use of electromagnetic waves for broadcasting, communication, etc. **2** device for receiving and amplifying radio signals. **3** communications device for sending and receiving messages using radio waves. **4** sound broadcasting. ▷ *v* **5** transmit (a message) by radio. ▷ *adj* **6** of, relating to, or using radio, e.g. *radio drama.* **radio-controlled** *adj* controlled by signals sent by radio. **radio telephone**

telephone which sends and receives messages using radio waves rather than wires. **radio telescope** instrument which picks up and analyses radio signals from space.

radio- *combining form* of radio, radiation, or radioactivity.

radioactive *adj* emitting radiation as a result of nuclear decay. **radioactivity** *n*.

radiocarbon *n* radioactive form of carbon used in calculating the age of very old objects.

radiography [ray-dee-**og**-ra-fee] *n* production of an image on a film or plate by radiation. **radiographer** *n*.

radioisotope *n* radioactive isotope.

radiology [ray-dee-**ol**-a-jee] *n* science of using x-rays in medicine. **radiologist** *n*.

radiotherapy *n* treatment of disease, esp. cancer, by radiation. **radiotherapist** *n*.

radish *n* small hot-flavoured root vegetable eaten raw in salads.

radium *n Chemistry* radioactive metallic element.

radius *n, pl* **radii, radiuses** **1** (length of) a straight line from the centre to the circumference of a circle. **2** outer of two bones in the forearm. **3** circular area of a specified size round a central point, e.g. *everyone within a two-mile radius.*

radon [ray-don] *n Chemistry* radioactive gaseous element.

RAF Royal Air Force.

raffia *n* prepared palm fibre for weaving mats etc.

raffish *adj* slightly disreputable.

raffle ❶ *n* **1** lottery with goods as prizes. ▷ *v* **2** offer as a prize in a raffle.

raft *n* floating platform of logs, planks, etc.

---

radiance *n* **1** = **happiness**, delight, gaiety, joy, pleasure, rapture, warmth **2** = **brightness**, brilliance, glare, gleam, glow, light, lustre, shine

radiant *adj* **1** = **happy**, blissful, delighted, ecstatic, glowing, joyful, joyous, on cloud nine (*inf*), rapturous **2** = **bright**, brilliant, gleaming, glittering, glowing, luminous, lustrous, shining

radiate *v* **1** = **spread out**, branch out, diverge, issue **3** = **emit**, diffuse, give

off *or* out, pour, scatter, send out, shed, spread

radical *adj* **1** = **fundamental**, basic, deep-seated, innate, natural, profound **2** = **extreme**, complete, drastic, entire, severe, sweeping, thorough **3** = **revolutionary**, extremist, fanatical ▷ *n* **4** = **extremist**, fanatic, militant, revolutionary

raffle *n* **1** = **draw**, lottery, sweep, sweepstake

rafter n one of the main beams of a roof.

rag¹ ⓘ n **1** fragment of cloth. **2** informal newspaper. ▷ pl **3** tattered clothing. **from rags to riches** from being extremely poor to being extremely wealthy. **ragged** [rag-gid] adj **1** dressed in shabby or torn clothes. **2** torn. **3** lacking smoothness. **ragbag** n confused assortment, jumble.

rag² v **ragging, ragged 1** tease. **2** play practical jokes on. ▷ adj, n **3** (of) events organized by students to raise money for charities.

ragamuffin ⓘ n ragged dirty child.

rage ⓘ n **1** violent anger or passion. **2** aggressive behaviour associated with a certain activity, e.g. traffic rage. ▷ v **3** speak or act with fury. **4** proceed violently and without check, e.g. a storm was raging. **all the rage** very popular.

raglan adj (of a sleeve) joined to a garment by diagonal seams from the neck to the underarm.

ragout [rag-**goo**] n richly seasoned stew of meat and vegetables.

ragtime n style of jazz piano music.

raid ⓘ n **1** sudden surprise attack or search. ▷ v **2** make a raid on. **3** sneak into (a place) in order to steal. **raider** n.

rail¹ ⓘ n **1** horizontal bar, esp. as part of a fence or track. **2** railway. **go off the rails** start behaving eccentrically or improperly. **railing** n fence made of rails supported by posts. **railcard** n card which pensioners, young people, etc. can buy, entitling them to cheaper rail travel. **railroad** n **1** US railway. ▷ v **2** informal force (a person) into an action with haste or by unfair means.

railway n **1** track of iron rails on which trains run. **2** company operating a railway.

rail² v (foll. by at or against) complain bitterly or loudly. **raillery** n teasing or joking.

rail³ n small marsh bird.

raiment n obs clothing.

rain ⓘ n **1** water falling in drops from the clouds. **2** large quantity of anything falling rapidly. ▷ v **3** fall or pour down as rain. **4** fall rapidly and in large quantities. **the rains** season in the tropics when there is a lot of rain. **rainy** adj **rainy day** future time of need, esp. financial need, e.g. saving some money for a rainy day. **rainbow** n arch of colours in the sky. **rainbow trout** freshwater trout with black spots and two red stripes. **raincoat** n water-resistant overcoat. **rainfall** n amount of rain. **rainforest** n dense forest in the tropics.

raise ⓘ v **1** lift up. **2** set upright. **3** increase in amount or intensity. **4** collect or levy. **5** bring up (a family). **6** grow (a crop). **7** put forward for consideration. **8** build. **9** end, e.g. raise a siege. ▷ n **10** US & Canad pay rise. **raised** adj higher than the surrounding area.

raisin n dried grape.

raison d'être [**ray**-zon **det**-ra] n, pl

r

ragamuffin n = **urchin**, guttersnipe

rage n **1** = **fury**, anger, frenzy, ire, madness, passion, rampage, wrath ▷ v **3** = **be furious**, blow one's top, blow up (inf), fly off the handle (inf), fume, go ballistic (sl, chiefly US), go up the wall (sl), lose it (inf), lose one's temper, lose the plot (inf), seethe, storm

ragged adj **1** = **shabby**, in rags, in tatters, tattered, tatty, threadbare, unkempt **2** = **torn 3** = **rough**, jagged, rugged, serrated, uneven, unfinished

raid n **1** = **attack**, foray, incursion, inroad, invasion, sally, sortie ▷ v **2** = **attack**, assault, foray, invade, pillage, plunder, sack

raider n = **attacker**, invader, marauder, plunderer, robber, thief

railing n = **fence**, balustrade, barrier, paling, rails

rain n **1** = **rainfall**, cloudburst, deluge, downpour, drizzle, fall, raindrops, showers **2** = **shower**, deluge ▷ v **3** = **pour**, bucket down (inf), come down in buckets (inf), drizzle, pelt (down), teem **4** = **fall**, deposit, drop, shower, sprinkle

rainy adj = **wet**, damp, drizzly, showery

raise v **1** = **lift**, elevate, heave, hoist, rear, uplift **3** = **increase**, advance, amplify, boost, enhance, enlarge, heighten, inflate, intensify, magnify, strengthen **4** = **collect**, assemble, form, gather, mass, obtain, rally, recruit **5** = **bring up**, develop, nurture, rear **6** = **grow**, produce **7** = **put forward**, advance, broach, introduce, moot, suggest **8** = **build**, construct, erect, put up

raisons d'être [**ray**-zon **det**-ra]*French* reason or justification for existence.

raita [**rye**-ta] *n* Indian dish of chopped cucumber, mint, etc., in yogurt, served with curries.

Raj *n* **the Raj** former British rule in India.

raja, rajah *n History* Indian prince or ruler.

rake¹ ❶ *n* **1** tool with a long handle and a crosspiece with teeth, used for smoothing earth or gathering leaves, hay, etc. ▷ *v* **2** gather or smooth with a rake. **3** search (through). **4** sweep (with gunfire). **rake it in** *informal* make a large amount of money. **rake-off** *n slang* share of profits, esp. illegal. **rake up** *v* revive memories of (a forgotten unpleasant event).

rake² ❶ *n* dissolute or immoral man.

rake³ *n* **1** slope, esp. backwards, of an object. ▷ *v* **2** slope from the vertical. **raked** *adj* (of a surface) sloping so that it is higher at the back than the front.

rakish ❶ [**ray**-kish] *adj* dashing or jaunty.

rally ❶ *n, pl* **-lies 1** large gathering of people for a meeting. **2** marked recovery of strength. **3** *Tennis, etc.* lively exchange of strokes. **4** car-driving competition on public roads. ▷ *v* **-lying, -lied 5** bring or come together after dispersal or for a common cause. **6** regain health or strength, revive. **rally round** *v* group together to help someone.

ram ❶ *n* **1** male sheep. **2** hydraulic machine. ▷ *v* **ramming, rammed 3** strike against with force. **4** force or drive. **5** cram or stuff. **ram (something) down someone's throat** put forward or emphasize (an idea or argument) with excessive force. **ram raid** *informal* raid on a shop in which a stolen car is driven into the window. **ram raider** *n*.

RAM *Computers* random access memory.

Ramadan *n* **1** 9th Muslim month. **2** strict fasting from dawn to dusk observed during this time.

ramble ❶ *v* **1** walk without a definite route. **2** talk incoherently. ▷ *n* **3** walk, esp. in the country. **rambler** *n* **1** person who rambles. **2** climbing rose. **rambling** *adj* **1** large and irregularly shaped. **2** (of speech or writing) confused and long-winded. ▷ *n* **3** activity of going for long walks in the country.

ramekin [**ram**-ik-in] *n* small ovenproof dish for a single serving of food.

ramifications *pl n* consequences resulting from an action.

ramp ❶ *n* **1** slope joining two level surfaces. **2** place where the level of a road surface changes because of road works. **3** mobile stairs by which passengers enter or leave an aircraft.

rampage ❶ *v* dash about violently. **on the rampage** behaving violently or destructively.

rampant ❶ *adj* **1** growing or spreading uncontrollably. **2** (of a heraldic beast) on its hind legs.

THESAURUS

rake¹ *v* **2** = **gather**, collect, remove **3** = **search**, comb, scour, scrutinize

rake² *n* = **libertine**, debauchee, lecher, playboy, roué, swinger (*sl*)

rakish *adj* = **dashing**, dapper, debonair, devil-may-care, jaunty, natty (*inf*), raffish, smart

rally *n* **1** = **gathering**, assembly, congress, convention, meeting **2** = **recovery**, improvement, recuperation, revival ▷ *v* **5** = **reassemble**, regroup, reorganize, unite **6** = **recover**, get better, improve, recuperate, revive

ram *v* **3** = **hit**, butt, crash, dash, drive, force, impact, smash **4, 5** = **cram**, crowd, force, jam, stuff, thrust

ramble *v* **1** = **walk**, range, roam, rove, saunter, stray, stroll, wander

2 = **babble**, rabbit (on) (*Brit inf*), waffle (*inf, chiefly Brit*), witter on (*inf*) ▷ *n* **3** = **walk**, hike, roaming, roving, saunter, stroll, tour

rambler *n* **1** = **walker**, hiker, rover, wanderer, wayfarer

rambling *adj* **2** = **long-winded**, circuitous, digressive, disconnected, discursive, disjointed, incoherent, wordy

ramifications *pl n* = **consequences**, developments, results, sequel, upshot

ramp *n* **1** = **slope**, gradient, incline, rise

rampage *v* = **go berserk**, rage, run amok, run riot, storm ▷ *n* **on the rampage** = **berserk**, amok, out of control, raging, riotous, violent, wild

rampant *adj* **1** = **widespread**, prevalent, profuse, rife, spreading like

r

rampart ❶ *n* mound or wall for defence.

ramrod *n* **1** long thin rod used for cleaning the barrel of a gun or forcing gunpowder into an old-fashioned gun. ▷ *adj* **2** (of someone's posture) very straight and upright.

ramshackle ❶ *adj* tumbledown, rickety, or makeshift.

ran *v* past tense of RUN.

ranch *n* large cattle farm in the American West. **rancher** *n*.

rancid ❶ *adj* (of butter, bacon, etc.) stale and having an offensive smell. **rancidity** *n*.

rancour ❶ *n* deep bitter hate. **rancorous** *adj*.

rand *n* monetary unit of S Africa.

R & B rhythm and blues.

R & D research and development.

random ❶ *adj* made or done by chance or without plan. **at random** haphazard(ly). **randomly** *adv*.

randy ❶ *adj* **randier**, **randiest** *informal* sexually aroused. **randiness** *n*.

ranee *n* same as RANI.

rang *v* past tense of RING¹.

range ❶ *n* **1** limits of effectiveness or variation. **2** distance that a missile or plane can travel. **3** distance of a mark

shot at. **4** difference in pitch between the highest and lowest note a voice or instrument can make. **5** whole set of related things. **6** chain of mountains. **7** place for shooting practice or rocket testing. **8** kitchen stove. ▷ *v* **9** vary between one point and another. **10** cover or extend over. **11** roam.

ranger *n* **1** official in charge of a nature reserve etc. **2** (**R-**) member of the senior branch of Guides.

rangefinder *n* instrument for finding how far away an object is.

rangy ❶ [**rain**-jee] *adj* **rangier**, **rangiest** having long slender limbs.

rani *n* wife or widow of a rajah.

rank¹ ❶ *n* **1** relative place or position. **2** status. **3** social class. **4** row or line. **5** *Brit* place where taxis wait to be hired. ▷ *v* **6** have a specific rank or position. **7** arrange in rows or lines. **rank and file** ordinary people or members. **the ranks** common soldiers.

rank² ❷ *adj* **1** complete or absolute, e.g. *rank favouritism*. **2** smelling offensively strong. **3** growing too thickly.

rankle ❶ *v* continue to cause resentment or bitterness.

ransack ❶ *v* **1** search thoroughly. **2** pillage, plunder.

wildfire, unchecked, uncontrolled, unrestrained **2** = **upright**, erect, rearing, standing

rampart *n* = **defence**, bastion, bulwark, fence, fortification, wall

ramshackle *adj* = **rickety**, crumbling, decrepit, derelict, flimsy, shaky, tumbledown, unsafe, unsteady

rancid *adj* = **rotten**, bad, fetid, foul, off, putrid, rank, sour, stale, strong-smelling, tainted

rancour *n* = **hatred**, animosity, bad blood, bitterness, hate, ill feeling, ill will

random *adj* = **chance**, accidental, adventitious, casual, fortuitous, haphazard, hit or miss, incidental **at random** = **haphazardly**, arbitrarily, by chance, randomly, unsystematically, willy-nilly

randy *adj Inf* = **lustful**, amorous, aroused, horny (*sl*), hot, lascivious, turned-on (*sl*)

range *n* **1** = **limits**, area, bounds, orbit, province, radius, reach, scope, sphere **5** = **series**, assortment, collection,

gamut, lot, selection, variety ▷ *v* **9** = **vary 10** = **extend**, reach, run, stretch **11** = **roam**, ramble, rove, traverse, wander

rangy *adj* = **long-limbed**, gangling, lanky, leggy, long-legged

rank¹ *n* **1, 2** = **status**, caste, class, degree, division, grade, level, order, position, sort, type **3** = **class**, caste **4** = **row**, column, file, group, line, range, series, tier ▷ *v* **7** = **arrange**, align, array, dispose, line up, order, sort **rank and file** = **general public**, majority, mass, masses

rank² *adj* **1** = **absolute**, arrant, blatant, complete, downright, flagrant, gross, sheer, thorough, total, utter **2** = **foul**, bad, disgusting, noisome, noxious, offensive, rancid, revolting, stinking **3** = **abundant**, dense, lush, luxuriant, profuse

rankle *v* = **annoy**, anger, gall, get on one's nerves (*inf*), irk, irritate, rile

ransack *v* **1** = **search**, comb, explore, go through, rummage, scour, turn inside out **2** = **plunder**, loot, pillage, raid, strip

ransom ❶ *n* **1** money demanded in return for the release of someone who has been kidnapped. ▷ *v* **2** pay money to obtain the release of a captive. **3** release a captive in return for money.

rant ❶ *v* talk in a loud and excited way. **ranter** *n* **ranting** *n*, *adj*.

ranunculus *n*, *pl* **-luses**, **-li** genus of plants including the buttercup.

rap ❶ *v* **rapping**, **rapped 1** hit with a sharp quick blow. **2** utter (a command) abruptly. **3** perform a rhythmic monologue with musical backing. ▷ *n* **4** quick sharp blow. **5** rhythmic monologue performed to music. **take the rap** *slang* suffer punishment for something whether guilty or not. **rapper** *n*.

rapacious ❶ *adj* greedy or grasping. **rapacity** *n*.

rape¹ ❶ *v* **1** force to submit to sexual intercourse. ▷ *n* **2** act of raping. **3** any violation or abuse. **rapist** *n*.

rape² *n* plant with oil-yielding seeds, also used as fodder.

rapid ❶ *adj* quick, swift. **rapids** *pl n* part of a river with a fast turbulent current. **rapidly** *adv* **rapidity** *n*.

rapier [**ray**-pyer] *n* fine-bladed sword.

rapine [**rap**-pine] *n* pillage or plundering.

rapport ❶ [rap-**pore**] *n* harmony or agreement.

rapprochement [rap-**prosh**-mong] *n* re-establishment of friendly relations, esp. between nations.

rapscallion *n* old-fashioned rascal or rogue.

rapt ❶ *adj* engrossed or spellbound. **rapture** *n* ecstasy. **rapturous** *adj*.

raptor *n* any bird of prey. **raptorial** *adj*.

rare¹ ❶ *adj* **1** uncommon. **2** infrequent. **3** of uncommonly high quality. **4** (of air at high altitudes) having low density, thin. **rarely** *adv* seldom. **rarity** *n*, *pl* **-ities**.

rare² ❶ *adj* (of meat) lightly cooked.

rarebit *n* see WELSH RAREBIT.

rarefied ❶ [**rare**-if-ide] *adj* **1** highly specialized, exalted. **2** (of air) thin.

raring ❶ *adj* **raring to** enthusiastic, willing, or ready to.

rascal ❶ *n* **1** rogue. **2** naughty (young) person. **rascally** *adj*.

rase *v* same as RAZE.

rash¹ ❶ *adj* hasty, reckless, or incautious. **rashly** *adv*.

---

ransom *n* **1** = **payment**, money, payoff, price

rant *v* = **shout**, cry, declaim, rave, roar, yell

rap *v* **1** = **hit**, crack, knock, strike, tap ▷ *n* **4** = **blow**, clout (*inf*), crack, knock, tap **take the rap** *Sl* = **rebuke**, blame, punishment, responsibility

rapacious *adj* = **greedy**, avaricious, grasping, insatiable, predatory, preying, voracious

rape¹ *v* **1** = **sexually assault**, abuse, force, outrage, ravish, violate ▷ *n* **2** = **sexual assault**, outrage, ravishment, violation **3** = **desecration**, abuse, defilement, violation

rapid *adj* = **quick**, brisk, express, fast, hasty, hurried, prompt, speedy, swift

rapport *n* = **bond**, affinity, empathy, harmony, link, relationship, sympathy, tie, understanding

rapt *adj* = **spellbound**, absorbed, engrossed, enthralled, entranced, fascinated, gripped

rapture *n* = **ecstasy**, bliss, delight, euphoria, joy, rhapsody, seventh heaven, transport

rapturous *adj* = **ecstatic**, blissful, euphoric, in seventh heaven, joyful, overjoyed, over the moon (*inf*), transported

rare¹ *adj* **1** = **uncommon**, few, infrequent, scarce, singular, sparse, strange, unusual **2** = **infrequent**, few, uncommon, unusual **3** = **superb**, choice, excellent, fine, great, peerless, superlative

rare² *adj* = **underdone**, bloody, half-cooked, half-raw, undercooked

rarefied *adj* **1** = **exalted**, elevated, high, lofty, noble, spiritual, sublime

rarely *adv* = **seldom**, hardly, hardly ever, infrequently

raring *adj* = **eager**, desperate, enthusiastic, impatient, keen, longing, ready

rarity *n* = **uncommonness**, infrequency, scarcity, shortage, sparseness, strangeness, unusualness

rascal *n* **1** = **rogue**, blackguard, devil, good-for-nothing, ne'er-do-well, scoundrel, villain **2** = **imp**, scamp

rash¹ *adj* = **reckless**, careless, foolhardy, hasty, heedless, ill-advised,

r

rash² ❶ *n* **1** eruption of spots or patches on the skin. **2** outbreak of (unpleasant) occurrences.

rasher *n* thin slice of bacon.

rasp *n* **1** harsh grating noise. **2** coarse file. ▷ *v* **3** speak in a grating voice. **4** make a scraping noise.

raspberry *n* **1** red juicy edible berry. **2** *informal* spluttering noise made with the tongue and lips, to show contempt.

Rastafarian *n*, *adj* (member) of a religion originating in Jamaica and regarding Haile Selassie as God (also **Rasta**).

rat *n* **1** small rodent. **2** *informal* contemptible person, esp. a deserter or informer. ▷ *v* **ratting**, **ratted** **3** *informal* inform (on). **4** hunt rats. **smell a rat** detect something suspicious. **ratty** *adj* **-tier**, **-tiest** *informal* bad-tempered, irritable. **rat race** continual hectic competitive activity.

ratafia [rat-a-**fee**-a] *n* **1** liqueur made from fruit. **2** almond-flavoured biscuit.

ratatouille [rat-a-**twee**] *n* vegetable casserole of tomatoes, aubergines, etc.

ratchet *n* set of teeth on a bar or wheel allowing motion in one direction only.

rate¹ ❶ *n* **1** degree of speed or progress. **2** proportion between two things. **3** charge. ▷ *pl* **4** local tax on business. **5** (in Australia and formerly in Britain) local tax on domestic property. ▷ *v* **6** consider or value. **7** estimate the value of. **8** be worthy of, deserve. **at any rate** in any case. **rateable** *adj* **1** able to be rated. **2** (of property) liable to payment of rates. **ratepayer** *n*.

rate² ❶ *v* scold or criticize severely.

rather ❶ *adv* **1** to some extent. **2** more truly or appropriately. **3** more willingly.

ratify ❶ *v* **-fying**, **-fied** give formal approval to. **ratification** *n*.

rating ❶ *n* **1** valuation or assessment. **2** classification. **3** noncommissioned sailor. ▷ *pl* **4** size of the audience for a TV programme.

ratio ❶ *n*, *pl* **-tios** relationship between two numbers or amounts expressed as a proportion.

ration ❶ *n* **1** fixed allowance of food etc. ▷ *v* **2** limit to a certain amount per person. **3** (often foll. by *out*) distribute a fixed amount of food etc. to each person in a group.

rational ❶ *adj* **1** reasonable, sensible. **2** capable of reasoning. **3** *Maths* (of a number) able to be expressed as a ratio of two integers. **rationally** *adv* **rationality** *n* **rationale** [rash-a-**nahl**] *n* reason for an action or decision.

— THESAURUS —

impetuous, imprudent, impulsive, incautious

rash² *n* **1** = **outbreak**, eruption **2** = **spate**, flood, outbreak, plague, series, wave

rate¹ *n* **1** = **speed**, pace, tempo, velocity **2** = **degree**, proportion, ratio, scale, standard **3** = **charge**, cost, fee, figure, price ▷ *v* **6** = **evaluate**, consider, count, estimate, grade, measure, rank, reckon, value **7** = **estimate**, evaluate, value **8** = **deserve**, be entitled to, be worthy of, merit **at any rate** = **in any case**, anyhow, anyway, at all events

rate² *v* = **scold**, bawl out (*inf*), berate, blame, carpet (*inf*), castigate, censure, chew out (*US & Canad inf*), chide, criticize severely, give a rocket (*Brit & NZ inf*), haul over the coals (*inf*), read the riot act, rebuke, reprimand, reprove, roast (*inf*), rouse on (*Aust*), take to task, tear into (*inf*), tear (someone) off a strip (*inf*), tell off (*inf*),

tongue-lash, upbraid

rather *adv* **1** = **to some extent**, a little, fairly, moderately, quite, relatively, somewhat, to some degree **3** = **preferably**, more readily, more willingly, sooner

ratify *v* = **approve**, affirm, authorize, confirm, endorse, establish, sanction, uphold

rating *n* **2** = **position**, class, degree, grade, order, placing, rank, rate, status

ratio *n* = **proportion**, fraction, percentage, rate, relation

ration *n* **1** = **allowance**, allotment, helping, measure, part, portion, quota, share ▷ *v* **2** = **limit**, budget, control, restrict

rational *adj* **1, 2** = **sensible**, intelligent, logical, lucid, realistic, reasonable, sane, sound, wise

rationale *n* = **reason**, grounds, logic, motivation, philosophy, principle, *raison d'être*, theory

rationalism n philosophy that regards reason as the only basis for beliefs or actions. **rationalist** n, adj **rationalistic** adj **rationalize** v
1 justify by plausible reasoning.
2 reorganize to improve efficiency or profitability. **rationalization** n.

rattan n climbing palm with jointed stems used for canes.

rattle ❶ v 1 give out a succession of short sharp sounds. 2 send, move or drive with such a sound. 3 shake briskly causing sharp sounds.
4 informal confuse or fluster. 5 (often foll. by off or out) recite perfunctorily or rapidly. 6 (often foll. by on or away) talk quickly and at length about something unimportant. ▷ n 7 short sharp sound. 8 instrument for making such a sound. **rattling** adv 1 informal, old-fashioned exceptionally, very. ▷ n 2 succession of short sharp sounds.
rattlesnake n poisonous snake with loose horny segments on the tail that make a rattling sound. **rattle through** v do very quickly.

raucous ❶ adj hoarse or harsh.

raunchy ❶ adj -chier, -chiest slang earthy, sexy.

ravage ❶ v cause extensive damage to. **ravages** pl n damaging effects.

rave ❶ v 1 talk wildly or with enthusiasm. ▷ n 2 informal enthusiastically good review. 3 slang large-scale party with electronic dance music. **raving** adj 1 delirious. 2 informal exceptional, e.g. a raving beauty.

ravel v -elling, -elled tangle or become entangled.

raven n 1 black bird like a large crow. ▷ adj 2 (of hair) shiny black.

ravening adj (of animals) hungrily searching for prey.

ravenous ❶ adj very hungry.

ravine ❶ [rav-**veen**] n narrow steep-sided valley worn by a stream.

ravioli pl n small squares of pasta with a savoury filling.

ravish ❶ v 1 enrapture. 2 lit rape. **ravishing** adj lovely or entrancing.

raw ❶ adj 1 uncooked. 2 not manufactured or refined. 3 (of the skin or a wound) painful, with the surface scraped away.
4 inexperienced, e.g. raw recruits.
5 chilly. **raw deal** unfair or dishonest treatment. **rawhide** n untanned hide.

ray¹ ❶ n 1 single line or narrow beam of light. 2 any of a set of radiating lines. 3 slight indication of something desirable, e.g. a ray of hope.

ray² n large sea fish with a flat body and a whiplike tail.

ray³ n Music (in tonic sol-fa) second note of any major scale.

rayon n (fabric made of) a synthetic fibre.

raze ❶ v destroy (buildings or a town) completely.

THESAURUS

rationalize v 1 = **justify**, account for, excuse, vindicate

rattle v 1 = **clatter**, bang, jangle **2, 3** = **shake**, bounce, jar, jolt, vibrate **4** Inf = **fluster**, disconcert, disturb, faze, perturb, shake, upset

raucous adj = **harsh**, grating, hoarse, loud, noisy, rough, strident

raunchy adj Sl = **sexy**, coarse, earthy, lusty, sexual, steamy (inf)

ravage v = **destroy**, demolish, despoil, devastate, lay waste, ransack, ruin, spoil

ravages pl n = **damage**, destruction, devastation, havoc, ruin, ruination, spoliation

rave v 1 a = **rant**, babble, be delirious, rage, roar b = **enthuse**, be mad about (inf), be wild about (inf), gush, praise

ravenous adj = **starving**, famished, starved

ravine n = **canyon**, defile, gorge, gulch (US & Canad), gully, pass

raving adj 1 = **mad**, crazed, crazy, delirious, hysterical, insane, irrational, wild

ravish v 1 = **enchant**, captivate, charm, delight, enrapture, entrance, fascinate, spellbind **2** Lit = **rape**, abuse, force, sexually assault, violate

ravishing adj = **enchanting**, beautiful, bewitching, charming, entrancing, gorgeous, lovely

raw adj 1 = **uncooked**, fresh, natural **2** = **unrefined**, basic, coarse, crude, natural, rough, unfinished, unprocessed **4** = **inexperienced**, callow, green, immature, new **5** = **chilly**, biting, bitter, cold, freezing, parky (Brit inf), piercing

ray¹ n 1 = **beam**, bar, flash, gleam, shaft

raze v = **destroy**, demolish, flatten, knock down, level, pull down, ruin

r

razor n sharp instrument for shaving.
razorbill n sea bird with a stout
sideways flattened bill. **razor shell**
(burrowing shellfish with) a long
narrow shell. **razor wire** strong wire
with pieces of sharp metal set across it
at intervals.

razzle-dazzle, razzmatazz n slang
showy activity.

Rb Chemistry rubidium.

RC 1 Roman Catholic. 2 Red Cross.

Rd Road.

re¹ ❶ prep with reference to, concerning.

re² n same as RAY³.

Re Chemistry rhenium.

RE religious education.

re- prefix again, e.g. re-enter; retrial.

reach ❶ v 1 arrive at. 2 make a
movement in order to grasp or touch.
3 succeed in touching. 4 make
contact or communication with.
5 extend as far as. ▷ n 6 distance that
one can reach. 7 range of influence.
▷ pl 8 stretch of a river. **reachable** adj.

react ❶ v 1 act in response (to). 2 (foll.
by against) act in an opposing or
contrary manner. 3 undergo a
chemical reaction. **reaction** n
1 physical or emotional response to a
stimulus. 2 any action resisting
another. 3 opposition to change.
4 chemical or nuclear change,
combination, or decomposition.
reactionary n, pl -aries adj (person)
opposed to change, esp. in politics.
reactance n Electricity resistance to
the flow of an alternating current
caused by the inductance or

capacitance of the circuit. **reactive**
adj chemically active. **reactor** n
apparatus in which a nuclear reaction
is maintained and controlled to
produce nuclear energy.

read ❶ v **reading, read** 1 look at and
understand or take in (written or
printed matter). 2 look at and say
aloud. 3 have a certain wording, e.g.
the statement reads as follows.
4 interpret the significance or
meaning of. 5 (of an instrument)
register. 6 make out the true mood of.
7 study. ▷ n 8 matter suitable for
reading, e.g. a good read. 9 spell of
reading. **readable** adj 1 enjoyable to
read. 2 legible. **reader** n 1 person
who reads. 2 textbook. 3 senior
university lecturer. **readership** n
readers of a publication collectively.
reading n.

readjust v adapt to a new situation.
readjustment n.

readmit v -mitting, -mitted let (a
person, country, etc.) back in to a
place or organization.

ready ❶ adj **readier, readiest**
1 prepared for use or action. 2 willing,
prompt. **readily** adv **readiness** n
ready-made adj for immediate use by
any customer. **ready money, the
ready, the readies** informal cash for
immediate use.

reaffirm v state again, confirm.
reaffirmation n.

reafforest v plant new trees in (an area
that was formerly forested).
reafforestation n.

—————————————————————————— THESAURUS ——

re¹ prep = **concerning**, about, apropos,
regarding, with reference to, with
regard to

reach v 1 = **arrive at**, attain, get to,
make 3, 5 = **touch**, contact, extend
to, grasp, stretch to 4 = **contact**,
communicate with, get hold of, get in
touch with, get through to ▷ n
6 = **range**, distance, extension,
extent, grasp, stretch 7 = **power**,
capacity, influence, mana (NZ), scope

react v 1 = **respond**, answer, reply

reaction n 1 = **response**, answer, reply
2 = **counteraction**, backlash, recoil
3 = **conservatism**, the right

reactionary n = **conservative**, die-hard,
right-winger ▷ adj = **conservative**,
right-wing

read v 1 = **look at**, comprehend,

construe, decipher, discover,
interpret, peruse, pore over, scan, see,
study, understand 5 = **register**,
display, indicate, record, show
7 = **study**, pore over

readable adj 1 = **enjoyable**,
entertaining, enthralling, gripping,
interesting 2 = **legible**, clear,
comprehensible, decipherable

reading n 2 = **recital**, lesson,
performance, sermon
4 = **interpretation**, grasp,
impression, version 7 = **perusal**,
examination, inspection, scrutiny,
study

ready adj 1 = **prepared**, accessible,
arranged, available, convenient, fit,
handy, near, organized, present,
primed, ripe, set 2 = **willing**,

reagent [ree-**age**-ent] *n* chemical substance that reacts with another, used to detect the presence of the other.

real ❶ *adj* **1** existing in fact. **2** actual. **3** genuine. **really** *adv* **1** very. **2** truly. ▷ *interj* **3** exclamation of dismay, doubt, or surprise. **reality** *n* state of things as they are. **reality TV** television programmes focusing on members of the public living in conditions created especially by the programme makers. **real ale** beer allowed to ferment in the barrel. **real estate** property consisting of land and houses. **real number** any rational or irrational number. **real tennis** old form of tennis played in a four-walled indoor court. **real-time** *adj* (of a computer system) processing data as it is received.

realistic ❶ *adj* seeing and accepting things as they really are, practical. **realistically** *adv* **realism** *n* **1** awareness or acceptance of things as they are. **2** style in art or literature that attempts to portray the world as it really is. **realist** *n*.

realize ❶ *v* **1** become aware or grasp the significance of. **2** achieve (a plan, hopes, etc.). **3** convert into money. **realization** *n*.

realm ❶ *n* **1** kingdom. **2** sphere of interest.

realtor *n US & Canad* agent, esp. accredited one who sells houses, etc.

for other people.

ream *n* **1** twenty quires of paper, generally 500 sheets. ▷ *pl* **2** *informal* large quantity (of written matter).

reap ❶ *v* **1** cut and gather (a harvest). **2** receive as the result of a previous activity. **reaper** *n*.

reappear *v* appear again. **reappearance** *n*.

reappraise *v* consider or review to see if changes are needed. **reappraisal** *n*.

rear¹ ❶ *n* **1** back part. **2** part of an army, procession, etc. behind the others. **bring up the rear** come last. **rearmost** *adj* **rearward** *adj*, *adv* **rear admiral** high-ranking naval officer. **rearguard** *n* troops protecting the rear of an army. **rear-view mirror** mirror inside a vehicle which allows the driver to see out of the rear window.

rear² ❶ *v* **1** care for and educate (children). **2** breed (animals). **3** (of a horse) rise on its hind feet.

rearm *v* **1** arm again. **2** equip with better weapons. **rearmament** *n*.

rearrange *v* organize differently, alter. **rearrangement** *n*.

reason ❶ *n* **1** cause or motive. **2** faculty of rational thought. **3** sanity. ▷ *v* **4** think logically in forming conclusions. **reason with** persuade by logical argument into doing something. **reasonable** *adj* **1** sensible. **2** not excessive. **3** logical. **reasonably** *adv*.

agreeable, alert, bright, clever, disposed, eager, glad, happy, inclined, keen, prompt, prone, quick

real *adj* **3** = **genuine**, actual, authentic, factual, rightful, sincere, true, unfeigned, valid

realistic *adj* = **practical**, common-sense, down-to-earth, level-headed, matter-of-fact, real, sensible

reality *n* = **truth**, actuality, fact, realism, validity, verity

realization *n* **1** = **awareness**, cognizance, comprehension, conception, grasp, perception, recognition, understanding **2** = **achievement**, accomplishment, fulfilment

realize *v* **1** = **become aware of**, comprehend, get the message, grasp, take in, understand **2** = **achieve**, accomplish, carry out *or* through,

complete, do, effect, fulfil, perform

really *adv* **2** = **truly**, actually, certainly, genuinely, in actuality, indeed, in fact, positively, surely

realm *n* **1** = **kingdom**, country, domain, dominion, empire, land **2** = **field**, area, branch, department, province, sphere, territory, world

reap *v* **1** = **collect**, bring in, cut, garner, gather, harvest **2** = **get**, acquire, derive, gain, obtain

rear¹ *n* **1** = **back**, end, rearguard, stern, tail, tail end

rear² *v* **1** = **bring up**, educate, foster, nurture, raise, train **2** = **breed 3** = **rise**

reason *n* **1** = **cause**, aim, goal, grounds, incentive, intention, motive, object, purpose **2** = **sense**, intellect, judgment, logic, understanding **3** = **sanity**, mind, rationality, soundness ▷ *v* **4** = **deduce**, conclude,

reassess *v* reconsider the value or importance of.

reassure ❶ *v* restore confidence to. **reassurance** *n* **reassuring** *adj*.

rebate ❶ *n* discount or refund.

rebel ❶ *v* **-belling, -belled 1** revolt against the ruling power. **2** reject accepted conventions. ▷ *n* **3** person who rebels. **rebellion** *n* **1** organized open resistance to authority. **2** rejection of conventions. **rebellious** *adj*.

rebirth *n* revival or renaissance. **reborn** *adj* active again after a period of inactivity.

rebore, reboring *n* boring of a cylinder to restore its true shape.

rebound ❶ *v* **1** spring back. **2** misfire so as to hurt the perpetrator of a plan or deed. ▷ *n* **3** act of rebounding. **on the rebound** *informal* while recovering from rejection.

rebuff ❶ *v* **1** reject or snub. ▷ *n* **2** blunt refusal, snub.

rebuke ❶ *v* **1** scold sternly. ▷ *n* **2** stern scolding.

rebus [**ree**-buss] *n, pl* **-buses** puzzle consisting of pictures and symbols representing words or syllables.

rebut ❶ *v* **-butting, -butted** prove that (a claim) is untrue. **rebuttal** *n*.

recalcitrant *adj* wilfully disobedient. **recalcitrance** *n*.

recall ❶ *v* **1** recollect or remember. **2** order to return. **3** annul or cancel. ▷ *n* **4** ability to remember. **5** order to return.

recant ❶ *v* withdraw (a statement or belief) publicly. **recantation** *n*.

recap *informal* ▷ *v* **-capping, -capped 1** recapitulate. ▷ *n* **2** recapitulation.

recapitulate ❶ *v* state again briefly, repeat. **recapitulation** *n*.

recapture *v* **1** experience again. **2** capture again.

recast *v* **-casting, -cast 1** organize or set out in a different way. **2** assign a part in a play or film to an actor other than the one originally intended.

recce *slang* ▷ *v* **-ceing, -ced** *or* **-ceed 1** reconnoitre. ▷ *n* **2** reconnaissance.

recede ❶ *v* **1** move to a more distant place. **2** (of the hair) stop growing at the front.

infer, make out, think, work out **reason with** = **persuade**, bring round (*inf*), prevail upon, talk into *or* out of, urge, win over

reasonable *adj* **1, 3** = **sensible**, logical, plausible, practical, sane, sober, sound, tenable, wise **2** = **fair**, equitable, fit, just, moderate, proper, right

reassure *v* = **encourage**, comfort, gee up, hearten, put *or* set one's mind at rest, restore confidence to

rebate *n* = **refund**, allowance, bonus, deduction, discount, reduction

rebel *v* **1** = **revolt**, mutiny, resist, rise up **2** = **defy** ▷ *n* **3** = **revolutionary**, insurgent, revolutionist, secessionist

rebellion *n* **1** = **resistance**, mutiny, revolt, revolution, rising, uprising **2** = **nonconformity**, defiance, heresy, schism

rebellious *adj* = **revolutionary**, defiant, disloyal, disobedient, disorderly, insurgent, mutinous, rebel, seditious, unruly

rebound *v* **1** = **bounce**, recoil, ricochet **2** = **misfire**, backfire, boomerang, recoil

rebuff *v* **1** = **reject**, cold-shoulder, cut, knock back (*sl*), refuse, repulse, slight, snub, spurn, turn down ▷ *n*

2 = **rejection**, cold shoulder, kick in the teeth (*sl*), knock-back (*sl*), refusal, repulse, slap in the face (*inf*), slight, snub

rebuke *v* **1** = **scold**, admonish, castigate, censure, chide, dress down (*inf*), give a rocket (*Brit & NZ inf*), haul (someone) over the coals (*inf*), reprimand, reprove, rouse on (*Aust*), tear (someone) off a strip (*inf*), tell off (*inf*) ▷ *n* **2** = **scolding**, admonition, censure, dressing down (*inf*), reprimand, row, telling-off (*inf*)

rebut *v* = **disprove**, confute, invalidate, negate, overturn, prove wrong, refute

recall *v* **1** = **recollect**, bring *or* call to mind, evoke, remember **3** = **annul**, cancel, countermand, repeal, retract, revoke, withdraw ▷ *n* **4** = **recollection**, memory, remembrance **5** = **repeal**, rescindment, retraction, withdrawal

recant *v* = **withdraw**, disclaim, forswear, renege, repudiate, retract, revoke, take back

recapitulate *v* = **restate**, outline, recap (*inf*), recount, repeat, summarize

recede *v* **1** = **fall back**, abate, ebb, regress, retire, retreat, return, subside, withdraw

receipt ❶ *n* **1** written acknowledgment of money or goods received. **2** receiving or being received.

receive ❶ *v* **1** take, accept, or get. **2** experience. **3** greet (guests). **4** have (an honour) bestowed. **5** admit (a person) to a society or condition. **6** convert radio or television signals into sound or vision. **7** support or sustain (the weight of something). **received** *adj* generally accepted. **receiver** *n* **1** part of telephone that is held to the ear. **2** equipment in a telephone, radio, or television that converts electrical signals into sound. **3** person appointed by a court to manage the property of a bankrupt. **4** person who handles stolen goods knowing they have been stolen. **receivership** *n* state of being administered by a receiver.

recent ❶ *adj* **1** having happened lately. **2** new. **recently** *adv*.

receptacle ❶ *n* object used to contain something.

reception ❶ *n* **1** area for receiving guests, clients, etc. **2** formal party. **3** manner of receiving. **4** welcome. **5** (in broadcasting) quality of signals received. **receptionist** *n* person who receives guests, clients, etc. **reception room** room in a house suitable for entertaining guests.

receptive ❶ *adj* willing to accept new ideas, suggestions, etc. **receptivity**, **receptiveness** *n*.

recess ❶ *n* **1** niche or alcove. **2** holiday between sessions of work. **3** secret hidden place. **recessed** *adj* hidden or placed in a recess.

recession ❶ *n* **1** period of economic difficulty when little is being bought or sold. **2** act of receding. **recessive** *adj* receding.

recharge *v* cause (a battery etc.) to take in and store electricity again. **rechargeable** *adj*.

recherché [rish-**air**-shay] *adj* **1** refined or elegant. **2** known only to experts.

recidivism *n* habitual relapse into crime. **recidivist** *n*.

recipe ❶ *n* **1** directions for cooking a dish. **2** method for achieving something.

recipient *n* person who receives something.

reciprocal ❶ [ris-**sip**-pro-kl] *adj* **1** mutual. **2** given or done in return. ▷ *n* **3** *Maths* number or quantity that gives a product of one when multiplied by a given number or quantity, e.g. *0.25 is the reciprocal of 4*. **reciprocally** *adv* **reciprocate** *v* **1** give or feel in return. **2** (of a machine part) move backwards and forwards. **reciprocation** *n* **reciprocity** *n*.

———————— THESAURUS ————————

receipt *n* **1** = **sales slip**, counterfoil, proof of purchase **2** = **receiving**, acceptance, delivery, reception

receive *v* **1** = **get**, accept, acquire, be given, collect, obtain, pick up, take **2** = **experience**, bear, encounter, suffer, sustain, undergo **3** = **greet**, accommodate, admit, entertain, meet, welcome **5** = **admit**, welcome

recent *adj* **1** = **late 2** = **new**, current, fresh, modern, novel, present-day, up-to-date

recently *adv* **1** = **lately**, latterly, not long ago, of late **2** = **newly**, currently, freshly

receptacle *n* = **container**, holder, repository

reception *n* **2** = **party**, function, soiree **3** = **response**, acknowledgment, greeting, reaction, treatment, welcome **4** = **welcome**, greeting

receptive *adj* = **open**, amenable, interested, open-minded, open to

suggestions, susceptible, sympathetic

recess *n* **1** = **alcove**, bay, corner, hollow, niche, nook **2** = **break**, holiday, intermission, interval, respite, rest, vacation

recession *n* = **depression**, decline, drop, slump

recipe *n* **1** = **directions**, ingredients, instructions **2** = **method**, formula, prescription, procedure, process, technique

reciprocal *adj* **1, 2** = **mutual**, alternate, complementary, correlative, corresponding, equivalent, exchanged, interchangeable

reciprocate *v* **1** = **return**, exchange, reply, requite, respond, swap, trade

recital *n* **1** = **performance**, rehearsal, rendering **2** = **recitation**, account, narrative, reading, relation, statement, telling

recitation *n* = **recital**, lecture, passage, performance, piece, reading

r

recite ❶ v **1** repeat (a poem etc.) aloud to an audience. **2** give a detailed account of. **recital** [ris-**site**-al] n **1** musical performance by a soloist or soloists. **2** act of reciting. **recitation** n recital, usu. from memory, of poetry or prose. **recitative** [ress-it-a-**teev**] n speechlike style of singing, used esp. for narrative passages in opera.

reckless ❶ adj heedless of danger. **recklessly** adv **recklessness** n.

reckon ❶ v **1** consider or think. **2** make calculations, count. **3** expect. **4** (foll. by with or without) take into account or fail to take into account. **5** (foll. by on or upon) rely on. **reckoning** n.

reclaim ❶ v **1** regain possession of. **2** make fit for cultivation. **3** recover (useful substances) from waste. **reclamation** n.

recline ❶ v rest in a leaning position. **reclining** adj.

recluse ❶ n person who avoids other people. **reclusive** adj.

recognize ❶ v **1** identify as (a person or thing) already known. **2** accept as true or existing. **3** treat as valid. **4** notice, show appreciation of.

recognition n **recognizable** adj **recognizance** [rik-**og**-nizz-anss] n undertaking before a court to observe some condition.

recoil ❶ v **1** jerk or spring back. **2** draw back in horror. **3** (of an action) go wrong so as to hurt the doer. ▷ n **4** backward jerk. **5** recoiling.

recollect ❶ v call back to mind, remember. **recollection** n.

recommend ❶ v **1** advise or counsel. **2** praise or commend. **3** make acceptable. **recommendation** n.

● **SPELLING TIP**
● If you wonder how many cs and
● ms to put in **recommend**, you
● are not alone. Most people who
● make the wrong decision go for
● single letters throughout (recomend
● and recomendation); they should,
● of course, double the m, as in
● **recommendation**.

recompense ❶ v **1** pay or reward. **2** compensate or make up for. ▷ n **3** compensation. **4** reward or remuneration.

reconcile ❶ v **1** harmonize (conflicting beliefs etc.). **2** bring back into friendship. **3** accept or cause to

---

recite v **1** = **repeat**, declaim, deliver, narrate, perform, speak

reckless adj = **careless**, hasty, headlong, heedless, imprudent, mindless, precipitate, rash, thoughtless, wild

reckon v **1** = **consider**, account, assume, believe, count, deem, esteem, guess (inf, chiefly US & Canad), imagine, judge, rate, regard, suppose, think **2** = **count**, add up, calculate, compute, figure, number, tally, total

reckoning n = **count**, addition, calculation, estimate

reclaim v **1** = **regain**, recapture, recover, redeem, retrieve **3** = **salvage**

recline v = **lean**, lie (down), loll, lounge, repose, rest, sprawl

recluse n = **hermit**, anchoress, anchorite, monk, solitary

reclusive adj = **solitary**, hermit-like, isolated, retiring, withdrawn

recognition n **1** = **identification**, discovery, recollection, remembrance **2** = **acceptance**, admission, allowance, confession **4** = **appreciation**, notice, respect

recognize v **1** = **identify**, know, notice, place, recall, recollect, remember, spot **2** = **acknowledge**, accept, admit, allow, concede, grant **4** = **appreciate**, notice, respect

recoil v **1** = **jerk back**, kick, react, rebound, spring back **2** = **draw back**, falter, quail, shrink **3** = **backfire**, boomerang, go pear-shaped (inf), misfire, rebound ▷ n **4** = **reaction**, backlash, kick, rebound, repercussion

recollect v = **remember**, place, recall, summon up

recollection n = **memory**, impression, recall, remembrance, reminiscence

recommend v **1** = **advise**, advance, advocate, counsel, prescribe, propose, put forward, suggest **2** = **commend**, approve, endorse, praise

recompense v **1** = **reward**, pay, remunerate **2** = **compensate**, make up for, pay for, reimburse, repay, requite, ress ▷ n **3** = **compensation**, amends, damages, payment, remuneration, reparation, repayment, requital, restitution **4** = **reward**, payment, return, wages

reconcile v **1** = **resolve**, adjust, compose, put to rights, rectify, settle, accept (an unpleasant situation). **reconciliation** n.

recondite ❶ adj difficult to understand.

recondition ❶ v restore to good condition or working order.

reconnaissance ❶ [rik-**kon**-iss-anss] n survey for military or engineering purposes.

● **SPELLING TIP**
● The Bank of English shows that
● the most common way to misspell
● **recon naissance** is to miss out an s,
● although there are examples where
● a n n has been missed out instead.
● Remember, there are two ns in the
● middle and two ss.

reconnoitre ❶ [rek-a-**noy**-ter] v make a reconnaissance of.

reconsider ❶ v think about again, consider changing.

reconstitute v 1 reorganize. 2 restore (dried food) to its former state by adding water. **reconstitution** n.

reconstruct ❶ v 1 rebuild. 2 use evidence to re-create. **reconstruction** n.

record ❶ n [**rek**-ord] 1 document or other thing that preserves information. 2 disc with indentations which a record player transforms into sound. 3 best recorded achievement. 4 known facts about a person's past. ▷ v [rik-**kord**] 5 put in writing. 6 preserve (sound, TV programmes, etc.) on plastic disc, magnetic tape, etc., for reproduction on a playback device. 7 show or register. **off the record** not for publication. **recorder** n 1 person or machine that records, esp. a video, cassette, or tape recorder. 2 type of flute, held vertically. 3 judge in certain courts. **recording** n **recorded delivery** postal service by which an official receipt is obtained for the posting and delivery of a letter or parcel. **record player** instrument for reproducing sound on records.

recount ❶ v tell in detail.

re-count v 1 count again. ▷ n 2 second or further count, esp. of votes.

recoup ❶ [rik-**koop**] v 1 regain or make good (a loss). 2 recompense or compensate.

recourse ❶ n source of help. **have recourse to** turn to a source of help or course of action.

recover ❶ v 1 become healthy again. 2 regain a former condition. 3 find

---

THESAURUS

square 2 = **make peace between**, appease, conciliate, propitiate, reunite 3 = **accept**, put up with (inf), resign oneself, submit, yield

reconciliation n = **pacification**, conciliation, reconcilement, reunion

recondite adj = **obscure**, arcane, concealed, dark, deep, difficult, hidden, mysterious, occult, profound, secret

recondition v = **restore**, do up (inf), overhaul, remodel, renew, renovate, repair, revamp

reconnaissance n = **inspection**, exploration, investigation, observation, recce (sl), scan, survey

reconnoitre v = **inspect**, case (sl), explore, investigate, observe, scan, spy out, survey

reconsider v = **rethink**, reassess, review, revise, think again

reconstruct v 1 = **rebuild**, recreate, regenerate, remake, remodel, renovate, restore 2 = **deduce**, build up, piece together

record n 1 = **document**, account, chronicle, diary, entry, file, journal, log, register, report 2 = **disc**, album,

LP, single, vinyl 4 = **background**, career, history, performance ▷ v 5 = **set down**, chronicle, document, enter, log, minute, note, register, take down, write down 6 = **make a recording of**, tape, tape-record, video, video-tape 7 = **register**, give evidence of, indicate, say, show **off the record** = **not for publication**, confidential, private, unofficial

recorder n 1 = **chronicler**, archivist, clerk, diarist, historian, scribe

recording n = **record**, disc, tape, video

recount v = **tell**, depict, describe, narrate, recite, relate, repeat, report

recoup v 1 = **regain**, recover, retrieve, win back 2 = **compensate**, make up for, refund, reimburse, repay, requite

recourse n = **option**, alternative, choice, expedient, remedy, resort, resource, way out

recover v 1 = **get better**, convalesce, get well, heal, improve, mend, rally, recuperate, revive 2-4 = **regain**, get back, recapture, reclaim, redeem, repossess, restore, retrieve

r

again. **4** get back (a loss or expense).
5 obtain (useful substances) from
waste. **recovery** n **recoverable** adj.
re-create v make happen or exist
again. **re-creation** n.
recreation ❶ n agreeable or refreshing
occupation, relaxation, or
amusement. **recreational** adj
recreational vehicle n chiefly US a
large vanlike vehicle equipped to be
lived in.
recrimination ❶ n mutual blame.
recriminatory adj.
recrudescence n outbreak of trouble
or a disease after a period of quiet.
recruit ❶ v **1** enlist (new soldiers,
members, etc.). ▷ n **2** newly enlisted
soldier. **3** new member or supporter.
recruitment n.
rectal adj see RECTUM.
rectangle n oblong four-sided
figure with four right angles.
rectangular adj.
rectify ❶ v **-fying**, **-fied 1** put right,
correct. **2** Chemistry purify by
distillation. **3** Electricity convert
(alternating current) into direct
current. **rectification** n **rectifier** n.
rectilinear [rek-tee-**lin**-ee-er] adj **1** in a
straight line. **2** characterized by
straight lines.
rectitude ❶ n moral correctness.
recto n, pl **-tos 1** right-hand page of a
book. **2** front of a sheet of paper.
rector n **1** clergyman in charge of a
parish. **2** head of certain academic
institutions. **rectory** n, pl **-ories**
rector's house.

rectum n, pl **-tums**, **-ta** final section of
the large intestine. **rectal** adj.
recumbent adj lying down.
recuperate ❶ v recover from illness.
recuperation n **recuperative** adj.
recur ❶ v **-curring**, **-curred** happen
again. **recurrence** n repetition.
recurrent adj **recurring decimal**
number in which a pattern of digits is
repeated indefinitely after the decimal
point.
recycle ❶ v reprocess (used materials)
for further use. **recyclable** adj.
red ❶ adj **redder**, **reddest 1** of a colour
varying from crimson to orange and
seen in blood, fire, etc. **2** flushed in
the face from anger, shame, etc. ▷ n
3 red colour. **4** (**R-**) informal
communist. **in the red** informal in
debt. **see red** informal be angry.
redness n **redden** v make or become
red. **reddish** adj **redback spider** small
venomous Australian spider with a red
stripe on the back of the abdomen.
red blood cell same as ERYTHROCYTE.
red-blooded adj informal vigorous or
virile. **redbrick** adj (of a university)
founded in the late 19th or early 20th
century. **red card** Soccer piece of red
pasteboard shown by a referee to
indicate that a player has been sent
off. **red carpet** very special welcome
for an important guest. **redcoat** n
1 History British soldier. **2** Canad
informal Mountie. **Red Crescent** name
and symbol used by the Red Cross in
Muslim countries. **Red Cross**
international organization providing

─────────────────────── THESAURUS ───────

r

recovery n **1** = **improvement**,
convalescence, healing, mending,
recuperation, revival **2-4** = **retrieval**,
reclamation, repossession,
restoration
recreation n = **pastime**, amusement,
diversion, enjoyment, entertainment,
fun, hobby, leisure activity, play,
relaxation, sport
recrimination n = **bickering**,
counterattack, mutual accusation,
quarrel, squabbling
recruit v **1** = **enlist**, draft, enrol, levy,
mobilize, muster, raise ▷ n
3 = **beginner**, apprentice, convert,
helper, initiate, learner, novice,
trainee
rectify v **1** = **correct**, adjust, emend,
fix, improve, redress, remedy, repair,

rectitude n = **morality**, decency,
goodness, honesty, honour, integrity,
principle, probity, virtue
recuperate v = **recover**, convalesce,
get better, improve, mend
recur v = **happen again**, come again,
persist, reappear, repeat, return,
revert
recurrent adj = **periodic**, continued,
frequent, habitual, recurring
recycle v = **reprocess**, reclaim, reuse,
salvage, save
red adj **1** = **crimson**, carmine, cherry,
coral, ruby, scarlet, vermilion
2 = **flushed**, blushing, embarrassed,
florid, shamefaced **in the red** Inf = **in
debt**, in arrears, insolvent, overdrawn
see red Inf = **lose one's temper**, be or

help for victims of war or natural disasters. **redcurrant** n small round edible red berry. **red flag 1** symbol of revolution. **2** danger signal. **red-handed** adj informal (caught) in the act of doing something wrong or illegal. **redhead** n person with reddish hair. **redheaded** adj **red herring** something which diverts attention from the main issue. **red-hot** adj **1** glowing red. **2** extremely hot. **3** very keen. **Red Indian** offens Native American. **red-letter day** memorably happy or important occasion. **red light 1** traffic signal to stop. **2** danger signal. **red-light district** area where prostitutes work. **red meat** dark meat, esp. beef or lamb. **red rag** something that infuriates or provokes. **redshank** n large sandpiper with red legs. **red shift** appearance of lines in the spectra of distant stars nearer the red end of the spectrum than on earth: used to calculate the velocity of objects in relation to the earth. **redskin** n informal, offens Native American. **redstart** n European bird of the thrush family, the male of which has an orange-brown tail and breast. **red tape** excessive adherence to official rules. **redwood** n giant Californian conifer with reddish bark.

redeem ❶ v **1** make up for. **2** reinstate (oneself) in someone's good opinion. **3** free from sin. **4** buy back. **5** pay off (a loan or debt). **the Redeemer** Jesus Christ. **redeeming** adj **redeemable** adj **redemption** n **redemptive** adj.

redeploy v assign to a new position or task. **redeployment** n.

redevelop v rebuild or renovate (an area or building). **redevelopment** n.

redirect v **1** send in a new direction or course. **2** send (mail) to a different address.

redolent adj **1** reminiscent (of). **2** smelling strongly (of). **redolence** n.

redouble v increase, multiply, or intensify.

redoubt n small fort defending a hilltop or pass.

redoubtable ❶ adj formidable.

redound v cause advantage or disadvantage (to).

redox n chemical reaction in which one substance is reduced and the other is oxidized.

redress ❶ v **1** make amends for. ▷ n **2** compensation or amends.

reduce ❶ v **1** bring down, lower. **2** lessen, weaken. **3** bring by force or necessity to some state or action. **4** slim. **5** simplify. **6** make (a sauce) more concentrated. **7** lose oxygen atoms in a chemical reaction. **reducible** adj **reduction** n.

redundant ❶ adj **1** (of a worker) no longer needed. **2** superfluous. **redundancy** n, pl **-cies**.

reduplicate v make double, repeat.

re-echo v **-echoing**, **-echoed** echo over and over again, resound.

reed n **1** tall grass that grows in swamps and shallow water. **2** tall straight stem of this plant. **3** Music vibrating cane or metal strip

——————— THESAURUS ———————

get pissed (off) (taboo sl), blow one's top, crack up (inf), fly off the handle (inf), go ballistic (sl, chiefly US), go mad (inf), lose it (inf)

red-blooded adj Inf = **vigorous**, lusty, robust, strong, virile

redeem v **1** = **make up for**, atone for, compensate for, make amends for **2** = **reinstate**, absolve, restore to favour **3** = **save**, deliver, free **4** = **buy back**, reclaim, recover, regain, repurchase, retrieve

redemption n **1** = **compensation**, amends, atonement, reparation **3** = **salvation**, deliverance **4** = **repurchase**, reclamation, recovery, repossession, retrieval

red-handed adj Inf = **in the act**, bang to rights (sl), (in) flagrante delicto

redoubtable adj = **formidable**, fearful, fearsome, mighty, powerful, strong

redress v **1** = **make amends for**, compensate for, make up for ▷ n **2** = **amends**, atonement, compensation, payment, recompense, reparation

reduce v **1, 2** = **lessen**, abate, curtail, cut, cut down, decrease, diminish, lower, moderate, shorten, weaken **3** = **degrade**, break, bring low, downgrade, humble

redundancy n = **unemployment**, joblessness, lay-off, the axe (inf), the sack (inf)

redundant adj **1** = **unemployed**, jobless, out of work **2** = **superfluous**, extra, inessential, supernumerary, surplus, unnecessary, unwanted

r

in certain wind instruments. **reedy** *adj* **reedier**, **reediest** **1** harsh and thin in tone. **2** full of reeds.

reef[1] *n* **1** ridge of rock or coral near the surface of the sea. **2** vein of ore.

reef[2] *n* **1** part of a sail which can be rolled up to reduce its area. ▷ *v* **2** take in a reef of. **reefer** *n* **1** short thick jacket worn esp. by sailors. **2** *old-fashioned slang* hand-rolled cigarette containing cannabis. **reef knot** two simple knots turned opposite ways.

reek ❶ *v* **1** smell strongly. ▷ *n* **2** strong unpleasant smell. **reek of** give a strong suggestion of.

reel[1] *n* **1** cylindrical object on which film, tape, thread, or wire is wound. **2** winding apparatus, as of a fishing rod. **3** roll of film. **reel in** *v* draw in by means of a reel. **reel off** *v* recite or write fluently or quickly.

reel[2] ❶ *v* stagger, sway, or whirl.

reel[3] *n* lively Scottish dance.

re-enter *v* **1** come back into a place, esp. a country. **2** (of a spacecraft) return into the earth's atmosphere. **re-entry** *n*.

ref *n informal* referee in sport.

refectory *n*, *pl* **-tories** room for meals in a college etc. **refectory table** long narrow dining table supported by two trestles.

refer ❶ *v* **-ferring**, **-ferred** (foll. by *to*) **1** allude (to). **2** be relevant (to). **3** send (to) for information. **4** direct (a patient) to another doctor. **5** submit (to) for decision. **referable**, **referrable** *adj* **referral** *n* **reference** *n* **1** act of referring. **2** citation or direction in a book. **3** written

testimonial regarding character or capabilities. **with reference to** concerning. **reference book** book, such as an encyclopedia or dictionary, containing information or facts. **reference library** library in which books may be consulted but not borrowed.

- **USAGE NOTE**
- Do not confuse a *reference* with
- a *testimonial*, which is an open
- letter of recommendation about
- someone.

referee ❶ *n* **1** umpire in sports, esp. football or boxing. **2** person willing to testify to someone's character etc. **3** arbitrator. ▷ *v* **-eeing**, **-eed** **4** act as referee of.

referendum ❶ *n*, *pl* **-dums**, **-da** direct vote of the electorate on an important question.

refill *v* **1** fill again. ▷ *n* **2** second or subsequent filling. **3** replacement supply of something in a permanent container.

refine ❶ *v* **1** purify. **2** improve. **3** separate (a mixture) into its components. **refined** *adj* **1** cultured or polite. **2** purified. **refinement** *n* **1** improvement or elaboration. **2** fineness of taste or manners. **3** subtlety. **refinery** *n*, *pl* **-eries** place where sugar, oil, etc. is refined.

refit *v* **1** make ready for use again by repairing or re-equipping. ▷ *n* **2** repair or re-equipping for further use.

reflation *n* increase in the supply of money and credit designed to encourage economic activity. **reflate** *v* **reflationary** *adj*.

THESAURUS

reek *v* **1** = **stink**, pong (*Brit inf*), smell ▷ *n* **2** = **stink**, fetor, odour, pong (*Brit inf*), smell, stench

reel[2] *v* = **stagger**, lurch, pitch, revolve, rock, roll, spin, sway, swirl, whirl

refer *v* (foll. by *to*) **1** = **allude**, bring up, cite, mention, speak of ▷ *v* **2** = **relate**, apply, belong, be relevant to, concern, pertain **3** = **consult**, apply, go, look up, turn to **4** = **direct**, guide, point, send

referee *n* **1** = **umpire**, adjudicator, judge, ref (*inf*) **3** = **arbitrator**, arbiter ▷ *v* **4 a** = **umpire**, adjudicate, judge **b** = **arbitrate**, mediate

reference *n* **2** = **citation**, allusion, mention, note, quotation

3 = **testimonial**, character, credentials, endorsement, recommendation

referendum *n* = **public vote**, plebiscite

refine *v* **1** = **purify**, clarify, cleanse, distil, filter, process **2** = **improve**, hone, perfect, polish

refined *adj* **1** = **cultured**, civilized, cultivated, elegant, polished, polite, well-bred **2** = **purified**, clarified, clean, distilled, filtered, processed, pure

refinement *n* **2** = **sophistication**, breeding, civility, courtesy, cultivation, culture, discrimination, gentility, good breeding, polish, taste **3** = **subtlety**, fine point, nicety, nuance

reflect ❶ v 1 throw back, esp. rays of light, heat, etc. 2 form an image of. 3 show. 4 consider at length. 5 bring credit or discredit upon. **reflecting telescope** telescope in which the initial image is formed by a concave mirror. **reflection** n 1 act of reflecting. 2 return of rays of heat, light, etc. from a surface. 3 image of an object given back by a mirror etc. 4 conscious thought or meditation. 5 attribution of discredit or blame. **reflective** adj 1 quiet, contemplative. 2 capable of reflecting images. **reflector** n 1 polished surface for reflecting light etc. 2 reflecting telescope.

reflex n 1 involuntary response to a stimulus or situation. ▷ adj 2 (of a muscular action) involuntary. 3 reflected. 4 (of an angle) more than 180°. **reflexive** adj Grammar 1 denoting a pronoun that refers back to the subject of a sentence or clause. 2 denoting a verb whose subject is the same as its object, e.g. dress oneself. **reflex camera** camera which uses a mirror to channel light from a lens to the viewfinder, so that the image seen is the same as the image photographed.

reflexology n foot massage as a therapy in alternative medicine.

reform ❶ n 1 improvement. ▷ v 2 improve. 3 abandon evil practices. **reformer** n **reformation** [ref-fer-**may**-shun] n 1 a reforming. 2 (R-) religious movement in 16th-century Europe that resulted in the establishment of the Protestant Churches. **reformatory** n, pl **-ries** (formerly) institution for reforming young offenders. **reformist** n, adj (person) seeking the reform of something rather than its abolition or overthrow.

refract v change the course of (light etc.) passing from one medium to another. **refraction** n **refractive** adj **refractor** n **refracting telescope** telescope in which the image is formed by a series of lenses (also **refractor**).

refractory adj 1 unmanageable or rebellious. 2 Medical resistant to treatment. 3 resistant to heat.

refrain¹ ❶ v **refrain from** keep oneself from doing.

refrain² ❶ n frequently repeated part of a song.

refresh ❶ v 1 revive or reinvigorate, as through food, drink, or rest. 2 stimulate (the memory). **refresher** n **refreshing** adj 1 having a reviving effect. 2 pleasantly different or new. **refreshment** n something that refreshes, esp. food or drink.

refrigerate ❶ v cool or freeze in order to preserve. **refrigeration** n **refrigerator** n full name for FRIDGE. **refrigerant** n 1 fluid capable of vaporizing at low temperatures, used in refrigerators. ▷ adj 2 refrigerating.

refuel v **-elling, -elled** supply or be supplied with fresh fuel.

refuge ❶ n (source of) shelter or protection. **refugee** n person who seeks refuge, esp. in a foreign country.

r

reflect v 1 = **throw back**, echo, return 2 = **mirror**, reproduce 3 = **show**, demonstrate, display, indicate, manifest, reveal 4 = **consider**, cogitate, meditate, muse, ponder, ruminate, think, wonder

reflection n 2 = **echo** 3 = **image**, mirror image 4 = **consideration**, cogitation, contemplation, idea, meditation, musing, observation, opinion, thinking, thought

reflective adj 1 = **thoughtful**, contemplative, meditative, pensive

reform n 1 = **improvement**, amendment, betterment, rehabilitation ▷ v 2 = **improve**, amend, correct, mend, rectify, restore 3 = **mend one's ways**, clean up one's act (inf), go straight (inf), pull one's socks up (Brit inf), shape up (inf), turn over a new leaf

refrain¹ v = **stop**, abstain, avoid, cease, desist, forbear, leave off, renounce

refrain² n = **chorus**, melody, tune

refresh v 1 = **revive**, brace, enliven, freshen, invigorate, revitalize, stimulate 2 = **stimulate**, jog, prompt, renew

refreshing adj 1 = **stimulating**, bracing, fresh, invigorating 2 = **new**, novel, original

refreshment n = **food and drink**, drink, snack, titbit

refrigerate v = **cool**, chill, freeze, keep cold

refuge n = **shelter**, asylum, haven,

refulgent *adj* shining, radiant.

refund ❶ *v* **1** pay back. ▷ *n* **2** return of money. **3** amount returned.

refurbish ❶ *v* renovate and brighten up. **refurbishment** *n*.

refuse¹ ❶ *v* **1** decline, deny, or reject. **2** (of a horse) be unwilling to jump a fence. **refusal** *n* denial of anything demanded or offered. **refusenik** *n* person who refuses to obey a law or cooperate with the government because of strong beliefs.

refuse² ❶ *n* rubbish or useless matter.

refute ❶ *v* disprove. **refutation** *n*.

regain ❶ *v* **1** get back or recover. **2** reach again.

regal ❶ *adj* of or like a king or queen. **regally** *adv* **regalia** *pl n* ceremonial emblems of royalty or high office.

regale ❶ *v* entertain (someone) with stories etc.

regard ❶ *v* **1** consider. **2** look at. **3** heed. ▷ *n* **4** respect or esteem. **5** attention. **6** look. ▷ *pl* **7** expression of goodwill. **as regards**, **regarding** in respect of, concerning. **regardless** *adj* **1** heedless. ▷ *adv* **2** in spite of

everything, e.g. *Carry on regardless*.

regatta *n* meeting for yacht or boat races.

regenerate ❶ *v* [ri-**jen**-er-ate] **1** (cause to) undergo spiritual, moral, or physical renewal. **2** reproduce or re-create. ▷ *adj* [ri-**jen**-er-it] **3** spiritually, morally, or physically renewed. **regeneration** *n* **regenerative** *adj*.

regent *n* **1** ruler of a kingdom during the absence, childhood, or illness of its monarch. ▷ *adj* **2** ruling as a regent, e.g. *prince regent*. **regency** *n*, *pl* **-cies** status or period of office of a regent.

reggae *n* style of Jamaican popular music with a strong beat.

regicide *n* **1** killing of a king. **2** person who kills a king.

regime ❶ [ray-**zheem**] *n* **1** system of government. **2** particular administration. **3** *Medical* regimen.

regimen *n* prescribed system of diet etc.

regiment *n* **1** organized body of troops as a unit of the army. **2** large number or group. **regimental** *adj* **regimentals** *pl n* military uniform. **regimentation** *n*

————————————————— THESAURUS —————————————————

hide-out, protection, retreat, sanctuary

refugee *n* = **exile**, displaced person, émigré, escapee

refund *v* **1** = **repay**, pay back, reimburse, restore, return ▷ *n* **2**, **3** = **repayment**, reimbursement, return

refurbish *v* = **renovate**, clean up, do up (*inf*), mend, overhaul, repair, restore, revamp

refusal *n* = **rejection**, denial, knock-back (*sl*), rebuff

refuse¹ *v* **1** = **reject**, decline, deny, say no, spurn, turn down, withhold

refuse² *n* = **rubbish**, garbage, junk (*inf*), litter, trash, waste

refute *v* = **disprove**, discredit, negate, overthrow, prove false, rebut

regain *v* **1** = **recover**, get back, recapture, recoup, retrieve, take back, win back **2** = **get back to**, reach again, return to

regal *adj* = **royal**, kingly or queenly, magnificent, majestic, noble, princely

regale *v* = **entertain**, amuse, delight, divert

regalia *pl n* = **trappings**, accoutrements, decorations, emblems, finery, paraphernalia

regard *v* **1** = **consider**, believe, deem, esteem, judge, rate, see, suppose, think, view **2** = **look at**, behold, check out (*inf*), clock (*Brit sl*), eye, eyeball (*US sl*), gaze at, observe, scrutinize, view, watch **3** = **heed**, attend, listen to, mind, pay attention to, take notice of ▷ *n* **4** = **respect**, care, concern, consideration, esteem, thought **5** = **heed**, attention, interest, mind, notice **6** = **look**, gaze, glance, scrutiny, stare ▷ *pl* **7** = **good wishes**, best wishes, compliments, greetings, respects **as regards**, **regarding** = **concerning**, about, in or with regard to, on the subject of, pertaining to, re, relating to, respecting, with reference to

regardless *adj* **1** = **heedless**, inconsiderate, indifferent, neglectful, negligent, rash, reckless, unmindful ▷ *adv* **2** = **in spite of everything**, anyway, in any case, nevertheless

regenerate *v* **1** = **renew**, breathe new life into, invigorate, reawaken, reinvigorate, rejuvenate, restore, revive

regime *n* **1, 2** = **government**, leadership, reign, rule, system

r

regimented adj very strictly controlled.

region ❶ n 1 administrative division of a country. 2 area considered as a unit but with no definite boundaries. 3 part of the body. **in the region of** approximately. **regional** adj **regionalism** n 1 division of a country or organization into geographical regions each having some autonomy. 2 loyalty to one's home region.

register ❶ n 1 (book containing) an official list or record of things. 2 range of a voice or instrument. ▷ v 3 enter in a register or set down in writing. 4 show or be shown on a meter or the face. 5 informal have an effect or make an impression. **registered** adj (of mail) insured against loss by the Post Office, e.g. a registered letter. **registration** n **registration document** document giving identification details of a vehicle, including its owner's name. **registration number** numbers and letters displayed on a vehicle to identify it. **registrar** n 1 keeper of official records. 2 senior hospital doctor, junior to a consultant. **registry** n, pl **-tries** 1 place where official records are kept. 2 registration of a ship's place of origin, e.g. a tanker of Liberian registry. **register office**, **registry office** place where births, marriages, and deaths are recorded.

Regius professor [**reej**-yuss] n professor appointed by the Crown to a university chair founded by a royal patron.

regress ❶ v revert to a former worse condition. **regression** n 1 act of regressing. 2 Psychology use of an earlier (inappropriate) mode of behaviour. **regressive** adj.

regret ❶ v **-gretting, -gretted** 1 feel sorry about. 2 express apology or distress. ▷ n 3 feeling of repentance, guilt, or sorrow. **regretful** adj **regrettable** adj **regrettably** adv.

regular ❶ adj 1 normal, customary, or usual. 2 symmetrical or even. 3 done or occurring according to a rule. 4 periodical. 5 employed continuously in the armed forces. ▷ n 6 regular soldier. 7 informal frequent customer. **regularity** n **regularize** v **regularly** adv.

regulate ❶ v 1 control, esp. by rules. 2 adjust slightly. **regulation** n 1 rule. 2 regulating. ▷ adj 3 in accordance with rules or conventions. **regulator** n device that automatically controls pressure, temperature, etc. **regulatory** adj.

regurgitate ❶ v 1 vomit. 2 (of some birds and animals) bring back (partly digested food) into the mouth. 3 reproduce (ideas, facts, etc.) without understanding them. **regurgitation** n.

THESAURUS

region n 1 = **area**, district, locality, part, place, quarter, section, sector, territory, tract, zone

regional adj = **local**, district, parochial, provincial, zonal

register n 1 = **list**, archives, catalogue, chronicle, diary, file, log, record, roll, roster ▷ v 3 = **record**, catalogue, chronicle, enlist, enrol, enter, list, note 4 = **show**, display, exhibit, express, indicate, manifest, mark, reveal

regress v = **revert**, backslide, degenerate, deteriorate, fall away or off, go back, lapse, relapse, return

regret v 1 = **feel sorry about**, bewail, deplore, lament 2 = **grieve**, bemoan, miss, mourn, repent, rue ▷ n 3 = **sorrow**, bitterness, compunction, contrition, penitence, remorse, repentance, ruefulness

regretful adj = **sorry**, apologetic, contrite, penitent, remorseful, repentant, rueful, sad, sorrowful

regrettable adj = **unfortunate**, disappointing, distressing, lamentable, sad, shameful

regular adj 1 = **normal**, common, customary, habitual, ordinary, routine, typical, usual 2 = **even**, balanced, flat, level, smooth, straight, symmetrical, uniform 3 = **systematic**, consistent, constant, even, fixed, ordered, set, stated, steady, uniform

regulate v 1 = **control**, direct, govern, guide, handle, manage, rule, run, supervise 2 = **adjust**, balance, fit, moderate, modulate, tune

regulation n 1 = **rule**, decree, dictate, edict, law, order, precept, statute 2 = **control**, direction, government, management, supervision

regurgitate v 1 = **vomit**, disgorge, puke (sl), sick up (inf), spew (out or up), throw up (inf)

r

rehabilitate ❶ v 1 help (a person) to readjust to society after illness, imprisonment, etc. 2 restore to a former position or rank. 3 restore the good reputation of. **rehabilitation** n.

rehash ❶ v 1 rework or reuse. ▷ n 2 old ideas presented in a new form.

rehearse ❶ v 1 practise (a play, concert, etc.). 2 repeat aloud. **rehearsal** n.

rehouse v provide with a new (and better) home.

Reich [**rike**] n German kingdom or regime. **Third Reich** Nazi dictatorship in Germany from 1933–45.

reign ❶ n 1 period of a sovereign's rule. 2 period when a person or thing is dominant, e.g. reign of terror. ▷ v 3 rule (a country). 4 be supreme.

reimburse ❶ v refund, pay back. **reimbursement** n.

rein ❶ v 1 check or manage with reins. 2 control or limit. **reins** pl n 1 narrow straps attached to a bit to guide a horse. 2 narrow straps attached to a harness to control a young child. 3 means of control. **give (a) free rein** allow a considerable amount of freedom.

reincarnation n 1 rebirth of a soul in successive bodies. 2 one of a series of such transmigrations. **reincarnate** v.

reindeer n, pl **-deer, -deers** deer of arctic regions with large branched antlers.

reinforce ❶ v 1 give added emphasis to. 2 strengthen with new support, material, or force. 3 strengthen with additional troops, ships, etc. **reinforcement** n **reinforced concrete** concrete strengthened by having steel mesh or bars embedded in it.

reinstate ❶ v restore to a former position. **reinstatement** n.

reiterate ❶ v repeat again and again. **reiteration** n.

reject ❶ v 1 refuse to accept or believe. 2 rebuff (a person). 3 discard as useless. 4 fail to accept (a tissue graft or organ transplant). ▷ n 5 person or thing rejected as not up to standard. **rejection** n.

rejig ❶ v **-jigging, -jigged** 1 re-equip (a factory or plant). 2 rearrange.

rejoice ❶ v feel or express great happiness. **rejoicing** n.

rejoin[1] v join again.

rejoin[2] ❶ v reply. **rejoinder** n answer, retort.

rejuvenate ❶ v restore youth or vitality to. **rejuvenation** n.

────────────────────── THESAURUS ──────────────

rehabilitate v 1 = **reintegrate**, adjust 3 = **redeem**, clear, reform, restore, save

rehash v 1 = **rework**, refashion, rejig (inf), reuse, rewrite ▷ n 2 = **reworking**, new version, rearrangement, rewrite

rehearsal n = **practice**, drill, preparation, rehearsing, run-through

rehearse v 1 = **practise**, drill, go over, prepare, run through, train 2 = **repeat**, recite

reign n 1 = **rule**, command, control, dominion, monarchy, power ▷ v 3 = **rule**, be in power, command, govern, influence 4 = **be supreme**, hold sway, predominate, prevail

reimburse v = **pay back**, compensate, recompense, refund, remunerate, repay, return

rein v 2 = **control**, check, curb, halt, hold back, limit, restrain, restrict ▷ pl n 3 = **control**, brake, bridle, check, curb, harness, hold, restraint

reinforce v 1 = **emphasize**, stress 2 = **support**, bolster, fortify, prop, strengthen, supplement, toughen

reinforcement n = **support**,
augmentation, brace, buttress, fortification, prop, stay, strengthening

reinstate v = **restore**, recall, re-establish, replace, return

reiterate v = **repeat**, do again, restate, say again

reject v 1 = **deny**, decline, disallow, exclude, renounce, repudiate, veto 2 = **rebuff**, jilt, refuse, repulse, say no to, spurn, turn down 3 = **discard**, eliminate, jettison, scrap, throw away or out ▷ n 5 = **castoff**, discard, failure, second

rejig v 2 = **rearrange**, alter, juggle, manipulate, reorganize, tweak

rejoice v = **be glad**, be happy, be overjoyed, celebrate, exult, glory

rejoicing n = **happiness**, celebration, elation, exultation, gladness, joy, jubilation, merrymaking

rejoin[2] v = **reply**, answer, respond, retort, riposte

rejoinder n = **reply**, answer, comeback (inf), response, retort, riposte

rejuvenate v = **revitalize**, breathe new life into, refresh, regenerate, renew, restore

r

rekindle *v* arouse former emotions or interests.

relapse ⊙ *v* **1** fall back into bad habits, illness, etc. ▷ *n* **2** return of bad habits, illness, etc.

relate ⊙ *v* **1** establish a relation between. **2** have reference or relation to. **3** have an understanding (of people or ideas). **4** tell (a story) or describe (an event). **related** *adj*.

relation ⊙ *n* **1** connection between things. **2** relative. **3** connection by blood or marriage. **4** act of relating (a story). ▷ *pl* **5** social or political dealings. **6** family. **7** *euphemistic* sexual intercourse. **relationship** *n* **1** dealings and feelings between people or countries. **2** emotional or sexual affair. **3** connection between two things. **4** association by blood or marriage, kinship, e.g. *my relationship with my parents*.

relative ⊙ *adj* **1** true to a certain degree or extent. **2** dependent on relation to something else, not absolute. **3** having reference or relation (to). **4** *Grammar* referring to a word or clause earlier in the sentence. ▷ *n* **5** person connected by blood or marriage. **relatively** *adv* **relativity** *n* **1** subject of two theories of Albert Einstein, dealing with relationships of space, time, and motion, and acceleration and gravity. **2** state of being relative.

relax ⊙ *v* **1** make or become looser, less tense, or less rigid. **2** ease up from effort or attention, rest. **3** be less strict about. **4** become more friendly. **relaxed** *adj* **relaxing** *adj* **relaxation** *n*.

relay ⊙ *n* **1** fresh set of people or animals relieving others. **2** *Electricity* device for making or breaking a local circuit. **3** broadcasting station receiving and retransmitting programmes. ▷ *v* **-laying, -layed 4** pass on (a message). **relay race** race between teams in which each runner races part of the distance.

release ⊙ *v* **1** set free. **2** let go or fall. **3** issue (a record, film, etc.) for sale or public showing. **4** emit heat, energy, etc. ▷ *n* **5** setting free. **6** statement to

—————————————— THESAURUS ——————————————

relapse *v* **1 a** = **lapse**, backslide, degenerate, fail, regress, revert, slip back **b** = **worsen**, deteriorate, fade, fail, sicken, sink, weaken ▷ *n* **2 a** = **lapse**, backsliding, regression, retrogression **b** = **worsening**, deterioration, turn for the worse, weakening

relate *v* **1** = **connect**, associate, correlate, couple, join, link **2** = **concern**, apply, be relevant to, have to do with, pertain, refer **4** = **tell**, describe, detail, narrate, recite, recount, report

related *adj* **1** = **akin**, kindred **2** = **associated**, affiliated, akin, connected, interconnected, joint, linked

relation *n* **1** = **connection**, bearing, bond, comparison, correlation, link **2** = **relative**, kin, kinsman *or* kinswoman **3** = **kinship**, affinity, kindred ▷ *pl* **5** = **dealings**, affairs, connections, contact, interaction, intercourse, relationship **6** = **family**, clan, kin, kindred, kinsfolk, kinsmen, relatives, tribe

relationship *n* **2** = **affair**, liaison **3** = **connection**, correlation, link, parallel, similarity, tie-up

relative *adj* **2** = **dependent**, allied, associated, comparative, contingent, corresponding, proportionate, related **3** = **relevant**, applicable, apposite, appropriate, apropos, germane, pertinent ▷ *n* **5** = **relation**, kinsman *or* kinswoman, member of one's *or* the family

relatively *adv* = **comparatively**, rather, somewhat

relax *v* **1** = **lessen**, abate, ease, ebb, let up, loosen, lower, moderate, reduce, relieve, slacken, weaken **2** = **be** *or* **feel at ease**, calm, chill out (*sl, chiefly US*), outspan (*S Afr*), take it easy, unwind **3** = **lighten up** (*sl*), chill out (*sl, chiefly US*), take it easy

relaxation *n* = **leisure**, enjoyment, fun, pleasure, recreation, rest

relaxed *adj* = **easy-going**, casual, comfortable, easy, free and easy, informal, laid-back (*inf*), leisurely

relay *n* **1** = **shift**, relief, turn ▷ *v* **4** = **pass on**, broadcast, carry, communicate, send, spread, transmit

release *v* **1** = **set free**, discharge, drop, extricate, free, liberate, loose, unbridle, undo, unfasten **3** = **issue**, circulate, distribute, launch, make known, make public, publish, put out

r

the press. **7** act of issuing for sale or publication. **8** newly issued film, record, etc.

relegate ❶ v **1** put in a less important position. **2** demote (a sports team) to a lower league. **relegation** n.

relent ❶ v give up a harsh intention, become less severe. **relentless** adj **1** unremitting. **2** merciless.

relevant ❶ adj to do with the matter in hand. **relevance** n.

- ● **SPELLING TIP**
- ● A common word in English,
- ● **relevant** is not always spelt
- ● correctly. The final syllable is the
- ● problem and sometimes appears
- ● incorrectly in the Bank of English
- ● as -ent.

reliable ❶ adj able to be trusted, dependable. **reliably** adv **reliability** n.

reliance ❶ n dependence, confidence, or trust. **reliant** adj.

relic ❶ n **1** something that has survived from the past. **2** body or possession of a saint, regarded as holy. ▷ pl **3** remains or traces. **relict** n obs **1** relic. **2** widow.

relief ❶ n **1** gladness at the end or removal of pain, distress, etc. **2** release from monotony or duty. **3** money or food given to victims of

disaster, poverty, etc. **4** freeing of a besieged city etc. **5** person who replaces another. **6** projection of a carved design from the surface. **7** any vivid effect resulting from contrast, e.g. comic relief. **relieve** v bring relief to. **relieve oneself** urinate or defecate. **relief map** map showing the shape and height of land by shading.

religion ❶ n system of belief in and worship of a supernatural power or god. **religious** adj **1** of religion. **2** pious or devout. **3** scrupulous or conscientious. **religiously** adv.

relinquish ❶ v give up or abandon. **relinquishment** n.

reliquary [rel-lik-wer-ee] n, pl -quaries case or shrine for holy relics.

relish ❶ v **1** enjoy, like very much. **2** anticipate eagerly. ▷ n **3** liking or enjoyment. **4** pleasurable anticipation. **5** appetizing savoury food, such as pickle. **6** zestful quality or flavour.

relive v experience (a sensation etc.) again, esp. in the imagination.

relocate v move to a new place to live or work. **relocation** n.

reluctant ❶ adj unwilling or disinclined. **reluctantly** adv **reluctance** n.

——————————— THESAURUS ———————————

▷ n **5** = **liberation**, deliverance, discharge, emancipation, freedom, liberty **6** = **proclamation 7** = **issue**, publication

relegate v **1, 2** = **demote**, downgrade

relent v = **be merciful**, capitulate, change one's mind, come round, have pity, show mercy, soften, yield

relentless adj **1** = **unremitting**, incessant, nonstop, persistent, unrelenting, unrelieved **2** = **merciless**, cruel, fierce, implacable, pitiless, remorseless, ruthless, unrelenting

relevant adj = **significant**, apposite, appropriate, apt, fitting, germane, pertinent, related, to the point

reliable adj = **dependable**, faithful, safe, sound, staunch, sure, true, trustworthy

reliance n = **trust**, belief, confidence, dependence, faith

relic n **1** = **remnant**, fragment, keepsake, memento, souvenir, trace, vestige

relief n **1** = **ease**, comfort, cure, deliverance, mitigation, release,

remedy, solace **2** = **rest**, break, breather (inf), relaxation, respite **3** = **aid**, assistance, help, succour, support

relieve v **a** = **ease**, alleviate, assuage, calm, comfort, console, cure, mitigate, outspan (S Afr), relax, soften, soothe **b** = **help**, aid, assist, succour, support, sustain

religious adj **2** = **devout**, devotional, faithful, godly, holy, pious, sacred, spiritual **3** = **conscientious**, faithful, meticulous, punctilious, rigid, scrupulous

relinquish v = **give up**, abandon, abdicate, cede, drop, forsake, leave, let go, renounce, surrender

relish v **1** = **enjoy**, delight in, fancy, like, revel in, savour ▷ n **3** = **enjoyment**, fancy, fondness, gusto, liking, love, partiality, penchant, predilection, taste **5** = **condiment**, sauce, seasoning **6** = **flavour**, piquancy, smack, spice, tang, taste, trace

reluctant adj = **unwilling**, disinclined, hesitant, loath, unenthusiastic

rely ❶ v **-lying**, **-lied 1** depend (on).
2 trust. **reliable** adj able to be trusted.
remain ❶ v **1** continue. **2** stay, be left
behind. **3** be left (over). **4** be left to be
done, said, etc. **remains** pl n **1** relics,
esp. of ancient buildings. **2** dead body.
remainder n **1** part which is left.
2 amount left over after subtraction
or division. **3** copy of a book sold
cheaply because it has been
impossible to sell at full price. ▷ v
4 offer (copies of a poorly selling book)
at reduced prices.
remand v send back into custody or
put on bail before trial. **on remand** in
custody or on bail before trial.
remand centre place where accused
people are detained awaiting trial.
remark ❶ v **1** make a casual comment
(on). **2** say. **3** observe or notice. ▷ n
4 observation or comment.
remarkable adj **1** worthy of note or
attention. **2** striking or unusual.
remarkably adv.
remarry v **-rying**, **-ried** marry again
following a divorce or the death of
one's previous husband or wife.
rematch n Sport second or return game
or contest between two players.
remedy ❶ n, pl **-edies 1** means of curing

pain or disease. **2** means of solving a
problem. ▷ v **-edying**, **-edied 3** put
right. **remediable** adj able to be put
right. **remedial** adj intended to correct
a specific disability, etc.
remember ❶ v **1** retain in or recall to
one's memory. **2** keep in mind. **3** give
money to, as in a tip or through a will.
remember to pass on someone's
greeting to, e.g. remember me to your
mother. **remembrance** n **1** memory.
2 token or souvenir. **3** honouring of
the memory of a person or event.
Remembrance Day, **Remembrance
Sunday** Sunday closest to November
11, on which the dead of both World
Wars are commemorated.
remind ❶ v **1** cause to remember.
2 put in mind (of). **reminder** n
1 something that recalls the past.
2 note to remind a person of
something not done.
reminisce ❶ v talk or write of past
times, experiences, etc. **reminiscence**
n **1** remembering. **2** thing recollected.
▷ pl **3** memoirs. **reminiscent** adj
reminding or suggestive (of).
remiss ❶ adj negligent or careless.
remission ❶ n **1** reduction in the
length of a prison term. **2** pardon or

THESAURUS

rely v **1** = **depend**, bank, bet, count ▷ n
2 = **trust**
remain v **1** = **continue**, abide, dwell,
endure, go on, last, persist, stand,
stay, survive **2** = **stay behind**, be left,
delay, linger, wait
remainder n **1** = **rest**, balance, excess,
leavings, remains, remnant, residue,
surplus
remaining adj = **left-over**, lingering,
outstanding, persisting, surviving,
unfinished
remains pl n **1** = **remnants**, debris,
dregs, leavings, leftovers, relics,
residue, rest **2** = **corpse**, body,
cadaver, carcass
remark v **1, 2** = **comment**, declare,
mention, observe, pass comment,
reflect, say, state **3** = **notice**, espy,
make out, mark, note, observe,
perceive, see ▷ n **4** = **comment**,
observation, reflection, statement,
utterance
remarkable adj **1** = **notable**,
outstanding **2** = **extraordinary**, rare,
singular, striking, surprising,
uncommon, unusual, wonderful

remedy n **1** = **cure**, medicine, nostrum,
treatment ▷ v **3** = **put right**, correct,
fix, rectify
remember v **1** = **recall**, call to mind,
commemorate, look back (on),
recollect, reminisce, think back
2 = **bear in mind**, keep in mind
remembrance n **1** = **memory**, recall,
recollection, reminiscence, thought
2 = **souvenir**, commemoration,
keepsake, memento, memorial,
monument, reminder, token
remind v **1** = **call to mind**, jog one's
memory, make (someone) remember,
prompt
reminisce v = **recall**, hark back, look
back, recollect, remember, think back
reminiscence n **1, 2** = **recollection**,
anecdote, memoir, memory, recall,
remembrance
reminiscent adj = **suggestive**,
evocative, similar
remiss adj = **careless**, forgetful,
heedless, lax, neglectful, negligent,
thoughtless
remission n **2** = **pardon**, absolution,
amnesty, discharge, exemption,

r

forgiveness. **3** easing of intensity, as of an illness.

remit ❶ v [rim-**mitt**] -**mitting, -mitted
1** send (money) for goods, services, etc., esp. by post. **2** cancel (a punishment or debt). **3** refer (a decision) to a higher authority or later date. ▷ n [**ree**-mitt] **4** area of competence or authority. **remittance** n money sent as payment.

remix v **1** change the relative prominence of each performer's part of (a recording). ▷ n **2** remixed version of a recording.

remnant ❶ n **1** small piece, esp. of fabric, left over. **2** surviving trace.

remonstrate ❶ v argue in protest. **remonstrance, remonstration** n.

remorse ❶ n feeling of sorrow and regret for something one did. **remorseful** adj **remorseless** adj **1** pitiless. **2** persistent. **remorselessly** adv.

remote ❶ adj **1** far away, distant. **2** aloof. **3** slight or faint. **remotely** adv **remote control** control of an apparatus from a distance by an electrical device.

remould v **1** change completely. **2** renovate (a worn tyre). ▷ n **3** renovated tyre.

remove ❶ v **1** take away or off. **2** get rid of. **3** dismiss from office. ▷ n **4** degree of difference. **removable** adj **removal** n removing, esp. changing residence.

remunerate ❶ v reward or pay. **remuneration** n **remunerative** adj.

renaissance ❶ n **1** revival or rebirth. **2** (**R-**) revival of learning in the 14th–16th centuries. ▷ adj **3** (**R-**) of the Renaissance.

renal [**ree**-nal] adj of the kidneys.

renascent adj becoming active or vigorous again.

rend ❶ v **rending, rent 1** tear or wrench apart. **2** (of a sound) break (the silence) violently.

render ❶ v **1** cause to become. **2** give or provide (aid, a service, etc.). **3** submit or present (a bill). **4** portray or represent. **5** cover with plaster. **6** melt down (fat).

rendezvous ❶ [**ron**-day-voo] n, pl -**vous 1** appointment. **2** meeting place. ▷ v **3** meet as arranged.

release, reprieve **3 = lessening,** abatement, alleviation, ebb, lull, relaxation, respite

remit v **1 = send,** dispatch, forward, mail, post, transmit **2 = cancel,** halt, repeal, rescind, stop **3 = postpone,** defer, delay, put off, shelve, suspend

remittance n **= payment,** allowance, fee

remnant n **1, 2 = remainder,** end, fragment, leftovers, remains, residue, rest, trace, vestige

remonstrate v **= protest,** argue, dispute, dissent, object, take issue

remorse n **= regret,** anguish, compunction, contrition, grief, guilt, penitence, repentance, shame, sorrow

remorseless adj **1 = pitiless,** callous, cruel, inhumane, merciless, ruthless **2 = relentless,** inexorable, persistent

remote adj **1 = distant,** far, inaccessible, in the middle of nowhere, isolated, out-of-the-way, secluded **2 = aloof,** abstracted, cold, detached, distant, reserved, standoffish, uncommunicative, withdrawn **3 = slight,** doubtful, dubious, faint, outside, slender, slim, small, unlikely

removal n **a = taking away** or **off** or **out,** dislodgment, ejection, elimination, eradication, extraction, uprooting, withdrawal **b = dismissal,** expulsion **c = move,** departure, flitting (Scot & N Eng dial), relocation, transfer

remove v **1, 2 = take away** or **off** or **out,** abolish, delete, detach, displace, eject, eliminate, erase, excise, extract, get rid of, wipe from the face of the earth, withdraw **3 = dismiss,** depose, dethrone, discharge, expel, oust, throw out

remunerate v **= pay,** compensate, recompense, reimburse, repay, requite, reward

renaissance n **1 = rebirth,** reappearance, reawakening, renewal, restoration, resurgence, revival

rend v **1 = tear,** rip, rupture, separate, wrench

render v **1 = make,** cause to become, leave **2 = provide,** furnish, give, hand out, pay, present, submit, supply, tender **4 = represent,** act, depict, do, give, perform, play, portray

rendezvous n **1 = appointment,** assignation, date, engagement,

rendition ❶ n **1** performance.
2 translation.

renegade ❶ n person who deserts a cause.

renege ❶ [rin-**nayg**] v go back (on a
promise etc.).

renew ❶ v **1** begin again. **2** make valid
again. **3** grow again. **4** restore to a
former state. **5** replace (a worn part).
6 restate or reaffirm. **renewable** adj
renewables pl n sources of alternative
energy such as wind, wave, and solar
power. **renewal** n.

rennet n substance for curdling milk to
make cheese.

renounce ❶ v **1** give up (a belief, habit,
etc.) voluntarily. **2** give up (a title or
claim) formally. **renunciation** n.

renovate ❶ v restore to good
condition. **renovation** n.

renown ❶ n widespread good
reputation. **renowned** adj famous.

rent¹ ❶ v **1** give or have use of in return
for regular payments. ▷ n **2** regular
payment for use of land, a building,
machine, etc. **rental** n **1** sum
payable as rent. ▷ adj **2** of or relating
to rent.

rent² ❶ n **1** tear or fissure. ▷ v **2** past
of REND.

rentier [**ron**-tee-ay] n French person
who lives off unearned income such as
rents or interest.

renunciation ❶ n see RENOUNCE.

reorganize v organize in a new and
more efficient way. **reorganization** n.

rep¹ n short for REPERTORY COMPANY.

rep² n short for REPRESENTATIVE.

repaid v past of REPAY.

repair¹ ❶ v **1** restore to good condition,
mend. ▷ n **2** act of repairing.
3 repaired part. **4** state or condition,
e.g. in good repair. **repairable** adj
reparation n something done or
given as compensation.

repair² ❶ v go (to).

repartee ❶ n **1** interchange of witty
retorts. **2** witty retort.

repast n meal.

repatriate v send (someone) back to his
or her own country. **repatriation** n.

repay ❶ v **repaying**, **repaid 1** pay
back, refund. **2** do something in
return for, e.g. repay hospitality.
repayable adj **repayment** n.

———————————————— THESAURUS ————————————————

meeting, tryst (arch) **2** = **meeting
place**, gathering point, venue ▷ v
3 = **meet**, assemble, come together,
gather, join up

rendition n **1** = **performance**,
arrangement, interpretation,
portrayal, presentation, reading,
rendering, version **2** = **translation**,
interpretation, reading, transcription,
version

renegade n = **deserter**, apostate,
defector, traitor, turncoat

renege v = **break one's word**, back
out, break a promise, default,
go back

renew v **1** = **recommence**, continue,
extend, recreate, reopen, repeat,
resume **4** = **restore**, mend,
modernize, overhaul, refit, refurbish,
renovate, repair **5** = **replace**, refresh,
replenish, restock **6** = **reaffirm**

renounce v **1, 2** = **give up**, abjure, deny,
disown, forsake, forswear, quit,
recant, relinquish, waive

renovate v = **restore**, do up (inf),
modernize, overhaul, recondition,
refit, refurbish, renew, repair

renown n = **fame**, distinction,
eminence, note, reputation,
repute

renowned adj = **famous**, celebrated,
distinguished, eminent, esteemed,
notable, noted, well-known

rent¹ v **1** = **hire**, charter, lease, let ▷ n
2 = **hire**, fee, lease, payment, rental

rent² n **1** = **tear**, gash, hole, opening,
rip, slash, slit, split

renunciation n = **giving up**,
abandonment, abdication, abjuration,
denial, disavowal, forswearing,
rejection, relinquishment, repudiation

repair¹ v **1** = **mend**, fix, heal, patch,
patch up, renovate, restore ▷ n
2, 3 = **mend**, darn, overhaul, patch,
restoration **4** = **condition**, form,
shape (inf), state

repair² v = **go**, betake oneself, head for,
leave for, move, remove, retire, set off
for, withdraw

reparation n = **compensation**,
atonement, damages, recompense,
restitution, satisfaction

repartee n **1** = **wit**, badinage, banter,
wittiness, wordplay **2** = **riposte**

repay v **1** = **pay back**, compensate,
recompense, refund, reimburse,
requite, return, square
2 = **reciprocate**, avenge, get even
with (inf), get one's own back on (inf),
hit back, retaliate, revenge

r

repeal ❶ *v* **1** cancel (a law) officially. ▷ *n* **2** act of repealing.

repeat ❶ *v* **1** say or do again. **2** happen again, recur. ▷ *n* **3** act or instance of repeating. **4** programme broadcast again. **5** *Music* passage that is identical to the one before it. **repeated** *adj* **repeatedly** *adv* **repeater** *n* firearm that may be discharged many times without reloading. **repetition** *n* act of repeating.

repel ❶ *v* **-pelling**, **-pelled 1** be disgusting to. **2** drive back, ward off. **3** resist. **repellent** *adj* **1** distasteful. **2** resisting water etc. ▷ *n* **3** something that repels, esp. a chemical to repel insects.

repent ❶ *v* feel regret for (a deed or omission). **repentance** *n* **repentant** *adj*.

repercussions *pl n* indirect effects, often unpleasant.

repertoire ❶ *n* **1** stock of plays, songs, etc. that a player or company can give. **2** range of things someone or something is capable of doing.

repertory *n, pl* **-ries** repertoire.

repertory company permanent theatre company producing a succession of plays.

repetition ❶ *n* **1** act of repeating. **2** thing repeated. **repetitive**, **repetitious** *adj* full of repetition.

rephrase *v* express in different words.

repine *v* fret or complain.

replace ❶ *v* **1** substitute for. **2** put back. **replacement** *n*.

replay *n* **1** (also **action replay**) immediate reshowing on TV of an incident in sport, esp. in slow motion. **2** second sports match, esp. one following an earlier draw. ▷ *v* **3** play (a match, recording, etc.) again.

replenish ❶ *v* fill up again, resupply. **replenishment** *n*.

replete ❶ *adj* filled or gorged. **repletion** *n*.

replica ❶ *n* exact copy. **replicate** *v* make or be a copy of. **replication** *n*.

reply ❶ *v* **-plying**, **-plied 1** answer or respond. ▷ *n, pl* **-plies 2** answer or response.

report ❶ *v* **1** give an account of. **2** make a report (on). **3** make a formal complaint about. **4** present oneself

---

repeal *v* **1** = **abolish**, annul, cancel, invalidate, nullify, recall, reverse, revoke ▷ *n* **2** = **abolition**, annulment, cancellation, invalidation, rescindment

repeat *v* **1** = **reiterate**, echo, replay, reproduce, rerun, restate, retell ▷ *n* **3** = **repetition**, echo, reiteration, replay, rerun

repeatedly *adv* = **over and over**, frequently, many times, often

repel *v* **1** = **disgust**, gross out (*US sl*), nauseate, offend, revolt, sicken **2**, **3** = **drive off**, fight, hold off, parry, rebuff, repulse, resist, ward off

repellent *adj* **1** = **disgusting**, abhorrent, hateful, horrid, loathsome, nauseating, noxious, offensive, repugnant, repulsive, revolting, sickening **3** = **proof**, impermeable, repelling, resistant

repent *v* = **regret**, be sorry, feel remorse, rue

repentance *n* = **regret**, compunction, contrition, grief, guilt, penitence, remorse

repentant *adj* = **regretful**, contrite, penitent, remorseful, rueful, sorry

repercussions *pl n* = **consequences**, backlash, result, sequel, side effects

repertoire *n* **1** = **range**, collection, list,

repertory, stock, store, supply

repetition *n* = **repeating**, echo, recurrence, reiteration, renewal, replication, restatement, tautology

repetitive, **repetitious** *adj* = **monotonous**, boring, dull, mechanical, recurrent, tedious, unchanging, unvaried

replace *v* **1** = **take the place of**, follow, oust, substitute, succeed, supersede, supplant, take over from **2** = **put back**, re-establish, reinstate, restore

replacement *n* = **successor**, double, proxy, stand-in, substitute, surrogate, understudy

replenish *v* = **refill**, fill, provide, reload, replace, restore, top up

replete *adj* = **filled**, crammed, full, full up, glutted, gorged, sated, stuffed

replica *n* = **duplicate**, carbon copy (*inf*), copy, facsimile, imitation, model, reproduction

replicate *v* = **copy**, duplicate, mimic, recreate, reduplicate, reproduce

reply *v* **1** = **answer**, counter, reciprocate, rejoin, respond, retaliate, retort ▷ *n* **2** = **answer**, counter, counterattack, reaction, rejoinder, response, retaliation, retort

report *v* **1, 2** = **communicate**,

r

(to). **5** be responsible (to). ▷ *n*
6 account or statement. **7** rumour.
8 written statement of a child's
progress at school. **9** bang.
reportedly *adv* according to rumour.
reporter *n* person who gathers news
for a newspaper, TV, etc. **reported
speech** report that gives the content
of what someone said but not the
actual words.
repose¹ ❶ *n* **1** peace. **2** composure.
3 sleep. ▷ *v* **4** lie or lay at rest. **5** lie
when dead.
repose² *v* place one's trust (in).
repository ❶ *n, pl* **-ries** place where
valuables are deposited for
safekeeping, store.
repossess *v* (of a lender) take back
property from a customer who is behind
with payments. **repossession** *n*.
reprehend ❶ *v* harshly criticize or find
fault with someone or something, e.g.
*He roundly reprehended the acts of the
terrorists.*

reprehensible ❶ *adj* open to criticism,
unworthy.
represent ❶ *v* **1** act as a delegate or
substitute for. **2** stand for.
3 symbolize. **4** make out to be.
5 portray, as in art. **representation** *n*
representational *adj* (of art)
portraying people or things, not
abstract. **representative** *n* **1** person
chosen to stand for a group.
2 (travelling) salesperson. ▷ *adj*
3 typical.
repress ❶ *v* **1** keep (feelings) in check.
2 restrict the freedom of. **repression** *n*
repressive *adj*.
reprieve ❶ *v* **1** postpone the execution
of (a condemned person). **2** give
temporary relief to. ▷ *n* **3** (document
granting) postponement or
cancellation of a punishment.
4 temporary relief.
reprimand ❶ *v* **1** blame (someone)
officially for a fault. ▷ *n* **2** official
blame.

THESAURUS

broadcast, cover, describe, detail,
inform of, narrate, pass on, recount,
relate, state, tell **4** = **present oneself**,
appear, arrive, come, turn up ▷ *n*
6 = **account**, communication,
description, narrative, news, record,
statement, word **7** = **rumour**, buzz,
gossip, hearsay, talk **9** = **bang**, blast,
boom, crack, detonation, discharge,
explosion, noise, sound
reporter *n* = **journalist**,
correspondent, hack (*derog*), journo
(*sl*), pressman, writer
repose¹ *n* **1** = **peace**, ease, quietness,
relaxation, respite, rest, stillness,
tranquillity **2** = **composure**,
calmness, poise, self-possession
3 = **sleep**, slumber ▷ *v* **4** = **rest**, lie, lie
down, recline, rest upon
repository *n* = **store**, depository,
storehouse, treasury, vault
reprehensible *adj* = **blameworthy**,
bad, culpable, disgraceful,
objectionable, shameful, unworthy
represent *v* **1, 2** = **stand for**, act for,
betoken, mean, serve as, speak for,
symbolize **3** = **exemplify**, embody,
epitomize, personify, symbolize, typify
5 = **depict**, denote, describe, illustrate,
outline, picture, portray, show
representation *n* **a** = **picture**,
illustration, image, likeness, model,
portrait **b** = **portrayal**, account,

depiction, description
representative *n* **1** = **delegate**,
agent, deputy, member, proxy,
spokesman *or* spokeswoman
2 = **salesman**, agent, commercial
traveller, rep ▷ *adj* **3** = **typical**,
archetypal, characteristic, exemplary,
symbolic
repress *v* **1** = **control**, bottle up, check,
curb, hold back, inhibit, restrain,
stifle, suppress **2** = **subdue**, quell,
subjugate
repression *n* = **subjugation**,
constraint, control, despotism,
domination, restraint, suppression,
tyranny
repressive *adj* = **oppressive**, absolute,
authoritarian, despotic, dictatorial,
tyrannical
reprieve *v* **1** = **grant a stay of
execution to**, let off the hook (*sl*),
pardon **2** = **relieve**, abate, allay,
alleviate, mitigate, palliate ▷ *n*
3 = **stay of execution**, amnesty,
deferment, pardon, postponement,
remission **4** = **relief**, alleviation,
mitigation, palliation, respite
reprimand *v* **1** = **blame**, censure, dress
down (*inf*), haul over the coals (*inf*),
rap over the knuckles (*inf*), rouse
on (*Aust*), scold, tear (someone) off a
strip (*Brit inf*) ▷ *n* **2** = **blame**, censure,
dressing-down (*inf*), rebuke, reproach,

reprint *v* **1** print further copies of (a book). ▷ *n* **2** reprinted copy.

reprisal ❶ *n* retaliation.

reproach ❶ *n*, *v* blame, rebuke. **reproachful** *adj* **reproachfully** *adv*.

reprobate [**rep**-roh-bate] *adj*, *n* depraved or disreputable (person). **reprobation** *n* disapproval or blame.

reproduce ❶ *v* **1** produce a copy of. **2** bring new individuals into existence. **3** re-create. **reproducible** *adj* **reproduction** *n* **1** process of reproducing. **2** facsimile, as of a painting etc. **3** quality of sound from an audio system. ▷ *adj* **4** made in imitation of an earlier style, e.g. *reproduction furniture*. **reproductive** *adj*.

reprove ❶ *v* speak severely to (someone) about a fault. **reproof** *n* severe blaming of someone for a fault.

reptile *n* cold-blooded egg-laying vertebrate with horny scales or plates, such as a snake or tortoise. **reptilian** *adj*.

republic *n* **1** form of government in which the people or their elected representatives possess the supreme power. **2** country in which a president is the head of state. **republican** *adj* **1** of or supporting a republic. ▷ *n* **2** person who supports or advocates a republic. **republicanism** *n* **Republican** *n*, *adj* **1** (member or supporter) of the Republican Party, the more conservative of the two main political parties in the US. **2** (member or supporter) of the Irish Republican Army. **Republicanism** *n*.

repudiate ❶ [rip-**pew**-dee-ate] *v* **1** reject the authority or validity of. **2** disown. **repudiation** *n*.

repugnant ❶ *adj* offensive or distasteful. **repugnance** *n*.

repulse ❶ *v* **1** be disgusting to. **2** drive (an army) back. **3** rebuff or reject. ▷ *n* **4** driving back. **5** rejection or rebuff. **repulsion** *n* **1** distaste or aversion. **2** *Physics* force separating two objects. **repulsive** *adj* loathsome, disgusting.

reputation ❶ *n* estimation in which a person is held. **reputable** [**rep**-pew-tab-bl] *adj* of good reputation, respectable. **repute** *n* reputation. **reputed** *adj* supposed. **reputedly** *adv*.

reproof, talking-to (*inf*)

reprisal *n* = **retaliation**, retribution, revenge, vengeance

reproach *n* = **blame**, censure, condemnation, disapproval, opprobrium, rebuke ▷ *v* = **blame**, censure, condemn, criticize, lambast(e), read the riot act, rebuke, reprimand, rouse on (*Aust*), scold, upbraid

reproduce *v* **1** = **copy**, duplicate, echo, imitate, match, mirror, recreate, repeat, replicate **2** = **breed**, multiply, procreate, propagate, spawn

reproduction *n* **1** = **breeding**, generation, increase, multiplication **2** = **copy**, duplicate, facsimile, imitation, picture, print, replica

reproof *n* = **rebuke**, blame, censure, condemnation, criticism, reprimand, scolding

reprove *v* = **rebuke**, berate, blame, censure, condemn, read the riot act, reprimand, rouse on (*Aust*), scold, tear into (*inf*), tear (someone) off a strip (*Brit inf*), tell off (*inf*)

repudiate *v* **1** = **reject**, deny, disavow, disclaim, renounce **2** = **disown**

repugnance *n* = **distaste**, abhorrence, aversion, disgust, dislike, hatred,

loathing

repugnant *adj* = **distasteful**, abhorrent, disgusting, loathsome, nauseating, offensive, repellent, revolting, sickening, vile

repulse *v* **1** = **disgust**, nauseate, offend, put off, repel, revolt, sicken, turn one's stomach **2** = **drive back**, beat off, fight off, rebuff, repel, ward off **3** = **reject**, rebuff, refuse, snub, spurn, turn down

repulsion *n* **1** = **disgust**, abhorrence, aversion, detestation, distaste, hatred, loathing, repugnance, revulsion

repulsive *adj* = **disgusting**, abhorrent, foul, loathsome, nauseating, repellent, revolting, sickening, vile

reputable *adj* = **respectable**, creditable, excellent, good, honourable, reliable, trustworthy, well-thought-of, worthy

reputation *n* = **name**, character, esteem, estimation, renown, repute, standing, stature

repute *n* = **reputation**, celebrity, distinction, eminence, fame, name, renown, standing, stature

reputed *adj* = **supposed**, alleged, believed, considered, deemed,

request ❶ v 1 ask. ▷ n 2 asking.
3 thing asked for.
Requiem [rek-wee-em] n 1 Mass for
the dead. 2 music for this.
require ❶ v 1 want or need. 2 demand.
requirement n 1 essential condition.
2 specific need or want.
requisite ❶ [rek-wizz-it] adj
1 necessary, essential. ▷ n 2 essential
thing.
requisition ❶ v 1 demand (supplies).
▷ n 2 formal demand, such as for
materials or supplies.
requite ❶ v return to someone (the
same treatment or feeling as
received). **requital** n.
reredos [rear-doss] n ornamental
screen behind an altar.
rerun n 1 film or programme that is
broadcast again, repeat. 2 race that is
run again. ▷ v 3 put on (a film or
programme) again. 4 run (a race)
again.
resale n selling of something purchased
earlier.
rescind ❶ v annul or repeal.

rescue ❶ v -cuing, -cued 1 deliver from
danger or trouble, save. ▷ n
2 rescuing. **rescuer** n.
research ❶ n 1 systematic
investigation to discover facts or
collect information. ▷ v 2 carry out
investigations. **researcher** n.
resemble ❶ v be or look like.
resemblance n.
resent ❶ v feel indignant or bitter
about. **resentful** adj **resentment** n.
reservation ❶ n 1 doubt. 2 exception
or limitation. 3 seat, room, etc. that
has been reserved. 4 area of land
reserved for use by a particular group.
5 (also **central reservation**) strip of
ground separating the two
carriageways of a dual carriageway or
motorway.
reserve ❶ v 1 set aside, keep for future
use. 2 obtain by arranging
beforehand, book. 3 retain. ▷ n
4 something, esp. money or troops,
kept for emergencies. 5 area of land
reserved for a particular purpose.
6 Sport substitute. 7 concealment of

THESAURUS

estimated, held, reckoned, regarded
request v 1 = **ask (for)**, appeal for,
demand, desire, entreat, invite, seek,
solicit ▷ n 2 = **asking**, appeal, call,
demand, desire, entreaty, suit
require v 1 = **need**, crave, desire, lack,
miss, want, wish 2 = **order**, ask, bid,
call upon, command, compel,
demand, exact, insist upon
requirement n 1 = **necessity**,
demand, essential, must, prerequisite,
stipulation 2 = **need**, lack, want
requisite adj 1 = **necessary**, called for,
essential, indispensable, needed,
needful, obligatory, required ▷ n
2 = **necessity**, condition, essential,
must, need, prerequisite, requirement
requisition v 1 = **demand**, call for,
request ▷ n 2 = **demand**, call, request,
summons
requital n = **return**, repayment
requite v = **return**, get even, give in
return, pay (someone) back in his or
her own coin, reciprocate, repay,
respond, retaliate
rescind v = **annul**, cancel,
countermand, declare null and void,
invalidate, repeal, set aside
rescue v 1 = **save**, deliver, get out,
liberate, recover, redeem, release,
salvage ▷ n 2 = **liberation**,

deliverance, recovery, redemption,
release, salvage, salvation, saving
research n 1 = **investigation**,
analysis, examination, exploration,
probe, study ▷ v 2 = **investigate**,
analyse, examine, explore, probe,
study
resemblance n = **similarity**,
correspondence, kinship, likeness,
parallel, sameness, similitude
resemble v = **be like**, bear a
resemblance to, be similar to, look
like, mirror, parallel
resent v = **be bitter about**, begrudge,
be pissed (off) about (taboo sl), grudge,
object to, take exception to, take
offence at
resentful adj = **bitter**, angry,
embittered, grudging, indignant,
miffed (inf), offended, piqued, pissed
(off) (taboo sl)
resentment n = **bitterness**,
animosity, bad blood, grudge, ill
feeling, ill will, indignation, pique,
rancour, umbrage
reservation n 1 = **doubt**, hesitancy,
scruple 2 = **condition**, proviso,
qualification, rider, stipulation
4 = **reserve**, sanctuary, territory
reserve v 1 = **keep**, hoard, hold, put by,
retain, save, set aside, stockpile, store

r

feelings or friendliness. **reservation** n
1 doubt. **2** exception or limitation.
3 seat, room, etc. that has been
reserved. **reserved** adj **1** not showing
one's feelings, lacking friendliness.
2 set aside for use by a particular
person. **reservist** n member of a
military reserve. **reserve price**
minimum price acceptable to the
owner of property being auctioned.

reservoir ❶ n **1** natural or artificial lake
storing water for community supplies.
2 store or supply of something.

reshuffle n **1** reorganization. ▷ v
2 reorganize.

reside ❶ v dwell permanently.
residence n **1** home or house.
2 (period of) living in a place. **in
residence** (of an artist) working for a
set period at a college, gallery, etc.,
e.g. writer in residence. **resident** n
1 person who lives in a place. **2** bird or
animal that does not migrate. ▷ adj
3 living in a place. **4** (of a bird or
animal) not migrating. **residential** adj
1 (of part of a town) consisting mainly
of houses. **2** providing living
accommodation.

residue ❶ n **1** what is left, remainder.
2 Law what is left of an estate after
debts have been paid and specific gifts

made. **residual** adj **residuum** n, pl **-ua**
residue.

resign ❶ v **1** give up office, a job, etc.
2 reconcile (oneself) to. **3** give up a
right, claim, etc. **resigned** adj content
to endure. **resignation** n **1** resigning.
2 passive endurance of difficulties.

resilient ❶ adj **1** (of a person)
recovering quickly from a shock etc.
2 able to return to normal shape after
stretching etc. **resilience** n.

resin [rezz-in] n **1** sticky substance
from plants, esp. pines. **2** similar
synthetic substance. **resinous** adj.

resist ❶ v **1** withstand or oppose.
2 refrain from despite temptation.
3 be proof against. **resistance** n **1** act
of resisting. **2** capacity to withstand
something. **3** Electricity opposition
offered by a circuit to the passage of a
current through it. **4** any force that
slows or hampers movement, e.g.
wind resistance. **5** (R-) illegal
organization fighting for national
liberty in a country under enemy
occupation. **resistant** adj **resistible**
adj **resistor** n component of an
electrical circuit producing resistance.

resit v **-sitting**, **-sat 1** take (an exam)
again. ▷ n **2** exam that has to be taken
again.

---

2 = **book**, engage, prearrange, secure
▷ n **4** = **store**, cache, fund, hoard,
reservoir, savings, stock, supply
5 = **reservation**, park, preserve,
sanctuary, tract **6** Sport = **substitute**
7 = **shyness**, constraint, reservation,
restraint, reticence, secretiveness,
silence, taciturnity
reserved adj **1** = **uncommunicative**,
restrained, reticent, retiring,
secretive, shy, silent, standoffish,
taciturn, undemonstrative **2** = **set
aside**, booked, engaged, held, kept,
restricted, retained, spoken for, taken
reservoir n **1** = **lake**, basin, pond, tank
2 = **store**, pool, reserves, source,
stock, supply
reside v = **live**, abide, dwell, inhabit,
lodge, stay
residence n **1** = **home**, abode,
domicile, dwelling, flat, habitation,
house, lodging, place
resident n **1** = **inhabitant**, citizen,
local, lodger, occupant, tenant
residual adj **1** = **remaining**, leftover,
unconsumed, unused, vestigial

residue n **1** = **remainder**, dregs,
excess, extra, leftovers, remains,
remnant, rest, surplus
resign v **1** = **quit**, abdicate, give in one's
notice, leave, step down (inf), vacate
2 = **accept**, acquiesce, give in, resign
oneself, submit, succumb, yield
3 = **give up**, abandon, forgo, forsake,
relinquish, renounce, surrender, yield
resignation n **1** = **leaving**,
abandonment, abdication, departure
2 = **acceptance**, acquiescence,
compliance, endurance,
nonresistance, passivity, patience,
submission, sufferance
resigned adj = **stoical**, compliant,
long-suffering, patient, subdued,
unresisting
resilient adj **1** = **tough**, buoyant,
hardy, irrepressible, strong
2 = **flexible**, elastic, plastic, pliable,
rubbery, springy, supple
resist v **1** = **oppose**, battle, combat,
defy, hinder, stand up to **2** = **refrain
from**, abstain from, avoid, forbear,
forgo, keep from **3** = **withstand**, be

r

resolute ❶ *adj* firm in purpose.
resolutely *adv* **resolution** *n*
1 firmness of conduct or character.
2 thing resolved upon. **3** decision of a
court or vote of an assembly. **4** act of
resolving. **5** ability of a television,
microscope, etc. to show fine detail.
resolve ❶ *v* **1** decide with an effort of
will. **2** form (a resolution) by a vote.
3 separate the component parts of.
4 make clear, settle. ▷ *n* **5** absolute
determination. **resolved** *adj*
determined.
resonance ❶ *n* **1** echoing, esp. with a
deep sound. **2** sound produced in one
object by sound waves coming from
another object. **resonant** *adj*
resonate *v* **resonator** *n*.
resort ❶ *v* **1** have recourse (to) for help
etc. ▷ *n* **2** place for holidays.
3 recourse.

resound ❶ [riz-**zownd**] *v* **1** echo or ring
with sound. **2** (of sounds) echo or
ring. **3** be widely known, e.g. *his fame
resounded through the land*. **resounding**
adj **1** echoing. **2** clear and emphatic.
resource ❶ *n* **1** thing resorted to for
support. **2** ingenuity. **3** means of
achieving something. ▷ *pl* **4** sources
of economic wealth. **5** stock that can
be drawn on, funds. **resourceful** *adj*
resourcefulness *n*.
respect ❶ *n* **1** consideration.
2 deference or esteem. **3** point or
aspect. **4** reference or relation, e.g.
with respect to. ▷ *pl* **5** polite greetings.
▷ *v* **6** treat with esteem. **7** show
consideration for. **respecter** *n*
respectful *adj* **respectfully** *adv*
respecting *prep* concerning.
respectable ❶ *adj* **1** worthy of respect.
2 having good social standing and

---

proof against
resistance *n* **1** = **fighting**, battle,
defiance, fight, hindrance,
impediment, obstruction, opposition,
struggle
resistant *adj* **1** = **opposed**,
antagonistic, hostile, intractable,
intransigent, unwilling
3 = **impervious**, hard, proof against,
strong, tough, unaffected by
resolute *adj* = **determined**, dogged,
firm, fixed, immovable, inflexible, set,
steadfast, strong-willed, tenacious,
unshakable, unwavering
resolution *n* **1** = **determination**,
doggedness, firmness, perseverance,
purpose, resoluteness, resolve,
steadfastness, tenacity, willpower
2 = **decision**, aim, declaration,
determination, intent, intention,
purpose, resolve
resolve *v* **1** = **decide**, agree, conclude,
determine, fix, intend, purpose
3 = **break down**, analyse, reduce,
separate **4** = **work out**, answer, clear
up, crack, fathom ▷ *n*
5 = **determination**, firmness,
resoluteness, resolution,
steadfastness, willpower
resonant *adj* = **echoing**, booming,
resounding, reverberating, ringing,
sonorous
resort *v* **1** = **have recourse to**, employ,
fall back on, turn to, use, utilize ▷ *n*
2 = **holiday centre**, haunt, retreat,
spot, tourist centre **3** = **recourse**,

reference
resound *v* **1, 2** = **echo**, re-echo,
resonate, reverberate, ring
resounding *adj* **1** = **echoing**, booming,
full, powerful, resonant, ringing,
sonorous
resource *n* **2** = **ingenuity**, ability,
capability, cleverness, initiative,
inventiveness **3** = **means**, course,
device, expedient, resort ▷ *pl*
4 = **assets**, capital, holdings, lolly
(*Aust & NZ sl*), money, riches, wealth
5 = **funds**, reserves, supplies
resourceful *adj* = **ingenious**, able,
bright, capable, clever, creative,
inventive
respect *n* **1** = **consideration**
2 = **regard**, admiration, deference,
esteem, estimation, honour,
recognition **3** = **particular**, aspect,
characteristic, detail, feature, matter,
point, sense, way **4** = **relation**,
bearing, connection, reference, regard
▷ *v* **6** = **think highly of**, admire, defer
to, esteem, have a good *or* high
opinion of, honour, look up to, value
7 = **abide by**, adhere to, comply with,
follow, heed, honour, obey, observe,
show consideration for
respectable *adj* **1, 2** = **honourable**,
decent, estimable, good, honest,
reputable, upright, worthy
3 = **reasonable**, ample, appreciable,
considerable, decent, fair, sizable *or*
sizeable, substantial
respectful *adj* = **polite**, civil,

r

reputation. **3** fairly good.
respectably adv **respectability** n.
respective ❶ adj relating separately to
each of those in question.
respectively adv.
respiration [ress-per-**ray**-shun] n
1 breathing. **2** process in plants and
animals of taking in oxygen and giving
out carbon dioxide. **3** breakdown of
complex organic substances by living
cells to produce energy and carbon
dioxide. **respirator** n apparatus worn
over the mouth and breathed through
as protection against dust, poison
gas, etc., or to provide artificial
respiration. **respiratory** adj **respire** v
breathe.
respite ❶ n **1** pause, interval of rest.
2 delay.
resplendent ❶ adj **1** brilliant or
splendid. **2** shining. **resplendence** n.
respond ❶ v **1** answer. **2** act in answer
to any stimulus. **3** react favourably.
respondent n Law defendant.
response n **1** answer. **2** reaction to a
stimulus. **3** (in some Christian
churches) words sung or recited in
reply to a priest during a service.
responsive adj readily reacting to
some influence. **responsiveness** n.
responsible ❶ adj **1** having control

and authority. **2** being the cause
(of some action). **3** reporting or
accountable (to). **4** sensible and
dependable. **5** involving
responsibility. **responsibly** adv
responsibility n, pl **-ties 1** state of
being responsible. **2** person or thing
for which one is responsible.
respray n new coat of paint applied to
a car, van, etc.
rest¹ ❶ n **1** freedom from exertion etc.
2 repose. **3** pause, esp. in music.
4 object used for support. ▷ v **5** take a
rest. **6** give a rest (to). **7** be
supported. **8** place on a support.
9 depend or rely, e.g. their hopes rested
on an early end to the dispute. **10** (of
someone's gaze) direct at or settle on,
e.g. her eyes rested on the dog. **restful**
adj **restless** adj.
rest² ❶ n **1** what is left. **2** others. ▷ v
3 remain, continue to be.
restaurant ❶ n commercial
establishment serving meals.
restaurateur [rest-er-a-**tur**] n person
who owns or runs a restaurant.
restaurant car railway coach where
meals are served.
restitution ❶ n **1** giving back.
2 reparation or compensation.
restive ❶ adj restless or impatient.

——————————————————— THESAURUS ——————

courteous, deferential, mannerly,
reverent, well-mannered
respective adj = **specific**, individual,
own, particular, relevant
respite n **1** = **pause**, break, cessation,
halt, interval, lull, recess, relief, rest
resplendent adj **1, 2** = **brilliant**, bright,
dazzling, glorious, radiant, shining,
splendid
respond v **1** = **answer**, counter,
reciprocate, rejoin, reply, retort,
return **2** = **react**
response n **1** = **answer**, feedback,
rejoinder, reply, retort, return
2 = **reaction**
responsibility n **1** = **accountability**,
answerability, blame, culpability,
fault, guilt, liability **2** = **duty**, care,
charge, liability, obligation, onus
responsible adj **1** = **in charge**, in
authority, in control **2** = **to blame**, at
fault, culpable, guilty
3 = **accountable**, answerable, liable
4 = **sensible**, dependable, level-
headed, rational, reliable,
trustworthy

responsive adj = **sensitive**, alive,
impressionable, open, reactive,
receptive, susceptible
rest¹ n **1** = **inactivity 2** = **relaxation**,
leisure, repose **3** = **pause**, break,
cessation, halt, interlude,
intermission, interval, lull, respite,
stop **4** = **support**, base, holder, prop,
stand ▷ v **5 a** = **relax**, be at ease, put
one's feet up, sit down, take it easy
b = **stop**, break off, cease, halt, have a
break, take a breather (inf) **7** = **be
supported**, lean, lie, recline, repose,
sit **8** = **place**, lean, lie, prop, sit
rest² n **1** = **remainder**, balance, excess,
remains, remnants, residue, surplus
2 = **others**
restaurant n = **café**, bistro, cafeteria,
diner (chiefly US & Canad), tearoom
restful adj = **relaxing**, calm, calming,
peaceful, quiet, relaxed, serene,
soothing, tranquil
restitution n **1** = **return**, restoration
2 = **compensation**, amends,
recompense, reparation, requital
restive adj = **restless**, edgy, fidgety,

restore ❶ v **1** return (a building, painting, etc.) to its original condition. **2** cause to recover health or spirits. **3** give back, return. **4** re-establish. **restoration** n **restorative** [rest-**or**-a-tiv] adj **1** restoring. ▷ n **2** food or medicine to strengthen etc. **restorer** n.

restrain ❶ v **1** hold (someone) back from action. **2** control or restrict. **restraint** n **1** something that restrains. **2** control, esp. self-control. **3** restraining. **restrained** adj not displaying emotion.

restrict ❶ v confine to certain limits. **restriction** n **restrictive** adj **restrictive practice** trading or industrial agreement which is against the interests of the public or other business interests.

restructure v reorganize.

result ❶ n **1** outcome or consequence. **2** score. **3** number obtained from a calculation. **4** exam mark or grade. ▷ v **5** (foll. by from) be the outcome or consequence (of). **6** (foll. by in) end (in). **resultant** adj **1** arising as a result. ▷ n **2** Maths, Physics sum of two or

more vectors, such as the force resulting from two or more forces acting on a single point.

resume ❶ v **1** begin again. **2** occupy or take again. **resumption** n.

résumé [**rezz**-yew-may] n summary.

resurgence ❶ n rising again to vigour. **resurgent** adj.

resurrect ❶ v **1** restore to life. **2** use once more (something discarded etc.), revive. **resurrection** n **1** rising again (esp. from the dead). **2** revival.

resuscitate ❶ [ris-**suss**-it-tate] v restore to consciousness. **resuscitation** n.

● **SPELLING TIP**
● There is a silent c in **resuscitate**, but
● only one: it comes after the second
● s, not after the first one.

retail n **1** selling of goods individually or in small amounts to the public. ▷ adj **2** of or engaged in such selling. ▷ adv **3** by retail. ▷ v **4** sell or be sold retail. **5** recount in detail. **retailer** n.

retain ❶ v **1** keep in one's possession. **2** be able to hold or contain. **3** engage the services of. **retainer** n **1** fee to retain someone's services. **2** payment

———— THESAURUS ————

impatient, jumpy, nervous, on edge, wired (sl)

restless adj **a** = **moving**, nomadic, roving, transient, unsettled, unstable, wandering **b** = **unsettled**, edgy, fidgeting, fidgety, jumpy, nervous, on edge, restive, wired (sl)

restore v **1** = **repair**, fix, mend, rebuild, recondition, reconstruct, refurbish, renew, renovate **2** = **revive**, build up, refresh, revitalize, strengthen **3** = **return**, bring back, give back, recover, reinstate, replace **4** = **reinstate**, re-establish, reintroduce

restrain v **1, 2** = **hold back**, check, constrain, contain, control, curb, curtail, hamper, hinder, inhibit, restrict

restrained adj = **controlled**, calm, mild, moderate, self-controlled, undemonstrative

restraint n **1** = **limitation**, ban, check, curb, embargo, interdict, limit, rein **2** = **self-control**, control, inhibition, moderation, self-discipline, self-possession, self-restraint

restrict v = **limit**, bound, confine, contain, hamper, handicap, inhibit, regulate, restrain

result n **1** = **consequence**, effect, end, end result, outcome, product, sequel, upshot ▷ v **5** (foll. by from) = **arise**, appear, derive, develop, ensue, follow, happen, issue, spring **6** (foll. by in) = **end**, culminate

resume v **1** = **begin again**, carry on, continue, go on, proceed, reopen, restart

résumé n = **summary**, précis, recapitulation, rundown, synopsis

resurgence n = **revival**, rebirth, re-emergence, renaissance, resumption, resurrection, return

resurrect v **1** = **restore to life**, raise from the dead **2** = **revive**, bring back, reintroduce, renew

resurrection n **1** = **raising** or **rising from the dead**, return from the dead **2** = **revival**, reappearance, rebirth, renaissance, renewal, restoration, resurgence, return

resuscitate v = **revive**, bring round, resurrect, revitalize, save

retain v **1** = **keep**, hold, maintain, preserve, reserve, save **2** = **hold 3** = **hire**, commission, employ, engage, pay, reserve

retainer n **1, 2** = **fee**, advance, deposit

to reserve a room or flat for future use.
3 old-established servant of a family.
retake *v* **-taking, -took, -taken**
1 recapture. **2** take something, such as
an examination, again. ▷ *n* **3** *Films* act
of rephotographing a scene.
retaliate ❶ *v* repay an injury or wrong
in kind. **retaliation** *n* **retaliatory** *adj*.
retard ❶ *v* delay or slow (progress or
development). **retarded** *adj*
underdeveloped, esp. mentally.
retardation *n*.
retch ❶ *v* try to vomit.
retention *n* **1** retaining. **2** ability to
remember. **3** abnormal holding of
something, esp. fluid, in the body.
retentive *adj* capable of retaining or
remembering.
rethink *v* consider again, esp. with a
view to changing one's tactics.
reticent ❶ *adj* uncommunicative,
reserved. **reticence** *n*.
retina *n, pl* **-nas, -nae** light-sensitive
membrane at the back of the eye.
retinue ❶ *n* band of attendants.
retire ❶ *v* **1** (cause to) give up office or
work, esp. through age. **2** go away or
withdraw. **3** go to bed. **retired** *adj*
having retired from work etc.
retirement *n* **retirement pension**
weekly pension paid by the
government to retired people over a
specified age. **retiring** *adj* shy.

retort¹ ❶ *v* **1** reply quickly, wittily, or
angrily. ▷ *n* **2** quick, witty, or angry
reply.
retort² *n* glass container with a bent
neck used for distilling.
retouch *v* restore or improve by new
touches, esp. of paint.
retrace *v* go back over (a route etc.)
again.
retract ❶ *v* **1** withdraw (a statement
etc.). **2** draw in or back. **retractable**,
retractile *adj* able to be retracted.
retraction *n*.
retread *v, n* same as REMOULD.
retreat ❶ *v* **1** move back from a
position, withdraw. ▷ *n* **2** act of or
military signal for retiring or
withdrawal. **3** place to which anyone
retires, refuge. **4** period of seclusion,
esp. for religious contemplation.
retrench *v* reduce expenditure, cut
back. **retrenchment** *n*.
retrial *n* second trial of a case or
defendant in a court of law.
retribution ❶ *n* punishment or
vengeance for evil deeds.
retributive *adj*.
retrieve ❶ *v* **1** fetch back again.
2 restore to a better state. **3** rescue or
save. **4** recover (information) from a
computer. **retrievable** *adj* **retrieval** *n*
retriever *n* dog trained to retrieve
shot game.

──────────────── THESAURUS ────────────────

3 = **servant**, attendant, domestic
retaliate *v* = **pay (someone) back**, get
even with (*inf*), get one's own back
(*inf*), hit back, reciprocate, strike back,
take revenge
retaliation *n* = **revenge**, an eye for an
eye, repayment, reprisal, requital,
vengeance
retard *v* = **slow down**, arrest, check,
delay, handicap, hinder, hold back *or*
up, impede, set back
retch *v* = **gag**, be sick, heave, puke (*sl*),
regurgitate, spew, throw up (*inf*),
vomit
reticent *adj* = **uncommunicative**,
close-lipped, quiet, reserved, silent,
taciturn, tight-lipped, unforthcoming
retinue *n* = **attendants**, aides,
entourage, escort, followers, servants
retire *v* **1** = **stop working**, give up work
2 = **withdraw**, depart, exit, go away,
leave **3** = **go to bed**, hit the hay (*sl*),
hit the sack (*sl*), turn in (*inf*)
retirement *n* = **withdrawal**, privacy,

retreat, seclusion, solitude
retiring *adj* = **shy**, bashful, quiet,
reserved, self-effacing, timid,
unassertive, unassuming
retort¹ *v* **1** = **reply**, answer, come back
with, counter, respond, return, riposte
▷ *n* **2** = **reply**, answer, comeback (*inf*),
rejoinder, response, riposte
retract *v* **1** = **withdraw**, deny, disavow,
disclaim, eat one's words, recant,
renege, renounce, revoke, take back
2 = **draw in**, pull back, pull in, sheathe
retreat *v* **1** = **withdraw**, back away,
back off, depart, draw back, fall back,
go back, leave, pull back ▷ *n*
2 = **withdrawal**, departure,
evacuation, flight, retirement
3 = **refuge**, haven, hideaway,
sanctuary, seclusion, shelter
retribution *n* = **punishment**, justice,
Nemesis, reckoning, reprisal,
retaliation, revenge, vengeance
retrieve *v* = **get back**, recapture,
recoup, recover, redeem, regain,

r

retro *adj* associated with or revived from the past, e.g. *retro fashion*.

retro- *prefix* back or backwards, e.g. *retroactive*.

retroactive *adj* effective from a date in the past.

retrograde ❶ *adj* **1** tending towards an earlier worse condition. **2** moving or bending backwards.

retrogress ❶ *v* go back to an earlier worse condition. **retrogression** *n* **retrogressive** *adj*.

retrorocket *n* small rocket engine used to slow a spacecraft.

retrospect *n* **in retrospect** when looking back on the past. **retrospective** *adj* **1** looking back in time. **2** applying from a date in the past. ▷ *n* **3** exhibition of an artist's life's work.

retroussé [rit-**troo**-say] *adj* (of a nose) turned upwards.

retsina *n* Greek wine flavoured with resin.

return ❶ *v* **1** go or come back. **2** give, put, or send back. **3** repay with something of equivalent value, e.g. *return the compliment*. **4** *Sport* hit, throw, or play (a ball) back. **5** reply. **6** elect. ▷ *n* **7** returning. **8** (thing) being returned. **9** profit. **10** official report, as of taxable income. **11** return ticket. ▷ *adj* **12** of or being a return, e.g. *a return visit*. **returnable** *adj*

returning officer person in charge of an election **return ticket** ticket allowing a passenger to travel to a place and back.

retweet *v* post (another user's Twitter post) for one's own followers.

reunify *v* bring together again something previously divided. **reunification** *n*.

reunion *n* meeting of people who have been apart. **reunite** *v* bring or come together again after a separation.

reuse *v* use again. **reusable** *adj*.

rev *informal* ▷ *n* **1** revolution (of an engine). ▷ *v* **revving, revved 2** (foll. by *up*) increase the speed of revolution of (an engine).

Rev., Revd Reverend.

revalue *v* adjust the exchange value of (a currency) upwards. **revaluation** *n*.

revamp ❶ *v* renovate or restore.

reveal ❶ *v* **1** make known. **2** expose or show. **revealing** *adj* **revelation** *n*.

reveille [riv-**val**-ee] *n* morning bugle call to waken soldiers.

revel ❶ *v* **-elling, -elled 1** take pleasure (in). **2** make merry. **revels** *pl n* merrymaking. **reveller** *n* **revelry** *n* festivity.

revenge ❶ *n* **1** retaliation for wrong done. ▷ *v* **2** make retaliation for. **3** avenge (oneself or another). **revenge porn** pornographic image posted on the internet without the

---

THESAURUS

restore, save, win back

retrograde *adj* **1 = deteriorating**, backward, declining, degenerative, downward, regressive, retrogressive, worsening

retrogress *v* **= deteriorate**, backslide, decline, go back, go downhill (*inf*), regress, relapse, worsen

return *v* **1 = come back**, go back, reappear, rebound, recur, retreat, revert, turn back **2 = put back**, re-establish, reinstate, replace, restore **3 = give back**, pay back, recompense, refund, reimburse, repay **5 = reply**, answer, respond, retort **6 = elect**, choose, vote in ▷ *n* **9 = profit**, gain, income, interest, proceeds, revenue, takings, yield **10 = statement**, account, form, list, report, summary

revamp *v* **= renovate**, do up (*inf*), overhaul, recondition, refurbish, restore

reveal *v* **1 = make known**, announce,

disclose, divulge, give away, impart, let out, let slip, make public, proclaim, tell **2 = show**, display, exhibit, manifest, uncover, unearth, unmask, unveil

revel *v* **1 revel in = enjoy**, delight in, indulge in, lap up, luxuriate in, relish, take pleasure in, thrive on **2 = celebrate**, carouse, live it up (*inf*), make merry **revels** *pl n* **= merrymaking**, carousal, celebration, festivity, party, spree

revelation *n* **= disclosure**, exhibition, exposé, exposure, news, proclamation, publication, uncovering, unearthing, unveiling

revelry *n* **2 = merrymaking**, carousal, celebration, festivity, fun, jollity, party, spree

revenge *n* **1 = retaliation**, an eye for an eye, reprisal, retribution, vengeance ▷ *v* **2, 3 = avenge**, get even, get one's own back for (*inf*),

consent of a participant, for vindictive reasons. **revengeful** adj.

revenue ⊙ n income, esp. of a state. **Inland Revenue** see INLAND.

reverberate ⊙ v echo or resound. **reverberation** n.

revere ⊙ v be in awe of and respect greatly. **reverence** n awe mingled with respect and esteem. **Reverend** adj title of respect for a clergyman. **reverent** adj showing reverence. **reverently** adv **reverential** adj marked by reverence.

reverie ⊙ n absent-minded daydream.

revers [riv-**veer**] n turned back part of a garment, such as the lapel.

reverse ⊙ v 1 turn upside down or the other way round. 2 change completely. 3 move (a vehicle) backwards. ▷ n 4 opposite. 5 back side. 6 change for the worse. 7 reverse gear. ▷ adj 8 opposite or contrary. **reverse the charges** make a telephone call at the recipient's expense. **reversal** n **reversible** adj **reverse gear** mechanism enabling a vehicle to move backwards.

reversing lights lights on the back of a motor vehicle that go on when the vehicle is moving backwards.

revert ⊙ v 1 return to a former state. 2 come back to a subject. 3 (of property) return to its former owner. **reversion** n 1 return to a former state, practice, or belief. 2 (of property) rightful passing to the owner, designated heir, etc.

review ⊙ n 1 critical assessment of a book, concert, etc. 2 publication with critical articles. 3 general survey. 4 formal inspection. ▷ v 5 hold or write a review of. 6 examine, reconsider, or look back on. 7 inspect formally. **reviewer** n writer of reviews.

revile ⊙ v be abusively scornful of.

revise ⊙ v 1 change or alter. 2 prepare a new edition of (a book etc.). 3 restudy (work) in preparation for an examination. **revision** n.

revive ⊙ v bring or come back to life, vigour, use, etc. **revival** n 1 reviving or renewal. 2 movement seeking to restore religious faith. 3 new

——————————————————— THESAURUS ———————————————

repay, retaliate, take revenge for

revenue n = **income**, gain, proceeds, profits, receipts, returns, takings, yield

reverberate v = **echo**, re-echo, resound, ring, vibrate

revere v = **be in awe of**, exalt, honour, look up to, respect, reverence, venerate, worship

reverence n = **respect**, admiration, awe, high esteem, honour, veneration, worship

reverent adj = **respectful**, awed, deferential, humble, reverential

reverie n = **daydream**, abstraction, brown study, woolgathering

reverse v 1 = **turn round**, invert, transpose, turn back, turn over, turn upside down, upend 2 = **change**, overthrow, overturn 3 = **go backwards**, back, back up, move backwards, retreat ▷ n 4 = **opposite**, contrary, converse, inverse 5 = **back**, other side, rear, underside, wrong side 6 = **misfortune**, adversity, affliction, blow, disappointment, failure, hardship, misadventure, mishap, reversal, setback ▷ adj 8 = **opposite**, contrary, converse

revert v 1, 2 = **return**, come back, go back, resume

review n 1 = **critique**, commentary, criticism, evaluation, judgment, notice 2 = **magazine**, journal, periodical 3 = **survey**, analysis, examination, scrutiny, study 4 = **inspection**, march past, parade ▷ v 5 = **assess**, criticize, evaluate, judge, study 6 = **look back on**, examine, inspect, reassess, recall, recollect, reconsider, re-evaluate, re-examine, reflect on, remember, rethink, revise, think over

reviewer n = **critic**, commentator, judge

revile v = **malign**, abuse, bad-mouth (sl, chiefly US & Canad), denigrate, knock (inf), reproach, run down, slag (off) (sl), vilify

revise v 1 = **change**, alter, amend, correct, edit, emend, redo, review, rework, update 3 = **study**, cram (inf), go over, run through, swot up (Brit inf)

revision n 1 = **change**, amendment, correction, emendation, updating 2 = **studying**, cramming (inf), homework, swotting (Brit inf)

revival n 1 = **renewal**, reawakening, rebirth, renaissance, resurgence, resurrection, revitalization

revive v = **revitalize**, awaken, bring

production of a play that has not been recently performed. **revivalism** n **revivalist** n.

revoke ❶ v cancel (a will, agreement, etc.). **revocation** n.

revolt ❶ n **1** uprising against authority. ▷ v **2** rise in rebellion. **3** cause to feel disgust. **revolting** adj disgusting, horrible.

revolution ❶ n **1** overthrow of a government by the governed. **2** great change. **3** spinning round. **4** complete rotation. **revolutionary** adj **1** advocating or engaged in revolution. **2** radically new or different. ▷ n, pl **-aries 3** person advocating or engaged in revolution. **revolutionize** v change considerably.

revolve ❶ v turn round, rotate. **revolve around** be centred on. **revolver** n repeating pistol.

revue n theatrical entertainment with topical sketches and songs.

revulsion ❶ n strong disgust.

reward ❶ n **1** something given in return for a service. **2** sum of money offered for finding a criminal or missing property. ▷ v **3** pay or give something to (someone) for a service, information, etc. **rewarding** adj giving

personal satisfaction, worthwhile.

rewind v run (a tape or film) back to an earlier point in order to replay.

rewire v provide (a house, engine, etc.) with new wiring.

rewrite v **1** write again in a different way. ▷ n **2** something rewritten.

Rh 1 Chemistry rhodium. **2** rhesus.

rhapsody ❶ n, pl **-dies 1** freely structured emotional piece of music. **2** expression of ecstatic enthusiasm. **rhapsodic** adj **rhapsodize** v speak or write with extravagant enthusiasm.

rhea [**ree**-a] n S American three-toed ostrich.

rhenium n Chemistry silvery-white metallic element with a high melting point.

rheostat n instrument for varying the resistance of an electrical circuit.

rhesus [**ree**-suss] n small long-tailed monkey of S Asia. **rhesus factor**, **Rh factor** antigen commonly found in human blood: the terms **Rh positive** and **Rh negative** are used to indicate its presence or absence.

rhetoric ❶ [**ret**-a-rik] n **1** art of effective speaking or writing. **2** artificial or exaggerated language. **rhetorical** [rit-**tor**-ik-kal] adj **1** (of a

round, come round, invigorate, reanimate, recover, refresh, rekindle, renew, restore

revoke v = **cancel**, annul, countermand, disclaim, invalidate, negate, nullify, obviate, quash, repeal, rescind, retract, reverse, set aside, withdraw

revolt n **1** = **uprising**, insurgency, insurrection, mutiny, rebellion, revolution, rising ▷ v **2** = **rebel**, mutiny, resist, rise **3** = **disgust**, gross out (US sl), make one's flesh creep, nauseate, repel, repulse, sicken, turn one's stomach

revolting adj = **disgusting**, foul, horrible, horrid, nauseating, repellent, repugnant, repulsive, sickening, yucky or yukky (sl)

revolution n **1** = **revolt**, coup, insurgency, mutiny, rebellion, rising, uprising **2** = **transformation**, innovation, reformation, sea change, shift, upheaval **4** = **rotation**, circle, circuit, cycle, lap, orbit, spin, turn

revolutionary adj **1** = **rebel**, extremist, insurgent, radical,

subversive **2** = **innovative**, different, drastic, ground-breaking, new, novel, progressive, radical

revolutionize v = **transform**, modernize, reform

revolve v = **go round**, circle, orbit, rotate, spin, turn, twist, wheel, whirl

revulsion n = **disgust**, abhorrence, detestation, loathing, repugnance, repulsion

reward n **1** = **payment**, bonus, bounty, compensation, premium, prize, recompense, repayment, return, wages ▷ v **3** = **compensate**, pay, recompense, remunerate, repay

rewarding adj = **satisfying**, beneficial, enriching, fruitful, fulfilling, productive, profitable, valuable, worthwhile

rhapsodize v = **enthuse**, go into ecstasies, gush, rave (inf)

rhetoric n **1** = **oratory**, eloquence **2** = **hyperbole**, bombast, grandiloquence, magniloquence, verbosity, wordiness

rhetorical adj **2** = **high-flown**, bombastic, grandiloquent, oratorical, verbose

r

question) not requiring an answer.
2 of, like, or using rhetoric.
rhetorically *adv*.

rheum [**room**] *n* watery discharge from the eyes or nose. **rheumy** *adj*.

rheumatism *n* painful inflammation of joints or muscles. **rheumatic** *n*, *adj* (person) affected by rheumatism. **rheumatoid** *adj* of or like rheumatism. **rheumatoid arthritis** chronic disease characterized by inflammation and swelling of the joints.

Rh factor *n* see RHESUS.

rhinestone *n* imitation diamond.

rhino *n*, *pl* **rhinos** short for RHINOCEROS.

rhinoceros *n*, *pl* **-oses**, **-os** large thick-skinned animal with one or two horns on its nose.

● **SPELLING TIP**
● The pronunciation of **rhinoceros**
● probably misleads some people
● into adding a *u* before the final *s*
● (*rhinocerous*).

rhizome *n* thick underground stem producing new plants.

rhodium *n* *Chemistry* hard metallic element.

rhododendron *n* evergreen flowering shrub.

rhombus *n*, *pl* **-buses**, **-bi** parallelogram with sides of equal length but no right angles, diamond-shaped figure. **rhomboid** *n* parallelogram with adjacent sides of unequal length.

rhubarb *n* garden plant of which the fleshy stalks are cooked as fruit.

rhyme ❶ *n* **1** sameness of the final sounds at the ends of lines of verse, or in words. **2** word identical in sound to another in its final sounds. **3** verse marked by rhyme. ▷ *v* **4** make a rhyme.

rhythm ❶ *n* **1** any regular movement or beat. **2** arrangement of the durations of and stress on the notes of

a piece of music, usu. grouped into a regular pattern. **3** (in poetry) arrangement of words to form a regular pattern of stresses. **rhythmic**, **rhythmical** *adj* **rhythmically** *adv*

rhythm and blues popular music, orig. Black American, influenced by the blues.

● **SPELLING TIP**
● The second letter of **rhythm** is a
● silent *h*, which people often forget
● in writing.

RI Rhode Island.

rib¹ *n* **1** one of the curved bones forming the framework of the upper part of the body. **2** cut of meat including the rib(s). **3** curved supporting part, as in the hull of a boat. **4** raised series of rows in knitting. ▷ *v* **ribbing**, **ribbed** **5** provide or mark with ribs. **6** knit to form a rib pattern. **ribbed** *adj* **ribbing** *n* **ribcage** *n* bony structure of ribs enclosing the lungs.

rib² *v* **ribbing**, **ribbed** *informal* tease or ridicule. **ribbing** *n*.

RIBA Royal Institute of British Architects.

ribald ❶ *adj* humorously or mockingly rude or obscene. **ribaldry** *n*.

ribbon *n* **1** narrow band of fabric used for trimming, tying, etc. **2** any long strip, for example of inked tape in a typewriter. **3** (also **riband**, **ribband**) small strip of coloured cloth worn as a badge or as the symbol of an award. ▷ *pl* **4** ragged strips or shreds. **ribbon development** *Brit & Aust* building of houses along a main road.

riboflavin [rye-boe-**flay**-vin] *n* form of vitamin B.

ribonucleic acid *n* see RNA.

rice *n* **1** cereal plant grown on wet ground in warm countries. **2** its seeds as food. **rice paper** thin edible paper.

rich ❶ *adj* **1** owning a lot of money or property, wealthy. **2** abounding. **3** fertile. **4** (of food) containing much fat or sugar. **5** mellow. **6** intense or

—————————————————————— THESAURUS ——————

rhyme *n* **3** = **poetry**, ode, poem, song, verse ▷ *v* **4** = **sound like**, harmonize

rhythm *n* **1** = **beat**, accent, cadence, lilt, metre, pulse, swing, tempo, time

ribald *adj* = **coarse**, bawdy, blue, broad, earthy, naughty, near the knuckle (*inf*), obscene, racy, rude, smutty, vulgar

rich *adj* **1** = **wealthy**, affluent, loaded (*sl*), moneyed, prosperous, well-heeled (*inf*), well-off, well-to-do **2** = **well-stocked**, full, productive, well-supplied **3** = **fruitful**, abounding, abundant, ample, copious, fertile, lush, luxurious, plentiful, productive, prolific **4** = **full-bodied**, creamy, fatty, luscious, succulent, sweet, tasty

vivid. **7** amusing. **riches** *pl n* wealth.
richly *adv* **1** elaborately. **2** fully.
richness *n*.

Richter scale *n* scale for measuring
the intensity of earthquakes.

rick¹ *n* stack of hay etc.

rick² *v*, *n* sprain or wrench.

rickets *n* disease of children marked by
softening of the bones, bow legs, etc.,
caused by vitamin D deficiency.

rickety ❶ *adj* shaky or unstable.

rickshaw *n* light two-wheeled man-
drawn Asian vehicle.

ricochet [**rik**-osh-ay] *v* **1** (of a bullet)
rebound from a solid surface. ▷ *n*
2 such a rebound.

rid ❶ *v* **ridding**, **rid** clear or relieve (of).
get rid of free oneself of (something
undesirable). **good riddance** relief at
getting rid of something or someone.

ridden *v* **1** past participle of RIDE. ▷ *adj*
2 afflicted or affected by the thing
specified, e.g. *disease-ridden*.

riddle¹ ❶ *n* **1** question made puzzling to
test one's ingenuity. **2** puzzling
person or thing. ▷ *v* **3** speak in riddles.

riddle² ❶ *v* **1** pierce with many holes.
▷ *n* **2** coarse sieve for gravel etc.
riddled with full of.

ride ❶ *v* **riding**, **rode**, **ridden 1** sit on
and control or propel (a horse, bicycle,
etc.). **2** go on horseback or in a
vehicle. **3** travel over. **4** be carried on
or across. **5** lie at anchor. ▷ *n*

6 journey on a horse etc., or in a
vehicle. **7** type of movement
experienced in a vehicle. **rider** *n*
1 person who rides. **2** supplementary
clause added to a document. **riding** *n*
art or practice of horsemanship. **ride
out** *v* survive (a period of difficulty or
danger) successfully. **ride up** *v* (of a
garment) move up from the proper
position.

ridge *n* **1** long narrow hill. **2** long
narrow raised part on a surface. **3** line
where two sloping surfaces meet.
4 *Meteorology* elongated area of high
pressure. **ridged** *adj*.

ridiculous ❶ *adj* deserving to be
laughed at, absurd. **ridicule** *n*
1 treatment of a person or thing as
ridiculous. ▷ *v* **2** laugh at, make fun of.

Riding *n* former administrative district
of Yorkshire.

riesling *n* type of white wine.

rife ❶ *adj* widespread or common. **rife
with** full of.

riff *n* Jazz, Rock short repeated melodic
figure.

riffle *v* flick through (pages etc.)
quickly.

riffraff ❶ *n* rabble, disreputable people.

rifle¹ *n* **1** firearm with a long barrel. ▷ *v*
2 cut spiral grooves inside the barrel of
a gun.

rifle² ❶ *v* **1** search and rob. **2** steal.

rift ❶ *n* **1** break in friendly relations.

———— THESAURUS ————

riches *pl n* = **wealth**, affluence, assets,
fortune, plenty, resources, substance,
treasure

richly *adv* **1** = **elaborately**, elegantly,
expensively, exquisitely, gorgeously,
lavishly, luxuriously, opulently,
splendidly, sumptuously **2** = **fully**,
amply, appropriately, properly,
suitably, thoroughly, well

rickety *adj* = **shaky**, insecure,
precarious, ramshackle, shonky (*Aust
& NZ inf*), tottering, unsound,
unsteady, wobbly

rid *v* = **free**, clear, deliver, disburden,
disencumber, make free, purge,
relieve, unburden **get rid of** = **dispose
of**, dump, eject, eliminate, expel,
remove, throw away *or* out

riddle¹ *n* **1, 2** = **puzzle**, conundrum,
enigma, mystery, poser, problem

riddle² *v* **1** = **pierce**, honeycomb,
pepper, perforate, puncture ▷ *n*
2 = **sieve**, filter, screen, strainer

ride *v* **1** = **control**, handle, manage
2 = **travel**, be carried, go, move ▷ *n*
6 = **journey**, drive, jaunt, lift, outing,
trip

ridicule *n* **1** = **mockery**, chaff, derision,
gibe, jeer, laughter, raillery, scorn ▷ *v*
2 = **laugh at**, chaff, deride, jeer, make
fun of, mock, poke fun at, sneer

ridiculous *adj* = **laughable**, absurd,
comical, farcical, funny, ludicrous,
risible, silly, stupid

rife *adj* = **widespread**, common,
frequent, general, prevalent,
rampant, ubiquitous, universal

riffraff *n* = **rabble**, hoi polloi, ragtag
and bobtail

rifle² *v* = **ransack**, burgle, go through,
loot, pillage, plunder, rob, sack, strip

rift *n* **1** = **breach**, disagreement,
division, falling out (*inf*), quarrel,
separation, split **2** = **split**, break, cleft,
crack, crevice, fault, fissure, flaw, gap,
opening

2 crack, split, or cleft. **rift valley** long narrow valley resulting from subsidence between faults.

rig ❶ v **rigging**, **rigged 1** arrange in a dishonest way. **2** equip, esp. a ship. ▷ n **3** apparatus for drilling for oil and gas. **4** way a ship's masts and sails are arranged. **5** (also **rigout**) informal outfit of clothes. **rigging** n ship's spars and ropes. **rig up** v set up or build temporarily.

right ❶ adj **1** just. **2** true or correct. **3** proper. **4** most favourable or convenient. **5** in a satisfactory condition. **6** of the side that faces east when the front is turned to the north. **7** of the outer side of a fabric. ▷ adv **8** correctly. **9** properly. **10** straight or directly. **11** on or to the right side. **12** all the way. **13** exactly or precisely. ▷ n **14** claim, title, etc. allowed or due. **15** what is just or due. **16** (R-) conservative political party or group. ▷ v **17** bring or come back to a normal or correct state. **18** bring or come back to a vertical position. **19** compensate for. **in the right** morally or legally correct. **right away** immediately. **rightly** adv **rightful** adj

rightfully adv **rightist** n, adj (person) on the political right. **right angle** angle of 90°. **right-handed** adj using or for the right hand. **right-hand man** person's most valuable assistant. **right-minded**, **right-thinking** adj having opinions or principles deemed acceptable by the speaker. **right of way 1** right of one vehicle to go before another. **2** legal right to pass over someone's land. **right-wing** adj **1** conservative or reactionary. **2** belonging to the more conservative part of a political party. **right-winger** n.

righteous ❶ [**rye**-chuss] adj **1** upright, godly, or virtuous. **2** morally justified. **righteousness** n.

rigid ❶ adj **1** inflexible or strict. **2** unyielding or stiff. **rigidly** adv **rigidity** n.

rigmarole ❶ n **1** long complicated procedure. **2** meaningless string of words.

rigor mortis n stiffening of the body after death.

rigour ❶ n **1** harshness, severity, or strictness. **2** hardship. **rigorous** adj harsh, severe, or stern.

---

rig v **1** = **fix** (inf), arrange, engineer, gerrymander, manipulate, tamper with **2** = **equip**, fit out, furnish, kit out, outfit, supply ▷ n **3** = **apparatus**, equipment, fittings, fixtures, gear, tackle **5** (also **rigout**) Inf = **outfit**, costume, dress, garb, gear (inf), get-up (inf), togs

right adj **1** = **just**, equitable, ethical, fair, good, honest, lawful, moral, proper **2** = **correct**, accurate, exact, factual, genuine, precise, true, valid **3** = **proper**, appropriate, becoming, desirable, done, fit, fitting, seemly, suitable ▷ adv **8** = **correctly**, accurately, exactly, genuinely, precisely, truly **9** = **suitably**, appropriately, aptly, fittingly, properly **10** = **straight**, directly, promptly, quickly, straightaway **13** = **exactly**, precisely, squarely ▷ n **14** = **prerogative**, authority, business, claim, due, freedom, liberty, licence, mana (NZ), permission, power, privilege **15** = **justice**, fairness, lawfulness, legality, righteousness, truth ▷ v **17** = **rectify**, correct, fix, put right,

redress, settle, sort out, straighten **right away** = **immediately**, at once, directly, forthwith, instantly, now, pronto (inf), straightaway

righteous adj **1** = **virtuous**, ethical, fair, good, honest, honourable, just, moral, pure, upright

rightful adj = **lawful**, due, just, legal, legitimate, proper, real, true, valid

rigid adj **1** = **strict**, exact, fixed, inflexible, rigorous, set, stringent, unbending, uncompromising **2** = **stiff**, inflexible, unyielding

rigmarole n **1** = **procedure**, bother, carry-on (inf, chiefly Brit), fuss, hassle (inf), nonsense, palaver, pantomime (inf), performance (inf) **2** = **twaddle**, gibberish

rigorous adj = **strict**, demanding, exacting, hard, harsh, inflexible, severe, stern, stringent, tough

rigour n **1** = **strictness**, harshness, inflexibility, rigidity, sternness, stringency **2** = **hardship**, ordeal, privation, suffering, trial

rig up v = **set up**, arrange, assemble, build, construct, erect, fix up,

r

rile ❶ v anger or annoy.

rill n small stream.

rim ❶ n 1 edge or border. 2 outer ring of a wheel. rimmed adj.

rime n lit hoarfrost.

rind ❶ n tough outer coating of fruits, cheese, or bacon.

ring¹ ❶ v ringing, rang, rung 1 give out a clear resonant sound, as a bell. 2 cause (a bell) to sound. 3 telephone. 4 resound. ▷ n 5 ringing. 6 telephone call. 7 inherent quality, e.g. the ring of truth. ring off v end a telephone call. ringtone n tune played by a cell phone when it receives a call. ring up v 1 telephone. 2 record on a cash register.

ring² ❶ n 1 circle of gold etc., esp. for a finger. 2 any circular band, coil, or rim. 3 circle of people. 4 circular course. 5 enclosed area, esp. a circle for a circus or a roped-in square for boxing. 6 group operating (illegal) control of a market. ▷ v 7 put a ring round. 8 mark (a bird) with a ring. 9 kill (a tree) by cutting the bark round the trunk. ringer n slang person or thing apparently identical to another (also dead ringer). ringlet n curly lock of hair. ring binder binder with metal rings that can be opened to insert perforated paper. ringdove n large pigeon with white patches on the wings and neck. ring finger third finger, esp. of the left hand, on which the wedding ring is worn. ringleader n instigator of a mutiny, riot, etc.

ringmaster n master of ceremonies in a circus. ring road main road that bypasses a town (centre). ringside n row of seats nearest a boxing or circus ring. ringtail n Aust possum with a curling tail used to grip branches while climbing. ringtone n tune played by a mobile phone when it receives a call. ringworm n fungal skin disease in circular patches.

rink n 1 sheet of ice for skating or curling. 2 floor for roller-skating. 3 building for ice-skating or roller-skating.

rinkhals n S African cobra that can spit venom.

rinse ❶ v 1 remove soap from (washed clothes, hair, etc.) by applying clean water. 2 wash lightly. ▷ n 3 rinsing. 4 liquid to tint hair.

riot ❶ n 1 disorderly unruly disturbance. 2 loud revelry. 3 profusion. 4 slang very amusing person or thing. ▷ v 5 take part in a riot. read the riot act reprimand severely. run riot 1 behave without restraint. 2 grow profusely. rioter n riotous adj 1 unrestrained. 2 unruly or rebellious.

rip ❶ v ripping, ripped 1 tear violently. 2 tear away. 3 informal rush. ▷ n 4 split or tear. let rip act or speak without restraint. ripcord n cord pulled to open a parachute. rip off v slang cheat by overcharging. rip-off n slang 1 overpriced article. 2 cheat or swindle. rip-roaring adj informal boisterous and exciting.

improvise, put together, put up

rile v = anger, aggravate (inf), annoy, get or put one's back up, irk, irritate

rim n 1 = edge, border, brim, brink, lip, margin, verge

rind n = skin, crust, husk, outer layer, peel

ring¹ v 1, 2 = chime, clang, peal, reverberate, sound, toll 3 = phone, buzz (inf, chiefly Brit), call, telephone ▷ n 5 = chime, knell, peal 6 = call, buzz (inf, chiefly Brit), phone call

ring² n 1, 2 = circle, band, circuit, halo, hoop, loop, round 5 = arena, circus, enclosure, rink 6 = gang, association, band, cartel, circle, group, mob, syndicate ▷ v 7 = encircle, enclose, gird, girdle, surround

rinse v 1, 2 = wash, bathe, clean, cleanse, dip, splash ▷ n 3 = wash,

bath, dip, splash

riot n 1 = disturbance, anarchy, confusion, disorder, lawlessness, strife, tumult, turbulence, turmoil, upheaval 2 = merrymaking, carousal, festivity, frolic, high jinks, revelry 3 = display, extravaganza, profusion, show, splash ▷ v 5 = rampage, go on the rampage run riot 1 = rampage, be out of control, go wild 2 = grow profusely, spread like wildfire

riotous adj 1 = unrestrained, boisterous, loud, noisy, uproarious, wild 2 = unruly, anarchic, disorderly, lawless, rebellious, rowdy, ungovernable, violent

rip v 1 = tear, burst, claw, cut, gash, lacerate, rend, slash, slit, split ▷ n 4 = tear, cut, gash, hole, laceration,

r

RIP rest in peace.

riparian [rip-**pair**-ee-an] *adj* of or on the banks of a river.

ripe ⊕ *adj* 1 ready to be reaped, eaten, etc. 2 matured. 3 ready or suitable. **ripen** *v* 1 grow ripe. 2 mature.

riposte ⊕ [rip-**posst**] *n* 1 verbal retort. 2 counterattack, esp. in fencing. ▷ *v* 3 make a riposte.

ripple *n* 1 slight wave or ruffling of a surface. 2 sound like ripples of water. ▷ *v* 3 flow or form into little waves (on). 4 (of sounds) rise and fall gently.

rise ⊕ *v* **rising**, **rose**, **risen** 1 get up from a lying, sitting, or kneeling position. 2 get out of bed. 3 move upwards. 4 (of the sun or moon) appear above the horizon. 5 reach a higher level. 6 (of an amount or price) increase. 7 rebel. 8 (of a court) adjourn. 9 have its source. ▷ *n* 10 rising. 11 upward slope. 12 increase, esp. of wages. **take a rise out of** *slang* provoke an angry reaction from. **give rise to** cause. **riser** *n* 1 person who rises, esp. from bed. 2 vertical part of a step. **rising** *n* 1 revolt. ▷ *adj* 2 increasing in rank or maturity.

risible [**riz**-zib-bl] *adj* causing laughter, ridiculous.

risk ⊕ *n* 1 chance of disaster or loss. 2 person or thing considered as a potential hazard. ▷ *v* 3 act in spite of the possibility of (injury or loss). 4 expose to danger or loss. **risky** *adj* **riskier**, **riskiest** full of risk, dangerous.

risotto *n*, *pl* **-tos** dish of rice cooked in stock with vegetables, meat, etc.

risqué ⊕ [**risk**-ay] *adj* bordering on indecency.

rissole *n* cake of minced meat, coated with breadcrumbs and fried.

rite ⊕ *n* formal practice or custom, esp. religious. **rite of passage** event that marks an important change in a person's life.

ritual ⊕ *n* 1 prescribed order of rites. 2 regular repeated action or behaviour. ▷ *adj* 3 concerning rites. **ritually** *adv* **ritualistic** *adj* like a ritual.

ritzy *adj* **ritzier**, **ritziest** *slang* luxurious or elegant.

rival ⊕ *n* 1 person or thing that competes with or equals another for favour, success, etc. ▷ *adj* 2 in the position of a rival. ▷ *v* **-valling**, **-valled**

---

rent, slash, slit, split

ripe *adj* **1, 2** = **mature**, mellow, ready, ripened, seasoned **3** = **suitable**, auspicious, favourable, ideal, opportune, right, timely

ripen *v* **1, 2** = **mature**, burgeon, develop, grow ripe, season

rip off *v Sl* = **cheat**, con (*inf*), defraud, fleece, rob, skin (*sl*), swindle

rip-off *n Sl* **2** = **cheat**, con (*inf*), con trick (*inf*), fraud, scam (*sl*), swindle, theft

riposte *n* **1** = **retort**, answer, comeback (*inf*), rejoinder, reply, response, sally ▷ *v* **3** = **retort**, answer, come back, reply, respond

rise *v* **1** = **get up**, arise, get to one's feet, stand up **3** = **go up**, ascend, climb **5** = **advance**, get on, progress, prosper **6** = **increase**, go up, grow, intensify, mount **7** = **rebel**, mutiny, revolt **9** = **originate**, happen, issue, occur, spring ▷ *n* **10** = **advancement**, climb, progress, promotion **11** = **upward slope**, ascent, elevation, incline **12** = **increase**, increment, pay increase, raise (*US*), upsurge, upswing,

upturn **give rise to** = **cause**, bring about, effect, produce, result in

risk *n* **1** = **danger**, chance, gamble, hazard, jeopardy, peril, pitfall, possibility ▷ *v* **3, 4** = **dare**, chance, endanger, gamble, hazard, imperil, jeopardize, venture

risky *adj* = **dangerous**, chancy (*inf*), dicey (*inf, chiefly Brit*), dodgy (*Brit, Aust & NZ inf*), hazardous, perilous, uncertain, unsafe

risqué *adj* = **suggestive**, bawdy, blue, improper, indelicate, naughty, near the knuckle (*inf*), racy, ribald

rite *n* = **ceremony**, custom, observance, practice, procedure, ritual

ritual *n* **1** = **ceremony**, observance, rite **2** = **custom**, convention, habit, practice, procedure, protocol, routine, tradition ▷ *adj* **3** = **ceremonial**, conventional, customary, habitual, routine

rival *n* **1** = **opponent**, adversary, competitor, contender, contestant ▷ *adj* **2** = **competing**, conflicting, opposing ▷ *v* **3** = **compete**, be a match

3 (try to) equal. **rivalry** n keen competition.

riven adj **1** split apart. **2** torn to shreds.

river ⊕ n **1** large natural stream of water. **2** plentiful flow.

rivet ⊕ [**riv**-vit] n **1** bolt for fastening metal plates, the end being put through holes and then beaten flat. ▷ v **riveting**, **riveted 2** fasten with rivets. **3** cause to be fixed, as in fascination. **riveting** adj very interesting and exciting.

rivulet n small stream.

Rn Chemistry radon.

RN Royal Navy.

RNA ribonucleic acid: substance in living cells essential for the synthesis of protein.

roach¹ n freshwater fish.

roach² n US same as COCKROACH.

road ⊕ n **1** way prepared for passengers, vehicles, etc. **2** route in a town or city with houses along it. **3** way or course, e.g. the road to fame. **4** roadstead. **on the road** travelling. **roadie** n informal person who transports and sets up equipment for a band. **roadblock** n barricade across a road to stop traffic for inspection etc. **road hog** informal selfish aggressive driver. **roadholding** n extent to which a vehicle does not skid on bends or wet surfaces. **roadhouse** n pub or restaurant on a country road. **road metal** broken stones used in building roads. **road rage** aggressive behaviour by a motorist in response to another motorist's driving. **road show** Radio live broadcast from a radio van taking a particular programme on a tour of the country.

roadside n, adj **roadstead** n Nautical partly sheltered anchorage. **road test** test of a vehicle etc. in actual use. **road-test** v test (a vehicle etc.) in actual use. **roadway** n the part of a road used by vehicles. **roadworks** pl n repairs to a road, esp. blocking part of the road. **roadworthy** adj (of a vehicle) mechanically sound.

roam ⊕ v wander about.

roan adj **1** (of a horse) having a brown or black coat sprinkled with white hairs. ▷ n **2** roan horse.

roar ⊕ v **1** make or utter a loud deep hoarse sound like that of a lion. **2** shout (something) as in anger. **3** laugh loudly. ▷ n **4** such a sound. **a roaring trade** informal brisk and profitable business. **roaring drunk** noisily drunk.

roast v **1** cook by dry heat, as in an oven. **2** make or be very hot. ▷ n **3** roasted joint of meat. ▷ adj **4** roasted. **roasting** informal ▷ adj **1** extremely hot. ▷ n **2** severe criticism or scolding.

rob ⊕ v **robbing, robbed 1** steal from. **2** deprive. **robber** n **robbery** n, pl **-beries**.

robe ⊕ n **1** long loose outer garment. ▷ v **2** put a robe on.

robin n small brown bird with a red breast.

robot ⊕ n **1** automated machine, esp. one performing functions in a human manner. **2** person of machine-like efficiency. **3** S Afr set of coloured lights at a junction to control the traffic flow. **robotic** adj **robotics** n science of designing and using robots.

robust ⊕ adj **1** very strong and healthy.

r

for, compare with, equal, match

rivalry n = **competition**, conflict, contention, contest, opposition

river n **1** = **stream**, brook, burn (Scot), creek, tributary, waterway **2** = **flow**, flood, rush, spate, torrent

riveting adj = **enthralling**, absorbing, captivating, engrossing, fascinating, gripping, hypnotic, spellbinding

road n **1** = **way**, course, highway, lane, motorway, path, pathway, roadway, route, track

roam v = **wander**, prowl, ramble, range, rove, stray, travel, walk

roar v **2** = **cry**, bawl, bellow, howl, shout, yell **3** = **guffaw**, hoot, laugh

heartily, split one's sides (inf) ▷ n **4** = **cry**, bellow, hoot, howl, outcry, shout, yell

rob v **1** = **steal from**, burgle, cheat, con (inf), defraud, dispossess, do out of (inf), hold up, loot, mug (inf), pillage, plunder, raid **2** = **deprive**, do out of

robbery n = **theft**, burglary, hold-up, larceny, mugging (inf), pillage, plunder, raid, rip-off (sl), stealing, stick-up (sl, chiefly US), swindle

robe n **1** = **gown**, costume, habit ▷ v **2** = **clothe**, dress, garb

robot n **1** = **machine**, android, automaton, mechanical man

robust adj **1, 2** = **strong**, fit, hale,

2 sturdily built. **3** requiring physical strength. **robustly** *adv* **robustness** *n*.

roc *n* monstrous bird of Arabian mythology.

rock¹ ❶ *n* **1** hard mineral substance that makes up part of the earth's crust, stone. **2** large rugged mass of stone. **3** *US & Aust* a stone. **4** hard sweet in sticks. **on the rocks 1** (of a marriage) about to end. **2** (of an alcoholic drink) served with ice. **rocky** *adj* **rockier**, **rockiest** having many rocks. **rockery** *n*, *pl* **-eries** mound of stones in a garden for rock plants. **rock bottom** lowest possible level. **rock cake** small fruit cake with a rough surface. **rock plant** any plant which grows on rocky ground. **rock salt** common salt as a naturally occurring mineral.

rock² ❶ *v* **1** (cause to) sway to and fro. **2** (cause to) feel shock, e.g. *the scandal rocked the government*. ▷ *n* **3** (also **rock music**) style of pop music with a heavy beat. ▷ *adj* **4** of or relating to rock music. **rocky** *adj* **rockier**, **rockiest** shaky or unstable. **rock and roll**, **rock'n'roll** style of pop music blending rhythm and blues and country music. **rocking chair** chair allowing the sitter to rock backwards and forwards. **rocking horse** toy horse on which a child can rock to and fro.

rocker *n* **1** rocking chair. **2** curved piece of wood etc. on which something may rock. **3** rock music performer, fan, or song. **off one's rocker** *informal* insane.

rocket *n* **1** self-propelling device powered by the burning of explosive contents (used as a firework, weapon, etc.). **2** vehicle propelled by a rocket engine, as a weapon or carrying a spacecraft. **3** *informal* severe reprimand. ▷ *v* **-eting**, **-eted 4** move fast, esp. upwards, like a rocket.

rock melon *n Aust, NZ & US* type of melon with sweet orange flesh.

rococo [rok-**koe**-koe] *adj* (of furniture, architecture, etc.) having much elaborate decoration in an early 18th-century style.

rod ❶ *n* **1** slender straight bar, stick. **2** cane.

rode *v* past tense of RIDE.

rodent *n* animal with teeth specialized for gnawing, such as a rat, mouse, or squirrel.

rodeo *n*, *pl* **-deos** display of skill by cowboys, such as bareback riding.

roe¹ *n* mass of eggs in a fish, sometimes eaten as food.

roe² *n* small species of deer.

roentgen [**ront**-gan] *n* unit measuring a radiation dose.

roger *interj* (used in signalling) message received and understood.

rogue ❶ *n* **1** dishonest or unprincipled person. **2** mischief-loving person. **3** inferior or defective specimen, esp. of a plant. ▷ *adj* **4** (of a wild beast) having a savage temper and living apart from the herd. **roguery** *n* **roguish** *adj*.

roister *v* make merry noisily or boisterously.

role, rôle ❶ *n* **1** task or function. **2** actor's part. **role model** person regarded by others, esp. younger people, as a good example to follow.

roll ❶ *v* **1** move by turning over and over. **2** move or sweep along. **3** wind

hardy, healthy, muscular, powerful, stout, strapping, sturdy, tough, vigorous

rock¹ *n* **2** = **stone**, boulder

rock² *v* **1** = **sway**, lurch, pitch, reel, roll, swing, toss **2** = **shock**, astonish, astound, shake, stagger, stun, surprise

rocky¹ *adj* = **rough**, craggy, rugged, stony

rocky² *adj* = **unstable**, rickety, shaky, unsteady, wobbly

rod *n* **1,2** = **stick**, bar, baton, cane, pole, shaft, staff, wand

rogue *n* **1** = **scoundrel**, blackguard, crook (*inf*), fraud, rascal, scally (*NW*

Eng dial), villain **2** = **scamp**, rascal

role, rôle *n* **1** = **job**, capacity, duty, function, part, position, post, task **2** = **part**, character, portrayal, representation

roll *v* **1** = **turn**, go round, revolve, rotate, spin, swivel, trundle, twirl, wheel, whirl **3** = **wind**, bind, enfold, envelop, furl, swathe, wrap **4** = **flow**, run, undulate **5** = **level**, even, flatten, press, smooth **6** = **toss**, lurch, reel, rock, sway, tumble ▷ *n* **10** = **turn**, cycle, reel, revolution, rotation, spin, twirl, wheel, whirl **13** = **register**, census, index, list, record **15** = **rumble**, boom, reverberation,

round. **4** undulate. **5** smooth out with a roller. **6** (of a ship or aircraft) turn from side to side about a line from nose to tail. **7** (of machinery) (begin to) operate. **8** (of a drum, thunder, etc.) make a continuous deep loud noise. **9** walk with a swaying gait. ▷ *n* **10** act of rolling over or from side to side. **11** piece of paper etc. rolled up. **12** small round individually baked piece of bread. **13** list or register. **14** complete rotation of an aircraft about a line from nose to tail. **15** continuous sound, as of drums, thunder, etc. **16** swaying unsteady movement or gait. **rolling** *adj* **1** (of hills) gently sloping, undulating. **2** (of a gait) slow and swaying. **roll call** calling out of a list of names, as in a school or the army, to check who is present. **rolled gold** metal coated with a thin layer of gold. **rolling pin** cylindrical roller for flattening pastry. **rolling stock** locomotives and coaches of a railway. **rolling stone** restless wandering person. **rollmop** *n* herring fillet rolled round onion slices and pickled. **roll-on/roll-off** *adj* denoting a ship allowing vehicles to be driven straight on and off. **roll-top** *adj* (of a desk) having a flexible lid sliding in grooves. **roll up** *v informal* appear or arrive. **roll-up** *n informal* cigarette made by the smoker from loose tobacco and cigarette paper.

roller *n* **1** rotating cylinder used for smoothing or supporting a thing to be moved, spreading paint, etc. **2** small tube around which hair is wound to make it curly. **3** long wave of the sea. **Rollerblade** *n* ® roller skate with the wheels set in one straight line. **roller coaster** (at a funfair) narrow railway with steep slopes. **roller skate** skate with wheels.

rollicking *adj* boisterously carefree.

roly-poly ❶ *adj* round or plump.

ROM *Computers* read only memory.

Roman *adj* of Rome or the Roman Catholic Church. **Roman alphabet** alphabet used for writing W European languages, including English. **Roman candle** firework that emits a steady stream of coloured sparks. **Roman Catholic** (member) of that section of the Christian Church that acknowledges the supremacy of the Pope. **Roman nose** nose with a high prominent bridge. **Roman numerals** the letters I, V, X, L, C, D, M, used to represent numbers. **roman type** plain upright letters in printing.

romance ❶ *n* **1** love affair. **2** love idealized for its purity or beauty. **3** mysterious or exciting quality. **4** novel or film dealing with love, esp. sentimentally. **5** story with scenes remote from ordinary life. ▷ *v* **6** exaggerate or fantasize. **romantic** *adj*.

Romance *adj* (of a language) developed from Latin, such as French or Spanish.

Romanesque *adj, n* (in) a style of architecture of the 9th–12th centuries, characterized by round arches.

romantic ❶ *adj* **1** of or dealing with love. **2** idealistic but impractical. **3** (of literature, music, etc.) displaying passion and imagination rather than order and form. ▷ *n* **4** romantic person or artist. **romantically** *adv* **romanticism** *n* **romanticize** *v* describe or regard in an idealized and unrealistic way.

Romany *n, pl* **-nies** *adj* Gypsy.

Romeo *n, pl* **Romeos** ardent male lover.

romp ❶ *v* **1** play wildly and joyfully. ▷ *n* **2** boisterous activity. **romp home** win easily. **rompers** *pl n* child's overalls.

rondavel *n S Afr* circular building, often thatched.

rondo *n, pl* **-dos** piece of music with a leading theme continually returned to.

roar, thunder

roly-poly *adj* = **plump**, buxom, chubby, fat, podgy, rounded, tubby

romance *n* **1** = **love affair**, affair, amour, attachment, liaison, relationship **3** = **excitement**, charm, colour, fascination, glamour, mystery **4, 5** = **story**, fairy tale, fantasy, legend, love story, melodrama, tale

romantic *adj* **1** = **loving**, amorous, fond, passionate, sentimental, tender **2** = **idealistic**, dreamy, impractical, starry-eyed, unrealistic ▷ *n* **4** = **idealist**, dreamer, sentimentalist

romp *v* **1** = **frolic**, caper, cavort, frisk, gambol, have fun, sport ▷ *n* **2** = **frolic**, caper, lark (*inf*) **romp home** = **win easily**, walk it (*inf*), win by a mile (*inf*),

roo n Aust informal kangaroo.

rood n 1 Christianity the Cross.
2 crucifix. **rood screen** (in a church) screen separating the nave from the choir.

roof n, pl **roofs** 1 outside upper covering of a building, car, etc. ▷ v
2 put a roof on. **roof rack** rack for carrying luggage attached to the roof of a car.

rooibos n S Afr tea prepared from the dried leaves of an African plant.

rook¹ n 1 bird of the crow family. ▷ v
2 old-fashioned slang swindle. **rookery** n, pl **-eries** colony of rooks, penguins, or seals.

rook² n chess piece shaped like a castle.

rookie n informal new recruit.

room ❶ n 1 enclosed area in a building.
2 unoccupied space. 3 scope or opportunity. ▷ pl 4 lodgings. ▷ v
5 US occupy or share a room. **roomy** adj **roomier**, **roomiest** spacious.

roost n 1 perch for fowls. ▷ v 2 perch.

rooster n US & Canad domestic cock.

root¹ ❶ n 1 part of a plant that grows down into the earth obtaining nourishment. 2 plant with an edible root, such as a carrot. 3 part of a tooth, hair, etc. below the skin.
4 source or origin. 5 form of a word from which other words and forms are derived. 6 Maths factor of a quantity which, when multiplied by itself the number of times indicated, gives the quantity. ▷ pl 7 person's sense of belonging. ▷ v 8 establish a root and start to grow. **rootless** adj having no sense of belonging. **root for** v informal cheer on. **root out** v get rid of completely. **rootstock** n rhizome.

root² **rootle** ❶ v 1 dig or burrow.
2 informal search vigorously but unsystematically.

rope ❶ n thick cord. **know the ropes** be thoroughly familiar with an activity. **rope in** v persuade to join in. **rope off** v enclose or divide with a rope.

ropey, ropy ❶ adj **ropier**, **ropiest** informal 1 inferior or inadequate. 2 not well.

Roquefort n strong blue-veined cheese made from ewes' or goats' milk.

rorqual n toothless whale with a dorsal fin.

rort n Aust informal dishonest scheme.

rosary n, pl **-saries** 1 series of prayers.
2 string of beads for counting these prayers.

rose¹ n 1 shrub or climbing plant with prickly stems and fragrant flowers.
2 flower of this plant. 3 perforated flat nozzle for a hose. 4 pink colour.
▷ adj 5 pink. **roseate** [roe-zee-ate] adj rose-coloured. **rose window** circular window with spokes branching from the centre. **rosewood** n fragrant wood used to make furniture.

rose² v past tense of RISE.

rosé [roe-zay] n pink wine.

rosehip n berry-like fruit of a rose plant.

rosemary n 1 fragrant flowering shrub. 2 its leaves as a herb.

rosette n rose-shaped ornament, esp. a circular bunch of ribbons.

Rosh Hashanah, Rosh Hashana n Hebrew Jewish New Year festival.

rosin [rozz-in] n 1 resin used for treating the bows of violins etc. ▷ v
2 apply rosin to.

r

THESAURUS

win hands down

room n 1 = **chamber**, apartment, office
2 = **space**, area, capacity, expanse, extent, leeway, margin, range, scope
3 = **opportunity**, chance, occasion, scope

roomy adj = **spacious**, ample, broad, capacious, commodious, extensive, generous, large, sizable or sizeable, wide

root¹ n 1 = **stem**, rhizome, tuber
4 = **source**, base, bottom, cause, core, foundation, heart, nucleus, origin, seat, seed ▷ pl 7 = **sense of belonging**, heritage, origins ▷ v
8 = **become established**, anchor, establish, fasten, fix, ground, implant,

moor, set, stick

root², rootle v 1 = **dig**, burrow, ferret

root out v = **get rid of**, abolish, do away with, eliminate, eradicate, exterminate, extirpate, remove, weed out

rope n = **cord**, cable, hawser, line, strand **know the ropes** = **be experienced**, be an old hand, be knowledgeable

rope in v = **persuade**, engage, enlist, inveigle, involve, talk into

ropey, ropy adj Inf 1 = **inferior**, deficient, inadequate, of poor quality, poor, substandard ▷ adj 2 = **unwell**, below par, crook (Aust & NZ sl), off

roster ⓘ *n* list of people and their turns of duty.

rostrum ⓘ *n, pl* **-trums, -tra** platform or stage.

rosy ⓘ *adj* **rosier, rosiest 1** pink-coloured. **2** hopeful or promising.

rot ⓘ *v* **rotting, rotted 1** decompose or decay. **2** slowly deteriorate physically or mentally. ▷ *n* **3** decay. **4** *informal* nonsense.

rota *n* list of people who take it in turn to do a particular task.

rotary ⓘ *adj* **1** revolving. **2** operated by rotation.

rotate ⓘ *v* **1** (cause to) move round a centre or on a pivot. **2** (cause to) follow a set sequence. **3** plant different crops from one year to the next to maintain the fertility of the soil. **rotation** *n*.

rote *n* mechanical repetition. **by rote** by memory.

rotisserie *n* rotating spit for cooking meat.

rotor *n* **1** revolving portion of a dynamo, motor, or turbine. **2** rotating device with long blades that provides thrust to lift a helicopter.

rotten ⓘ *adj* **1** decaying. **2** *informal* very bad. **3** corrupt. **rottenness** *n*.

rotter ⓘ *n slang* despicable person.

Rottweiler [**rot**-vile-er] *n* large sturdy dog with a smooth black and tan coat and usu. a docked tail.

rotund ⓘ [roe-**tund**] *adj* **1** round and plump. **2** sonorous. **rotundity** *n*.

rotunda *n* circular building or room, esp. with a dome.

rouble [**roo**-bl] *n* monetary unit of Russia, Belarus, and Tajikistan.

roué [**roo**-ay] *n* man given to immoral living.

rouge *n* **1** red cosmetic used to colour the cheeks. ▷ *v* **2** apply rouge to.

rough ⓘ *adj* **1** uneven or irregular. **2** not careful or gentle. **3** difficult or unpleasant. **4** approximate. **5** violent, stormy, or boisterous. **6** in preliminary form. **7** lacking refinement. ▷ *v* **8** make rough. ▷ *n* **9** rough state or area. **10** sketch. **rough it** live without the usual comforts etc. **roughen** *v* **roughly** *adv* **roughness** *n* **roughage** *n* indigestible constituents of food which aid digestion. **rough-and-ready** *adj*

THESAURUS

colour, under the weather (*inf*)

roster *n* = **rota**, agenda, catalogue, list, register, roll, schedule, table

rostrum *n* = **stage**, dais, platform, podium, stand

rosy *adj* **1** = **pink**, red **2** = **promising**, auspicious, bright, cheerful, encouraging, favourable, hopeful, optimistic

rot *v* **1** = **decay**, crumble, decompose, go bad, moulder, perish, putrefy, spoil **2** = **deteriorate**, decline, waste away ▷ *n* **3** = **decay**, blight, canker, corruption, decomposition, mould, putrefaction **4** *Inf* = **nonsense**, claptrap (*inf*), codswallop (*Brit sl*), drivel, garbage (*chiefly US*), hogwash, kak (*S Afr sl*), poppycock (*inf*), rubbish, trash, tripe (*inf*), twaddle

rotary *adj* **1** = **revolving**, rotating, spinning, turning

rotate *v* **1** = **revolve**, go round, gyrate, pivot, reel, spin, swivel, turn, wheel **2** = **follow in sequence**, alternate, switch, take turns

rotten *adj* **1** = **decaying**, bad, corrupt, crumbling, decomposing, festering, mouldy, perished, putrescent, rank, sour, stinking **2** *Inf* = **despicable**, base, contemptible, dirty, mean, nasty **3** = **corrupt**, crooked (*inf*), dishonest, dishonourable, immoral, perfidious

rotter *n Sl* = **scoundrel**, blackguard, bounder (*old-fashioned Brit sl*), cad (*Brit inf*), rat (*inf*)

rotund *adj* **1** = **plump**, chubby, corpulent, fat, fleshy, globular, podgy, portly, rounded, spherical, stout, tubby

rough *adj* **1** = **uneven**, broken, bumpy, craggy, irregular, jagged, rocky, stony **2** = **harsh**, cruel, hard, nasty, tough, unfeeling, unpleasant, violent **3** = **unpleasant**, arduous, difficult, hard, tough, uncomfortable **4** = **approximate**, estimated, general, imprecise, inexact, sketchy, vague **5** = **stormy**, choppy, squally, turbulent, wild **6** = **basic**, crude, imperfect, incomplete, rudimentary, sketchy, unfinished, unpolished, unrefined **7** = **ungracious**, blunt, brusque, coarse, impolite, rude, unceremonious, uncivil, uncouth, unmannerly ▷ *n* **10** = **outline**, draft, mock-up, preliminary sketch

rough-and-ready *adj* = **makeshift**,

hastily prepared but adequate. **rough-and-tumble** n playful fight. **rough-hewn** adj roughly shaped.
roughhouse n slang fight. **roughneck** n slang **1** violent person. **2** worker on an oil rig. **rough out** v prepare (a sketch or report) in preliminary form.
roughcast n **1** mixture of plaster and small stones for outside walls. ▷ v **2** coat with this.
roughshod adv **ride roughshod over** act with total disregard for.
roulette n gambling game played with a revolving wheel and a ball.
round ❶ adj **1** spherical, cylindrical, circular, or curved. **2** complete or whole, e.g. round numbers. ▷ adv, prep **3** indicating an encircling movement, presence on all sides, etc., e.g., tied round the waist; books scattered round the room. ▷ v **4** move round. ▷ n **5** round shape. **6** recurrent duties. **7** customary course, as of a milkman. **8** game (of golf). **9** stage in a competition. **10** one of several periods in a boxing match etc. **11** number of drinks bought at one time. **12** bullet or shell for a gun. **13** part song in which singers join at equal intervals. **14** circular movement. **15** set of sandwiches. **roundly** adv thoroughly. **rounders** n bat-and-ball team game. **round on** v attack angrily. **round robin** petition signed with names in a circle to conceal the order. **round**

table meeting of people on equal terms for discussion. **round-the-clock** adj throughout the day and night. **round trip** journey out and back again. **round up** v gather (people or animals) together. **roundup** n.
roundabout ❶ n **1** road junction at which traffic passes round a central island. **2** revolving circular platform on which people ride for amusement. ▷ adj **3** not straightforward.
roundel n small disc. **roundelay** n simple song with a refrain.
Roundhead n History supporter of Parliament against Charles I in the English Civil War.
rouse¹ ❶ v **1** wake up. **2** provoke or excite. **rousing** adj lively, vigorous.
rouse² [rhymes with **mouse**] v (foll. by on) Aust scold or rebuke.
roustabout n labourer on an oil rig.
rout ❶ n **1** overwhelming defeat. **2** disorderly retreat. ▷ v **3** defeat and put to flight.
route ❶ n **1** roads taken to reach a destination. **2** chosen way. ▷ v **3** send by a particular route. **routemarch** n long military training march.
routine ❶ n **1** usual or regular method of procedure. **2** set sequence. ▷ adj **3** ordinary or regular.
roux [roo] n fat and flour cooked together as a basis for sauces.
rove ❶ v wander. **rover** n.

——— THESAURUS ———

crude, improvised, provisional, sketchy, stopgap, unpolished, unrefined
rough out v = **outline**, draft, plan, sketch
round adj **1** = **spherical**, circular, curved, cylindrical, globular, rotund, rounded ▷ v **4** = **go round**, bypass, circle, encircle, flank, skirt, turn ▷ n **5** = **sphere**, ball, band, circle, disc, globe, orb, ring **7** = **course**, beat, circuit, routine, schedule, series, tour **9** = **stage**, division, lap, level, period, session, turn
roundabout adj **3** = **indirect**, circuitous, devious, discursive, evasive, oblique, tortuous
round up v = **gather**, collect, drive, group, herd, marshal, muster, rally
roundup n = **gathering**, assembly, collection, herding, marshalling, muster, rally

rouse¹ v **1** = **wake up**, awaken, call, rise, wake **2** = **excite**, agitate, anger, animate, incite, inflame, move, provoke, stimulate, stir
rousing adj = **lively**, exciting, inspiring, moving, spirited, stimulating, stirring
rout n **1** = **defeat**, beating, debacle, drubbing, overthrow, pasting (sl), thrashing ▷ v **3** = **defeat**, beat, conquer, crush, destroy, drub, overthrow, thrash, wipe the floor with (inf)
route n **2** = **way**, beat, circuit, course, direction, itinerary, journey, path, road
routine n **1** = **procedure**, custom, method, order, pattern, practice, programme ▷ adj **3** = **usual**, customary, everyday, habitual, normal, ordinary, standard, typical
rove v = **wander**, drift, ramble, range,

r

row¹ ❶ [rhymes with **go**] *n* straight line of people or things. **in a row** in succession.

row² [rhymes with **go**] *v* **1** propel (a boat) by oars. ▷ *n* **2** spell of rowing. **rowing boat** boat propelled by oars.

row³ ❶ [rhymes with **now**] *informal* ▷ *n* **1** dispute. **2** disturbance. **3** reprimand. ▷ *v* **4** quarrel noisily.

rowan *n* tree producing bright red berries, mountain ash.

rowdy ❶ *adj* **-dier**, **-diest 1** disorderly, noisy, and rough. ▷ *n, pl* **-dies 2** person like this.

rowel [rhymes with **towel**] *n* small spiked wheel on a spur.

rowlock [**rol**-luk] *n* device on a boat that holds an oar in place.

royal ❶ *adj* **1** of, befitting, or supported by a king or queen. **2** splendid. ▷ *n* **3** *informal* member of a royal family. **royally** *adv* **royalist** *n* supporter of monarchy. **royalty** *n* **1** royal people. **2** rank or power of a monarch. **3** *pl* **-ties** payment to an author, musician, inventor, etc. **royal blue** deep blue.

RPI retail price index: measure of change in the average level of prices.

rpm revolutions per minute.

RR Right Reverend.

RSI repetitive strain injury.

RSPCA Royal Society for the Prevention of Cruelty to Animals.

RSS Rich Site Summary *or* Really Simple Syndication: way of allowing internet users to receive updates from selected websites.

RSVP please reply.

Rt Hon. Right Honourable.

Ru *Chemistry* ruthenium.

rub ❶ *v* **rubbing**, **rubbed 1** apply pressure and friction to (something) with a circular or backwards-and-forwards movement. **2** clean, polish, or dry by rubbing. **3** chafe or fray through rubbing. ▷ *n* **4** act of rubbing. **5** difficulty. **rub it in** emphasize an unpleasant fact. **rub along** *v* have a friendly relationship. **rub off** *v* affect through close association. **rub out** *v* remove with a rubber.

rubato *adv, n Music* (with) expressive flexibility of tempo.

rubber¹ *n* **1** strong waterproof elastic material, orig. made from the dried sap of a tropical tree, now usu. synthetic. **2** piece of rubber used for erasing writing. ▷ *adj* **3** made of or producing rubber. **rubberize** *v* coat or treat with rubber. **rubbery** *adj* **rubberneck** *v US* stare with unthinking curiosity. **rubber plant** house plant with glossy leaves. **rubber stamp 1** device for imprinting the date, a name, etc. **2** automatic authorization.

rubber² *n* **1** match consisting of three games of bridge, whist, etc. **2** series of matches.

rubbish ❶ *n* **1** waste matter. **2** anything worthless. **3** nonsense. ▷ *v* **4** *informal* criticize. **rubbishy** *adj*.

rubble *n* fragments of broken stone, brick, etc.

rubella [roo-**bell**-a] *n* same as GERMAN MEASLES.

rubicund [**roo**-bik-kund] *adj* ruddy.

rubidium [roo-**bid**-ee-um] *n Chemistry* soft highly reactive radioactive element.

rubric [**roo**-brik] *n* **1** set of rules for behaviour. **2** heading or explanation inserted in a text.

ruby *n, pl* **-bies 1** red precious

r

THESAURUS

roam, stray, traipse (*inf*)

row¹ *n* = **line**, bank, column, file, range, series, string **in a row** = **consecutively**, one after the other, successively

row³ *Inf n* **1** = **quarrel**, brawl, dispute, squabble, tiff, trouble **2** = **disturbance**, commotion, noise, racket, rumpus, tumult, uproar ▷ *v* **4** = **quarrel**, argue, dispute, fight, squabble, wrangle

rowdy *adj* **1** = **disorderly**, loud, noisy, rough, unruly, wild ▷ *n* **2** = **hooligan**, lout, ruffian, tearaway (*Brit*), yob *or* yobbo (*Brit sl*)

royal *adj* **1** = **regal**, imperial, kingly, princely, queenly, sovereign **2** = **splendid**, grand, impressive, magnificent, majestic, stately

rub *v* **1** = **stroke**, caress, massage **2** = **polish**, clean, scour, shine, wipe **3** = **chafe**, abrade, fray, grate, scrape ▷ *n* **4** = **massage**, caress, kneading, polish, shine, stroke, wipe

rubbish *n* **1, 2** = **waste**, garbage (*chiefly US*), junk (*inf*), litter, lumber, refuse, scrap, trash **3** = **nonsense**, claptrap (*inf*), codswallop (*Brit sl*), garbage (*chiefly US*), hogwash, hot air (*inf*), kak (*S Afr sl*), rot, tommyrot, trash, tripe

gemstone. ▷ adj 2 deep red. **ruby wedding** fortieth wedding anniversary.

ruche n pleat or frill of lace etc. as a decoration.

ruck¹ n 1 rough crowd of common people. 2 Rugby loose scrummage.

ruck² n, v wrinkle or crease.

rucksack n large pack carried on the back.

ructions ❶ pl n informal noisy uproar.

rudder n vertical hinged piece at the stern of a boat or at the rear of an aircraft, for steering.

ruddy ❶ adj **-dier, -diest** 1 of a fresh healthy red colour. ▷ adv, adj 2 slang bloody.

rude ❶ adj 1 impolite or insulting. 2 coarse, vulgar, or obscene. 3 unexpected and unpleasant. 4 roughly-made. 5 robust. **rudely** adv **rudeness** n.

rudiments ❶ pl n simplest and most basic stages of a subject. **rudimentary** adj basic, elementary.

rue¹ ❶ v **ruing, rued** feel regret for.

rueful adj regretful or sorry. **ruefully** adv.

rue² n plant with evergreen bitter leaves.

ruff¹ n 1 starched and frilled collar. 2 natural collar of feathers, fur, etc. on certain birds and animals. 3 kind of sandpiper.

ruff² n, v Cards same as TRUMP¹.

ruffian ❶ n violent lawless person.

ruffle ❶ v 1 disturb the calm of. 2 annoy, irritate. ▷ n 3 frill or pleat.

rufous adj reddish-brown.

rug n 1 small carpet. 2 thick woollen blanket.

rugby n form of football played with an oval ball which may be handled by the players.

rugged ❶ [rug-gid] adj 1 rocky or steep. 2 uneven and jagged. 3 strong-featured. 4 tough and sturdy.

rugger n informal rugby.

ruin ❶ v 1 destroy or spoil completely. 2 impoverish. ▷ n 3 destruction or decay. 4 loss of wealth, position, etc. 5 broken-down unused building. **ruination** n 1 act of ruining. 2 state

———————————————————— THESAURUS —————

(inf), twaddle

rub out v = **erase**, cancel, delete, efface, obliterate, remove, wipe out

ructions pl n Inf = **row**, commotion, disturbance, fracas, fuss, hue and cry, trouble, uproar

ruddy adj 1 = **rosy**, blooming, fresh, glowing, healthy, radiant, red, reddish, rosy-cheeked

rude adj 1 = **impolite**, abusive, cheeky, discourteous, disrespectful, ill-mannered, impertinent, impudent, insolent, insulting, uncivil, unmannerly 2 = **vulgar**, boorish, brutish, coarse, graceless, loutish, oafish, rough, uncivilized, uncouth, uncultured 3 = **unpleasant**, abrupt, harsh, sharp, startling, sudden 4 = **roughly-made**, artless, crude, inartistic, inelegant, makeshift, primitive, raw, rough, simple

rudimentary adj = **basic**, early, elementary, fundamental, initial, primitive, undeveloped

rudiments pl n = **basics**, beginnings, elements, essentials, foundation, fundamentals

rue¹ v = **regret**, be sorry for, kick oneself for, lament, mourn, repent

rueful adj = **regretful**, contrite, mournful, penitent, remorseful, repentant, sorrowful, sorry

ruffian n = **thug**, brute, bully, heavy (sl), hoodlum, hooligan, rough (inf), tough

ruffle v 1 = **disarrange**, dishevel, disorder, mess up, rumple, tousle, muss (US & Canad) 2 = **annoy**, agitate, fluster, irritate, nettle, peeve (inf), upset

rugged adj 1 = **rocky**, craggy 2 = **uneven**, broken, bumpy, craggy, difficult, irregular, jagged, ragged, rough 3 = **strong-featured**, rough-hewn, weather-beaten 4 = **tough**, brawny, burly, husky (inf), muscular, robust, strong, sturdy, well-built

ruin v 1 = **destroy**, blow (sl), botch, crush, damage, defeat, demolish, devastate, lay waste, make a mess of, mess up, screw up (inf), smash, spoil, wreck 2 = **bankrupt**, impoverish, pauperize ▷ n 3 = **disrepair**, decay, disintegration, ruination, wreckage 4 = **destruction**, breakdown, collapse, defeat, devastation, downfall, fall, undoing, wreck b = **bankruptcy**, destitution,

of being ruined. **3** cause of ruin.
ruinous *adj* **1** causing ruin. **2** more
expensive than can be afforded.
ruinously *adv.*
rule ❶ *n* **1** statement of what is
allowed, for example in a game or
procedure. **2** what is usual.
3 government, authority, or control.
4 measuring device with a straight
edge. ▷ *v* **5** govern. **6** be pre-eminent.
7 give a formal decision. **8** mark with
straight line(s). **9** restrain. **as a rule**
usually. **ruler** *n* **1** person who governs.
2 measuring device with a straight
edge. **ruling** *n* formal decision. **rule of
thumb** practical but imprecise
approach. **rule out** *v* exclude.
rum¹ *n* alcoholic drink distilled from
sugar cane.
rum² *adj informal* odd, strange.
rumba *n* lively ballroom dance of Cuban
origin.
rumble *v* **1** make a low continuous
noise. **2** *informal* discover the
(disreputable) truth about. ▷ *n* **3** deep
resonant sound.
rumbustious *adj* boisterous or unruly.
ruminate ❶ *v* **1** chew the cud.
2 ponder or meditate. **ruminant** *adj, n*
cud-chewing (animal, such as a cow,
sheep, or deer). **rumination** *n* quiet
meditation and reflection.

ruminative *adj* **ruminatively** *adv.*
rummage ❶ *v* **1** search untidily and at
length. ▷ *n* **2** untidy search through a
collection of things.
rummy *n* card game in which players
try to collect sets or sequences.
rumour ❶ *n* **1** unproved statement.
2 gossip or common talk. **rumoured**
adj suggested by rumour.
rump ❶ *n* **1** buttocks. **2** rear of an
animal.
rumple *v* make untidy, crumpled, or
dishevelled.
rumpus ❶ *n, pl* **-puses** noisy
commotion.
run ❶ *v* **running, ran, run 1** move with
a more rapid gait than walking. **2** go
quickly (across). **3** compete in a race,
election, etc. **4** operate a vehicle.
5 travel according to schedule.
6 function. **7** manage. **8** continue in a
particular direction or for a specified
period. **9** expose oneself to (a risk).
10 flow. **11** spread. **12** (of stitches)
unravel. **13** (of a newspaper) publish
(a story). **14** smuggle (goods, esp.
arms). ▷ *n* **15** act or spell of running.
16 ride in a car. **17** unrestricted access.
18 continuous period. **19** sequence.
20 heavy demand. **21** series of
unravelled stitches, ladder. **22** steep
snow-covered course for skiing.

————————— **THESAURUS** —————————

insolvency
ruinous *adj* **1** = **destructive**,
calamitous, catastrophic,
devastating, dire, disastrous,
shattering **2** = **extravagant**,
crippling, immoderate, wasteful
rule *n* **1** = **regulation**, axiom, canon,
decree, direction, guideline, law,
maxim, precept, principle, tenet
2 = **custom**, convention, habit,
practice, procedure, routine, tradition
3 = **government**, authority,
command, control, dominion,
jurisdiction, mana (*NZ*), mastery,
power, regime, reign ▷ *v* **5** = **govern**,
be in authority, be in power,
command, control, direct, reign
7 = **decree**, decide, judge, pronounce,
settle **as a rule** = **usually**, generally,
mainly, normally, on the whole,
ordinarily
rule out *v* = **exclude**, ban, debar,
dismiss, disqualify, eliminate, leave
out, preclude, prohibit, reject
ruler *n* **1** = **governor**, commander,

controller, head of state, king *or*
queen, leader, lord, monarch,
potentate, sovereign **2** = **measure**,
rule, yardstick
ruling *n* = **decision**, adjudication,
decree, judgment, pronouncement,
verdict
ruminate *v* **2** = **ponder**, cogitate,
consider, contemplate, deliberate,
mull over, muse, reflect, think, turn
over in one's mind
rummage *v* **1** = **search**, delve, forage,
hunt, ransack, root
rumour *n* **2** = **story**, buzz, dirt (*US sl*),
gossip, hearsay, news, report, talk,
whisper, word
rump *n* = **buttocks**, backside (*inf*),
bottom, bum (*Brit sl*), butt (*US & Canad
inf*), hindquarters, posterior, rear, rear
end, seat
rumpus *n* = **commotion**, disturbance,
furore, fuss, hue and cry, noise, row,
uproar
run *v* **1** = **race**, bolt, dash, gallop, hare
(*Brit inf*), hurry, jog, leg it (*inf*), lope,

r

23 enclosure for domestic fowls. **24** migration of fish upstream to spawn. **25** score of one at cricket. **run across** v meet by chance. **run away** v make one's escape, flee. **runaway** n person or animal that runs away. **run down** v **1** be rude about. **2** reduce in number or size. **3** stop working. **rundown** n **run-down** adj **1** exhausted. **2** dilapidated. **run in** v **1** run (an engine) gently. **2** informal arrest. **run-in** n informal argument. **run into** v meet. **run-of-the-mill** adj ordinary. **run out** v be completely used up. **run over** v knock down (a person) with a moving vehicle. **run up** v incur (a debt). **run-up** n time just before an event.

rune n **1** any character of the earliest Germanic alphabet. **2** obscure piece of writing using mysterious symbols. **runic** adj.

rung[1] n crossbar on a ladder.

rung[2] v past participle of RING[1].

runnel n small brook.

runner ❶ n **1** competitor in a race. **2** messenger. **3** smuggler. **4** part underneath an ice skate etc., on which it slides. **5** slender horizontal stem of a plant, such as a strawberry, running along the ground and forming new roots at intervals. **6** long strip of carpet or decorative cloth. **runner bean** seeds and pod of a climbing bean plant. **runner-up** n person who comes second in a competition.

running ❶ adj **1** continuous. **2** consecutive. **3** (of water) flowing. ▷ n **4** act of moving or flowing quickly. **5** management of a business etc. **in, out of the running** having or not having a good chance in a competition.

runny ❶ adj **-nier, -niest 1** tending to flow. **2** exuding moisture.

runt n **1** smallest animal in a litter. **2** undersized person.

runway n hard level roadway where aircraft take off and land.

rupee n monetary unit of India and Pakistan.

rupture ❶ n **1** breaking, breach. **2** hernia. ▷ v **3** break, burst, or sever.

rush, scurry, sprint **2 = move**, course, glide, go, pass, roll, skim **3 = compete**, be a candidate, contend, put oneself up for, stand, take part **6 = work**, function, go, operate, perform **7 = manage**, administer, be in charge of, control, direct, handle, head, lead, operate **8 = continue**, extend, go, proceed, reach, stretch **10 = flow**, discharge, go, gush, leak, pour, spill, spout, stream **11 = melt**, dissolve, go soft, liquefy **13 = publish**, display, feature, print **14 = smuggle**, bootleg, traffic in ▷ n **15 = race**, dash, gallop, jog, rush, sprint, spurt **16 = ride**, drive, excursion, jaunt, outing, spin (inf), trip **19 = sequence**, course, period, season, series, spell, stretch, string **23 = enclosure**, coop, pen

run away v **= flee**, abscond, bolt, do a runner (sl), escape, fly the coop (US & Canad inf), make a run for it, scram (inf), take to one's heels

runaway n **= fugitive**, deserter, escapee, refugee, truant

run down v **1 = criticize**, bad-mouth (sl, chiefly US & Canad), belittle, decry, denigrate, disparage, knock (inf), rubbish (inf), slag (off) (sl) **2 = reduce**, curtail, cut, cut back, decrease, trim

run-down adj **1 = exhausted**, below par, debilitated, drained, enervated, unhealthy, weak, weary, worn-out **2 = dilapidated**, broken-down, decrepit, ramshackle, seedy, shabby, worn-out

runner n **1 = athlete**, jogger, sprinter **2 = messenger**, courier, dispatch bearer, errand boy

running adj **1, 2 = continuous**, constant, incessant, perpetual, unbroken, uninterrupted **3 = flowing**, moving, streaming ▷ n **5 = management**, administration, control, direction, leadership, organization, supervision

runny adj **1 = flowing**, fluid, liquefied, liquid, melted, watery

run-of-the-mill adj **= ordinary**, average, bog-standard (Brit & Irish sl), mediocre, middling, passable, tolerable, undistinguished, unexceptional

run out v **a = be used up**, be exhausted, dry up, fail, finish, give out **b = expire**, end, terminate

run over v **= knock down**, hit, knock over, run down

rupture n **1 = break**, breach, burst,

r

rural ❶ *adj* in or of the countryside.

ruse ❶ [**rooz**] *n* stratagem or trick.

rush¹ ❶ *v* **1** move or do very quickly.
2 force (someone) to act hastily.
3 make a sudden attack upon (a person or place). ▷ *n* **4** sudden quick or violent movement. **5** sudden demand. ▷ *pl* **6** first unedited prints of a scene for a film. ▷ *adj* **7** done with speed, hasty. **rush hour** period at the beginning and end of the working day, when many people are travelling to or from work.

rush² *n* marsh plant with a slender pithy stem. **rushy** *adj* full of rushes.

rusk *n* hard brown crisp biscuit, used esp. for feeding babies.

russet *adj* **1** reddish-brown. ▷ *n* **2** apple with rough reddish-brown skin.

Russian *adj* **1** of Russia. ▷ *n* **2** person from Russia. **3** official language of Russia and, formerly, of the Soviet Union. **Russian roulette** act of bravado in which a person spins the cylinder of a revolver loaded with only one cartridge and presses the trigger with the barrel against his or her own head.

rust ❶ *n* **1** reddish-brown coating formed on iron etc. that has been exposed to moisture. **2** disease of plants which produces rust-coloured spots. ▷ *adj* **3** reddish-brown. ▷ *v* **4** become coated with rust.

5 deteriorate through lack of use.
rusty *adj* **rustier**, **rustiest 1** coated with rust. **2** of a rust colour. **3** out of practice.

rustic ❶ *adj* **1** of or resembling country people. **2** rural. **3** crude, awkward, or uncouth. **4** (of furniture) made of untrimmed branches. ▷ *n* **5** person from the country. **rusticity** *n*.

rusticate *v* **1** banish temporarily from university as a punishment. **2** retire to the country.

rustle¹ ❶ *v, n* (make) a low whispering sound.

rustle² *v US* steal (cattle). **rustler** *n US* cattle thief. **rustle up** *v* prepare at short notice.

rut¹ ❶ *n* **1** furrow made by wheels. **2** dull settled habits or way of living.

rut² *n* **1** recurrent period of sexual excitability in male deer. ▷ *v* **rutting**, **rutted 2** be in a period of sexual excitability.

rutabaga *n* the US and Canadian name for SWEDE.

ruthenium *n Chemistry* rare hard brittle white element.

ruthless ❶ *adj* pitiless, merciless. **ruthlessly** *adv* **ruthlessness** *n*.

rye *n* **1** kind of grain used for fodder and bread. **2** *US* whiskey made from rye.

rye-grass *n* any of several grasses cultivated for fodder.

THESAURUS

crack, fissure, rent, split, tear ▷ *v*
3 = **break**, burst, crack, separate, sever, split, tear

rural *adj* = **rustic**, agricultural, country, pastoral, sylvan

ruse *n* = **trick**, device, dodge, hoax, manoeuvre, ploy, stratagem, subterfuge

rush¹ *v* **1** = **hurry**, bolt, career, dash, fly, hasten, race, run, shoot, speed, tear
2 = **push**, hurry, hustle, press
3 = **attack**, charge, storm ▷ *n* **4**
a = **hurry**, charge, dash, haste, race, scramble, stampede, surge
b = **attack**, assault, charge, onslaught ▷ *adj* **7** = **hasty**, fast, hurried, quick, rapid, swift, urgent

rust *n* **1** = **corrosion**, oxidation
2 = **mildew**, blight, mould, must, rot
▷ *v* **4** = **corrode**, oxidize

rustic *adj* **1, 2** = **rural**, country, pastoral, sylvan **3** = **uncouth**, awkward, coarse, crude, rough ▷ *n* **5** = **yokel**, boor, bumpkin, clod, clodhopper (*inf*), hick (*inf, chiefly US & Canad*), peasant

rustle¹ *v* = **crackle**, crinkle, whisper ▷ *n* = **crackle**, crinkling, rustling, whisper

rusty *adj* **1** = **corroded**, oxidized, rust-covered, rusted **2** = **reddish-brown**, chestnut, coppery, reddish, russet, rust-coloured **3** = **out of practice**, stale, unpractised, weak

rut¹ *n* **1** = **groove**, furrow, indentation, track, trough, wheel mark **2** = **habit**, dead end, pattern, routine, system

ruthless *adj* = **merciless**, brutal, callous, cruel, harsh, heartless, pitiless, relentless, remorseless

r

s second(s).

S 1 South(ern). **2** *Chemistry* sulphur.

SA 1 Salvation Army. **2** South Africa South Australia.

Sabbath *n* day of worship and rest: Saturday for Jews, Sunday for Christians. **sabbatical** *adj, n* (denoting) leave for study.

sable *n* **1** dark fur from a small weasel-like Arctic animal. ▷ *adj* **2** black.

sabot [**sab**-oh] *n* wooden shoe, clog.

sabotage ❶ *n* **1** intentional damage done to machinery, systems, etc. ▷ *v* **2** damage intentionally. **saboteur** *n* person who commits sabotage.

sabre *n* **1** curved cavalry sword. **2** light fencing sword.

sac *n* pouchlike structure in an animal or plant.

saccharin ❶ *n* artificial sweetener. **saccharine** *adj* **1** excessively sweet. **2** of or like sugar.

sacerdotal *adj* of priests.

sachet *n* **1** small envelope or bag containing a single portion. **2** small bag of perfumed powder for scenting clothing.

sack¹ ❶ *n* **1** large bag made of coarse material. **2** *informal* dismissal. **3** *slang* bed. ▷ *v* **4** *informal* dismiss. **sacking** *n*

rough woven material used for sacks. **sackcloth** *n* coarse fabric used for sacks, formerly worn as a penance.

sack² ❶ *n* **1** plundering of a captured town. ▷ *v* **2** plunder (a captured town).

sacrament *n* ceremony of the Christian Church, esp. Communion. **sacramental** *adj*.

sacred ❶ *adj* **1** holy. **2** connected with religion. **3** set apart, reserved. **sacred cow** person, custom, etc. regarded as being beyond criticism.

sacrifice ❶ *n* **1** giving something up. **2** thing given up. **3** making of an offering to a god. **4** thing offered. ▷ *v* **5** offer as a sacrifice. **6** give (something) up. **sacrificial** *adj*.

sacrilege ❶ *n* misuse or desecration of something sacred. **sacrilegious** *adj*.

- **SPELLING TIP**
- It may sound as if **sacrilegious** has
- something to do with the word
- 'religious', which might explain why
- the most common misspelling of
- the word in the Bank of English is
- *sacreligious*. But it should be spelt
- **sacrilegious**.

sacristan *n* person in charge of the contents of a church. **sacristy** *n*, *pl* **-ties** room in a church where sacred objects are kept.

sacrosanct ❶ *adj* regarded as sacred, inviolable, e.g. *For many people, Christmas celebrations are still sacrosanct.* **sacrosanctity** or **sacrosanctness** *n*.

sacrum [**say**-krum] *n*, *pl* **-cra** wedge-shaped bone at the base of the spine.

sad ❶ *adj* **sadder**, **saddest 1** sorrowful, unhappy. **2** causing or expressing

————————————————————————————— THESAURUS —————

sabotage *n* **1** = **damage**, destruction, disruption, subversion, wrecking ▷ *v* **2** = **damage**, destroy, disable, disrupt, incapacitate, subvert, vandalize, wreck

saccharine *adj* **1** = **oversweet**, cloying, honeyed, nauseating, sickly

sack¹ *n* **2** *Inf* = **dismissal**, discharge, the axe (*inf*), the boot (*sl*), the push (*sl*) ▷ *v* **4** *Inf* = **dismiss**, axe (*inf*), discharge, fire (*inf*), give (someone) the push (*inf*)

sack² *n* **1** = **plundering**, looting, pillage ▷ *v* **2** = **plunder**, loot, pillage, raid, rob, ruin, strip

sacred *adj* **1** = **holy**, blessed, divine, hallowed, revered, sanctified **2** = **religious**, ecclesiastical, holy

3 = **inviolable**, protected, sacrosanct

sacrifice *n* **1** = **surrender**, loss, renunciation **3, 4** = **offering**, oblation ▷ *v* **5** = **offer**, immolate, offer up **6** = **give up**, forego, forfeit, let go, lose, say goodbye to, surrender

sacrilege *n* = **desecration**, blasphemy, heresy, impiety, irreverence, profanation, violation

sacrilegious *adj* = **profane**, blasphemous, desecrating, impious, irreligious, irreverent

sacrosanct *adj* = **inviolable**, hallowed, inviolate, sacred, sanctified, set apart, untouchable

sad *adj* **1** = **unhappy**, blue, dejected, depressed, doleful, down, low,

sorrow. **3** deplorably bad. **sadden** *v* make sad. **sadly** *adv* **sadness** *n*.

saddle ❶ *n* **1** rider's seat on a horse or bicycle. **2** joint of meat. ▷ *v* **3** put a saddle on (a horse). **4** burden (with a responsibility). **saddler** *n* maker or seller of saddles. **saddlery** *n*.

sadism ❶ [**say**-dizz-um] *n* gaining of (sexual) pleasure from inflicting pain. **sadist** *n* **sadistic** *adj* **sadistically** *adv*.

sadomasochism *n* combination of sadism and masochism. **sadomasochist** *n*.

s.a.e. stamped addressed envelope.

safari *n*, *pl* **-ris** expedition to hunt or observe wild animals, esp. in Africa. **safari park** park where lions, elephants, etc. are kept uncaged so that people can see them from cars.

safe ❶ *adj* **1** secure, protected. **2** uninjured, out of danger. **3** not involving risk. **4** not dangerous, e.g. *the beef is safe to eat.* ▷ *n* **5** strong lockable container. **safely** *adv* **safe-conduct** *n* permit allowing travel through a dangerous area. **safe deposit** place where valuables can be stored safely. **safekeeping** *n* protection.

safeguard ❶ *v* **1** protect. ▷ *n* **2** protection.

safety ❶ *n*, *pl* **-ties** state of being safe. **safety belt** same as SEAT BELT. **safety lamp** miner's lamp designed to prevent it from igniting gas. **safety**

net net to catch performers on a trapeze or high wire if they fall. **safety pin** pin with a spring fastening and a guard over the point when closed. **safety valve 1** valve that allows steam etc. to escape if pressure becomes excessive. **2** harmless outlet for emotion.

safflower *n* thistle-like plant with flowers used for dye and oil.

saffron *n* **1** orange-coloured flavouring obtained from a crocus. ▷ *adj* **2** orange.

sag ❶ *v* **sagging, sagged 1** sink in the middle. **2** tire. **3** (of clothes) hang loosely. ▷ *n* **4** droop.

saga ❶ [**sah**-ga] *n* **1** legend of Norse heroes. **2** any long story.

sagacious *adj* wise. **sagacity** *n*.

sage¹ ❶ *n* **1** very wise man. ▷ *adj* **2** *lit* wise. **sagely** *adv*.

sage² *n* aromatic herb with grey-green leaves.

sagebrush *n* aromatic plant of West N America.

Sagittarius *n* (the archer) ninth sign of the zodiac.

sago *n* starchy cereal from the powdered pith of the sago palm tree.

sahib *n* Indian term of address placed after a man's name as a mark of respect.

said *v* past of SAY.

sail ❶ *n* **1** sheet of fabric stretched to catch the wind for propelling a sailing

---

THESAURUS

low-spirited, melancholy, mournful, woebegone **2** = **tragic**, depressing, dismal, grievous, harrowing, heart-rending, moving, pathetic, pitiful, poignant, upsetting **3** = **deplorable**, bad, lamentable, sorry, wretched

sadden *v* = **upset**, deject, depress, distress, grieve, make sad

saddle *v* **4** = **burden**, encumber, load, lumber (*Brit inf*)

sadistic *adj* = **cruel**, barbarous, brutal, ruthless, vicious

sadness *n* = **unhappiness**, dejection, depression, despondency, grief, melancholy, misery, poignancy, sorrow, the blues

safe *adj* **1** = **secure**, impregnable, in safe hands, out of danger, out of harm's way, protected, safe and sound **2** = **unharmed**, all right, intact, O.K. or okay (*inf*), undamaged, unhurt, unscathed **3** = **risk-free**, certain,

impregnable, secure, sound ▷ *n* **5** = **strongbox**, coffer, deposit box, repository, safe-deposit box, vault

safeguard *v* **1** = **protect**, defend, guard, look after, preserve ▷ *n* **2** = **protection**, defence, guard, security

safely *adv* = **in safety**, in one piece, safe and sound, with impunity, without risk

safety *n* = **security**, impregnability, protection

sag *v* **1** = **sink**, bag, dip, droop, fall, give way, hang loosely, slump **2** = **tire**, droop, flag, wane, weaken, wilt

saga *n* **2** = **tale**, epic, narrative, story, yarn

sage¹ *n* **1** = **wise man**, elder, guru, master, philosopher ▷ *adj* **2** *Lit* = **wise**, judicious, sagacious, sapient, sensible

sail *v* **5** = **embark**, set sail **6** = **pilot**, steer **7** = **glide**, drift, float, fly, skim, soar, sweep, wing

boat. **2** journey by boat. **3** arm of a windmill. ▷ *v* **4** travel by water. **5** begin a voyage. **6** navigate a vessel. **7** move smoothly. **sailor** *n* **1** member of a ship's crew. **2** person considered as liable or not liable to seasickness, e.g. *a bad sailor*; *a good sailor*. **sailboard** *n* board with a mast and single sail, used for windsurfing. **sailcloth** *n* **1** fabric for making sails. **2** light canvas for making clothes.

saint ❶ *n* **1** *Christianity* person venerated after death as specially holy. **2** exceptionally good person. **saintly** *adj* **saintliness** *n* **sainthood** *n*.

saithe *n* dark-coloured edible sea fish.

sake¹ ❶ *n* **1** benefit. **2** purpose. **for the sake of 1** for the purpose of. **2** to please or benefit (someone).

sake², **saki** [**sah**-kee] *n* Japanese alcoholic drink made from fermented rice.

salaam [sal-**ahm**] *n* **1** low bow of greeting among Muslims. ▷ *v* **2** make a salaam.

salacious ❶ *adj* excessively concerned with sex.

salad *n* dish of raw vegetables, eaten as a meal or part of a meal. **salad days** period of youth and inexperience. **salad dressing** sauce of oil and vinegar or mayonnaise.

salamander *n* amphibian which looks like a lizard.

salami *n* highly spiced sausage.

salary ❶ *n*, *pl* **-ries** fixed regular payment, usu. monthly, to an employee. **salaried** *adj*.

sale ❶ *n* **1** exchange of goods for money. **2** amount sold. **3** selling of goods at unusually low prices. **4** auction. ▷ *pl* **5** department that sells its company's products. **saleable** *adj* fit or likely to be sold. **saleroom** *n* place where goods are sold by auction.

salesman, **saleswoman**, **salesperson** *n* person who sells goods. **salesmanship** *n* skill in selling.

salient ❶ [**say**-lee-ent] *adj* **1** prominent, noticeable. ▷ *n* **2** *Military* projecting part of a front line.

saline [**say**-line] *adj* containing salt. **salinity** *n*.

saliva [sal-**lie**-va] *n* liquid that forms in the mouth, spittle. **salivary** *adj* **salivate** *v* produce saliva.

sallee *n* *Aust* (also **snow gum**) **1** SE Australian eucalyptus with a pale grey bark. **2** acacia tree.

sallow ❶ *adj* of an unhealthy pale or yellowish colour.

sally *n*, *pl* **-lies 1** witty remark. **2** sudden brief attack by troops. ▷ *v* **-lying**, **-lied** (foll. by *forth*) **3** rush out. **4** go out.

salmon *n* **1** large fish with orange-pink flesh valued as food. **2** any of several unrelated fish. ▷ *adj* **3** orange-pink.

salmonella *n*, *pl* **-lae** bacterium causing food poisoning.

salon *n* **1** commercial premises of a hairdresser, beautician, etc. **2** elegant reception room for guests. **3** informal gathering of important people.

saloon *n* **1** car with a fixed roof. **2** large public room, as on a ship. **3** *US* bar serving alcoholic drinks. **saloon bar** more expensive bar in a pub.

salt ❶ *n* **1** white crystalline substance used to season food. **2** chemical compound of acid and metal. **3** liveliness, wit. ▷ *pl* **4** mineral salts used as a medicine. ▷ *v* **5** season or preserve with salt. **6** scatter salt over (an icy road) to melt the ice. **old salt** experienced sailor. **with a pinch of salt** allowing for exaggeration. **worth one's salt** efficient. **salty** *adj* **salt away** *v* hoard or save. **saltbush** *n*

— THESAURUS —

sailor *n* **1** = **mariner**, marine, sea dog, seafarer, seaman

saintly *adj* = **virtuous**, godly, holy, pious, religious, righteous, saintlike

sake¹ *n* **1** = **benefit**, account, behalf, good, interest, welfare **2** = **purpose**, aim, end, motive, objective, reason

salacious *adj* = **lascivious**, carnal, erotic, lecherous, lewd, libidinous, lustful

salary *n* = **pay**, earnings, income, wage, wages

sale *n* **1** = **selling**, deal, disposal, marketing, transaction

salient *adj* **1** = **prominent**, conspicuous, important, noticeable, outstanding, pronounced, striking

sallow *adj* = **wan**, anaemic, pale, pallid, pasty, sickly, unhealthy, yellowish

salt *n* **1** = **seasoning**, flavour, relish, savour, taste **with a pinch of salt** = **sceptically**, cynically, disbelievingly, suspiciously, with reservations

shrub that grows in alkaline desert regions. **saltcellar** *n* small container for salt at table. **saltwater** *adj* living in the sea.

saltpetre *n* compound used in gunpowder and as a preservative.

salubrious ❶ *adj* favourable to health.

Saluki *n* tall hound with a silky coat.

salutary ❶ *adj* producing a beneficial result.

salute ❶ *n* **1** motion of the arm as a formal military sign of respect. **2** firing of guns as a military greeting of honour. ▷ *v* **3** greet with a salute. **4** make a salute. **5** acknowledge with praise. **salutation** *n* greeting by words or actions.

salvage ❶ *n* **1** saving of a ship or other property from destruction. **2** property so saved. ▷ *v* **3** save from destruction or waste. **4** gain (something beneficial) from a failure.

salvation ❶ *n* **1** fact or state of being saved from harm or the consequences of sin. **2** person or thing that preserves from harm.

salve ❶ *n* **1** healing or soothing ointment. ▷ *v* **2** soothe or appease, e.g. *salve one's conscience*.

salver *n* (silver) tray on which something is presented.

salvia *n* plant with blue or red flowers.

salvo *n, pl* **-vos, -voes 1** simultaneous discharge of guns etc. **2** burst of applause or questions.

sal volatile [sal vol-**at**-ill-ee] *n* preparation of ammonia, used to revive a person who feels faint.

SAM surface-to-air missile.

Samaritan *n* person who helps people in distress.

samarium *n Chemistry* silvery metallic element.

samba *n* lively Brazilian dance.

same ❶ *adj* **1** identical, not different, unchanged. **2** just mentioned. **all the same, just the same** nevertheless. **sameness** *n*.

samovar *n* Russian tea urn.

Samoyed *n* dog with a thick white coat and tightly curled tail.

sampan *n* small boat with oars used in China.

samphire *n* plant found on rocks by the seashore.

sample ❶ *n* **1** part taken as representative of a whole. ▷ *n* **2** *Music* short extract from an existing recording mixed into a backing track to produce a new recording. ▷ *v* **3** take and test a sample of. **sampler** *n* piece of embroidery showing the embroiderer's skill. **sampling** *n*.

samurai *n, pl* **-rai** member of an ancient Japanese warrior caste.

sanatorium *n, pl* **-riums, -ria 1** institution for invalids or convalescents. **2** room for sick pupils at a boarding school.

sanctify ❶ *v* **-fying, -fied 1** make holy. **2** approve as religiously binding.

sanctimonious ❶ *adj* pretending to be religious and virtuous.

sanction ❶ *n* **1** permission, authorization. **2** coercive measure or

---

salty *adj* = **salt**, brackish, briny, saline

salubrious *adj* = **health-giving**, beneficial, good for one, healthy, wholesome

salutary *adj* = **beneficial**, advantageous, good for one, profitable, useful, valuable

salute *n* **1** = **salutation** ▷ *v* **3** = **greet**, acknowledge, address, hail, welcome **5** = **honour**, acknowledge, pay tribute *or* homage to, recognize

salvage *v* **3** = **save**, recover, rescue, retrieve **4** = **redeem**

salvation *n* **1** = **saving**, deliverance, escape, preservation, redemption, rescue

salve *n* **1** = **ointment**, balm, cream, lotion

same *adj* **1 a** = **identical**, alike,

corresponding, duplicate, equal, twin **b** = **unchanged**, changeless, consistent, constant, invariable, unaltered, unvarying **2** = **aforementioned**, aforesaid

sample *n* **1** = **specimen**, example, instance, model, pattern ▷ *v* **2** = **test**, experience, inspect, taste, try

sanctify *v* **1** = **consecrate**, cleanse, hallow

sanctimonious *adj* = **holier-than-thou**, hypocritical, pious, self-righteous, smug

sanction *n* **1** = **permission**, approval, authority, authorization, backing (*inf*), mana (*NZ*), O.K. *or* okay, stamp *or* seal of approval **2** = **ban**, boycott, coercive measures, embargo, penalty ▷ *v* **3** = **permit**, allow, approve, authorize, endorse

S

penalty. ▷ v **3** allow, authorize.

sanctity ❶ n sacredness, inviolability.

sanctuary ❶ n, pl **-aries 1** holy place.
2 part of a church nearest the altar.
3 place of safety for a fugitive. **4** place where animals or birds can live undisturbed.

sanctum n, pl **-tums, -ta 1** sacred place. **2** person's private room.

sand n **1** substance consisting of small grains of rock, esp. on a beach or in a desert. ▷ pl **2** stretches of sand forming a beach or desert. ▷ v **3** smooth with sandpaper. **4** fill with sand. **sander** n power tool for smoothing surfaces.
sandy adj **1** covered with sand. **2** (of hair) reddish-fair. **sandbag** n **1** bag filled with sand, used as protection against gunfire or flood water. ▷ v **2** protect with sandbags. **sandbank** n bank of sand below the surface of a river or sea. **sandblast** v, n (clean with) a jet of sand blown from a nozzle under pressure. **sand castle** model of a castle made from sand. **sandpaper** n **1** paper coated with sand for smoothing a surface. ▷ v **2** smooth with sandpaper. **sandpiper** n shore bird with a long bill and slender legs. **sandstone** n rock composed of sand. **sandstorm** n desert wind that whips up clouds of sand.

sandal n light shoe consisting of a sole attached by straps.

sandalwood n sweet-scented wood.

sandwich n **1** two slices of bread with a layer of food between. ▷ v **2** insert between two other things. **sandwich board** pair of boards hung over a person's shoulders to display advertisements in front and behind. **sandwich course** course consisting of alternate periods of

study and work.

sane ❶ adj **1** of sound mind. **2** sensible, rational. **sanity** n.

sang v past tense of SING.

sang-froid [sahng-**frwah**] n French composure and calmness.

sangria n Spanish drink of wine and fruit juice.

sanguinary adj **1** accompanied by bloodshed. **2** bloodthirsty.

sanguine ❶ adj **1** cheerful, optimistic. **2** ruddy.

Sanhedrin [**san**-id-rin] n Judaism highest court of the ancient Jewish nation.

sanitary ❶ adj **1** promoting health by getting rid of dirt and germs. **2** hygienic. **sanitation** n sanitary measures, esp. drainage or sewerage. **sanitary towel** absorbent pad worn externally during menstruation.

sank v past tense of SINK.

Sanskrit n ancient language of India.

Santa Claus n legendary patron saint of children, who brings presents at Christmas.

sap¹ ❶ n **1** moisture that circulates in plants. **2** informal gullible person. **sappy** adj.

sap² ❶ v **sapping, sapped 1** undermine. **2** weaken. ▷ n **3** trench dug to undermine an enemy position. **sapper** n soldier in an engineering unit.

sapient [**say**-pee-ent] adj lit wise, shrewd. **sapience** n.

sapling n young tree.

sapphire n **1** blue precious stone. ▷ adj **2** deep blue.

saprophyte n plant that lives on dead organic matter.

sarabande, saraband n slow stately Spanish dance.

sanctity n = **holiness**, godliness, goodness, grace, inviolability, piety, sacredness

sanctuary n **1** = **church**, temple **2** = **shrine**, altar **3** = **protection**, asylum, haven, refuge, retreat, shelter **4** = **reserve**, conservation area, national park, nature reserve

sane adj **1** = **of sound mind**, all there (inf), compos mentis, in one's right mind, mentally sound **2** = **sensible**, balanced, judicious, level-headed, rational, reasonable, sound

sanguine adj **1** = **cheerful**, buoyant, confident, hopeful, optimistic

sanitary adj **2** = **hygienic**, clean, germ-free, healthy, wholesome

sanity n **1** = **mental health**, normality, rationality, reason, saneness **2** = **good sense**, common sense, level-headedness, rationality, sense

sap¹ n **1** = **vital fluid**, essence, lifeblood **2** Inf = **fool**, idiot, jerk (sl, chiefly US & Canad), ninny, simpleton, twit (inf), wally (sl)

sap² v **1** = **undermine 2** = **weaken**, deplete, drain, exhaust

s

Saracen *n History* Arab or Muslim who opposed the Crusades.

sarcasm ❶ *n* (use of) bitter or wounding ironic language. **sarcastic** *adj* **sarcastically** *adv*.

sarcoma *n, pl* **-mata, -mas** malignant tumour beginning in connective tissue.

sarcophagus *n, pl* **-gi, -guses** stone coffin.

sardine *n* small fish of the herring family, usu. preserved in tightly packed tins.

sardonic ❶ *adj* mocking or scornful. **sardonically** *adv*.

sardonyx *n* brown-and-white gemstone.

sargassum, sargasso *n* type of floating seaweed.

sari, saree *n* long piece of cloth draped around the body and over one shoulder, worn by Hindu women.

sarmie *n S Afr slang* sandwich.

sarong *n* long piece of cloth tucked around the waist or under the armpits, worn esp. in Malaysia.

sarsaparilla *n* soft drink, orig. made from the root of a tropical American plant.

sartorial *adj* of men's clothes or tailoring.

SAS Special Air Service.

sash¹ *n* decorative strip of cloth worn round the waist or over one shoulder.

sash² *n* wooden frame containing the panes of a window. **sash window** window consisting of two sashes that can be opened by sliding one over the other.

sassafras *n* American tree with aromatic bark used medicinally.

Sassenach *n Scot* English person.

sat *v* past of SIT.

Sat. Saturday.

Satan ❶ *n* the Devil. **satanic** *adj* **1** of Satan. **2** supremely evil. **Satanism** *n* worship of Satan.

satay, saté [sat-ay] *n* Indonesian and Malaysian dish consisting of pieces of chicken, pork, etc., grilled on skewers and served with peanut sauce.

satchel *n* bag, usu. with a shoulder strap, for carrying school books.

sate *v* satisfy (a desire or appetite) fully.

satellite *n* **1** man-made device orbiting in space. **2** heavenly body that orbits another. **3** country that is dependent on a more powerful one. ▷ *adj* **4** of or used in the transmission of television signals from a satellite to the home.

satiate ❶ [say-she-ate] *v* provide with more than enough, so as to disgust. **satiable** *adj* **satiety** [sat-tie-a-tee] *n* feeling of having had too much.

satin *n* silky fabric with a glossy surface on one side. **satiny** *adj* of or like satin. **satinwood** *n* tropical tree yielding hard wood.

satire ❶ *n* **1** use of ridicule to expose vice or folly. **2** poem or other work that does this. **satirical** *adj* **satirist** *n* **satirize** *v* ridicule by means of satire.

satisfy ❶ *v* **-fying, -fied 1** please, content. **2** provide amply for (a need

---

sarcasm *n* = **irony**, bitterness, cynicism, derision, mockery, ridicule, satire

sarcastic *adj* = **ironical**, acid, biting, caustic, cutting, cynical, mocking, sardonic, sarky (*Brit inf*), satirical

sardonic *adj* = **mocking**, cynical, derisive, dry, ironical, sarcastic, sneering, wry

Satan *n* = **The Devil**, Beelzebub, Lord of the Flies, Lucifer, Mephistopheles, Old Nick (*inf*), Prince of Darkness, The Evil One

satanic *adj* **2** = **evil**, black, demonic, devilish, diabolic, fiendish, hellish, infernal, wicked

satiate *v* **2** = **glut**, cloy, gorge, jade, nauseate, overfill, stuff, surfeit

satire *n* **1** = **mockery**, irony, ridicule **2** = **parody**, burlesque, caricature, lampoon, take off, travesty

satirical *adj* = **mocking**, biting, caustic, cutting, incisive, ironical

satirize *v* = **ridicule**, burlesque, deride, lampoon, parody, pillory

satisfaction *n* **1** = **contentment**, comfort, content, enjoyment, happiness, pleasure, pride **2** = **assuaging**, gratification, repletion, satiety **4** = **fulfilment**, achievement

satisfactory *adj* = **adequate**, acceptable, all right, average, fair, good enough, passable, sufficient

satisfy *v* **1** = **content**, assuage, gratify, indulge, pacify, pander to, please, quench, sate, slake **2** = **be sufficient**, answer, be enough, do, fulfil, meet, serve, suffice **3** = **convince**, assure, persuade, reassure

S

or desire). **3** convince, persuade.
4 fulfil the requirements of.
satisfaction n **satisfactory** adj.

satnav n Motoring informal satellite
navigation.

satsuma n kind of small orange.

saturate ❶ v **1** soak thoroughly.
2 cause to absorb the maximum
amount of something. **saturation** n
saturation point point at which
some capacity is at its fullest.

Saturday n seventh day of the week.

Saturn ❶ n **1** Roman god of
agriculture. **2** sixth planet from the
sun. **saturnine** adj gloomy in
temperament or appearance.
saturnalia n wild party or orgy.

saturnine ❶ adj gloomy in
temperament or appearance.

satyr n **1** woodland god, part man,
part goat. **2** lustful man.

sauce ❶ n **1** liquid added to food to
enhance flavour. **2** informal
impudence. **saucy** adj **1** impudent.
2 pert, jaunty. **saucily** adv **saucepan** n
cooking pot with a long handle.

saucer n small round dish put under
a cup.

sauerkraut n shredded cabbage
fermented in brine.

sauna n Finnish-style steam bath.

saunter ❶ v **1** walk in a leisurely
manner, stroll. ▷ n **2** leisurely walk.

saurian adj of or like a lizard.

sausage n minced meat in an edible
tube-shaped skin. **sausage roll**
skinless sausage covered in pastry.

sauté [so-tay] v **-téing** or **-téeing**,
-téed fry quickly in a little fat.

savage ❶ adj **1** wild, untamed. **2** cruel
and violent. **3** uncivilized, primitive.
▷ n **4** uncivilized person. ▷ v **5** attack
ferociously. **6** criticize violently.
savagely adv **savagery** n.

savannah, savanna n extensive open
grassy plain in Africa.

savant n learned person.

save ❶ v **1** rescue or preserve from
harm, protect. **2** avoid the waste or
loss of. **3** keep for the future. **4** set
aside (money). **5** prevent the
necessity for. **6** Sport prevent the
scoring of (a goal). ▷ n **7** Sport act of
preventing a goal. ▷ prep **8** old-
fashioned except. **saver** n **saving** n
1 economy. ▷ pl **2** money put by
for future use. ▷ prep **3** except.
saving grace good quality that
prevents a person from being
worthless.

saveloy n spicy smoked sausage.

saviour ❶ n **1** person who rescues
another. **2** (S-) Christ.

savoir-faire ❶ [sav-wahr-**fair**] n French
ability to do and say the right thing in
any situation.

savory n aromatic herb used in
cooking.

————————————————————————— THESAURUS —————————

saturate v **1** = **soak**, drench, imbue,
souse, steep, suffuse, waterlog, wet
through

saturnine adj = **gloomy**, dour, glum,
grave, morose, sombre

saucy adj **1** = **impudent**, cheeky
(inf), forward, impertinent,
insolent, pert, presumptuous, rude
2 = **jaunty**, dashing, gay, natty (inf),
perky

saunter v **1** = **stroll**, amble, meander,
mosey (inf), ramble, roam, wander ▷
2 = **stroll**, airing, amble, ramble, turn,
walk

savage adj **1** = **wild**, feral, rough,
rugged, uncultivated,
undomesticated, untamed **2** = **cruel**,
barbarous, bestial, bloodthirsty,
brutal, ferocious, fierce, harsh,
ruthless, sadistic, vicious
3 = **primitive**, rude, uncivilized,
unspoilt ▷ n **4** = **lout**, boor, yahoo, yob
(Brit sl) ▷ v **5** = **attack**, lacerate,

mangle, maul

savagery n = **cruelty**, barbarity,
brutality, ferocity, ruthlessness,
viciousness

save v **1 a** = **rescue**, deliver, free,
liberate, recover, redeem, salvage
b = **protect**, conserve, guard, keep
safe, look after, preserve, safeguard **3,
4** = **keep**, collect, gather, hoard, hold,
husband, lay by, put by, reserve, set
aside, store

saving n **1** = **economy**, bargain,
discount, reduction pl **2** = **nest
egg**, fund, reserves, resources,
store

saviour n **1** = **rescuer**, defender,
deliverer, liberator, preserver,
protector, redeemer **2** (S-) = **Christ**,
Jesus, Messiah, Redeemer

savoir-faire n French = **social know-
how** (inf), diplomacy, discretion,
finesse, poise, social graces, tact,
urbanity

savour ❶ *v* **1** enjoy, relish. **2** (foll. by *of*) have a flavour or suggestion of. ▷ *n* **3** characteristic taste or odour. **4** slight but distinctive quality. **savoury** *adj* **1** salty or spicy. **2** pleasant or acceptable. ▷ *n, pl* **-vouries 3** savoury dish served before or after a meal.

savoy *n* variety of cabbage.

savvy *slang* ▷ *v* **-vying, -vied 1** understand. ▷ *n* **2** understanding, intelligence.

saw¹ *n* **1** cutting tool with a toothed metal blade. ▷ *v* **sawing, sawed, sawed** *or* **sawn 2** cut with a saw. **3** move (something) back and forth. **sawyer** *n* person who saws timber for a living. **sawdust** *n* fine wood fragments made in sawing. **sawfish** *n* fish with a long toothed snout. **sawmill** *n* mill where timber is sawn into planks.

saw² *v* past tense of SEE¹.

saw³ *n* wise saying, proverb.

sax *n informal* short for SAXOPHONE.

saxifrage *n* alpine rock plant with small flowers.

Saxon *n* **1** member of the W Germanic people who settled widely in Europe in the early Middle Ages. ▷ *adj* **2** of the Saxons.

saxophone *n* brass wind instrument with keys and a curved body. **saxophonist** *n*.

say ❶ *v* **saying, said 1** speak or utter. **2** express (an idea) in words. **3** give as one's opinion. **4** indicate or show. **5** suppose as an example or possibility. ▷ *n* **6** right or chance to speak. **7** share in a decision. **saying** *n* maxim, proverb. **say-so** *n informal* permission.

SAYE save as you earn: system by which regular payments are made into a savings account from a salary.

Sb *Chemistry* antimony.

Sc *Chemistry* scandium.

SC South Carolina.

scab *n* **1** crust formed over a wound. **2** *offens* blackleg. **3** disease of plants and animals. **scabby** *adj* **1** covered with scabs. **2** *informal* despicable.

scabbard *n* sheath for a sword or dagger.

scabies [**skay**-beez] *n* itchy skin disease.

scabrous [**skay**-bruss] *adj* **1** rough and scaly. **2** indecent.

scaffold *n* **1** temporary platform for workmen. **2** gallows. **scaffolding** *n* (materials for building) scaffolds.

scalar *n, adj* (variable quantity) having magnitude but no direction.

scald *v* **1** burn with hot liquid or steam. **2** sterilize with boiling water. **3** heat (liquid) almost to boiling point. ▷ *n* **4** injury by scalding.

scale¹ ❶ *n* **1** one of the thin overlapping plates covering fishes and reptiles. **2** thin flake. **3** coating which forms in kettles etc. due to hard water. **4** tartar formed on the teeth. ▷ *v* **5** remove scales from. **6** come off in scales. **scaly** *adj*.

scale² *n* (often *pl*) weighing instrument.

scale³ ❶ *n* **1** graduated table or sequence of marks at regular intervals, used as a reference in making measurements. **2** ratio of size between a thing and a representation of it. **3** graded system, e.g. *a wage scale*. **4** relative degree or extent. **5** fixed series of notes in music.

---

savour *v* **1** = **enjoy**, appreciate, delight in, luxuriate in, relish, revel in **2** (foll. by *of*) = **suggest**, be suggestive of, show signs of, smack of ▷ *n* **3** = **flavour**, piquancy, relish, smack, smell, tang, taste **4** = **trace**, distinctive quality

savoury *adj* **1** = **spicy**, full-flavoured, piquant, rich **2** = **palatable**, appetizing, lekker (*S Afr sl*), luscious, mouthwatering, tasty

say *v* **1** = **speak**, announce, express, mention, pronounce, remark, state, utter, voice **2** = **express**, communicate, convey, imply **3** = **declare**, affirm, assert, maintain

5 = **suppose**, assume, conjecture, estimate, guess, imagine, presume, surmise ▷ *n* **6** = **chance to speak**, voice, vote **7** = **influence**, authority, clout (*inf*), mana (*NZ*), power, weight

saying *n* = **proverb**, adage, aphorism, axiom, dictum, maxim

scale¹ *n* = **flake**, lamina, layer, plate

scale³ *n* **1, 3** = **graduation**, gradation, hierarchy, ladder, progression, ranking, sequence, series, steps **2** = **ratio**, proportion **4** = **degree**, extent, range, reach, scope ▷ *v* **7** = **climb**, ascend, clamber, escalade, mount, surmount **scale up, down** *v* = **adjust**, proportion, regulate

S

6 notation of a number system. ▷ v
7 climb. **scale up, down** v increase or
decrease proportionally in size.
scalene adj (of a triangle) with three
unequal sides.
scallion n spring onion.
scallop n **1** edible shellfish with two
fan-shaped shells. **2** one of a series of
small curves along an edge. **scalloped**
adj decorated with small curves along
the edge.
scallywag n informal scamp, rascal.
scalp n **1** skin and hair on top of the
head. **2** part of this taken as a trophy
from a slain person by a Native
American. ▷ v **3** cut off the scalp of.
scalpel n small surgical knife.
scamp ❶ n mischievous child.
scamper ❶ v **1** run about hurriedly or
in play. ▷ n **2** scampering.
scampi pl n large prawns.
scan ❶ v **scanning, scanned**
1 scrutinize carefully. **2** glance over
quickly. **3** examine or search (an area)
by passing a radar or sonar beam over
it. **4** (of verse) conform to metrical
rules. ▷ n **5** scanning. **scanner** n
electronic device used for scanning.
scansion n metrical scanning of verse.
scandal ❶ n **1** disgraceful action or
event. **2** shame or outrage.
3 malicious gossip. **scandalize** v
shock by scandal. **scandalmonger** n
person who spreads gossip.

scandalous adj **scandalously** adv.
Scandinavian n, adj (inhabitant or
language) of Scandinavia (Norway,
Denmark, Sweden, Finland, and
Iceland).
scandium n Chemistry rare silvery-
white metallic element.
scant ❶ adj barely sufficient, meagre.
scanty ❶ adj **scantier, scantiest**
barely sufficient or not sufficient.
scantily adv **scantiness** n.
scapegoat ❶ n person made to bear
the blame for others.
scapula n, pl **-lae, -las** shoulder blade.
scapular adj of the scapula.
scar[1] ❶ n **1** mark left by a healed
wound. **2** permanent emotional
damage left by an unpleasant
experience. ▷ v **scarring, scarred**
3 mark or become marked with a scar.
scar[2] n bare craggy rock formation.
scarab n sacred beetle of ancient
Egypt.
scarce ❶ adj **1** insufficient to meet
demand. **2** not common, rarely found.
make oneself scarce informal go
away. **scarcely** adv **1** hardly at
all. **2** definitely or probably not.
scarcity n.
scare ❶ v **1** frighten or be frightened.
2 (foll. by away or off) drive away by
frightening. ▷ n **3** fright, sudden
panic. **4** period of general alarm.
scary adj informal frightening.

— THESAURUS —

scamp n = **rascal**, devil, imp, monkey,
rogue, scallywag (inf)
scamper v **1** = **run**, dart, dash, hasten,
hurry, romp, scoot, scurry, scuttle
scan v **1** = **scrutinize**, check, check out
(inf), examine, eye, eyeball (sl),
investigate **2** = **glance over**, look
through, run one's eye over, run over,
skim **3** = **survey**, scour, search,
sweep
scandal n **1** = **crime**, disgrace,
embarrassment, offence, sin,
wrongdoing **2** = **shame**, defamation,
discredit, disgrace, dishonour,
ignominy, infamy, opprobrium, stigma
3 = **gossip**, aspersion, dirt, rumours,
slander, talk, tattle
scandalize v = **shock**, affront, appal,
horrify, offend, outrage
scandalous adj **1** = **shocking**,
disgraceful, disreputable, infamous,
outrageous, shameful, unseemly
3 = **slanderous**, defamatory, libellous,

scurrilous, untrue
scant adj = **meagre**, barely sufficient,
little, minimal, sparse
scanty adj = **meagre**, bare, deficient,
inadequate, insufficient, poor, scant,
short, skimpy, sparse, thin
scapegoat n = **whipping boy**, fall guy
(inf)
scar[1] n **1** = **mark**, blemish, injury,
wound ▷ v **3** = **mark**, damage,
disfigure
scarce adj **1** = **in short supply**, few,
few and far between, infrequent,
insufficient **2** = **rare**, uncommon
scarcely adv **1** = **hardly**, barely
2 = **definitely not**, hardly
scarcity n = **shortage**, dearth,
deficiency, insufficiency, lack, paucity,
rareness, want
scare v **1** = **frighten**, alarm, dismay,
intimidate, panic, shock, startle,
terrify ▷ n **3** = **fright**, panic, shock,
start, terror

scarecrow *n* **1** figure dressed in old clothes, set up to scare birds away from crops. **2** raggedly dressed person. **scaremonger** *n* person who spreads alarming rumours.

scarf¹ *n, pl* **scarves**, **scarfs** piece of material worn round the neck, head, or shoulders.

scarf² *n* **1** joint between two pieces of timber made by notching the ends and fastening them together. ▷ *v* **2** join in this way.

scarify *v* **-fying**, **-fied 1** scratch or cut slightly all over. **2** break up and loosen (topsoil). **3** criticize mercilessly. **scarification** *n*.

scarlatina *n* scarlet fever.

scarlet *adj, n* brilliant red. **scarlet fever** infectious fever with a scarlet rash.

scarp *n* steep slope.

scarper ❶ *v slang* run away.

scat¹ *v* **scatting**, **scatted** *informal* go away.

scat² *n* jazz singing using improvised vocal sounds instead of words.

scathing ❶ *adj* harshly critical.

scatological *adj* preoccupied with obscenity, esp. with references to excrement. **scatology** *n*.

scatter ❶ *v* **1** throw about in various directions. **2** disperse. ▷ *n* **3** scattering. **scatterbrain** *n* empty-headed person.

scatty *adj* **-tier**, **-tiest** *informal* empty-headed.

scavenge *v* search for (anything usable) among discarded material. **scavenger** *n* **1** person who scavenges. **2** animal that feeds on decaying matter.

SCE Scottish Certificate of Education.

scenario ❶ *n, pl* **-rios 1** summary of the plot of a play or film. **2** imagined sequence of future events.

scene ❶ *n* **1** place of action of a real or imaginary event. **2** subdivision of a play or film in which the action is continuous. **3** scenery. **4** view of a place. **5** display of emotion. **6** *informal* specific activity or interest, e.g. *the fashion scene*. **behind the scenes 1** backstage. **2** in secret. **scenery** *n* **1** natural features of a landscape. **2** painted backcloths or screens used on stage to represent the scene of action. **scenic** *adj* **1** picturesque. **2** of stage scenery.

scent ❶ *n* **1** pleasant smell. **2** smell left in passing, by which an animal can be traced. **3** series of clues. **4** perfume. ▷ *v* **5** detect by smell. **6** suspect. **7** fill with fragrance.

sceptic ❶ [**skep**-tik] *n* person who habitually doubts generally accepted beliefs. **sceptical** *adj* **sceptically** *adv* **scepticism** *n*.

sceptre *n* ornamental rod symbolizing royal power.

THESAURUS

scarper *v Sl* = **run away**, abscond, beat it (*sl*), clear off (*inf*), disappear, flee, run for it, scram (*inf*), take to one's heels

scary *adj Inf* = **frightening**, alarming, chilling, creepy (*inf*), horrifying, spine-chilling, spooky (*inf*), terrifying

scathing *adj* = **critical**, biting, caustic, cutting, harsh, sarcastic, scornful, trenchant, withering

scatter *v* **1** = **throw about**, diffuse, disseminate, fling, shower, spread, sprinkle, strew **2** = **disperse**, disband, dispel, dissipate

scatterbrain *n* = **featherbrain**, butterfly, flibbertigibbet

scenario *n* **1** = **story line**, outline, résumé, summary, synopsis

scene *n* **1** = **site**, area, locality, location, place, position, setting, spot **2** = **act**, division, episode, part **3** = **setting**, backdrop, background, set **4** = **view**, landscape, panorama, prospect, vista **5** = **fuss**, carry-on (*inf, chiefly Brit*), commotion, exhibition, performance, row, tantrum, to-do **6** *Inf* = **world**, arena, business, environment

scenery *n* **1** = **landscape**, surroundings, terrain, view, vista **2** = **set**, backdrop, flats, setting, stage set

scenic *adj* **1** = **picturesque**, beautiful, panoramic, spectacular, striking

scent *n* **1** = **aroma**, bouquet, odour, smell **2** = **trail**, spoor, track **4** = **fragrance**, perfume ▷ *v* **5** = **detect**, discern, nose out, sense, smell, sniff

sceptic *n* = **doubter**, cynic, disbeliever, doubting Thomas

sceptical *adj* = **doubtful**, cynical, disbelieving, dubious, incredulous, mistrustful, unconvinced

scepticism *n* = **doubt**, cynicism, disbelief, incredulity, unbelief

S

schedule ❶ *n* **1** plan of procedure for a project. **2** list. **3** timetable. ▷ *v* **4** plan to occur at a certain time. **5** make or place in a schedule.

schema *n*, *pl* **-mata** overall plan or diagram. **schematic** *adj* presented as a plan or diagram. **schematize** *v* arrange in a scheme.

schematic *adj* presented as a plan or diagram.

scheme ❶ *n* **1** systematic plan. **2** systematic arrangement. **3** secret plot. ▷ *v* **4** plan in an underhand manner. **schemer** *n* **scheming** *adj*, *n*.

scherzo [skairt-so] *n*, *pl* **-zos, -zi** brisk lively piece of music.

schilling *n* former monetary unit of Austria.

schism ❶ [skizz-um] *n* (group resulting from) division in an organization. **schismatic** *adj*, *n*.

schist [skist] *n* crystalline rock which splits into layers.

schizo [skit-so] *adj*, *n*, *pl* **-os** *offens* schizophrenic (person).

schizoid *adj* **1** abnormally introverted. **2** *informal* contradictory. ▷ *n* **3** *offens* schizoid person.

schizophrenia *n* **1** mental disorder involving deterioration of or confusion about the personality. **2** *informal* contradictory behaviour or attitudes. **schizophrenic** *adj*, *n*.

schmaltz *n* excessive sentimentality.

schmaltzy *adj*.

schnapps *n* strong alcoholic spirit.

schnitzel *n* thin slice of meat, esp. veal.

scholar ❶ *n* **1** learned person. **2** student receiving a scholarship. **3** pupil. **scholarly** *adj* learned. **scholarship** *n* **1** learning. **2** financial aid given to a student because of academic merit. **scholastic** *adj* of schools or scholars.

school¹ ❶ *n* **1** place where children are taught or instruction is given in a subject. **2** staff and pupils of a school. **3** department specializing in a subject. **4** group of artists, thinkers, etc. with shared principles or methods. ▷ *v* **5** educate or train. **scholar** *n* **1** learned person. **2** student receiving a scholarship. **3** pupil. **schooling** *n* education. **schoolboy**, **schoolgirl** *n* child attending school. **schoolteacher**, **schoolmaster**, **schoolmistress** *n* person who teaches in a school.

school² *n* shoal of fish, whales, etc.

schooner *n* **1** sailing ship rigged fore-and-aft. **2** large glass.

schottische *n* type of slow polka.

sciatica *n* severe pain in the large nerve in the back of the leg. **sciatic** *adj* **1** of the hip. **2** of or afflicted with sciatica.

science ❶ *n* **1** systematic study and knowledge of natural or physical phenomena. **2** branch of this

———————————— THESAURUS ————————————

schedule *n* **1** = **plan**, agenda **2** = **list**, calendar, catalogue, inventory **3** = **timetable**, programme ▷ *v* **4** = **plan**, appoint, arrange, book, organize, programme

scheme *n* **1** = **plan**, programme, project, proposal, strategy, system, tactics **2** = **diagram**, blueprint, chart, draft, layout, outline, pattern **3** = **plot**, conspiracy, intrigue, manoeuvre, ploy, ruse, stratagem, subterfuge ▷ *v* **4** = **plot**, collude, conspire, intrigue, machinate, manoeuvre

scheming *adj* = **calculating**, artful, conniving, cunning, sly, tricky, underhand, wily

schism *n* = **division**, breach, break, rift, rupture, separation, split

scholar *n* **1** = **intellectual**, academic, savant **3** = **student**, disciple, learner, pupil, schoolboy *or* schoolgirl

scholarly *adj* = **learned**, academic,

bookish, erudite, intellectual, lettered, scholastic

scholarship *n* **1** = **learning**, book-learning, education, erudition, knowledge **2** = **bursary**, fellowship

scholastic *adj* = **learned**, academic, lettered, scholarly

school¹ *n* **1** = **academy**, college, faculty, institute, institution, seminary **4** = **group**, adherents, circle, denomination, devotees, disciples, faction, followers, set ▷ *v* **5** = **train**, coach, discipline, drill, educate, instruct, tutor

schooling *n* = **teaching**, coaching, drill, education, instruction, training, tuition

science *n* **2** = **discipline**, body of knowledge, branch of knowledge **3** = **skill**, art, technique

scientific *adj* **2** = **systematic**, accurate, controlled, exact, mathematical, precise

knowledge. **3** skill or technique.
scientific *adj* **1** of science.
2 systematic. **scientifically** *adv*
scientist *n* person who studies or
practises a science. **science fiction**
stories making imaginative use of
scientific knowledge. **science park**
area where scientific research and
commercial development are carried
on in cooperation.

sci-fi *n* short for SCIENCE FICTION.

scimitar *n* curved oriental sword.

scintillate ❶ *v* give off sparks.
scintillating *adj* very lively and
amusing. **scintillation** *n*.

scintillating ❶ *adj* very lively and
amusing.

scion [**sy**-on] *n* **1** descendant or heir.
2 shoot of a plant for grafting.

scissors *pl n* cutting instrument with
two crossed pivoted blades.

sclerosis *n, pl* **-ses** abnormal hardening
of body tissues.

scoff¹ ❶ *v* **1** express derision. ▷ *n*
2 mocking expression.

scoff² ❶ *v informal* eat rapidly.

scold ❶ *v* **1** find fault with, reprimand.
▷ *n* **2** person who scolds. **scolding** *n*.

scollop *n* same as SCALLOP.

sconce *n* bracket on a wall for holding
candles or lights.

scone *n* small plain cake baked in an
oven or on a griddle.

scoop ❶ *n* **1** shovel-like tool for ladling
or hollowing out. **2** news story
reported in one newspaper before all
its rivals. ▷ *v* **3** take up or hollow out
with or as if with a scoop. **4** beat (rival
newspapers) in reporting a news item.

scoot *v slang* leave or move quickly.
scooter *n* **1** child's vehicle propelled
by pushing on the ground with one
foot. **2** light motorcycle.

scope ❶ *n* **1** opportunity for using
abilities. **2** range of activity.

scorch ❶ *v* **1** burn on the surface.
2 parch or shrivel from heat. ▷ *n*
3 slight burn. **scorcher** *n informal* very
hot day.

score ❶ *n* **1** points gained in a game or
competition. **2** twenty. **3** written
version of a piece of music showing
parts for each musician. **4** mark or cut.
5 record of amounts due. **6** reason.
7 grievance, e.g. *settle old scores.* ▷ *pl*
8 lots. ▷ *v* **9** gain (points) in a game.
10 keep a record of points. **11** mark or
cut. **12** (foll. by *out*) cross out.
13 arrange music (for). **14** achieve a
success. **score off** *v* gain an advantage
at someone else's expense.

scorn ❶ *n* **1** open contempt. ▷ *v*
2 despise. **3** reject with contempt.
scornful *adj* **scornfully** *adv*.

Scorpio *n* (the scorpion) eighth sign of
the zodiac.

—— THESAURUS ——

scientist *n* = **inventor**, boffin (*inf*)
scintillating *adj* = **brilliant**, animated,
bright, dazzling, exciting, glittering,
lively, sparkling, stimulating
scoff¹ *v* **1** = **scorn**, belittle, deride,
despise, jeer, knock (*inf*), laugh at,
mock, pooh-pooh, ridicule, sneer
scoff² *v Inf* = **gobble (up)**, bolt, devour,
gorge oneself on, gulp down, guzzle,
wolf
scold *v* **1** = **reprimand**, berate,
castigate, censure, find fault with,
give (someone) a dressing-down,
lecture, rebuke, reproach, reprove,
rouse on (*Aust*), tell off (*inf*), tick off
(*inf*), upbraid ▷ *n* **2** = **nag**, shrew,
termagant (*rare*)
scolding *n* = **rebuke**, dressing-down
(*inf*), lecture, row, telling-off (*inf*),
ticking-off (*inf*)
scoop *n* **1** = **ladle**, dipper, spoon
2 = **exclusive**, exposé, revelation,
sensation ▷ *v* **3 a** = **lift**, gather up,
pick up, take up **b** = **hollow**, bail, dig,

empty, excavate, gouge, shovel
scope *n* **1** = **opportunity**, freedom,
latitude, liberty, room, space
2 = **range**, area, capacity, orbit,
outlook, reach, span, sphere
scorch *v* **1** = **burn**, roast, sear, singe
2 = **shrivel**, parch, wither
score *n* **1** = **points**, grade, mark,
outcome, record, result, total
6 = **grounds**, basis, cause, ground,
reason **7** = **grievance**, grudge, injury,
injustice, wrong ▷ *pl* **8** = **lots**,
hundreds, masses, millions,
multitudes, myriads, swarms ▷ *v*
9 = **gain**, achieve, chalk up (*inf*),
make, notch up (*inf*), win **10** = **keep
count**, count, record, register, tally
11 = **cut**, deface, gouge, graze, mark,
scrape, scratch, slash **12** (foll. by *out*)
= **cross out**, cancel out, delete,
obliterate, strike out **13** = **arrange**,
adapt, orchestrate, set
scorn *n* **1** = **contempt**, derision,
disdain, disparagement, mockery,

S

scorpion *n* small lobster-shaped animal with a sting at the end of a jointed tail.

Scot *n* person from Scotland. **Scottish** *adj* of Scotland, its people, or their languages. **Scots** *adj* 1 Scottish. ▷ *n* 2 English dialect spoken in Scotland. **Scotsman**, **Scotswoman** *n*.

- **USAGE NOTE**
- *Scotch* is used only in certain fixed
- expressions like *Scotch egg*. The
- use of *Scotch* for *Scots* or *Scottish* is
- otherwise felt to be incorrect, esp.
- when applied to people.

Scotch *n* whisky distilled in Scotland. **Scotch broth** thick soup of beef or lamb and vegetables. **Scotch egg** hard-boiled egg encased in sausage meat and breadcrumbs.

scotch *v* 1 put an end to. 2 wound without killing.

scot-free *adj* without harm or punishment.

Scotland Yard *n* headquarters of the police force of metropolitan London.

scoundrel ❶ *n old-fashioned* cheat or deceiver.

scour¹ ❶ *v* 1 clean or polish by rubbing with something rough. 2 clear or flush out. ▷ *n* 3 scouring. **scourer** *n* small rough nylon pad used for cleaning pots and pans.

scour² ❶ *v* 1 search thoroughly and energetically. 2 move swiftly over.

scourge ❶ *n* 1 person or thing causing severe suffering. ▷ *v* 3 cause severe suffering to. 4 whip.

Scouse *informal* ▷ *n* 1 (also **Scouser**) person from Liverpool. 2 dialect of Liverpool. ▷ *adj* 3 of Liverpool, its people, or their dialect.

scout ❶ *n* 1 person sent out to reconnoitre. 2 (S-) member of the Scout Association, an organization for boys which aims to develop character and promotes outdoor activities. ▷ *v* 3 act as a scout. 4 reconnoitre. **Scouter** *n* leader of a troop of Scouts.

scow *n* unpowered barge.

scowl ❶ *v*, *n* (have) an angry or sullen expression.

scrabble ❶ *v* 1 scrape at with the hands, feet, or claws. ▷ *n* 2 (S-) ® board game in which words are formed by letter tiles.

scrag ❶ *n* 1 thin end of a neck of mutton. 2 scrawny person or animal. **scraggy** *adj* thin, bony.

scram¹ ❶ *v* **scramming**, **scrammed** *informal* go away quickly.

scram² *n* 1 emergency shutdown of a nuclear reactor. ▷ *v* **scramming**, **scrammed** 2 (of a nuclear reactor) shut or be shut down in an emergency.

scramble ❶ *v* 1 climb or crawl hastily or awkwardly. 2 struggle with others

——————————————— THESAURUS ———————————

sarcasm ▷ *v* 2 = **despise**, be above, deride, disdain, scoff at 3 = **reject**, flout, slight, spurn

scornful *adj* = **contemptuous**, derisive, disdainful, haughty, jeering, mocking, sarcastic, sardonic, scathing, scoffing, sneering

scoundrel *n Old-fashioned* = **rogue**, bastard (*offens*), blackguard, good-for-nothing, heel (*sl*), miscreant, ne'er-do-well, rascal, reprobate, rotter (*sl*, *chiefly Brit*), scally (*NW Eng dial*), scamp, swine, villain

scour¹ *v* 1 = **rub**, abrade, buff, clean, polish, scrub 2 = **wash**, cleanse

scour² *v* 1 = **search**, beat, comb, hunt, ransack

scourge *n* 1 = **affliction**, bane, curse, infliction, misfortune, pest, plague, terror, torment 2 = **whip**, cat, lash, strap, switch, thong ▷ *v* 3 = **afflict**, curse, plague, terrorize, torment 4 = **whip**, beat, cane, flog, horsewhip, lash, thrash

scout *n* 1 = **vanguard**, advance guard, lookout, outrider, precursor, reconnoitrer ▷ *v* 3, 4 = **reconnoitre**, investigate, observe, probe, recce (*sl*), spy, survey, watch

scowl *v* = **glower**, frown, lour *or* lower ▷ *n* = **glower**, black look, dirty look, frown

scrabble *v* 1 = **scrape**, claw, scramble, scratch

scraggy *adj* = **scrawny**, angular, bony, lean, skinny

scram¹ *v Inf* = **go away**, abscond, beat it (*sl*), clear off (*inf*), get lost (*inf*), leave, make oneself scarce (*inf*), make tracks, scarper (*Brit sl*), vamoose (*sl*, *chiefly US*)

scramble *v* 1 = **struggle**, climb, crawl, scrabble, swarm 2 = **strive**, contend, jostle, push, run, rush, vie ▷ *n* 8 = **climb**, trek 9 = **struggle**, commotion, competition, confusion, mêlée, race, rush, tussle

(for). **3** mix up. **4** cook (eggs beaten up with milk). **5** (of an aircraft or aircrew) take off hurriedly in an emergency. **6** make (transmitted speech) unintelligible by the use of an electronic device. ▷ *n* **7** scrambling. **8** rough climb. **9** disorderly struggle. **10** motorcycle race over rough ground. **scrambler** *n* electronic device that makes transmitted speech unintelligible.

scrap¹ ❶ *n* **1** small piece. **2** waste metal collected for reprocessing. ▷ *pl* **3** leftover food. ▷ *v* **scrapping**, **scrapped 4** discard as useless. **scrappy** *adj* fragmentary, disjointed. **scrapbook** *n* book with blank pages in which newspaper cuttings or pictures are stuck.

scrap² ❶ *n, v* **scrapping**, **scrapped** *informal* fight or quarrel.

scrape ❶ *v* **1** rub with something rough or sharp. **2** clean or smooth thus. **3** rub with a harsh noise. **4** economize. ▷ *n* **5** act or sound of scraping. **6** mark or wound caused by scraping. **7** *informal* awkward situation. **scraper** *n* **scrape through** *v* succeed in or obtain with difficulty.

scratch ❶ *v* **1** mark or cut with claws, nails, or anything rough or sharp. **2** scrape (skin) with nails or claws to relieve itching. **3** cross out.

4 withdraw from a race or competition. ▷ *n* **5** wound, mark, or sound made by scratching. ▷ *adj* **6** put together at short notice. **7** *Sport* with no handicap allowed. **from scratch** from the very beginning. **up to scratch** up to standard. **scratchy** *adj* **scratchcard** *n* ticket that reveals whether or not the holder has won a prize when the surface is removed by scratching.

scrawl ❶ *v* **1** write carelessly or hastily. ▷ *n* **2** scribbled writing.

scrawny ❶ *adj* **scrawnier**, **scrawniest** thin and bony.

scream ❶ *v* **1** utter a piercing cry, esp. of fear or pain. **2** utter with a scream. ▷ *n* **3** shrill piercing cry. **4** *informal* very funny person or thing.

scree *n* slope of loose shifting stones.

screech ❶ *v, n* (utter) a shrill cry. **screech owl** barn owl.

screed *n* long tedious piece of writing.

screen ❶ *n* **1** surface of a television set, VDU, etc., on which an image is formed. **2** white surface on which films or slides are projected. **3** movable structure used to shelter, divide, or conceal something. ▷ *v* **4** shelter or conceal with or as if with a screen. **5** examine (a person or group) to determine suitability for a task or to detect the presence of disease or

---

THESAURUS

scrap¹ *n* **1** = **piece**, bit, crumb, fragment, grain, morsel, part, particle, portion, sliver, snippet **2** = **waste**, junk, offcuts ▷ *pl* **3** = **leftovers**, bits, leavings, remains ▷ *v* **4** = **get rid of**, abandon, discard, ditch (*sl*), drop, jettison, throw away *or* out, write off

scrap² *n Inf* = **fight**, argument, battle, disagreement, dispute, quarrel, row, squabble, wrangle ▷ *v Inf* = **fight**, argue, row, squabble, wrangle

scrape *v* **1** = **rub**, bark, graze, scratch, scuff **2** = **scour**, clean, erase, remove, rub, skin **3** = **grate**, grind, rasp, scratch, squeak **4** = **scrimp**, pinch, save, skimp, stint ▷ *n* **7** *Inf* = **predicament**, awkward situation, difficulty, dilemma, fix (*inf*), mess, plight, tight spot **scrape through** *v* = **get by** (*inf*), just make it, struggle

scrappy *adj* = **incomplete**, bitty, disjointed, fragmentary, piecemeal, sketchy, thrown together

scratch *v* **1** = **mark**, claw, cut, damage, etch, grate, graze, lacerate, score, scrape **3** = **erase**, cancel, cross out, delete, eliminate **4** = **withdraw**, pull out ▷ *n* **5** = **mark**, blemish, claw mark, gash, graze, laceration, scrape ▷ *adj* **6** = **improvised**, impromptu, rough-and-ready **up to scratch** = **adequate**, acceptable, satisfactory, sufficient, up to standard

scrawl *v, n* **1, 2** = **scribble**, doodle, squiggle

scrawny *adj* = **thin**, bony, gaunt, lean, scraggy, skin-and-bones (*inf*), skinny, undernourished

scream *v* **1, 2** = **cry**, bawl, screech, shriek, yell ▷ *n* **3** = **cry**, howl, screech, shriek, yell, yelp

screech *v, n* = **cry**, scream, shriek

screen *n* **3 a** = **cover**, awning, canopy, guard, mesh, net, shade, shelter, shield **b** = **partition**, room divider **c** = **cloak** ▷ *v* **4 a** = **protect**, defend, guard, shelter, shield **b** = **cover**,

S

weapons. **6** show (a film). **the screen** cinema generally. **screenplay** n script for a film. **screen saver** *Computers* a changing image on a monitor when the computer is operative but idle.

screw ❶ n **1** metal pin with a spiral ridge along its length, twisted into materials to fasten them together. **2** *slang* prison guard. ▷ v **3** turn (a screw). **4** twist. **5** fasten with screw(s). **6** *informal* extort. **screwy** *adj* *informal* crazy or eccentric.
screwdriver n tool for turning screws. **screw up** v **1** *informal* bungle. **2** distort. **3** summon up (courage).

scribble ❶ v **1** write hastily or illegibly. **2** make meaningless or illegible marks. ▷ n **3** something scribbled.

scribe ❶ n **1** person who copied manuscripts before the invention of printing. **2** *Bible* scholar of the Jewish Law.

scrimmage n **1** rough or disorderly struggle. ▷ v **2** engage in a scrimmage.

scrimp ❶ v be very economical.

scrip n certificate representing a claim to stocks or shares.

script ❶ n **1** text of a film, play, or TV programme. **2** particular system of writing, e.g. *Arabic script.* **3** candidate's answer paper in an exam. **4** handwriting. ▷ v **5** write a script for.

scripture ❶ n **1** sacred writings of a religion. **2** (**S-**) Old and New Testaments. **scriptural** *adj.*

scrofula n tuberculosis of the lymphatic glands. **scrofulous** *adj.*

scroll n **1** roll of parchment or paper. **2** ancient book in scroll form. **3** ornamental carving shaped like a scroll. ▷ v **4** move (text) up or down on a VDU screen.

Scrooge n miserly person.

scrotum n, pl **-ta, -tums** pouch of skin containing the testicles.

scrounge ❶ v *informal* get by cadging or begging. **scrounger** n.

scrub¹ ❶ v **scrubbing, scrubbed 1** clean by rubbing, often with a hard brush and water. **2** *informal* delete or cancel. ▷ n **3** scrubbing.

scrub² n **1** stunted trees. **2** area of land covered with scrub. **scrubby** *adj* **1** covered with scrub. **2** stunted. **3** *informal* shabby. **scrub turkey** same AS MEGAPODE.

scruff¹ n nape (of the neck).

scruff² ❶ n *informal* untidy person. **scruffy** *adj* unkempt or shabby.

scrum, scrummage n **1** *Rugby* restarting of play in which opposing packs of forwards push against each other to gain possession of the ball. **2** disorderly struggle.

scrump v *Brit dialect* steal (apples) from an orchard or garden.

scrumptious ❶ *adj* *informal* delicious.

scrumpy n rough dry cider.

scrunch v **1** crumple or crunch or be crumpled or crunched. ▷ n **2** act or sound of scrunching.

━━━━━━━━━━━━━━━━━━━━━━━━━ THESAURUS ━━━━━

cloak, conceal, hide, mask, shade, veil **5** = **vet**, evaluate, examine, filter, gauge, scan, sift, sort **6** = **broadcast**, present, put on, show

screw v **3** = **turn**, tighten **4** = **twist 6** *Inf* = **extort**, extract, wrest, wring

screw up v **1** *Inf* = **bungle**, botch, make a hash of (*inf*), make a mess of (*sl*), mess up, mishandle, spoil **2** = **contort**, distort, pucker, wrinkle

screwy *adj* *Inf* = **crazy**, crackpot (*inf*), eccentric, loopy (*inf*), nutty (*sl*), odd, off-the-wall (*sl*), out to lunch (*inf*), round the bend (*Brit sl*), weird

scribble v **1** = **scrawl**, dash off, jot, write

scribe n **1** = **copyist**, amanuensis, writer

scrimp v = **economize**, be frugal, save, scrape, skimp, stint, tighten one's belt

script n **1** = **text**, book, copy, dialogue,

libretto, lines, words **4** = **handwriting**, calligraphy, penmanship, writing

Scripture n **2** = **The Bible**, Holy Bible, Holy Scripture, Holy Writ, The Good Book, The Gospels, The Scriptures

scrounge v *Inf* = **cadge**, beg, blag (*sl*), bludge (*Aust & NZ*), bum (*inf*), freeload (*sl*), sponge (*inf*)

scrounger *adj* *Inf* = **cadger**, freeloader (*sl*), parasite, sponger (*inf*)

scrub¹ v **1** = **scour**, clean, cleanse, rub **2** *Inf* = **cancel**, abolish, call off, delete, drop, forget about, give up

scruffy *adj* = **tatty**, ill-groomed, mangy, messy, ragged, run-down, seedy, shabby, unkempt, untidy

scrumptious *adj* *Inf* = **delicious**, appetizing, delectable, luscious, mouthwatering, succulent, yummy (*sl*)

scrunchie n loop of elastic covered loosely with fabric, used to hold the hair in a ponytail.

scruple ❶ n **1** doubt produced by one's conscience or morals. ▷ v **2** have doubts on moral grounds. **scrupulous** adj **1** very conscientious. **2** very careful or precise. **scrupulously** adv.

scrutiny ❶ n, pl -**nies 1** close examination. **2** searching look. **scrutinize** v examine closely.

scuba diving n sport of swimming under water using cylinders containing compressed air attached to breathing apparatus.

scud v **scudding, scudded 1** move along swiftly. **2** run before a gale.

scuff v **1** drag (the feet) while walking. **2** scrape (one's shoes) by doing so. ▷ n **3** mark caused by scuffing.

scuffle ❶ v **1** fight in a disorderly manner. ▷ n **2** disorderly struggle. **3** scuffling sound.

scull n **1** small oar. ▷ v **2** row (a boat) using sculls.

scullery n, pl -**leries** small room where washing-up and other kitchen work is done.

sculpture ❶ n **1** art of making figures or designs in wood, stone, etc. **2** product of this art. ▷ v **3** (also **sculpt**) represent in sculpture. **sculptor, sculptress** n **sculptural** adj.

scum ❶ n **1** impure or waste matter on the surface of a liquid. **2** worthless

people. **scummy** adj.

scungy adj -**ier, -iest** Aust & NZ informal sordid or dirty.

scupper¹ ❶ v informal defeat or ruin.

scupper² n drain in the side of a ship.

scurf n flaky skin on the scalp. **scurfy** adj.

scurrilous ❶ adj untrue and defamatory.

scurry ❶ v -**rying, -ried 1** move hastily. ▷ n **2** act or sound of scurrying.

scurvy n **1** disease caused by lack of vitamin C. ▷ adj **2** mean and despicable.

scut n short tail of the hare, rabbit, or deer.

scuttle¹ n fireside container for coal.

scuttle² ❶ v **1** run with short quick steps. ▷ n **2** hurried run.

scuttle³ v make a hole in (a ship) to sink it.

scythe n **1** long-handled tool with a curved blade for cutting grass. ▷ v **2** cut with a scythe.

SD South Dakota.

Se Chemistry selenium.

SE southeast(ern).

sea ❶ n **1** mass of salt water covering three quarters of the earth's surface. **2** particular area of this. **3** vast expanse. **at sea 1** in a ship on the ocean. **2** confused or bewildered. **sea anemone** sea animal with suckers like petals. **seaboard** n coast. **sea dog** experienced sailor. **seafaring** adj

———————————————————— THESAURUS ————————————————————

scruple n **1** = **misgiving**, compunction, doubt, hesitation, qualm, reluctance, second thoughts, uneasiness ▷ v **2** = **have misgivings about**, demur, doubt, have qualms about, hesitate, think twice about

scrupulous adj **1** = **moral**, conscientious, honourable, principled, upright **2** = **careful**, exact, fastidious, meticulous, precise, punctilious, rigorous, strict

scrutinize v = **examine**, explore, inspect, investigate, peruse, pore over, probe, scan, search, study

scrutiny n **1** = **examination**, analysis, exploration, inspection, investigation, perusal, search, study

scuffle v **1** = **fight**, clash, grapple, jostle, struggle, tussle ▷ n **2** = **fight**, brawl, commotion, disturbance, fray, scrimmage, skirmish, tussle

sculpture v **3** (also **sculpt**) = **sculpt**,

carve, chisel, fashion, form, hew, model, mould, shape

scum n **1** = **impurities**, dross, film, froth **2** = **rabble**, dregs of society, riffraff, trash (chiefly US & Canad)

scupper¹ v Inf = **destroy**, defeat, demolish, put paid to, ruin, torpedo, wreck

scurrilous adj = **slanderous**, abusive, defamatory, insulting, scandalous, vituperative

scurry v **1** = **hurry**, dart, dash, race, scamper, scoot, scuttle, sprint ▷ n **2** = **flurry**, scampering, whirl

scuttle² v **1** = **run**, bustle, hasten, hurry, rush, scamper, scoot, scurry

sea n **1** = **ocean**, main, the deep, the waves **3** = **expanse**, abundance, mass, multitude, plethora, profusion **at sea 2** = **bewildered**, baffled, confused, lost, mystified, puzzled

S

working or travelling by sea. **seafood** n edible saltwater fish or shellfish. **seagoing** adj built for travelling on the sea. **seagull** n gull. **sea horse** small sea fish with a plated body and horselike head. **sea legs** ability to keep one's balance at sea and resist seasickness. **sea level** average level of the sea's surface in relation to the land. **sea lion** kind of large seal. **seaman** n sailor. **seaplane** n aircraft designed to take off from and land on water. **seascape** n picture of a scene at sea. **seashell** n empty shell of a mollusc. **seasick** adj suffering from nausea caused by the motion of a ship. **seasickness** n **seaside** n area, esp. a holiday resort, on the coast. **sea urchin** sea animal with a round spiky shell. **seaweed** n plant growing in the sea. **seaworthy** adj (of a ship) in fit condition for a sea voyage.

seal[1] **⊙** n **1** piece of wax, lead, etc. with a special design impressed upon it, attached to a letter or document as a mark of authentication. **2** device for making such an impression. **3** device or material used to close an opening tightly. ▷ v **4** close with or as if with a seal. **5** make airtight or watertight. **6** affix a seal to or stamp with a seal. **7** decide (one's fate) irrevocably. **sealant** n any substance used for sealing. **sealing wax** hard material which softens when heated, used to make a seal. **seal off** v enclose or isolate (a place) completely.

seal[2] n **1** amphibious mammal with flippers as limbs. ▷ v **2** hunt seals.

sealskin n skin of a seal.

seam **⊙** n **1** line where two edges are joined, as by stitching. **2** thin layer of coal or ore. ▷ v **3** mark with furrows or wrinkles. **seamless** adj **seamy** adj sordid.

seamstress n woman who sews.

seance [say-anss] n meeting at which spiritualists attempt to communicate with the dead.

sear **⊙** v scorch, burn the surface of. **searing** adj **1** (of pain) very sharp. **2** highly critical.

search **⊙** v **1** examine closely in order to find something. **2** make a search. ▷ n **3** searching. **searching** adj keen or thorough, e.g. a searching look. **search engine** Computers internet service enabling users to search for items of interest. **searchlight** n powerful light with a beam that can be shone in any direction. **search warrant** document permitting the entry and search of premises.

season **⊙** n **1** one of four divisions of the year, each of which has characteristic weather conditions. **2** period during which a thing happens or is plentiful. **3** any definite or indefinite period, e.g. the busy season. **4** fitting or proper time. ▷ v **5** flavour with salt, herbs, etc. **6** dry (timber) till ready for use. **seasonable** adj **1** appropriate for the season. **2** timely or opportune. **seasonal** adj depending on or varying with the seasons. **seasoned** adj experienced. **seasoning** n salt, herbs, etc. added to food to enhance flavour. **season ticket** ticket

━━━━━━━━━━━━━━━━━━━━━━━━━ THESAURUS ━━━━━

seafaring adj = **nautical**, marine, maritime, naval

seal[1] n **1** = **authentication**, confirmation, imprimatur, insignia, ratification, stamp ▷ v **5** = **close**, bung, enclose, fasten, plug, shut, stop, stopper, stop up
6 = **authenticate**, confirm, ratify, stamp, validate **7** = **settle**, clinch, conclude, consummate, finalize **seal off** v = **isolate**, put out of bounds, quarantine, segregate

seam n **1** = **joint**, closure **2** = **layer**, lode, stratum, vein

sear v = **scorch**, burn, sizzle

search v **1, 2** = **look**, comb, examine, explore, fossick (Aust & NZ), hunt, inspect, investigate, ransack, scour,

scrutinize ▷ n **3** = **look**, examination, exploration, hunt, inspection, investigation, pursuit, quest

searching adj = **keen**, close, intent, penetrating, piercing, probing, quizzical, sharp

season n **3** = **period**, spell, term, time ▷ v **5** = **flavour**, enliven, pep up, salt, spice

seasonable adj **2** = **appropriate**, convenient, fit, opportune, providential, suitable, timely, well-timed

seasoned adj = **experienced**, hardened, practised, time-served, veteran

seasoning n = **flavouring**, condiment, dressing, relish, salt and pepper, sauce, spice

for a series of journeys or events within a specified period.

seat ❶ *n* **1** thing designed or used for sitting on. **2** part of a chair on which one sits. **3** place to sit in a theatre, esp. one that requires a ticket. **4** buttocks. **5** part of a garment covering the buttocks. **6** place in which something is based. **7** country house. **8** membership of a legislative or administrative body. ▷ *v* **9** cause to sit. **10** provide seating for. **seating** *n* supply or arrangement of seats. **seat belt** belt worn in a car or aircraft to prevent a person being thrown forward in a crash.

sebaceous *adj* of, like, or secreting fat or oil.

sec¹ *adj* (of wines) dry.

sec² *n informal* second (of time).

sec. 1 second (of time). **2** secondary. **3** secretary.

secateurs *pl n* small pruning shears.

secede ❶ *v* withdraw formally from a political alliance or federation. **secession** *n* **secessionist** *n*.

seclude ❶ *v* keep (a person) from contact with others. **secluded** *adj* private, sheltered. **seclusion** *n*.

second¹ ❶ *adj* **1** coming directly after the first. **2** alternate, additional.

3 inferior. ▷ *n* **4** person or thing coming second. **5** attendant in a duel or boxing match. ▷ *pl* **6** inferior goods. ▷ *v* **7** express formal support for (a motion proposed in a meeting). **secondly** *adv* **second-best** *adj* next to the best. **second-class** *adj* **1** inferior. **2** cheaper, slower, or less comfortable than first-class. **second-hand** *adj* **1** bought after use by another. **2** not from an original source. **second nature** something so habitual that it seems part of one's character. **second-rate** *adj* not of the highest quality. **second sight** supposed ability to predict events. **second thoughts** revised opinion on a matter already considered. **second wind** renewed ability to continue effort.

second² ❶ *n* **1** sixtieth part of a minute of an angle or time. **2** moment.

second³ [si-**kawnd**] *v* transfer (a person) temporarily to another job. **secondment** *n*.

secondary ❶ *adj* **1** of less importance. **2** coming after or derived from what is primary or first. **3** relating to the education of people between the ages of 11 and 18.

secret ❶ *adj* **1** kept from the knowledge of others. **2** secretive. ▷ *n*

THESAURUS

seat *n* **1** = **chair**, bench, pew, settle, stall, stool **6** = **centre**, capital, heart, hub, place, site, situation, source **7** = **mansion**, abode, ancestral hall, house, residence **8** = **membership**, chair, constituency, incumbency, place ▷ *v* **9** = **sit**, fix, install, locate, place, set, settle **10** = **hold**, accommodate, cater for, contain, sit, take

seating *n* = **accommodation**, chairs, places, room, seats

secede *v* = **withdraw**, break with, leave, pull out, quit, resign, split from

secluded *adj* = **private**, cloistered, cut off, isolated, lonely, out-of-the-way, sheltered, solitary

seclusion *n* = **privacy**, isolation, shelter, solitude

second¹ *adj* **1** = **next**, following, subsequent, succeeding **2** = **additional**, alternative, extra, further, other **3** = **inferior**, lesser, lower, secondary, subordinate ▷ *n* **5** = **supporter**, assistant, backer, helper ▷ *v* **7** = **support**, approve, assist, back, endorse, go along with

second² *n* **2** = **moment**, flash, instant, jiffy (*inf*), minute, sec (*inf*), trice

secondary *adj* **1** = **subordinate**, inferior, lesser, lower, minor, unimportant **2** = **resultant**, contingent, derived, indirect

second-class *adj* **1** = **inferior**, indifferent, mediocre, second-best, second-rate, undistinguished, uninspiring

second-hand *adj* **1** = **used**, hand-me-down (*inf*), nearly new

secondly *adv* = **next**, in the second place, second

second-rate *adj* = **inferior**, low-grade, low-quality, mediocre, poor, rubbishy, shoddy, substandard, tacky (*inf*), tawdry, two-bit (*US & Canad sl*)

secrecy *n* **1** = **mystery**, concealment, confidentiality, privacy, silence **2** = **secretiveness**, clandestineness, covertness, furtiveness, stealth

secret *adj* **1** = **concealed**, close, confidential, disguised, furtive, hidden, undercover, underground, undisclosed, unknown, unrevealed

S

3 something kept secret. **4** mystery. **5** underlying explanation, e.g. *the secret of my success.* **in secret** without other people knowing. **secretly** *adv* **secrecy** *n* **secretive** *adj* inclined to keep things secret. **secretiveness** *n* **secret agent** spy. **secret service** government department concerned with spying.

secretariat *n* administrative office or staff of a legislative body.

secretary *n, pl* **-ries 1** person who deals with correspondence and general clerical work. **2** (**S-**) head of a state department, e.g. *Home Secretary.* **3** person who keeps records for a company. **secretarial** *adj* **Secretary of State** head of a major government department.

secrete¹ ❶ *v* (of an organ, gland, etc.) produce and release (a substance). **secretion** *n* **secretory** [sek-**reet**-or-ee] *adj.*

secrete² ❶ *v* hide or conceal.

sect ❶ *n* subdivision of a religious or political group, esp. one with extreme beliefs. **sectarian** *adj* **1** of a sect. **2** narrow-minded. **sectarianism** *n.*

section ❶ *n* **1** part cut off. **2** part or subdivision of something. **3** distinct part of a country or community. **4** cutting. **5** drawing of something as

if cut through. ▷ *v* **6** cut or divide into sections. **sectional** *adj.*

sector ❶ *n* **1** part or subdivision. **2** part of a circle enclosed by two radii and the arc which they cut off. **3** portion of an area for military operations.

secular ❶ *adj* **1** worldly, as opposed to sacred. **2** not connected with religion or the church. **secularism** *n* belief that religion should have no place in education. **secularize** *v* remove from the influence of the Church.

secure ❶ *adj* **1** free from danger. **2** free from anxiety. **3** firmly fixed. **4** reliable. ▷ *v* **5** obtain. **6** make safe. **7** make firm. **8** guarantee payment of (a loan) by giving something as security. **securely** *adv* **security** *n, pl* **-ties 1** precautions against theft, espionage, or other danger. **2** state of being secure. **3** certificate of ownership of a share, stock, or bond. **4** something given or pledged to guarantee payment of a loan.

sedan *n US & Aust* saloon car. **sedan chair** *History* enclosed chair for one person, carried on poles by two bearers.

sedate¹ ❶ *adj* **1** calm and dignified. **2** slow or unhurried. **sedately** *adv.*

sedate² ❶ *v* give a sedative drug to. **sedation** *n* **sedative** *adj* **1** having a

——————————— THESAURUS ———————

2 = **stealthy**, secretive, sly, underhand ▷ *n* **3** = **enigma**, code, key
4 = **mystery in secret** = **secretly**, slyly, surreptitiously

secrete¹ *v* = **give off**, emanate, emit, exude

secrete² *v* = **hide**, cache, conceal, harbour, stash (*inf*), stow

secretive *adj* = **reticent**, close, deep, reserved, tight-lipped, uncommunicative

secretly *adv* = **in secret**, clandestinely, covertly, furtively, privately, quietly, stealthily, surreptitiously

sect *n* = **group**, camp, denomination, division, faction, party, schism

sectarian *adj* = **narrow-minded**, bigoted, doctrinaire, dogmatic, factional, fanatical, limited, parochial, partisan

section *n* **1** = **slice 2** = **part**, division, fraction, instalment, passage, piece, portion, segment **3** = **district**, area, region, sector, zone

sector *n* **1** = **part**, division **3** = **zone**, area

secular *adj* **1** = **worldly**, earthly, nonspiritual, temporal **2** = **lay**, civil

secure *adj* **1** = **safe**, immune, protected, unassailable **2** = **sure**, assured, certain, confident, easy, reassured **3** = **fixed**, fast, fastened, firm, immovable, stable, steady ▷ *v* **5** = **obtain**, acquire, gain, get, procure, score (*sl*) **7** = **fasten**, attach, bolt, chain, fix, lock, make fast, tie up

security *n* **1** = **precautions**, defence, protection, safeguards, safety measures **2 a** = **safety**, care, custody, refuge, safekeeping, sanctuary **b** = **assurance**, certainty, confidence, conviction, positiveness, reliance, sureness **4** = **pledge**, collateral, gage, guarantee, hostage, insurance, pawn, surety

sedate¹ *adj* **1** = **calm**, collected, composed, cool, dignified, serene, tranquil **2** = **unhurried**, deliberate, slow-moving

sedative *adj* **1** = **calming**, anodyne, relaxing, soothing, tranquillizing

S

soothing or calming effect. ▷ *n*
2 sedative drug.
sedentary ❶ [**sed**-en-tree] *adj* done
sitting down, involving little
exercise.
sedge *n* coarse grasslike plant growing
on wet ground. **sedgy** *adj*.
sediment ❶ *n* **1** matter which settles
to the bottom of a liquid. **2** material
deposited by water, ice, or wind.
sedimentary *adj*.
sedition ❶ *n* speech or action
encouraging rebellion against the
government. **seditious** *adj*.
seduce ❶ *v* **1** persuade into sexual
intercourse. **2** tempt into
wrongdoing. **seducer**, **seductress** *n*
seduction *n* **seductive** *adj*.
sedulous *adj* diligent or persevering.
sedulously *adv*.
sedum *n* rock plant.
see¹ ❶ *v* **seeing**, **saw**, **seen** **1** perceive
with the eyes or mind. **2** understand.
3 watch. **4** find out. **5** make sure (of
something). **6** consider or decide.
7 have experience of. **8** meet or visit.

9 interview. **10** frequent the company
of. **11** accompany. **seeing** *n* **1** use of
the eyes. ▷ *conj* **2** in view of the fact
that. **see about** *v* attend to. **see off** *v*
be present at the departure of. **see
through** *v* **1** perceive the true nature
of. **2** remain with until the end. **see-
through** *adj* transparent.
see² ❶ *n* diocese of a bishop.
seed ❶ *n* **1** mature fertilized grain of a
plant. **2** such grains used for sowing.
3 origin. **4** *obs* offspring.
5 *Sport* player ranked according to his
or her ability. ▷ *v* **6** sow with seed.
7 produce seeds. **8** remove seeds
from. **9** arrange (the draw of a sports
tournament) so that the outstanding
competitors will not meet in the early
rounds. **go, run to seed 1** (of plants)
produce or shed seeds after flowering.
2 lose vigour or usefulness. **seedling** *n*
young plant raised from a seed. **seedy**
adj **1** shabby. **2** *informal* unwell. **3** full
of seeds.
seek ❶ *v* **seeking**, **sought 1** try to find
or obtain. **2** try (to do something).

━━━━━━ **THESAURUS** ━━━━━━

▷ *n* **2** = **tranquillizer**, anodyne,
downer *or* down (*sl*)
sedentary *adj* = **inactive**, desk, desk-
bound, seated, sitting
sediment *n* **1** = **dregs**, deposit,
grounds, lees, residue
sedition *n* = **rabble-rousing**,
agitation, incitement to riot,
subversion
seditious *adj* = **revolutionary**,
dissident, mutinous, rebellious,
refractory, subversive
seduce *v* **1** = **corrupt**, debauch,
deflower, deprave, dishonour
2 = **tempt**, beguile, deceive, entice,
inveigle, lead astray, lure, mislead
seduction *n* = **corruption**,
enticement, lure, snare,
temptation
seductive *adj* = **alluring**, attractive,
bewitching, enticing, inviting,
provocative, tempting
seductress *n* = **temptress**,
enchantress, *femme fatale*, siren, vamp
(*inf*)
see¹ *v* **1** = **perceive**, behold, catch sight
of, discern, distinguish, espy, eyeball
(*sl*), glimpse, look, make out, notice,
sight, spot, witness **2** = **understand**,
appreciate, comprehend, fathom, feel,
follow, get, grasp, realize **3** = **observe**

4 = **find out**, ascertain, determine,
discover, learn **5** = **make sure**, ensure,
guarantee, make certain, see to it
6 = **consider**, decide, deliberate,
reflect, think over **8** = **visit**, receive
9 = **speak to**, confer with, consult,
interview **10** = **go out with**, court,
date (*inf, chiefly US*), go steady with
(*inf*) **11** = **accompany**, escort, lead,
show, usher, walk
see² *n* = **diocese**, bishopric
seed *n* **1, 2** = **grain**, germ, kernel, pip,
spore **3** = **origin**, beginning, germ,
nucleus, source, start **4** *Obs*
= **offspring**, children, descendants,
issue, progeny **go, run to seed**
2 = **decline**, decay, degenerate,
deteriorate, go downhill (*inf*), go to
pot, let oneself go
seedy *adj* **1** = **shabby**, dilapidated,
grotty (*sl*), grubby, mangy, run-down,
scruffy, sleazy, squalid, tatty **2** *Inf*
= **unwell**, crook (*Aust & NZ sl*), ill, off
colour, out of sorts, poorly (*inf*), under
the weather (*inf*)
seeing *conj* **2** = **since**, as, inasmuch as,
in view of the fact that
seek *v* **1** = **look for**, be after, follow,
hunt, pursue, search for **2** = **try**, aim,
aspire to, attempt, endeavour, essay,
strive

S

seem ⓘ v 1 appear to be. 2 have the impression. **seeming** adj apparent but not real. **seemingly** adv.

seemly ⓘ adj -lier, -liest proper or fitting.

seen v past participle of SEE¹.

seep ⓘ v trickle through slowly, ooze. **seepage** n.

seer ⓘ n prophet.

seersucker n light cotton fabric with a slightly crinkled surface.

seesaw ⓘ n 1 plank balanced in the middle so that two people seated on either end ride up and down alternately. ▷ v 2 move up and down.

seethe ⓘ v **seething**, **seethed** 1 be very agitated. 2 (of a liquid) boil or foam.

segment ⓘ n 1 one of several sections into which something may be divided. 2 part of a circle cut off by an intersecting line. ▷ v 3 divide into segments. **segmentation** n.

segregate ⓘ v 1 set apart. 2 keep (a racial or minority group) apart from the rest of the community. **segregation** n.

seigneur n feudal lord.

seine [sane] n large fishing net that hangs vertically from floats.

seismic adj relating to earthquakes. **seismology** n study of earthquakes. **seismological** adj **seismologist** n **seismograph**, **seismometer** n instrument that records the strength of earthquakes.

seize ⓘ v 1 take hold of forcibly or quickly. 2 take immediate advantage of. 3 take legal possession of. 4 understand quickly. 5 (usu. foll. by up) (of mechanical parts) stick tightly through overheating. **seizure** n 1 sudden violent attack of an illness. 2 seizing or being seized.

seldom ⓘ adv not often, rarely.

select ⓘ v 1 pick out or choose. ▷ adj 2 chosen in preference to others. 3 restricted to a particular group, exclusive. **selection** n 1 selecting. 2 things that have been selected. 3 range from which something may be selected. **selective** adj chosen or choosing carefully. **selectively** adv **selectivity** n **selector** n.

selenium n Chemistry nonmetallic element with photoelectric properties.

self ⓘ n, pl **selves** 1 distinct individuality or identity of a person or thing. 2 one's basic nature. 3 one's own welfare or interests. **selfie** n informal

---

THESAURUS

seem v 1 = **appear**, assume, give the impression, look

seemly adj = **fitting**, appropriate, becoming, decent, decorous, fit, proper, suitable

seep v = **ooze**, exude, leak, permeate, soak, trickle, well

seer n = **prophet**, sibyl, soothsayer

seesaw v 2 = **alternate**, fluctuate, oscillate, swing

seethe v 1 = **be furious**, be livid, be pissed (off) (taboo sl), fume, go ballistic (sl, chiefly US), rage, see red (inf), simmer 2 = **boil**, bubble, fizz, foam, froth

see through v 1 = **be undeceived by**, be wise to (inf), fathom, not fall for, penetrate 2 **a** = **persevere (with)**, keep at, persist, stick out (inf) **b** = **help out**, stick by, support

segment n 1 = **section**, bit, division, part, piece, portion, slice, wedge

segregate v 1 = **set apart**, dissociate, isolate, separate 2 = **discriminate against**

segregation n 1 = **separation**, isolation 2 = **apartheid**, discrimination

seize v 1 = **grab**, catch up, clutch, grasp, grip, lay hands on, snatch, take 3 = **confiscate**, impound, take possession of

seizure n 1 = **attack**, convulsion, fit, paroxysm, spasm 2 = **taking**, annexation, commandeering, confiscation, grabbing

seldom adv = **rarely**, hardly ever, infrequently, not often

select v 1 = **choose**, opt for, pick, single out ▷ adj 2 = **choice**, excellent, first-class, hand-picked, special, superior, top-notch (inf) 3 = **exclusive**, cliquish, elite, privileged

selection n 1 = **choice**, choosing, option, pick, preference 3 = **range**, assortment, choice, collection, medley, variety

selective adj = **particular**, careful, discerning, discriminating

self-centred adj = **selfish**, egotistic, narcissistic, self-seeking

self-confidence n = **self-assurance**, aplomb, confidence, nerve, poise

self-confident adj = **self-assured**, assured, confident, poised, sure of oneself

S

photograph taking by pointing the camera at oneself. **selfish** *adj* caring too much about oneself and not enough about others. **selfishly** *adv* **selfishness** *n* **selfless** *adj* unselfish.

self- ❶ *prefix* used with many main words to mean: **1** of oneself or itself. **2** by, to, in, due to, for, or from the self. **3** automatic(ally). **self-addressed** *adj* addressed to the sender. **self-assertion** *n* putting forward one's opinions, esp. aggressively. **self-assertive** *adj* **self-assured** *adj* confident. **self-catering** *adj* (of accommodation) for people who provide their own food. **self-centred** *adj* totally preoccupied with one's own concerns. **self-coloured** *adj* having only a single colour. **self-confessed** *adj* according to one's own admission. **self-confidence** *n* belief in one's own abilities. **self-confident** *adj* **self-conscious** *adj* embarrassed at being the object of others' attention. **self-contained** *adj* **1** containing everything needed, complete. **2** (of a flat) having its own facilities. **self-control** *n* ability to control one's feelings and reactions. **self-defence** *n* defending of oneself or one's property. **self-determination** *n* the right of a nation to decide its own form of government. **self-effacing** *adj* unwilling to draw attention to oneself. **self-employed** *adj* earning a living from one's own business. **self-esteem** *n* favourable opinion of oneself. **self-evident** *adj* obvious

without proof. **self-government** *n* government of a nation or community by its own people. **self-help** *n* **1** use of one's own abilities to solve problems. **2** practice of solving one's problems within a group of people with similar problems. **self-important** *adj* having an unduly high opinion of one's importance. **self-importance** *n* **self-indulgent** *adj* tending to indulge one's desires. **self-interest** *n* one's own advantage. **self-made** *adj* having achieved wealth or status by one's own efforts. **self-opinionated** *adj* clinging stubbornly to one's own opinions. **self-possessed** *adj* having control of one's emotions, calm. **self-raising** *adj* (of flour) containing a raising agent. **self-respect** *n* sense of one's dignity and integrity. **self-righteous** *adj* thinking oneself more virtuous than others. **selfsame** *adj* the very same. **self-satisfied** *adj* conceited. **self-seeking** *adj, n* seeking to promote only one's own interests. **self-service** *adj* denoting a shop, café, or garage where customers serve themselves and then pay a cashier. **self-styled** *adj* using a title or name that one has taken without right. **self-sufficient** *adj* able to provide for oneself without help. **self-willed** *adj* stubbornly determined to get one's own way.

sell ❶ *v* **selling**, **sold 1** exchange (something) for money. **2** stock, deal in. **3** (of goods) be sold. **4** (foll. by *for*) have a specified price. **5** promote.

━━━━━━━━━━━━━━ THESAURUS ━━━━━━━━━━━━━━

self-conscious *adj* = **embarrassed**, awkward, bashful, diffident, ill at ease, insecure, nervous, uncomfortable
self-control *n* = **willpower**, restraint, self-discipline, self-restraint
self-esteem *n* = **self-respect**, confidence, faith in oneself, pride, self-assurance, self-regard
self-evident *adj* = **obvious**, clear, incontrovertible, inescapable, undeniable
self-important *adj* = **conceited**, bigheaded, cocky, full of oneself, pompous, swollen-headed
selfish *adj* = **self-centred**, egoistic, egoistical, egotistic, egotistical, greedy, self-interested, ungenerous
selfless *adj* = **unselfish**, altruistic,

generous, self-denying, self-sacrificing
self-possessed *adj* = **self-assured**, collected, confident, cool, poised, unruffled
self-respect *n* = **pride**, dignity, morale, self-esteem
self-righteous *adj* = **sanctimonious**, complacent, holier-than-thou, priggish, self-satisfied, smug, superior
self-satisfied *adj* = **smug**, complacent, pleased with oneself, self-congratulatory
self-seeking *adj* = **selfish**, careerist, looking out for number one (*inf*), out for what one can get, self-interested, self-serving
sell *v* **1** = **trade**, barter, exchange **2** = **deal in**, handle, market, peddle, retail, stock, trade in, traffic in

S

6 be in demand. **7** *informal* persuade (someone) to accept (something). **8** give up for a price or reward. ▷ *n* **9** manner of selling. **seller** *n* **sell-by date** date printed on packaged food specifying the date after which the food should not be sold. **past one's sell-by date** *informal* beyond one's prime. **sell out** *v* **1** dispose of (something) completely by selling. **2** *informal* betray. **sellout** *n* **1** performance of a show etc. for which all the tickets are sold. **2** *informal* betrayal. **sell up** *v* sell all one's goods.

Sellotape *n* **1** ® type of adhesive tape. ▷ *v* **2** stick with Sellotape.

selvage, selvedge *n* edge of cloth, woven so as to prevent unravelling.

selves *n* plural of SELF.

semantic *adj* relating to the meaning of words. **semantics** *n* study of linguistic meaning.

semaphore *n* system of signalling by holding two flags in different positions to represent letters of the alphabet.

semblance ❶ *n* outward or superficial appearance.

semen *n* sperm-carrying fluid produced by male animals.

semester *n* either of two divisions of the academic year.

semi *n informal* semidetached house.

semi- *prefix* used with many main words to mean: **1** half, e.g. *semicircle*. **2** partly or almost, e.g. *semiprofessional*. **3** occurring twice in a specified period, e.g. *semiweekly*.

semibreve *n* musical note four beats long.

semicircle *n* half of a circle. **semicircular** *adj*.

semicolon *n* the punctuation mark (;).

semiconductor *n* substance with an electrical conductivity that increases with temperature.

semidetached *adj* (of a house) joined to another on one side.

semifinal *n* match or round before the final. **semifinalist** *n*.

seminal ❶ *adj* **1** original and influential. **2** capable of developing. **3** of semen or seed.

seminar *n* meeting of a group of students for discussion.

seminary *n, pl* **-ries** college for priests.

semiotics *n* study of human communications, esp. signs and symbols.

semiprecious *adj* (of gemstones) having less value than precious stones.

semiquaver *n* musical note half the length of a quaver.

semiskilled *adj* partly trained but not for specialized work.

Semite *n* member of the group of peoples including Jews and Arabs. **Semitic** *adj*.

semitone *n* smallest interval between two notes in Western music.

semolina *n* hard grains of wheat left after the milling of flour, used to make puddings and pasta.

Senate *n* **1** upper house of some parliaments. **2** governing body of some universities. **senator** *n* member of a Senate. **senatorial** *adj*.

send ❶ *v* **sending, sent 1** cause (a person or thing) to go to or be taken or transmitted to a place. **2** (foll. by *for*) issue a request for. **3** bring into a specified state or condition. **sender** *n* **send down** *v* **1** expel from university. **2** *informal* send to jail. **sendoff** *n* demonstration of good wishes at a person's departure. **send up** *v informal* make fun of by imitating. **send-up** *n informal* imitation.

senescent *adj* growing old. **senescence** *n*.

──────────────────────── THESAURUS ──────────

seller *n* = **dealer**, agent, merchant, purveyor, retailer, salesman *or* saleswoman, supplier, vendor

sell out *v* **1** = **dispose of**, be out of stock of, get rid of, run out of **2** *Inf* = **betray**, double-cross (*inf*), sell down the river (*inf*), stab in the back

semblance *n* = **appearance**, aspect, facade, mask, pretence, resemblance, show, veneer

seminal *adj* **1** = **influential**, formative, ground-breaking, important, innovative, original

send *v* **1** = **dispatch**, convey, direct, forward, remit, transmit **2** (foll. by *for*) = **summon**, call for, order, request

sendoff *n* = **farewell**, departure, leave-taking, start, valediction

send up *v Inf* = **imitate**, burlesque, lampoon, make fun of, mimic, mock, parody, satirize, spoof (*inf*), take off (*inf*)

send-up *n Inf* = **imitation**, parody, satire, skit, spoof (*inf*), take-off (*inf*)

senile ❶ *adj* mentally or physically weak because of old age. **senility** *n*.

senior ❶ *adj* **1** superior in rank or standing. **2** older. **3** of or for older pupils. ▷ *n* **4** senior person. **seniority** *n* **senior citizen** old person, esp. a pensioner.

senna *n* **1** tropical plant. **2** its dried leaves or pods used as a laxative.

señor [sen-**nyor**] *n*, *pl* **-ores** Spanish term of address equivalent to *sir* or *Mr*. **señora** [sen-**nyor**-a] *n* Spanish term of address equivalent to *madam* or *Mrs*. **señorita** [sen-nyor-**ee**-ta] *n* Spanish term of address equivalent to *madam* or *Miss*.

sensation ❶ *n* **1** ability to feel things physically. **2** physical feeling. **3** general feeling or awareness. **4** state of excitement. **5** exciting person or thing. **sensational** *adj* **1** causing intense shock, anger, or excitement. **2** *informal* very good. **sensationalism** *n* deliberate use of sensational language or subject matter. **sensationalist** *adj*, *n*.

sense ❶ *n* **1** any of the faculties of perception or feeling (sight, hearing, touch, taste, or smell). **2** ability to perceive. **3** feeling perceived through one of the senses. **4** awareness. **5** moral discernment. **6** (sometimes pl) sound practical judgment or intelligence. **7** reason or purpose. **8** specific meaning. ▷ *v* **9** perceive. **senseless** *adj* **1** foolish. **2** unconscious.

sensible ❶ *adj* **1** having or showing good sense. **2** practical, e.g. *sensible shoes*. **3** capable of being perceived by the senses. **4** (foll. by *of*) aware. **sensibly** *adv* **sensibility** *n* **1** ability to experience deep feelings. **2** (usu. pl) tendency to be influenced or offended.

sensitive ❶ *adj* **1** easily hurt or offended. **2** responsive to external stimuli. **3** (of a subject) liable to arouse controversy or strong feelings. **4** (of an instrument) responsive to slight changes. **sensitively** *adv* **sensitivity** *n* **sensitize** *v* make sensitive.

sensor *n* device that detects or measures the presence of something, such as radiation.

THESAURUS

senile *adj* = **doddering**, decrepit, doting, in one's dotage

senility *n* = **dotage**, decrepitude, infirmity, loss of one's faculties, senile dementia

senior *adj* **1** = **higher ranking**, superior **2** = **older**, elder, major (*Brit*)

senior citizen *n* = **pensioner**, O.A.P., old age pensioner, old *or* elderly person, retired person

seniority *n* = **superiority**, precedence, priority, rank

sensation *n* **3** = **feeling**, awareness, consciousness, impression, perception, sense **4** = **excitement**, commotion, furore, stir, thrill

sensational *adj* **1** = **exciting**, amazing, astounding, dramatic, melodramatic, shock-horror (*facetious*), shocking, thrilling **2** *Inf* = **excellent**, fabulous (*inf*), impressive, marvellous, mean (*sl*), mind-blowing (*inf*), out of this world (*inf*), smashing (*inf*), superb

sense *n* **1** = **faculty 3** = **feeling**, sensation **4** = **feeling**, atmosphere, aura, awareness, consciousness, impression, perception **6** (sometimes pl) = **intelligence**, brains (*inf*), cleverness, common sense, judgment, reason, sagacity, sanity, sharpness, understanding, wisdom, wit(s) **8** = **meaning**, drift, gist, implication, import, significance ▷ *v* **9** = **perceive**, be aware of, discern, feel, get the impression, pick up, realize, understand

senseless *adj* **1** = **stupid**, asinine, crazy, daft (*inf*), foolish, idiotic, illogical, inane, irrational, mad, mindless, nonsensical, pointless, ridiculous, silly **2** = **unconscious**, insensible, out, out cold, stunned

sensibility *n* **1** = **sensitivity**, responsiveness, sensitiveness, susceptibility **2** (usu. pl) = **feelings**, emotions, moral sense, sentiments, susceptibilities

sensible *adj* **1** = **wise**, canny, down-to-earth, intelligent, judicious, prudent, rational, realistic, sage, sane, shrewd, sound **2** = **practical 4** (foll. by *of*) = **aware of**, conscious of, mindful of, sensitive to

sensitive *adj* **1** = **easily hurt**, delicate, easily offended, easily upset, tender, thin-skinned, touchy **2** = **susceptible**, easily affected, impressionable, responsive **4** = **precise**, acute, fine, keen, responsive

S

sensory *adj* of the senses or sensation.
sensual ❶ *adj* **1** giving pleasure to the body and senses rather than the mind. **2** having a strong liking for physical pleasures. **sensually** *adv* **sensuality** *n* **sensualist** *n*.
sensuous ❶ *adj* pleasing to the senses. **sensuously** *adv*.
sent *v* past of SEND.
sentence ❶ *n* **1** sequence of words capable of standing alone as a statement, question, or command. **2** punishment passed on a criminal. ▷ *v* **3** pass sentence on (a convicted person).
sententious ❶ *adj* **1** trying to sound wise. **2** pompously moralizing. **sententiously** *adv*.
sentient ❶ [**sen**-tee-ent] *adj* capable of feeling. **sentience** *n*.
sentiment ❶ *n* **1** thought, opinion, or attitude. **2** feeling expressed in words. **3** exaggerated or mawkish emotion. **sentimental** *adj* excessively romantic or nostalgic. **sentimentalism** *n* **sentimentality** *n* **sentimentalize** *v* make sentimental.
sentinel ❶ *n* sentry.
sentry *n*, *pl* **-tries** soldier on watch.

sepal *n* leaflike division of the calyx of a flower.
separate ❶ *v* **1** act as a barrier between. **2** distinguish between. **3** divide up into parts. **4** sever or be severed. **5** (of a couple) stop living together. ▷ *adj* **6** not the same, different. **7** set apart. **8** not shared, individual. **separately** *adv*
separation *n* **1** separating or being separated. **2** *Law* living apart of a married couple without divorce.
separable *adj* **separatist** *n* person who advocates the separation of a group from an organization or country. **separatism** *n*.
● **SPELLING TIP**
● There are 101 examples of *seperate* in
● the Bank of English, which makes
● it the most popular misspelling of
● **separate**.
sepia *adj*, *n* reddish-brown (pigment).
sepoy *n* (formerly) Indian soldier in the service of the British.
sepsis *n* poisoning caused by pus-forming bacteria.
sept *n* clan, esp. in Ireland or Scotland.
Sept. September.
September *n* ninth month of the year.

———————————————————————————————— THESAURUS ————————————————————————————————

sensitivity *n* **1** = **delicacy**
2 = **sensitiveness**, receptiveness, responsiveness, susceptibility
sensual *adj* **1** = **physical**, animal, bodily, carnal, fleshly, luxurious, voluptuous **2** = **erotic**, lascivious, lecherous, lewd, lustful, raunchy (*sl*), sexual
sensuality *n* = **eroticism**, carnality, lasciviousness, lecherousness, lewdness, sexiness (*inf*), voluptuousness
sensuous *adj* = **pleasurable**, gratifying, hedonistic, sybaritic
sentence *n* **2** = **punishment**, condemnation, decision, decree, judgment, order, ruling, verdict ▷ *v* **3** = **condemn**, doom, penalize
sententious *adj* **2** = **pompous**, canting, judgmental, moralistic, preachifying (*inf*), sanctimonious
sentient *adj* = **feeling**, conscious, living, sensitive
sentiment *n* **1** = **opinion**, attitude, belief, feeling, idea, judgment, view **3** = **sentimentality**, emotionalism, mawkishness, romanticism
sentimental *adj* = **romantic**,

emotional, maudlin, nostalgic, overemotional, schmaltzy (*sl*), slushy (*inf*), soft-hearted, touching, weepy (*inf*)
sentimentality *n* = **romanticism**, corniness (*sl*), emotionalism, mawkishness, nostalgia, schmaltz (*sl*)
sentinel *n* = **guard**, lookout, sentry, watch, watchman
separable *adj* = **distinguishable**, detachable, divisible
separate *v* **2** = **single out**, isolate, segregate **3** = **divide 4** = **sever**, come apart, come away, detach, disconnect, disjoin, remove, split, sunder **5** = **part**, break up, disunite, diverge, divorce, estrange, part company, split up ▷ *adj* **7** = **unconnected**, detached, disconnected, divided, divorced, isolated, unattached **8** = **individual**, alone, apart, distinct, particular, single, solitary
separately *adv* = **individually**, alone, apart, severally, singly
separation *n* **1** = **division**, break, disconnection, dissociation, disunion, gap **2** *Law* = **split-up**, break-up, parting, rift, split

S

septet *n* **1** group of seven performers. **2** music for such a group.

septic ❶ *adj* **1** (of a wound) infected. **2** of or caused by harmful bacteria. **septic tank** tank in which sewage is decomposed by the action of bacteria.

septicaemia [sep-tis-**see**-mee-a] *n* infection of the blood.

septuagenarian *n* person aged between seventy and seventy-nine.

septum *n, pl* **-ta** dividing partition between two tissues or cavities in the body, such as in the nose.

sepulchre ❶ [**sep**-pull-ker] *n* tomb or burial vault. **sepulchral** [sip-**pulk**-ral] *adj* gloomy.

sequel ❶ *n* **1** novel, play, or film that continues the story of an earlier one. **2** thing that follows something else. **3** consequence.

sequence ❶ *n* **1** arrangement of two or more things in successive order. **2** the successive order of two or more things. **3** section of a film showing a single uninterrupted episode. **sequential** *adj*.

sequester *v* **1** seclude. **2** sequestrate.

sequestrate *v* confiscate (property) until its owner's debts are paid or a court order is complied with. **sequestration** *n*.

sequin *n* small ornamental metal disc on a garment. **sequined** *adj*.

sequoia *n* giant Californian coniferous tree.

seraglio [sir-**ah**-lee-oh] *n, pl* **-raglios** **1** harem of a Muslim palace. **2** Turkish sultan's palace.

seraph *n, pl* **-aphs**, **-aphim** member of the highest order of angels. **seraphic** *adj*.

Serbian, Serb *adj* **1** of Serbia. ▷ *n* **2** person from Serbia. **3** dialect of Serbo-Croat spoken in Serbia. **Serbo-Croat, Serbo-Croatian** *adj, n* (of) the chief official language of Serbia and Croatia.

serenade *n* **1** music played or sung to a woman by a lover. **2** piece of music for a small orchestra. ▷ *v* **3** sing or play a serenade to (someone).

serendipity *n* gift of making fortunate discoveries by accident.

serene ❶ *adj* **1** calm, peaceful. **2** (of the sky) clear. **serenely** *adv* **serenity** *n*.

serf *n* medieval farm labourer who could not leave the land he worked on. **serfdom** *n*.

serge *n* strong woollen fabric.

sergeant *n* **1** noncommissioned officer in the army. **2** police officer ranking between constable and inspector. **sergeant at arms** parliamentary or court officer with ceremonial duties. **sergeant major** highest rank of noncommissioned officer in the army.

serial *n* **1** story or play produced in successive instalments. ▷ *adj* **2** of or forming a series. **3** published or presented as a serial. **serialize** *v* publish or present as a serial. **serial killer** person who commits a series of murders.

series ❶ *n, pl* **-ries** **1** group or succession of related things, usu. arranged in order. **2** set of radio or TV programmes about the same subject or characters.

serious ❶ *adj* **1** giving cause for concern. **2** concerned with important matters. **3** not cheerful, grave. **4** sincere, not joking. **5** *informal*

———————————— THESAURUS ————————————

septic *adj* **1** = **infected**, festering, poisoned, putrefying, putrid, suppurating

sepulchre *n* = **tomb**, burial place, grave, mausoleum, vault

sequel *n* **2** = **follow-up**, continuation, development **3** = **consequence**, conclusion, end, outcome, result, upshot

sequence *n* **1, 2** = **succession**, arrangement, chain, course, cycle, order, progression, series

serene *adj* **1** = **calm**, composed, peaceful, tranquil, unruffled, untroubled

serenity *n* = **calmness**, calm, composure, peace, peacefulness, quietness, stillness, tranquillity

series *n* **1** = **sequence**, chain, course, order, progression, run, set, string, succession, train

serious *adj* **1** = **grave**, acute, critical, dangerous, severe **2** = **important**, crucial, fateful, grim, momentous, no laughing matter, pressing, significant, urgent, worrying **3** = **solemn**, grave, humourless, sober, unsmiling **4** = **sincere**, earnest, genuine, honest, in earnest

seriously *adv* **1** = **badly**, acutely, critically, dangerously, gravely, severely **3** = **gravely** **4** = **sincerely**, in earnest

impressive, e.g. *serious money*.
seriously *adv* **seriousness** *n*.
sermon ❶ *n* **1** speech on a religious or moral subject by a clergyman in a church service. **2** long moralizing speech. **sermonize** *v* make a long moralizing speech.
serpent *n* snake. **serpentine** *adj* twisting like a snake.
serrated *adj* having a notched or sawlike edge. **serration** *n*.
serried *adj* in close formation.
serum [**seer**-um] *n* **1** watery fluid left after blood has clotted. **2** this fluid from the blood of immunized animals used for inoculation or vaccination.
serval *n* feline African mammal.
servant ❶ *n* person employed to do household work for another.
serve ❶ *v* **1** work for (a person, community, or cause). **2** perform official duties. **3** attend to (customers). **4** provide with food or drink. **5** present (food or drink). **6** provide with a service. **7** be a member of the armed forces. **8** spend (time) in prison. **9** be useful or suitable. **10** *Tennis, etc.* put (the ball) into play. **11** deliver (a legal document) to (a person). ▷ *n* **12** *Tennis, etc.* act of serving the ball. **servant** *n* person employed to do household work for another. **serve someone right** *informal* be what someone deserves for doing something wrong. **serving** *n* portion of food.
service ❶ *n* **1** serving. **2** system that provides something needed by the public. **3** department of public employment and its employees.

4 maintenance of goods provided by a dealer after sale. **5** availability for use. **6** overhaul of a machine or vehicle. **7** set of dishes etc. for serving a meal. **8** formal religious ceremony. **9** *Tennis, etc.* act, manner, or right of serving the ball. ▷ *pl* **10** armed forces. ▷ *adj* **11** serving the public rather than producing goods, e.g. *service industry*. ▷ *v* **12** provide a service or services to. **13** overhaul (a machine or vehicle). **serviceable** *adj* **1** useful or helpful. **2** able or ready to be used. **service area** area beside a motorway with garage, restaurant, and toilet facilities. **service charge** additional cost on a restaurant bill to pay for service. **service flat** flat where domestic services are provided. **serviceman**, **servicewoman** *n* member of the armed forces. **service road** narrow road giving access to houses and shops. **service station** garage selling fuel for motor vehicles.
serviette *n* table napkin.
servile ❶ *adj* **1** too eager to obey people, fawning. **2** suitable for a slave. **servility** *n*.
servitude *n* bondage or slavery.
sesame [**sess**-am-ee] *n* plant cultivated for its seeds and oil, which are used in cooking.
session ❶ *n* **1** period spent in an activity. **2** meeting of a court, parliament, or council. **3** series or period of such meetings. **4** academic term or year.
set¹ ❶ *v* **setting**, **set 1** put in a specified position or state. **2** make ready. **3** make or become firm or rigid. **4** put

——————— THESAURUS ———————

S

seriousness *n* **2** = **importance**, gravity, significance, urgency **4** = **solemnity**, earnestness, gravity
sermon *n* **1, 2** = **homily**, address
servant *n* = **attendant**, domestic, help, maid, retainer, skivvy (*chiefly Brit*), slave
serve *v* **1** = **work for**, aid, assist, help **2** = **perform**, act, complete, discharge, do, fulfil **3** = **attend to**, minister to, wait on **4, 6** = **provide**, supply **5** = **present**, deliver, dish up, set out **9** = **be adequate**, answer the purpose, be acceptable, do, function as, satisfy, suffice, suit
service *n* **1** = **help**, assistance, avail, benefit, use, usefulness **3** = **work**,

business, duty, employment, labour, office, yakka (*Aust & NZ inf*) **6** = **overhaul**, check, maintenance **8** = **ceremony**, observance, rite, worship ▷ *v* **13** = **overhaul**, check, fine tune, go over, maintain, tune (up)
serviceable *adj* **1** = **useful**, beneficial, helpful, practical, profitable, utilitarian **2** = **usable**, functional, operative
servile *adj* **1** = **subservient**, abject, fawning, grovelling, obsequious, sycophantic, toadying
session *n* **1** = **period 2** = **meeting**, discussion, hearing, sitting **3** = **congress**, assembly, conference
set¹ *v* **1** = **put**, deposit, lay, locate, place, plant, position, rest, seat, situate,

(a broken bone) or (of a broken bone) be put into a normal position for healing. **5** adjust (a clock) to a particular position. **6** establish, arrange. **7** prescribe, assign. **8** arrange (hair) while wet, so that it dries in position. **9** place (a jewel) in a setting. **10** put to music. **11** arrange (type) for printing. **12** (of the sun) go down. **13** (of plants) produce (fruit or seeds). **14** (of a gun dog) face game. ▷ *n* **15** setting or being set. **16** bearing or posture. **17** scenery used in a play or film. ▷ *adj* **18** fixed or established beforehand. **19** rigid or inflexible. **20** conventional or stereotyped. **21** determined (to do something). **22** ready. **set back** *v* **1** hinder. **2** cost. **setback** *n* anything that delays progress. **set off** *v* **1** embark on a journey. **2** cause to begin. **3** cause to explode. **4** act as a contrast to. **set square** flat right-angled triangular instrument used for drawing angles. **set to** *v* begin working. **set-to** *n* brief fight. **set up** *v* arrange or establish. **setup** *n* way in which anything is organized or arranged.

set² ❶ *n* **1** number of things or people grouped or belonging together. **2** *Maths* group of numbers or objects that satisfy a given condition or share a property. **3** television or radio

receiver. **4** *Sport* group of games in a match. **5** series of songs performed by a musician or group. **set theory** branch of mathematics concerned with the properties of sets.

sett, set *n* **1** badger's burrow. **2** small paving stone.

settee *n* couch.

setter *n* long-haired gun dog.

setting ❶ *n* **1** background or surroundings. **2** time and place where a film, book, etc. is supposed to have taken place. **3** music written for the words of a text. **4** decorative metalwork in which a gem is set. **5** plates and cutlery for a single place at table. **6** position or level to which the controls of a machine can be adjusted.

settle¹ ❶ *v* **1** arrange or put in order. **2** come to rest. **3** establish or become established as a resident. **4** colonize. **5** make quiet, calm, or stable. **6** pay (a bill). **7** dispose of, conclude. **8** bestow (property) legally. **9** end (a dispute). **settlement** *n* **1** act of settling. **2** place newly colonized. **3** subsidence (of a building). **4** property bestowed legally. **settler** *n* colonist. **settle down** *v* **1** make or become calm. **2** (foll. by *to*) concentrate on. **3** adopt a routine way of life. **settle for** *v* accept in spite of dissatisfaction.

THESAURUS

---

station, stick **2** = **prepare**, arrange, lay, make ready, spread **3** = **harden**, cake, congeal, crystallize, solidify, stiffen, thicken **6** = **arrange**, appoint, decide (upon), determine, establish, fix, fix up, resolve, schedule, settle, specify **7** = **assign**, allot, decree, impose, ordain, prescribe, specify **12** = **go down**, decline, dip, disappear, sink, subside, vanish ▷ *n* **16** = **position**, attitude, bearing, carriage, posture **17** = **scenery**, scene, setting, stage set ▷ *adj* **18** = **fixed**, agreed, appointed, arranged, decided, definite, established, prearranged, predetermined, scheduled, settled **19** = **inflexible**, hard and fast, immovable, rigid, stubborn **20** = **conventional**, stereotyped, traditional, unspontaneous
set² *n* **1 a** = **series**, assortment, batch, collection, compendium **b** = **group**, band, circle, clique, company, coterie, crowd, faction, gang

set back *v* **1** = **hold up**, delay, hinder, impede, retard, slow
setback *n* = **hold-up**, blow, check, defeat, disappointment, hitch, misfortune, reverse
set off *v* **1** = **leave**, depart, embark, start out **3** = **detonate**, explode, ignite
setting *n* **1** = **surroundings**, backdrop, background, location, scene, scenery, set, site **2** = **context**
settle¹ *v* **1** = **put in order**, adjust, order, regulate, straighten out, work out **2** = **land**, alight, come to rest, descend, light **3** = **move to**, dwell, inhabit, live, make one's home, put down roots, reside, set up home, take up residence **4** = **colonize**, people, pioneer, populate **5** = **calm**, lull, outspan (*S Afr*), pacify, quell, quiet, quieten, reassure, relax, relieve, soothe **6** = **pay**, clear, discharge, square (up) **7** = **decide**, agree, confirm, determine, establish, fix

S

settle² n long wooden bench with high back and arms.

seven adj, n one more than six. **seventh** adj, n (of) number seven in a series. **seventeen** adj, n ten and seven. **seventeenth** adj, n **seventy** adj, n ten times seven. **seventieth** adj, n.

sever ❶ v **1** cut through or off. **2** break off (a relationship). **severance** n **severance pay** compensation paid by a firm to an employee who leaves because the job he or she was appointed to do no longer exists.

several ❶ adj **1** some, a few. **2** various, separate. **3** distinct or different. **severally** adv separately.

severe ❶ adj **1** strict or harsh. **2** very intense or unpleasant. **3** strictly restrained in appearance. **severely** adv **severity** n.

sew v **sewing**, **sewed**, **sewn** or **sewed** **1** join with thread repeatedly passed through with a needle. **2** make or fasten by sewing.

sewage n waste matter or excrement carried away in sewers. **sewer** n drain to remove waste water and sewage. **sewerage** n system of sewers.

sewn v a past participle of SEW.

sex ❶ n **1** state of being male or female. **2** male or female category. **3** sexual intercourse. **4** sexual feelings or behaviour. ▷ v **5** find out the sex of. **sexy** adj **1** sexually exciting or attractive. **2** informal exciting or trendy. **sexism** n discrimination on the basis of a person's sex. **sexist** adj, n **sexual** adj **sexually** adv **sexuality** n **sexual intercourse** sexual act in which the male's penis is inserted into the female's vagina. **sex up** v informal make (something) more exciting.

sexagenarian n person aged between sixty and sixty-nine.

sextant n navigator's instrument for measuring angles, as between the sun and horizon, to calculate one's position.

sextet n **1** group of six performers. **2** music for such a group.

sexton n official in charge of a church and churchyard.

sextuplet n one of six children born at one birth.

SF science fiction.

SFA Scottish Football Association.

Sgt. Sergeant.

sh interj be quiet!

⸻ THESAURUS ⸻

9 = **resolve**, clear up, decide, put an end to, reconcile

settlement n **1** = **agreement**, arrangement, conclusion, confirmation, establishment, working out **2** = **colony**, community, encampment, outpost

settler n = **colonist**, frontiersman, immigrant, pioneer

set up v **a** = **build**, assemble, construct, erect, put together, put up, raise **b** = **establish**, arrange, begin, found, initiate, institute, organize, prearrange, prepare

setup n = **arrangement**, conditions, organization, regime, structure, system

sever v **1** = **cut**, cut in two, detach, disconnect, disjoin, divide, part, separate, split **2** = **discontinue**, break off, dissociate, put an end to, terminate

several adj **1** = **some**, many **2** = **various**, sundry **3** = **different**, diverse, manifold

severe adj **1** = **strict**, austere, cruel, drastic, hard, harsh, oppressive, rigid, unbending **2** = **intense**, acute,

extreme, fierce **3 a** = **grim**, forbidding, grave, serious, stern, tight-lipped, unsmiling **b** = **plain**, austere, classic, restrained, simple, Spartan, unadorned, unembellished, unfussy

severely adv **1** = **strictly**, harshly, sharply, sternly **2** = **seriously**, acutely, badly, extremely, gravely

severity n = **strictness**, hardness, harshness, severeness, sternness, toughness

sex n **1, 2** = **gender 3** = **(sexual) intercourse**, coition, coitus, copulation, fornication, lovemaking, sexual relations

sexual adj **3** = **reproductive**, genital, procreative, sex **4** = **carnal**, erotic, intimate, sensual, sexy

sexual intercourse n = **copulation**, bonking (inf), carnal knowledge, coition, coitus, sex (inf), union

sexuality n = **desire**, carnality, eroticism, lust, sensuality, sexiness (inf)

sexy adj **1** = **erotic**, arousing, naughty, provocative, seductive, sensual, sensuous, suggestive, titillating

S

shabby ❶ *adj* **-bier**, **-biest 1** worn or dilapidated in appearance. **2** mean or unworthy, e.g. *shabby treatment*. **shabbily** *adv* **shabbiness** *n*.

shack ❶ *n* rough hut. **shack up with** *v slang* live with (one's lover).

shackle ❶ *n* **1** one of a pair of metal rings joined by a chain, for securing a person's wrists or ankles. **2** anything that restricts freedom. ▷ *v* **3** fasten with shackles. **4** hinder.

shad *n* herring-like fish.

shade ❶ *n* **1** relative darkness. **2** place sheltered from sun. **3** screen or cover used to protect from a direct source of light. **4** depth of colour. **5** slight amount. **6** *lit* ghost. ▷ *pl* **7** *slang* sunglasses. ▷ *v* **8** screen from light. **9** darken. **10** represent (darker areas) in drawing. **11** change slightly or by degrees. **shady** *adj* **1** situated in or giving shade. **2** of doubtful honesty or legality. **in the shade** in a position of relative obscurity.

shadow ❶ *n* **1** dark shape cast on a surface when something stands between a light and the surface. **2** patch of shade. **3** slight trace. **4** threatening influence. **5** inseparable companion. **6** person who secretly trails another. ▷ *v* **7** cast a shadow over. **8** follow secretly. **shadowy** *adj* **shadow-boxing** *n*

boxing against an imaginary opponent for practice. **Shadow Cabinet** members of the main opposition party in Parliament who would be ministers if their party were in power.

shaft ❶ *n* **1** long narrow straight handle of a tool or weapon. **2** ray of light. **3** revolving rod that transmits power in a machine. **4** vertical passageway, as for a lift or a mine. **5** one of the bars between which an animal is harnessed to a vehicle. **6** something directed like a missile, e.g. *shafts of wit*. **7** middle part of a column.

shag¹ ❶ *n* **1** coarse shredded tobacco. **2** tangled hair or wool. ▷ *adj* **3** (of a carpet) having a long pile. **shaggy** *adj* **1** covered with rough hair or wool. **2** tousled, unkempt. **shaggy-dog story** long anecdote with a humorous twist at the end.

shag² *n* kind of cormorant.

shagreen *n* **1** sharkskin. **2** rough grainy untanned leather.

shah *n* formerly, ruler of Iran.

shake ❶ *v* **shaking**, **shook**, **shaken 1** move quickly up and down or back and forth. **2** make unsteady. **3** tremble. **4** grasp (someone's hand) in greeting or agreement. **5** shock or upset. **6** undermine or weaken. ▷ *n* **7** shaking. **8** vibration. **9** *informal*

shabby *adj* **1** = **tatty**, dilapidated, mean, ragged, run-down, scruffy, seedy, tattered, threadbare, worn **2** = **mean**, cheap, contemptible, despicable, dirty, dishonourable, low, rotten (*inf*), scurvy

shack *n* = **hut**, cabin, shanty

shackle *n* **1** = **fetter**, bond, chain, iron, leg-iron, manacle ▷ *v* **3** = **fetter**, bind, chain, manacle, put in irons

shade *n* **1** = **dimness**, dusk, gloom, gloominess, semidarkness, shadow **3** = **screen**, blind, canopy, cover, covering, curtain, shield, veil **4** = **hue**, colour, tinge, tint, tone **5** = **dash**, hint, suggestion, trace **6** *Lit* = **ghost**, apparition, phantom, spectre, spirit ▷ *v* **8** = **cover**, conceal, hide, obscure, protect, screen, shield, veil **9** = **darken**, cloud, dim, shadow

shadow *n* **2** = **dimness**, cover, darkness, dusk, gloom, shade **3** = **trace**, hint, suggestion, suspicion **4** = **cloud**, blight, gloom, sadness ▷ *v*

7 = **shade**, darken, overhang, screen, shield **8** = **follow**, stalk, tail (*inf*), trail

shadowy *adj* **2** = **dark**, dim, dusky, gloomy, murky, shaded, shady **3** = **vague**, dim, dreamlike, faint, ghostly, nebulous, phantom, spectral, unsubstantial

shady *adj* **1** = **shaded**, cool, dim **2** = **crooked**, disreputable, dodgy (*Brit, Aust & NZ inf*), dubious, questionable, shifty, suspect, suspicious, unethical

shaft *n* **1** = **handle**, pole, rod, shank, stem **2** = **ray**, beam, gleam

shaggy *adj* **1** = **hairy**, hirsute, long-haired **2** = **unkempt**, rough, tousled, unshorn

shake *v* **1** = **wave**, brandish, flourish **2** = **jolt**, bump, jar, rock **3** = **tremble**, quake, quiver, shiver, totter, vibrate **5** = **upset**, distress, disturb, frighten, rattle (*inf*), shock, unnerve ▷ *n* **7** = **quaking**, agitation, convulsion, jerk, jolt, shiver, shudder, trembling **8** = **vibration**, tremor

S

short period of time. **shaker** n container in which drinks are mixed or from which powder is shaken. **shaky** adj **1** unsteady. **2** uncertain or questionable. **shakily** adv **shake off** v **1** remove. **2** escape from. **shake up** v **1** mix by shaking. **2** reorganize drastically. **3** shock.

shale n flaky sedimentary rock.

shall v, past tense **should** used as an auxiliary to make the future tense or to indicate intention, obligation, or inevitability.

- **USAGE NOTE**
- The use of shall with I and we is a
- matter of preference, not rule. Shall
- is commonly used for questions in
- southern England but less often in
- the north and Scotland.

shallot [shal-**lot**] n kind of small onion.

shallow ⊕ adj **1** not deep. **2** lacking depth of character or intellect. **3** (of breathing) consisting of short breaths. **shallows** pl n area of shallow water. **shallowness** n.

sham ⊕ n **1** thing or person that is not genuine. ▷ adj **2** not genuine. ▷ v **shamming**, **shammed 3** fake, feign.

shamble v walk in a shuffling awkward way.

shambles ⊕ n **1** disorderly event or place. **2** slaughterhouse. **shambolic** adj informal completely disorganized.

shame ⊕ n **1** painful emotion caused by awareness of having done something dishonourable or foolish. **2** capacity to feel shame. **3** disgrace. **4** cause of shame. **5** cause for regret. ▷ v **6** cause to feel shame. **7** disgrace. **8** compel by shame, e.g. she was shamed into helping. **shameful** adj causing or deserving shame. **shamefully** adv **shameless** adj with no sense of shame. **shamefaced** adj looking ashamed. **put to shame** vb show up as being inferior by comparison.

shammy n, pl **-mies** informal piece of chamois leather.

shampoo n **1** liquid soap for washing hair, carpets, or upholstery. **2** process of shampooing. ▷ v **3** wash with shampoo.

shamrock n clover leaf, esp. as the Irish emblem.

shandy n, pl **-dies** drink made of beer and lemonade.

shanghai v **-haiing**, **-haied** force or trick (someone) into doing something. ▷ n Aust & NZ catapult.

shank n **1** lower leg. **2** shaft or stem.

shan't shall not.

shantung n soft Chinese silk with a knobbly surface.

shanty¹ ⊕ n, pl **-ties** shack or crude dwelling. **shantytown** n slum consisting of shanties.

— THESAURUS —

shake up v **1** = **stir (up)**, agitate, churn (up), mix **2** = **reorganize**, overturn, turn upside down **3** = **upset**, disturb, shock, unsettle

shaky adj **1** = **unsteady**, faltering, precarious, quivery, rickety, trembling, unstable, weak **2** = **uncertain**, dubious, iffy (inf), questionable, suspect

shallow adj **1** = **superficial**, empty, slight, surface, trivial **2** = **unintelligent**, foolish, frivolous, ignorant, puerile, simple

sham n **1** = **phoney** or **phony** (inf), counterfeit, forgery, fraud, hoax, humbug, imitation, impostor, pretence ▷ adj **2** = **false**, artificial, bogus, counterfeit, feigned, imitation, mock, phoney or phony (inf), pretended, simulated ▷ v **3** = **fake**, affect, assume, feign, pretend, put on, simulate

shambles n **1** = **chaos**, confusion, disarray, disorder, havoc, madhouse, mess, muddle

shame n **1** = **embarrassment**, abashment, humiliation, ignominy, mortification **3** = **disgrace**, blot, discredit, dishonour, disrepute, infamy, reproach, scandal, smear ▷ v **6** = **embarrass**, abash, disgrace, humble, humiliate, mortify **7** = **dishonour**, blot, debase, defile, degrade, smear, stain

shamefaced adj = **embarrassed**, abashed, ashamed, humiliated, mortified, red-faced, sheepish

shameful adj **a** = **embarrassing**, cringe-making (Brit inf), humiliating, mortifying **b** = **disgraceful**, base, dishonourable, low, mean, outrageous, scandalous, wicked

shameless adj = **brazen**, audacious, barefaced, flagrant, hardened, insolent, unabashed, unashamed

shanty¹ n = **shack**, cabin, hut, shed

shanty² n, pl **-ties** sailor's traditional song.

shape ❶ n **1** outward form of an object. **2** way in which something is organized. **3** pattern or mould. **4** condition or state. ▷ v **5** form or mould. **6** devise or develop. **shapeless** adj **shapely** adj having an attractive shape. **shape up** v informal develop satisfactorily.

shard n broken piece of pottery or glass.

share¹ ❶ n **1** part of something that belongs to or is contributed by a person. **2** one of the equal parts into which the capital stock of a public company is divided. ▷ v **3** give or take a share of (something). **4** join with others in doing or using (something). **5** divide and distribute. **shareholder** n.

share² n blade of a plough.

shark n **1** large usu. predatory sea fish. **2** person who cheats others.

sharkskin n stiff glossy fabric.

sharp ❶ adj **1** having a keen cutting edge or fine point. **2** not gradual. **3** clearly defined. **4** mentally acute. **5** clever but underhand. **6** shrill. **7** bitter or sour in taste. **8** Music above the true pitch. ▷ adv **9** promptly. **10** Music too high in pitch. ▷ n **11** Music symbol raising a note one semitone above natural pitch. **sharply** adv **sharpness** n **sharpen** v make or become sharp or sharper.

sharpener n **sharper** n person who cheats. **sharpshooter** n marksman.

shatter ❶ v **1** break into pieces. **2** destroy completely. **shattered** adj informal **1** completely exhausted. **2** badly upset.

shave ❶ v **shaving**, **shaved**, **shaved** or **shaven 1** remove (hair) from (the face, head, or body) with a razor or shaver. **2** pare away. **3** touch lightly in passing. ▷ n **4** shaving. **close shave** informal narrow escape. **shaver** n electric razor. **shavings** pl n parings.

shawl n piece of cloth worn over a woman's head or shoulders or wrapped around a baby.

she pron refers to: **1** female person or animal previously mentioned. **2** something regarded as female, such as a car, ship, or nation.

sheaf n, pl **sheaves 1** bundle of papers. **2** tied bundle of reaped corn. ▷ v **3** tie into a sheaf.

shear v **shearing**, **sheared**, **sheared** or **shorn 1** clip hair or wool from. **2** cut through. **3** cause (a part) to break or (of a part) break through strain or twisting. **shears** pl n large scissors or a cutting tool shaped like these. **shearer** n.

sheath n **1** close-fitting cover, esp. for a knife or sword. **2** condom. **sheathe** v **1** put into a sheath. **2** cover with a sheath.

---

shape n **1** = **form**, build, contours, figure, lines, outline, profile, silhouette **2** = **configuration 3** = **pattern**, frame, model, mould **4** = **condition**, fettle, health, state, trim ▷ v **5** = **form**, create, fashion, make, model, mould, produce **6** = **develop**, adapt, devise, frame, modify, plan

shapeless adj = **formless**, amorphous, irregular, misshapen, unstructured

shapely adj = **well-formed**, curvaceous, elegant, graceful, neat, trim, well-proportioned

share¹ n **1** = **part**, allotment, allowance, contribution, due, lot, portion, quota, ration, whack (inf) ▷ v **3** = **divide**, assign, distribute, split **4** = **partake**, participate, receive **5** = **go halves**, go fifty-fifty (inf)

sharp adj **1** = **keen**, acute, jagged, pointed, serrated, spiky **2** = **sudden**, abrupt, distinct, extreme, marked **3** = **clear**, crisp, distinct, well-defined **4** = **quick-witted**, alert, astute, bright, clever, discerning, knowing, penetrating, perceptive, quick **5** = **cunning**, artful, crafty, dishonest, sly, unscrupulous, wily **7** = **sour**, acid, acrid, hot, piquant, pungent, tart ▷ adv **9** = **promptly**, exactly, on the dot, on time, precisely, punctually

sharpen v = **whet**, edge, grind, hone

shatter v **1** = **smash**, break, burst, crack, crush, pulverize **2** = **destroy**, demolish, ruin, torpedo, wreck

shattered adj Inf **1** = **exhausted**, all in (sl), dead beat (inf), done in (inf), drained, knackered (sl), ready to drop, tired out, worn out ▷ adj **2** = **devastated**, crushed, gutted (sl)

shave v **1, 2** = **trim**, crop, pare, shear

S

sheaves *n* plural of SHEAF.

shebeen *n Irish, S Afr & Scot* place where alcohol is sold illegally.

shed¹ ❶ *n* building used for storage or shelter or as a workshop.

shed² ❶ *v* **shedding, shed 1** get rid off. **2** pour forth (tears). **3** cast off (skin, hair, or leaves).

sheen ❶ *n* glistening brightness on the surface of something.

sheep *n, pl* **sheep 1** ruminant animal bred for wool and meat. **2** timid person. **sheep-dip** *n* liquid disinfectant in which sheep are immersed. **sheepdog** *n* dog used for herding sheep. **sheepskin** *n* skin of a sheep with the fleece still on, used for clothing or rugs.

sheepish ❶ *adj* embarrassed because of feeling foolish. **sheepishly** *adv*.

sheer¹ ❶ *adj* **1** absolute, complete, e.g. *sheer folly*. **2** perpendicular, steep. **3** (of material) so fine as to be transparent. ▷ *adv* **4** steeply.

sheer² *v* **1** change course suddenly. **2** avoid an unpleasant person or thing.

sheet¹ ❶ *n* **1** large piece of cloth used as an inner bed cover. **2** broad thin piece of any material. **3** large expanse. **sheeting** *n* material from which sheets are made. **sheet lightning** lightning that appears to flash across a large part of the sky at once.

sheet² *n* rope for controlling the position of a sail. **sheet anchor 1** strong anchor for use in an emergency. **2** person or thing relied on.

sheikh, sheik [**shake**] *n* Arab chief.

sheikhdom, sheikdom *n*.

sheila *n Aust slang* girl or woman.

shekel *n* **1** monetary unit of Israel. ▷ *pl* **2** *informal* money.

shelf *n, pl* **shelves 1** board fixed horizontally for holding things. **2** ledge. **on the shelf** past the age where marriage is likely. **shelf life** time a packaged product will remain fresh.

shell ❶ *n* **1** hard outer covering of an egg, nut, or certain animals. **2** external frame of something. **3** explosive projectile fired from a large gun. **4** light rowing boat. ▷ *v* **5** take the shell from. **6** fire at with artillery shells. **shellfish** *n* sea-living animal, esp. one that can be eaten, with a shell. **shell out** *v informal* pay out or hand over (money). **shell shock** nervous disorder caused by exposure to battle conditions. **shell suit** lightweight tracksuit made of a waterproof nylon layer over a cotton layer.

shellac *n* **1** resin used in varnishes. ▷ *v* **-lacking, -lacked 2** coat with shellac.

shelter ❶ *n* **1** structure providing protection from danger or the weather. **2** protection. ▷ *v* **3** give shelter to. **4** take shelter.

shelve¹ ❶ *v* **1** put aside or postpone. **2** provide with shelves. **shelving** *n* (material for) shelves.

shelve² *v* slope.

shelves *n* plural of SHELF.

shenanigans *pl n informal* **1** mischief or nonsense. **2** trickery.

———————————————————————— THESAURUS ————————

shed¹ *n* = **hut**, outhouse, shack

shed² *v* **1** = **cast**, drop **2** = **spill**, emit, give, give out, radiate, scatter, shower **3** = **cast off**, discard, moult, slough

sheen *n* = **shine**, brightness, gleam, gloss, lustre, polish

sheepish *adj* = **embarrassed**, abashed, ashamed, mortified, self-conscious, shamefaced

sheer¹ *adj* **1** = **total**, absolute, complete, downright, out-and-out, pure, unmitigated, utter **2** = **steep**, abrupt, precipitous **3** = **fine**, diaphanous, gauzy, gossamer, see-through, thin, transparent

sheet¹ *n* **2** = **coat**, film, lamina, layer, overlay, panel, plate, slab, stratum, surface, veneer **3** = **expanse**, area, blanket, covering, stretch, sweep

shell *n* **1** = **case**, husk, pod **2** = **frame**, framework, hull, structure ▷ *v* **6** = **bomb**, attack, blitz, bombard, strafe

shell out *v Inf* = **pay out**, fork out (*sl*), give, hand over

shelter *n* **1** = **cover**, screen **2** = **protection**, asylum, defence, guard, haven, refuge, retreat, safety, sanctuary, security ▷ *v* **3** = **protect**, cover, defend, guard, harbour, hide, safeguard, shield **4** = **take shelter**, hide, seek refuge

shelve¹ *v* **1** = **postpone**, defer, freeze, put aside, put on ice, put on the back burner (*inf*), suspend, take a rain check on (*US & Canad inf*)

shepherd ● n **1** person who tends sheep. ▷ v **2** guide or watch over (people). **shepherdess** n fem **shepherd's pie** baked dish of mince covered with mashed potato.

sherbet n fruit-flavoured fizzy powder.

sheriff n **1** (in the US) chief law enforcement officer of a county. **2** (in England and Wales) chief executive officer of the Crown in a county. **3** (in Scotland) chief judge of a district.

Sherpa n member of a people of Tibet and Nepal.

sherry n, pl **-ries** pale or dark brown fortified wine.

Shetland pony n very small sturdy breed of pony.

shibboleth n slogan or principle, usu. considered outworn, characteristic of a particular group.

shied v past of SHY.

shield ● n **1** piece of armour carried on the arm to protect the body from blows or missiles. **2** anything that protects. **3** sports trophy in the shape of a shield. ▷ v **4** protect.

shift ● v **1** move. **2** transfer (blame or responsibility). **3** remove or be removed. ▷ n **4** shifting. **5** group of workers who work during a specified period. **6** period of time during which they work. **7** loose-fitting straight underskirt or dress. **shiftless** adj lacking in ambition or initiative. **shifty** adj evasive or untrustworthy. **shiftiness** n.

shih-tzu, **shitzu** n small dog with a long straight dense coat.

shillelagh [shil-**lay**-lee] n (in Ireland) a cudgel.

shilling n **1** former British coin, replaced by the 5p piece. **2** monetary

unit in some E African countries.

shillyshally v **-lying, -lied** informal be indecisive.

shimmer ● v, n (shine with) a faint unsteady light.

shin n **1** front of the lower leg. ▷ v **shinning, shinned 2** climb by using the hands or arms and legs. **shinbone** n tibia.

shindig n informal **1** noisy party. **2** brawl.

shine ● v **shining, shone 1** give out or reflect light. **2** aim (a light). **3** polish. **4** excel. ▷ n **5** brightness or lustre. **take a shine to** informal take a liking to (someone). **shiny** adj **shiner** n informal black eye.

shingle¹ n **1** wooden roof tile. ▷ v **2** cover (a roof) with shingles.

shingle² n coarse gravel found on beaches.

shingles n disease causing a rash of small blisters along a nerve.

Shinto n Japanese religion in which ancestors and nature spirits are worshipped. **Shintoism** n.

shinty n game like hockey.

ship ● n **1** large seagoing vessel. **2** airship or spaceship. ▷ v **shipping, shipped 3** send or transport by carrier, esp. a ship. **4** bring or go aboard a ship. **5** informal send away. **6** be hired to work on a ship. **shipment** n **1** act of shipping cargo. **2** consignment of goods shipped. **shipping** n **1** freight transport business. **2** ships collectively. **shipmate** n sailor serving on the same ship as another. **shipshape** adj orderly or neat. **shipwreck** n **1** destruction of a ship through storm or collision. **2** ruin or destruction. ▷ v **3** cause to

shepherd n **1** = **herdsman**, drover, grazier, stockman ▷ v **2** = **guide**, conduct, herd, steer, usher

shield n **2** = **protection**, cover, defence, guard, safeguard, screen, shelter ▷ v **4** = **protect**, cover, defend, guard, safeguard, screen, shelter

shift v **1** = **move**, budge, displace, move around, rearrange, relocate, reposition ▷ n **4** = **move**, displacement, rearrangement, shifting

shiftless adj = **lazy**, aimless, good-for-nothing, idle, lackadaisical, slothful, unambitious, unenterprising

shifty adj = **untrustworthy**, deceitful,

devious, evasive, furtive, slippery, sly, tricky, underhand

shimmer v = **gleam**, glisten, scintillate, twinkle ▷ n = **gleam**, iridescence

shine v **1** = **gleam**, beam, flash, glare, glisten, glitter, glow, radiate, sparkle, twinkle **3** = **polish**, brush, buff, burnish **4** = **be outstanding**, be conspicuous, excel, stand out ▷ n **5** = **brightness**, glare, gleam, gloss, light, lustre, polish, radiance, sheen, shimmer, sparkle

shiny adj = **bright**, gleaming, glistening, glossy, lustrous, polished

ship n **1** = **vessel**, boat, craft

S

undergo shipwreck. **shipyard** n place where ships are built.

shire n county.

shire horse n large powerful breed of horse.

shirk ❶ v avoid (duty or work). **shirker** n.

shirt n garment for the upper part of the body. **shirtsleeves** pl n **in one's shirtsleeves** not wearing a jacket.

shirty adj **-tier, -tiest** slang bad-tempered or annoyed.

shish kebab n meat and vegetable dish cooked on a skewer.

shit taboo ▷ v **shitting, shitted, shit** or **shat 1** defecate. ▷ n **2** excrement. **3** slang nonsense. **4** slang worthless person. ▷ interj **5** slang exclamation of anger or disgust. **shitty** adj.

shiver¹ ❶ v **1** tremble, as from cold or fear. ▷ n **2** shivering. **shivery** adj.

shiver² ❶ v **1** splinter into pieces. ▷ n **2** splintered piece.

shoal¹ n **1** large number of fish swimming together. **2** large group of people.

shoal² n **1** stretch of shallow water. **2** sandbank.

shock¹ ❶ v **1** horrify, disgust, or astonish. ▷ n **2** sudden violent emotional disturbance. **3** sudden violent blow or impact. **4** something causing this. **5** state of bodily collapse caused by physical or mental shock. **6** pain and muscular spasm caused by an electric current passing through the body. **shocker** n **shocking** adj **1** causing horror, disgust, or astonishment. **2** informal very bad.

shock absorber device on a car for reducing the effects of travelling over bumps. **shock therapy** electroconvulsive therapy.

shock² n bushy mass (of hair).

shod v past of SHOE.

shoddy ❶ adj **-dier, -diest** made or done badly.

shoe n **1** outer covering for the foot, ending below the ankle. **2** horseshoe. ▷ v **shoeing, shod 3** fit with a shoe or shoes. **shoehorn** n smooth curved implement inserted at the heel of a shoe to ease the foot into it. **shoelace** n cord for fastening shoes. **shoestring** n **on a shoestring** using a very small amount of money. **shoetree** n piece of metal, wood, or plastic inserted in a shoe to keep its shape.

shone v past of SHINE.

shonky adj **-kier, -kiest** Aust & NZ informal unreliable or unsound.

shoo interj **1** go away! ▷ v **2** drive away as by saying 'shoo'.

shook v past tense of SHAKE.

shoot ❶ v **shooting, shot 1** hit, wound, or kill with a missile fired from a weapon. **2** fire (a missile from) a weapon. **3** hunt. **4** send out or move rapidly. **5** (of a plant) sprout. **6** photograph or film. **7** Sport take a shot at goal. ▷ n **8** new branch or sprout of a plant. **9** hunting expedition. **10** informal photographic assignment. **shooting star** meteor. **shooting stick** stick with a spike at one end and a folding seat at the other.

---

shipshape adj = **tidy**, neat, orderly, spick-and-span, trim, well-ordered, well-organized

shirk v = **dodge**, avoid, evade, get out of, skive (Brit sl), slack

shirker n = **slacker**, clock-watcher, dodger, idler, piker (Aust & NZ sl), skiver (Brit sl)

shiver¹ v **1** = **tremble**, quake, quiver, shake, shudder ▷ n **2** = **trembling**, flutter, quiver, shudder, tremor

shiver² v **1** = **splinter**, break, crack, fragment, shatter, smash, smash to smithereens

shivery adj = **shaking**, chilled, chilly, cold, quaking, quivery

shock v **1 a** = **horrify**, appal, disgust, nauseate, revolt, scandalize, sicken **b** = **astound**, jolt, shake, stagger, stun, stupefy ▷ n **2** = **upset**, blow, bombshell, distress, disturbance, stupefaction, stupor, trauma, turn (inf) **3** = **impact**, blow, clash, collision

shocking adj **1** = **dreadful**, appalling, atrocious, disgraceful, disgusting, ghastly, horrifying, nauseating, outrageous, revolting, scandalous, sickening

shoddy adj = **inferior**, cheap, poor, rubbishy, second-rate, slipshod, tawdry, trashy

shoot v **1** = **hit**, blast (sl), bring down, kill, open fire, plug (sl) **2** = **fire**, discharge, emit, fling, hurl, launch, project, propel **4** = **speed**, bolt, charge, dart, dash, fly, hurtle, race, rush, streak, tear ▷ n **8** = **sprout**, branch, bud, offshoot, sprig

S

shop ❶ n 1 place for sale of goods and services. 2 workshop. ▷ v **shopping**, **shopped** 3 visit a shop or shops to buy goods. 4 *slang* inform against (someone). **talk shop** discuss one's work, esp. on a social occasion. **shopper** n **shopping** n 1 act of going to shops and buying things. 2 things bought. **shopping centre** area or building with many shops. **shop around** v visit various shops to compare goods and prices. **shop assistant** person serving in a shop. **shop floor** 1 production area of a factory. 2 workers in a factory. **shoplifter** n person who steals from a shop. **shopsoiled** adj soiled or faded from being displayed in a shop. **shop steward** trade-union official elected to represent his or her fellow workers.

shore¹ ❶ n 1 edge of a sea or lake. 2 land.

shore² ❶ v 1 (foll. by *up*) prop or support. ▷ n 2 prop set under or against something as a support.

shorn v a past participle of SHEAR.

short ❶ adj 1 not long. 2 not tall. 3 not lasting long, brief. 4 deficient, e.g. *short of cash*. 5 abrupt, rude. 6 (of a drink) consisting chiefly of a spirit. 7 (of pastry) crumbly. ▷ adv 8 abruptly. ▷ n 9 drink of spirits. 10 short film. 11 *informal* short circuit. ▷ pl 12 short trousers. ▷ v 13 short-circuit. **shortage** n deficiency. **shorten** v make or become shorter. **shortly** adv 1 soon. 2 rudely. **shortbread**, **shortcake** n crumbly biscuit made

with butter. **short-change** v 1 give (someone) less than the correct amount of change. 2 *slang* swindle. **short circuit** faulty or accidental connection in a circuit, which deflects current through a path of low resistance. **short-circuit** v 1 develop a short circuit. 2 bypass. **shortcoming** n failing or defect. **short cut** quicker route or method. **shortfall** n deficit. **shorthand** n system of rapid writing using symbols to represent words. **short-handed** adj not having enough workers. **short list** selected list of candidates for a job or prize, from which the final choice will be made. **short-list** v put on a short list. **short-lived** adj lasting a short time. **short shrift** brief and unsympathetic treatment. **short-sighted** adj 1 unable to see distant things clearly. 2 lacking in foresight. **short-tailed shearwater** same as MEGAPODE. **short-tempered** adj easily angered. **short-term** adj of or lasting a short time. **short wave** radio wave with a wavelength of less than 60 metres.

shot¹ ❶ n 1 shooting. 2 small lead pellets used in a shotgun. 3 person with specified skill in shooting. 4 *slang* attempt. 5 *Sport* act or instance of hitting, kicking, or throwing the ball. 6 photograph. 7 uninterrupted film sequence. 8 *informal* injection. 9 *informal* drink of spirits. **shotgun** n gun for firing a charge of shot at short range. **shotgun wedding** wedding enforced because the bride is pregnant.

THESAURUS

shop n 1 = **store**, boutique, emporium, hypermarket, supermarket

shore¹ n 1 = **beach**, coast, sands, seashore, strand (*poet*)

shore² v 1 (foll. by *up*) = **support**, brace, buttress, hold, prop, reinforce, strengthen, underpin

short adj 1 = **concise**, brief, compressed, laconic, pithy, succinct, summary, terse 2 = **small**, diminutive, dumpy, little, petite, squat 3 = **brief**, fleeting, momentary 4 = **lacking**, deficient, limited, low (on), scant, scarce, wanting 5 = **abrupt**, brusque, curt, discourteous, impolite, sharp, terse, uncivil ▷ adv 8 = **abruptly**, suddenly, without warning

shortage n = **deficiency**, dearth, insufficiency, lack, paucity, scarcity, want

shortcoming n = **failing**, defect, fault, flaw, imperfection, weakness

shorten v = **cut**, abbreviate, abridge, curtail, decrease, diminish, lessen, reduce

shortly adv 1 = **soon**, before long, in a little while, presently

short-sighted adj 1 = **near-sighted**, myopic 2 = **unthinking**, ill-advised, ill-considered, impolitic, impractical, improvident, imprudent, injudicious

short-tempered adj = **quick-tempered**, hot-tempered, impatient, irascible, ratty (*Brit & NZ inf*), testy

shot¹ n 1 = **throw**, discharge, lob, pot shot 2 = **pellet**, ball, bullet, lead, projectile, slug 3 = **marksman**, shooter 4 *Sl* = **attempt**, effort, endeavour, go (*inf*), stab (*inf*), try, turn

S

shot² ❶ v **1** past of SHOOT. ▷ adj
2 woven to show changing colours,
e.g. shot silk. **3** streaked with colour.
shot put n athletic event in which
contestants hurl a heavy metal ball as
far as possible. **shot-putter** n.
should v past tense of **shall** used as an
auxiliary to make the subjunctive
mood or to indicate obligation or
possibility.
shoulder ❶ n **1** part of the body to
which an arm, foreleg, or wing is
attached. **2** cut of meat including the
upper foreleg. **3** part of a garment
which covers the shoulder. **4** side of a
road. ▷ v **5** bear (a burden or
responsibility). **6** push with one's
shoulder. **7** put on one's shoulder.
shoulder blade large flat triangular
bone at the shoulder.
shouldn't should not.
shout ❶ n **1** loud cry. ▷ v **2** cry out
loudly. **3** Aust & NZ informal treat
(someone) to (something, such as a
drink). **shout down** v silence
(someone) by shouting.
shove ❶ v **1** push roughly. **2** informal
put. ▷ n **3** rough push. **shove off** v
informal go away.
shovel ❶ n **1** tool for lifting or moving
loose material. ▷ v **-elling, -elled 2** lift
or move as with a shovel.
show ❶ v **showing, showed, shown** or
showed 1 make, be, or become
noticeable or visible. **2** exhibit or
display. **3** indicate. **4** instruct by
demonstration. **5** prove. **6** guide.
7 reveal or display (an emotion). ▷ n

8 public exhibition. **9** theatrical or
other entertainment. **10** mere display
or pretence. **11** slang thing or affair.
showy adj **1** gaudy. **2** ostentatious.
showily adv **showing** n **1** exhibition.
2 manner of presentation. **show
business** the entertainment industry.
showcase n **1** situation in which
something is displayed to best
advantage. **2** glass case used to
display objects. **showdown** n
confrontation that settles a dispute.
showjumping n competitive sport of
riding horses to demonstrate skill in
jumping. **showman** n man skilled at
presenting anything spectacularly.
showmanship n **show off** v **1** exhibit
to invite admiration. **2** informal
behave flamboyantly in order to
attract attention. **show-off** n informal
person who shows off. **showpiece** n
excellent specimen shown for display
or as an example. **showroom** n room
in which goods for sale are on display.
show up v **1** reveal or be revealed
clearly. **2** expose the faults or defects
of. **3** informal embarrass. **4** informal
arrive.
shower ❶ n **1** kind of bath in which a
person stands while being sprayed
with water. **2** wash in this. **3** short
period of rain, hail, or snow. **4** sudden
abundant fall of objects, e.g. shower of
sparks. ▷ v **5** wash in a shower.
6 sprinkle with or as if with a shower.
7 bestow (things) or present
(someone) with things liberally.
showery adj.

━━━━━━━━━━━━━━━━━━━ **THESAURUS** ━━━

shot² adj **2 = iridescent**, moiré,
opalescent, watered
shoulder v **5 = bear**, accept, assume,
be responsible for, carry, take on
6 = push, elbow, jostle, press, shove
shout n **1 = cry**, bellow, call, roar,
scream, yell ▷ v **2 = cry (out)**, bawl,
bellow, call (out), holler (inf), roar,
scream, yell
shout down v **= silence**, drown, drown
out, overwhelm
shove v **1 = push**, drive, elbow, impel,
jostle, press, propel, thrust
shovel v **2 = move**, dredge, heap, ladle,
load, scoop, toss
shove off v Inf **= go away**, clear off
(inf), depart, leave, push off (inf),
scram (inf)
show v **1 = be visible**, appear

2 = present, display, exhibit
3 = indicate, demonstrate, display,
manifest, register, reveal **4 = instruct**,
demonstrate, explain, teach **5 = prove**,
clarify, demonstrate, elucidate, point
out **6 = guide**, accompany, attend,
conduct, escort, lead ▷ n **8 = exhibition**,
array, display, fair, parade, sight,
spectacle **9 = entertainment**, pageant,
presentation, production
10 = pretence, affectation, air,
appearance, display, illusion, parade,
pose
showdown n **= confrontation**, clash,
face-off (sl)
shower n **3, 4 = deluge**, barrage,
stream, torrent, volley ▷ v
7 = inundate, deluge, heap, lavish,
pour, rain

S

shown *v* a past participle of SHOW.

shrank *v* a past tense of SHRINK.

shrapnel *n* **1** artillery shell filled with pellets which scatter on explosion. **2** fragments from this.

shred ❶ *n* **1** long narrow strip torn from something. **2** small amount. ▷ *v* **shredding**, **shredded** *or* **shred 3** tear to shreds.

shrew ❶ *n* **1** small mouselike animal. **2** bad-tempered nagging woman. **shrewish** *adj*.

shrewd ❶ *adj* clever and perceptive. **shrewdly** *adv* **shrewdness** *n*.

shriek ❶ *n* **1** shrill cry. ▷ *v* **2** utter (with) a shriek.

shrike *n* songbird with a heavy hooked bill.

shrill ❶ *adj* **1** (of a sound) sharp and high-pitched. ▷ *v* **2** utter shrilly. **shrillness** *n* **shrilly** *adv*.

shrimp *n* **1** small edible shellfish. **2** *informal* small person. **shrimping** *n* fishing for shrimps.

shrine *n* **1** place of worship associated with a sacred person or object. **2** container for holy relics.

shrink ❶ *v* **shrinking**, **shrank** *or* **shrunk**, **shrunk** *or* **shrunken 1** become or make smaller. **2** recoil or withdraw. ▷ *n* **3** *slang* psychiatrist.

shrinkage *n* decrease in size, value, or weight.

shrivel ❶ *v* **-elling**, **-elled** shrink and wither.

shroud ❶ *n* **1** piece of cloth used to wrap a dead body. **2** anything which conceals. ▷ *v* **3** conceal.

Shrove Tuesday *n* day before Ash Wednesday.

shrub *n* woody plant smaller than a tree. **shrubbery** *n*, *pl* **-beries** area planted with shrubs.

shrug *v* **shrugging**, **shrugged 1** raise and then drop (the shoulders) as a sign of indifference, ignorance, or doubt. ▷ *n* **2** shrugging. **shrug off** *v* dismiss as unimportant.

shrunk *v* a past of SHRINK.

shrunken *v* a past participle of SHRINK.

shudder ❶ *v* **1** shake or tremble violently, esp. with horror. ▷ *n* **2** shaking or trembling.

shuffle ❶ *v* **1** walk without lifting the feet. **2** jumble together. **3** rearrange. ▷ *n* **4** shuffling. **5** rearrangement.

shun ❶ *v* **shunning**, **shunned** avoid.

shunt *v* **1** move (objects or people) to a different position. **2** move (a train) from one track to another. ▷ *n* **3** shunting. **4** railway point.

THESAURUS

showman *n* = **performer**, entertainer

show off *v* **1** = **exhibit**, demonstrate, display, flaunt, parade **2** *Inf* = **boast**, blow one's own trumpet, brag, skite (*Aust & NZ*), swagger

show-off *n Inf* = **exhibitionist**, boaster, braggart, poseur

show up *v* **1** = **stand out**, appear, be conspicuous, be visible **2** = **reveal**, expose, highlight, lay bare **3** *Inf* = **embarrass**, let down, mortify, put to shame **4** *Inf* = **arrive**, appear, come, turn up

showy *adj* **1** = **gaudy**, garish, loud **2** = **ostentatious**, brash, flamboyant, flash (*inf*), flashy, over the top (*inf*)

shred *n* **1** = **strip**, bit, fragment, piece, scrap, sliver, tatter **2** = **particle**, atom, grain, iota, jot, scrap, trace

shrew *n* **2** = **nag**, harpy, harridan, scold, spitfire, vixen

shrewd *adj* = **clever**, astute, calculating, canny, crafty, cunning, intelligent, keen, perceptive, perspicacious, sharp, smart

shrewdness *n* = **cleverness**, astuteness, canniness, discernment, judgment, perspicacity, quick wits, sharpness, smartness

shriek *v*, *n* **1, 2** = **cry**, scream, screech, squeal, yell

shrill *adj* **1** = **piercing**, high, penetrating, sharp

shrink *v* **1** = **decrease**, contract, diminish, dwindle, grow smaller, lessen, narrow, shorten **2** = **recoil**, cower, cringe, draw back, flinch, quail

shrivel *v* = **wither**, dehydrate, desiccate, shrink, wilt, wizen

shroud *n* **1** = **winding sheet**, grave clothes **2** = **covering**, mantle, pall, screen, veil ▷ *v* **3** = **conceal**, blanket, cloak, cover, envelop, hide, screen, veil

shudder *v* **1** = **shiver**, convulse, quake, quiver, shake, tremble ▷ *n* **2** = **shiver**, quiver, spasm, tremor

shuffle *v* **1** = **scuffle**, drag, scrape, shamble **2** = **jumble**, disarrange, disorder, mix **3** = **rearrange**

shun *v* = **avoid**, keep away from, steer clear of

S

shush *interj* **1** be quiet! ▷ *v* **2** quiet by saying 'shush'.

shut ❶ *v* **shutting, shut 1** bring together or fold, close. **2** prevent access to. **3** (of a shop etc.) stop operating for the day. **shutter** *n* **1** hinged doorlike cover for closing off a window. **2** device in a camera letting in the light required to expose a film. ▷ *v* **3** close or equip with a shutter. **shut down** *v* close or stop (a factory, machine, or business). **shutdown** *n* **shuteye** *n slang* sleep. **shut up** *v* **1** *informal* stop talking. **2** confine.

shuttle ❶ *n* **1** vehicle going to and fro over a short distance. **2** instrument which passes the weft thread between the warp threads in weaving. **3** small thread-holding device in a sewing machine. ▷ *v* **4** travel by or as if by shuttle.

shuttlecock *n* small light cone with feathers stuck in one end, struck to and fro in badminton.

shy¹ ❶ *adj* **1** not at ease in company. **2** timid. **3** (foll. by *of*) cautious or wary. **4** reluctant, e.g. *workshy*. ▷ *v* **shying, shied 5** start back in fear. **6** (foll. by *away from*) avoid (doing something) through fear or lack of confidence. **shyly** *adv* **shyness** *n*.

shy² ❶ *v* **shying, shied 1** throw. ▷ *n, pl* **shies 2** throw.

Si *Chemistry* silicon.

SI *French* Système International (d'Unités), international metric system of units of measurement.

Siamese *adj* of Siam, former name of Thailand. **Siamese cat** breed of cat with cream fur, dark ears and face, and blue eyes. **Siamese twins** twins born joined to each other at some part of the body.

sibilant *adj* **1** hissing. ▷ *n* **2** consonant pronounced with a hissing sound.

sibling *n* brother or sister.

sibyl *n* (in ancient Greece and Rome) prophetess.

sic *Latin* thus: used to indicate that an odd spelling or reading is in fact accurate.

sick ❶ *adj* **1** vomiting or likely to vomit. **2** physically or mentally unwell. **3** *informal* amused by something sadistic or morbid. **4** (foll. by *of*) *informal* disgusted (by) or weary (of). ▷ *n* **5** *informal* vomit. **sickness** *n* **sicken** *v* **1** make nauseated or disgusted. **2** become ill. **sickly** *adj* **1** unhealthy, weak. **2** looking pale and ill. **3** causing revulsion or nausea. **sickbay** *n* place for sick people, such as that on a ship.

sickle *n* tool with a curved blade for cutting grass or grain.

side ❶ *n* **1** line or surface that borders anything. **2** either of two halves into which something can be divided.

━━━━━━━━━━━━━━━━━━━━━━━━━━━━━━━━━━ **THESAURUS** ━━━━━━

shut *v* **1** = **close**, fasten, seal, secure, slam

shut down *v* **a** = **close**, shut up **b** = **stop**, halt, switch off

shuttle *v* **4** = **go back and forth**, alternate, commute, go to and fro

shut up *v* **1** *Inf* = **be quiet**, fall silent, gag, hold one's tongue, hush, silence **2** = **confine**, cage, coop up, immure, imprison, incarcerate

shy¹ *adj* **1, 2** = **timid**, bashful, coy, diffident, retiring, self-conscious, self-effacing, shrinking **3** (foll. by *of*) = **cautious of**, chary of, distrustful of, hesitant about, suspicious of, wary of ▷ *v* **5** (foll. by *away from*) = **recoil**, balk, draw back, flinch, start

shy² *v* **1** = **throw**, cast, fling, hurl, pitch, sling, toss

shyness *n* = **timidity**, bashfulness, diffidence, lack of confidence, self-consciousness, timidity, timorousness

sick *adj* **1** = **nauseous**, ill, nauseated, queasy **2** = **unwell**, ailing, crook (*Aust & NZ sl*), diseased, indisposed, poorly (*inf*), under the weather **3** *Inf* = **morbid**, black, ghoulish, macabre, sadistic **4** (foll. by *of*) *Inf* = **tired**, bored, fed up, jaded, weary

sicken *v* **1** = **disgust**, gross out (*US sl*), nauseate, repel, revolt, turn one's stomach **2** = **fall ill**, ail, take sick

sickly *adj* **1** = **unhealthy**, ailing, delicate, faint, feeble, infirm, weak **2** = **pallid**, peaky, wan **3** = **nauseating**, cloying, mawkish

sickness *n* **1** = **nausea**, queasiness, vomiting **2** = **illness**, affliction, ailment, bug (*inf*), complaint, disease, disorder, malady

side *n* **1** = **border**, boundary, division, edge, limit, margin, perimeter, rim, sector, verge **3** = **surface**, facet **8** = **part**, aspect, face, flank, hand, view **9** = **party**, camp, cause, faction,

3 either surface of a flat object.
4 slope of a hill. **5** right or left part of the body. **6** area immediately next to a person or thing. **7** region. **8** aspect or part. **9** one of two opposing groups or teams. **10** line of descent through one parent. **11** *slang* conceit. ▷ *adj* **12** at or on the side. **13** subordinate. **on the side 1** as an extra. **2** unofficially. **siding** *n* short stretch of railway track on which trains or wagons are shunted from the main line. **sidebar** *n* (on a website) short article placed alongside a longer one. **sideboard** *n* piece of furniture for holding plates, cutlery, etc. in a dining room. **sideburns, sideboards** *pl n* man's side whiskers. **sidecar** *n* small passenger car on the side of a motorcycle. **side effect** additional undesirable effect. **sidekick** *n informal* close friend or associate. **sidelight** *n* either of two small lights on the front of a vehicle. **sideline** *n* **1** subsidiary interest or source of income. **2** *Sport* line marking the boundary of a playing area. **sidelong** *adj* **1** sideways. ▷ *adv* **2** obliquely. **side-saddle** *n* saddle designed to allow a woman rider to sit with both legs on the same side of the horse. **sideshow** *n* entertainment offered along with the main show. **sidestep** *v* **1** dodge (an issue). **2** avoid by stepping sideways. **sidetrack** *v* divert from the main topic. **sideways** *adv* **1** to or from the side. **2** obliquely. **side with** *v* support (one side in a dispute).
sidereal [side-**eer**-ee-al] *adj* of or

determined with reference to the stars.
sidewalk *n US & Canad* paved path for pedestrians.
sidle ❶ *v* move in a furtive manner.
SIDS sudden infant death syndrome, cot death.
siege *n* surrounding and blockading of a place.
siemens *n* SI unit of electrical conductance.
sienna *n* reddish- or yellowish-brown pigment made from natural earth.
sierra *n* range of mountains in Spain or America with jagged peaks.
siesta ❶ *n* afternoon nap, taken in hot countries.
sieve ❶ [siv] *n* **1** utensil with mesh through which a substance is sifted or strained. ▷ *v* **2** sift or strain through a sieve.
sift ❶ *v* **1** remove the coarser particles from a substance with a sieve. **2** examine (information or evidence) to select what is important.
sigh *n* **1** long audible breath expressing sadness, tiredness, relief, or longing. ▷ *v* **2** utter a sigh. **sigh for** *v* long for.
sight ❶ *n* **1** ability to see. **2** instance of seeing. **3** range of vision. **4** thing seen. **5** *informal* unsightly thing. **6** device for guiding the eye while using a gun or optical instrument. **7** thing worth seeing. **8** *informal* a lot. ▷ *v* **9** catch sight of. **10** aim (a weapon) using a sight. **sightless** *adj* blind. **sight-read** *v* play or sing printed music without previous preparation. **sightseeing** *n* visiting places of interest. **sightseer** *n*.
sign ❶ *n* **1** indication of something not immediately or outwardly observable.

sect, team **11** *Sl* = **conceit**, airs, arrogance ▷ *adj* **13** = **subordinate**, ancillary, incidental, lesser, marginal, minor, secondary, subsidiary **side with** *v* = **support**, ally with, favour, go along with, take the part of
sidelong *adj* **1** = **sideways**, covert, indirect, oblique
sidestep *v* **1** = **avoid**, circumvent, dodge, duck (*inf*), evade, skirt
sidetrack *v* = **distract**, deflect, divert
sideways *adv* **1** = **obliquely**, edgeways, laterally, sidelong, to the side
sidle *v* = **edge**, creep, inch, slink, sneak, steal
siesta *n* = **nap**, catnap, doze, forty winks (*inf*), sleep, snooze (*inf*)

sieve *n* **1** = **strainer**, colander ▷ *v* **2** = **sift**, separate, strain
sift *v* **1** = **sieve**, filter, separate **2** = **examine**, analyse, go through, investigate, research, scrutinize, work over
sight *n* **1** = **vision**, eye, eyes, eyesight, seeing **3** = **view**, range of vision, visibility **4** = **spectacle**, display, exhibition, pageant, scene, show, vista **5** *Inf* = **eyesore**, mess, monstrosity ▷ *v* **9** = **spot**, behold, catch sight of, discern, distinguish, espy, glimpse, make out, observe, perceive, see
sign *n* **1** = **indication**, clue, evidence, gesture, hint, mark, proof, signal, symptom, token **2** = **symbol**, badge,

S

2 gesture, mark, or symbol conveying a meaning. **3** notice displayed to advertise, inform, or warn. **4** visible indication. **5** omen. ▷ v **6** write (one's name) on (a document or letter) to show its authenticity or one's agreement. **7** communicate using sign language. **8** make a sign or gesture. **9** engage by signing a contract. **sign language** system of communication by gestures, as used by deaf people (also **signing**). **sign on** v **1** register as unemployed. **2** sign a document committing oneself to a job, course, etc. **signpost** n **1** post bearing a sign that shows the way. ▷ v **2** mark with signposts.

signal ❶ n **1** sign or gesture to convey information. **2** sequence of electrical impulses or radio waves transmitted or received. ▷ adj **3** formal very important. ▷ v **-nalling, -nalled 4** convey (information) by signal. **signally** adv **signal box** building from which railway signals are operated. **signalman** n railwayman in charge of signals and points.

signatory [sig-na-tree] n, pl **-ries** one of the parties who sign a document.

signature n **1** person's name written by himself or herself in signing something. **2** identifying characteristic. **3** sign at the start of a piece of music to show the key or tempo. **signature tune** tune used to introduce a particular television or radio programme.

signet n small seal used to authenticate documents. **signet ring** finger ring bearing a signet.

significant ❶ adj **1** important. **2** having or expressing a meaning. **significantly** adv **significance** n.

signify ❶ v **-fying, -fied 1** indicate or suggest. **2** be a symbol or sign for. **3** be important. **signification** n meaning.

signor [see-**nyor**] n Italian term of address equivalent to sir or Mr. **signora** [see-**nyor**-a] n Italian term of address equivalent to madam or Mrs. **signorina** [see-nyor-**ee**-na] n Italian term of address equivalent to madam or Miss.

Sikh [**seek**] n member of an Indian religion having only one God. **Sikhism** n.

silage [**sile**-ij] n fodder crop harvested while green and partially fermented in a silo.

silence ❶ n **1** absence of noise or speech. **2** refusal or failure to speak or communicate. ▷ v **3** make silent. **4** put a stop to. **silent** adj **silently** adv **silencer** n device to reduce the noise of an engine exhaust or gun.

silhouette ❶ n **1** outline of a dark shape seen against a light background. **2** outline drawing of a profile. ▷ v **3** show in silhouette.

silica n hard glossy mineral found as quartz and in sandstone. **silicosis** n lung disease caused by inhaling silica dust.

---

device, emblem, logo, mark **3** = **notice**, board, placard, warning **5** = **omen**, augury, auspice, foreboding, portent, warning ▷ v **6** = **autograph**, endorse, initial, inscribe **8** = **gesture**, beckon, gesticulate, indicate, signal

signal n **1** = **sign**, beacon, cue, gesture, indication, mark, token ▷ v **4** = **gesture**, beckon, gesticulate, indicate, motion, sign, wave

significance n **1** = **importance**, consequence, moment, relevance, weight **2** = **meaning**, force, implication(s), import, message, point, purport, sense

significant adj **1** = **important**, critical, material, momentous, noteworthy, serious, vital, weighty **2** = **meaningful**, eloquent, expressive, indicative, suggestive

signify v **1, 2** = **indicate**, be a sign of, betoken, connote, denote, imply, intimate, mean, portend, suggest **3** = **matter**, be important, carry weight, count

silence n **1** = **quiet**, calm, hush, lull, peace, stillness **2** = **muteness**, dumbness, reticence, taciturnity ▷ v **3** = **quieten**, deaden, gag, muffle, quiet, stifle, still, suppress **4** = **cut off**, cut short

silent adj **1** = **quiet**, hushed, muted, noiseless, soundless, still **2** = **mute**, dumb, speechless, taciturn, voiceless, wordless

silently adv = **quietly**, inaudibly, in silence, mutely, noiselessly, soundlessly, without a sound, wordlessly

silhouette n **1** = **outline**, form, profile, shape ▷ v **3** = **outline**, etch, stand out

silicate n compound of silicon, oxygen, and a metal.

silicon n *Chemistry* brittle nonmetallic element widely used in chemistry and industry. **silicone** n tough synthetic substance made from silicon and used in lubricants, paints, and resins. **silicon chip** tiny wafer of silicon processed to form an integrated circuit.

silk ❶ n **1** fibre made by the larva (**silkworm**) of a certain moth. **2** thread or fabric made from this. **take silk** become a Queen's (or King's) Counsel. **silky**, **silken** adj of or like silk.

sill n ledge at the bottom of a window or door.

silly ❶ adj **-lier**, **-liest** foolish. **silliness** n.

silo n, pl **-los 1** pit or airtight tower for storing silage. **2** underground structure in which nuclear missiles are kept ready for launching.

silt ❶ n **1** mud deposited by moving water. ▷ v **2** (foll. by *up*) fill or be choked with silt.

silvan adj same as SYLVAN.

silver n **1** white precious metal. **2** coins or articles made of silver. ▷ adj **3** made of or of the colour of silver. ▷ v **4** coat with silver. **silvery** adj **1** like silver. **2** having a clear ringing sound. **silverbeet** n *Aust & NZ* leafy green vegetable with white stalks. **silver birch** tree with silvery-white bark. **silverfish** n small wingless silver-coloured insect. **silver medal** medal given to the runner-up in a competition or race. **silver-plated** adj covered with a thin layer of silver.

silverside n cut of beef from below the rump and above the leg.

silversmith n person who makes articles of silver. **silver wedding** twenty-fifth wedding anniversary.

silviculture n cultivation of forest trees.

sim n computer game that simulates an activity such as flying or playing a sport.

simian adj, n (of or like) a monkey or ape.

similar ❶ adj alike but not identical. **similarity** n **similarly** adv.

● **USAGE NOTE**
● Do not confuse *similar* and *same*.
● *Similar* is 'alike but not identical';
● *same* means 'identical'.

simile [**sim**-ill-ee] n figure of speech comparing one thing to another, using 'as' or 'like', e.g. *as blind as a bat*.

similitude n similarity, likeness.

simmer ❶ v **1** cook gently at just below boiling point. **2** be in a state of suppressed rage. **simmer down** v *informal* calm down.

simnel cake n fruit cake covered with marzipan.

simper ❶ v **1** smile in a silly or affected way. **2** utter (something) with a simper. ▷ n **3** simpering smile.

simple ❶ adj **1** easy to understand or do. **2** plain or unpretentious. **3** not

━━━━ **THESAURUS** ━━━━

silky, silken adj = **smooth**, sleek, velvety

silly adj = **foolish**, absurd, asinine, daft, fatuous, idiotic, inane, ridiculous, senseless, stupid, unwise

silt n **1** = **sediment**, alluvium, deposit, ooze, sludge ▷ v **2** (foll. by *up*) = **clog up**, choke up, congest

similar adj = **alike**, analogous, close, comparable, like, resembling

similarity n = **resemblance**, affinity, agreement, analogy, closeness, comparability, correspondence, likeness, sameness

simmer v **2** = **fume**, be angry, be pissed (off) (*taboo sl*), rage, seethe, smoulder

simmer down v *Inf* = **calm down**, control oneself, cool off *or* down

simper v **1** = **smile coyly**, smile affectedly, smirk

simple adj **1** = **uncomplicated**, clear, easy, intelligible, lucid, plain, straightforward, understandable, uninvolved **2** = **plain**, classic, homely, humble, modest, naked, natural, stark, unembellished, unfussy, unpretentious, unsophisticated **3** = **pure**, elementary, unalloyed, uncombined, unmixed **4** = **sincere**, artless, bald, childlike, direct, frank, guileless, honest, ingenuous, innocent, naive, natural, plain, unaffected **5** = **feeble-minded**, dumb (*inf*), foolish, half-witted, moronic, slow, stupid

simple-minded adj = **feeble-minded**, backward, dim-witted, foolish, idiot, idiotic, moronic, retarded, simple, stupid

simpleton n = **halfwit**, dullard, fool, idiot, imbecile (*inf*), moron, numskull *or* numbskull

combined or complex. **4** sincere or frank. **5** feeble-minded. **simply** adv **1** in a simple manner. **2** merely. **3** absolutely. **simplicity** n **simplify** v **-fying, -fied** make less complicated. **simplification** n **simplistic** adj too simple or naive. **simple fraction** fraction in which the numerator and denominator are whole numbers. **simple-minded** adj unsophisticated. **simpleton** n foolish or half-witted person.

simulate ❶ v **1** make a pretence of. **2** imitate the conditions of (a particular situation). **3** have the appearance of. **simulation** n **simulator** n.

simultaneous ❶ adj occurring at the same time. **simultaneity** n **simultaneously** adv.

sin¹ ❶ n **1** breaking of a religious or moral law. **2** offence against a principle or standard. ▷ v **sinning, sinned 3** commit a sin. **sinful** adj **1** guilty of sin. **2** being a sin. **sinfully** adv **sinner** n.

sin² Maths sine.

since prep **1** during the period of time after. ▷ conj **2** from the time when. **3** for the reason that. ▷ adv **4** from that time.

sincere ❶ adj without pretence or deceit. **sincerely** adv **sincerity** n.

sine n (in trigonometry) ratio of the length of the opposite side to that of the hypotenuse in a right-angled triangle.

sinecure ❶ [**sin**-ee-cure] n paid job with minimal duties.

sine die [**sin**-ay **dee**-ay] adv Latin with no date fixed for future action.

sine qua non [**sin**-ay kwah **non**] n Latin essential requirement.

sinew n **1** tough fibrous tissue joining muscle to bone. **2** muscles or strength. **sinewy** adj.

sing ❶ v **singing, sang, sung 1** make musical sounds with the voice. **2** perform (a song). **3** make a humming or whistling sound. **singer** n **singing telegram** service in which a messenger presents greetings to a person by singing. **singsong** n **1** informal singing session. ▷ adj **2** (of the voice) repeatedly rising and falling in pitch.

singe ❶ v **singeing, singed 1** burn the surface of. ▷ n **2** superficial burn.

single ❶ adj **1** one only. **2** distinct from others of the same kind. **3** unmarried. **4** designed for one user. **5** formed of only one part. **6** (of a ticket) valid for

— THESAURUS —

simplicity n **1** = **ease**, clarity, clearness, straightforwardness **2** = **plainness**, lack of adornment, purity, restraint **4** = **artlessness**, candour, directness, innocence, naivety, openness

simplify v = **make simpler**, abridge, disentangle, dumb down, reduce to essentials, streamline

simply adv **1** = **plainly**, clearly, directly, easily, intelligibly, naturally, straightforwardly, unpretentiously **2** = **just**, merely, only, purely, solely **3** = **totally**, absolutely, completely, really, utterly, wholly

simulate v **1, 2** = **pretend**, act, affect, feign, put on, sham

simultaneous adj = **coinciding**, at the same time, coincident, concurrent, contemporaneous, synchronous

simultaneously adv = **at the same time**, concurrently, together

sin¹ n **1, 2** = **wrongdoing**, crime, error, evil, guilt, iniquity, misdeed, offence, transgression ▷ v **3** = **transgress**, err, fall, go astray, lapse, offend

sincere adj = **honest**, candid, earnest, frank, genuine, guileless, heartfelt, real, serious, true, unaffected

sincerely adv = **honestly**, earnestly, genuinely, in earnest, seriously, truly, wholeheartedly

sincerity n = **honesty**, candour, frankness, genuineness, seriousness, truth

sinecure n = **cushy number** (inf), gravy train (sl), money for jam or old rope (inf), soft job (inf), soft option

sinful adj **1** = **wicked**, bad, corrupt, criminal, erring, guilty, immoral, iniquitous

sing v **1, 2** = **warble**, carol, chant, chirp, croon, pipe, trill, yodel **3** = **hum**, buzz, purr, whine

singe v **1** = **burn**, char, scorch, sear

singer n = **vocalist**, balladeer, chorister, crooner, minstrel, soloist

single adj **1** = **one**, individual, lone, only, separate, sole, solitary **2** = **individual**, distinct, exclusive, separate, undivided, unshared **3** = **unmarried**, free, unattached,

S

an outward journey only. ▷ *n* **7** single thing. **8** thing intended for one person. **9** record with one short song or tune on each side. **10** single ticket. ▷ *pl* **11** game between two players. ▷ *v* **12** (foll. by *out*) pick out from others. **singly** *adv* **single-breasted** *adj* (of a garment) having only slightly overlapping fronts and one row of buttons. **single file** (of people or things) arranged in one line. **single-handed** *adj* without assistance. **single-minded** *adj* having one aim only.

singlet *n* sleeveless vest.

singular ❶ *adj* **1** (of a word or form) denoting one person or thing. **2** remarkable, unusual. ▷ *n* **3** singular form of a word. **singularity** *n* **singularly** *adv*.

Sinhalese, Singhalese *n, adj* (member or language) of a people living mainly in Sri Lanka.

sinister ❶ *adj* threatening or suggesting evil or harm.

sink ❶ *v* **sinking, sank, sunk** *or* **sunken 1** submerge (in liquid). **2** descend or cause to descend. **3** decline in value or amount. **4** become weaker in health. **5** seep or penetrate. **6** dig or drill (a hole or shaft). **7** invest (money). **8** *Golf, Snooker* hit (a ball) into a hole or pocket. ▷ *n* **9** fixed basin with a water supply and drainage pipe. **sinker** *n* weight for a fishing line. **sink in** *v* penetrate the mind. **sinking fund** money set aside regularly to repay a long-term debt.

Sino- *combining form* Chinese.

sinuous *adj* **1** curving. **2** lithe. **sinuously** *adv*.

sinus [**sine**-uss] *n* hollow space in a bone, esp. an air passage opening into the nose. **sinusitis** *n* inflammation of a sinus membrane.

sip ❶ *v* **sipping, sipped 1** drink in small mouthfuls. ▷ *n* **2** amount sipped.

siphon *n* **1** bent tube which uses air pressure to draw liquid from a container. ▷ *v* **2** draw off thus. **3** redirect (resources).

sir *n* **1** polite term of address for a man. **2** (**S-**) title of a knight or baronet.

sire *n* **1** male parent of a horse or other domestic animal. **2** respectful term of address to a king. ▷ *v* **3** father.

siren *n* **1** device making a loud wailing noise as a warning. **2** dangerously alluring woman.

sirloin *n* prime cut of loin of beef.

sirocco *n, pl* **-cos** hot wind blowing from N Africa into S Europe.

sis *interj* S Afr informal exclamation of disgust.

sisal [**size**-al] *n* (fibre of) plant used in making ropes.

siskin *n* yellow-and-black finch.

sissy ❶ *adj, n, pl* **-sies** weak or cowardly (person).

sister *n* **1** girl or woman with the same parents as another person. **2** female fellow-member of a group. **3** senior nurse. **4** nun. ▷ *adj* **5** closely related, similar. **sisterhood** *n* **1** state of being

---

unwed **5 = simple**, unblended, unmixed ▷ *v* **12** (foll. by *out*) **= pick**, choose, distinguish, fix on, pick on *or* out, select, separate, set apart

single-minded *adj* **= determined**, dedicated, dogged, fixed, unswerving

singly *adv* **= one by one**, individually, one at a time, separately

singular *adj* **1 = single**, individual, separate, sole **2 a = remarkable**, eminent, exceptional, notable, noteworthy, outstanding **b = unusual**, curious, eccentric, extraordinary, munted (*NZ sl*), odd, peculiar, queer, strange

singularly *adv* **a = remarkably**, especially, exceptionally, notably, outstandingly, particularly **b = unusually**, uncommonly

sinister *adj* **= threatening**, dire, disquieting, evil, malign, menacing, ominous

sink *v* **1 = submerge**, founder, go under **2 = descend**, dip, drop, fall, go down, lower, plunge, subside **3 = fall**, abate, collapse, drop, lapse, slip, subside **4 = decline**, decay, decrease, deteriorate, diminish, dwindle, fade, fail, flag, lessen, weaken, worsen **6 = dig**, bore, drill, drive, excavate

sink in *v* **= be understood**, get through to, penetrate, register (*inf*)

sip *v* **1 = drink**, sample, sup, taste ▷ *n* **2 = swallow**, drop, taste, thimbleful

sissy *adj* **= wimpish** *or* **wimpy**, cowardly, effeminate, feeble, namby-pamby, soft (*inf*), unmanly, weak, wet (*Brit inf*) ▷ *n* **= wimp**, coward, milksop, mummy's boy, namby-pamby, softie (*inf*), weakling, wet (*Brit inf*)

S

a sister. **2** group of women united by common aims or beliefs. **sisterly** *adj* **sister-in-law** *n*, *pl* **sisters-in-law 1** sister of one's husband or wife. **2** wife of one's sibling.

sit ❶ *v* **sitting, sat 1** rest one's body upright on the buttocks. **2** cause to sit. **3** perch. **4** (of a bird) incubate (eggs) by sitting on them. **5** be situated. **6** pose for a portrait. **7** occupy an official position. **8** (of an official body) hold a session. **9** fit or hang as specified. **10** take (an examination). **sit tight** *informal* wait patiently without taking action. **sitter** *n* **1** baby-sitter. **2** person posing for a picture. **sitting** *n* **1** time when a meal is served. **2** meeting of an official body. ▷ *adj* **3** current. **4** seated. **sitting room** room in a house where people sit and relax. **sit down** *v* (cause to) adopt a sitting posture. **sit-in** *n* protest in which demonstrators occupy a place and refuse to move. **sit on** *v informal* delay action on. **sit out** *v* endure to the end.

sitar *n* Indian stringed musical instrument.

sitcom *n informal* situation comedy.

site ❶ *n* **1** place where something is, was, or is intended to be located. ▷ *n* **2** same as WEBSITE. ▷ *v* **3** provide with a site.

situate ❶ *v* place. **situation** *n* **1** state of affairs. **2** location and surroundings. **3** position of employment. **situation comedy** radio or television series involving the same characters in various situations.

six *adj*, *n* one more than five. **sixth** *adj*, *n* (of) number six in a series. **sixteen** *adj*, *n* six and ten. **sixteenth** *adj*, *n* **sixty** *adj*, *n* six times ten. **sixtieth** *adj*, *n* **sixpence** *n* former British coin worth

six pennies. **sixth sense** perception beyond the five senses.

size¹ ❶ *n* **1** dimensions, bigness. **2** one of a series of standard measurements of goods. ▷ *v* **3** arrange according to size. **sizeable, sizable** *adj* quite large. **size up** *v informal* assess.

size² *n* **1** gluey substance used as a protective coating. ▷ *v* **2** treat with size.

sizzle ❶ *v* **1** make a hissing sound like frying fat. ▷ *n* **2** hissing sound.

SK Saskatchewan.

skanky *adj slang* dirty or unattractive.

skate¹ *n* **1** boot with a steel blade or sets of wheels attached to the sole for gliding over ice or a hard surface. ▷ *v* **2** glide on or as if on skates. **skateboard** *n* board mounted on small wheels for riding on while standing up. **skate over, round** *v* avoid discussing or dealing with (a matter) fully.

skate² *n* large marine flatfish.

skean-dhu *n* dagger worn in the stocking as part of the Highland dress.

skedaddle *v informal* run off.

skein *n* **1** yarn wound in a loose coil. **2** flock of geese in flight.

skeleton ❶ *n* **1** framework of bones inside a person's or animal's body. **2** essential framework of a structure. **3** skinny person or animal. **4** outline of bare essentials. ▷ *adj* **5** reduced to a minimum. **skeletal** *adj* **skeleton key** key which can open many different locks.

skerry *n*, *pl* **-ries** rocky island or reef.

sketch ❶ *n* **1** rough drawing. **2** brief description. **3** short humorous play. ▷ *v* **4** make a sketch (of). **sketchy** *adj* incomplete or inadequate. **sketch out** *v* make a brief description of.

————————————————————— THESAURUS —————

sit *v* **1-3, 5** = **rest**, perch, settle **7** = **officiate**, preside **8** = **convene**, assemble, deliberate, meet

site *n* **1** = **location**, place, plot, position, setting, spot ▷ *v* **3** = **locate**, install, place, position, set, situate

situation *n* **1** = **state of affairs**, case, circumstances, condition, equation, plight, state **2** = **location**, place, position, setting, site, spot **3** = **job**, employment, office, place, position, post

size¹ *n* **1** = **dimensions**, amount, bulk, extent, immensity, magnitude, mass,

proportions, range, volume

sizeable, sizable *adj* = **large**, considerable, decent, goodly, largish, respectable, substantial

size up *v Inf* = **assess**, appraise, evaluate, take stock of

sizzle *v* **1** = **hiss**, crackle, frizzle, fry, spit

skeleton *n* **2** = **framework**, frame, outline, structure **4** = **bare bones**, draft, sketch

sketch *n* **1** = **drawing**, delineation, design, draft, outline, plan ▷ *v* **4** = **draw**, delineate, depict, draft, outline, represent, rough out

S

skew v **1** make slanting or crooked. ▷ adj **2** slanting or crooked. **skewed** adj distorted or biased because of lack of information. **skewwhiff** adj informal slanting or crooked.

skewbald n, adj (horse) marked with patches of white and another colour.

skewer n **1** pin to hold meat together during cooking. ▷ v **2** fasten with a skewer.

ski n **1** one of a pair of long runners fastened to boots for gliding over snow or water. ▷ v **skiing**, **skied** or **ski'd 2** travel on skis. **skier** n.

skid v **skidding**, **skidded 1** (of a moving vehicle) slide sideways uncontrollably. ▷ n **2** skidding. **skid row** US slang dilapidated part of a city frequented by down-and-outs.

skiff n small boat.

skill ❶ n **1** special ability or expertise. **2** something requiring special training or expertise. **skilful** adj having or showing skill. **skilfully** adv **skilled** adj.

● **SPELLING TIP**
● When you make an adjective
● from **skill**, you should drop an l to
● make **skilful**. This is not the case
● in American English, and this is
● probably why there are over 100
● examples of skillful in the Bank of
● English.

skillet n small frying pan or shallow cooking pot.

skim ❶ v **skimming**, **skimmed 1** remove floating matter from the surface of (a liquid). **2** glide smoothly over. **3** throw across a surface. **4** read quickly. **skimmed**, **skim milk** milk from which the cream has been removed.

skimp ❶ v not invest enough time, money, material, etc. **skimpy** adj scanty or insufficient.

skin ❶ n **1** outer covering of the body. **2** complexion. **3** outer layer or covering. **4** film on a liquid. **5** animal skin used as a material or container. ▷ v **skinning**, **skinned 6** remove the skin of. **7** graze. **8** slang swindle. **skinless** adj **skinny** adj thin. **skindeep** adj superficial. **skin diving** underwater swimming using flippers and light breathing apparatus. **skindiver** n **skinflint** n miser. **skinhead** n youth with very short hair. **skintight** adj fitting tightly over the body.

skint adj slang having no money.

skip¹ ❶ v **skipping**, **skipped 1** leap lightly from one foot to the other. **2** jump over a rope as it is swung under one. **3** informal pass over, omit. **4** change quickly from one subject to another. ▷ n **5** skipping.

skip² n **1** large open container for builders' rubbish. **2** cage used as a lift in mines.

skipper n, v captain.

skirl n sound of bagpipes.

skirmish ❶ n **1** brief or minor fight or argument. ▷ v **2** take part in a skirmish.

skirt ❶ n **1** woman's garment hanging from the waist. **2** part of a dress or coat below the waist. **3** circular hanging part. **4** cut of beef from the flank. ▷ v **5** border. **6** go round. **7** avoid dealing with (an issue).

THESAURUS

sketchy adj = **incomplete**, cursory, inadequate, perfunctory, rough, scrappy, skimpy, superficial

skilful adj = **expert**, able, adept, adroit, clever, competent, dexterous, masterly, practised, professional, proficient, skilled

skill n **1** = **expertise**, ability, art, cleverness, competence, craft, dexterity, facility, knack, proficiency, skilfulness, talent, technique

skim v **1** = **separate**, cream **2** = **glide**, coast, float, fly, sail, soar **4** = **scan**, glance, run one's eye over

skimp v = **stint**, be mean with, be sparing with, cut corners, scamp, scrimp

skin n **3** = **coating**, casing, crust, film, husk, outside, peel, rind **5** = **hide**, fell, pelt ▷ v **6** = **peel**, flay, scrape

skinflint n = **miser**, meanie or meany (inf, chiefly Brit), niggard, pennypincher (inf), Scrooge

skinny adj = **thin**, emaciated, lean, scrawny, undernourished

skip¹ v **1** = **hop**, bob, bounce, caper, dance, flit, frisk, gambol, prance, trip **3** Inf = **pass over**, eschew, give (something) a miss, leave out, miss out, omit

skirmish n **1** = **fight**, battle, brush, clash, conflict, encounter, fracas, scrap (inf) ▷ v **2** = **fight**, clash, collide

skirt v **5** = **border**, edge, flank **6**, **7** = **avoid**, circumvent, evade, steer clear of

skirting board narrow board round the bottom of an interior wall.

skit ❶ *n* brief satirical sketch.

skite *v, n Aust & NZ* boast.

skittish ❶ *adj* **1** playful or lively. **2** (of a horse) easily frightened.

skittle *n* **1** bottle-shaped object used as a target in some games. ▷ *pl* **2** game in which players try to knock over skittles by rolling a ball at them.

skive ❶ *v informal* evade work or responsibility.

skivvy *n, pl* **-vies** female servant who does menial work.

skookum ❶ *adj Canad* powerful or big.

skua *n* large predatory gull.

skulduggery ❶ *n informal* trickery.

skulk ❶ *v* **1** move stealthily. **2** lurk.

skull *n* **1** bony framework of the head. **2** *informal* brain or mind. **skullcap** *n* close-fitting brimless cap.

skunk *n* **1** small black-and-white N American mammal which emits a foul-smelling fluid when attacked. **2** *slang* despicable person.

sky ❶ *n, pl* **skies 1** upper atmosphere as seen from the earth. ▷ *v* **skying, skied 2** *informal* hit high in the air. **skydiving** *n* sport of jumping from an aircraft and performing manoeuvres before opening one's parachute. **skylark** *n* lark that sings while soaring at a great height. **skylight** *n* window in a roof or ceiling. **skyline** *n* outline of buildings, trees, etc. against the sky. **skyscraper** *n* very tall building.

slab ❶ *n* broad flat piece.

slack¹ ❶ *adj* **1** not tight. **2** negligent. **3** (of water) moving slowly. **4** not busy. ▷ *n* **5** slack part. **6** slack period. ▷ *pl* **7** informal trousers. ▷ *v* **8** neglect one's work or duty. **9** loosen or slacken. **slackness** *n* **slacken** *v* make or become slack. **slacker** *n*.

slack² *n* coal dust or small pieces of coal.

slag ❶ *n* **1** waste left after metal is smelted. **2** *Brit slang* a sexually immoral woman. ▷ *v* **slagging, slagged 3** (foll. by *off*) *slang* criticize. **slag heap** pile of waste from smelting or mining.

slain *v* past participle of SLAY.

slake ❶ *v* **1** satisfy (thirst or desire). **2** combine (quicklime) with water.

slalom *n* skiing or canoeing race over a winding course.

slam ❶ *v* **slamming, slammed 1** shut, put down, or hit violently and noisily. **2** *informal* criticize harshly. ▷ *n* **3** act or sound of slamming. **grand slam** see GRAND.

slander ❶ *n* **1** false and malicious statement about a person. **2** crime of making such a statement. ▷ *v* **3** utter slander about. **slanderous** *adj*.

slang *n* very informal language. **slangy** *adj* **slanging match** abusive argument.

———————————— THESAURUS ————————————

skit *n* = **parody**, burlesque, sketch, spoof (*inf*), takeoff (*inf*)

skittish *adj* **1** = **lively**, wired (*sl*) **2** = **nervous**, excitable, fidgety, highly strung, jumpy, restive

skive *v Inf* = **slack**, idle, malinger, shirk, swing the lead

skookum *adj Canad* = **powerful**, influential, big, dominant, controlling, commanding, supreme, prevailing, authoritative

skulduggery *n Inf* = **trickery**, double-dealing, duplicity, machinations, underhandedness

skulk *v* **1** = **sneak**, creep, prowl, slink **2** = **lurk**, lie in wait, loiter

sky *n* **1** = **heavens**, firmament

slab *n* = **piece**, chunk, lump, portion, slice, wedge

slack¹ *adj* **1** = **loose**, baggy, lax, limp, relaxed **2** = **negligent**, lax, neglectful, remiss, slapdash, slipshod **3** = **slow**, quiet, slow-moving, sluggish **4** = **inactive**, idle, lazy ▷ *n* **5** = **room**, excess, give (*inf*), leeway ▷ *v* **8** = **shirk**, dodge, idle, skive (*Brit sl*)

slacken *v* = **lessen**, abate, decrease, diminish, drop off, moderate, reduce, relax

slacker *n* = **layabout**, dodger, idler, loafer, piker (*Aust & NZ sl*), shirker, skiver (*Brit sl*)

slag *v* **3** (foll. by *off*) *Sl* = **criticize**, abuse, deride, insult, malign, mock, slander, slate

slake *v* **1** = **satisfy**, assuage, quench, sate

slam *v* **1 a** = **bang**, crash, smash **b** = **throw**, dash, fling, hurl

slander *n* **1** = **defamation**, calumny, libel, scandal, smear ▷ *v* **3** = **defame**, blacken (someone's) name, libel, malign, smear

slanderous *adj* = **defamatory**, damaging, libellous, malicious

slant ❶ v 1 lean at an angle, slope.
2 present (information) in a biased
way. ▷ n 3 slope. 4 point of view, esp.
a biased one. **slanting** adj.

slap ❶ n 1 blow with the open hand or a
flat object. ▷ v **slapping**, **slapped**
2 strike with the open hand or a flat
object. 3 informal place forcefully or
carelessly. **slapdash** adj careless and
hasty. **slap-happy** adj informal
cheerfully careless. **slapstick** n
boisterous knockabout comedy. **slap-
up** adj (of a meal) large and luxurious.

slash ❶ v 1 cut with a sweeping stroke.
2 gash. 3 reduce drastically.
4 criticize harshly. ▷ n 5 sweeping
stroke. 6 gash.

slat n narrow strip of wood or metal.

slate¹ n 1 rock which splits easily into
thin layers. 2 piece of this for covering
a roof or, formerly, for writing on. ▷ v
3 cover with slates. 4 US plan or
arrange. ▷ adj 5 dark grey.

slate² ❶ v informal criticize harshly.
slating n.

slattern n old-fashioned slovenly
woman. **slatternly** adj.

slaughter ❶ v 1 kill (animals) for food.
2 kill (people) savagely or
indiscriminately. ▷ n 3 slaughtering.
slaughterhouse n place where

animals are killed for food.

Slav n member of any of the peoples of
E Europe or the former Soviet Union
who speak a Slavonic language.
Slavonic n 1 language group
including Russian, Polish, and Czech.
▷ adj 2 of this language group.

slave ❶ n 1 person owned by another for
whom he or she has to work. 2 person
dominated by another or by a habit.
3 drudge. ▷ v 4 work like a slave. **slaver**
n person or ship engaged in the slave
trade. **slavery** n 1 state or condition of
being a slave. 2 practice of owning
slaves. **slavish** adj 1 of or like a slave.
2 imitative. **slave-driver** n person who
makes others work very hard.

slaver [slav-ver] v 1 dribble saliva from
the mouth. ▷ n 2 saliva dribbling from
the mouth.

slay ❶ v **slaying**, **slew**, **slain** kill.

sleazy ❶ adj **-zier**, **-ziest** run-down or
sordid. **sleaze** n.

sledge¹, **sled** n 1 carriage on runners
for sliding on snow. 2 light wooden
frame for sliding over snow. ▷ v
3 travel by sledge.

sledge², **sledgehammer** n heavy
hammer with a long handle.

sleek ❶ adj 1 glossy, smooth, and shiny.
2 elegantly dressed.

slant v 1 = **slope**, bend, bevel, cant,
heel, incline, lean, list, tilt 2 = **bias**,
angle, colour, distort, twist ▷ n
3 = **slope**, camber, gradient, incline,
tilt 4 = **bias**, angle, emphasis, one-
sidedness, point of view, prejudice

slanting adj = **sloping**, angled, at an
angle, bent, diagonal, inclined,
oblique, tilted, tilting

slap n 1 = **smack**, blow, cuff, spank,
swipe ▷ v 2 = **smack**, clap, cuff, spank,
swipe

slapdash adj = **careless**, clumsy, hasty,
hurried, messy, slipshod, sloppy (inf),
untidy

slap-up adj = **luxurious**, lavish,
magnificent, splendid, sumptuous,
superb

slash v 1, 2 = **cut**, gash, hack, lacerate,
rend, rip, score, slit 3 = **reduce**, cut,
drop, lower ▷ n 6 = **cut**, gash, incision,
laceration, rent, rip, slit

slate² v Inf = **criticize**, censure,
rebuke, rouse on (Aust), scold, tear
into (inf)

slaughter v 2 = **slay**, butcher, kill,

massacre, murder ▷ n 3 = **slaying**,
bloodshed, butchery, carnage, killing,
massacre, murder

slaughterhouse n = **abattoir**,
butchery

slave n 1 = **servant**, serf, vassal
3 = **drudge**, skivvy (chiefly Brit) ▷ v
4 = **toil**, drudge, slog

slavery n 1 = **servitude**, bondage,
captivity 2 = **enslavement**,
subjugation

slavish adj 1 = **servile**, abject, base,
cringing, fawning, grovelling,
obsequious, submissive, sycophantic
2 = **imitative**, second-hand,
unimaginative, unoriginal

slay v = **kill**, butcher, massacre, mow
down, murder, slaughter

sleaze n = **corruption**, bribery,
dishonesty, extortion, fraud,
unscrupulousness, venality

sleazy adj = **sordid**, disreputable, low,
run-down, scungy (Aust & NZ sl),
seedy, squalid

sleek adj 1 = **glossy**, lustrous, shiny,
smooth

S

sleep ⊕ *n* **1** state of rest characterized by unconsciousness. **2** period of this. ▷ *v* **sleeping**, **slept** **3** be in or as if in a state of sleep. **4** have sleeping accommodation for (a specified number). **sleeper** *n* **1** railway car fitted for sleeping in. **2** beam supporting the rails of a railway. **3** ring worn in a pierced ear to stop the hole from closing up. **4** person who sleeps. **sleepy** *adj* **1** needing sleep. **2** without activity or bustle. **sleepily** *adv* **sleepiness** *n* **sleepless** *adj* **sleep in** *v* sleep longer than usual. **sleeping bag** padded bag for sleeping in. **sleeping partner** business partner who does not play an active role. **sleeping sickness** African disease spread by the tsetse fly. **sleepout** *n* NZ small building for sleeping in. **sleepover** *n chiefly US* occasion when a person stays overnight at a friend's house. **sleepwalk** *v* walk while asleep. **sleepwalker** *n* **sleep with, together** *v* have sexual intercourse (with).

sleet *n* **1** rain and snow or hail falling together. ▷ *v* **2** fall as sleet.

sleeve *n* **1** part of a garment which covers the arm. **2** tubelike cover. **3** gramophone record cover. **up one's sleeve** secretly ready. **sleeveless** *adj*.

sleigh *n*, *v* sledge.

sleight of hand [**slite**] *n* skilful use of the hands when performing conjuring tricks.

slender ⊕ *adj* **1** slim. **2** small in amount.

slept *v* past of SLEEP.

sleuth ⊕ [**slooth**] *n* detective.

slew¹ *v* past tense of SLAY.

slew² *v* twist or swing round.

slice ⊕ *n* **1** thin flat piece cut from something. **2** share. **3** kitchen tool with a broad flat blade. **4** *Sport* hitting of a ball so that it travels obliquely. ▷ *v* **5** cut into slices. **6** cut (through). **7** *Sport* hit (a ball) with a slice.

slick ⊕ *adj* **1** persuasive and glib. **2** skilfully devised or carried out. **3** well-made and attractive, but superficial. ▷ *n* **4** patch of oil on water. ▷ *v* **5** make smooth or sleek.

slide ⊕ *v* **sliding**, **slid** **1** slip smoothly along (a surface). **2** pass unobtrusively. **3** go into or become (something) by degrees, e.g. *the states slid into barbarism.* ▷ *n* **4** sliding. **5** piece of glass holding an object to be viewed under a microscope. **6** photographic transparency. **7** surface or structure for sliding on or down. **8** ornamental hair clip. **9** sliding curved part of a trombone. **slide rule** mathematical instrument formerly used for rapid calculations. **sliding scale** variable scale according to which things such as wages alter in response to changes in other factors.

slight ⊕ *adj* **1** small in quantity or extent. **2** not important. **3** slim and delicate. ▷ *v*, *n* **4** snub. **slightly** *adv*.

slim ⊕ *adj* **slimmer**, **slimmest** **1** not heavy or stout, thin. **2** slight. ▷ *v* **slimming**, **slimmed** **3** make or become slim by diet and exercise. **slimmer** *n*.

slime ⊕ *n* unpleasant thick slippery substance. **slimy** *adj* **slimier**,

━━━━━━━━━━━━━━━━━━━━━━━━━━ THESAURUS ━━━━━

S

sleep *n* **1, 2** = **slumber(s)**, doze, forty winks (*inf*), hibernation, nap, siesta, snooze (*inf*), zizz (*Brit inf*) ▷ *v* **3** = **slumber**, catnap, doze, drowse, hibernate, snooze (*inf*), take a nap

sleepless *adj* = **wakeful**, insomniac, restless

sleepy *adj* **1** = **drowsy**, dull, heavy **2** = **inactive**, lethargic, sluggish

slender *adj* **1** = **slim**, lean, narrow, slight, willowy **2** = **meagre**, little, scant, scanty, small

sleuth *n* = **detective**, private eye (*inf*), (private) investigator

slice *n* **1, 2** = **piece**, cut, helping, portion, segment, share, sliver, wedge ▷ *v* **5, 6** = **cut**, carve, divide, sever

slick *adj* **1** = **glib**, plausible, polished,

smooth, specious **2** = **skilful**, adroit, deft, dexterous, polished, professional ▷ *v* **5** = **smooth**, plaster down, sleek

slide *v* **1** = **slip**, coast, glide, skim, slither

slight *adj* **2** = **small**, feeble, insignificant, meagre, measly, minor, paltry, scanty, trifling, trivial, unimportant **3** = **slim**, delicate, feeble, fragile, lightly-built, small, spare ▷ *v*, *n* **4** = **snub**, affront, disdain, ignore, insult, rebuff, scorn, slap in the face (*inf*)

slightly *adv* **1** = **a little**, somewhat

slim *adj* **1** = **slender**, lean, narrow, slight, svelte, thin, trim **2** = **slight**, faint, poor, remote, slender ▷ *v* **3** = **lose weight**, diet, reduce

slimiest 1 of, like, or covered with slime. **2** ingratiating.

sling¹ ❶ *n* **1** bandage hung from the neck to support an injured hand or arm. **2** rope or strap for lifting something. **3** strap with a string at each end for throwing a stone. ▷ *v* **slinging, slung 4** throw. **5** carry, hang, or throw with or as if with a sling. **slingback** *n* shoe with a strap that goes around the back of the heel.

**sling² ** *n* sweetened drink with a spirit base, e.g. *gin sling*.

slink ❶ *v* **slinking, slunk** move furtively or guiltily. **slinky** *adj* **slinkier, slinkiest** (of clothes) figure-hugging.

slip¹ ❶ *v* **slipping, slipped 1** lose balance by sliding. **2** move smoothly, easily, or quietly. **3** place quickly or stealthily. **4** (foll. by *on* or *off*) put on or take off easily or quickly. **5** pass out of (the mind). **6** become worse. **7** dislocate (a bone). ▷ *n* **8** slipping. **9** mistake. **10** petticoat. **11** *Cricket* fielding position behind and to the offside of the wicketkeeper. **give someone the slip** escape from someone. **slippy** *adj informal* slippery. **slipknot** *n* knot tied so that it will slip along the rope round which it is made. **slip-on** *adj* (of a garment or shoe) made to be put on easily. **slipped disc** painful condition in which one of the

discs connecting the bones of the spine becomes displaced. **slip road** narrow road giving access to a motorway. **slipshod** *adj* (of an action) careless. **slipstream** *n* stream of air forced backwards by a fast-moving object. **slip up** *v* make a mistake. **slipway** *n* launching slope on which ships are built or repaired.

slip² ❶ *n* **1** small piece (of paper). **2** cutting from a plant. **3** slender person.

slip³ *n* clay mixed with water used for decorating pottery.

slipper *n* light shoe for indoor wear.

slippery ❶ *adj* **1** so smooth or wet as to cause slipping or be difficult to hold. **2** (of a person) untrustworthy.

slit ❶ *n* **1** long narrow cut or opening. ▷ *v* **slitting, slit 2** make a long straight cut in.

slither ❶ *v* **1** slide unsteadily. **2** move in a twisting way.

sliver ❶ [sliv-ver] *n* **1** small thin piece. ▷ *v* **2** cut into slivers.

slob ❶ *n informal* lazy and untidy person. **slobbish** *adj*.

slobber ❶ *v* **1** dribble or drool. **2** behave in a gushy way. **slobbery** *adj*.

sloe *n* sour blue-black fruit.

slog ❶ *v* **slogging, slogged 1** work hard and steadily. **2** make one's way with difficulty. **3** hit hard. ▷ *n* **4** long and exhausting work or walk.

slimy *adj* **1** = **viscous**, clammy, glutinous, oozy **2** = **obsequious**, creeping, grovelling, oily, servile, smarmy (*Brit inf*), unctuous

sling¹ *v* **4** = **throw**, cast, chuck (*inf*), fling, heave, hurl, lob (*inf*), shy, toss **5** = **hang**, dangle, suspend

slink *v* = **creep**, prowl, skulk, slip, sneak, steal

slinky *adj* = **figure-hugging**, clinging, close-fitting, skintight

slip¹ *v* **1** = **fall**, skid **2** = **slide**, glide, skate, slither **3** = **sneak**, conceal, creep, hide, steal ▷ *n* **9** = **mistake**, blunder, error, failure, fault, lapse, omission, oversight **give someone the slip** = **escape from**, dodge, elude, evade, get away from, lose (someone) **slip up** *v* = **make a mistake**, blunder, err, miscalculate

slip² *n* **1** = **strip**, piece, sliver **2** = **cutting**, offshoot, runner, scion, shoot, sprig, sprout

slippery *adj* **1** = **smooth**, glassy,

greasy, icy, slippy (*inf*), unsafe **2** = **untrustworthy**, crafty, cunning, devious, dishonest, evasive, shifty, tricky

slipshod *adj* = **careless**, casual, slapdash, sloppy (*inf*), slovenly, untidy

slit *n* **1** = **cut**, gash, incision, opening, rent, split, tear ▷ *v* **2** = **cut (open)**, gash, knife, lance, pierce, rip, slash

slither *v* **1** = **slide**, glide, slink, slip **2** = **undulate**, snake

sliver *n* **1** = **shred**, fragment, paring, shaving, splinter

slob *n Inf* = **layabout**, couch potato (*sl*), good-for-nothing, idler, loafer, lounger

slobber *v* **1** = **drool**, dribble, drivel, salivate, slaver

slobbish *adj Inf* = **messy**, slovenly, unclean, unkempt, untidy

slog *v* **1** = **work**, labour, plod, plough through, slave, toil **2** = **trudge**, tramp, trek **3** = **hit**, punch, slug, sock (*sl*), strike, thump, wallop (*inf*)

S

slogan ❶ *n* catchword or phrase used in politics or advertising.

sloop *n* small single-masted ship.

slop ❶ *v* **slopping, slopped 1** splash or spill. ▷ *n* **2** spilt liquid. **3** liquid food. ▷ *pl* **4** liquid refuse and waste food used to feed animals. **sloppy** *adj* **-pier, -piest 1** careless or untidy. **2** gushingly sentimental.

slope ❶ *v* **1** slant. ▷ *n* **2** sloping surface. **3** degree of inclination. ▷ *pl* **4** hills. **slope off** *v informal* go furtively.

slosh *v* **1** pour carelessly. **2** splash carelessly. **3** *slang* hit hard. ▷ *n* **4** splashing sound. **sloshed** *adj slang* drunk.

slot ❶ *n* **1** narrow opening for inserting something. **2** *informal* place in a series or scheme. ▷ *v* **slotting, slotted 3** make a slot or slots in. **4** fit into a slot. **slot machine** automatic machine worked by placing a coin in a slot.

sloth ❶ [rhymes with **both**] *n* **1** slow-moving animal of tropical America. **2** laziness. **slothful** *adj* lazy or idle.

slouch ❶ *v* **1** sit, stand, or move with a drooping posture. ▷ *n* **2** drooping posture. **be no slouch** *informal* be very good or talented.

slough¹ [rhymes with **now**] *n* bog.

slough² [**sluff**] *v* **1** (of a snake) shed (its skin) or (of a skin) be shed. ▷ *n* **2** outer covering that has been shed. **slough off** *v* get rid of (something unwanted

or unnecessary).

Slovak *adj, n* **1** (person) from Slovakia. ▷ *n* **2** language of Slovakia.

sloven ❶ *n* habitually dirty or untidy person. **slovenly** *adj* **1** dirty or untidy. **2** careless.

Slovene *adj, n* **1** (also **Slovenian**) (person) from Slovenia. ▷ *n* **2** language of Slovenia.

slovenly ❶ *adj* **1** dirty or untidy. **2** careless.

slow ❶ *adj* **1** taking a longer time than is usual or expected. **2** not fast. **3** (of a clock or watch) showing a time earlier than the correct one. **4** stupid. **5** dull or uninteresting. ▷ *adv* **6** slowly. ▷ *v* **7** reduce the speed (of). **slowly** *adv* **slowness** *n* **slowcoach** *n informal* person who moves or works slowly. **slow motion** movement on film made to appear much slower than it actually is.

slowworm *n* small legless lizard.

sludge ❶ *n* **1** thick mud. **2** sewage.

slug¹ ❶ *n* land snail with no shell. **sluggish** *adj* slow-moving, lacking energy. **sluggishly** *adv* **sluggishness** *n* **sluggard** *n* lazy person.

slug² *n* **1** bullet. **2** *informal* mouthful of an alcoholic drink.

slug³ *v* **slugging, slugged 1** hit hard. ▷ *n* **2** heavy blow.

sluice *n* **1** channel carrying off water. **2** sliding gate used to control the flow

──────────────────────────────── THESAURUS ──────────

▷ *n* **4 a** = **labour**, effort, exertion, struggle **b** = **trudge**, hike, tramp, trek

slogan *n* = **catch phrase**, catchword, motto, tag-line

slop *v* **1** = **spill**, overflow, slosh (*inf*), splash

slope *v* **1** = **slant**, drop away, fall, incline, lean, rise, tilt ▷ *n* **2** = **incline**, ramp, rise, slant, tilt **3** = **inclination**, gradient **slope off** *v Inf* = **slink away**, creep away, slip away

sloppy *adj* **1** *Inf* = **careless**, messy, slipshod, slovenly, untidy **2** = **sentimental**, gushing, icky (*inf*), mawkish, slushy (*inf*), soppy (*Brit inf*)

slot *n* **1** = **opening**, aperture, groove, hole, slit, vent **2** *Inf* = **place**, opening, position, space, time, vacancy ▷ *v* **4** = **fit in**, fit, insert

sloth *n* **2** = **laziness**, idleness, inactivity, inertia, slackness, sluggishness, torpor

slothful *adj* = **lazy**, idle, inactive,

indolent, skiving (*Brit sl*), workshy

slouch *v* **1** = **slump**, droop, loll, stoop

slovenly *adj* **1** = **untidy**, disorderly **2** = **careless**, negligent, slack, slapdash, slipshod, sloppy (*inf*)

slow *adj* **1** = **late**, backward, behind, delayed, lingering, long-drawn-out, prolonged, protracted, tardy **2** = **unhurried**, dawdling, gradual, lackadaisical, laggard, lazy, leisurely, ponderous, sluggish **4** = **stupid**, braindead (*inf*), dense, dim, dozy (*Brit inf*), dull-witted, obtuse, retarded, thick ▷ *v* **7** = **reduce speed**, brake, decelerate, handicap, hold up, retard, slacken (off)

slowly *adv* = **gradually**, leisurely, unhurriedly

sludge *n* **1** = **sediment**, mire, muck, mud, ooze, residue, silt, slime

sluggish *adj* = **inactive**, dull, heavy, indolent, inert, lethargic, slothful, slow, torpid

S

of water in this. **3** water controlled by a sluice. ▷ v **4** pour a stream of water over or through.

slum ❶ n **1** squalid overcrowded house or area. ▷ v **slumming**, **slummed** **2** temporarily and deliberately experience poorer places or conditions than usual. **slummy** adj.

slumber ❶ v, n lit sleep.

slump ❶ v **1** (of prices or demand) decline suddenly. **2** sink or fall heavily. ▷ n **3** sudden decline in prices or demand. **4** time of substantial unemployment.

slung v past of SLING¹.

slunk v past of SLINK.

slur ❶ v **slurring**, **slurred** **1** pronounce or utter (words) indistinctly. **2** disparage. **3** Music sing or play (notes) smoothly without a break. **4** treat carelessly. ▷ n **5** slurring of words. **6** remark intended to discredit someone. **7** Music slurring of notes. **8** curved line indicating notes to be slurred.

slurp informal ▷ v **1** eat or drink noisily. ▷ n **2** slurping sound.

slurry n, pl **-ries** muddy liquid mixture.

slush n **1** watery muddy substance. **2** sloppy sentimental talk or writing. **slushy** adj **slush fund** fund for financing bribery or corruption.

slut ❶ n offens dirty or immoral woman. **sluttish** adj.

sly ❶ adj **slyer**, **slyest** or **slier**, **sliest** **1** crafty. **2** secretive and cunning. **3** roguish. **on the sly** secretly. **slyly** adv **slyness** n.

Sm Chemistry samarium.

smack¹ ❶ v **1** slap sharply. **2** open and close (the lips) loudly in enjoyment or anticipation. ▷ n **3** sharp slap. **4** loud kiss. **5** slapping sound. ▷ adv **6** informal squarely or directly, e.g. smack in the middle. **smacker** n slang **1** loud kiss. **2** pound note or dollar bill.

smack² n **1** slight flavour or trace. **2** slang heroin. ▷ v **3** have a slight flavour or trace (of).

smack³ n small single-masted fishing boat.

small ❶ adj **1** not large in size, number, or amount. **2** unimportant. **3** mean or petty. ▷ n **4** narrow part of the lower back. ▷ pl **5** informal underwear. ▷ adv **6** into small pieces. **smallness** n **small change** coins of low value. **smallholding** n small area of farming land. **small hours** hours just after midnight. **small-minded** adj intolerant, petty. **smallpox** n contagious disease with blisters that leave scars. **small talk** light social conversation. **small-time** adj insignificant or minor.

smarmy ❶ adj **smarmier**, **smarmiest** informal unpleasantly suave or flattering.

smart ❶ adj **1** well-kept and neat. **2** astute. **3** witty. **4** fashionable.

---

slum n **1** = **hovel**, ghetto

slumber v Lit = **sleep**, doze, drowse, nap, snooze (inf), zizz (Brit inf)

slump v **1** = **fall**, collapse, crash, plunge, sink, slip **2** = **sag**, droop, hunch, loll, slouch ▷ n **3** = **fall**, collapse, crash, decline, downturn, drop, reverse, trough **4** = **recession**, depression

slur n **6** = **insult**, affront, aspersion, calumny, innuendo, insinuation, smear, stain

slut n Offens = **tart**, scrubber (Brit & Aust sl), slag (Brit sl), slapper (Brit sl), trollop

sly adj **1,2** = **cunning**, artful, clever, crafty, devious, scheming, secret, shifty, stealthy, subtle, underhand, wily **3** = **roguish**, arch, impish, knowing, mischievous **on the sly** = **secretly**, covertly, on the quiet, privately, surreptitiously

smack¹ v **1** = **slap**, clap, cuff, hit, spank, strike, swipe ▷ n **3** = **slap**, blow, swipe ▷ adv **6** Inf = **directly**, exactly, precisely, right, slap (inf), squarely, straight

small adj **1** = **little**, diminutive, mini, miniature, minute, petite, pygmy or pigmy, teeny, teeny-weeny, tiny, undersized, wee **2** = **unimportant**, insignificant, minor, negligible, paltry, petty, trifling, trivial **3** = **petty**, base, mean, narrow

small-minded adj = **petty**, bigoted, intolerant, mean, narrow-minded, ungenerous

small-time adj = **minor**, insignificant, of no account, petty, unimportant

smarmy adj Inf = **obsequious**, crawling, ingratiating, servile, smooth, suave, sycophantic, toadying, unctuous

smart adj **1** = **neat**, spruce, trim **2** = **astute**, acute, bright, canny,

S

5 brisk. **6** causing a stinging pain. ▷ *v* **7** feel or cause stinging pain. ▷ *n* **8** stinging pain. **smartly** *adv* **smartness** *n* **smart aleck** *informal* irritatingly clever person. **smart card** plastic card used for storing and processing computer data. **smarten** *v* make or become smart. **smartphone** *n* mobile phone which allows the user to access the internet and send and receive e-mails.

smash ❶ *v* **1** break violently and noisily. **2** throw (against) violently. **3** collide forcefully. **4** destroy. ▷ *n* **5** act or sound of smashing. **6** violent collision of vehicles. **7** *informal* popular success. **8** *Sport* powerful overhead shot. ▷ *adv* **9** with a smash. **smasher** *n informal* attractive person or thing. **smashing** *adj informal* excellent.

smattering ❶ *n* slight knowledge.

smear ❶ *v* **1** spread with a greasy or sticky substance. **2** rub so as to produce a dirty mark or smudge. **3** slander. ▷ *n* **4** dirty mark or smudge. **5** slander. **6** *Medical* sample of a secretion smeared on to a slide for examination under a microscope. **smear test** *Medical* examination of stained cells in a specimen taken from the neck or lining of the womb for detection of cancer.

smell ❶ *v* **smelling**, **smelt** *or* **smelled** **1** perceive (a scent or odour) by means of the nose. **2** have or give off a smell. **3** have an unpleasant smell. **4** detect by instinct. **5** (foll. by *of*) indicate, suggest. ▷ *n* **6** ability to perceive

odours by the nose. **7** odour or scent. **8** smelling. **smelly** *adj* having a nasty smell. **smelling salts** preparation of ammonia used to revive a person who feels faint.

smelt¹ *v* extract (a metal) from (an ore) by heating. **smelter** *n*.

smelt² *n* small fish of the salmon family.

smelt³ *v* a past of SMELL.

smile *n* **1** turning up of the corners of the mouth to show pleasure, amusement, or friendliness. ▷ *v* **2** give a smile. **3** express by a smile. **smile on, upon** *v* regard favourably.

smirch *v*, *n* disgrace.

smirk ❶ *n* **1** smug smile. ▷ *v* **2** give a smirk.

smite ❶ *v* **smiting**, **smote**, **smitten** **1** *old-fashioned* strike hard. **2** affect severely.

smith *n* worker in metal. **smithy** *n* blacksmith's workshop.

smithereens *pl n* shattered fragments.

smitten ❶ *v* **1** past participle of SMITE. ▷ *adj* **2** affected by love.

smock *n* **1** loose overall. **2** woman's loose blouselike garment. ▷ *v* **3** gather (material) by sewing in a honeycomb pattern. **smocking** *n*.

smog *n* mixture of smoke and fog.

smoke *n* **1** cloudy mass that rises from something burning. **2** act of smoking tobacco. **3** *informal* cigarette or cigar. ▷ *v* **4** give off smoke. **5** inhale and expel smoke of (a cigar, cigarette, or pipe). **6** do this habitually. **7** cure (meat, fish,

━━━━━━━━━━━━━━━━━━━━━━━━━━━━━ THESAURUS ━━━━━━━━━━━

clever, ingenious, intelligent, keen, shrewd **3** = **sharp**, quick **4** = **chic**, elegant, natty (*inf*), snappy, stylish **5** = **brisk**, lively, quick, vigorous ▷ *v* **7** = **sting**, burn, hurt ▷ *n* **8** = **sting**, pain, soreness

smart aleck *n Inf* = **know-all** (*inf*), clever-clogs (*inf*), smarty pants (*inf*), wise guy (*inf*)

smarten *v* = **tidy**, groom, put in order, put to rights, spruce up

smash *v* **1** = **break**, crush, demolish, pulverize, shatter **3** = **collide**, crash **4** = **destroy**, lay waste, ruin, trash (*sl*), wreck ▷ *n* **5** = **destruction**, collapse, downfall, failure, ruin **6** = **collision**, accident, crash

smashing *adj Inf* = **excellent**, awesome (*sl*), brilliant (*inf*), cracking (*Brit inf*), fabulous (*inf*), fantastic (*inf*), great (*inf*), magnificent, marvellous,

mean (*sl*), sensational (*inf*), super (*inf*), superb, terrific (*inf*), wonderful

smattering *n* = **modicum**, bit, rudiments

smear *v* **1** = **spread over**, bedaub, coat, cover, daub, rub on **2** = **dirty**, smudge, soil, stain, sully **3** = **slander**, besmirch, blacken, malign ▷ *n* **4** = **smudge**, blot, blotch, daub, splotch, streak **5** = **slander**, calumny, defamation, libel

smell *v* **1** = **sniff**, scent **3** = **stink**, pong (*Brit inf*), reek ▷ *n* **7** = **odour**, aroma, bouquet, fragrance, perfume, scent

smelly *adj* = **stinking**, fetid, foul, foul-smelling, malodorous, noisome, reeking

smirk *n* **1** = **smug look**, simper

smitten *adj* **2** = **infatuated**, beguiled, bewitched, captivated, charmed, enamoured

S

or cheese) by treating with smoke.
smokeless *adj* **smoker** *n* **smoky** *adj*
smoke out *v* drive out of hiding, esp. by
using smoke. **smoke screen** something
said or done to hide the truth.
smokestack *n* tall chimney of a factory.

smolt *n* young salmon at the stage
when it migrates to the sea.

smooch *informal* ▷ *v* **1** kiss and cuddle.
▷ *n* **2** smooching.

smooth ❶ *adj* **1** even in surface,
texture, or consistency. **2** without
obstructions or difficulties.
3 charming and polite but possibly
insincere. **4** free from jolts. **5** not
harsh in taste. ▷ *v* **6** make smooth.
7 calm. **smoothly** *adv*.

smorgasbord *n* buffet meal of
assorted dishes.

smote *v* past tense of SMITE.

smother ❶ *v* **1** suffocate or stifle.
2 surround or overwhelm (with).
3 suppress. **4** cover thickly.

smoulder ❶ *v* **1** burn slowly with
smoke but no flame. **2** (of feelings)
exist in a suppressed state.

SMS short message system: used for
sending data to mobile phones.

smudge ❶ *v* **1** make or become
smeared or soiled. ▷ *n* **2** dirty mark.
3 blurred form. **smudgy** *adj*.

smug ❶ *adj* **smugger**, **smuggest** self-
satisfied. **smugly** *adv* **smugness** *n*.

smuggle ❶ *v* **1** import or export
(goods) secretly and illegally. **2** take
somewhere secretly. **smuggler** *n*.

smut ❶ *n* **1** obscene jokes, pictures,
etc. **2** speck of soot or dark mark left
by soot. **3** fungal disease of cereals.
smutty *adj*.

Sn *Chemistry* tin.

snack ❶ *n* light quick meal. **snack bar**
place where snacks are sold.

snaffle *n* **1** jointed bit for a horse. ▷ *v*
2 *slang* steal.

snag ❶ *n* **1** difficulty or disadvantage.
2 sharp projecting point. **3** hole in
fabric caused by a sharp object. ▷ *v*
snagging, **snagged 4** catch or tear
on a point.

snail *n* slow-moving mollusc with a
spiral shell. **snail mail** *informal*
conventional post, as opposed to
e-mail. **snail's pace** very slow speed.

snake *n* **1** long thin scaly limbless
reptile. ▷ *v* **2** move in a winding course
like a snake. **snake in the grass**
treacherous person. **snaky** *adj* twisted
or winding.

snap ❶ *v* **snapping**, **snapped 1** break
suddenly. **2** (cause to) make a sharp
cracking sound. **3** move suddenly.
4 bite (at) suddenly. **5** speak sharply
and angrily. **6** take a snapshot of. ▷ *n*
7 act or sound of snapping. **8** fastener
that closes with a snapping sound.
9 *informal* snapshot. **10** thin crisp
biscuit. **11** sudden brief spell of cold
weather. **12** card game in which the
word `snap' is called when two similar
cards are put down. ▷ *adj* **13** made on
the spur of the moment. ▷ *adv* **14** with
a snap. **snappy** *adj* **1** (also **snappish**)
irritable. **2** *slang* quick. **3** *slang* smart

smooth *adj* **1** = **even**, flat, flush,
horizontal, level, plane **2** = **easy**,
effortless, well-ordered **3** = **suave**,
facile, glib, persuasive, slick, smarmy
(*Brit inf*), unctuous, urbane
4 = **flowing**, regular, rhythmic, steady,
uniform **5** = **mellow**, agreeable, mild,
pleasant ▷ *v* **6** = **flatten**, iron, level,
plane, press **7** = **ease**, appease,
assuage, calm, mitigate, mollify,
soften, soothe

smother *v* **1 a** = **suffocate**, choke,
strangle **b** = **extinguish**, snuff, stifle
3 = **suppress**, conceal, hide, muffle,
repress, stifle

smoulder *v* **2** = **seethe**, boil, fume,
rage, simmer

smudge *v* **1** = **smear**, daub, dirty, mark,
smirch ▷ *n* **2** = **smear**, blemish, blot

smug *adj* = **self-satisfied**, complacent,
conceited, superior

smuggler *n* **1** = **trafficker**, bootlegger,
runner

smutty *adj* = **obscene**, bawdy, blue,
coarse, crude, dirty, indecent,
indelicate, scungy (*Aust & NZ sl*),
suggestive, vulgar

snack *n* = **light meal**, bite, refreshment(s)

snag *n* **1** = **difficulty**, catch,
complication, disadvantage,
downside, drawback, hitch, obstacle,
problem ▷ *v* **4** = **catch**, rip, tear

snap *v* **1** = **break**, crack, separate
2 = **crackle**, click, pop **4** = **bite at**,
bite, nip, snatch **5** = **speak sharply**,
bark, jump down (someone's) throat
(*inf*), lash out at ▷ *n* **7** = **crackle**, pop
▷ *adj* **13** = **instant**, immediate, spur-
of-the-moment, sudden

snappy *adj* **1** (also **snappish**) = **irritable**,

and fashionable. **snapdragon** n plant with flowers that can open and shut like a mouth. **snapper** n food fish of Australia and New Zealand with a pinkish body covered with blue spots. **snapshot** n informal photograph. **snap up** v take eagerly and quickly.

snare¹ ❶ n 1 trap with a noose. ▷ v 2 catch in or as if in a snare.

snare² n Music set of gut strings wound with wire fitted across the bottom of a drum to increase vibration. **snare drum** cylindrical double-headed drum with snares.

snarl¹ v 1 (of an animal) growl with bared teeth. 2 speak or utter fiercely. ▷ n 3 act or sound of snarling.

snarl² ❶ n 1 tangled mess. ▷ v 2 make tangled. **snarl-up** n informal confused situation such as a traffic jam.

snatch ❶ v 1 seize or try to seize suddenly. 2 take (food, rest, etc.) hurriedly. 3 remove suddenly. ▷ n 4 snatching. 5 fragment.

snazzy adj -zier, -ziest informal stylish and flashy.

sneak ❶ v 1 move furtively. 2 bring, take, or put furtively. 3 informal tell tales. ▷ n 4 cowardly or underhand person. **sneaking** adj 1 slight but persistent. 2 secret. **sneaky** adj.

sneakers pl n US & Canad canvas shoes with rubber soles.

sneer ❶ n 1 contemptuous expression or remark. ▷ v 2 show contempt by a sneer.

sneeze v 1 expel air from the nose suddenly, involuntarily, and noisily. ▷ n 2 act or sound of sneezing. **sneeze at** v informal dismiss lightly.

snib n Scot catch of a door or window.

snick v, n (make) a small cut or notch.

snicker n, v same as SNIGGER.

snide ❶ adj critical in an unfair and nasty way.

sniff ❶ v 1 inhale through the nose in short audible breaths. 2 smell by sniffing. ▷ n 3 act or sound of sniffing. **sniffle** v 1 sniff repeatedly, as when suffering from a cold. ▷ n 2 slight cold. **sniff at** v express contempt for. **sniffer dog** police dog trained to detect drugs or explosives by smell.

snifter n informal small quantity of alcoholic drink.

snigger ❶ n 1 sly disrespectful laugh, esp. one partly stifled. ▷ v 2 utter a snigger.

snip ❶ v **snipping**, **snipped** 1 cut in small quick strokes with scissors or shears. ▷ n 2 informal bargain. 3 act or sound of snipping. 4 piece snipped off. **snippet** n small piece.

snipe ❶ n 1 wading bird with a long straight bill. ▷ v 2 (foll. by at) shoot at (a person) from cover. 3 make critical remarks about. **sniper** n.

———————————————— THESAURUS ————————————————

cross, edgy, pissed (taboo sl), pissed off (taboo sl), ratty (Brit & NZ inf), testy, tetchy, touchy 3 Sl = **smart**, chic, dapper, fashionable, natty (inf), stylish

snap up v = **take advantage of**, grab, pounce upon, seize

snare¹ n 1 = **trap**, gin, net, noose, wire ▷ v 2 = **trap**, catch, entrap, net, seize, wire

snarl² v 2 = **tangle**, entangle, entwine, muddle, ravel

snarl-up n Inf = **tangle**, confusion, entanglement, muddle

snatch v 1 = **seize**, clutch, grab, grasp, grip 2 = **grab** ▷ n 5 = **bit**, fragment, part, piece, snippet

sneak v 1 = **slink**, lurk, pad, skulk, slip, steal 2 = **slip**, smuggle, spirit 3 Inf = **inform on**, grass on (Brit sl), shop (sl, chiefly Brit), tell on (inf), tell tales ▷ n 4 = **informer**, telltale

sneaking adj 1 = **nagging**, persistent, uncomfortable, worrying 2 = **secret**,

hidden, private, undivulged, unexpressed, unvoiced

sneaky adj = **sly**, deceitful, devious, dishonest, double-dealing, furtive, low, mean, shifty, untrustworthy

sneer n 1 = **scorn**, derision, gibe, jeer, mockery, ridicule ▷ v 2 = **scorn**, deride, disdain, jeer, laugh, mock, ridicule

snide adj = **nasty**, cynical, disparaging, hurtful, ill-natured, malicious, sarcastic, scornful, sneering, spiteful

sniff v 1, 2 = **inhale**, breathe, smell

snigger n, v 1, 2 = **laugh**, giggle, snicker, titter

snip v 1 = **cut**, clip, crop, dock, shave, trim ▷ n 2 Inf = **bargain**, giveaway, good buy, steal (inf) 4 = **bit**, clipping, fragment, piece, scrap, shred

snipe v 3 = **criticize**, carp, denigrate, disparage, jeer, knock (inf), put down

snippet n = **piece**, fragment, part, scrap, shred

S

snitch *informal* ▷ *v* **1** act as an informer. **2** steal. ▷ *n* **3** informer.

snivel ❶ *v* **-elling, -elled 1** cry in a whining way. **2** have a runny nose.

snob ❶ *n* **1** person who judges others by social rank. **2** person who feels smugly superior in his or her tastes or interests. **snobbery** *n* **snobbish** *adj*.

snog *v* **snogging, snogged** *informal* kiss and cuddle.

snood *n* pouch, often of net, loosely holding a woman's hair at the back.

snook *n* **cock a snook at** show contempt for.

snooker *n* **1** game played on a billiard table. ▷ *v* **2** leave (a snooker opponent) in a position such that another ball blocks the target ball. **3** *informal* put (someone) in a position where he or she can do nothing.

snoop ❶ *informal* ▷ *v* **1** pry. ▷ *n* **2** snooping. **snooper** *n*.

snooty *adj* **snootier, snootiest** *informal* haughty.

snooze ❶ *informal* ▷ *v* **1** take a brief light sleep. ▷ *n* **2** brief light sleep.

snore *v* **1** make snorting sounds while sleeping. ▷ *n* **2** sound of snoring.

snorkel *n* **1** tube allowing a swimmer to breathe while face down on the surface of the water. **2** device supplying air to a submarine when under water. ▷ *v* **-kelling, -kelled 3** swim using a snorkel.

snort *v* **1** exhale noisily through the nostrils. **2** express contempt or anger by snorting. **3** say with a snort. ▷ *n* **4** act or sound of snorting. **5** *informal* small drink of alcohol.

snot *n* *slang* mucus from the nose. **snotty** *adj* *slang* **1** covered with mucus from the nose. **2** haughty.

snout *n* animal's projecting nose and jaws.

snow *n* **1** frozen vapour falling from the sky in flakes. **2** *slang* cocaine. ▷ *v* **3** fall as or like snow. **be snowed under** be overwhelmed, esp. with paperwork. **snowy** *adj* **snowball** *n* **1** snow pressed into a ball for throwing. ▷ *v* **2** increase rapidly. **snow-blind** *adj* temporarily blinded by the brightness of the sun on snow. **snowboard** *n* board on which a person stands to slide across the snow. **snowboarding** *n* **snowbound** *adj* shut in by snow. **snowdrift** *n* bank of deep snow. **snowdrop** *n* small white bell-shaped spring flower. **snowflake** *n* single crystal of snow. **snow gum** same as SALLEE. **snow line** (on a mountain) height above which there is permanent snow. **snowman** *n* figure shaped out of snow. **snowplough** *n* vehicle for clearing away snow. **snowshoes** *pl n* racket-shaped shoes for travelling on snow.

SNP Scottish National Party.

snub ❶ *v* **snubbing, snubbed 1** insult deliberately. ▷ *n* **2** deliberate insult. ▷ *adj* **3** (of a nose) short and blunt. **snub-nosed** *adj*.

snuff¹ *n* powdered tobacco for sniffing up the nostrils.

snuff² *v* extinguish (a candle). **snuff it** *informal* die. **snuff out** *v* *informal* put an end to.

snuff³ *v* take in air through the nose.

snuffle *v* **1** breathe noisily or with difficulty. **2** speak through the nose.

snug ❶ *adj* **snugger, snuggest 1** warm and comfortable. **2** comfortably close-fitting. ▷ *n* **3** small room in a pub. **snugly** *adv*.

snuggle ❶ *v* nestle into a person or thing for warmth or from affection.

so¹ *adv* **1** to such an extent. **2** in such a manner. **3** very. **4** also. **5** thereupon. ▷ *conj* **6** in order that. **7** with the result that. **8** therefore. ▷ *interj* **9** exclamation of surprise, triumph, or

---

snivel *v* **1** = **whine**, cry, grizzle (*inf, chiefly Brit*), moan, whimper, whinge (*inf*) **2** = **sniffle**

snob *n* **1, 2** = **elitist**, highbrow, prig

snobbery *n* = **arrogance**, airs, pretension, pride, snobbishness

snobbish *adj* = **superior**, arrogant, patronizing, pretentious, snooty (*inf*), stuck-up (*inf*)

snoop *Inf* ▷ *v* **1** = **pry**, interfere, poke one's nose in (*inf*), spy

snooper *n* = **nosy parker** (*inf*),

busybody, meddler, snoop (*inf*)

snooze *Inf* ▷ *v* **1** = **doze**, catnap, nap, take forty winks (*inf*) ▷ *n* **2** = **doze**, catnap, forty winks (*inf*), nap, siesta

snub *v* **1** = **insult**, cold-shoulder, cut (*inf*), humiliate, put down, rebuff, slight ▷ *n* **2** = **insult**, affront, put-down, slap in the face

snug *adj* **1** = **cosy**, comfortable, comfy (*inf*), warm

snuggle *v* = **nestle**, cuddle, nuzzle

realization. **or so** approximately. **so-and-so** n 1 *informal* person whose name is not specified. **2** unpleasant person or thing. **so-called** adj called (in the speaker's opinion, wrongly) by that name. **so long** goodbye. **so that** in order that.

so² n *Music* same as SOH.

soak ⊕ v 1 make wet. **2** put or lie in liquid so as to become thoroughly wet. **3** (of liquid) penetrate. ▷ n **4** soaking. **5** *slang* drunkard. **soaking** n, adj **soak up** v absorb.

soap n 1 compound of alkali and fat, used with water as a cleaning agent. **2** *informal* soap opera. ▷ v **3** apply soap to. **soapy** adj **soapbox** n crate used as a platform for speech-making. **soap opera** radio or television serial dealing with domestic themes.

soapstone n soft mineral used for making table tops and ornaments.

soar ⊕ v 1 rise or fly upwards. **2** increase suddenly.

sob ⊕ v **sobbing, sobbed 1** weep with convulsive gasps. **2** utter with sobs. ▷ n **3** act or sound of sobbing. **sob story** tale of personal distress told to arouse sympathy.

sober ⊕ adj 1 not drunk. **2** temperate. **3** serious. **4** (of colours) plain and dull. ▷ v **5** make or become sober. **soberly** adv **sobriety** n.

sobriquet [so-brik-ay] n nickname.

Soc. Society.

soccer n football played by two teams of eleven kicking a spherical ball.

sociable ⊕ adj 1 friendly or companionable. **2** (of an occasion) providing companionship. **sociability** n **sociably** adv.

social ⊕ adj 1 living in a community. **2** of society or its organization. **3** of the behaviour of people living in groups. **4** sociable. ▷ n **5** *informal* gathering. **socially** adv **socialize** v **1** meet others socially. **2** prepare for life in society. **socialite** n member of fashionable society. **social democrat** socialist who believes in the gradual transformation of capitalism into democratic socialism. **social media** websites and applications that allow users to interact with each other. **social networking site** website that allows users to converse and share text, photographs, videos, etc. **social science** scientific study of society and its relationships. **social security** state provision for the unemployed, aged, or sick. **social services** welfare services provided by the local authorities. **social work** work which involves helping people with serious financial or family problems.

socialism n political system which advocates public ownership of industries, resources, and transport. **socialist** n, adj.

society ⊕ n, pl **-ties 1** human beings considered as a group. **2** organized

---

THESAURUS

soak v **1, 2** = **wet**, bathe, damp, drench, immerse, moisten, saturate, steep **3** = **penetrate**, permeate, seep **soak up** v = **absorb**, assimilate

soaking adj = **soaked**, drenched, dripping, saturated, sodden, sopping, streaming, wet through, wringing wet

soar v **1** = **ascend**, fly, mount, rise, wing **2** = **rise**, climb, escalate, rocket, shoot up

sob v **1** = **cry**, howl, shed tears, weep

sober adj **2** = **abstinent**, abstemious, moderate, temperate **3** = **serious**, composed, cool, grave, level-headed, rational, reasonable, sedate, solemn, staid, steady **4** = **plain**, dark, drab, quiet, sombre, subdued

sobriety n **2** = **abstinence**, abstemiousness, moderation, nonindulgence, soberness, temperance **3** = **seriousness**, gravity, level-headedness, solemnity,

staidness, steadiness

so-called adj = **alleged**, pretended, professed, self-styled, supposed

sociable adj **1** = **friendly**, affable, companionable, convivial, cordial, genial, gregarious, outgoing, social, warm

social adj **2** = **communal**, collective, common, community, general, group, public ▷ n **5** = **get-together** (*inf*), gathering, party

socialize v **1** = **mix**, fraternize, get about *or* around, go out

society n **1** = **civilization**, humanity, mankind, people, the community, the public **4** = **organization**, association, circle, club, fellowship, group, guild, institute, league, order, union **5** = **upper classes**, beau monde, elite, gentry, high society **6** = **companionship**, company, fellowship, friendship

community. **3** structure and institutions of such a community. **4** organized group with common aims and interests. **5** upper-class or fashionable people collectively. **6** companionship.

sociology *n* study of human societies. **sociological** *adj* **sociologist** *n*.

sock¹ *n* cloth covering for the foot.

sock² *slang* ▷ *v* **1** hit hard. ▷ *n* **2** hard blow.

socket *n* hole or recess into which something fits.

sod¹ *n* (piece of) turf.

sod² *n slang* obnoxious person.

soda *n* **1** compound of sodium. **2** soda water. **soda water** fizzy drink made from water charged with carbon dioxide.

sodden ❶ *adj* **1** soaked. **2** dulled, esp. by drink.

sodium *n Chemistry* silvery-white metallic element. **sodium bicarbonate** white soluble compound used in baking powder. **sodium hydroxide** white alkaline substance used in making paper and soap.

sodomy *n* anal intercourse. **sodomite** *n* person who practises sodomy.

sofa ❶ *n* couch.

soft ❶ *adj* **1** easy to shape or cut. **2** not hard, rough, or harsh. **3** (of a breeze or climate) mild. **4** (too) lenient. **5** easily influenced or imposed upon. **6** feeble or silly. **7** not robust. **8** (of drugs) not liable to cause addiction. **9** *informal* easy. **10** (of water) containing few mineral salts. ▷ *adv* **11** softly. **softly** *adv* **soften** *v* **1** make or become soft or softer. **2** make or become more gentle. **softie, softy** *n informal* person who is easily upset. **soft drink** nonalcoholic drink. **soft furnishings** curtains, rugs, lampshades, and

furniture covers. **soft option** easiest alternative. **soft-pedal** *v* deliberately avoid emphasizing something. **soft-soap** *v informal* flatter. **soft touch** *informal* person easily persuaded, esp. to lend money.

software *n* computer programs.

softwood *n* wood of a coniferous tree.

soggy ❶ *adj* **-gier, -giest 1** soaked. **2** moist and heavy. **sogginess** *n*.

soh *n Music* (in tonic sol-fa) fifth degree of any major scale.

soigné (*fem*) **soignée** [swah-nyay] *adj* well-groomed, elegant.

soil¹ ❶ *n* **1** top layer of earth. **2** country or territory.

soil² ❶ *v* **1** make or become dirty. **2** disgrace. ▷ *n* **3** soiled spot. **4** refuse.

soiree [swah-ray] *n* evening party or gathering.

sojourn [soj-urn] *n* **1** temporary stay. ▷ *v* **2** stay temporarily.

sol *n Music* same as SOH.

solace ❶ [sol-iss] *n, v* comfort in distress.

solar *adj* **1** of the sun. **2** using the energy of the sun. **solar plexus 1** network of nerves at the pit of the stomach. **2** this part of the stomach. **solar system** the sun and the heavenly bodies that go round it.

solarium *n, pl* **-lariums, -laria** place with beds and ultraviolet lights used for acquiring an artificial suntan.

sold *v* past of SELL.

solder *n* **1** soft alloy used to join two metal surfaces. ▷ *v* **2** join with solder. **soldering iron** tool for melting and applying solder.

soldier ❶ *n* **1** member of an army. ▷ *v* **2** serve in an army. **soldierly** *adj* **soldier on** *v* persist doggedly.

───────── THESAURUS ─────────

sodden *adj* **1** = **soaked**, drenched, saturated, soggy, sopping, waterlogged

sofa *n* = **couch**, chaise longue, divan, settee

soft *adj* **1** = **pliable**, bendable, elastic, flexible, gelatinous, malleable, mouldable, plastic, pulpy, spongy, squashy, supple, yielding **3** = **mild**, balmy, temperate **4** = **lenient**, easy-going, indulgent, lax, overindulgent, permissive, spineless **7** = **out of condition**, effeminate, flabby, flaccid, limp, weak **9** *Inf* = **easy**, comfortable, cushy (*inf*), undemanding

soften *v* **2** = **lessen**, allay, appease, cushion, ease, mitigate, moderate, mollify, still, subdue, temper

soggy *adj* **1, 2** = **sodden**, dripping, moist, saturated, soaked, sopping, waterlogged

soil¹ *n* **1** = **earth**, clay, dirt, dust, ground **2** = **land**, country

soil² *v* **1, 2** = **dirty**, befoul, besmirch, defile, foul, pollute, spot, stain, sully, tarnish

solace *n* = **comfort**, consolation, relief ▷ *v* = **comfort**, console

soldier *n* **1** = **fighter**, man-at-arms, serviceman, squaddie *or* squaddy (*Brit sl*), trooper, warrior

S

sole¹ ❶ *adj* **1** one and only. **2** not shared, exclusive. **solely** *adv* **1** only, completely. **2** alone.

sole² *n* **1** underside of the foot. **2** underside of a shoe. **3** lower surface of something. ▷ *v* **4** provide (a shoe) with a sole.

sole³ *n* small edible flatfish.

solecism [**sol**-iss-izz-um] *n* **1** minor grammatical mistake. **2** breach of etiquette.

solemn ❶ *adj* **1** serious, deeply sincere. **2** formal. **3** glum. **solemnly** *adv* **solemnity** *n* **solemnize** *v* **1** celebrate or perform (a ceremony). **2** make solemn.

solenoid [**sole**-in-oid] *n* coil of wire magnetized by passing a current through it.

sol-fa *n* system of syllables used as names for the notes of a scale.

solicit *v* **-iting, -ited 1** request. **2** (of a prostitute) offer (a person) sex for money. **solicitation** *n*.

solicitor *n* lawyer who advises clients and prepares documents and cases.

solicitous ❶ *adj* **1** anxious about someone's welfare. **2** eager. **solicitude** *n*.

solid ❶ *adj* **1** (of a substance) keeping its shape. **2** not liquid or gas. **3** not hollow. **4** of the same substance throughout. **5** strong or substantial. **6** sound or reliable. **7** having three dimensions. ▷ *n* **8** three-dimensional shape. **9** solid substance. **solidly** *adv* **solidify** *v* make or become solid or

firm. **solidity** *n*.

solidarity ❶ *n* agreement in aims or interests, total unity.

solidus *n, pl* **-di** short oblique stroke (/) used to separate items in text.

soliloquy *n, pl* **-quies** speech made by a person while alone, esp. in a play. **soliloquize** *v* utter a soliloquy.

solipsism *n* doctrine that the self is the only thing known to exist. **solipsist** *n*.

solitaire *n* **1** game for one person played with pegs set in a board. **2** gem set by itself. **3** *US* card game for one person.

solitary ❶ *adj* **1** alone, single. **2** (of a place) lonely. ▷ *n, pl* **-aries 3** hermit. **solitude** *n* state of being alone. **solitary confinement** isolation of a prisoner in a special cell.

solo *n, pl* **-los 1** music for one performer. **2** any act done without assistance. ▷ *adj* **3** done alone. ▷ *adv* **4** by oneself, alone. **soloist** *n*.

solstice *n* either the shortest (in winter) or longest (in summer) day of the year.

soluble *adj* **1** able to be dissolved. **2** able to be solved. **solubility** *n*.

solution ❶ *n* **1** answer to a problem. **2** act of solving a problem. **3** liquid with something dissolved in it. **4** process of dissolving.

solve ❶ *v* find the answer to (a problem). **solvable** *adj*.

solvent *adj* **1** having enough money to pay one's debts. ▷ *n* **2** liquid capable of dissolving other substances.

——————————————— THESAURUS ———————

sole¹ *adj* **1** = **only**, individual, one, single, solitary **2** = **alone**, exclusive

solely *adv* **1** = **only**, completely, entirely, merely **2** = **alone**, exclusively

solemn *adj* **1** = **serious**, earnest, grave, sedate, sober, staid **2** = **formal**, ceremonial, dignified, grand, grave, momentous, stately

solemnity *n* **1** = **seriousness**, earnestness, gravity **2** = **formality**, grandeur, impressiveness, momentousness

solicitous *adj* **1** = **concerned**, anxious, attentive, careful

solicitude *n* = **concern**, anxiety, attentiveness, care, consideration, regard

solid *adj* **1** = **firm**, compact, concrete, dense, hard **5** = **strong**, stable, sturdy, substantial, unshakable **6** = **reliable**,

dependable, genuine, good, pure, real, sound, trusty, upright, upstanding, worthy

solidarity *n* = **unity**, accord, cohesion, concordance, like-mindedness, team spirit, unanimity, unification

solidify *v* = **harden**, cake, coagulate, cohere, congeal, jell, set

solitary *adj* **1** = **single**, alone, lone, sole **2** = **isolated**, hidden, lonely, out-of-the-way, remote, unfrequented

solitude *n* = **isolation**, loneliness, privacy, retirement, seclusion

solution *n* **1** = **answer**, explanation, key, result **3** = **mixture**, blend, compound, mix, solvent

solve *v* = **answer**, clear up, crack, decipher, disentangle, get to the bottom of, resolve, suss (out) (*sl*), unravel, work out

solvency n **solvent abuse** deliberate inhaling of intoxicating fumes from certain solvents.

somatic adj of the body, as distinct from the mind.

sombre ❶ adj dark, gloomy.

sombrero n, pl **-ros** wide-brimmed Mexican hat.

some ❶ adj **1** unknown or unspecified. **2** unknown or unspecified quantity or number of. **3** considerable number or amount of. **4** a little. **5** informal remarkable. ▷ pron **6** certain unknown or unspecified people or things. **7** unknown or unspecified number or quantity. ▷ adv **8** approximately. **somebody** pron **1** some person. ▷ n **2** important person. **somehow** adv in some unspecified way. **someone** pron somebody. **something** pron **1** unknown or unspecified thing or amount. **2** impressive or important thing. **sometime** adv **1** at some unspecified time. ▷ adj **2** former. **sometimes** adv from time to time, now and then. **somewhat** adv to some extent, rather. **somewhere** adv in, to, or at some unspecified or unknown place.

somersault n **1** leap or roll in which the trunk and legs are turned over the head. ▷ v **2** perform a somersault.

somnambulist n person who walks in his or her sleep. **somnambulism** n.

somnolent adj drowsy. **somnolence** n.

son n **1** male offspring. **2** man who comes from a certain place or is connected with a certain thing. **son-in-law** n, pl **sons-in-law** daughter's or son's husband.

sonar n device for detecting underwater objects by the reflection of sound waves.

sonata n piece of music in several movements for one instrument with or without piano. **sonatina** n short sonata.

son et lumière [**sawn** eh **loo**-mee-er] n French night-time entertainment with lighting and sound effects, telling the story of the place where it is staged.

song ❶ n **1** music for the voice. **2** tuneful sound made by certain birds. **3** singing. **for a song** very cheaply. **songster**, **songstress** n singer. **songbird** n any bird with a musical call.

sonic adj of or producing sound. **sonic boom** loud bang caused by an aircraft flying faster than sound.

sonnet n fourteen-line poem with a fixed rhyme scheme.

sonny n informal term of address to a boy.

sonorous adj **1** (of sound) deep or resonant. **2** (of speech) pompous. **sonorously** adv **sonority** n.

soon ❶ adv in a short time. **as soon as** at the very moment that. **sooner** adv rather, e.g. I'd sooner go alone. **sooner or later** eventually.

soot n black powder formed by the incomplete burning of an organic substance. **sooty** adj.

soothe ❶ v **1** make calm. **2** relieve (pain etc.).

soothsayer ❶ n seer or prophet.

sop ❶ n **1** concession to pacify someone. ▷ pl **2** food soaked in liquid. ▷ v **sopping**, **sopped 3** mop up or absorb (liquid). **sopping** adj completely soaked. **soppy** adj informal oversentimental.

sophist n person who uses clever but invalid arguments. **sophistry**, **sophism** n clever but invalid argument.

S

THESAURUS
---

sombre adj = **gloomy**, dark, dim, dismal, doleful, drab, dull, grave, joyless, lugubrious, mournful, sad, sober

somebody n **2** = **celebrity**, dignitary, household name, luminary, megastar (inf), name, notable, personage, star

somehow adv = **one way or another**, by fair means or foul, by hook or (by) crook, by some means or other, come hell or high water (inf), come what may

sometimes adv = **occasionally**, at times, now and then

song n **1** = **ballad**, air, anthem, carol, chant, chorus, ditty, hymn, number, psalm, tune

soon adv = **before long**, in the near future, shortly

soothe v **1** = **calm**, allay, appease, hush, lull, mollify, pacify, quiet, still **2** = **relieve**, alleviate, assuage, ease

soothsayer n = **prophet**, diviner, fortune-teller, seer, sibyl

sophisticate ❶ *v* **1** make less natural or innocent. **2** make more complex or refined. ▷ *n* **3** sophisticated person.
sophisticated *adj* **1** having or appealing to refined or cultured tastes and habits. **2** complex and refined. **sophistication** *n*.
sophistry, sophism *n* clever but invalid argument.
sophomore *n* US student in second year at college.
soporific ❶ *adj* **1** causing sleep. ▷ *n* **2** drug that causes sleep.
soprano *n*, *pl* **-pranos 1** (singer with) the highest female or boy's voice. **2** highest pitched of a family of instruments.
sorbet *n* flavoured water ice.
sorcerer ❶ *n* magician. **sorceress** *n fem* **sorcery** *n* witchcraft or magic.
sordid ❶ *adj* **1** dirty, squalid. **2** base, vile. **3** selfish and grasping. **sordidly** *adv* **sordidness** *n*.
sore ❶ *adj* **1** painful. **2** causing annoyance. **3** resentful. **4** (of need) urgent. ▷ *n* **5** painful area on the body.

▷ *adv* **6** *obs* greatly. **sorely** *adv* greatly. **soreness** *n*.
sorghum *n* kind of grass cultivated for grain.
sorority *n*, *pl* **-ties** US society for female students.
sorrel *n* bitter-tasting plant.
sorrow ❶ *n* **1** grief or sadness. **2** cause of sorrow. ▷ *v* **3** grieve. **sorrowful** *adj* **sorrowfully** *adv*.
sorry ❶ *adj* **-rier, -riest 1** feeling pity or regret. **2** pitiful or wretched. **3** of poor quality.
sort ❶ *n* **1** group all sharing certain qualities or characteristics. **2** *informal* type of character. ▷ *v* **3** arrange according to kind. **4** mend or fix. **out of sorts** slightly unwell or bad-tempered. **sort out** *v* **1** find a solution. **2** put in order. **3** *informal* scold or punish.
sortie *n* **1** relatively short return trip. **2** raid into enemy territory. **3** operational flight made by military aircraft.
SOS *n* **1** international code signal of distress. **2** call for help.

——————— THESAURUS ———————

sophisticated *adj* **1** = **cultured**, cosmopolitan, cultivated, refined, urbane, worldly **2** = **complex**, advanced, complicated, delicate, elaborate, intricate, refined, subtle
sophistication *n* = **savoir-faire**, finesse, poise, urbanity, worldliness, worldly wisdom
soporific *adj* **1** = **sleep-inducing**, sedative, somnolent, tranquillizing ▷ *n* **2** = **sedative**, narcotic, opiate, tranquillizer
soppy *adj Inf* = **sentimental**, icky (*inf*), overemotional, schmaltzy (*sl*), slushy (*inf*), weepy (*inf*)
sorcerer, sorceress *n* = **magician**, enchanter, necromancer, warlock, witch, wizard
sorcery *n* = **black magic**, black art, enchantment, magic, necromancy, witchcraft, wizardry
sordid *adj* **1** = **dirty**, filthy, foul, mean, scungy (*Aust & NZ sl*), seedy, sleazy, squalid, unclean **2** = **base**, debauched, degenerate, low, shabby, shameful, vicious, vile **3** = **mercenary**, avaricious, covetous, grasping, selfish
sore *adj* **1** = **painful**, angry, burning, inflamed, irritated, raw, sensitive, smarting, tender **2** = **annoying**, severe, sharp, troublesome

3 = **annoyed**, aggrieved, angry, cross, hurt, irked, irritated, pained, pissed (*US taboo sl*), pissed off (*taboo sl*), resentful, stung, upset **4** = **urgent**, acute, critical, desperate, dire, extreme, pressing
sorrow *n* **1** = **grief**, anguish, distress, heartache, heartbreak, misery, mourning, regret, sadness, unhappiness, woe **2** = **affliction**, hardship, misfortune, trial, tribulation, trouble, woe ▷ *v* **3** = **grieve**, agonize, bemoan, be sad, bewail, lament, mourn
sorrowful *adj* = **sad**, dejected, dismal, doleful, grieving, miserable, mournful, sorry, unhappy, woebegone, woeful, wretched
sorry *adj* **1** = **regretful**, apologetic, conscience-stricken, contrite, penitent, remorseful, repentant, shamefaced **2** = **wretched**, mean, miserable, pathetic, pitiful, poor, sad **3** = **deplorable**
sort *n* **1** = **kind**, brand, category, class, ilk, make, nature, order, quality, style, type, variety ▷ *v* **3** = **arrange**, categorize, classify, divide, grade, group, order, put in order, rank
sort out *v* **1** = **resolve**, clarify, clear up **2** = **organize**, tidy up

so-so *adj* **1** *informal* mediocre. ▷ *adv* **2** in an average way.

sot *n* habitual drunkard.

sotto voce [sot-toe **voe**-chay] *adv* in an undertone.

sou *n* **1** former French coin. **2** small amount of money.

soubriquet [so-brik-ay] *n* same as SOBRIQUET.

soufflé [soo-flay] *n* light fluffy dish made with beaten egg whites and other ingredients.

sough [rhymes with **now**] *v* (of the wind) make a sighing sound.

sought [sawt] *v* past of SEEK.

souk [sook] *n* marketplace in Muslim countries, often open-air.

soul ❶ *n* **1** spiritual and immortal part of a human being. **2** essential part or fundamental nature. **3** deep and sincere feelings. **4** person regarded as typifying some quality. **5** person. **6** (also **soul music**) type of Black music combining blues, pop, and gospel. **soulful** *adj* full of emotion. **soulless** *adj* **1** lacking human qualities, mechanical. **2** (of a person) lacking sensitivity. **soul-destroying** *adj* extremely monotonous. **soul-searching** *n* deep examination of one's actions and feelings.

sound¹ ❶ *n* **1** something heard, noise. **2** vibrations travelling in waves through air, water, etc. ▷ *v* **3** make or cause to make a sound. **4** seem to be as specified. **5** announce by a sound. **6** pronounce. **sound barrier** *informal* sudden increase in air resistance against an object as it approaches the speed of sound. **soundproof** *adj* **1** not penetrable by sound. ▷ *v* **2** make

soundproof. **soundtrack** *n* recorded sound accompaniment to a film.

sound² ❶ *adj* **1** in good condition. **2** firm, substantial. **3** financially reliable. **4** showing good judgment. **5** ethically correct. **6** (of sleep) deep. **7** thorough. **soundly** *adv*.

sound³ ❶ *v* **1** find the depth of (water etc.). **2** examine (the body) by tapping or with a stethoscope. **3** ascertain the views of. **soundings** *pl n* measurements of depth taken by sounding. **sounding board** person or group used to test a new idea.

sound⁴ ❶ *n* channel or strait.

soup *n* liquid food made from meat, vegetables, etc. **soupy** *adj* **soup kitchen** place where food and drink is served to needy people. **souped-up** *adj* (of an engine) adjusted so as to be more powerful than normal.

soupçon [soop-sonn] *n* small amount.

sour ❶ *adj* **1** sharp-tasting. **2** (of milk) gone bad. **3** (of a person's temperament) sullen. ▷ *v* **4** make or become sour. **sourly** *adv* **sourness** *n* **sour cream** cream soured by bacteria for use in cooking. **sour grapes** attitude of claiming to despise something when one cannot have it oneself.

source ❶ *n* **1** origin or starting point. **2** person, book, etc. providing information. **3** spring where a river or stream begins.

souse *v* **1** plunge (something) into liquid. **2** drench. **3** pickle. **soused** *adj* *slang* drunk.

soutane [soo-tan] *n* Roman Catholic priest's cassock.

soul *n* **1** = **spirit**, essence, life, vital force **2** = **essence**, embodiment, epitome, personification, quintessence, type **5** = **person**, being, body, creature, individual, man *or* woman

sound¹ *n* **1** = **noise**, din, report, reverberation, tone ▷ *v* **3** = **resound**, echo, reverberate **4** = **seem**, appear, look **5, 6** = **pronounce**, announce, articulate, declare, express, utter

sound² *adj* **1** = **perfect**, fit, healthy, intact, solid, unhurt, unimpaired, uninjured, whole **4** = **sensible**, correct, logical, proper, prudent,

rational, reasonable, right, trustworthy, valid, well-founded, wise **6** = **deep**, unbroken, undisturbed, untroubled

sound³ *v* **1** = **fathom**, plumb, probe

sound⁴ *n* = **channel**, arm of the sea, fjord, inlet, passage, strait, voe

sour *adj* **1** = **sharp**, acetic, acid, bitter, pungent, tart **2** = **gone off**, curdled, gone bad, turned **3** = **ill-natured**, acrimonious, disagreeable, embittered, ill-tempered, peevish, tart, ungenerous, waspish

source *n* **1** = **origin**, author, beginning, cause, derivation, fount, originator **2** = **informant**, authority

S

south *n* **1** direction towards the South Pole, opposite north. **2** area lying in or towards the south. ▷ *adj* **3** to or in the south. **4** (of a wind) from the south. ▷ *adv* **5** in, to, or towards the south. **southerly** *adj* **southern** *adj* **southerner** *n* person from the south of a country or area. **southward** *adj, adv* **southwards** *adv* **southeast** *n, adj, adv* (in or to) direction between south and east. **southwest** *n, adj, adv* (in or to) direction between south and west. **southpaw** *n informal* left-handed person, esp. a boxer. **South Pole** southernmost point on the earth's axis.

souvenir ❶ *n* keepsake, memento.

sou'wester *n* seaman's waterproof hat covering the head and back of the neck.

sovereign ❶ *n* **1** king or queen. **2** former British gold coin worth one pound. ▷ *adj* **3** (of a state) independent. **4** supreme in rank or authority. **5** excellent. **sovereignty** *n*.

soviet *n* **1** formerly, elected council at various levels of government in the USSR. ▷ *adj* **2** (**S-**) of the former USSR.

sow¹ ❶ [rhymes with **know**] *v* **sowing**, **sowed**, **sown** *or* **sowed** **1** scatter or plant (seed) in or on (the ground). **2** implant or introduce.

sow² [rhymes with **cow**] *n* female adult pig.

soya *n* plant whose edible bean (**soya bean**) is used for food and as a source of oil. **soy sauce** sauce made from fermented soya beans, used in Chinese and Japanese cookery.

sozzled *adj slang* drunk.

spa *n* resort with a mineral-water spring.

space ❶ *n* **1** unlimited expanse in which all objects exist and move. **2** interval. **3** blank portion. **4** unoccupied area. **5** the universe beyond the earth's atmosphere. ▷ *v* **6** place at intervals. **spacious** *adj* having a large capacity or area. **spacecraft**, **spaceship** *n* vehicle for travel beyond the earth's atmosphere. **space shuttle** manned reusable vehicle for repeated space flights. **space station** artificial satellite used as a base for people travelling and researching in space. **spacesuit** *n* sealed pressurized suit worn by an astronaut.

spacious ❶ *adj* having a large capacity or area.

spade¹ ❶ *n* tool for digging. **spadework** *n* hard preparatory work.

spade² *n* playing card of the suit marked with black leaf-shaped symbols.

spaghetti *n* pasta in the form of long strings.

spam *Computers sl.* ▷ *v* **spamming**, **spammed** **1** send unsolicited e-mail or text messages to multiple recipients. ▷ *n* **2** unsolicited e-mail or text messages.

span ❶ *n* **1** space between two points. **2** complete extent. **3** distance from thumb to little finger of the expanded hand. ▷ *v* **spanning**, **spanned** **4** stretch or extend across.

spangle *n* **1** small shiny metallic ornament. ▷ *v* **2** decorate with spangles.

Spaniard *n* person from Spain.

spaniel *n* dog with long ears and silky hair.

Spanish *n* **1** official language of Spain and most countries of S and Central

S

─────────────────────── THESAURUS ───────────────────────

souvenir *n* = **keepsake**, memento, reminder

sovereign *n* **1** = **monarch**, chief, emperor *or* empress, king *or* queen, potentate, prince *or* princess, ruler ▷ *adj* **4** = **supreme**, absolute, imperial, kingly *or* queenly, principal, royal, ruling **5** = **excellent**, effectual, efficacious, efficient

sovereignty *n* = **supreme power**, domination, kingship, primacy, supremacy

sow¹ *v* **1** = **scatter**, plant, seed **2** = **implant**

space *n* **1** = **expanse**, extent **2** = **interval**,

capacity, duration, elbowroom, leeway, margin, period, play, room, scope, span, time, while **3** = **gap**, blank, distance, interval, omission

spacious *adj* = **roomy**, ample, broad, capacious, commodious, expansive, extensive, huge, large, sizable *or* sizeable

spadework *n* = **preparation**, donkey-work, groundwork, labour

span *n* **1** = **period**, duration, spell, term **2** = **extent**, amount, distance, length, reach, spread, stretch ▷ *v* **4** = **extend across**, bridge, cover, cross, link, traverse

America. ▷ *adj* **2** of Spain or its language or people.

spank ❶ *v* **1** slap with the open hand, on the buttocks or legs. ▷ *n* **2** such a slap.

spanking *adj* **1** *informal* outstandingly fine or smart. **2** quick.

spanner *n* tool for gripping and turning a nut or bolt.

spar¹ *n* pole used as a ship's mast, boom, or yard.

spar² ❶ *v* **sparring**, **sparred 1** box or fight using light blows for practice. **2** argue (with someone). ▷ *n* **3** argument.

spare ❶ *adj* **1** extra. **2** in reserve. **3** (of a person) thin. **4** very plain or simple. **5** *slang* upset or angry. ▷ *n* **6** duplicate kept in case of damage or loss. ▷ *v* **7** refrain from punishing or harming. **8** protect (someone) from (something unpleasant). **9** afford to give. **to spare** in addition to what is needed. **sparing** *adj* economical. **spare ribs** pork ribs with most of the meat trimmed off. **spare tyre** *informal* roll of fat at the waist.

spark ❶ *n* **1** fiery particle thrown out from a fire or caused by friction. **2** flash of light produced by an electrical discharge. **3** trace or hint (of a particular quality). **4** liveliness or humour. ▷ *v* **5** give off sparks. **6** initiate. **sparkie** *n* NZ *informal* electrician. **spark plug** device in an engine that ignites the fuel by producing an electric spark.

sparkle ❶ *v* **1** glitter with many points of light. **2** be vivacious or witty. ▷ *n* **3** sparkling points of light. **4** vivacity or wit. **sparkler** *n* hand-held firework that emits sparks. **sparkling** *adj* (of wine or mineral water) slightly fizzy.

sparrow *n* small brownish bird. **sparrowhawk** *n* small hawk.

sparse ❶ *adj* thinly scattered. **sparsely** *adv* **sparseness** *n*.

spartan ❶ *adj* strict and austere.

spasm ❶ *n* **1** involuntary muscular contraction. **2** sudden burst of activity or feeling. **spasmodic** *adj* occurring in spasms. **spasmodically** *adv*.

spastic *n* *old-fashioned, offensive* **1** person with cerebral palsy. ▷ *adj* **2** *old-fashioned, offensive* suffering from cerebral palsy. **3** affected by spasms.

spat¹ *n* slight quarrel.

spat² *v* past of SPIT¹.

spate ❶ *n* **1** large number of things happening within a period of time. **2** sudden outpouring or flood.

spathe *n* large sheathlike leaf enclosing a flower cluster.

spatial *adj* of or in space.

spats *pl n* coverings formerly worn over the ankle and instep.

spatter *v* **1** scatter or be scattered in drops over (something). ▷ *n* **2** spattering sound. **3** something spattered.

spatula *n* utensil with a broad flat blade for spreading or stirring.

spawn *n* **1** jelly-like mass of eggs of fish, frogs, or molluscs. ▷ *v* **2** (of fish,

---

THESAURUS

---

spank *v* **1** = **smack**, cuff, slap

spar² *v* **2** = **argue**, bicker, row, scrap (*inf*), squabble, wrangle

spare *adj* **1** = **extra**, additional, free, leftover, odd, over, superfluous, surplus, unoccupied, unused, unwanted **3** = **thin**, gaunt, lean, meagre, wiry ▷ *v* **7** = **have mercy on**, be merciful to, go easy on (*inf*), leave, let off (*inf*), pardon, save from **9** = **afford**, do without, give, grant, let (someone) have, manage without, part with

sparing *adj* = **economical**, careful, frugal, prudent, saving, thrifty

spark *n* **1** = **flicker**, flare, flash, gleam, glint **3** = **trace**, atom, hint, jot, scrap, vestige ▷ *v* **6** = **start**, inspire, precipitate, provoke, set off, stimulate, trigger (off)

sparkle *v* **1** = **glitter**, dance, flash, gleam, glint, glisten, scintillate, shimmer, shine, twinkle ▷ *n* **3** = **glitter**, brilliance, flash, flicker, gleam, glint, twinkle **4** = **vivacity**, dash, élan, life, liveliness, spirit, vitality

sparse *adj* = **scattered**, few and far between, meagre, scanty, scarce

spartan *adj* = **austere**, ascetic, disciplined, frugal, plain, rigorous, self-denying, severe, strict

spasm *n* **1** = **convulsion**, contraction, paroxysm, twitch **2** = **burst**, eruption, fit, frenzy, outburst, seizure

spasmodic *adj* = **sporadic**, convulsive, erratic, fitful, intermittent, irregular, jerky

spate *n* **2** = **flood**, deluge, flow, outpouring, rush, torrent

S

frogs, or molluscs) lay eggs.
3 generate.

spay v remove the ovaries from (a female animal).

speak ❶ v **speaking**, **spoke**, **spoken**
1 say words, talk. **2** communicate or express in words. **3** give a speech or lecture. **4** know how to talk in (a specified language). **speaker** n
1 person who speaks, esp. at a formal occasion. **2** loudspeaker. **3** (**S-**) official chairman of a body. **speak out**, **speak up** v **1** state one's beliefs firmly.
2 speak more loudly.

spear¹ ❶ n **1** weapon consisting of a long shaft with a sharp point. ▷ v
2 pierce with or as if with a spear.
spearhead v **1** lead (an attack or campaign). ▷ n **2** leading force in an attack or campaign.

spear² n slender shoot.

spearmint n type of mint.

spec n **on spec** informal as a risk or gamble.

special ❶ adj **1** distinguished from others of its kind. **2** for a specific purpose. **3** exceptional. **4** particular.
▷ n **5** product, programme, etc. which is only available at a certain time.
specially adv **specialist** n expert in a particular activity or subject.
speciality n **1** special interest or skill.
2 product specialized in. **specialize** v

be a specialist. **specialization** n
Special Branch British police department concerned with political security.

specie n coins as distinct from paper money.

species ❶ n, pl **-cies** group of plants or animals that are related closely enough to interbreed naturally.

specific ❶ adj **1** particular, definite.
2 relating to a particular thing. ▷ n
3 drug used to treat a particular disease. ▷ pl **4** particular details.
specifically adv **specification** n detailed description of something to be made or done. **specify** v **1** refer to or state specifically. **2** state as a condition. **specific gravity** ratio of the density of a substance to that of water.

specimen ❶ n **1** individual or part typifying a whole. **2** sample of blood etc. taken for analysis. **3** informal person.

specious [**spee**-shuss] adj apparently true, but actually false.

speck ❶ n small spot or particle.
speckle n **1** small spot. ▷ v **2** mark with speckles.

specs pl n informal short for SPECTACLES.

spectacle ❶ n **1** strange, interesting, or ridiculous sight. **2** impressive public show. ▷ pl **3** pair of glasses for

—————————————————————————— THESAURUS ——————————

speak v **1, 2** = **talk**, articulate, converse, express, pronounce, say, state, tell, utter **3** = **lecture**, address, declaim, discourse, hold forth

speaker n **1** = **orator**, lecturer, public speaker, spokesman or spokeswoman, spokesperson

speak out, **speak up** v **1** = **speak one's mind**, have one's say, make one's position plain

spearhead v **1** = **lead**, head, initiate, launch, pioneer, set in motion, set off

special adj **1, 2, 4** = **specific**, appropriate, distinctive, individual, particular, precise **3** = **exceptional**, extraordinary, important, memorable, significant, uncommon, unique, unusual

specialist n = **expert**, authority, buff (inf), connoisseur, consultant, fundi (S Afr), guru, mana (NZ), master, professional

speciality n **1** = **forte**, bag (sl), métier, pièce de résistance, specialty

species n = **kind**, breed, category, class, group, sort, type, variety

specific adj **1** = **particular**, characteristic, distinguishing, special

specification n = **requirement**, condition, detail, particular, qualification, stipulation

specify v **1** = **state**, define, designate, detail, indicate, mention, name
2 = **stipulate**

specimen n **1** = **example**, exemplification, instance, model, pattern, representative, sample, type
2 = **sample**

speck n = **particle**, atom, bit, blemish, dot, fleck, grain, iota, jot, mark, mite, mote, shred, speckle, spot, stain

spectacle n **1** = **sight**, curiosity, marvel, phenomenon, scene, wonder
2 = **show**, display, event, exhibition, extravaganza, pageant, performance

spectacular adj **1** = **impressive**, dazzling, dramatic, grand, magnificent, sensational, splendid,

correcting faulty vision. **spectacular** adj **1** impressive. ▷ n **2** spectacular public show. **spectacularly** adv.

spectate ❶ v watch. **spectator** n person viewing anything, onlooker.

spectre ❶ n **1** ghost. **2** menacing mental image. **spectral** adj.

spectrum n, pl **-tra 1** range of different colours, radio waves, etc. in order of their wavelengths. **2** entire range of anything. **spectroscope** n instrument for producing or examining spectra.

speculate ❶ v **1** guess, conjecture. **2** buy property, shares, etc. in the hope of selling them at a profit. **speculation** n **speculative** adj **speculator** n.

speculum n, pl **-la**, **-lums** medical instrument for examining body cavities.

sped v a past of SPEED.

speech ❶ n **1** act, power, or manner of speaking. **2** utterance. **3** talk given to an audience. **4** language or dialect. **speechify** v make speeches, esp. boringly. **speechless** adj unable to speak because of great emotion. **speech therapy** treatment of people with speech problems.

speed ❶ n **1** swiftness. **2** rate at which something moves or acts. **3** measure of the light sensitivity of photographic film. **4** slang amphetamine. ▷ v **speeding**, **sped** or **speeded 5** go quickly. **6** drive faster than the legal

limit. **speedy** adj **1** prompt. **2** rapid. **speedily** adv **speedboat** n light fast motorboat. **speed limit** maximum legal speed for travelling on a particular road. **speedometer** n instrument to show the speed of a vehicle. **speed up** v accelerate. **speedway** n track for motorcycle racing. **speedwell** n plant with small blue flowers.

speleology n study and exploration of caves. **speleologist** n.

spell¹ ❶ v **spelling**, **spelt** or **spelled 1** give in correct order the letters that form (a word). **2** (of letters) make up (a word). **3** indicate. **spellcheck** v use a computer program to check that a piece of writing is spelt correctly. **spelling** n **1** way a word is spelt. **2** person's ability to spell. **spell out** v make explicit.

spell² ❶ n **1** formula of words supposed to have magic power. **2** effect of a spell. **3** fascination. **spellbound** adj entranced.

spell³ ❶ n period of time of weather or activity.

spelt v a past of SPELL¹.

spend ❶ v **spending**, **spent 1** pay out (money). **2** use or pass (time). **3** use up completely. **spendthrift** n person who spends money wastefully.

sperm n **sperms** or **sperm 1** male reproductive cell. **2** semen. **spermicide** n substance that kills sperm. **sperm whale** large toothed whale.

THESAURUS

striking, stunning (inf) ▷ n **2 = show**, display, spectacle

spectator n = **onlooker**, bystander, looker-on, observer, viewer, watcher

spectre n **1 = ghost**, apparition, phantom, spirit, vision, wraith

speculate v **1 = conjecture**, consider, guess, hypothesize, suppose, surmise, theorize, wonder **2 = gamble**, hazard, risk, venture

speech n **1 = communication**, conversation, dialogue, discussion, talk **3 = talk**, address, discourse, homily, lecture, oration, spiel (inf) **4 = language**, articulation, dialect, diction, enunciation, idiom, jargon, parlance, tongue

speechless adj = **astounded**, aghast, amazed, dazed, shocked

speed n **1 = swiftness**, haste, hurry, pace, quickness, rapidity, rush, velocity ▷ v **5 = race**, career, bomb (along), gallop, hasten, hurry, make

haste, rush, tear, zoom

speed up v = **accelerate**, gather momentum, increase the tempo

speedy adj **1 = prompt**, immediate, precipitate **2 = quick**, express, fast, hasty, headlong, hurried, rapid, swift

spell¹ v **3 = indicate**, augur, imply, mean, point to, portend, signify

spell² n **1 = incantation**, charm **2, 3 = enchantment**, allure, bewitchment, fascination, glamour, magic

spell³ n = **period**, bout, course, interval, season, stretch, term, time

spellbound adj = **entranced**, bewitched, captivated, charmed, enthralled, fascinated, gripped, mesmerized, rapt

spend v **1 = pay out**, disburse, expend, fork out (sl) **2 = pass**, fill, occupy, while away **3 = use up**, consume, dissipate, drain, empty, exhaust, run through, squander, waste

S

spermaceti [sper-ma-**set**-ee] *n* waxy solid obtained from the sperm whale.

spermatozoon [sper-ma-toe-**zoe**-on] *n*, *pl* **-zoa** sperm.

spew ❶ *v* **1** vomit. **2** send out in a stream.

sphagnum *n* moss found in bogs.

sphere ❶ *n* **1** perfectly round solid object. **2** field of activity. **3** social class. **spherical** *adj*.

sphincter *n* ring of muscle which controls the opening and closing of a hollow organ.

Sphinx *n* **1** statue in Egypt with a lion's body and human head. **2** (**s-**) enigmatic person.

spice ❶ *n* **1** aromatic substance used as flavouring. **2** something that adds zest or interest. ▷ *v* **3** flavour with spices. **4** add zest or interest to. **spicy** *adj* **1** flavoured with spices. **2** *informal* slightly scandalous.

spick-and-span *adj* neat and clean.

spider *n* small eight-legged creature which spins a web to catch insects for food. **spidery** *adj*.

spiel *n* speech made to persuade someone to do something.

spigot *n* stopper for, or tap fitted to, a cask.

spike¹ ❶ *n* **1** sharp point. **2** sharp pointed metal object. ▷ *pl* **3** sports shoes with spikes for greater grip. ▷ *v* **4** put spikes on. **5** pierce or fasten with a spike. **6** add alcohol to (a drink). **spike someone's guns** thwart someone. **spiky** *adj*.

spike² *n* **1** long pointed flower cluster. **2** ear of corn.

spill¹ ❶ *v* **spilling**, **spilt** *or* **spilled 1** pour from or as if from a container. **2** come out of a place. **3** shed (blood). ▷ *n* **4** fall. **5** amount spilt. **spill the**

beans *informal* give away a secret. **spillage** *n*.

spill² *n* thin strip of wood or paper for lighting pipes or fires.

spin ❶ *v* **spinning**, **spun 1** revolve or cause to revolve rapidly. **2** draw out and twist (fibres) into thread. **3** (of a spider) form (a web) from a silky fibre from the body. **4** grow dizzy. ▷ *n* **5** revolving motion. **6** continuous spiral descent of an aircraft. **7** spinning motion given to a ball in sport. **8** *informal* short drive for pleasure. **9** *informal* presenting of information in a way that creates a favourable impression. **spin a yarn** tell an improbable story. **spinner** *n* **spin doctor** *informal* person who provides a favourable slant to a news item or policy on behalf of a politician or a political party. **spin-dry** *v* dry (clothes) in a spin-dryer. **spin-dryer** *n* machine in which washed clothes are spun in a perforated drum to remove excess water. **spinning wheel** wheel-like machine for spinning, worked by hand or foot. **spin-off** *n* incidental benefit. **spin out** *v* prolong.

spina bifida *n* condition in which part of the spinal cord protrudes through a gap in the backbone, often causing paralysis.

spinach *n* dark green leafy vegetable.

spindle *n* **1** rotating rod that acts as an axle. **2** weighted rod rotated for spinning thread by hand. **spindly** *adj* long, slender, and frail.

spindrift *n* spray blown up from the sea.

spine ❶ *n* **1** backbone. **2** edge of a book on which the title is printed. **3** sharp point on an animal or plant. **spinal** *adj* of the spine. **spinal cord** cord of

S

————————————————————————————— THESAURUS —————————

spendthrift *n* = **squanderer**, big spender, profligate, spender, waster

spew *v* **1** = **vomit**, disgorge, puke (*sl*), regurgitate, throw up (*inf*)

sphere *n* **1** = **ball**, circle, globe, globule, orb **2** = **field**, capacity, department, domain, function, patch, province, realm, scope, territory, turf (*US sl*)

spherical *adj* = **round**, globe-shaped, globular, rotund

spice *n* **1** = **seasoning**, relish, savour **2** = **excitement**, colour, pep, piquancy, zest, zing (*inf*)

spicy *adj* **1** = **hot**, aromatic, piquant,

savoury, seasoned **2** *Inf* = **scandalous**, hot (*inf*), indelicate, racy, ribald, risqué, suggestive, titillating

spike¹ *n* **1** = **point**, barb, prong, spine ▷ *v* **5** = **impale**, spear, spit, stick

spill¹ *v* **1** = **pour**, discharge, disgorge, overflow, slop over ▷ *n* **4** = **fall**, tumble

spin *v* **1** = **revolve**, gyrate, pirouette, reel, rotate, turn, twirl, whirl **4** = **reel**, swim, whirl ▷ *n* **5** = **revolution**, gyration, roll, whirl **8** *Inf* = **drive**, joy ride (*inf*), ride

spine *n* **1** = **backbone**, spinal column, vertebrae, vertebral column **3** = **barb**,

nerves inside the spine, which connects the brain to the nerves in the body. **spineless** *adj* lacking courage. **spiny** *adj* covered with spines. **spine-chiller** *n* terrifying film or story.

spinet *n* small harpsichord.

spinnaker *n* large sail on a racing yacht.

spinneret *n* organ through which silk threads come out of a spider.

spinney *n* small wood.

spinster *n* unmarried woman.

spiral ⊙ *n* **1** continuous curve formed by a point winding about a central axis at an ever-increasing distance from it. **2** steadily accelerating increase or decrease. ▷ *v* **-ralling, -ralled 3** move in a spiral. **4** increase or decrease with steady acceleration. ▷ *adj* **5** having the form of a spiral.

spire *n* pointed part of a steeple.

spirit¹ ⊙ *n* **1** nonphysical aspect of a person concerned with profound thoughts. **2** nonphysical part of a person believed to live on after death. **3** prevailing feeling. **4** mood or attitude. **5** temperament or disposition. **6** liveliness. **7** courage. **8** essential meaning as opposed to literal interpretation. **9** ghost. ▷ *pl* **10** emotional state. ▷ *v* **-iting, -ited 11** carry away mysteriously. **spirited** *adj* **1** lively. **2** characterized by the mood specified, e.g. *low-spirited*.

spirit² *n* liquid obtained by distillation. **spirit level** glass tube containing a bubble in liquid, used to check whether a surface is level.

spiritual ⊙ *adj* **1** relating to the spirit. **2** relating to sacred things. ▷ *n* **3** type of religious folk song originating among Black slaves in America. **spiritually** *adv* **spirituality** *n* **spiritualism** *n* belief that the spirits of the dead can communicate with the living. **spiritualist** *n*.

spit¹ ⊙ *v* **spitting, spat 1** eject (saliva or food) from the mouth. **2** throw out particles explosively. **3** rain slightly. **4** utter (words) in a violent manner. ▷ *n* **5** saliva. **spitting image** *informal* person who looks very like another. **spittle** *n* fluid produced in the mouth, saliva. **spittoon** *n* bowl to spit into.

spit² *n* **1** sharp rod on which meat is skewered for roasting. **2** long strip of land projecting into the sea.

spite ⊙ *n* **1** deliberate nastiness. ▷ *v* **2** annoy or hurt from spite. **in spite of** in defiance of. **spiteful** *adj* **spitefully** *adv*.

spitfire *n* person with a fiery temper.

spiv *n slang* smartly dressed man who makes a living by shady dealings.

splash ⊙ *v* **1** scatter liquid on (something). **2** scatter (liquid) or (of liquid) be scattered in drops. **3** print (a story or photograph) prominently in a

---

THESAURUS

needle, quill, ray, spike, spur

spineless *adj* = **weak**, cowardly, faint-hearted, feeble, gutless (*inf*), lily-livered, soft, weak-kneed (*inf*)

spin out *v* = **prolong**, amplify, delay, drag out, draw out, extend, lengthen

spiral *n* **1** = **coil**, corkscrew, helix, whorl ▷ *adj* **5** = **coiled**, helical, whorled, winding

spirit¹ *n* **2** = **life force**, life, soul, vital spark **3** = **feeling**, atmosphere, gist, tenor, tone **4, 5** = **temperament**, attitude, character, disposition, outlook, temper **6** = **liveliness**, animation, brio, energy, enthusiasm, fire, force, life, mettle, vigour, zest **7** = **courage**, backbone, gameness, grit, guts (*inf*), spunk (*inf*) **8** = **intention**, essence, meaning, purport, purpose, sense, substance **9** = **ghost**, apparition, phantom, spectre ▷ *pl* **10** = **mood**, feelings, frame of mind, morale ▷ *v*

11 = **remove**, abduct, abstract, carry away, purloin, seize, steal, whisk away

spirited *adj* **1** = **lively**, active, animated, energetic, feisty (*inf, chiefly US & Canad*), mettlesome, vivacious

spiritual *adj* **1** = **nonmaterial**, immaterial, incorporeal **2** = **sacred**, devotional, divine, holy, religious

spit¹ *v* **1** = **eject**, expectorate, splutter **2** = **throw out** ▷ *n* **5** = **saliva**, dribble, drool, slaver, spittle

spite *n* **1** = **malice**, animosity, hatred, ill will, malevolence, spitefulness, spleen, venom ▷ *v* **2** = **annoy**, harm, hurt, injure, vex **in spite of** = **despite**, (even) though, notwithstanding, regardless of

splash *v* **1, 2** = **scatter**, shower, slop, spatter, spray, sprinkle, wet **3** = **publicize**, broadcast, tout, trumpet ▷ *n* **6** = **dash**, burst, patch, spattering, touch **7** = **display**, effect, impact, sensation, stir

S

newspaper. ▷ *n* **4** splashing sound. **5** amount splashed. **6** patch (of colour or light). **7** extravagant display. **8** small amount of liquid added to a drink. **splashdown** *n* landing of a spacecraft on water. **splash out** *v informal* spend extravagantly.

splatter *v, n* splash.

splay *v* spread out, with ends spreading in different directions.

spleen *n* **1** abdominal organ which filters bacteria from the blood. **2** bad temper. **splenetic** *adj* spiteful or irritable.

splendid ❶ *adj* **1** excellent. **2** brilliant in appearance. **splendidly** *adv* **splendour** *n*.

splice *v* join by interweaving or overlapping ends. **get spliced** *slang* get married.

splint *n* rigid support for a broken bone.

splinter ❶ *n* **1** thin sharp piece broken off, esp. from wood. ▷ *v* **2** break into fragments. **splinter group** group that has broken away from an organization.

split ❶ *v* **splitting, split 1** break into separate pieces. **2** separate. **3** separate because of disagreement. **4** share. **5** (foll. by *on*) *slang* inform. ▷ *n* **6** splitting. **7** crack or division caused by splitting. **8** dessert of sliced fruit, ice cream, and cream. ▷ *pl* **9** act of sitting with the legs outstretched in opposite directions. **splitting** *adj* (of a headache) very painful. **split-level** *adj* (of a house or room) having the ground floor on different levels. **split personality 1** tendency to change

mood rapidly. **2** *informal* schizophrenia. **split second** very short period of time.

splotch, splodge *n, v* splash, daub.

splurge *v* **1** spend money extravagantly. ▷ *n* **2** bout of extravagance.

splutter *v* **1** utter with spitting or choking sounds. **2** make hissing spitting sounds. ▷ *n* **3** spluttering.

spoil ❶ *v* **spoiling, spoilt** *or* **spoiled 1** damage. **2** harm the character of (a child) by giving it all it wants. **3** rot, go bad. **spoils** *pl n* **1** booty. **2** benefits of public office. **spoiling for** eager for. **spoiler** *n* device on an aircraft or car to increase drag. **spoilsport** *n* person who spoils the enjoyment of others.

spoke¹ *v* past tense of SPEAK.

spoke² *n* bar joining the hub of a wheel to the rim.

spoken *v* past participle of SPEAK.

spokesman, spokeswoman spokesperson *n* person chosen to speak on behalf of a group.

spoliation *n* plundering.

sponge ❶ *n* **1** sea animal with a porous absorbent skeleton. **2** skeleton of a sponge, or a substance like it, used for cleaning. **3** type of light cake. **4** rub with a wet sponge. ▷ *v* **5** wipe with a sponge. **6** live at the expense of others. **sponger** *n slang* person who sponges on others. **spongy** *adj* **sponge bag** small bag for holding toiletries.

sponsor ❶ *n* **1** person who promotes something. **2** person who agrees to give money to a charity on completion

——————————————————— THESAURUS ———————

splendid *adj* **1** = **excellent**, cracking (*Brit inf*), fantastic (*inf*), first-class, glorious, great (*inf*), marvellous, wonderful **2** = **magnificent**, costly, gorgeous, grand, impressive, lavish, luxurious, ornate, resplendent, rich, sumptuous, superb

splinter *n* **1** = **sliver**, chip, flake, fragment ▷ *v* **2** = **shatter**, disintegrate, fracture, split

split *v* **1** = **break**, burst, come apart, come undone, crack, give way, open, rend, rip **2** = **separate**, branch, cleave, disband, disunite, diverge, fork, part **3** = **separate**, break up, divorce, part **4** = **share out**, allocate, allot, apportion, distribute, divide, halve, partition ▷ *n* **6** = **division**, breach, break-up, discord, dissension,

estrangement, rift, rupture, schism **7** = **crack**, breach, division, fissure, gap, rent, rip, separation, slit, tear

spoil *v* **1** = **ruin**, damage, destroy, disfigure, harm, impair, injure, mar, mess up, trash (*sl*), wreck **2** = **overindulge**, coddle, cosset, indulge, mollycoddle, pamper **3** = **go bad**, addle, curdle, decay, decompose, go off (*Brit inf*), rot, turn

spoils *pl n* **1** = **booty**, loot, plunder, prey, swag (*sl*)

spoilsport *n Inf* = **killjoy**, damper, dog in the manger, misery (*Brit inf*), wet blanket (*inf*)

spongy *adj* **2** = **porous**, absorbent

sponsor *n* **1** = **backer**, patron, promoter ▷ *v* **5** = **back**, finance, fund, patronize, promote, subsidize

S

of a specified activity by another.
3 godparent. **4** person who pays the costs of a programme in return for advertising. ▷ v **5** act as a sponsor for. **sponsorship** n.

spontaneous ❶ adj **1** not planned or arranged. **2** occurring through natural processes without outside influence. **spontaneously** adv **spontaneity** n.

spoof ❶ n **1** mildly satirical parody. **2** trick.

spook ❶ n informal ghost. **spooky** adj.

spool n cylinder round which something can be wound.

spoon n **1** shallow bowl attached to a handle for eating, stirring, or serving food. ▷ v **2** lift with a spoon. **spoonful** n **spoon-feed** v **1** feed with a spoon. **2** give (someone) too much help. **spoonbill** n wading bird of warm regions with a long flat bill.

spoonerism n accidental changing over of the initial sounds of a pair of words, such as *half-warmed fish* for *half-formed wish*.

spoor n trail of an animal.

sporadic ❶ adj intermittent, scattered. **sporadically** adv.

spore n minute reproductive body of some plants.

sporran n pouch worn in front of a kilt.

sport ❶ n **1** activity for pleasure, competition, or exercise. **2** such activities collectively. **3** enjoyment.

4 playful joking. **5** person who reacts cheerfully. ▷ v **6** wear proudly.

sporting adj of sport. **2** behaving in a fair and decent way. **sporting chance** reasonable chance of success.

sporty adj **sportive** adj playful. **sports car** fast low-built car, usu. open-topped. **sports jacket** man's casual jacket. **sportsman**, **sportswoman** n **1** person who plays sports. **2** person who plays fair and is good-humoured when losing. **sportsmanlike** adj **sportsmanship** n **sport utility vehicle** n chiefly US powerful four-wheel drive vehicle for rough terrain.

spot ❶ n **1** small mark on a surface. **2** pimple. **3** location. **4** informal small quantity. **5** informal awkward situation. **6** part of a show assigned to a performer. ▷ v **spotting**, **spotted 7** notice. **8** mark with spots. **9** watch for and take note of. **10** rain lightly. **on the spot 1** at the place in question. **2** immediately. **3** in an awkward predicament. **spotless** adj absolutely clean. **spotlessly** adv **spotted** adj **spotty** adj **1** with spots. **2** inconsistent. **spot check** random examination. **spotlight** n **1** powerful light illuminating a small area. **2** centre of attention. ▷ v **3** draw attention to. **spot-on** adj informal absolutely accurate.

spouse ❶ n husband or wife.

---

spontaneous adj **1** = **unplanned**, impromptu, impulsive, instinctive, natural, unprompted, voluntary, willing

spoof n Inf **1** = **parody**, burlesque, caricature, mockery, satire, send-up (Brit inf), take-off (inf)

spooky adj = **eerie**, chilling, creepy (inf), frightening, scary (inf), spine-chilling, uncanny, unearthly, weird

sporadic adj = **intermittent**, irregular, occasional, scattered, spasmodic

sport n **1, 2** = **game**, amusement, diversion, exercise, pastime, play, recreation **4** = **fun**, badinage, banter, jest, joking, teasing ▷ v **6** = **wear**, display, exhibit, show off

sporting adj **2** = **fair**, game (inf), sportsmanlike

sporty adj **1** = **athletic**, energetic, outdoor

spot n **1** = **mark**, blemish, blot, blotch,

scar, smudge, speck, speckle, stain
2 = **pimple**, pustule, zit (sl) **3** = **place**, location, point, position, scene, site **5** Inf = **predicament**, difficulty, hot water (inf), mess, plight, quandary, tight spot, trouble ▷ v **7** = **see**, catch sight of, detect, discern, espy, make out, observe, recognize, sight **8** = **mark**, dirty, fleck, mottle, smirch, soil, spatter, speckle, splodge, splotch, stain

spotless adj = **clean**, flawless, gleaming, immaculate, impeccable, pure, shining, unblemished, unstained, unsullied, untarnished

spotlight n **2** = **attention**, fame, limelight, public eye ▷ v **3** = **highlight**, accentuate, draw attention to

spotted adj = **speckled**, dappled, dotted, flecked, mottled

spouse n = **partner**, consort, husband or wife, mate, significant other (US inf)

S

spout ❶ v 1 pour out in a stream or jet. 2 *slang* utter (a stream of words) lengthily. ▷ n 3 projecting tube or lip for pouring liquids. 4 stream or jet of liquid. **up the spout** *slang* ruined or lost.

sprain v 1 injure (a joint) by a sudden twist. ▷ n 2 such an injury.

sprang v a past tense of SPRING.

sprat n small sea fish.

sprawl ❶ v 1 lie or sit with the limbs spread out. 2 spread out in a straggling manner. ▷ n 3 part of a city that has spread untidily over a large area.

spray¹ ❶ n 1 (device for producing) fine drops of liquid. 2 number of small objects flying through the air. ▷ v 3 scatter in fine drops. 4 cover with a spray. **spray gun** device for spraying paint etc.

spray² ❶ n 1 branch with buds, leaves, flowers, or berries. 2 ornament like this.

spread ❶ v **spreading, spread 1** open out or be displayed to the fullest extent. 2 extend over a larger expanse. 3 apply as a coating. 4 send or be sent in all directions. ▷ n 5 spreading. 6 extent. 7 *informal* large meal. 8 soft food which can be spread. 9 two facing pages in a magazine or book. **spread-eagled** *adj* with arms and legs outstretched. **spreadsheet** n computer program for manipulating figures.

spree ❶ n session of overindulgence, usu. in drinking or spending money.

sprig n 1 twig or shoot. 2 design like this. **sprigged** *adj*.

sprightly ❶ *adj* **-lier, -liest** lively and brisk. **sprightliness** n.

spring ❶ v **springing, sprang** or **sprung, sprung 1** move suddenly upwards or forwards in a single motion, jump. 2 cause to happen unexpectedly. 3 develop unexpectedly. 4 originate (from). 5 provide with springs. 6 *informal* arrange the escape of (someone) from prison. ▷ n 7 season between winter and summer. 8 jump. 9 coil which can be compressed, stretched, or bent and returns to its original shape when released. 10 natural pool forming the source of a stream. 11 elasticity. **springy** *adj* elastic. **springboard** n 1 flexible board used to gain height or momentum in diving or gymnastics. 2 thing acting as an impetus. **spring-clean** v clean (a house) thoroughly. **spring onion** onion with a tiny bulb and long green leaves. **spring tide** high tide at new or full moon. **springtime** n season of spring.

springbok n S African antelope.

springer n small spaniel.

sprinkle ❶ v 1 scatter (liquid or powder) in tiny drops or particles over (something). 2 distribute over. **sprinkler** n **sprinkling** n small quantity or number.

sprint ❶ n 1 short race run at top speed. 2 fast run. ▷ v 3 run a short distance at top speed. **sprinter** n.

---

spout v 1 = **stream**, discharge, gush, shoot, spray, spurt, surge

sprawl v 1 = **loll**, flop, lounge, slouch, slump 2 = **spread**, ramble, straggle, trail

spray¹ n 1 = **aerosol**, atomizer, sprinkler 2 = **droplets**, drizzle, fine mist ▷ v 3 = **scatter**, diffuse, shower, sprinkle

spray² n 1 = **sprig**, branch 2 = **corsage**, floral arrangement

spread v 1 = **open (out)**, broaden, dilate, expand, extend, sprawl, stretch, unfold, unroll, widen 4 = **circulate**, broadcast, disseminate, make known, propagate ▷ n 5 = **increase**, advance, development, dispersal, dissemination, expansion, proliferation 6 = **extent**, span, stretch, sweep

spree n = **binge** (*inf*), bacchanalia, bender (*inf*), carousal, fling, orgy, revel

sprightly *adj* = **lively**, active, agile, brisk, energetic, nimble, spirited, spry, vivacious

spring v 1 = **jump**, bounce, bound, leap, vault **2, 3** = **appear**, develop, mushroom, shoot up 4 = **originate**, arise, come, derive, descend, issue, proceed, start, stem ▷ n 8 = **jump**, bound, leap, vault 11 = **elasticity**, bounce, buoyancy, flexibility, resilience

springy *adj* = **elastic**, bouncy, buoyant, flexible, resilient

sprinkle v 1 = **scatter**, dredge, dust, pepper, powder, shower, spray, strew

sprinkling n = **scattering**, dash, dusting, few, handful, sprinkle

sprint v 3 = **race**, dart, dash, hare (*Brit inf*), shoot, tear

S

sprit *n* small spar set diagonally across a sail to extend it. **spritsail** *n* sail extended by a sprit.

sprite *n* elf.

sprocket *n* wheel with teeth on the rim, that drives or is driven by a chain.

sprout ❶ *v* **1** put forth shoots. **2** begin to grow or develop. ▷ *n* **3** shoot. **4** short for BRUSSELS SPROUT.

spruce¹ *n* kind of fir.

spruce² ❶ *adj* neat and smart. **spruce up** *v* make neat and smart.

sprung *v* a past of SPRING.

spry ❶ *adj* **spryer**, **spryest** *or* **sprier**, **spriest** active or nimble.

spud *n informal* potato.

spume *n, v* froth.

spun *v* past of SPIN.

spunk *n informal* courage, spirit. **spunky** *adj*.

spur ❶ *n* **1** stimulus or incentive. **2** spiked wheel on the heel of a rider's boot used to urge on a horse. **3** projection. ▷ *v* **spurring**, **spurred 4** urge on, incite (someone). **on the spur of the moment** on impulse.

spurge *n* plant with milky sap.

spurious ❶ *adj* not genuine.

spurn ❶ *v* reject with scorn.

spurt ❶ *v* **1** gush or cause to gush out in a jet. ▷ *n* **2** short sudden burst of activity or speed. **3** sudden gush.

sputnik *n* early Soviet artificial satellite.

sputter *v, n* same as SPLUTTER.

sputum *n, pl* **-ta** spittle, usu. mixed with mucus.

spy ❶ *n, pl* **spies 1** person employed to obtain secret information. **2** person who secretly watches others. ▷ *v* **spying**, **spied 3** act as a spy. **4** catch sight of. **spyglass** *n* small telescope. **spyware** *n Computers* software that gathers and transmits information about the user.

Sq. Square.

squab *n* young bird yet to leave the nest.

squabble ❶ *v, n* (engage in) a petty or noisy quarrel.

squad ❶ *n* small group of people working or training together.

squadron *n* division of an air force, fleet, or cavalry regiment.

squalid ❶ *adj* **1** dirty and unpleasant. **2** morally sordid. **squalor** *n* disgusting dirt and filth.

squall¹ *n* sudden strong wind.

squall² *v* **1** cry noisily, yell. ▷ *n* **2** harsh cry.

squander ❶ *v* waste (money or resources).

square ❶ *n* **1** geometric figure with four equal sides and four right angles. **2** open area in a town in this shape. **3** product of a number multiplied by itself. ▷ *adj* **4** square in shape. **5** denoting a measure of area.

THESAURUS

sprout *v* **1, 2** = **grow**, bud, develop, shoot, spring

spruce² *adj* = **smart**, dapper, natty (*inf*), neat, trim, well-groomed, well turned out

spruce up *v* = **smarten up**, tidy, titivate

spry *adj* = **active**, agile, nimble, sprightly, supple

spur *n* **1** = **stimulus**, impetus, impulse, incentive, incitement, inducement, motive **2** = **goad**, prick ▷ *v* **4** = **incite**, animate, drive, goad, impel, prick, prod, prompt, stimulate, urge **on the spur of the moment** = **on impulse**, impromptu, impulsively, on the spot, without planning

spurious *adj* = **false**, artificial, bogus, fake, phoney *or* phony (*inf*), pretended, sham, specious, unauthentic

spurn *v* = **reject**, despise, disdain, rebuff, repulse, scorn, slight, snub

spurt *v* **1** = **gush**, burst, erupt, shoot, squirt, surge ▷ *n* **2** = **burst**, fit, rush, spate, surge

spy *n* **1** = **undercover agent**, mole, nark (*Brit, Aust & NZ sl*) ▷ *v* **4** = **catch sight of**, espy, glimpse, notice, observe, spot

squabble *v* = **quarrel**, argue, bicker, dispute, fight, row, wrangle ▷ *n* = **quarrel**, argument, disagreement, dispute, fight, row, tiff

squad *n* = **team**, band, company, crew, force, gang, group, troop

squalid *adj* = **dirty**, filthy, scungy (*Aust & NZ sl*), seedy, sleazy, slummy, sordid, unclean

squalor *n* = **filth**, foulness, sleaziness, squalidness

squander *v* = **waste**, blow (*sl*), expend, fritter away, misspend, misuse, spend

square *adj* **7** = **honest**, above board, ethical, fair, genuine, kosher (*inf*), on the level (*inf*), straight ▷ *v* **12** = **pay**

S

6 straight or level. **7** fair and honest.
8 with all accounts or debts settled.
9 *informal* old-fashioned. ▷ *v*
10 multiply (a number) by itself.
11 make square. **12** settle (a debt).
13 level the score. **14** be or cause to be
consistent. ▷ *adv* **15** squarely, directly.
squarely *adv* **1** in a direct way. **2** in an
honest and frank manner. **square
dance** formation dance in which the
couples form squares. **square meal**
substantial meal. **square root**
number of which a given number is
the square. **square up to** *v* prepare to
confront (a person or problem).
squash¹ ❶ *v* **1** crush flat. **2** suppress.
3 push into a confined space.
4 humiliate with a crushing retort. ▷ *n*
5 sweet fruit drink diluted with water.
6 crowd of people in a confined space.
7 (also **squash rackets**) game played
in an enclosed court with a rubber
ball and long-handled rackets.
squashy *adj*.
squash² *n* marrow-like vegetable.
squat *v* **squatting**, **squatted 1** crouch
with the knees bent and the weight on
the feet. **2** occupy unused premises to
which one has no legal right. ▷ *n*
3 place where squatters live. ▷ *adj*
4 short and broad. **squatter** *n* illegal
occupier of unused premises.
squaw *n offens* Native American
woman.
squawk ❶ *n* **1** loud harsh cry. **2** loud
complaint. ▷ *v* **3** utter a squawk.
squeak ❶ *n* **1** short shrill cry or sound.
▷ *v* **2** make or utter a squeak. **narrow
squeak** *informal* narrow escape.
squeaky *adj*.
squeal ❶ *n* **1** long shrill cry or sound.
▷ *v* **2** make or utter a squeal. **3** *slang*
inform on someone to the police.

squeamish ❶ *adj* easily sickened or
shocked.
squeegee *n* tool with a rubber blade
for clearing water from a surface.
squeeze ❶ *v* **1** grip or press firmly.
2 crush or press to extract liquid.
3 push into a confined space. **4** hug.
5 obtain (something) by force or great
effort. ▷ *n* **6** squeezing. **7** amount
extracted by squeezing. **8** hug.
9 crush of people in a confined space.
10 restriction on borrowing.
squelch *v* **1** make a wet sucking sound,
as by walking through mud. ▷ *n*
2 squelching sound.
squib *n* small firework that hisses
before exploding.
squid *n* sea creature with a long soft
body and ten tentacles.
squiffy *adj informal* slightly drunk.
squiggle *n* wavy line. **squiggly** *adj*.
squint ❶ *v* **1** have eyes which face in
different directions. **2** glance
sideways. ▷ *n* **3** squinting condition of
the eye. **4** *informal* glance. ▷ *adj*
5 crooked.
squire *n* **1** country gentleman, usu. the
main landowner in a community.
2 *History* knight's apprentice. ▷ *v* **3** (of
a man) escort (a woman).
squirm ❶ *v* **1** wriggle, writhe. **2** feel
embarrassed. ▷ *n* **3** wriggling
movement.
squirrel *n* small bushy-tailed tree-living
animal.
squirt *v* **1** force (a liquid) or (of a liquid)
be forced out of a narrow opening.
2 squirt liquid at. ▷ *n* **3** jet of liquid.
4 *informal* small or insignificant person.
squish *v, n* (make) a soft squelching
sound. **squishy** *adj*.
Sr 1 Senior. **2** Señor.
3 *Chemistry* strontium.

━━━━━━━━━━━━━━━━━━ THESAURUS ━━━━━━━━

off, settle **13** = **even up**, level
14 = **match**, agree, correspond, fit,
reconcile, tally
squash¹ *v* **1** = **crush**, compress, distort,
flatten, mash, press, pulp, smash
4 = **suppress**, annihilate, crush,
humiliate, quell, silence
squashy *adj* = **soft**, mushy, pulpy,
spongy, yielding
squawk *v* **3** = **cry**, hoot, screech
squeak *v* **2** = **peep**, pipe, squeal
squeal *n* **1** = **scream**, screech, shriek,
wail, yell ▷ *v* **2** = **scream**, screech,
shriek, wail, yell

squeamish *adj* = **fastidious**, delicate,
nauseous, prudish, queasy, sick,
strait-laced
squeeze *v* **1** = **press**, clutch, compress,
crush, grip, pinch, squash, wring
3 = **cram**, crowd, force, jam, pack,
press, ram, stuff **4** = **hug**, clasp,
cuddle, embrace, enfold **5** = **extort**,
milk, pressurize, wrest ▷ *n* **8** = **hug**,
clasp, embrace **9** = **crush**, congestion,
crowd, jam, press, squash
squint *adj* **5** = **crooked**, askew, aslant,
awry, cockeyed, skew-whiff (*inf*)
squirm *v* **1** = **wriggle**, twist, writhe

SRN State Registered Nurse.
SS 1 Schutzstaffel: Nazi paramilitary security force. **2** steamship.
SSE south-southeast.
SSW south-southwest.
St 1 Saint. **2** Street.
st. stone (weight).
stab ❶ v **stabbing, stabbed 1** pierce with something pointed. **2** jab (at). ▷ n **3** stabbing. **4** sudden unpleasant sensation. **5** *informal* attempt.
stabilize v make or become stable. **stabilization** n **stabilizer** n device for stabilizing a child's bicycle, an aircraft, or a ship.
stable¹ n **1** building in which horses are kept. **2** establishment that breeds and trains racehorses. **3** establishment that manages or trains several entertainers or athletes. ▷ v **4** put or keep (a horse) in a stable.
stable² ❶ adj **1** firmly fixed or established. **2** firm in character. **3** *Science* not subject to decay or decomposition. **stability** n.
staccato [stak-**ah**-toe] adj, adv **1** *Music* with the notes sharply separated. ▷ adj **2** consisting of short abrupt sounds.
stack ❶ n **1** ordered pile. **2** large amount. **3** chimney. ▷ v **4** pile in a stack. **5** control (aircraft waiting to land) so that they fly at different altitudes.
stadium n, pl **-diums, -dia** sports arena with tiered seats for spectators.
staff¹ ❶ n **1** people employed in an organization. **2** stick used as a weapon, support, etc. ▷ v **3** supply

with personnel. **staff nurse** qualified nurse of the rank below a sister.
staff² n, pl **staves** set of five horizontal lines on which music is written.
stag n adult male deer. **stag beetle** beetle with large branched jaws. **stag night, party** party for men only.
stage ❶ n **1** step or period of development. **2** platform in a theatre where actors perform. **3** scene of action. **4** portion of a journey. ▷ v **5** put (a play) on stage. **6** organize and carry out (an event). **the stage** theatre as a profession. **stagey** adj overtheatrical. **stagecoach** n large horse-drawn vehicle formerly used to carry passengers and mail. **stage door** theatre door leading backstage. **stage fright** nervousness felt by a person about to face an audience. **stagehand** n person who moves props and scenery on a stage. **stage-manage** v arrange from behind the scenes. **stage-manager** n stage **whisper** loud whisper intended to be heard by an audience.
stagger ❶ v **1** walk unsteadily. **2** astound. **3** set apart to avoid congestion. ▷ n **4** staggering. **staggering** adj.
stagnant ❶ adj **1** (of water or air) stale from not moving. **2** not growing or developing. **stagnate** v be stagnant. **stagnation** n.
staid ❶ adj sedate, serious, and rather dull.
stain ❶ v **1** discolour, mark. **2** colour with a penetrating pigment. ▷ n **3** discoloration or mark. **4** moral

———————————— THESAURUS ————————————

stab v **1** = **pierce**, impale, jab, knife, spear, stick, thrust, transfix, wound ▷ n **3** = **wound**, gash, incision, jab, puncture, thrust **4** = **twinge**, ache, pang, prick **5** *Inf* = **attempt**, endeavour, go, try
stable² adj **1** = **firm**, constant, established, fast, fixed, immovable, lasting, permanent, secure, sound, strong **2** = **steady**, reliable, staunch, steadfast, sure
stack n **1, 2** = **pile**, berg (*S Afr*), heap, load, mass, mound, mountain ▷ v **4** = **pile**, accumulate, amass, assemble, heap up, load
staff¹ n **1** = **workers**, employees, personnel, team, workforce **2** = **stick**, cane, crook, pole, rod, sceptre,

stave, wand
stage n **1** = **step**, division, juncture, lap, leg, level, period, phase, point
stagger v **1** = **totter**, lurch, reel, sway, wobble **2** = **astound**, amaze, astonish, confound, overwhelm, shake, shock, stun, stupefy **3** = **alternate**, overlap, step
stagnant adj = **stale**, quiet, sluggish, still
stagnate v = **vegetate**, decay, decline, idle, languish, rot, rust
staid adj = **sedate**, calm, composed, grave, serious, sober, solemn, steady
stain v **1** = **mark**, blemish, blot, dirty, discolour, smirch, soil, spot, tinge **2** = **dye**, colour, tint ▷ n **3** = **mark**, blemish, blot, discoloration, smirch,

S

blemish or slur. **5** penetrating liquid used to colour things. **stainless** adj **stainless steel** steel alloy that does not rust.

stairs pl n flight of steps between floors, usu. indoors. **stair** n one step in a flight of stairs. **staircase**, **stairway** n flight of stairs with a handrail or banisters.

stake¹ ❶ n **1** pointed stick or post driven into the ground as a support or marker. ▷ v **2** support or mark out with stakes. **stake a claim to** claim a right to. **stake out** v slang (of police) keep (a place) under surveillance.

stake² ❶ n **1** money wagered. **2** interest, usu. financial, held in something. ▷ pl **3** prize in a race or contest. ▷ v **4** wager, risk. **5** support financially. **at stake** being risked. **stakeholder** n person who has a concern or interest in something, esp. a business.

stalactite n lime deposit hanging from the roof of a cave.

stalagmite n lime deposit sticking up from the floor of a cave.

stale ❶ adj not fresh. **2** lacking energy or ideas through overwork or monotony. **3** uninteresting from overuse. **staleness** n.

stalemate n **1** Chess position in which any of a player's moves would put his king in check, resulting in a draw. **2** deadlock, impasse.

stalk¹ n plant's stem.

stalk² ❶ v **1** follow or approach stealthily. **2** pursue persistently and, sometimes, attack (a person with whom one is obsessed). **3** walk in a

stiff or haughty manner. **stalking-horse** n pretext.

stall¹ n **1** small stand for the display and sale of goods. **2** compartment in a stable. **3** small room or compartment. ▷ pl **4** ground-floor seats in a theatre or cinema. **5** row of seats in a church for the choir or clergy. ▷ v **6** stop (a motor vehicle or engine) or (of a motor vehicle or engine) stop accidentally.

stall² ❶ v employ delaying tactics.

stallion n uncastrated male horse.

stalwart ❶ [**stawl**-wart] adj **1** strong and sturdy. **2** dependable. ▷ n **3** stalwart person.

stamen n pollen-producing part of a flower.

stamina ❶ n enduring energy and strength.

stammer ❶ v **1** speak or say with involuntary pauses or repetition of syllables. ▷ n **2** tendency to stammer.

stamp ❶ n **1** (also **postage stamp**) piece of gummed paper stuck to an envelope or parcel to show that the postage has been paid. **2** act of stamping. **3** instrument for stamping a pattern or mark. **4** pattern or mark stamped. **5** characteristic feature. ▷ v **6** bring (one's foot) down forcefully. **7** walk with heavy footsteps. **8** characterize. **9** impress (a pattern or mark) on. **10** stick a postage stamp on. **stamping ground** favourite meeting place. **stamp out** v suppress by force.

stampede ❶ n **1** sudden rush of frightened animals or of a crowd. ▷ v **2** (cause to) take part in a stampede.

———————————————————————————————— THESAURUS ———————

spot **4** = **stigma**, disgrace, dishonour, shame, slur **5** = **dye**, colour, tint

stake¹ n **1** = **pole**, pale, paling, palisade, picket, post, stick

stake² n **1** = **bet**, ante, pledge, wager **2** = **interest**, concern, investment, involvement, share ▷ v **4** = **bet**, chance, gamble, hazard, risk, venture, wager

stale adj **1** = **old**, decayed, dry, flat, fusty, hard, musty, sour **2,** **3** = **unoriginal**, banal, hackneyed, overused, stereotyped, threadbare, trite, worn-out

stalk² v **1, 2** = **pursue**, follow, haunt, hunt, shadow, track

stall² v = **play for time**, hedge,

stonewall, temporize

stalwart adj **1** = **strong**, stout, strapping, sturdy **2** = **loyal**, dependable, reliable, staunch

stamina n = **staying power**, endurance, energy, force, power, resilience, strength

stammer v **1** = **stutter**, falter, hesitate, pause, stumble

stamp n **3** = **imprint**, brand, earmark, hallmark, mark, signature ▷ v **6** = **trample**, crush **8** = **identify**, brand, categorize, label, mark, reveal, show to be **9** = **imprint**, impress, mark, print

stampede n **1** = **rush**, charge, flight, rout

stance ❶ *n* **1** attitude. **2** manner of standing.

stanch ❶ [stahnch] *v* same as STAUNCH².

stanchion *n* upright bar used as a support.

stand ❶ *v* **standing**, **stood** **1** be in, rise to, or place in an upright position. **2** be situated. **3** be in a specified state or position. **4** remain unchanged or valid. **5** tolerate. **6** survive. **7** offer oneself as a candidate. **8** *informal* treat to. ▷ *n* **9** stall for the sale of goods. **10** structure for spectators at a sports ground. **11** firmly held opinion. **12** *US & Aust* witness box. **13** rack or piece of furniture on which things may be placed. **14** act of standing. **15** halt to counter-attack. **standing** *adj* **1** permanent, lasting. **2** used to stand in. ▷ *n* **3** reputation or status. **4** duration. **stand by** *v* **1** be available and ready. **2** watch without taking any action. **3** be faithful to. **stand-by** *n* person or thing ready to be used in an emergency. **stand down** *v* resign or withdraw. **stand for** *v* **1** represent or mean. **2** *informal* tolerate. **stand in** *v* act as a substitute. **stand-in** *n* substitute.

standing order instruction to a bank to pay a stated sum at regular intervals. **standoffish** *adj* reserved or haughty. **stand out** *v* be distinctive. **stand up** *v* **1** rise to one's feet. **2** *informal* fail to keep an appointment. **3** withstand examination. **stand up for** *v* support or defend. **stand up to** *v* **1** confront and resist. **2** withstand and endure.

standard ❶ *n* **1** level of quality. **2** example against which others are judged or measured. **3** moral principle. **4** distinctive flag. **5** upright pole. ▷ *adj* **6** usual, regular, or average. **7** of recognized authority. **8** accepted as correct. **standardize** *v* cause to conform to a standard. **standardization** *n* **standard-bearer** *n* leader of a movement. **standard lamp** lamp attached to an upright pole on a base.

standpipe *n* tap attached to a water main to provide a public water supply.

standpoint ❶ *n* point of view.

standstill *n* complete halt.

stank *v* a past tense of STINK.

stanza *n* verse of a poem.

———————————— **THESAURUS** ————————————

stamp out *v* = **eliminate**, crush, destroy, eradicate, put down, quell, scotch, suppress

stance *n* **1** = **attitude**, position, stand, standpoint, viewpoint **2** = **posture**, bearing, carriage, deportment

stanch SEE STAUNCH².

stand *v* **1** **a** = **be upright**, be erect, be vertical, rise **b** = **put**, mount, place, position, set **4** = **exist**, be valid, continue, hold, obtain, prevail, remain **5** = **tolerate**, abide, allow, bear, brook, countenance, endure, handle, put up with (*inf*), stomach, take ▷ *n* **9** = **stall**, booth, table **11** = **position**, attitude, determination, opinion, stance **13** = **support**, base, bracket, dais, platform, rack, stage, tripod

standard *n* **1** = **level**, gauge, grade, measure **2** = **criterion**, average, benchmark, example, guideline, model, norm, yardstick **3** = **principles**, ethics, ideals, morals **4** = **flag**, banner, ensign ▷ *adj* **6** = **usual**, average, basic, customary, normal, orthodox, regular, typical **7, 8** = **accepted**, approved, authoritative, definitive, established, official, recognized

standardize *v* = **bring into line**, institutionalize, regiment

stand by *v* **1** = **be prepared**, wait **3** = **support**, back, be loyal to, champion, take (someone's) part

stand for *v* **1** = **represent**, betoken, denote, indicate, mean, signify, symbolize **2** *Inf* = **tolerate**, bear, brook, endure, put up with

stand in *v* = **be a substitute for**, cover for, deputize for, represent, take the place of

stand-in *n* = **substitute**, deputy, locum, replacement, reserve, stopgap, surrogate, understudy

standing *adj* **1** = **permanent**, fixed, lasting, regular ▷ *n* **3** = **status**, eminence, footing, position, rank, reputation, repute **4** = **duration**, continuance, existence

standoffish *adj* = **reserved**, aloof, cold, distant, haughty, remote, unapproachable, unsociable

stand out *v* = **be conspicuous**, be distinct, be obvious, be prominent

standpoint *n* = **point of view**, angle, position, stance, viewpoint

S

staple¹ *n* **1** U-shaped piece of metal used to fasten papers or secure things. ▷ *v* **2** fasten with staples. **stapler** *n* small device for fastening papers together.

staple² ❶ *adj* **1** of prime importance, principal. ▷ *n* **2** main constituent of anything.

star ❶ *n* **1** hot gaseous mass in space, visible in the night sky as a point of light. **2** star-shaped mark used to indicate excellence. **3** asterisk. **4** celebrity in the entertainment or sports world. ▷ *pl* **5** astrological forecast, horoscope. ▷ *v* **starring**, **starred 6** feature or be featured as a star. **7** mark with a star or stars. ▷ *adj* **8** leading, famous. **stardom** *n* status of a star in the entertainment or sports world. **starlet** *n* young actress presented as a future star. **starry** *adj* full of or like stars. **starry-eyed** *adj* full of naive optimism. **starfish** *n* star-shaped sea creature. **Stars and Stripes** national flag of America. **star sign** sign of the zodiac under which a person was born.

starboard *n* **1** right-hand side of a ship, when facing forward. ▷ *adj* **2** of or on this side.

starch *n* **1** carbohydrate forming the main food element in bread, potatoes, etc., and used mixed with water for stiffening fabric. ▷ *v* **2** stiffen (fabric) with starch. **starchy** *adj* **1** containing starch. **2** stiff and formal.

stare ❶ *v* **1** look or gaze fixedly (at). ▷ *n* **2** fixed gaze.

stark ❶ *adj* **1** harsh, unpleasant, and plain. **2** desolate, bare. **3** absolute. ▷ *adv* **4** completely. **stark-naked** *adj* completely naked.

starling *n* songbird with glossy black speckled feathers.

start ❶ *v* **1** take the first step, begin. **2** set or be set in motion. **3** make a sudden involuntary movement from fright. **4** establish or set up. ▷ *n* **5** first part of something. **6** place or time of starting. **7** advantage or lead in a competitive activity. **8** sudden movement made from fright. **starter** *n* **1** first course of a meal. **2** device for starting a car's engine. **3** person who signals the start of a race. **start-up** *n* recently launched project or business enterprise.

startle ❶ *v* slightly surprise or frighten.

starve *v* **1** die or suffer or cause to die or suffer from hunger. **2** deprive of something needed. **starvation** *n*.

stash *informal* ▷ *v* **1** store in a secret place. ▷ *n* **2** secret store.

state ❶ *n* **1** condition of a person or thing. **2** sovereign political power or its territory. **3** (**S-**) the government.

⸺⸺⸺⸺⸺⸺⸺⸺⸺⸺⸺ THESAURUS ⸺⸺

stand up for *v* = **support**, champion, defend, stick up for (*inf*), uphold

staple² *adj* **1** = **principal**, basic, chief, fundamental, key, main, predominant

star *n* **1** = **heavenly body**
4 = **celebrity**, big name, luminary, main attraction, megastar (*inf*), name ▷ *adj* **8** = **leading**, brilliant, celebrated, major, prominent, well-known

stare *v* **1** = **gaze**, eyeball (*sl*), gape, gawk, gawp (*Brit sl*), goggle, look, watch

stark *adj* **1, 2** = **harsh**, austere, bare, barren, bleak, grim, hard, plain, severe
3 = **absolute**, blunt, downright, out-and-out, pure, sheer, unmitigated, utter ▷ *adv* **4** = **absolutely**, altogether, completely, entirely, quite, utterly, wholly

start *v* **1** = **begin**, appear, arise, commence, embark upon, issue, make a beginning, originate, set about, take the first step **2** = **set in motion**,

activate, get going, initiate, instigate, kick-start, open, originate, trigger
3 = **jump**, flinch, jerk, recoil, shy
4 = **establish**, begin, create, found, inaugurate, initiate, institute, launch, pioneer, set up ▷ *n* **5, 6** = **beginning**, birth, dawn, foundation, inception, initiation, onset, opening, outset
7 = **advantage**, edge, head start, lead
8 = **jump**, convulsion, spasm

startle *v* = **surprise**, frighten, make (someone) jump, scare, shock

starving *adj* = **hungry**, famished, ravenous, starved

state *n* **1** = **condition**, attitude, circumstances, equation, frame of mind, humour, mood, position, predicament, shape, situation, spirits
2 = **country**, commonwealth, federation, kingdom, land, nation, republic, territory **5** = **ceremony**, display, glory, grandeur, majesty, pomp, splendour, style ▷ *v*
8 = **express**, affirm, articulate, assert,

S

4 *informal* excited or agitated condition. **5** pomp. ▷ *adj* **6** of or concerning the State. **7** involving ceremony. ▷ *v* **8** express in words. **the States** United States of America.

stately *adj* dignified or grand.

statehouse *n NZ* publicly-owned house rented to a low-income tenant.

statement *n* **1** something stated. **2** printed financial account.

stateroom *n* **1** private cabin on a ship. **2** large room in a palace, used for ceremonial occasions. **statesman**, **stateswoman** *n* experienced and respected political leader. **statesmanship** *n*.

static ❶ *adj* **1** stationary or inactive. **2** (of a force) acting but producing no movement. ▷ *n* **3** crackling sound or speckled picture caused by interference in radio or television reception. **4** (also **static electricity**) electric sparks produced by friction. **statics** *n* branch of mechanics dealing with the forces producing a state of equilibrium.

statin *n Medical* drug used to lower cholesterol.

station ❶ *n* **1** place where trains stop for passengers. **2** headquarters or local offices of the police or a fire brigade. **3** building with special equipment for a particular purpose, e.g. *power station.* **4** television or radio channel. **5** place or position assigned to a person. **6** position in society. **7** large Australian sheep or cattle ranch. ▷ *v* **8** assign (someone) to a particular place. **stationmaster** *n* official in charge of a railway station.

stationary ❶ *adj* not moving.

● **SPELLING TIP**
● The words **stationary** and
● **stationery** are completely
● different in meaning and should not
● be confused.

stationery *n* writing materials such as paper and pens. **stationer** *n* dealer in stationery.

station wagon *n US & Canad* automobile with a rear door and luggage space behind the rear seats.

statistic *n* numerical fact collected and classified systematically. **statistics** *n* science of classifying and interpreting numerical information. **statistical** *adj* **statistically** *adv* **statistician** *n* person who compiles and studies statistics.

statue ❶ *n* large sculpture of a human or animal figure. **statuary** *n* statues collectively. **statuesque** [stat-yoo-**esk**] *adj* (of a woman) tall and well-proportioned. **statuette** *n* small statue.

stature ❶ *n* **1** person's height. **2** reputation of a person or their achievements.

status ❶ *n* **1** social position. **2** prestige. **3** person's legal standing. **status quo** existing state of affairs. **status symbol** possession regarded as a sign of position or wealth.

statute *n* written law. **statutory** *adj* required or authorized by law.

staunch¹ ❶ *adj* loyal, firm.

staunch² ❶ stanch *v* stop (a flow of blood).

stave *n* **1** one of the strips of wood forming a barrel. **2** *Music* same as STAFF². **3** thick stick. **4** stanza. **stave in** *v* **staving**, **stove** burst a hole in. **stave off** *v* **staving**, **staved** ward off.

--- THESAURUS ---

declare, expound, present, say, specify, utter, voice

stately *adj* = **grand**, august, dignified, lofty, majestic, noble, regal, royal

statement *n* **1** = **account**, announcement, communication, communiqué, declaration, proclamation, report

static *adj* **1** = **stationary**, fixed, immobile, motionless, still, unmoving

station *n* **2** = **headquarters**, base, depot **5** = **place**, location, position, post, seat, situation **6** = **position**, post, rank, situation, standing, status ▷ *v* **8** = **assign**, establish, install, locate, post, set

stationary *adj* = **motionless**, fixed, parked, standing, static, stock-still, unmoving

statuesque *adj* = **well-proportioned**, imposing, Junoesque

stature *n* **2** = **importance**, eminence, prestige, prominence, rank, standing

status *n* **1, 2** = **position**, condition, consequence, eminence, grade, prestige, rank, standing

staunch¹ *adj* = **loyal**, faithful, firm, sound, stalwart, steadfast, true, trusty

staunch², stanch *v* = **stop**, check, dam, halt, stay, stem

S

staves n plural of STAFF² or STAVE.

stay¹ ❶ v **1** remain in a place or condition. **2** reside temporarily. **3** endure. ▷ n **4** period of staying in a place. **5** postponement. **staying power** stamina.

stay² ❶ n **1** prop or buttress. ▷ pl **2** corset.

stay³ n rope or wire supporting a ship's mast.

STD 1 sexually transmitted disease. **2** subscriber trunk dialling.

stead n **in someone's stead** in someone's place. **stand someone in good stead** be useful to someone.

steadfast ❶ adj firm, determined. **steadfastly** adv.

steady ❶ adj **steadier**, **steadiest 1** not shaky or wavering. **2** regular or continuous. **3** sensible and dependable. ▷ v **steadying**, **steadied 4** make steady. ▷ adv **5** in a steady manner. **steadily** adv **steadiness** n.

steak n **1** thick slice of meat, esp. beef. **2** slice of fish.

steal ❶ v **stealing**, **stole**, **stolen 1** take unlawfully or without permission. **2** move stealthily.

stealth ❶ n **1** moving carefully and quietly. **2** secret or underhand behaviour. ▷ adj **3** (of technology) able to render an aircraft almost invisible to radar. **4** disguised or hidden, e.g. stealth taxes. **stealthy** adj **stealthily** adv.

steam n **1** vapour into which water changes when boiled. **2** power,

energy, or speed. ▷ v **3** give off steam. **4** (of a vehicle) move by steam power. **5** cook or treat with steam. **steamer** n **1** steam-propelled ship. **2** container used to cook food in steam. **steamy** adj **steamier**, **steamiest 1** full of steam. **2** informal erotic. **steam engine** engine worked by steam. **steamroller** n **1** steam-powered vehicle with heavy rollers, used to level road surfaces. ▷ v **2** use overpowering force to make (someone) do what one wants.

steatite [**stee**-a-tite] n same as SOAPSTONE.

steed n lit horse.

steel n **1** hard malleable alloy of iron and carbon. **2** steel rod used for sharpening knives. **3** hardness of character or attitude. ▷ v **4** prepare (oneself) for something unpleasant. **steely** adj **steel band** band of people playing on metal drums, popular in the West Indies.

steep¹ ❶ adj **1** sloping sharply. **2** informal (of a price) unreasonably high. **steeply** adv **steepness** n.

steep² ❶ v soak or be soaked in liquid. **steeped in** filled with, e.g. steeped in history.

steeple n church tower with a spire. **steeplejack** n person who repairs steeples and chimneys.

steeplechase n **1** horse race with obstacles to jump. **2** track race with hurdles and a water jump.

———————————————— THESAURUS ————————————————

stay¹ v **1** = **remain**, abide, continue, halt, linger, loiter, pause, stop, tarry, wait ▷ n **4** = **visit**, holiday, sojourn, stop, stopover **5** = **postponement**, deferment, delay, halt, stopping, suspension

stay² n **1** = **support**, brace, buttress, prop, reinforcement, shoring, stanchion

steadfast adj = **firm**, faithful, fast, fixed, intent, loyal, resolute, stalwart, staunch, steady, unswerving, unwavering

steady adj **1** = **firm**, fixed, safe, secure, stable **2** = **continuous**, ceaseless, consistent, constant, incessant, nonstop, persistent, regular, unbroken, uninterrupted **3** = **dependable**, balanced, calm, equable, level-headed, reliable, sensible, sober ▷ v **4** = **stabilize**,

brace, secure, support

steal v **1** = **take**, appropriate, embezzle, filch, lift (inf), misappropriate, nick (sl, chiefly Brit), pilfer, pinch (inf), purloin, thieve **2** = **sneak**, creep, slink, slip, tiptoe

stealth n **1, 2** = **secrecy**, furtiveness, slyness, sneakiness, stealthiness, surreptitiousness, unobtrusiveness

stealthy adj = **secret**, furtive, secretive, sneaking, surreptitious

steep¹ adj **1** = **sheer**, abrupt, precipitous **2** Inf = **high**, exorbitant, extortionate, extreme, overpriced, unreasonable

steep² v = **soak**, drench, immerse, marinate (Cookery), moisten, souse, submerge **steeped in** = **saturated**, filled with, imbued, infused, permeated, pervaded, suffused

steer¹ ❶ v **1** direct the course of (a vehicle or ship). **2** direct (one's course). **steerage** n cheapest accommodation on a passenger ship. **steering wheel** wheel turned by the driver of a vehicle in order to steer it.

steer² n castrated male ox.

stein [**stine**] n earthenware beer mug.

stellar adj of stars.

stem¹ ❶ n **1** long thin central part of a plant. **2** long slender part, as of a wineglass. **3** part of a word to which inflections are added. ▷ v **stemming**, **stemmed 4 stem from** originate from.

stem² ❶ v **stemming**, **stemmed** stop (the flow of something).

stench ❶ n foul smell.

stencil n **1** thin sheet with cut-out pattern through which ink or paint passes to form the pattern on the surface below. **2** pattern made thus. ▷ v **-cilling, -cilled 3** make (a pattern) with a stencil.

stenographer n shorthand typist.

stentorian adj (of a voice) very loud.

step ❶ v **stepping, stepped 1** move and set down the foot, as when walking. **2** walk a short distance. ▷ n **3** stepping. **4** distance covered by a step. **5** sound made by stepping. **6** foot movement in a dance. **7** one of a sequence of actions taken in order to achieve a goal. **8** degree in a series or scale. **9** flat surface for placing the foot on when going up or down. ▷ pl **10** stepladder. **11** flight of stairs. **step in** v intervene. **stepladder** n folding portable ladder with supporting frame. **stepping stone 1** one of a series of stones for stepping on in crossing a stream. **2** means of progress towards a goal. **step up** v increase (something) by stages.

step- prefix denoting a relationship created by the remarriage of a parent, e.g. stepmother.

steppes pl n wide grassy treeless plains.

stereo adj **1** short for STEREOPHONIC. ▷ n **2** stereophonic record player. **3** stereophonic sound.

stereophonic adj using two separate loudspeakers to give the effect of naturally distributed sound.

stereoscopic adj having a three-dimensional effect.

stereotype ❶ n **1** standardized idea of a type of person or thing. **2** monotonously familiar idea. ▷ v **3** form a stereotype of.

sterile ❶ adj **1** free from germs. **2** unable to produce offspring or seeds. **3** lacking inspiration or vitality. **sterility** n **sterilize** v make sterile. **sterilization** n.

sterling ❶ n **1** British money system. ▷ adj **2** genuine and reliable. **sterling silver** alloy with 92.5 per cent silver.

stern¹ ❶ adj severe, strict. **sternly** adv **sternness** n.

stern² n rear part of a ship.

sternum n, pl **-na, -nums** same as BREASTBONE.

steroid n organic compound containing a carbon ring system, such as many hormones.

stertorous adj (of breathing) laboured and noisy.

stet interj instruction to ignore an alteration previously made by a proofreader.

S

steer¹ v **1 = drive**, control, direct, guide, handle, pilot

stem¹ n **1 = stalk**, axis, branch, shoot, trunk ▷ v **4 stem from = originate from**, arise from, be caused by, derive from

stem² v **= stop**, check, curb, dam, hold back, staunch

stench n **= stink**, foul smell, pong (Brit inf), reek, whiff (Brit sl)

step v **1 = walk**, move, pace, tread ▷ n **3 = footstep**, footfall, footprint, pace, print, stride, track **7 = action**, act, deed, expedient, means, measure, move **8 = degree**, level, rank

step in v Inf **= intervene**, become involved, take action

step up v Inf **= increase**, intensify, raise

stereotype n **1 = formula**, pattern ▷ v **3 = categorize**, pigeonhole, standardize, typecast

sterile adj **1 = germ-free**, aseptic, disinfected, sterilized **2 = barren**, bare, dry, empty, fruitless, unfruitful, unproductive

sterilize v **= disinfect**, fumigate, purify

sterling adj **2 = excellent**, fine, genuine, sound, superlative, true

stern¹ adj **= severe**, austere, forbidding, grim, hard, harsh, inflexible, rigid, serious, strict

stethoscope *n* medical instrument for listening to sounds made inside the body.

Stetson *n* ® tall broad-brimmed hat, worn mainly by cowboys.

stevedore *n* person who loads and unloads ships.

stew *n* 1 food cooked slowly in a closed pot. 2 *informal* troubled or worried state. ▷ *v* 3 cook slowly in a closed pot.

steward *n* 1 person who looks after passengers on a ship or aircraft. 2 official who helps at a public event such as a race. 3 person who administers another's property. **stewardess** *n fem*.

stick¹ ❶ *n* 1 long thin piece of wood. 2 such a piece of wood shaped for a special purpose, e.g. *hockey stick*. 3 something like a stick, e.g. *stick of celery*. 4 *slang* verbal abuse, criticism. **the sticks** *informal* remote country area. **stick insect** tropical insect resembling a twig.

stick² ❶ *v* **sticking, stuck** 1 push (a pointed object) into (something). 2 fasten or be fastened by or as if by pins or glue. 3 (foll. by *out*) extend beyond something else, protrude. 4 *informal* put. 5 jam. 6 come to a standstill. 7 remain for a long time. 8 *slang* tolerate, abide. **sticker** *n* adhesive label or sign. **sticky** *adj* 1 covered with an adhesive substance. 2 *informal* difficult, unpleasant.

3 (of weather) warm and humid. **stick around** *v informal* remain in a place. **stick-in-the-mud** *n* person who does not like anything new. **stick-up** *n slang* robbery at gunpoint. **stick up for** *v informal* support or defend.

stickleback *n* small fish with sharp spines on its back.

stickler ❶ *n* person who insists on something, e.g. *stickler for detail*.

stiff ❶ *adj* 1 not easily bent or moved. 2 moving with pain. 3 difficult. 4 severe, e.g. *stiff punishment*. 5 unrelaxed or awkward. 6 firm in consistency. 7 strong, e.g. *a stiff drink*. ▷ *n* 8 *slang* corpse. **stiffly** *adv* **stiffness** *n* **stiffen** *v* make or become stiff. **stiff-necked** *adj* haughtily stubborn.

stifle ❶ *v* 1 suppress. 2 feel difficulty in breathing. 3 suffocate. **stifling** *adj* uncomfortably hot and stuffy.

stigma ❶ *n*, *pl* **-mas**, **-mata** 1 mark of social disgrace. 2 part of a plant that receives pollen. **stigmata** *pl n* marks resembling the wounds of the crucified Christ. **stigmatize** *v* mark as being shameful.

stile *n* set of steps allowing people to climb a fence.

stiletto *n*, *pl* **-tos** 1 (also **stiletto heel**) high narrow heel on a woman's shoe. 2 small slender dagger.

still¹ ❶ *adv* 1 now or in the future as before. 2 up to this or that time.

———— THESAURUS ————

stick¹ *n* **1, 2** = **cane**, baton, crook, pole, rod, staff, twig **4** *Sl* = **abuse**, criticism, flak (*inf*)

stick² *v* **1** = **poke**, dig, jab, penetrate, pierce, prod, puncture, spear, stab, thrust, transfix **2** = **fasten**, adhere, affix, attach, bind, bond, cling, fix, glue, hold, join, paste, weld **3** (foll. by *out*) = **protrude**, bulge, extend, jut, obtrude, poke, project, show **4** *Inf* = **put**, deposit, lay, place, set **7** = **stay**, linger, persist, remain **8** *Sl* = **tolerate**, abide, stand, stomach, take

stickler *n* = **fanatic**, fusspot (*Brit inf*), perfectionist, purist

stick up for *v Inf* = **defend**, champion, stand up for, support

sticky *adj* **1** = **tacky**, adhesive, clinging, gluey, glutinous, gooey (*inf*), gummy, icky (*inf*), viscid, viscous **2** *Inf* = **difficult**, awkward, delicate, embarrassing, nasty, tricky,

unpleasant **3** = **humid**, clammy, close, muggy, oppressive, sultry, sweltering

stiff *adj* **1** = **inflexible**, firm, hard, inelastic, rigid, solid, taut, tense, tight, unbending, unyielding **3** = **difficult**, arduous, exacting, hard, tough **4** = **severe**, drastic, extreme, hard, harsh, heavy, strict **5** = **awkward**, clumsy, constrained, forced, formal, graceless, inelegant, jerky (*inf*), stilted, ungainly, ungraceful, unnatural, unrelaxed

stiffen *v* = **brace**, reinforce, tauten, tense

stifle *v* **1** = **suppress**, check, hush, repress, restrain, silence, smother, stop **2** = **choke 3** = **suffocate**, asphyxiate, choke, smother, strangle

stigma *n* **1** = **disgrace**, dishonour, shame, slur, smirch, stain

still¹ *adj* **6** = **motionless**, calm, peaceful, restful, serene, stationary,

3 even or yet, e.g. *still more insults*.
4 nevertheless. **5** quietly or without movement. ▷ *adj* **6** motionless.
7 silent and calm, undisturbed. **8** (of a drink) not fizzy. ▷ *n* **9** calmness.
10 photograph from a film scene. ▷ *v*
11 make still. **12** relieve or end.
stillness *n* **stillborn** *adj* born dead.
still life painting of inanimate objects.

still² *n* apparatus for distilling alcoholic drinks.

stilted ❶ *adj* stiff and formal in manner.

Stilton *n* ® strong-flavoured cheese.

stilts *pl n* **1** pair of poles with footrests for walking raised from the ground.
2 long posts supporting a building above ground level.

stimulus ❶ *n, pl* **-li** something that rouses a person or thing to activity.
stimulant *n* something, such as a drug, that acts as a stimulus.
stimulate *v* act as a stimulus (on).
stimulation *n*.

sting ❶ *v* **stinging**, **stung 1** (of certain animals or plants) wound by injecting with poison. **2** feel or cause to feel sharp physical or mental pain.
3 incite. **4** *slang* cheat (someone) by overcharging. ▷ *n* **5** wound or pain caused by or as if by stinging.
6 mental pain. **7** sharp pointed organ of certain animals or plants by which poison can be injected. **stingray** *n* flatfish capable of inflicting painful wounds.

stingy ❶ *adj* **-gier**, **-giest** mean or miserly. **stinginess** *n*.

stink ❶ *n* **1** strong unpleasant smell.
2 *slang* unpleasant fuss. ▷ *v* **stinking**, **stank** or **stunk**, **stunk 3** give off a strong unpleasant smell. **4** *slang* be very unpleasant. **stinker** *n informal* difficult or unpleasant person or thing. **stinking** *informal* ▷ *adj*
1 unpleasant. ▷ *adv* **2** extremely.

stint ❶ *v* **1** (foll. by *on*) be miserly with (something). ▷ *n* **2** allotted amount of work.

stipend [*sty*-pend] *n* regular allowance or salary, esp. that paid to a clergyman. **stipendiary** *adj* receiving a stipend.

stipple *v* paint, draw, or engrave using dots.

stipulate ❶ *v* specify as a condition of an agreement. **stipulation** *n*.

stir ❶ *v* **stirring**, **stirred 1** mix up (a liquid) by moving a spoon etc. around in it. **2** move. **3** excite or stimulate (a person) emotionally. ▷ *n* **4** a stirring.
5 strong reaction, usu. of excitement.
stir up *v* instigate.

stirrup *n* metal loop attached to a saddle for supporting a rider's foot.

stitch *n* **1** link made by drawing thread through material with a needle.
2 loop of yarn formed round a needle or hook in knitting or crochet. **3** sharp pain in the side. ▷ *v* **4** sew. **in stitches** *informal* laughing uncontrollably. **not a stitch** *informal* no clothes at all.

——————————— THESAURUS ———————————

tranquil, undisturbed **7** = **silent**, hushed, quiet ▷ *v* **11** = **quieten**, allay, calm, hush, lull, pacify, quiet, settle, silence, soothe

stilted *adj* = **stiff**, constrained, forced, unnatural, wooden

stimulant *n* = **pick-me-up** (*inf*), restorative, tonic, upper (*sl*)

stimulate *v* = **encourage**, arouse, fire, gee up, impel, incite, inspire, prompt, provoke, rouse, spur

stimulus *n* = **incentive**, encouragement, fillip, geeing-up, goad, impetus, incitement, inducement, spur

sting *v* **2** = **hurt**, burn, pain, smart, tingle, wound **4** *Sl* = **cheat**, defraud, do (*sl*), fleece, overcharge, rip off (*sl*), swindle

stingy *adj* = **mean**, miserly, niggardly, parsimonious, penny-pinching (*inf*), tightfisted, ungenerous

stink *n* **1** = **stench**, fetor, foul smell, pong (*Brit inf*) ▷ *v* **3** = **reek**, pong (*Brit inf*)

stint *v* **1** (foll. by *on*) = **be mean**, be frugal, be sparing, hold back, skimp on ▷ *n* **2** = **share**, period, quota, shift, spell, stretch, term, time, turn

stipulate *v* = **specify**, agree, contract, covenant, insist upon, require, settle

stipulation *n* = **condition**, agreement, clause, precondition, proviso, qualification, requirement, specification

stir *v* **1** = **mix**, agitate, beat, shake
3 = **stimulate**, arouse, awaken, excite, incite, move, provoke, rouse, spur ▷ *v*
5 = **commotion**, activity, bustle, disorder, disturbance, excitement, flurry, fuss

S

stoat *n* small mammal of the weasel family, with brown fur that turns white in winter.

stock ❶ *n* **1** total amount of goods available for sale in a shop. **2** supply stored for future use. **3** financial shares in, or capital of, a company. **4** livestock. **5** lineage. **6** handle of a rifle. **7** liquid produced by boiling meat, fish, bones, or vegetables. **8** fragrant flowering plant. **9** standing or status. ▷ *pl* **10** *History* instrument of punishment consisting of a wooden frame with holes into which the hands and feet of the victim were locked. ▷ *adj* **11** kept in stock, standard. **12** hackneyed. ▷ *v* **13** keep for sale or future use. **14** supply (a farm) with livestock or (a lake etc.) with fish. **stockist** *n* dealer who stocks a particular product. **stocky** *adj* (of a person) broad and sturdy. **stockbroker** *n* person who buys and sells stocks and shares for customers. **stock car** car modified for a form of racing in which the cars often collide. **stock exchange, market** institution for the buying and selling of shares. **stock in trade** thing constantly used as part of a profession. **stockpile** *v* **1** store a large quantity of (something) for future use. ▷ *n* **2** accumulated store. **stock-still** *adj* motionless. **stocktaking** *n* counting and valuing of the goods in a shop. **stockyard** *n* yard where farm animals are sold.

stockade *n* enclosure or barrier made of stakes.

stockinette *n* machine-knitted elastic fabric.

stocking *n* close-fitting covering for the foot and leg. **stocking stitch** alternate rows of plain and purl in knitting.

stodgy ❶ *adj* **stodgier, stodgiest 1** (of food) heavy and starchy. **2** (of a person) serious and boring. **stodge** *n* heavy starchy food.

stoep [**stoop**] *n* S Afr verandah.

stoic ❶ [**stow**-ik] *n* **1** person who suffers hardship without showing his or her feelings. ▷ *adj* **2** (also **stoical**) suffering hardship without showing one's feelings. **stoically** *adv* **stoicism** [**stow**-iss-izz-um] *n*.

stoke *v* feed and tend (a fire or furnace). **stoker** *n*.

stole¹ *v* past tense of STEAL.

stole² *n* long scarf or shawl.

stolen *v* past participle of STEAL.

stolid ❶ *adj* showing little emotion or interest. **stolidity** *n* **stolidly** *adv*.

stomach ❶ *n* **1** organ in the body which digests food. **2** front of the body around the waist. **3** desire or inclination. ▷ *v* **4** put up with.

stomp *v informal* tread heavily.

stone ❶ *n* **1** material of which rocks are made. **2** piece of this. **3** gem. **4** piece of rock for a specific purpose. **5** hard central part of a fruit. **6** unit of weight equal to 14 pounds or 6.350 kilograms. **7** hard deposit formed in the kidney or bladder. ▷ *v* **8** throw stones at. **9** remove stones from (a fruit). **stoned** *adj slang* under the influence of alcohol or drugs. **stony** *adj* **1** of or like stone. **2** unfeeling or hard. **stony-broke** *adj slang* completely penniless. **stonily** *adv* **Stone Age** prehistoric period when tools were made of stone.

──────────── THESAURUS ────────────

stock *n* **1** = **goods**, array, choice, commodities, merchandise, range, selection, variety, wares **2** = **supply**, fund, hoard, reserve, stockpile, store **3** = **property**, assets, capital, funds, investment **4** = **livestock**, beasts, cattle, domestic animals ▷ *adj* **11** = **standard**, conventional, customary, ordinary, regular, routine, usual **12** = **hackneyed**, banal, overused, trite ▷ *v* **13** = **sell**, deal in, handle, keep, supply, trade in **14** = **provide with**, equip, fit out, furnish, supply

stocky *adj* = **thickset**, chunky, dumpy, solid, stubby, sturdy

stodgy *adj* **1** = **heavy**, filling, leaden, starchy **2** = **dull**, boring, fuddy-duddy (*inf*), heavy going, staid, stuffy, tedious, unexciting

stoic *adj* **2** (also **stoical**) = **resigned**, dispassionate, impassive, long-suffering, philosophic, phlegmatic, stolid

stolid *adj* = **apathetic**, dull, lumpish, unemotional, wooden

stomach *n* **2** = **belly**, abdomen, gut (*inf*), pot, tummy (*inf*) **3** = **inclination**, appetite, desire, relish, taste ▷ *v* **4** = **bear**, abide, endure, swallow, take, tolerate

stony *adj* **2** = **cold**, blank, chilly, expressionless, hard, hostile, icy, unresponsive

stone-cold *adj* completely cold.
stone-deaf *adj* completely deaf.
stonewall *v* obstruct or hinder discussion. **stoneware** *n* hard kind of pottery fired at a very high temperature. **stonework** *n* part of a building made of stone.

stood *v* past of STAND.

stooge *n* **1** actor who feeds lines to a comedian or acts as the butt of his jokes. **2** *slang* person taken advantage of by a superior.

stool *n* **1** chair without arms or back. **2** piece of excrement.

stool pigeon *n* informer for the police.

stoop ❶ *v* **1** bend (the body) forward and downward. **2** carry oneself habitually in this way. **3** degrade oneself. ▷ *n* **4** stooping posture.

stop ❶ *v* **stopping**, **stopped 1** cease or cause to cease from doing (something). **2** bring to or come to a halt. **3** prevent or restrain. **4** withhold. **5** block or plug. **6** stay or rest. **7** instruct a bank not to honour (a cheque). ▷ *n* **8** stopping or being stopped. **9** place where something stops. **10** device that prevents, limits, or ends the motion of a mechanism. **11** full stop. **12** knob on an organ that is pulled out to allow a set of pipes to sound. **stoppage time** same as INJURY TIME. **stopper** *n* plug for closing a bottle etc. **stopcock** *n* valve to control or stop the flow of fluid in a pipe. **stopgap** *n* temporary substitute. **stopover** *n* short break in a journey. **stop press** news item put into a newspaper after printing has been started. **stopwatch** *n* watch which can be stopped instantly for exact timing of a sporting event.

store ❶ *v* **1** collect and keep (things) for future use. **2** put (furniture etc.) in a warehouse for safekeeping. **3** stock (goods). **4** *Computers* enter or retain (data). ▷ *n* **5** shop. **6** supply kept for future use. **7** storage place, such as a warehouse. ▷ *pl* **8** stock of provisions. **in store** about to happen. **set great store by** value greatly. **storage** *n* **1** storing. **2** space for storing. **storage heater** electric device that can accumulate and radiate heat generated by off-peak electricity.

storey *n* floor or level of a building.

stork *n* large wading bird.

storm ❶ *n* **1** violent weather with wind, rain, or snow. **2** strongly expressed reaction. **3** heavy shower of missiles. ▷ *v* **4** attack or capture (a place) suddenly. **5** shout angrily. **6** rush violently or angrily. **stormy** *adj* **1** characterized by storms. **2** involving violent emotions. **storm trooper** member of the Nazi militia.

story ❶ *n, pl* **-ries 1** description of a series of events told or written for entertainment. **2** plot of a book or film. **3** news report. **4** *informal* lie.

stoup [stoop] *n* small basin for holy water.

---

stoop *v* **1** = **bend**, bow, crouch, duck, hunch, lean **3** = **lower oneself by**, descend to, resort to, sink to ▷ *n* **4** = **slouch**, bad posture

stop *v* **1, 2** = **halt**, cease, conclude, cut short, desist, discontinue, end, finish, pause, put an end to, quit, refrain, shut down, terminate **3** = **prevent**, arrest, forestall, hinder, hold back, impede, repress, restrain **5** = **plug**, block, obstruct, seal, staunch, stem **6** = **stay**, lodge, rest ▷ *n* **8** = **end**, cessation, finish, halt, standstill **9** = **station**, depot, terminus

stopgap *n* = **makeshift**, improvisation, resort, substitute

stoppage *n* = **stopping**, arrest, close, closure, cutoff, halt, shutdown, standstill

store *v* **1, 2** = **put by**, deposit, garner, hoard, keep, put aside, reserve, save, stockpile ▷ *n* **5** = **shop**, market, mart, outlet **6** = **supply**, accumulation, cache, fund, hoard, quantity, reserve, stock, stockpile **7** = **repository**, depository, storeroom, warehouse

storm *n* **1** = **tempest**, blizzard, gale, hurricane, squall **2** = **outburst**, agitation, commotion, disturbance, furore, outbreak, outcry, row, rumpus, strife, tumult, turmoil ▷ *v* **4** = **attack**, assail, assault, charge, rush **5** = **rage**, bluster, rant, rave, thunder **6** = **rush**, flounce, fly, stamp

stormy *adj* **1** = **wild**, blustery, inclement, raging, rough, squally, turbulent, windy

story *n* **1** = **tale**, account, anecdote, history, legend, narrative, romance, yarn **3** = **report**, article, feature, news, news item, scoop

S

stout ❶ adj 1 fat. 2 thick and strong. 3 brave and resolute. ▷ n 4 strong dark beer. **stoutly** adv.

stove[1] n apparatus for cooking or heating.

stove[2] v a past of STAVE.

stow ❶ v pack or store. **stowage** n space or charge for stowing goods. **stowaway** n person who hides on a ship or aircraft in order to travel free. **stow away** v hide as a stowaway.

straddle v have one leg or part on each side of (something).

strafe v attack (an enemy) with machine guns from the air.

straggle v 1 go or spread in a rambling or irregular way. 2 linger behind. **straggler** n **straggly** adj.

straight ❶ adj 1 not curved or crooked. 2 level or upright. 3 orderly. 4 honest or frank. 5 in continuous succession. 6 (of spirits) undiluted. 7 Theatre serious. 8 slang heterosexual. 9 slang conventional. ▷ adv 10 in a straight line. 11 immediately. 12 in a level or upright position. 13 uninterruptedly. ▷ n 14 straight part, esp. of a racetrack. **go straight** informal reform after being a criminal. **straighten** v **straightaway** adv immediately. **straight face** serious facial expression concealing a desire to laugh. **straightforward** adj 1 honest, frank. 2 (of a task) easy.

strain[1] ❶ v 1 subject to mental tension. 2 cause (something) to be used or tested beyond its limits. 3 make an intense effort. 4 injure by overexertion. 5 sieve. 6 draw or be drawn taut. ▷ n 7 tension or tiredness. 8 force exerted by straining. 9 injury from overexertion. 10 great demand on strength or resources. 11 melody or theme. **strained** adj 1 not natural, forced. 2 not relaxed, tense. **strainer** n sieve.

strain[2] ❶ n 1 breed or race. 2 trace or streak.

strait ❶ n 1 narrow channel connecting two areas of sea. ▷ pl 2 position of acute difficulty. **straitjacket** n strong

——————————— THESAURUS ———————————

stout adj 1 = **fat**, big, bulky, burly, corpulent, fleshy, heavy, overweight, plump, portly, rotund, tubby 2 = **strong**, able-bodied, brawny, muscular, robust, stalwart, strapping, sturdy 3 = **brave**, bold, courageous, fearless, gallant, intrepid, plucky, resolute, valiant

stow v = **pack**, bundle, load, put away, stash (inf), store

straight adj 1 = **direct**, near, short 2 a = **level**, aligned, even, horizontal, right, smooth, square, true b = **upright**, erect, plumb, vertical 3 = **orderly**, arranged, in order, neat, organized, shipshape, tidy 4 a = **honest**, above board, fair, honourable, just, law-abiding, reliable, respectable, trustworthy, upright b adj = **frank**, blunt, bold, candid, forthright, honest, outright, plain, straightforward 5 = **successive**, consecutive, continuous, nonstop, running, solid 6 = **undiluted**, neat, pure, unadulterated, unmixed 9 Sl = **conventional**, bourgeois, conservative ▷ adv 11 = **directly**, at once, immediately, instantly

straightaway adv = **immediately**, at once, directly, instantly, now, right away

straighten v = **neaten**, arrange, order, put in order, tidy (up)

straightforward adj 1 = **honest**, candid, direct, forthright, genuine, open, sincere, truthful, upfront (inf) 2 = **simple**, easy, elementary, routine, uncomplicated

strain[1] v 3 = **strive**, bend over backwards (inf), endeavour, give it one's best shot (inf), go for it (inf), knock oneself out (inf), labour, struggle 4 = **overexert**, injure, overtax, overwork, pull, sprain, tax, tear, twist, wrench 5 = **sieve**, filter, purify, sift 6 = **stretch**, distend, draw tight, tauten, tighten ▷ n 7 = **stress**, anxiety, burden, pressure, tension 8 = **exertion**, effort, force, struggle 9 = **injury**, pull, sprain, wrench

strain[2] n 1 = **breed**, ancestry, blood, descent, extraction, family, lineage, race 2 = **trace**, streak, suggestion, tendency

strained adj 1 = **forced**, artificial, false, put on, unnatural 2 = **tense**, awkward, difficult, embarrassed, stiff, uneasy

strait n 1 = **channel**, narrows, sound ▷ pl 2 = **difficulty**, dilemma, extremity, hardship, plight, predicament

jacket with long sleeves used to bind the arms of a violent person. **strait-laced**, **straight-laced** *adj* prudish or puritanical.

straitened *adj* **in straitened circumstances** not having much money.

strand¹ ❶ *v* **1** run aground. **2** leave in difficulties. ▷ *n* **3** *poetic* shore.

strand² ❶ *n* **1** single thread of string, wire, etc. **2** element of something.

strange ❶ *adj* **1** odd or unusual. **2** not familiar. **3** inexperienced (in) or unaccustomed (to). **strangely** *adv* **strangeness** *n* **stranger** *n* person who is not known or is new to a place or experience.

strangle ❶ *v* **1** kill by squeezing the throat. **2** prevent the development of. **strangler** *n* **strangulation** *n* strangling. **stranglehold** *n* **1** strangling grip in wrestling. **2** powerful control.

strap ❶ *n* **1** strip of flexible material for lifting, fastening, or holding in place. ▷ *v* **strapping**, **strapped 2** fasten with a strap or straps. **strapping** *adj* tall and sturdy.

strata *n* plural of STRATUM.

stratagem ❶ *n* clever plan, trick.

strategy ❶ *n*, *pl* **-gies 1** overall plan. **2** art of planning in war. **strategic** [strat-**ee**-jik] *adj* **1** advantageous. **2** (of weapons) aimed at an enemy's homeland. **strategically** *adv*

strategist *n* **strategize** *v.*

strathspey *n* Scottish dance with gliding steps.

stratosphere *n* atmospheric layer between about 15 and 50 kilometres above the earth.

stratum [**strah**-tum] *n*, *pl* **strata 1** layer, esp. of rock. **2** social class. **stratified** *adj* divided into strata. **stratification** *n.*

straw *n* **1** dried stalks of grain. **2** single stalk of straw. **3** long thin tube used to suck up liquid into the mouth. **straw-coloured** *adj* pale yellow. **straw poll** unofficial poll taken to determine general opinion.

strawberry *n* sweet fleshy red fruit with small seeds on the outside. **strawberry mark** red birthmark.

stray ❶ *v* **1** wander. **2** digress. **3** deviate from certain moral standards. ▷ *adj* **4** having strayed. **5** scattered, random. ▷ *n* **6** stray animal.

streak ❶ *n* **1** long band of contrasting colour or substance. **2** sudden flash. **3** quality or characteristic. **4** short stretch (of good or bad luck). ▷ *v* **5** mark with streaks. **6** move rapidly. **7** *informal* run naked in public. **streaker** *n* **streaky** *adj.*

stream ❶ *n* **1** small river. **2** steady flow, as of liquid, speech, or people. **3** schoolchildren grouped together because of similar ability. ▷ *v* **4** flow

strait-laced, straight-laced *adj* = **puritanical**, moralistic, narrow-minded, prim, proper, prudish, strict

strand² *n* **1** = **filament**, fibre, string, thread

stranded *adj* **1** = **beached**, aground, ashore, grounded, marooned, shipwrecked **2** = **helpless**, abandoned, high and dry

strange *adj* **1** = **odd**, abnormal, bizarre, curious, extraordinary, munted (*NZ sl*), peculiar, queer, uncommon, weird, wonderful **2** = **unfamiliar**, alien, exotic, foreign, new, novel, unknown, untried

stranger *n* = **newcomer**, alien, foreigner, guest, incomer, outlander, visitor

strangle *v* **1** = **throttle**, asphyxiate, choke, strangulate **2** = **suppress**, inhibit, repress, stifle

strap *n* **1** = **belt**, thong, tie ▷ *v*

2 = **fasten**, bind, buckle, lash, secure, tie

strapping *adj* = **well-built**, big, brawny, husky (*inf*), powerful, robust, sturdy

stratagem *n* = **trick**, device, dodge, manoeuvre, plan, ploy, ruse, scheme, subterfuge

strategy *n* **1** = **plan**, approach, policy, procedure, scheme

stray *v* **1** = **wander**, drift, err, go astray **2** = **digress**, deviate, diverge, get off the point ▷ *adj* **4** = **lost**, abandoned, homeless, roaming, vagrant **5** = **random**, accidental, chance

streak *n* **1** = **band**, layer, line, slash, strip, stripe, stroke, vein **3** = **trace**, dash, element, strain, touch, vein ▷ *v* **6** = **speed**, dart, flash, fly, hurtle, sprint, tear, whizz (*inf*), zoom

stream *n* **1** = **river**, bayou, beck, brook, burn (*Scot*), rivulet, tributary **2** = **flow**,

steadily. **5** move in unbroken
succession. **6** float in the air. **7** group
(pupils) in streams. **streamer** n **1** strip
of coloured paper that unrolls when
tossed. **2** long narrow flag.

streamline ⊙ v **1** make more efficient
by simplifying. **2** give (a car, plane,
etc.) a smooth even shape to offer least
resistance to the flow of air or water.

street ⊙ n public road, usu. lined with
buildings. **streetwalker** n prostitute.
streetwise adj knowing how to
survive in big cities.

streetcar n US & Canad public
transport vehicle powered by an
overhead wire and running on rails
laid in the road.

strength ⊙ n **1** quality of being strong.
2 quality or ability considered an
advantage. **3** degree of intensity.
4 total number of people in a group.
on the strength of on the basis of.
strengthen v.

strenuous ⊙ adj requiring great energy
or effort. **strenuously** adv.

streptococcus [strep-toe-**kok**-uss] n, pl
-cocci bacterium occurring in chains,
many species of which cause disease.

streptomycin n antibiotic drug.

stress ⊙ n **1** tension or strain.
2 emphasis. **3** stronger sound in
saying a word or syllable.
4 Physics force producing strain. ▷ v

5 emphasize. **6** put stress on (a word
or syllable). **stressed-out** adj informal
suffering from tension. **stressful** adj.

stretch ⊙ v **1** extend or be extended.
2 be able to be stretched. **3** extend the
limbs or body. **4** pull tight. **5** strain
(resources or abilities) to the utmost.
▷ n **6** stretching. **7** continuous
expanse. **8** period. **9** informal term of
imprisonment. **stretchy** adj **stretcher**
n frame covered with canvas, on
which an injured person is carried.

strew v **strewing**, **strewed**, **strewed**
or **strewn** scatter (things) over a
surface.

striation n **1** scratch or groove.
2 pattern of scratches or grooves.
striated adj.

stricken adj seriously affected by
disease, grief, pain, etc.

strict ⊙ adj **1** stern or severe.
2 adhering closely to specified rules.
3 complete, absolute. **strictly** adv
strictness n.

stricture n severe criticism.

stride v **striding**, **strode**, **stridden**
1 walk with long steps. ▷ n **2** long
step. **3** regular pace. ▷ pl **4** progress.

strident ⊙ adj loud and harsh.
stridently adv **stridency** n.

strife ⊙ n conflict, quarrelling.

strike ⊙ v **striking**, **struck 1** cease
work as a protest. **2** hit. **3** attack

———————————————— THESAURUS ————————————————

course, current, drift, run, rush, surge,
tide, torrent ▷ v **4, 5** = **flow**, cascade,
flood, gush, issue, pour, run, spill,
spout

streamlined adj **1** = **efficient**,
organized, rationalized, slick, smooth-
running

street n = **road**, avenue, lane, roadway,
row, terrace

strength n **1** = **might**, brawn, courage,
fortitude, muscle, robustness,
stamina, sturdiness, toughness
2 = **strong point**, advantage, asset
3 = **power**, effectiveness, efficacy,
force, intensity, potency, vigour

strengthen v = **fortify**, augment,
bolster, brace, brace up, build up,
buttress, consolidate, gee up, harden,
intensify, invigorate, reinforce,
restore, stiffen, support, toughen

strenuous adj = **demanding**, arduous,
hard, laborious, taxing, tough, uphill

stress n **1** = **strain**, anxiety, burden,
pressure, tension, trauma, worry

2 = **emphasis**, force, significance,
weight **3** = **accent**, accentuation,
beat, emphasis ▷ v **5** = **emphasize**,
accentuate, dwell on, underline

stretch v **1** = **extend**, cover, put forth,
reach, spread, unroll **2** = **distend**,
draw out, elongate, expand, strain,
tighten **4** = **tighten**, pull **5** = **strain**
▷ n **7** = **expanse**, area, distance,
extent, spread, tract **8** = **period**,
space, spell, stint, term, time

strict adj **1** = **severe**, authoritarian,
firm, harsh, stern, stringent
2 = **exact**, accurate, close, faithful,
meticulous, precise, scrupulous, true
3 = **absolute**, total, utter

strident adj = **harsh**, discordant,
grating, jarring, raucous, screeching,
shrill

strife n = **conflict**, battle, clash,
discord, dissension, friction, quarrel

strike v **1** = **walk out**, down tools,
mutiny, revolt **2** = **hit**, beat, clobber
(sl), clout (inf), cuff, hammer, knock,

S

suddenly. **4** ignite (a match) by friction. **5** sound (a note) on a musical instrument. **6** (of a clock) indicate (a time) by sounding a bell. **7** affect in a particular way. **8** enter the mind of. **9** render. **10** afflict. **11** discover (gold, oil, etc.). **12** agree (a bargain). **13** take up (a posture). **14** make (a coin) by stamping it. ▷ *n* **15** stoppage of work as a protest. **16** striking. **17** military attack. **18** discovery of gold, oil, etc. **strike camp** dismantle and pack up tents. **strike home** have the desired effect. **striker** *n* **1** striking worker. **2** attacking footballer. **striking** *adj* **1** impressive. **2** noteworthy. **strikebreaker** *n* person who works while others are on strike. **strike off, out** *v* cross out. **strike up** *v* **1** begin (a conversation or friendship). **2** begin to play music.

string ❶ *n* **1** thin cord used for tying. **2** set of objects threaded on a string. **3** series of things or events. **4** stretched wire or cord on a musical instrument that produces sound when vibrated. ▷ *pl* **5** restrictions or conditions. **6** section of an orchestra consisting of stringed instruments. ▷ *v* **stringing, strung 7** provide with a string or strings. **8** thread on a string. **9** extend in a line. **pull strings** use one's influence. **stringed** *adj* (of a musical instrument) having strings that are plucked or played with a bow. **stringy** *adj* **1** like string. **2** (of meat) fibrous. **stringy-bark** *n Aust* eucalyptus with a fibrous bark. **string along** *v* **1** *informal* accompany. **2** deceive over a period of time. **string up** *v informal* kill by hanging.

stringent ❶ [**strin**-jent] *adj* strictly controlled or enforced. **stringently** *adv* **stringency** *n*.

strip¹ ❶ *v* **stripping, stripped 1** take (the covering or clothes) off. **2** take a title or possession away from (someone). **3** remove (paint) from (a surface). **4** dismantle (an engine). ▷ *n* **5** act of stripping. **stripper** *n* person who performs a striptease. **striptease** *n* entertainment in which a performer undresses to music.

strip² *n* **1** long narrow piece. **2** clothes a football team plays in. **strip cartoon** sequence of drawings telling a story.

stripe *n* **1** long narrow band of contrasting colour or substance. **2** chevron on a uniform to indicate rank. **striped, stripy, stripey** *adj*.

stripling *n* youth.

strive ❶ *v* **striving, strove, striven** make a great effort.

strobe *n* short for STROBOSCOPE.

stroboscope *n* instrument producing a very bright flashing light.

strode *v* past tense of STRIDE.

stroke ❶ *v* **1** touch or caress lightly with the hand. ▷ *n* **2** light touch or caress with the hand. **3** rupture of a blood vessel in the brain. **4** blow. **5** action or occurrence of the kind specified, e.g. *a stroke of luck*. **6** chime of a clock. **7** mark made by a pen or paintbrush. **8** hitting of the ball in some sports. **9** style or method of swimming. **10** single pull on the oars in rowing.

stroll ❶ *v* **1** walk in a leisurely manner. ▷ *n* **2** leisurely walk.

stroller *n US & Canad* chair-shaped carriage for a baby.

THESAURUS

punch, slap, smack, swipe, thump, wallop (*inf*) **3 = attack**, assail, assault, hit **7 = affect**, hit, register (*inf*) **8 = occur to**, come to, dawn on or upon, hit, register (*inf*)
striking *adj* **1 = impressive**, conspicuous, dramatic, jaw-dropping, noticeable, outstanding
string *n* **1 = cord**, fibre, twine **3 = series**, chain, file, line, procession, row, sequence, succession
stringent *adj* **= strict**, inflexible, rigid, rigorous, severe, tight, tough
stringy *adj* **2 = fibrous**, gristly, sinewy, tough
strip¹ *v* **1 = undress**, disrobe, unclothe

2 = divest, plunder, rob
strip² *n* **1 = piece**, band, belt, shred
strive *v* **= try**, attempt, bend over backwards (*inf*), break one's neck (*inf*), do one's best, give it one's best shot (*inf*), go all out (*inf*), knock oneself out (*inf*), labour, make an all-out effort (*inf*), struggle, toil
stroke *v* **1 = caress**, fondle, pet, rub ▷ *n* **3 = apoplexy**, attack, collapse, fit, seizure **4 = blow**, hit, knock, pat, rap, swipe, thump
stroll *v* **1 = walk**, amble, promenade, ramble, saunter ▷ *n* **2 = walk**, breath of air, constitutional, promenade, ramble

strong ❶ *adj* **1** having physical power.
2 not easily broken. **3** great in degree
or intensity. **4** having moral force.
5 having a powerful taste or smell.
6 having a specified number, e.g.
twenty strong. **going strong** *informal*
thriving. **strongly** *adv* **strong-arm** *adj*
involving violence. **stronghold** *n*
1 area of predominance of a particular
belief. **2** fortress. **strong point** thing
at which one excels. **strongroom** *n*
room designed for the safekeeping of
valuables.

strontium *n Chemistry* silvery-white
metallic element. **strontium-90** *n*
radioactive isotope present in the
fallout of nuclear explosions.

strop *n* leather strap for sharpening
razors.

stroppy *adj* **-pier, -piest** *slang* angry or
awkward.

strove *v* past tense of STRIVE.

struck *v* past of STRIKE.

structure ❶ *n* **1** complex construction.
2 manner or basis of construction or
organization. ▷ *v* **3** give a structure to.
structural *adj* **structuralism** *n*
approach to literature, social sciences,
etc., which sees changes in the subject
as caused and organized by a hidden
set of universal rules. **structuralist** *n*,
adj.

strudel *n* thin sheet of filled dough
rolled up and baked, usu. with an
apple filling.

struggle ❶ *v* **1** work, strive, or make
one's way with difficulty. **2** move
about violently in an attempt to get
free. **3** fight (with someone). ▷ *n*
4 striving. **5** fight.

strum *v* **strumming, strummed** play
(a guitar or banjo) by sweeping the
thumb or a plectrum across the
strings.

strumpet *n old-fashioned* prostitute.

strung *v* past of STRING.

strut ❶ *v* **strutting, strutted 1** walk
pompously, swagger. ▷ *n* **2** bar
supporting a structure.

strychnine [**strik**-neen] *n* very
poisonous drug used in small
quantities as a stimulant.

stub ❶ *n* **1** short piece left after use.
2 counterfoil of a cheque or ticket. ▷ *v*
stubbing, stubbed 3 strike (the toe)
painfully against an object. **4** put out
(a cigarette) by pressing the end
against a surface. **stubby** *adj* short
and broad.

stubble *n* **1** short stalks of grain left in
a field after reaping. **2** short growth of
hair on the chin of a man who has not
shaved recently. **stubbly** *adj*.

stubborn ❶ *adj* **1** refusing to agree or
give in. **2** difficult to deal with.
stubbornly *adv* **stubbornness** *n*.

stucco *n* plaster used for coating or
decorating walls. **stuccoed** *adj*.

stuck ❶ *v* past of STICK². **stuck-up** *adj*
informal conceited or snobbish.

——————————————— THESAURUS ———————————————

strong *adj* **1** = **powerful**, athletic,
brawny, burly, hardy, lusty, muscular,
robust, strapping, sturdy, tough
2 = **durable**, hard-wearing, heavy-
duty, sturdy, substantial, well-built
3 = **intense**, acute, deep, fervent,
fervid, fierce, firm, keen, vehement,
violent, zealous **4** = **persuasive**,
compelling, convincing, effective,
potent, sound, telling, weighty, well-
founded **5** = **distinct**, clear, marked,
overpowering, unmistakable

stronghold *n* **2** = **fortress**, bastion,
bulwark, castle, citadel, fort

structure *n* **1** = **building**,
construction, edifice, erection
2 = **arrangement**, configuration,
construction, design, form, formation,
make-up, organization ▷ *v*
3 = **arrange**, assemble, build up,
design, organize, shape

struggle *v* **1** = **strive**, exert oneself,

give it one's best shot (*inf*), go all out
(*inf*), knock oneself out (*inf*), labour,
make an all-out effort (*inf*), strain,
toil, work **3** = **fight**, battle, compete,
contend, grapple, wrestle ▷ *n*
4 = **effort**, exertion, labour, pains,
scramble, toil, work, yakka (*Aust & NZ
inf*) **5** = **fight**, battle, brush, clash,
combat, conflict, contest, tussle

strut *v* **1** = **swagger**, parade, peacock,
prance

stub *n* **1** = **butt**, dog-end (*inf*), end,
remnant, stump, tail, tail end
2 = **counterfoil**

stubborn *adj* **1, 2** = **obstinate**, dogged,
headstrong, inflexible, intractable,
obdurate, pig-headed, recalcitrant,
tenacious, unyielding

stubby *adj* = **stocky**, chunky, dumpy,
short, squat, thickset

stuck *adj* = **fastened**, cemented, fast,
fixed, glued, joined

stud¹ ❶ n 1 small piece of metal attached to a surface for decoration. 2 disc-like removable fastener for clothes. 3 one of several small round objects fixed to the sole of a football boot to give better grip. ▷ v **studding**, **studded** 4 set with studs.

stud² n 1 male animal, esp. a stallion, kept for breeding. 2 (also **stud farm**) place where horses are bred. 3 *slang* virile or sexually active man.

student ❶ n person who studies a subject, esp. at university.

studio ❶ n, pl **-dios** 1 workroom of an artist or photographer. 2 room or building in which television or radio programmes, records, or films are made. **studio flat** one-room flat with a small kitchen and bathroom.

study ❶ v **studying**, **studied** 1 be engaged in learning (a subject). 2 investigate by observation and research. 3 scrutinize. ▷ n, pl **studies** 4 act or process of studying. 5 room for studying in. 6 book or paper produced as a result of study. 7 sketch done as practice or preparation. 8 musical composition designed to improve playing technique. **student** n person who studies a subject, esp. at university. **studied** adj carefully practised or planned. **studious** [styoo-dee-uss]

adj 1 fond of study. 2 careful and deliberate. **studiously** adv.

stuff ❶ n 1 substance or material. 2 collection of unnamed things. 3 raw material of something. 4 subject matter. 5 woollen fabric. ▷ v 6 pack, cram, or fill completely. 7 fill (food) with a seasoned mixture. 8 fill (an animal's skin) with material to restore the shape of the live animal. **stuff oneself** informal eat large quantities. **stuffing** n 1 seasoned mixture with which food is stuffed. 2 padding.

stuffy ❶ adj **stuffier**, **stuffiest** 1 lacking fresh air. 2 informal dull or conventional.

stultifying adj very boring and repetitive.

stumble ❶ v 1 trip and nearly fall. 2 walk in an unsure way. 3 make frequent mistakes in speech. ▷ n 4 stumbling. **stumble across** v discover accidentally. **stumbling block** obstacle or difficulty.

stump ❶ n 1 base of a tree left when the main trunk has been cut away. 2 part of a thing left after a larger part has been removed. 3 *Cricket* one of the three upright sticks forming the wicket. ▷ v 4 baffle. 5 *Cricket* dismiss (a batsman) by breaking his wicket with the ball. 6 walk with heavy steps. **stumpy** adj short and thick.

———————— THESAURUS ————————

stuck-up adj Inf = **snobbish**, arrogant, bigheaded (inf), conceited, haughty, proud, snooty (inf), toffee-nosed (sl, chiefly Brit)

stud¹ v 4 = **ornament**, dot, spangle, spot

student n = **learner**, apprentice, disciple, pupil, scholar, trainee, undergraduate

studied adj = **planned**, conscious, deliberate, intentional, premeditated

studio n 1 = **workshop**, atelier

studious adj 1 = **scholarly**, academic, assiduous, bookish, diligent, hard-working, intellectual

study v 1 = **learn**, cram (inf), mug up (Brit sl), read up, swot (up) (Brit inf) 2 = **contemplate**, consider, examine, go into, ponder, pore over, read 3 = **examine**, analyse, investigate, look into, research, scrutinize, survey ▷ n 4 a = **learning**, application, lessons, reading, research, school work, swotting (Brit inf)

b = **examination**, analysis, consideration, contemplation, inquiry, inspection, investigation, review, scrutiny, survey

stuff n 1 = **substance**, essence, matter 2 = **things**, belongings, effects, equipment, gear, kit, objects, paraphernalia, possessions, tackle 5 = **material**, cloth, fabric, textile ▷ v 6 = **cram**, crowd, fill, force, jam, pack, push, ram, shove, squeeze

stuffing n 2 = **filling**, packing, wadding

stuffy adj 1 = **airless**, close, frowsty, heavy, muggy, oppressive, stale, stifling, sultry, unventilated 2 Inf = **staid**, dreary, dull, pompous, priggish, prim, stodgy

stumble v 1 = **trip**, fall, falter, lurch, reel, slip, stagger ▷ v **stumble across** = **discover**, chance upon, come across, find

stump v 4 = **baffle**, bewilder, confuse, flummox, mystify, nonplus, perplex, puzzle

S

stump up v informal give (the money required).

stun ❶ v **stunning**, **stunned 1** shock or overwhelm. **2** knock senseless. **stunner** n informal beautiful person or thing. **stunning** adj very attractive or impressive.

stung v past of STING.

stunk v a past of STINK.

stunt¹ ❶ v prevent or impede the growth of. **stunted** adj.

stunt² ❶ n **1** acrobatic or dangerous action. **2** anything spectacular done to gain publicity.

stupefy ❶ v **-fying**, **-fied 1** make insensitive or lethargic. **2** astound. **stupefaction** n.

stupendous ❶ adj very large or impressive. **stupendously** adv.

stupid ❶ adj **1** lacking intelligence. **2** silly. **3** in a stupor. **stupidity** n **stupidly** adv.

stupor ❶ n dazed or unconscious state.

sturdy ❶ adj **-dier**, **-diest 1** healthy and robust. **2** strongly built. **sturdily** adv.

sturgeon n fish from which caviar is obtained.

stutter ❶ v **1** speak with repetition of initial consonants. ▷ n **2** tendency to stutter.

sty n, pl **sties** pen for pigs.

stye, sty n, pl **styes**, **sties** inflammation at the base of an eyelash.

Stygian [**stij**-jee-an] adj lit gloomy.

style ❶ n **1** shape or design. **2** manner of writing, speaking, or doing something. **3** elegance, refinement. **4** prevailing fashion. **5** part of a flower that bears the stigma. ▷ v **6** shape or design. **7** name or call. **stylish** adj smart, elegant, and fashionable. **stylishly** adv **stylist** n **1** hairdresser. **2** person who writes or performs with great attention to style. **stylistic** adj of literary or artistic style. **stylize** v cause to conform to an established stylistic form.

stylus n needle-like device on a record player that rests in the groove of the record and picks up the sound signals.

stymie v **-mieing**, **-mied** hinder or thwart.

styptic n, adj (drug) used to stop bleeding.

— THESAURUS —

stumpy adj = **stocky**, dumpy, short, squat, stubby, thickset

stun v **1** = **overcome**, astonish, astound, bewilder, confound, confuse, overpower, shock, stagger, stupefy **2** = **knock out**, daze

stunning adj = **wonderful**, beautiful, dazzling, gorgeous, impressive, jaw-dropping, lovely, marvellous, sensational (inf), spectacular, striking

stunt² n **1, 2** = **feat**, act, deed, exploit, trick

stunted adj = **undersized**, diminutive, little, small, tiny

stupefy v **2** = **astound**, amaze, daze, dumbfound, shock, stagger, stun

stupendous adj **a** = **wonderful**, amazing, astounding, breathtaking, jaw-dropping, marvellous, overwhelming, sensational (inf), staggering, superb **b** = **huge**, colossal, enormous, gigantic, mega (sl), vast

stupid adj **1** = **unintelligent**, brainless, dense, dim, half-witted, moronic, obtuse, simple, simple-minded, slow, slow-witted, thick **2** = **silly**, asinine, daft (inf), foolish, idiotic, imbecilic, inane, nonsensical, pointless, rash, senseless, unintelligent **3** = **dazed**, groggy, insensate, semiconscious, stunned, stupefied

stupidity n **1** = **lack of intelligence**, brainlessness, denseness, dimness, dullness, imbecility, obtuseness, slowness, thickness **2** = **silliness**, absurdity, fatuousness, folly, foolishness, idiocy, inanity, lunacy, madness

stupor n = **daze**, coma, insensibility, stupefaction, unconsciousness

sturdy adj **1** = **robust**, athletic, brawny, hardy, lusty, muscular, powerful **2** = **substantial**, durable, solid, well-built, well-made

stutter v **1** = **stammer**, falter, hesitate, stumble

style n **1** = **design**, cut, form, manner **2** = **manner**, approach, method, mode, technique, way **3** = **elegance**, affluence, chic, comfort, ease, élan, flair, grandeur, luxury, panache, polish, smartness, sophistication, taste **4** = **fashion**, mode, rage, trend, vogue ▷ v **6** = **design**, adapt, arrange, cut, fashion, shape, tailor **7** = **call**, designate, dub, entitle, label, name, term

stylish adj = **smart**, chic, dressy (inf), fashionable, modish, trendy (Brit inf), voguish

S

suave ❶ [swahv] *adj* smooth and sophisticated in manner. **suavely** *adv*.

sub *n* 1 subeditor. 2 submarine. 3 subscription. 4 substitute. 5 *informal* advance payment of wages or salary. ▷ *v* **subbing**, **subbed** 6 act as a substitute. 7 grant advance payment to.

sub- *prefix* used with many main words to mean: 1 under or beneath, e.g. *submarine*. 2 subordinate, e.g. *sublieutenant*. 3 falling short of, e.g. *subnormal*. 4 forming a subdivision, e.g. *subheading*.

subaltern *n* army officer below the rank of captain.

subatomic *adj* of or being one of the particles which make up an atom.

subcommittee *n* small committee formed from some members of a larger committee.

subconscious ❶ *adj* 1 happening or existing without one's awareness. ▷ *n* 2 *Psychoanalysis* that part of the mind of which one is not aware but which can influence one's behaviour. **subconsciously** *adv*.

subcontinent *n* large land mass that is a distinct part of a continent.

subcontract *n* 1 secondary contract by which the main contractor for a job puts work out to others. ▷ *v* 2 put out (work) on a subcontract. **subcontractor** *n*.

subcutaneous [sub-cute-**ayn**-ee-uss] *adj* under the skin.

subdivide *v* divide (a part of something) into smaller parts. **subdivision** *n*.

subdue ❶ *v* **-duing**, **-dued** 1 overcome.

2 make less intense.

subeditor *n* person who checks and edits text for a newspaper or magazine.

subhuman *adj* less than human.

subject ❶ *n* 1 person or thing being dealt with or studied. 2 figure, scene, etc. portrayed by an artist or photographer. 3 *Grammar* word or phrase that represents the person or thing performing the action of the verb in a sentence. 4 person under the rule of a monarch or government. ▷ *adj* 5 being under the rule of a monarch or government. ▷ *v* (foll. by *to*) 6 cause to undergo. 7 bring under the control (of). **subject to** 1 liable to. 2 conditional upon. **subjection** *n* **subjective** *adj* based on personal feelings or prejudices. **subjectively** *adv*.

sub judice [sub **joo**-diss-ee] *adj Latin* before a court of law.

subjugate ❶ *v* bring (a group of people) under one's control. **subjugation** *n*.

subjunctive *Grammar* ▷ *n* 1 mood of verbs used when the content of the clause is doubted, supposed, or wished. ▷ *adj* 2 in or of that mood.

sublet *v* **-letting**, **-let** rent out (property rented from someone else).

sublieutenant *n* naval officer of the lowest rank.

sublimate *v Psychology* direct the energy of (a strong desire, esp. a sexual one) into socially acceptable activities. **sublimation** *n*.

sublime ❶ *adj* 1 of high moral, intellectual, or spiritual value.

THESAURUS

suave *adj* = **smooth**, charming, courteous, debonair, polite, sophisticated, urbane

subconscious *adj* 1 = **hidden**, inner, intuitive, latent, repressed, subliminal

subdue *v* 1 = **overcome**, break, conquer, control, crush, defeat, master, overpower, quell, tame, vanquish 2 = **moderate**, mellow, quieten down, soften, suppress, tone down

subdued *adj* 1 = **quiet**, chastened, crestfallen, dejected, downcast, down in the mouth, sad, serious 2 = **soft**, dim, hushed, muted, quiet, subtle, toned down, unobtrusive

subject *n* 1 = **topic**, affair, business,

issue, matter, object, point, question, substance, theme 4 = **citizen**, national, subordinate ▷ *adj* 5 = **subordinate**, dependent, inferior, obedient, satellite ▷ *v* (foll. by *to*) 6 = **put through**, expose, lay open, submit, treat **subject to** 1 = **liable to**, prone to 2 = **conditional on**, contingent on, dependent on

subjective *adj* = **personal**, biased, nonobjective, prejudiced

subjugate *v* = **conquer**, enslave, master, overcome, overpower, quell, subdue, suppress, vanquish

sublime *adj* 1 = **noble**, elevated, exalted, glorious, grand, great, high, lofty

S

2 unparalleled, supreme. ▷ *v*
3 *Chemistry* change from a solid to a vapour without first melting. **sublimely** *adv*.

subliminal *adj* relating to mental processes of which the individual is not aware.

sub-machine-gun *n* portable machine gun with a short barrel.

submarine *n* **1** vessel which can operate below the surface of the sea. ▷ *adj* **2** below the surface of the sea.

submerge ❶ *v* **1** put or go below the surface of water or other liquid. **2** involve totally. **submersion** *n* **submersible** *n, adj* (vehicle) able to work under water.

submit ❶ *v* **-mitting, -mitted**
1 surrender. **2** put forward for consideration. **3** be (voluntarily) subjected to a process or treatment. **submission** *n* **1** submitting. **2** something submitted for consideration. **3** state of being submissive. **submissive** *adj* meek and obedient.

subnormal *adj* less than normal, esp. in intelligence.

subordinate ❶ *adj* **1** of lesser rank or importance. ▷ *n* **2** subordinate person or thing. ▷ *v* **3** make or treat as subordinate. **subordination** *n*.

suborn *v formal* bribe or incite

(a person) to commit a wrongful act.

subpoena [sub-**pee**-na] *n* **1** writ requiring a person to appear before a lawcourt. ▷ *v* **2** summon (someone) with a subpoena.

sub rosa [sub **rose**-a] *adv Latin* in secret.

subscribe ❶ *v* **1** pay (a subscription). **2** give support or approval (to). **subscriber** *n* **subscription** *n* **1** payment for issues of a publication over a period. **2** money contributed to a charity etc. **3** membership fees paid to a society.

subscript *n, adj* (character) printed below the line.

subsection *n* division of a section.

subsequent ❶ *adj* occurring after, succeeding. **subsequently** *adv*.

subservient ❶ *adj* submissive, servile. **subservience** *n*.

subside ❶ *v* **1** become less intense. **2** sink to a lower level. **subsidence** *n* act or process of subsiding.

subsidiarity *n* principle of taking political decisions at the lowest practical level.

subsidiary ❶ *adj* **1** of lesser importance. ▷ *n, pl* **-aries 2** subsidiary person or thing.

subsidize ❶ *v* help financially. **subsidy** *n, pl* **-dies** any financial aid, grant, or contribution.

——————————————————————————————— THESAURUS ————

submerge *v* **1** = **immerse**, deluge, dip, duck, engulf, flood, inundate, overflow, overwhelm, plunge, sink, swamp

submission *n* **1** = **surrender**, assent, capitulation, cave-in (*inf*), giving in, yielding **2** = **presentation**, entry, handing in, tendering **3** = **meekness**, compliance, deference, docility, obedience, passivity, resignation

submissive *adj* = **meek**, accommodating, acquiescent, amenable, compliant, docile, obedient, passive, pliant, tractable, unresisting, yielding

submit *v* **1** = **surrender**, accede, agree, capitulate, cave in (*inf*), comply, endure, give in, succumb, tolerate, yield **2** = **present**, hand in, proffer, put forward, table, tender

subordinate *adj* **1** = **lesser**, dependent, inferior, junior, lower, minor, secondary, subject ▷ *n*
2 = **inferior**, aide, assistant,

attendant, junior, second

subordination *n* = **inferiority**, inferior *or* secondary status, servitude, subjection

subscribe *v* **1** = **contribute**, donate, give **2** = **support**, advocate, endorse

subscription *n* **2** = **contribution**, donation, gift **3** = **membership fee**, annual payment, dues

subsequent *adj* = **following**, after, ensuing, later, succeeding, successive

subsequently *adv* = **later**, afterwards

subservient *adj* = **servile**, abject, deferential, obsequious, slavish, submissive, sycophantic

subside *v* **1** = **decrease**, abate, diminish, ease, ebb, lessen, quieten, slacken, wane **2** = **collapse**, cave in, drop, lower, settle, sink

subsidiary *adj* **1** = **lesser**, ancillary, auxiliary, minor, secondary, subordinate, supplementary

subsidize *v* = **fund**, finance, promote, sponsor, support

subsist *v* manage to live.
subsistence *n*.

subsoil *n* earth just below the surface soil.

subsonic *adj* moving at a speed less than that of sound.

substance ❶ *n* **1** physical composition of something. **2** solid, powder, liquid, or paste. **3** essential meaning of something. **4** solid or meaningful quality. **5** wealth. **substantial** *adj* **1** of considerable size or value. **2** (of food or a meal) sufficient and nourishing. **3** solid or strong. **4** real. **substantially** *adv* **substantiate** *v* support (a story) with evidence. **substantiation** *n* **substantive** *n* **1** noun. ▷ *adj* **2** of or being the essential element of a thing.

substitute ❶ *v* **1** take the place of or put in place of another. ▷ *n* **2** person or thing taking the place of (another). **substitution** *n*.

subsume *v* include (an idea, case, etc.) under a larger classification or group.

subterfuge ❶ *n* trick used to achieve an objective.

subterranean *adj* underground.

subtitle *n* **1** secondary title of a book. ▷ *pl* **2** printed translation at the bottom of the picture in a film with foreign dialogue. ▷ *v* **3** provide with a subtitle or subtitles.

subtle ❶ *adj* **1** not immediately obvious. **2** delicate. **3** having or requiring ingenuity. **subtly** *adv* **subtlety** *n*.

subtract ❶ *v* take (one number or quantity) from another. **subtraction** *n*.

subtropical *adj* of the regions bordering on the tropics.

suburb *n* residential area on the outskirts of a city. **suburban** *adj* **1** of or inhabiting a suburb. **2** narrow or unadventurous in outlook. **suburbanite** *n* **suburbia** *n* suburbs and their inhabitants.

subvention *n* formal subsidy.

subvert ❶ *v* overthrow the authority of. **subversion** *n* **subversive** *adj*, *n*.

subway *n* **1** passage under a road or railway. **2** *US & Canad* underground railway.

succeed ❶ *v* **1** accomplish an aim. **2** turn out satisfactorily. **3** come next in order after (something). **4** take over a position from (someone). **success** *n* **1** achievement of something attempted. **2** attainment of wealth, fame, or position. **3** successful person or thing. **successful** *adj* having success. **successfully** *adv* **succession** *n* **1** series of people or things following one another in order. **2** act or right by which one person succeeds another in a position. **successive** *adj* consecutive. **successively** *adv* **successor** *n* person who succeeds someone in a position.

● **SPELLING TIP**
● The Bank of English evidence shows
● that people are able to remember
● the double s at the end of **success**
● more easily than the double c in the
● middle.

─────── **THESAURUS** ───────

subsidy *n* = **aid**, allowance, assistance, grant, help, support

substance *n* **1** = **material**, body, fabric, stuff **3** = **meaning**, essence, gist, import, main point, significance **4** = **reality**, actuality, concreteness **5** = **wealth**, assets, estate, means, property, resources

substantial *adj* **1** = **big**, ample, considerable, large, significant, sizable *or* sizeable

substantiate *v* = **support**, authenticate, confirm, establish, prove, verify

substitute *v* **1** = **replace**, change, exchange, interchange, swap, switch ▷ *n* **2** = **replacement**, agent, deputy, locum, proxy, reserve, sub, surrogate

subterfuge *n* = **trick**, deception, dodge, manoeuvre, ploy, ruse, stratagem

subtle *adj* **1** = **faint**, delicate, implied, slight, understated **2** = **sophisticated**, delicate, refined **3** = **crafty**, artful, cunning, devious, ingenious, shrewd, sly, wily

subtract *v* = **take away**, deduct, diminish, remove, take from, take off

subversive *adj* = **seditious**, riotous, treasonous ▷ *n* = **dissident**, fifth columnist, saboteur, terrorist, traitor

subvert *v* = **overturn**, sabotage, undermine

succeed *v* **1, 2** = **make it** (*inf*), be successful, crack it (*inf*), do well, flourish, make good, make the grade

S

succinct ❶ *adj* brief and clear. **succinctly** *adv*.

succour ❶ *v, n* help in distress.

succulent ❶ *adj* 1 juicy and delicious. 2 (of a plant) having thick fleshy leaves. ▷ *n* 3 succulent plant. **succulence** *n*.

succumb ❶ *v* 1 (foll. by *to*) give way (to something overpowering). 2 die of (an illness).

such *adj* 1 of the kind specified. 2 so great, so much. ▷ *pron* 3 such things. **such-and-such** *adj* specific, but not known or named. **suchlike** *pron* such or similar things.

suck ❶ *v* 1 draw (liquid or air) into the mouth. 2 take (something) into the mouth and moisten, dissolve, or roll it around with the tongue. 3 (foll. by *in*) draw in by irresistible force. ▷ *n* 4 sucking. **sucker** *n* 1 *slang* person who is easily deceived or swindled. 2 organ or device which adheres by suction. 3 shoot coming from a plant's root or the base of its main stem. **suck up to** *v informal* flatter (someone) for one's own profit.

suckle *v* feed at the breast. **suckling** *n* unweaned baby or young animal.

sucrose [**soo**-kroze] *n* chemical name for sugar.

suction *n* 1 sucking. 2 force produced by drawing air out of a space to make a vacuum that will suck in a substance from another space.

sudden ❶ *adj* done or occurring quickly and unexpectedly. **all of a sudden** quickly and unexpectedly. **suddenly** *adv* **suddenness** *n* **sudden death** *Sport* period of extra time in which the first competitor to score wins.

sudoku [soo-**doh**-koo] *n* logic puzzle involving the insertion of numbers into each row, column, and individual grid of a larger square so that none is repeated.

sudorific [syoo-dor-**if**-ik] *n, adj* (drug) causing sweating.

suds *pl n* froth of soap and water.

sue ❶ *v* **suing, sued** start legal proceedings against.

suede *n* leather with a velvety finish on one side.

suet *n* hard fat obtained from sheep and cattle, used in cooking.

suffer ❶ *v* 1 undergo or be subjected to. 2 tolerate. **sufferer** *n* **suffering** *n* **sufferance** *n* **on sufferance** tolerated with reluctance.

suffice ❶ [suf-**fice**] *v* be enough for a purpose. **sufficiency** *n* adequate amount. **sufficient** *adj* enough, adequate. **sufficiently** *adv*.

suffix *n* letter or letters added to the end of a word to form another word.

suffocate ❶ *v* 1 kill or be killed by deprivation of oxygen. 2 feel

(*inf*), prosper, thrive, triumph, work 3 = **follow**, come next, ensue, result 4 = **take over**, accede, assume the office of, come into, come into possession of, inherit

success *n* 1, 2 = **favourable outcome**, fame, fortune, happiness, luck, prosperity, triumph 3 = **hit** (*inf*), celebrity, megastar (*inf*), sensation, smash (*inf*), star, winner

successful *adj* = **thriving**, booming, flourishing, fortunate, fruitful, lucky, profitable, rewarding, top, victorious

succession *n* 1 = **series**, chain, course, cycle, order, progression, run, sequence, train 2 = **taking over**, accession, assumption, inheritance

successive *adj* = **consecutive**, following, in succession

succinct *adj* = **brief**, compact, concise, laconic, pithy, terse

succour *v* = **help**, aid, assist ▷ *n* = **help**, aid, assistance

succulent *adj* 1 = **juicy**, luscious, lush, moist, mouthwatering

succumb *v* 1 (foll. by *to*) = **surrender**, capitulate, cave in (*inf*), give in, submit, yield 2 = **die**, cark (*Aust & NZ sl*), fall

sucker *n* 1 *Sl* = **fool**, dupe, mug (*Brit sl*), pushover (*sl*), victim

sudden *adj* = **quick**, abrupt, hasty, hurried, rapid, rash, swift, unexpected

sue *v* = **take (someone) to court**, charge, indict, prosecute, summon

suffer *v* 1 = **undergo**, bear, endure, experience, go through, sustain 2 = **tolerate**, put up with (*inf*)

suffering *n* = **pain**, agony, anguish, discomfort, distress, hardship, misery, ordeal, torment

suffice *v* = **be enough**, be adequate, be sufficient, do, meet requirements, serve

sufficient *adj* = **adequate**, enough, satisfactory

suffocate *v* 1 = **choke**, asphyxiate, smother, stifle 2 = **stifle**, choke

uncomfortable from heat and lack of air. **suffocation** n.

suffragan n bishop appointed to assist an archbishop.

suffrage n right to vote in public elections. **suffragette** n (in Britain in the early 20th century) a woman who campaigned militantly for the right to vote.

suffuse v spread through or over (something). **suffusion** n.

sugar n **1** sweet crystalline carbohydrate found in many plants and used to sweeten food and drinks. ▷ v **2** sweeten or cover with sugar. **sugary** adj **sugar beet** beet grown for the sugar obtained from its roots. **sugar cane** tropical grass grown for the sugar obtained from its canes. **sugar daddy** slang elderly man who gives a young woman money and gifts in return for sexual favours. **sugar glider** common Australian phalanger that glides from tree to tree feeding on insects and nectar.

suggest ❶ v **1** put forward (an idea) for consideration. **2** bring to mind by the association of ideas. **3** give a hint of. **suggestible** adj easily influenced. **suggestion** n **1** thing suggested. **2** hint or indication. **suggestive** adj **1** suggesting something indecent. **2** conveying a hint (of). **suggestively** adv.

suicide n **1** killing oneself intentionally. **2** person who kills himself intentionally. **3** self-inflicted ruin of one's own prospects or interests. **suicidal** adj liable to commit suicide. **suicidally** adv.

suit ❶ n **1** set of clothes designed to be worn together. **2** outfit worn for a specific purpose. **3** one of the four sets into which a pack of cards is divided. **4** lawsuit. ▷ v **5** be appropriate for. **6** be acceptable to. **suitable** adj appropriate or proper. **suitably** adv **suitability** n **suitcase** n portable travelling case for clothing.

suite ❶ n **1** set of connected rooms in a hotel. **2** matching set of furniture. **3** set of musical pieces in the same key.

suitor ❶ n old-fashioned man who is courting a woman.

sulk ❶ v **1** be silent and sullen because of resentment or bad temper. ▷ n **2** resentful or sullen mood. **sulky** adj **sulkily** adv **sulkiness** n.

sullen ❶ adj unwilling to talk or be sociable. **sullenly** adv **sullenness** n.

sully ❶ v **-lying, -lied 1** ruin (someone's reputation). **2** make dirty.

sulphate n salt or ester of sulphuric acid.

sulphide n compound of sulphur with another element.

sulphite n salt or ester of sulphurous acid.

sulphonamide [sulf-**on**-a-mide] n any of a class of drugs that prevent the growth of bacteria.

sulphur n Chemistry pale yellow nonmetallic element. **sulphuric**, **sulphurous** adj of or containing sulphur. **sulphuric acid** colourless corrosive liquid used for making explosives. **sulphurous acid** acid used for bleaching and as a preservative.

sultan n sovereign of a Muslim country. **sultana** n **1** kind of raisin. **2** sultan's wife, mother, or daughter. **sultanate** n territory of a sultan.

THESAURUS

suggest v **1** = **recommend**, advise, advocate, prescribe, propose **2** = **bring to mind**, evoke **3** = **hint**, imply, indicate, intimate

suggestion n **1** = **recommendation**, motion, plan, proposal, proposition **2** = **hint**, breath, indication, intimation, trace, whisper

suggestive adj **1** = **smutty**, bawdy, blue, indelicate, racy, ribald, risqué, rude

suit n **2** = **outfit**, clothing, costume, dress, ensemble, habit **4** = **lawsuit**, action, case, cause, proceeding, prosecution, trial ▷ v **5** = **befit**, agree, become, go with, harmonize, match, tally **6** = **be acceptable to**, do, gratify, please, satisfy

suitable adj = **appropriate**, apt, becoming, befitting, fit, fitting, proper, right, satisfactory

suite n **1** = **rooms**, apartment

suitor n Old-fashioned = **admirer**, beau, young man

sulky adj = **huffy**, cross, disgruntled, in the sulks, moody, petulant, querulous, resentful, sullen

sullen adj = **morose**, cross, dour, glowering, moody, sour, sulky, surly, unsociable

sully v **1** = **dishonour**, besmirch, disgrace, ruin, smirch **2** = **defile**, stain, tarnish

sultry ❶ *adj* **-trier, -triest 1** (of weather or climate) hot and humid. **2** passionate, sensual.

sum ❶ *n* **1** result of addition, total. **2** problem in arithmetic. **3** quantity of money. **4** gist of a matter. **sum total** complete or final total. **sum up** *v* **summing, summed 1** summarize. **2** form a quick opinion of.

summary ❶ *n, pl* **-ries 1** brief account giving the main points of something. ▷ *adj* **2** done quickly, without formalities. **summarily** *adv* **summarize** *v* make or be a summary of (something). **summation** *n* **1** summary. **2** adding up.

summer *n* warmest season of the year, between spring and autumn. **summery** *adj* **summerhouse** *n* small building in a garden. **summer school** academic course held during the summer. **summertime** *n* period or season of summer.

summit ❶ *n* **1** top of a mountain or hill. **2** highest point. **3** conference between heads of state.

summon ❶ *v* **1** order (someone) to come. **2** send for (someone) to appear in court. **3** call upon (someone) to do something. **4** gather (one's courage, strength, etc.). **summons** *n* **1** command summoning someone. **2** order requiring someone to appear in court. ▷ *v* **3** order (someone) to appear in court.

sumo *n* Japanese style of wrestling.

sump *n* **1** container in an internal-combustion engine into which oil can drain. **2** hollow into which liquid drains.

sumptuous ❶ *adj* lavish, magnificent. **sumptuously** *adv*.

sun ❶ *n* **1** star around which the earth and other planets revolve. **2** any star around which planets revolve. **3** heat and light from the sun. ▷ *v* **sunning, sunned 4** expose (oneself) to the sun's rays. **sunless** *adj* **sunny** *adj* **1** full of or exposed to sunlight. **2** cheerful. **sunbathe** *v* lie in the sunshine in order to get a suntan. **sunbeam** *n* ray of sun. **sunburn** *n* painful reddening of the skin caused by overexposure to the sun. **sunburnt, sunburned** *adj* **sundial** *n* device showing the time by means of a pointer that casts a shadow on a marked dial. **sundown** *n* sunset. **sunflower** *n* tall plant with large golden flowers. **sunglasses** *pl n* dark glasses to protect the eyes from the sun. **sun lamp** lamp that gives off ultraviolet rays. **sunrise** *n* **1** daily appearance of the sun above the horizon. **2** time of this. **sunroof** *n* panel in the roof of a car that opens to let in air. **sunset** *n* **1** daily disappearance of the sun below the horizon. **2** time of this. **sunshine** *n* light and warmth from the sun. **sunspot** *n* **1** dark patch appearing temporarily on the sun's surface. **2** *Aust* small area of skin damage caused by exposure to the sun. **sunstroke** *n* illness caused by prolonged exposure to intensely hot sunlight. **suntan** *n* browning of the skin caused by exposure to the sun. **sun-up** *n US* sunrise.

Sun. Sunday.

sundae *n* ice cream topped with fruit etc.

Sunday *n* first day of the week and the Christian day of worship. **Sunday school** school for teaching children about Christianity.

sundry ❶ *adj* several, various. **sundries** *pl n* several things of various sorts. **all and sundry** everybody.

sung *v* past participle of SING.

sunk *v* a past participle of SINK.

                  THESAURUS

sultry *adj* **1** = **humid**, close, hot, muggy, oppressive, sticky, stifling **2** = **seductive**, provocative, sensual, sexy (*inf*)

sum *n* **1** = **total**, aggregate, amount, tally, whole

summarize *v* = **sum up**, abridge, condense, encapsulate, epitomize, précis

summary *n* **1** = **synopsis**, abridgment, outline, précis, résumé, review, rundown

summit *n* **1, 2** = **peak**, acme, apex, head, height, pinnacle, top, zenith

summon *v* **1** = **send for**, bid, call, invite **4** = **gather**, draw on, muster

sumptuous *adj* = **luxurious**, gorgeous, grand, lavish, opulent, splendid, superb

sum up *v* **1** = **summarize**, put in a nutshell, recapitulate, review

sundry *adj* = **various**, assorted, different, miscellaneous, several, some

S

sunken ● *v* **1** a past participle of SINK. ▷ *adj* **2** unhealthily hollow. **3** situated at a low level. **4** underwater.

sup *v* **supping, supped 1** take (liquid) by sips. ▷ *n* **2** sip.

super ● *adj informal* excellent.

super- *prefix* used with many main words to mean: **1** above or over, e.g. *superimpose*. **2** outstanding, e.g. *superstar*. **3** of greater size or extent, e.g. *supermarket*.

superannuation *n* **1** regular payment by an employee into a pension fund. **2** pension paid from this. **superannuated** *adj* discharged with a pension, owing to old age or illness.

superb ● *adj* excellent, impressive, or splendid. **superbly** *adv*.

superbug *n informal* bacterium resistant to antibiotics.

supercharged *adj* (of an engine) having a supercharger. **supercharger** *n* device that increases the power of an internal-combustion engine by forcing extra air into it.

supercilious ● *adj* showing arrogant pride or scorn.

superconductor *n* substance which has almost no electrical resistance at very low temperatures. **superconductivity** *n*.

superficial ● *adj* **1** not careful or thorough. **2** (of a person) without depth of character, shallow. **3** of or on the surface. **superficially** *adv* **superficiality** *n*.

superfluous ● [soo-**per**-flew-uss] *adj* more than is needed. **superfluity** *n*.

supergrass *n* person who acts as a police informer on a large scale.

superhuman ● *adj* beyond normal human ability or experience.

superimpose *v* place (something) on or over something else.

superintend ● *v* supervise (a person or activity). **superintendent** *n* **1** senior police officer. **2** supervisor.

superior ● *adj* **1** greater in quality, quantity, or merit. **2** higher in position or rank. **3** believing oneself to be better than others. ▷ *n* **4** person of greater rank or status. **superiority** *n*.

superlative ● [soo-**per**-lat-iv] *adj* **1** of outstanding quality. **2** *Grammar* denoting the form of an adjective or adverb indicating *most*. ▷ *n* **3** *Grammar* superlative form of a word.

superman *n* man with great physical or mental powers.

THESAURUS
---

sunken *adj* **2** = **hollow**, drawn, haggard **3** = **lower**, buried, recessed **4** = **submerged**

sunny *adj* **1** = **bright**, clear, fine, radiant, summery, sunlit, unclouded **2** = **cheerful**, buoyant, cheery, happy, joyful, light-hearted

sunrise *n* **1, 2** = **dawn**, break of day, cockcrow, daybreak

sunset *n* **1, 2** = **nightfall**, close of (the) day, dusk, eventide

super *adj Inf* = **excellent**, cracking (*Brit inf*), glorious, magnificent, marvellous, outstanding, sensational (*inf*), smashing (*inf*), superb, terrific (*inf*), wonderful

superb *adj* = **splendid**, excellent, exquisite, fine, first-rate, grand, magnificent, marvellous, superior, superlative, world-class

supercilious *adj* = **scornful**, arrogant, contemptuous, disdainful, haughty, lofty, snooty (*inf*), stuck-up (*inf*)

superficial *adj* **1** = **hasty**, casual, cursory, desultory, hurried, perfunctory, sketchy, slapdash **2** = **shallow**, empty-headed, frivolous, silly, trivial **3** = **surface**, exterior, external, on the surface, slight

superfluous *adj* = **excess**, extra, left over, redundant, remaining, spare, supernumerary, surplus

superhuman *adj* = **heroic**, paranormal, phenomenal, prodigious, supernatural

superintendent *n* **2** = **supervisor**, chief, controller, director, governor, inspector, manager, overseer

superior *adj* **1 a** = **better**, grander, greater, higher, surpassing, unrivalled **b** = **first-class**, choice, de luxe, excellent, exceptional, exclusive, first-rate **3** = **supercilious**, condescending, disdainful, haughty, lofty, lordly, patronizing, pretentious, snobbish ▷ *n* **4** = **boss** (*inf*), chief, director, manager, principal, senior, supervisor

superiority *n* = **supremacy**, advantage, ascendancy, excellence, lead, predominance

superlative *adj* **1** = **supreme**, excellent, outstanding, unparalleled, unrivalled, unsurpassed

S

supermarket n large self-service store selling food and household goods.

supermodel n famous and highly-paid fashion model.

supernatural ❶ adj of or relating to things beyond the laws of nature. **the supernatural** supernatural forces, occurrences, and beings collectively.

supernova n, pl **-vae, -vas** star that explodes and briefly becomes exceptionally bright.

supernumerary adj **1** exceeding the required or regular number. ▷ n, pl **-ries 2** supernumerary person or thing.

superpower n extremely powerful nation.

superscript n, adj (character) printed above the line.

supersede ❶ v replace, supplant.

> ● **SPELLING TIP**
> ● Although there is a word 'cede', spelt
> ● with a c, the word **supersede** must
> ● have an s in the middle.

supersonic adj of or travelling at a speed greater than the speed of sound.

superstar n very famous entertainer or sportsperson.

superstition n **1** belief in omens, ghosts, etc. **2** idea or practice based on this. **superstitious** adj.

superstore n large supermarket.

superstructure n **1** structure erected on something else. **2** part of a ship above the main deck.

supertanker n large fast tanker.

supertax n extra tax on incomes above a certain level.

supervene v occur as an unexpected development. **supervention** n.

supervise ❶ v watch over to direct or check. **supervision** n **supervisor** n **supervisory** adj.

supine [**soo**-pine] adj lying flat on one's back.

supper n light evening meal.

supplant ❶ v take the place of, oust.

supple ❶ adj **1** (of a person) moving and bending easily and gracefully. **2** bending easily without damage. **suppleness** n.

supplement ❶ n **1** thing added to complete something or make up for a lack. **2** magazine inserted into a newspaper. **3** section added to a publication to supply further information. ▷ v **4** provide or be a supplement to (something). **supplementary** adj.

supplication ❶ n humble request. **supplicant** n person who makes a humble request.

supply ❶ v **-plying, -plied 1** provide with something required. ▷ n, pl **-plies 2** supplying. **3** amount available. **4** Economics willingness and ability to provide goods and services. ▷ pl **5** food or equipment. ▷ adj **6** acting as a temporary substitute. **supplier** n.

support ❶ v **1** bear the weight of. **2** provide the necessities of life for. **3** give practical or emotional help to.

————————— THESAURUS —————————

supernatural adj = **paranormal**, ghostly, miraculous, mystic, occult, psychic, spectral, uncanny, unearthly

supersede v = **replace**, displace, oust, supplant, take the place of, usurp

supervise v = **oversee**, control, direct, handle, look after, manage, run, superintend

supervision n = **superintendence**, care, charge, control, direction, guidance, management

supervisor n = **boss** (inf), administrator, chief, foreman, inspector, manager, overseer

supplant v = **replace**, displace, oust, supersede, take the place of

supple adj **1** = **flexible**, limber, lissom(e), lithe **2** = **pliant**, pliable

supplement n **1** = **addition**, add-on, extra **2** = **pull-out**, insert

3 = **appendix**, postscript ▷ v **4** = **add**, augment, extend, reinforce

supplementary adj = **additional**, add-on, ancillary, auxiliary, extra, secondary

supplication n Formal = **plea**, appeal, entreaty, petition, prayer, request

supply v **1** = **provide**, contribute, endow, equip, furnish, give, grant, produce, stock, yield ▷ n **3** = **store**, cache, fund, hoard, quantity, reserve, source, stock ▷ pl **5** = **provisions**, equipment, food, materials, necessities, rations, stores, tucker (Aust & NZ inf)

support v **1** = **bear**, brace, buttress, carry, hold, prop, reinforce, sustain **2** = **provide for**, finance, fund, keep, look after, maintain, sustain **3** = **help**, aid, assist, back, champion, defend,

S

4 take an active interest in (a sports team, political principle, etc.). **5** help to prove (a theory etc.). **6** speak in favour of. **7** play a subordinate part. ▷ *n* **8** supporting. **9** means of support. **supporter** *n* person who supports a team, principle, etc. **supportive** *adj*.

suppose ❶ *v* **1** presume to be true. **2** consider as a proposal for the sake of discussion. **3** presuppose. **supposed** *adj* presumed to be true without proof, doubtful. **supposed to 1** expected or required to, e.g. *you were supposed to phone me*. **2** permitted to, e.g. *we're not supposed to swim here*. **supposedly** *adv* **supposition** *n* **1** supposing. **2** something supposed. **suppositious** *adj* deduced from an idea or statement believed or assumed to be true.

suppository *n, pl* **-ries** solid medication inserted into the rectum or vagina and left to melt.

suppress ❶ *v* **1** put an end to. **2** prevent publication of (information). **3** restrain (an emotion or response). **suppression** *n*.

suppurate *v* (of a wound etc.) produce pus.

supreme ❶ *adj* highest in authority, rank, or degree. **supremely** *adv* extremely. **supremacy** *n* **1** supreme power. **2** state of being supreme.

supremo *n informal* person in overall authority.

surcharge *n* additional charge.

surd *n Maths* number that cannot be expressed in whole numbers.

sure ❶ *adj* **1** free from uncertainty or doubt. **2** reliable. **3** inevitable. **4** physically secure. ▷ *adv, interj* **5** *informal* certainly. **for sure** without a doubt. **surely** *adv* it must be true that. **sure-fire** *adj informal* certain to succeed. **sure-footed** *adj* unlikely to slip or stumble.

surety *n, pl* **-ties** person who takes responsibility, or thing given as a guarantee, for the fulfilment of another's obligation.

surf *n* **1** foam caused by waves breaking on the shore. ▷ *v* **2** take part in surfing. **3** move quickly through a medium such as the internet. **surfing** *n* sport of riding towards the shore on a surfboard on the crest of a wave. **surfer** *n* **surfboard** *n* long smooth board used in surfing.

surface ❶ *n* **1** outside or top of an object. **2** material covering the

--- THESAURUS ---

second, side with **5** = **bear out**, confirm, corroborate, substantiate, verify ▷ *n* **8** = **help**, aid, assistance, backing, encouragement, loyalty **9** = **prop**, brace, foundation, pillar, post

supporter *n* = **follower**, adherent, advocate, champion, cobber (*Aust or old-fashioned NZ inf*), fan, friend, helper, patron, sponsor, well-wisher

suppose *v* **1** = **presume**, assume, conjecture, expect, guess (*inf, chiefly US & Canad*), imagine, think **2** = **imagine**, conjecture, consider, hypothesize, postulate, pretend

supposed *adj* = **presumed**, accepted, alleged, assumed, professed **supposed to 1** = **meant**, expected, obliged, required

supposedly *adv* = **presumably**, allegedly, hypothetically, ostensibly, theoretically

supposition *n* **2** = **guess**, conjecture, hypothesis, presumption, speculation, surmise, theory

suppress *v* **1** = **stop**, check, conquer, crush, overpower, put an end to, quash, quell, subdue **3** = **restrain**, conceal, contain, curb, hold in *or* back, repress, silence, smother, stifle

supremacy *n* **1, 2** = **domination**, mastery, predominance, primacy, sovereignty, supreme power, sway

supreme *adj* = **highest**, chief, foremost, greatest, head, leading, paramount, pre-eminent, prime, principal, top, ultimate

supremo *n Inf* = **head**, boss (*inf*), commander, director, governor, leader, master, principal, ruler

sure *adj* **1** = **certain**, assured, confident, convinced, decided, definite, positive **2** = **reliable**, accurate, dependable, foolproof, infallible, undeniable, undoubted, unerring, unfailing **3** = **inevitable**, assured, bound, guaranteed, inescapable

surely *adv* = **undoubtedly**, certainly, definitely, doubtlessly, indubitably, unquestionably, without doubt

surface *n* **1** = **outside**, exterior, face, side, top **2** = **covering**, veneer **3** = **veneer** ▷ *v* **5** = **appear**, arise,

S

surface of an object. **3** superficial appearance. **4** top level of the land or sea. ▷ v **5** become apparent. **6** rise to the surface. **7** put a surface on.

surfeit ❶ n excessive amount.

surge ❶ n **1** sudden powerful increase. **2** strong rolling movement, esp. of the sea. ▷ v **3** increase suddenly. **4** move forward strongly.

surgeon n doctor who specializes in surgery. **surgery** n **1** treatment in which the patient's body is cut open in order to treat the affected part. **2** pl **-geries** place where, or time when, a doctor, dentist, MP, etc. can be consulted. **surgical** adj **surgically** adv **surgical spirit** spirit used for sterilizing and cleaning.

surly ❶ adj **-lier**, **-liest** ill-tempered and rude. **surliness** n.

surmise ❶ v, n guess, conjecture.

surmount v **1** overcome (a problem). **2** be on top of (something). **surmountable** adj.

surname n family name.

surpass ❶ v be greater than or superior to.

surplice n loose white robe worn by clergymen and choristers.

surplus ❶ n **1** amount left over in excess of what is required. ▷ adj **2** extra.

surprise ❶ n **1** unexpected event. **2** amazement and wonder. **3** act of taking someone unawares. ▷ v **4** cause to feel amazement or wonder. **5** come upon, attack, or catch suddenly and unexpectedly. **take someone by surprise** catch someone unprepared.

surrealism n movement in art and literature involving the combination of incongruous images, as in a dream. **surreal** adj bizarre. **surrealist** n, adj **surrealistic** adj.

surrender ❶ v **1** give oneself up. **2** give (something) up to another. **3** yield (to a temptation or influence). ▷ n **4** surrendering.

surreptitious ❶ adj done secretly or stealthily. **surreptitiously** adv.

surrogate ❶ n substitute. **surrogate mother** woman who gives birth to a child on behalf of a couple who cannot have children.

surround ❶ v **1** be, come, or place all around (a person or thing). ▷ n **2** border or edging. **surroundings** pl n area or environment around a person, place, or thing.

surtax n extra tax on incomes above a certain level.

surveillance ❶ n close observation.

survey ❶ v **1** view or consider in a general way. **2** make a map of (an area). **3** inspect (a building) to assess

——————————— THESAURUS ———————————

come to light, come up, crop up (inf), emerge, materialize, transpire

surfeit n = **excess**, glut, plethora, superfluity

surge n **1** = **rush**, flood, flow, gush, outpouring **2** = **wave**, billow, roller, swell ▷ v **3** = **rush**, gush, rise **4** = **roll**, heave

surly adj = **ill-tempered**, churlish, cross, grouchy (inf), morose, sulky, sullen, uncivil, ungracious

surmise v = **guess**, conjecture, imagine, presume, speculate, suppose ▷ n = **guess**, assumption, conjecture, presumption, speculation, supposition

surpass v = **outdo**, beat, eclipse, exceed, excel, outshine, outstrip, transcend

surplus n **1** = **excess**, balance, remainder, residue, surfeit ▷ adj **2** = **extra**, excess, odd, remaining, spare, superfluous

surprise n **1** = **shock**, bombshell, eye-opener (inf), jolt, revelation **2** = **amazement**, astonishment, incredulity, wonder ▷ v **4** = **amaze**, astonish, stagger, stun, take aback **5** = **catch unawares** or **off-guard**, discover, spring upon, startle

surrender v **1** = **give in**, capitulate, cave in (inf), give way, submit, succumb, yield **2** = **give up**, abandon, cede, concede, part with, relinquish, renounce, waive, yield **3** = **yield**, give in ▷ n **4** = **submission**, capitulation, cave-in (inf), relinquishment, renunciation, resignation

surreptitious adj = **secret**, covert, furtive, sly, stealthy, underhand

surrogate n = **substitute**, proxy, representative, stand-in

surround v **1** = **enclose**, encircle, encompass, envelop, hem in, ring

surroundings pl n = **environment**, background, location, milieu, setting

surveillance n = **observation**, inspection, scrutiny, supervision, watch

survey v **1** = **look over**, contemplate, examine, inspect, observe, scrutinize,

S

its condition and value. **4** find out the incomes, opinions, etc. of (a group of people). ▷ *n* **5** surveying. **6** report produced by a survey. **surveyor** *n*.

survive ❶ *v* **1** continue to live or exist after (a difficult experience). **2** live after the death of (another). **survival** *n* **1** condition of having survived. **2** thing that has survived from an earlier time. **survivor** *n*.

susceptible ❶ *adj* liable to be influenced or affected by. **susceptibility** *n*.

suspect ❶ *v* **1** believe (someone) to be guilty without having any proof. **2** think (something) to be false or questionable. **3** believe (something) to be the case. ▷ *adj* **4** not to be trusted. ▷ *n* **5** person who is suspected.

suspend ❶ *v* **1** hang from a high place. **2** cause to remain floating or hanging. **3** cause to cease temporarily. **4** remove (someone) temporarily from a job or team. **suspenders** *pl n* **1** straps for holding up stockings. **2** *US* braces. **suspended sentence** prison sentence that is not served unless the offender commits another crime during a specified period.

suspense ❶ *n* state of uncertainty while awaiting news, an event, etc.

suspension ❶ *n* **1** suspending or being suspended. **2** system of springs and shock absorbers supporting the body

of a vehicle. **3** mixture of fine particles of a solid in a fluid. **suspension bridge** bridge hanging from cables attached to towers at each end.

suspicion ❶ *n* **1** feeling of not trusting a person or thing. **2** belief that something is true without definite proof. **3** slight trace. **suspicious** *adj* feeling or causing suspicion. **suspiciously** *adv*.

suss out *v slang* work out using one's intuition.

sustain ❶ *v* **1** maintain or prolong. **2** keep up the vitality or strength of. **3** suffer (an injury or loss). **4** support. **5** confirm. **sustenance** *n* food.

suture [**soo**-cher] *n* stitch joining the edges of a wound.

SUV sport utility vehicle.

suzerain *n* **1** state or sovereign with limited authority over another self-governing state. **2** feudal lord. **suzerainty** *n*.

svelte *adj* attractively or gracefully slim.

SW southwest(ern).

swab *n* **1** small piece of cotton wool used to apply medication, clean a wound, etc. ▷ *v* **swabbing**, **swabbed** **2** clean (a wound) with a swab. **3** clean (the deck of a ship) with a mop.

swaddle *v* wrap (a baby) in swaddling clothes. **swaddling clothes** long strips of cloth formerly wrapped round a newborn baby.

——————— **THESAURUS** ———————

view **2** = **plot**, measure, plan, size up **3** = **estimate**, appraise, assess ▷ *n* **5** = **examination**, inspection, scrutiny **6** = **study**, report, review

survive *v* **1, 2** = **remain alive**, endure, last, live on, outlast, outlive

susceptible *adj* = **liable**, disposed, given, impressionable, inclined, prone, receptive, responsive, sensitive, subject, suggestible, vulnerable

suspect *v* **1** = **believe**, consider, feel, guess, speculate, suppose **2** = **distrust**, doubt, mistrust ▷ *adj* **4** = **dubious**, doubtful, iffy (*inf*), questionable

suspend *v* **1** = **hang**, attach, dangle **3** = **postpone**, cease, cut short, defer, discontinue, interrupt, put off, shelve

suspense *n* = **uncertainty**, anxiety, apprehension, doubt, expectation, insecurity, irresolution, tension

suspension *n* **1** = **postponement**, abeyance, break, breaking off,

deferment, discontinuation, interruption

suspicion *n* **1** = **distrust**, doubt, dubiety, misgiving, mistrust, qualm, scepticism, wariness **2** = **idea**, guess, hunch, impression, notion **3** = **trace**, hint, shade, *soupçon*, streak, suggestion, tinge, touch

suspicious *adj* **a** = **distrustful**, doubtful, sceptical, unbelieving, wary **b** = **suspect**, dodgy (*Brit, Aust & NZ inf*), doubtful, dubious, fishy (*inf*), questionable

sustain *v* **1** = **maintain**, continue, keep up, prolong, protract **2** = **keep alive**, aid, assist, help, nourish **3** = **suffer**, bear, endure, experience, feel, undergo, withstand **4** = **support**, bear, uphold

sustained *adj* = **continuous**, constant, nonstop, perpetual, prolonged, steady, unremitting

S

swag *n slang* stolen property.
swagman *n Aust* tramp who carries his belongings in a bundle on his back.

swagger ❶ *v* **1** walk or behave arrogantly. ▷ *n* **2** arrogant walk or manner.

swain *n poetic* **1** suitor. **2** country youth.

swallow¹ ❶ *v* **1** cause to pass down one's throat. **2** make a gulping movement in the throat, as when nervous. **3** *informal* believe (something) gullibly. **4** refrain from showing (a feeling). **5** engulf or absorb. ▷ *n* **6** swallowing. **7** amount swallowed.

swallow² *n* small migratory bird with long pointed wings and a forked tail.

swam *v* past tense of SWIM.

swamp ❶ *n* **1** watery area of land, bog. ▷ *v* **2** cause (a boat) to fill with water and sink. **3** overwhelm. **swampy** *adj*.

swan *n* **1** large usu. white water bird with a long graceful neck. ▷ *v* **swanning, swanned 2** *informal* wander about idly. **swan song** person's last performance before retirement or death.

swank *slang* ▷ *v* **1** show off or boast. ▷ *n* **2** showing off or boasting. **swanky** *adj slang* expensive and showy, stylish.

swap ❶ *v* **swapping, swapped 1** exchange (something) for something else. ▷ *n* **2** exchange.

sward *n* stretch of short grass.

swarm¹ ❶ *n* **1** large group of bees or other insects. **2** large crowd. ▷ *v* **3** move in a swarm. **4** (of a place) be crowded or overrun.

swarm² *v* (foll. by *up*) climb (a ladder or rope) by gripping with the hands and feet.

swarthy ❶ *adj* **-thier, -thiest** dark-complexioned.

swashbuckling ❶ *adj* having the exciting behaviour of pirates, esp. those depicted in films. **swashbuckler** *n*.

swastika *n* symbol in the shape of a cross with the arms bent at right angles, used as the emblem of Nazi Germany.

swat *v* **swatting, swatted 1** hit sharply. ▷ *n* **2** sharp blow.

swatch *n* sample of cloth.

swath [swawth] *n* see SWATHE.

swathe ❶ *v* **1** wrap in bandages or layers of cloth. ▷ *n* **2** long strip of cloth wrapped around something. **3** (also **swath**) the width of one sweep of a scythe or mower. **4** strip cut in one sweep.

sway ❶ *v* **1** swing to and fro or from side to side. **2** waver or cause to waver in opinion. ▷ *n* **3** power or influence. **4** swaying motion.

swear ❶ *v* **swearing, swore, sworn 1** use obscene or blasphemous language. **2** state or promise on oath. **3** state earnestly. **swear by** *v* have complete confidence in. **swear in** *v* cause to take an oath. **swearword** *n* word considered obscene or blasphemous.

sweat ❶ *n* **1** salty liquid given off through the pores of the skin. **2** *slang*

— THESAURUS —

swagger *v* **1** = **show off** (*inf*), boast, brag, parade, skite (*Aust & NZ*)

swallow¹ *v* **1** = **gulp**, consume, devour, drink, eat, swig (*inf*)

swamp *n* **1** = **bog**, fen, marsh, mire, morass, quagmire, slough, muskeg (*Canad*) ▷ *v* **2** = **flood**, capsize, engulf, inundate, sink, submerge **3** = **overwhelm**, engulf, flood, inundate, overload, submerge

swap *v* **1** = **exchange**, barter, interchange, switch, trade

swarm¹ *n* **2** = **multitude**, army, crowd, flock, herd, horde, host, mass, throng ▷ *v* **3** = **crowd**, flock, mass, stream, throng **4** = **teem**, abound, bristle, crawl

swarthy *adj* = **dark-skinned**, black, brown, dark, dark-complexioned, dusky

swashbuckling *adj* = **dashing**, bold, daredevil, flamboyant

swathe *v* **1** = **wrap**, bundle up, cloak, drape, envelop, shroud

sway *v* **1** = **bend**, lean, rock, roll, swing **2** = **influence**, affect, guide, induce, persuade ▷ *n* **3** = **power**, authority, clout (*inf*), control, influence, mana (*NZ*)

swear *v* **1** = **curse**, be foul-mouthed, blaspheme **2** = **vow**, attest, promise, testify **3** = **declare**, affirm, assert

swearing *n* = **bad language**, blasphemy, cursing, foul language, profanity

swearword *n* = **oath**, curse, expletive, four-letter word, obscenity, profanity

sweat *n* **1** = **perspiration 2** *Sl* = **labour**, chore, drudgery, toil **3** *Inf* =

S

drudgery or hard labour. **3** *informal* state of anxiety. ▷ *v* **4** have sweat coming through the pores. **5** be anxious. **sweaty** *adj* **sweatband** *n* strip of cloth tied around the forehead or wrist to absorb sweat. **sweatshirt** *n* long-sleeved cotton jersey. **sweatshop** *n* place where employees work long hours in poor conditions for low pay.

sweater *n* (woollen) garment for the upper part of the body.

swede *n* **1** kind of turnip. **2** (**S-**) person from Sweden. **Swedish** *n*, *adj* (language) of Sweden.

sweep ❶ *v* **sweeping**, **swept 1** remove dirt from (a floor) with a broom. **2** move smoothly and quickly. **3** spread rapidly. **4** move majestically. **5** carry away suddenly or forcefully. **6** stretch in a long wide curve. ▷ *n* **7** sweeping. **8** sweeping motion. **9** wide expanse. **10** curving line. **11** sweepstake. **12** chimney sweep. **sweeping** *adj* **1** wide-ranging. **2** indiscriminate. **sweepstake** *n* lottery in which the stakes of the participants make up the prize.

sweet ❶ *adj* **1** tasting of or like sugar. **2** kind and charming. **3** agreeable to the senses or mind. **4** (of wine) with a high sugar content. ▷ *n* **5** shaped piece of food consisting mainly of sugar. **6** dessert. **sweetly** *adv*

sweetness *n* **sweeten** *v* **sweetener** *n* **1** sweetening agent that does not contain sugar. **2** *slang* bribe. **sweetie** *n informal* **1** lovable person. **2** sweet. **sweetbread** *n* animal's pancreas used as food. **sweet corn** type of maize with sweet yellow kernels, eaten as a vegetable. **sweetheart** *n* lover. **sweetmeat** *n old-fashioned* sweet delicacy such as a small cake. **sweet pea** climbing plant with bright fragrant flowers. **sweet potato** tropical root vegetable with yellow flesh. **sweet-talk** *v informal* coax or flatter. **sweet tooth** strong liking for sweet foods. **sweet william** garden plant with clusters of scented flowers.

swell ❶ *v* **swelling**, **swelled**, **swollen** *or* **swelled 1** expand or increase. **2** (of an emotion) become more intense. **3** (of a sound) become gradually louder. ▷ *n* **4** swelling or being swollen. **5** movement of waves in the sea. **6** *old-fashioned slang* fashionable person. ▷ *adj* **7** *US slang* excellent or fine. **swelling** *n* enlargement of part of the body, caused by injury or infection.

sweltering ❶ *adj* uncomfortably hot. **swelter** *v*.

swept *v* past of SWEEP.

swerve ❶ *v* **1** turn aside from a course sharply or suddenly. ▷ *n* **2** swerving.

swift ❶ *adj* **1** moving or able to move quickly. **2** performed or happening

worry, agitation, anxiety, distress, panic, strain ▷ *v* **4** = **perspire**, glow **5** = **worry**, agonize, fret, suffer, torture oneself

sweaty *adj* = **perspiring**, clammy, sticky

sweep *v* **1** = **clear**, brush, clean, remove **2** = **sail**, fly, glide, pass, skim, tear, zoom ▷ *n* **8** = **stroke**, move, swing **9** = **extent**, range, scope, stretch **10** = **arc**, bend, curve

sweeping *adj* **1** = **wide-ranging**, all-embracing, all-inclusive, broad, comprehensive, extensive, global, overarching, wide **2** = **indiscriminate**, blanket, exaggerated, overstated, unqualified, wholesale

sweet *adj* **1** = **sugary**, cloying, icky (*inf*), saccharine **2** = **charming**, appealing, engaging, kind, likable *or* likeable, lovable, winning **3** = **fragrant**, agreeable, aromatic, clean, fresh, pure

▷ *n* **5** = **confectionery**, bonbon, candy (*US*), lolly (*Aust & NZ inf*) **6** = **dessert**, pudding

sweeten *v* = **sugar**

sweetheart *n* = **love**, beloved, boyfriend *or* girlfriend, darling, dear, lover

swell *v* **1** = **expand**, balloon, bloat, bulge, dilate, distend, enlarge, grow, increase, rise **2** = **increase**, heighten, intensify, mount, surge ▷ *n* **5** = **wave**, billow, surge

swelling *n* = **enlargement**, bulge, bump, distension, inflammation, lump, protuberance

sweltering *adj* = **hot**, boiling, burning, oppressive, scorching, stifling

swerve *v* **1** = **veer**, bend, deflect, deviate, diverge, stray, swing, turn, turn aside

swift *adj* **1, 2** = **quick**, fast, hurried, prompt, rapid, speedy

swiftly *adv* = **quickly**, fast, hurriedly, promptly, rapidly, speedily

quickly. ▷ *n* **3** fast-flying bird with pointed wings. **swiftly** *adv* **swiftness** *n*.

swig *n* **1** large mouthful of drink. ▷ *v* **swigging, swigged 2** drink in large mouthfuls.

swill *v* **1** drink greedily. **2** rinse (something) in large amounts of water. ▷ *n* **3** sloppy mixture containing waste food, fed to pigs. **4** deep drink.

swim *v* **swimming, swam, swum 1** move along in water by movements of the limbs. **2** be covered or flooded with liquid. **3** float on a liquid. **4** reel, e.g. *her head was swimming.* ▷ *n* **5** act or period of swimming. **swimmer** *n* **swimmingly** *adv* successfully and effortlessly. **swimming costume**, **swimsuit** *n* swimming garment that leaves the arms and legs bare. **swimming pool** (building containing) an artificial pond for swimming in.

swindle ❶ *v* **1** cheat (someone) out of money. ▷ *n* **2** instance of swindling. **swindler** *n*.

swine *n* **1** contemptible person. **2** pig.

swing ❶ *v* **swinging, swung 1** move to and fro, sway. **2** turn, as on a hinge. **3** move in a curve. **4** (of an opinion or mood) change sharply. **5** hit out with a sweeping motion. **6** *slang* be hanged. **7** *informal* manipulate or influence. ▷ *n* **8** swinging. **9** suspended seat on which a child can swing to and fro. **10** style of popular dance music played by big bands in the 1930s. **11** sudden or extreme change.

swingeing ❶ [**swin**-jing] *adj* punishing, severe.

swipe ❶ *v* **1** strike (at) with a sweeping blow. **2** *slang* steal. **3** pass (a credit card) through a machine which electronically reads information stored in the card. ▷ *n* **4** hard blow.

swirl ❶ *v* **1** turn with a whirling motion. ▷ *n* **2** whirling motion. **3** twisting shape.

swish *v* **1** move with a whistling or hissing sound. ▷ *n* **2** whistling or hissing sound. ▷ *adj* **3** *informal* fashionable, smart.

Swiss *adj* **1** of Switzerland or its people. ▷ *n, pl* **Swiss 2** person from Switzerland. **swiss roll** sponge cake spread with jam or cream and rolled up.

switch ❶ *n* **1** device for opening and closing an electric circuit. **2** abrupt change. **3** exchange or swap. **4** flexible rod or twig. ▷ *v* **5** change abruptly. **6** exchange or swap. **switchback** *n* road or railway with many sharp hills or bends. **switchboard** *n* installation in a telephone exchange or office where telephone calls are connected. **switch on, off** *v* turn (a device) on *or* off by means of a switch.

swivel ❶ *v* **-elling, -elled 1** turn on a central point. ▷ *n* **2** coupling device that allows an attached object to turn freely.

swizz, swiz *n* *Brit informal* swindle or disappointment.

swizzle stick *n* small stick used to stir cocktails.

swollen ❶ *v* a past participle of SWELL.

swoon *v, n* faint.

swoop ❶ *v* **1** sweep down or pounce on suddenly. ▷ *n* **2** swooping.

---

swiftness *n* = **speed**, promptness, quickness, rapidity, speediness, velocity

swindle *v* **1** = **cheat**, con, defraud, do (*sl*), fleece, rip (someone) off (*sl*), skin (*sl*), sting (*inf*), trick ▷ *n* **2** = **fraud**, con trick (*inf*), deception, fiddle (*Brit inf*), racket, rip-off (*sl*), scam (*sl*)

swindler *n* = **cheat**, con man (*inf*), fraud, rogue, shark, trickster

swing *v* **1** = **sway**, oscillate, rock, veer, wave **2** = **turn**, pivot, rotate, swivel **3** = **curve 6** *Sl* = **hang** ▷ *n* **8** = **swaying**, oscillation

swingeing *adj* = **severe**, drastic, excessive, harsh, heavy, punishing, stringent

swipe *v* **1** = **hit**, lash out at, slap, strike, wallop (*inf*) **2** *Sl* = **steal**, appropriate, filch, lift (*inf*), nick (*sl, chiefly Brit*), pinch (*inf*), purloin ▷ *n* **4** = **blow**, clout (*inf*), cuff, slap, smack, thump, wallop (*inf*)

swirl *v* **1** = **whirl**, churn, eddy, spin, twist

switch *n* **2** = **change**, reversal, shift **3** = **exchange**, substitution, swap ▷ *v* **5** = **change**, deflect, deviate, divert, shift **6** = **exchange**, substitute, swap

swivel *v* **1** = **turn**, pivot, revolve, rotate, spin

swollen *adj* = **enlarged**, bloated, distended, inflamed, puffed up

swoop *v* **1** = **pounce**, descend, dive, rush, stoop, sweep ▷ *n* **2** = **pounce**,

swop ❶ v **swopping**, **swopped** n same as SWAP.

sword n weapon with a long sharp blade. **sword dance** Highland dance performed over swords on the ground. **swordfish** n large fish with a very long upper jaw. **swordsman** n person skilled in the use of a sword.

swore v past tense of SWEAR.

sworn v **1** past participle of SWEAR. ▷ adj **2** bound by or as if by an oath, e.g. sworn enemies.

swot ❶ informal ▷ v **swotting**, **swotted** **1** study hard. ▷ n **2** person who studies hard.

swum v past participle of SWIM.

swung v past tense of SWING.

sybarite [sib-bar-ite] n lover of luxury. **sybaritic** adj.

sycamore n tree with five-pointed leaves and two-winged fruits.

sycophant ❶ n person who uses flattery to win favour from people with power or influence. **sycophantic** adj **sycophancy** n.

syllable n part of a word pronounced as a unit. **syllabic** adj.

syllabub n dessert of beaten cream, sugar, and wine.

syllabus ❶ n, pl -**buses**, -**bi** list of subjects for a course of study.

syllogism n form of logical reasoning consisting of two premises and a conclusion. **syllogistic** adj.

sylph n **1** slender graceful girl or woman. **2** imaginary being supposed to inhabit the air. **sylphlike** adj.

sylvan adj lit relating to woods, trees, and forests, e.g. a sylvan setting.

symbiosis n close association of two species living together to their mutual benefit. **symbiotic** adj.

symbol ❶ n sign or thing that stands for something else. **symbolic** adj **symbolically** adv **symbolism** n **1** representation of something by symbols. **2** movement in art and literature using symbols to express abstract and mystical ideas. **symbolist** n, adj **symbolize** v **1** be a symbol of. **2** represent with a symbol.

symmetry ❶ n **1** state of having two halves that are mirror images of each other. **2** beauty resulting from a balanced arrangement of parts. **symmetrical** adj **symmetrically** adv.

sympathy ❶ n, pl -**thies 1** compassion for someone's pain or distress. **2** agreement with someone's feelings or interests. **3** feelings of loyalty and support for an idea. **sympathetic** adj **1** feeling or showing sympathy. **2** likeable or appealing. **sympathetically** adv **sympathize** v **1** feel or express sympathy. **2** agree with. **sympathizer** n.

symphony n, pl -**nies 1** composition for orchestra, with several movements. **2** visually pleasing arrangement. **symphonic** adj.

symposium n, pl -**siums**, -**sia** **1** conference for discussion of a particular topic. **2** collection of essays on a topic.

THESAURUS

descent, drop, lunge, plunge, rush, stoop, sweep

swop see SWAP.

swot v Inf **1** = **study**, cram (inf), mug up (Brit sl), revise

sycophant n = **crawler**, bootlicker (inf), fawner, flatterer, toady, yes man

sycophantic adj = **obsequious**, crawling, fawning, flattering, grovelling, ingratiating, servile, smarmy (Brit inf), toadying, unctuous

syllabus n = **course of study**, curriculum

symbol n = **sign**, badge, emblem, figure, image, logo, mark, representation, token

symbolic adj = **representative**, allegorical, emblematic, figurative

symbolize v **2** = **represent**, denote,

mean, personify, signify, stand for, typify

symmetrical adj = **balanced**, in proportion, regular

symmetry n **2** = **balance**, evenness, order, proportion, regularity

sympathetic adj **1** = **caring**, compassionate, concerned, interested, kind, pitying, supportive, understanding, warm **2** = **like-minded**, agreeable, companionable, compatible, congenial, friendly

sympathize v **1** = **feel for**, commiserate, condole, pity **2** = **agree**, side with, understand

sympathy n **1** = **compassion**, commiseration, pity, understanding **2** = **affinity**, agreement, fellow feeling, rapport

S

symptom ❶ *n* **1** sign indicating the presence of an illness. **2** sign that something is wrong. **symptomatic** *adj*.

synagogue *n* Jewish place of worship and religious instruction.

sync, synch *informal* ▷ *n* **1** synchronization. ▷ *v* **2** synchronize.

synchromesh *adj* (of a gearbox) having a device that synchronizes the speeds of gears before they engage.

synchronize *v* **1** (of two or more people) perform (an action) at the same time. **2** set (watches) to show the same time. **3** match (the soundtrack and action of a film) precisely. **synchronization** *n* **synchronous** *adj* happening or existing at the same time.

syncopate *v Music* stress the weak beats in (a rhythm) instead of the strong ones. **syncopation** *n*.

syncope [**sing**-kop-ee] *n Medical* a faint.

syndicate *n* **1** group of people or firms undertaking a joint business project. **2** agency that sells material to several newspapers. ▷ *v* **3** publish (material) in several newspapers. **4** form a syndicate. **syndication** *n*.

syndrome *n* **1** combination of symptoms indicating a particular disease. **2** set of characteristics indicating a particular problem.

synergy *n* potential ability for people or groups to be more successful working together than on their own.

synod *n* church council.

synonym *n* word with the same meaning as another. **synonymous** *adj*.

synopsis *n, pl* **-ses** summary or outline.

syntax *n Grammar* way in which words are arranged to form phrases and sentences. **syntactic** *adj*.

synthesis ❶ *n, pl* **-ses 1** combination of objects or ideas into a whole. **2** artificial production of a substance. **synthesize** *v* produce by synthesis. **synthesizer** *n* electronic musical instrument producing a range of sounds. **synthetic** *adj* **1** (of a substance) made artificially. **2** not genuine, insincere. **synthetically** *adv*.

syphilis *n* serious sexually transmitted disease. **syphilitic** *adj*.

syphon *n, v* same as SIPHON.

Syrian *adj* **1** of Syria, its people, or their dialect of Arabic. ▷ *n* **2** person from Syria.

syringe *n* **1** device for withdrawing or injecting fluids, consisting of a hollow cylinder, a piston, and a hollow needle. ▷ *v* **2** wash out or inject with a syringe.

syrup *n* **1** solution of sugar in water. **2** thick sweet liquid. **3** sugar solution containing medicine. **syrupy** *adj* **1** thick and sweet. **2** excessively sentimental.

system ❶ *n* **1** method or set of methods. **2** orderliness. **3** scheme of classification or arrangement. **4** network or assembly of parts that form a whole. **5** body considered as a whole. **the system** society or government regarded as oppressive and exploitative. **systematic** *adj* **systematically** *adv* **systematize** *v* organize using a system. **systematization** *n* **systemic** *adj* affecting the entire animal or body. **systemically** *adv*.

systole [**siss**-tol-ee] *n* regular contraction of the heart as it pumps blood. **systolic** *adj*.

S

━━━━━━━━━━━━━━━━━━━━━━━━━ THESAURUS ━━━━━━━━

symptom *n* **2** = **sign**, expression, indication, mark, token, warning

synthetic *adj* **1** = **artificial**, fake, man-made **2** = **fake**, artificial

system *n* **1** = **method**, practice, procedure, routine, technique **3** = **arrangement**, classification, organization, scheme, structure

t tonne.

T *n* **to a T 1** in every detail. **2** perfectly.

t. ton.

ta *interj informal* thank you.

Ta *Chemistry* tantalum.

TA Territorial Army.

tab *n* small flap or projecting label. **keep tabs on** *informal* watch closely.

tabard *n* short sleeveless tunic decorated with a coat of arms, worn in medieval times.

Tabasco *n* ® very hot red pepper sauce.

tabby *n, pl* **-bies** *adj* (cat) with dark stripes on a lighter background.

tabernacle *n* **1** portable shrine of the Israelites. **2** Christian place of worship not called a church. **3** *RC Church* receptacle for the consecrated Host.

tabla *n, pl* **-bla, -blas** one of a pair of Indian drums played with the hands.

table ❶ *n* **1** piece of furniture with a flat top supported by legs. **2** arrangement of information in columns. ▷ *v* **3** submit (a motion) for discussion by a meeting. **4** *US* suspend discussion of (a proposal). **tablecloth** *n* cloth for covering the top of a table, esp. during meals. **tableland** *n* high plateau. **tablespoon** *n* large spoon for serving food. **table tennis** game like tennis played on a table with small bats and a light ball.

tableau ❶ [**tab**-loh] *n, pl* **-leaux** silent motionless group arranged to represent some scene.

table d'hôte [**tah**-bla **dote**] *n, pl* **tables d'hôte** *adj* (meal) having a set number of dishes at a fixed price.

tablet *n* **1** pill of compressed medicinal substance. **2** flattish cake of soap etc. **3** inscribed slab of stone etc. **4** handheld personal computer operated by a touch screen.

tabloid *n* small-sized newspaper with many photographs and a concise, usu. sensational style.

taboo ❶ *n, pl* **-boos 1** prohibition resulting from religious or social conventions. ▷ *adj* **2** forbidden by a taboo.

tabor *n* small drum, used esp. in the Middle Ages.

tabular *adj* arranged in a table. **tabulate** *v* arrange (information) in a table. **tabulation** *n*.

tachograph *n* device for recording the speed and distance travelled by a motor vehicle.

tachometer *n* device for measuring speed, esp. that of a revolving shaft.

tacit ❶ [**tass**-it] *adj* implied but not spoken. **tacitly** *adv*.

taciturn ❶ [**tass**-it-turn] *adj* habitually uncommunicative. **taciturnity** *n*.

tack¹ ❶ *n* **1** short nail with a large head. **2** long loose stitch. ▷ *v* **3** fasten with tacks. **4** stitch with tacks. **tack on** *v* append.

tack² ❶ *n* **1** course of a ship sailing obliquely into the wind. **2** course of action. ▷ *v* **3** sail into the wind on a zigzag course.

tack³ *n* riding harness for horses.

tackies, takkies *pl n, sing* **tacky** *S Afr informal* tennis shoes or plimsolls.

THESAURUS

table *n* **1** = **counter**, bench, board, stand **2** = **list**, catalogue, chart, diagram, record, register, roll, schedule, tabulation ▷ *v* **3** = **submit**, enter, move, propose, put forward, suggest

tableau *n* = **picture**, representation, scene, spectacle

taboo *n* **1** = **prohibition**, anathema, ban, interdict, proscription, restriction ▷ *adj* **2** = **forbidden**, anathema, banned, outlawed, prohibited, proscribed, unacceptable, unmentionable

tacit *adj* = **implied**, implicit, inferred, undeclared, understood, unexpressed, unspoken, unstated

taciturn *adj* = **uncommunicative**, quiet, reserved, reticent, silent, tight-lipped, unforthcoming, withdrawn

tack¹ *n* **1** = **nail**, drawing pin, pin ▷ *v* **3** = **fasten**, affix, attach, fix, nail, pin **4** = **stitch**, baste, sew **tack on** *v* = **append**, add, attach, tag

tack² *n* **2** = **course**, approach, direction, heading, line, method, path, plan, procedure, way

t

tackle ❶ v **1** deal with (a task).
2 confront (an opponent).
3 *Sport* attempt to get the ball from
(an opposing player). ▷ n **4** *Sport* act of
tackling an opposing player.
5 equipment for a particular activity.
6 set of ropes and pulleys for lifting
heavy weights.

tacky¹ ❶ adj **tackier**, **tackiest** slightly
sticky. **tackiness** n.

tacky² ❶ adj **tackier**, **tackiest**
1 *informal* vulgar and tasteless.
2 shabby. **tackiness** n.

taco [**tah**-koh] n, pl **tacos** *Mexican
cookery* tortilla fried until crisp, served
with a filling.

tact ❶ n skill in avoiding giving offence.
tactful adj **tactfully** adv **tactless** adj
tactlessly adv **tactlessness** n.

tactics ❶ n art of directing military
forces in battle. **tactic** n method or
plan to achieve an end. **tactical** adj
tactically adv **tactician** n.

tactile adj of or having the sense of
touch.

tadpole n limbless tailed larva of a frog
or toad.

taffeta n shiny silk or rayon fabric.

tag¹ ❶ n **1** label bearing information.
2 pointed end of a cord or lace. **3** trite
quotation. ▷ v **tagging**, **tagged**
4 attach a tag to. **tag along** v
accompany someone, esp. if uninvited.

tag² n **1** children's game where the
person being chased becomes the
chaser upon being touched. ▷ v
tagging, **tagged 2** touch and catch in
this game.

tagliatelle n pasta in long narrow
strips.

tail ❶ n **1** rear part of an animal's body,
usu. forming a flexible appendage.
2 rear or last part or parts of
something. **3** *informal* person
employed to follow and spy on
another. ▷ pl **4** *informal* tail coat. ▷ adj
5 at the rear. ▷ v **6** *informal* follow
(someone) secretly. **turn tail** run
away. **tailless** adj **tails** adv with the
side of a coin uppermost that does not
have a portrait or tail of a head on it.

tailback n queue of traffic stretching
back from an obstruction. **tailboard** n
removable or hinged rear board on a
lorry etc. **tail coat** man's coat with a
long back split into two below the
waist. **tail off**, **away** v diminish
gradually. **tailplane** n small stabilizing
wing at the rear of an aircraft. **tailspin**
n uncontrolled spinning dive of an
aircraft. **tailwind** n wind coming from
the rear.

tailor ❶ n **1** person who makes men's
clothes. ▷ v **2** cut or style (a garment)
to specific requirements. **3** adapt to
suit a purpose. **tailored** adj made to fit

————————————— THESAURUS —————————————

tackle v **1** = **deal with**, attempt, come
or get to grips with, embark upon, get
stuck into (*inf*), have a go or stab at
(*inf*), set about, undertake
2 = **confront**, challenge, grab, grasp,
halt, intercept, seize, stop ▷ n **4** *Sport* =
challenge, block **5** = **equipment**,
accoutrements, apparatus, gear,
paraphernalia, tools, trappings

tacky¹ adj = **sticky**, adhesive, gluey,
gummy, wet

tacky² adj **1** *Inf* = **vulgar**, cheap, naff
(*Brit sl*), sleazy, tasteless **2** = **shabby**,
seedy, shoddy, tatty

tact n = **diplomacy**, consideration,
delicacy, discretion, sensitivity,
thoughtfulness, understanding

tactful adj = **diplomatic**, considerate,
delicate, discreet, polite, politic,
sensitive, thoughtful, understanding

tactic n = **policy**, approach,
manoeuvre, method, move, ploy,
scheme, stratagem ▷ pl n = **strategy**,
campaigning, manoeuvres, plans

tactical adj = **strategic**, cunning,
diplomatic, shrewd, smart

tactician n = **strategist**, general,
mastermind, planner, schemer

tactless adj = **insensitive**, impolite,
impolitic, inconsiderate, indelicate,
indiscreet, thoughtless, undiplomatic,
unsubtle

tag¹ n **1** = **label**, flap, identification,
mark, marker, note, slip, tab, ticket ▷ v
4 = **label**, mark **tag along** v =
accompany, attend, follow, shadow,
tail (*inf*), trail

tail n **1, 2** = **extremity**, appendage,
end, rear end, tailpiece ▷ v **6** *Inf* =
follow, shadow, stalk, track, trail **turn
tail** = **run away**, cut and run, flee,
retreat, run off, take to one's
heels

tailor n **1** = **outfitter**, clothier,
costumier, couturier, dressmaker,
seamstress ▷ v **2** = **style**, alter
3 = **adapt**, adjust, customize, fashion,
modify, mould, shape

close to a particular person's body.
tailor-made *adj* **1** made by a tailor.
2 perfect for a purpose.

taint ❶ *v* **1** spoil with a small amount of decay, contamination, or other bad quality. ▷ *n* **2** something that taints.

take ❶ *v* **taking**, **took**, **taken 1** remove from a place. **2** carry or accompany. **3** use. **4** get possession of, esp. dishonestly. **5** capture. **6** select. **7** require (time, resources, or ability). **8** assume. **9** accept. **10** perform, do, or make. **11** write down. **12** subtract or deduct. ▷ *n* **13** one of a series of recordings from which the best will be used. **take place** happen. **taking** *adj* charming. **takings** *pl n* money received by a shop. **take after** *v* look or behave like (a parent etc.). **take against** *v* start to dislike. **take away** *v* remove or subtract. **takeaway** *adj* **1** (of food) sold for consumption away from the premises. ▷ *n* **2** shop or restaurant selling meals for eating elsewhere. **3** meal bought at a takeaway. **take in** *v* **1** understand. **2** deceive or swindle. **3** make (clothing) smaller. **take off** *v* **1** (of an aircraft) leave the ground.

2 *informal* depart. **3** *informal* become successful. **4** *informal* parody. **takeoff** *n* **takeover** *n* act of taking control of a company by buying a large number of its shares. **take up** *v* **1** occupy or fill (space or time). **2** adopt the study or activity of. **3** shorten (a garment). **4** accept (an offer).

talc *n* **1** talcum powder. **2** soft mineral of magnesium silicate. **talcum powder** powder, usu. scented, used to dry or perfume the body.

tale ❶ *n* **1** story. **2** malicious piece of gossip.

talent ❶ *n* **1** natural ability. **2** *informal* attractive members of the opposite sex. **3** ancient unit of weight or money. **talented** *adj*.

talisman ❶ *n*, *pl* **-mans** object believed to have magic power. **talismanic** *adj*.

talk ❶ *v* **1** express ideas or feelings by means of speech. **2** utter. **3** discuss, e.g. *let's talk business*. **4** reveal information. **5** (be able to) speak in a specified language. ▷ *n* **6** speech or lecture. **7** conversation. **talker** *n* **talkative** *adj* fond of talking. **talk back** *v* answer impudently. **talkback** *n*

THESAURUS

taint *v* **1** = **spoil**, blemish, contaminate, corrupt, damage, defile, pollute, ruin, stain, sully, tarnish ▷ *n* **2** = **stain**, black mark, blemish, blot, defect, demerit, fault, flaw, spot

take *v* **2** = **carry**, accompany, bear, bring, conduct, convey, convoy, escort, ferry, fetch, guide, haul, lead, transport, usher **4** = **obtain**, acquire, appropriate, catch, get, grasp, grip, misappropriate, pinch (*inf*), pocket, purloin, secure, seize, steal **5** = **capture**, seize **7** = **require**, call for, demand, necessitate, need **8** = **assume**, believe, consider, perceive, presume, regard, understand **9** = **accept**, accommodate, contain, have room for, hold **12** = **subtract**, deduct, eliminate, remove

take in *v* **1** = **understand**, absorb, assimilate, comprehend, digest, get the hang of (*inf*), grasp **2** = **deceive**, cheat, con (*inf*), dupe, fool, hoodwink, mislead, swindle, trick

takeoff *n* **1, 2** = **departure**, launch, liftoff **4** *Inf* = **parody**, caricature, imitation, lampoon, satire, send-up (*Brit inf*), spoof (*inf*)

take off *v* **1** = **lift off**, take to the air

2 *Inf* = **depart**, abscond, decamp, disappear, go, leave, slope off **4** *Inf* = **parody**, caricature, imitate, lampoon, mimic, mock, satirize, send up (*Brit inf*)

takeover *n* = **merger**, coup, incorporation

take up *v* **1** = **occupy**, absorb, consume, cover, extend over, fill, use up **2** = **start**, adopt, become involved in, engage in

taking *adj* = **charming**, attractive, beguiling, captivating, enchanting, engaging, fetching (*inf*), lekker (*S Afr sl*), likable *or* likeable, prepossessing

takings *pl n* = **revenue**, earnings, income, proceeds, profits, receipts, returns, take

tale *n* **1** = **story**, account, anecdote, fable, legend, narrative, saga, yarn (*inf*)

talent *n* **1** = **ability**, aptitude, capacity, flair, genius, gift, knack

talented *adj* **1** = **gifted**, able, brilliant

talisman *n* = **charm**, amulet, fetish, lucky charm, mascot

talk *v* **1, 2** = **speak**, chat, chatter, communicate, converse, gossip, natter, utter **3** = **discuss**, confabulate,

NZ broadcast in which telephone comments or questions from the public are transmitted live. **talking-to** *n informal* telling-off. **talk into** *v* persuade (someone) to do something by talking. **talk out of** *v* dissuade (someone) from doing something by talking.

tall ❶ *adj* **1** higher than average. **2** of a specified height. **tall order** difficult task. **tall story** unlikely and probably untrue tale.

tallboy *n* high chest of drawers.

tallow *n* hard animal fat used to make candles.

tally ❶ *v* **-lying, -lied 1** (of two things) correspond. ▷ *n, pl* **-lies 2** record of a debt or score.

tally-ho *interj* huntsman's cry when the quarry is sighted.

Talmud *n* body of Jewish law. **Talmudic** *adj*.

talon *n* bird's hooked claw.

tamarind *n* **1** tropical tree. **2** its acid fruit.

tamarisk *n* evergreen shrub with slender branches and feathery flower clusters.

tambourine *n* percussion instrument like a small drum with jingling metal discs attached.

tame ❶ *adj* **1** (of animals) brought under human control. **2** (of animals) not afraid of people. **3** meek or submissive. **4** uninteresting. ▷ *v* **5** make tame. **tamely** *adv* **tamer** *n*.

Tamil *n* **1** member of a people of Sri Lanka and S India. **2** their language.

tam-o'-shanter *n* brimless wool cap with a bobble in the centre.

tamp *v* pack down by repeated taps.

tamper ❶ *v* (foll. by *with*) interfere.

tampon *n* absorbent plug of cotton wool inserted into the vagina during menstruation.

tan *n* **1** brown coloration of the skin from exposure to sunlight. ▷ *v* **tanning, tanned 2** (of skin) go brown from exposure to sunlight. **3** convert (a hide) into leather. ▷ *adj* **4** yellowish-brown. **tannery** *n, pl* **-eries** place where hides are tanned.

tandem *n* bicycle for two riders, one behind the other. **in tandem** together.

tandoori *adj* (of food) cooked in an Indian clay oven.

tang ❶ *n* **1** strong taste or smell. **2** trace or hint. **tangy** *adj* **tangier, tangiest**.

tangent *n* **1** line that touches a curve without intersecting it. **2** (in trigonometry) ratio of the length of the opposite side to that of the adjacent side of a right-angled triangle. **go off at a tangent** suddenly take a completely different line of thought or action. **tangential** *adj* **1** of superficial relevance only. **2** of a tangent. **tangentially** *adv*.

tangerine *n* small orange-like fruit of an Asian citrus tree.

        THESAURUS

confer, negotiate, parley **4 = inform**, blab, give the game away, grass (*Brit sl*), let the cat out of the bag, tell all ▷ *n* **6 = speech**, address, discourse, disquisition, lecture, oration, sermon

talkative *adj* **= loquacious**, chatty, effusive, garrulous, gossipy, long-winded, mouthy, verbose, voluble, wordy

talker *n* **= speaker**, chatterbox, conversationalist, lecturer, orator

talking-to *n Inf* **= reprimand**, criticism, dressing-down (*inf*), lecture, rebuke, reproach, reproof, scolding, telling-off (*inf*), ticking-off (*inf*)

tall *adj* **1 = high**, big, elevated, giant, lanky, lofty, soaring, towering **tall order = difficult**, demanding, hard, unreasonable, well-nigh impossible **tall story = implausible**, absurd, cock-and-bull (*inf*), exaggerated, far-

fetched, incredible, preposterous, unbelievable

tally *v* **1 = agree**, accord, coincide, concur, conform, correspond, fit, harmonize, match, square ▷ *n* **2 = record**, count, mark, reckoning, running total, score, total

tame *adj* **1 = broken**, amenable, disciplined, docile, gentle, obedient, tractable **2 = domesticated 3 = submissive**, compliant, docile, manageable, meek, obedient, subdued, unresisting **4 = unexciting**, bland, boring, dull, humdrum, insipid, uninspiring, uninteresting, vapid ▷ *v* **5 a = domesticate**, house-train, train **b = subdue**, break in, master

tamper *v* (foll. by *with*) **= interfere with**, alter, fiddle with (*inf*), fool about with (*inf*), meddle with, mess about with, tinker with

t

tangible ❶ *adj* **1** able to be touched. **2** clear and definite. **tangibly** *adv* **tangibility** *n*.

tangle ❶ *n* **1** confused mass or situation. ▷ *v* **2** twist together in a tangle. **3** (often foll. by *with*) come into conflict.

tango *n*, *pl* **-gos 1** S American dance. ▷ *v* **2** dance a tango.

tank *n* **1** container for liquids or gases. **2** armoured fighting vehicle moving on tracks. **tanker** *n* ship or lorry for carrying liquid in bulk.

tankard *n* large beer-mug, often with a hinged lid.

tannin, tannic acid *n* vegetable substance used in tanning.

Tannoy *n* ® type of public-address system.

tansy *n*, *pl* **-sies** yellow-flowered plant.

tantalize ❶ *v* torment by showing but withholding something desired. **tantalizing** *adj* **tantalizingly** *adv*.

tantalum *n Chemistry* hard greyish-white metallic element.

tantamount ❶ *adj* **tantamount to** equivalent in effect to.

tantrum ❶ *n* childish outburst of temper.

Taoism [**tow**-iz-zum] *n* system of religion and philosophy advocating a simple, honest life and noninterference with the course of natural events. **Taoist** *n*, *adj*.

tap¹ ❶ *v* **tapping, tapped 1** knock lightly and usu. repeatedly. ▷ *n* **2** light knock. **tap dancing** style of dancing in which the feet beat out an elaborate rhythm.

tap² ❶ *n* **1** valve to control the flow of liquid from a pipe or cask. ▷ *v* **tapping, tapped 2** listen in on (a telephone call) secretly by making an illegal connection. **3** obtain something useful or desirable from (something). **4** draw off with or as if with a tap. **on tap 1** *informal* readily available. **2** (of beer etc.) drawn from a cask.

tape ❶ *n* **1** narrow long strip of material. **2** (recording made on) a cassette containing magnetic tape. **3** string stretched across a race track to mark the finish. ▷ *v* **4** record on magnetic tape. **5** bind or fasten with tape. **have a person, situation taped** *informal* have full understanding and control of a person *or* situation. **tape measure** tape marked off in centimetres or inches for measuring. **tape recorder** device for recording and reproducing sound on magnetic tape. **tapeworm** *n* long flat parasitic worm living in the intestines of vertebrates.

taper ❶ *v* **1** become narrower towards one end. ▷ *n* **2** long thin candle. **3** narrowing. **taper off** *v* become gradually less.

tapestry *n*, *pl* **-tries** fabric decorated with coloured woven designs.

tapioca *n* beadlike starch made from cassava root, used in puddings.

tapir [**tape**-er] *n* piglike mammal of tropical America and SE Asia, with a long snout.

tappet *n* short steel rod in an engine,

THESAURUS

tangible *adj* **1** = **palpable**, actual, concrete, material, real **2** = **definite**, perceptible, positive

tangle *n* **1 a** = **knot**, coil, entanglement, jungle, twist, web **b** = **confusion**, complication, entanglement, fix (*inf*), imbroglio, jam, mess, mix-up ▷ *v* **2** = **twist**, coil, entangle, interweave, knot, mat, mesh, ravel **3** (often foll. by *with*) = **come into conflict with**, come up against, contend with, contest, cross swords with, dispute with, lock horns with

tangy *adj* **1** = **sharp**, piquant, pungent, spicy, tart

tantalize *v* = **torment**, frustrate, lead on, taunt, tease, torture

tantamount *adj* **tantamount to** = **equivalent to**, commensurate with,

equal to, synonymous with

tantrum *n* = **outburst**, fit, flare-up, hysterics, temper

tap¹ *v* **1** = **knock**, beat, drum, pat, rap, strike, touch ▷ *n* **2** = **knock**, pat, rap, touch

tap² *n* **1** = **valve**, stopcock, faucet (*US & Canad*) ▷ *v* **2** = **listen in on**, bug (*inf*), eavesdrop on **4** = **draw off**, bleed, drain, siphon off **on tap 1** *Inf* = **available**, at hand, in reserve, on hand, ready **2** = **on draught**

tape *n* **1** = **strip**, band, ribbon ▷ *v* **4** = **record**, tape-record, video **5** = **bind**, seal, secure, stick, wrap

taper *v* **1** = **narrow**, come to a point, thin **taper off** *v* = **decrease**, die away, dwindle, fade, lessen, reduce, subside, wane, wind down

transferring motion from one part to another.

taproot n main root of a plant, growing straight down.

tar n 1 thick black liquid distilled from coal etc. ▷ v **tarring, tarred 2** coat with tar.

taramasalata n creamy pink pâté made from fish roe.

tarantella n 1 lively Italian dance. **2** music for this.

tarantula n large hairy spider with a poisonous bite.

tardy adj **tardier, tardiest** slow or late. **tardily** adv **tardiness** n.

tare¹ n 1 weight of the wrapping or container of goods. **2** unladen weight of a vehicle.

tare² n 1 type of vetch plant. **2** Bible weed.

target ❶ n 1 object or person a missile is aimed at. **2** goal or objective. **3** object of criticism. ▷ v **-geting, -geted 4** aim or direct.

● **SPELLING TIP**
● Lots of people put an extra t into
● *targetting* and *targetted*, but they are
● wrong: the words are **targeting** and
● **targeted**.

tariff ❶ n 1 tax levied on imports. **2** list of fixed prices.

Tarmac n 1 ® mixture of tar, bitumen, and crushed stones used for roads etc. **2** (**t-**) airport runway.

tarn n small mountain lake.

tarnish ❶ v 1 make or become stained or less bright. **2** damage or taint. ▷ n **3** discoloration or blemish.

tarot [**tarr**-oh] n special pack of cards used mainly in fortune-telling. **tarot card** card in a tarot pack.

tarpaulin n (sheet of) heavy waterproof fabric.

tarragon n aromatic herb.

tarry v **-rying, -ried** old-fashioned

1 linger or delay. **2** stay briefly.

tarsus n, pl **-si** bones of the heel and ankle collectively.

tart¹ ❶ n pie or flan with a sweet filling.

tart² ❶ adj sharp or bitter. **tartly** adv **tartness** n.

tart³ ❶ n informal sexually provocative or promiscuous woman. **tart up** v informal dress or decorate in a smart or flashy way.

tartan n 1 design of straight lines crossing at right angles, esp. one associated with a Scottish clan. **2** cloth with such a pattern.

tartar¹ n 1 hard deposit on the teeth. **2** deposit formed during the fermentation of wine.

tartar² n fearsome or formidable person.

Tartar, Tatar n 1 member of a Mongoloid people who established a powerful state in central Asia in the 13th century. **2** descendant of this people. ▷ adj **3** of the Tartars.

tartare sauce n mayonnaise sauce mixed with chopped herbs and capers, served with seafood.

tartrazine [**tar**-traz-zeen] n artificial yellow dye used in food etc.

TAS Tasmania.

task ❶ n (difficult or unpleasant) piece of work to be done. **take to task** criticize or scold. **task force** (military) group formed to carry out a specific task. **taskmaster** n person who enforces hard work.

Tasmanian devil n small carnivorous marsupial found in Tasmania.

Tasmanian tiger same as THYLACINE.

tassel n decorative fringed knot of threads.

taste ❶ n 1 sense by which the flavour of a substance is distinguished in the mouth. **2** distinctive flavour. **3** small amount tasted. **4** brief experience of

───────────────── THESAURUS ─────────────────

target n 2 = **goal**, aim, ambition, end, intention, mark, object, objective **3** = **victim**, butt, scapegoat

tariff n 1 = **tax**, duty, excise, levy, toll **2** = **price list**, menu, schedule

tarnish v 1 = **stain**, blemish, blot, darken, discolour **2** = **damage**, blacken, smirch, sully, taint ▷ n **3** = **stain**, blemish, blot, discoloration, spot, taint

tart¹ n = **pie**, pastry, tartlet

tart² adj = **sharp**, acid, bitter, piquant,

pungent, sour, tangy, vinegary

tart³ n Inf = **slut**, call girl, floozy (sl), prostitute, trollop, whore

task n = **job**, assignment, chore, duty, enterprise, exercise, mission, undertaking **take to task** = **criticize**, blame, censure, rebuke, reprimand, reproach, reprove, rouse on (Aust), scold, tell off (inf), upbraid

taste n 2 = **flavour**, relish, savour, smack, tang **3** = **bit**, bite, dash, morsel, mouthful, sample, soupçon,

something. **5** liking. **6** ability to appreciate what is beautiful or excellent. ▷ *v* **7** distinguish the taste of (a substance). **8** take a small amount of (something) into the mouth. **9** have a specific taste. **10** experience briefly. **tasteful** *adj* having or showing good taste. **tastefully** *adv* **tasteless** *adj* **1** bland or insipid. **2** showing bad taste. **tastelessly** *adv* **tasty** *adj* pleasantly flavoured. **taste bud** small organ on the tongue which perceives flavours.

tat *n* tatty or tasteless article(s).

Tatar *n, adj* same as TARTAR.

tattered *adj* ragged or torn. **in tatters** in ragged pieces.

tattle *v, n* gossip or chatter.

tattletale ❶ *n Chiefly US & Canad* a scandalmonger or gossip.

tattoo¹ *n* **1** pattern made on the body by pricking the skin and staining it with indelible inks. ▷ *v* **-tooing, -tooed** **2** make such a pattern on the skin. **tattooist** *n*.

tattoo² *n* **1** military display or pageant. **2** drumming or tapping.

tatty ❶ *adj* **-tier, -tiest** shabby or worn out.

taught *v* past of TEACH.

taunt ❶ *v* **1** tease with jeers. ▷ *n*

2 jeering remark.

taupe *adj* brownish-grey.

Taurus *n* (the bull) second sign of the zodiac.

taut ❶ *adj* **1** drawn tight. **2** showing nervous strain. **tauten** *v* make or become taut.

tautology *n, pl* **-gies** use of words which merely repeat something already stated. **tautological** *adj*.

tavern ❶ *n old-fashioned* pub.

tawdry ❶ *adj* **-drier, -driest** cheap, showy, and of poor quality.

tawny *adj* **-nier, -niest** yellowish-brown.

tax ❶ *n* **1** compulsory payment levied by a government on income, property, etc. to raise revenue. ▷ *v* **2** levy a tax on. **3** make heavy demands on. **taxable** *adj* **taxation** *n* levying of taxes. **taxing** *adj* demanding, onerous. **tax-free** *adj* (of goods and services) not taxed. **taxpayer** *n* **tax relief** reduction in the amount of tax a person or company has to pay. **tax return** statement of personal income for tax purposes.

taxi *n* **1** (also **taxicab**) car with a driver that may be hired to take people to any specified destination. ▷ *v* **taxiing, taxied** **2** (of an aircraft) run along the

---

THESAURUS

spoonful, titbit **5** = **liking**, appetite, fancy, fondness, inclination, partiality, penchant, predilection, preference **6** = **refinement**, appreciation, discernment, discrimination, elegance, judgment, sophistication, style ▷ *v* **7** = **distinguish**, differentiate, discern, perceive **8** = **sample**, savour, sip, test, try **9** = **have a flavour of**, savour of, smack of **10** = **experience**, encounter, know, meet with, partake of, undergo

tasteful *adj* = **refined**, artistic, cultivated, cultured, discriminating, elegant, exquisite, in good taste, polished, stylish

tasteless *adj* **1** = **insipid**, bland, boring, dull, flat, flavourless, mild, thin, weak **2** = **vulgar**, crass, crude, gaudy, gross, inelegant, naff (*Brit sl*), tacky (*inf*), tawdry

tasty *adj* = **delicious**, appetizing, delectable, full-flavoured, lekker (*S Afr sl*), luscious, palatable, savoury, scrumptious (*inf*), toothsome

tattletale *noun chiefly US & Canad* =

gossip, busybody, babbler, bigmouth (*sl*), scandalmonger, gossipmonger

tatty *adj* = **shabby**, bedraggled, dilapidated, down at heel, neglected, ragged, run-down, scruffy, threadbare, worn

taunt *v* **1** = **jeer**, deride, insult, mock, provoke, ridicule, tease, torment ▷ *n* **2** = **jeer**, derision, dig, gibe, insult, provocation, ridicule, sarcasm, teasing

taut *adj* **1** = **tight**, flexed, rigid, strained, stressed, stretched, tense

tavern *n Old-fashioned* = **inn**, alehouse (*arch*), bar, hostelry, pub (*inf, chiefly Brit*), public house, beer parlour (*Canad*), beverage room (*Canad*)

tawdry *adj* = **vulgar**, cheap, gaudy, gimcrack, naff (*Brit sl*), tacky (*inf*), tasteless, tatty

tax *n* **1** = **charge**, duty, excise, levy, tariff, tithe, toll ▷ *v* **2** = **charge**, assess, rate **3** = **strain**, burden, exhaust, load, stretch, test, try, weaken, weary

taxing *adj* = **demanding**, exacting, onerous, punishing, sapping, stressful, tiring, tough, trying

t

ground before taking off or after landing. **taximeter** n meter in a taxi that registers the fare. **taxi rank** place where taxis wait to be hired.

taxidermy n art of stuffing and mounting animal skins to give them a lifelike appearance. **taxidermist** n.

taxonomy n classification of plants and animals into groups. **taxonomic** adj **taxonomist** n.

Tb Chemistry terbium.

TB tuberculosis.

T-bone steak n steak cut from the sirloin of beef, containing a T-shaped bone.

tbs., tbsp. tablespoon(ful).

Tc Chemistry technetium.

te n Music (in tonic sol-fa) seventh degree of any major scale.

Te Chemistry tellurium.

tea n 1 drink made from infusing the dried leaves of an Asian bush in boiling water. 2 leaves used to make this drink. 3 main evening meal. 4 light afternoon meal of tea, cakes, etc. 5 drink like tea, made from other plants. **tea bag** small porous bag of tea leaves. **tea cosy** covering for a teapot to keep the tea warm. **teapot** n container with a lid, spout, and handle for making and serving tea. **teaspoon** n small spoon for stirring tea. **tea towel**, **tea cloth** towel for drying dishes. **tea tree** tree of Australia and New Zealand that yields an oil used as an antiseptic.

teach ❶ v **teaching**, **taught** 1 tell or show (someone) how to do something. 2 give lessons in (a subject). 3 cause to learn or understand. **teacher** n **teaching** n.

teak n very hard wood of an E Indian tree.

teal n kind of small duck.

team ❶ n 1 group of people forming one side in a game. 2 group of people or animals working together. **teamster** n US lorry driver. **team spirit** willingness to cooperate as part of a team. **team up** v make or join a team. **teamwork** n cooperative work by a team.

tear¹, **teardrop** ❶ n drop of fluid appearing in and falling from the eye. **in tears** weeping. **tearful** adj weeping or about to weep. **tear gas** gas that stings the eyes and causes temporary blindness. **tear-jerker** n informal excessively sentimental film or book.

tear² ❶ v **tearing**, **tore**, **torn** 1 rip a hole in. 2 rip apart. 3 rush. 4 remove by force. ▷ n 5 hole or split. **tearaway** n wild or unruly person.

tease ❶ v 1 make fun of (someone) in a provoking or playful way. ▷ n 2 person who teases. **teaser** n annoying or difficult problem. **teasing** adj, n **tease out** v remove tangles from (hair etc.) by combing.

teasel, **teazel**, **teazle** n plant with prickly leaves and flowers.

teat n 1 nipple of a breast or udder. 2 rubber nipple of a feeding bottle.

tech n informal technical college.

techie informal ▷ n 1 person who is skilled in the use of technology. ▷ adj 2 relating to or skilled in the use of technology.

technetium [tek-**neesh**-ee-um] n Chemistry artificially produced silvery-grey metallic element.

━━━━━━━━━━━━━━━━━━━━━━━━━━━━━━━━━━━ THESAURUS ━━━━━━

t

teach v = **instruct**, coach, drill, educate, enlighten, guide, inform, show, train, tutor

teacher n = **instructor**, coach, educator, guide, lecturer, master or mistress, mentor, schoolteacher, trainer, tutor

team n 1 = **side**, line-up, squad 2 = **group**, band, body, bunch, company, gang, set **team up** = **join**, band together, cooperate, couple, get together, link, unite, work together

teamwork n = **cooperation**, collaboration, coordination, esprit de corps, fellowship, harmony, unity

tear¹ n **in tears** = **weeping**, blubbering, crying, distressed, sobbing

tear² v 1 = **rip**, rend, rupture, scratch, shred, split 2 = **pull apart**, claw, lacerate, mangle, mutilate 3 = **rush**, bolt, charge, dash, fly, hurry, race, run, speed, sprint, zoom ▷ n 5 = **hole**, laceration, rent, rip, rupture, scratch, split

tearaway n = **hooligan**, delinquent, good-for-nothing, rowdy, ruffian

tearful adj = **weeping**, blubbering, crying, in tears, lachrymose, sobbing, weepy (inf), whimpering

tease v 1 = **mock**, goad, provoke, pull someone's leg (inf), taunt, torment

technical ❶ *adj* **1** of or specializing in industrial, practical, or mechanical arts and applied sciences. **2** skilled in technical subjects. **3** relating to a particular field. **4** according to the letter of the law. **5** showing technique, e.g. *technical brilliance*. **technically** *adv* **technicality** *n, pl* **-ties** petty point based on a strict application of rules. **technician** *n* person skilled in a particular technical field. **technical college** higher educational institution with courses in art and technical subjects. **technique** *n* **1** method or skill used for a particular task. **2** technical proficiency.

Technicolor *n* ® system of colour photography used for the cinema.

technique ❶ *n* **1** method or skill used for a particular task. **2** technical proficiency.

techno *n* type of electronic dance music with a very fast beat.

technocracy *n, pl* **-cies** government by technical experts. **technocrat** *n*.

technology *n* **1** application of practical or mechanical sciences to industry or commerce. **2** scientific methods used in a particular field. **technological** *adj* **technologist** *n*.

tectonics *n* study of the earth's crust and the forces affecting it.

teddy *n, pl* **-dies** **1** teddy bear. **2** combined camisole and knickers. **teddy bear** soft toy bear.

teddy boy *n* youth who wore mock Edwardian fashions in Britain esp. in the mid-1950s.

Te Deum [tee **dee**-um] *n* ancient Latin hymn of praise.

tedious ❶ *adj* causing fatigue or boredom. **tediously** *adv* **tedium** *n* monotony.

tee *n* **1** small peg from which a golf ball can be played at the start of each hole. **2** area of a golf course from which the first stroke of a hole is made.

tee off *v* make the first stroke of a hole in golf.

teem[1] *v* be full of.

teem[2] *v* rain heavily.

teenage ❶ *adj* of the period of life between the ages of 13 and 19. **teenager** *n* person aged between 13 and 19.

teens *pl n* period of being a teenager.

teeny *adj* **-nier, -niest** *informal* extremely small.

teepee *n* same as TEPEE.

tee-shirt *n* same as T-SHIRT.

teeter ❶ *v* wobble or move unsteadily.

teeth *n* plural of TOOTH.

teethe *v* (of a baby) grow his or her first teeth. **teething troubles** problems during the early stages of something.

teetotal ❶ *adj* drinking no alcohol. **teetotaller** *n*.

TEFL Teaching of English as a Foreign Language.

Teflon *n* ® substance used for nonstick coatings on saucepans etc.

telecommunications *n* communications using telephone, radio, television, etc.

telegram *n* formerly, a message sent by telegraph.

telegraph *n* **1** formerly, a system for sending messages over a distance along a cable. ▷ *v* **2** communicate by telegraph. **telegraphic** *adj* **telegraphist** *n* **telegraphy** *n* science or use of a telegraph.

telekinesis *n* movement of objects by thought or willpower.

Telemessage *n* ® message sent by telephone or telex and delivered in printed form.

telemetry *n* use of electronic devices to record or measure a distant event and transmit the data to a receiver.

teleology *n* belief that all things have a predetermined purpose. **teleological** *adj*.

t

———————— THESAURUS ————————

technical *adj* **1, 2** = **scientific**, hi-tech *or* high-tech, skilled, specialist, specialized, technological

technique *n* **1** = **method**, approach, manner, means, mode, procedure, style, system, way **2** = **skill**, artistry, craft, craftsmanship, execution, performance, proficiency, touch

tedious *adj* = **boring**, drab, dreary, dull, humdrum, irksome, laborious, mind-numbing, monotonous, tiresome, wearisome

tedium *n* = **boredom**, drabness, dreariness, dullness, monotony, routine, sameness, tediousness

teenager *n* = **youth**, adolescent, boy, girl, juvenile, minor

teeter *v* = **wobble**, rock, seesaw, stagger, sway, totter, waver

teetotaller *n* = **abstainer**, nondrinker

telepathy ❶ n direct communication between minds. **telepathic** adj **telepathically** adv.

telephone ❶ n **1** device for transmitting sound over a distance along wires. ▷ v **2** call or talk to (a person) by telephone. **telephony** n **telephonic** adj **telephonist** n person operating a telephone switchboard.

telephoto lens n camera lens producing a magnified image of a distant object.

teleprinter n apparatus like a typewriter for sending and receiving typed messages by wire.

Teleprompter n ® device under a television camera enabling a speaker to read the script while appearing to look at the camera.

telesales n selling of a product or service by telephone.

telescope ❶ n **1** optical instrument for magnifying distant objects. ▷ v **2** shorten. **telescopic** adj.

television ❶ n **1** system of producing a moving image and accompanying sound on a distant screen. **2** device for receiving broadcast signals and converting them into sound and pictures. **3** content of television programmes. **televise** v broadcast on television. **televisual** adj.

teleworking n use of home computers, telephones, etc., to enable a person to work from home while maintaining contact with colleagues or customers. **teleworker** n.

telex n **1** international communication service using teleprinters. **2** machine used in such a service. **3** message sent by telex. ▷ v **4** transmit by telex.

tell ❶ v **telling**, **told 1** make known in words. **2** order or instruct. **3** give an account of. **4** discern or distinguish. **5** have an effect. **6** informal reveal secrets. **teller** n **1** narrator. **2** bank cashier. **3** person who counts votes. **telling** adj having a marked effect. **tell off** v reprimand. **telling-off** n **telltale** n **1** person who reveals secrets. ▷ adj **2** revealing.

tellurium n Chemistry brittle silvery-white nonmetallic element.

telly n, pl **-lies** informal television.

temerity ❶ [tim-**merr**-it-tee] n boldness or audacity.

temp informal ▷ n **1** temporary employee, esp. a secretary. ▷ v **2** work as a temp.

temp. 1 temperature. **2** temporary.

temper ❶ n **1** outburst of anger. **2** tendency to become angry. **3** calm mental condition, e.g. I lost my temper. **4** frame of mind. ▷ v **5** make less

———————————————— THESAURUS ————————————————

telepathy n = **mind-reading**, sixth sense

telephone n **1** = **phone**, dog and bone (sl), handset, line, mobile (phone) ▷ v **2** = **call**, dial, phone, ring (chiefly Brit)

telescope n **1** = **glass**, spyglass ▷ v **2** = **shorten**, abbreviate, abridge, compress, condense, contract, shrink

television n **2** = **TV**, small screen (inf), telly (Brit inf), the box (Brit inf), the tube (sl)

tell v **1** = **inform**, announce, communicate, disclose, divulge, express, make known, notify, proclaim, reveal, state **2** = **instruct**, bid, call upon, command, direct, order, require, summon **3** = **describe**, chronicle, depict, narrate, portray, recount, relate, report **4** = **distinguish**, differentiate, discern, discriminate, identify **5** = **have** or **take effect**, carry weight, count, make its presence felt, register, take its toll, weigh

telling adj = **effective**, considerable, decisive, forceful, impressive, influential, marked, powerful, significant, striking

telling-off n = **reprimand**, criticism, dressing-down (inf), lecture, rebuke, reproach, reproof, scolding, talking-to, ticking-off (inf)

tell off v = **reprimand**, berate, censure, chide, haul over the coals (inf), lecture, read the riot act, rebuke, reproach, rouse on (Aust), scold

temerity n = **audacity**, boldness, cheek, chutzpah (US & Canad inf), effrontery, front, impudence, nerve (inf), rashness, recklessness

temper n **1** = **rage**, bad mood, fury, passion, tantrum **2** = **irritability**, hot-headedness, irascibility, passion, petulance, resentment, surliness **3** = **self-control**, calmness, composure, cool (sl), equanimity **4** = **frame of mind**, constitution, disposition, humour, mind, mood,

t

extreme. **6** strengthen or toughen (metal).

tempera n painting medium for powdered pigments.

temperament ➊ n person's character or disposition. **temperamental** adj **1** having changeable moods. **2** informal erratic and unreliable. **temperamentally** adv.

temperate ➊ adj **1** (of climate) not extreme. **2** self-restrained or moderate. **temperance** n **1** moderation. **2** abstinence from alcohol.

temperature n **1** degree of heat or cold. **2** informal abnormally high body temperature.

tempest ➊ n violent storm. **tempestuous** adj **1** violent or stormy. **2** extremely emotional or passionate. **tempestuously** adv.

template n pattern used to cut out shapes accurately.

temple¹ ➊ n building for worship.

temple² n region on either side of the forehead.

tempo n, pl **-pi**, **-pos** **1** rate or pace. **2** speed of a piece of music.

temporal adj **1** of time. **2** worldly rather than spiritual.

temporary ➊ adj lasting only for a short time. **temporarily** adv.

temporize v **1** gain time by negotiation or evasiveness. **2** adapt to circumstances.

tempt ➊ v entice (a person) to do something wrong. **tempt fate** take foolish or unnecessary risks. **tempter**, **temptress** n **temptation** n **1** tempting. **2** tempting thing. **tempting** adj attractive or inviting.

ten adj, n one more than nine. **tenth** adj, n (of) number ten in a series.

tenable ➊ adj able to be upheld or maintained.

tenacious ➊ adj **1** holding fast. **2** stubborn. **tenaciously** adv **tenacity** n.

THESAURUS

---

nature, temperament ▷ v **5** = **moderate**, assuage, lessen, mitigate, mollify, restrain, soften, soothe, tone down **6** = **strengthen**, anneal, harden, toughen

temperament n **a** = **nature**, bent, character, constitution, disposition, humour, make-up, outlook, personality, temper **b** = **excitability**, anger, hot-headedness, moodiness, petulance, volatility

temperamental adj **1** = **moody**, capricious, emotional, excitable, highly strung, hypersensitive, irritable, sensitive, touchy, volatile **2** Inf = **unreliable**, erratic, inconsistent, inconstant, unpredictable

temperance n **1** = **moderation**, continence, discretion, forbearance, restraint, self-control, self-discipline, self-restraint **2** = **teetotalism**, abstemiousness, abstinence, sobriety

temperate adj **1** = **mild**, calm, cool, fair, gentle, moderate, pleasant **2** = **moderate**, calm, composed, dispassionate, even-tempered, mild, reasonable, self-controlled, self-restrained, sensible

tempest n = **storm**, cyclone, gale, hurricane, squall, tornado, typhoon

tempestuous adj **1** = **stormy**, blustery, gusty, inclement, raging, squally, turbulent, windy

2 = **passionate**, boisterous, emotional, furious, heated, intense, stormy, turbulent, violent, wild

temple¹ n = **shrine**, church, sanctuary

temporarily adv = **briefly**, fleetingly, for the time being, momentarily, pro tem

temporary adj = **impermanent**, brief, ephemeral, fleeting, interim, momentary, provisional, short-lived, transitory

tempt v = **entice**, coax, invite, lead on, lure, seduce, tantalize

temptation n **1** = **enticement**, allurement, inducement, lure, pull, seduction, tantalization **2** = **appeal**, attraction

tempting adj = **inviting**, alluring, appetizing, attractive, enticing, lekker (S Afr sl), mouthwatering, seductive, tantalizing

tenable adj = **sound**, arguable, believable, defensible, justifiable, plausible, rational, reasonable, viable

tenacious adj **1** = **firm**, clinging, forceful, immovable, iron, strong, tight, unshakable **2** = **stubborn**, adamant, determined, dogged, obdurate, obstinate, persistent, resolute, steadfast, unswerving, unyielding

tenacity n **2** = **perseverance**, application, determination,

t

tenant ❶ *n* person who rents land or a building. **tenancy** *n*.

tench *n, pl* **tench** freshwater game fish of the carp family.

tend¹ ❶ *v* **1** be inclined. **2** go in the direction of. **tendency** *n* inclination to act in a certain way. **tendentious** *adj* biased, not impartial.

tend² ❶ *v* take care of.

tender¹ ❶ *adj* **1** not tough. **2** gentle and affectionate. **3** vulnerable or sensitive. **tenderly** *adv* **tenderness** *n* **tenderize** *v* soften (meat) by pounding or treatment with a special substance. **tenderizer** *n* **tenderloin** *n* tender cut of pork or other meat from between the sirloin and the ribs.

tender² ❶ *v* **1** offer. **2** make a formal offer to supply goods or services at a stated cost. ▷ *n* **3** such an offer. **legal tender** currency that must, by law, be accepted as payment.

tender³ *n* **1** small boat that brings supplies to a larger ship in a port. **2** carriage for fuel and water attached to a steam locomotive.

tendon *n* strong tissue attaching a muscle to a bone.

tendril *n* slender stem by which a climbing plant clings.

tenement *n* building divided into several flats.

tenet [**ten**-nit] *n* doctrine or belief.

tenner *n informal* ten-pound note.

tennis *n* game in which players use rackets to hit a ball back and forth over a net.

tenon *n* projecting end on a piece of wood fitting into a slot in another piece.

tenor *n* **1** (singer with) the second highest male voice. **2** general meaning. ▷ *adj* **3** (of a voice or instrument) between alto and baritone.

tenpin bowling *n* game in which players try to knock over ten skittles by rolling a ball at them.

tense¹ ❶ *adj* **1** emotionally strained. **2** stretched tight. ▷ *v* **3** make or become tense.

tense² *n Grammar* form of a verb showing the time of action.

tensile *adj* of tension. **tensile strength** measure of the ability of a material to withstand lengthways stress.

tension ❶ *n* **1** hostility or suspense. **2** emotional strain. **3** degree of stretching.

tent *n* portable canvas shelter.

tentacle *n* flexible organ of many invertebrates, used for grasping, feeding, etc.

tentative ❶ *adj* **1** provisional or experimental. **2** cautious or hesitant. **tentatively** *adv*.

——————————————————— THESAURUS ———————

doggedness, obduracy, persistence, resolve, steadfastness, stubbornness

tenancy *n* = **lease**, occupancy, possession, renting, residence

tenant *n* = **leaseholder**, inhabitant, lessee, occupant, occupier, renter, resident

tend¹ *v* **1** = **be inclined**, be apt, be liable, gravitate, have a tendency, incline, lean **2** = **go**, aim, bear, head, lead, make for, move, point

tend² *v* = **take care of**, attend, cultivate, keep, look after, maintain, manage, nurture, watch over

tendency *n* = **inclination**, disposition, leaning, liability, proclivity, proneness, propensity, susceptibility

tender¹ *adj* **2** = **gentle**, affectionate, caring, compassionate, considerate, kind, loving, sympathetic, tenderhearted, warm-hearted **3** = **sensitive**, bruised, inflamed, painful, raw, sore, vulnerable

tender² *v* **1** = **offer**, give, hand in,

present, proffer, propose, put forward, submit, volunteer ▷ *n* **3** = **offer**, bid, estimate, proposal, submission

tenderness *n* **2** = **gentleness**, affection, care, compassion, consideration, kindness, love, sentimentality, sympathy, warmth **3** = **soreness**, inflammation, pain, sensitivity

tense¹ *adj* **1** = **nervous**, anxious, apprehensive, edgy, jumpy, keyed up, on edge, on tenterhooks, strained, uptight (*inf*), wired (*sl*) **2** = **tight**, rigid, strained, stretched, taut ▷ *v* **3** = **tighten**, brace, flex, strain, stretch

tension *n* **1** = **hostility**, apprehension, suspense **2** = **strain**, anxiety, nervousness, pressure, stress, unease **3** = **tightness**, pressure, rigidity, stiffness, stress, stretching, tautness

tentative *adj* **1** = **unconfirmed**, conjectural, experimental, indefinite, provisional, speculative, unsettled **2** = **hesitant**, cautious, diffident,

tenterhooks *pl n* **on tenterhooks** in anxious suspense.

tenuous ❶ *adj* slight or flimsy. **tenuously** *adv*.

tenure *n* **1** (period of) the holding of an office or position. **2** legal right to live in a building or use land for a period of time.

tenuto *adj, adv Music* (of a note) to be held for or beyond its full time value.

tepee [**tee**-pee] *n* cone-shaped tent, formerly used by Native Americans.

tepid ❶ *adj* **1** slightly warm. **2** half-hearted.

tequila *n* Mexican alcoholic drink.

terbium *n Chemistry* rare metallic element.

tercentenary *adj, n, pl* **-naries** (of) a three hundredth anniversary.

term ❶ *n* **1** word or expression. **2** fixed period. **3** period of the year when a school etc. is open or a lawcourt holds sessions. ▷ *pl* **4** conditions. **5** mutual relationship. ▷ *v* **6** name or designate.

termagant *n* unpleasant and bad-tempered woman.

terminal ❶ *adj* **1** (of an illness) ending in death. **2** at or being an end. ▷ *n* **3** place where people or vehicles begin or end a journey. **4** point where current enters or leaves an electrical device. **5** keyboard and VDU having input and output links with a computer. **terminally** *adv* **terminal velocity** *Physics* maximum velocity reached by a body falling under gravity.

terminate ❶ *v* bring or come to an end. **termination** *n* **terminable** *adj* capable of being terminated.

terminology ❶ *n* technical terms relating to a subject. **terminological** *adj*.

terminus ❶ *n, pl* **-ni, -nuses** railway or bus station at the end of a line.

termite *n* white antlike insect that destroys timber.

tern *n* gull-like sea bird with a forked tail and pointed wings.

ternary *adj* **1** consisting of three parts. **2** *Maths* (of a number system) to the base three.

Terpsichorean *adj* of dancing.

terrace *n* **1** row of houses built as one block. **2** paved area next to a building. **3** level tier cut out of a hill. ▷ *pl* **4** (also **terracing**) tiered area in a stadium where spectators stand. ▷ *v* **5** form into or provide with a terrace.

terracotta *adj, n* **1** (made of) brownish-red unglazed pottery. ▷ *adj* **2** brownish-red.

terra firma *n Latin* dry land or solid ground.

terrain ❶ *n* area of ground, esp. with reference to its physical character.

terrapin *n* small turtle-like reptile.

terrarium *n, pl* **-raria, -rariums** enclosed container for small plants or animals.

terrazzo *n, pl* **-zos** floor of marble chips set in mortar and polished.

terrestrial ❶ *adj* **1** of the earth. **2** of or living on land.

---

doubtful, faltering, timid, uncertain, undecided, unsure

tenuous *adj* = **slight**, doubtful, dubious, flimsy, insubstantial, nebulous, shaky, sketchy, weak

tepid *adj* **1** = **lukewarm**, warmish **2** = **half-hearted**, apathetic, cool, indifferent, lukewarm, unenthusiastic

term *n* **1** = **word**, expression, name, phrase, title **2** = **period**, duration, interval, season, span, spell, time, while ▷ *v* **6** = **call**, designate, dub, entitle, label, name, style

terminal *adj* **1** = **fatal**, deadly, incurable, killing, lethal, mortal **2** = **final**, concluding, extreme, last, ultimate, utmost ▷ *n* **3** = **terminus**, depot, end of the line, station

terminate *v* = **end**, abort, cease, close, complete, conclude, discontinue, finish, stop

termination *n* = **ending**, abortion, cessation, completion, conclusion, discontinuation, end, finish

terminology *n* = **language**, jargon, nomenclature, phraseology, terms, vocabulary

terminus *n* = **end of the line**, depot, garage, last stop, station

terms *pl n* **4** = **conditions**, particulars, provisions, provisos, qualifications, specifications, stipulations **5** = **relationship**, footing, relations, standing, status

terrain *n* = **ground**, country, going, land, landscape, topography

terrestrial *adj* **1** = **earthly**, global, worldly

t

terrible ⊕ *adj* **1** very serious. **2** *informal* very bad. **3** causing fear. **terribly** *adv*.

terrier *n* any of various breeds of small active dog.

terrific ⊕ *adj* **1** great or intense. **2** *informal* excellent.

terrify ⊕ *v* **-fying, -fied** fill with fear. **terrified** *adj* **terrifying** *adj* **terrifyingly** *adv*.

terrine [terr-**reen**] *n* **1** earthenware dish with a lid. **2** pâté or similar food.

territory ⊕ *n, pl* **-ries** **1** district. **2** area under the control of a particular government. **3** area inhabited and defended by an animal. **4** area of knowledge. **5** (**T-**) region of a country, esp. of a federal state, that does not enjoy full rights. **territorial** *adj* **Territorial Army** reserve army. **territorial waters** parts of the sea over which a country exercises control, esp. with regard to fishing rights.

terror ⊕ *n* **1** great fear. **2** terrifying person or thing. **3** *informal* troublesome person or thing. **terrorism** *n* use of violence and intimidation to achieve political ends. **terrorist** *n, adj* **terrorize** *v* force or oppress by fear or violence.

terry *n* fabric with small loops covering both sides, used esp. for making towels.

terse ⊕ *adj* **1** neat and concise. **2** curt;

abrupt. **tersely** *adv*.

tertiary [**tur**-shar-ee] *adj* third in degree, order, etc.

Terylene *n* ® synthetic polyester yarn or fabric.

tessellated *adj* paved or inlaid with a mosaic of small tiles. **tessera** *n, pl* **-serae** small square tile used in mosaics.

test ⊕ *v* **1** try out to ascertain the worth, capability, or endurance of. **2** carry out an examination on. ▷ *n* **3** critical examination. **4** Test match. **testing** *adj* **test case** lawsuit that establishes a precedent. **Test match** one of a series of international cricket or rugby matches. **test pilot** pilot who tests the performance of new aircraft. **test tube** narrow round-bottomed glass tube used in scientific experiments. **test-tube baby** baby conceived outside the mother's body.

testament ⊕ *n* **1** proof or tribute. **2** *Law* will. **3** (**T-**) one of the two main divisions of the Bible.

testate *adj* having left a valid will. **testacy** *n* **testator** [test-**tay**-tor], (*fem*) **testatrix** [test-**tay**-triks] *n* maker of a will.

testicle *n* either of the two male reproductive glands.

testify ⊕ *v* **-fying, -fied** give evidence under oath. **testify to** be evidence of.

---

terrible *adj* **1** = **serious**, dangerous, desperate, extreme, severe **2** *Inf* = **bad**, abysmal, awful, dire, dreadful, poor, rotten (*inf*) **3** = **fearful**, dreadful, frightful, horrendous, horrible, horrifying, monstrous, shocking, terrifying

terribly *adv* **1** = **extremely**, awfully (*inf*), decidedly, desperately, exceedingly, seriously, thoroughly, very

terrific *adj* **1** = **great**, enormous, fearful, gigantic, huge, intense, tremendous **2** *Inf* = **excellent**, amazing, brilliant, fantastic (*inf*), magnificent, marvellous, outstanding, sensational (*inf*), stupendous, superb, wonderful

terrified *adj* = **frightened**, alarmed, appalled, horrified, horror-struck, panic-stricken, petrified, scared

terrify *v* = **frighten**, alarm, appal, horrify, make one's hair stand on end, scare, shock, terrorize

territory *n* **1** = **district**, area, country,

domain, land, patch, province, region, zone

terror *n* **1** = **fear**, alarm, anxiety, dread, fright, horror, panic, shock **2** = **scourge**, bogeyman, bugbear, devil, fiend, monster

terrorize *v* = **oppress**, browbeat, bully, coerce, intimidate, menace, threaten

terse *adj* **1** = **concise**, brief, condensed, laconic, monosyllabic, pithy, short, succinct **2** = **curt**, abrupt, brusque, short, snappy

test *v* **1** = **try out**, experiment, put to the test **2** = **check**, analyse, assess, examine, investigate, research ▷ *n* **3** = **examination**, acid test, analysis, assessment, check, evaluation, investigation, research, trial

testament *n* **1** = **proof**, demonstration, evidence, testimony, tribute, witness **2** *Law* = **will**, last wishes

testify *v* = **bear witness**, affirm, assert, attest, certify, corroborate, state, swear, vouch

testimony ❶ *n, pl* **-nies 1** declaration of truth or fact. **2** evidence given under oath. **testimonial** *n* **1** recommendation of the worth of a person or thing. **2** tribute for services or achievement.

● **USAGE NOTE**
● A *testimonial* is an open letter of
● recommendation about someone.
● A *reference* is a confidential report
● that is not read by the person who is
● the subject.

testis *n, pl* **-tes** testicle.
testosterone *n* male sex hormone secreted by the testes.
testy *adj* **-tier, -tiest** irritable or touchy. **testily** *adv* **testiness** *n*.
tetanus *n* acute infectious disease producing muscular spasms and convulsions.
tetchy *adj* **tetchier, tetchiest** cross and irritable.
tête-à-tête *n, pl* **-têtes, -tête** private conversation.
tether ❶ *n* **1** rope or chain for tying an animal to a spot. ▷ *v* **2** tie up with rope. **at the end of one's tether** at the limit of one's endurance.
tetragon *n* figure with four angles and four sides. **tetragonal** *adj*.
tetrahedron [tet-ra-**heed**-ron] *n, pl* **-drons, -dra** solid figure with four faces.
tetralogy *n, pl* **-gies** series of four related works.
tetrameter [tet-**tram**-it-er] *n* **1** line of poetry with four metrical feet. **2** verse composed of such lines.
Teutonic [tew-**tonn**-ik] *adj* of or like the (ancient) Germans.

text ❶ *n* **1** main body of a book as distinct from illustrations etc. **2** any written material. **3** passage of the Bible as the subject of a sermon. **4** novel or play studied for a course. **5** text message. ▷ *v* **6** send a text message to (someone). **textual** *adj*
textbook *n* **1** standard book on a particular subject. ▷ *adj* **2** perfect, e.g. *a textbook landing*. **text message** message sent in text form, esp. by means of a cell phone.
textile *n* **1** fabric or cloth, esp. woven. ▷ *adj* **2** of (the making of) fabrics.
texture ❶ *n* structure, feel, or consistency. **textured** *adj* **textural** *adj*.
Th *Chemistry* thorium.
Thai *adj* **1** of Thailand. ▷ *n, pl* **2 Thais, Thai** person from Thailand. **3** language of Thailand.
thalidomide [thal-**lid**-oh-mide] *n* drug formerly used as a sedative, but found to cause abnormalities in developing fetuses.
thallium *n* *Chemistry* highly toxic metallic element.
than *conj, prep* used to introduce the second element of a comparison.
thane *n* *History* Anglo-Saxon or medieval Scottish nobleman.
thank ❶ *v* **1** express gratitude to. **2** hold responsible. **thanks** *pl n* **1** words of gratitude. ▷ *interj* **2** (also **thank you**) polite expression of gratitude. **thanks to** because of. **thankful** *adj* grateful. **thankless** *adj* unrewarding or unappreciated. **Thanksgiving Day** autumn public holiday in Canada and the US.

testimonial *n* = **tribute**, commendation, endorsement, recommendation, reference
testimony *n* **1** = **proof**, corroboration, demonstration, evidence, indication, manifestation, support, verification **2** = **evidence**, affidavit, deposition, statement, submission
testing *adj* = **difficult**, arduous, challenging, demanding, exacting, rigorous, searching, strenuous, taxing, tough
tether *n* **1** = **rope**, chain, fetter, halter, lead, leash ▷ *v* **2** = **tie**, bind, chain, fasten, fetter, secure **at the end of one's tether** = **exasperated**, at one's wits' end, exhausted

text *n* **1** = **contents**, body **2** = **words**, wording
texture *n* = **feel**, consistency, grain, structure, surface, tissue
thank *v* **1** = **say thank you**, show one's appreciation
thankful *adj* = **grateful**, appreciative, beholden, indebted, in (someone's) debt, obliged, pleased, relieved
thankless *adj* = **unrewarding**, fruitless, unappreciated, unprofitable, unrequited
thanks *pl n* **1** = **gratitude**, acknowledgment, appreciation, credit, gratefulness, recognition **thanks to** = **because of**, as a result of, due to, owing to, through

t

that *adj, pron* **1** used to refer to something already mentioned or familiar, or further away. ▷ *conj* **2** used to introduce a noun clause. ▷ *pron* **3** used to introduce a relative clause.

thatch *n* **1** roofing material of reeds or straw. ▷ *v* **2** roof (a house) with reeds or straw. **thatched** *adj*.

thaw ❶ *v* **1** make or become unfrozen. **2** become more relaxed or friendly. ▷ *n* **3** thawing. **4** weather causing snow or ice to melt.

the *adj* the definite article, used before a noun.

theatre ❶ *n* **1** place where plays etc. are performed. **2** hospital operating room. **3** drama and acting in general. **4** region in which a war takes place. **theatrical** *adj* **1** of the theatre. **2** exaggerated or affected. **theatricals** *pl n* (amateur) dramatic performances. **theatrically** *adv* **theatricality** *n*.

thee *pron obs* objective form of THOU.

theft ❶ *n* act or an instance of stealing.

their *adj* of or associated with them. **theirs** *pron* (thing or person) belonging to them.

> ● **SPELLING TIP**
> ● Do not confuse **their** and **theirs**,
> ● which do not have apostrophes,
> ● with **they're** and **there's**, which do
> ● because letters have been missed
> ● out where two words have been
> ● joined together.

theism [thee-iz-zum] *n* belief in a God or gods. **theist** *n*, *adj* **theistic** *adj*.

them *pron* refers to people or things other than the speaker or those addressed. **themselves** *pron* emphatic and reflexive form of THEY or THEM.

theme ❶ *n* **1** main idea or subject being discussed. **2** recurring idea in literature, art, etc. **3** recurring melodic figure in music. **thematic** *adj* **thematically** *adv* **theme park** leisure area in which all the activities and displays are based on a single theme. **theme tune, song** tune or song used to introduce a television or radio programme.

then *adv* **1** at that time. **2** after that. **3** that being so.

thence *adv* **1** from that place or time. **2** therefore.

theocracy *n, pl* **-cies** government by a god or priests. **theocratic** *adj*.

theodolite [thee-**odd**-oh-lite] *n* surveying instrument for measuring angles.

theology ❶ *n, pl* **-gies** study of religions and religious beliefs. **theologian** *n* **theological** *adj* **theologically** *adv*.

theorem *n* proposition that can be proved by reasoning.

theory ❶ *n, pl* **-ries 1** set of ideas to explain something. **2** abstract knowledge or reasoning. **3** idea or opinion. **in theory** in an ideal or hypothetical situation. **theoretical** *adj* based on theory rather than practice or fact. **theoretically** *adv* **theorist** *n* **theorize** *v* form theories, speculate.

theosophy *n* religious or philosophical system claiming to be based on intuitive insight into the divine nature. **theosophical** *adj*.

therapy ❶ *n, pl* **-pies** curing treatment. **therapist** *n* **therapeutic** [ther-rap-**pew**-tik] *adj* curing. **therapeutics** *n* art of curing.

THESAURUS

thaw *v* **1** = **melt**, defrost, dissolve, liquefy, soften, unfreeze, warm

theatrical *adj* **1** = **dramatic**, Thespian **2** = **exaggerated**, affected, dramatic, histrionic, mannered, melodramatic, ostentatious, showy, stagy

theft *n* = **stealing**, embezzlement, fraud, larceny, pilfering, purloining, robbery, thieving

theme *n* **1** = **subject**, idea, keynote, subject matter, topic **2, 3** = **motif**, leitmotif

theological *adj* = **religious**, doctrinal, ecclesiastical

theoretical *adj* = **abstract**, academic, conjectural, hypothetical, notional, speculative

theorize *v* = **speculate**, conjecture, formulate, guess, hypothesize, project, propound, suppose

theory *n* **3** = **hypothesis**, assumption, conjecture, presumption, speculation, supposition, surmise, thesis

therapeutic *adj* = **beneficial**, corrective, curative, good, healing, remedial, restorative, salutary

therapist *n* = **healer**, physician

therapy *n* = **remedy**, cure, healing, treatment

therefore *adv* = **consequently**, accordingly, as a result, ergo, hence, so, then, thence, thus

there ❶ adv **1** in or to that place. **2** in that respect. **thereby** adv by that means. **therefore** adv consequently, that being so. **thereupon** adv immediately after that.

● **SPELLING TIP**
● Do not confuse **there**, which is
● closely connected in meaning and in
● spelling with 'here', and **their**, which
● means 'belonging to them'.

therm n unit of measurement of heat. **thermal** adj **1** of heat. **2** hot or warm. **3** (of clothing) retaining heat. ▷ n **4** rising current of warm air.

thermionic valve n electronic valve in which electrons are emitted from a heated rather than a cold cathode.

thermodynamics n scientific study of the relationship between heat and other forms of energy.

thermoelectric adj of or relating to the conversion of heat energy to electrical energy.

thermometer n instrument for measuring temperature.

thermonuclear adj **1** involving nuclear fusion. **2** involving atomic weapons.

thermoplastic adj (of a plastic) softening when heated and resetting on cooling.

Thermos n ® vacuum flask.

thermosetting adj (of a plastic) remaining hard when heated.

thermostat n device for automatically regulating temperature. **thermostatic** adj **thermostatically** adv

thesaurus [thiss-**sore**-uss] n, pl **-ruses** book containing lists of synonyms and related words.

these adj, pron plural of THIS.

thesis ❶ n, pl **theses 1** written work submitted for a degree. **2** opinion supported by reasoned argument.

thespian n **1** actor or actress. ▷ adj **2** of the theatre.

they pron refers to: **1** people or things other than the speaker or people addressed. **2** people in general. **3** informal he or she.

thiamine n vitamin found in the outer coat of rice and other grains.

thick ❶ adj **1** of great or specified extent from one side to the other. **2** having a dense consistency. **3** informal stupid or insensitive. **4** (of an accent) very noticeable. **5** informal friendly. **a bit thick** informal unfair or unreasonable. **the thick** busiest or most intense part. **thick with** full of. **thicken** v make or become thick or thicker. **thickener** n substance used to thicken liquids. **thickly** adv **thickness** n **1** state of being thick. **2** dimension through an object. **3** layer. **thickset** adj **1** stocky in build. **2** set closely together. **thick-skinned** adj insensitive to criticism or hints.

thicket ❶ n dense growth of small trees.

thief ❶ n, pl **thieves** person who steals. **thieve** v steal. **thieving** adj.

thigh n upper part of the human leg.

thimble n cap protecting the end of the finger when sewing.

thin ❶ adj **thinner, thinnest 1** not thick. **2** slim or lean. **3** sparse or meagre. **4** of low density. **5** poor or unconvincing. ▷ v **thinning, thinned**

——— **THESAURUS** ———

thesis n **1** = **dissertation**, essay, monograph, paper, treatise **2** = **proposition**, contention, hypothesis, idea, opinion, proposal, theory, view

thick adj **1** = **wide**, broad, bulky, fat, solid, substantial **2** = **dense**, close, compact, concentrated, condensed, heavy, impenetrable, opaque **3** Inf = **stupid**, brainless, dense, dopey (inf), moronic, obtuse, slow, thickheaded **5** Inf = **friendly**, close, devoted, familiar, inseparable, intimate, pally (inf) **a bit thick** Inf = **unreasonable**, unfair, unjust

thicken v = **set**, clot, coagulate, condense, congeal, jell

thicket n = **wood**, brake, coppice, copse, covert, grove

thickset adj **1** = **stocky**, bulky, burly, heavy, muscular, strong, sturdy, well-built

thief n = **robber**, burglar, embezzler, housebreaker, pickpocket, pilferer, plunderer, shoplifter, stealer

thieve v = **steal**, filch, nick (sl, chiefly Brit), pilfer, pinch (inf), purloin, rob, swipe (sl)

thin adj **1** = **narrow**, attenuated, fine **2** = **slim**, bony, emaciated, lean, scrawny, skeletal, skinny, slender, slight, spare, spindly **3** = **meagre**, deficient, scanty, scarce, scattered, skimpy, sparse, wispy **4** = **fine**, delicate, diaphanous, filmy, flimsy, gossamer, sheer, unsubstantial

6 make or become thin. **thinly** adv **thinness** n **thin-skinned** adj sensitive to criticism or hints.

thine pron, adj obs (something) of or associated with you (thou).

thing ❶ n **1** material object. **2** object, fact, or idea considered as a separate entity. **3** informal obsession. ▷ pl **4** possessions, clothes, etc.

think ❶ v **thinking**, **thought** **1** consider, judge, or believe. **2** make use of the mind. **3** be considerate enough or remember to do something. **thinker** n **thinking** adj, n **think-tank** n group of experts studying specific problems. **think up** v invent or devise.

third adj **1** of number three in a series. **2** rated or graded below the second level. ▷ n **3** one of three equal parts. **third degree** violent interrogation. **third party** (applying to) a person involved by chance or only incidentally in legal proceedings, an accident, etc. **Third World** developing countries of Africa, Asia, and Latin America.

thirst ❶ n **1** desire to drink. **2** craving or yearning. ▷ v **3** feel thirst. **thirsty** adj **thirstier**, **thirstiest**. **thirstily** adv.

thirteen adj, n three plus ten. **thirteenth** adj, n.

thirty adj, n three times ten. **thirtieth** adj, n.

this adj, pron **1** used to refer to a thing or

person nearby, just mentioned, or about to be mentioned. ▷ adj **2** used to refer to the present time, e.g. this morning.

thistle n prickly plant with dense flower heads. **thistledown** n mass of feathery plumed seeds produced by thistles.

thither adv obs to or towards that place.

tho', tho conj, adv short for THOUGH.

thole, tholepin n wooden pin set in the side of a rowing boat to serve as a fulcrum for rowing.

thong n **1** thin strip of leather etc. **2** skimpy article of underwear or beachwear that leaves the buttocks bare.

thorax n, pl **thoraxes**, **thoraces** part of the body between the neck and the abdomen. **thoracic** adj.

thorium n Chemistry radioactive metallic element.

thorn ❶ n **1** prickle on a plant. **2** bush with thorns. **thorn in one's side**, **flesh** source of irritation. **thorny** adj **1** covered with thorns. **2** (of a problem, subject) difficult or unpleasant.

thorough ❶ adj **1** complete. **2** careful or methodical. **thoroughly** adv **thoroughness** n **thoroughbred** n, adj (animal) of pure breed. **thoroughfare** n way through from one place to another. **thoroughgoing** adj extremely thorough.

——————————————————————————— THESAURUS ———————————————

5 = **unconvincing**, feeble, flimsy, inadequate, lame, poor, superficial, weak

thing n **1, 2** = **object**, article, being, body, entity, something, substance **3** Inf = **obsession**, bee in one's bonnet, fetish, fixation, hang-up (inf), mania, phobia, preoccupation ▷ pl n **4** = **possessions**, belongings, clobber (Brit sl), effects, equipment, gear, luggage, stuff

think v **1** = **believe**, consider, deem, estimate, imagine, judge, reckon, regard, suppose **2** = **ponder**, cerebrate, cogitate, contemplate, deliberate, meditate, muse, obsess, reason, reflect, ruminate

thinking adj = **thoughtful**, contemplative, intelligent, meditative, philosophical, rational, reasoning, reflective ▷ n = **reasoning**, conjecture, idea, judgment, opinion, position, theory, view

think up v = **devise**, come up with,

concoct, contrive, create, dream up, invent, visualize

thirst n **1** = **thirstiness**, drought, dryness **2** = **craving**, appetite, desire, hankering, keenness, longing, passion, yearning

thirsty adj **1** = **parched**, arid, dehydrated, dry **2** = **eager**, avid, craving, desirous, greedy, hungry, itching, longing, yearning

thorn n **1** = **prickle**, barb, spike, spine

thorny adj **1** = **prickly**, barbed, bristly, pointed, sharp, spiky, spiny

thorough adj **1** = **complete**, absolute, out-and-out, outright, perfect, total, unmitigated, unqualified, utter **2** = **careful**, assiduous, conscientious, efficient, exhaustive, full, in-depth, intensive, meticulous, painstaking

thoroughbred adj = **purebred**, pedigree

thoroughfare n = **road**, avenue, highway, passage, passageway, street, way

those adj, pron plural of THAT.

thou pron obs singular form of YOU.

though ❶ conj 1 despite the fact that. ▷ adv 2 nevertheless.

thought ❶ v 1 past of THINK. ▷ n 2 thinking. 3 concept or idea. 4 ideas typical of a time or place. 5 consideration. 6 intention or expectation. **thoughtful** adj 1 considerate. 2 showing careful thought. 3 pensive or reflective. **thoughtfully** adv **thoughtless** adj inconsiderate. **thoughtlessly** adv.

thousand adj, n 1 ten hundred. 2 large but unspecified number. **thousandth** adj, n (of) number one thousand in a series.

thrall n state of being in the power of another person.

thrash ❶ v 1 beat, esp. with a stick or whip. 2 defeat soundly. 3 move about wildly. 4 thresh. **thrashing** n severe beating. **thrash out** v solve by thorough argument.

thread ❶ n 1 fine strand or yarn. 2 unifying theme. 3 spiral ridge on a screw, nut, or bolt. ▷ v 4 pass thread through. 5 pick (one's way etc.). **threadbare** adj 1 (of fabric) with the nap worn off. 2 hackneyed. 3 shabby.

threat ❶ n 1 declaration of intent to harm. 2 strong possibility of something dangerous happening. 3 dangerous person or thing. **threaten** v 1 make or be a threat to. 2 be a menacing indication of. **threatening** adj **threateningly** adv.

three adj, n one more than two. **threefold** adj, adv (having) three times as many or as much. **threesome** n

---

THESAURUS

thoroughly adv 1 = **completely**, absolutely, downright, perfectly, quite, totally, to the hilt, utterly 2 = **carefully**, assiduously, conscientiously, efficiently, exhaustively, from top to bottom, fully, intensively, meticulously, painstakingly, scrupulously

though conj 1 = **although**, even if, even though, notwithstanding, while ▷ adv 2 = **nevertheless**, for all that, however, nonetheless, notwithstanding, still, yet

thought n 2 = **thinking**, cogitation, consideration, deliberation, meditation, musing, reflection, rumination 3 = **idea**, concept, judgment, notion, opinion, view 5 = **consideration**, attention, heed, regard, scrutiny, study 6 a = **intention**, aim, design, idea, notion, object, plan, purpose b = **expectation**, anticipation, aspiration, hope, prospect

thoughtful adj 1 = **considerate**, attentive, caring, helpful, kind, kindly, solicitous, unselfish 2 = **well-thought-out**, astute, canny, prudent 3 = **reflective**, contemplative, deliberative, meditative, pensive, ruminative, serious, studious

thoughtless adj = **inconsiderate**, impolite, insensitive, rude, selfish, tactless, uncaring, undiplomatic, unkind

thrash v 1 = **beat**, belt (inf), cane, flog, give (someone) a (good) hiding (inf), scourge, spank, whip 2 = **defeat**, beat, crush, drub, rout, run rings around (inf), slaughter (inf), trounce, wipe the floor with (inf) 3 = **thresh**, flail, jerk, toss and turn, writhe

thrashing n = **beating**, belting (inf), flogging, hiding (inf), punishment, whipping

thrash out v = **settle**, argue out, debate, discuss, have out, resolve, solve, talk over

thread n 1 = **strand**, fibre, filament, line, string, yarn 2 = **theme**, direction, drift, plot, story line, train of thought ▷ v 4 = **string** 5 = **pass**, ease, pick (one's way), squeeze through

threadbare adj 2 = **hackneyed**, commonplace, conventional, familiar, overused, stale, stereotyped, tired, trite, well-worn 3 = **shabby**, down at heel, frayed, old, ragged, scruffy, tattered, tatty, worn

threat n 1 = **menace**, threatening remark 2 = **warning**, foreboding, foreshadowing, omen, portent, presage, writing on the wall 3 = **danger**, hazard, menace, peril, risk

threaten v 1 a = **intimidate**, browbeat, bully, lean on (sl), menace, pressurize, terrorize b = **endanger**, imperil, jeopardize, put at risk, put in jeopardy, put on the line 2 = **foreshadow**, forebode, portend, presage

threatening adj 1 = **menacing**, bullying, intimidating 2 = **ominous**, forbidding, grim, inauspicious, sinister

t

group of three. **three-dimensional**, **3-D** *adj* having three dimensions. **three-ply** *adj* having three layers or strands. **three-point turn** complete turn of a motor vehicle using forward and reverse gears. **three-quarter** *adj* being three quarters of something.

threnody *n, pl* **-dies** lament for the dead.

thresh *v* beat (wheat etc.) to separate the grain from the husks and straw. **thresh about** move about wildly.

threshold ❶ *n* **1** bar forming the bottom of a doorway. **2** entrance. **3** starting point. **4** point at which something begins to take effect.

threw *v* past tense of THROW.

thrice *adv lit* three times.

thrift ❶ *n* **1** wisdom and caution with money. **2** low-growing plant with pink flowers. **thrifty** *adj* **thriftier**, **thriftiest**.

thrill ❶ *n* **1** sudden feeling of excitement. ▷ *v* **2** (cause to) feel a thrill. **thrilling** *adj*.

thriller *n* book, film, etc. with an atmosphere of mystery or suspense.

thrive ❶ *v* **thriving**, **thrived** *or* **throve**, **thrived** *or* **thriven 1** flourish or prosper. **2** grow well.

throat *n* **1** passage from the mouth and nose to the stomach and lungs. **2** front of the neck. **throaty** *adj* (of the voice) hoarse.

throb ❶ *v* **throbbing**, **throbbed 1** pulsate repeatedly. **2** vibrate rhythmically. ▷ *n* **3** throbbing.

throes *pl n* violent pangs or pains. **in the throes of** struggling to cope with.

thrombosis *n, pl* **-ses** forming of a clot in a blood vessel or the heart.

throne *n* **1** ceremonial seat of a monarch or bishop. **2** sovereign power.

throng ❶ *n, v* crowd.

throstle *n* song thrush.

throttle ❶ *n* **1** device controlling the amount of fuel entering an engine. ▷ *v* **2** strangle.

through ❶ *prep* **1** from end to end or side to side of. **2** because of. **3** during. ▷ *adj* **4** finished. **5** (of transport) going directly to a place. **through and through** completely. **throughout** *prep, adv* in every part (of). **throughput** *n* amount of material processed.

throve *v* a past tense of THRIVE.

throw ❶ *v* **throwing**, **threw**, **thrown 1** hurl through the air. **2** move or put suddenly or carelessly. **3** bring into a specified state, esp. suddenly. **4** move (a switch, lever, etc.). **5** shape (pottery) on a wheel. **6** give (a party). **7** *informal* baffle or disconcert. **8** direct (a look, light, etc.). **9** project

---

threshold *n* **2** = **entrance**, door, doorstep, doorway **3** = **start**, beginning, brink, dawn, inception, opening, outset, verge **4** = **minimum**, lower limit

thrift *n* **1** = **economy**, carefulness, frugality, parsimony, prudence, saving, thriftiness

thrifty *adj* **1** = **economical**, careful, frugal, parsimonious, provident, prudent, saving, sparing

thrill *n* **1** = **pleasure**, buzz (*sl*), kick (*inf*), stimulation, tingle, titillation ▷ *v* **2** = **excite**, arouse, electrify, move, stimulate, stir, titillate

thrilling *adj* **1** = **exciting**, electrifying, gripping, riveting, rousing, sensational, stimulating, stirring

thrive *v* **1** = **prosper**, boom, develop, do well, flourish, get on, increase, succeed **2** = **grow**

throb *v* **1** = **pulsate**, beat, palpitate, pound, pulse, thump **2** = **vibrate** ▷ *n* **3** = **pulse**, beat, palpitation, pounding,

pulsating, thump, thumping, vibration

throng *n* = **crowd**, crush, horde, host, mass, mob, multitude, pack, swarm ▷ *v* = **crowd**, congregate, converge, flock, mill around, pack, swarm around

throttle *v* **2** = **strangle**, choke, garrotte, strangulate

through *prep* **1** = **from one side to the other of**, between, by, past **2** = **because of**, by means of, by way of, using, via **3** = **during**, in, throughout ▷ *adj* **4** = **completed**, done, ended, finished **through and through** = **completely**, altogether, entirely, fully, thoroughly, totally, utterly, wholly

throughout *prep* = **through the whole of**, all over, everywhere in, right through ▷ *adv* = **from start to finish**, right through

throw *v* **1**, **2** = **hurl**, cast, chuck (*inf*), fling, launch, lob (*inf*), pitch, send, sling, toss **7** *Inf* = **confuse**, astonish, baffle, confound, disconcert,

(the voice) so that it seems to come from elsewhere. ▷ *n* **10** throwing. **11** distance thrown. **throwaway** *adj* **1** done or said casually. **2** designed to be discarded after use. **throwback** *n* person or thing that reverts to an earlier type. **throw up** *v* vomit.

thrum *v* **thrumming**, **thrummed 1** strum rhythmically but without expression on (a musical instrument). **2** make a low beating or humming sound.

thrush¹ *n* brown songbird.

thrush² *n* fungal disease of the mouth or vagina.

thrust ❶ *v* **thrusting**, **thrust 1** push forcefully. ▷ *n* **2** forceful stab. **3** force or power. **4** essential part. **5** intellectual or emotional drive.

thud ❶ *n* **1** dull heavy sound. ▷ *v* **thudding**, **thudded 2** make such a sound.

thug ❶ *n* violent man, esp. a criminal. **thuggery** *n* **thuggish** *adj*.

thulium *n* *Chemistry* malleable ductile silvery-grey element.

thumb *n* **1** short thick finger set apart from the others. ▷ *v* **2** touch or handle with the thumb. **3** signal with the thumb for a lift in a vehicle. **thumb through** flick through (a book or magazine). **thumb index** series of notches cut into the edge of a book to allow quick reference.

thumbtack *n* the US and Canadian name for DRAWING PIN.

thump ❶ *n* **1** (sound of) a dull heavy blow. ▷ *v* **2** strike heavily. **thumping** *adj* *informal* huge or excessive.

thunder ❶ *n* **1** loud noise accompanying lightning. **2** any loud sound. ▷ *v* **3** rumble with thunder. **4** shout. **5** move fast, heavily, and noisily. **thunderous** *adj* **thundery** *adj* **thunderbolt** *n* **1** lightning flash. **2** something sudden and unexpected. **thunderclap** *n* peal of thunder. **thunderstorm** *n* storm with lightning and thunder. **thunderstruck** *adj* amazed.

Thurs. Thursday.

Thursday *n* fifth day of the week.

thus ❶ *adv* **1** therefore. **2** in this way.

thwack *v*, *n* whack.

thwart ❶ *v* **1** foil or frustrate. ▷ *n* **2** seat across a boat.

thy *adj* *obs* of or associated with you (thou). **thyself** *pron* *obs* emphatic form of THOU.

thylacine *n* extinct doglike Tasmanian marsupial.

thyme [time] *n* aromatic herb.

thymol *n* substance obtained from thyme, used as an antiseptic.

thymus *n*, *pl* **-muses**, **-mi** small gland at the base of the neck.

thyroid *adj*, *n* (of) a gland in the neck controlling body growth.

ti *n* *Music* same as TE.

Ti *Chemistry* titanium.

tiara *n* semicircular jewelled headdress.

tibia *n*, *pl* **tibiae**, **tibias** inner bone of the lower leg. **tibial** *adj*.

tic *n* spasmodic muscular twitch.

THESAURUS

dumbfound, faze ▷ *n* **10** = **toss**, fling, heave, lob (*inf*), pitch, sling

throwaway *adj* **1** = **casual**, careless, offhand, passing, understated

thrust *v* **1** = **push**, drive, force, jam, plunge, propel, ram, shove ▷ *n* **2** = **push**, drive, lunge, poke, prod, shove, stab **3** = **momentum**, impetus

thud *n*, *v* **1**, **2** = **thump**, crash, knock, smack

thug *n* = **ruffian**, bruiser (*inf*), bully boy, gangster, heavy (*sl*), hooligan, tough

thump *n* **1 a** = **thud**, bang, clunk, crash, thwack **b** = **blow**, clout (*inf*), knock, punch, rap, smack, swipe, wallop (*inf*), whack ▷ *v* **2** = **strike**, beat, clobber (*sl*), clout (*inf*), hit, knock, pound, punch, smack, swipe, wallop (*inf*), whack

thunder *n* **2** = **rumble**, boom, crash, explosion ▷ *v* **3** = **rumble**, boom, crash, peal, resound, reverberate, roar **4** = **shout**, bark, bellow, roar, yell

thunderous *adj* **2** = **loud**, booming, deafening, ear-splitting, noisy, resounding, roaring, tumultuous

thunderstruck *adj* = **amazed**, astonished, astounded, dumbfounded, flabbergasted (*inf*), open-mouthed, shocked, staggered, stunned, taken aback

thus *adv* **1** = **therefore**, accordingly, consequently, ergo, for this reason, hence, on that account, so, then **2** = **in this way**, as follows, like this, so

thwart *v* **1** = **frustrate**, foil, hinder, obstruct, outwit, prevent, snooker, stymie

t

tick¹ ❶ *n* **1** mark (✓) used to check off or indicate the correctness of something. **2** recurrent tapping sound, as of a clock. **3** *informal* moment. ▷ *v* **4** mark with a tick. **5** make a ticking sound. **tick off** *v* **1** mark with a tick. **2** reprimand. **tick over** *v* **1** (of an engine) idle. **2** function smoothly. **ticktack** *n* bookmakers' sign language.

tick² *n* tiny bloodsucking parasitic animal.

tick³ ❶ *n informal* credit or account.

ticket ❶ *n* **1** card or paper entitling the holder to admission, travel, etc. **2** label, esp. showing price. **3** official notification of a parking or traffic offence. **4** declared policy of a political party. ▷ *v* **-eting**, **-eted 5** attach or issue a ticket to.

ticking *n* strong material for mattress covers.

tickle *v* **1** touch or stroke (a person) to produce laughter. **2** itch or tingle. **3** please or amuse. ▷ *n* **4** tickling. **ticklish** *adj* **1** sensitive to tickling. **2** requiring care or tact.

tiddly¹ *adj* **-dlier**, **-dliest** tiny. **tiddler** *n informal* very small fish.

tiddly² *adj* **-dlier**, **-dliest** *informal* slightly drunk.

tiddlywinks *n* game in which players try to flip small plastic discs into a cup.

tide ❶ *n* **1** rise and fall of the sea caused by the gravitational pull of the sun and moon. **2** current caused by this. **3** widespread feeling or tendency. **tidal** *adj* **tidal wave** large destructive wave. **tideline** *n* mark left by the highest or lowest point of the tide. **tide over** *v* help (someone) temporarily.

tidings *pl n* news.

tidy ❶ *adj* **-dier**, **-diest 1** neat and orderly. **2** *informal* considerable. ▷ *v* **-dying**, **-died 3** put in order. **tidily** *adv* **tidiness** *n*.

tie ❶ *v* **tying**, **tied 1** fasten or be fastened with string, rope, etc. **2** make (a knot or bow) in (something). **3** restrict or limit. **4** score the same as another competitor. ▷ *n* **5** long narrow piece of material worn knotted round the neck. **6** bond or fastening. **7** match in an eliminating competition. **8** drawn game or contest. **tied** *adj* **1** (of a pub) allowed to sell only the beer of a particular brewery. **2** (of a cottage etc.) rented to the tenant only as long as he or she is employed by the owner. **tie-break**, **tie-breaker** *n* extra game or question that decides the result of a contest ending in a draw.

tier ❶ *n* one of a set of rows placed one above and behind the other.

tiff *n* petty quarrel.

tiger *n* large yellow-and-black striped Asian cat. **tigress** *n* **1** female tiger. **2** *informal* fierce woman. **tiger snake** *n* highly venomous brown-and-yellow Australian snake.

tight ❶ *adj* **1** stretched or drawn taut. **2** closely fitting. **3** secure or firm. **4** cramped. **5** (of a situation) difficult

---

tick¹ *n* **1** = **mark**, dash, stroke **2** = **tapping**, clicking, ticktock **3** *Inf* = **moment**, flash, instant, minute, second, split second, trice, twinkling ▷ *v* **4** = **mark**, check off, indicate **5** = **tap**, click, ticktock

tick³ *n Inf* = **credit**, account, the slate (*Brit inf*)

ticket *n* **1** = **voucher**, card, certificate, coupon, pass, slip, token **2** = **label**, card, docket, marker, slip, sticker, tab, tag

tide *n* **2** = **current**, ebb, flow, stream, tideway, undertow **3** = **tendency**, direction, drift, movement, trend

tidy *adj* **1** = **neat**, clean, methodical, orderly, shipshape, spruce, well-kept, well-ordered **2** *Inf* = **considerable**, ample, generous, goodly, handsome, healthy, large, sizable *or* sizeable, substantial ▷ *v* **3** = **neaten**, clean, groom, order, spruce up, straighten

tie *v* **1** = **fasten**, attach, bind, connect, join, knot, link, secure, tether **3** = **restrict**, bind, confine, hamper, hinder, limit, restrain **4** = **draw**, equal, match ▷ *n* **6 a** = **bond**, affiliation, allegiance, commitment, connection, liaison, relationship **b** = **fastening**, bond, cord, fetter, knot, ligature, link **8** = **draw**, dead heat, deadlock, stalemate

tier *n* = **row**, bank, layer, level, line, rank, storey, stratum

tight *adj* **1** = **taut**, rigid, stretched **2** = **close-fitting**, close **3** = **secure**, fast, firm, fixed **4** = **cramped**, constricted, narrow, snug **6** *Inf* = **miserly**, grasping, mean, niggardly, parsimonious, stingy, tightfisted

or dangerous. **6** *informal* not generous. **7** (of a match or game) very mean. **8** *informal* drunk. **tights** *pl n* one-piece clinging garment covering the body from the waist to the feet. **tightly** *adv* **tighten** *v* make or become tight or tighter. **tight-fisted** *adj* very mean. **tight-lipped** *adj* **1** secretive. **2** with lips pressed tightly together, as through anger. **tightrope** *n* rope stretched taut on which acrobats perform.

tikka *adj Indian cookery* marinated in spices and dry-roasted, e.g. *chicken tikka*.

tilde *n* mark (~) used in Spanish to indicate that the letter 'n' is to be pronounced in a particular way.

tile *n* **1** flat piece of ceramic, plastic, etc. used to cover a roof, floor, or wall. ▷ *v* **2** cover with tiles. **tiled** *adj* **tiling** *n* tiles collectively.

till¹ *conj, prep* until.

till² ❶ *v* cultivate (land). **tillage** *n*.

till³ ❶ *n* drawer for money, usu. in a cash register.

tiller *n* lever to move a rudder of a boat.

tilt ❶ *v* **1** slant at an angle. **2** *History* compete against in a jousting contest. ▷ *n* **3** slope. **4** *History* jousting contest. **5** attempt. **at full tilt** at full speed or force.

tilth *n* (condition of) land that has been tilled.

timber ❶ *n* **1** wood as a building material. **2** trees collectively. **3** wooden beam in the frame of a house, boat, etc. **timbered** *adj* **timber line** (esp on a mountain) limit beyond which trees will not grow.

timbre ❶ [**tam**-bra] *n* distinctive quality of sound of a voice or instrument.

time ❶ *n* **1** past, present, and future as a continuous whole. **2** specific point in time. **3** unspecified interval. **4** instance or occasion. **5** period with specific features. **6** musical tempo. **7** *slang* imprisonment. ▷ *v* **8** note the time taken by. **9** choose a time for. **timeless** *adj* **1** unaffected by time. **2** eternal. **timely** *adj* at the appropriate time. **times** *prep* multiplied by. **timing** *n* ability to judge when to do or say something so as to make the best effect. **time-honoured** *adj* sanctioned by custom. **time-lag** *n* period between cause and effect. **timepiece** *n* watch or clock. **timeserver** *n* person who changes his or her views to gain support or favour. **time sharing 1** system of part ownership of a holiday property for a specified period each year. **2** system enabling users at different terminals of a computer to use it at the same time. **time signature** *Music* sign that indicates the number and length of beats in the bar. **timetable** *n* plan showing the times when something takes place, the departure and arrival times of trains or buses, etc. **time zone** region throughout which the same standard time is used.

timid ❶ *adj* **1** easily frightened. **2** shy, not bold. **timidly** *adv* **timidity** *n* **timorous** [**tim**-mor-uss] *adj* timid.

timpani [**tim**-pan-ee] *pl n* set of kettledrums. **timpanist** *n*.

THESAURUS

7 = **close**, even, evenly-balanced, well-matched **8** *Inf* = **drunk**, inebriated, intoxicated, paralytic (*inf*), plastered (*sl*), tipsy, under the influence (*inf*)
tighten *v* = **squeeze**, close, constrict, narrow
till² *v* = **cultivate**, dig, plough, work
till³ *n* = **cash register**, cash box
tilt *v* **1** = **slant**, heel, incline, lean, list, slope, tip ▷ *n* **3** = **slope**, angle, inclination, incline, list, pitch, slant **4** *Hist* = **joust**, combat, duel, fight, lists, tournament **(at) full tilt** = **full speed**, for dear life, headlong
timber *n* **1** = **wood**, boards, logs, planks **2** = **trees**, forest **3** = **beam**
timbre *n* = **tone**, colour, resonance, ring

time *n* **3** = **period**, duration, interval, season, space, span, spell, stretch, term **4** = **occasion**, instance, juncture, point, stage **6** = **tempo**, beat, measure, rhythm ▷ *v* **9** = **schedule**, set
timeless *adj* **1** = **changeless**, ageless **2** = **eternal**, enduring, everlasting, immortal, lasting, permanent
timely *adj* = **opportune**, appropriate, convenient, judicious, propitious, seasonable, suitable, well-timed
timetable *n* = **schedule**, agenda, calendar, curriculum, diary, list, programme
timid *adj* **1** = **fearful**, apprehensive, faint-hearted, shrinking, timorous **2** = **shy**, bashful, coy, diffident

t

tin n 1 soft metallic element.
2 (airtight) metal container. **tinned** adj
(of food) preserved by being sealed in a
tin. **tinny** adj (of sound) thin and
metallic. **tinpot** adj informal worthless
or unimportant.

tincture n medicinal extract in a
solution of alcohol.

tinder n dry easily-burning material
used to start a fire. **tinderbox** n
formerly, small box for tinder, esp. one
fitted with a flint and steel.

tine n prong of a fork or antler.

ting n high metallic sound, as of a small
bell.

tinge ❶ n 1 slight tint. 2 trace. ▷ v
tingeing, tinged 3 give a slight tint or
trace to.

tingle ❶ v, n (feel) a prickling or stinging
sensation.

tinker ❶ n 1 travelling mender of pots
and pans. 2 Scot & Irish Gypsy. ▷ v
3 fiddle with (an engine etc.) in an
attempt to repair it.

tinkle v 1 ring with a high tinny sound
like a small bell. ▷ n 2 this sound or
action.

tinsel n 1 decorative metallic strips or
threads. 2 anything cheap and gaudy.

tint ❶ n 1 (pale) shade of a colour. 2 dye
for the hair. ▷ v 3 give a tint to.

tintinnabulation n act or instance of

the ringing or pealing of bells.

tiny ❶ adj **tinier, tiniest** very small.

tip¹ ❶ n 1 narrow or pointed end of
anything. 2 small piece forming an
end. ▷ v **tipping, tipped** 3 put a tip on.

tip² ❶ n 1 money given in return for
service. 2 helpful hint or warning.
3 piece of inside information. ▷ v
tipping, tipped 4 give a tip to. **tipster**
n person who sells tips about races.

tip³ ❶ v **tipping, tipped** 1 tilt or
overturn. 2 dump (rubbish). ▷ n
3 rubbish dump.

tipple ❶ v 1 drink alcohol habitually,
esp. in small quantities. ▷ n 2 alcoholic
drink. **tippler** n.

tipsy adj **-sier, -siest** slightly drunk.

tiptoe v **-toeing, -toed** walk quietly
with the heels off the ground.

tiptop adj of the highest quality or
condition.

tirade ❶ n long angry speech.

tire ❶ v 1 reduce the energy of, as by
exertion. 2 weary or bore. **tired** adj
1 exhausted. 2 bored. 3 hackneyed or
stale. **tiring** adj **tireless** adj energetic
and determined. **tirelessly** adv
tiresome adj boring and irritating.

tissue n 1 substance of an animal body
or plant. 2 piece of thin soft paper
used as a handkerchief etc.
3 interwoven series, e.g. a tissue of lies.

timorous adj = **timid**, apprehensive,
bashful, coy, diffident, faint-hearted,
fearful, shrinking, shy

tinge n 1 = **tint**, colour, shade 2 = **bit**,
dash, drop, smattering, sprinkling,
suggestion, touch, trace ▷ v 3 = **tint**,
colour, imbue, suffuse

tingle v = **prickle**, have goose pimples,
itch, sting, tickle ▷ n = **quiver**, goose
pimples, itch, pins and needles (inf),
prickling, shiver, thrill

tinker v 3 = **meddle**, dabble, fiddle (inf),
mess about, play, potter

tint n 1 = **shade**, colour, hue, tone
2 = **dye**, rinse, tincture, tinge, wash ▷ v
3 = **dye**, colour

tiny adj = **small**, diminutive,
infinitesimal, little, microscopic,
miniature, minute, negligible, petite,
slight

tip¹ n 1 = **end**, extremity, head, peak,
pinnacle, point, summit, top ▷ v
3 = **cap**, crown, finish, surmount, top

tip² n 1 = **gratuity**, gift 2 = **hint**,
pointer, suggestion ▷ v 4 **a** = **reward**,

remunerate **b** = **advise**, suggest

tip³ v 1 = **tilt**, incline, lean, list, slant
2 = **dump**, empty, pour out, unload ▷ n
3 = **dump**, refuse heap, rubbish heap

tipple v 1 = **drink**, imbibe, indulge (inf),
quaff, swig, tope ▷ n 2 = **alcohol**,
booze (inf), drink, liquor

tirade n = **outburst**, diatribe,
fulmination, harangue, invective,
lecture

tire v 1 = **exhaust**, drain, fatigue, wear
out, weary 2 = **bore**, exasperate, irk,
irritate, weary

tired adj 1 = **exhausted**, drained,
drowsy, fatigued, flagging, sleepy,
weary, worn out 2 = **bored**, fed up,
sick, weary 3 = **hackneyed**, clichéd,
corny (sl), old, outworn, stale,
threadbare, trite, well-worn

tireless adj = **energetic**, indefatigable,
industrious, resolute, unflagging,
untiring, vigorous

tiresome adj = **boring**, dull, irksome,
irritating, tedious, trying, vexatious,
wearing, wearisome

tit¹ *n* any of various small songbirds.

tit² *n* slang female breast.

titanic *adj* huge or very important.
titan *n* person who is huge, strong, or very important.

titanium *n* Chemistry strong light metallic element used to make alloys.

titbit ❶ *n* **1** tasty piece of food.
2 pleasing scrap of scandal.

tit-for-tat *adj* done in retaliation.

tithe *n* **1** esp. formerly, one tenth of one's income or produce paid to the church as a tax. ▷ *v* **2** charge or pay a tithe.

Titian [**tish**-an] *adj* (of hair) reddish-gold.

titillate ❶ *v* excite or stimulate pleasurably. **titillating** *adj* **titillation** *n*.

titivate *v* smarten up. **titivation** *n*.

title ❶ *n* **1** name of a book, film, etc.
2 book or periodical. **3** name signifying rank or position. **4** formal designation, such as *Mrs*.
5 Sport championship. **6** Law legal right of possession. **titled** *adj* aristocratic. **title deed** legal document of ownership. **titleholder** *n* person who holds a title, esp. a sporting championship. **title role** role of the character after whom a film or play is named.

titration *n* Chemistry operation in which a measured amount of one solution is added to a known quantity of another solution until the reaction between the two is complete.

titter ❶ *v* **1** laugh in a suppressed way. ▷ *n* **2** suppressed laugh.

tittle-tattle *n, v* gossip.

titular *adj* **1** in name only. **2** of a title.

tizzy *n, pl* **-zies** informal confused or agitated state.

Tl Chemistry thallium.

Tm Chemistry thulium.

TN Tennessee.

TNT *n* trinitrotoluene, a powerful explosive.

to *prep* **1** indicating movement towards, equality or comparison, etc., e.g. *walking to school; forty miles to the gallon*. **2** used to mark the indirect object or infinitive of a verb. ▷ *adv* **3** to a closed position, e.g. *pull the door to*.
to and fro back and forth.

toad *n* animal like a large frog.

toad-in-the-hole *n* sausages baked in batter.

toadstool *n* poisonous fungus like a mushroom.

toady ❶ *n, pl* **toadies 1** ingratiating person. ▷ *v* **toadying, toadied 2** be ingratiating.

toast¹ ❶ *n* **1** sliced bread browned by heat. ▷ *v* **2** brown (bread) by heat.
3 warm or be warmed. **toaster** *n* electrical device for toasting bread.

toast² ❶ *n* **1** tribute or proposal of health or success marked by people raising glasses and drinking together.
2 person or thing so honoured. ▷ *v* **3** drink a toast to.

tobacco *n, pl* **-cos, -coes** plant with large leaves dried for smoking.
tobacconist *n* person or shop selling tobacco, cigarettes, etc.

toboggan *n* **1** narrow sledge for sliding over snow. ▷ *v* **-ganing, -ganed 2** ride a toboggan.

toby jug *n* mug in the form of a stout seated man.

toccata [tok-**kah**-ta] *n* rapid piece of music for a keyboard instrument.

today *n* **1** this day. **2** the present age. ▷ *adv* **3** on this day. **4** nowadays.

toddle *v* walk with short unsteady steps. **toddler** *n* child beginning to walk.

t

---

tiring *adj* **1** = **exhausting**, arduous, demanding, exacting, laborious, strenuous, tough, wearing

titbit *n* **1** = **delicacy**, dainty, morsel, snack, treat

titillate *v* = **excite**, arouse, interest, stimulate, tantalize, tease, thrill

title *n* **1** = **name**, designation, handle (sl), term **5** Sport = **championship**, crown **6** Law = **ownership**, claim, entitlement, prerogative, privilege, right

titter *v* **1** = **snigger**, chortle (inf), chuckle, giggle, laugh

toady *n* **1** = **sycophant**, bootlicker (inf), crawler (sl), creep (sl), flatterer, flunkey, hanger-on, lackey, minion, yes man ▷ *v* **2** = **fawn on**, crawl, creep, cringe, flatter, grovel, kowtow to, pander to, suck up to (inf)

toast¹ *v* **2** = **brown**, grill, roast **3** = **warm**, heat

toast² *n* **1** = **tribute**, compliment, health, pledge, salutation, salute **2** = **favourite**, darling, hero or heroine ▷ *v* **3** = **drink to**, drink (to) the health of, salute

toddy *n, pl* **-dies** sweetened drink of spirits and hot water.

to-do *n, pl* **-dos** fuss or commotion.

toe *n* **1** digit of the foot. **2** part of a shoe or sock covering the toes. ▷ *v* **toeing, toed 3** touch or kick with the toe. **toecap** *n* strengthened covering for the toe of a shoe. **toehold** *n* **1** small space on a mountain for supporting the toe of the foot in climbing. **2** means of gaining access or advantage. **toerag** *n slang* contemptible person. **toe the line** conform.

toff *n slang* well-dressed or upper-class person.

toffee *n* chewy sweet made of boiled sugar. **toffee-apple** *n* apple fixed on a stick and coated with toffee. **toffee-nosed** *adj informal* snobbish.

tofu *n* soft food made from soya-bean curd.

tog *n* **1** unit for measuring the insulating power of duvets. ▷ *pl* **2** *informal* clothes.

toga [**toe**-ga] *n* garment worn by citizens of ancient Rome.

together ❶ *adv* **1** in company. **2** simultaneously. ▷ *adj* **3** *informal* organized.

toggle *n* **1** small bar-shaped button inserted through a loop for fastening. **2** switch used to turn a machine or computer function on or off.

toil ❶ *n* **1** hard work. ▷ *v* **2** work hard. **3** progress with difficulty.

toilet ❶ *n* **1** (room with) a bowl connected to a drain for receiving and disposing of urine and faeces. **2** washing and dressing. **toiletry** *n, pl* **-ries** object or cosmetic used to clean or groom oneself. **toilet paper** thin absorbent paper used for cleaning oneself after defecation. **toilet water** light perfume.

token ❶ *n* **1** sign or symbol. **2** voucher exchangeable for goods of a specified value. **3** disc used as money in a slot machine. ▷ *adj* **4** nominal or slight. **tokenism** *n* policy of making only a token effort, esp. to comply with a law.

told *v* past of TELL.

tolerate ❶ *v* **1** allow to exist or happen. **2** endure patiently. **tolerable** *adj* **1** bearable. **2** *informal* quite good. **tolerably** *adv* **tolerance** *n* **1** acceptance of other people's rights to their own opinions or actions. **2** ability to endure something. **tolerant** *adj* **tolerantly** *adv* **toleration** *n*.

toll¹ ❶ *v* **1** ring (a bell) slowly and regularly, esp. to announce a death. ▷ *n* **2** tolling.

toll² ❶ *n* **1** charge for the use of a bridge or road. **2** total loss or damage from a disaster.

---

together *adv* **1** = **collectively**, as one, hand in glove, in concert, in unison, jointly, mutually, shoulder to shoulder, side by side **2** = **at the same time**, at one fell swoop, concurrently, contemporaneously, simultaneously ▷ *adj* **3** *Inf* = **self-possessed**, composed, well-adjusted, well-balanced

toil *n* **1** = **hard work**, application, drudgery, effort, elbow grease (*inf*), exertion, graft (*inf*), slog, sweat ▷ *v* **2** = **labour**, drudge, graft (*inf*), slave, slog, strive, struggle, sweat (*inf*), work, work one's fingers to the bone

toilet *n* **1** = **lavatory**, bathroom, convenience, gents *or* ladies (*Brit inf*), ladies' room, latrine, loo (*Brit inf*), privy, urinal, water closet, W.C.

token *n* **1** = **symbol**, badge, expression, indication, mark, note, representation, sign ▷ *adj* **4** = **nominal**, hollow, minimal, perfunctory, superficial, symbolic

tolerable *adj* **1** = **bearable**, acceptable, allowable, endurable, sufferable, supportable **2** *Inf* = **fair**, acceptable, adequate, all right, average, O.K. *or* okay (*inf*), passable

tolerance *n* **1** = **broad-mindedness**, forbearance, indulgence, open-mindedness, permissiveness **2** = **endurance**, fortitude, hardiness, resilience, resistance, stamina, staying power, toughness

tolerant *adj* **1** = **broad-minded**, catholic, forbearing, liberal, long-suffering, open-minded, understanding, unprejudiced

tolerate *v* **1** = **allow**, accept, brook, condone, permit, put up with (*inf*), take **2** = **endure**, put up with (*inf*), stand, stomach, take

toll¹ *v* **1** = **ring**, chime, clang, knell, peal, sound, strike ▷ *n* **2** = **ringing**, chime, clang, knell, peal

toll² *n* **1** = **charge**, duty, fee, levy, payment, tariff, tax **2** = **damage**, cost, loss, penalty

toluene *n* colourless volatile flammable liquid obtained from petroleum and coal tar.

tom *n* male cat.

tomahawk *n* fighting axe of the Native Americans.

tomato *n, pl* **-toes** red fruit used in salads and as a vegetable.

tomb ❶ *n* **1** grave. **2** monument over a grave. **tombstone** *n* gravestone.

tombola *n* lottery with tickets drawn from a revolving drum.

tomboy *n* girl who acts or dresses like a boy.

tome *n* large heavy book.

tomfoolery ❶ *n* foolish behaviour.

Tommy *n, pl* **-mies** *Brit informal* private soldier in the British army.

Tommy gun *n* light sub-machine-gun.

tomorrow *adv, n* **1** (on) the day after today. **2** (in) the future.

tom-tom *n* drum beaten with the hands.

ton *n* unit of weight equal to 2240 pounds or 1016 kilograms (**long ton**) or, in the US, 2000 pounds or 907 kilograms (**short ton**). **tonnage** *n* weight capacity of a ship.

tone ❶ *n* **1** sound with reference to its pitch, volume, etc. **2** *US* musical note. **3** *Music* (also **whole tone**) interval of two semitones. **4** quality of a sound or colour. **5** general character. **6** healthy bodily condition. ▷ *v* **7** harmonize (with). **8** give tone to. **tonal** *adj Music* written in a key. **tonality** *n* **toneless** *adj* **tone-deaf** *adj* unable to perceive subtle differences in pitch. **tone down** *v* make or become more moderate. **tone up** *v* make or become more healthy.

tongs *pl n* large pincers for grasping and lifting.

tongue ❶ *n* **1** muscular organ in the mouth, used in speaking and tasting. **2** language. **3** animal tongue as food. **4** thin projecting strip. **5** flap of leather on a shoe. **tonguing** *n* technique of playing a wind instrument by obstructing and uncovering the air passage through the lips with the tongue. **tongue-tied** *adj* speechless, esp. with shyness or embarrassment. **tongue twister** sentence or phrase that is difficult to say quickly.

tonic ❶ *n* **1** medicine to improve body tone. **2** anything that is strengthening or cheering. **3** tonic water. **4** *Music* first note of a scale. ▷ *adj* **5** invigorating. **tonic water** mineral water containing quinine.

tonight *adv, n* (in or during) the night or evening of this day.

toning table *n* exercise table with mechanically moving parts, which is programmed to repeat certain movements for a set time, in order to exercise specific parts of the body of the person lying on it.

tonne [**tunn**] *n* unit of weight equal to 1000 kilograms.

tonsil *n* small gland in the throat. **tonsillectomy** *n* surgical removal of the tonsils. **tonsillitis** *n* inflammation of the tonsils.

tonsure *n* **1** shaving of all or the top of the head as a religious or monastic practice. **2** shaved part of the head. **tonsured** *adj*.

too ❶ *adv* **1** also, as well. **2** to excess. **3** extremely.

took *v* past tense of TAKE.

tool ❶ *n* **1** implement used by hand. **2** person used by another to perform

---

THESAURUS

tomb *n* = **grave**, catacomb, crypt, mausoleum, sarcophagus, sepulchre, vault

tombstone *n* = **gravestone**, headstone, marker, memorial, monument

tomfoolery *n* = **foolishness**, buffoonery, clowning, fooling around (*inf*), horseplay, shenanigans (*inf*), silliness, skylarking (*inf*)

tone *n* **1** = **pitch**, inflection, intonation, modulation, timbre **4** = **colour**, hue, shade, tinge, tint **5** = **character**, air, attitude, feel, manner, mood, spirit, style, temper ▷ *v* **7** = **harmonize**, blend, go well with, match, suit

tone down *v* = **moderate**, play down, reduce, restrain, soften, subdue, temper

tongue *n* **2** = **language**, dialect, parlance, speech

tonic *n* **2** = **stimulant**, boost, fillip, pick-me-up (*inf*), restorative, shot in the arm (*inf*)

too *adv* **1** = **also**, as well, besides, further, in addition, likewise, moreover, to boot **2, 3** = **excessively**, extremely, immoderately, inordinately, overly, unduly, unreasonably, very

tool *n* **1** = **implement**, appliance, contraption, contrivance, device,

unpleasant or dishonourable tasks. ▷ v **3** work on with a tool. **toolbar** n Computers row of buttons displayed on a computer screen, allowing the user to select various functions.

toonie, twonie n inf Canadian two-dollar coin.

toot n **1** short hooting sound. ▷ v **2** (cause to) make such a sound.

tooth n, pl **teeth 1** bonelike projection in the jaws of most vertebrates for biting and chewing. **2** toothlike prong or point. **sweet tooth** strong liking for sweet food. **toothless** adj **1** lacking teeth. **2** (of an official body) lacking power or influence. **toothpaste** n paste used to clean the teeth. **toothpick** n small stick for removing scraps of food from between the teeth.

top¹ ❶ n **1** highest point or part. **2** lid or cap. **3** highest rank. **4** garment for the upper part of the body. ▷ adj **5** at or of the top. ▷ v **topping, topped 6** form a top on. **7** be at the top of. **8** exceed or surpass. **topping** n sauce or garnish for food. **topless** adj (of a costume or woman) with no covering for the breasts. **topmost** adj highest or best. **top brass** most important officers or leaders. **top-dress** v spread fertilizer on the surface of the land. **top dressing** layer of fertilizer spread on the surface of land. **top hat** man's tall cylindrical hat. **top-heavy** adj unstable through being overloaded at the top. **top-notch** adj excellent, first-class. **top-secret** adj (of military or government information) classified as needing the highest level of secrecy and security. **topsoil** n surface layer of soil.

top² n toy which spins on a pointed base.

topaz [**toe**-pazz] n semiprecious stone in various colours.

tope¹ v drink alcohol regularly.

tope² n small European shark.

topee, topi [**toe**-pee] n lightweight hat worn in tropical countries.

topiary [**tope**-yar-ee] n art of trimming trees and bushes into decorative shapes. **topiarist** n.

topic ❶ n subject of a conversation, book, etc. **topical** adj relating to current events. **topicality** n.

topography n, pl **-phies** (science of describing) the surface features of a place. **topographer** n **topographical** adj.

topology n geometry of the properties of a shape which are unaffected by continuous distortion. **topological** adj.

topple ❶ v **1** (cause to) fall over. **2** overthrow (a government etc.).

topsy-turvy ❶ adj **1** upside down. **2** in confusion.

toque [**toke**] n small round hat.

tor n high rocky hill.

Torah n body of traditional Jewish teaching.

torch n **1** small portable battery-powered lamp. **2** wooden shaft dipped in wax and set alight. ▷ v **3** informal deliberately set (a building) on fire. **carry a torch for** be in love with (someone).

tore v past tense of TEAR².

toreador [**torr**-ee-a-dor] n bullfighter.

torment ❶ v **1** cause (someone) great suffering. **2** tease cruelly. ▷ n **3** great

━━━━━━━━━━━━━━━━━ THESAURUS ━━━━━

gadget, instrument, machine, utensil **2** = **puppet**, cat's-paw, hireling, lackey, minion, pawn, stooge (sl)

top¹ n **1** = **peak**, apex, crest, crown, culmination, head, height, pinnacle, summit, zenith **2** = **lid**, cap, cover, stopper **3** = **first place**, head, lead ▷ adj **5** = **leading**, best, chief, elite, finest, first, foremost, head, highest, pre-eminent, principal, uppermost ▷ v **6** = **cover**, cap, crown, finish, garnish **7** = **lead**, be first, head **8** = **surpass**, beat, better, eclipse, exceed, excel, outstrip, transcend

topic n = **subject**, issue, matter, point, question, subject matter, theme

topical adj = **current**, contemporary,

newsworthy, up-to-date, up-to-the-minute

topmost adj = **highest**, dominant, foremost, leading, paramount, principal, supreme, top, uppermost

topple v **1** = **fall over**, collapse, fall, keel over, overbalance, overturn, totter, tumble **2** = **overthrow**, bring down, bring low, oust, overturn, unseat

topsy-turvy adj **1** = **upside-down 2** = **disorganized**, chaotic, confused, disorderly, inside-out, jumbled, messy, mixed-up

torment v **1** = **torture**, crucify, distress, rack **2** = **tease**, annoy, bother, harass, hassle (inf), irritate, nag, pester, vex

suffering. **4** source of suffering.
tormentor n.

torn ❶ v past participle of TEAR².

tornado ❶ n, pl **-dos, -does** violent
whirlwind.

torpedo n, pl **-does 1** self-propelled
underwater missile. ▷ v **-doing, -doed
2** attack or destroy with or as if with
torpedoes.

torpid ❶ adj sluggish and inactive.
torpor n torpid state.

torque [**tork**] n **1** force causing
rotation. **2** Celtic necklace or armband
of twisted metal.

torrent ❶ n **1** rushing stream. **2** rapid
flow of questions, abuse, etc.
torrential adj (of rain) very heavy.

torrid ❶ adj **1** very hot and dry. **2** highly
emotional.

torsion n twisting of a part by equal
forces being applied at both ends but
in opposite directions.

torso n, pl **-sos 1** trunk of the human
body. **2** statue of a nude human trunk.

tort n Law civil wrong or injury for which
damages may be claimed.

tortilla n thin Mexican pancake.

tortoise n slow-moving land reptile
with a dome-shaped shell.
tortoiseshell n **1** mottled brown shell
of a turtle, used for making
ornaments. ▷ adj **2** having brown,
orange, and black markings.

tortuous ❶ adj **1** winding or twisting.
2 not straightforward.

torture ❶ v **1** cause (someone) severe
pain or mental anguish. ▷ n **2** severe
physical or mental pain. **3** torturing.
torturer n.

Tory n, pl **Tories 1** member of the
Conservative Party in Great Britain or
Canada. ▷ adj **2** of Tories. **Toryism** n.

toss ❶ v **1** throw lightly. **2** fling or be
flung about. **3** coat (food) by gentle
stirring or mixing. **4** (of a horse) throw
(its rider). **5** move (one's head)
suddenly backwards. **6** throw up (a
coin) to decide between alternatives
by guessing which side will land
uppermost. ▷ n **7** tossing. **toss up** v
toss a coin. **toss-up** n even chance or
risk.

tot¹ ❶ n **1** small child. **2** small drink of
spirits.

tot² ❶ v **totting, totted. tot up** add
(numbers) together.

total ❶ n **1** whole, esp. a sum of parts.
▷ adj **2** complete. **3** of or being a total.
▷ v **-talling, -talled 4** amount to.
5 add up. **totally** adv **totality** n
totalizator n machine operating a
betting system in which money is paid
out to the winners in proportion to
their stakes.

totalitarian ❶ adj of a dictatorial one-
party government. **totalitarianism** n.

THESAURUS

▷ n **3** = **suffering**, agony, anguish,
distress, hell, misery, pain, torture

torn adj **2** = **cut**, lacerated, ragged,
rent, ripped, slit, split

tornado n = **whirlwind**, cyclone, gale,
hurricane, squall, storm, tempest,
typhoon

torpor n = **inactivity**, apathy,
drowsiness, indolence, laziness,
lethargy, listlessness, sloth,
sluggishness

torrent n **1** = **stream**, cascade, deluge,
downpour, flood, flow, rush, spate,
tide

torrid adj **1** = **arid**, dried, parched,
scorched **2** = **passionate**, ardent,
fervent, intense, steamy (inf)

tortuous adj **1** = **winding**, circuitous,
convoluted, indirect, mazy,
meandering, serpentine, sinuous,
twisting **2** = **complicated**,
ambiguous, convoluted, devious,
indirect, involved, roundabout, tricky

torture v **1** = **torment**, afflict, crucify,

distress, persecute, put on the
rack, rack ▷ n **2** = **agony**, anguish,
distress, pain, persecution, suffering,
torment

toss v **1** = **throw**, cast, fling, flip, hurl,
launch, lob (inf), pitch, sling
2 = **thrash**, rock, roll, shake, wriggle,
writhe ▷ n **7** = **throw**, lob (inf), pitch

tot¹ n **1** = **infant**, baby, child, mite,
toddler **2** = **measure**, dram, finger,
nip, shot (inf), slug, snifter (inf)

tot² v **tot up** = **add up**, calculate, count
up, reckon, tally, total

total n **1** = **whole**, aggregate, entirety,
full amount, sum, totality ▷ adj
2, 3 = **complete**, absolute,
comprehensive, entire, full, gross,
overarching, thoroughgoing,
undivided, utter, whole ▷ v
4 = **amount to**, come to, mount up to,
reach **5** = **add up**, reckon, tot up

totalitarian adj = **dictatorial**,
authoritarian, despotic, oppressive,
tyrannous, undemocratic

tote[1] *v* carry (a gun etc.).

tote[2] *n* short for TOTALIZATOR.

totem *n* tribal badge or emblem. **totem pole** post carved or painted with totems by Native Americans.

totter ❶ *v* **1** move unsteadily. **2** be about to fall.

toucan *n* tropical American bird with a large bill.

touch ❶ *v* **1** come into contact with. **2** tap, feel, or stroke. **3** affect. **4** move emotionally. **5** eat or drink. **6** equal or match. **7** *slang* ask for money. ▷ *n* **8** sense by which an object's qualities are perceived when they come into contact with part of the body. **9** contact with the body. **10** gentle tap, push, or caress. **11** small amount. **12** characteristic style. **13** detail. **touch and go** risky or critical. **touched** *adj* **1** emotionally moved. **2** slightly mad. **touching** *adj* emotionally moving. **touchy** *adj* easily offended. **touch base** make contact, renew communication. **touch down** *v* (of an aircraft) land. **touchline** *n* side line of the pitch in some games. **touch on** *v* refer to in passing. **touch-type** *v* type without looking at the keyboard.

touchy-feely *adj informal, sometimes offens.* sensitive and caring.

touché [**too**-shay] *interj* acknowledgment of the striking home of a remark or witty reply.

touchstone ❶ *n* standard by which a judgment is made.

tough ❶ *adj* **1** strong or resilient. **2** difficult to chew or cut. **3** firm and determined. **4** rough and violent. **5** difficult. **6** *informal* unlucky or unfair. ▷ *n* **7** *informal* rough violent person. **toughness** *n* **toughen** *v* make or become tough or tougher.

toupee [**too**-pay] *n* small wig.

tour ❶ *n* **1** journey visiting places of interest along the way. **2** trip to perform or play in different places. ▷ *v* **3** make a tour (of). **tourism** *n* tourist travel as an industry. **tourist** *n* person travelling for pleasure. **touristy** *adj informal, often derogatory* full of tourists or tourist attractions.

tour de force *n, pl* **tours de force** *French* brilliant stroke or achievement.

tourmaline *n* crystalline mineral used for optical instruments and as a gem.

---

totality *n* **1** = **whole**, aggregate, entirety, sum, total

totally *adv* **2** = **completely**, absolutely, comprehensively, entirely, fully, one hundred per cent, thoroughly, utterly, wholly

totter *v* **1** = **falter** **2** = **stagger**, lurch, reel, stumble, sway, wobble

touch *v* **1** = **come into contact**, abut, adjoin, be in contact, border, contact, graze, impinge upon, meet **2** = **handle**, brush, caress, contact, feel, finger, fondle, stroke, tap **3** = **affect**, impress, influence, inspire **4** = **move**, disturb, stir **5** = **consume**, drink, eat, partake of **6** = **match**, compare with, equal, hold a candle to (*inf*), parallel, rival ▷ *n* **8** = **feeling**, handling, physical contact **9** = **contact**, brush, caress, stroke **10** = **tap**, pat **11** = **bit**, dash, drop, jot, small amount, smattering, *soupçon*, spot, trace **12** = **style**, manner, method, technique, trademark, way **touch on** = **refer to**, allude to, bring in, cover, deal with, mention, speak of

touch and go *adj* = **risky**, close, critical, near, nerve-racking, precarious

touching *adj* = **moving**, affecting, emotive, pathetic, pitiable, poignant, sad, stirring

touchstone *n* = **standard**, criterion, gauge, measure, norm, par, yardstick

touchy *adj* = **oversensitive**, irascible, irritable, querulous, quick-tempered, testy, tetchy, thin-skinned

tough *adj* **1** = **resilient**, durable, hard, inflexible, leathery, resistant, rugged, solid, strong, sturdy **3** = **firm**, hard, hardy, resolute, seasoned, stern, stout, strapping, strong, sturdy, unbending, vigorous **4** = **rough**, hard-bitten, merciless, pugnacious, ruthless, violent **5** = **difficult**, arduous, exacting, hard, laborious, strenuous, troublesome, uphill **6** *Inf* = **unlucky**, lamentable, regrettable, unfortunate ▷ *n* **7** *Inf* = **ruffian**, bruiser (*inf*), bully, hooligan, roughneck (*sl*), thug

tour *n* **1** = **journey**, excursion, expedition, jaunt, outing, trip ▷ *v* **3** = **visit**, explore, go round, journey, sightsee, travel through

tourist *n* = **traveller**, excursionist, globetrotter, holiday-maker, sightseer, tripper, voyager

tournament ❶ *n* **1** sporting competition with several stages to decide the overall winner. **2** *History* contest between knights on horseback.

tourniquet [**tour**-nick-kay] *n* something twisted round a limb to stop bleeding.

tousled *adj* ruffled and untidy.

tout [rhymes with **shout**] *v* **1** seek business in a persistent manner. **2** recommend (a person or thing). ▷ *n* **3** person who sells tickets for a popular event at inflated prices.

tow¹ ❶ *v* **1** drag, esp. by means of a rope. ▷ *n* **2** towing. **in tow** following closely behind. **on tow** being towed. **towbar** *n* metal bar on a car for towing vehicles. **towpath** *n* path beside a canal or river, originally for horses towing boats. **towrope** *n* rope or cable used for towing a vehicle or vessel.

tow² *n* fibre of hemp or flax.

towards, toward ❶ *prep* **1** in the direction of. **2** with regard to. **3** as a contribution to.

towel *n* **1** cloth for drying things. ▷ *v* **-elling, -elled 2** dry or wipe with a towel. **towelling** *n* material used for making towels. **throw in the towel** give up completely.

tower ❶ *n* tall structure, often forming part of a larger building. **towering** *adj* very tall or impressive. **tower block** tall building divided into flats or offices. **tower of strength** person who supports or comforts. **tower over** *v* be much taller than.

town *n* **1** group of buildings larger than a village. **2** central part of this. **3** people of a town. **township** *n* **1** small town. **2** (in S Africa) urban settlement of Black or Coloured people. **town hall** large building used for council meetings, concerts, etc. **town planning** comprehensive planning of the physical and social development of a town.

toxaemia [tox-**seem**-ya] *n* **1** blood poisoning. **2** high blood pressure in pregnancy.

toxic ❶ *adj* **1** poisonous. **2** caused by poison. **toxicity** *n* **toxicology** *n* study of poisons. **toxin** *n* poison of bacterial origin.

toy ❶ *n* **1** something designed to be played with. ▷ *adj* **2** designed to be played with. **3** (of a dog) of a variety much smaller than is normal for that breed. **toy with** *v* play or fiddle with.

toy-toy *S Afr* ▷ *n* **1** dance of political protest. ▷ *v* **2** perform this dance.

trace ❶ *v* **1** locate or work out (the cause of something). **2** track down and find. **3** follow the course of. **4** copy exactly by drawing on a thin sheet of transparent paper set on top of the original. ▷ *n* **5** track left by something. **6** minute quantity. **7** indication. **traceable** *adj* **tracer** *n* projectile which leaves a visible trail. **tracery** *n* pattern of interlacing lines. **tracing** *n* traced copy. **trace element** chemical element occurring in very small amounts in soil etc.

traces *pl n* strap by which a horse pulls a vehicle. **kick over the traces** escape or defy control.

trachea [track-**kee**-a] *n, pl* **tracheae** windpipe. **tracheotomy** [track-ee-**ot**-a-mee] *n* surgical incision into the trachea.

track ❶ *n* **1** rough road or path. **2** mark or trail left by the passage of anything.

tournament *n* **1** = **competition**, contest, event, meeting, series

tow¹ *v* **1** = **drag**, draw, haul, lug, pull, tug, yank

towards *prep* **1** = **in the direction of**, en route for, for, on the way to, to **2** = **regarding**, about, concerning, for, with regard to, with respect to

tower *n* = **column**, belfry, obelisk, pillar, skyscraper, steeple, turret

towering *adj* **a** = **tall**, colossal, elevated, high, lofty, soaring **b** = **impressive**, imposing, magnificent

toxic *adj* **1** = **poisonous**, deadly, harmful, lethal, noxious, pernicious, pestilential, septic

toy *n* **1** = **plaything**, doll, game ▷ *v* (with *with*) = **play**, amuse oneself with, dally with, fool (about *or* around) with, trifle

trace *v* **2** = **find**, detect, discover, ferret out, hunt down, track, unearth **3** = **outline**, draw, sketch **4** = **copy** ▷ *n* **5** = **track**, footmark, footprint, footstep, path, spoor, trail **6** = **bit**, drop, hint, shadow, suggestion, suspicion, tinge, touch, whiff **7** = **remnant**, evidence, indication, mark, record, sign, survival, vestige

track *n* **1** = **path**, course, line, orbit, pathway, road, trajectory, way

t

3 railway line. **4** course for racing. **5** separate section on a record, tape, or CD. **6** course of action or thought. **7** endless band round the wheels of a tank, bulldozer, etc. ▷ *v* **8** follow the trail or path of. **track down** *v* hunt for and find. **track event** athletic sport held on a running track. **track record** past accomplishments of a person or organization. **track shoe** light running shoe fitted with spikes for better grip. **tracksuit** *n* warm loose-fitting suit worn by athletes etc., esp. during training.

tract¹ ❶ *n* **1** wide area. **2** *Anat* system of organs with a particular function.

tract² ❷ *n* pamphlet, esp. a religious one.

tractable *adj* easy to manage or control.

traction ❶ *n* **1** pulling, esp. by engine power. **2** *Medical* application of a steady pull on an injured limb by weights and pulleys. **3** grip of the wheels of a vehicle on the ground. **traction engine** old-fashioned steam-powered vehicle for pulling heavy loads.

tractor *n* motor vehicle with large rear wheels for pulling farm machinery.

trade ❶ *n* **1** buying, selling, or exchange of goods. **2** person's job or craft. **3** (people engaged in) a particular industry or business. ▷ *v* **4** buy and sell. **5** exchange. **6** engage in trade.

trader *n* **trading** *n* **trade-in** *n* used article given in part payment for a new one. **trademark** *n* (legally registered) name or symbol used by a firm to distinguish its goods. **trade-off** *n* exchange made as a compromise. **trade secret** secret formula, technique, or process known and used to advantage by only one manufacturer. **tradesman** *n* **1** skilled worker. **2** shopkeeper. **trade union** society of workers formed to protect their interests. **trade wind** wind blowing steadily towards the equator.

tradescantia [trad-dess-**kan**-shee-a] *n* widely cultivated plant with striped variegated leaves.

tradition ❶ *n* **1** handing down from generation to generation of customs and beliefs. **2** body of beliefs, customs, etc. handed down from generation to generation. **3** custom or practice of long standing. **traditional** *adj* **traditionally** *adv* **traditionalist** *n* person who supports established customs or beliefs. **traditionalism** *n*.

traduce *v* slander.

traffic ❶ *n* **1** vehicles coming and going on a road. **2** (illicit) trade. ▷ *v* **-ficking**, **-ficked 3** trade, usu. illicitly. **trafficker** *n* **traffic lights** set of coloured lights at a junction to control the traffic flow. **traffic warden** person employed to control the movement and parking of traffic.

———————————————————— THESAURUS ————————————————————

2 = **trail**, footmark, footprint, footstep, mark, path, spoor, trace, wake **3** = **line**, permanent way, rails ▷ *v* **8** = **follow**, chase, hunt down, pursue, shadow, stalk, tail (*inf*), trace, trail

track down *v* = **find**, dig up, discover, hunt down, run to earth *or* ground, sniff out, trace, unearth

tract¹ *n* **1** = **area**, district, expanse, extent, plot, region, stretch, territory

tract² *n* = **treatise**, booklet, dissertation, essay, homily, monograph, pamphlet

traction *n* **1** = **pulling**, pull **3** = **grip**, friction, purchase, resistance

trade *n* **1** = **commerce**, barter, business, dealing, exchange, traffic, transactions, truck **2** = **job**, business, craft, employment, line of work, métier, occupation, profession ▷ *v* **4** = **deal**, bargain, cut a deal, do business, have dealings, peddle,

traffic, transact, truck **5** = **exchange**, barter, swap, switch

trader *n* = **dealer**, merchant, purveyor, seller, supplier

tradesman *n* **1** = **craftsman**, artisan, journeyman, workman **2** = **shopkeeper**, dealer, merchant, purveyor, retailer, seller, supplier, vendor

tradition *n* **2** = **lore**, folklore **3** = **custom**, convention, habit, institution, ritual

traditional *adj* **3** = **customary**, accustomed, conventional, established, old, time-honoured, usual

traffic *n* **1** = **transport**, freight, transportation, vehicles **2** = **trade**, business, commerce, dealings, exchange, peddling, truck ▷ *v* **3** = **trade**, bargain, cut a deal, deal, do business, exchange, have dealings, peddle

tragedy ❶ *n, pl* **-dies 1** shocking or sad event. **2** serious play, film, etc. in which the hero is destroyed by a personal failing in adverse circumstances. **tragedian** [traj-**jee**-dee-an], **tragedienne** [traj-jee-dee-**enn**] *n* person who acts in or writes tragedies. **tragic** *adj* of or like a tragedy. **tragically** *adv* **tragicomedy** *n* play with both tragic and comic elements.

trail ❶ *n* **1** path, track, or road. **2** tracks left by a person, animal, or object. ▷ *v* **3** drag along the ground. **4** lag behind. **5** follow the tracks of. **trailer** *n* **1** vehicle designed to be towed by another vehicle. **2** extract from a film or programme used to advertise it. **trailer park** *n US* site for parking mobile homes.

train ❶ *v* **1** instruct in a skill. **2** learn the skills needed to do a particular job or activity. **3** prepare for a sports event etc. **4** aim (a gun etc.). **5** cause (an animal) to perform or (a plant) to grow in a particular way. ▷ *n* **6** line of railway coaches or wagons drawn by an engine. **7** sequence or series. **8** long trailing back section of a dress. **trainer** *n* **1** person who trains an athlete or sportsman. **2** person who trains racehorses. **3** piece of equipment employed in training, such as a simulated aircraft cockpit. **4** sports shoe. **trainee** *n* person being trained. **train spotter** person who collects the numbers of railway trains.

traipse ❶ *v informal* walk wearily.

trait ❶ *n* characteristic feature.

traitor ❶ *n* person guilty of treason or treachery. **traitorous** *adj*.

trajectory ❶ *n, pl* **-ries** line of flight, esp. of a projectile.

tram *n* public transport vehicle powered by an overhead wire and running on rails laid in the road. **tramlines** *pl n* track for trams.

tramp ❶ *v* **1** travel on foot, hike. **2** walk heavily. ▷ *n* **3** homeless person who travels on foot. **4** hike. **5** sound of tramping. **6** cargo ship available for hire. **7** *US & Aust slang* promiscuous woman.

trample ❶ *v* tread on and crush.

trampoline *n* **1** tough canvas sheet attached to a frame by springs, used by acrobats etc. ▷ *v* **2** bounce on a trampoline.

trance ❶ *n* unconscious or dazed state.

tranche *n* portion of something large, esp. a sum of money.

tranquil ❶ *adj* calm and quiet. **tranquilly** *adv* **tranquillity** *n* **tranquillize** *v* make calm. **tranquillizer** *n* drug which reduces anxiety or tension.

THESAURUS

tragedy *n* **1** = **disaster**, adversity, calamity, catastrophe, misfortune

tragic *adj* = **distressing**, appalling, calamitous, catastrophic, deadly, dire, disastrous, dreadful, miserable, mournful, pathetic, sad, unfortunate

trail *n* **1** = **path**, footpath, road, route, track, way **2** = **tracks**, footprints, marks, path, scent, spoor, trace, wake ▷ *v* **3** = **drag**, dangle, draw, haul, pull, tow **4** = **lag**, dawdle, follow, hang back, linger, loiter, straggle, traipse (*inf*) **5** = **follow**, chase, hunt, pursue, shadow, stalk, tail (*inf*), trace, track

train *v* **1** = **instruct**, coach, drill, educate, guide, prepare, school, teach, tutor **3** = **exercise**, prepare, work out **4** = **aim**, direct, focus, level, point ▷ *n* **7** = **sequence**, chain, progression, series, set, string, succession

trainer *n* **1** = **coach**

traipse *v Inf* = **trudge**, drag oneself, slouch, trail, tramp

trait *n* = **characteristic**, attribute, feature, idiosyncrasy, mannerism, peculiarity, quality, quirk

traitor *n* = **betrayer**, apostate, back-stabber, defector, deserter, Judas, quisling, rebel, renegade, turncoat

trajectory *n* = **path**, course, flight path, line, route, track

tramp *v* **1** = **hike**, march, ramble, roam, rove, slog, trek, walk **2** = **trudge**, plod, stump, toil, traipse (*inf*) ▷ *n* **3** = **vagrant**, derelict, down-and-out, drifter **4** = **hike**, march, ramble, slog, trek **5** = **tread**, footfall, footstep

trample *v* = **crush**, flatten, run over, squash, stamp, tread, walk over

trance *n* = **daze**, abstraction, dream, rapture, reverie, stupor, unconsciousness

tranquil *adj* = **calm**, peaceful, placid, quiet, restful, sedate, serene, still, undisturbed

tranquillize *v* = **calm**, lull, outspan (*S Afr*), pacify, quell, quiet, relax, sedate, settle one's nerves, soothe

t

trans- *prefix* across, through, or beyond.

transact ❶ *v* conduct or negotiate (a business deal). **transaction** *n* business deal transacted.

transatlantic *adj* on, from, or to the other side of the Atlantic.

transceiver *n* transmitter and receiver of radio or electronic signals.

transcend ❶ *v* 1 rise above. 2 be superior to. **transcendence** *n* **transcendent** *adj* **transcendental** *adj* 1 based on intuition rather than experience. 2 supernatural or mystical. **transcendentalism** *n*.

transcribe ❶ *v* 1 write down (something said). 2 record for a later broadcast. 3 arrange (music) for a different instrument. **transcript** *n* copy.

transducer *n* device that converts one form of energy to another.

transept *n* either of the two shorter wings of a cross-shaped church.

transfer ❶ *v* **-ferring**, **-ferred** 1 move or send from one person or place to another. ▷ *n* 2 transferring. 3 design which can be transferred from one surface to another. **transferable** *adj* **transference** *n* transferring.

transfigure *v* change in appearance. **transfiguration** *n*.

transfix ❶ *v* 1 astound or stun. 2 pierce through.

transform ❶ *v* change the shape or character of. **transformation** *n* **transformer** *n* device for changing the voltage of an alternating current.

transfusion *n* injection of blood into the blood vessels of a patient. **transfuse** *v* 1 give a transfusion to. 2 permeate or infuse.

transgress ❶ *v* break (a moral law). **transgression** *n* **transgressor** *n*.

transient ❶ *adj* lasting only for a short time. **transience** *n*.

transistor *n* 1 semiconducting device used to amplify electric currents. 2 portable radio using transistors. **transistorized** *adj*.

transit ❶ *n* movement from one place to another. **transition** *n* change from one state to another. **transitional** *adj* **transitive** *adj Grammar* (of a verb) requiring a direct object. **transitory** *adj* not lasting long.

translate ❶ *v* turn from one language into another. **translatable** *adj*

---

tranquillizer *n* = **sedative**, barbiturate, bromide, downer (*sl*), opiate

transaction *n* = **deal**, bargain, business, enterprise, negotiation, undertaking

transcend *v* 1 = **rise above** 2 = **surpass**, eclipse, exceed, excel, go beyond, outdo, outstrip

transcendent *adj* 2 = **unparalleled**, consummate, incomparable, matchless, pre-eminent, sublime, unequalled, unrivalled

transcribe *v* 1 = **write out**, copy out, reproduce, take down, transfer

transcript *n* = **copy**, duplicate, manuscript, record, reproduction, transcription

transfer *v* 1 = **move**, change, convey, hand over, pass on, relocate, shift, transplant, transport, transpose ▷ *n* 2 = **move**, change, handover, relocation, shift, transference, translation, transmission, transposition

transfix *v* 1 = **stun**, engross, fascinate, hold, hypnotize, mesmerize, paralyse 2 = **pierce**, impale, puncture, run through, skewer, spear

transform *v* = **change**, alter, convert, remodel, revolutionize, transmute

transformation *n* = **change**,

alteration, conversion, metamorphosis, revolution, sea change, transmutation

transgress *v* = **break**, break the law, contravene, disobey, exceed, go beyond, infringe, offend, overstep, sin, trespass, violate

transgression *n* = **crime**, contravention, infraction, infringement, misdeed, misdemeanour, offence, sin, trespass, violation

transient *adj* = **brief**, ephemeral, fleeting, impermanent, momentary, passing, short-lived, temporary, transitory

transit *n* = **movement**, carriage, conveyance, crossing, passage, transfer, transport, transportation

transition *n* = **change**, alteration, conversion, development, metamorphosis, passing, progression, shift, transmutation

transitory *adj* = **short-lived**, brief, ephemeral, fleeting, impermanent, momentary, passing, short, temporary, transient

translate *v* = **interpret**, construe, convert, decipher, decode, paraphrase, render

translation *n* **1** piece of writing or speech translated into another language. **2** *Maths* transformation in which the origin of a coordinate system is moved to another position so that each axis retains the same direction. **translator** *n*.

transliterate *v* convert to the letters of a different alphabet. **transliteration** *n*.

translucent *adj* letting light pass through, but not transparent. **translucency, translucence** *n*.

transmigrate *v* (of a soul) pass into another body. **transmigration** *n*.

transmit ❶ *v* **-mitting, -mitted 1** pass (something) from one person or place to another. **2** send out (signals) by radio waves. **3** broadcast (a radio or television programme). **transmission** *n* **1** transmitting. **2** shafts and gears through which power passes from a vehicle's engine to its wheels. **transmittable** *adj* **transmitter** *n* **1** piece of equipment used for broadcasting radio or television programmes. **2** person or thing that transmits.

transmogrify *v* **-fying, -fied** *informal* change completely.

transmute *v* change the form or nature of. **transmutation** *n*.

transom *n* **1** horizontal bar across a window. **2** bar separating a door from the window over it.

transparent ❶ *adj* **1** able to be seen through, clear. **2** easily understood or recognized. **transparently** *adv* **transparency** *n* **1** transparent quality. **2** *pl* **-cies** colour photograph on transparent film that can be viewed by means of a projector.

transpire ❶ *v* **1** become known. **2** *informal* happen. **3** give off water vapour through pores. **transpiration** *n*.

transplant ❶ *v* **1** transfer (an organ or tissue) surgically from one part or body to another. **2** remove and transfer (a plant) to another place. ▷ *n* **3** surgical transplanting. **4** thing transplanted. **transplantation** *n*.

transport ❶ *v* **1** convey from one place to another. **2** *History* exile (a criminal) to a penal colony. **3** enrapture. ▷ *n* **4** business or system of transporting. **5** vehicle used in transport. **6** ecstasy or rapture. **transportation** *n* **transporter** *n* large goods vehicle.

transpose ❶ *v* **1** interchange two things. **2** put (music) into a different key. **3** *Maths* move (a term) from one side of an equation to the other with a corresponding reversal in sign. **transposition** *n*.

transsexual, transexual *n* **1** person of one sex who believes his or her true identity is of the opposite sex. **2** person who has had a sex-change operation.

THESAURUS

translation *n* **1** = **interpretation**, decoding, paraphrase, rendering, rendition, version

transmission *n* **1 a** = **transfer**, conveyance, dissemination, sending, shipment, spread, transference **b** = **broadcasting**, dissemination, putting out, relaying, sending, showing

transmit *v* **1** = **pass on**, bear, carry, convey, disseminate, hand on, impart, send, spread, transfer **3** = **broadcast**, disseminate, radio, relay, send out

transparency *n* **1** = **clarity**, clearness, limpidity, pellucidness, translucence **2** = **photograph**, slide

transparent *adj* **1** = **clear**, crystalline, diaphanous, limpid, lucid, see-through, sheer, translucent **2** = **obvious**, evident, explicit, manifest, patent, plain, recognizable,

unambiguous, undisguised

transpire *v* **1** = **become known**, come out, come to light, emerge **2** *Inf* = **happen**, arise, befall, chance, come about, occur, take place

transplant *v* **2** = **transfer**, displace, relocate, remove, resettle, shift, uproot

transport *v* **1** = **convey**, bear, bring, carry, haul, move, take, transfer **2** *Hist* = **exile**, banish, deport **3** = **enrapture**, captivate, delight, enchant, entrance, move, ravish ▷ *n* **4** = **transference**, conveyance, shipment, transportation **5** = **vehicle**, conveyance, transportation **6** = **ecstasy**, bliss, delight, enchantment, euphoria, heaven, rapture, ravishment

transpose ❶ *v* **1** = **interchange**, alter, change, exchange, move, reorder, shift, substitute, swap, switch, transfer

t

transubstantiation n Christianity doctrine that the bread and wine consecrated in Communion changes into the substance of Christ's body and blood.

transuranic [tranz-yoor-**ran**-ik] adj (of an element) having an atomic number greater than that of uranium.

transverse adj crossing from side to side.

transvestite n person who seeks sexual pleasure by wearing the clothes of the opposite sex. **transvestism** n.

trap ❶ n 1 device for catching animals. 2 plan for tricking or catching a person. 3 situation from which it is difficult to escape. 4 bend in a pipe containing liquid to prevent the escape of gas. 5 stall in which greyhounds are enclosed before a race. 6 two-wheeled carriage. 7 slang mouth. ▷ v **trapping**, **trapped** 8 catch. 9 trick. **trapper** n person who traps animals for their fur. **trapdoor** n door in floor or roof. **trapdoor spider** spider that builds a silk-lined hole in the ground closed by a hinged door of earth and silk.

trapeze n horizontal bar suspended from two ropes, used by circus acrobats.

trapezium n, pl -ziums, -zia quadrilateral with two parallel sides of unequal length. **trapezoid** [**trap**-piz-zoid] n 1 quadrilateral with no sides parallel. 2 Chiefly US trapezium.

trappings ❶ pl n accessories that symbolize an office or position.

Trappist n member of an order of Christian monks who observe strict silence.

trash ❶ n 1 anything worthless. 2 US & Canad rubbish. **trashy** adj.

trauma ❶ [**traw**-ma] n 1 emotional shock. 2 injury or wound. **traumatic** adj **traumatically** adv **traumatize** v.

travail n lit labour or toil.

travel ❶ v -elling, -elled 1 go from one place to another, through an area, or for a specified distance. ▷ n 2 travelling, esp. as a tourist. ▷ pl 3 (account of) travelling. **traveller** n person who makes a journey or travels a lot. **travelogue** n film or talk about someone's travels. **travel agency** agency that arranges holidays. **traveller's cheque** cheque sold by a bank to the bearer, who signs it on purchase and cashes it abroad by signing it again.

traverse ❶ v move over or back and forth over.

travesty ❶ n, pl -ties 1 grotesque imitation or mockery. ▷ v -tying, -tied 2 make or be a travesty of.

trawl n 1 net dragged at deep levels behind a fishing boat. ▷ v 2 fish with such a net. **trawler** n trawling boat.

tray n 1 flat board, usu. with a rim, for carrying things. 2 open receptacle for office correspondence.

——————————————————— THESAURUS ———————

trap n 1 = **snare**, ambush, gin, net, noose, pitfall 2 = **trick**, ambush, deception, ruse, stratagem, subterfuge, wile ▷ v 8 = **catch**, corner, enmesh, ensnare, entrap, snare, take 9 = **trick**, ambush, beguile, deceive, dupe, ensnare, inveigle

trappings pl n = **accessories**, accoutrements, equipment, finery, furnishings, gear, panoply, paraphernalia, things, trimmings

trash n 1 = **nonsense**, drivel, hogwash, kak (S Afr sl), moonshine, poppycock (inf), rot, rubbish, tripe (inf), twaddle 2 US = **litter**, dross, garbage, junk (inf), refuse, rubbish, waste

trashy adj 1 = **worthless**, cheap, inferior, rubbishy, shabby, shoddy, tawdry

trauma n 1 = **shock**, anguish, ordeal, pain, suffering, torture 2 = **injury**, agony, damage, hurt, wound

traumatic adj 1 = **shocking**, disturbing, painful, scarring, upsetting 2 = **wounding**, agonizing, damaging, hurtful, injurious

travel v 1 = **go**, journey, move, progress, roam, tour, trek, voyage, wander ▷ pl n 3 = **journey**, excursion, expedition, globetrotting, tour, trip, voyage, wandering

traveller n = **voyager**, explorer, globetrotter, gypsy, holiday-maker, tourist, wanderer, wayfarer

traverse v = **cross**, go over, span, travel over

travesty n 1 = **mockery**, burlesque, caricature, distortion, lampoon, parody, perversion ▷ v 2 = **mock**, burlesque, caricature, lampoon, make a mockery of, parody, ridicule

treacherous adj 1 = **disloyal**, deceitful, double-dealing, duplicitous, faithless,

treachery ❶ n, pl **-eries** wilful betrayal.
treacherous adj **1** disloyal.
2 unreliable or dangerous.
treacherously adv.

treacle n thick dark syrup produced when sugar is refined. **treacly** adj.

tread ❶ v **treading**, **trod**, **trodden** or **trod 1** set one's foot on. **2** crush by walking on. ▷ n **3** way of walking or dancing. **4** upper surface of a step. **5** part of a tyre or shoe that touches the ground. **tread water** stay afloat in an upright position by moving the legs in a walking motion. **treadmill** n **1** History cylinder turned by treading on steps projecting from it. **2** dreary routine.

treadle [**tred**-dl] n lever worked by the foot to turn a wheel.

treason ❶ n **1** betrayal of one's sovereign or country. **2** treachery or disloyalty. **treasonable**, **treasonous** adj.

treasure ❶ n **1** collection of wealth, esp. gold or jewels. **2** valued person or thing. ▷ v **3** prize or cherish. **treasurer** n official in charge of funds. **treasury** n **1** storage place for treasure. **2** (**T-**) government department in charge of finance. **treasure-trove** n treasure found with no evidence of ownership.

treat ❶ v **1** deal with or regard in a certain manner. **2** give medical treatment to. **3** subject to a chemical or industrial process. **4** provide (someone) with (something) as a treat. ▷ n **5** pleasure, entertainment, etc. given or paid for by someone else. **treatment** n **1** medical care. **2** way of treating a person or thing.

treatise ❶ [**treat**-izz] n formal piece of writing on a particular subject.

treaty ❶ n, pl **-ties** signed contract between states.

treble adj **1** triple. **2** Music high-pitched. ▷ n **3** (singer with or part for) a soprano voice. ▷ v **4** increase three times. **trebly** adv.

tree n large perennial plant with a woody trunk. **treeless** adj **tree kangaroo** tree-living kangaroo of New Guinea and N Australia. **tree surgery** repair of damaged trees. **tree surgeon**.

trefoil [**tref**-foil] n **1** plant, such as clover, with a three-lobed leaf. **2** carved ornament like this.

trek ❶ n **1** long difficult journey, esp. on foot. **2** S Afr migration by ox wagon. ▷ v **trekking**, **trekked 3** make such a journey.

trellis n framework of horizontal and vertical strips of wood.

THESAURUS

false, perfidious, traitorous, unfaithful, untrustworthy
2 = **dangerous**, deceptive, hazardous, icy, perilous, precarious, risky, slippery, unreliable, unsafe, unstable

treachery n = **betrayal**, disloyalty, double-dealing, duplicity, faithlessness, infidelity, perfidy, treason

tread v **1** = **step**, hike, march, pace, stamp, stride, walk **2** = **crush underfoot**, squash, trample ▷ n **3** = **step**, footfall, footstep, gait, pace, stride, walk

treason n = **disloyalty**, duplicity, lese-majesty, mutiny, perfidy, sedition, traitorousness, treachery

treasure n **1** = **riches**, cash, fortune, gold, jewels, money, valuables, wealth **2** = **darling**, apple of one's eye, gem, jewel, nonpareil, paragon, pride and joy ▷ v **3** = **prize**, adore, cherish, esteem, hold dear, idolize, love, revere, value

treasury n **1** = **storehouse**, bank, cache, hoard, repository, store, vault

treat v **1** = **behave towards**, act towards, consider, deal with, handle, look upon, manage, regard, use **2** = **take care of**, attend to, care for, nurse **4** = **provide**, entertain, lay on, regale, stand (inf) ▷ n **5 a** = **pleasure**, delight, enjoyment, fun, joy, satisfaction, surprise, thrill **b** = **entertainment**, banquet, celebration, feast, gift, party, refreshment

treatise n = **paper**, dissertation, essay, monograph, pamphlet, study, thesis, tract, work

treatment n **1** = **care**, cure, healing, medication, medicine, remedy, surgery, therapy **2** = **handling**, action, behaviour, conduct, dealing, management, manipulation

treaty n = **agreement**, alliance, compact, concordat, contract, entente, pact

trek n **1** = **journey**, expedition, hike, march, odyssey, safari, slog, tramp ▷ v **3** = **journey**, hike, march, slog, traipse (inf), tramp, trudge

tremble ❶ v 1 shake or quiver. 2 feel fear or anxiety. ▷ n 3 trembling. **trembling** adj.

tremendous ❶ adj 1 huge. 2 informal great in quality or amount. **tremendously** adv.

tremolo n, pl **-los** Music quivering effect in singing or playing.

tremor ❶ n 1 involuntary shaking. 2 minor earthquake.

tremulous adj trembling, as from fear or excitement. **tremulously** adv.

trench ❶ n long narrow ditch, esp. one used as a shelter in war. **trench coat** double-breasted waterproof coat.

trenchant adj 1 incisive. 2 effective.

trencher n History wooden plate for serving food. **trencherman** n hearty eater.

trend ❶ n 1 general tendency or direction. 2 fashion. **trendy** adj, n informal consciously fashionable (person). **trendiness** n **trendsetter** n person or thing that creates, or may create, a new fashion. **trendsetting** adj.

trepidation ❶ n fear or anxiety.

trespass ❶ v 1 go onto another's property without permission. ▷ n 2 trespassing. 3 old-fashioned sin or wrongdoing. **trespasser** n **trespass on** v take unfair advantage of (someone's friendship, patience, etc.).

tresses pl n long flowing hair.

trestle n board fixed on pairs of spreading legs, used as a support.

trevally n, pl **-lies** Aust & NZ any of various food and game fishes.

trews pl n close-fitting tartan trousers.

tri- combining form three.

triad n 1 group of three. 2 (**T-**) Chinese criminal secret society.

trial ❶ n 1 Law investigation of a case before a judge. 2 trying or testing. 3 thing or person straining endurance or patience. ▷ pl 4 sporting competition for individuals. **trial and error** method of discovery based on practical experience and experiment rather than theory.

triangle n 1 geometric figure with three sides. 2 triangular percussion instrument. 3 situation involving three people. **triangular** adj.

tribe ❶ n group of clans or families believed to have a common ancestor. **tribal** adj **tribalism** n loyalty to a tribe.

tribulation n great distress.

tribunal ❶ n 1 board appointed to inquire into a specific matter. 2 lawcourt.

tribune n people's representative, esp. in ancient Rome.

tributary n, pl **-taries** 1 stream or river flowing into a larger one. ▷ adj 2 (of a stream or river) flowing into a larger one.

tribute ❶ n 1 sign of respect or admiration. 2 tax paid by one state to another.

— THESAURUS —

tremble v 1 = **shake**, quake, quiver, shiver, shudder, totter, vibrate, wobble ▷ n 3 = **shake**, quake, quiver, shiver, shudder, tremor, vibration, wobble

tremendous adj 1 = **huge**, colossal, enormous, formidable, gigantic, great, immense, stupendous, terrific 2 Inf = **excellent**, amazing, brilliant, exceptional, extraordinary, fantastic (inf), great, marvellous, sensational (inf), wonderful

tremor n 1 = **shake**, quaking, quaver, quiver, shiver, trembling, wobble 2 = **earthquake**, quake (inf), shock

trench n = **ditch**, channel, drain, excavation, furrow, gutter, trough

trend n 1 = **tendency**, bias, current, direction, drift, flow, inclination, leaning 2 = **fashion**, craze, fad (inf), mode, rage, style, thing, vogue

trendy adj Inf = **fashionable**, in fashion, in vogue, modish, stylish, voguish, with it (inf)

trepidation n = **anxiety**, alarm, apprehension, consternation, disquiet, dread, fear, nervousness, uneasiness, worry

trespass v 1 = **intrude**, encroach, infringe, invade, obtrude ▷ n 2 = **intrusion**, encroachment, infringement, invasion, unlawful entry

trespasser n = **intruder**, interloper, invader, poacher

trial n 1 Law = **hearing**, litigation, tribunal 2 = **test**, audition, dry run (inf), experiment, probation, test-run 3 = **hardship**, adversity, affliction, distress, ordeal, suffering, tribulation, trouble

tribe n = **race**, clan, family, people

tribunal n 2 = **hearing**, court, trial

tribute n 1 = **accolade**, commendation, compliment, eulogy, panegyric,

trice *n* **in a trice** instantly.

triceps *n* muscle at the back of the upper arm.

trichology [trick-**ol**-a-jee] *n* study and treatment of hair and its diseases. **trichologist** *n*.

trick ❶ *n* **1** deceitful or cunning action or plan. **2** joke or prank. **3** feat of skill or cunning. **4** deceptive illusion. **5** mannerism. **6** cards played in one round. ▷ *v* **7** cheat or deceive. **trickery** *n* **trickster** *n* **tricky** *adj* **1** difficult, needing careful handling. **2** crafty.

trickle ❶ *v* **1** (cause to) flow in a thin stream or drops. **2** move gradually. ▷ *n* **3** gradual flow.

tricolour [**trick**-kol-lor] *n* three-coloured striped flag.

tricycle *n* three-wheeled cycle.

trident *n* three-pronged spear.

triennial *adj* happening every three years.

trifle ❶ *n* **1** insignificant thing or amount. **2** dessert of sponge cake, fruit, custard, and cream. **trifling** *adj* insignificant. **trifle with** *v* toy with.

trigger ❶ *n* **1** small lever releasing a catch on a gun or machine. **2** action that sets off a course of events. ▷ *v*

3 (usu. foll. by *off*) set (an action or process) in motion. **trigger-happy** *adj* too quick to use guns.

trigonometry *n* branch of mathematics dealing with relations of the sides and angles of triangles.

trike *n informal* tricycle.

trilateral *adj* having three sides.

trilby *n*, *pl* **-bies** man's soft felt hat.

trill *n* **1** *Music* rapid alternation between two notes. **2** shrill warbling sound made by some birds. ▷ *v* **3** play or sing a trill.

trillion *n* **1** one million million, 10^{12}. **2** *Brit* (formerly) one million million million, 10^{18}.

trilobite [**trile**-oh-bite] *n* small prehistoric sea animal.

trilogy [**trill**-a-jee] *n*, *pl* **-gies** series of three related books, plays, etc.

trim ❶ *adj* **trimmer**, **trimmest 1** neat and smart. **2** slender. ▷ *v* **trimming**, **trimmed 3** cut or prune into good shape. **4** decorate with lace, ribbons, etc. **5** adjust the balance of (a ship or aircraft) by shifting the cargo etc. **6** adjust the sails of a ship to take advantage of the wind. ▷ *n* **7** decoration. **8** upholstery and decorative facings in a car. **9** trim

recognition, testimonial **2** = **tax**, charge, homage, payment, ransom

trick *n* **1** = **deception**, fraud, hoax, manoeuvre, ploy, ruse, stratagem, subterfuge, swindle, trap, wile **2** = **joke**, antic, jape, leg-pull (*Brit inf*), practical joke, prank, stunt **3** = **secret**, hang (*inf*), knack, know-how (*inf*), skill, technique **4** = **sleight of hand**, legerdemain **5** = **mannerism**, characteristic, foible, habit, idiosyncrasy, peculiarity, practice, quirk, trait ▷ *v* **7** = **deceive**, cheat, con (*inf*), dupe, fool, hoodwink, kid (*inf*), mislead, swindle, take in (*inf*), trap

trickery *n* **1** = **deception**, cheating, chicanery, deceit, dishonesty, guile, jiggery-pokery (*inf, chiefly Brit*), monkey business (*inf*)

trickle *v* **1** = **dribble**, drip, drop, exude, ooze, run, seep, stream ▷ *n* **3** = **dribble**, drip, seepage

tricky *adj* **1** = **difficult**, complicated, delicate, knotty, problematic, risky, thorny, ticklish **2** = **crafty**, artful, cunning, deceitful, devious, scheming, slippery, sly, wily

trifle *n* **1** = **knick-knack**, bagatelle, bauble, plaything, toy **trifle with** *v* = **toy with**, dally with, mess about, play with

trifling *adj* = **insignificant**, measly, negligible, paltry, trivial, unimportant, worthless

trigger *v* **3** = **set off**, activate, cause, generate, produce, prompt, provoke, spark off, start

trim *adj* **1** = **neat**, dapper, natty (*inf*), shipshape, smart, spruce, tidy, well-groomed **2** = **slender**, fit, shapely, sleek, slim, streamlined, svelte, willowy ▷ *v* **3** = **cut**, clip, crop, even up, pare, prune, shave, tidy **4** = **decorate**, adorn, array, beautify, deck out, dress, embellish, ornament ▷ *n* **7** = **decoration**, adornment, border, edging, embellishment, frill, ornamentation, piping, trimming **9** = **condition**, fettle, fitness, health, shape (*inf*), state, wellness **10** = **cut**, clipping, crop, shave, tidying up

trimming *n* **1** = **decoration**, adornment, border, edging, embellishment, frill, ornamentation,

state. **10** haircut that neatens the existing style. **trimming** n **1** decoration. ▷ pl **2** usual accompaniments, e.g. *turkey with all the trimmings*.

trimaran [**trime**-a-ran] n three-hulled boat.

trinitrotoluene n full name for TNT.

trinity n, pl **-ties 1** group of three. **2** (**T-**) *Christianity* union of three persons, Father, Son, and Holy Spirit, in one God.

trinket ❶ n small or worthless ornament or piece of jewellery.

trio ❶ n, pl **trios 1** group of three. **2** piece of music for three performers.

trip ❶ n **1** journey to a place and back, esp. for pleasure. **2** stumble. **3** act of causing someone to stumble. **4** *informal* hallucinogenic drug experience. **5** switch on a mechanism. ▷ v **tripping, tripped 6** (cause to) stumble. **7** (often foll. by *up*) catch (someone) in a mistake. **8** move or tread lightly. **9** *informal* experience the hallucinogenic effects of a drug. **tripper** n tourist.

tripartite adj involving or composed of three people or parts.

tripe n **1** stomach of a cow used as food. **2** *informal* nonsense.

triple ❶ adj **1** having three parts. **2** (of musical time or rhythm) having three beats in each bar. **3** three times as great or as many. ▷ v **4** increase three times. **triplet** n one of three babies

born at one birth. **triple jump** athletic event in which competitors make a hop, a step, and a jump as a continuous movement.

triplicate adj triple. **in triplicate** in three copies.

tripod [**tripe**-pod] n three-legged stand, stool, etc.

tripos [**tripe**-poss] n final examinations for an honours degree at Cambridge University.

triptych [**trip**-tick] n painting or carving on three hinged panels, often forming an altarpiece.

trite ❶ adj (of a remark or idea) commonplace and unoriginal.

tritium n radioactive isotope of hydrogen.

triumph ❶ n **1** (happiness caused by) victory or success. ▷ v **2** be victorious or successful. **3** rejoice over a victory. **triumphal** adj celebrating a triumph. **triumphant** adj feeling or showing triumph. **triumphantly** adv.

triumvirate [try-**umm**-vir-rit] n group of three people in joint control.

trivalent adj *Chemistry* **1** having a valency of three. **2** having three valencies. **trivalency** n.

trivet [**triv**-vit] n metal stand for a pot or kettle.

trivial ❶ adj of little importance. **trivially** adv **trivia** pl n trivial things or details. **triviality** n **trivialize** v make (something) seem less important or complex than it is.

THESAURUS

piping ▷ pl n **2 = extras**, accessories, accompaniments, frills, ornaments, paraphernalia, trappings

trinket n **= ornament**, bagatelle, bauble, knick-knack, toy, trifle

trio n **1 = threesome**, triad, trilogy, trinity, triumvirate

trip n **1 = journey**, errand, excursion, expedition, foray, jaunt, outing, run, tour, voyage **2 = stumble**, fall, misstep, slip ▷ v **6 = stumble**, fall, lose one's footing, misstep, slip, tumble **7 = catch out**, trap **8 = skip**, dance, gambol, hop

triple adj **1 = threefold**, three-way, tripartite ▷ v **4 = treble**, increase threefold

trite adj **= unoriginal**, banal, clichéd, commonplace, hackneyed, stale, stereotyped, threadbare, tired

triumph n **1 a = joy**, elation, exultation, happiness, jubilation,

pride, rejoicing **b = success**, accomplishment, achievement, attainment, conquest, coup, feat, victory ▷ v **2 = succeed**, overcome, prevail, prosper, vanquish, win **3 = rejoice**, celebrate, crow, exult, gloat, glory, revel

triumphant adj **a = victorious**, cock-a-hoop, conquering, elated, exultant, proud, successful, winning **b = celebratory**, jubilant

trivia pl n **= minutiae**, details, trifles, trivialities

trivial adj **= unimportant**, incidental, inconsequential, insignificant, meaningless, minor, petty, small, trifling, worthless

trivialize v **= undervalue**, belittle, laugh off, make light of, minimize, play down, scoff at, underestimate, underplay

trod v past tense and a past participle of TREAD.

trodden v a past participle of TREAD.

troglodyte n cave dweller.

troika n **1** Russian vehicle drawn by three horses abreast. **2** group of three people in authority.

Trojan adj **1** of Ancient Troy. ▷ n **2** person from ancient Troy. **3** hardworking person. **Trojan Horse** trap intended to undermine an enemy.

troll[1] n giant or dwarf in Scandinavian folklore.

troll[2] v **1** fish by dragging a baited hook through the water. **2** post a deliberately provocative comment online in order to generate a response. ▷ n **3** person who posts deliberately provocative comments online.

trolley n **1** small wheeled table for food and drink. **2** wheeled cart for moving goods. **trolley bus** bus powered by electricity from an overhead wire but not running on rails.

trollop n promiscuous or slovenly woman.

trombone n brass musical instrument with a sliding tube. **trombonist** n.

troop ❶ n **1** large group. **2** artillery or cavalry unit. **3** Scout company. ▷ pl **4** soldiers. ▷ v **5** move in a crowd. **6** Brit Military parade (the colour or flag of a regiment) ceremonially. **trooper** n cavalry soldier.

trope n figure of speech.

trophy ❶ n, pl **-phies 1** cup, shield, etc. given as a prize. **2** memento of success.

tropic ❶ n **1** either of two lines of latitude at 23½°N (**tropic of Cancer**) or 23½°S (**tropic of Capricorn**). ▷ pl **2** part of the earth's surface between these lines. **tropical** adj **1** of or in the tropics. **2** (of climate) very hot.

tropism n tendency of a plant or animal to turn or curve in response to an external stimulus.

troposphere n lowest layer of the earth's atmosphere.

trot ❶ v **trotting, trotted 1** (of a horse) move at a medium pace, lifting the feet in diagonal pairs. **2** (of a person) move at a steady brisk pace. ▷ n **3** trotting. **trotter** n pig's foot. **trot out** v repeat (old ideas etc.) without fresh thought.

troth [rhymes with **growth**] n obs pledge of devotion, esp. a betrothal.

Trotskyist, Trotskyite n, adj (supporter) of the theories of Leon Trotsky, Russian communist writer.

troubadour [**troo**-bad-oor] n medieval travelling poet and singer.

trouble ❶ n **1** (cause of) distress or anxiety. **2** disease or malfunctioning. **3** state of disorder or unrest. **4** care or effort. ▷ v **5** (cause to) worry. **6** exert oneself. **7** cause inconvenience to. **troubled** adj **troublesome** adj **troublemaker** n person who causes trouble, esp. between people. **troubleshooter** n person employed to locate and deal with faults or problems. **trouble spot** place where there is frequent fighting or violence.

trough ❶ [troff] n **1** long open container, esp. for animals' food or water. **2** narrow channel between two

——————————— THESAURUS ———————————

troop n **1** = **group**, band, body, crowd, horde, multitude, team, unit **2** = **company**, squad ▷ pl **4** = **soldiers**, armed forces, army, men, servicemen, soldiery ▷ v **5** = **flock**, march, stream, swarm, throng, traipse (inf)

trophy n **1** = **prize**, award, booty, cup **2** = **memento**, laurels, souvenir, spoils

tropical adj **2** = **hot**, steamy, stifling, sultry, sweltering, torrid

trot v **1, 2** = **run**, canter, jog, lope, scamper ▷ n **3** = **run**, canter, jog, lope

trouble n **1** = **distress**, anxiety, disquiet, grief, misfortune, pain, sorrow, torment, woe, worry **2** = **ailment**, complaint, defect, disease, disorder, failure, illness, malfunction **3** = **disorder**, agitation, bother (inf), commotion, discord, disturbance, strife, tumult, unrest **4** = **effort**, care, exertion, inconvenience, labour, pains, thought, work ▷ v **5** = **bother**, disconcert, distress, disturb, pain, perturb, plague, sadden, upset, worry **6** = **take pains**, exert oneself, make an effort, take the time **7** = **inconvenience**, bother, burden, disturb, impose upon, incommode, put out

troublesome adj **1** = **bothersome**, annoying, demanding, difficult, inconvenient, irksome, taxing, tricky, trying, vexatious, worrying **3** = **disorderly**, rebellious, rowdy, turbulent, uncooperative, undisciplined, unruly, violent

trough n **1** = **manger**, water trough **2** = **channel**, canal, depression, ditch, duct, furrow, gully, gutter, trench

t

waves or ridges. **3** low point in a cycle.
4 *Meteorology* area of low pressure.

trounce ❶ *v* defeat utterly.

troupe ❶ [troop] *n* company of
performers. **trouper** *n*.

trousers *pl n* two-legged outer
garment with legs reaching usu. to the
ankles. **trouser** *adj* of trousers.

trousseau [troo-so] *n, pl* **-seaux**,
-seaus bride's collection of clothing
etc. for her marriage.

trout *n* game fish related to the salmon.

trowel *n* hand tool with a wide blade for
spreading mortar, lifting plants, etc.

troy weight, troy *n* system of weights
used for gold, silver, and jewels.

truant ❶ *n* pupil who stays away from
school without permission. **play
truant** stay away from school without
permission. **truancy** *n*.

truce ❶ *n* temporary agreement to stop
fighting.

truck¹ *n* **1** railway goods wagon. **2** lorry.

truck² *n* **have no truck with** refuse to
be involved with.

trucker *n US & Canad* truck driver.

truckle bed *n* low bed on wheels,
stored under a larger bed.

truculent [truck-yew-lent] *adj*
aggressively defiant. **truculence** *n*.

trudge ❶ *v* **1** walk heavily or wearily. ▷ *n*
2 long tiring walk.

true ❶ *adj* **truer, truest 1** in accordance
with facts. **2** genuine. **3** faithful.
4 exact. **truly** *adv* **1** in a true manner.
2 really. **truism** *n* self-evident truth.
truth *n* **1** state of being true.
2 something true. **truthful** *adj*

1 honest. **2** exact. **truthfully** *adv* **true-
blue** *adj* fiercely loyal. **true
blue** *Brit* staunch Royalist or
Conservative.

truffle *n* **1** edible underground fungus.
2 sweet flavoured with chocolate.

trug *n* long shallow basket used by
gardeners.

trump¹ *n, adj* **1** (card) of the suit
outranking the others. ▷ *v* **2** play a
trump card on (another card). ▷ *pl n*
3 suit outranking the others. **turn up
trumps** achieve an unexpected
success. **trumped up** invented or
concocted.

trump² *n lit* (sound of) a trumpet.

trumpery *n, pl* **-eries 1** something
useless or worthless. ▷ *adj* **2** useless or
worthless.

trumpet *n* **1** valved brass instrument
with a flared tube. ▷ *v* **-peting, -peted
2** proclaim loudly. **3** (of an elephant)
cry loudly. **trumpeter** *n*.

truncate ❶ *v* cut short.

truncheon *n* small club carried by a
policeman.

trundle *v* move heavily on wheels.

trunk ❶ *n* **1** main stem of a tree. **2** large
case or box for clothes etc. **3** person's
body excluding the head and limbs.
4 elephant's long nose. **5** *US* car boot.
▷ *pl* **6** man's swimming shorts. **trunk
call** long-distance telephone call.
trunk road main road.

truss ❶ *v* **1** tie or bind up. ▷ *n* **2** device
for holding a hernia in place.
3 framework supporting a roof, bridge,
etc.

trounce *v* = **defeat utterly**, beat,
crush, drub, give a hiding (*inf*),
hammer (*inf*), rout, slaughter (*inf*),
thrash, wipe the floor with (*inf*)

troupe *n* = **company**, band, cast

truancy *n* = **absence**, absence without
leave, malingering, shirking, skiving
(*Brit sl*)

truant *n* = **absentee**, malingerer, piker
(*Aust & NZ sl*), runaway, shirker, skiver
(*Brit sl*)

truce *n* = **ceasefire**, armistice,
cessation, let-up (*inf*), lull,
moratorium, peace, respite

trudge *v* **1** = **plod**, lumber, slog, stump,
traipse (*inf*), tramp, trek ▷ *n* **2** = **tramp**,
hike, march, slog, traipse (*inf*), trek

true *adj* **1** = **correct**, accurate, factual,
precise, right, truthful, veracious

2 = **genuine**, authentic, real
3 = **faithful**, dedicated, devoted,
dutiful, loyal, reliable, staunch, steady,
trustworthy **4** = **exact**, accurate, on
target, perfect, precise, spot-on (*Brit
inf*), unerring

truism *n* = **cliché**, axiom, bromide,
commonplace, platitude

truncate *v* = **shorten**, abbreviate,
curtail, cut short, dock, lop, pare,
prune, trim

trunk *n* **1** = **stem**, bole, stalk **2** = **chest**,
box, case, casket, coffer, crate
3 = **body**, torso

truss *v* **1** = **tie**, bind, fasten, make fast,
secure, strap, tether ▷ *n* **2** = **support**,
bandage **3** = **joist**, beam, brace,
buttress, prop, stanchion, stay, strut,
support

t

trust ❶ v **1** believe in and rely on. **2** consign to someone's care. **3** expect or hope. ▷ n **4** confidence in the truth, reliability, etc. of a person or thing. **5** obligation arising from responsibility. **6** arrangement in which one person administers property, money, etc. on another's behalf. **7** property held for another. **8** *Brit* self-governing hospital or group of hospitals within the National Health Service. **9** group of companies joined to control a market. **trustee** n person holding property on another's behalf. **trustful**, **trusting** adj inclined to trust others. **trustworthy** adj reliable or honest. **trusty** adj faithful or reliable. **trust fund** money or securities held in trust.

truth ❶ n see TRUE.

try ❶ v **trying**, **tried 1** make an effort or attempt. **2** test or sample. **3** put strain on, e.g. *he tries my patience*. **4** investigate (a case). **5** examine (a person) in a lawcourt. ▷ n, pl **tries 6** attempt or effort. **7** *Rugby* score gained by touching the ball down over the opponent's goal line. **try it on** *informal* try to deceive or fool someone. **trying** adj *informal* difficult or annoying.

tryst n arrangement to meet.

tsar, czar [**zahr**] n *History* Russian emperor.

tsetse fly [**tset**-see] n bloodsucking African fly whose bite transmits disease, esp. sleeping sickness.

T-shirt n short-sleeved casual shirt or top.

tsp. teaspoon.

T-square n T-shaped ruler.

tsunami n, pl **-mis, -mi** tidal wave, usu. caused by an earthquake under the sea.

TT teetotal.

tub ❶ n **1** open, usu. round container. **2** bath. **tubby** adj (of a person) short and fat.

tuba [**tube**-a] n valved low-pitched brass instrument.

tube n **1** hollow cylinder. **2** flexible cylinder with a cap to hold pastes. **the tube** underground railway, esp. the one in London. **tubing** n **1** length of tube. **2** system of tubes. **tubular** [**tube**-yew-lar] adj of or shaped like a tube.

tuber [**tube**-er] n fleshy underground root of a plant such as a potato. **tuberous** adj.

tubercle [**tube**-er-kl] n small rounded swelling.

tuberculosis [tube-berk-yew-**lohss**-iss] n infectious disease causing tubercles, esp. in the lungs. **tubercular** adj **tuberculin** n extract from a bacillus used to test for tuberculosis.

TUC Trades Union Congress.

tuck ❶ v **1** push or fold into a small space. **2** thrust the loose ends or sides of (a shirt etc.) into a space. **3** stitch in

━━━━━━━━━━ THESAURUS ━━━━━━━━━━

trust v **1** = **believe in**, bank on, count on, depend on, have faith in, rely upon **2** = **entrust**, assign, commit, confide, consign, delegate, give **3** = **expect**, assume, hope, presume, suppose, surmise ▷ n **4** = **confidence**, assurance, belief, certainty, conviction, credence, credit, expectation, faith, reliance

trustful, trusting adj = **unsuspecting**, credulous, gullible, naive, unsuspicious, unwary

trustworthy adj = **dependable**, honest, honourable, principled, reliable, reputable, responsible, staunch, steadfast, trusty

trusty adj = **reliable**, dependable, faithful, solid, staunch, steady, strong, trustworthy

truth n = **truthfulness**, accuracy, exactness, fact, genuineness, legitimacy, precision, reality, validity, veracity

truthful adj **1** = **honest**, candid, frank, sincere, straight, true, trustworthy **2** = **true**, accurate, correct, precise

try v **1** = **attempt**, aim, endeavour, have a go, make an effort, seek, strive, struggle **2** = **test**, appraise, check out, evaluate, examine, investigate, put to the test, sample, taste ▷ n **6** = **attempt**, crack (*inf*), effort, go (*inf*), shot (*inf*), stab (*inf*), whack (*inf*)

trying adj *Inf* = **annoying**, bothersome, difficult, exasperating, hard, stressful, taxing, tiresome, tough, wearisome

tubby adj = **fat**, chubby, corpulent, obese, overweight, plump, portly, stout

tuck v **1** = **push**, fold, gather, insert ▷ n **4** = **fold**, gather, pinch, pleat **5** *Inf* = **food**, grub (*sl*), nosh (*sl*)

folds. ▷ *n* **4** stitched fold. **5** *informal* food. **tuck away** *v* **1** eat (a large amount of food). **2** store in a safe place.

tucker *n Aust & NZ informal* food.

Tudor *adj* **1** of the English royal house ruling from 1485–1603. **2** in an architectural style characterized by half-timbered buildings.

Tues. Tuesday.

Tuesday *n* third day of the week.

tufa [**tew**-fa] *n* porous rock formed as a deposit from springs.

tuffet *n* small mound or seat.

tuft ❶ *n* bunch of feathers, grass, hair, etc. held or growing together at the base. **tufted** *adj*.

tug ❶ *v* **tugging**, **tugged 1** pull hard. ▷ *n* **2** hard pull. **3** (also **tugboat**) small ship used to tow other vessels. **tug of war** contest in which two teams pull against one another on a rope.

tuition ❶ *n* instruction, esp. received individually or in a small group.

tulip *n* plant with bright cup-shaped flowers.

tulle [**tewl**] *n* fine net fabric of silk etc.

tumble ❶ *v* **1** (cause to) fall, esp. awkwardly or violently. **2** roll or twist, esp. in play. **3** rumple. ▷ *n* **4** fall. **5** somersault. **tumbler** *n* **1** stemless drinking glass. **2** acrobat. **3** spring catch in a lock. **tumbledown** *adj* dilapidated. **tumble dryer**, **drier** machine that dries laundry by rotating it in warm air. **tumble to** *v informal* realize, understand.

tumbril, **tumbrel** *n* farm cart used during the French Revolution to take prisoners to the guillotine.

tumescent [tew-**mess**-ent] *adj* swollen or becoming swollen.

tummy *n*, *pl* **-mies** *informal* stomach.

tumour ❶ [**tew**-mer] *n* abnormal growth in or on the body.

tumult ❶ [**tew**-mult] *n* uproar or commotion. **tumultuous** [tew-**mull**-tew-uss] *adj*.

tumulus [**tew**-mew-luss] *n*, *pl* **-li** [-lie] burial mound.

tun *n* large beer cask.

tuna [**tune**-a] *n* large marine food fish.

tundra *n* vast treeless Arctic region with permanently frozen subsoil.

tune ❶ *n* **1** (pleasing) sequence of musical notes. **2** correct musical pitch, e.g. *she sang out of tune*. ▷ *v* **3** adjust (a musical instrument) so that it is in tune. **4** adjust (a machine) to obtain the desired performance. **tuneful** *adj* **tunefully** *adv* **tuneless** *adj* **tuner** *n* part of a radio or television receiver for selecting channels. **tune in** *v* adjust (a radio or television) to receive (a station or programme). **tuning fork** small steel instrument which produces a note of a fixed musical pitch when struck.

tungsten *n Chemistry* greyish-white metal.

tunic *n* **1** close-fitting jacket forming part of some uniforms. **2** loose knee-length garment.

tunnel ❶ *n* **1** underground passage. ▷ *v* **-nelling**, **-nelled 2** make a tunnel (through). **tunnel vision 1** condition in which a person is unable to see things that are not straight in front of him or her. **2** narrowness of viewpoint caused by concentration on a single idea or opinion.

tunny *n*, *pl* **-nies**, **-ny** same as TUNA.

tup *n* male sheep.

tupik, **tupek** *n Canad* (esp. in the Arctic) a tent of animal skins, a traditional type of Inuit dwelling.

──────────────────────── THESAURUS ────────────────────

t

tuft *n* = **clump**, bunch, cluster, collection, knot, tussock

tug *v* **1** = **pull**, jerk, wrench, yank ▷ *n* **2** = **pull**, jerk, yank

tuition *n* = **training**, education, instruction, lessons, schooling, teaching, tutelage, tutoring

tumble *v* **1** = **fall**, drop, flop, plummet, stumble, topple ▷ *n* **4** = **fall**, drop, plunge, spill, stumble, trip

tumbledown *adj* = **dilapidated**, crumbling, decrepit, munted (*NZ sl*), ramshackle, rickety, ruined

tumour *n* = **growth**, cancer, carcinoma

(*Path*), lump, sarcoma (*Med*), swelling

tumult *n* = **commotion**, clamour, din, hubbub, pandemonium, riot, row, turmoil, upheaval, uproar

tune *n* **1** = **melody**, air, song, strain, theme **2** = **concord**, consonance, euphony, harmony, pitch ▷ *v* **3** = **adjust**, adapt, attune, harmonize, pitch, regulate

tunnel *n* **1** = **passage**, burrow, channel, hole, passageway, shaft, subway, underpass ▷ *v* **2** = **dig**, burrow, excavate, mine, scoop out

turban *n* Muslim, Hindu, or Sikh man's head covering, made by winding cloth round the head.

turbid *adj* muddy, not clear.

turbine *n* machine or generator driven by gas, water, etc. turning blades.

turbocharger *n* device that increases the power of an internal-combustion engine by using the exhaust gases to drive a turbine.

turbofan *n* engine in which a large fan driven by a turbine forces air rearwards to increase the thrust.

turboprop *n* gas turbine for driving an aircraft propeller.

turbot *n* large European edible flatfish.

turbulence ❶ *n* **1** confusion, movement, or agitation. **2** atmospheric instability causing gusty air currents. **turbulent** *adj*.

tureen *n* serving dish for soup.

turf ❶ *n, pl* **turfs, turves 1** short thick even grass. **2** square of this with roots and soil attached. ▷ *v* **3** cover with turf. **the turf 1** racecourse. **2** horse racing. **turf accountant** bookmaker. **turf out** *v informal* throw out.

turgid [**tur**-jid] *adj* **1** (of language) pompous. **2** swollen and thick. **turgidity** *n*.

turkey *n* large bird bred for food.

Turkish *adj* **1** of Turkey, its people, or their language. ▷ *n* **2** Turkish

language. **Turkish bath** steam bath. **Turkish delight** jelly-like sweet coated with icing sugar.

turmeric *n* yellow spice obtained from the root of an Asian plant.

turmoil ❶ *n* agitation or confusion.

turn ❶ *v* **1** change the position or direction (of). **2** move around an axis, rotate. **3** (usu. foll. by *into*) change in nature or character. **4** reach or pass in age, time, etc., e.g. *she has just turned twenty*. **5** shape on a lathe. **6** become sour. ▷ *n* **7** turning. **8** opportunity to do something as part of an agreed succession. **9** direction or drift. **10** period or spell. **11** short excursion. **12** slight attack of an illness. **13** short theatrical performance. **good, bad turn** helpful *or* unhelpful act. **turner** *n* **turning** *n* road or path leading off a main route. **turncoat** *n* person who deserts one party or cause to join another. **turn down** *v* **1** reduce the volume or brightness (of). **2** refuse or reject. **turn in** *v* **1** go to bed. **2** hand in. **turning circle** smallest circle in which a vehicle can turn. **turning point** moment when a decisive change occurs. **turn off** *v* stop (something) working by using a knob etc. **turn on** *v* **1** start (something) working by using a knob etc. **2** become aggressive towards. **3** *informal* excite, esp.

---

turbulence *n* **1** = **confusion**, agitation, commotion, disorder, instability, tumult, turmoil, unrest, upheaval

turbulent *adj* **1** = **agitated**, foaming, furious, raging, tumultuous **2** = **blustery**, choppy, rough, tempestuous

turf *n* **1, 2** = **grass**, sod, sward **the turf 2** = **horse-racing**, racing, the flat

turmoil *n* = **confusion**, agitation, chaos, commotion, disarray, disorder, tumult, upheaval

turn *v* **1** = **change course**, move, shift, swerve, switch, veer, wheel **2** = **rotate**, circle, go round, gyrate, pivot, revolve, roll, spin, twist, whirl **3** (usu. foll. by *into*) = **change into**, alter, convert, mould, mutate into, remodel, shape, transform into **5** = **shape**, fashion, frame, make, mould **6** = **go bad**, curdle, go off (*Brit inf*), sour, spoil, taint ▷ *n* **7** = **rotation**, circle, cycle, gyration, revolution, spin, twist, whirl **8** = **opportunity**, chance,

crack (*inf*), go, stint, time, try **9** = **direction**, drift, heading, tendency, trend

turncoat *n* = **traitor**, apostate, backslider, defector, deserter, renegade

turn down *v* **1** = **lower**, lessen, muffle, mute, quieten, soften **2** = **refuse**, decline, rebuff, reject, repudiate, spurn

turn in *v* **1** = **go to bed**, go to sleep, hit the sack (*sl*) **2** = **hand in**, deliver, give up, hand over, return, submit, surrender, tender

turning *n* = **turn-off**, bend, crossroads, curve, junction, side road, turn

turning point *n* = **crossroads**, change, crisis, crux, moment of truth

turn off *v* = **stop**, cut out, put out, shut down, switch off, turn out, unplug

turn on *v* **1** = **start**, activate, ignite, kick-start, start up, switch on **2** = **attack**, assail, assault, fall on, round on **3** *Inf* = **arouse**, attract, excite, please, stimulate, thrill, titillate

t

sexually. **turnout** n number of people appearing at a gathering. **turn out** v **1** produce or create. **2** be discovered. **3** end up or result. **turnover** n **1** total sales made by a business over a certain period. **2** small pastry. **3** rate at which staff leave and are replaced. **turnpike** n road where a toll is collected at barriers. **turnstile** n revolving gate for admitting one person at a time. **turntable** n revolving platform. **turn up** v **1** arrive or appear. **2** find or be found. **3** increase the volume or brightness (of). **turn-up** n **1** turned-up fold at the bottom of a trouser leg. **2** informal unexpected event.

turnip n root vegetable with orange or white flesh.

turpentine n (oil made from) the resin of certain trees. **turps** n turpentine oil.

turpitude n wickedness.

turquoise adj **1** blue-green. ▷ n **2** blue-green precious stone.

turret n **1** small tower. **2** revolving gun tower on a warship or tank. **turreted** adj.

turtle n sea tortoise. **turn turtle** capsize. **turtledove** n small wild dove. **turtleneck** n (sweater with) a round high close-fitting neck.

tusk n long pointed tooth of an elephant, walrus, etc.

tussle ❶ n, v fight or scuffle.

tussock n tuft of grass.

tutelage [**tew**-till-lij] n **1** instruction or guidance, esp. by a tutor. **2** state of being supervised by a guardian or tutor. **tutelary** [**tew**-till-lar-ee] adj.

tutor ❶ n **1** person teaching individuals or small groups. ▷ v **2** act as a tutor to. **tutorial** n period of instruction with a tutor.

tutti adj, adv Music to be performed by the whole orchestra or choir.

tutti-frutti n ice cream or other sweet food containing small pieces of candied or fresh fruits.

tutu n short stiff skirt worn by ballerinas.

tuxedo n, pl **-dos** US & Canad dinner jacket.

TV television.

twaddle ❶ n silly or pretentious talk or writing.

twain n obs two.

twang n **1** sharp ringing sound. **2** nasal speech. ▷ v **3** (cause to) make a twang. **twangy** adj.

tweak ❶ v **1** pinch or twist sharply. ▷ n **2** tweaking.

twee adj informal too sentimental, sweet, or pretty.

tweed n **1** thick woollen cloth. ▷ pl **2** suit of tweed. **tweedy** adj **1** of or made of tweed. **2** showing a fondness for country life, often associated with wearers of tweed.

tweet n **1** chirp. **2** post a short message on the Twitter website. ▷ n **3** chirp. **4** short message posted on the Twitter website. **tweeter** n loudspeaker reproducing high-frequency sounds.

tweezers pl n small pincer-like tool.

twelve adj, n two more than ten. **twelfth** adj, n (of) number twelve in a series.

twenty adj, n two times ten. **twentieth** adj, n **twenty-four-seven**, 24/7 adv informal all the time.

twerp n informal silly person.

twice adv two times.

twiddle v fiddle or twirl in an idle way. **twiddle one's thumbs** be bored, have nothing to do.

twig[1] ❶ n small branch or shoot.

———————————— THESAURUS ————————————

turnout n = **attendance**, assembly, audience, congregation, crowd, gate, number, throng

turnover n **1** = **output**, business, productivity **3** = **movement**, change, coming and going

turn up v **1** = **arrive**, appear, attend, come, put in an appearance, show one's face, show up (inf) **2 a** = **find**, dig up, disclose, discover, expose, reveal, unearth **b** = **come to light**, crop up (inf), pop up **3** = **increase**, amplify, boost, enhance, intensify, raise

tussle n = **fight**, battle, brawl, conflict, contest, scrap (inf), scuffle, struggle

▷ v = **fight**, battle, grapple, scrap (inf), scuffle, struggle, vie, wrestle

tutor n **1** = **teacher**, coach, educator, guardian, guide, guru, instructor, lecturer, mentor ▷ v **2** = **teach**, coach, drill, educate, guide, instruct, school, train

twaddle n = **nonsense**, claptrap (inf), drivel, garbage (inf), gobbledegook (inf), kak (S Afr sl), poppycock (inf), rubbish, waffle (inf, chiefly Brit)

tweak v, n **1, 2** = **twist**, jerk, pinch, pull, squeeze

twig[1] n = **branch**, shoot, spray, sprig, stick

twig² ❶ v **twigging, twigged** *informal* realize or understand.

twilight ❶ n **1** soft dim light just after sunset. **2** period in which strength or importance is gradually declining. **twilit** *adj*.

twill n fabric woven to produce parallel ridges.

twin ❶ n **1** one of a pair, esp. of two children born at one birth. ▷ v **twinning, twinned 2** pair or be paired. **twin town** *Brit* town that has cultural and social links with a foreign town.

twine ❶ n **1** string or cord. ▷ v **2** twist or coil round.

twinge ❶ n sudden sharp pain or emotional pang.

twinkle ❶ v **1** shine brightly but intermittently. ▷ n **2** flickering brightness. **in the twinkling of an eye** in a very short time.

twirl ❶ v **1** turn or spin around quickly. **2** twist or wind, esp. idly.

twist ❶ v **1** turn out of the natural position. **2** distort or pervert. **3** wind or twine. ▷ n **4** twisting. **5** twisted thing. **6** unexpected development in the plot of a film, book, etc. **7** bend or curve. **8** distortion. **twisted** *adj* (of a person) cruel or perverted. **twister** n *informal* swindler.

twit¹ v **twitting, twitted** poke fun at or tease (someone).

twit² ❶ n *informal* foolish person.

twitch ❶ v **1** move spasmodically. **2** pull sharply. ▷ n **3** nervous muscular spasm. **4** sharp pull.

twitter v **1** (of birds) utter chirping sounds. **2** talk nervously. ▷ n **3** act or sound of twittering. **4** (**T-**) ® website where people can post short messages, up to 140 characters in length.

two ❶ *adj, n* one more than one. **two-edged** *adj* (of a remark) having both a favourable and an unfavourable interpretation. **two-faced** *adj* deceitful, hypocritical. **two-ply** *adj* having two layers or strands. **two-stroke** *adj* (of an internal-combustion engine) making one explosion to every two strokes of the piston. **two-time** v *informal* deceive (a lover) by having an affair with someone else. **two-way** *adj* **1** moving in, or allowing movement in, two opposite directions. **2** involving mutual involvement or cooperation. **3** (of a radio or transmitter) capable of both transmission and reception of messages.

TX Texas.

tycoon ❶ n powerful wealthy businessman.

tyke n *informal* small cheeky child.

tympanum n, pl **-nums, -na 1** cavity of the middle ear. **2** tympanic membrane. **3** *Architecture* space between the arch and the lintel above

---

THESAURUS

twig² v *Inf* = **understand**, catch on (*inf*), comprehend, fathom, find out, get, grasp, make out, rumble (*Brit inf*), see, tumble to (*inf*)

twilight n **1** = **dusk**, dimness, evening, gloaming (*Scot or poet*), gloom, half-light, sundown, sunset

twin n **1** = **double**, clone, counterpart, duplicate, fellow, likeness, lookalike, match, mate ▷ v **2** = **pair**, couple, join, link, match, yoke

twine n **1** = **string**, cord, yarn ▷ v **2** = **coil**, bend, curl, encircle, loop, spiral, twist, wind

twinge n = **pain**, pang, prick, spasm, stab, stitch

twinkle v **1** = **sparkle**, blink, flash, flicker, gleam, glint, glisten, glitter, shimmer, shine ▷ n **2** = **sparkle**, flash, flicker, gleam, glimmer, shimmer, spark

twirl v **1** = **turn**, pirouette, pivot, revolve, rotate, spin, wheel, whirl **2** = **twist**, wind

twist v **1** = **screw**, curl, spin, swivel, wrap, wring **2** = **distort**, contort, screw up **3** = **wind**, coil ▷ n **4** = **wind**, coil, curl, spin, swivel **6** = **development**, change, revelation, slant, surprise, turn, variation **7** = **curve**, arc, bend, meander, turn, undulation, zigzag **8** = **distortion**, defect, deformation, flaw, imperfection, kink, warp

twit² n *Inf* = **fool**, ass, chump (*inf*), halfwit, idiot, nincompoop, numbskull *or* numskull, prat (*sl*), twerp *or* twirp (*inf*)

twitch v **1** = **jerk**, flutter, jump, squirm **2** = **pull**, pluck, tug, yank ▷ n **3** = **jerk**, flutter, jump, spasm, tic

two-faced *adj* = **hypocritical**, deceitful, dissembling, duplicitous, false, insincere, treacherous, untrustworthy

tycoon n = **magnate**, baron, capitalist, fat cat (*sl, chiefly US*), financier, industrialist, mogul, plutocrat

t

a door. **tympanic** *adj* **tympanic membrane** thin membrane separating the external ear from the middle ear.

type ❶ *n* **1** class or category. **2** *informal* person, esp. of a specified kind. **3** block with a raised character used for printing. **4** printed text. ▷ *v* **5** print with a typewriter or word processor. **6** typify. **7** classify. **typist** *n* person who types with a typewriter or word processor. **typecast** *v* continually cast (an actor or actress) in similar roles. **typeface** *n Printing* style of the type. **typescript** *n* typewritten document. **typewriter** *n* machine which prints a character when the appropriate key is pressed.

typhoid fever *n* acute infectious feverish disease.

typhoon ❶ *n* violent tropical storm.

typhus *n* infectious feverish disease.

typical ❶ *adj* true to type, characteristic. **typically** *adv* **typify** *v* **-fying, -fied** be typical of.

typography *n* art or style of printing. **typographical** *adj* **typographer** *n*.

tyrannosaurus [tirr-ran-oh-**sore**-uss] *n* large two-footed flesh-eating dinosaur.

tyrant ❶ *n* **1** oppressive or cruel ruler. **2** person who exercises authority oppressively. **tyrannical** *adj* like a tyrant, oppressive. **tyrannize** *v* exert power (over) oppressively or cruelly. **tyrannous** *adj* **tyranny** *n* tyrannical rule.

tyre *n* rubber ring, usu. inflated, over the rim of a vehicle's wheel to grip the road.

tyro *n, pl* **-ros** novice or beginner.

tzar *n* same as TSAR.

tzetze fly *n* same as TSETSE FLY.

⸺ THESAURUS ⸺

type *n* **1** = **kind**, category, class, genre, group, order, sort, species, style, variety

typhoon *n* = **storm**, cyclone, squall, tempest, tornado

typical *adj* = **characteristic**, archetypal, average, model, normal, orthodox, representative, standard, stock, usual

typify *v* = **represent**, characterize, embody, epitomize, exemplify, illustrate, personify, sum up, symbolize

tyrannical *adj* = **oppressive**, authoritarian, autocratic, cruel, despotic, dictatorial, domineering, high-handed, imperious, overbearing, tyrannous

tyranny *n* = **oppression**, absolutism, authoritarianism, autocracy, cruelty, despotism, dictatorship, high-handedness, imperiousness

tyrant *n* = **dictator**, absolutist, authoritarian, autocrat, bully, despot, martinet, oppressor, slave-driver

t

U *Chemistry* uranium.

UB40 *n Brit* registration card issued to an unemployed person.

ubiquitous ❶ [yew-**bik**-wit-uss] *adj* being or seeming to be everywhere at once. **ubiquity** *n*.

U-boat *n* German submarine.

udder *n* large baglike milk-producing gland of cows, sheep, or goats.

UDI Unilateral Declaration of Independence.

UEFA Union of European Football Associations.

UFO unidentified flying object.

ugh [**uhh**] *interj* exclamation of disgust.

ugly ❶ *adj* **uglier**, **ugliest 1** of unpleasant appearance. **2** ominous or menacing. **ugliness** *n*.

UHF ultrahigh frequency.

UHT (of milk or cream) ultra-heat-treated.

UK United Kingdom.

ukulele, ukelele [yew-kal-**lay**-lee] *n* small guitar with four strings.

ulcer ❶ *n* open sore on the surface of the skin or mucous membrane. **ulcerated** *adj* made or becoming ulcerous. **ulceration** *n* **ulcerous** *adj* of, like, or characterized by ulcers.

ulna *n*, *pl* **-nae**, **-nas** inner and longer of the two bones of the human forearm.

ulster *n* man's heavy double-breasted overcoat.

ulterior ❶ [ult-**ear**-ee-or] *adj* (of an aim, reason, etc.) concealed or hidden, e.g. *ulterior motives*.

ultimate ❶ *adj* **1** final in a series or process. **2** highest or supreme. **3** most extreme. **ultimately** *adv*.

ultimatum [ult-im-**may**-tum] *n* final warning stating that action will be taken unless certain conditions are met.

ultra- *prefix* **1** beyond a specified extent, range, or limit, e.g. *ultrasonic*. **2** extremely, e.g. *ultramodern*.

ultrahigh frequency *n* radio frequency between 3000 and 300 megahertz.

ultramarine *adj* vivid blue.

ultrasonic *adj* of or producing sound waves with a higher frequency than the human ear can hear.

ultrasound *n* ultrasonic waves, used in medical diagnosis and therapy and in echo sounding.

ultraviolet *adj*, *n* (of) light beyond the limit of visibility at the violet end of the spectrum.

ululate [**yewl**-yew-late] *v* howl or wail. **ululation** *n*.

umbel *n* umbrella-like flower cluster with the stalks springing from the central point. **umbelliferous** *adj* denoting a plant with flowers in umbels.

umber *adj* dark brown to reddish-brown.

umbilical [um-**bill**-ik-al] *adj* of the navel. **umbilical cord** long flexible tube of blood vessels that connects a fetus with the placenta.

umbra *n*, *pl* **-brae**, **-bras** shadow, esp. the shadow cast by the moon onto the earth during a solar eclipse.

umbrage *n* **take umbrage** feel offended or upset.

umbrella *n* **1** portable device used for protection against rain, consisting of a folding frame covered in material attached to a central rod. **2** single organization, idea, etc. that contains or covers many different organizations, ideas, etc.

———————— **THESAURUS** ————————

ubiquitous *adj* = **everywhere**, ever-present, omnipresent, pervasive, universal

ugly *adj* **1** = **unattractive**, distasteful, homely (*chiefly US*), horrid, ill-favoured, plain, unlovely, unpleasant, unprepossessing, unsightly **2** = **ominous**, baleful, dangerous, menacing, sinister

ulcer *n* = **sore**, abscess, boil, gumboil, peptic ulcer, pustule

ulterior *adj* = **hidden**, concealed, covert, secret, undisclosed

ultimate *adj* **1** = **final**, end, last **2, 3** = **supreme**, extreme, greatest, highest, paramount, superlative, utmost

ultimately *adv* **1** = **finally**, after all, at last, eventually, in due time, in the end, sooner or later

umiak [oo-mee-ak] *n* Inuit boat made of skins.

umlaut [oom-lowt] *n* mark (¨) placed over a vowel, esp. in German, to indicate a change in its sound.

umpire ❶ *n* **1** official who rules on the playing of a game. ▷ *v* **2** act as umpire in (a game).

umpteen *adj informal* very many. **umpteenth** *n, adj.*

UN United Nations.

un- *prefix* **1** not, e.g. *unidentified*. **2** denoting reversal of an action, e.g. *untie*. **3** denoting removal from, e.g. *unthrone*.

unabated *adv* without any reduction in force, e.g. *the storm continued unabated*.

unable ❶ *adj* **unable to** lacking the necessary power, ability, or authority to (do something).

unaccountable ❶ *adj* **1** unable to be explained. **2** (foll. by *to*) not answerable to. **unaccountably** *adv*.

unadulterated *adj* with nothing added, pure.

unaffected ❶ *adj* **1** unpretentious, natural, sincere. **2** not influenced or moved by something.

unanimous ❶ [yew-**nan**-im-uss] *adj* **1** in complete agreement. **2** agreed by all. **unanimously** *adv* **unanimity** *n*.

unannounced *adv* without warning, e.g. *he turned up unannounced*.

unapproachable ❶ *adj* discouraging friendliness, aloof.

unarmed ❶ *adj* without weapons.

unassailable ❶ *adj* unable to be attacked or disputed.

unassuming ❶ *adj* modest or unpretentious.

unattached ❶ *adj* **1** not connected with any specific group or organization. **2** not married or involved in a steady relationship.

unavailing *adj* useless or futile.

unavoidable ❶ *adj* unable to be avoided or prevented. **unavoidably** *adv*.

unaware ❶ *adj* not aware or conscious, e.g. *unaware of the danger*. **unawares** *adv* **1** by surprise, e.g. *caught unawares*. **2** without knowing.

unbalanced ❶ *adj* **1** biased or one-sided. **2** mentally deranged.

unbearable ❶ *adj* not able to be endured. **unbearably** *adv*.

———————— THESAURUS ————————

umpire *n* **1** = **referee**, arbiter, arbitrator, judge ▷ *v* **2** = **referee**, adjudicate, arbitrate, judge

unable *adj* **unable to** = **incapable**, impotent, ineffectual, powerless, unfit, unqualified

unaccountable *adj* **1** = **inexplicable**, baffling, mysterious, odd, puzzling, unexplainable, unfathomable **2** (foll. by *to*) = **not answerable to**, exempt, not responsible to

unaffected *adj* **1** = **natural**, artless, genuine, plain, simple, sincere, unpretentious **2** = **impervious**, proof, unmoved, unresponsive, untouched

unanimity *n* **1** = **agreement**, accord, assent, concord, concurrence, consensus, harmony, like-mindedness, unison

unanimous *adj* **1** = **agreed**, common, concerted, harmonious, in agreement, like-minded, united

unanimously *adv* **2** = **without exception**, nem. con., with one accord

unapproachable *adj* = **unfriendly**, aloof, chilly, cool, distant, remote, reserved, standoffish

unarmed *adj* = **defenceless**, exposed, helpless, open, unprotected, weak

unassailable *adj* = **impregnable**, invincible, invulnerable, secure

unassuming *adj* = **modest**, humble, quiet, reserved, retiring, self-effacing, unassertive, unobtrusive, unpretentious

unattached *adj* **1** = **free**, independent **2** = **single**, available, not spoken for, unengaged, unmarried

unavoidable *adj* = **inevitable**, certain, fated, inescapable

unaware *adj* = **ignorant**, not in the loop (*inf*), oblivious, unconscious, uninformed, unknowing

unawares *adv* **1** = **by surprise**, off guard, suddenly, unexpectedly **2** = **unknowingly**, accidentally, by accident, inadvertently, unwittingly

unbalanced *adj* **1** = **biased**, one-sided, partial, partisan, prejudiced, unfair **2** = **deranged**, crazy, demented, disturbed, eccentric, insane, irrational, mad, *non compos mentis*, not all there, unhinged, unstable

unbearable *adj* = **intolerable**, insufferable, too much (*inf*), unacceptable

unbecoming ⊙ *adj* unattractive or unsuitable.

unbeknown *adv* **unbeknown to** without the knowledge of (a person).

unbelievable ⊙ *adj* **1** too unlikely to be believed. **2** *informal* marvellous, amazing. **3** *informal* terrible, shocking. **unbelievably** *adv*.

unbend ⊙ *v informal* become less strict or more informal in one's attitudes or behaviour.

unbending ⊙ *adj* rigid or inflexible.

unbidden *adj* not ordered or asked.

unborn ⊙ *adj* not yet born.

unbosom *v* relieve (oneself) of (secrets or feelings) by telling someone.

unbridled ⊙ *adj* (of feelings or behaviour) not controlled in any way.

unburden ⊙ *v* relieve (one's mind or oneself) of a worry by confiding in someone.

uncalled-for ⊙ *adj* not fair or justified.

uncanny ⊙ *adj* weird or mysterious. **uncannily** *adv*.

unceremonious *adj* **1** relaxed and informal. **2** abrupt or rude.

unceremoniously *adv*.

uncertain ⊙ *adj* **1** not able to be accurately known or predicted. **2** not able to be depended upon. **3** changeable. **uncertainty** *n*.

uncharacteristic *adj* not typical. **uncharacteristically** *adv*.

uncharitable *adj* unkind or harsh. **uncharitably** *adv*.

un-Christian *adj* not in accordance with Christian principles.

uncivilized ⊙ *adj* **1** (of a tribe or people) not yet civilized. **2** lacking culture or sophistication.

uncle *n* **1** brother of one's father or mother. **2** husband of one's aunt.

unclean ⊙ *adj* lacking moral, spiritual, or physical cleanliness.

uncomfortable ⊙ *adj* **1** not physically relaxed. **2** anxious or uneasy. **uncomfortably** *adv*.

uncommon ⊙ *adj* **1** not happening or encountered often. **2** in excess of what is normal, e.g. *an uncommon liking for honey*. **uncommonly** *adv*.

uncompromising ⊙ *adj* not prepared to compromise. **uncompromisingly** *adv*.

THESAURUS

unbecoming *adj* = **unattractive**, unbefitting, unflattering, unsightly, unsuitable

unbelievable *adj* **1** = **incredible**, astonishing, far-fetched, implausible, impossible, improbable, inconceivable, jaw-dropping, preposterous, unconvincing **2** *Inf* = **wonderful**, excellent, fabulous (*inf*), fantastic (*inf*), great (*inf*), splendid, superb, terrific (*inf*)

unbending *adj* = **inflexible**, firm, intractable, resolute, rigid, severe, strict, stubborn, tough, uncompromising

unborn *adj* = **expected**, awaited, embryonic

unbridled *adj* = **unrestrained**, excessive, intemperate, licentious, riotous, unchecked, unruly, wanton

unburden *v* = **confess**, confide, disclose, get (something) off one's chest (*inf*), reveal

uncalled-for *adj* = **unnecessary**, gratuitous, needless, undeserved, unjustified, unwarranted

uncanny *adj* = **weird**, mysterious, strange, supernatural, unearthly, unnatural

uncertain *adj* **1** = **unpredictable**, doubtful, indefinite, questionable, risky, speculative **2** = **unsure**, dubious, hazy, irresolute, unclear, unconfirmed, undecided, vague

uncertainty *n* **1** = **unpredictability**, ambiguity **2** = **doubt**, confusion, dubiety, hesitancy, indecision

uncivilized *adj* **1** = **primitive**, barbarian, savage, wild **2** = **uncouth**, boorish, coarse, philistine, uncultivated, uneducated

unclean *adj* = **dirty**, corrupt, defiled, evil, filthy, foul, impure, polluted, soiled, stained

uncomfortable *adj* **1** = **painful**, awkward, cramped, rough **2** = **uneasy**, awkward, discomfited, disturbed, embarrassed, troubled

uncommon *adj* **1** = **rare**, infrequent, munted (*NZ sl*), novel, odd, peculiar, queer, scarce, strange, unusual **2** = **extraordinary**, distinctive, exceptional, notable, outstanding, remarkable, special

uncommonly *adv* **1** = **rarely**, hardly ever, infrequently, occasionally, seldom **2** = **exceptionally**, particularly, very

uncompromising *adj* = **inflexible**, firm, inexorable, intransigent, rigid,

unconcerned ⊙ *adj* lacking in concern or involvement. **unconcernedly** [un-kon-**sern**-id-lee] *adv*.

unconditional ⊙ *adj* without conditions or limitations. **unconditionally** *adv*.

unconscionable *adj* **1** having no principles, unscrupulous. **2** excessive in amount or degree.

unconscious ⊙ *adj* **1** lacking normal awareness through the senses. **2** not aware of one's actions or behaviour. ▷ *n* **3** part of the mind containing instincts and ideas that exist without one's awareness. **unconsciously** *adv* **unconsciousness** *n*.

unconventional ⊙ *adj* not conforming to accepted rules or standards.

uncooperative *adj* not willing to help other people with what they are doing.

uncouth ⊙ *adj* lacking in good manners, refinement, or grace.

uncover ⊙ *v* **1** reveal or disclose. **2** remove the cover, top, etc., from.

unction *n* act of anointing with oil in sacramental ceremonies.

unctuous *adj* pretending to be kind and concerned.

undecided ⊙ *adj* **1** not having made up one's mind. **2** (of an issue or problem) not agreed or decided upon.

undeniable ⊙ *adj* unquestionably true. **undeniably** *adv*.

under ⊙ *prep, adv* **1** indicating movement to or position beneath the underside or base. ▷ *prep* **2** less than. **3** subject to.

under- *prefix* **1** below, e.g. *underground*. **2** insufficient or insufficiently, e.g. *underrate*.

underachieve *v* fail to achieve a performance appropriate to one's age or talents. **underachiever** *n*.

underage *adj* below the required or standard age.

underarm *adj* **1** *Sport* denoting a style of throwing, bowling, or serving in which the hand is swung below shoulder level. **2** of or denoting the armpit. ▷ *adv* **3** *Sport* in an underarm style.

undercarriage *n* **1** landing gear of an aircraft. **2** framework supporting the body of a vehicle.

underclass *n* class consisting of the most disadvantaged people, such as the long-term unemployed.

undercoat *n* coat of paint applied before the final coat.

undercover ⊙ *adj* done or acting in secret.

undercurrent ⊙ *n* **1** current that is not apparent at the surface. **2** underlying opinion or emotion.

undercut *v* charge less than (a competitor) to obtain trade.

underdeveloped *adj* **1** immature or undersized. **2** (of a country) lacking the finance, industries, and organization necessary to advance.

———————— THESAURUS ————————

strict, tough, unbending
unconcerned *adj* = **indifferent**, aloof, apathetic, cool, detached, dispassionate, distant, uninterested, unmoved

unconditional *adj* = **absolute**, complete, entire, full, outright, positive, total, unlimited, unqualified, unreserved

unconscious *adj* **1** = **senseless**, insensible, knocked out, out, out cold, stunned **2 a** = **unintentional**, accidental, inadvertent, unwitting **b** = **unaware**, ignorant, oblivious, unknowing

unconventional *adj* = **unusual**, eccentric, individual, irregular, nonconformist, odd, offbeat, original, outré, unorthodox

uncouth *adj* = **coarse**, barbaric, boorish, crude, graceless, ill-mannered, loutish, oafish, rough, rude, vulgar

uncover *v* **1** = **reveal**, disclose, divulge, expose, make known **2** = **open**, bare, show, strip, unwrap

undecided *adj* **1** = **unsure**, dithering, hesitant, in two minds, irresolute, torn, uncertain **2** = **unsettled**, debatable, iffy (*inf*), indefinite, moot, open, unconcluded, undetermined

undeniable *adj* = **certain**, clear, incontrovertible, indisputable, obvious, sure, unquestionable

under *prep* **1** = **below**, beneath, underneath **3** = **subject to**, governed by, secondary to, subordinate to ▷ *adv* **1** = **below**, beneath, down, lower

undercover *adj* = **secret**, concealed, covert, hidden, private

undercurrent *n* **1** = **undertow**, riptide **2** = **undertone**, atmosphere, feeling,

u

underdog ❶ n person or team in a weak or underprivileged position.

underdone adj not cooked enough.

underestimate ❶ v 1 make too low an estimate of. 2 not realize the full potential of.

underfelt n thick felt laid under a carpet to increase insulation.

underfoot adv under the feet.

undergarment n any piece of underwear.

undergo ❶ v experience, endure, or sustain.

undergraduate n person studying in a university for a first degree.

underground ❶ adj 1 occurring, situated, used, or going below ground level. 2 secret. ▷ n 3 electric passenger railway operated in underground tunnels. 4 movement dedicated to overthrowing a government or occupation forces.

undergrowth ❶ n small trees and bushes growing beneath taller trees in a wood or forest.

underhand ❶ adj sly, deceitful, and secretive.

underlay n felt or rubber laid beneath a carpet to increase insulation and resilience.

underlie ❶ v 1 lie or be placed under. 2 be the foundation, cause, or basis of. **underlying** adj fundamental or basic.

underline ❶ v 1 draw a line under. 2 state forcibly, emphasize.

underling n subordinate.

undermine ❶ v 1 weaken gradually. 2 (of the sea or wind) wear away the base of (cliffs).

underneath prep, adv 1 under or beneath. ▷ adj, n 2 lower (part or surface).

underpants pl n man's undergarment for the lower part of the body.

underpass n section of a road that passes under another road or a railway line.

underpin v give strength or support to.

underprivileged ❶ adj lacking the rights and advantages of other members of society.

underrate ❶ v not realize the full potential of. **underrated** adj.

underseal n coating of tar etc. applied to the underside of a motor vehicle to prevent corrosion.

undersecretary n senior civil servant or junior minister in a government department.

underside n bottom or lower surface.

undersized ❶ adj smaller than normal.

underskirt n skirtlike garment worn under a skirt or dress, petticoat.

understand ❶ v 1 know and comprehend the nature or meaning of. 2 realize or grasp (something).

THESAURUS

hint, overtone, sense, suggestion, tendency, tinge, vibes (sl)

underdog n = **weaker party**, little fellow (inf), outsider

underestimate v 2 = **underrate**, belittle, minimize, miscalculate, undervalue

undergo v = **experience**, bear, endure, go through, stand, suffer, sustain

underground adj 1 = **subterranean**, buried, covered 2 = **secret**, clandestine, covert, hidden ▷ n 3 = **the tube**, the metro, the subway 4 = **the Resistance**, partisans

undergrowth n = **scrub**, bracken, briars, brush, underbrush

underhand adj = **sly**, crafty, deceitful, devious, dishonest, furtive, secret, sneaky, stealthy

underline v 1 = **underscore**, mark 2 = **emphasize**, accentuate, highlight, stress

underlying adj = **fundamental**, basic, elementary, intrinsic, primary, prime

undermine v 1 = **weaken**, disable, sabotage, sap, subvert

underprivileged adj = **disadvantaged**, deprived, destitute, impoverished, needy, poor

underrate v = **underestimate**, belittle, discount, undervalue

undersized adj = **stunted**, dwarfish, miniature, pygmy or pigmy, small

understand v 2 = **comprehend**, conceive, fathom, follow, get, grasp, perceive, realize, see, take in 3 = **believe**, assume, gather, presume, suppose, think

understandable adj 2 = **reasonable**, justifiable, legitimate, natural, to be expected

understanding n 1 = **perception**, appreciation, awareness, comprehension, discernment, grasp, insight, judgment, knowledge, sense 2 = **interpretation**, belief, idea, judgment, notion, opinion,

u

3 assume, infer, or believe.
understandable *adj* **understandably**
adv **understanding** *n* **1** ability to
learn, judge, or make decisions.
2 personal interpretation of a subject.
3 mutual agreement, usu. an informal
or private one. ▷ *adj* **4** kind and
sympathetic.
understate *v* **1** describe or represent
(something) in restrained terms.
2 state that (something, such as a
number) is less than it is.
understatement *n*.
understudy **❶** *n* **1** actor who studies a
part in order to be able to replace the
usual actor if necessary. ▷ *v* **2** act as
an understudy for.
undertake **❶** *v* **1** agree or commit
oneself to (something) or to do
(something). **2** promise. **undertaking**
n **1** task or enterprise. **2** agreement to
do something.
undertaker *n* person whose job is to
prepare corpses for burial or
cremation and organize funerals.
undertone **❶** *n* **1** quiet tone of voice.
2 underlying quality or feeling.
undertow *n* strong undercurrent
flowing in a different direction from
the surface current.

underwater **❶** *adj, adv* (situated,
occurring, or for use) below the
surface of the sea, a lake, or a river.
underwear **❶** *n* clothing worn under
the outer garments and next to the
skin.
underworld **❶** *n* **1** criminals and their
associates. **2** *Greek & Roman
myth* regions below the earth's surface
regarded as the abode of the dead.
underwrite **❶** *v* **1** accept financial
responsibility for (a commercial
project). **2** sign and issue (an
insurance policy), thus accepting
liability. **underwriter** *n*.
undesirable **❶** *adj* **1** not desirable or
pleasant, objectionable. ▷ *n*
2 objectionable person.
undies *pl n informal* underwear, esp.
women's.
undistinguished *adj* not particularly
good or bad, mediocre.
undo **❶** *v* **1** open, unwrap. **2** reverse
the effects of. **3** cause the downfall of.
undone *adj* **undoing** *n* cause of
someone's downfall.
undoubted **❶** *adj* certain or
indisputable. **undoubtedly** *adv*.
undress **❶** *v* **1** take off the clothes of
(oneself or another person). ▷ *n* **2** in a

—————————— THESAURUS ——————————

perception, view **3** = **agreement**,
accord, pact ▷ *adj* **4** = **sympathetic**,
compassionate, considerate, kind,
patient, sensitive, tolerant
understudy *n* **1** = **stand-in**,
replacement, reserve, substitute
undertake *v* **1** = **agree**, bargain,
contract, engage **2** = **promise**,
guarantee, pledge
undertaking *n* **1** = **task**, affair,
attempt, business, effort, endeavour,
enterprise, operation, project, venture
2 = **promise**, assurance, commitment,
pledge, vow, word
undertone *n* **1** = **murmur**, whisper
2 = **undercurrent**, hint, suggestion,
tinge, touch, trace
underwater *adj* = **submerged**,
submarine, sunken
underwear *n* = **underclothes**,
lingerie, undergarments, underthings,
undies (*inf*)
underworld *n* **1** = **criminals**, gangland
(*inf*), gangsters, organized crime
2 *Greek & Roman myth* = **nether world**,
Hades, nether regions
underwrite *v* **1** = **finance**, back, fund,

guarantee, insure, sponsor, subsidize
2 = **sign**, endorse, initial
undesirable *adj* **1** = **objectionable**,
disagreeable, distasteful,
unacceptable, unattractive,
unsuitable, unwanted, unwelcome
undo *v* **1** = **open**, disentangle, loose,
unbutton, unfasten, untie
2 = **reverse**, annul, cancel, invalidate,
neutralize, offset **3** = **ruin**, defeat,
destroy, overturn, quash, shatter,
subvert, undermine, upset, wreck
undoing *n* = **ruin**, collapse, defeat,
disgrace, downfall, overthrow,
reversal, shame
undone *adj* **3** = **ruined**, betrayed,
destroyed, forlorn, hapless, munted
(*NZ sl*), overcome, prostrate, wretched
undoubted *adj* = **certain**,
acknowledged, definite, indisputable,
indubitable, sure, undisputed,
unquestioned
undoubtedly *adv* = **certainly**,
assuredly, definitely, doubtless, surely,
without doubt
undress *v* **1** = **strip**, disrobe, shed, take
off one's clothes ▷ *n* **2** **in a state of**

u

state of undress naked or nearly naked.

undue ⊕ *adj* greater than is reasonable, excessive. **unduly** *adv*.

undulate *v* move in waves. **undulation** *n*.

undying ⊕ *adj* never ending, eternal.

unearned income *n* income from property or investments rather than work.

unearth ⊕ *v* **1** reveal or discover by searching. **2** dig up out of the earth.

unearthly ⊕ *adj* **1** ghostly or eerie. **2** ridiculous or unreasonable, e.g. *an unearthly hour*.

uneasy ⊕ *adj* **1** (of a person) anxious or apprehensive. **2** (of a condition) precarious or uncomfortable. **uneasily** *adv* **uneasiness** *n* **unease** *n* **1** feeling of anxiety. **2** state of dissatisfaction.

unemployed ⊕ *adj* **1** out of work. ▷ *pl n* **2 the unemployed** people who are out of work. **unemployment** *n*.

unequivocal ⊕ *adj* completely clear in meaning. **unequivocally** *adv*.

unerring ⊕ *adj* never mistaken, consistently accurate.

UNESCO United Nations Educational, Scientific, and Cultural Organization.

uneven ⊕ *adj* **1** not level or flat. **2** not consistent in quality, e.g. *an uneven performance*. **3** not fairly matched, e.g. *an uneven race*.

unexceptionable *adj* beyond criticism or objection.

unexceptional ⊕ *adj* ordinary or normal.

unexpected ⊕ *adj* surprising or unforeseen. **unexpectedly** *adv*.

unfailing ⊕ *adj* continuous or reliable. **unfailingly** *adv*.

unfair ⊕ *adj* not right, fair, or just. **unfairly** *adv* **unfairness** *n*.

unfaithful ⊕ *adj* **1** having sex with someone other than one's regular partner. **2** not true to a promise or vow. **unfaithfulness** *n*.

unfathomable ⊕ *adj* too strange or too complicated to be understood.

THESAURUS

undress = **naked**, nude

undue *adj* = **excessive**, extreme, improper, inappropriate, needless, uncalled-for, unnecessary, unwarranted

unduly *adv* = **excessively**, overly, unnecessarily, unreasonably

undying *adj* = **eternal**, constant, deathless, everlasting, infinite, permanent, perpetual, unending

unearth *v* **1** = **discover**, expose, find, reveal, uncover **2** = **dig up**, dredge up, excavate, exhume

unearthly *adj* **1** = **eerie**, ghostly, phantom, spectral, spooky (*inf*), strange, supernatural, uncanny, weird

uneasiness *n* **1** = **anxiety**, disquiet, doubt, misgiving, qualms, trepidation, worry

uneasy *adj* **1** = **anxious**, disturbed, edgy, nervous, on edge, perturbed, troubled, uncomfortable, worried **2** = **precarious**, awkward, insecure, shaky, strained, tense, uncomfortable

unemployed *adj* **1** = **out of work**, idle, jobless, laid off, redundant

unequivocal *adj* = **clear**, absolute, certain, definite, explicit, incontrovertible, indubitable, manifest, plain, unambiguous

unerring *adj* = **accurate**, exact, infallible, perfect, sure, unfailing

uneven *adj* **1** = **rough**, bumpy, lopsided **2** = **variable**, broken, fitful, irregular, jerky, patchy, spasmodic **3** = **unequal**, ill-matched, unfair

unexceptional *adj* = **ordinary**, commonplace, conventional, mediocre, normal, pedestrian, run-of-the-mill, undistinguished, unremarkable

unexpected *adj* = **unforeseen**, abrupt, chance, fortuitous, sudden, surprising, unanticipated, unlooked-for, unpredictable

unfailing *adj* **a** = **continuous**, boundless, endless, persistent, unflagging **b** = **reliable**, certain, dependable, faithful, loyal, staunch, sure, true

unfair *adj* **a** = **unscrupulous**, dishonest, unethical, unsporting, wrongful **b** = **biased**, bigoted, one-sided, partial, partisan, prejudiced, unjust

unfaithful *adj* **1** = **faithless**, adulterous, inconstant, two-timing (*inf*), untrue **2** = **disloyal**, deceitful, faithless, false, traitorous, treacherous, untrustworthy

unfathomable *adj* = **baffling**, deep, impenetrable, incomprehensible, indecipherable, inexplicable, profound

u

unfavourable ❶ *adj* **1** unlikely to produce the desired outcome, inauspicious, e.g. *unfavourable weather conditions*. **2** disapproving, e.g. *an unfavourable opinion*. **unfavourably** *adv*.

unfeeling ❶ *adj* without sympathy.

unfit ❶ *adj* **1** unqualified or unsuitable. **2** in poor physical condition.

unflappable ❶ *adj informal* not easily upset. **unflappability** *n*.

unfold ❼ *v* **1** open or spread out from a folded state. **2** reveal or be revealed.

unfollow *v* stop following (a person) on a social networking site.

unforeseen *adj* surprising because not expected.

unforgettable *adj* impossible to forget, memorable. **unforgettably** *adv*.

unfortunate ❶ *adj* **1** unlucky, unsuccessful, or unhappy. **2** regrettable or unsuitable. ▷ *n* **3** unlucky person. **unfortunately** *adv*.

unfounded ❶ *adj* not based on facts or evidence.

unfriend *v* remove (a person) as a friend on a social networking site.

unfrock *v* deprive (a priest in holy orders) of his priesthood.

unfurl *v* unroll or unfold.

ungainly ❶ *adj* **-lier, -liest** lacking grace when moving. **ungainliness** *n*.

ungodly ❶ *adj* **1** *informal* unreasonable or outrageous, e.g. *an ungodly hour*. **2** wicked or sinful. **ungodliness** *n*.

ungovernable *adj* not able to be disciplined or restrained.

ungrateful *adj* not grateful or thankful.

unguarded ❶ *adj* **1** not protected. **2** incautious or careless.

unguent [**ung**-gwent] *n lit* ointment.

unhand *v old-fashioned or lit* release from one's grasp.

unhappy ❶ *adj* **1** sad or depressed. **2** unfortunate or wretched. **unhappily** *adv* **unhappiness** *n*.

unhealthy ❶ *adj* **1** likely to cause poor health. **2** not fit or well. **3** morbid, unnatural.

unheard-of ❶ *adj* **1** without precedent. **2** highly offensive or shocking.

unhinge *v* derange or unbalance (a person or his or her mind).

———————————— THESAURUS ————————————

unfavourable *adj* **1** = **adverse**, contrary, inauspicious, unfortunate, unlucky, unpropitious **2** = **hostile**, inimical, negative, unfriendly

unfeeling *adj* = **callous**, apathetic, cold, cruel, hardhearted, heartless, insensitive, pitiless, uncaring

unfit *adj* **1 a** = **incapable**, inadequate, incompetent, ineffective, no good, useless **b** = **unsuitable**, unqualified, unsuited **2** = **out of shape**, feeble, flabby, in poor condition, unhealthy

unflappable *adj Inf* = **imperturbable**, calm, collected, composed, cool, impassive, level-headed, self-possessed

unfold *v* **1** = **open**, expand, spread out, undo, unfurl, unravel, unroll, unwrap **2** = **reveal**, disclose, divulge, make known, present, show, uncover

unfortunate *adj* **1 a** = **unlucky**, cursed, doomed, hapless, ill-fated, unhappy, wretched **b** = **disastrous**, adverse, calamitous, unsuccessful **c** = **deplorable**, lamentable **2** = **regrettable**, unsuitable

unfounded *adj* = **groundless**, baseless, false, idle, spurious, unjustified

ungainly *adj* = **awkward**, clumsy,

inelegant, lumbering, ungraceful

ungodly *adj* **1** *Inf* = **unreasonable**, dreadful, intolerable, outrageous, unearthly **2** = **wicked**, corrupt, depraved, godless, immoral, impious, irreligious, profane, sinful

unguarded *adj* **1** = **unprotected**, defenceless, undefended, vulnerable **2** = **careless**, heedless, ill-considered, imprudent, incautious, rash, thoughtless, unthinking, unwary

unhappiness *n* **1** = **sadness**, blues, dejection, depression, despondency, gloom, heartache, low spirits, melancholy, misery, sorrow, wretchedness

unhappy *adj* **1** = **sad**, blue, dejected, depressed, despondent, downcast, melancholy, miserable, mournful, sorrowful **2** = **unlucky**, cursed, hapless, ill-fated, unfortunate, wretched

unhealthy *adj* **1** = **harmful**, detrimental, insalubrious, insanitary, unwholesome **2** = **sick**, ailing, crook (*Aust & NZ sl*), delicate, feeble, frail, infirm, invalid, sickly, unwell

unheard-of *adj* **1** = **unprecedented**, inconceivable, new, novel, obscure, singular, unfamiliar, unique, unknown **2** = **shocking**, disgraceful, outrageous, preposterous

unholy ❶ *adj* **1** immoral or wicked. **2** *informal* unnatural or outrageous, e.g. *an unholy mess*.

uni- *combining form* of, consisting of, or having only one, e.g. *unicellular*.

UNICEF *n* agency of United Nations that funds education and children's health.

unicorn *n* imaginary horselike creature with one horn growing from its forehead.

uniform ❶ *n* **1** special identifying set of clothes for the members of an organization, such as soldiers. ▷ *adj* **2** regular and even throughout, unvarying. **3** alike or like. **uniformly** *adv* **uniformity** *n*.

unify ❶ *v* **-fying, -fied** make or become one. **unification** *n*.

unilateral *adj* made or done by only one person or group. **unilaterally** *adv*.

unimpeachable *adj* completely honest and reliable.

uninterested ❶ *adj* having or showing no interest in someone or something.

union ❶ *n* **1** uniting or being united. **2** short for TRADE UNION. **3** association or confederation of individuals or groups for a common purpose. **unionist** *n* member or supporter of a trade union. **unionism** *n* **unionize** *v* organize (workers) into a trade union. **unionization** *n* **Union Jack, Flag** national flag of the United Kingdom.

unique ❶ [yoo-**neek**] *adj* **1** being the only one of a particular type. **2** without equal or like. **unique to** concerning or belonging to a particular person, thing, or group. **uniquely** *adv*.

unisex *adj* designed for use by both sexes.

unison ❶ *n* **1** complete agreement. **2** *Music* singing or playing of the same notes together at the same time. **in unison** at the same time as another person or other people.

UNISON *n* British trade union consisting mainly of council and hospital workers.

unit ❶ *n* **1** single undivided entity or whole. **2** group or individual regarded as a basic element of a larger whole. **3** fixed quantity etc., used as a standard of measurement. **4** piece of furniture designed to be fitted with other similar pieces, e.g. *kitchen units*. **unit trust** investment trust that issues units for public sale and invests the money in many different businesses.

Unitarian *n* person who believes that God is one being and rejects the Trinity. **Unitarianism** *n*.

unitary *adj* **1** consisting of a single undivided whole. **2** of a unit or units.

unite ❶ *v* **1** make or become an integrated whole. **2** (cause to) enter into an association or alliance.

unity ❶ *n* **1** state of being one. **2** mutual agreement.

THESAURUS

unholy *adj* **1** = **evil**, corrupt, profane, sinful, ungodly, wicked

unification *n* = **union**, alliance, amalgamation, coalescence, coalition, confederation, federation, uniting

uniform *n* **1** = **outfit**, costume, dress, garb, habit, livery, regalia, suit ▷ *adj* **2** = **unvarying**, consistent, constant, even, regular, smooth, unchanging **3** = **alike**, equal, like, same, similar

uniformity *n* **2, 3** = **regularity**, constancy, evenness, invariability, sameness, similarity

unify *v* = **unite**, amalgamate, combine, confederate, consolidate, join, merge

uninterested *adj* = **indifferent**, apathetic, blasé, bored, listless, unconcerned

union *n* **1** = **uniting**, accord, agreement, amalgamation, blend, combination, concord, conjunction, fusion, harmony, joining, mixture, unanimity, unison, unity **3** = **alliance**, association, coalition, confederacy, federation, league

unique *adj* **1** = **single**, lone, only, solitary **2** = **unparalleled**, matchless, unequalled, unmatched, without equal

unison *n* **1** = **agreement**, accord, concert, concord, harmony, unity

unit *n* **1** = **item**, entity, whole **2** = **part**, component, constituent, element, member, section, segment **3** = **measure**, measurement, quantity

unite *v* **1** = **join**, amalgamate, blend, combine, couple, fuse, link, merge, unify **2** = **cooperate**, ally, band, collaborate, join forces, pool

unity *n* **1** = **wholeness**, entity, integrity, oneness, singleness, union

u

universe ❶ n 1 whole of all existing matter, energy, and space. 2 the world. **universal** adj 1 of or typical of the whole of mankind or of nature. 2 existing everywhere. **universally** adv **universality** n.

university n, pl **-ties** institution of higher education with the authority to award degrees.

unkempt ❶ adj 1 (of the hair) not combed. 2 slovenly or untidy.

unkind ❶ adj unsympathetic or cruel. **unkindly** adv **unkindness** n.

unknown ❶ adj 1 not known. 2 not famous. ▷ n 3 unknown person, quantity, or thing.

unleaded adj (of petrol) containing less tetraethyl lead, in order to reduce environmental pollution.

unleash ❶ v set loose or cause (something bad).

unleavened [un-**lev**-vend] adj (of bread) made without yeast.

unless conj except under the circumstances that.

unlike ❶ adj 1 dissimilar or different. ▷ prep 2 not like or typical of.

unlikely ❶ adj improbable.

unload ❶ v 1 remove (cargo) from (a ship, lorry, or plane). 2 tell someone your problems or worries. 3 remove the ammunition from (a firearm).

unlooked-for ❶ adj unexpected or unforeseen.

unlucky ❶ adj 1 having bad luck, unfortunate. 2 ill-omened or inauspicious.

unman v cause to lose courage or nerve.

unmanned adj having no personnel or crew.

unmask ❶ v 1 remove the mask or disguise from. 2 (cause to) appear in true character.

unmentionable ❶ adj unsuitable as a topic of conversation.

unmistakable, unmistakeable ❶ adj not ambiguous, clear. **unmistakably, unmistakeably** adv.

unmitigated ❶ adj 1 not reduced or lessened in severity etc. 2 total and complete.

unmoved adj not affected by emotion, indifferent.

2 = **agreement**, accord, assent, concord, consensus, harmony, solidarity, unison
universal adj 1 = **widespread**, common, general, overarching, total, unlimited, whole, worldwide
universally adv 2 = **everywhere**, always, invariably, without exception
universe n 1 = **cosmos**, creation, macrocosm, nature
unkempt adj 1 = **uncombed**, shaggy, tousled 2 = **untidy**, dishevelled, disordered, messy, scruffy, slovenly, ungroomed
unkind adj = **cruel**, hardhearted, harsh, malicious, mean, nasty, spiteful, uncharitable, unfeeling, unfriendly, unsympathetic
unknown adj 1 **a** = **unidentified**, anonymous, nameless, uncharted, undiscovered, unexplored, unnamed **b** = **hidden**, concealed, dark, mysterious, secret, unrevealed **c** = **strange**, alien, new 2 = **obscure**, humble, unfamiliar
unleash v = **release**, free, let go, let loose
unlike adj 1 = **different**, dissimilar, distinct, diverse, not alike, opposite, unequal

unlikely adj = **improbable**, doubtful, faint, implausible, incredible, questionable, remote, slight, unbelievable
unload v 1 = **empty**, discharge, dump, lighten, relieve, unpack
unlooked-for adj = **unexpected**, chance, fortuitous, surprising, unanticipated, unforeseen, unpredicted
unlucky adj 1 = **unfortunate**, cursed, hapless, luckless, miserable, unhappy, wretched 2 = **ill-fated**, doomed, inauspicious, ominous, unfavourable
unmask v 1, 2 = **reveal**, disclose, discover, expose, lay bare, uncover
unmentionable adj = **taboo**, forbidden, indecent, obscene, scandalous, shameful, shocking, unspeakable
unmistakable, unmistakeable adj = **clear**, certain, distinct, evident, manifest, obvious, plain, sure, unambiguous
unmitigated adj 1 = **unrelieved**, intense, persistent, unalleviated, unbroken, undiminished 2 = **complete**, absolute, arrant, downright, outright, sheer, thorough, utter

u

unnatural ❶ adj **1** strange and frightening because not usual. **2** not in accordance with accepted standards of behaviour. **unnaturally** adv **not unnaturally** as one would expect.

unnecessary ❶ adj not essential, or more than is essential. **unnecessarily** adv.

unnerve ❶ v cause to lose courage, confidence, or self-control. **unnerving** adj.

unnumbered adj **1** countless. **2** not counted or given a number.

UNO United Nations Organization.

unobtrusive adj not drawing attention to oneself or itself, inconspicuous. **unobtrusively** adv.

unorthodox adj **1** (of ideas, methods, etc.) unconventional and not generally accepted. **2** (of a person) having unusual opinions or methods.

unpack v **1** remove the contents of (a suitcase, trunk, etc.). **2** take (something) out of a packed container.

unpalatable adj **1** (of food) unpleasant to taste. **2** (of a fact, idea, etc.) unpleasant and hard to accept.

unparalleled ❶ adj not equalled, supreme.

unpick v undo (the stitches) of (a piece of sewing).

unpleasant ❶ adj not pleasant or agreeable. **unpleasantly** adv **unpleasantness** n.

unpopular ❶ adj generally disliked or disapproved of. **unpopularity** n.

unprecedented ❶ adj never having happened before, unparalleled.

unprepossessing adj unattractive in appearance.

unpretentious adj modest, unassuming, and down-to-earth.

unprincipled ❶ adj lacking moral principles, unscrupulous.

unprintable adj unsuitable for printing for reasons of obscenity or libel.

unprofessional ❶ adj contrary to the accepted code of a profession. **unprofessionally** adv.

unprofitable adj **1** not making a profit. **2** not helpful or beneficial.

unqualified ❶ adj **1** lacking the necessary qualifications. **2** total or complete.

unquestionable ❶ adj not to be doubted, indisputable. **unquestionably** adv.

unquote interj expression used to indicate the end of a quotation that was introduced with the word 'quote'.

unravel ❶ v **-elling, -elled 1** reduce (something knitted or woven) to separate strands. **2** become unravelled. **3** explain or solve.

unreadable adj **1** unable to be read or

---

unnatural adj **1** = **strange**, extraordinary, freakish, outlandish, queer **2** = **false**, affected, artificial, feigned, forced, insincere, phoney or phony (inf), stiff, stilted

unnecessary adj = **needless**, expendable, inessential, redundant, superfluous, unneeded, unrequired

unnerve v = **intimidate**, demoralize, discourage, dishearten, dismay, faze, fluster, frighten, psych out (inf), rattle (inf), shake, upset

unparalleled adj = **unequalled**, incomparable, matchless, superlative, unique, unmatched, unprecedented, unsurpassed

unpleasant adj = **nasty**, bad, disagreeable, displeasing, distasteful, horrid, objectionable

unpopular adj = **disliked**, rejected, shunned, unwanted, unwelcome

unprecedented adj = **extraordinary**, abnormal, munted (NZ sl), new, novel,

original, remarkable, singular, unheard-of

unprincipled adj = **dishonest**, amoral, crooked, devious, dishonourable, immoral, underhand, unethical, unscrupulous

unprofessional adj **a** = **unethical**, improper, lax, negligent, unprincipled **b** = **amateurish**, cowboy (inf), incompetent, inefficient, inexpert

unqualified adj **1** = **unfit**, ill-equipped, incapable, incompetent, ineligible, unprepared **2** = **total**, absolute, complete, downright, outright, thorough, utter

unquestionable adj = **certain**, absolute, clear, conclusive, definite, incontrovertible, indisputable, sure, undeniable, unequivocal, unmistakable

unravel v **1** = **undo**, disentangle, free, separate, untangle, unwind **3** = **solve**, explain, figure out (inf), resolve, work out

u

deciphered. **2** too difficult or dull to read.

unreal ● *adj* **1** (as if) existing only in the imagination. **2** insincere or artificial. **unreality** *n*.

unreasonable ● *adj* **1** immoderate or excessive. **2** refusing to listen to reason. **unreasonably** *adv*.

unremitting *adj* never slackening or stopping. **unremittingly** *adv*.

unrequited *adj* not returned, e.g. *unrequited love*.

unreserved ● *adj* completely, without reservation. **unreservedly** [un-re-**zerv**-id-lee] *adv*.

unrest ● *n* rebellious state of discontent.

unrivalled ● *adj* having no equal.

unroll *v* open out or unwind (something rolled or coiled) or (of something rolled or coiled) become opened out or unwound.

unruffled *adj* **1** calm and unperturbed. **2** smooth and still.

unruly ● *adj* **-lier, -liest** difficult to control or organize.

unsaturated *adj* **1** (of an organic compound) containing a double or triple bond and therefore capable of combining with other substances.

2 (of a fat, esp. a vegetable fat) containing a high proportion of fatty acids with double bonds.

unsavoury ● *adj* distasteful or objectionable.

unscathed ● *adj* not harmed or injured.

unscrupulous ● *adj* prepared to act dishonestly, unprincipled.

unseasonable *adj* inappropriate or unusual for the time of year. **unseasonably** *adv*.

unseat ● *v* **1** throw or displace from a seat or saddle. **2** depose from an office or position.

unseemly ● *adj* not according to expected standards of behaviour.

unsettled ● *adj* **1** lacking order or stability. **2** disturbed and restless. **3** constantly changing or moving from place to place.

unshakable, unshakeable *adj* (of beliefs) completely firm, not wavering. **unshakably, unshakeably** *adv*.

unsightly ● *adj* unpleasant to look at.

unsocial ● *adj* **1** (also **unsociable**) avoiding the company of other people. **2** falling outside the normal working day, e.g. *unsocial hours*.

unsound ● *adj* **1** unhealthy or

---

unreal *adj* **1** = **imaginary**, dreamlike, fabulous, fanciful, illusory, make-believe, visionary **2** = **fake**, artificial, false, insincere, mock, pretended, sham

unreasonable *adj* **1** = **excessive**, extortionate, immoderate, undue, unfair, unjust, unwarranted **2** = **biased**, blinkered, opinionated

unreserved *adj* = **total**, absolute, complete, entire, full, unlimited, wholehearted

unrest *n* = **discontent**, agitation, discord, dissension, protest, rebellion, sedition, strife

unrivalled *adj* = **unparalleled**, beyond compare, incomparable, matchless, supreme, unequalled, unmatched, unsurpassed

unruly *adj* = **uncontrollable**, disobedient, mutinous, rebellious, wayward, wild, wilful

unsavoury *adj* = **distasteful**, nasty, nauseating, obnoxious, offensive, repellent, repulsive, revolting, sickening, unpleasant

unscathed *adj* = **unharmed**, safe,

unhurt, uninjured, unmarked, whole

unscrupulous *adj* = **unprincipled**, corrupt, dishonest, dishonourable, immoral, improper, unethical

unseat *v* **1** = **throw**, unhorse, unsaddle **2** = **depose**, dethrone, displace, oust, overthrow, remove

unseemly *adj* = **improper**, inappropriate, indecorous, unbecoming, undignified, unsuitable

unsettled *adj* **1** = **unstable**, disorderly, insecure, shaky, unsteady **2** = **restless**, agitated, anxious, confused, disturbed, flustered, restive, shaken, tense **3** = **inconstant**, changing, uncertain, variable

unsightly *adj* = **ugly**, disagreeable, hideous, horrid, repulsive, unattractive

unsocial *adj* **1** (also **unsociable**) = **unfriendly**, chilly, cold, distant, hostile, retiring, unforthcoming, withdrawn

unsound *adj* **1** = **unhealthy**, ailing, crook (*Aust & NZ sl*), defective, diseased, ill, unbalanced, unstable, unwell, weak **2** = **invalid**, defective,

unstable. **2** not based on truth or fact.

unspeakable ❶ *adj* indescribably bad or evil. **unspeakably** *adv*.

unstable ❶ *adj* **1** lacking stability or firmness. **2** having abrupt changes of mood or behaviour.

unsteady ❶ *adj* **1** not securely fixed. **2** shaky or staggering. **unsteadily** *adv*.

unstinting *adj* generous, gladly given, e.g. *unstinting praise*.

unstructured *adj* without formal or systematic organization.

unstuck *adj* **come unstuck** *informal* fail badly.

unstudied *adj* natural or spontaneous.

unsuccessful *adj* not achieving success. **unsuccessfully** *adv*.

unsuitable *adj* not right or appropriate for a particular purpose. **unsuitably** *adv*.

unsuited *adj* **1** not appropriate for a particular task or situation. **2** (of a couple) having different personalities or tastes and unlikely to form a lasting relationship.

unsung *adj* not acclaimed or honoured, e.g. *unsung heroes*.

unswerving ❶ *adj* firm, constant, not changing.

unsympathetic *adj* **1** not feeling or showing sympathy. **2** unpleasant, not

likeable. **3** (foll. by *to*) opposed to.

untapped *adj* not yet used, e.g. *untapped resources*.

untenable ❶ *adj* (of a theory, idea, etc.) incapable of being defended.

unthinkable ❶ *adj* out of the question, inconceivable.

untidy ❶ *adj* messy and disordered. **untidily** *adv* **untidiness** *n*.

untie ❶ *v* **1** open or free (something that is tied). **2** free from constraint.

until *conj* **1** up to the time that. ▷ *prep* **2** in or throughout the period before. **not until** not before (a time or event).

untimely ❶ *adj* **1** occurring before the expected or normal time. **2** inappropriate to the occasion or time. **untimeliness** *n*.

unto *prep old-fashioned* to.

untold ❶ *adj* **1** incapable of description. **2** incalculably great in number or quantity.

untouchable *adj* **1** above reproach or suspicion. **2** unable to be touched. ▷ *n* **3** member of the lowest Hindu caste in India.

untoward ❶ *adj* causing misfortune or annoyance.

untrue ❶ *adj* **1** incorrect or false. **2** disloyal or unfaithful. **untruth** *n* statement that is not true, lie. **untruthful** *adj* **untruthfully** *adv*.

fallacious, false, flawed, illogical, shaky, specious, unreliable, weak

unspeakable *adj* **a** = **indescribable**, inconceivable, unbelievable, unimaginable **b** = **dreadful**, abominable, appalling, awful, heinous, horrible, monstrous, shocking

unstable *adj* **1** = **insecure**, precarious, shaky, tottering, unsettled, unsteady, wobbly **2** = **changeable**, capricious, erratic, fitful, fluctuating, inconsistent, inconstant, irrational, temperamental, unpredictable, variable, volatile

unsteady *adj* **1** = **unstable**, infirm, insecure, precarious, unsafe **2** = **shaky**, wobbly

unswerving *adj* = **constant**, firm, resolute, single-minded, staunch, steadfast, steady, true, unwavering

untenable *adj* = **unsustainable**, groundless, illogical, indefensible, insupportable, shaky, unsound, weak

unthinkable *adj* **a** = **impossible**, absurd, out of the question,

unreasonable **b** = **inconceivable**, implausible, incredible, unimaginable

untidy *adj* = **messy**, chaotic, cluttered, disarrayed, disordered, jumbled, littered, muddled, shambolic, unkempt

untie *v* **1** = **undo**, free, loosen, release, unbind, unfasten, unlace

untimely *adj* **1** = **early**, premature, unseasonable **2** = **ill-timed**, awkward, inappropriate, inconvenient, inopportune, mistimed

untold *adj* **1** = **indescribable**, inexpressible, undreamed of, unimaginable, unthinkable, unutterable **2** = **countless**, incalculable, innumerable, myriad, numberless, uncountable

untoward *adj* **a** = **unfavourable**, adverse, inauspicious, inopportune, unlucky **b** = **troublesome**, annoying, awkward, inconvenient, irritating, unfortunate

untrue *adj* **1** = **incorrect**, erroneous, false, inaccurate, mistaken, wrong

u

unusual ❶ *adj* uncommon or extraordinary. **unusually** *adv*.

unutterable *adj* incapable of being expressed in words. **unutterably** *adv*.

unvarnished *adj* not elaborated upon, e.g. *the unvarnished truth*.

unveil ❶ *v* **1** ceremonially remove the cover from (a new picture, plaque, etc.). **2** make public (a secret). **unveiling** *n*.

unwarranted ❶ *adj* not justified, not necessary.

unwell ❶ *adj* not healthy, ill.

unwieldy ❶ *adj* too heavy, large, or awkward to be easily handled.

unwind ❶ *v* **1** relax after a busy or tense time. **2** slacken, undo, or unravel.

unwitting ❶ *adj* **1** not intentional. **2** not knowing or conscious. **unwittingly** *adv*.

unwonted *adj* out of the ordinary.

unworthy ❶ *adj* **1** not deserving or worthy. **2** lacking merit or value. **unworthy of** beneath the level considered befitting (to).

unwrap *v* remove the wrapping from (something).

unwritten ❶ *adj* **1** not printed or in writing. **2** operating only through custom, e.g. *an unwritten rule*.

up *prep, adv* **1** indicating movement to or position at a higher place. ▷ *adv* **2** indicating readiness, intensity or completeness, etc. e.g., *warm up*; *drink up*. ▷ *adj* **3** of a high or higher position. **4** out of bed. ▷ *v* **upping, upped 5** increase or raise. **up against** having to cope with. **up and** *informal* do something suddenly, e.g. *he upped and left*. **ups and downs** alternating periods of good and bad luck. **up to 1** engaged in (usu. something shady, secretive, or mischievous). **2** the responsibility of, e.g. *it's up to you to lock the doors*. **3** equal to or capable of (doing something). **what's up?** *informal* what is wrong? **upward** *adj* **1** directed or moving towards a higher place or level. ▷ *adv* **2** (also **upwards**) from a lower to a higher place, level, or condition.

up-and-coming *adj* likely to be successful in the future.

upbeat ❶ *adj* **1** *informal* cheerful and optimistic. ▷ *n* **2** *Music* unaccented beat.

upbraid ❶ *v* scold or reproach.

upbringing ❶ *n* education of a person during the formative years.

— THESAURUS —

2 = unfaithful, deceitful, deceptive, dishonest, disloyal, faithless, false, inconstant, lying, treacherous, untrustworthy

untruth *n* = **lie**, deceit, falsehood, fib, pork pie (*Brit sl*), porky (*Brit sl*), story

untruthful *adj* = **dishonest**, deceitful, deceptive, false, lying, mendacious

unusual *adj* = **extraordinary**, curious, different, exceptional, odd, queer, rare, remarkable, singular, strange, uncommon, unconventional

unveil *v* **2** = **reveal**, disclose, divulge, expose, make known, uncover

unwarranted *adj* = **unnecessary**, gratuitous, groundless, indefensible, inexcusable, uncalled-for, unjustified, unprovoked

unwell *adj* = **ill**, ailing, crook (*Aust & NZ sl*), sick, sickly, under the weather (*inf*), unhealthy

unwieldy *adj* **a** = **bulky**, clumsy, hefty, massive, ponderous **b** = **awkward**, cumbersome, inconvenient, unmanageable

unwind *v* **1** = **relax**, loosen up, take it easy, wind down **2** = **unravel**, slacken, uncoil, undo, unroll, untwine, untwist

unwitting *adj* **1** = **unintentional**, accidental, chance, inadvertent, involuntary, unplanned **2** = **unknowing**, ignorant, innocent, unaware, unconscious, unsuspecting

unworthy *adj* **1** = **undeserving**, not fit for, not good enough **2** = **dishonourable**, base, contemptible, degrading, discreditable, disgraceful, disreputable, ignoble, shameful **unworthy of** = **unbefitting**, beneath, inappropriate, unbecoming, unfitting, unseemly, unsuitable

unwritten *adj* **1** = **oral**, vocal **2** = **customary**, accepted, tacit, understood

upbeat *adj* **1** *Inf* = **cheerful**, cheery, encouraging, hopeful, optimistic, positive

upbraid *v* = **scold**, admonish, berate, rebuke, reprimand, reproach, reprove

upbringing *n* = **education**, breeding, raising, rearing, training

u

update ❶ v bring up to date.

upend v turn or set (something) on its end.

upfront adj 1 open and frank. ▷ adv, adj 2 (of money) paid out at the beginning of a business arrangement.

upgrade ❶ v promote (a person or job) to a higher rank. **upgrading** n.

upheaval ❶ n strong, sudden, or violent disturbance.

uphill ❶ adj 1 sloping or leading upwards. 2 requiring a great deal of effort. ▷ adv 3 up a slope. ▷ n 4 S Afr difficulty.

uphold ❶ v 1 maintain or defend against opposition. 2 give moral support to. **upholder** n.

upholster v fit (a chair or sofa) with padding, springs, and covering. **upholstered** adj **upholsterer** n **upholstery** n soft covering on a chair or sofa.

upkeep ❶ n act, process, or cost of keeping something in good repair.

upland adj of or in an area of high or relatively high ground. **uplands** pl n area of high or relatively high ground.

uplift ❶ v 1 raise or lift up. 2 raise morally or spiritually. ▷ n 3 act or process of improving moral, social, or cultural conditions. **uplifting** adj.

upload v 1 transfer (data) from one computer system to a larger one. ▷ n 2 file transferred in such a way.

up-market adj expensive and of superior quality.

upon prep 1 on. 2 up and on.

upper ❶ adj 1 higher or highest in physical position, wealth, rank, or status. ▷ n 2 part of a shoe above the sole. **on one's uppers** destitute. **uppermost** adj 1 highest in position, power, or importance. ▷ adv 2 in or into the highest place or position. **upper case** capital letters. **upper class** highest social class. **upper-class** adj **upper crust** informal upper class. **uppercut** n short swinging upward punch delivered to the chin. **upper hand** position of control.

uppish, uppity ❶ adj informal snobbish, arrogant, or presumptuous.

upright ❶ adj 1 vertical or erect. 2 honest or just. ▷ adv 3 vertically or in an erect position. ▷ n 4 vertical support, such as a post. **uprightness** n.

uprising ❶ n rebellion or revolt.

uproar ❶ n disturbance characterized by loud noise and confusion. **uproarious** adj 1 very funny. 2 (of laughter) loud and boisterous. **uproariously** adv.

THESAURUS

update v = **bring up to date**, amend, modernize, renew, revise

upgrade v = **promote**, advance, better, elevate, enhance, improve, raise

upheaval n = **disturbance**, disorder, disruption, revolution, turmoil

uphill adj 1 = **ascending**, climbing, mounting, rising 2 = **arduous**, difficult, exhausting, gruelling, hard, laborious, strenuous, taxing, tough

uphold v 1 = **defend**, maintain, sustain 2 = **support**, advocate, aid, back, champion, endorse, promote

upkeep n a = **maintenance**, keep, repair, running, subsistence b = **running costs**, expenditure, expenses, overheads

uplift v 1 = **raise**, elevate, hoist, lift up 2 = **improve**, advance, better, edify, inspire, raise, refine ▷ n 3 = **improvement**, advancement, edification, enhancement, enlightenment, enrichment, refinement

upper adj 1 a = **higher**, high, loftier, top, topmost b = **superior**, eminent, greater, important

upper-class adj = **aristocratic**, blue-blooded, highborn, high-class, noble, patrician

upper hand n = **control**, advantage, ascendancy, edge, mastery, supremacy

uppermost adj 1 a = **top**, highest, loftiest, topmost b = **supreme**, chief, dominant, foremost, greatest, leading, main, principal

uppish, uppity adj Inf = **conceited**, bumptious, cocky, full of oneself, impertinent, self-important

upright adj 1 = **vertical**, erect, perpendicular, straight 2 = **honest**, conscientious, ethical, good, honourable, just, principled, righteous, virtuous

uprising n = **rebellion**, disturbance, insurgence, insurrection, mutiny, revolt, revolution, rising

uproar n = **commotion**, din, furore, mayhem, noise, outcry, pandemonium, racket, riot, turmoil

uproarious adj 1 = **hilarious**,

uproot ❶ v **1** pull up by or as if by the roots. **2** displace (a person or people) from their native or usual surroundings.

upset ❶ adj **1** emotionally or physically disturbed or distressed. ▷ v **2** tip over. **3** disturb the normal state or stability of. **4** disturb mentally or emotionally. **5** make physically ill. ▷ n **6** unexpected defeat or reversal. **7** disturbance or disorder of the emotions, mind, or body. **upsetting** adj.

upshot ❶ n final result or conclusion.

upside down ❶ adj **1** turned over completely. **2** informal confused or jumbled. ▷ adv **3** in an inverted fashion. **4** in a chaotic manner.

upstage adj **1** at the back half of the stage. ▷ v **2** informal draw attention to oneself from (someone else).

upstairs adv **1** to or on an upper floor of a building. ▷ n **2** upper floor. ▷ adj **3** situated on an upper floor.

upstanding ❶ adj of good character.

upstart ❶ n person who has risen suddenly to a position of power and behaves arrogantly.

upstream adv, adj in or towards the higher part of a stream.

upsurge n rapid rise or swell.

uptake n **quick, slow on the uptake** informal quick or slow to understand or learn.

uptight ❶ adj informal nervously tense, irritable, or angry.

up-to-date ❶ adj modern or fashionable.

uptown US & Canad ▷ adj, adv **1** towards, in, or relating to some part of a town that is away from the centre. ▷ n **2** such a part of a town, esp. a residential part.

upturn ❶ n upward trend or improvement. **upturned** adj facing upwards.

uranium [yew-**rain**-ee-um] n Chemistry radioactive silvery-white metallic element, used chiefly as a source of nuclear energy.

Uranus n **1** Greek myth god of the sky. **2** seventh planet from the sun.

urban ❶ adj **1** of or living in a city or town. **2** denoting modern pop music of African-American origin, such as hip-hop. **urbanize** v make (a rural area) more industrialized and urban. **urbanization** n.

urbane ❶ adj characterized by courtesy, elegance, and sophistication. **urbanity** n.

urchin ❶ n mischievous child.

Urdu [**oor**-doo] n language of Pakistan.

ureter [yew-**reet**-er] n tube that conveys urine from the kidney to the bladder.

THESAURUS

hysterical, killing (inf), rib-tickling, rip-roaring (inf), side-splitting, very funny **2** = **boisterous**, loud, rollicking, unrestrained

uproot v **1** = **pull up**, dig up, rip up, root out, weed out **2** = **displace**, exile

upset adj **1 a** = **distressed**, agitated, bothered, dismayed, disturbed, grieved, hurt, put out, troubled, worried **b** = **sick**, ill, queasy ▷ v **2** = **tip over**, capsize, knock over, overturn, spill **3** = **mess up**, change, disorder, disorganize, disturb, spoil **4** = **distress**, agitate, bother, disconcert, disturb, faze, fluster, grieve, perturb, ruffle, trouble ▷ n **6** = **reversal**, defeat, shake-up (inf) **7 a** = **distress**, agitation, bother, disturbance, shock, trouble, worry **b** = **illness**, bug (inf), complaint, disorder, malady, sickness

upshot n = **result**, culmination, end, end result, finale, outcome, sequel

upside down adj **1** = **inverted**,

overturned, upturned **2** Inf = **confused**, chaotic, disordered, higgledy-piggledy (inf), muddled, topsy-turvy

upstanding adj = **honest**, ethical, good, honourable, incorruptible, moral, principled, upright

upstart n = **social climber**, arriviste, nouveau riche, parvenu

uptight adj Inf = **tense**, anxious, edgy, on edge, uneasy, wired (sl)

up-to-date adj = **modern**, current, fashionable, in vogue, stylish, trendy (Brit inf), up-to-the-minute

upturn n = **rise**, advancement, improvement, increase, recovery, revival, upsurge, upswing

urban adj = **civic**, city, dorp (S Afr), metropolitan, municipal, town

urbane adj = **sophisticated**, cultivated, cultured, debonair, polished, refined, smooth, suave, well-bred

urchin n = **ragamuffin**, brat, gamin, waif

urethra [yew-**reeth**-ra] *n* canal that carries urine from the bladder out of the body.

urge ● *n* **1** strong impulse, inner drive, or yearning. ▷ *v* **2** plead with or press (a person to do something). **3** advocate earnestly. **4** force or drive onwards.

urgent ● *adj* requiring speedy action or attention. **urgency** *n* **urgently** *adv*.

uric acid *n* white odourless crystalline acid present in the blood and urine.

urine *n* pale yellow fluid excreted by the kidneys to the bladder and passed as waste from the body. **urinary** *adj* **urinate** *v* discharge urine. **urination** *n* **urinal** *n* sanitary fitting used by men for urination.

URL uniform resource locator: a standardized address of a location on the internet.

urn *n* **1** vase used as a container for the ashes of the dead. **2** large metal container with a tap, used for making and holding tea or coffee.

ursine *adj* of or like a bear.

us *pron* objective case of WE.

US, USA United States (of America).

USB Universal Serial Bus: standard for connecting sockets on computers.

use ● *v* **1** put into service or action. **2** take advantage of, exploit.

3 consume or expend. ▷ *n* **4** using or being used. **5** ability or permission to use. **6** usefulness or advantage. **7** purpose for which something is used. **usable** *adj* able to be used.

usage *n* **1** regular or constant use. **2** way in which a word is used in a language. **use-by date** *Aust, NZ, S Afr & US* date on packaged food after which it should not be sold. **used** *adj* second-hand. **used to** *adj* **1** accustomed to. ▷ *v* **2** used as an auxiliary to express past habitual or accustomed actions, e.g. *I used to live there*. **useful** *adj* **1** able to be used advantageously or for several different purposes. **2** *informal* commendable or capable, e.g. *a useful day's work*. **usefully** *adv* **usefulness** *n*

useless *adj* **1** having no practical use. **2** *informal* ineffectual, weak, or stupid, e.g. *useless at maths*. **uselessly** *adv* **uselessness** *n* **user** *n* **user-friendly** *adj* easy to familiarize oneself with, understand, and use.

username *n Computers* name entered into a computer for identification purposes.

- **SPELLING TIP**
- The Bank of English shows
- that it's very common to write
- *usualy*, forgetting the double *l* of
- **usually**.

THESAURUS

urge *n* **1** = **impulse**, compulsion, desire, drive, itch, longing, thirst, wish, yearning ▷ *v* **2** = **beg**, beseech, entreat, exhort, implore, plead **3** = **advocate**, advise, counsel, recommend, support **4** = **drive**, compel, encourage, force, gee up, goad, impel, incite, induce, press, push, spur

urgency *n* = **importance**, extremity, gravity, hurry, necessity, need, pressure, seriousness

urgent *adj* = **crucial**, compelling, critical, immediate, imperative, important, pressing, top-priority

usable *adj* = **serviceable**, available, current, functional, practical, utilizable, valid, working

usage *n* **1** = **practice**, convention, custom, habit, method, mode, procedure, regime, routine

use *v* **1** = **employ**, apply, exercise, exert, operate, practise, utilize, work **2** = **take advantage of**, exploit,

manipulate **3** = **consume**, exhaust, expend, run through, spend ▷ *n* **4** = **usage**, application, employment, exercise, handling, operation, practice, service **6** = **good**, advantage, avail, benefit, help, point, profit, service, usefulness, value **7** = **purpose**, end, object, reason

used *adj* = **second-hand**, cast-off, nearly new, shopsoiled

used to *adj* **1** = **accustomed to**, familiar with

useful *adj* **1** = **helpful**, advantageous, beneficial, effective, fruitful, practical, profitable, serviceable, valuable, worthwhile

usefulness *n* **1** = **helpfulness**, benefit, convenience, effectiveness, efficacy, practicality, use, utility, value, worth

useless *adj* **1** = **worthless**, fruitless, futile, impractical, ineffectual, pointless, unproductive, vain, valueless **2** *Inf* = **inept**, hopeless, incompetent, ineffectual, no good

u

usher ❶ *n* **1** official who shows people to their seats, as in a church. ▷ *v* **2** conduct or escort. **usherette** *n* female assistant in a cinema who shows people to their seats.

USSR (formerly) Union of Soviet Socialist Republics.

usual ❶ *adj* of the most normal, frequent, or regular type. **as usual** as happens normally. **usually** *adv* most often, in most cases.

usurp ❶ [yewz-**zurp**] *v* seize (a position or power) without authority. **usurpation** *n* **usurper** *n*.

usury *n* practice of lending money at an extremely high rate of interest. **usurer** [**yewz**-yoor-er] *n*.

UT Utah.

utensil *n* tool or container for practical use.

uterus [**yew**-ter-russ] *n* womb. **uterine** *adj*.

utilitarian *adj* **1** useful rather than beautiful. **2** of utilitarianism. **utilitarianism** *n* doctrine that the right action is the one that brings about the greatest good for the greatest number of people.

utility ❶ *n* **1** usefulness. **2** *pl* **-ties** public service, such as electricity. ▷ *adj*

3 designed for use rather than beauty.

utility room room used for large domestic appliances and equipment.

utility truck *Aust & NZ* small truck with an open body and low sides.

utilize ❶ *v* make practical use of. **utilization** *n*.

utmost ❶ *adj, n* (of) the greatest possible degree or amount.

Utopia ❶ [yew-**tope**-ee-a] *n* any real or imaginary society, place, or state considered to be perfect or ideal. **Utopian** *adj*.

utter¹ ❶ *v* express (something) in sounds or words. **utterance** *n* **1** something uttered. **2** act or power of uttering.

utter² ❶ *adj* total or absolute. **utterly** *adv*.

uttermost *adj, n* same as UTMOST.

U-turn *n* **1** turn, made by a vehicle, in the shape of a U, resulting in a reversal of direction. **2** complete change in policy.

UV ultraviolet.

uvula [**yew**-view-la] *n* small fleshy part of the soft palate that hangs in the back of the throat.

uxorious [ux-**or**-ee-uss] *adj* excessively fond of or dependent on one's wife.

━━━━━━━━━━━━━━━━━━━━━━━ **THESAURUS** ━━━━━━━

usher *n* **1** = **attendant**, doorkeeper, doorman, escort, guide ▷ *v* **2** = **escort**, conduct, direct, guide, lead

usual *adj* = **normal**, common, customary, everyday, general, habitual, ordinary, regular, routine, standard, typical

usually *adv* = **normally**, as a rule, commonly, generally, habitually, mainly, mostly, on the whole

usurp *v* = **seize**, appropriate, assume, commandeer, take, take over, wrest

utility *n* **1** = **usefulness**, benefit, convenience, efficacy, practicality, serviceableness

utilize *v* = **use**, avail oneself of, employ, make use of, put to use, take advantage of, turn to account

utmost *adj* **a** = **greatest**, chief, highest, maximum, paramount,

pre-eminent, supreme **b** = **farthest**, extreme, final, last ▷ *n* = **greatest**, best, hardest, highest

Utopia *n* = **paradise**, bliss, Eden, Garden of Eden, heaven, Shangri-la

Utopian *adj* = **perfect**, dream, fantasy, ideal, idealistic, imaginary, romantic, visionary

utter¹ *v* = **express**, articulate, pronounce, say, speak, voice

utter² *adj* = **absolute**, complete, downright, outright, sheer, thorough, total, unmitigated

utterance *n* **1** = **speech**, announcement, declaration, expression, remark, statement, words

utterly *adv* = **totally**, absolutely, completely, entirely, extremely, fully, perfectly, thoroughly

u

Vv

V 1 *Chemistry* vanadium. **2** volt. **3** the Roman numeral for five.

v. 1 verb. **2** versus. **3** very.

VA Virginia.

vacant ❶ *adj* 1 (of a toilet, room, etc.) unoccupied. **2** without interest or understanding. **vacantly** *adv*
vacancy *n, pl* **-cies** 1 unfilled job. **2** unoccupied room in a guesthouse. **3** state of being unoccupied.

vacate ❶ *v* 1 cause (something) to be empty by leaving. **2** give up (a job or position). **vacation** *n* 1 time when universities and law courts are closed. **2** *US & Canad* holiday.

vaccinate *v* inject with a vaccine. **vaccination** *n* **vaccine** *n* substance designed to cause a mild form of a disease to make a person immune to the disease itself.

vacillate [**vass**-ill-late] *v* keep changing one's mind or opinions. **vacillation** *n*.

vacuous ❶ *adj* not expressing intelligent thought. **vacuity** *n*.

vacuum ❶ *n, pl* **vacuums**, **vacua** 1 empty space from which all or most air or gas has been removed. **2** same as VACUUM CLEANER. ▷ *v* **3** clean with a vacuum cleaner. **vacuum cleaner** electrical appliance which sucks up dust and dirt from carpets and upholstery. **vacuum flask** double-walled flask with a vacuum between the walls that keeps drinks hot or cold. **vacuum-packed** *adj* contained in packaging from which the air has been removed.

vagabond ❶ *n* person with no fixed home, esp. a beggar.

vagary [**vaig**-a-ree] *n, pl* **-garies** 1 unpredictable change. **2** whim.

vagina [vaj-**jine**-a] *n, pl* **-nas**, **-nae** (in female mammals) passage from the womb to the external genitals. **vaginal** *adj*.

vagrant ❶ [**vaig**-rant] *n* 1 person with no settled home. ▷ *adj* **2** wandering. **vagrancy** *n*.

vague ❶ *adj* 1 not clearly explained. **2** deliberately withholding information. **3** unable to be seen or heard clearly. **4** absent-minded. **vaguely** *adv*.

vain ❶ *adj* 1 excessively proud, esp. of one's appearance. **2** bound to fail, futile. **in vain** unsuccessfully.

vainglorious *adj lit* boastful.

valance [**val**-lenss] *n* piece of drapery round the edge of a bed.

vale *n lit* valley.

valedictory [val-lid-**dik**-tree] *adj* (of a speech, performance, etc.) intended as a farewell. **valediction** *n* farewell speech.

valence [**vale**-ence] *n* molecular bonding between atoms.

valency *n, pl* **-cies** power of an atom to make molecular bonds.

valentine *n* (person to whom one sends) a romantic card on Saint Valentine's Day, February 14.

valerian *n* herb used as a sedative.

valet *n* man's personal male servant.

THESAURUS

vacancy *n* 1 = **job**, opening, opportunity, position, post, situation
vacant *adj* 1 = **unoccupied**, available, empty, free, idle, unfilled, untenanted, void **2** = **blank**, absent-minded, abstracted, dreamy, idle, inane, vacuous, vague
vacate *v* 1 = **leave**, evacuate, quit
vacuous *adj* = **unintelligent**, blank, inane, stupid, uncomprehending, vacant
vacuum *n* 1 = **emptiness**, gap, nothingness, space, vacuity, void
vagabond *n* = **vagrant**, beggar, down-and-out, itinerant, rover, tramp

vagrant *n* 1 = **tramp**, drifter, hobo (*US*), itinerant, rolling stone, wanderer ▷ *adj* **2** = **itinerant**, nomadic, roaming, rootless, roving, unsettled, vagabond
vague *adj* 1 = **unclear**, hazy, imprecise, indefinite, loose, uncertain, unspecified, woolly **3** = **indistinct**, hazy, ill-defined, indeterminate, nebulous, unclear
vain *adj* 1 = **proud**, arrogant, conceited, egotistical, narcissistic, self-important, swaggering **2** = **futile**, abortive, fruitless, idle, pointless, senseless, unavailing, unprofitable,

valetudinarian [val-lit-yew-din-**air**-ee-an] *n* **1** person with a long-term illness. **2** person overconcerned about his or her health.

valiant ❶ *adj* brave or courageous. **valiantly** *adv*.

valid ❶ *adj* **1** soundly reasoned. **2** having legal force. **validate** *v* make valid. **validation** *n* **validity** *n*.

valise [val-**leez**] *n* old-fashioned small suitcase.

Valium *n* ® drug used as a tranquillizer.

valley ❶ *n* low area between hills, often with a river running through it.

valour ❶ *n lit* bravery.

value ❶ *n* **1** importance, usefulness. **2** monetary worth. **3** satisfaction, e.g. *value for money*. **4** *Maths* particular number represented by a figure or symbol. ▷ *pl* **5** moral principles. ▷ *v* **valuing, valued 6** assess the worth or desirability of. **7** have a high regard for. **valuable** *adj* having great worth. **valuables** *pl n* valuable personal property. **valuation** *n* assessment of worth. **valueless** *adj* **valuer** *n* **value-added tax** *Brit* see VAT. **value judgment** opinion based on personal belief.

valve *n* **1** device to control the movement of fluid through a pipe. **2** *Anat* flap in a part of the body allowing blood to flow in one direction only. **3** *Physics* tube containing a vacuum, allowing current to flow from a cathode to an anode. **4** *Zoology* one of the hinged shells of an oyster or clam. **5** *Music* device on brass instruments to lengthen the tube. **valvular** *adj* **1** of or having valves. **2** like valves.

vamp¹ *n informal* sexually attractive woman who seduces men.

vamp² *v* **vamp up** make (a story, piece of music, etc.) seem new by inventing additional parts.

vampire *n* (in folklore) corpse that rises at night to drink the blood of the living. **vampire bat** tropical bat that feeds on blood.

van¹ *n* **1** motor vehicle for transporting goods. **2** *Brit & Aust* railway carriage for goods, luggage, or mail.

van² *n* short for VANGUARD.

vanadium *n Chemistry* metallic element, used in steel.

vandal ❶ *n* person who deliberately damages property. **vandalism** *n* **vandalize** *v*.

vane *n* flat blade on a rotary device such as a weathercock or propeller.

vanguard ❶ *n* **1** unit of soldiers leading an army. **2** most advanced group or position in a movement or activity.

vanilla *n* seed pod of a tropical climbing orchid, used for flavouring.

vanish ❶ *v* **1** disappear suddenly or mysteriously. **2** cease to exist.

———————————————————————— THESAURUS ——————

useless, worthless **in vain = to no avail**, fruitless(ly), ineffectual(ly), unsuccessful(ly), useless(ly), vain(ly)

valiant *adj* = **brave**, bold, courageous, fearless, gallant, heroic, intrepid, lion-hearted

valid *adj* **1** = **sound**, cogent, convincing, good, logical, telling, well-founded, well-grounded **2** = **legal**, authentic, bona fide, genuine, lawful, legitimate, official

validate *v* = **confirm**, authenticate, authorize, certify, corroborate, endorse, prove, ratify, substantiate

validity *n* **1** = **soundness**, cogency, force, power, strength, weight **2** = **legality**, authority, lawfulness, legitimacy, mana (*NZ*), right

valley *n* = **hollow**, dale, dell, depression, glen, vale

valour *n Lit* = **bravery**, boldness, courage, fearlessness, gallantry, heroism, intrepidity, spirit

valuable *adj* **a** = **useful**, beneficial, helpful, important, prized, profitable, worthwhile **b** = **precious**, costly, dear, expensive, high-priced ▷ *pl n* = **treasures**, heirlooms

value *n* **1** = **importance**, advantage, benefit, desirability, merit, profit, usefulness, utility, worth **2** = **cost**, market price, rate ▷ *pl* **5** = **principles**, ethics, (moral) standards ▷ *v* **6** = **evaluate**, appraise, assess, estimate, price, rate, set at **7** = **regard highly**, appreciate, cherish, esteem, hold dear, prize, respect, treasure

vandal *n* = **hooligan**, delinquent, rowdy, yob *or* yobbo (*Brit sl*)

vanguard *n* **2** = **forefront**, cutting edge, forerunners, front line, leaders, spearhead, trailblazers, trendsetters, van

vanish *v* **1** = **disappear**, dissolve, evanesce, evaporate, fade (away), melt (away)

vanity ❶ *n, pl* **-ties** (display of) excessive pride. **vanity case** small bag for carrying cosmetics.

vanquish ❶ *v lit* defeat (someone) utterly.

vantage *n* **vantage point** position that gives one an overall view.

vapid ❶ *adj* lacking character, dull. **vapidity** *n*.

vapour ❶ *n* **1** moisture suspended in air as steam or mist. **2** gaseous form of something that is liquid or solid at room temperature. **vaporize** *v* change into a' vapour. **vaporizer** *n* **vaporous** *adj*.

variable ❶ *adj* **1** not always the same, changeable. ▷ *n* **2** something that is subject to variation. **3** *Maths* expression with a range of values. **variability** *n*.

variant ❶ *adj* **1** differing from a standard or type. ▷ *n* **2** something that differs from a standard or type. **at variance** in disagreement.

variation ❶ *n* **1** something presented in a slightly different form. **2** difference in level, amount, or quantity. **3** *Music* repetition in different forms of a basic theme.

varicose veins *pl n* knotted and swollen veins, esp. in the legs.

variegated *adj* having patches or streaks of different colours. **variegation** *n*.

variety ❶ *n, pl* **-ties 1** state of being diverse or various. **2** different things of the same kind. **3** particular sort or kind. **4** light entertainment composed of unrelated acts.

various ❶ *adj* of several kinds. **variously** *adv*.

varnish ❶ *n* **1** solution of oil and resin, put on a surface to make it hard and glossy. ▷ *v* **2** apply varnish to.

varsity *n Brit informal* university.

vary ❶ *v* **varying**, **varied 1** change. **2** cause differences in. **varied** *adj*.

vascular *adj Biology* relating to vessels.

vas deferens *n, pl* **vasa deferentia** *Anat* sperm-carrying duct in each testicle.

vase *n* ornamental jar, esp. for flowers.

vasectomy *n, pl* **-mies** surgical removal of part of the vas deferens, as a contraceptive method.

Vaseline *n* ® thick oily cream made from petroleum, used in skin care.

vassal *n* **1** *History* man given land by a lord in return for military service. **2** subordinate person or nation. **vassalage** *n*.

vast ❶ *adj* extremely large. **vastly** *adv* **vastness** *n*.

vat *n* large container for liquids.

VAT *Brit* value-added tax: tax on the difference between the cost of materials and the selling price.

Vatican *n* **1** the Pope's palace. **2** authority of the Pope.

vaudeville *n* variety entertainment of songs and comic turns.

———————— THESAURUS ————————

vanity *n* = **pride**, arrogance, conceit, conceitedness, egotism, narcissism

vanquish *v Lit* = **defeat**, beat, conquer, crush, master, overcome, overpower, overwhelm, triumph over

vapid *adj* = **dull**, bland, boring, flat, insipid, tame, uninspiring, uninteresting, weak, wishy-washy (*inf*)

vapour *n* **1** = **mist**, exhalation, fog, haze, steam

variable *adj* **1** = **changeable**, flexible, fluctuating, inconstant, mutable, shifting, temperamental, uneven, unstable, unsteady

variant *adj* **1** = **different**, alternative, divergent, modified ▷ *n* **2** = **variation**, alternative, development, modification **at variance** = **in disagreement**, at loggerheads, at odds, at sixes and sevens (*inf*), conflicting, out of line

variation *n* **1** = **difference**, change, departure, deviation, diversity, innovation, modification, novelty, variety

variety *n* **1** = **diversity**, change, difference, discrepancy, diversification, multifariousness, variation **2** = **range**, array, assortment, collection, cross section, medley, miscellany, mixture **3** = **type**, brand, breed, category, class, kind, sort, species, strain

various *adj* = **different**, assorted, disparate, distinct, diverse, miscellaneous, several, sundry, varied

varnish *n, v* **1, 2** = **lacquer**, glaze, gloss, polish

vary *v* **1** = **change**, alter, fluctuate **2** = **alternate**

vast *adj* = **huge**, boundless, colossal, enormous, gigantic, great, immense, massive, monumental, wide

V

vault¹ ❶ *n* **1** secure room for storing valuables. **2** underground burial chamber. **vaulted** *adj* having an arched roof.

vault² ❶ *v* **1** jump over (something) by resting one's hand(s) on it. ▷ *n* **2** such a jump.

vaunt *v* describe or display (success or possessions) boastfully. **vaunted** *adj*.

VC 1 Vice Chancellor. **2** Victoria Cross.

VCR video cassette recorder.

VD venereal disease.

VDU visual display unit.

veal *n* calf meat.

vector *n* **1** *Maths* quantity that has size and direction, such as force. **2** animal, usu. an insect, that carries disease.

veer ❶ *v* change direction suddenly.

vegan [**vee**-gan] *n* **1** person who eats no meat, fish, eggs, or dairy products. ▷ *adj* **2** suitable for a vegan. **veganism** *n*.

vegetable *n* **1** edible plant. **2** *informal* severely brain-damaged person. ▷ *adj* **3** of or like plants or vegetables.

vegetarian *n* **1** person who eats no meat or fish. ▷ *adj* **2** suitable for a vegetarian. **vegetarianism** *n*.

vegetate ❶ *v* live a dull boring life with no mental stimulation.

vegetation *n* plant life of a given place. **vegetative** *adj* of plant life or growth.

vehement ❶ *adj* expressing strong feelings. **vehemence** *n* **vehemently** *adv*.

vehicle ❶ *n* **1** machine, esp. with an engine and wheels, for carrying people or objects. **2** something used to achieve a particular purpose or as a means of expression. **vehicular** *adj*.

veil ❶ *n* **1** piece of thin cloth covering the head or face. **2** something that masks the truth, e.g. *a veil of secrecy*. ▷ *v* **3** cover with or as if with a veil. **take the veil** become a nun. **veiled** *adj* disguised.

vein ❶ *n* **1** tube that takes blood to the heart. **2** line in a leaf or an insect's wing. **3** layer of ore or mineral in rock. **4** streak in marble, wood, or cheese. **5** feature of someone's writing or speech, e.g. *a vein of humour*. **6** mood or style, e.g. *in a lighter vein*. **veined** *adj*.

Velcro *n* ® fastening consisting of one piece of fabric with tiny hooked threads and another with a coarse surface that sticks to it.

veld, veldt *n* high grassland in southern Africa.

vellum *n* **1** fine calfskin parchment. **2** type of strong good-quality paper.

velocity ❶ [vel-**loss**-it-ee] *n, pl* **-ties** speed of movement in a given direction.

velour, velours [vel-**loor**] *n* fabric similar to velvet.

velvet ❶ *n* fabric with a thick soft pile. **velvety** *adj* soft and smooth. **velveteen** *n* cotton velvet.

venal [**vee**-nal] *adj* **1** easily bribed. **2** characterized by bribery. **venally** *adv*.

vend *v* sell. **vendor** *n* **vending machine** machine that dispenses goods when coins are inserted.

— THESAURUS —

vault¹ *n* **1** = **strongroom**, depository, repository **2** = **crypt**, catacomb, cellar, charnel house, mausoleum, tomb, undercroft

vault² *v* **1** = **jump**, bound, clear, hurdle, leap, spring

veer *v* = **change direction**, change course, sheer, shift, swerve, turn

vegetate *v* = **stagnate**, deteriorate, go to seed, idle, languish, loaf

vehemence *n* = **forcefulness**, ardour, emphasis, energy, fervour, force, intensity, passion, vigour

vehement *adj* = **strong**, ardent, emphatic, fervent, fierce, forceful, impassioned, intense, passionate, powerful

vehicle *n* **1** = **transport**, conveyance, transportation **2** = **medium**, apparatus, channel, means, mechanism, organ

veil *n* **1** = **cover**, blind, burka, burqa, cloak, curtain, disguise, film, hejab, hijab, mask, niqab, screen, shroud ▷ *v* **3** = **cover**, cloak, conceal, disguise, hide, mask, obscure, screen, shield

veiled *adj* = **disguised**, concealed, covert, hinted at, implied, masked, suppressed

vein *n* **1** = **blood vessel 3** = **seam**, lode, stratum **4** = **streak**, stripe **6** = **mood**, mode, note, style, temper, tenor, tone

velocity *n* = **speed**, pace, quickness, rapidity, swiftness

velvety *adj* = **soft**, delicate, downy, smooth

vendetta ❶ *n* **1** long-lasting quarrel between people or organizations in which they attempt to harm each other. **2** prolonged quarrel between families, esp. one involving revenge killings.

veneer ❶ *n* **1** thin layer of wood etc. covering a cheaper material. **2** superficial appearance, e.g. *a veneer of sophistication*.

venerable ❶ *adj* worthy of deep respect. **venerate** *v* hold (a person) in deep respect. **veneration** *n*.

venereal disease [ven-**ear**-ee-al] *n* disease transmitted sexually.

Venetian *adj* **1** of Venice, port in NE Italy. ▷ *n* **2** native or inhabitant of Venice. **Venetian blind** window blind made of thin horizontal slats that turn to let in more or less light.

vengeance ❶ *n* revenge. **with a vengeance** to an excessive degree. **vengeful** *adj* wanting revenge.

venial [**veen**-ee-al] *adj* (of a sin or fault) easily forgiven.

venison *n* deer meat.

venom ❶ *n* **1** malice or spite. **2** poison produced by snakes etc. **venomous** *adj* **venomously** *adv*.

venous [**vee**-nuss] *adj Anat* of veins.

vent¹ ❶ *n* **1** outlet releasing fumes or fluid. ▷ *v* **2** express (an emotion) freely. **give vent to** release (an emotion) in an outburst.

vent² *n* vertical slit in a jacket.

ventilate *v* **1** let fresh air into. **2** discuss (ideas or feelings) openly.

ventilation *n* **ventilator** *n* device to let fresh air into a room or building.

ventral *adj* relating to the front of the body.

ventricle *n Anat* one of the four cavities of the heart or brain.

ventriloquist *n* entertainer who can speak without moving his or her lips, so that a voice seems to come from elsewhere. **ventriloquism** *n*.

venture ❶ *n* **1** risky undertaking, esp. in business. ▷ *v* **2** do something risky. **3** dare to express (an opinion). **4** go to an unknown place. **venture capital** money provided for investment in new commercial enterprises. **venturesome** *adj* daring.

venue *n* place where an organized gathering is held.

Venus *n* **1** planet second nearest to the sun. **2** Roman goddess of love. **Venus flytrap**, **Venus's flytrap** plant that traps and digests insects between hinged leaves.

veracious *adj* habitually truthful. **veracity** *n*.

verandah, veranda *n* open porch attached to a house.

verb ❶ *n* word that expresses the idea of action, happening, or being. **verbal** *adj* **1** spoken. **2** of a verb. **verbally** *adv* **verbalize** *v* express (something) in words.

verbatim ❶ [verb-**bait**-im] *adv, adj* word for word.

verbena *n* plant with sweet-smelling flowers.

verbiage *n* excessive use of words.

THESAURUS

vendetta *n* **2** = **feud**, bad blood, quarrel

veneer *n* **1** = **layer**, finish, gloss **2** = **mask**, appearance, facade, front, guise, pretence, semblance, show

venerable *adj* = **respected**, august, esteemed, honoured, revered, sage, wise, worshipped

venerate *v* = **respect**, adore, esteem, honour, look up to, revere, reverence, worship

vengeance *n* = **revenge**, reprisal, requital, retaliation, retribution

venom *n* **1** = **malice**, acrimony, bitterness, hate, rancour, spite, spleen, virulence **2** = **poison**, bane, toxin

venomous *adj* **1** = **malicious**, hostile, malignant, rancorous, savage, spiteful, vicious, vindictive **2** = **poisonous**, mephitic, noxious, toxic, virulent

vent¹ *n* **1** = **outlet**, aperture, duct, opening, orifice ▷ *v* **2** = **express**, air, discharge, emit, give vent to, pour out, release, utter, voice

venture *n* **1** = **undertaking**, adventure, endeavour, enterprise, gamble, hazard, project, risk ▷ *v* **2** = **risk**, chance, hazard, speculate, stake, wager **3** = **dare**, hazard, make bold, presume, take the liberty, volunteer **4** = **go**, embark on, plunge into, set out

verbal *adj* **1** = **spoken**, oral, unwritten, word-of-mouth

verbatim *adv* = **word for word**, exactly, precisely, to the letter

verbose ❶ [verb-**bohss**] adj speaking at tedious length. **verbosity** n.

verdant ❶ adj lit covered in green vegetation.

verdict ❶ n **1** decision of a jury. **2** opinion formed after examining the facts.

verdigris [**ver**-dig-riss] n green film on copper, brass, or bronze.

verdure n lit flourishing green vegetation.

verge ❶ n grass border along a road. **on the verge of** having almost reached (a point or condition). **verge on** v be near to (a condition).

verger n C of E church caretaker.

verify ❶ v -**ifying**, -**ified** check the truth or accuracy of. **verifiable** adj **verification** n.

verily adv obs in truth.

verisimilitude n appearance of being real or true.

veritable adj rightly called, without exaggeration, e.g. a veritable feast. **veritably** adv.

verity n, pl -**ties** true statement or principle.

vermicelli [ver-me-**chell**-ee] n **1** fine strands of pasta. **2** tiny strands of chocolate.

vermiform adj shaped like a worm. **vermiform appendix** Anat same as APPENDIX.

vermilion adj orange-red.

vermin pl n **1** animals, esp. insects and rodents, that spread disease or cause damage. **2** people who are considered dangerous or harmful to others. **verminous** adj.

vermouth [**ver**-muth] n wine flavoured with herbs.

vernacular ❶ [ver-**nak**-yew-lar] n **1** most widely spoken language of a particular people or place. ▷ adj **2** in or using the vernacular.

vernal adj occurring in spring.

vernier [**ver**-nee-er] n movable scale on a graduated measuring instrument for taking readings in fractions.

veronica n plant with small blue, pink, or white flowers.

verruca [ver-**roo**-ka] n wart, usu. on the foot.

versatile ❶ adj having many skills or uses. **versatility** n.

verse ❶ n **1** group of lines forming part of a song or poem. **2** poetry as distinct from prose. **3** subdivision of a chapter of the Bible. **versed in** knowledgeable about. **versify** v -**fying**, -**fied** write in verse. **versification** n.

version ❶ n **1** form of something, such as a piece of writing, with some differences from other forms. **2** account of an incident from a particular point of view.

verso n, pl -**sos** **1** left-hand page of a book. **2** back of a sheet of printed paper.

versus prep **1** in opposition to or in contrast with. **2** Sport, Law against.

vertebra [**ver**-tib-ra] n, pl **vertebrae** [**ver**-tib-ree] one of the bones that form the spine. **vertebral** adj **vertebrate** n, adj (animal) having a spine.

vertex n, pl -**texes**, -**tices** **1** Maths point on a geometric figure where the sides form an angle. **2** highest point of a triangle.

— THESAURUS —

verbose adj = **long-winded**, circumlocutory, diffuse, periphrastic, prolix, tautological, windy, wordy

verbosity n = **long-windedness**, loquaciousness, prolixity, verboseness, wordiness

verdant adj Lit = **green**, flourishing, fresh, grassy, leafy, lush

verdict n = **decision**, adjudication, conclusion, finding, judgment, opinion, sentence

verge n = **border**, boundary, brim, brink, edge, limit, margin, threshold **verge on** v = **come near to**, approach, border

verification n = **proof**, authentication, confirmation, corroboration,

substantiation, validation

verify v = **check**, authenticate, bear out, confirm, corroborate, prove, substantiate, support, validate

vernacular n **1** = **dialect**, idiom, parlance, patois, speech

versatile adj = **adaptable**, adjustable, all-purpose, all-round, flexible, multifaceted, resourceful, variable

versed in adj = **knowledgeable about**, acquainted with, conversant with, experienced in, familiar with, practised in, proficient in, seasoned in, well informed about

version n **1 a** = **form**, design, model, style, variant **b** = **adaptation**,

vertical ❶ *adj* **1** straight up and down. ▷ *n* **2** vertical direction. **vertically** *adv*.

vertigo ❶ *n* dizziness, usu. when looking down from a high place. **vertiginous** *adj*.

vervain *n* plant with spikes of blue, purple, or white flowers.

verve ❶ *n* enthusiasm or liveliness.

very ❶ *adv* **1** more than usually, extremely. ▷ *adj* **2** absolute, exact, e.g. *the very top; the very man*.

vesicle *n Biology* sac or small cavity, esp. one containing fluid.

vespers *pl n RC Church* (service of) evening prayer.

vessel ❶ *n* **1** ship. **2** *lit* container, esp. for liquids. **3** *Biology* tubular structure in animals and plants that carries body fluids, such as blood or sap.

vest ❶ *n* **1** undergarment worn on the top half of the body. **2** *US & Aust* waistcoat. ▷ *v* **3** (foll. by *in* or *with*) give (authority) to (someone). **vested interest** interest someone has in a matter because he or she might benefit from it.

vestal *adj* pure, chaste. **vestal virgin** (in ancient Rome) one of the virgin priestesses dedicated to the goddess Vesta and to maintaining the sacred fire in her temple.

vestibule ❶ *n* small entrance hall.

vestige ❶ [**vest**-ij] *n* small amount or trace. **vestigial** [vest-**ij**-ee-al] *adj*.

vestments *pl n* priest's robes.

vestry *n, pl* **-tries** room in a church used as an office by the priest or minister.

vet¹ ❶ *n* **1** short for VETERINARY SURGEON. ▷ *v* **vetting**, **vetted 2** check the suitability of.

vet² *n US & Aust* military veteran.

vetch *n* climbing plant with a beanlike fruit used as fodder.

veteran ❶ *n* **1** person with long experience in a particular activity, esp. military service. ▷ *adj* **2** long-serving. **veteran car** car built before 1919, esp. before 1905.

veterinarian *n US* veterinary surgeon.

veterinary *adj* concerning animal health. **veterinary surgeon** medical specialist who treats sick animals.

veto ❶ [**vee**-toe] *n, pl* **-toes 1** official power to cancel a proposal. ▷ *v* **-toing**, **-toed 2** enforce a veto against.

vex ❶ *v* frustrate, annoy. **vexation** *n* **1** something annoying. **2** being annoyed. **vexatious** *adj* **vexed question** much debated subject.

VHF very high frequency: radio frequency band between 30 and 300 MHz.

VHS ® Video Home System: format for recording on video.

VI Vancouver Island.

via *prep* by way of.

viable ❶ *adj* **1** able to be put into practice. **2** *Biology* able to live and grow independently. **viability** *n*.

portrayal, rendering **2** = **account**, interpretation

vertical *adj* **1** = **upright**, erect, on end, perpendicular

vertigo *n* = **dizziness**, giddiness, light-headedness

verve *n* = **enthusiasm**, animation, energy, gusto, liveliness, sparkle, spirit, vitality

very *adv* **1** = **extremely**, acutely, decidedly, deeply, exceedingly, greatly, highly, profoundly, really, uncommonly, unusually ▷ *adj* **2** = **exact**, precise, selfsame

vessel *n* **1** = **ship**, boat, craft **2** *Lit* = **container**, pot, receptacle, utensil

vest *v* **3** (foll. by *in* or *with*) = **place in**, bestow upon, confer on, consign to, endow with, entrust with, invest with, settle on

vestibule *n* = **hall**, anteroom, foyer, lobby, porch, portico

vestige *n* = **trace**, glimmer, indication, remnant, scrap, suspicion

vet¹ *v* **2** = **check**, appraise, examine, investigate, review, scrutinize

veteran *n* **1** = **old hand**, old stager, past master, warhorse (*inf*) ▷ *adj* **2** = **long-serving**, battle-scarred, old, seasoned

veto *n* **1** = **ban**, boycott, embargo, interdict, prohibition ▷ *v* **2** = **ban**, boycott, disallow, forbid, prohibit, reject, rule out, turn down

vex *v* = **annoy**, bother, distress, exasperate, irritate, plague, trouble, upset, worry

vexation *n* **1** = **problem**, bother, difficulty, hassle (*inf*), headache (*inf*), nuisance, trouble, worry **2** = **annoyance**, chagrin, displeasure, dissatisfaction, exasperation, frustration, irritation, pique

viable *adj* **1** = **workable**, applicable, feasible, operable, practicable, usable

V

viaduct *n* bridge over a valley.
Viagra *n* ® drug used to treat impotence in men.
vial *n* same as PHIAL.
viands *pl n obs* food.
viaticum *n*, *pl* **-ca**, **-cums** Holy Communion given to a person who is dying or in danger of death.
vibes *pl n informal* **1** emotional reactions between people. **2** atmosphere of a place. **3** short for VIBRAPHONE.
vibrant ❶ [**vibe**-rant] *adj* **1** vigorous in appearance, energetic. **2** (of a voice) resonant. **3** (of a colour) strong and bright. **vibrancy** *n*.
vibraphone *n* musical instrument with metal bars that resonate electronically when hit.
vibrate ❶ *v* **1** move back and forth rapidly. **2** (cause to) resonate. **vibration** *n* **vibrator** *n* device that produces vibratory motion, used for massage or as a sex aid. **vibratory** *adj*.
vibrato *n*, *pl* **-tos** *Music* rapid fluctuation in the pitch of a note.
viburnum [vie-**burn**-um] *n* subtropical shrub with white flowers and berry-like fruits.
VIC Victoria (Australian state).
vicar *n C of E* clergyman in charge of a parish. **vicarage** *n* vicar's house.
vicarious ❶ [vick-**air**-ee-uss] *adj* **1** felt indirectly by imagining what another person experiences. **2** delegated. **vicariously** *adv*.
vice¹ ❶ *n* **1** immoral or evil habit or action. **2** habit regarded as a weakness in someone's character. **3** criminal immorality, esp. involving sex.
vice² *n* tool with a pair of jaws for holding an object while working on it.
vice³ *adj* serving in place of.
vice chancellor *n* chief executive of a university.
vice president *n* officer ranking immediately below the president and serving as his or her deputy. **vice-presidency** *n*.
viceroy *n* governor of a colony who represents the monarch. **viceregal** *adj*.
vice versa ❶ [vie-see **ver**-sa] *adv Latin* conversely, the other way round.
Vichy water [**vee**-shee **waw**-ter] *n* mineral water from Vichy in France, reputed to be good for the health.
vicinity ❶ [viss-**in**-it-ee] *n* surrounding area.
vicious ❶ *adj* cruel and violent. **viciously** *adv* **vicious circle, cycle** situation in which an attempt to resolve one problem creates new problems that recreate the original one.
vicissitudes [viss-**iss**-it-yewds] *pl n* changes in fortune.
victim ❶ *n* **1** person or thing harmed or killed. **2** person who has suffered because of misfortune or other people's actions. **victimize** *v* **1** punish unfairly. **2** discriminate against. **victimization** *n*.
victor ❶ *n* person who has defeated an opponent, esp. in war or sport. **victorious** *adj* **victory** *n*, *pl* **-tories**

━━━━━━━━━━━━━━━━━━ THESAURUS ━━━━━━━━

vibrant *adj* **1** = **energetic**, alive, animated, dynamic, sparkling, spirited, storming, vigorous, vivacious, vivid
vibrate *v* **1** = **shake**, fluctuate, judder (*inf*), oscillate, pulsate, quiver, sway, throb, tremble **2** = **reverberate**
vibration *n* **1** = **shake**, judder (*inf*), oscillation, pulsation, quiver, throbbing, trembling, tremor **2** = **reverberation**
vicarious *adj* **1** = **indirect**, at one remove, substituted, surrogate **2** = **delegated**, deputed
vice¹ *n* **1** = **wickedness**, corruption, depravity, evil, immorality, iniquity, sin, turpitude **2** = **fault**, blemish, defect, failing, imperfection, shortcoming, weakness

vice versa *adv Latin* = **conversely**, contrariwise, in reverse, the other way round
vicinity *n* = **neighbourhood**, area, district, environs, locality, neck of the woods (*inf*), proximity
vicious *adj* **a** = **malicious**, cruel, mean, spiteful, venomous, vindictive **b** = **savage**, barbarous, cruel, ferocious, violent
victim *n* **1** = **casualty**, fatality, sufferer **2** = **sacrifice**, martyr, scapegoat
victimize *v* **2** = **persecute**, discriminate against, have it in for (someone) (*inf*), pick on
victor *n* = **winner**, champion, conqueror, prizewinner, vanquisher
victorious *adj* = **winning**, champion,

winning of a battle or contest.

victoria *n* large sweet plum, red and yellow in colour.

Victoria Cross *n* Brit highest award for bravery.

Victorian *adj* **1** of or in the reign of Queen Victoria (1837–1901). **2** characterized by prudery or hypocrisy. ▷ *n* **3** person who lived during Victoria's reign.

victuals [**vit**-tals] *pl n old-fashioned* food and drink. **victual** *v* **victualling**, **victualled** *old-fashioned* supply with or obtain victuals. **victualler** *n*.

vicuña [vik-**koo**-nya] *n* **1** S American animal like the llama. **2** fine cloth made from its wool.

vide [**vie**-dee] *Latin* see.

videlicet [vid-**deal**-ee-set] *Latin* namely.

video *n, pl* **-os 1** short for VIDEO CASSETTE (RECORDER). ▷ *v* **videoing**, **videoed 2** record (a TV programme or event) on video. ▷ *adj* **3** relating to or used in producing television images. **video game** game that can be played using an electronic control to manipulate objects on a VDU. **video nasty** horrific or pornographic film, usu. made for video.

video cassette *n* cassette containing video tape. **video cassette recorder** tape recorder for recording and playing back TV programmes and films.

video tape *n* **1** magnetic tape used to record video-frequency signals in TV production. **2** magnetic tape used to record programmes when they are broadcast. **videotape** *v* record (a TV programme) on video tape. **video tape recorder** tape recorder for vision signals, used in TV production.

vie ❶ *v* **vying, vied** compete (with someone).

Vietnamese *adj* **1** of Vietnam, in SE Asia. ▷ *n* **2** *pl* **-ese** native of Vietnam. **3** language of Vietnam.

view ❶ *n* **1** opinion or belief. **2** understanding of or outlook on something. **3** everything that can be seen from a given place. **4** picture of this. ▷ *v* **5** think of (something) in a particular way. **6** see or watch. **in view of** taking into consideration. **on view** exhibited to the public. **viewer** *n* **1** person who watches television. **2** hand-held device for looking at photographic slides. **viewfinder** *n* window on a camera showing what will appear in a photograph.

vigil ❶ [**vij**-ill] *n* night-time period of staying awake to look after a sick person, pray, etc. **vigilant** *adj* watchful in case of danger. **vigilance** *n*.

vigilante [vij-ill-**ant**-ee] *n* person, esp. as one of a group, who takes it upon himself or herself to enforce the law.

vignette [vin-**yet**] *n* **1** concise description of the typical features of something. **2** small decorative illustration in a book.

vigour ❶ *n* physical or mental energy. **vigorous** *adj* **vigorously** *adv*.

Viking *n History* seafaring raider and settler from Scandinavia.

vile ❶ *adj* **1** very wicked. **2** disgusting. **vilely** *adv* **vileness** *n*.

conquering, first, prizewinning, successful, triumphant, vanquishing

victory *n* = **win**, conquest, success, triumph

vie *v* = **compete**, contend, strive, struggle

view *n* **1** = **opinion**, attitude, belief, conviction, feeling, point of view, sentiment **2** = **impression 3** = **scene**, landscape, outlook, panorama, perspective, picture, prospect, spectacle, vista ▷ *v* **5** = **regard**, consider, deem, look on

viewer *n* **1** = **watcher**, observer, onlooker, spectator

vigilance *n* = **watchfulness**, alertness, attentiveness, carefulness, caution,
circumspection, observance

vigilant *adj* = **watchful**, alert, attentive, careful, cautious, circumspect, on one's guard, on the lookout, wakeful

vigorous *adj* = **energetic**, active, dynamic, forceful, lively, lusty, powerful, spirited, strenuous, strong

vigorously *adv* = **energetically**, forcefully, hard, lustily, strenuously, strongly

vigour *n* = **energy**, animation, dynamism, forcefulness, gusto, liveliness, power, spirit, strength, verve, vitality

vile *adj* **1** = **wicked**, corrupt, degenerate, depraved, evil, nefarious,

V

vilify ❶ [**vill**-if-fie] *v* **-ifying, -ified** attack the character of. **vilification** *n*.

villa *n* **1** large house with gardens. **2** holiday home, usu. in the Mediterranean.

village *n* **1** small group of houses in a country area. **2** rural community. **villager** *n*.

villain ❶ *n* **1** wicked person. **2** main wicked character in a play. **villainous** *adj* **villainy** *n*.

villein [**vill**-an] *n History* peasant bound in service to his lord.

vim *n informal* force, energy.

vinaigrette *n* salad dressing of oil and vinegar.

vindicate ❶ *v* **1** clear (someone) of guilt. **2** provide justification for. **vindication** *n*.

vindictive ❶ *adj* maliciously seeking revenge. **vindictiveness** *n* **vindictively** *adv*.

vine *n* climbing plant, esp. one producing grapes. **vineyard** [**vinn**-yard] *n* plantation of grape vines, esp. for making wine.

vinegar *n* acid liquid made from wine, beer, or cider. **vinegary** *adj*.

viniculture *n* process or business of growing grapes and making wine.

vino [**vee**-noh] *n informal* wine.

vintage ❶ *n* **1** wine from a particular harvest of grapes. ▷ *adj* **2** best and most typical. **vintage car** car built between 1919 and 1930.

vintner *n* dealer in wine.

vinyl [**vine**-ill] *n* type of plastic, used in mock leather and records.

viol [**vie**-oll] *n* early stringed instrument preceding the violin.

viola[1] [vee-**oh**-la] *n* stringed instrument lower in pitch than a violin.

viola[2] [**vie**-ol-la] *n* variety of pansy.

violate ❶ *v* **1** break (a law or agreement). **2** disturb (someone's privacy). **3** treat (a sacred place) disrespectfully. **4** rape. **violation** *n* **violator** *n*.

violence ❶ *n* **1** use of physical force, usu. intended to cause injury or destruction. **2** great force or strength in action, feeling, or expression. **violent** *adj* **violently** *adv*.

violet *n* **1** plant with bluish-purple flowers. ▷ *adj* **2** bluish-purple.

violin *n* small four-stringed musical instrument played with a bow. **violinist** *n*.

violoncello [vie-oll-on-**chell**-oh] *n*, *pl* **-los** same as CELLO.

VIP ❶ very important person.

viper *n* poisonous snake.

virago [vir-**rah**-go] *n*, *pl* **-goes, -gos** aggressive woman.

---

perverted **2** = **disgusting**, foul, horrid, nasty, nauseating, offensive, repugnant, repulsive, revolting, sickening

vilify *v* = **malign**, abuse, berate, denigrate, disparage, revile, slander, smear

villain *n* **1** = **evildoer**, blackguard, criminal, miscreant, reprobate, rogue, scoundrel, wretch **2** = **antihero**, baddy (*inf*)

villainous *adj* **1** = **wicked**, bad, cruel, degenerate, depraved, evil, fiendish, nefarious, vicious, vile

villainy *n* **1** = **wickedness**, delinquency, depravity, devilry, iniquity, turpitude, vice

vindicate *v* **1** = **clear**, absolve, acquit, exculpate, exonerate, rehabilitate **2** = **justify**, defend, excuse

vindication *n* **1** = **exoneration**, exculpation **2** = **justification**, defence, excuse

vindictive *adj* = **vengeful**, implacable, malicious, resentful, revengeful, spiteful, unforgiving, unrelenting

vintage *adj* **2** = **best**, choice, classic, prime, select, superior

violate *v* **1** = **break**, contravene, disobey, disregard, infringe, transgress **2** = **encroach upon 3** = **desecrate**, abuse, befoul, defile, dishonour, pollute, profane **4** = **rape**, abuse, assault, debauch, ravish

violation *n* **1** = **infringement**, abuse, breach, contravention, infraction, transgression **2** = **trespass**, encroachment **3** = **desecration**, defilement, profanation, sacrilege, spoliation

violence *n* **1** = **force**, bloodshed, brutality, cruelty, ferocity, fighting, savagery, terrorism **2** = **intensity**, abandon, fervour, force, severity, vehemence

violent *adj* **1** = **destructive**, brutal, cruel, hot-headed, murderous, riotous, savage, uncontrollable, unrestrained, vicious

VIP *n* = **celebrity**, big hitter (*inf*), big

viral [**vie**-ral] *adj* of or caused by a virus. **go viral** (of a story, video, etc.) spread quickly among internet users via social media, e-mail, etc.

virgin ❶ *n* **1** person, esp. a woman, who has not had sexual intercourse. ▷ *adj* **2** not having had sexual intercourse. **3** not yet exploited or explored. **virginal** *adj* **1** like a virgin. **2** extremely pure or fresh. ▷ *n* **3** early keyboard instrument like a small harpsichord. **virginity** *n* **the Virgin**, **the Virgin Mary** *Christianity* Mary, the mother of Christ.

Virginia creeper *n* climbing plant that turns red in autumn.

Virgo *n* (the virgin) sixth sign of the zodiac.

virile ❶ *adj* having the traditional male characteristics of physical strength and a high sex drive. **virility** *n*.

virology *n* study of viruses.

virtual ❶ *adj* **1** having the effect but not the form of. **2** of or relating to virtual reality. **virtual reality** computer-generated environment that seems real to the user. **virtually** *adv* practically, almost.

virtue ❶ *n* **1** moral goodness. **2** positive moral quality. **3** merit. **by virtue of** by reason of. **virtuous** *adj* morally good. **virtuously** *adv*.

virtuoso ❶ *n*, *pl* **-sos**, **-si** person with impressive esp. musical skill. **virtuosity** *n*.

virulent ❶ [**vir**-yew-lent] *adj* **1** extremely bitter or hostile. **2** very infectious. **3** violently harmful. **virulently** *adv* **virulence** *n*.

virus *n* **1** microorganism that causes disease in humans, animals, and plants. **2** *Computers* program that propagates itself, via disks and electronic networks, to cause disruption.

visa *n* permission to enter a country, granted by its government and shown by a stamp on one's passport.

visage [**viz**-zij] *n* lit face.

vis-à-vis [veez-ah-**vee**] *prep* in relation to, regarding.

viscera [**viss**-er-a] *pl n* large abdominal organs. **visceral** *adj* **1** instinctive. **2** of or relating to the viscera.

viscid [**viss**-id] *adj* sticky.

viscose *n* synthetic fabric made from cellulose.

viscount [**vie**-count] *n* British nobleman ranking between an earl and a baron. **viscountcy** *n*, *pl* **-cies**.

viscountess [**vie**-count-iss] *n* **1** woman holding the rank of viscount in her own right. **2** wife or widow of a viscount.

viscous ❶ *adj* thick and sticky. **viscosity** *n*.

visible ❶ *adj* **1** able to be seen. **2** able to be perceived by the mind. **visibly** *adv* **visibility** *n* range or clarity of vision.

vision ❶ *n* **1** ability to see. **2** mental image of something. **3** foresight.

THESAURUS

name, heavy hitter (*inf*), luminary, somebody, star

virgin *n* **1** = **maiden**, girl (*arch*) ▷ *adj* **2** = **pure**, chaste, immaculate, uncorrupted, undefiled, vestal, virginal

virginity *n* **2** = **chastity**, maidenhood

virile *adj* = **manly**, lusty, macho, manlike, masculine, red-blooded, strong, vigorous

virility *n* = **masculinity**, machismo, manhood, vigour

virtual *adj* **1** = **practical**, essential, in all but name

virtually *adv* = **practically**, almost, as good as, in all but name, in effect, in essence, nearly

virtue *n* **1**, **2** = **goodness**, incorruptibility, integrity, morality, probity, rectitude, righteousness, uprightness, worth **3** = **merit**, advantage, asset, attribute, credit, good point, plus (*inf*), strength

virtuosity *n* = **mastery**, brilliance, craft, expertise, flair, panache, polish, skill

virtuoso *n* = **master**, artist, genius, maestro, magician

virtuous *adj* = **good**, ethical, honourable, incorruptible, moral, praiseworthy, righteous, upright, worthy

virulent *adj* **3** = **deadly**, lethal, pernicious, poisonous, toxic, venomous

viscous *adj* = **thick**, gelatinous, sticky, syrupy

visible *adj* **1** = **apparent**, clear, discernible, evident, in view, manifest, observable, perceptible, unconcealed

vision *n* **1** = **sight**, eyesight, perception, seeing, view **2** = **image**, concept, conception, daydream, dream, fantasy, idea, ideal **3** = **foresight**, discernment, farsightedness, imagination, insight,

V

4 hallucination. **visionary** *adj* **1** showing foresight. **2** idealistic but impractical. ▷ *n*, *pl* **-aries 3** visionary person.

visit ❶ *v* **-iting, -ited 1** go or come to see. **2** stay temporarily with. **3** (foll. by *upon*) *lit* afflict. ▷ *n* **4** instance of visiting. **5** official call. **visitor** *n* **visitation** *n* **1** formal visit or inspection. **2** catastrophe seen as divine punishment.

visor [**vize**-or] *n* **1** transparent part of a helmet that pulls down over the face. **2** eyeshade, esp. in a car. **3** peak on a cap.

vista ❶ *n* (beautiful) extensive view.

visual ❶ *adj* **1** done by or used in seeing. **2** designed to be looked at. **visualize** *v* form a mental image of. **visualization** *n* **visual display unit** device with a screen for displaying data held in a computer.

vital ❶ *adj* **1** essential or highly important. **2** lively. **3** necessary to maintain life. **vitals** *pl n* bodily organs necessary to maintain life. **vitally** *adv* **vitality** *n* physical or mental energy. **vital statistics 1** statistics of births, deaths, and marriages. **2** *informal* woman's bust, waist, and hip measurements.

vitamin *n* one of a group of substances that are essential in the diet for specific body processes.

vitiate [**vish**-ee-ate] *v* spoil the effectiveness of. **vitiation** *n*.

viticulture *n* cultivation of grapevines.

vitreous *adj* like or made from glass. **vitreous humour** gelatinous substance that fills the eyeball.

vitrify *v* **-ifying, -ified** change or be changed into glass or a glassy substance. **vitrification** *n*.

vitriol ❶ *n* **1** language expressing bitterness and hatred. **2** sulphuric acid. **vitriolic** *adj*.

vituperative [vite-**tyew**-pra-tiv] *adj* bitterly abusive. **vituperation** *n*.

viva¹ *interj* long live (a person or thing).

viva² *n* examination in the form of an interview.

vivace [viv-**vah**-chee] *adv Music* in a lively manner.

vivacious ❶ *adj* full of energy and enthusiasm. **vivacity** *n*.

vivarium *n*, *pl* **-iums, -ia** place where animals are kept in natural conditions.

viva voce [**vive**-a **voh**-chee] *adv* **1** by word of mouth. ▷ *n* **2** same as VIVA².

vivid ❶ *adj* **1** very bright. **2** conveying images that are true to life. **vividly** *adv* **vividness** *n*.

vivify *v* **-ifying, -ified** animate, inspire.

viviparous [viv-**vip**-a-russ] *adj* producing live offspring.

vivisection *n* performing surgical

---

intuition, penetration, prescience **4 = hallucination**, apparition, chimera, delusion, illusion, mirage, revelation

visionary *adj* **1 = prophetic**, mystical **2 = idealistic**, impractical, quixotic, romantic, speculative, starry-eyed, unrealistic, unworkable, utopian ▷ *n* **3 = idealist**, daydreamer, dreamer, mystic, prophet, seer

visit *v* **1 = call on**, drop in on (*inf*), look (someone) up, stop by **2 = stay with** ▷ *n* **4 = call**, sojourn, stay, stop

visitation *n* **1 = inspection**, examination, visit **2 = catastrophe**, blight, calamity, cataclysm, disaster, ordeal, punishment, scourge

visitor *n* **1 = caller**, company **2 = guest**

vista *n* = **view**, panorama, perspective, prospect

visual *adj* **1 = optical**, ocular, optic **2 = observable**, discernible, perceptible, visible

visualize *v* = **picture**, conceive of, envisage, imagine

vital *adj* **1 = essential**, basic, fundamental, imperative, indispensable, necessary, requisite **2 = lively**, animated, dynamic, energetic, spirited, vibrant, vigorous, vivacious, zestful **3 = important**, critical, crucial, decisive, key, life-or-death, significant, urgent

vitality *n* = **energy**, animation, exuberance, life, liveliness, strength, vigour, vivacity

vitriolic *adj* **1 = bitter**, acerbic, caustic, envenomed, sardonic, scathing, venomous, virulent, withering

vivacious *adj* = **lively**, bubbling, ebullient, high-spirited, sparkling, spirited, sprightly, upbeat (*inf*), vital

vivacity *n* = **liveliness**, animation, ebullience, energy, gaiety, high spirits, sparkle, spirit, sprightliness

vivid *adj* **1 = bright**, brilliant, clear, colourful, glowing, intense, rich

v

experiments on living animals. **vivisectionist** n.

vixen n **1** female fox. **2** informal spiteful woman.

viz. (introducing specified items) namely.

vizier [viz-**zeer**] n high official in certain Muslim countries.

vizor n same as VISOR.

VLF, vlf Radio very low frequency.

vlog n video journal uploaded to the internet. **vlogger** n **vlogging** n.

V neck n neck on a garment shaped like the letter 'V'. **V-neck, V-necked** adj.

vocabulary ⊙ n, pl **-aries 1** all the words that a person knows. **2** all the words in a language. **3** specialist terms used in a given subject. **4** list of words in another language with their translation.

vocal ⊙ adj **1** relating to the voice. **2** outspoken. **vocals** pl n singing part of a piece of pop music. **vocally** adv **vocalist** n singer. **vocalize** v express with or use the voice. **vocalization** n **vocal cords** membranes in the larynx that vibrate to produce sound.

vocation ⊙ n **1** profession or trade. **2** occupation that someone feels called to. **vocational** adj directed towards a particular profession or trade.

vocative n (in some languages) case of nouns used when addressing a person.

vociferate v exclaim, cry out. **vociferation** n.

vociferous ⊙ adj shouting, noisy. **vociferously** adv.

vodka n (Russian) spirit distilled from potatoes or grain.

vogue ⊙ n **1** popular style. **2** period of popularity. **in vogue** fashionable.

voice ⊙ n **1** (quality of) sound made when speaking or singing. **2** expression of opinion by a person or group. **3** property of verbs that makes them active or passive. ▷ v **4** express verbally. **voiceless** adj **voice mail** electronic system for the storage of telephone messages. **voice-over** n film commentary spoken by someone off-camera.

void ⊙ adj **1** not legally binding. **2** empty. ▷ n **3** feeling of deprivation. **4** empty space. ▷ v **5** make invalid. **6** empty.

voile [**voyl**] n light semitransparent fabric.

vol. volume.

volatile ⊙ [**voll**-a-tile] adj **1** liable to sudden change, esp. in behaviour. **2** evaporating quickly. **volatility** n.

vol-au-vent [**voll**-oh-von] n small puff-pastry case with a savoury filling.

volcano n, pl **-noes, -nos** mountain with a vent through which lava is ejected. **volcanic** adj.

vole n small rodent.

volition ⊙ n ability to decide things for oneself. **of one's own volition** through one's own choice.

volley ⊙ n **1** simultaneous discharge of ammunition. **2** burst of questions or critical comments. **3** Sport stroke or kick at a moving ball before it hits the ground. ▷ v **4** discharge (ammunition)

2 = **clear**, dramatic, graphic, lifelike, memorable, powerful, realistic, stirring, telling, true to life

vocabulary n **2** = **words**, dictionary, glossary, language, lexicon

vocal adj **1** = **spoken**, oral, said, uttered, voiced **2** = **outspoken**, articulate, eloquent, expressive, forthright, frank, plain-spoken, strident, vociferous

vocation n **1** = **profession**, career, job, pursuit, trade **2** = **calling**, mission

vociferous adj = **noisy**, clamorous, loud, outspoken, strident, uproarious, vehement, vocal

vogue n **1** = **fashion**, craze, custom, mode, style, trend, way **in vogue** = **popular**, accepted, current, in favour, in use, prevalent

voice n **1** = **sound**, articulation, tone,

utterance **2** = **say**, view, vote, will, wish ▷ v **4** = **express**, air, articulate, declare, enunciate, utter

void adj **1** = **invalid**, ineffective, inoperative, null and void, useless, vain, worthless **2** = **empty**, bare, free, tenantless, unfilled, unoccupied, vacant ▷ n **4** = **emptiness**, blankness, gap, lack, space, vacuity, vacuum ▷ v **5** = **invalidate**, cancel, nullify, rescind **6** = **empty**, drain, evacuate

volatile adj **1 a** = **changeable**, erratic, explosive, inconstant, unsettled, unstable, unsteady, up and down (inf), variable **b** = **temperamental**, fickle, mercurial

volition n = **free will**, choice, choosing, discretion, preference, will

volley n **1** = **barrage**, blast, bombardment, burst, cannonade,

v

in a volley. **5** hit or kick (a ball) in a volley. **volleyball** *n* team game where a ball is hit with the hands over a high net.

volt *n* unit of electric potential. **voltaic** *adj* same as GALVANIC (sense 1). **voltage** *n* electric potential difference expressed in volts. **voltmeter** *n* instrument for measuring voltage.

volte-face [volt-**fass**] *n* reversal of opinion.

voluble ⊕ *adj* talking easily and at length. **volubility** *n* **volubly** *adv*.

volume ⊕ *n* **1** size of the space occupied by something. **2** amount. **3** loudness of sound. **4** control on a radio or TV for adjusting this. **5** book, esp. one of a series. **voluminous** *adj* **1** (of clothes) large and roomy. **2** (of writings) extensive. **volumetric** *adj* relating to measurement by volume.

voluntary ⊕ *adj* **1** done by choice. **2** done or maintained without payment. **3** (of muscles) controlled by the will. ▷ *n, pl* **-taries 4** organ solo in a church service. **voluntarily** *adv*.

volunteer ⊕ *n* **1** person who offers voluntarily to do something. **2** person who voluntarily undertakes military service. ▷ *v* **3** offer one's services. **4** give (information) willingly. **5** offer the services of (another person).

voluptuous ⊕ *adj* **1** (of a woman) sexually alluring through fullness of figure. **2** sensually pleasurable. **voluptuary** *n, pl* **-aries** person

devoted to sensual pleasures.

volute *n* spiral or twisting turn, form, or object.

vomit ⊕ *v* **-iting, -ited 1** eject (the contents of the stomach) through the mouth. ▷ *n* **2** matter vomited.

voodoo *n* religion involving ancestor worship and witchcraft, practised by Black people in the West Indies, esp. in Haiti.

voracious ⊕ *adj* **1** craving great quantities of food. **2** insatiably eager. **voraciously** *adv* **voracity** *n*.

vortex ⊕ *n, pl* **-texes, -tices 1** whirlpool. **2** situation which people are drawn into against their will.

votary *n, pl* **-ries** person dedicated to religion or to a cause.

vote ⊕ *n* **1** choice made by a participant in a shared decision, esp. in electing a candidate. **2** right to this choice. **3** total number of votes cast. **4** collective voting power of a given group, e.g. *the Black vote.* ▷ *v* **5** make a choice by a vote. **6** authorize (something) by vote. **voter** *n*.

votive *adj* done or given to fulfil a vow.

vouch ⊕ *v* **vouch for 1** give one's personal assurance about. **2** provide evidence for.

voucher ⊕ *n* **1** ticket used instead of money to buy specified goods. **2** record of a financial transaction, receipt.

vouchsafe *v* **1** *old-fashioned* give, entrust. **2** offer assurances about.

---

fusillade, hail, salvo, shower

voluble *adj* = **talkative**, articulate, fluent, forthcoming, glib, loquacious

volume *n* **1** = **capacity**, compass, dimensions **2** = **amount**, aggregate, body, bulk, mass, quantity, total **5** = **book**, publication, title, tome, treatise

voluminous *adj* **1** = **large**, ample, capacious, cavernous, roomy, vast

voluntarily *adv* **1** = **willingly**, by choice, freely, off one's own bat, of one's own accord

voluntary *adj* **1** = **unforced**, optional, spontaneous, willing **2** = **discretionary**, free

volunteer *v* **3** = **offer**, step forward

voluptuous *adj* **1** = **buxom**, ample, curvaceous (*inf*), enticing, seductive, shapely **2** = **sensual**, epicurean, hedonistic, licentious, luxurious,

self-indulgent, sybaritic

vomit *v* **1** = **be sick**, disgorge, emit, heave, regurgitate, retch, spew out *or* up, throw up (*inf*)

voracious *adj* **1** = **gluttonous**, greedy, hungry, insatiable, omnivorous, ravenous **2** = **avid**, hungry, insatiable, rapacious, uncontrolled, unquenchable

vortex *n* **1** = **whirlpool**, eddy, maelstrom

vote *n* **1** = **poll**, ballot, franchise, plebiscite, referendum, show of hands ▷ *v* **5** = **cast one's vote**, elect, opt

voucher *n* **1** = **ticket**, coupon, token

vouch for *v* **1** = **guarantee**, answer for, certify, give assurance of, stand witness, swear to **2** = **confirm**, affirm, assert, attest to, support, uphold

vow ❶ *n* **1** solemn and binding promise. ▷ *pl* **2** formal promises made when marrying or entering a religious order. ▷ *v* **3** promise solemnly.

vowel *n* **1** speech sound made without obstructing the flow of breath. **2** letter representing this.

vox pop *n* interviews with members of the public on TV or radio.

vox populi *n* public opinion.

voyage ❶ *n* **1** long journey by sea or in space. ▷ *v* **2** make a voyage. **voyager** *n*.

voyeur *n* person who obtains pleasure from watching people undressing or having sex. **voyeurism** *n* **voyeuristic** *adj*.

vs versus.

V-sign *n* **1** offensive gesture made by sticking up the index and middle fingers with the palm inwards. **2** similar gesture, with the palm outwards, meaning victory or peace.

VSO Voluntary Service Overseas.

VSOP (of brandy or port) very superior old pale.

VT Vermont.

VTOL vertical takeoff and landing.

VTR video tape recorder.

vulcanize *v* strengthen (rubber) by treating it with sulphur. **vulcanization** *n* **vulcanite** *n* vulcanized rubber.

vulgar ❶ *adj* showing lack of good taste, decency, or refinement. **vulgarly** *adv* **vulgarity** *n* **vulgarian** *n* vulgar (rich) person. **vulgarism** *n* coarse word or phrase. **vulgarize** *v* make vulgar or too common. **vulgarization** *n* **vulgar fraction** simple fraction.

Vulgate *n* fourth-century Latin version of the Bible.

vulnerable ❶ *adj* **1** liable to be physically or emotionally hurt. **2** exposed to attack. **3** financially weak and likely to fail. **vulnerability** *n*.

vulpine *adj* of or like a fox.

vulture *n* large bird that feeds on the flesh of dead animals.

vulva *n* woman's external genitals.

vying *v* present participle of VIE.

THESAURUS

vow *n* **1** = **promise**, oath, pledge ▷ *v* **3** = **promise**, affirm, pledge, swear

voyage *n* **1** = **journey**, crossing, cruise, passage, trip

vulgar *adj* = **crude**, coarse, common, impolite, indecent, ribald, risqué, rude, tasteless, uncouth, unrefined

vulgarity *n* = **crudeness**, bad taste, coarseness, indelicacy, ribaldry, rudeness, tastelessness

vulnerable *adj* **1** = **susceptible**, sensitive, tender, thin-skinned, weak **2** = **exposed**, accessible, assailable, defenceless, unprotected, wide open

V

W 1 *Chemistry* tungsten. **2** watt.
3 West(ern).

WA 1 Washington. **2** Western Australia.

wacky *adj* **wackier**, **wackiest** *informal* eccentric or funny. **wackiness** *n*.

wad ❶ *n* **1** small mass of soft material. **2** roll or bundle, esp. of banknotes. **wadded** *adj* **wadding** *n* soft material used for padding or stuffing.

waddle ❶ *v* **1** walk with short swaying steps. ▷ *n* **2** swaying walk.

wade ❶ *v* **1** walk with difficulty through water or mud. **2** proceed with difficulty. **wader** *n* **1** long-legged water bird. ▷ *pl* **2** angler's long waterproof boots.

wadi [**wod**-dee] *n, pl* **-dies** (in N Africa and Arabia) river which is dry except in the wet season.

wafer *n* **1** thin crisp biscuit. **2** thin disc of unleavened bread used at Communion. **3** thin slice. **wafer-thin** *adj* extremely thin.

waffle¹ ❶ *informal* ▷ *v* **1** speak or write in a vague wordy way. ▷ *n* **2** vague wordy talk or writing.

waffle² *n* square crisp pancake with a gridlike pattern.

waft ❶ *v* **1** drift or carry gently through the air. ▷ *n* **2** something wafted.

wag ❶ *v* **wagging**, **wagged 1** move rapidly from side to side. ▷ *n* **2** wagging movement. **3** *old-fashioned* humorous witty person. **waggish** *adj* **wagtail** *n* small long-tailed bird.

Wag *n informal* wife or girlfriend of a famous sportsperson.

wage ❶ *n* **1** (often *pl*) payment for work done, esp. when paid weekly. ▷ *v* **2** engage in (an activity).

wager ❶ *n, v* bet on the outcome of something.

waggle ❶ *v* move with a rapid shaking or wobbling motion. **waggly** *adj*.

wagon, waggon *n* **1** four-wheeled vehicle for heavy loads. **2** railway freight truck.

wahoo *n* food and game fish of tropical seas.

waif ❶ *n* young person who is, or seems, homeless or neglected.

wail ❶ *v* **1** cry out in pain or misery. ▷ *n* **2** mournful cry.

wain *n poetic* farm wagon.

wainscot, wainscoting *n* wooden lining of the lower part of the walls of a room.

waist *n* **1** part of the body between the ribs and hips. **2** narrow middle part. **waistband** *n* band of material sewn on to the waist of a garment to strengthen it. **waistcoat** *n* sleeveless garment which buttons up the front, usu. worn over a shirt and under a jacket. **waistline** *n* (size of) the waist of a person or garment.

wait ❶ *v* **1** remain inactive in expectation (of something). **2** be ready (for something). **3** delay or be

---

THESAURUS

wad *n* **1** = **mass**, hunk **2** = **roll**, bundle

waddle *v* **1** = **shuffle**, sway, toddle, totter, wobble

wade *v* **1** = **walk through**, ford, paddle, splash **2** = **plough through**, drudge at, labour at, peg away at, toil at, work one's way through

waffle¹ *Inf* ▷ *v* **1** = **prattle**, blather, jabber, prate, rabbit (on) (*Brit inf*), witter on (*inf*) ▷ *n* **2** = **verbosity**, padding, prolixity, verbiage, wordiness

waft *v* **1** = **carry**, bear, convey, drift, float, transport

wag *v* **1** = **wave**, bob, nod, quiver, shake, stir, vibrate, waggle, wiggle ▷ *n* **2** = **wave**, bob, nod, quiver, shake, vibration, waggle, wiggle **3** *Old-fashioned* = **joker**, card (*inf*), clown,

comedian, comic, humorist, jester, wit

wage *n* **1** (often *pl*) = **payment**, allowance, emolument, fee, pay, recompense, remuneration, reward, stipend ▷ *v* **2** = **engage in**, carry on, conduct, practise, proceed with, prosecute, pursue, undertake

wager *n* = **bet**, flutter (*Brit inf*), gamble, punt (*chiefly Brit*) ▷ *v* = **bet**, chance, gamble, lay, risk, speculate, stake, venture

waggle *v* = **wag**, flutter, oscillate, shake, wave, wiggle, wobble

waif *n* = **stray**, foundling, orphan

wail *v* **1** = **cry**, bawl, grieve, howl, lament, weep, yowl ▷ *n* **2** = **cry**, complaint, howl, lament, moan, weeping, yowl

wait *v* **1** = **remain**, hang fire, hold back,

delayed. **4** serve in a restaurant etc.
▷ n **5** act or period of waiting. **waiter**
n man who serves in a restaurant etc.
waitress n fem **waiting list** list of
people who have applied for
something that is not immediately
available. **waiting-room** n room for
waiting in, as at a station or surgery.

waive ❶ v refrain from enforcing (a law,
right, etc.). **waiver** n (written
statement of) this act.

wake¹ ❶ v **waking**, **woke**, **woken**
1 rouse from sleep or inactivity. ▷ n
2 vigil beside a corpse the night before
the funeral. **wake up to** become
aware of. **waken** v wake. **wakeful** adj
wakefulness n.

wake² ❶ n track left by a moving ship.
in the wake of following, often as a
result.

walk ❶ v **1** move on foot with at least
one foot always on the ground. **2** pass
through or over on foot. **3** escort or
accompany on foot. ▷ n **4** short
journey on foot, usu. for pleasure.
5 act or instance of walking.
6 distance walked. **7** manner of
walking. **8** place or route for walking.
walk of life social position or
profession. **walker** n **walkabout** n
informal walk among the public by
royalty etc. **walkie-talkie** n portable
radio transmitter and receiver.
walking stick stick used as a support
when walking. **walk into** v meet with

unwittingly. **Walkman** n ® small
portable cassette player with
headphones. **walk-on** adj (of a part in
a film or play) small and not involving
speaking. **walkout** n **1** strike. **2** act of
leaving as a protest. **walkover** n easy
victory.

wall ❶ n **1** structure of brick, stone, etc.
used to enclose, divide, or support.
2 something having the function or
effect of a wall. ▷ v **3** enclose or seal
with a wall or walls. **go to the wall** be
ruined, esp. financially. **wall-to-wall**
adj (of carpeting) completely covering
a floor. **wallflower** n **1** fragrant
garden plant. **2** (at a dance) woman
who remains seated because she
has no partner. **wallpaper** n
decorative paper to cover interior
walls.

wallaby n, pl **-bies** marsupial like a
small kangaroo.

wallaroo n large stocky Australian
kangaroo of rocky regions.

wallet ❶ n small folding case for paper
money, documents, etc.

walleye n fish with large staring eyes
(also **dory**).

walleyed adj having eyes with an
abnormal amount of white showing
due to a squint.

wallop ❶ informal ▷ v **-loping**, **-loped**
1 hit hard. ▷ n **2** hard blow.
walloping informal ▷ n **1** thrashing.
▷ adj **2** large or great.

THESAURUS
---

linger, pause, rest, stay, tarry ▷ n
3 = **delay**, halt, hold-up, interval,
pause, rest, stay

waive v = **set aside**, abandon, dispense
with, forgo, give up, relinquish, remit,
renounce

wake¹ v **1 a** = **awaken**, arise, awake,
bestir, come to, get up, rouse, stir
b = **activate**, animate, arouse, excite,
fire, galvanize, kindle, provoke,
stimulate, stir up ▷ v **2** = **vigil**,
deathwatch, funeral, watch

wake² n = **slipstream**, aftermath,
backwash, path, track, trail, train,
wash, waves

waken v = **awaken**, activate, arouse,
awake, rouse, stir

walk v **1, 2** = **go**, amble, hike, march,
move, pace, step, stride, stroll
3 = **escort**, accompany, convoy, take
▷ n **4** = **stroll**, hike, march,
promenade, ramble, saunter, trek,

trudge **7** = **gait**, carriage, step
8 = **path**, alley, avenue, esplanade,
footpath, lane, promenade, trail **walk
of life** = **profession**, calling, career,
field, line, trade, vocation

walker n = **pedestrian**, hiker, rambler,
wayfarer

walkout n **1** = **strike**, industrial action,
protest, stoppage

walkover n = **pushover**, breeze (US &
Canad inf), cakewalk (inf), child's play
(inf), doddle (Brit sl), picnic (inf), piece
of cake (inf)

wall n **1** = **partition**, enclosure, screen
2 = **barrier**, fence, hedge,
impediment, obstacle, obstruction

wallet n = **holder**, case, pouch, purse

wallop Inf ▷ v **1** = **hit**, batter, beat,
clobber (sl), pound, pummel, slug,
swipe, thrash, thump, whack ▷ n
2 = **blow**, bash, punch, slug, smack,
swipe, thump, thwack, whack

w

wallow ❶ *v* **1** revel in an emotion. **2** roll in liquid or mud. ▷ *n* **3** act or instance of wallowing. **4** muddy place where animals wallow.

wally *n, pl* **-lies** *slang* stupid person.

walnut *n* **1** edible nut with a wrinkled shell. **2** tree it grows on. **3** its wood, used for making furniture.

walrus *n, pl* **-ruses, -rus** large sea mammal with long tusks.

waltz *n* **1** ballroom dance. **2** music for this. ▷ *v* **3** dance a waltz. **4** *informal* move in a relaxed confident way.

wampum *n US & Canad* shells woven together, formerly used by N American Indians for money and ornament.

wan ❶ [rhymes with **swan**] *adj* **wanner, wannest** pale and sickly looking.

wand ❶ *n* thin rod, esp. one used in performing magic tricks.

wander ❶ *v* **1** move about without a definite destination or aim. **2** go astray, deviate. **3** (of the mind) lose concentration. ▷ *n* **4** act or instance of wandering. **wanderer** *n* **wanderlust** *n* great desire to travel.

wane ❶ *v* **1** decrease gradually in size or strength. **2** (of the moon) decrease in size. **on the wane** decreasing in size, strength, or power.

wangle ❶ *v informal* get by devious methods.

want ❶ *v* **1** need or long for. **2** desire or wish. ▷ *n* **3** act or instance of wanting. **4** thing wanted. **5** lack or absence, e.g. *a want of foresight*. **6** state of being in need, poverty. **wanted** *adj* sought by the police. **wanting** *adj* **1** lacking. **2** not good enough.

wanton ❶ *adj* **1** without motive, provocation, or justification. **2** maliciously and unnecessarily cruel. **3** *old-fashioned* (of a woman) sexually unrestrained or immodest. **wantonly** *adv*.

WAP Wireless Application Protocol.

wapiti [**wop**-pit-tee] *n, pl* **-tis** large N American and NZ deer.

war ❶ *n* **1** fighting between nations. **2** conflict or contest. ▷ *adj* **3** of, like, or caused by war. ▷ *v* **warring, warred 4** conduct a war. **warring** *adj* **warlike** *adj* **1** of or relating to war. **2** hostile and eager to have a war. **on the warpath** *informal* angry and prepared for conflict. **war crime** crime, such as killing, committed during a war in violation of accepted conventions. **war criminal** person who has committed war crimes. **war cry 1** shout used in battle. **2** slogan for rallying support for a cause. **warfare** *n* fighting or hostilities. **warhead** *n* explosive front part of a missile. **warmonger** *n* person who

---

wallow *v* **1** = **revel**, bask, delight, glory, luxuriate, relish, take pleasure **2** = **roll about**, splash around

wan *adj* = **pale**, anaemic, ashen, pallid, pasty, sickly, washed out, white

wand *n* = **stick**, baton, rod

wander *v* **1** = **roam**, drift, meander, ramble, range, rove, stray, stroll **2** = **deviate**, depart, digress, diverge, err, go astray, swerve, veer ▷ *n* **4** = **excursion**, cruise, meander, ramble

wane *v* **1** = **decline**, decrease, diminish, dwindle, ebb, fade, fail, lessen, subside, taper off, weaken **on the wane** = **declining**, dwindling, ebbing, fading, obsolescent, on the decline, tapering off, weakening

wangle *v Inf* = **contrive**, arrange, engineer, fiddle (*inf*), fix (*inf*), manipulate, manoeuvre, pull off

want *v* **1** = **need**, call for, demand, lack, miss, require **2** = **desire**, covet, crave, hanker after, hope for, hunger for, long

for, thirst for, wish, yearn for ▷ *n* **3** = **wish**, appetite, craving, desire, longing, need, requirement, yearning **5** = **lack**, absence, dearth, deficiency, famine, insufficiency, paucity, scarcity, shortage **6** = **poverty**, destitution, neediness, penury, privation

wanting *adj* **1** = **lacking**, absent, incomplete, missing, short, shy **2** = **inadequate**, defective, deficient, faulty, imperfect, poor, substandard, unsound

wanton *adj* **1** = **unprovoked**, arbitrary, gratuitous, groundless, motiveless, needless, senseless, uncalled-for, unjustifiable, wilful **3** *Old-fashioned* = **promiscuous**, dissipated, dissolute, immoral, lecherous, libidinous, loose, lustful, shameless, unchaste

war *n* **1, 2** = **fighting**, battle, combat, conflict, enmity, hostilities, struggle, warfare ▷ *v* **4** = **fight**, battle, campaign against, clash, combat, take up arms, wage war

encourages war. **warmongering** n, adj **warship** n ship designed and equipped for naval combat.

warble ❶ v sing in a trilling voice. **warbler** n any of various small songbirds.

ward ❶ n 1 room in a hospital for patients needing a similar kind of care. 2 electoral division of a town. 3 child under the care of a guardian or court. **warder** n prison officer. **wardress** n fem **wardship** n state of being a ward. **ward off** v avert or repel. **wardroom** n officers' quarters on a warship.

warden ❶ n 1 person in charge of a building and its occupants. 2 official responsible for the enforcement of regulations.

wardrobe ❶ n 1 cupboard for hanging clothes in. 2 person's collection of clothes. 3 costumes of a theatrical company.

ware ❶ n 1 articles of a specified type or material, e.g. silverware. ▷ pl 2 goods for sale. **warehouse** n building for storing goods prior to sale or distribution.

warlock n man who practises black magic.

warm ❶ adj 1 moderately hot. 2 providing warmth. 3 (of a colour) predominantly yellow or red. 4 affectionate. 5 enthusiastic. ▷ v 6 make or become warm. **warmly** adv **warmth** n 1 mild heat. 2 cordiality. 3 intensity of emotion. **warm-blooded** adj 1 Zoology (of mammals and birds) having a constant body temperature, usu. higher than the surroundings. 2 passionate. **warm up** v 1 make or become warmer. 2 do preliminary exercises before a race or more strenuous exercise. 3 make or become more lively. **warm-up** n.

warn ❶ v 1 make aware of possible danger or harm. 2 caution or scold. 3 inform (someone) in advance. **warning** n 1 something that warns. 2 scolding or caution. **warn off** v advise (someone) not to become involved with.

warp ❶ v 1 twist out of shape. 2 pervert. ▷ n 3 state of being warped. 4 lengthwise threads on a loom.

warrant ❶ n 1 (document giving) official authorization. ▷ v 2 make necessary. 3 guarantee. **warranty** n, pl **-ties** (document giving) a guarantee. **warrant officer** officer in certain armed services with a rank between a commissioned and noncommissioned officer.

warren n 1 series of burrows in which rabbits live. 2 overcrowded building or part of a town.

THESAURUS

warble v = **sing**, chirp, trill, twitter

ward n 1 = **room**, apartment, cubicle 2 = **district**, area, division, precinct, quarter, zone 3 = **dependant**, charge, minor

warden n 1 = **keeper**, administrator, caretaker, curator, custodian, guardian, ranger, superintendent

warder, wardress n = **jailer**, custodian, guard, prison officer, screw (sl)

ward off v = **repel**, avert, avoid, deflect, fend off, parry, stave off

wardrobe n 1 = **clothes cupboard**, closet 2 = **clothes**, apparel, attire

warehouse n = **store**, depository, depot, stockroom, storehouse

wares pl n = **goods**, commodities, merchandise, produce, products, stock, stuff

warfare n = **war**, arms, battle, combat, conflict, fighting, hostilities

warlike adj 2 = **belligerent**, aggressive, bellicose, bloodthirsty, hawkish, hostile, martial, warmongering

warm adj 1 = **heated**, balmy, lukewarm, pleasant, sunny, tepid, thermal 4 = **affectionate**, amorous, cordial, friendly, hospitable, kindly, loving, tender ▷ v 6 = **heat**, heat up, melt, thaw, warm up

warmth n 1 = **heat**, hotness, warmness 2 = **affection**, amorousness, cordiality, heartiness, kindliness, love, tenderness

warn v 1 = **alert**, tip off 2 = **caution** 3 = **forewarn**, advise, apprise, give notice, inform, make (someone) aware, notify

warning n 1 = **caution**, advice, alarm, alert, notification, omen, sign, tip-off

warp v 1 = **twist**, bend, contort, deform, distort ▷ n 3 = **twist**, bend, contortion, distortion, kink

warrant n 1 = **authorization**, authority, licence, mana (NZ), permission, permit, sanction ▷ v 2 = **call for**, demand, deserve, excuse, justify, license, necessitate, permit, require, sanction 3 = **guarantee**,

w

warrigal *Aust* ▷ *n* **1** dingo. ▷ *adj* **2** wild.
warrior ❶ *n* person who fights in a war.
wart *n* small hard growth on the skin.
warty *adj* **wart hog** kind of African
wild pig.
wary ❶ [ware-ree] *adj* **warier**, **wariest**
watchful or cautious. **warily** *adv*
wariness *n*.
was *v* first and third person singular
past tense of BE.
wash ❶ *v* **1** clean (oneself, clothes, etc.)
with water and usu. soap. **2** be
washable. **3** flow or sweep over or
against. **4** *informal* be believable or
acceptable, e.g. *that excuse won't wash*.
▷ *n* **5** act or process of washing.
6 clothes washed at one time. **7** thin
coat of paint. **8** disturbance in the
water after a ship has passed by.
washable *adj* **washer** *n* ring put under
a nut or bolt or in a tap as a seal.
washing *n* clothes to be washed.
washing machine electric machine
for washing clothes and linen.
washing-up *n* (washing of) dishes
and cutlery needing to be cleaned
after a meal. **wash away** *v* carry or be
carried off by moving water.
washbasin *n* basin for washing the
face and hands. **washout** *n informal*
complete failure. **washed-out** *adj*
1 exhausted. **2** faded. **wash up** *v* wash
dishes and cutlery after a meal.

wasp *n* stinging insect with a slender
black-and-yellow striped body.
waspish *adj* bad-tempered.
Wasp, WASP *n US derogatory* White
Anglo-Saxon Protestant.
wassail *n* **1** formerly, festivity when
much drinking took place. ▷ *v* **2** drink
health of (a person) at a wassail.
waste ❶ *v* **1** use pointlessly or
thoughtlessly. **2** fail to take advantage
of. ▷ *n* **3** act of wasting or state of
being wasted. **4** anything wasted.
5 rubbish. ▷ *pl* **6** desert. ▷ *adj*
7 rejected as worthless or surplus to
requirements. **8** not cultivated or
inhabited. **waste away** (cause to)
decline in health or strength. **wastage**
n **1** loss by wear or waste. **2** reduction
in size of a workforce by not filling
vacancies. **wasted** *adj* **1** unnecessary
or unfruitful. **2** pale, thin, and
unhealthy. **wasteful** *adj* extravagant.
wastefully *adv* **waster**, **wastrel** *n*
layabout. **wasteland** *n* barren or
desolate area of land. **wastepaper
basket** container for discarded paper.
watch ❶ *v* **1** look at closely. **2** look
after. **3** maintain a careful interest in.
4 guard or supervise. ▷ *n* **5** portable
timepiece for the wrist or pocket.
6 (period of) watching. **7** sailor's spell
of duty. **watchable** *adj* **watcher** *n*
watchful *adj* vigilant or alert.

——————————————————— THESAURUS ———————

affirm, attest, certify, declare, pledge,
vouch for
warranty *n* = **guarantee**, assurance,
bond, certificate, contract, covenant,
pledge
warrior *n* = **soldier**, combatant,
fighter, gladiator, man-at-arms
wary *adj* = **cautious**, alert, careful,
chary, circumspect, distrustful,
guarded, suspicious, vigilant, watchful
wash *v* **1** = **clean**, bathe, cleanse,
launder, rinse, scrub **3** = **sweep away**,
bear away, carry off, move **4** *Inf* =
be plausible, bear scrutiny, be
convincing, carry weight, hold up,
hold water, stand up, stick ▷ *n*
5 = **cleaning**, cleansing, laundering,
rinse, scrub **7** = **coat**, coating, film,
layer, overlay **8** = **swell**, surge, wave
washout *n Inf* = **failure**,
disappointment, disaster, dud (*inf*),
fiasco, flop (*inf*)
waste *v* **1** = **squander**, blow (*sl*),
dissipate, fritter away, lavish, misuse,

throw away ▷ *n* **3** = **squandering**,
dissipation, extravagance, frittering
away, misuse, prodigality,
wastefulness **5** = **rubbish**, debris,
dross, garbage, leftovers, litter,
refuse, scrap, trash ▷ *pl* **6** = **desert**,
wasteland, wilderness ▷ *adj*
7 = **unwanted**, leftover, superfluous,
supernumerary, unused, useless,
worthless **8** = **uncultivated**, bare,
barren, desolate, empty, uninhabited,
unproductive, wild **waste away** =
decline, atrophy, crumble, decay,
dwindle, fade, wane, wear out, wither
wasteful *adj* = **extravagant**, lavish,
prodigal, profligate, spendthrift,
thriftless, uneconomical
waster, wastrel *n* = **layabout**, good-
for-nothing, idler, loafer, ne'er-do-
well, piker (*Aust & NZ sl*), shirker, skiver
(*Brit sl*)
watch *v* **1** = **look at**, contemplate, eye,
eyeball (*sl*), observe, regard, see, view
2, 4 = **guard**, keep, look after, mind,

watchfully *adv* **watchfulness** *n*
watchdog *n* **1** dog kept to guard property. **2** person or group guarding against inefficiency or illegality.
watch for *v* be keenly alert to or cautious about. **watchman** *n* man employed to guard a building or property. **watchword** *n* word or phrase that sums up the attitude of a particular group.

water ❶ *n* **1** clear colourless tasteless liquid that falls as rain and forms rivers etc. **2** body of water, such as a sea or lake. **3** level of the tide. **4** urine. ▷ *v* **5** put water on or into. **6** (of the eyes) fill with tears. **7** (of the mouth) salivate. **watery** *adj* **water buffalo** oxlike Asian animal. **water closet** *old-fashioned* (room containing) a toilet flushed by water. **watercolour** *n* **1** paint thinned with water. **2** painting done in this. **watercourse** *n* bed of a stream or river. **watercress** *n* edible plant growing in clear ponds and streams. **water down** *v* dilute, make less strong. **waterfall** *n* place where the waters of a river drop vertically. **waterfront** *n* part of a town alongside a body of water. **waterhole** *n* pond or pool in a dry area where animals drink. **water ice** ice cream made from frozen fruit-flavoured syrup. **watering place 1** place where drinking water may be obtained for people or animals. **2** resort or spa. **water lily** water plant with large floating leaves. **waterline** *n* level to which a ship's hull will be immersed when afloat. **waterlogged** *adj* saturated with water. **watermark**

n faint translucent design in a sheet of paper. **watermelon** *n* melon with green skin and red flesh. **water polo** team game played by swimmers with a ball. **waterproof** *adj* **1** not letting water through. ▷ *n* **2** waterproof garment. ▷ *v* **3** make waterproof.
watershed *n* **1** important period or factor serving as a dividing line. **2** line separating two river systems. **water-skiing** *n* sport of riding over water on skis towed by a speedboat. **watertight** *adj* **1** not letting water through. **2** with no loopholes or weak points. **water wheel** large wheel which is turned by flowing water to drive machinery.

watt [wott] *n* unit of power. **wattage** *n* electrical power expressed in watts.
wattle [wott-tl] *n* **1** branches woven over sticks to make a fence. **2** Australian acacia with flexible branches formerly used for making fences. **3** fold of skin hanging from the neck of certain birds.

wave ❶ *v* **1** move the hand to and fro as a greeting or signal. **2** direct (someone) to move in a particular direction by waving. **3** move or flap to and fro. ▷ *n* **4** moving ridge on water. **5** curve(s) in the hair. **6** prolonged spell of something, e.g. *the recent wave of violence.* **7** gesture of waving. **8** vibration carrying energy through a medium. **wavy** *adj* **wavier**, **waviest**. **wavelength** *n* distance between the same points of two successive waves.
waver ❶ *v* **1** hesitate or be irresolute. **2** be or become unsteady. **waverer** *n* **wavering** *adj*.

THESAURUS

protect, superintend, take care of, tend ▷ *n* **5** = **wristwatch**, chronometer, timepiece **6** = **lookout**, observation, surveillance, vigil
watchdog *n* **1** = **guard dog 2** = **guardian**, custodian, monitor, protector, scrutineer
watchful *adj* = **alert**, attentive, observant, on the lookout, suspicious, vigilant, wary, wide awake
watchman *n* = **guard**, caretaker, custodian, security guard
watchword *n* = **motto**, battle cry, byword, catch phrase, catchword, maxim, rallying cry, slogan, tag-line
water *n* **1** = **liquid**, H2O ▷ *v* **5** = **moisten**, dampen, douse, drench, hose, irrigate, soak, spray

water down *v* = **dilute**, thin, water, weaken
waterfall *n* = **cascade**, cataract, fall
waterlogged *adj* = **soaked**, drenched, dripping, saturated, sodden, sopping, streaming, wet through, wringing wet
watertight *adj* **1** = **waterproof**, sound **2** = **foolproof**, airtight, flawless, impregnable, sound, unassailable
wave *v* **1** = **signal**, gesticulate, gesture, sign **2** = **direct**, beckon, indicate **3** = **flap**, brandish, flourish, flutter, oscillate, shake, stir, swing, wag ▷ *n* **4** = **ripple**, billow, breaker, ridge, roller, swell, undulation **6** = **outbreak**, flood, rash, rush, stream, surge, upsurge
waver *v* **1** = **hesitate**, dither, falter, fluctuate, hum and haw, seesaw,

wax¹ *n* **1** solid shiny fatty or oily substance used for sealing, making candles, etc. **2** similar substance made by bees. **3** waxy secretion of the ear. ▷ *v* **4** coat or polish with wax. **waxed** *adj* **waxen** *adj* made of or like wax. **waxy** *adj* **waxier**, **waxiest**. **waxwork** *n* **1** lifelike wax model of a (famous) person. ▷ *pl* **2** place exhibiting these.

wax² ❶ *v* **1** increase in size or strength. **2** (of the moon) get gradually larger.

way ❶ *n* **1** manner or method. **2** characteristic manner. **3** route or direction. **4** track or path. **5** distance. **6** room for movement or activity, e.g. *you're in the way.* **7** passage or journey. **8** *informal* state or condition, e.g. *in a bad way.* ▷ *pl* **9** habits or customs. **wayfarer** *n* traveller. **waylay** *v* lie in wait for and accost or attack. **way-out** *adj informal* extremely unconventional. **wayside** *adj, n* (situated by) the side of a road.

wayward ❶ *adj* erratic, selfish, or stubborn. **waywardness** *n*.

Wb *Physics* weber.

WC water closet.

we *pron* (used as the subject of a verb) **1** the speaker or writer and one or more others. **2** people in general.

3 formal word for 'I' used by editors and monarchs.

weak ❶ *adj* **1** lacking strength. **2** liable to give way. **3** unconvincing. **4** lacking flavour. **weaken** *v* make or become weak. **weakling** *n* feeble person or animal. **weakly** *adv* **1** feebly. ▷ *adj* **2** weak or sickly. **weakness** *n* **1** being weak. **2** failing. **3** self-indulgent liking. **weak-kneed** *adj informal* lacking determination.

weal¹ *n* raised mark left on the skin by a blow.

weal² *n obs* prosperity or wellbeing, esp. in *the common weal*.

wealth ❶ *n* **1** state of being rich. **2** large amount of money and valuables. **3** great amount or number. **wealthy** *adj* **wealthier**, **wealthiest**.

wean *v* **1** accustom (a baby or young mammal) to food other than mother's milk. **2** coax (someone) away from former habits.

weapon *n* **1** object used in fighting. **2** anything used to get the better of an opponent. **weaponry** *n* weapons collectively.

wear ❶ *v* **wearing**, **wore**, **worn 1** have on the body as clothing or ornament. **2** show as one's expression. **3** have (the hair) in a particular style.

—————————————— THESAURUS ——————————————

vacillate **2** = **tremble**, flicker, quiver, shake, totter, wobble

wax² *v* **1** = **increase**, develop, enlarge, expand, grow, magnify, swell

way *n* **1** = **method**, fashion, manner, means, mode, procedure, process, system, technique **2** = **style**, custom, habit, manner, nature, personality, practice, wont **3** = **route**, channel, course, direction **4** = **track**, path, pathway, road, trail **5** = **distance**, length, stretch **7** = **journey**, approach, march, passage

wayward *adj* **a** = **erratic**, capricious, inconstant, unpredictable **b** = **unmanageable**, ungovernable, unruly

weak *adj* **1** = **feeble**, debilitated, effete, fragile, frail, infirm, puny, sickly, unsteady **2** = **unsafe**, defenceless, exposed, helpless, unguarded, unprotected, vulnerable **3** = **unconvincing**, feeble, flimsy, hollow, lame, pathetic, unsatisfactory **4** = **tasteless**, diluted, insipid, runny, thin, watery

weaken *v* **a** = **lessen**, diminish, dwindle, fade, flag, lower, moderate, reduce, sap, undermine, wane **b** = **dilute**, thin out, water down

weakling *n* = **sissy**, drip (*inf*), wet (*Brit inf*), wimp (*inf*)

weakness *n* **1** = **frailty**, decrepitude, feebleness, fragility, infirmity, powerlessness, vulnerability **2** = **failing**, blemish, defect, deficiency, fault, flaw, imperfection, lack, shortcoming **3** = **liking**, fondness, inclination, partiality, passion, penchant, soft spot

wealth *n* **2** = **riches**, affluence, capital, fortune, lolly (*Aust & NZ sl*), money, opulence, prosperity **3** = **plenty**, abundance, copiousness, cornucopia, fullness, profusion, richness

wealthy *adj* **1** = **rich**, affluent, flush (*inf*), moneyed, opulent, prosperous, well-heeled (*inf*), well-off, well-to-do

wear *v* **1** = **be dressed in**, don, have on, put on, sport (*inf*) **2** = **show**, display, exhibit **4** = **deteriorate**, abrade, corrode, erode, fray, grind, rub ▷ *n*

4 (cause to) deteriorate by constant use or action. **5** *informal* tolerate. **6** endure constant use. ▷ *n* **7** clothes suitable for a particular time or purpose, e.g. *beach wear*. **8** damage caused by use. **9** ability to endure constant use. **wearable** *adj* **wearer** *n* **wearing** *adj* tiring and sometimes trying. **wear and tear** damage or loss from ordinary use. **wear off** *v* gradually decrease in intensity. **wear on** *v* (of time) pass slowly. **wear out** *v* **1** make or become useless through wear. **2** exhaust or tire.

weary ❶ *adj* **-rier, -riest 1** tired or exhausted. **2** tiring. ▷ *v* **-rying, -ried 3** make or become weary. **wearily** *adv* **weariness** *n* **wearisome** *adj* tedious. **wearying** *adj*.

weasel *n* small carnivorous mammal with a long body and short legs.

weather ❶ *n* **1** day-to-day atmospheric conditions of a place. ▷ *v* **2** (cause to) be affected by the weather. **3** come safely through. **under the weather** *informal* slightly ill. **weather-beaten** *adj* worn, damaged, or (of skin) tanned by exposure to the weather. **weathercock, weathervane** *n* device that revolves to show the direction of the wind. **weatherman** *n informal* person who forecasts the weather on television or radio.

weave ❶ *v* **weaving, wove** *or* **weaved,**

woven *or* **weaved 1** make (fabric) by interlacing (yarn) on a loom. **2** compose (a story). **3** move from side to side while going forwards. **weaver** *n* **weaving** *n*.

web ❶ *n* **1** net spun by a spider. **2** anything intricate or complex, e.g. *web of deceit*. **3** skin between the toes of a duck, frog, etc. **the Web** short for WORLD WIDE WEB. **webbed** *adj* **webbing** *n* strong fabric woven in strips. **webcam** *n* camera that transmits images over the internet. **webcast** *n* broadcast of an event over the internet. **weblog** *n* person's online journal (also **blog**). **website** *n* group of connected pages on the World Wide Web.

weber [**vay**-ber] *n* SI unit of magnetic flux.

wed ❶ *v* **wedding, wedded** *or* **wed 1** marry. **2** unite closely. **wedded** *adj* **1** of marriage. **2** firmly in support of an idea or institution. **wedding** *n* act or ceremony of marriage. **wedlock** *n* marriage.

Wed. Wednesday.

wedge ❶ *n* **1** piece of material thick at one end and thin at the other. ▷ *v* **2** fasten or split with a wedge. **3** squeeze into a narrow space. **wedge-tailed eagle** large brown Australian eagle with a wedge-shaped tail.

THESAURUS

7 = **clothes**, apparel, attire, costume, dress, garb, garments, gear (*inf*), things **8** = **damage**, abrasion, attrition, corrosion, deterioration, erosion, wear and tear
weariness *n* **1** = **tiredness**, drowsiness, exhaustion, fatigue, languor, lassitude, lethargy, listlessness
wearing *adj* = **tiresome**, exasperating, fatiguing, irksome, oppressive, trying, wearisome
wearisome *adj* = **tedious**, annoying, boring, exhausting, fatiguing, irksome, oppressive, tiresome, troublesome, trying, wearing
wear off *v* = **subside**, decrease, diminish, disappear, dwindle, fade, peter out, wane
weary *adj* **1** = **tired**, done in (*inf*), drained, drowsy, exhausted, fatigued, flagging, jaded, sleepy, worn out **2** = **tiring**, arduous, laborious,

tiresome, wearisome ▷ *v* **3** = **tire**, drain, enervate, fatigue, sap, take it out of (*inf*), tax, tire out, wear out
weather *n* **1** = **climate**, conditions ▷ *v* **3** = **withstand**, brave, come through, endure, overcome, resist, ride out, stand, survive
weave *v* **1** = **knit**, braid, entwine, interlace, intertwine, plait **2** = **create**, build, construct, contrive, fabricate, make up, put together, spin **3** = **zigzag**, crisscross, wind
web *n* **1** = **spider's web**, cobweb **2** = **network**, lattice, tangle
wed *v* **1** = **marry**, get married, take the plunge (*inf*), tie the knot (*inf*) **2** = **unite**, ally, blend, combine, interweave, join, link, merge
wedding *n* = **marriage**, nuptials, wedlock
wedge *n* **1** = **block**, chunk, lump ▷ *v* **3** = **squeeze**, cram, crowd, force, jam, lodge, pack, ram, stuff, thrust

W

Wednesday n fourth day of the week.
wee adj small.
weed ❶ n 1 plant growing where undesired. 2 informal thin ineffectual person. ▷ v 3 clear of weeds. **weedy** adj **weedier**, **weediest** 1 informal (of a person) thin and weak. 2 full of or like weeds. **weed out** v remove or eliminate (what is unwanted).
weeds pl n obs widow's mourning clothes.
week n 1 period of seven days, esp. one beginning on a Sunday. 2 hours or days of work in a week. **weekly** adj, adv 1 happening, done, etc. once a week. ▷ n, pl **-lies** 2 newspaper or magazine published once a week. **weekday** n any day of the week except Saturday or Sunday. **weekend** n Saturday and Sunday.
weep ❶ v **weeping**, **wept** 1 shed tears. 2 ooze liquid. ▷ n 3 spell of weeping. **weepy** adj **weepier**, **weepiest** liable to cry. **weeping willow** willow with drooping branches.
weevil n small beetle which eats grain etc.
weft n cross threads in weaving.
weigh ❶ v 1 have a specified weight. 2 measure the weight of. 3 consider carefully. 4 be influential. 5 be burdensome. **weigh anchor** raise a ship's anchor or (of a ship) have its anchor raised. **weighbridge** n machine for weighing vehicles by means of a metal plate set into the road.

weight ❶ n 1 heaviness of an object. 2 unit of measurement of weight. 3 object of known mass used for weighing. 4 heavy object. 5 importance or influence. ▷ v 6 add weight to. 7 slant (a system) so that it favours one side rather than another. **weightless** adj **weightlessness** n **weightlifting** n sport of lifting heavy weights. **weightlifter** n **weight training** physical exercise using weights to improve muscles.
weighting n extra allowance paid in special circumstances.
weighty ❶ adj **weightier**, **weightiest** 1 important or serious. 2 very heavy. **weightily** adv.
weir n river dam.
weird ❶ adj 1 strange or bizarre. 2 unearthly or eerie. **weirdly** adv.

● **SPELLING TIP**
● The pronunciation of **weird** possibly
● leads people to spell it with the
● vowels the wrong way round. The
● Bank of English shows that wierd is a
● common misspelling.

weirdo n, pl **-dos** informal peculiar person.
welch v same as WELSH.
welcome ❶ v **-coming**, **-comed** 1 greet with pleasure. 2 receive gladly. ▷ n 3 kindly greeting. ▷ adj 4 received gladly. 5 freely permitted.
weld ❶ v 1 join (pieces of metal or plastic) by softening with heat. 2 unite closely. ▷ n 3 welded joint. **welder** n.

——————————————— THESAURUS ———————

wedlock n = **marriage**, matrimony
weed out v = **eliminate**, dispense with, eradicate, get rid of, remove, root out, uproot
weedy adj 1 Inf = **weak**, feeble, frail, ineffectual, namby-pamby, puny, skinny, thin
weep v 1 = **cry**, blubber, lament, mourn, shed tears, snivel, sob, whimper
weigh v 1 = **have a weight of**, tip the scales at (inf) 3 = **consider**, contemplate, deliberate upon, evaluate, examine, meditate upon, ponder, reflect upon, think over 4 = **matter**, carry weight, count
weight n 1 = **heaviness**, load, mass, poundage, tonnage 5 = **importance**, authority, consequence, impact, import, influence, mana (NZ), power,

value ▷ v 6 = **load**, freight 7 = **bias**, load, slant, unbalance
weighty adj 1 = **important**, consequential, crucial, grave, momentous, portentous, serious, significant, solemn 2 = **heavy**, burdensome, cumbersome, hefty (inf), massive, ponderous
weird adj 1 = **strange**, bizarre, freakish, odd, queer, unnatural 2 = **eerie**, creepy (inf), mysterious, spooky (inf)
welcome v 1 = **greet**, embrace, hail, meet 2 = **receive** ▷ n 3 = **greeting**, acceptance, hospitality, reception, salutation ▷ adj 4 = **acceptable**, agreeable, appreciated, delightful, desirable, gratifying, pleasant, refreshing 5 = **free**, under no obligation
weld v 1 = **solder**, fuse 2 = **unite**, bind, bond, connect, join, link

w

welfare ❶ n 1 wellbeing. 2 help given to people in need. **welfare state** system in which the government takes responsibility for the wellbeing of its citizens.

well¹ ❶ adv **better**, **best** 1 satisfactorily. 2 skilfully. 3 completely. 4 prosperously. 5 suitably. 6 intimately. 7 favourably. 8 considerably. 9 very likely. ▷ adj 10 in good health. 11 satisfactory. ▷ interj 12 exclamation of surprise, interrogation, etc.

well² ❶ n 1 hole sunk into the earth to reach water, oil, or gas. 2 deep open shaft. ▷ v 3 flow upwards or outwards.

wellbeing n state of being well, happy, or prosperous.

well-built adj strong and muscular.

well-disposed adj inclined to be friendly or sympathetic.

well-done adj 1 accomplished satisfactorily. 2 (of food, esp. meat) thoroughly cooked.

well-heeled adj informal wealthy.

wellies pl n informal wellingtons.

wellingtons pl n high waterproof rubber boots.

well-known ❶ adj famous.

well-meaning adj having good intentions.

well-nigh adv almost.

well-off ❶ adj 1 moderately wealthy. 2 in a fortunate position.

well-spoken adj speaking in a polite or articulate way.

well-to-do ❶ adj moderately wealthy.

well-worn ❶ adj 1 (of a word or phrase) stale from overuse. 2 so much used as to be affected by wear.

welsh v fail to pay a debt or fulfil an obligation.

Welsh adj 1 of Wales. ▷ n 2 language or people of Wales. **Welsh rarebit, rabbit** dish of melted cheese on toast.

welt ❶ n 1 raised mark on the skin produced by a blow. 2 raised or strengthened seam.

welter n jumbled mass.

welterweight n boxer weighing up to 147lb (professional) or 67kg (amateur).

wen n cyst on the scalp.

wench n facetious young woman.

wend v go or travel.

wensleydale n type of white cheese of flaky texture.

went v past tense of GO.

wept v past of WEEP.

were v 1 form of the past tense of **be** used after we, you, they, or a plural noun. 2 subjunctive of BE.

we're we are.

weren't were not.

werewolf n (in folklore) person who can turn into a wolf.

west n 1 (direction towards) the part of the horizon where the sun sets. 2 region lying in this direction. 3 (**W-**) western Europe and the US. ▷ adj 4 to or in the west. 5 (of a wind) from the west. ▷ adv 6 in, to, or towards the west. **westerly** adj **western** adj 1 of or in the west. ▷ n 2 film or story about cowboys in the western US.

westerner n person from the west of

THESAURUS

welfare n 1 = **wellbeing**, advantage, benefit, good, happiness, health, interest, prosperity

well¹ adv 1 = **satisfactorily**, agreeably, nicely, pleasantly, smoothly, splendidly, successfully 2 = **skilfully**, ably, adeptly, adequately, admirably, correctly, efficiently, expertly, proficiently, properly 3 = **fully**, thoroughly 4 = **prosperously**, comfortably 5 = **suitably**, fairly, fittingly, justly, properly, rightly 6 = **intimately**, deeply, profoundly 7 = **favourably**, approvingly, glowingly, highly, kindly, warmly 8 = **considerably**, abundantly, amply, fully, greatly, heartily, highly, substantially, thoroughly, very much ▷ adj 10 = **healthy**, fit, in fine fettle,

sound 11 = **satisfactory**, agreeable, fine, pleasing, proper, right

well² n 1, 2 = **hole**, bore, pit, shaft ▷ v 3 = **flow**, gush, jet, pour, spout, spring, spurt, surge

well-known adj = **famous**, celebrated, familiar, noted, popular, renowned

well-off adj 1 = **rich**, affluent, comfortable, moneyed, prosperous, wealthy, well-heeled (inf), well-to-do

well-to-do adj = **rich**, affluent, comfortable, moneyed, prosperous, wealthy, well-heeled (inf), well-off

well-worn adj 1 = **stale**, banal, commonplace, hackneyed, overused, stereotyped, trite

welt n 1 = **mark**, contusion, streak, stripe, wale, weal

a country or area. **westernize** v adapt to the customs and culture of the West. **westward** adj, adv **westwards** adv.

wet ❶ adj **wetter**, **wettest** 1 covered or soaked with water or another liquid. 2 not yet dry, e.g. wet paint. 3 rainy. 4 informal (of a person) feeble or foolish. ▷ n 5 moisture or rain. 6 informal feeble or foolish person. 7 Brit moderate Conservative politician. ▷ v **wetting**, **wet** or **wetted** 8 make wet. **wetly** adv **wetness** n **wet blanket** informal person who has a depressing effect on others. **wetland** n area of marshy land. **wet nurse** woman employed to breast-feed another's child. **wet suit** close-fitting rubber suit worn by divers etc.

whack ❶ v 1 strike with a resounding blow. ▷ n 2 such a blow. 3 informal share. 4 informal attempt. **whacked** adj exhausted. **whacking** adj informal huge.

whale n large fish-shaped sea mammal. **a whale of a time** informal a very enjoyable time. **whaling** n hunting of whales. **whaler** n ship or person involved in whaling. **whalebone** n horny substance hanging from the upper jaw of toothless whales.

wham interj expression indicating suddenness or forcefulness.

wharf ❶ n, pl **wharves**, **wharfs** platform at a harbour for loading and unloading ships. **wharfie** n Aust person employed to load and unload ships.

what pron 1 which thing. 2 that which. 3 request for a statement to be repeated. ▷ interj 4 exclamation of anger, surprise, etc. ▷ adv 5 in which way, how much, e.g. what do you care? **what for?** why? **whatever** pron 1 everything or anything that. 2 no matter what. **whatnot** n informal similar unspecified things. **whatsoever** adj at all.

wheat n 1 grain used in making flour, bread, and pasta. 2 plant producing this. **wheaten** adj made of the grain or flour of wheat. **wheatear** n small songbird. **wheatgerm** n vitamin-rich embryo of the wheat kernel. **wheatmeal** adj, n (made with) brown, but not wholemeal, flour.

wheedle ❶ v coax or cajole.

wheel ❶ n 1 disc that revolves on an axle. 2 something repeated in cycles, e.g wheel of life. 3 pivoting movement. ▷ v 4 push or pull (something with wheels). 5 turn as if on an axis. 6 turn round suddenly. **wheeling and dealing** use of shrewd and sometimes unscrupulous methods to achieve success. **wheeler-dealer** n **wheelie** n manoeuvre on a bike in which the front wheel is raised off the ground. **wheelie bin** large container for household rubbish, mounted on wheels for easy movement. **wheelbarrow** n shallow box for carrying loads, with a wheel at the front and two handles. **wheelbase** n distance between a vehicle's front and back axles. **wheelchair** n chair mounted on wheels for use by people who cannot walk. **wheel clamp** immobilizing device fixed to one wheel of an illegally parked car. **wheelwright** n person who makes or mends wheels as a trade.

THESAURUS

wet adj 1 = **damp**, dank, moist, saturated, soaking, sodden, soggy, sopping, waterlogged, watery 3 = **rainy**, drizzling, pouring, raining, showery, teeming 4 Inf = **feeble**, effete, ineffectual, namby-pamby, soft, spineless, timorous, weak, weedy (inf) ▷ n 5 = **moisture**, condensation, damp, dampness, drizzle, humidity, liquid, rain, water, wetness 6 Inf = **weakling**, drip (inf), weed (inf), wimp (inf) ▷ v 8 = **moisten**, dampen, douse, irrigate, saturate, soak, spray, water

whack v 1 = **strike**, bang, belt (inf), clobber (sl), hit, smack, swipe, thrash, thump, thwack, wallop (inf) ▷ n 2 = **blow**, bang, belt (inf), hit, smack, stroke, swipe, thump, thwack, wallop (inf) 3 Inf = **share**, bit, cut (inf), part, portion, quota 4 Inf = **attempt**, bash (inf), crack (inf), go (inf), shot (inf), stab (inf), try, turn

wharf n = **dock**, jetty, landing stage, pier, quay

wheedle v = **coax**, cajole, entice, inveigle, persuade

wheel n 3 = **circle**, gyration, pivot, revolution, rotation, spin, turn ▷ v 5, 6 = **turn**, gyrate, pirouette, revolve, rotate, spin, swing, swivel, twirl, whirl

w

wheeze ❶ v **1** breathe with a hoarse whistling noise. ▷ n **2** wheezing sound. **3** informal trick or plan. **wheezy** adj **wheezier**, **wheeziest**.

whelk n edible snail-like shellfish.

whelp n **1** pup or cub. **2** offens youth. ▷ v **3** (of an animal) give birth.

when adv **1** at what time? ▷ conj **2** at the time that. **3** although. **4** considering the fact that. ▷ pron **5** at which time. **whenever** adv, conj at whatever time.

whence adv, conj obs from what place or source.

where ❶ adv **1** in, at, or to what place? ▷ pron **2** in, at, or to which place. ▷ conj **3** in the place at which. **whereabouts** n **1** present position. ▷ adv **2** at what place. **whereas** conj but on the other hand. **whereby** pron by which. **wherefore** obs ▷ adv **1** why. ▷ conj **2** consequently. **whereupon** conj at which point. **wherever** conj, adv at whatever place. **wherewithal** n necessary funds, resources, etc.

whet ❶ v **whetting**, **whetted** sharpen (a tool). **whet someone's appetite** increase someone's desire. **whetstone** n stone for sharpening tools.

whether conj used to introduce an indirect question or a clause expressing doubt or choice.

whew interj exclamation expressing relief, delight, etc.

whey [way] n watery liquid that separates from the curd when milk is clotted.

which adj, pron **1** used to request or refer to a choice from different possibilities. ▷ pron **2** used to refer to a thing already mentioned. **whichever** adj, pron **1** any out of several. **2** no matter which.

whiff ❶ n **1** puff of air or odour. **2** trace or hint.

Whig n member of a British political party of the 18th–19th centuries that sought limited reform.

while conj **1** at the same time that. **2** during the time that. **3** whereas. ▷ n **4** period of time. **whilst** conj while. **while away** v pass (time) idly but pleasantly.

whim ❶ n sudden fancy. **whimsy** n, pl **-sies 1** capricious idea. **2** light or fanciful humour. **whimsical** adj unusual, playful, and fanciful.

whimper ❶ v **1** cry in a soft whining way. ▷ n **2** soft plaintive whine.

whin n gorse.

whine ❶ n **1** high-pitched plaintive cry. **2** peevish complaint. ▷ v **3** make such a sound. **whining** n, adj.

whinge ❶ informal ▷ v **1** complain. ▷ n **2** complaint.

whinny v **-nying**, **-nied 1** neigh softly. ▷ n, pl **-nies 2** soft neigh.

whip ❶ n **1** cord attached to a handle, used for beating animals or people. **2** politician responsible for organizing and disciplining fellow party members. **3** call made on members of Parliament to attend for important votes. **4** dessert made from beaten cream or egg whites. ▷ v **whipping**, **whipped 5** strike with a whip, strap, or cane. **6** informal pull, remove, or move quickly. **7** beat (esp. eggs or

---

wheeze v **1** = **gasp**, cough, hiss, rasp, whistle ▷ n **2** = **gasp**, cough, hiss, rasp, whistle **3** Inf = **trick**, idea, plan, ploy, ruse, scheme, stunt

whereabouts n **1** = **position**, location, site, situation

wherewithal n = **resources**, capital, funds, lolly (Aust & NZ sl), means, money, supplies

whet v **1** = **sharpen**, hone **whet someone's appetite** = **stimulate**, arouse, awaken, enhance, excite, kindle, quicken, rouse, stir

whiff n **1** = **smell**, aroma, hint, odour, scent, sniff

whim n = **impulse**, caprice, fancy, notion, urge

whimper v **1** = **cry**, moan, snivel, sob, weep, whine, whinge (inf) ▷ n **2** = **sob**, moan, snivel, whine

whimsical adj = **fanciful**, curious, eccentric, freakish, funny, odd, playful, quaint, unusual

whine n **1** = **cry**, moan, sob, wail, whimper **2** = **complaint**, gripe (inf), grouch (inf), grouse, grumble, moan, whinge (inf) ▷ v **3** = **cry**, moan, sniffle, snivel, sob, wail, whimper

whinge Inf ▷ v **1** = **complain**, bleat, carp, gripe (inf), grouse, grumble, moan ▷ n **2** = **complaint**, gripe (inf), grouch, grouse, grumble, moan, whine

whip n **1** = **lash**, birch, cane, cat-o'-nine-tails, crop, scourge ▷ v **5** = **lash**, beat, birch, cane, flagellate, flog, scourge, spank, strap, thrash

w

cream) to a froth. **8** rouse into a particular condition. **9** *informal* steal. **whip bird** *Aust* bird with a whistle ending in a whipcrack note. **whip hand** advantage. **whiplash injury** neck injury caused by a sudden jerk to the head, as in a car crash. **whipping boy** scapegoat. **whip-round** *n informal* collection of money.

whippet *n* racing dog like a small greyhound.

whirl ❶ *v* **1** spin or revolve. **2** be dizzy or confused. ▷ *n* **3** whirling movement. **4** bustling activity. **5** confusion or giddiness. **whirlpool** *n* strong circular current of water. **whirlwind** *n* **1** column of air whirling violently upwards in a spiral. ▷ *adj* **2** much quicker than normal.

whirr, whir *n* **1** prolonged soft buzz. ▷ *v* **whirring, whirred 2** (cause to) make a whirr.

whisk ❶ *v* **1** move or remove quickly. **2** beat (esp. eggs or cream) to a froth. ▷ *n* **3** quick movement. **4** egg-beating utensil.

whisker *n* **1** any of the long stiff hairs on the face of a cat or other mammal. ▷ *pl* **2** hair growing on a man's face. **by a whisker** *informal* only just. **whiskered, whiskery** *adj*.

whisky *n, pl* **-kies** spirit distilled from fermented cereals. **whiskey** *n, pl* **-keys** Irish or American whisky.

whisper ❶ *v* **1** speak softly, without vibration of the vocal cords. **2** rustle. ▷ *n* **3** soft voice. **4** *informal* rumour. **5** rustling sound.

whist *n* card game in which one pair of players tries to win more tricks than another pair. **whist drive** social event

at which whist is played.

whistle *v* **1** produce a shrill sound, esp. by forcing the breath through pursed lips. **2** signal by a whistle. ▷ *n* **3** whistling sound. **4** instrument blown to make a whistling sound. **blow the whistle on** *informal* inform on or put a stop to. **whistling** *n, adj*.

whit *n* **not a whit** not the slightest amount.

white ❶ *adj* **1** of the colour of snow. **2** pale. **3** light in colour. **4** (of coffee) served with milk. ▷ *n* **5** colour of snow. **6** clear fluid round the yolk of an egg. **7** white part, esp. of the eyeball. **8** (**W-**) member of the race of people with light-coloured skin. **whiten** *v* make or become white or whiter. **whiteness** *n* **whitish** *adj* **white ant** same as TERMITE. **white blood cell** same as LEUCOCYTE. **white-collar** *adj* denoting professional and clerical workers. **white elephant** useless or unwanted possession. **white fish** any sea fish with white flesh used as food. **white flag** signal of surrender or truce. **white goods** large household appliances such as cookers and fridges. **white-hot** *adj* very hot. **White House 1** official residence of the US president. **2** US presidency. **white lie** minor unimportant lie. **white paper** report by the government, outlining its policy on a matter. **white sauce** thick sauce made from butter, flour, and milk or stock.

whitebait *n* small edible fish.

whitewash ❶ *n* **1** substance for whitening walls. **2** attempt to conceal unpleasant facts. ▷ *v* **3** cover with

—————————————————————— THESAURUS ——————

6 *Inf* = **dash**, dart, dive, fly, rush, shoot, tear, whisk **7** = **whisk**, beat **8** = **incite**, agitate, drive, foment, goad, spur, stir, work up

whirl *v* **1** = **spin**, pirouette, revolve, roll, rotate, swirl, turn, twirl, twist **2** = **feel dizzy**, reel, spin ▷ *n* **3** = **revolution**, pirouette, roll, rotation, spin, swirl, turn, twirl, twist **4** = **bustle**, flurry, merry-go-round, round, series, succession **5** = **confusion**, daze, dither, giddiness, spin

whirlwind *n* **1** = **tornado**, waterspout ▷ *adj* **2** = **rapid**, hasty, quick, short, speedy, swift

whisk *v* **1** = **flick**, brush, sweep, whip

2 = **beat**, fluff up, whip ▷ *n* **3** = **flick**, brush, sweep, whip **4** = **beater**

whisper *v* **1** = **murmur**, breathe **2** = **rustle**, hiss, sigh, swish ▷ *n* **3** = **murmur**, undertone **4** *Inf* = **rumour**, gossip, innuendo, insinuation, report **5** = **rustle**, hiss, sigh, swish

white *adj* **2** = **pale**, ashen, pallid, pasty, wan

white-collar *adj* = **clerical**, nonmanual, professional, salaried

whiten *v* = **pale**, blanch, bleach, fade

whitewash *n* **2** = **cover-up**, camouflage, concealment, deception ▷ *v* **4** = **cover up**, camouflage,

whitewash. **4** conceal or gloss over unpleasant facts.

whither adv obs to what place.

whiting [white-ing] n edible sea fish.

whitlow n inflamed sore on a finger or toe, esp. round a nail.

Whitsun, Whitsuntide n Christian festival celebrating the descent of the Holy Spirit to the apostles.

whittle ❶ v cut or carve (wood) with a knife. **whittle down, away** v reduce or wear away gradually.

whizz, whiz v **whizzing, whizzed** **1** make a loud buzzing sound. **2** informal move quickly. ▷ n, pl **whizzes** **3** loud buzzing sound. **4** informal person skilful at something. **whizz kid**, **whiz kid** informal person who is outstandingly able for his or her age.

who pron **1** which person. **2** used to refer to a person or people already mentioned. **whoever** pron **1** any person who. **2** no matter who.

WHO World Health Organization.

whoa interj command used, esp. to horses, to stop or slow down.

whodunnit, whodunit [hoo-**dun**-nit] n informal detective story, play, or film.

whole ❶ adj **1** containing all the elements or parts. **2** uninjured or undamaged. ▷ n **3** complete thing or system. **on the whole** taking everything into consideration. **wholly** adv **wholefood** n food that has been processed as little as possible. **wholehearted** adj sincere or enthusiastic. **wholemeal** adj **1** (of flour) made from the whole wheat

grain. **2** made from wholemeal flour.

whole number number that does not contain a fraction.

wholesale ❶ adj, adv **1** dealing by selling goods in large quantities to retailers. **2** on a large scale. **wholesaler** n.

wholesome ❶ adj physically or morally beneficial.

whom pron objective form of WHO.

whoop v, n shout or cry to express excitement.

whoopee interj informal cry of joy.

whooping cough n infectious disease marked by convulsive coughing and noisy breathing.

whoops interj exclamation of surprise or of apology.

whopper ❶ n informal **1** anything unusually large. **2** huge lie. **whopping** adj.

whore ❶ [hore] n prostitute.

whorl n **1** ring of leaves or petals. **2** one turn of a spiral. **3** something coiled.

whose pron of whom or of which.

why adv **1** for what reason. ▷ pron **2** because of which.

WI 1 Wisconsin. **2** Brit Women's Institute.

wick n cord through a lamp or candle which carries fuel to the flame.

wicked ❶ adj **1** morally bad. **2** mischievous. **3** dangerous. **4** slang very good. **wickedly** adv **wickedness** n.

wicker adj made of woven cane. **wickerwork** n.

wicket n **1** set of three cricket stumps and two bails. **2** ground between the two wickets on a cricket pitch.

──────────── THESAURUS ────────────

conceal, gloss over, suppress

whittle v = **carve**, cut, hew, pare, shape, shave, trim

whittle down, away v = **reduce**, consume, eat away, erode, wear away

whole adj **1** = **complete**, entire, full, total, unabridged, uncut, undivided **2** = **undamaged**, in one piece, intact, unbroken, unharmed, unscathed, untouched ▷ n **3** = **totality**, ensemble, entirety **on the whole** = **all in all**, all things considered, by and large

wholehearted adj = **sincere**, committed, dedicated, determined, devoted, enthusiastic, unstinting, zealous

wholesale adj = **extensive**, broad,

comprehensive, far-reaching, indiscriminate, mass, sweeping, wide-ranging ▷ adv = **extensively**, comprehensively, indiscriminately

wholesome adj **a** = **healthy**, beneficial, good, nourishing, nutritious, salubrious **b** = **moral**, decent, edifying, improving

whopper n Inf **1** = **giant**, colossus, crackerjack (inf), jumbo (inf), leviathan, mammoth, monster **2** = **big lie**, fabrication, falsehood, tall story (inf), untruth

whore n = **prostitute**, call girl, streetwalker, tart (inf)

wicked adj **1** = **bad**, corrupt, depraved, devilish, evil, fiendish, immoral, sinful, vicious, villainous **2** = **mischievous**,

w

wicketkeeper *n* fielder positioned directly behind the wicket.

wide ● *adj* **1** large from side to side. **2** having a specified width. **3** spacious or extensive. **4** far from the target. **5** opened fully. ▷ *adv* **6** to the full extent. **7** over an extensive area. **8** far from the target. **widely** *adv* **widen** *v* make or become wider. **wide-awake** *adj* fully awake. **wide-eyed** *adj* **1** naive or innocent. **2** surprised or frightened. **widespread** *adj* affecting a wide area or a large number of people.

widgeon *n* same as WIGEON.

widow *n* woman whose spouse is dead and who has not remarried. **widowed** *adj* **widowhood** *n* **widower** *n* man whose spouse is dead and who has not remarried.

width ● *n* **1** distance from side to side. **2** quality of being wide.

wield ● *v* **1** hold and use (a weapon). **2** have and use (power).

wife ● *n, pl* **wives** woman to whom a person is married. **wifely** *adj*.

Wi-Fi *n* system of wireless access to the internet.

wig *n* artificial head of hair.

wigeon *n* duck found in marshland.

wigging *n Brit slang* reprimand.

wiggle ● *v* **1** move jerkily from side to side. ▷ *n* **2** wiggling movement.

wiggly *adj* **wigglier**, **wiggliest**.

wigwam *n* Native American's tent.

wiki *n Computers* website that can be edited by anyone.

wilco *interj* expression in telecommunications etc., indicating that the message just received will be complied with.

wild ● *adj* **1** (of animals) not tamed or domesticated. **2** (of plants) not cultivated. **3** not civilized. **4** lacking restraint or control. **5** violent or stormy. **6** *informal* excited. **7** *informal* furious. **8** random. **wilds** *pl n* desolate or uninhabited place. **wildly** *adv* **wildness** *n* **wild-goose chase** search that has little chance of success. **Wild West** western US, which was lawless during settlement.

wildcat *n* European wild animal like a large domestic cat. **wildcat strike** sudden unofficial strike.

wildebeest *n* gnu.

wilderness ● *n* **1** uninhabited uncultivated region. **2** state of no longer being in a prominent position.

wildfire *n* **spread like wildfire** spread quickly and uncontrollably.

wildlife *n* wild animals and plants collectively.

wiles ● *pl n* tricks or ploys. **wily** *adj* **wilier**, **wiliest** crafty or sly.

impish, incorrigible, naughty, rascally, roguish

wide *adj* **1** = **broad**, expansive, extensive, far-reaching, immense, large, overarching, sweeping, vast **3** = **spacious**, baggy, capacious, commodious, full, loose, roomy **4** = **distant**, off course, off target, remote **5** = **expanded**, dilated, distended, outspread, outstretched ▷ *adv* **6** = **fully**, completely **8** = **off target**, astray, off course, off the mark, out

widen *v* = **broaden**, dilate, enlarge, expand, extend, spread, stretch

widespread *adj* = **common**, broad, extensive, far-reaching, general, pervasive, popular, universal

width *n* **1** = **breadth**, compass, diameter, extent, girth, scope, span, thickness

wield *v* **1** = **brandish**, employ, flourish, handle, manage, manipulate, ply, swing, use **2** = **exert**, exercise, have, maintain, possess

wife *n* = **spouse**, better half (*hum*), bride, mate, partner

wiggle *v, n* **1, 2** = **jerk**, jiggle, shake, shimmy, squirm, twitch, wag, waggle, writhe

wild *adj* **1** = **untamed**, feral, ferocious, fierce, savage, unbroken, undomesticated **2** = **uncultivated**, natural **3** = **uncivilized**, barbaric, barbarous, brutish, ferocious, fierce, primitive, savage **4** = **uncontrolled**, disorderly, riotous, rowdy, turbulent, undisciplined, unmanageable, unrestrained, unruly, wayward **5** = **stormy**, blustery, choppy, raging, rough, tempestuous, violent **6** *Inf* = **excited**, crazy (*inf*), enthusiastic, hysterical, raving ▷ *pl n* **wilds** = **wilderness**, back of beyond (*inf*), desert, middle of nowhere (*inf*), wasteland

wilderness *n* **1** = **desert**, jungle, wasteland, wilds

wiles *pl n* = **trickery**, artfulness, chicanery, craftiness, cunning, guile, slyness

W

wilful ❶ *adj* **1** headstrong or obstinate. **2** intentional. **wilfully** *adv* **wilfulness** *n*.

will¹ ❶ *v*, *past* **would** used as an auxiliary to form the future tense or to indicate intention, ability, or expectation.

● **USAGE NOTE**
● *Will* is normal for discussing
● the future. The use of *shall* with
● *I* and *we* is a matter of preference,
● not of rule. *Shall* is commonly used
● for questions in Southern England
● but less often in the North and
● Scotland.

will² ❶ *n* **1** strong determination. **2** desire or wish. **3** directions written for disposal of one's property after death. ▷ *v* **4** use one's will in an attempt to do (something). **5** wish or desire. **6** leave (property) by a will. **willing** *adj* **1** ready or inclined (to do something). **2** keen and obliging. **willingly** *adv* **willingness** *n* **willpower** *n* ability to control oneself and one's actions.

willies *pl n* **give someone the willies** *slang* cause nervousness or fright.

will-o'-the-wisp *n* **1** elusive person or thing. **2** pale light sometimes seen over marshes at night.

willow *n* **1** tree with thin flexible branches. **2** its wood, used for making cricket bats. **willowy** *adj* slender and graceful.

willy-nilly *adv* whether desired or not.

wilt ❶ *v* (cause to) become limp or lose strength.

wimp ❶ *n informal* feeble ineffectual person.

wimple *n* garment framing the face, worn by medieval women and now by nuns.

win ❶ *v* **winning**, **won 1** come first in (a competition, fight, etc.). **2** gain (a prize) in a competition. **3** get by effort. ▷ *n* **4** victory, esp. in a game. **winner** *n* **winning** *adj* **1** gaining victory. **2** charming. **winnings** *pl n* sum won, esp. in gambling. **win over** *v* gain the support or consent of (someone).

wince ❶ *v* **1** draw back, as if in pain. ▷ *n* **2** wincing.

winch *n* **1** machine for lifting or hauling using a cable wound round a drum. ▷ *v* **2** lift or haul using a winch.

wind¹ ❶ *n* **1** current of air. **2** hint or suggestion. **3** breath. **4** flatulence. **5** idle talk. ▷ *v* **6** render short of breath. **windy** *adj* **windier**, **windiest**. **windward** *adj*, *n* (of or in) the direction from which the wind is blowing. **windbag** *n slang* person who talks much but uninterestingly. **windbreak** *n* fence or line of trees providing shelter from the wind. **windfall** *n* **1** unexpected good luck. **2** fallen fruit. **wind farm** collection of wind-driven turbines for generating electricity. **wind instrument** musical instrument

———— THESAURUS ————

wilful *adj* **1** = **obstinate**, determined, headstrong, inflexible, intransigent, obdurate, perverse, pig-headed, stubborn, uncompromising
2 = **intentional**, conscious, deliberate, intended, purposeful, voluntary

will² *n* **1** = **determination**, purpose, resolution, resolve, willpower
2 = **wish**, desire, fancy, inclination, mind, preference, volition
3 = **testament**, last wishes ▷ *v*
5 = **wish**, desire, prefer, see fit, want
6 = **bequeath**, confer, give, leave, pass on, transfer

willing *adj* **1** = **ready**, agreeable, amenable, compliant, consenting, game (*inf*), inclined, prepared

willpower *n* = **self-control**, determination, drive, grit, resolution, resolve, self-discipline, single-mindedness

wilt *v* **a** = **droop**, sag, shrivel, wither
b = **weaken**, fade, flag, languish, wane

wily *adj* = **cunning**, artful, astute, crafty, guileful, sharp, shrewd, sly, tricky

wimp *n Inf* = **weakling**, coward, drip (*inf*), mouse, sissy, softy *or* softie

win *v* **1** = **triumph**, come first, conquer, overcome, prevail, succeed, sweep the board **3** = **gain**, achieve, acquire, attain, earn, get, land, obtain, procure, secure ▷ *n* **4** = **victory**, conquest, success, triumph

wince *v* **1** = **flinch**, blench, cower, cringe, draw back, quail, recoil, shrink, start ▷ *n* **2** = **flinch**, cringe, start

wind¹ *n* **1** = **air**, blast, breeze, draught, gust, zephyr **2** = **hint**, inkling, notice, report, rumour, suggestion, warning, whisper **3** = **breath**, puff, respiration

W

played by blowing. **windmill** *n* machine for grinding or pumping driven by sails turned by the wind. **windpipe** *n* tube linking the throat and the lungs. **windscreen** *n* front window of a motor vehicle. **windscreen wiper** device that wipes rain etc. from a windscreen. **windsock** *n* cloth cone on a mast at an airfield to indicate wind direction. **windsurfing** *n* sport of riding on water using a surfboard propelled and steered by a sail. **windswept** *adj* exposed to the wind.

wind² ❶ *v* **winding, wound 1** coil or wrap around. **2** tighten the spring of (a clock or watch). **3** move in a twisting course. **wind up** *v* **1** bring to or reach an end. **2** tighten the spring of (a clock or watch). **3** *informal* make tense or agitated. **4** *slang* tease.

windlass *n* winch worked by a crank.

window *n* **1** opening in a wall to let in light or air. **2** glass pane or panes fitted in such an opening. **3** display area behind the window of a shop. **4** area on a computer screen that can be manipulated separately from the rest of the display area. **5** period of unbooked time in a diary or schedule. **window-dressing** *n* **1** arrangement of goods in a shop window. **2** attempt to make something more attractive than it really is. **window-shopping** *n* looking at goods in shop windows without intending to buy. **windowsill** *n* ledge below a window.

windshield *n* the US and Canadian name for WINDSCREEN.

wine *n* **1** alcoholic drink made from fermented grapes. **2** similar drink made from other fruits. ▷ *adj* **3** of a dark purplish-red colour. **wine and dine** entertain or be entertained with fine food and drink.

wing ❶ *n* **1** one of the limbs or organs of a bird, insect, or bat that are used for flying. **2** one of the winglike supporting parts of an aircraft. **3** projecting side part of a building. **4** faction of a political party. **5** part of a car body surrounding the wheels. **6** *Sport* (player on) either side of the pitch. ▷ *pl* **7** sides of a stage. ▷ *v* **8** fly. **9** wound slightly in the wing or arm. **winged** *adj* **winger** *n Sport* player positioned on a wing. **wing commander** middle-ranking commissioned air-force officer. **wingspan** *n* distance between the wing tips of an aircraft, bird, or insect.

wink ❶ *v* **1** close and open (an eye) quickly as a signal. **2** twinkle. ▷ *n* **3** winking. **4** smallest amount of sleep.

winkle *n* shellfish with a spiral shell. **winkle out** *v informal* extract or prise out.

winnow *v* **1** separate (chaff) from (grain). **2** examine to select desirable elements.

winsome *adj* charming or winning.

winter ❶ *n* **1** coldest season. ▷ *v* **2** spend the winter. **wintry** *adj* **wintrier, wintriest 1** of or like winter. **2** cold or unfriendly. **winter sports** open-air sports held on snow or ice.

⸻ THESAURUS ⸻

4 = **flatulence**, gas **5** = **talk**, babble, bluster, boasting, hot air
wind² *v* **1** = **coil**, curl, encircle, loop, reel, roll, spiral, twist **3** = **meander**, bend, curve, ramble, snake, turn, twist, zigzag
windfall *n* **1** = **godsend**, bonanza, find, jackpot, manna from heaven
wind up *v* **1** = **end**, close, conclude, finalize, finish, settle, terminate, wrap up **3** *Inf* = **excite**, put on edge, work up
windy *adj* **1** = **breezy**, blowy, blustery, gusty, squally, stormy, wild, windswept
wing *n* **4** = **faction**, arm, branch, group, section ▷ *v* **8** = **fly**, glide, soar = **wound**, clip, hit

wink *v* **1** = **blink**, bat, flutter **2** = **twinkle**, flash, gleam, glimmer, sparkle ▷ *n* **3** = **blink**, flutter
winner *n* **1** = **victor**, champ (*inf*), champion, conqueror, master
winning *adj* **1** = **victorious**, conquering, successful, triumphant **2** = **charming**, alluring, attractive, cute, disarming, enchanting, endearing, engaging, lekker (*S Afr sl*), likable *or* likeable
winnings *pl n* = **spoils**, gains, prize, proceeds, profits, takings
win over *v* = **convince**, bring *or* talk round, convert, influence, persuade, prevail upon, sway
wintry *adj* **1** = **cold**, chilly, freezing, frosty, frozen, icy, snowy

w

wipe ❶ v 1 clean or dry by rubbing.
2 erase (a tape). ▷ n 3 wiping. **wipe
out** v destroy completely.

wire ❶ n 1 thin flexible strand of metal.
2 length of this used to carry electric
current. 3 wire or cable connecting
points in a telephone or telegraph
system. 4 obs telegram. ▷ v 5 fasten
with wire. 6 equip with wires. **wired**
adj slang 1 excited or nervous. 2 using
computers and the internet to send
and receive information. **wiring** n
system of wires. **wiry** adj **wirier**,
wiriest 1 lean and tough. 2 like wire.
wire-haired adj (of a dog) having a
stiff wiry coat. **wire netting** net made
of wire, used for fences.

wireless n 1 old-fashioned same as
RADIO. ▷ adj 2 communicating
without connecting wires.

wisdom ❶ n 1 good sense and
judgment. 2 accumulated
knowledge. **wisdom tooth** any of the
four large molar teeth that come
through usu. after the age of twenty.

wise¹ ❶ adj having intelligence and
knowledge. **wisely** adv **wiseacre** n
person who wishes to seem wise.

wise² n obs manner.

-wise adv suffix 1 indicating direction or
manner, e.g. clockwise; likewise. 2 with
reference to, e.g. businesswise.

wisecrack ❶ informal ▷ n 1 clever,
sometimes unkind, remark. ▷ v
2 make a wisecrack.

wish ❶ v 1 want or desire. 2 feel or
express a hope about someone's
wellbeing, success, etc. ▷ n

3 expression of a desire. 4 thing
desired. **wishful** adj too optimistic.
wishful thinking interpretation of
the facts as one would like them to be,
rather than as they are. **wishbone** n
V-shaped bone above the breastbone
of a fowl. **wish list** list of things a
person wants.

wishy-washy adj informal insipid or
bland.

wisp n 1 light delicate streak. 2 twisted
bundle or tuft. **wispy** adj **wispier**,
wispiest.

wisteria n climbing shrub with blue or
purple flowers.

wistful ❶ adj sadly longing. **wistfully**
adv **wistfulness** n.

wit¹ ❶ n 1 ability to use words or ideas
in a clever and amusing way. 2 person
with this ability. 3 (sometimes pl)
practical intelligence. **witless** adj
foolish.

wit² v **to wit** that is to say; namely.

witch ❶ n 1 person, usu. female, who
practises (black) magic. 2 ugly or
wicked woman. **witchcraft** n use of
magic. **witch doctor** (in certain
societies) a man appearing to cure or
cause injury or disease by magic.
witch-hunt n campaign against
people with unpopular views.

with prep indicating presence alongside,
possession, means of performance,
characteristic manner, etc. e.g. walking
with his dog; a man with two cars; hit with
a hammer; playing with skill. **within**
prep, adv in or inside. **without** prep not
accompanied by, using, or having.

THESAURUS

wipe v 1 = **clean**, brush, mop, rub,
sponge, swab 2 = **erase**, remove ▷ n
3 = **rub**, brush

wipe out v = **destroy**, annihilate,
eradicate, erase, expunge,
exterminate, massacre, obliterate

wiry adj 1 = **lean**, sinewy, strong, tough

wisdom n 1 = **understanding**,
discernment, enlightenment, erudition,
insight, intelligence, judgment, sense
2 = **knowledge**, learning

wise¹ adj = **sensible**, clever, discerning,
enlightened, erudite, intelligent,
judicious, perceptive, prudent, sage

wisecrack Inf ▷ n 1 = **joke**, jest, jibe,
quip, witticism ▷ v 2 = **joke**, jest, jibe,
quip

wish v 1 = **want**, aspire, crave, desire,
hanker, hope, long, yearn ▷ n

3 = **desire**, aspiration, hope,
intention, urge, want, whim, will

wistful adj = **melancholy**,
contemplative, dreamy, longing,
meditative, pensive, reflective,
thoughtful

wit¹ n 1 = **humour**, badinage, banter,
drollery, jocularity, raillery, repartee,
wordplay 2 = **humorist**, card (inf),
comedian, joker, wag 3 (sometimes
pl) = **cleverness**, acumen, brains,
common sense, ingenuity, intellect,
sense, wisdom

witch n 1 = **enchantress**, crone, hag,
magician, sorceress

witchcraft n = **magic**, black magic,
enchantment, necromancy, occultism,
sorcery, the black art, voodoo,
wizardry

w

withdraw ❶ v -**drawing**, -**drew**, -**drawn** take or move out or away. **withdrawal** n **withdrawn** adj unsociable.

wither ❶ v 1 wilt or dry up. 2 fade or waste. **withering** adj (of a look or remark) scornful.

withers pl n ridge between a horse's shoulder blades.

withhold ❶ v -**holding**, -**held** refrain from giving.

withstand ❶ v -**standing**, -**stood** oppose or resist successfully.

witness ❶ n 1 person who has seen something happen. 2 person giving evidence in court. 3 person who confirms that a document is genuine by signing it. 4 evidence or testimony. ▷ v 5 see at first hand. 6 be the scene of. 7 sign (a document) to certify that it is genuine. **witness box** place in a court where a witness stands to give evidence.

witter ❶ v chatter pointlessly or at unnecessary length.

wittingly adv intentionally.

witty ❶ adj **wittier**, **wittiest** clever and amusing. **wittily** adv **witticism** n witty remark.

wives n plural of WIFE.

wizard ❶ n 1 magician. 2 person with outstanding skill in a particular field. **wizardry** n.

wizened ❶ [**wiz**-zend] adj shrivelled or wrinkled.

WMD weapon(s) of mass destruction.

woad n blue dye obtained from a plant.

wobble ❶ v 1 move unsteadily. 2 shake. ▷ n 3 wobbling movement or sound. **wobbly** adj **wobblier**, **wobbliest**.

wodge n informal thick lump or chunk.

woe ❶ n grief. **woeful** adj 1 extremely sad. 2 pitiful. **woefully** adv **woebegone** adj looking miserable.

wok n bowl-shaped Chinese cooking pan, used for stir-frying.

woke v past tense of WAKE¹. **woken** v past participle of WAKE¹.

wold n high open country.

wolf n, pl **wolves** 1 wild predatory canine mammal. ▷ v 2 eat ravenously. **cry wolf** raise a false alarm. **wolfhound** n very large breed of dog. **wolf whistle** whistle by a man indicating that he thinks a woman is attractive.

wolverine n carnivorous mammal of Arctic regions.

woman ❶ n, pl **women** 1 adult human female. 2 women collectively. **womanhood** n **womanish** adj

————————— THESAURUS —————————

withdraw v = **remove**, draw back, extract, pull out, take away, take off

withdrawal n = **removal**, extraction

wither v 1 = **wilt**, decline, perish, shrivel 2 = **fade**, decay, disintegrate, waste

withering adj = **scornful**, devastating, humiliating, hurtful, mortifying, snubbing

withhold v = **keep back**, conceal, hide, hold back, refuse, reserve, retain, suppress

withstand v = **resist**, bear, cope with, endure, hold off, oppose, stand up to, suffer, tolerate

witness n 1 = **observer**, beholder, bystander, eyewitness, looker-on, onlooker, spectator, viewer, watcher 2 = **testifier**, corroborator ▷ v 5 = **see**, note, notice, observe, perceive, view, watch 7 = **sign**, countersign, endorse

witter v = **chatter**, babble, blather, chat, gabble, jabber, prate, prattle, waffle (inf, chiefly Brit)

witticism n = **quip**, bon mot, one-liner, pun, riposte

witty adj = **humorous**, amusing, clever, droll, funny, piquant, sparkling, whimsical

wizard n 1 = **magician**, conjuror, magus, necromancer, occultist, shaman, sorcerer, warlock, witch

wizened adj = **wrinkled**, dried up, gnarled, lined, shrivelled, shrunken, withered

wobble v 1 = **sway**, rock, teeter, totter 2 = **shake**, tremble ▷ n 3 = **unsteadiness**, shake, tremble, tremor

wobbly adj = **unsteady**, rickety, shaky, teetering, tottering, uneven

woe n = **grief**, agony, anguish, distress, gloom, misery, sadness, sorrow, unhappiness, wretchedness

woeful adj 1 = **sad**, deplorable, dismal, distressing, grievous, lamentable, miserable, pathetic, tragic, wretched 2 = **pitiful**, abysmal, appalling, bad, deplorable, dreadful, feeble, pathetic, poor, sorry

woman n 1 = **lady**, female, girl

womanizer n = **philanderer**,

w

effeminate. **womanly** *adj* having qualities traditionally associated with a woman. **womanizing** *n* practice of indulging in casual affairs with women. **womanizer** *n* **Women's Liberation** movement for the removal of inequalities between women and men (also **women's lib**).

womb *n* hollow organ in female mammals where babies are conceived and develop.

wombat *n* small heavily-built burrowing Australian marsupial.

won *v* past of WIN.

wonder ❶ *v* **1** be curious about. **2** be amazed. ▷ *n* **3** wonderful thing. **4** emotion caused by an amazing or unusual thing. ▷ *adj* **5** spectacularly successful, e.g. *a wonder drug*. **wonderful** *adj* **1** very fine. **2** remarkable. **wonderfully** *adv* **wonderment** *n* **wondrous** *adj* old-fashioned wonderful. **wonderland** *n* real or imaginary place full of wonders.

wonky ❶ *adj* **-kier, -kiest** *informal* **1** shaky or unsteady. **2** insecure or unreliable.

wont [rhymes with **don't**] *adj* **1** accustomed. ▷ *n* **2** custom.

won't will not.

woo ❶ *v* **1** try to persuade. **2** *old-fashioned* try to gain the love of.

wood ❶ *n* **1** substance trees are made of, used in carpentry and as fuel. **2** area where trees grow.

3 long-shafted golf club, usu. with wooden head. ▷ *adj* **4** made of or using wood. **wooded** *adj* covered with trees. **wooden** *adj* **1** made of wood. **2** without expression. **woody** *adj* **woodier, woodiest. woodbine** *n* honeysuckle. **woodcock** *n* game bird. **woodcut** *n* (print made from) an engraved block of wood. **woodland** *n* forest. **woodlouse** *n* small insect-like creature with many legs. **woodpecker** *n* bird which searches tree trunks for insects. **woodwind** *adj*, *n* (of) a type of wind instrument made of wood. **woodwork** *n* **1** parts of a room or building made of wood. **2** skill of making things in wood. **woodworm** *n* insect larva that bores into wood.

woof¹ *n* cross threads in weaving.

woof² *n* barking noise made by a dog. **woofer** *n* loudspeaker reproducing low-frequency sounds.

wool ❶ *n* **1** soft hair of sheep, goats, etc. **2** yarn spun from this. **woollen** *adj* **woolly** *adj* **woollier, woolliest 1** of or like wool. **2** vague or muddled. ▷ *n*, *pl* **-lies 3** knitted woollen garment. **woolgathering** *n* daydreaming.

woozy *adj* **woozier, wooziest** *informal* weak, dizzy, and confused.

wop-wops *pl n NZ informal* remote rural areas.

word ❶ *n* **1** smallest single meaningful unit of speech or writing. **2** chat or

---

THESAURUS

Casanova, Don Juan, lady-killer, lecher, seducer

womanly *adj* = **feminine**, female, ladylike, matronly, motherly, tender, warm

wonder *v* **1** = **think**, conjecture, meditate, ponder, puzzle, query, question, speculate **2** = **be amazed**, be astonished, gape, marvel, stare ▷ *n* **3** = **phenomenon**, curiosity, marvel, miracle, prodigy, rarity, sight, spectacle **4** = **amazement**, admiration, astonishment, awe, bewilderment, fascination, surprise, wonderment

wonderful *adj* **1** = **excellent**, brilliant, fabulous (*inf*), fantastic (*inf*), great (*inf*), magnificent, marvellous, outstanding, superb, terrific, tremendous **2** = **remarkable**, amazing, astonishing, extraordinary,

incredible, jaw-dropping, miraculous, phenomenal, staggering, startling, unheard-of

wonky *adj Inf* **1** = **shaky**, unsteady, wobbly

woo *v* **1** = **court**, cultivate, pursue

wood *n* **1** = **timber**, planks **2** = **woodland**, coppice, copse, forest, grove, thicket

wooden *adj* **1** = **woody**, ligneous, timber **2** = **expressionless**, deadpan, lifeless, unresponsive

wool *n* **1** = **fleece**, hair **2** = **yarn**

woolly *adj* **1** = **fleecy**, hairy, shaggy, woollen **2** = **vague**, confused, hazy, ill-defined, indefinite, indistinct, muddled, unclear

word *n* **1** = **term**, expression, name **2** = **chat**, confab (*inf*), consultation, discussion, talk, tête-à-tête **3** = **remark**, comment, utterance

discussion. **3** brief remark.
4 message. **5** promise. **6** command.
▷ *v* **7** express in words. **wordless** *adj*
wordy *adj* **wordier**, **wordiest** using
too many words. **wording** *n* choice
and arrangement of words. **word-
perfect** *adj* (of a speaker or actor)
knowing one's speech or role
perfectly. **word processor**
keyboard, microprocessor, and VDU
for electronic organization and
storage of text. **word
processing**.

wore *v* past tense of WEAR.

work ❶ *n* **1** physical or mental effort
directed to making or doing
something. **2** paid employment.
3 duty or task. **4** something made or
done. ▷ *pl* **5** factory. **6** total of a
writer's or artist's achievements.
7 *informal* full treatment.
8 mechanism of a machine. ▷ *adj* **9** of
or for work. ▷ *v* **10** (cause to) do work.
11 be employed. **12** (cause to) operate.
13 (of a plan etc.) be successful.
14 cultivate (land). **15** manipulate,
shape, or process. **16** (cause to) reach
a specified condition. **work-to-rule** *n*
protest in which workers keep strictly
to all regulations to reduce the rate of
work. **workable** *adj* **worker** *n*

workaday *adj* ordinary. **workaholic** *n*
person obsessed with work.
workforce *n* total number of workers.
workhorse *n* person or thing that
does a lot of dull or routine work.
workhouse *n History* institution
where the poor were given food and
lodgings in return for work. **working
class** social class consisting of wage
earners, esp. manual workers.
working-class *adj* **working party**
committee investigating a specific
problem. **workman** *n* manual
worker. **workmanship** *n* skill
with which an object is made. **work
out** *v* **1** solve by reasoning or
calculation. **2** happen in a particular
way. **3** take part in physical
exercise. **workout** *n* session of
physical exercise for training or
fitness. **workshop** *n* **1** room or
building for a manufacturing
process. **2** session of group study or
practice of a subject. **work station**
area in an office where one person
works. **worktop** *n* surface in a
kitchen, used for food preparation.
work up *v* **1** make angry or excited.
2 build up.

world ❶ *n* **1** the planet earth.
2 mankind. **3** society of a particular

---

4 = **message**, communiqué, dispatch,
information, intelligence, news,
notice, report **5** = **promise**,
assurance, guarantee, oath, pledge,
vow **6** = **command**, bidding, decree,
mandate, order ▷ *v* **7** = **express**,
couch, phrase, put, say, state,
utter
wording *n* = **phraseology**, language,
phrasing, terminology, words
wordy *adj* = **long-winded**, diffuse,
prolix, rambling, verbose, windy
work *n* **1** = **effort**, drudgery, elbow
grease (*facetious*), exertion, industry,
labour, sweat, toil **2** = **employment**,
business, duty, job, livelihood,
occupation, profession, trade
3 = **task**, assignment, chore,
commission, duty, job, stint,
undertaking **4** = **creation**,
achievement, composition,
handiwork, opus, piece, production
▷ *v* **10** = **labour**, drudge, exert oneself,
[slog] away, slave, slog (away), sweat,
[11] = **be employed**, be in work
[12] = **operate**, control, drive, handle,

manage, manipulate, move, run, use
14 = **cultivate**, dig, farm, till
15 = **manipulate**, fashion, form,
knead, mould, shape
worker *n* **2** = **employee**, artisan,
craftsman, hand, labourer,
tradesman, workman
workman *n* = **labourer**, artisan,
craftsman, employee, hand,
journeyman, mechanic, operative,
tradesman, worker
workmanship *n* = **skill**, artistry,
craftsmanship, expertise, handiwork,
technique
work out *v* **1** = **solve**, calculate, figure
out, find out **2** = **happen**, develop,
evolve, result, turn out **3** = **exercise**,
practise, train, warm up
works *pl n* **5** = **factory**, mill, plant,
workshop **6** = **writings**, canon,
oeuvre, output **8** = **mechanism**,
action, machinery, movement, parts,
workings
workshop *n* **1** = **studio**, factory, mill,
plant, workroom
world *n* **1** = **earth**, globe **2** = **mankind**,

area or period. **4** sphere of existence. ▷ *adj* **5** of the whole world. **worldly** *adj* **1** not spiritual. **2** concerned with material things. **3** wise in the ways of the world. **world-weary** *adj* no longer finding pleasure in life. **worldwide** *adj* applying or extending throughout the world. **World Wide Web** global network of linked computer files.

worm *n* **1** small limbless invertebrate animal. **2** *informal* wretched or spineless person. **3** shaft with a spiral thread forming part of a gear system. **4** *Computers* type of virus. ▷ *pl* **5** illness caused by parasitic worms in the intestines. ▷ *v* **6** rid of worms. **worm one's way 1** crawl. **2** insinuate (oneself). **wormy** *adj* **wormier**, **wormiest**. **wormcast** *n* coil of earth excreted by a burrowing worm. **worm-eaten** *adj* eaten into by worms. **worm out** *v* extract (information) craftily.

wormwood *n* bitter plant.

worn ❶ *v* past participle of WEAR. **worn-out** *adj* **1** threadbare, valueless, or useless. **2** completely exhausted.

worry ❶ *v* **-rying, -ried 1** (cause to) be anxious or uneasy. **2** annoy or bother. **3** (of a dog) chase and try to bite (sheep etc.). ▷ *n*, *pl* **-ries 4** (cause of) anxiety or concern. **worried** *adj* **worrying** *adj*, *n*.

worse ❶ *adj*, *adv* comparative of BAD *or* BADLY. **worst** *adj*, *adv* **1** superlative of BAD *or* BADLY. ▷ *n* **2** worst thing. **worsen** *v* make or grow worse.

worship ❶ *v* **-shipping, -shipped 1** show religious devotion to. **2** love and admire. ▷ *n* **3** act or instance of worshipping. **4** (**W-**) title for a mayor or magistrate. **worshipper** *n* **worshipful** *adj* worshipping.

worsted [**wooss**-tid] *n* type of woollen yarn or fabric.

worth ❶ *prep* **1** having a value of. **2** meriting or justifying. ▷ *n* **3** value or price. **4** excellence. **5** amount to be had for a given sum. **worthless** *adj* **worthy** *adj* **-thier, -thiest 1** deserving admiration or respect. ▷ *n*, *pl* **-thies 2** *informal* notable person. **worthy of** deserving of. **worthily** *adv* **worthiness** *n* **worthwhile** *adj* worth the time or effort involved.

THESAURUS

everybody, everyone, humanity, humankind, man, the public
4 = sphere, area, domain, environment, field, realm
worldly *adj* **1 = earthly**, physical, profane, secular, temporal, terrestrial **2 = materialistic**, grasping, greedy, selfish **3 = worldly-wise**, blasé, cosmopolitan, experienced, knowing, sophisticated, urbane
worldwide *adj* **= global**, general, international, omnipresent, pandemic, ubiquitous, universal
worn *adj* **= ragged**, frayed, shabby, tattered, tatty, the worse for wear, threadbare
worn-out *adj* **1 = run-down**, on its last legs, ragged, shabby, threadbare, used-up, useless, worn **2 = exhausted**, all in (*sl*), done in (*inf*), fatigued, fit to drop, spent, tired out, weary
worry *v* **1 = be anxious**, agonize, brood, fret, obsess **2 = trouble**, annoy, bother, disturb, perturb, pester, unsettle, upset, vex ▷ *n* **4 a = problem**, bother, care, hassle (*inf*), trouble **b = anxiety**,

apprehension, concern, fear, misgiving, trepidation, trouble, unease
worsen *v* **a = aggravate**, damage, exacerbate **b = deteriorate**, decay, decline, degenerate, get worse, go downhill (*inf*), sink
worship *v* **1 = praise**, adore, exalt, glorify, honour, pray to, revere, venerate **2 = love**, adore, idolize, put on a pedestal ▷ *n* **3 = praise**, adoration, adulation, devotion, glory, honour, regard, respect, reverence
worth *n* **3 = value**, cost, price, rate, valuation **4 = importance**, excellence, goodness, merit, quality, usefulness, value, worthiness
worthless *adj* **a = useless**, ineffectual, rubbishy, unimportant, valueless **b = good-for-nothing**, contemptible, despicable, vile
worthwhile *adj* **= useful**, beneficial, constructive, expedient, helpful, productive, profitable, valuable
worthy *adj* **1 = praiseworthy**, admirable, creditable, deserving, laudable, meritorious, valuable, virtuous, worthwhile

would ❶ *v* used as an auxiliary to express a request, describe a habitual past action, or form the past tense or subjunctive mood of WILL¹. **would-be** *adj* wishing or pretending to be.

wouldn't would not.

wound¹ ❶ *n* **1** injury caused by violence. **2** injury to the feelings. ▷ *v* **3** inflict a wound on.

wound² *v* past of WIND².

wove *v* a past tense of WEAVE. **woven** *v* a past participle of WEAVE.

wow *interj* **1** exclamation of astonishment. ▷ *n* **2** *informal* astonishing person or thing. ▷ *v* **3** *informal* be a great success with.

wowser *n Aust & NZ slang* **1** puritanical person. **2** teetotaller.

wpm words per minute.

WRAC Women's Royal Army Corps.

wrack *n* seaweed.

WRAF Women's Royal Air Force.

wraith *n* ghost.

wrangle ❶ *v* **1** argue noisily. ▷ *n* **2** noisy argument.

wrap ❶ *v* **wrapping, wrapped 1** fold (something) round (a person or thing) so as to cover. ▷ *n* **2** garment wrapped round the shoulders. **3** sandwich made by wrapping a filling in a tortilla. **wrapper** *n* cover for a product. **wrapping** *n* material used to wrap. **wrap up** *v* **1** fold paper round. **2** put warm clothes on. **3** *informal* finish or settle (a matter).

wrasse *n* colourful sea fish.

wrath ❶ [roth] *n* intense anger. **wrathful** *adj*.

wreak *v* **wreak havoc** cause chaos. **wreak vengeance on** take revenge on.

wreath ❶ *n* twisted ring or band of flowers or leaves used as a memorial or tribute. **wreathed** *adj* surrounded or encircled.

wreck ❶ *v* **1** destroy. ▷ *n* **2** remains of something that has been destroyed or badly damaged, esp. a ship. **3** person in very poor condition. **wrecker** *n* formerly, person who lured ships onto the rocks in order to plunder them. **wreckage** *n* wrecked remains.

wren *n* **1** small brown songbird. **2** Australian warbler.

Wren *n* *informal* member of the Women's Royal Naval Service.

wrench ❶ *v* **1** twist or pull violently. **2** sprain (a joint). ▷ *n* **3** violent twist or pull. **4** sprain. **5** difficult or painful parting. **6** adjustable spanner.

wrest ❶ *v* **1** twist violently. **2** take by force.

wrestle ❶ *v* **1** fight, esp. as a sport, by grappling with and trying to throw down an opponent. **2** struggle hard with. **wrestler** *n* **wrestling** *n*.

THESAURUS

would-be *adj* = **budding**, self-appointed, self-styled, unfulfilled, wannabe (*inf*)

wound¹ *n* **1** = **injury**, cut, gash, hurt, laceration, lesion, trauma (*Path*) **2** = **insult**, offence, slight ▷ *v* **3 a** = **injure**, cut, gash, hurt, lacerate, pierce, wing **b** = **offend**, annoy, cut (someone) to the quick, hurt, mortify, sting

wrangle *v* **1** = **argue**, bicker, contend, disagree, dispute, fight, quarrel, row, squabble ▷ *n* **2** = **argument**, altercation, bickering, dispute, quarrel, row, squabble, tiff

wrap *v* **1** = **cover**, bind, bundle up, encase, enclose, enfold, pack, package, shroud, swathe ▷ *n* **2** = **cloak**, cape, mantle, shawl, stole

wrapper *n* = **cover**, case, envelope, jacket, packaging, wrapping

wrap up *v* **1** = **giftwrap**, bundle up, pack, package **3** *Inf* = **end**, conclude, finish off, polish off, round off, terminate, wind up

wrath *n* = **anger**, displeasure, fury, indignation, ire, rage, resentment, temper

wreath *n* = **garland**, band, chaplet, crown, festoon, ring

wreck *v* **1** = **destroy**, break, demolish, devastate, ruin, shatter, smash, spoil ▷ *n* **2** = **shipwreck**, hulk

wreckage *n* = **remains**, debris, fragments, pieces, rubble, ruin

wrench *v* **1** = **twist**, force, jerk, pull, rip, tear, tug, yank **2** = **sprain**, rick, strain ▷ *n* **3** = **twist**, jerk, pull, rip, tug, yank **4** = **sprain**, strain, twist **5** = **blow**, pang, shock, upheaval **6** = **spanner**, adjustable spanner

wrest *v* **2** = **seize**, extract, force, take, win, wrench

wrestle *v* **1** = **fight**, battle, combat, grapple, scuffle, struggle, tussle

wretch ❶ n 1 despicable person.
2 pitiful person. **wretched** [retch-id]
adj 1 miserable or unhappy.
2 worthless. **wretchedly** adv
wretchedness n.

wrier adj a comparative of WRY. **wriest**
adj a superlative of WRY.

wriggle ❶ v 1 move with a twisting
action. 2 manoeuvre oneself by
devious means. ▷ n 3 wriggling
movement.

wright n maker, e.g. wheelwright.

wring ❶ v **wringing, wrung** 1 twist,
esp. to squeeze liquid out of. 2 clasp
and twist (the hands). 3 obtain by
forceful means.

wrinkle ❶ n 1 slight crease, esp. one in
the skin due to age. ▷ v 2 make or
become slightly creased. **wrinkled** adj
wrinkly adj.

wrist n joint between the hand and the
arm. **wristwatch** n watch worn on
the wrist.

writ ❶ n written legal command.

write ❶ v **writing, wrote, written**
1 mark paper etc. with symbols or
words. 2 set down in words.
3 communicate by letter. 4 be the
author or composer of. **writing** n

writer n 1 author. 2 person who has
written something specified.

write-off n informal something
damaged beyond repair.

write-up n published account of
something.

writhe ❶ v twist or squirm in or as if in
pain.

WRNS Women's Royal Naval Service.

wrong ❶ adj 1 incorrect or mistaken.
2 immoral or bad. 3 not intended or
suitable. 4 not working properly.
▷ adv 5 in a wrong manner. ▷ n
6 something immoral or unjust. ▷ v
7 treat unjustly. 8 malign.
wrongly adv **wrongful** adj
wrongfully adv **wrongdoing** n
immoral or illegal behaviour.
wrongdoer n.

wrote v past tense of WRITE.

wrought [rawt] v 1 lit past of WORK.
▷ adj 2 (of metals) shaped by
hammering or beating.
wrought iron pure form of
iron used for decorative
work.

wrung v past of WRING.

WRVS Women's Royal Voluntary
Service.

THESAURUS

---

wretch n 1 = **scoundrel**, good-for-
nothing, miscreant, rascal, rogue,
swine, worm

wretched adj 1 = **unhappy**, dejected,
depressed, disconsolate, downcast,
forlorn, hapless, miserable,
woebegone 2 = **worthless**, inferior,
miserable, paltry, pathetic, poor,
sorry

wriggle v 1 = **crawl**, jerk, jiggle, slink,
snake, squirm, turn, twist, waggle,
wiggle, worm, writhe, zigzag
2 = **manoeuvre**, dodge, extricate
oneself ▷ n 3 = **twist**, jerk, jiggle,
squirm, turn, waggle, wiggle

wring v 1 = **twist**, squeeze 3 = **force**,
extract, screw

wrinkle n 1 = **crease**, corrugation,
crinkle, crow's-foot, crumple, fold,
furrow, line ▷ v 2 = **crease**, corrugate,
crumple, fold, furrow, gather, pucker,
rumple

writ n = **summons**, court order, decree,
document

write v 1, 2 = **record**, draft, draw up,
inscribe, jot down, pen, scribble, set
down

writer n 1 = **author**, hack, novelist,

penpusher, scribbler, scribe,
wordsmith

writhe v = **squirm**, jerk, struggle,
thrash, thresh, toss, twist, wiggle,
wriggle

writing n 1 = **script**, calligraphy, hand,
handwriting, penmanship, scrawl,
scribble 4 = **document**, book,
composition, opus, publication,
work

wrong adj 1 = **incorrect**, erroneous,
fallacious, false, inaccurate,
mistaken, untrue, wide of the mark
2 = **bad**, criminal, dishonest, evil,
illegal, immoral, sinful, unjust,
unlawful, wicked, wrongful
3 = **inappropriate**, incongruous,
incorrect, unacceptable, unbecoming,
undesirable, unseemly, unsuitable
4 = **defective**, amiss, askew, awry,
faulty ▷ adv 5 = **incorrectly**, badly,
erroneously, inaccurately, mistakenly,
wrongly ▷ n 6 = **offence**, crime, error,
injury, injustice, misdeed, sin,
transgression ▷ v 7 = **mistreat**,
cheat, oppress, take advantage
of 8 = **malign**, abuse, dishonour,
harm, hurt

wry ❶ *adj* **wrier**, **wriest** *or* **wryer**, **wryest 1** drily humorous, e.g. *a wry response* **2** (of a facial expression) contorted. **wryly** *adv*.

wt. weight.

wuss [**wooce**] *n slang, chiefly US* feeble or effeminate person.

WV West Virginia.
WWI World War One.
WWII World War Two.
WWW World Wide Web.
WY Wyoming.
wych-elm *n* elm with large rough leaves.

wry *adj* **1** = **ironic**, droll, dry, mocking, sarcastic, sardonic **2** = **contorted**, crooked, twisted, uneven

w

X 1 indicating an error, a choice, or a kiss. **2** indicating an unknown, unspecified, or variable factor, number, person, or thing. **3** the Roman numeral for ten.

X-chromosome *n* sex chromosome that occurs in pairs in the females of many animals, and as one of a pair with the Y-chromosome in males.

Xe *Chemistry* xenon.

xenon *n Chemistry* colourless odourless gas found in very small quantities in the air.

xenophobia [zen-oh-**fobe**-ee-a] *n* fear or hatred of people from other countries. **xenophobic** *adj*.

Xerox [**zeer**-ox] *n* **1** ® machine for copying printed material. **2** ® copy made by a Xerox machine. ▷ *v* **3** copy (a document) using such a machine.

Xmas ❶ [**eks**-mass] *n informal* Christmas.

X-ray, x-ray *n* **1** stream of radiation that can pass through some solid materials. **2** picture made by sending X-rays through someone's body to examine internal organs. ▷ *v* **3** photograph, treat, or examine using X-rays.

xylem [**zy**-lem] *n* plant tissue that conducts water and minerals from the roots to all other parts.

xylophone [**zile**-oh-fone] *n* musical instrument made of a row of wooden bars played with hammers.

THESAURUS

Xmas *n Inf* = **Christmas**, Noel, Yule (*arch*)

X

Y *Chemistry* yttrium.

Y2K *n informal* name for the year 2000 AD (esp. referring to the millennium bug).

ya *interj S Afr* yes.

yacht [**yott**] *n* **1** large boat with sails or an engine, used for racing or pleasure cruising. ▷ *v* **2** sail in a yacht. **yachting** *n* **yachtsman**, **yachtswoman** *n*.

yahoo *n* crude coarse person.

yak¹ *n* Tibetan ox with long shaggy hair.

yak² *v* **yakking, yakked** *slang* talk continuously about unimportant matters.

yakka *n Aust & NZ informal* work.

Yale lock *n* ® cylinder lock using a flat serrated key.

yam *n* tropical root vegetable.

yank ❶ *v* **1** pull or jerk suddenly. ▷ *n* **2** sudden pull or jerk.

Yankee, Yank *n slang* **1** person from the United States. **2** *US* person from the Northern United States.

yap *v* **yapping, yapped 1** bark with a high-pitched sound. **2** *informal* talk continuously. ▷ *n* **3** high-pitched bark.

yard¹ ❶ *n* **1** unit of length equal to 36 inches or equal to 91.4 centimetres. **2** spar slung across a ship's mast to extend the sail. **yardarm** *n* outer end of a ship's yard. **yardstick** *n* standard against which to judge other people or things.

yard² *n* **1** enclosed area, usu. next to a building and often used for a particular purpose, e.g. *builder's yard*. **2** *US* garden of a house.

yarmulke [**yar**-mull-ka] *n* skullcap

worn by Jewish men.

yarn ❶ *n* **1** thread used for knitting or making cloth. **2** *informal* long involved story.

yashmak *n* veil worn by a Muslim woman to cover her face in public.

yaw *v* (of an aircraft or ship) turn to one side or from side to side while moving.

yawl *n* two-masted sailing boat.

yawn ❶ *v* **1** open the mouth wide and take in air deeply, often when sleepy or bored. **2** (of an opening) be large and wide. ▷ *n* **3** act of yawning. **yawning** *adj*.

yaws *n* infectious tropical skin disease.

Yb *Chemistry* ytterbium.

Y-chromosome *n* sex chromosome that occurs as one of a pair with the X-chromosome in the males of many animals.

yd yard.

ye [**yee**] *pron obs* you.

yea *interj old-fashioned* yes.

yeah *interj informal* yes.

year ❶ *n* **1** time taken for the earth to make one revolution around the sun, about 365 days. **2** twelve months from January 1 to December 31. **3** any period of twelve months. **4** group of people who have started a course at the same time. ▷ *pl* **5** a long time. **6** age. **yearly** *adj, adv* (happening) every year or once a year. **yearling** *n* animal between one and two years old. **yearbook** *n* reference book published annually containing details of the previous year's events.

yearn ❶ *v* **1** want (something) very much. **2** feel tenderness. **yearning** *n, adj*.

yeast *n* fungus used to make bread rise and to ferment alcoholic drinks. **yeasty** *adj*.

yebo *interj S Afr informal* yes.

yell ❶ *v* **1** shout or scream in a loud or piercing way. ▷ *n* **2** loud cry of pain, anger, or fear.

—— THESAURUS ————

yank *v, n* = **pull**, hitch, jerk, snatch, tug, wrench

yardstick *n* = **standard**, benchmark, criterion, gauge, measure, par, touchstone

yarn *n* **1** = **thread**, fibre **2** *Inf* = **story**, anecdote, cock-and-bull story (*inf*), fable, tale, tall story, urban legend, urban myth

yawning *adj* **2** = **gaping**, cavernous, vast, wide

yearly *adj* = **annual** ▷ *adv* = **annually**, every year, once a year, per annum

yearn *v* **1** = **long**, ache, covet, crave, desire, hanker, hunger, itch

yell *v* **1** = **scream**, bawl, holler (*inf*), howl, screech, shout, shriek, squeal ▷ *n*

yellow *n* **1** the colour of gold, a lemon, etc. ▷ *adj* **2** of this colour. **3** *informal* cowardly. ▷ *v* **4** make or become yellow. **yellow belly** *Aust* freshwater food fish with yellow underparts. **yellow card** *Soccer* piece of yellow pasteboard shown by a referee to indicate that a player has been booked. **yellow fever** serious infectious tropical disease. **yellowhammer** *n* European songbird with a yellow head and body. **Yellow Pages®** telephone directory which lists businesses under the headings of the type of service they provide.

yelp ❶ *v, n* (give) a short sudden cry.

yen¹ *n, pl* **yen** main unit of currency in Japan.

yen² ❶ *n informal* longing or desire.

yeoman [**yo**-man] *n, pl* **-men** *History* farmer owning and farming his own land. **yeomanry** *n* **1** yeomen. **2** (in Britain) former volunteer cavalry force. **yeoman of the guard** member of the ceremonial bodyguard of the British monarchy.

yes ❶ *interj* **1** expresses consent, agreement, or approval. **2** used to answer when one is addressed. ▷ *n* **3** answer or vote of yes. **yes man** person who always agrees with their superior.

yesterday *adv, n* **1** (on) the day before today. **2** (in) the recent past.

yet ❶ *conj* **1** nevertheless, still. ▷ *adv* **2** up until then or now. **3** still. **4** now. **5** eventually.

yeti *n* same as ABOMINABLE SNOWMAN.

yew *n* evergreen tree with needle-like leaves and red berries.

YHA Youth Hostels Association.

Yiddish *adj, n* (of or in) a language of German origin spoken by many Jews in Europe and elsewhere.

yield ❶ *v* **1** produce or bear. **2** give up control of, surrender. **3** give in. **4** agree (to). **5** grant or allow. ▷ *n* **6** amount produced. **yielding** *adj* **1** submissive. **2** soft or flexible.

yippee *interj* exclamation of joy or pleasure.

YMCA Young Men's Christian Association.

yob, yobbo ❶ *n slang* bad-mannered aggressive youth.

yodel *v* **-delling, -delled** sing with abrupt changes between a normal and a falsetto voice. **yodelling** *n*.

yoga *n* Hindu method of exercise and discipline aiming at spiritual, mental, and physical wellbeing. **yogi** *n* person who practises yoga.

yogurt, yoghurt *n* slightly sour custard-like food made from milk that has had bacteria added to it, often sweetened and flavoured with fruit.

yoke *n* **1** wooden bar put across the necks of two animals to hold them together. **2** frame fitting over a person's shoulders for carrying buckets. **3** *lit* oppressive force, e.g. *the yoke of the tyrant*. **4** fitted part of a garment to which a fuller part is attached. ▷ *v* **5** put a yoke on. **6** unite or link.

yokel ❶ *n offens* person who lives in the country and is usu. simple and old-fashioned.

yolk *n* yellow part of an egg that provides food for the developing embryo.

THESAURUS

2 = **scream**, cry, howl, screech, shriek, whoop

yelp *v* = **cry**, yap, yowl

yen² *n Inf* = **longing**, ache, craving, desire, hankering, hunger, itch, passion, thirst, yearning

yes man *n* = **sycophant**, bootlicker (*inf*), crawler (*sl*), minion, timeserver, toady

yet *conj* **1** = **nevertheless**, however, notwithstanding, still ▷ *adv* **2** = **so far**, as yet, thus far, until now, up to now **3** = **still**, besides, in addition, into the bargain, to boot **4** = **now**, just now, right now, so soon

yield *v* **1** = **produce**, bear, bring forth, earn, generate, give, net, provide,

return, supply **2, 3** = **surrender**, bow, capitulate, cave in (*inf*), give in, relinquish, resign, submit, succumb ▷ *n* **6** = **profit**, crop, earnings, harvest, income, output, produce, return, revenue, takings

yielding *adj* **1** = **submissive**, accommodating, acquiescent, biddable, compliant, docile, flexible, obedient, pliant **2** = **soft**, elastic, pliable, spongy, springy, supple, unresisting

yob, yobbo *n Inf* = **thug**, hooligan, lout, roughneck (*sl*), ruffian

yokel *n Offens* = **peasant**, (country) bumpkin, countryman, hick (*inf, chiefly US & Canad*), hillbilly, rustic

Yom Kippur *n* annual Jewish religious holiday.

yon *adj old-fashioned or dialect* that or those over there.

yonder *adj, adv* (situated) over there.

yonks *pl n informal* very long time.

yoo-hoo *interj* call to attract attention.

yore *n lit* **of yore** a long time ago.

yorker *n Cricket* ball that pitches just under the bat.

Yorkshire pudding *n* baked batter made from flour, milk, and eggs.

you *pron* refers to: **1** the person or people addressed. **2** an unspecified person or people in general.

young ❶ *adj* **1** in an early stage of life or growth. ▷ *pl n* **2** young people in general. **3** offspring, esp. young animals. **youngish** *adj* **youngster** *n* young person.

your *adj* **1** of, belonging to, or associated with you. **2** of, belonging to, or associated with an unspecified person or people in general. **yours** *pron* something belonging to you. **yourself** *pron.*

youth ❶ *n* **1** time of being young. **2** state of being young. **3** boy or young man. **4** young people as a group. **youthful** *adj* **youthfulness** *n* **youth**

club club that provides leisure activities for young people. **youth hostel** inexpensive lodging place for young people travelling cheaply.

yowl *v, n* (produce) a loud mournful cry.

yo-yo *n, pl* **-yos** toy consisting of a spool attached to a string, by which it is repeatedly spun out and reeled in.

YT Yukon Territory.

ytterbium [it-**terb**-ee-um] *n Chemistry* soft silvery element.

yttrium [**it**-ree-um] *n Chemistry* silvery metallic element used in various alloys.

yucca *n* tropical plant with spikes of white leaves.

yucky *adj* **yuckier, yuckiest** *slang* disgusting, nasty.

Yugoslav *n* **1** person from the former Yugoslavia. ▷ *adj* **2** of the former Yugoslavia.

Yule *n lit* Christmas (season).

yummy *adj* **-mier, -miest** *informal* delicious.

yuppie *n* **1** young highly-paid professional person, esp. one who has a fashionable way of life. ▷ *adj* **2** typical of or reflecting the values of yuppies.

YWCA Young Women's Christian Association.

——————— THESAURUS ———————

young *adj* **1** = **immature**, adolescent, callow, early, fledgling, green, infant, junior, juvenile, little, new, recent, undeveloped, youthful ▷ *pl n*
3 = **offspring**, babies, brood, family, issue, litter, progeny

youngster *n* = **youth**, boy, girl, juvenile, kid (*inf*), lad, lass, teenager

youth *n* **1** = **immaturity**, adolescence, boyhood, girlhood, salad days
3 = **boy**, adolescent, kid (*inf*), lad, stripling, teenager, young man, youngster

youthful *adj* **2** = **young**, boyish, childish, girlish, immature, inexperienced, juvenile

Z *Chemistry* atomic number.

zany ❶ [**zane**-ee] *adj* **zanier**, **zaniest** comical in an endearing way.

zap *v* **zapping**, **zapped** **1** *slang* kill (by shooting). **2** change TV channels rapidly by remote control. **3** move quickly.

zeal ❶ *n* great enthusiasm or eagerness. **zealot** [**zel**-lot] *n* fanatic or extreme enthusiast. **zealous** [**zel**-luss] *adj* extremely eager or enthusiastic. **zealously** *adv*.

zebra *n* black-and-white striped African animal of the horse family. **zebra crossing** pedestrian crossing marked by black and white stripes on the road.

zebu [**zee**-boo] *n* Asian ox with a humped back and long horns.

Zen *n* Japanese form of Buddhism that concentrates on learning through meditation and intuition.

zenith ❶ *n* **1** highest point of success or power. **2** point in the sky directly above an observer.

zephyr [**zef**-fer] *n* soft gentle breeze.

zeppelin *n History* large cylindrical airship.

zero ❶ *n, pl* **-ros**, **-roes** **1** (symbol representing) the number 0. **2** point on a scale of measurement from which the graduations commence. **3** lowest point. **4** nothing, nil. ▷ *adj* **5** having no measurable quantity or size. **zero hour** time at which something is set to happen. **zero in on** *v* **1** aim at. **2** *informal* concentrate on.

zest ❶ *n* **1** enjoyment or excitement. **2** interest, flavour, or charm. **3** peel of an orange or lemon.

zigzag *n* **1** line or course having sharp turns in alternating directions. ▷ *v* **-zagging**, **-zagged** **2** move in a zigzag. ▷ *adj* **3** formed in or proceeding in a zigzag. ▷ *adv* **4** in a zigzag manner.

zilch *n slang* nothing.

zinc *n Chemistry* bluish-white metallic element used in alloys and to coat metal.

zing *n informal* quality in something that makes it lively or interesting.

Zionism *n* movement to found and support a Jewish homeland in Israel. **Zionist** *n, adj*.

zip ❶ *n* **1** fastener with two rows of teeth that are closed or opened by a small clip pulled between them. **2** *informal* energy, vigour. **3** short whizzing sound. ▷ *v* **zipping**, **zipped** **4** fasten with a zip. **5** move with a sharp whizzing sound. **6** rush.

zircon *n* mineral used as a gemstone and in industry.

zirconium *n Chemistry* greyish-white metallic element that is resistant to corrosion.

zither *n* musical instrument consisting of strings stretched over a flat box and plucked to produce musical notes.

zloty *n, pl* **-tys**, **-ty** monetary unit of Poland.

Zn *Chemistry* zinc.

zodiac *n* imaginary belt in the sky within which the sun, moon, and planets appear to move, divided into twelve equal areas, called signs of the zodiac, each named after a constellation.

zombie, zombi *n* **1** person who appears to be lifeless, apathetic, or totally lacking in independent

---

————— THESAURUS —————

zany *adj* = **comical**, clownish, crazy, eccentric, goofy (*inf*), madcap, wacky (*sl*)

zeal *n* = **enthusiasm**, ardour, eagerness, fanaticism, fervour, gusto, keenness, passion, spirit, verve, zest

zealot *n* = **fanatic**, bigot, enthusiast, extremist, militant

zealous *adj* = **enthusiastic**, ardent, devoted, eager, fanatical, fervent, impassioned, keen, passionate

zenith *n* **1** = **height**, acme, apex, apogee, climax, crest, high point, peak, pinnacle, summit, top

zero *n* **1** = **nothing**, nil, nought **2** = **nought 3** = **bottom**, nadir, rock bottom **4** = **nil**, nothing

zest *n* **1** = **enjoyment**, appetite, gusto, keenness, relish, zeal **2** = **flavour**, charm, interest, piquancy, pungency, relish, spice, tang, taste

zip *n* **2** *Inf* = **energy**, drive, gusto, liveliness, verve, vigour, zest ▷ *v*

judgment. **2** corpse brought back to life by witchcraft.

zone ❶ *n* **1** area with particular features or properties. **2** one of the divisions of the earth's surface according to temperature. ▷ *v* **3** divide into zones. **zonal** *adj*.

zoo *n, pl* **zoos** place where live animals are kept for show.

zoology *n* study of animals. **zoologist** *n* **zoological** *adj* **zoological garden** zoo.

zoom ❶ *v* **1** move or rise very rapidly.

2 make or move with a buzzing or humming sound. **zoom lens** lens that can make the details of a picture larger or smaller while keeping the picture in focus.

Zr *Chemistry* zirconium.

zucchini [zoo-**keen**-ee] *n, pl* **-ni**, **-nis** the US and Canadian name for COURGETTE.

Zulu *n* **1** member of a tall Black people of southern Africa. **2** language of this people.

zygote *n* fertilized egg cell.

─────────────────────────────── THESAURUS ──────────

6 = **speed**, flash, fly, shoot, whizz (*inf*), zoom

zone *n* **1** = **area**, belt, district, region, section, sector, sphere

zoom *v* **1** = **speed**, dash, flash, fly, hurtle, pelt, rush, shoot, whizz (*inf*)

[handwritten notes:]

Name person Dear mrs John

Yours Sincerely

Unname — Dear sir or maadam
Yours faithfully